Contents

◄◄ Diner on Route 66 ◄ Glacier National Park

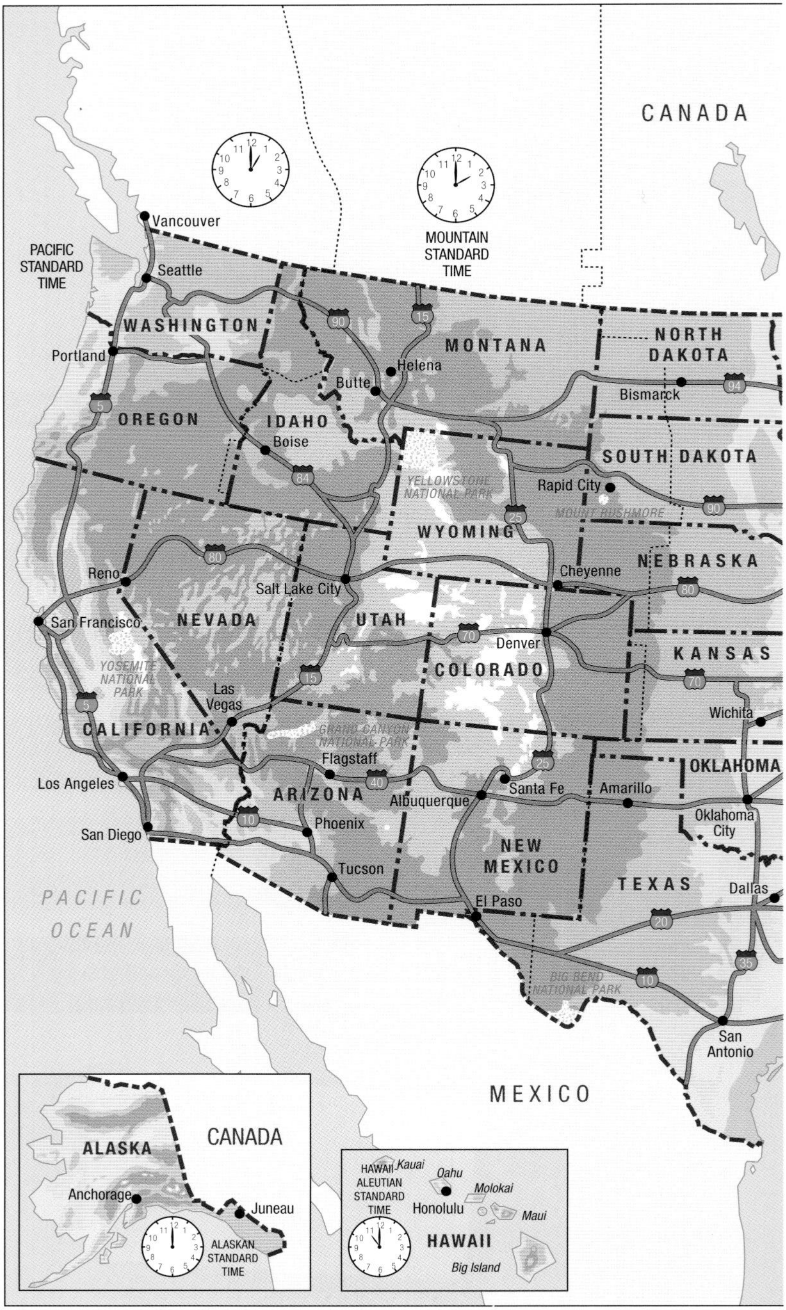
CANADA
PACIFIC STANDARD TIME
MOUNTAIN STANDARD TIME
Vancouver
Seattle
WASHINGTON
Portland
OREGON
IDAHO
Boise
MONTANA
Helena
Butte
NORTH DAKOTA
Bismarck
SOUTH DAKOTA
Rapid City
MOUNT RUSHMORE
YELLOWSTONE NATIONAL PARK
WYOMING
Cheyenne
NEBRASKA
Reno
Salt Lake City
NEVADA
UTAH
San Francisco
YOSEMITE NATIONAL PARK
Denver
COLORADO
KANSAS
Wichita
Las Vegas
CALIFORNIA
GRAND CANYON NATIONAL PARK
Flagstaff
OKLAHOMA
Los Angeles
ARIZONA
Albuquerque
Santa Fe
Amarillo
Oklahoma City
San Diego
Phoenix
Tucson
NEW MEXICO
TEXAS
Dallas
El Paso
BIG BEND NATIONAL PARK
San Antonio
PACIFIC OCEAN
MEXICO
ALASKA
CANADA
Anchorage
Juneau
ALASKAN STANDARD TIME
HAWAII ALEUTIAN STANDARD TIME
Kauai
Oahu
Molokai
Honolulu
Maui
HAWAII
Big Island
5
90
15
94
84
25
80
70
40
10
20
35

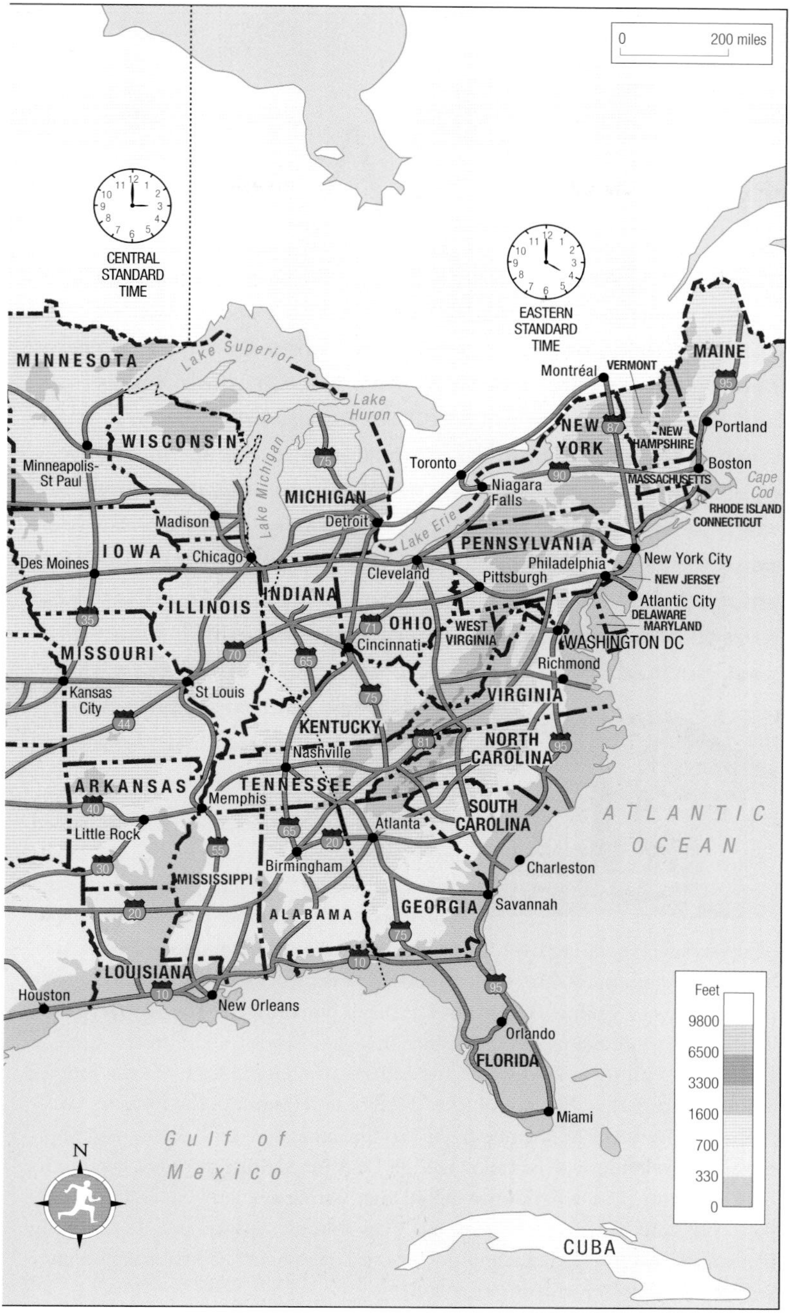

0 200 miles
CENTRAL STANDARD TIME
EASTERN STANDARD TIME
Lake Superior
Lake Huron
Lake Michigan
Lake Erie
MINNESOTA
WISCONSIN
MICHIGAN
IOWA
ILLINOIS
INDIANA
OHIO
MISSOURI
KENTUCKY
TENNESSEE
ARKANSAS
MISSISSIPPI
ALABAMA
GEORGIA
LOUISIANA
FLORIDA
SOUTH CAROLINA
NORTH CAROLINA
VIRGINIA
WEST VIRGINIA
PENNSYLVANIA
NEW YORK
VERMONT
NEW HAMPSHIRE
MAINE
MASSACHUSETTS
RHODE ISLAND
CONNECTICUT
NEW JERSEY
DELAWARE
MARYLAND
WASHINGTON DC
Minneapolis-St Paul
Madison
Chicago
Des Moines
Kansas City
St Louis
Detroit
Toronto
Niagara Falls
Montréal
Portland
Boston
Cape Cod
New York City
Philadelphia
Atlantic City
Pittsburgh
Cleveland
Cincinnati
Richmond
Nashville
Memphis
Little Rock
Atlanta
Birmingham
Charleston
Savannah
New Orleans
Houston
Orlando
Miami
ATLANTIC OCEAN
Gulf of Mexico
CUBA
N
Feet
9800
6500
3300
1600
700
330
0

Introduction to

the USA

As the twenty-first century unfolds, the eyes of the world continue to be drawn towards the United States. For over five hundred years, travelers have brought their hopes and dreams to America. The first European explorers were followed by millions of immigrants, escaping the hidebound societies of the Old World. Eventually, they were joined as free citizens by the Native Americans – the continent's true pioneers –and the slaves who had been shipped over from Africa and the Caribbean. Together they formed a nation that not only offered something genuinely new, but has continued to re-invent itself in the face of each fresh challenge, with a capacity to inspire that remains undiminished.

The images of the country that named itself after a continent are embedded in the mind of every traveler: endless highways cutting through shimmering deserts; forests of skyscrapers towering over urban jungles; acres of beaches dotted with surfboards and suntanned skin; high mountain peaks and green river valleys; magnificent feats of engineering, from the Brooklyn Bridge to the Hoover Dam. The country's emblems are so familiar that they constitute as much a part of the world's culture as its own – Lady Liberty, the Grand Canyon, the Empire State Building, the US Capitol, the "Hollywood" sign . . . the list goes on.

The combination of a shoot-from-the-hip mentality with *laissez-faire* capitalism and religious fervor can make the USA maddening at times, even to its own residents. But what's most surprising, perhaps, is how such an initially daunting land can prove so enticing – its vibrant mix of peoples, striking landscapes and city skylines, and rich musical, cinematic, and culinary heritage seduce almost every visitor in the end.

▲ Lincoln Memorial, Washington DC

And for all of its pride and bluster, the USA can be a land of quiet nuances: snow falling on a country lane in Vermont, cherry trees blooming under Washington memorials, alligators swimming through the bayou. You could easily plan a trip that focuses on the out-of-the-way hamlets, remote wilderness, eerie ghost towns, and forgotten byways that are every bit as "American" as its showpiece icons and monuments. Putting aside the sheer size of the place, deciding exactly what version of America you want to see may be the hardest decision of all.

For all of its pride and bluster, the USA can be a land of quiet nuances

Fact file

- The US government is divided into three branches: the executive, headed by the president; the legislative, which comprises the Senate and the House of Representatives; and the judicial, with the Supreme Court as its highest office.
- Despite New York's status as the cultural and economic center of the US, the federal capital is in Washington DC, which doesn't even rank among the top twenty cities in terms of population (though officially, it is a district, not a city).
- The population of the US (some 300 million) owns 200 million cars and trucks (roughly 1 vehicle for every 1.4 people), with more than 5.7 million miles of paved highway on which to drive them.
- With an area of 9.6 million square kilometers, the US is the third-largest country in the world (ranking behind Russia and Canada).
- The US is the only country that contains all six major climate zones: tropical humid, dry, mild mid-latitude, severe mid-latitude, polar, and highland.
- With its Aleutian Islands crossing the Greenwich Meridian, Alaska is technically home to both the easternmost and westernmost points in the US. Alaska also has the highest point in the US, Mount McKinley (20,320ft), and is the largest state by area (Rhode Island is the smallest).

Traveling through American history

To explore the United States is to explore its **history**. Some early European settlements, such as St Augustine, Florida, and Santa Fe, New Mexico, founded by the Spanish in 1565 and 1609 respectively, remain thriving to this day. Others, like Roanoke Island in North Carolina, home to Sir Walter Raleigh's ill-fated "Lost Colony" of 1585; Jamestown, Virginia, established in 1607; and Plimoth Plantation in Massachusetts, where the Pilgrims landed in 1620, are now preserved as fascinating living-history parks.

Other sites commemorate the two major conflicts fought on US soil: the Revolutionary War and the Civil War. Among Revolutionary landmarks are a plaque (and replica ship and museum) honoring 1773's legendary "Tea Party" in Boston, Massachusetts; Minute Man National Park in nearby Lexington, where the "shot heard 'round the world" was fired in 1775; and Philadelphia's Independence Hall, which hosted the signing of the Declaration of Independence in 1776. Civil War flashpoints scattered throughout the South, Capital, and mid-Atlantic regions include Harpers Ferry, West Virginia, site of John Brown's infamous (and ill-fated) raid in 1859; Fort Sumter, off Charleston, South Carolina, where the war's first shots were fired in 1861; and Gettysburg, Pennsylvania, scene, in 1863, of the bloodiest battle of all, as well as Abraham Lincoln's immortal address.

Pilgrims also flock to the scenes of tragedies that have shaped US history over the last century, like the spot in Dallas, Texas, where President John F. Kennedy was assassinated in 1963, and the motel (now a museum) in Memphis, Tennessee, where Dr Martin Luther King Jr was gunned down in 1968. The only two sites where the US has been attacked on its own soil receive throngs of visitors each year as well: Pearl Harbor, Hawaii, which was bombed on December 7, 1941, and Ground Zero, in New York City, where the World Trade Center stood before it was destroyed by terrorists on September 11, 2001.

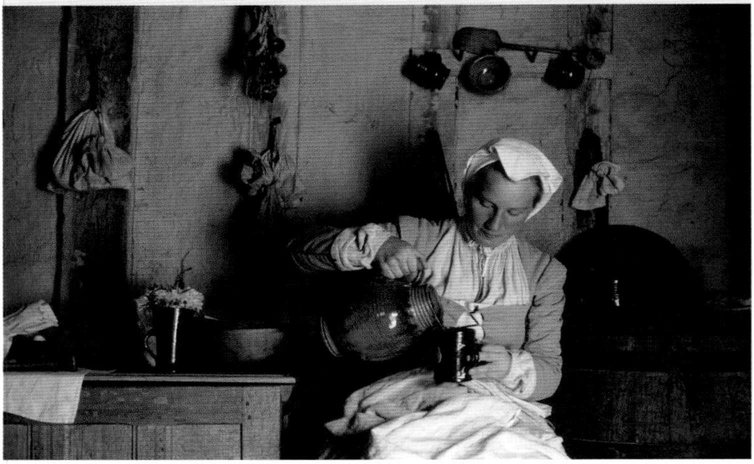

Where to go

▼ Brown bear, Katmai National Park, Alaska

Traveling in the United States is extremely easy; in a country where everyone seems to be forever on the move, there's rarely any problem finding a room for the night, and you can almost invariably depend on being able to eat well and inexpensively. The development of transportation has played a major role in the growth of the nation; the railroad opened the way for transcontinental migrations, while the automobile has been responsible for shaping most of the great cities. Your experience of the country will be very much flavored by how you choose to get around.

By far the best way to explore the country is to **drive your own vehicle**: it takes a long time before the sheer pleasure of cruising down the highway, with the radio blaring blues or country music, and the signs to Chicago, Memphis, or Monument Valley flashing past, begins to pall. Car rental is reasonable, and every main road is lined with budget motels charging around $60 per night for a good room.

We also give detailed **public transportation** options throughout; you can pretty much get to wherever you choose by a nationwide network of air, bus, and rail. However, if you do travel this way, there's a real temptation to see America as a succession of big **cities**. True enough, **New York** and **Los Angeles** have an exhilarating dynamism and excitement, and among their worthy rivals are **New Orleans**, the wonderfully decadent home of jazz, **Chicago**, a showcase of modern architecture, and **San Francisco**, on the beautiful Pacific bay. Few other cities – with the possible, and idiosyncratic, exception of **Las Vegas**, shimmering in the desert – can quite match this level of interest, however, and following a heavily urban itinerary will cut you off from the astonishing **landscapes** that make the USA truly distinctive. Especially in the vast open spaces of the West, the scenery is often breathtaking. The glacial splendor of **Yosemite**, the thermal wonderland of **Yellowstone**, the awesome red-rock **canyons** of Arizona and Utah, and the spectacular **Rocky Mountains** are among many of the treasures preserved and protected in the excellent national park system. Once you reach such wilderness, the potential for **hiking** and **camping** is magnificent – but it's usually essential to have a car to get near these spots.

There can be few places where strangers can feel so confident of a warm reception

Above all, travelers can enjoy the

The Wild West

Nowhere in the US is imbued with myth and history quite like the Wild West, much of which remains unchanged since the days of pioneers, prospectors, and, of course, "cowboys and Indians." In Lincoln, New Mexico, you can trace the footsteps of Billy the Kid; in Tombstone, Arizona, you can relive the gunfight at the OK Corral; and at Little Bighorn, Montana, you can climb the windswept hillside where General Custer made his "Last Stand." Colorado and California still abound with ghost towns abandoned when the gold and silver mines played out, while the great cattle drives are commemorated in Dodge City, Kansas, and Fort Worth, Texas. Above all, many Native Americans continue to inhabit their ancestral lands, especially in the Southwest, where the Hopi and the Ácomans survive in remote mesa-top villages, the Navajo ride through Monument Valley, and the Havasupai still farm alongside magical waterfalls deep in the Grand Canyon.

sheer thrill of experiencing American popular culture in the places where it began. Rock 'n' roll place-names spring to life; panoramas etched on our consciousness from a century of movies spread across the horizon; and road trips taken by your favorite literary characters are still there to be traveled.

For **music** fans, the chance to hear country music in Nashville or rhythm and blues in New Orleans, to shake it in a Mississippi jook-joint, or to visit Elvis's grave in Memphis, verges on a religious experience; readers brought up on the **books** of Mark Twain can ride a sternwheeler on the Mississippi; and **movie-goers** can live out their Wild West fantasies in the rugged Utah deserts.

The United States is all too often dismissed, even by its own inhabitants, as a land almost devoid of **history**. Though mainstream America tends to trace its roots back to the Pilgrims and Puritans of New England, the land itself has a longer history, stretching back way beyond the French culture of Louisiana and the Spanish presence in California to the majestic cliff palaces built by the Ancestral Puebloans in the Southwest a thousand years ago. There are also any number of fascinating strands to America's post-revolutionary history: relics of the Gold Rush in California, of the Civil Rights years in the South, or of the Civil War anywhere east of the Mississippi.

Though we've had to structure this book regionally, the most invigorating expeditions are those that take in more than one area. You do not, however, have to cross the entire continent from shore to shore in order to appreciate its amazing diversity, or to be impressed by the way in which such an extraordinary range of topography and people has been melded into one nation. It would take a long time to see the whole country, and the more time you spend on the road simply getting from place to place – no matter how enjoyable in itself that can be – the less time you'll have to savor the small-town pleasures and back-road oddities that may well provide your strongest memories. It will hit you early on that there is no such thing as a typical American person, any more than there is a typical American landscape, but there can be few places where strangers can feel so confident of a warm reception.

When to go

All US cities are pretty much year-round destinations (though Fairbanks, Alaska, in winter and Houston, Texas, in summer can be less than ideal), national parks and mountain ranges sometimes less so.

The US **climate** is characterized by wide variations, not just from region to region and season to season, but also day to day and hour to hour. Even setting aside far-flung Alaska and Hawaii, the main body of the US is subject to dramatically shifting weather patterns, most notably produced by westerly winds sweeping across the continent from the Pacific. As a general rule, however, temperatures tend to rise the further south you go, and to fall the higher you climb, while the climate along either coast is, on the whole, milder and more uniform than inland.

▲ Celebrating Mardi Gras, New Orleans

▲ Looking down on New York City from the Empire State Building

The **Northeast**, from Maine down to Washington DC, experiences relatively low precipitation as a rule, but temperatures can range from bitterly cold in winter to uncomfortably hot (made worse by humidity) in the short summer. Farther south, summers get warmer and longer. **Florida**'s air temperatures are not necessarily dramatically high in summer, being kept down by the proximity of the sea both east and west; in the winter, the state is warm and sunny enough to attract visitors from all over the country.

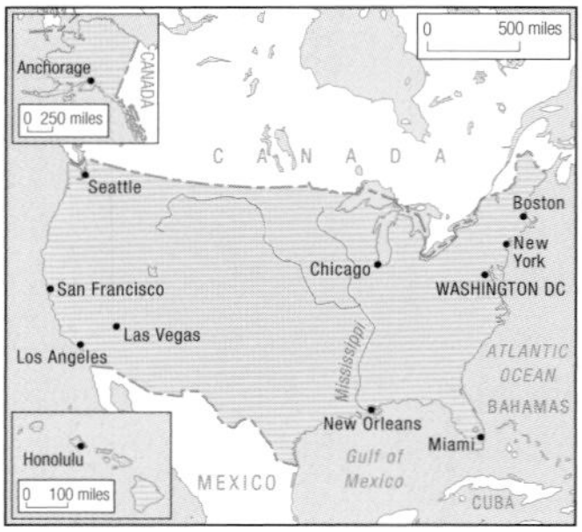

The **Great Plains**, which for climatic purposes can be said to extend from the Appalachians to the Rockies, are alternately exposed to icy Arctic winds streaming down from Canada and humid tropical airflows from the Caribbean and the Gulf of Mexico. Winters in the north, around the Great Lakes and Chicago, can be abjectly

Average temperature (°F) and rainfall

To convert °F to °C, subtract 32 and multiply by 5/9

	Jan	Feb	Mar	Apr	May	June	July	Aug	Sept	Oct	Nov	Dec
Anchorage												
av. max temp	19	27	33	44	54	62	65	64	57	43	30	20
av. min temp	5	9	13	27	36	44	49	47	39	29	15	6
days of rain	7	6	5	4	5	6	10	15	14	12	7	6
Chicago												
av. max temp	32	34	43	55	65	75	81	79	73	61	47	36
av. min temp	18	20	29	40	50	60	66	65	58	47	34	23
days of rain	11	10	12	11	12	11	9	9	9	9	10	11
Honolulu												
av. max temp	76	76	77	78	80	81	82	83	83	82	80	78
av. min temp	69	67	67	68	70	72	73	74	74	72	70	69
days of rain	14	11	13	12	11	12	14	13	13	13	13	15
Las Vegas												
av. max temp	60	67	72	81	89	99	103	102	95	84	71	61
av. min temp	29	34	39	45	52	61	68	66	57	47	36	30
days of rain	2	2	2	1	1	1	2	2	1	1	1	2
Los Angeles												
av. max temp	65	66	67	70	72	76	81	82	81	76	73	67
av. min temp	46	47	48	50	53	56	60	60	58	54	50	47
days of rain	6	6	6	4	2	1	0	0	1	2	3	6
Miami												
av. max temp	74	75	78	80	84	86	88	88	87	83	78	76
av. min temp	61	61	64	67	71	74	76	76	75	72	66	62
days of rain	9	6	7	7	12	13	15	15	18	16	10	7
New Orleans												
av. max temp	62	65	71	77	83	88	90	90	86	79	70	64
av. min temp	47	50	55	61	68	74	76	76	73	64	55	48
days of rain	10	12	9	7	8	13	15	14	10	7	7	10
New York City												
av. max temp	37	38	45	57	68	77	82	80	79	69	51	41
av. min temp	24	24	30	42	53	60	66	66	60	49	37	29
days of rain	12	10	12	11	11	10	12	10	9	9	9	10
San Francisco												
av. max temp	55	59	61	62	63	66	65	65	69	68	63	57
av. min temp	45	47	48	49	51	52	53	53	55	54	51	47
days of rain	11	11	10	6	4	2	0	0	2	4	7	10
Seattle												
av. max temp	45	48	52	58	64	69	72	73	67	59	51	47
av. min temp	36	37	39	43	47	52	54	55	52	47	41	38
days of rain	18	16	16	13	12	9	4	5	8	13	17	19
Washington DC												
av. max temp	42	44	53	64	75	83	87	84	78	67	55	45
av. min temp	27	28	35	44	54	63	68	66	58	48	38	29
days of rain	11	10	12	11	12	11	11	11	8	8	9	10

cold, with driving winds and freezing rain. It can freeze or even snow in winter as far south as the Gulf of Mexico, though spring and fall get progressively longer and milder farther south through the Plains. Summer is much the wettest season in the **South** as a whole, the time when thunderstorms are most likely to strike. One or two hurricanes each year rage across Florida and/or the Southeast, from obscure origins in the Gulf of Mexico on the way to extinction out in the Atlantic. Tornadoes (or "twisters") are usually a much more local phenomenon, tending to cut a narrow swath of destruction in the wake of violent spring or summer thunderstorms. Average rainfall dwindles to lower and lower levels the further west you head across the Plains.

Temperatures in the **Rockies** correlate closely with altitude; beyond the mountains in the south lie the extensive arid and inhospitable deserts of the **Southwest**. Much of this area is within the rain shadow of the California ranges. In cities such as Las Vegas and Phoenix, the mercury regularly soars above 100°F, though the atmosphere is not usually humid enough to be as enervating as that might sound.

West of the barrier of the Cascade Mountains, the fertile **Pacific Northwest** is the only region of the country where winter is the wettest season, and throughout the year the European-style climate is wet, mild, and seldom hot. **California** weather more or less lives up to the popular idyllic image, though the climate is markedly hotter and drier in the south than in the north, where there's enough snow to make the mountains a major skiing destination. San Francisco is kept milder and colder than the surrounding district by the propensity of the Bay Area to attract sea fog, while the Los Angeles basin is prone to filling up with smog, as fog and pollution become trapped beneath a layer of warm air.

32

things not to miss

It's not possible to see everything that the USA has to offer in one trip – and we don't suggest you try. What follows is a selective and subjective taste of the country's highlights: unforgettable cities, spectacular drives, magnificent parks, spirited celebrations, and stunning natural phenomena. They're arranged in five color-coded categories to help you find the very best things to see, do, and experience. All highlights have a page reference to take you straight into the Guide, where you can find out more.

01 **Monument Valley, AZ** Page **905** • Massive sandstone monoliths stand sentinel in this iconic southwestern landscape.

02 Going to a baseball game Pages **200 & 332** • America's summer pastime is a treat to watch wherever you are, from Chicago's ivy-clad Wrigley Field to Boston's Fenway Park, the oldest in the country.

03 Pike Place Market, Seattle, WA Page **1082** • Piled high with salmon, lobster, clams, and crab, the oldest public market in the nation is also home to some great seafood restaurants.

04 Savannah, GA Page **492** • Mint juleps on wide verandas, horse-drawn carriages on cobbled streets, and lush foliage draped with Spanish moss; this historic cotton port remains the South's loveliest town.

05 Mardi Gras, New Orleans, LA Page **648** • Crazy, colorful, debauched, and historic – this is the carnival to end them all.

06 Yellowstone National Park, WY Page **812** • The national park that started it all has it all, from steaming fluorescent hot springs and spouting geysers to sheer canyons and meadows filled with wildflowers and assorted grazing beasts.

07 Rock and Roll Hall of Fame, OH Page **281** • Housed inside this striking glass pyramid is an unparalleled collection of rock music's finest mementos, recordings, films, and exhibitions.

08 Walt Disney World, Orlando, FL Page **597** • Though each of Orlando's theme parks strives to outdo the rest, Walt Disney World remains the one to beat.

09 Aurora borealis, AK Page **1167** • Winter visitors to Alaska just might see the skies ablaze with the shimmering veils of the Northern Lights.

11 American food **See *American food* color section** • From cheese steaks in Philadelphia and thin-crust pizza in New York, to Cajun crawfish in Louisiana and Texas barbecues, sampling food is the best way to get a feel for the USA.

10 Chicago's modern architecture, IL
Page **319** • The history of modern architecture is writ large on Chicago's skyline, site of the world's first skyscraper.

12 Niagara Falls, NY Page **139** • The sheer power of Niagara Falls is even more overwhelming when seen from below, aboard the Maid of the Mist.

13 Crazy Horse Memorial, SD Page **758** • A staggering monument to the revered Sioux leader, this colossal statue continues to be etched into the Black Hills of South Dakota.

14 Burning Man Page **943** • Every summer a temporary community takes life in the middle of the Nevada desert and hosts an art and music festival wholly unlike any other.

15 Swamps Pages **615** & **659** • From the steamy Everglades of Florida to the ghostly bayous of Louisiana's Cajun country, America's swamplands are hauntingly beautiful.

16 Sweet Auburn, Atlanta, GA Page **485** • This historic district holds the birthplace of Dr Martin Luther King Jr, the Center for Nonviolent Social Change, and other spots honoring King's legacy.

17 Graceland, Memphis, TN Page **516** • Pilgrims from all over the world pay homage to the King by visiting his gravesite and endearingly modest home.

18 Skiing in the Rocky Mountains Pages **789, 802 & 841** • The Rockies make for some of the best skiing anywhere, with their glitzy resorts and atmospheric mining towns.

19 Ancestral Puebloan sites Page **861** • Scattered through desert landscapes like Colorado's magnificent Mesa Verde National Park, the dwellings of the Ancestral Puebloans afford glimpses of an ancient and mysterious world.

20 The National Mall, Washington DC Page **377** • From the Lincoln Memorial to the US Capitol by way of the towering Washington Monument – the National Mall is an awesome showcase of American culture and history.

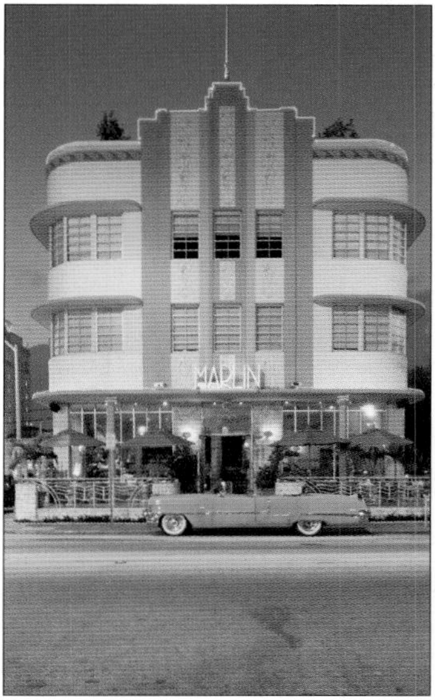

22 Miami's Art Deco, FL Page **562** • This flamboyant city is deservedly famed for the colorful pastel architecture of its restored South Beach district.

21 Hiking in the Grand Canyon Page **895** • Explore the innermost secrets of this wondrous spot on many of its superb hiking trails at the heart of California's best-loved park.

23 Las Vegas, NV Page **931** • From the Strip's erupting volcanoes, Eiffel Tower, and Egyptian pyramid to its many casinos, Las Vegas will blow your mind as well as your wallet.

24 Glacier National Park, MT

Page **836** • Montana's loveliest park holds not only fifty glaciers, but also two thousand lakes, a thousand miles of rivers, and the exhilarating Going-to-the-Sun road.

25 South by Southwest, TX

Page **688** • This thriving ten-day music festival in Austin is one of the nation's best and plays hosts to bands from around the world – and Texas, too.

26 Hawaii's volcanoes

Page **1185** • Hawaii's Big Island grows bigger by the minute, as the world's most active volcano pours molten lava into the ocean.

27 Driving Highway 1 Page **1017** • The rugged Big Sur coastline, pounded by Pacific waves, makes an exhilarating route between San Francisco and LA.

28 New England in the fall Page **181** • The Northeast's breathtaking fall foliage presents an ever-changing palette of color and light.

29 Yosemite Valley, CA Page **1009** • Enclosed by near-vertical, mile-high cliffs, and laced with hiking trails and climbing routes, the dramatic geology of Yosemite Valley is at the heart of California's best-loved park.

30 San Francisco, CA Page **1024** • Enchanting, fog-bound San Francisco remains bohemian and individualistic at heart.

31 **Rodeos** Page **805** • Relive the Old West with cowboys and cowgirls at rodeos like Cheyenne Frontier Days and countless smaller ones.

32 **New York City** Page **69** • With world-class museums, restaurants, nightlife, and shops aplenty, the Big Apple is in a league of its own.

Basics

Basics

Getting there

Anyone traveling to the US from abroad should start by deciding which area to explore first; the country is so vast that it makes a huge difference which airport you fly into. Once you've chosen whether to hit the swamps of Florida, the frozen tundra of Alaska, the summer heat of the South, or the splendor of the Rockies and Southwest, you can then buy a flight to the nearest hub city.

In general, ticket prices are highest from July to September, and around Easter and Christmas. Fares drop during the shoulder seasons – April to June, and October – and even more so in low season, from November to March (excluding Easter, Christmas, and New Year). Prices depend more on when Americans want to head overseas than on the demand from foreign visitors. Flying on weekends usually costs significantly more; prices quoted below assume midweek travel.

Flights from the UK and Ireland

More than twenty US cities are accessible by **nonstop** flights from the **UK**. At these gateway cities, you can connect with onward domestic flights. **Direct** services (which may land once or twice on the way, but are called direct if they keep the same flight number throughout their journey) fly from Britain to nearly every other major US city.

Nonstop flights to Los Angeles from London take eleven or twelve hours; the London–Miami flight takes eight hours; and flying time to New York is seven or so hours. Following winds ensure that return flights take an hour or two less. One-stop direct flights to destinations beyond the East Coast add time to the journey, but can work out cheaper than nonstop flights. They can even save you time, because customs and immigration are cleared on first touchdown into the US rather than the final destination, which may be a busy international gateway.

Four airlines run nonstop scheduled services to the US from **Ireland**. Flights depart from both Dublin and Shannon airports, and the journey times are very similar to those from London.

As for **fares**, Britain remains one of the best places in Europe to obtain flight bargains, though prices vary widely. In low or shoulder season, you should be able to find a return flight to East Coast destinations such as New York for under £300, or to California for under £400, while high-season rates can easily double. Things may change if, as repeatedly rumoured, a budget airline such as Ryanair starts low-cost services to the US from London Stansted.

With an **open-jaw** ticket, you can fly into one city and out of another. Remember to check whether there is a high drop-off fee for returning a rental car in a different state from the one where you picked it up (see p.35). An air pass can be a good idea if you want to see a lot of the country. These are available only to non-US residents, and must be bought before reaching the US (see p.34).

Nonstop flights

From London (Heathrow or Gatwick)

Atlanta BMI, British Airways, Delta
Boston American Airlines, British Airways, Virgin Atlantic
Charlotte BMI, US Airways
Chicago Air India, American Airlines, British Airways, United, Virgin Atlantic
Cincinnati Delta
Dallas/Fort Worth American Airlines, British Airways
Denver British Airways
Detroit Northwest
Houston British Airways, Continental
Las Vegas Virgin Atlantic
Los Angeles Air New Zealand, American Airlines, British Airways, United, Virgin Atlantic
Miami American Airlines, British Airways, Virgin Atlantic

Minneapolis Northwest
New York Air France, Air India, American Airlines, British Airways, Delta, Kuwait Airways, Virgin Atlantic
Orlando British Airways, Virgin Atlantic
Philadelphia BMI, British Airways, US Airways
Phoenix British Airways
Raleigh/Durham American Airlines
San Francisco British Airways, United, Virgin Atlantic
Seattle British Airways
Washington DC British Airways, United, Virgin Atlantic

From Manchester

Atlanta Delta
Chicago American Airlines, British Airways
New York Continental, Delta
Orlando Virgin Atlantic
Philadelphia US Airways

From Edinburgh

New York Delta

From Glasgow

New York Continental
Orlando Virgin Atlantic
Philadelphia US Airways

From Dublin/Shannon

Atlanta Delta
Boston Aer Lingus
Chicago Aer Lingus, American Airlines
New York Aer Lingus, Continental, Delta
Orlando Aer Lingus
Washington Aer Lingus

Flights from Australia, New Zealand, and South Africa

If you're traveling from Australasia to the US, the most expensive time to fly is during the northern summer (mid-May to end Aug) and over the Christmas period (Dec to mid-Jan);

Six steps to a better kind of travel

At Rough Guides we are passionately committed to travel. We feel strongly that only through travelling do we truly come to understand the world we live in and the people we share it with – plus tourism has brought a great deal of benefit to developing economies around the world over the last few decades. But the extraordinary growth in tourism has also damaged some places irreparably, and of course climate change is exacerbated by most forms of transport, especially flying. This means that now more than ever it's important to travel thoughtfully and responsibly, with respect for the cultures you're visiting – not only to derive the most benefit from your trip but also in order to preserve the best bits of the planet for everyone to enjoy. At Rough Guides we feel there are six main areas in which you can make a difference:

- Consider what you're contributing to the local economy, and indeed how much the services you use do the same, whether it's through employing local workers and guides or sourcing locally grown produce and local services.
- Consider the environment on holiday as well as at home. Water is scarce in many developing destinations, and the biodiversity of local flora and fauna can be adversely affected by tourism. Patronise businesses that take account of this rather than those that trash the local environment for short-term gain.
- Give thought to how often you fly and what you can do to redress any harm that your trips create. Reduce the amount you travel by air; avoid short hops by air and more harmful night flights.
- Consider alternatives to flying, travelling instead by bus, train, boat and even by bike or on foot where possible. Take time to enjoy the journey itself as well as your final destination.
- Think about making all the trips you take "climate neutral" via a reputable carbon offset scheme. All Rough Guide flights are offset, and every year we donate money to a variety of charities devoted to combating the effects of climate change.
- Travel with a purpose, not just to tick off experiences. Consider spending longer in a place, and really getting to know it and its people – you'll find it much more rewarding than dashing from place to place.

shoulder seasons cover March to mid-May and September, while the rest of the year is low season.

Los Angeles is the main US gateway airport for flights from **Australia**: in low season, the regular Air New Zealand, Qantas, and United flights cost around Aus$1800 from the eastern states, or Aus$2100 from Western Australia, including tax; flying all the way through to New York can cost little extra. During peak season, however, fares to the US West Coast start at more like Aus$2250, and to New York at Aus$2750.

From **New Zealand**, fares from Auckland or Christchurch to LA or San Francisco start at around NZ$2000 in low season, and range closer to NZ$3000 for a flight to New York in summer.

Various add-on fares and air passes valid in the continental US are available with your main ticket, allowing you to fly to destinations across the States. These must be bought before you go.

Airlines, agents and operators

Online booking

Ⓦ **www.expedia.co.uk** (in UK), Ⓦ **www.expedia.com** (in US)
Ⓦ **www.expedia.ca** (in Canada)
Ⓦ **www.lastminute.com** (in UK)
Ⓦ **www.opodo.co.uk** (in UK)
Ⓦ **www.orbitz.com** (in US)
Ⓦ **www.travelocity.co.uk** (in UK), Ⓦ **www.travelocity.com** (in US), Ⓦ **www.travelocity.ca** (in Canada)
Ⓦ **www.travelonline.co.za** (in South Africa)
Ⓦ **www.zuji.com.au** (in Australia), Ⓦ **www.travelocity.co.nz** (in New Zealand)

Packages and tours

Although you can often do things cheaper independently, countless flight and accommodation **packages** to all the major American cities allow you to leave the organizational hassles to someone else. Drawbacks include the loss of flexibility and the fact that you'll probably have to stay in relatively expensive hotels. A typical package might be a round-trip flight plus mid-range Midtown hotel accommodation for three nights in New York City, starting at around £550 per person in low season and more like £800 at peak periods. Pre-booked accommodation schemes, where you buy vouchers for use in a specific group of hotels as you travel around, are not normally good value.

Fly-drive deals, which give cut-rate (sometimes free) car rental when a traveler buys a transatlantic ticket from an airline or tour operator, are always cheaper than renting on the spot, and give great value if you intend to do a lot of driving. They're readily available through general online booking agents such as Expedia and Travelocity, as well as through specific airlines.

Several of the operators listed here go one stage further and book accommodation for **self-drive tours**; some travelers consider having their itineraries planned and booked by experts to be a real boon. Bon Voyage, for example, arranges tailor-made packages in the Southwest; the cost of twelve nights in Arizona, Utah, and Nevada, flying into Las Vegas and out from Phoenix, and staying in standard hotels, starts at around £1100 per person.

A simple and exciting way to see a chunk of America's great outdoors, without being hassled by too many practical considerations, is to take a specialist touring and **adventure package**, which includes transportation, accommodation, food, and a guide. Companies such as TrekAmerica carry small groups around on minibuses and use a combination of budget hotels and camping. Most concentrate on the West – ranging from Arizona to Alaska, and lasting from seven days to five weeks; cross-country treks and Eastern adventures that take in New York or Florida are also available. Typical rates for a week– excluding transatlantic flights – range from £580 in low season up to £850 in midsummer. Trips to Alaska cost a good bit more. For another touring and adventure package option, see the box on Green Tortoise, p.33.

Airlines

Aer Lingus ⓦ www.aerlingus.com
Air Canada ⓦ www.aircanada.com
Air France ⓦ www.airfrance.com
Air India ⓦ www.airindia.com
Air New Zealand ⓦ www.airnewzealand.com
Air Pacific ⓦ www.airpacific.com
Airtran ⓦ www.airtran.com
Alaska Airlines ⓦ www.alaskaair.com
Alitalia ⓦ www.alitalia.com
America West ⓦ www.usairways.com
American Airlines ⓦ www.aa.com
BMI ⓦ www.flybmi.com
British Airways ⓦ www.britishairways.com
Continental Airlines ⓦ www.continental.com
Delta Airlines ⓦ www.delta.com
Frontier Airlines ⓦ www.frontierairlines.com
Great Lakes Airlines ⓦ www.greatlakesav.com
Hawaiian Airlines ⓦ www.hawaiianair.com
Horizon Airlines ⓦ www.horizonair.com
JetBlue ⓦ www.jetblue.com
KLM ⓦ www.klm.com
Lufthansa ⓦ www.lufthansa.com
Malaysia Airlines ⓦ www.malaysiaairlines.com
Mesa Airlines ⓦ www.mesa-air.com
Mexicana ⓦ www.mexicana.com
Midwest Airlines ⓦ www.midwestairlines.com
Northwest ⓦ www.nwa.com
Qantas ⓦ www.qantas.com.au
SAS ⓦ www.flysas.com
Scenic Airlines ⓦ www.scenic.com
Skywest ⓦ www.skywest.com
Southwest ⓦ www.southwest.com
Swiss ⓦ www.swiss.com
United Airlines ⓦ www.united.com
US Airways ⓦ www.usairways.com
Virgin Atlantic ⓦ www.virgin-atlantic.com

Agents and operators

Adventure World Australia ⓣ 1300/363 055, ⓦ www.adventureworld.com.au, New Zealand ⓣ 09/524 5118, ⓦ www.adventureworld.co.nz
American Holidays Northern Ireland ⓣ 028/9031 0000, Republic of Ireland ⓣ 01/673 3840 ⓦ www.american-holidays.com
Bon Voyage UK ⓣ 0800/435 282, ⓦ www.bon-voyage.co.uk
British Airways Holidays ⓦ www.baholidays.co.uk
Exodus UK ⓣ 0845/863 9600, ⓦ www.exodus.co.uk
Explore Worldwide UK ⓣ 0845/013 1537, ⓦ www.explore.co.uk
Jetsave UK ⓣ 0871/2312 295, ⓦ www.jetsave.com
North America Travel Service UK ⓣ 0207/569 6710, ⓦ www.northamericatravelservice.co.uk
North South Travel UK ⓣ 01245/608 291,

ⓦ www.northsouthtravel.co.uk.
Titan HiTours UK ⓣ 0800/988 5823, ⓦ www.titantravel.co.uk
travel.com.au Australia ⓣ 1300/130 482, ⓦ www.travel.com.au
Travelsphere UK ⓣ 0870/240 2426, ⓦ www.travelsphere.co.uk
TrekAmerica UK ⓣ 0870/444-8735, ⓦ www.trekamerica.co.uk

Rail and bus contacts

Amtrak US ⓣ 1-800/872-7245, ⓦ www.amtrak.com.
Green Tortoise US ⓣ 1/800-867-8647, ⓦ www.greentortoise.com.
Greyhound US ⓣ 1/800-231-2222, ⓦ www.greyhound.com.
Peter Pan US ⓣ 1/800/343-9999, ⓦ www.peterpanbus.com.
STA Travel US ⓣ 1-800/781-4040, ⓦ www.statravel.com; UK ⓣ 0871/2300 040, ⓦ www.statravel.co.uk.

Getting around

Distances in the US are so great that it's essential to plan in advance how you'll get from place to place. Amtrak provides a skeletal but often scenic rail service, and there are usually good bus links between the major cities. Even in rural areas, by advance planning, you can usually reach the main points of interest without too much trouble by using local buses and charter services.

That said, travel between cities is almost always easier if you have a **car**. Many worthwhile and memorable US destinations are far from the cities: even if a bus or train can take you to the general vicinity of one of the great national parks, for example, it would be of little use when it comes to enjoying the great outdoors.

By rail

Traveling by **rail** is rarely the fastest way to get around, though if you have the time it can be a pleasant and relaxing experience. As you will see from our map, on p.32, the Amtrak system isn't comprehensive – East Coast states from Virginia northward are well-covered with rail routes, but some Western states are left out altogether. What's more, the cross-country routes tend to be served by one or at most two trains per day, so in large areas of the nation the only train of the day passes through at three or four in the morning. A number of small local train services connect stops on the Amtrak lines with towns and cities not on the main grid. Amtrak also runs the coordinated, but still limited, Thruway bus service that connects some cities that their trains don't reach.

For any one specific journey, the train can be more **expensive** than taking a Greyhound bus, or even a plane – the

Historic railroads

While Amtrak has a monopoly on long-distance rail travel, a number of historic or **scenic railways**, some steam-powered or running along narrow-gauge mining tracks, bring back the glory days of train travel. Many are purely tourist attractions, doing a full circuit through beautiful countryside in two or three hours, though some can drop you off in otherwise hard-to-reach wilderness areas. Fares vary widely according to the length of your trip. We've covered the most appealing options in the relevant guide chapters.

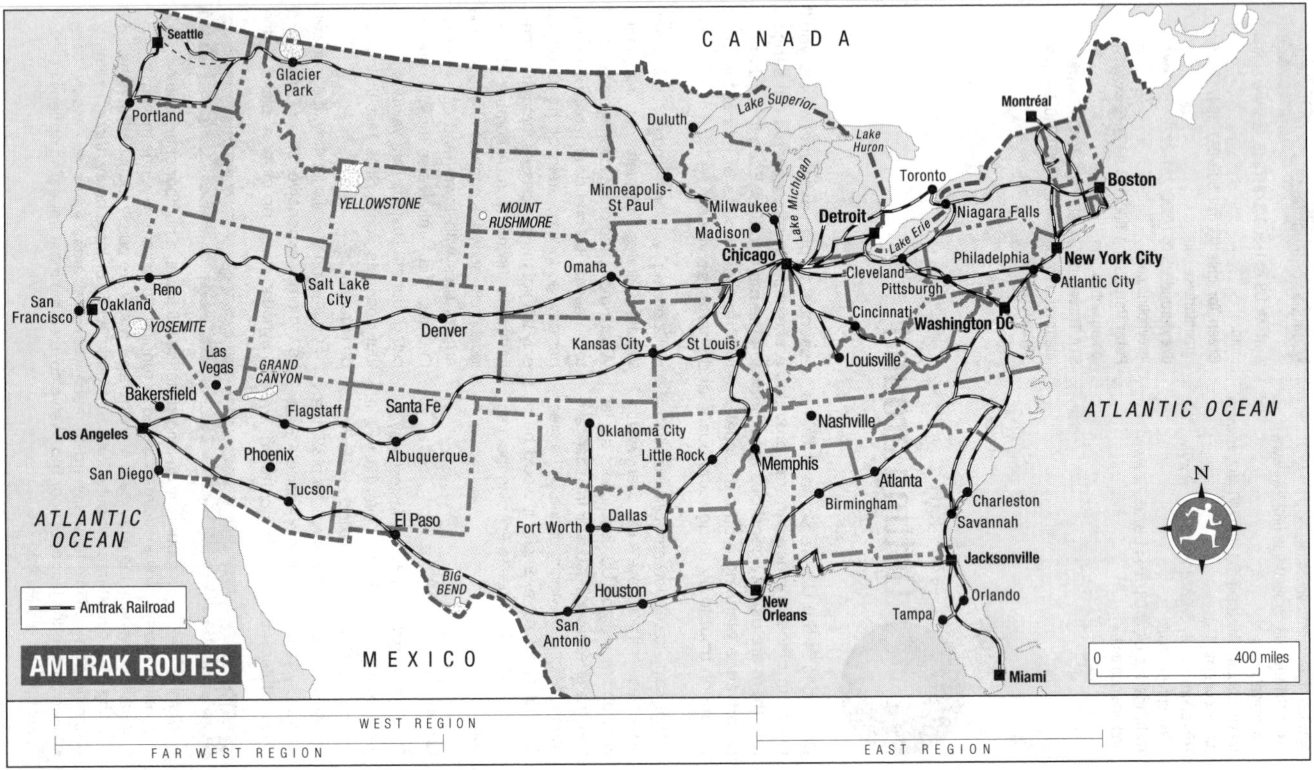
AMTRAK ROUTES
Amtrak Railroad
CANADA
MEXICO
ATLANTIC OCEAN
ATLANTIC OCEAN
N
0
400 miles
Seattle
Portland
Glacier Park
Duluth
Lake Superior
Lake Huron
Lake Michigan
Lake Erie
Montréal
Boston
Toronto
Niagara Falls
New York City
Atlantic City
Philadelphia
Detroit
Minneapolis-St Paul
Milwaukee
Madison
Chicago
Cleveland
Pittsburgh
Cincinnati
Washington DC
Louisville
YELLOWSTONE
MOUNT RUSHMORE
San Francisco
Oakland
Reno
Salt Lake City
Omaha
Denver
YOSEMITE
Kansas City
St Louis
Las Vegas
GRAND CANYON
Bakersfield
Flagstaff
Santa Fe
Nashville
Los Angeles
Oklahoma City
Phoenix
Albuquerque
Little Rock
Memphis
San Diego
Tucson
Atlanta
Birmingham
Charleston
Savannah
Dallas
Fort Worth
El Paso
Jacksonville
BIG BEND
Houston
New Orleans
Orlando
Tampa
San Antonio
Miami
WEST REGION
FAR WEST REGION
EAST REGION

Green Tortoise

One alternative to long-distance bus torture is the fun, countercultural **Green Tortoise**, whose buses, complete with foam cushions, bunks, fridges, and rock music, mostly ply the West and the Northwest of the country, but can go as far as New Orleans, Washington DC and New York. Highlights include a national park loop (16 days; $1060), the coast-to-coast USA Explorer (34 days; $1790), and a gung-ho, month-long Alaska Expedition (27 days; $1730); all prices include food and park admissions. There are more than 30 seductive options, each allowing plenty of stops for hiking, river-rafting, bathing in hot springs and the like.

Green Tortoise's main office is at 494 Broadway, San Francisco, CA 94133 (Ⓣ415/956-7500 or 1-800/867-8647, Ⓦwww.greentortoise.com).

standard rail fare from New York to Los Angeles, for example, is around $230 single – though special deals, especially in the off-peak seasons (Sept–May, excluding Christmas), bring the cost of a coast-to-coast round-trip to around $370. **Booking online** can also yield bargains, and there are also two categories of money-saving passes available. Fifteen-, thirty-, and 45-day **USA Rail Passes** allow travel across the entire continent, for $389–749, depending on length of pass, while the **California Rail Pass** buys you seven days' travel in a 21-day period for $159.

Even with a pass, you should always **reserve** as far in advance as possible; all passengers must have seats, and some trains, especially between major East Coast cities, are booked solid. Sleeping compartments start at around $300 per night, including three full meals, in addition to your seat fare, for one or two people, and private bedrooms cost $800 more. However, even standard Amtrak quarters are surprisingly spacious compared to airplane seats, and there are additional dining cars and lounge cars (with full bars and sometimes glass-domed 360° viewing compartments). Finally, if you want to make your journey in a hurry, hop aboard the speedy Acela service in the Northeast, which can shave anywhere from thirty minutes to an hour off your trip, though tends to cost from $25–100 more than a fare on a standard Amtrak train.

Beautiful East Coast Amtrak trips include the Hudson River Valley north of New York City (on several routes); along the Potomac River at Harpers Ferry, West Virginia (on the *Capitol Limited* out of Washington DC); and the New River Gorge (on the *Cardinal*). In the West, the *California Zephyr*, which runs between Chicago and San Francisco, follows a stunning route west of Denver over the Rockies, rivaled a day later by the towering Sierra Nevada, and the *Coast Starlight* gives unsurpassed views of the California coast and Northwest mountains on its journey between Seattle and Los Angeles. Confirm when you book your journey that the train in question passes through the scenic splendor during daylight hours.

By bus

If you're traveling on your own and plan on making a lot of stops, **buses**, by far the cheapest way to get around, make sense. The main long-distance operator, **Greyhound** (Ⓣ1-800/231-2222, Ⓦwww.greyhound.com, international customers without toll-free access can also call Ⓣ214/849-8100 from 5am–1am CST), links all major cities and many towns. Out in the country, buses are fairly scarce, sometimes appearing only once a day, if at all. However, along the main highways, buses run around the clock to a full timetable, stopping only for meal breaks (almost always fast-food chains) and driver changeovers.

To avoid possible hassle, travelers should take care to sit as near to the driver as possible, and to arrive during daylight hours – many bus stations are in dodgy areas. It used to be that any sizeable community would have a Greyhound station; now, in some places, the post office or a gas station doubles as the

Pre-trip planning for overseas travelers

Amtrak USA Rail Passes

USA Rail Passes (15-day/$389, 30-day/$579, 45-day/$749) cover the areas shown on the map on p.4. Passes can be bought from the Amtrak website (Ⓦwww.amtrak.com).

Greyhound Discovery Passes

Foreign visitors, especially those inclined to venture beyond the major destinations, can buy a **Greyhound Discovery Pass** either online (give yourself at least 14 days before you leave home) or at any of the major Greyhound terminals and agencies in the States. The pass offers unlimited travel within a set time period. A seven-day pass costs $329; a fifteen-day pass $483; thirty days $607; and sixty days $750. No daily extensions are available.

Each time you travel, you'll need to present your pass at the ticket counter to receive a boarding ticket. For more information go to Ⓦwww.greyhound.com.

Air passes

The main American airlines offer **air passes** for visitors who plan to fly a lot within the US. These must be bought in advance, and are often sold with the proviso that you cross the Atlantic with the same airline or group of airlines (such as One World Alliance). Each deal will involve the purchase of a certain number of flights, air miles, or coupons. Other plans entitle foreign travelers to **discounts** on regular US domestic fares, again with the proviso that you buy the ticket before you leave home. Check with the individual airlines to see what they offer and the overall range of prices. However you do it, flying within the US is only a wise choice for travel in regions where fares are low anyway; flights within Florida, for example, are very expensive.

bus stop and ticket office, and in many others the bus service has been canceled altogether. Reservations, which can be made in person at the station, online, or on the toll-free number, are not essential, but recommended – if a bus is full, and you don't have a reservation, you may be forced to wait until the next one, sometimes overnight or longer.

Fares on shorter journeys average out at about 25¢ per mile, but for longer hauls there are plenty of savings available. Check the website's discounts page. Buying your ticket even a few days in advance of travel will save money, as will traveling between Monday and Thursday. For long-haul travel though, considering the time expended (around 65 hours coast-to-coast, if you eat and sleep on the bus) and the steep price of gas (built into the bus fare), riding the bus is not necessarily a much better deal than flying, unless you plan to make a lot of stops using a Discovery Pass (see above).

By plane

Despite the presence of good-value discount airlines – namely Southwest and JetBlue – airplane travel is a much less appealing way of getting around the country than it used to be. With air fuel costs escalating even faster than gasoline costs, and airlines cutting routes, demanding customers pay for routine services, and jacking up prices across the board, the days of using jet travel as a spur to vacation adventuring are long gone. To get any kind of break on price, you'll have to reserve well ahead of time (at least three weeks), preferably not embark in the high season, and be firm in your plans in buying a "non-refundable" fare – which if changed can incur costs of $100 or more.

Nonetheless, if you arrange your trip properly, flying can still cost less than the train – especially if you take into account how much you save not paying for food and drink while on the move – though a bit more

Driving for foreigners

Foreign nationals from English-speaking countries can drive in the US using their **full domestic driving licenses.** (International Driving Permits are not always regarded as sufficient.) Fly-drive deals are good value if you want to **rent** a car (see below), though you can save up to fifty percent simply by booking in advance with a major firm. If you choose not to pay until you arrive, be sure you take a written confirmation of the price with you. Remember that it's safer not to drive right after a long transatlantic flight – and that most standard rental cars have **automatic transmissions.**

than the bus. In those examples where flying can make sense for short local hops, we mention such options wherever appropriate throughout this guide. Otherwise, phone the airlines or visit their websites to find out routes and schedules.

By car

For many, the concept of cruising down the highway, preferably in a convertible with the radio blasting, is one of the main reasons to set out on a tour of the US. The romantic images of countless road movies are not far from the truth, though you don't have to embark on a wild spree of drinking, drugs, and sex to enjoy **driving** across America. Apart from anything else, a car makes it possible to choose your own itinerary and to explore the astonishing wide-open landscapes that may well provide your most enduring memories of the country.

Driving in the cities, on the other hand, is not exactly fun, and can be hair-raising. Yet in the larger places a car is by far the most convenient way to make your way around, especially as public transportation tends to be spotty outside the major cities. Many urban areas, especially in the west, have grown up since cars were invented. As such, they sprawl for so many miles in all directions – Los Angeles and Houston are classic examples – that your hotel may be fifteen or twenty miles from the sights you came to see, or perhaps simply on the other side of a freeway that can't be crossed on foot. In some centralized cities – mostly in the Northeast, plus Chicago, San Francisco, Portland and Seattle – the main attractions and facilities are concentrated within walking distance of each other.

To **rent a car**, you must have held your license for at least one year. Drivers under 25 may encounter problems and have to pay higher than normal insurance premiums. Rental companies expect customers to have a credit card; if you don't, they may let you leave a cash deposit (at least $200), but don't count on it. All the major **rental companies** have outlets at the main airports. Reservations are handled centrally, so the best way to shop around is either online, or by calling their national toll-free numbers. Potential variations are endless; certain cities and states are consistently cheaper than others, while individual travelers may be eligible for corporate, frequent-flier, or AAA discounts. In low season you may find a tiny car (a "subcompact") for as little as $150 per week, but a typical budget rate would be more like $40 per day or $200 per week including taxes.

You can get some good deals from strictly local operators, though it can be risky as well. Make reading up on such inexpensive vendors part of your pre-trip planning. Even between the major operators – who tend to charge $50–150 per week more than the local competition – there can be a big difference in the quality of cars. Industry leaders like Alamo, Hertz, and Avis tend to have newer, lower-mileage cars, often with air-conditioning and stereo CD players as standard – no small consideration on a thousand-mile desert drive. Always be sure to get **unlimited mileage**, and remember that leaving the car in a

Hitchhiking

Hitchhiking in the United States is a **bad idea**, making you a potential victim both inside (you never know whom you're traveling with) and outside the car, as the odd fatality may occur from hitchers getting a little too close to the highway lanes. At a minimum, in the many states where the practice is illegal, you can expect a steep fine from the police and, on occasion, an overnight stay in the local jail.

different city to the one where you rented it can incur a drop-off charge of $200 or more.

When you rent a car, read the small print carefully for details on **Collision Damage Waiver** (CDW), sometimes called **Liability Damage Waiver** (LDW). This form of insurance specifically covers the car that you are driving yourself – you are in any case insured for damage to other vehicles. At $12–20 a day, it can add substantially to the total cost, but without it you're liable for every scratch to the car – even those that aren't your fault. Increasing numbers of states are requiring that this insurance be included in the weekly rental rate and are regulating the amounts charged to cut down on rental-car company profiteering. Some credit card companies offer automatic CDW coverage to customers using their card; contact your issuing company for details.

The **American Automobile Association**, or AAA (ⓣ1-800/222-4357; ⓦwww.aaa.com), provides free maps and assistance to its members and to members of affiliated associations overseas, such as the British AA and RAC. If you **break down** in a rented car, call one of these services if you have towing coverage, or the emergency number pinned to the dashboard.

Car rental agencies

Alamo US ⓣ1-800/GO-ALAMO, ⓦwww.alamo.com

Avis US ⓣ1-800/230-4898, ⓦwww.avis.com

Budget US ⓣ1-800/527-0700, ⓦwww.budget.com
Dollar US ⓣ1-800/800-3665, ⓦwww.dollar.com.
Enterprise Rent-a-Car US ⓣ1-800/261-7331, ⓦwww.enterprise.com
Hertz US ⓣ1-800/654-3131, ⓦwww.hertz.com
Holiday Autos US ⓣ1-866/392-9288, ⓦwww.holidayautos.com
National US ⓣ1-800/CAR-RENT, ⓦwww.nationalcar.com
Thrifty US and Canada ⓣ1-800/847-4389, ⓦwww.thrifty.com

Cycling

Typically, **cycling** is a cheap and healthy way to get around the big cities, an increasing number of which have cycle lanes and local buses equipped to carry bikes (strapped to the outside). In country areas, roads have wide shoulders and fewer passing motorists. Bikes can be rented for $15–35 per day, or at discounted weekly rates, from outlets that are usually found close to beaches, university campuses, and good cycling areas. Rates in heavily visited areas can be higher. Local visitor centers have details.

The national nonprofit **Adventure Cycling Association**, based in Missoula, Montana (ⓣ406/721-1776 or 1-800/755-2453, ⓦwww.adventurecycling.org), publishes maps of several lengthy routes, detailing campgrounds, motels, restaurants, bike shops, and sites of interest. Many individual states issue their own cycling guides; contact the tourist offices listed on p.63. Before setting out on a long-distance cycling trip, you'll need a good-quality, multispeed bike, panniers, tools and spares, maps, padded shorts, and a helmet (legally required in many states and localities). Plan a route that avoids interstate highways (on which cycling is unpleasant and usually illegal) and sticks to well-maintained, paved rural roads. Of problems you'll encounter, the main one is traffic – RVs, huge eighteen-wheelers, logging trucks – that scream past and create intense backdrafts capable of pulling you out into the middle of the road.

Backroads Bicycle Tours (ⓦwww.backroads.com), and the HI-AYH hosteling group (see p.39) arrange multi-day cycle tours, with camping or stays in country inns; we've also mentioned local firms that offer this where appropriate.

Greyhound, Amtrak, and major airlines will carry passengers' bikes – dismantled and packed into a box – for a small fee.

Accommodation

The cost of accommodation is significant for any traveler exploring the US – in part, because the standards of comfort and service are usually fairly high. Wherever you travel, you're almost certain to find a good-quality, reasonably priced motel or hotel, while if you're prepared to pay a little extra, wonderful historic hotels and lodges can offer truly memorable experiences.

Typical room rates in motels and hotels start at around $50 per night in rural areas, and more like $75 in cities. Many hotels will set up a third single bed for around $20 extra, reducing costs for three people sharing. For lone travelers, on the other hand, a "single room" is usually a double room at an only slightly reduced rate. A dorm bed in a hostel usually costs $16–32 per night, but standards of cleanliness and security can be low, and for groups of two or more the saving compared to a motel is often minimal. In certain parts of the US, camping makes a cheap – and exhilarating – alternative, costing around $10–25 per night.

Wherever you stay, you'll be expected to pay in advance, at least for the first night and perhaps for further nights, too. Most hotels ask for a credit card imprint when you arrive, but some still accept cash or US dollar travelers' checks. Reservations – essential in busy areas in summer – are held only until 5 or 6pm, unless you've said you'll be arriving late.

Hotels and motels

Hotels and **motels** are essentially the same thing, although motels tend to be found beside the main roads away from city centers, and are thus much more accessible to drivers. The budget ones can be pretty basic, but in general standards of comfort are uniform – each room comes with a double bed (often two), a TV and phone, and an attached bathroom – and you don't get a much better deal by paying, say, $80 instead of $55. Over $80 or so, the room and its fittings simply get bigger and more luxurious, and there'll probably be a swimming pool (in the warmer states, you'll tend to get a pool in even the cheaper motels, though it may be tiny and in full view of the roaring traffic). The great majority of motels these days

Accommodation price codes

Throughout this book, **accommodation prices** have been graded with the symbols below, according to the cost of the least expensive double room throughout most of the year.

However, except at interstate budget motels, there's rarely such a thing as a set rate for a room. A basic motel in a seaside or mountain resort may quadruple its prices according to the season, while a big-city hotel that charges "rack rates" of $200 per room during the week will often slash its rate on the weekend. Online rates can throw up considerable savings, and because the high and low seasons for tourists vary widely across the country, astute planning can also save a lot of money. Watch out too for local events – Mardi Gras in New Orleans, Spring Break in Myrtle Beach, college football games – which might raise rates far above normal. Only where we explicitly say so do these room rates include local **taxes**.

❶ up to $35
❷ $36–50
❸ $51–75
❹ $76–100
❺ $101–130
❻ $131–160
❼ $161–200
❽ $201–250
❾ $251+

offer wi-fi, albeit sometimes available in the lobby only.

The least expensive properties tend to be family-run, independent "mom'n'pop" motels, but these are rarer and rarer nowadays, and, in the big urban areas at least, can be pretty insalubrious. When you're driving along the main interstates there's a lot to be said for paying a few dollars more to stay in motels belonging to the national chains. These range from the ever-reliable and cheap *Super 8* (❷–❸) through the mid-range *Days Inn* (❸–❹) up to the relatively luxurious *Holiday Inn Express* and *Marriott* (❺–❻).

During off-peak periods, many motels and hotels struggle to fill their rooms, and it's worth bargaining to get a few dollars off the asking price. Staying in the same place for more than one night may bring further reductions. Also, look for discount coupons, especially in the free magazines distributed by local visitor centers and interstate Welcome Centers. These can offer amazing value – but read the small print first.

Few budget hotels or motels bother to compete with the ubiquitous diners by offering full breakfasts, although most will provide free self-service coffee, sticky buns, and if you are lucky, fruit or cereal, collectively referred to as "continental breakfast."

Bed-and-breakfasts

Staying in a **bed-and-breakfast** is a popular, and often luxurious, alternative to conventional hotels. Some B&Bs consist of no more than a couple of furnished rooms in someone's home, and even the larger establishments tend to have fewer than ten rooms, sometimes without TV or phone, but often laden with potpourri, chintzy cushions, and an almost over-contrived homey atmosphere.

The price you pay for a B&B – which varies from around $80 to $250 for a double room – always includes breakfast (sometimes a buffet on a sideboard, but more often a full-blown cooked meal). The crucial determining factor is whether each room has an en-suite bathroom; most B&Bs provide private bath facilities, although that can damage the authenticity of a fine old house. At the top end of the spectrum, the distinction between a hotel and a "bed-and-breakfast inn" may amount to no more than that the B&B is owned by a private individual rather than a chain. In many areas, B&Bs have united to form central booking agencies, making it much easier to find a room at short notice; we've given contact information for these where appropriate.

Historic hotels and lodges

Throughout the country, but especially out west, many towns still hold **historic hotels**, whether dating from the arrival of the railroads or from the heyday of Route 66 in the 1940s and 1950s. So long as you accept that not all will have up-to-date facilities to match their period charm, these can make wonderfully characterful places to spend a night or two. Those that are exceptionally well preserved or restored may charge $200 or more per room, but a more typical rate for a not overly luxurious but atmospheric, antique-furnished room would be more like $120.

In addition, several **national parks** feature long-established and architecturally distinguished hotels, traditionally known as **lodges**, that can be real bargains thanks to their federally controlled rates. The only drawback is that all rooms tend to be reserved far in advance. Among the best are *El Tovar* and *Grand Canyon Lodge* on the south and north rims, respectively, of the Grand Canyon; the *Old Faithful Inn* in Yellowstone; and *Glacier Park Lodge* in Glacier

Hostels

Hostel-type accommodation is not as plentiful in the US as it is in Europe, but provision for backpackers and low-budget travelers does exist. Unless you're traveling alone, most hostels work out little cheaper than motels; stay in them only if you prefer their youthful ambiance and sociability. Many are not accessible on public transportation, or convenient for sightseeing in the towns and cities, let alone in rural areas.

These days, most hostels are independent, with no affiliation to HI-AYH (Hosteling International–American Youth Hostels) network. Many are no more than converted motels, where the "dorms" consist of a couple of sets of bunkbeds in a musty room, which is also let out as a private unit on demand; others may be purpose-built rural properties, or at least converted and modernized to a high standard. Most expect guests to bring sheets or sleeping bags. Rates range from $15 to about $24 for a dorm bed, from perhaps $35 for a double room. Those few hostels that do belong to HI-AYH tend to impose curfews and limit daytime access hours, and segregate dormitories by sex.

Youth hostel associations

US and Canada

Hostelling International–American Youth Hostels US ⓣ1-301/495-1240, ⓦwww.hiayh.org
Hostelling International Canada ⓣ1-800/663-5777, ⓦwww.hihostels.ca

UK and Ireland

Youth Hostel Association (YHA) UK ⓣ01629/592 700, ⓦwww.yha.org.uk
Scottish Youth Hostel Association UK ⓣ0870/155 3255, ⓦwww.syha.org.uk
Irish Youth Hostel Association Republic of Ireland ⓣ01/830 4555, ⓦwww.anoige.ie
Hostelling International Northern Ireland Northern !reland ⓣ028/9032 4733, ⓦwww.hini.org.uk

Australia, New Zealand, and South Africa

Australia Youth Hostels Association Australia ⓣ02/9281 9444, ⓦwww.yha.com.au
Youth Hostelling Association New Zealand New Zealand ⓣ0800/278 299 or 03/379 9970, ⓦwww.yha.co.nz

Food and drink

In addition to all-American fast food, the country has numerous choices for food and drink: regional cuisines are on offer everywhere, and international food turns up regularly in the big cities, and in more unexpected places. Many farming and ranching regions—Nevada and central California in particular—have a number of Basque restaurants; Portuguese restaurants, dating from whaling days, line the New England coast; and old-fashioned Welsh pasties can be found in the mining towns of Montana.

When it comes to **Asian food**, Indian cuisine is usually better in the cities, though there are exceptions. Chinese cooking is sometimes top-notch, and can often be cheap — though look out for the dismal-tasting "chop suey" and "chow mein" joints in suburbs and small towns. Japanese, found on the coasts and in cities, is rather more expensive and fashionable, though sushi restaurants come in all sizes and price ranges, from candlelit affairs done up like French restaurants to the lowest-end diners where you grab color-coded plates of raw fish from a moving belt. Thai and Vietnamese fare, meanwhile, provide some of the best, cheapest, and most exciting cooking available, sometimes in diners mixing the two, but always with an excellent range of savory soups and noodle dishes, and occasionally "fusion" cooking with other Asian cuisines (ie "pan-Asian," as it's known).

French cuisine is almost always expensive, typically nouvelle, and associated with high-end hotels and ultra-chic, jacket-only affairs. That said, country French dining and French sub-styles (like Cajun and French Canadian) offer a much cheaper variant on Gallic cooking, and are often excellent as well.

Coping as a vegetarian

In the big US cities at least, being a **vegetarian**—or even a vegan—presents few problems. However, don't be too surprised in rural areas if you find yourself restricted to a diet of eggs, cheese sandwiches (you might have to ask them to leave the ham out), salads, and biscuits. In the Southeast, most soul-food cafés offer great-value vegetable plates (four different vegetables, including potatoes) for around $5, but these are often cooked with pork fat. Similarly, baked beans, and the nutritious-sounding red beans and rice, usually contain bits of diced pork. If all else fails, you can always make up a nice repast from what you find at a supermarket or, better yet, farmers' market.

Italian fare is even broader in its range; the top-shelf restaurants in major cities tend to focus on the northern end of the boot, with careful presentation, subtle flavors, and high prices, while the tomato-heavy, gut-busting portions associated with southern Italian cooking are still, in America at least, confined to lower-end, checkered-tablecloth diners with massive portions and pictures of Frank and Dino on the walls. Pizza restaurants occupy a similar range from high-end gourmet eateries to cheap and tasty dives—New Yorkers and Chicagoans can argue for days over which of their respective cities makes the best kind, either Gotham's shingle-flat "slices" or the Windy City's overstuffed wedges that actually resemble slices of meat pie.

Eating out

In the big cities, you can pretty much eat whatever you want, whenever you want, thanks to the ubiquity of restaurants, 24-hour diners, and bars and street carts selling food well into the night. Also, along all the highways and on virtually every town's main street, restaurants, fast-food joints and coffeeshops try to outdo one another with flashing neon signs as well as bargains and special offers.

Whatever you eat and wherever you eat, service is usually prompt and attentive – thanks in large part to the institution of **tipping**. Waiters depend on tips for the bulk of their earnings; fifteen to twenty percent is the standard rate, with anything less sure to draw a sneer or even an insult.

Regional cuisines

While the predictably enormous steaks, burgers, and piles of ribs or half-chickens, served up with salads, cooked vegetables, and bread, are found everywhere, it's more rewarding to explore the diverse **regional and ethnic cuisines** around the US. Steaks and other beef are prominent in the Midwest and Texas, while fish and seafood dominate the menus in Florida, Louisiana, around Chesapeake Bay in Maryland, and in the Pacific Northwest. Shellfish, such as the highly rated dungeness crab and the Chesapeake's unique soft-shell crab, highly spiced and eaten whole, is popular, too. Maine lobsters and steamers (clams), eaten alone or mixed up in a chowder, are reason alone to visit New England.

Cajun fare, which originated in the bayous of Louisiana as a way to use up leftovers, is centered on red beans and rice, enlivened with unusual seafood like crawfish and catfish, and always highly spiced. (The oft-misunderstood distinction between Cajun and Creole cooking is explained in our "Louisiana" chapter, on p.643.)

Southern cooking – sometimes known as "**soul food**" – is not always easy to find outside the South, but is worth seeking out for everything from grits to collard greens, from fried chicken to pralines, and more exotic offerings like hogjaw (meat from the mouth of a pig) and chitlins (pork intestines). **Barbecue** is also very popular in the South, where a mouth-watering plate, with sides, can be had for usually less than $10. (Generally, the more ramshackle the restaurant, the better the food.) There's also great barbecue outside of the South, in places like Kansas City and Chicago.

California Cuisine is geared toward health and aesthetics. It's basically a development of French nouvelle cuisine, pioneered in the 1970s and utilizing a wide mix of fresh, local ingredients in season and offered as small but beautifully presented portions, with accompanying high prices: expect to pay $50 a head (or much more) for a full dinner with wine. California's culinary experiments have since branched out into what's called the **New American Cuisine,** which is essentially California cooking transplanted to different regions – New Southern, New England, Northwest, Southwestern and Western (or Midwestern) are but a few manifestations of this trend.

Although technically ethnic, **Mexican food** is so common it might as well be an indigenous cuisine, especially in southern California. In the US, Mexican food is different from that found south of the border, focusing more on frying and on a standard set of staples. The essentials, however, are the same: lots of rice and black or pinto beans, often served refried (boiled, mashed, and fried), with variations on the tortilla, a thin corn or flour pancake that can be wrapped around fillings and eaten by hand (a burrito); folded and filled (a taco); rolled, filled, and baked in sauce (an enchilada); or fried flat and topped with a stack of filling (a tostada). In Texas and the Southwest, beef and bean chili con carne is the distinguishing dish of **Tex-Mex** cuisine. Day or night, this is the cheapest type of food to eat: even a full dinner with a few drinks will rarely be more than $10 anywhere except in more upmarket establishments.

Finally, there are also regional variations on **American staples.** You can get plain old burgers and hot dogs anywhere, but for a truly American experience, grab a piping-hot "Philly cheesesteak" sandwich, gooey with cheese and thin-sliced beef from a diner in eastern Pennsylvania, or one of New York's signature Coney Island hot dogs – or the LA version of the frankfurter, rolled in a tortilla and stuffed with cheese and chili. Almost every Eastern state has at least one spot claiming to have invented the hamburger, and regardless of where you go, you can find a good range of authentic diners where the buns are fresh, the patties are large, handcrafted, and tasty, and the dressings and condiments are inspired. Needless to say, although we list the better of these locations in the Guide, almost none of them can be found along the interstate, under massive signs advertising their wares for 99 cents.

Drink

Across the country, bars and cocktail lounges are often dimly lit spots with long counters, a few customers perched on stools before a bartender-cum-guru, and tables and booths for those who don't want to join in the drunken barside debates. New York, Baltimore, Chicago, New Orleans, and San Francisco are the consummate boozing towns – filled with tales of plastered, famous authors indulging in famously bad behavior – but almost anywhere you shouldn't have to search very hard for a comfortable place to drink. You need to be 21 years old to buy and consume alcohol in the US, and it's likely you'll be asked for ID if you look under 30.

"Blue laws" – archaic statutes that restrict when, where, and under what conditions alcohol can be purchased – are held by many states, and prohibit the sale of alcohol on Sundays; on the extreme end of the scale, some counties (known as "dry") don't allow any alcohol, ever. The famous whiskey and bourbon distilleries of Tennessee and Kentucky, including Jack Daniel's (see p.527), can be visited—though maddeningly, several are in dry counties, so they don't offer samples. A few states – Vermont, Oklahoma, and Utah (which, being predominantly Mormon, has the most byzantine rules) – restrict the alcohol content in beer to just 3.2 percent, almost half the usual strength. Rest assured, though, that in a few of the more liberal parts of the country (New York City, for one), alcohol can be bought and drunk any time between 6am and 4am, seven days a week.

The most popular American beers are still fizzy, insipid lagers from national brands, but there is no lack of alternatives. The craze for microbreweries started in northern California several decades ago, and even today Anchor Steam—once at the vanguard—is still an excellent choice for sampling. The West Coast continues to be, to a large extent, the center of the microbrewing movement, and even the smaller towns have their own share of decent handcrafted beers. The town with the most such breweries, per capita or raw quantity, is Portland, Oregon, which enthusiasts from across the country (or world for that matter) have been known to visit just to sample draughts of its notable brewers. Los Angeles, San Diego, Seattle, the Bay Area, Denver, and other Western cities rank up there, too, and you can even find excellent brews in tiny spots such as Whitefish, Montana, where the beers of Great Northern Brewing are well worth seeking out.

On the East Coast look for Boston-based Samuel Adams and its mix of mainstream and alternative brews, the top-notch offerings of Pennsylvania's Victory Brewing, or stop in to Washington DC's great beer-tasting spot, the Brickskeller, to sample a broad array of the country's finest potables—some eight hundred different kinds. Elsewhere, the Texas brand Lone Star has its dedicated followers, Indiana's best beverages come from Three Floyds Brewing, and Pete's Wicked Ales in Minnesota can be found throughout the US. Indeed, microbreweries and brewpubs can now be found in virtually every sizeable US city and college town. Almost all serve a wide range of good-value, hearty food to help soak up the drink.

California and, to a lesser extent, Oregon, Washington, and a few other states, are famous for their wines. In California, it's the Napa and Sonoma valleys that boast the finest grapes, and beefy reds such as Merlot, Pinot Noir, and Cabernet Sauvignon as well as crisp or buttery whites like Chardonnay and Sauvignon Blanc all do very well up here. Many tourists make a pilgrimage to these valleys for "wine-tasting" jags, where you can sip (or slurp) at sites ranging from downhome country farms with tractors and hayrides to upper-crust estates thick with modern art and yuppies in designer wear. Elsewhere, Oregon's Willamette Valley and other areas in the state are becoming known for excellent vino, especially pinot noir, while Washington State has its prime vineyards in places like the Yakima Valley, Columbia River Gorge and Walla Walla area, among others. Beyond this, a broad variety of states from Arizona to Virginia have established wineries, typically of varying quality, though there are always a few standouts in each state that may merit a taste while you're on your journey. Throughout this book, you'll find details of tours and tastings where relevant.

Festivals

Someone, somewhere, is always celebrating something in the US – although, apart from national holidays, few festivities are shared throughout the country. Instead, there is a diverse multitude of engaging local events: arts-and-crafts shows, county fairs, ethnic celebrations, music festivals, rodeos, sandcastle-building competitions, chili cook-offs, and countless others.

Certain festivities, such as **Mardi Gras** in New Orleans, are well worth planning your vacation around – obviously other people will have the same idea, so visiting during these times requires an extra amount of advance effort.

On July 4, **Independence Day,** almost everyone in the country takes time out to picnic, drink, salute the flag, and watch or participate in fireworks displays, marches, beauty pageants, eating contests, and more, all in commemoration of the signing of the Declaration of Independence in 1776.

Halloween (October 31) is also immensely popular, although it lacks any such patriotic overtones, and is not a public holiday. Masked kids run around the streets banging on doors and demanding "trick or treat," returning home with heaping piles of candy. In some bigger cities Halloween has evolved into a massive celebration: in LA's West Hollywood, New York's Greenwich Village, New Orleans' French Quarter, and San Francisco's Castro district, the night is marked by colorful parades, mass cross-dressing, huge block parties, and wee-hours partying.

Thanksgiving Day, on the fourth Thursday in November, is more sedate. Relatives return to the nest to share a meal (traditionally, roast turkey and stuffing, cranberry sauce, and all manner of delicious pies) and give thanks for family and friends. Ostensibly, the holiday recalls the first harvest of the Pilgrims in Massachusetts, though Thanksgiving was a national holiday before anyone thought to make that connection.

Annual festivals and events

For further details of the festivals and events listed below, including more precise dates, see the relevant page of the *Guide*, or access their websites. The state tourist boards listed on p.00 can provide more complete calendars for each area.

January

Cowboy Poetry Gathering Elko, NV ⓦwww.westernfolklife.org
St Paul, MN Winter Carnival ⓦwww.winter-carnival.com

February

Daytona 500 Daytona Beach, FL stock-car race ⓦwww.daytona500.com
Mardi Gras New Orleans, LA (the six weeks before Lent) ⓦwww.mardigrasneworleans.com

March

South by Southwest Music Festival Austin, TX ⓦsxsw.com
Championship Crawfish Étouffée Cookoff Eunice, LA World ⓦwww.eunice-la.com
Ice Festival Fairbanks, AK ⓦwww.icealaska.com
Academy Awards (the "Oscars") Los Angeles, CA ⓦwww.oscars.org
St Joseph's Day and the Mardi Gras Indians' "Super Sunday" New Orleans, LA ⓦwww.mardigrasindians.com

April

Patriots' Day Marathon Boston, MA ⓦwww.bostonmarathon.org
Festival International de Louisiane Lafayette, LA ⓦwww.festivalinternational.com
Arkansas Folk Festival Mountain View, AR ⓦwww.magically.org
French Quarter Festival New Orleans, LA ⓦwww.fqfi.org
Jazz and Heritage Festival New Orleans, LA (into May) ⓦwww.nojazzfest.com
Fiesta San Antonio San Antonio, TX ⓦwww.fiesta-sa.org

May

Leaf Festival Black Mountain, NC ⓦwww.theleaf.com
Crawfish Festival Breaux Bridge, LA ⓦwww.bbcrawfest.com
Spoleto Festival Charleston, SC (into June) ⓦwww.spoletousa.org
Indianapolis 500 Indianapolis, IN ⓦwww.indy500.com
Folk Festival Kerrville, TX ⓦwww.kerrvillefolkfestival.com
Kentucky Derby Louisville, KY ⓦwww.kentuckyderby.com
Memphis in May International Festival Memphis, TN ⓦwww.memphisinmay.org
San Antonio, TX Tejano Conjunto Festival ⓦwww.guadalupeculturalarts.org

June

Little Bighorn Days Hardin, MT ⓦwww.custerslaststand.org
CMA Music Festival Nashville, TN ⓦwww.cmafest.com
Texas Folklife Festival San Antonio, TX ⓦwww.texancultures.com
Bluegrass Festival Telluride, CO ⓦwww.bluegrass.com

July

Highland Games Blowing Rock, NC ⓦwww.gmhg.org
Cheyenne Frontier Days Cheyenne, WY ⓦwww.cfdrodeo.com
National Basque Festival Elko, NV ⓦwww.elkobasque.com
Eskimo/Indian Olympics Fairbanks, AK ⓦwww.weio.org

Hopi Marketplace Flagstaff, AZ Ⓦ www.musnaz.org
Powwow and rodeo Fort Totten, ND Ⓦ www.powwows.com
Satchmo music festival New Orleans, LA (into Aug) Ⓦ www.fqfi.org
Taste of Minnesota St Paul, MN Ⓦ www.tasteofmn.org
Moose Dropping Festival Talkeetna, AK Ⓦ www.talkeetnachamber.org
Cherry Festival Traverse City, MI Ⓦ www.cherryfestival.org

August

Mountain Dance and Folk Festival Asheville, NC Ⓦ www.folkheritage.org
Burning Man Black Rock City, NV Ⓦ www.burningman.com
Augusta Festival of Appalachian Culture Elkins, WV Ⓦ www.augustaheritage.com
Inter-Tribal Indian Ceremonial Gallup, NM Ⓦ gallup-ceremonial.org
Anniversary of Elvis's death Memphis, TN Ⓦ www.elvis.com
olk and jazz festivals Newport, RI FⓌ www.festivalnetwork.com
Indian Market Santa Fe, NM Ⓦ www.swaia.org
Sturgis, SD Motorcycle Rally and Races Ⓦ www.sturgis.com

September

Bluegrass and Chili Festival Claremore, OK Ⓦ www.claremore.org
International Jazz Festival Detroit, MI Ⓦ www.detroitjazzfest.com
Delta Blues Festival Greenville, MS Ⓦ www.deltablues.org
Panhandle South Plains Fair Lubbock, TX Ⓦ www.southplainsfair.com
Memphis Music and Heritage Festival Memphis, TN Ⓦ www.southernfolklore.com
Monterey Jazz Festival Monterey, CA Ⓦ www.montereyjazzfestival.org
Southern Decadence New Orleans, LA Ⓦ www.southerndecadence.com
Festa di San Gennaro New York, NY Ⓦ www.littleitalynyc.com
Zydeco Festival Opelousas, LA Ⓦ www.zydeco.org
Pendleton, OR Pendleton Round-Up Ⓦ pendletonroundup.com
Fiestas de Santa Fe Santa Fe, NM Ⓦ www.santafefiesta.org

October

International Balloon Fiesta Albuquerque, NM Ⓦ www.balloonfiesta.com
Moja Arts Festival Charleston, SC Ⓦ www.mojafestival.com
Buffalo Roundup Custer State Park, SD Ⓦ www.sdgfp.info
Pumpkin Festival Half Moon Bay, CA Ⓦ www.miramarevents.com
Blues and Heritage Festival Helena, AR Arkansas Ⓦ www.bluesandheritage.com
Festivals Acadiens et Créoles Lafayette, LA Ⓦ www.festivalsacadiens.com
Louisiana Yambilee Opelousas, LA Ⓦ www.yambilee.com
Helldorado Days Tombstone, AZ Ⓦ www.helldoradodays.com

November

Ozark Folk Festival Eureka Springs, AR Ⓦ www.ozarkfolkfestival.com

Sports and the outdoors

As well as being good fun, catching a baseball game at Chicago's Wrigley Field on a summer afternoon or joining the screaming throngs at a Steelers football game in Pittsburgh can give visitors an unforgettable insight into a town and its people. Professional teams almost always put on the most spectacular shows, but big games between college rivals, minor league baseball games, and even Friday night high-school football games provide an easy and enjoyable way to get on intimate terms with a place.

Specific details for the most important teams in all the sports are given in the various city accounts. They can also be found through the major league websites: Ⓦwww.mlb.com (baseball); Ⓦwww.nba.com (basketball); Ⓦwww.nfl.com (football); Ⓦwww.nhl.com (ice hockey); and Ⓦwww.mlsnet.com (soccer).

Baseball, because the major league teams play so many games (162 in total, usually five or so a week throughout the summer), is probably the easiest sport to catch when traveling. The ballparks – such as Boston's historic Fenway Park, LA's glamorous Dodger Stadium, or Baltimore's evocative Camden Yards – are great places to spend time. It's also among the cheapest sports to watch (from around $10 a seat), and tickets are usually easy to come by.

Pro football, the American variety, is quite the opposite. Tickets are exorbitantly expensive and almost impossible to obtain (if the team is any good), and most games are played in anonymous municipal bunkers; you'll do better stopping in a bar to watch it on TV. **College football** is a whole lot better and more exciting, with chanting crowds, cheerleaders, and cheaper tickets. Although New Year's Day games such as the Rose Bowl or the Orange Bowl are all but impossible to see live, big games like Nebraska vs Oklahoma, Michigan vs Ohio State, or Notre Dame vs anybody are not to be missed if you're anywhere nearby.

Basketball also brings out intense emotions. The protracted – though invariably thrilling – pro playoffs run well into June. The men's month-long college playoff tournament, called "March Madness," is acclaimed by many as the nation's most exciting sports extravaganza.

Ice hockey, usually referred to simply as hockey, was long the preserve of Canada and cities in the far north of the US, but now penetrates the rest of the country. Tickets, particularly for successful teams, are hard to get and not cheap.

Soccer, meanwhile, remains much more popular as a participant sport, especially for kids, than a spectator one and those Americans that are interested in it usually follow foreign matches like England's Premier League, rather than their home-grown talent. The good news for international travelers is that any decent-sized city will have one or two pubs where you can catch games from England, other European countries, or Latin America; check out Ⓦwww.livesoccertv.com for a list of such establishments and match schedules.

Skiing is the biggest mass-market participant sport, and downhill resorts can be found all over the US. The Eastern resorts of Vermont and New York State, however, pale by comparison with those of the Rockies, such as Vail and Aspen in Colorado, and the Sierra Nevada in California. Expect to pay $40–100 per day (depending on the quality and popularity of the resort) for lift tickets, plus another $25 or more per day to rent equipment.

A cheaper option is **cross-country skiing**, or ski touring. Back country ski lodges dot mountainous areas along both coasts and in the Rockies. They offer a range of rustic accommodation, equipment rental, and lessons, from as little as $20 a day for skis, boots, and poles, up to about $200 for an all-inclusive weekend tour.

The other sporting events that attract national interest involve four legs or four wheels. The **Kentucky Derby**, held in Louisville on the first Saturday in May (see p.000), is the biggest date on the horseracing calendar. Also in May, the NASCAR **Indianapolis 500**, the world's largest motor-racing event, fills that city with visitors throughout the month, with practice sessions and carnival events building up to the big race.

National parks

Coated by dense forests, cut by deep canyons, and capped by great mountains, the US is blessed with fabulous back-country and wilderness areas. Even the heavily populated East Coast has its share of open space, notably along the Appalachian Trail, which winds from Mount Katahdin in Maine to the southern Appalachians in Georgia – some two thousand miles of untrammeled woodland. To experience the full breathtaking sweep of America's wide-open stretches, however, head west: to the Rockies, the red-rock deserts of the Southwest, or right across the continent to the amazing wild spaces of the West Coast. On the down side, be warned that in many coastal areas, the shoreline can be disappointingly hard to access, with a high proportion under private ownership.

National parks and monuments

The **National Park Service** administers both national parks and national monuments. Its rangers do a superb job of providing information and advice to visitors, maintaining trails, and organizing such activities as free guided hikes and campfire talks.

In principle, a **national park** preserves an area of outstanding natural beauty, encompassing a wide range of terrain and prime examples of particular landforms and wildlife. Thus Yellowstone has boiling geysers and herds of elk and bison, while Yosemite offers towering granite walls and cascading waterfalls. A **national monument** is usually much smaller, focusing perhaps on just one archeological site or geological phenomenon, such as Devil's Tower in Wyoming. Altogether, the national park system comprises around four hundred units, including national seashores, lakeshores, battlefields, and other historic sites.

While national parks tend to be perfect places to **hike** – almost all have extensive trail networks – all are far too large to tour entirely on foot. (Yellowstone, for example, is bigger than Delaware and Rhode Island combined.) Even in those rare cases where you can use public transportation to reach a park, you'll almost certainly need some sort of vehicle to explore it once you're there. The Alaska parks are mostly howling wilderness, with virtually no roads or facilities for tourists – you're on your own.

Most parks and monuments charge admission fees, ranging from $5 to $25, which cover a vehicle and all its occupants for up to a week. For anyone on a touring vacation, it may well make more sense to buy the annual National Parks Pass for $80, available at all federal parks and monuments, or online at Ⓦstore.usgs.gov/pass. It grants unrestricted access for a year to the bearer, and any accompanying passengers, to all national parks and monuments, as well as sites managed by such agencies as the US Fish and Wildlife Service, the Forest Service, and the BLM (see below). It does not however cover or reduce additional fees like charges for camping in official park campgrounds, or permits for back-country hiking or rafting.

Two further passes, obtainable at any park but not online, grant free access for life to all national parks and monuments, again to the

The Park Service website, ⓦ www.nps.gov, details the main attractions of the national parks, plus opening hours, the best times to visit, admission fees, hiking trails, and visitor facilities.

holder and any accompanying passengers, and also provide a fifty percent discount on camping fees. The Senior Pass is available to any US citizen or permanent resident aged 62 or older for a one-time fee of $10, while the Access Pass is issued free to blind or permanently disabled US citizens or permanent residents.

While hotel-style **lodges** are found only in major parks, every park or monument tends to have at least one well-organized **campground**. Often, a cluster of motels can be found not far outside the park boundaries. With appropriate permits – subject to restrictions in popular parks – backpackers can also usually camp in the back country (a general term for areas inaccessible by road).

Other public lands

National parks and monuments are often surrounded by tracts of **national forest** – also federally administered but much less protected. These too usually hold appealing rural campgrounds but, in the words of the slogan, each is a "Land Of Many Uses," and usually allows logging and other land-based industry (thankfully, more often ski resorts than strip mines).

Other government departments administer wildlife refuges, national scenic rivers, recreation areas, and the like. The **Bureau of Land Management** (BLM) has the largest holdings of all, most of it open rangeland, such as in Nevada and Utah, but also including some enticingly out-of-the-way reaches. Environmentalist groups engage in endless running battles with developers, ranchers, and the extracting industries over uses – or alleged misuses – of federal lands.

While state parks and **state monuments**, administered by individual states, preserve sites of more limited, local significance, many are explicitly intended for recreational use, and thus hold better campgrounds than their federal equivalents.

Camping and backpacking

The ideal way to see the great outdoors – especially if you're on a low budget – is to tour by car and **camp** in state and federal campgrounds. Typical public campgrounds range in price from free (usually when there's no water available, which may be seasonal) to around $15 per night. Fees at the generally less scenic commercial campgrounds – abundant near major towns, and often resembling open-air hotels, complete with shops and restaurants – are more like $15–25. If you're camping in high season, either reserve in advance or avoid the most popular areas.

Back-country camping in the national parks is usually free, by permit only. Before you set off on anything more than a half-day hike, and whenever you're headed for anywhere at all isolated, be sure to inform a ranger of your plans, and ask about weather conditions and specific local tips. Carry sufficient food and drink to cover emergencies, as well as all the necessary equipment and maps. Check whether fires are permitted; even if they are, try to use a camp stove in preference to local materials. In wilderness areas, try to camp on previously used sites. Where there are no toilets, bury human waste at least six inches into the ground and a hundred feet from the nearest water supply and campground.

Backpackers should never drink from rivers and streams; you never know what acts people – or animals – have performed further upstream. **Giardia** – a water-borne bacteria that causes an intestinal disease characterized by chronic diarrhea, abdominal cramps, fatigue, and weight loss – is a serious problem. Water that doesn't come from a tap should be boiled for at least five minutes, or cleansed with an iodine-based purifier or a giardia-rated filter.

Hiking at lower elevations should present few problems, though swarms of **mosquitoes** near water can drive you crazy; Avon Skin-so-soft, or anything containing DEET, are fairly reliable repellents. **Ticks** – tiny beetles that plunge their heads into your skin and swell up – are another hazard. They sometimes leave their heads inside, causing blood clots or infections, so get advice from a ranger if you've been bitten. One species of tick causes **Lyme Disease**, a serious condition that can even affect the brain. Nightly inspections of your skin are strongly recommended.

Beware, too, of **poison oak**, which grows throughout the west, usually among oak trees. Its leaves come in groups of three (the middle one on a short stem) and are distinguished by prominent veins and shiny surfaces. If you come into contact with it, wash your skin (with soap and cold water) and clothes as soon as possible – and don't scratch. In serious cases, hospital emergency rooms can give antihistamine or adrenaline shots. A comparable curse is **poison ivy**, found throughout the country. For both plants, remember the sage advice, "Leaves of three, let it be."

Mountain hikes

Take special care hiking at higher elevations, for instance in the 14,000ft peaks of the Rockies, or in California's Sierra Nevada (and certainly in Alaska). Late snows are common, and in spring avalanches are a real danger, while meltwaters make otherwise simple stream crossings hazardous. Weather conditions can also change abruptly. **Altitude sickness** can affect even the fittest of athletes: take it easy for your first few days above seven thousand feet. Drink lots of water, avoid alcohol, eat plenty of carbohydrates, and protect yourself from the sun.

Desert hikes

If you intend to hike in the **desert**, tell someone where you are going, and write down all pertinent information, including your expected time of return. Carry an extra two days' food and water and never go anywhere without a map. Cover most of your ground in early morning: the midday heat is too debilitating. If you get lost, find some shade and wait. As long as you've registered, the rangers will eventually come looking for you.

At any time of year, you'll stay cooler during the day if you wear full-length sleeves and trousers, while a wide-brimmed hat and good sunglasses will spare you the blinding headaches that can result from the desert light. You may also have to contend with **flash floods**, which can appear from nowhere. Never camp in a dry wash, and don't attempt to cross flooded areas until the water has receded.

It's essential to carry – and drink – large quantities of **water** in the desert. An eight-hour hike in typical summer temperatures above 100°F would require you to drink a phenomenal thirty pints of water. Loss of appetite and thirst are early symptoms of heat exhaustion, so it's possible to become seriously dehydrated without feeling thirsty. Watch out for signs of dizziness or nausea; if you feel weak and stop sweating, it's time to get to the doctor. Check whether water is available on your trail; ask a ranger, and carry at least a quart per person even if it is.

When **driving** in the desert, carry two gallons of water per person in the car, and take along an emergency pack with flares, a first-aid kit and snakebite kit, matches, and a compass. A shovel, tire pump, and extra gas are always a good idea. If the engine overheats, don't turn it off; instead, try to cool it quickly by turning the front end of the car towards the wind. Carefully pour some water on the front of the radiator, and turn the air conditioning off and the heat up full blast. In an emergency, never panic and leave the car: you'll be harder to find wandering around alone.

Adventure travel

The opportunities for **adventure travel** in the US are all but endless, from whitewater rafting down the Colorado River, to mountain biking in the volcanic Cascades, canoeing down the headwaters of the Mississippi River, horseback riding in Big Bend on the Rio Grande in Texas, and Big Wall rock-climbing on the sheer granite monoliths of Yosemite Valley.

While an exhaustive listing of the possibilities could fill another volume, certain places have an especially high concentration of adventure opportunities, such as Moab, Utah (p.000), or New Hampshire's White Mountains (p.0000). Throughout the book we recommend guides, outfitters, and local adventure-tour operators.

Wildlife

Watch out for bears, deer, moose, mountain lions, and rattlesnakes in the back country,

1 Olympic, WA
2 North Cascades, WA
3 Mount Rainier, WA
4 Crater Lake, OR
5 Glacier, MT
6 Yellowstone, WY
7 Grand Teton, WY
8 T. Roosevelt (north), ND
9 T. Roosevelt (south), ND
10 Wind Cave, SD
11 Badlands, SD
12 Redwood, CA
13 Lassen Volcanic, CA
14 Yosemite, CA
15 Kings Canyon, CA
16 Sequoia, CA
17 Death Valley, CA
18 Joshua Tree, CA
19 Great Basin, NV
20 Zion, UT
21 Bryce Canyon, UT
22 Capitol Reef, UT
23 Canyonlands, UT
24 Arches, UT

25 Grand Canyon, AZ
26 Petrified Forest, AZ
27 Saguaro, AZ
28 Mesa Verde, CO
29 Black Canyon of the Gunnison, CO
30 Rocky Mountain, CO
31 Great Sand Dunes, CO
32 Carlsbad Caverns, NM
33 Guadalupe Mtns, TX
34 Big Bend, TX
35 Haleakala, HI
36 Hawaii Volcanoes, HI
37 Glacier Bay, AK
38 Wrangell-St Elias, AK
39 Kenai Fjords, AK
40 Denali, AK
41 Gates of the Arctic, AK
42 Voyageurs, MN
43 Isle Royale, MI
44 Acadia, ME
45 Mammoth Cave, KY
46 Great Smoky Mtns, TN
47 Shenandoah, VA
48 Hot Springs, AR
49 Everglades, FL

and consider the effect your presence can have on their environment.

Other than in a national park, you're highly unlikely to encounter a **bear**. Even there, it's rare to stumble across one in the wilderness. If you do, don't run, just back away slowly. Most fundamentally, it will be after your food, which should be stored in airtight containers when camping. Ideally, hang both food and garbage from a high but slender branch some distance from your camp. Never attempt to feed bears, and never get between a mother and her young. Young animals are cute; irate mothers are not.

Snakes and creepy-crawlies

Though the deserts in particular are home to a wide assortment of poisonous creatures, these are rarely aggressive towards humans. To avoid trouble, observe obvious precautions. Don't attempt to handle wildlife; keep your eyes open as you walk, and watch where you put your hands when scrambling over obstacles; shake out shoes, clothing, and bedding before use; and back off if you do spot a creature, giving it room to escape.

If you are bitten or stung, current medical thinking rejects the concept of cutting yourself open and attempting to suck out the venom. Whether snake, scorpion, or spider is responsible, apply a cold compress to the wound, constrict the area with a tourniquet to prevent the spread of venom, drink lots of water, and bring your temperature down by resting in a shady area. Stay as calm as possible and seek medical help immediately.

Traveling with children

Traveling with kids in the United States is relatively problem-free. Children are readily accepted – indeed welcomed – in public places across the country. Hotels and motels are quite accustomed to them, most state and national parks organize children's activities, every town or city has clean and safe playgrounds, and, of course, Disneyland in California and Disney World in Florida provide the ultimate in kids' entertainment, while lesser theme parks are scattered nationwide.

Many, if not most, restaurants encourage parents to bring in their offspring. All the national chains provide highchairs and a special kids' menu, packed with huge, low-priced (if not necessarily healthful) meals – cheeseburger and fries for 99¢, and so on. Virtually all museums and tourist attractions offer reduced rates for kids. Most large cities have natural history museums or aquariums, and quite a few also have hands-on children's museums.

State tourist offices can provide more specific information, while the *Rough Guide to Travel with Babies and Young Children* (2008; $15.99), is packed with valuable advice for parents.

Getting around

Children under two years old fly free on domestic routes and for ten percent of the adult fare on international flights – though that doesn't mean they get a seat, let alone frequent-flier miles. Kids aged between two and twelve years old are usually entitled to half-price tickets.

Traveling by bus may be the cheapest way to go, but it's also the most uncomfortable for kids. Under-twos travel (on your lap) for free. Children under twelve are charged half the standard fare.

Taking the train is by far the best option for long journeys – not only does everyone get to enjoy the scenery, but you can get up and walk around. Most cross-country trains have sleeping compartments, which may be quite expensive, but are likely to be seen by the kids as a great adventure. Children's discounts are much the same as for bus or plane travel.

All that said, most families choose to travel by car. If you hope to enjoy a driving vacation with your kids, make plans. Don't set unrealistic targets; pack sensible snacks and drinks; stop every couple of hours; arrive at your destination before sunset; and avoid traveling through big cities during rush hour.

Car rental companies usually provide kids' car seats – which are required by law for children under the age of four – for around $10 a day. You would, however, be advised to check, or bring your own; they are not always available.

Recreational vehicles (RVs) are a good option for families, combining the convenience of kitchens and bedrooms with the freedom of the road (see "Getting around," p.00).

Travel essentials

Costs

When it comes to **average costs** for traveling expenses, much depends on where you've chosen to go. A jaunt around the barbeque shacks of Texas and the Deep South won't cost you much in accommodation, dining, or souvenir-buying, but gas prices, although back under $2 per gallon at the time of writing, will add to the expense. By contrast, getting around a centralized city such as Boston, New York, or Chicago will be relatively cheap, but you'll pay much more for your hotel, meals, and shopping purchases. A simple rule of thumb is, prices will vary directly with the size and glamour of the location. Also keep in mind that added to the cost of most items you purchase is a state – but not federal – **sales tax**, anywhere from less than three percent (in Colorado) to more than eight percent (in New York), and big cities may add on another point or two to that rate. (Alaska, Delaware, Montana, New Hampshire, and Oregon have no state sales tax.) Additionally, some cities – probably the ones you most want to visit – tack on a **hotel tax** that makes the total tax for accommodation around fifteen percent.

Unless you're camping or staying in a hostel, **accommodation** will be your greatest expense while in the US. Adequate lodging is rarely available for under $60, outside of bare-bones roadside motels and off-season cabins. A halfway decent room will run anywhere from $75–100, with fancier hotels costing much, much more – upwards of $200–350 in many of the big cities.

Unlike accommodation, prices for good **food** don't automatically take a bite out of your wallet, and you can indulge anywhere from the lowliest (but still scrumptious) burger shack to the chicest restaurant helmed by a celebrity chef. You can get by on as little as $20 a day, but realistically you should aim for around $50–60.

Public transit options are usually affordable, with the best deals being the multi-day or week-long **transit passes** offered by most cities for riding on buses, light rail, and subways. Renting a car, at around $120–200 per week, is a far more efficient way to explore the broader part of the country, and, for a group of two or more, it's no more expensive, either. Keep in mind, though, that for those under 25 years of age, there are often supplements of $20 a day tacked onto car rental fees.

For attractions in the Guide, prices are quoted for adults, with children's rates listed if they are more than a few dollars less; at some spots, kids get in for half price, or for free if they're under 6.

Tipping

Tipping is expected for all bar and restaurant service. Expect to tip about fifteen percent of the bill before tax to waiters in most restaurants (unless the service is truly wretched), and twenty percent for good service. In the US, this is where most of a waiter's income comes from, and not leaving a fair amount is seen as an insult. About fifteen percent should also be added to taxi fares; round up to the nearest 50¢ or dollar, as well. A hotel porter should get $1–2 per bag; if he's lugged your suitcases up several flights of stairs, make it $3–5. Chambermaids get $1–2 per guest for each day; valet attendants get $2.

Crime and personal safety

No one could pretend that America is crime-free, although away from the urban centers crime is often remarkably low. Even the lawless reputations of Miami, Detroit, or Los Angeles are far in excess of the truth, and most parts of these cities, by day at least, are safe; at night, however, some areas are completely off-limits. All the major tourist areas and the main nightlife zones in cities are invariably brightly lit and well policed. By planning carefully and taking good care of your possessions, you should, generally speaking, have few problems.

Car crime

Crimes committed against tourists driving rented cars aren't as common as they once were, but it still pays to be cautious. In major urban areas, any car you rent should have nothing on it – such as a particular license plate – that makes it easy to spot as a rental car. When driving, under no circumstances should you stop in any unlit or seemingly deserted urban area – and especially not if someone is waving you down and suggesting that there is something wrong with your car. Similarly, if you are accidentally rammed by the driver behind you, do not stop immediately, but proceed on to the nearest well-lit, busy area and call ⓣ911 for assistance. Hide any valuables out of sight, preferably locked in the trunk or in the glove compartment.

Dental treatment

For a free referral to the nearest **dentist**, call the national Dental Society Referral Service (ⓣ415/421-1435 or 1-800/511-8663).

Electricity

Electricity runs on 110V AC. All plugs are two-pronged and rather insubstantial. Some travel plug adapters don't fit American sockets.

Entry requirements

Although regulations have been continually tightening up since 9/11, citizens of 27 countries, including the UK, Ireland, Australia, New Zealand, and most Western European countries, visiting the United States for a period of less than ninety days can still enter the country on the **Visa Waiver Scheme.** The requisite visa waiver form (I-94W) is provided by the airline during check-in or on the plane, and presented to an immigration official on arrival.

However, even with an I-94W form, each traveler must undergo the US-VISIT process at immigration, where both index fingers are digitally scanned and a digital headshot is also taken for file. What's more, all passports accompanying an I-94W must now be **machine readable** and any issued after October 2006 must include a digital **chip** containing biometric data (these are now automatically issued by most countries but check). Anybody with an old passport will require some sort of **visa** for even a short stay in America and anybody planning to stay over three months will: check ⓦwww.dhs.gov for updates and the list of Visa Waiver Scheme countries.

Canadian citizens, used to being able to make an oral declaration, have also had to provide documentation since January 2008, although an enhanced secure driver's license is still an acceptable alternative to a passport. This may change though so again, check for updates.

Prospective visitors from other parts of the world not mentioned above require a valid passport and a non-immigrant **visitor's visa** for a maximum ninety-day stay. How you obtain a visa depends on what country you're in and your status on application, so contact your nearest US embassy or consulate. Whatever your nationality, visas are not issued to convicted felons and anybody who owns up to being a communist, fascist, or drug dealer.

On arrival, the date stamped on your passport is the latest you're legally allowed to stay. The Department of Homeland Security (DHS) has toughened its stance on anyone violating their visa status, so even **overstaying** by a few days can result in a protracted interrogation from officials. Overstaying may also cause you to be turned away next time you try to enter the US.

To get an **extension** before your time is up, apply at the nearest Department of Homeland Security office, whose address will be under the Federal Government Offices listings at the front of the phone book. In San Francisco, the office is at 630 Sansome St at Washington, Jackson Square (Ⓣ1-800/375-5283; Ⓦwww.dhs.gov). INS officials will assume that you're working in the US illegally, and it's up to you to convince them otherwise by providing evidence of ample finances. If you can, bring along an upstanding American citizen to vouch for you. You'll also have to explain why you didn't plan for the extra time initially.

US embassies and consulates

In Australia

Online Ⓦusembassy-australia.state.gov
Canberra Moonah Place, Yarralumla, ACT 2600 Ⓣ02/6214 5600
Melbourne 553 St Kilda Rd, PO Box 6722, Vic 3004 Ⓣ03/9526 5900
Perth 16 St George's Terrace, 13th floor, WA 6000 Ⓣ08/9202 1224
Sydney MLC Centre, 59th floor, 19–29 Martin Place, NSW 2000 Ⓣ02/9373 9200

In Canada

Online Ⓦwww.ottawa.usembassycanada.gov
Calgary 615 Macleod Trail SE, Room 1000, AB T2G 4T8 Ⓣ403/266-8962
Halifax Suite 910, Purdy's Wharf Tower II, 1969 Upper Water St, NS B3J 3R7 Ⓣ902/429-2480
Montréal 1155 Rue de St Alexandre, Québec, H3B 1Z1 Ⓣ514/398-9695
Ottawa 490 Sussex Drive, ON K1N 1G8 Ⓣ613/238-5335
Québec City 2 Rue de la Terrasse-Dufferin, Québec, G1R 4T9 Ⓣ418/692-2095
Toronto 360 University Ave, ON M5G 1S4 Ⓣ416/595-1700
Vancouver 1075 W Pender St, BC V6E 2M6 Ⓣ604/685-4311
Winnipeg 201 Portage Ave, Manitoba, R3B 3K6 Ⓣ204/940-1800

In Ireland

Dublin 42 Elgin Rd, Ballsbridge Ⓣ01/668 8777 Ⓦdublin.usembassy.gov

In New Zealand

Online Ⓦnewzealand.usembassy.gov
Auckland Citibank Building, 3rd floor, 23 Customs St Ⓣ09/303 2724
Wellington 29 Fitzherbert Terrace, Thorndon Ⓣ04/462 6112

In South Africa

Online Ⓦsouthafrica.usembassy.gov
Cape Town 2 Reddam Ave, Westlake 7945 Ⓣ021/421 4280
Durban Old Mutual Building, 31st floor, 303 West St 4001 Ⓣ031/305 7600
Johannesburg 1 River St, Killarney 2041 Ⓣ011/644 8000
Pretoria 877 Pretorius St, Arcadia 0083 Ⓣ012/431 4000

In the UK

Online Ⓦwww.usembassy.org.uk
Belfast Danesfort House, 223 Stranmillis Rd, Belfast BT9 5GR Ⓣ028/9038 6100
Edinburgh 3 Regent Terrace EH7 5BW Ⓣ0131/556 8315
London 24 Grosvenor Square W1A 1AE Ⓣ020/7499 9000; visa hotline (£1.50/min) Ⓣ0906 150 0590

Foreign embassies and consulates in the US

Australia

Embassy 1601 Massachusetts Ave NW, Washington DC 20036 Ⓣ202/797-3000, Ⓦwww.austemb.org

Canada

Embassy 501 Pennsylvania Ave NW, Washington DC 20001 Ⓣ202/682-1740,Ⓦcanadianembassy.org

Consulates Boston: Three Copley Place, Suite 400, MA 02216 ⓣ617/262-3760
Chicago: Two Prudential Plaza, 180 N Stetson Ave, Suite 2400, IL 60601 ⓣ312/616-1860
Los Angeles: 550 S Hope St, 9th floor, CA 90071–2627 ⓣ213/346-2700
Miami: First Union Financial Center, 200 S. Biscayne Blvd, FL 33131 ⓣ305/579-1600
New York: 1251 Avenue of the Americas, NY 10020–1175 ⓣ212/596-1628
San Francisco: 580 California St, 14th Floor, CA 94104 ⓣ415/834-3180

Ireland

Embassy 2234 Massachusetts Ave NW, Washington DC 20008 ⓣ202/462-3939, ⓦwww.irelandemb.org

New Zealand

Embassy 37 Observatory Circle NW, Washington DC 20008 ⓣ202/328 4800, ⓦwww.nzembassy.com

South Africa

Embassy 3051 Massachusetts Ave NW, Washington DC 20008 ⓣ202/232-4400, ⓦwww.saembassy.org

UK

Embassy 3100 Massachusetts Ave NW, Washington DC 20008 ⓣ202/588-7800, ⓦwww.britainusa.com/consular/embassy
Consulates Atlanta: Georgia Pacific Centre, Suite 3400, 133 Peachtree St NE, GA 30303 ⓣ404/954-7700, ⓦwww.britainusa.com/atlanta
Boston: One Memorial Drive, Suite 1500, Cambridge, MA 02142 ⓣ617/245-4500, ⓦwww.britainusa.com/boston
Chicago: 13th floor, The Wrigley Building, 400 N Michigan Ave, IL 60611 ⓣ312/970-3800, ⓦwww.britainusa.com/chicago
Denver: Suite 1030, World Trade Center, 1675 Broadway, CO 80202 ⓣ303/592-5200, ⓦwww.britainusa.com/denver
Houston: Wells Fargo Plaza, 1000 Louisiana, 19th Floor, TX 77002 ⓣ713/659-6270, ⓦwww.britainusa.com/houston
Los Angeles: 11766 Wilshire Blvd, Suite 1200, CA 90025 ⓣ310/481-0031, ⓦwww.britainusa.com/la
Miami: Brickell Bay Office Tower, 1001 Brickell Bay Drive, Suite 2800, FL 33131 ⓣ305/374-1522, ⓦwww.britainusa.com/miami
New York: 845 Third Ave, NY 10022 ⓣ212/745-0202, ⓦwww.britainusa.com/ny
San Francisco: 1 Sansome St, Suite 850, CA 94104 ⓣ415/617-1300, ⓦwww.britainusa.com/sf
Seattle: 900 Fourth Ave, Suite 3001, WA 98164 ⓣ206/622-9255, ⓦwww.britainusa.com/seattle

Gay and lesbian travelers

The gay scene in America is huge, albeit heavily concentrated in the major cities. San Francisco, where between a quarter and a third of the voting population is reckoned to be gay or lesbian, is arguably the world's premier gay city. New York runs a close second, and up and down both coasts gay men and women enjoy the kind of visibility and influence those in other places can only dream about. Gay officeholders and police officers are no longer a novelty. Resources, facilities, and organizations are endless.

Virtually every major city has a predominantly gay area and we've tried to give an overview of local resources, bars, and clubs in each large urban area. In the rural heartland, however, life can look more like the Fifties – homosexuals are still oppressed and commonly reviled. Gay travelers need to watch their step to avoid hassles and possible aggression.

National publications are available from any good bookstore. Bob Damron in San Francisco (ⓣ415/255-0404 or 1-800/462-6654, ⓦwww.damron.com) produces the best and sells them at a discount online. These include the *Men's Travel Guide*, a pocket-sized yearbook listing hotels, bars, clubs, and resources for gay men ($21.95); the *Women's Traveler*, which provides similar listings for lesbians ($18.95); the *Damron City Guide*, which details lodging and entertainment in major cities ($22.95); and *Damron Accommodations*, which lists 1000 accommodations for gays and lesbians worldwide ($23.95).

Gayellow Pages in New York (ⓣ212/674-0120, ⓦwww.gayellowpages.com) publishes a useful directory of businesses in the US and Canada ($24.95, CD-ROM edition $10), plus regional directories for New England, New York, and the South. *The Advocate*, based in Los Angeles ($3; ⓦwww.advocate.com) is a bimonthly national gay news magazine, with features, general info, and classified ads. Finally, the International Gay & Lesbian Travel Association in Fort Lauderdale

FL (☎1-954/776-2626, Ⓦwww.iglta.org), is a comprehensive, invaluable source for gay and lesbian travelers.

Health

If you have a serious accident while in the US, emergency medical services will get to you quickly and charge you later. For emergencies or ambulances, dial ☎911, the nationwide emergency number.

Should you need to see a doctor, consult the *Yellow Pages* telephone directory under "Clinics" or "Physicians and Surgeons." The basic consultation fee is $50–100, payable in advance. Tests, X-rays, etc are much more. Medications aren't cheap either – keep all your receipts for later claims on your insurance policy.

Foreign visitors should bear in mind that many pills available over the counter at home – most codeine-based painkillers, for example – require a prescription in the US. Local brand names can be confusing; ask for advice at the pharmacy in any drugstore.

In general, inoculations aren't required for entry to the US.

Medical resources for travelers

CDC Ⓦwww.cdc.gov/travel. Official US government travel health site.

International Society for Travel Medicine Ⓦwww.istm.org. Full listing of travel health clinics.

Insurance

In view of the high cost of medical care in the US, all travelers visiting the US from overseas should be sure to buy some form of travel insurance. American and Canadian citizens should check that you're not already covered – some homeowners' or renters' policies are valid on vacation, and credit cards such as American Express often include some medical or other insurance; most Canadians are covered for medical mishaps overseas by their provincial health plans. If you only need trip cancellation/interruption coverage (to supplement your existing plan), this is generally available at about $6 per $100.

Internet

Due to the fact that nearly eighty percent of American homes are now online, **cyber-cafés**, where you can get plugged in to the web for around $2–5 per hour, are not as common as they were, though many places have wi-fi to hook up your own laptop. Hotels may offer free or cheap **high-speed internet access**, and nearly all **public libraries** provide free Internet access, though often there's a wait and machine time is limited.

A useful website – Ⓦwww.kropla.com – has information on how to plug in a laptop when abroad, as well as useful worldwide communications info. For a database of internet cafés and public internet access points worldwide, go to Ⓦwww.cybercaptive.com.

Living in the USA

Study and work programs

AFS Intercultural Programs US ☎1-800/237-4636, Canada ☎1-800/361-7248 or 514/288-3282, UK ☎0113/242 6136, Australia ☎1300/131 736 or ☎02/9215-0077, NZ ☎0800/600 300 or 04/494 6020, international inquiries ☎+1-212/807-8686, Ⓦwww.afs.org.

Rough Guides travel insurance

Rough Guides has teamed up with Columbus Direct to offer you tailor-made **travel insurance.** Products include a low-cost **backpacker** option for long stays; a **short break** option for city getaways; a typical **holiday package** option; and others. There are also annual **multi-trip** policies for those who travel regularly. Different sports and activities (trekking, skiing, etc) can usually be included.

See our website (Ⓦww.roughguides.com/website/shop) for eligibility and purchasing options. Alternatively, UK residents can call ☎0870/033 9988; Australians ☎1300/669 999 and New Zealanders ☎0800/559 911. All other nationalities should call ☎+44 870/890 2843.

Global UN-recognized organization running summer programs to foster international understanding.

From the US and Canada

American Institute for Foreign Study ⓣ1-866/906-2437, ⓦwww.aifs.com. Language study and cultural immersion, as well as au pair and Camp America programs.

Council on International Educational Exchange (CIEE) ⓣ1-800/40-STUDY or ⓣ1/207-533-7600, ⓦwww.ciee.org. Leading NGO offering study programs and volunteer projects around the world.

Earthwatch Institute ⓣ1-800/776-0188 or 978/461-0081, ⓦwww.earthwatch.org. International non-profit that does research projects in over fifty countries all over the world.

From the UK and Ireland

BTCV (British Trust for Conservation Volunteers) ⓣ01302/572 244, ⓦwww.btcv.org.uk. One of the largest environmental charities in Britain, with a program of national and international working holidays (as a paying volunteer).

BUNAC (British Universities North America Club) ⓣ020/7251 3472, ⓦwww.bunac.co.uk. Organizes working holidays in the US and other destinations for students.

Camp America Camp America ⓣ020/7581 7373, ⓦwww.campamerica.co.uk.

Earthwatch Institute ⓣ01865/318 838, ⓦwww.uk.earthwatch.org. Long-established international charity with environmental and archeological research projects worldwide.

From Australia and New Zealand

AFS Intercultural Programs Australia ⓣ1300/131 736 or 02/9215 0088, NZ ⓣ0800/600 300 or 04/494 6020, ⓦwww.afs.org.au, ⓦwww.afsnzl.org.nz. Runs summer experiential programs aimed at fostering international understanding for teenagers and adults.

From South Africa

AFS Intercultural Programs ⓣ011/339 2741, ⓦwww.afs.org/southafrica. Non-profit, self-funded and volunteer-based NGO organization..

Mail

Post offices are usually open Monday to Friday from 9am to 5pm, and Saturday from 9am to noon, and there are blue mail boxes on many street corners. At time of publication, first class mail within the US costs 42¢ for a letter weighing up to an ounce, 72¢ for Canada and 94¢ for the rest of the world. Air mail between the US and Europe may take a week to be received.

In the US, the last line of the address includes the city or town and an abbreviation denoting the state (California is "CA" and Texas is "TX"). The last line also includes a five-digit number – the **zip code** – denoting the local post office. It is very important to include this, though the additional four digits that you will sometimes see appended are not essential. You can check zip codes on the US Postal Service website, at ⓦwww.usps.com.

Rules on sending **parcels** are very rigid: packages must be in special containers bought from post offices and sealed according to their instructions, which are given at the start of the *Yellow Pages*. To send anything out of the country, you'll need a green customs declaration form, available from a post office.

Maps

The free **road maps** distributed by each state through its tourist offices and welcome centres are usually fine for general driving and route planning. In addition, Rough Guides makes rip-proof, waterproof maps for numerous **cities, states, and regions** in the US, such as New York, California, New England, and much more.

Rand McNally produces maps for each state, bound together in the *Rand McNally Road Atlas*, and you're apt to find even cheaper state and regional maps at practically any gas station along the major highways for around $3–7. Britain's best source for maps is Stanfords, at 12–14 Long Acre, London WC2E 9LP (ⓣ020/7836 1321, ⓦwww.stanfords.co.uk), which also has a mail-order service.

The American Automobile Association, or AAA ("Triple A"; ⓣ1-877/244-9790, ⓦwww.aaa.com) provides free maps and assistance to its members, and to British members of the AA and RAC. Call the main number to get the location of a branch near you; bring your membership card, or at least a copy of your membership number.

If you're really after **detailed maps** that go far beyond the usual fold-out, try Thomas Guides ($20–40), though they only cover places in the western US. Highly detailed **park, wilderness**, and **topographical maps** are available through the Bureau of Land Management for the West (Ⓦblm.gov) and for the entire country through the Forest Service (Ⓦwww.fs.fed.us/maps). The best supplier of detailed, large-format map books for travel through the American outback is **Benchmark Maps**, whose elegantly designed depictions are easy to follow and make even the most remote dirt roads look appealing.

Money

The US dollar, the country's currency, comes in $1, $5, $10, $20, $50 and $100 **denominations**. One dollar comprises one hundred cents, made up of combinations of one-cent pennies, five-cent nickels, ten-cent dimes, and 25-cent quarters. You can check current exchange rates at Ⓦwww.xe.com/ucc; at the time of writing one pound sterling will buy $1.45–1.50 and a Euro $1.25–1.35.

Bank hours are generally from 9am to 5pm Monday to Thursday, and until 6pm on Friday; the big bank names are Wells Fargo, US Bank, and Bank of America. With an **ATM card**, you'll be able to withdraw cash just about anywhere, though you'll be charged $1.50–4 per transaction for using a different bank's network. Foreign cash-dispensing cards linked to international networks, such as Plus or Cirrus, are also widely accepted – ask your home bank or credit card company which branches you can use. To find the location of the nearest ATM, call AmEx Ⓣ1-800/227-4669; Cirrus Ⓣ1-800/424-7787; The Exchange Ⓣ1-800/237-2867; or Plus Ⓣ1-800/843-7587.

Credit and **debit cards** are the most widely accepted form of payment at major hotels, restaurants, and retailers, even though some smaller merchants still do not accept them. You'll be asked to show some plastic when renting a car, bike, or other such item, or to start a "tab" at hotels for incidental charges; in any case, you can always pay the bill in cash when you return the item or check out of your room.

US **traveler's checks** are the safest way for overseas visitors to carry money, and the better-known checks, such as those issued by American Express and Visa, are treated as cash in most shops.

Opening hours and public holidays

Government offices (including post offices) and banks will be closed on the following national **public holidays**:

Jan 1 New Year's Day
Third Mon in Jan Martin Luther King Jr's Birthday
Third Mon in Feb Presidents' Day
Last Mon in May Memorial Day
July 4 Independence Day
First Mon in Sept Labor Day
Second Mon in Oct Columbus Day
Nov 11 Veterans' Day
Fourth Thurs in Nov Thanksgiving Day
December 25 Christmas Day

Phones

The US currently has well over one hundred area codes – three-digit numbers that must precede the seven-figure number if you're

Wiring money

Having money **wired** from home is never cheap, and should be considered a last resort. If you must, the quickest way is to have someone take cash to the nearest **American Express Moneygram** office (call Ⓣ1-800/543-4080 for locations; also available at participating Travelex branches) and have it instantaneously wired to you, minus a ten-percent commission. For similar, if slightly pricier, services, **Western Union** also has offices throughout the country (Ⓣ1-800/325-6000 in the US; Ⓣ0800/833 833 in the UK; and Ⓣ1800/649 565 in Australia; Ⓦwww.westernunion.com), with credit-card payments subject to an additional $10 fee.

Calling home from abroad

Note that the initial zero is omitted from the area code when dialing the UK, Ireland, Australia, and New Zealand from abroad.
US and Canada international access code + 1 + area code.
Australia international access code + 61 + city code.
New Zealand international access code + 64 + city code.
UK international access code + 44 + city code.
Republic of Ireland international access code + 353 + city code.
South Africa international access code + 27 + city code.
For codes not listed here, dial 0 for the operator, consult any phone directory or log onto Ⓦwww.countrycallingcodes.com.

calling from abroad (following the 001 international access code) or from a different area code, in which case you prefix the ten digits with a 1. It can get confusing, especially as certain cities have several different area codes within their boundaries; for clarity, in this book, we've included the local area codes in all telephone numbers. Note that some cities require you to dial all ten digits, even when calling within the same code.

The cheapest way to make **long-distance** and **international** calls is by purchasing a **prepaid phonecard**, commonly found in $5 and $10 denominations in newsagents or minimarkets, especially in urban areas. These are cheaper than the similar cards issued by the big phone companies that are usually on sale in pharmacy outlets and chain stores. The rate using such cards from the USA to most European and other western countries is only 2/3¢ per minute; they also provide the lowest rates to developing countries. Such cards can be used from any touchpad phone but there is usually a surcharge for using them from a payphone. You can also usually arrange with your local telecom provider to have a **chargecard** account with a freephone access in the US, so that any calls you make are billed to your home. This may be convenient, but it's far more expensive than using prepaid cards.

If you are planning to take a **mobile phone** (universally known as cell phones in America) from outside of the USA, you'll need to check with your service provider whether it will work in the country. Unless you have a **tri-band** or **quad-band** phone, it is unlikely that a mobile bought for use outside the US will work there. If you do have such a phone, you'll have to contact your service provider's customer care department to ensure it is enabled for international calls. Be aware that you will incur hefty **roaming charges** for making calls and also be charged extra for incoming calls, as the people calling you will be paying the usual rate. If you want to retrieve messages while you're away, ask your provider for a new access code, as your home one is unlikely to work abroad. As the cost of using mobiles abroad is still fairly prohibitive, you may want to rent or buy a phone if you're traveling to the US; pay-as-you-go phones are inexpensive from major electrical shops. For a comprehensive overview of the capabilities of various phones and a useful database of roaming charges, check out Ⓦwww.mediacells.com.

Senior travelers

Anyone over age 62 (with appropriate ID) can enjoy a vast range of discounts in the US. Both Amtrak and Greyhound offer (smallish) percentage reductions on fares to older passengers, and any US citizen or permanent resident 62 or over is entitled to free admission for life to all national parks, monuments, and historic sites using a Golden Age Passport (issued for a one-time fee of $10 at any such site). This free admission applies to all accompanying travelers in the same vehicle and also gives a fifty percent reduction on park user fees, such as camping charges.

Membership in the AARP (formerly the American Association of Retired Persons), based in Washington DC (Ⓣ202/434-2277 or 1-888/687-2277, Ⓦwww.aarp.org), is open

Clothing and shoe sizes

Women's dresses and skirts

American	4	6	8	10	12	14	16	18
British	8	10	12	14	16	18	20	22
Continental	38	40	42	44	46	48	50	52

Women's blouses and sweaters

American	6	8	10	12	14	16	18
British	30	32	34	36	38	40	42
Continental	40	42	44	46	48	50	52

Women's shoes

American	5	6	7	8	9	10	11
British	3	4	5	6	7	8	9
Continental	36	37	38	39	40	41	42

Men's suits

American	34	36	38	40	42	44	46	48
British	34	36	38	40	42	44	46	48
Continental	44	46	48	50	52	54	56	58

Men's shirts

American	14	15	15.5	16	16.5	17	17.5	18
British	14	15	15.5	16	16.5	17	17.5	18
Continental	36	38	39	41	42	43	44	45

Men's shoes

American	7	7.5	8	8.5	9.5	10	10.5	11	11.5
British	6	7	7.5	8	9	9.5	10	11	12
Continental	39	40	41	42	43	44	44	45	46

to US residents 50 or over for an annual $12.50 fee; the organization plans group travel for seniors and can provide discounts on accommodation and vehicle rental.

Elderhostel, in Boston (ⓣ1-800/454-5768, ⓦwww.elderhostel.org), runs an extensive network of educational and activity programs for people over 60 throughout the US, at prices broadly in line with those of commercial tours. Saga Holidays, also based in Boston (ⓣ1-800/343-0723, ⓦwww.sagaholidays.com) offers some domestic tours too.

Shopping

Not surprisingly, the US has some of the greatest **shopping** opportunities in the world – from the luxury-lined blocks of Fifth Avenue in New York, the Miracle Mile in Chicago, and Rodeo Drive in Beverly Hills, to the local markets found in both big cities and small, offering everything from fruits and vegetables to handmade local crafts.

When buying clothing and accessories, international visitors will need to convert their sizes into American equivalents (see box). For almost all purchases, state taxes will be applied (see "Costs," p.53).

Time

The continental US covers four **time zones**, and there's one each for Alaska and Hawaii as well. The Eastern zone is five hours behind Greenwich Mean Time (GMT), so 3pm London time is 10am in New York (see below for the one-week exceptions). The Central zone, starting approximately on a line down from Chicago and spreading west to Texas and across the Great Plains, is an hour behind the East (10am in New York is 9am in Dallas). The Mountain zone, which covers the Rocky Mountains and most of the Southwest, is two hours behind the East Coast (10am in New York is 8am in Denver). The Pacific zone includes the three coastal states and Nevada, and is three hours behind New York (10am in the Big Apple is 7am in San Francisco). Lastly, most of Alaska (except for the St Lawrence Islands, which are with Hawaii) is nine hours behind GMT (10am in New York is 6am in Anchorage), while Hawaii is ten hours behind GMT (10am in New York is 5am in Honolulu). The US puts its clocks forward to daylight saving time on the first Sunday in April and turns them back on the first Sunday in November (a week later than the EU in both cases).

Tourist information

Each state has its own tourist office, as listed in the box on p.000. These offer prospective visitors a colossal range of free maps, leaflets, and brochures on attractions from overlooked wonders to well-trod tourist traps. You can either contact the offices before you set off, or, as you travel around the country, look for the state-run "welcome centers," usually along main highways close to the state borders. In heavily visited states, these often have piles of discount coupons for cut-price accommodation and food. In addition, visitor centers in most towns and cities—often known as the "Convention and Visitors Bureau," or CVB, and listed throughout this book—provide details on the area, as do local Chambers of Commerce in almost any town of any size.

Tourist offices and government sites

Australian Department of Foreign Affairs ⓦwww.dfat.gov.au, ⓦwww.smartraveller.gov.au.
British Foreign & Commonwealth Office ⓦwww.fco.gov.uk.
Canadian Department of Foreign Affairs ⓦwww.dfait-maeci.gc.ca.
Irish Department of Foreign Affairs ⓦwww.foreignaffairs.gov.ie.
New Zealand Ministry of Foreign Affairs ⓦwww.mft.govt.nz.
US State Department ⓦwww.travel.state.gov.

Travelers with disabilities

By international standards, the US is exceptionally accommodating for travelers with mobility concerns or other physical disabilities. All public buildings, including hotels and restaurants, must be wheelchair accessible and provide suitable toilet facilities. Almost all street corners have dropped curbs, and most public transportation systems include subway stations with elevators and buses that "kneel" to let wheelchaired passengers board.

Getting around

The Americans with Disabilities Act (1990) obliges all air carriers to make the majority of their services accessible to travelers with disabilities, and most airlines will usually let attendants of more seriously disabled people accompany them at no extra charge.

Almost every Amtrak train includes one or more coaches with accommodation for handicapped passengers. Guide dogs travel free and may accompany blind, deaf, or disabled passengers. Be sure to give 24 hours' notice. Hearing-impaired passengers can get information on ⓣ1-800/523-6590 (though it can take a while to get through; the service is poorly staffed).

Greyhound, however, is not recommended. Buses are not equipped with lifts for wheelchairs, though staff will assist with boarding (intercity carriers are required by law to do this), and the "Helping Hand" policy offers two-for-the-price-of-one tickets to passengers unable to travel alone (carry a doctor's certificate). The American Public Transportation Association, in Washington DC (ⓣ202/496-4800, ⓦwww.apta.com), provides information about the accessibility of public transportation in cities.

The American Automobile Association (ⓣ1-877/244-9790, ⓦwww.aaa.com) produces the *Handicapped Driver's Mobility Guide*, while the larger car-rental companies provide cars with hand controls at no extra charge, though only on their full-sized (ie most expensive) models; reserve well in advance.

Resources

Most state tourism offices provide information for disabled travelers (see p.000). In addition, SATH, the Society for Accessible Travel and Hospitality, in New York (ⓣ212/447-7284, ⓦwww.sath.org), is a not-for-profit travel-industry group of travel agents, tour operators,

State tourism information

Alabama ⓣ 1-800/252-2262, ⓦ www.alabama.travel
Alaska ⓣ 1-800/862-5275, ⓦ www.travelalaska.com
Arizona ⓣ 1-866/275-5816, ⓦ www.arizonaguide.com
Arkansas ⓣ 1-800/628-8725, ⓦ www.arkansas.com
California ⓣ 1-800/TO-CALIF, ⓦ www.visitcalifornia.com
Colorado ⓣ 1-800/COLORADO, ⓦ www.colorado.com
Connecticut ⓣ 1-888/288-4748, ⓦ www.ctvisit.com
Delaware ⓣ 1-866/284-7483, ⓦ www.visitdelaware.com
Florida ⓣ 1-888/735-2872, ⓦ www.visitflorida.com
Georgia ⓣ 1-800/847-4842, ⓦ www.exploregeorgia.org
Hawaii ⓣ 1-800/GO-HAWAII, ⓦ www.gohawaii.com
Idaho ⓣ 1-800/VISIT-ID, ⓦ www.visitidaho.org
Illinois ⓣ 1-800/226-6632, ⓦ www.enjoyillinois.com
Indiana ⓣ 1-888/365-6946, ⓦ www.visitindiana.com
Iowa ⓣ 1-800/345-IOWA, ⓦ www.traveliowa.com
Kansas ⓣ 1-800/252-6727, ⓦ www.travelks.com
Kentucky ⓣ 1-800/225-8747, ⓦ www.kentuckytourism.com
Louisiana ⓣ 1-800/99-GUMBO, ⓦ www.louisianatravel.com
Maine ⓣ 1-888/624-6345, ⓦ www.visitmaine.com
Maryland ⓣ 1-800/634-7386, ⓦ www.visitmaryland.org
Massachusetts ⓣ 1-800/227-6277, ⓦ www.massvacation.com
Michigan ⓣ 1-888/784-7328, ⓦ www.michigan.org
Minnesota ⓣ 1-800/657-3700, ⓦ www.exploreminnesota.com
Mississippi ⓣ 1-866/733-6477, ⓦ www.visitmississippi.org
Missouri ⓣ 1-800/519-2100, ⓦ www.visitmo.com
Montana ⓣ 1-800/847-4868, ⓦ www.visitmt.com
Nebraska ⓣ 1-800/228-4307, ⓦ www.visitnebraska.org
Nevada ⓣ 1-800/237-0774, ⓦ www.travelnevada.com
New Hampshire ⓣ 1-800/386-4664, ⓦ www.visitnh.gov
New Jersey ⓣ 1-800/847-4865, ⓦ www.visitnj.org
New Mexico ⓣ 1-800/545-2070, ⓦ www.newmexico.org
New York ⓣ 1-800/I-LOVE-NY, ⓦ www.iloveny.com
North Carolina ⓣ 1-800/847-4862, ⓦ www.visitnc.com
North Dakota ⓣ 1-800/435-5663, ⓦ www.ndtourism.com
Ohio ⓣ 1-800/BUCKEYE, ⓦ www.discoverohio.com
Oklahoma ⓣ 1-800/652-6552, ⓦ www.travelok.com
Oregon ⓣ 1-800/547-7842, ⓦ www.traveloregon.com
Pennsylvania ⓣ 1-800/847-4872, ⓦ www.visitpa.com
Rhode Island ⓣ 1-800/556-2484, ⓦ www.visitrhodeisland.com
South Carolina ⓣ 1-888/727-6453, ⓦ www.discoversouthcarolina.com
South Dakota ⓣ 1-800/732-5682, ⓦ www.travelsd.com
Tennessee ⓣ 1-800/462-8366, ⓦ www.tnvacation.com
Texas ⓣ 1-800/888-8839, ⓦ www.traveltex.com
Utah ⓣ 1-800/882-4386, ⓦ www.utah.com
Vermont ⓣ 1-800/VERMONT, ⓦ www.vermontvacation.com
Virginia ⓣ 1-800/847-4882, ⓦ www.virginia.org
Washington ⓣ 1-800/544-1800, ⓦ www.experiencewa.com
Washington DC ⓣ 1-800/422-8644, ⓦ www.washington.org
West Virginia ⓣ 1-800/225-5982, ⓦ www.wvtourism.com
Wisconsin ⓣ 1-800/432-8747, ⓦ www.travelwisconsin.com
Wyoming ⓣ 1-800/225-5996, ⓦ www.wyomingtourism.org

hotel and airline management, and people with disabilities. They pass on any inquiry to the appropriate member, though you should allow plenty of time for a response. Mobility International USA, in Eugene OR (T 541/343-1284, W www.miusa.org), offers travel tips and operates exchange programs for disabled people. They also serve as a national information center on disability. If you'd like to plan a specific itinerary for your trip, contact the Directions Unlimited travel agency in New York (T 914/241-1700 or 1-800/533-5343), which has a department for disabled travelers.

Disabled Outdoors is a quarterly magazine specializing in facilities for disabled travelers who wish to explore the great outdoors. The useful publications by Twin Peaks Press, *Travel for the Disabled* and *Wheelchair Vagabond*, are both out of print but widely available online.

The Golden Access Passport, issued without charge to permanently disabled or blind US citizens, gives free lifetime admission to all national parks. It can only be obtained in person at a federal area where an entrance fee is charged; you'll have to show proof of permanent disability, or that you are eligible for receiving benefits under federal law.

Women travelers

A woman traveling alone in America is not usually made to feel conspicuous, or liable to attract unwelcome attention. Cities can feel a lot safer than you might expect from recurrent media images of demented urban jungles, simply because there are so many people around. Like anywhere, though, particular care must be taken at night: walking through unlit, empty streets is never a good idea, and, if there's no bus service, take a taxi. Women who look confident are less likely to encounter trouble; those who stand around looking lost and a bit scared are prime targets.

In the major urban centers, if you stick to the better parts of town, going into bars and clubs alone should pose few problems: there's generally a pretty healthy attitude toward women who do so, and your privacy will be respected. Lesbian bars are usually a trouble-free and welcoming alternative.

However, small towns may lack the same liberal or indifferent attitude toward lone women travelers. People seem to jump immediately to the conclusion that your car has broken down, or that you've suffered some strange misfortune; you may get fed up with well-meant offers of help. If your vehicle does break down on heavily traveled roads, wait in the car for a police or highway patrol car to arrive. You should also rent a mobile phone with your car, for a small charge – a potential lifesaver.

Women – even more so than for men – should never hitchhike in the US. It's just asking for trouble. Similarly, you should never pick up anyone who's trying to hitchhike. If someone is waving you down on the road, ostensibly to get help with a broken-down vehicle, just drive on by – the highway patrol will be along soon enough to see what the trouble is.

Avoid traveling at night by public transportation – deserted bus stations, if not actually threatening, will do little to make you feel secure. Where possible, team up with a fellow traveler. On Greyhound buses, sit near the driver.

Should disaster strike, all major towns have some kind of rape counseling service; if not, the local sheriff's office will arrange for you to get help and counseling, and, if necessary, get you home. The National Organization for Women (W www.now.org) is a leader in seeking to advance issues of importance to women. NOW branches, listed in local phone directories and on the website, can provide information on rape crisis centers, counseling services, feminist bookstores, and lesbian bars.

Resources and specialists

Gutsy Women Travel Glenside PA T 215/572-7676 or 1-866/464-8879, W www.gutsywomentravel.com. International agency that provides practical support, as well as organising trips for lone female travelers.

Womanship Annapolis MD T 410/267-6661 or 1-800/342-9295, W www.womanship.com. Live-aboard, learn-to-sail cruises for women of all ages. Destinations include Chesapeake Bay, Florida, the Pacific Northwest, and Mystic, Connecticut.

The Women's Travel Club Bloomfield NJ T 1-800/480-4448, W www.womenstravelclub.com. Arranges vacations, itineraries, room-sharing and various activities for women.

Guide

Guide

1

New York City

CHAPTER 1 Highlights

- **Ellis Island** Once the first stop for millions of prospective immigrants from all over the world, and now the site of a moving museum. See p.76
- **Empire State Building** Enjoy the mind-blowing views from the top of the most iconic skyscraper in the city. 87 p.000
- **Central Park** A massive, gorgeous, green space, filled with countless bucolic amusements; familiar from countless movies, it's one of the greatest urban parks in America. See p.91
- **The Metropolitan Museum of Art** The museum's mammoth collection could keep you busy for days. See p.94
- **Coney Island** Soak up the sun, stroll the boardwalk, and savor the most famous hot dogs in America at this beachside amusement park. See p.100
- **A baseball game at the new Yankee Stadium** Between April and October, it would be a shame not to take in a Bronx Bombers ballgame. See p.115
- **New York delis** The city's culinary delights range from bagels and pizza slices to global haute cuisine, but Katz's and Zabar's delis are essential New York. See p.102

▲ Central Park

1

New York City

The most beguiling city in the world, **New York City** is an adrenaline-charged, history-laden place that holds immense romantic appeal for visitors. Whether gazing at the flickering lights of the Midtown skyscrapers as you speed across the Queensboro Bridge, experiencing the 4am half-life in the Village, or just whiling the day away in Central Park, you really would have to be made of stone not to be moved by it all. There's no place quite like it.

New York City comprises the central island of **Manhattan** and the four outer boroughs – **Brooklyn**, **Queens**, the **Bronx**, and **Staten Island**. Manhattan, to many, *is* New York; certainly, this is where you're likely to stay and spend most of your time. The island is broadly divided into three areas: **Downtown** (below 14th St), **Midtown** (from 14th St to Central Park/59th St), and **Uptown** (north of 59th St). Though you could spend weeks here and still barely scratch the surface, there are some key attractions and pleasures that you won't want to miss. These include the different **ethnic neighborhoods**, like Chinatown, and the more artsy concentrations of SoHo and the East and West villages. Of course, there is the celebrated **architecture** of Midtown and the Financial District, as well as many fabulous **museums** – not just the Metropolitan and MoMA, but countless other smaller collections that afford weeks of happy wandering. In between sights, you can **eat** just about anything, at any time, cooked in any style; you can **drink** in any kind of company; and enjoy any number of obscure **movies**. The more established arts – **dance**, **theater**, and **music** – are superbly presented. For the avid consumer, the choice of **shops** is vast, almost numbingly exhaustive, in this heartland of the great capitalist dream.

Manhattan is a hard act to follow, and the four **outer boroughs**, essentially residential in character, inevitably pale in comparison. Parts of **Brooklyn** have changed dramatically since the 1990s, with gentrification spreading across the East River and places like **Williamsburg** absorbing a hip and youthful exodus from Manhattan's high prices – you'll find some of the city's coolest bars here. Beyond nightlife, **Brooklyn Heights** is one of the city's most beautiful neighborhoods; **Long Island City** and **Astoria**, both in Queens, hold a couple of innovative museums; and a visit to the **Bronx Zoo** is sure to be rewarding. Last but not least, a free trip on the **Staten Island Ferry** is not to be missed; a sea-sprayed, refreshing good time, it provides excellent views of the city.

Some history

The first European to see Manhattan Island, then inhabited by the Lenape Indians, was the Italian navigator Giovanni da Verrazano, in 1524. Dutch colonists established the settlement of **New Amsterdam** exactly one hundred years later. The

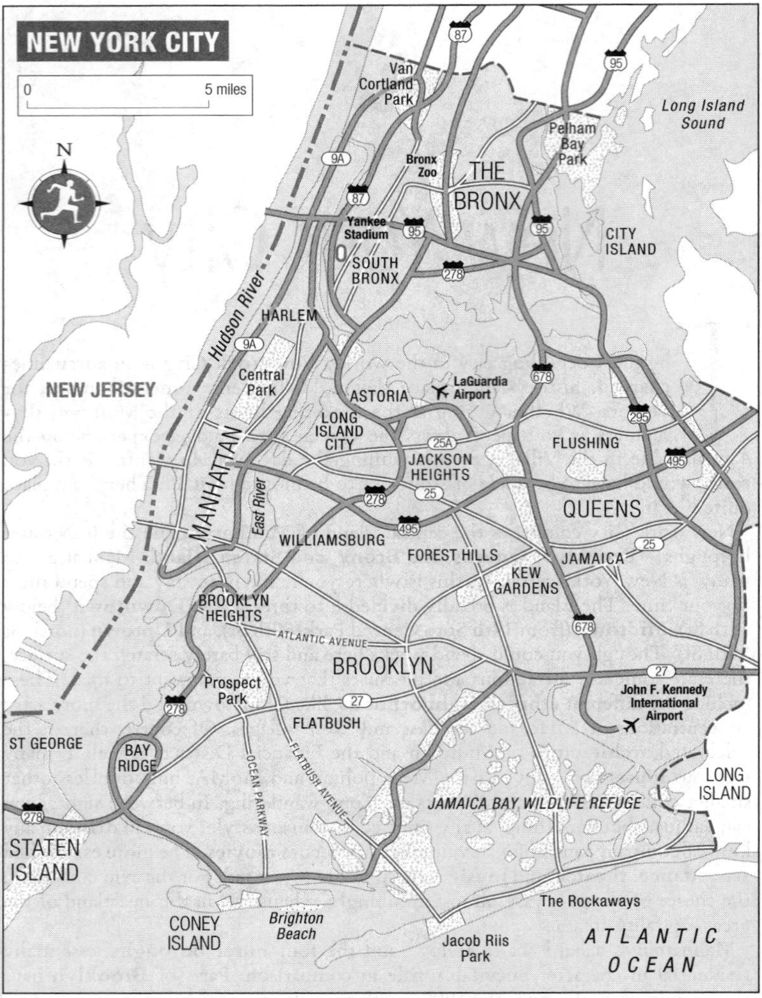

first governor, Peter Minuit, was the man who famously bought the whole island for a handful of trinkets. Though we don't know for sure who "sold" the island (it was probably a northern branch of the Lenni Lenape), the other side of the story (and the part you never hear), was that the concept of owning land was utterly alien to Native Americans – they had merely agreed to support Dutch claims to *use* the land, as they did. By the time the British laid claim to the area in 1664, the heavy-handed rule of governor **Peter Stuyvesant** had so alienated its inhabitants that the Dutch relinquished control without a fight.

Renamed **New York**, the city prospered and grew, its population reaching 33,000 by the time of the American Revolution. The opening of the **Erie Canal** in 1825 facilitated trade farther inland, spurring the city to become the economic powerhouse of the nation, the base later in the century of **tycoons** such as Cornelius Vanderbilt and **financiers** like J.P. Morgan. The **Statue of Liberty** arrived from France in 1886, a symbol of the city's role as the gateway for generations of immigrants, and the early twentieth century saw the sudden proliferation of Manhattan's extraordinary **skyscrapers**, which cast New York as the city of the future in the eyes of an astonished world.

Almost a century later, the events of **September 11, 2001**, which destroyed the World Trade Center, shook New York to its core. Yet the Financial District has bounced back with a comprehensive redevelopment plan, ensuring that by 2011 a new array of glitzy skyscrapers, including the **Freedom Tower** (see box, p.78), will dominate the Downtown skyline.

Arrival, information, and city transportation

New York City is served by three major **airports**: **John F. Kennedy**, or **JFK**, in Queens, **LaGuardia**, also in Queens, and **Newark**, in New Jersey.

From JFK, the New York Airport Service (ⓣ212/875-8200) runs **buses** to Grand Central Terminal, Port Authority Bus Terminal, and Penn Station (every 15–20min 6.15am–11.10pm; 45–60min; $15 single, $27 round-trip). The AirTrain (24hr daily; ⓦwww.panynj.gov/airtrain; $5) runs between JFK and the Jamaica and Howard Beach **subway** stations in Queens; at Jamaica you can connect to the subway lines E, J, or Z, and at Howard Beach, to the A subway line, into Manhattan (from both stations: 1hr; $2). Alternatively, the Long Island Railroad runs **trains** from the Jamaica station to Penn Station (20min; $5.25 off-peak).

From LaGuardia, New York Airport Service **buses** take 45 minutes to get to Grand Central and Port Authority (every 15–30min 7.20am–11pm; $12 single, $21 round-trip). Alternatively, for $2, you can take the #M60 bus to 106th Street in Manhattan, where you can transfer to Downtown-bound subway lines.

From Newark, Newark Airport Express (ⓣ877/863-9275) runs **buses** to Grand Central Station, Port Authority Bus Terminal, and Penn Station (every 20–30min 4am–12.45am; $15 single, $25 round-trip). Alternatively, you can use the **AirTrain** service, which runs for free between all Newark terminals, parking lots, and the Newark Airport Train Station, where you can connect with NJ Transit or Amtrak trains into New York Penn Station. It usually takes about twenty minutes, and costs $15 single (every 20–30min 6am–midnight).

Taxis are pricey from the airports; reckon on paying $20 to $30 from LaGuardia to Manhattan, a flat rate of $45 from JFK, and $45 to $55 from Newark; you'll also be responsible for the turnpike and tunnel tolls – an extra $5 or so – as well as a fifteen- to twenty-percent tip for the driver. You should only use official yellow taxis that wait at designated ranks – just follow the signs out of the terminal.

Greyhound buses pull in at the Port Authority Bus Terminal, 42nd Street and Eighth Avenue. **Amtrak** trains come in to Penn Station, at Seventh Avenue and 33rd Street. From either Port Authority or Penn Station, various subway lines will take you where you want to go.

If **arriving by car**, you have multiple options: Rte-495 transects Midtown Manhattan from New Jersey through the Lincoln Tunnel ($6) and from the east through the Queens-Midtown Tunnel ($5). From the southwest, I-95 (the New Jersey Turnpike) and I-78 serve Canal and Spring streets (near SoHo) via the Holland Tunnel ($6). From the north, I-87 (New York State Thruway) and I-95 serve

Manhattan's loop roads. Be prepared for **delays** at tunnels and bridges. Also, when **parking** your car in Manhattan, try for a garage as near to the rivers as possible to avoid high fees.

Information

The best place for information is **NYC & Company**, 810 Seventh Ave at 53rd Street (Mon–Fri 8.30am–6pm, Sat & Sun 9am–5pm; Ⓣ212/484-1222, Ⓦwww.nycvisit.com). It has leaflets on what's going on in the arts, bus and subway maps, and information on accommodation – though they can't actually book anything for you.

City transportation

Few cities equal New York for sheer street-level stimulation, and **walking** is the most exciting way to explore. However, it's also exhausting, so at some point you'll need to use some form of **public transportation**. Citywide subway and bus system **maps** – the subway map is especially invaluable – are available from all subway station booths, tourist information centers (see above), the concourse office at Grand Central, or online at Ⓦwww.mta.nyc.ny.us.

The subway

The fastest way to get from point A to point B in Manhattan and the boroughs is the **subway**, open 24hr a day. A number or letter identifies each train and route; every trip, whether on the **express** lines, which stop only at major stations, or the **locals**, which stop at all stations, costs $2. All riders must use a **MetroCard**, available at station booths or credit/debit/ATM card-capable vending machines. MetroCards can be purchased in any amount from a $2 single ride to $80; a $20 purchase provides $23 worth of rides. Unlimited rides are available with a 24hr "Fun Pass" ($7.50), a seven-day pass ($25), and a thirty-day pass ($80).

Once you get past the turnstile, forget everything you've seen in the movies. New York City subways are generally **quite safe**, in part because they are almost always busy, but always use the more crowded center subway cars late at night.

Buses

New York's **bus system** is clean, efficient, and fairly frequent. Its one disadvantage is that it can be extremely slow – in peak hours almost down to walking pace – but it can be your best bet for traveling crosstown. Buses leave their route terminal points at five- to ten-minute intervals, and stop every two or three blocks. The $2 fare is payable on entry with a MetroCard (the same one used for the subway) or

City streets and orientation

The first part of Manhattan to be settled was what is now Downtown; this is why the streets here have names (as opposed to numbers) and are somewhat randomly arranged. Often you will hear of places referred to as being either on the **West Side** or the **East Side**; this refers to whether the place lies west or east of **Fifth Avenue**, which begins at the arch in Washington Square Park and runs north to cut along the east side of Central Park. On the East Side above Houston Street (pronounced "Howstun"), and on the West Side above 14th, the streets follow a **grid pattern**, progressing northward one by one. When looking for a specific **address**, keep in mind that on streets, house numbers increase as you walk away from Fifth in either direction; on avenues, house numbers increase as you move north.

Walking tours

Big Onion Walking Tours ⓣ212/439-1090, ⓦwww.bigonion.com. The Onion guides peel off the many layers of the city's history (all guides hold advanced degrees in American history). Tours are $15; call or visit the website for schedules and meeting places.

City Hunt ⓣ877/HUNT-FUN, ⓦwww.cityhunt.org. Innovative scavenger hunts and urban "safaris" like the "Da Vinci Hunt," which begins at the Met, and private pub crawls ($20–30).

Harlem Heritage Tours ⓣ212/280-7888, ⓦwww.harlemheritage.com. Cultural walking tours of Harlem, general and specific (such as Harlem jazz clubs). Reservations are recommended and can be booked online (average $25–40).

in cash, but with exact change only; you can **transfer** for free within two hours of swiping your MetroCard. Keep in mind, though, that transfers can only be used to continue on in your original direction, not for return trips on the same bus line.

Taxis

Taxis are relatively good value for short journeys (fares start at $2.50), convenient, and can be caught just about anywhere. You should only use official yellow taxis.

Guided tours

Countless businesses and individuals compete to help you make sense of the city, offering all manner of **guided tours**. One of the more original – and least expensive – ways to get oriented is with Big Apple Greeter, 1 Centre St, suite 2035 (ⓣ212/669-8159, ⓦwww.bigapplegreeter.org). This not-for-profit group matches you with a local volunteer and points you to places that interest you. It's free, so get in touch well ahead of time.

Gray Line, the biggest operator of guided **bus tours** in the city, have an office at the Port Authority Bus Terminal (ⓣ1-800/669-0051, ⓦwww.graylinenewyork.com). Double-decker bus tours offer an unlimited hop-on, hop-off service, taking in the main sights of Manhattan, for around $45. Tours are bookable through any travel agent, or directly at the bus stops. If you're not happy with your tour guide (quality can vary widely), you can hop off the bus and wait another fifteen minutes for the next bus.

A good way to see the city skyline is with the **Circle Line Ferry** (ⓣ212/563-3200, ⓦwww.circleline42.com), which sails from Pier 83 at W 42nd Street and Twelfth Avenue, circumnavigating Manhattan with live commentary; the three-hour tour runs year-round ($31, $26 seniors, $18 under-12s). Alternatively, the **Staten Island Ferry** (p.79) provides a beautiful panorama of the Downtown skyline for free.

For a bird's-eye view, Liberty Helicopter Tours, at the west end of 30th Street (ⓣ212/967-6464, ⓦwww.libertyhelicopters.com), offers **helicopter flights** from around $110 (6–8min) to $204 (16–20min) per person.

Accommodation

Prices for **accommodation** in New York are well above the norm for the US as a whole. Most hotels charge more than $200 a night (although exceptions for under $100 a night do exist), and for anything better than four stars you'll be lucky to pay less than $400. Most of New York's **hotels** are in Midtown Manhattan – a good enough location, though you may well want to travel downtown for less expensive (and usually better) food and nightlife. **Booking ahead** is strongly advised; at certain times of the year – Christmas, early summer, and the fall in particular – everything is likely to be full. Phone the hotels directly, or at no extra charge contact a booking service, such as CRS (ⓣ407/740-6442 or 1-800/555-7555, ⓦwww.crshotels.com) or Quikbook (Mon–Sat ⓣ1-800/789-9887 inside the US, ⓣ212/779-7666 outside the US, ⓦwww.quikbook.com). The **price codes** given at the end of each review reflect the cost of the cheapest double room during the high season.

Apartment stays and **bed-and-breakfasts** are an attractive alternative. Staying in a New Yorker's spare room or subletting an apartment is an increasingly popular and somewhat less expensive option. Reservations are normally arranged through an agency such as New York Stay (ⓦwww.newyorkstay.com). Rates start at around $140 for a double, but prices come down the longer you stay.

Hostels offer still more savings, and run the gamut in terms of quality, safety, and amenities. It pays to do research ahead of time to ensure satisfaction upon arrival; most of the city's best cheap sleeps have websites. Average hostel rates range from $30 to $60.

Hotels

60 Thompson 60 Thompson St, between Spring and Broome strs ⓣ212/431-0400, ⓦwww.60thompson.com. This boutique property oozes sophistication and tempts guests with countless amenities, including gourmet minibars, DVD players, and a summertime rooftop lounge overlooking the SoHo skyline. All this fabulousness comes at a price, though. ❾

Algonquin 59 W 44th St, between 5th and 6th aves ⓣ212/840-6800, ⓦwww.algonquinhotel.com. At New York's classic literary hangout, you'll find cabaret performances, and suites with silly names. The decor remains little changed since its Round Table heyday, though the bedrooms have been refurbished to good effect, and the lobby restored. Ask about summer and weekend specials. ❾

Amsterdam Inn 340 Amsterdam Ave, at 76th St ⓣ212/579-7500, ⓦwww.nyinns.com. Within easy walking distance of Central Park, Lincoln Center, and the American Museum of Natural History. Rooms are basic but clean, with TVs, phones, and maid service. The staff is friendly and there's a 24hr concierge. ❻

The Chelsea Hotel 222 W 23rd St, between 7th and 8th aves ⓣ212/243-3700, ⓦwww.hotelchelsea.com. One of New York's most noted landmarks, this aging neo-Gothic building boasts a notorious past (see p.000). Ask for a renovated room, with wood floors, log-burning fireplaces, and plenty of space for a few extra friends. ❽

Dylan 52 E 41st St, between Park and Madison aves ⓣ212/338-0500 or 1-866/55-DYLAN, ⓦwww.dylanhotel.com. The hardwood floors, warm light, and vaguely lemony-tasting air in the lobby are indicative of the whole experience at Dylan – classy and clever. If you can afford it, book the Alchemy Suite, a one-of-a-kind Gothic bedchamber with a vaulted ceiling and unusual stained-glass windows. ❾

Edison 228 W 47th St, between Broadway and 8th Ave ⓣ212/840-5000, ⓦwww.edisonhotelnyc.com. The most striking thing about the funky 1000-room Edison, a good value for Midtown, is its beautiful Art-Deco lobby. The rooms are not as fancy. ❽

Gramercy Park 2 Lexington Ave, at E 21st St ⓣ212/475-4320, ⓦwww.gramercyparkhotel.com. In a lovely location, this hotel reopened in 2006 after Ian Schrager (co-founder of Studio 54) made great bohemian renovations. The lobby is like stepping into a 3D painting. Guests get a key to the adjacent private park (see p.000). ❾

Larchmont 27 W 11th St, between 5th and 6th aves ⓣ212/989-9333, ⓦwww.larchmonthotel.com. This budget hotel, with a terrific location on a tree-lined street in Greenwich Village, has small but nice, clean rooms - it's a bargain, but the bathrooms are shared. Slightly more expensive on weekends. ❺

Lucerne 201 W 79th St, at Amsterdam Ave ⓣ212/875-1000 or 1-800/492-8122, ⓦwww.newyorkhotel.com. This beautifully restored 1904 brownstone, with its extravagantly Baroque red terracotta entrance, charming rooms, and friendly, helpful staff, is just a block from the American Museum of Natural History and close to the liveliest stretch of the Columbus Ave scene. ❾

Mercer 147 Mercer St, at Prince St ⓣ212/966-6060, ⓦwww.mercerhotel.com. Housed in a landmark Romanesque Revival building, this hot SoHo hotel has been the choice of many celebs since 1998. Some loft-like guest rooms also have massive baths with ninety square feet for splashing around, and the *Mercer Kitchen* restaurant garners rave reviews. ⑨

Milburn 242 W 76th St, between Broadway and West End aves ⓣ212/362-1006, ⓦwww.milburnhotel.com. This welcoming and well-situated hotel is great for families. ⑦

The Pod 230 E 51st St, between 2nd and 3rd aves ⓣ212/355-0300, ⓦwww.thepodhotel.com. This stylish budget hotel is one of the best deals in Midtown, with cramped but extremely hip doubles, singles, and bunks set against the glass-enclosed private bathrooms. You get free Wi-Fi, LCD TVs, and yes, iPod docking stations. ⑥

Roger Smith 501 Lexington Ave, at E 47th St ⓣ212/755-1400, ⓦwww.rogersmith.com. One of the best Midtown hotels. Plusses include individually decorated rooms, a great restaurant, helpful service, and artwork on display in public spaces. Breakfast is included. ⑨

Royalton 44 W 44th St, between 5th and 6th aves ⓣ212/869-4400, ⓦwww.royaltonhotel.com. Attempting to capture the market for the arbiters of style, the Philippe Starck–designed Royalton has tiny, nautical-themed rooms that are comfortable and quiet, affording a welcome escape from the bustle of Midtown. Stop in just to see the elegant lobby, which runs the length of a city block. ⑨

Hotel 17 225 E 17th St, between 2nd and 3rd aves ⓣ212/475-2845, ⓦwww.hotel17ny.com. Seventeen's rooms feature a/c, cable TV, and phones, though they still have shared baths. It's clean, friendly, and nicely situated on a pleasant tree-lined street minutes from Union Square and the East Village. Check out the excellent weekly rates. ⑧

Soho Grand 310 W Broadway, at Grand St ⓣ212/965-3000, ⓦwww.sohogrand.com. In a great location at the edge of SoHo, this hotel draws guests of the model/media-star/actor variety. Its appeal includes small but stylish rooms, a good bar, restaurant, and fitness center. Call for info about its sleek sister property, the Tribeca Grand. ⑨

Wales 1295 Madison Ave, between 92nd and 93rd streets ⓣ212/876-6000, ⓦwww.waleshotel.com. Just steps from NYC's "Museum Mile" (see p.000), rooms are attractive with antique details, thoughtful in-room amenities, and some views of Central Park. There's also a rooftop terrace, fitness studio, and live harp music during breakfast. ⑨

Washington Square 103 Waverly Place, at Washington Square Park ⓣ212/777-9515, ⓦwww.washingtonsquarehotel.com. Located in the heart of Greenwich Village, a stone's throw from the NYU campus. Don't be deceived by the posh-looking lobby – the rooms are surprisingly simple for the price (ask for a renovated room). Tends to fill up months in advance, regardless. ⑨

Bed-and-breakfast agents

Affordable New York City 21 E 10th St ⓣ212/533-4001, ⓦwww.affordablenyc.com. Detailed descriptions are provided for this established network of 120 properties (B&Bs and apartments) around the city. B&B accommodations (four-night minimum) with shared or private bath run ④–⑥, studios are ⑥–⑦ , and one-bedroom apartments are ⑦–⑧. Apartments accept cash or traveler's checks only and have a five-night minimum.

Bed and Breakfast Network of New York 130 Barrow St ⓣ212/645-8134 or 1-800/ 900-8134, ⓦwww.bedandbreakfastnetny.com. Call at least a month in advance, and ask about weekly and monthly specials. Hosted doubles ⑦

CitySonnet.com ⓣ212/614-3034, ⓦwww.citysonnet.com. This small, personalized, artist-run B&B and short-term apartment agency offers accommodations all over the city, but specializes in Greenwich Village. Singles, doubles, and unhosted studio apartments. ⑦

Colby International 139 Round Hey, Liverpool L28 1RG, England UK ⓣ0151/220 5848, ⓦwww.colbyinternational.com. Guaranteed B&B accommodations can be arranged from the UK. Book at least two weeks ahead in high season for these great value double apartments (from ⑨) and studios (⑦), though charging in UK pounds definitely benefits the sellers (while the US dollar remains low).

Hostels

Chelsea International Hostel 251 W 20th St, between 7th and 8th aves ⓣ212/647-0010, ⓦwww.chelseahostel.com. In the heart of Chelsea, this is a smart Downtown choice: beds are $32–36 a night (with tax), with four or six sharing the clean, rudimentary rooms. Private double rooms are $80 a night. Guests must leave a $10 key deposit. No curfew; passport required.

Gershwin 7 E 27th St, between 5th and Madison aves ⓣ212/545-8000, ⓦwww.gershwinhotel.com. This hostel and hotel geared toward young travelers offers Pop Art decor and dormitories with two, six, or ten beds per room (from $40 a night) and private rooms from $109. Reservations recommended for both room types.

Hostelling International-New York 891 Amsterdam Ave, at W 103rd St ⓣ212/932-2300, ⓦwww.hinewyork.org. Dorm beds cost $41 (in ten-bed rooms) to $45 (in four-bed rooms); members pay a few dollars less per night. The massive facilities – 624 beds in all – include a restaurant, library, travel shop, TV room, laundry, and kitchen. Reserve well in advance – this hostel is very popular.

Jazz on the Park 36 W 106th St, at Central Park West ⓣ212/932-1600, ⓦwww.jazzonthepark.com. This groovy bunkhouse boasts a TV and games room, the Java Joint Café, and lots of activities, including live jazz on weekends. Rooms sleep between two and fourteen people, are clean, bright, with a/c, and range from $32 to $62 per night. Reserve at least one week in advance.

West Side YMCA 5 W 63rd St, at Central Park West ⓣ212/441-8800, ⓦwww.ymcanyc.org. The "Y," just steps from Central Park, houses two floors of renovated rooms, an inexpensive restaurant, swimming pool, gym, and laundry. All rooms are a/c. Singles $92, doubles $112 with semi-private bath.

Whitehouse Hotel of New York 340 Bowery ⓣ212/477-5623, ⓦwww.whitehousehotelofny.com. This is the only hostel in the city that offers single and double rooms at dorm rates. Also popular for its Downtown location, and amenities such as a/c, ATMs, cable TV, and linens. Private singles start at $28, private doubles at $54.

Downtown Manhattan

The patchwork of neighborhoods below 14th Street, **DOWNTOWN MANHATTAN**, runs the gamut from high finance and cutting-edge cool to Old World charm; it's truly one of the most vibrant, exciting parts of the city. Downtown's interest actually begins in New York Harbor, which holds the compulsory attractions of the **Statue of Liberty** and **Ellis Island**. The southernmost neighborhood on the mainland is the **Financial District**, with Wall Street at its center; less than a half-mile north, the buildings of the **Civic Center** transition into the jangling street life of **Chinatown**, which is fast encroaching upon the once-authentic, now-touristy **Little Italy**. East of Chinatown and Little Italy, the **Lower East Side** marks the traditional point of entry into the city for many different immigrant groups. These days, it's very trendy, with chic bars and restaurants opening up weekly.

West of Chinatown and Little Italy, respectively, the one-time industrial area of **SoHo** is now an expensive residential and shopping district. The smallish area known as **Nolita** takes in numerous boutiques and hip restaurants in its few well-manicured blocks. North of Houston Street, the activity picks up even more in the **West Village** (also known as Greenwich Village) and **East Village**, two former bohemian enclaves that remain great fun despite ongoing gentrification, the former for its charming backstreets and brownstones, the latter for its energetic nightlife.

The Statue of Liberty and Ellis Island

Standing tall and proud in the middle of New York Harbor, the **Statue of Liberty** has for more than a century served as a symbol of the American Dream. Depicting Liberty throwing off her shackles and holding a beacon to light the world, the monument was the creation of the French sculptor Frédéric Auguste Bartholdi, in recognition of fraternity between the French and American people. The statue, designed by Gustave Eiffel, of Eiffel Tower fame, was built in Paris between 1874 and 1884 and formally dedicated by President Grover Cleveland on October 28, 1886.

Just across the water, **Ellis Island** was the first stop for more than twelve million prospective immigrants. It became an immigration station in 1892, mainly to handle the massive influx from southern and eastern Europe, and remained open until 1954, when it was left to fall into an atmospheric ruin. In the turreted central building, the **Ellis Island Immigration Museum** (daily 9.30am–5.15pm;

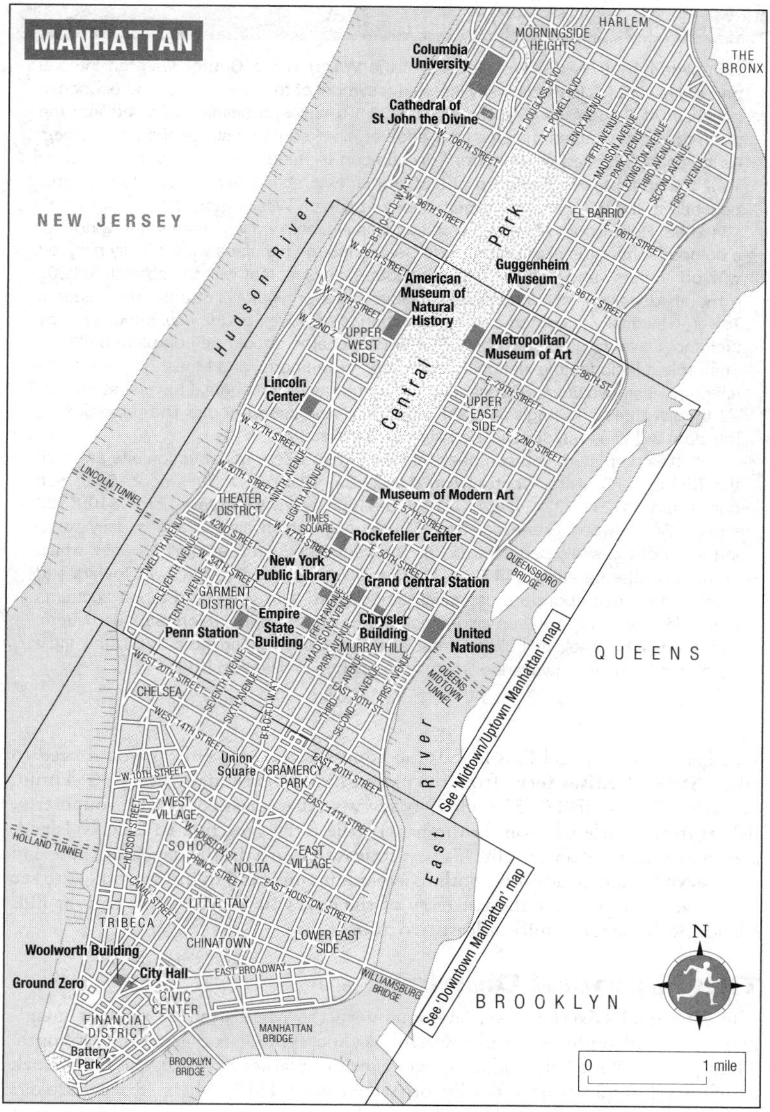

Ⓣ212/363-3200, Ⓦwww.nps.gov/elis; free) eloquently recaptures the spirit of the place with artifacts, photographs, maps, and personal accounts that tell the story of the immigrants who passed through. "Peopling of America" chronicles four centuries of immigration, offering a statistical portrait of those who arrived here, while the huge, vaulted **Registry Room** on the second floor, scene of so much immigrant trepidation, elation, and despair, has been left imposingly bare, with just a couple of inspectors' desks and American flags.

September 11 and its aftermath

Completed in 1973, the Twin Towers of the **World Trade Center** were an integral part of New York's legendary skyline, and a symbol of the city's social and economic success. At 8.46am on September 11, 2001, a hijacked airliner slammed into the north tower; seventeen minutes later another hijacked plane struck the south tower. As thousands looked on in horror – in addition to hundreds of millions viewing on TV – the south tower collapsed at 9.50am, its twin at 10.30am. In all, 2996 people perished at the WTC and the simultaneous attack on Washington DC.

In 2003, Polish-born American architect Daniel Libeskind was named the winner of a competition for the new World Trade Center, though his plans were initially plagued with controversy and he's had little subsequent involvement with the project. In 2006 a modified design, still incorporating Libeskind's original 1776-foot-high Freedom Tower, was finally accepted and construction is now well-under way, supervised by architect David Childs. The whole $12-billion scheme should be complete by 2013. The project includes the National September 11 Memorial and Museum; the memorial comprises two voids representing the footprints of the original towers, surrounded by oak trees and rings of water falling into illuminated pools. The underground museum will use artifacts and exhibits to tell the story of 9/11.

Until it's completed, you can peek into the Ground Zero construction site and visit the Tribute WTC Visitor Center (Mon & Wed–Sat 10am–6pm, Tues noon–6pm, Sun noon–5pm; Ⓣ212/422-3520 or 212/393-9160, Ⓦwww.tributewtc.org; $10), 120 Liberty St (between Greenwich and Church sts), which also arranges daily walking tours of the site's perimeter ($10). The center houses five small galleries which commemorate the attacks of 9/11, beginning with a model of the Twin Towers and a moving section about the day itself, embellished with video and taped accounts of real-life survivors. You can also check out St Paul's Chapel (Mon–Sat 10am–6pm, Sun 9am–4pm; free), at Fulton Street and Broadway, dating from 1766; the main attraction inside is Unwavering Spirit, a poignant exhibition on 9/11.

To get to Liberty and Ellis islands (no admission fees for either), you'll need to take a **Statue Cruises ferry** from the pier in Battery Park (daily every 30–45min, 9.30am–3.30pm; Ⓣ877/523-9849, Ⓦwww.statuecruises.com; $12 round-trip, tickets from Castle Clinton, in the park)); the ferry goes first to Liberty Island, and then continues on to Ellis. It's best to leave as early in the day as possible and to **reserve tickets** in advance, both to avoid long lines and to insure you get to see both islands; if you take the last ferry of the day, you won't be able to visit Ellis Island. Both islands require at least two hours.

The Financial District

The **Financial District** is synonymous with the Manhattan of popular imagination, its tall buildings and powerful skyline symbols of economic strength. Though New York City had an active securities market by 1790, the **New York Stock Exchange** wasn't officially organized until 1817, when 28 stockbrokers adopted their own constitution and established membership rules. It's been one of the world's great financial centers ever since.

Wall Street and around

The narrow canyon of **Wall Street** gained its name from the Dutch stockade built in the 1650s to protect New Amsterdam from the English colonies to the north. Today, behind the Neoclassical mask of the **New York Stock Exchange**, at Broad and Wall streets, the purse strings of the world are pulled. Due to security concerns, however, the public can no longer observe the frenzied trading on the floor of the exchange.

The **Federal Hall National Memorial**, at 26 Wall St, was once the Customs House, but the exhibits inside (Mon–Fri 9am–5pm; ⓣ212/825-6888, ⓦwww.nps.gov/feha; free) relate to the headier days of 1789, when George Washington was sworn in as president from a balcony on this site. At Wall Street's western end, on Broadway, between Rector and Church streets, **Trinity Church** (Mon–Fri 7am–6pm, Sat 8am–4pm, Sun 7am–4pm; free), is a knobbly neo-Gothic structure erected in 1846, and the city's tallest building for fifty years. The place has much the air of an English church, especially in its sheltered graveyard, which is the resting place of early luminaries including the first Secretary of the Treasury (and the man on the ten-dollar bill) Alexander Hamilton, who was killed in a duel by then-Vice President Aaron Burr.

Just down from Trinity Church, the **Sports Museum of America** (Mon–Fri 9am–7pm, Sat & Sun 9am–9pm; ⓦwww.sportsmuseum.com; $27), opened in 2008 at 26 Broadway (entrance on Beaver St), showcasing every major American sport through a combination of video, information boards, and rare memorabilia.

Broadway comes to a gentle end at **Bowling Green Park**, an oval of turf used for the game (of bowling) by eighteenth-century colonial Brits, in the shadow of Cass Gilbert's 1907 **US Custom House**. The Custom House contains the superb **National Museum of the American Indian** (Fri–Wed 10am–5pm, Thurs 10am–8pm; ⓣ212/514-3700, ⓦwww.americanindian.si.edu; free), a fascinating assembly of artifacts from almost every tribe native to the Americas, including large wood and stone carvings from the Pacific Northwest and elegant featherwork from Amazonia.

Battery Park and around

Across State Street from the Custom House, Downtown Manhattan lets out its breath in **Battery Park**, where the nineteenth-century Castle Clinton (daily 8.30am–5pm) once protected the southern tip of Manhattan and now sells ferry tickets to the Statue of Liberty and Ellis Island (see p.000). The spruced-up park stretches for blocks up the west side and is dotted with piers, cool corners, a restaurant, and some inventive landscaping.

Further toward the tip of the island, in the adjacent Robert F. Wagner Park and just a few feet from the Hudson River, the **Museum of Jewish Heritage**, 36 Battery Place (Sun–Tues & Thurs 10am–5.45pm, Wed 10am–8pm, Fri 10am–5pm; closed Jewish holidays; ⓣ646/437-4200, ⓦwww.mjhnyc.org; $10) is essentially a memorial of the Holocaust, and has three floors of exhibits on twentieth-century Jewish history. The moving and informative collection features objects from everyday Eastern European Jewish life, prison garb that survivors wore in Nazi concentration camps, photographs, personal belongings, and multimedia presentations.

Staten Island Ferry

The **Staten Island ferry** (ⓣ718/727-2508, ⓦwww.siferry.com) sails from a modern terminal on the east side of Battery Park, built directly above the South Ferry subway station. Departures are frequent, from every 15–20 minutes during weekday rush hours (7–9am and 5–7pm), to every 60 minutes late at night (the ferry runs 24hr). The 25-minute ride is truly New York's best bargain: it's absolutely free, offering wide-angle views of the city and the Statue of Liberty that become more spectacular as you retreat. Most visitors get the next boat straight back to Manhattan, as there's not much to detain you on **Staten Island** itself.

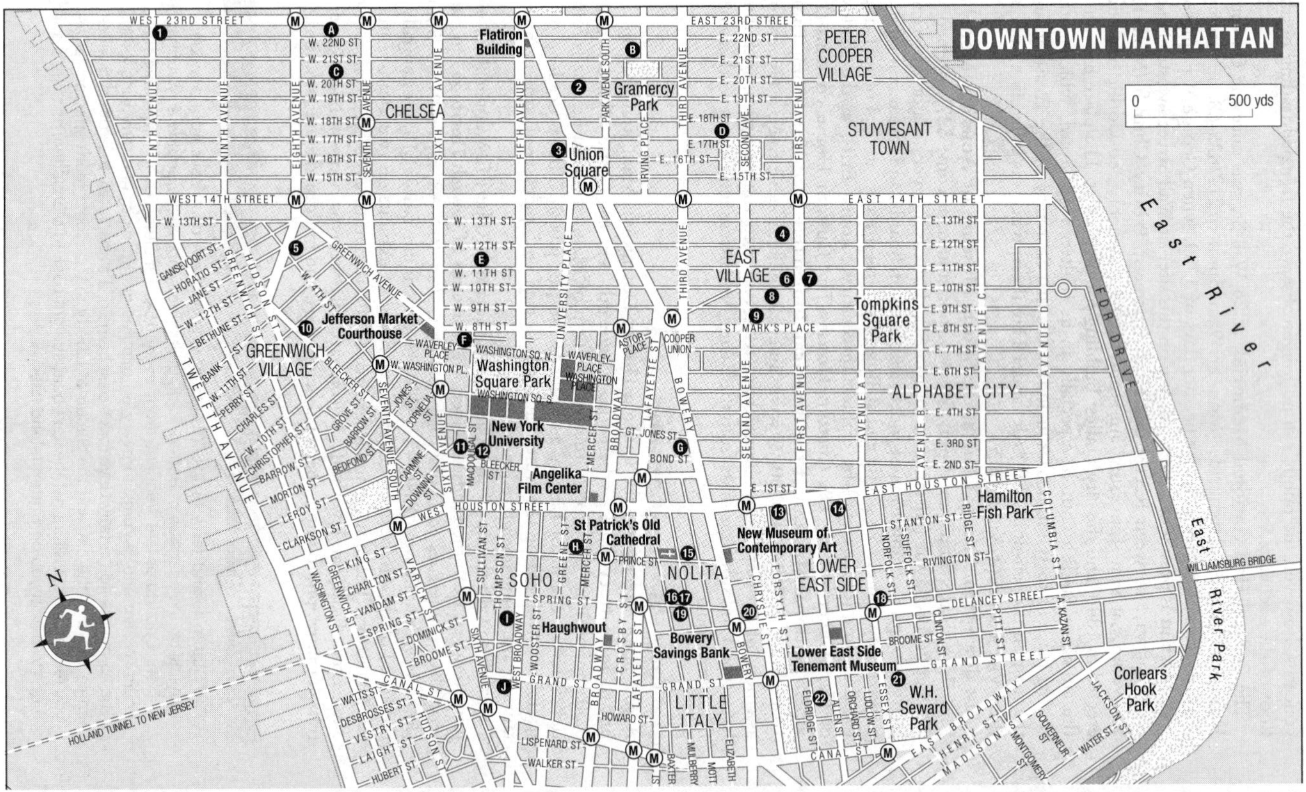
DOWNTOWN MANHATTAN
0
500 yds
N
East River
FDR DRIVE
East River Park
WILLIAMSBURG BRIDGE
HOLLAND TUNNEL TO NEW JERSEY
WEST 23RD STREET
EAST 23RD STREET
WEST 14TH STREET
EAST 14TH STREET
EAST HOUSTON STREET
WEST HOUSTON STREET
TENTH AVENUE
NINTH AVENUE
EIGHTH AVENUE
SEVENTH AVENUE
SIXTH AVENUE
FIFTH AVENUE
PARK AVENUE SOUTH
IRVING PLACE
THIRD AVENUE
SECOND AVE.
SECOND AVENUE
FIRST AVENUE
AVENUE A
AVENUE B
AVENUE C
AVENUE D
UNIVERSITY PLACE
BROADWAY
LAFAYETTE ST
BOWERY
TWELFTH AVENUE
GREENWICH AVENUE
SEVENTH AVENUE SOUTH
CANAL ST
GRAND STREET
DELANCEY STREET
EAST BROADWAY
HENRY ST
MADISON ST
PETER COOPER VILLAGE
STUYVESANT TOWN
CHELSEA
Flatiron Building
Gramercy Park
Union Square
EAST VILLAGE
Tompkins Square Park
ALPHABET CITY
GREENWICH VILLAGE
Jefferson Market Courthouse
Washington Square Park
New York University
Angelika Film Center
St Patrick's Old Cathedral
SOHO
NOLITA
Haughwout
Bowery Savings Bank
LITTLE ITALY
New Museum of Contemporary Art
LOWER EAST SIDE
Hamilton Fish Park
Lower East Side Tenement Museum
W.H. Seward Park
Corlears Hook Park
ST MARK'S PLACE
ASTOR PLACE
COOPER UNION
WASHINGTON SQ. N.
WASHINGTON SQ. S.
WAVERLEY PLACE
WASHINGTON PLACE
W. WASHINGTON PL.
BLEECKER ST
MACDOUGAL ST
MERCER ST
GREENE ST
WOOSTER ST
WEST BROADWAY
THOMPSON ST
SULLIVAN ST
SPRING ST
PRINCE ST
CROSBY ST
BOND ST
GT. JONES ST
HOWARD ST
LISPENARD ST
WALKER ST
BAXTER ST
MULBERRY
MOTT
ELIZABETH
CHRYSTIE ST
FORSYTH ST
ELDRIDGE ST
ALLEN ST
ORCHARD ST
LUDLOW ST
ESSEX ST
NORFOLK ST
SUFFOLK ST
CLINTON ST
RIDGE ST
PITT ST
COLUMBIA ST
A. KAZAN ST
STANTON ST
RIVINGTON ST
BROOME ST
JACKSON ST
GOUVERNEUR ST
MONTGOMERY ST
WATER ST
HUDSON ST
GREENWICH ST
WASHINGTON ST
VARICK ST
KING ST
CHARLTON ST
VANDAM ST
DOMINICK ST
WATTS ST
DESBROSSES ST
VESTRY ST
LAIGHT ST
HUBERT ST
CLARKSON ST
LEROY ST
MORTON ST
BARROW ST
CHRISTOPHER ST
W. 10TH ST
CHARLES ST
PERRY ST
W. 11TH ST
BANK ST
BETHUNE ST
W. 12TH ST
JANE ST
HORATIO ST
GANSEVOORT ST
W. 4TH ST
GROVE ST
BEDFORD ST
CARMINE ST
DOWNING ST
JONES ST
CORNELIA ST
W. 22ND ST
W. 21ST ST
W. 20TH ST
W. 19TH ST
W. 18TH ST
W. 17TH ST
W. 16TH ST
W. 15TH ST
W. 13TH ST
W. 12TH ST
W. 11TH ST
W. 10TH ST
W. 9TH ST
W. 8TH ST
E. 22ND ST
E. 21ST ST
E. 20TH ST
E. 19TH ST
E. 18TH ST
E. 17TH ST
E. 16TH ST
E. 15TH ST
E. 13TH ST
E. 12TH ST
E. 11TH ST
E. 10TH ST
E. 9TH ST
E. 8TH ST
E. 7TH ST
E. 6TH ST
E. 4TH ST
E. 3RD ST
E. 2ND ST
E. 1ST ST

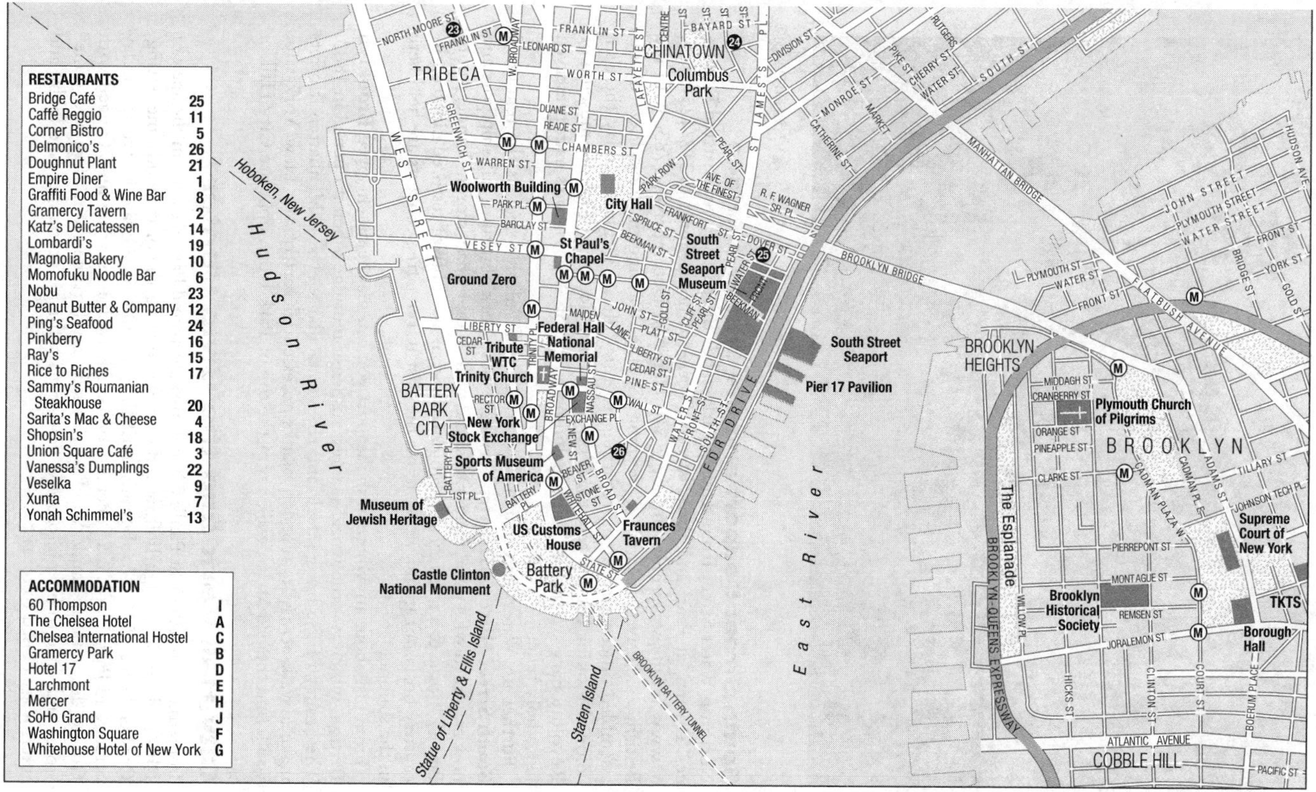
RESTAURANTS
Bridge Café 25
Caffè Reggio 11
Corner Bistro 5
Delmonico's 26
Doughnut Plant 21
Empire Diner 1
Graffiti Food & Wine Bar 8
Gramercy Tavern 2
Katz's Delicatessen 14
Lombardi's 19
Magnolia Bakery 10
Momofuku Noodle Bar 6
Nobu 23
Peanut Butter & Company 12
Ping's Seafood 24
Pinkberry 16
Ray's 15
Rice to Riches 17
Sammy's Roumanian Steakhouse 20
Sarita's Mac & Cheese 4
Shopsin's 18
Union Square Café 3
Vanessa's Dumplings 22
Veselka 9
Xunta 7
Yonah Schimmel's 13
ACCOMMODATION
60 Thompson I
The Chelsea Hotel A
Chelsea International Hostel C
Gramercy Park B
Hotel 17 D
Larchmont E
Mercer H
SoHo Grand J
Washington Square F
Whitehouse Hotel of New York G
TRIBECA
CHINATOWN
Columbus Park
Woolworth Building
City Hall
St Paul's Chapel
South Street Seaport Museum
Ground Zero
Federal Hall National Memorial
Tribute WTC
Trinity Church
New York Stock Exchange
BATTERY PARK CITY
Sports Museum of America
Museum of Jewish Heritage
US Customs House
Fraunces Tavern
Castle Clinton National Monument
Battery Park
South Street Seaport
Pier 17 Pavilion
Hudson River
East River
Hoboken, New Jersey
Statue of Liberty & Ellis Island
Staten Island
BROOKLYN BATTERY TUNNEL
FDR DRIVE
BROOKLYN BRIDGE
MANHATTAN BRIDGE
BROOKLYN HEIGHTS
BROOKLYN
Plymouth Church of Pilgrims
The Esplanade
BROOKLYN-QUEENS EXPRESSWAY
Brooklyn Historical Society
Supreme Court of New York
TKTS
Borough Hall
COBBLE HILL
FLATBUSH AVENUE
ATLANTIC AVENUE
WEST STREET

▲ Brooklyn Bridge

South Street Seaport and the Brooklyn Bridge

North up Water Street from Battery Park stands the partly reconstructed **Fraunces Tavern**, at Pearl and Broad streets (Tues–Sat noon–5pm; ⓣ212/425-1778, ⓦwww.fraucestavernmuseum.org; $4). Here, on December 4, 1783, with the British conclusively beaten, a weeping George Washington took leave of his assembled officers, intent on returning to rural life in Virginia. Today there's a colonial-looking bar and restaurant on the ground floor, and a quirky museum of Revolutionary artifacts upstairs, including a lock of Washington's hair, preserved like a holy relic.

Further up Water Street, at the eastern end of Fulton Street, is the renovated **South Street Historic District**, formerly New York's bustling sail-ship port and now crammed with pubs, restaurants, and well-known chain stores. Wander out to Pier 17, home to a touristy shopping mall and an assembly of restored nineteenth-century boats, for grand views across the East River – free concerts are held here in the summer.

From just about anywhere in the seaport you can see the much-loved **Brooklyn Bridge**, which was the world's largest suspension bridge when it opened in 1883. The beauty of the bridge itself and the spectacular views of Manhattan it offers make a walk across its wooden planks an essential part of any New York trip; you'll find the pedestrian walkway at the top of Park Row, opposite City Hall.

City Hall Park and the Civic Center

Immediately north of St Paul's Chapel, Broadway and Park Row form the apex of **City Hall Park**, a brightly flowered triangle now worthy of its handsome setting. Cass Gilbert's 1913 **Woolworth Building**, at 233 Broadway, between Barclay Street and Park Place, is a venerable onlooker, with its soaring lines fringed with Gothic decoration. Frank Woolworth made his fortune from "five and dime" stores and, true to his philosophy, he paid cash for his skyscraper (the lobby and interior are closed to tourists).

At the top of the park stands **City Hall**, which was completed in 1812. Inside, it's an elegant meeting of arrogance and authority, with the sweeping spiral staircase delivering you to the precise geometry of the Governor's Room. **Free guided tours** (Wed noon) are the only way inside: sign up at the **NYC Heritage Tourism Center** booth (Mon–Fri 9am–6pm, Sat & Sun 10am–5pm) opposite the Woolworth Building.

Chinatown, Little Italy, and Nolita

A short stroll northeast from City Hall leads into **Chinatown**, Manhattan's most thriving ethnic neighborhood, which over recent years has extended north across Canal Street into Little Italy and northeast into the Lower East Side. There aren't many sights; rather, the appeal of the neighborhood lies simply in its unbridled energy, in the hordes of people coursing the sidewalk all day long – and, of course, for its excellent **Chinese food** (see p.102). Today, **Mott Street** is the most vibrant thoroughfare, and the streets around – Canal, Pell, Bayard, Doyers, and Bowery – host a positive glut of restaurants, tea and rice shops, grocers, and vendors selling everything from jewelry to toy robots.

On the north side of Canal Street, **Little Italy** is light years away from the solid ethnic enclave of old. Originally settled by the huge nineteenth-century influx of Italian immigrants, the neighborhood has far fewer Italians living here now and the restaurants (of which there are plenty), tend to have high prices and a touristy feel. However, some original bakeries and *salumerias* (specialty food stores) do survive, and you can still indulge yourself with a good cappuccino and a tasty pastry. During September's ten-day **Festa di San Gennaro**, a wild and raucous party held in honor of the patron saint of Naples, Italians from all over the city converge on **Mulberry Street**, transforming Little Italy's main strip with food outlets and street stalls.

North of Little Italy, the trendy enclave of **Nolita** runs from Grand to Houston streets, between Bowery and Lafayette street. Brimming with chic boutiques and restaurants, the district surrounds **St Patrick's Old Cathedral** (on Mott and Prince st), once the spiritual heart of Little Italy and the oldest Catholic cathedral in the city. If you're not interested in shopping, you should definitely check out the **New Museum of Contemporary Art**, 235 Bowery, opposite Prince Street (Wed, Sat, & Sun noon-6pm, Thurs & Fri noon–10pm; Ⓣ212/219-1222, Ⓦwww.newmuseum.org; $12), a powerful symbol of the **Bowery**'s rebirth, which until recently was the city's original skid row. The building itself, a stack of seven shimmering aluminum boxes designed by Japanese architects, is as much the attraction as the avant-garde work inside.

SoHo

Since the early 1980s, SoHo, the grid of streets that runs *so*uth of *Ho*uston Street, has been all about fashion chic, urbane shopping, and cosmopolitan art galleries. For the first half of the twentieth century, this area was a wasteland of manufacturers and warehouses, but as rising rents drove artists out of Greenwich Village in the 1940s and 1950s, SoHo suddenly became "in." In the 1960s, largely due to the area's magnificent cast-iron architecture, SoHo was declared a historic district. Following this, yuppification – albeit an ultra-trendy strain of it – set in, bringing the fashionable boutiques, hip restaurants, and tourist crowds that are SoHo's signature today. The landmark Apple Store occupies the former post office on the corner of Greene and Prince streets, while the best example of cast-iron architecture, the flamboyant **Haughwout Building**, can be found at the northeast corner of Broome Street and Broadway. You should also check out **72–76 Greene**

Street, a neat extravagance whose Corinthian portico stretches the whole five stories, all in painted metal, and the strongly composed elaborations of its sister building at nos. 28–30.

The West Village

For many visitors, the **West Village** (also known as Greenwich Village, or simply "the Village") is the most-loved neighborhood in New York, despite having lost any radical edge long ago. Its bohemian image endures well enough if you don't live in the city, and it still sports many attractions that brought people here in the first place: a busy streetlife that lasts later than in many other parts of the city; more restaurants per head than anywhere else; and bars cluttering every corner.

Greenwich Village grew up as a rural retreat from the early and frenetic nucleus of New York City. Refined Federal and Greek Revival townhouses lured some of the city's highest society names, and later, at the start of World War I, the Village proved fertile ground for struggling artists and intellectuals, who were attracted to the area's cheap rents and growing community of free-thinking residents. The **Beat movement** flourished here after World War II, laying the path for rebellious, countercultural groups and activities in the 1960s, particularly **folk music**, with Bob Dylan a resident for much of his early career. The natural heart of the Village, **Washington Square Park**, is not exactly elegant, though it does retain its northern edging of red-brick rowhouses – the "solid, honorable dwellings" of Henry James's novel *Washington Square* – and Stanford White's imposing **Washington Arch**, built in 1892 to commemorate the centenary of George Washington's inauguration. The park is also the heart of the truly urban campus of New York University. As soon as the weather gets warm, the park becomes a sports field, performance space, chess tournament, protest site, and social club, feverish with life.

From the bottom of the park, follow **MacDougal Street** south and you hit **Bleecker Street** – the Village's main drag, packed with shops, bars, people, and restaurants. Walk right (west) onto Bleecker, then right again (north) on Sixth Avenue, until you see the unmistakable clock tower of the beautiful nineteenth-century **Jefferson Market Courthouse**, at W 10th Street. This imposing High Victorian-style edifice first served as an indoor market, but later went on to be a firehouse, a gaol, and finally a women's detention center before enjoying its current incarnation as a public library.

West of here, in the brownstone-lined side streets off Seventh Avenue, such as Bedford and Grove, you'll glimpse one of the city's most desirable living areas. Bedford Street is particularly attractive, and is the site of the oldest house in the Village, at no. 77 (from 1799), while 17 Grove St (from 1822) is the most complete wood-frame house in the city. Nearby, **Christopher Street** joins Seventh Avenue at **Sheridan Square**, home of the *Stonewall Inn*'s gay bar where, in 1969, a police raid precipitated a siege that lasted the best part of an hour. If not a victory for gay rights, it was the first time that gay men had stood up to the police en masse, and as such represents a turning point in the struggle for equal rights. The event is honored by the **Annual Gay Pride Parade**, typically held on the last Sunday in June (starting at 5th Ave and 52nd St, and ending around Sheridan Sq).

The East Village

The **East Village**, sandwiched between 14th and Houston streets, to the east of Third Avenue, differs quite a bit from its western counterpart. Once, like the adjacent Lower East Side, the neighborhood was a refuge for immigrants and solidly working-class people. Home to New York's nonconformist intelligentsia in the early twentieth century, it later became the haunt of **the Beats** – Kerouac,

Burroughs, Ginsberg, et al – who would get together at Ginsberg's house on East Seventh Street for declamatory poetry readings. Later, Andy Warhol debuted the Velvet Underground here; the *Fillmore East* hosted almost every band under the sun; and Richard Hell, Patti Smith, and The Ramones invented punk rock at a hole-in-the-wall club called **CBGB**, which closed its doors after 33 years in October 2006 (it's now a John Varvatos fashion boutique).

Much of the East Village has changed since the economic boom of the mid-1980s and the 1990s, not the least of which has been escalating rents and gentrification, stripping it of its former status as a hotbed of dissidence and creativity. Nevertheless, the area's main drag, the vaudevillian **St Mark's Place** (8th St), is still one of Downtown's more vibrant strips, even if the thrift shops, panhandlers, and political hustlers have given way to more sanitized forms of rebellion and a cluster of *Starbucks*.

Astor Place, at the western end of St Mark's Place, was one of the city's most desirable neighborhoods in the 1830s. The now-undistinguished Lafayette Street was home to such wealthy names as John Jacob Astor, a hideously greedy New York tycoon.

Nearby, **Cooper Square** is dominated by the seven-story brownstone mass of **Cooper Union**, erected in 1859 by the industrialist Peter Cooper as a college for the poor and now a prestigious art and architecture school. Early in 1860, Abraham Lincoln wowed top New Yorkers here with his "right makes might" speech, in which he boldly criticized the pro-slavery South and helped propel himself to the Republican nomination for president.

Further east, **Tompkins Square Park**, between avenues A and B, and Seventh and Tenth streets, has long been a focus for the East Village community, scene of the notorious 1988 riots that partly inspired the musical *Rent*. These days things are far more relaxed, and the surrounding area sports some of the most enticing bars and restaurants in the city.

The Lower East Side

Below the eastern stretch of Houston Street, the **Lower East Side** began life toward the end of the nineteenth century as an insular slum for roughly half a million Jewish immigrants. Since then it has changed considerably, with many Dominican and Chinese inhabitants, followed by a recent influx of well-off students, artists, designers, and the like. It's all made the neighborhood quite cool, and the hotbed for trendy shops, bars, and restaurants, with **Stanton** and **Clinton streets** as the epicenter.

You can still **buy** just about anything cut-price in the Lower East Side, especially on Sunday mornings, when **Orchard Street** is filled with stalls and stores selling hats, clothes, and designer labels at hefty discounts. Next to this melee is the excellent **Lower East Side Tenement Museum**, 90 Orchard St, between Broome and Delancey streets (Tues–Fri 11am–6pm, Sat & Sun 10.45am–6pm; ⓣ212/431-0233, ⓦwww.tenement.org; $17 tours), which is housed in a nineteenth-century tenement and chronicles the neighborhood's immigrant and impoverished past. To get a feel for the area's Jewish roots, make for the absorbing **Museum at Eldridge Street** (Sun–Thurs 10am–4pm; ⓣ212/219-0888, ⓦwww.eldridgestreet.org; $10), just south of Canal Street, at 12 Eldridge St. Built in 1887 as the first synagogue constructed by Eastern European Orthodox Jews in the city (and still a functioning house of worship), half-hourly guided tours take you upstairs to the main sanctuary and provide a thorough introduction to the history of the building.

Midtown Manhattan

MIDTOWN MANHATTAN encompasses everything from the East to the Hudson rivers, between 14th Street and 59th Street, the southern border of Central Park. New York's most glamorous (and most expensive) thoroughfare, **Fifth Avenue**, cuts through Midtown's heart, with the neon theater strip of **Broadway** running just to the west for much of the way. The character of Midtown is very different depending on which side of Fifth you find yourself. On the avenue itself and to the east are corporate businesses and prestigious skyscrapers – including the Empire State, Chrysler, and Seagram buildings – as well as Grand Central Station and the UN. Here you'll also find the residential neighborhoods of **Murray Hill** and elegant **Gramercy Park**. Just below Gramercy's eponymous park, busy **Union Square** is always great for people-watching. Meanwhile, west of Fifth, **Chelsea** is home to many quality art galleries, and bordered by the **Garment District**, where apparel-shop employees still roll racks of clothing through the streets. Around 42nd Street, the **Theater District** heralds a cleaned-up, frenetic area of entertainment that culminates at **Times Square**. West of Broadway in the 40s and low 50s, colorful **Hell's Kitchen** is now more or less wholly gentrified.

Union Square and Gramercy Park

Downtown Manhattan ends at 14th Street, which slices across from the housing projects of the East Side through rows of cut-price shops to the meatpacking warehouses on the Hudson River. In the middle is **Union Square**, its shallow steps enticing passers-by to sit and watch the motley assortment of skateboarders, Whole Foods shoppers, and NYU students or to stroll the cool, tree-shaded paths and lawns. The shopping that once dominated the stretch of **Broadway** north of here, formerly known as Ladies' Mile for its fancy stores and boutiques, has been moved to Fifth Avenue, where chain stores now cover virtually every block in the mid-teens through the 20s.

East from here, between 20th and 21st streets, where Lexington Avenue becomes Irving Place, Manhattan's clutter suddenly breaks into the ordered, open space of **Gramercy Park**. This former swamp, reclaimed in 1831, is one of the city's best parks, its center tidily planted and, most noticeably, completely empty for much of the day – principally because the only people who can gain access are those rich enough to live here and possess keys to the gate. (There is, however, another way: guests at the *Gramercy Park Hotel* are allowed into the park; see p.74.)

Broadway and Fifth Avenue meet at 23rd Street at **Madison Square**, with a serene, well-manicured **park** to take the edge off, enhanced by the celebrated burgers of *Shake Shack* (see p.104). Most notable among the elegant structures nearby is the **Flatiron Building**, 175 Fifth Ave, between 22nd and 23rd streets; the 1902 Beaux Arts structure is known for its unusual narrow corners and six-and-a-half-feet-wide rounded tip.

Chelsea and the Garment District

Home to a thriving **gay community**, and considered the heart of the New York art market because of its many renowned **art galleries** (check out West 24th St, between Tenth and Eleventh avenues), the center of **Chelsea** lies west of Broadway between 14th and 23rd streets. During the nineteenth century, this was New York's theater district. Nothing remains of that now, but the hotel that put up all the actors, writers, and attendant entourages – the **Hotel Chelsea** – remains a New York landmark, with an Edwardian grandeur all its own (see p.74). Mark Twain and Tennessee Williams lived here, Dylan Thomas staggered in and out of the hotel, and in 1951 Jack Kerouac, armed with a customized typewriter (and a lot of Benzedrine), typed the first draft of *On the Road* nonstop onto a 120-foot-long roll of paper in one of its rooms. Perhaps most famously, however, Sid Vicious, of the Sex Pistols, stabbed his girlfriend Nancy Spungen to death in their suite in October 1978, a few months before he died of a heroin overdose. Whilst in Chelsea you should also check out one of New York's most ambitious urban regeneration projects, the **High Line** (Ⓦ www.thehighline.org), which runs from Gansevoort Street to West 20th Street, west of Ninth and Tenth avenues; it's a unique city park, slicing through the highrises on a former elevated rail line.

The **Garment District**, a loosely defined patch north of Chelsea between 34th and 42nd streets and Sixth and Eighth avenues, produces three-fourths of all the women's and children's clothes in America. You'd never guess it, though; the outlets are strictly wholesale, with no need to woo customers. Retail stores abound, however: **Macy's**, the largest department store in the world, is on **Herald Square** at 34th Street and Seventh Avenue. Dominant landmarks nearby include the **Penn Station** and **Madison Square Garden** complex, which swallows up millions of commuters in its train station below and accommodates the Knicks and Liberty basketball teams, as well as the Rangers hockey team, up top.

The Empire State Building

Up Fifth Avenue is the **Empire State Building**, at 34th Street and Fifth Avenue (daily 8am–2am, last trip up at 1.15am; Ⓣ 212/736-3100, Ⓦ www.esbnyc.com; $19, bring photo ID), which has been a muscular 102-storey symbol of New York since it was completed in 1931. After the terrorist attacks of September 11th, it became, as it once was, the city's tallest building. An elevator takes you to the 86th floor, which was the summit of the building before the radio and TV mast was added. The views from the outside walkways here are as stunning as you'd expect (you can continue up to the tiny 102nd floor observatory for an extra $15, but the view is about the same). For the best experience, you should try to time your visit so that you'll reach the top at sunset. (Be advised that during peak season, wait times to ascend are often upwards of an hour.)

Forty-second Street

On the corner of **42nd Street** and Fifth Avenue stands the Beaux Arts **New York Public Library** (Mon 11am–6pm, Tues & Wed 11am–7.30pm, Thurs–Sat 11am–6pm; Ⓣ 212/930-0830, Ⓦ www.nypl.org), boasting one of the five largest collections of books in the world. Leon Trotsky worked occasionally in the large coffered Reading Room at the back of the building during his brief sojourn in New York, just prior to the 1917 Russian Revolution. It's worth going inside just to appreciate its reverent, church-like atmosphere.

East on 42nd Street at Park Avenue, the huge bulk of **Grand Central Terminal** was completed in 1913 around a basic iron frame but features a dazzling Beaux Arts facade. The structure's immense size is now dwarfed by the MetLife building behind it. Regardless, the main station's **concourse** is a sight to behold – 470-feet long and 150-feet high, it boasts a barrel-vaulted ceiling speckled like a Baroque church with a painted representation of the winter night sky. The 2500 stars are shown back to front – "as God would have seen them," the painter is reputed to have explained.

You can explore Grand Central on your own, or you can take the Municipal Arts Society's excellent **free tour** (Wed 12.30pm). For the best view of the concourse – as well as the flow of commuters and commerce – climb up to the catwalks that span the sixty-foot-high windows on the Vanderbilt Avenue side. After that, seek

▲ Chrysler Building

out the station's more esoteric reaches, including the *Oyster Bar* – one of the city's most highly regarded seafood restaurants, deep in the terminal's bowels and jam-packed every lunchtime.

The equally famous **Chrysler Building**, at 405 Lexington Ave, dates from a time (1930) when architects carried off prestige with grace and style. For a short while, this was the world's tallest building; today, it's one of Manhattan's best-loved structures. The lobby, once a car showroom, with its opulently inlaid elevators, walls covered in African marble, and murals depicting airplanes, machines, and the brawny builders who worked on the tower, is for the moment all you can see of the building.

At the eastern end of 42nd Street, the **United Nations** complex comprises the glass-curtained **Secretariat**, the curving sweep of the **General Assembly**, and, connecting them, the low-rising **Conference Wing**. Guided **tours** leave from the General Assembly lobby (daily every 20–30min Mon–Fri 9.45am–4.45pm; Ⓣ212/963-8687, Ⓦwww.un.org/MoreInfo/pubsvs.html; 45min; $12.50, bring ID) and take in the UN conference chambers and its constituent parts. Note that tours may vary depending on official room usage.

Times Square and the Theater District

Forty-second Street meets Broadway at the southern margin of **Times Square**, center of the **Theater District** and a top tourist attraction. Here, countless monolithic advertisements for Coke, Budweiser, NBC, and the like jostle brightly for attention from the crowds of gawking visitors. It wasn't always this way: traditionally a melting pot of debauchery, depravity, and fun, Times Square was cleaned up in the 1990s and turned into a largely sanitized universe of popular consumption, with refurbished theaters and blinking signage.

North of Times Square, along Seventh Avenue at 154 W 57th St, **Carnegie Hall** (Sept–June only, tours available Mon–Fri at 11.30am, 2pm, & 3pm, Sat 11.30am & 12.30pm, Sun 12.30pm; general info Ⓣ212/903-9600, tours Ⓣ212/903-9765, tickets Ⓣ212/247-7800, Ⓦwww.carnegiehall.org; $10) is a world-famous venue for opera and concerts. Tchaikovsky conducted the program on opening night and Mahler, Rachmaninov, Toscanini, Frank Sinatra, and Judy Garland have played here. Even if you don't have time for a show, it's worth taking the tour to admire the vast interior.

East of Seventh Avenue, **Sixth Avenue** is named "the Avenue of the Americas," though no New Yorker ever calls it this, and the name's only manifestations are the Central and South American flags that still fly on some of the avenue's blocks. At 1260 Sixth Ave, at 50th Street, **Radio City Music Hall** (tours daily 11am–3pm; Ⓣ212/307-7171, Ⓦwww.radiocity.com; 1hr; $17) is the last word in 1930s luxury. The staircase is regally resplendent, with the world's largest chandeliers, and the huge auditorium looks like an extravagant scalloped shell. Surely, however, Radio City is best know for the Rockettes, whose Christmas shows and kicklines have dazzled the masses since 1932.

Fifth Avenue and around

Fifth Avenue has been a great thoroughfare for as long as New York has been a great city, and its very name evokes wealth and opulence. All who consider themselves suave and cosmopolitan end up here, and the stores showcase New York's most conspicuous consumerism. That the shopping is beyond the means of most people needn't put you off, for Fifth Avenue has some of the city's best architecture, too.

At the heart of the glamour is **Rockefeller Center**, built between 1932 and 1940 by John D. Rockefeller Jr, son of the oil magnate. One of the finest pieces of urban planning anywhere, the Center balances office space with cafés, a theater, underground concourses, and rooftop gardens that work together with a rare intelligence and grace. The **GE Building** here rises 850ft; the "Top of the Rock" observation deck offers another mesmerizing view of the Manhattan skyline (daily 8am–midnight, last entry 11pm; Ⓣ212/698-2000, Ⓦwww.topoftherocknyc.com; $18). At its foot, the **Lower Plaza** holds a sunken restaurant in summer, linked visually by Paul Manship's sparkling *Prometheus*; in winter, the plaza becomes a small **ice rink**, allowing skaters to show off their skills to passers-by. Inside, the Center is no less impressive. In the GE lobby, José Maria Sert's murals, *American Progress* and *Time*, are a little faded but eagerly in tune with the 1930s Art-Deco ambiance. A leaflet available from the lobby desk details a **self-guided tour** of the Center. Among the GE Building's many offices are the **NBC Studios** (every 30min Mon–Thurs 8.30am–4.30pm, every 15min Fri & Sat 9.30am–5.30pm, every 15min Sun 9.30am–4.30pm; reservations at the NBC Experience Store Tour Desk; ⓣ212/664-7174; $18.50, $15.50 for children). If you're a TV fan, pick up a free ticket for a **show recording** from the mezzanine lobby or out on the street. Keep in mind that the most popular tickets evaporate before 9am. The glass-enclosed **Today Show** studio is at the southwest corner of the plaza at 49th Street, surrounded in the early morning by avid fans waiting to get on TV by way of the cameras that obligingly pan the crowds from time to time.

Almost opposite Rockefeller Center, on 50th Street and Fifth Avenue, **St Patrick's Cathedral**, designed by James Renwick and completed in 1888, seems the result of a painstaking academic tour of the Gothic cathedrals of Europe.

Continuing north, **Trump Tower** at 57th Street is the last word in Fifth Avenue extravagance, with an outrageously over-the-top atrium filled with designer stores. Perfumed air, polished marble paneling, and a five-storey waterfall are calculated to knock you senseless with somewhat garish taste. But the building is clever: a neat little outdoor garden is squeezed high in a corner, and each of the 230 apartments above the atrium gets views in three directions.

East of Fifth, **Madison Avenue** makes for pleasant strolling, and is filled with expensive galleries, haute couture shops, and elegantly dressed Eastsiders. The next avenue east, **Park Avenue**, was said in 1929 to be the place "where wealth is so swollen that it almost bursts." Things haven't changed much: corporate headquarters and four-star hotels jostle in triumphal procession, led by the massive New York Central Building (now the **Helmsley Building**) that literally sits above Park Avenue at 46th Street and boasts a lewdly excessive Rococo lobby. In its day this formed a skillful punctuation mark to the avenue, but its thunder was stolen in 1963 by the **MetLife Building**, 200 Park Ave at 45th Street, which looms behind it.

Crouched behind the Art Deco **Waldorf Astoria Hotel**, on Park between 49th and 50th streets, is **St Bartholomew's Church**, a striking, low-slung Byzantine hybrid that adds immeasurably to the street and gives the lumbering skyscrapers a much-needed sense of scale. The spiky-topped **General Electric Building** behind seems like a wild extension of the church, its slender shaft rising to a meshed crown of abstract sparks and lightning bolts that symbolizes the radio waves used by its original owner, RCA. The lobby (entrance at 570 Lexington) is yet another Deco delight.

Overshadowing all this is the **Museum of Modern Art**, at 11 W 53rd St, between Fifth and Sixth avenues, offering the finest collection of late nineteenth- and twentieth-century art anywhere, and an essential stop. Nineteenth-century highlights include Van Gogh's *Starry Night*, Cézanne's *Foliage*, and Munch's *Madonna*, while the modern period is represented by works such as Picasso's *Demoiselles d'Avignon*, Jasper Johns' *Flag*, and Warhol's soup cans (Sat–Mon, Wed & Thurs 10.30am–5.30pm, Fri 10.30am–8pm; ⓣ212/708-9400, ⓦwww.moma.org; $20, $16 for seniors, $12 for students, free Fri 4–8pm; ticket includes admission to P.S. 1 Contemporary Arts Center in Queens, if visited within 30 days).

Uptown Manhattan

UPTOWN MANHATTAN begins above 59th Street, where the businesslike bustle of Midtown gives way to the comfortable domesticity of the Upper East and West sides. In between, people come to **Central Park**, the city's giant backyard, to play, jog, and escape Midtown's crowds in a particularly intelligent piece of urban landscaping.

The **Upper East Side** is at its most opulent in the several blocks just east of Central Park, and at its most distinguished in the Metropolitan and other great museums of "Museum Mile," from 82nd to 104th streets along Fifth Avenue. The predominantly residential **Upper West Side** is somewhat less refined, though there are certainly plenty of expensive townhouses and apartment buildings. The northern reaches embrace the monolithic Cathedral of St John the Divine and Columbia University. North and east from here, **Harlem**, the cultural capital of black America, is experiencing a new renaissance. Still farther north, in the Washington Heights area, you'll find one of the city's most intriguing museums, the medieval arts collection of The Cloisters.

Central Park

Completed in 1876, smack in the middle of Manhattan, **Central Park** extends from 59th to 110th streets, and provides residents (and street-weary tourists) with a much-needed refuge from the harshness of big-city life. The poet and newspaper editor William Cullen Bryant had the idea for an open public space in 1844, and spent seven years trying to persuade City Hall to carry it out. Eventually, 840 desolate and swampy acres north of the city limits, then occupied by a shantytown of squatters, were set aside. The two architects commissioned to design the landscape, **Frederick Law Olmsted** and **Calvert Vaux**, planned to create a rural paradise, a complete illusion of the countryside in the heart of Manhattan – even then growing at a fantastic rate. Today, although the skyline has changed greatly, and some of the open space has been turned into asphalted playgrounds, the sense of captured nature that they intended largely survives. For general park **information**, call ⓣ212/310-6600, or visit ⓦwww.centralparknyc.org.

One of the best ways to explore the park is to rent a **bicycle** from either the Loeb Boathouse, between 74th and 75th streets (daily 10am–dusk; $9–15 for the first hour, $5–10/hr thereafter), or Metro Bicycles, on Lexington Avenue at 88th Street (daily 10am–6pm; ⓣ212/427-4450; $7/hr, $35/day). Otherwise, it's easy to get around **on foot**, along the many paths that crisscross the park. There's little chance of getting lost, but to know exactly where you are, find the nearest lamppost: the first two figures signify the number of the nearest street. After dark, however, you'd be well advised not to enter on foot.

Most places of interest in the park lie in its southern reaches. Near **Grand Army Plaza**, the main entrance at Fifth Avenue and 59th Street, is the **Central Park Zoo**, which tries to keep caging to a minimum and the animals as close to the viewer as possible (April–Oct Mon–Fri 10am–5pm, Sat & Sun 10am–5.30pm; Nov–March daily 10am–4.30pm; ⓣ212/439-6500; $8, $3 ages 3–12, free under 3). Beyond here, the **Dairy**, once a ranch building intended to provide milk for nursing mothers, now houses a **visitor's center** (Tues–Sun 10am–5pm; ⓣ212/794-6564), which distributes free leaflets and maps, sells books, and puts on exhibitions. Also, weekend **walking tours** often leave from here; call for times.

Nearby, the Trump-owned **Wollman Rink**, 63rd Street at mid-park (Mon & Tues 10am–2.30pm, Wed & Thurs 10am–10pm, Fri & Sat 10am–11pm, Sun 10am–9pm; ⓣ212/439-6900; $9.50–12), is a lovely place to skate in winter, or to

1, 2, 3, A, B, The Cloisters, Columbia University, Cathedral of St John the Divine, & Studio Museum in Harlem
C, Cooper Hewitt Museum of the City of New York, & Museo del Barrio
ACCOMMODATION
Algonquin K
Amsterdam Inn F
Dylan M
Edison J
Hostelling International-New York B
Jazz on the Park A
Lucerne D
Milburn E
The Pod H
Roger Smith I
Royalton L
Wales C
West Side YMCA G
RESTAURANTS
Amy Ruth's 1
Artisanal 21
Big Nick's Burger Joint 8
Boathouse Café in 9
Café Sabarsky 4
Carmine's 18
Carnegie Deli 15
Gray's Papaya 10
Heidelburg 6
Hell's Kitchen 16
Joe Allen Restaurant 17
La Caridad 78 7
Oyster Bar 20
Pinkberry 13
Rosa Mexicano 11
Russian Tea Room 14
Serendipity 3 12
Shake Shack 22
Sylvia's Restaurant 2
Tavern on the Green 5
Terrace in the Sky 3
Virgil's Real BBQ 19
Jacqueline Onassis Reservoir
Great Lawn
Turtle Pond
Delacorte Theater
Belvedere Castle
The Ramble
Loeb Boathouse
Rowboat Lake
Bow Bridge
Strawberry Fields
Central Park
Sheep Meadow
Dairy
Zoo
Wollman Rink
Plaza Hotel
Grand Army Plaza
Guggenheim Museum
Metropolitan Museum of Art
Whitney Museum
The Frick Collection
Temple Emanu-El
Seventh Regiment Armory
Bloomingdale's
Gracie Mansion
Carl Schurz Park
John Jay Park
UPPER EAST SIDE
UPPER WEST SIDE
American Museum of Natural History
New-York Historical Society
The Dakota
Lincoln Center
Columbus Circle
Riverside Park
Riverside Drive
Freedom Place
Roosevelt Island
Roosevelt Island Tram
Queensboro Bridge
FDR Drive
Central Park South
Transverse Road No. 3
Transverse Road No. 2
Broadway
Amsterdam Avenue
Central Park West
Columbus Ave.
Eleventh Avenue
Tenth Avenue
Eighth Avenue
Fifth Avenue
Madison Ave.
Park Avenue
Third Avenue
Second Avenue
First Avenue
York Avenue
East End Avenue

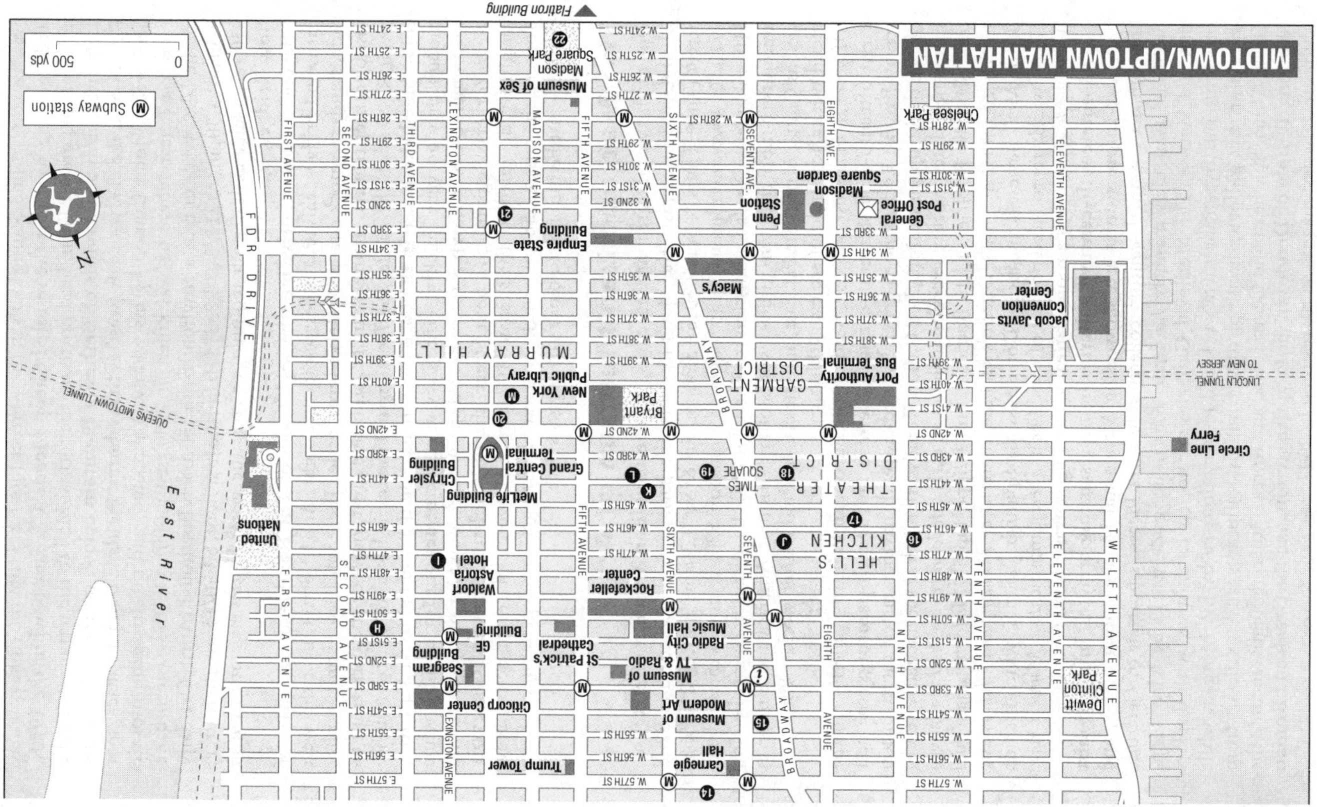
MIDTOWN/UPTOWN MANHATTAN
Subway station
0
500 yds
N
East River
QUEENS MIDTOWN TUNNEL
F D R DRIVE
FIRST AVENUE
SECOND AVENUE
THIRD AVENUE
LEXINGTON AVENUE
MADISON AVENUE
FIFTH AVENUE
SIXTH AVENUE
SEVENTH AVENUE
BROADWAY
EIGHTH AVENUE
NINTH AVENUE
TENTH AVENUE
ELEVENTH AVENUE
TWELFTH AVENUE
United Nations
Trump Tower
Citicorp Center
Seagram Building
GE Building
Waldorf Astoria Hotel
St Patrick's Cathedral
Rockefeller Center
MetLife Building
Chrysler Building
Grand Central Terminal
New York Public Library
MURRAY HILL
Empire State Building
Museum of Sex
Madison Square Park
Flatiron Building
Carnegie Hall
Museum of Modern Art
Museum of TV & Radio
Radio City Music Hall
Bryant Park
Macy's
HELL'S KITCHEN
THEATER DISTRICT
TIMES SQUARE
GARMENT DISTRICT
Port Authority Bus Terminal
Penn Station
Madison Square Garden
General Post Office
Chelsea Park
Jacob Javits Convention Center
Dewitt Clinton Park
Circle Line Ferry
LINCOLN TUNNEL TO NEW JERSEY
E. 57TH ST
E. 56TH ST
E. 55TH ST
E. 54TH ST
E. 53RD ST
E. 52ND ST
E. 51ST ST
E. 50TH ST
E. 49TH ST
E. 48TH ST
E. 47TH ST
E. 46TH ST
E. 44TH ST
E. 43RD ST
E. 42ND ST
E. 40TH ST
E. 39TH ST
E. 38TH ST
E. 37TH ST
E. 36TH ST
E. 35TH ST
E. 34TH ST
E. 33RD ST
E. 32ND ST
E. 31ST ST
E. 30TH ST
E. 29TH ST
E. 28TH ST
E. 27TH ST
E. 26TH ST
E. 25TH ST
E. 24TH ST
W. 57TH ST
W. 56TH ST
W. 55TH ST
W. 54TH ST
W. 53RD ST
W. 52ND ST
W. 51ST ST
W. 50TH ST
W. 49TH ST
W. 48TH ST
W. 47TH ST
W. 46TH ST
W. 45TH ST
W. 44TH ST
W. 43RD ST
W. 42ND ST
W. 41ST ST
W. 40TH ST
W. 39TH ST
W. 38TH ST
W. 37TH ST
W. 36TH ST
W. 35TH ST
W. 34TH ST
W. 33RD ST
W. 32ND ST
W. 31ST ST
W. 30TH ST
W. 29TH ST
W. 28TH ST
W. 27TH ST
W. 26TH ST
W. 25TH ST
W. 24TH ST

practice your in-line skating skills in the warmer months. From the rink, you may wish to swing west past the restored **Sheep Meadow**, a dust bowl in the 1970s, now emerald green. Then, head north up the formal Mall to the terrace, with the sculptured birds and animals of **Bethesda Fountain** below, on the shore of the **Rowboat Lake**. To your left (west) is **Strawberry Fields**, a tranquil, shady spot dedicated to John Lennon by his widow, Yoko Ono, and the **Imagine mosaic** – both are near where he was killed in 1980 (see p.000). On the eastern bank of the lake, you can rent a **rowboat** from the Loeb Boathouse (April–Oct daily 9.30am–5.30pm; ⓣ212/517-2233; $10 for the first hour, $2.50/15min thereafter; $30 refundable cash deposit required) or cross the water by the elegant cast-iron **Bow Bridge**.

Beyond the bridge, delve into the wild woods of **The Ramble** along a maze of paths and bridges; this area is best avoided at night. At 81st Street, near the West Side, stands the mock citadel of **Belvedere Castle** (Tues–Sun 10am–5pm) another visitor center that has nature exhibits and boasts great views of the park from its terraces. Next to the castle, the **Delacorte Theater** is home to the thoroughly enjoyable **Shakespeare in the Park** performances in the summer (tickets are free, though they go very quickly; visit ⓦwww.publictheater.org for details), while the immense **Great Lawn** is the preferred sprawling ground for many sun-loving New Yorkers. Beginning at 86th Street, the **Jacqueline Onassis Reservoir** (originally designed in 1862) spans 107 acres. A favored place for active New Yorkers, the raised 1.58-mile track is a great place to get 360-degree views of the skyline – just be sure not to block any jogger's path.

The Metropolitan Museum of Art

One of the world's great art museums, the **Metropolitan Museum of Art** (usually referred to as just "the Met") juts into the park at Fifth Avenue and 82nd Street (Tues–Thurs & Sun 9.30am–5.30pm, Fri & Sat 9.30am–9pm; ⓣ212/535-7710, ⓦwww.metmuseum.org; suggested donation $20, seniors $15, students $10; includes same-day admission to The Cloisters). Its all-embracing collection amounts to more than two million works of art, spanning America and Europe as well as China, Africa, the Far East, and the classical and Islamic worlds. You could spend weeks here and not see everything.

If you can make just one visit, head for the **European Painting** galleries. Of the early (fifteenth- and sixteenth-century) **Flemish and Dutch paintings**, the best are by Jan van Eyck, who is generally credited with having started the tradition of North European realism. The **Italian Renaissance** is less spectacularly represented here, but a worthy selection includes an early *Madonna and Child Enthroned with Saints* by Raphael, a late Botticelli, and Filippo Lippi's *Madonna and Child Enthroned with Two Angels*. Duccio's sublime masterpiece *Madonna and Child* is one of the Met's newest acquisitions. Don't miss the **Spanish** galleries, which include Goya's widely reproduced portrait of a toddler in a red jumpsuit, *Don Manuel Osorio Manrique de Zuniga*, and a room of freaky, dazzling canvases by El Greco.

The **nineteenth-century galleries** house a startling array of **Impressionist** and **post-Impressionist** art, showcasing Manet and Monet among others, and the compact twentieth-century collection features Picasso's portrait of Gertrude Stein and Gauguin's masterly *La Orana Maria*, alongside works by Klee, Hopper, and Matisse. The **Medieval Galleries** are no less exhaustive, with displays of sumptuous Byzantine metalwork and jewelry donated by J.P. Morgan, while the **Asian Art galleries** house plenty of murals, sculptures, and textile art from Japan, China, Southeast and Central Asia, and Korea. Other highlights include the imposing **Temple of Dendur** in the Egyptian section, and the **Greek** and **Roman** sculpture galleries, magnificently restored in 2007.

The Upper East Side

A two-square-mile grid, the **Upper East Side** has wealth as its defining characteristic, as you'll appreciate if you've seen any of the many Woody Allen movies set here. The area's stretch of **Fifth Avenue** has been the patrician face of Manhattan since the opening of Central Park attracted the Carnegies, Astors, and Whitneys to migrate north and build fashionable residences. **Grand Army Plaza**, at Central Park South and Fifth Avenue, flanked by the extended chateau of the swanky **Plaza Hotel**, and glowing with the gold statue of the Civil War's General William Tecumseh Sherman, serves as the introduction.

On the corner of Fifth Avenue and 65th Street, America's largest reform synagogue, the **Temple Emanu-El**, strikes a sober tone (Sun–Thurs 10am–4.30pm, Fri 10am–3pm; Ⓣ212/744-1400, Ⓦwww.emanuelnyc.org; free). The brooding Romanesque-Byzantine cavern manages to be bigger inside than it seems from outside, and, as you enter, the interior appears to melt away into darkness, making you feel very small indeed.

At 70th Street, you'll find Henry Clay Frick's house, a handsome spread and now the tranquil home of the **Frick Collection** (Tues–Sat 10am–6pm, Sun 11am–5pm; Ⓣ212/288-0700, Ⓦwww.frick.org; $15). One of many prestigious museums in the area, the Frick is perhaps the most enjoyable of the big New York galleries; it is made up of the art treasures hoarded by Frick during his years as probably the most ruthless of New York's robber barons. The collection includes paintings by Rembrandt, Reynolds, Hogarth, Gainsborough (*St James's Park*), and Bellini, whose *St Francis* suggests his vision of Christ by means of pervading light, a bent tree, and an enraptured stare. Above the fireplace, El Greco's *St Jerome* reproachfully surveys the riches all around, looking out to the South Hall, where one of Boucher's intimate depictions of his wife hangs near an early Vermeer, *Officer and Laughing Girl*.

Just a few blocks north, over on Madison Avenue at 75th Street, the **Whitney Museum of American Art** (Wed, Thurs, Sat, & Sun 11am–6pm, Fri 1–9pm; Ⓣ212/570-3676, Ⓦwww.whitney.org; $15) boasts a pre-eminent collection of twentieth-century American art and a superb exhibition locale. Every other year the museum mounts the Whitney Biennial show of contemporary American art – an event that has become a lightning rod for critical abuse since the 1995 show, when a giant mound of cooking fat presented as sculpture set right-wing aesthetes into a frenzy. When that's not on, enjoy the prominent Abstract Expressionists collection, with great works by high priests Pollock and De Kooning, leading on to Rothko and the Color Field painters and the later Pop Art works of Warhol, Johns, and Oldenburg. The museum is especially strong on Hopper, O'Keeffe, and Calder, with galleries concentrating on each.

A ten-minute walk north from the Whitney, the **Guggenheim Museum**, Fifth Avenue at 89th Street (Sat–Wed 10am–5.45pm, Fri 10am–7.45pm, closed Thurs; Ⓣ212/423-3500, Ⓦwww.guggenheim.org; $18, seniors & students $15, pay what you wish Fri 5.45–7.15pm), is better known for the building than its collection. Designed by Frank Lloyd Wright, this unique structure caused a storm of controversy when it was unveiled in 1959. Its centripetal spiral ramp, which wends you continuously all the way to its top floor (affording a vertiginous view of the lobby at the center) or, alternatively, from the top to the bottom, is still thought by some to favor Wright's talents over those of the exhibited artists. Much of the building is still given over to temporary exhibitions, but the permanent collection includes work by Chagall, Léger, the major Cubists and, most completely, Kandinsky. Additionally, there are some late nineteenth-century paintings, not least the exquisite Degas' *Dancers*, Modigliani's *Jeanne Héburene with Yellow Sweater*, and some sensitive early Picassos.

Two blocks up, at Fifth Avenue and 91st Street, lies the Smithsonian-run **Cooper Hewitt National Design Museum** (Mon–Thurs 10am–5pm, Fri 10am–9pm, Sat 10am–6pm, Sun noon–6pm; ⓣ212/849-8400, ⓦcooperhewitt.org; $15). This wonderful institution is the only museum in the US devoted exclusively to historic and contemporary design. Founded in 1897, it's housed in the magnificent mansion once owned by Andrew Carnegie and functions as a research center as well as museum. The **Museo del Barrio**, 1230 Fifth Avenue at 104th Street (Wed–Sun 11am–5pm; ⓣ212/831-7272, ⓦwww.elmuseo.org; $6 suggested donation), showcases Latin American and Caribbean art and culture – it should reopen after a major renovation in the fall of 2009. The museum takes its name from **El Barrio or** Spanish Harlem, which collides head-on with the affluence of the Upper East Side around here. Traditionally the center of a large Puerto Rican community, it remains one of the rougher parts of Manhattan.

About a thirty-minute walk away, at the far eastern end of 88th Street overlooking the East River, **Gracie Mansion** (tours Wed 10am, 11am, 1pm, & 2pm; $7), is one of the best-preserved colonial buildings in the city. Built in 1799, it has been the official residence of the mayor of New York City since 1942, when Fiorello LaGuardia, "man of the people" that he was, reluctantly set up house here – though "mansion" is a bit overblown for what's a rather cramped clapboard cottage.

The Upper West Side

Above 59th Street, Manhattan's West Side becomes less commercial, fading north of Lincoln Center into a lively residential area. This is the **Upper West Side**, now one of the city's more desirable addresses, though in truth an area long favored by artists and intellectuals.

Broadway shears north from Columbus Circle to the **Lincoln Center for the Performing Arts**, a marble assembly of buildings put up in the early 1960s on the site of some of the city's worst slums. Home to the Metropolitan Opera, the New York Philharmonic, the prestigious Juilliard School, and a host of other companies (see p.109), the center is worth seeing even if you don't catch a performance (tours daily 10.30am–4.30pm, leaving from the main concourse under the Center; ⓣ212/875-5350 to reserve; $15). At the center of the complex, behind a large fountain, the **Metropolitan Opera House** is an impressive marble and glass structure, with murals by Marc Chagall behind each of its high front windows.

The most famous of the monumental apartment buildings of **Central Park West** is the **Dakota**, a grandiose Renaissance-style mansion on 72nd Street, completed in 1884. Over the years, big-time tenants have included Lauren Bacall and Leonard Bernstein, and in the late 1960s the building was used as the setting for Roman Polanski's film *Rosemary's Baby*. Now, though, most people know it as the former home of **John Lennon** – and (still) of his wife Yoko Ono, who owns a number of the apartments. Outside the Dakota, on the night of December 8, 1980, Lennon was murdered, shot to death by a man who professed to be one of his greatest admirers (see p.000 to read about the nearby Lennon memorial in Central Park).

North up Central Park West, at 77th Street, the often-overlooked **New York Historical Society** (Tues–Sat 10am–6pm, Sun 11am–5.45pm, open Fri till 8pm; ⓣ212/873-3400, ⓦwww.nyhistory.org; $10, students $6, children under 12 free) is more a museum of American than of New York history. Its collection includes paintings by James Audubon, the Harlem naturalist who specialized in lovingly detailed watercolors of birds; a broad sweep of nineteenth-century American portraiture (including the picture of Alexander Hamilton that found its way onto the $10 bill); Hudson River School landscapes; and a glittering display of Tiffany glass.

Up the street looms the **American Museum of Natural History**, on Central Park West at 79th Street (daily 10am–5.45pm; ⓣ212/769-5200 for tickets or 212/769-5100 for general info, ⓦwww.amnh.org; suggested donation $15, students $11, children $8.50; IMAX films, Hayden Planetarium & special exhibits extra). This, the largest such museum in the world, is a strange architectural blend of heavy Neoclassical and rustic Romanesque styles covering four city blocks. The museum boasts superb nature dioramas and anthropological collections, interactive and multimedia displays, lively signage, and an awesome assemblage of bones, fossils, and models.

Top attractions include the **Dinosaur Halls**, the massive totems in the **Hall of African Peoples**, the taxidermic marvels in **North American Mammals** (including a vividly staged bull and moose fight), and the two thousand gems in the **Hall of Meteorites**, among them a dazzling two-ton hunk of raw copper. The **Hall of Ocean Life** features a replica of, among other aquatic beings, a 94-foot long blue whale.

The **Rose Center for Earth and Space**, comprising the **Hall of the Universe** and the **Hayden Planetarium**, boasts all the latest technology and a truly innovative design, with open construction, spiral ramps, and dramatic glass walls on three sides of the facility. The Planetarium screens a dramatic 30-minute film "Cosmic Collisions," narrated by Robert Redford (throughout the day; $24, students $18, children $14, includes museum). For a head-trip of a different sort, check out SonicVision (Fri & Sat 7.30pm & 8.30pm; $15), a "digitally animated alternative music show" featuring animated graphics and songs by bands such as Radiohead and Coldplay, as mixed by Moby.

After Central Park West, the Upper West Side's second-best address is **Riverside Drive**, which weaves its way from 72nd Street up the western edge of Manhattan, flanked by palatial townhouses put up in the early twentieth century and by **Riverside Park**, landscaped in 1873 by Frederick Law Olmsted, of Central Park fame. Riverside Drive makes the most pleasant route up to prestigious **Columbia University**, whose campus fills seven blocks between 114th and 121st streets and Amsterdam Avenue and Morningside Drive. The campus plazas were designed in grand Beaux Arts style. Regular guided **tours** (Mon–Fri 1pm; free) start from the visitors center in room 213 of the stately Low Library, in the heart of the campus.

At Amsterdam Avenue and 112th Street, one of New York's lesser-known gems, the **Cathedral Church of St John the Divine** (Mon–Sat 7am–6pm, Sun 7am–7pm; free), rises up with a solid kind of majesty. A curious, somewhat eerie mix of Romanesque and Gothic styles, the church was begun in 1892, though building stopped with the outbreak of war in 1939 and only sporadically resumed in the early 1990s; today, it's still barely two-thirds finished. On completion (which is unlikely before 2050), it will be the largest cathedral structure in the world, its floorspace – 600-feet long, and 320-feet wide at the transepts – big enough to swallow both the cathedrals of Notre Dame and Chartres whole.

Harlem

Home to a culturally and historically – if not economically – rich black community, **Harlem** is still a focus of black activism and culture, and well worth seeing. Up until recently, because of a near-total lack of support from federal and municipal funds, Harlem formed a self-reliant and inward-looking community. For many downtown Manhattanites, white and black, 125th Street was a physical and mental border not willingly crossed. Today, the fruits of a co-operative effort involving businesses, residents, and City Hall are manifest in new housing, retail, and community projects, and much has been made of former president Bill Clinton's new offices here as well. But while brownstones triple in value and Harlem's physical proximity to the Upper West Side is touted, poverty and unemployment are still evident in large patches. The safest areas are 125th Street, 145th Street, Convent Avenue, and Malcolm X Boulevard; at night, stick to the clubs and restaurants.

Harlem's sights are very spread out; it's not a bad idea to get acquainted with the area via a **guided tour** (see p.73), and follow that up with further trips. Harlem's working center is 125th Street, between Broadway and Fifth Avenue, anchored by the famous **Apollo Theater**, 253 W 125th St, for many years the center of black entertainment in the Northeast (tours Mon, Tues, Thurs & Fri 11am, 1pm & 3pm, Wed 11am, Sat & Sun 11am–1pm; Ⓣ212/531-5337; $16–18). Almost all the great figures of jazz and the blues played here – James Brown recorded his seminal *Live at the Apollo* album here in 1962 – though a larger attraction today is the Wednesday Amateur Night, open to all (7.30pm; Ⓣ212/531-5300). At 144 W 125th St, the **Studio Museum in Harlem** (Wed–Fri & Sun noon–6pm, Sat 10am–6pm; Ⓣ212/864-4500, Ⓦwww.studiomuseum.org; $7) is a small but vibrant collection of African and African-American art from all eras.

One avenue block east, the **Schomburg Center for Research in Black Culture**, 515 Malcolm X Blvd at 135th Street (Mon–Wed noon–8pm, Thurs & Fri 11am–6pm, Sat 10am–5pm; Ⓣ212/491-2200, Ⓦwww.nypl.org/research/sc; free), has displays on black history, and literally millions of artifacts, manuscripts, artwork, and photographs in its archives. Meanwhile, just north, at 132 W 138th St, is the **Abyssinian Baptist Church**, famed for its revival-style Sunday morning services and a gospel choir of gut-busting vivacity. Cross over west to 138th Street, between Powell Boulevard and Eighth Avenue, and you're in what many consider the finest block of rowhouses in Manhattan – **Strivers' Row** – commissioned during the 1890s housing boom and designed by three sets of architects. Within the burgeoning black community at the turn of the last century, this came to be the desirable place for ambitious professionals to reside – hence its moniker.

Washington Heights and the Cloisters

North of Harlem, starting from West 145th Street or so, is the neighborhood of **Washington Heights**, an area that evolved from poor farmland to highly sought-after real estate in the early part of the twentieth century. Today, the area is home to the largest Dominican population in the US, and while its points of interest are safely accessed during daylight hours, it's advisable to stay clear of the area after dark.

A real surprise lies on 160th Street, between Amsterdam and Edgecombe avenues: the **Morris–Jumel Mansion**, the oldest house in Manhattan (Wed–Sun 10am–4pm; Ⓣ212/923-8008, Ⓦwww.morrisjumel.org; $4). The house, with its proud Georgian outlines, faced by a later Federal portico, was built as a rural retreat in 1765 by Colonel Roger Morris, and served briefly as George Washington's headquarters, before it fell to the British. Later, wine merchant Stephen Jumel bought the mansion and refurbished it for his wife Eliza, formerly a prostitute and his mistress. When Jumel died in 1832, Eliza married ex-vice president Aaron Burr, twenty years her senior. The marriage lasted six months before old Burr took off, to die on the day of their divorce. Eliza battled on to the age of 91, and on the top floor of the house you'll find her obituary, a magnificently fictionalized account of a "scandalous" life.

It's worth continuing up to the northern tip of Manhattan for **The Cloisters** in Fort Tryon Park. This reconstructed monastic complex houses the pick of the Metropolitan Museum's (see p.000) medieval collection – take subway A to 190th St–Ft Washington Ave (Tues–Thurs & Sun 9.30am–5.30pm, Fri & Sat 9.30am–9pm; Ⓣ212/923-3700, Ⓦwww.metmuseum.org; suggested donation

$20, students $10, includes admission to the Metropolitan Museum on the same day). Among its larger artifacts are a monumental Romanesque Hall made up of French remnants, and a frescoed Spanish Fuentiduena Chapel, both from thirteenth century.

The outer boroughs

Many visitors to New York don't stray off Manhattan, but if you're staying a while, choose to investigate the **outer boroughs** and you'll be well rewarded. **Brooklyn** is certainly worth a trip, primarily for Brooklyn Heights just across the East River, bucolic Prospect Park, and the Brooklyn Museum. For inveterate nostalgics, Coney Island and its Russian neighbor, Brighton Beach, lie at the far end of the subway line. Few indeed make it to **Queens**, though the borough holds the bustling Greek community of Astoria, the increasingly hip neighborhood of Long Island City, and the Museum of the Moving Image. The **Bronx**, renowned for the desolate and bleak environs of its southern reaches, which are in fact slowly improving, has the city's largest zoo, Yankee Stadium, and another glorious botanical garden. **Staten Island** is primarily a sleepy residential community, with little in the way of sights (see p.79 for the **Staten Island** ferry).

Brooklyn

Until the early 1800s, **Brooklyn** was no more than a group of autonomous towns and villages, but Robert Fulton's steamship service across the East River changed all that, starting with the establishment of a leafy retreat at Brooklyn Heights. What really transformed things, though, was the opening of the Brooklyn Bridge on May 24, 1883. Thereafter, development spread deeper inland, as housing was needed to service a more commercialized Manhattan. By 1900, Brooklyn was fully established as part of the newly incorporated New York City, and its fate as Manhattan's perennial kid brother was sealed.

Brooklyn Heights (#2, #3, #4, #5, M, N, R, or W to Court St–Borough Hall, or simply walk from Manhattan over the Brooklyn Bridge), one of New York City's most beautiful neighborhoods, has little in common with the rest of the borough. Begin your tour at the **Esplanade** – more commonly known as the **Promenade** – with its fine Manhattan views across the water. **Pierrepoint** and **Montague** streets, the Heights' main arteries, are studded with delightful brownstones, restaurants, bars, and shops.

Farther into Brooklyn, Flatbush Avenue leads to **Grand Army Plaza** (#2 or #3 train to the eponymous subway station), a grandiose junction laid out by Calvert Vaux (co-designer of Central Park) in the late nineteenth century as a dramatic entry-point to the newly unveiled Prospect Park just beyond. The triumphal **Soldiers and Sailors' Memorial Arch** was added thirty years later, topped with *Victory*, a sculpture by Frederick William MacMonnies with a rider, chariot, four horses, and two heralds, in tribute to the Union triumph in the Civil War.

The enormous swath of green that rolls forth from behind the arch is **Prospect Park**. Landscaped in the early 1890s, the park remains an ideal place for exercise, picnics, and family gatherings. During the day it's perfectly safe, but it's best to stay clear of the park at night. The adjacent **Brooklyn Botanic Garden** (March–Oct Tues–Fri 8am–6pm, Sat & Sun 10am–6pm; Nov–Feb Tues–Fri 8am–4.30pm, Sat & Sun 10am–4.30pm; ⓣ718/623-7200, ⓦwww.bbg.org; $8, students $4, free all day Tues & Sat 10am–noon), one of the city's most enticing park and garden spaces, is smaller and more immediately likeable than its more celebrated cousin in the Bronx. Sumptuous but not overplanted, its 52 acres comprise a Rose Garden, Japanese Garden, Shakespeare Garden, and delightful lawns draped with weeping willows and beds of flowering shrubs.

Though doomed to stand in the shadow of the Met, the **Brooklyn Museum of Art**, 200 Eastern Parkway (#2 or #3 train to Eastern Parkway; Wed–Fri 10am–5pm, Sat & Sun 11am–6pm, first Sat of every month 11am–11pm; ⓣ718/638-5000, ⓦwww.brooklynart.org; $8, students $4), is a major museum and a good reason to forsake Manhattan for an afternoon. Highlights include the ethnographic department on the ground floor, the arts and applied arts from Oceania and the Americas and the classical and Egyptian antiquities on the second floor, and the evocative American period rooms on the fourth floor. Pastoral canvases by William Sidney Mount, alongside the heavily romantic Hudson River School and paintings by Eastman Johnson (such as the curious *Not at Home*) and John Singer Sargent lead up to twentieth-century work by Charles Sheeler and Georgia O'Keeffe. European artists on display include Degas, Cézanne, Toulouse-Lautrec, Monet, Dufy, and Rodin.

Generations of working-class New Yorkers came to relax at one of Brooklyn's farthest points, **Coney Island** (ⓦwww.coneyislandusa.com), reachable from Manhattan on the Q, W, F, or N subway lines (45min–1hr). Though it's one of the city's poorest districts, the **Astroland Amusement Park** (ⓦwww.astroland.com) was slated for closure in 2008 to make way for an ambitious (and controversial) resort development, and the lively boardwalk is always jam-packed on summer weekends. An undeniable highlight is the 1927 wooden roller coaster, the **Cyclone** – whatever happens at Astroland, this Coney Island icon is likely to remain open. The beach, a broad swath of golden sand, is beautiful, although it is often crowded on hot days and the water might be less than clean. In late June, catch the **Mermaid Parade**, one of the country's oddest and glitziest small-town fancy dress parades, which culminates here. Meanwhile, the **New York Aquarium** on the boardwalk opened in 1896 and is still going strong, displaying fish and invertebrates from the world over in its darkened halls, along with frequent open-air shows of marine mammals (June–Aug Mon–Fri 10am–6pm, Sat & Sun 10am–7pm; April–May & Sept–Oct Mon–Fri 10am–5pm, Sat & Sun 10am–5.30pm; Nov–March daily 10am–4.30pm; ⓣ718/265-3474, ⓦwww.nyaquarium.com; $13).

Farther east along the boardwalk, **Brighton Beach**, or "Little Odessa," is home to the country's largest community of Russian émigrés and a long-established and now largely elderly Jewish population who, much to the surprise of visiting Russians, still live as if they were in a 1970s Soviet republic. Livelier than Coney Island, it's also more prosperous, especially along its main drag, **Brighton Beach Avenue**, which runs underneath the Q subway line in a hodgepodge of food shops and appetizing restaurants. In the evening, the restaurants really heat up, becoming a near-parody of a rowdy Russian night out, with loud live music and the frenzied knocking back of vodka.

Queens

Named in honor of the wife of Charles II of England, **Queens** was one of the rare places where post-war immigrants could buy their own homes and establish their own communities (**Astoria**, for example, holds the world's largest concentration of Greeks outside Greece). Other than exploring the ethnic neighborhoods here, the major attraction in Queens is the **American Museum of the Moving Image**, in the old Paramount complex in Astoria, at 35th Avenue and 36th Street (R or V train to Steinway; Tues–Thurs 10am–4pm, Fri

10am–6.30pm; ⓣ718/784-0077, ⓦwww.ammi.org; $7.50). The museum is devoted to the history of film, video, and TV. In addition to viewing posters and kitsch movie souvenirs from the 1930s and 1940s, you can listen in on directors explaining sequences from famous movies; watch fun short films made up of well-known clips; add your own sound effects to movies; and see some original sets and costumes. A wonderful, mock-Egyptian pastiche of a 1920s movie theater shows kids' movies and TV classics. Note that until the museum completes a **major renovation** in 2010, opening times and entry fees may change – check the website or call before your visit.

Nearby in Long Island City, the MoMA-affiliated **P.S. 1 Contemporary Art Center**, 22-25 Jackson Ave at 46th Street (Thurs–Mon noon–6pm; ⓣ718/784-2084, ⓦwww.ps1.org; $5, free with a MoMA ticket from the last 30 days), is one of the oldest and biggest organizations in the US devoted exclusively to contemporary art and leading emerging artists.

The Bronx

The city's northernmost and only mainland borough, **The Bronx** was for a long time believed to be its toughest and most crime-ridden district. In fact, it's not much different from the other outer boroughs, though geographically it has more in common with Westchester County to the north than it does with the island regions of New York City: steep hills, deep valleys, and rocky outcroppings to the west, and marshy flatlands along Long Island Sound to the east. Settled in the seventeenth century by the Swede Jonas Bronk, it became, like Brooklyn, part of New York proper around the end of the nineteenth century. Its main thoroughfare, **Grand Concourse**, was lined with luxurious Art-Deco apartment houses; many, though greatly rundown, still stand.

The **Bronx Zoo** (Mon–Fri 10am–5pm, Sat & Sun 10am–5.30pm; ⓣ718/220-5100, ⓦwww.bronxzoo.com; $15, kids $11, pay-what-you-wish every Wed) is accessible either by its main gate on Fordham Road or by a second entrance on

▲ Bronx Zoo

Bronx Park South. The latter is the entrance to use if you come directly here by subway (#2 or #5 to E Tremont Ave). With over four thousand animals, it's the largest urban zoo in the US, and is better than most; it was one of the first institutions of its kind to realize that animals both looked and felt better out in the open. The "Wild Asia" exhibit is an almost forty-acre wilderness through which tigers, elephants, and deer roam relatively free, visible from a monorail (May–Oct; $4). Look in also on the "World of Darkness," which holds nocturnal species, the "Himalayan Highlands," with endangered species such as the red panda and snow leopard, and the "Tiger Mountain" exhibit, which allows visitors the opportunity to get up close and personal with six Siberian tigers.

Across the road from the zoo's main entrance is the back turnstile of the **New York Botanical Gardens** (April–Oct Tues–Sun 10am–6pm; Nov–March 10am–5pm; ⓣ718/817-8700, ⓦwww.nybg.org; $20, gardens only $6, free Wed & Sat 10am–noon), in parts is as wild as anything you're likely to see upstate. Don't miss its Enid A. Haupt Conservatory, a landmark, turn-of-the-century crystal palace featuring a stunning 90-foot dome, beautiful reflecting pool, lots of tropical plants, and seasonal displays.

The original **Yankee Stadium**, at 161st Street and River Avenue (ⓣ718/293-6000, ⓦwww.yankees.com), was home to the most winning team in professional sports – the 26-time World Series champions called the New York Yankees. The new stadium stands just north of the old location, between 161st and 164th streets, and is part of a larger Bronx redevelopment project that also includes a hotel and a conference center.

Eating

There isn't anything you can't eat in New York, and New Yorkers take their food very seriously, obsessed with new cuisines, new dishes, and new restaurants. Certain areas are pockets of ethnic restaurants – **Chinatown** (including Malaysian, Thai, and Vietnamese) below Canal Street; and **Indian Row**, on 6th Street between First and Second avenues – but you can generally find whatever you want, wherever (and whenever) you want. The **outer boroughs** of Brooklyn, the Bronx, and Queens all have excellent dining opportunities worth seeking out, in neighborhoods such as Jackson Heights, Astoria, Williamsburg, and Flushing.

Downtown Manhattan (below 14th St)

Bridge Café 279 Water St, at Dover St ⓣ212/227-3344. This is the city's oldest surviving tavern, opening in 1847 (the building is 50 years older), but now an upscale restaurant. The crabcakes are excellent, as is the list of microbrew beers. Entrees $20–30.

Caffè Reggio 119 MacDougal St, between Bleecker and W 3rd sts ⓣ212/475-9557. One of the first Village coffeehouses, dating back to 1927, embellished with all sorts of Italian antiques and paintings; excellent espresso and cannoli.

Corner Bistro 331 W 4th St, at Jane St ⓣ212/242-9502. This down-home tavern serves some of the best burgers and fries in town. An excellent place to unwind and refuel in a friendly neighborhood atmosphere, it's also a longstanding literary haunt; can get quite crowded.

Delmonico's 56 Beaver St, at William St ⓣ212/509-1144. Many a million-dollar deal has been made at this 1837 landmark steakhouse (check out the pillars from Pompeii). Patrons tend to come more for its historic charms – including classic dishes like Lobster Newburg and Baked Alaska (which was invented here) – than its pricey Porterhouses. Closed Sat.

Doughnut Plant 379 Grand St, between Essex and Clinton sts ⓣ212/505-3700. Serious (and seriously delicious) doughnuts; make sure to sample the seasonal flavors and glazes, including pumpkin and passion fruit.

Graffiti Food & Wine Bar 244 E 10th St, between 1st and 2nd aves ⓣ212/677-0695. Chef Jehangir Mehta cooks up a fusion of Chinese, American, and Indian flavors in this artsy space, with just four tables and courses ranging

$7–12: chili pork dumplings, grapefruit confit, and a cumin-eggplant wrap grace the menu. Closed Mon.

Katz's Delicatessen 205 E Houston St, at Ludlow St ☎212/254-2246. Venerable Lower East Side Jewish deli serving archetypal overstuffed pastrami and corned-beef sandwiches. Best known as the site of the orgasm scene in When Harry Met Sally.

Lombardi's 32 Spring St, between Mott and Mulberry sts ☎212/941-7994. The oldest pizzeria in Manhattan serves some of the best pie in town, including an amazing clam pizza; no slices, though. Ask for roasted garlic on the side.

Magnolia Bakery 401 Bleecker St, at W 11th St ☎212/462-2572. There are lots of baked goods on offer here, but everyone comes for the heavenly and deservedly famous multi-colored cupcakes (celebrated in both Sex and the City and Saturday Night Live), $2.25 each. Lines can stretch around the block.

Momofuku Noodle Bar 171 First Ave, between E 10th and E 11th sts ☎212/777-7773. Celebrated chef David Chang's first restaurant, where his simplest creations are still the best: silky steamed pork buns, laced with hoisin sauce and pickled cucumbers ($9), or steaming bowls of chicken and pork ramen noodles ($10).

Nobu 105 Hudson St, at Franklin St ☎212/219-0500. Superlative Japanese cuisine such as black cod with miso ($23) and chilled sake served in hollow bamboo trunks. Reservations are hard to get; you can also try the somewhat cheaper Next Door Nobu, literally next door.

Peanut Butter & Company 240 Sullivan St, between Bleecker and W 3rd sts ☎212/677-3995. Peanut butter heaven. Try the "Elvis" – a grilled peanut butter and honey sandwich with bananas, or the slightly more adventurous "Spicy Peanut Butter Sandwich," made with pineapple jam and grilled chicken. Sandwiches are $5–6.50.

Ping's Seafood 22 Mott St, between Chatham Square and Pell sts ☎212/602-9988. While this Hong Kong–style seafood restaurant is good any time, it's most enjoyable on weekends for dim sum, when carts of tasty, bite-size delicacies whir by every thirty seconds.

Pinkberry 41 Spring St, between Mott and Mulberry sts ☎212/274-8696; also 330 W 58th St, between 8th and 9th aves at Columbus Circle ☎212/397-0412. This LA chain is known as "crackberry" for good reason; its delicious non-fat, low-cal frozen yoghurt comes in original, green tea and coffee flavors, with a vast range of fruit and nut toppings. One of eleven outlets in the city.

Ray's 27 Prince St, between Mott and Elizabeth sts ☎212/966-1960. While countless pizzerias in the city claim to be the "original Ray's," this Little Italy mainstay is perhaps the most distinctive and unchain-like of the bunch (note, though: it's not actually a chain). The thick Sicilian slices ($2.50) are particularly good.

Rice to Riches 37 Spring St, between Mott and Mulberry sts ☎212/274-0008. Rice pudding made hip and utterly irresistible, served up in this funky take-out space, from peanut butter and choc chip, to mango and cinnamon flavors. Bowls start at $5.50.

Sammy's Roumanian Steakhouse 157 Chrystie St, at Delancey St ☎212/673-0330. This basement Jewish steakhouse gives diners more than they bargained for: schmaltzy songs, delicious-but-heartburn-inducing food (topped off by homemade *rugelach* and egg creams for dessert), and chilled vodka in blocks of ice. Keep track of your tab, if you can.

Sarita's Mac & Cheese 345 E 12th St between 2nd and 1st aves ☎212/358-7912. Indulge your macaroni and cheese cravings at this homey joint, with ten creative varieties on offer, blending cheddar, gruyère, brie and goat's cheese with herbs and meats. Pick your portion sizes: nosh, major munch or mongo ($4.25–12.50).

Shopsin's Essex St Market, 120 Essex St (no phone). Something of a New York institution, Kenny Shopsin ran his famously idiosyncratic diner in the West Village for years (no cell phones or parties of five), but was forced down here by high rents. His addictive creations – like peanut-butter filled pancakes – have a loyal following. Closed Sun & Mon.

Vanessa's Dumplings 118A Eldridge St, between Grand and Broome sts ☎212/625-8008. This always busy Chinese eatery knocks out various combinations of steamed or fried pork, shrimp, and vegetable dumplings at the bargain price of $1 for four – the crispy sesame pancake with pork is just as addictive.

Veselka 144 2nd Ave, at 9th St ☎212/228-9682. The terrific grilled kielbasa, vegetarian stuffed cabbage, and Ukrainian pierogi at Eastern European Veselka are all great for sopping up alcohol and killing hunger pangs at 4am. Open 24hr.

Xunta 174 1st Ave, between 10th and 11th sts ☎212/614-0620. This East Village gem buzzes with hordes of young people perched on rum barrels, downing pitchers of sangria and choosing from the dizzying tapas menu – try the mussels in fresh tomato sauce, or shrimp with garlic. You can eat (and drink) very well for around $20.

Yonah Schimmel's 137 E Houston St, between Forsyth and Eldridge sts ☎212/477-2858. The traditional knishes here, rounds of vegetable- or meat-stuffed dough, are baked fresh on the premises, as are the wonderful bagels.

Midtown Manhattan (14th St to 59th St)

Artisanal 2 Park Ave, at 32nd St ⓣ212/725-8585. Cheese is the name of the game here – there's a cave with 700 varieties. If you don't want the full experience, grab a small table at the bar and try the gougere (gruyère puffs) with one of the excellent wines on offer.

Carmine's 200 W 44th St, between Broadway and 8th Ave ⓣ212/221-3800; also, 2450 Broadway, between W 90th and W 91st sts ⓣ212/362-2200. Mountainous portions of tasty, homestyle, Southern Italian food are made to share at this large, loud favorite. Be prepared to wait; only parties of six or more can make reservations after 6pm.

Carnegie Deli 854 7th Ave, between W 54th and 55th sts ⓣ212/757-2245. The most generously stuffed corned-beef sandwiches in the city are served by the rudest of waiters at this famous Jewish deli. Still, it's a must-have experience, if you can stand the inflated prices.

Empire Diner 210 10th Ave, at 22nd St ⓣ212/243-2736. Spangled in silver, this all-night diner charms with its festive vibe and moderately priced food.

Gramercy Tavern 42 E 20th St, between Broadway and Park Ave ⓣ212/477-0777. By many accounts, NYC's best and most-beloved restaurant; its neo-colonial decor, exquisite New American cuisine, and perfect service make for a memorable meal. The lively front room is a great place to drop in for a drink, or a more casual (and cheaper) meal.

Hell's Kitchen 679 9th Ave, between W 46th and 47th sts ⓣ212/977-1588. Features six different kinds of frozen margaritas and creative renderings of Mexican cuisines. The caramelized banana empanadas are mouth-watering.

Joe Allen Restaurant 326 W 46th St, between 8th and 9th aves ⓣ212/581-6464. The tried-and-true formula of checkered tablecloths, old-fashioned barroom feel, and reliable American food at moderate prices works excellently at this popular pre-theater spot. Make a reservation, unless you plan to arrive after 8pm.

Oyster Bar lower level, Grand Central Station ⓣ212/490-6650. This wonderfully atmospheric old place, down in the vaulted dungeons of Grand Central, features a staggering menu of daily catches – she-crab bisque, steamed Maine lobster, and sweet Kumamoto oysters. Prices are moderate to expensive; you can eat more cheaply at the bar.

Rosa Mexicano 1063 1st Ave, at 58th St ⓣ212/753-7407; also, 61 Columbus Ave, at 62nd St ⓣ212/977-7700. Festive decor, authentic dishes such as *bisteca al hongos* (beef with creamy mushroom sauce), and pomegranate margaritas make this the best Mexican restaurant in NYC. Not surprisingly, it's pricey.

Russian Tea Room 150 W 57th St, between 6th and 7th aves ⓣ212/581-7100. In its third incarnation, this celebrated restaurant still looks fabulous, with a superb Russian menu (the stroganoff and the chicken kiev are faves). Dinner entrees from $30 – Sunday brunch is better value.

Shake Shack Madison Square Park ⓣ212/889-6600. Wildly popular food kiosk, with long lines for the perfectly grilled burgers and frozen-custard shakes. You can also buy beer and wine to sip outside, with everything around $5 or less. Closes at 7pm in winter; until 11pm the rest of the year.

Union Square Café 21 E 16th St, between 5th Ave and Union Square W ⓣ212/243-4020. Choice California-style dining in a classy but comfortable atmosphere. No one does salmon like the chefs here, and the polenta with gorgonzola is incredible. Meals aren't cheap – prices average $100 and up for two – but the creative menu is a real treat.

Virgil's Real BBQ 152 W 44th St, between 6th and 7th aves ⓣ212/921-9494. Virgil's, one of New York's earliest entries in the BBQ game, is one of the few Times Square eateries that's not just for tourists. All the food groups – Memphis, Carolina, Texas, even Maryland (ham) – are well represented, and you'll likely be able to skip breakfast in the morning.

Uptown Manhattan (60th St and above)

Amy Ruth's 113 W 116th St, between Lenox and 7th aves ⓣ212/280-8779. The honey-dipped fried chicken is reason enough to travel to this casual, family restaurant in Harlem. The place gets especially busy after church on Sun.

Big Nick's Burger Joint 2175 Broadway, between 76th and 77th sts ⓣ212/362-9238. This welcoming greasy spoon with gargantuan portions is heaven for hungry diners, be it after-hours or early in the morning.

Boathouse Café In Central Park (enter from 72nd St), at Central Park Drive N ⓣ212/517-2233. While the New American cuisine here is fine, it's the picturesque setting that makes the pumped-up prices worth every penny, especially at sunset. If you don't feel like splurging, go for a drink at the water's edge.

Café Sabarsky in the Neue Galerie 1048 5th Ave, at E 86th St ☎212/288-0665. The lavish parlor of the former Vanderbilt mansion has been transformed into this Old Vienna Kaffeehaus. The menu includes superb pastries, like Klimt torte and strudels, and small sandwiches, many made with cured meats.

Gray's Papaya 2090 Broadway, at 72nd St; also, 402 6th Ave, at W 8th St. Open 24/7, this insanely popular hot-dog joint is an NYC institution, selling crispy hot dogs ($1.25) and fresh papaya drinks (gimmicky, but delicious). Three locations in the city.

Heidelburg 1648 2nd Ave, between E 85th and 86th sts ☎212/628-2332. At one of the last Yorkville German joints, the food is the real deal, with excellent liver dumpling soup, *Bauernfruestuck* omelets and pancakes (both sweet and potato). Have a huge, boot-shaped glass of Weissbeer with anything.

La Caridad 78 2199 Broadway, at W 78th St ☎212/874-2780. Plentiful and inexpensive Cuban-Chinese food (the Cuban dishes are better) is doled out at this neighborhood institution. Bring your own beer and expect to wait.

Serendipity 3 225 E 60th St, between 2nd and 3rd aves ☎212/838-3531. The long-established eatery and ice cream parlor serves out-of-this-world frozen hot chocolate; the wealth of ice cream offerings are a real treat, too.

Sylvia's Restaurant 328 Lenox Ave, between W 126th and 127th sts ☎212/996-0660. Celebrated Southern soul-food restaurant in Harlem – so famous that Sylvia herself even has her own packaged-food line. The fried chicken and candied yams are exceptional.

Tavern on the Green Central Park W ☎212/873-3200. This fantastical, tacky tourist trap remains a New York institution. The American and Continental cuisine is dependable if ordinary, but you can also come for a drink on the terrace overlooking the park – special cocktails from $12.

Terrace in the Sky 400 W 119th St, between Amsterdam Ave and Morningside Drive ☎212/666-9490. Enjoy harp music, marvelous Mediterranean fare, and great views of Morningside Heights in this romantic Uptown spot.

The outer boroughs

Diner 85 Broadway, at Berry St, Williamsburg, Brooklyn ☎718/486-3077. A fave with artists and hipsters, this groovy eatery (in a Pullman diner car) serves tasty American bistro grub (hangar steaks, roasted chicken, fantastic fries) at good prices. Stays open late, with an occasional DJ spinning.

Elias Corner 24-02 31st St, at 24th Ave, Astoria, Queens ☎718/932-1510. Pay close attention to the seafood on display as you enter, because this Astoria institution doesn't have menus and meals are prepared based on availability. Serves some of the best Greek food and freshest fish you'll find; try the marinated grilled octopus, if on offer.

Grocery 195 Smith St, Carroll Gardens, Brooklyn ☎718/596-3335. Smith St has become a Brooklyn dining destination, and this tiny eatery, featuring a seasonal menu full of unique, New American dishes, is the best of the bunch. Entrees $21–35; call well in advance for reservations.

Jackson Diner 37-47 74th St, between 37th Rd and 37th Ave, Jackson Heights, Queens ☎718/672-1232. Come here hungry and stuff yourself silly with amazingly light and reasonably priced Indian fare. The samosas and mango lassis are not to be missed.

Mario's 2342 Arthur Ave, between 184th and 186th sts, Bronx ☎718/584-1188. Pricey but impressive Neapolitan cooking, from pizzas to pastas and beyond, enticing even die-hard Manhattanites to the Belmont section of the Bronx.

Nathan's 1310 Surf Ave at Schweiker's Walk, Coney Island, Brooklyn ☎718/946-2202. Home of the "famous Coney Island hot dog," served since 1916, *Nathan's* is not to be missed (unless you're a vegetarian). Its annual Hot Dog Eating Contest is held on July 4.

Peter Luger's Steak House 178 Broadway, at Driggs Ave, Williamsburg, Brooklyn ☎718/387-7400. Catering to carnivores since 1873, Peter Luger's may just be the city's finest steakhouse. The service is surly and the decor plain, but the porterhouse steak – the only cut served – is divine. Cash only, and very expensive; expect to pay at least $75 a head.

Primorski 282 Brighton Beach Ave, between 2nd and 3rd sts, Brighton Beach, Brooklyn ☎718/891-3111. Perhaps the best of Brighton Beach's Russian hangouts, with a huge menu of authentic Russian dishes, including blintzes and stuffed cabbage, at absurdly cheap prices. Live music in the evening.

Drinking

New York's best **bars** are in **Downtown Manhattan** – the West and East villages, SoHo, and the Lower East Side. The **Midtown** places tend to be geared to tourists and an after-hours office crowd and (with a few exceptions) are pricey and rather dull. **Uptown** bars can be fun, and it's worth spending at least one night in Brooklyn – **Williamsburg** is easy to reach. Most of the bars listed below serve food of some kind and have happy hours sometime between 4pm and 8pm during the week. See also the bars listed in "Gay New York," p.112.

Downtown Manhattan (to 14th St)

Barramundi 67 Clinton St, between Stanton and Rivington sts ⓣ212/529-6900. The magical, fairy-lit garden makes this bar a blessed sanctuary from the painfully hip Lower East Side.

Blind Tiger Ale House 281 Bleecker St, at Jones St ⓣ212/462-4682. This wood-paneled pub is the home of serious ale connoisseurs, with 28 rotating drafts, a couple of casks, and loads of bottled beers – they also serve cheese plates from Murray's (see p.000). The prime location means it tends to get packed.

Bourgeois Pig 111 E 7th St, between 1st Ave and Ave A ⓣ212/475-2246. The decadent Versailles theme at this funky wine bar, replete with wall-size mirrors, chandeliers, and crimson satin couches, is backed by an extensive cocktail menu (using just wines, beers and champagne).

d.b.a 41 1st Ave, between E 2nd and 3rd sts ⓣ212/475-5097. A beer-lover's paradise, *d.b.a.* has at least 60 bottled beers, 14 brews on tap, and an authentic hand-pump. Garden seating (with a small smoking section) is available in the summer.

Ear Inn 326 Spring St, between Washington and Greenwich sts ⓣ212/226-9060. This historic pub, a stone's throw from the Hudson River, opened in 1890 (the building dates from 1817). Its creaky (and some claim, haunted) interior is as cozy as a Cornish inn, with a good mix of beers on tap and basic, reasonably priced American food.

Grassroots Tavern 20 St Mark's Place, between 2nd and 3rd aves ⓣ212/475-9443. This roomy, wooden, and wonderful underground den has Brooklyn beers for $3, an extended happy hour, and at least three animals roaming around at any hour of the day or night.

Happy Ending Lounge 302 Broome St, between Eldridge and Forsyth sts ⓣ212/334-9676. A former erotic massage parlor has been reborn as an exceptionally cool bar and club, with the original tiled sauna rooms downstairs converted to cozy booths. Drinks $8–12.

Hogs & Heifers 859 Washington St, at W 13th St ⓣ212/929-0655. It's honky-tonk cheesy but fun; a raucous Meatpacking District watering hole that has inspired thousands of women to dance on the bar, as well as donate their bras to the growing collection that adorns the joint.

McSorley's Old Ale House 15 E 7th St, between 2nd and 3rd aves ⓣ212/472-9148. Yes, it's touristy and often full of local frat boys, but you'll be drinking in history at a landmark that served its first beer in 1854.

Other Room 143 Perry St, between Washington and Greenwich sts ⓣ212/645-9758. The cozy-cool atmosphere, excellent drink menu, and "way-West" location of this wine and beer bar has guaranteed it a special place in locals' hearts.

St Dymphna's 118 St Marks Place, between 1st Ave and Ave A ⓣ212/254-6636. With a tempting pub menu and some of the city's best Guinness, Dymphna's is great place to warm up on a cold winter's night.

Temple Bar 332 Lafayette St, between Bleecker and Houston sts ⓣ212/925-4242. One of the most discreet and romantic spots for a drink Downtown, this sumptuous, dark lounge evokes the 1940s. They take their martinis very seriously here.

White Horse Tavern 567 Hudson St, at W 11th St ⓣ212/989-3956. A Greenwich Village institution, opening in 1880: Dylan Thomas supped his last here before being carted off to hospital, while Norman Mailer and Hunter S. Thompson were also regulars.

Midtown Manhattan (14th St to 59th St)

Campbell Apartment Southwest balcony, Grand Central Terminal ⓣ212/953-0409. The former home of businessman John W. Campbell – built to look like a Florentine palace – has been given a snappy refit by designer Nina Campbell, and is now one of New York's most distinctive cocktail bars. Go early, bring a chunk of cash, and don't wear sneakers.

Hudson Bar in the Hudson Hotel 356 W 58th St, between 8th and 9th aves ⓣ212/554-6000. Philippe Starck mixes French Rococo decor and modern lighting here, with spectacular results.

Drinks are fun: try the lemongrass cocktails. The high prices reflect the banker clientele, and it can be hard to get in – it's one of those places.

Jimmy's Corner 140 W 44th St, between Broadway and 6th Ave ⓣ212/221-9510. The walls of this long, narrow corridor of a bar, one of the most characterful dives in the city, are a virtual boxing hall of fame; it's owned by ex-fighter and trainer Jimmy Glenn.

Lever House 390 Park Ave, at 53rd St ⓣ212/888-2700. An NYC power-drinking stalwart in a 1950s landmark. The interior strikes a balance between retro and futuristic; though this is primarily a posh restaurant, it's worth a look and a martini or two at the white-glass bar.

Old Town Bar & Restaurant 45 E 18th St, between Broadway and Park Ave ⓣ212/529-6732. An atmospheric Flatiron District pub that's popular with publishing types, photographers, and the staff of the New York Observer. Originally opened in 1892, much of the creaking interior is original.

Pete's Tavern 129 E 18th St, at Irving Place ⓣ212/473-7676. This former speakeasy, which opened in 1864, has hosted such illustrious patrons as John F. Kennedy Jr and O. Henry, who allegedly wrote "*Gift of the Magi*" in his regular booth here. A fun and often raucous spot to grab a pint near Gramercy Park.

Russian Vodka Room 265 W 52nd St, between Broadway and 8th Ave ⓣ212/307-5835. As you might expect, they serve 53 different types of vodka here, as well as their own fruit-flavored and sublime garlic-infused concoctions. Office workers mingle with Russian expats; you'll be laughed out the bar if you ask for a mixer.

Uptown Manhattan (60th St and above)

Dead Poet 450 Amsterdam Ave, between 81st and 82nd sts ⓣ212/595-5670. You'll wax poetical and then drop dead if you stay for the duration of this sweet little bar's happy hour: it lasts from 4 to 8pm and offers draft beer at $3 a pint. The backroom has armchairs, books, and a pool table.

Ding Dong Lounge 929 Columbus Ave, between 105th and 106th sts ⓣ212/663-2600. A punk bar with a DJ and occasional live bands that attracts a vibrant mix of graduate students, neighborhood Latinos, and stragglers from the nearby youth hostel.

Metropolitan Museum of Art 1000 5th Ave at 82nd St ⓣ212/535-7710. It's hard to imagine a more romantic spot to sip a glass of wine and kick off the evening, whether on the Roof Garden Café (open May–Oct), which has some of the best views in the city, or in the Balcony Bar overlooking the Great Hall. Bars close at 8.30pm Fri–Sat.

Prohibition 503 Columbus Ave, between 84th and 85th sts ⓣ212/579-3100. A pool table, live jazz, and outdoor tables combine to make *Prohibition* one of the liveliest singles scenes on the Upper West Side.

Subway Inn 143 E 60th St, at Lexington Ave ⓣ212/223-8929. This neighborhood dive bar, across from Bloomingdale's, has been serving customers since 1937, and is great for a late-afternoon beer.

The outer boroughs

Bohemian Hall and Beer Garden 29-19 24th Ave, at 29th St, Astoria, Queens ⓣ718/721-4226. This old Czech bar is the real deal, catering to old-timers and serving a good selection of pilsners, hard-to-find brews, and burgers and sausages. In back, there's a very large beer garden, complete with picnic tables, trees, and a bandshell for polka and non-polka groups alike.

Brooklyn Brewery 1 Brewers Row, 79 N 11th St, Williamsburg, Brooklyn ⓣ718/486-7422. New York's best-known microbrewery, open Fri nights only (6–11pm), for "happy hour" (beers $3).

Brooklyn Inn 148 Hoyt St, at Bergen St, Boerum Hill, Brooklyn ⓣ718/625-9741. Locals – and their dogs – gather at this convivial favorite with high ceilings and a friendly bar staff. Great place for a daytime buzz or shooting pool in the back room.

Floyd 131 Atlantic Ave, between Clinton and Henry sts, Brooklyn Heights, Brooklyn ⓣ718/858-5810. Tricked out with antique couches and comfy leather chairs, the main draws here are the cheap draft beers (includes Brooklyn Lager), popular indoor bocce court, and live English Premier League games.

Pete's Candy Store 709 Lorimer St, between Frost and Richardson sts, Williamsburg, Brooklyn ⓣ718/302-3770, ⓦwww.petescandystore.com. This terrific little spot to drink was once a real candy store. There's free live music every night, poetry on Mon, Scrabble and bingo nights, and even an organized "Stitch and Bitch" knitting group.

Stonehome Wine Bar 87 Lafayette Ave, between S Portland Ave and S Elliot Place, Fort Greene, Brooklyn ⓣ718/624-9443. Stylish wine bar with the added bonus of a backyard patio, perfect for spring and summer evenings (and smokers). The bar itself is a gorgeous, curving, cherry-wood masterpiece, and the carefully crafted wine list is impressively long.

Nightlife and entertainment

You'll never be at a loss for something fun or culturally enriching to do while in New York. The **live music** scene, in particular, well reflects New York's diversity: on any night of the week, you can hear pretty much any type of music, from thumping hip-hop to raging punk, and, of course, plenty of jazz. There are also quite a few **dance clubs**, where you can move to hard-hitting house or cheesy tunes from the 1970s and 80s.

Home to Broadway and 42nd Street (as well as off-Broadway and the Fringe Festival), New York is also one of the world's great **theater** centers, with productions that range from lavish, over-the-top musicals to experimental productions in converted garages. **Classical music**, **opera**, and **dance** are all very well-represented, too. As for **film**, you couldn't hope for better pickings: the city has several large indie theaters, numerous revival and art-house cinemas, and countless Hollywood-blockbuster multiplexes. Last but not least, NYC has many excellent **comedy** clubs, as well as a healthy **spoken-word** and **poetry slam** scene.

For **listings** of what's on during any particular week, check out *Time Out New York* ($3.99; available from newsstands citywide) or *The Village Voice* (free; available in newspaper boxes and many other spots around town). Useful **websites** include Ⓦwww.ohmyrockness.com (for indie rock), Ⓦwww.thelmagazine.com and Ⓦwww.timeout.com (for general listings).

Clubs and live music

New York has plenty of great **live music venues**, from the cutting-edge *Knitting Factory* to *S.O.B.'s*, which caters to world music and more eclectic fare. Numerous **jazz clubs**, ranging in quality from passable to sublime, keep the black-clad, turtleneck-wearing set happy. **Cover charges** at any of these smaller places will run you from $10 to $25 or so. There are also many larger music venues, which attract touring bands from around the world; here, a ticket can cost anywhere from $25 to $100. If the show's not sold out, tickets are usually available at the door. For advance tickets, go to the venue's box office, or visit **Ticketmaster** (Ⓣ212/307-4100 or 1-800/755-4000 outside NY, Ⓦwww.ticketmaster.com), or **Ticketweb** (Ⓦwww.ticketweb.com).

As for **clubs**, things change at a rapid pace, so be sure to check the listings in *The Village Voice* or *Time Out* before you make any plans. Though the city's nightclubs have largely recovered from a string of police raids in the winter of 2006, West Chelsea bore the brunt of the crackdown and is no longer the center of the scene. You'll find the action much more spread out, with the Lower East Side, the East and West villages and Brooklyn offering as many venues as the **Meatpacking District**, now the city's premier, if slightly overrated, nightlife hub. New York's DJs rely on a varied diet of house music, electro-house and techno, though there's a growing cadre of inventive hip-hop, retro soul, indie rock, and Latin-jazz venues. **Cover charges** range from $15 to $50, though most average out at around $20; always bring photo **ID**.

Theater

Even if you're not normally a **theater** buff, going to see a play or a musical while in New York is virtually de rigueur. The various theater venues are referred to as **Broadway**, **Off-Broadway**, or **Off-Off Broadway**, representing a descending order of ticket price, production polish, elegance, and comfort. Broadway offerings consist primarily of large-scale musicals, comedies, and dramas with big-name actors, while Off-Broadway theaters tend to combine high production qualities with a greater willingness to experiment. Off-Off Broadway is the fringe – drama on a shoestring. As for **location**, most Broadway theaters are just east or west of Broadway, between 40th and 52nd streets; the rest are sprinkled throughout Manhattan, with a concentration in the East and West villages, Union Square, Chelsea, and the 40s and 50s west of the Theater District. Check out *Time Out New York* for the latest shows.

On Broadway, **ticket prices** run $60–200; Off-Broadway, expect to pay $25–75; Off-Off is usually $12–20. The prices of Broadway and Off-Broadway shows can be cut considerably if you can wait in line on the day of the performance at the red-and-white **TKTS** booth in Times Square (Mon–Sat 3–8pm, Sun 3pm–until 30min before latest show, also Wed & Sat 10am–2pm for 2pm matinees). The booth has tickets for many Broadway and Off-Broadway shows, at 25- to 50-percent off (plus a $4 per ticket service charge), payable in **cash or traveler's checks only**. Keep in mind that you may have to wait in line for a couple of hours, and that the show you want to see may be sold out by the time you get to the front of the line.

If you're prepared to pay **full price**, you can go directly to the theater box office, or use **Telecharge** (ⓣ212/239-6200 or 1-800/432-7250 outside NY, ⓦwww.telecharge.com) or **Ticketmaster**. For these ticket agencies, you will need a credit card and should expect to pay a $7 surcharge per ticket. For Off-Broadway shows, **Ticket Central** (ⓣ212/279-4200, ⓦwww.ticketcentral.com) sells tickets to many of these online, and at their office at 416 W 42nd St, between 9th and 10th avenues (daily noon to 8pm; ⓣ212/279-4200). For Off-Off Broadway productions, check out **SmartTix** (ⓣ212/868-4444, ⓦwww.smarttix.com) or **TheaterMania** (ⓦwww.theatermania.com, ⓣ212/352-0255).

Classical music, opera, and dance

The **Lincoln Center**, located on Broadway between W 62nd and W 66th streets (ⓣ212/875-5456, ⓦwww.lincolncenter.org), is New York's powerhouse of performing arts. The complex comprises some twenty venues in all, including the **Avery Fisher Hall** (ⓣ212/875-5656), the permanent base of the New York Philharmonic (box office Mon–Sat 10am–6pm, Sun noon–6pm; ⓦwww.newyorkphilharmonic.org), and the 120-year-old **Metropolitan Opera**, New York City's premier venue for opera. The soaring theater has pitch-perfect acoustics and regularly draws big crowds who come to hear sopranos, baritones, and tenors from around the world. It hosts the Metropolitan Opera Company from September to April, as well as the American Ballet Theater from May to June. Tickets are outrageously expensive and difficult to get, though 175 standing-room tickets ($12–16) go on sale every Saturday morning at 10am (the line has been known to form at dawn). Contact the Met Ticket Service (ⓣ212/362-6000, ⓦwww.metopera.org).

The **New York State Theater**, also in the Lincoln Center (ⓣ212/870-5570) is home to the **New York City Ballet** six months a year, considered by many to be the greatest dance company in existence. Tickets must be purchased through the company's website (ⓦwww.nycballet.com), or through Ticketmaster. This accessible venue is also where the New York City Opera (ⓦwww.nycopera.com) plays David to the Met's Goliath. Seats go for less than half the Met's, and standing-room tickets are available if a performance sells out.

Besides the **Lincoln Center**, the most important venue is **Carnegie Hall**, 154 W 57th St, at Seventh Avenue (ⓣ212/247-7800, ⓦwww.carnegiehall.org), where the greatest names from all schools of music have performed.

When it comes to **dance**, Lincoln Center once again serves as a showcase, though a number of other venues regularly host events. The **Brooklyn Academy of**

Music (or **BAM**), at 30 Lafayette St in Brooklyn, between Ashland Place and St Felix Street (ⓣ718/636-4100, ⓦwww.bam.org), is America's oldest performing arts academy and one of the most daring producers in New York – definitely worth crossing the river for. Meanwhile, back in Manhattan, the **New York City Center**, 131 W 55th St, between Sixth and Seventh avenues (ⓣ212/581-1212, ⓦwww.citycenter.org), is home to some of the country's leading dance companies, including Alvin Ailey American Dance Theater (ⓣ212/405-9000, ⓦwww.alvinailey.org), American Ballet Theatre (ⓣ212/477-3030, ⓦww.abt.org), and the Paul Taylor Dance Company (ⓣ212/431-5562, ⓦwww.ptdc.org). For small and mid-sized companies, the most important space in Manhattan is the **Joyce Theater**, 175 8th Ave, at 19th Street (ⓣ212/242-0800, ⓦwww.joyce.org). The Joyce hosts companies from around the world, and also has a small Downtown satellite – Joyce SoHo – at 155 Mercer St, between Houston and Prince streets (ⓣ212/431-9233).

Rock, pop and multi-genre

Arlene's Grocery 95 Stanton St, between Ludlow and Orchard sts ⓣ212/358-1633, ⓦwww.arlene-grocery.com. This intimate, erstwhile bodega hosts free gigs by local indie talent during the week. Mon is "Punk/Heavy Metal Karaoke" night, where you can wail along (with a live band, no less) to your favorite songs.

The Bowery Ballroom 6 Delancey St, at Bowery ⓣ212/533-2111, ⓦwww.boweryballroom.com. A minimum of attitude, great sound, and even better sightlines make this a local favorite to see well-known indie-rock bands. Shows $12–25. Pay in cash at the Mercury Lounge box office (see below), at the door, or by credit card through Ticketweb.

The Fillmore NY at Irving Plaza 17 Irving Place, between E 15th and E 16th sts ⓣ212/777-6800, ⓦwww.irvingplaza.com. Once home to Off-Broadway musicals, this venue now hosts an impressive array of rock, electronic music, and techno acts – a good place to see popular bands in a manageable setting. Tickets $20-50.

Joe's Pub At the Public Theater, 425 Lafayette St, between Astor Place and E 4th St ⓣ212/539-8770, ⓦwww.publictheater.org. The word "pub" is a misnomer for this swanky nightspot, which features a vast array of musical, cabaret, and dramatic performances. Star spottings abound. Shows nightly at 7 or 7.30pm, 9.30pm, and 11pm. Covers range from $12 to $50 depending on the performer.

Knitting Factory 74 Leonard St, between Church St and Broadway ⓣ212/219-3006, ⓦwww.knittingfactory.com. At this intimate Downtown space, you can hear all kinds of aural experimentation, from art rock and avant-garde jazz to electronica and indie-rock. Highly recommended. Cover prices vary wildly, so call ahead.

The Mercury Lounge 217 E Houston St, between Ludlow and Essex sts ⓣ212/260-4700, ⓦwww.mercuryloungenyc.com. The dark, medium-sized, innocuous space showcases a mix of local, national, and international pop and rock acts. It's owned by the same crew as Bowery Ballroom, which usually gets the better-known bands. Purchase tickets (around $10–20) in cash at the box office, at the door, or via Ticketweb.

Music Hall of Williamsburg 66 N 6th St, between Wythe and Kent aves, Williamsburg, Brooklyn ⓣ718/486-5400, ⓦwww.musichallofwilliamsburg.com. A large performance space with excellent acoustics, set in an old factory. One of Brooklyn's really great venues and another in the Bowery Ballroom stable – expect the same kind of acts. Tickets $10–20.

S.O.B.'s 204 Varick St, at W Houston St ⓣ212/243-4940. Short for "Sounds of Brazil," this lively club-restaurant, with regular Caribbean, salsa, and world music acts, puts on two performances a night. Admission ranges $10–20, depending on the act. No cover, however, for those with dinner reservations pre 7pm. Be sure to check out Samba Saturday, the venue's hottest night.

Southpaw 125 5th Ave, between Sterling Place and Douglass St, Park Slope, Brooklyn ⓣ718/230-0236. ⓦwww.spsounds.com. Brooklyn's premier live venue, with 5000 square feet of space and a wide range of acts and DJs from almost every genre. Admission varies, but is rarely more than $10–12, while a cab from lower Manhattan costs around $10–15.

Jazz venues

Arthur's Tavern 57 Grove St, between Bleecker St and 7th Ave ⓣ212/675-6879, ⓦwww.arthurstavernnyc.com. This low-key, 50-year-old club is housed in a landmark building and features the Grove Street Stompers, who've been playing every Monday for the past forty years. Jazz 7–9.30pm, blues and funk 10pm–3.30am. No cover; one-drink minimum.

Birdland 315 W 44th St, between 8th and 9th aves ⓣ212/581-3080, ⓦwww.birdlandjazz.com. Not the original place where Charlie Parker played, but nonetheless an established jazz club that plays host to some big names. Sets nightly at 9 and 11pm. Music charge of $20–50; at a table, you'll need to spend a minimum of $10 or more on food or drink, while at the bar, the cover includes your first drink.

Lenox Lounge 288 Lenox Ave, at 125th St ⓣ212/427-0253, ⓦwww.lenoxlounge.com. Entertaining Harlem since the 1930s, this historic jazz lounge has an over-the-top Art-Deco interior (check out the Zebra Room). Three sets nightly at 9pm, 10.45pm, & 12.30am. Cover $15, with a one-drink minimum.

Smoke 2751 Broadway, at 106th St ⓣ212/864-6662, ⓦwww.smokejazz.com. This Upper West Side joint is a real neighborhood treat. Sets start at 9pm, 11pm, & 12.30am; stop by for happy hour and $5 cocktails daily 5–8pm. Cover varies.

Village Vanguard 178 7th Ave S, between W 11th and Perry streets ⓣ212/255-4037, ⓦwww.villagevanguard.com. This jazz landmark still lays on a regular diet of big names. Mon–Thurs admission is $30, while Sat & Sun entry is $35; both tickets include a $10 drink credit. Cash only.

Zinc Bar 90 W Houston St, at La Guardia Place ⓣ212/477-8337, ⓦwww.zincbar.com. New talent, as well as established greats such as Max Roach and Grant Green, perform at this great jazz venue with strong drinks and loyal regulars. The Ron Affit Trio plays four sets on Mon, and throughout the week there's a mix of Brazilian and African jazz. Cover is $5 with a one- or two-drink minimum.

Larger music venues

Beacon Theater 2124 Broadway, at W 74th St ⓣ212/496-7070. A beautiful restored theater that caters to a more mature rock crowd; Scorsese's 2008 movie of a Rolling Stones concert, Shine a Light, was filmed here. Tickets $50–300, sold through Ticketmaster.

Madison Square Garden W 31st–33rd sts, between 7th and 8th aves ⓣ212/465-6741, ⓦwww.madisonsquaregarden.com. New York's principal large stage plays host to big rock acts. However, it's not the most atmospheric place to see a band, with seating for yourself and 20,000 of your closest friends. Tickets are sold through Ticketmaster.

Radio City Music Hall 1260 6th Ave, at 50th St ⓣ212/247-4777, ⓦwww.radiocity.com. Although not as prestigious a venue as it once was, the building is a star in its own right. Here, you can see everyone from rock stars to the famous high-kicking Rockettes. Tickets are sold at the box office or through Ticketmaster.

Roseland Ballroom 239 W 52nd St, between Broadway and 8th Ave ⓣ212/247-0200, ⓦwww.roselandballroom.com. This venue has retained the grand ballroom feel of its heyday and is a good place to catch big names before they hit the arena and stadium circuit. The box office only sells tickets the day of the show, otherwise tickets can be purchased through Ticketmaster.

Clubs and discos

Cielo 18 Little W 12th St, between 9th Ave and Washington St ⓣ212/645-5700, ⓦwww.cieloclub.com. Plan for a night of glam-meets-underground here, where the main attractions are the sunken dance floor and audio system, which pumps house, global, and nu jazz beats. Cover $10–20.

Pacha 618 W 46th St ⓣ212/209-7500, ⓦwww.pachanyc.com. New York outpost of the chain of Ibiza superclubs. Sprawling over 30,000 square feet, and featuring a spine-tingling, high-tech sound system, three floors, palm trees, and mosaic-mirrors, this is the place for a big, corporate club experience, and a generally non-local clientele – expect big (sweaty) crowds. Cover $30.

Sapphire Lounge 249 Eldridge St, at Houston St ⓣ212/777-5153, ⓦwww.sapphirenyc.com. DJ bar and lounge, with an arty, sexy vibe, created by the dark lights and enhanced by the moody Lower East Side regulars. Expect music of almost every genre on different nights – it's open seven days, and the cover is usually minimal ($5–12).

Sullivan Room 218 Sullivan St, at Bleecker St ⓣ212/252-2151, ⓦwww.sullivanroom.com. Basement club for serious dancing. Fri and Sat, popular with students from nearby NYU, are best for house music. The only downside: two bathrooms for the whole place. Thurs–Sat 10pm–4am. Cover $10–15.

Film

Angelika Film Center 18 W Houston St, at Mercer St ⓣ212/995-2000, ⓦwww.angelikafilmcenter.com. The latest indie offerings, as well as European art-house movies.

Anthology Film Archives 32-34 2nd Ave, at 2nd St ⓣ212/505-5181, ⓦwww.anthologyfilmarchives.org. Expect any and every kind of indie film here, from animated shorts to riveting documentaries.

Film Forum 209 W Houston St, between Varick and 6th Ave ⓣ212/727-8110, ⓦwww.filmforum.com.

Offers the best in independent film and documentary, as well as themed revivals.

Landmark Sunshine Cinema 143 E Houston St, between Forsyth and Eldridge sts ⓣ212/358-7709. This former synagogue and vaudeville theater is now one of the plushest art-house movie theaters in town, with fun midnight screenings of cult classics.

Museum of Modern Art 11 W 53rd St, between 5th and 6th aves ⓣ212/708-9400, ⓦwww.moma.org. A vast collection of well-chosen films, from Sundance selections to abstract moving images to hand-painted Super 8; entry is free with museum admission (see p.000).

Poetry slams and literary readings

Bowery Poetry Club 308 Bowery, at Bleecker St ⓣ212/614-0505, ⓦwww.bowerypoetry.com. Terrifically welcoming joint featuring the Urbana Poetry Slam every Tues night at 7pm ($7). This event is dedicated to showcasing the city's most innovative voices in poetry.

NuYorican Poet's Café 236 E 3rd St, between aves B and C ⓣ212/505-8183, ⓦwww.nuyorican.org. The godfather of all slam venues, established by New York-based Puerto Ricans in the 1970s. SlamOpen on Wed (except the first Wed of every month) is $7 and the Friday Night Slam is $10, both highly recommended.

Poetry Project At St Mark's Church, 131 E 10th St, at 2nd Ave ⓣ212/674-0910, ⓦwww.poetryproject.com. Founded in the 1960s and closely linked with the late Allen Ginsberg, entry to the twice-weekly reading series (Mon and Wed at 8pm) is $8. Closed July & Aug.

Comedy clubs

Caroline's 1626 Broadway, between W 49th and 50th streets ⓣ212/757-4100, ⓦwww.carolines.com. Some of the best acts in town (and Hollywood) appear at this glitzy spot. $15–35 cover, with a two-drink minimum; more expensive on weekends.

Comic Strip Live East 1568 2nd Ave, between E 81st and E 82nd streets ⓣ212/861-9386, ⓦwww.comicstriplive.com. This famed showcase draws stand-up comics going for the big time. Two shows Fri & Sat, one show Sun-Thurs. Cover $20–22, with two-drink minimum.

Gotham Comedy Club 208 W 23rd St, between 7th and 8th aves ⓣ212/367-9000, ⓦwww.gothamcomedyclub.com. A stylish club that has been building a reputation for cutting-edge stand-up acts since the 1990s, hosting the likes of Dave Chapelle and Lewis Black, as well as a live Comedy Central cable show. Daily, cover $15–20.

Gay New York

There are few places in America where **gay culture** thrives as it does in New York. **Chelsea** (centered on 8th Ave, between 14th and 23rd streets) and the **East Village** have replaced the **West Village** as the hubs of gay New York, although a strong presence still lingers around Christopher Street. The other haven is Brooklyn's **Park Slope,** though perhaps more for women than for men. Up-to-the-minute news can be found in *HomoXtra* (*HX*) or *Blade* (ⓦwww.nyblade.com), both free, provocative weekly listings magazines.

Resources

Bluestockings 172 Allen St, between Stanton and Rivington streets ⓣ212/777-6028, ⓦwww.bluestockings.com. Collectively run radical bookstore (with a focus on gay and feminist titles), and organic café on the Lower East Side. Daily 11am–11pm.

Gay Men's Health Crisis (GMHC) 119 W 24th St, between 6th and 7th aves ⓣ212/367-1000 or 1-800/243-7692 (hotline), ⓦwww.gmhc.org. Despite the name, this organization – the oldest and largest not-for-profit AIDS organization in the world – provides information and referrals to everyone, no matter their sex or sexual orientation.

Gayellow Pages ⓦwww.gayellowpages.com. Available for $24.95 online or from the bookstores listed above and below, this is a good all-in-one resource; New York is in the East & South edition.

The Lesbian, Gay, Bisexual & Transgender Community Center 208 W 13th St, at 7th Ave ⓣ212/620-7310, ⓦwww.gaycenter.org. The LGBT Community Center, which houses countless organizations (including ACT UP, the Center for Mental Health, and even the Metro Gay Wrestling Alliance), also sponsors workshops, dances, movie nights, guest speakers, youth services, programs for parents and kids, an archive and library, the annual Center Garden Party, and lots more.

The Oscar Wilde Memorial Bookshop 15 Christopher St, between 6th and 7th aves ⓣ 212/255-8097, ⓦ www.oscarwildebooks.com. The first gay bookstore in the US. Unbeatable. Daily 11am–7pm.

Bars and clubs

Barracuda 275 W 22nd St, between 8th and 9th aves ⓣ 212/645-8613. A favorite spot in New York's gay scene, though as un-sceney as you'll find in Chelsea. Check out the two-for-one happy hour 4–9pm during the week, crazy drag shows, and the sweet hideaway lounge out back.

Duplex 61 Christopher St, at 7th Ave ⓣ 212/255-5438, ⓦ www.theduplex.com. This Village cabaret is popular with a gay crowd but entertaining for all, and features occasional bitchy barb routines from Joan Rivers, among others. Cover varies, from free to $15.

Ginger's 363 5th Ave, between 5th and 6th sts, Park Slope, Brooklyn ⓣ 718/788-0924. A dark and moody addition to Park Slope's sapphic scene, with a great happy hour from 5 to 8pm.

Henrietta Hudson 438 Hudson St, at Morton St ⓣ 212/924-3347. This lesbian hangout serves food and gets fairly brimming at night. The lounge, pool, and dancing areas are all separate, and guys are welcome, too.

Rubyfruit Bar & Grill 531 Hudson St, between Charles and W 10th streets ⓣ 212/929-3343. A cozy, friendly place for grown-up dykes, *Rubyfruit* is all about couches, cheap drinks, and good company.

Stonewall 53 Christopher St, between Waverly Place and 7th Ave ⓣ 212/463-0950. The site of the seminal 1969 riot is mostly refurbished and flies the pride flag like they own it – which, one supposes, they do.

Shopping

When it comes to consumerism, New York leaves all other cities behind. Shopping can be extraordinarily cheap, but move further uptown and it can also be phenomenally expensive. **Midtown Manhattan** is mainstream territory, with the department stores, big-name clothes designers, and branches of the larger chains. Downtown plays host to a wide variety of more offbeat stores – **SoHo** is perhaps the most popular shopping neighborhood in these parts, and generally the most expensive. Affordable alternatives for the young and trendy are available in the **Lower East Side**, and good vintage clothing can be found there, in the East Village, and in Williamsburg, Brooklyn.

Department stores

Barney's 660 Madison Ave, at 61st St ⓣ 212/826-8900, ⓦ www.barneys.com. The hippest and most fashion-forward of the big NYC department stores. Check the website for dates of its famous semi-annual warehouse sales, where couture bargains abound.

Bergdorf Goodman 754 5th Ave, at 58th St ⓣ 212/753-7300, ⓦ www.bergdorfgoodman.com. Housed in what used to be a Vanderbilt mansion, this venerable department store caters to the city's wealthiest clientele. Even if you can't afford to shop, it's still fun to browse and dream.

Bloomingdale's 1000 3rd Ave, between 59th and 60th sts ⓣ 212/705-2000, ⓦ www.bloomingdales.com. Perhaps Manhattan's most beloved department store, Bloomingdale's is packed with designer clothes, perfume concessions, and the like.

Macy's 151 W 34th St, at Broadway ⓣ 212/695-4400, ⓦ www.macys.com. The world's largest department store embraces two buildings, two million square feet of floor space, and ten floors.

Boutique and vintage shops

Beacon's Closet 88 N 11th St, Williamsburg, Brooklyn ⓣ 718/486-0816, ⓦ www.beaconscloset.com. Vast 5500-square-foot used-clothing paradise, specializing in modern fashions and vintage attire.

Century 21 22 Cortlandt St, at 61st St ⓣ 212/227-9092, ⓦ www.c21stores.com. One of a chain of stylish discount department stores, where you can pick up designer labels at bargain prices.

Edith Machinist 104 Rivington St ⓣ 212/979-9992. Treasure trove of chic vintage women's fashion, especially shoes and leather; you'll also find designer gems here, and plenty of fur.

Opening Ceremony 35 Howard St, SoHo ⓣ 212/219-2688, ⓦ www.openingceremony.us.

▲ Saks

Cutting-edge, uber-hip, and astronomically expensive, this is the place to find the hottest global indie fashion labels – many items can only be bought here.

Bookstores

Asian American Writers' Workshop Suite 10A, 16 W 32nd St, at 5th Ave ⓣ212/494-0061, ⓦwww.aaww.org. In addition to its list of classes, speakers, and readings, the adjacent bookstore carries the nation's largest selection of literary works by Asian-American authors, both established and on-the-rise.

Drama Book Shop 250 W 40th St, between 7th and 8th aves ⓣ1-800/322-0595. The best theater and film bookstore around, with more than 50,000 titles and a very knowledgeable staff.

Housing Works Used Books Café 126 Crosby St, between Houston and Prince sts ⓣ212/334-3324. Very cheap books in a spacious and comfy environment. Proceeds benefit AIDS charities.

Partners & Crime 44 Greenwich Ave, at Charles St ⓣ212/243-0440, ⓦwww.crimepays.com. Superb, informed shop with 4000 mystery titles. Author signings, a lending library, authoritative staff recommendations, and radio play re-enactments the first Sat of every month (6pm & 8pm; $5) make it a find for devout mystery fans.

Strand Bookstore 828 Broadway, at 12th St ⓣ212/473-1452, ⓦwww.strandbooks.com. With about eight miles of books and a stock of more than 2.5 million, this is the largest book operation in the city. Recent review copies and new books show up at half price; older books are from 50¢ up.

Record stores

Breakbeat Science Halcyon at 57 Pearl St, Dumbo, Brooklyn ⓣ212/995-2592. The first drum'n'bass-only store to open in the US is still going strong as part of the Halcyon design boutique and gallery complex.

Etherea 66 Ave A, between 4th and 5th sts ⓣ212/358-1126. Specializing in indie rock and electronica, both domestic and import, CD and vinyl, this is one of the best shops in the city. Good used selection.

Generation Records 210 Thompson St, between Bleecker and W 3rd sts ⓣ212/254-1100. The focus here is on hardcore, metal, and punk, with some indie thrown in. New CDs and vinyl are upstairs, while the used records are downstairs.

Other Music 15 E 4th St, between Broadway and Lafayette ⓣ212/477-8150. This excellent small shop has perhaps the most engaging and curious indie-rock and avant-garde collection in the city. Records here are divided into categories like "In," "Out," and "Then." Definitely worth a visit. Great used selection.

Vinyl Mania 60 Carmine St, between Bedford St and 7th Ave ⓣ212/924-7223. First port of call for DJs seeking the newest, rarest releases and imports.

Food

Chelsea Market 75 9th Ave, between 15th and 16th sts. A wonderful array of food shops line this former Nabisco factory warehouse's ground floor; go for pad thai, fresh produce, lobster rolls, panini,

Sports in New York

Seeing either of New York's two **baseball** teams involves a trip to the outer boroughs. The **Yankees** play in the Bronx, at the new **Yankee Stadium**, between 161st and 164th streets and River Avenue (ⓣ718/293-6000, ⓦwww.yankees.com). Get there on the B, D, or #4 subway lines direct to the 161st Street station. The **Mets** are based in Queens, at the equally new Citi Field, 126th Street and Roosevelt Avenue, Willets Point, Queens (ⓣ718/507-8499, ⓦmets.mlb.com). Take the #7 train, direct to Willets Point. Tickets are priced between $5 and over $200, depending on the team (Yankee tickets are generally more expensive) and where you sit.

New York's football teams – the **Jets** and 2008 Super Bowl champions the **Giants** – play at the **New Jersey Meadowlands Sports Complex**, East Rutherford, New Jersey (ⓣ201/935-3900, ⓦwww.meadowlands.com). Both teams are expected to move to the New Meadowlands Stadium in 2010, presently under construction near the current complex. Buses from the Port Authority Bus Terminal, 42nd Street at Eighth Avenue (ⓣ1-800/772-2222) serve the stadium. Tickets for both teams are always officially sold out well in advance, but you can often pick up tickets (legally) from secondary-broker websites such as ⓦwww.ticketliquidator.com. Prices fluctuate according to supply and demand.

Basketball's two New York pro teams are the NBA **Knicks** (ⓦwww.nba.com/knicks) and the WNBA **Liberty** (ⓦwww.wnba.com/liberty). Both play at **Madison Square Garden**, W 33rd Street at Seventh Avenue (ⓣ212/465-6741, ⓦwww.thegarden.com), which is served by the #1, #2, #3, A, C, and E trains. Tickets for the Knicks are very expensive, and, due to impossibly high demand, available in only limited numbers, if at all. The women's games are fairly exciting and cheaper ($10–65). Another area team, the **New Jersey Nets**, plays in an arena at the Meadowlands Complex; tickets range from $10 to over $200, and are relatively easy to procure. New York's hockey team, the **Rangers** (ⓦwww.newyorkrangers.com), also plays at Madison Square Garden; tickets range from $40 to $254.

chewy breads, sinful brownies, kitchenware, or simply to browse.

Murray's Cheese Shop 254 Bleecker St, between 6th and 7th aves ☎212/243-3289 or 1-888/692-4339. The city's number-one stop for cheese lovers; go to learn about the cheese-making process, sample the wares, or pick up a pungent sandwich.

Russ & Daughters 179 E Houston St, between Allen and Orchard sts ☎212/475-4880. This small family-run shop has been serving fine Jewish edibles such as smoked whitefish, chopped liver, and herring soaked in schmaltz since 1914. A must-visit.

Union Square Greenmarket In Union Square, at 16th St. A bit of country in the city: an open-air market that offers local seasonal produce and natural goods sold by regional farmers and purveyors (Mon, Wed, Fri, & Sat 8am–6pm). You'll find hand-carded wools, wildflowers, and infused honeys, too.

Zabar's 2245 Broadway, at 80th St ☎212/787-2000. Beloved family store offers a quintessential taste of New York: bagels, lox, all manner of schmears (cream cheeses), not to mention a dizzying selection of gourmet goods at reasonable prices. Fine kitchenware is sold upstairs.

2

The Mid-Atlantic

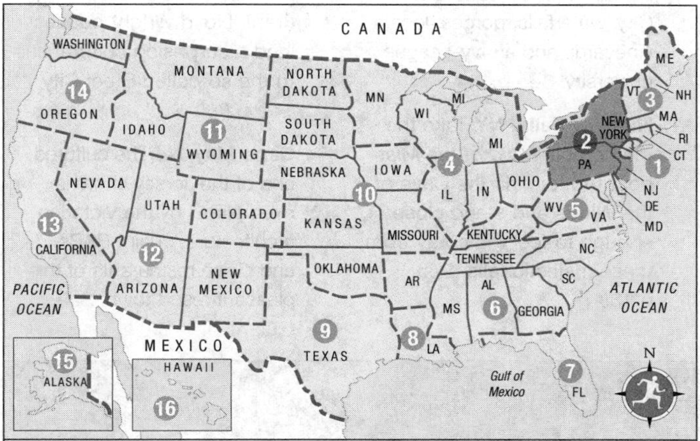

AL - ALABAMA	IN - INDIANA	MN - MINNESOTA	RI - RHODEISLAND
AR - ARKANSAS	LA - LOUISIANA	MS - MISSISSIPPI	SC - SOUTH CAROLINA
CT - CONNECTICUT	MA - MASSACHUSETTS	NC - NORTH CAROLINA	VA - VIRGINIA
DE - DELAWARE	MD - MARYLAND	NH - NEW HAMPSHIRE	VT - VERMONT
FL- FLORIDA	ME - MAINE	NJ - NEW JERSEY	WI - WISCONSIN
IL - ILLINOIS	MI - MICHIGAN	PA - PENNSYLVANIA	WV - WEST VIRGINIA

CHAPTER 2

Highlights

* **The Adirondacks, NY** A vast and rugged alpine wilderness offering superb hiking, skiing, fishing, and mountain-climbing opportunities. See p.130

* **Ithaca, NY** This lovely Finger Lakes' town has a solar-powered library, its own legal tender, more restaurants per capita than New York City, waterfalls, gorges, local vineyards and an Ivy-League university. See p.134

* **Niagara Falls, NY** Take the memorable *Maid of the Mist* boat trip, or visit the Cave of the Winds and stand close enough to feel the spray from these majestic falls. See p.139

* **History in Philadelphia, PA** See the Liberty Bell and trace the steps of Benjamin Franklin in the city of brotherly love, where the Declaration of Independence was signed. See p.000

* **Art and architecture, Pittsburgh, PA** The Warhol Museum, Cathedral of Learning, and two outlying Frank Lloyd Wright houses lend a surprising cultural flair to the so-called Steel City. See p.000

* **Cape May, NJ** The cultured end of the Jersey shore is exemplified by the Victorian architecture, quaint B&Bs, and swish restaurants of this pleasant resort town. See p.000

▲ Taughannock Falls

2

The Mid-Atlantic

The three **MID-ATLANTIC** states – New York, Pennsylvania, and New Jersey – stand at the heart of the most populated and industrialized corner of the US. Although dominated in the popular imagination by the gray smokestacks of New Jersey and steel factories of Pennsylvania,, these states actually encompass beaches, mountains, islands, lakes, forests, rolling green countryside, and many worthwhile small cities and towns.

European settlement here was characterized by considerable shifts and turns: the **Dutch**, who arrived in the 1620s, were methodically squeezed out by the **English**, who in turn fought off the **French** challenge to secure control of the region by the mid-eighteenth century. The Native American population, including the **Iroquois Confederacy** and Lenni Lenape Indians, had sided with the French against the English, and were soon confined to reservations or pushed north into Canada. At first, the economy depended on the fur trade, though by the 1730s English **Quakers**, along with **Amish** and **Mennonites** from Germany, plus a few Presbyterian **Irish**, had made farming a significant force, their holdings extending to the western limits of Pennsylvania and New York.

All three states were important during the **Revolution**: over half the battles were fought here, including major American victories at **Trenton** and **Princeton**, in New Jersey. Upstate New York was geographically crucial, as the British forces knew that American control of the Hudson River would effectively divide New England from the other colonies; and the long winter spent by the rag-tag Continental Army at **Valley Forge** outside Philadelphia turned it into a well-organized force. After the Revolution, industry became the region's prime economic force, with **mill towns** springing up along the numerous rivers. By the mid-1850s the large **coalfields** of northeast Pennsylvania were powering the smoky steel mills of Pittsburgh, and the discovery of high-grade **crude oil** in 1859 marked the beginning of the automobile age. Though still significant, especially in the regions near New York City, heavy industry has now largely been replaced by tourism as the economic engine.

Although many travelers to the East Coast do not venture much further than New York City itself, the region offers varied attractions, from the crashing Atlantic surf of **Long Island**, through the wooded **Catskill Mountains** that line the Hudson River and the imposing **Adirondack Mountains** spread over a quarter of the state, to the cultured and pastoral **Finger Lakes**. In the northwest corner of the state, beyond the more industrialized **Erie Canal cities** along I-90, awesome **Niagara Falls** and artsy post-industrial **Buffalo** hug the Canadian border. **Pennsylvania** is best known for the fertile **Pennsylvania Dutch** country and the two great cities of **Philadelphia** and **Pittsburgh**. **New Jersey**, often pictured as one big industrial carbuncle, offers shameless tourist pleasures along the shore

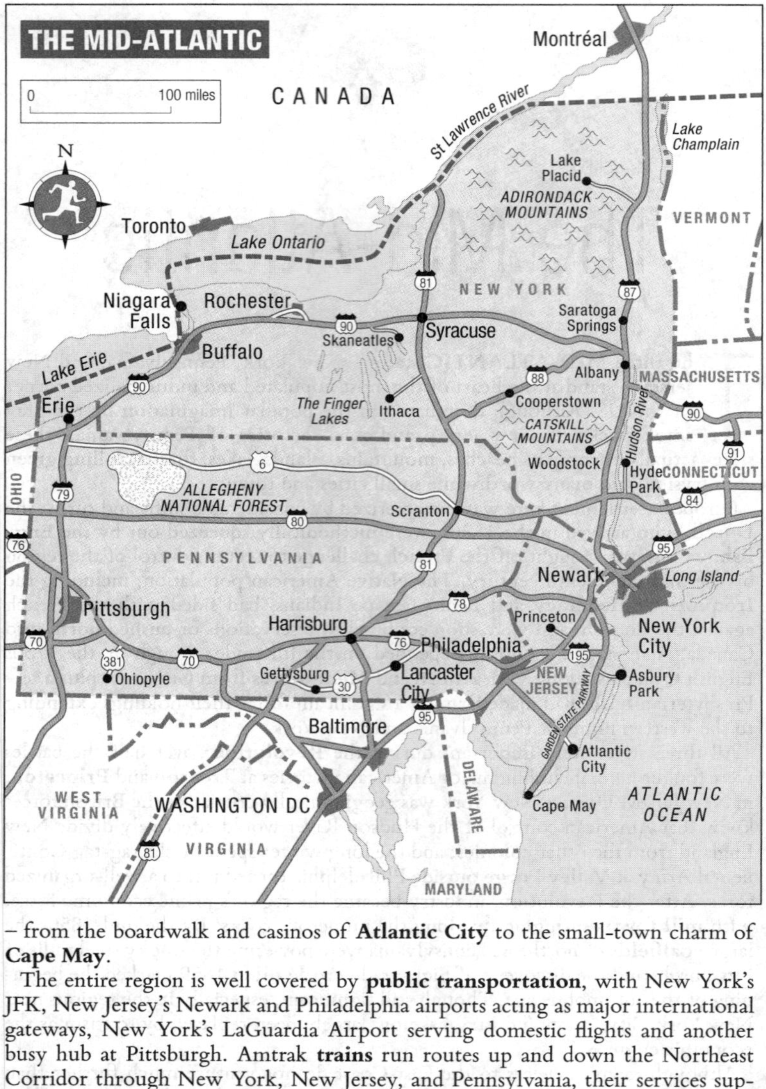

– from the boardwalk and casinos of **Atlantic City** to the small-town charm of **Cape May**.

The entire region is well covered by **public transportation**, with New York's JFK, New Jersey's Newark and Philadelphia airports acting as major international gateways, New York's LaGuardia Airport serving domestic flights and another busy hub at Pittsburgh. Amtrak **trains** run routes up and down the Northeast Corridor through New York, New Jersey, and Pennsylvania, their services supplemented by New Jersey Transit, Metro-North and the Long Island Railroad. Greyhound **buses** follow the major interstates, with a few subsidiary lines running to more out-of-the-way places.

New York State

However much exists to attract visitors, the vast state of **NEW YORK** stands inevitably in the shadow of America's most celebrated city. The words "New York" bring to mind soaring skyscrapers and congested streets, not the beaches of **Long Island** to the east or 50,000 square miles of rolling dairy farmland, colonial villages, workaday towns, lakes, waterfalls, and towering mountains that fan out north and west from New York City and constitute **upstate New York**. Just an hour's drive north of Manhattan, the valley of the **Hudson River**, with the moody **Catskill Mountains** rising stealthily from the west bank, offers a respite from the intensity of the city. Much wilder and more rugged are the peaks of the vast **Adirondack Mountains** further north, which hold some of eastern America's most enticing scenery. To the west, the slender **Finger Lakes** and endless miles of dairy farms and vineyards occupy the central portion of the state. Of the larger cities, only **Buffalo** and **Rochester** hold much of interest, but some of the smaller towns, like Ivy-League **Ithaca** and the venerable spa town of **Saratoga Springs**, can be quite captivating.

In the seventeenth and eighteenth centuries semi-feudal **Dutch landowning dynasties** such as the Van Rensselaers held sway upstate. Their control over tens of thousands of tenant farmers was barely affected by the transfer of colonial power from Holland to Britain, or even by American independence. Only with the completion of the **Erie Canal** in 1825, linking New York City with the Great Lakes, did the interior start to open up; improved opportunities for trade enabled canal-side cities like **Syracuse**, Rochester, and especially Buffalo to undergo massive expansion.

Getting around New York State

From New York City, the **Long Island Railroad** (leaving from Penn Station) and **Metro North** (leaving from Grand Central Station) shuttle commuters to and from the suburbs of Long Island and Westchester, Putnam, and Dutchess counties, respectively. For journeys further north, Amtrak operates a **train** service along the beautiful Hudson Valley to the state capital, Albany; from there, trains continue north to Montréal, via the Adirondacks, and west along the Erie Canal to Buffalo and Niagara Falls. Greyhound and Adirondack Trailways **buses** also run to all the major towns. **Car rental** in and around New York City is expensive; lower rates can be found by taking public transportation away from the metropolitan area. Be aware as well that the New York State Thruway (I-87) is a toll road, around $20 end-to-end. **Cycling** is best enjoyed as a means of exploring areas such as the Finger Lakes or Catskills.

Long Island

Just east of New York City, **Long Island** unfurls for 125 miles of lush farmland and broad sandy beaches, and is most often explored as an excursion of a few days from the metropolis. Its western end abuts the urban boroughs of Brooklyn and Queens, and for a good while continues as a suburban sprawl of strip malls and fast-food outlets; but further east, the settlements begin to thin out and the countryside can get surprisingly remote. The **north** and **south shores** differ greatly – the former more immediately beautiful, its cliffs topped with luxurious mansions and estates, while the South Shore is fringed by almost continuous sand, interspersed with vacation spots such as **Jones Beach** and **Fire Island**. At its far end, Long Island splits in two, the **North Fork** retaining a marked rural aspect while the **South Fork**, much of which is known as **the Hamptons**, sets itself apart as an enclave of New York's richest and most famous.

The quickest way to reach Long Island is via the reliable if rather worn **Long Island Railroad** from Penn Station (T 718/217-5477 in NYC, T 718/558-3022 from elsewhere, W www.mta.nyc.ny.us/lirr), which runs ten routes to over a hundred destinations on Long Island. You can also arrive via **ferry** from New England: Cross Sound Ferry makes the trip from New London, CT to Orient Point, Long Island (T 860/443-5281 in New England, T 631/323-2525 on Long Island, W www.longislandferry.com). Numerous **bus services** (operated by the usual major companies, as well as Hampton Jitney; T 1-800/936-0440, W www.hamptonjitney.com) cover most destinations. Summer **parking permits** for most of Long Island's beaches are issued only to local residents, so on the whole it works out to be less expensive to head to the beach on public transport. If you are **driving** to Long Island, you'll take the Brooklyn–Queens Expressway (the BQE) to I-495 East. Be aware that **accommodation** prices all over the island rise dramatically during the summer season, rigidly demarcated by Memorial and Labor days, so visit at other times if possible.

The South Shore and Fire Island

Long Island's **South Shore** merges gently with the wild Atlantic, with shallow, creamy sand beaches and rolling dunes – two of the most popular options are **Long Beach** and **Jones Beach**, which together run along fifty miles of seashore, getting less crowded the further east you go. **Ocean Parkway** leads along the narrow offshore strand from Jones Beach to **Captree**, from where the **Robert Moses Causeway** crosses back to **Bay Shore**, or heads south to pristine **Robert Moses State Park**, at the western tip of Fire Island. This way you can bypass the sprawling mess of **Amityville**, famous for its 1974 "horror"; the house in which a mysterious supernatural force is said to have victimized the occupants still stands as a private residence at 108 Ocean Ave.

Fire Island

A slim spit of land parallel to the South Shore, **Fire Island** is in many ways a microcosm of New York City and on the summer weekends half of Manhattan seems to be holed up in its tiny settlements, including the primarily gay enclaves of **Cherry Grove** and **The Pines** (check out the *Fire Island Q News*; W www.fireislandqnews.com for what's on), lively **Ocean Beach**, exclusive **Point O'Woods** and **Sunken Forest** (aka Sailor's Haven), which attracts a mixed crowd.

There are various **ferry crossings**, which anybody planning to stay must use, as driving between the two road access points at either end of the island is restricted to island business owners. Ferry schedules are subject to change; Fire Island Ferries (30–45min; $8 single; T 631/665-3600, W www.fireislandferries.com) run from Bay Shore, the Sayville Ferry Service (25–45min; $6.50–12 single; T 631/589-0810, W www.sayvilleferry.com) from Sayville, and the Davis Park Ferries (25–35min; $8.50 single; T 631/475-1665, W www.pagelinx.com/dpferry) from Patchogue.

All **accommodation** should be booked well in advance during summer, when rates can be six times more than the off-season ones quoted here; options include the hopping *Grove Hotel*, Bayview Walk and Holly Walk, Cherry Grove (Ⓣ631/597-6600, Ⓦwww.grovehotel.com; ❸); *Cleggs Hotel*, 478 Bayberry Walk, Ocean Beach (open May–Oct only; Ⓣ631/583-5399, Ⓦwww.cleggshotel.com; ❻), which, along with regular rooms, offers garden apartments with full kitchens and baths; and the *Fire Island Hotel & Resort*, at 25 Cayuga Walk, in nearby Ocean Bay Park (Ⓣ631/583-8000, Ⓦwww.fireislandhotel.com; ❼), which used to be a Coast Guard station. If you'd like to splash out on a **meal**, try nearby *Matthew's*, 935 Bay Walk (Ⓣ631/583-8016), for its terrific fish specials for around $30. At weekends, the *Ice Palace*, at the *Grove Hotel*, and *Flynn's*, at 1 Cayuga St in Ocean Beach (Ⓣ631/583-5000), are good for riotous boozing and dancing.

The North Shore and North Fork

Along the rugged **North Shore**, Long Island drops to the sea in a series of bluffs, coves, and wooded headlands. The expressway beyond Queens leads straight onto the ultra exclusive **Gold Coast**, where **Great Neck** was F. Scott Fitzgerald's West Egg in *The Great Gatsby*. The motley French Norman–style buildings at Falaise in **Sands Point**, a nature preserve located on the next peninsula, were once owned by the Guggenheims and now house a self-celebratory **museum** (May–Oct Thurs–Sun tours hourly noon–3pm; $6; Ⓣ516/571-7900, Ⓦwww.sandspointpreserve.org). In Old Westbury, at 71 Old Westbury Rd, **Old Westbury Gardens** is a classier attraction: a Georgian mansion with beautiful, well-tended gardens and some pleasant works of art, including a few Gainsboroughs (late April–Oct Wed–Mon 10am–5pm; $10; Ⓣ516/333-0048, Ⓦwww.oldwestburygardens.org).

Sagamore Hill, on the coast road in Oyster Bay, twelve miles north of Old Westbury, is the heavily touristed former country retreat where **Teddy Roosevelt** lived for thirty-odd years (May–Sept daily, rest of year Wed–Sun 10am–5pm; hourly tours $5; Ⓣ516/922-4788, Ⓦwww.nps.gov/sahi). Its 23 rooms are adorned with hunting trophies, while the Old Orchard Museum (same days 9am–5pm; free), set withing the same gorgeous grounds, recounts Teddy's political and personal life. Nearby **COLD SPRING HARBOR** grew up as a whaling port, and retains some of its looks. A fully equipped whaleboat and a 400-piece assembly of scrimshaw work help its **Whaling Museum** (Tues–Sun 11am–5pm; $5; Ⓣ631/367-3418, Ⓦwww.cshwhalingmuseum.org) to recapture that era.

After fifty more miles of bluffs and parks, the less touristed **North Fork** – once an independent colony – boasts typical wild Atlantic coastal scenery. In **GREENPORT**, its most picturesque town, a spacious wooden boardwalk encloses a harbor pierced by the masts of visiting yachts. At one end there's the small **East End Seaport Museum and Marine Foundation** (mid-May to June & Sep Sat & Sun 11am–5pm; July & Aug Mon & Wed–Fri 11am–5pm, Sat & Sun 9.30am–5pm; free; Ⓣ631/477-2100, Ⓦwww.eastendseaport.org). Plentiful **accommodation** includes Victorian B&Bs like the ten-room *Bartlett House Inn*, 503 Front St (Ⓣ631/477-0371, Ⓦwww.bartletthouseinn.com; ❼) and you can get a decent seafood meal at the *Chowder Pot Pub*, 102 3rd St (Ⓣ631/477-1345), opposite the ferry terminal. Regular **ferries** connect the North Fork (pedestrians $2 single, cars including driver $9 single, $13 round-trip; Ⓣ631/749-0139, Ⓦwww.northferry.com) with pleasant **Shelter Island** (Ⓦwww.shelter-island.org) and on to the South Fork (pedestrians $1 single, cars including passengers $12 single, $15 round-trip; Ⓣ631/749-1200, Ⓦwww.southferry.com).

The South Fork

The US holds few wealthier quarters than the small towns of Long Island's **South Fork**, where huge mansions lurk among the trees or stand boldly on the flats behind the dunes. Nowhere is consumption as deliberately conspicuous as in **the Hamptons**, among the oldest communities in the state, while **Sag Harbor**, on the north coast of the fork, is cuter but also expensive, while easterly **Montauk** offers the best value, though still overpriced in high summer.

The Hamptons

Long association with the smart set has left **SOUTHAMPTON** unashamedly upper class. Its streets are lined with galleries and clothing and jewelry stores, but the nearby beaches are superb. The **visitor center** at 76 Main St (Mon–Fri 10am–4pm, Sat & Sun 11am–4pm; Ⓣ631/283-0402, Ⓦwww.southamptonchamber.com) has lists of pricey **B&Bs**. You can get marvelous fresh seafood in a number of **restaurants**, notably *Barrister's*, at 36 Main St (Ⓣ631/283-6206), and the venerable brewpub-restaurant *Southampton Publick House*, at 40 Bowden Square (Ⓣ631/283-2800). **EAST HAMPTON** is the trendiest of the Hamptons, filled with the mansions of celebrities like Renée Zellweger, Jerry Seinfeld, and Steven

▲ East Hampton Beach

Spielberg – as well as obnoxiously chic shops and restaurants. Nightlife venues in the Hamptons are expensive and notoriously changeable; pick up *Dan's Hamptons* (Ⓦwww.danshamptons.com) to find out the latest on what's happening.

Sag Harbor

Historic **SAG HARBOR**, in its heyday a port second only to that of New York, was designated first Port of Entry to the New Country by George Washington; the **Old Custom House** (May–June & Sept–Oct Sat & Sun 10am–5pm; July & Aug daily 10am–5pm; $5; Ⓣ631/692-4664) dates from this era. The **Whaling Museum** on Main Street (mid-May–Oct Mon–Sat 10am–5pm, Sun 1–5pm; $5; Ⓣ631/725-0770, Ⓦwww.sagharborwhalingmuseum.org) commemorates the town's brief whaling days with guns and scrimshaw. The windmill where John Steinbeck once lived serves as a **visitor center** (May–June & Sept–Oct Fri–Sun; July–Aug daily 10am–4pm; Ⓣ631/725-0011, Ⓦwww.sagharborchamber.com). You can get a luxurious **room** at the *Baron's Cove Inn*, at 31 W Water St (Ⓣ631/725-2100, Ⓦwww.baronscove.com; ⑦), but at the well-heeled *American Hotel* on Main Street (Ⓣ631/725-3535, Ⓦwww.theamericanhotel.com; ⑧) you can also get a splendid French meal. There are several good, less expensive **restaurants** along Main Street, such as the superb sushi bar *Sen* at no. 23 (Ⓣ631/725-1774).

Montauk

Blustery, wind-battered **MONTAUK**, on the farthest tip of Long Island, isn't chic or quaint – but real people actually live here, and it provides access to the rocky wilds of **Montauk Point**, whose rare beauty figures in all the tourist brochures. A **lighthouse** – New York State's oldest, dating from 1796 – forms an almost symbolic finale to this stretch of the American coast. **Motels** in the town center, such as *Sands Motel*, as you enter on Rte-27 (Ⓣ631/668-5100, Ⓦwww.montauksands.com; ④), offer refreshingly reasonable room prices; for something fancier, try *Gurney's Inn* on Old Montauk Highway (Ⓣ631/668-2345, Ⓦwww.gurneysinn.com; ⑧). The ultimate Montauk **dining** experience is *The Lobster Roll*, halfway back towards East Hampton on Rte-27 (Ⓣ631/267-3740), which serves excellent fresh seafood. Other good options include the moderately priced *Shagwong* on Main Street (Ⓣ631/668-3050) and the delicious sushi at *West Lake Clam & Chowder House* (Ⓣ631/668-6252).

The Hudson Valley and the Catskills

You only need to travel a few miles north of Manhattan before the Hudson River Valley takes on a Rhine-like charm, with prodigious historic homes rising from its steep and thickly wooded banks. A little further on come the forests of the **Catskill Mountains**, whose brilliant fall colors rival anything to be seen in New England. Few of the cities along the Hudson, including the large but lackluster state capital of **Albany**, hold much to attract the visitor, though many of the small towns are worth checking out, such as regional historic and culinary mecca **Hyde Park**.

The east bank

Heading north of New York City on US-9, the urban sprawl suddenly gives way to rustic scenery and you soon find yourself in the pleasant environs of **Tarrytown**, **Irvington** and, a little further up, **Ossining**, each meriting a quick pit stop in their own way. It's probably not worth spending the night, however, until you reach **Hyde Park** or **Rhinebeck**.

The lower valley

A mere 25 miles north of central New York City on the Hudson's east bank, the leafy town of **TARRYTOWN** and village of **IRVINGTON** were the original settings for Washington Irving's tales of *Rip Van Winkle* and *The Legend of Sleepy Hollow*. In 1835 the author rebuilt a farm cottage on West Sunnyside Lane (off Broadway/US-9) and renamed it **Sunnyside**. Tours squeeze through its cozy rooms, and are enjoyable even if you've never read a word of Irving (April–Nov Wed–Mon, Dec Sat & Sun 10am–5pm; $10; Ⓣ914/591-8763). The charming Main Streets of Irvington and Tarrytown have a range of good **food** options, from cheap, delicious *Irvington Pizza*, 106 Main St (Ⓣ914/591-7050), to upscale Italian, Spanish, and American restaurants. Irvington's riverside **Hudson Park** makes for a scenic picnic or after-dinner stroll. About ten miles north of Tarrytown along US-9, the town of **OSSINING** holds two impressive mid-Victorian creations: one is a huge bridge carrying the **Old Croton Aqueduct**, New York City's first water supply; the other, just south of town, is **Sing Sing Prison**, which for over 150 years has been the place where New York City criminals get sent "up the river."

Hyde Park and Rhinebeck

HYDE PARK, set on a peaceful plateau on the east bank of the Hudson twenty miles north of Beacon, is worth a stop for the homes of **Franklin D.** and **Eleanor Roosevelt**. Well-signposted off US-9, the homes, a Vanderbilt mansion (see below) and a couple of minor attractions all come under the aegis of the new **Henry A. Wallace Visitor and Education Center** (April–Oct daily 8.45am–6.30pm; Nov–March 8.45am–5.30pm). The house where the "New Deal" president was born and spent much of his adult life is preserved here along with a library and a good **museum** (daily 9am–5pm; museum and guided house tour $14; Ⓣ845/486-7770, Ⓦwww.nps.gov/hofr). The museum contains extensive photos and artifacts, including the intriguing specially adapted car FDR drove after being struck down by polio in 1921, and the letter from Einstein that led to the development of the atomic bomb. FDR lies buried in the Rose Garden, beside his wife (and distant cousin) Eleanor, one of the first women to play a prominent role in politics, especially women's and workers' rights. After FDR's death in 1945, Eleanor moved to **Val-Kill** (May–Oct daily 9am–5pm; Nov–April Thurs–Mon 9am–5pm; tours $8; Ⓦwww.nps.gov/elro), the nearby cottage retreat where she carried on her work until her death in 1962. The grounds to both homes are open from dawn to dusk and there is no charge.

A three-mile-long cliff-top **path** along the Hudson from the Roosevelt complex winds up at the Beaux Arts **Vanderbilt Mansion** (daily 9am–5pm; $8; Ⓦwww.nps.gov/vama). This virtual palace is, believe it or not, the smallest of the family's residences, built for Frederick, a grandson of railroad baron Cornelius. The furnishings are quite garish, but the formal gardens are very pretty and offer a fine view of the Hudson River. The grounds are open year-round from 7am to dusk, at no charge. Apart from these historic homes, Hyde Park has one other huge tourist draw: the excellent restaurants and fascinating campus of the **Culinary Institute of America**, the most prestigious cooking school in the country, which stands along US-9, south of Hyde Park at 1946 Campus Drive. The outstanding restaurants here (lunch and dinner Mon–Sat; Ⓣ845/471-6608 or Ⓦwww.ciachef.edu for reservations) have trained some of America's best chefs; classes and **tours** (Mon 10am & 4pm, Wed & Thurs 4pm; $5) can also be booked. Bargain **accommodation** in Hyde Park is available at the *Golden Manor Motel* (Ⓣ845/229-2157, Ⓦwww.goldenmanorhydepark.com; ❸), located on US-9 almost opposite the Roosevelt complex.

Six miles north of Hyde Park, **RHINEBECK** is the location of **America's oldest hotel** in continuous operation. The lovely, white colonial *Beekman*

Arms on Rte-9 has been hosting and feeding travelers in its warm, wood-paneled rooms since 1766 (Ⓣ845/876-7077, Ⓦwww.beekmandelamaterinn.com; ⑥). Among a number of good places to **eat** are the *Calico Restaurant & Patisserie*, 6384 Mill St (Ⓣ845/876-2749; closed Mon & Tues), which has a menu featuring Italian and French influences, and the all-American *Foster's Coachhouse Tavern*, 6411 Montgomery St (Ⓣ845/876-8052). Rhinebeck is also home to the New Agey **Omega Institute for Holistic Studies**, which runs a spa and offers a wide range of health and wellness workshops at a large campus east of town on Lake Drive (Ⓣ1-800/944-1001, Ⓦwww.eomega.org).

The west bank and Catskill Mountains

Rising above the west bank of the Hudson River, the magnificent crests of the **Catskills**, cloaked with maple and beech that turn orange, ochre, and gold each fall, have a rich and absorbing beauty. This dislocated branch of the Appalachians is inspiring country, filled with amenities – campgrounds, hiking, fishing, and, especially, skiing.

Woodstock

Around fifty miles further north, Hwy-28 meanders into the Catskills, looping past the lovely Ashokan Reservoir where Hwy-375 branches off to **WOODSTOCK**. The village, carved out of the lush deciduous woodlands and cut by fast-rushing creeks, was not actually the venue of the famed **psychedelic picnic** of August 1969. That was some sixty miles southwest in Bethel, where a monument at Herd and West Shore roads marks the site on the farm owned by Max Yasgur where the first festival was held. However, Woodstock has enjoyed a bohemian reputation since the foundation in 1903 of the **Byrdcliffe Arts Colony** (which runs summer residency courses; Ⓣ845/679-2079, Ⓦwww.woodstockguild.org), and during the 1960s it was a favorite stomping ground for the likes of Dylan, Hendrix, and Van Morrison. The town still trades on its **hippie** past: shops sell crystals and tie-dyed T-shirts, and there's even the odd commune out in the woods. Woodstock's galleries and craft shops command a regional reputation and the village is also a hub for the performing arts: the **Maverick Concert** series (late June to Aug; $20 per concert/$5 students; Ⓣ845/679-8217, Ⓦwww.maverickconcerts.org) has played host to some of the world's finest chamber musicians since 1906.

Woodstock is a great base for exploring the Catskills, and the best option for **accommodation** is the cozy *Twin Gables Guest House*, 73 Tinker St (Ⓣ845/679-9479, Ⓦwww.twingableswoodstockny.com; ④). If this is full, try the equally central *Getaway-on-the-Falls* at 5 Waterfall Way (Ⓣ845/679-2568, Ⓦwww.tinkervillagewoodstock.com; ⑥). Between Woodstock and Saugerties, which offers a string of chain motels ten miles northeast, are *Bed by the Stream* (Ⓣ845/246-2979, Ⓦwww.bedbythestream.com; ⑥), a lovely rustic B&B, and *Rip Van Winkle* **campgrounds** (May–Oct; $30 per tentsite; Ⓣ845/246-8334), both signposted off Rte-212. Apart from the town's favorite café, *Joshua's*, at 51 Tinker St (Ⓣ845/679-5533), the best **places to eat** are a little way out of the village: the menu at the *New World Home Cooking Company*, towards Saugerties at 1411 Rte-212 (April–Oct; Ⓣ845/246-0900), has Caribbean and Creole-influenced dishes for under $20, while two miles west on Rte-212 in tiny **Bearsville**, the lively *Bear Café* (Ⓣ845/679-5555) serves excellent French bistro cuisine. Several daily **buses** take two and a half hours to reach Woodstock from New York City's Port Authority Bus Terminal (Adirondack Trailways; Ⓣ1-800/858-8555, Ⓦwww.trailwaysny.com). For more **information**, visit the Chamber of Commerce booth on Rock City Road, just off the village green (Ⓣ845/679-6234, Ⓦwww.woodstockchamber.com).

On through Catskill Park

Seven miles west of Woodstock, in the hamlet of **MOUNT TREMPER**, the **Emerson Place Kaleidoscope** (Sun–Thurs 10am–5pm, Fri & Sat 10am–7pm; $8) claims to be the world's largest, created by a local hippie artist in a 60ft-high converted grain silo. It plays ten-minute sound and light shows on request throughout the day and is part of the constantly expanding upscale *Emerson Place Resort & Spa*, 146 Mt Pleasant Rd (Ⓣ845/688-2828 or 1-877/688-2828, Ⓦwww.emersonplace.com; ❼), which offers spacious suites and soothing holistic treatments. As you continue along Hwy-28, the picturesque village of **PHOENICIA**, in a hollow to the right of the road, is an ideal resting place and a great base for hiking trails in the area. You can catch the circular **Catskill Mountain Railroad** (late May to late Oct Sat, Sun & holidays 11.15am, 1.15pm & 3.15pm; $14 round-trip; Ⓣ845/688-7400, Ⓦwww.catskillmtrailroad.com) through scenic Esopus Creek. The *Phoenicia Belle*, 73 Main St (Ⓣ845/688-7226, Ⓦwww.phoeniciabelle.com; ❺), is a very decent value lodge with optional breakfast. A few doors along is the ever-popular café *Sweet Sue's* (Ⓣ845/688-7852), while the *Phoenicia Diner* is another good option back on Hwy-28 (Ⓣ845/688-9957).

A few miles further west, Hwy-49A affords a good vista of the rambling Catskills from the parking lot of the Belleayre ski resort. The return route to I-90, along Hwy-23A, includes a breathtaking view of the dramatic **gorge** between the villages of Hunter and Catskill, along with the area's premier **ski runs** on Hunter Mountain (Ⓣ518/263-4223, Ⓦwww.huntermtn.com). The resort's Skyride chair lifts also operate after the snow has melted (late June to Oct Sat & Sun 10am–5pm; $8). Accommodation rates rise significantly during the ski season: *Scribner Hollow Lodge*, half a mile from the mountain on Hwy-23A (Ⓣ518/263-4211, Ⓦwww.scribnerhollow.com; ❽), boasts 37 deluxe rooms, a fine-dining restaurant with great views, and a multi-pool swimming grotto. Rooms in the hamlet of Catskill, such as in the *Red Ranch Motel* at 4555 Rte-32 (April–Dec; Ⓣ518/678-3380 or 1-800/962-4560, Ⓦwww.redranchmotel.com; ❸), are much more basic, but more affordable.

Albany

Founded by Dutch fur-trappers in the early seventeenth century, **ALBANY** made its money by controlling trade along the Erie Canal, and its reputation by being capital of the state. It's not an unpleasant town, just rather boring, though there are a few livelier areas on the fringes. A good place to start a tour is the **Quackenbush House**, the city's oldest building, built along the river in 1736 and now serving as part of the **Albany Urban Culture Park**. The modern **visitor center**, next door at Broadway and Clinton (Mon–Fri 9am–4pm, Sat & Sun 10am–4pm; Ⓣ518/434-0405, Ⓦwww.albany.org), has free maps and can provide details of **tours** of the imposing Neoclassical **Capitol** and the downtown area, where a number of Revolutionary-era homes survive.

Uphill from the waterfront, the ugly complex of Nelson A. Rockefeller's **Empire State Plaza** has one redeeming feature: the view from **Corning Tower**'s 42nd-floor observation deck (daily 10am–2.30pm; free) looks out far across the state, beyond the twisting Hudson River to the Adirondack foothills, the Catskills, and the Berkshires in Massachusetts. It also peers down on the neighboring Performing Arts Center, known locally as **"The Egg"** (Ⓣ518/478-1845, Ⓦwww

.theegg.org) – which adds the only curves to the Plaza's harsh angularity. The **New York State Museum** (daily 9.30am–5pm; ⓣ518/474-5877, ⓦwww.nysm.nysed.gov; $2 suggested donation), one level down at the south end of the plaza, reveals everything you could want to know about New York State in imaginative, if static, tableaux. The excellent section on New York City history is better than anything like it in Manhattan itself, with absorbing exhibits and the original set of *Sesame Street*.

The most engaging part of Albany is the few blocks west of the plaza, a neighborhood full of the same sort of nineteenth-century brick-built homes Rockefeller had pulled down to build his Empire State Plaza. The **Albany Institute of History and Art**, 125 Washington Ave (Wed–Sat 10am–5pm, Sun noon–5pm; $10; ⓣ518/463-4478, ⓦwww.albanyinstitute.org), has a good range of Hudson River School paintings.

Practicalities

Arrive by Greyhound or Adirondack Trailways (ⓣ1-800/858-8555, ⓦwww.trailwaysny.com) and it's a short, hilly walk to the heart of downtown; come in via Amtrak and you face a two-mile bus ride. If you intend to **stay** the night, it's mainly a choice between suburban chain motels at $60 a night and downtown standards like the *Ramada Inn*, 300 Broadway (ⓣ518/434-4111, ⓦwww.ramada.com; ❺). For more atmosphere, try the *Mansion Hill Inn*, 115 Philip St (ⓣ518/465-2038 or 1-888/299-0455, ⓦwww.mansionhill.com; ❻), a lovely B&B in a restored home just down the hill from the state governor's mansion; it also has a fine restaurant. Other good **places to eat** are located on or near **Lark Street**, a few blocks west of the plaza; which is also the hub of the local gay scene. *Justin's*, at no. 301 (ⓣ518/436-7008), and *Café Hollywood*, at no. 275 (ⓣ518/472-9043), serve good, progressive American food at moderate prices, while the welcoming *Mamoun's*, 206 Washington Ave (ⓣ518/434-3901), has great inexpensive lamb, chicken, and vegetarian dishes. Two of the most popular **nightlife** haunts are *Jillian's*, 59 N Pearl St (ⓣ518/432-1997), which has live music and DJs, and the *Lark Tavern*, 453 Madison Ave (ⓣ518/463-7875), an Irish bar. Or head across the river to the college town of **Troy**.

North through the Adirondacks

Mountaineers, skiers, and dedicated hikers form the majority of visitors to the vast northern region between Albany and the Canadian border. Outdoor pursuits are certainly the main attractions in the rugged wilderness of the **Adirondack Mountains**, though a few small resorts, especially the former Winter Olympic venue of **Lake Placid**, offer creature comforts in addition to breathtaking scenery; and the elegant spa town of **Saratoga Springs** nestles invitingly in the delicate countryside of the southern foothills.

Saratoga Springs

Saratoga was fast, man, it was real fast. It was up all night long.

Hattie Gray, founder of *Hattie's*

For well over a century, **SARATOGA SPRINGS**, just 42 miles north of Albany on I-87, was very much the place to be seen for the Northeast's richest and most glittering names. At first, the town's curative waters were the main attraction; then John Morrisey, an Irish boxer, transformed things by opening a **racetrack** and

casino here during the 1860s. During the August horse-racing season, Saratoga Springs retains the feel of an exclusive vintage resort – but for the rest of the summer it is accessible, affordable, and fun.

Broadway, the main axis, and the few blocks just east of it are where you'll find most of the action. The carefully cultivated **Congress Park**, off South Broadway, remains a shady retreat from town-center traffic. Three of the original mineral springs still flow up to the surface here, funneled out into drinking fountains. Also here is the original **casino**, which when built formed part of a whole city block. The **racetrack** (late July to early Sept, post time 1pm; $3–5; ⓣ518/584-6200, ⓦwww. nyra.com/index_saratoga.html) still functions in a rather grand, old-fashioned manner, though there is no longer such a strict dress code. There's no such pretension at the **harness track**, aka the Equine Sports Center, on nearby Crescent Avenue (evening races several times a week May–Nov; $2; ⓣ518/584-2110). If you can't get to either, visit the array of paintings, trophies, and audiovisual displays at the **National Museum of Racing and Hall of Fame**, on Union Avenue at Ludlow Street (Mon–Sat 10am–4pm, Sun noon–4pm, during race meet open daily 9am–5pm; $7; ⓣ518/584-0400, ⓦwww.racingmuseum.org).

On the southern edge of town, green **Saratoga Spa State Park** (daily 8am–dusk; $6 per car; ⓣ518/584-2535) presents opportunities to swim in great old Victorian pools, picnic, hike, or even "take the waters," ie, take a hot bath in the tingly, naturally carbonated stuff and receive a variety of spa treatments. The nearby **Saratoga Performing Arts Center** (June to early Sept; ⓣ518/587-3330, ⓦwww.spac.org) – or SPAC – is home to the New York City Ballet in July, the Philadelphia Orchestra in August, and hosts other quality festivals.

Practicalities

Central Saratoga Springs is easily explored on foot. **Accommodation** is only a problem during August's race season, or if there's a big gig on at SPAC, when prices can more than double. One good central motel is the *Turf and Spa*, 140 Broadway (April–Oct; ⓣ518/584-2550 or 1-800/972-1229, ⓦwww.saratogaturfandspa.com; ❷). Both the lavishly restored landmark *Adelphi Hotel*, 365 Broadway (May–Oct; ⓣ518/587-4688, ⓦwww.adelphihotel.com; ❺), and the grand *Gideon Putnam Hotel*, located right in Saratoga Spa State Park (ⓣ518/584-3000, ⓦwww.gideonputnam.com; ❽), have more character. The **Chamber of Commerce**, 28 Clinton St (ⓣ518/584-3255, ⓦwww.saratoga.org), has full lists of accommodations.

Eating is also easy. One longtime favorite is the soul food at *Hattie's*, 45 Phila St (ⓣ518/584-4790), where huge entrees cost around $15; another good bet is *Wheat Fields*, 440 Broadway (ⓣ518/587-0534), with good salads and pasta served on an outdoor patio. *Beverly's*, 47 Phila St (ⓣ518/583-2755), serves great but pricey breakfasts. There's usually good Irish **music** at the *Parting Glass Pub*, 40 Lake Ave (ⓣ518/583-1916). *9 Maple Avenue*, logically enough at 9 Maple Ave (ⓣ518/583-2582), offers live jazz and blues until the early hours, while folksy non-profit *Caffé Lena*, 47 Phila St (Thurs–Sun; ⓣ518/583-0022, ⓦwww.caffelena.org) is where Don McLean first inflicted "American Pie" on the world.

The Adirondacks

The **Adirondacks**, which cover an area larger than Connecticut and Rhode Island combined, are said by locals to be named after an Iroquois insult for enemies they'd driven into the forests and left to become "bark eaters." Until recent decades the area was almost the exclusive preserve of loggers, fur trappers, and a few select New York millionaires. For sheer grandeur, the region is hard to beat: 46 peaks

▲ Black Brook, the Adirondacks

reach to over 4000ft; in summer the purple-green mountains span far into the distance in shaggy tiers, in fall the trees form a russet-red kaleidoscope.

Though Adirondack Trailways buses serve the area, you'll find it hard-going without a **car**. General **information** and some special deals can be had from the Adirondack Region tourist office (Ⓣ1-800/487-6867, Ⓦwww.visitadirondacks.com). The Adirondack Mountain Club (Ⓣ518/668-4447, Ⓦwww.adk.org) and the Adirondack Park Visitor Interpretive Centers (daily 9am–5pm; Ⓣ518/327-3000, Ⓦwww.adkvic.org), can provide details on **hiking** and **camping**.

Blue Mountain Lake

It is better to press on past over-commercialized Lake George and the eastern fringes of the Adirondacks and drive the extra hour northwest along Hwy-28 to where the headwaters of the Hudson River announce the tiny resort of **BLUE MOUNTAIN LAKE**. A handful of **motels** and lakeside **cabins** provide accommodation, and you can swim at the pretty little **beach** that fronts the village center. Just north of Blue Mountain Lake on Hwy-30, the otherwise rather bland twenty-building **Adirondack Museum** (late May to mid-Oct daily 10am–5pm; $16; Ⓦwww.adkmuseum.org) is perhaps most memorable for its grand views out over the lake and surrounding mountains.

Lake Placid

The winter sports center of **LAKE PLACID**, twice the proud host of the Winter Olympics, lies thirty miles west of I-87 on Hwy-73. In winter there's thrilling alpine skiing at imposing Whiteface Mountain and all manner of Nordic disciplines at Mount Van Hoevenberg; in summer you can watch luge athletes practice on refrigerated runs, freestyle skiers somersaulting off dry slopes into swimming pools, and top amateur ice hockey games. The mountain slopes also provide challenging terrain for hikers and cyclists; good **mountain bikes**, maps of local trails, and **guided tours** are available from High Peaks Cyclery, 2733 Main St (ⓣ518/523-3764). The **Olympic Summer Passport** (June–Oct; $25; ⓣ518/523-1655, ⓦwww.orda.org) allows you on the chair lift to the top of the 393ft ski jump and eight miles up the sheer Whiteface Mountain toll road and back again, on the Whiteface gondola, and into the Olympic museum (see below). A similar winter passport is also available. At the **Olympic Sports Complex** on Mount Van Hoevenburg (ⓣ518/523-4436), you can do a blood-curdling bobsled run ($65) or bike the extensive trail network ($25 bike rental; $6 trail fee).

The town itself is set on two lakes: **Mirror Lake**, which you can sail on in summer and skate on in winter, and larger **Lake Placid**, just to the west, on which you can take a narrated **cruise** in summer ($11; ⓣ518/523-9704). Other attractions include the **Olympic Center** on Main Street, which houses four ice rinks and the informative **1932 and 1980 Lake Placid Winter Olympic Museum** (self-guided audio tour $5; ⓣ518/523-1655). Outside the village on Hwy-73, the **John Brown Farm State Historic Site** was where the famous abolitionist brought his family in 1849 to aid a small colony of black farmers and where he conceived his ill-fated raid on Harper's Ferry in an attempt to end slavery. The house is less interesting than his story (see p.132; late May to late Oct Wed–Sun 10am–5pm; $2; ⓣ518/523-3900); the grounds, which include Brown's grave, are open year-round.

Practicalities

Lake Placid's **information center** is located on 49 Pakside Drive, by the public beach (ⓣ518/523-2445 or 1-800/447-5224, ⓦwww.lakeplacid.com), and offers 15 minutes of free online access. **Accommodation** in town ranges from the somewhat economical to the opulent. The casually elegant *Mirror Lake Inn Resort & Spa*, 77 Mirror Lake Drive (ⓣ518/523-2544, ⓦwww.mirrorlakeinn.com; ❾), has over 120 rooms, the best of them palatial, and an array of facilities, while the nearby *Interlaken Inn*, 39 Interlaken Ave (ⓣ518/523-3180, ⓦwww.theinterlakeninn.com; ❼), is a slightly cheaper but equally upscale B&B, with an excellent restaurant. *Edelweiss Motel*, on the east side of town at 2806 Wilmington Rd, has clean if somewhat dated rooms (ⓣ518/523-3821; ❹). The *Keene Valley Hostel*, in nearby Keene Valley (ⓣ518/576-2030; dorm beds $20; ❷), is a great base to be within walking distance of all the best hiking trails.

It's possible to **eat** well, with a view, for relatively little here. *Blues Berry Bakery*, 2436 Main St (ⓣ518/523-4539), is much-loved for its apple strudel, while *Nicola's* (ⓣ518/523-4430), nearby at no. 2617, does Greek and Italian dinners, including good wood-fired pizza. On the east side of town, the *Station Street Bar & Grille*, 1 Station St (ⓣ518/523-9963), is undoubtedly the friendliest place for a night out with the locals and serves delicious ribs and other dishes, occasionally accompanied by acoustic strumming. Main Street's buzzing *Zig Zags Pub* (ⓣ518/523-8221) is the main place for **live music** on the weekends.

Saranac Lake

SARANAC LAKE, ten miles northwest of Lake Placid, is a smaller, more laid-back and cheaper base for the region. The tranquil lakeshore is lined with lovely gingerbread cottages, most of them built during the late 1800s, when this was a popular middle-class retreat and spa. **Robert Louis Stevenson** spent the winter of 1888 in a small cottage on the east side of town at 44 Stevenson Lane; it's now preserved as a **museum** (July–Sept Tues–Sun 9.30am–noon & 1–4.30pm; rest of year by appointment; $5; ⓣ518/891-1462). Set in quiet rustic grounds at 371 Park Ave, the *Saranac Club & Inn* (ⓣ518/891-7212 or 1-866/595-9800, ⓦwww.saranacclubandinn.com; ⑤) is a spacious B&B which offers far better value than its Lake Placid equivalents. Downtown the *Hotel Saranac*, 100 Main St (ⓣ518/891-2200 or 1-800/937-0211, ⓦwww.hotelsaranac.com; ③), also has a friendly **bar**. *Eat-n-Meet*, 139 Broadway (ⓣ518/891-3149) is a quirky and laid-back little **restaurant**, serving inexpensive home-cooking at very fair prices.

The Thousand Islands

Beyond the Adirondacks, on the broad St Lawrence River (which forms the border with Canada), there are 1800 barely populated hunks of earth known as the **Thousand Islands**, which supposedly gave their name to the salad dressing after a c.1900 visitor, George Boldt, president of New York's *Waldorf-Astoria* hotel, asked the steward on his yacht to concoct something different for a special luncheon. For **information** about the area, contact the Thousand Islands International Tourism Council (ⓣ1-800/847-5263, ⓦwww.visit1000islands.com). From both Alexandria Bay and the smaller fishing port of Clayton, **boat excursions** set out to explore the waterway; the tiny craft are all but swamped by the huge passing cargo ships, larger than many of the islands. For departure times, contact Uncle Sam Boat Tours (May–Oct daily; $10–40; ⓣ315/482-2611 or 1-800/253-9229, ⓦwww.usboattours.com).

The Finger Lakes

At the heart of the state, southwest of Syracuse on the far side of the Catskills from New York City, are the eleven **Finger Lakes**, narrow channels gouged out by glaciers that have left tell-tale signs in the form of drumlins, steep gorges, and a number of waterfalls. With the exception of progressive, well-to-do **Ithaca** and tiny **Skaneateles**, few towns compete with the lakeshore scenery. That said, the area as a whole is a relaxing place to spend some time, particularly if you enjoy sampling **wine**: the Finger Lakes region – and much of upstate New York – produces a number of good vintages.

Skaneateles and Seneca Falls

SKANEATELES (pronounced "Skinny-Atlas"), crouching at the neck of Skaneateles Lake, is perhaps the prettiest Finger Lakes town. It's also the best place to go swimming in the region: just a block from the town center, and lined by huge resort homes, the appealing bay sports a **beach** (summer daily; $3) and the Skaneateles Marina, where you can rent watersports equipment (ⓣ315/685-5095) and take boat trips, from Mid-Lakes Navigation ($11 for 1hr; ⓣ315/685-8500, ⓦwww.midlakesnav.com). **Accommodation** options include the *Colonial Motel*, one mile west on Hwy-20 (ⓣ315/685-5751, ⓦwww.colonialmotelonline.com; ③), and, overlooking the lake, the elegant *1899 Lady of the Lake* B&B, 2 W Lake St (ⓣ1-888/685-7997, ⓦwww.ladyofthelake.net; ⑦), and the *Sherwood Inn*, 26 W Genesee St (ⓣ315/685-3405, ⓦwww.thesherwoodinn.com; ⑤), featuring a good dining room and tavern. Cheaper but still scrumptious **meals** can be had at the ever-popular *Doug's Fish Fry*, 8 Jordan St (ⓣ315/685-3288), while the spot for a classy blowout is *Krebs 1899*, 53 W Genesee St (ⓣ315/685-5714), which does an excellent American home-cooking buffet for under $50 per person and has a bar with snacks upstairs.

At **SENECA FALLS**, just west of the northern tip of Cayuga Lake, Elizabeth Cady Stanton and a few colleagues held the first Women's Rights Convention in

1848 – well before female suffrage in 1920. On the site of the **Wesleyan Chapel**, 136 Fall St, where the first campaign meeting was held, is the terrific **Women's Rights National Historical Park** (daily 9am–5pm; ⓣ315/568-2991, ⓦwww.nps.gov/wori), which sets the early and contemporary women's movements in their historical contexts, with a strong emphasis on the connection with the African-American civil rights movements. A block east, at 76 Fall St, the **National Women's Hall of Fame** (May–Sept Mon–Sat 10am–5pm, Sun noon–5pm; Oct–April Wed–Sat 11am–5pm; $3; ⓣ315/568-8060, ⓦwww.greatwomen.org), honors about two hundred women, including Emily Dickinson and Sojourner Truth, for their efforts in various fields. If you want to stop over, the best **place to stay** is the *Hubbell House* B&B, at 42 Cayuga St (ⓣ315/568-9690, ⓦwww.hubbellhousebb.com; ❻). There are several places to eat, such as *Jeremy's Café*, 77 Fall Street (ⓣ315/568-1614). Hwy-89, between Seneca Falls and Ithaca, has been dubbed the **Cayuga Wine Trail**, with dozens of small wineries operating along the west shore of the largest of the Finger Lakes, such as Sheldrake Point and Thirsty Owl; both offer tastings for $1.

Ithaca

Cayuga Lake comes to a halt at its southern end at picturesque **ITHACA**, piled like a diminutive San Francisco above the lakeshore and culminating in the towers, sweeping lawns, and shaded parks of Ivy-League **Cornell University**. On campus, which is cut by striking gorges, creeks, and lakes, the sleek, I.M. Pei–designed **Herbert F. Johnson Museum of Art** (Tues–Sun 10am–5pm; free; ⓣ607/255-6464, ⓦwww.museum.cornell.edu), across the street from the gorge-straddling **suspension bridge**, merits a visit more for its fifth-floor view of the town and lake than for the moderate collection of Asian and contemporary art. Adjacent to campus lie the **Cornell Plantations** (daily: dawn to dusk; free; ⓣ607/255-2400, ⓦwww.plantations.cornell.edu), the extensive botanical gardens and arboretum run by the university.

The pick of the countless **waterfalls** within a few miles of town are the slender **Taughannock Falls**, ten miles north of town just off Hwy-89 and with swimming beach; they are taller than Niagara at a height of 215ft. **Buttermilk Falls State Park**, two miles south of town on Rte-13, is a delightful spot, and the dangerous-looking Lucifer Falls, at lush **Robert H. Treman State Park**, three miles further south, should not be missed. Parking is $7 for the day, which covers all three parks. Cayuga Lake provides excellent **boating** and **windsurfing** opportunities; boards and boats can be rented from several places, including Cayuga Boat Rentals (ⓣ607/277-5072), in Cass Park, off Hwy-89.

Practicalities

Greyhound and other **buses** operate out of the terminal at W State and N Fulton. Free **internet** access is available at the huge, partially solar-powered library on Cayuga Avenue next to the Ithaca Commons. The helpful **visitor center** is at 904 East Shore Drive, off Hwy-34 N (Mon–Fri 9am–5pm, Sat 10am–5pm, Sun 10am–4pm, longer in summer; ⓣ607/272-1313 or 1-800/284-8422, ⓦwww.visitithaca.com). **Accommodation** is, on the whole, reasonably priced. Try the *Cottage Garden Inn*, a cosy B&B at 107 Crescent Place (ⓣ607/277-7561, ⓦwww.cottagegardeninn.com; ❹), or the *Statler Hotel*, on East Avenue within the campus proper (ⓣ1-800/541-2501, ⓦwww.statlerhotel.cornell.edu; ❼), which makes a pleasant option, particularly out of term. Ithaca boasts two **dining** and **entertainment** zones. **Downtown**, centered on the vehicle-free Commons, is the larger and better of the two. Here DeWitt Mall, on the corner of Cayuga and Seneca streets, features the top-rated vegetarian restaurant of cookbook fame, *Moosewood* (Ⓣ607/273-9610), as well as the *Café DeWitt* (Ⓣ607/273-3473), which offers healthy and filling salads at lunchtime. A block away, *Just a Taste*, 116 N Aurora St (Ⓣ607/277-9463), is a lively wine and tapas bar. Numerous cheap student-oriented places to eat line the streets of **Collegetown**; check out *The Nines*, 311 College Ave (Ⓣ607/272-1888), which serves up the best deep-dish pizza around and has live music. *Common Ground* (Ⓣ607/273-1505) is a gay-friendly **bar** down Route 96B with ping-pong, billiards, and a gorgeous patio. The Kitchen Theatre produces new and avant-garde **plays** in its intimate auditorium (Ⓣ607/272-0403, Ⓦwww.kitchentheatre.com); for news of the lively **music** scene, pick up the free *Ithaca Times* (Ⓦwww.ithacatimes.com).

Toward Niagara Falls: the Erie Canal towns

The fertile farming country stretching from Albany at the head of the Hudson to the growing tourist destination of **Buffalo** on Lake Erie, along the route of the **Erie Canal**, comprises the agricultural heartland of New York State. The eastern parts – also known as **Central Leatherstocking**, after the protective leggings worn by the area's first settlers – are well off the conventional tourist trails, with exception of the lovely village of **Cooperstown**. In their haste to reach **Niagara Falls**, one of the continent's biggest crowd-pullers, many travellers also bypass the northwestern reaches of the state, although the industrial towns of **Syracuse** and **Rochester** possess some worthy attractions and a few exploratory detours will pay dividends in the shape of the quaint canal-side villages scattered between the two and some deserted lakeside beaches up on the lake.

Cooperstown

Seventy miles west of Albany, sitting gracefully on the wooded banks of tranquil Otsego Lake, is pleasant **COOPERSTOWN**, christened "Glimmerglass" by novelist James Fenimore Cooper, son of the town's founder. The birth of baseball, said to have originated here on Doubleday Field, is commemorated by the inspired and spacious **National Baseball Hall of Fame**, on Main Street (daily 9am–5pm, summer until 9pm; $16.50; Ⓣ607/547-7200, Ⓦwww.baseballhalloffame.org), enjoyable even for the uninitiated. The delightful **Fenimore Art Museum**, just north of town on Lake Road/Rte-80 (April to mid-May & mid-Oct to Dec Tues–Sun 10am–4pm; mid-May to mid-Oct daily 10am–5pm; $11; Ⓣ1-888/547-1450, Ⓦwww.fenimoreartmuseum.org), has innovative special exhibits and a fine collection of folk and North American Indian art. In summer, Cooperstown hosts **classical concerts** and the **Glimmerglass Opera** at Alice Busch Opera Theater, north on Hwy-80 by the lake (Ⓣ607/547-5704, Ⓦwww.glimmerglass.org).

If you drive here in summer, park in one of the free lots on the edge of town and take the **trolley** around the various sights (8am–9pm; $3 all-day pass). The local chamber of commerce runs a helpful **visitor center** at 31 Chestnut St (summer daily 9am–6pm, winter Mon–Sat 9am–5pm; Ⓣ607/547-9983, Ⓦwww.cooperstownchamber.org); their website is an excellent way to arrange **accommodation**. Rooms in the town itself are expensive during summer at classy establishments such as *The Inn At Cooperstown*, 16 Chestnut St (Ⓣ607/547-5756, Ⓦwww.innatcooperstown.com; ❺), but there's a cluster of clean motels right on pretty Otsego Lake, a few miles north on Rte-80; the *Lake 'N Pines* (Ⓣ607/547-

2790 or 1-800/615-5253, ⓦwww.lakenpinesmotel.com; ❸; closed Dec–March) offers superb value. Further north on Rte-80, the *Blue Mingo Grill* (ⓣ607/547-7496), where fusion and New American dishes change nightly, is one of the area's best and most creative **restaurants**. For a quick bite in town away from the crowds, try the *Cooperstown Diner*, 136 1/2 Main St (ⓣ607/547-9201), open until 2pm for breakfast and burgers.

Syracuse

A lively but largely unattractive modern city, busy **SYRACUSE** made its name first for the production of salt and, more importantly, for its central position on the Erie Canal. There's little to see, though the presence of Syracuse University gives downtown an active and youthful feel. The redevelopment of **Armory Square**, around Franklin and Fayette streets, as an area of specialty shops, galleries, and cafés has also added some character to the city center. The **Erie Canal Museum** (Tues–Sat 10am–5pm, Sun 10am–3pm; suggested donation $4; ⓣ315/471-0593, ⓦwww.eriecanalmuseum.org), housed in an 1850s weighing station at 318 E Erie Blvd, tells the story of the planning, construction, and operation of the canal, which began in 1810. Designed to link the Great Lakes with New York City via the Hudson and thus cut hefty transportation costs, when it finally opened in 1825 after considerable cost and loss of life, prosperous towns quickly sprung up alongside the canal.

The city's small **visitor center** is in the Erie Canal Museum (same hours and contact information). Excellent **rooms** can be found in the lakeside *Ancestors Inn*, just outside of town in Liverpool (ⓣ315/461-1226 or 1-888/866-8591, ⓦwww.ancestorsinn.com; ❺). The fairly central *HI-Downing International Hostel*, 535 Oak St (ⓣ315/472-5788; ❷), has dorm beds from $15. For **food**, *Pastabilities*, 311 S Franklin St (ⓣ315/474-1153), is popular for its delicious pasta, while *Lemon Grass*, 238 W Jefferson St (ⓣ315/475-1111), is a great but pricey Thai place. Student numbers ensure a lively **music** scene; consult the free *Syracuse New Times* (ⓦwww.syracusenewtimes.com) for what's happening. Good hangouts include the loud, bluesy *Dinosaur BBQ*, 246 W Willow St (ⓣ315/476-1662).

Rochester

In contrast to its sprawling suburbs, downtown **ROCHESTER** is a salubrious place, with its central office-block area bordered by well-heeled mansions on spacious boulevards. High-tech companies such as Bausch & Lomb, Xerox, and Kodak have created a thriving local economy throughout the years, despite national and regional economic downturns. Kodak's (and its founder, George Eastman's) legacies throughout the metropolitan area include Kodak Park, the Eastman Theater, and above all the **International Museum of Photography** at George Eastman House, two miles from downtown at 900 East Ave (Tues–Sat 10am–5pm, Thurs until 8pm, Sun 1–5pm; $8; ⓣ585/271-3361, ⓦwww.eastmanhouse.org). In the modern annex, a first-rate exhibition of photographic history ranges from high-quality Civil War prints to modern experimental works. There's also a space for temporary exhibitions and an arthouse cinema but the house itself is only mildly interesting, surpassed in glory by its superbly maintained gardens. A few blocks back towards downtown at 657 East Ave, the **Rochester Museum & Science Center** (Mon–Sat 9am–5pm, Sun noon–5pm; $9; ⓣ585/271-4320, ⓦwww.rmsc.org) houses interesting interactive displays on science, natural history, native Indians, and local history. Nearby at 500 University Ave, the **Memorial Art Gallery** (Wed–Sun 11am–5pm, Thurs until 9pm; $10; ⓣ585/473-7720, ⓦwww.mag.rochester.edu) houses a surprisingly extensive collection that includes three Monets and a Rembrandt.

An obsessive collector of anything and everything, local bigwig Margaret Woodbury Strong (1897–1969) bequeathed her estate to the city and today it is the **Strong National Museum of Play** on Manhattan Square (Mon–Sat 10am–5pm, Fri until 8pm, Sun noon–5pm; $9.50, kids $7.50; Ⓣ585/263-2700, Ⓦwww.strongmuseum.org). Half devoted to a history of the American family, and half obsessed with a history of American children's pop culture, it features interactive kid-oriented exhibits such as a history of *Sesame Street* and a fully working 1920s carousel. There's also a stunning indoor butterfly garden. The theme of celebrating former Rochester residents continues at the **Susan B. Anthony House** at 17 Madison St, where this renowned suffragist lived from 1866 to 1906 (Tues–Sun 10am–5pm; $6; Ⓣ585/235-6124, Ⓦwww.susanbanthonyhouse.org).

Practicalities

Greyhound drops off at Broad and Chestnut streets downtown. The Amtrak station, 320 Central Ave, is on the north side beyond the I-490 inner loop road; it's served by Regional Transit Service (RTS) public **buses** (Ⓣ585/288-1700, Ⓦwww.rgrta.com). Rochester's **visitor center** is at 45 East Ave between Chestnut and Main (Mon–Fri 8.30am–5pm, Sat 10am–3pm; Ⓣ1-800/677-7282, Ⓦwww.visitrochester.com). **Accommodation** is somewhat expensive downtown, where choices include the excellent *428 Mt Vernon B&B* (Ⓣ716/271-0792 or 1-800/836-3159, Ⓦwww.428mtvernon.com; ⑥), at the entrance to lush Highland Park, with private baths in all rooms. Among budget options in the south of the city is the *Red Roof Inn*, 4820 W Henrietta Rd, off I-90 exit 46 (Ⓣ585/359-1100, Ⓦwww.redroof.com; ③).

Popular **places to eat** downtown include *Aladdin's Natural Eatery*, 646 Monroe Ave (Ⓣ585/442-5000), serving inexpensive Middle Eastern food, and *Nick Tahou Hots* at 320 W Main St (Ⓣ585/436-0184), famous for its "Garbage Plate" – a local hotch-potch of meats, eggs, and vegetables. In the university area, *Jine's Restaurant*, 658 Park Ave (Ⓣ585/461-1280), is good-value for breakfast, and *Esan*, 696 Park Ave (Ⓣ585/271-2271), is the place for authentically spicy and inexpensive Thai food. In the up-and-coming area known as South Wedge the *Beale St Café*, 689 South Ave (Ⓣ585/271-4650), serves fine heapings of Southern and Cajun cooking, complemented by live blues four nights a week.

Buffalo

As I-90 sweeps down into the state's second largest city, **BUFFALO**, downtown looms up in a cluster of Art Deco spires and glass-box skyscrapers – Manhattan in miniature on Lake Erie. The city's early twentieth-century prosperity, which busted while many other American cities were booming, and thus exempted Buffalo's historic buildings from destruction and replacement, is reflected in such architecturally significant structures as the towering 1928 **City Hall** (the tallest in the country; free observation deck on the top floor) and the deep red terracotta relief of Louis Sullivan's **Guaranty Building** on Church Street. The massive abandoned **grain elevators**, which rise proudly along the Erie waterfront like wonders of the industrial world, provide an interesting architectural counterpoint. Because of its proximity to the Canadian border, Buffalo also has numerous Underground Railroad sites.

That Buffalo's wealthy merchants were a cultured lot is apparent in the excellent **Albright-Knox Art Gallery**, 1285 Elmwood Ave (Wed, Sat & Sun 10am–5pm, Thurs & Fri 10am–10pm; $10; Ⓣ716/882-8700, Ⓦwww.albrightknox.org), two miles north of downtown amid the green spaces of the Frederick Law Olmsted–designed **Delaware Park**. One of the top modern collections in the world, it's especially strong on recent American and European art with Pollock, Rothko,

Warhol, and Rauschenberg among the names. Other highlights are a Surrealism collection and pieces by earlier artists such as Matisse, Picasso, and Monet. The area around Delaware Park is Buffalo's choicest neighborhood; it features several homes designed by **Frank Lloyd Wright**, most notably the Darwin D. Martin House Complex (tour times and lengths vary, reservations required; $15–40; ⓣ716/947-9217, ⓦwww.darwinmartinhouse.org). Between here and downtown is **Allentown**, a National Historic District and Buffalo's most bohemian quarter. Its leafy streets are lined with lovely Victorian homes and numerous good cafés, bars, restaurants – as well as most of Buffalo's gay and lesbian venues.

As a traditionally blue-collar city, Buffalo loves its professional **sports** teams: football's Bills (ⓣ1-877/228-4257, ⓦwww.buffalobills.com), ice hockey's Sabres (ⓣ1-888/467-2273, ⓦwww.sabres.nhl.com), and minor-league baseball's Bisons (ⓣ1-888/223-6000, ⓦwww.bisons.com), who, as the top farm team for the New York Mets, attract huge crowds to downtown's pleasant ballpark.

Arrival and information

Greyhound, Metro Bus, and Metro Rail, the city's tramway (both Metros ⓣ716/855-7211, ⓦwww.nfta.com/metro), all operate from the downtown depot at Ellicott and Church streets. Several routes go to **Niagara Falls** (see p.139). Amtrak **trains** stop some six blocks away, at Exchange Street, as well as in the eastern suburb of Depew, eight miles from town but close to the **airport** (ⓣ716/630-6020, ⓦwww.nfta.com/airport). There's a helpful **visitor center** at 617 Main St (Mon–Thurs 9am–5pm, Fri 9am–4pm, Sat 10am–2pm; ⓣ716/852-0511 or 1-800/283-3256, ⓦwww.visitbuffaloniagara.com), which offers a wealth of information.

Accommodation

Buffalo has no shortage of good **places to stay**, many of which are n the heart of downtown

Beau Fleuve 242 Linwood Ave ⓣ716/882-6116 or 1-800/278-0245, ⓦwww.beaufleuve.com. Extremely comfortable, well-appointed B&B with great breakfasts. ❺

Hampton Inn & Suites 220 Delaware Ave ⓣ716/855-2223, ⓦwww.hamptoninnbuffalo.com. A safe bet in the heart of the nightlife district downtown, with free breakfasts. ❺

HI-Buffalo Hostel 667 Main St ⓣ716/852-5222, ⓦwww.hostelbuffalo.com. Very central hostel with beds for $25. Best budget option for the Buffalo/Niagara area. No lock-out. ❶

Lenox Hotel & Suites 140 North St ⓣ716/884-1700 or 1-800/825-3669, ⓦwww.roycroftinn.com. Rather drab brick building but centrally located and the simple rooms are good value. ❸

The Mansion on Delaware Avenue 414 Delaware Ave ⓣ716/886-3300, ⓦwww.mansionondelaware.com. Centrally located luxury inn, with all modern amenities and gourmet breakfasts. ❼

Eating, drinking, and nightlife

The heart of Buffalo's downtown centers on Chippewa and Main; plenty of restaurants are within easy reach and there's ample parking. For a quick snack, the cheap food stalls and tiny Polish cafés of ancient **Broadway Market**, 999 Broadway, are well worth perusing. The main **nightlife** drag, along Chippewa from Delaware Avenue to Main Street, has plenty of sports bars and nightclubs. The majority of theaters and venues that house the city's burgeoning **arts scene** are handily grouped nearby along Main between Chippewa and Tupper streets. Asbury Hall, inside Ani DiFranco's *Babeville*, 341 Delaware Ave (ⓣ716/852-3835, ⓦwww.babevillebuffalo.com), hosts leftfield gigs and other events. For details of what's on, pick up the free weekly *Art Voice* (ⓦwww.artvoice.com), or the gay and lesbian *Outcome* (ⓦwww.outcomebuffalo.com).

Anchor Bar 1047 Main St ⓣ716/886-8920, ⓦwww.anchorbar.com. The city's specialty of buffalo (spicy chicken) wings with blue cheese and celery dressing is said to have been invented here.

Bacchus Wine Bar & Restaurant 54 W Chippewa St ⓣ716/854-9463. A good late-night bar and restaurant, with jazz, blues, folk, and world music.

Cole's 1104 Elmwood Ave, Allentown ⓣ716/886-1449. Lively diner-style joint that rustles up a tasty and inexpensive array of appetisers, salads, burgers, wraps, and chicken dishes, as well as decent beers.

India Gate 1116 Elmwood Ave ⓣ716/886-4000. Good, inexpensive Indian restaurant with generous lunch buffet.

Nietzsche's 248 Allen St ⓣ716/886-8539, ⓦwww.nietzsches.com. Bar with friendly staff and cheap drinks, hosting a wide variety of live acts seven days a week; there's room for dancing in the back.

Spot Coffee 227 Delaware Ave ⓣ716/856-BREW; 765 Elmwood Ave ⓣ716/332-5288, ⓦwww.spotcoffee.com. Lively, happening neighborhood institution serving basic food and good drinks. The location on Elmwood is connected to New World Records, one of the best music stores in Buffalo.

Niagara Falls

Every second almost three quarters of a million gallons of water explode over the knife-edge **NIAGARA FALLS**, right on the border with Canada some twenty miles north of Buffalo on I-190. This awesome spectacle is made even more impressive by the variety of methods laid on to help you get closer to it: boats, catwalks, observation towers, and helicopters all push as near to the curtains of gushing water as they dare. At night, the falls are lit up, and the colored waters tumble dramatically into blackness, while in winter the whole scene changes as the falls freeze to form gigantic razor-tipped icicles.

Some visitors will, no doubt, find the whole experience a bit too gimmicky; corporate big-hitters like the *Hard Rock Café* and various casinos on both sides have pushed the place closer to an aquatic Vegas, although the green fringes of the state park provide some bucolic getaways. Don't expect too much from the touristy small city of **Niagara Falls**, **New York**, or the more developed tinseltown of **Niagara Falls, Ontario**. Once you've seen the falls, from as many different angles as you can manage, and traced the **Niagara Gorge**, you'll have a better time heading back to Buffalo.

Arrival, information, and getting around

Amtrak **trains**, en route between New York City and Toronto, stop a long two miles from downtown Niagara Falls at 27th Street and Lockwood Road. **Buses** stop downtown at 303 Rainbow Boulevard, ten minutes' walk from the falls. Arriving **by car**, follow the signs to the main parking lot, which is right next to the falls and costs $10 – avoid being steered into privately owned, high-priced lots outside the park. **Information** is available at the Niagara Tourism & Convention Corporation, 345 3rd St (ⓣ716/282-8992 or 1-800/325-5787, ⓦwww.niagara-usa.com) and from the Niagara Falls State Park Visitors' Center (ⓣ716/278-1796) near the falls. As for **getting around**, local Metro Transit System **buses** ($1.50 base fare, plus 25¢/zone; ⓣ716/285-9319, ⓦwww.nfta.com) run to all areas of the city and to Buffalo (see p.137).

Accommodation

Places to stay in central Niagara can be quite expensive if you don't plan ahead, but huge competition keeps rates down overall. US-62 (Niagara Falls Blvd), east of

Whirlpool Rapids & Niagara Power Project ▲

CANADA

RESTAURANTS
Como Restaurant 2
Hard Rock Café 4
The Orchard Grill 1
Sadar Sahib 3
Top of the Falls 5

Helicopter Rides

Maid of the Mist Boat Dock

Prospect Point Observation Tower

American Falls

Luna Island

Bridal Veil Falls

Cave of the Winds

Terrapin Point

Horseshoe Falls

Goat Island

Green Island

Three Sisters Islands

0 400 yds

Seneca Niagara Casino

USA

Niagara River

ACCOMMODATION
Crowne Plaza C
HI-Niagara Falls B
Park Place B&B A
Red Coach Inn D
Seneca Niagara
 Casino & Hotel E

N

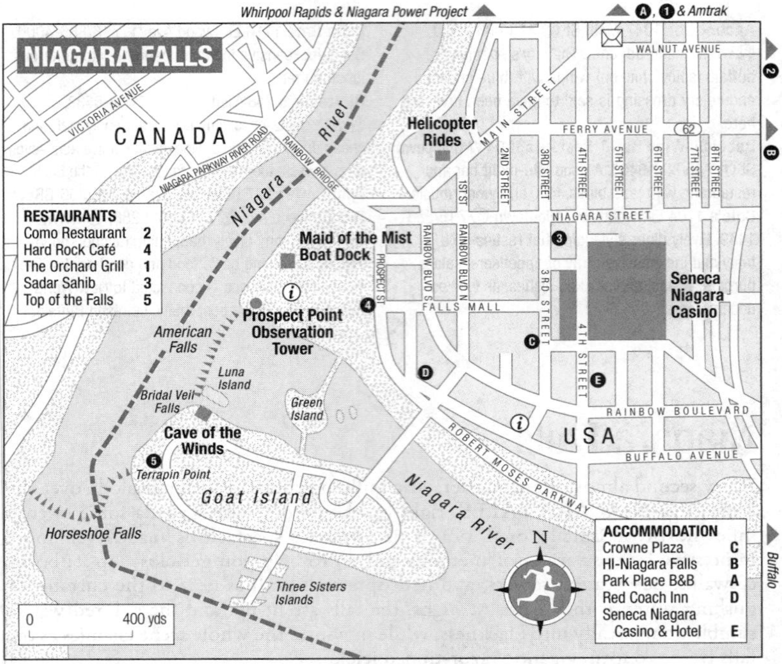

I-190, is lined with dozens of inexpensive motels, some being rather tacky honeymoon spots. The closest place to **camp** is six miles from downtown at *Niagara Falls Campground & Lodging* at 2405 Niagara Falls Blvd (April–Oct; ☏716/731-3434, Ⓦ www.niagarafallscampground.net; from $35 per site).

Crowne Plaza 300 3rd St ☏716/285-3361 or 1-800/953-2557, Ⓦ www.crowneplaza.com/niagarafalls. Typical of the chain hotels that dominate downtown and overcharge at peak times. ⑤
HI-Niagara Falls 1101 Ferry Ave ☏716/282-3700, Ⓔ niagarahostel@gmail.com. Friendly, well-run hostel with dorm beds from $18, singles from $44 and larger rooms. Preference is given to HI members and reservations are necessary in summer. ③
Park Place B&B 740 Park Place ☏716/282-4626 or 1-800/510-4626, Ⓦ www.parkplacebb .com. Comfortable spot near downtown, with full

breakfast and afternoon pastries. ④
Red Coach Inn 2 Buffalo Ave ☏716/282-1459 or 1-866/719-2070, Ⓦ www.redcoach.com. Popular, well-appointed mock Tudor B&B with views of the falls. ④
Seneca Niagara Casino & Hotel 310 4th St ☏716/299-1100 or 1-877/873-6322, Ⓦ www .senecaniagaracasino.com. Luxury pad whose interiors are about as garish as the flashy neon entrance. Rates vary considerably – look out for online promotions. Several highly rated restaurants on the premises. ⑥

The Falls

Niagara Falls comprises three distinct cataracts. The tallest are the **American** and **Bridal Veil falls** on the American side, separated by tiny Luna Island and plunging over jagged rocks in a 180ft drop; the broad **Horseshoe Falls** which curve their way over to Canada are far more majestic. Together, they date back a mere twelve thousand years, when the retreat of melting glaciers allowed water trapped in Lake Erie to gush north to Lake Ontario. Back then the falls were seven miles downriver, but constant erosion has cut them back to their present site.

▲ Niagara Falls

Getting around Niagara Falls State Park is easy, thanks to the convenient but twee **Niagara Scenic Trolley** ($2) which connects all parking lots and the major sightseeing points. The best views on the American side are from the **Observation Tower** (daily 10am–5pm; $1), and from the area at its base where the water rushes past. In the middle of the river, Terrapin Point on **Goat Island** has similar views of Horseshoe Falls. Near here, the nineteenth-century tightrope-walker Blondin crossed the Niagara repeatedly, and even carried passengers across on his back. Other suicidal fools over the years have taken the plunge in barrels – or less (see box, p.142). The reason such craziness has long been banned becomes self-evident when you approach the towering cascade on the not-to-be-missed **Maid of the Mist** boat trip, which leaves from the foot of the observation tower (May–Oct daily 9.15am–7.30pm every 15 min; $12.50, kids $7.50; ⓣ716/284-8897, ⓦwww.maidofthemist.com). Another excellent way to see the falls is the **Cave of the Winds** tour (mid-May to late Oct daily 8am–10pm; $10, kids $7; ⓣ716/278-1730), which leads from Goat Island by elevator down to the base of the falls. Bringing you to within almost touching distance of the water, the tour can provide a magical nighttime view, as it runs well into the evening. A "**Discovery Pass**" for these and other attractions costs $30 for adults, or $23 for children at the Visitor Center.

For a bird's eye view, Rainbow Air Inc **helicopter** tours, 454 Main St (9am–dusk; prices vary; ⓣ716/284-2800) are heart-stopping both scenically and financially. To check out the superior view from Niagara, Ontario, it's a twenty-minute walk across the **Rainbow Bridge** to the Canadian side (50¢ to Canada, free to US; passports required). Driving across is inadvisable: discounting the $3.25 toll, parking on the other side is expensive and increased security checks make delays more likely.

Maniacs and miracles

Fifteen people have taken the plunge over Niagara's 170-foot **Horseshoe Falls** – and, remarkably, ten of them survived the fall. The first daredevil was 63-year-old Annie Taylor in 1901, who rode in a wooden barrel and suffered only minor bruises from her journey. Since then, thrillseekers have followed her lead, using everything from giant rubber balls to water tanks as craft. The last successful navigation of the falls was in 2003, by a man who claimed he was trying to commit suicide; after surviving the plunge, the man decided life was worth living. Those less lucky include Red Hill, killed in 1945 while using a vessel he called "The Thing," built of little more than inner tubes and netting. Other deaths have been equally pointless: from a would-be stuntman in a kayak, who refused a helmet for fear it would obscure his face on film, to a jet-skier whose parachute, improperly packed, failed to open when he overshot the falls.

The most miraculous survival story, though, is that of Roger Woodward, a seven-year-old on a boat trip with his teenage sister in the upper Niagara River in the summer of 1960. When the boat developed motor trouble and capsized, they were thrown into the river. His sister was plucked from the water, but Roger and the captain, James Honeycutt, went over the falls wearing nothing but swimsuits and life preservers. Honeycutt was killed, but the boy surfaced near a tour boat at the base of the falls, bruised and concussed but alive, making him the only person ever to survive an unprotected trip over the falls.

Eating and drinking

Though most of the **eating options** in Niagara Falls are fast-food joints of indifferent quality, there are a few decent local bars and restaurants – with some better places over in Canada.

Como Restaurant 2200 Pine Ave ⓣ716/285-9341. A good, posh option with huge portions of Italian cuisine and a reasonably priced deli.

Hard Rock Café 333 Prospect St ⓣ716/282-0007. Although a bit cliched and expensive, this branch of the rock-homage American-food chain restaurant has a lively, dependable bar.

The Orchard Grill 1217 Main St ⓣ716/282-8079. Large portions of all-American classics are served at this unpretentious spot with a pleasant outdoor patio.

Sadar Sahib 431 3rd St ⓣ716/282-0444. Authentic and inexpensive curry house with an emphasis on Punjabi dishes.

Top Of The Falls Goat Island, Niagara Falls State Park ⓣ716/278-0340. The food is adequate standard American fare but the setting is unrivalled. Floor to ceiling windows ensure everyone gets a great view across the falls.

Pennsylvania

PENNSYLVANIA was explored by the Dutch in the early 1600s, settled by the Swedes forty years later, and claimed by the British in 1664. Charles II of England, who owed a debt to the Penn family, rid himself of the potentially troublesome young **William Penn**, an enthusiastic advocate of religious freedom, by granting him land in the colony in 1682. Penn Jr immediately established a "holy experiment" of "brotherly love" and tolerance, naming the state for his father and setting a good example by signing a peaceful cohabitation treaty with the Native Americans. Most of the early agricultural settlers were religious refugees, Quakers like Penn himself and Mennonites from Germany and Switzerland, to be joined by Irish Catholics during the potato famines of the nineteenth century.

"The Keystone State" was crucial in the development of the United States. Politicians and thinkers like **Benjamin Franklin** congregated in Philadelphia – home of both the Declaration of Independence and the Constitution – and were prominent in articulating the ideas behind the Revolution. Later, the battle in Gettysburg, in south Pennsylvania – best remembered for Abraham Lincoln's immortal **Gettysburg Address** – marked a turning point in the Civil War. Pennsylvania was also vital industrially: Pittsburgh, in the west, was the world's leading steel producer in the nineteenth century, and nearly all the nation's anthracite coal is still mined here.

The two great urban centers of **Philadelphia** and **Pittsburgh**, both lively and vibrant tourist destinations, are at opposite ends of the state. The three hundred miles between them, though predominantly agricultural, are topographically diverse. There are over one hundred state parks, with green rolling countryside in the east and brooding forests in the west. **Lancaster County**, home to traditional Amish farmers, the **Gettysburg** battlefield and the **Hershey** chocolate factory, minutes away from state capital **Harrisburg**, all draw visitors by the thousands. Finally, in the far northwest, **Lake Erie** provides the state's only waterfront, centered upon the eponymous town.

Getting around Pennsylvania

If you organize your trip carefully, **public transporation** is adequate to navigate Pennsylvania – although it's best to have a **car**. Both I-76 (the Pennsylvania Turnpike) and I-80 sweep all the way across to Ohio, over four hundred miles east to west. US-30 (the Lincoln Highway) also runs east–west between Philadelphia and Pittsburgh, past Lancaster City, York, and Gettysburg. **Amtrak** crosses daily from Philadelphia to Pittsburgh, stopping at Lancaster City, Harrisburg, and other smaller towns. **Greyhound** covers all the major cities and some small towns not served by rail.

Philadelphia

The original capital of the nation, **PHILADELPHIA** was laid out by William Penn Jr in 1682, on a grid system that was to provide the pattern for most American cities. It was envisaged as a "greene countrie towne," traces of which are still discernable. Just a few blocks away from the noise and crowds of downtown, shady cobbled alleys stand lined with red-brick colonial houses, while the peace and quiet of huge Fairmount Park make it easy to forget you're in a major metropolis. Settled by **Quakers**, Philadelphia prospered swiftly on the back of trade and commerce, and by the 1750s had become the second largest city in the British Empire. Economic power fueled strong revolutionary feeling, and the city was the capital for most of the **War of Independence** and the US capital until 1800, while Washington DC, was being built. The **Declaration of Independence** was written, signed, and first publicly read here in 1776, as was the **US Constitution** ten years later. Philadelphia was also a hotbed of new ideas in the arts and sciences, as epitomized by the scientist, philosopher, statesman, inventor, and printer **Benjamin Franklin**.

Philadelphia, which means "City of Brotherly Love" in Greek, is in fact one of the most **ethnically mixed** US cities, with substantial communities of Italians, Irish, Eastern Europeans, and Asians living side-by-side among the large **African-American** population. Many of the city's black residents are descendants of the migrants who flocked here after the Civil War when Philadelphia was seen as a bastion of tolerance and liberalism. A century later it voted in the nation's first black mayor, and erected the country's best museum of African-American history and culture. Philly also retains its Quaker heritage, with large "meetings" or congregations of **The Society of Friends**. On the downside, Philadelphia is also the place where in 1985, as part of a huge police effort to dislodge the black separatist group MOVE, a bomb dropped from a helicopter set fire to entire city blocks, killing men, women, and children, and leaving many hundreds homeless. Once known as "Filthydelphia," the city underwent a remarkable resurgence preparing for the nation's bicentennial celebrations in 1976. Philadelphia's strength today is its great energy – fueled by history, strong cultural institutions, and grounded in its many staunchly traditional neighborhoods. The city's mood was lifted above the general economic gloom of October 2008 by the Phillies' triumph in baseball's World Series.

Arrival and information

Philadelphia's **International Airport** (Ⓣ215/937-6800, Ⓦwww.phl.org) is seven miles southwest of the city off I-95. **Taxis** into town cost around $30 (try Yellow Cab; Ⓣ215/829-4222), and the South East Pennsylvania Transit Authority (**SEPTA**) runs trains from the airport every thirty minutes (4.30am–11.30pm; $6; see "City transportation," below) to five downtown destinations: Eastwick Station, University City, 30th Street near the university, Suburban Station near City Hall, and Market East, adjacent to the Greyhound terminal at 11th and Filbert streets. The very grand 30th Street **Amtrak** station, one of the busiest in the US, is just across the Schuylkill River in the university area (free transfer downtown on SEPTA). SEPTA connects to **NJ Transit**, and between the two commuter rail systems you can travel to the Jersey shore, Princeton, suburban Pennsylvania, and New York City for a fraction of the price of Amtrak.

The excellent **Independence Visitor Center**, at 6th and Market streets (daily: late June to Aug 8.30am–5pm; rest of year 8.30am–7pm; Ⓣ215/965-7676 or 1-800/537-7676; Ⓦwww.independencevisitorcenter.com), contains a staggering wealth of information, and should be the first stop on any downtown or Independence National Historic Park itinerary. It is also an outlet for the good-value **Philadelphia Pass**, which allows entry to over thirty city attractions (valid 1–5 days; $47–88; Ⓦwww.philadelphiapass.com). There is a smaller visitor center branch downtown in City Hall room 121 (Mon–Fri 9am–5pm; Ⓣ215/686-2840).

City transportation and tours

SEPTA (Ⓣ215/580-7800, Ⓦwww.septa.org) runs an extensive **bus** system and a **subway**. The most useful subway lines cross the city east–west (Market–Frankford line) and north–south (Broad Street line); the handiest bus route is **#76**, which runs from Penn's Landing and the Independence Hall area out along Market Street past City Hall to the museums and Fairmount Park. Bus and subway services require exact fares of $2 (tokens, purchased in batches of two or more, cost only $1.45); **day passes**, also good for the airport, go for $6. Bright purple **PHLASH** buses run a handy downtown loop in summer (June–Oct daily 10am–8pm; $2; day pass $5; Ⓣ215/474-5274, Ⓦwww.phillyphlash.com).

Philadelphia offers a wealth of **tours** focusing on a wide range of subjects. For general orientation, the Big Bus Company (Ⓣ215/389-8687, Ⓦwww.phillytour

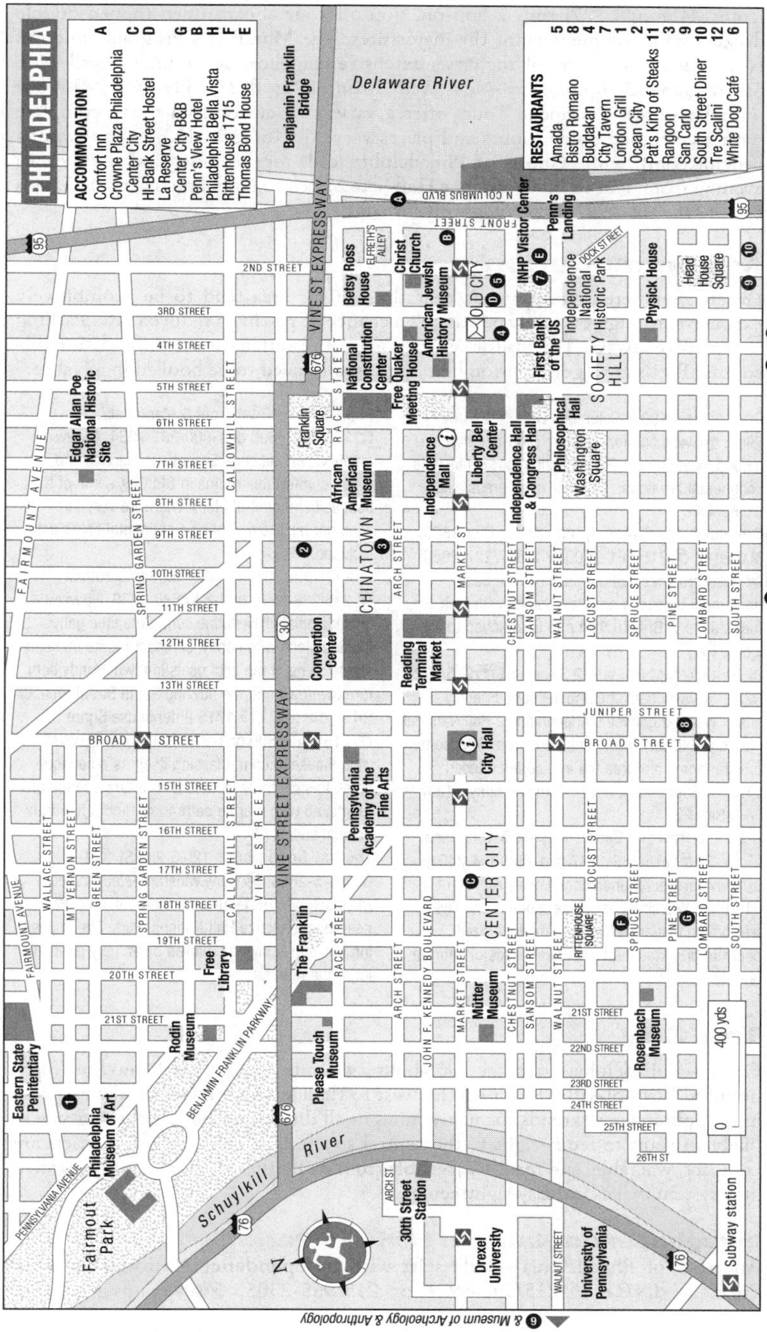
PHILADELPHIA
ACCOMMODATION
Comfort Inn A
Crowne Plaza Philadelphia Center City C
HI-Bank Street Hostel D
La Reserve G
Center City B&B B
Penn's View Hotel H
Philadelphia Bella Vista F
Rittenhouse 1715 E
Thomas Bond House
RESTAURANTS
Amada 5
Bistro Romano 8
Buddakan 4
City Tavern 7
London Grill 1
Ocean City 2
Pat's King of Steaks 11
Rangoon 3
San Carlo 9
South Street Diner 10
Tre Scalini 12
White Dog Café 6
Delaware River
Benjamin Franklin Bridge
VINE ST EXPRESSWAY
VINE STREET EXPRESSWAY
N COLUMBUS BLVD
FRONT STREET
2ND STREET
3RD STREET
4TH STREET
5TH STREET
6TH STREET
7TH STREET
8TH STREET
9TH STREET
10TH STREET
11TH STREET
12TH STREET
13TH STREET
BROAD STREET
15TH STREET
16TH STREET
17TH STREET
18TH STREET
19TH STREET
20TH STREET
21ST STREET
22ND STREET
23RD STREET
24TH STREET
25TH STREET
26TH ST
FAIRMOUNT AVENUE
SPRING GARDEN STREET
CALLOWHILL STREET
RACE STREET
ARCH STREET
MARKET ST
CHESTNUT STREET
SANSOM STREET
WALNUT STREET
LOCUST STREET
SPRUCE STREET
PINE STREET
LOMBARD STREET
SOUTH STREET
JUNIPER STREET
WALLACE STREET
MT VERNON STREET
GREEN STREET
VINE STREET
JOHN F. KENNEDY BOULEVARD
BENJAMIN FRANKLIN PARKWAY
PENNSYLVANIA AVENUE
ARCH ST
DOCK STREET
Edgar Allan Poe National Historic Site
Franklin Square
Betsy Ross House
ELFRETH'S ALLEY
Christ Church
National Constitution Center
Free Quaker Meeting House
American Jewish History Museum
OLD CITY
INHP Visitor Center
Penn's Landing
First Bank of the US
Independence National Historic Park
SOCIETY HILL
Physick House
Head House Square
African American Museum
Independence Mall
Liberty Bell Center
Independence Hall & Congress Hall
Philosophical Hall
Washington Square
CHINATOWN
Convention Center
Reading Terminal Market
City Hall
Pennsylvania Academy of the Fine Arts
CENTER CITY
The Franklin
Free Library
RITTENHOUSE SQUARE
Rodin Museum
Mütter Museum
Rosenbach Museum
Please Touch Museum
Eastern State Penitentiary
Philadelphia Museum of Art
Fairmount Park
Schuylkill River
30th Street Station
Drexel University
University of Pennsylvania
Italian Market
11 & 12
6 & Museum of Archeology & Anthropology
400 yds
Subway station
N
95
676
30
76

.com; 24hr pass $27) runs a hop-on, hop-off tour aboard open-topped double deckers with commentary of the major sites. The Mural Arts Program conducts two-hour trolley tours of the city's extensive neighborhood murals (April–Nov Sat & Sun 12.30pm, May–Nov Wed 10am; $25; Ⓣ215/389-8687, Ⓦwww.muralarts.org). Centipede Tours offer a variety of customized tours, complete with a costumed guide (hours and prices vary; Ⓣ215/735-3123, Ⓦwww.centipedeinc.com), while Ghosts of Philadelphia leads morbid historical tours every evening from next to Independence Hall (late March to Nov, hours vary; $17, kids $8; Ⓣ215/413-1997, Ⓦwww.ghosttour.com).

Accommodation

Hotels anywhere downtown or near the historic area tend to be prohibitively expensive, though on weekends there's a chance of getting a reduced rate. Parking is expensive always. The visitor center is a great resource for accommodation discounts; B&Bs are a good option here, but usually need to be booked in advance.

Comfort Inn 100 N Columbus Blvd Ⓣ215/627-7900, Ⓦwww.comfortinn.com. High-rise hotel in a good location near Penn's Landing; rates include continental breakfast. Cheaper rates are available online. 6

Crowne Plaza Philadelphia Center City 1800 Market St Ⓣ215/561-7500 or 1-877/227-6963, Ⓦwww.crowneplaza.com. One of the best downtown business-oriented hotels, with lush furnishings. A British-style pub is attached to the lobby. 9

HI-Bank Street Hostel 32 S Bank St Ⓣ215/922-0222, Ⓦwww.bankstreethostel.com. Friendly hostel wedged between Independence Hall National Park and Old City, with bunk beds from $27, some private rooms and free tea and coffee. Closed 11am–4.30pm; curfew 12.30am weekdays, 1am Fri & Sat. 3

La Reserve Center City B&B 1804 Pine St Ⓣ215/735-1137 or 1-800/354-8401, Ⓦwww.lareservebandb.com. Lovely rooms, of which the two cheapest share a bathroom. The welcoming owner dishes up a modest-sized gourmet breakfast and dispenses loads of information. 5

Penn's View Hotel Front & Market sts Ⓣ215/922-7600 or 1-800/331-7634, Ⓦwww.pennsviewhotel.com. Exceptional service and clean, comfortable rooms in Old City, some of the best value in central Philly. There's a very fine wine bar next to the lobby. Continental breakfast included. 6

Philadelphia Bella Vista 752 South 10th St Ⓣ215/238-1270 or 1-800/680-1270, Ⓦwww.philadelphiabellavistabnb.com. Cute little gaily painted place with comfy, compact rooms that constitute some of the best deals in town. Handy both for downtown and the buzzing South Street area. 4

Rittenhouse 1715 1715 Rittenhouse Sqare St Ⓣ215/546-6500 or 1-877/791-6500, Ⓦwww.rittenhousebb.com. Classing itself as a boutique hotel, this centrally located B&B offers a range of rooms, all with marble bathrooms, and a few truly palatial suites. 8

Thomas Bond House 129 S 2nd St Ⓣ1-800/845-2663, Ⓦwww.winston-salem-inn.com/philadelphia. Thirteen-room restored 1769 B&B near Independence Hall National Park. The imposing building is slightly marred by an ugly parking lot at the rear. 5

The City

Central Philadelphia stretches for about two miles from the Schuylkill (pronounced "school-kill") River on the west to the Delaware River on the east; the metropolitan area extends for many miles in all directions, but everything you're likely to want to see is right in the central swath. The city's central districts are compact, walkable, and readily accessible from each other; Penn's sensibly planned grid system makes for easy sightseeing.

Independence National Historic Park

Any tour of Philadelphia should start with **Independence National Historic Park**, or **INHP** (Ⓣ215/597-8974 or 215/965-2305, Ⓦwww.nps.gov/inde),

"America's most historic square mile." Though the park covers a mere four blocks just west of the Delaware River, between Walnut and Arch streets, it can take more than a day to explore in full. The solid red-brick buildings here, not all of which are open to the public, epitomize the Georgian (and after the Revolution, Federalist) obsession with balance and symmetry.

All INHP sites (unless otherwise specified) are open 365 days a year and admission is free; hours are usually 9am to 5pm, sometimes longer in summer. Free **tours** set off from the rear of the east wing of Independence Hall, the single most important site. Throughout the day, costumed actors perform patchy but informative skits in various locations across the site – pick up a free copy of *The Gazette* newssheet for listings and a useful map. It's best to reach **Independence Hall** early, to avoid the hordes of tourists and school parties. In peak season, free tickets must be obtained at the Independence Visitor Center. Built in 1732 as the Pennsylvania State House, this was where the Declaration of Independence was prepared, signed, and, after the pealing of the Liberty Bell, given its first public reading on July 8, 1776. Today, in the room in which Jefferson et al drafted and signed the United States Constitution, you can see George Washington's high-backed chair with the half-sun on the back – Franklin, in optimistic spirit, called it "the rising sun."

The **Liberty Bell** itself hung in Independence Hall from 1753, ringing to herald vital announcements such as victories and defeats in the Revolutionary War. Stories as to how it received its famous crack vary but one thing's for sure; it rang publicly for the very last time on George Washington's birthday in 1846. Later in the century, the bell's inscription from Leviticus, advocating liberty, made it an anti-slavery symbol for the New England abolitionists – the first to call it the Liberty Bell. After the Civil War, the silent bell was adopted as a symbol of freedom and reconciliation and embarked on a national rail tour. The iconic lump of metal now rests in a shrine-like space in the new multimedia **Liberty Bell Center** in INHP.

Next door to Independence Hall, on 6th and Chestnut streets, **Congress Hall**, built in 1787 as Philadelphia County Courthouse, is where members of the new United States Congress first took their places, and where all the patterns for today's US government were established. The **First Bank of the United States**, at 3rd and Chestnut streets, was established in 1797 to formalize the new union's currency – a vital task given the multiple forms of currency hitherto in use. In 1774, delegates of the first Continental Congress – predecessor of the US Congress – chose defiantly to meet at **Carpenter's Hall**, 320 Chestnut St, to air their grievances against the English king. Today the building exhibits early tools and furniture (Tues–Sun 10am–4pm). Directly north, **Franklin Court**, 313 Market St, is a tribute to Benjamin Franklin on the site of his home, which no longer stands. An underground museum has hilarious dial-a-quote recordings of his pithy sayings and the musings of his contemporaries, as well as a working printshop. The **B Free Franklin Post Office**, 316 Market St, sells stamps and includes a small postal museum.

Other buildings in the park include the original **Free Quaker Meeting House**, two blocks north of Market at 5th and Arch, built in 1783 by the small group of Quakers who actually fought in the Revolutionary War. There's also the **Philosophical Hall**, 104 S 5th St (March–Sept Wed–Sun 10am–4pm; rest of year Thurs–Sun 10am–4pm; free), still used today by the nation's first philosophical debating society, also founded by Franklin. Although most of the building is closed to the public, a handful of exhibitions provide insights into the history of American science. The must-see **National Constitution Center**, 525 Arch St (Sun–Fri 9.30am–5pm, Sat 9.30am–6pm; $12; ⓣ1-866/917-1787 or ⓣ215/409-

6600, Ⓦwww.constitutioncenter.org), a modern, interactive, and provocative museum dedicated to the nation's best-known document, offers a wealth of information on the venerated document.

Old City

Immediately north of INHP lies **Old City**, Philadelphia's earliest commercial area, above Market Street near the riverfront. Washington, Franklin, and Betsy Ross all worshiped at **Christ Church**, on 2nd Street just north of Market. Dating from 1727, it is surrounded by the gravestones of signatories to the Declaration of Independence (tour times vary; Ⓣ215/922-1695, Ⓦwww.christchurchphila.org). The church's official burial ground, two blocks west at 5th and Arch, includes **Benjamin Franklin's grave**. At 239 Arch St, the **Betsy Ross House** (April–Oct daily 10am–5pm; Nov–March Tues–Sun 10am–5pm; $3; Ⓣ215/686-1252, Ⓦwww.betsyrosshouse.org), by means of unimpressive wax dummies, salutes the woman credited, probably apocryphally, with making the first American flag.

The claim of **Elfreth's Alley** – a pretty little cobbled way off 2nd Street between Arch and Race streets – to be the "oldest street in the United States" is somewhat dubious, though it has been in continuous residential use since 1727; its thirty houses, notable for their wrought-iron gates, water pumps, wooden shutters, and attic rooms, date from later in the eighteenth century. At no. 126 is the **Elfreth's Alley Museum** (March–Oct Tues & Sun noon–5pm, Wed–Sat 10am–5pm; Nov–Feb Thurs–Sat 10am–5pm, Sun noon–5pm; $5; Ⓣ215/574-0560, Ⓦwww.elfrethsalley.org); the house was built by blacksmith Jeremiah Elfreth in 1762.

The area north of Market Street also holds two excellent museums: the **National Museum of American Jewish History**, 55 N 5th St (Mon–Thurs 10am–5pm, Fri 10am–3pm, Sun noon–5pm; free; Ⓣ215/923-3811, Ⓦwww.nmajh.org), which is dedicated to the experiences of Jews in the States and includes a synagogue and a Statue of Religious Liberty; and the emotive and politically informed **African American Museum in Philadelphia**, 7th and Arch streets (Tues–Sat 10am–5pm, Sun noon–5pm; $8; Ⓣ215/574-0380, Ⓦwww.aampmuseum.org). The latter tells the stories of the thousands of blacks who migrated north to Philadelphia after Reconstruction and in the early twentieth century. As well as lectures, films, and concerts, there are photos, personal memorabilia, poems by black poet Langston Hughes, and a piped-in Billie Holiday soundtrack. The Old City is also home to a number of **art galleries**, clustered around N 2nd and 3rd streets, and to September's annual Philadelphia Fringe Festival, a popular experimental theater series (Ⓣ215/413-9006, Ⓦwww.pafringe.org).

Penn's Landing

Just east of Old City along the Delaware River, where William Penn stepped off in 1682, spreads the huge and heavily industrialized port of Philadelphia. Along the port's southern reaches, on the river side of the I-95 freeway, the old docklands have been renovated as part of the **Penn's Landing** development, the most interesting feature of which is the **Independence Seaport Museum** (daily 10am–5pm; $10, free Sun 10am–noon; Ⓣ215/925-5439, Ⓦwww.phillyseaport.org). Admission includes entry into two **historical ships**: the flagship USS *Olympia* and the World War II submarine *Becuna*. All along the riverfront promenade are food stalls, landscaped pools, and fountains, and regular outdoor concerts and festivals are held here. The seasonal Riverlink **ferry** crosses the Delaware (May–Sept hourly 10am–6pm; $6 round-trip; Ⓣ215/925-5465, Ⓦwww.riverlinkferry.org) to the down-at-heel town of **Camden**, where the main attraction is the **Adventure Aquarium** (daily 9.30am–5pm; $18.95; Ⓣ856/365-3300, Ⓦwww.adventureaquarium.com) – good for kids but otherwise eminently missable.

Society Hill

Society Hill, an elegant residential area west of the Delaware and directly south of INHP, spreads between Walnut and Lombard streets. Though it is indeed Philadelphia's high society that lives here now, the area was named for its first inhabitants, the Free Society of Traders. After falling into disrepair, the Hill itself was flattened in the early 1970s to provide a building site for I.M. Pei's twin skyscrapers, Society Hill Towers. Luckily, the rest of the neighborhood has been restored to form one of the city's most picturesque districts: cobbled gas-lit streets are lined with immaculately kept colonial, Federal, and Georgian homes, often featuring the state's namesake keystones on their window frames. One of the few buildings open to the public is the **Physick House**, 321 S 4th St, home to Dr Philip Syng Physick, "the Father of American Surgery," and filled with eighteenth- and nineteenth-century decorative arts (Thurs–Sat noon–5pm; $5; Ⓣ215/925-7866, Ⓦwww.philalandmarks.org).

Center City

Center City, Philadelphia's main business and commercial area, stretches from 8th Street west to the Schuylkill River, dominated by the endearing baroque wedding cake of **City Hall** and its 37ft bronze statue of Penn. Before ascending thirty stories to the **observation deck** (Mon–Fri 9.30am–4.30pm; free) at Penn's feet, check out the quirky sculptures and carvings around the building, including the cats and mice at the south entrance. A couple of blocks north at Broad and Cherry streets, the **Pennsylvania Academy of the Fine Arts** (Tues–Sat 10am–5pm, Sun 11am–5pm; $10; Ⓣ215/972-7600, Ⓦwww.pafa.org), housed in an elaborate, multicolored Victorian pile, exhibits three hundred years of American art, including works by Mary Cassatt, Thomas Eakins, and Winslow Homer.

Beginning at 8th Street, **Chinatown**, marked by the gorgeous 40ft Friendship Gate at 10th and Arch, has some of the best inexpensive food in the city. A few blocks over on 12th Street is the century-old **Reading Terminal Market** (daily 9am–4pm; Ⓣ215/922-2317, Ⓦwww.readingterminalmarket.org), where many Amish farmers come to the city to sell their produce. It's always good for a lively time and makes a great lunch spot.

Rittenhouse Square

Grassy **Rittenhouse Square**, one of Penn's original city squares, is in a very fashionable part of town. On one side it borders chic Walnut Street, on the other a residential area of solid brownstones with beautifully carved doors and windows. The red-brick 1860 **Rosenbach Museum**, 2010 Delancey Place, holds over thirty thousand rare books, as well as James Joyce's original hand-scrawled manuscripts of *Ulysses* (Tues–Sun 10am–5pm, Wed until 8pm; $10, inc house tour; Ⓣ215/732-1600, Ⓦwww.rosenbach.org). On summer evenings there are free outdoor jazz and R&B concerts in the square.

Three blocks northwest from the square, the **Mütter Museum**, 19 S 22nd St in the College of Physicians (daily 10am–5pm; $12; Ⓣ215/563-3737, Ⓦwww.collphyphil.org), is not for the squeamish. Filled with weird pathological and medical oddities – including sickeningly lifelike wax models of tumors and skin infections, alongside closets full of skeletons, syphilitic skulls, pickled internal organs, and the death cast of a pair of Siamese twins – it's unique to say the least.

Museum Row and Fairmount Park

The mile-long Benjamin Franklin Parkway, known as Museum Row, sweeps northwest from City Hall to the colossal Museum of Art in **Fairmount Park**, an area of countryside annexed by the city in the nineteenth century. Spanning nine hundred scenic acres on both sides of the Schuylkill River, this is one of the world's largest landscaped city parks, with jogging, biking, and hiking trails, early American homes, an all-wars memorial to the state's black soldiers, and a zoo – the country's first – at 3400 W Girard Ave (March–Nov 9.30am–5pm; $17.95; Dec–Feb 9.30am–4pm; $12.95; ⓣ215/243-1100, ⓦwww.phillyzoo.org). In the late 1960s, local resident **Joe Frazier** and **Muhammad Ali** all but brought the city to a standstill with the announcement one afternoon that they were heading to Fairmount for an informal slug-out.

Sylvester Stallone later immortalized the steps of the **Philadelphia Museum of Art**, 26th St and Franklin Parkway (Tues–Thurs, Sat & Sun 10am–5pm, Fri 10am–8.45pm; $12, Sun donation; ⓣ215/763-8100, ⓦwww.philamuseum.org), by running up them in the film *Rocky*. Inside are some of the finest treasures in the US, with a twelfth-century French cloister, **Renaissance** art, a complete Robert Adam interior from a 1765 house in London's Berkeley Square, **Rubens** tapestries, Pennsylvania Dutch crafts and Shaker furniture, a strong **Impressionist** collection, and the world's most extensive collection of the works of Marcel Duchamp.

A few blocks back towards Center City, at Franklin Parkway and 22nd Street, the exquisite **Rodin Museum** (Tues–Sun 10am–5pm; $3 suggested donation; ⓣ215/763-8100, ⓦwww.rodinmuseum.org), marble-walled and set in a shady garden with a green pool, holds the largest collection of Rodin's Impressionistic sculptures and casts outside of Paris, including *The Burghers of Calais*, *The Thinker*, and *The Gates of Hell*. Diagonally across the road, within the vast edifice of **The Franklin**, N 20th St and Benjamin Franklin Parkway (daily 9.30am–5pm; $14.25, $19.75 including one Imax show; ⓣ215/448-1200, ⓦwww.fi.edu), are a Planetarium, the Tuttleman IMAX Theater (film only $9), and the Mandell Futures Center. Continuing the educational theme, the nearby **Academy of Natural Sciences** exhibits dinosaurs, mummies, and gems (Mon–Fri 10am–4.30pm, Sat, Sun & holidays 10am–5pm; $10; ⓣ215/299-1000, ⓦwww.ansp.org). Among the rare items at the **Free Library of Philadelphia**, 19th and Vine streets (Mon–Wed 9am–9pm, Thurs–Sat 9am–5pm, Sun 1–5pm; tours at 11am; free; ⓣ215/686-5322, ⓦwww.library.phila.gov), are cuneiform tablets from 3000 BC, medieval manuscripts, and first editions of Dickens and Poe.

Just a short walk northeast of the museums, occupying two full blocks of Fairmount Avenue between 20th and 22nd streets, stand the gloomy Gothic fortifications of the **Eastern State Penitentiary** (daily 10am–5pm, last entry 4pm; $12; ⓣ215/236-3300, ⓦwww.easternstate.org), one of Philadelphia's most significant historic sites, which embodies a complete history of attitudes toward crime and punishment in the US. Since it opened in 1829, the Quaker-inspired prison's radical efforts to rehabilitate inmates via isolation and reflection, rather than use physical abuse and capital punishment, attracted curious social commentators from around the world; when Charles Dickens came to America in 1842, he wanted to see two things, this prison and Niagara Falls. After a period of decay following its closure in 1970, the bulk of the Panopticon-style radial prison has been restored. Informative **audio tours** point out the prison's many novel architectural features, as well as its old synagogue and the upmarket cell where Al Capone cooled his heels.

West Philadelphia

Across the Schuylkill River, **West Philadelphia** is home to the Ivy-League **University of Pennsylvania**, where Franklin established the country's first medical school. The compact but extremely pleasant campus has some great museums: the small **Institute of Contemporary Art**, 118 S 36th St (Wed–Fri noon–8pm, Sat & Sun 11am–5pm; free; ⓣ215/898-5911, ⓦwww.icaphila.org) displays cutting-edge traveling exhibitions in an airy space; the intriguing **Arthur Ross Gallery**,

220 S 34th St (Tues–Fri 10am–5pm, Sat & Sun noon–5pm; free; ⓣ215/898-2083, ⓦwww.upenn.edu/ARG) features changing exhibits, particularly of international and colorful, innovative work; finally, the superlative **Museum of Archeology and Anthropology**, 33rd and Spruce streets (Tues–Sat 10am–4.30pm; Sept–May also Sun 1–5pm; $8, free Sun; ⓣ215/898-4000, ⓦwww.museum.upenn.edu) is the university's top draw. Regarded by experts as one of the world's finest science museums, its exhibits span all the continents and their major epochs – from Nigerian Benin bronzes to Chinese crystal balls. Most astonishing is the priceless twelve-ton granite Sphinx of Rameses II, c.1293–1185 BC, in the Lower Egyptian Gallery.

South Philadelphia

Staunchly blue-collar **South Philadelphia**, center of Philadelphia's black community since the Civil War, is also home to many of the city's Italians; opera singer **Mario Lanza** and pop stars Fabian and Chubby Checker grew up here. It's also where to come for an authentic – and very messy – **Philly cheesesteak** (see "Eating," below), and to rummage through the wonderful **Italian Market** (another *Rocky* location), which runs along 9th Street south from Christian Street. One of the last surviving urban markets in the US, the wooden market stalls that have stood here for generations are packed to overflowing with bric-a-brac and various produce, such as live seafood, and, most famously, mozzarella. **South Street**, the original boundary of the city, is now one of Philadelphia's main **nightlife** districts, with dozens of cafés, bars, restaurants, and nightclubs lined up along the few blocks west from Front Street; there are also many good book, record, and clothing **shops** for browsing by day or night.

Eating

Eating out in Philadelphia is a real treat: the ubiquitous street stands sell **soft pretzels** with mustard for 50¢, Chinatown and the Italian Market are good for ethnic food, while Reading Terminal Market offers bargain lunches of various cuisines in Center City. South Street has plenty of good, if well-touristed, eateries, while pricier, trendier restaurants cluster along S 2nd Street in the Old City. The South Philly **cheesesteak**, a hot sandwich of wafer-thin roast beef topped with melted cheese (aka Cheez Whiz), varies from place to place around town; some of the best are to be found around 9th and Passyunk in South Philadelphia (see *Pat's*, below).

Amada 217 Chestnut St ⓣ215/625-2450. A dash of Spanish inspiration in Old City, with over 60 tapas dishes, great paella, and fine red or white sangria, all at reasonable prices.

Bistro Romano 120 Lombard St ⓣ215/925-8880. Quality Italian food is served in a converted 18th-century granary, with authentic pastas and other dishes costing under $20. There is a piano bar on Fri & Sat evenings.

Buddakan 325 Chestnut St ⓣ215/574-9440. Delicious pan-Asian fusion food and a family atmosphere make this a firm Philly favorite. Admire the 10ft gilded Buddha while dining.

City Tavern 138 S 2nd St ⓣ215/413-1443. Reconstructed 1773 tavern in INHP, familiar to the city's founders, and called by John Adams "the most genteel tavern in America." Chef Walter Staib cooks and costumed staff serve "olde style" food (pasties, turkey rarebit) to a harpsichord accompaniment – dinner entrees are mostly $20 and up.

London Grill 2301 Fairmount Ave ⓣ215/978-4545. This sophisticated establishment in the museum district serves delicious American and European cuisine at fair prices, with dishes such as duck confit going for $17.

Ocean City 234-6 N 9th St ⓣ215/829-0688. Huge Chinatown space specialising in fresh seafood, which is on display in tanks; also excellent dim sum before 3pm.

Pat's King of Steaks 1237 E Passyunk Ave ⓣ215/468-1546. At this delightfully decrepit, outdoor-seating-only cheesesteak joint, take care to order correctly (there's a sign to help "rookies") or prepare yourself to be sent to the back of the line. The cheesesteaks here are the real deal. Open 24hr.

Rangoon 112 N 9th St Ⓣ215/829-8939. Friendly and intimate Burmese joint, serving an authentic selection of curries and rice and noodle dishes at around $10–12; try the cheap lunch specials.
San Carlo 214 South St Ⓣ215/592-9777. Excellent fresh pasta dishes, nice atmosphere, and attentive – if pushy – service at reasonable prices.
South Street Diner 140 South St Ⓣ215/627-5258. Huge menu with great three-course dinner specials from $7.50. Open 24hr.
Tre Scalini 1533 S 11th St Ⓣ215/551-3870. A taste of traditional South Philly Italian, with reasonably priced dishes and a low-key atmosphere.
White Dog Café 3420 Sansom St Ⓣ215/386-9224. Delicious, creative food in three Victorian brownstones near the universities. Artsy, student crowd; lunch entrees $11–13, dinner double that; happy hour Sun–Thurs 10pm–midnight.

Drinking

The most popular place for bar-hopping is **South Street** and around **2nd Street** in the Old City, although the **Northern Liberties** area, about eight blocks north, beyond the flyovers, is rapidly up-and-coming for trendy bars and clubs. Local brews are popular and inexpensive; try any ale by Yards or Yuengling if you prefer lager. Philly's growing number of **cafés** are spread around the city; South Street, 2nd Street, and Center City have the densest concentrations.

The Artful Dodger 400 S 2nd St Ⓣ215/922-1790. Lively bar that gets livelier late on, especially if the 2008 world champion Phillies are playing baseball on TV. Reasonable ales and music too.
Dark Horse 421 S 2nd St Ⓣ215/928-9307. Unpretentious British-style boozer with a fine range of beer and the added bonus of soccer on TV for visitors from the old continent.
Dirty Frank's 347 S 13th St Ⓣ215/732-5010. Popular with a very mixed crowd, this Philly institution touts itself as "one of the few places in the world where you can drink a $2.50 pint of Yuengling underneath oil paintings by nationally recognized artists."
Lounge 125 125 S 2nd St Ⓣ215/351-9026. Lively nightclub that features dance and trance music that packs in the college crowd most nights. ID required.
The Mean Bean Co. 1112 Locust St Ⓣ215/925-2010. Coffeeshop serving a mixed gay and straight crowd, with outdoor seating next to the lovely Sartain St private community garden.
Skinner's Dry Goods 226 Market St Ⓣ215/922-0522. Friendly Old City bar with decent ale, good music, and screens to keep an eye on important sports events.
Sugar Mom's Church Street Lounge 225 Church St Ⓣ215/925-8219. Popular basement bar where the jukebox ranges from Tony Bennett to Sonic Youth, with a dozen international beers on tap.

Live music and entertainment

Few reminders are left of the 1970s "Sound of Philadelphia." Instead, in recent times the city has produced the likes of pop starlet Pink, while its active underground scene features psych bands like Bardo Pond and The Asteroid #4. Philadelphia is a good place to see rock bands, as most of the names that play New York perform here for half the price. The world-famous **Philadelphia Orchestra** performs at the smart modern Kimmel Center for the Performing Arts (Ⓣ215/893-1999, Ⓦwww.kimmelcenter.org). Philadelphia's other great strength is its **theater** scene, where small venues abound. Check the **listings** in the free *City Paper* (Ⓦwww.citypaper.net) or *Philadelphia Weekly* (Ⓦwww.philadelphiaweekly.com) newspapers, or visit the Theatre Alliance website at Ⓦwww.theatrealliance.org, which features the StageTix discount ticket program.

The Khyber 56 S 2nd St Ⓣ215/238-5888, Ⓦwww.thekhyber.com. Small rock venue with a gargoyle-lined bar, bluesy jukebox, and casual young clientele. Cover is mostly $8–10 when bands are on. A bar with no cover is upstairs.
Painted Bride Art Center 230 Vine St Ⓣ215/925-9914, Ⓦwww.paintedbride.org. Art gallery with live jazz, dance, and theater performances after dark.

Theater of Living Arts 334 South St ⓣ215/922-1011, ⓦwww.thetla.com. Converted movie palace that's one of the best places to catch mid-size rock bands.

Tin Angel 20 S 2nd St ⓣ215/928-0770, ⓦwww.tinangel.com. Intimate upstairs bar and coffeehouse, featuring top local and nationally known folk, jazz, blues and acoustic acts.

Trocadero 1003 Arch St ⓣ215/922-5483, ⓦwww.thetroc.com. Trendy downtown music venue, sometimes featuring big-name alternative bands. Cover varies, and ID is essential.

Zanzibar Blue 200 S Broad St in the *Bellevue Hotel* ⓣ215/732-4500, ⓦwww.zanzibarblue.com. Classy restaurant and club with contemporary New York–style jazz nightly, often by famous names; expect a hefty cover charge and two-drink minimum.

Central Pennsylvania

Central Pennsylvania, cut north to south by the broad **Susquehanna River**, has no major cities – though the state capital, **Harrisburg**, is an excellent base from which to explore sights that include the **Hershey** chocolate empire and the rolling Amish farmlands of **Lancaster County** to the east, and the Civil War site of **Gettysburg** on the state's southern border. To the north, lie some mighty forests around Williamsport but the further back east you go leads into the industrial mediocrity of towns like Scranton, whose dullness got it chosen as the setting for the US version of *The Office*.

Lancaster County: Pennsylvania Dutch Country

Lancaster County, fifty miles west of Philadelphia, stretches for about 45 miles from Churchtown in the east to the Susquehanna River in the west. Although tiny, uncosmopolitan Lancaster City, ten miles east of the river, was US capital for a day in September 1777, the region is famed more for its preponderance of agricultural religious communities, known collectively as the **Pennsylvania Dutch**. They actually have no connection to the Netherlands; the name is a mistaken derivation of Deutsch (German). A touristy place even before it was brought to international fame by the movie *Witness*, most of Lancaster County has maintained its natural beauty in the face of encroaching commercialization. It is a region of gentle countryside and fertile farmlands, eccentric-sounding place names such as **Intercourse**, horse-drawn buggies, tiny roadside bakeries crammed with jams and pies, and Amish children wending their way between immaculate, flower-filled farmhouses and one-room schoolhouses. Tragically, the innocence of this idyll was shattered on October 2, 2006, when a non-Amish gunman entered a schoolhouse in **Nickel Mines** and shot ten girls, killing half of them.

Indeed, attempting to live a simple life away from the pressures of the outside world has proved too much for many Pennsylvania Dutch. A few (mainly Mennonites) have succumbed to commercial need by offering rides in their buggies and meals in their homes, while members of the stricter orders have moved away to communities in less touristed Ohio, Indiana, Minnesota, and Iowa. When visiting, remember that Sunday is a day of rest for the Amish, so many attractions, restaurants, and other amenities will be closed.

Arrival, information, and getting around

The best route through the concentrated Amish communities is US-30, which runs east–west. **Amtrak** arrives at the train station at 53 McGovern Ave, Lancaster City, as do buses from Capital Trailways (ⓣ717/397-4861) and Greyhound. The

▲ Amish bakery

bustling **Pennsylvania Dutch Convention and Visitors Bureau**, just off US-30 at 501 Greenfield Rd (daily 8.30am–5pm, until 6pm in summer; ⓣ717/299-8901 or 1-800/723-8824, ⓦwww.padutchcountry.com), does an excellent job of providing orientation and advice on accommodation. Visitors keen to learn about Pennsylvania Dutch culture should head to the **Mennonite Information Center** (April–Oct Mon–Sat 8am–5pm; Nov–March Mon–Sat 8.30am–4.30pm; ⓣ717/299-0954 or 1-800/858-8320, ⓦwww.mennoniteinfoctr.com), off US-30 at 2209 Millstream Rd, which shows a short film entitled *Who Are the Amish?* and also organizes lodging with Mennonite families. If you call at least two hours ahead, a guide can take you on a two-hour, $44 tour in your car.

Although a **car** will get you to the quieter back roads that the tour buses miss, it's more fun to ride a **bike**, which gives the benefits of all that fresh air and shows more consideration for the ubiquitous horse-drawn buggies. For self-guided **bike tours**, contact Lancaster Bicycle Club in Lancaster City (ⓦwww.lancasterbikeclub.org). The Amish Experience, on US-30 at Plain & Fancy Farm (ⓣ717/768-3600 ext 210, ⓦwww.amishexperience.com), operates, among various attractions, two-hour **bus tours** (Mon–Sat 10.30am & 1.45pm, Sun 11.30am only) for $28.95, though some accommodations (see the *Village Inn*, p.155) offer a similar service for free. AAA Buggy Rides offer lolloping three-mile countryside excursions for $10 (ⓣ717/989-2829, ⓦwww.aaabuggyrides.com) from the *Kitchen Kettle Village* in Intercourse.

Accommodation

Accommodation options in Pennsylvania Dutch Country range from reasonably priced **hotels** and **B&Bs**, which can be arranged through a central agency (ⓣ1-800/552-2632, ⓦwww.authenticbandb.com), to **farm vacations** (ask at the visitors bureau; see above) to **campgrounds**. *White Oak Campground*, 372 White Oak Rd, Quarryville, four miles north of Strasburg (ⓣ717/687-6207, ⓦwww.whiteoak-campground.com; sites from $24), overlooks the heart of the Dutch farmlands.

The Pennsylvania Dutch

The people now known as the Pennsylvania Dutch originated as **Anabaptists** in sixteenth-century Switzerland, under the leadership of Menno Simons. His unorthodox advocacy of adult baptism and literal interpretation of the Bible led to the order's persecution; they were invited by William Penn to settle in Lancaster County in the 1720s. Today the twenty or so orders of Pennsylvania Dutch include the "plain" Old Order **Amish** (a strict order that originally broke away from Simons in 1693) and freer-living **Mennonites**, as well as the "fancy" **Lutheran** groups (distinguished by the colorful circular "hex" signs on their barns). Living by an unwritten set of rules called Amish Ordnung, which includes absolute pacifism, the Amish are the strictest and best-known: the men with their wide-brimmed straw hats and beards (but no "military" mustaches), the women in bonnets, plain dresses (with no fripperies like buttons), and aprons. Shunning electricity and any exposure to the corrupting influence of the outside world, the Amish power their farms with generators, and travel (at roughly ten miles per hour) in handmade horse-drawn buggies. For all their insularity, the Amish are very friendly and helpful; resist the temptation to photograph them, however, as the making of "graven images" offends their beliefs.

Cameron Estate Inn & Restaurant 1855 Mansion Lane, Mount Joy ⓣ717/492-0111 or 1-800/422-6376, ⓦwww.cameronestateinn.com. Out-of-the-way gay-friendly inn on fifteen acres with sparkling, comfortable rooms (one with jacuzzi), free full breakfast and a restaurant. ❺

Countryside Motel 134 Hartman Bridge Rd, Ronks ⓣ717/687-8431. Clean and simple place six miles east of Lancaster City on Hwy-896. ❸

Historic Strasburg Inn 1400 Historic Drive, Strasburg ⓣ717/687-7691 or 1-800/872-0201, ⓦwww.historicinnofstrasburg.com. Over a hundred luxury rooms, plus a hot tub and a sauna, tucked away on sixty rolling acres. Great value. ❹

O'Flaherty's Dingeldein House 1105 E King St, Lancaster City ⓣ717/293-1723 or 1-800/779-7765, ⓦwww.dingeldeinhouse.com. Friendly rustic eight-room B&B. Rates include a large country breakfast. ❹

Village Inn & Suites 2695 Old Philadelphia Pike, Bird-in-Hand ⓣ1-800/665-8780, ⓦwww.bird-in-hand.com/villageinn. Excellent old inn with modern amenities, large breakfast, deck, lawn, and back pasture. Price includes 2hr tour of Amish Country and use of the adjacent motel's pool. Book ahead. ❹

Touring Pennsylvania Dutch Country

Though useful for a general overview and historical insight, the attractions that interpret Amish culture tend toward overkill. It's far more satisfying just to explore the countryside for yourself. Here, among the streams with their covered bridges and fields striped with corn, alfalfa, and tobacco, the reality hits you – these aren't actors recreating an ancient lifestyle, but real people, part of a living, working community. On Sunday, for example, commercial actibities are suspended but you may see a large gathering of buggies outside one of the farms, indicating an Amish church service (in High German) or a "visiting day." Such social gatherings sometimes take place on weekdays too.

Among the widely spread formal attractions, the **Ephrata Cloister**, 632 W Main St, **Ephrata** (on US-272 and 322), recreates the eighteenth-century settlement of German Protestant celibates that acted, amongst other things, as an early publishing and printing center (Mon–Sat 9am–5pm, Sun noon–5pm, Jan & Feb closed Mon; $7; ⓣ717/733-6600, ⓦwww.ephratacloister.org). Further south, about three miles northeast of Lancaster City, the **Landis Valley Museum**, 2451 Kissell Hill Rd (Tues–Sat 9am–5pm, Sun noon–5pm; $10; ⓣ717/569-0401, ⓦwww.landisvalleymuseum.org), is a living history museum of rural life, with demonstrations of local crafts. At **Strasburg**, a mixture of tourist kitsch and historical authenticity southeast of Lancaster City on US-896, the **Strasburg Railroad** (daily, hours and tours vary; from $12, kids $6; ⓣ717/687-7522, ⓦwww.strasburgrailroad.com) offers round-trip rides in original steam train **Paradise**, which, dissappointingly, holds no heavenly delights, although there are good views of the patchwork farmland on the way. The oldest building in the county, the **Hans Herr House**, 1849 Hans Herr Drive, five miles south of downtown Lancaster City off US-222 (April–Nov Mon–Sat 9am–4pm; $5; ⓣ717/464-4438, ⓦwww.hansherr.org), is a 1719 Mennonite church with a pretty garden and orchard, a medieval German facade, and exhibits on early farm life.

Eating, drinking, and entertainment

Lancaster County **food** is delicious, Germanic, and served in vast quantities. There are no Amish-owned restaurants, but Amish roadside stalls sell fresh home-made root beer, jams, pickles, breads, and pies. The huge "all-you-care-to-eat" **tourist restaurants** on US-30 and US-340 may look off-putting, all pseudo-rusticism with costumed waitresses, but most serve good meals, for under $20, "family-style" – you share long tables with other out-of-towners. Typical fare includes fried chicken, hickory-smoked ham, *schnitz und knepp* (apple, ham, and dumpling stew), sauerkraut, pickles, cottage cheese and apple butter, shoo-fly pie, and the like. None stays open later than 8pm, though a few regular **diners** in busier areas do open later. Rural Lancaster County is, unsurprisingly, not known for its nightlife – though there are a couple of very friendly **bars** in downtown Lancaster City worth checking out. The Fulton Opera House, 12 N Prince St (ⓣ717/394-7133, ⓦwww.fultontheatre.org), is a plush red-and-gold restored Victorian **theater**, hosting dance, plays, and special events.

Central Market Penn Square, Lancaster City. Covered market selling fresh local farm produce and lunch to loyal Lancastrians and tourists alike. Tues & Fri 6am–4pm, Sat 6am–2pm.

Good 'n' Plenty East Brook Rd, US-896, Smoketown ⓣ717/394-7111. Not Amish-owned, though Amish women cook and serve food in this, the best of the family-style restaurants. Open early Feb to mid-Dec Mon–Sat.

Lancaster Brewing Co. 302 N Plum St, Lancaster City ⓣ717/391-6258, ⓦwww.lancasterbrewing.com. Brewpub serving good bar food and five different microbrews. Tours given Fri & Sat by appointment. Open daily.

Lancaster Dispensing Co. 33-35 N Market St, Lancaster City ⓣ717/299-4602. Downtown Lancaster's trendiest, friendliest bar, with live weekend jazz and blues, plus overstuffed sandwiches for around $7.

Lapp's 2270 Lincoln Hwy E (US-30), near Lancaster City ⓣ717/394-1606. A solid diner with family atmosphere and ample Germanic food typical of Lancaster County; open daily.

Molly's Pub 253 E Chestnut St, Lancaster City ⓣ717/396-0225. Neighborhood bar with lively atmosphere and good burgers. Closed Sun.

Plain and Fancy 3121 Old Philadelphia Pike (Rte-340), Bird-in-Hand ⓣ717/768-4400. Standard family-style restaurant; only one in the area open on Sun.

Harrisburg and Hershey

HARRISBURG, Pennsylvania's capital, lies on the Susquehanna River thirty or so miles northwest of Lancaster City. It's a surprisingly attractive small city, its lush waterfront lined with shuttered colonial buildings, and is well-complemented by its kitschy Chocolatetown neighbor **Hershey**. Harrisburg is also known as the site of the **Three Mile Island** nuclear facility, which suffered a famous meltdown in the 1970s and stands along the river on the east side of town.

The ornate, attractive Italian Renaissance **capitol** at Third and State streets has a dome modeled after St Peter's in Rome (tours Mon–Fri 8.30am–4pm; Sat, Sun & holidays at 9am, 11am, 1pm, & 3pm; free; ⓣ1-800/868-7672, ⓦwww.thecapitol.com). The complex includes the four-floor **State Museum of Pennsylvania** at

Third and North (Tues–Sat 9am–5pm, Sun noon–5pm; free; ⓣ717/787-4980, ⓦwww.statemuseumpa.org), a cylindrical building that holds a planetarium (Sat & Sun only), archeological and military artifacts, decorative arts, tools and machinery. Undoubtedly the real attraction is the excellent **National Civil War Museum**, roughly two miles east of downtown at the summit of hilly Reservoir Park (Mon–Sat 9am–5pm, Sun noon–5pm; closed Mon & Tues Sept to March; $8; ⓣ717/260-1861 or 1-866/258-4729, ⓦwww.nationalcivilwarmuseum.org), with fine city views. Almost 730,000 Americans were killed in the Civil War – more than in all other conflicts since the Revolution combined – and the museum offers an intelligent analysis of the reasons for, and results of, the war. Especially evocative are the fictionalized monologues, playing on video screens in every gallery, which focus on the human cost of the conflict.

HERSHEY, ten miles east, was built in 1903 by candy magnate Milton S. Hershey for his chocolate factory – so it has streets named Chocolate and Cocoa avenues and streetlamps in the shape of Hershey's Chocolate Kisses. **Hershey's Chocolate World** (daily 9am–5pm, later in summer months; ⓣ717/534-4900, ⓦwww.hersheyschocolateworld.com) offers a free mini-train ride through a romanticized simulated chocolate factory, a 3D chocolate show ($5.95), and a cheesy musical/historical trolley ride around town ($10.75). Nearby **Hersheypark** (mid-May to Sept, hours vary; $43.95; ⓣ717/534-3090 or 1-800/437-7439, ⓦwww.hersheypark.com) is a hugely popular amusement park, with stomach-churning roller coasters and various other rides; cheaper special events take place for Halloween and Christmas. The adjacent **Hershey Museum** (daily 9am–5pm, later in summer months; $10; ⓣ717/534-3439, ⓦwww.hersheymuseum.org) has exhibits on the Pennsylvania Dutch and tells the Milton S. Hershey story.

Practicalities

Amtrak **trains** share the central station at Fourth and Chestnut streets with Greyhound, whose **buses** also stop in Hershey at 337 W Chocolate St. Harrisburg's **visitor center** (ⓣ717/231-7788, ⓦwww.visithhc.com) is not open to walk-ins, but can be contacted for good local and regional information. In leafy Camp Hill, just across the river from Harrisburg, the *Radisson Penn Harris* (ⓣ717/763-7117, ⓦwww.radisson.com; ④) has good-value rooms in relaxing surroundings. Options in Hershey include the standard *Spinners Inn*, 845 E Chocolate Ave (ⓣ717/533-9157, ⓦwww.spinnersinn.com; ④), which has a very good restaurant, while luxury lodging is available at the palatial *Hotel Hershey*, Hotel Road (ⓣ717/533-2171, ⓦwww.thehotelhershey.com; ⑨), complete with an on-site spa offering chocolate-based beauty treatments. The best **campsite** in the region is *Hershey Highmeadow Campground*, 1200 Matlack Rd, Hummellstown, on the Harrisburg side of Hershey (ⓣ717/534-8999 or 1-800/437-7439, ⓦwww.hersheycamping.com), which has sites from $27.50 off-season to $38 in summer. Budget **restaurants** line Second Street in downtown Harrisburg, the best being *Fisaga's*, at Locust and N Second streets (ⓣ717/441-1556), which serves good basic sandwiches and pasta. *Scott's*, 212 Locust St (ⓣ717/234-7599), is a popular bar and grill, with live music some nights.

Gettysburg

The small town of **GETTYSBURG**, thirty miles south of Harrisburg near the Maryland border, gained tragic notoriety in July 1863 for the cataclysmic **Civil War** battle in which fifty thousand men died. There were more casualties during these three days than in any American battle before or since – a full third of those who fought were killed or wounded – and entire regiments were wiped out when the tide finally turned against the South.

Four months later, on November 19, Abraham Lincoln delivered his **Gettysburg Address** at the dedication of the National Cemetery. His two-minute speech, in memory of all the soldiers who died, is acknowledged as one of the most powerful orations in American history. Gettysburg, by far the most baldly commercialized of all the Civil War sites, is overwhelmingly geared toward **tourism**, relentlessly replaying the most minute details of the battle. Fortunately, it is perfectly feasible to avoid the crowds and commercial overkill and explore for yourself the rolling hills of the battlefield (now a national park) and the tidy town streets with their shuttered historic houses. The town's largely old-fashioned museums, however, are mostly quite missable.

Information and getting around

Gettysburg **CVB**, 102 Carlisle St (daily 8.30am–5pm; ⓣ717/334-6274, ⓦwww.gettysburg.travel), is housed next door to the tiny historic train depot where Lincoln disembarked in November 1863 and should be the first stop on any visit. Though the town is compact and easy to walk around, there is no public transportation, and a car helps when touring the huge battlefield. Two-hour double decker **Battlefield Bus Tours**, running through the town and making numerous stops, depart from 778 Baltimore St (up to eight tours daily; $22.95 for audio, $25.95 for live guide; ⓣ717/334-6296, ⓦwww.gettysburgbattlefieldtours.com).

Accommodation

There is plenty of lodging in and around Gettysburg, including many **B&Bs**. The most central place to **camp** is at *Artillery Ridge Resort*, 610 Taneytown Rd (ⓣ717/334-1288, ⓦwww.artilleryridge.com; sites from $29.50; open April–Oct).

Baladerry Inn 40 Hospital Rd ⓣ717/337-1342, ⓦwww.baladerryinn.com. Historic hospital turned B&B, with nine en-suite rooms. ❻

Doubleday Inn 104 Doubleday Ave ⓣ717/334-9119, ⓦwww.doubledayinn.com. A memorabilia-packed luxury B&B, and the only one within the battlefield itself. ❺

Gettysburg Travelodge 613 Baltimore St ⓣ717/334-9281, ⓦwww.travelodge.com. Standard motel between downtown and the battlefield. ❹

HI-Gardners 1212 Pine Grove Rd, Gardners ⓣ717/486-7575, ⓦwww.hiayh.org. Located on the Appalachian Trail in remote Pine Grove Furnace State Park, over 20 miles away. Busiest during ski season. Beds from $15.

Historic Farnsworth House Inn 401 Baltimore St ⓣ717/334-8838, ⓦwww.farnsworthhouseinn.com. An 1810 townhouse, used as Union HQ in the war and still riddled with bullet holes. Includes 10 rooms, a tavern, and a theater. ❺

The battleground

It takes most of a day to see the 3500-acre **Gettysburg National Military Park**, which surrounds the town (daily 6am–10pm; free; ⓦwww.nps.gov/gett). The stunning new **visitor center**, just over a mile south of downtown at 1175 Baltimore Pike (daily: summer 8am–7pm, rest of year 8am–6pm; ⓣ717/334-1124) now rivals Harrisburg's (see p.156) as the best Civil War **museum** in the state, possibly the country. It is beautifully designed, with tons of memorabilia such as photos, guns, uniforms, surgical and musical instruments, tents and flags, as well as exhaustive written information. Five repeating ten-minute videos, insterspersed throughout the chronological sequence of the museum, chronicle the early part of the war, the three days of the battle, and the war's conclusion. The star exhibit is the moving **Cyclorama**, a 356ft circular painting of Pickett's Charge, the suicidal Confederate thrust across open wheatfields in broad daylight. This is also the place to pick up details of a self-guided **driving route**, or a **guide** will join you in your car for a personalized two-hour tour ($55).

Not far from the visitor center, the **Gettysburg National Cemetery** contains thousands of graves arranged in a semicircle around the Soldiers' National Monument, on the site where Lincoln gave the Gettysburg Address. Most stirring of all are the hundreds of small marble gravestones marked only with numbers. A short walk away, the battlegrounds themselves, golden fields reminiscent of an English country landscape, are peaceful now except for their names: **Valley of Death**, **Bloody Run**, **Cemetery Hill**. Uncanny statues of key figures stand at appropriate points, while heavy stone monuments honor different regiments.

Other attractions

The one sight worth a peek in town, at 528 Baltimore Street, is the **Jennie Wade House** (daily: June–Aug 9am–9pm, Sept 9am–7pm, Oct, Nov & March–May 9am–5pm; $7.95; ⓣ717/334-4100), the former home of the only civilian to die in the battle; Wade was killed by a stray bullet as she made bread for the Union troops in her sister's kitchen. Today, the residence looks more or less as it did on July 3, 1863, with bullet holes in the front door and on the bedpost, an artillery shell hole ripped through a wall, and a macabre model of Jennie's corpse lying under a sheet in the cellar. To the west of the park, President Eisenhower, who retired to Gettysburg, is commemorated at the **Eisenhower National Historic Site** (daily 9am–4pm; $6.50; ⓣ717/338-9114, ⓦwww.nps.gov/eise), where his Georgian-style mansion holds an array of memorabilia. The site is accessible only on shuttle-bus tours from the National Park Visitor Center (see p.158).

Eating and entertainment

Evenings in Gettysburg tend to be quiet once the tour buses have gone home. However, there are some good **restaurants**, many in historically important buildings.

Blue Parrot Bistro 35 Chambersburg St ⓣ717/337-3739. Pasta and steaks with a good choice of sauces. Like most restaurants in town, things wind down soon after 8.30pm.

Dobbin House Tavern 89 Steinwehr Ave ⓣ717/334-2100. The oldest house in the city, dating from 1776 and once a hideout for former slaves on the Underground Railroad. Lunch from around $10; candlelit dinners are more expensive. Food veers between Pennsylvania Dutch, early American, and contemporary.

Gettysbrew Restaurant & Brewery 248 Hunterstown Rd ⓣ717/337-1001. Also a pub and historic site. Brews five beers, plus its own root beer and soda.

Mayflowers 533 Steinwehr Ave ⓣ717/337-3377. Huge modern Chinese restaurant that does a high-quality evening buffet for $9.99 and à la carte sushi.

Western Pennsylvania

Western Pennsylvania, a key point for frontier trade and an important thoroughfare to the West, was the focus of the fighting between the English and the French in the seven-year French and Indian War for colonial and maritime power (1756–63). This region grew to industrial prominence in the nineteenth century, with the exploitation of its coal resources gathering pace after the Civil War, and the opening of the world's first oil well at Titusville (now Drake Well Memorial Park) in northwestern Pennsylvania in 1859.

Today, tourism in western Pennsylvania is concentrated around the surprisingly appealing city of **Pittsburgh**. To the south of the city, the **Laurel Highlands** features Frank Lloyd Wright's not-to-be-missed architectural masterpiece, **Fallingwater**, as well as nearby **Ohiopyle State Park**. In the overwhelming rural northwest corner of the state, another great wilderness area to explore is the lush **Allegheny National Forest**, which begins twenty miles north of I-80. The region's only major conurbation, **Erie**, is located on the eponymous great lake and includes **Presque Isle State Park**, well worth a visit for its sandy lake beaches and wooded hiking trails.

Pittsburgh

The appealing ten-block district known as the **Golden Triangle**, at the heart of downtown **PITTSBURGH**, stands at the confluence of the Monongahela, Allegheny, and Ohio rivers; this area was once bitterly fought over as the gateway to the West. The French built Fort Duquesne on the site in 1754, only for it to be destroyed four years later by the British, who replaced it with **Fort Pitt**. Industry began with the development of iron foundries in the early 1800s, and by the time of the Civil War, Pittsburgh was producing half of the iron and one third of the glass in the US. Soon after, the city became the world's leading producer of steel, thanks to the vigorous expansion programs of **Andrew Carnegie**, who by 1870 was the richest man in the world. Present-day Pittsburgh is dotted with his cultural bequests, along with those of other wealthy forefathers, including the Mellon bankers, the Frick coal merchants, and the Heinz food producers.

The city has gradually ditched its Victorian reputation for dirt and pollution since its transformation began in the 1960s and has now established itself as one of America's most attractive and most liveable cities, a destination to be reckoned with. The face-lift involved large-scale demolition of abandoned steel mills, which freed up much of the downtown waterfront to make way for sleek skyscapers and green spaces. That said, all-out sanitization has been kept in check by the student population, the small-town feel of the older areas to the north and south, and the effects of economic downturn. Each of Pittsburgh's close-knit neighborhoods – the **South Side** and **Mount Washington**, across the Monongahela River from the Golden Triangle, the **North Side** across the Allegheny River, and the **East End**, especially the university area of **Oakland** – has an individual feel and attests in its own way to the city's history and its resurgence.

Arrival, information, and getting around

Greyhound pulls in beside the Monongahela River at 990 2nd Ave, a good fifteen-minute walk from downtown, whereas the Amtrak station is far more central, at 1100 Liberty Ave. From the modern, efficient **Pittsburgh International Airport**, fifteen miles west (Ⓣ412/472-3525, Ⓦwww.pitairport.com), several shuttle services run to Pittsburgh. Almost as quick, more frequent, and significantly cheaper, the excellent PAT bus #28X runs roughly every twenty minutes between the airport and twelve Pittsburgh stops, including downtown, Oakland, and the universities (daily 5am–midnight; $2.25).

Pittsburgh's main **Welcome Center** is downtown on Liberty Avenue, adjacent to the Gateway Center (Mon–Fri 8am–4pm, Sat 9am–5pm, Sun 10am–3pm; Ⓣ412/281-7711 or 1-800/366-0093, Ⓦwww.visitpittsburgh.com), with subsidiary branches at the airport and at the Senator John Heinz Pittsburgh Regional History Center.

Though Pittsburgh is a city of distinct districts, **transportation** between them is simple. **Buses** through town (free–$2.75), the Monongahela and Duquesne Heights trolley inclines ($1.75), and a small "T" **subway** system (free downtown; further out the fare runs up to $3.25 at rush hour) are all excellent transportation options; **PAT**, the area transit authority (Ⓣ412/442-2000, Ⓦwww.portauthority.org), has a downtown service center at 534 Smithfield St (Mon–Thurs 7.30am–5.30pm, Fri 7.30am–5pm), where you can pick up timetables. Fifty-cent transfers, which must be bought simultaneously with your fare if needed, allow

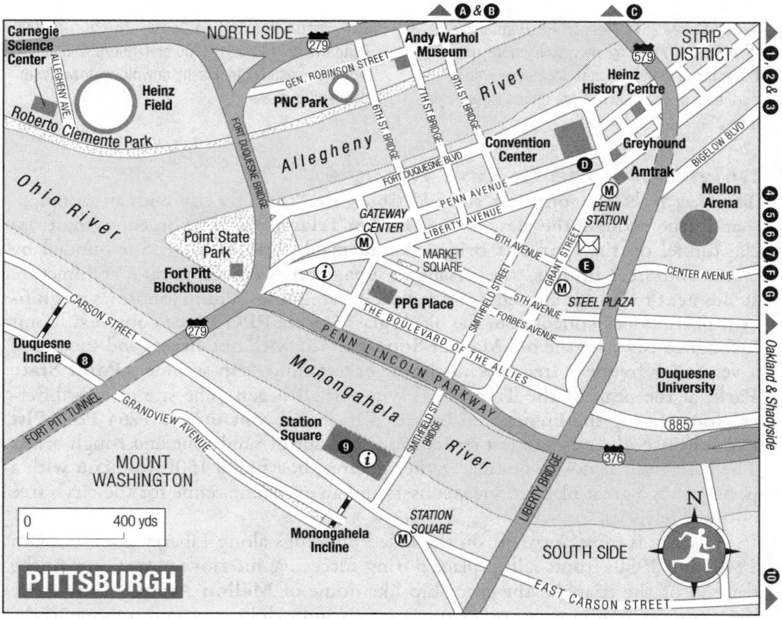

ACCOMMODATION				RESTAURANTS			
Doubletree Hotel Pittsburgh City Center	E	The Inn on Negley	F	The Church Brew Works	3	Kaya	1
Hampton Inn University Center	G	The Priory–A City Inn	A	Grand Concourse	9	La Feria	5
The Inn on the Mexican War Streets	B	Valley Motel	C	Grandview Saloon	8	Mallorca	10
		The Westin Convention Center Pittsburgh	D	Gullifty's	4	Thai Gourmet	2
				India Garden	6	Yumwok/Lulu's Noodles	7

you to connect with any of the system's vehicles within three hours. For **taxis**, call Yellow Cab (Ⓣ412/665-8100).

Accommodation

Pittsburgh's **hotels** and few **B&Bs** are generally pricey, although weekend packages at luxury downtown hotels can bring rates down to not too much above $100. **Oakland** has a couple of reasonably priced business hotels, and you can check out all of the Pittsburgh area's B&Bs at Ⓦwww.pittsburghbnb.com.

Doubletree Hotel Pittsburgh City Center One Bigelow Square Ⓣ412/281-5800, 1-800/225-5858, Ⓦwww.doubletree.hilton.com. Convenient downtown highrise chain hotel offering suites with kitchens; look for advance internet rates. ❽

Hampton Inn University Center 3315 Hamlet St Ⓣ412/681-1000 or 1-800/426-7866, Ⓦwww.hamptoninn.com. Welcoming branch of chain in Oakland offering a generous self-service continental breakfast bar, plus free shuttle to downtown and surrounding areas. ❺

The Inn on Negley 703 S Negley Ave, Shadyside Ⓣ412/661-0631, Ⓦwww.theinnsonnegley.com. Friendly, upmarket establishment with eight elegantly furnished rooms and suites, several with jacuzzi. As well as the complimentary gourmet breakfasts, quality teas and sweets are served noon–4pm. ❼

The Inn on the Mexican War Streets 604 W North Ave Ⓣ412/231-6544, Ⓦwww.innonthemexicanwarstreets.com. Eight tastefully refurbished rooms in one of the North Side's trendiest areas. The less expensive rooms are great value. ❻

The Priory–A City Inn 614 Pressley St Ⓣ412/231-3338, Ⓦwww.thepriory.com. Restored 1880s inn, originally built to house traveling Benedictine monks; now, it's the North Side's nicest B&B. Room rates include continental breakfast, evening wine, weekday limo service, and use of fitness room. ❻

Valley Motel 2571 Freeport Rd, Harmarville ⓣ412/828-7100, ⓦwww.valleymotel.net. Basic motel with low rates, located eleven miles northeast of downtown. A fair option if you have a car. ❷

The Westin Convention Center Pittsburgh 1000 Penn Ave ⓣ412/281-3700 or 1-800/937-8461, ⓦwww.westin.com. Flashy downtown tower with pool and gym. ❼

Downtown: the Golden Triangle

The *New York Times* once described Pittsburgh as "the only city with an entrance" – and, true enough, the view of the **Golden Triangle** skyline on emerging from the tunnel on the Fort Pitt Bridge is undeniably breathtaking. Surrounded by water and steel bridges, the Triangle's imaginative contemporary architecture stands next to Gothic churches and redbrick warehouses. Philip Johnson's magnificent postmodern concoction, the black-glass Gothic **PPG Place** complex, looms incongruously over the old **Market Square**, lined with restaurants and shops and a venue for frequent free live lunchtime entertainment in summer. **Point State Park**, at the peak of the Triangle, is where it all began. The site of five different forts during the French and Indian War, it still contains the 1764 **Fort Pitt Blockhouse**, the city's oldest structure, a lookout of sandstone and rough brick. The park itself is now a popular gathering area, boasting a 150ft fountain with a pool, and is a great place to view sunsets and an excellent venue for the city's free outdoor festivals.

History is most apparent on the faded buildings along Liberty Avenue, with 1940s and 1950s fronts left in place during successive interior renovations. At the flat end of the triangle, the spaceship-like dome of **Mellon Arena** looms above the transport stations – it hosts large concerts and exhibitions, and is home to the **Pittsburgh Penguins** ice hockey team (ⓣ412/642-7367, ⓦwww.pittsburghpenguins.com). Northeast of downtown, along Penn Avenue past the vast new Convention Center, the characterful **Strip District** has a bustling early-morning fresh produce market, as well as bargain shops by day and lively night-time venues. The seven-floor **Senator John Heinz Pittsburgh Regional History Center**, at

▲ The Golden Triangle

1212 Smallman St (daily 10am–5pm; $9; ⓣ412/454-6000, ⓦwww.pghhistory.org), does a good job of telling the city's story, paying particular attention to immigrants of various eras.

The South Side

In the nineteenth century, 400ft **Mount Washington**, across the Monongahela River, was the site of most of the city's coal mines. No longer dominated by belching steel mills and industry, the **South Side**, banked by the green "mountain," is an area of many churches, colorful houses nestled on steep hills, and old neighborhoods. These days, only two survive of the twelve cable cars which, at the height of steel production, used to carry both freight and passengers up the trolley inclines. The 1877 **Duquesne Incline**, from 1197 W Carson St to 1220 Grandview Ave, is a working cable-car system ($1.75 single; ⓣ412/381-1665, ⓦwww.incline.cc) whose upper station contains a small **museum**: old photos show the city blanketed in pitch-black midday smog. The outdoor observation platform, surrounded by mainly expensive bars and restaurants, is a prime spot for **views** over the Golden Triangle to the hills on the horizon, which are especially awesome after dark.

The best way to get to the South Side is across the 1883 blue-and-cream **Smithfield Street Bridge**, the oldest of fifteen downtown bridges and the most unusual-looking, thanks to its elliptical "fisheye" truss. Just to the west of the bridge stands red-brick **Station Square**, a food and shopping complex converted from old railroad warehouses and the beautiful stained glass and marble waiting room of the Pittsburgh and Lake Erie train. In front stands the jetty for the enjoyable hour-long narrated Just Ducky Tours **river cruises** (April–Oct daily, Nov Sat & Sun 10.30am–6pm, earlier in Oct & Nov; $19, kids $15; tours every 90min; ⓣ412/402-3825, ⓦwww.justduckytours.com).

Heading east along the banks of the Monongahela, **East Carson Street** is the main commercial drag of South Side, where a longstanding community of Polish and Ukrainian steelworkers has gradually absorbed an offbeat mix of artsy residents, along with the attendant cafés, bars, and bookstores. Onion-domed churches poke out behind thrift stores and galleries, and the narrow backstreets are lined with brick rowhouses. This is far and away Pittsburgh's most extensive and varied **nightlife** center (see p.166).

The North Side

The star attraction on the **North Side**, annexed by Pittsburgh only in 1907, is undoubtedly the **Andy Warhol Museum**, 117 Sandusky St, just over the Seventh

The guru of pop art

Born in Pittsburgh in 1928, **Andy Warhol** (born Andrew Warhola, the youngest son of working-class Slovakian immigrants) moved to New York City at the age of 21, after graduating from Carnegie-Mellon University. After a decade as a successful commercial artist, by the early 1960s he was leading the vanguard of the new pop art, shooting 16mm films such as *Chelsea Girls*, and by 1967 had developed the "Exploding Plastic Inevitable" multimedia show, featuring erotic dancers and music by The Velvet Underground, whom he managed. After founding *Interview* magazine in 1969, Warhol became transfixed with the rich and famous and, up until his death in 1987, was perhaps best known for his celebrity portraits and his appearances at society events. Ironically, he always disowned his gritty hometown, which didn't fit with NYC cool, and would probably turn in his grave that his main shrine is located back there, as are his mortal remains, in Bethel cemetery.

Street Bridge from downtown (Tues–Sun 10am–5pm, Fri until 10pm; $15, Fri 5–10pm $7.50; ⓣ412/237-8300, ⓦwww.warhol.org). The museum documents the life and work of Pittsburgh's most celebrated son (see box, p.163) over seven floors of a spacious Victorian warehouse; it claims to be the largest museum in the world devoted to a single artist.

Although the majority of Warhol's most famous pieces are in the hands of private collectors, the museum boasts an impressive and ever-changing selection of exhibits, with over five hundred items on display at any one time, including pop art (Campbell's soup cans) and portraiture (Elvis, Marilyn Monroe, Jackie Kennedy). It pays equal attention to archival material, and chronological **self-guided tours** give a good idea of Warhol's artistic development and his eventful lifestyle. At any given time, two or three non-Warhol exhibits show work related in some way to Warhol themes. There's an excellent, informative Archives Study and occasional workshops take place. During "**Good Fridays**" (5–10pm) there is free entrance to the lobby, which has a cash bar, and often buzzes with live bands or other performance arts.

Elsewhere on the North Side, revitalization centers around the intriguingly named **Mexican War Streets**, on the northern edge of Allegheny Commons. In this unevenly restored, tree-lined area of nineteenth-century gray-brick and limestone terraces, old families, descendants of German and Scandinavian immigrants, live in an uneasy truce alongside young professionals. The excellent and highly unusual **Mattress Factory**, 500 Sampsonia Way (Tues–Sat 10am–5pm, Sun 1–5pm, closed Aug; $10, Thurs $5; ⓣ412/231-3169, ⓦwww.mattress.org), has contemporary installations by top mixed-media artists, and is a must on any visit to the city. The **National Aviary**, Allegheny Commons West (daily 9am–5pm; $8; ⓣ412/323-7235, ⓦwww.aviary.org), is a huge indoor bird sanctuary with over two hundred species, including foul-mouthed parrots, fluttering inside a thirty-foot glass dome. Nearby, **The Children's Museum of Pittsburgh**, 10 Children's Way, Allegheny Square (Mon–Sat 10am–5pm, Sun noon–5pm; $10, kids $9, Thurs $6 for all; ⓣ412/322-5058, ⓦwww.pittsburghkids.org), offers a plethora of games, events, and special exhibitions.

Heading northwest along the river, the huge, state-of-the-art **Carnegie Science Center**, 1 Allegheny Ave (daily 10am–5pm, Sat until 7pm; $14, kids $10; ⓣ412/237-3400, ⓦwww.carnegiesciencecenter.org), is also predominantly aimed at children, with, among other exhibits, an interactive engineering play-space, a miniature railroad, and a planetarium. The center contains an impressive OMNIMAX theater ($8–10 for one show, $13–15 for two); various combination tickets are available. Outside by the water, you can visit the **USS Requin** (included in admission), a 1945 submarine. Next door to the Science Center, the gargantuan edifice of **Heinz Field** is home to football's **Pittsburgh Steelers** (ⓣ412/323-1200, ⓦwww.steelers.com), one of only three teams to have won five Superbowls, most recently in 2009. Further along the river toward the Sixth Street Bridge is **PNC Park**, the home of the **Pittsburgh Pirates** baseball team (ⓣ1-800/289-2827, ⓦwww.pirates.com). Beautifully constructed so that from most seats you get a sweeping view of the Allegheny and downtown, it's a real treat to watch a game here on a balmy summer night, even though the team is a laughing stock.

Oakland and the East End

Oakland, Pittsburgh's university area, is totally dominated by the campuses of **Carnegie-Mellon University**, the **University of Pittsburgh** (always known as "Pitt"), and several other colleges. At Fifth Avenue and Bigelow Boulevard, the 42-story, 2529-window Gothic Revival **Cathedral of Learning** is a university building with a difference: among its classrooms the 26 **Nationality Rooms** are furnished with antiques and specially crafted items donated by the city's different ethnic groups, from Lithuanian to Chinese. These can be visited on ninety-minute **guided tours** (Mon–Sat 9am–2.30pm, Sun 11am–2.30pm; $3; ⓣ412/624-6000, www.pitt.edu/~natrooms). On the grounds behind the Cathedral of Learning is the French Gothic **Heinz Memorial Chapel** (Mon–Fri 9am–5pm, Sun 1–5pm; free), notable for its long, narrow, stained-glass windows depicting political, literary, and religious figures.

Across from the cathedral at 4400 Forbes Ave, the **Carnegie** cultural complex holds two great museums – the **Museum of Natural History**, famed for its extensive dinosaur relics and sparkling gems, and the **Museum of Art**, with Impressionist, Post-Impressionist and American regional art, as well as an excellent modern collection (both museums Tues–Sat 10am–5pm, Thurs until 8pm, Sun noon–5pm; $15; ⓣ412/622-3131, ⓦwww.carnegiemuseums.org). Nearby, Schenley Park includes the colorful flower gardens of **Phipps Conservatory** (daily 9.30am–5pm, Fri until 10pm; $10; ⓣ412/622-6814 ⓦwww.phipps.conservatory.org) and wild wooded areas beyond.

The stretch of Fifth Avenue from around the Cathedral of Learning up to **Shadyside** is lined with important and architecturally beautiful academic buildings, places of worship, and the former mansions of the early industrialists. The imposing **Soldiers and Sailors Memorial**, 4141 Fifth Ave (Mon–Sat 10am–4pm; tours $5; ⓣ412/621-4253), also serves as a museum, and is filled with military paraphernalia and historic exhibits. Further on, opposite the exquisite external mural of the Byzantine Catholic **Church of the Holy Spirit**, is the humble broadcasting complex of **WQED**, notable for being the first publicly-funded TV station when it opened in April 1954 and home to the long-running kids' show *Mr Rogers' Neighborhood*. Shadyside itself is an upmarket, trendy neighborhood containing the particularly chic commercial section of Walnut Street. Continuing along Fifth Avenue, the **Pittsburgh Center for the Arts**, at no. 6300, in the corner of Mellon Park, showcases innovative Pittsburgh art in various media (Tues–Sat 10am–5pm, Sun noon–5pm; suggested donation $5; ⓣ412/361-0873, ⓦwww.pittsburgharts.org). A short way to the southeast, **Squirrel Hill** is another lively area, housing a mixture of students and the city's largest Jewish community, with a fine selection of shops and restaurants lining Murray and Forbes avenues.

Further east, the **Frick Art and Historical Center** complex, 7227 Reynolds St (Tues–Sun 10am–5pm; free; ⓣ412/371-0600, ⓦwww.frickart.org) includes the **Frick Art Museum**, which displays Italian, Flemish, and French art from the fifteenth to the nineteenth centuries, as well as two of Marie Antoinette's chairs; the self-explanatory **Car & Carriage Museum**; and the **Clayton mansion** (obligatory guided tours $10) where Frick lived. Frick and family are buried just south of here in **Homewood Cemetery**, which also holds the tombs of H.J. Heinz (of the ketchup and baked beans fortune) and sundry Mellons. Three miles north, bordering the Allegheny River, the green expanse of **Highland Park** contains the nicely landscaped and enjoyable **Pittsburgh Zoo and PPG Aquarium** (daily: summer 9am–6pm, spring & fall 9am–5pm, winter 9am–4pm; April–Nov $12, Dec–March $9; ⓣ412/665-3640, ⓦwww.zoo.pgh.pa.us), which has the distinction of owning a Komodo dragon and having successfully bred two baby elephants.

Eating

Eating in downtown Pittsburgh can prove expensive, and the area is rather deserted at night. It's better to head for the **Strip District** or along and around **East Carson Street** on the South Side. **Station Square** and **Mount Washington**

cater to a more upmarket crowd, while **Oakland** is, as you might expect, home to an array of cheap student hangouts. Also in the East End, **Bloomfield**, **Shadyside** and **Squirrel Hill** all have a number of good inexpensive and mid-priced places.

The Church Brew Works 3525 Liberty Ave ⓣ 412/688-8200. Vast establishment located between downtown and Bloomfield, serving American cuisine and fine ales brewed on-site. Housed in a grand, converted old church where vats have replaced the organ.

Grand Concourse 1 Station Square ⓣ 412/261-1717. Pricey, plush seafood restaurant in a gorgeous setting, where you can feast on delights such as coconut macadamia encrusted shrimp. Expect to pay at least $50 per head.

Grandview Saloon 1212 Grandview Ave ⓣ 412/431-1400. Relaxed Mt Washington restaurant, usually packed with a young crowd enjoying huge plates of pasta. Arrive early for a deck table with a view.

Gullifty's 1922 Murray Ave ⓣ 412/521-8222. Longstanding Squirrel Hill favorite serving fine pasta, meat dishes, and sumptuous sweets. Look out for the twice-yearly Garlic Festival (usually held in April and Oct).

India Garden 328 Atwood St ⓣ 412/682-3000. North Indian restaurant and bar in Oakland, serving tasty curries and creamy *lassi*. Good-value buffet during lunch and on Sun evenings. Catch a cricket game on the TV.

Kaya 2000 Smallman St ⓣ 412/261-6565. Stylish Caribbean restaurant in the Strip District with a varied vegetarian selection, as well as a huge range of beers, rums, and cocktails.

La Feria 5527 Walnut St ⓣ 412/682-4501. Colorful upstairs Peruvian shop-cum-restaurant in Shadyside, offering a limited but tasty selection of inexpensive specials from the Andes. BYOB.

Mallorca 2228 E Carson St ⓣ 412/488-1818. This smart South Side restaurant serves excellent paella and Mediterranean dishes, as well as fine sangria. Ask if they have the delicious goat in red-wine sauce – at under $30 it's enough for two.

Thai Gourmet 4505 Liberty Ave ⓣ 412/681-4373. Intimate and friendly Bloomfield spot with unbeatably authentic and inexpensive Southeast Asian fare, such as their wonderful Penang curry. BYOB.

Yumwok/Lulu's Noodles 400 S Craig St ⓣ 412/687-7777. Combined Oakland establishment serving filling noodles and good standard pan-Asian cuisine at bargain prices. Justifiably popular with students. BYOB.

Nightlife and entertainment

Pittsburgh's **nightlife** offers rich pickings in everything from the classics to jazz and alternative rock. The nationally regarded City Theatre, 57 S 13th St (ⓣ 412/431-4400, ⓦ www.citytheatrecompany.org), puts on groundbreaking productions in a converted South Side church. The widely traveled **Pittsburgh Symphony Orchestra** plays at the Heinz Hall, 600 Penn Ave (ⓣ 412/392-4900, ⓦ www.pittsburghsymphony.org), and the city's ballet, dance, and opera companies perform at the downtown **Benedum Center for the Performing Arts**, 719 Liberty Ave (ⓣ 412/456-6666, ⓦ www.pgharts.org/venues/benedum.aspx). *City Paper*, a free weekly newspaper published on Wednesdays (ⓦ www.pghcitypaper.com), has extensive **listings**.

31st St Pub 3101 Penn Ave ⓣ 412/391-8334, ⓦ www.31stpub.com. It won't win any prizes for decor, but this place draws a crowd to hear up-and-coming local indie and hardcore bands, plus the odd underground celebrity act from out of town.

Brillobox 4104 Penn Ave ⓣ 412/621-4900. Two prodigal Pittsburghers returning from New York have created a unique bar that's both chic and a fun local spot for watching sports. There's a good jukebox downstairs and a performance space for mostly obscure acts above.

Club Café 56–58 S 12th St ⓣ 412/431-4950, ⓦ www.clubcafelive.com. Laid-back South Side club with regular live music, including rock, folk, and salsa.

Dee's 1314 E Carson St ⓣ 412/431-5400. This South Side institution has a great jukebox, pool, darts, and a lively crowd.

Kelly's 6012 Penn Circle S, E Liberty ⓣ 412/363-6012. Just east of Shadyside, this popular bar offers good beer such as East End Big Hop and eclectic recorded music. Check out punk night on alternate Wed.

Mr Small's Theatre 400 Lincoln Ave, Millvale ⓣ 1-800/594-8499, ⓦ www.mrsmalls.com. Several miles northeast of downtown off US-28, this converted church hosts most of the mid-sized US and foreign indie rock acts.

Piper's Pub 1828 E Carson St ⓣ 412/431-6757, ⓦ www.piperspub.com. One of the South Side's most convivial bars and the place for soccer, rugby, and Gaelic football on TV. Imported and US beers are available and the food is decent, especially the breakfasts.

Rex Theatre 1602 E Carson St ⓣ412/381-6811, ⓦwww.ticketmaster.com/venue/180366. This former cinema hosts mainly rock shows.

Around Pittsburgh

Just over an hour southeast of Pittsburgh, the **Laurel Highlands** takes in seventy miles of rolling wooded hills and valleys. The main reasons to come this way down Hwy-381 are to see one of Frank Lloyd Wright's most unique creations, **Fallingwater**, and to take advantage of some prime outdoor opportunities around the small town of **Ohiopyle**.

Falling Water

You do not need to be an architecture buff to appreciate Wright's **Fallingwater** (mid-March to late Nov Tues–Sun 10am–4pm; Dec & early March Sat & Sun 11.30am–3pm; tour $16; ⓣ724/329-8501, ⓦwww.fallingwater.org), which was built in the late 1930s for the Kaufmann family, owners of Pittsburgh's premier department store. Signposted off Hwy-381, some twenty miles south of I-70, it is set on Bear Run Creek in the midst of the gorgeous deciduous forest that constitutes the 5000-acre Bear Run Nature Reserve. It is the only one of Wright's buildings to be on display exactly as it was designed, and for good reason – it's built right into a set of cliffside waterfalls. Wright used a cantilever system to make the multi-tiered structure "cascade down the hill like the water down the falls;" the house's almost precarious position is truly stunning, and it is remarkable how well its predominantly rectangular shapes blend in with nature's less uniform lines. Among the house's pioneering features is a lack of load-bearing walls, which gives an extra sense of space, and natural skylights.

Ohiopyle

Five miles south of Fallingwater, tiny **OHIOPYLE** is the most convenient base from which to enjoy the wilds of **Ohiopyle State Park** or activities like whitewater rafting on the **Youghiogheny River**. The park fans out around the town and river, offering a maze of trails for hiking or biking, and natural delights such as **Cucumber Falls** and the unique habitat of the **Ferncliff Peninsula**, known for its wildflowers. A small **visitor center** dispenses local information (daily 10am–4.30pm; ⓣ724/329-8591). Just beyond it the *Ohiopyle House Café*, 144 Grant St (ⓣ724/329-1122), serves up tasty dishes like lobster ravioli and caramel pudding, while a couple of seasonal canteens and a general store sell basic snacks and provisions. The *Yough Plaza Motel* on Sherman Street (ⓣ1-800/992-7238, ⓦwww.youghplaza.com; ④) has reasonable standard units and efficiency apartments; even better for budget travelers is camping or renting a cabin in the park itself (ⓣ1-888/727-2757). For **rafting**, White Water Adventurers at 6 Negley St (ⓣ1-800/992-7238, ⓦwww.wwaraft.com) is one of several outfits that rent equipment and give instruction.

Allegheny National Forest

Occupying over half a million acres and a sizeable portion of four counties, the pristine **Allegheny National Forest** affords a bounty of opportunities for engaging in outdoor pursuits like hiking, fishing, snowmobiling, and, best of all, admiring the **fall foliage**, which rivals any in New England. In the north, there are several points of interest within easy access of Hwy-6, the major route through the forest. Just north of the highway, it is worth a stop to admire the views from the

▲ Allegheny National Forest

Kinzua Viaduct railroad bridge, the highest and longest in the world when constructed in 1882. The dominant feature of the forest's northern section is the huge **Kinzua Reservoir**, created by a dam at the southern end. Swimming is possible at **Kinzua** and **Kiasutha beaches** or you can enjoy a picnic at **Rimrock Overlook** or at **Willow Bay** in the very north. The summer-only Kinzua Point Information Center on Hwy-59 (Ⓣ814/726-1291) has details on trails and private cabins and campgrounds around the forest, or you can can **camp** in any of the twenty state-run campsites (Ⓣ1-877/444-6777, Ⓦwww.reserveusa.com).

Erie

The focal point of Pennsylvania's forty-mile slice of Lake Erie waterfront is the pleasant city of **ERIE** itself. It bears no resemblance to the major urban centers of Pittsburgh or Philadelphia, being entirely low-rise and extremely leafy. There are several places of cultural interest in the city, all within walking distance of the square, including the Neoclassical **Court House** and several **museums** devoted to history, art, and science. Better than these, the **Erie Maritime Museum** at 150 E Front St in the Bayfront Historical District (April–Dec Mon–Sat 9am–5pm, Sun noon–5pm, Jan–March closed Mon–Wed; $6, $4 if Brig is absent; Ⓣ814/452-2744, Ⓦwww.brigniagara.org) has a fascinating display on the geological and ecological development of the Great Lakes and also focuses on warships of different periods; the elegant **US Brig Niagara**, usually moored outside, is part of the museum.

Undoubtedly, Erie's main attraction is the elongated comma-shaped peninsula of **Presque Isle State Park**, which bends east from its narrow neck three miles west of downtown until it almost touches the city's northernmost tip. The park is maintained as a nature preserve and has wide sandy **beaches** good for swimming, backed by thick woods offering a series of trails. Rangers at the Park Office (daily 8am–4pm; Ⓣ814/833-7424, Ⓦwww.presqueisle.org) provide general information and a map, but the main visitors' center is the **Stull Interpretive Center and**

American food

Food is big in America – a country where a deli sandwich can be a meal for two and where all-you-can-eat buffets are destinations in themselves. Still, it's not all about quantity. There's something irresistible about sitting in a vintage diner, munching on a simple grilled-cheese sandwich while a gum-chewing waitress with big hair pours endless coffee refills and calls you darlin'. Such quintessentially American experiences are there for the taking, along with a host of other intriguing dining opportunities, and – those buffets notwithstanding – some of the

Barbecue chicken ▲

Biting into a hamburger ▼

Lobster dinner ▼

Burgers, barbecue, and seafood

No one knows who invented the **burger**, but it's an American staple that's set to stay. Fans of the Golden Arches may not recognize the infinitely tastier home-made versions served in regional restaurants – a Happy Meal will never seem the same again. Famous **hot dog** spots include New York City, where every July 4 *Nathan's* in Coney Island holds a hot-dog-eating contest, and Chicago, where the dog is served in a poppy-seed bun and *never* with ketchup. Other meaty takeout treats include the **Philly cheesesteak**, a dripping sandwich of hot sliced beef and rich melted cheese born on the streets of Philadelphia, and New Orleans's **muffuletta**, in which spicy Italian cured meats are combined with piquant olives and cheese and crammed into a colossal bun.

Emotions run high when it comes to **barbecue** – smoked pork or beef shredded and drenched in tangy sauces – with the southern states and the cities of Memphis, Kansas City, and Chicago hotly claiming to serve the world's best. Texas is where you'll find the best **chili** – and scores of passionately fought chili cookoffs. If you fancy a really big **steak** head for Texas or Western states like Montana and Wyoming. This is cattle-rearing country, so the slab of beef on your plate couldn't be fresher – or bigger.

Crab is king along the Mid-Atlantic shore, with steamed blue crabs and spicy soft-shells around Chesapeake Bay, and stone-crab claws abounding in Florida. New Englanders feast on giant Maine **lobsters** and **steamers** (clams), perhaps in a creamy **chowder**, while any trip to Louisiana should see you slurping back raw **oysters** and mounds of juicy mudbugs (**crawfish**) boiled with spices.

Florida offers **conch**, a meaty mollusc, while the firm-fleshed, tasty **catfish** is a staple in the south. Hawaii, meanwhile, is home to some of the world's finest **Pacific Rim** restaurants, fusing Asian, Pacific, and Californian cuisine and centering on local fish like **mahi mahi** (dorado).

Regional cuisine

The complex pattern of immigration in the US is writ large in its food. In the soggy swamplands of southern Louisiana, for example, the French-speaking population cooks up a spicy stew called **gumbo** – made with okra, garlic, and bell peppers, and filled out with anything from chicken or pork sausage to crawfish – that was heavily influenced by the cooking of West African slaves. This **Cajun** cooking, as rustic as it is, has similarities with **Creole cuisine**, its urban cousin, and you'll find gumbos served in grand New Orleans restaurants alongside shrimp *étouffé* ("smothered" in a flavorful sauce).

Southern cooking, or **soul food**, is the perfect comfort food, if often quirkily named. Take unappetizing-sounding grits, for example (in fact a tasty, steaming hot gloop of ground corn cooked with butter and salt) – not to mention collard greens (cabbage), chitlins (pork sweetmeats), Hoppin' John (black-eyed beans and rice) and hush puppies (fried corn balls).

Tex-Mex, spicier than Mexican food, adds guacamole, melted cheese, and chopped tomatoes with cilantro to staples like pinto beans and tortillas. Originally Mexican, **tamales**, wads of soft crumbly corn dough filled with shredded pork and chicken, cheese, and vegetables steamed in a cornhusk, have spread throughout the southern states. In the health-conscious 1980s, California created its own take on nouvelle cuisine,

▲ Shrimp *étouffé*

▼ Hoppin' John

▼ Tex-Mex burritos

producing tiny plates of highly designed, healthy food. This fad spread nationwide, evolving into **New American Cuisine** – a style of cooking that can be applied to any regional dish with a modern edge. In the **Southwest**, local ingredients – chili peppers, *jicama*, *piñons* – give Tex-Mex a creative twist. Another Southwestern staple is **Navajo frybread**, which is similar to a taco, served with minced beef and chili, or, in New Mexico, with honey butter.

Katz's Delicatessen ▲

Galatoire's ▼

The best...

If you're looking for the very best food in the US, pay a visit to one – or more, ideally – of the restaurants listed below.

▸▸ **All-you-can-eat buffet** *The Bellagio*, Las Vegas, NV (p.937)
▸▸ **BBQ** *Fresh Air*, Jackson, GA (p.492)
▸▸ **Cajun** *Prejean's*, Lafayette, LA (p.657)
▸▸ **California cuisine** *Chez Panisse*, Berkeley, CA (p.1051)
▸▸ **Crab** *Obrycki's*, Baltimore, MD (p.433)
▸▸ **Creole** *Galatoire's*, New Orleans, LA (p.643)
▸▸ **Delicatessen** *Katz's*, New York, NY (p.103)
▸▸ **Diner** *Moody's Diner,* Waldoboro, ME (p.261)
▸▸ **Hot dog** *Nathan's*, Brooklyn, NY (p.105)
▸▸ **Lobster** *Lobster Shack at Two Lights*, Cape Elizabeth, ME (p.258)
▸▸ **New American** *Alpenglow Stube*, Keystone, CO (p.786)
▸▸ **Pacific Rim** *Roy's Poipu Bar & Grill*, Poipu, HI (p.1193)
▸▸ **Soul food** *Four Way Grill*, Memphis, TN (p.519)
▸▸ **Southern** *Mrs Wilkes' Dining Room*, Savannah, GA (p.497)
▸▸ **Southwestern** *Turquoise Room*, Winslow, AZ (p.890)
▸▸ **Steak** *Cattleman's Steak House*, Fort Worth, TX (p.721)
▸▸ **Tex-Mex** *Boudro's*, San Antonio, TX (p.683)

Nature Shop (spring & fall 10am–4pm; summer 10am–5pm; Ⓣ814/836-9107). Those without a vehicle can hop on the Port of Erie **water taxi** (late May to mid-Oct Mon noon–6pm, Tues–Sun 10am–6pm; $4 single, $6 round-trip; Ⓣ814/881-2502), which leaves on the hour from Dobbins Landing on the Erie Bayfront.

Practicalities

Erie has frequent Greyhound **bus** connections to Pittsburgh, Cleveland, and Buffalo; the station is at 5759 Peach St (Ⓣ814/864-5949), some three miles out of downtown, and is served by local bus #9 to Mill Creek Mall. The **CVB**, downtown at 208 E Bayfront Drive (Mon–Fri 9am–5pm; Ⓣ814/454-7191 or 1-800/524-3743, Ⓦwww.visiteriepa.com), is the place to go for information.

Accommodation is often twice as expensive in the summer as in the off-season. The centrally located *Holiday Inn Erie-Downtown*, 18 W 18th St (Ⓣ814/456-2961 or 1-800/832-9101, Ⓦwww.holiday-inn.com; ❺), provides the usual amenities, but the elegant *Boothby Inn B&B*, at 311 W 6th St (Ⓣ814/456-1888 or 1-866/266-8429, Ⓦwww.theboothbyinn.com; ❺), makes for a far more pleasant stay. Numerous functional **motels** also line Peninsula Drive. The well-sited *Sara's Campground*, 50 Peninsula Drive (Ⓣ814/833-4560, Ⓦwww.sarascampground.com; from $23), is just before the entrance to Presque Isle. Nearby in Sara Coyne Plaza, *Sally's Diner* (Ⓣ814/833-1957) serves up hearty breakfasts and meals; downtown, try the *Marketplace Grill*, 319 State St (Ⓣ814/455-7272), for steaks and a filling pizza-and-pasta lunchtime buffet, or the cheap Chinese food at *Happy Garden*, 418 State St (Ⓣ814/452-4488).

New Jersey

The skinny coastal state of **NEW JERSEY** has been at the heart of US history since the Revolution, when a battle was fought at **Princeton**, and George Washington spent two bleak winters at Morristown. As the Civil War came, the state's commitment to an industrial future ensured that, despite its border location along the Mason–Dixon Line, it fought with the Union.

That commitment to industry has doomed New Jersey in modern times. Most travelers only see "the Garden State," so called for the rich market garden territory at the state's heart, from the stupendously ugly New Jersey Turnpike toll road, which is always heavy with truck traffic. Even the songs of **Bruce Springsteen**, **Asbury Park**'s golden boy, paint his home state as a gritty urban wasteland of empty lots, gray highways, lost dreams, and blue-collar heartache. The majority of the refineries and factories actually hug only a mere fifteen-mile-wide swath along the turnpike, but bleak cities like **Newark**, home to the major airport, and Trenton, the forgettable capital, reinforce the dour image. But there is more to New Jersey than factories and pollution. Alongside its revolutionary history, the northwest corner near the Delaware Water Gap is traced with picturesque lakes, streams, and woodlands while, in the south, the town of **Princeton** adds architectural elegance to the interior with the grand buildings of its Ivy League university. Best of all perhaps, the Atlantic shore offers many bustling resorts, from the compelling tattered glitz of **Atlantic City** to the old world charm of **Cape May**.

Getting around New Jersey

With a **car**, New Jersey is easily accessible from New York City, via I-95, while the New Jersey Turnpike (a $6.45 toll end-to-end) sweeps from the northeast down to Philadelphia. The Garden State Parkway runs parallel to the Atlantic from New York to Cape May (with a 35–70¢ toll every twenty miles or so), and gives easy access to the shoreline resorts. **Newark Liberty International Airport** (Ⓣ973/961-6000, Ⓦwww.newarkairport.com) is served by all the major international carriers. **PATH trains** connect northern New Jersey to New York City (Ⓣ1-800/234-7284, Ⓦwww.panynj.gov/path), while New Jersey Transit (Ⓣ973/762-5100 or 1-800/772-2222, Ⓦwww.njtransit.com) provides good, inexpensive train and bus service from New Jersey hubs to Philadelphia, New York, and the coast. Numerous **Amtrak** trains pass through Newark, Princeton, and Trenton, en route between Philadelphia, New York, and Washington DC. Greyhound covers most of the state, while New Jersey's south coast is connected to Delaware by the Cape May–Lewes **ferry** (see p.176).

Inland New Jersey

Visitors most often travel from New York to northern New Jersey for the great **shopping**: from huge malls and designer outlet stores to ethnic emporiums like Mitsuwa Marketplace, the Japanese shopping center in Edgewater (Ⓣ201/941-9113, Ⓦwww.mitsuwa.com), both prices and taxes are lower than across the Hudson River. The well-off towns along the river also contain some fine Italian and Asian restaurants, while Hoboken offers a spillover of Manhattan subculture. Traveling southwest on the interstates from the shore or from New York City, however, visitors see the New Jersey of popular imagination: a heavily industrialized cultural desert peppered with run-down cities like Trenton, Paterson and Newark. The one place that holds interest in inland New Jersey is **Princeton**, an Ivy-League town that makes a pretty afternoon stopoff.

Princeton

Self-satisfied **PRINCETON**, on US-206 eleven miles north of Trenton, is home to **Princeton University** – the nation's fourth oldest, after having broken away from the overly religious Yale in 1756. It began its days inauspiciously as Stony Brook in the late 1600s and then in 1724 became known as Princes Town, a coach stop between New York and Philadelphia. In January 1777, a week after Washington's triumph against the British at Trenton, the **Battle of Princeton** occurred southwest of town. This victory, a turning point in the Revolutionary effort, bolstered the morale of Washington's troops before their long winter encampment at Morristown to the north. After the war, in 1783, the **Continental Congress**, fearful of potential attack from incensed unpaid veterans in Philadelphia, met here for four months; the leafy, well-kept town was then left in peace to follow its academic pursuits. Alumni of Princeton University include actor James Stewart, Jazz-Age writer F. Scott Fitzgerald, actress Brooke Shields, and presidents Wilson and Madison. Today, there is little to do here other than tour the university and see the historic sites.

Arrival, information, and getting around

A shuttle **bus**, the Princeton Airporter, makes the run from Newark airport to town (daily: every hour 7.15am–8.15pm; 1hr 30mins trip; $30, students $25; Ⓣ609/587-6600, Ⓦwww.goairporter.com). On their New York–Philadelphia runs, Amtrak and NJ Transit stop at Princeton Junction, three miles south of Princeton. From there, you can take a SEPTA shuttle (Ⓣ215/580-7800, Ⓦwww.septa.com) to Princeton's train terminal, on-campus at University Place, a block north of Alexander Road. You must buy a ticket for the shuttle ahead of time, preferably as a connecting ticket from your point of origin. Suburban Transit **buses** from New York's Port Authority bus station (Ⓣ1-800/222-0492, Ⓦwww.suburbantransit.com) stop every thirty minutes from 6am to 11pm at Palmer Square.

Information is available from the Frist Campus Center at the university (Ⓣ609/258-1766, Ⓦwww.princeton.edu/frist) or from the **Chamber of Commerce** at 9 Vandeventer Ave (Mon–Fri 8.30am–5pm; Ⓣ609/924-1776, Ⓦwww.princetonchamber.org). The **Historical Society Museum**, 158 Nassau St (Tues–Sun noon–4pm; Ⓣ609/921-6748, Ⓦwww.princetonhistory.org), organizes **walking tours** through town (Sun 2pm; $7) and also provides **maps** so you can do it yourself. Central Princeton is easily **navigable on foot**, but weather extremes in the winter and summer, as well as the distance of accommodation options from downtown, may make you glad to have a **car**.

The Town and the university

Mercer Street, the long road that sweeps southwest past the university campus to Nassau Street, is lined with elegant colonial houses, graced with shutters, columns, and wrought-iron fences. The **Princeton Battlefield State Park**, a mile and a half out, includes the **Thomas Clarke House**, 500 Mercer St, a Quaker farmhouse that served as a hospital during the battle. The simple house at 112 Mercer, back toward town, is where **Albert Einstein** lived while teaching at the Institute of Advanced Study. Unfortunately, the house is not open to the public.

Princeton University's tranquil and shaded campus is a beautiful place for a stroll. Just inside the main gates on Nassau Street, **Nassau Hall**, a vault-like historic building containing numerous portraits of famous graduates and one of King George II, was the largest stone building in the nation when constructed in 1756; its 26-inch-thick walls, now patterned with plaques and patches of ivy placed by graduating classes, withstood American and British fire during the Revolution. It was also the seat of government during Princeton's brief spell as national capital in 1783. The 1925 **chapel**, based on one at Kings College, Cambridge University, in England, has stained-glass windows showing scenes from works by Dante, Shakespeare, and Milton, as well as the Bible. Across campus, the **Prospect Gardens**, a flowerbed in the shape of the university emblem, are a blaze of orange in summer. Somewhat smug student-led **tours** (during term Mon–Sat 10am, 11am, 1.30pm, & 3.30pm, Sun 1.30pm & 3.30pm; hours vary during vacations; free; Ⓣ609/258-1766) take you around to all of these sights, leaving from the Frist Campus Center.

In the middle of the campus, fronted by the Picasso sculpture *Head of a Woman*, the **University Art Museum**, not included on the standard tours, is well worth a look for its collection from the Renaissance to the present, including works by Modigliani, Van Gogh, and Warhol, as well as Asian and pre-Columbian art (Tues–Sat 10am–5pm, Sun 1–5pm; free; Ⓣ609/258-3788, Ⓦwww.princetonart-museum.org).

Accommodation, eating, and drinking

The only **hotels** in the center of Princeton are the ersatz-colonial *Nassau Inn* on Palmer Square (Ⓣ609/921-7500 or 1-800/862-7728, Ⓦwww.nassauinn.com; ❾) and the *Peacock Inn* (Ⓣ609/924-1707, Ⓦwww.peacockinn.com; ❼), tucked in a quieter spot at 20 Bayard Lane. Budget **motels** can be found along US-1 and in the suburb of **Lawrenceville** a few miles south of town; one such is the functional *Red Roof Inn*, 3203 US-1 (Ⓣ609/896-3388, Ⓦwww.redroof.com; ③).

Despite its affluence, Princeton is by no means the culinary capital of New Jersey. There's cheap diner-type **food** along Witherspoon Street; *Teresa's*, 19–23 Palmer Square E (Ⓣ609/921-1974), serves creative, good-value Italian food; and *Mediterra*, at 29 Hulfish St (Ⓣ609/252-9680), is an upscale Mediterranean restaurant with a welcoming atmosphere and well-prepared food. **Nightlife** is limited, especially when school is out, but the *Triumph Brewery*, 138 Triumph St (Ⓣ609/942-7855), has good, home-brewed beers and is popular with a mixed crowd; meanwhile, the old *Yankee Doodle Tap Room* bar, downstairs at the *Nassau Inn*, is usually full of ancient revelers drinking, reminiscing, and enjoying live jazz.

The New Jersey shore

New Jersey's Atlantic coast, a 130-mile stretch of almost uninterrupted **resorts** – some rowdy, some run-down, some undeveloped and peaceful – has long been reliant on farming and tourism, in the absence of a major port. In the late 1980s, the whole coastline suffered severe and well-publicized pollution from ocean dumping. But today, the beaches, if occasionally somewhat crowded, are safe and clean: sandy, broad, and lined by characteristic wooden **boardwalks**, some of which, in an attempt to maintain their condition, charge admission during the summer. The rowdy, sleazy glitz of **Atlantic City** is perhaps the shore's best-known attraction, though there are also quieter resorts like **Spring Lake** and Victorian **Cape May**.

Spring Lake and Asbury Park

SPRING LAKE, an elegant Victorian resort about twenty miles down the Jersey coast, is one of the smallest, most uncommercial communities on the shore, a gentle respite on the road south to Atlantic City. You can walk the undeveloped two-mile **boardwalk** and watch the crashing ocean from battered gazebos, swim and bask on the white beaches (in summer, compulsory beach tags, badges that provide admission to the beach, cost a small fee), or sit in the shade by the town's namesake, **Spring Lake** itself. Wooden footbridges, swans, geese, and the grand St Catharine Roman Catholic Church on the banks of the lake give it the feel of a country village. What little activity there is centers on the upmarket shops of Third Avenue.

Bruce Springsteen fans can use the town as a base for visiting nearby **ASBURY PARK**, a decaying old seaside town where The Boss lived for many years and played his first gigs. Almost nothing remains of the carousels and seaside arcades that Springsteen wrote about on early albums such as his debut, *Greetings from Asbury Park*. The **Stone Pony**, 913 Ocean Ave (Ⓣ732/502-0600, Ⓦwww.stoneponyonline.com), where Springsteen played dozens of times in the mid-1970s and has returned occasionally since, has survived and is the one obligatory stop for devotees.

Practicalities

Spring Lake is accessible by US-34 from the New Jersey Turnpike, and served by New Jersey Transit from New York. The Chamber of Commerce, 302 Washington Ave (Ⓣ732/449-0577, Ⓦwww.springlake.org), keeps erratic hours but the Spring Lake Hotel and B&B Association (Ⓣ732/449-6685) can help find lodging, especially on summer weekends. There are no cheap **motels**, and **B&Bs** can be expensive; the

Chateau Inn, 500 Warren Ave (ⓣ732/974-2000 or 1-877/974-5253, ⓦwww.chateauinn.com; ❽), is typical. Adjacent to Asbury Park, in the less exclusive Victorian resort of **Ocean Grove**, friendly *Lillagaard B&B*, 5 Abbot Ave (ⓣ732/988-1216, ⓦwww.lillagaard.com; ❺), is right on the beach. Most of Spring Lake's **restaurants** are in the elegant Victorian hotels along the seafront and can be pricey. *Who's On Third*, 1300 Third Ave (ⓣ732/449-4233), is a no-nonsense café serving breakfast and lunch. For a blowout, *The Sandpiper*, 7 Atlantic Ave (BYOB; ⓣ732/449-4700), serves superb fresh fish and seafood in elegant, candlelit surroundings. In Asbury Park, *Red Fusion* (ⓣ732/775-1008), at 660 Cookman Ave, serves excellent Asian/American fusion food in a unique space that is part art gallery, part sports bar.

Atlantic City

What they wanted was Monte Carlo. They didn't want Las Vegas. What they got was Las Vegas. We always knew that they would get Las Vegas.

Stuart Mendelson, *Philadelphia Journal*

ATLANTIC CITY, on Absecon Island just off the midpoint of the Jersey shoreline, has been a tourist magnet since 1854, when Philadelphia speculators created it as a rail terminal resort. In 1909, at the peak of the seaside town's popularity, Baedeker wrote "there is something colossal about its vulgarity" – a glitzy, slightly monstrous quality that it sustains today. The real-life model for the modern version of the board game **Monopoly**, it has an impressive popular history, boasting the nation's first **boardwalk** (1870), the world's first **Ferris wheel** (1892), the first color **postcards** (1893), and the first **Miss America Beauty Pageant** (1921 – it only moved to Las Vegas in 2006). During Prohibition and the Depression, Atlantic City was a center for rum-running, packed with speakeasies and illegal gambling dens. Thereafter, in the face of increasing competition from Florida, it slipped into a steep decline, until desperate city officials decided in 1976 to open up the decrepit resort to legal **gambling**, now its mainstay.

Arrival, information, and getting around

The **bus terminal** at Atlantic and Michigan is served by NJ Transit and Greyhound. NJ Transit trains stop at the **train station** next to the Convention Center, at 1 Miss America Way, and are connected by free shuttle service to all casinos. **Atlantic City International Airport** in Pomona (ⓣ609/645-7895, ⓦwww.acairport.com) has direct flights to Philadelphia, as well as some flights further afield; from the airport, cabs cost around $30 to downtown. For maps and information, head for the Atlantic City Convention & Visitors Authority's helpful **boardwalk information center** inside Boardwalk Hall at 2314 Pacific Ave (daily 9.30am–5.30pm, summer Thurs–Sun until 8pm; ⓣ609/449-7130 or 1-888/228-4748, ⓦwww.atlanticcitynj.com). Atlantic City is easy to **walk** around, though it's unwise to stray further from the five-mile boardwalk along the ocean than the parallel Pacific, Atlantic, and Arctic avenues, as other parts of the city can be **dangerous** at night and are not that savory by day. Ventnor and Margate, to the south on Absecon Island, are served by **buses** along Atlantic Avenue. Pale blue Jitneys ($2.25, exact change required; ⓣ609/344-8642, ⓦwww.jitneys.net) offer a 24-hour minibus service the length of Pacific Avenue. Along the boardwalk, various **bike rental** stands and rickshaw-like **rolling chairs** (ⓣ609/347-7148) provide alternative means of transportation.

Accommodation

Atlantic City is not Vegas – there's no chance of getting a $40 room at one of the casinos. The already high **accommodation** rates rise on weekends and in summer, though rates plunge off-season; if you book ahead online and business is slow, many places will offer discounted **package deals**, with $200 suites going for around half-price. Alternatively, reasonably priced **motels** line Pacific and Atlantic avenues behind the boardwalk, and things are cheaper in quiet Ocean City, a family resort around ten miles south.

Bally's Atlantic City Park Place and Boardwalk ⓣ609/340-2000, ⓦwww.harrahs.com/ballys. One of the big midtown theme casinos, *Bally's* offers a full-service spa, fifteen restaurants and four bars, not to mention all the gambling opportunities, all under one roof. ❺

EconoLodge Boardwalk 117 S Kentucky Ave ⓣ609/344-9093, ⓦwww.choicehotels.com. Standard chain motel next to the boardwalk and the *Sands Casino*. ❸

The Irish Pub Inn 164 St James Place ⓣ609/344-9063, ⓦwww.theirishpub.com. Basic, cheap rooms above one of the town's best bars. Great single rates from $25. Hotel operation only open May–Sept. ❸

Quality Inn Beach Block 119 S South Carolina Ave ⓣ609/345-7070, ⓦwww.choicehotels.com. Chain motel housed in a converted school. The lobby and shared areas are rather shabby, but the clean, newly refurbished rooms make up for it. Prices double on weekends. ❸

Resorts Atlantic City Casino Hotel 1133 Boardwalk ⓣ1-800/336-6378, ⓦwww.resortsac.com. The most pleasant of the huge casino hotels, with pool and spa. ❺

Rodeway Inn 124 S North Carolina Ave ⓣ609/345-0155, ⓦwww.choicehotels.com. Clean, basic, reasonably priced rooms close to the boardwalk. ❸

The Town

Atlantic City's wooden **boardwalk** was originally built as a temporary walkway, raised above the beach so that vacationers could take a seaside stroll without treading sand into the grand hotels. Alongside the brash 99¢ shops and exotically named palm-readers, a few beautiful Victorian buildings that survived the wrecking ball invoke past elegance, despite the fact that many now house fast-food joints. Early in the morning, when the breezes from the ocean are at their most pleasant, the boardwalk is peaceful, peopled only by keen cyclists and a few lost souls down on their luck. The **Central Pier** offers all the fun of a fair, with rides and old-fashioned games. A few blocks south, another pier has been remodeled into an ocean-liner-shaped shopping center. The small and faded **Atlantic City Arts Center** (summer daily 10am–4pm, closed Mon off-season; free; ⓣ609/347-5837, ⓦwww.acartcenter.org), on the Garden Pier at the quiet northern end of the boardwalk, has a free collection of seaside memorabilia, postcards, photos, a special exhibit on Miss America, and hosts traveling art shows. A block off the boardwalk, where Pacific and Rhode Island avenues meet, and at the heart of some of the city's worst deprivation, stands the **Absecon Lighthouse**. Active until 1933, it's now fully restored and offers a terrific view from its 167ft tower (July & Aug daily 10am–5pm; rest of year Thurs–Mon 11am–4pm; $7; ⓣ609/449-1360, ⓦwww.abseconlighthouse.org).

Atlantic City's **beach** is free, family-filled, and surprisingly clean, considering its proximity to the boardwalk. Beaches at well-to-do **Ventnor**, a Jitney ride away, are quieter, while three miles south of Atlantic City, New Jersey's beautiful people pose on the beaches of **Margate** (both beaches charge a nominal fee), watched over by **Lucy the Elephant** at 9200 Atlantic Ave. A 65ft wood-and-tin Victorian oddity, Lucy was built as a seaside attraction in 1881 and used variously as a tavern and a hotel. Today, her huge belly contains a museum (June to early Sept Mon–Sat 10am–8pm, Sun 10am–5pm; $5; ⓣ609/823-6473, ⓦwww.lucytheelephant.org) filled with Atlantic City memorabilia, as well as photos and artifacts from her own history.

The casinos of Atlantic City

Each of Atlantic City's dozen **casinos**, which also act as luxury hotels, conference centers, and concert halls, has a slightly different image, though you might not guess it among the apparent uniformity of vast, richly ornamented halls, slot machines, relentless flashing lights and incessant noise, chandeliers, mirrors, and a disorienting absence of clocks or windows. The casinos are divided into four areas: **uptown**, **midtown** and **downtown** occupy the north, central and south sections of the boardwalk respectively, while the **marina** enclave towers over a spit of land in the northwest of the city.

The most outwardly ostentatious, unsurprisingly, is Donald Trump's **Taj Mahal**. Occupying nearly twenty acres and over forty stories high, dotted with glittering minarets and onion domes, this gigantic but oddly anticlimactic piece of Far Eastern kitsch stands uptown, opposite the arcade-packed Steel Pier. **Bally's** charmingly garish midtown Wild West Casino is much more outlandish and fun, and also offers complete access to the games and memberships of adjacent Roman-themed **Caesar's**, the smaller **Showboat** uptown and **Hilton** downtown, although garish **Tropicana** is the more amusing of the two casinos down at that end. All casinos are **open 24 hours**, including holidays, and have a strict minimum **age requirement**, so be prepared to show ID that proves you're 21 or older.

Eating

One effect of Atlantic City's rabid commercialization is an abundance of **fast food**. The boardwalk is lined with pizza, burger, and sandwich joints, while the diners on Atlantic and Pacific avenues serve soul food and cheap breakfasts. All the large casinos boast several restaurants, ranging in price and menu but all of average quality, as well as all-you-can-eat **buffets** – most cost around $15 for lunch, and around $20 for dinner. Some of the casinos offer half-price buffets to "members" or "VIPs" – all you have to do to join is fill out a form and give some proof of address. If money's running low after too many days in the casino, there are bargain buffets on the boardwalk for around $5 – but inevitably, you get what you pay for.

Dune 9510 Ventnor Ave, Margate Ⓣ609/487-7450. Specializing in tasty and fresh, if a little pricey, seafood. Entrees of quality fish like grouper, black bass, and Arctic char run around $25–30.

Hunan Chinese Restaurant 2323 Atlantic Ave Ⓣ609/348-5946. Reasonably priced Chinese food two blocks from the boardwalk. Combination plates cost $7–12.

Los Amigos 1926 Atlantic Ave Ⓣ609/344-2293. Great for cheap, late-night food, this pleasant but average Mexican restaurant and bar across from the bus station is open until 3am Fri and Sat.

Pappa T's Pizza 445 Boardwalk Ⓣ609/348-5030. One of the better cheap boardwalk joints, with pizza and breakfast from $5.

White House Sub Shop 2301 Arctic Ave Ⓣ609/345-1564. This bright and super-efficient Atlantic City institution is where the submarine sandwich was born; definitely worth a visit.

Entertainment and nightlife

Atlantic City sells itself as the fun night-time city, but the **nightlife** centers on the casinos and boardwalk amusements. Once you get bored with slot machines there is little else to do. Big-name entertainers perform regularly at the casinos, but you'll be lucky to find tickets much under $100 – the free weekly *Atlantic City Weekly* (Ⓦwww.acweekly.com) has listings. For cheaper informal fun, try the friendly, dark-paneled *Irish Pub*, 164 St James Place (Ⓣ609/344-9063, Ⓦwww.theirishpub.com), which serves extremely cheap food and often has live Irish music.

Cape May

CAPE MAY was founded in 1620 by the Dutch Captain Mey, on the small hook at the very southern tip of the Jersey coast, jutting out into the Atlantic and washed by the Delaware Bay on the west. After being briefly settled by New England whalers in the late 1600s, it turned in the eighteenth century to more profitable farming and, soon after, to tourism. In 1745 the first advertisement for Cape May's restorative air and fine accommodation appeared in the Philadelphia press, heralding a period of great prosperity, when Southern plantation owners, desiring cool sea breezes without having to venture into Yankee land, flocked to the fashionable boarding houses of this genteel "resort of Presidents."

The Victorian era was Cape May's finest; nearly all its gingerbread architecture dates from a mass rebuilding after a severe fire in 1878. Suffering from the fact that increased car travel made it easier to head south and competition from Atlantic City to the north, during the 1950s Cape May began to dust off its most valuable commodity: its history. Today, the whole town is a National Historic Landmark, with over six hundred **Victorian buildings**, tree-lined streets and beautifully kept **gardens**, and a lucrative B&B industry. It teeters dangerously on self-parody at times, thanks to its glut of cutesy "olde shoppes," but if you avoid the main drags and wander through the backstreets, you'll enjoy the historical authenticity. The town also boasts good **beaches**.

Arrival, information, and getting around

New Jersey Transit runs an express **bus** to Cape May from Philadelphia and the south Jersey coast, as well as services from New York and Atlantic City. Greyhound also stops at the terminal, opposite the corner of Lafayette and Ocean Street. **Ferries** connect the town to Lewes, Delaware ($7–9.50 per person, $28–41 per car; schedules on ⓣ1-800/643-3779, ⓦwww.capemaylewesferry.com). Maps, **information** and help with accommodation are available from the **Welcome Center** (daily 9am–4.30pm; ⓣ609/884-9562, ⓦwww.capemaynj.com), attached to the bus terminal.

Though Cape May itself is best enjoyed on foot, to venture out a bit further rent a **bike** from the Village Bike Shop near the bus terminal, at 609 Lafayette ($5 per hour, $12 per day; ⓣ609/884-8500). The Cape May Whale Watcher, at Second Avenue and Wilson Drive (ⓣ609/884-5445 or 1-800/786-5445, ⓦwww.capemaywhalewatcher.com), offers three trips (daily March–Dec) around Cape May Point: two **dolphin-watches** (2hr; 10am & 6.30pm; $27) and a **whale & dolphins voyage** (3hr; 1pm; $38).

Accommodation

Many of Cape May's pastel Victorian homes have been converted to pricey **B&Bs** or **guesthouses**, and the resort is so popular that choice plummets on summer weekends. During July and August even old motor inns can command over $100 a night; June and September rates are often around half that. Standard **hotels** front the ocean on Beach Drive, and you can **camp** at the expensive *Seashore Campsites*, 720 Seashore Rd (sites from $45 in summer, $20 off-season; ⓣ609/884-4010 or 1-800/313-2267, ⓦwww.seashorecampsites.com).

Cape Harbor Motor inn 715 Pittsburgh Ave ⓣ609/884-3352, ⓦwww.capeharbormotorinn.com. Comfortable motel, situated in a residential street seven blocks from the beach; cheaper than most places but rates soar in summer. ❸–❼

The Chalfonte 301 Howards St ⓣ609/884-8409, ⓦwww.chalfonte.com. Classy and spacious 1876 mansion with wraparound verandas, three blocks from the beach. ❺–❽

Inn of Cape May 7 Ocean St ⓣ1-800/582-5933, ⓦwww.innofcapemay.com. This once-fashionable Victorian shorefront hotel now has a small adjoining modern motel wing. The cheapest rooms are those with shared baths in the main building. Open daily April–Oct, weekends only late Oct to Dec. 3–7

Manor House 612 Hughes St Ⓣ609/884-4710, Ⓦwww.manorhouse.net. Great breakfasts and a relaxing porch in the heart of the historic district. 4–8

Queen Victoria 102 Ocean St Ⓣ609/884-8702, Ⓦwww.queenvictoria.com. Twenty-one rooms in four buildings, including a cottage and a carriage house. Rates include bicycle loans, beach chairs, breakfast (in bed, if desired), and afternoon tea. 6–8

Summer Cottage Inn 613 Columbia Ave Ⓣ609/884-4948, Ⓦwww.summercottageinn.com. 1867 inn with verandas and a cupola. Wide range of rates include good-value deals. 5–8

The Town and the beaches

Cape May's brightly colored houses were built by nouveaux riches Victorians with a healthy disrespect for subtlety. Cluttered with cupolas, gazebos, balconies, and "widow's walks," the houses follow no architectural rules except excess. They were known as "patternbook homes," with designs and features chosen from catalogs and thrown together in accordance with the owner's taste. The Victorian obsession with the Near East is everywhere: Moorish arches and onion domes sit comfortably next to gingerbread- and Queen Anne-style turrets. The **Emlen Physick Estate**, 1048 Washington St (tour hours vary; $10; Ⓣ609/884-5404, Ⓦwww.capemaymac.org), was built by the popular Philadelphia architect Frank Furness. It has been restored to its 1879 glory, with whimsical "upside-down" chimneys, a mock Tudor half-timbered facade, and much original furniture. West of town, where the Delaware Bay and the ocean meet, the 1859 **Cape May Lighthouse**, visible from 25 miles out at sea, offers great views from a gallery below the lantern (199 steps up) and a small exhibit on its history at ground level (daily April–Nov, winter weekends, hours vary; $5; Ⓣ609/884-8656, Ⓦwww.capemaymac.org). Three miles north of town on US-9, **Historic Cold Spring Village**, 720 Rte-9 (late May through mid-June & Sept Sat & Sun 10am–4.30pm; June–Aug Tues–Sun 10am–4.30pm; $8; Ⓣ609/898-2300, Ⓦwww.hcsv.org), depicts a typical nineteenth-century south Jersey farming community. Restored buildings from the region house a jail, school, inn, and shops, and there are various craft shows and special events.

Cape May's excellent **beaches** literally sparkle with quartz pebbles. Beach tags ($4 per day, $13 per week, $25 for a seasonal pass purchased before Memorial Day) must be worn from 10am until 6pm in the summer, and are available at the beach, from official vendors, or from **City Hall**, 643 Washington St (Ⓣ609/884-9525, Ⓦwww.capemaycity.com).

Eating

Cape May lacks the usual boardwalk snack bars, but it has plenty of cheap **lunch** places. **Dinner**, however, is far more expensive. Cape May's liquor laws are stringent, which means that many restaurants are BYO – call to check.

Wildwood

The traditionally blue-collar resort of nearby **Wildwood**, on a barrier island east of Rte-47, offers a counterpoint to the old-world fakery (pretty though it may be) of Cape May. Its 1950s architecture, left lovingly intact, includes dozens of gaudy and fun-looking hotels with names like *Pink Orchid*, *Waikiki*, and *The Shalimar*, all still featuring plastic palm trees, kidney-shaped swimming pools, and plenty of aqua, orange, and pink paint. To best appreciate the town's brash charm, take a stroll along the boardwalk and stop along the wide, throbbing, free beaches. Additionally, check out the local amusement rides and waterparks, such as Morey's Piers, Raging Waters, and Splash Zone.

Bellevue Tavern 7 S Main St ⓣ 609/463-1738. Functional early twentieth-century bar serving crab cakes and inexpensive hot sandwiches; dinners of steak, veal, and seafood average nearly $20.

Depot Market Café 409 Elmira St ⓣ 609/884-8030. Opposite the bus terminal, offering filling sandwiches, salads, and hoagies; dinners around $10.

Gecko's Carpenter's Lane ⓣ 609/898-7750. A good lunch stop with a tasty Southwestern menu and great desserts. Patio seating available.

The Lemon Tree 101 Liberty Way ⓣ 609/884-2704. The cheesesteaks at this cheap, cheerful deli are Philly-quality; a nice antidote to the coffeeshops along the street.

Mad Batter 19 Jackson St ⓣ 609/884-5970. Splash out on meat and fresh fish dishes, served by candlelight in the garden. Lunch is $9–15, dinner $18–30.

Nightlife and entertainment

Cape May is a friendly and laid-back place to be after dark; the day-trippers have gone home and the **bars** and **music venues** are enjoyed by locals and tourists alike. If you're after something a bit more lively, head a few miles north to the raucous nightclubs of **Wildwood**, such as *H2O*. Again, because of the liquor laws, remember that you may have to travel a little farther than you expect to find a drink.

Cabana's 429 Beach Ave ⓣ 609/884-4800. Two-level bar that often hosts live music downstairs; upstairs is a low-key cocktail lounge.

Carney's 401 Beach Ave ⓣ 609/884-4424. Spacious and relaxed Irish bar, with raucous live music.

Ugly Mug Washington St Mall and Decatur St ⓣ 609/884-3459. This friendly bar is a local favorite and serves chowder, sandwiches, and seafood.

3

New England

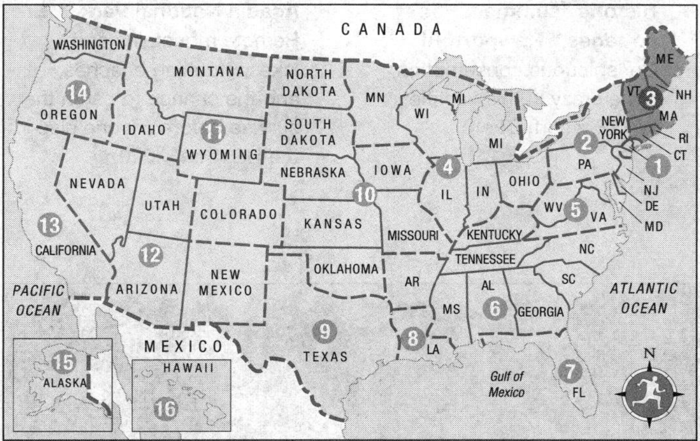

AL - ALABAMA	IN - INDIANA	MN - MINNESOTA	RI - RHODE ISLAND
AR - ARKANSAS	LA - LOUISIANA	MS - MISSISSIPPI	SC - SOUTH CAROLINA
CT - CONNECTICUT	MA - MASSACHUSETTS	NC - NORTH CAROLINA	VA - VIRGINIA
DE - DELAWARE	MD - MARYLAND	NH - NEW HAMPSHIRE	VT - VERMONT
FL - FLORIDA	ME - MAINE	NJ - NEW JERSEY	WI - WISCONSIN
IL - ILLINOIS	MI - MICHIGAN	PA - PENNSYLVANIA	WV - WEST VIRGINIA

CHAPTER 3

Highlights

* **Boston, MA** Revolutionary history comes to life around every charming corner, in one of America's most storied, walkable cities. See p.184
* **Provincetown, MA** Wild beaches, lovely flower-filled streets, and an alternative vibe on the outer reaches of Cape Cod. See p.209
* **Historic "summer cottages," Newport, RI** Conspicuous consumption gone crazy in this yachtie WASP resort. See p.224
* **White Mountains, NH** Ski, hike or just soak up the scenery on Mount Washington or Franconia Notch. See p.000
* **Montpelier, VT** Relaxed, friendly, and relatively tourist-free, pretty Montpelier is bounded by rivers and a forest of tall trees. See p.000
* **Acadia National Park, ME** Remote mountains and lakes, stunning beaches, and the chance to catch the sunrise before anyone else in the US. See p.000

▲ Acadia National Park

3

New England

The six **NEW ENGLAND** states of Massachusetts, Rhode Island, Connecticut, New Hampshire, Vermont, and Maine like to view themselves as the repository of all that is intrinsically American. In this version of history, the tangled streets of old Boston, the farms of Connecticut, and the village greens of Vermont are the cradle of the nation. Although nostalgia is at the root of the region's tourist trade, with innumerable small towns dolled-up to recapture a past that is at best wishful, and at times purely fictional, this is undeniably one of the most historic parts of the United States; a landscape studded with aging clapboard houses, Revolutionary War sites and white-spired churches set upon immaculate rolling greens. The region was home to, and inspiration for, some of the seminal figures of American literature, from Mark Twain and Henry Thoreau, to Emily Dickinson and Jack Kerouac.

The **Ivy League** colleges – Harvard, Yale, Brown, Dartmouth, et al – are the oldest in the country and remain hugely influential, dominating towns like Hanover and Amherst, attracting vast numbers of bright students from all over the world and setting a decidedly liberal tone throughout the region; though New Hampshire is something of a swing state, New England has voted solidly for Democratic presidential candidates since the 1980s.

Much of the Northeast is conspicuously wealthy. Indeed, the genteel seaside towns of modern Cape Cod and Rhode Island are a far cry from the first ragtag European settlements in New England. As the fortunes of industry magnates soared in the mid-nineteenth century, the coastline came increasingly to be viewed as prime real estate, to be lined with grand patrician homes, from the Vanderbilt mansions of Newport to the presidential compounds of the Bush and Kennedy families.

New England can still be a rather pricey place to visit, especially in late September and October, when visitors flock to see the magnificent **fall foliage**. Its tourist facilities are aimed at weekenders from the big cities as much as outsiders; places like **Cape Cod** and the **Berkshires** make convenient short breaks for locals. **Connecticut** and **Rhode Island** form part of the great East Coast megalopolis, but off I-95 you'll find plenty of tranquil pockets. **Boston** is a vibrant and stimulating city from which to set off north, where population is thin on the ground (and the **seafood** gets even better). The rest of **Massachusetts** is rich in historical and literary sights, while further inland, the lakes and mountains of **New Hampshire** and particularly **Maine** offer rural wildernesses to rival any in the nation. **Vermont** is slightly less diverse, but its country roads offer pleasant wandering through tiny villages and serene forests.

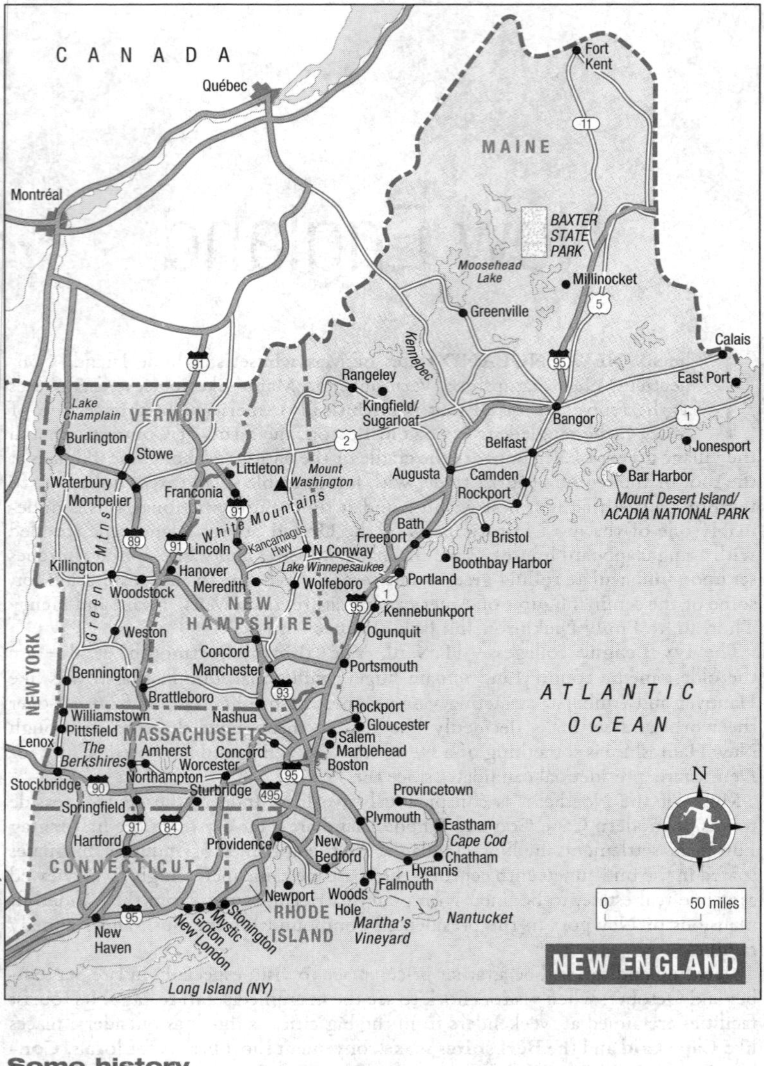

Some history

The Algonquin, **Native Americans** who first inhabited the northeast shoreline, were composed of several tribes and subgroups with different dialects. They shared a lifestyle of farming and fishing along the coast in summer, retreating with their animals to the relative warmth of the inland valleys in winter.

Six years after Columbus's first voyage, John Cabot nosed by in 1498, in search of the Northwest Passage. Over the next century, European fishermen began to return each year, though it was not until the early 1600s that the French and English attempted to found permanent colonies, in what is now Maine. The name – New England – was given in 1614 by surveyor-cum-explorer **John Smith**, who particularly appreciated the plentiful lobsters. By 1619 three-fourths of the native population had been killed by epidemics.

Even for the new arrivals, this was not promising land: without precious metals to be mined, or the potential to grow lucrative crops, the first major impetus for emigration was **religion**. Refugees from intolerance – notably the Puritans, beginning with the **Pilgrims** in 1620 – made the arduous voyage to search for the freedom to build their own communities. The Pilgrims only survived at first thanks to the Indians: they were aided by a certain Squanto, who had been kidnapped, sold as a slave in Spain, and returned home via England. In thanks, the Pilgrims forced the natives from the terraces they had farmed for generations.

The possibility of a serious Native American threat was eliminated in **King Philip's War** of 1675–76, in which a leader of the Wampanoag Indians (known as Philip) persuaded feuding native groups to bury their differences in one last, and ultimately hopeless, stand against the settlers. By then, though, white colonization had gathered an unstoppable momentum. The **Salem witch trials** of 1692 provided a salutary lesson on the potential dangers of fanaticism, and as immigration became less English-based, with influxes of Huguenots after 1680 and Irish in 1708, Puritan domination decreased and a definite class structure began to emerge.

While the strand of history that began with the Pilgrims is just one among many in the colonization of America – the Spanish were in Santa Fe before the Pilgrims ever left England – the metropolis of **Boston** deserves to be celebrated as the place where the great project of **American independence** first captured the popular imagination. This leading port of colonial America was always the likeliest focus of resentment against the latest impositions of the British government, and was ready to take up the challenge thrown down by British Chancellor Townshend in 1767: "I dare tax America." So many of the seminal moments of the **Revolutionary War** took place here: the Boston Massacre of 1770, the Boston Tea Party of 1773, and the first shots in nearby Lexington and Concord in 1775.

Once nationhood was secured by the signing of the **Declaration of Independence** on July 4, 1776, New England's prosperity was ironically hit hard by the loss of trade with England, and Boston was slowly eclipsed by Philadelphia, New York, and the new capital, Washington. The **Triangular Trade** in slaves, sugar, and rum provided one substitute source of income, the brief heyday of **whaling** another. New England was also momentarily at the forefront of the **Industrial Revolution**, when water-powered mills created a booming textile industry, most of which quickly moved south where wages were scandalously cheaper. Yet despite the continued presence of old money, recent diversification, and the development of some high-tech industries, New England today contains some pockets of poverty; in rural Vermont and New Hampshire, and also in towns such as Worcester, Providence, and Hartford, which have struggled since the decline of manufacturing industries. The region has been dominated by the **Democratic Party** since the early 1960s and has often led the country when it comes to liberal policies; Vermont was the first state to allow same-sex civil unions (2000) and Massachusetts was the first to allow **same-sex marriage** in 2004.

Massachusetts

To the first colonists of the **Massachusetts Bay Company**, their arrival near the site of modern Salem in 1629 marked a crucial moment in history. **Puritans** who had decided to leave England before it was engulfed by civil war saw their purpose, in the words of Governor John Winthrop, as the establishment of a utopian "**City upon a hill.**" Their new colony of **MASSACHUSETTS** was to be a beacon to the rest of humanity, an exemplar of sober government along sound spiritual principles.

In their own terms, the Puritans were not successful: as waves of immigration brought all kinds of dissenters and free thinkers from Europe, society in New England inevitably became secular. However, their **influence** remained. A clarity of thought and forcefulness of purpose can be traced from the foundation of Harvard College in 1636, through the intellectual impetus behind the Revolution and the crusade against slavery, to the nineteenth-century achievements of **writers** such as Melville, Emerson, Hawthorne, and Thoreau.

Other traditions, too, have helped shape the state – migrants from **Ireland** and **Italy**, freed and escaped **slaves** from the Southern states, **Portuguese** seamen – even if they have not always been welcome.

Spending a few days in **Boston** is strongly recommended. While its history is often visible, there's a great deal of modern life and energy besides, thanks in part to the presence of **Cambridge**, the home of Harvard University and MIT (Massachusetts Institute of Technology), just across the river. Several historic towns are within easy reach – **Salem** to the north, **Concord** and **Lexington** just inland, and **Plymouth** to the south. **Provincetown**, a ninety-minute ferry ride across the bay at the tip of Cape Cod, is great fun to visit, and the rest of the Cape offers old towns and lovely beaches – with the requisite huge crowds. Except for a handful of college towns such as **Amherst**, **western Massachusetts** is much quieter; its settlements are naturally concentrated where the land is fertile, such as along the Connecticut River Valley and in the **Berkshires** to the west.

Getting around Massachusetts

Massachusetts is an easy state to tour on **public transportation**: planes, trains, and buses all radiate out from Boston; connections to **Cape Cod** in particular are legion. The **Amtrak** line that connects Boston with New York, Philadelphia, and Washington DC is the best regional **train** service in the nation, while the *Vermonter* gives access to Vermont and Connecticut, and (via Springfield) Chicago and Toronto. The affable *Downeaster* service follows a scenic route that links Boston to Portland, Maine. **Buses** from Boston are also plentiful. The main east–west artery across the state is I-90 (or "MassPike"); the major north–south route is I-95, which circumnavigates the greater Boston area and affords entry points for its many suburbs.

Boston

Although the metropolitan area of **BOSTON** has long since expanded to fill the shoreline of **Massachusetts Bay**, and stretches for miles inland as well, the seventeenth-century port at its heart is still discernible. The tangled roads (former cow paths) clustered around **Boston Common** are a reminder of how the nation started out, and the city is enjoyably walkable in scale.

Boston was, until 1755, the biggest city in America; as the one most directly affected by the whims of the British Crown, it was the natural birthplace for the opposition that culminated in the **Revolutionary War**. Numerous evocative sites from that era are preserved along the downtown **Freedom Trail**. Since then, however, Boston has in effect turned its back on the sea. As the third busiest port in the British Empire (after London and Bristol), it stood on a narrow peninsula. What is now Washington Street provided the only access by land, and when the British set off to Lexington in 1775 they embarked in ships from the Common itself. During the nineteenth century, the Charles River marshlands were filled in to create the posh Back Bay residential area. Central Boston is now slightly set back from the water, and until recently, was divided by the hideous John Fitzgerald Expressway that carried I-93 across downtown. In 2006 the city successfully routed the traffic underground and disposed of this eyesore – a project more than a decade in the making, known as "the **Big Dig**."

Echoes of the "Brahmins" of a century ago can be seen in the stately brick enclaves and purple windowpanes of the city's posher districts. But this is by no means just a city of WASPs: the Irish who began to arrive in large numbers after the Great Famine had produced their first mayor as early as 1885, and the president of the entire nation within a hundred years. The liberal tradition that spawned the Kennedys remains very much alive, fed in part by the presence in the city of more than one hundred universities and colleges, the most famous of which – **Harvard University** – is actually in the contiguous city of Cambridge, just across the Charles River.

The slump of the Depression seemed to linger in Boston for years – in the 1950s, the population was actually dwindling – but these days the place has a bright, rejuvenated feel. The aesthetic effects of the Big Dig have completely reshaped the city – most notably with the elegant, skyline-boosting Zakim Bridge, the central Rose Kennedy Greenway, and the beautification of the HarborWalk. With its busy street life, imaginative museums, eminent architecture, and palpable history, Boston is one destination in New England there's no excuse for missing.

Arrival and information

Boston is the center of New England's transportation networks. It provides many visitors arriving by air from Europe with their first taste of America, while efficient rail and bus services from New York, Chicago, and further afield make this an obvious starting point.

By air

Logan Airport (Ⓣ617/561-1800 or 1-800/23-LOGAN), busy with both international and domestic services, is a mere three miles from downtown Boston. A **taxi** into town costs around $30, plus an extra $7.50 in fees and tolls; the trip should take twenty minutes at its best. Between 4am and 1am, free **shuttle buses** run every few minutes from all airport terminals to the airport **subway** station on the MBTA Blue line (see "City transportation and tours," p.186), from where it's an easy ten-minute ride to the city center.

By train

Amtrak (Ⓣ1-800/USA-RAIL, Ⓦwww.amtrak.com) trains along the Northeast Corridor from Providence, Washington DC, and New York, and from Chicago and Canada via Springfield, arrive a short walk from downtown Boston near the waterfront at **South Station**, on Summer Street at Atlantic Avenue. The station houses information booths, newsstands, restaurants, and a fantastic old clock, though no currency exchange. The Red subway line inside the station can whisk you to the center of town or out to Cambridge. Some Amtrak services also make an extra stop at **Back Bay Station**, 145 Dartmouth St, on the Orange subway line near Copley Square. **North Station** is used by MBTA commuter trains as well as the amiable *Downeaster*, which connects Boston to Portland, Maine, with a number of Maine and New Hampshire stops along the way.

By bus

Several **bus** companies provide direct links between the rest of New England and Boston. Greyhound (Ⓣ1-800/231-2222, Ⓦwww.greyhound.com) covers western Massachusetts, New Hampshire's White Mountains, Vermont, and Montréal in addition to a nationwide service; while Concord Coach (Ⓣ1-800/639-3317, Ⓦwww.concordcoachlines.com) runs to New Hampshire and up the Maine coast; it also has shuttle service to Logan Airport. Heading south, Peter Pan Bus Lines (Ⓣ1-800/343-9999, Ⓦwww.peterpanbus.com) connects Providence and Newport, Cape Cod, and New York City, as well as western Massachusetts. The popular Fung Wah bus offers an hourly service to Canal Street in New York City (Ⓣ617/345-8000, Ⓦwww.fungwahbus.com) for a mere $15 dollars each way, while the Bolt Bus (no telephone, Ⓦwww.boltbus.com) takes you from South Station to midtown Manhattan for $20 or less and has the added benefit of wireless internet. Plymouth and Brockton Bus Co. (Ⓣ508/746-0378, Ⓦwww.p-b.com), serves Cape Cod as well as access to Martha's Vineyard and Nantucket and has buses that leave from Logan Airport as well as South Station; all other buses leave from South Station (see "By train," p.185).

Information

The most convenient place to get advice and maps is the **Visitor Information Center** (Mon–Sat 8.30am–5pm, Sun 10am–6pm; Ⓣ617/536-4100 or 1-888/SEE-BOSTON, Ⓦwww.bostonusa.com) near the Park Street subway stop on the Tremont Street side of Boston Common. Across the street from the Old State House, at 15 State St, is an excellent information center maintained by rangers from the National Park Service (daily 9am–5pm; Ⓣ617/242-5642), as well as bathrooms and a bookstore. There are also information kiosks in **Quincy Market** and at the **Prudential Center** (in Back Bay). For advance information, the **Boston By Phone** service (Ⓣ1-888/SEE-BOSTON) allows visitors anywhere in North America to connect directly with a wide range of hotels and services. The city's main **post office**, 25 Dorchester Ave, is located behind South Station and is open 24hr (Ⓣ617/654-5302).

City transportation and tours

Much of the pleasure of visiting Boston comes from being in a city that was built long before cars were invented. Walking around town can be a joy; conversely, driving is an absolute nightmare. The freeways won't take you where you want to go, signage is bad, the one-way traffic systems can have you circling for hours, and if you ever do arrive, parking lots can be very expensive. There's no point renting a car in Boston until the day you leave, especially since the city's public transportation is good and the local drivers notoriously crazy.

Subways and trolleys

The Massachusetts Bay Transportation Authority (MBTA, known as the "**T**") is responsible for Boston's **subway** system and **trolleys**. The subway, which opened in 1897, is the oldest in the US; its first station, **Park Street**, remains its center (any train marked "inbound" is headed here). Four lines – Red, Green, Blue, and Orange – operate daily from 5am until 12.30am, although certain routes begin to shut down earlier. The four lines are supplemented by a bus rapid transit (BRT) route, the **Silver Line**, which runs aboveground along Washington Street and cuts through the heart of the South End and has additional access to the airport and the new Seaport District. While maps are posted at each station, it's a good idea to pick up the widely available transport maps for reference. Trains are fast and safe; only some parts of the Orange line might be said to be unsafe after dark.

Boston has recently installed a new and somewhat confusing system for subway fares. Within the city, the standard fare is $2, payable by the purchase of a "Charlie Ticket," which can be purchased at any of the ATM-like machines in the station. If you pick up a "CharlieCard" – with more of a credit card thickness and a longer lifespan – from a station attendant - your fare begins at only $1.70 per ride. Your safest (and simplest) bet is the **visitor's pass** which seamlessly covers all subway and local bus journeys (as well as the ferry to Charlestown) at a cost of $9 a day or $15 a week. For MBTA **information** call Ⓣ617/222-3200 or 1-800/392-6100, or visit Ⓦwww.mbta.com.

Buses

The normal fare on MBTA's **local buses** is $1.50 (exact change or CharlieTicket or Card), but longer distances, such as out to Salem or Marblehead, cost up to $5. MBTA also runs **commuter rail lines**, extending as far as Salem, Concord, and Providence, Rhode Island, some with wi-fi on board; destinations north leave from **North Station** (Ⓣ617/222-3200) on Causeway Street, under the TD Banknorth Garden; destinations south leave from (you guessed it) **South Station** (Ⓣ617/222-3200) on Summer Street at Atlantic Avenue, by the waterfront.

Cycling

In and around Boston are some eighty miles of **bike trails**. Bicycles can be rented from Boston Bicycle, 842 Beacon St (Ⓣ617/236-0752, Ⓦwww.cambridgebicycle.com) or at their sister location, Cambridge Bicycle, in Cambridge (259 Massachusetts Avenue; near MIT; Ⓣ617/876-6555, Ⓦwww.cambridgebicycle.com), and from Boston Bike Tours and Rentals, near the Visitor Information Center on Boston Common (Ⓣ617/308-5902, Ⓦwww.bostonbiketours.com). Rentals are around $25 per day.

City tours

It's easy enough to get to know Boston on foot by following the **Freedom Trail** (see p.192). The National Park Service, 15 State St (Ⓣ617/242-5642, Ⓦwww.nps.gov/bost), conducts free, ranger-led tours centering on a number of Freedom Trail hotspots as well as the Black Heritage Trail. Other standout walking tours include those offered by North End Market Tours ($48–60; Ⓣ617/523-6032, advance tickets required, Ⓦwww.northendmarkettours.com), which conduct great tasting tours of the North End and Chinatown neighborhoods.

If you prefer to see the city while comfortably seated, narrated trips run throughout the day aboard the hundred-minute Old Town Trolley Tours (Ⓣ617/269-7150, Ⓦwww.trolleytours.com; $34, kids aged 3–12, $13; discounted price if purchased online). But nothing is as popular (or as novel) as a Boston Duck Tour (adults $29, kids 3–11 $19; Ⓣ617/267-DUCK, Ⓦwww.bostonducktours.com) or its newbie rival Super Duck Tours (adults $29, kids 3–11 $17; Ⓣ1-877/34DUCKS, Ⓦwww.superduckexcursions.com), entertaining romps by land and by sea aboard a real WWII amphibious landing vehicle or Hydra-Terra. The former departs from the Prudential Center as well as the Museum of Science, while the latter leaves from Gate 1 of the Charlestown Navy Yard, March through November. Another well-recommended, more specialized tour is the Gondola di

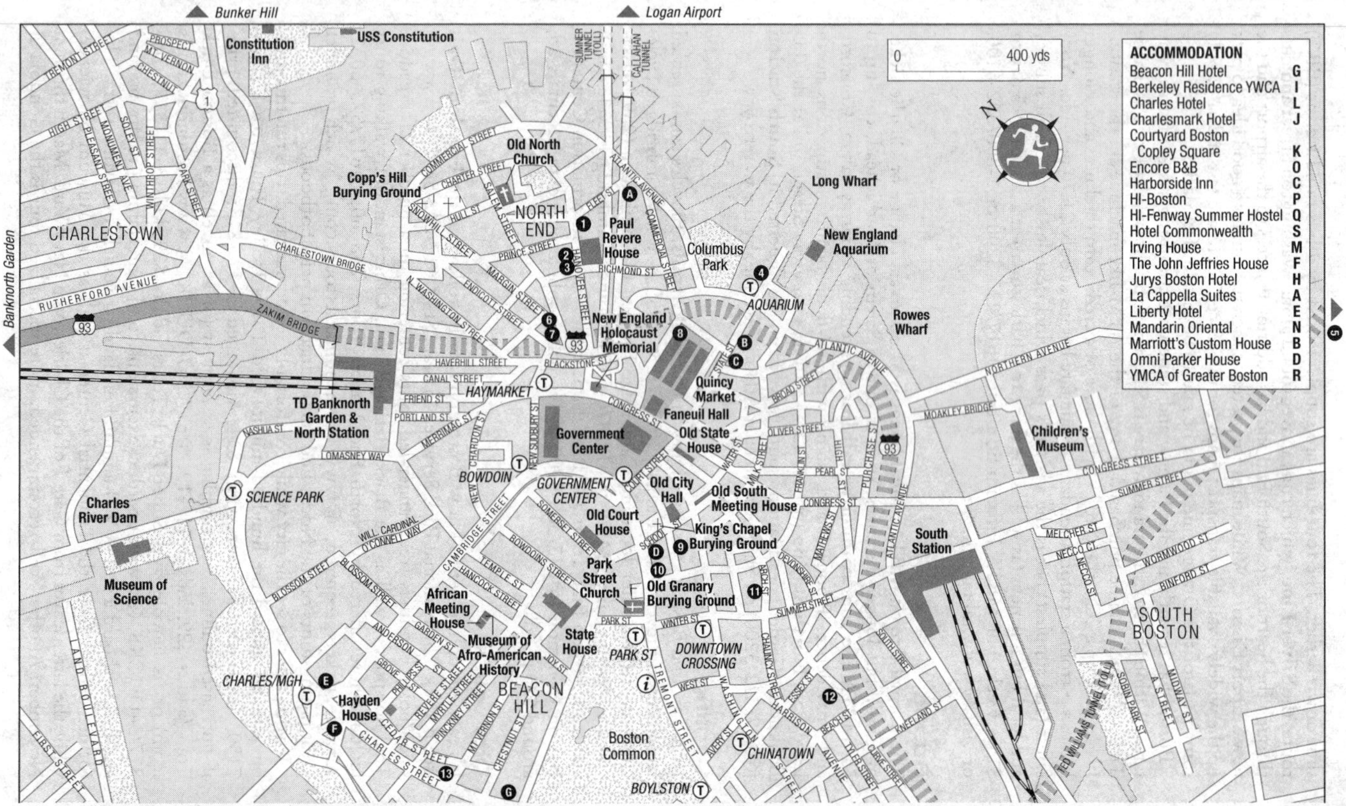
Bunker Hill
Logan Airport
Banknorth Garden
5
ACCOMMODATION
Beacon Hill Hotel G
Berkeley Residence YWCA I
Charles Hotel L
Charlesmark Hotel J
Courtyard Boston Copley Square K
Encore B&B O
Harborside Inn C
HI-Boston P
HI-Fenway Summer Hostel Q
Hotel Commonwealth S
Irving House M
The John Jeffries House F
Jurys Boston Hotel H
La Cappella Suites A
Liberty Hotel E
Mandarin Oriental N
Marriott's Custom House B
Omni Parker House D
YMCA of Greater Boston R
0
400 yds
N
CHARLESTOWN
Constitution Inn
USS Constitution
Copp's Hill Burying Ground
Old North Church
NORTH END
Paul Revere House
Columbus Park
New England Aquarium
Long Wharf
Rowes Wharf
AQUARIUM
New England Holocaust Memorial
Quincy Market
Faneuil Hall
Old State House
TD Banknorth Garden & North Station
HAYMARKET
Government Center
GOVERNMENT CENTER
BOWDOIN
SCIENCE PARK
Charles River Dam
Museum of Science
Old City Hall
Old South Meeting House
King's Chapel Burying Ground
Old Court House
Park Street Church
Old Granary Burying Ground
State House
PARK ST
DOWNTOWN CROSSING
African Meeting House
Museum of Afro-American History
BEACON HILL
CHARLES/MGH
Hayden House
Boston Common
BOYLSTON
CHINATOWN
South Station
Children's Museum
SOUTH BOSTON
ZAKIM BRIDGE
SUMNER TUNNEL (TOLL)
CALLAHAN TUNNEL
TED WILLIAMS TUNNEL (TOLL)
TREMONT STREET
PROSPECT
MT VERNON
CHESTNUT
HIGH STREET
PLEASANT STREET
MONUMENT AVE
SOLEY ST
WINTHROP STREET
PARK STREET
CHARLESTOWN BRIDGE
RUTHERFORD AVENUE
COMMERCIAL STREET
CHARTER STREET
SALEM STREET
HULL ST
SNOWHILL STREET
PRINCE STREET
HANOVER STREET
FLEET ST
ATLANTIC AVENUE
RICHMOND ST
MARGIN STREET
ENDICOTT STREET
N. WASHINGTON STREET
HAVERHILL STREET
BLACKSTONE ST
CANAL STREET
FRIEND ST
PORTLAND ST
MERRIMAC ST
NASHUA ST
LOMASNEY WAY
NEW CHARDON ST
NEW SUDBURY ST
CONGRESS ST
STATE ST
BROAD STREET
OLIVER STREET
FRANKLIN ST
HIGH ST
PURCHASE ST
PEARL ST
WATER ST
MILK STREET
COURT STREET
SCHOOL ST
MATHEWS ST
DEVONSHIRE ST
ARCH ST
SUMMER STREET
WINTER ST
WEST ST
WASHINGTON
CHAUNCY STREET
ESSEX ST
AVERY ST
HARRISON AVENUE
BEACH ST
KNEELAND ST
SOUTH STREET
TYLER STREET
CURVE STREET
MOAKLEY BRIDGE
NORTHERN AVENUE
CONGRESS STREET
MELCHER ST
NECCO CT
NECCO ST
WORMWOOD ST
BINFORD ST
SOBIN PARK ST
A STREET
MIDWAY ST
CAMBRIDGE STREET
SOMERSET STREET
BOWDOIN STREET
TEMPLE ST
HANCOCK STREET
JOY ST
WILL CARDINAL O'CONNELL WAY
BLOSSOM STREET
ANDERSON
GARDEN ST
GROVE
PHILLIPS ST
REVERE STREET
MYRTLE STREET
PINCKNEY STREET
MT VERNON ST
CHESTNUT ST
CEDAR STREET
CHARLES STREET
FIRST STREET
LAND BOULEVARD

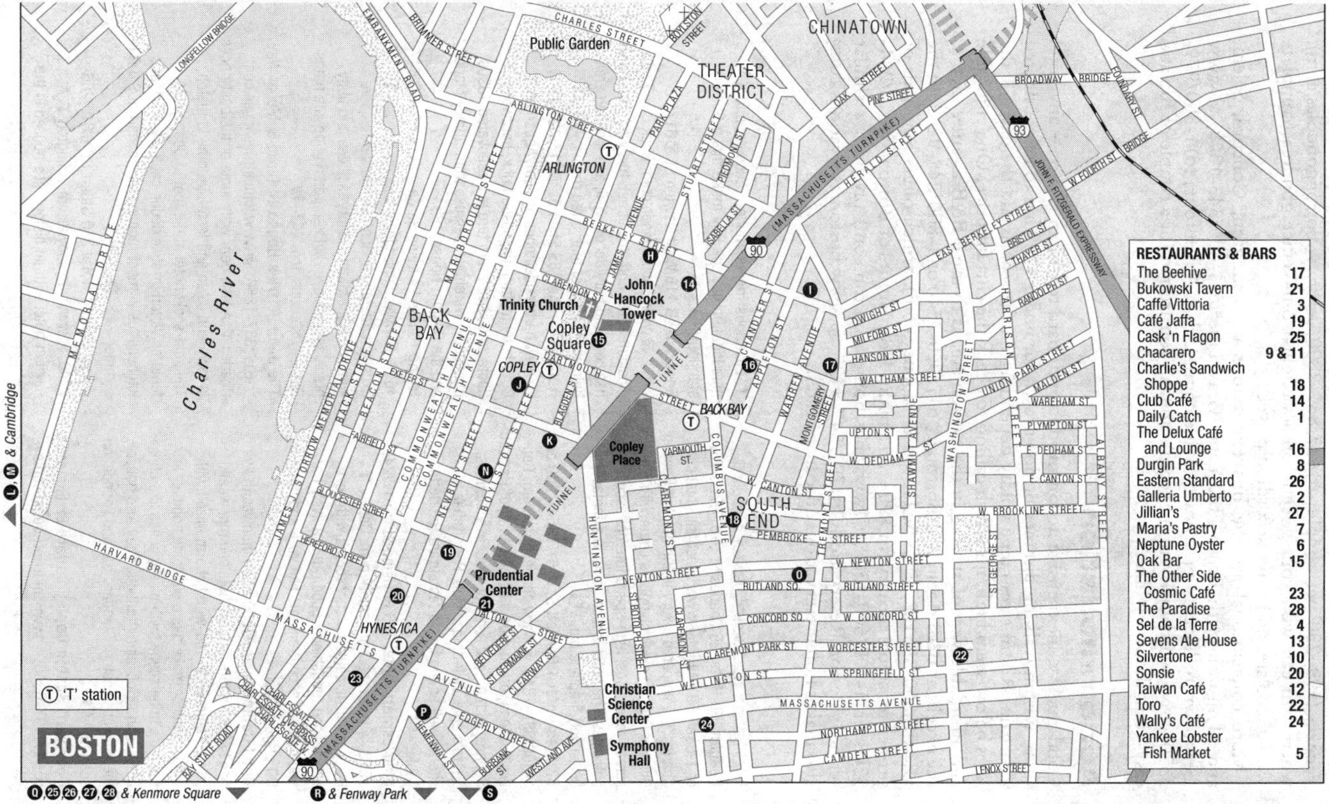
BOSTON
T 'T' station
RESTAURANTS & BARS
The Beehive 17
Bukowski Tavern 21
Caffe Vittoria 3
Café Jaffa 19
Cask 'n Flagon 25
Chacarero 9 & 11
Charlie's Sandwich Shoppe 18
Club Café 14
Daily Catch 1
The Delux Café and Lounge 16
Durgin Park 8
Eastern Standard 26
Galleria Umberto 2
Jillian's 27
Maria's Pastry 7
Neptune Oyster 6
Oak Bar 15
The Other Side Cosmic Café 23
The Paradise 28
Sel de la Terre 4
Sevens Ale House 13
Silvertone 10
Sonsie 20
Taiwan Café 12
Toro 22
Wally's Café 24
Yankee Lobster Fish Market 5
Charles River
Public Garden
CHINATOWN
THEATER DISTRICT
BACK BAY
SOUTH END
ARLINGTON
COPLEY
BACK BAY
HYNES/ICA
Trinity Church
John Hancock Tower
Copley Square
Copley Place
Prudential Center
Christian Science Center
Symphony Hall
MASSACHUSETTS TURNPIKE
JOHN F. FITZGERALD EXPRESSWAY
TUNNEL
MEMORIAL DRIVE
JAMES J. STORROW MEMORIAL DRIVE
HARVARD BRIDGE
LONGFELLOW BRIDGE
COMMONWEALTH AVENUE
BOYLSTON STREET
HUNTINGTON AVENUE
COLUMBUS AVENUE
TREMONT STREET
WASHINGTON STREET
MASSACHUSETTS AVENUE
L, M & Cambridge
0, 25, 26, 27, 28 & Kenmore Square
R & Fenway Park
S

Venezia ($99–230 per couple; ⓣ617/867-2800, ⓦwww.bostongondolas.com), where you can woo your sweetie on a straight-from-Venice gondola (complete with chocolates and a live accordion player).

More conventional are the **bus excursions** to Lexington, Concord, Salem, and Plymouth with Brush Hill Tours/Gray Line (ⓣ1-800/343-1328, ⓦwww.beantowntrolley.com or www.grayline.com). Urban Adventours (ⓣ1-800/979-3370, ⓦwww.urbanadventours.com) can take you around for a couple of fun and easy-going hours by bike.

Accommodation

Good-quality, inexpensive **accommodation** is hard to find in Boston – any hotel room within walking distance of downtown for under $200 has to be considered a bargain. Room rates range wildly depending on the season and the day – if the rates below seem high, it's worth calling to check the current price. One enjoyable and affordable way of staying in the Boston area is to use a **B&B agency** such as the excellent B&B Agency of Boston (ⓣ617/720-3540 or 1-800/248-9262; in the UK ⓣ0800/895128, ⓦwww.boston-bnbagency.com), which offers hundreds of properties across the city for $90–180 a night. Host Homes of Boston (ⓣ617/244-1308 or 1-800/600-1308, ⓦwww.hosthomesofboston.com) provides a similar service; Boston Reservations (ⓣ781/547-5427, ⓦwww.bostonreservations.com) also makes hotel reservations at reduced rates.

Hotels, motels, and B&Bs

Beacon Hill Hotel 25 Charles St ⓣ617/723-7575 or 1-888/959-BHHB, ⓦwww.beaconhillhotel.com; Charles **T**. Pampered luxury in the heart of Beacon Hill; the thirteen sleek chambers come with flat-screen televisions, high-speed internet access, and balconies. The hotel is also home to a fantastic bistro and fireplace bar. 9

Charles Hotel 1 Bennett St ⓣ617/864-1200 or 1-800/882-1818, ⓦwww.charleshotel.com; Copley **T**. Clean, bright rooms in the center of Harvard Square, with a good array of modern amenities. There's an excellent jazz club, Regattabar, on-site as well as the iconic restaurant Henrietta's Table. 9

Charlesmark Hotel 655 Boylston St ⓣ617/247-1212, ⓦwww.thecharlesmark.com; Copley **T**. Forty smallish, contemporary rooms with cozy beechwood furnishings, good rates, a lively bar, and modern accoutrements like wi-fi and in-room CD players. 6–9

Hotel Commonwealth 500 Commonwealth Ave ⓣ617/933-5000, ⓦwww.hotelcommonwealth.com; Kenmore **T**. Old-world charm mixed with modern decor make this a welcome addition to Boston's hotel scene, with nice touches like choice linens and L'Occitaine products. They also house the fabulous Eastern Standard bar and Foundation Lounge. 9

Courtyard Boston Copley Square 88 Exeter St ⓣ617/437-9300, ⓦwww.marriott.com; Copley **T**. Luxurious rooms, modern accents, and a nice location in Back Bay make this a Boston standout. 9

Encore B&B 116 West Newton St ⓣ617/266-7200, ⓦwww.encorebandb.com; Back Bay **T**. On a pleasant South End side street, this well-loved B&B has contemporary decor, wi-fi, and a sitting area or balcony in each of their three rooms. 6–8

Harborside Inn 185 State St ⓣ617/723-7500, ⓦwww.harborsideinnboston.com; Aquarium **T**. Cozy hotel featuring exposed brick, hardwood floors, and cherry furniture in a renovated 1890s mercantile warehouse; across from Quincy Market and the Custom House. 5–9

Irving House 24 Irving St, Cambridge ⓣ617/547-4600, ⓦwww.cambridgeinns.com; Harvard **T**. Excellent, friendly option near Harvard Square with (coin-operated) laundry facilities and tasty breakfast included; both shared and private baths. Birthday specials, too. 5–7

The John Jeffries House 14 David G. Mugar Way ⓣ617/367-1866, ⓦwww.johnjeffrieshouse.com; Charles **T**. A little gem with some of the best prices in town and clean and tasteful rooms to match. This mid-scale hotel at the foot of Beacon Hill features Victorian-style decor, cable TV, wi-fi, and kitchenettes in most rooms; singles start at $109 in summer. 5–7

Jurys Boston Hotel 350 Stuart St ⓣ617/266-7200, ⓦwww.jurysdoyle.com; Arlington **T**. A modern hotel with an historic (it's housed in the former Boston police headquarters), Irish bent, Jurys features stylish rooms equipped with wireless internet, a fitness center, and the swanky Stanhope Grille. ⑨

La Cappella Suites 290 North St ⓣ617/523-9020, ⓦwww.lacappellasuites.com; Haymarket **T**. Accommodation has opened up in the North End with this lovely new arrival – three cozy, modern rooms with wi-fi, cable TV, and a nice public seating area. Two of the rooms have private balconies. Be prepared for a five-floor walk-up. ⑤–⑧

Liberty Hotel 215 Charles St ⓣ617/224-4000, ⓦwww.libertyhotel.com; Charles **T**. The Liberty Hotel has taken over the labyrinthine digs of an 1851 prison in Beacon Hill and fashioned it with stylish furnishings and lush details, such as same-day laundry service, a fitness and business center, and overnight shoe shines. They also house the Clink restaurant and the Alibi lounge, currently the places to see and be seen In Boston. ⑨

Mandarin Oriental 776 Boylston St ⓣ617/535-8888, ⓦwww.mandarinoriental.com/boston; Copley **T**. Boston is all abuzz with the opening of this glamorous hotel slated to change the already pretty face of Back Bay. Rooms – which are frightfully expensive (starting at $675) – offer luxuries such as silk window treatments, personal trainers, an indulgent spa, and a spacious layout. Back Bay's L'Espalier restaurant, long a darling of Boston's restaurant scene, will be accompanying the Mandarin and is moving from its landmark brownstone digs into the hotel. ⑨

Marriott's Custom House 3 McKinley Square ⓣ617/310-6300, ⓦwww.marriott.com; Aquarium **T**. While it's no longer the tallest skyscraper in New England (a title it held in the nineteenth century), it continues to have gorgeous, jaw-dropping views of the harbor, historic, elegantly appointed rooms, high-speed internet, great service, and a fantastic location. ⑨

Omni Parker House 60 School St ⓣ617/227-8600 or 1-800/843-6664, ⓦwww.omniparkerhouse.com; Park **T**. The oldest continuously running hotel in the US (as well as the originators of Boston cream pie), the Omni Parker House features a gorgeous, gilded lobby, modern renovations (including high-speed internet), an amazing central location, and some of downtown's better room rates. ⑧–⑨

Hostels

Berkeley Residence YWCA 40 Berkeley St ⓣ617/375-2524, ⓦwww.ywcaboston.org/berkeley; Back Bay **T**. Clean and simple rooms next door to a police station. All rates include breakfast; dinner is an additional $7.50. Singles are ($60), doubles ($90), and triples ($105) in a convenient South End location. Longer-term accommodation only available to women.

HI-Boston 12 Hemenway St ⓣ617/536-1027, ⓦwww.bostonhostel.org; Hynes **T**. Located in the Fenway area, close to the hip end of Newbury St and the Lansdowne St clubs, this is one of Boston's better hostel options. Internet access and a safe, clean environment. Dorm beds are $32–39 a night. In summer, book ahead, or check in at 8am, to be sure of a place.

HI-Fenway Summer Hostel 575 Commonwealth Ave ⓣ617/536-9455, ⓦwww.bostonhostel.org; Kenmore **T**. A summer-only hostel (June 1–mid-Aug) that functions as a BU dorm in winter months. Spacious rooms and a great location within walking distance of nightclubs and Fenway Park. Members $36, nonmembers $39.

YMCA of Greater Boston 316 Huntington Ave ⓣ617/536-7800 ⓦwww.ymcaboston.org/huntington; Northeastern **T**. Good budget rooms, and access to the Y's pool and weight room. Singles are $50, but you can get a four-person room for $100. Co-ed June–Sept, otherwise men-only. Ten-day maximum stay.

The City

Boston has grown up around **Boston Common**, a utilitarian chunk of green established for public use and "the feeding of cattell" in 1634. A good starting point for a tour of the city, it is also one of the links in the string of nine parks (six of which were designed by Frederick Law Olmsted, America's foremost landscape architect) known as Boston's **Emerald Necklace**. Another piece is the lovely **Public Garden**, across Charles Street from the Common, where Boston's iconic swan boats ($2.75; ⓣ617/522-1966, ⓦwww.swanboats.com), paddle the main pond amidst tulip-strewn greenery.

The visitor center, which marks the start of the **Freedom Trail**, is near the tapering east end of the Common. As you stand here, facing up Tremont Street with the State House away to your left, the main shopping district, **Quincy Market**, and the **waterfront** are slightly ahead (a 12min walk) and down to the right. The modern concrete structures of **Government Center** are straight up Tremont

▲ Public Gardens

Street, with the beloved **North End** beyond – first Irish, then Jewish, and now a very Italian enclave. A short way behind you on the left rises lofty **Beacon Hill**, every bit as elegant as when Henry James called Mount Vernon Street "the most prestigious address in America" (far removed from its eighteenth-century nickname of "Mount Whoredom"). Heading away from the center down Tremont Street brings you to **Chinatown** and the **Theater District**, while grand boulevards such as Commonwealth Avenue lead west from the Public Garden into the **Back Bay**, where Harvard Bridge runs across the Charles River into **Cambridge**.

The Freedom Trail

Probably the best way to orient yourself in downtown Boston – and to appreciate the city's role in American history – is to walk some or all of the **Freedom Trail**. You can pick up or leave this easy self-guided route anywhere – a line of red bricks (or red paint) marking the trail is embedded in the pavement – but technically it begins on Boston Common at the **Visitor Information Center**.

From here, head for the golden dome of the **Massachusetts State House** (free tours Mon–Fri 10am–3.30pm); a Charles Bulfinch design completed in 1798. It remains the seat of Massachusetts' government; its most famous feature, a carved fish dubbed the "Sacred Cod," symbolizes the wealth Boston accrued from maritime trade. Politicos take this symbol so seriously that when Harvard pranksters stole it in the 1930s the House didn't reconvene until it was recovered.

Though **Park Street Church**, on the corner of Park and Tremont Street, (July & Aug Tues–Sat 8.30am–3.30pm; rest of year by appointment; free) is by no means "the most interesting mass of bricks and mortar in America," as Henry James once claimed, its ornate white steeple is undeniably impressive. It was here, on July 4, 1829, that orator William Lloyd Garrison delivered his first public address calling for the nationwide abolition of slavery. Just around the corner, the atmospheric **Old Granary Burying Ground** (daily 9am–5pm; free) includes the Revolutionary remains of Paul Revere, Samuel Adams, and John Hancock, as well as those of the so-called Mother Goose, née Elizabeth Vergoose (or Vertigoose), said to have collected nursery rhymes for her grandchildren. A block or so north on Tremont is the ethereal **King's Chapel Burying Ground** (daily 9.30am–5pm; free), final resting place for seventeenth-century luminaries such as Mary Chilton, woman of the *Mayflower,* and Boston's first governor, John Winthrop. Nearby on School Street, a statue of Benjamin Franklin marks the site of **Boston Latin School**, America's first public school, attended by Franklin (who later dropped out) and Samuel Adams. Malcolm X and Ho Chi Minh are both former employees of the **Omni Parker House Hotel** (not officially on the Trail), the longest continuously operating luxury hotel in the nation and home of the first-ever Boston cream pie.

Next come two of the Trail's more striking and significant buildings. The **Old South Meeting House** (daily: April–Oct 9.30am–5pm; Nov–March 10am–4pm; $5) is where Samuel Adams pronounced "this meeting can do nothing more to save the country" – the signal that triggered the Boston Tea Party on December 16, 1773. Considered to be the first major act of rebellion preceding the Revolutionary War, it was a carefully-planned event wherein one hundred men, mostly dressed in Indian garb, solemnly threw enough British tea into the harbor to make 24 million cuppas. The elegant **Old State House**, built in 1712, was the seat of colonial government, and from its balcony the Declaration of Independence was first publicly-read in Boston on July 18, 1776; two hundred years later to the day, Queen Elizabeth II made a speech from that same balcony. Inside is a neat **museum** of Boston history that includes a dapper jacket belonging to John Hancock (daily 9am–5pm; $5). Outside, a circle of cobblestones set on a traffic island at the intersection of Devonshire and State streets marks the site of the **Boston Massacre** on March 5, 1770, when British soldiers fired on a crowd that was pelting them with stone-filled snowballs, and killed five, including Crispus Attucks, a former slave.

Lively **Quincy Market** and **Faneuil Hall Marketplace** (a 10min walk northeast from here; daily 10am–8pm; free) is where to refuel at restaurants and takeaway food stalls or shop for souvenirs. The market is a pioneer example of successful urban renewal (by the same developer who transformed London's Covent Garden). Faneuil Hall (daily 9am–5pm; free) was, however, once known as the "Cradle of Liberty," a meeting place for revolutionaries and, later, abolitionists. Nearby on Union Street, step off the Freedom Trail to visit **The New England Holocaust Memorial** – lofty, hollow glass pillars etched with six million numbers recalling the tattoos the Nazis gave its victims. Its smokestack design is particularly striking at night, when the steam that rises from the pillars is lit up from within.

Passing over pleasant greenery and splash-worthy fountains of the new Rose Kennedy Greenway (formerly a massive, aboveground expressway) and into the **North End**, you reach **Paul Revere House**, 19 North Square, Boston's last surviving seventeenth-century house (daily: mid-April to Oct 9.30am–5.15pm; Nov to mid-April Tues–Sun 9.30am–4.15pm; $3), built after the Great Fire of 1676, and home to Paul Revere – patriot, silversmith, Freemason, and father of sixteen children – from 1770 until 1800. When Revere embarked upon his famous **ride** of April 18, 1775, to warn Samuel Adams and John Hancock (as well as the residents of Lexington, MA) that the British were assembling for an attack, two lanterns were hung from the belfry of **Old North Church**, 193 Salem St (daily: June–Oct 9am–6pm; Nov–May 9am–5pm; free), to alert Charlestown in case he got caught. Up the hill on Hull Street, from **Copp's Hill Burial Ground** (daily 9am–5pm; free), you can see across the harbor to Charlestown; as indeed could the British, who planted their artillery here for the Battle of Bunker Hill. As you exit the cemetery, keep an eye out for the **narrowest house** at 44 Hull St; a private residence merely ten feet in width.

Next, the Freedom Trail crosses the Charlestown Bridge, a fairly long - but scenic - walk. Its final two sites are also reached by the frequent **ferries** from Long

Wharf to Charlestown Navy Yard (Mon–Fri every 15–30mins 6.30am–8pm, Sat & Sun every 15min 10am–6pm; $1.70 each way).

The celebrated **USS Constitution**, also known as "Old Ironsides," is the oldest commissioned warship still afloat in the world. Launched in Boston in 1797, she earned her nickname during the War of 1812, when advancing cannonballs bounced off her hull; she subsequently saw 33 battles without ever losing one. Free tours of the ship are led every half-hour (April–Oct Tues–Sun 10am–5.50pm, Nov–March Thurs–Sun 10am–3.50pm; Ⓦwww.ussconstitution.navy.mil). Across the way, the **USS Constitution Museum** (daily: summer 9am–6pm; rest of year 10am–5pm; free) houses well-tailored displays on the history of the ship; upstairs is more fun-oriented, with hands-on sailorly exhibits testing your ability to balance on a footrope and helping to pinpoint whether your comrades have scurvy or gout. Beyond the museum, the **Bunker Hill Monument** sits on Breed's Hill, the actual site of the battle fought on June 17, 1775, which, while technically won by the British, invigorated the patriots, whose strong showing felled nearly half the British troops. A spiral staircase of 294 steps leads to sweeping views at the top; a new **museum** (daily 9am–4.30pm; free) at the base has interesting exhibits on the battle as well as the history of Charlestown. In summer there's usually an ice cream truck to reward your hike to the top, and the park makes a nice spot for picnicking.

The waterfront and Seaport District

Boston's **waterfront** has recently seen major revitalization efforts – inviting fountains, well-maintained green spaces, and historic signage have all started popping up – making it a great spot for a warm weather stroll. Wisteria-laden **Columbus Park**, next to the *Marriott Long Wharf Hotel*, is a pretty place to lounge and picnic.

The Black Heritage Trail

Massachusetts was the first state to declare slavery illegal, in 1783 – partly as a result of black participation in the Revolutionary War – and a large community of free blacks and escaped slaves swiftly grew in the North End and on Beacon Hill. Very few blacks live in either place today, but the **Black Heritage Trail** traces Beacon Hill's key role in local and national black history – perhaps the most important historical site in America devoted to pre-Civil War African-American history and culture.

Pick up the Trail at 46 Joy St, where the **Abiel Smith School** contains a **Museum of African American History** (Mon–Sat 10am–4pm; free), and rotates a number of well-tailored exhibits centered on abolitionism and African-American history and talks from well-informed rangers. Built in 1806 as the country's first African-American church, this became known as "Black Faneuil Hall" during the abolitionist campaign; Frederick Douglass issued his call here for all blacks to take up arms in the Civil War. Among those who responded were the volunteers of the **Massachusetts 54th Regiment**, commemorated by a monument at the edge of Boston Common, opposite the State House, which depicts their farewell march down Beacon Street. Robert Lowell won a Pulitzer Prize for his poem, "For the Union Dead," about this monument, and the regiment's tragic end at Fort Wagner was depicted in the movie *Glory*.

From the monument, the Trail winds around Beacon Hill, and includes a stop at the **Lewis and Harriet Hayden House**. Once a stop on the famous "Underground Railroad," the Haydens sheltered hundreds of runaway slaves from bounty-hunters in pursuit.

While it's easy enough to traverse it on your own, the best way to experience the Trail is by taking a National Park Service **walking tour** (Mon–Sat 10am, noon, & 2pm; call to reserve; free; Ⓣ617/742-5415 or Ⓣ617/720-2991, Ⓦwww.nps.gov/boaf).

Faneuil Hall originally stood at the head of **Long Wharf**, which stuck out nearly two thousand feet into the harbor; it also served as the site of the final British evacuation on March 17, 1776. Later, a thousand-foot expanse of the waterfront was filled in, and the **Custom House Tower**, once the tallest skyscraper in New England, was erected to mark the end of the wharf. It too now finds itself inland; although its observation deck offers terrific harbor views (3 McKinley Square; ⓣ617/310-6300; free).

Close by on Central Wharf, the **New England Aquarium** (July & Aug Mon–Thurs & Sun 9am–6pm, Fri & Sat 9am–7pm; Sept–June Mon–Fri 9am–5pm, Sat & Sun 9am–6pm; $19.95, kids $11.95; ⓣ617/973-5200) has an outdoor pool of basking sea otters. Inside, a colossal, three-story glass cylindrical tank is packed with giant sea turtles, moray eels, and sharks as well as a range of other ocean exotica that swim by in unsettling proximity. Scuba divers hand-feed the fish five times a day, and sea lion shows are held in a floating amphitheater alongside. The Aquarium also runs excellent **whale-watching** trips (early April to late Oct; 3-4hr, call for times; $36, kids $30; ⓣ617/973-5206).

The waterfront is also the base for **ferries** to Provincetown, MA on Cape Cod (see p.209; ⓣ617/227-4321), Salem, MA (see p.202; ⓣ978/741-0220) and day trips to the Harbor Islands, including Spectacle and George's Island (ⓣ617/223-8666). All of these trips are highly recommended.

It's hard to miss the newly-updated **Children's Museum**, 300 Congress St (Mon–Thurs, Sat & Sun 10am–5pm, Fri 10am–9pm; $10, kids $8; Fri 5–9pm $1; ⓣ617/426-8855) marked as it is by a whimsical Boston icon: a forty-foot tall Hood **milk bottle** (it doubles as a food stand). The museum's three floors of educational exhibits are craftily designed to trick kids into learning about a huge array of topics, from musicology to the engineering of a humongous bubble. Before leaving, check out the Recycle Shop where industrial leftovers are transformed into appealing craft-fodder.

Looking like a glamorous glass ice-cube perched above a chilly Boston Harbor, the **Institute of Contemporary Art**, 100 Northern Ave (Tues & Wed 10am–5pm, Thurs & Fri 10am–9pm, Sat & Sun 10-5pm, closed Mon; $12, kids 17 and under free; free for families the last Sat of the month; Courthouse **T**; ⓣ617/478-3100) gives you a show before you've even stepped inside. Complementing the museum's collection of contemporary artworks is the building's dramatic cantilever shape that extends eighty feet into the water's edge. From the interior, this extended section functions as the "Founders Gallery," a meditative, enclosed ledge where, if you look down from the gallery's wall of glass, you'll find yourself standing directly above a jellyfish-laden Boston Harbor.

The Museum of Science

At the northern end of the waterfront, clear across the Boston peninsula from the Children's Museum, the beloved **Museum of Science** (July to early Sept Sat–Thurs 9am–7pm, Fri 9am–9pm; Sept–June Sat–Thurs, 9am–5pm, Fri 9am–9pm; $19, kids $16; Science Park **T**; ⓣ617/723-2500) has several floors of interactive exhibits illustrating basic principles of natural and physical science. An impressive IMAX cinema takes up the full height of one end of the building, and the Hayden Planetarium pays its way with semi-rocking laser shows including the infamous "Laser Floyd: Dark Side of the Moon" ($9; call ⓣ617/723-2500 for showtimes); the museum's **3D Theater** provides a chance to wear those retro-cool 3D glasses.

Back Bay and beyond

Beginning in 1857, the spacious boulevards and elegant houses of **Back Bay** were fashioned along gradually filled-in portions of former Charles River marshland.

Thus a walk through the area from east to west provides an impressive visual timeline of Victorian architecture. One of the most architecturally significant of its buildings is the Romanesque **Trinity Church**, 206 Clarendon St (Mon–Sat 9am–5.30pm, Sun 1–5pm; $6), whose stunning interior was built to feel like "walking into a living painting." Towering over the church is Boston's signature skyscraper, the **John Hancock Tower**, an elegant wedge designed by I.M. Pei. Nearby **Newbury Street** is an atmospheric and inviting stretch of swanky boutiques, cafés, and art galleries.

The **Christian Science Center** at Huntington and Massachusetts avenues is the "Mother Church" of the First Church of Christ Scientist, and the home of the *Christian Science Monitor* newspaper; Nelson Mandela made a point of paying a personal visit in 1990 to thank the paper for its support of his release from prison. The complex houses the marvelous **Mapparium** (Tues–Sun 10am–4pm; $6), a curious, 30ft stained-glass globe through which you can walk on a footbridge. The globe's best feature is its lack of sound absorption, which enables a tiny whisper spoken at one end of the bridge to be easily heard by someone at the other.

Further south, beyond the boundaries of Back Bay and a long enough walk to warrant taking the "**T**'s" green line (take the train marked "E" to the "Museum" stop), is the **Museum of Fine Arts** at 465 Huntington Ave (Mon, Tues, Sat & Sun 10am–4.45pm, Wed–Fri 10am–9.45pm; $17, which includes a free repeat visit within 30 days; Wed after 4pm suggested donation only; ⓣ617/267-9300, ⓦwww.mfa.org). From its magnificent collections of Asian and ancient Egyptian art onwards, the MFA (as it's known) holds sufficient marvels to detain you all day - but be forewarned, the museum is currently undergoing a major expansion (including the addition of a new wing and central courtyard); even the best-loved galleries have been known to close down for periods of time. High points include Renoir's *Dance at Bougival*; Gauguin's sumptuous display of existential angst *Where do we come from? What are we? Where are we going?*; a saxophone made by Adolphe Sax himself (Musical Instruments room); and Botero's voluptuous *Venus*, bold sentinel of the West Wing.

Less broad in its collection, but more distinctive and idiosyncratic than the MFA, is the **Isabella Stewart Gardner Museum**, just down the road at 280 The Fenway (Tues–Sun 11am–5pm; $12; free admission for those named "Isabella"; ⓣ617/566-1401, ⓦwww.gardnermuseum.org). Styled after a fifteenth-century Venetian villa, the Gardner brims with a dazzling hodgepodge of works meant to "fire the imagination." While it's best known for its spectacular central courtyard, the museum's greatest successes are its show-stopping pieces by John Singer Sargent, including a stunning portrait of Isabella herself. Weekend concerts are held on select Friday nights as well as on Sunday afternoons; tickets $23 (includes museum admission).

Cambridge

The excursion across the Charles River to **Cambridge** merits at least half a day, and begins with a fifteen-minute ride on the Red **T** line to **Harvard Square**. This is not so much a square as a number of interlocking streets, filled with small shopping malls and bookstores, at the point where Massachusetts Avenue runs into JFK and Brattle streets. It's an exceptionally lively area, filled with students from nearby Harvard University and MIT, and in the summer, street musicians are a common sight. The **Cambridge Visitor Information Booth** here (Mon–Sat 9am–5pm; ⓣ617/441-2884) sporadically organizes walking tours in summer, and sells local maps and guides. Additional info (as well as free internet access) is available from the **Holyoke Center**, 1350 Massachusetts Ave

(Mon–Sat 9am–5pm; ⓣ617/495-1573), which also arranges student-led tours of the campus.

Feel free to wander into **Harvard Yard** and around the core of the university, founded in 1636; its enormous Widener Library (named for a victim of the *Titanic*) boasts a Gutenberg Bible and a first folio of Shakespeare. Five minutes' walk west along Brattle Street (at no. 105) is the best known of the Brattle Street mansions, the **Longfellow House** (May Thurs–Sat 10am-4pm, June–Sept Wed–Sun 10am–4.30pm, tours hourly 10.30am–11.30am & 1–4pm; $3; ⓣ617/876-4491), named after the author of *Hiawatha*, who lived here until 1882. Its halls and walls are festooned with Longfellow's furniture and art collection, best of which are the stunning pieces culled from the Far East. Dexter Pratt, immortalized in Longfellow's "Under the spreading chestnut tree, the village smithy stands," lived at 56 Brattle St; a marker on the corner of Brattle and Story streets commemorates the exalted tree.

Cambridge has several first-class museums, with a few engaging exhibits of note. Unfortunately, the **Harvard University Art Museums** are currently closed for a major renovation and are slated to reopen as a single museum in 2013. Once open, the new **Harvard Art Museum** will encompass over 150,000 works of art, including highlights of Harvard's substantial collection of Western art, a small yet excellent selection of German Expressionists and Bauhaus works, and sensuous Buddhas and gilded bodhisattvas from its Asian and Islamic art collection. During the renovation, you can check out a selection of the museum's holdings at 485 Broadway, the former home of the **Arthur M. Sackler Museum** (Mon–Sat 10am–5pm, Sun 1–5pm, free on Sat before noon; $9; ⓣ617/495-9400). The stellar **Harvard Museum of Natural History**, 26 Oxford St (daily 9am–5pm; $9), features a number of freakishly huge dinosaur fossils as well as a visually stunning collection of flower models constructed entirely from glass.

A couple of miles southeast of Harvard Square is the **Massachusetts Institute of Technology** (MIT), whose very cool **MIT Museum**, 265 Massachusetts Ave (daily 10am–5pm; $7.50; ⓣ617/253-5927) is filled with hypnotizing mini-machines, like a walking wishbone that swaggers forward, pulling behind it a mass of wiry wheels.

Eating

Boston is brimming with a hearty range of culinary options. Above all, there's **seafood**, lobsters (boiled red or handpicked into lobster rolls), scrod (a generic term for young, white-fleshed fish), clams (served steamed and dipped in butter, or as creamy chowder), and oysters (some of the world's best come fresh daily from Wellfleet and other Cape Cod spots). You could base a day's tour of the different neighborhoods around the foods on offer: breakfast in the cafés of **Beacon Hill**; lunch in the food plazas of **Quincy Market** or **The Garage** on JFK Street in Cambridge, or dim sum in **Chinatown**; for dinner, a budget **Indian** restaurant in Cambridge, an **Italian** place around Hanover Street in the North End, one of the South End's stylish foodie hangouts, or seafood overlooking the Harbor.

The central aisle of **Quincy Market**, lined with restaurants and brasseries, is superb for all kinds of takeout, including fresh clams and lobster, ethnic dishes, fruit cocktails, and cookies, which you can buy from different vendors and eat in the central seating area.

Chinatown, where restaurants stay open until 2 or 3am, is the best place for **late-night dining**.

Boston

Café Jaffa 48 Gloucester St ☎617/536-0230; Hynes **T**. One of Back Bay's best inexpensive dining options, with great Middle Eastern fare served up in an inviting space. They're known for their falafel and locally-famous lamb chops, but you can't really go wrong here.

Chacarero 26 Province St ☎617/367-1167; Downtown Crossing **T**. Fabulous and fresh, the chacarero is a Chilean sandwich built upon warm, soft bread and filled with avocado, chicken, green beans, muenster cheese, and hot sauce. Closed weekends, cash only.

Charlie's Sandwich Shoppe 429 Columbus Ave ☎617/536-7669; Back Bay **T**. The long lines out front should tell you – *Charlie's* is widely regarded as the best breakfast in Boston, with greasy spoon fare (and famous turkey hash) served up in delightful vintage diner environs. Closed Sun, cash only.

Daily Catch 323 Hanover St ☎617/523-8567 and 261 Northern Ave ☎617/338-3093; Haymarket **T** and South Station **T**. Ocean-fresh seafood, notably calamari and shellfish – Sicilian-style, with megadoses of garlic – draws big lines to this tiny storefront restaurant.

The Delux Café and Lounge 100 Chandler St ☎617/338-5258; Back Bay **T**. This retro hideaway has all the fixings of a great dive: fantastic kitschy decor, constant cartoon viewing, and a Christmas-lit Elvis shrine. The menu is funky American fusion with old standbys like grilled cheese sandwiches and split pea soup. Cash only.

Durgin Park 340 Faneuil Hall Marketplace ☎617/227-2038; State **T**. A Boston landmark in operation since 1827, *Durgin Park* has a waitstaff known for their surly charm as well as iconic New England foods like roast beef, baked beans, and warm Indian pudding. The downstairs bar is cheaper and livelier.

Galleria Umberto 289 Hanover St ☎617/227-5709; Haymarket **T**. North End nirvana. There are fewer than a dozen items on the menu, but the lines are consistently to the door for *Umberto's* perfect pizza slices and *arancini*. Lunch only, and get there early – they always sell out. Cash only; very inexpensive.

Maria's Pastry 46 Cross St ☎617/523-1196; Haymarket **T**. The best pastries in the North End, and inexplicably underrated; the chocolate cannoli with fresh ricotta filling will make your day.

Neptune Oyster 63 Salem St ☎617/742-3474; Haymarket **T**. Snazzy little raw bar filled with devoted fans who swoon over the fantastic shucked shellfish. Closed Mon and Tues.

The Other Side Cosmic Café 407 Newbury St ☎617/536-8437; Hynes **T**. This ultracasual hipster hangout on "the other side" of Newbury St offers gourmet sandwiches, tasty salads, and fresh juices. They also have pitchers of good beer. Open late.

Sel de la Terre 255 State St ☎617/720-1300; Aquarium **T**. *Sel de la Terre* serves up rustic Provençal fare like hearty bouillabaisse and roasted lamb and eggplant as well as what are perhaps the best french fries in town.

Silvertone 69 Bromfield St ☎617/338-7887; Park **T**. Nostalgia runs high at this bustling basement bar and eatery with standout comfort foods like mashed potatoes and meatloaf and a super-cheesy mac and cheese. Good beers on tap. Closed Sun.

Sonsie 327 Newbury St ☎617/351-2500, Hynes **T**. This Newbury St staple is good for contemporary bistro fare, particularly the swanky sandwiches, pastries, and chocolate bread pudding.

Taiwan Café 34 Oxford St ☎617/426-8181; Chinatown **T**. Locals swoon over this busy, authentic Taiwanese eatery which serves up mustard greens with *edamame* (soybean) and steamed pork buns done just right. Open late. Cash only.

Toro 1704 Washington St ☎617/536-4300; Back Bay **T**. A hip and lively tapas bar brimming with white and red sangria and inventive tapas plates such as the grilled corn with lime and aged cheese or the citrus and soy tuna.

Yankee Lobster Fish Market 300 Northern Ave ☎617/345-9799; World Trade Center **T**. Right on the water in the Seaport District, this low-key lobster shack serves up fresh seafood (the lobster roll is particularly noteworthy) from its takeout window. It's a hike from downtown – you might want to hop on the Silver Line.

Cambridge

Central Kitchen 567 Massachusetts Ave, ☎617/491-5599; Central **T**. Hip Central Square bistro with a delightful chalkboard menu offering European classics (moules frites) and contemporary American twists (mushroom ragout with ricotta dumplings) in a stylish, intimate setting.

Charlie's Kitchen 10 Eliot St ☎617/492-9646; Harvard **T**. Marvelously atmospheric local hangout in the heart of Harvard Square, with red vinyl booths, an outdoor beer garden, and great cheeseburger specials. The bar upstairs is equally cool, particularly during Tuesday's karaoke nights.

Chez Henri 1 Shepard St ☎617/354-8980; Harvard or Porter **T**. Fantastic French fare with a strong Cuban accent, and some of Cambridge's best cuisine. If you're looking to spend less cash, head to the adjacent bar for the Cuban pressed sandwich – amazing.

Darwin's Ltd 148 Mt Auburn St ☎617/354-5233; 1629 Cambridge St ☎617/491-2999; both Harvard

T. Two locations, both housing fantastic delis with wonderfully inventive sandwich combinations. Cash only.

East Coast Grill 1271 Cambridge St, Inman Square ⓣ617/491-6568; Harvard or Central **T**. A festive and funky atmosphere – think shades of Miami Vice – in which to enjoy fresh seafood and Caribbean side dishes. The Sunday serve-yourself Bloody Mary bar is reason enough to visit.

Emma's Pizza 40 Hampshire St ⓣ617/864-8534; Kendall **T**. Consistently listed at or near the top of Boston's "best of" lists, this tasty, local pizzeria has signature thin pies and slices with fun toppings like roasted sweet potatoes and ricotta.

The Garage 36 JFK St; Harvard **T**. A "mall" with hipstery types of stores (think records, tattoos, and hemp clothing), this landmark spot also has good cheap eats – pizza, Mexican, Vietnamese, and ice cream.

Mr Bartley's Burger Cottage 1246 Massachusetts Ave, ⓣ617/354-6559; Harvard **T**. A Cambridge must-visit. Perhaps the best burgers on the planet washed down with raspberry lime rickeys amongst Americana-festooned environs. Good veggie burgers, too. Cash only.

Bars, clubs, and live music

Boston has a lively **nightlife** scene that offers the best of both old and new, from tried-and-true neighborhood taverns to young, trendy lounges. The **live music** circuit in Boston and Cambridge is dominated by the very best local and touring indie bands. The free weeklies *Boston Phoenix* (ⓦwww.thephoenix.com) and *Boston's Weekly Dig* (ⓦwww.weeklydig.com) are the best source for up-to-date **listings**. Key nightlife zones include **Lansdowne Street**, an entire block of nightclubs next to Fenway Park; **Boylston Street**, on the south side of Boston Common; and Cambridge's **Central Square** district. Note that most establishments are unusually officious in demanding **ID**.

Boston

The Beehive 541 Tremont St ⓣ617/423-0069; Back Bay **T**. With chandeliers dripping from the ceiling, a red-curtained stage, and knock-you-down cocktails, the *Beehive* exudes a vaudeville vibe, complete with jazz, cabaret, or burlesque shows playing nearly every night of the week.

Bukowski Tavern 50 Dalton St ⓣ617/437-9999; Hynes **T**. Boston's best dive bar, this parking garage watering hole has views over the MassPike and a beer selection so vast it prompted a homemade "wheel of indecision" – spun by the waitstaff for indecisive patrons.

Caffe Vittoria 296 Hanover St ⓣ617/227-7606; Haymarket **T**. A Boston institution, the *Vittoria's* atmospheric original section, with its dark wood panelling, pressed-tin ceilings, and Sinatra-blaring Wurlitzer, is vintage North End. There's also a subterranean cigar bar.

Cask 'n Flagon 62 Brookline Ave ⓣ617/536-4840; Kenmore **T**. An iconic neighborhood bar located right by Fenway Park, the *Cask 'n Flagon* is a popular place for the Red Sox faithful to warm up before games and drown their sorrows after.

Club Café 209 Columbus Ave ⓣ617/536-0966; Back Bay **T**. Popular combination restaurant/video gay bar with a back lounge, *Moonshine*, showing the latest videos amidst dancing and DJs.

Eastern Standard 528 Commonwealth Ave ⓣ617/532-9100; Kenmore **T**. Set inside a gorgeous, spacious dining room, this Boston favorite pulls in a nice mix of clientele, both age-wise and style-wise. The bartenders really know what they're doing, and are just as quick to make you a swanky highball as they are to pour you a pint. There's also a nice patio in the summer.

Jillian's 145 Ipswich St ⓣ617/437-0300; Kenmore **T**. Massive entertainment club complex housing an arcade, a raucous, spacious dance club, and a Lucky Strike bowling alley.

Oak Bar in the Fairmont Copley Plaza, 138 St James Ave ⓣ617/267-5300; Copley **T**. Rich wood panelling, high ceilings, and excellent martinis are the highlights of this swanky Back Bay drinkery.

The Paradise 967-969 Commonwealth Ave, Allston ⓣ617/562-8800; Pleasant Street **T**. One of Boston's classic rocking venues (many greats have played here), and it's still happening after 25 years.

Sevens Ale House 77 Charles St, Beacon Hill ⓣ617/523-9074; Charles **T**. This unpolished gem of a neighborhood pub provides local flavor in the midst of upscale Beacon Hill; far more authentic than the nearby *Bull and Finch Pub*.

Wally's Café 427 Massachusetts Ave ⓣ617/424-1408; Massachusetts Ave **T**. Founded in 1947, this is one of the oldest jazz clubs around, and some folks think it's one of Boston's best assets.

Cambridge

B-Side Lounge 92 Hampshire St ⓣ617/354-0766; Kendall **T**. It's a hipster bar, but not in an alienating way. Lots of live tunes, a great drinks menu, and tasty and creative bar food.
Club Passim 47 Palmer St ⓣ617/492-7679; Harvard **T**. A four-decades-old, intimate "coffeehouse" that has been a noted folk/blues venue since Joan Baez performed here as an unknown 17-year-old. They also house the tasty *Veggie Planet*, with good pizza and vegetarian items.
Enormous Room 577 Massachusetts Ave ⓣ617/491-5550; Central **T**. Walking into this comfy, tiny lounge is tantamount to entering a swanky slumber party – the clientele lounges along myriad couches, and sways to the tune of a local DJ.
Lizard Lounge 1667 Massachusetts Ave ⓣ617/547-0759; Harvard or Porter **T**. An intimate rock and jazz venue, and one of Boston's best. Fairly nominal cover charges.
Middle East 472 Massachusetts Ave ⓣ617/492-9181; Central **T**. Local and regional progressive rock acts regularly stop in at this Cambridge institution. Downstairs hosts bigger bands; smaller ones ply their stuff in a tiny upstairs space.
Miracle of Science 321 Massachusetts Ave ⓣ617/868-ATOM; Central **T**. Surprisingly hip despite its status as an MIT hangout. There's a Table of Elements-minded decor and a laidback, unpretentious crowd. The bar stools will conjure up memories of high school chemistry class.
Regattabar in the *Charles Hotel*, 1 Bennett St ⓣ617/661-5000; Harvard **T**. The *Regattabar* draws top national jazz acts, although, as its location in the swish *Charles Hotel* might suggest, the atmosphere is a bit sedate. Dress nicely and prepare to pay around a $25 cover.
Shay's 58 JFK St ⓣ617/864-9161; Harvard **T**. Unwind with grad students over wine and quality beer at *Shay's*, a relaxed contrast to the crowded student-oriented bars found elsewhere in Harvard Square.
T.T. the Bear's 10 Brookline St ⓣ617/492-BEAR; Central **T**. Highly esteemed, intimate venue, showcasing cutting-edge live music seven nights a week.
Western Front 343 Western Ave ⓣ617/492-7772; Central **T**. This former jazz and blues club is now dedicated to reggae, with live music Fri and Sat nights, cheap drinks, and delectably authentic Jamaican food served up on the weekends.

Performing arts

Mainstream Boston's pride and joy, the **Boston Symphony Orchestra** is based at Symphony Hall, 301 Massachusetts Ave (ⓣ617/266-1200, ⓦwww.bso.org), which Stravinsky called the best auditorium in the world. The orchestra's winter season is supplemented by the **Boston Pops** concerts in May, June, and on July 4.

The city's **theater** scene divides into the safe productions of the Theater District (often Broadway cast-offs) and more experimental companies in Cambridge. The **BosTix** ticket kiosks (ⓣ617/482-BTIX, ⓦwww.artsboston.org) at Faneuil Hall and in Copley Square sell tickets for all major events – as well as tours, **T** passes, and so on – with some half-price same-day tickets (cash only). They're open Tuesday through Saturday 10am to 6pm and Sunday 11am to 4pm; the Copley Square location is also open on Monday 10am to 6pm.

Sports

Baseball is treated with reverence in Boston, so it's fitting that the Red Sox play at storied Fenway Park (Kenmore subway stop on the Green **T** line; tickets $12–325; information ⓣ1-877/REDSOX9, tickets ⓣ617/482-4769, ⓦwww.redsox.com). Built in 1912 and squeezed into an odd-shaped plot just off Brookline Avenue, the stadium is famed for its crazy caroms and awkward quirks, particularly the 37-foot wall in left field known as the **"Green Monster."** The very popular Fenway Park **tours** (ⓣ617/226-6666; $12) are well recommended.

Basketball's Celtics and **hockey**'s Bruins both play at the TD Banknorth Garden, 150 Causeway St near North Station; Celts tickets will run you $10–700, Bruins tickets $10–176 (box office open daily 10am–5pm; call Ticketmaster for tickets by phone ⓣ617/931-2000, ⓦwww.tdbanknorthgarden.com).

The cheer-worthy 26.2-mile **Boston Marathon**, first run in 1897, is held on the third Monday in April, and finishes on Boylston Street at Copley Square (Ⓣ617/236-1652, Ⓦwww.bostonmarathon.org).

Every October features the annual **Head of the Charles** river regatta crew race (Ⓣ617/868-6200, Ⓦww.hocr.org) that draws thousands of exuberant, picnicking fans to the shorelines.

Lexington and Concord

On the night of April 18, 1775, **Paul Revere** rode down what is now Massachusetts Avenue from Boston, racing through Cambridge and Arlington on his way to warn the American patriots gathered at **Lexington** (eleven miles to the west) of an impending British attack. Close behind him was a force of more than seven hundred British soldiers, intent on seizing the supplies that they knew the local militia had hoarded at **Concord**, further north.

Although much of Revere's route has been turned into major freeways, the various settings of the first military confrontation of the Revolutionary War – "the shot heard 'round the world" – remain much as they were then. The triangular **Town Common** at Lexington was where the British encountered their first opposition. Captain John Parker ordered his 77 American "**Minutemen**" to "stand your ground. Don't fire unless fired upon, but if they mean to have a war let it begin here." No one knows who fired the first shot, but the eight soldiers that died are buried beneath a surprisingly affecting memorial at the southeast end of the park. Guides in period costume lead tours of the **Buckman Tavern** (April–Oct daily 10am–4pm; $6; Ⓣ781/862-5598), where the Minutemen waited for the British to arrive; the **Hancock-Clarke House**, a quarter of a mile north, where Samuel Adams and John Hancock were awakened by Paul Revere, is now a museum (opening in 2009 after a major restoration). Two-house combo tickets are $8.

By the time the British soldiers marched on Concord, on the morning after the encounter in Lexington, the surrounding countryside was up in arms, and the Revolutionary War was in full swing. In running battles in the town itself, and along the still-evocative **Battle Road** leading back toward Boston, 73 British soldiers and 49 colonials were killed over the next two days. The relevant sites now form the **Minuteman National Historic Park**, with visitor centers at the scenic North Bridge, 174 Liberty St, in Concord (daily: end March to end Oct 9am–5pm; end Oct to Nov 9am–4pm; Dec–March 11am–3pm), and on Massachusetts Avenue (Rte-2A) west of Lexington (daily: end March to end Oct 9am–5pm; end-Oct to Nov 9am–4pm; Dec–March closed; Ⓣ978/318-7832).

After a morning spent denouncing eighteenth-century British rule, it's customary to indulge in a quintessential British activity – high tea – at the historic Concord Inn (Fri–Sun 3–5pm; $10.95–24.95; Ⓣ978/369-2372; reservations recommended). Just outside Concord, the area's rich **literary heritage** is the focus at **Orchard House** (April–Oct Mon–Sat 10am–4.30pm, Sun 1–4.30pm; Nov–March Mon–Fri 11am–3pm, Sat 10am–4.30pm, Sun 1–4.30pm; closed Jan 1–15; entry by guided tour only, $9; Ⓣ978/369-4118, Ⓦwww.louisamayalcott.org) 399 Lexington Rd, where Louisa May Alcott lived from 1858 to 1877 and wrote *Little Women*.

South of Concord, **Walden Pond** was where Henry David Thoreau conducted the experiment in solitude and self-sufficiency described in his 1854 book *Walden*. The site where his log cabin once stood is marked with stones, and at dawn you can still watch the pond "throwing off its nightly clothing of mist" (at midday, it's a great spot for swimming and hiking). Thoreau is interred, along with Ralph

Waldo Emerson, Nathaniel Hawthorne, and Louisa May Alcott, atop a hill in **Sleepy Hollow Cemetery**, just east of the center of Concord.

As well as guided bus tours from Boston (see p.186), **buses** (25min) run to Lexington from Alewife Station (15min; $1.50), at the northern end of the Red **T** line, and **trains** to Concord run from North Station (40-45min; $6.25).

The north shore

As you head northward out of Boston, you pass through a succession of rich little ports that have been all but swallowed up by the suburbs. **Salem** and neighboring **Marblehead** make for an enticing day-trip, and if you have the time, the atmospheric old fishing ports of **Gloucester** and **Rockport**, further out on Cape Ann, are also worth a look. This area is also the best place on the East Coast for **whale-watching** trips. Cape Ann Whale Watch (Ⓣ978/283-5110 or 1-800/877-5110, Ⓦwww.caww.com) offers trips from Gloucester (May–Oct; 3–4hr; $42).

Salem

SALEM is remembered less as the site where the colony of Massachusetts was first established than as the place where, sixty years later, Puritan self-righteousness reached its apogee in the horrific **witch trials** of 1692. Nineteen Salem women were hanged as witches (and one man, Giles Corry, was pressed to death with a boulder), thanks to a group of impressionable teenage girls who reported as truth a garbled mixture of fireside tales told by a West Indian slave, Tituba, and scare stories published by Cotton Mather, a pillar of the Puritan community. That this unpleasant history is now the basis of a child-oriented tourist industry – all black hats and broomsticks – is a bit unsettling. However, if you can overlook the contrived, witchy vibe (and the shops selling corsets and fairy clothing) this pretty, historic town proves to be an enjoyable visit.

The **Salem Witch Museum** in Washington Square (daily: July & Aug 10am–7pm; Sept–June 10am–5pm; $8; Ⓣ978/744-1692) draws parallels with modern racism and political persecution, but is at its heart a rather tacky show of illuminated dioramas and prerecorded commentary. Innumerable other witch-related attractions in town are best ignored. Salem's crown jewel is the **Peabody Essex Museum** at 161 Essex St (daily 10am–5pm; $15; Ⓣ978/745-9500), whose vast, modern space incorporates more than thirty galleries filled with remarkable *objets* brought home by voyaging New Englanders. Founded by a ship captain in 1799, the museum has stellar Asian and Oceanic displays, most notably the **Yin Yu Tang**, a stunning sixteen-room Qing dynasty merchants' house reassembled here in Salem.

The remnants of Salem's original waterfront have been preserved as the **Salem Maritime National Historic Site** (visitors' center at 174 Derby St daily 9am–5pm; Ⓣ978/740-1650). The chief sights – opulent Derby House and the imposing Customs House, where Nathaniel Hawthorne once worked as a surveyor – can only be visited on daily one-hour tours ($5). The nearby **House of Seven Gables** at 115 Derby St, the star of Hawthorne's eponymous novel, is a rambling old mansion beside the sea (daily: July–Oct 10am–7pm, Nov–June 10am–5pm, closed first half of Jan; $12; Ⓣ978/744-0991). Hour-long guided tours of the complex also take in the author's birthplace, moved here from its original site on Union Street.

Practicalities

Regular MBTA **buses** run to Salem from Boston's Haymarket station (every 30min; $3.50). Frequent **trains** also leave from North Station (weekdays 2–3 an hour, weekends hourly; $5.25). For **accommodation**, the well-run *Hawthorne Hotel*, 18 Washington Square W (ⓣ978/744-4080, ⓦwww.hawthornehotel.com; ⑤–⑨) is right in the heart of things, while *Morning Glory Bed and Breakfast*, 22 Hardy St (ⓣ978/741-1703 or 1-800/446-2995, ⓦwww.morningglorybb.com; ⑥) has home-made goodies in the morning and great views of the water. The atmospheric *Red's Sandwich Shop*, 15 Central St (ⓣ978/745-3527), features cheap and hearty breakfast fare, while the *Grapevine*, 26 Congress St (ⓣ978/745-9335), is a more upscale, expensive restaurant with creative dishes like brook trout pasta and tasty vegetarian options (entrees $21-27). Heading south out of town on Rte-1A, *Salem Diner*, 70 Loring Ave (ⓣ978/741-7918), is a must-visit for road-trip aficionados, housed in an original 1941 Sterling Streamliner car, one of only four remaining in the US.

Marblehead

Five miles south and east along the bay from Salem is **MARBLEHEAD**, a lovely waterfront village whose historic homes date back as far as the mid-1700s, and which is known as the birthplace of the US Navy – George Washington's first five vessels were built here. Free walking-tour **maps** are available from the information booth in the center (late May to early Sept Mon–Fri 9am–5pm, Sat & Sun 10am–6pm; ⓣ781/639-8469, ⓦwww.visitmarblehead.com), while 250-year-old **Fort Sewall**, jutting into the harbor, gives pretty views. The best of the central hotels is the elegant *Harbor Light Inn*, 58 Washington St (ⓣ781/631-2186, ⓦwww.harborlightinn.com; ⑥–⑨), which has a heated outdoor pool in summer, while the gorgeous *Fox Pond B&B*, 31 Arthur Ave (ⓣ781/631-1370, ⓦwww.foxpondbnb.com; ⑤–⑥), is a romantic hideaway a short drive inland. *Flynnie's on the Avenue*, 28 Atlantic Ave (ⓣ781/639-2100), serves fresh, inexpensive **seafood**, as does *Lime Rickey's* (ⓣ781/631-6700) at Devereux Beach.

The south shore

Heading south, it can take a while to get clear of Boston, especially on summer weekends, when the traffic down to Cape Cod can be horrendous. Two historic towns, one north and one west of the Cape, are worth exploring: **Plymouth** and **New Bedford**.

Plymouth

"America's Hometown," little **PLYMOUTH**, on the south shore of Massachusetts Bay, forty miles south of Boston, is given over to commemorating, in various degrees of taste, the landing of the 102 **Pilgrims** in December of 1620.

By the sea, a solemn pseudo-Greek temple encloses the nondescript **Plymouth Rock**, where the Pilgrims are said to have first touched land. Given that the rock was only identified in 1741, and that the Pilgrims had already spent two months on Cape Cod before settling here, it is of symbolic importance only.

Two worthier memorials make no claim to authenticity, but meticulously reproduce the experience of the Pilgrims. Both the replica of the **Mayflower** in town (the *Mayflower II*), and **Plimoth Plantation** three miles south, are staffed by costumed "interpreters," each of whom acts out the part of a specific Pilgrim, Wampanoag Indian, or sailor (both attractions: April–Nov daily 9am–5pm; *Mayflower II* alone $10, Plantation alone $24, together $28; ⓣ508/746-1622, ⓦwww.plimoth.org). The charade visitors are obliged to perform – pretending to have stepped back into the seventeenth century – can be a little tiresome, but ultimately the sheer depth of detail in both endeavors makes them fascinating. At the Plantation, everything you see in the Pilgrim Village of 1627, and the Wampanoag Indian Settlement, has been created using traditional techniques.

Practicalities

Plymouth's **Visitor Information Center** is on the waterfront at 130 Water St (daily: summer 8am–8pm; winter 9am–5pm; ⓣ508/747-7525 or 1-800/USA-1620, ⓦwww.visit-plymouth.com). Plymouth & Brockton provides a regular **bus** service to and from Boston ($14 single, $25 round-trip; ⓣ508/746-0378, ⓦwww.p-b.com). There are also express ferries from Plymouth to Provincetown (see p.209). A good standard **motel** option is the clean and comfortable *Best Western Cold Spring*, 188 Court St (closed mid-Jan to mid-Feb; ⓣ508/746-2222 or 1-800/678-8667; ❼). *By The Sea*, 22 Winslow St (ⓣ508/830-9643, ⓦwww.bytheseabedandbreakfast.com; ❻–❼), is a harborview B&B with two spacious suites and private bath. America's hometown has a few favorable **food** options. Right on the waterfront, *Ziggy's*, 120 Water St (ⓣ508/746-5411), is a no-frills shack selling cheap but tasty ice cream, shakes and fast food, while the *All American Diner*, 60 Court St (ⓣ508/747-4763) is the best place for breakfasts and standard diner fare. *Hearth 'n' Kettle*, in the *John Carver Inn*, 25 Summer St, has well-priced New England seafood (ⓣ508/746-7100).

New Bedford

The old whaling port of **NEW BEDFORD**, 45 miles due south of Boston, was immortalized at the start of Herman Melville's *Moby Dick*, and is still home to one of the nation's most prosperous fishing fleets. Much of the downtown and waterfront area is preserved within the **New Bedford Whaling National Historic Park**, (visitor center at 33 Williams St, daily 9am–5pm; ⓣ508/996-4095), the centerpiece of which is the impressive **New Bedford Whaling Museum** at 18 Johnny Cake Hill (daily 9am–5pm, every second Thurs of the month to 9pm; $10), featuring a 66-foot blue whale skeleton, collections of scrimshaw and harpoons, and an evocative half-sized whaling vessel replica. More affecting is the **Seamen's Bethel** directly opposite the museum; the chapel really does have the ship-shaped pulpit described in *Moby Dick*, though this one was rebuilt after a fire in 1866.

One good place to **stay** is *Melville House*, 100 Madison St (ⓣ508/990-1566, ⓦwww.melvillehouse.net; ❺–❻), the home of Melville's sister and a regular haunt of the author in the 1860s. A favorite local place to **eat** is the Portuguese *Antonio's*, 267 Coggeshall St (ⓣ508/990-3636), where long lines often stretch out the door. Right by the museum, *Freestone's*, 41 Williams St (ⓣ508/993-7477), serves excellent chowder and microbrews in a restored 1877 bank.

Cape Cod and the islands

One of the most celebrated slices of real estate in America, **Cape Cod** boasts a dazzling, three-hundred mile coastline with some of the best beaches in New England. Unsurprisingly, this means that the Cape's main haunts are packed in the summer, and it's barely worth turning up on weekends, especially between June and August. The best strategy is to visit mid-week in May or September, when hotel prices are much lower, the crowds have thinned, and the weather is usually very pleasant.

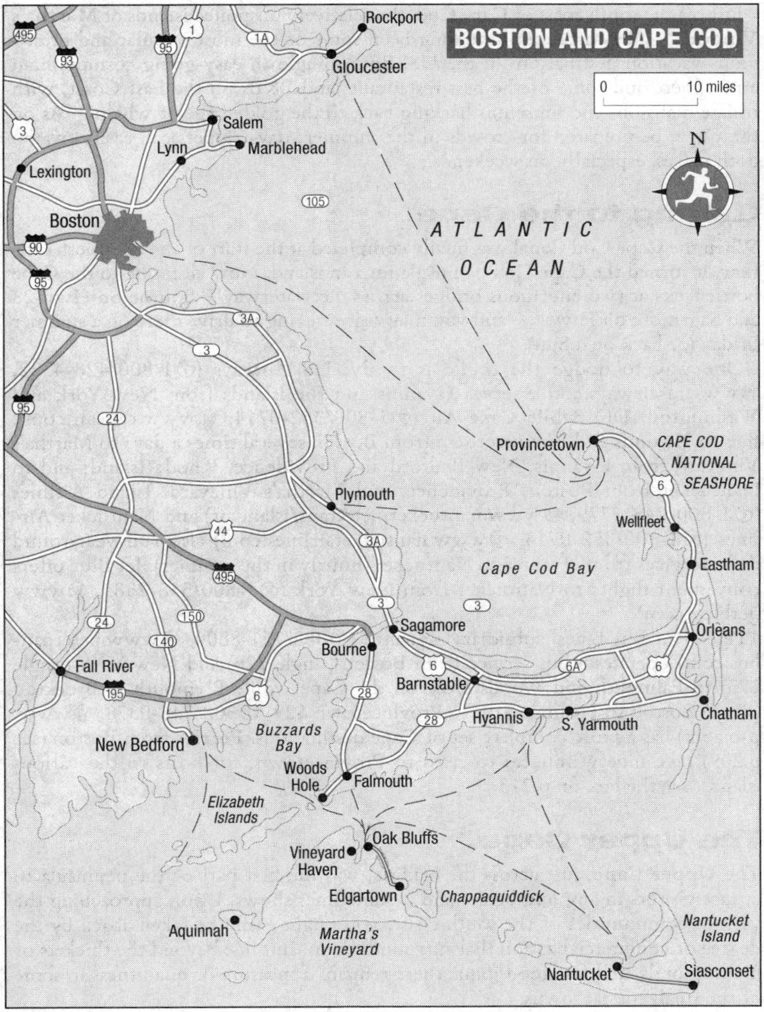

Cape Cod was named by Bartholomew Gosnold in 1602, on account of the prodigious quantities of cod caught by his crew off Provincetown. Less than twenty years later the Pilgrims landed nearby, before moving on to Plymouth. Today, much of the land on the Cape, from its salt marshes to its ever-eroding dunes, is considered a fragile and endangered ecosystem – though this designation hasn't especially dampened the persistence of developers. Much of the worst beachfront development lies along the southern shore, and Hwy-28, running from Falmouth via Hyannis to Chatham, gets especially clogged. Only once you head north to the **Outer Cape**, past the spectacular dunes of **Cape Cod National Seashore**, do you get a feeling for why this narrow spit of land still has a reputation as a seaside wilderness. **Provincetown**, right at the tip, is the one town on the Cape that can be unreservedly recommended.

Just off the south coast of Cape Cod, the relatively unspoiled islands of **Martha's Vineyard** and **Nantucket** have long been some of the most popular and prestigious vacation destinations in the US. Both mingle an easy-going cosmopolitan atmosphere and some of the best restaurants and B&Bs on the East Coast, with ornate mansions and museums harking back to the golden age of whaling. As on the Cape, be prepared for crowds in the summer; day-trippers can easily swamp both places, especially on weekends.

Getting to the Cape

When the Cape Cod Canal was finally completed at the start of the twentieth century, it turned the Cape Cod peninsula into an island. Now all traffic to the Cape bottlenecks at two enormous bridges across the waterway – Bourne on Hwy-28 and Sagamore on Hwy-6 – and you may regret trying to drive there on a summer Friday (or back on a Sun).

One way to dodge the traffic is to fly. US Airways (ⓣ1-800/428-4322, ⓦwww.usairways.com), serves Hyannis and the islands from New York and Washington, DC, while Cape Air (ⓣ1-800/352-0714, ⓦwww.capeair.com), flies to Hyannis and Provincetown from Boston several times a day; to Martha's Vineyard from Hyannis, New Bedford and Providence, Rhode Island; and to Nantucket from Boston, Providence, and Martha's Vineyard. Island Airlines (ⓣ1-800/248-7779, ⓦwww.nantucket.net/trans/islandair) and Nantucket Airlines (ⓣ1-800/352-0714, ⓦwww.nantucketairlines.com) also run year-round daily services from Hyannis to Nantucket (hourly in the summer). Jet Blue offers convenient flights to Nantucket from New York (ⓣ1-800/538-2583, ⓦwww.jetblue.com).

Peter Pan Bus Lines' subsidiary Bonanza (ⓣ888/751-8800, ⓦwww.peterpanbus.com) operates a bus service from Boston (single $26) and New York (single $73) to Falmouth and Woods Hole on the Cape, while Plymouth & Brockton (single Boston to Hyannis $19, to Provincetown $29; ⓣ508/746-0378, ⓦwww.p-b.com) has a more complete set of Cape destinations. **Ferries** from Boston (see p.209) take ninety minutes to cross to Provincetown; for boats to the various islands, see the box on p.213.

The Upper Cape

The **Upper Cape**, just across the bridges, was the first part of the peninsula to attract visitors in any numbers – and it sometimes shows. Upon approaching the various communities of the south coast, you might easily be taken aback by the degree of commercialization that surrounds them. But just beyond the thickets of malls, motels, and fast-food joints there remains a measure of quaintness in some of the small coastal towns.

Falmouth and Woods Hole

One obvious base for catching a **ferry** to the islands is **FALMOUTH**, where cozy accommodation includes the *Beach Breeze Inn,* 321 Shore St (ⓣ508/548-1765, ⓦwww.beachbreezeinn.com; ❼–❾), a 1858 Victorian house with sea views, beautiful grounds and super-clean rooms, or the *Woods Hole Passage*, at 186 Woods Hole Rd (ⓣ508/548-9575, ⓦwww.woodsholepassage.com; ❺–❼), with brightly painted chambers equipped with wireless internet. The *Sippewissett Campground & Cabins*, a couple of miles out at 836 Palmer Ave (ⓣ508/548-2542, ⓦwww.sippewissett.com; peak season $29; off-season $25; plus $8 for each additional camper year-round), offers a free shuttle service to the ferries and beaches.

▲ Lobster shack, Cape Cod

Restaurants abound in Falmouth, though with the possible exception of *Betsy's Diner*, 457 Main St (Ⓣ508/540-0060), an authentic 1950s diner beckoning you to "eat heavy," the best meals are to be found in the assorted moderately priced seafood places along the waterfront at **WOODS HOLE**, four miles southwest. The *Fishmonger's Café*, 56 Water St (Ⓣ508/540-5376), is a natural-foods restaurant that serves eggs, granola, and the like at breakfast, with seafood specials at lunch and dinner. As for sights, the **Woods Hole Oceanographic Institution's exhibit center**, at 15 School St, near Little Harbor (May–Oct Mon–Sat 10am–4.30pm; Nov & Dec Tues–Fri 10am–4.30pm; $2; Ⓣ508/457-2034, Ⓦwww.whoi.edu), focuses on the Institution's underwater research, including their sensational finding of the *Titanic* in 1986. If you're looking to get out on the water, Ocean Quest runs informative, hands-on **ocean cruises** in summer (July & Aug Mon–Fri 10am, noon, 2pm & 4pm, Sat noon & 2pm; $22; Ⓣ1-800/37-OCEAN, Ⓦwww.oceanquestonline.org).

Hyannis

It stands to reason that **HYANNIS** – the largest port on the Cape, and its main commercial hub – would be a little less charming than Falmouth and Woods Hole. Nevertheless, it still clings to the glamour it earned when the **Kennedy compound** at Hyannisport placed it at the center of world affairs. Hence the existence of the **John F. Kennedy Museum**, 397 Main St (mid-April to mid-May Mon–Sat 10am–4pm, Sun noon–4pm; mid-May to late-Oct Mon–Sat 9am–5pm, Sun noon–5pm; Nov, Dec & mid-Feb to mid-April Thurs–Sat 10am–4pm, Sun noon-4pm; $5; Ⓣ508/790-3077), which shows photographs, news clippings, and film footage of the days JFK spent on the Cape.

If you have a boat to catch and need to stay in Hyannis, options include the friendly, neat, and affordable Sea Beach Inn, 388 Sea St (Ⓣ508/775-4612, Ⓦwww.capecodtravel.com/seabeach; ❹–❻). A great B&B in Hyannisport is the Simmons Homestead Inn, 288 Scudder Ave (Ⓣ508/778-4999 or 1-800/637-1649,

ⓦ www.simmonshomesteadinn.com; ❽). For **food** and entertainment stick to Main Street: *Harry's*, at no. 700 (ⓣ 508/778-4188), is a Cajun spot serving up spicy jambalaya, barbecued ribs, and live blues music most days of the week (especially Wed); The Egg & I, at no. 521 (ⓣ 508/771-1596), is a great spot for big breakfasts, while Alberto's Ristorante, no. 360 (ⓣ 508/778-1770), offers tasty Italian meals. See p.213 for ferry information.

The Mid-Cape

The middle stretch of Cape Cod holds some of its prettiest, most unspoiled places. Time-worn fishing communities like Wellfleet and Chatham, along with dozens of carefully maintained, mildly touristy hamlets along the many winding roads, are what most people hope to find when they come to the Cape. Cutting across the middle, the **Cape Cod Rail Trail** follows a paved-over railroad track from Dennis to Eastham, through forests and cranberry bogs. It makes a good **cycling** trip; bikes can be rented in all the main towns.

One desirable destination is the whitewashed old town of **CHATHAM**, tucked away in a protected harbor between Nantucket Sound and the open Atlantic Ocean. Hang out at the **Fish Pier** on Shore Road and wait for the fleet to come in during the mid-afternoon, or head a mile south on Hwy-28 to **Chatham Light**, one of many lighthouses built to protect mariners from the treacherous shoals. Tour **maps** are available from the information booth at 533 Main St (May–Oct Mon–Sat 10am–5pm, Sun noon-5pm; ⓣ 508/945-5199, ⓦ www.chathamcapecod.org). Good **seafood** abounds at the *Chatham Squire*, 487 Main St (ⓣ 508/945-0945), a low-key, local institution. Also, be sure to stop by *Marion's Pie Shop*, 2022 Main St, Rte-28 (ⓣ 508/432-9439), for a life-changing bumbleberry pie. If you're going to **stay** in chic Chatham, you might as well indulge; the fantastic *Carriage House Inn*, 407 Old Harbor Rd (ⓣ 508/945-0127, ⓦ www.captainshouseinn.com; ❽), is a gorgeous old whaling captain's home with rambling gardens and afternoon tea, while the *Pleasant Bay Village Resort*, 1191 Orleans Rd (ⓣ 508/945-1133, ⓦ www.pleasantbayvillage.com; ❼) has lovely grounds and more affordable digs.

The **place to stay** in the resort community of **EASTHAM** is the romantic *Whalewalk Inn*, at 220 Bridge Rd (ⓣ 508/255-0617 or 1-800/440-1281, ⓦ www.whalewalkinn.com; ❽–❾). Rates for the secluded B&B rooms include use of their fabulous spa facilities. Right around the corner is the *Mid-Cape American Youth Hostel*, 75 Goody Hallet Drive, (ⓣ 508/255-2785; open May–Sept; $32 dorm beds), a collection of woodsy cabins.

For **food**, join those obsessed with the onion rings at *Arnold's Lobster and Clam Bar*, 3580 Rte-6 (ⓣ 508/255-2575), a popular seafood **restaurant** and beer garden. *Box Lunch*, 4205 Rte-6 (ⓣ 508/255-0799), as its name suggests, is the place to go for packed pitta sandwiches to take to the beach.

Cape Cod National Seashore

After the bustle of Cape Cod's towns, the **Cape Cod National Seashore** really does come as a proverbial breath of fresh air. These protected lands, spared by President Kennedy from the rampant development further south, take up virtually the entire Atlantic side of the Cape, from Chatham north to Provincetown. Most of the way you can park by the road, sometimes for a fee, and strike off across the dunes to windswept, seemingly endless beaches – though in places parking is limited to local residents. A program of grass-planting helps to hold the whole place together: three feet of the sands south of the National Seashore are washed away each year.

Displays and movies at the main **Salt Pond Visitor Center**, on US-6 just north of Eastham (daily 9am–4.30pm, closes 5pm in summer; ⓣ 508/255-3421,

Ⓦ www.nps.gov/caco), trace the geology and history of the Cape. A road and a hiking and cycling trail head east to the sands of **Coast Guard Beach** and **Nauset Light Beach**, both of which offer excellent swimming. Another fine beach is the **Head of the Meadow**, halfway between Truro and Provincetown, on the northeast shore (beach parking $15). The inviting *HI-Truro* **hostel**, at 111 North Pamet Rd in Truro (Ⓣ 508/349-3889, Ⓦ www.capecodhostels.org; mid-June to early Sept), has dorms beds for $29 in a breezy former Coast Guard station, offering spectacular views of the seashore and the dunes.

Provincetown

The compact fishing village of **PROVINCETOWN** (or, as it's popularly known, "P-Town") is a gorgeous place, with silvery clapboard houses and gloriously unruly gardens lining the town's tiny, winding streets. Bohemians and artists have long flocked here for the dazzling light and vast beaches; in 1914 Eugene O'Neill established the Provincetown Playhouse in a small hut. Since the Beatnik 1950s, the town has also been a **gay** center, and today its population of five thousand rises tenfold in the summer. Commercialism, though rampant, tends to be countercultural: gay, environmentalist, and feminist gift shops join arty galleries, restaurants, and bars on the aptly named **Commercial Street**. However, strict zoning ensures that there are few new buildings in town. Albeit crowded and raucous from July through September, P-Town remains a place where history, natural beauty, and, above all, difference, are respected and celebrated.

Arrival and information

Provincetown lies 120 miles from Boston by land, but less than fifty miles by sea, nestled in the New England coast's largest natural harbor. By far the nicest way to arrive is on one of the passenger **ferries**. Bay State Cruise Company (Ⓣ 617/748-1428, Ⓦ www.baystatecruisecompany.com) runs a daily express ferry in the summer from Boston's World Trade Center pier (90min express round-trip $71), and a standard ferry on the weekends (3hr; round-trip $33), while Boston Harbor Cruises (Ⓣ 617/227-4320, Ⓦ www.bostonharborcruises.com), does two express services a day from Boston's Long Wharf (May-Oct; 90min; $71), and also runs once a day (July & Aug) from Gloucester for $80 round-trip. By far the cheapest option is the Plymouth to Provincetown ferry, run by Captain John's Boats (July & Aug daily 10am; 90min; round-trip $37; Ⓣ 508/746-2400 or 1-800/242-2469, Ⓦ www.provincetownferry.com).

A slower option is the Plymouth & Brockton **bus**, which runs to Provincetown four times daily from Boston via Hyannis ($29 single from Boston; $10 single from Hyannis; 3hr 45min; Ⓣ 508/746-0378, Ⓦ www.p-b.com).

The tiny **visitor center**, in the Chamber of Commerce at the end of the wharf, 307 Commercial St (May–Oct daily 9am–5pm; Nov–April Mon–Sat 9.30am–4.30pm; Ⓣ 508/487-3424, Ⓦ www.ptownchamber.com), has a wealth of information on area attractions.

It couldn't be easier to **walk** around tiny P-Town, though many visitors prefer to **cycle** the narrow streets, hills, and the undulating Province Lands Bike Trail, a beguiling six-mile route with great vistas. One good bike-rental outlet in town is Arnold's, 329 Commercial St (Ⓣ 508/487-0844); they charge about $20 a day.

If you're in need of transport, the Cape Cod Regional Transit Authority (Ⓣ 1-800/352-7155, Ⓦ www.thebreeze.info) runs frequent Flex route buses (6am–8pm) connecting P-Town with other villages on the Cape such as Truro; simply flag them down on the side of the road and cough up $2.

Narrated **tours** are run by Provincetown Trolley, from the town hall on Commercial Street (daily every 30min 10am–4pm, or until 7pm in season; 40min; $11;

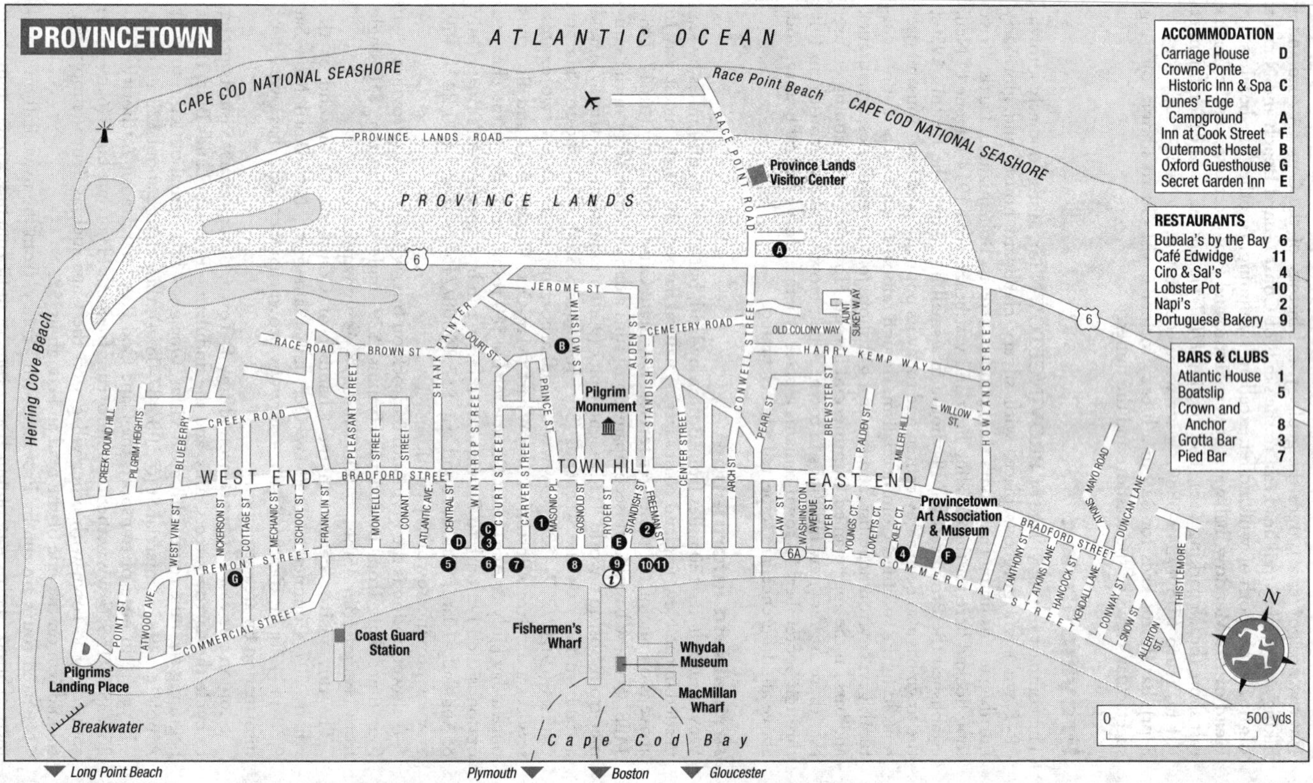
PROVINCETOWN
ATLANTIC OCEAN
CAPE COD NATIONAL SEASHORE
Race Point Beach
PROVINCE LANDS ROAD
RACE POINT ROAD
Province Lands Visitor Center
PROVINCE LANDS
Herring Cove Beach
Pilgrims' Landing Place
Breakwater
Coast Guard Station
Fishermen's Wharf
Whydah Museum
MacMillan Wharf
Cape Cod Bay
Pilgrim Monument
Provincetown Art Association & Museum
WEST END
TOWN HILL
EAST END
BRADFORD STREET
COMMERCIAL STREET
TREMONT STREET
HARRY KEMP WAY
CEMETERY ROAD
JEROME ST
WINSLOW ST
SHANK PAINTER
CREEK ROAD
RACE ROAD
BROWN ST
HOWLAND STREET
CONWELL STREET
OLD COLONY WAY
AUNT SUKEY WAY
Long Point Beach
Plymouth
Boston
Gloucester
HI-Truro
ACCOMMODATION
Carriage House D
Crowne Ponte Historic Inn & Spa C
Dunes' Edge Campground A
Inn at Cook Street F
Outermost Hostel B
Oxford Guesthouse G
Secret Garden Inn E
RESTAURANTS
Bubala's by the Bay 6
Café Edwidge 11
Ciro & Sal's 4
Lobster Pot 10
Napi's 2
Portuguese Bakery 9
BARS & CLUBS
Atlantic House 1
Boatslip 5
Crown and Anchor 8
Grotta Bar 3
Pied Bar 7
0
500 yds

ⓣ508/487-9483, ⓦwww.provincetowntrolley.com), while the more isolated dunes and moors are accessed by Art's Sand Dune Tours, based at Commercial and Standish streets (April–Oct 10am–dusk; $25 for 1hr tours; ⓣ508/487-1950 or 1-800/894-1951, ⓦwww.artsdunetours.com). **Whale-watching cruises** leave from MacMillan Wharf between April and October 31; one of the main cruise operators is the Dolphin Fleet Whale Watch; $37 (ⓣ1-800/826-9300, ⓦwww.whalewatch.com).

Accommodation

Besides the few motels on the outskirts, every second picturesque cottage in town seems to be a **guesthouse**. Prices are reasonable until mid-June, and during the off-season you can find some real bargains. As for **camping**, the welcoming *Dunes' Edge Campground*, on Hwy-6 just east of the central stoplights (May–Sept; ⓣ508/487-9815, ⓦwww.dunes-edge.com), charges $30–40 for its wooded sites.

Carriage Guest House 7 Central St ⓣ508/487-8855, ⓦwww.thecarriagehse.com. Fabulously maintained rooms, some with private decks, and all with VCR and CD players; stylish breakfasts and large hot tub and sauna are soothing extras. ⑨

Crowne Pointe Historic Inn & Spa 7 Winthrop St ⓣ508/487-6767 or 1-877/276-9631, ⓦwww.crownepointe.com. Provincetown's most luxurious digs: gorgeous rooms, a fancy restaurant, and unbelievable spa treatments. ⑨

Inn at Cook Street 7 Cook St ⓣ508/487-3894, ⓦwww.innatcookstreet.com. A quiet, lovingly-maintained inn with lots of breezy spaces and freshly-baked brownies. ⑧

Outermost Hostel 28 Winslow St ⓣ508/487-4378, ⓦwww.outermosthostel.com. Cheapest rates in town: thirty $25 beds in five cramped dorm cabins, includes kitchen access and parking. Closed Nov–April.

Oxford Guesthouse 8 Cottage St ⓣ508/487-9103, ⓦwww.oxfordguest-house.com. Seven elegantly-styled rooms and suites, with classical drapes and patterned wall-paper adding to the Victorian ambiance – you get fresh, continental breakfast, cookies in the afternoons, and a civilized "wine hour" every evening. CDs, DVDs, and w-fi available. ⑦

Secret Garden Inn 300a Commercial St ⓣ1-866/786-9646 or 508/487-9027, ⓦwww.secretgardenptown.com. This is a relative bargain; seven quaint rooms in a house with a verandah, done up in country furnishings, with modern touches like TVs and a/c. Big breakfast included. ④–⑤

The town and the beaches

Provincetown's tiny core is centered on the three narrow miles of **Commercial Street**. **MacMillan Wharf**, always busy with charters, yachts, and fishing boats (which unload their catch each afternoon), splits the town in half. Somewhat out from the center, on Commercial Street, are scores of quaint art galleries, as well as the delightful **Provincetown Art Association and Museum**, at no. 460 (mid-May to Sept Mon–Thurs 11am–8pm, Fri 11am–10pm, Sat & Sun 11am–5pm; Oct to mid-May Thurs–Sun noon–5pm; $5; ⓣ508/487-1750), with displays of local artists.

Looming above the center of P-Town, the **Pilgrim Monument and Provincetown Museum** on High Pole Hill (daily: April to mid-June & mid-Sept to Nov 9am–5pm, mid-June to mid-Sept 9am–7pm; $7; ⓣ508/487-1310), has permanent exhibits giving a fairly romantic account of the Pilgrim story and subsequent history of the town, along with a 252-foot granite tower with an observation deck (only accessible by 116 stairs) that looks out over the whole of the Cape.

A little way beyond the town's narrow strip of sand, undeveloped **beaches** are marked only by dunes and a few shabby beach huts. You can swim in the clear water from the uneven rocks of the two-mile breakwater, where the sea bed crunches with soft-shell clams, or head through scented wild roses and beach plums to find blissful isolation on undeveloped beaches nearby. West of town, **Herring**

Cove Beach, easily reached by bike or through the dunes, is more crowded, but never unbearably so. In the wild **Province Lands**, at the Cape's northern tip, vast sweeping moors and bushy dunes are buffeted by Cape Cod's deadly sea, the site of one thousand known shipwrecks. The **visitor center** (May–Oct daily 9am–5pm; ⓣ508/487-1256), in the middle of the dunes on Race Point Road, has videos and displays highlighting the exceptionally fragile environment here.

Eating

Great **food** options abound in P-Town. Portuguese bakeries, relics of early settlement, can be found along Commercial Street; beware the bland family restaurants that are often found nearby.

Bubala's By the Bay 183 Commercial St ⓣ508/487-0773. Perhaps the freshest seafood in P-Town at a fun hangout right on the water; good non-fish fare as well; open all day.

Café Edwige 333 Commercial St ⓣ508/487-2008. Breakfast's the thing at this popular second-floor spot; try the home-made Danish pastries and fresh fruit pancakes. Creative bistro fare at dinnertime. Closed Tues.

Ciro & Sal's 4 Kiley Court ⓣ508/487-6444. Traditional Northern Italian cooking with plenty of veal and seafood; a bit on the pricey side, but worth it.

Lobster Pot 321 Commercial St ⓣ508/487-0842. Its landmark neon sign is like a beacon for those who come from far and wide for the ultra-fresh crustaceans. Affordable and family-oriented, with a great outdoor deck. Closed Dec–March.

Napi's 7 Freeman St ⓣ508/487-1145. Popular dishes at this art-strewn spot include pastas and its celebrated soups: thick Portuguese fish stews and clam chowders (from $5.95). They have a less expensive menu on week nights.

Portuguese Bakery 299 Commercial St ⓣ508/487-1803. This old standby is the place to come for cheap baked goods, particularly the tasty fried *rabanada*, akin to portable French toast.

Nightlife and entertainment

Each weekend, boatloads of revelers from the mainland seek out P-Town's notoriously wild **nightlife**. Heavily geared towards a **gay** clientele, resulting in ubiquitous tea dances, drag shows, and video bars, some establishments have terrific waterfront locations and terraces to match, making them ideal spots to sit out with a drink at sunset.

Atlantic House 6 Masonic Place, behind Commercial St ⓣ508/487-3821. The "A-House" – a dark drinking hole favored by Tennessee Williams and Eugene O'Neill – is now a trendy gay club and bar.

Boatslip 161 Commercial St ⓣ508/487-1669. The Sunday tea dances at this resort are legendary (4–7pm); you can either dance away on a long wooden deck overlooking the water, or cruise inside under a disco ball and flashing lights.

Crown and Anchor 247 Commercial St ⓣ508/487-1430, ⓦwww.onlyatthecrown.com. A massive complex housing several bars, including The Vault, P-town's only gay leather bar, Wave, a video-karaoke bar, and Paramount, a cabaret with nightly acts.

Grotta Bar *Enzo Hotel*, 186 Commercial St ⓣ508/487-7555. One the newer bars in town, with campy live entertainment, bands, DJs, a 46-inch plasma TV, and zesty martinis. Live piano Tues, Fri, and Sun.

Pied Bar 193 Commercial St ⓣ508/487-1527. Though largely a lesbian club (it's the oldest in the country), the outdoor deck and inside dancefloor at this trendy waterfront space attract a good dose of men, too, for their longstanding After Tea T-Dance (daily 6.30pm).

Martha's Vineyard

The largest offshore island in New England, twenty-mile-long **MARTHA'S VINEYARD** encompasses more physical variety than Nantucket, with hills and pastures providing scenic counterpoints to the beaches and wild, windswept moors on the separate island of **Chappaquiddick**. Though the seminal movie *Jaws* was filmed here in 1974, don't worry – shark attacks are extremely rare in these waters (though Great Whites do occasionally prowl the beaches), and, ironically, the movie actually boosted tourism on the island.

Martha's Vineyard's most genteel town is **Edgartown**, all prim and proper with its freshly-painted, white clapboard Colonial homes, museums and manicured gardens. The other main settlement, **Vineyard Haven**, is more commercial and one of the island's ferry ports. **Oak Bluffs**, in between the two (and the other docking point for ferries), has an array of whimsical wooden gingerbread cottages and inviting eateries. Be aware of island terminology: heading "Up-Island" takes you southwest to the cliffs at **Aquinnah** (formerly known as Gay Head); conversely, "Down-Island" refers to the triumvirate of easterly towns mentioned above.

The island has an increasingly frequent and reliable **bus** system that connects the main towns and villages, from around 7am to 12.45am daily (Ⓣ508/639-9440, Ⓦwww.vineyardtransit.com); tickets cost $2 per ride, or $6 per day. Bringing a car over is expensive and generally pointless, as the island is jam-packed with vehicles

Ferries to Martha's Vineyard and Nantucket

Unless otherwise specified, all the **ferries** below run several times daily in midsummer (mid-June to mid-Sept). Most have fewer services from May to mid-June, and between mid-September and October. There is at least a skeleton service to each island year-round, though not on all routes. To discourage clogging of the roads, round-trip costs for cars are prohibitively high in the peak season (mid-May to mid-Sept; Woods Hole ferry only), while costs for bikes are just $6 each way. Be sure to call in advance for reservations as spaces do sell out.

To Martha's Vineyard

Falmouth to Oak Bluffs (about 35min): pedestrians only; $16 round-trip; the *Island Queen* ferry Ⓣ508/548-4800, Ⓦwww.islandqueen.com.
Falmouth to Edgartown (1hr): pedestrians only; $50 round-trip; Falmouth Ferry Service Ⓣ508/548-9400, Ⓦwww.falmouthferry.com.
Hyannis to Oak Bluffs (about 1hr 35min; fast ferry about 55min): pedestrians only; $39 round-trip, fast ferry $63 round-trip; Hy-Line Ⓣ508/778-2600 in Hyannis, Ⓣ508/693-0112 on Martha's Vineyard, Ⓦwww.hy-linecruises.com.
New Bedford to Oak Bluffs or Vineyard Haven (1hr): pedestrians only; $72 round-trip; New England Fast Ferry Ⓣ1-866/453-6800, Ⓦwww.nefastferry.com.
Quanset Point, Rhode Island, to Oak Bluffs (1hr 30min): pedestrians only; $80 round-trip; Vineyard Fast Ferry (Ⓣ401/295-4040, Ⓦwww.vineyardfastferry.com). Shuttles provided to Kingston Amtrak station ($18) and Providence airport ($15).
Woods Hole to Vineyard Haven and Oak Bluffs (45min): pedestrians $7.50 round-trip; May–Oct vehicles $135 roundtrip; off-season vehicles $85 round-trip; Steamship Authority Ⓣ508/477-8600, Ⓦwww.steamshipauthority.com.

To Nantucket

From Hyannis: pedestrians $33 round-trip (2hr journey); pedestrians $65 round-trip (1hr journey); May–Oct vehicles $380 round-trip; off-season vehicles $260 round-trip; Steamship Authority Ⓣ508/477-8600 for auto reservations, Ⓣ508/771-4000 on the mainland, Ⓣ508/228-0262 on Nantucket, Ⓦwww.steamshipauthority.com. Also Hy-Line Cruises, pedestrians only; 2hr journey $39 round-trip; 1hr journey $71 round-trip; Ⓣ508/778-2600, Ⓦwww.hy-linecruises.com.
In summer, the Hy-Line ferry company also runs a **connecting service** between Oak Bluffs, Martha's Vineyard, and Nantucket (one departure daily; pedestrians only; $28.50 single; Ⓣ508/778-2600). The trip takes 1hr 10min.

throughout the summer, and you can easily get around by bus or **bike**; rent one at the rental places lined up by the ferry dock ($25/day). The best bike ride is along the State Beach Park between Oak Bluffs and Edgartown, with the dunes to one side and marshy Sengekontacket Pond to the other; purpose-built cycle routes continue to the youth hostel at West Tisbury.

Trips around the west side of the island are decidedly bucolic, with nary a peep of the water beyond the rolling hills and private estates; however, you do eventually come to the **lighthouse** at **Aquinnah**, where the multicolored clay was once the main source of paint for the island's houses – now, anyone caught removing any clay faces a sizeable fine. From Moshup beach below, you can get great views of this spectacular formation.

Martha's Vineyard brims with beautiful **beaches**. Highlights include the secluded, gorgeous Wasque, at the end of Wasque Road in Chappaquiddick, and South Beach, at the end of Katama Road south of Edgartown, known for its "good waves and good bodies." The gentle State Beach, along Beach Road between Oak Bluffs and Edgartown, is more family-oriented.

Accommodation

If accommodation is booked up, as is very likely, the main **Chamber of Commerce** office, at 24 Beach Rd in Vineyard Haven (Mon–Fri 9am–5pm, Sat 10am–4pm; ⓣ508/693-0085, ⓦwww.mvy.com), may be able to help. There is a **campground** in Vineyard Haven, at 569 Edgartown Rd (May–Oct; ⓣ508/693-3772, ⓦwww.campmv.com); tent sites cost $48 per day for two people and include water and electricity hook-ups.

Crocker House Inn 12 Crocker Ave, Vineyard Haven ⓣ1-800/772-0206, ⓦwww.crockerhouseinn.com. Elegant and accommodating, the Crocker House features pretty rooms, free wi-fi, good proximity to shops, and lots of home-made goodies. ❼

HI-Martha's Vineyard 525 Edgartown–West Tisbury Rd ⓣ508/693-2665, ⓦwww.usahostels.org. In an appealing setting at the forest's edge and away from town; near the island's main bike path, and right on the bus route. Free wi-fi. Open April to mid-Nov. Dorm beds $32–35 a night.

Jonathan Munroe House 100 Main St, Edgartown ⓣ877/468-6763 or 508/627-5536, ⓦwww.jonathanmunroe.com. Enchanting eighteenth-century house with just six lovely rooms, and a great wraparound porch; the carafes of sherry in each room, and evening wine and cheese, are nice touches. ❽

Menemsha Inn & Cottages and Beach Plum Inn North Road, Menemsha ⓣ508/645-9454 or 1-800/901-2087, ⓦwww.menemshainn.com and ⓦwww.beachpluminn.com. These adjacent properties are beautifully maintained. Within walking distance of the Menemsha beach, they also include private beach access. ❾

Oak Bluffs Inn 64 Circuit Ave, Oak Bluffs ⓣ508/693-7171, ⓦwww.oakbluffsinn.com. One of the most alluring hotels on the island, with a convenient location, cozy, clean Victorian-style rooms, wi-fi, wide porch, free cookies, and a great host. ❽–❾

The Oak House 79 Seaview Ave, Oak Bluffs ⓣ866/693-5805, ⓦwww.vineyardinns.com. Another wonderful Victorian B&B, with stupendous sea views and beachside rooms decked out like luxurious ship cabins; afternoon tea is served on the porch. ❾

The Winnetu Inn & Resort South Beach, south of Edgartown ⓣ508/627-4747, ⓦwww.winnetu.com. This family-friendly resort hotel is just a short walk from a private stretch of South Beach, but you really need a car to stay here; very well-appointed rooms, many with kitchenettes. ❽

Eating and drinking

Eating is one of the principal pleasures of Martha's Vineyard; fresh lobster, quahogs (large clams), and fresh fish are particularly abundant. Only in Edgartown and Oak Bluffs can you order alcohol with meals, but you can bring your own elsewhere.

ArtCliff Diner 39 Beach Rd, Vineyard Haven Ⓣ508/693-1224. Perfect for a pre-ferry send-off breakfast with the likes of almond-crusted French toast and chorizo, egg, and pepperjack sandwiches. Open 7am–2pm, closed Wed.

The Bite 29 Basin Rd, Menemsha Ⓣ508/645-9239. Roadside, seaside nirvana. Some of the juiciest fried belly clams you'll ever taste (from $13.95), served up in a tiny seafood shack. Good chowder, too. Cash only.

The Black Dog Bakery 11 Water St, Vineyard Haven Ⓣ508/693-4786. Skip the overrated *Black Dog Tavern* next door and stock up on delicious muffins and breads for the ferry ride back.

Chilmark Chocolates 19 State Rd, Chilmark Ⓣ508/645-3013. People line up for *Chilmark's* island-grown berries dipped in unbelievably tasty organic chocolate. Closed Mon.

Chilmark Store 7 State Rd, Chilmark Ⓣ866/904-0819. Another island institution, but not for seafood; lines form here for the perfectly fired slices of pizza ($3.95), which come in four flavors with freshly-made olive oil and pesto bases – try the whole wheat.

Détente Nevin Sq, off Winter St (between N Water St and N Summer St), Edgartown Ⓣ508/627-8810. Of the fancier restaurants on the island, this one's your best bet for a great meal. Seasonal menus showcase local ingredients, ranging from halibut to lamb shank.

Larsen's Fish Market 56 Basin Rd, Menemsha Ⓣ508/645-2680. For about $20 you can pick out your very own lobster and then eat it on low-key flats overlooking the harbor. Best lobster roll on the East Coast, too ($11).

Offshore Ale Company 30 Kennebec Ave, Oak Bluffs Ⓣ508/693-2626. Local brewpub with wooden booths, toss-on-the-floor peanut shells, and lots of live shows. If you're there at night, be sure to stop by *Back Door Donuts* (behind *Martha's Vineyard Gourmet Café*, Ⓣ508/693-3688; daily 9pm–12.30am) for one of their life-changing apple fritters – it's a Martha's Vineyard must-do.

Nantucket

The thirty-mile, two-hour sea crossing to **NANTUCKET** may not be an ocean odyssey, but it does set the "Little Gray Lady" apart from her larger, shore-hugging sister, Martha. Nantucket's smaller size adds to its palpable sense of identity, as does the architecture; the "gray" epithet refers not only to the winter fogs, but to the austere gray clapboard and shingle applied uniformly to buildings across the island.

The tiny cobbled carriageways of **Nantucket Town** itself, once one of the largest cities in Massachusetts, were frozen in time by economic decline 150 years ago. Today, this area of delightful old restored houses – the town has more buildings on the National Register of Historic Places than Boston – is very much the island hub. From the moment you get off the ferry you're besieged by bike rental places and tour companies. **Straight Wharf** leads directly onto **Main Street**, with its shops and restaurants; the **information office** – which has a daily list of accommodation vacancies, but doesn't make reservations – is nearby at 25 Federal St (April–Dec 9am–6pm; Jan–March Mon–Sat 9am–5pm; Ⓣ508/228-0925, Ⓦwww.nantucket.net). The **Chamber of Commerce**, Zero Main St, 2/F (Mon–Fri 9am–5pm; Ⓣ508/228-1700, Ⓦwww.nantucketchamber.org), carries the best range of island information.

The excellent **Whaling Museum**, 13 Broad St, at the head of Steamboat Wharf (late May to mid-Oct daily 10am–5pm, every first and third Wed until 9pm; $15; Ⓣ508/228-1894, Ⓦwww.nha.org), houses an outstanding collection of seafaring exotica, including a gallery of entrancing, delicately-engraved scrimshaw and a 46-foot sperm whale skeleton washed ashore in 1998. Look for the rotted tooth on its jaw; officials believe a tooth infection brought on the whale's demise.

Beyond the town, Nantucket remains surprisingly wild, a mixture of moors, marshes and heathland, though the main draw remains its untrammeled sandy **beaches**. One of the best can be found at **Siaconset** (pronounced 'Sconset), seven flat, bike-friendly miles east of the town, where venerable cottages stand literally encrusted with salt; meander back across the heaths and moorland via Polpis Road. **Bikes** can be rented from Young's Bicycle Shop, 6 Broad St (around $25 for a full day; ⓣ508/228-1151). **Buses** also link Nantucket Town and 'Sconset: NRTA (ⓣ508/228-7025) runs shuttles from late May through early October ($2 each way).

Accommodation

But for the youth hostel, accommodation on Nantucket is somewhat expensive; most **B&Bs** and **guesthouses** charge well over $200 in the summer.

Hawthorn House 2 Chestnut St ⓣ508/228-1468, ⓦwww.hawthornhouse.com. Central, well-appointed guesthouse with a friendly, helpful staff and ten handsome rooms outfitted with antique furnishings. ❼

HI-Nantucket Surfside Beach 31 Western Ave ⓣ508/228-0433, ⓦwww.usahostels.org. Dorm beds ($32–35 a night) a stone's throw from Surfside Beach, just over three miles south of town. Lock-out 10am–5pm, curfew 11pm. Open mid-May–Sept.

Martin House Inn 61 Centre St ⓣ508/228-0678, ⓦwww.martinhouseinn.com. Thirteen lovely rooms offer good value in this 1803 seaman's house; close to shops and ferries. ❽

Union Street Inn 7 Union St ⓣ888/517-0707, ⓦwww.unioninn.com. This luxurious B&B boasts a central location, hearty breakfasts, and dazzling rooms, with thick rugs, drapes, and period wallpaper – it's pricey, and is thus much better value off-season. ❾

Veranda House 3 Step Lane ⓣ508/228-0695, ⓦwww.theverandahouse.com. This boutique hotel adds a refreshingly contemporary take on the island's traditional Victorian-style B&Bs; rooms are stylishly designed, most with harbor views, and come with free wi-fi. ❾

Eating and drinking

Nantucket abounds in first-rate **restaurants**, most of them located in or around Nantucket Town. Dinner can be exceptionally expensive, however, easily costing $30 to $40 for an entree. You'll find a bevy of cheaper take-out options on Broad Street near Steamboat Wharf.

Nantucket

In 1659, a sober group of twenty-seven Quaker and Presbyterian families arrived on Nantucket and set about imposing order on the haphazard business of **whaling**. Whales had always beached themselves on the treacherous sandy shoals all around – up to a dozen might be washed ashore in a major storm – and the local **Wampanoags** had become skilled in hunting them in nearby waters. As the years went by, the colonists began sending large ships out to pursue their prey. The Wampanoags remained an integral part of the process: the actual kill was effected by two rowboats working in tandem, and at least five of each thirteen-man crew, usually including the crucial **harpooneer**, would be Native American. The common occurrence when an injured whale would speed away, dragging a boat helter-skelter behind it for endless terrifying hours, was known as a **"Nantucket Sleighride."**

The early chronicler Crèvecoeur provides an extensive account of Nantucket as it was in 1782 in his *Letters from an American Farmer*. Although perturbed by the islanders' universal habit of taking a dose of opium every morning, he held them up as a model of diligence and good self-government. Whaling was a disciplined profession, and to feed themselves and equip their ships the islanders kept up a shrewd and extensive trade with the mainland. At that time, there were already more than a hundred ships. The whalers were not paid; instead each had a share (a "lay") of the final proceeds of the voyage. Ambitious Nantucketers even reached the Pacific – see p.000 in Chapter 16, "Hawaii," for an account of their experiences there. The great days of Nantucket were immortalized by Herman Melville, but by the time *Moby Dick* was published in 1851, Nantucket's fortunes had gone into an abrupt decline.

Black Eyed Susan's 10 India St ⓣ508/325-0308. Beloved little brunch spot with inventive egg scrambles and delectable buttermilk pancakes. Cash only.

Chicken Box 14 Dave St ⓣ508/228-9717. Every summer night, people of all stripes pack into "the Box" for great live shows and low-key drinking environs. Shuffleboard and pool tables, too. Cash only; an ATM is inside.

Company of the Cauldron 5 India St ⓣ508/228-4016. A romantic, vine-covered, candlelit haven with live harp music thrice weekly. Both seatings of a shifting prix-fixe menu ($58) sell out quickly, so make reservations.

Downyflake 18 Sparks Ave ⓣ508/228-4533. The island's best diner, a bit out of the way on the edge of town, but worth a visit for the reasonably priced plates of comfort food and the freshly-made doughnuts (get them to go).

Juice Bar 12 Broad St ⓣ508/228-5799. The fresh juices are the healthiest options on offer at this small takeout shop, but in summer expect long lines for the luscious home-made ice cream (try "crantucket"), served in cups or giant waffle cones ($3.30–4.50).

Sayle's Seafood 99 Washington St Extension ⓣ508/228-4599. Breezy, very casual seafood shack serving chowder ($3.25), fried shellfish, fresh lobster, and fried clams (at market prices) – get it to go for a picnic or munch on the veranda.

Central and western Massachusetts

The 150 miles of Massachusetts that stretch inland to the west of Boston have always been obliged to play second fiddle to the state capital. Just three years after the end of the Revolutionary War, the farmers who struggled to make a living from this indifferent soil rose in **Shay's Rebellion** to prevent eastern creditors from seizing their property; their pitchforks were no match for the guns of the new nation.

These days, the west is known best to vacationers for the **Berkshires,** which host the celebrated **Tanglewood** summer music festival and boast museum-filled towns such as **North Adams** and **Williamstown** – both in the far northwest corner of the state, at the end of the incredibly scenic **Mohawk Trail. Amherst** and **Northampton** are stimulating college towns in the verdant **Pioneer Valley**, with all the cafés, restaurants, and bookstores you could want. Culture of a more popular variety is on offer at the Basketball Hall of Fame in **Springfield**.

Springfield

Basketball was invented in **SPRINGFIELD**, an otherwise dreary industrial center ninety miles from Boston at the southern border of the Pioneer Valley. The city has an odd assortment of claims to fame, including being the home of the Springfield rifle as well as children's author Dr Seuss, but it's the 1891 invention of Dr James Naismith that brings a steady stream of visitors. First opened in 1959, the **Basketball Hall of Fame**, at 1000 W Columbus Ave, next to the river just south of Memorial Bridge (Sun–Fri 10am–6pm, Sat 9am–5pm; $16.99; ⓣ413/781-6500 or 1-877/4HOOPLA, ⓦwww.hoophall.com), includes movies, videos, memorabilia, and interactive gadgets that test your skills.

Springfield's Amtrak **train** station is very central, at 66 Lyman St (ⓣ413/785-4230). Peter Pan Trailways (ⓣ413/781-2900 or 1-800/237-8747, ⓦwww.peterpanbus.com) provides daily **bus** services to and from Boston and New York City, the Pioneer Valley, and the Berkshires from the nearby bus station at 1776 Main St (ⓣ413/781-3320). The **Convention & Visitors Bureau** is downtown at 1441 Main St (Mon–Fri 9am–5pm; ⓣ413/787-1548 or 1-800/723-1548, ⓦwww.valleyvisitor.com). Downtown **lodging** includes the expensive but super-convenient *Sheraton Springfield*, 1 Monarch Place (ⓣ413/781-1010; 7), and the cheaper

Old Sturbridge Village

Halfway between Worcester and Springfield on US-20, near the junction of I-90 and I-84, the restored and reconstructed **Old Sturbridge Village** (April to late Oct daily 9.30am–5pm, late Oct to March Tues–Sun 9.30am–4pm; $20; ⓣ508/347-3362 or 1-800/SEE-1830, ⓦwww.osv.org), made up of preserved buildings brought from all over the region, gives a somewhat idealized but engaging portrait of a small New England town of the 1830s. Costumed interpreters act out roles – working in blacksmiths' shops, planting and harvesting vegetables, tending cows, and the like – but they pull it off in an unusually convincing manner. The 200-acre site itself, with mature trees, ponds, and dirt footpaths, is very pretty, and worth a half-day visit. Nearby *Sturbridge Host Hotel*, 366 Main St (ⓣ508/347-7993, ⓦwww.sturbridgehosthotel.com; ⑤), is a pretty **place to stay**, situated on nine groomed acres with a heated indoor swimming pool and access to beautiful Cedar Lake.

Super 8 Motel, 1500 Riverdale St, US-5 (ⓣ413/736-8080; 3), across the river in West Springfield. Take a break from New England fare with authentic Louisiana home-cooking at *Chef Wayne's Big Mamou*, 53 Liberty St (ⓣ413-732-1011), where simmering pots of gumbo and catfish poboys go for under $10.

Amherst and Northampton

North of Springfield, the Pioneer Valley is a verdant corridor created by the Connecticut River, home to the college towns of **AMHERST** and **NORTHAMPTON**, both good places to kick back for a few days, hang out in cafés, and browse bookstores in one of New England's most liberal and progressive areas.

Amtrak **trains** stop in Amherst at 13 Railroad St, while you can catch Peter Pan Trailways **buses** at 1 Roundhouse Plaza in Northampton (ⓣ413/586-1030) and 8 Main St in Amherst (ⓣ413/256-1547). Good **accommodation** is available at Northampton's historic *Hotel Northampton*, 36 King St (ⓣ413/584-3100 or 1-800/547-3529, ⓦwww.hotelnorthampton.com; ⑦), or the *Allen House Victorian Inn*, 599 Main St, Amherst (ⓣ413/253-5000, ⓦwww.allenhouse.com; ④–⑦), a quintessentially New England inn. Among the numerous places to **eat**, *Sylvester's*, 111 Pleasant St (ⓣ413/586-5343), serves up tasty fare, including delightful breakfast treats such as banana-bread, French toast and waffles, while *Herrell's Ice Cream*, 8 Old South St (ⓣ413/586-9700) is the home base of a small but irresistible chain of ice cream stores. *Amherst Chinese Food*, 62 Main St, Amherst (ⓣ413/253-7835), serves healthy Chinese specialties made with organic veggies plucked from their own garden.

The Berkshires

A rich cultural history, world-class summer arts festivals, and a bucolic landscape of forests and verdant hills make the **Berkshires**, at the extreme western edge of Massachusetts; ideal for warm weather exploration.

While you're in the area, try to visit the excellent **Berkshire Visitors Bureau**, 3 Hoosac St (Rte-8) in Adams (Mon–Fri 8.30am–5pm; ⓣ413/743-4500 or 1-800/237-5747, ⓦwww.berkshires.org), the best source for information on the area.

The Mohawk Trail: North Adams and Williamstown

In the northwest corner of the region, the **Mohawk Trail** passes through **NORTH ADAMS** and **WILLIAMSTOWN**, following the very scenic route the Native Americans used to travel between the valleys of the Connecticut and

Hudson rivers. North Adams is home to the glorious **Mass MoCA** (Massachusetts Museum of Contemporary Art), 87 Marshall St (July & Aug daily 10am–6pm; Sept–June Mon & Wed–Sun 11am–5pm; $15; ⓣ413/662-2111, ⓦwww.massmoca.org), a sprawling, neo-funhouse collection of modern art installations, contemporary videos, and upside-down trees gathered in a captivating old mill site. Williamstown has two worthy art museums: the highlight of the **Sterling and Francine Clark Art Institute**, 225 South St (Tues–Sun 10am–5pm, July & Aug daily 10am–5pm; $12.50 June–Oct, rest of year free; ⓣ413/458-2303, ⓦwww.clarkart.edu), is the thirty-strong collection of Renoir paintings, while the **Williams College Museum of Art**, 15 Lawrence Hall Drive (Tues–Sat 10am–5pm, Sun 1–5pm; free; ⓣ413/597-2429, ⓦwww.wcma.org), has good exhibits of ancient Middle Eastern and modern American art in a beautiful Neoclassical space. The ultra-modern *Porches Inn,* 231 River St, right around the corner from Mass MoCA (ⓣ413/664-0400, ⓦwww.porches.com; ⑧–⑨), is *the* place to **stay** in the area, featuring high-speed internet, DVD players, and contemporary, stylish decor. For **food,** head to hip *Café Latino,* at Mass MoCA (Wed-Sat; ⓣ413/662-2004) for crispy calamari and *caipirinhas,* or to its sister restaurant, *Mezze,* at 16 Water St in Williamstown (ⓣ413/458-0123), for outstanding New American flavors in a gracious, airy space.

Stockbridge

STOCKBRIDGE, just south of I-90 and fifty miles west of Springfield, started out as "Indian Town," when the remaining Mohican Indians in the region were re-settled here in 1736. The Reverend John Sergeant built the simple wooden **Mission House**, now located on Main Street, in 1739 in an attempt to live in close proximity with the Mohicans and convert them to Christianity.

That Stockbridge today looks like the archetypal New England small town – most of all when there's snow on the ground – is due largely to the artist **Norman Rockwell**, who lived here for 25 years until his death in 1978. Many of his *Saturday Evening Post* covers, whose sentimentality was made palatable by his sharp wit, featured the town; a collection of covers can be seen at the **museum** on Rte-183 (May–Oct daily 10am–5pm; Nov–April Mon–Fri 10am–4pm, Sat & Sun 10am–5pm; $15; ⓣ413/298-4100, ⓦwww.nrm.org). Some of the tour guides modeled for Rockwell as children and recall that for every few minutes they managed to hold still he'd slip them a coin from his large pile of nickels.

Magnificent houses in the hills around Stockbridge include **Chesterwood**, half a mile south of the Norman Rockwell Museum at 4 Williamsville Rd (May–Oct daily 10am–5pm; $12; ⓣ413/298-3579, ⓦwww.chesterwood.org), the luxurious home and studio of Daniel Chester French, sculptor of the Lincoln Memorial, and **Naumkeag**, on Prospect Hill Road, Rte-7 (late May to mid-Oct daily 10am–5pm; $12; ⓣ413/298-3239), which was the first modernist garden estate in the country.

The slightly frou-frou *Red Lion Inn* is one of the grander edifices on Main Street (ⓣ413/298-5545, ⓦwww.redlioninn.com; 5); their **restaurant** has big portions of reliable American cuisine, with standout burgers and steaks.

Lenox and around

Roughly five miles north of Stockbridge on US-7, well-heeled tourists flock to **LENOX** each year for the summer season of the Boston Symphony Orchestra at **Tanglewood**, 297 West St (for ticket info, call ⓣ413/637-1666 or visit ⓦwww.bso.org). Open-air orchestral concerts are held on weekends from July to late August, with chamber music and recitals given on other days; covered seats are pricey and often hard to get, but you can sit and picnic on the lush lawns for an admission fee of around $17. Some midweek rehearsals are also open to the public, and there's a **jazz** festival on Labor Day weekend (the first weekend of Sept). On Rte-20 between Becket and Lee, **Jacob's Pillow** (Ⓣ413/243-0745 or visit Ⓦwww.jacobspillow.org; June to Aug) hosts one of the most famous contemporary dance festivals in the country.

Further north on US-7, **Arrowhead** (late May to Oct daily 9.30am–4pm; $12; Ⓣ413/442-1793, Ⓦwww.mobydick.org), in Pittsfield, was Herman Melville's home while he wrote *Moby Dick*; declining sales of his books eventually forced him to sell his house and move to New York. The **Hancock Shaker Village**, five miles west of Pittsfield (daily: mid-April to late May 10am–4pm, late May to late Oct 10am–5pm; rest of year by guided tour only, Mon-Fri 1pm, Sat & Sun 11am & 1pm; summer and fall $15, rest of year $12.50; Ⓣ413/443-0188, Ⓦwww.hancockshakervillage.org), was a going concern from 1783 to 1960. Its legacy includes the large dwelling-place, in which almost one hundred people slept and ate, and a round stone barn for their cattle. You can **stay** in total luxury at *Blantyre*, Blantyre Road; Ⓣ413/637-3556, Ⓦwww.blantyre.com; ❾), one of the country's most plush (and expensive) resorts. *Walker House*, 64 Walker St (Ⓣ413/637-1271, Ⓦwww.walkerhouse.com; ❺) is an informal eight-room B&B set in an attractive 1804 Federal-style mansion, and much cheaper. For **food,** head over to *Church Street Café,* 69 Church St in Lenox (Ⓣ413/637-2745) for standout New England fare, or linger over a martini at the atmospheric *Bistro Zinc,* around the corner at 56 Church St (Ⓣ413/637-8800). *Berkshire Bagel,* 18 Franklin St, just off Rte-7A (Ⓣ413/637-1500) is a rare budget option in the center of town, with a huge range of bagels and smears ($2–5).

Rhode Island

A mere 48 miles long by 37 miles wide, **RHODE ISLAND** is the smallest state in the Union, yet it had a disproportionately large influence on national life: it enacted the first law against slavery in North America; it was the first of the thirteen colonies to declare independence from Britain; it helped to foster the nation's tradition of religious freedom; and it also saw the beginning of the **Industrial Revolution** in America. Today, Rhode Island is a prime tourist destination, boasting nearly four dozen National Historic Landmarks and four hundred miles of spectacular coastline.

Over thirty tiny islands make up the state, including Hope, Despair, and the bay's largest, Rhode Island (also known by its Native American name "Aquidneck"), which gives the state its name. **Narragansett Bay** has long been a determining factor in Rhode Island's economic development and strategic military importance, as the **Ocean State** developed through sea trade, whaling, and smuggling before shifting to manufacturing in the nineteenth century. Today, the state's principal destinations are its two original ports: the colonial college town of **Providence**, and well-heeled **Newport**, yachting capital of the world, with lavish mansions along its gorgeous shores.

Rhode Island is tiny enough to make **getting around** very easy. Major interstate I-95 runs through **Providence** on its way from Massachusetts to Connecticut, while the more scenic US-1 follows the coast of Narragansett Bay. **Newport** is accessible from Hwy-138. It is possible to get around on **public transportation**, with Amtrak stopping in Providence and local RIPTA buses and ferries connecting Providence and Newport (Ⓣ401/781-9400, Ⓦwww.ripta.com).

Providence

Splayed across seven hills on the Providence and Seekonk rivers, **PROVIDENCE** was Rhode Island's first settlement, founded in 1636 "in commemoration of God's providence" on land granted to Roger Williams by the Narragansett Indians. Despite its roots in celebrating freedom, the city flourished as one of the most important ports of call in the notorious "triangle trade," where New England rum was exchanged for African slaves, who were then sold for West Indian molasses. With Slater's invention of the textile mill, industry along with port trade became the mainstays of Providence's economy.

The state's capital since 1901, Providence is today one of New England's three largest cities. Ivy League **Brown University** and the **Rhode Island School of Design** (RISD, or "Rizdee") give the place a certain cultural verve, while the many original colonial homes on **Benefit Street** and around **College Hill** emanate an atmospheric, historic feel. The city's ethnic diversity is showcased west of downtown by the large Italian community on **Federal Hill**, with bustling restaurants and traditional appeal.

Arrival, information, and getting around

T.F. Green Airport in Warwick, nine miles south of Providence, connects to all major US cities. The **Amtrak station** (Ⓣ1-800/USA-RAIL) is in a domed building at 100 Gaspee St; here you can also catch the commuter rail to Boston (1hr; Ⓣ617/222-3200). Greyhound (Ⓣ1-800/231-2222) and Peter Pan (Ⓣ1-888/751-8800) **buses** stop downtown at the Kennedy Plaza hub.

The well-stocked **Visitors' Center**, in the rotunda lobby of the Rhode Island Convention Center, 1 Sabin St (Mon–Sat 9am–5pm; Ⓣ401/751-1177 or 1-800/233-1636), provides maps and brochures. The **Rhode Island Historical Society**, 110 Benevolent St (Ⓣ401/331-8575 or Ⓣ401/273-7507, Ⓦwww.rihs.org) leads walking tours through the city.

There is good **bus transportation** within the city, provided by RIPTA ($1.75, tickets sold onboard; Ⓣ401/781-9400, Ⓦwww.ripta.com), which has a hub at Kennedy Plaza. Also from here, a trolley runs to the **ferry** docks at Providence Piers, 180 Allens Ave, where you can catch ferries to Newport (May–Oct up to 6 daily; 1hr; $12; Ⓣ401/453-6800, Ⓦwww.providencefastferry.com).

Accommodation

Downtown Providence is largely geared to the business traveler and has few budget rooms, but **B&B**s are a viable option. Motorists can take advantage of the mid-priced **motels** along I-95 north towards Pawtucket, and south near the airport at Warwick.

Annie Brownell House B&B 400 Angell St Ⓣ401/454-2934, Ⓦwww.anniebrownellhouse.com. A handful of guestrooms in a lovely 1899 Colonial Revival house near Thayer St. Full hot breakfasts. ❺

Comfort Inn 1940 Post Rd, Warwick Ⓣ401/732-0470, Ⓦwww.choicehotels.com. Adequate lodging right by the airport. Also a branch at 2 George St, in Pawtucket (Ⓣ401/723-6700). ❺

Hotel Dolce Villa 63 DePasquale Sq Ⓣ401/383-7031, Ⓦwww.dolcevillari.com. Elegant white suites in Federal Hill's choice boutique hotel; also has a classic Italian villa. Suites ❼, villa ❽

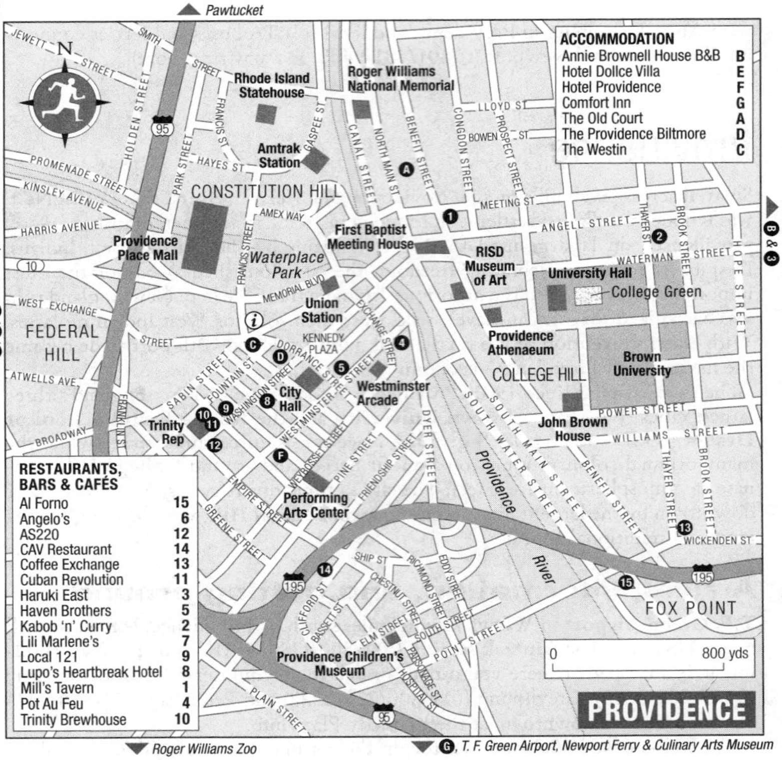

The Old Court 144 Benefit St ⓣ401/751-2002, ⓦwww.oldcourt.com. Appealing ten-room Victorian B&B in an old rectory near RISD. ❻

Hotel Providence 311 Westminster St ⓣ401/861-8000 or 1-800/861-8990, ⓦwww.thehotelprovidence.com. Eighty plush and colorful rooms, with trendy restaurant downstairs. ❼

The Providence Biltmore 11 Dorrance St ⓣ401/421-0700 or 1-800/294-7709, ⓦwww.providencebiltmore.com. A Providence landmark since 1922, featuring Old World elegance in the heart of downtown. ❻

The Westin 1 W Exchange St ⓣ401/598-8000 or 1-800/937-8461, ⓦwww.westin.com. Deluxe modern rooms in a palatial Downcity landmark. ❽

The City

The hub of downtown ("**Downcity**") is the transportation center at Kennedy Plaza, surrounded by new, modern buildings, with the notable exception of the 1878 **City Hall** at its western end. Though no longer used as a train terminal, the nearby 1898 Beaux Arts **Union Station** is another fine example of the historic restoration at which the city excels. A few blocks south, the still functional 1828 **Westminster Arcade** is the oldest indoor shopping mall in the nation.

North of Downcity, **Roger Williams National Memorial**, at N Main and Smith streets, is the site of the city-founder's original settlement, while to its west at the top of **Constitution Hill**, the magnificent white-marble **Rhode Island State House** boasts purportedly the fourth-largest dome in the world and the original Rhode Island Charter of 1663 (call ahead for tour schedule; ⓣ401/222-2357).

Just south of Downcity in the Jewelry District is the **Providence Children's Museum**, at 100 South St (April–Aug daily 9am–6pm, Sept–March Tues–Sun 9am–6pm; $6.50; ⓣ401/273-5437, ⓦwww.childrenmuseum.org), where the range of interactive displays includes a time-traveling adventure through Rhode Island's history. Further south near the Cranston city line, the **Culinary Arts Museum**, 315 Harborside Blvd (Tues–Sun 10am–5pm; $7; ⓣ401/598-2805, ⓦwww.culinary.org), features a wealth of food history, including ancient utensils and recipes, on the satellite campus of Johnson & Wales University, one of the country's premier culinary colleges.

Two miles south of downtown, the 430-acre **Roger Williams Park** is home to the marvelous **Roger Williams Zoo**, the third oldest zoo in the country with 130 species of animals and imaginative exhibits (daily: April–Sept 9am–5pm, rest of year 9am–4pm; $12; ⓣ401/785-3510, ⓦwww.rogerwilliamsparkzoo.org).

College Hill and Federal Hill

Across the river from Downcity, laidback **College Hill** is an attractive district of colonial buildings and museums. The white clapboard **First Baptist Meeting House**, at the foot of the hill at 75 N Main St, dates from 1775, and testifies to the state's origins as a "lively experiment" in religious freedom. Nearby **Benefit Street** is Providence's "**mile of history**," lined with beautifully restored former homes of merchants and sea captains. The street was once a dirt path leading to graveyards until it was improved in the nineteenth century for the "benefit of the people of Providence" – hence its name. One of the few homes open to the public, the elegant **John Brown House**, 52 Power St, at Benefit Street (call for tours; $8; ⓣ401/273-7507), was the first house built on the hill and home to the patriot and entrepreneur (also uncle to the man the university is named after) who prospered from the slave trade and trade with China.

The leafy, historic campus of Ivy League **Brown University** sets the tone for this three-centuries-old district; for free tours, contact the admissions office, 45 Prospect St (ⓣ401/863-2378, ⓦwww.brown.edu). In the same area, the smaller RISD campus is home to the **RISD Museum of Art**, 224 Benefit St (Tues–Sun 10am–5pm; $8; ⓣ401/454-6500, ⓦwww.risd.edu), featuring 45 galleries, including superb European and American decorative arts collections and an outstanding Asian collection with more than six hundred Japanese woodblock prints and a Heian Buddha. Also here, the Greek Revival **Providence Athenaeum**, 251 Benefit St (Mon–Thurs 9am–7pm, Fri & Sat 9am–5pm, Sun 1–5pm; closed Sun in summer; free; ⓣ401/421-6970, ⓦwww.providenceathenaeum.org) is one of America's oldest libraries, where Edgar Allan Poe once courted Sarah Whitman. East and south of College Hill, **Thayer** and **Wickenden Streets** buzz with an assortment of bookstores and cafés.

Federal Hill, west of Downcity, is Providence's **Little Italy**, greeting visitors with the traditional symbol of welcome, a bronze pinecone, on the entrance arch on Atwells Avenue. This is one of the friendliest areas in the city, alive with cafés, delis, bakeries, and bars, and with a lively piazza around the Italianate fountain in **DePasquale Square**.

Slater Mill Historic Site

Just north of Providence, Pawtucket is home to the **Slater Mill Historic Site**, 67 Roosevelt Ave, exit 28 off I-95 (March & April Sat & Sun 11am–3pm, May–June & Oct–Nov Tues–Sat 10am–3pm, July–Sept Tues–Sat 10am–5pm; $9; ⓣ401/725-8638, ⓦwww.slatermill.org), which illustrates America's move to the industrial age led by Samuel Slater, who imported the technology from

England in 1790. Highlights include the **Old Slater Mill**, with rare textile machines dating from 1838; the 1810 **Wilkinson Mill**, where a machine shop still operates; and the **Sylvanus Brown House**, a worker's home with replica early-1800s furnishings.

Eating

Providence boasts excellent **food** options. **Thayer Street** is lined with inexpensive eateries popular with students, while nearby **Wickenden Street** has a more mature clientele. Or head to **Federal Hill**, where you can find great Italian food at reasonable prices.

Al Forno 577 S Main St ⓣ401/273-9760. Famed wood-grilled pizzas, meats, and other treats at one of the best restaurants in the country. Dinner only, closed Sun & Mon.

Angelo's 141 Atwells Ave ⓣ401/621-8171. A staple in Federal Hill since 1924, with homey, no-frills, affordable Italian cooking.

CAV Restaurant 14 Imperial Place ⓣ401/751-9164. A contemporary American mid-priced menu in an atmospheric historic loft.

Coffee Exchange 207 Wickenden St ⓣ401/273-1198. Fair Trade, shade-grown, organic coffees and a delectable vegetarian menu in a relaxed café setting.

Haruki East 172 Wayland Ave ⓣ401/223-0332. Known as one of the best Japanese places around, with mid-priced, finely presented dishes.

Haven Brothers Diner-on-wheels since 1893, with classic hot dogs, burgers, and fries. Parked outside City Hall every night 4.30pm–5am.

Kabob 'n' Curry 261 Thayer St ⓣ401/273-8844. Above-average Indian meals on lively Thayer St, with fun twists like "naninis" ($6–8).

Local 121 121 Washington St ⓣ401/274-2121. Elegant dining setting, with a mission to serve local, fresh, and sustainable cuisine.

Mill's Tavern 101 N Main St ⓣ401/272-3331. Contemporary, upscale American cuisine, with special wood-fired dishes. Dinner only.

Pot Au Feu 44 Custom House St ⓣ401/273-8953. Expensive salon dining upstairs, moderately priced bistro downstairs, and excellent French dishes in both.

Nightlife and entertainment

Providence has a rich and varied **performing arts** and **film** scene. The Avon Rep Cinema at 260 Thayer St (ⓣ401/421-3315) shows independent and art **films**, as does the love-seat filled Cable Car Cinema at 204 S Main St (ⓣ401/272-3970). In Downcity, Trinity Rep, 201 Washington St (ⓣ401/351-4242, ⓦwww.trinityrep.com) is one of America's foremost regional theaters, while the **Providence Performing Arts Center**, 220 Weybosset St (ⓣ401/421-2787, ⓦwww.ppacri.org), hosts **musicals** in a grand old Art Deco movie house. On Gallery Night (March–Nov, third Thurs of the month, 5–9pm; ⓣ401/490-2042, ⓦwww.gallerynight.info), free Art Buses leave from behind Citizens Plaza (near Waterplace Park) and stop along many of the city's **galleries** and museums, where admission is also free for the evening.

In the warmer months, the unusual event known as **WaterFire** (several times a month, May–Oct; ⓦwww.waterfire.org) sees nearly one hundred small bonfires set at sunset in the center of the Providence River starting at Waterplace Park, tended by gondoliers and accompanied by rousing music. Complete entertainment listings can be found in the free weekly *Providence Phoenix* and the *Providence Journal*'s Thursday edition.

The city's **nightlife** bustles around Empire and Washington streets, south of Kennedy Plaza in Downcity, and along **Thayer Street** near Brown University during term-time.

AS220 115 Empire St ⓣ401/831-9327. Hip, lively, anti-establishment establishment that operates as a café/bar/gallery, showcasing eclectic local art and diverse nightly performances.
Cuban Revolution 50 Aborn St ⓣ401/331-8829. Cuban beer and tropical cocktails in a laid-back atmosphere; you can also munch on assorted tapas, sushi, and Che fries.
Lili Marlene's 422 Atwells Ave ⓣ401/751-4996. Small, dark, low-key bar, with red-leather booths, a pool table, and late-night snacks, tucked out of the way in Federal Hill.
Lupo's Heartbreak Hotel 79 Washington St ⓣ401/272-5876. This is the spot in town to see nationally recognized bands rock out. Tickets around $10–40, cheaper in advance.
Trinity Brewhouse 186 Fountain St ⓣ401/453-2337. Hang out here after a Providence Bruins (minor league hockey) or Friars (college basketball) game; fresh brews on tap.

Newport

NEWPORT, nicknamed "America's First Resort," is a place out of a picture book, distinct for its polished yacht fleets, rose-colored sunsets, and long-time association with America's fine and fabulous. The Kennedys were married here (Jackie was a local girl); and during his presidency Eisenhower spent time here at the Naval War College, which continues to introduce a uniformed presence to the lively streets. Tourists come today for the opulent fin-de-siècle mansions that line Bellevue Avenue – huge tree-lined estates and ornate palaces, former summer homes of the likes of the Astors and Vanderbilts.

Stroll beyond the extravagant facades, though, and you'll find much more, including many original eighteenth-century homes that sit among downtown's restaurants, boutiques, and shops. The town's prime seaside location also means that the views are often, if not always, free – a short drive and you're greeted by unrivalled shores, with rugged seascapes and long swaths of sand.

Arrival and information

There are three towns on Aquidneck Island: **Portsmouth**, **Middletown**, and **Newport**. The mainland (and I-95) is connected to the island by US-138, which passes over the **Jamestown Bridge** to Jamestown, and from there by the **Newport Bridge** to Newport.

Newport is easy to **walk** around, with Thames (pronounced "Thaymz") Street as the main thoroughfare. Just north of downtown, at 23 America's Cup Ave, the **Gateway Visitor Center** is a hub of information (daily 9am–5pm; ⓣ401/845-9123 or 1-800/976-5122, ⓦwww.gonewport.com). It also serves as the terminal for **Bonanza** (ⓣ401/846-1820) and **RIPTA** buses, as well as an **airport shuttle**.

Bikes are available for rent at Ten Speed Spokes, 18 Elm St ($6/hr, $30/day; ⓣ401/847-5609). On foot, the Newport Historical Society and Newport Restoration Foundation organize walking **tours** through downtown, departing from the Brick Market Museum, 127 Thames St ($12; ⓣ401/841-8770, ⓦwww.newportrestoration.com/histours). But easily the most relaxing way of seeing Newport is on one of a number of **cruises**; try the beautiful schooner *Madeleine* (ⓣ401/847-0298, ⓦwww.cruisenewport.com), with ninety-minute tours in the summer departing from Bannister's Wharf ($27).

Accommodation

Accommodation in Newport, mostly inns and B&Bs, is not cheap, and prices skyrocket during summer weekends. Chain motels and **campgrounds** can be found just a few miles north in Middletown and Portsmouth. If you're stuck, try the Visitor Center, or, alternatively, Bed & Breakfast Newport (Ⓣ401/846-5408 or 1-800/800-8765; Ⓦwww.bbnewport.com).

The Almondy 25 Pelham St Ⓣ401/848-7202 or 1-800/478-6155, Ⓦwww.almondyinn.com. 1890s B&B, with harbor views, jacuzzi baths, and gourmet breakfasts. ❽

Chart House Inn 16 Clarke St Ⓣ401/207-6418, Ⓦwww.charthouseinn.com. Eight sunlit, airy rooms in centrally located B&B. All rooms with private bath, but some in hallway. ❻

Hotel Viking 1 Bellevue Ave Ⓣ401/847-3300, Ⓦwww.hotelviking.com. Luxurious, 222-room hotel originally built in 1926 to accommodate spill-over mansion guests. ❾

Melville House 39 Clarke St Ⓣ401/847-0640, Ⓦwww.melvillehouse.com. Colonial B&B with seven cozy rooms; private and shared baths. ❻

The Old Beach Inn 19 Old Beach Rd Ⓣ401/849-3479 or 1-888/303-5033, Ⓦwww.oldbeachinn.com. Secluded, old-fashioned retreat down the street from the Newport Art Museum, with garden and porch. ❻

William Gyles Guesthouse 16 Howard St Ⓣ401/369-0243, Ⓦwww.newporthostel.com. Welcoming hostel in the heart of downtown. Private accommodation also available. In-season dorm beds $59/night weekends, $35–39 weekdays.

The Town

Newport's palatial nineteenth-century **mansions** are its main draw; when you tire of the opulence, head to the shoreline, to enjoy some spectacular **beaches**.

The mansions

When sociologist Thorstein Veblen visited Newport at the turn of the twentieth century, he was so horrified by the extravagance that he coined the phrase "conspicuous consumption." Beginning in the 1870s, Newport was an arena for the New York elite, where the industrial magnates and their families competed to outdo each other in building lavish estates. Many of the mansions fell to bleak fates just a few

▲ The Breakers

decades later; the **Preservation Society of Newport County**, 424 Bellevue Ave (Ⓣ401/847-1000, Ⓦwww.newportmansions.org; mansions open April–Jan) maintains the bulk of the dozen or so houses open for public viewing today.

The mansions each boast their own version of Gilded Age excess: **Marble House**, with its golden ballroom and adjacent Chinese teahouse; **Rosecliff**, with a colorful rose garden and heart-shaped staircase; the ornate French **The Elms**, known for its gardens; and Cornelius Vanderbilt's **The Breakers**, an Italian Renaissance palace overlooking the ocean and the grandest of the lot. Besides those, a number of earlier, smaller houses, including the quirky Gothic Revival cottage **Kingscote**, may well make for a more interesting excursion. Admission to the Breakers is $16.50; visit with one other property and it's $23; and a combo ticket to five is $31. Note that many houses operate on hourly tours; unless you're a mansion nut, viewing one or two should suffice to get a glimpse of the opulence.

Independent from the Preservation Society mansions, the Astors' **Beechwood**, 580 Bellevue Ave (Feb to mid-May Fri–Sun 10am–4pm, mid-May to Dec daily 10am–4pm, closed Jan; $15; Ⓣ401/846-3772, Ⓦwww.astors-beechwood.com) is an entertaining antidote to the drier historical drills given on other tours, with costumed actors leading you into their set. **Belcourt Castle**, also on Bellevue at no. 657 (summer and fall daily 10am–4pm, other months times vary; $12; Ⓣ401/846-0669, Ⓦwww.belcourtcastle.com), is unusual in that it is still inhabited by its owners.

One way to see the mansions on the cheap is to peer in the back gardens from the **Cliff Walk**, which begins on Memorial Boulevard where it meets First (Easton) Beach. This spectacular three-and-a-half-mile oceanside path alternates from pretty stretches lined by jasmine and wild roses to rugged rocky passes.

Downtown Newport

Colonial Newport's political and business center, **Washington Square**, lies just south of the Gateway Center, beginning where Thames Street meets the **Brick Market**. Here, the **Brick Market Museum** (Mon–Thurs 10am–6pm, Fri & Sat 10am–8pm, Sun 10am–5pm; $4 suggested donation; Ⓣ401/841-8770) features exhibits on Newport's past. Across the square, the **Old Colony House** is a pre-Revolutionary brick building which held the state's seat of government from 1739 to 1900. Here, in May of 1776, Rhode Island became the first colony to declare independence from Britain.

The oldest religious building in town is the 1699 Quaker **Great Friends Meeting House**, at Marlborough and Farewell streets, restored to its nineteenth-century appearance and completely free of adornment (tours by appointment; Ⓣ401/846-0813). Indeed, the state's penchant for religious tolerance is echoed by the nearby **Touro Synagogue**, 85 Touro St, the oldest house of Jewish worship in America, founded by descendants of Jews fleeing the Spanish Inquisition ($5 tours; Ⓣ401/847-4794, Ⓦwww.tourosynagogue.org). Tolerance even extended to the Anglicans, who founded the 1726 **Trinity Church** in Queen Anne Square, while **St Mary's Church**, at Spring Street and Memorial Boulevard, is the oldest Catholic Church in Rhode Island (Ⓣ401/847-0475). Perhaps most enigmatic of all, though, is what's known as the **Viking Tower** in Touro Park, a stone structure with mysterious, purportedly Norse, origins.

Apart from the mansions, Bellevue Avenue also has two museums of note. The **Newport Art Museum**, at no. 76, is housed in the 1864 mock-medieval Griswold House, and exhibits New England art from the last two centuries (late May to mid-Oct Mon–Sat 10am–5pm, Sun noon–5pm; rest of year Mon–Sat 10am–4pm, Sun noon–4pm; $8; Ⓣ401/848-8200, Ⓦwww.newportartmuseum.org). At no. 194, the grand **Newport Casino** was an early country club, which held the first national tennis championship in 1881. It now houses the **International Tennis**

Hall of Fame Museum, with a vast collection of tennis-related memorabilia (ⓣ401/849-3990, ⓦwww.tennisfame.com).

The beaches

The attraction of Newport's shoreline, with its many coves and gently sloping sands, is indubitably its beaches. Small **Gooseberry Beach** is surrounded by grand houses, while **First Beach** is the lively town beach at the eastern end of Memorial Boulevard; further out, **Second (Sachuest) Beach**, with its quiet, long sandy swaths, is where you really want to go, while calmer waters can be found at Third Beach. Most beaches have summer parking fees of $10–15 per car. If you want spectacular views without getting wet, bike along the several miles of **Ocean Drive**, leading to **Brenton Point State Park** (open daily sunrise–sunset; free), a great sunset spot where you'll find panoramic views of Narragansett Bay.

Eating

Many of Newport's **restaurants** are geared to tourists and overpriced, though with a little hunting you can find some marvelous exceptions. Note that many of the restaurants listed below have seasonal hours.

Asterisk 599 Thames St ⓣ401/841-8833. Upscale French bistro in a former car garage, with mouthwatering breakfasts, desserts, and dinner dishes of sole meuniere and chicken scallopini.
The Black Pearl Bannisters Wharf ⓣ401/846-5264. Newport institution famous for its chunky clam chowder; informal patio as well as formal dining available.
Firehouse Pizza 595 Thames St ⓣ401/846-1199. An old firehouse with kooky hand-painted booths and twelve-inch pan pizzas.
Flo's Clam Shack 4 Wave Ave ⓣ401/847-8141. Hugely popular joint across from First Beach, famed for cheap chowder and the usual clam shack faves.
Salvation Café 140 Broadway ⓣ401/847-2620. Funky spot off the main drag, with exotic concoctions like Moroccan chicken and Thai shrimp cakes, at reasonable prices. Dinner daily.
Scales & Shells 527 Thames St ⓣ401/846-3474. Casual restaurant known for its fresh seafood – raw, broiled, or mesquite-grilled. Dinner only.
Smokehouse Café America's Cup Ave and Scotts Wharf ⓣ401/848-9800. Giant BBQ combos and baby back ribs at affordable prices in a lively atmosphere.
White Horse Tavern Marlborough and Farewell Sts ⓣ401/849-3600. Dine by candlelight at one of the oldest taverns in America, since 1687. Continental cuisine with a New England touch; more affordably priced at lunchtime.

Festivals and nightlife

There is always something afoot in Newport, particularly in the summer for the **Newport Folk Festival** (ⓣ877/655-4849, ⓦwww.newportfolk.com) or the **JVC Jazz Festival** (ⓣ877/655-4849, ⓦjazz.jvc.com). The **Newport Music Festival** (ⓣ401/846-1133, ⓦwww.newportmusic.org) boasts classical music performed at the mansions, while the **Irish Waterfront Festival** is one of the city's biggest Irish events (ⓣ401/646-1600, ⓦwww.newportfestivals.com). **Nightlife** also bustles during the summer, with lively bars lining the waterfront.

Billy Goode's 23 Marlborough St ⓣ401/848-5013. Get a feel for the speakeasy days at this old joint in the former sailor's district. Live country music Wed nights.
The Boom-Boom Room at the *Clarke Cooke House*, Bannister's Wharf ⓣ401/849-2900. Popular disco attracting a mixed crowd with standards, oldies, and Top-40.
Mudville Pub 8 W Marlborough St ⓣ401/849-1408. Irish pub and sports bar above Cardines Field, with an extensive beer list.
Newport Blues Café 286 Thames St ⓣ401/841-5510. Come watch the legends and future acts in this laid-back venue; live blues and jazz nightly.
One Pelham East Thames and Pelham Sts ⓣ401/847-9460. Popular venue that has hosted live bands since 1975; there's a dance club upstairs.

Connecticut

New England's southernmost state, **CONNECTICUT**, was named *Quinnehtukqut* ("great tidal river") by the Native Americans after the river that bisects it and spills into Long Island Sound. First settled by white settlers in the 1630s, Connecticut is one of the oldest colonies of the Union, playing crucial roles during the Revolutionary War (hence named "**the provisions state**") and in the country's founding - its original 1639 charter helped to inspire the American Constitution (hence also named "**the Constitution state**"). During the eighteenth and nineteenth centuries, the state prospered from steady industrialization and lucrative whaling along the coast. Today, much of the old industry has withered away, leaving areas of green countryside and idyllic villages that typify New England's quaint image.

While predominantly rural, Connecticut is densely populated along the coast, with a vibrant southwestern corner exuding the cosmopolitan air of neighbouring New York City, and the at once industrial and intellectual **New Haven**, home to Yale University. Further east, **Mystic** and **New London** still maintain intimate ties to their maritime past, while inland, the old architecture scattered around the state capital of **Hartford** tells of the city's more glorious days.

Getting around Connecticut

Connecticut is well-connected by major **roads**: I-95 runs from New York to Rhode Island along the coast, while I-91 weaves its way north along the Connecticut River to Vermont. Greyhound and Peter Pan (Ⓣ1-800/343-9999, Ⓦwww.peterpanbus.com) run **buses** to most of the main towns. CT Transit (Ⓣ860/522-8101) provides **local bus** transport in metro Hartford and New Haven. Metro North (Ⓣ1-800/638-7646) **trains** carry passengers between New Haven and New York City; Amtrak's line runs between New York City and Boston, with various stops along the shore and a connection to Hartford.

Southeastern Connecticut

The much-visited **southeastern coast** of Connecticut spans 25 miles from Stonington in the east to Niantic in the west. The old whaling port of **Mystic** is a big draw with its restored nineteenth-century seaport and huge aquarium, while **New London** is home to the US Coast Guard Academy. Further east is the picturesque seaside village of **Stonington**.

Mystic

As purists will tell you, the town of **MYSTIC**, right on I-95, does not really exist; **Old Mystic** comprises a couple of quaint streets north of the highway, while tourists are drawn to the maritime recreations at **Mystic Seaport**, a couple of miles south, and its bustling downtown just across the Mystic River. The drawbridge leading downtown is still raised hourly and on request for some magnificent taller ships sailing through.

The area's biggest draw is the **Mystic Aquarium & Institute for Exploration**, exit 90 off I-95 (Jan & Feb Mon–Fri 10am–5pm, Sat & Sun 9am–6pm, March–Dec daily 9am–6pm; adults $24, children 3–17 $18; Ⓣ860/572-5955, Ⓦwww.ife.org), home to over twelve thousand weird and wonderful marine specimens, including penguins, sea lions, piranhas, and the only Beluga whales in New England.

Whether you think it's authentic or tacky, **Mystic Seaport**, also known as the Museum of America & the Sea (daily: April–Oct 9am–5pm, rest of year 10am–4pm; $18.50, children $13; ⓣ860/572-5315, ⓦwww.mysticseaport.org), is the area's other big draw, where more than sixty buildings house old-style workshops and stores reflecting life in a nineteenth century seafaring village. In the **Preservation Shipyard**, watch the restoration and maintenance of a vast collection of wooden ships, among them the 1841 *Charles W. Morgan*, the last wooden whaling ship in the world.

Practicalities

Mystic's main **information office** lies in the tacky Olde Mistick Village Shopping Mall (Mon–Sat 9am–5pm, Sun 10am–5pm; ⓣ860/536-1641), with a smaller branch office (daily 10am–4pm, ⓣ860/572-1102) at the Amtrak **train station** (ⓣ1-800/872-7245). **Accommodation** options include the *Steamboat Inn*, 73 Steamboat Wharf (ⓣ860-536-8300, ⓦwww.steamboatinnmystic.com; ❽), overlooking the water with eleven elegant rooms in the heart of downtown. Near I-95 are a handful of chain motels, including *Best Western Mystic*, 9 Whitehall Ave (ⓣ860/536-4281; ❹); also here, the pretty *Whitehall Mansion*, 42 Whitehall Ave (ⓣ860/572-7280 or 1-800/572-3993; ❻) is a restored 1771 house with five guestrooms. The Seaport **campground**, off Rte-184 in Old Mystic (ⓣ860/536-4044, ⓦwww.seaportcampground.com; $45/site), has 130 sites.

Mystic's excellent **restaurants** include *Bravo Bravo*, 20 E Main St (ⓣ860/536-3228), serving inspired pastas and fine Italian classics in an unpretentious space, and *S&P Oyster Company*, 1 Holmes St (ⓣ860/536-2674), serving fine seafood on the waterfront. The small, family-run *Mystic Pizz*a, at 56 W Main St (ⓣ860/536-3700), unruffled by its movie-title status, serves huge pies for $10–16.

Stonington

STONINGTON, just south of I-95 near the state's eastern border, is a pretty old fishing village, originally settled in 1649 and still very much New England with its whitewashed cottages and peaceful waterfront. Its main road, **Water Street**, is dotted with restaurants and shops. At no. 7, the **Old Lighthouse Museum** (May–Nov daily 10am–5pm; $8; ⓣ860-535-1440), relays fine textures of town life through the last centuries in six small rooms of exhibits. The view from the top, as from the entrance, is endless on a sunny day. Museum admission includes access to the Italianate **Captain Nathaniel B. Palmer House**, 40 Palmer St (May–Nov Wed–Sun 10am–5pm; $8; ⓣ860-535-8445), at the north end of town, celebrating Stonington's premier seafarer credited with one of the earliest sightings of Antarctica.

For **accommodation**, the *Orchard Street Inn,* 41 Orchard St (ⓣ860/535-2681, ⓦwww.orchardstreetinn.com; ❼) has three rooms in a quiet cottage. In neighbouring Pawcatuck, the *Cove Ledge Inn & Marina*, on Rte-1 at Whewell Circle (ⓣ860/599-4130, ⓦwww.coveledgeinn.com; ❹), offers twenty rooms close to the water. For **food**, try *Noah's*, 113 Water St (ⓣ860/535-3925; closed Mon), known for fine homestyle cooking, featuring eclectic choices ranging from Korean pancakes to fresh local catch. Alternatively, *Skipper's Dock*, 66 Water St (ⓣ860/535-0111), offers mid-priced seafood dishes complemented by fantastic water views.

Groton

Seven miles west of Mystic Seaport, **GROTON** is a suitably unpleasant name for the hometown of the **US Naval Submarine Base**, headquarters for the North Atlantic fleet and a crucial fixture in the local economy since 1916. While the naval base is off limits to the public, the **Submarine Force Museum** (mid-May to Oct Wed–Mon 9am–5pm, Tues 1–5pm; Nov to mid-May Wed–Mon 9am–4pm; free; ⓣ1-800/343-0079) welcomes visitors to trace the history of submersibles from as early as the Revolutionary era to the 1954 **USS Nautilus**, America's first nuclear-powered submarine and the first vessel to sail under the polar icecap. Wind your way through narrow, claustrophobic passages down to the crew's quarters, where things look pretty much as they did in the 1950's, complete with pin-ups of Marilyn Monroe.

New London

NEW LONDON, opposite Groton on the west side of the Thames River, is the most populated city along this stretch of the coast, spreading over six square miles. Originally settled in 1646, it was a wealthy whaling port in the nineteenth century. Today, it's home to the **US Coast Guard Academy**, off I-95 at 31 Mohegan Ave, on an attractive sloping campus overlooking the Thames. Visitors are welcome to take a self-guided tour (daily 9am–4.30pm; ID required; free), with walking maps available from the admissions office in Waesche Hall (ⓣ860/444-8500). Here, the **US Coast Guard Museum** (open daily, call for hours; free; ⓣ860/444-8511) explores two centuries of coast guard history, and you can also visit the USS *Eagle* when it's docked here (ⓣ860/444-8595).

From the Southeastern Connecticut **CVB** at 32 Huntington St (ⓣ860/444-2206), you can pick up a self-guided walking tour map of downtown, and continue down the formerly prosperous Huntington Street, past the Greek Revival mansions known as **Whale Oil Row**. The city boasts a number of historic houses open to the public, among them the **Shaw-Perkins Mansion**, 11 Blinman St (Wed–Fri 1–4pm, Sat 10am–4pm; $5; ⓣ860/443-1209), a stone house built in 1756 for wealthy ship-owner and trader Nathaniel Shaw, and the **Monte Cristo Cottage**, 325 Pequot Ave (June to Sept Tues–Sat 10am–5pm, Sun 1–3pm; $7; ⓣ860/443-5378 ext 290), childhood home of boozy, Nobel-winning playwright **Eugene O'Neill**. The Eugene O'Neill Theater Center, 305 Great Neck Rd (exit 82 off I-95) in nearby **Waterford,** is an acclaimed testing-ground for emerging playwrights and actors (ⓣ860/443-5378, ⓦwww.oneilltheatercenter.org).

South of downtown, **Ocean Beach Park**, at 1225 Ocean Ave, has a sugar-sand beach and huge saltwater pool, as well as a wooden boardwalk, mini-golf and arcade (open summer daily till late; $14–18 parking; additional fees for activities; ⓣ860/447-3031).

Practicalities

You can arrive in New London by **ferry** from Orient Point on Long Island (via Cross Sound Ferry, 2 Ferry St, ⓣ860/443-5281, ⓦwww.longislandferry.com; reservations recommended). The city is also served well by Amtrak **train** and Greyhound **buses**.

Information is available at the **Trolley Station**, on Eugene O'Neill Drive (May & Oct Fri–Sun 10am–4pm, June–Sept daily 10am–4pm; ⓣ860/444-7264). A number of motels are scattered along I-95, including the *Holiday Inn*, 269 N Frontage Rd (ⓣ860/442-0631; ❻). For a more atmospheric stay, try *Lighthouse Inn Resort*, 6 Guthrie Place (ⓣ860/443-8411, ⓦwww.lighthouseinn-ct.com; ❺), with elegant rooms on the former country estate of steel magnate Charles S. Guthrie.

The inn's classy restaurant, *Timothy's*, serves a variety of seafood from its vantage point on Long Island Sound. Downtown, the French café *Mangetout,* 140 State St (Mon–Sat 8am–4pm, Sun 11am–4pm, ⓣ860/444-2066) offers fresh, organic meals and delicious desserts.

Hartford

The town that Mark Twain once described as "the best built and handsomest...I have ever seen" is today hardly recognizable as such. Rather, the modern capital of Connecticut, **HARTFORD**, is best known as the insurance center of the United States. Though the city itself has fallen on rather hard times, the old architecture scattered around town continues to tell many a history. Highlights include the gold-domed **state capitol**, in Bushnell Park (free tours hourly Mon–Fri 9.15am–1.15pm, July & Aug additional tour at 2.15pm; also April–Oct Sat 10.15am–2.15pm), an 1878 mixture of Gothic, Classical, and Second Empire styles, emanating an ecclesiastical ambience. Also in the park, the 1914 antique wooden merry-go-round still gives jangling rides for a mere $1 (mid-May to Oct, closed Mon).

Hartford's pride and joy is the Greek Revival **Wadsworth Atheneum**, at 600 Main St (Wed–Fri 11am–5pm, Sat & Sun 10am–5pm; $10; ⓣ860/278-2670, ⓦwww.wadsworthatheneum.org), founded by Daniel Wadsworth in 1842 and the nation's oldest continuously operating public art museum. The world-class collection, spanning over five thousand years, includes a distinguished collection of American paintings and sculpture, Renaissance and Baroque masterpieces, and a significant contemporary collection.

A mile west of downtown, the hilltop community known as Nook Farm was home in the 1880s to next-door neighbors **Mark Twain** and **Harriet Beecher Stowe**. Their Victorian homes, furnished much as they were then, are both open for tours. Twain lived at 351 Farmington Ave from 1874 until 1891, writing many of his classic works in this ornate house, complete with elaborate brickwork and Tiffany interiors (April–Dec Mon–Sat 9.30am–5.30pm, Sun noon–5.30pm; rest of year closed Tues; $14; ⓣ860/247-0998, ⓦwww.marktwainhouse.org).

Next door, the much less flamboyant **Harriet Beecher Stowe Center**, 77 Forest St (May–Oct Mon–Sat 9.30am–4.30pm, Sun noon–4.30pm; rest of year same hours but closed Mon; $8; ⓣ860/522-9258, ⓦwww.harrietbeecherstowecenter.org), celebrates one of America' most important female activists. The white Victorian Gothic home is a fine example of the nineteenth-century "cottage," with a hint of the romantic villa, and you can see Stowe's writing table.

Other town highlights include the beautiful campus of **Trinity College**, at 300 Summit St, located on a hundred acres at the highest point in the city. Founded in 1823, the college hosts an array of stunning Victorian Gothic architecture, including its magnificent college **chapel**. West on Prospect and Asylum avenues, **Elizabeth Park** (daily dawn–dusk; free; ⓦwww.elizabethpark.org) is the first municipal rose garden in the nation. June is the best time to visit to see the more than eight hundred varieties of roses in bloom, but in addition there are rock gardens, greenhouses (ⓣ860/231-9443; Mon–Fri 8am–3pm), and miles of tranquil walking paths.

Practicalities

Hartford, which lies at the junction of I-91 and I-84, is easily accessible by car. Greyhound, Peter Pan, and Bonanza **buses**, and Amtrak **trains**, all pull into Union

Station, just north of Bushnell Park. Twelve miles north of town lies Connecticut's **Bradley International Airport** (Ⓣ860/292-2000, Ⓦwww.bradleyairport.com), served by a CT Transit **shuttle** to the Old State House in downtown. For **information**, visit the Greater Hartford Welcome Center, 45 Pratt St (Mon–Fri 9am–5pm; Ⓣ860/244-0253, Ⓦwww.hartford.com).

Hartford has a limited range of **lodging** options, with a handful of pricey downtown hotels catering mainly to business travelers, with weekend deals, including the *Goodwin Hotel*, Goodwin Square, 1 Haynes St (Ⓣ860/246-7500; ❻), a 124-room luxury hotel opposite the Civic Center. Budget motels can be found along I-91, including the above-average *Super 8,* exit 33 (Ⓣ860/246-8888; ❹), a half-mile from downtown. More charming options are available in Wethersfield and Farmington, just a few miles from town – try the spacious, elegant *Farmington Inn*, 827 Farmington Ave, in Farmington (Ⓣ860/677-2821, Ⓦwww.farmingtoninn.com; ❻).

A popular **restaurant** is *Black Eyed Sally's*, 350 Asylum St (Ⓣ860/278-7427), where hearty Cajun cooking is complemented by live blues bands. *Trumbull Kitchen*, 150 Trumbull St (Ⓣ860/493-7417), offers a cross-cultural menu in a modern setting, while *Peppercorn's Grill*, 357 Main St Ⓣ860/547-1714 serves outstanding contemporary Italian dishes. For an exotic touch, visit the *Abyssinian,* 535 Farmington Ave Ⓣ860/218-2231, offering authentic Ethiopian stews, salads, fish, and breads, with plentiful vegetarian options.

New Haven

Don't be put off by the grubby initial impression you get when you arrive in **NEW HAVEN**. Tucked away among the grimy factories and architecturally nondescript office blocks are some of the best restaurants, most exciting nightspots, and diverting cultural activities in all of New England. Founded in 1638 by a group of wealthy Puritans from London, New Haven became the seat of Yale University in 1716, the third oldest college in the nation. Today, its leafy campus and magnificent Gothic architecture continue to exert a veritable historical presence. The tensions between the city's two very different facets (tension-ridden urbanity and Ivy League idyll) once made New Haven an uneasy place, though an active symbiosis has thrived since the early 1990s. The city has been undergoing a major downtown development, which will yield new residential, cultural, and commercial spaces.

Arrival, information, and getting around

New Haven lies where interstates I-91 and I-95 fork, and is well served by Greyhound **buses** and Amtrak **trains**. **Union Station**, on Union Avenue six blocks southeast of the Yale campus downtown, is the main terminal. From New York, the Metro-North Commuter Railroad (Ⓣ1-800/638-7646) is a better deal than Amtrak. If you arrive at night, you may want to grab a **taxi**; try Metro Taxi (Ⓣ203/777-7777).

Public transportation is provided by Connecticut Transit, 470 James St ($1.25; Ⓣ203/624-0151, Ⓦwww.cttransit.com), which also runs a daytime **shuttle** between Union Station and Temple Plaza, across from the Omni Hotel downtown. An **INFO New Haven** office is located just off the Green at 1000 Chapel St (Mon–Thurs 10am–9pm, Fri & Sat 10am–10pm, Sun noon–5pm; Ⓣ203/773-9494, Ⓦwww.infonewhaven.com), with a helpful staff.

Accommodation

New Haven has surprisingly few **hotels** for a city of its size. Given the shortage of rooms downtown, make sure to book well in advance if you intend to visit around Yale graduation in June, around start of term in late August, and during Parents' Weekend in October.

Courtyard by Marriott at Yale 30 Whalley Ave ⓣ203/777-6221 or 1-888/522-1186, ⓦwww.courtyard.com. Comfy rooms conveniently located just west of campus, with weekend deals. ❻

Farnum Guesthouse 616 Prospect St ⓣ203/562-7121 or 1-888/562-7121, ⓦwww.farnamguesthouse.com. Seven charming rooms close to Yale Divinity School. ❹

Historic Mansion Inn 600 Chapel St ⓣ203/865-8324 or 1-888-512-6278, ⓦwww.thehistoricmansioninn.com. 1830 Greek Revival house near Wooster Street. ❼

Hotel Duncan 1151 Chapel St ⓣ203/787-1273. Centrally located, good-value rooms in an old-fashioned hotel built in 1894. ❹

New Haven Hotel 229 George St ⓣ203/498-3100 ⓦwww.newhavenhotel.com. Adequate downtown rooms, some of which have been recently renovated. ❺

Omni New Haven Hotel at Yale 155 Temple St ⓣ203/772-6664, ⓦwww.omnihotels.com. Over three hundred deluxe units in New Haven's plush downtown landmark. ❾

The City

Downtown, centered on the **Green**, retains a historic atmosphere. Laid out in 1638, the Green was the site of the city's original settlement and also functioned as a meeting area and burial ground. In its center, the 1812 **Center Church** (ⓣ203/787-0121) holds tombs dating back to 1687 in its crypt. Surrounding the Green is a number of stately government buildings, including the 1861 High Victorian **City Hall**. Bordering the Green, lively, student-filled **College Street** and **Chapel Street** are lined with bookstores, shops, cafés and bars.

At the opposite end of the Green, Yale University's 1750 **Connecticut Hall** is the oldest surviving building in New Haven, guarded by a statue of Yale alum and Revolutionary War hero Nathan Hale. The nearby 1895 **Phelps Gate** allows access to the cobbled courtyards of Yale's **Old Campus**. While you're free to wander at will, you may want to consider the free hour-long student-led **tours** setting off daily (Mon–Fri at 10.30am & 2pm, Sat & Sun at 1.30pm) from the **Yale Visitor Information Center** at 149 Elm St (ⓣ203/432-2300, ⓦwww.yale.edu/visitor), as many of the key sights have restricted access. Tour highlights include the magnificent, modern Gothic-style **Sterling Memorial Library**, the university's largest library.

Among Yale's notable museums, the modernist **Yale Center for British Art**, 1080 Chapel St (Tues–Sat 10am–5pm, Sun noon–5pm; free) boasts the most comprehensive collection of British art outside of the UK. Opposite, the **Yale University Art Gallery**, 1111 Chapel St (Tues–Sat 10am–5pm, Sun 1–6pm; free) holds the nation's most venerable university art collection, with more than 100,000 objects from around the world, ranging from Etruscan vases and African masks to Baroque masterpieces and contemporary art. North at 170 Whitney Ave, the huge **Peabody Museum of Natural History**, 170 Whitney Ave (Mon–Sat 10am–5pm, Sun noon–5pm; $7; ⓣ203/432-5050, ⓦwww.peabody.yale.edu) holds an impressive collection of artifacts from the natural world, including a Brontosaurus skeleton.

Another source of New Haven affection and pride is its close-knit **Italian District**, based since 1900 among the well-kept brownstones and colorful window boxes of **Wooster Square** (just beyond Crown Street southeast of the Green). This was where the city's original Italian immigrants settled when they came to work on the railroad. There's little to see here, but there are some incredibly popular restaurants, and it's well worth stopping by when there's a festival on.

Eating

New Haven offers a rich and eclectic range of **restaurants**, many located around the Green and on Chapel and College streets. Savor the university town's intellectual atmosphere at one of many fine downtown **cafés**, and don't leave town without trying the **pizza**, available at the family-run Italian restaurants in Wooster Square.

Atticus Bookstore Café 1082 Chapel St ⓣ203/776-4040. Sandwiches, scones, and great coffee in a relaxed atmosphere.

Claire's Corner Copia 1000 Chapel St ⓣ203/562-3888. The local vegetarian spot for thirty years, serving moderately priced casual fare.

Frank Pepe's Pizzeria 157 Wooster St ⓣ203/865-5762. A Wooster St institution since 1925, drawing crowds with its coal-fired pies.

Geronimo 271 Crown St ⓣ203/777-7700. Moderately-priced, inspired Southwestern fare, with a range of specialty cocktails and tequilas to accompany.

Ibiza 39 High St ⓣ203/865-1933. Upscale Spanish restaurant serving traditional specialties, with a fine list of Spanish wines.

Louis' Lunch 261–263 Crown St ⓣ203/562-5507. Small, dark, ancient burger institution which claims to have served America's first hamburger, circa 1900. No ketchup; cash only.

Miso 15 Orange St ⓣ203/848-6472. Upmarket Japanese restaurant, famed for sushi.

Tre Scalini 100 Wooster St ⓣ203/777-3373. Fine Italian dining in an elegant setting.

Union League Café 1032 Chapel St ⓣ203/562-4299. Expensive French bistro, known as one of the finest restaurants around.

Performing arts and nightlife

New Haven's rich **cultural scene** is especially strong in **theater**. The Yale Repertory Theater, 1120 Chapel St (ⓣ203/432-1234, ⓦwww.yalerep.org), which boasts among its eminent past members Jodie Foster and Meryl Streep, turns out consistently good shows during term-time. The Shubert Performing Arts Center, 247 College St (ⓣ203/562-5666, ⓦwww.shubert.com) is known for musicals.

As you'd expect with such a large student population, there are plenty of excellent **bars** and **clubs**, mostly concentrated around Chapel and College streets. The *New Haven Advocate*, a free weekly news and arts paper, has detailed **listings**.

Bar 254 Crown St ⓣ203/495-8924. A simple name for a not-so-simple spot that's a combination pizzeria, brewery, bar, and nightclub.

Café Nine 250 State St ⓣ203/789-8281. Intimate club with live music every night, from punk to jazz and R&B. Cover $5–10.

The Playwright 144 Temple St ⓣ203/752-0450. Four bars, ranging from boisterous pub to dance club, in a massive space with reassembled church interiors from Ireland.

Prime 16 172 Temple St, ⓣ203/782-1616. Temple St hot spot with creative gourmet burgers and two dozen beers on tap.

Rudy's 372 Elm St ⓣ203/865-1242. A favorite local dive-bar with great jukebox and legendary frites. Cash only.

Toad's Place 300 York St ⓣ203/562-5589, ⓦwww.toadsplace.com. Mid-sized live-music venue, where Bruce Springsteen and the Stones used to "pop in" to play impromptu gigs. Some shows 21 and over.

New Hampshire

Long after sailors, fishermen, and agricultural colonists had domesticated the entire coastline of New England, the harsh, glacier-scarred interior of **NEW HAMPSHIRE**, with its dense forests and forbidding mountains, remained the exclusive preserve of the Abenaki Indians. Only the few miles of seashore held sizeable seventeenth-century communities of European settlers, such as the one at **Portsmouth**.

Even when the Indians were finally driven back, the settlers could make little agricultural impact on the rocky terrain of this "granite state," and it wasn't until the Industrial Revolution made possible the development of water-powered **textile mills** that the economy took off. For a while, ruthless **timber** companies looked set to strip all northern New Hampshire bare, but they were brought under control when the state recognized that the pristine landscape of the **White Mountains** might turn out to be its greatest asset. Large-scale **tourism** began towards the end of nineteenth century; at one time fifty trains daily brought travelers up to Mount Washington.

Ever since becoming the first American state to declare independence, in January 1776, New Hampshire has been proud to go its own idiosyncratic way. The absence of a sales tax, or even a personal income tax, is seen as a fulfillment of the state motto, "Live Free or Die." The state has long gained inordinate political clout as the venue of the first **primary election** of each presidential campaign, with its villages well used to playing host to would-be world leaders.

Beyond the charming coastal town of Portsmouth, the major destinations are **Lake Winnipesaukee**, **Conway**, **Lincoln**, and **Franconia Notch** in the White Mountains. To see the bucolic rural scenery more usually associated with New England, take a detour off the main roads up the Merrimack Valley, to **Canterbury Shaker Village** near Concord or the **Robert Frost Farm** close to Nashua.

Getting around New Hampshire

Three **Interstate highways** run through New Hampshire: I-89 connects the state capital, Concord, with Vermont; I-95 runs along the short stretch of New Hampshire coastline that separates Massachusetts and Maine; and I-93 is the main north–south road, giving southern New England access to the White Mountains.

Concord Coach Lines (Ⓣ1-800/639-3317, Ⓦwww.concordcoachlines.com), C&J Trailways (Ⓣ603/430-1100 or 1-800/258-7111, Ⓦwww.cjtrailways.com), and Greyhound (Ⓣ1-800/231-2222, Ⓦwww.greyhound.com) all run from Boston to either the Nashua–Concord corridor or the coast. Only a few services on Concord Coach Lines continue north to the Lakes Region and the White Mountains. **Train** service is limited to Amtrak's *Downeaster*, which links Boston to Portland, Maine, stopping in New Hampshire at the sleepy towns of Exeter, Durham, and Dover.

The coast

Of all the US states with ocean access, New Hampshire has the shortest coastline – just eighteen miles. Skip the tacky family-oriented resort of **Hampton Beach**, and keep driving on Rte-1A to **NORTH HAMPTON BEACH**, which is far more pleasant. The beach here is usually quieter, with abundant metered parking, though it still catches a bit of the slough from its brash neighbor. Popular with surfers and families alike, **Jenness State Beach**, a few miles north, has a long, curving stretch of sand with a smallish parking lot ($1.50/hr). Finally, beyond Rye Harbor, lies **Wallis Sands State Beach** ($15/car), even more serene and the best place for swimming and sunning.

Portsmouth

New Hampshire's oldest community, **PORTSMOUTH** blends small-town accessibility with the enthusiasm of a rejuvenated city. Its position at the mouth of the Piscataqua River has always made it an important port – it was the state capital until 1808 – but it has barely grown, and the spire of **North Church** in the central **Market Square**, dating from 1854, remains the tallest structure in town.

Portsmouth is home to eight painstakingly restored **colonial homes**, which, during the summer, are open to the public. The 1758 gambrel-roofed, boxy, yellow **John Paul Jones House**, 43 Middle St, at State Street (daily late May–mid-Oct 11am–5pm; $8, self-guided tours only; Ⓣ603/436-8420), is the most distinctive, home to the Portsmouth Historical Society's museum (Ⓦwww.portsmouthhistory.org). Jones, America's first great naval commander, stayed here in 1777 while his ships were being outfitted in the harbor. You should also check out the **Moffatt-Ladd House**, 154 Market St (mid-June–Oct Mon–Sat 11am–5pm, Sun 1–5pm; $6; Ⓦwww.moffattladd.org), completed in 1763 and particularly notable for its Great Hall.

Strawbery Banke

Although historic buildings can be found all over Portsmouth, for a more concentrated look at American architecture over the last three centuries, visit the **Strawbery Banke Museum**, 64 Marcy St (May–Oct daily 10am–5pm; Nov by guided tour only, offered on the hour Sat & Sun 10am–2pm; Ⓣ603/433-1100, Ⓦwww.strawberybanke.org; $15; tickets good for two consecutive days), a fenced-off, ten-acre neighborhood of forty meticulously restored and maintained old wooden buildings (though some can only be viewed from the outside). The area began life as the residence of wealthy shipbuilders, and was successively the lair of privateers and a red-light district before turning into respectable – and, in the 1950s, ultimately decaying – suburbia. It was then decided to recreate its former appearance, mainly by clearing away the newer buildings.

Each building is shown in its most interesting former incarnation, whether that be 1695 or 1955. The 1766 **Pitt Tavern** holds the most historic significance, having served as a meeting place during the Revolution for patriots and loyalists. Traditional crafts can be viewed in the **Dinsmore Shop**, where an infinitely patient cooper manufactures barrels with the tools and methods of 1800.

Practicalities

Greyhound **buses** (Ⓣ603/433-3210) run from Boston three times daily, stopping outside 55 Hanover St, a short walk from Market Square. You can pick up **information** from the **visitor center** at 500 Market St, a fifteen-minute walk from Market Square (June–Sept Mon–Fri 8.30am–5pm, Sat & Sun 10am–5pm; Oct–May Mon–Fri 8.30am–5pm; Ⓣ603/436-1118, Ⓦwww.portsmouthchamber.org), or from the kiosk in Market Square (May–Oct daily 10am–5pm). Portsmouth Harbor Cruises (Ⓣ603/436-8084 or 1-800/776-0915, Ⓦwww.portsmouthharbor.com) is one of several operators offering **boat trips**, from $12.

Accommodation in the town center is restricted to expensive places such as the grand *Sise Inn*, 40 Court St (Ⓣ603/433-1200 or 1-877/747-3466, Ⓦwww.siseinn.com; ❼), a beautifully preserved Queen Anne–style house with large rooms; the peaceful, rambling seven-room *Inn at Strawbery Banke*, 314 Court St (Ⓣ603/436-7242 or 1-800/428-3933, Ⓦwww.innatstrawberybanke.com; ❼); and the waterfront *Bow Street Inn*, 121 Bow St (Ⓣ603/431-7760, Ⓦwww.bowstreetinn.com; ❼). Cheaper motels near the traffic circle, where I-95 and Rte-1 intersect, include the good-value *Port Inn*, Rte-1 Bypass South (Ⓣ1-800/282-PORT, Ⓦwww.theportinn.com; ❺).

Portsmouth likes to bill itself, with some justification, as the "food capital of New England." Of the in-town **restaurants**, *Jumpin' Jay's Seafood Café,* 150 Congress St, (Ⓣ603/766-3474), offers the best seafood in town. *Ristorante Massimo*, 59 Penhallow St (Ⓣ603/436-4000), is a gourmet Italian restaurant with a strong wine list, and funky *Friendly Toast*, 121 Congress St (Ⓣ603/430-2154), makes for an inexpensive breakfast and lunch spot, with generous portions.

At night, the *Portsmouth Brewery*, 56 Market St (Ⓣ603/431-1115, Ⓦwww.portsmouthbrewery.com), serves up exceptional microbrews and occasional live music, while *The Press Room*, 77 Daniel St (Ⓣ603/431-5186, Ⓦwww.pressroomnh.com), has jazz, blues, folk, or bluegrass performances every night. Those searching for caffeine rather than alcohol will be happy at *Breaking New Grounds* (Ⓣ603/436-9555) in Market Square.

The Merrimack Valley

The financial and political heartland of New Hampshire is the **Merrimack Valley**, which – first by water and now by road – has always been the main thoroughfare north to the White Mountains and Québec. None of its towns is of any great interest to tourists, though all are equipped with relatively inexpensive motels.

About twenty miles north of state capital Concord, off I-95, exit 18, **Canterbury Shaker Village**, 288 Shaker Rd (daily: May–Oct 10am–5pm; Nov to early-Dec Fri–Sun 10am–5pm; Ⓣ603/783-9511, Ⓦwww.shakers.org; $15, good two consecutive days), was founded in 1774, and was three-hundred-strong by 1860; three different hour-long tours explain the Shaker way of life. There are craft demonstrations (such as basket-making) and even frequent all-day craft workshops if you're so inclined. The *Shaker Table* near the village entry serves delicious and imaginative Shaker-inspired food. South of Concord, outside Derry just off Rte-28 (take exit 4 from I-93), the **Robert Frost Farm** (May–June & Sept to mid-Oct Wed–Sun 10am–5pm; July & Aug daily 10am–5pm; entry free, tour $7; Ⓣ603/432-3091, Ⓦrobertfrostfarm.org) has been evocatively restored to its condition when New England's poet laureate lived here from 1900 to 1911. Displays in the barn highlight his work, and a half-mile "poetry nature trail" leads past the sites that inspired many of his best-known poems.

The Lakes Region

Of the literally hundreds of lakes occupying the state's central corridor, the biggest by far is **Lake Winnipesaukee**, which forms the center of the vacation-oriented Lakes Region. Long segments of its three-hundred-mile shoreline, especially in the east, consist of thick forests sweeping down to waters dotted with little islands, which are disturbed only by pleasure craft. The most sophisticated of the towns along the shoreline is **Wolfeboro**; the most fun has to be **Weirs Beach**.

▲ Lake Winnipesaukee

Ideally, you would bring your own small boat here and get thoroughly lost in the maze of small channels and islets. Failing that, the **cruise ship** *Mount Washington*, a 230-foot monster of a boat, departs from the dock in the center of Weirs Beach several times a day to sail to Wolfeboro, on the western side of the lake (mid-May to Oct; from $22; ⓣ603/366-5531 or 1-888/843-6686, ⓦwww.cruisenh.com). The ship also sets sail for dinner and dance cruises several times per week (from $43). The same company offers cruises from Weirs Beach on the smaller *M/V Doris* E (late June to early Sept daily; $15) and the US mail boat, *M/V Sophie C* (mid-June to mid-Sept Mon–Sat; $22), from which you can view some of the lake's many islands as the boat delivers the mail.

Wolfeboro

Because Governor Wentworth of New Hampshire built his summer home nearby in 1768, tiny **WOLFEBORO** claims to be "the oldest summer resort in America." Sandwiched between lakes Winnipesaukee and Wentworth, it's a relaxing place to spend a few hours, especially along the short but bustling main street, next to the quay where the *Mount Washington* (see above) comes in.

For **accommodation**, the 1812 *Wolfeboro Inn*, 90 N Main St (ⓣ603/569-3016 or 1-800/451-2389, ⓦwww.wolfeboroinn.com; ❼), stands in a dignified waterfront position just a few yards from the town proper. The *Tuc' Me Inn B&B*, 118 N Main St (ⓣ603/569-5702, ⓦwww.tucmeinn.com; ❻), is a homey place with tastefully furnished rooms, close to both the town and lake. *Wolfeboro Campground* is on Haines Hill Road (ⓣ603/569-9881, ⓦwww.wolfeborocamp.delectual.com; $25–28), and is open from mid-May to mid-October. For **food**, *Wolfe's Tavern*, at the *Wolfeboro Inn*, serves good-value steaks, seafood, burgers, and sandwiches, while *Bailey's Bubble*, on Railroad Avenue (ⓣ603/569-3612), serves luscious local ice cream to enjoy on the quayside; *Lydia's Café*, 33 N Main St (daily until 2.30pm; ⓣ603/569-3991), is an excellent, veggie-oriented place for breakfast, lunch, or smoothies.

Weirs Beach

The short boardwalk at **WEIRS BEACH**, the very essence of seaside tackiness (even if it is fifty miles inland), is the social center of the Lakes Region in the summer. Its little wooden jetty throngs with vacationers, the amusement arcades jingle with cash, and there's even a neat little crescent of sandy beach, suitable for family swimming. A quieter diversion here is the **Winnipesaukee Railroad** (late May–early June & Sept–Oct weekends; mid-June to Aug daily; $12 for 1hr, $13 for 2hr; ⓣ603/279-5253, ⓦwww.hoborr.com), which operates scenic trips along the lakeshore between Weirs Beach and Meredith.

Meredith

Four miles north of Weirs Beach, **MEREDITH** enjoys a peaceful location and has an upscale character, making it the best place to stay on the lake's western shore. The *Inns at Mill Falls*, which is actually four separate hotels (ⓣ1-800/622-6455, ⓦwww.millfalls.com), are the best choice for **accommodation**. Choose from the *Inn at Mill Falls* (❻) and the *Chase House* (❽), both on the hill overlooking the lake, or the *Inn at Bay Point* (❽) or the new *Church Landing* (❾), directly on the water and offering unrivalled lake views. *Town Docks*, on US-3 just south of the intersection with Rte-25 (ⓣ603/279-3445), is a solid choice for seafood.

The White Mountains

Thanks to their accessibility from both Montréal to the north and Boston to the south, the **White Mountains** have become a year-round tourist destination, popular with both summer hikers and winter skiers. Commercialized they may be, but the great granite massifs retain most of their majesty and power. **Mount Washington**, the highest peak in the northeast, can claim some of the most severe weather in the world, and conditions are harsh enough for the timberline to lie at four thousand feet (compared to the Rockies' norm of ten thousand).

Just a few high passes – here called "**notches**" – pierce the range, and the roads through these gaps, such as the **Kancamagus Highway** between Lincoln and Conway, make for enjoyable driving (compulsory **parking permits** are $3 for one day, or $5 for seven consecutive days). However, you won't really have made the most of the White Mountains unless you also set off, on foot or on skis, across the long expanses of thick evergreen forest that separate them, with snowcapped peaks poking out in all directions. The best sources of **information** in the region are the White Mountains Visitor Center, at I-93 exit 32, in North Woodstock (July–Sept 8.30am–6pm; Oct–June 8.30am–5.30pm; ⓣ603/745-8720 or 1-800/FIND-MTS, ⓦwww.visitwhitemountains.com), and the Pinkham Notch Visitor Center on Rte-16 (daily 6.30am–10pm; ⓣ603/466-2721, ⓦwww.outdoors.org), north of Jackson.

Accommodation

Thanks to the influx of young hikers and skiers to the White Mountains, there's a relative abundance of **budget** accommodation in the area. Keep in mind, too, that

Hiking, skiing, and cycling in the White Mountains

Hiking in the White Mountains is coordinated by the **Appalachian Mountain Club** (AMC), whose chain of information centers, hostels, and huts along the Appalachian Trail, traversing the region from northeast to southwest, is detailed below. Call ⓣ603/466-2725 for trail and weather information, and pick up a copy of the *AMC White Mountain Guide* ($24.95) before you attempt any serious expedition.

Downhill and cross-country **skiers** can choose from several resorts that double up as summertime activity centers. Both the Waterville Valley Resort (ⓣ603/236-8311 or 1-800/468-2553, ⓦwww.waterville.com) and Loon Mountain (ⓣ603/745-8111 or 1-800/229-LOON, ⓦwww.loonmtn.com), both just east of I-93, are good for downhill, while Jackson (ⓣ603/383-9355, ⓦwww.jacksonxc.org), about fifteen miles north of Conway on Rte-16, has some of the finest cross-country skiing trails in the northeast. General information on the skiing centers is available from Ski NH (ⓣ603/745-9396 or 1-800/88SKI-NH, ⓦwww.skinh.com).

In the summer, the cross-country skiing trails can make for strenuous but exhilarating **biking** (you can take lifts up the slopes and ride back down). Bikes can be rented for around $30 per day from All Seasons Adventures at 134 Main St in Lincoln (ⓣ603/745-8600), and from Joe Jones Sports at 2709 Main St in North Conway (ⓣ603/356-9411, ⓦwww.joejonessports.com).

rates vary dramatically between seasons, and even from weekday to weekend.

Along the Appalachian Trail itself, there are eight **Appalachian Mountain Club huts**, which can only be reached on foot. In summer, each hut provides meals and bedding for between forty and ninety people. Prices range from $27–98 a night, according to the amount of privacy, luxury, and food you're after (and depending on whether or not you're an AMC member; individual membership is $50; see ⓦwww.outdoors.org for details). **Reservations** are strongly recommended (call ⓣ603/466-2727, or visit the website), and you'll be expected to pay in full when you book the accommodation.

Campers can pitch their tents anywhere below the treeline and away from the roads in the White Mountains National Forest, provided they show consideration for the environment. There are also numerous official campgrounds ($18–30/night), particularly along the Kancamagus Highway.

The AMC runs two scheduled **shuttle van services** ($16) for hikers between major trailheads and the lodges daily from June to mid-September, with weekend service through mid-October.

AMC lodges

Highland Center US-302, Crawford Notch ⓣ603/466-2727, ⓦwww.outdoors.org. This innovatively designed and environmentally friendly building offers beds in a shared room for $40–64 or double rooms (cheapest with shared bath) for $81–141, breakfast and dinner included (peak season rates). Open year-round.

Joe Dodge Lodge Hwy-16, Pinkham Notch ⓣ603/466-2727, ⓦwww.outdoors.org. Filled with hikers, this second AMC lodge-cum-hostel has bunks or double rooms with shared bath and meals for $64 ($51 without meals). Near the Mount Washington Auto Road. Open year-round.

Motels, hotels, and B&Bs

Adair Country Inn 80 Guider Lane, Bethlehem ⓣ603/444-2600 or 1-888/444-2600, ⓦwww.adairinn.com. Deluxe antique-furnished rooms, with sweeping views of the landscaped grounds, and an impeccable staff, all reflected in the steep prices. ❼

Balsams Dixville Notch ⓣ1-800/255-0800 in NH or 1-800/255-0600 outside NH, ⓦwww.thebalsams.com. Like the Mount Washington, Balsams is another of the last grand, red-roofed resort hotels. Opened in the 1860s (under a different name and since expanded in 1918), the hotel has year-round activities (skiing, golf, tennis, boating), light and airy rooms, and delicious meals (cooking classes are available). ❾

Boulder Motor Court 5 Harmony Hill Rd, Rte-302 (junction with US-3), Twin Mountain ⓣ603/846-5437, ⓦwww.bouldermotorcourt.com. Bargain one- and two-bedroom cottages with kitchens, fireplaces, and other amenities. ❹

Eagle Mountain House 2 Carter Notch Rd, Jackson ⓣ603/383-9111 or 1-800/966-5779, ⓦwww.eaglemt.com. Highly atmospheric inn with a roaring fireplace in the lobby and a wraparound porch filled with rocking chairs, far above the bustle of North Conway. Has its own nine-hole golf course. ❹

Franconia Inn Easton Rd/Hwy-116, Franconia ⓣ603/823-5542 or 1-800/473-5299, ⓦwww.franconiainn.com. Comfortable 32-room inn two miles south of town, with great views. Makes for a good cross-country ski base. ❺

Mount Washington Hotel Rte-302, Bretton Woods ⓣ603/278-1000 or 1-800/314-1752, ⓦwww.mtwashington.com. Beautiful hotel dating from 1902, with a quarter-mile terrace, stellar views, indoor pool, and a complete range of activities (including golf, horseback riding, and skiing) and pricing packages. Also runs the less-fancy Bretton Arms, on the same property, which is a bit cheaper (❼), though rooms are still spacious. ❽

Thayer's Inn 111 Main St, Littleton ⓣ603/444-6469 or 1-800/634-8179, ⓦwww.thayersinn.com. Creaky but comfortable and classy old inn since 1850, which has hosted guests such as Ulysees S. Grant and Richard Nixon. ❹–❺

Franconia Notch

Ten miles beyond **Lincoln,** I-93, which speeds up towards northern Vermont, briefly merges with the more leisurely US-3, to pass through **Franconia Notch State Park**. **Franconia Notch** itself is a slender valley crammed between two great walls of stone. From the Flume Visitor Center (May to late Oct daily 10am–5pm; ⓣ603/745-8391), you can walk along a two-mile boardwalk-cum-nature trail to the Pemigewasset River as it rages through the narrow, rock-filled Flume gorge ($12). Alternatively, take a $12 cable-car ride up the sheer granite face of Cannon Mountain (late May to mid-Oct daily 9am–5pm; ⓣ603/823-8800, ⓦwww.cannonmt.com), or hike the various, well-marked trails up to panoramic views for free.

Further on, one mile south of the friendly village of **FRANCONIA**, the **Frost Place** on Ridge Road (late May to early July Sat & Sun 1–5pm; early July to early Oct Wed–Mon 1–5pm; $5 suggested donation; ⓣ603/823-5510, ⓦwww.frostplace.org) is another former home of poet Robert Frost, memorable largely for an inspiring panorama of unspoiled mountains. Each summer the poet-in-residence will often give poetry readings during visiting hours.

Mount Washington

From the awe-inspiring peak of 6288-foot **Mount Washington** you can, on a clear day, see all the way to the Atlantic and into Canada. But the real interest in making the ascent lies in the extraordinary severity of the weather up here, which results from the summit's position right in the path of the principal storm tracks and air-mass routes affecting the northeastern US. The wind here exceeds hurricane strength on more than a hundred days of the year, and in 1934 it reached the highest speed ever recorded anywhere in the world – 231mph. At the top, you'll see the remarkable spectacle of buildings actually held down with great chains; many have been blown away over the years, including the old observatory, said to be the strongest wooden building ever constructed. Up here you'll also find a **visitor center** (mid-May to mid-Oct 8am–6pm; ⓣ603/466-3347), the new observatory with small museum (daily 9am–6pm; $3), a large viewing platform and **Tip Top House**, once a hotel for wealthy travelers and now a basic museum (June-Oct daily 10am–4pm; free).

On the way to the top, you pass through four distinct climatic zones, starting with century-old fir and ash trees so stunted as to be below waist-height and ending with Arctic tundra. The drive up the **Mount Washington Auto Road** (early May to late Oct, weather permitting 8am–4pm; ⓣ603/466-3988 for weather conditions, ⓦwww.mtwashingtonautoroad.com) isn't as hair-raising as you might expect, though the hairpin bends and lack of guardrails certainly keep you alert. There is a $20 **toll** for cars and driver (plus $7 for each additional adult and $5 for kids), which comes with an audio tape or CD detailing the road's history. You can also take a **narrated tour** in a specially-adapted minibus (daily 8.30am–5pm; $26).

Last but far from least, you can also ride to the top on the coal-fired steam train of the **Mount Washington Cog Railway**, which noisily climbs the exposed flank of the mountain, ascending grades of up to 38 degrees on a track completed in 1869. It's truly a unique experience, as you inch up the steep wooden trestles while trying to avoid descending showers of coal smut. The three-hour round-trip costs $59 ($39 for kids), and trains leave hourly (mid-May–early Nov daily, weather permitting; ⓣ603/278-5404 or 1-800/922-8825 for other dates and times and to reserve, ⓦwww.thecog.com) from a station off Rte-302 six miles northeast of Bretton Woods. The Cog also runs uphill in the winter season (Nov–March) to access groomed, mile-long downhill ski trails ($31).

North Conway

A few miles south of Mount Washington, US-302 and Hwy-16 enter **NORTH CONWAY** by first passing through a hodgepodge of shopping malls, fast-food joints, and kiddie theme parks such as Story Land (ⓣ603/383-4186; $24). More useful is the **White Mountain National Forest Saco Ranger Station**, 33 Kancamagus Hwy near Rte-16 in Conway (Mon 9am–4.30pm, Tues–Sun 8am–4.30pm; ⓣ603/447-5448), which sells books, maps, and the mandatory National Forest parking permits ($3 for one day, $5 for seven consecutive days). It also provides a ton of resources for area planning and handles back country cabin rentals.

The Kancamagus Highway

The **Kancamagus Highway** (Hwy-112), connecting North Conway and Lincoln, is the least busy road through the mountains, and makes for a very pleasant 34-mile drive. Several campgrounds are situated in the woods to either side, and various walking trails are signposted. The half-mile hike to **Sabbaday Falls**, off to the south roughly halfway along the highway, leads up a narrow rocky cleft in the forest to a succession of idyllic waterfalls. If you plan on a picnic, though, take note: there is no food or gas available along the highway.

Eating and drinking

Family **restaurants** and fast-food joints line the main drags of major centers such as North Woodstock and North Conway. The best places are in less conspicuous areas and worth rooting out. Some of the hotels and B&Bs recommended on p.241 also serve food.

1785 Inn & Restaurant 3582 Hwy-16, just north of North Conway ⓣ603/356-9025 or 1-800/421-1785. Original appetizers, gourmet meals such as apple-wood-smoked rabbit, and fine wines, with prices to match. Entrees $18–30.

Flying Moose Café 2 W Main St, Littleton ⓣ603/444-2661. Intimate bistro serving a mix of classic cuisines with contemporary flair, such as braised lamb shank over polenta.

Polly's Pancake Parlor I-93 exit 38, Rte-117, Sugar Hill ⓣ603/823-5575. Yes, it's in the middle of nowhere, but it's a scenic nowhere and well worth the trip if you love pancakes ($6.99 for three). Open early May–Oct 7am–3pm.

Red Parka Pub US-302, Glen ⓣ603/383-4344. Evening-only steakhouse with bar until 12.30am. Live rock music on weekends, and open-mike night Mon.

Yesterday's Rte-16A, next to Wildcat Inn, Jackson ⓣ603/383-4457. Big, cheap American breakfasts are the order of the day here. Daily 7am–3pm.

Hanover

HANOVER, just across the Connecticut River from Vermont, is home to the venerable and elegant **Dartmouth College**, founded in this remote spot in 1769. The main attraction here is the small **Hood Museum of Art** on the college green (Mon, Tues, Thurs, & Fri 10am–4pm, Wed 10am–9pm, Sat & Sun 10am–5pm; free; ⓣ603/646-2808, ⓦhoodmuseum.dartmouth.edu), which has works by Picasso and Monet alongside Assyrian bas-reliefs.

Hanover itself is enjoyable to wander around, with lively places to **eat and drink**, such as *Murphy's on the Green*, 11 S Main St (ⓣ603/643-4075), the best place for a beer and some healthy food, and the always-busy *Lou's Restaurant & Bakery*, 30 S Main St (ⓣ603/643-3321), good for breakfast. The finest **accommodation** is at the expensive and luxurious *Hanover Inn*, overlooking Dartmouth Green from the corner of Main and Wheelock streets (ⓣ603/643-4300 or 1-800/443-7024, ⓦwww.hanoverinn.com; ❾). The *Chieftain Motor Inn*, at 84 Lyme Rd (ⓣ603/643-2550, ⓦwww.chieftaininn.com; ❻), represents the best budget option you'll find in this generally expensive area.

Seven miles east of Hanover, one secluded and memorable place to stay is *Moose Mountain Lodge* (Jan & Feb, June, & Sept–mid-Oct; ⓣ603/643-3529, ⓦwww.themoosemountainlodge.com; ❻, with a minimum two-night stay required), high in the hills above **Etna**, overlooking Vermont. All year it feels blissfully remote from the world below, but it really comes into its own in winter for **cross-country skiing**.

Vermont

VERMONT comes closer than any other New England state to realizing the quintessential image of small-town America, with its white churches and red barns, covered bridges and clapboard houses, snowy woods and maple syrup. The largest city, **Burlington**, approaches a population of just forty thousand, and the chief tourist attraction is **Ben & Jerry's** ice-cream factory in Waterbury. Though rural, the landscape is not all that agricultural, as much of it is covered by mountainous forests (the state's name comes from the French *vert mont*, or "green mountain").

This was the last area of New England to be settled, early in the eighteenth century. The leader of the New Hampshire settlers, the now-legendary **Ethan Allen**, formed his **Green Mountain Boys** in 1770, and during the Revolutionary War, this all-but-autonomous force helped to win the decisive Battle of Bennington. By 1777, Vermont was an independent republic, with the first constitution in the world explicitly forbidding slavery and granting universal (male) suffrage, but it eventually joined the Union in 1791. A more recent example of Vermont's progressive attitude occurred in 2000, when former governor Howard Dean signed the **civil union** bill into law, making Vermont the first state in the US to sanction same-sex marriage.

With the occasional exception, such as the extraordinary assortment of Americana at the **Shelburne Museum** near Burlington, there are few specific goals for tourists. Visitors come in great numbers during two well-defined seasons: to see the **fall foliage** in the first two weeks of October, and to **ski** in the depths of winter, when the resorts of **Killington**, and **Stowe** further north (home of *The Sound of Music*'s Von Trapp family), spring into life. For the rest of the year, you might just as well explore any of the state's minor roads, confident that some picturesque village will appear around the next corner.

Getting around

Vermont's main north–south road is I-91, hugging the edge of New Hampshire. I-89 traverses the center of the state, passing Montpelier and Burlington on its way from New Hampshire to Canada. Greyhound **buses** (Ⓣ 1-800/231-2222, Ⓦ www.greyhound.com) connect towns such as Burlington, Montpelier, and Brattleboro with their national network. Amtrak's *Vermonter* **train** (Ⓣ 1-800/872-7245), which runs between Washington, D.C. and St Albans, stops at Brattleboro, Montpelier, Waterbury, and Burlington. The main **airport** is in Burlington.

The Green Mountains

The weather in the **Green Mountains**, which form the backbone of Vermont, is not as harsh as in New Hampshire's White Mountains – though the forests here are invariably buried in snow for most of the winter, and the higher roads are liable to be blocked for long periods. Routes north from **Bennington**, **Brattleboro**, and along scenic **Hwy-100** offer unspoiled mountain views and the best of small-town New England.

In summer, hikers take up the challenge of the **Long Trail** along the central ridge, leading 265 miles from the Massachusetts border all the way to Québec. This trail predates the Appalachian Trail, which now follows its southern portion, and is looked after by the **Green Mountain Club** (Ⓣ 802/244-7037, Ⓦ www.greenmountainclub.org), whose *Long Trail Guide* ($18.95) is invaluable.

Bennington

In the past two hundred years, little has happened in **BENNINGTON** to match the excitement of the days when Ethan Allen's Green Mountain Boys were based here. A 306-foot hilltop obelisk (mid-April–Oct daily 9am–5pm; $2) commemorates the **Battle of Bennington** of 1777, in which the Boys were a crucial factor in defeating the British under General Burgoyne (though the battle itself was fought just across the border in New York). You should also check out the **Bennington Museum**, 75 Main St (daily except Wed 10am–5pm; $9; Ⓣ 802/447-1571, Ⓦ www.benningtonmuseum.org), which contains a memorable array of Americana and the largest collection of paintings by folk artist Grandma Moses. For fine hand-crafted ceramics visit **Bennington Potters**, 324 County St (Mon–Sat 9.30am–6pm, Sun 10am–5pm; Ⓣ 1-800/205-8033, Ⓦ www.benningtonpotters.com).

The *Paradise Motor Inn,* 141 West Main St (Ⓣ 802/442-8351, Ⓦ www.theparadisemotorinn.com; ❹–❺), is one of several downtown **motels** on this stretch. More stylish digs can be found at the *Four Chimneys Inn* on Rte-9, also called West Road (Ⓣ 802/447-3500, Ⓦ www.fourchimneys.com; ❻–❾). As for **food**, students from the small and exclusive arty Bennington College crowd into the *Madison Brewing Company,* 428 Main St (Ⓣ 1-800/44BREWS) or the *Blue Benn Diner*, 102 Hunt St (Ⓣ 802/442-5140).

North from Brattleboro

Driving north from **BRATTLEBORO**, noted for its lively local arts scene and student-driven nightlife, routes 30 and 35 offer a less-traveled alternative into central Vermont. Few places come closer to the iconic image of rural New England than **GRAFTON**, a truly gorgeous ensemble of brilliant white clapboard buildings, shady trees and a bubbling brook in the center. Stop in at the **Grafton Village Cheese Company** on Townshend Road (Mon–Fri 8am–5pm, Sat & Sun 10am–5pm; ⓣ802/843-2221 or 1-800/472-3866, ⓦwww.graftonvillagecheese.com). Further north, sleepy **CHESTER** blends prototypical Vermont clapboard houses with more ornate, Victorian architecture, laid out charmingly where Rte-11 runs along a narrow green. Here you can jump aboard the **Green Mountain Flyer** (1 departure at 12.30pm: July & Aug Sat & Sun; mid-Sept to mid-Oct daily; $19; ⓦwww.rails-vt.com), a sightseeing train that runs two-hour round-trips from Chester Depot down to Bellows Falls and back.

Practicalities

The most popular place to **stay** in Brattleboro is the Art Deco *Latchis Hotel*, 50 Main St (ⓣ802/254-6300, ⓦwww.latchis.com; ❹). In Grafton, try the upmarket *Old Tavern*, 92 Main St (ⓣ1-800/843-1801, ⓦwww.old-tavern.com; ❽), which has an excellent **restaurant**. The best place in Chester is *Inn Victoria*, 321 Main St (ⓣ802/875-4288 or 1-800/732-4288, ⓦwww.innvictoria.com; ❺–❾).

In Brattleboro you can't go wrong **eating** at the *Riverview Café*, 36 Bridge St (ⓣ802/254-9841), which overlooks the Connecticut River. The best **beer** resides at the rough-around-the-edges *McNeill's Brewery*, 90 Elliot St (ⓣ802/254-2553). The nearby *Mole's Eye Cafe*, at 4 High St (ⓣ802/257-0771, ⓦwww.themoleseyecafe.com), is an established nightspot with **live music** every night and a bar menu that includes a smattering of Mexican and Italian dishes.

Hwy-100 Scenic Drive: Weston

One of the prettiest villages along Hwy-100 is **WESTON**, which spreads out beside a little river and centers on a perfect green. The **Vermont Country Store**, south of the green, is larger than it looks from its modest facade. For all its seeming quaintness, this Vermont institution is actually part of a chain. Opposite, the **Weston Village Store** is more authentic – and cheaper – with a range of vaguely rural and domestic articles, such as local maple syrup and cheeses.

Weston's best **accommodation** is the lovely *Inn at Weston*, on Hwy-100, near the village green (ⓣ802/824-6789, ⓦwww.innweston.com; ❼), with homey rooms, an excellent **restaurant**, and a cozy pub. Another appealing B&B is the *Darling Family Inn* (ⓣ802/824-3223; ❹–❻), north of the green on Hwy-100. A small but magnificent soda fountain dominates the 1885 mahogany bar of the *Bryant House* restaurant, next door to the Vermont Country Store on Main Street (dinner on Fri & Sat only, closed Sun; ⓣ802/824-6287), whose lunch menu includes country fare, including "johnnycakes." The best bet for entertainment is the attractive **Weston Playhouse**, which offers summer and fall performances (Tues–Sun; $39–52; ⓣ802/824-5288, ⓦwww.westonplayhouse.org).

Killington

The ski resort of **KILLINGTON** (ⓣ802/422-6200 for the resort or 1-800/621-6867 for other area reservations; ⓣ802/422-3261 for 24-hour taped skiing information, ⓦwww.killington.com), in the center of the Green Mountains, thirty miles north of Weston, has grown exponentially since 1958. The resort sprawls over seven mountains (Pico Mountain is the best for skiers of mid-range ability), and is notorious for its rowdy nightlife. For hikers, the Long and Appalachian trails meet just north of here. In summer and fall, you can still take the **K-1 Gondola** ($10 single, $15 round-trip) up to the observation deck and cafeteria on Killington Peak (4241ft). Choose your way back down: hike or mountain bike (rentals are available at the base).

In winter, the Killington Road up from US-4 is humming with crowded **bars and restaurants**: *Wobbly Barn Steakhouse* (Nov–April; ⓣ802/422-6171) is good for beef in all forms, and lively entertainment, and the *Pickle Barrel* (ⓣ802/422-3035) is a rowdy bar that gets crazier on winter weekends. The *Inn of the Six Mountains*, 2617 Killington Rd (ⓣ802/422-4302, ⓦwww.sixmountains.com ❹–❻), is the best place to stay within the resort, offering reduced summer rates; the *Inn at Long Trail*, on Sherburne Pass (ⓣ802/775-7181 or 1-800/325-2540; ⓦwww.innatlongtrail.com; ❹), is perfectly located for Long Trail hikers (see p.245).

Woodstock

Since its settlement in the 1760s, beautiful **WOODSTOCK**, a few miles west of the Connecticut River up US-4, has been one of Vermont's more refined centers. Its distinguished houses cluster around an oval green, now largely taken over by art galleries and tearooms (don't confuse it with Woodstock, New York, of music festival fame).

Woodstock's main paying attraction is the **Billings Farm and Museum**, Rte-12, at River Road (May–Oct daily 10am–5pm; Nov–Dec Sat & Sun 10am–4pm; $11; ⓣ802/457-2355, ⓦwww.billingsfarm.org): part modern dairy farm, part museum of farm life, it puts on demonstrations of antiquated skills and shows an excellent biographical film of the farm's various owners. **Hiking trails**, accessible from the town center, are great for a leisurely stroll, as are the forest trails of the **Marsh-Billings-Rockefeller National Historical Park** (year-round; visitor center open late-May to Oct daily 10am–5pm; ⓣ802/457-3368, ⓦwww.nps.gov/mabi; free), which are also groomed for winter skiing and snowshoeing.

The friendly staff at the centrally-located **Woodstock Welcome Center** on Mechanic Street (daily 9am–5pm; ⓣ802/432-1100, ⓦwww.woodstockvt.com) has extensive information on lodging, dining, and other area attractions. Options include the well-refurbished *Shire Riverview*, 46 Pleasant St (ⓣ802/457-2211, ⓦwww.shiremotel.com; ❹–❼) the upscale *Woodstock Inn and Resort*, 14 The Green, US-4, in the center of the village (ⓣ802/457-1100 or 1-800/448-7900, ⓦwww.woodstockinn.com; ❾), and the cozy *Applebutter Inn*, four miles east of town on US-4, in Taftsville (ⓣ802/457-4158, ⓦwww.applebutterinn.com; ❹–❼).

Of the several places to **eat** in Woodstock, *Bentley's*, 3 Elm St (ⓣ802/457-3232), has a range of microbrews and upscale versions of traditional bistro food, and the *Kedron Valley Inn*, on Rte-106 in South Woodstock (ⓣ802/457-1473), serves more expensive but superb American standards. Comfort food breakfasts and lunches are on offer at *Mountain Creamery*, 33 Central St (daily 7am–3pm; ⓣ802/457-1715), while *Wasp's Snack Bar*, 57 Pleasant St (ⓣ802/457-3334), is a no-frills local institution, specializing in home-cooked breakfasts (Tues–Sat 6–11am).

Quechee

Six miles east of Woodstock, **QUECHEE** is off the main US-4 highway, a combination of quaint Vermont village and expensive new condos. The main highlight here lies on US-4 itself, **Quechee Gorge State Park**, which preserves the splendors of the **Quechee Gorge**. A delicate bridge spans the 165-foot chasm of the Ottauquechee River, and hiking trails lead down from the **visitor center** (daily 9am–5pm; ⓣ802/295-6852). You can **camp** at the park at one of Vermont's many state-run campgrounds (Ⓣ802/295-2990 or 1-888/409-7579; $14–23/night, with a two-night minimum stay;). If you'd rather not rough it, the *Quality Inn* (Ⓣ802/295-7600 or 1-800/732-4376, Ⓦwww.qualityinnquechee.com; ⑤) on US-4, between the gorge and the tourist shops of the Quechee Gorge Village, offers the best-value **accommodation**.

The river spins the turbines of the **Simon Pearce Glass Mill** (daily 10am–9pm; Ⓣ802/295-2711, Ⓦwww.simonpearce.com), housed in a former wool mill along Main Street back in Quechee. Here, you can watch glass bowls and plates being blown (10am–5pm), and then eat from them at the on-site **restaurant** (overlooking a waterfall) which serves, among other dishes, seared Arctic char, ancho-cured pork, and crispy roast duck ($22–30 dinner entrees, about $15 for lunch); reservations are recommended (Ⓣ802/295-1470).

Montpelier

Some fifty-five miles north up I-89, **MONTPELIER** is the smallest state capital in the nation, with fewer than ten thousand inhabitants. Surrounded by leafy gardens, the golden domed **State House** (Mon–Fri 7.45am–4.15pm) is well worth a free tour for its marble-floored and mural-lined hallways (July to mid-Oct Mon–Fri 10am–3.30pm, Sat 11am–2.30pm; Ⓣ802/828-2228). Copious information on accommodation, here and throughout the state, is available from

▲ The State House, Montpelier

the **Capitol Region Visitors Center**, opposite the State House at 134 State St (Mon–Fri 6am–6pm, Sat & Sun 10am–6pm; ⓣ802/828-5981 or 1-800/VERMONT, ⓦwww.vermontvacation.com). Good **B&B rooms** can be had at the central yet quiet *Betsy's Bed & Breakfast*, 74 E State St (ⓣ802/229-0466, ⓦwww.betsysbnb.com; ❻). For more luxurious digs, try the *Capitol Plaza Hotel*, 100 State St (ⓣ802/223-5252, ⓦwww.capitolplaza.com; ❽).

For **food**, students from the local New England Culinary Institute run the *Main St Grill & Bar* at 118 Main St (closed Mon; ⓣ802/223-3188), serving excellent, inexpensive, experimental dishes from all over the world. *Coffee Corner*, on Main Street at State (ⓣ802/229-9060), has been serving dirt-cheap diner food for over sixty years, while *Capitol Grounds*, 45 State St (ⓣ802/223-7800), is definitely tops for your morning coffee or tea fix.

There are several options for live music; *Langdon Street Café*, 4 Langdon St (ⓣ802/223-8667, ⓦwww.langdonstreetcafe.com), has a homey feel, with live music nightly and beer, wine, and coffee, while *Black Door Bar*, 44 Main St (closed Sun; ⓣ802/223-7070, ⓦwww.blackdoorvt.com), is a bit fancier, with jazz or zydeco ($3 cover).

Waterbury

Few people paid much attention to **WATERBURY** before 1978; even then, the opening of a home-made ice cream stand run by a pair of hippies on the forecourt of a gas station excited little interest. However, **Ben & Jerry's Ice Cream Factory**, one mile north of I-89 on Rte-100 in the center of Waterbury, on the way up to Stowe, has grown so huge, so fast, that it is now the number-one tourist destination in Vermont. Half-hour tours (daily: July to mid-Aug 9am–8pm; late-Aug to mid-Oct 9am–6pm; late Oct to June 10am–5pm; $3, under 12 free; every 30min; ⓣ802/882-1240 or 1-866/BJ-TOURS, ⓦwww.benjerry.com) include a short film, a view of the workforce from an observation platform (weekdays only), and a free mini-scoop of the stuff that made it all possible – you can buy more at the counter outside.

Stowe

At the foot of Vermont's highest mountain, the 4393-foot **Mount Mansfield**, lies the popular summer- and wintertime resort of **STOWE**. There is still a beautiful nineteenth-century village at the town's heart – with a white-spired meeting house and a pretty green – though a century's worth of catering to skiers and outdoor enthusiasts has swamped the approach road to the main ski area with equipment stores, resort spas, and sprawling condo complexes. Nevertheless, Stowe's setting remains spectacular.

Stowe's **visitor center** on Main Street, near the intersection with Mountain Road (Mon–Sat 9am–8pm, Sun 9am–5pm; ⓣ802/253-7321 or 1-877/GO-STOWE, ⓦwww.gostowe.com), provides information on skiing conditions and accommodation. **Bikes** for the Recreation Path, a paved trail that twists through 5.3 miles of scenery, can be rented from the Mountain Sports & Bike Shop, 580 Mountain Rd (ⓣ802/253-7919, ⓦwww.skiershop.com).

Hwy-108 – **Mountain Road** – leads up to the main Stowe Mountain Resort (ⓦwww.stowe.com) and beyond, through the dramatic **Smugglers' Notch** pass. The resort on the other side (ⓣ1-800/451-8752, ⓦwww.smuggs.com) is a less crowded, more family-orientated alternative to Stowe. Weather permitting, you can get to the top of Mount Mansfield either by driving four and a half miles up the **Toll Road**, which itself starts seven miles up Mountain Road (late May to mid-Oct daily 9am–4pm; $23/car), or by taking the **Gondola Skyride** (mid-June to mid-Oct daily 10am–5pm; $16 single, $22 round-trip; ⓣ802/253-7311) up to the *Cliff House Restaurant* (lunch only), which, at an elevation of 3660ft, is an extremely strenuous 0.7-mile hike from the summit. What really made Stowe's name as a **cross-country ski resort** was its connection to the **Von Trapp family**, of *The Sound of Music* fame. After fleeing Austria, they came here in 1941 to establish the *Trapp Family Lodge* at 700 Trapp Hill Rd (ⓣ802/253-8511 or 1-800/826-7000, ⓦwww.trappfamily.com; ⑨). The original lodge, where Maria von Trapp held her singing camps, has burned down, and she herself died in 1987, but an equally luxurious building has taken its place: its *Austrian Tea Room* serves incredibly heavy Germanic cakes and pastries (daily 11am–5pm). Almost 150km of back-country and groomed cross-country ski trails lead out from the lodge.

Practicalities

The best of the plentiful accommodation (save the lodge above) includes the sumptuous *Stowe Mountain Lodge*, 7412 Mountain Rd (ⓣ1-888/478-6938 or ⓣ802/253-3560, ⓦwww.stowemountainlodge.com; ⑨), right next to the Spruce Peak ski area; and the historic *Green Mountain Inn*, 18 Main St (ⓣ802/253-7301 or 1-800/253-7302, ⓦwww.greenmountaininn.com; ⑥–⑦). Cheaper rooms are available at the *Riverside Inn*, 1965 Mountain Rd (ⓣ802/253-4217 or 1-800/966-4217, ⓦwww.rivinn.com; ④). *Gold Brook Campground* is two miles south on Hwy-100 (ⓣ802/253-7683; $23).

There are plenty of places to **eat** on Mountain Road. *McCarthy's* (ⓣ802/253-8626), at no. 2043, is best for breakfast; the *Shed Restaurant & Brew Pub*, at no. 1859 (ⓣ802/253-4364), has moderately-priced American food and good beer; and the always-crowded *Pie Casso*, at no. 1899 (ⓣ802/253-5100), serves excellent pizza and pasta dishes. A more upscale option for dinner is the *Blue Moon Café*, at 35 School St in the main village (ⓣ802/253-7006), which offers an innovative menu including Vermont rabbit and venison, as well as a good wine list.

Burlington

Lakeside **BURLINGTON**, Vermont's largest "city," with a population near forty thousand, is one of the most enjoyable towns in New England. A hip, relaxed fusion of Montréal, eighty miles to the north, and Boston, over two hundred miles southeast, it's always looked as much to Canada as to the south. Burlington faces 150-mile-long **Lake Champlain**, which forms the boundary between Vermont and New York State; shipping connections with the St Lawrence River were far easier than the land routes across the mountains, and the harbor became a major supply center. The city's founders included Ethan Allen and family, but far from being some impoverished Robin Hood figure, Ethan was in fact a wealthy landowner, and his brother Ira founded the University of Vermont. As the home of the university, Burlington is the definitive youthful, outward-looking college town. Downtown is easily strolled by foot, notably around the **Church Street Marketplace**.

Arrival, information, and getting around

Greyhound **buses** stop in downtown Burlington, at 345 Pine St, four blocks south of Main Street. The Amtrak **train** station is an inconvenient five miles northeast, in the small community of Essex Junction (connecting buses $1.25). The **airport**, Vermont's largest, is a few miles east of town along US-2.

Information and help with accommodation is available from the **Lake Champlain Regional Chamber of Commerce**, 60 Main St (July–Sept Mon–Fri 8.30am–5pm, Sat & Sun 9am–5pm; Oct–June Mon–Fri 8.30am–5pm; Ⓣ802/863-3489 or 1-877/686-5253, Ⓦwww.vermont.org).

The local CCTA **bus** company (Ⓣ802/864-2282, Ⓦwww.cctaride.org) runs a free shuttle (every 15–30min Mon–Fri 6.30am–7pm; late-May to mid-Oct additionally Sat & Sun 9am–9pm; no service July & Aug) connecting the university campus, downtown, and the waterfront.

Lake Champlain Ferries (see below) leave from the jetty at the end of King Street. If you're looking to actually get on the water, convivial *Spirit of Ethan Allen III* (Ⓣ802/862-8300, Ⓦwww.soea.com; $14.49 narrated tour, $19.25–47 lunch and evening theme and lobster dinner cruises) sets out from the dock at the end of College Street. North Star Sports, 100 Main St (Ⓣ802/863-3832), and Skirack, 85 Main St (Ⓣ802/658-3313), rent **bikes** from $28 per day.

If your onward travel plans require it, **Lake Champlain Ferries** (Ⓣ802/864-9804, Ⓦwww.ferries.com) crosses the lake from Vermont to New York from **Burlington** (to Port Kent; $17.50), **Charlotte** (to Essex; $9.50), and **Grand Isle** (to Plattsburgh; $9.50). All these rates are single for a car and driver; additional passengers, cyclists, and walk-ons pay $3.75 to $5.95.

Accommodation

Burlington has no shortage of moderately priced **accommodation**, especially along Shelburne Road between Burlington and Shelburne, while for **camping** the lakeside *North Beach Campground* (Ⓣ802/862-0942 or 1-800/571-1198; $24–33) is less than two miles north on Institute Road.

Courtyard Burlington Harbor 25 Cherry St Ⓣ802/864-4700, Ⓦwww.marriott.com. Best hotel downtown, with fabulous location near the waterfront and new, luxurious rooms and amenities; buffet breakfast, indoor pool, and LCD TVs included. ❽

G.G.T. Tibet Inn 1860 Shelburne Rd, South Burlington Ⓣ802/863-7110, Ⓦwww.ggt-tibetinn.com. Popular motel run by amiable Tibetan emigres; rooms, though small and simple, are a great value (each with cable TV, fridge, and microwave), but it's the extra touches, including arts and crafts, a Tibetan library, and prayer flags, that make it so memorable. ❹

Sunset House B&B 78 Main St Ⓣ802/864-3790, Ⓦwww.sunsethousebb.com. Centrally located, homely B&B with shared bathrooms. ❹–❻

Willard Street Inn 349 S Willard St Ⓣ802/651-8710, or 1-800/577-8712, Ⓦwww.willardstreetinn.com. A few blocks south of the town center, this gorgeously restored home comes with a relaxing garden, pantry, and filling breakfasts. ❼–❾

The City

The **waterfront** of Burlington is a surprisingly undeveloped area, though Battery Park at its northern end makes a good place to watch the sun go down over the Adirondacks – especially when there's a band playing, as there often is at weekends.

A better place to explore is the pedestrianized **Church Street Marketplace**, a few blocks back, which holds Burlington's finest old buildings and its modern cafés and boutiques. The **Robert Hull Fleming Museum** on Colchester Avenue (May to early Sept Tues–Fri noon–4pm, Sat & Sun 1–5pm; early Sept to April Tues, Thurs & Fri 9am–4pm, Wed 9am–8pm, Sat & Sun 1–5pm; Ⓣ802/656-0750, Ⓦwww.flemingmuseum.org; $5), at the University of Vermont, has an interesting collection of art and artifacts from all over the world, including pre-Columbian pieces. North on Rte-127, the **Ethan Allen Homestead** (June–Oct Mon–Sat 10am–4pm, Sun 1–4pm; $5; Ⓣ802/865-4556, Ⓦwww.ethanallenhomestead.org) offers a multifaceted look at the life and times of Vermont's controversial founding father.

The Shelburne Museum

It takes a whole day, if not more, to fully appreciate the remarkable fifty-acre collection of unalloyed **Americana** gathered at the **Shelburne Museum**, on US-7 in Shelburne, three miles south of Burlington (May–Oct daily 10am–5pm; $18, valid for two successive days; ⓣ802/985-3346, ⓦwww.shelburnemuseum.org). Created in 1947 by heiress Electra Webb, the museum is built around her parents' French Impressionist paintings, including works by Degas and Monet, displayed in a careful reconstruction of their New York City apartment. However, Electra's own interests ranged far wider, and she put together what is probably the nation's finest celebration of its own inventions outside of the Smithsonian Institution. More than thirty buildings, some original and some constructed specially for the museum, focus on aspects of everyday American life over the past two centuries. The village includes a general store and an apothecary, a railroad station, and even an enormous **steam paddlewheeler** from Lake Champlain, the *SS Ticonderoga*, with its own rock-surrounded lighthouse.

Eating, drinking, and entertainment

When school is in session, the presence of ten thousand students insures that Burlington has many inexpensive and good **restaurants**, as well as some pretty raucous nightspots.

American Flatbread 115 St Paul St ⓣ802/861-2999. Wildly popular place with all natural and organic pizzas, many made with locally-farmed produce.

Club Metronome/Nectar's 188 Main St ⓣ802/658-4771, ⓦwww.clubmetronome.com. Club Metronome is a very hip club with some live acts, but mainly house and techno music. Downstairs, Nectar's (ⓦwww.liveatnectars.com) is a retro lounge, which gave birth to the jam band Phish. Cover charge weekends (usually $5).

Muddy Waters 184 Main St ⓣ802/658-0466. Eclectic woody interior and colorful clientele distinguish this popular coffeehouse. The caffeine beverages pack quite a punch.

Shanty on the Shore 181 Battery St ⓣ802/864-0238. Truly fresh seafood in a laid-back setting, with views of Lake Champlain.

Smokejack's 156 Church St ⓣ802/658-1119. Creative meat and seafood dishes smoked over an oak-wood grill, all of which go down easier with the spicy Bloody Marys, custom martinis, or beers on tap.

Vermont Pub and Brewery 144 College St ⓣ802/865-0500. Roomy, convivial brewpub with a good menu of burgers, sandwiches, and other American-style food and occasional live music.

Maine

Celebrated as "the way life should be," spectacular **MAINE** lives up to its laurels. As large as the other five New England states combined, Maine has barely the population of Rhode Island. In theory, therefore, there's plenty of room for its exuberant influx of summer visitors; in practice, the majority of these head for the extravagantly corrugated **coast**. You only really begin to appreciate the size and space of the state, however, farther north or inland, where vast tracts of mountainous forest are dotted with lakes and barely pierced by roads – more like the Alaskan interior than the RV-cluttered roads of the Vermont and New Hampshire mountains. This region is ideal territory for hiking and canoeing (and spotting moose), particularly in **Baxter State Park**, home to the northern terminus of the Appalachian Trail.

North America's first agricultural **colonies** took root in Maine: de Champlain's **French** Protestants near Mount Desert Island in 1604, and an **English** group that survived one winter at the mouth of the Kennebec River three years later. At first considered part of Massachusetts, Maine became a separate entity only in 1820, when the Missouri Compromise made Maine a free, and Missouri a slave, state. Today, the **economy** remains heavily centered on the sea. Thanks to careful planning amongst Maine's hearty lobstering community, lobster fishing in particular has defied gloomy predictions and boomed again, as evidenced by the many thriving **lobster pounds**.

Maine's climate is famously harsh. In **winter**, the state gets quite snowy and the landscape is marked by snowshoes, buzzing snowmobiles, and the peaceful criss-crossing of skis. Officially, summer is spread between two long weekends: Memorial Day, (the last Monday in May) and Labor Day (the first Mon in September). This is Maine's most popular season, and heralded by sweet corn and lively lobster shacks; its end is marked by tasty wild blueberry crops – ninety percent of the nation's harvest comes from Maine – and the cheery blue berries show up in everything from pies to pancakes to chicken dishes. Brilliant **fall colors** begin to spread from the north in late September – when, unlike elsewhere in New England, off-season prices apply – and the frosty sweater weather is great for apple picking, leef peeping, or simply curling up with a blanket and a book.

Getting around Maine

By far the best way to see Maine is by **car**. The most enjoyable route to follow is Rte-1, which runs within a few miles of the coast all the way to Canada, with innumerable turnoffs to secluded seaside villages. If you're in a hurry, I-95, initially the (tolled) Maine Turnpike, offers speedy access to the Portland area and beyond. In the **interior**, the roads are quiet and the views spectacular; many of the northernmost routes are graveled and belong to the lumber companies. At any time of the year, bad weather can render these roads suddenly impassable; be sure to check before setting off.

While many touristed spots offer extensive in-town shuttle bus services, **public transportation** between Maine towns can fall a long way short of meeting travelers' needs. There are three daily Greyhound buses (Ⓣ1-800/231-2222, Ⓦwww.greyhound.com) from Boston to Portland; Greyhound also accesses Wiscasset, Brunswick, Bath, Rockland and Camden, as well as a number of other mid to northern Maine towns. Concord Coach (which makes it all the way down east to Bangor; Ⓣ1-800/639-3317, Ⓦwww.concordcoachlines.com) has the best access to the **coast**, and also runs a shuttle from Portland to Logan Airport (in Boston). The CYR bus lines (Ⓣ207/827-2335) trek up to the far north (culminating at Fort Kent) via Bangor. Amtrak has the amiable *Downeaster* (Ⓣ1-800/USA-RAIL, Ⓦwww.amtrakdowneaster.com), which leaves from Boston's North Station and terminates in Portland (making stops along the way in Wells, Biddeford, and Old Orchard Beach); it's great value at $24 each way.

The Maine coast

Although the water is chilly, the **beaches** of southern Maine are unequivocally beautiful, and there are plenty of rocky coastal footpaths and harbor villages to explore. The liveliest destinations are **Portland** and **Bar Harbor** (at the edge of

Acadia National Park); there's a wide choice of smaller seaside towns, such as **Wiscasset** and **Blue Hill**, if you're looking for a more peaceful base. **Beaches** are more common (and the sea warmer) further south, for example at **Ogunquit**.

The best way to see the coast itself is by **boat**: ferries and excursions operate from even the smallest harbors, with major routes including the ferries to Canada from Portland and Bar Harbor, shorter trips to **Monhegan** island via Port Clyde, Boothbay Harbor, and New Harbor; and **Vinalhaven** via Rockland.

South of Portland

I-95 crosses from Portsmouth, New Hampshire (see p.237) into an area of Maine so dense with little communities that Mark Twain alleged one couldn't "throw a brick without danger of disabling a postmaster." Three miles over the Maine border, at the intersection with Rte-1, an **information center** at **Kittery** provides copious details on the whole state (daily: summer 8am–6pm; rest of year 9am–5.30pm; ⓣ207/439-1319). For a fun fish dinner overlooking the water, stop into the *Chauncey Creek Lobster Pier* (ⓣ207/439-1030), 16 Chauncey Creek Rd in Kittery Point, while you're here.

If you want to avoid the tolls on the interstate and follow more scenic Rte-1 instead (both head north, but Rte-1 hugs the coast), you'll soon find yourself in pleasant **YORK**, which was in 1642 the first English city to be chartered in North America. Its seventeenth-century **Old Gaol** ("Old Jail") now serves as a museum, commemorating its colorful, criminal past – dating from 1653, it was used as Maine's primary prison until the Revolutionary War. As well as its historical attractions, York is home to several fine beaches, a vintage arcade (the endearing "Fun-O-Rama"), and a number of invigorating cliff walks. Head beyond Old York, for example, towards **Nubble Light**, at the end of Shore Road, off Rte-103, at York Beach, where you'll find one of Maine's most striking lighthouses, situated on an island of its own and observable from a rocky promontory. People love to line up for *Flo's* **hot dogs**, just north of here in Cape Neddick, Rte-1 across from Mountain Road (closed Wed), a crowd-pleasing institution since 1959, while *Stonewall Kitchen's* flagship *Company Store,* 2 Stonewall Lane, right behind the Chamber of Commerce just off Rte-1 (ⓣ207/351-2712) has fresh lobster BLTs and salads to take to the beach alongside its signature displays of mustards, jams, and chocolate sauces.

Ogunquit and around

The three-mile spit of sand that shields gay-friendly **OGUNQUIT** from the open ocean is one of Maine's finest **beaches**, a long stretch of sugary sand and calm surf that is ideal for leisurely strolls. The summer season at the **Ogunquit Playhouse** (ⓣ207/646-5511) usually attracts a few big-name performers. The late director of the Met in New York called the **Ogunquit Museum of American Art** (ⓣ207/646-4909; $7) "the most beautiful little museum in the world." Its tiny space is blessed with a strong collection of seascapes, further enhanced by the museum's sweeping ocean views.

One great place to **stay** in Ogunquit is the *Terrace by the Sea*, 11 Wharf Lane (ⓣ207/646-3232, ⓦwww.terracebythesea.com; ❺–❽) with lovely gardens and a location right on the water's edge. The *Beachmere Inn*, Shore Road (ⓣ207/646-2021, ⓦwww.beachmereinn.com; ❻–❾), has newly-refurbished rooms in a quirky, turreted old wooden hotel that overlooks the ocean. The nearest campground, *Pinederosa*, is north of town at 128 North Village Rd (May–Sept; ⓣ207/646-2492, ⓦwww.pinederosa.com; $28 for two adults); it operates a free shuttle to Ogunquit Beach in July and August. Back downtown, the misnamed Marginal Way, a scenic clifftop path, leads from central Ogunquit to pretty **Perkins Cove**, a mile south. *The Blue Water Inn,* 11 Beach St (Ⓣ207/646-5559) is right on the water and serves up fresh **seafood** at amazing prices, while *Joshua's Restaurant*, 1637 Rte-1 (Ⓣ207/646-3355) just north in **Wells**, has the best dinners in the area; many of the dishes use ingredients from their own local farm.

Kennebunkport

There's a reason former presidents **George Herbert Walker Bush** (known locally as "41") and **George "W" Bush** summer in **Kennebunkport** – it's beautiful, historical, and full of eats even Barbara approves of. Although the town can feel a bit snooty, it has (fortunately) been blessed with beaches as well as bluebloods. Neighboring Kennebunk is home to a lovely trio of beaches: Kennebunk, Mother's, and Gooch's, all located on Beach Street, grab a permit from HB Provisions (6am–10pm, Ⓣ207/967-5762; $15 a day), 15 Western Ave. A fun place to hang out and eat seafood is *Alisson's*, at 8 Dock Square (Ⓣ207/967-4841), or the low-key *Clam Shack*, just before the bridge into town (Ⓣ207/967-3321).

An intriguing diversion is the tiny Tom's of Maine outlet store at 52 Main St, Kennebunk (Ⓣ207/985-6331); the pleasantly aromatic space sells slightly-dinged toothpaste "seconds" for only $2.

Portland

The largest city in Maine, **PORTLAND** was founded in 1632 in a superb position on the Casco Bay Peninsula, and quickly prospered, building ships and exporting great inland pines for use as masts. A long line of wooden **wharves** stretched along the seafront, with the merchants' houses on the hillside above.

From its earliest days, Portland was a cosmopolitan city, with a large free black population that traditionally worked as longshoremen; great bitterness arose when Irish immigrants began to muscle in on the scene in the 1830s. When the **railroads** came, the Canada Trunk Line had its terminus right on Portland's quayside, bringing the produce of Canada and the Great Plains one hundred miles closer to Europe than it would have been at any other major US port. Some of the wharves are now taken up by sleek condo developments, though **Custom House Wharf** remains much as it must have looked when Anthony Trollope passed through in 1861 and said, "I doubt whether I ever saw a town with more evident signs of prosperity." Most of what he saw of the town was destroyed by an accidental **fire** in 1866 (Native Americans in 1675, and the British in 1775, had previously burned Portland deliberately).

Grand Trunk Station was torn down in 1966, and downtown Portland appeared to be in terminal decline – until, that is, a group of committed residents undertook the energetic redevelopment of the area now known as the **Old Port**. Their success has revitalized the city, keeping it at the heart of Maine life – though you shouldn't expect a hive of energy. Portland is quite simply a pleasant, sophisticated, and very attractive town, where one can experience the benefits of a large city at a lesser cost and without the hassle of crowds.

Arrival, information, and getting around

Both I-95 and Rte-1 skirt the promontory of Portland, within a few miles of the city center, while I-295 runs directly through it and offers access to downtown. **Portland International Jetport** is next to I-95, and is connected with downtown by regular city buses. Congress Street is the main central thoroughfare, while Commercial Street is prettier and runs along the harbor. Concord Coach

(Ⓣ207/828-1151, Ⓦwww.concordcoachlines.com) and Greyhound are the principal **bus** operators along the coast, with frequent service to Boston, as well as north to Bangor (and, in summer, Bar Harbor). Greyhound (see p.31) also runs to Montréal, New Hampshire, and Vermont, as well as destinations within Maine; the station is at 950 Congress St, on the eastern edge of downtown. The **visitor center** is at 245 Commercial St (Mon–Fri 8am–5pm, Sat 10am–3pm; Ⓣ207/772-5800, Ⓦwww.visitportland.com), and friendly staffers can help you with city's ins and outs.

Though served by public **buses** ($1.25), downtown Portland is compact enough to stroll or bike around; Cyclemania, at 59 Federal St (Ⓣ207/774-2933), rents **bicycles** for $25 a day. You can also take a **land & sea tour** of the city with the affable Mainely/Eagle Island Tours, 170 Commercial St ($29; Ⓣ207/774-0808), or the amphibious Downeast Duck Adventures, at 177 Commercial St ($24; Ⓣ207/774-DUCK), which whisks you through historical Old Port and then takes you into Casco Bay to view the Calendar Islands.

Four mornings a week between late May and mid-October, the high-speed *Cat* **ferry** (Ⓣ1-877/359-3760, Ⓦwww.catferry.com) leaves Portland for **Yarmouth** in Nova Scotia at 8am; the trip takes about six hours each way. High-season fare is $99 per person single, and there are various discount and excursion fares; single vehicle fares begin at $164. You will need your birth certificate or an up-to-date passport to make the trip, however.

Accommodation

Finding a room in Portland is no great problem, although you should book in advance for summer and fall. A number of **budget motels** cluster around exit 48 off I-95. The closest **campground** is *Wassamki Springs*, west of Portland off Rte-22 towards Westbrook (May to mid-Oct only; Ⓣ207/839-4276; $43).

The Chadwick 140 Chadwick St Ⓣ207/774-5141, Ⓦwww.thechadwick.com. Tucked away in Portland's West End, this delightful B&B has four cozy rooms decked out in warm tones, a welcoming innkeeper, excellent breakfasts, wi-fi, and happy guests. ❺–❼

Hilton Garden Inn 65 Commercial St Ⓣ207/780-0780, Ⓦwww.hiltongardeninn.com. Fitness center, saltwater pool, and wireless internet, all in a snappy location that overlooks the harbor. A bit overpriced, but a good spot. ❾

Inn at Park Spring 135 Spring St Ⓣ207/774-1059 or 1-800/437-8511, Ⓦwww.innatparkspring.com. A charming B&B from 1835 in the Arts District and convenient to the restaurant and shops of Old Port. Friendly innkeepers and delicious breakfasts. ❻–❼

Inn at St John 939 Congress St Ⓣ207/773-6481 or 1-800/636-9127, Ⓦwww.innatstjohn.com. Located just outside of downtown in a slightly dodgy area, this elegant Victorian mainstay offers reasonably priced, comfortable rooms, some with shared baths. No elevator. ❺–❼

Morrill Mansion B&B 249 Vaughan St Ⓣ207/774-6900, Ⓦwww.morrillmansion.com. Well-appointed, West End B&B with cozy, stylish rooms, refrigerators, DVD players, free internet access, and a helpful, well-informed innkeeper. ❻–❽

Portland Harbor Hotel 468 Fore St Ⓣ207/775-9090 or 1-888/798-9090, Ⓦwww.theportlandharborhotel.com. Pretty, but not exceptional rooms, in a great location near the waterfront; many rooms overlook the English garden. ❾

Portland Regency Hotel 20 Milk St Ⓣ207/774-4200, Ⓦwww.theregency.com. Fancy rooms – some with bay views – in a beautiful renovated brick armory building not far from the Old Port. ❾

The City

Thanks to the several fires, not much of old Portland survives, though grand mansions can be seen along Congress and Danforth streets. The **Wadsworth-Longfellow House/Maine Historical Society**, at 485–489 Congress St (May–Oct & Dec Mon–Sat 10am–4pm, Sun noon–4pm; Nov Sat only, 10am–4pm; $7 includes museum, below; 45min tour on the hour), was Portland's first brick house when built in 1785 by Peleg Wadsworth. However, the house owes its fame primarily to Wadsworth's grandson, the poet Henry Wadsworth Longfellow, who spent his boyhood here. Next door, the **Historical Society Museum** (Mon–Sat 10am–5pm, Sun noon–5pm; $4; ⓣ207/879-0427) has changing displays of state history and art.

The **Portland Museum of Art** at 7 Congress Square, was built in 1988 by the renowned I.M. Pei partnership (Tues–Thurs, Sat & Sun 10am–5pm, Fri 10am–9pm; June to mid-Oct Mon 10am–5pm; $10, free Friday 5–9pm; ⓣ207/775-6148, ⓦwww.portlandmuseum.org). It's a stellar exhibition space, brimming with maritime pieces such as Winslow Homer's "*Weatherbeaten*" and other affecting seascapes. The lower stories usually hold temporary exhibitions while the second floor displays classic New England scenes. Upstairs is a bit more lively, with a strong collection of fantastic modern works such as Brian White's "mussel dress" – entirely composed of well-worn mussel shells.

The restored **Old Port** near the quayside, between Exchange and Pearl streets, can be quite entertaining, with all sorts of red-brick antiquarian shops, bookstores, boutique clothing spots (especially on Exchange Street), and other esoterica. Several companies operate **boat trips** from the nearby wharves: The Portland Schooner Co. has two vintage schooners that sail around the harbor and to the Casco Bay islands and lighthouses from the Maine State Pier, adjacent to Casco Bay Lines on Commercial Street (daily in summer; 2hr trip $35, overnight trips $240; ⓣ207/766-2500 or 1-87/SCHOONER, ⓦwww.portlandschooner.com). With Lucky Catch Cruises, at 170 Commercial St ($22; ⓣ207/761-0941, ⓦwww.luckycatch.com) you can throw on a pair of lobsterman overalls and gloves and head out to catch your very own lobster. Casco Bay Lines runs a twice-daily mail boat all year, and additional cruises in summer, to seven of the innumerable **Calendar Islands** in Casco Bay, from its terminal at 56 Commercial St at Franklin (single direct trip $7.75–11.50, scenic cruises $12–22.50; ⓣ207/774-7871, ⓦwww.cascobaylines.com). **Long**, **Peaks**, and **Cliff islands** all have accommodation or camping facilities.

If you follow Portland's waterfront to the end of the peninsula, you'll come to the **Eastern Promenade**, a remarkably peaceful two-mile harbor trail that connects to East End Beach, below the headland. Above the promenade, at the top of Munjoy Hill, at 138 Congress St, is the eight-sided, shingled 1807 **Portland Observatory** (June to mid-Oct daily 10am–5pm; $7; ⓣ207/774-5561); you can climb its 103 steps for an exhilarating view of the bay.

Eating

Portland is stuffed with outstanding **restaurants**, and most of its bars (see p.258) serve good food as well. The bountiful **Farmer's Market**, in Monument Square (open Wed, 7am–2pm, May–Nov) offers the perfect opportunity to sample local produce.

Asmara 51 Oak St ⓣ207/253-5122. Amazing, low-key Ethiopian and Eritrean food with the likes of *tsebhi hamli* (collard greens and kale mildly curried and served on injera bread). Closed Mon.

Aurora Provisions 64 Pine St ⓣ207/871-9060. Upscale market/deli with mouthwatering sandwiches, a full selection of coffee, drinks, pastries, salads, desserts, and a small seating area. Perfect for picnic fare. Closed Sun.

Becky's Diner 390 Commercial St ⓣ207/773-7070. A vintage Maine breakfast spot with a newly-expanded upper deck serving hearty American portions, including home-made muffins and pies, from 4am (for the fishermen) until 9pm.

Flatbread Company 72 Commercial St ⓣ207/772-8777. Tasty pizza, made with flatbread dough, their own sauce, and all-natural ingredients, in a hip waterfront location.

Herbs Gully 55 Oak St ⓣ207/780-8080. Tasty, creatively constructed burritos ("hand-rolled fatties"), quesadillas, and side dishes; they also mix drinks like the "kind buzz" (banana, honey, vanilla, and bee pollen).

Lobster Shack at Two Lights 225 Two Lights Rd ⓣ207/799-1677. Perhaps the best seafood-eating scenery in all of Maine – lighthouse to the left, unruly ocean to the right, and a scrumptious lobster roll on the plate in front of you.

Market Street Eats 36 Market St ⓣ207/773-3135. You won't find any frou-frou juice drinks on the menu at this subterranean sandwich joint serving awesome lunch fare like the Red Rooster wrap (chicken, bacon, provolone, spicy Thai mayo and red onion, $6.75).

Shays Grill Pub 18 Monument Square ⓣ207/772-2626. Home to what is Portland's best burger and onion strings; good martinis and beer in a relaxed ambience right on Monument Square.

Street and Co. 33 Wharf St ⓣ207/775-0887. A great special-occasion seafood spot where the cuts are grilled, blackened, or broiled to perfection amidst an intimate, noisy dining room. There are a few good non-fish items as well. Reservations recommended.

Walter's Cafe 15 Exchange St ⓣ207/871-9258. New American cuisine in a sophisticated, high-ceilinged dining room right on Exchange St. Entrees are $15–20; lunch is less expensive and just as good.

Nightlife and entertainment

Performing arts in town include chamber music, opera, dance, and touring theater, some as part of PCA Great Performances held at City Hall's Merrill Auditorium (tickets ⓣ207/842-0800, ⓦwww.pcagreatperformances.org); larger productions are put on by the Portland Stage Company at the Portland Stage Co., 25A Forest Ave (ⓣ207/774-0465). Portland Parks and Recreation (ⓣ207/756-8130, ⓦwww.ci.portland.me.us) sponsors free outdoor noontime and evening **jazz** and **blues concerts** throughout the city during the summer. The free *Portland Phoenix* has weekly **listings** of events.

Portland's **bar scene** is rowdier than you might expect, with pubs packing it in on the weekend with lively, beer-drinking fun seekers.

Great Lost Bear 540 Forest Ave ⓣ207/772-0300, ⓦwww.greatlostbear.com. Outside of downtown Portland proper, it's a great beer bar that's worth the trek, especially if you have a thing for hops. Try one from their 65 taps, including fifteen state microbrews. Decent pub grub, too.

Gritty McDuff's 396 Fore St ⓣ207/772-2739. Portland's first brewpub, making Portland Head Pale Ale and Black Fly Stout. Food, folk music, long wooden benches, and a friendly atmosphere, which can get rowdy on Sat nights.

Novare Res Bier Café 4 Canal Plaza, Suite 1 (enter through alleyway on lower Exchange St, by Keybank sign) ⓣ207/761-2437. A little tricky to find, this very cool Old Port beer spot sports over 200 brews with fifteen on tap, outdoor and indoor picnic tables, and tasty meat and cheese accompaniments.

The Port Hole 16 Custom House Wharf ⓣ207/780-6533. Right on the water, this sea-breezy Portland fixture has all sorts of cool features, including a great daily breakfast. Their summertime Sun reggae shows, held on a sunny deck in the harbor, are seriously bumping.

RiRa 72 Commercial St ⓣ207/761-4446. Lively Irish pub with great food and a hip waterfront location.

Rivalries 10 Cotton St ⓣ207/774-6044. Packed with energetic sports fans, this recent addition to Portland's scene is a clean, hip two-story bar.

SPACE Gallery 538 Congress St ⓣ207/828-5600, ⓦwww.space538.org. Cool, artsy space which displays contemporary artworks and always has something interesting going on, whether it's films, music, art shows, or local bands.

Top of the East Lounge In the Eastland Park Hotel 157 High St ⓣ207/775-5411. Sophisticated rooftop lounge, with swanky martinis and great views of the city.

North from Portland: the mid-coast

The coastal towns immediately north of Portland are no less commercialized than those to the south; **Freeport**, for example, is basically just an outdoor mall (albeit a good one). However, soon after **Brunswick**, I-95 veers inland toward Augusta, and Rte-1 is left to run on alone, parallel to the ocean. From here, things become much less frenetic, and prices a whole lot lower; even on the main road you'll find pleasant communities such as **Bath** and **Belfast**; the many headlands can be even more peaceful.

Eartha at the DeLorme Headquarters

If you're driving north on I-95 from Portland up to L.L. Bean in Freeport, you might notice an enormous, lit-up globe just by the highway at Exit 17. That's **Eartha**, iconic symbol for the *DeLorme Headquarters* and at 41.5 in diameter, the largest rotating globe in the world. The place is very much worth a stop for the great selection of maps (including the indispensable Maine Atlas & Gazetteer) or just to watch Eartha's spellbinding turns mimic the true rotation of the earth (Sun–Thurs 9am–6pm, Fri & Sat 9am–7pm; ⓣ1-800/642-0970).

Freeport

Much of the current prosperity of **FREEPORT**, fifteen miles north of Portland, rests on the invention by Leon L. Bean, in 1912, of a funky-looking rubber-soled fishing boot. That original boot is still selling (there's now an enormous replica at the entrance), and **L.L. Bean** has grown into a multi-national clothing conglomerate, with an enormous clothing store on Main Street that literally never closes. Originally, this was so pre-dawn hunting expeditions could stock up; all the relevant equipment is available for rent or sale, and the store runs regular workshops to teach backcountry activities and survival skills. In practice, though, the late-night hours seem more geared toward high school students, who attempt to fall asleep in the tents without being noticed by store personnel. L.L. Bean is now more of a fashion emporium (it's Maine's most-visited destination) and Freeport has expanded to include a mile-long stretch of top-name **factory outlets** (such as the Gap, Banana Republic, and Cole Haan), most of which do give genuine reductions on the standard retail prices.

Freeport is not an ideal place to stay – everything falls quiet once the shoppers have gone home – but if you need **accommodation**, the *Harraseeket Inn* at 162 Main St (ⓣ207/865-9377 or 1-800/342-6423, ⓦwww.harraseeketinn.com; ❽–❾) is a wonderful clapboard B&B inn with some eighty rooms. There is also the *Applewood Inn,* 8 Holbrook St (ⓣ207/865-9705, ⓦwww.applewoodusa.com; ❼–❾), a great B&B just behind L.L. Bean. A few miles north of town, the lovely *Maine Idyll Motor Court*, at 1411 Rte-1 N (ⓣ207/865-4201, ⓦwww.maineidyll.com; ❸–❺), provides basic but romantic cottages in a pretty, woodsy setting.

The best **food** in Freeport is south of town at *Conundrum Wine Bistro,* 117 Rte-1 S (ⓣ207/865-0303); most people come for the swanky martinis, then they get hooked on the fresh, eclectic seasonal entrees, such as butternut squash ravioli with sage cream sauce. Right downtown, the *Mediterranean Grill*, 10 School St (ⓣ207/865-1688) has really good authentic Lebanese food (like *gyro* kebabs) at lunch and dinner. For a scenic change of pace, head a mile south of Freeport (on Rte-1) to the sea, where the *Harraseeket Lunch & Lobster Co* (ⓣ207/865-4888), extending on its wooden jetty into the peaceful bay, makes a great outdoor lunch spot. The very green promontory visible just across the water is **Wolfe's Neck Woods State Park**. In summer, for $3, you can follow hiking and nature trails along the unspoiled fringes of the headland (daily 9am–6pm; ⓣ207/865-4465).

Bath and around

Eight miles on, the charming small town of **BATH** has an exceptionally long history of **shipbuilding**: the first vessel to be constructed and launched here was the *Virginia* in 1607, by Sir George Popham's short-lived colony. **Bath Iron Works**, founded in 1833, attracted job-seeking Irishmen in such numbers as to provoke a mob of anti-immigrant "**Know-Nothings**" to burn down the local Catholic church in July 1854. The works continues to produce ships – during World War II, more destroyers were built here than in all Japan. At the stellar **Maine Mari-**

▲ Maine Maritime Museum

time Museum, 243 Washington St, next to the Iron Works two miles south of the town center (daily 9.30am–5pm; $10 for two days; ⓣ207/443-1316), you can take a tour of the Iron Works (reservations recommended, $26), explore several visiting historic vessels, or browse the museum's intriguing collection of ship-related paintings, photographs, and artifacts. There's even a mini-pirate ship for little buccaneers to climb around on.

A pretty fourteen-mile drive south along Rte-209 leads to gorgeous **Popham Beach** ($4; ⓣ207/389-1335) at the end of the Phippsburg Peninsula, where you can explore scenic sands as well as the hulking **Fort Popham** – a nineteenth-century granite fort.

The *Inn at Bath*, 969 Washington St (ⓣ207/443-4294 or 1-800/423-0964, ⓦwww.innatbath.com; ❼), is a great **B&B** with beautiful gardens and all the amenities, while the *Kismet Inn*, 44 Summer (ⓣ207/443-3399, ⓦwww.kismetinnmaine.com; ❽–❾), has bright rooms, luxurious soaking tubs, body scrubs, and yoga classes.

Places to eat in the area include *Solo Bistro*, 128 Front St (ⓣ207/443-3373) which serves hip, tasty fare in contemporary environs and hosts live jazz some nights; and *Beale Street Barbecue & Grill*, at 215 Water St (ⓣ207/442-9514), offering slow-smoked chicken, pulled pork, and ribs, to stay or to go. *The Cabin*, 552 Washington St (ⓣ207/443-6224) has great pizza. *The Sea Basket,* right onRte-1 N in Wiscasset (ⓣ207/882-6581), has great fried seafood; while eating at *Red's Eats* (ⓣ207/882-6128), just further on Rte-1 N, is a bit of a culinary rite of passage – people line up and down the block just to get their hands on one of his famous lobster rolls.

Boothbay Harbor

BOOTHBAY HARBOR, at the southern tip of Hwy-27, twelve miles south from Rte-1, is a crowded, yet undeniably pretty, resort town that's right on the water. The town lays on boat trips of all kinds, including Balmy Days Cruises (ⓣ207/633-2284 or 1-800/298-2284), which offers all-day trips to Monhegan Island for $32, and harbor tours for $14. Cap'n Fish's affable "Puffin nature cruises" (☎207/633-3244 or 1-800/636-3244; $24 for a 2hr 30m tour) offer glimpses of the brightly-beaked birds who inhabit Eastern Egg Rock; bring binoculars. The Coastal Maine Botanical Gardens (call for the best directions; daily 9am–5pm; $10; ☎207/633-4333, www.mainegardens.org) has pretty, bloom-filled trails that wind along the Sheepscot River.

If you want to **stay** in Boothbay, look no further than the stylish *Topside Inn*, 60 McKown St (☎207/633-5404, www.topsideinn.com; ❺), with pleasant rooms in an old sea captain's house and great views of the harbor. The *Lobster Dock,* across the footbridge at 49 Atlantic Ave (☎207/633-7120), dishes up ultrafresh lobster rolls and seafood dinners at low prices, while the *Boathouse Bistro,* Pier 1 (☎207/633-0400), has excellent tapas and a sunny rooftop deck and bar. Lastly, *The Thistle Inn*, 55 Oak St, serves up stellar New American fare at dinnertime and also has lovely rooms (☎207/633-3541, www.thethistleinn.com; ❺). Back on Rte-1 N (about ten miles north of Boothbay) in Waldoboro, the legendary *Moody's Diner* (☎207/832-7785) has been a Maine institution for more than fifty years. *Moody's* is the real deal, open late and oozing nostalgia, with vinyl booths, inexpensive daily specials, and fourteen types of freshly made pie – their four-berry is a must-have.

Rockland and Monhegan Island

ROCKLAND, where Rte-1 reaches Penobscot Bay, has historically been Maine's largest distributor of **lobsters**, boasting one of the busiest working harbors in the state, and more recently, it has grown into one of Maine's hippest, most liveable places. The town is home to the annual Maine Lobster Festival (held on the first weekend of Aug; ☎1-800/LOB-CLAW, www.mainelobsterfestival.com) as well as the North Atlantic Blues Festival (held mid-July; ☎207/596-6055, www.northatlanticbluesfestival.com), and it's cultural centerpiece is the outstanding **Farnsworth Art Museum**, 352 Main St (late May to mid-Oct daily 10am–5pm; rest of year Tues–Sun 10am–5pm; $10; ☎207/596-6457, www.farnsworthmuseum.org). The collection spans two centuries of American art, much of it Maine-related, and spreads over several buildings. The **Wyeth Center**, a beautiful gallery in a converted old church, holds two floors' worth of works by Jamie and N.C. Wyeth. Rockland's other star attraction is the lush Art Deco **Strand Theatre**, 345 Main St (tickets $8.50; ☎207/594-0070, www.rocklandstrand.com), showing film classics as well as contemporary indie fare.

A fun day-trip is the **Maine Eastern Railroad** (☎1-866/637-2457, www.maineeasternrailroad.com; $40 round-trip), which provides scenic two-hour coastal trips between Rockland and Brunswick (including stops in Bath and Wiscasset), in its restored Art Deco railcars.

For **dining**, one of the best of the area's traditional lobster pounds is *Miller's* (☎207/594-7406), on the shore of Wheeler's Bay in an isolated cove at Spruce Head on Hwy-73, open from 10am until 7pm in season. The *Brass Compass Café*, 305 Main St (☎207/596-5960), does a standout breakfast and lunch. The best dinners in town can be had at funky and perennially crowded *Café Miranda*, tucked away at 15 Oak St, just off Main Street (☎207/594-2034), with an array of moderately priced international entrees, while *Primo*, 2 S Main St (☎207/596-0770), serves some of the best food in the state (for less moderate prices) from its scenic Victorian digs. A great place to **stay** is the turreted *LimeRock Inn*, 96 Limerock St (☎207/594-2257, www.limerockinn.com; ❻–❽), with fantastic innkeepers, free wi-fi and cozy decor, while the bright, petite *Ripples Inn,* 16 Pleasant St (☎207/594-5771, www.ripplesinnattheharbor.com; ❻–❽) is another appealing option.

Monhegan Island

South of Rockland, the pretty **St George Peninsula**, in particular the village of Tenants Harbor, inspired writer Sarah Orne Jewett's classic Maine novel *Country of the Pointed Firs*. At the tip of the peninsula, boats leave from the hamlet of Port Clyde for tiny **Monhegan Island**, eleven miles off the coast and with a year-round population of less than a hundred residents. The island makes a great day-trip away from the tourist bustle of the mainland; you can get there (in about an hour) via Monhegan Boat Lines (May–Oct daily; Nov–April Mon, Wed & Fri; three sailings a day in summer, fewer at other times; $30 round-trip; Ⓣ207/372-8848, Ⓦwww.monheganboat.com).

On this rocky outcrop, **lobsters** are the main business, though the stunning cliffs and isolated coves have long attracted artists as well – including Edward Hopper. Fifteen miles of **hiking trails** twist through the wilderness and past a magnificent 1824 lighthouse. **Accommodation** – such as the *Island Inn,* well-sited overlooking the harbor right by the ferry dock (Ⓣ207/596-0371, Ⓦwww.islandinnmonhegan.com; ❻–❾) – is generally pricey; you may want to try the simple comfort of *Trailing Yew* (Ⓣ207/596-6194, Ⓦwww.trailingyew.com; ❸).

Camden and Rockport

The adjacent communities of **CAMDEN** and **ROCKPORT** split into two separate towns in 1891, in a dispute over who should pay for a new bridge over the Goose River between them. Rockport is now a quiet working port, among the prettiest on the Maine coast, home to lobster boats, pleasure cruisers, and little else; Camden has clearly won the competition for tourists. The one essential stop in the area is **Camden Hills State Park**, two miles north of Camden ($3), where you can hike or drive up to a tower that affords one of the best views of the Maine coastline; on a clear day it's possible to see as far as Acadia National Park.

Camden and Rockport specialize in organizing sailing expeditions of up to six days in the large schooners known as **windjammers**. Expeditions sail from late May into mid-October. Vessels include the *Appledore* (Ⓣ207/236-8353), which does two-hour cruises for $30 from Camden. Contact the Maine Windjammer Association (Ⓣ1-800/807-WIND) for information and schedules for longer three- to six-day trips out of the area. Maine Sport Outfitters in Rockport (Ⓣ207/236-7120, Ⓦwww.mainesport.com) rents **kayaks** and **bikes**. Camden's **information** office is at the Public Landing (Ⓣ207/236-4404, Ⓦwww.camdenme.org).

Don't underestimate the magnetism of the Belted Galloway cows at **Aldermere Farm**, on Russell Avenue in Rockport (Ⓣ207/236-2739, Ⓦwww.aldermere.org). These quirky, endearing "Oreo cookie cows" (so named for the funny white stripe of fur that's sandwiched between their black front and back) have been amusing passersby for ages. The farm doesn't currently have any public programming, per se, but the cows are nearly always in plain view.

A great **place to stay** in town is the beautiful *Camden Maine Stay Inn*, 22 High St (Ⓣ207/236-9636, Ⓦwww.camdenmainestay.com; ❼–❽), a cozy 1813 white-clapboard inn. *The Belmont*, 6 Belmont Ave (Ⓣ1-800/238-8053, Ⓦwww.thebelmontinn.com; ❼), has a lovely porch and grounds and is decked out in conservative elegance. The *Ducktrap Motel*, just north on Hwy-1 in Lincolnville (Ⓣ207/789-5400 or 1-877/977-5400; ❹), is a cute budget option.

Among busy **eating** and **drinking** spots in Camden are the *Camden Deli*, 37 Main St (Ⓣ207/236-8343), with gourmet, bulging sandwiches and harbor views from the upstairs patio. Tea-lit *Francine*, 55 Chestnut St (Ⓣ207/230-0083), serves excellent French bistro fare amidst romantic environs. The *Lobster Pound Restaurant,* Rte-1 N in Lincolnville (Ⓣ207/789-5550) is a wildly popular seaside restaurant serving heaps of the bright-red crustaceans.

Belfast and around

Beloved **BELFAST** feels like one of the most lived-in and liveable towns along the Maine coast. Here, eighteen miles from Camden, the shipbuilding boom is long since over (and the chicken-processing plant that regularly turned the bay blood-red has also gone). In recent years, the town has declared the waterfront a historic district; as you stroll around, look out for any number of whitewashed Greek Revival houses, particularly between Church and Congress streets. Belfast was a lively center in the 1960s, a fact still reflected in its food co-op and festivals; nowadays it has a strong creative bent, with many inviting galleries lining Main Street and a Gallery Walk every Friday in summer. Searsport, five miles north on Rte-1, is home to the atmospheric **Penobscot Marine Museum,** Rte-1 at Church Street (Mon–Sat 10am–5pm, Sun noon–5pm; $8; ⓣ207/548-2529), which features marine artworks and nautical artifacts that are spread between a number of historic buildings, including a nineteenth-century sea captain's home (which includes among its furnishings a very cool vintage record player and a piano with mother-of-pearl keys).

For **accommodation**, try the *Jeweled Turret Inn*, 40 Pearl St (ⓣ207/338-2304 or 1-800/696-2304, ⓦwww.jeweledturret.com; ❺–❻), a beautiful Victorian house with free wireless internet, or the *Penobscot Bay Inn*, 192 Northport Ave (ⓣ207/338-5715 or 1-800/335-2370, ⓦwww.penobscotbayinn.com; ❹–❻). There's also an oceanfront **campground**, *Searsport Shores Camping Resort*, at 216 W Main St (Rte-1) in Searsport (ⓣ207/548-6059; $38–55 per tentsite).

Belfast has some great **eating** establishments. *Chase's Daily*, 96 Main St (ⓣ207/338-0555), has fresh eats like breakfast burritos and peach smoothies with ginger and lime as well as take-home flower bouquets from their farm. *Three Tides*, at 2 Pinchy Lane (ⓣ207/338-1707) is a hip tapas spot right on the water that brews its own beer (and root beer); on-site, their *Ship to Shore* harbor store features lobster rolls and provisions to take on a picnic or ship. Across the bay, *Young's Lobster Pound* (ⓣ207/338-1160) serves fresh-boiled lobster dinners – some of the best in the state – with sunset views.

The Blue Hill Peninsula

It used to be that the **Blue Hill Peninsula**, reaching south from Bucksport, was a sleepy expanse of land, too far off the primary roads to attract much attention. But word is slowly getting out about this beautiful area, blanketed with fields of wild blueberries and their pinkish-white flowers, and dotted with both dignified towns like **Blue Hill** and hardcore fishing villages like **Stonington** and **Deer Isle**. Even farther off the established tourist trail, **Isle au Haut** is a remote outpost accessible only by mailboat. As you might expect, the main draw down here is the quiet tranquility that comes with isolation, and while the area presents ample opportunities for exploration, you might find yourself content with a good book, an afternoon nap, and a night in a posh B&B.

Accommodation

If you need help finding **accommodation**, the Blue Hill Peninsula Chamber of Commerce, at 28 Water St, (ⓣ207/374-3242), can point you in the right direction.

Blue Hill Inn 40 Union St, Blue Hill ⓣ207/374-2844 or 1-800/826-7415, ⓦwww.bluehillinn.com. Romantic 1830 inn with inviting rooms and decor. Guests are treated to outstanding gourmet breakfasts and a tasty evening wine hour. A small apartment, Cape House, is available in winter for

$165 per night, two-night minimum. May to Nov only. ❼–❽

Boyce's Motel 44 Main Street, Stonington ⓣ207/367-2421 or 1-800/224-2421. Centrally located, basic, clean rooms complemented by a very cool owner. They also have full apartments, with kitchens and living rooms, for $540–780 per week. ❸

Deer Isle Homestead Hostel 65 Tennis Rd, Deer Isle ⓣ207/348-2308, ⓦwww.deerislehostel.com. This beautiful hostel, set amidst spruce trees and organic gardens, is slated to open in July 2009. Crafted from scratch by the owners, it's a no-frills lodging, with a woodstove for cooking, solar showers, and an indoor composting toilet; it's also accessible to 3–4 miles of walking trails on the shore and nearby canoeing launch spots. Dorm beds $25 a night.

Inn on the Harbor Main St, Stonington ⓣ1-800/942-2420. Stonington's fanciest (and priciest) place to stay, with beautiful rooms and good amenities (wi-fi, TVs, binoculars) throughout. It also has the best location, with a fine view of the harbor. Breakfast included. ❻–❽

Pres du Port B&B W Main St at Highland Ave, Stonington ⓣ207/367-5007. Brightly wallpapered, whimsically furnished B&B with a great view from the rooftop deck – literally on the peak of the roof. Also has one endearing little room for only $40. No credit cards. June to Oct only. ❷–❺

Blue Hill

Plenty of folks come to **BLUE HILL**, at the intersection of routes 172, 176, and 15 adjacent to the Blue Hill Harbor, simply to relax in the quietude. Still, there are livelier activities available, particularly with the town's bustling music scene – it runs a well-loved chamber music festival every summer (ⓦwww.kneisel.org), in addition to being the "Steel Drum Capital of Downeast Maine" (ⓦwww.peninsulapan.org). The best time to visit is Labor Day weekend (the last weekend in Aug), when oxen pulling, sheep dog trials, fireworks, and carnival rides are all in effect at the Blue Hill Fair ($5; ⓦwww.bluehillfair.com). The fairground was also the basis for the county fair featured in E.B. White's beloved *Charlotte's Web* – White was a longtime resident of the area.

It's a 30 to 45 minute walk up to the top of **Blue Hill Mountain**, from which you can see across the Blue Hill Bay to the dramatic ridges of Mount Desert Island. The trailhead is not difficult to find, halfway down Mountain Road between Rte-15 and Rte-172. South on Rte-175, **Blue Hill Falls** is a good spot to give kayaking a try: the Activity Shop in Blue Hill at no. 61 Rte-172 (ⓣ207/374-3600, ⓦwww.theactivityshop.com) has canoe and kayak rentals that they'll even deliver to your door ($25 a day and up; reservations recommended). In summer, the Marine Environmental Research Institute (**MERI**) at 55 Main St (ⓣ207/374-2135) runs eco-cruises ($40 for adults, $20 for kids) and island excursions ($60 for adults, $40 for kids) where you might spot a seal or pull lobster traps from a people-free shoreline.

Stonington and Isle au Haut

The **Deer Isle** peninsula is one of the most beautiful regions in a state that's known for its beauty. Clear down at the end of Rte-15, it doesn't get much more remote than gorgeous, lies seaside **STONINGTON**, a working fishing village whose residents have long had a reputation for superior seamanship (many pirates and smugglers reputedly made port here in the late nineteenth century). Over the past hundred years, the place has found hard-earned prosperity in the sardine canning and granite quarrying businesses; now it has turned to lobstering. Old Quarry Ocean Adventures (ⓣ207/367-8977, ⓦwww.oldquarry.com) runs excellent kayaking, boating, and camping trips as well as the highly recommended Puffin Boat Trip. For nightlife, the restored, more-than-one-hundred-year-old Opera House (ⓣ207/367-2788, ⓦwww.operahousearts.org) always has something cool to see, be it a jazzfest, Shakespeare performance, or contemporary film.

Mailboats headed for **ISLE AU HAUT** ("I'll ah hoe") depart from the Stonington landing several times daily (ⓣ207/367-5193 or 207/367-6516; $16 single).

On this lonely island, you can explore the trails of the less-visited part of **Acadia National Park** – highlighted by the rocky shoreline, bogs, and dense stands of spruce trees. If you are looking to spend more time here, there is one place to **stay** on the island: the *Inn at Isle au Haut*, an endearing B&B that whisks you up from the ferry dock and transports you the 2.5 miles east to the inn (Ⓣ207/335-5141, Ⓦwww.innatisleauhaut.com; ⑨).

Eating and drinking

There's a lot of good **food** to be had on the peninsula, but keep in mind that distances between towns are deceptively large. The appealing Blue Hill **farmer's market** is held Saturday mornings at the Blue Hill Fairgrounds (Rte-172), on Fridays in summer.

El El Frijoles 41 Caterpillar Hill Rd (Rte-15), Sargentville Ⓣ207/359-2486. Worth visiting for the name alone (it's a riff on "L.L. Bean"), this casual, California-style taqueria serves up wicked good tacos, burritos, and house-made agua fresca. Open Wed–Sat 11am–8pm, breakfast Fri–Sun 8–11am.

Fish Net 162 Main St, Blue Hill Ⓣ207/374-5240. Soft serve ice cream and really good lobster rolls, right in the middle of town.

Harbor Café Main St, Stonington Ⓣ207/367-5099. A salty ambiance – it's where the fishermen come in the morning – with sandwiches, coffee, and muffins; right in the center of town.

Lily's Café and Wine Bar 450 Airport Rd at Rte-15, Stonington Ⓣ207/367-5936. The sunny, bloom-filled gardens welcome you in to this local lunch and breakfast spot where you can munch on fresh sandwiches and home-made soups on tables made from windows. Closed weekends.

The Wescott Forge 66 Main St, Blue Hill Ⓣ207/374-9909. The best of both worlds: fabulous fine dining on a sunny deck and a plush bar that's open late. Lunch is less expensive and just as good; they also have a tasty Sunday brunch.

Mount Desert Island

Considering that five million visitors come to **MOUNT DESERT ISLAND** each year; that it contains most of New England's only national park; and that it boasts not only a genuine fjord but also the highest headland on the entire Atlantic coast north of Rio de Janeiro, it is an astonishingly small place, measuring just sixteen miles by thirteen. It is, of course, simply one among innumerable rugged granite islands along the Maine coast; the reason to come here is that it is the most accessible, linked to the mainland by bridge since 1836, and has the best facilities.

The island was named *Monts Deserts* (bare mountains) by Samuel de Champlain in 1604 and fought over by the French and English for the rest of the century. Although all existing settlements date from long after the final defeat

The Bucksport Observatory

Named after founder Colonel Jonathan Buck, who's buried at the Bucksport Cemetery near the Verona Bridge, quiet yet up-and-coming **BUCKSPORT** was first settled as a trading post in 1762. These days, it's known for its **Penobscot Narrows Observatory** (on the bridge on Rte-1 across from Bucksport, get tickets at nearby Ft Knox on Rte-174; daily 9am–5pm, summer 9am–7pm; $5; Ⓣ207/469-7719), which whisks gleeful viewers up inside a 420-foot viewing station. On a clear day you can see out to Mount Desert Island and Katahdin, but even if it's cloudy, it's still a thrill to look down and see the traffic moving on the bridge 400ft below you.

of the French, the name remains, still pronounced in French (more like *dessert*, actually).

The social center, **Bar Harbor**, has accommodation and restaurants to suit all pocketbooks, while you'll find lower-key communities all over the island. **Acadia National Park**, which covers much of the island, offers active travelers plenty of outdoor opportunities, including camping, cycling, canoeing, kayaking, and birdwatching.

Getting there and getting around

Mount Desert is easy to reach by **car**, traveling along Hwy-3 off Rte-1. In high summer, though, roads on the island get congested – the horse-drawn tours don't help – and the 55 miles from Belfast seem much longer.

There are a number of ways to get around Mount Desert via **public transportation**. Before setting out, check out the excellent Island Explorer services (ⓣ207/667-5796, ⓦwww.exploreacadia.com/guide.html), which include the free **shuttle buses** that travel through Acadia to Bar Harbor, and even out to the airport. Nearby Hancock City/Bar Harbor Airport (ⓣ207/667-7432) has a limited service run by Colgan Air (reservations via US Airways ⓣ1-800/428-4322); Bangor International Airport, 45 miles away, is served by Northwest, Delta, Continental, US Airways Express, and Allegiant Air, and there is a **shuttle**

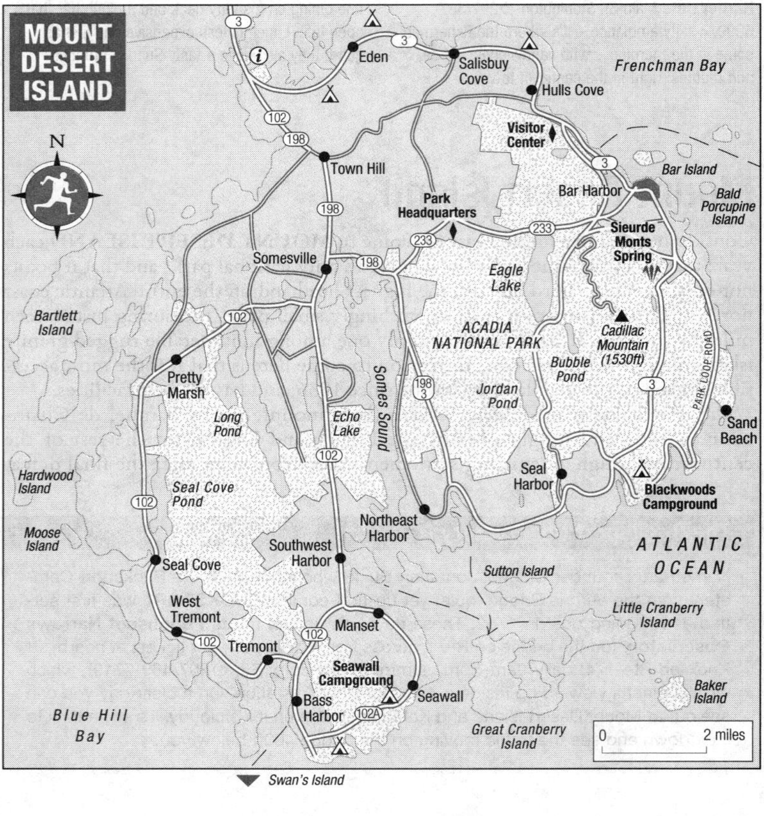

bus that links Bar Harbor and Bangor ($30 and up, cash only; ⓣ207/479-5911). The *Cat* **high-speed catamaran** takes under three hours to link Bar Harbor with Yarmouth, Nova Scotia (June–early Oct $69). For reservations and schedules, contact Bay Ferries (ⓣ1-888/249-7245, ⓦwww.catferry.com).

Accommodation

Hwy-3 into and out of Bar Harbor (which becomes Main Street on the way south) is lined with budget **motels** to satisfy the enormous demand for accommodation. Many places are open May to October only, and rates increase drastically in July and August; anywhere offering sea views will cost a whole lot more, as well. If possible, make your reservations in advance.

Bar Harbor Hostel 321 Main St, Bar Harbor ⓣ207/288-5587, ⓦwww.barharborhostel.com. Clean, safe hostel right near the center of town. Dorm beds $25 a night (linens included), private room $80. They also have three tent platforms for $10 per person.

Coach Stop Inn 715 Acadia Highway, Bar Harbor ⓣ207/288-9886 or 1-800/927-3097, ⓦwww.coachstopinn.com. A Bar Harbor standout with lovely innkeepers, great rooms, and lots of outstanding food – including life-changing blueberry fritters. ❺–❻

Emery's Cottages on the Shore Sand Point Rd, five miles north of Bar Harbor ⓣ207/288-3432 or 1-888/240-3432, ⓦwww.emeryscottages.com. Sweet little cottages with kitchenettes (many with wi-fi) on a private pebble beach just off Hwy-3. Weekly stays in high season cost $550 and up. ❹

Hearthside B&B 7 High St, Bar Harbor ⓣ207/288-4533, ⓦwww.hearthsideinn.com. It has a bit of a frilly look, but guests rave about the stellar innkeepers, cozy rooms, great breakfasts, and proximity to shops and restaurants. ❺–❼

Lindenwood Inn 118 Clark Point Rd, Southwest Harbor ⓣ207/244-5335 or 1-800/307-5335, ⓦwww.lindenwoodinn.com. This first-class inn, built in 1904, offers tastefully decorated rooms and African accents in a stylish former sea captain's home. ❻–❾

Ullikana B&B 16 The Field, Bar Harbor ⓣ207/288-9552, ⓦwww.ullikana.com. Sited on a secluded byway just off Main St, this is the place to go in town for a romantic splurge; nicely decorated rooms and unbelievably sumptuous breakfasts on a terrace overlooking the water. They also own the *Yellow House*, just across the way. ❼–❾

Bar Harbor

The town of **BAR HARBOR** began life as an exclusive resort, summer home to the Vanderbilts and the Astors; the great fire of October 1947 that destroyed their opulent "cottages" changed the direction of the town's growth. It's now firmly geared towards tourists, though it's by no means downmarket.

Bar Harbor's main **tourist information** office is at the ferry terminal (ⓣ207/288-5103). In summer, there's another in the Municipal Building at 93 Cottage Street. Both offices offer many free and comprehensive maps of the area. In high season, up to 21 different **sea trips** set off each day, ranging from deep-sea fishing to cocktail cruises. Among the most popular are the **whale-watching,** puffin, and seal cruises offered by Bar Harbor Whale Watch Company, 1 West St (June–Oct at least twice daily; ⓣ207/288-2386, ⓦwww.barharborwhales.com), and the two-hour cruises on the impressive **four-masted schooner** *Margaret Todd* from the *Bar Harbor Inn* (daily June–Oct; $32; ⓣ207/288-4585, ⓦwww.downeastwindjammer.com). Lulu Lobster Boat Rides ($27; ⓣ207/963-2341, ⓦwww.lululobsterboat.com) offers authentic **lobstering** trips where Captain John raises his lobstering traps and woos riders with seafaring folklore and lighthouse sightings.

The native Wapanaki heritage is preserved in the Robert **Abbe Museum**, 26 Mount Desert St (mid-May to Oct daily 10am–6pm; rest of year Thurs–Sat 10am–4pm; $6, admission includes entrance to the original Sieur de Monts location; ⓣ207/288-3519, ⓦwww.abbemuseum.org), which has gorgeously constructed exhibit spaces full of light and pale wood panelling. Although the opening displays on Wapanaki culture are well put together, the Abbe's knockout piece is the "Circle of the Four Directions," a contemplative, circular space built of cedar panels. The museum even has an original piece from glass wizard Dale Chihuly, his personal gift to the museum. The museum's original location, just off Park Loop Road, relates the history of the institution and is included in the admission price (daily mid-May to mid-Oct 9am–4pm).

Acadia National Park

ACADIA NATIONAL PARK, sprawled out over most of Mount Desert Island, the Schoodic Peninsula to the east, and Isle au Haut to the south, is the most visited natural place in Maine. It's visually stunning, with all you could want in terms of mountains and lakes for secluded rambling, and **wildlife** such as seals, beavers, and bald eagles. The two main geographical features are the narrow fjord of **Somes Sound**, which almost splits the island in two, and lovely **Cadillac Mountain**, 1530ft high, which offers tremendous ocean views. The summit can be reached either by a moderately strenuous climb or by a very leisurely drive, winding up a low-gradient road.

Open all year, the park has the Hulls Cove **visitor center** near the entrance to the Loop Road north of Bar Harbor (mid-April to Oct daily 8am–4.30pm, open until 6pm July & Aug; Ⓣ207/288-3338), and its headquarters at Eagle Lake (daily 8am–4.30pm; same number as above). The entrance fee is $20 per vehicle or $5 per motorcycle or bike; good for seven days. There are two official **campgrounds**: *Blackwoods*, five miles south of Bar Harbor, off Rte-3 (reserve through the National Park Service at Ⓣ1–800/365-2267 or Ⓦwww.reservations.nps.gov; $20 per tentsite), and *Seawall* on Hwy-102A, four miles south of Southwest Harbor (Ⓣ207/288-3338; tentsites $14–20). Both are in woods, near the ocean, and have full facilities in summer; only *Blackwoods* is open in winter, with minimal facilities.

Once here, the free Island Explorer (Ⓦwww.exploreacadia.com) **shuttle buses** travel through Acadia to Bar Harbor. However, the most enjoyable way to explore the park is to ride a rented **bicycle** around the fifty miles of gravel-surfaced "**carriage roads**," built by John D. Rockefeller to protest the 1913 vote allowing "infernal combustion engines" onto the island. Three Bar Harbor companies rent mountain bikes at less than $30 a day: Bar Harbor Bicycle Shop, at 141 Cottage St, on the edge of town (Ⓣ207/288-3886), Acadia Bike & Canoe, across from the post office at 48 Cottage St (Ⓣ1-800/526-8615), and Southwest Cycle, on Main Street in Southwest Harbor (Ⓣ207/244-5856). All outlets provide excellent **maps**. Be sure to carry water, as there are very few refreshment stops inside the park. You can take a 4hr guided **kayak tour** ($48) from mid-May to mid-October with National Park Sea Kayak Tours, 39 Cottage St (Ⓣ1-800/347-0940, Ⓦwww.acadiakayak.com). Another popular tour operator, Coastal Kayaking Tours (Ⓣ207/288-9605, Ⓦwww.acadiafun.com), has the same location as Acadia Bike.

The one and only sizeable beach, five miles south of Bar Harbor, is a stunner: called simply **Sand Beach**, it's a gorgeous strand bounded by twin headlands, with restrooms, a parking lot, and a few short hiking trails. The water, sadly, is usually arctic.

Eating, drinking, and nightlife

Mount Desert's most memorable **eating** experiences are to be found near the many **lobster pounds** all over the island. For nightlife (such as it is), Bar Harbor is where the people are. Cottage Street is a much more promising area to look for food and evening atmosphere than the surprisingly subdued waterfront. The Art Deco **Criterion cinema** at 35 Cottage St (Ⓣ207/288-3441) shows current films, while ImprovAcadia at 15 Cottage St, 2nd floor ($15; Ⓣ207/288-2503) has nightly comedy shows in summer.

Beal's Lobster Pier 182 Clark Point Rd, Southwest Harbor ☎207/244-7178. Fresh seafood for under $10, on a rickety wooden pier. You can pick out your own lobster from a tank, or choose from a small menu of other seafood choices.

Café This Way 14 ½ Mt Desert St, Bar Harbor ☎207/288-4483. Fresh, creative breakfast options like the café Monte Cristo (a French toast sandwich with eggs, ham, cheddar cheese, and syrup on the side). Very busy in summer. They also serve dinner.

Eden 78 West St, Bar Harbor ☎207/288-4422. A well-loved dinner spot with inventive, international vegetarian fare and an emphasis on organic, locally-grown produce.

Havana 318 Main St, Bar Harbor ☎207/288-CUBA. American dining with a Latin sensibility, which translates into dishes like lemon and cilantro cured local salmon. Cool modern ambiance, sometimes with low-key live music.

Jordan Pond Park Loop Rd, Acadia National Park ☎207/276-3316. Light meals, ice cream, and popovers (light, puffy egg muffins). Afternoon tea, a longtime Acadia tradition, is served in the beautiful lakeside garden from 11.30am–5.30pm; reservations recommended.

Lompoc Café & Brewpub 36 Rodick St, Bar Harbor ☎207/288-9392. A healthy Middle Eastern menu for $14–20, with local Bar Harbor Blueberry Ale and other Atlantic Brewing Company beers on draft, complemented by a woodsy outdoor dining area and bocce ball court. Live music every Fri and Sat night, Open 11.30am–1am.

Maggie's Restaurant 6 Summer St, Bar Harbor ☎207/288-9007. In a little blue house away from downtown, Maggie's serves locally-fresh, well-composed seafood entrees such as lobster crêpes and salmon with cucumber mint salsa. Closed Sun.

Morning Glory Bakery 39 Rodick St, Bar Harbor ☎207/288-3041. Fabulous fresh-baked breads, coffee, and pastries served at a purple-trimmed cottage. Good lunch options, too. Closed Sun.

XYZ Restaurant end of Bennett Lane, off of Seawall Rd (Rte 102-A), Manset ☎207/244-5221. Slamming, legitimate Mexican entrees served in a bright, folk-artsy interior that will make you long for the southlands. Reservations (as well as the margaritas) are strongly recommended, dinner only, closed Sun.

Downeast Maine: the coast to Canada

Few travelers venture into the hundred miles of Maine lying east beyond Acadia National Park, mainly because it is almost entirely unpopulated, windswept, and remote. In summer, though, the weather is marked by mesmerizing fogs, and the coastal drive is exhilarating – it runs next to the Bay of Fundy, home to the highest tides in the nation. **Downeast Maine** is also marked by its wild **blueberry** crops – ninety percent of the nation's harvest comes from this corner of the state.

A short way northeast of Acadia, a loop road leads from Rte-1 to the rocky outcrop of **Schoodic Point**, which offers good birdwatching, great views, and a splendid sense of solitude. Each village has one or two B&Bs and well-priced restaurants. **MACHIAS**, almost forty miles further once you rejoin Rte-1 at Gouldsboro, is quite picturesque, with a little waterfall right in the middle of town. The town was the unlikely scene of the first naval battle of the Revolutionary War, in 1775: the townsfolk commandeered the British schooner *Margaretta* and proceeded to terrorize all passing British shipping, an attack they planned in the still-standing, gambrel-roofed **Burnham Tavern** on Rte-192, just off Rte-1 (mid-June to early Sept Mon–Fri 9.30am–4pm; $2.50; ☎207/255-6930). Perhaps the best place to **eat** in town is the *Artist's Café*, 3 Hill St (☎207/255-8900), with its moderately priced and frequently changing menu; chicken parmesan and lobster linguini are typical offerings. Meals are also good at the bluesy and fresh *Fat Cat Deli*, 50 Main St (Rte-1) (☎207/255-6777), and you have to try the blueberry pie from Maine landmark *Helen's*, 28 E Main St (Rte-1) (☎207/255-8433). Run by the owners of *Helen's*, The *Inn at Schoppee Farm*, Rte-1 in Machias (☎207/255-4648, Ⓦwww.schoppeefarm.com; ❺–❾), overlooks the Machias River and has two beautiful rooms as well as a family-sized guesthouse set in a restored barn.

West Quoddy Head and around

With a distinctive, candy-striped **lighthouse** dramatically signaling its endpoint, **WEST QUODDY HEAD** is the easternmost point of the US, jutting defiantly into the stormy Atlantic. Just beyond the turnoff for Quoddy Head, tiny **LUBEC** was once home to more than twenty sardine-packing plants. They're all gone now, but the restored McCurdy's Fish Company, on Water Street, now gives lively tours ($3); you might spot a seal as you stroll the main drag. Lubec also hosts the dynamic adult music summer camp The Summer Keys (Ⓦwww.summerkeys.com) and is the gateway to **Campobello Island**, in New Brunswick, Canada, where President Franklin D. Roosevelt summered from 1909 to 1921, and to which he occasionally returned during his presidency. His barn-red cottage (mid-May to mid-Oct daily 9am–5pm; free) is now open to the public, furnished just as the Roosevelts left it – although keep in mind you will need a birth certificate or valid passport to make the border crossing. The rest of **Roosevelt Campobello International Park** (daily sunrise–sunset; free; Ⓦwww.fdr.net), located on Canadian soil but established jointly with the United States, is good for a couple of hours of wandering – the coastal trails and the drive out to **Liberty Point** are worth the effort. The *Peacock House*, 27 Summer St (Ⓣ207/733-2403, Ⓦwww.peacockhouse.com; ❹–❻) is a fantastic place to **stay**; it offers friendly B&B accommodations with stylish yet cozy furnishings.

The border between the United States and Canada weaves through the center of Passamaquoddy Bay; the towns to either side get on so well that they refused to fight against each other in the War of 1812, and promote themselves jointly to tourists as the **Quoddy Loop** (Ⓦwww.quoddyloop.com). It's perfectly feasible to take a "two-nation vacation," but each passage through customs and immigration between **Calais** (pronounced "callous") in the States (fifty miles north of Lubec) and **St Stephen** in Canada does take a little while – and be aware, also, that the towns are in different time zones. If you have the driving stamina, **Eastport**, some forty miles up the road, is one of the coolest places you'll ever see, with an edge-of-the-earth seaside feel and unbelievable views of the Canadian shoreline. Eastport has some good **eats**, particularly at the *Pickled Herring* 32 Water St (Ⓣ207/853-2323) and the *Eastport Chowderhouse*, 169 Water St (Ⓣ207/853-4700). *Katie's on the Cove* (Ⓣ207/454-8446), a Maine institution north of town on Rte-1, doles out unbelievably good confections from a little canary-yellow house. *The Commons*, 51 Water St (Ⓣ207/853-4123, Ⓦwww.thecommonseastport.com; weekly rentals $700 per week, sometimes they'll do a shorter stay for you if it's not filled up) offers two inviting, year-round suites above an art gallery, and is one of the best **stays** in Maine; each comes with two bedrooms, a kitchen, dining room, internet access, laundry, and a front porch with barbecue set-up and jaw-dropping views of the harbor and into Canada.

Inland and western Maine

The vast expanses of the **Maine interior**, stretching up into the cold far north, consist mostly of evergreen forests of pine, spruce, and fir, interspersed with the white birches and maples responsible for the spectacular fall colors.

Distances here are large. Once you get away from the two largest cities – **Augusta** and **Bangor** – it's roughly two hundred miles by road to the northern border at **Fort Kent**, while to drive between the two most likely inland bases, **Greenville** and **Rangeley**, takes three hours or more. Driving (there's no public transportation) through this mountainous scenery can be a great pleasure – it smells like

Christmas trees as you go – but be aware that beyond Millinocket many roads are tolled access routes belonging to the lumber companies: gravel-surfaced, vulnerable to bad weather, and in any case often not heading anywhere in particular.

This is great territory in which to **hike** – the **Appalachian Trail** culminates its two thousand-mile course up from Georgia at the top of Mount Katahdin, and in August you'll often run into hikers celebrating with champagne at the terminus – or raft on the **Allagash Wilderness Waterway**. Especially around **Baxter State Park**, the forests are home to deer, beaver, a few bears, some recently introduced caribou – and plenty of **moose**. These endearingly gawky creatures are virtually blind and tend to be seen at early morning or dusk; you may spot them feeding in shallow water. They can cause major havoc on the roads, particularly at night, and each year several drivers (and moose) are killed in collisions.

Baxter State Park and the far north

Driving through northern Maine can feel as though you're trespassing on the private fiefdoms of the logging companies; only **Baxter State Park** is public land. However, you're pretty much free to hike, camp, and explore anywhere you like, so long as you let people know what you're doing.

About seventy miles from Bangor, **MILLINOCKET** is a genuine company town, built on a wilderness site by the Great Northern Paper Company in 1899–1900. The hundred-year-old manufacturing facilities still churn out nearly twenty-percent of the newsprint produced in the United States.

Next to **Millinocket Lake**, ten miles northwest, the splendidly ramshackle old *Big Moose Inn* (Ⓣ207/723-8391, Ⓦwww.bigmoosecabins.com; ❷) makes a great place to stay, with cabins and an inn, and a wide range of activities. There's also an adjacent campground ($10 per person). A more standard place to stay is the jacuzzi-enhanced *America's Best Value Heritage Inn,* 935 Central St (Rte-11) (Ⓣ207/723-9777, Ⓦwww.heritageinnmaine.com; ❹), or the clean *Gateway Inn*, Rte-11/157 just off I-95 at the Medway exit (Ⓣ207/746-3193, Ⓦwww.medwaygateway.com; ❸), where many rooms have decks with views of Katahdin. New England Outdoor Center (Ⓣ1-800/766-7238, Ⓦwww.neoc.com) conducts day **rafting** and **canoeing** expeditions, as well as "**moose safaris**" and snowmobile vacations and rentals, according to the season. For **food**, head over to the *Appalachian Trail Café,* 210 Penobscot Ave, (Ⓣ207/723-6720) for a hot meal before heading into the park.

By now you're approaching the southern end of sprawling (200,000 acres) and unspoiled **BAXTER STATE PARK** (Ⓣ207/723-5140; $13 per car) itself. On a clear day the 5268ft peak of **Katahdin** (or "greatest mountain," in the language of the local Penobscot tribe) is visible from afar. The area's **chamber of commerce** resides in Millinocket at 1029 Central St (Rte-11/157) (Ⓣ207/723-4443, Ⓦwww.katahdinmaine.com); the **Baxter State Park Authority** is at 64 Balsam Drive next to *McDonald's* (Ⓣ207/723-5140).

North to Canada

The northernmost tip of Maine is taken up by Aroostook County, which covers an area larger than several individual states. Although its main activity is the large-scale cultivation of potatoes, it is also the location of the **Allagash Wilderness Waterway**; this is where most of the **whitewater rafting** companies in this area actually carry out their expeditions. Raft Maine (Ⓣ1-800/723-8633, Ⓦwww.raftmaine.com) is an association comprised of several outfitters and can help get you out on the water.

Britain and the United States all but went to war over Aroostook in 1839; at **Fort Kent**, the northern terminus of Rte-1 (which runs all the way from Key

West, Florida), the main sight is the solid cedar **Fort Kent Blockhouse**, built to defend American integrity and looking like a throwback to pioneer days. People come from all around to eat at *Eureka Hall* (33 miles south, off Rte-161 in Stockholm, ⓣ207/896-3196), an institution of Aroostook County that serves up homestyle meals and incredible desserts.

Greenville

GREENVILLE, at the southern end of Moosehead Lake, is quite pretty and quite small and well positioned for exploring the Maine woods. The main attraction is the lake – an enormous ink blot of serenity that looks silver at night. You can get out on the water via the restored **steamboat** *Katahdin*, which tours the lake and serves as a floating Marine Museum exhibit – but watch out ladies, no high heels or smoking on the ship (call for cruise times; $30–35; ⓣ207/695-2716).

The **Chamber of Commerce,** just south of town on Rte-6/15 (Mon–Sat 10am–4pm; ⓣ207/695-2702, ⓦwww.greenvilleme.com), has details on **accommodation**, including the lovely *Pleasant Street Inn,* 26 Pleasant St (ⓣ207/695-3400, ⓦwww.pleasantstinn.com; ❺–❼), or the almost unbelievably well-appointed *Blair Hill Inn*, 351 Lily Bay Rd (ⓣ207/695-0224, ⓦwww.blairhill.com; ❾ and up) complete with lavish rooms, fabulous views of the lake, incredible fine dining (lit with original Tiffany lamps), and even an excellent summer concert series. Among local **rafting** companies, which charge $80–135 for a day in the water, is Wilderness Expeditions (ⓣ1-800/825-WILD), associated with the *Birches Resort* in North Rockwood (ⓣ207/268-4330), where you can stay in the main lodge (❹–❺), a cabin (❼–❾), or a yurt (❷). For **food**, head to the *Rod-N-Reel* (ⓣ207/695-0388) at 77 Pritham Avenue for fresh fish entrees on an outdoor patio, or the *Stress Free Moose Pub & Café* (ⓣ207/695-3100), at 65 Moosehead Lake Rd, for tasty pub grub and good beers on tap.

Moose are indigenous to the area and there is nary a business around here that doesn't somehow incorporate the animal into its name. For several weeks in June, there's even an annual celebration, creatively named MooseMainea (call ⓣ207/695-2702 for more information). The town is also the largest **seaplane** base in New England; contact Currier's Flying Service (ⓣ207/695-2778) or Jack's Air Service (ⓣ207/695-3020) for scenic tours over the lake.

Rangeley

RANGELEY is only just in Maine, a little way east of New Hampshire and an even shorter distance south of the border with Québec. Furthermore, as the sign on Main Street boldly declares, it's equidistant (at 3107.5 miles) from the North Pole and the Equator. That doesn't mean it's on the main road to anywhere, although if you're avoiding the coast altogether you can get here direct from the northern side of the White Mountains via Rte-17 – one of the prettiest drives in the state. It has always been a resort, served in 1900 by two train lines and several steamships (though now you have to get here on your own), with the main attraction then being the fishing in the spectacularly named Mooselookmeguntic Lake.

This small and very cozy one-street town, nestling amid a complex system of lakes and waterways, serves as a base for summer explorations, and in winter as the nearest town to the **ski** area at **Saddleback Mountain**. Rangeley also has one unlikely tourist attraction, on Dodge Pond Road, about halfway along the north side of Rangeley Lake, a mile up a side track off Rte-16. The remote **Wilhelm Reich Museum** (July & Aug Wed–Sun 1–5pm; Sept Sun 1–5pm; $6; ⓣ207/864-3443) is where Wilhelm Reich eventually made his American home after fleeing Germany in 1933. An associate of Sigmund Freud and author of the acclaimed

Mass Psychology of Fascism, Reich is best remembered for developing the orgone energy accumulator, which he claimed could concentrate atmospheric energy; skeptical authorities focused on the rather unspecific way in which it was said to collect and harness human sexual energy. He is buried here, amid the neat lawns and darting hummingbirds, and his house remains a museum for the reflection of his work.

Practicalities

The *Rangeley Inn,* at 343 Main St (ⓣ207/864-3341, ⓦwww.rangeleyinn.com; ④), stands between Rangeley Lake and the smaller bird sanctuary of Haley Pond, so you can stay right in town and have a room that backs onto a scene of utter tranquility; there's also a gorgeous old wooden dining room. *Pleasant Street Inn*, at 104 Pleasant St (ⓣ207/864-5916, ⓦwww.pleasantstreetinnbb.com; ⑥), is a great second choice – ask for Room #5. For **food**, head to *The Shed*, 2647 Main St (Thurs–Sun, ⓣ207/864-2277), where pit boss Martin gets up at stupid o' clock to smoke his excellent pulled pork and ribs – "it's done when it's ready." The best food in the area is at the *Porterhouse Restaurant*, in Eustis (take Rte-16E to Rte-27N, it's four miles up on Rte-27N ⓣ207/246-7932). Set in a 1908 farmhouse, they offer exquisitely prepared entrees and an award-winning wine list.

Just south of the *Porterhouse,* on Eustis Road, is the pretty *Cathedral Pines* **campground** (ⓣ207/246-3491; $22 per site). Twenty miles north of Rangeley, the peaceful *Grant's Kennebago Camps* beside Kennebago Lake (ⓣ1-800/633-4815) arranges fly fishing, canoeing, and windsurfing, with accommodation in comfortable cabins, including all meals, costing around $185 per person per day; there are slightly lower weekly rates. Rangeley Lakes' **Chamber of Commerce**, down by Lakeside Park (ⓣ207/864-5364 or 1-800/MT-LAKES, ⓦwww.rangeleymaine.com), has details of various activities, including snowmobiling and dawn moose-watching **canoeing** expeditions.

4

The Great Lakes

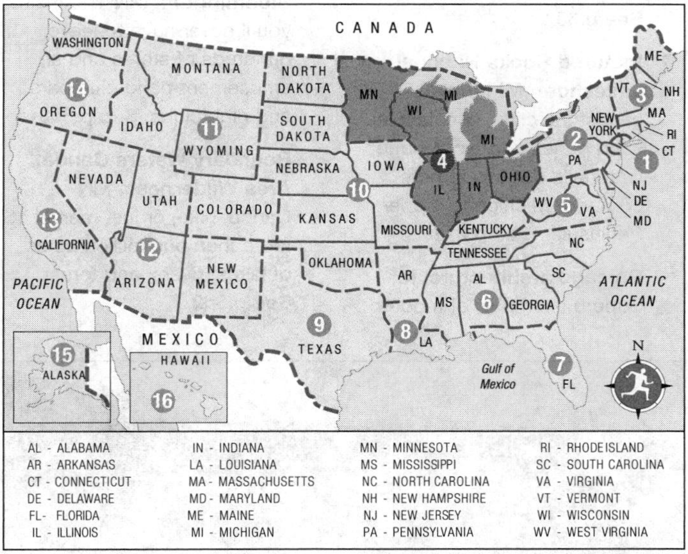

AL - ALABAMA	IN - INDIANA	MN - MINNESOTA	RI - RHODE ISLAND
AR - ARKANSAS	LA - LOUISIANA	MS - MISSISSIPPI	SC - SOUTH CAROLINA
CT - CONNECTICUT	MA - MASSACHUSETTS	NC - NORTH CAROLINA	VA - VIRGINIA
DE - DELAWARE	MD - MARYLAND	NH - NEW HAMPSHIRE	VT - VERMONT
FL - FLORIDA	ME - MAINE	NJ - NEW JERSEY	WI - WISCONSIN
IL - ILLINOIS	MI - MICHIGAN	PA - PENNSYLVANIA	WV - WEST VIRGINIA

CHAPTER 4 Highlights

- **Rock and Roll Hall of Fame and Museum, Cleveland, OH** From rockabilly to Motown to punk – it's all here inside this striking museum. See p.281
- **The Henry Ford Museum, Detroit, MI** Home to such oddities as the car JFK was riding in when he was shot. See p.302
- **Pictured Rocks National Lakeshore, MI** Multi-hued sandstone cliffs, spectacular sand dunes and picuresque waterfalls dot this remote corner of Michigan's Upper Peninsula. See p.311
- **Chicago architecture, IL** Superb examples of modern architecture make up the city's distinctive skyline. See p.319
- **Wrigley Field, Chicago, IL** Soak in the sun with a cold beer and a hot dog at this storied ivy-covered ballpark. See p.332
- **The Mall of America, Bloomington, MN** The mall you'll never have to leave: hundreds of stores and an amusement park, plus bars and nightclubs. See p.358
- **Boundary Waters Canoe Area Wilderness, MN** Canoe, hike, or just marvel at more than one million acres of lakes, rivers, and forest. See p.362

▲ Boundary Waters Canoe Area Wilderness

4

The Great Lakes

Swept by tumultuous storms and traversed by fleets of ocean-going tankers, the interconnected **Great Lakes** form the largest body of fresh water in the world; Lake Superior alone is more than three hundred miles from east to west. The shores of these inland seas can rival any coastline: Superior and the northern reaches of Lake Michigan offer stunning rocky peninsulas, craggy cliffs, tree-covered islands, mammoth dunes, and deserted beaches. However, for lengthy stretches along Lake Erie, and the bottom lips of lakes Michigan and Huron, sluggish waters lap against large cities and decaying ports.

To varying degrees, the principal states that line the American side of the lakes – **Ohio**, **Michigan**, **Indiana**, **Illinois**, **Wisconsin**, and **Minnesota** – share this mixture of natural beauty and aging industry. Cities such as **Chicago** and **Detroit**, for all their pros and cons, do not characterize the entire region, although the former's magnificent architecture, museums, music, and restaurants make it an unmissable destination. Within the first hundred miles or so of the lakeshores, especially in Wisconsin and Minnesota, tens of thousands of smaller lakes and tumbling streams are scattered through a luxuriant rural wilderness; beyond that, you are soon in the heart of the **Corn Belt**, where you can drive for hours and encounter nothing more than a succession of crossroads communities, grain silos, and giant barns.

Some history

The first foreigner to reach the Great Lakes, the French explorer Champlain, found the region in 1603 inhabited mostly by tribes of Huron, Iroquois, and Algonquin. France soon established a network of military forts, Jesuit missions, and fur-trading posts here, which entailed treating the native people as allies rather than subjects. After the **French and Indian War** with Britain from 1754 to 1761, however, the victorious British felt under no constraints to deal equitably with the Native Americans, and things grew worse with large-scale American settlement after independence. The **Black Hawk War** of 1832 put a bloody end to traditional Native American life.

Settlers from the east were followed to Wisconsin and Minnesota by waves of **Scandinavians** and **Germans**, while the lower halves of Illinois and Indiana attracted **Southerners**, who attempted to maintain slavery here and resisted Union conscription during the Civil War. These areas still have more in common with neighboring Kentucky and Tennessee than with the industrial cities of their own states.

The impetus given to **industry** by the Civil War was encouraged by abundant supplies of ores and fuel, as well as efficient transportation by water and rail. As lakeshore cities like Chicago, Detroit, and Cleveland grew, their populations

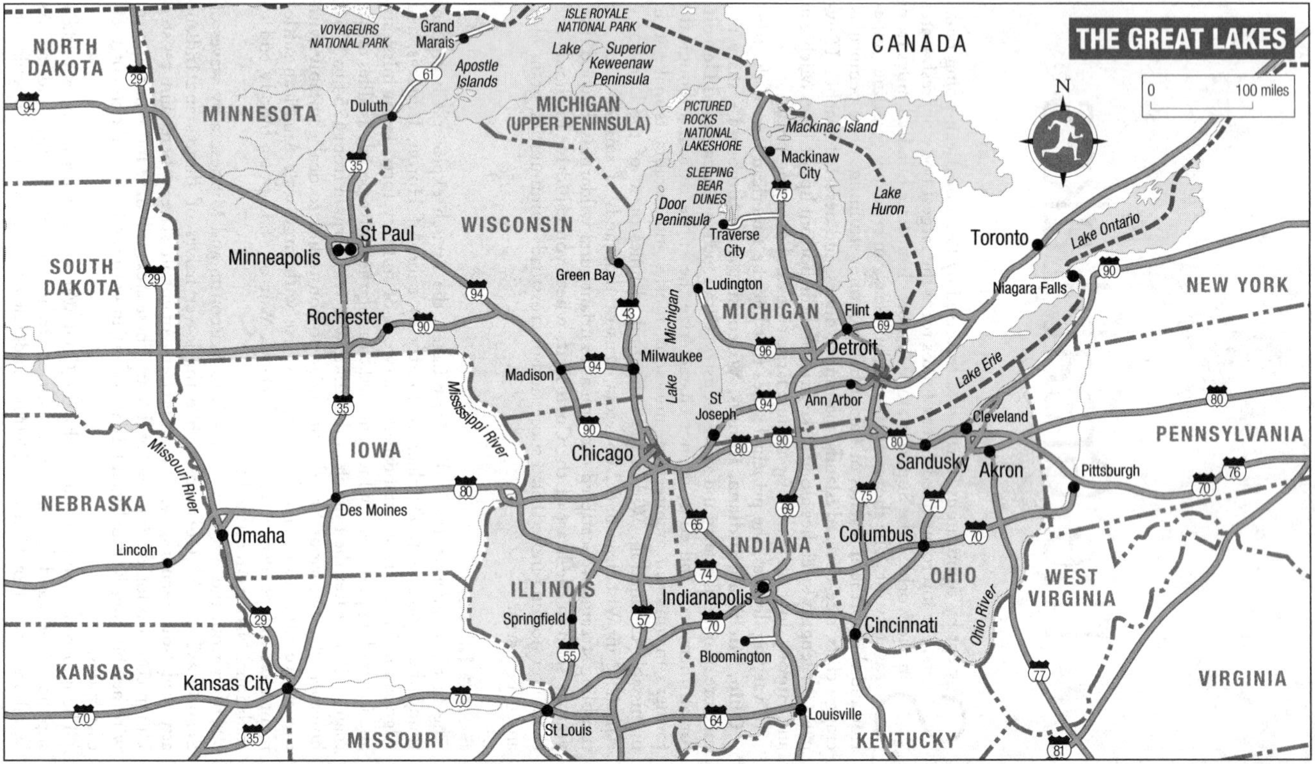
THE GREAT LAKES
0 100 miles
N
CANADA
NORTH DAKOTA
SOUTH DAKOTA
NEBRASKA
KANSAS
MINNESOTA
IOWA
MISSOURI
WISCONSIN
MICHIGAN (UPPER PENINSULA)
MICHIGAN
ILLINOIS
INDIANA
OHIO
KENTUCKY
WEST VIRGINIA
VIRGINIA
PENNSYLVANIA
NEW YORK
VOYAGEURS NATIONAL PARK
ISLE ROYALE NATIONAL PARK
Lake Superior
Keweenaw Peninsula
Apostle Islands
Grand Marais
Duluth
PICTURED ROCKS NATIONAL LAKESHORE
SLEEPING BEAR DUNES
Door Peninsula
Mackinac Island
Mackinaw City
Lake Huron
Lake Michigan
Lake Ontario
Lake Erie
Toronto
Niagara Falls
Traverse City
Ludington
Green Bay
St Paul
Minneapolis
Rochester
Madison
Milwaukee
Flint
Detroit
Ann Arbor
St Joseph
Chicago
Cleveland
Sandusky
Akron
Pittsburgh
Des Moines
Omaha
Lincoln
Kansas City
Indianapolis
Columbus
Springfield
Cincinnati
Bloomington
Louisville
St Louis
Mississippi River
Missouri River
Ohio River
94
29
61
35
90
43
69
96
75
94
80
65
74
57
55
70
64
71
76
77
81

Great Lakes' climate

During the summer, breezes coming off the Great Lakes keep the **temperature** down to a comfortable average of 70°F, though heat waves can push temperatures over 100°F. Even in spring and fall, **freezing** occurs in the northern reaches of the region, where winter readings of 50°F are not uncommon, and parts of the lakes are frozen solid.

swelled with hundreds of thousands of poor blacks who migrated from the Deep South in search of jobs. But a lack of planning, inadequate housing, and mass layoffs at times of low demand bred conditions that led to the riots of the late 1960s and continuing inner-city deprivation. Depression in the 1970s ravaged the economy – especially the **automobile** industry, on which so much else depended – and gave the area the unwanted title of "**Rust Belt**." Since then, cities such as **Cleveland** have revived their fortunes to some degree, although the current economic crisis has hit the region especially hard.

Ohio

OHIO, the easternmost of the Great Lakes states, lies to the south of shallow Lake Erie. This is one of the nation's most industrialized regions, but the industry is largely concentrated in the east, near the Ohio River. To the south the landscape becomes less populated and more forested.

Enigmatic traces of Ohio's earliest inhabitants exist at the **Great Serpent Mound**, a grassy state park sixty miles east of Cincinnati, where a cleared hilltop high above a river was reshaped to look like a giant snake swallowing an egg, possibly by the Adena Indians around 800 BC. When the French claimed the area in 1699, it was inhabited by the **Iroquois**, in whose language Ohio means "something great." In the eighteenth century, the territory's prime position between Lake Erie and the Ohio River made it the subject of fierce contention between the French and British. Once the British acquired control of most land east of the Mississippi, settlers from New England began to establish communities along both the Ohio River and the Iroquois War Trail paths on the shores of the lake.

During the Civil War, Ohio was at the forefront of the struggle, producing two great Union generals, **Ulysses Grant** and **William Tecumseh Sherman**, and sending more than twice its quota of volunteers to fight for the North. Its progress thereafter has followed the classic "Rust Belt" pattern: rapid industrialization, aided by its natural resources and crucial location, followed by 1970s post-industrial gloom and a period of steady revitalization that has been stopped in its tracks by the current credit crunch.

Although the state is dominated by its triumvirate of "C" towns (**Cleveland**, **Columbus**, and **Cincinnati**), the **Lake Erie Islands** are its most visited holiday destination, attracting thousands of partying mainlanders. Cincinnati and Cleveland have both undergone major face-lifts and are surprisingly attractive, as is the comparatively unassuming state capital of Columbus.

Getting around Ohio

Amtrak **trains** between New York or Washington in the east and Chicago to the west stop at either Cincinnati or Cleveland and Toledo. Ohio is well served by Greyhound **buses**, and there are major **airports** at Cleveland and Cincinnati. I-71 is the major interstate linking Cincinnati, Columbus, and Cleveland, while I-70 bisects the state from west to east, passing through Columbus as well. The 325-mile Ohio to Erie **biking trail** (Ⓦwww.ohiotoerietrail.org), following former railroad and canal routes, is slowly nearing completion; when finished, it will link the three "C" towns.

Cleveland and around

Today, the great industrial port of **CLEVELAND** – for so long the butt of jokes after the heavily polluted Cuyahoga River caught fire in 1969 – is no longer the "Mistake on the Lake." Although the path back from acute recession is by no means complete on a city-wide basis, areas like **the Warehouse District, East Fourth Street**, and **University Circle** are now hubs of energy. Cleveland boasts a sensitive restoration of the Lake Erie and Cuyahoga River waterfront, a superb constellation of museums, a growing culinary scene, and new downtown super-stadiums. Add to that the now well-established **Rock and Roll Hall of Fame** and there's an unmistakable buzz about the place.

Founded in 1796, thirty years later Cleveland profited greatly from the opening of the **Ohio Canal** between the Ohio River and Lake Erie. During the city's heyday, which began with the Civil War and lasted until the 1920s, its vast iron and coal supplies made it one of the most important **steel** and **shipbuilding centers** in the world. **John D. Rockefeller** made his billions here, as did the many others whose restored old mansions line "Millionaires' Row." West of the city lie the quaint lakeshore community of **Vermilion** and tiny college sanctuary of **Oberlin**, while way to the south **Holmes County** has a huge Amish population.

Arrival, information, and getting around

Cleveland Hopkins International Airport is ten miles southwest of downtown. The twenty-minute **taxi** ride into town costs around $20, but the Regional Transit Authority (RTA; Ⓣ216/621-9500, Ⓦwww.gcrta.org) **train** is only $1.75 and takes just ten minutes longer. Greyhound arrives at 1465 Chester Ave, at the back of Playhouse Square, while the Amtrak station is on the lakefront at 200 Cleveland Memorial Shoreway NE.

Maps and **information** can be ordered or picked up from **Positively Cleveland**, suite 100, 100 Public Square (summer daily 9am–5pm, rest of year Mon–Fri 9am–5pm; Ⓣ216/875-6680 or 1-800/321-1001, Ⓦwww.positivelycleveland.com); or try the booth on the baggage level of the airport (hours vary).

Cleveland is generally safe, though its size makes getting around easiest by **car**. The RTA runs an efficient **bus** service ($1.75 single or $3.50 for an unlimited day-pass) and a small train line ($1.75), known locally as "the Rapids," until about 12.30am. A **light rail** system – the Waterfront Line – connects Terminal Tower, the Flats, the Rock and Roll Hall of Fame, and other downtown sights (every 15min 6.15am– midnight; $1.75).

Accommodation

Travelers without cars in Cleveland tend to stay at the downtown **hotels**, which include some reasonable deals – most offer packages that include admission to the

Rock and Roll Hall of Fame or other attractions. **B&Bs** can be booked through Ⓦwww.positivelycleveland.com or Ⓦwww.bedandbreakfast.com/cleveland.

Comfort Inn Downtown 1800 Euclid Ave Ⓣ216/861-0001, Ⓦwww.comfortinn.com. This chain hotel is on the edge of downtown, a fair walk from most bars and restaurants but with some of the best rates around. ❹

Glidden House 1901 Ford Drive Ⓣ216/231-8900 or 1-800/759-8358, Ⓦwww.gliddenhouse.com. Sixty rooms are housed in a Gothic mansion situated in University Circle. Large continental breakfast is included. ❻

Holiday Inn Select City Center Lakeshore 1111 Lakeside Ave Ⓣ216/241-5100 or 1-888/425-3835, Ⓦwww.holiday-inn.com. Unbeatable online rates, great lake views, and proximity to the Rock and Roll Hall of Fame make this an excellent choice. ❸

Hyatt Regency at The Arcade 420 Superior Ave, University Circle Ⓣ216/575-1234, Ⓦwww.cleveland.hyatt.com. Set behind the imposing facade of The Arcade, a historic landmark, this hotel provides all the usual upscale comforts and services. ❻

Wyndham Cleveland at Playhouse Square 1260 Euclid Ave Ⓣ216/615-7500 or 1-800/996-3426, Ⓦwww.wyndham.com. The best option in the downtown theater district, Playhouse Square, providing luxury accommodations at mid-range prices. ❺

The City

The main streets in Cleveland lead to the stately nineteenth-century Beaux Arts **Public Square**, at the very center of downtown, and dominated in its southwestern corner by the landmark **Terminal Tower**. **Ontario Street**, which runs north–south through the Square, divides the city into east and west. Cleveland's most interesting areas are at two opposite ends of the spectrum: the revived industrial romance of the **Flats** and **Warehouse District** in the northwest, and the cultural institutions of **University Circle**, east of the river.

Downtown and around

Downtown Cleveland is once again a bustling place, and its recent redevelopment has seen the emergence of several distinct subsections. In its traditional heart, among the banks and corporate headquarters, stand a couple of glamorous shopping malls. One, the **Avenue at Tower City**, is located in the Terminal Tower. Another, the **Arcade**, is a skylit hall built in 1890. Twelve blocks away, at 1501 Euclid Ave, the **Playhouse Square** (see p.285) is an impressive complex of four renovated old theaters; the small Ohio Theater, with its gorgeous starlit-sky lobby ceiling, is worth a look.

Just to the southwest is the **Gateway District**, where new restaurants and bars surround **Jacobs Field** stadium, home of the Indians baseball team (Ⓣ216/420-4200, Ⓦwww.indians.com), and the equally modern, multipurpose **Quicken Loans Arena** (Ⓣ216/420-2000, Ⓦwww.theqarena.com), aka "The Q," which hosts the Cavaliers basketball team, along with major sporting and entertainment events.

Northwest of The Q, at the riverfront, one of the nation's busiest waterways shares space with excellent bars, clubs, and restaurants, all strung out along a boardwalk. On the west bank of the Cuyahoga River, the Flats, long known for its nightlife, has an atmospheric, still industrial setting, set among some remaining grimy buildings and no less than fourteen bridges.

A short but steep walk back across the river from the Flats leads to the historic **Warehouse District**, a nicely developing stretch of nineteenth-century commercial buildings between West Third and West Ninth streets, given over to shops, galleries, cafés, and trendy restaurants. North of here, on the other side of the busy Cleveland Memorial Shoreway (Hwy-2), the waters of Lake Erie lap gently into **North Coast Harbor**, a showpiece of Midwest regeneration. To see the city from the water, try a two-hour cruise on the *Goodtime III* (Ⓣ216/861-5110; $15) from the dock at East Ninth Street Pier, just beyond the **Rock and Roll Hall of**

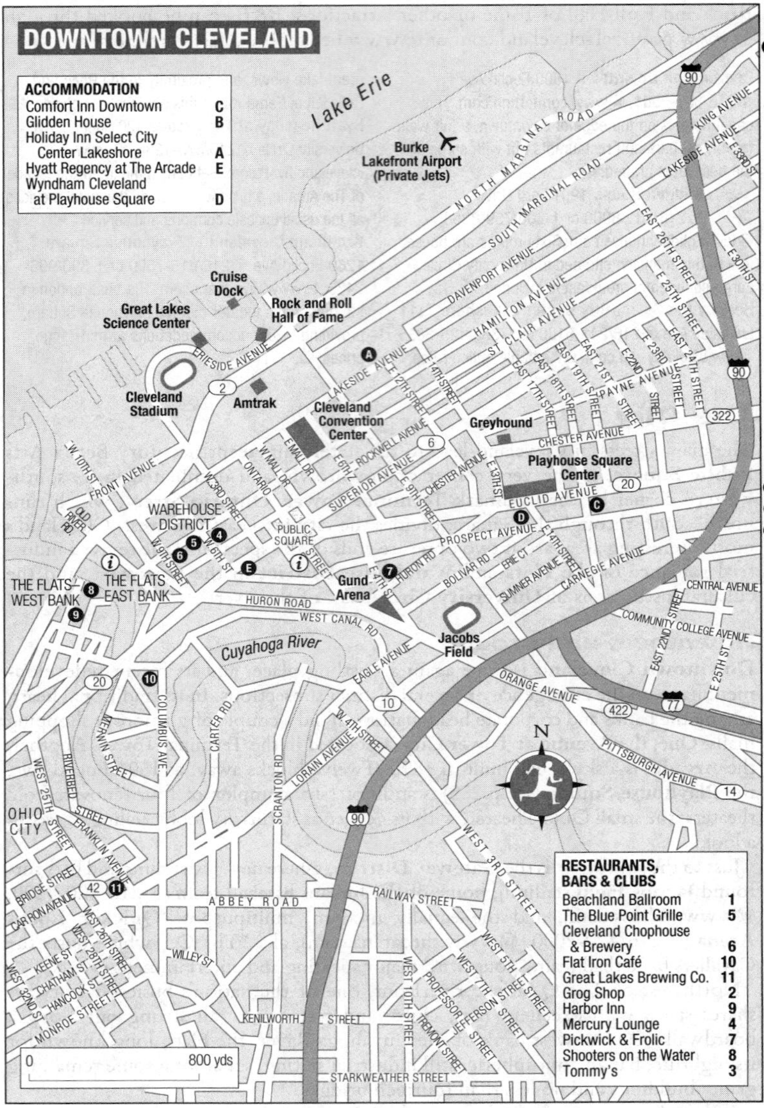

Fame (see box, p.283). Next door to the Rock Hall – as Clevelanders refer to it – is the giant **Great Lakes Science Center** (daily; ⓣ216/696-4941, ⓦwww.greatscience.com; $9.50, $14.95 OMNIMAX combo-ticket), one of America's largest interactive science museums, which cleverly outlines the interdependency of science, technology, and the environment, with emphasis on the lakes region. Across the road, the futuristic, 72,000-seat **Cleveland Stadium** is the home of the Browns pro football team (ⓣ440/891-5000, ⓦwww.clevelandbrowns.com).

The Rock and Roll Hall of Fame

Cleveland, not the most obvious candidate, convincingly won a hotly contested bid to host the **Rock and Roll Hall of Fame** largely because **Alan Freed**, a local disc jockey, popularized the phrase "rock and roll" here back in 1951. Since then, Cleveland has hardly produced a roll call of rock icons – Joe Walsh, Pere Ubu, and Nine Inch Nails are the biggest names. Ignoring criticism that it bought victory by stumping up most cash, the city embraced the idea of the museum with enthusiasm and few now argue with the choice.

The museum's octogenarian architect – **I.M. Pei** – wanted the building "to echo the energy of rock and roll." One of Pei's trademark tinted-glass pyramids (a smaller version of the one he did at the Louvre), this white structure of concrete, steel, and glass strikes a bold pose on the shore of Lake Erie, especially when illuminated at night. The base of the pyramid extends into an impressive entrance plaza shaped like a turntable, complete with a stylus arm attachment.

The museum is much more than an array of **mementos** and artifacts. Right from the start, with the excellent twelve-minute **films** *Mystery Train* and *Kick Out the Jams*, the emphasis is on the contextualization of rock. The exhibits chart the art form's evolution and progress, acknowledging influences ranging from the blues singers of the Delta to the hillbilly wailers of the Appalachians. Elsewhere in the subterranean main exhibition hall, there's an in-depth look at seven crucial **rock genres** through the cities that spawned them: rockabilly (Memphis), R&B (New Orleans), Motown (Detroit), psychedelia (San Francisco), punk (London and New York), hip-hop (New York), and grunge (Seattle). Much space is taken up by exhibits on what the museum sees as the key rock artists of all time, including Elvis Presley, the Beatles, Jimi Hendrix, the Rolling Stones, and U2. All inductees to the hall are selected annually by an international panel of rock "experts," but only performers who have released a record 25 years prior to their nomination are eligible.

Escalators lead to a level devoted to Freed, **studio techniques**, and a great **archive** of rare live recordings, which you can listen to on headphones. The third floor houses the **Hall of Fame** itself, where an hourly video presentation of all inductees unfolds on three vast screens; the upper stories contain the museum's **temporary exhibitions**.

The museum is at North Coast Harbor (daily 10am–5.30pm, Wed also until 9pm; summer Sat until 9pm; $22; reservations Ⓣ216/781-7625 or 1-800/493-7655, Ⓦwww.rockhall.com). As weekends get very crowded, it's much better to go on a weekday.

To the west of the river, **Ohio City** is one of Cleveland's more hip neighborhoods, with junk stores, Victorian clapboard houses, and the busy **West Side Market**, at Lorain Avenue and West 25th Street (Mon & Wed 7am–4pm, Fri & Sat 7am–6pm), which sells all manner of ethnic foods and stocks the exotic local eateries. It's easily spotted by its red-brick clock tower. Nearby **Tremont** is another up and coming area.

Out from downtown

Four miles east of downtown, **University Circle** is a cluster of more than seventy cultural and medical institutions, and is also home to several major performing arts companies (see p.285) as well as Frank Gehry's twisted-steel Weatherhead School of Management building at Case Western University. The eclectic **Museum of Art**, fronted by a lagoon at 11150 East Blvd (Tues, Thurs, Sat, & Sun 10am–5pm, Wed & Fri 10am–9pm; free; Ⓣ216/421-7340, Ⓦwww.clevelandart.org), and currently undergoing major expansion, has a collection that ranges from Renaissance armor to African art, with a good café. Also nota-

▲ Outside the Rock and Roll Hall of Fame

ble is the **Museum of Natural History**, Wade Oval (Mon–Sat 10am–5pm, Sun noon–5pm; summer Tues–Thurs until 7pm; Sept–May Wed until 10pm; $7.50, planetarium $4; ⓣ1-800/317-9155, ⓦwww.cmnh.org), with exhibits on dinosaurs and Native American culture. The **Cleveland Botanical Garden**, 11030 East Blvd (daily 10am–5pm; ⓣ1-888/853-7091, ⓦwww.cbgarden.org; $7.50), has a glass house that features a cloud forest, a desert ecosystem, free-roaming chameleons and butterflies, a waterfall, and a treetop walkway. Meanwhile, dotted along East and Martin Luther King Jr boulevards in Rockefeller Park, 24 small landscaped cultural **gardens** are dedicated to and tended by Cleveland's diverse ethnic groups, including Croatians, Estonians, and Finns. Adjacent to University Circle, **Murray Hill** is Cleveland's Little Italy; beyond this attractive area of brick streets, small delis, and galleries is the trendy neighborhood of **Coventry Village**.

Five miles southwest of downtown via I-71 (exit at W 25th or Fulton Rd), the **Cleveland Metroparks Zoo**, 3900 Wildlife Way (summer Mon–Fri 9am–5pm, Sat & Sun 9am–7pm; rest of year daily 10am–5pm; rainforest also open Wed until 8pm; $10; ⓣ216/661-6500, ⓦwww.clemetzoo.com), features a "Wolf Wilderness," while the spectacular 164-acre rainforest building is populated by some seven thousand plants and 118 species of animals, including orang-utans, American crocodiles, and Madagascan hissing cockroaches. During summer, the RTA runs special **buses** from downtown to the zoo.

Eating

The city has a range of culinary delights, many of them ethnic. The excellent **West Side Market** (Mon & Wed 7am–4pm, Fri & Sat 7am–6pm) in Ohio City abounds with cheap, unusual picnic food, while there are some excellent fine-dining restaurants downtown. Little Italy and Coventry Village are worth exploring for authentic Italian food and coffee bars, respectively.

The Blue Point Grille 700 W St Clair Ave ⓣ216/875-7827. Warehouse District favorite, serving the best seafood in town, with specials such as Nagshead grouper with lobster mashed potatoes.

Cleveland Chophouse and Brewery 824 W St Clair ⓣ216/623-0909. Try the mashed potatoes at this spacious, casual brewery and steakhouse – they're fantastic.

Flat Iron Café 1114 Center St ⓣ216/696-6968. Landmark Irish-American tavern on the east (downtown) bank of the Flats, serving up good sandwiches, salads, and desserts, plus a smooth pint of Guinness.

Pickwick & Frolic 2035 E 4th St ⓣ216/241-7425. Cavernous restaurant with champagne lounge and martini bar. You can enjoy cabaret and stand-up comedy while dining on a huge range of pizza, rustic American cuisine, and oddities like Cheddar Ale Soup.

Shooters on the Water 1148 Main Ave ⓣ216/861-6900. Watch ships coming and going on the Cuyahoga while eating seafood and classic American dishes.

Tommy's 1824 Coventry Rd ⓣ216/321-7757. Great-value food, much of it Middle Eastern and vegetarian, dished up in a trendy, bright setting in lively Coventry Village. Try the famous shakes and check out the adjoining used-book store.

Nightlife and entertainment

The **Warehouse District** and **E 4th Street** boast the greatest conglomeration of drinking, live music, and dancing venues, although those in the know head across the river to more bohemian **Tremont**. Under five miles east, both **University Circle** and youthful **Coventry Village** have good bars. Cleveland's **rave** scene remains strong and mostly underground; if you're interested, look for flyers at Record Revolution, 1832 Coventry Rd (ⓣ216/321-7661).

For more refined entertainment, **Playhouse Square** (ⓣ216/241-6000, ⓦwww.playhousesquare.com) is home to the **Cleveland Opera** and **Ballet**, as well as comedy, musicals, concerts, and the Great Lakes Theatre Festival. The well-respected **Cleveland Orchestra** (ⓣ216/231-1111, ⓦwww.clevelandorchestra.com) is based in University Circle at Severance Hall, 11001 Euclid Ave, close to the leading regional theater of the **Cleveland Play House** (ⓣ216/795-7000, ⓦwww.clevelandplayhouse.com). For **listings** information, try one of Cleveland's two free weeklies: the well-written *Free Times* covers all of the arts, while *Scene* concentrates mostly on music.

Beachland Ballroom 15711 Waterloo Rd ⓣ216/383-1124, ⓦwww.beachlandballroom.com. Over ten miles east of downtown, but this buzzing venue still draws the top indie and rock bands.

Great Lakes Brewing Co. 2516 Market Ave, Ohio City ⓣ216/771-4404. At this famous old joint, Cleveland's best brewpub, the huge mahogany bar still bears the bullet holes made during a 1920s shoot-out involving lawman Elliot Ness.

Grog Shop 2785 Euclid Heights Blvd, Cleveland Heights ⓣ216/321-5588. Near Coventry Village, the Grog Shop is a fun, sweaty, collegiate punk and alternative venue.

Harbor Inn 1219 Main Ave ⓣ216/241-3232. A great old-fashioned bar amid the hyped chain outfits of the Flats, with 180 beers, a few video games, and lots of character.

Mercury Lounge 1392 W 6th St ⓣ216/566-8840. In the Warehouse District, this hip martini lounge tends to attract Cleveland's fashionable set.

Around Cleveland

Less than an hour from the city are a couple of small towns well worth exploring. **VERMILION**, beyond the western suburbs, is also known as Harbor Town, for its attractive lakeside area, which has thrived since 1837. Today it's a quaint old hamlet lined with clapboard houses, cedar trees, and tidy gardens. Old-style galleries and shops hug the small downtown, a stone's throw from the dockside. The **Inland Seas Maritime Museum**, 480 Main St (daily 10am–5pm; $6; ⓣ1-800/893-1485, ⓦwww.inlandseas.org), does a worthy job of exploring shipping on the Great Lakes. Vermilion's **Chamber of Commerce** is at 5495 Liberty Ave (summer Mon–Fri 10am–4pm; rest of year Mon–Fri 10am–3pm, closed Wed; ⓣ440/967-4477, ⓦwww.vermilionohio.com). The best place to **stay** in town is the comfortable *Motel Plaza*, 4645 Liberty Ave (ⓣ440/967-3191; ❸).

Some twenty miles southeast of Vermilion, the famously liberal college town of **OBERLIN** clusters around the green acres of Tappan Square. Founded in 1834, **Oberlin College**, on the square's north and east sides, was America's first co-ed university, and one of the first to enroll black students. From the start, it played a pivotal role in facilitating the movement of black slaves from the Deep South to Canada via the Underground Railroad. A **sculpture** of railroad tracks emerging from the earth, opposite the Conservatory of Music on South Professor Street, is one of several such commemorative sights detailed in a fascinating **walking tour** leaflet available from the **Chamber of Commerce**, on the second floor at 13 S Main St (Mon–Thurs 10am–3pm, Fri 9am–noon; ⓣ440/774-6262, ⓦwww.oberlin.org). Also of interest is the **Allen Memorial Art Museum**, 87 N Main St (Tues–Sat 10am–5pm, Sun 1–5pm; free; ⓦwww.oberlin.edu/allenart). Recognized as one of the best college art museums in the US, it holds more than fourteen thousand objects, from ancient African icons to Japanese scroll paintings, plus a fine array of contemporary art. As for **accommodation**, try the pleasant *Oberlin Inn*, 7 N Main St (ⓣ440/775-1111 or 1-800/376-4173, ⓦwww.oberlininn.com; ❹). Oberlin also boasts half a dozen hip coffeehouses and bars.

Over eighty miles south of Cleveland, beyond Akron, the home of New Wave band Devo, the world's largest Amish community resides in **HOLMES COUNTY**, a meandering section of hills, farms, and backroads. **Berlin** is the commercial center of Amish country, a somewhat saccharine arts-and-crafts center. A good dose of Amish simplicity is better found in the surrounding countryside. At **Yoder's Amish Home**, between the towns of Walnut Creek and Trail, on Rte-515 (mid-April–Oct Mon–Sat 10am–5pm; $5; ⓣ330/893-2541, ⓦwww.yodersamishhome.com), visitors can tour two Amish homes and a barn, and add on a schoolhouse tour and a ride in a horse-drawn carriage for a few dollars more.

The Lake Erie Islands

The **LAKE ERIE ISLANDS** – **Kelleys Island** and the three **Bass Islands** further north – were early stepping stones for the **Iroquois** on the route to what is now Ontario. French attempts to claim the islands in the 1640s met with considerable hostility, and they were left more or less in peace until 1813, when the Americans established their control over the Great Lakes by destroying the entire English fleet in the **Battle of Lake Erie**.

A boom in **wine production** brought the islands prosperity in the 1860s; nearly every available acre was planted with grapes and tourism arrived almost simultaneously. However, the economy was hit hard by Prohibition, the emergence of the California wineries, the advent of the automobile and, finally, the lake's appalling pollution. Thankfully, the clean-up of recent decades has worked; today the islands are again a popular summer destination, with fishing, swimming, and partying as the main attractions. Various mainland towns off Rte-2, such as **Sandusky** and **Port Clinton**, act as jump-off points to the islands.

The mainland

The large coal-shipping port of **SANDUSKY**, fifty miles west of Cleveland on US-2, is probably the most visited of the lakeshore towns, thanks to **Cedar Point Amusement Park**, five miles southeast of town (early-May–Aug daily hours

Getting to the islands

Ferries to Kelleys Island are operated by Kelleys Island Ferry Boat Line from Main Street in **Marblehead** year-round, when weather permits, as frequently as every half hour at peak times (Ⓣ419/798-9763, Ⓦwww.kelleysislandferry.com; $13 round-trip, bikes $6 extra). Jet Express runs summer **catamaran** services from their dock at 101 West Shoreline Dr, Sandusky (Ⓣ1-800/245-1538, Ⓦwww.jet-express.com) to Kelleys Island ($24 round-trip) and **South Bass Island** ($32 round-trip), and to the latter only from 5 N Jefferson St, Port Clinton ($24 round-trip). South Bass Island is also served by Miller Ferry (Ⓣ1-800/500-2421, Ⓦwww.millerferry.com; $12 round-trip, bicycle $4) from late-March to late-November. **Flights** to both Kelleys Island and South Bass Island leave daily from Sandusky and cost $40 one-way. Contact Griffing Airlines (Ⓣ419/626-5161).

vary; Sept–early Nov weekends; $42.95, after 4 or 5pm $25.95; Ⓣ419/627-2350, Ⓦwww.cedarpoint.com). The largest ride park in the nation – and considered by many to be the best in the world – Cedar Point boasts no less than seventeen roller coasters. The neighboring **Soak City** water park (June–Aug daily 10am–9pm; $28, after 4 or 5pm $15.95) provides a good way to cool off, with eighteen acres of water slides and a wave pool. Aquatic fun continues through the winter a few miles further southeast at **Kalahari Waterpark** (daily 10am–8pm; $39–42, after 5pm $29–32; Ⓣ1-877/525-2477, Ⓦwww.kalahariresorts.com), America's largest indoor water park; there's even a surf-making pool.

The smaller resort town of **PORT CLINTON**, twelve miles west across the Sandusky Bay Bridge, is another departure point for the islands. Its pleasant lakefront is dotted with decent cafés and jet-ski rental outlets. Try not to leave the area without exploring the rest of the peninsula, which has some glorious views, particularly around little **Marblehead**, fourteen miles east of Port Clinton.

Practicalities

Amtrak **trains** pass through Sandusky once daily en route between Chicago and the east coast. The unstaffed station, at North Depot and Hayes avenues, is in a dodgy area. Greyhound **buses** stop way out at 6513 Milan Rd (US-250). Sandusky's **visitor center** is at 4424 Milan Rd (summer Mon–Fri 8am–8pm, Sat 9am–8pm, Sun 10am–4pm; rest of year Mon–Fri 8.30am–5.30pm; Ⓣ419/625-2984 or 1-800/255-3743, Ⓦwww.sanduskycounty.org).

Accommodation prices in Sandusky shoot up in high season, with simple motel rooms costing $200-plus on peak weekends – the theme parks described above can be better value at such times. Along the main drag of Cleveland Road (US-6), the *Best Western Cedar Point*, no. 1530 (Ⓣ419/625-9234, Ⓦwww.bestwestern.com; ❺), has a pool. **Camping** is available at *KOA*, 2311 Cleveland Rd (Ⓣ419/625-7906 or 1-800/962-3786, Ⓦwww.mhdcorp.com; from $19–50). **Port Clinton** has the *Sunnyside Tower*, 3612 NW Catawba Rd (Ⓣ419/797-9315 or 1-888/831-1263, Ⓦwww.sunnysidetower.com ❺), a Victorian-style B&B. For a good **meal** and **live music** in fun surroundings (there's an on-site waterfall), head for *Margaritaville* in Sandusky, at the junction of highways 6 and 2 (Ⓣ419/627-8903).

Kelleys Island

About nine miles north of Sandusky, **KELLEYS ISLAND** (Ⓦwww.kelleysisland.com) lies in the western basin of Lake Erie. Seven miles across at its widest, it's the largest American island on the lake, but it's also one of the most peaceful and picturesque, home to under two hundred permanent residents. The whole island

– green, sleepy, and with few buildings less than a century old – is a National Historic District. Its seventy-plus archeological sites include **Inscription Rock**, a limestone slab carved with 400-year-old pictographs; you can find it east of the dock on the southern shore. The **Glacial Grooves State Memorial**, on the west shore, is a 400-foot trough of solid limestone, scoured with deep ridges by the glacier that carved out the Great Lakes.

Settled in the 1830s, Kelleys was initially a working island, its economy based on lumber, then wine, and later limestone quarrying. All but the last have collapsed, though a steady **tourist industry** has developed.

Practicalities

The Kelleys Island **Chamber of Commerce** is on Division Street, straight up from the dock (summer daily 10am–5pm; Ⓣ419/746-2360, Ⓦwww.kelleysislandchamber.com). Getting around the island is easy; cars are heavily discouraged and most people, when not strolling, use **bikes** ($3.50/hr or $15/day) or **golf carts** ($15/hr or $80/day), available from Caddy Shack Square, also on Division Street (Ⓣ419/746-2221). One comfortable **accommodation** option is *The Inn on Kelleys Island*, 317 W Lakeshore Drive (Ⓣ1-866/878-2135, Ⓦwww.kelleysisland.com/theinn; ❹), a restored nineteenth-century Victorian home with a great lake view and a private beach; ask about other options at the Chamber of Commerce. You can **camp** for $17 at the first-come, first-served state park on the north bay near the beach. The jovial *Village Pump*, 103 W Lakeshore Drive (Ⓣ419/746-2281), serves good home-style **food and drink** until 2am, while the menu at the *Kelleys Island Brewery*, 504 W Lakeshore Drive (Ⓣ419/746-2314), includes several choices for vegetarians.

South Bass Island

SOUTH BASS ISLAND is the largest and southernmost of the Bass Island chain, three miles from the mainland and northwest of Kelleys Island; the islands are named for the excellent bass fishing in the surrounding waters. Also referred to as **Put-in-Bay** (the name of its one and only village), this is the most visited of the American Lake Erie Islands, with its permanent population of 450 swelling to ten times that in the summer.

Just a year after its first white settlers arrived, British troops invaded the island during the War of 1812. The Battle of Lake Erie, which took place off the island's southeastern edge, is commemorated by **Perry's Victory and International Peace Memorial**, set in a 25-acre park where the island dramatically nips in at the waist. You can see the battle site, ten miles away, from an observation deck near the top of a 352-foot stone column (May–Oct daily 10am–7pm; $3). All this history is well documented at the **Lake Erie Islands Historical Society**, 441 Catawba Ave (May–Oct daily 10am–5pm, until 6pm July & Aug; $2; Ⓣ419/285-2804, Ⓦwww.leihs.org), which features dozens of model ships, exhibits on the shipping and fishing industries, and memorabilia of life on the islands. After the war, with the lake safe from Canadian invasion, South Bass Island grew as a port, wine-growing area and tourist destination.

Practicalities

Put-in-Bay's **visitor center** on Harbor Square, is just next to the northern dock (summer daily 9am–6pm; rest of year hours vary; Ⓣ419/285-2832, Ⓦwww.put-in-bay.com). To get around, as on Kelleys Island, most people rent either **golf carts** from Baycarts Rental, Harbor Square ($10–20/hr; Ⓣ419/285-5785), or **bikes** from Island Bike Rental, at both docks ($10/day; Ⓣ419/285-2016). A **shuttle bus** runs between the northern dock and the state park ($1).

Hotel rooms are heavily booked on weekends and during the summer, and **B&Bs** often require a two-night minimum stay on weekends. The *Arbor Inn B&B*, 511 Trenton Ave (ⓣ419/285-2306, ⓦwww.arborinnpib.com; ❹), and the *Commodore Motel*, 272 Delaware Ave (ⓣ419/285-3101; ❹), which has a pool, offer some of the most competitive rates. You can **camp** for $16 in the state park or at the *Fox's Den Campground*, on the southern shore (ⓣ419/285-5001; $29).

Food on the island is expensive. The grill meals and seafood sandwiches at The Boardwalk (summer only; ⓣ419/285-3695) are no exception, but this is the only downtown restaurant directly on the water. Just across the street, Frosty's (ⓣ419/285-3278) does good pizza. Put-in-Bay's wild nightlife – it really does get raucous – pulls in partiers from the other islands and the mainland. Numerous live music venues include the *Beer Barrel Saloon* (ⓣ419/285-2337, ⓦwww.beerbarrelpib.com) – said to have the longest uninterrupted bar in the world, complete with 160 bar stools – and the appropriately named *Round House* (ⓣ419/285-4595, ⓦwww.theroundhousebar.com).

Columbus

Ohio's largest city, state capital, and home to the massive Ohio State University, **COLUMBUS** is a likeable place to visit. Its position in the rural heart of the state also makes it the only center of culture for a good two-hour drive in any direction.

Ohio became a state in 1803 and legislators designated this former patch of rolling farmland, on the high east bank of the Scioto River, its capital in 1812. The fledgling city was built from scratch, and its considered town planning is evident today in broad thoroughfares and green spaces. Statues form a significant part of the cityscape, with many of them portraying the city's namesake, **Christopher Columbus**; there's even a replica of his ship, the *Santa Maria*, docked downtown on the Scioto River.

Though Columbus has more people, it always seems to lag behind Cincinnati or Cleveland in terms of public recognition. As such, the place is best enjoyed for what it is – a lively college city with some good **museums**, gorgeous Germanic **architecture**, and a particularly vibrant **nightlife**. Surprisingly, it boasts one of the country's most active **gay scenes**. The spacious, orderly, and easy-going **downtown** area holds several attractions, along with the new **Arena District** entertainment zone. The main nightlife areas –bohemian **Short North Arts District** and more mainstream **Brewery District** – are on the north and south fringes of the center, respectively.

Arrival, information, and getting around

Port Columbus International Airport is seven miles northeast of downtown. Central Ohio Transit Authority's (COTA; ⓣ614/228-1776, ⓦwww.cota.com) express route bus #52 runs from there through downtown for $2, while **taxis** cost around $25. **Greyhound** stops at 111 East Town St. The most central **visitor center** is at 90 N High St (Mon–Fri 9am–5pm; ⓣ614/221-2489 or 1-800/345-4386, ⓦwww.experiencecolumbus.com). COTA's good, citywide **bus service** connects all points of interest; a day-pass costs $3.50.

Accommodation

Compared with other cities in the region, Columbus offers a good choice of convenient mid-range places to **stay**. Downtown rates are good, while even more savings can be had by staying in the German Village and Brewery District locales.

German Village Inn 920 S High St ⓣ614/443-6506, ⓦwww.germanvillageinn.net. This family-run motel, on the south edge of the German Village/Brewery District, is one of the best deals going. ④

The Lofts Hotel 55 E Nationwide Blvd ⓣ614/461-2663, ⓦwww.55lofts.com. Luxury New York-style loft conversions, within easy walking distance of the Arena and the downtown areas. ⑧

Red Roof Inn Nationwide Arena 111 E Nationwide Blvd ⓣ614/224-6539, ⓦwww.redroof.com. Cut above average motel chain with comfortable rooms only half a mile north of downtown. ④

Short North B&B 50 E Lincoln St ⓣ614/299-5050 or 1-800/516-9664, ⓦwww.columbus-bed-breakfast.com. Enjoy a warm welcome and lavish furnishings in one of the seven rooms of this grand Short North house. ⑥

The Westin Great Southern 310 S High St ⓣ614/228-3800 or 1-888/627-7088, ⓦwww.greatsouthernhotel.com. Columbus's grand downtown Victorian hotel, with surprisingly moderate rates for some rooms. ⑤

Downtown

As good a place as any to start a walking tour of downtown is the **Ohio Statehouse**, pleasantly set in ten acres of park at the intersection of Broad and High streets, the two main downtown arteries (Mon–Fri 7am–6pm, Sat & Sun 11am–5pm; hourly tours Mon–Fri 10am–3pm, Sat & Sun noon–3pm; free; ⓣ1-888/644-6123, ⓦwww.statehouse.state.oh.us). Highlights of this 1839 Greek Revival structure – one of the very few state capitols without a dome – are the ornate Senate and House chambers.

From here, most places of interest lie a few blocks east and west along Broad Street. **COSI**, housed in a streamlined structure across the river, at 333 W Broad St (Mon–Sat 10am–5pm, Sun noon–6pm; $12.50, kids $7.50; ⓣ614/228-2674 or 1-877/257-2674, ⓦwww.cosi.org), boasts more than 300,000 square feet of exhibit space, most of it geared toward familiarizing children with science and shows related movies ($7.50)

About a mile east, a giant Henry Moore sculpture stands at the entrance to the inviting **Columbus Museum of Art**, 480 E Broad St (Tues–Sun 10am–5.30pm, Thurs until 8.30pm; $8, free Sun; ⓣ614/221-6801, ⓦwww.columbusmuseum.org). Indoors, this airy space holds particularly good collections of Western and modernist art.

In the northwest corner of downtown, the area surrounding the impressive Nationwide Arena, home to NHL's Columbus Blue Jackets (ⓣ1-800/645-2637, ⓦwww.bluejackets.com), dubbed the **Arena District**, has attracted a number of restaurants and nightspots. Just above it, left off High Street, is the restored Victorian warehouse of **North Market** (see "Eating" p.291), while on the right side the strikingly deconstructivist **Greater Columbus Convention Center** is a massive pile of angled blocks designed by Peter Eisenman and completed in 1993.

German Village and Brewery District

Just six blocks south of the Statehouse, I-70 separates downtown from the delightful **German Village** neighborhood. During the mid-nineteenth century, thousands of German immigrants settled in this part of Columbus, building neat red-brick homes, the most lavish of which surround the 23-acre **Schiller Park**. Their descendants gradually dwindled in numbers by the 1950s and the area became increasingly run-down until it won a place on the National Register of Historic Places. The best way to explore its brick-paved streets, corner bars, old-style restaurants, Catholic churches, and grand homes is to stop in at the German Village Meeting Haus, 588 S 3rd St (Mon–Fri 9am–4pm, Sat 10am–2pm; ⓣ614/221-8888, ⓦwww.germanvillage.com), where popular walking tours run by the German Village Society start with a twelve-minute video presentation.

The Society also oversees the immensely popular Haus und Garten Tour on the last Sunday in June, and the Oktoberfest celebrations in late September. Booklovers will adore the Book Loft, 631 S 3rd St (daily 10am–11pm; ⓣ614/464-1774), whose books, many of them discounted, are crammed into 32 rooms of one grand building.

Just across High Street (US-23) are the warehouses of the **Brewery District**, where, until Prohibition, the German immigrants brewed beer by traditional methods. Many of the original buildings still stand, but today the beer is produced by a handful of microbreweries. These brewpubs are typical of the area's more mainstream **nightlife**.

North of downtown

Across Nationwide Boulevard at the top end of downtown is the **Short North Arts District**, a former red-light district that's now Columbus's most vibrant enclave. Standing on either side of High Street – the main north–south thoroughfare – its entrance is marked by the iron gateways of The Cap at Union Station. Thereafter starts the trail of galleries, bars, and restaurants that makes the area so popular with locals; it is also the heart of the gay community. The first Saturday of each month sees the **Gallery Hop**, when local art dealers throw open their doors – complementing the artworks with wine, snacks, and occasional performance pieces – and the socializing goes on well into the evening (ⓦwww.shortnorth.org).

Businesses become a little more low-rent for a mile before High Street cuts through the **university campus** and suddenly sprouts cheap eating places and funky shopping. For bargain vinyl, head to Used Kids Records, 1980 N High St (ⓣ614/421-9455). On the other side of the road, the **Wexner Center for the Arts**, North High Street at 15th Avenue (Tues, Wed, & Sun 10am–6pm; free, Thurs–Sat 10am–8pm; free; ⓣ614/292-3535, ⓦwww.wexarts.org), is another Eisenman construction, even more extreme than the Convention Center (p.290).

Eating

The Short North and German Village neighborhoods are crammed with places to **eat**, be they bottom-dollar snack bars or stylish and adventurous bistros. For a wide range of ethnic and organic snacks during the day, try the **North Market**, downtown at 59 Spruce St (Tues–Fri 9am–7pm, Sat 8am–5pm, Sun noon–5pm; ⓣ614/463-9664), which also sells fresh produce.

Haiku 800 N High St, Short North ⓣ614/294-8168. Excellent Japanese restaurant with a huge range of sushi, noodle, and rice dishes.

Katzinger's 475 S 3rd St, German Village ⓣ614/228-3354. A mesmerizing range of sandwiches, Jewish delicacies, and cheesecakes, though prices are high for a deli.

Marcella's 615 N High St, Short North ⓣ614/223-2100. Buzzing Italian restaurant with a lively bar. The food is a a range of moderately upscale pizzas, pasta, salads and main dishes like veal milanese.

Schmidt's 240 E Kossuth St, German Village ⓣ614/444-6808. This Columbus landmark (since 1886) serves a range of sausages, schnitzel, and strudel in a former slaughterhouse, served by waitresses in German garb.

Surly Girl Saloon 1126 N High St, Short North ⓣ614/294-4900. Heapings of Tex-Mex, Cajun, and other cuisines are served in this quirky joint where Western bordello meets Pirates of the Caribbean. Fine microbrews on tap help the place get rowdy late on.

Nightlife

This youthful university town has a rich source of local **bands**, from country revivalists to experimental alternative acts. The **gay scene** is concentrated in the Short North, with a few additional bars and clubs downtown – the weekly *Outlook* has complete listings. The *Other Paper* and *Columbus Alive* provide fuller free details of what's happening around town.

Axis Night Club 775 N High St ⓣ614/291-4008. Very popular gay nightspot that gets steamier as the night wears on, as people gyrate to the latest disco and trance vibes.

Dick's Den 2417 N High St ⓣ614/268-9573. This campus dive bar has good jazz on the weekends.

Oldfield's On High 2590 N High St ⓣ614/784-0477, ⓦwww.oldfieldsonhigh.com. Campus bar with live music across a broad range of genres. No cover.

Short North Tavern 674 N High St, Short North ⓣ614/221-2432. The oldest bar in the neighborhood, with live bands playing on the weekend.

Skully's Music-Diner 1151 N High St, Short North ⓣ614/291-8856, ⓦwww.skullys.org. Classic 1950s-style diner whose happy hour (4–9pm) is often followed by cool indie-rock shows.

Tommy Keegans Irish Pub 456 S Front St, Brewery District ⓣ614/221-9444. Friendly pub with a decent jukebox and soccer from Europe on TV.

Cincinnati

CINCINNATI, just across the Ohio River from Kentucky, is a dynamic commercial metropolis with a definite European flavor and a sense of the South. Its tidy center, rich in architecture and culture, lies within a few minutes' walk of the arty **Mount Adams** district, the attractive **riverfront**, and the lively **Over-the-Rhine** area, in the north end of downtown.

The city was founded in 1788 at the point where a Native American trading route crossed the river. Its name comes from a group of Revolutionary War admirers of the Roman general Cincinnatus, who saved Rome in 458 BC and then returned to his small farm, refusing to accept any reward. Cincinnati quickly became an important supply point for pioneers heading west on flatboats and rafts, and its population skyrocketed with the establishment of a major steamboat **riverport** in 1811. Tens of thousands of **German** immigrants poured in during the 1830s.

Loyalties were split by the **Civil War**. Despite the loss of some important markets, the city decided that its future lay with the Union. In the prosperous post-war decade, Cincinnati acquired Fountain Square, the country's first professional baseball team, the **Reds**; they, along with the **Bengals** football team, remain a great source of pride.

Arrival, information, and getting around

Cincinnati–Northern Kentucky International Airport is twelve miles south of downtown, in Covington, Kentucky. **Taxis** to the city center (ⓣ859/586-5236) cost $32. The **Greyhound** station is on the eastern fringe of the city center, just off Broadway, at 1005 Gilbert Ave. Amtrak **trains** arrive a mile northwest of downtown at the Union Terminal museum complex, which is on the daytime, citywide SORTA/Metro **bus** network (ⓣ513/621-4455, ⓦwww.sorta.com; $1). Buses on the Kentucky side are run by TANK (ⓣ859/331-8265, ⓦwww.tankbus.org; $1), including shuttle buses across to Cincinnati. Extraordinarily for a city of its size, there is no walk-in visitors office, though **info** can be obtained by phone or online from the CincinnatiUSA Regional Tourism Network (ⓣ859/589-2260, ⓦwww.cincinnatiusa.com).

Accommodation

Although Cincinnati's quality **hotels** are reasonable by big-city standards, budget travelers may have problems finding affordable downtown rooms. Uptown

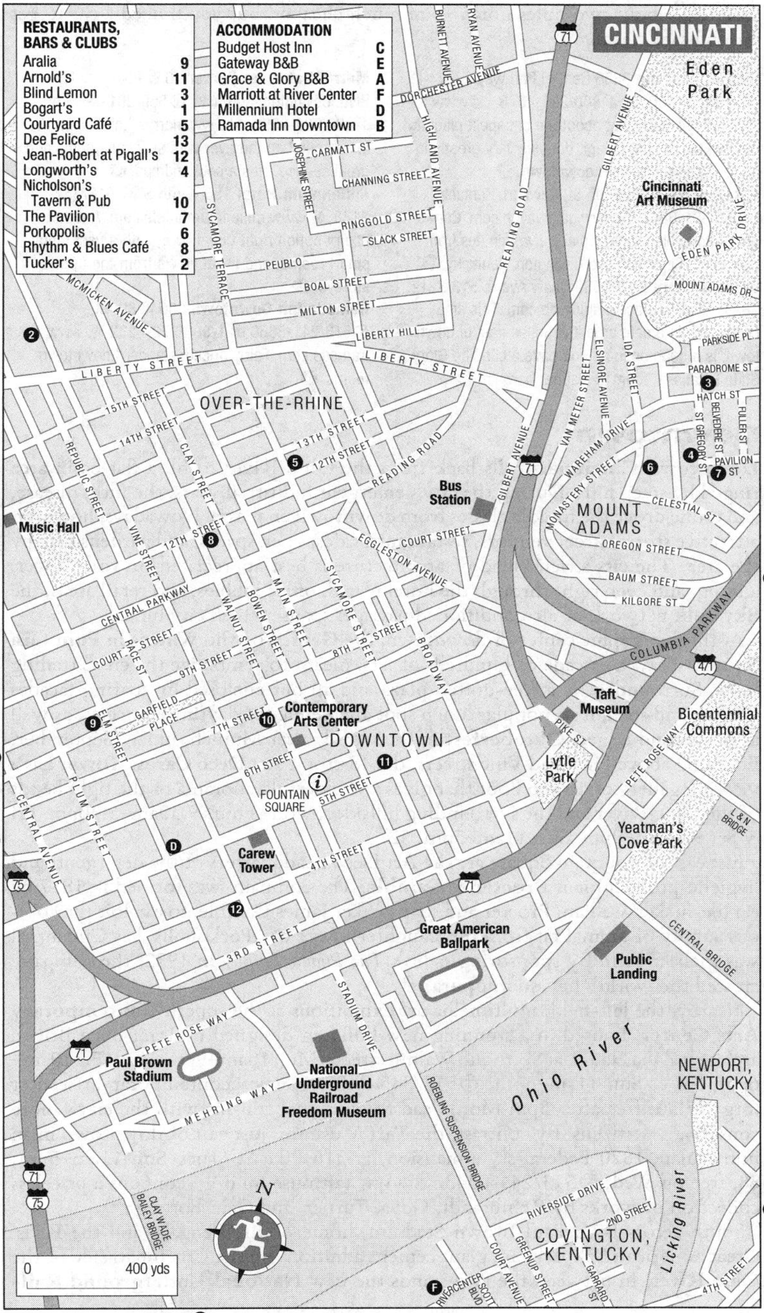
CINCINNATI
RESTAURANTS, BARS & CLUBS
Aralia 9
Arnold's 11
Blind Lemon 3
Bogart's 1
Courtyard Café 5
Dee Felice 13
Jean-Robert at Pigall's 12
Longworth's 4
Nicholson's Tavern & Pub 10
The Pavilion 7
Porkopolis 6
Rhythm & Blues Café 8
Tucker's 2
ACCOMMODATION
Budget Host Inn C
Gateway B&B E
Grace & Glory B&B A
Marriott at River Center F
Millennium Hotel D
Ramada Inn Downtown B
Eden Park
Cincinnati Art Museum
OVER-THE-RHINE
DOWNTOWN
MOUNT ADAMS
Music Hall
Museum Center
1 & Zoo
Bus Station
Contemporary Arts Center
FOUNTAIN SQUARE
Carew Tower
Taft Museum
Lytle Park
Bicentennial Commons
Yeatman's Cove Park
Great American Ballpark
Public Landing
Paul Brown Stadium
National Underground Railroad Freedom Museum
Ohio River
Licking River
NEWPORT, KENTUCKY
COVINGTON, KENTUCKY
CLAY WADE BAILEY BRIDGE
ROEBLING SUSPENSION BRIDGE
CENTRAL BRIDGE
L & N BRIDGE
LIBERTY STREET
CENTRAL PARKWAY
COLUMBIA PARKWAY
READING ROAD
GILBERT AVENUE
EGGLESTON AVENUE
PETE ROSE WAY
MEHRING WAY
STADIUM DRIVE
RIVERSIDE DRIVE
71
75
471
N
0 400 yds

motels – about two miles north – are much cheaper, but you'll need a car to get around safely at night.

Budget Host Inn 3356 Central Parkway ⓣ513/559-1600 or 1-800/283-4678, ⓦwww.budgethost.com. Just about the cheapest place in uptown Cincinnati, though doubles vary greatly in price. Three miles from downtown. ❸

Gateway B&B 326 E 6th St, Newport, Kentucky ⓣ859/581-6447, ⓦwww.gatewaybb.com. Comfortable, affordable Victorian place, five minutes from downtown Cincinnati and Covington, Kentucky. ❺

Grace & Glory B&B 3539 Shaw Ave ⓣ513/321-2824, ⓦwww.graceandglorybb.com. This small cozy place in a safe area, five miles east of downtown, is a good option if you have a car. The Glory Suite Extension room is a super bargain. ❸

Marriott at River Center 10 W River Center Blvd, Covington, Kentucky ⓣ859/261-2900 or 1-800/228-9290, ⓦwww.marriotthotels.com. A luxury hotel on the river with spacious rooms and great service, plus a pool and spa. ❻

Millennium Hotel 150 W 5th St ⓣ513/352-2188, ⓦwww.millenniumhotels.com. Another luxury option right downtown, with a vast lobby, smart rooms, and great views from the upper storeys. ❻

Ramada Inn Downtown 800 W 8th St ⓣ513/241-8660 or 1-800/272-6232, ⓦwww.ramada.com. Fairly priced, standard downtown rooms. ❹

Downtown

Downtown Cincinnati rolls back from the Ohio River to fill a flat basin area ringed by steep hills. During the city's emergent industrial years, the filth, disease, and crime drove the middle classes from downtown en masse. Nowadays, however, attractive stores, street vendors, restaurants, cafés, open spaces, and gardens occupy the area. The city's rich blend of architecture is best appreciated **on foot**. Over, among, and even right through the hotel plazas, office lobbies, and retail areas, the **Skywalk** network of air-conditioned passages spans sixteen city blocks.

At the geographic center of downtown, the **Genius of the Waters** in **Fountain Square** sprays a cascade of hundreds of jets, meant to symbolize the city's trading links. Surrounded by a tree-dotted plaza and all but enclosed by soaring facades of glass and steel, it's a popular lunch spot and venue for daytime concerts, as well as the second largest **Oktoberfest** in the world, after Munich, in late September. Looming above Fifth and Vine streets, the 48-story, Art Deco **Carew Tower** has a viewing gallery on its top floor that gives a wonderful panorama of the tight bends of the Ohio River and the surrounding hillsides (Mon–Thurs 9.30am–5.30pm, Fri & Sat 9.30am–9pm, Sun 11am–5pm; $2).

Just east of Fountain Square are the Art Deco headquarters of the detergents and hygiene-product giant **Procter & Gamble**. The company was formed in 1837 by candle-maker William Procter and soap-maker James Gamble, to exploit the copious supply of animal fat from the slaughterhouses of "Porkopolis," as Cincinnati was then known. By sponsoring radio's *The Puddle Family* in 1932, the company created the world's first **soap opera**.

Nearby, the left-field, multimedia art exhibitions at the superb **Contemporary Arts Center**, housed in a stunning new building designed by Iraqi-born British architect Zaha Hadid, at Sixth and Walnut streets (Mon 10am–9pm, Wed–Fri 10am–6pm, Sat & Sun 11am–6pm; ⓣ513/345-8400, ⓦwww.contemporaryartscenter.org; $7.50; free after 5pm Mon), lead to continual run-ins with the city's more conservative citizens. By contrast, the **Taft Museum**, just east of downtown in an immaculate 1820 Federal-style mansion, at 316 Pike St (Tues–Sun 11am–5pm; $8, free on Wed; ⓣ513/241-0343, ⓦwww.taftmuseum.org), contains a priceless collection of works by Rembrandt, Goya, Turner, and Gainsborough.

South across I-71, Paul Brown Stadium, home of the Bengals, and the Reds' Great American Ballpark, are giant cement additions on the Cincinnati side of the Ohio River. In between the two stands the new **National Underground Rail-**

road Freedom Museum (Tues–Sun 11am–5pm; $12; ⓣ513/333-7500, ⓦwww.freedomcenter.org), whose light and airy space chronicles the city's role in the emancipation of slaves as well as other worldwide struggles for freedom. A mile-long **riverside walk** begins at **Public Landing**, at the bottom of Broadway, and stretches east past painted showboats and the **Bicentennial Commons**, a 200th-birthday present from the city to itself in 1988.

North of downtown

Just over a mile northeast from downtown, the land rises suddenly and the streets start to conform to the contours of **Mount Adams**. Here, century-old townhouses coexist with avant-garde galleries, stylish boutiques, international restaurants, and trendy bars. To explore these and enjoy unparalleled views of the river, take a taxi or the #49 bus from downtown.

Adjacent to this tightly packed neighborhood are the rolling lawns, verdant copses, and scenic overlooks of **Eden Park**. A loop road at the western end of the park leads to the **Cincinnati Art Museum**, on Art Museum Drive (Tues–Sun 11am–5pm, Wed until 9pm; free; ⓣ513/639-2984, ⓦwww.cincinnatiartmuseum.org). Its one hundred labyrinthine galleries span five thousand years, taking in an excellent Islamic collection as well as a solid selection of European and American paintings by the likes of Matisse, Monet, Picasso, Edward Hopper, and Grant Wood.

Meanwhile, northwest from downtown, Cincinnati's **Museum Center** is housed in the magnificent Art Deco **Union Terminal**, approached via a stately driveway off Ezzard Charles Drive (Mon–Sat 10am–5pm, Sun 11am–6pm; museums $7.25 each, any two $10.25, all three $13.25, with OMNIMAX $16.25 or $19.25 for two shows; ⓣ513/287-7000, ⓦwww.cincymuseum.org). Highlights of the **Museum of Natural History** are dioramas of Ice Age Cincinnati and "The Cavern," which houses a living bat colony. The **Historical Society** holds a succession of well-presented, short-term exhibitions, and the **Cinergy Children's Museum** has a two-story treehouse and eight other interactive exhibit areas.

Covington and Newport, Kentucky

Covington, directly across the Ohio River on the Kentucky side, is regarded as the southern side of Cincinnati. It can be reached from downtown Cincinnati by walking over the bright blue, 355-yard **John A. Roebling Suspension Bridge**, at the bottom of Walnut Street, which was built in 1867 and served as a prototype for the Brooklyn Bridge. A ten-minutes walk southwest of the bridge brings you to the attractive, narrow, tree-lined streets and nineteenth-century houses of **MainStrasse Village**. It's a Germanic neighborhood of antique shops, bars, and restaurants that plays host to the lively **Maifest** on the third weekend of each May, and is the centerpiece of the citywide **Oktoberfest** on the weekend after Labor Day. At 6th and Philadelphia streets, 21 mechanical figures accompanied by glockenspiel music toll the hour on the German Gothic **Carroll Chimes Bell Tower**. Further south en route to the airport off I-275, one of the area's newest attractions is the multi-million dollar **Creation Museum** (Mon–Thurs 10am–6pm, Fri 10am–9pm, Sat 9am–6pm, Sun noon–6pm; ⓣ1-888/582-4253, ⓦwww.creationmuseum.org; $21.95). A truly "only in America" experience, the state of the art dioramas, video show, and planetarium ($7) argue an uncompromising creationist case and make Darwin out to be little short of Lucifer himself.

Across the Licking River from Covington, the subdued town of **Newport** has gotten a lot livelier since the opening of a large shopping complex and the impressive **Newport Aquarium**, One Aquarium Way (daily: summer 10am–7pm, Sat until 9pm; rest of year 10am–6pm; $17.95; ⓣ859/491-3467 or 1-800/406-3474, ⓦwww.newportaquarium.com). Clear underwater tunnels and see-through floors allow visitors to be literally surrounded by sharks and snapping gators.

Eating

Cincinnati boasts excellent home-grown gourmet and continental **restaurants**. It's also famous for fast-food **Cincinnati chili**, a combination of spaghetti noodles, meat, cheese, onions, and kidney beans, served at chains such as *Skyline Chili*, open all day at more than forty locations, including one at Vine and 7th streets, downtown.

Aralia 815 Elm St ⓣ513/723-1217. Excellent Sri Lankan curries in a convenient downtown location.
Courtyard Café 1211 Main St, Over-the-Rhine ⓣ513/723-1119. Good grill food, burgers, and desserts, at value-for-money prices.
Dee Felice 529 Main St, Covington, Kentucky ⓣ859/261-2365. This small and atmospheric spot specializes in Cajun cuisine, with lots of fresh seafood dishes, and doubles as a jazz venue.
Jean–Robert at Pigall's 127 W 4th St ⓣ513/721-1345. Generally considered the city's premier fine dining location, serving Parisian food with a little New York style. A three-course *prix-fixe* menu of the day costs $74.
Longworth's 1108 St Gregory St, Mount Adams ⓣ513/651-2253. Good hamburgers, sandwiches, salads, and pizzas at attractive prices in a delightful garden setting. Food is served all day until midnight, with music until 2.30am.
Nicholson's Tavern & Pub 625 Walnut St ⓣ513/564-9111. Scottish and other European fare, as well as decent ale, can be enjoyed amid the appealing wooden decor.
Porkopolis 1077 Celestial St, Mount Adams ⓣ513/721-5456. Steaks and sandwiches are served in the building that once produced the city's celebrated pottery.
Tucker's 1637 Vine St ⓣ513/721-7123; also 18 E 13th St, Over-the-Rhine ⓣ513/241-3354. Get a perfect start on your day with traditional and gourmet breakfasts in a 1950s setting.

Nightlife and entertainment

After dark, the hottest area with the widest appeal is the **Over-the-Rhine** district, which fans out from Main Street around 12th and 14th streets, and buzzes every night – though be careful where you park or walk, as it backs onto some unsafe areas. The next liveliest areas are ritzier **Mount Adams** and more collegiate **Corryville**, a five-minute drive northwest from downtown. Entertainment **listings** for the whole city can be found in the free *Cincinnati CityBeat* (ⓦwww.citybeat.com).

For classical music and the like, **Music Hall**, 1243 Elm St (ⓣ513/744-3344, ⓦwww.cincinnatiarts.org), an 1870s conglomeration of spires, arched windows, and cornices, is said to have near-perfect acoustics. Home to Cincinnati's Opera and Symphony Orchestra, it also hosts the May Festival of choral music. The **Cincinnati Playhouse in the Park**, in Eden Park (ⓣ513/421-3888, ⓦwww.cincyplay.com), puts on drama, musicals, and comedies, with performances throughout the year.

Arnold's 210 E 8th St ⓣ513/421-6234. A fun and funky downtown spot, it's a favorite with jazz fans, though it also puts on acoustic acts. Good restaurant upstairs.
Blind Lemon 936 Hatch St, Mount Adams ⓣ513/241-3885. Beyond the intimate, low-ceilinged bar, you'll find a relaxed patio crowd. Music (mostly acoustic) nightly at 9.30pm.
Bogart's 2621 Vine St, Corryville ⓣ513/281-8400, ⓦwww.bogarts.com. Established indie acts play this mid-sized venue a couple of miles north of downtown
The Pavilion 949 Pavilion St, Mount Adams ⓣ513/744-9200. From its terraced outdoor deck, you'll have great views of the city and the Ohio River.
Rhythm & Blues Café 1142 Main St, Over-the-Rhine ⓣ513/684-0080. Good food and great atmosphere. Live rock, blues, and various genres Wed through Sat nights.

Michigan

Mention **MICHIGAN** and most people think of cars, heavy industry, and inner-city Detroit. Midwesterners prefer to focus on the state's magnificent scenery. The beaches, dunes, and cliffs along the 3200-mile shoreline of its two vividly contrasting **peninsulas** – bordering four of the five Great Lakes – rival many an oceanfront state.

The mitten-shaped **Lower Peninsula** is dominated from its southeastern corner by the industrial giant of **Detroit**, surrounded by satellite cities heavily devoted to the automotive industry. In the west, the scenic 350-mile Lake Michigan shoreline drive passes through likeable little ports before reaching the stunning **Sleeping Bear Dunes** and resort towns such as **Traverse City**, in the peninsula's balmy northwest corner. The desolate, dramatic, and thinly populated **Upper Peninsula**, reaching out from Wisconsin like a claw to separate lakes Superior and Michigan, is a far cry indeed from the cosmopolitan south.

In the mid-seventeenth century, **French explorers** forged a successful trading relationship with the Chippewa, Ontario, and other Native American tribes. The **British**, who acquired control after 1763, were far more brutal. Governor Henry Hamilton, the "Hair Buyer of Detroit," advocated taking scalps rather than prisoners. Ever since, Michigan's economy has developed in waves, the eighteenth-century fur, timber, and copper booms culminating in the state establishing itself at the forefront of the nation's manufacturing capacity, thanks to its abundant raw materials, good transportation links, and the genius of innovators such as **Henry Ford**. Despite the slumps of the Seventies and Eighties, **automobile production** remains the major source of Michigan income – though tourism is now a four-season money-spinner, too.

Getting around Michigan

Greyhound buses run regularly throughout Michigan's south, but services elsewhere are less frequent, and the few buses that serve the remote Upper Peninsula do so at night. Amtrak trains between New York and Chicago stop at Detroit, Dearborn, and Ann Arbor. Michigan's principal airport is just outside Detroit. Cycling is both feasible and rewarding, particularly with the abundance of bike paths in and around Traverse City; the League of Michigan Bicyclists in Lansing (Ⓣ1-888/642-4537, Ⓦwww.lmb.org) organizes tours and provides info.

Detroit

DETROIT, the birthplace of the mass-production auto industry and the Motown sound, has long had an image problem. The city boasts a billion-dollar downtown development, ultramodern motor-manufacturing plants, some excellent museums, and one of the nation's biggest art galleries – but since the 1960s, media attention has dwelt instead on its huge tracts of urban wasteland, where for block after block there's nothing but the occasional heavily fortified loan shop or grocery store. This characterization incurs the wrath of many Detroiters, and, though their city has unarguably suffered and continues to face tremendous challenges – perhaps none more paramount than the dire state of the auto industry – their claims of exaggeration or exploitation by the media do carry weight.

Founded in 1701 by **Antoine de Mothe Cadillac**, as a trading post for the French to do business with the Chippewa, Detroit was no more than a medium-sized port two hundred years later. Then **Henry Ford**, **Ransom Eli Olds**, the **Chevrolets**, and the **Dodge** brothers began to build their automobile empires. Thanks to the introduction of the mass assembly line, Detroit boomed in the 1920s, but the auto barons sponsored the construction of segregated neighborhoods and unceremoniously dispensed with workers during times of low demand. Such policies created huge ghettos, resulting, in July 1967, in the bloodiest **riot** in the US in fifty years. More than forty people died and thirteen hundred buildings were destroyed. The **inner city** was left to fend for itself, while the all-important motor industry was rocked by the oil crises and Japanese competition. Today, though scarred and bruised, Detroit is not the mess some would have it, and suburban residents have started to return to the city's festivals, theaters, clubs, and restaurants.

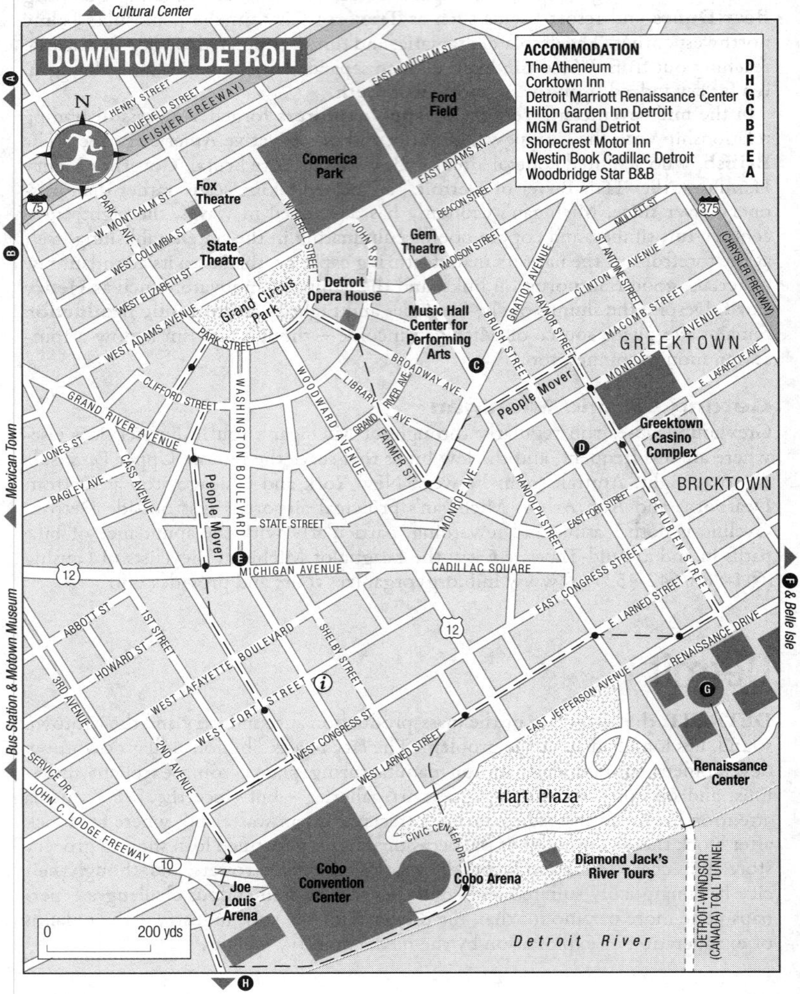

As for orientation, it makes sense to think of Detroit as a region rather than a concentrated city – and, with some planning and wheels, it holds plenty to see and do. For the moment, **downtown** is not so much the heart of the giant as just another segment. Other interesting areas include the huge **Cultural Center**, free-wheeling **Royal Oak**, posh **Birmingham**, the Ford-town of **Dearborn**, nearby **Windsor, Ontario**, and the college town of **Ann Arbor**, a short drive west.

Arrival, information, and getting around

Flights come into **Detroit Metropolitan Wayne County Airport** in Romulus, eighteen miles southwest of downtown and a hefty $40-plus taxi ride (Metro Airport Taxi ⓣ1-800/745-5191 cost $41 while Checker Sedan Taxis ⓣ800/351-5466 are $55), though SMART ($1.50; ⓣ866/962-5515, ⓦwww.smartbus.org) bus #125 goes downtown from Smith terminal.

The main **Greyhound** (1001 Howard Ave) and **Amtrak** (11 W Baltimore Ave) terminals are in areas where it's inadvisable to walk around at night. Amtrak also stops ten miles out at 16121 Michigan Ave, Dearborn, near the Henry Ford Museum and several mid-range motels, and at unstaffed suburban stations at Birmingham, Pontiac, and Royal Oak.

Detroit's main **visitor center** is downtown at 211 W Fort St, on the tenth floor (Mon–Fri 9am–5pm; ⓣ313/202-1800 or 1-800/338-7648, ⓦwww.visitdetroit.com). The main **post office** is at 1401 W Fort St, at Eighth St (Mon–Fri 8.30am–5pm, Sat 8am–noon).

Downtown, the People Mover elevated **railway** loops around thirteen art-adorned stations (Mon–Thurs 6:30am–midnight, Fri 6:30am–2am, Sat 9am–2am, Sun noon–midnight; 50¢). Further out, public transportation is just about adequate. SMART serves the entire metro region, while DDOT **buses** ($1.50; ⓣ313/933-1300, ⓦwww.detroitmi.gov/ddot) run a patchier inner-city service. Getting around in the Motor City, however, remains geared firmly toward the **car**.

Accommodation

Downtown Detroit caters well for expense-account travelers – its top-range **hotels** are as secure as any city's – but if your budget is restricted it's harder to find lodging that is both cheap and safe at night. A fifteen-percent tax comes tacked onto room bills.

The Atheneum 1000 Brush St ⓣ313/962-2323 or 1-800/772-2323, ⓦwww.atheneumsuites.com. At this swish all-suite hotel in Greektown, some units fetch more than $300 a night; others are a third of that price. ❻–❾

The Cork Town Inn 1331 Trumbull St ⓣ313/496-1400, ⓦwww.corktowninn.com. A recently renovated *Holiday Inn* in historic Cork Town. Clean, simple and close to both stadiums; thirty minutes from the airport. ❹

Detroit Marriott Renaissance Center Renaissance Center ⓣ313/568-8000 or 1-800/228-9290, ⓦwww.marriotthotels.com. A fun place to stay, it towers over the city by the river – ask for a room on the upper floors. ❻

Hilton Garden Inn Detroit 351 Gratiot Ave ⓣ313/967-0900, ⓦwww.hiltongardeninn.hilton.com. Smack in the center of downtown life, near Commercial Park. Warm and relaxed atmosphere and is pet friendly. Safe, full service hotel comes with free internet access. ❻

MGM Grand Hotel and Casino 1777 Third St ⓣ877/888-1212 or 1-888/MGM-DETR, ⓦwww.mgmgranddetroit.com. A bit at odds with its surroundings, this swanky new resort is dripping with luxury and loaded with amenities. ❻–❽

Shorecrest Motor Inn 1316 E Jefferson Ave ⓣ313/568-3000 or 1-800/992-9616, ⓦwww.shorecrestmi.com. Friendly, family-run place in lively Rivertown, with clean rooms and specials for Greyhound passengers. ❹

Westin Book Cadillac Detroit 1114 Washington Blvd ⓣ313/442-1600, ⓦwww.bookcadillacwestin.com. Listed on the National

Registry of Historic Places, the *Book Hotel* has been recently renovated and taken over by the Westin chain. Elegant rooms and a full range of amenities. ❼–❾

Woodbridge Star Bed and Breakfast 3985 Trumbull Ave ⓣ 313/831-9668, ⓦ www.woodbridgestar.com. Friendly, more affordable option, with good-value rooms just west of the Theater District. ❹–❻

Downtown

Futuristic glass-box office buildings and a tastefully revamped park overlook the sea glass-green **Detroit River**, but for the most part downtown seems rather empty – even in the middle of the day, its streets are quiet and uncrowded. One reason is that most offices and stores are squeezed into the six gleaming towers of the **Renaissance Center**, a virtual city within a city. Zooming up 73 stories from the riverbank, the towers offer a great view of the metropolis from their free observation deck. This giant business, convention, and retail center, known locally as the RenCen, was one of many complexes developed by **Detroit Renaissance** (a joint public/private sector project) to rejuvenate downtown in the aftermath of the 1967 riot, although it was criticized for forcing out small businesses. Nevertheless, it's an attractive public space and the soaring glass atrium known as the "Winter Garden" is particularly impressive.

Rare greenspace is found among the fountains and sculptures of **Hart Plaza**, which rolls down to the river in the shade of the RenCen. The plaza hosts free lunchtime concerts and lively weekend ethnic festivals all summer long. The US leg of the annual **Ford-Detroit International Jazz Festival**, the largest free jazz festival in the world, takes place here over Labor Day weekend and now spreads up to the Campus Martius square. Across the plaza from the RenCen is the Cobo Convention Center; next to this is **Joe Louis Arena**, home of the beloved Red Wings hockey team (see p.305).

Ten blocks north of the RenCen up Woodward Avenue is the **Theater District**, downtown's prime nightlife spot. Highlights are the magnificently restored Siamese-Byzantine **Fox Theatre** (see p.305) a huge old movie palace that is the city's top concert, drama, and film venue, and the grand Italian Renaissance **State Theatre** next door. This area is at the center of the city's massive **Columbia Street** redevelopment project, home to the new baseball and football stadiums (see p.305), as well as microbreweries, coffeehouses, and the inevitable themed restaurants, including a *Hard Rock Café*.

Three miles east of the RenCen, **Belle Isle Park** is an inner-city island retreat with twenty miles of walkways, sports facilities, a marina, and free attractions including an aquarium, a Great Lakes Museum, and elaborate gardens. It is quiet during the week but can attract crowds on the weekend. Belle Isle Park is also home to the annual **Detroit Grand Prix** Indy car race. To see the island, use Diamond Jack's River Tours (early June to early Sept; $15; ⓣ 313/843-9376, ⓦ www.diamondjack.com), which depart from Hart Plaza downtown, last two hours, and loop round Belle Isle, or just take DOT bus #25 and transfer at MacArthur Bridge to the #12.

The Detroit Cultural Center

Three miles northwest of downtown, next to Wayne State University, the top-class museums of the **Detroit Cultural Center** are clustered within easy walking distance of one another; you can easily spend a whole day here.

One of America's most prestigious art museums and newly refurbished, the colossal **Detroit Institute of Arts**, 5200 Woodward Ave (Wed & Thurs 10am–4pm, Fri 10am–10pm, Sat & Sun 10am–5pm; $8; ⓣ 313/833-7900, ⓦ www.dia.org), traces the history of civilization through one hundred galleries, most notably

Chinese, Persian, Egyptian, Greek, Roman, Dutch, and American collections – not to mention the largest Italian collection outside of Italy. The museum has masterpieces such as a Van Gogh self-portrait and Joos Van Cleeve's *Adoration of the Magi*, as well as Diego Rivera's enormous, show-stealing, 1933 *Detroit Industry* mural. The DIA also presents live music every Friday from 6–10pm (free with museum admission).

The impressive Charles H. Wright **Museum of African American History**, 315 E Warren St (Tues–Sat 9am–5pm, Sun 1–5pm; $8; Ⓣ313/494-5800, Ⓦwww.maah-detroit.org), is the largest African-American museum in the world. Its massive core exhibit covers six hundred years of history in eight distinct segments, starting with a chilling sculpture of a slave boat, before moving through the Civil War, the Depression, and the work of Dr Martin Luther King Jr and Malcolm X, finally settling on contemporary African-American society.

Also in the Cultural Center, the **Detroit Historical Museum**, 5401 Woodward Ave (Wed–Fri 9.30am–3pm, Sat 10am–5pm, Sun noon–5pm; $6; Ⓣ313/833-1805, Ⓦwww.detroithistorical.org), interprets the city's past through its "**Streets of Old Detroit**" display of reconstructed shops dating from the 1840s to the 1900s. The most interesting exhibit, not surprisingly, examines the automobile, with an automated display of the "body drop" process on an assembly line, in which a car's frame is lowered onto its chassis.

The Motown Museum

Unlike cities such as Memphis, Nashville, and New Orleans, Detroit is devoid of the bars, clubs, and homes of its musical heroes. The golden age of Motown was

The Motown sound

The legend that is Tamla Motown started in 1959 when Ford worker and part-time songwriter **Berry Gordy Jr** borrowed $800 to set up a studio. From his first hit onward – the prophetic "Money (That's What I Want)" – he set out to create a crossover style, targeting his records at white and black consumers alike.

Early Motown hits were pure formula. Gordy softened the blue notes of most contemporary black music in favor of a more danceable, poppy beat, with **gospel**-influenced singing and clapping. Prime examples of the early approach featured all-female groups like the **Marvelettes** ("Needle in a Haystack"), the **Supremes** ("Baby Love"), and **Martha Reeves and the Vandellas** ("Nowhere to Run"), as well as the all-male **Miracles** ("Tracks of My Tears"), featuring the sophisticated love lyrics of lead singer **Smokey Robinson**. Gordy's "Quality Control Department" scrutinized every beat, playing all recordings through speakers modeled on cheap transistor radios before the final mix.

The Motown organization was an intense, close-knit community: **Marvin Gaye** married Gordy's sister, while "Little" **Stevie Wonder** was the baby of the family. The label did, however, move with the times, utilizing such innovations as the wah-wah pedal and synthesizer. By the late 1960s its output had acquired a harder sound, crowned by the acid soul productions of Norman Whitfield with the versatile **Temptations**. In 1968 the organization outgrew its premises on Grand Avenue; four years later it abandoned Detroit altogether for LA. Befitting the MOR tastes of the 1970s, the top sellers were then the high-society soul of **Diana Ross** and the ballads of the **Commodores**. This saw many top artists, dissatisfied with Gordy's constant intervention, leave the label, although the crack songwriting team of Holland-Dozier-Holland, responsible for most of the **Four Tops**' hits, stayed in Detroit to produce the seminal **Chairmen of the Board** ("Gimme Just A Little More Time"), along with **Aretha Franklin** and **Jackie Wilson**. Today, Motown is owned by the giant **Universal Music Group**.

very much confined to a specific time and a place, and, disappointingly, only at the **Motown Museum**, 2648 W Grand Blvd (Tues–Sat 10am–6pm; $10; ⓣ313/875-2264, ⓦwww.motownmuseum.com), can Tamla fans pay homage to one of the world's most celebrated record labels. The museum, run as a not-for-profit organization, is housed in the small white-and-blue clapboard house, Hitsville USA, which served as Motown's recording studio from 1959 to 1972. On the ground floor, Studio A remains just as it was left: battered instruments stand piled up against the nicotine-stained acoustic wall-tiles, and a well-scuffed Steinway piano all but fills the room. Upstairs are the former living quarters of label founder **Berry Gordy**, while in the adjoining room record sleeves, gold and platinum discs, and other memorabilia are displayed. The enthusiastic and knowledgeable staff will quite happily give one person the full **tour**.

The Henry Ford Museum, Greenfield Village, and the Automotive Hall of Fame

The enormous **Henry Ford Museum**, ten miles from downtown at 20900 Oakwood Blvd, Dearborn (daily 9.30am–5pm; $15, for Greenfield Village; $22; ⓣ313/271-6001 or 1-800/835-5237, ⓦwww.thehenryford.org; accessible on

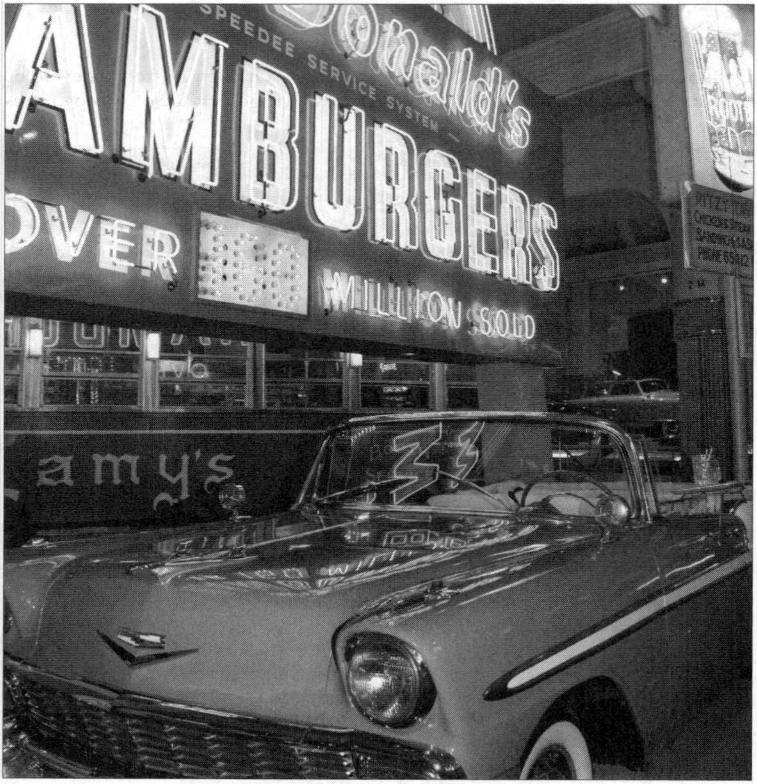

▲ Henry Ford Museum

SMART bus routes #200 and #250), pays fulsome tribute to its founder, an inveterate collector of Americana, as a brilliant industrialist and do-gooder. The former is certainly true. The hero of the "second industrial revolution" and inventor of the assembly line didn't succeed by being a philanthropist. His Service Department of 3500 private policemen prompted the *New York Times* in 1928 to call him "an industrialist fascist – the Mussolini of Detroit." Despite considering unions "the worst things that ever struck the earth," Ford was forced to let the United Auto Workers (UAW) into his factories in 1943, after only 34 out of 78,000 workers voted against joining. Ford also bowed to the economic necessity of employing blacks, though he banned them from the model communities he built for his white workers. Instead, the company constructed a separate town, which he sardonically named Inkster.

In addition to the massive **"The Automobile in American Life"** exhibit ranging from early Ford models and postal carriages to NASCAR vehicles and electric cars, the twelve-acre museum amounts to a giant curiosity shop, holding planes, trains, and row upon row of domestic inventions and non-technological collectibles. Real oddities include the chair Lincoln was sitting in and the car Kennedy was riding in when each was shot, the bus Rosa Parks was riding when she refused to give up her seat, and even a test tube holding Edison's last breath. One pertinent item not on view is the Iron Cross that Hitler presented to Ford (a notorious anti-Semite) in 1938. Down the street from the main museum complex, **Greenfield Village** is a collection of homes owned by famous Americans, relocated from across the country to this site by Ford (same hours as museum; $22, or $26 with Ford Museum). Among the 240 buildings, you'll find Ford's own birthplace, the Wright Brothers' cycle shop, Edison's laboratory, and Firestone's farm. Costumed hosts demonstrate everything from weaving to puncture-repairing.

Directly next door to the Ford sprawl, the **Automotive Hall of Fame**, 21400 Oakwood Blvd (daily 9am–5pm; $8; Ⓣ313/240-4000, Ⓦwww.automotivehalloffame.org), is more interesting than it might at first sound. In paying homage to the innovators and inventors of the global (not just the Detroit) auto industry, the interactive exhibits let visitors see how they would have handled problems encountered by Buick, Honda, and the like. It's not just for mechanical types, either – there's a chance to pit your wits against the dealmakers who set up General Motors.

Windsor, Ontario

The riverside cafés of the easygoing Canadian city of **WINDSOR**, due south of Detroit across the Detroit River, offer pleasant views of their larger neighbor's skyline. Like Detroit, Windsor's main industry is auto manufacturing, but it's much smaller and more relaxed, and makes a good place simply to hang out. The newly renovated **Caesars Casino** (Ⓦwww.caesarswindsor.com) brings shows and a touch of Vegas to town, while the **Hiram Walker Distillery** provides a diverting booze-oriented attraction. Here, Canadian Club whiskey is distilled and stands just a short stroll from downtown at Riverside and Walker (free tours and samplings Mon–Sat 10am–6pm; Ⓣ519/255-9192).

Transit Windsor **buses** (Ⓣ519/944-4111) connect the downtowns of Detroit and Windsor for $2.75 each way. Bring proper identification/passports for customs and immigration officials. To **drive**, take the Windsor Tunnel ($3.75 toll) or the less claustrophobic Ambassador Bridge ($3.75 toll). Windsor has two **visitor centers**, one across the Ambassador Bridge at 1235 Huron Church Rd, and one at 110 Park St E in the city center (both open daily 8.30am–4.30pm; Ⓣ519/973-1338 or 1-800/265-3633, Ⓦwww.visitwindsor.com).

Eating

Detroit's **ethnic** restaurants dish up the best (and least expensive) food in the city. **Greektown**, basically one block of Monroe Avenue between Beaubien and St Antoine streets, is crammed with authentic Greek places; it also contains Trappers Alley, a small mall brimming with good stalls and shops. Less commercial, but offering just as high a standard, are the bakeries, bars, and cantinas of **Mexican Town**, five minutes from downtown. **Royal Oak**, ten miles north, has a wide range of vaguely alternative wholefood places and is the liveliest suburban hang-out in this sprawling metropolis.

Atwater Block Brewery 237 Joseph Campau St ⓣ313/393-2073. This spacious Rivertown brewpub serves up excellent beer-battered fish, mushrooms, mussels, wings, and whatever else the chefs can think of.

Fishbone's Rhythm Kitchen Café 400 Monroe Ave, Greektown ⓣ313/965-4600. Noisy, fun, and often-packed, chain restaurant is a Cajun joint with whiskey ribs, crawfish, gumbo, sushi and lots more.

Golden Fleece 525 Monroe St, Greektown ⓣ313/962-7093. Laid-back Greek diner serves the most authentic gyros in town. Moderate prices.

Pronto! 608 S Washington, Royal Oak ⓣ248/544-7900. Big salads and a huge selection of sandwiches are the specialties in this soothing pastel space.

Rattlesnake Club 300 River Place ⓣ313/567-4400. Owned by creative Detroit master chef Jimmy Schmidt, the *Rattlesnake Club* has a setting in Rivertown to match the exquisite food. Dinner will set you back $30–40 per main course, lunch a lot less. Closed Sun & Mon.

SaltWater in the *MGM Grand* (see p.299) ⓣ313/465-1777. Casual, chic, and quiet dining tucked amidst the lively casino gamblers. Dishes like Misto glazed sea bass are a tad expensive but well worth it.

Slows Bar BQ 2138 Michigan Ave ⓣ313/962-9828. A lively, affordable restaurant and bar that brings the Southern flavor. Located in Corktown, it has the best mac and cheese around.

Xochimilco 3409 Bagley Ave ⓣ313/843-0179. The cornerstone restaurant of Detroit's authentic Mexican Town, bustling *Xochimilco* delivers on huge portions, great service, and superb value. Open till 2am.

Nightlife

There's a lot to do at night in Detroit – the city where the **techno** beat originated and is still going strong. The bars and clubs of the **Theater District** are ever popular, while the **Rivertown** area is renowned for its chic bistros and funky jazz and blues bars. The suburbs of upmarket **Birmingham** and youthful **Royal Oak** are good places to hang out, while there are a couple of fun establishments in the blue-collar neighborhood of **Hamtramck**. Way up on the northern fringe, once-deserted **Pontiac** now has a range of well-attended rock venues, dance clubs, and lounges. Canadian **Windsor** also has some good nightlife, with a drinking age of 19 as opposed to Michigan's 21. For event **listings** in Detroit, Ann Arbor, and Windsor, pick up the free weekly *Metro Times*.

Baker's Keyboard Lounge 20510 Livernois Ave, Royal Oak ⓣ313/345-6300. Mostly local jazz musicians jam in what claims to be the world's oldest jazz club.

Gusoline Alley 309 S Center St, Royal Oak ⓣ248/545-2235. Cramped and dark with a loaded jukebox, this is a legend among Detroit bars serving beers from all over the globe. Go early for a seat; the wildly mixed crowd is a people-watcher's dream.

Magic Bag 22920 Woodward Ave, Ferndale ⓣ248/544-3030, ⓦwww.themagicbag.com. About two miles south of Royal Oak, this popular club boasts a huge range of beers, top jazz and blues artists, and regular roots acts. All shows are 18+ or 21+ with a cover charge at the door.

Magic Stick 4120 Woodward Ave ⓣ313/833-9700, ⓦwww.majesticdetroit.com/stick.asp. This great venue incorporates billiards, bands, and, of course, alcoholic beverages. It's part of the Majestic Theater complex, a venue for big rock shows and huge techno nights.

Saint Andrew's Hall/Shelter 431 E Congress St ⓣ313/961-6358. This cramped downtown club promotes top bands on the alternative circuit. It only holds 800 people, so get a ticket in advance.

Downstairs is the *Shelter* club, with lesser-known touring bands followed by dance music.

Tonic 29 S Saginaw St, Pontiac ⓣ248/334-7411, ⓦwww.tonicdetroit.com. Open Friday through Sun until 2am, the over-18 crowd *Tonic* bills itself as the premiere concert after-party: three levels of dancing and all the DJ vibe you can handle. Hip dress code.

The performing arts

Most of Detroit's major arts venues are handily grouped together in the northwest section of downtown. A sweeping staircase and giant chandeliers are part of the splendor at the **Detroit Opera House**, 1526 Broadway (ⓣ313/237-SING, ⓦwww.detroitoperahouse.com). Close by, the **Music Hall Center for Performing Arts**, 350 Madison Ave (ⓣ313/887-8500, ⓦwww.musichall.org), is the primary venue for **dance** in the city; it also hosts rock concerts, youth theater, and Broadway shows. In the Theater District, the gorgeous Fox Theatre, 2211 Woodward Ave (ⓣ313/983-6611, ⓦwww.olympiaentertainment.com), is the biggest draw, hosting big Broadway shows, while the cozy 450-seater **Gem Theatre**, 333 Madison Ave (ⓣ313/963-9800, ⓦwww.gemtheatre.com), is also worth a visit. A little further on toward the Cultural Center, the **Detroit Symphony Orchestra** performs at the **Max M Fisher Music Center**, 3711 Woodward Ave (ⓣ313/576-5111, ⓦwww.detroitsymphony.com).

Sports

Detroit is one of the few cities with franchises competing at the professional level in all four major team sports. **Hockey**'s Red Wings are arguably the town favorites, and tickets are hard to get; they play downtown at the Joe Louis Arena (ⓣ313/983-6606, ⓦwww.detroitredwings.com). **Baseball**'s Tigers (ⓣ313/962-4000, ⓦwww.detroit.tigers.mlb.com) call the snazzy Comerica Park, or COPA, home, while the Lions play **football** at adjacent Ford Field (ⓣ313/262-2003, ⓦwww.detroitlions.com). Lastly, the Pistons (ⓣ248/377-0100, ⓦwww.nba.com/pistons) play **basketball** in the Palace of Auburn Hills, twenty-five miles north.

Around Detroit: Ann Arbor

Although its population just tops 114,000, **ANN ARBOR**, 45 minutes' drive west of Detroit along I-94, offers a greater choice of restaurants, live music venues, and cultural activities than most towns ten times its size. The **University of Michigan** has shaped the economy and character of the town ever since it was moved here from Detroit in 1837, providing the city with a very conspicuous radical edge.

The best thing to do in Ann Arbor is to stroll around downtown and the campus, which meet at South State and Liberty streets. Downtown's twelve blocks of brightly painted shops and sidewalk cafés offer all you would expect from a college town, with forty bookshops and more than a dozen record stores. Don't miss the huge flagship store of Borders Books at 612 E Liberty St. Though the huge university campus doesn't look particularly appealing, it does engender a sense of excitement, especially around the central meeting place of the **Diag** (or Diagonal Walkway).

Practicalities

Frequent **Greyhound** services from Detroit stop at 116 W Huron St; **Amtrak** is on the north edge of downtown at 325 Depot St; and the **visitor center** is at 120 W Huron St (Mon–Fri 8.30am–5pm; ⓣ734/995-7281 or 1-800/888-9487, ⓦwww.annarbor.org). There are dozens of national **hotel** chains as well as cozy intimate options. The choice place to stay is the *Campus Inn*, right downtown at 615 E Huron St (T 734/769-2200 or 1-800/666-8693, W www.campusinn.com; 6). A good central B&B is the *Burnt Toast Inn*, 415 W William St (T 734/669-6685, W www.burnttoastinn.com; 4–5) and bargain *Eighth Street Trekkers' Lodge*, 120 Eighth St (T 734/369-3107, W www.ofglobalinterest.net; 3), run by an inveterate trekker.

Restaurants worth seeking out include *The Original Cottage Inn*, 512 E William St. (T 734/663-3379) for delicious pizza and *Zingerman's*, 422 Detroit St (T 734/663-DELI), an excellent (if expensive) deli. A more fine dining experience can be had at *Gandy Dancer*, 401 E Depot St (T 734/769-0592).

Ann Arbor's **live music** scene enjoys a nationwide reputation. Unlike many college towns, the place doesn't go to sleep during the summer, either. For news of gigs, grab a copy of *Current*, a free monthly. Likely venues include the *Blind Pig*, 208 S First St (T 734/996-8555, W www.blindpigmusic.com), the best place to watch live rock, alternative, and blues, while *The Ark*, 316 S Main St (T 734/761-1451, W www.a2ark.org), is an important venue for folk, acoustic, and roots music. From time to time there are also live bands at the beautiful Art Deco Michigan Theater, 603 E Liberty St (T 734/668-TIME, W www.michtheater.org), otherwise a great place to watch movies on the cheap.

Festivals are also a key part of Ann Arbor life. In June, the orchestral Summer Festival kicks off activities with music and film (W www.annarborsummerfestival.org); July sees the hectic Ann Arbor Art Fairs with hundreds of stalls; and mid-September brings the recently revived Ann Arbor Blues and Jazz Festival.

The rest of the Lower Peninsula

From Ann Arbor, you will travel a little over 150 miles west along I-94 before you reach Lake Michigan and the quaint town of St Joseph, just the first of many small ports along the lake's 350-mile eastern shoreline. North from St Joseph along Hwy-31, the northwest reaches of the lower peninsula attract sportspeople and tourists from all over the Midwest. Here, out on the unspoiled **Leelanau Peninsula** you'll find the beautiful **Sleeping Bear Dunes**, as well as the charming towns of **Harbor Springs**, **Charlevoix**, and **Petoskey**; all are within striking distance of larger **Traverse City**. At the northern tip of the lower peninsula, revitalized **Mackinaw City** is the departure point for the state's major tour-bus attraction, Old-World **Mackinac Island**.

Along Lake Michigan

Less than thirty miles north of Indiana, **ST JOSEPH** lies just north of "Harbor Country" – a string of adorable small towns offering good swimming, boating, and fishing opportunities. St Joseph's neat, icecream parlor-riddled downtown perches on a high bluff, from which steep steps lead down to sandy Silver Beach and two lighthouses atop two piers. You can enjoy great **food** such as nachos, steak salad, and pasta on the waterfront at *Clementine's Too*, 1235 Broad St (T 269/983-0990). **Places to stay** include the stately lakeside *Boulevard Inn*, 521 Lake Blvd (T 269/983-6600, W www.theboulevardinn.com; 5), where all the rooms are suites, and the good-value *Holiday Inn Express*, at 3019 Lakeshore Drive (T 269/982-0004, W www.sjhiexpress.com; 3–4). For general information on the area, stop in at the **welcome center**, just off I-94 exit 29 (summer Mon–Sat 9am–5pm; rest of year closed Sat; T 269/925-6301).

Fifty miles north, **HOLLAND** was settled in 1847 by Dutch religious dissidents. Today's residents lose no opportunity to let visitors know of their roots: tens of thousands of tulips brighten the town in early summer, while the Holland museum, a Dutch village, a clog factory, and the inevitable windmill all attract tourist dollars. You can **stay** in the Hope College favorite *Haworth Inn* (Ⓣ616/395-7200 or 1-800/903-9142, Ⓦwww.haworthinn.com; ❹), 225 College Ave, and go for a pint of fine ale at *The Curragh* (Ⓣ616/393-6340), 73 E 8th St, which also serves up bar **food**. Twenty miles farther up the shoreline, **GRAND HAVEN** boasts one of the largest and most appealing sandy beaches on the Great Lakes, best seen on a leisurely stroll along the one-and-a-half-mile largely concrete boardwalk.

Just under one hundred miles farther north, a string of pleasant small villages starts with **LUDINGTON**, where a long stretch of public beach precedes **Ludington State Park**, eight miles north on Hwy-116, which offers great hiking and sightseeing amid sweeping sand dunes and virgin pine forests; admission is $8 per car. **Camping** in some beautiful sites cost around $29 a night, though sites for the summer tend to fill up a year in advance (Ⓣ301/784-9090 or 1-800/447-2757). The **visitor center** is on the east side of town at 5827 US-10 (Mon–Fri 8am–5pm; Ⓣ231/845-0324 or 1-800/542-4600, Ⓦwww.visitludington.com). From downtown, the **Lake Michigan Car Ferry** departs for Manitowoc, Wisconsin ($67 per adult, $70 per car, not including driver; Ⓣ231/845-5555 or 1-800/841-4243, Ⓦwww.ssbadger.com) – worth it to avoid Chicago traffic. There are countless places to **stay overnight**, from national chains to cottage rentals; a great option is *Snyder's Shoreline Inn*, 903 W Ludington Ave (May–Oct Ⓣ231/845-1261 or 1-800/843-2177, Ⓦwww.snydersshoreinn.com; ❹), the only downtown property with uninterrupted views of the lakeshore. *House of Flavors*, 402 W Ludington Ave (Ⓣ231/845-5785), is a chrome-heavy **diner** with breakfasts, burgers, and a huge range of ice cream.

Surrounded by forest 32 miles to the north, **MANISTEE** boasts an attractive Victorian downtown and a mile-long **boardwalk** that runs alongside the Manistee River onto Lake Michigan. One of several pretty lakeside areas is **Douglas Park** – with a good sandy beach, small marina, and picnic area. The **Chamber of Commerce** is at 11 Cypress St (Mon–Fri 9am–5pm; Ⓣ231/723-2575, Ⓦwww.manistee.com).

The Leelanau Peninsula

The southwestern edge of the heavily wooded **Leelanau Peninsula** is occupied by the **Sleeping Bear Dunes National Lakeshore**, (Ⓦwww.sleepingbeardunes.com) a constantly resculptured area of towering dunes and precipitous 400ft drops; admission is $10 per car. The area was named by the Chippewa, who saw the mist-shrouded North and South Manitou islands as the graves of two drowned bear cubs, and the massive mainland dune, covered with dark trees, as their grieving mother. Fierce winds off Lake Michigan cause the dunes to edge inland, burying trees that reappear years later stripped of foliage, while the continual attack of high water undercuts the massive sand banks, occasionally sending huge chunks into the lake. Stunning overlooks can be had along the hilly, nine-mile loop of the **Pierce Stocking Scenic Drive**, off Hwy-109. You can also clamber up the strenuous but enjoyable **Dune Climb**, four miles farther north on Hwy-109.

The **visitor center**, south of the dunes at 9922 Front St (Hwy-72) in Empire (daily: summer 8am–6pm; rest of year 8.15am–4pm; Ⓣ231/326-5134, Ⓦwww.nps.gov/slbe), provides details on trails, campgrounds, and beaches. Fifteen miles north, **LELAND** makes a great base to visit the dunes. Its harbor holds a quaint collection of well-weathered sheds, known as **Fishtown**, where the day's catch was once hauled in for gutting and smoking; most are now touristy knick-knack shops. The *Leland Lodge*, 565 Pearl St (Ⓣ231/256-9848, Ⓦwww.lelandlodgeresort.com; ❹) has some of the cheaper rooms in the whole peninsula, while *The Stone House Café & Bread,* 407 S Main St, makes excellent sandwiches on freshly baked bread. **Ferries** from Leland ($30 round-trip; Ⓣ231/256-9061, Ⓦwww.leelanau.com/manitou) go to the uninhabited North and South Manitou islands.

Traverse City

Smooth beaches and striking bay views help make lively **TRAVERSE CITY**, the favorite in-state resort for Michigan natives. A town of fifteen thousand year-round residents, it was saved from the stagnation that overtook many communities when their lumber mills closed down, because the stripped fields proved to be ideal for fruit-growing. Today, the area's claim to be **"Cherry Capital of the World"** is no idle boast. Thousands of acres of cherry orchards envelop the town, their wispy, pink blossoms bringing a delicate beauty each May. At the **National Cherry Festival**, held during the first full week in July, visitors can watch parades, fireworks, and concerts, while sampling every imaginable cherry product.

Traverse City's neat **downtown** rests along the bottom of the west arm of **Grand Traverse Bay**, below the Old Mission Peninsula. This slender seventeen-mile strip of land, which divides the bay into two inlets, makes for a pleasant short driving tour along narrow roads with tremendous simultaneous views of the bay on either side. Five sandy public beaches and a small harbor can be found around the town itself. Various companies offer boat, windsurfer, jet-ski, and mountain bike rental. There are 36 **golf courses** in the immediate area, as well – some of them among the most beautiful in the country.

Practicalities

Greyhound stops near downtown at 3233 Cass Rd. The **visitor center**, downtown at 101 Grandview Parkway (Mon–Fri 9am–5pm, Sat 9am–3pm; Ⓣ231/947-1120 or 1-800/872-8377, Ⓦwww.visittraversecity.com), can help with finding **accommodation**, though prices anywhere near downtown soar in summer. The attractive little *Bayshore Resort*, near downtown at 833 E Front St (Ⓣ231/935-4400, Ⓦwww.bayshore-resort.com; ❺), has a private beach and nice rooms. The very central *Park Place Hotel*, 300 E State St (Ⓣ231/946-5000 or 1-800/748-0133, Ⓦwww.park-place-hotel.com; ❻), is reliable, as are the well-maintained *Days Inn & Suites*, 420 Munson Ave (Ⓣ231/941-0208, Ⓦwww.tcdaysinn.com; ❺). There's **camping** at Traverse City State Park, just outside town at 1132 US-31 N (Ⓣ231/922-5270; $15–29/night).

Affordable **places to eat** in Traverse City are easy to find. Big breakfasts with home-baked bread are served at *Mabel's*, 472 Munson Ave (Ⓣ231/947-0252), while *Mode's Bum Steer*, 125 E State St (Ⓣ231/947-9832), is a ribs joint. The best bet for a meal, though, particularly in the evening, is to drive north onto the Old Mission Peninsula where the *Boathouse*, 14039 Peninsula Drive (Ⓣ231/223-4030), dishes up fresh seafood, pasta, and vegetarian food right by the lake. The *North Peak Brewing Company*, 400 W Front St (Ⓣ231/941-7325), is a fine downtown **bar**; it also serves up great burgers, pizza, salmon, and salads.

North to Mackinaw City

On its way north from Traverse City, scenic Hwy-31 skims along Lake Michigan through **Charlevoix** and other pretty lakeside towns. The northern tip of the peninsula is occupied by **Mackinaw City**, where ferries take excursionists to much-hyped **Mackinac Island** – billboards advertise its attractions for fifty miles before you arrive.

Charlevoix, Petoskey, and Harbor Springs

CHARLEVOIX boasts a positively idyllic setting, fronting onto three separate lakes: Michigan, Charlevoix, and the beautiful, bowl-shaped Round Lake. Petunia-lined **Bridge Street**, the two-block downtown, looks over a picturesque, almost landlocked harbor on Round Lake, hemmed in on the other sides by terraced ridges. Though an undeniably beautiful place, in recent years the town has become a bit too fancy. Beaver Island Boat Company, 103 Bridge Park Drive, runs **ferries** to **Beaver Island**, the most remote inhabited island in the Great Lakes (April–Dec; $38 round-trip; 2hr crossing; ⓣ231/547-2311 or 1-888/446-4095, ⓦwww.bibco.com).

Charlevoix's helpful **visitor center** is at 109 Mason St (ⓣ231/547-2101 or 1-800/367-8557, ⓦwww.charlevoixlodging.com). Lakeside **hotels**, such as the turreted *Weathervane Terrace*, 111 Pine River Lane (ⓣ231/547-9955, ⓦwww.weathervane-chx.com; ❼), charge over $300 a night on peak weekends. One of the best-value **B&Bs**, the *MacDougall House*, 109 Petoskey Ave (ⓣ231/547-5788 or 1-800/753-5788 ⓦwww.michiganbandb.com; ❸), has a garden and huge breakfasts. As for **food**, *Tapawingor*, 9502 Lake St, Ellsworth (ⓣ231/588-7971), is worth the twenty-minute-drive south for richly prepared, if expensive, dishes like roasted pheasant.

In bigger and busier **PETOSKEY**, high above Lake Michigan sixteen miles north along US-31, grand Victorian houses encircle the downtown's nicely restored **Gaslight District**. Ernest Hemingway spent many of his teenage summers here and alludes to the town in his novel *The Torrents of Spring*. The **visitor center** is at 401 E Mitchell St (Mon–Fri 8am–5pm, Sat 10am–4pm, summer Sun noon–4pm; ⓣ1-800/845-2828, ⓦwww.boynecountry.com). For an affordable **place to stay**, try the *Comfort Inn*, 1314 US 31 North (ⓣ231/347-3220 or 1-877/228-5150, ⓦwww.comfortinn.com/hotel/mi412; ❺), or the venerable *Stafford's Perry Hotel*, centrally located at Bay and Lewis streets (ⓣ231/347-4000 or 1-800/737-1899, ⓦwww.staffords.com; ❹); its *Noggin Room Pub* has good snacks and pizza. Other options for **something to eat** include a Hemingway haunt, *Jesperson's*, 312 Howard St (ⓣ231/347-3601), which still does great pies and sandwiches (closed during winter). *Roast & Toast Café & Coffee*, 309 Lake St (ⓣ231/347-7767) an eclectic coffee shop and café serves soups and sandwiches and homemade potpies.

Twelve miles up Hwy-119, **HARBOR SPRINGS** is a favorite with the Midwestern elite. The charming Main Street and small shaded beach of this "Cornbelt Riviera" resort are certainly captivating. The comfy *Colonial Inn*, at 210 Artesian Ave (ⓣ231/526-2111; ❹–❺), has the only reasonably affordable rooms in town; much pricier is the new and luxurious *Hotel Janelle*, 266 Main St (ⓣ231-526-2537, ⓦwww.hoteljanelle.com; ❾). From Harbor Springs, the **"Tunnel of Trees"** scenic drive follows a section of Hwy-119 to Mackinaw City. Along this narrow winding road, occasional breaks in the overhanging trees afford views of Lake Michigan and Beaver Island.

Mackinaw City

Forty miles northeast of Petoskey, **MACKINAW CITY** has long enjoyed a steady tourist trade as the major embarkation point for Mackinac Island and, though the streets have been landscaped and visitors flock to **Mackinaw Crossings**, a mall-cum-entertainment zone on South Huron Street, that remains its real raison d'être, as well as being the last stop en route to the Upper Peninsula.

The **visitor center** is located at 10800 S US-23 (Mon–Fri 8am–5pm; Ⓣ800/666-0160, Ⓦwww.mackinawcity.com). Several mid-priced **hotels** have been built alongside the shore, among them the *Best Western Dockside Waterfront,* 505 S Huron Ave (Ⓣ231/436-5001, Ⓦwww.bestwestern.com; ❺). More rooms can be found at the *Clarion Hotel Beachfront*, 905 S Huron (Ⓣ231/436-5539, Ⓦwww.clarionhotel.com; ❺–❻).

To reach Mackinac Island, contact Arnold Transit (May–Oct, schedule varies; $25 for pedestrians, $8 for bikes; Ⓣ906/847-3351 or 1-800/542-8528, Ⓦwww.arnoldline.com) or Shepler's Ferry (late April to mid-Oct, schedule varies; $23 and $8 for bikes; Ⓣ231/436-5023 or 1-800/828-6157, Ⓦwww.sheplersferry.com); both companies offer **high-speed catamaran crossings** from the Ferry Terminal in Mackinaw City, and do not require reservations.

Mackinac Island

Viewed from an approaching boat, the tree-blanketed rocky limestone outcrop of **MACKINAC ISLAND** (pronounced "Mackinaw"), suddenly thrusting out from the swirling waters, is an unforgettable sight. As you near the harbor, large Victorian houses come into view, dappling the hillsides with white and pastel. The most conspicuous is the imposing, $300-a-night *Grand Hotel* (Ⓣ906/847-3331 or 1-800/334-7263, Ⓦwww.grandhotel.com; ❾), where just to enter the foyer costs $10. On disembarking, you'll see rows of horses and buggies (all motorized transportation is banned from the island, except for emergency vehicles) and inhale the omnipresent smell of fresh manure. Also ubiquitous on the island is **fudge**, relentlessly marketed as a Mackinac "delicacy."

Mackinac's crowded **Main Street** can get irritating, but the island is worth visiting, not least for the ferry ride over and the chance to cycle along the hilly back roads. Underneath the tourist trimmings is a rich history. French priests established a mission to the Huron Indians here during the winter of 1670–71. The French built a fort here in 1715, but within fifty years had lost control of the island to the British. The government acknowledged the island's beauty by designating it as the country's second national park, two years after Yellowstone in 1875, though it was handed over to the state of Michigan twenty years later. To get a feel for the history, hike or cycle up to the whitewashed stone **Fort Mackinac**, a US Army outpost until 1890. Its ramparts afford a great view of the village and lake below, though admission is a steep $8 (May to mid-Oct 9.30am–6.30pm).

On Main Street, an **information kiosk** (daily 9am–5pm; Ⓣ906/847-3783, Ⓦwww.mackinac.com) provides full details of accommodation and other facilities. The less costly **hotel** is *Murray Hotel* (Ⓣ906/847-3360 or 1-800/462-2546, Ⓦwww.4mackinac.com; ❺), which serves a large continental breakfast buffet. Unpretentious **B&Bs** dot the island. **Places to eat** include *Pink Pony Bar & Grill* (Ⓣ906/847-3341), which has a great harbor view and lively atmosphere, and *Horn's Gaslight Bar* (Ⓣ906/847-6154), which also has nightly live music.

The Upper Peninsula

From the map, it would seem logical for Michigan's **Upper Peninsula**, separated from the rest of the state by the **Mackinac Straits**, to be part of Wisconsin. However, when Michigan entered the Union in 1837, its legislators, eyeing the peninsula's huge mineral wealth, incorporated it into their new state before Wisconsin existed.

Previously UP, as it's commonly known, figured prominently in French plans to create an empire in North America. Father Jacques Marquette and other missionaries made peace with the native people and established settlements, including the port of Sault Ste Marie in 1688. The French hoped to press further south, but before they could get much past Detroit, the British inflicted a severe military defeat in 1763.

Vast, lonesome, and wild, the Upper Peninsula is full of stunning landmarks, exemplified by the **Pictured Rocks National Lakeshore**. Most of the eastern section is marked by low-lying, sometimes swampy land between softly undulating limestone hills. Infamous for its bitter winters (1997 saw 272 inches of snow), the northwest corner is the most desolate, especially the rough and broken **Keweenaw Peninsula** and **Isle Royale National Park**, fifty miles offshore. The UP's only real city is **Marquette**, a college town with a quiet buzz and a good base for exploration. Until 1957 you could get to the UP from lower Michigan only by ferry. Today, the five-mile **Mackinac Bridge** ($3 toll), lit up beautifully at night, stretches elegantly across the bottleneck Mackinac Straits.

Pictured Rocks National Lakeshore

The 42 miles between the attractive fishing villages of Grand Marais and Munising form the **Pictured Rocks National Lakeshore**, a splendid array of multicolored

▲ Pictured Rocks National Lakeshore

cliffs, rolling dunes, and secluded sandy beaches. Rain, wind, ice, and sun have carved and gouged arches, columns, and caves into the face of the lakeshore, all stained different hues. Hiking trails run along the clifftops, and Hwy-58 takes you close to the water, but the best way to see the cliffs is by **boat**. Pictured Rocks Cruises offers a three-hour narrated **tour** that leaves from the City Pier in Munising (late May to early Oct 2–8 trips daily; $30; ⓣ906/387-3386, ⓦwww.picturedrocks.com). Less than a mile farther along the lake, at 1204 Commercial St, Shipwreck Tours gives two-hour narrated cruises in a glass-bottomed boat, with surprisingly clear views of three shipwrecks – one intact (June to early Oct 2–3 trips daily; $28; ⓣ906/387-4477, ⓦwww.shipwrecktours.com). Those in a hurry can get a glimpse of the cliffs by visiting the **Miners Castle Overlook**, twelve miles east of Munising, or **Munising Falls**, one of a half-dozen nearby waterfalls, near the village's well-signposted **visitors bureau** (Mon–Fri 9am–5pm; ⓣ906/387-2138, ⓦwww.munising.org). In Munising, *Scotty's Motel*, 415 Cedar St (ⓣ906/387-2449; ❸), and the *Munising Motel*, 332 E Onota St (ⓣ906/387-3187; ❹), are fairly comfortable places to stay. At 101 E Munising Ave, *The Navigator* (ⓣ906/387-1555) is the only **restaurant** in Munising with a view of Lake Superior, and serves breakfast any time along with steaks, seafood, pizza, and burgers.

Marquette

Forty miles west of Munising is the unofficial capital of the UP, the low-key college town of **MARQUETTE**, also the center of the area's massive ore industry. The helpful **state welcome center**, just south of town at 2201 US-41 S (daily: summer 9am–6pm; rest of year 9am–5pm; ⓣ906/249-9066, ⓦwww.marquettecountry.org), has vouchers for local hotel discounts and lots of information about Marquette's sights. Premier among them is rugged **Presque Isle Park**, north of town on Lakeshore Boulevard, almost completely surrounded by Lake Superior and with stunning views of the lake. Back in town, at East Ridge Street and Lakeshore, the **Marquette Maritime Museum** (mid-May to late Oct daily 10am–5pm; $4; ⓣ906/226-2006, ⓦwww.mqtmaritimemuseum.com) has exhibits on the fishing and freighting industries, as well as a video about the fabled Superior wrecking of the *Edmund Fitzgerald*. The area's most curious sight is the **Superior Dome**, on Northern Michigan University's campus at 1401 Presque Isle Ave, the largest wooden dome in the world.

By far the nicest place to **stay** is the grand *Landmark Inn*, 230 N Front St (ⓣ906/228-2580, ⓦwww.thelandmarkinn.com; ❺), which has rooms overlooking the lake, although a host of cheaper motels cluster west of town on US-41. You can **camp** at the *Tourist Park Campground* on Sugarloaf Avenue (ⓣ906/228-0465; $15). *JJ's Shamrock*, downtown at 113 S Front St (ⓣ906/226-6734), serves basic bar **food** along with occasional live music. For a more formal dining experience, locals favor the *Northwoods Supper Club*, just west of town off US-41 (ⓣ906/228-4343), with a meat-and-potatoes menu in a rustic setting. One popular watering hole is *Remie's Bar*, 111 Third St (ⓣ906/226-9133), with a rowdy local crowd and live music on Wednesdays.

Isle Royale National Park

Much closer to Canada than the US, the 45-mile sliver of **Isle Royale National Park**, fifty miles out in Lake Superior, is in a double sense as far as you can get in Michigan from Detroit. All cars are banned and, instead of freeways, 166 miles of hiking trails lead past windswept trees, swampy lakes, and grazing moose. Aside from other outdoors types, the only traces of human life you're likely to see are ancient mineworks, possibly two millennia old, shacks left behind by commercial fishermen in the 1940s, and a few lighthouses and park buildings. Hiking, canoeing, fishing, and scuba-diving among shipwrecks are the principal leisure activities.

The park is open from mid-May until the end of September. **Camping** is free, though you should visit the **park headquarters** at 800 E Lakeshore Drive in Houghton (Mon–Fri 8am–4.30pm; ⓣ906/482-0984, ⓦwww.nps.gov/isro) before you leave the mainland, for advice on water purity, mosquitoes, and temperatures that can drop well below freezing even in summer. Aside from camping, you can stay in a self-catering cottage or a luxury lodge room at the *Rock Harbor Lodge* (ⓣ906/337-4993, Oct–April ⓣ866/644-2003, ⓦwww.isleroyaleresort.com; ❻–❾). The lodge rents canoes and motorboats for $30 and $64 per day, respectively, and offers cruises for $30.

Ferries to Isle Royale leave from Copper Harbor ($52–60 single; ⓣ906/289-4437, ⓦwww.isleroyale.com), Houghton ($54 single; ⓣ906/482-0984, ⓦwww.nps.gov/isro), and Grand Portage, Minnesota ($40–55 single; ⓣ715/392-2100, ⓦwww.grand-isle-royale.com). If you are in a hurry, you can hop over by **plane** with the Isle Royale Seaplane Service in Houghton ($250 round-trip; ⓣ906/482-8850, ⓦwww.royaleairservice.com).

Indiana

Thanks to an influx of northward migrants early in the nineteenth century – including the family of Abraham Lincoln, who lived for fourteen years near the present village of Santa Claus before moving to Illinois – much of **INDIANA** bears the influence of the easygoing South. Unlike the abolitionist Lincolns, many former Southerners brought slaves to this new territory, and thousands rioted against being drafted into the Union army when the Civil War broke out. However, massive industrialization since the 1870s has firmly integrated Indiana into the regional economy. On a national level, this sports-happy state is best known these days for automobile racing and high school basketball.

Despite some beautiful dunes and beaches, the most lasting memories provided by Indiana's fifty-mile **lakeshore** (by far the shortest of the Great Lakes states) are of the grimy steel mills and poverty-stricken neighborhoods of towns like Gary and East Chicago. In northern Indiana, the area in and around Elkhart and Goshen contains one of the nation's largest **Amish settlements**. The central plains are characterized by small market towns, except for the sprawling capital, **Indianapolis**, which makes a nice enough stopover. Hilly southern Indiana, at its most appealing in the fall, is a welcome contrast to the central cornbelt, boasting several quaint towns such as Nashville, while thriving Columbus exhibits a great array of contemporary architecture for such a small city.

Getting around Indiana

Nine interstates, five of which slice through Indianapolis, provide boring but fast ways to traverse Indiana. Greyhound runs frequent services, particularly on I-65 between Chicago and Louisville, and I-70 between the Eastern US and St Louis, while **Indianapolis**, **Michigan City**, and **South Bend** are the major stops on the state's three different Amtrak routes. Flights from most Midwestern and Eastern cities land at **Indianapolis International Airport**.

Indianapolis and around

INDIANAPOLIS began life in 1821, when a tract of barely inhabited marshes was designated the state capital. While its location in the middle of Indiana's rich farmland bore immense commercial advantages, the absence of a navigable river prohibited the transportation of bulky materials such as coal and iron to sustain heavy industry. Though home to more than sixty car manufacturers by 1910, the city never seriously threatened Detroit's supremacy. Nevertheless, it's now one of the biggest cities in the world that's not accessible by water, having attracted food, paper, and pharmaceutical industries, including the giant Eli Lilly Corporation.

Although Indianapolis continues its focus on sports – in recent years, it has constructed several world-class sports arenas, including the retro-styled **Conseco Fieldhouse** downtown – there is more to the city than could perhaps once be said. Along with new hotels, a gaggle of top-class museums, and a zoo, its old downtown landmarks have become cultural, shopping, and dining complexes. No longer is it (quite) true that nothing happens here except for the glamorous **Indianapolis 500 car race** each May.

Arrival and information

Indianapolis International Airport is ten miles southwest of downtown, on the #8 IndyGo bus route ($1.50; ⓣ317/635-3344), IndyGo's Green Line Downtown/Airport Express route provides non-stop service from the airport to downtown and the Convention Center (daily 5am–9pm; $7). A **taxi** into the center costs around $33; try Yellow Cabs (ⓣ317/487-7777). Both Greyhound **buses** and Amtrak **trains** arrive at 350 S Illinois St (ⓣ317/267-3071), next to the fairly central Union Station complex. Useful **visitor centers** can be found at 201 S Capitol St, beside the RCA Dome (Mon–Fri 8.30am–5.30pm; ⓣ1-800/323-4639, ⓦwww.indy.org), and in the glass pavilion at 100 W Washington St (Mon–Sat 10am–9pm, Sun noon–6pm; ⓣ317/624-2563).

Accommodation

Indianapolis has plenty of quality **places to stay**, with budget options about five miles from downtown. Prices can double during the race months of May, August, and September.

Canterbury Hotel 123 S Illinois St ⓣ317/204-2569 or 1-877/866-0837, ⓦwww.canterburyhotel.com. Much the classiest downtown option, this landmark hotel was rebuilt in 1928 and offers a hundred opulent and expensive rooms. ❼–❽

Crowne Plaza Union Station 123 W Louisiana St ⓣ317/631-2221 or 1-877/227-6963, ⓦwww.crowneplaza.com/ind-downtown. Regular hotel rooms plus some much more exciting suites in converted railway carriages. ❻–❼

Days Inn Downtown 401 E Washington St ⓣ317/637-6464 or 1-800/329-7466, ⓦwww.daysinn.com. Centrally located lodgings in a reliable chain motel. ❹

Indy Hostel 4903 Winthrop Ave ⓣ317/727-1696, ⓦwww.indyhostel.us. Appealing small-scale hostel in a former family home, in a friendly neighborhood six miles from downtown. Dorm beds for $22 weekdays, $25 weekends, plus basic private rooms. Bike hire available. ❶–❷

The Villa Inn 1456 N Delaware St ⓣ317/916-8500 or 1-866/626-8500, ⓦwww.thevillainn.com. Castellated six-room luxury B&B inn with the feel of a hotel, two miles north of downtown, and offering a spa and restaurant. The same owners run two other local B&Bs. ❽

Downtown

The nerve center of Indianapolis's spacious, relaxed downtown is the reasonably tasteful **Circle Centre** shopping and entertainment complex. Suspended over the busy Washington and Illinois intersection, the spectacular **Indianapolis Artsgarden** is an eight-story glass rotunda illuminated with twinkling lights. A performance and exhibition space, it doubles as a walkway to Circle Centre and several downtown hotels. One block north, streets radiate from **Monument Circle**, the starting point for a lengthy series of memorials and plazas dedicated to war veterans. Many visitors climb the 330 steps of the renovated 284ft **Soldiers and Sailors Monument** (daily 10am–7pm; walk up free, elevator $1) – the tiny elevator can seldom cope with the demand – but in truth the view of the city from the top is nothing special.

▲ The Indianapolis 500

The Indianapolis 500

Seven miles northwest of downtown, the **Indianapolis Motor Speedway** stages three events each year; one is the legendary **Indianapolis 500**, held on the last Sunday in May, the others are July's prestigious NASCAR Brickyard 400 and August's Red Bull Indianapolis GP.

The Indy 500 is preceded by two weeks of qualification runs that whittle the hopeful entrants down to a final field of 33 drivers, one of whom will scoop the million-dollar first prize. The two-and-a-half-mile circuit was built as a test track for the city's motor manufacturers. The first 500-mile race – held in 1911 and won in a time of 6hr 42min, at an average speed of 74.6mph – was a huge success, vindicating the organizers' belief that the distance was the optimum length for spectators' enjoyment. Cars now hit 235mph, though the official times of the winners are reduced by delays caused by accidents. While the technology is marvelous, the true legends in the eyes of their fans are such championship drivers as A.J. Foyt, Mario Andretti, and members of the Unser dynasty. The big race crowns one of the nation's largest festivals, attended by almost half a million spectators. Seats for the race usually sell out well in advance ($70–90; ⓣ1-800/822-4639, ⓦwww.imstix.com), but you may gain admittance to the infield ($20), for a tailgate style, rowdy atmosphere and limited viewing.

Adjoining the track, the impressive display of race-car history at the **Indianapolis Motor Speedway Hall of Fame Museum**, 4790 W 16th St (daily 9am–5pm, extended hours around race time; $3; ⓣ317/492-6700, ⓦwww.indy500.com), provides a good background to the hysteria. To an irregular schedule, it's also possible to join a 90-minute behind-the-scenes **Grounds Tour** ($25 inc museum admission).

Five blocks east, starting at New York and East streets, the serene tree-shaded **Lockerbie Square Historic District** is a small enclave of picturesque residences that were home to nineteenth-century artisans and business leaders. Small wood-frame cottages line the cobblestone streets, many of them painted in bright pinks, blues, and yellows, and fronted by ornately carved porches.

Several blocks west of Monument Circle, the **Indiana State Museum**, 650 W Washington St (Mon–Sat 9am–5pm, Sun 11am–5pm; $7; ⓣ317/232-1637, ⓦwww.indianamuseum.org), gives a useful insight into the state's history through exhibits on everything from geology to sport. The **Eiteljorg Museum of American Indians and Western Art** is nearby at 500 W Washington St, on the western edge of downtown (Mon–Sat 10am–5pm, Sun noon–5pm; tours at 1pm; $8; ⓣ317/636-9378, ⓦwww.eiteljorg.org). Harrison Eiteljorg, an industrialist who went West in the 1940s to speculate in minerals, fell so deeply in love with the art of the region that he brought as much of it back with him as possible, especially from Taos, New Mexico. On display are works by Frederic Remington, Charles M. Russell, and Georgia O'Keeffe, as well as tribal artifacts from all over North America and a 38ft Haida totem pole on the grounds. There are also superb touring exhibits and a gorgeous gift shop. The Eiteljorg stands amid the rolling greenery of **White River State Park**, which is also home to the sizeable **Indianapolis Zoo** (summer Mon–Thurs 9am–5pm, Fri–Sun 9am–6pm; rest of year daily 9am–4pm; $13.50; ⓣ317/630-2001, ⓦwww.indyzoo.com). In the park's southeast corner stands the superb **Victory Field**, home of the Indianapolis Indians (ⓣ317/269-3545), the farm team for baseball's Cincinnati Reds.

Out from downtown

Although the bodies of former president Benjamin Harrison and Hoosier poet James Whitcomb Riley lie in the enormous **Crown Hill Cemetery**, at 38th Street and Michigan, the most visited grave belongs to 1930s bank robber **John Dillinger**, at Section 44 Lot 94. Designated Public Enemy Number One, Dillinger completed thirteen bank raids – killing four policemen, three FBI agents, one sheriff, and an undetermined number of innocent bystanders – in a single-year career. Something of a folk hero, he escaped from jail twice, but was eventually ambushed by the FBI outside a Chicago theater in 1934 (see p.332) – that said, some researchers allege that another man was killed in his place.

Opposite the cemetery at 1200 W 38th St, more than 150 lush wooded acres accommodate the capacious **Indianapolis Museum of Art** (Tues, Wed, & Sat 11am–5pm, Thurs & Fri 11am–9pm; ⓣ317/923-1331, ⓦwww.imamuseum.org). The main building is surrounded by a lake, botanical garden, sculpture courtyard, and a concert terrace. Inside, the exceptional displays include the largest collection of Turner paintings outside Britain and an array of paintings and prints from Gauguin's Pont Aven school; collections from around the globe include an extensive assortment of masks, figures, jewelry, and household items from northern Africa.

The **Children's Museum of Indianapolis**, 3000 N Meridian St, four miles north of downtown off I-65 (daily 10am–5pm; closed Mon late Sept to late March; $13.50, under-18s $8.5; ⓣ317/334-3322, ⓦwww.childrensmuseum.org), is arguably the best of its kind in the country. Its most popular exhibit is the Dinosphere, in which visitors can dig for genuine fossils, while All Aboard! is an entertaining romp through the Age of Steam.

Eating

The swish **Circle Centre** mall houses dozens of **places to eat**, but most are chains. You'd do better to stick to the more established restaurants downtown or head up to **Broad Ripple Village** (bus #17) at College Avenue and 62nd Street, which is packed with bars and cafés (along with galleries and shops).

3 Sisters Café 334 N Guilford Ave ⓣ317/257-5556. Stop in for a laidback atmosphere and a healthy dose of vegetarian fare.

Bazbeaux 6360 Massachusetts Ave, downtown ⓣ 317/636-7662 and 811 E Westfield Blvd, Broad Ripple Village ⓣ 317/255-5711. The best (thin-crust) pizzas in town, with a range of exotic toppings.

Elbow Room 605 N Pennsylvania St ⓣ317/635-3354. This pub serves specialty sandwiches and lots of import beers.

H20 Sushi 1912 Broad Ripple Ave ⓣ317/254-0677. This restaurant and sushi bar has successfully married a traditional mix of sushi with a more modern choice of savory combos. Closed Sun & Mon.

St Elmo Steak House 127 S Illinois St ⓣ317/635-0636. One of the most famous steak restaurants in the meat-mad Midwest. It can be rather pompous, and it's certainly expensive ($40–50 per person), but there's no denying the quality.

Shapiro's 808 S Meridian St ⓣ317/631-4041. Landmark deli just a few blocks off downtown, where you can fill up on lox, tongue, and other specialties in an old-style cafeteria atmosphere for around $8. Leave room for the huge desserts.

Yat's Cajun and Creole 659 Massachusetts Ave ⓣ317/686-6380; also at 5463 N College Ave ⓣ317/253-8817. Wildly popular Louisiana-flavored cafeteria, offering a changing menu of inexpensive daily specials in two locations (entrees $4.50–6.50).

Nightlife and entertainment

The **nightlife** area in downtown is Massachusetts Avenue, where along with some good bars and restaurants, the 3000-seat **Murat Centre**, a former Masonic shrine at 502 N New Jersey St (ⓣ317/231-0000, ⓦwww.murat.com), hosts headliners and Broadway musicals. Otherwise, head north to chic **Broad Ripple Village**. Check the free weekly *NUVO* (ⓦwww.nuvo.net) "Indy's alternative voice," for full details of gigs and events.

On the **performing arts** scene, the 1927 Spanish Baroque Indiana Repertory Theatre, 140 W Washington St (Ⓣ317/635-5252, Ⓦwww.irtlive.com), puts on dramatic productions between September and May, while the Indianapolis Symphony Orchestra has weekly concerts at the equally elaborate 1916 Hilbert Circle Theatre, 45 Monument Circle (Ⓣ317/639-4300, Ⓦwww.indyorch.org).

Broad Ripple Brew Pub 842 E 65th St Ⓣ317/253-2739. Atmospheric brewpub located six miles north of downtown Indianapolis.

Chatterbox 435 Massachusetts Ave Ⓣ317/636-0584, Ⓦwww.chatterboxjazz.com. Ever-busy local bar, hosting live jazz nightly for the past 25 years.

Madame Walker Theatre Center 617 Indiana Ave Ⓣ317/236-2099, Ⓦwww.walkertheatre.com. Black cultural and heritage center putting on Jazz on the Avenue every 4th Friday, plus regular dance events, plays, and concerts.

Rathskeller Restaurant 401 E Michigan St Ⓣ317/636-0396. German beer hall in the basement of the historic Atheneum building that also serves food. Live music and a three-season Biergarten.

Slippery Noodle 372 S Meridian St Ⓣ317/631-6974. Indiana's oldest bar, established in 1850, is next to Union Station. Cheap beer Mon and Tues, and live blues every night starting at 8:15pm.

Vogue 6259 N College Ave Ⓣ317/259-7029, Ⓦwww.thevogue.ws. Popular Broad Ripple rock and indie venue in a former movie theater, and featuring retro club nights.

Bloomington

BLOOMINGTON, a college town, is by far the liveliest small city in Indiana, just 45 miles southwest of Indianapolis on Hwy-37. It owes its vibrancy to the main campus of Indiana University, east of downtown. The I.M. Pei–designed **Indiana University Art Museum** on East Seventh Street (Tues–Sat 10am–5pm, Sun noon–5pm; free) holds a fine international collection of painting and sculpture. Across the street from the pastoral campus, Indiana native and law student, Hoagy Carmichael composed *Stardust* on the piano of a popular hangout. The architecturally rich downtown also features a host of good shops.

Practicalities

Bloomington Shuttle, 3200 Venture Blvd, (Ⓣ812/332-6004 or 1-800/589-6004), runs a **bus** service to Indianapolis. Bloomington's friendly **visitor center** can be found at 2855 N Walnut St (Mon–Fri 8.30am–5pm, Sat 9am–4pm; Ⓣ812/334-8900,Ⓦwww.visitbloomington.com).

If you need **to stay**, the conveniently located *Hampton Inn,* 2100 N Walnut St (Ⓣ812/334-2100; ❹–❺), is a friendly, clean choice. The cozy and also very central Victorian *Grant Street Inn*, 310 N Grant St (Ⓣ812/334-2353 or 1-800/328-4350, Ⓦwww.grantstreetinn.com; ❻–❼), offers more luxury. Among student bars and cafés lining Kirkwood Avenue is the vegetarian *Laughing Planet*, at no. 322 E Kirkwood (Ⓣ812/323-2233), renowned for its burritos, while local **restaurant** *FARMbloomington*, 108 E Kirkwood Ave (Ⓣ 812/323-0002) offers real food right from the farm. The *Brewpub at Lennie's*, 1795 E Tenth St (Ⓣ812/339-2256), is the liveliest drinking spot around.

Illinois

Nearly everything in the agricultural powerhouse state of **ILLINOIS** revolves around **Chicago**, the largest and most exciting city in the Great Lakes region. Perched in the state's northeastern corner, on the shores of **Lake Michigan**, Chicago has a fabulous skyline, plus top-rated museums, restaurants, and cafés, and dozens of nightspots that send forth blues, jazz, and rock into the night. Seventy-five percent of the state's twelve-million-strong population lives within commuting distance of the Windy City. The contrast between Illinois' quiet rural hinterlands and its buzzing urban center could hardly be greater.

Illinois was first explored and settled by the French, though in 1763 the territory was sold to the English. Granted statehood in 1818, Illinois remained a distant frontier until the mid-1830s; only once the native **Sauk** were subjugated, after a series of uprisings, did settlers arrive in sizeable numbers. Among them were the first followers of Joseph Smith, founder of the Mormon Church, who established a large colony along the Mississippi at Nauvoo. The **Mormons** met with suspicion and persecution and, after Smith was murdered by a lynch mob in 1844, fled west to Utah. Other early immigrants included the young **Abraham Lincoln**, who practiced law from 1837 onward in **Springfield**. Now the state capital, it's home to a wide range of Lincolniana, including his restored home, his law offices, and various other period buildings and artifacts, as well as his monumental tomb and new presidential library. Hence Illinois' self-proclaimed nickname, "Land of Lincoln."

Getting around Illinois

Chicago is the site of **O'Hare Airport** and the hub of the national Amtrak **train** network. If you plan to spend time in the rest of Illinois, Amtrak, numerous commuter railroads, and, to a lesser extent, Greyhound, provide reasonable public transportation. **Cycling** is also generally easy on these endless flat plains. Half a dozen **interstates** fan out across the country from Chicago.

Chicago

CHICAGO is in many ways the nation's last great city. Sarah Bernhardt called it "the pulse of America" and, though long eclipsed by Los Angeles as the nation's second most populous city after New York, Chicago really does have it all, with less hassle and fewer infrastructural problems than its coastal rivals.

Founded in the early 1800s, Chicago had a population of just fifty in 1830. Its expansion was triggered first by the opening of the Erie Canal in 1825, and then by the arrival of the first locomotive in 1848; by 1860 it was the largest railroad center in the world, serving as the main connection between the established East Coast cities and the frontier that stretched over 2000 miles west to the Pacific Ocean. That position on the sharp edge between civilization and wilderness made it a crucible of innovation. Many aspects of modern life, from skyscrapers to suburbia, had their start, and perhaps their finest expression, here on the shores of Lake Michigan.

Despite burning to the ground in 1871, Chicago boomed thereafter, doubling in population every decade and by 1900 the city was home to over two million people,

many of whom made their way on crowded ships from Ireland and Eastern Europe. In the early years of the twentieth century, it cemented its reputation as a place of apparently limitless opportunity, with jobs aplenty for those willing and not averse to strenous physical labor and largely monotonous tasks. The attraction was strongest among **blacks** from the Deep South: African-Americans poured into the city, with more than 75,000 arriving during the war years of 1916–18 alone.

During the Roaring Twenties, Chicago's self-image as a no-holds-barred free market was pushed to the limit by a new breed of entrepreneur. Criminal syndicates, ruthlessly run by the likes of **gangsters** such as Al Capone and Bugsy Moran, took advantage of Prohibition to sell bootleg alcohol. Shootouts in the street between sharp-suited, Tommy-gun-wielding mobsters were not as common as legend would have it, but the backroom dealing and iron-handed control they pioneered was later perfected by politicians such as former mayor **Richard Daley** – father of the present mayor – who ran Chicago single-handedly from the 1950s until his death in 1976. These days, the tourist authorities play down the mobster era; few traces of the hoodlum years exist, and those that do owe more to Hollywood than contemporary Chicago.

Most visitors to Chicago are immediately bowled over by its magnificent urban **skyline**, adorned with one of the world's finest assemblages of **modern architecture**, ranging from Mies van der Rohe's masterpieces to the 110-story **Sears Tower**. The city is also rightfully quite proud of the wonderful new Millennium Park and the extraordinary treasures of the **Art Institute of Chicago**, as well as several other excellent **museums**, along with restaurants, sports, and highbrow cultural activities. Perhaps its strongest suit, however, is **live music**, with a phenomenal array of **jazz** and **blues** clubs packed into the back rooms of its amiable bars and cafés. The **rock** scene is also healthy, having spawned such bands as Smashing Pumpkins and Wilco during the 1990s. And almost everything is noticeably less expensive than in other US cities – **eating out**, for example, costs much less than in New York or LA, but is every bit as good. Two great ways to get a real feel for the city are to head out to ivy-covered **Wrigley Field** on a sunny summer afternoon to catch baseball's Cubs in action, or take a cruise boat under the bridges of the Chicago River at sunset.

Arrival, information, and getting around

Chicago's **O'Hare International Airport** (Ⓦwww.ohare.com), the national headquarters for United, American, and several other airlines, is seventeen miles northwest of downtown Chicago. It is connected to the city center by 24-hour CTA (Blue Line) **trains** from the station under Terminal 4 (around 40min; $2). **Midway Airport** is smaller than O'Hare and primarily used by domestic airlines. Midway is eleven miles southwest of downtown, and you can take one of CTA's Midway (Orange Line) trains from right outside of the terminal (30min; $2). **Taxis** into town from O'Hare cost up to $40 (there's also a ride-share program with a flat rate of $22), and take thirty minutes to an hour. From Midway the fare is about $30 and the journey time is twenty to forty minutes. Another option is Airport Express's **express bus and van service** between the airports and downtown hotels (around $27 from O'Hare, $22 from Midway; 1-888/284-3826, Ⓦwww.airportexpress.com).

Chicago is the hub of the nationwide **Amtrak** rail system, and almost every cross-country route passes through **Union Station**, west of the Loop at Canal and Adam streets. Greyhound and a number of regional bus companies pull into the large 24-hour **bus station** at 630 W Harrison St (Ⓣ312/408-5800), three blocks southwest of Union Station.

Arriving in Chicago **by car**, racing towards the gleaming glass towers of the Loop, can be memorable. Bear in mind, though, that traffic on the expressways to and from downtown can be bumper-to-bumper during rush hours. **Parking** can also be a problem. Meters are expensive (60¢ for 10min) and usually have a 2-hour limit. Check street signs for additional restrictions, which are rigidly enforced – violations may result in your car being towed and impounded. Perhaps the best

CityPass

For significant **discounts** at five of the city's major tourist and cultural attractions – the Hancock Observatory, the Field Museum, Shedd Aquarium, Adler Planetarium & Astronomy Museum, and the Museum of Science and Industry – you can purchase a **CityPass** ($59, ages 4–11 $49; Ⓣ1-888/330-5008, Ⓦwww.citypass.com). Valid for nine days, it allows you to skip most lines and save (up to $49, if you visit all five sights). CityPasses are sold at each of the attractions, or via the website.

Guided tours

The best **guided tours** of Chicago have to be the wide range offered by the **Chicago Architecture Foundation**, based in the Archicenter in the Santa Fe Building at 224 S Michigan Ave (Ⓣ312/922-3432, Ⓦwww.architecture.org). Expert guides point out the city's many architectural treasures and explain their role in Chicago's history and development. Most popular of all are the superb Architecture River Cruises, ninety-minute **boat trips** along the Chicago River that leave from Michigan Avenue and Lower Wacker Drive (late April to early June Mon–Fri 3 departures, Sat & Sun 5 departures; early June to Sept Mon–Fri 10 deps, Sat & Sun 13 deps; Oct Mon–Fri 5 deps, Sat & Sun 6 deps; Nov Fri–Sun 3 deps; Mon–Fri $28, Sat & Sun $30). The Foundation also runs several **walking tours** of the Loop, departing from the Archicenter on a complicated schedule of at least two different 2-hour tours daily throughout the year ($15 for one tour), and a daily 45-minute, $5 lunchtime tour of downtown landmarks at 12.15pm. Their longer-range **bus tours** operate mainly in summer, focusing principally on the works of Frank Lloyd Wright ($52) and the socially-minded "Roots of Reform" tour ($35), though the 3-hour 30-minute "highlights" tour ($40) leaves at 9.30am on Saturdays and Wednesdays all year. Finally, the Foundation also operates the free **Loop Tour Train** in the summer, and it is a unique way to get a first overview of downtown Chicago, in which a special "El" train makes a couple of slow but non-stop commentated circuits around the Loop. Tickets, on the day of the tour only, are available first-come, first-served from the visitor center at 77 E Randolph St.

Among the many other tour operators in the city are **Untouchable Tours**, which run wise-cracking, gangster-themed bus tours of Prohibition-era haunts ($27; Ⓣ773/881-1195; Ⓦwww.gangstertour.com); the **Chicago Trolley**, which makes regular circuits of downtown (daily 9.30am–5pm; $29 for one day, $40.50 for three days, hop on and off; Ⓣ773/663-0260, Ⓦwww.chicagotrolley.com); and **Shoreline Sightseeing Tours**, which specializes in lake cruises, starting from Navy Pier and the Shedd Aquarium, and also runs a simple Water Taxi service between the two (architectural cruises $24-26, lake cruises $14; Ⓣ312/222-9328, Ⓦwww.shorelinesightseeing.com).

place to leave a car in the downtown area is in the garage under Grant Park, at Columbus Street and Monroe Drive, close to the east side of the Art Institute ($22 for 24hr).

Information

Pick up information and maps from the **Chicago Office of Tourism**, in the lobby of the Chicago Cultural Center, 77 E Randolph St (Mon–Thurs 8am–7pm, Fri 8am–6pm, Sat 9am–6pm, Sun 10am–6pm; Ⓣ1-800/877-CHICAGO, Ⓦwww.explorechicago.org). There are also **information centers** in the Historic Water Tower, 800 N Michigan Ave on the Magnificent Mile (Mon–Thurs 8am–7pm, Fri 8am–6pm, Sat 9am–6pm, Sun 10am–6pm)) and in the Northwest Exelon Pavilion at Millennium Park (daily 10am–4pm).

Chicago's main **post office**, the largest in the world, is at 433 W Harrison St (open 24hr). There's a downtown branch at 211 S Clark St (Mon–Fri 7am–6pm).

City transportation

Getting around Chicago is simple and quick, thanks to buses and the "El," a system of elevated trains operated 24 hours a day by the Chicago Transit Authority (CTA; Ⓣ312/836-7000, Ⓦwww.transitchicago.com). Pick up a CTA System Map, available at most subway stations and visitor centers, or from CTA headquarters west of the Chicago River at 567 W Lake St. **Buses** run every five to fifteen minutes

ACCOMMODATION

Allegro	H	Hampton Inn & Suites	E	Monaco	G	Trump International Hotel & Tower	F
The Drake	B	HI-Chicago	J	Palmer House Hilton	I	Wheeler Mansion	K
Gold Coast Guest House	A	Holiday Inn Express- Hotel Cass	D	Sofitel Chicago Water Tower	C		

during rush hours and every eight to twenty minutes at most other times. **Rapid transit trains** run every five to fifteen minutes during the day and every fifteen to sixty minutes all night. Lines are color-coded and denoted by route rather than destination. The Howard–Dan Ryan is the Red Line; Lake–Englewood–Jackson Park is the Green Line; the O'Hare–Congress–Douglas is the Blue Line; the Ravenswood is the Brown Line (whose trains circle the Loop, giving the area its name); the Evanston Express is the Purple Line; the Midway–Loop is the Orange Line; the Pink Line (which runs from the Loop to the suburb of Cicero), and the Skokie Swift is the Yellow Line.

The CTA no longer accepts tokens; instead, riders purchase a "**Chicago card**" (available in all El stations) and add value to it. One ride costs $2.00; two more rides within two hours costs just 25¢. Passes good for one ($5), two ($9), three ($12), or five ($18) days of unlimited rides on both buses and the El are sold at O'Hare and Midway airports as well as Union Station, the visitor center, and other locations. In addition, **Metra Commuter Trains** run from various points downtown to and from the suburbs and outlying areas, including Oak Park and Hyde Park. One ride is $2.15.

Chicago's **taxis** cost $2.25 at the drop of the flag, and $1.80 per mile. They can be hailed anytime in the Loop and other central neighborhoods; otherwise call Yellow (ⓣ312/829-4222) or Checker taxis (ⓣ312/243-2537).

Finally, **bicycles** are available for rent at Millennium Park's multi-level bike park at 239 E Randolph St.

Accommodation

Most central **accommodation** is oriented toward business and convention trade rather than tourism, but there are still plenty of moderately priced rooms in and around the Loop, to say nothing of the myriad of establishments that are scattered alongside major interstates.. Even top-class downtown hotels are, comparatively, not that expensive. Note, however, that a **room tax** of just over fifteen percent is added to all bills, while overnight **parking** can cost $25 at a modest downtown hotel, and as much as $45 at a fancy one.

If you're stuck, Hot Rooms is a reservation service offering hotel rooms at discount rates (ⓣ773/468-7666 or 1-800/468-3500; ⓦwww.hotrooms.com). While they're not as prominent as elsewhere, **bed-and-breakfast** rooms are available from around $80 per night; the Chicago B&B Association maintains full listings (ⓦwww.chicago-bed-breakfast.com).

Allegro 179 W Randolph St ⓣ312/236-0123 or 1-800/643-1500, ⓦwww.allegrochicago.com. With a colorful, updated Art Deco design, this boutique hotel is sure to delight. Luxury amenities throughout. ❽

Arlington House International Hostel 616 W Arlington Place ⓣ773/929-5380 or 1-800/467-8355, ⓦwww.arlingtonhouse.com. Easygoing hostel close to loads of good bars and Wrigley Field, with segregated dorms ($31) and private rooms with and without en-suite facilities. Open 24hr. ❶–❸

Comfort Inn & Suites Downtown 15 E Ohio St ⓣ312/894-0900 or 1-888/775-9223, ⓦwww.chicagocomfortinn.com. This high-rise chain hotel is given considerable charm by its restored Art Deco lobby. The rooms are well equipped, and complemented by fitness and sauna facilities. Rates include continental breakfast. ❻

Days Inn Lincoln Park North 644 W Diversey Parkway at Clark ⓣ773/525-7010 or 1-888/576-3287, ⓦwww.lpndaysinn.com. This good, friendly motel is popular with visiting musicians and a convenient base for North Side nightlife. Free continental breakfast. ❺

The Drake 140 E Walton Place ⓣ312/787-2200 or 1-800/553-7253, ⓦwww.thedrakehotel.com. Chicago's society hotel, just off the Magnificent Mile, has been modernized without sacrificing its sedate charms. Its well-appointed rooms feature high-speed internet access and jacuzzis. You can always just pop in for a drink at the elegant Palm Court Lounge. ❽–❾

Gold Coast Guest House 113 W Elm St ⓣ312/337-0361, ⓦwww.bbchicago.com. Inconspicuous 1870s rowhouse that's been beautifully converted to offer four high-class en-suite B&B rooms, with a friendly atmosphere and plenty of useful advice from the knowledgeable hostess. ⑤

Hampton Inn & Suites 33 W Illinois Ave ⓣ312/832-0330, ⓦwww.hamptoninnchicago.com. Clean high-rise chain hotel (built in 1988 but "Frank-Lloyd-Wright-inspired") in a good River North location, four blocks east of the Magnificent Mile. ⑥

HI-Chicago – The J. Ira & Nicki Harris Family Hostel 24 E Congress St ⓣ312/360-0300 or 1-800/909-4776 code 244, ⓦwww.hichicago.org. Huge, very central hostel, where beds in the clean and spacious dorms cost $28-34 for members, $31-37 for non-members. Open 24hr, with internet access and full kitchen and laundry facilities. ①

Holiday Inn Express Mag Mile-Hotel Cass 640 N Wabash Ave ⓣ312/787-4030 or 1-800/799-4030, ⓦwww.casshotel.com. Budget hotel with complimentary wi-fi and a breakfast buffet. Basic, but a solid lodging option. ④

House of Two Urns 1239 N Greenview Ave, Wicker Park ⓣ773/235-1408 or 1-877/896-8767, ⓦwww.twourns.com. This rambling, artist-owned B&B, three blocks from the El and close to Wicker Park, is filled with contemporary art; the five guest rooms have a quirky flair, but some share facilities. Three- and four-room apartments are also available. Rooms ④, apartments ⑦–⑨.

The Inn at Lincoln Park 601 W Diversey Parkway ⓣ773/348-2810 or 1-866/774-7275, ⓦwww.innlp.com. Medium-sized motel, with free continental breakfast, in the accommodation-starved Lincoln Park district. ⑥

Monaco 225 N Wabash Ave ⓣ312/960-8500 or 1-800/397-7661, ⓦwww.monaco-chicago.com. A stylish and luxurious French Deco hotel with a 24hr fitness room. ⑧

Palmer House Hilton 17 E Monroe St ⓣ312/726-7500 or 1-800/445-8667. ⓦwww.chicagohilton.com/hotels_palmer.aspx. One of the city's most storied hotels, the Palmer House is in the center of the Loop, and perfect for visits to Millennium Park and the Art Institute of Chicago. ⑥

Sofitel Chicago Water Tower 20 E Chestnut St ⓣ312/324-4000 or 1-800/763-4835, ⓦwww.sofitel.com. Stunning 32-story glass prism, just off the Magnificent Mile, that offers elegant, ultra-chic accommodation plus gourmet French food in its *Café des Architectes*. ⑧

Trump International Hotel & Tower 401 N Wabash Ave ⓣ312/588-8000 or 1-877/458-7867, ⓦwww.trumpchicagohotel.com. New York's favorite real estate developer has made his mark in the Windy City with this 92-story hotel. Every room has floor-to ceiling windows, and there are a number of kid-friendly amenities, such as in-room video game systems and children's robes.

Wheeler Mansion 2020 S Calumet Ave ⓣ312/945-2020, ⓦwww.wheelermansion.com. A very grand mansion that's been converted into a plush, formal, but romantic B&B that's a hit with business travelers. In the Prairie Avenue Historic District, in close proximity to Soldier Field. ⑧

The City

Chicago's visitor-friendly street grid is numbered from **State Street** – "that great street" in Sinatra's song – at zero east and west, and **Madison Street** at zero north and south. **Lake Michigan**, which gives the city some of its most attractive open space (twenty miles of lakeshore lie within the city limits), makes a clear point of reference to the east of the urban grid. **Michigan Avenue** is the main thoroughfare, running between the lakeside museums and parklands, the densely packed skyscrapers of downtown, and the diverse low-rise neighborhoods that spread to the north, south, and west.. The nickname "**Windy City**" was coined by a New York newspaper editor describing the boastful claims of the city's promoters when attempting to lure investors from the eastern United States. The **Chicago River**, which cuts through the heart of downtown, separates the business district from the shopping and entertainment areas of the North Side, including the upscale **Near North** and **Gold Coast** neighborhoods; the artists' lofts and galleries of **River North**; the modestly charming area of **Old Town**; and the young professional enclaves of **Lincoln Park**, **Wrigleyville**, and **Lakeview**, as well as hip **Wicker Park**.

In contrast to the wealth and prosperity of the North Side, the **South Side** contains some very stark contrasts between the very wealthy and the tremendously poor. A few of its corners are well worth visiting – particularly the Gothic and

▲ The Chicago skyline

well-landscaped campus of the **University of Chicago** which sits in **Hyde Park**, site of the **Museum of Science and Industry**. Other than **Oak Park** to the west, which holds the childhood home of **Ernest Hemingway** and more than a dozen well-maintained examples of the influential architecture of **Frank Lloyd Wright**, suburban Chicago has little to offer.

Millennium Park

Until the late 1990s, the area that is downtown's **Millennium Park** was a rather poorly used bit of dreary looking real estate, albeit well-located. Now, however, thanks to a highly ambitious (and hugely expensive, to the tune of almost $500 million) renovation project that long overran its original 2000 completion date, it's a showcase for all that's best in the city. Its twin artistic centerpieces are equally compelling. First is a stunning, seamless, stainless-steel sculpture officially titled **Cloud Gate** but universally known as "The Bean," by the Indian-born, British-based artist Anish Kapoor. Inspired by liquid mercury, it invites viewers to walk around, beside, and even underneath it to enjoy spectacular and endlessly intriguing reflections of both the city and the sky above it. Nearby, **Crown Fountain** consists of two glass-brick towers set to either side of a black granite plaza; giant video images of the faces of ordinary Chicagoans play across them both, and water spurts from them in summer at unexpected intervals to form a lake that's usually filled with playing children. Further back, the **Jay Pritzker Pavilion** is an amazing open-air auditorium designed by Frank Gehry, who used mighty swirls and flourishes of steel to improve its acoustics. If you're heading for the lakefront, follow Gehry's sinuous, intriguing, wood-and-steel BP Pedestrian Bridge across Columbus Drive.

Downtown Chicago: The Loop

Downtown Chicago puts on what is perhaps the finest display of **modern architecture** in the world, from the prototype skyscrapers of the 1890s to Mies van der Rohe's "less is more" modernist masterpieces, and the fourth tallest building in the world, the quarter-mile-high **Sears Tower**.

The compact heart of Chicago is known as **the Loop**, because it's circled by the elevated tracks of the CTA "El" trains. The best way to get your bearings downtown is on one of the many excellent **city tours** detailed on p.322; whether you take a river cruise, ride the "El", or join a walking tour, you'll get a sense of the major architectural landmarks and their assorted histories.

Once you're ready to explore by yourself, start by calling in at the **Chicago Cultural Center** at 77 E Randolph St, which not only holds the city's main visitor center, as described on p.322, but is worth admiring in its own right. Built in 1897 as the original Chicago Public Library, it's a splendid Beaux-Arts palace filled with opulent detail, including the 38-foot Tiffany Dome on the fourth floor; it also stages all manner of temporary exhibitions.

The Loop holds two of Chicago's grandest century-old **department stores**. The best looking, the 1899 **Carson Pirie Scott** building (the store went out of business in 2007), at 1 S State St, boasts a magnificent ironwork facade that blends botanic and geometric forms in an intuitive version of Art Moderne. Its architect, Louis Sullivan, was also responsible for the gorgeous spherical bronze clocks suspended from the corners of the **Macy's** department store (Mon–Thurs 9am–9pm, Fri & Sat 9am–9pm, Sun 11am–6pm), two blocks north at State and Washington. The comparatively bland exterior masks one of the world's great stores, with seven floors of merchandise. Make sure and pop in to see the elaborate Tiffany ceiling, which is made up of over one million pieces of iridescent glass.

Half the world's wheat and corn (and pork-belly futures) are bought and sold amid the cacophonic roar of the **Chicago Board of Trade**, housed in a gorgeous Art Deco tower, appropriately topped by a 30ft stainless steel statue of Ceres, the Roman goddess of grain. It's no longer possible to watch the action inside, but if you're interested in learning more about the similarly energetic ballet that goes on within the **Chicago Mercantile Exchange**, three blocks away at 30 S Wacker Drive, a high-tech visitor center in the lobby explains all (Mon–Fri 8am–4.30pm; free). Precious metals, currencies, and commodities are bought and sold here to the tune of some $50 billion a day.

Half a block from the Board of Trade, **The Rookery**, 209 S LaSalle St, built in 1886 by Burnham and Root, is one of the city's most celebrated and photographed edifices. Its forbidding Moorish Gothic exterior gives way to a wonderfully airy lobby, decked out with cool Italian marble and gold leaf during a major 1905 remodeling by Frank Lloyd Wright; the spiral cantilever staircase rising from the second floor must be seen to be appreciated. A couple of doors down toward the Board of Trade, check out the **Continental Illinois Bank** lobby, with its 28 Ionic marble columns and intricate murals.

Looking up at the proud facade of the **Reliance Building**, 32 N State St, you'd be forgiven for thinking it dates from the Art Deco Thirties, but it was in fact completed way back in 1895 by Daniel Burnham, who did much to shape the face of Chicago through his buildings. His **Fisher Building**, with its tongue-in-cheek, aquatic-inspired ornamental terracotta, stands at 343 S Dearborn St. A block farther south, the 1890 **Manhattan Building** was the world's first tall all-steel-frame building, and is generally acknowledged as the progenitor of the modern curtain-walled skyscraper. Now converted into luxury apartments, it preserves some noteworthy exterior ornament.

A resurrected stretch of the riverfront walk follows the west bank of the river, with open-air cafés and gardens. Farther south, and back on the Loop side at South Wacker Drive and Adams Street, is the 1468ft **Sears Tower**, which was the tallest building in the world until 1998, when Malaysia's Petronas Towers nudged it from the top by the length of an antenna; both have since been eclipsed by further construction projects in southeast Asia and Taiwan. Various companies occupy the tower (Sears has moved to the suburbs), and it's so huge that it has more than one hundred elevators. Two ascend, in little more than a minute, from the ground-level shopping mall to the 103rd-floor **Skydeck Observatory** (daily: May–Sept 10am–10pm, Oct–April 10am–8pm; $12.95), for breathtaking views that on a clear day take in four states – Illinois, Michigan, Wisconsin, and Indiana. Look east for the distinctive triangular **Metropolitan Detention Center**, where prisoners exercise on the grassy roof beneath wire netting to ensure they don't get whisked away by helicopter.

The Chicago River

The Loop is usually said to end at the "El" tracks, but the blocks beyond this core, to either side of the Chicago River, hold plenty of interest. Broad, double-decked **Wacker Drive**, parallel to the water, was designed as a sophisticated promenade, lined by benches and obelisk-shaped lanterns, by Daniel Burnham in 1909. Though never completed, and despite the almost constant intrusion of construction works, it makes for a nice extended walk. The direction of the river itself was reversed a century ago, in an engineering project more extensive than the digging of the Panama Canal. As a result, rather than letting its sewage and industrial waste flow east into Lake Michigan, Chicago now sends it all south into the Corn Belt.

A **boat tour** from beneath the Michigan Avenue Bridge gives magnificent views of downtown (see p.322). However, half an hour's walk, especially at lunchtime when the office workers are out in force, will do the trick nearly as well. Burnham's promenade runs along both sides of the river, crossing back and forth over the twenty-odd drawbridges that open and close to let barges and the occasional sailboat pass. The **State Street Bridge** makes a superb vantage point. On the south bank, at 35 E Wacker Drive, the elegant Beaux Arts **Jewelers Building** was built in 1926 and is capped on the seventeenth floor by a domed rotunda that once housed Al Capone's favorite speakeasy. Across the river stands what's commonly considered Ludwig Mies van der Rohe's masterpiece – the 1971 **IBM Building**, 330 N Wabash Ave. The gentle play of light and shadow across the detailed bronze and smoked-glass facade has been the model for countless other less considered copies worldwide. The building is so huge that it acts as a funnel for winter winds off Lake Michigan, and heavy ropes sometimes must be tied across the broad plaza at its base to protect people from getting blown away.

Perhaps Chicago's most successful and acclaimed building of recent years stands four blocks west at **333 W Wacker Drive**. Towering over a broad bend in the river, and bowed to follow its curve, the green glass facade reflects the almost fluorescent green of the river (now upgraded from "toxic" to merely " very polluted"). On the lower floors, a more classically detailed stone base actively addresses its stalwart elder neighbors.

The Art Institute of Chicago

The **Art Institute of Chicago** ranks as one of the greatest art museums in the world, thanks to a magnificent collection that includes, and extends way beyond, Impressionist and Post-Impressionist paintings, Asian art, photography, and architectural drawings (Mon–Wed & Fri 10.30am–5pm, Thurs 10.30am–8pm, Sat & Sun 10am–5pm; suggested donation $12, free Thurs from 5–8pm; Ⓣ312/443-3600, Ⓦwww.artic.edu). While the Neoclassical facade of the main entrance, on the lake side of South Michigan Avenue, does its best to look dignified, the numerous added-on wings can make it hard to find your way around inside.

Most visitors head straight upstairs to the Impressionist works, which include a wall full of Monet's *Haystacks* captured in various lights, next to Seurat's immediately familiar pointillist *Sunday Afternoon on La Grande Jatte*. A handful of Post-

Impressionist masterpieces by Van Gogh, Gauguin, and Matisse are arrayed nearby. Beyond that, the rooms seem to stretch away forever; it takes at least half a day to get even a basic sense of what's here and where it is. Specific highlights include the pitchfork-holding farmer of Grant Woods' oft-parodied *American Gothic*, which he painted as a student at the Art Institute school, and sold to the museum for $300 in 1930; El Greco's 1577 *Assumption of the Virgin*; Edward Hopper's lonely *Nighthawks*; Pablo Picasso's melancholy *Old Guitarist*, one of the definitive masterpieces of his Blue Period; a tortured, tuxedoed self-portrait that was Max Beckmann's last Berlin painting before fleeing the Nazis; canvases by Jackson Pollock and Mark Rothko; and several works by Georgia O'Keeffe, such as a 1926 depiction of New York's *Shelton Hotel*, where she was living.

Be sure to look for the beautiful pre-Columbian ceramics from what's now the Southwest USA; the ornate carved stone used for the coronation of the Aztec ruler Motecuhzoma II on July 15, 1503; and the delightful seventh-century Indonesian-sculptured stone monkeys in the Southeast Asia collections, displayed around the McKinlock Court Garden, which in summer is employed as an **open-air café**. Also here, in the east end of the complex, is the immaculately reconstructed Art Moderne trading room of the Chicago Stock Exchange, designed by Louis Sullivan in 1893 and moved here in the 1970s. Finally, the Art Institute's delightful store is worth perusing, and the quality of goods here is on par with the masterworks on the walls inside.

Grant Park

East of the Art Institute toward Lake Michigan, **Grant Park** is an urban oasis that's become a bit overshadowed by the high-profile Millennium Park (see p.326) immediately northwest. In any case, wandering through the park requires traversing some busy roads, so casual rambling can be frustrating.

The major attractions are gathered in its landscaped southern half, known as the **Museum Campus**. The extensive and engaging **Field Museum of Natural History**, 1200 S Lake Shore Drive, at Roosevelt Road (June daily 8am–5pm; July & Aug Mon–Thurs 8am–5pm, Fri–Sun 7.30am–5pm; Sept–May daily 9am–5pm; last admission always 4pm; $14, plus extra for temporary exhibitions; Ⓦwww.fieldmuseum.org), is ten minutes' walk south of the Art Institute, in a huge, marble-clad, Daniel Burnham–designed Greek temple. It's quite an erratic sort of institution, in which the exhibits vary enormously in their age and sophistication; as a rule, its temporary exhibitions tend to be the most compelling, but cost a hefty additional premium on the already high entrance fee. "Natural history" is taken to include anything non-white and non-European, so as well as a hall of stupendous dinosaurs, including "Sue," the most complete *T-rex* fossil ever found, the permanent collection ranges from Egyptian tombs – the entire burial chamber of the son of a Fifth Dynasty pharaoh was brought here in 1908 – to the man-eating lions of Tsavo, and some fascinating displays on the islands of the Pacific. Best of all for young kids is the "Underground Adventure," a simulated environment that "shrinks" visitors to a hundredth of their normal size and propels them into a world of giant animatronic spiders and crayfish.

Just across busy Lake Shore Drive, on the shores of Lake Michigan, the **Shedd Aquarium** (first three weeks of June daily 9am–6pm; late June to Aug Mon–Wed & Fri 9am–6pm, Thurs 9am–10pm; Sept–May Mon–Fri 9am–5pm, Sat & Sun 9am–6pm; $16 wild reef and aquarium, $18 oceanarium and aquarium, $23 for all exhibits; Ⓣ312/939-2438, Ⓦwww.sheddaquarium.org) proclaims itself the largest indoor aquarium in the world. The 1920s structure is rather old-fashioned, but the lighthearted and often tongue-in-cheek displays – some use *Far Side* cartoons – are informative and entertaining. The central exhibit, a 90,000-gallon recreation of a coral reef, complete with sharks (who are fed at 11am and 2pm daily), turtles, and thousands of tropical fish, is surrounded by more than a hundred lesser tanks. Highlights include the new wild reef exhibit, which features floor-to-ceiling living reefs, tropical fish, sharks, and rays. The **Oceanarium** provides an enormous contrast, with its modern lake-view home for marine mammals such as Pacific dolphins and beluga whales. Designed to replicate a rocky Alaskan coastline, it's a carefully disguised amphitheater for demonstrations of the animals' "natural behavior," such as jumping out of the water and fetching plastic rings. Performances are four times daily; at other times, watch from underwater galleries as the animals cruise around the tank, and listen to the clicks, beeps, and whistles they use to communicate with each other. Get to the Shedd early to beat the long lines and school groups.

At the tip of the Museum Campus peninsula, the **Adler Planetarium** (late May to early Sept daily 9.30am–6pm, rest of year daily 9.30am–4.30pm, first Fri of month always 9.30am–10pm; $10–25, determined by exhibits entered, free Tues, Sept–Feb only; ⓣ312/922-STAR, ⓦwww.adlerplanetarium.org) has an interactive 360-degree movie theater and offers one of the best views of the city skyline.

The Near North Side

While Chicago's **Near North Side** has few marquee attractions, it's great for simply wandering around, chancing upon odd **shops**, neighborhood bars, and historic sites in a generally low-rise tangle containing some of the city's most characteristic corners.

When the Michigan Avenue Bridge was built over the Chicago River in 1920, the warehouse district along its north bank quickly changed into one of the city's most upmarket quarters, now known as the **Magnificent Mile**, famed for its fashionable shops and department stores. Throughout the Roaring Twenties one glitzy tower after another was thrown up along Michigan Avenue. At the north end, the opulent **Drake Hotel** rose off Lincoln Park. To the south, the white terracotta, wedding-cake colossus of the **Wrigley Building** was put up just over the river at no. 400; it's spectacularly lit up at night. Built by the Chicago-based chewing-gum magnate, it was eclipsed almost immediately by the "Mag Mile's" most famous structure, the **Tribune Tower**. Still housing the editorial offices of Chicago's morning newspaper, as well as, on the ground floor, the studios of its main AM radio station, WGN (you can peer in from the street and watch the DJs in action), the tower was completed in 1925. Its flying buttresses and Gothic detailing turn their back on the then-prevalent Moderne style. Look closely at its lower floors and you'll see embedded chunks of historic buildings – like the Parthenon and the Great Pyramid – pilfered from around the world by *Tribune* staffers.

While the Tribune Tower anchors its southern end, the Mag Mile's northern reaches are dominated by the cross-braced steel **John Hancock Center** at 875 N Michigan Ave. Though it's about 325 feet shorter than the Sears Tower, the 360-degree panorama on a clear day from its 94th-floor **Skydeck Observatory** (daily 9am–11pm; $15) is unforgettable. It's worth pointing out that taking the elevator to the swanky Signature Lounge on the 96th floor costs nothing, and you can use that extra money to buy a libation of your choice. If you prefer quality over quantity, the Hancock Observatory is a better, less trafficked experience than the Sears.

Back at ground level, you're right at the heart of Chicago's prime **shopping district**. Stores like Neiman-Marcus and Tiffany & Co front onto Michigan Avenue, but most of the shops are enclosed within multistory complexes, or "vertical shopping malls." The oldest of these – and still the best – is **Water Tower Place**, 835

N Michigan Ave, with more than a hundred stores on seven floors, plus a bustling food court. The **900 N Michigan Avenue** mall offers a less-cramped space and more upscale shops, anchored by Bloomingdale's.

Across from Water Tower Place, at the center of this consumer paradise, stands the **Historic Water Tower** – a whimsically Gothic stone castle, topped by a 100ft tower, that was built in 1869 and is one of the very few structures to have survived the 1871 fire. Inside the Water Tower is a tiny, yet compelling gallery that features rotating photographic exhibits by Chicago-based artists. The **Museum of Contemporary Art**, one block east at 220 E Chicago Ave (Tues 10am–8pm, Wed–Sun 10am–5pm; free on Tues, $10; ⓣ312/280-2660; ⓦwww.mcachicago.org), is a spare space that holds photography, video, and installation works, as well as a permanent collection featuring pieces by Calder, Nauman, Warhol, and others. At the rear is a lake-view patio where a Wolfgang Puck café serves good coffee and bistro food; additionally, the museum store is well worth a browse. Away from the Magnificent Mile, the area along the river between Michigan Avenue and the lake has seen dramatic redevelopment since **Navy Pier**, at East Illinois Street (ⓦwww.navypier.com), underwent a major facelift in 1995. The pier attracts more than eight million visitors annually to its shops, chain restaurants, IMAX theater, and fifteen-story Ferris wheel. Three floors are taken up by the imaginative interactive exhibits of the **Chicago Children's Museum** (Sun–Wed & Fri 10am–5pm, Thurs & Sat 10am–8pm; also Fri 5–8pm mid-June to Aug; $9, no reduction for children; free Thurs 5–8pm; ⓣ312/527-1000, ⓦwww.chichildrensmuseum.org). The pier also serves as a venue for concerts and weekend festivals in summer, and an embarkation point for several boat tours, including those run by Shoreline Sightseeing (see p.322).

The Gold Coast and Old Town

As its name suggests, the **Gold Coast**, stretching north from the Magnificent Mile along the lakeshore, is one of Chicago's wealthiest and most desirable neighborhoods. This residential district is primarily notable for Chicago's most central (and style-conscious) beach. The broad strand of **Oak Street Beach** is accessible via a walkway under Lake Shore Drive, across from the *Drake Hotel*. After dark, the summertime crowds are apt to be found in the myriad bars of Rush and Division streets. The more northerly reaches of the Gold Coast, approaching Lincoln Park, are also its most exclusive, especially in the stretch of Astor Street running south from the park. **Old Town**, west of LaSalle Street to either side of North Avenue, has a much more lived-in look. Originally a German immigrant community based around the 1873 **St Michael's Church**, it now boasts a broad ethnic and cultural mix. **Wells Street**, the main drag, emerged in the late 1960s as a mini-Haight-Ashbury. Although almost all signs of that era have vanished, at least one survivor, the *Second City* comedy club (see p.331), is still going strong. The rest of the neighborhood is packed with bars, galleries, and barbecue joints, and makes for a diverting afternoon's wander. Especially noteworthy is the House of Glunz, 1206 N Wells St, a wine shop dating to 1888.

Lincoln Park and Wrigleyville

In summer, Chicago's largest greenspace, **Lincoln Park**, gives visitors and locals a much-needed respite from the gridded pavements of the rest of the city. Unlike Grant Park to the south, Lincoln Park is packed with leafy nooks and crannies, monuments and sculptures, and has a couple of friendly, family-oriented **beaches**, at the eastern ends of North and Fullerton avenues. Near the small **zoo** at the heart of the park (late May–Oct Mon–Fri 9am–6pm, Sat & Sun 9am–7pm; Nov–March daily 9am–5pm; free), renowned for its menagerie of African apes, you can rent paddleboats or bikes. If the weather's bad, head for sauna-level conditions at the **conservatory**, 2400 N Stockton Drive (daily 9am–5pm; free), or bone up on Chicago's captivating past at the **Chicago History Museum**, at the south end of the park at 1601 N Clark St (Mon–Wed and Fri & Sat 9.30am–4.30pm,Thurs 9.30am–8pm, Sun noon–5pm; $14, free on Mon; ⓣ312/642-4600, ⓦwww.chicagohistory.org), where the comprehensive displays on regional and national history were fully upgraded in 2006.

The Lincoln Park neighborhood, inland from the lake, centers on **Lincoln Avenue** and **Clark Street**, which run diagonally from near the Historical Society Museum; **Halsted Street**, with its blues bars and nightclubs, runs north–south through the neighborhood's heart. Any of these main roads merits an extended stroll, with forays into the many book and record stores. Look for the **Biograph Theatre** movie house, 2433 N Lincoln Ave, where **John Dillinger** was ambushed and killed by the FBI in 1934, thanks to a tip from his companion, the legendary Lady in Red.

Chicago spreads north from Lincoln Park for block after low-rise block of houses and shops, many of which date from the late 1800s, when thousands of German immigrants settled in what was then the separate enclave of Lakeview. This area is now called **Wrigleyville** in honor of **Wrigley Field**, 1060 W Addison St at N Clark Street, the ivy-covered 1920s stadium of baseball's much-loved Cubs, and one of the best places to get a real feel for the game – the club is so traditional that it fought the installation of floodlights (for night games) until 1988. There are few more pleasant and relaxing ways to spend an afternoon than drinking beer, eating hot dogs, and watching a ballgame in the sunshine, among the Cubs' faithful; see p.339 for ticket information. Two-hour **Field tours** run from May through September on select days every half-hour from 10am to 4pm, and cost $25.

Wicker Park and Bucktown

Three miles northwest of the Loop, **Wicker Park/Bucktown** is Chicago's newest neighborhood. Once a Polish and German community referred to as the "Polish Gold Coast," it is now a trendy, upscale enclave of shopping, clubbing, and Victorian mansions. Stylish health-food cafés, galleries, tattoo parlors, smoky clubs, boutiques, and alternative bookstores follow Damen Street north to Bucktown.

The West Side and Oak Park

West of the Chicago River, Chicago's **West Side** was where the **Great Fire of 1871** started – supposedly when Mrs O'Leary's cow kicked over a lantern. The flames spread quickly east to engulf the entire central city, which was built of wood and fed the fire for three full days. Appropriately enough, the O'Leary cottage is now the site of the Chicago Fire Department training academy. The West Side also saw 1886's **Haymarket Riots**, when striking workers assembled at the old city market at Desplaines and Randolph streets; after a peaceful demonstration, as police began to break up the crowd, a bomb exploded, killing an officer. Six more policemen and four workers died in the resulting panic. Four labor leaders were later found guilty of murder and hanged, although none had been present at the event. Though the West Side has little to see compared with the rest of the city, it does provide a good look at its day-to-day realities, having served as the port of entry for Chicago's myriad ethnic groups, now congregated in its distinct neighborhoods.

Nine miles west of the Loop, the affluent and attractive nineteenth century suburb of **Oak Park** is easily accessible by public transportation: take the Green Line west to the Harlem Avenue stop. The area's **visitor center**, just over two blocks east of the station at 158 N Forest Ave (daily 10am–3.30pm; ⓣ708/848-1500, ⓦwww.visitoakpark.com), provides an excellent architectural **walking tour map**.

Ernest Hemingway was born and raised in Oak Park, editing his high school newspaper and living a normal middle-class life. His birthplace at 339 N Oak Park Ave, where he lived until the age of six, is now preserved as a shrine to the author, and is run in conjunction with a museum of his life two blocks south at 200 N Oak Park Ave (Sun-Fri 1–5pm, Sat 10am–5pm; $8; ⓣ708/848-2222, ⓦwww.ehfop.org).

In 1889, a decade before Hemingway's birth, an ambitious young architect named **Frank Lloyd Wright** arrived in Oak Park, which he used for the next twenty years as a testing ground for his innovative design theories. Most of the 25 buildings he put up here are in keeping with conventional Victorian design, and few are open to the public; fortunately, however, his most interesting and groundbreaking edifices are maintained as monuments. His ideal of an "organic architecture," in which all aspects of the design derive from a single unifying concept – quite at odds with the fussy "gingerbread" style popular at the time – is exemplified by the **Unity Temple** at 875 Lake St (Mon–Fri 10.30am–4.30pm, Sat & Sun 1–4pm, $8; ⓣ708/383-8873, ⓦwww.unitytemple-utrf.org). Though the simplicity of this angular, reinforced-concrete structure was largely dictated by economics, its unembellished surfaces contribute to a masterful manipulation of space, especially in the skylit interior, where the subtle interplay of overlapping planes creates a dynamic spatial flow.

Wright built his small, brown-shingled **home and studio** nearby at 951 Chicago Ave at Forest, aged 22 in 1889, and remodeled it repeatedly for the next twenty years. It shows all his hallmarks: large fireplaces to symbolize the heart of the home and family; free-flowing, open-plan rooms; and the visual linking of interior and exterior spaces. The furniture of the kitchen and dining rooms is Wright's own design; he added a two-story studio in 1898, with a mezzanine drafting area suspended by chains from the roof beams. You can see the house itself on a 45-minute guided tour (Mon–Fri 11am, 1pm & 3pm, Sat & Sun every 20min 11am–3.30pm; $12; ⓣ708/848-1976, ⓦwww.wrightplus.org). Lengthier, self-guided audio walking tours ($12) take in the dozen other Wright-designed houses within a two-block radius.

The South Side

The **South Side** of Chicago has always had a raw deal, cursed with the presence of bad-neighbor heavy industries like the sprawling **Chicago Stockyards**, the slaughterhouses and meatpackers that Upton Sinclair exposed in his 1906 novel *The Jungle*, and whose oppressive odors covered most of the South Side until the 1950s. Parts of the South Side failed to benefit from the economic uplift of the 1990s, but there remain a number of thriving districts: not just the **Prairie Avenue** and **Hyde Park** districts described below, but also the buzzing **Chinatown** around Wentworth Avenue and 22nd Street; the artsy, predominantly Mexican **Pilsen** district, a few blocks north and west; and the largely Irish, blue-collar **Bridgeport**, formerly known by the evocative name "Hardscrabble," around Halsted and 37th – Mayor Daley's old fiefdom, the home of baseball's White Sox (see p.339).

Two blocks east of Michigan Avenue, a mile from the Loop and only a quarter of a mile from the lake, **Prairie Avenue** started life as an exclusive suburb. It's best reached by taxi, bus, or train, as the walk south from the Loop just isn't that interesting. As the one part of Chicago to remain unscathed in the Great Fire of 1871, this area had a brief moment of glory as the city's finest address. However, by 1900 the railroads had cut it off from Lake Michigan, and the wealthy fled back to their traditional North Side haunts. One of the few structures to have survived is the Romanesque 1887 **Glessner House**, Chicago's only surviving H.H. Richardson–designed house, standing sentry at Prairie Avenue and 18th. Behind the forbidding stone facade, the house opens onto a garden court, its interior filled with Arts and Crafts furniture, and swathed in William Morris fabrics and wall coverings. The Chicago Architecture Foundation gives guided tours (Wed–Sun 1 and 3pm; $10; ⓣ312/326-1480, ⓦwww.glessnerhouse.org).

Six miles south, **Hyde Park**, the most attractive and sophisticated South Side neighborhood, is also one of Chicago's more racially integrated areas. Of course, these days, the neighborhood has received additional attention for being the home of President Barack Obama prior to his arrival in the White House. The **University of Chicago**, endowed by Rockefeller in 1892, has encouraged a college-town atmosphere, with bookshops and cafés surrounding its compact campus, especially along East 57th Street. On the campus itself, two buildings are well worth searching out: the massive Collegiate Gothic pile of the **Rockefeller Memorial Chapel**, 59th Street and Woodlawn Avenue (daily 9am–4pm; free), and the Prairie-style, Frank Lloyd Wright-designed **Robie House**, two blocks north at 5757 S Woodlawn Ave (tours Sat, 11am-3pm; $12; ⓦwww.wrightplus.org).

Washington Park wraps around the south side of the campus to join the long green strip of the **Midway** – one of the few reminders that Chicago was the site of the **World's Fair Columbian Exposition**. Attracting some thirty million spectators in the summer of 1893 (at the time, 45 percent of the US population), the Midway was then filled with full-sized model villages from around the globe, including an Irish market town and a mock-up of Cairo, complete with belly dancers. These days it's used mainly by joggers and students tossing Frisbees.

A short stroll east, in Jackson Park, the cavernous **Museum of Science and Industry**, 57th Street at Lake Shore Drive (Mon–Sat 9.30am–4pm, Sun 11am–4pm; $13; ⓣ773/684-1414, ⓦwww.msichicago.org), was Chicago's single most popular tourist destination (and ranked second in the US) until it started charging admission in 1991. Besides interactive computer displays, the best of which explores the inner workings of the brain and heart, exhibits include a captured German U-boat, a trip down a replica coal mine, the Apollo 8 command module, and a simulated space-shuttle journey. It's fun for kids, but adults may not feel like staying very long. The complex also hosts a giant OMNIMAX movie dome; admission is $7 extra.

East of the museum, **Promontory Point** juts into Lake Michigan, giving great views of the Chicago skyline, including a close-up look at Mies van der Rohe's first highrise, the Promontory Apartments at 5530 S Lake Shore Drive.

Eating

Chicago's cosmopolitan make-up is reflected in its plethora of ethnic restaurants. **Italian** food, ranging from hearty **deep-dish pizza** (developed in 1943 at *Pizzeria Uno*; see p.336) to delicately crafted creations presented at stylish trattorias, continues to dominate a very dynamic scene. In recent years there's been a surge of popularity for **New American** cuisine. **Thai** restaurants still thrive, as do ones with a broad **Mediterranean** slant, many of which serve tapas; and there are still plenty of opportunities to sample more longstanding Chicago cuisines – Eastern European, German, Mexican, Chinese, Indian, even Burmese and Ethiopian. Of course, a number of establishments serve good old-fashioned **barbecue ribs**, a legacy of Chicago's days as the nation's meatpacker. And no visit is complete without sampling a messy Italian beef sandwich, or a Chicago-style hot dog, laden with tomatoes, onions, hot peppers, and a pickle.

The largest concentration of restaurants is found north and west of the **Loop**. To the west, **Greektown**, around Halsted Street at Jackson Boulevard, and **Little Italy**, on and around Taylor Street, are worth a look, while the **Near North** and **River North** areas harbor a good number of upscale places.

The Loop

Billy Goat Tavern 430 N Michigan Ave at Kinzie ⓣ312/222-1525. This legendary journalists' haunt opens early and closes late, serving the "cheezborgers" made famous by John Belushi's comedy skit. Very reasonable.
Everest One Financial Place, 440 S LaSalle St at Congress ⓣ312/663-8920. Take in the stunning vista from the 40th floor and tuck into chef Jean Joho's French/Alsatian cuisine, in dishes like wild mushroom consommé and Casco Bay sea scallops. Very expensive. Closed Sun & Mon.
Italian Village 71 W Monroe St at Clark ⓣ312/332-7005. Three Italian establishments flourish under one roof. *The Village* has traditional Italian-American food and a world-class wine cellar; the basement *Cantina Enoteca* serves chicken Vesuvio, a Chicago creation, among its reasonably priced dishes; and the expensive *Vivere* has an adventurous menu, a mesmerizing wine list, and a large pre-theater crowd (meaning it's best to arrive after 8pm). *The Village* is open daily, but the other two establishments are closed Sun.
Lou Mitchell's 565 W Jackson Ave at Clinton ⓣ312/939-3111. Near Union Station, Lou's has been around since 1923, serving terrific omelets, waffles, and hash browns all day long. Try the pecan-laden cookies.
Marché 833 W Randolph St at Halsted ⓣ312/226-8399. Creative French cuisine served in an eclectic atmosphere in the Market District. Entrees $16–40.
Russian Tea Time 77 E Adams St at Michigan ⓣ312/360-0000. This Midwestern nod to New York's Russian Tea Room offers a (pricey) sampling of authentic fare from the former Soviet empire.
Trattoria No. 10 10 N Dearborn St ⓣ312/984-1718. This charming surprise, in a series of underground rooms, serves up delicious ravioli, grilled sea scallops, and risotto. Closed Sun.

The West Side: Greektown and Little Italy

Francesca's on Taylor 1400 W Taylor St ⓣ312/829-2828. Assorted Francesca-family restaurants dot Chicago. This relatively subdued example offers some of the best Italian food in the city, at moderate prices. Don't be surprised to find a crowd here all day.
Parthenon 314 S Halsted St at Jackson ⓣ312/726-2407. One of the oldest places in Greektown, but still deservedly popular: saganaki (fried cheese doused with Metaxa brandy and ignited) was invented here.
Pegasus 130 S Halsted St at Adams ⓣ312/226-3377. Lively Greek option, where true hospitality and evocative wall murals add to the appeal. Stuffed squid and pastitsio (macaroni, meat, and cheese casserole) are recommended. During the summer the rooftop garden has a superb view of the Loop skyline.
Santorini 800 W Adams St at Halsted ⓣ312/829-8820. The decor recreates a Greek island village, and the food is beguiling, too; grilled octopus and lamb *exohiko* (wrapped in filo pastry and fried) are highlights.

South Loop and the South Side

Dixie Kitchen 5225 S Harper, Harper Court ⓣ773/363-4943. Great soul food here includes pulled-pork sandwiches, breaded oysters with chili sauce, and desserts like peach cobbler and pecan pie.
Emperor's Choice 2238 S Wentworth Ave at 23rd ⓣ312/225-8800. This attractive storefront serves delicious egg rolls and well-priced seafood dishes. Try the steamed clams, poached shrimp, or lobster.
Gioco 1312 S Wabash Ave at 13th ⓣ312/939-3870. Immensely popular (and somewhat expensive) place, whose classic, meticulously prepared Italian cuisine is drawing a hip crowd to the rapidly gentrifying South Loop district.
The Medici 1327 E 57th St ⓣ773/667-7394. Hyde Park institution close to the University of Chicago that serves up a mix of salads, pizza, and quality hamburgers.
Opera 1301 S Wabash Ave at 13th ⓣ312/461-0161. High-class, high-concept, high-priced but very funky new-Chinese restaurant, housed in an opulent former film studio in the South Loop that holds a few private dining booths.

Near North Side and River North

Bistrot Zinc 1131 N State St at Elm ⓣ312/337-1131. Very friendly, intimate neighborhood bistro, offering a quintessential French menu prepared and served just the way it should be, at good prices.
Club Lago 331 W Superior St at N Orleans ⓣT312/337-9444. Best described as a post-World

War II American take on Northern Italian, this low-key restaurant is a good place for a drink or a plate of baked clams.

Frontera Grill & Topolobampo 445 N Clark St at Illinois ⓣ312/661-1434. Wildly imaginative Mexican food: *Frontera Grill* is crowded and boisterous; *Topolobampo* is more refined and pricier. The front door and bar are shared between the two. Closed Sun & Mon.

Gino's East 633 N Wells St at Ontario ⓣ312/943-1124. Despite its relocation into larger but meticulously aged premises, this remains a Chicago tradition, with huge deep-dish pizzas and graffiti-covered walls. Expect a considerable wait to get in, and at least 40 minutes for your pizza to cook.

Le Colonial 937 N Rush St at Walton ⓣ312/255-0088. This atmospheric evocation of some colonial outpost in Indochina, with its palm trees and rattan furniture, serves zestful French-influenced Vietnamese food at reasonable prices, and has outdoor seating in summer.

Nacional 27 325 W Huron St at Franklin ⓣ312/664-2727. This popular Latin place draws its menu from every imaginable Central American cuisine, and has salsa dancing on weekends.

Pizzeria Uno 29 E Ohio St at Wabash ⓣ312/321-1000. The original outlet of the chain that put Chicago deep-dish pizza on the map.

Portillo's 100 W Ontario St at La Salle ⓣ312/587-8930. Much-loved local chain that serves delicious Chicago hot dogs and the best Italian beef sandwich in the city.

Star of Siam 11 E Illinois St at State ⓣ312/670-0100. Terrific Thai food served in a spacious, inviting setting. The tom yum soup, pad Thai, and curries are top-notch.

SushiSamba Rio 504 N Wells St at Illinois ⓣ312/595-2300. Very fancy restaurant-cum-bar offering a gimmicky but nonetheless delicious melding of Japanese (sushi) and South American (*ceviche*) cuisine; lots of fish, naturally, but also tender meats. High prices, but memorable atmosphere.

Lincoln Park and Old Town

Boka 1729 N Halsted St near Willow ⓣ773/337-6070. Stylish option close to the Steppenwolf Theatre, serving inventive and tasty dishes from around the world on a changing weekly menu that offers small ($8–12) and large ($21–37) portions, depending on your appetite.

Charlie Trotter's 816 W Armitage Ave at Halsted ⓣ773/248-6228. Prepare for a superb experience: Chef Trotter is a true artist, and his daring creations, such as caviar-stuffed quail eggs or Maine salmon with blood sausage, are constantly evolving. The prices are appropriately high; you can only choose between two set menus, at $115 (vegetarian) or $135. Closed Sun & Mon.

Hema's Kitchen II 2411 N Clark St ⓣ773-529-1705. Bustling Indian restaurant that's well regarded for its garlic nan, curried fish, and tandoori chicken. As an added bonus, you can bring your own beer or wine.

Old Jerusalem 1411 N Wells St at Evergreen ⓣ312/944-3304. This long-time favorite serves reasonable Middle Eastern dishes; the falafel is great. Bring your own beer or wine.

RJ Grunts 2056 Lincoln Park W at Clark ⓣ773/929-5363. Check out the great burgers and a top-notch salad bar – purported to be the nation's first – in a casual neighborhood atmosphere.

Topo Gigio 1516 N Wells St at Burton ⓣ312/266-9355. Well-prepared, moderately priced Italian cuisine, served by very friendly staff in a peaceful garden amid the Old Town bustle. The homemade tiramisu is fabulous.

Wicker Park

Café Absinthe 1954 W North Ave at Milwaukee ⓣ773/278-4488. Fine French dining in a romantic, casual setting. One of the city's best restaurants, with prices to match.

Earwax Cafe 1561N Milwaukee Ave at North ⓣ773/772-4019. Bustling, inexpensive coffeehouse in a happening neighborhood, with an extensive menu of light vegetarian meals as well as meaty deli sandwiches.

Hot Chocolate 1747 N Damen Ave near St Paul ⓣ773/489-1747 Priding themselves on a mix of "sweet" and "savory" offerings, the weekend brunch is a good bet, and their chocolate desserts are miniature masterpieces.

Irazu 1865 N Milwaukee Ave near Armitage ⓣ773/252-5687. Very cheap but wonderful Costa Rican diner, serving great burritos plus a small selection of authentic main courses. Closed Sun.

Drinking

Chicago is a consummate boozer's town, and is one of the best US cities for **bars**, catering to just about every group and interest, with many open until 3, 4, or even 5am. The city's drinking areas include the touristy **Division Street**, the post-college melange that is **Wrigleyville**, and a clutch of places in tweedy **Hyde Park**. **Wicker Park** is the trendiest hangout zone, while Halsted Street between Belmont and Addison is known as **Boystown** for its gay bars and clubs.

The hundred-plus **cafés and coffeehouses** across the city may not have taken the place of the traditional taverns, but they're a growing alternative.

Saloons, pubs, and bars

Cavanaugh's 53 W Jackson St ⓣ312/939-3125. Visit this Loop favorite in the historic Monadnock Building for an after-work drink. Experience the warm interior with antique woodwork, Harp on draft, and a full menu.

Delilah's 2771 N Lincoln Ave ⓣ773/472-2771. At this dimly lit bar (playing underground records – from rock to alt-country – at night), choose from a great selection of beers (150) and whiskeys.

Goose Island Brewing Co. 1800 N Clybourn Ave ⓣ312/915-0071. Forty ales and lagers, including the popular Honker's Ale, are brewed on the premises at this lively Lincoln Park haunt, which ranks as Chicago's best brewpub.

Green Door Tavern 678 N Orleans St ⓣ312/664-5496. In an unlikely spot near the galleries of River North, this historic place is chock-full of Chicago memorabilia: some pure kitsch, others genuine antiques. Drink at the long bar or settle into a cozy back room to sample home-style cooking.

John Barleycorn 658 W Belden Ave ⓣ773/348-8899. A dimly lit Lincoln Park pub dating to 1890. This former speakeasy and John Dillinger haunt has retained many of its original nautical-themed fixtures. The lovely garden is open in summer.

Matchbox 770 N Milwaukee Ave ⓣ312/666-9292. All kinds of Chicago characters squeeze into this phenomenally narrow little neighborhood hangout on the West Side.

Old Town Ale House 219 W North Ave ⓣ312/944-7020. An eclectic crowd of scruffy regulars and yuppies mingle in this convivial haunt, complete with a pinball machine and a library of paperbacks.

Rainbo Club 1150 N Damen Ave ⓣ773/489-5999. Busy Wicker Park bar and hangout for indie-rock types.

Signature Room 875 N Michigan Ave ⓣ312/787-7230. Slightly down-at-the-heel but nonetheless unmissable cocktail lounge on the 96th floor of the John Hancock Building, with the city's best skyline views.

Twin Anchors 1655 N Sedgwick St at North ⓣ312/266-1616. You'll wait for a seat in this neighborhood spot, famed for its BBQ ribs, but the interesting clientele and 1950s-style bar make it worthwhile.

Woodlawn Tap 1172 E 55th St at Woodawn ⓣ773/643-5516. In the center of Hyde Park, this place features cheap cold beer and conversation that alternates between the White Sox and Wittgenstein.

Gay and lesbian bars

Big Chicks 5024 N Sheridan Rd, Andersonville ⓣ773/728-5511. A friendly place for a mixed crowd, with a no-charge jukebox and free barbecues out back on summer Sun.

The Closet 3325 N Broadway ⓣ773/477-8533. A tiny, cramped but congenial lesbian bar that attracts gay men as well.

Gentry 440 N State St ⓣ773/836-0933. Cabaret and piano bar popular with corporate types after work.

Sidetrack 3349 N Halsted St ⓣ773/477-9189. One of the most popular bars along Halsted's gay strip in Lakeview. Theme nights include Sun, which is dedicated to showtunes.

Nightlife and entertainment

From its earliest frontier days, Chicago has had some of the best **nightlife** in the US. Blues fans who celebrate Chicago as the birthplace of Muddy Waters' **urban blues** will be disappointed that the original South-Side headquarters of Chess Records, at 2120 S Michigan Ave (immortalized in a Rolling Stones song recorded on site), has yet to become a museum. However, the city remains proud of its blues traditions, and continues to innovate in other genres, such as the energetic dance beat of 1980s **house music** as well as the groundbreaking **jazz** of the Art Ensemble of Chicago.

Nightclubs aplenty can be found all over town, especially along Halsted Street, Lincoln Avenue, and Clark Street on the North Side. **Uptown**, at the intersection of North Broadway and Lawrence, has a couple of excellent venues for jazz and rock. The best **gay clubs** congregate in the Boystown area, which is a mile north of Lincoln Park. Highbrow pursuits are also well provided for: Chicago's **classical music**, **dance**, and **theater** are world-class.

For **what's-on information**, Chicagoans pick up free weeklies like the excellent *Chicago Reader* (available Thurs afternoon), the *New City*, and the gay and lesbian *Windy City Times*. Full listings also appear in the Friday issues of the *Chicago Sun-Times* and the *Chicago Tribune*, while *Time Out Chicago* has useful arts, music, theater, and movie listings.

Blues

B.L.U.E.S. 2519 N Halsted St ⓣ773/528-1012, ⓦwww.chicagobluesbar.com. Opened in the 1970s, *B.L.U.E.S.* is still going strong, though it's a bit touristy. The tiny stage has been graced by all the greats.

Buddy Guy's Legends 754 S Wabash Ave ⓣ312/427-0333, ⓦwww.buddyguys.com. South Loop club owned by veteran bluesman Buddy Guy, with great acoustics and atmosphere, aims to present the very best local and national acts. Not as touristy as other downtown blues clubs.

Kingston Mines 2548 N Halsted St ⓣ773/477-4646. Top-notch local and national acts on two stages play to an up-for-it, partying crowd.

Rosa's Lounge 3420 W Armitage Ave ⓣ773/342-0452, ⓦwww.rosaslounge.com. Run by Mama Rosa and her son, this West-Side club is undoubtedly the friendliest blues joint around. For real aficionados. Closed Sun & Mon.

Jazz

Andy's 11 E Hubbard St ⓣ312/642-6805. Very popular with the after-work crowd; informal with moderate prices.

The Cotton Club 1710 S Michigan Ave ⓣ312/341-9787. A sophisticated live-music venue and disco, The Cotton Club attracts a well-dressed, mellow crowd.

Green Dolphin Street 2200 N Ashland Ave ⓣ773/395-0066, ⓦwww.jazzitup.com. This swanky, pricey restaurant and jazz club offers a solid line-up of regular performers. Closed Mon.

The Green Mill 4802 N Broadway ⓣ773/878-5552. One of the best – and most beautiful – rooms for local and national talent. Located in the Uptown neighborhood, and proud of its checkered Prohibition-era past.

Jazz Showcase 806 S Plymouth Court ⓣ312/360-0234, ⓦwww.jazzshowcase.com. A classy, dressy room that hosts premier jazz by top names.

Velvet Lounge 67 E Cermak Rd ⓣ312/791-9050. Avant-garde and free jazz are the usual sounds at this South Side mainstay.

Rock

Cubby Bear 1059 W Addison St ⓣ773/327-1662, ⓦwww.cubbybear.com. A sports bar during the day – right next to Wrigley Field – this place transforms itself after dark into one of the city's most boisterous and eclectic live venues. Popular with aging dinosaurs more than new bands, but still fun.

Double Door 1572 N Milwaukee Ave ⓣ773/489-3160, ⓦwww.doubledoor.com. Former biker bar turned hip music venue in the Wicker Park/Bucktown neighborhood. Indie bands play almost every night.

Elbo Room 2871 N Lincoln Ave ⓣ773/549-5549, ⓦwww.elboroomchicago.com. Easygoing venue specializing in emerging bands, whether indie, pop, funk, or ska.

Empty Bottle 1035 N Western Ave ⓣ773/276-3600, ⓦwww.emptybottle.com. Loud hole-in-the-wall club where you might hear just about anything: experimental jazz, alternative rock, hip-hop, house, dub, and progressive country.

House of Blues 329 N Dearborn St ⓣ312/527-2583, ⓦwww.hob.com. Despite its name, this Near North chain venue puts on all kinds of music, including a popular gospel brunch on Sun.

Metro 3730 N Clark St ⓣ773/549-0203, ⓦwww.metrochicago.com. Arguably the top spot in the city, this club, in an old cinema building, regularly hosts young British bands trying to break the States, plus DJ mixes.

Folk, country, and world music

Fitzgerald's 6615 W Roosevelt, Berwyn ⓣ708/788-2118, ⓦwww.fitzgeraldsnightclub.com. In the western suburb of Berwyn, an excellent venue for alt-country, Americana, Cajun, and zydeco. Accessible by the CTA's Blue Line.

Old Town School of Folk Music 4544 N Lincoln Ave. Established in 1959, this place presents about eighty concerts a year, including just about every type of folk and world music, and also offers great classes.

Schubas Tavern 3159 N Southport Ave, Lakeview ⓣ773/525-2508, ⓦwww.schubas.com. A quirky roster of up-and-coming acts, from rock to alt-country or roots, appear at this intimate, all-but-perfect neighborhood venue.

Dance

Excalibur 632 N Dearborn St ⓣ312/266-1944. City institution blasting out rock and R&B on several floors to a predominantly out-of-town crowd.
Funky Buddha Lounge 728 W Grand Ave ⓣ312/666-1695, ⓦwww.funkybuddha.com. Small West-Side club where the resident DJs attract a devoted young crowd.
Sidetrack 3349 N Halsted St ⓣ773/477-9189. Huge, very glitzy Wrigleyville club, with a garden bar and rooftop deck, that's Chicago's biggest gay venue. Open every night of the week.
Smartbar 3730 N Clark St, underneath the Metro (see opposite) ⓣ773/549-0203, ⓦwww.smartbarchicago.com. Great techno and house on the weekend in post-industrial Wrigleyville surroundings. Weekdays see a mix of punk, goth, and Eighties. The whole complex is open late – until 5am Fri and Sat.

Theater and comedy

While it was once every Chicago actor and playwright's ambition to end up in New York, many are now perfectly happy to remain here. The city supports numerous **theater** companies, several of which boast reputations as good as any in the US. Best known of all is Steppenwolf, with alumni like John Malkovich and Gary Sinise, based at 1650 N Halsted St (ⓣ312/335-1650, ⓦwww.steppenwolf.org), while others include the Court Theatre, 5535 S Ellis St (ⓣ773/753-4472, ⓦwww.courttheatre.org), and the Goodman Theatre, 170 N Dearborn St (ⓣ312/443-3800, ⓦwww.goodman-theatre.org). **Comedy**, too, is particularly vibrant; Chicago's improvisational scene is considered the best in the nation, with the troupe at **Second City** – who now spread their activities across three separate auditoriums centered on 1616 N Wells St (ⓣ312/337-3992, ⓦwww.secondcity.com) – especially heralded.

Classical music, opera, and dance

The world-famous **Chicago Symphony Orchestra** is based at Symphony Center, 220 S Michigan Ave (ⓣ312/294-3000, ⓦwww.chicagosymphony.org), but spends part of the year on tour. The 186-member **Symphony Chorus** performs both classical and contemporary choral works with the CSO, specifically in summer at the open-air **Ravinia Festival**, 25 miles north of downtown Chicago (ⓦwww.ravinia.org). Home for the **Lyric Opera of Chicago** is the beautiful Civic Opera House, 20 N Wacker Drive (ⓣ312/332-2244, ⓦwww.lyricopera.org); its season is from mid-September to early February, and most performances end up being sold out. Chicago can also boast two world-class dance companies: the classically oriented **Joffrey Ballet**, based at 70 E Lake St (ⓣ312/739-0120, ⓦwww.joffrey.com), and the more contemporary **Hubbard Street Dance Chicago**, 1147 W Jackson Blvd (ⓣ312/850-9744, ⓦwww.hubbardstreetdance.com).

Sports

Staunchly blue-collar Chicago must be among the best US cities for watching **sports**, as Chicagoans are, for better or worse, loyally supportive of their teams. The city's most successful outfit in recent memory was the Michael Jordan–led **Bulls** basketball team, winner of six NBA championships in the 1990s (ⓣ312/559-1212, ⓦwww.nba.com/bulls). Now, though, with the Jordan era long gone, Bulls fans have little to cheer about, though the team's fortunes have improved in recent years. The team plays in the ultramodern United Center, 1901 W Madison St, as do hockey's **Blackhawks** (same phone, ⓦwww.chicagoblackhawks.com). The **Bears** football team (ⓣ312/295-6600, ⓦwww.chicagobears.com) can be seen at the 66,000-capacity Soldier Field, 425 E McFetridge Drive, at the south end of Grant Park. As for baseball, neither Chicago team had won a World Series since 1917 until the **White Sox** finally broke the streak in 2005. Perhaps the destruction of their Comiskey Park home had something to do with it, though its replacement, the US Cellular Field stadium, which stands alongside at 333 W 35th St on the South Side, feels pretty soulless (ⓣ312/831-1SOX, ⓦchicago.whitesox.mlb.com). The long-suffering **Cubs** still call grand old Wrigley Field home (ⓣ312/831-CUBS, ⓦchicago.cubs.mlb.com).

Central Illinois

Interstates 55 and 57 slice south through the Corn Belt of **central Illinois** from Chicago. Parallel to I-55, the legendary **Route 66** began its run here, cutting through the state before running all the way to the Pacific Coast – you might try to catch a glimpse of it, as some old-time diners and other Americana still stand. One worthwhile stop, reachable by either interstate, is the state capital, **Springfield**, which commemorates president and former resident **Abraham Lincoln**. Otherwise, if you're on your way south, the college towns of **Bloomington-Normal** and **Champaign-Urbana** are the only good urban stops, while if you're heading west from Chicago spare the time to pause at the delightful Civil War, river town of **Galena**.

Springfield

Two hundred miles south of Chicago, the Illinois state capital of **SPRINGFIELD** spreads out from a neat, downtown grid. Abraham Lincoln honed his legal and political skills here, and tourists flock to his old homes, haunts, and final resting place. What they find is neither tacky nor pompous, but rather sites that illuminate not only the life of the sixteenth president of the USA, but also the uncertainty and turmoil of a nation on the brink of civil war.

The number one Lincoln attraction is the only house he ever owned, and which he shared with his wife, Mary Todd from 1844 to 1861. For a free narrated tour, pick up tickets at the **Lincoln Home Visitor Center**, 426 S Seventh St (daily 8.30am–5pm; ⓣ217/492-4241, ⓦwww.nps.gov/liho). Assorted displays and a brief film help to pass the time while you wait for the next available tour.

Four blocks north, at 212 N Sixth St, the **Abraham Lincoln Presidential Library and Museum** (daily 9am–5pm; Library is free, Museum $10; ⓣ217/782-5764, ⓦwww.alplm.org) is a state-of-the-art new facility that covers Lincoln's career in exhaustive detail, with fascinating original documents and interactive displays, as well as some simple mock-ups aimed largely at kids.

In the restored Greek Revival **Old State Capitol**, at Sixth and Adams nearby (mid-April to Aug daily 9am–5pm; Sept to mid-April Tues–Sat 9am–5pm; free; ⓣ217/785-7960), Lincoln attended at least 240 Supreme Court hearings, and proclaimed in 1858, "A house divided against itself cannot stand. I believe this government cannot endure permanently, half slave and half free." Objects, busts, and papers relating to Lincoln and the Democrat Stephen A. Douglas, whom he debated (and subsequently lost to) in Illinois' 1858 US Senate election, and whom he defeated in the 1860 presidential race, can be found throughout the building. At the tastefully renovated **Lincoln Depot** on Tenth and Monroe streets (April–Aug daily 10am–4pm; free), the newly elected president said goodbye to Springfield in February 1861 and boarded a train for his inauguration in Washington, DC (a video illustrates the twelve-day journey). The next time he returned was in his funeral train. **Lincoln's Tomb**, an 117ft-tall obelisk, stands in beautiful Oak Ridge Cemetery on the north side of town. The vault, adorned with busts and statuettes, is open to the public (June–Aug Tues 7pm–8pm; March–Oct Tues–Sat 9am–5pm and June to Aug Tues 7–8pm; Nov–Feb daily 9am–4pm; free). Inside are inscribed the words, "Now he belongs to the ages."

The **Illinois State Museum**, at 502 South Spring and Edwards on the south side of the complex of the current Illinois State Capitol, is crammed with natural history and Native American and contemporary art exhibits, along with the interactive "**At Home in the Heartland**" display, which traces Illinois family life from 1700 to 1970 (Mon–Sat 8.30am–5pm, Sun noon–5pm; free). Just south of Springfield, along Springfield Lake sits **The Lincoln Memorial Gardens**, 2301 E Lake Drive (daily; free; ⓣ217/529-1111, ⓦwww.lmgnc.org). Designed by famous landscape architect Jens Jensen, the hundred-acre site is home to hordes of arbour, plant, and bird life, all native to the states where Lincoln spent his young life. Completed in 1904, the **Dana-Thomas House**, 301 E Lawrence Ave (open for special events and private functions only; ⓣ217/782-6776), survives as the best preserved and most completely furnished example of **Frank Lloyd Wright**'s early Prairie house, with more than four hundred pieces of glasswork, original art, and light fixtures. A museum ripe for amateur photographers is just north of town, at 2075 Peoria Rd, where Bill Shea proudly displays fifty years' worth of road signs, gas pumps, and Route 66 memorabilia at **Shea's Gas Station Museum** (Tues–Fri 7am–4pm, Sat 8am–noon; free).

Twenty miles northwest of Springfield on Hwy-97, **Lincoln's New Salem State Historic Site** marks where the future president first lived in this area, from 1831 to 1837. In this backwoods clearing he clerked in a store, volunteered for the Black Hawk War, served as postmaster, and failed in business before taking up legal studies and moving to Springfield to pursue his political career. Today the recreated village features simple homes, workshops, a store, and a tavern. The **visitor center** hosts a worthwhile exhibit on pioneer lifestyles (Wed–Sun 9am–5pm, calling in advance is recommended, hours change periodically; suggested donation adults $4, children $2; ⓣ217/632-4000, ⓦwww.lincolnsnewsalem.com).

Practicalities

Abraham Lincoln Capital Airport (ⓣ217/788-1060, ⓦwww.flyspi.com) currently has two major airlines serving Springfield (United Airlines and American Airlines). Amtrak **trains** from Chicago and St Louis roll in at Third and Washington streets downtown, at manageable times. Greyhound drops off two miles east of downtown at 2351 S Dirksen Parkway. The **Convention and Visitors Bureau**, 109 N Seventh St (Mon–Fri 8.30am–5pm; ⓣ217/789-2360 or 1-800/545-7300, ⓦwww.visit-springfieldillinois.com), has brochures and maps.

The best selection of **accommodation** includes the full-service *President Abraham Lincoln Hotel and Convention Center*, 701 East Adams St (ⓣ217/544-8800 or 1/866-7888-1860, ⓦwww.presidentabrahamlincolnhotel.com; ❹) and the *Mansion View Inn*, 529 S Fourth St (ⓣ217/544-7411 or 1-800/252-1083, ⓦwww.mansionview.com; ❹). *The Inn at 835*, 835 S Second St (ⓣ217/523-4466, ⓦwww.innat835.com; ❺), is a charming ten-room B&B converted from a 1909 downtown apartment block.

Springfield's **cafés** are the origin of a phenomenon known as the **Horseshoe** – simply said, a meat sandwich, but fried, covered in melted cheese, and very tasty. *D'Arcy's Pint Restaurant*, 661 W Stanford Ave. (ⓣ217/492-8800) serves up the ultimate Horseshoe, however, first timers should steer toward the smaller Ponyshoe version ($6.50). The *Cozy Dog Drive-In*, 2935 S Sixth St (ⓣ217/525-1992) claims to be the birthplace of the **Cozy Dog** (also known as the corn dog), a deep-fried, batter-drenched hot dog on a stick (closed Sun). At the other end of the health spectrum, *Augie's Front Burner*, 109 S Fifth St (ⓣ217/544-6979), serves up good California-style and vegetarian meals.

Galena

The charming town of **GALENA**, a few miles short of both Iowa and Wisconsin in the far northwest corner of Illinois, has changed little since its nineteenth-century heyday. Thanks to its sheltered location just a few miles up the Galena River, it was a major port of call for Mississippi River steamboats. These days, the main foot traffic comes from weekend travelers who step back in time strolling along the gentle crescent of Main Street. Its impeccable redbrick facades and graceful skyline of spires and crosses place it among the most attractive river towns in the US. Outdoor adventurers kayak and canoe down the Mississippi back waters or bike the winding roads that boast Illinois highest elevations. Fever River Outfitters has canoe, kayak, bicycle and scooter rentals and offer a variety of well-planned trips: kayak and canoe birdwatching ($26–54), scooter rides to the local vineyard ($45–85) and a paddle/run/bike triathlon every summer (Ⓣ815/777-9425, Ⓦwww.feverriveroutfitters.com).

Galena boasts of having contributed nine generals to the Union army during the Civil War, the most significant of whom was **Ulysses S. Grant**. Grant moved to the town in 1860, working with his brothers as a clerk in a leather store owned by his father. His West Point education encouraged the townspeople to appoint him as colonel when they raised the 21st Illinois regiment on the outbreak of war. When he came home, in August 1865, it was as overall commander of the victorious Union army.

The grateful citizens of Galena presented Grant with a **house**, a couple of blocks up Bouthillier Street on the far side of the river (Wed–Sun 9am–4:15pm; suggested donation $3; Ⓣ815/777-0248; it is best to phone before arriving). It was there, in the drawing room that Grant received the news of his election as president in 1868. Although he went on to serve two terms, he is commonly agreed to have been a better general than president. His administrations were plagued by scandal, and he lost all his own money through unwise investments. The family fortunes were restored just before his death in 1885, when Mark Twain first persuaded Grant to write, and then published, his bestselling *Memoirs*.

Practicalities

The 1857 Railroad Museum, across the river from the town proper at 101 Bouthillier St, serves as the local **visitor center** (daily 9am–5pm; Ⓣ815/777-4390 or 1-877/464-2536, Ⓦwww.galena.org). The gracefully restored 1850's *Victorian Mansion*, 301 High St (Ⓣ815/777-0675, Ⓦwww.victorianmansion.com; ❺), is an elegant eight-room B&B where President Grant gave his farewell speech to the town before heading off to the White House. If your budget won't stretch that far, the *Grant Hills Motel*, a mile east on highway 20 (Ⓣ815/777-2116 or 1-877/421-0924, Ⓦwww.granthills.com; ❷), makes a good-value option. As for a local spot to **eat**, *Railway Café'*, 100 Bouthillier St. (Ⓣ815/777-0047) serves organic breakfasts and lunches and has live music. *Backstreets Steak and Chophouse,* 216 S Commerce St (Ⓣ815/777-4800) serves up delicious meats the Midwest makes famous or try *Fried Green Tomatoes*, 213 N Main St (Ⓣ815/777-3938), a reliable Italian alternative.

Wisconsin

Nearly as many cows as humans call **WISCONSIN** home; over five million of each reside in this rich, rolling farmland. However, America's self-proclaimed "Dairyland" is more than just one giant pasture. Beyond the massive hills, red barns and silvery silos lie endless pine forests, some fifteen thousand sky-blue lakes, postcard-pretty valleys, and dramatic bluffs. The state, whose Ojibway name means "gathering of the waters," is bordered by Lake Michigan to the east, Lake Superior in the north and, to the west, the Mississippi and St Croix rivers.

The **history** of Wisconsin exemplifies the standard formula for westward expansion. Seventeenth-century French and British explorers began by trading with the Native Americans and soon ousted them from their land. The European settlers who followed – predominantly Germans, Scandinavians, and Poles – tended to be liberal and progressive; such major national social programs as labor laws for women and children, assistance for the elderly and the disabled, and unemployment compensation were rooted here.

Wisconsin today is best known for its liquids. The **milk** from all those cattle yields cheeses of all kinds, while the **beer**, as the song says, is what made **Milwaukee** famous. Sparkling Madison apart, Wisconsin's other cities – **La Crosse**, **Green Bay**, **Oshkosh** – can veer toward the dull side, but they're also clean, safe, and amiable, while the smaller towns can be distinctive and charming.

Getting around Wisconsin

You'll be hard put to explore Wisconsin's remote north, or key locales like the Door County peninsula, without a vehicle. Public transportation is better in the south. Milwaukee and, to a lesser extent, Madison are hubs for Greyhound and Amtrak. Five **trains** daily connect Milwaukee and Chicago, a ninety-minute journey, while one crosses the state in the south en route for Seattle, via Columbus (near Madison), Portage, Wisconsin Dells, Tomah, and La Crosse.

Milwaukee

Just ninety miles north of Chicago, bustling **MILWAUKEE** is the largest city in Wisconsin and is a combination of the down-home Midwest and its stylish urban counterparts. Known for its lakeside and ethnic **festivals** and huge **breweries**, Milwaukee is reshaping its image. Visually it's a mix of elegant architecture, rambling Victorian warehouses, and revamped waterfront developments. Its prime position on the shores of Lake Michigan, at the confluence of three rivers, made it a meeting place for Native American groups long before white settlers moved in, while the opulent mansions lining the lake commemorate the industrialists who helped make this Wisconsin's economic and manufacturing capital. By 1850, less than two decades old and with a population of twenty thousand, Milwaukee already had a dozen breweries and 225 saloons.

Arrival, information, and getting around

Milwaukee is well served by air, rail, and bus. Mitchell **airport**, eight miles south of downtown at 5300 S Howell Ave, is connected with the city center by bus #80 ($2), and by shared-ride van service ($15). A taxi will set you back about $30. Amtrak is at 433 W St Paul Ave, while Greyhound (Ⓣ414/272-2156) which has several locations and Wisconsin Coach (Ⓣ262/542-8864; Ⓦwww.wisconsincoach.com), serving southeastern Wisconsin, operate out of the same terminal at 606 N James Lovell Drive. Badger Bus (Ⓣ414/276-7490, Ⓦwww.badgerbus.com), across the street at no. 635, runs to Madison and points between (six daily; $40 round-trip). Take care in and around the stations at night, which can be dodgy.

Milwaukee's **Visitor Center** is at Discovery World, at Pier Wisconsin (daily 8am–5pm; Ⓣ414/273-7222 or 1-800/554-1448, Ⓦwww.visitmilwaukee.org), and has details on such **festivals** as the eleven-day Summerfest (late-June to early July), also known as "The Big Gig," and the Wisconsin State Fair (early Aug).

Getting around Milwaukee is easy and inexpensive via the county's extensive **transportation system** (flat fare $2; 24hr info Ⓣ414/344-6711). The Milwaukee Loop is a special trolley service connecting 25 stops in the city center (June–Aug, Wed–Sat 11am–10pm; free).

Accommodation

Accommodation in Milwaukee runs the gamut from low-budget motels to upmarket chains and luxury hotels. Staying a few miles outside of town will reduce your rates drastically.

Brumder Mansion 3046 W Wisconsin Ave Ⓣ414/342-9767 or 866/793-3676; Ⓦwww.brumdermansion.com. Fabulously decorated, enormous B&B with an in-house theater, just minutes from downtown. Rooms include antiques, marble, rich draperies, and stained glass. ④

Comfort Inn & Suites Downtown Lakeshore 916 E State St Ⓣ414/276-8800 or 1-800/328-7275, Ⓦwww.comfortinn.com. Clean, very comfortable rooms in a nice part of downtown. ④

Holiday Inn Express W177 N 9675 Riverbend Lane, Germantown (Ⓣ877/654-0232). Located twenty minutes NW of Milwaukee, this basic hotel is comfortable and affordable, with convenient highway access. ③

Hotel Metro 411 East Madison St Ⓣ414/272-1937 or 1-877/638-7620; Ⓦwww.hotelmetro.com. This retro Art Deco hotel has an historic feeling with a modern twist. Updated and eco-friendly, it's worth the extra cash you might need to lay down for the fireplace and jacuzzi that sit in the center of the room. A little forward planning might secure a discounted package. ⑦

The Pfister Hotel 424 E Wisconsin Ave Ⓣ414/273-822, Ⓦwww.pfisterhotel.com. Sits nestled like a Victorian Grande Dame in the heart of downtown. Replenish yourself in the spa or visit the 23rd floor martini lounge. There is even a world-class Victorian art collection. It will cost a bit more, but often you can grab a special package for considerably less. ⑦–⑨

The City

Downtown Milwaukee, split north to south by the Milwaukee River, is only a mile long and a few blocks wide. Handsome old buildings and gleaming, modern steel-and-glass structures are comfortably corralled together on three sides by spaghetti-like strands of freeway, with Lake Michigan forming the fourth boundary. To bolster the allure of downtown, the city has successfully poured millions into its **Riverwalk** development along the Milwaukee River, now something of a nightlife center and the site of many public entertainment events. East of the river on the lakefront, the **Milwaukee Art Museum**, 700 N Art Museum Drive (Tues & Wed and Fri–Sun 10am–5pm, Thurs 10am–8pm; $8; Ⓣ414/224-3200, Ⓦwww.mam.org), contains works by European masters and twentieth-century Americans. One wing – with stunning views of the lake – is devoted to a comprehensive collection of Post-Impressionist paintings. Architect Santiago Calatrava's spectacular expansion is an attraction in itself, the white wings of the building flapping up and down three times each day to reduce heat gain and glare. Close by, **Dis-**

covery World at Pier Wisconsin,** 500 N Harbor Drive (Tues–Sun 9am–5pm; $15.95; ⓣ414/765-9966, ⓦwww.discoveryworld.org), features popular hands-on exhibits and the S/V *Denis Sullivan* schooner. Downtown at 800 W Wells St are the **Milwaukee Public Museum** (Mon–Sat 9am–5pm, Sun 10am–6pm; $11; ⓣ414/278-2702 or 1-888-700-9069, ⓦwww.mpm.edu), where the intertwined histories and mysteries of the earth, nature, and humankind are imaginatively presented through dioramas such as "A Sense of Wonder," and the **Humphrey IMAX Dome Theater**, which has a giant, wraparound screen (show times vary; $8–10, $16 for a combo ticket; ⓣ414/319-4629, ⓦwww.mpm.edu/imax).

West of downtown, the 37-room **Pabst Mansion**, at 2000 W Wisconsin Ave (Feb–Oct Mon–Sat 10am–4pm, Sun noon–4pm; closed Mon mid-Jan through Feb; $8-12; ⓣ414/931-0808, ⓦwww.pabstmansion.com), was completed in 1893 as the castle of a local beer baron and is a knockout example of ornate Flemish Renaissance architecture, featuring exquisite wood-, glass-, and ironwork. Although the Pabst Brewery here has shut down, the **Miller Brewing Company**, five miles west of downtown at 4251 W State St, still offers free behind-the-scenes tours (Mon–Sat, usually 10:30am–3:30pm but times change frequently; ⓣ414/931-2337 or 1-800/931-BEER), culminating in generous samples for over-21s. The shiny new museum responsible for Milwaukee's other legendary brand name, **Harley-Davidson**, located at 400 Canal St. (May–Oct Mon–Fri 9am–6pm, Nov–April Mon–Fri 10am–5pm, Sat & Sun 9am–6pm; ⓣ877/436-8738, ⓦwww.hdmuseum.com; $16) is geared squarely toward Harley devotees; for those more interested in Harley chic, there's ample opportunity to purchase all kinds of merchandise at the shop or throughout Milwaukee.

Eating

The Germans who first settled in Milwaukee determined its **eating** style – heavy on bratwurst, rye bread, and beer. Subsequent immigrants threw the collective kitchen wide open, making for a culinary cornucopia. With Lake Michigan lapping the city's feet, freshwater fish can hardly be overlooked, especially on a Friday night when legendary fish fries break out all over the place. Wherever you go, portions tend to be big.

Bacchus 925 E Wells ⓣ414/765-1166. Located in the historic Cudahy Tower and featuring fresh seafood and handmade pastas, this place drips with taste and style.

Carnevor 724 N Milwaukee St ⓣ414/223-2200. The art of fine dining and outstanding cuts of meat are in full swing at this chic and contemporary steakhouse. Closed Sun.

Eddie Martini's 8612 W Watertown Plank Rd ⓣ414/771-6680. Energetic atmosphere with inventive takes on American classics.

Mimma's Café 1307 E Brady St ⓣ414/264-6640. This unmissable, twenty-year-old Italian restaurant is classy yet casual, with imaginative, mouthwatering cuisine, like fried eggplant and artichoke ravioli, and an extensive wine list.

Rudy's 1122 N Edison St ⓣ414/223-1122. Family-friendly and affordable Mexican from 11am–11pm daily. Try the house special combo platters.

Trocadero 1758 N Water St ⓣ414/272-0205. Parisian-styled eastside spot that serves small plates and great continental dishes like grilled tuna and saffron shrimp.

Nightlife and entertainment

The concept of neighborhoods is vital to Milwaukee's nightlife. On the east side, **Brady Street**, a counterculture haven in the 1960s, is now filled with Italian restaurants and bars. **Walker's Point**, on the edge of downtown, has all sorts of watering holes, while the Polish locals can be found farther south. Downtown gets busy on the weekend, especially either side of the river on **Water** and **Old World Third** streets between Juneau and State.

Live theater and high culture in downtown Milwaukee revolves around the **Marcus Center for the Performing Arts**, 929 N Water St (ⓣ414/273-7121 or 1-888/612-3500, ⓦwww.marcuscenter.org). The plush, historic **Pabst Theater**, 144 E Wells St (ⓣ414/286-3663), and the **Riverside Theater**, 116 W Wisconsin Ave (ⓣ414/286-3663), host well-known bands, while the **Milwaukee Repertory Theater**, 108 E Wells St (ⓣ414/224-9490, ⓦwww.milwaukeerep.com), has a reputation for staging risk-taking productions in addition to classics like "A Christmas Carol." The **Third Ward**, a restored warehouse district on the edge of downtown full of shops and cafés, is home to the **Broadway Theater Center**, 158 N Broadway (ⓣ414/291-7800), which in turn holds the adventurous **Skylight Opera** (ⓦwww.skylightopera.com), **Chamber Theatre** (ⓦwww.chamber-theatre.com) and **Renaissance Theaterworks** (ⓦwww.r-t-w.com).

Café Vecchio 1137 N Old World Third St ⓣ414/273-5700. Upscale European-style coffee/wine bar featuring a one-hundred-plus wine list, espresso drinks, and a myriad of martinis.
Milwaukee Ale House 233 N Water St ⓣ414/226-BEER. Milwaukee's sole all-grain, old-style brewpub serves filling food and its own beer.
Safe House 779 N Front St ⓣ414/271-2007, ⓦwww.safe-house.com. This unique, tongue-in-cheek nightclub seems to come straight out of a spy film. Hint: enter through the "International Exports Ltd" office.
Up and Under Pub 1216 E Brady St ⓣ414/276-2677. Milwaukee's top blues bar.
Von Trier 2235 N Farwell Ave ⓣ414/272-1775. Black Forest decor and lots of imported beers – the Weise is a house specialty.

Wisconsin's eastern shores

North of Milwaukee, **eastern Wisconsin** is a melange of the industrial and the maritime, shaped by its proximity to **Lake Michigan** and the smaller **Lake Winnebago**. Of its towns, **Green Bay**, home to the legendary Packers, is best seen as a prelude to the most romanticized part of the state, **Door County**.

Green Bay

Few cities are as closely associated with a sports team as **GREEN BAY** is with the football Packers: 108 miles north of Milwauke; a small city with a big market. **The Green Bay Packer Hall of Fame**, 1265 Lombardi Ave (daily 8am–9pm; $10; ⓣ920/569-7500), celebrates the dynastic years of the 1960s when the Pack won Superbowls I and II, as well as more recent stars such as Antonio Freeman and Brett Favre. Stuffed with hands-on displays, movie theaters, and memorabilia, the museum offers more than enough to satisfy any football fan. The Hall of Fame is located in an atrium inside the Packers' **Lambeau Field** stadium, which you can also tour (times vary; $11, or $19 combination ticket with Hall of Fame; ⓦwww.packers.com). West on Hwy-172, opposite the airport, stands Wisconsin's biggest casino, **Oneida Bingo & Casino** ⓣ920/494-4500, ⓦwww.oneidabingoandcasino.net). Ten miles northwest of downtown Green Bay is the **New Zoo** 4378 Reforestation Rd, (ⓣ920/434-7841, ⓦwww.newzoo.org). Sitting within 1560 acres of the Brown County Reforestation Camp, New Zoo has miles of hiking, biking, and nature trails available in addition to its live animals. (daily 9am–4pm; $5).

The city's **CVB** (ⓣ920/494-9507 or 1-888/867-3342, ⓦwww.packercountry.com) sits in the shadow of the football stadium, off Lombardi Avenue, at 1901 S Oneida St. Nearby, the *Best Western Midway Hotel*, 780 Armed Forces Drive (ⓣ920/499-3161 or 1-800/528-1234, ⓦwww.bestwestern.com; ❹–❺), has standard rooms and an indoor pool. *Titletown Brewing Company*, 200 Dousman St

(Ⓣ920/437-2337), has a great setting for drinks in a former railroad depot downtown, while *Brett Favre's Steakhouse*, 1004 Brett Favre Pass (Ⓣ920/499-MVP4), is an upscale family restaurant/sports bar serving Southern cuisine.

Door County

From Sturgeon Bay, 140 miles north of Milwaukee, **Door County** sticks into Lake Michigan like a gradually tapering candle for 42 miles. A charming collection of small towns, tiny villages, and an island, its 300 miles of shoreline smacks more of New England than the Midwest. Prices can be a little steep in the summer, but you get what you pay for – a small sliver of America devoid, for the most part, of crude billboards, sloppy diners, bland chain motels, and tacky amusements. Activities include browsing around galleries and attending arts festivals, as well as hiking, fishing, and boating. Renting a **bicycle** gives you the chance to follow an excellent **cycle trail**; try Fish Creek's Nor Door Cyclery (Ⓣ920/868-2275, Ⓦwww.nordoorsports.com), on Hwy-42 just north of the entrance to Peninsula State Park (see below), which has the best models. Winter is considerably quieter, with ice fishing, cross-country skiing, and snowmobiling being the predominant outdoor activities.

Pick up road and trail maps at the **visitor center** on Hwy-42/57 upon entering Sturgeon Bay (lobby open 24 hours; staffed times vary; Ⓣ920/743-4456 or 1-800/52-RELAX, Ⓦwww.doorcounty.com), where you can also phone local lodgings for free.

Exploring Door County

Door County's only sizeable town, **Sturgeon Bay**, is a pleasant enough shipbuilding community, if not exactly abundant in small-town splendor. Ten miles north on Hwy-57 you find one of five state parks, the rolling **Whitefish Dunes State Park**, with its wispy sand dunes and popular mile-long beach (daily; $7 per car, $10 with out-of-state plates). A short trail beginning at the park's Nature Center leads to the spectacular rocky **Cave Point County Park** (free), studded with wind- and wave-sculptured caves that are particularly dramatic in winter. In general beaches are better this side of the peninsula; you can also swim in several placid inland lakes.

Over on the western side, biking and hiking trails traverse the thickly forested hills of **Peninsula State Park** (situated between tiny Fish Creek and enchanting **Ephraim**, with its picturesque white-clapboard architecture). Peninsula Park is one of the most popular parks in Wisconsin and summer camping reservations usually book up in January. Just outside it on Hwy-42, the old-fashioned Skyway Drive-In movie theater (Ⓣ920/854-9938) offers a couple of hours' diversion on a warm night. Northeast of Ellison Bay near the peninsula's tip, **Newport State Park** is one of Wisconsin's least visited parks, with hiking, mountain biking, cross-country skiing, and backpack camping opportunities.

Washington Island, off the peninsula's northern tip, is a tiny dollop of land that offers a different cultural perspective. During Prohibition, the Icelandic community here convinced authorities that (40 percent alcohol) bitters were an ancient cure for rheumatism and dyspepsia. Cases of the stuff were shipped in, and the habit stuck; drop into the historic *Nelsen's Hall Bitters Pub and Restaurant* (Ⓣ920/847-2496, T877/NESLENS), about two miles from the Detroit Harbor dock for a taste. **Motel rooms** are available on Washington, but there's no such luxury on the primitive neighboring 950-acre **Rock Island**. Once the private estate of a millionaire, it's dotted with stark, stone buildings; no cars are allowed, so see it by foot or bike.

The islands are served by the Washington Island Ferry from Northport at the tip of the peninsula (daily; $11 round-trip, cars $24, bikes $4; ⓣ920/847-2546 or 1-800/223-2094, ⓦwww.wisferry.com) and the Rock Island Ferry out of Jackson Harbor (May to early Oct daily; $9 round-trip for foot traffic only; ⓣ920/847-3322).

Accommodation

Door County has a full range of **accommodation**, including some overpriced resorts. Prices given are for shoulder seasons (the best time to come); expect to pay up to 25 percent extra at the grander hotels in July and August, and a small weekend premium. Camping is idyllic. State park sites cost $12–17 (plus $10 reservation fee and $7 daily admission or $10 for out-of-state residents; ⓣ1-888/947-2757). Among the best of the private campgrounds is the pet-friendly *Path of Pines*, County Road F off Hwy-42, near Fish Creek (mid-May to mid-Oct; $20; ⓣ920/868-3332 or 1-800/868-7802).

Brichwood Lodge 337 Hwy 57, Sister Bay ⓣ920/854-7195, ⓦwww.birchwoodlodge.com. A pleasant lodge with a variety of accommodation options. European designed suites with a modern touch ❺–❼

French Country Inn 3052 Spruce Lane, Ephraim ⓣ920/854-4001. This charming B&B close to the water offers seven rooms (two with private baths) in the summer and four in the winter. Breakfast features organic, local produce when possible. ❸–❹

Peninsula Park-View Resort 3397 Hwy-42 ⓣ920/854-2633, ⓦwww.peninsulaparkview.com. Friendly motel conveniently situated on the edge of Fish Creek at the quiet entrance of Peninsula State Park. Offers standard rooms as well as suites and cottages. Guests have free use of bikes; one room is pet friendly. ❹

Settlement Courtyard Inn & Lavender Spa 9126 Hwy 42, Fish Creek ⓣ920/868-3524 or 1-877/398-9308, ⓦwww.settlement.com. The *Settlement*'s location on a 200-acre estate makes it an ideal year-round destination with four miles of trails for biking, hiking, or cross country skiing. Clean and comfortable, breakfast included. ❺

White Gull Inn 4225 Main St, Fish Creek ⓣ920/868-3517 or 1-888/364-9542, ⓦwww.whitegullinn.com. The county's crown jewel, this elegant old inn, next to delightful Sunset Park, was built in 1896. Rooms are decorated in antiques, and some have fireplaces and double whirlpools. The inn is also known for its good restaurant (breakfast is included) and fish boil (see below) every night in summer. ❻–❾

Eating

One reward of a midsummer visit to Door County is the chance to sample the cherry in all its guises. Another traditional treat is the **fish boil**, a delicious outdoor ritual involving whitefish steaks, potatoes, and onions cooked in a cauldron over a wood fire. Rounded off with coleslaw and cherry pie, it's widely available for between $12 and $18.

Al Johnson's Swedish Restaurant Hwy-42, Sister Bay ⓣ920/854-2626. Swedish pancakes, meatballs, and other fine Scandinavian dishes make this spot unmissable. Be sure and look up to see goats grazing atop the sod roof.

C & C Supper Club Hwy-42, Corner of Spruce and Main St ⓣ920/868-3412. Get your supper club fix at *C & C's* and set aside room for the delicious apple cobbler.

Square Rigger Galley 6332 Hwy-57, Jacksonport ⓣ920/823-2408 or ⓣ1-866/439-4578. This cocktail lounge and restaurant, on a private sandy beach, serves one of the county's best fish boils.

Wilson's 9990 Water St, Ephraim ⓣ920/854-2041. The old-fashioned red and white striped awnings beckon you in for burgers, sandwiches, and (along with the Door County Ice Cream Factory in Sister Bay) the top ice cream on the peninsula (open May–Oct).

Northern Wisconsin

Sparsely settled **northern Wisconsin** has no large cities (and few small ones), and no interstates. It's a lake-studded wilderness, covered by enormous tracts of forest. Canoe its rivers, fish for record-breakers, or ski or snowmobile cross-country trails without having to fight for space. **Bayfield**, **Madeline Island**, and the **Apostle Islands** in the northwest are the obvious destinations.

The Apostle Islands

All but one of the 22 islands scattered off **Bayfield Peninsula** in Lake Superior are part of the **Apostle Islands National Lakeshore** – a prized preserve for outdoors enthusiasts seeking to recharge depleted spiritual batteries.

The jumping-off point for the islands, **BAYFIELD**, once a lumbering and fishing village, is now a pleasant soft-sell tourist trap. Its sumptuous *Old Rittenhouse Inn*, 301 Rittenhouse Ave (Ⓣ715/779-5111 or 1-800/779-2129, Ⓦwww.rittenhouseinn.com; ❺–❻), offers gourmet meals and well-appointed **rooms**. *Tree Top House*, 225 N Fourth St (Ⓣ715/779-3293; ❷), features clean, simple doubles, while *Island View B&B*, 86720 Island View Lane (Ⓣ715/779-5307 or 1-888/309-5307, Ⓦwww.islandviewbandb.com; ❻), has secluded cottages and B&B-style accommodation a mile outside of town. Lodges and cottages are the centerpiece for the thirty gorgeous lakeside acres of *Rocky Run* (Ⓣ715/373-2551; ❹), a resort outside **Washburn** eleven miles south. Bayfield's **visitor center** is at 42 S Broad St (Ⓣ715/779-3335 or 1-800/447-4094; Ⓦwww.bayfield.org). Campers heading for the islands require permits from the visitor center (ask about permit fees) at 415 Washington Ave (summer daily; weekdays in winter; Ⓣ715/779-3397). Getting around the islands is straightforward: Apostle Island's Cruise Services boats ($32.95; Ⓣ715/779-3925, Ⓦwww.apostleisland.com) wend their way past all of the islands, and will set down and pick up campers.

Madeline Island

By the fifteenth century **Madeline Island** was known to the Ojibway as Moningwunakauning – home of the golden-shafted woodpecker. Frenchman Michel Cadotte founded a fur-trading post there for the British in 1793, and subsequently married Equaysayway, daughter of a tribal leader, who took the name the island bears today. Madeline is now the only commercially developed Apostle Island, but it remains pretty low-key. Cadotte is buried in an overgrown cemetery in its sole town, **LA POINTE**.

La Pointe is accessible in summer via the twenty-minute ride on the Madeline Island Ferry Line from Bayfield (every 30min in peak season; cars $16.50 single, $33 round-trip; passengers $5, $10; bikes $2.50, $5; Ⓣ715/747-2051, Ⓦwww.madferry.com). Its 180 year-round residents maintain an interesting little **historical museum** (May–Oct daily 10am–5pm; $5.50), and assorted sandy beaches, wide bays, scenic points, and forests can also be explored along 45 miles of sometimes rough road in the area. The Ferry Line conducts two-hour bus tours of the island (July & Aug, Mon–Sat, 1.30pm; $11).

The **visitor center** on Main Street (Ⓣ715/747-2801 or 1-888/475-3386, Ⓦwww.madelineisland.com) can offer advice on **places to stay**; the *Madeline Island Motel* (Ⓣ715/747-3000; ❹) and *The Island Inn* (Ⓣ715/747-2000; ❺), both near the ferry dock, are probably the best value. A wooden footbridge from La Pointe across the lagoon leads to **Big Bay State Park** where the campgrounds share a splendid mile-long beach. Camping sites, on top of a bluff and close to caves in the park (Ⓣ1-888/947-2757), cost $10–14, plus a $10 reservation fee and a $7–10 vehicle fee. **Eating options** include the pub in *The Inn on Madeline Island* resort (Ⓣ715/747-6322 or 1-800/822-6315, Ⓦwww.madisland.com; ❹–❻) where homes, cottages, and condominiums can also be rented along a private beach.

Southern Wisconsin

Assorted highways and back roads lace up **southern Wisconsin**, passing over rolling hills and deep dales. The main urban center of Wisconsin's most populated region is the immensely likeable lakeside college town of **Madison**, which doubles as the state capital. Cozy Madison-area communities like New Glarus or Mount Horeb, and historic settlements like Little Norway have cute, walkable downtowns. Further north, a kid's dream town, Wisconsin Dells has a picturesque setting, but may appeal only to those who revel in tacky attractions and T-shirts shops. Undulating down the state's western border, alongside the Mississippi River, the scenic highway designated as **The Great River Road** runs from near Canada to the Gulf of Mexico.

Madison and around

The history books record that **MADISON**, just over an hour west of Milwaukee, was little more than a wooded, mosquito-infested swamp when it was selected to be the political nucleus of the Wisconsin Territory in 1836. Today this stimulating, youthful metropolis is one of the most beautifully set cities in the US, with a handful of diverting museums, great restaurants, and a student-fueled nightlife scene.

Arrival, information, and accommodation

Greyhound **buses** run regularly to Milwaukee, Green Bay, and beyond, while Badger Coaches makes six trips daily from downtown Milwaukee ($17.50 single/$31 round-trip; Ⓣ608/255-6771, Ⓦwww.badgerbus.com). Both operate out of the terminal at 2 S Bedford St. Van Galder/Coach USA buses depart from the Memorial Union to Chicago's O'Hare Airport (10 daily; $29 single, $58 round-trip; Ⓣ608/752-5407 or 1-800/747-0994, Ⓦwww.coachusa.com/vangalder). Madison also has a recently renovated airport, (Ⓣ608/246-3380), offering flights all over the Midwest and further afield. The **visitor center** is at 21 N Park St (Mon–Fri 9am–4.30pm, Sat 11am–2pm, closed Sun; Ⓣ608/262-4636, Ⓦwww.visitmadison.com).

Accommodation can be found throughout the city, though the budget chains lie to the east, off I-90/94. *Madison Concourse Hotel*, 1 W Dayton St (Ⓣ608/257-6000 or 1-800/356-8293, Ⓦwww.concoursehotel.com; ❺–❻) has spacious, well-appointed rooms steps from State Street. Right on Capitol Square, you can stay in one of the comfortable rooms at *The Best Western Inn on the Park*, 22 S Carroll St (Ⓣ608/257-8811 or 1-800/279-8811; ❺). There's also a Hostelling International location at 141 S Butler St (Ⓣ608/441-0144, Ⓦwww.madisonhostel.org), with 28 beds ($22 members/$25 non-members, 5 private rooms ($44 members/$47 non-members), and all the usual amenities: kitchen, laundry, internet access, storage, and lockers.

The Town

Downtown is neatly laid out on an isthmus between lakes Mendota and Monona, with the white-granite **State Capitol** (tours Mon–Sat 9am–3pm excluding noon,

Sun 1–3pm; ⓣ608/266-0382) sitting on a hill at its center, surrounded by shady trees, lawns, and park benches. The State Capitol square is the site of a nationally renowned **farmers' market** (late April–early Nov Sat 6am–2pm), where you can browse the local produce, and arts-and-crafts. Nearby, the brand-new, glassy **Overture Center**, 201 State St, hosts touring musicians, Broadway plays, and other cultural events (box office ⓣ608/258-4141, ⓦwww.overturecenter.com); inside, the **Madison Museum of Contemporary Art** 227 State St (Tues & Wed 11am–5pm, Thurs & Fri 11am–8pm, Sat 10am–8pm, Sun noon–5pm, closed Mon; free; ⓣ608/257-0158; ⓦwww.mmoca.org), features touring exhibits.

Frank Lloyd Wright designed the **Unitarian Meeting House**, 900 University Bay Drive, in the late 1940s. Its sweeping, dramatically curved ceiling and triangle motif are definitely worth a look (May–Oct Mon–Fri 10am–4pm, Sat 9am–noon; $3). The lakeside **Monona Terrace Community and Convention Center**, 1 John Nolen Drive, is a more recently realized example of Wright's grand vision (daily tours at 1pm; $3). Surprisingly intimate and full of architectural detail, the Center, with its curves, arches, and domes, echoes the State Capitol building just a few blocks away.

If the capitol is the city's governmental heart, the 46,000-student **University of Wisconsin** is its spirited, liberal-thinking head, now mellowed since its protest heyday in the late 1960s. The **Memorial Union**, 800 Langdon St (ⓣ608/262-1583), holds a cafeteria and pub, the *Rathskeller*, with tables strewn beneath huge, vaulted ceilings and live music most nights. Out back, the spacious **UW Terrace** offers beautiful sunset views over Lake Mendota. Capitol and campus are arterially connected by State Street, eight tree-lined, pedestrianized blocks of restaurants, cafés, bars, and funky stores.

Eating, drinking, and entertainment

State Street is a veritable smorgasbord of food and drink, and the **Capital Square** and **King St** areas have also seen a spate of great new restaurants open in recent years. For details of what's on, check the free weekly *Isthmus*, which comes out on Thursdays and carries full listings.

Café Continental 108 King St ⓣ608/251-488. Upscale European bistro atmosphere with a bar serving over fifty wines by the glass. Open weekends for brunch.

Great Dane Pub & Brewing Co 123 E Doty St ⓣ608/284-0000. Billiards and brew complement fresh hearty fare in this inviting pub.

Marigold Kitchen 118 S Pinckney St ⓣ608/661-5559. Charming, sunny spot serving delicious, creative breakfast and lunch dishes – such as *challah* french toast and chile poached eggs – focusing on local, organic ingredients.

Oceans Grille 117 Martin Luther King, Jr. Blvd ⓣ608/285-2582. Terrific seafood and an extensive wine list in a lively, festive atmosphere.

The Old Fashioned 23 N Pinckney St ⓣ 608/310-4545, ⓦwww.theoldfashioned.com. Named for the state's signature brandy cocktail, this homey restaurant serves the traditional food that made Wisconsin famous, like fried cheese curds and a killer version of its eponymous cocktail.

Spring Green

During his seventy-year career, Wisconsin-born architect and social philosopher **Frank Lloyd Wright** designed such monumental structures as New York's spiraling Guggenheim Museum and Tokyo's earthquake-proof *Imperial Hotel*. Three miles south of **SPRING GREEN**, itself forty miles west of Madison on Hwy-14, stand more intimate examples of his work: Wright's magnificent former residence, **Taliesin**, and his **Hillside Home School**. His studio is imposing, and there's also a theater space on the estate. Extensive and varied tours are available of the house and the school (May–Oct daily; reservations recommended; $16–75). Tours leave from the **Frank Lloyd Wright Visitor Center** (ⓣ608/588-7900 or 1-877/588-

7900, ⓦ www.taliesinpreservation.org), which was designed by Wright in 1953 as a restaurant; it now features displays, a café, and a bookstore. Among numerous other Wright-influenced buildings in Spring Green are the bank and the pharmacy.

From 1944 onward, Alex Jordan built the **House on the Rock**, six miles south of Taliesin on Hwy-23, on and out of a natural, 60ft, chimney-like rock – for no discernible reason. He certainly never lived in it, nor did he intend it to become Wisconsin's number one tourist attraction (mid-March to Oct daily 9am–dusk, $12.50 per section or $26.50 for all three; Nov & Dec Christmas tours Thurs–Mon 9am–5pm; $21.50; ⓣ 800/947-2799, ⓦ www.thehouseontherock.com). Only the first section of this multilevel series of furnished nooks and chambers bears any resemblance to a house of any kind. With its low ceilings, indirect lighting, indoor pools, waterfalls, trees, and pervasive shag carpeting, the style brings to mind Frank Lloyd Wright meets *The Flintstones*. The rest of the house is a logic-free labyrinth, containing Jordan's astounding collection of collections (antiques, an enormous carousel and pneumatic music machines, miniature circuses, dolls and dolls' houses, maritime memorabilia, armor and firearms, ad infinitum). The net effect is overwhelming and disorienting, alternately great fun and ghastly. Highlights include the **Infinity Room**, comprising three thousand small glass panels tapering to a point and cantilevered several hundred feet above the Wyoming Valley.

Practicalities

Spring Green is a pretty place to stay, but prices can be high in summer. If you're looking to **stay overnight** in the area, a great bet is the *Castle of Spring Green,* 2247 State Rd 133 in nearby Blue River. Built to resemble a French chateau and set on 500 acres, the *Castle* doesn't disappoint with its ornate furnishings and luxurious rooms. Full castle and grounds rentals available as well as nightly rates (ⓣ 847/543-1452; ❹–❽). For a **bite to eat**, follow the locals to *The Shed* (ⓣ 608/588-9049), an easygoing diner and bar at 123 N Lexington St in downtown Spring Green.

Minnesota

Though **MINNESOTA** is more than a thousand miles from either coast, it's virtually a seaboard state, thanks to **Lake Superior**, connected to the Atlantic via the St Lawrence Seaway. The glaciers that, millions of years ago, flattened all but its southeast corner also gouged out more than fifteen thousand **lakes**, and major **rivers** run along the eastern and western borders. Ninety-five percent of the population lives within ten minutes of a body of water, and the very name Minnesota is a Sioux word meaning "land of sky-tinted water."

French explorers in the sixteenth century encountered prairies to the south and, in the north, dense forests whose abundant waterways were an ideal breeding ground for beavers and muskrats. **Fur trading**, **fishing**, and **lumbering** flourished, and the Ojibway and Sioux were eased out by waves of French, British, and American immigrants. Admitted to the Union in 1858, the new state of Minnesota was at first settled by Germans and Scandinavians, who farmed in the west and south. Other ethnic groups followed, many drawn by the massive **iron ore** deposits of north central Minnesota, which are expected to hold out for two more centuries.

More than half of Minnesota's hardy inhabitants, who endure some of the fiercest winters in the nation, live in the southeast, around the so-called Twin Cities of **Minneapolis** and **St Paul**. These attractive and basically friendly rivals together rank as the Midwest's great civic double act for their combined cultural, recreational, and business opportunities. Smaller cities include the northern shipping port of **Duluth**, the gateway to the Scenic Hwy-61 lakeshore drive, and **Rochester**, near pretty river towns like Red Wing and Winona. The tranquil waters of **Voyageurs National Park** lie halfway along the state's boundary with Canada.

Getting around Minnesota

Minneapolis/St Paul **airport** is home base for Northwest Airlines and, with eighteen passenger airlines, it easily handles routes to Europe as well as domestic flights. Amtrak **trains** cross the state once a day east and west from Chicago and Seattle, with stops in Winona, Red Wing, St Paul, St Cloud, Staples, and Detroit Lakes. Greyhound is the largest of the several **bus** companies plying Minnesota's roads. Seven buses per day make the nine-hour journey to Chicago from the Twin Cities. Duluth, St Louis, and Kansas City are also served several times daily from the state's major metropolises.

Minneapolis and St Paul

Commonly known as the **Twin Cities**, **MINNEAPOLIS** (a hybrid Sioux/Greek word meaning "water city") and **ST PAUL** are competitive yet complementary. Fraternally rather than identically twinned, they may be even better places to live than they are to visit, thanks to their cleanliness, cultural activity, social awareness, and relatively low crime rates. Life for a majority of Twin City residents seems so vibrantly wholesome that the most significant threat would appear to be their own creeping complacency.

Only a twenty-minute expressway ride separates the respective downtowns, but each has its own character, style, and strengths. **St Paul**, the state capital – originally called Pig's Eye, after a scurrilous French-Canadian fur trader who sold whisky at a Mississippi River landing in the 1840s – is the staid, slightly older sibling, careful to preserve its buildings and traditions. The compact but stately downtown is built, like Rome, on seven hills: the **Capitol** and the **Cathedral** occupy one each, both august monuments that keep the city mindful of its responsibilities.

Minneapolis, founded on money generated by the Mississippi's hundreds of flour and saw mills, is livelier, artier, and more modern, with up-to-date architecture and an upbeat attitude. The residents are spread over wider ground than in St Paul, and dozens of lakes and parks underscore the city's appeal.

Arrival, information, and getting around

Twin Cities International Airport lies about ten miles south of either city in suburban Bloomington. Super Shuttle Minneapolis (Ⓣ612/827-7777) takes travelers between the airport and major hotels for around $13, while some lodgings provide their own transportation. **Taxis** to Minneapolis will set you back close to $40, and to St Paul $30. You can also take the new light rail system (Ⓣ612/373-3333) into Minneapolis (daily 4am–1am: $1.75–2.25), or bus #54 to St Paul (4am–1am: $1.75–2.25). Amtrak is midway between the cities at 730 Transfer Rd, off University Avenue. The Greyhound terminals, both in convenient downtown locations, are at 950 Hawthorne Ave (ⓣ612/371-3325) in Minneapolis and the less-used 166 W University Ave location (ⓣ651/222-0507) in St Paul. Metro Transit **buses** (ⓣ612/341-4287 or 612/373-3333) make both cities relatively easy to explore without a car. Old-style **trolleys** run through downtown Minneapolis from May to November (ⓦwww.trollyride.org).

In Minneapolis, the **visitor center** is at 250 Marquette Ave (Mon–Fri 8am–5pm; ⓣ612/767-8000 or 1-888/676-MPLS, ⓦwww.minneapolis.org). In St Paul, it's at 175 W Kellogg Blvd, suite 502 (ⓣ651/265-4900 or 1-800/627-6101, ⓦwww.visitsaintpaul.com). The main Minneapolis **post office** is on First Street and Marquette Avenue; St Paul's is at 180 Kellogg Blvd E.

Accommodation

You're likely to pay more for lodgings downtown than in the suburbs, where dozens of cheap **motels** line I-494 near the airport, though some of the pricier central hotels offer reduced rates and special package deals on weekends. The pretty riverside community of **Stillwater**, 25 miles from St Paul via I-35 N and Hwy-36 E, has many grand old B&Bs and motels (ⓣ651/439-4001 for information). For **bed-and-breakfast** options in the Twin Cities, consult ⓦwww.bedandbreakfast.com, as many B&Bs do not have their own websites.

Minneapolis

Birdhouse Inn & Gardens 371 Water St, Excelsior ⓣ952/474-0196. This suburban B&B a few blocks from Lake Minnetonka offers good prices and a homey atmosphere. ❹

The Depot 225 Third Ave S ⓣ612/375-1700, ⓦwww.thedepotminneapolis.com. The historic Depot building recently underwent massive renovations and now boasts an enormous indoor water park, luxury accommodations, dining and even an ice rink. It is best to check for any packages or specials to keep the cost down. ❻–❼

Evelo's B&B 2301 Bryant Ave S ⓣ612/374-9656. Three comfortable rooms in a well-preserved Victorian home near bus lines, lakes, and downtown. Non-smoking only. ❹

Hilton Minneapolis 1001 Marquette Ave ⓣ612/376-1000, ⓦwww.minneapolis.hilton.com. Elegant downtown spot with a great gym and pool. Weekend rates are considerably less. ❻–❽

Historic Heights B&B 3980 5th St NE (ⓣ612/475-1950, ⓦwww.thehistoricheights.com). Six simple rooms priced well. Guests use shared bathrooms but are allowed to use laundry facilities. ❸–❹

Le Blanc House 302 University Ave NE ⓣ612/379-2570, ⓦwww.leblanchouse.com. Fancy Victorian home just minutes from downtown. Serves gourmet breakfasts on the weekend and continental fare during the week. ❺

Minneapolis International House 2400 Stevens Ave ⓣ612/874-0407, ⓦwww.minneapolishostel.com. This conveniently situated independent hostel has $35–75 private rooms and $25 dorm beds.

Nicollet Island Inn 95 Merriam St ⓣ612/331-1800, ⓦwww.nicolletislandinn.com. Pricey, mid-river establishment with the edge on other downtown hotels because of its delightful location and excellent restaurant. ❽–❾

St Paul

Best Western Bandana Square 1010 Bandana Blvd W ⓣ651/647-1637, ⓦwww.book.bestwestern.com. Straightforward rooms and a nice indoor pool and sauna housed in a former railroad car repair shop. ❺

The Covington Inn Pier 1, Harriet Island ⓣ651/292-1411, ⓦwww.covingtoninn.com. A one-of-a-kind B&B in a converted towboat facing downtown. ❻–❽

Embassy Suites 175 E 10th St ⓣ651/224-5400 or 1-800/EMBASSY, ⓦwww.embassystpaul.com. The tropical atrium is the outstanding feature of this comfortable chain hotel on the edge of downtown. ❻

The Saint Paul Hotel 350 Market St ⓣ651/292-9292 or 1-800/292-9292, ⓦwww.stpaulhotel.com. This grand, 1910 establishment is Minnesota's top hotel. Rooms tend to be smaller than those of other luxury hotels, but the staff and atmosphere make up for it. The *St Paul Grill*, in the hotel, provides some of the city's finest dining, while the classy bar has tons of great scotches and cognacs. ❻

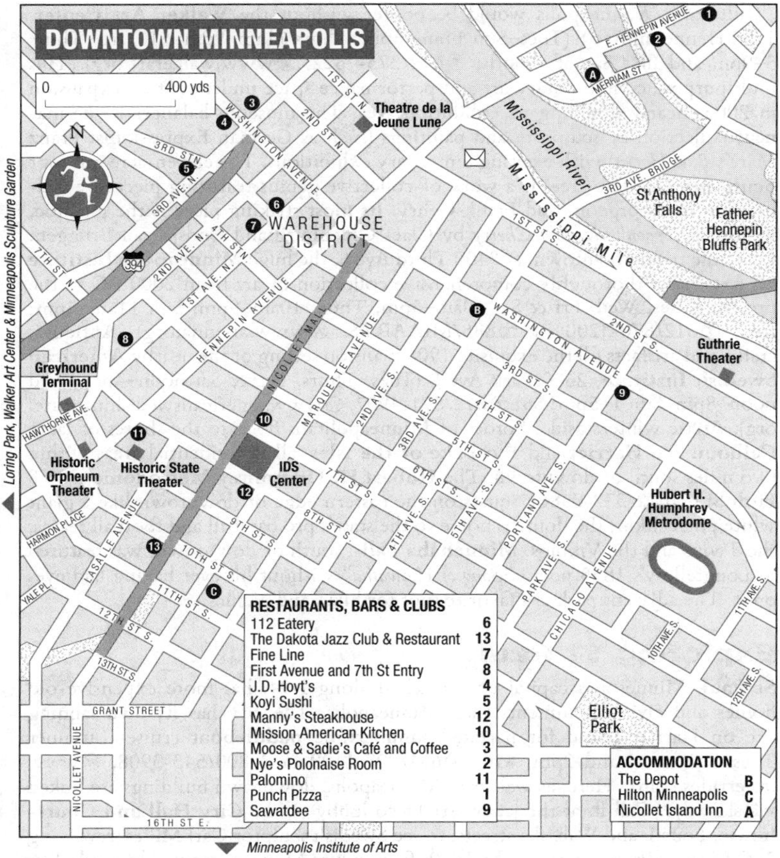

Exploring Minneapolis

Downtown Minneapolis is laid out on a simple grid. The riverfront, dubbed the **Mississippi Mile**, continues to be developed as a place for strolling, dining, and entertainment. The vast Third Avenue Bridge makes an ideal vantage point for viewing **St Anthony Falls**, a controlled torrent in a wide stretch of the river. The missionary Father Hennepin discovered the falls in 1680, but it wasn't until the early nineteenth century that the first permanent settlement of present-day Minneapolis was begun nearby.

Downtown's major stores line up along the pedestrianized **Nicollet Mall**. **Hennepin Avenue**, the other main drag, is a block west. It has been revitalized as an entertainment district in recent years thanks, in part, to the beautifully restored **Orpheum** and **State theaters**, twin hosts to top-quality Broadway shows and concerts. The ultra-modern **Guthrie Theater**, 818 S Second St (Ⓣ612/377-2224 or 1-877/44-STAGE; Ⓦwww.guthrietheater.org), opened in 2006 on the riverfront. Even if you can't make it to one of the classic or brand-new stage productions, presented on one of the venue's three stages, the building itself is still worth a look.

Culturally, Minneapolis would be poorer without the **Walker Art Center**, 1750 Hennepin Ave S (Tues–Sun 11am–5pm, Thurs 11am–9pm; $10, free Thurs 5–9pm and first Sat of month; ⓣ612/375-7622, ⓦwww.walkerart.org). This multipurpose contemporary art and performance space underwent an expansion in 2005, nearly doubling its exhibition area. The museum balances its permanent collection of sculpture and paintings (such as German Expressionist Franz Marc's *Blue Horses*) with exciting temporary exhibitions. The eleven-acre outdoor **Sculpture Garden** (free) is a work of collective genius featuring pieces by Calder, Louise Bourgeois, and Frank Gehry. Its most striking piece is the gigantic, whimsical *Spoonbridge and Cherry* by Claes Oldenburg and Coosje van Bruggen. One mile from downtown, at 2400 Third Ave S, the huge **Minneapolis Institute of Arts** has a thoroughly comprehensive collection of art from 2000 BC to the present (Tues, Wed, Fri & Sat 10am–5pm, Thurs 10am–9pm, Sun 11am–5pm; free; ⓣ612/870-3200 or ⓣ888/MIAARTS, ⓦwww.artsmia.org). Antiques, crafts, and artifacts fill the exquisite 1908 mansion setting of the nearby **American Swedish Institute**, 2600 Park Ave S (Tues, Thurs, Fri, & Sat noon–4pm, Wed noon–8pm, Sun 1–5pm; $6; ⓣ612/871-4907, ⓦwww.americanswedishinstitute.org). Arctic winters aside, hordes of Minneapolitans flock to the shores of lakes **Calhoun** and **Harriet** and also **Lake of the Isles**, all in residential areas within two miles south of downtown. The **Hubert H. Humphrey Metrodome**, 900 S Fifth St (ⓣ612/332-0386), squats on the eastern edge of downtown like a giant white pincushion; the dome is home to the state's pro baseball and football teams, the Twins and the Vikings. **Minnehaha Falls**, south of downtown, was featured in Longfellow's 1855 poem "*Song of Hiawatha*" without his ever having laid eyes on it. The adjacent park is a favorite spot for hikes and picnics.

Exploring St Paul

St Paul, Minnesota's capital city, reached along I-94, has more expensive old homes and civic monuments than Minneapolis. The city has its own landing site on Harriet Island for narrated summertime **paddleboat** cruises (summer Tues–Sun noon and 2pm; $16; ⓣ651/227-1100 or 1-800/543-3908, ⓦwww.riverrides.com). Here, as well as in Minneapolis, downtown buildings are linked via skyways. Call in at the jazzy Art Deco lobby of the **City Hall and Courthouse**, Fourth and Wabasha streets, to see Swedish sculptor Carl Milles' revolving 36ft *Vision of Peace*, carved in the 1930s from white Mexican onyx. The castle-like **Landmark Center**, a couple of blocks away at Fifth and Market streets, and the glittering **Ordway Center for the Performing Arts** both overlook Rice Park, probably the prettiest little square in either city. A sculpture garden with characters from Charles Schulz's "Peanuts" comic strip, the artist himself a St Paul native, has been added to **Schulz Park** next to the Landmark Center. A few blocks east, **Town Square Park** is a lush, multilevel indoor garden in a shopping complex at Minnesota and Sixth streets. The gorgeous granite and limestone **Minnesota History Center**, 345 W Kellogg Blvd (Tues 10am–8pm, Wed–Sat 10am–5pm, Sun noon–5pm; open Mon in summer; $10; ⓣ651/259-3000 or ⓣ888/727-8386, ⓦwww.mnhs.org), with its extensive research facilities and some inventive exhibits for the more casual visitor, is the best place to grasp the state's story. An immense steel iguana is the doorkeeper at the exciting hands-on **Science Museum of Minnesota**, 120 W Kellogg Blvd (Mon–Wed 9.30am–5pm, Thurs–Sun 9.30am–9pm; $16; ⓣ651/221-9444, ⓦwww.smm.org), which also has a domed Omnitheater (entry included in ticket) where you can see giant-screen films. Or check out the **Minnesota Children's Museum**, 10 W Seventh St (Tues–Thurs and Sat & Sun 9am–5pm, Fri till 8pm; open Mon 9am–5pm summer only; $8.95;

ⓣ651/225-6000, ⓦwww.mcm.org), where even big kids will be diverted by the interactive galleries.

A well-preserved five-mile Victorian boulevard, Summit Avenue, leads away from downtown. **F. Scott Fitzgerald**, who was born close by, finished his first success, *This Side of Paradise*, in 1918 while living in a modest rowhouse at no. 599. He disparaged the avenue as a "museum of American architectural failures." Look for the coffin atop no. 465, once the home of an undertaker, and visit the **James J. Hill House** at no. 240, a railroad baron's sumptuous mansion from around 1891 (tours every half-hour Wed–Sat 10am–3.30pm and Sun 1–3:30pm; $8; reservations recommended; ⓣ651/297-2555). Minnesota's first territorial governor **Alexander Ramsey**'s house, nearby at 265 S Exchange St, remains a showcase of Victorian high style (tours on the hour Fri & Sat 10am–3pm, summer also Tues–Thurs 1pm; $8; ⓣ651/296-8760; reservations recommended).

The costumed staff does a fine job of interpreting Minnesota's frontier past at **Fort Snelling** (May, Sept, Oct Sat 10am–5pm, Sun noon–5pm, June–Aug Mon–Sat 10am–5pm, Sun noon–5pm; $10; ⓣ612/726-1171), near the airport off highways 5 and 55. Built between 1819 and 1825 on a strategic bluff at the confluence of the Mississippi and Minnesota rivers, this was Minnesota's first permanent structure – a successful attempt by the US government to establish an official presence in the wilderness that had recently been won from Great Britain. Another good bet is the venerable and picturesque **Como Park Zoo and Conservatory**, reached by taking I-94 to the Lexington Avenue exit, then continuing north on Lexington for about three miles (daily: April–Sept 10am–6pm; rest of year 10am–4pm; $2 donation requested; ⓣ651/487-8200). Farther afield, in suburban Apple Valley, off Hwy-775 is the spacious, highly regarded **Minnesota Zoo** (daily June–Sept 9am–6pm, rest of the year 9am–4pm; $14, $5 parking fee; ⓣ952/431-9200, ⓦwww.mnzoo.org), where the animals reside in reconstructions of their natural habitats. The Komodo dragon exhibit, Imation IMAX Theater, and Discovery Bay aquatic center, in particular, are outstanding.

Annual celebrations in St Paul include the **Taste of Minnesota** (tons of food, live entertainment, rides, and fireworks) running from late June to July 4 on Harriet Island and the nation's largest **State Fair** (end of Aug to early Sept). The **Winter Carnival** (late Jan to early Feb) is a frosty gala designed to make the most of the season with ice and snow sculpturing, hot-air ballooning, team sports, parades, and more.

The Mall of America

Shopping addicts make the pilgrimage to the **Mall of America** from all over the Midwest – and far beyond, including parties from as far away as Japan. Opened in 1992, this mind-boggling 4.2-million-square-foot, four-story monument to consumerism tallied 42 million visits in a recent year. It incorporates more than five hundred stores, with a seven-acre Nickelodeon Universe theme park. Featured rides include **UnderWater Adventures** ($18.95), with 1.2 million gallons of water and amazing Gulf of Mexico and Caribbean aquariums. Evidence of the Mall's all-under-one-roof convenience is provided by the **Chapel of Love** retail store, where more than five thousand couples have legitimately tied the knot. The mall is open Monday through Saturday 10am–9.30pm, Sunday 11am–7pm, (ⓣ952/883-8800, ⓦwww.mallofamerica.com).

The Mall is twenty minutes south of the cities on I-494 at 24th Avenue, Bloomington. Take bus #54M from St Paul's West Sixth Street at Cedar, the #5E bus or the light rail from downtown Minneapolis; catch the train from 5th Street on Nicollet Mall.

Eating

Preconceptions of Midwestern blandness are swiftly put to rest by an almost bewildering array of **restaurants** in the Twin Cities. In **Minneapolis**, head for the downtown warehouse district, the southerly Nicollet neighborhood, the funky Uptown, and Lyn-Lake areas, or the university's Dinkytown. In **St Paul**, try Galtier Plaza downtown, the Asian restaurants on University Avenue, or the horde of ethnic options all along Grand Avenue.

Minneapolis

112 Eatery 112 N 3rd St ⓣ612/343-7696. This small, upscale café serves an inventive mix of American and Continental dishes, from pork tenderloin to sauteed sweetbreads.

Bryant-Lake Bowl 810 W Lake St ⓣ612/825-3737. Bowling and fantastic food rarely go hand-in-hand, but this Lyn-Lake institution manages to do both well, turning out such creative dishes as organic chicken wings and a bison Philly sandwich.

Emily's Lebanese Deli 641 University Ave NE ⓣ612/379-4069. Friendly, low-cost local place for Lebanese staples.

Fugaise 308 E Hennepin Ave ⓣ612/436-0777. An exceptional French dining experience in the Old St Anthony neighborhood.

J.D. Hoyts 301 Washington Ave N ⓣ612/338-1560. A traditional supper club serving down-home food at good prices.

Koyi Sushi 122 Fourth St N ⓣ612/375-9811. Modern spot in the warehouse district. Creative rolls and fresh fish are the mark here.
Manny's Steakhouse 821 Marquette Ave ⓣ612/215-3700. Dry-aged, hand-trimmed and every other master butcher delicacy you can imagine at this local favorite.
Mission American Kitchen 77 S 7th St ⓣ612/339-1000. This great lunch and dinner spot serves delicious and creative starters like Truffle Cream Cheese Wontons and Deviled Eggs.
Moose & Sadie's Café and Coffee 212 3rd Ave ⓣ612/371-0464. This great breakfast and lunch spot in the warehouse district has yummy baked goods and soups like coconut milk curry.
Palomino 825 Hennepin Ave ⓣ612/339-3800. Inviting, popular bistro specializing in Mediterranean fare.
Punch Pizza 210 Hennepin Ave ⓣ612/3623-8114. Stylish wood-fired ovens produce these popular Neapolitan pizzas.

St Paul

Acropol Inn 748 Grand Ave ⓣ651/312-1299. Mom-and-pop-styled diner serving authentic Greek fare.
Downtowner Woodfire Grill 253 W 7th St ⓣ651/228-9500. Great neighbourhood restaurant if you plan to catch a Wild game or just dinner. Weekends have live jazz music starting at 8pm.
Mickey's Dining Car 36 W 7th St ⓣ651/698-0259. Landmark 24hr diner in a 1930s dining car.
St Paul Grill 350 Market St ⓣ651/224-7455. Traditional American fare in a classic downtown hotel.
Trattoria DaVinci 400 Sibley St ⓣ651/222-4050. Exceptional Northern Italian cuisine served in an Italian Renaissance-inspired setting.
Sakura 350 Saint Peter St ⓣ651/224-0185. Fresh sushi in a relaxing environment. Great long sushi bar and smooth vibe perfect the dining experience.
W.A. Frost 374 Selby Ave and Western Ave ⓣ651/224-5715. This former pharmacy and F. Scott Fitzgerald hangout has been converted into a plush restaurant with a garden patio. The menu spans Mediterranean, Asian, and Middle Eastern cuisines and features dishes like mushroom Wellington and squash ravioli; the wine cellar stocks some 3000 bottles.

Entertainment and nightlife

The Greater Twin Cities have been dubbed a "cultural Eden on the prairie," where 2.5 million people support upwards of one hundred **theater** companies, more than forty **dance** troupes, twenty **classical music** ensembles, and more than a hundred art galleries. Sir Tyrone Guthrie began the theatrical boom back in 1963, enrolling large-scale local assistance to establish the classical repertory company named for him. The cities now have more theaters per capita than anywhere in the US apart from New York City.

Unusually, **nightlife** in Minneapolis (and, to a lesser extent, St Paul) hasn't been siphoned off by suburbia – one hundred thousand students ensure a vibrant club scene. For complete entertainment **information and listings**, check out the ubiquitous free weekly *City Pages*.

Minneapolis and St Paul theaters

Chanhassen Dinner Theater 501 W 78th St, Chanhassen ⓣ952/934-1525 or 1-800/362-3515. Mainstream musicals, popular comedies, and drama on four stages, plus meals. Thirty minutes from downtown.
Fitzgerald Theater 10 E Exchange St, St Paul ⓣ651/290-1200, ⓦwww.fitzgeraldtheater.org. Best known as the venue for Garrison Keillor's weekly A Prairie Home Companion performance, it also hosts other concerts and lectures.
Great American History Theater 30 E 10th St, St Paul ⓣ651/292-4323, ⓦwww.historytheatre.com. Original plays deal with events and personalities from the region's past.
Jungle Theater 2951 S Lyndale Ave S, Minneapolis ⓣ612/822-7063, ⓦwww.jungletheater.com. Theater/cabaret putting on an eclectic mix of classic and contemporary plays.
Park Square 20 W 7th Place, St Paul ⓣ651/291-7005, ⓦwww.parksquaretheatre.org. The venue for well-executed classic and contemporary plays.
Penumbra 270 N Kent St, St Paul ⓣ651/224-3180, ⓦwww.penumbratheatre.org. African-American theater company focusing on works by African-American playwrights.
Theatre de la Jeune Lune 1st St and 1st Ave, Minneapolis ⓣ612/333-6200, ⓦwww.jeunelune.org. A unique ensemble of Parisians and Minneapolitans offer dynamic, highly physical productions based on commedia dell'arte, vaudeville, and the like.

Minneapolis bars and clubs

The Dakota Jazz Club and Restaurant 1010 Nicollet Mall ⓣ612/332-1010, ⓦwww.dakotacooks.com. Gourmet Midwestern food and great local and national jazz acts downtown.

Fine Line 318 1st Ave N ⓣ612/338-8100. Sleek, small, and musically eclectic downtown club.

First Avenue and 7th St Entry 701 1st Ave ⓣ612/338-8388 or 332-1775,ⓦwww.first-avenue.com. The landmark rock venue where Prince's Purple Rain was shot still packs them in with top bands and dance music.

Muddy Pig 162 N Dale St ⓣ651/254-1030. A hip neighborhood joint with good bar food and a wide selection of microbrews.

Nye's Polonaise Room 112 E Hennepin Ave ⓣ651/379-2021. Experience old-European atmosphere at the piano and polka bars and in the Polish-American restaurant.

O'Gara's Bar and Grill 164 N Snelling Ave ⓣ651/644-3333, ⓦwww.ogaras.com. Dimly lit bar/restaurant with its own handcrafted beers. Draws a mixed clientele and hosts live bands in the adjoining *Garage*.

Tom Reid's Hockey City Pub 258 W 7th St ⓣ651/292-9916. This pre- and post-game hangout is where locals gather to honor the state's favorite sport.

Northern and southern Minnesota

Minnesota's substantial **northern** half, covered with forested lakes, remains much as it was when the Europeans first traded with the Indians. The northeast – **the Arrowhead**, poking into Lake Superior – holds the greatest charm: most visitors choose secluded outdoor vacations centered on fishing, canoeing, and snowmobiling, but there's infinite potential for driving tours in a wilderness comparable to the Alaskan interior.

The Arrowhead is anchored by busy **Duluth**. From here, **Scenic Hwy-61** skirts the clifftops around Lake Superior, passing waterfalls, state parks, and neat little towns on the way northeast to the Canadian border. Sleepy **Grand Marais** is poised at the edge of the wild **Boundary Waters Canoe Area Wilderness** and the **Gunflint Trail**, while inland, the **Iron Range** makes a scenic route north to the idyllic **Voyageurs National Park**. To the southwest, in **Itasca State Park**, the Mississippi River begins its great roll down to the Gulf of Mexico; you can cross the headwaters on stepping-stones. Everywhere you'll find campgrounds and mom-and-pop lakeside **resorts**, havens of homey simplicity dedicated to soothing urban-ravaged souls.

Southern Minnesota is split between high plains, timbered ravines, and slow-flowing Mississippi tributaries in the east, and the drier, flatter prairie and checkerboard farmland of the west. In the scenic **southeast**, spared a grinding-down by the last glacial advance, attractive small towns sit along the Mississippi, or on bluffs above it, in the ninety-mile **Hiawatha Valley**. Mississippi shipping helped sustain easygoing communities like Winona, Red Wing, Lake City, and Wabasha, all of which share well-preserved old homes and hotels. **Rochester** occupies the rolling farmland to the west.

Duluth

DULUTH, at the western extremity of Lake Superior, 150 miles north of Minneapolis and St Paul, forms a long crescent at the base of the Arrowhead. Named for a seventeenth-century French officer, Daniel Greysolon, Sieur du Luth (1636–1710), the town cascades down from the granite bluffs surrounding **Skyline Drive** (an exhilarating thirty-mile route) to a busy **harbor**, shared with Superior, Wisconsin. Together these "twin ports" constitute the largest inland harbor in the US.

In the 1980s, Duluth had a face-lift and began to encourage tourism. The main drawback is that it's bitingly **cold** here. The seaway is frozen through the winter, and even spring and fall evenings can be chilly. Temperatures are always significantly cooler near the lake – the location of nearly all the attractions and activities.

From the Convention and Visitors Bureau (see below), a short walk down Lake Avenue leads to the free **Marine Museum** (June to early Oct daily 10am–9pm; rest of year times vary; ⓣ218/727-2497, ⓦwww.lsmma.com) in Canal Park, a vantage point for watching big boats from around the world pass under the delightfully archaic Aerial Lift Bridge. Originating at Canal Park, Duluth's **Lakewalk** is the free way to take in the view, though in summer you can also take ninety-min **harbor cruises** ($14; ⓣ218/722-6218 or 1-877/883-4002; ⓦwww.vistafleet.com). Also worthwhile is a visit to the stately lakeside Jacobean Revival mansion **Glensheen**, 3300 London Rd (May–Oct daily 9.30am–4pm; Nov–April Sat & Sun 11am–2pm; $12; ⓣ218/726-8910 or 1-888/454-GLEN). The vast interior features finely crafted original furnishings, and the grounds are immaculate.

Rail excursions along the Superior shoreline to the busy harbor community **Two Harbors** run from **The Depot** complex at 506 W Michigan St (early May to mid-Oct; ⓣ218/722-1273 or 1-800/423-1273, ⓦwww.lsrm.org). The Depot (summer 9.30am–6pm; winter 10am–5pm; $10) also houses the Lake Superior Railroad Museum, a children's museum, cultural heritage center, and art museum; at night, it's home to performing arts companies. From the parking lot at Grand Avenue and 71st Avenue W, across from the zoo, the historic **Lake Superior and Mississippi Railroad** takes a ninety-min journey along the scenic St Louis River (mid-June to early Oct; ⓣ218/624-7549, ⓦwww.lsmrr.org). Duluth's Spirit Mountain **ski area** (ⓣ1-800/642-6377, ⓦwww.spiritmt.com) boasts the best downhill runs in the Midwest.

Practicalities

Greyhound **buses** pull into town four miles south of town just off I-35 at 4426 Grand Ave. The **Convention and Visitors Bureau** is at 21 W Superior St suite 100 (Mon–Fri 8:30am–5pm; ⓣ218/722-4011 or 1-800/4-DULUTH, ⓦwww.visitduluth.com). For a **place to stay**, the *Charles Weiss Inn*, 1615 E Superior St (ⓣ218/724-7016 or 1-800/525-5243, ⓦwww.acweissinn.com; ❺–❻), is a nice Victorian-styled **B&B**, while better **motels** include the *Edgewater Resort and Waterpark*, 2400 London Rd (ⓣ218/728-3601 or 1-800/777-7925; ⓦwww.duluthwaterpark.com; ❹–❺), which has a new indoor water park. Keep in mind that accommodation rates and availability fluctuate in summer. *Indian Point* **campground**, west off Hwy-23 at 75th Street and Grand Avenue (ⓣ218/624-5637), has summer bayside tent sites for $21; full hook-ups are also available for $32.

Two of the best **dining** options in town are the revolving *Top of the Harbor*, which serves American cuisine atop the *Radisson Hotel* at 505 W Superior St (ⓣ218/727-8981), and the lovely *Bennett's on the Lake*, 600 E Superior St (ⓣ218/722-2829), where you can dine on steaks and seafood with a superb view of the lake.

North from Duluth: Highway 61

Memorialized on vinyl by Minnesota native Bob Dylan, stunning **Scenic Highway 61** follows Lake Superior for 150 miles northeast from Duluth to the US/Canadian border, its precipitous cliffs interspersed with pretty little ports and picture-postcard picnic sites.

At **Gooseberry River State Park**, forty miles along from Duluth, the river splashes over volcanic rock through waterfalls and cascades to its outlet in Lake

Superior. Like all but one of the seven other state parks along Hwy-61, it provides access to the rugged three-hundred-mile **Superior Hiking Trail** (ⓣ218/834-2700), divided into easily manageable segments for day-trekkers. To camp at any of the state parks, reserve at ⓣ1-866/857-2757.

Just beyond **Cascade River State Park**, the road dips into the somnolent little port of **GRAND MARAIS**, where a walk around the photogenic Circular Harbor will soon cure car-stiff legs. The **visitor center**, 13 N Broadway (ⓣ218/387-2524 or 1-888/922-5000, ⓦwww.grandmarais.com), has lists of **outfitters** for those going into the Boundary Waters Canoe Area Wilderness (see below). The town of **GRAND PORTAGE**, just below the Canadian border, is at the lake end of the historic 8.5-mile portage route – so vital to the nineteenth-century fur trade – now preserved in the form of **Grand Portage National Monument**, where a clutch of fur-trade era buildings has been superbly reconstructed. In town, residents of the Grand Portage Indian Reservation operate a **casino**. In summer, ferries run daily to remote **Isle Royale National Park** (see p.312).

Boundary Waters Canoe Area Wilderness and the Gunflint Trail

The huge **Boundary Waters Canoe Area Wilderness**, west of Grand Marais, is one of the most heavily used wilderness areas in the country. It's accessible from Tofte, Cook, and especially from easygoing **Ely**, home of the intriguing **International Wolf Center** (hours vary; ⓣ218/365-4695; $7.50). The wilderness is a paradise for canoeing, backpacking, and fishing. Overland trails, or "portages," link more than a thousand lakes; in winter you can ski and dogsled cross-country. The unpaved sixty-mile **Gunflint Trail** from Grand Marais cuts the wilderness in two; otherwise there are no roads in this outback, let alone electricity or telephones. Most lakes remain motor-free, and stringent rules limit entry to the wilderness: in summer you need a date-specific **permit** that local outfitters can issue. For the following year, permit applications may be submitted by website, fax, or mail. Phone reservations are accepted ($12 reservation fee and a $20 deposit; ⓣ1-877/550-6777, ⓕ518/885-9951, ⓦwww.bwcaw.org). For those who don't want to rough it, several rustic lodges lie strung out along the trail; the **Gunflint Trail Association** (ⓣ218/387-3191 or 1-800/338-6932,ⓦwww.gunflint-trail.com) can offer good advice.

The Iron Range

In the **Iron Range**, a few miles west of Ely, which is itself about one hundred miles west of Grand Marais, a number of fabulously rich mines continue to function more than a century after their construction. If you're interested in surveying old workings, it's possible to descend 2300ft at the **Soudan Underground Mine State Park** on Hwy-169 (summer daily 10am–4pm; admission and vehicle fee).

Eighty miles southwest on Hwy-169 is **Hibbing** – a plain little community, of interest mainly as the birthplace of Bob Dylan (born Robert Zimmerman) in 1941. Oddly enough, the museum in City Hall has no exhibits on him.

Voyageurs National Park

Set along the border lakes between Minnesota and Canada, **VOYAGEURS NATIONAL PARK** is like no other in the US national park system. To see it properly, or indeed to grasp its immense beauty at all, you need to leave your car behind and venture into the wild by boat. Once out on the lakes, you're in a great,

▲ Voyageurs National Park

silent world. Kingfishers, osprey, and eagles swoop down for their share of the abundant walleye; moose and bear stalk the banks.

The park's name comes from the intrepid eighteenth-century French-Canadian trappers, who needed almost a year to get their pelts back to Montréal in primitive birch bark canoes. Their "customary waterway" became so established that the treaty of 1783 ending the American Revolution specified it as the international border.

You can't do Voyageurs justice on a day-trip, though daily cruises from the **Rainy Lake visitor center** (open daily mid-May–Sept 9am–5pm, Oct–mid-May Wed–Sun 9am–5pm; from $12-20 for a range of tours; Ⓣ218/286-5258 Ⓦwww.nps.gov/voya) do at least allow a peek at the lake country. If you're here for a few days, rent a **boat** (reckon on $50 a day) and camp out. It's easy to get lost in this maze of islands and rocky outcrops, and unseen sandbanks lurk beneath the surface. If you're at all unsure, hire a guide from one of the resorts for the first day (around $250 per 8hr day). During **freeze-up** – usually from December until March – the park takes on a whole new aura, as a prime destination for skiers and snowmobilers.

Practicalities

Most travelers access Voyageurs from Hwy-53, which runs northwest from Duluth. After just over one hundred miles, at Orr, Hwy-53 intersects with Rte-23, which runs northeast toward **Crane Lake**, at the eastern end of the park. About 28 and 31 miles past Hwy-53's junction with Rte-23, highways 129 and 122 lead, respectively, to the **visitor centers** at **Ash River** (May–Sept daily 9am–5pm; Ⓣ218/374-3221) and **Kabetogama Lake** (same hours; Ⓣ218/875-2111). Another prime visitor center is at **Rainy Lake**, at the westernmost entrance, 36 miles farther on via International Falls.

Once inside the park, you need to take a few **precautions**. Check (natural) mercury levels in fish before eating them, don't pick wild rice (only Native Americans may do this), be wary of Lyme Disease (a tick-induced gastric illness), boil drinking water, and watch out for bears. Discuss such matters along with customs procedures, in case you plan to paddle into Canadian waters, with a ranger before venturing out.

The definitive way to experience the park is to **camp** on one of its many scattered islands, most plentiful around Crane Lake (if you don't have your own boat, cruise operators can drop you off and pick you up at a later date). There are also first-come, first-served state-owned campgrounds on the mainland at Ash River and Woodenfrog, near Kabetogama. However, most visitors stay in one of more than sixty **resorts**. Basically family-run cottages, these usually cater for weekly stays, with all meals, though you can rent rooms nightly. Kayak in or take a boat taxi to *Kettle Falls Hotel*, a perfectly rustic way to experience Voyagers. They have a wide range of lodging options and day-trips (Ⓦ www.kettlefallshotel.com; open seasonally ❷–❽).

5

The Capital Region

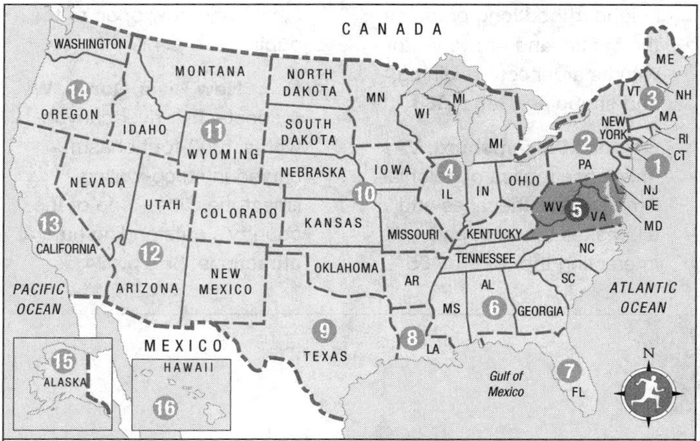

AL - ALABAMA	IN - INDIANA	MN - MINNESOTA	RI - RHODEISLAND
AR - ARKANSAS	LA - LOUISIANA	MS - MISSISSIPPI	SC - SOUTH CAROLINA
CT - CONNECTICUT	MA - MASSACHUSETTS	NC - NORTH CAROLINA	VA - VIRGINIA
DE - DELAWARE	MD - MARYLAND	NH - NEW HAMPSHIRE	VT - VERMONT
FL- FLORIDA	ME - MAINE	NJ - NEW JERSEY	WI - WISCONSIN
IL - ILLINOIS	MI - MICHIGAN	PA - PENNSYLVANIA	WV - WEST VIRGINIA

CHAPTER 5 Highlights

* **National Gallery of Art, Washington DC** One of the country's premier institutions for art and culture, laid out in spacious, elegant surroundings on the National Mall. See p.381

* **Georgetown, Washington DC** Though now part of Washington, this eighteenth-century neighborhood long predates the capital and draws visitors with its architecture, dining, and shopping. See p.388

* **Colonial Williamsburg, VA** This close replica of colonial America, apothecaries and all, makes for a fun and interesting trip. See p.405

* **Monticello, VA** Thomas Jefferson's home is for many as much an architectural icon as it is a symbol of democracy. See p.413

* **The du Pont Mansions, DE** Wilmington is the site of some of the East Coast's greatest, most palatial mansions, once owned by the industrialist du Pont family, and now open to the public. See p.422

* **New River Gorge, WV** A spectacular river canyon with a 1000-foot chasm carved in steep-walled limestone cliffs – one of the country's outstanding natural attractions. See p.424

△ Mount Vernon

5

The Capital Region

The city of Washington, in the District of Columbia, and the four surrounding states of Virginia, West Virginia, Maryland, and Delaware are collectively known as the **CAPITAL REGION**. Since the days of the first American colonies, US history has been shaped here, from the Jamestown landings to agitation for independence, to the battles of the Revolutionary and Civil wars to 1960s Civil Rights milestones, to protest movements on issues including war, abortion, and gay rights.

Early in the seventeenth century, the first British settlements began to take root along the rich estuary of the **Chesapeake Bay**; the colonists hoped for gold but found their fortunes in tobacco. Virginia, the first settlement, was the largest and most populous. Fully half of its people were **slaves**, brought from Africa to do the backbreaking work of harvesting tobacco. Despite its central position on the East Coast, almost all of the region lies below the Mason-Dixon Line – the symbolic border between North and South, drawn up in 1763 as the boundary between free and unfree states. Slaves helped build the Capitol, and until the Civil War one of the country's busiest slave markets was just two blocks from the White House.

Tensions between North and South finally erupted into the **Civil War**, of which traces are still visible everywhere. The hundred miles between the capital of the Union – Washington DC – and that of the Confederacy – Richmond, Virginia – were a constant and bloody battleground for four long years.

Washington DC, itself, with its magnificent monumental architecture, is an essential stop on any tour of the region, or of the country in general. **Virginia**, to the south, is home to hundreds of historic sites, from the estates of revolutionary leaders and early politicians to the Colonial capital of **Williamsburg**, as well as the narrow forested heights of **Shenandoah National Park**, along the crest of the Blue Ridge Mountains. Much greater expanses of wilderness, crashing whitewater rivers, and innumerable backwoods villages await you in less-visited **West Virginia**.

Most tourists come to **Maryland** for the maritime traditions of Chesapeake Bay, though many of its quaint old villages have been gentrified by weekend pleasure-boaters. **Baltimore** is full of character, enjoyably unpretentious if a bit ramshackle (it has a phenomenal concentration of bars in its grand old Fell's Point district), while **Annapolis**, the pleasant state capital, is linked by bridge and ferry to the Eastern Shore, where **Assateague Island** remains an Atlantic paradise. **New Castle**, across the border in **Delaware**, is a perfectly preserved colonial-era town; nearby are some of the East Coast's best and least crowded beaches.

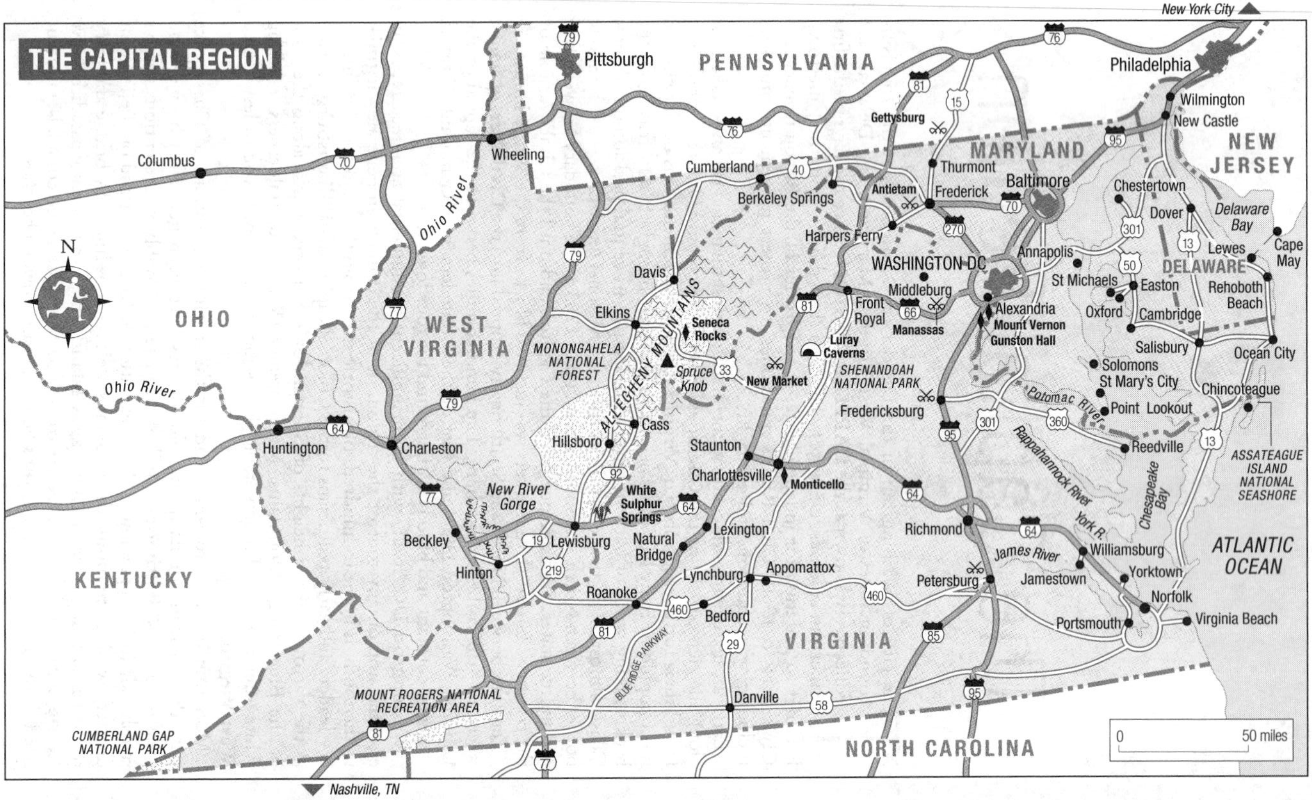
THE CAPITAL REGION
New York City
Nashville, TN
PENNSYLVANIA
MARYLAND
NEW JERSEY
DELAWARE
OHIO
WEST VIRGINIA
VIRGINIA
KENTUCKY
NORTH CAROLINA
ATLANTIC OCEAN
Pittsburgh
Philadelphia
Wilmington
New Castle
Columbus
Wheeling
Cumberland
Berkeley Springs
Gettysburg
Thurmont
Antietam
Frederick
Baltimore
Chestertown
Dover
Delaware Bay
Lewes
Cape May
Harpers Ferry
WASHINGTON DC
Annapolis
St Michaels
Easton
Rehoboth Beach
Oxford
Cambridge
Salisbury
Ocean City
Davis
Elkins
Seneca Rocks
Middleburg
Front Royal
Manassas
Alexandria
Mount Vernon
Gunston Hall
Luray Caverns
SHENANDOAH NATIONAL PARK
New Market
Spruce Knob
ALLEGHENY MOUNTAINS
MONONGAHELA NATIONAL FOREST
Ohio River
Solomons
St Mary's City
Point Lookout
Potomac River
Chincoteague
Fredericksburg
Cass
Hillsboro
Huntington
Charleston
Staunton
Charlottesville
Monticello
Reedville
ASSATEAGUE ISLAND NATIONAL SEASHORE
Rappahannock River
Chesapeake Bay
New River Gorge
White Sulphur Springs
York R.
Richmond
Beckley
Lewisburg
Natural Bridge
Lexington
Williamsburg
James River
Hinton
Lynchburg
Appomattox
Petersburg
Jamestown
Yorktown
Norfolk
Roanoke
Bedford
Portsmouth
Virginia Beach
BLUE RIDGE PARKWAY
MOUNT ROGERS NATIONAL RECREATION AREA
Danville
CUMBERLAND GAP NATIONAL PARK
0 50 miles
N

Washington DC

WASHINGTON, DISTRICT OF COLUMBIA (the boundaries of the two are identical) – also known as **"The District"** – can be unbearably hot and humid in summer, and bitterly cold in winter. It was chosen as the site of the **capital** of the newly independent United States of America because such an unpleasant climate, it was hoped, would discourage elected leaders from making government a full-time job. The other side of DC, with a majority black population, is run as a virtual colony of Congress, where residents have only non-voting representation and couldn't vote in presidential elections until the 23rd amendment was passed in 1961 – the city's official license plate reads "Taxation Without Representation."

The best times to come are during April's National Cherry Blossom Festival and the more temperate months (May–June and Sept). The nation's showcase puts on quite a display for its guests, and, best of all, admission to all major attractions on the **National Mall** is free.

The most famous sites are concentrated along the Mall, including the White House, memorials to four of the greatest presidents, and the superb museums of the Smithsonian Institution. In recent years, even the once-blighted area known as **Old Downtown** (north of the eastern side of the Mall), has had a dramatic uptick in visitors and nightlife around its **Penn Quarter**. Still, you're more likely to spend your evenings in the hotels and restaurants of the city's most vibrant neighborhoods: historic **Georgetown**, arty **Dupont Circle**, and funky **Adams Morgan**.

Some history

The national capital was established here because of the site's location between the Northern and Southern states, its accessibility from the sea, and the cheapness of its land: Maryland and Virginia ceded sovereignty of a diamond-shaped tract to the federal government (though a half-century later Virginia demanded its land back). Although George Washington's baroque, radial plan of the city was laid out in 1791 by a Frenchman, **Pierre L'Enfant**, few buildings were put up, apart from the actual houses of government, until near the end of the century. Charles Dickens, visiting in 1842, found "spacious avenues that begin in nothing and lead nowhere." After the Civil War, thousands of Southern **blacks** arrived in search of a sanctuary from racial oppression; to some extent, they found one. By the 1870s African-Americans made up more than a third of the 150,000 population, but as poverty and squalor became endemic, official **segregation** was reintroduced in 1920. After World War II, the city's economy and population boomed. Segregation of public facilities was declared illegal in the 1950s, and Martin Luther King Jr gave a famous 1963 speech on the steps of the Lincoln Memorial. When King was killed five years later, large sections of the city's ghettos burned, and are only now being rebuilt, as gentrified, higher-rent neighborhoods. Indeed, skyrocketing real-estate values have led to newly paved roads and a revitalized downtown, where chic restaurants and cultural and sports events have begun to attract visitors to areas once considered urban wastelands.

Arrival, information, and getting around

Washington DC is served by three major **airports**, two on the outskirts and one right in the city center. **Dulles International Airport**, 26 miles west in northern Virginia (IAD; ⓣ703/572-2700, ⓦwww.mwaa.com/dulles), and **Baltimore-**

Washington International Airport (BWI), halfway between DC and Baltimore (BWI; ⓣ410/859-7111, ⓦwww.bwiairport.com), get the majority of the international traffic. By far the most convenient, **Ronald Reagan Washington National Airport**, west across the Potomac River from the Mall (DCA; ⓣ703/417-8000, ⓦwww.mwaa.com/national), is mostly used by domestic flights.

You can take a **taxi** downtown from BWI or Dulles ($55-60), while SuperShuttle (ⓣ1-800/BLUE-VAN, ⓦwww.supershuttle.com) offers **door-to-door** service from Dulles (45min; $27), BWI (1hr; $35), and National (15min; $12). Cheaper are the express **buses** that run every half-hour from both airports to nearby Metro subway stations. From Dulles, take the Washington Flyer Express Bus (ⓣ1-888/WASH-FLY, ⓦwww.washfly.com) to the West Falls Church Metro station (30min; $9, round-trip $16). From BWI, a free shuttle service connects the airport with the BWI rail terminal (10–15min). The most economical choice is the southbound Penn Line of the **Maryland Rail Commuter Service** (MARC; ⓣ410/539-5000, ⓦwww.mtamaryland.com; $6 single), providing frequent peak-hour departures to Washington's Union Station, a forty-minute trip. The station is also reached from BWI by the quicker daily **Amtrak** trains (ⓦwww.amtrak.com; $12 single), which take a half-hour with regular service. National Airport conveniently has its own subway stop and is just a short ride from the city center. A **taxi** downtown from National costs around $20.

By **train**, you arrive amid the gleaming, Neoclassical specter of **Union Station**, 50 Massachusetts Ave NE, three blocks north of the US Capitol and with a connecting Metro station. Greyhound and other **buses** stop at a modern terminal at 1005 First St NE, in a fairly dodgy part of the city, a few blocks north of the Union Station Metro; take a cab, especially at night. **Driving** into DC is a sure way to experience some of the worst traffic on the East Coast – the main I-95 and I-495 freeways circle Washington on the **Beltway** and are jammed eighteen hours a day.

Once in the city, stop at the **DC Chamber of Commerce Visitor Center**, Ronald Reagan Building, 1300 Pennsylvania Ave NW (Mon–Fri 8am–5.30pm, Sat–Sun 9am-4pm; ⓣ1-866/324-7386, ⓦwww.dcchamber.com), which can help with maps, tours, bookings, and information. The **White House Visitor Information Center**, not located at the president's mansion but downtown at 1450 Pennsylvania Ave NW (daily 7.30am–4pm; ⓣ202/208-1631, ⓦwww.nps.gov/whho), supplies free maps and handy guides to museums and attractions.

The central **Benjamin Franklin Post Office**, 1200 Pennsylvania Ave NW (Mon–Fri 7.30am–5.30pm, Sat 8am–12.30pm; ⓣ202/842-1444), has the latest hours of the area post offices.

City transportation

Getting around DC is easy. Most places downtown, including the museums, monuments, and White House, are within walking distance of each other, and an excellent **public transit** system reaches outlying sights and neighborhoods. The expansive **Metro subway** (ⓣ202/637-7000, ⓦwww.wmata.com) is clean and efficient (trains run Mon–Thurs 5am–midnight, Fri 5am–3am, Sat 7am–3am, & Sun 7am–midnight). Single fares start at $1.35; during rush hours the fare is $1.65 (5.30am–9.30am & 3–7pm); and if you're going out to the suburbs the one-way fare can be up to $4.50. **Day passes** cost $7.80 and are valid weekdays (from 9.30am on) and all day on weekends. **Weekly passes** are $26.40 – good for fares of up to $2.65 during weekday rush hours and all fares at other times. The standard fare on the extensive **bus** network is $1.35, or $3 for express buses. **Taxis** are a good alternative: if traveling in the downtown core, most fees are around $10, and most crosstown fares are no more than $20. There are taxi stands at major hotels and transportation terminals (like Union Station). For more information, call the **DC Taxicab Commission** at ⓣ202/645-6018 or visit ⓦdctaxi.dc.gov.

There's also the special "**DC Circulator**" (ⓣ202/962-1423, ⓦwww.dccirculator.com), which will take you from Union Station to Georgetown, or, alternatively, from the Convention Center to the Southwest waterfront; a third shuttle route loops around the museums of the Mall itself (museum loop Sat & Sun 10am–4pm; all other routes daily 7am–9pm; $1 all routes).

Tours

During the day, **Tourmobiles** (daily 9.30am–4.30pm; ⓣ202/554-5100, ⓦwww.tourmobile.com; $24-30) connect the major museums and sights, allowing you to stop for as long as you choose at fifteen to twenty different locations.

If you want to **cycle** or **cruise** along the Potomac River or the historic C&O Canal, both Thompson's Boat Center, 2900 Virginia Ave NW at Rock Creek Parkway (mid-March–Sept daily 8am–6pm; ⓣ202/333-9543), near Georgetown, and Fletcher's Boat House, 4940 Canal Rd NW, two miles farther up the canal towpath (daily 9am–7pm; ⓣ202/244-0461), rent touring bikes, rowboats, and canoes (bikes $5–10/hr, $15–50/day; boats $10–12/hr, $25–30/day). You could also get to know the city on a three-hour cycling trip with Bike the Sites (ⓣ202/842-BIKE, ⓦwww.bikethesites.com; $30–40 per person including bike and helmet), or call Better Bikes (daily 24hr; ⓣ202/293-2080, ⓦwww.betterbikesinc.com), which will deliver rental bikes anywhere in DC ($38–48/day). For **walking tours** of the city, DC Heritage (ⓣ202/828-9255, ⓦwww.culturaltourismdc.org) has information on the many options for viewing aspects of local history, while Washington Walks (ⓣ202/484-1565, ⓦwww.washingtonwalks.com; $10 per person) provides a number of easy treks around the area's more notable sights.

Accommodation

Most DC **hotels** cater to business travelers and political lobbyists, and during the week are quite expensive. At weekends, however, many cut their rates by up to fifty percent, or up to $100 or so. For a list of vacancies, call WDCA Hotels (ⓣ202/289-2220 or 1-800/503-3330, ⓦwww.wdcahotels.com), which provides a hotel-reservation and travel-planning service.

Similarly, a number of **B&B** agencies offer comfortable doubles starting from $60 in the low season: try Capitol Reservations (ⓣ202/452-1270 or 1-800/847-4832, ⓦwww.capitolreservations.com) or Bed & Breakfast Accommodations, Ltd (ⓣ1-877/893-3233, ⓦwww.bedandbreakfastdc.com). There's no good **camping** anywhere near DC, but Catholic University (ⓣ202/319-5277), Georgetown University (ⓣ202/687-4560, ⓦhousing.georgetown.edu), American University (ⓣ202/885-3370), and George Washington University (ⓣ202/994-2552, ⓦgwired.gwu.edu/gwhousing) offer **budget rooms** (starting at $30) in the summer; these must be arranged well in advance and may have minimum-stay requirements – often one to three weeks. Wherever you go, make sure the facility has **air conditioning**; DC can be unbearably stifling in the summer without it.

Adam's Inn 1744 Lanier Place NW ⓣ202/745-3600 or 1-800/578-6807, ⓦwww.adamsinn.com. Three adjoining Victorian townhouses with simple B&B rooms in Adams Morgan. No in-room TVs, but free internet access, breakfast, garden patio, and laundry facilities. Sharing a bath saves you $30. Near the zoo. ⑤

❶▲ ❷.❸.❹.❺.❻.Ⓐ.Ⓑ.Ⓒ.Ⓓ Adams-Morgan, National Zoo ▲ ❼▲Ⓔ▲ ❽.❾.❿.⓫.⓬&⓭
& Washington National Cathedral

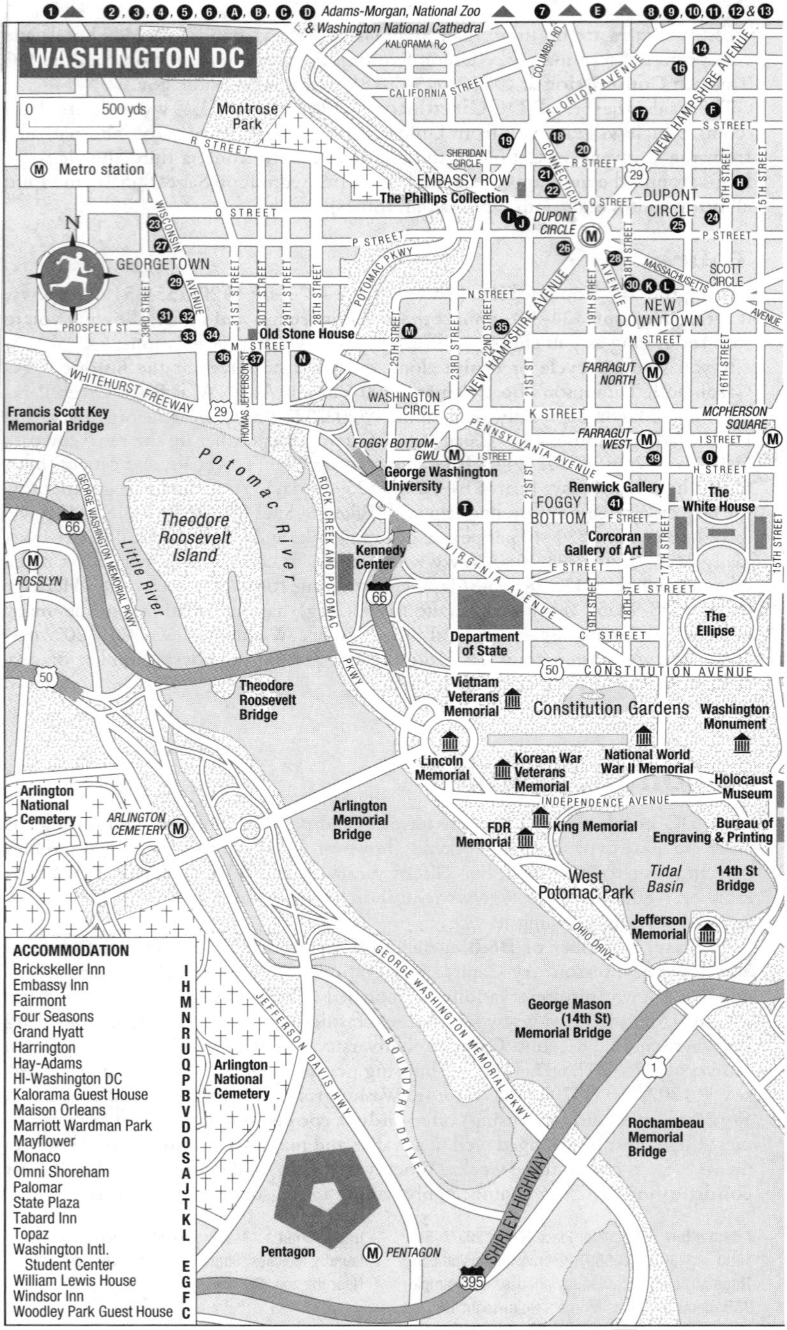

WASHINGTON DC

0	500 yds

Ⓜ Metro station

KALORAMA RD

KALORAMA ROAD

CALIFORNIA STREET

Montrose Park

R STREET

SHERIDAN ❶❾
CIRCLE
EMBASSY ROW ❶❽ ❷⓿
The Phillips Collection ❷❷ ❷❶
R STREET

S STREET

Ⓕ

Ⓗ

R STREET

Q STREET

Q STREET ❷❸
Ⓘ
Ⓙ
DUPONT
CIRCLE

❷❻ Ⓜ

DUPONT
CIRCLE ❷❹
❷❺
P STREET

SCOTT
CIRCLE

GEORGETOWN ❷❼
❷❾

P STREET

P STREET

N STREET

Ⓜ

❸⓿ Ⓚ Ⓛ
NEW
DOWNTOWN

MASSACHUSETTS AVENUE

Old Stone House ❸❹ ❸❸
❸❻ ❸❼
Ⓝ

PROSPECT ST ❸❶
❸❸

M STREET ❸❺
Ⓜ

FARRAGUT
NORTH
Ⓜ

Ⓞ

MCPHERSON
SQUARE

WHITEHURST FREEWAY

WASHINGTON
CIRCLE

K STREET

FARRAGUT
WEST Ⓜ Ⓜ

Francis Scott Key
Memorial Bridge

FOGGY BOTTOM-
GWU Ⓜ

PENNSYLVANIA AVENUE

I STREET
❸❾ Ⓠ

H STREET

George Washington
University
Ⓣ

FOGGY
BOTTOM ❹❶

Renwick Gallery
The
White House

Potomac River

Theodore
Roosevelt
Island

Little River

Kennedy
Center

VIRGINIA AVENUE

F STREET
Corcoran
Gallery of Art

E STREET

ROSSLYN Ⓜ

Theodore
Roosevelt
Bridge

Department
of State

E STREET

C STREET

The
Ellipse

CONSTITUTION AVENUE

Vietnam
Veterans
Memorial 🏛

Constitution Gardens

Washington
Monument 🏛

Arlington
National
Cemetery

ARLINGTON
CEMETERY Ⓜ

Arlington
Memorial
Bridge

Lincoln
Memorial 🏛

Korean War
Veterans
Memorial 🏛

National World
War II Memorial 🏛

Holocaust
Museum

INDEPENDENCE AVENUE

FDR
Memorial 🏛 King Memorial 🏛

Bureau of
Engraving & Printing

West
Potomac Park

Tidal
Basin

14th St
Bridge

Jefferson
Memorial 🏛

GEORGE WASHINGTON MEMORIAL PARKWAY

OHIO DRIVE

George Mason
(14th St)
Memorial Bridge

Rochambeau
Memorial
Bridge

ACCOMMODATION

Brickskeller Inn	I
Embassy Inn	H
Fairmont	M
Four Seasons	N
Grand Hyatt	R
Harrington	U
Hay-Adams	Q
HI-Washington DC	P
Kalorama Guest House	B
Maison Orleans	V
Marriott Wardman Park	D
Mayflower	O
Monaco	S
Omni Shoreham	A
Palomar	J
State Plaza	T
Tabard Inn	K
Topaz	L
Washington Intl.	
Student Center	E
William Lewis House	G
Windsor Inn	F
Woodley Park Guest House	C

Arlington
National
Cemetery

Pentagon

Ⓜ PENTAGON

SHIRLEY HIGHWAY

395

National Airport & Alexandria ▼

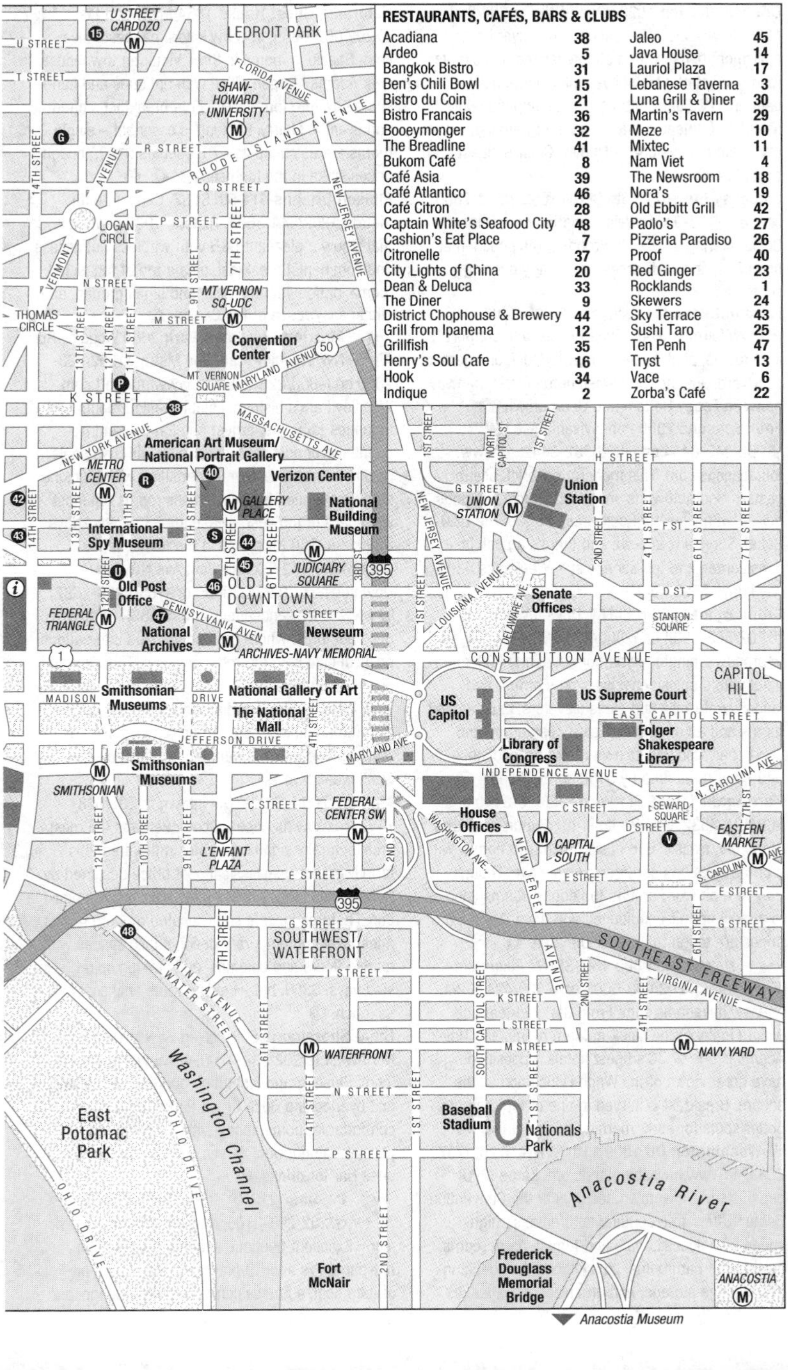

RESTAURANTS, CAFÉS, BARS & CLUBS

Acadiana	38	Jaleo	45
Ardeo	5	Java House	14
Bangkok Bistro	31	Lauriol Plaza	17
Ben's Chili Bowl	15	Lebanese Taverna	3
Bistro du Coin	21	Luna Grill & Diner	30
Bistro Francais	36	Martin's Tavern	29
Booeymonger	32	Meze	10
The Breadline	41	Mixtec	11
Bukom Café	8	Nam Viet	4
Café Asia	39	The Newsroom	18
Café Atlantico	46	Nora's	19
Café Citron	28	Old Ebbitt Grill	42
Captain White's Seafood City	48	Paolo's	27
Cashion's Eat Place	7	Pizzeria Paradiso	26
Citronelle	37	Proof	40
City Lights of China	20	Red Ginger	23
Dean & Deluca	33	Rocklands	1
The Diner	9	Skewers	24
District Chophouse & Brewery	44	Sky Terrace	43
Grill from Ipanema	12	Sushi Taro	25
Grillfish	35	Ten Penh	47
Henry's Soul Cafe	16	Tryst	13
Hook	34	Vace	6
Indique	2	Zorba's Café	22

Brickskeller Inn 1523 22nd St NW ⓣ202/293-1885, ⓦwww.lovethebeer.com. A converted apartment house with a stately facade and simple rooms, most of which have sinks; some have a bath and TV. Funky, ultra-basic lodging is mainly useful if you need a crash pad after partying, since it's located above one of Dupont Circle's oldest and best bars. ❺

Embassy Inn 1627 16th St NW ⓣ202/234-7800 or 1-800/423-9111. Welcoming inn near Dupont Circle offering good-value rooms, free continental breakfast, and wi-fi access, and early evening sherry. ❼

Fairmont 2401 M St NW ⓣ202/429-2400, ⓦwww.fairmont.com. Classy oasis with comfortable rooms, pool, health club, whirlpool, and garden courtyard. Just north of Washington Circle, midway between Foggy Bottom and Georgetown. ❾

Four Seasons 2800 Pennsylvania Ave NW ⓣ202/342-0444 or 1-800/332-3442, ⓦwww.fourseasons.com. This modern red-brick pile in eastern Georgetown is one of DC's most luxurious hotels, with views of Rock Creek Park or the C&O Canal. Service is superb, and there's a pool, fitness center, and full-service spa. Weekends $395, weekdays $595. ❾

Grand Hyatt 1000 H St NW, Downtown ⓣ202/582-1234 or 1-800/233-1234, ⓦgrandwashington.hyatt.com. A nearly 900-room hotel with a splashy twelve-storey atrium and lagoon, waterfalls and glass elevators, plus tasteful rooms and an on-site deli-café, restaurant, and sports bar. Also has its own Metro connection. $499, but rates drop by $100 on weekends. ❾

Harrington 1100 E St NW ⓣ202/628-8140 or 1-800/424-8532, ⓦwww.hotel-harrington.com. One of the old, classic, and basic Downtown hotels, with a prime location near Pennsylvania Ave. Though they're a bit worn around the edges, rooms (singles to quads) are air-conditioned and have TV, plus the prices are tough to beat for the area. ❺

Hay-Adams 800 16th St NW, Foggy Bottom ⓣ202/638-6600 or 1-800/424-5054, ⓦwww.hayadams.com. From the gold-leaf and walnut lobby to the sleek modern rooms, the Hay-Adams is one of DC's finest hotels. Upper floors have great views of the White House across the square. Breakfast is served in one of the District's better spots for early-morning power dining. ❾

HI-Washington DC 1009 11th St NW ⓣ202/737-2333, ⓦwww.hiwashingtondc.org. Large (270 beds), clean, Downtown hostel near the Convention Center. Offers free continental breakfast, high-speed web access, male and female dorm rooms, and shared bathrooms, plus kitchen, lounge, laundry, luggage storage, and organized activities. ❶

Kalorama Guest House 1854 Mintwood Place NW ⓣ202/667-6369, ⓦwww.kaloramaguesthouse.com. Spacious rooms in three Victorian townhouses near Adams Morgan, filled with antiques and handsome furniture (but no TV). Free breakfast, coffee, and evening sherry. Booking is essential – single rooms are as cheap as $70, doubles $100, though prices spike in the high season. ❹–❻

Maison Orleans 414 5th St SE, Capitol South Metro ⓣ202/544-3694. Historic 1902 rowhouse that's now a pleasant B&B with wireless net access and continental breakfast, plus a trio of functional rooms, patio with fountains, and small garden, and within easy reach of the Capitol. ❻

Marriott Wardman Park 2660 Woodley Rd NW, Woodley Park–Zoo Metro ⓣ202/328-2000 or 1-800/228-9290, ⓦwww.marriott.com. Woodley Park's historic, celebrity-filled monument manages to be the largest hotel in DC (and frequent site of political fundraisers), with two pools, a health club, and restaurants bristling with cracking staff. Convention business keeps rooms full most weekdays of the year. Weekends $329, weekdays $399; add $50 for rooms in the tower. ❾

Mayflower 1127 Connecticut Ave NW, New Downtown ⓣ202/347-3000 or 1-800/228-7697, ⓦwww.renaissancehotels.com/WASSH. If there's one spot in DC where the national and international political elite come to roost, this is it. This sumptuous Washington classic has a promenade – a vast, imperial hall – and smart rooms with subtle, tasteful furnishings; the terrific Café Promenade restaurant is much in demand. $499 weekends, $665 weekdays. ❾

Monaco 700 F St NW, Downtown ⓣ202/628-7177, ⓦwww.monaco-dc.com. Perhaps the most architecturally significant hotel in the area, this former grand, Neoclassical post office designed by Robert Mills today houses ultra-chic accommodation. Features include sophisticated modern rooms, minimalist contemporary decor, public spaces with marble floors and columns, and striking spiral stairways. $369, but weekend rates only cost half as much. ❾

Omni Shoreham 2500 Calvert St NW, Upper Northwest ⓣ202/234-0700, ⓦwww.omnihotels.com. Plush, grand institution bursting with history and overlooking Rock Creek Park. Offers swank, comfortable rooms, many with a view of the park, plus an outdoor pool, tennis courts, and the Marquee Bar for drinks. ❾

Palomar 2121 P St NW, Dupont Circle ⓣ202/293-3100, ⓦwww.hotelpalomar-dc.com. Excellent boutique accommodation with flat-panel TVs and CD players in the rooms, an on-site pool, a fitness center, a stylish lounge, and an evening "wine hour" for schmoozing with other guests. $219 weekends, $329 weekdays. ❽–❾

State Plaza 2117 E St NW, Foggy Bottom ⓣ202/861-8200 or 1-800/424-2859, ⓦwww.stateplaza.com. Commodious, stylish suites with fully equipped kitchens and a dining area, plus a rooftop sundeck, health club, and good café. $149 weekends, $249 weekdays (sometimes with three-night minimum stay). ❻–❽

Tabard Inn 1739 N St NW ⓣ202/785-1277, ⓦwww.tabardinn.com. Three converted Victorian townhouses near Dupont Circle, with forty unique, antique-stocked rooms. Comfortable lounges and romantic fireplaces, a courtyard, and a fine restaurant. Rates include breakfast and a pass to the nearby YMCA. ❺; ❻ with private bath

Topaz 1733 N St NW, Dupont Circle ⓣ202/393-3000, ⓦwww.topazhotel.com. Boutique hotel whose vibrant rooms have padded headboards with polka dots, striped wallpaper, and arty furniture; several also have space for yoga – or treadmills, stationary bikes, and elliptical machines. Weekends $263, weekdays $399. ❾

Washington International Student Center 2451 18th St NW ⓣ202/667-7681 or 1-800/567-4150, ⓦwww.washingtondchostel.com. Backpacker accommodation in plain dorms in Adams Morgan, with internet access, lockers, and free pickup from bus and train stations (advance reservation required). This is downtown DC's cheapest bed, so book at least two weeks in advance. ❶

William Lewis House 1309 R St NW ⓣ202/462-7574 or 1-800/465-7574, ⓦwww.wlewishouse.com. Elegantly decorated, gay-friendly B&B set in two century-old townhouses north of Logan Circle. All ten antique-filled rooms have shared bath and net access. Out back there's a roomy porch and a hot tub set in a garden. Rates include continental breakfast on weekdays and a full American breakfast on weekends. It's ultra-cheap for what you get, so reservations are essential. ❹

Windsor Inn 1842 16th St NW ⓣ202/667-0300 or 1-800/423-9111, ⓦwww.windsor-inn-dc.com. Not too far from Dupont Circle, with units in twin, brick, 1920s houses and spacious suites. Some rooms have fridges; ground-floor rooms look onto a terrace. Free wi-fi access and continental breakfast served in the attractive lobby. ❺–❼ by season.

Woodley Park Guest House 2647 Woodley Rd NW, Upper Northwest ⓣ202/667-0218 or 1-866/667-0218, ⓦwoodleyparkguesthouse.com. Eighteen cozy rooms (the cheapest share facilities) that come with free continental breakfast. Close to the zoo, the Metro, and plenty of good restaurants. ❺, add $50 for double occupancy with private bath.

The City

Washington's **city plan** is easy to grasp: with the US Capitol as the center of the street grid, the District is divided into four **quadrants** – northeast, northwest, southeast, and southwest. Dozens of broad **avenues**, named after states, run diagonally across a standard grid of **streets**, meeting up at monumental traffic circles like Dupont Circle. North–south streets are numbered, east–west ones are lettered. (J Street was intentionally skipped to avoid confusion with I Street, which is often written Eye Street.) Be sure to note the relevant two-letter code in any **address** (NW, NE, SW, SE), which shows its quadrant; 1600 Pennsylvania Ave NW is a long way from 1600 Pennsylvania Ave SE.

Almost all the most famous sights are on **Capitol Hill** or, running two miles west, the broad, green **National Mall**, which holds monuments to famous presidents, as well as the **White House**, official home of the current president. Also here are the bulk of the city's many fine museums, including the peerless collections of the **Smithsonian Institution**.

Between the Mall and the main spine of **Pennsylvania Avenue** – the route connecting Capitol Hill to the White House – the Neoclassical buildings of the **Federal Triangle** are home to agencies forming the hub of the national bureaucracy. North and east of here, **Old Downtown** features splashy new plazas, galleries, and restaurants – especially around the **Verizon Center** – alongside traditional attractions like the Old Post Office and Ford Theatre, where Abraham Lincoln was shot. West of the White House, **Foggy Bottom** is another cornerstone of the federal bureaucracy, but further northwest is the city's oldest area, **Georgetown**, where popular bars and restaurants line M Street and Wisconsin Avenue above the **Potomac River**. Georgetown is a fifteen-minute walk from the Foggy Bottom–GWU Metro, but its Federal-era and Victorian townhouses and the towpath along the **C&O Canal** make it a fine target for a day's poking around. Other neighborhoods to check out – especially for hotels, restaurants, and bars – are **Dupont Circle** at Massachusetts, Connecticut, and New Hampshire avenues, and the gentrifying community of **Adams Morgan**, a favored destination of the weekend party crowd. More gung-ho visitors may also want to follow the Red Line Metro out to the genteel precinct of **Upper Northwest**, which offers some interesting historical neighborhoods, along with the National Zoo. Most tourists also walk or take the short Metro ride to **Arlington** in Virginia to see the National Cemetery, burial place of John F. Kennedy.

Capitol Hill

Although there's more than one hill in Washington DC, when people talk about what's happening on **"The Hill,"** they mean **Capitol Hill** – a shallow knoll topped by the giant white dome of the US Capitol, rising at the official center of the city. Home of both the legislature – **Congress** – and the judiciary – the **Supreme Court** – this is still the place where the law of the land is made and interpreted; in addition, it holds the esteemed **Library of Congress** and **Folger Shakespeare Library**.

US Capitol

The **US Capitol**, at the east end of the National Mall, between Constitution and Independence avenues (tour information ⓣ202/225-6827, general information ⓣ202/224-3121, ⓦwww.aoc.gov), provides an opportunity to appreciate the immense power wielded by the nation's elected officials.

George Washington laid the building's cornerstone in 1793 in a ceremony rich with Masonic symbolism, and though the Capitol was torched by the British during the War of 1812, it was later rebuilt and repeatedly expanded over the ensuing centuries. Ten presidents – most recently Gerald Ford – have lain in state in the impressive **Rotunda**, which, capped by a massive cast-iron dome 180-feet high and 96-feet across, links the two halves of the Capitol – the **Senate** in the north wing, the **House of Representatives** in the south. When the "Tholos" lantern above the dome is lit, Congress is in session.

Tight security means that walk-up access to the Capitol is limited to **guided tours** that leave every thirty minutes (9am–4.30pm; 35min; free). Since advance tickets are unavailable, arrive early at the Capitol Guide Service kiosk (near 1st St SW and Independence Ave). Tickets are distributed starting at 9am, and lines can form as early as 7am; before your scheduled tour, you can expect to wait in a lengthy queue south of the building at the South Visitor Receiving Facility. US citizens who want to see the legislative chambers must arrange to get a pass through their representatives. Visitors from other countries should bring a passport or photo ID and first go to the receiving facility, where they can obtain international passes. The East Front is being completely reconstructed to make way for the new **underground visitor center**. The completion of this $550-million showpiece has been long overdue (planned for late 2008 or 2009) and the project has run well over budget.

Library of Congress

With 128-million books, manuscripts, microfilm rolls, and photographs kept on 530 miles of shelves, the **Library of Congress** is the largest library in the world. Housed east of the Capitol in the Jefferson, Madison, and John Adams buildings between 1st and 3rd streets SE and E Capitol and C streets SE (Mon–Sat 10am–5.30pm; Ⓣ202/707-8000, Ⓦwww.loc.gov; free), the library was set up to serve members of Congress in 1800. In 1870, the library became the national copyright repository, and in time it outgrew its original home. The exuberantly eclectic **Thomas Jefferson Building** opened in 1897, complete with a domed octagonal **Reading Room**, and hundreds of mosaics, murals, and sculptures in its stunning Great Hall. The library's huge collection is showcased on the second floor in the **main gallery**, where periodic exhibitions are based around broad subjects. It's hard to predict exactly what you'll see, but previous displays have included items such as Walt Whitman's Civil War notebooks, the original typescript of Martin Luther King Jr's "I Have a Dream" speech, and a copy of Francis Scott Key's "Star-Spangled Banner." Free **tours** depart Monday to Saturday at 10.30am, 11.30am, 1.30pm, 2.30pm, and 3.30pm (with the latter tour time not available on Sat).

Supreme Court

The **Supreme Court**, across from the US Capitol, at First Street NE and Maryland Avenue NE (Mon–Fri 9am–4.30pm; Ⓣ202/479-3211, Ⓦwww.supremecourtus.gov; free), is the nation's final arbiter of what is and isn't legal. The federal judiciary dates to 1787, but the court didn't receive its own building until 1935, when Cass Gilbert – architect of New York's Woolworth Building – designed this Greek Revival masterpiece. The Court is in session from October through June. Between the beginning of October and the end of April, oral arguments are heard every Monday, Tuesday, and Wednesday from 10am to noon, and 1pm to 3pm on occasion. The sessions, which almost always last one hour per case, are open to the public on a first-come, first-served basis. Arrive by 8.30am if you really want one of the 150 seats.

Folger Shakespeare Library

The renowned **Folger Shakespeare Library**, 201 E Capitol St (Mon–Sat 10am–4pm; tours Mon–Fri 11am, Sat 11am & 1pm; Ⓦwww.folger.edu), on the south side of the Supreme Court, was founded in 1932 and today holds more than 350,000 books, manuscripts, paintings, and engravings related to Shakespeare's work and background. The dark-oak Great Hall – with its carved lintels, stained glass, Tudor roses, and sculpted ceiling – displays changing exhibitions about the playwright and Elizabethan themes. The reproduction Elizabethan Theater hosts lectures and readings as well as medieval and Renaissance music concerts, and an Elizabethan garden on the east lawn grows herbs and flowers common in the sixteenth century.

The National Mall – monuments

One of the central features of L'Enfant's grand plan for Washington, the elegant, two-mile-long **National Mall** stretches from the Capitol to the Lincoln Memorial and is DC's most popular green space, used for summer softball games and Fourth of July concerts. When there's a protest gesture to be made, the Mall is the place to make it. What the Mall is perhaps best known for, however, is its quartet of presidential **monuments**, along with the White House and the powerful **memorials** to veterans of the twentieth century's various wars.

Washington Monument

The Mall's most prominent feature, the **Washington Monument**, is an unadorned marble obelisk built in memory of George Washington. At 555ft, it's the tallest all-masonry structure in the world, towering over the city from its hilltop perch at 15th Street NW and Constitution Avenue (daily 9am–5pm; free; ⓣ202/426-6841, ⓦwww.nps.gov/wamo). To visit the monument pick up a free ticket from the 15th Street kiosk, just south of Constitution Avenue on Madison Drive (8am–4.30pm), which allows you to turn up at a fixed time later in the day. The kiosk is first-come, first-served; tickets run out early during the peak season. You can also book a ticket in advance with the National Park Service (ⓣ1-877/444-6777; $1.50). Once you gain access, a seventy-second **elevator ride** whisks you past the honorary stones in the (closed) stairwell and deposits you at a level where the views are, of course, tremendous (though the windows could use some cleaning).

The White House

For nearly two hundred years, the **White House** has been the residence and office of the president of the United States. Standing at the edge of the Mall, due north from the Washington Monument at America's most famous address, 1600 Pennsylvania Ave NW, this grand, Neoclassical edifice was completed in 1800 by Irish immigrant James Hoban, who modeled it on the Georgian manors of Dublin. Security at the White House is every bit as tight as you'd imagine. In the wake of 9/11, White House **tours** (ⓣ202/456-7041, ⓦwww.whitehouse.gov; free) have become much more restricted: to gain access, you must be part of a group of ten and contact your congressional representative at least a month in advance (foreign visitors can contact their embassies or consulates). Tours are offered Tuesday through Saturday, from 7.30am to 12.30pm. If you're interested in the history of the place and its occupants, walk a few blocks southeast to the **visitor center** at 1450 Pennsylvania Ave (daily 7.30am–4pm; ⓣ202/208-1631, ⓦwww.nps.gov/whho).

National World War II Memorial

In 2004 the **National World War II Memorial**, 17th Street SW at Independence Avenue (daily 24hr, staffed 9.30am–11.30pm; ⓣ202/426-6841, ⓦwww.nps.gov/nwwm; free), just west of the Washington Monument, is a moving statement of duty and sacrifice. Two arcs on each side of a central fountain have a combined total of 56 stone pillars (representing the number of US states and territories at the time of the war) that are decorated with bronze wreaths. In the middle of each arc stands a short tower, one called "Atlantic" and the other "Pacific," and within each tower are four interlinked bronze eagles and a sculpted wreath. Beyond the carefully considered architecture and the FDR and Eisenhower quotes chiseled on the walls, a concave wall of four thousand golden stars reminds you of the 400,000 fallen US soldiers – a number matched only by the colossal carnage of the Civil War.

Lincoln Memorial

The **Lincoln Memorial**, with its stately Doric columns, anchors the west end of the Mall (daily 24hr, staffed 9.30am–11.30pm; ⓦwww.nps.gov/linc; free), a fitting tribute to the sixteenth US president, who preserved the Union through the Civil War, and provided the first step toward ending slavery in the country with his Emancipation Proclamation in 1863. During the Civil Rights March on Washington in 1963, Martin Luther King Jr delivered his epic "I Have a Dream" speech here, and on-site protests against the Vietnam War in the 1960s fueled the growing antiwar feeling in the country. Inside the monument, an enormous, craggy likeness of Lincoln sits firmly grasping the arms of his throne-like chair, deep in thought. Inscriptions of his two most celebrated speeches – the Gettysburg Address and the Second Inaugural Address – are carved on the south and north walls.

Vietnam Veterans Memorial

A striking wedge of black granite, slashed into the green lawn of the Mall at Constitution Avenue and 21st Street NW, the **Vietnam Veterans Memorial** (daily 24hr, staffed 9.30am–11.30pm; Ⓦ www.nps.gov/vive; free) serves as a somber and powerful reminder of the 58,000 US soldiers who died in Vietnam. The pathway that slopes down from the grass forms a gash in the earth, its increasing depth symbolizing the increasing involvement of US forces in the war. The polished surface is carved with the names of every soldier who died, in chronological order from 1959 to 1975, and you can often find family members taking paper rubbings of the names of the departed.

Korean War Veterans Memorial

The **Korean War Veterans Memorial**, southeast of the Lincoln Memorial (daily 24hr, staffed 8am–11.45pm; Ⓦ www.nps.gov/kwvm; free), has as its centerpiece a Field of Remembrance, featuring nineteen life-sized, armed combat troops sculpted from stainless steel. The troops advance across a triangular plot with alternating rows of stones and plant life and head toward the Stars and Stripes positioned at the vertex. A reflecting black granite wall, with the inscription "Freedom is not

▲ Korean War Veterans Memorial

free," and an etched mural, depicting military support crew and medical staff, flank the ensemble.

Jefferson Memorial and Tidal Basin

Completed in 1943 and loosely modeled on his country home, Monticello (see p.413), the **Jefferson Memorial**, just south of the Mall near 14th Street SW and Ohio Drive (daily 24hr, staffed 9.30am–11.30pm; Ⓦwww.nps.gov/thje; free), has a shallow dome hovering over a huge bronze statue of Thomas Jefferson, the author of the Declaration of Independence and the third US president. Just out front, the picturesque **Tidal Basin** stretches up to the Mall and offers one of the best places in town to take a break from sightseeing. The reflections off the Tidal Basin are especially pretty in spring when the rows of **Japanese cherry trees** come out in full bloom (usually early- to mid-April).

FDR and King Memorials

Alongside the Tidal Basin, the **FDR Memorial**, just west of the Jefferson Memorial at West Basin Drive SW and Ohio Drive (daily 24hr, staffed 9.30am–11.30pm; Ⓦwww.nps.gov/fdrm; free), spreads across a seven-acre site made up of a series of interlinking granite outdoor galleries – called "rooms" – punctuated by waterfalls, statuary, sculpted reliefs, groves of trees, and shaded alcoves and plazas. It's among the most successful and popular of DC's memorials, and has an almost Athenian quality to its open spaces, resting-places, benches, and inspiring texts. Note that by the end of 2010, the **Martin Luther King Jr National Memorial** (details at Ⓦwww.mlkmemorial.org) will be unveiled on the northern flank of the FDR Memorial, between it and the Lincoln Memorial, commemorating the various heroes and victims of the civil rights struggle up to the present day.

The National Mall – museums

In contrast to the memorials and monuments of its western half, the National Mall's eastern side is dominated by museums, most of which are part of the spectacular **Smithsonian Institution**. The Smithsonian was endowed in 1846 by Englishman James Smithson; the Institution's original home, the stately 1855 structure known as **The Castle**, 1000 Jefferson Drive SW, is in the center of the Mall's south side and now acts as the main **visitor center** (daily 8.30am–5.30pm; Ⓣ202/633-1000). Unless otherwise stated below, all Smithsonian museums and galleries are **open daily** all year (except December 25) from 10am until 5.30pm, with summer hours until 7.30 or 8pm, and admission is **free**. For details on current exhibitions and events, call the visitor center or visit the Smithsonian's website at Ⓦwww.si.edu.

National Museum of American History

One of the prime repositories of US cultural artifacts is the **National Museum of American History**, located at 14th Street NW and Constitution Avenue (Ⓣ202/633-1000, Ⓦwww.americanhistory.si.edu), deservedly one of the country's most popular museums, with objects taken from nearly four hundred years of American and pre-American history. You're apt to find anything from George Washington's wooden teeth to Jackie Kennedy's designer dresses to Judy Garland's ruby slippers from The Wizard of Oz. You could easily spend a full day poking around the displays, but three to four hours would be a reasonable compromise – and to stick to this time frame, you'll have to be selective. The museum's biggest draw is the battered red, white, and blue flag that inspired the US national anthem – the **Star-Spangled Banner** itself, which survived the British bombardment of Baltimore Harbor during the War of 1812.

National Museum of Natural History

Continuing eastward toward the Capitol, on the north side of the Mall, at Tenth Street NW and Constitution Avenue, lies the imposing, three-story entrance rotunda of the **National Museum of Natural History** (Ⓣ202/633-1000, Ⓦwww.mnh.si.edu), which traces evolution from fossilized four-billion-year-old plankton to dinosaurs' eggs and beyond. In fact, the "Dinosaurs" section is the most popular part of the museum, with hulking skeletons reassembled in imaginative poses. The museum also boasts a truly exceptional array of gemstones, including the legendary 45-carat Hope Diamond that once belonged to Marie Antoinette, and the Gem and Mineral Hall, which features natural and reconstructed environments, interactive exhibits, and hands-on specimens. Elsewhere, the Hall of Mammals has some three hundred replicas focusing on mostly fur-wearing, milk-producing creatures, and the 25,000-square-foot Ocean Hall uses hundreds of displays and specimens – among them, a 50-foot-long whale model – to explain the world of the sea.

National Gallery of Art

The visually stunning **National Gallery of Art**, just east on Constitution Avenue, between Third and Ninth streets NW (Mon–Sat 10am–5pm, Sun 11am–6pm; Ⓣ202/737-4215, Ⓦwww.nga.gov; free), is one of the most important museums in the US. The original Neoclassical gallery, designed by John Russell Pope and opened in 1941, is now called the **West Building** and holds the bulk of the permanent collection. Galleries to the west on the main floor display major works by early- and high-Renaissance and Baroque masters, arranged by nationality: half a dozen Rembrandts fill the **Dutch** gallery, including a glowing, mad portrait of **Lucretia**, Van Eyck and Rubens dominate the **Flemish**, and El Greco, Goya and Velázquez face off in the **Spanish**. In the voluminous **Italian** galleries, there's the only **da Vinci** in the Americas, the 1474 **Ginevra de' Benci**, painted in oil on wood; **Titian**'s vivid image of **Saint John the Evangelist** on Patmos and **Venus with a Mirror**; and **Raphael's** renowned **Alba Madonna** (1510). The other half of the West Building holds an exceptional collection of nineteenth-century paintings – a couple of Van Goghs, some Monet studies of Rouen Cathedral and water lilies, Cézanne still lifes, and the like. For British art, you can find genteel portraits by Gainsborough and Reynolds, but even more evocative hazy land- and waterscapes by **J.M.W. Turner**. **Augustus St Gaudens'** magisterial battle sculpture **Memorial to Robert Gould Shaw and the Massachusetts 54th Regiment** takes up a whole gallery to itself.

The National Gallery's **East Building** (same hours and admission) was opened in 1978 with an audaciously modern **I.M. Pei** design, dominated by a huge atrium. European highlights of the permanent collection include **Pablo Picasso**'s Blue Period pieces **The Tragedy** and **Family of Saltimbanques**, along with his cubist **Nude Woman**; and **Henri Matisse**'s exuberant **Pianist** and **Checker Players**. Andy Warhol's works are as familiar as they come, with classic serial works **32 Soup Cans**, **Let Us Now Praise Famous Men**, and **Green Marilyn**. Notable Abstract Expressionist works include large, hovering slabs of blurry color by Mark Rothko, the thirteen stations of the cross by Barnett Newman, and Jackson Pollock's **Number 1, 1950 (Lavender Mist)**. There's also Robert Rauschenberg's splattered, stuffed-bird sculpture known as **Canyon**, and Jasper Johns's **Targets**, among his most influential works.

National Museum of the American Indian

Continuing clockwise around the Mall, skirting the Capitol Reflecting Pool and heading back west along Jefferson Drive, the Smithsonian's **National Museum**

of the American Indian (Ⓣ202/633-1000, Ⓦwww.nmai.si.edu) is instantly recognizable by its curvaceous modern form, with undulating walls the color of yellow earth – designed to represent the natural American landscape – plus a terraced facade and surrounding replicas of forest and wetland landscapes. The collection – which reaches back thousands of years and incorporates nearly a million objects from nations spread out from Canada to Mexico – features fascinating ceramics, textiles, and other artifacts from civilizations such as the Olmec, Maya, and Inca.

National Air and Space Museum

The **National Air and Space Museum**, further west between Fourth and Seventh streets SW (Ⓣ202/633-1000, Ⓦwww.nasm.si.edu) is DC's most popular attraction. The entry hall, known as "Milestones of Flight," is a huge atrium filled with all kinds of flying machines, rockets, satellites, and assorted aeronautic gizmos, highlighted by Charles Lindbergh's **Spirit of St Louis**. Elsewhere, the "Space Race" exhibit traces the development of space flight, including an array of space suits from different eras, while nearby, "Rocketry and Space Flight" outlines the history of rocketry. The whimsically labeled "Wright Cycle Co." is devoted to the siblings who pioneered aeronautics; the focus is the handmade Wright Flyer, in which the Wrights made the first powered flight in December 1903. However, "Apollo to the Moon" is the most popular and crowded room in the museum, centering on the **Apollo 11** (1969) and **17** (1972) missions, the first and last US flights to the moon. Finally, the most hardcore of aeronautics buffs should inquire about the museum's **Steven F. Udvar-Hazy Center** in suburban Virginia, where you can get a look at flying craft too big even to fit into the main museum's capacious digs, including a Concorde and space shuttle.

Hirshhorn Museum

Continuing west, the **Hirshhorn Museum**, Independence Avenue at 7th Street SW (Ⓣ202/633-4674, Ⓦwww.hirshhorn.si.edu), with its concrete facade and monumental scale, is a perfect example of late-modernist architecture at its most inhuman. If the museum has one recognized strength, it's sculpture: bronzes by Henri Matisse, masks and busts by Pablo Picasso and Brancusi's **Torso of a Young Man**, resembling a cylindrical brass phallus. The Hirshhorn's cache of modern paintings has several strengths (de Kooning, Bacon) and starts with figurative paintings from the late nineteenth and early twentieth century and winds its way toward Abstract Expressionism and Pop Art. Along the way, separate rooms showcase the various major currents of the past century, from the surrealism of Salvador Dalí, Max Ernst, and Joan Miró to the organic abstractions of Alexander Calder.

National Museum of African Art

Further on, the domed **National Museum of African Art**, 950 Independence Ave SW (Ⓣ202/633-4600, Ⓦwww.nmafa.si.edu), holds more than six thousand sculptures and artifacts from the cultures of sub-Saharan Africa. The permanent collection ranges widely, and there are plenty of rotating exhibits, which may include headrests, mostly carved from wood using an adze, as well as assorted ivory snuff containers, carved drinking horns, combs, pipes, spoons, baskets, and cups. For many shows you're apt to see a wide variety of ceramic bowls (perfectly round, despite being hand-formed), including one with a hippo head for a spout, and carved legs and delicate ivory animal figures from the ceremonial beds used to carry the dead to the cemetery for burial.

Arthur M. Sackler Gallery

The angular and pyramidal **Arthur M. Sackler Gallery**, 1050 Independence Ave SW (Ⓣ202/633-4880, Ⓦwww.asia.si.edu), along with the Freer Gallery (see below), is part of the National Museum of Asian Art. Among its permanent exhibitions, which are on the first level, "The Arts of China" is the most prominent, featuring 3000-year-old Chinese bronzes, ritual wine containers decorated with the faces and tails of dragons, intricate jade pendants, remarkably well-preserved carved wooden cabinets and book stands, and Qing imperial porcelain embellished with symbolic figures and motifs. "**Sculpture of South and Southeast Asia**" traces the spread of devotional sculpture across the continent. Hindu temple sculpture from India includes bronze, brass, and granite representations of Brahma, Vishnu, and Shiva; there's also a superb thirteenth-century stone carving of the elephant-headed Ganesha.

Freer Gallery of Art

From the day it opened in 1923, the **Freer Gallery**, on Jefferson Drive at 12th Street NW, has been one of the more unusual Smithsonian museums (Ⓣ202/357-4880, Ⓦwww.asia.si.edu), containing more than one thousand prints, drawings, and paintings by London-based American artist James McNeil Whistler – the largest collection of his works anywhere – highlighted by the magnificent Peacock Room, with a ceiling covered with imitation gold leaf and walls painted with blue and gold peacocks and feather patterns. The museum also includes Chinese jades and bronzes, Byzantine illuminated manuscripts, Buddhist wall sculptures, and pieces of Persian metalwork, all of which were collected under Whistler's tutelage. Among other works are pieces by Whistler's contemporaries, Winslow Homer and John Singer Sargent.

United States Holocaust Memorial Museum

The sizeable **United States Holocaust Memorial Museum**, just south of the National Mall at 100 Raoul Wallenburg Place SW (Ⓣ202/488-0400, Ⓦwww.ushmm.org), recalls the persecution and murder of six million Jews by the Nazis and personalizes the suffering of individual victims. Newspapers and newsreels documenting Nazi activities from the early 1930s through the "Final Solution" are on display, plus replicas and, in many cases, actual relics, of Warsaw Ghetto streets, railroad cattle-cars, and other artifacts on the top floors. The staggering number of people killed is chillingly evoked throughout, first by a room filled with shoes stolen from deportees, and later by piles of blankets, umbrellas, scissors, cutlery, and other personal effects taken from the hundreds of thousands who arrived at the various camps expecting to be forced to work, but were most often gassed within hours instead.

Tickets for specific entry times are available free of charge from 10am each day – with a limit of four per person – at the 14th Street entrance. You can also reserve in advance (Ⓣ1-800/400-9373).

The Bureau of Engraving and Printing

The **Bureau of Engraving and Printing**, one block south of the Mall at 14th and C streets SW (Ⓣ202/874-2330, Ⓦwww.moneyfactory.com; free), is the federal agency for designing and printing all US currency, government securities, and postage stamps; it's also host to one of DC's most popular tours, netting a half-million visitors annually. Between May and August you must pick up **tickets** in advance for tours from 9am to 2pm; you can, and should, start waiting in line at 8am, as tickets are often gone by 11.30am. The rest of the year, you can just show up without tickets, though you'll still have to wait in line. Note that a more in-depth, forty-minute Congressional/VIP tour is offered for those who make arrangements for it through their representative's office (Mon–Fri 8.15am & 8.45am). If you care only to drop by the **visitor center** – perhaps to purchase an overpriced bag of shredded currency to send to the folks back home – it's open daily from 8.30am to 3.30pm.

Corcoran Gallery of Art

The **Corcoran Gallery of Art**, just north of the Mall, at 17th Street NW and New York Avenue (Wed–Sun 10am–5pm, Thurs closes 9pm; Ⓦwww.corcoran.org; $6), is one of the oldest and most respected art museums in the US. The gallery possesses a fine collection of landscapes, including masterpieces by Frederic Edwin Church and Albert Bierstadt, and portraits by John Singer Sargent, Thomas Eakins, and Mary Cassatt, among others. Some of the most familiar names hang in the **Clark Landing**, a two-tier, wood-paneled gallery accessed from the Rotunda on the second floor. Here you're likely to find mid-level paintings by Degas, Renoir, Monet, Sisley, and Pissarro, as well as works by the likes of Rousseau and Corot. In the **Salon Doré** (Gilded Room), an eighteenth-century Parisian interior has been re-created to stunning effect, with floor-to-ceiling hand-carved paneling, gold-leaf decor, and ceiling murals.

Downtown and around

Those whose patience grows thin with the hordes of people on the Mall may enjoy a trip through Washington DC's **Downtown** district, which was damaged during the 1968 riots but has in the last fifteen years seen new boutiques, restaurants, and hotels spring up in the so-called **Penn Quarter**. Adjacent to Downtown is the wedge-shaped **Federal Triangle**, home to countless government agencies and a few major attractions, such as the National Archives, while, to the northwest, the **New Downtown** area, known for its lobbyist-rich K Street, has numerous swanky shops and restaurants.

National Archives

On display at the **National Archives**, 700 Pennsylvania Ave NW (research room daily 9am–5pm, rotunda and exhibit hall daily 10am-5.30pm, spring and summer closes 7pm; last admission 30min before closing; Ⓣ202/501-5205, Ⓦwww.archives.gov; free), are the three short texts upon which the United States was founded: the **Declaration of Independence**, the **Constitution**, and the **Bill of Rights**. These three original sheets of parchment, drafted respectively in 1776, 1787, and 1789, are secured in bomb-proof, argon-filled, glass-and-titanium containers that slide into a vault in case of fire or other threats. The impressive Neoclassical Greek building – designed by John Russell Pope – also houses temporary exhibitions with fascinating documents such as the Louisiana Purchase, the Marshall Plan, Nixon's resignation letter, the Emancipation Proclamation, and the Japanese surrender from World War II. As the official repository of all US national records – census data, treaties, passport applications – the Archives also attracts thousands of visitors who come here each year in search of their own genealogical, military, or other records. Among the holdings are seven million pictures; 125,000 reels of film; 200,000 sound recordings; eleven million maps and charts; and a quarter of a million other artifacts.

National Portrait Gallery and American Art Museum

In the center of the Penn Quarter, the **Old Patent Office** – a Neoclassical gem dating from 1836 – houses two of the city's major art displays: the Smithsonian's

National Portrait Gallery and **American Art Museum** (both daily 11.30am–7pm; ⓣ202/633-8300, ⓦwww.npg.si.edu; free). In the Portrait Gallery, striking images of figures from the performing arts include Paul Robeson as Othello; photographs of Gloria Swanson and Boris Karloff; a rough-hewn wooden head of Bob Hope; and an almost three-dimensional metallic study of Ethel Merman as Annie Oakley. Also worth a look are the presidential portraits – one for every man to occupy the office, from Gilbert Stuart's George Washington, an imperial study of an implacable leader, to Norman Rockwell's overly flattering portrait of Richard Nixon. Elsewhere are portraits of both colonial and Native Americans, including a painting of Pocahontas in English attire.

The other major museum to occupy the Old Patent Office building, the **American Art Museum**, holds one of the more enduring of the city's art collections, which dates back to the early nineteenth century. The museum contains almost four hundred paintings by George Catlin, who spent six years touring the Great Plains, painting portraits and scenes of Native American life as well as lush landscapes. There are also notable twentieth-century modern pieces – items by Robert Motherwell, Willem de Kooning, Robert Rauschenberg, Clyfford Still, Ed Kienholz, and Jasper Johns – but none more vibrant than Nam June Paik's jaw-dropping **Electronic Superhighway**, a huge, neon-outlined map of the US. Another branch of the American Art Museum, the **Renwick Gallery**, located near the White House, at 17th Street and Pennsylvania Avenue (daily 10am–5.30pm; ⓣ202/633-2850; free), offers overflow space for the museum's treasures, as well as rotating exhibits focussing on the decorative arts.

International Spy Museum

The **International Spy Museum**, 800 F St NW (hours vary, usually summer daily 9am–7pm; rest of year daily 10am–8pm; ⓦwww.spymuseum.org; $18), is a hugely popular DC attraction – tickets sell out days in advance during the high season – celebrating espionage in all forms, from feudal Japan's silent and deadly ninjas, to surveillance pigeons armed with cameras from World War I, to infamous modern-day CIA moles like Aldrich Ames. The museum's standouts are undoubtedly its artifacts from the height of the Cold War in the 1950s and 1960s, presented in glass cases and broken down by theme – "training," "surveillance," and so on. Some of the many highlights include tiny pistols disguised as lipstick holders, cigarette cases, pipes, and flashlights; oddments like invisible-ink writing kits and a Get Smart!-styled shoe phone; a colorful and active model of James Bond's Aston Martin spy car; ricin-tipped poison umbrellas used to kill dissidents; and a rounded capsule containing a screwdriver, razor, and serrated knife – ominously marked, "rectal tool kit."

Ford's Theatre and Petersen House

Ford's Theatre National Historic Site, 511 Tenth St NW (daily 9am–5pm, closed during rehearsals and matinees; ⓣ202/347-4833, ⓦwww.nps.gov/foth; free), is a beautiful restoration of the nineteenth-century playhouse, which continues to stage regular productions of contemporary and period drama (see p.394). It was here, on April 14, 1865, a mere five days after the end of the Civil War, that **Abraham Lincoln** was shot by the actor and Confederate partisan John Wilkes Booth during a performance of Our American Cousin.

However, all public operations are suspended for the moment while the site is fully renovated in advance of the bicentennial of Lincoln's birth, in February 2009 (more general info at ⓦwww.lincoln200.gov). At that time, a new **Lincoln Campus** will open with the site as its centerpiece, and you'll once again be able to see the damask-furnished presidential box in which Lincoln sat in his rocking chair, and, on the lower level, a **Lincoln Museum** displaying impressive items like the actual murder weapon (a .44 Derringer), a bloodstained piece of Lincoln's overcoat, and Booth's knife, keys, compass, boot and diary. After he was shot, the mortally wounded president was carried across the street to the **Petersen House**, where he died the next morning. That, too, is open to the public (daily 9am–5pm; ⓣ202/426-6924), who troop through its gloomy parlor rooms to see a replica of Lincoln's death bed.

National Museum of Women in the Arts

Housed in a converted Masonic Temple at 1250 New York Ave NW, the **National Museum of Women in the Arts** is the country's only major museum dedicated to female artists (Mon–Sat 10am–5pm, Sun noon–5pm; ⓣ202/783-5000, ⓦwww.nmwa.org; $10). The collection is arranged chronologically, starting with works from the Renaissance, like those of Sofonisba Anguissola, who was considered the most important female artist of her day. A century or so later, Dutch and Flemish women like Clara Peeters, Judith Leyster, and Rachel Ruysch were producing still lifes and genre scenes – witness the vivacity of Peeters's *Still Life of Fish and Cat*. Twentieth-century works include the classical sculpture of Camille Claudel, the paintings of Georgia O'Keeffe and Tamara de Lempicka, linocuts by Hannah Höch, and, most boldly, a cycle of prints depicting the hardships of working-class life by the socialist Käthe Kollwitz. Frida Kahlo appears dressed in a peasant's outfit and clutching a note to Trotsky, but more fetching is **Itzcuintli Dog with Me**, in which she poses next to a truly tiny, strangely adorable mutt.

The Newseum

The **Newseum**, on 6th Street at Pennsylvania Avenue (daily 9am–5pm; ⓣ1-800/NEWSEUM, ⓦwww.newseum.org; $20), is a new "edutainment" colossus that opened to the public in 2008 and provides a flashy look at the greatest hits of the news biz. There's certainly a lot of space to fill for the purpose: with a quarter-million square feet and seven levels, the Newseum is chock full of information. On the various levels, you'll see how modern news is gathered and transmitted, witness pivotal moments in journalism through docudrama re-enactments, bone up on the freedoms of speech and press, and get a look at the history of news as provided by the News Corporation, owner of controversial **FOX News**.

National Building Museum

First known as the Pension Building, the **National Building Museum**, 401 F Street NW (Mon–Sat 10am–5pm, Sun 11am–5pm; ⓦwww.nbm.org; $5), housed various federal offices before its current function as a stirring museum of architecture, presenting changing exhibitions that cover topics like urban renewal, high-rise technology, and environmental concerns. The best feature of the museum, though, is the interior space itself: the majestic **Great Hall** is a stadium-sized expanse centered on a working fountain, and one of the greatest interior spaces anywhere in DC. The eight supporting columns are 8ft across at the base and more than 75ft high; each is made up of 70,000 bricks, plastered and painted to resemble Siena marble.

Dupont Circle to Upper Northwest

Washington's other key attractions are spaced out among various neighbourhoods, but they are nevertheless worth taking the time to visit. Many lie near Connecticut Avenue, on the stretch that runs from the increasingly swanky shopping and dining area of **Dupont Circle** up to the elite precinct of **Upper Northwest** – both areas conveniently accessed by subway. Less convenient, just to the northeast, is the funky urban district of **Adams-Morgan** – a draw for its diners, clubs, and bars.

Phillips Collection

The oldest part of the Georgian Revival brownstone housing the **Phillips Collection**, just northwest of Dupont Circle, at 1600 21st St NW (Tues–Sat 10am–5pm, Thurs until 8.30pm, Sun 11am–6pm; ⓣ202/387-2151, ⓦwww.phillipscollection .org; free admission weekdays, $10 weekends, $12-15 special exhibitions), is one of DC's key museums, and has expanded considerably in the last several years, with its main building, the Goh Annex, next door on 21st Street, and a new underground wing, the Sant Building, which focusses on more contemporary pieces. On display are works by everyone from Renoir to Rothko (and several by non-modern artists like Giorgione and El Greco). Highlights include signature pieces by Willem de Kooning and Richard Diebenkorn, Blue Period Picassos, Matisse's *Studio, Quai St-Michel*, a Cézanne still life, and no fewer than four van Goghs, including the powerful *Road Menders*. Top billing generally goes to *The Luncheon of the Boating Party* by Renoir, where straw-hat-wearing dandies linger over a feast.

Embassy Row

An intriguing strip that is unique to Washington DC among American cities, **Embassy Row** starts in earnest a few paces northwest up Massachusetts Avenue from Dupont Circle, where the **Indonesian Embassy** at no. 2020 (closed to the public) occupies the magnificent Art Nouveau Walsh-McLean House, built in 1903 for gold baron Thomas Walsh. It's a superb building – with colonnaded loggia and intricate, carved windows – and saw regular service as one of Washington society's most fashionable venues. Nearby, the **Anderson House**, no. 2118 (free guided tours Tues–Sat 1.15pm, 2.15pm, & 3.15pm; ⓣ202/785-2040; free admission), is a veritable palace, finished in 1905 with a gray-stone exterior sporting twin arched entrances, heavy wooden doors, and colonnaded portico. Inside there's a grand ballroom, and original furnishings include cavernous fireplaces, inlaid marble floors, Flemish tapestries, and diverse murals. Check out ⓦwww .embassyevents.com for a listing of art shows, lectures, food fairs, films, and displays taking place at selected embassies here and elsewhere in town.

The National Zoo

Continuing well north, into the hilly district of Upper Northwest, at 3001 Connecticut Ave NW (luckily a short walk from the Metro), is the Smithsonian's **National Zoo** (buildings: daily April–Oct 10am–6pm; Nov–March 10am–4.30pm; grounds: daily April–Oct 6am–8pm; Nov–March 6am–6pm; ⓦwww .natzoo.si.edu; free), founded way back in 1889. **Amazonia** is a re-creation of a tropical river and rainforest habitat – piranhas included – while the **Small Mammal House** showcases some of the zoo's lovable oddballs like golden tamarind monkeys, armadillos, meerkats, and porcupines. Further along, orang-utans are encouraged to leave the confines of the **Great Ape House** and commute to the "**Think Tank**," where scientists and four-legged primates come together to hone their communications skills and discuss world events. Between the Ape House and Think Tank is the **Reptile Discovery Center**, with a full roster of snakes, turtles, crocodiles, alligators, lizards, and frogs. Here you can ponder the remarkable Komodo dragons, one of which was the first to be born in captivity outside Indonesia. If all else fails, there's always the **giant pandas**, who have been amusing visitors since their arrival in 1972. Nearby, the **Asia Trail** displays such curious beasts as the sloth bear, a fishing cat, a somewhat grotesque Japanese giant salamander, and the formidable clouded leopard.

▲ Giant panda, National Zoo

Washington National Cathedral

The twin towers of **Washington National Cathedral**, the world's sixth-largest cathedral, are visible long before you reach the heights of Mount St Alban where the church sits, a good walk from the subway line in Upper Northwest (Mon–Fri 10am–5.30pm, Sat 10am–4.30pm, Sun 8am–6.30pm; Ⓦ www.cathedral.org/cathedral; donation). Built from Indiana limestone and modeled entirely in the medieval English Gothic style, the Protestant cathedral took 83 years to build and measures more than a tenth of a mile from the west end of the nave to the high altar at the opposite end. Among other things, you'll find the sarcophagus of **Woodrow Wilson**, the only president to be buried in the District – though presidents including Ford and Reagan have lain in state here – and the **Space Window** commemorating the flight of Apollo 11, whose stained glass incorporates a sliver of moon rock.

Georgetown

Although it is, unfortunately, a good hike from the nearest subway stop (though taking the DC Circulator helps; see p.371), **Georgetown** is the quintessential DC neighborhood, enlivened by a main drag – M Street – where chic new restaurants and boutiques are housed in 200-year-old buildings, and the old C&O Canal (which you can tour on a historic boat ride; see p.371) runs parallel to the south. There are few conventional attractions along M, though the **Old Stone House**, no. 3051 (Wed–Sun noon–5pm; Ⓦ www.nps.gov/olst; free), comes close, as the only surviving pre-Revolutionary home in the city. Built in 1765 by a Pennsylvania carpenter, it retains its rugged, rough-hewn appearance, the craggy rocks used for the three-feet-thick walls being quarried from blue fieldstone.

In the hillier part of the district, there are two spots that definitely merit a visit: Tudor Place and Dumbarton Oaks. **Tudor Place**, 1644 31st St NW (tours Tues–Fri 10am–2.30pm, Sat 10am–3pm, Sun noon-3pm; Ⓦwww.tudorplace.org; $6), was once the estate of Martha Washington's granddaughter and, with its Federal-style architecture and Classical domed portico, has remained virtually untouched since it was built in 1816. **Dumbarton Oaks** (gardens: mid-March–Oct Tues–Sun 2–6pm; Nov–early March Tues–Sun 2–5pm; Ⓦwww.doaks.org; $8) encompasses a marvelous red-brick, Georgian mansion surrounded by gardens and woods. In 1944 this was the site of a meeting that led to the founding of the United Nations the following year. Its **Bliss Collection** (closed for renovation until 2009) is excellent for its pre-Columbian gold, jade, and polychromatic carvings, sculpture, and pendants, as well as ceremonial axes, jewelry made from spondylus shells, stone masks of unknown significance, and sharp jade "celts" possibly used for human sacrifice.

Arlington National Cemetery and around

Across the Potomac River west of the National Mall, the vast sea of identical white headstones on the hillsides of Virginia's **Arlington National Cemetery** (daily: April–Sept 8am–7pm; Oct–March 8am–5pm; Ⓦwww.arlingtoncemetery.org; free) stands in poignant contrast to the grand monuments of the capital across the river. The country's most honored final resting place was first used during the Civil War, when the land belonged to Confederate general **Robert E. Lee**. Some 350,000 US soldiers and others – from presidents to Supreme Court justices – now lie here. An eternal flame marks the grave of **President John F. Kennedy**, who lies next to his wife, Jacqueline Kennedy Onassis, and a short distance from his brother, Robert (the only grave marked with a simple white cross). At the **Tomb of the Unknowns**, visitors can watch a solemn Changing of the Guard ceremony every thirty minutes (hourly Oct–March). The cemetery's prominent Neoclassical **Arlington House** (same hours; free) is Lee's modest mansion which his family was forced to sell after the war, as the proximity of the nation's war dead created a less than ideal setting for the country home.

Unless you have strong legs and lots of time, the best way to see the vast cemetery is by Tourmobile (see p.371), which leaves from the visitor center at the entrance. You can also walk here from the Lincoln Memorial, across the Arlington Bridge, or take the Blue Line Metro. Finally, beyond the gates of the cemetery are notable **memorials** to the **Marine Corps**, on Arlington Boulevard at Meade Street (daily 24hr; Ⓦwww.nps.gov/gwmp/usmc.htm), based around the Iwo Jima Statue, commemorating the bloody World War II battle where 6800 lives were lost; and to the **Air Force**, on Columbia Pike off Washington Boulevard (daily: April-Sept 8am-11pm; Oct-March 8am-9pm; Ⓦwww.airforcememorial.org.), immediately recognizable by its three giant steel arcs, which twist 270ft out into the sky.

Eating

Restaurants may come and go more quickly in Washington DC than anywhere else in the US. Certain neighborhoods – Connecticut Avenue around Dupont Circle, 18th Street and Columbia Road in Adams–Morgan, M Street in Georgetown, and downtown's Seventh Street and Chinatown – always seem to hold a satisfying range of dining options. A few citywide chains like **Teaism** and **Firehook** offer good coffee and quick snacks; otherwise, the cafés in the main museums are good for downtown lunch breaks. Likewise, you'll find convenient food courts in Union Station and at the Old Post Office.

Downtown

Acadiana 901 New York Ave NW ⓣ202/408-8848. Chic Cajun spot near the convention center that serves up mid-priced catfish, shrimp poboys, and crawfish pies for lunch, then saves the big-ticket veal medallions, roasted duck, and grilled swordfish for dinner.

The Breadline 1751 Pennsylvania Ave NW ⓣ202/822-8900. DC's best sandwiches, made with DC's best bread. This superb open bakery also turns out pizza, empanadas, flatbreads, salads, and smoothies, using organic ingredients whenever possible.

Café Asia 1720 I St NW ⓣ202/659-2696. Breezy Pan-Asian restaurant that's good for sushi and sashimi, or try the grilled chicken soup, satay, or Thai noodles.

Café Atlantico 405 8th St NW ⓣ202/393-0812. Upscale nuevo Latino treat with spicy spins on traditional cuisine, but really best for its Minibar, a six-seat counter famed for its "molecular gastronomy" – the likes of beet "tumbleweeds," olive oil bon bons, and lobster injections (into the mouth). Reserve a month in advance and expect to pay $120 a head.

Captain White's Seafood City 1100 Maine Ave SW ⓣ202/484-2722. South of downtown at the Fish Wharf, a fine vendor hawking catfish, oysters, crab, and other delicious choices, which you can get fresh to go or fried up in a tasty platter or sandwich.

District Chophouse & Brewery 509 7th St NW ⓣ202/347-3434. This somewhat pricey joint delivers a hearty, meat-and-potatoes grillhouse menu (along with some solid crab cakes), and good house beers on tap.

Grillfish 1200 New Hampshire Ave NW ⓣ202/331-7310. Industrial-chic eatery offering casual dining and well-cooked fish and seafood; the daily catch options might include sea bass, tuna, snapper, trout, mahi-mahi, shark, or calamari.

Jaleo 480 7th St NW ⓣ202/628-7949. Renowned, upscale tapas bar-restaurant with flamenco dancing to accompany its fine seafood and plentiful sangria, plus supreme paella. Limited reservation policy makes for long waits during peak hours.

Old Ebbitt Grill 675 15th St NW ⓣ202/347-4801. A plush re-creation of a nineteenth-century tavern, with mahogany bar (serving microbrews), gas chandeliers, leather booths, and gilt mirrors. Swanky clientele feasts on everything from burgers to oysters.

Proof 775 G St NW ⓣ202/737-7663. A delicious, upscale, grab bag of flavors and styles, with a fine wine selection to boot. Try the charcuterie plates to start, then move on to a huge range of cheeses, sashimi, ceviche, and King salmon or sablefish.

Sky Terrace Hotel Washington, 515 15th St NW ⓣ202/638-5900. A romantic spot to enjoy a sweeping view of the city, along with seafood or sandwiches. The food is nothing special, but it's a bargain considering the outdoor perch above the White House. May–Oct only.

Ten Penh 1001 Pennsylvania Ave NW ⓣ202/393-4500. High-profile Asian-fusion restaurant serving up expensive but delicious dishes like Kobe beef tartar, citrus-glazed salmon, and five-spice, tea-rubbed beef tenderloin.

Dupont Circle

Bistro du Coin 1738 Connecticut Ave NW ⓣ202/234-6969. Classic bistro with a superb bar, boisterous atmosphere, and genuine, affordable French food – goat cheese salad, steamed mussels, pâté and rabbit stew, among other offerings.

Café Citron 1343 Connecticut Ave NW ⓣ202/530-8844. Trendy restaurant serving tasty Caribbean-influenced Latin food – try the ceviche or fill up on one of their popular fajitas. The scene becomes a salsa- and samba-fueled meat market later at night.

City Lights of China 1731 Connecticut Ave NW ⓣ202/265-6688. Enjoyable Chinese restaurant, with spicy Szechuan and Hunan specialties and a strong emphasis on seafood – try the Hunan shrimp. Also good for veggie fare like steamed dumplings and garlic eggplant.

Java House 1645 Q St NW ⓣ202/387-6622. A local favorite arguably serving the neighborhood's best coffee. A good spot to read a book, have an afternoon chat, or fire up the laptop for wi-fi access. Desserts, bagels, salads, and sandwiches are on offer, too.

Luna Grill & Diner 1301 Connecticut Ave NW ⓣ202/835-2280. Inexpensive diner with bright decor and wholesome blue-plate specials, "green plate" (vegetarian) dishes, and organic coffees and teas. The crab cake sandwich, meatball sub, and sirloin and veggie burgers are worth a taste.

The Newsroom 1803 Connecticut Ave NW ⓣ202/332-1489. Coffee, snacks, and pastries are served at this newsstand, which carries reasonable selections of hipster magazines, British and French imports, and hard-to-find newspapers.

Nora's 2132 Florida Ave NW ⓣ202/462-5143. Top-notch place to eat, with prices to match. The all-organic fare includes wild mushroom risotto, Amish pork roast, braised short ribs, and a French brie tart.

Pizzeria Paradiso 2029 P St NW ⓣ202/223-1245. Supreme pizzeria, with famously tasty pies such as the enormous Siciliana, potato-and-pesto

Genovese, and ultra-peppery, spicy Atomica. Expect to wait in line.

Skewers 1633 P St NW ☎202/387-7400. Mouth-watering Middle Eastern that's tops for kebabs – plus eggplant, seafood, and oddball items like ravioli and angel-hair pancakes – not to mention belly dancing.

Sushi Taro 1503 17th St NW ☎202/462-8999. Plenty of fine sushi, sashimi, tempura, and teriyaki, with moderate to expensive prices. If raw fish isn't your thing, choose from the selection of steak and pork cutlets.

Zorba's Café 1612 20th St NW ☎202/387-8555. Filling and cheap Greek combo platters, kebabs, pizzas, and pitta-bread sandwiches, as well as daily specials and traditional dishes like bean casserole and spinach pie.

Adams Morgan and Shaw

Ben's Chili Bowl 1213 U St NW, Shaw ☎202/667-0909. Worth the trip for the legendary chili dogs, milk shakes, and cheese fries.

Bukom Café 2442 18th St NW, Adams Morgan ☎202/265-4600. Serves delicious West African dishes like oxtail or okra soup, *egusi*, a broth of goat meat with ground melon seeds and spinach, and chicken *yassa*, baked with onions and spices, for around $10.

Cashion's Eat Place 1819 Columbia Rd NW, Adams Morgan ☎202/797-1819. New Southern cuisine, in which old-time casseroles, tarts, corn cakes, grits, sweet potatoes, and fruit and nut pies are transformed into taste-bud-altering delights – at a rather high price.

The Diner 2453 18th St NW, Adams Morgan ☎202/232-8800. More a stylish café than a grungy dive, good and greasy classics adorn the egg-, pancake-, and sandwich-rich menu nonetheless. 24hr.

Grill from Ipanema 1858 Columbia Rd NW, Adams Morgan ☎202/986-0757. Brazilian staples highlighted by the *feijoada* (meat stew), shrimp dishes, and scrumptious weekend brunch. Try the baked clams and watch your caipirinha (rum cocktail) intake.

Henry's Soul Cafe 1704 U St NW, Shaw ☎202/265-3336. One of the District's hotspots for authentic soul food. The fried chicken wings, fillet of trout, meatloaf, beef liver, and chitterlings give a savory taste of the Deep South for $10.

Lauriol Plaza 1835 18th St NW, Adams Morgan ☎202/387-0035. Serves scrumptious, affordable Tex-Mex grilled meats, shrimp, and fajitas, plus Cuban steak and roasted chicken. But the place does get packed with tourists and partiers, and the service can be spotty.

Meze 2437 18th St NW, Adams Morgan ☎202/797-0017. A wide array of cheap and delicious Turkish *meze* (Middle Eastern tapas) is served in a fashionable restaurant-lounge setting. A sausage-and-pastrami omelet and Istanbul burger are among the highlights.

Mixtec 1792 Columbia Rd NW, Adams Morgan ☎202/332-1011. Drab setting, but solid, low-priced Mexican food including some very fine tacos, plus roasted chicken and mussels steamed with chilis, and dozens of tequila varieties on offer.

Tryst 2459 18th St NW, Adams Morgan ☎202/232-5500. Very popular hangout where you can enjoy decent pastries, sandwiches, and gourmet drinks, but also slurp down wine, beer, and even morning cocktails. Also has internet access.

Georgetown

Bangkok Bistro 3251 Prospect St NW ☎202/337-2424. In a stylish, often crowded, dining room, this mid-priced gem has old favorites (tom yum, pad thai, shrimp cakes, and satay) offered alongside coconut shrimp, duck noodles, spicy beef curries and chili prawns.

Bistro Francais 3128 M St NW ☎202/338-3830. Renowned for its (affordable) French cooking, from simple steak frites, baked mussels, and beef tenderloin to lamb steak and liver mousse; open until 3am or 4am weekends.

Booeymonger 3265 Prospect St NW ☎202/333-4810. Crowded deli-coffee shop, excellent for its inventive sandwiches like the Gatsby Arrow (roast beef and brie) and the Patty Hearst (turkey and bacon with Russian dressing).

Citronelle In the *Latham Hotel*, 3000 M St ☎202/625-2150. Huge player on the DC dining scene, serving up French-inspired cuisine and set-price food and wine pairings starting at $235. Reserve in advance, dress chic, and bring plenty of attitude.

Dean & DeLuca 3276 M St NW ☎202/342-2500. Superior self-service café in one of M Street's most handsome and historic red-brick buildings. Good for croissants, cappuccinos, designer salads, pastas, and sandwiches.

Hook 3241 M St NW ☎202/625-4488. Hard to do better for the catch of the day than this centrally located seafood favorite, which serves up a mean blackfin tuna, sunburst trout, and King salmon at upper-end prices..

Martin's Tavern 1264 Wisconsin Ave NW ☎202/333-7370. Old-fashioned, clubby diner featuring succulent steaks and chops, great burgers, linguine with clam sauce, and oyster platters.

Paolo's 1303 Wisconsin Ave NW ☎202/333-7353. Mid-level Italian dining with a few hotly contested tables open to the sidewalk. Gourmet pizzas and even better pastas are specialties.

Red Ginger 1564 Wisconsin Ave NW ⓣ202/965-7009. Lamb shank, "mojo" curry chicken, and shrimp and grits are just some of the dishes at this hybrid Caribbean-African restaurant, with spicy flavors.

Rocklands 2418 Wisconsin Ave NW ⓣ202/333-2558. A bit north of the main action, but still worth the trek to enjoy some of DC's best pork sandwiches, ribs, beans, sausage, and other staples of the barbecue scene, all for cheap prices.

Upper Northwest

Ardeo 3311 Connecticut Ave NW ⓣ202/244-6750. Ultra-trendy but not too expensive spot where you can get your fill of a well-prepared selection of lamb loin, scallops and mussels, pan-roasted shrimp with sweetbreads, and other mid-Atlantic favorites.

Indique 3512 Connecticut Ave NW ⓣ202/244-6600. Recipes from all over India come together with a modern twist at this stylish and affordable restaurant. Don't miss the tasty shrimp curry or tikka makhani, or the piquant lamb vindaloo.

Lebanese Taverna 2641 Connecticut Ave NW ⓣ202/265-8681. Delicious Middle Eastern joint with dark decor. Sample something from the assortment of kebabs and grilled-meat platters, or go straight for the leg of lamb. Five other area locations.

Nam Viet 3419 Connecticut Ave NW ⓣ202/237-1015. No-frills Vietnamese eatery where you can enjoy good soups, caramel pork, barbecued shrimp, and grilled chicken and fish.

Vace 3315 Connecticut Ave NW ⓣ202/363-1999. Grab a slice of the excellent designer or traditional pizzas – some of DC's best – and tasty sub sandwiches, focaccia, or pasta, or pack a picnic from the selection of sausages, salads, and olives, then head to the zoo.

Nightlife

Peak times for **drinking** in DC tend to be during rush hour, but for solid late-night imbibing, the well-worn haunts of collegiate **Georgetown**, yuppified **Dupont Circle**, and boisterous **Adams Morgan** will do nicely – and in the suit-and-tie spots on **Capitol Hill**, you can even spot a politician or two. For clubs, expect to pay a cover of $5 to $25 (highest on weekends); ticket prices for most gigs run the same amount, unless you're seeing a major name. Check the free weekly **CityPaper** (ⓦwww.washingtoncitypaper.com) for up-to-date **listings** of music, theater, and other events in the area, in addition to good alternative features and reporting. **Gay** and **lesbian** life is at its most outgoing in Dupont Circle.

Bars

Aroma 3417 Connecticut Ave NW ⓣ202/244-7995. With a smart, mildly smug atmosphere, Cleveland Park's stylish cigar-and-martini bar has a sizeable touch of chic, though it still feels like a neighborhood watering hole despite the gloss.

Bedrock Billiards 1841 Columbia Rd NW ⓣ202/667-7665. A comfortable, lively subterranean setting, solid bartenders, and loyal clientele set this funky pool hall apart from Adams Morgan's more frenzied, dance-oriented spots.

Birreria Paradiso 2029 P St NW ⓣ202/223-1245. Downstairs at a branch of Dupont Circle's famed *Pizzeria Paradiso* (see p.390) is this supreme touchstone for beer lovers, who come to sample some eighty bottled beers and various US and European brews, among them some excellent Belgian ales, lambics, stouts and porters.

Brickskeller 1523 22nd St NW, Dupont Circle ⓣ202/293-1885. Renowned brick-lined basement saloon serving "the world's largest selection of beer": as many as a thousand different types, including dozens from US microbreweries – though only a fraction are typically available. Also has an inexpensive inn upstairs (see p.374).

Bullfeathers 410 First St SE ⓣ202/543-5005. Pol watchers just may catch a sighting at this old-time Hill favorite, a dark and clubby spot with affordable beer that was named for one of Teddy Roosevelt's favorite euphemisms during his White House years.

Capitol City Brewing Co 2 Massachusetts Ave NE ⓣ202/842-2337. Prime microbrewing turf near Union Station, highlighted by Amber Waves Ale, German-styled Capitol Kolsch, and Prohibition Porter.

Capitol Lounge 229 Pennsylvania Ave SE Ⓣ202/547-2098. Signature brick-walled saloon on the Hill for drinking and partying, with pool tables, inexpensive beer, three bars on two levels, and scads of Congressional staffers looking to get wasted.

D.A.'s RFD Washington 810 7th St NW Ⓣ202/289-2030. The leader in Downtown DC microbreweries, with three hundred bottled beers and forty locally crafted and international brews on tap. Centrally located near the Verizon Center, so watch for heavy post-game crowds.

The Dubliner 520 N Capitol St NW, in the Phoenix Park Hotel Ⓣ202/737-3773. A wooden-vaulted, good-time Irish pub with draft Guinness, boisterous conversation, and live Irish music catering to the more refined Hill set. The patio is a solid summer hangout.

Fox and Hounds 1537 17th St NW, Dupont Circle Ⓣ202/232-6307. Smack in the middle of the 17th Street scene, this easy-going bar draws a diverse crowd, all here to enjoy the stiff and cheap rail drinks and the solid jukebox.

Garrett's 3003 M St NW Ⓣ202/333-1033. Amid its brick-and-wood interior, *Garrett's* features a pumping jukebox that keeps the young crowd in a party mood, and nightly drink specials, along with a few microbrews.

Hawk 'n Dove 329 Pennsylvania Ave SE Ⓣ202/543-3553. Iconic DC pub (a bit tatty at the edges now) decorated with bottles and bric-a-brac. Attracts Hill interns for its cheap food, half-price food, and football.

Nanny O'Brien's 3319 Connecticut Ave NW Ⓣ202/686-9189. An authentic Irish pub in Upper Northwest, with live music from (or in the style of) the Emerald Isle, several nights a week.

Clubs and live music venues

The Black Cat 1811 14th St NW, Shaw Ⓣ202/667-7960. Part-owned by Foo Fighter Dave Grohl, this indie institution provides a showcase for up-and-coming rock, punk, and garage bands and veteran alternative acts alike. Connected to the *Red Room Bar*.

Blues Alley 1073 Wisconsin Ave NW (rear) Ⓣ202/337-4141. Small, celebrated Georgetown jazz bar, in business for over forty years, that attracts top names. Shows usually at 8pm and 10pm, plus midnight some weekends; cover can run up to $45. Book in advance.

Bohemian Caverns 2003 11th St NW, Shaw district Ⓣ202/299-0800. Legendary DC jazz supper club, set in a basement grotto below the stylish ground-level restaurant. Cover runs to $15 or more, with a limited number of reserved tickets for bigger acts.

Chief Ike's Mambo Room 1725 Columbia Rd NW, Adams Morgan Ⓣ202/332-2211. Ramshackle mural-clad bar with live bands playing rock, reggae, and R & B, or DJs hosting theme nights. An unpretentious, fun spot to dance.

Eighteenth Street Lounge 1212 18th St, Dupont Circle Ⓣ202/466-3922. Ultra-stylish spot housed in Teddy Roosevelt's former mansion. While the attitude can be a bit thick at times, the beats – mostly techno, house, and dub – are a big draw, along with superstar DJs. Look for the unmarked door and dress smart.

Habana Village 1834 Columbia Rd NW Ⓣ202/462-6310. Intoxicating Latin dance joint (tango and salsa lessons are available) infused with an eclectic spirit. A good downstairs bar serves a fine mojito.

HR-57 1610 14th St NW, Logan Circle Ⓣ202/667-3700. Small but authentic club where jazz in various manifestations – classic, hard bop, free, and cool – is performed by ardent professionals as well as newcomers on their way up.

IOTA 2832 Wilson Blvd, Arlington, VA Ⓣ703/522-8340. One of the area's better choices for nightclubbing, this warehouse-style music joint has nightly performances by local and national indie, folk, and blues bands. Has a great bar, and attached restaurant, too.

Madam's Organ 2461 18th St NW Ⓣ202/667-5370. Self-consciously divey spot that has a fine rep for showcasing a variety of driving live blues, grinding, raw R & B, and the odd bluegrass band, plus some solidly rib-sticking soul food and generous cocktails.

9:30 Club 815 V St NW, Shaw Ⓣ202/265-0930. Top musicians love to play at this spacious yet intimate club, deservedly famous as DC's best venue for live acts, from indie rock and pop to reggae and rap.

Rumba Café 2443 18th St NW, Adams Morgan Ⓣ202/588-5501. This Latin oasis, a sliver of a café-bar, its walls decked out with paintings and photographs, is a good bet for a night of sipping caipirinhas and grooving to live Brazilian bossa nova and Afro-Cuban rhythms.

Performing arts

The **performing-arts** heavyweight in town, the **Kennedy Center**, 2700 F St NW (Ⓣ202/467-4600, Ⓦwww.kennedy-center.org), next to the Watergate complex, hosts most of the capital's highbrow cultural events, including National Symphony Orchestra and Washington National Opera performances. Otherwise, some of the more notable arts venues are noted below.

Arena Stage Ⓣ202/488-3300, Ⓦwww.arenastage.org. Highly regarded, often pioneering site that puts on contemporary theater and performance pieces, though check ahead since the current facility is being renovated and performances take place in Arlington, Virginia.

Ford's Theatre 511 Tenth St NW, Downtown Ⓣ202/347-4833, Ⓦwww.fordstheatre.org. Historic venue with a family-friendly program of mainstream musicals and dramas, frequently historical in nature,

Shakespeare Theatre 450 Seventh St NW, Downtown Ⓣ202/547-1122, Ⓦwww.shakespearedc.org. Celebrated troupe stages ten productions a year, plus free summer performances in Rock Creek Park.

National Theatre 1321 Pennsylvania Ave NW, Downtown Ⓣ202/628-6161, Ⓦwww.nationaltheatre.org. Offers big-name touring musicals and other crowd-pleasers.

Woolly Mammoth Theatre 641 D St NW, Downtown Ⓣ202/289-2443, Ⓦwww.woollymammoth.net. Experimental theatre showcases budget- and mid-priced contemporary and off-the-wall plays.

Studio Theatre 1501 14th St NW, Logan Circle Ⓣ202/332-3300, Ⓦwww.studiotheatre.org. Good venue that's a staple of DC's alternative theater scene.

Wolf Trap Farm Park outside the Beltway between Rte-7 and Rte-267, at 1624 Trap Rd, Vienna, Virginia Ⓣ703/255-1868, Ⓦwww.wolftrap.org. Presents American music in all its native forms, like bluegrass, jazz, ragtime, Cajun, zydeco, etc., at the outdoor Filene Center or the indoor Barns. There's a Metro shuttle bus service from West Falls Church station for most performances (Ⓣ202/637-7000 or Ⓦwww.wmata.com for details).

Spectator sports

Tickets to Washington Redskins **football** games at FedEx Field in Landover, Maryland (Ⓣ301/276-6050, Ⓦwww.redskins.com), are sold on a season-ticket basis only and are often impossible to get unless you have a connection. Somewhat easier to obtain are tickets to DC's new Washington Nationals **baseball** team, which plays at the splashy Nationals Park on the Anacostia waterfront (Ⓣ202/675-NATS, Ⓦnationals.mlb.com; tickets $10-90). East of Capitol Hill, at RFK Stadium, is the DC United **soccer** squad (Ⓣ202/587-5000, Ⓦwww.dcunited.com; tickets $20–50), which plays in the pro MLS league. The huge downtown Verizon Center (Ⓦwww.verizoncenter.com) hosts home games of the men's pro **basketball** Washington Wizards (Ⓣ202/661-5050, Ⓦwww.nba.com/wizards; tickets $10–105) and women's Mystics (tickets $10-60; Ⓣ202/397-SEAT, Ⓦwww.wnba.com/mystics), as well as the pro **hockey** Capitals (Ⓣ202/397-SEAT, Ⓦwww.washingtoncapitals.com; tickets $10–95).

Virginia

VIRGINIA is the oldest American colony and has arguably had the most direct influence on the early development of the United States. Its recorded history famously began at **Jamestown**, just off the Chesapeake Bay, with the establishment in 1607 of the first successful British colony in North America. Though the first colonists hoped to find gold, it was **tobacco** that made their fortunes. To grow and harvest tobacco required both an immense amount of land and labor – so Native Americans were driven off their land and **slaves** were imported from Africa. Many of them wealthy planters, Virginians had an enormous impact on the foundation of the United States: George Mason, Thomas Jefferson, and James Madison wrote the Declaration of Independence and the Constitution, and four of the first five US presidents were from Virginia (excepting John Adams). Later, as the confrontation between North and South over slavery and related issues grew more divisive, Virginia was caught in the middle, but joined the Confederacy when the **Civil War** broke out, providing the Confederate capital, Richmond, and its military leader, Robert E. Lee. Four long years later, Virginia was ravaged, its towns and cities wrecked, its farmlands ruined, and most of its youth dead.

Richmond itself was largely destroyed in the war; today it's a small city with some good museums, the best ones historical in nature. The bulk of the colonial sites are concentrated just east, in what is known as the **Historic Triangle**, where **Jamestown**, the original colony, **Williamsburg**, the restored colonial capital, and **Yorktown**, site of the final battle of the Revolutionary War, lie within half an hour's drive of each other on the Colonial Parkway. Another historic center, **Charlottesville** – famously home to Thomas Jefferson's Monticello – sits at the foot of the gorgeous **Blue Ridge Mountains**, an hour west of Richmond. It's also within easy reach of the natural splendor of **Shenandoah National Park** and the little towns of the western valleys. **Northern Virginia**, often visited as a day-trip from Washington DC, features several posh suburbs, a number of restored historic homes, the antique architecture of **Alexandria**, and **Manassas**, the scene of two important Civil War battles.

Getting around Virginia

Virginia is an easy place to explore. Seven north–south **Amtrak** routes cross the central and eastern side of the state – one of them an "Auto Train" connecting Lorton, Virginia, with Sanford, Florida, which allows you to bring a car along. In addition, the daily Cardinal line runs east from Washington DC to Charlottesville and on to Chicago. Greyhound **buses** reach dozens of smaller towns. **Drivers** heading south can take the stunning Blue Ridge Parkway along the Appalachians. If you've got the time, there is ample opportunity for **cycling**, whether on quiet country roads or up in the mountains, and **hiking** or **walking** are also compelling options.

Northern Virginia

Despite its longstanding conservative pedigree, **Northern Virginia** has in recent years become one large suburban enclave with a decidedly liberal bent, due to the number of former residents of Washington DC taking residence there, including a high proportion of US senators. **Alexandria**, nestled on the Potomac just beyond the limits of the nation's capital (but not beyond its Metro system), seems at least two centuries removed from the modern political whirl. Further afield, this heartland of the landed gentry – often called "Hunt Country" for the love of horses and fancy-dress blood sports – holds well-preserved estates, cottages, churches, barns, and taverns tucked away along the quiet back roads. It's all very popular with tourists, nowhere more so than **Mount Vernon**, the longtime home of George Washington, while **Manassas** to the west was the site of the bloody battles of Bull Run.

Alexandria

Extending a good half-mile west of the Potomac, the **Old Town** of **ALEXANDRIA** is a must, especially for those who are staying in Washington DC but don't have time to venture very far into Virginia. Originally an important colonial trading post and a busy port named after the pioneer John Alexander, the town was part of the District of Columbia in 1801, but Virginia demanded it and the surrounding land back in 1847.

In earlier days, George Washington maintained close ties with Alexandria, owning property here and attending gatherings at the famous **Gadsby's Tavern**, 134 N Royal St (tours: April–Oct Tues–Sat 10am–5pm, Sun & Mon 1–5pm; Nov–March Wed–Sat 11am–4pm, Sun 1–4pm; Ⓣ703/838-4242, Ⓦwww.gadsbystavern.org; $4), which occupies two stately Georgian buildings: the **City Hotel** from 1792 and the tavern itself from 1785. Downstairs, there's a working restaurant, complete with colonial food and costumed staff. Among other restored buildings open to the public are the **Carlyle House**, 121 N Fairfax St (tours Tues–Sat 10am–4pm, Sun noon–4:30pm; Ⓣ703/549-2997, Ⓦwww.carlylehouse.org; $4), a 1752 sandstone manor that was home to five royal governors, and the **Lee-Fendall House**, 614 Oronoco

▲ King Street, Alexandria

St (Tues & Thurs–Sat 10am–4pm, Wed & Sun 1–4pm; ⓣ703/548-1789, ⓦwww.leefendallhouse.org; $4), a splendid clapboard mansion built in 1785 by Phillip Fendall, a cousin of Robert E. Lee's father. South of King Street, the **Lyceum**, 201 S Washington St (Mon–Sat 10am–5pm, Sun 1–5pm; ⓣ703/838-4994, ⓦwww.alexandriahistory.org), houses the town's history museum in a magisterial, 1839 Greek Revival building designed to be a centerpiece for the town's cultural affairs.

The Georgian **Christ Church**, 118 N Washington St (Mon–Sat 9am–4pm, Sun 2–4pm; ⓦwww.historicchristchurch.org), was built in 1773 and often counted George Washington among its worshippers. Patent medicines for the general were concocted behind the tiny yellow windows of the **Stabler-Leadbeater Apothecary Shop**, 105 S Fairfax St (April–Oct Tues–Sat 10am–5pm, Sun & Mon 1–5pm; Nov–March Wed–Sat 11am–4pm, Sun 1–4pm; ⓣ703/838-3852, ⓦwww.apothecarymuseum.org; $4), which was founded in 1792 and remained in business until the 1930s. It still displays herbs, potions, and medical paraphernalia – some eight thousand items in all.

Down on the waterfront, a former munitions factory houses the **Torpedo Factory Art Center**, 105 N Union St (daily 10am–5pm; ⓣ703/838-4565, ⓦwww.torpedofactory.org; free), where you can watch artists at work in more than two hundred studios and browse numerous galleries. In the same building, the **Alexandria Archaeology Museum** (Tues–Fri 10am–3pm, Sat 10am–5pm, Sun 1–5pm; ⓣ703/838-4399, ⓦwww.alexandriaarchaeology.org; free) displays aspects of 250 years of the town's history and prehistory.

Next to the Amtrak and King Street subway station stands the 333-foot obelisk of the **George Washington National Masonic Memorial**, 101 Callahan Drive (daily 9am–5pm; ⓣ703/683-2007, ⓦwww.gwmemorial.org; free), which is visible for miles around; inside, there's a 17-foot bronze **statue** of the founding father, sundry Masonic memorabilia, and dioramas depicting events from his life.

Practicalities

The **Metro** station for Old Town Alexandria is King Street (25min from downtown DC; yellow and blue lines), a mile or so from most of the sights; alternatively, you can pick up the local **DASH** bus (ⓣ703/370-3274, ⓦwww.dashbus.com; $1), which runs down King Street, and get off at Fairfax Street; or, if you prefer, you can make the twenty-minute walk from the station instead. The friendly **visitor center** is located in the **Ramsay House**, the town's oldest, at 221 King St (daily 9am–5pm; ⓣ703/838-5005, ⓦwww.funside.com), where you can get the usual tourist information as well as details on walking tours.

Good places to **stay** include **Best Western Old Colony Inn**, 1101 N Washington St (ⓣ703/739-2222, ⓦwww.bestwestern.com; ❼), with free breakfast and high-speed internet access; **Morrison House**, 116 S Alfred St (ⓣ703/838-8000, ⓦwww.morrisonhouse.com; ❾), a faux Federal-era townhouse (built in 1985) with modern comforts like high-speed internet and designer linens; and **Hotel Monaco**, 480 King St (ⓣ703/549-6080, ⓦwww.monaco-alexandria.com; ❾), boasting designer decor, free wi-fi, wine tastings, and chic rooms and suites that variously offer jetted tubs, flat-screen TVs, and wet bars.

There's a great range of **places to eat**. Try the elite **Restaurant Eve**, 110 S Pitt St (ⓣ703/706-0450), a nouveau American bistro offering expensive five- and nine-course meals drawn from a rotating menu of seafood, game, and beef ($95 or $125); the **Fish Market**, 105 King St (ⓣ703/836-5676), a brick building with a terrace just one block from the water, serving oysters and chowder at the bar and fried-fish platters, pastas, and fish entrees; and **The Majestic**, 911 King St (ⓣ703/837-9117), a fine upscale diner, with seafood stew, rib chops, meatloaf, and liver among the tastier offerings.

Mount Vernon

Set on a bluff overlooking the Potomac River, eight miles south of Alexandria, at 3200 George Washington Memorial Parkway, **Mount Vernon** (daily: April–Aug 8am–5pm; March, Sept, & Oct 9am–5pm; Nov–Feb 9am–4pm; Ⓣ703/780-2000, Ⓦwww.mountvernon.org; $13) is the country estate built by **George Washington**. With five hundred acres of landscaped and planted grounds, it has been restored to the year 1799, the last year of the general's life. Fifteen miles from downtown DC, it's close enough to be reached as a day-trip on the city's Tourmobile (see p.371), or by the Fairfax Connector bus #101 from the Huntington Metro station (hourly; Ⓦwww.fairfaxcounty.gov/connector; $1).

In the house itself, the furnishings and decoration reflect Washington's preference for plain living. Among the items on display include a reading chair with a built-in fan and a key to the destroyed Bastille, presented by Thomas Paine on behalf of Lafayette. The four-poster bed upon which he died stands in an upstairs bedroom. Outside is a renovated **slave quarters**, built to house the ninety slaves who lived and worked on the grounds alone. Washington and his wife, Martha, are buried in a simple tomb on the south side of the house. For the full background on the site, the fancy modern **Reynolds Museum** has interactive displays, models of Washington, and assorted short films. It also traces Washington's ancestry and displays porcelain from the house, medals, weapons, silver, and a series of striking miniatures.

Three miles away stands the restored **grist mill**, Route 235 S (April-Oct daily 10am-5pm; $4, or $2 extra with Mount Vernon admission), that Washington built as a water-powered testament to the future of American industry. Today colonial re-enactors go about the laborious work of crushing grain into flour and cornmeal. The **distillery**, a more recent reconstruction on the site, features copper stills, a boiler, and mash tubs, and a short movie about Washington's role in the whiskey-making process.

Gunston Hall

Gunston Hall, the 1755 Georgian brick home of Washington's contemporary, **George Mason**, is a twenty-minute drive south of Washington DC near highways 1 and 95 (daily 9.30am–5pm; Ⓣ703/550-9220, Ⓦwww.gunstonhall.org; $8). Mason, in writing the Virginia Declaration of Rights, inspired Thomas Jefferson when he later wrote the Declaration of Independence. Though one of the framers of the US Constitution, Mason subsequently refused to support it because it neither included a Bill of Rights nor abolished slavery – ironic, considering he himself was a slaveholder. One of the most impressive works of architecture in Virginia, his home's masterful interiors, particularly in the drawing room, feature exquisite carved ornamentation, and the house fronts a large formal garden, beyond which lie extensive grounds surrounded by a riverfront state park and wildlife refuge.

Manassas National Battlefield Park

Manassas National Battlefield Park extends over grassy hills at the western fringes of the Washington DC suburbs, just off I-66. The first major land battle of the Civil War – known in the North as the **Battle of Bull Run** – was fought here on the morning of July 21, 1861. Expecting an easy victory, some 25,000 Union troops attacked a Confederate detachment that controlled a vital railroad link to the Shenandoah Valley, and spectators came to see what they imagined would be rousing entertainment. But the rebels proved powerful opponents, and their strength in battle earned their commander, Thomas Jackson, the famous nickname "Stonewall." He and General Lee also masterminded a second, even more demoralizing Union loss here in late August 1862.

Displays in the small **visitor center** at the entrance, at 6511 Sudley Rd (June–Aug Mon–Fri 8.30am–5pm, Sat & Sun 8.30am–6pm; Sept–May daily 8.30am–5pm; Ⓣ703/361-1339, Ⓦwww.nps.gov/mana; $3 park admission) describe how the battles took shape, and detail other aspects of the war.

Richmond and the tidewater

At the very heart of Virginia, **Richmond** and the **Chesapeake Bay tidewater** make up a fairly compact area that holds some of the country's most important surviving colonial- and Civil War-era sites. The greatest interest is to be found in the fascinating **Historic Triangle**, east of Richmond, and in **Fredericksburg**, to the north, around which several crucial battles were waged.

Fredericksburg

Only a mile off the I-95 highway, halfway to Richmond from Washington DC, **FREDERICKSBURG** is one of Virginia's prettiest historic towns, where elegant downtown streets are backed by residential avenues lined with white picket fences. In colonial days, this was an important inland port, in which tobacco and other plantation commodities were loaded onto boats that sailed down the Rappahannock River. Dozens of stately early-American buildings along the waterfront now hold antique stores and boutiques.

In the 1816 town hall, the **Fredericksburg Area Museum**, 907 Princess Anne St (Mon–Sat 10am–5pm, Sun 1–4pm; Ⓣ540/371-3037, Ⓦwww.famcc.org; $7), has a range of displays tracing local history, from Native American settlements to the Civil Rights era. The **Rising Sun Tavern**, 1304 Caroline St, was built as a home in 1760 by George Washington's brother, Charles. As an inn, it became a key meeting place for patriots and a hotbed of sedition. It is now a small **museum** (March–Nov Mon–Sat 9am–5pm, Sun 11am–5pm; Dec–Feb Mon–Sat 10am–4pm, Sun noon–4pm; Ⓣ540-371-1494; $5), where costumed guides take visitors around a collection of pub games and antique pewter. Guides are also on hand to explain eighteenth-century medicine at **Hugh Mercer's Apothecary Shop**, 1020 Caroline St (same hours as above; $5), which often involved treating patients with the likes of leeches and crab claws. If you're more interested in George Washington, you can venture out to his family's **Ferry Farm**, 268 Kings Hwy (daily 10am–5pm, except Jan & Feb Sat & Sun only; Ⓣ540/370-0732, Ⓦwww.kenmore.org; $5), where he grew up and which still maintains a bucolic setting and gardens appropriate for the era

Fredericksburg's strategic location made it vital during the **Civil War**, and the land around the town was heavily contested. More than 100,000 men lost their lives in the major battles of Fredericksburg, Chancellorsville, Spotsylvania, and countless bloody skirmishes. The **visitor center**, 702 Caroline St (daily: summer 9am–7pm; rest of year 9am–5pm; Ⓣ540/373-1776, Ⓦwww.fredericksburgva.com), has informative exhibits and can lead you out to **Fredericksburg and Spotsylvania National Battlefield Park** (dawn–dusk; Ⓦwww.nps.gov/frsp; free), south of town. Contact the center or the above website for information on the other major battlefields, **Wilderness** and **Chancellorsville**, both west of town, as well as the various manors and shrines in the area.

Practicalities

The **Amtrak** station is at 200 Lafayette Blvd and the **Greyhound** station at 1400 Jefferson Davis Hwy. Fredericksburg has many good, old-fashioned **B&Bs**, including the 1812 **Kenmore Inn**, 1200 Princess Anne St (Ⓣ540/371-7622, Ⓦwww.kenmoreinn.com; ⑤), which has stylish rooms with internet access and a cozy pub in the basement, occasionally featuring live music. The **Richard Johnston Inn**, 711 Caroline St (Ⓣ540/899-7606 or 877-557-0770, Ⓦwww.therichardjohnstoninn.com), is an elegant, eighteenth-century B&B with plush rooms and a broad range of prices, from ④–⑧. One worthwhile motel to try is the **Inn at the Olde Silk Mill**, 1707 Princess Anne St (Ⓣ540/371-5666, Ⓦwww.fci1.com; ④), known for its rooms stocked with antiques. For close access to the battlefields, there's **On Keegan Pond**, 11315 Gordon Rd (Ⓣ540/785-4662; ④), in a pleasant rural setting, also with antique-laden rooms.

The town has several good places to **eat** and **drink**. **Sammy T's**, 801 Caroline St (Ⓣ540/371-2008), is a popular bar and diner with substantial sandwiches, salads, and pastas, and a huge range of bottled beers. The **Virginia Deli**, 101 Williams St (Ⓣ540/371-2233), doles out hefty sandwiches with names like the Stonewall Jackson (salami and two kinds of ham) and the Blue & Grey (hot chicken, ham, and swiss cheese). The **Colonial Tavern**, 406 Lafayette Blvd (Ⓣ540/373-1313), is the place to fill up on Irish food, music, and beer.

Richmond and around

Founded in 1737 at the furthest navigable point on the James River, **RICHMOND** remained a small outpost until just before the end of the colonial era, when Virginians, realizing that their capital at Williamsburg was open to British attack, shifted it fifty miles further inland. When war broke out it was named the **capital of the Confederacy**. For four years the city was the focus of Southern defenses and Union attacks, but despite a near constant state of siege, it held on almost until the very end. After the war, Richmond was devastated. Much of its downtown was burned by fleeing Confederates who wanted to keep its stores of weapons and its warehouses full of tobacco out of the victors' hands. Today's Richmond has an extensive inventory of architecturally significant older buildings alongside its modern office towers, while **tobacco** is still a major industry. Finally, it may surprise some visitors to find that Richmond is relatively liberal. In 2003, a statue was even unveiled at Tredagar, the old Confederate munitions plant, of the town's former arch-enemy, Abraham Lincoln.

Arrival, information, and getting around

Two hours by car from Washington DC, via I-95, which cuts through the east side of downtown, Richmond is also served by **Amtrak**, which pulls into 1500 E Main St, on a regional route that connects Newport News, Virginia, with Washington DC and Boston. (Further out of town, the station at 7519 Staples Mill Rd covers that route as well as the Silver Service/Palmetto line connecting Miami, Washington DC, and New York City.) **Greyhound**, which stops just off I-64 at 2910 N Blvd, is a good way from the center of town. The **airport**, ten miles east of downtown, is served by major carriers and has a small visitor center (Mon–Fri 9.30am–4.30pm; Ⓣ804/236-3260; Ⓦwww.flyrichmond.com) in the arrivals terminal. The **main visitor center**, 403 N 3rd St (daily 9am–5pm; Ⓣ804/782-2777 or 1-888/RICHMOND, Ⓦwww.visit.richmond.com), provides discounts on area hotels and advises on tours. Much of Richmond is compact enough to walk around, but to get to outlying places you can take a GRTC **bus** (Ⓣ804/358-GRTC, Ⓦwww.ridegrtc.com; $1.25, $1.75 express routes).

Accommodation

Finding well-priced **accommodation** in Richmond isn't difficult, with plenty of chain hotels downtown catering to the business and government trade. If you prefer to get a feel for the old city, stay the night in a **B&B** in one of the historic quarters.

The Berkeley 1200 E Cary St ⓣ804/780-1300 or 1-888/780-4422, ⓦwww.berkeleyhotel.com. Elegant small hotel with boutique touches, and suites with private terraces, on the historic Shockoe Slip. 8

Grace Manor Inn 1853 W Grace St ⓣ804/353-4334, ⓦwww.thegracemanorinn.com. Stately B&B housing three tasteful suites in a grand 1910 building. Rooms are rich with antique decor; some have fireplaces and claw-foot tubs. 7

Henry Clay Inn 114 N Railroad Ave, Ashland, Virginia ⓣ804/798-3100, ⓦwww.henryclayinn.com. Though eleven miles out of town, this excellent B&B has sixteen antique-filled rooms, a proper parlor, and a majestic veranda. Some are suites with jacuzzis. 4

The Jefferson 101 W Franklin St ⓣ804/788-8000 or 1-800/424-8014, ⓦwww.jefferson-hotel.com. A beautifully maintained grand hotel, with a fabulous marble-columned lobby, marble baths, high-speed internet access, and stylish rooms. 9

Linden Row Inn 100 E Franklin St ⓣ804/783-7000 or 1-800/348-7424, ⓦwww.lindenrowinn.com. A magnificent row of red-brick Georgian terraced houses, now a comfortable modern hotel with antique furnishings, high-speed internet access, and complimentary continental breakfast. 5

Richmond Marriott 500 E Broad St ⓣ804/643-3400, ⓦwww.marriott.com. Smart chain accommodation offering high-speed internet and a good downtown location. 6

William Catlin House 2304 E Broad St ⓣ804/780-3746. B&B dating from 1845 that offers a mix of seven antebellum and Victorian rooms and suites, sited in the Church Hill district, not too far from downtown and the Shockoe Slip. 5

Downtown Richmond

Richmond's **downtown** centers on a few blocks rising up from the James River to either side of Broad Street. Modern office towers front onto a riverside park, while up the hill in the **Court End District**, dozens of well-preserved antebellum homes provide a suitable backdrop for some important museums and historic sites.

The **Virginia State Capitol**, 910 Capitol St, houses the oldest legislative body still in existence in the US; the site has been in continuous use since 1788 as the state (and, briefly, Confederate) legislature. Thomas Jefferson had a hand in the design, and the domed central rotunda (not visible from outside) holds the only marble statue of George Washington modeled from life (by master sculptor Jean-Antoine Houdon), and busts of Jefferson and the seven other Virginia-born US presidents line the walls. Two hundred years later, the Capitol has reopened after a lengthy and beautiful restoration (tours Mon–Sat 8.30am–5pm, Sun 1–4pm; ⓣ804/698-1788, ⓦlegis.state.va.us; free).

Also on Capitol Square is the Federal-style **Governor's Mansion**, 901 E Grace St, which, like the capitol, is the oldest of its kind in the US, dating to 1813 (ⓣ804/371-2642 for tours). Much less reserved, across from Capitol Square, is the huge Victorian artifact of **Old City Hall**, 1001 E Broad St, designed in 1894 in a retro-Gothic style and so visually busy it makes your head spin. Just two blocks north of the capitol, the **Museum of the Confederacy**, 1201 E Clay St (ⓦwww.moc.org; $8), covers the history of the Civil War through weapons, uniforms, and the like. Personal effects of Confederate leaders include J.E.B. Stuart's plumed hat, the tools used to amputate Stonewall Jackson's arms at Chancellorsville (he died regardless), and Robert E. Lee's revolver and the pen he used to sign the surrender. Next door, the **White House of the Confederacy** (Mon–Sat 10am–5pm, Sun noon–5pm; $8, $11 combo ticket), an 1818 Neoclassical mansion where Jefferson Davis lived as Confederate president, has been restored to its 1860s appearance.

Two blocks west, the 1812 **Wickham House** now forms part of the excellent **Valentine Richmond History Center**, at 1015 E Clay St (Tues–Sat 10am–5pm, Sun noon–5pm; ⓣ804/649-0711, ⓦwww.richmondhistorycenter.com; $10). This Federal-style monolith houses a small local history museum, focusing on the experience of working-class and black Americans, as well as an extensive array of furniture and pre–Civil War clothing such as whalebone corsets and other **Gone With the Wind**–era apparel.

Jackson Ward

West of the Convention Center on Sixth Street is a neighborhood of early-nineteenth-century houses, **Jackson Ward**, filling a dozen blocks around First and Clay streets. This National Historic Landmark District has been the center of Richmond's African American community since well before the Civil War, when Richmond had the largest free black population in the US. As well as covering local history, the **Maggie L. Walker House**, 110 E Leigh St (Mon–Sat 9am–5pm; ⓣ804/771-2017, ⓦwww.nps.gov/mawa; free), traces the working life of the physically disabled, black Richmond woman who, during the 1920s, was the first woman in the US to found and run a bank, now the Consolidated Bank and Trust. Nearby, the **Black History Museum**, at 00 Clay St (Tues–Sat 10am–5pm; ⓦwww.blackhistorymuseum.org; $5), contains displays on Richmond's role as a center of Southern black society, and includes a well-presented gallery of artifacts of the Civil Rights movement as well as textiles from different peoples in Africa and America.

Canal Walk and around

A nice example of urban revitalization is the landscaping of a 1.25-mile stretch of waterfront into **Canal Walk**, which runs between downtown and Shockoe Bottom. **Canal boat rides** depart from around 14th and Virginia streets (April–Nov Fri & Sat noon–7pm, Sun noon–5pm; also June–Aug Wed & Thurs noon–7pm; ⓣ804/649-2800; $5), providing a leisurely and pleasant half-hour jaunt. For insight into the Confederate period, you can start or end your stroll at the **American Civil War Center**, 490 Tredegar St (daily 9am–5pm; ⓣ804-771-2145, ⓦwww.nps.gov/rich; $8), at the refurbished **Tredegar Iron Works**, a munitions plant whose foundry churned out tons of Confederate materiel. The center has multimedia presentations about Civil War history and three floors of exhibits. Tredagar is also the main visitor center for **Richmond National Battlefield Park**, a collection of dozens of Civil War sites, which can all be accessed on an eighty-mile drive. Four other local visitor centers are also in operation, the most interesting being the **Chimborazo Medical Museum**, a few miles east at 3215 E Broad St (daily 9am–5pm; ⓣ804/226-1981; free), which has disturbing displays on the medicine and technology available (or not) to help wounded soldiers of the era. Those who weren't so lucky ended up just west of Tredagar at **Hollywood Cemetery**, 412 S Cherry St (daily 8am–5pm; ⓣ804/648-8501, ⓦwww.hollywoodcemetery.org), where a 90-foot-tall granite **pyramid** commemorates the 18,000 Confederate troops killed nearby.

Shockoe Bottom, the Poe Museum, and Church Hill

Split down the middle by the raised I-95 freeway, the gentrified riverfront warehouse district of **Shockoe Bottom** still holds a few reminders of Richmond's industrial past among the restaurants and nightclubs on its cobblestone streets. From **Shockoe Slip**, a fetching old wharf rebuilt in the 1890s after being destroyed in the Civil War, Cary Street runs east along the waterfront, lined by a wall of brick warehouses – now being converted into chic lofts and condos – known as **Tobacco Row**.

Nearby, Richmond's oldest building, an appropriately gloomy 250-year-old stone house, holds the **Edgar Allan Poe Museum**, 1914 E Main St (Tues–Sat 10am–5pm, Sun 11am–5pm; ⓣ804/648-5523, ⓦwww.poemuseum.org; $6). Poe spent much of his youth in Richmond and considered it his home town. The museum displays Poe memorabilia and relics, including his walking stick and a lock of his hair, plus a model of Richmond as it was in Poe's time.

Church Hill, a few blocks northeast, is one of Richmond's oldest surviving districts, its decorative eighteenth-century houses looking out over the James River (it's also the site of the Chimborazo Museum; see p.402). Capping the hill at the heart of the neighborhood, **St John's Church**, 2401 E Broad St (tours Mon–Sat 10am–3.30pm, Sun 1–3.30pm; ⓦwww.historicstjohnschurch.org; $6), dates back to 1741 and is best known as the place where, during a 1775 debate, future state governor **Patrick Henry** made the impassioned plea, "Give me liberty or give me death." His speech, along with the debate itself, is re-created by actors in period dress every Sunday at 2pm in summer.

The Fan District and Carytown

The **Fan District**, so named because its tree-lined avenues fan out at oblique angles, is an interesting Richmond neighborhood surrounding the campus of Virginia Commonwealth University. The district spreads west from the downtown area, beyond Belvidere Street (US-1), and its centerpiece, **Monument Avenue**, is lined with garish Victorian and historic-revival mansions from the turn of the twentieth century. South of Monument Avenue, at 2800 Grove Ave, stands the **Virginia Museum of Fine Arts** (Wed–Sun 11am–5pm; ⓦwww.vmfa.museum; $5 donation). An extensive collection of Impressionist and post-Impressionist paintings is displayed alongside American paintings ranging from Charles Willson Peale's acclaimed portraits to George Catlin's romantic images of Plains Indians to the pop art creations of Roy Lichtenstein and Claes Oldenburg. Other galleries contain such items as Frank Lloyd Wright furniture, Lalique jewelry, Hindu and Buddhist sculpture from the Himalayas, and four jewel-encrusted Fabergé Easter eggs, crafted in the 1890s for the Russian czars.

Just beyond the Fan District, **Carytown** is a thriving nine-block area of trendy shops offering Asian art, tarot readings, and holistic medicines. Here, too, is the **Byrd Theatre**, 2908 W Cary St (ⓦwww.byrdtheatre.com; tickets $2-5), one of the grandest cinemas in the region, dating from 1928 and rich with European marble and crystal chandeliers; it still shows movies, some accompanied by its grand Wurlitzer organ.

Eating and drinking

Richmond has a good choice of **eating** options at both ends of the price spectrum, with barbecue and the higher-priced New Southern cuisine being specialties.

Border Chophouse 1501 W Main St, Fan District ⓣ804/355-2907. Western-style spot that serves up pasta, veal, and lamb dishes, but whose specialty is barbecue, be it beef ribs, pork, or chicken.

Cabo's Corner Bistro 2053 W Broad St, Fan District ⓣ804/355-1144. Swanky spot that offers creative steak, seafood, and pasta dishes, as well as taste-bud-tingling desserts and nightly live jazz.

Millie's Diner 2603 E Main St ⓣ804/643-5512. Refurbished diner, complete with mini-jukeboxes on each table, a bit out of downtown beyond Shockoe Bottom. The changing menu includes fairly expensive but delicious seafood and steak, plus rack of lamb and duck breast, and there's also a nice range of brews.

O'Neill's Penny Lane Pub 421 E Franklin St, Downtown ⓣ804/780-1682. British-style joint with solid grilled food and other affordable pub grub, including a mean steak-and-Guinness pie, plus a full range of English and other beers, and European soccer on TV.

Richbrau Brewing Co 1214 E Cary St, Shockoe Slip ⓣ804/644-3018. The place to go in town for hearty, handcrafted microbrews, as well as good

Southern fare, steak, and fish and chips, along with dancing, pool, and darts.

Strawberry Street Café 421 N Strawberry St ☎804/353-6860. Casual and comfortable Fan District café offering mainly inexpensive quiches, pasta, and salads, but also jambalaya and crab cakes, and a salad bar nestled in an old bathtub.

Third Street Diner 218 E Main St, Downtown ☎804/788-4750. Relaxed 24hr diner with cheap and solid breakfasts and pork chops, omelets, grits, barbecue, and sausage platters. Draws a stylish student crowd, especially at night when it's also a bar.

The Tobacco Company 1201 E Cary St, Shockoe Slip ☎804/782-9555. Inventive New American food in a stunningly restored three-storey tobacco warehouse, complete with antique elevator. Affordable sandwiches and burgers for lunch; pricier steak and seafood for dinner.

Nightlife

Richmond's main **nightlife** spots are concentrated around the **Shockoe Slip** and **Shockoe Bottom** areas, just east of Downtown. A good bet for mainstream **theater** is the Barksdale Theatre, 1601 Willow Lawn Drive (☎804/282-2620, Ⓦwww.barksdalerichmond.org; $35–38), while the Chamberlayne Actors Theatre, 319 N Wilkinson Rd (☎804/262-9760, Ⓦwww.cattheatre.com; $15), offers fringe works that are more daring and contemporary. For details on music and events, check the free **Style Weekly** newspaper or Ⓦwww.arts.Richmond.com.

The Historic Triangle

The **Historic Triangle**, on the peninsula that stretches southeast of Richmond between the James and York rivers, holds the richest concentration of colonial-era sites in the US. **Jamestown**, founded in 1607, was Virginia's first settlement; **Williamsburg** is a detailed replica of the colonial capital; and **Yorktown** was the site of the climactic battle in the Revolutionary War. All are within an hour's drive from Richmond, and Williamsburg is accessible by Amtrak.

Although I-64 is the quickest way to cover the fifty miles from Richmond to Williamsburg, a far more pleasing drive along US-5 rolls through **plantation** country, where many eighteenth-century mansions are open to the public. Once you're in the Historic Triangle, the best way to get around is along the wooded **Colonial Parkway**, which winds west to Jamestown and east to Yorktown, twenty miles in all. Most of the area's numerous tourist facilities are to be found around Williamsburg; a few suggestions are listed under "Historic Triangle practicalities" on p.407.

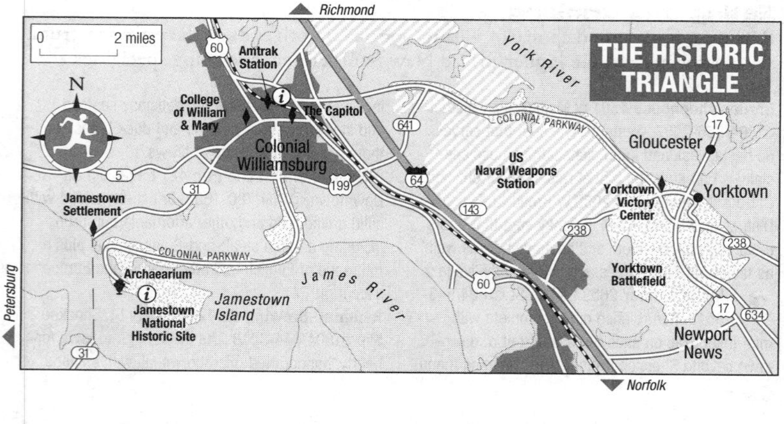

Jamestown

Jamestown is the place where England first got its feet wet in the New World, a trade and military outpost whose lore is still being celebrated four hundred years later, with recent archeological discoveries adding new insights and perspectives. You'll want to visit both the original location and the re-created site by taking the scenic Colonial Parkway, or highways 5 and 31 from Williamsburg. The one bit of seventeenth-century Jamestown to survive, protected within the **Jamestown National Historic Site** on Jamestown Island, is the 50-foot tower of the first brick church, built around 1650 (the rest was destroyed by fire in 1698), which makes it one of the oldest extant English structures in the US.

The area is roughly divided into two sections: the **New Towne** is where the colonists relocated after the 1620s to erect businesses, establish permanent residences, build livestock pens, and so on. Much of what's visible are replicas of the original brick foundations buried below (to protect from weather damage). More interesting is the site of the **Old Towne** – the location most of us associate with the colony – which includes ruins from the original triangular 1607 fort. Here you'll see dozens of archeologists working behind a perimeter, and you can also drop in on the **Archaearium**, where some of the many treasures discovered here – everything from glassware to utensils to the skeleton of a colonist who died a violent death – are on display (also online at Ⓦwww.historicjamestowne.org).

At the end of the Colonial Parkway, the **visitor center** (daily 9am–5pm; Ⓣ757/229-1733, Ⓦwww.nps.gov/jame; $10 per car, includes Yorktown battlefield, see p.406), features drawings and audiovisual exhibits that conjure up the past, and, closer to the park entrance, you can watch artisans making old-fashioned **glassworks** and purchase some of their creations, as well as see the brick remnants of a seventeenth-century kiln.

If looking at dusty artifacts isn't enough for you, head to the adjacent **Jamestown Settlement** (daily 9am–5pm; Ⓣ757/253-4838, Ⓦwww.historyisfun.org; $13.50, $19.25 with Yorktown Victory Center), a complex of museums and actual-size replicas that provide details of what went on here, the reconstructed buildings staffed by guides in period costume weaving, making pottery, and so on. Full-sized replicas of the three **ships** that carried the first settlers are moored on the James River.

Colonial Williamsburg

Providing details on what the eighteenth-century capital of Virginia may have been like, **Colonial Williamsburg** is an essential tourist experience for anyone with a flair for American history. While you have to buy a pricey ticket to look inside the restored buildings, the entire historic area is open all the time, and you can wander freely down the cobblestone streets and across the green commons.

From the Wren Building on the William and Mary campus, separated from Colonial Williamsburg by a mock-historic shopping center, **Duke of Gloucester Street** runs east through the historic area to the old Capitol. The first of its eighteenth-century buildings, a hundred yards along, is the Episcopalian **Bruton Parish Church**, where all the big names of the revolutionary period were known to visit. Behind the church, the broad **Palace Green** spreads north to the Governor's Palace (see below). West of the church, the 1771 **courthouse** and the octagonal **powder magazine**, protected by a guardhouse, face each other in the midst of Market Square. Further along, **Chowning's Tavern**, a reconstruction of an alehouse that stood here in 1766, is one of four functioning pubs in the district, with lively entertainment nightly.

The real architectural highlight is the **Capitol**, a monumental edifice at the east end of Duke of Gloucester Street. The current building, a 1945 reconstruction of

▲ Colonial Williamsburg

the 1705 original, has an open-air ground-floor **arcade** linking two keyhole-shaped wings. One wing housed the elected, legislative body of the Colonial government, the **House of Burgesses**, while the other held the chambers of the **General Court** – where alleged felons, including thirteen of Blackbeard's pirates, were tried.

The gift shops along Duke of Gloucester Street have been done up as eighteenth-century apothecaries, cobblers, and silversmiths. The **Raleigh Tavern** here was where the independence-minded colonial government reconvened after being dissolved by the loyalist governors in 1769 and again in 1774; the original burned down in 1859. Finally, the imposing two-story **Governor's Palace**, at the north end of the Palace Green, has a grand ballroom and opulent furnishings, and must have served as a telling declaration of royal power, no doubt enforced by the startling display of swords, muskets, and other deadly weaponry interlaced on the walls of the foyer.

For those still in need of further immersion into the re-created past, as well as a heavy dose of theme-park (sur)reality, the park presents **"Revolutionary City,"** a two-hour daily spectacle on the east end of the area, in which costumed actors on the streets act out the highlights of the 1770s and 1780s, sweeping up tourists in the rebellious fervor of the day with a flurry of angry speeches and shouting matches.

Yorktown

YORKTOWN, along the York River on the north side of the peninsula, gave its name to the decisive final major battle of the **Revolutionary War**. Yorktown was little more than farmland when, on October 18, 1781, overwhelmed and besieged British (and German mercenary) troops under the command of Charles, Lord Cornwallis, surrendered here to the joint American and French forces commanded by George Washington. At the heart of the namesake battlefield that surrounds the town, a **visitor center** (daily 9am–5pm; ⓣ757/898-2410; ⓦwww.nps.gov/yonb; $10 per car for seven-day pass, good also for admission to Jamestown

Tickets for Colonial Williamsburg

To set foot inside any of the buildings that have been restored or rebuilt as part of Colonial Williamsburg, you need to buy a ticket, either from the main **visitor center** (daily 9am–5pm; ⓣ1-800/HISTORY, ⓦwww.history.org), north of the center off the Colonial Parkway, or from a smaller office at the west end of Duke of Gloucester Street. Most buildings in the park are open daily from 9am to 5pm, but about a third of them may have special hours and days they're open; check the website for details.

There are several types of **tickets**, which include an introductory guided walk and free parking at the visitor center. The basic **Capital City Pass** ($36, kids $18), valid for one day only, gets you into many of the lesser buildings but excludes the Governor's Palace; the better-value **Key-to-the-City Pass** ($49, kids $24) includes the palace and lasts two days; the **Freedom Pass** ($59, kids $29) is the same as the latter but lasts for an entire year; and the less appealing **Independence Pass** ($79, kids $39) is almost the same as the Freedom Pass, but throws in a ticket to the nightly shows as well. Aside from these, there are additional charges for the special programs and events offered by Colonial Williamsburg, such as staged courthouse trials, holiday spectacles, and candlelit walking tours.

National Historic Site) has interpretive displays, including a replica, walk-through fighting ship, military artifacts, and a short audiovisual presentation on the war, and also provides several guided tours of the area. A dozen original buildings survive from the era, along with the earthworks manned by the troops. The **Siege Line Overlook** (at the visitor center) has good views of strategic points, while maps and an audio tour are available if you want to explore in greater detail.

The town itself – within the historic site – also has a handful of interesting old structures worth looking at. These include the handsome homes of local gentry, a customhouse, and, best of all, the archeological remains of the workshop of the **Poor Potter** – who, contrary to his name, was a prosperous merchant and one of the first businessmen in the colonies to produce quality ceramics and glassworks to rival those imported from England.

Note that, as at Jamestown, the state of Virginia and National Park Service have constructed a mini–theme park nearby – this time a re-created Continental Army encampment – as part of the **Yorktown Victory Center** (daily 9am–5pm; ⓦwww.historyisfun.org; $9.25, $19.25 with Jamestown Settlement, see p.405), west of the battlefield on US-17. The museum covers both sides of the conflict, and two outdoor museums portray life on a middle-class farm and in a Revolutionary War camp.

Historic Triangle practicalities

Of the three main sites, only Williamsburg is easily reached without a car. Amtrak **trains** and Greyhound **buses** stop at 468 N Boundary St, two blocks from the Governor's Palace. The Colonial Parkway makes an excellent, scenic cycling route to Jamestown (12 miles away) or Yorktown (14 miles); rent a **bike** from Bikes Unlimited at 759 Scotland St in Williamsburg (ⓣ757/229-4620, ⓦwww.bikewilliamsburg.com; $15-20/day). In Colonial Williamsburg, ticket-holders can use the hop-on, hop-off **shuttle buses** (every 10min 9am–5.30pm) that leave from the visitor center and stop at convenient points in the historic area. You can also pick up the **Historic Triangle Shuttle**, which is free and stops at all the major attractions (March–Oct daily every 30min 9.30am–4pm).

For **accommodation**, the Williamsburg Hotel/Motel Association (ⓣ757/220-3330 or 1-800/221-7165, ⓦwww.gowilliamsburg.com) can find you a bed at no extra charge. West of the center, US-60 is lined with endless motels, and there are also several cheap options just a few blocks east of the capitol, including the basic **Bassett Motel**, 800 York St (Ⓣ757/229-5175, Ⓦwww.bassettmotel.com; ③), and the clean and conveniently located **Quarterpath Inn**, 620 York St (Ⓣ1-800/446-9222, Ⓦwww.quarterpathinn.com; ③). The **Duke of York Motel**, 508 E Water St in Yorktown (Ⓣ757/898-3232, Ⓦwww.dukeofyorkmotel.com; ③), has beachfront units, some with kitchenettes, fridges, and jacuzzis, along the York River. For a bit more luxury, **Marriott's Manor Club at Ford's Colony**, 101 St Andrews Drive (Ⓣ757/258-5705, Ⓦwww.marriott.com; ⑧), is four miles outside of town and has expensive villas as well as entry-level units with DVD players, fireplaces, and patios. Finally, there are several **campgrounds** along US-5 and US-60, west of Williamsburg ($25–35 per tent).

The various **restaurants** and taverns along Duke of Gloucester Street in Colonial Williamsburg feature good (if overpriced) pub food; some operate on a seasonal basis only (often April–Oct) and all except **Chowning's Tavern** should be reserved in advance (Ⓣ1-800/HISTORY). West of the historic area, in the Merchants Square shopping mall, the excellent **Trellis Café** (Ⓣ757/229-8610) serves pricey seafood and steak entrees for dinner, but affordable sandwiches and burgers for lunch, and across the street the **Cheese Shop** (Ⓣ757/220-0298) has great deli sandwiches, but expect a wait during peak hours. For even fancier fare, try the **Whitehall**, 1325 Jamestown Rd (Ⓣ757/229-4677), which offers elegant, upmarket French dining with a focus on seafood and beef. There is also a clutch of solid restaurants near the William and Mary campus, including the **Green Leafe Café**, 765 Scotland St (Ⓣ757/220-3405), offering solid chili, burgers, pizza, and pasta, and thirty brews on tap.

The Atlantic coast

One of the busiest of the East Coast ports, **Norfolk** sits midway along the coast at the point where the Chesapeake Bay empties into the Atlantic Ocean. Virginia's only heavily industrial center, it is not a particularly pretty place, but it does have a rich maritime and naval heritage, as well as the Chrysler Museum, one of the region's best art galleries. Fifteen miles east of Norfolk, along the open Atlantic, **Virginia Beach** draws summer sun-seekers to the state's busiest seashore.

The rest of Virginia's Atlantic coast is on its isolated and sparsely populated **Eastern Shore**, where the attractive little island town of **Chincoteague** serves as the headquarters of a wildlife refuge that straddles the Maryland border and forms part of the Assateague Island National Seashore.

Norfolk and Portsmouth

Along with Hampton Roads and Newport News on the north side of the James River, **NORFOLK** is home to the largest US naval base, with some 60,000 seamen based here and all manner of gray-steel behemoths cruising past regularly. The waterfront features Norfolk's premier attraction, **Nauticus: The National Maritime Center** (June–Aug daily 10am–5pm; Sept–May Tues–Sat 10am–5pm, Sun noon–5pm; Ⓣ757/664-1000, Ⓦwww.nauticus.org; $11), which has oceanography exhibits, shallow pools for touching tidal creatures and innocuous nurse sharks, larger aquariums, large-screen films, and a deep-sea submersible. On the second floor, the **Hampton Roads Naval Museum** (June–Aug daily 10am–5pm; Sept–May Tues–Sat 10am–5pm, Sun noon–5pm; Ⓦwww.hrnm.navy.mil; free) documents historical naval operations in the area; across from the center, you can tour the decks of the **USS Wisconsin** (same hours; free).

A small **paddlewheel ferry** (hours vary, usually weekdays 7.15am-11.30pm, weekends 10.15am-11.45pm; Ⓦwww.hrtransit.org; $1) shuttles from nearby **Waterside Park** across the harbor to the historic city of **PORTSMOUTH**. Here, if you're sufficiently fired up by all the naval hardware on view, you can dig into more local history at the **Norfolk Naval Shipyard Museum**, 2 High St, on the waterfront (Mon–Sat 10am-5pm, Sun 1–5pm; Sept-May closed Mon; Ⓣ757/393-8591, Ⓦwww.portsnavalmuseums.com; $3), whose tourable highlight is a century-old **lightship** (same hours, but closed Dec–Feb) that once acted as a floating lighthouse for the harbor. Away from the docks, Portsmouth's brick-lined streets are flanked by charming early American houses, and the fetching 1846 Colonial Revival **courthouse**, on High and Court streets (Tues–Sat 10am-5pm, Sun 1–5pm; Ⓦwww.courthousegalleries.com; free), now an art gallery.

Back in Norfolk, an extraordinary array of Asian antiquities is displayed in the intimate Tudor-style home now known as the **Hermitage Foundation Museum**, by the Lafayette River at 7637 N Shore Rd (45min guided tours only; Mon–Sat 10am–5pm, Sun 1–5pm; Ⓣ757/423-2052, Ⓦwww.hermitagefoundation.org; $5), including Persian rugs, medieval tapestries, ancient Chinese ceremonial vessels, and Roman glass. There are also tours of the gardens ($6) and of some of the related buildings on the site (summer, by reservation only; $40).

The city's biggest-name institution, the **Chrysler Museum**, half a mile north of the Norfolk waterfront, 245 W Olney Rd at Mowbray Arch (Wed 10am–9pm, Thurs–Sat 10am–5pm, Sun 1–5pm; Ⓣ757/664-6200, Ⓦwww.chrysler.org; $7, free on Wed), holds the eclectic collection of car magnate Walter Chrysler Jr, comprising ancient Greek statuary, French Impressionist paintings, Franz Klein abstractions, and Mayan funerary objects, as well as world-class Tiffany and Lalique glassware. For a glimpse of bourgeois life in the area c.1800, check out the museum's **Moses Myers House**, on Bank Street at E Freemason Street (Wed–Sat 10am–4pm, Sun 1–4pm; free), the elegant home of one of Norfolk's most prominent Jewish residents, adorned with portraits by Gilbert Stuart and Thomas Sully, and the **Norfolk History Museum**, 601 E Freemason St (Wed-Sar 10am-4pm, Sun noon-4pm; Ⓣ757/441-1526; free), which apart from its selection of historical objects and exhibits is most interesting for the sturdy 1794 Georgian manor it's housed in.

Practicalities

Airport Connection (Ⓣ757/963-0433) connects downtown Norfolk with **Norfolk International Airport** ($21), five miles northeast. Amtrak **bus** connections from Newport News stop at W Bute Street at York Street, and Greyhound stops at 701 Monticello Avenue. Norfolk's downtown **visitor center** is at the Nauticus Center, 232 E Main St (daily 9am–5pm; Ⓣ757/664-6620 or 1-800/368-3097, Ⓦwww.norfolkcvb.com); drivers can go to a convenient visitor center with easy parking at exit 273 off I-64, at 9401 Fourth View St (daily 9am–5pm; Ⓣ757/441-1852). Free **NET buses** provide transportation to major sites (Mon–Fri 6am–11pm, Sat noon–midnight, Sun noon–8pm; Ⓦwww.norfolk.gov/Visitors/net.asp).

With far better **accommodation** options available nearby in Virginia Beach (see p.410), there should be no need to resort to the usual chain hotels in Norfolk. Two exceptions are the pleasant **Freemason Inn**, 411 W York St (Ⓣ757/963-7000, Ⓦwww.freemasoninn.com; ❻), a four-unit B&B whose rooms offer fireplaces, poster beds, and jacuzzi tubs, and the stately **Governor Dinwiddie**, 506 Dinwiddie St (Ⓣ757/392-1330, Ⓦwww.hawthorn.com; ❻), a classic, recently remodeled fixture in Portsmouth, with rooms and suites variously offering DVD players, kitchens, and wet bars. For **dining**, there are savory tapas and zesty cocktails at **Bardo**, 430 W 21st St (Ⓣ757/622-7362), and eclectic fare – crab cakes, noodle dishes, steak, and hearty sandwiches – at **The 219**, 219 Granby St (Ⓣ757/627-2896). For a cheap taste of Americana, stop by **Doumar's**, a 1950s-era drive-in restaurant at 1919 Monticello Ave (Ⓣ757/627-4163), where white-hatted wait-staff bring the food to your car; it's tops for barbecue, burgers, and waffle-cone ice cream. Finally, in downtown Norfolk, the ornate 1913 **Wells Theater**, 110 E Tazewell St (Ⓣ757/627-1234, Ⓦwww.vastage.com) puts on plays, musicals, and the odd vaudeville show.

Virginia Beach

The massive resort of **VIRGINIA BEACH** has grown to become the largest city in the state, with nearly half a million people. Although the oceanfront commercial activity can be a monument to tackiness, and there are still many testosterone-filled surfer bars, the relaxed atmosphere actually leads some to stay longer than planned.

The city's focus is its long, sandy **beach**, lined with the usual hotels and motels, and backed by a boardwalk strip of bars, restaurants, and nightclubs. Virginia Beach is also a major **surf center**, hosting the **East Coast Surfing Championships** in late August (Ⓣ1-800/861-SURF, Ⓦwww.surfecsc.com/index.html). You can rent surf and boogie boards at Wave Riding Vehicles, on Cypress Avenue at 19th Street (Ⓣ757/422-8823). Away from the sands, most of the action is along Atlantic Avenue, the main beachfront drag.

High-tech exhibits and an IMAX theater are featured at the **Virginia Aquarium and Marine Science Center**, 717 General Booth Blvd (daily: summer 9am–7pm; rest of year 9am–5pm; Ⓣ757/385-FISH, Ⓦwww.vmsm.com; $12, $17 with IMAX show), which explores all things aquatic, including tanks devoted to sharks, rays, sea turtles, and jellyfish, and has a short, pleasant nature trail through the **Owls Creek salt marsh**, and an aviary displaying dozens of native species. The museum also organizes **dolphin-watching** expeditions (April–Oct; 90min; $18) and **whale-watching** cruises (2hr 30min; late-Dec–mid-March; $28), for which you should reserve in advance.

Heading north, the eccentric **A.R.E. Center** at the headquarters of the Association for Research and Enlightenment, 215 67th St at Atlantic Avenue (Mon–Sat 9am–8pm, Sun noon–8pm; Ⓦwww.edgarcayce.org/visit_are; free), focuses on **Edgar Cayce** (1877–1945), known as "the sleeping prophet" because of his alleged ability, while in a trance, to diagnose and heal the ailments of individuals anywhere in the world. Visitors can use an enormous metaphysical library, take in a lecture on various New Age subjects (daily 3.30pm), or test their own personal ESP (Sat & Sun 1pm). Close by the center, the woodland of **First Landing State Park** was the site where the first English settlers touched land in 1607 before moving on to Jamestown; it's Virginia's most popular state park, good for boating, cycling and campgrounds (some with electricity; Ⓣ1-800/933-PARK; $24–30), with a beach on the Chesapeake Bay. About eight miles inland from the park is one of the city's many historic relics (for the various others, inquire at the visitor center), the **Adam Thoroughgood House**, 1636 Parish Rd (Tues–Sat 9am–5pm, Sun 11am–5pm; Ⓣ757/460-7588; $4), the squat brick home of a colonial leader and militiaman who started out in the New World as a servant; his story, and that of the era, is told through the 1636 house's antiques and displays.

Elsewhere, a few miles up and down the coast are some beautiful and peaceful stretches of golden sand. To the south lies the 9000-acre, four-mile-long **Back Bay National Wildlife Refuge** (daily dawn–dusk; Ⓦwww.fws.gov/backbay; $5 per car, $2 per hiker or cyclist), where you can walk, bike, or fish (but not swim), and **False Cape State Park**, a mile-wide barrier spit that connects to North Carolina and is one of the region's last undisturbed coastlines – though you'll have to arrive by foot, bike, or boat (cars are banned), and only primitive camping is available (Ⓣ1-800/933-PARK; $11 per night).

Practicalities

Greyhound stops at 1017 Laskin Rd, off 31st Street, while the Amtrak **bus** connection from Newport News arrives at 19th Street and Pacific Avenue. The **visitor center**, 2100 Parks Ave (daily 9am–5pm; Ⓣ1-800/822-3224, Ⓦwww.vbfun.com), is at the east end of I-264, half a mile west of the beach at 21st Street. Beach **trolleys** called The Wave (June–Aug daily 8am–2am; Ⓣ757/222-6100, Ⓦwww.hrtransit.org; $1) are the easiest way to get around (though there are also buses, at $1.50 per ride); there are three different trolley routes covering the city, the most useful being up and down Atlantic Avenue (#30; runs May-Oct).

Virginia Beach has great **hotels** for budget travelers. Just a block from the ocean, **Angie's Guest Cottage**, 302 24th St (April–Oct; Ⓣ757/491-1830, Ⓦwww.angiescottage.com), has dorm beds from $17–21, private rooms from ❷, and bargain B&B units for ❹ and up (there's a two-night minimum for the latter). Typical rates at the seafront hotels tend to approach $200 in summer. Cheaper options can be found at **The Capes Ocean Resort**, 2001 Atlantic Avenue (March–Oct; Ⓣ757/428-5421, Ⓦwww.capeshotel.com; ❸), which offers a broad range of rooms, though all come with oceanfront balconies and fridges (rates can reach $150 in the summer, however), and the **Cavalier**, on Atlantic Ave at 42nd Street (Ⓣ1-800/446-8199, Ⓦwww.cavalierhotel.com; ❻), a stately 1927 beachfront pile whose facilities include two pools, a gym, and tennis courts, and rooms with fridges and microwaves, or jacuzzis for $60 more.

The town also offers some great **restaurants** and a decent **nightlife**. Among the best are the **Tilted Table**, 2181 Upton Drive (Ⓣ757/563-8458), for its nice array of affordable pasta dishes, pricier steaks, and delicious raw bar offerings, and the elite **One Fish-Two Fish**, 2109 W Great Neck Rd (Ⓣ757/496-4350), which has a fine range of seafood, as well as steak and rack of lamb. On the main drag, the choices are inconsistent, but **Catch 31**, 3001 Atlantic Ave (Ⓣ757/213-3472), does have decent burgers and surf-and-turf, with a waterside view, and **Baja Cantina**, 206 23rd St (Ⓣ757/437-2920), is a friendly bar featuring serviceable Mexican food at cheap prices. For **live music**, try the **Jewish Mother**, 3108 Pacific Ave (Ⓣ757/422-5430), a daytime deli and late-night bar with blues and roots music, sometimes from notable names (tickets for shows $5–20).

The Eastern Shore

Virginia's longest and least-visited stretch of Atlantic coastline, the **Eastern Shore**, lies separated from the rest of the state on the distant side of the Chesapeake Bay. Only the southernmost segment of what's known as the Delmarva Peninsula belongs to Virginia, by which point it has narrowed to become a flat spit of sand protected by a fringe of low-lying islands.

US-13, which runs straight down the center of the peninsula and provides a handy short cut from Philadelphia or points north, crosses seventeen miles of open sea at the mouth of the Chesapeake Bay via the **Chesapeake Bay Bridge-Tunnel** (Ⓦwww.cbbt.com; $12 per car single, $17 round-trip within 24hrs). For most of its 23-mile length, the roadway runs just a few yards above the water, twice burrowing beneath the surface, before reaching its southern extremity halfway between Norfolk and Virginia Beach. To either side of US-13, little villages and fishing harbors such as Nassawadox, Assawoman, and Accomac are tucked away on rambling back roads.

Chincoteague and Assateague Island National Seashore

The most appealing destination on the Eastern Shore, **Chincoteague** occupies a beautiful seven-mile-long barrier island just south of the Maryland border. Little more than a village, the town is attracting new migrants and condo developments, but still makes a relaxed base for exploring **Assateague Island National Seashore** (ⓣ757/336-6577, ⓦwww.nps.gov/asis; $15 week-long vehicle pass, $5 per day), whose northern half holds several good hiking trails and can only be reached from Maryland (see p.426); there are several types of first-come, first-served **campgrounds** available on the Maryland side, on the bay- or oceanfront (mid-Oct–mid-April; ⓣ410/641-3030; $16). The southern half of the seashore, just a mile onwards from Chincoteague, is taken up by the 14,000-acre **Chincoteague National Wildlife Refuge** (daily: May–Sept 5am–10pm; Oct 6am-8pm; Nov–April 6am–6pm; $10 seven-day vehicle pass), notable for its seabirds and wild ponies. Call in at the **visitor center** (ⓣ757/336-6122, ⓦchinco.fws.gov) for information on the fifteen miles of trails through the dunes and marshes, or the pleasant beach at **Tom's Cove**. If you're in Chincoteague on the last Wednesday of July, don't miss the annual **Pony Swim**, when the 300 wild ponies that roam Assateague Island to the north are herded together and directed on a swim through the channel to Chincoteague Memorial Park. Here the foals are sold by auction to help the local community.

Solid **accommodation** options in Chincoteague include the grand **Island Manor House**, 4160 Main St (ⓣ1-800/852-1505, ⓦwww.islandmanor.com; ❺), a smart, antique-furnished B&B with eight quaint rooms; the **Refuge Inn**, 7058 Maddox Blvd (ⓣ757/336-5511, ⓦwww.refugeinn.com; ❹), providing an assortment of charming rooms and suites with private patios and balconies (though rates double in summer); and the **Cedar Gables Seaside Inn**, 6095 Hopkins Lane (ⓣ1-888/491-2944, ⓦwww.cedargable.com; ❼), a homey B&B whose four suites have fireplaces, jacuzzis, CD players, and fridges. The best of the seafood eateries, **Bill's Seafood**, 4040 Main St (ⓣ757/336-5831), is a fine **restaurant** serving delicious crab, oysters, clams, and shrimp at reasonable prices.

Charlottesville and the Shenandoah Valley

The densely forested but fairly low peaks of the **Blue Ridge Mountains** form the eastern front of the four-hundred-mile-long crest of the **Appalachian Mountains**. The British crown marked the mountains as an official, but still porous, settlement boundary to try to prevent American settlers from encroaching on Indian lands (and treaties) during the colonial period. At the geographical center of the state sits the friendly college town of **Charlottesville**, which holds two monuments to Thomas Jefferson. South of here, **Appomattox Court House** is where Robert E. Lee surrendered his Confederate army, while to the west, **Shenandoah National Park** culminates in the 5729-foot Mount Rogers. On the far side of the mountains, the lush **Shenandoah Valley** was once a vital Civil War battleground.

The main highway through the Shenandoah Valley, I-81, can be reached in the north via I-66 from Washington DC, and in the middle via I-64 from Richmond through Charlottesville. Numerous scenic routes are slower but more worthwhile, such as **Skyline Drive** and the **Blue Ridge Parkway** – both weave along the mountain crest, which typically reaches 4000ft or so. You'll need a car to get the most out of the region, though cycling is a good option along the many backroads and, for hikers, the **Appalachian Trail** runs right down the middle.

Charlottesville

Seventy miles west of Richmond, **CHARLOTTESVILLE** holds some of the finest examples of early American architecture; it's worth strolling its compact, low-rise center, crisscrossed by magnolia-shaded streets, particularly in the pedestrianized blocks of **Main Street**. However pleasant the town, the most compelling attraction is Thomas Jefferson's home and memorial, **Monticello**, which sits atop a hill just east of town, overlooking the beautiful Neoclassical campus of the University of Virginia, which he also designed.

The University of Virginia

Though he wrote the Declaration of Independence and served as the third US president, Thomas Jefferson took more pride in having established the **University of Virginia** than in any of his other achievements, as he designed every building down to the most minute detail, planned the curriculum, and selected the faculty. Unlike the theology-based universities of the time, the University of Virginia was not rooted in religion (theology was indeed banned from the classroom), but emphasized instead a broad liberal arts education – not surprising, as Jefferson had been one of the prime proponents of the separation of church and state.

The highlight of the campus is the red-brick, white-domed **Rotunda**, modeled on the Pantheon and completed in 1821 to house the library and classrooms (though reconstructed in 1976). A basement gallery tells the history of the university, while upstairs a richly decorated central hall links three elliptical classrooms. A staircase winds up to the **Dome Room**, where paired Corinthian columns rise to an ocular skylight. From the Rotunda, 45-minute guided tours of the campus begin (daily 10am, 11am, 2pm, 3pm, & 4pm, except during holidays; free). Twin colonnades stretch along either side of a lushly landscaped quadrangle – **The Lawn** – linking single-storey student apartments with ten taller pavilions in which professors live and hold tutorials.

Parallel to the quadrangle buildings, two further rows of dormitory buildings, the East and West ranges, front on to serpentine walled gardens. **Edgar Allan Poe** stayed in one of these dorms while studying at the university in 1826, but was forced to drop out after he couldn't pay his gambling debts. His room in the West Range – Number 13, of course –is now restored to how it would have looked during his occupancy: a rather spartan, bleak affair (the honorary Ravens Society maintains the unit; Ⓦ www.uvaravensociety.com).

Monticello

One of America's most familiar buildings – it graces the back of the nickel – **Monticello**, three miles southeast of Charlottesville on Hwy-53, was the home of Thomas Jefferson for most of his life. It is surrounded by acres of beautiful hilltop grounds, which once made up an enormous plantation, with fine views out over the Virginia countryside. The symmetrical brick facade, centered upon a white Doric portico, belies the quirks of the interior, still furnished as it was when Jefferson lived here.

You can see Monticello on a **guided tour** (daily: March–Oct 8am–5pm; Nov–Feb 9am–4.30pm; Ⓣ 434/984-9822, Ⓦ www.monticello.org; $15); from the outside, it looks like an elegant, Palladian-style country home, but as soon as you enter the domed entrance hall, with its animal hides, native craftworks, and fossilized bones and elk antlers (from Lewis and Clark's epic 1804 journey across North America, which Jefferson sponsored as president), you begin to see a differ-

▲ Monticello

ent side of Jefferson. His love of gadgets and clever contraptions is evidenced by an elaborate dual-pen device he used to make automatic copies of all his letters, and a weather vane over the front porch, connected to a dial so he could measure wind direction without stepping outside, among others. In his **private chambers**, he slept in a cramped alcove that linked his dressing room and his study, and would get up on the right side of the bed if he wanted to make some late-night notes, on the left if he wanted to get dressed.

With the price of a ticket to the main house you can also tour the **gardens** (April–Oct 9am–4pm), in which extensive flower and vegetable gardens spread to the south and west, and other parts of the plantation site (10am–3pm), focusing on the remains of **Mulberry Row**, Monticello's slave quarters. Despite calling slavery an "abominable crime," he owned almost two hundred slaves and recent research indicates he probably had one or more children with one of them, Sally Hemings. At the south end of Mulberry Row, a grove of ancient hardwood trees surrounds Jefferson's gravesite, marked by a simple stone **obelisk**; the epitaph, which lists his major accomplishments, does not mention his having been president.

Practicalities

Amtrak **trains** from DC stop at 810 W Main St, and Greyhound pulls in at 310 W Main St. Once you arrive, you can get to everything on foot, including the downtown **visitor center**, 610 E Main St (Mon–Sat 10am–5pm, Sun 11am–3pm; ⓣ434/293-6789 or 1-877/386-1103, ⓦwww.pursuecharlottesville.com). Another visitor center (daily 9am–5pm; ⓣ434/977-1783), well-signposted on Hwy-20, just south of I-64, houses a superb free exhibit of four hundred items called "Thomas Jefferson at Monticello," and is an excellent starting point for a trip there.

Charlottesville has a good range of **accommodation**. Most places are of the familiar chain variety, but for better digs, try the **English Inn**, 2000 Morton Drive (ⓣ434/971-9900, ⓦwww.englishinncharlottesville.com; ❺), a large, mock-Tudor motel with clean and functional rooms, some of which have fridges and microwaves. Good-value **B&B rooms** are available at the two restored, antique-laden houses of the **200 South Street Inn**, 200 South St (Ⓣ434/979-0200, Ⓦwww.southstreetinn.com; ❻), some of whose units have fireplaces and whirlpool tubs. Similar amenities are available at the handsome **Inn at Court Square**, 410 E Jefferson St (Ⓣ434/295-2800, Ⓦwww.innatcourtsquare.com; ❻), which has nine rooms as well as excellent Southern cuisine on offer. You can also arrange a stay in a B&B through Guesthouses (Ⓣ434/979-7264, Ⓦwww.va-guesthouses.com).

The best **eating** and **drinking** can be found near the university and the downtown mall. Just north of the downtown mall, the upscale **Tastings**, 502 E Market St (Ⓣ434/293-3663), offers steak, fricassees, and crab casseroles, plus a fine selection of wine – including many from local vineyards. A sizeable selection of beers (more than a hundred in all) can be sampled along with solid pub grub a block further north at the affordable, English-styled **Court Square Tavern**, 500 Court Square (Ⓣ434/296-6111). The **C&O Restaurant**, 515 E Water St (Ⓣ434/971-7044), housed in an old railroad engineers' building, offers bistro-style food in its humming bar and more upscale New Southern cuisine in the upstairs dining room.

Appomattox Court House

Set amid the pleasant, rolling hills of central Virginia, some sixty miles south of Charlottesville on US-460 and Hwy-24, the village of **APPOMATTOX COURT HOUSE** was where Robert E. Lee and Ulysses S. Grant met on April 9, 1865, for the former to sign surrender papers for his Army of Northern Virginia, effectively ending the Civil War after four bloody years. Final papers were signed in the home of the **McLean family**, who, ironically, had moved here after the war's first major battle – Bull Run – was fought on their property in Manassas. Details of the surrender are given in **Appomattox Court House National Historical Park** (daily 8.30am–5pm; Ⓦwww.nps.gov/apco; $3–4 per person by season). The village has been handsomely restored, and the McLean home is now a museum.

The nearest **accommodation** is available in the newer burg of **Appomattox**, a few miles west. Here, the cozy **Longacre B&B**, 1670 Church St (Ⓣ434/352-9251 or 1-800/758-7730, Ⓦwww.longacreva.com; ❹), is nestled among century-old boxwoods and includes a lap pool. **Spring Grove Farm**, several miles northwest of town along Rte-613, at 3440 Spring Grove Rd (Ⓣ434/352-7429, Ⓦwww.springgrovefarm.com; ❺), is set on a 200-acre, 1842 plantation where the twelve rooms and suites (some with fireplaces) have whirlpool tubs and tasteful, early American decor.

Shenandoah National Park

The dark forests, deep rocky ravines, and pleasant waterfalls of **SHENANDOAH NATIONAL PARK**, far from being untouched wilderness, were created when hundreds of small family farms and homesteads were condemned by the state and federal governments during the Depression, and the land was left to revert to its natural state. So it's no surprise that Shenandoah, meaning "river of high mountains," has one of the most scenic byways in the US, **Skyline Drive**, a thin, 105-mile ribbon of pavement curving along the crest of the Blue Ridge Mountains. It starts just off I-66 near the town of **Front Royal**, 75 miles west of DC, and winds south through the park, giving great views over the area.

Week-long **admission** to the park is $15 for cars and $8 for pedestrians ($10 for cars and $5 for pedestrians during the winter). Any time of year you can get the best of what the park has to offer by following one of the many **hiking trails** that split off from the ridge; most are two to six miles long. One begins near Byrd visitor center and winds along to tumbling **Dark Hollow Falls**; another trail, leaving Skyline Drive at mile marker 45, climbs up a treacherous incline to the top of **Old Rag Mountain** for panoramic views out over the whole of Virginia and the Allegheny Mountains in the west. More ambitious hikers, or those who want to spend the night out in the back country, head for the **Appalachian Trail**. Details on any of these hikes, and free overnight camping permits, can be picked up at the following **visitor centers**: Dickey Ridge, milepost 4.6, Harry F. Byrd Sr, milepost 51, and Loft Mountain, milepost 79 (daily 8.30am–5pm; Ⓣ540/999-3500, Ⓦwww.nps.gov/shen).

Park **accommodation** (Ⓣ1-888/896-3833, Ⓦwww.visitshenandoah.com) includes the 1894 **Skyland Lodge**, at milepost 41.7, with cabins and hotel rooms (❻), as well as a large restaurant with panoramic views; **Big Meadows Lodge**, at milepost 51.2, with similar facilities (❻); and **Lewis Mountain Cabins**, at milepost 57.5, with cozy, rustic accommodation (❹). There are also four campgrounds in the park ($15–17 per night); reserve online at Ⓦwww.recreation.gov or by calling Ⓣ1-877/444-6777.

The Shenandoah Valley

Many of the small, colorful towns of the **SHENANDOAH VALLEY**, down below Skyline Drive, were left in ruins after the Civil War – the region changed hands over seventy times at a cost of some 100,000 dead or maimed – but have since been restored to their original antebellum states. Numerous monuments and cemeteries line the backroads, surrounded by horse farms and apple orchards. Some eight major battlefields can be found here, along with their requisite visitor centers, antique weapons, and museums, and the region is marked as an official **National Historic Area**; for more details on following the military campaigns on foot or by car, see Ⓦwww.shenandoahatwar.org.

Besides its martial history, the northern Shenandoah Valley also holds half a dozen of Virginia's many **limestone caverns**, which tend to be privately owned and touristy, and cost between $15 and $20 to explore. One of the largest is **Luray Caverns**, twelve miles east of New Market off Hwy-211 (daily: April–mid-June & Sept–Oct 9am–6pm; mid-June–Aug 9am–7pm; Nov–March 9am–4pm; Ⓦwww.luraycaverns.com; $19), featuring an underground "organ" with stalagmites as "pipes," which you can see on the one-hour guided tours. Further south, off Hwy-250 northwest of the town of **STAUNTON**, the **Frontier Culture Museum of Virginia** (daily: winter 10am–4pm; rest of year 9am–5pm; Ⓦwww.frontiermuseum.org; $10) showcases six different kinds of immigrant farms and the labors involved in tending to each. Since the buildings were mostly imported (and rebuilt) from Europe, it's more of a historic theme park than an authentic cultural experience, but still worth a look to see how backbreaking it must have once been to live the rural life. By contrast, the **Woodrow Wilson Presidential Library**, 18–24 N Coalter St (daily: March–Oct 9am–5pm; Nov–Feb 10am–4pm, opens at noon Sun; Ⓦwww.woodrowwilson.org; $12), commemorates the 28th president of the US, whose decision to enter World War I and assorted moral crusades remain controversial. Find out more about his academic and political life in the museum's galleries, then take a look at his chic Pierce-Arrow presidential limousine and his birthplace next door.

Lexington

With horse-drawn carriages moving along its quiet, brick-lined streets, the small valley town of **Lexington** is rich in languid country life and wartime memories. One of its most engaging sites, the somber **Lee Chapel and Museum** (April–Oct Mon–Sat 9am–5pm, Sun 1–5pm; Nov–March Mon–Sat 9am–4pm, Sun 1–4pm; Ⓦwww.chapelapps.wlu.edu; free), is on the imposing colonnaded campus of

Washington and Lee University, just north of the town center. The Confederate icon taught here after the war – when it was known as Washington University – and, along with his family, is interred in the chapel's crypt; his horse Traveler is buried just outside. East of the chapel, on the far end of the parade ground of the arch **Virginia Military Institute**, the **George C. Marshall Museum** (Mon–Sat 9am–5pm, Sun 1–5pm; ⓣ540/463-7103, ⓦwww.marshallfoundation.org; $5) documents the life of World War II US general, and later secretary of state, George C. Marshall.

In the town center, another big-name warrior is commemorated at the **Stonewall Jackson House**, 8 E Washington St (Mon–Sat 9am–5pm, Sun 1-5pm; ⓦwww.stonewalljackson.org; $6), where the Confederate general and VMI professor lived before he rode off to war (he died at the battle of Chancellorsville, felled by friendly fire). His spartan 1801 brick townhouse is furnished as it was when he lived there. Nearby, Jackson is buried, with 144 of his fellow rebels, in the **Stonewall Jackson Memorial Cemetery**, on S Main Street at White Street (daily dawn–dusk; free).

For a break from military history, take a trip fifteen miles north of town, off Rte-606, to **Cyrus McCormick's Farm** (daily 8.30am–5pm; ⓣ540/377-2255; free), where the famed inventor of the industrial reaper is honored in an antique setting that includes a gristmill, blacksmith's forge, smokehouse, and museum. For a further taste of the bucolic life, the **Virginia Horse Center**, a few miles north of town on Rte-39 (ⓣ540/464-2950, ⓦwww.horsecenter.org), sits on six hundred acres, with eight barns and eighteen rings and arenas for displays of equine gallantry – horse-and-carriage shows, dressage, show-jumping, and so on. Some are free, some cost between $5 and $12 and require advance tickets (ⓣ540/464-2956 to reserve).

Twenty miles south of Lexington on US-11 is the spectacular **Natural Bridge** (daily 8am until dark; ⓦwww.naturalbridgeva.com; $12), a 215-foot limestone arch slowly carved by a creek; George Washington allegedly carved his initials into the rock (though it takes a keen eye to see them), and Thomas Jefferson was so impressed that he bought the site to preserve it and owned it for fifty years.

Practicalities

Lexington is also a good place to visit for its dozens of fine old homes; pick up a walking-tour map at the **visitor center**, 106 E Washington St (daily: June–Aug 8.30am–6pm; Sept–May 9am–5pm; ⓣ540/463-3777, ⓦwww.lexingtonvirginia.com). For distinctive **accommodation, Historic Country Inns** operates some of the most appealing B&Bs, spread over five stately old structures with 43 total units, some with fireplaces, jacuzzis, and wet bars (ⓣ1-877/283-9680, ⓦwww.lexingtonhistoricinns.com; ❹–❼ per night). Otherwise, the **Magnolia House Inn**, 501 S Main St (ⓣ540/463-2567, ⓦwww.magnoliahouseinn.com; ❺), has five comfortable units with tasteful furnishings in a pleasant garden setting. Just a few miles north of town, the **Hummingbird Inn**, 30 Wood Lane, (ⓣ540/997-9065, ⓦwww.hummingbirdinn.com; ❻), has five quaint rooms, with the added appeal of a renovated c.1780 farmhouse with fine dining, a solarium, veranda, and wireless internet access.

For **food**, the **Southern Inn Restaurant**, right in the center of town, at 37 S Main St (ⓣ540/463-3612), has fine regional cuisine, like meatloaf and fried chicken, plus steak, seafood, and pasta. The pricey **Sheridan Livery Inn**, 35 N Main St (ⓣ540/464-1887), offers some of the best food around, from the barbecued shrimp and crab cake sandwiches to the succulent strip steak, paella, and various international dishes. For delicious burgers, seafood, and Mexican food at more affordable prices, the **Bistro on Main**, 8 N Main St (ⓣ540/464-4888), is a solid choice.

Along the Blue Ridge Parkway

Once it wends its way out of Shenandoah National Park, Skyline Drive becomes the **Blue Ridge Parkway**, a beautiful route heading southwest along the crest of the Appalachians. However, **I-81**, sweeping along the flank of the mountains, is a more efficient way of getting from Virginia to North Carolina and on to the Great Smoky Mountains (see p.470). Call ⓣ828/271-4779 or visit ⓦwww.nps.gov/blri for information on the various **campgrounds** ($16) and **visitor centers** along the Parkway. From May to November, the **Rocky Knob Cabins** (ⓣ540/593-3503, ⓦwww.blueridgeresort.com; ❸), on milepost 174, offers a memorable stay in the idyllic Meadows of Dan, with units featuring kitchenettes and fireplaces. Alternatively, the handsome **Peaks of Otter Lodge**, twenty miles north of Roanoke, VA at milepost 86 (ⓣ1-800/542-5927, ⓦwww.peaksofotter.com; ❺), is open year-round, with clean, simple rooms and a view overlooking a lake.

Roanoke

Of the nearby towns, **ROANOKE**, between I-81 and the Parkway, is the largest in western Virginia, known for its historic **farmers' market**, dating to 1882, on Campbell Avenue at Market Street (Mon–Sat 8am–5pm, Sun 10am–4pm; ⓣ540/342-2028). Fascinating castoffs are on view at the **History Museum of Western Virginia**, 1 Market Square (Tues–Fri 10am–4pm, Sat 10am–5pm, Sun 1–5pm; ⓦwww.history-museum.org; $3), which records settlement of the region and holds everything from Victorian fashions to documents signed by Thomas Jefferson to war relics, and at the **Virginia Museum of Transportation**, 303 Norfolk Ave (Tues–Sat 10am–5pm, Sun 1–5pm; ⓦwww.vmt.org; $8), home to the South's largest collection of diesel locomotives, plus antique buggies, buses, and fire trucks. The **visitor center**, 101 Shenandoah Ave NE (daily 9am–5pm; ⓣ540/342-6025 or 1-800/635-5535, ⓦwww.visitroanokeva.com), has walking-tour maps of the town and information on historic homes, plantations, and other tourable sites. Finally, for sweeping views of the valley, make the fifteen-minute drive from the farmers' market up Mill Mountain to the **Roanoke Star**, an 89-foot, neon-lit star built in 1949 (ask at the visitor center for directions), which gives the town its nickname, "Star City."

Unlike many towns in the region, Roanoke boasts one fine **hotel**, the ★**Hotel Roanoke**, 110 Shenandoah Ave (ⓣ540/985-5900, ⓦwww.hotelroanoke.com; ❼), an upscale, mock-Tudor structure built in 1882, whose units feature comfortable amenities and high-speed net access, plus on-site pools and a fitness center. For cheaper digs near the airport, the **Roanoke Plaza**, 2801 Hershberger Rd (ⓣ540/563-9300, ⓦwww.roanokeplaza.com; ❺), has been recently renovated, featuring a pool, gym, and sauna, and rooms with high-speed internet. Check the visitor center for details on local **B&Bs**.

You'll find a number of appealing **restaurants** in Roanoke, including the rib-stuffing fare of the **Texas Tavern**, 114 W Church Ave (ⓣ540/342-4825), a longtime diner favorite where you can load up on tasty sandwiches, burgers, and of course, chili; **Stephen's**, 2926 Franklin Rd SW (ⓣ540/344-7203), with pricey (but still excellent) oysters Rockefeller and entrees of rockfish, salmon, and steak; and **Grace's Place**, 1316 Grandin Rd (ⓣ540/981-1340), which has a savory array of pizzas, pastas, and sandwiches for affordable prices.

Bedford and Lynchburg

War buffs who've had enough Civil War history might want to call in at **BEDFORD**, about twenty miles east of Roanoke, which lost 21 men (out of 35) at Omaha Beach during the Allied invasion of Normandy, the highest per capita loss anywhere in the US. Thus, Bedford was chosen as the site of the **National D-Day Memorial**, signposted just off US-460 (daily 10am-5pm; ⓣ540/586-DDAY,

ⓦwww.dday.org; $5), a hilltop site with monuments, statues, and structures depicting the beach landing culminating in the 44-foot arch of Victory Plaza. Some twenty miles east of Bedford, **LYNCHBURG** is a busy little town that boasts the **Poplar Forest**, off Rte-460 on Rte-661 (April–Nov Wed–Mon 10am–4pm; ⓦwww.poplarforest.org; $9), Thomas Jefferson's **other** Virginia retreat, an 1806 octagonal creation with classical Palladian elements, slowly being restored along with its fifty-acre grounds (originally a hundred times as large).

West Virginia

Generally poor and almost entirely rural, **WEST VIRGINIA** is known for its timber and coal mining industries, which thrive thanks to the state's rich natural resources. Rightly called "the Mountain State," it boasts the longest whitewater rivers and most extensive wilderness in the eastern US; for these reasons, the state has become a popular destination for hikers and outdoors enthusiasts, as the moonshiners of old have been replaced by ski instructors and mountain-bike guides.

Freed from the British-imposed settlement boundary of the Appalachian Mountains, German and Scots-Irish pioneers started to cross into western Virginia in major numbers after the Revolution. They farmed small plots of land themselves, and thus had little in common with the slave-holding tidewater planters of eastern Virginia. When the Civil War broke out, the area voted to set up a rival Virginia government, loyal to the Union. Statehood was formalized by Congress in 1863, and then eight years later by the Supreme Court. Around 1900, when railroads first reached into the rugged interior, timber companies clear-cut great expanses of forests, setting up mill towns and dismantling them when they moved onto somewhere new. Later, coal-mining conglomerates perfected the "**company town**" approach, wherein workers were paid a little bit less each month than the amount they owed for their company-provided food and lodging, a policy which ultimately led to great resentment and the rise of one of America's most powerful unions, the United Mine Workers.

The state's most popular destination, the restored 1850s town of **Harpers Ferry**, is barely in West Virginia at all, standing just across the broad rivers that form its Maryland and Virginia borders. To the west, the **Allegheny Mountains** stretch for over 150 miles, their million-plus acres of hardwood forest rivaling New England's for brilliant autumnal color. West Virginia's oldest town, **Lewisburg**, sits just off I-64 at the mountains' southern foot, while the capital, **Charleston**, lies in the comparatively flat Ohio River Valley of the west.

Getting around West Virginia

Since the state is wholly built around mountains and rivers, straight, flat roads are virtually nonexistent and **getting around** via any means other than driving can be a challenge. Greyhound's service is limited, mostly traveling the western side of the state along Hwy-77, while Amtrak's Cardinal line crosses the southeast part from White Sulphur Springs through Charleston to Huntington (as part of a DC-to-Chicago route), and the Capitol Limited goes from DC to Harper's Ferry and Martinsburg on to the Great Lakes. Otherwise, plan on driving narrow, serpentine roads endlessly up and down, and allow yourself lots of time.

John Brown and Harpers Ferry

George Washington set up the country's first national munitions factory at **Harpers Ferry** to arm his young republic, and by the mid-1800s it was a thriving industrial complex, home to some five thousand workers and linked to the capital by the B&O Railroad and the Chesapeake & Ohio Canal. The 1859 **raid** on its huge arsenal by militant **John Brown** rocked the already fragmented nation and was the clearest foreshadowing of the Civil War, which broke out just eighteen months later. In the hope of fomenting a widespread slave revolt, Brown and 21 other abolitionists, including two of his sons and five black men, seized the munitions factory and its large store of weapons on the night of October 16. They held out for two days before US troops, under the command of **Robert E. Lee**, stormed the buildings, killing many of the raiders and capturing Brown. He was taken to nearby Charles Town, put on trial just nine days later, and convicted of treason; by the time he was hanged on December 2, he was far from alone in regarding himself as a martyr to the abolitionist cause.

Harpers Ferry

HARPERS FERRY, a ruggedly sited eighteenth-century town restored as a **national historic park**, clings to steep hillsides above the rocky confluence of the Potomac and Shenandoah rivers. After suffering the ravages of the Civil War (see box above) and torrential floods, the town was all but abandoned, but has since been reconstructed as an outdoor museum, combining historical importance and natural beauty, especially in the fall, when the leaves blaze with color.

Shuttle buses drop off at the end of gas-lit Shenandoah Street in the heart of the restored **Lower Town**, or Old Town, whose buildings include a blacksmith's shop, clothing and dry-goods stores, tavern, and boardinghouse – as well as the **Master Armorer's House**, once occupied by the chief gunsmith. Museums housing exhibits on the Civil War and black history, line both sides of High Street as it climbs away from the river. In the vicinity, a set of stone steps leads to the 1782 **Harper House**, the oldest in town.

A footpath continues uphill, past overgrown churchyards hemmed in by drystone walls, to **Jefferson Rock**, a huge gray boulder affording a great view over the two rivers. For a longer hike, several trails lead onwards into the surrounding forest: the **Appalachian Trail** – linking Maine to Georgia – continues from Jefferson Rock across the Shenandoah River into the Blue Ridge Mountains of Virginia, while the **Maryland Heights Trail** makes a four-mile round-trip around the headlands of the Potomac River. You can also float down the Shenandoah in a **raft** or inner-tube provided by one of the many outfitters along the rivers east and south of town.

Practicalities

Harpers Ferry makes a popular excursion from Washington DC and is served by several trains daily on the Maryland Rail Commuter network (Ⓣ 1-800/325-7245, Ⓦ www.mtamaryland.com) and by one daily Amtrak service, the Capitol Limited. Otherwise, you'll need to drive here. Parking is virtually banned in the Old Town area, though you can get there via the shuttle buses that run from the large national park **visitor center** on US-340 (site and center daily 8am–5pm; Ⓣ 304/535-6029, Ⓦ www.nps.gov/hafe; park entry $4 per person, $6 per car).

If you want to spend the night, appealing **B&Bs** are sprinkled throughout the area, among them the **Ledge House**, 280 Henry Clay St (Ⓣ 304/582-2443, Ⓦ www.theledgehouse.com; ❺), whose simple, pleasant units have balconies, with on-site wireless internet. The cozy **Laurel Lodge**, 844 E Ridge St (Ⓣ 304/535-

2886, Ⓦwww.laurellodge.com; ❺), has three rooms with wireless internet and smart antique decor. The **Angler's Inn**, 867 W Washington St (Ⓣ340/535-1239, Ⓦwww.theanglersinn.com; ❻, save $30 on weekdays), provides the requisite B&B amenities, plus the opportunity to go on a full-day fishing expedition on local rivers (combo packages start at $400). Another option is the **Harpers Ferry Hostel**, seven miles east at 19123 Sandy Hook Rd in Knoxville, Maryland (Ⓣ301/834-7652, Ⓦwww.harpersferryhostel.org; dorm beds from $23, private rooms $50). The park's visitor center and the **Jefferson County tourist bureau**, 37 Washington Court (Ⓣ304/535-2627, Ⓦwww.hello-wv.com), have details on area camping.

Around Harpers Ferry

CHARLES TOWN, four miles south of Harpers Ferry on US-340, is where John Brown was tried and hanged; the **Jefferson County Museum**, at Washington and Samuel streets (March–Dec Tues-Sat 11am–4pm; Ⓣ304/725-8628, Ⓦjeffctywvmuseum.org; free) tells the story of his trial, which took place at the still-functional, 1836 Greek Revival gem of the **Jefferson County Courthouse**, 100 E Washington St (Mon–Fri 9am–5pm), as well as his conviction and execution. Drop by the museum for walking tours of the town's fetching antique homes, which include a half-dozen owned by the family of George Washington. **SHEPHERDSTOWN**, a cozy village along the Potomac, ten miles to the north, is even better for wandering, with quaint shops and cafés looking across the river to Maryland's infamous **Antietam Battlefield** (see p.435). Sited in a 1786 red-brick edifice with plenty of Victorian furnishings and antiques, the **Historic Shepherdstown Museum**, 129 E German St (April–Oct Sat 11am–5pm, Sun 1–4pm; Ⓦwww.historicshepherdstown.com; donation), displays war relics and a replica of a steamboat.

Further afield, **BERKELEY SPRINGS** (also known as Bath) is preserved as a state historic park, thirty miles west of Harpers Ferry on Hwy-9 and seven miles south of I-70, and was a favorite summer retreat of the colonial elite – among them George Washington. Assorted massage and steam-bath treatments are still available. You can take a soak in the old **Roman Baths**, 2 S Washington St (daily 10am–6pm; Ⓣ304/258-2711 for reservations, Ⓦwww.berkeleyspringssp.com; $20 per 30min soak or $45 with massage), in active use since 1815; the spring's waters are 74°F year-round but heated to 102°F for bathers. The town's leafy and green **central square** has footpaths fanning out in all directions; one of these climbs the hill up to the crenellated, medieval-looking **Berkeley Castle**, a private estate built in 1885. Among the better **B&Bs** here are the **Highlawn Inn**, 171 Market St (Ⓣ304/258-5700 or 1-888/290-4163, Ⓦwww.highlawninn.com; ❹), spread over three buildings, including some rooms with whirlpool tubs featuring the area's famed waters, and the **Manor Inn**, 234 Fairfax St (Ⓣ304/258-1552, Ⓦwww.bathmanorinn.com; ❹), where the simple, pleasant rooms are some of the more affordable in the area.

The Allegheny Mountains

The **Allegheny Mountains**, West Virginia's segment of the Appalachian chain, spread along a 140-mile crest protected as part of the **Monongahela National Forest**, within which numerous state parks contain the most spectacular sights. There are no cities and few towns, public transportation is nonexistent, and not much goes on after dark, but if you like to backpack, hike, cycle, climb, or canoe, the Alleghenies are well worth a visit. For maps and more detailed information, contact the state tourist office (see p.63) or the Monongahela National Forest Supervisor, 200 Sycamore St, Elkins, West Virginia (Mon–Fri 8am–4.45pm; Ⓣ304/636-1800, Ⓦwww.fs.fed.us/r9/mnf).

The Northern Monongahela

Some of the most beautiful stretches of the Monongahela National Forest are in the **northern** part of the state, where the thundering torrents of the **Blackwater Falls** pour over a sixty-foot limestone cliff before crashing down through a steeply walled canyon, its water amber from the presence of darkish tannins. South from here spreads the dense forest of broad **Canaan Valley**, while to the east rise the highlands of the **Dolly Sods Wilderness**, vividly marked with rocky topography and murky bogs. The whole area is crisscrossed by hiking, cycling, and skiing trails.

Rising up at the south end of the Canaan Valley, the state's highest point, 4861-foot **Spruce Knob**, stands out over the headwaters of the Potomac River – you can actually drive all the way to the summit. Even more impressive views can be had from the top of **Seneca Rocks**, some twenty miles to the northeast, whose craggy 1000-foot cliffs present what is widely considered the most challenging rockclimb on the East Coast. If you want to take the easy way up, a good trail leads in around the back of the North Peak, and takes well under an hour to the top. Get more information at the **Seneca Rocks Discovery Center**, near the junction of highways 33 and 55 (April–Oct daily 9am–4.30pm; ⓣ304/567-2827; free). **Yokum's** (ⓣ304/567-2351 or 1-800/772-8342, ⓦwww.yokum.com), close to the base of the rocks, has a cheap **motel** ($40), self-service **cabins** ($80), and a pretty riverside **campground** (from $5 per person). Just northwest is **Smoke Hole Canyon**, whose river has cut a nearly half-mile-deep chasm into the sheer rock walls, out of which sometimes rise mist and fog for a truly spellbinding sight. For the hardy, the **North Fork Mountain Trail** follows the canyon for 24 miles, and the **Big Bend Campground** is available seasonally (April–Oct; ⓣ304/257-4488 or 1-877/444-6677; $16).

The tiny logging town of **DAVIS**, just east of US-219 at the north end of the Canaan Valley, makes a convenient **base**: the **Bright Morning Inn** on William Avenue (ⓣ304/259-5119, ⓦwww.brightmorninginn.com; ❹) is an 1896 boarding house with somewhat twee rooms, while the **Meyer House**, Third Street at Thomas Avenue (ⓣ304/259-5451, ⓦwww.meyerhousebandb.com; ❹), built in 1885, has four tasteful rooms with period decor and DVD players. Among local **outdoor guides and outfitters**, Blackwater Outdoor Adventures, twenty miles away on Rte-72 at St George (ⓣ304/478-3775, ⓦwww.blackwateroutdoors.com), runs rafting, kayaking, and canoeing trips and rents out bikes. **Timberline Resort** (ⓣ304/866-4801 or 1-800/SNOWING, ⓦwww.timberlineresort.com; $57 lift tickets) operates one of the state's largest downhill ski areas several miles southeast of town, while off Route 32 N, the **Canaan Valley Resort** (ⓣ1-800/622-4121, ⓦwww.canaanresort.com) offers a broad range of activities, plus hotel rooms (❺), campsites ($25), and cabins and cottages, the latter two usually with three-night minimums ($417). For more information on the region, contact the **visitor center** at 1401 Main St (ⓣ1-800/782-2775, ⓦwww.canaanvalley.org).

Elkins and the Augusta Festival

Just west of the Canaan Valley, **ELKINS** is the biggest town in northern West Virginia and home to the **Augusta Heritage Center**, located at Davis and Elkins College at 100 Campus Drive (ⓣ304/637-1209, ⓦwww.augustaheritage.com). It holds concerts and events in the summer, including dulcimer-playing in April and fiddle music in October, but its major showcase is mid-August's **Augusta Festival**, offering banjo-playing, blacksmithing, quilt-making, and folk dancing; after dark, performers get together for a spirited nightly hoedown, featuring storytellers and bluegrass bands.

Elkins' **visitor center**, 1035 N Randolph Ave (ⓣ1-800/422-3304, ⓦwww.randolphcountywv.com), has details on **accommodation**, including the **Cheat**

River Lodge, six miles from Elkins on Rte-33 (ⓣ304/636-2301, ⓦwww.cheatriverlodge.com), which has a lovely riverside setting, though drab facilities, at the main lodge (❹) and modern cabins (❽). Better is the **Graceland Inn**, at Davis and Elkins College (ⓣ1-800/624-3157, ⓦwww.gracelandinn.com; ❻), a chicly decorated, eleven-unit converted 1893 mansion with smart Victorian rooms. To **eat**, the **Kissel Stop Café**, 21 Third St, one block from the visitor center (ⓣ304/636-8810), serves tasty sandwiches and coffee amid railroad-car decor.

The Southern Monongahela

The **southern half** of the Monongahela National Forest is, like most of the Alleghenies, a mountainous, semi-inaccessible region – two roads, US-219 and Hwy-92, wind north to south, with a handful of minor roads twisting between them – offering outstanding recreation as well as great scenic vistas. The **visitor center** in Marlinton, 8th Street at 4th Avenue (ⓣ1-800/336-7009; ⓦwww.pocahontascountywv.com), has maps of the area.

One signature sight is the state-run **Cass Scenic Railroad**, a restored, steam-powered logging railroad built in 1902, which carries visitors on a five-hour trip up to the top of 4842-foot Bald Knob (schedule varies; ⓣ304/456-4300 or 1-800/CALL-WVA, ⓦwww.cassrailroad.com; $22-25), starting at the old lumber-mill company town of **CASS**, five miles west of Hwy-28 near the town of Greenbank, now preserved in its entirety as a historic park. You can **stay the night** in one of thirteen rail-employees' two-storey cottages built in 1902; the cottages have been converted into self-service accommodation and sleep four to ten people (ⓣ1-800/CALL-WVA; ❺). At the same number, you can also rent a historic 1920s **caboose**, with clean and basic furnishings, for a day-trip up the mountain ($139–199), or an overnight stay as well (❹ plus train fare).

Just outside of Greenbank, it's impossible to miss the gigantic white dish of the **Robert C. Byrd Green Bank Telescope** – named for the long-serving US senator – which, at sixteen million tons, is the largest steerable object on the planet. You can join free hourly tours of it on a shuttle bus (June–Aug daily 9am–6pm; Sept & Oct Wed–Sun 9am–6pm; Nov–May Wed-Sun 10am–5pm; ⓣ304/456-2011, ⓦwww.gb.nrao.edu).

A rigorous five-mile walk downhill from Cass leads along the tracks to the start of the bicycle-friendly **Greenbrier River Trail** (ⓦwww.greenbrierrivertrail.com), which follows the river and the railroad for 79 miles, coming out near Lewisburg (see p.424). You can also rent a **mountain bike** from Elk River Touring Center (ⓣ1-866/572-3771, ⓦwww.ertc.com), fifteen miles north of Marlinton, off US-219 in the hamlet of **Slatyfork**. The center runs a shuttle service to the trailheads and organizes fly-fishing and cycling trips, and ski tours in winter, and has a somewhat pricey restaurant serving trout, seafood, and pasta. It also operates basic **lodging** in an inn (❺) and farmhouse (❹) and four cabins with more amenities (❼); weekends require a two-night stay.

Five miles west of the junction with the exquisite Highland Scenic Highway (Rte-150) is **Cranberry Glades Botanical Area**, where a half-mile boardwalk is set out around a patch of peat bog swamp – one of four such bogs occupying 750 acres. Further information can be obtained from the Cranberry Mountain Nature Center (late-April–Oct Thurs–Mon 9am–4.30pm; ⓣ304/653-4826) at the junction of highways 39 and 55. Further along, the **Highland Scenic Highway** merits a leisurely trip to explore its 43 miles of eye-catching views, several fine campgrounds, and 150 miles of hiking trails that branch off from it. Contact the Marlington Ranger District (ⓣ304/799-4334) for more information.

Lewisburg and the Greenbrier Resort

Just off I-64, south of the Monongahela National Forest, **LEWISBURG** is best known as the site for August's **West Virginia State Fair**, 107 W Fair St (Ⓣ304/645-1090, Ⓦwww.wvstatefair.com), though its **Washington Street** is lined by brick-faced, early-nineteenth-century houses, and makes for pleasant wandering. The **visitor center**, 540 N Jefferson St (Ⓣ1-800/833-2068, Ⓦwww.greenbrierwv.com), hands out walking tour maps and can suggest driving tours around Greenbrier Valley. It can also put you in touch with various cozy **hotels**, such as the **General Lewis Inn**, 301 E Washington St (Ⓣ304/645-2600 or 1-800/628-4454, Ⓦwww.generallewisinn.com; ❻), which has two dozen comfortable Victorian rooms and a fine, moderately priced **restaurant** serving all-American cuisine.

Just east of Lewisburg, **WHITE SULPHUR SPRINGS** is a historic resort town mainly known for its **Greenbrier** hotel and resort, 300 W Main St (Ⓣ304/536-1110 or 1-800/453-4858, Ⓦwww.greenbrier.com; $379), the grandest hotel in the state with a pillared entrance hall, 6500 lush acres, 850 units, golf courses, and fine restaurants (reserve ahead). Two dozen US presidents have stayed here, perhaps thanks in part to the hotel's extensive, deep-underground Cold War-era **bunker**, which, having been decommissioned, is now open for fascinating tours (daily: April–Oct 9.30am, 11.30am, 1.30pm, & 3.30pm; Nov–March 1.30pm; Ⓣ304/536-7810; $30).

The New River Gorge

One of West Virginia's most spectacular river canyons, the **New River Gorge** (daily 9am–5pm; Ⓦwww.nps.gov/neri; free), lies just thirty miles west of Lewisburg along I-64. Stretching for over fifty miles, and protected as a national park, the thousand-foot chasm was carved through the limestone mountains by the New River – ironically one of the oldest in North America. Apart from one daily Amtrak train, there's no easy access to most of the gorge; to see it, you have to get out on the water, with the help of any of over fifty professional rafting companies. For details on the cycling, climbing, hiking, and rafting options available, visit the gorge's southern **Sandstone Visitor Center**, located where Hwy-64 crosses the river (Ⓣ304/466-0417), or the **Canyon Rim visitor center**, seven miles north of Oak Hill on Hwy-19 (Ⓣ304/574-2115), which sits alongside the **New River Gorge Bridge**, dramatically rising nine hundred feet above the river.

HINTON, on the southern end of the gorge (and another Amtrak stop), is an almost perfectly preserved company town, beautifully sited, with brick-lined streets angling up from the water, lined by dozens of grand civic buildings as well as rows of old worker housing. A walking tour map is available from the **visitor center**, 206 Temple St (Mon–Fri 10am–4pm; Ⓣ304/466-5420, Ⓦwww.threeriverswv.com), also the site of a railroad museum. There are the usual budget **motels**, highlighted by the **New River Falls Lodge**, 110 Cliff Island Drive (Ⓣ304/466-5710, Ⓦwww.newriverfallslodge.com), offering six basic B&B rooms (❹) and four two-bedroom cottages with kitchens and fireplaces (❼). Cantrell Ultimate Rafting, on Hwy-20, just south of town (Ⓣ1-800/470-RAFT, Ⓦwww.ultimaterafting.com), charges $49-100 per person for **river rafting**, depending on the type of raft and the destination.

Charleston

CHARLESTON, West Virginia's state capital and largest city, holds few major attractions, but does have a nice selection of Victorian-era buildings, which you

▲ New River Gorge Bridge

can see on a walking tour provided by the **visitor center**, 200 Civic Center Drive (Mon–Fri 9am–5pm; ⓣ304/344-5075, ⓦwww.charlestonwv.com). The riverfront **state capitol**, 1900 Kanawha Blvd (Mon–Sat 9am–7pm, Sun noon–7pm; tours Mon–Fri 9am–3.30pm; ⓣ304/558-4839), designed by Lincoln Memorial and US Supreme Court architect Cass Gilbert, is a stately Renaissance Revival structure from 1932 that has an impressively large, gold-leafed dome. The **West Virginia Cultural Center** (Mon–Thurs 9am–8pm, Fri & Sat 9am–6pm, Sun noon–6pm; free; ⓣ304/558-0220, ⓦwww.wvculture.org), in the same compound, has extensive displays on coal mining, geology, forestry, war, and state history. The main showcase of traditional West Virginian culture takes place here during the **Vandalia Festival**, Appalachia's largest celebration of arts and crafts, held on Memorial Day weekend and featuring lively bluegrass and folk music as well as tall-tale contests.

If you want distinctive **accommodation** in Charleston, try the **Brass Pineapple**, 1611 Virginia St E (ⓣ304/344-0748, ⓦbrasspineapple.com; ❺), a Victorian-styled B&B with plenty of antique, flowery decor, or **Tikvah's Kosher Bed-and-Breakfast**, 1564 Virginia St E (ⓣ304/345-8511, ⓦwww.tikvahskosherbandb.com; ❹), with comfortable rooms and food that's certified kosher by an area rabbi. For **dining** choices, the **Southern Kitchen**, 5240 MacCorkle Ave SE (ⓣ304/925-3154), dishes up regional favorites like ham-and-gravy and fried chicken at affordable prices, while the Art-Deco **Blossom Dairy and Soda Fountain Cafe**, 904 Quarrier St (ⓣ304/345-2233), has tasty sandwiches, burgers, and sundaes for lunch, and expensive steak, seafood, and regional fare for dinner.

Maryland

Founded as the sole Catholic colony in strongly Protestant America, and, in the nineteenth century, isolated as the northernmost slave state, **MARYLAND** has always been unique. Within its small, irregularly shaped area, its attractions range from the frantic boardwalk beaches of **Ocean City** to the sleepy fishing villages of the **Chesapeake Bay** to the bustling urban center of **Baltimore**. The Chesapeake Bay's legendary **blue crabs** and sweet rockfish are another highlight, eaten by the weekend boaters who cruise between the Bay's colonial-era towns.

Maryland boasts a number of firsts for the United States, including the first Catholic cathedral, gas-lit street, and telegraph line (between Baltimore and Washington DC), while Kent Island on Maryland's **Eastern Shore** was the third permanent English settlement (behind Jamestown and Plymouth Rock), founded in 1631.

Maryland's largest city is the busy port of **Baltimore**, a quirky metropolis with a revitalized urban waterfront, thriving cultural scene, and eclectic neighborhoods. **Western Maryland** stretches over a hundred miles to the Appalachian foothills, its rolling farmlands notable chiefly for the Civil War killing grounds at **Antietam**. Just twenty miles south of Baltimore, picturesque **Annapolis** has served as Maryland's capital since 1694. Some of the state's most worthwhile destinations, from the pretty fishing and yachting town of **St Michaels** to the untouched wilderness of **Assateague Island**, are across the Chesapeake Bay on the Eastern Shore, connected to the rest of the state by the US-50 bridge but still a world apart.

Getting around Maryland

The best ways to get around Maryland are by **car** and, if you can rent one, **boat**, sailing around the gorgeous Chesapeake Bay. **Cycling** is also a good option, especially on the Eastern Shore, where the roads are wide-shouldered and little traveled, and wind from one hamlet to another. The state tourist office (see p.63) puts out an excellent free map of the safest and most scenic routes. Baltimore is on the main Amtrak route between New York, Philadelphia, and Washington DC, and is linked by regular buses with Annapolis and elsewhere.

Baltimore

Thanks to TV's potent **The Wire, BALTIMORE** has a reputation as a city in deep decline, its glory days of port industry now distant, and its various criminals fighting desperate wars of survival. While it's true that there are places in town worth avoiding, Baltimore is still among the more enjoyable stops on the East Coast, and its closely knit neighborhoods and historic quarters provide an engaging backdrop to many diverse attractions, especially those along its celebrated **waterfront**. The city also boasts top-rated **museums**, which cover everything from fine arts to black history to urban archeology. It's also been home to such diverse figures as writers Edgar Allan Poe and H.L. Mencken, and civil rights icons Frederick Douglass and Thurgood Marshall.

Arrival, information, and getting around

Baltimore-Washington International Airport (Ⓣ410/859-7111, Ⓦwww.bwiairport.com) is ten miles south of the city center. The cheapest way to get into the city is on the **MTA commuter rail system** (ⓣ410/539-5000 or 1-800/RIDE-MTA, ⓦwww.mtamaryland.com; 25min; $1.60), which connects BWI to the restored **Pennsylvania Station**, half a mile north of downtown, at 1515 N Charles St. Penn station is also the arrival point of Amtrak **trains** (ⓣ1-800/USA-RAIL); because it's in a dicey neighborhood, you should either take a cab downtown or get on the Penn-Camden **light-rail shuttle** (Mon–Sat 6am–11pm, Sun 11am–7pm; $1.60 single), which stops downtown. **Shuttle vans** from the airport go to downtown Baltimore, including Super Shuttle (ⓣ1-800/BLUE VAN, ⓦwww.supershuttle.com; 20min; $35 single). Greyhound **buses** stop south of downtown, at 2110 Haines St, though this is in a grim area, too; take a taxi downtown or bus #27.

Pick up free **maps** and **guides** at the Baltimore Area Convention and Visitors Association, 401 Light Street, near the Maryland Science Center (April–Oct 9am–6pm; Nov–March 9.30am-4.30pm; ⓣ410/837-7024 or 1-877/BALTIMORE, ⓦwww.baltimore.org), or from its booths at the airport and train station.

City transportation

Because the city is compact, you can cover a lot of territory on foot. The **MTA**'s bus, subway, and light-rail lines ($1.60, day-pass $3.50; ⓣ410/539-5000, ⓦwww.mtamaryland.com) cover many locations, though the subway and light rail are limited to one main route each. On buses, have exact change ready. **Taxi** companies include Yellow Cab (ⓣ410/685-1212) and Royal Cab (ⓣ410/327-0330). **Water taxis** link the Inner Harbor and sixteen area attractions, including the National Aquarium, Fell's Point, and Fort McHenry (schedule varies, usually runs every 15–20min summer Mon–Sat 10am–11pm, Sun 10am–9pm; rest of year daily 11am–6pm; ⓣ410/563-3901 or 1-800/658-8947, ⓦwww.thewatertaxi.com; $8 all-day pass).

Accommodation

Baltimore has the usual chain **hotels** available downtown, along with a few local institutions, while the **B&Bs** clustered around the historic waterfront area of Fell's Point make for a pleasant alternative. The Convention and Visitors office (ⓣ410/837-7024 or 1-877/BALTIMORE, ⓦwww.baltimore.org) can help with reservations.

Admiral Fell Inn 888 S Broadway ⓣ410/522-7377 or 1-866/583-4162, ⓦwww.harbormagic.com. Chic historic hotel spread over seven buildings (some dating to the 1770s) in the heart of Fell's Point. Rooms have vaulted ceilings and fireplaces; some have jacuzzis and balconies as well. ❽

Celie's Waterfront Inn 1714 Thames St ⓣ410/522-2323 or 1-800/432-0184, ⓦwww.baltimore-bed-breakfast.com. Nine exquisite rooms and suites, some with private balconies. A rooftop deck has superb views of Fell's Point harbor. ❼

Henderson's Wharf Inn 1000 Fell St ⓣ410/522-7087, ⓦwww.hendersonswharf.com. Prominent waterside spot with modern rooms that include boutique furnishings, refrigerators, and internet access. Continental breakfast and on-site gym as well. ❽

HI-Baltimore 17 W Mulberry St ⓣ410/576-8880 ⓦwww.baltimorehostel.org. Set in a sturdy 1850s brownstone, this boasts four dozen dorm beds, with antiques, deck and patio, wi-fi access, karaoke, and laundry, plus movie screenings and pasta feeds. ❶

The Inn at Government House 1125 N Calvert St ⓣ410/539-0566, ⓦwww.baltimorecity.gov/visitor/inn@gh. Elaborate 1889 Victorian mansion with antique-filled rooms, grand music and dining rooms, detailed woodwork, and breakfast and parking included. ❺

Mount Vernon 24 W Franklin St ⓣ410/727-2000 or 1-800/245-5256, ⓦwww.mountvernonbaltimore.com. Large, stately hotel has comfortable rooms with free high-speed net access and complimentary breakfast, plus a central location. ❹

Peabody Court 612 Cathedral St ⓣ410/727-7101, ⓦwww.peabodycourthotel.com. Luxury hotel in a handsome, converted 1928 apartment building set in a historic neighborhood. Has marble bathrooms and upscale decor, plus internet access. Pet-friendly. ❽

Pier 5 711 Eastern Ave ⓣ410/539-2000, ⓦwww.harbormagic.com. Centrally located, upscale boutique hotel with plenty of style, offering smart, modern rooms with CD players and suites with fridges, microwaves, and wet bars. ❾

Downtown Baltimore

Enlivened by new restaurants and bars, **downtown Baltimore** makes for a pleasant stroll along the brick-lined waterfront and features a bevy of nautical and science-oriented attractions. It's also within walking distance of the two sports stadiums, which makes it a convenient spot for fans to meet for dinner or a drink.

The main cluster of restaurants and cafés is found west of **Charles Street**, in Baltimore's original shopping district, now coming back after a long decline. One Baltimore landmark here, dating from 1782, is the oldest and loudest of the city's covered markets, **Lexington Market**, 400 W Lexington St (Mon–Sat 8.30am–6pm; ⓣ410/685-6169, ⓦwww.lexingtonmarket.com), with more than a hundred food stalls, including **Faidley's** (see p.433). Safe during the day, the area can become more dicey after dark.

Just south of the market, **Westminster Church**, 519 W Fayette St, was built in 1852 atop the main Baltimore cemetery. Among the prominent figures entombed here is **Edgar Allan Poe**, who lived in town for three years in the 1830s, marrying his 13-year-old cousin and starting a career in journalism before moving on to Richmond, Virginia. In 1849, while passing through Baltimore, Poe was found incoherent near a polling place and died soon after. In 1875 his remains were moved from a pauper's grave and entombed within the stone memorial that stands along Green Street on the north side of the church. Every January 19, a mysterious figure clad in black appears at Poe's grave to offer a toast of cognac and three red roses in honor of his birthday.

Despite the notoriety of the Poe site, most visitors come to visit **Oriole Park at Camden Yards**, five blocks south, the baseball stadium of the Baltimore Orioles (ⓣ1-888/848-BIRD, ⓦwww.theorioles.com; $8–80 tickets). Open-faced and city-oriented, the park was one of the first to reintroduce a historic flair to stadium design, in contrast to the concrete boxes that had dominated pro sports for a generation. Just next door, looking very much like a newly landed alien spaceship, is the 68,400-seat **M&T Bank Stadium**, built in 1998 and home to the **Baltimore Ravens** football team, who were named after Edgar Allan Poe's most (in)famous character (ⓣ410/547-SEAT, ⓦwww.baltimoreravens.com; $50–115 tickets).

The Inner Harbor

By most estimates, the **Inner Harbor** is a success story of urban revitalization. The rotting wharves and derelict warehouses that stood here through the 1970s have been replaced by the sparkling steel-and-glass **Harborplace** shopping mall (Mon–Sat 10am–9pm, Sun noon–6pm; ⓣ410/332-4191, ⓦwww.harborplace.com), though the businesses inside aren't too different from what you'll find in any other consumer zone. Sweeping views of the entire city and beyond can be admired from the 27th-storey Top of the World observation deck at Baltimore's own **World Trade Center**, on the north pier (May–Sept 10am–9pm; Oct–April Wed–Sun 10am–6pm; ⓣ410/837-VIEW, ⓦwww.viewbaltimore.org; $5). Nothing in the Inner Harbor dates from before its rebuilding, but to lend an air of authenticity, the graceful **USS Constellation** (April–Oct 10am–5.30pm; Nov–March 10am–4.30pm; ⓣ410/539-1797, ⓦwww.constellation.org; $8.75)

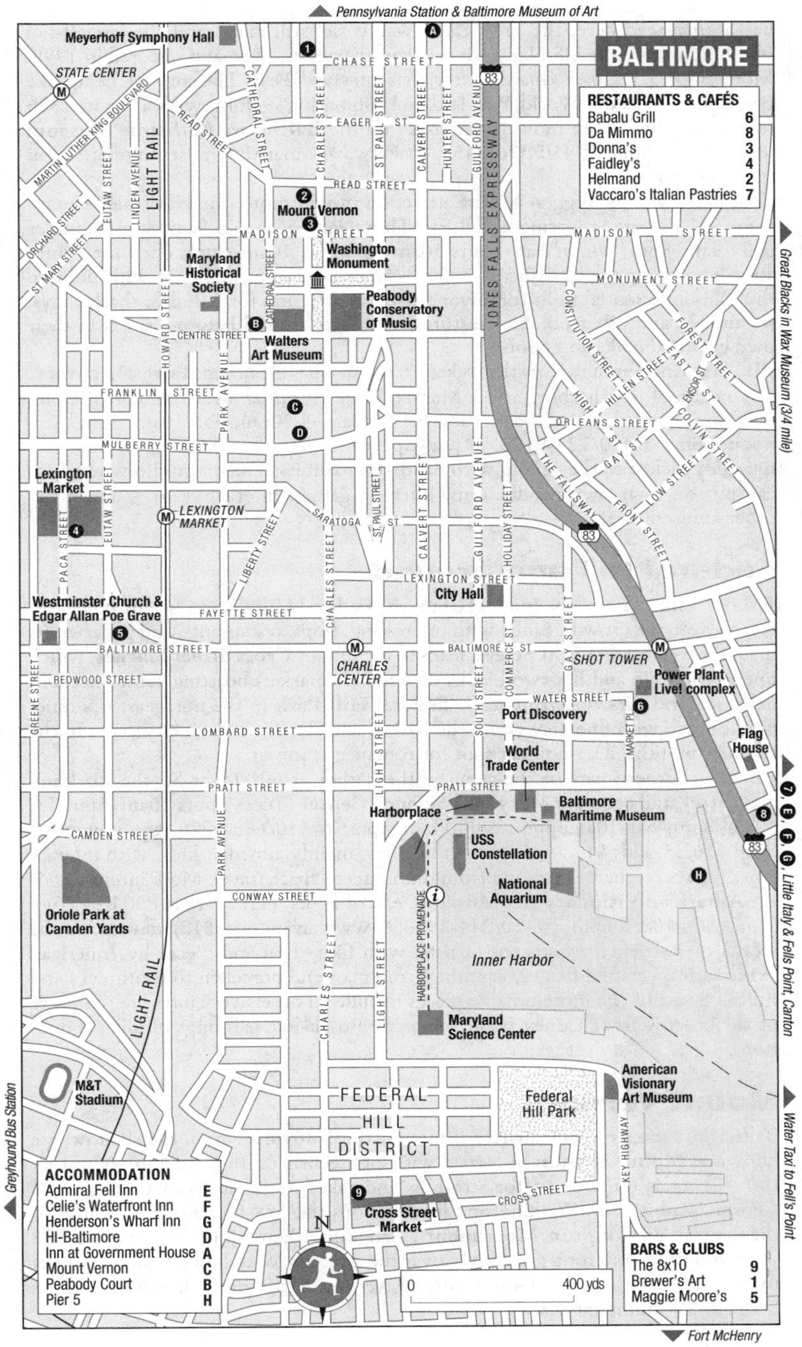
Pennsylvania Station & Baltimore Museum of Art
BALTIMORE
RESTAURANTS & CAFÉS
Babalu Grill 6
Da Mimmo 8
Donna's 3
Faidley's 4
Helmand 2
Vaccaro's Italian Pastries 7
Meyerhoff Symphony Hall
STATE CENTER
CHASE STREET
EAGER ST
READ STREET
MADISON STREET
MONUMENT STREET
CENTRE STREET
FRANKLIN STREET
MULBERRY STREET
SARATOGA ST
LEXINGTON STREET
FAYETTE STREET
BALTIMORE STREET
BALTIMORE ST
REDWOOD STREET
WATER STREET
LOMBARD STREET
PRATT STREET
CAMDEN STREET
CONWAY STREET
CROSS STREET
MARTIN LUTHER KING BOULEVARD
ORCHARD STREET
ST MARY STREET
EUTAW STREET
LINDEN AVENUE
LIGHT RAIL
HOWARD STREET
PARK AVENUE
CATHEDRAL STREET
CHARLES STREET
ST PAUL STREET
CALVERT STREET
HUNTER STREET
GUILFORD AVENUE
HOLLIDAY STREET
JONES FALLS EXPRESSWAY
CONSTITUTION STREET
FOREST STREET
HILLEN STREET
EAST ST
ENSOR ST
COLVIN STREET
HIGH ST
ORLEANS STREET
GAY ST
THE FALLSWAY
FRONT STREET
LOW STREET
PACA STREET
GREENE STREET
LIBERTY STREET
SOUTH STREET
COMMERCE ST
GAY STREET
MARKET PL
LIGHT STREET
HARBORPLACE PROMENADE
KEY HIGHWAY
83
Mount Vernon
Washington Monument
Maryland Historical Society
Peabody Conservatory of Music
Walters Art Museum
Lexington Market
LEXINGTON MARKET
Westminster Church & Edgar Allan Poe Grave
City Hall
CHARLES CENTER
SHOT TOWER
Power Plant Live! complex
Port Discovery
World Trade Center
Flag House
Harborplace
Baltimore Maritime Museum
USS Constellation
National Aquarium
Inner Harbor
Oriole Park at Camden Yards
Maryland Science Center
M&T Stadium
FEDERAL HILL DISTRICT
Federal Hill Park
American Visionary Art Museum
Cross Street Market
Great Blacks in Wax Museum (3/4 mile)
7, E, F, G, Little Italy & Fells Point, Canton
Water Taxi to Fell's Point
Greyhound Bus Station
Fort McHenry
ACCOMMODATION
Admiral Fell Inn E
Celie's Waterfront Inn F
Henderson's Wharf Inn G
HI-Baltimore D
Inn at Government House A
Mount Vernon C
Peabody Court B
Pier 5 H
BARS & CLUBS
The 8x10 9
Brewer's Art 1
Maggie Moore's 5
N
0
400 yds

has been placed here, the only Civil War vessel still afloat and the last all-sail warship built by the US Navy – it was constructed in 1854 and restored in 1999. More ships – a Coast Guard cutter that survived Pearl Harbor, a Chesapeake Bay lightship, and a World War II diesel submarine – along with a squat, 1856 lighthouse that's been moved here make up the **Baltimore Maritime Museum** (daily 10am–5pm; ⓣ410/396-3453, ⓦwww.baltomaritimemuseum.org; $6) on the next pier.

Far and away the biggest tourist attraction in Baltimore, the **National Aquarium**, 501 E Pratt St (spring & fall Sat–Thurs 9am–5pm, Fri 9am–8pm; summer daily 9am–8pm; winter Sat–Thurs 10am–5pm, Fri 10am–8pm; open for 90min after last admission; ⓣ410/576-3800, ⓦwww.aqua.org; $22, $26 with dolphin show), is an essential sight for anyone with an affection for jellyfish, sharks, rays, sea turtles, and other oceanic creatures, who dart around before visitors in their own enclosed tanks and pools.

If this isn't enough for the tykes, try out the gleaming **Port Discovery**, just north of the harbor, at 35 Market Place (summer Mon–Sat 10am–5pm, Sun noon–5pm; rest of year Tues–Fri 9.30am–4.30pm, Sat 10am–5pm, Sun noon–5pm; ⓣ410/727-8120, ⓦwww.portdiscovery.org; $10.75), a children's museum packed to the ceiling with hands-on exhibits, a media studio where kids can put on their own productions, learning games, interactive toys, and many other amusements.

Federal Hill and around

A short walk south of the Inner Harbor, the **Federal Hill** district is a great place to escape from the crowds. Lined with interesting shops, restaurants, and galleries, its main thoroughfare, **Light Street**, leads to the indoor **Cross Street Market**, which opened in 1875 and has two blocks of open-air markets boasting some excellent delis, seafood bars, and fruit stalls. **Federal Hill Park** in the northeast is a quiet public space with fine views over the harbor and the downtown cityscape. In the summer months, it's a popular spot for romance at sunset.

In the northern part of the area, by the harbor at 601 Light St, the sparkling glass, steel, and concrete **Maryland Science Center** (Tues–Thurs 10am–5pm, Fri 10am–8pm, Sat 10am–6pm, Sun 11am–5pm; ⓣ410/685-5225, ⓦwww.mdsci.org; $16.25, kids $11.75, IMAX show $8) is mainly aimed at kids, with interactive displays on themes ranging from dinosaurs to space travel. More interesting is the **American Visionary Art Museum**, east of Federal Hill Park at 800 Key Hwy (Tues–Sun 10am–6pm; ⓣ410/244-1900, ⓦwww.avam.org; $12), devoted to the works of untrained or amateur artists, with four thousand pieces by American "visionaries," crafted from everything from glass and porcelain to toothpicks and tinfoil. Some of the more notable pieces include an obsessively intricate sculpture of the boardwalk of Coney Island and eerie Bosch-like paintings of alien abductions.

Mount Vernon

Baltimore's most elegant quarter is just north of downtown on the shallow rise known as **Mount Vernon**. Adorned with eighteenth-century brick townhouses, this district is quite good for strolling and takes its name from the home of George Washington. Washington's likeness tops the 178-foot marble column of the central **Washington Monument** (Wed–Sun 10am–5pm; free), whose 228 steps you can climb for a great view over the city. It's located in a small park next to the spire of the sham-Gothic Mount Vernon Methodist Church at Charles Street and Monument Place.

Across the street, a solemn stone facade of the **Peabody Conservatory of Music** hides one of the city's best interior spaces: the beautiful, skylit atrium of the **Peabody Library**, 17 E Mount Vernon Place (Tues–Fri 9am–5pm, Sat 9am–1pm; ⓣ410/659-8179), an 1878 Victorian delight rich with cast-iron balconies, soaring columns, and glass skylights. The ground floor features displays of various history books, among them a wonderful illustrated 1555 edition of Boccaccio's **Decameron**, and a 1493 printing of the **Nuremburg Chronicles**. Two blocks west, the **Maryland Historical Society** museum, 201 W Monument St (Wed–Sun 10am–5pm; ⓣ410/685-3750, ⓦwww.mdhs.org; $8), traces the path of local history through portraits of the old Maryland elite and key documents, and its antique-filled chambers give a sense of the maritime wealth created here through nineteenth-century trade.

A block south of the Washington Monument, the **Walters Art Museum**, 600 N Charles St (Wed–Sun 11am–5pm; ⓣ410/547-9000, wwww.thewalters.org; $12), is set around a large sculpture court, modeled on an Italian Renaissance palazzo, beyond which modern galleries show off Egyptian jewelry and sarcophagi, including an intact mummy, Greek and Roman antiquities, medieval illuminated manuscripts, Islamic ceramics, Byzantine silver, pre-Columbian artifacts, and French Impressionist works.

The Flag House and Star-Spangled Banner Museum, and Little Italy

A quarter of a mile east of downtown and the Inner Harbor is the intriguing **Flag House and Star-Spangled Banner Museum**, 844 E Pratt St (Tues–Sat 10am–4pm; last tour at 3.30pm; ⓣ410/837-1793, ⓦwww.flaghouse.org; $7), where in 1813 Mary Pickersgill sewed the 30-foot-by-45-foot US flag, whose presence at the British attack on Baltimore Harbor the following year inspired Francis Scott Key to write "The Star-Spangled Banner." The house is full of patriotic tributes, as well as various antiques from the era, and there's a less interesting **War of 1812 Museum** (same hours and admission) that covers that conflict with costumes and military relics.

The densely tangled streets of **Little Italy**, still a strongly Italian neighborhood with dozens of good restaurants and cafés, spread to the east of downtown. The area is built around the 1881 **St Leo the Great** church, 227 S Exeter St, and holds plenty of Baltimore's trademark stone-fronted **rowhouses**, almost all with highly polished steps quarried from local marble, the same also used to construct the stone monuments of Washington DC.

Fell's Point, Canton and Greektown

Southeast of Little Italy stands Baltimore's oldest and liveliest quarter, **Fell's Point**, whose position on deep water made it the heart of the city's extensive shipbuilding industry. The shipyards are long gone, but many old bars and earthy pubs – the highest concentration in the city – have hung on to form one of the better nightlife districts on the East Coast, set in and around handsome nineteenth-century buildings. To pick up a healthy snack, the area's **Broadway Market**, 610 S Broadway (ⓣ410/675-1466), is always a favorite stopping point. The Fell's Point **visitor center**, 808 S Ann St (daily noon–4pm; ⓣ410/675-6750), provides good self-guided walking maps and tours of the 1765 **Robert Long House**, the oldest surviving urban residence in Baltimore, a handsome Colonial structure dating to 1765.

Other interesting sights include the **Fell's Point Maritime Museum**, 1724 Thames St (Thurs–Mon 10am–5pm; ⓣ410/732-0278; $4), originally a trolley barn and warehouse, now converted into an exhibition space outlining the area's nautical history as a shipping point for fruit and tobacco, as well as slaves and opium. A different perspective on that history is provided by the **Frederick Douglass Isaac Myers Maritime Park**, 1417 Thames St (Mon & Wed–Fri 11am–5pm, Sat & Sun noon–5pm; ⓣ410/685-0295, ⓦwww.douglassmyers.org; $5), a historical museum named after the pioneering black leaders who were active in the area. Exhibits focus on their backgrounds, the history of the local port – including the slave trade – and a re-creation of a late-nineteenth-century shipyard that employed African Americans.

East of Fell's Point and two miles southeast of downtown, **Canton** is another district full of historic rowhouses, some of which date back to the Civil War, and is being revitalized with new restaurants and nightlife. A mile east, **Greektown** is still a thriving Hellenic community, after almost a century, and boasts its share of authentic bakeries, diners, and groceries. The area's centerpiece is the sturdy brick edifice of **St Nicholas Greek Orthodox Church**, at Eastern Avenue and Ponca Street.

Fort McHenry

Linked by water taxi from Fell's Point, but on the opposite side of the harbor, **Fort McHenry National Monument**, 2400 E Fort Ave (summer daily 8am–8pm; rest of year daily 8am–5pm; ⓣ410/962-4290, ⓦwww.nps.gov/fomc; $7 seven-day pass), is a star-shaped fort that the British bombed during the War of 1812 to penetrate the harbor to attack Baltimore. The attack failed, and when he saw "the bombs bursting in air," Francis Scott Key was moved to write the poem "The Star-Spangled Banner," first known as "The Defense of Fort McHenry." Over the next century, the fort was used as a prison for Confederate soldiers and pro-Southern political prisoners. You can tour the fort's old barracks, officers' and enlisted men's quarters and guardhouse, and see military hardware and relics of different eras.

Further north

About a mile northeast of the city center, in an old fire station off Broadway at 1601 E North Ave, the **Great Blacks in Wax Museum** (summer Tues–Sat 9am–6pm, Sun noon–6pm; winter Tues–Sat 9am–5pm, Sun noon–5pm; ⓣ410/563-7809, ⓦwww.ngbiwm.com; $12) uses wax models in posed dioramas to illustrate black history, from Egyptian pharaohs and early Muslims through to Dr Martin Luther King Jr, Marcus Garvey, Rosa Parks, and Malcolm X. The neighborhood is a bit dicey, so drive or take a cab. Further out on the north side, two miles from downtown, is the Charles Village district that is enjoyable for its early-twentieth-century rowhouses and walkable streets. Here, at the top of Charles Street is the **Baltimore Museum of Art**, 10 Art Museum Drive (Wed–Fri 11am–5pm, Sat & Sun 11am–6pm; ⓣ443/573-1700, ⓦwww.artbma.org; free). As well as Italian and Dutch works by Botticelli, Raphael, Rembrandt, and Van Dyck, the museum holds Chardin's **A Game of Knucklebones**, played by a smiling scamp, drawings by Durer and Goya, and photographs from Weston, Stieglitz, and others. The highlight is the **Cone Collection** of works by Delacroix, Degas, Cézanne, and Picasso, as well as over a hundred drawings and paintings by Matisse, among them his signature **Large Reclining Nude** and **Seated Odalisque**.

Eating

Baltimore's restaurants tend to be unpretentious, family oriented, and reasonably priced, with particularly appealing fresh **seafood** places offering top-notch **steamed crabs**, as well as the usual diners and more than a dozen good restaurants side by side in Little Italy. Fell's Point boasts numerous vegetarian, seafood, and other types of restaurants.

Babalu Grill 332 Market Place, just north of Inner Harbor ⓣ410/234-9898. Popular restaurant serving well-priced traditional Cuban and *Nuevo Latino* cuisine in a lively setting. Good for its ceviche, ham croquettes, lamb shank, and Cuban sandwich with fried yuca.

Bertha's 734 S Broadway ⓣ410/327-5795. Casual and inexpensive (yet stylish) seafood restaurant, tucked away behind a tiny Fell's Point bar. Known for its delicious mussels, crab cakes, high tea, and nightly live blues, jazz, and Dixieland.

Black Olive 814 S Bond St, Fell's Point ⓣ410/276-7141. Expensive but succulent Mediterranean restaurant that has affordable *meze* (small plates) like grilled octopus salad, calamari, and pan-seared zucchini, as well as pricier entrees like rack of lamb and lobster tail.

Da Mimmo 217 S High St ⓣ410/727-6876. Intimate, upscale Little Italy café, with a wide-ranging menu that includes favorites like clams, *saltimbocca*, gnocchi, and pasta fagioli, live piano music, and a romantic ambiance.

Donna's 800 N Charles St ⓣ410/385-0180. Delicious sandwiches and burgers for lunch, and savory, mid-priced pasta, steak, and seafood for dinner in an elegant Mount Vernon locale.

Faidley's 203 N Paca, downtown ⓣ410/727-4898. Located in Lexington Market, the best and cheapest of many outlets serving oysters, clams, and other catches from the Chesapeake Bay, including terrific crab cakes – a business dating back to 1886. Stand-up dining only.

Helmand 806 N Charles St ⓣ410/752-0311. Inexpensive but chic dinner-only Afghan restaurant in Mount Vernon, with plenty of lamb dishes as well as *aushak* (leek-filled vegetarian ravioli) and the delicious *kaddo borawni* (a fried-pumpkin appetizer).

Matthew's Pizza 3131 Eastern Ave, west of Greektown ⓣ410/276-8755. Old-line hole in the wall that still boasts the city's best slices – rich and tangy, with a solid crust and traditional ingredients, or nuovo toppings like crab.

Obrycki's 1727 E Pratt St, just north of Fell's Point ⓣ410/732-6399. Baltimore's longest-established seafood restaurant, with delicious steamed, soft-shell, and broiled crabs at premium prices, as well as other excellent seafood. Closed in winter.

Peter's Inn 504 S Ann St, Fell's Point ⓣ410/675-7313. Top-notch but casual restaurant with a fine, rotating menu, where you can get anything from shrimp bisque to seared tuna to a New York strip steak, for $14–28 per entree. Also has an enjoyable bar on-site.

Vaccaro's Italian Pastries 222 Albemarle St, Little Italy ⓣ410/685-4905. Great spot to load up on cheesecakes, cookies, and other sweets, and to indulge in the kind of delicious gelato they make in the Old Country.

Drinking and nightlife

Baltimore has plenty of places to **drink**, and **Fell's Point** may well have the most. One bar after another lines up along Broadway and the many smaller side streets, and almost all feature some sort of entertainment. The **Power Plant Live!** complex, next to the Inner Harbor, at 34 Market Place (ⓣ410-727-LIVE, ⓦwww.powerplantlive.com), offers a wide selection of dining and mainstream entertainment. The city's highbrow culture is concentrated northwest of the center, in the Mount Royal Avenue area, including the **Meyerhoff Symphony Hall**, 1212 Cathedral St (ⓣ410/783-8000, ⓦwww.bsomusic.org), and the **Lyric Opera House**, 110 W Mount Royal Ave (ⓣ410/727-6000, ⓦwww.baltimoreopera.com). For a rundown of what's on, pick up a copy of the excellent and free **City Paper** (ⓦwww.citypaper.com) or check out ⓦwww.Baltimore.org.

The 8x10 10 E Cross St, Federal Hill ⓣ410/625-2000. Solid bar and live-music venue that features an eclectic mix of bands, from jazz to indie rock and electronica, often for a cover charge.

Brewer's Art 1106 N Charles St, Mount Vernon ⓣ410/547-9310. The place anyone with a yen for microbrews must visit – a local landmark for beer-making that's tops for its "Ozzy" Belgian-style, dark "Proletary Ale" and good old "Charm City Sour Cherry."

Cat's Eye Pub 1730 Thames St, Fell's Point ⓣ410/276-9085. Cozy, crowded bar, offering a good range of beers and live music nightly, from blues and jazz to bluegrass and folk.

Looney's Pub 2900 O'Donnell St ⓣ410/675-9235. This animated hangout, serving up a variety of snacks and beers to the tune of guest DJs, is one of Canton's most popular watering holes.

Lulu's Off Broadway 1703 Aliceanna St, Fell's Point ⓣ410/537-LULU. Jumping joint where you can dine on BBQ ribs, meatloaf, and lobster sandwiches – as well as vegetarian fare – or knock back a glass of wine or a microbrew while listening to guest DJs on weekends.

Maggie Moore's 21 N Eutaw St, north of Inner Harbor ⓣ410/837-2100. Smart and appealing Irish pub with handsome decor and nice, dark brews, as well as fare such as leg-of-lamb sandwich and beef-and-Guinness stew.

Max's on Broadway 735 S Broadway ⓣ410/675-6297. Huge corner venue with a very long bar – doling out some three hundred kinds of beer in bottles, and rotating more than seventy on tap – pool tables, and, upstairs, a leather-upholstered cigar lounge.

Wharf Rat Bar 801 S Ann St, Fell's Point ⓣ410/276-9034. This friendly bar, well stocked with English ales, other European imports, and regional microbrews, packs in a trendy and discerning crowd.

Western Maryland

Western Maryland ranges for some two hundred miles east to west, but is in places only two miles north to south. The further west you go the more hilly and rural it becomes, similar to West Virginia.

Apart from the Civil War battlefield at **Antietam**, west of the only sizeable town, **Frederick**, the best reason to come to this part of the state is to cycle or hike the footpath of the restored old **Chesapeake and Ohio Canal**, which winds along the Maryland side of the Potomac River from Washington DC for over 180 miles to **Cumberland** in the western mountains. Even further west is the state's largest fresh-water lake, **Deep Creek Lake**, popular with watersports enthusiasts. It also has more than 70,000 acres of public parks and forests surrounding it, some of which make for smooth cross-country skiing during the winter.

Frederick and around

One of the first towns settled in northwestern Maryland, **FREDERICK**, less than an hour west of Baltimore, at the junction of I-70 and I-270, was laid out in 1745 by German farmers and grew to become a main stopover on the route west to the Ohio Valley; the bulk of today's tidy town survives from the early 1800s. Frederick is also a good base for exploring Antietam (see p.435) and Harpers Ferry (see p.420).

The **visitor center**, 19 E Church St (daily 9am–5pm; ⓣ301/600-2888 or 1-800/999-3613, ⓦwww.fredericktourism.org), has walking-tour maps of the town highlights, some of which include the **Schifferstadt House**, just off US-15 (April to mid-Dec Thurs–Sun noon–4pm; ⓣ301/668-6088; $3), a stone-walled farmhouse built in 1756 and largely unaltered since; the **Roger Taney House**, 121 S Bentz St (Sat 10am–4pm, Sun 1–4pm; ⓣ301/663-1188; $3), owned by the US Supreme Court chief justice best known for presiding over the infamous **Dred Scott** case, which helped lead to the Civil War; and the **Beatty-Cramer House**, 9010 Liberty Rd on Rte-26 (donation; tours by appointment at ⓣ301/668-2086), a collection of three farm buildings that contains the area's oldest, still-standing structure, from 1732.

The tiny **Barbara Fritchie House**, 154 W Patrick St (tours by appointment at ⓣ301/698-8992), is the place where 95-year-old Barbara Fritchie was said to have defiantly waved the US flag while Confederate soldiers marched past her home. Although this is probably myth, the house is a well-preserved piece of Americana, with a historic flag still hanging from the pitched roof. A short walk east, the **National Museum of Civil War Medicine**, 48 E Patrick St (Mon–Sat 10am–5pm, Sun 11am–5pm; ⓦwww.civilwarmed.org; $6.50) offers intriguing exhibits on mid-nineteenth-century military medicine, including grisly amputation tools and battlefield triage.

In the outskirts north of Frederick, **Cunningham Falls State Park** (8am–sunset) and the **Catoctin Mountain Park** (open dawn to dusk; free) hold seemingly endless hardwood forests – great for fall color – in the midst of which are preserved remnants of early homesteads. Pick up details on hiking and camping at the main **visitor center**, off Hwy-77 two miles west of US-15 (Mon–Thurs 10am–4.30pm, Fri 10am–5pm, Sat & Sun 8.30pm–5pm; Ⓣ301/663-9330, Ⓦwww.nps.gov/cato). You can also **camp** here ($20 a night), and **rent cabins** of various size ($40–80).

There are **motels** along both I-70 and US-15, but the town's major **B&Bs** are better options: the **Hill House**, 12 W Third St (Ⓣ301/682-4111; ❺), has artfully decorated rooms that feature antiques and balconies, and **Hollerstown Hill**, 4 Clarke Place (Ⓣ301/228-3630, Ⓦwww.hollerstownhill.com; ❺), has four pleasant rooms in historic buildings from the late nineteenth century. If you plan on visiting Antietam (see below), try the **Jacob Rohrbach Inn**, 138 W Main St, Sharpsburg (Ⓣ301/432-5079, Ⓦwww.jacob-rohrbach-inn.com; ❺), with four well-appointed rooms and suites and one detached cottage, all decorated in a style appropriate for a 200-year-old homestead.

For a bite to **eat**, try **Monocacy Crossing**, 4424 Urbana Pike (Ⓣ301/846-4204), for its fine sandwiches and seafood at lunchtime, or mid-priced ribs, crab cakes, and other top-shelf Atlantic cuisine for dinner. Also worthwhile are the same, slightly cheaper entrees at **Barley & Hops**, 5473 Urbana Pike (Ⓣ301/668-5555), with good microbrewed pales ales and stouts, and the nice range of handcrafted beer on tap at **Brewer's Alley**, 124 N Market St (Ⓣ301/631-0089).

Antietam National Battlefield

The site of the single bloodiest battle in the Civil War – causing more American deaths than any other single-day battle in US history – **Antietam National Battlefield** spreads over unaltered farmlands outside the village of **Sharpsburg**, fifteen miles west of Frederick. Here, on the morning of September 17, 1862, forty thousand troops faced a Union army twice that number. Hours later, 23,000 men from both sides lay dead or dying. The fiercest fighting, and the worst bloodshed, occurred in cornfields to the north.

For all the carnage, the battle wasn't tactically decisive, but the Confederates' lack of success lost them the support of their would-be ally Great Britain, while the Union performance encouraged Lincoln to issue the Emancipation Proclamation. Pick up a brochure and driving-tour map of the park at the **visitor center**, a mile north of Sharpsburg off Hwy-65 (hours vary, usually daily 8.30am–6pm; Ⓣ301/432-5124, Ⓦwww.nps.gov/anti; $4 three-day pass).

Cumberland and the C&O Canal

The only large town in the far west of Maryland, sandwiched between West Virginia and Pennsylvania in a part of the state only eight miles wide, **CUMBERLAND** started life as a coal-mining center in the late 1700s, and became the terminus of the **C&O (Chesapeake and Ohio) Canal**, an impressive engineering feat begun in 1813 but not completed until 1850, by which time the railroads had already made it obsolete (the Cumberland Amtrak station is at E Harrison Street at Queen City Street).

There are six **visitor centers** along the canal: the westernmost is in Cumberland, at 13 Canal St (daily 9am–5pm; Ⓣ301/722-8226, Ⓦwww.nps.gov/choh). One visitor center, at 11710 MacArthur Blvd, in Potomac, Maryland (Ⓣ301/767-3714), is located in **Great Falls** Park; admission ($3 per pedestrian, $5 per car for three days) is required to enter the park. All centers provide information on hiking, cycling, canoeing, and camping, which can prove valuable if you're interested in traveling the entire 184.5 miles along the **canal towpath**, one of the longest and loveliest contiguous trails in the US. In summer, the historic trains of the **Western Maryland Scenic Railroad** leave from here to make the three-hour trip to Frostburg through the surrounding mountains (all trips at 11:30 am: May–Sept Fri–Sun; Oct Thurs–Sun; Nov–mid-Dec Sat & Sun; ⓣ301/759-4400 or 1-800/872-4650, ⓦwww.wmsr.com; $25). Look for the tiny black-and-white log cabin where George Washington served his first commission in the 1750s, standing directly opposite the station on the other side of the canal.

Accommodation in Cumberland is limited, but one good choice is the **Bruce House Inn**, 201 Fayette St (ⓣ301/777-8860, ⓦwww.brucehouseinn.com; ⑤), an 1840 charmer that appeals for its four B&B rooms with stylish furnishings and high-speed net access.

About thirty miles east of Cumberland, I-68 slices straight through a 1600-foot wedge of sedimentary rock, exposing a dramatic rock formation (called a syncline) that can be viewed from a platform at the excellent **Sideling Hill Exhibit Center**, part of Fort Frederick State Park (daily 9am–5pm; ⓣ301/842-2155), where there's a special geological exhibit and stunning views all around.

Annapolis and southern Maryland

Maryland's capital since 1694, **Annapolis** has changed little in size and appearance over the centuries, its charmingly narrow, time-worn streets making it among the more engaging small US cities. If you want to get a better feel for the Chesapeake Bay region, head south to places like **St Mary's City** – the first capital of Maryland, reconstructed in the 1960s – or **Solomons Island**, one of many small bay towns that seem timeless.

Annapolis

At the center of **ANNAPOLIS**, overlooking the town's dense web of streets, the **Maryland State House** (Mon–Fri 9am–5pm, Sat & Sun 10am–4pm; tours at 11am & 3pm; ⓣ410/974-3400; free) was completed in 1779. For six months, between 1783 and 1784, it served as the official capitol of the US; it remains the nation's oldest statehouse still in use. The **Old Senate Chamber**, off the grand entrance hall, is where the Treaty of Paris was ratified in 1784, officially ending the Revolutionary War. A statue of George Washington stands here on the spot where, three weeks before the treaty signing, he resigned his commission as head of the Continental Army. Also on the grounds of the State House is the cottage-sized **Old Treasury**, built in 1735 to hold colonial Maryland's currency reserves.

Many grand late-eighteenth-century brick homes line the streets of Annapolis. The red-brick villa of the **Hammond-Harwood House**, two blocks west of the State House at 19 Maryland Ave, off King George Street (April–Oct Tues–Sun noon–5pm, last tour at 4pm; ⓦwww.hammondharwoodhouse.org; $6), was built in 1774 and is notable for its beautifully carved woodwork and intricate front doorway. The 1774 **Chase-Lloyd House**, 22 Maryland Ave (Mon–Sat 2–4pm; donation; ⓣ410/263-2723), is a three-storey Georgian brick townhouse with grand stairway, interior Ionic columns, and intricate ornamentation. Finally, the 1765 **William Paca House**, 186 Prince George St (winter Fri–Sun noon–5pm; rest of year Mon–Sat 10am–5pm, Sun noon–5pm; ⓣ410/267-7619; $8 including tour), is named for one of the state's governors and signers of the Declaration of Independence and decorated in warm, rich colors and ornate furniture. The splendid formal garden has French-styled geometry and lovely topiary and boasts a nice viewing pavilion. Besides such elite manors, dozens of eighteenth-century clapboard cottages and warehouses fill the narrow streets that run down to the waterfront. The **Historic Annapolis Foundation**, housed in a c.1715 tavern at 18 Pinkney St (Ⓣ410/267-7619, Ⓦwww.annapolis.org), can provide information on self-guided tours of many of them.

For a different insight into Maryland history, stop by the **Banneker-Douglass Museum**, 84 Franklin St, a few blocks northeast of the capitol (Tues–Sat 10am–4pm; Ⓣ410/216-6180, Ⓦwww.marylandhistoricaltrust.net/bdm.html; free), named after two of the most prominent black leaders and home to the state's largest holding of African-American art and artifacts.

The waterfront and US Naval Academy

Few colonial sites survive on the **Chesapeake Bay waterfront**, save the 1850s dockside **Market House**, 25 Market Place (hours vary; Ⓦwww.annapolismarkethouse.com), a replacement of a colonial warehouse that was used by the Revolutionary army but today is home to a drab handful of food vendors. Among the boat-supply shops and harborside bars, the gray stone walls of the **US Naval Academy** house four thousand crew-cut young men and a handful of women who spend four rigid years here before embarking on careers as naval officers. Superb guided tours leave from **Armel-Leftwich Visitor Center** (daily: March–Dec 9am–5pm; Jan & Feb 9am–4pm; Ⓣ410/293-8687, Ⓦwww.navyonline.com; $8.50) in Halsey Field House, through Gate 1 at the end of King George Street, and take in the elaborate crypt and marble sarcophagus of early-American naval hero John Paul Jones.

Practicalities

Annapolis is easy to reach: Greyhound stops at 308 Chinquapin Round Road, and you can access Amtrak and MARC trains (Ⓣ 1-800/RIDE-MTA Ⓦwww.mtamaryland.com) at BWI Airport via the North Star (C-60) Route on Annapolis's ADOT bus system (Ⓣ410/263-7964; $4). By road, it's only about half an hour from Washington DC (via US-50) or Baltimore (via I-97). Central, historic Annapolis is very walkable, and the city's **visitor center**, 26 West St (daily 9am–5pm; Ⓣ410/280-0445, Ⓦwww.visit-annapolis.org), can provide free maps and practical information about walking, minibus, and water tours.

Finding a **place to stay** is not usually a problem. There's a free accommodations bureau (Ⓣ410/263-3262, Ⓦwww.stayannapolis.com). Playing off their charms, the city's **B&Bs** are expensive; the best, and best-value, are the four rooms and one suite of the **Flag House Inn**, 26 Randall St (Ⓣ410/280-2721 or 1-800/437-4825, Ⓦwww.flaghouseinn.com; ❼), and the **Royal Folly**, 65 College Ave (Ⓣ410/263-3999, Ⓦwww.royalfolly.com; ❽), whose sizeable and elegant suites variously come with fireplaces, jacuzzis, and patios. Also, the three supremely elegant suites of the **Annapolis Inn**, 114 Prince George St (Ⓣ410/295-5200, Ⓦwww.annapolisinn.com; ❾), and the three stylish buildings of the **Historic Inns of Annapolis**, 58 State Circle (Ⓣ410/263-2641, Ⓦwww.historicinnsofannapolis.com; ❻), all provide smart accommodation options in classic Georgian structures.

Worthwhile **dining** options include the no-frills **Chick and Ruth's Delly**, 165 Main St (Ⓣ410/269-6737), which offers monster breakfasts and huge sandwiches; the ritzier **Harry Browne's**, 66 State Circle (Ⓣ410/263-4332), popular with politicos and expense-account lobbyists for its upscale steak and seafood; and the exquisite Atlantic fare of the **Wild Orchid Cafe**, 909 Bay Ridge Ave (Ⓣ410/268-8009), featuring fine seafood, rack of lamb, and a good fixed-price menu ($39).

Southern Maryland

The winding backroads of **southern Maryland** in many ways resemble the rural South. Along both main routes, US-301 from Baltimore and Hwy-2 from Annapolis, lie fields of corn and tobacco, dotted with aging wooden barns. Narrow, tree-lined country lanes branch off to rivers or coves of the broad Chesapeake Bay. One of the more interesting side-trips, on an inlet of the Patuxent River, about 45 miles south of Annapolis off Hwy-2, is the hundred-acre **Battle Creek Cypress Swamp Sanctuary** (Tues–Sat 10am–4.30pm, Sun 1–4.30pm; ⓣ410/535-5327; free), a towering stand of ancient cypress trees, whose gnarly roots have "knees" that poke out of the muck to absorb oxygen; you can take in the bizarre surroundings on the third-of-a-mile elevated walkway.

The old shipbuilding community of **SOLOMONS ISLAND** – not actually an island but a narrow two-mile peninsula between the Patuxent River and Back Creek Bay – lies sixty miles south of Annapolis via Hwy-2. The best reason to stop here is the **Calvert Marine Museum**, on Hwy-2 at the north end of town (daily 10am–5pm; ⓦwww.calvertmarinemuseum.com; $7), which focuses on the Patuxent River and the Chesapeake Bay tidal ecosystem, with two protected marshland wildlife areas, one saltwater and one fresh-water. Your admission also gains you access and entry to the nearby **Drum Point Lighthouse**, a small, wooden, colonial cottage perched above the water on spindly iron legs. The waterfront is dotted with cozy **B&Bs**, among them the **Back Creek Inn**, 210 Alexander Lane (ⓣ410/326-2022, ⓦwww.backcreekinnbnb.com; $115), which has nicely decorated rooms, a pair of suites, and a cottage; and the seven quaint units of the **Solomons Victorian Inn**, 125 Charles St (ⓣ410/326-4811, ⓦwww.solomons-victorianinn.com; $100), some of which offer bayside views and whirlpool tubs. Fresh **seafood** includes the upscale lobster tail and crab cakes of the **Captain's Table**, 275 Lore St (ⓣ410/326-2772), with pleasant waterfront dining, and the mid-priced burgers, seafood, and pasta of the **CD Cafe**, 14350 Solomons Island Rd (ⓣ410/326-3877).

Just a few miles north of the island, **Calvert Cliffs State Park**, 2750 Sweden Point Rd (dawn–dusk; ⓣ301/743-7613; free), is a thousand-acre preserve rich with woods and wetlands and eroding sedimentary cliffs, from which some six hundred different kinds of fossils have been excavated. A two-mile hike leads to a beachside stretch where you're legally allowed to poke around for ancient shark teeth and the like.

The Eastern Shore

The rambling back roads of Maryland's **Eastern Shore** cross over half of the broad Delmarva (**Del**aware, **Mar**yland, **V**irgini**a**) peninsula that protects the Chesapeake from the open Atlantic, its country lanes passing the odd wooden farmhouse or dilapidated tobacco barn. The US-50 bridge, built across the Chesapeake Bay in the early 1960s, may have made the Eastern Shore more accessible, but the area off the main roads still has a sleepy air. Branching off from US-50 as the highway races down to the beach resort of **Ocean City**, quiet country lanes lead to 200-year-old bayside towns like **Chestertown** and **St Michaels**.

Chestertown

A prime Chesapeake port in colonial days, **CHESTERTOWN** stretches west along High Street from the Chester River. It is surprisingly intact, with fine old riverfront homes and a courthouse square lined with ornate wooden cottages. Although the town is rich with historic edifices, like the grand 1769 Georgian mansion **Widehall**, 101 N Water St, the only house regularly open to the public is the contemporaneous **Geddes-Piper House**, 101 Church Alley (Tues–Fri 10am–4pm; tours May–Oct Sat 1–4pm; ⓣ410/778-3499; $4), which has a good collection of kitchen tools and eighteenth-century furnishings.

Many of the old houses have been converted into charming **B&Bs**, like the **Widow's Walk Inn**, 402 High St (ⓣ410/778-6455 or 1-888/778-6455, ⓦwww.chestertown.com/widow; ❺); the dozen refined and elegant rooms of **Great Oak Manor**, 10568 Cliff Rd (ⓣ1-800/504-3098, ⓦwww.greatoak.com; ❽), some of which come with fireplaces and antique decor; and the **Imperial Hotel**, 208 High St (ⓣ410/778-5000, ⓦwww.imperialchestertown.com; ❼), which has a central location and Wi-Fi access, along with the **Front Room restaurant**, serving fine steak and seafood. Across the street, the top-notch **Feast of Reason**, 203 High St (ⓣ410/778-3828), has quality soups and sandwiches for lunch. The **visitor center**, 122 North Cross St (Mon–Fri 9am–5pm, Sat & Sun 10am–4pm (2pm in fall & winter); ⓣ410/778-9737, ⓦwww.chestertown.com), has information on the town's historic features, walking and cycling tours, and a two-hour cruise on the **Sultana**, a replica eighteenth-century schooner, (April–Sept; ⓣ410/778-5954, ⓦwww.sultanaprojects.org; 2hr; $30).

To the west of town, fifteen miles of country lanes lead down to the wharves and dockside restaurants of **ROCK HALL**, an old fishing port where you can watch the day's catch being unloaded while chewing on tasty crab legs at the barebones **Waterman's Crabhouse**, 21055 Sharp St (ⓣ410/639-2261), on the main pier.

St Michaels

The fetching harbor of **ST MICHAELS**, twelve miles west of US-50 on Hwy-33, is one of the Chesapeake Bay's oldest ports. Founded during the mid-1600s, it grew into one of colonial America's prime shipbuilding centers. Since the 1960s it has been revitalized, its old buildings now gentrified into art galleries, boutiques, and cozy B&Bs.

The old town green, **St Mary's Square**, sits a block off Talbot Street on Mulberry Street, while north along the docks is the extensive and modern **Chesapeake Bay Maritime Museum** (daily April–May & Oct 10am–5pm; June–Sept 10am–6pm; Nov–Jan 10am–4pm; ⓦwww.cbmm.org; $13). The complex focuses on the restored 1879 **Hooper Strait Lighthouse** (which you can tour), at the foot of which float several Chesapeake Bay sailboats, designed to make the most of the bay's shallow waters. If you want to get out on the bay, Patriot Cruises (daily at 11am, 12.30pm, 2.30pm, & 4pm; ⓣ410/745-3100, ⓦwww.patriotcruises.com; 60–90min; $22.50) runs **excursions**, while other companies operate shorter (and cheaper) trips.

B&Bs include the 1883 Victorian splendor of the **Parsonage Inn**, (ⓣ410/745-5519, ⓦwww.parsonage-inn.com; ❼), where the rooms have graceful period decor, and some have fireplaces; and the three grand buildings of the **Old Brick Inn**, 401 Talbot St (ⓣ410/745-3323, ⓦwww.saintmichaelsmdbedandbreakfast.com; ❼), whose artful rooms variously feature Wi-Fi access, flat-screen TVs, and jacuzzis; they tend to be fully booked in the high season, so call well ahead. Among local **restaurants**, **Bistro St Michaels**, 403 S Talbot St (ⓣ410/745-9111), has some of the best steamed mussels, salmon, and shrimp around, at a premium price, while the **Key Lime Cafe**, 207 N Talbot St (ⓣ410/745-3158), is tops for its clams, oysters, salads, and ribs, with a nice selection of fresh fish, too.

If you want to explore more of the rural life, seven miles south of St Michaels, in the sleepy waterside hamlet of Oxford, the 1710 **Robert Morris Inn**, 314 N Morris St (ⓣ410/226-5111, ⓦwww.robertmorrisinn.com; $150), has some lovely period appointments and elegant rooms with wi-fi access, while its restaurant serves fine crab cakes.

Tilghman Island

The declining fishing port of **TILGHMAN ISLAND**, west of St Michaels across the Knapps Narrows drawbridge, mainly appeals for its **seafood**. Drop in on **Dogwood Harbor**, on the east side of the island, during the fall and winter harvest when the rusty skipjacks unload at Harrison Oyster Packing Company (ⓣ410/886-2530), a wholesaler at the foot of the bridge. You can buy oysters fresh off the boat here, or sample them at two good restaurants on either side of the bridge: **Bay Hundred**, 6176 Tilghman Island Rd (ⓣ410/886-2126), with a solid, mid-priced array of surf-and-turf, and **The Bridge**, 6136 Tilghman Island Rd (ⓣ410/886-2330), with some decent chowders and fried seafood. Many locals and weekend fishermen head for **Harrison's Chesapeake House,** 21551 Chesapeake House Drive (ⓣ410/886-2121), two miles south of town, for an affordable, traditional Eastern Shore dinner with corn on the cob and fried chicken; you can also stay in the basic, on-site **B&B** (ⓦwww.chesapeakehouse.com; ❻).

Ocean City

With more than ten miles of broad Atlantic beach, a boisterous boardwalk, amusement park, and hordes of visitors, **OCEAN CITY** is Maryland's number one summer resort, accessible across the Eastern Shore via US-50. If you're after a quiet weekend by the sea, avoid it like the plague and take extra care to avoid college Spring Break.

The Greyhound terminal is at Second Street and Philadelphia Avenue, and the city has two helpful **visitor centers**: the Chamber of Commerce, on US-50 as you approach the city (daily 9am–5pm; ⓣ410/213-0552, ⓦwww.oceancity.org), and another at 4001 Coastal Hwy (daily 9am–5pm; ⓣ1-800/626-2326, ⓦwww.ococean.com); both have the usual brochures and can help with accommodation.

Places to **stay** are plentiful except on summer weekends, and off-season rates are at least half the prime-time ones. The **Crystal Beach Hotel**, 2500 N Baltimore Ave (ⓣ1-866/BEACH-21, ⓦwww.crystalbeachhotel.com; ❸–❾), has rooms with Wi-Fi access ($6/day), kitchenettes, and balconies, while cheaper are the more basic units of the **Sea Hawk Motel**, 12410 Coastal Hwy (ⓣ1-800/942-9042, ⓦwww.seahawkmotel.com; ❸–❻ by season), and those of the **Commander Hotel**, on the boardwalk at 14th Street (ⓣ410/289-6166 or 1-888/289-6166, ⓦwww.commanderhotel.com; ❸–❽), with its variety of rooms, suites, and apartments. The good **eating** options amid the national chains include the **PGN Crab House**, 2906 Philadelphia Ave (ⓣ410/289-8380), for its succulent crab cakes, and the pricier seafood and pasta, with fine views, at **Macky's Bayside Bar and Grill**, 5311 Coastal Hwy (ⓣ410/723-5565). **Nightspots** include the frenetic, college-oriented **Big Kahuna**, 18th and Coastal Highway (ⓣ410/289-6331), and **Shenanigan's**, 4th and Boardwalk (ⓣ410/289-7181), an Irish pub with a full menu and live music.

Assateague Island National Seashore

Just nine miles down the coast, **Assateague Island National Seashore** – a 37-mile stretch of undeveloped beach and marshland – is a great escape from Ocean City. Its main **visitor center** (daily 9am–5pm; ⓣ410/641-1441, ⓦwww.nps.gov/asis) is eight miles from Ocean City, just before the bridge across to the island

($15 entry per car, valid one week, or $5/day; free for pedestrians and cyclists). The park's three main **trails** variously lead through boardwalks over low-lying leeward wetlands, or thick white sands just back from the beach. Most visitors, however, come strictly for the beaches themselves. Seashore and bayside **camping** on Assateague Island is available (mid-Oct–mid-April; ⓣ410/641-3030; $16), but if you want a bit more comfort, the best **lodging** is to be found near the southern half of the island, across the Virginia border in **Chincoteague** (see p.412).

Delaware

Founded in 1631, **DELAWARE** was once part of neighboring Pennsylvania – Philadelphia is only ten miles north – until separating itself off in 1776. In 1787 it was the first former colony to ratify the Constitution and become a state. Much of Delaware's fortunes can be traced to the **du Pont family**, who, fleeing the wrath of revolutionary France, set up a gunpowder mill that became the main supplier of conventional explosives to the US government. The family built huge mansions in the **Brandywine Valley** north of Wilmington, near the perfectly preserved old colonial capital, **New Castle**, on the Delaware Bay, five miles south of I-95. Further south, **Dover**, the capital, may not detain you long, but beyond it, the small and amiable resorts of **Lewes** and **Rehoboth Beach** mark the northern extent of over twenty miles of rather unspoiled Atlantic beaches.

Getting around Delaware

Apart from Wilmington, which is on the main East Coast **train** and **bus** lines, Delaware is hard to get around without a car. Greyhound stops only at Wilmington and Dover, and I-95 and the New Jersey Turnpike converge at Wilmington, from where US-13 runs south through the state. More often called the **Du Pont Highway**, it was paid for and constructed by the industrialists so that they could ride in comfort between their Wilmington mansions and Dover. A direct car **ferry** connects Cape May, the southern tip of New Jersey, and Lewes, at the mouth of the Delaware Bay (see p.445).

Wilmington and around

Pleasant **WILMINGTON** boasts decent art museums and some pretty waterside parks, and the surrounding Brandywine Valley holds the manor homes and gardens (and factories) of the du Ponts, providing an inside look at the first state's First Family.

Amtrak pulls in at 100 S French St, and Greyhound at 101 N French St, both on the dicey south side of the city (Wilmington has a fair amount of crime for a city its size). From here, the two main streets, Market and King, run north for about a mile to the Brandywine River, holding stores and other businesses, as well as a handful of restored eighteenth-century structures, including the **Old Town Hall**, 500 Market St (special events only; ⓣ302/655-7161 for details), a graceful 1798 Federal mansion.

A short walk north of the downtown commercial district, at the top end of Market Street, **Brandywine Park** is filled with grassy knolls lining both banks of the

Brandywine River. The nearby **Delaware Art Museum**, 2301 Kentmere Parkway (Tues–Sat 10am–4pm, Sun noon–4pm; Ⓦ www.delart.org; $10, free Sun), focuses on American art from the nineteenth and twentieth centuries and has a number of emblematic images from key figures like Frederic Church, Winslow Homer, Edward Hopper, and Augustus Saint Gaudens. For those with a yen for the archly modern, the **Delaware Center for the Contemporary Arts**, back downtown at 200 S Madison St (Tues & Thurs–Sat 10am–5pm, Wed & Sun noon–5pm; Ⓦ www.thedcca.org; $5), is best known for its dozens of yearly rotating exhibits that showcase regional and national artists.

Most of Wilmington's colonial sites are hidden away amid the shambling, industrialized waterfront east of downtown. These include the **Hendrickson House Museum**, at 606 Church St, a c.1690 pinewood residence with furnishings from various eras, and **Old Swedes Church**, one of the oldest houses of worship in the US, built in 1698 (both: Wed–Sat 10am–4pm; Ⓣ 302/652-5629; $2). Several miles north, near I-95 in Rockwood Park, the Gothic Revival **Rockwood Mansion**, 610 Shipley Rd (park and gardens daily 6am–10pm, mansion tours Tues–Sun 10am–3pm; Ⓦ www.rockwood.org; $5 tours), was built in 1854 in the style of a rural English estate, its elegant rooms now restored to their Gilded Age appearance. Groups can take high tea (noon Tues–Sat; reserve at Ⓣ 302/761-4340; $18) in the richly decorated **Butler's Pantry**, which otherwise serves coffee and pastries.

Practicalities

The downtown **CVB**, 100 W 10th St (Mon–Fri 9am–5pm; Ⓣ 1-800/489-6664, Ⓦ www.VisitWilmingtonDe.com), has walking and driving tour maps and practical information. The DART **bus** system runs around the county (Ⓣ 302/652-3278, Ⓦ www.dartfirststate.com; tickets $1.15). To **spend the night**, the splendidly ornate, 1913 **Hotel du Pont**, 100 W 11th St (Ⓣ 302/594-3100 or 1-800/441-9019, Ⓦ www.hoteldupont.com; ❽), has well-appointed rooms and suites that are the height of contemporary chic, and **Brandywine Suites**, 707 King St (Ⓣ 1-800/756-0700, Ⓦ www.brandywinesuites.com; ❹), offers affordable, spacious units with microwaves, fridges, and free high-speed net access. A good choice for **eating** is the happening Trolley Square area northwest of downtown, where **Moro**, 1307 N Scott St (Ⓣ 302/777-1800), has upscale Atlantic cuisine like maple-glazed salmon and truffle-roasted oysters, plus several fixed-price menus. Elsewhere, **Attilio's**, 1900 Lancaster Ave (Ⓣ 302/428-0909), is a smallish spot with some of the state's best old-style Italian eats, while the **Washington Street Ale House**, 1205 Washington St (Ⓣ 302/658-2537), has serviceable pasta and seafood, but the main draw is its copious microbrew selection.

The du Pont mansions

A short distance up I-95 from the Rockwood Mansion, the first of the **du Pont mansions** is accessible in **Bellevue State Park**, 800 Carr Rd (daily 8am–dusk; free). William du Pont Jr converted a Gothic Revival mansion into his own version of James Madison's Neoclassical home and called it **Bellevue Hall**. You can't get inside, but can visit the grounds and see the ponds, woodlands, gardens, and tennis courts.

Twenty minutes northwest of Wilmington, various generations of the du Pont family built opulent homes in the rural Brandywine Valley. The **Hagley Museum**, off Hwy-141 just north of Wilmington (mid-March–Dec daily 9.30am–4.30pm; Jan–mid-March Sat & Sun 9.30am–4.30pm; Ⓦ www.hagley.org; $11), showcases their 1802 founding of a small water-powered gunpowder mill, which grew over the next century to include ever-larger steam- and electricity-powered factories

– most of which are still in working order. Also make sure to tour the luxurious du Pont mansion, Eleutherian Mills, the centerpiece of the 235-acre estate.

The newly restored, enormous, dusty-pink **Nemours Mansion**, just a mile away at 1600 Rockland Rd (reserve a tour at ⓣ1-800/651-6912, ⓦwww.Nemours.org/mansion.html), was built by Alfred du Pont in 1910 and named for the family's ancestral home in France, and is surrounded by a three-hundred-acre, French-style garden. Inside the mansion, you'll find plenty of lavish rooms including those devoted to fitness, bowling, and ice-making, and a collection of early twentieth-century automobiles. Two miles northwest, off Hwy-52, the one-time du Pont family estate of **Winterthur** (Tues–Sun 10am–5pm; ⓦwww.winterthur.org; tours $20–30, gardens and galleries $15) now displays American decorative arts, from 1640 to 1860, each of its 175 rooms showcasing styles ranging from a simple Shaker cottage to a beautiful three-storey elliptical staircase taken from a North Carolina plantation. Separately, the estate galleries present a selection of furniture, textiles, ceramics, paintings, and glass in a more conventional museum setting.

New Castle

Delaware's original capital, **NEW CASTLE**, fronts the broad Delaware River, just six miles south of Wilmington via Hwy-141. Founded in the 1650s by the Dutch and taken over by the British in 1664, New Castle has managed to survive intact, its quiet cobbled streets and immaculate eighteenth-century brick houses shaded by ancient hardwood trees.

The heart of New Castle is the tree-filled **town green** that spreads east from the shops of Delaware Street, and dominated by the stalwart tower of the **Immanuel Episcopal Church**, on Harmony Street at The Strand, built in 1703 and bordered by tidy rows of eighteenth-century gravestones. On the west edge of the green, the **Old Court House**, 211 Delaware St (Tues–Sat 10am–3.30pm, Sun 1.30–4.30pm; free), was built in 1732 and served as the first state capitol until 1881. Its dainty cupola provided the vista from which surveyors determined the state's arcing northern border, drawn up when Delaware seceded from Pennsylvania in 1776.

Fine colonial houses fill the blocks around the town green. The largest is the **George Read II House**, two blocks south along the river at 42 The Strand (winter Sat 10am-4pm & Sun 11am–4pm; rest of year Tues–Fri & Sun 11am–4pm, Sat 10am-4pm; ⓦwww.hsd.org/read.htm; $5), a sumptuous replica of a c.1800 house, with marble fireplaces, brightly painted walls, elaborately carved woodwork, Federal-style plaster ornament, and picturesque gardens. Another collection of classic edifices lies several blocks north along Third and Fourth streets: the **Amstel House**, 2 E Fourth St (April-Dec Wed–Sat 11am–4pm, Sun 1–4pm; ⓦwww.newcastlehistory.org; $4), a 1730 early-Georgian mansion that hosted prominent Revolutionary-era figures; the hexagonal brick bauble of the **Old Library Museum**, 40 E Third St (March–Dec Sat & Sun 1–4pm; free), housing the historical society's collection; and the **Dutch House**, 32 E Third St (April–Dec Wed–Sat 11am-4pm, Sun 1–4pm; $4), a simple c.1700 residence with authentic decor and artifacts including a cherry-wood cupboard, duck-footed wooden chairs, and polychromed Delft ceramics.

Practicalities

To pick up the self-guided **walking tour** map, drop by the **visitor center** at 211 Delaware St, in the Old Court House (ⓣ302/323-4453), or call the **Historic New Castle Visitor's Bureau** (ⓣ1-800/758-1550). Good **B&Bs** include the **William Penn Guest House**, 206 Delaware St (ⓣ302/328-7736; ❼), with four cozy units in a building dating from 1682 (its namesake even visited here) and the **Terry House**, 130 Delaware St (ⓣ302/322-2505, ⓦwww.terryhouse.com; ❹), a townhouse dating from the Civil War with four simple, tastefully decorated rooms. The better **restaurants** serve colonial-style food, such as crabs, clams, and shepherd's pie, as at the popular **Jessop's Tavern**, 114 Delaware St (ⓣ302/322-6111). More refined taste buds will enjoy the Continental-influenced seafood dishes at the grand **Arsenal at Old New Castle**, next to the Episcopal Church at 30 Market St (ⓣ302/328-1290).

Dover

Located in Delaware's mostly agricultural center, just west of US-13, the capital **DOVER** is a small town hemmed in by suburban houses. South of **Lockerman Street**, the main route through town, the 1792 **Old State House**, 25 The Green, is the state's onetime judicial and legislative chambers, now a museum furnished with early American antiques (Mon–Sat 9am–4.30pm, Sun 1.30–4.30pm; ⓣ302/739-4266; free). To the west, around the oval **town green**, lawyers and insurance brokers have taken over a number of eighteenth- and nineteenth-century buildings.

In the same building as the **visitor center** (Mon–Sat 9am–4.30pm, Sun 1.30–4.30pm; ⓣ302/739-4266), at the corner of Duke of York and Federal streets next to the Old State House, the impressive **Biggs Museum of American Art** (same hours; ⓦwww.biggsmuseum.org; free) has historical and decorative art, including colonial-era furniture, paintings by the likes of Benjamin West and Gilbert Stuart, silver and porcelain services, and grand landscapes from Albert Bierstadt and Thomas Cole. The **Delaware State Museums**, 316 S Governors Ave (Mon–Sat 9am–4.30pm, Sun 1.30–4.30pm; ⓦhistory.delaware.gov; free), comprise a quaint trio just west of the green: the **Archaeology Museum** traces the area's history from the end of the Ice Age, showing such items as native spear points, shards of pottery, and everyday colonial-era objects; the **Museum of Small Town Life** is a pleasant hodgepodge of century-old mementos and relics, including a general store, post office, pharmacy, and print shop; and the **Johnson Victrola Museum**, dedicated to the inventor of the Victrola, has dozens of "talking machines," from early wind-ups to prototype jukeboxes, period recordings, and amusing photographs showing pre-electric recording techniques.

For more than fifty years, **Spence's Bazaar**, two blocks south on Queen Street at 550 S New St (Tues & Fri 7.30am–6.30pm; ⓣ302/734-3441; free), has hosted a **flea market** that all of Dover turns out for, including dozens of local **Amish**, who ride here in their old horse-drawn buggies to sell home-grown fruits and vegetables.

A few miles outside town, the eighteen-acre **John Dickinson Plantation**, off Rte-9 at 340 Kitts Hummock Rd (Tues–Sat 10am–3.30pm, Sun 1.30–4.30pm; ⓣ302/739-3277; free), is where costumed re-enactors of colonial residents, including slaves, go about farming, cooking, and gardening; both the estate's grounds and 1740 brick mansion are viewable on various tours, lasting ninety minutes to two hours.

Practicalities

Appealing **B&Bs** include the **Little Creek Inn**, 2623 N Little Creek Rd, off Hwy 8 (ⓣ302/730-1300, ⓦwww.littlecreekinn.com; ❺), an attractive 1860 estate, with five rooms (some with jacuzzis) featuring period appointments, as well as a pool, gym, and bocce court; and the similar amenities of the **State Street Inn**, 228 N State St (ⓣ302/734-2294, ⓦwww.statestreetinn.com; ❺), more centrally located, but with rooms that are a bit smaller. As for **eating**, most of Dover's restaurants are concentrated on Lockerman and State streets in the town center, just north of the green. **W.T. Smithers**, 140 State St (ⓣ302/674-8875), offers reasonably priced steaks, sandwiches, and seafood; further out, some of the cheapest decent fare around can be had at **Kirby and Holloway's**, 656 N Dupont Hwy (ⓣ302/734-7133), known for their filling steaks, chicken and dumplings, and turkey platters, most below $10.

The Delaware coast

The thirty-mile-long Delaware coast is one of the little-known jewels of the East Coast, aside from the summer resort **Rehoboth Beach**. The historic fishing community of **Lewes** is an attractive stopover, but what sets the area apart are the long, isolated stretches of sand. Much has been preserved as open space, most extensively at **Delaware Seashore State Park**, which stretches south to the Maryland border.

Lewes

Accessible via Hwy-1, the natural harbor at the mouth of Delaware Bay at **LEWES** has attracted seafarers ever since a Dutch whaling company set up a small colony here in 1631, a history outlined in the mock-Dutch **Zwaanendael Museum**, Savannah Road at Kings Highway (Tues–Sat 10am–4.30pm, Sun 1.30–4.30pm; ⓣ302/645-1148; free). The **tourist office** next door (ⓣ302/645-8073, ⓦwww.leweschamber.com), housed inside a gambrel-roofed 1730s farmhouse, has walking-tour maps of the town and its numerous eighteenth-century homes. Don't miss the **Lewes Historic Complex**, three blocks north at 110 Shipcarpenter St (May–mid-June Sat 11am–4pm; mid-June–mid-Sept Mon–Sat 11am–4pm; ⓣ302/645-7670, ⓦwww.historiclewes.org; $7), a collection of twelve classic properties dating from the early-colonial to late-Victorian eras, including a crude plank-house, doctor's office, store, and boathouse. On Front Street, **Memorial Park** is decorated by an array of cannons, and commemorates an 1813 British attack, which resulted in spotty cannonball damage around town.

There's a popular, extensive **beach** along the Delaware Bay at the foot of town, while three-thousand-acre, four-mile-long **Cape Henlopen State Park** (ⓣ302/645-8983), where the bay meets the open ocean just a mile east of the town center, offers the chance to **camp** ($30–32 per night) beside the biggest sand dunes north of Cape Hatteras, and hike worthwhile trails, including one to a World War II-era observation tower. You can also ride the **ferry** across Delaware Bay from beside the state park to Cape May, New Jersey (times vary by day and season; ⓣ1-800/64-FERRY, ⓦwww.cmlf.com; 80min; $34 per car, $9.50 per person, Nov–March $28/$7; see also p.176).

You can walk most places in town, or **rent a bike** from Lewes Cycle Sports, 526 Savannah Rd (ⓣ302/645-4544). Thanks to its proximity to Rehoboth Beach, in summer **accommodation** prices can be steep. There are cheap motels along Savannah Road, but try instead **Hotel Blue**, 110 Anglers Rd (ⓣ302/645-4880, ⓦwww.hotelblue.info; by season ❺–❽), whose rooms and suites come with flat-panel TVs, boutique decor, fireplaces, and internet access. Continuing the azure theme, the **Blue Water House** (ⓣ302/645-7832, ⓦwww.lewes-beach.com; ❻–❽, two-night minimum), is a B&B with warm and comfortable rooms and a suite, all with net access and watersports rentals. For **dining**, **Stripper Bites**, 107 Savannah Rd (ⓣ302/645-4657), has affordable seafood, sandwiches, and burgers (though dinner prices double), and **Cafe Azafran**, 109 Market St (ⓣ302/644-4446), has a nice assortment of tapas (including seafood items) for a range of prices. **The Buttery**, 2nd Street at Savannah Road (Ⓣ302/645-7755), is a fine French bistro that has mid-priced crab cakes, burgers, and seafood sandwiches for lunch, and pricey steak and rack of lamb for dinner.

Rehoboth Beach

A nonstop parade of motels and malls along the six miles of Hwy-1 links Lewes with **REHOBOTH BEACH**, Delaware's largest and liveliest beach resort, which merges into **Dewey Beach** at its southern end.

The resort's wooden **boardwalk** is one of the last ones left on the East Coast, stretching along the Atlantic to either side of Rehoboth Avenue – **"The Avenue"** – which acts as the main drag, its four short blocks clogged with T-shirt vendors and seaside kitsch. Most of the **restaurants** and **nightspots** are concentrated here, though you're better off sticking to Lewes for dining. Exceptions include the **Back Porch Café**, 59 Rehoboth Ave (Ⓣ302/227-3674), with its upscale selection of softshell crab, guinea fowl, salmon, and rabbit, and **Dogfish Head**, 320 Rehoboth Ave (Ⓣ302/226-2739), which has fine microbrews, weekend live bands, and an on-site distillery.

Rehoboth's **motels** (very pricey in July and Aug) include the **Sandcastle**, 123 Second St (April–Oct; Ⓣ302/227-0400 or 1-800/372-2112, Ⓦwww.thesandcastlemotel.com; ❸–❼by season), with pool and sundeck, and the **Crosswinds**, 312 Rehoboth Ave (Ⓣ302/227-7997, Ⓦwww.crosswindsmotel.com; ❸–❽), whose rooms have fridges and wireless internet. Among area **B&Bs**, try the **Corner Cupboard Inn**, 50 Park Ave (Ⓣ302/227-8553, Ⓦwww.cornercupboardinn.com; ❹–❽), with clean and basic units, or the **Rehoboth Guest House**, 40 Maryland Ave (Ⓣ302/227-4117, Ⓦwww.rehobothguesthouse.com; ❹–❻), with porch and shaded backyard, and basic rooms (add $35 for private bath). The **tourist office**, 501 Rehoboth Ave (Ⓣ302/227-2233 or 1-800/441-1329, Ⓦwww.beach-fun.com), has more details.

South of Rehoboth, **Delaware Seashore State Park** (Ⓣ302/227-2800, Ⓦwww.destateparks.com) stretches for miles along a thin, sandy peninsula, split by Hwy-1 and bounded by the ocean and fresh-water marshlands, and good for its fishing and surfing. South of the park, as you approach the Maryland border, you'll pass the concrete tower blocks of **Bethany Beach** and the pleasant barrier island of **Fenwick Island State Park** (Ⓣ302/227-2800), a three-mile stretch that offers good swimming and the opportunity for **"surf fishing"** – parking on the beach itself and casting a line from your car.

6

The South

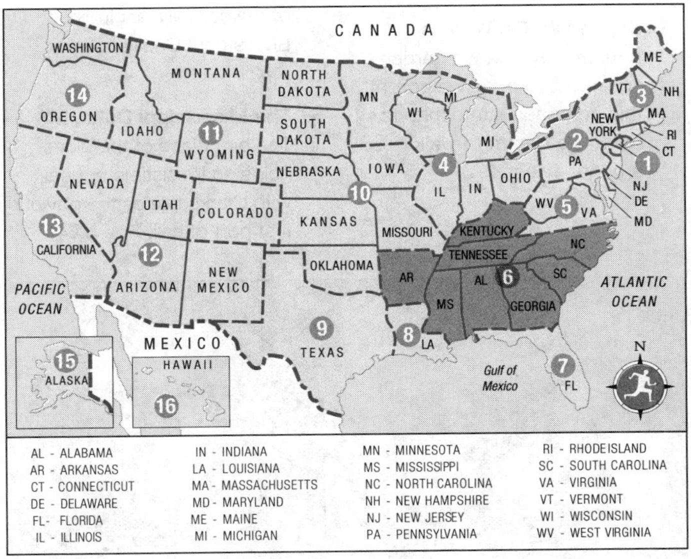
CANADA
WASHINGTON
MONTANA
NORTH DAKOTA
MN
MI
ME
VT
NH
3
14
OREGON
WI
MA
NEW YORK
SOUTH DAKOTA
IDAHO
11
WYOMING
MI
2
RI
CT
PA
1
4
NEBRASKA
IOWA
OHIO
NEVADA
IL
IN
NJ
10
DE
UTAH
COLORADO
WV
5
VA
MD
KANSAS
13
KENTUCKY
MISSOURI
CALIFORNIA
12
TENNESSEE
NC
OKLAHOMA
NEW MEXICO
AR
SC
PACIFIC OCEAN
ARIZONA
AL
6
ATLANTIC OCEAN
MS
GEORGIA
9
8
LA
MEXICO
TEXAS
15
HAWAII
ALASKA
16
Gulf of Mexico
7
FL
N
AL - ALABAMA
AR - ARKANSAS
CT - CONNECTICUT
DE - DELAWARE
FL- FLORIDA
IL - ILLINOIS
IN - INDIANA
LA - LOUISIANA
MA - MASSACHUSETTS
MD - MARYLAND
ME - MAINE
MI - MICHIGAN
MN - MINNESOTA
MS - MISSISSIPPI
NC - NORTH CAROLINA
NH - NEW HAMPSHIRE
NJ - NEW JERSEY
PA - PENNSYLVANIA
RI - RHODEISLAND
SC - SOUTH CAROLINA
VA - VIRGINIA
VT - VERMONT
WI - WISCONSIN
WV - WEST VIRGINIA

CHAPTER 6 Highlights

* **Blue Ridge Parkway, NC** A tortuous but exhilarating wilderness highway that makes a destination in itself. See p.466

* **Martin Luther King Birth Home, Atlanta, GA** Engaging tours take you around King's childhood home, in the South's most dynamic city. See p.485

* **Savannah, GA** With its romantic overgrown garden squares and busy waterfront, this gorgeous, atmospheric town is a dream to walk around. See p.492

* **Memphis, TN** Especially exciting for music fans, who could spend days checking out Beale Street, Sun Studio, the Stax Museum, Al Green's church, and, of course, Graceland. See p.510

* **Country Music Hall of Fame, Nashville, TN** At once a fascinating interactive museum and a treasure trove of memorabilia, including Elvis's gold Cadillac. See p.524

* **The Mississippi Delta, MS** The birthplace of the blues holds an irresistible appeal, with Clarksdale as the obvious first port of call. See p.540

Graceland

6

The South

Mark Twain put it best, as early as 1882: "In the South, the [Civil] war is what AD is elsewhere; they date everything from it." Several generations later, the legacies of slavery and "The War Between the States" remain evident throughout the southern states of North Carolina, South Carolina, Georgia, Kentucky, Tennessee, Alabama, Mississippi, and Arkansas. It's impossible to travel through the region without experiencing constant jolting reminders of the two epic historical clashes that have shaped its destiny: the Civil War, and the civil rights movement of the 1950s and 1960s.

Although it's debatable whether the much-vaunted "New South" truly exists, the last few decades have unquestionably seen considerable change. The inspirational campaigns that finally secured black participation in Southern elections have resulted not only in the prominence of black political leaders but also in the emergence of liberal white counterparts like Jimmy Carter and Bill Clinton. High-tech industries have moved in, luring considerable inward migration, while urban centers such as **Atlanta**, the birthplace of Dr Martin Luther King Jr and venue for the 1996 Olympics, are booming.

That said, it's misleading in any case to generalize too much about "the South." Even during the Civil War there were substantial pockets of pro-Union support, particularly in the mountains, while during the long century of segregation that followed, certain states, such as Mississippi and Alabama, were far more brutally oppressive than others. These days, inequities within the South, between for example the industrialized "Sun Belt" centers of North Carolina and northern Alabama and the much poorer rural backwaters of southern Georgia, Mississippi, or Tennessee, are just as significant as those between the South and the rest of the nation, and are no longer so clearly demarcated along racial lines.

For many travelers, the most exciting aspect of a visit to the South has to be its **music**. Fans flock to the homelands of Elvis Presley, Hank Williams, Robert Johnson, Dolly Parton, and Otis Redding, heading to the country and blues meccas of **Nashville** and **Memphis**, or seeking out backwoods barn dances in Appalachia and blues jook joints in the Mississippi Delta or South Carolina. The Southern experience is also reflected in a rich regional **literature**, documented by the likes of William Faulkner, Carson McCullers, Eudora Welty, Margaret Mitchell, and Harper Lee.

Other major destinations for visitors include the elegant coastal cities of **Charleston** and **Savannah**, frenzied beach resorts such as **Myrtle Beach**, college towns like **Athens** and **Chapel Hill**, and the historic Mississippi River ports of **Natchez** and **Vicksburg**. Away from the urban areas, much Southern scenery consists of fertile but sun-baked farmlands, the undulating hillsides dotted with wooden shacks and rust-red barns, and broken by occasional forests. Highlights

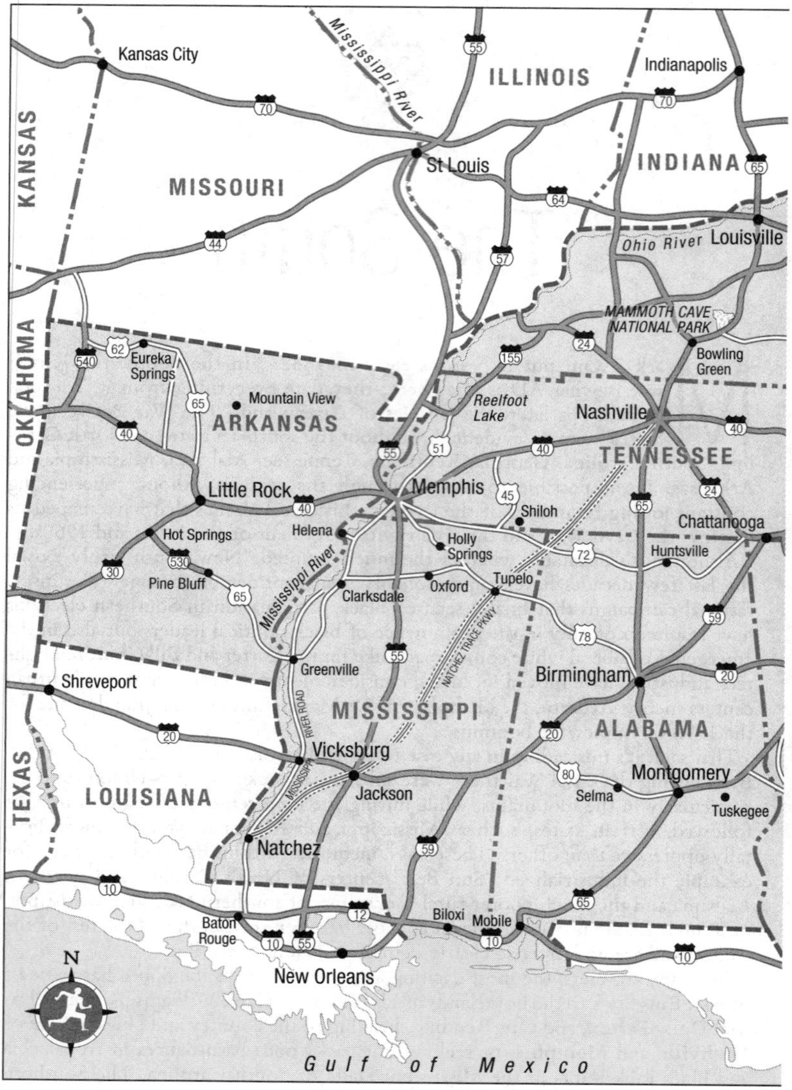

include the misty Appalachian **mountains** of Kentucky, Tennessee, and North Carolina; the subtropical **beaches** and tranquil **barrier islands** along the Atlantic and Gulf coasts; and the river road through the tiny settlements of the flat Mississippi Delta.

Unless your primary goal is the coastline, where the beaches offer a less expensive alternative to neighboring Florida, it's better to avoid visiting during midsummer. In July and August, the daily high **temperature** is mostly a very humid 90°F, and while almost every public building is air-conditioned, the heat can be debilitating.

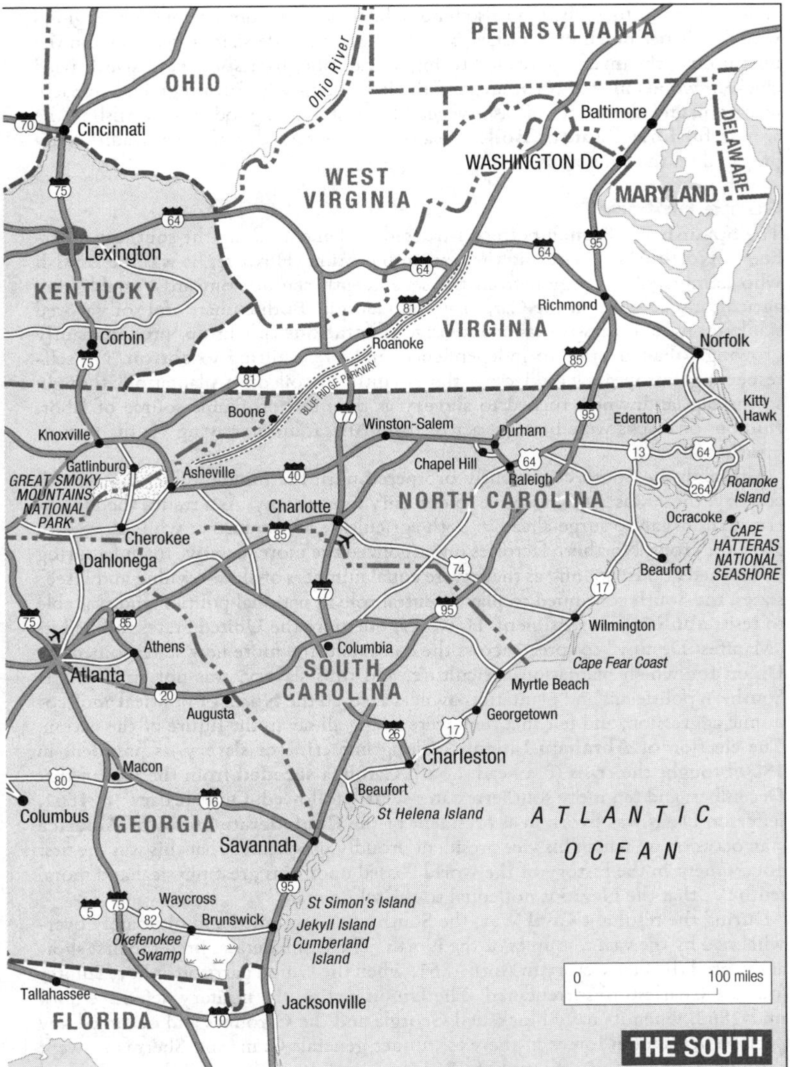

May and June are more bearable, and tend to see a lot of local festivals, while the fall colors in the mountains – just as beautiful and a lot less expensive and congested than New England – are at their headiest during October.

Public transportation in rural areas is poor. In any case, it's best to take things at your own pace – you'll find things to see and do in the most unlikely places – so **renting a car** is the best idea. **Accommodation** in the South is generally good value. Motels are everywhere, while abundant B&Bs offer a chance to sample the much-vaunted Southern hospitality – though unless you share a broadly Confederate view of history, they can also tend to be socially uncomfortable. The region's varied **cuisine**, much of it dished out at simple roadside shacks, ranges from the ubiquitous grits (maize porridge) to highly calorific, irresistible **soul food**: fried chicken, wood-smoked barbecue, and the like, along with turnip greens, spinach, macaroni, and all manner of tasty vegetables. Fish is also good, from catfish to the wonderful **Low Country Boils** – seafood stews served with rice, traditionally prepared on the sea islands.

Some history

The **Spanish** and **French** both constructed settlements along the southern coastline of North America during the sixteenth century. However, it was the **British** who dominated the region from the seventeenth century onwards, establishing agricultural colonies in the Carolinas and Georgia. Both climate and soil favored staple crops, and massive labor-intensive **plantations** sprang up, predominantly growing **tobacco** prior to independence, and later shifting to **cotton**. No self-respecting European would cross the Atlantic to toil on a plantation, though, so the big landowners turned to **slavery** as the most profitable source of labor. Millions of blacks were brought across from Africa, most arriving via the port of Charleston.

Although the South consistently prospered until the middle of the nineteenth century, there was little incentive to diversify its economy. As a result, the Northern states began to surge ahead in both agriculture and industry; while the South grew the crops, Northern factories monopolized the more lucrative manufacturing of finished goods. So long as there were equal numbers of slave-owning and "free" states, the South continued to play a central role in national politics, and was able to resist **abolitionist** sentiment. However, the more the United States fulfilled its "Manifest Destiny" to spread across the continent, the more new states joined the Union for which plantation agriculture, and thus slavery, was not appropriate. Southern politicians and plantation owners accused the North of political and economic aggression, and felt that they were losing all say in the future of the nation. The election of **Abraham Lincoln**, a longtime critic of slavery, as president in 1860 brought the crisis to a head. South Carolina **seceded** from the Union that December, and ten more southern states swiftly followed. On February 18, 1861, Jefferson Davis was sworn in as president of the **Confederate States of America** – an occasion on which his vice president proudly proclaimed that this was the first government in the history of the world "based upon this great physical and moral truth . . . that the Negro is not equal to the white man."

During the resultant **Civil War**, the South was outgunned and ultimately overwhelmed by the vast resources of the North. The Confederates fired the first shots and scored the first victory in April 1861, when the Union garrison at Fort Sumter (outside Charleston) surrendered. The Union was on the military defensive until mid-1862, when its navy blockaded Georgia and the Carolinas and occupied key ports. Then Union forces in the west, under generals Grant and Sherman, swept through Tennessee. By the end of 1863 the North had taken Vicksburg, the final Confederate-held port on the Mississippi, as well as the strategic mountain-locked town of Chattanooga on the Tennessee–Georgia border. Grant proceeded north to Virginia, while Sherman captured the transportation nexus of Atlanta and began a bloody and ruthless march to the coast, burning everything in his path. With 258,000 men dead, the Confederacy's defeat was total, and General Robert E. Lee **surrendered** on April 9, 1865, at Appomattox in Virginia.

The war left the South in chaos. A quarter of the South's adult white male population had been killed, and two-thirds of Southern wealth destroyed. From controlling thirty percent of the nation's assets in 1860, the South was down to twelve percent in 1870, while the spur the war gave to industrialization meant that the North was booming. For a brief period of **Reconstruction**, the South was occupied by Union troops. Newly freed Southern blacks were able to vote, and black representatives were elected to both state and federal office. However, unrepentant former Confederates thwarted any potential for change, and by the end of the century the Southern states were firmly back under white Democratic control. "**Jim Crow**" segregation laws were imposed, backed by the terror of the **Ku Klux Klan**, and poll taxes, literacy tests, and property qualifications disenfranchised virtually all blacks. Many found themselves little better off as **sharecroppers** – in which virtually all they could earn from raising crops went to pay their landlords – than they had been as slaves, and there were mass migrations to cities like Memphis and Atlanta, as well as to the North.

Not until the Supreme Court outlawed segregation in schools in 1954 was there any sign that the federal authorities in Washington might concern themselves with inequities in the South. Even then, individual Southern states proved extremely reluctant to effect the required changes. In the face of institutionalized white resistance, non-violent black protestors coalesced to form the **civil rights movement**, and broke down segregation through their own mass action. After tackling such issues as public transportation, as in the Montgomery bus boycott and the Freedom Rides, and segregated dining facilities, as in the Greensboro lunch-counter sit-in, the campaign culminated in finally restoring full black voter registration. One obvious itinerary for modern travelers is to trace the footsteps of **Dr Martin Luther King Jr**, from his birthplace in Atlanta, through his church in Montgomery, to the site of his assassination in Memphis.

The dispossession of the **Native Americans** is often the forgotten chapter of Southern history. Colonial powers at best tolerated the Indians, for the most part peaceful agrarian tribes, and used them as allies in their imperialist wars with each other. However, after the Revolution, pressure from plantation owners and small farmers led to the forced removal in the 1830s of the "five civilized tribes" – the Cherokee, Creek, Choctaw, Chickasaw, and Seminole – to malarial Oklahoma. Today only a few thousand Native Americans live in the South.

North Carolina

NORTH CAROLINA, the most industrialized of the Southern states, holds nine million people spread over an area larger than England. Geographically, it has three distinct areas – the coast, the Piedmont, and the mountains. The **coast** promises stunning beaches, beautiful landscapes, and a fascinating history. The inner coast consists largely of the less developed **Albemarle Peninsula**, with colonial **Edenton** nearby. The central **Piedmont** is dominated by manufacturing cities and the academic institutions of the prestigious "Research Triangle": **Raleigh**, the state capital, is home to North Carolina State University; Durham has Duke; and the University of North Carolina is in trendy **Chapel Hill**. **Winston-Salem** combines tobacco culture and Moravian heritage, while **Charlotte** is distinguished by little but its downtown skyscrapers. In the **Appalachian Mountains**, the only towns of any size, **Asheville** and **Boone**, are enjoyable places to stop along the spectacular **Blue Ridge Parkway**; **Great Smoky Mountains National Park** overlaps the border with Tennessee.

Getting around North Carolina

North Carolina's major **airports** are at Charlotte (an arrival point for transatlantic flights), Raleigh-Durham, and Wilmington, all of which will connect you with several major US cities. A tiny airport at Manteo in the Outer Banks (Ⓣ252/475-5570, Ⓦwww.fly2mqi.com) runs charter flights to the barrier islands, but driving is easier. Charlotte, Raleigh, Durham, and Greensboro (with an express bus link to Winston-Salem) are served by **Amtrak**, but unfortunately there is no coastal route. Plenty of **buses** run within the Piedmont. The state also has a good network of **cycling** routes along quiet country roads; for information, contact the Department of Transportation (Ⓣ919/807-0777, Ⓦwww.ncdot.org).

The North Carolina coast

The **North Carolina coast**, which ranges through salt marshes, beaches, and barrier islands, holds many **historic sites**. Among these are **Roanoke Island**, where the continent's earliest English colonists vanished in 1590, and **Kill Devil Hills**, where the Wright brothers achieved the first powered flight just over three centuries later. As for scenic beauty, the **Outer Banks**, the long reef of barrier islands that stretch down from Virginia, are in places unspoiled, though elsewhere they're downright tacky.

Edenton and the Albemarle

The huge **Albemarle Peninsula** remains largely unexploited. Local towns try to make much of their **Colonial history** – but often there's not a lot left to see. The area is rewarding to explore if you like to travel off the beaten path, its sleepy old towns and remote plantations set in wide swathes of rural farmland and endless marshes that eventually give way to water.

Edenton

EDENTON, set along the majestic Albemarle Sound waterfront, was established as North Carolina's first state capital in 1722 and was a major center of unrest in the American Revolution. Nowadays, if you like peace and quiet, it makes a nice little base for explorations of the coast, with some good B&Bs and restaurants with a small-town ambiance.

The town's main road, **Broad Street,** has grand Victorian facades and old-fashioned stores. The Historic Edenton **Visitor Center**, 108 N Broad St (April–Oct Mon–Sat 9am–5pm, Sun 1–5pm; Nov–March Mon–Sat 10am–4pm, Sun 1–4pm; Ⓣ252/482-2637), runs **trolley tours** that take in all the major sites, including a fine collection of Colonial and pre–Civil War houses.

The visitor center provides an **African-American history** walking-tour map; among other important figures, Edenton was home to **Harriet Jacobs**, a runaway slave who hid for seven years in her grandmother's attic. In 1842, she escaped to the North, and was eventually reunited in Boston with the two children she had with a white man in Edenton. She wrote her autobiography as *Incidents in the Life of a Slave Girl*. None of the buildings mentioned in the book are still standing, but the tours give you an idea of where places were.

Luxurious **B&Bs** include the peaceful *Trestle House Inn*, set in seven acres overlooking a nature refuge on a lake; it's five miles south of town, off Hwy-32, at 632 Soundside Rd (T 252/482-2282, W www.trestlehouseinn.com; 5). A few minutes' walk from the waterfront, the *Governor Eden Inn*, 304 N Broad St (T 252/482-2072; 4), offers appealing rooms and a huge veranda. Edenton has a gratifying number of good places to **eat**. *Chero's*, 112 W Water St (T 252/482-5525), is a funky, colorful place serving delicious Mediterranean and regional food, while the fishy *Waterman's Grill*, 427 S Broad St (T 252/482-7733), gets packed with locals at dinnertime.

Exploring the Albemarle

Albemarle **plantation life** is brought alive in tours of **Hope**, the home of David Stone, a state governor and US senator of the Revolutionary and Federal periods. You'll find it off Hwy-308, a few miles west of **Windsor**, which is about 25 miles southwest of Edenton (tours: April–Oct Mon–Sat 10am–5pm, Sun 2–5pm; Nov–March 10am–4pm, Sun 2–5pm; $8; W www.hopeplantation.org). The main house, dating from 1803, was built to an English template.

At Creswell, 25 miles southeast of Edenton on US-64, a vivid picture of slave life is painted by **Somerset Place State Historic Site** (April–Oct Mon–Sat 9am–5pm, Sun 1–5pm; Nov–March Tues–Sat 10am–4pm, Sun 1–4pm; free). The museum here tells the history of the plantation, from its origins in the 1780s to its growth, by 1860, into a 2000-acre enterprise, and its demise after the Civil War.

The southern shore of the Albemarle Peninsula holds less to see, though the marshy countryside roads make for a pleasant drive. **Lake Mattamuskeet Wildlife Refuge** (T 252/926-4021) is an amazing sight in winter, when thousands of swans migrate here from Canada. The refuge's entrance is on Hwy-94, about a mile north of its intersection with US 264. South of Mattamuskeet, you can catch a **ferry** from **Swan Quarter** to Ocracoke on the Outer Banks (see p.458).

The Outer Banks

The **OUTER BANKS** are a string of skinny barrier islands, the remnants of ancient sand dunes, which stretch about 180 miles from the Virginia border to Cape Lookout, near Beaufort. This is a great region to meander, with some wonderful wild beaches, otherworldly marshes, and attractive small towns. Note that when Outer Banks hotels describe themselves as "**waterfront**," it simply means they are on the coastal side of the road, not that they necessarily have ocean views. There is **no public transportation** on the Outer Banks, apart from the ferries between islands and to the mainland.

If you come in on the main road from the north, US-158, stop at the well-stocked Cape Hatteras National Park Service **visitor center** (daily: June–Aug 9am–6pm, Sept–May 9am–5pm; T 252/473-2111, W www.nps.gov/caha). South along US-158 and the parallel shoreline Beach Road, the coastal towns of **Kitty Hawk**, **Kill Devil Hills**, and **Nags Head** nestle closely together where the **beaches** are lined with motels, restaurants, and huge vacation "cottages." Arriving from the west on Hwy-64, you'll come to another useful **visitor center** (daily 9am–5.30pm; T 252/473-2138, W www.outerbanks.org) on **Roanoke Island**. The island, site of the first English settlement in the US, has obvious historical interest; its village, **Manteo**, is perhaps the nicest on the Outer Banks.

Kill Devil Hills and Nags Head

The main feature of the **Wright Brothers National Memorial** (daily: June–Aug 9am–6pm, Sept–May 9am–5pm; $4; T 252/473-2111, W www.nps.gov/wrbr), just off the main road at **KILL DEVIL HILLS**, is the Wright Brothers Monu-

▲ Wright Brothers National Monument

ment, a 60ft granite fin atop a 90ft dune (which is in fact *the* Kill Devil Hill). The memorial commemorates Orville Wright's **first powered flight**, on December 17, 1903. A boulder next to the memorial's **visitor center** marks where Orville's first aircraft hit the ground, and numbered markers show the distance of each of his three subsequent flights. A **museum** in the visitor center records the brothers' various experiments.

A few miles south in **NAGS HEAD**, at Mile 12 on Hwy-158, **Jockey's Ridge State Park** (Ⓣ252/441-7132, Ⓦwww.jockeysridgestatepark.com) boasts the largest sand dunes on the east coast. The park has summer nature programs and instructors from Kitty Hawk Kites (Ⓣ252/441-2426 or 1-877/359-8477, Ⓦwww.kittyhawk.com) can teach you the basics of **hang-gliding** (from $99). It's a beautiful place to be at sunset.

Motels line the beaches north of Oregon Inlet, which separates Bodie Island and Cape Hatteras National Seashore. The *First Colony Inn*, a luxurious **B&B** at 6720 S Virginia Dare Trail, Nags Head (Ⓣ252/441-2343 or 1-800/368-9390, Ⓦwww.firstcolonyinn.com; ❺–❽), is housed in a 1930s beach hotel, with verandas and a pool. The standard of **food** varies considerably, but *the Flying Fish Café*, at 2003 S. Croatan Hwy in Kill Devil Hills (Ⓣ252/441-6894), serves Mediterranean-influenced cuisine, with seafood or meat entrees at $17–24. In Nags Head, *Tortugas Lie*, at Mile 11.5 on Beach Road (Ⓣ252/441-7299), is a funky place for creative shellfish and Tex-Mex.

Roanoke Island and Manteo

ROANOKE ISLAND, between the mainland and Bodie Island, is accessible from both by bridges. This was the **first English settlement** in North America, founded in 1585, and makes much of its status as Sir Walter Raleigh's so-called "Lost Colony" (see box, opposite).

Nothing authentic survives of the settlement, though **Fort Raleigh National Historic Site**, three miles north of Manteo off US-64, contains a tiny reconstruction of the colonists' earthwork fort, set in a wooded glade (daily: June–Aug

American music

Some of the world's greatest musical genres took root in cities across America: Chicago, birthplace of the blues; New Orleans, with unrivalled jazz and R&B scenes; Nashville, synonymous with country; and Memphis, home to seminal record labels and the ultimate rock'n'roll shrine, Graceland. Outside the cities, rural Appalachia brims with backwoods fiddlers; Louisiana's sleepy bayous are alive with Cajun and zydeco; and Mississippi Delta hamlets enrapture blues purists. In short, music runs through the veins of the USA.

Rehearsing bluegrass ▲

Gillian Welch ▼

John Lee Hooker ▼

Rural beginnings

American **folk music** can be traced back to the Europeans – particularly those from England and the Celtic lands – who settled in the Appalachian mountain region. Over the centuries, traditional songs and ballads mixed with various influences from other parts of the world and evolved into the guitar-twanging **country-and-western** music that is today associated with the American South. It wasn't until the mid-twentieth century, however, that country music broke into the mainstream, when the plain cowboy style of Roy Rogers and the harmonies of the Carter Family found a home with a wide audience, and honky-tonk hero Hank Williams performed six encores in his Grand Ole Opry debut.

Bluegrass is another sub-genre of American folk music, and many regard its banjo- and fiddle-based sound to be the purest form of country there is. It's enjoyed a bit of a revival in the past decade, with newfound popularity for traditionalists like Ralph Stanley and more modern practitioners Alison Krauss and Gillian Welch, who surprisingly grew up in Los Angeles and Boston respectively.

The Mississippi sounds

Both jazz and the blues grew out of African-American culture, with the latter inextricably linked to the experiences of slavery and poverty. Forged from a combination of African and gospel sounds into a simple twelve-bar form during the late nineteenth century, by the 1930s the **blues** had gained widespread popularity, spreading along a path that followed the Mississippi River through Memphis, then on to northern urban centres (namely Chicago), which were relatively safe havens for the descendants of freed slaves. Thanks to mainstream icons like Leadbelly, Muddy Waters, and BB King, the genre not only solidified its own stature but – as the saying goes – had a baby and named it Rock'n'Roll.

Jazz remains forever associated with the Deep South and, more specifically, the Creole culture of New Orleans and the Mississippi Delta. The most complex of all modern musical styles, jazz blends African traditions with western techniques, favouring saxophones, trumpets, the double bass, and piano to create a distinctive American sound. Miles Davis is the figure most responsible for raising jazz to a high art form; he first made his mark in New York City's mid-twentieth-century club scene.

Rock of ages

Rock has come a long way since its blues-based infancy, when Elvis Presley swivelled his hips in 1950s Memphis, Bill Haley rocked around the clock, and Chuck Berry told Beethoven it was time to roll over. The amorphous new form would absorb a host of influences, from Bob Dylan's folk protest songs to the pop that followed the Beatles-led British invasion, through the drug- and sitar-tinged psychedelic revolution of bands like the Grateful Dead in the late 1960s. Since then, spiky New York punk, quirky Ohio industrial, furious LA hardcore, slacker Seattle grunge, and spaced-out neo-psychedelia are but a few of the sounds that have thrown up modern-day rock icons like Patti Smith, Black Flag, Nirvana, and REM.

From soul to hip-hop

As the black social experience diversified over the course of the twentieth century, various forms of music sprang up to give it voice. In the 1960s, the heartfelt **soul** of masters like Otis Redding preceded the explosion of talent that came to define the Motown era, which was born in Detroit. As soul went mainstream in the 1970s, progressive mavericks like Parliament and Funkadelic paved the way for the transition to 1980s **rap** culture: loaded with attitude, street-style, and political savvy, rappers from Run DMC to NWA, mostly based in New York and

▲ Miles Davis

▼ Ginger Reyes of the Smashing Pumpkins

Mary J. Blige and Jay-Z ▲

BB King's Blues Club ▼

Preservation Hall ▼

LA, stood at the forefront of a dynasty that would eventually include **hip-hop** and **R&B**. Other major current centers of hip-hop include Philadelphia, Atlanta, and Detroit, to name just a few.

Ten great music venues

▶▶ **924 Gilman**, Berkeley CA. Punk, indie, and experimental bands such as Green Day have emerged from this squat-like community hangout. p.1052

▶▶ **BB King's Blues Club**, Memphis TN. Blues stronghold founded and owned by the legend himself, who still makes the odd appearance. p.520

▶▶ **The Fillmore Auditorium**, San Francisco, CA. This legendary theatre with superb design features and walls of 60s posters still hosts rock and alt-rock acts. p.1044

▶▶ **Knitting Factory**, New York, NY. Cutting edge sounds, from art-rock to electronica can be sampled in the club's two spaces. p.110

▶▶ **Preservation Hall**, New Orleans, LA. One of the finest venues in the country for trad jazz. p.647

▶▶ **Continental Club**, Austin, TX. Laid back outlet for interesting country and folk acts in the music capital of Texas. p.688

▶▶ **Rosa's Lounge**, Chicago, IL. Intimate and welcoming blues club that offers a variety of great local talent. p.338

▶▶ **Ryman Auditorium**, Nashville, TN. The classic seated theatre is one of the best spots to sample country and western. p.525

▶▶ **The Stone Pony**, Asbury Park, NJ. The unassuming bar that helped launch Springsteen maintains its tradition of promoting local talent. p.172

▶▶ **Whisky-a-Go-Go**, Los Angeles, CA. The former stomping ground of the Doors now tends to showcase harder edged outfits. p.989

9am–6pm, Sept–May 9am–5pm; free; ⓣ252/473-5772, ⓦwww.nps.gov/fora). A museum covers the history of the expeditions and colonization, and an amphitheater hosts performances of *The Lost Colony* (June to late Aug Sun–Fri 8.30pm; $16–20; ⓣ252/473-3414, ⓦwww.thelostcolony.org). Outside, a simple monument commemorates the Underground Railroad and the **Freedmen's Colony** that formed here during the Civil War. Adjacent to the fort, the **Elizabethan Gardens** are elegantly landscaped with walkways and statues (June–Aug Mon–Fri 9am–8pm, Sat 9am–7pm; April, May, Sept & Oct daily 9am–6pm; March daily 9am–5pm; Nov daily 9am–5pm; Dec–Feb daily 10am–4pm; $8; ⓣ252/473-3234, ⓦwww.elizabethangardens.org).

Just across from the waterfront at **Manteo**, the **Roanoke Island Festival Park** has a slew of historical attractions (daily: April to mid-June & mid-Aug to Oct 10am–6pm; mid-June to mid-Aug 10am–7pm; Nov–Dec & mid-Feb to March 10am–5pm; $9 tickets valid for two consecutive days; ⓣ252/475-1500, ⓦwww.

Roanoke: The Lost Colony

According to popular myth, the first English attempt to settle in North America – Sir Walter Raleigh's colony at **Roanoke** – remains an unsolved mystery, in which the "Lost Colony" disappeared without trace.

Sir Walter himself never visited North America. The original patent to establish a colony was granted by Queen Elizabeth I to his half-brother, Sir Humphrey Gilbert, but Gilbert died following an abortive landfall in Newfoundland in 1583. Raleigh directed subsequent explorations further south. A 1584 expedition pinpointed Roanoke Island, behind the Outer Banks of North Carolina. The English named the region **Virginia**, in honor of the Virgin Queen.

A party led by Ralph Lane in 1585 was interested in searching for gold; their hopes of finding a fortune were quickly dashed, however, and the following year they sailed home with Sir Francis Drake, who visited on his way up from the West Indies. In 1587, 117 more colonists set off from England, intending to farm a more fertile site beside Chesapeake Bay; but, fearing Spanish attack, the ships that carried them dumped them at Roanoke once again. Their leader, **John White**, who went home to fetch supplies a month later, was stranded in England when war broke out with Spain, and the Spanish Armada set sail. When he finally managed to persuade a reluctant sea captain to carry him back to Roanoke in 1590, he found the island abandoned. Even so, he was reassured by the absence of the agreed-upon distress signal (a carved Maltese cross), while the word "**Croatoan**" inscribed on a tree seemed a clear message that the colonists had moved south to the eponymous island. However, fearful of both the Spanish and of the approaching hurricane season, White's crew refused to take him any further.

There the story usually ends, with the colonists never seen again. In fact, during the next decade, several reports reached the subsequent, more durable colony of Jamestown (in what's now Virginia), of English settlers being dispersed as slaves among the Native American tribes of North Carolina. Rather than admit their inability to rescue their fellow countrymen, and thus expose a vulnerability that might deter prospective settlers or investors, the Jamestown colonists seem simply to have written their predecessors out of history.

Roanoke Island gained and lost another colony during the **Civil War**. After it was captured by Union forces in February 1862, so many freed and runaway slaves made their way here through Confederate lines that the federal government formally declared it to be a "**Freedmen's Colony**." Around four thousand blacks were living on Roanoke by the end of the war, and many of the men served in the Union army. During Reconstruction, the government returned all land to its former owners, and the colony was disbanded. Roanoke retains a substantial black population to this day.

roanokeisland.com). Highlights include the **adventure museum**, an interactive exhibit on the history of the Outer Banks, the **settlement site**, a living museum peopled with "Elizabethan" soldiers and craftsmen, and the *Elizabeth II*, a reconstruction of a sixteenth-century English ship.

If you're after fine **dining** on the Outer Banks, Manteo is the place. *Clara's Seafood Grill* (Ⓣ252/473-1727), right on the waterfront, offers creative shellfish dishes, while the *Full Moon Café*, across from the waterfront at the corner of Sir Walter Raleigh and Queen Elizabeth streets (Ⓣ252/473-6666), is more casual, serving chowder, gourmet sandwiches, and quiche. Manteo also has a range of places to **stay**. *The Outdoors Inn*, 406 Uppowoc St (Ⓣ252/473-1356, Ⓦwww.theoutdoorsinn.com; ❺), has two stylish, brightly decorated en-suite **B&B** rooms in an airy home. The *Island Guesthouse*, on Hwy-64 (Ⓣ252/473-2434, Ⓦwww.theislandmotel.com; ❺), is more of a **motel**, with fully equipped rooms and a sociable atmosphere.

Cape Hatteras National Seashore

CAPE HATTERAS NATIONAL SEASHORE stretches south from South Nags Head on Bodie Island to **Hatteras** and **Ocracoke** islands, with forty miles of unspoiled beaches. Even in high season you can pull off the road and walk across the dunes to deserted beaches. The salt marshes on the western side are also beautiful. At the northern end of Hatteras Island, the **Pea Island National Wildlife Refuge** (Ⓣ252/987-2394, Ⓦwww.fws.gov/peaisland) offers guided canoe tours, trails, and observation platforms for exemplary bird-watching.

At the south end of Hatteras Island, not far from the early nineteenth-century black-and-white-striped **Cape Hatteras Lighthouse**, a **visitor center** (daily: summer 9am–6pm; rest of year 9am–5pm) has exhibits on the island's maritime history. The 208ft lighthouse, which you can climb (mid-April to mid-Oct; $7), was moved 2900ft inland from its original location to protect it from encroaching waters. Further south, at the village of **Frisco**, the **Native American Museum** is a loving collection of arts and crafts from around the US, including a drum from a Hopi *kiva*, or prayer chamber. The museum also offers several acres of forested **nature** trails (Tues–Sun 11am–5pm, Mon by appointment; $5; Ⓣ252/995-4440, Ⓦwww.nativeamericanmuseum.org).

In **Hatteras**, next to the Ocracoke ferry landing, the **Graveyard of the Atlantic Museum** (Mon–Fri 10am–4pm; free; Ⓦwww.graveyardoftheatlantic.com) tells the stories of the explorers, pirates, and Civil War blockade-runners who perished along this wild stretch of coast.

Various **motels**, food shops, and **restaurants** are scattered through the fly-blown settlements along Hwy-12. The *Cape Hatteras Motel* in Buxton, a mile from the lighthouse (Ⓣ252/995-5611, Ⓦwww.capehatterasmotel.com; ❹–❼), has comfy oceanfront rooms and a pool. A good place for breakfast and seafood is *Diamond Shoals*, also in Buxton on Hwy-12 (Ⓣ252/995-5611), while on the waterfront at Hatteras, *Austin Creek Grill* serves stylish salads, shellfish, and pasta nightly (Ⓣ252/986-1511). **Camping** is best at one of the first-come, first-served National Park Service campgrounds (Ⓣ252/473-2111, Ⓦwww.nps.gov/caha; $20 per night); they're located at Frisco and Oregon Inlet on Bodie Island (both early April to mid-Oct); and at Cape Point near Buxton (late May to Aug).

Ocracoke Island

Peaceful, undeveloped **OCRACOKE ISLAND** is forty minutes by free ferry from Hatteras (see box opposite). This sixteen-mile ribbon of land is bisected by Hwy-12, where it's possible to pull over anywhere and enjoy a deserted patch of beach. Despite the crowds of tourists in the village of **Ocracoke** the island has maintained its easy-going atmosphere. It's perfect for catching rays, taking a stroll, or enjoying a cycle ride; a number of places, including hotels, **rent bikes**.

Hotels and **B&Bs** in Ocracoke village fill up in summer and are fairly expensive; as elsewhere on the Outer Banks, rates drop come September. The *Anchorage Inn*, on Hwy-12 (Ⓣ252/928-1101, Ⓦwww.theanchorageinn.com; ❺), is comfortable, with sea views, a pool, and complimentary continental breakfast. Or you could sleep in one of the unusual "crow's-nest" rooms in the 1901 *Island Inn and Dining Room*, on Hwy-12 (Ⓣ1-877/456-3466, Ⓦwww.ocracokeislandinn.com; ❸–❻), whose **restaurant** is renowned for its crabcakes (Ⓣ252/928-7821). Other, less expensive restaurants include the *Back Porch*, on Back Road (Ⓣ252/928-6401), which serves great fish, and the lively *Howard's Pub & Raw Bar*, a mile north of the village on Hwy-12 (Ⓣ252/928-4441), which offers more than two hundred beers. It's one of the few places on the island that's open all year. The fairly isolated Park Service **campground** tends to be the first of the Outer Banks sites to fill up; unlike the others, it accepts reservations (Ⓣ1-800/365-2267; $23 per night; open early-April to late-Oct).

Cape Lookout National Seashore

The mainland between Cedar Island and Beaufort (see p.460) is a rural backwater, sparsely settled and hardly touched by tourists. The most likely reason to pass through is to get to the all-but-deserted **CAPE LOOKOUT NATIONAL SEASHORE**, a narrow ribbon of sand stretching south of Ocracoke Island along three Outer Banks with no roads or habitation. The seashore is only accessible by **ferry** (mid-March to early Dec) or private boat, and its few visitors share a total of around 56 miles of beach along all three islands. The **visitor center** is at the eastern end of the mainland settlement of **Harker's Island** (daily 9am–5pm; Ⓣ252/728-2250, Ⓦwww.nps.gov/calo).

At the northern tip of the first island, **North Core Banks**, stand the eerie ruins of the abandoned village of **Portsmouth**, whose last two residents left in 1971. Ferries arrive in Portsmouth from Ocracoke (around $16 round-trip; call Island Boat Tours on Ⓣ252/928-4361). The ferry from **Atlantic**, south of Cedar Island

Ocracoke ferries

In summer, free **ferries** run **between Hatteras and Ocracoke** (40min). There's room for only thirty cars, and it's loaded on a first-come, first-served basis.

Hatteras–Ocracoke May–Oct every 30min 7.30am–7pm, hourly 5–7am & 7pm–midnight; Nov–April hourly 5am–midnight.

Ocracoke–Hatteras May–Oct every 30min 8am–7pm, hourly 5–7am & 7pm–midnight; Nov–April hourly 5am–midnight.

Ferries **from Ocracoke** also head south down the coast to **Cedar Island** on the mainland (2hr 15min; $1 pedestrian, $3 bike, $10 motorbike, $15 car) and to **Swan Quarter** on the Albemarle Peninsula (2hr 30min; same fares). Both require **reservations** in summer, preferably a day or two in advance (Ocracoke Ⓣ1-800/345-1665, Cedar Island Ⓣ1-800/856-0343, Swan Quarter Ⓣ1-800/773-1094); at short notice you should be able to get the day you want, if not the time.

Between Ocracoke and Cedar Island spring & summer seven or eight departures 7am–7.30pm; fall & winter four departures 7am–5pm

Ocracoke–Swan Quarter late May to early Sept 6.30am, 10am, 12.30pm, 4pm; no 4pm sailing rest of year.

Swan Quarter–Ocracoke late May to early Sept 7am, 9.30am, 4pm; no 7am sailing rest of year.

For **further information** contact Ⓣ1-800/BY-FERRY or Ⓦwww.ncferry.org.

on the mainland ($14 per person or $75 per vehicle round-trip; call Morris Marina on ⓣ252/225-4261), lands at **Long Point**, seventeen miles south of Portsmouth, which you can only reach on foot. **Cabins** on the island are operated by Morris Marina (starting at $100 per night for up to six people); otherwise there's only primitive **camping**.

South Core Banks is served by private ferry from **Davis**, south of Atlantic on the mainland ($14 round-trip; ⓣ1-877/956-6568). Here, too, the ferry company manages more than twenty **cabins**, all with showers (❸–❻). Three passenger ferries run to the southern tip of the south island from Beaufort (see below) and from Harker's Island, to within two or three miles of **Cape Lookout** itself and its lighthouse.

To get to the peaceful **Shackleford Banks**, inhabited by wild mustangs since the early 1500s, when they are thought to have swum ashore from shipwrecks, you can catch ferries from Beaufort and Morehead City (see below).

Beaufort

BEAUFORT, about 150 miles southeast of Raleigh, is probably the nicest of North Carolina's coastal towns. A good base for visiting the nearby beaches, it has an attractive waterfront that's particularly lively at night.

North Carolina's third-oldest town, Beaufort also has an appealing twelve-block **historical district**, centering on Turner Street, off the waterfront. Here you'll find handsome old houses, an apothecary, and the city jail; the town **welcome center**, 130 Turner St (daily: March–Nov 9.30am–5pm; Dec–Feb 10am–4pm; ⓣ252/728-5225, ⓦwww.historicbeaufort.com), offers a number of tours.

Ferries to **Shackleford Banks** (see opposite) are run by Island Ferry Adventures (mid-March to mid-Oct; round-trip $15; minimum two adults, ⓣ252/728-7555, ⓦwww.islandferryadventures.com), Mystery Tours (from $16; ⓣ252/728-7827, ⓦwww.mysteryboattours.com), and Outer Banks Ferry Service (ⓣ252/728-3576), which are all on the waterfront. You can also get there from **Morehead City**, a couple of miles down the coast (Waterfront Ferry Service ⓣ252/726-7678). Beaufort Inlet Watersports, next to the Outer Banks Ferry Service at 328 Front St (ⓣ252/728-7607), offers **parasailing** for around $50 single, $90 tandem.

Among the many historic **B&Bs** on the residential streets off Turner, *Langdon House*, 135 Craven St (ⓣ252/728-5499, ⓦwww.langdonhouse.com; ❺), is friendly and relaxed; the *Cedars Inn*, 305 Front St (ⓣ252/728-7036, ⓦwww.cedarsinn.com; ❻), is rather plush. The *Inlet Inn*, on the waterfront at 601 Front St (ⓣ252/728-3600 or 1-800/554-5466, ⓦwww.inlet-inn.com; ❺), has huge rooms and serves continental breakfast in your room. Morehead City and the Bogue Banks boast plenty of **motels**.

As for **eating and nightlife**, Beaufort's waterfront is vibrant at night, with locals and vacationers drinking, listening to live music at the *Dock House* (ⓣ252/728-4506), and simply strolling. Decent bars and restaurants line the wooden **boardwalk**, with other good options a block or so inland. The *Beaufort Grocery Co*, 117 Queen St (closed Tues; ⓣ252/728-3899), prides itself on inventive dishes made from superbly fresh ingredients, while the buzzy *Aqua*, 114 Middle Lane (ⓣ252/728-7777; dinner only, closed Sun & Mon), offers Carolina-style tapas and big desserts.

The beaches

South of Beaufort, the **beaches** along the twenty-mile offshore **Bogue Banks**, especially Atlantic Beach at the east end, are always pretty crowded. On **Bear**

Island to the south – reached from **Swansboro** by boat taxi or ferry (April–Oct, hours vary; $5; ⓣ910/326-4881) – the stunning **Hammocks Beach State Park** has high sand dunes, a wooded shore, and perfect beaches. To **camp** ($9), you need to register at the small park center (daily: Sept–May 8am–6pm; June–Aug 8am–7pm; ⓣ910/326-4881). No camping is permitted in turtle season (March and April), when **loggerhead sea turtles** come ashore to lay their eggs.

Wilmington

Though it's the largest town on North Carolina's coast, **WILMINGTON**, set back along the **Cape Fear River**, fifty miles short of the state's southern border, has a laid-back feel. During the Civil War, it was briefly the Confederacy's most important harbor, exporting cotton all over the world. "**Blockade-runners**" would attempt to outrun the Union navy, racing into the safety of Fort Fisher's guns.

Wilmington today is attractive, friendly, and energized. Its notoriety as a popular **movie location** has earned it the nickname "Wilmywood," and the influx of creative types has led to a certain gentrification that feels very different from the rest of the coast.

While Wilmington's extravagant houses, ornate **City Hall** and lovely **Thalian Hall** demonstrate its former wealth, the streets of the weathered, boardwalked **waterfront**, dotted with cafés and restaurants, are the real draw. **Chandler's Wharf**, an upmarket mall in a restored warehouse, is typical of the area's revitalization, while the **Cotton Exchange**, 321 N Front St, sells crafts and food in a group of buildings that once housed a grain mill, warehouse, and cotton business. At the foot of Market Street, at the small **Riverfront Park**, you can pick up a horse-drawn **carriage tour** (ⓣ910/251-8889; $11); a **harbor cruise** (ⓣ910/343-1611, ⓦwww.cfrboats.com; from $10); or a **river taxi** to the battleship USS *North Carolina*, which participated in every naval offensive in the Pacific during World War II. At 814 Market St, the **Cape Fear Museum** (summer Mon–Sat 9am–5pm, Sun 1–5pm; rest of year closed Mon; $6; ⓦwww.capefearmuseum.com) gives a lively account of local history.

To get a sense of how Wilmywood works, take a tour of **EUE/Screen Gems Studios**, 1223 N 23rd St, the site of productions as diverse as David Lynch's *Blue Velvet* and TV hit *Dawson's Creek* (call for seasonal hours; $12; ⓣ910/343-3500, ⓦwww.screengemsstudios.com).

Twenty miles south of Wilmington on Hwy-421, near Kure Beach, **Fort Fisher State Historic Site** commands a rocky position overlooking both the sea and the mouth of the Cape Fear River. A small **museum** focuses on its days as a Confederate stronghold, with relics from sunken blockade-runners (April–Oct Mon–Sat 9am–5pm, Sun 1–5pm; Nov–March Tues–Sat 10am–4pm; free; ⓣ910/458-5538).

Practicalities

The **bus station** is at 201 Harnett St, a mile north of downtown off Third Street. Wilmington's **visitor center**, 24 N Third St (Mon–Fri 8.30am–5pm, Sat 9am–4pm, Sun 10am–4pm; ⓣ1-877/406-2356, ⓦwww.cape-fear.nc.us), has maps and walking tours, including a good African-American site map and a *Dawson's Creek* FAQ sheet. The funniest overviews are given by Adventure Walking Tours, which leave from the flagpole at Market and Water streets (April–Oct 10am & 2pm; $12; ⓣ910/763-1785).

Cheap motels line Market Street for the last few miles into Wilmington, and there are also some lovely **B&Bs**: movie stars stay at the lavish *Graystone Inn*, on Third and Dock (ⓣ910/763-2000, ⓦwww.graystoneinn.com; ❼). At the nonsmoking *Best Western Coastline Inn*, on the riverfront at 503 Nutt St (Ⓣ910/763-2800 or 1-800/617-7732, Ⓦwww.coastlineinn.com; ④), rates include breakfast served in your room.

The central blocks of downtown hold an abundance of swanky, often Asian-flavored **restaurants**, such as *Deluxe* at 114 Market St (Ⓣ910/251-0333), where entrees like rare seared garam masala-spiced ahi tuna fillet will cost you $27. But you can eat well for less at local restaurants like the *Dock Street Oyster Bar*, 12 Dock St (Ⓣ910/762-2827), a little place serving cheap raw oysters and seafood.

Wilmington has a thriving **nightlife** as well; for **listings**, pick up a copy of the free weekly *Encore*. The *Soapbox*, 266 N Front St (Ⓣ910/251-5800), hosts the best in local and national indie music while the *Barbary Coast*, 116 S Front St (Ⓣ910/762-8996), is a hole-in-the-wall that has gained some cachet from being Mickey Rourke's favorite bar in town. For a little art and wine try the edgy *Bottega Gallery and Art Bar*, 208 N Front St (Tues–Sun 1pm–late; Ⓣ910/763-3737, Ⓦwww.bottegagallery.com). Built in 1858, *Thalian Hall*, 310 Chestnut St (Ⓣ1-800/523-2820, Ⓦwww.thalianhall.com), hosts music, theater, and movies.

The North Carolina Piedmont

North Carolina's **PIEDMONT** is an industrialized area of textile and tobacco towns seeing downtown revitalization. The main area of interest is the **Research Triangle** trio of neighboring college towns: **Raleigh**, the state capital; relaxed **Durham**, with its strong black community; and countercultural **Chapel Hill**. **Winston-Salem**, famous for its tobacco industry, boasts Old Salem village.

Raleigh

Founded as North Carolina's capital in 1792, **RALEIGH** focuses around the central **Capitol Square**, where the **North Carolina Museum of History**, 5 E Edenton St (Mon–Sat 9am–5pm, Sun noon–5pm; free; Ⓣ919/807-7900), provides a far-reaching chronology through the state's history. Opposite is the **North Carolina Museum of Natural Sciences**, 11 W Jones St (Mon–Sat 9am–5pm, Sun noon–5pm; free), which looks at local geology, as well as animal and plant life back to the dinosaur age.

South of the capitol, the four-block **City Market**, a lamp-lit, cobbled enclave at the intersection of Blount and Martin streets, holds a number of good shops and restaurants. Check out the local artists at work in **Artspace**, 201 E Davie St (Tues–Sat 10am–6pm; Ⓦwww.artspacenc.org). Seventeenth US President **Andrew Johnson** was born in a tiny home just north of where the capitol now stands; his birthplace has since been moved to **Mordecai Historic Park**, north of town at the corner of Wake Forest Rd and Mimosa St (Tues–Sat 10am–4pm, Sun 1–4pm; 1hr tours begin on the hour, with last tour at 3pm; $5).

A little way out to the northwest via I-40, the impressive **North Carolina Museum of Art**, 2110 Blue Ridge Rd (Tues–Thurs & Sat 9am–5pm, Fri 9am–9pm, Sun 10am–5pm; tours daily 1.30pm; free except for special exhibitions), has an eclectic display of works from the ancient world, Africa, Europe, and the US, along with a great restaurant (see below).

Practicalities

Raleigh-Durham **airport** (Ⓦwww.rdu.com) is off I-40, fifteen minutes northwest of town. The **taxi** ride into town costs around $30, while a circuitous **shuttle service** will set you back $25. Amtrak drops you off at 320 W Cabarrus St, while the Greyhound station is in a seedy part of downtown at 314 W Jones St. The **visitor center**, 220 Fayetteville St (Mon–Sat 10am–5pm, Sun 12pm–4pm; Ⓦwww.visitraleigh.com), has the usual racks of leaflets.

If you want to **stay here**, avoid the more anonymous downtown hotels and instead head out to Hillsborough Street, near North Carolina State University, where the *Velvet Cloak Inn* at no. 1505 offers comfortable rooms and an indoor pool (Ⓣ919/828-0333, Ⓦwww.velvetcloakinn.com; ❺). For **food**, *Big Ed's*, in the City Market at 220 Wolfe St (closed Sun; Ⓣ919/836-9909), serves fabulous Southern breakfasts. The huge *42nd St Oyster Bar*, downtown at 508 Jones St (Ⓣ919/831-2811), is a popular spot for fresh fish and seafood. The art museum boasts the contemporary *Blue Ridge Restaurant* (Tues–Sun lunch, Sun brunch; Ⓣ919/664-6838). Newly renovated Fayetteville Street features destinations for the professional set, including *The Mint*, at no. 219 (Ⓣ919/821-0011), with entrees such as kurobuta pork chop paired with watermelon gazpacho.

Hillsborough Street, lined with bars and restaurants, is the epicenter of Raleigh's student **nightlife**. *The Brewery*, at no. 3009 (Ⓣ919/838-6788, Ⓦwww.brewerync.com), hosts the best regional rock and alternative bands. Away from Hillsborough, *Berkeley Café*, 217 W Martin (Ⓣ919/821-0777), specializes in roots, alt-country, and rock.

Durham

Twenty miles northwest of Raleigh, **DURHAM** found itself at the center of the nation's tobacco industry after farmer Washington Duke came home from the Civil War with the idea of producing cigarettes. By 1890 he and his three sons had formed the **American Tobacco Company**. The **Duke Homestead Historical Site**, north of I-85 at 2828 Duke Homestead Rd (Tues–Sat 9am–5pm; free), covers the social history of tobacco farming.

In 1924, the Duke family's $40 million endowment to the Trinity College enabled it to expand into a world-respected medical research facility that became **Duke University**. On campus, the **Nasher Museum of Art** at 2001 Campus Drive (Tues, Wed, Fri & Sat 10am–5pm, Thurs 10am–9pm, Sun noon–5pm; $5; Ⓣ919/684-5135, Ⓦwww.nasher.duke.edu) has good African, pre-Columbian, medieval, and Asian collections.

Downtown Durham has little of interest, though **Brightleaf Square**, an upbeat shopping area of restored tobacco warehouses at Gregson and Main streets, is worth a stroll to browse its galleries, bookstores, and specialty stores.

Durham takes pride in its vibrant **black heritage**. Seven miles north of town, in Treyburn Park, the fascinating **Historic Stagville** (Tues–Sat 10am–4pm; free; Ⓣ919/620-0120, Ⓦwww.historicstagvillefoundation.org) illustrates North Carolina plantation life, in particular the slave experience, from the early 1800s to Reconstruction. The grounds have preserved the small two-story houses they lived in, as well as the plantation owners' house and a colossal barn built by skilled slave carpenters.

Practicalities

Greyhound **buses** stop at 412 W. Chapel Hill St. Pick up maps and local information from the Durham **visitor center**, 101 E Morgan St (Mon–Fri 8.30am–5pm, Sat 10am–2pm; Ⓣ919/687-0288 or 1-800/446-8604, Ⓦwww.durham-nc.com). The *Arrowhead Inn*, 106 Mason Rd (Ⓣ919/477-8430, Ⓦwww.arrowheadinn.com; ❺), which dates back to 1775, offers lovely **B&B** rooms.

For **food**, try places around Brightleaf Square: *Fowler's*, 112 S Duke St (Ⓣ919/683-2555), serves organic gourmet sandwiches and coffee, while

Anotherthyme, 109 N Gregson St (dinner only; ⓣ919/682-5225), specializes in creative seafood and tapas.

Chapel Hill

Hip **CHAPEL HILL**, on the southwest outskirts of Durham, is nationally renowned as the home of such bands as Superchunk and musicians like Ben Folds and Ryan Adams, not to mention James Taylor. A pleasant town to wander, it has a multitude of laid-back bars and coffeehouses along **Franklin Street**, which fringes the north side of campus. Franklin continues west into the adjacent city of **Carrboro**, where it becomes **Main Street**; bars and restaurants here have a slightly post-collegiate edge.

The **University of North Carolina**, dating from 1789, was the nation's first state university. The earliest of its fine eighteenth-century buildings is **Old East**, its original brick painted a fashionable tan in the 1840s. Evidence of the university's wealth can be seen at the **Morehead Planetarium** on E Franklin St (Mon–Thurs 10am–3.30pm, Fri–Sat 10am–3.30pm & 6.30–8.45pm, Sun 1–5pm; $6; ⓦwww.moreheadplanetarium.org), which served as an early NASA training center, and at the **Ackland Art Museum**, South Columbia and Franklin streets (Wed–Sat 10am–5pm, Sun 1–5pm; free; ⓦwww.ackland.org), which is particularly strong on Asian art and antiquities.

Practicalities

The Chapel Hill/Orange County **visitors bureau** is at 501 W Franklin (Mon–Fri 8.30am–5pm, Sat 10am–2pm; ⓣ1-888/968-2060, ⓦwww.chocvb.org). Chapel Hill has few places to **stay**; one of the most popular spots is the very swanky, university-owned *Carolina Inn*, on campus at 211 Pittsboro St (ⓣ919/933-2001 or 1-800/962-8519, ⓦwww.carolinainn.com; ❻). Five miles northeast of town, the *Sheraton*, 1 Europa Drive (ⓣ919/968-4900; ❺), has stylish, ultra-comfy rooms, while the nearby *Hampton Inn*, 1740 Fordham Blvd (ⓣ919/968-3000; ❹), is cheaper.

Chapel Hill has no shortage of great **restaurants**. The minimalist *Lantern*, 423 W Franklin St, dishes up fabulous pan-Asian food until late (closed Sun; ⓣ919/969-8846), and has an atmospheric bar. At 610 W Franklin, *Crooks Corner* (closed Mon; ⓣ919/929-7643) offers a daily changing menu of delicious, stylish Southern cooking. *Elmo's Diner*, in the Carr Mill Mall in Carrboro, 200 N Greensboro St (ⓣ919/929-2909), does great breakfasts, tasty veggie choices, and daily specials. At *Southern Rail*, 201 E Main St (ⓣ919/967-1967), dine on eclectic fare in refurbished railcars and check out live music many nights.

For **nightlife**, stay on Franklin and Main streets. *Orange County Social Club*, 108 E Main St, Carrboro (ⓣ919/933-0669, ⓦwww.orangecountysocialclub.com), is a hip, laid-back **bar** with vintage decor, a pool table, a great jukebox, and a garden. Most **music** venues have an eclectic booking policy: *Local 506*, 506 W Franklin St (ⓣ919/942-5506, ⓦwww.local506.com), features indie bands, open-mike and hip-hop, while over in Carrboro, the *Cat's Cradle*, 300 E Main St (ⓣ919/967-9053, ⓦwww.catscradle.com), books the best bands on the national touring circuit. Check **listings** in the free *Independent Weekly* (ⓦwww.indyweek.com).

Winston-Salem

Though synonymous with the brand names of its cigarettes, **WINSTON-SALEM**, eighty miles west of Chapel Hill, owes its spot on the tourist itinerary to **Old Salem**. These twenty preserved blocks of homes honor the heritage of the city's first Moravian settlers. Escaping religious persecution in what are now the Czech and

Slovak republics, the first Moravians settled in the Piedmont in the mid-seventeenth century. They soon established trading links with the frontier settlers and founded the town of Salem on a communal basis – they permitted only those of the same religious faith to live here. The demand for their crafts helped establish the adjacent community of Winston, which, accruing tremendous wealth from tobacco, soon outgrew the older community. The two merged in 1913 to form Winston-Salem.

Visitors are free to stroll or drive the streets of Old Salem, or by touring ten **restored buildings** (Jan & Feb Tues–Sat 9.30am–4.30pm, Sun 1–5pm; March–Dec Mon–Sat 9.30am–4.30pm, Sun 1–5pm; $21, or $24 for two days). Start at the huge **visitor center** on Academy and Old Salem Rd (Jan & Feb Tues–Sat 9am–5.30pm, Sun 12.30–5.30pm; March–Dec Mon–Sat 9am–5.30pm, Sun 12.30–5pm). Worth a stop is **St Philips Moravian Church**, an African-American church originally built in 1823. Admission includes entrance to the **Museum of Early Southern Decorative Arts** (Jan & Feb Tues–Sat 9.30am–4.30pm, Sun 1–5pm; March–Dec Mon–Sat 9.30am–4.30pm, Sun 1–5pm), the **Children's Museum**, (Jan–Feb Tues–Sat 9.30am–4.30pm, Sun 1–5pm; March–Dec Mon–Sat 9.30am–4.30pm, Sun 1–5pm; $6 for the two if not part of Old Salem ticket), and the **Toy Museum** (Jan & Feb Tues–Sat 9.30am–4.30pm, Sun 1–5pm; March–Dec Mon–Sat 9.30am–4.30pm, Sun 1–5pm), which has thousands of antique toys dating from 225 AD. Large lunches and dinners, and beer, are served at the *Old Salem Tavern*, 736 S Main (Ⓣ336/748-8585), where the costumed waiters carry dishes like the $7.50 Moravian chicken pie to diners on the spacious patio.

Three miles northwest of downtown, the **Reynolda House Museum of American Art**, 2250 Reynolda Rd (Tues–Sat 9.30am–4.30pm, Sun 1.30–4.30pm; $10), features pieces by top American artists from the eighteenth century to the present day, in what was the home of tobacco baron Richard Joshua Reynolds. The mansion, designed by Charles Barton Keen, is set in lush, landscaped gardens, with a number of its surrounding buildings converted into fancy stores and restaurants known collectively as **Reynolda Village**.

Practicalities

Winston-Salem's **visitor center** is a few blocks from Old Salem, at 200 Brookstown Ave (Ⓣ336/728-4200, Ⓦwww.visitwinstonsalem.com). Next door, the *Brookstown Inn* (Ⓣ336/725-1120, Ⓦwww.brookstowninn.com; ❻), is a lovely small **hotel** in a former textile mill.

Finding a place to eat in town isn't all that exciting a prospect though *Hutch & Harris*, 420 W Fourth St (closed Mon Ⓣ336/721-1336), serves good regional and international cuisine. *Tumeric Indian Restaurant & Bar*, 3088 Healey Drive, dishes up reasonably priced, and mostly spicy, entrees from across the spectrum of regions of India.

Charlotte

The banking and transportation center of **CHARLOTTE**, where I-77 and I-85 meet near the South Carolina border, is the largest city in the state, although tourist offerings are minimal. The busy downtown thoroughfare **Tryon Street** is an unlovely mass of tall buildings and concrete known as "uptown." A few blocks away, the excellent **Museum of the New South**, 200 E Seventh St (Mon–Sat 10am–5pm, Sun noon–5pm; $6; Ⓦwww.museumofthenewsouth.org), looks at the growth of the region from Reconstruction onwards. **Discovery Place**, 301 N Tryon St, is a kids-oriented science museum with an indoor rainforest, an IMAX theater, and a planetarium (Mon–Fri 9am–5pm, Sat 9am–6pm, Sun noon–6pm; $10, IMAX $11, combo ticket $19; Ⓦwww.discoveryplace.org).

Practicalities

Charlotte/Douglas International Airport, seven miles west of town on Old Dowd Road or I-85, is served by the #5 **bus** ($1.75), which runs hourly from the Charlotte Transportation Center, uptown on Brevard Street, between Fourth and Fifth streets, to the airport; **taxis** cost about $25. Greyhound stops centrally at 601 W Trade St, while Amtrak trains pull in at 1914 N Tryon St. The huge **visitor center** is at 330 S Tryon St (Mon–Fri 8.30am–5pm, Sat 9am–3pm; ⓣ704/331-2753 or 1-800/231-4636, ⓦwww.charlottecvb.org). A recently added light rail makes getting around the city easier.

Most of Charlotte's **hotels** are aimed at the conference trade, though the 1929 *Dunhill Hotel*, 237 N Tryon St (ⓣ704/332-4141, ⓦwww.dunhillhotel.com; ⑥), possesses an Old World elegance. The *Days Inn*, 601 N Tryon St (ⓣ704/333-4733; ③), is a cheaper central alternative. Good **restaurants** include trendy *Providence Café*, 110 Perrin Place (ⓣ704/376-2008), for vegetarian and New American cuisine and *La Vecchia's Seafood Grille*, 225 E Sixth St (ⓣ704/370-6776; closed Sun). Charlotte's lively **nightlife** is concentrated between the easily walkable grid of Tryon, College, Seventh, and Fifth streets, and in the South End, southwest of uptown. Check **listings** in the free weekly *Creative Loafing* (ⓦcharlotte.creativeloafing.com).

The North Carolina mountains

The best way to see the **mountains** of North Carolina is from the exhilarating **Blue Ridge Parkway**, which runs across the northwest of the state from Virginia to the **Great Smoky Mountains National Park**. The panoramic expanses of forested hillside may astonish travelers fresh from the crowded centers of the east coast. The region has been a breeding ground since the early twentieth century for **bluegrass music**, which you will still find performed regularly throughout the region. Laid-back **Asheville** is a good place to see more experimental reinventions of the traditional mountain sounds.

The helpful **visitor center** at 1700 Blowing Rock Rd in Boone (ⓣ1-800/438-7500, ⓦwww.mountainsofnc.com), services most of the mountain area.

The Blue Ridge Parkway

The peak tourist season for the **BLUE RIDGE PARKWAY** is October, when the leaves of the deciduous trees turn vivid shades of yellow, gold, and orange.

Mountain activities

Organized **outdoor pursuits** available along the Blue Ridge Parkway include **white-water rafting** and **canoeing**, most of it on the Nolichucky River near the Tennessee border, south of Johnson City, Tennessee, but also on the Watauga River and Wilson Creek. Companies running trips include Nantahala Outdoor Center (ⓣ1-888/905-7238, ⓦwww.noc.com) and High Mountain Expeditions (ⓣ1-800/262-9036, ⓦwww.highmountainexpeditions.com), who also offer biking, hiking, and caving trips. Expect to pay around $75 per person for a full day of rafting.

Winter sees **skiing** at a number of slopes and resorts, particularly around **Banner Elk**, twelve miles southwest of Boone. Resort accommodation is expensive, ski passes less so. Appalachian Ski Mountain (ⓣ1-800/322-2373, ⓦwww.appskimtn.com) is near Blowing Rock, and Ski Beech (ⓣ828/898-4521, ⓦwww.skibeech.com), the highest ski area in the east, is at Beech Mountain. You can pick up full listings at visitor centers, or check ⓦwww.skithehighcountry.com.

▲ The Blue Ridge Parkway

Year-round, however, this twisting mountain road – largely built in the 1930s by President Roosevelt's Civilian Conservation Corps volunteers – is a worthwhile vacation destination in itself, peppered with state-run campgrounds, short hiking trails, and dramatic overlooks. Although the Parkway is closed to commercial vehicles, the constant curves make it hard to average anything approaching the 45mph speed limit.

Boone

BOONE is the most obvious northern base for exploring the mountains. Corny family entertainments dot US-321, while pretty backroads hold offbeat settlements such as **Valle Crucis**, off US-194, where the 1883 Mast General Store (summer Mon–Sat 7am–6.30pm, Sun noon–6pm; winter hours vary; ⓣ828/963-6511) is well worth a look for its cast-iron cookware, fresh coffee beans, rustic furniture, and outdoor gear.

Boone's **visitor center** is downtown at 208 Howard St (ⓣ828/262-3516 or 1-800/852-9506, ⓦwww.visitboonenc.com). For clean **hotel** rooms, head for the *High Country Inn*, 1785 Hwy-105 (ⓣ828/264-1000 or 1-800/334-5605, ⓦwww.highcountryinn.com; ❸), which also has a decent café and bar; good **B&Bs** include the *Lovill House Inn*, at 404 Old Bristol Rd (ⓣ1-800/849-9466, ⓦwww.lovillhouseinn.com; ❻). Walk along King Street for plenty of options for **eating** and **drinking**. *Earth Fare*, no. 178 (ⓣ828/263-8138), is a natural foods store, with a café and juice bar, while nearby *Cafe Portofino*, at 970 Rivers St, (ⓣ828/264-7772), features homemade breads and an eclectic blend of Eurasian, Italian, and seafood dishes.

South along the Parkway

Eight miles south of Boone, **BLOWING ROCK** is a pleasant, if touristy, resort just south of the Blue Ridge Parkway. The "Blowing Rock" itself, a high cliff from which light objects thrown over the side will simply blow back up, is nowhere near as impressive as photos suggest. The three-mile steam-driven

Tweetsie Railroad, now the center of a family theme park on Hwy-321, is all that remains of a train line that used to cross the mountains to Johnson City, Tennessee (June–Aug daily 9am–6pm; May, Sept & Oct Fri–Sun 9am–6pm; $30; ⓦwww.tweetsie.com).

Blowing Rock's **visitor center** (Mon–Sat 9am–5pm; ⓣ828/295-4636; ⓦwww.blowingrock.com) is on Valley Boulevard. On Main Street you'll find **hotels** such as the *Boxwood Lodge* at no. 671 (ⓣ828/295-9984, ⓦwww.boxwoodlodge.com; ④). At *Woodlands* (ⓣ828/295-3651), on the Hwy-321 bypass, the pork **barbecue** is excellent; it's also a good spot to drink beer, as is the comfy back porch of *The Canyons*, Hwy-321 (ⓣ828/295-7661), which dishes up contemporary Southwestern and regional cuisine.

The Canyons has a fine view of the privately owned **Grandfather Mountain** (5964ft), fifteen miles south of Blowing Rock, with access at milepost 305 (daily: spring & fall 8am–6pm; summer 8am–7pm; winter 9am–5pm; $14; ⓦwww.grandfather.com). The price may be high, but the owners make a genuine attempt to protect this unique environment.

Rough Ridge, near milepost 301, is one of several access points to the 13.5-mile **Tanawha Trail**, which runs along the ridge above the Parkway from Beacon Heights to Julian Price Park, looking out over the dense forests to the east. Another good hiking destination is the **Linville Gorge Wilderness**, near milepost 316 a couple of miles outside Linville Falls village. There are two main trails; one is a steep, 1.6 mile round-trip climb to the top of the high and spectacular **Linville Falls** themselves. Breathtaking views from either side of the gorge look down 2000ft to the **Linville River** below. An easier walk leads to the base of the falls. You can also climb **Hawksbill** or **Table Rock** mountains from the nearest forest road, which leaves Hwy-181 south of the village of Jonas Ridge (signposted "Gingercake Acres," with a small, low sign to Table Rock). The amiable villages of **Linville** and **Linville Falls** have the usual **motels** and restaurants; Linville Falls also has a **campground** (ⓣ828/765-2681, ⓦwww.linvillefalls.com; $28 per night), and *Spears Restaurant*, Hwy-221 (ⓣ828/765-2658), is worth a detour for its hickory-smoked pork barbecue.

The views from the Parkway in the **Mount Mitchell State Park** (ⓣ828/675-4611) area, south toward Asheville, are tremendous. Sadly, however, this is largely because the trees around the summit of Mount Mitchell – the highest point in the eastern US, at 6684ft – have been ravaged by acid rain from coal-burning industries and the large barren patches leave the horizon clear.

Asheville

Encircled by a ring of interstates, and skirted to the east and south by the Parkway, artsy **ASHEVILLE**, roughly one hundred miles southwest of Boone, retains an appealing 1920s downtown core. With a strong student community from UNC, it's also become quite an alternative center, studded with cafés, galleries, and vintage shops. Vibrant yet laid-back, it's a nice place to walk around, with a number of handsome **Art Deco** buildings. **Woolworth Walk**, 25 Haywood St, is a quirky space, exhibiting more than one hundred local artists in a vintage Woolworth store, while Malaprop's Bookstore, 55 Haywood, has a great selection of titles. Ninety-minute offbeat tours are available through the purple LaZoom buses, run on bio-diesel, which depart from 60 Biltmore Ave (daily May–Oct, check for holiday schedule, ⓣ828/225-6932, ⓦwww.lazoomtours.com). Twentieth-century novelist Thomas Wolfe memorialized the town in the autobiographical novel, *Look Homeward, Angel*. Wolfe's childhood home, a bright yellow Victorian pile that also served as a boarding house called Old Kentucky Home, has been preserved as a memorial (Tues–Sat 9am–5pm, Sun 1–5pm, $1, ⓣ828/253-8304).

Two miles south of town on Biltmore Avenue, the **Biltmore Estate** is the largest private mansion in the US, with 250 rooms (daily: April–Dec 8.30am–5pm; Jan–March 9am–5pm; prices vary, typically Sun–Fri $47, Sat $51; Ⓦwww.biltmore.com). Built in the late nineteenth century by George Vanderbilt and loosely modelled on a Loire chateau, it's a wild piece of nouveau riche folly. You could spend an entire day here, taking a tour, enjoying tastings at the winery, renting a raft or bike to explore the 250 acres of grounds, eating at the four restaurants, and maybe even staying at the 213-room "inn" (Ⓣ1-800-411-3812; ❽).

Asheville's **Greyhound/Trailways** terminal is inconveniently located at 2 Tunnel Rd, two miles out of downtown; take bus #13 or #4 stopping at the Innsbruck Mall. There's a good **visitor center** at 36 Montford Ave, reached via exit 4C off I-240 (Mon–Fri 8.30am–5.30pm, Sat & Sun 9am–5pm; Ⓣ828/258-6101, Ⓦwww.exploreasheville.com). Central **motels** include the *Days Inn*, 120 Patton Ave (Ⓣ828/254-9661; ❸), and there's another *Days Inn* near the Asheville Mall, at 201 Tunnel Rd (Ⓣ828/252-4000, Ⓦwww.daysinnashevillemall.com; ❸). For a bit of pampering, head to the luxurious *Cedar Crest* **B&B**, set in four acres three blocks from the Biltmore Estate, at 674 Biltmore Ave (Ⓣ828/252-1389 or 1-877/251-1389, Ⓦwww.cedarcrestvictorianinn.com; ❻). The nearest **campground** is *Bear Creek RV Park*, 81 S Bear Creek Rd, off I-40 to the west (Ⓣ1-800/833-0798, Ⓦwww.ashevillebearcreek.com; $38).

Asheville has by far the best **places to eat** in the region, with lots of ethnic and organic food. The fabulous *Laughing Seed Café*, 40 Wall St (Ⓣ 828/252-3445; closed Tues), dishes up really good vegetarian cuisine from around the world. Locavores chow down on market-driven seasonal American fare at the minimalist *Table*, 48 College St (closed Tues, Ⓣ828/254-8980). The best breakfast in town is served at the *Over Easy Cafe*, 32 Broadway St (Wed–Sat 9am–2pm, Ⓣ828/236-3533). In the up-and-coming river arts district, where artist lofts and galleries are opening, *12 Bones Smokehouse,* at 5 Riverside Drive (Mon–Fri, lunch only; Ⓣ828/253-4499), serves up mouth-watering ribs to a line out the door.

There's a lively **nightlife** scene, too; *Jack of the Wood*, an enjoyable bar at 95 Patton Ave (under the *Laughing Seed*; Ⓣ828/252-5445), and the *Grey Eagle*, 185 Clingman Ave (Ⓣ828/232-5800), both feature regular live bluegrass, folk, and newgrass. For national touring acts check out the *Orange Peel*, 101 Biltmore Ave (Ⓣ828/225-5851). For a drink with a view visit the *Sky Bar*, 18 Battery Park Avenue (Ⓣ828/225-6998), where cocktails are served on the spacious outdoor stairwell for a stunning panorama of the city. Catch a drag show at *LaRue's Backdoor,* aka *'Cookie's',* situated in the back of a warehouse at 237 Haywood St (Wed–Sat, Ⓣ828/252-1014), where owner *Cookie's* image hangs behind the over-the-top kitsch bar. Check local listings in the free *Mountain Xpress* (Ⓦwww.mountainx.com).

Black Mountain and Chimney Rock

BLACK MOUNTAIN, fourteen miles east of Asheville on I-40, is home to the hugely enjoyable **Leaf Festival** (Ⓦwww.theleaf.com). This folk music and arts and crafts gathering, held in mid-May and October, showcases Appalachian and world folk music, and usually attracts major European and African musicians. There's little to do in Black Mountain otherwise, but the clear fresh air, pretty views, and relaxed pace make a visit worthwhile.. The *Monte Vista*, at 308 W State St (Ⓣ828/669-2119 or 1-888/804-8438, Ⓦwww.montevistahotel.com; ❹), is a small, old-fashioned **hotel**; *Dripolator*, nearby at 221 W State St (Ⓣ828/669-0999), serves coffee, smoothies, and desserts.

Twenty-five miles southeast of the Parkway on US-64/74A, the natural granite tower of **Chimney Rock** sticks out from the almost-sheer side of Hickory

Nut Gorge (daily: summer 8.30am–5.30pm; rest of year 8.30am–4.30pm; park stays open 90 min past last ticket sale; $14; Ⓣ828/625-9611 or 1-800/277-9611, Ⓦwww.chimneyrockpark.com). After taking the elevator twenty-six stories up through the body of the mountain, you can walk along protected walkways above the impressive cliffs. Many of the climactic moments of *The Last of the Mohicans* were filmed here; you may recognize the mighty **Hickory Nut Falls**, which tumble 400ft from the western end of the gorge.

Great Smoky Mountains National Park

West of Asheville, **GREAT SMOKY MOUNTAINS NATIONAL PARK** is the most visited national park in the US. It straddles the border with Tennessee, and is covered in more detail – with a map – in our Tennessee section. In summer and fall accommodation can be booked up weeks in advance.

The largest base for touring the park is **CHEROKEE**, where a few Cherokee managed to hang on when the tribe was "removed" along the Trail of Tears to Oklahoma in 1838 (see p.532). Now known as the "Eastern Band of the Cherokee Nation," they have a small reservation on the edge of the park, which derives its main income from tourism. As a result, Cherokee itself has its fair share of moccasin retailers and themed attractions along with the requisite casino.

Away from the kitsch however, the impressive **Museum of the Cherokee Indian**, Hwy-441 at Drama Road (daily 9am–5pm; $9; Ⓦwww.cherokeemuseum.org), has archaeological and interactive displays on Cherokee arts and history – including Sequoyah's invention of a syllabary in 1821. Qualla Arts and Crafts, across the street, is a Cherokee-owned co-operative selling high-quality traditional **crafts** (June–Aug: Mon–Sat 8am–7pm, Sun 8am–5pm; Sept–May: daily 8am–5pm; Ⓣ828/497-3103). Nearby, the **Oconaluftee Indian Village** (mid-May to late Oct daily 9am–5.30pm; $15) is a reconstruction of a mid-eighteenth-century Cherokee village. Amid the log cabins, you can see demonstrations of dugout canoe construction and blowpipe hunting. During summer, at the Mountainside Theater on Hwy-441, an outdoor drama, *Unto these Hills*, re-enacts the Cherokee plight from Hernando De Soto's arrival to the Trail of Tears (mid-June to late Aug, Mon–Sat 8pm; $16–18; Ⓣ1-866/554-4557).

The **visitor center** (daily: Nov to late Aug 8am–9pm; late Aug–Oct 8am–5pm; 1-800/438-1601, Ⓦwww.cherokee-nc.com), on Hwy-441 by the river, has lots of information on the National Park and the Parkway. There are reasonable motels – but you might just as well stay in Maggie Valley (see below). You'll do fine for **eating** if you like fast food and buffets – and note that as a reservation town, Cherokee is entirely dry.

The **Oconaluftee visitor center**, the headquarters of the North Carolina side of the park, is two miles north of Cherokee on US-441 (daily: June–Aug 8am–6pm; Sept–Oct 8.30am–6pm; Nov–April 8.30am–4.30pm; May 8.30am–5pm Ⓣ828/497-1904).

Fifteen miles east, the small community of **MAGGIE VALLEY** boasts a string of motels with peaceful views – one of the cheapest, the *Riverlet*, on US-19 (Ⓣ828/926-1900 or 1-800/691-9952, Ⓦwww.riverlet.com; ❸), commands prospects of two streams. Tourism focuses on hillbilly culture, with lots of hoedowns and the like; the nearby **Ghost Town in the Sky** is an extraordinary piece of kitsch, with a chairlift that sweeps you up into a Wild West–style theme park (summer daily; fall Fri–Sun only; $30, children $22; Ⓦwww.ghosttowninthesky.com). During the last fortnight in July, Maggie Valley hosts North Carolina's **International Folk Festival** (Ⓦwww.folkmootusa.org).

South Carolina

The relatively small state of **SOUTH CAROLINA** remains, with Mississippi, one of the poorest and most rural in the US; it holds no truly substantial urban centers, and though the pockets of prime real estate along its coast have been developed into exclusive golf courses and tennis clubs, these are self-contained enclaves that make little impression on the rest of the state. **Politics** in South Carolina, the first state to secede from the Union in 1860, have traditionally been conservative. Reconstruction was mired in Klan violence, while demagogues openly espoused lynching and enforced "Jim Crow" laws with frightening zeal. Today, the state is home to a surprising number of universities including the football-fixated Clemson, Christian Bob Jones University in Greenville, a training-ground for the fundamentalist right, The Citadel military academy, South Carolina State University, a historically black college, and the largest in the state, the University of South Carolina.

However the state has a lot to offer for tourists. Its main fascination lies in the subtropical coastline, also called the **Low Country**, and its **sea islands**. Great beaches, swampy marshes, and lush palmetto groves preserve traces of a virtually independent black culture (featuring the unique patois, "Gullah"), dating back to when enslaved Africans escaped here from the mainland plantations. There are no interstates along the coast, so journeys take longer than you might expect, and the pace of life definitely feels slower. Beyond the grand old peninsular port of **Charleston** – with its pastel-colored old buildings, appealing waterfront, and magnificent, tree-lined avenues – restored plantations stretch as far north as **Georgetown**, en route toward **Myrtle Beach**. Inland, the rolling Piedmont and flat coastal plain hold little to see.

Getting around South Carolina

Charleston has South Carolina's biggest **airport**, with flights to and from major towns on the east coast. Three Amtrak routes cut through the state, stopping at Greenville and Clemson in the west, Columbia and other towns in the center, and Charleston on the coast. **Buses** run along I-85 between Charlotte, North Carolina, and Atlanta, while a less regular service operates along the coast, stopping at Myrtle Beach and Charleston.

Myrtle Beach and the north coast

MYRTLE BEACH is an unmitigated stretch of commercial seaside development twenty miles down the coast from the North Carolina border. Predominantly a family resort, it's packed fit during mid-term vacations with students drinking and partying themselves into a frenzy. Fans of elaborate mini-golf, water parks, factory outlet malls, funfairs, and parasailing will be in heaven, and the **beach** itself isn't at all bad. The widest stretch is at North Myrtle Beach, a chain of small communities among which Ocean Boulevard is the center.

South of Myrtle Beach lies **Murrells Inlet**, a fishing port with lots of good seafood restaurants, and **Pawleys Island**, a secluded resort once favored by plantation owners and today retaining a far slower pace than its neighbors. Between the two on Hwy-17 is the beautifully landscaped **Brookgreen Gardens** (daily: Jan–Nov

9.30am–5pm; Dec 9.30am–5pm; admission $12, valid for a week; ⓣ1-800/849-1931, ⓦwww.brookgreen.org), a former rice and indigo plantation with an outdoor display of American figurative sculpture, and the setting for many of Julia Peterkin's novels of Gullah life. There's also a wildlife sanctuary, where you can often see alligator and deer.

Practicalities

US- or Hwy-17 (also called Kings Highway) is Myrtle Beach's main traffic thoroughfare; the parallel Ocean Boulevard is lined with hotels and motels. Greyhound **buses** from Charleston and Wilmington come in at 511 7th Ave N. Great American Trolley runs a route along Ocean Boulevard from 29th Ave S to Broadway at the beach (March–Oct; ⓣ843/236-0337). The main **visitor center** at 1200 N Oak St (ⓣ843/626-7444 or 1-800/356-3016, ⓦwww.myrtlebeachinfo.com) provides bus timetables, events listings, and brochures.

Accommodation rates increase dramatically in summer; it may be cheaper to stay in **Conway**, about eleven miles to the west of US-501, where there's another visitor center at 2090 Hwy-501 E. In Myrtle Beach, the vast *Compass Cove Resort*, 2311 S Ocean Blvd (ⓣ1-800/331-0934, ⓦwww.compasscove.com; ❼), features around twenty pools, plus ocean views from the more expensive tower rooms; *Serendipity Inn*, near the sea at 407 71st Ave N (ⓣ843/449-5268, ⓦwww.serendipityinn.com; ❹), is an old Spanish-Mission-style motel that's been converted into a B&B.

So long as you crave surf 'n' turf, burgers, or diner food, you'll have no problem finding somewhere to **eat**. Creative seafood can be had at the classy *Sea Captain's House*, 3002 N Ocean Blvd (ⓣ843/448-8082), or at a number of similar establishments in Murrells Inlet; for a Mediterranean-influenced meal in a colorful atmosphere, stop by the *Collector's Café*, 7726 N Kings Hwy (ⓣ843/449-9370).

Myrtle Beach **nightlife** focuses around elaborate themed bars and music venues. There's a *House of Blues* at Barefoot Landing, 4640 Hwy-17 (ⓣ843/272-3000, ⓦwww.hob.com), which attracts top national bands. More kitschy are the glut of **country music variety shows**; the longest-running is the *Carolina Opry*, Hwy-17 N (ⓣ843/913-4000, ⓦwww.thecarolinaopry.com), where powerful singers belt out family-oriented rock'n'roll, country, gospel, and bluegrass. Next door at the Dolly Parton–owned *Dixie Stampede*, 8901-B Hwy-17 N (ⓣ1-800/433-4401, ⓦwww.dixiestampede.com), you can see a patriotic, surreal take on the Civil War.

South to Charleston: Georgetown and the plantations

The peaceful waterfront community of **GEORGETOWN** – the first town in forty miles beyond Myrtle Beach that's anything more than a beach resort – makes a refreshing contrast. It's hard to imagine today, but in the eighteenth century Georgetown was the center of a thriving network of Low Country rice plantations; by the 1840s the surrounding area produced nearly half the rice grown in the United States.

Georgetown's 32-block **historic district** features many fine eighteenth-century and antebellum houses; the **visitor center**, 531 Front St (Mon–Sat 9am–5pm; ⓣ843/546-8436 or 1-800/777-7705, ⓦwww.georgetownchamber.com), has maps for self-guided walking tours. The **Rice Museum**, in the Clock Tower at 633 Front St (Mon–Sat 10am–4.30pm; $7; ⓦwww.ricemuseum.org), tells of the Low Country's long history of rice cultivation and its dependence on a constant supply of enslaved Africans brought over for their expertise. Hop on the *Jolly*

Rover sailing ship (Mon–Sat; two-hour tours starting at $26; ⓣ843/546-8812) for a historic tour of the coastline. Choose from themed tours, including a Pirate's Adventure.

If you want to **stay** here, the *Carolinian Inn*, 706 Church St (ⓣ843/546-5191 or 1-800/722-4667, ⓦwww.carolinianinn.com; ③), which has a pool, is the best bet. There's a shortage of good places to **eat**, but the *Kudzu Bakery*, 120 King St (ⓣ843/546-1847), offers light lunches and pastries.

Hopsewee Plantation, the grand 1740 mansion home of Thomas Lynch, a signatory of the Declaration of Independence, is set in Spanish-moss-draped grounds, twelve miles south of Georgetown on US-17 (Feb–Nov 10am–4pm; $15; ⓦwww.hopsewee.com). **Hampton Plantation State Historic Site**, further south, two miles off US-17 on Hwy-857, is more typical of a plantation. The grounds (9am–6pm; free) are attractive, but the house (March–Oct Tues–Sat noon–4pm; Nov–Feb Thurs–Sun noon–4pm; $4) is most impressive. An eighteenth-century Neoclassical monolith built by Huguenots with a restored exterior, the inside is relatively bare. The plantation itself is isolated in the heart of the dense **Francis Marion National Forest**. This heavily African-American area is particularly known for its sweetgrass basket-weaving, a craft that originated with the slaves in West Africa.

Further south, beyond the forest and a few miles north of Charleston on US-17, is the much-publicized **Boone Hall Plantation** (April to early Sept Mon–Sat 8.30am–6.30pm, Sun 1–5pm; early Sept to March Mon–Fri 9am–5pm, Sun 1–4pm; $17.50; ⓦwww.boonehallplantation.com). Though the plantation dates from the late seventeenth century, the house is a twentieth-century reconstruction.

Charleston

CHARLESTON stands roughly halfway between Myrtle Beach to the north and Savannah, Georgia, to the south, one hundred miles from either. It's a compelling place to visit, its **historic district** lined with tall, narrow houses of peeling, multicolored stucco, adorned with wooden shutters and wide piazzas. The Caribbean feel is augmented by palm trees and the tropical climate, while the town's hidden gardens, leafy patios, and ironwork balconies evoke the romance of New Orleans.

Founded by a group of English aristocrats in 1670, Charles Towne swiftly boomed as a **port** serving the rice and cotton plantations. It became the region's commercial and cultural center with immigrants including French, Germans, Jews, Italians, and Irish, as well as the English majority. One-third of the nation's **enslaved Africans** passed through Charleston, sold at the market on the riverfront and bringing with them their ironworking, building, and farming skills. The town had a sizeable **free black** community too. Nevertheless there was still slave unrest, culminating in the abortive Veysey revolt of 1823, after which the city built the Citadel armory and later the military university.

Charleston was practically ruined by the **Civil War**, which started on its very doorstep, at **Fort Sumter** in the harbor. Fire swept through in 1861 and Union bombardment was relentless. Union forces took the city in February 1865. After the war, the decline of the plantation economy and slump in cotton prices led to an economic crash, made worse by a catastrophic earthquake in 1886. As the upcountry industrialized, capital steadily deserted the city, and it only really recovered when World War II restored its importance as a port and naval base. Since then,

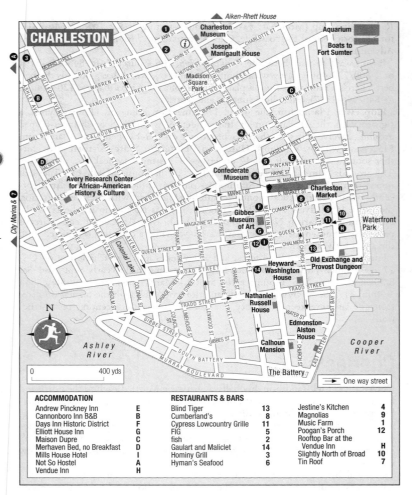

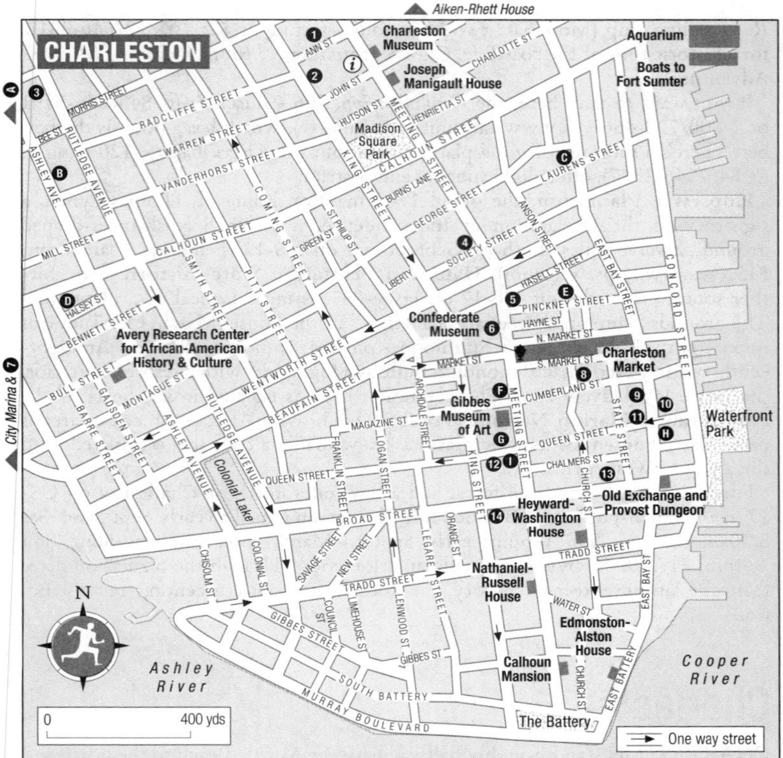

ACCOMMODATION	
Andrew Pinckney Inn	E
Cannonboro Inn B&B	B
Days Inn Historic District	F
Elliott House Inn	G
Maison Dupre	C
Merhaven Bed, no Breakfast	D
Mills House Hotel	I
Not So Hostel	A
Vendue Inn	H

RESTAURANTS & BARS	
Blind Tiger	13
Cumberland's	8
Cypress Lowcountry Grille	11
FIG	5
fish	2
Gaulart and Maliclet	14
Hominy Grill	3
Hyman's Seafood	6
Jestine's Kitchen	4
Magnolias	9
Music Farm	1
Poogan's Porch	12
Rooftop Bar at the Vendue Inn	H
Slightly North of Broad	10
Tin Roof	7

a steady program of preservation and restoration has made **tourism** Charleston's main focus. Downtown there's a genteel air about the place and prices tend to be high, whether you're looking for a room, a quick lunch, or a beer. Despite the gentrification, Charleston has kept its charming atmosphere, while maintaining all the energy and life of a functioning town. The traditions of the sea islands are a tangible presence here, too: many residents – both black and white – speak the distinctive **Gullah** dialect.

Arrival and information

Charleston International Airport is about twelve miles north of downtown, off I-526 (Ⓦwww.chs-airport.com); the airport **shuttle** (Ⓣ843/767-1100) costs $12, while a **taxi** ride with Yellow Cabs (Ⓣ843/577-6565) costs around $30. Local **public transportation** isn't bad: CARTA buses ($1.25 exact change; Ⓦwww

Guided tours

Charleston is ideal for **walking tours**; the visitor center has details on scores of them. For a lively, informed overview, set off from the circular fountain in Waterfront Park with **Tour Charleston LLC** (Mon–Sat 10am & 2pm; $18; ⓣ843/723-1670, ⓦwww.tourcharleston.com). The same company offers popular **pirate tours** (10am & 4pm; $18) and **ghost tours** (5pm, 7.30pm & 9.30pm; $18). Reservations are necessary. The **Civil War Walking Tour** sets out from the *Mills House Hotel*, 115 Meeting St (March–Dec daily 9am; $17; private tours available all year; ⓣ843/722-7033). **Architectural Walking Tours of Charleston** run two 2hr tours, starting at the *Meeting Street Inn*, 173 Meeting St – the morning tour covers the eighteenth century, the afternoon tour the nineteenth (Mon & Wed–Sat 10am & 2pm; $20; ⓣ843/893-2327 or 1-800/931-7761, ⓦwww.architecturalwalkingtoursofcharleston.com). In fall, the **Preservation Society**, 147 King St (ⓣ843/722-4630), organizes candlelit tours of the historic district, visiting a few private old homes (Sept & Oct Thurs–Sat 7–10pm; $45; ⓦwww.preservationsociety.org).

There are two good **black history tours. Al Miller**'s van tours include material on slave uprisings, the Civil War, and the lives of the freed slaves; they leave from the visitor center (1hr/2hr; $13/18; ⓣ843/762-0051, ⓦwww.sitesandinsightstours.com). **Gullah Tours**, which depart from Gallery Chuma, 43 John St, diagonally across from the visitor center, include folktales told in Gullah (Mon–Fri 11am & 1pm, Sat 11am, 1pm & 3pm; $18; ⓣ843/763-7551, ⓦwww.gullahtours.com).

Horse and carriage rides provide a lively and leisurely overview of the town. Try **Old South Carriage Co**, which leaves regularly between 9am and 5pm from 14 Anston St (1hr; $21, children $9; ⓣ843/723-9712, ⓦwww.oldsouthcarriagetours.com).

.ridecarta.com) cover most areas, including nearby beaches as well as the Amtrak station at 4565 Gaynor Ave, eight miles north of downtown (take a cab at night) and Greyhound station, in a similarly unsafe area at 3610 Dorchester Rd, out near I-26. The Downtown Area Shuttles (DASH; $1.25 exact change) comprise four useful trolley routes, three of which stop at the visitor center. You can buy **passes** that cover both buses and trolleys (day-pass $4, three-day pass $9, ten-ride pass $10).

Charleston's huge **visitor center**, 375 Meeting St (daily: March–Oct 8.30am–5.30pm; Nov–Feb 8.30am–5pm; ⓣ843/853-8000, ⓦwww.charlestoncvb.com), has discount coupons, leaflets, maps, and bus passes.

Accommodation

Though Charleston accommodation is pricey, it's worth budgeting to stay within walking distance of downtown. Many historic district houses serve as **B&Bs**, with prices starting at around $100 a night; agencies include Historic Charleston B&B, 60 Broad St (ⓣ843/722-6606 or 1-800/743-3583, ⓦwww.historiccharlestonbedandbreakfast.com). There's also a good **hostel** not far from downtown. Further out, the usual **motels** cluster around US-17 in West Ashley and Mount Pleasant, and along I-26 in North Charleston.

Andrew Pinckney Inn 40 Pinckney St ⓣ843/937-8800 or 1-800/505-8983, ⓦwww.andrewpinckneyinn.com. Stylish, Caribbean-style rooms in this boutique inn located beside Charleston's historic market. Continental breakfast served on the rooftop terrace overlooking the city. ⑤

Cannonboro Inn B&B 184 Ashley Ave, Cannonboro ⓣ843/723-8572 or 1-800/235-8039, ⓦwww.charleston-sc-inns.com. Fine columned house with attractive patio and garden. Six very comfortable non-smoking rooms and delicious breakfasts. ⑥

Days Inn Historic District 155 Meeting St ⓣ843/722-8411, ⓦwww.the.daysinn.com

/charleston05262. This two-story motel makes an unlikely sight so close to the market, but its rooms are surprisingly spacious and comfortable, with attractive wrought-iron balconies, A pool and free off-street parking as well make this downtown's best bargain. ④–⑥

Elliott House Inn 78 Queen St ⓣ843/723-1855 or 1-800/729-1855, ⓦwww.elliotthouseinn.com. Built in 1861 as a residence, today the *Elliott House* holds 24 plush, antique-furnished guest rooms. Complimentary wine and afternoon tea are served in a pretty courtyard, which also has a jacuzzi. Free bicycle use and a good continental breakfast. ⑤–⑦

Maison Dupre 317 E Bay St ⓣ843/723-8691 or 1-800/844-4667, ⓦwww.maisondupre.com. Beautiful inn with 15 rooms set in a crumbling 1804 European-style building and assorted other period structures. An idyllic garden holds fountains and a wishing well. Complimentary high teas plus a good continental breakfast. ⑥–⑧

Merhaven Bed, no Breakfast 16 Halsey St ⓣ843/577-3053. Two simple but light and comfortable rooms, with shared bath, and, obviously, no breakfast, in a comfy family home with a little courtyard. No credit cards. ④–⑤

Mills House Hotel 115 Meeting St ⓣ843/577-2400 or 1-800/874-9600, ⓦwww.millshouse.com. Large, very elegant, and very central hotel, in business since 1853 and true to its traditions despite total renovations. Guest rooms combine period furnishings with modern comfort, while the nice lounge bar features occasional live music. ⑥–⑧

Not So Hostel 156 Spring St ⓣ843/722-8383, ⓦwww.notsohostel.com. Appealing hostel in a double-porched 1850 house. Rates include internet access and breakfast. Regular live music on a small stage in the back yard. Dorms $21 per night. There are also private rooms available starting at $60. ①/③

Vendue Inn 19 Vendue Range ⓣ843/577-7970, ⓦwww.vendueinn.com. A luxurious, French provincial B&B right on the waterfront. Their *Rooftop Bar & Restaurant* (see p.479) has a stunning view of the harbor. ⑥–⑧

The City

Charleston's **historic district** is a predominantly residential area of weathered colors and exquisite hidden courtyards bounded by Calhoun Street to the north and East Bay Street by the river. The further south of Broad you head, the posher and more residential the streets become. The district is best taken in by strolling at your own pace. Attractive spots to pause in the shade include the swinging benches at **Waterfront Park**, a exquisitely landscaped piazza with fountains and boardwalks leading out over the river, and **White Point Gardens**, by the Battery on the tip of the peninsula, where the flower-filled lawns have good views across the water.

Most of the city's fine **houses** are private, and can only be admired from the outside; some, however, are available for **tours**. The late nineteenth-century **Calhoun Mansion**, just up from Battery Park at 16 Meeting St, is over-the-top, with ornate plaster and woodwork, hand-painted porcelain ballroom chandeliers, and similar extravagances (tours depart 11am–5pm, call 843/722-8205 for seasonal schedule; $15). Nearby, the antebellum **Edmonston-Alston House** overlooks the harbor at 21 E Battery St (Tues–Sat 10am–4.30pm, Sun & Mon 1.30–4.30pm; $10). This was one of the first houses built on the Battery in 1825. The Neoclassical **Nathaniel-Russell House**, 51 Meeting St (Mon–Sat 10am–5pm, Sun 2–5pm; $10), is noted for its flying staircase, which soars unsupported for three floors. The Charleston Museum's $22 combination ticket (see below) gets you into the 1803 **Joseph Manigault House**, a Neoclassical structure built by descendants of Huguenot settlers, and the 1772 **Heyward-Washington House**, at the south end of the peninsula at 87 Church St, which was built by Thomas Heyward, a rice baron and signatory of the Declaration of Independence. (George Washington stayed here for a month in 1791, thus the name.) Admission to each separately is $10 (Mon–Sat 9am–5pm, Sun 1–5pm). North of downtown, at the antebellum **Aiken-Rhett House**, 48 Elizabeth St, the mansion retains its original decor and furnishings (Mon–Sat 10am–5pm, Sun 2–5pm; $10).

Built in 1771 as the Customs House and used as a prison during the Revolutionary War, the **Old Exchange and Provost Dungeon**, 122 E Bay St (daily 9am–5pm; $7), remains as a significant Colonial structure. Today the upper floors

▲ Street in Charleston's historic district

are given over to exhibits detailing the history of the building and the city. The tone changes in the dank confines below, where spot-lit dummies recount tales of revolutionaries and gentlemen pirates.

Charleston's **market area** runs from Meeting Street to East Bay Street, focusing on a long, narrow line of enclosed, low-roofed, nineteenth-century sheds. Undeniably touristy, this is one of the liveliest spots in town.

The vast **Charleston Museum**, opposite the visitor center at 360 Meeting St (Mon–Sat 9am–5pm, Sun 1–5pm; Ⓦ www.charlestonmuseum.org; $10, $16 with the Joseph Manigault House or the Heyward-Washington House, $22 with both), is filled with a wealth of city memorabilia, with videos on subjects from rice-growing to the Huguenots, and strong sections on Native Americans, architecture, and the devastation of the Civil War.

A good source for black history is the **Avery Research Center for African-American History and Culture**, based in what was once a prestigious African-American private school, west of the market at 125 Bull St (tours Mon–Fri 10am–5pm, Sat noon–5pm; donation suggested; Ⓦ www.cofc.edu/avery/). Focused on an archive of personal papers, photographs, oral histories, and art, the center also shows periodic films, lectures, and exhibitions.

The high-quality **Gibbes Museum of Art**, a couple of blocks south of the market at 135 Meeting St (Tues–Sat 10am–5pm, Sun 1–5pm; Ⓦ www.gibbesmuseum.org; $9), places a strong emphasis on Charleston itself, providing a quick history of the city through art.

At the end of Calhoun Street, overlooking the harbour, you'll find Charleston's **Aquarium** (mid-Aug to end March Mon–Sat 9am–5pm, Sun noon–5pm; April to mid-Aug Mon–Sat 9am–6pm, Sun noon–6pm; last ticket sold 1hr before closing; $17). It's a well-designed space, with a 40ft-deep tank at the core and open, eye-level exhibits.

Fort Sumter National Monument

The first shots of the Civil War were fired on April 12, 1861, at **Fort Sumter**, a redoubtable federal garrison that entirely occupied a small artificial island at the entrance to Charleston Harbor. After secession, the federal government had to decide whether to reprovision its forts in the south. When a relief expedition was sent to Fort Sumter, Confederate General Pierre Beauregard demanded its surrender. After a relentless barrage, the garrison gave in the next day.

Fort Sumter may only be seen on regular **boat tours** that leave from alongside the Aquarium at the eastern end of Calhoun Street (departures vary daily; $15; ⓣ843/881-7337 or 1-800/789-3678, ⓦwww.fortsumtertours.com). Only one of the fort's original three stories is left standing, thanks not to the assault that started the war, but to its subsequent siege and bombardment by Union troops, who finally recaptured it on Good Friday 1865, the very day Lincoln was assassinated. A comprehensive museum back at the Fort Sumter visitor center on the mainland recounts the history not only of the fort but also of Charleston, and the build-up to the conflict (daily 8.30am–5pm; free).

Eating

Historic Charleston's elegant ambiance lends itself very well to classy **New Southern cooking** served up in a variety of innovative restaurants. There are also plenty of international restaurants and cafés that line Market and King streets.

Cypress - a Lowcountry Grille 167 E Bay St ⓣ843/727-0111. Exquisite Southern/Pan-Asian fusion food – raw and baked oysters, grouper with okra and herb broth, tuna sashimi – in a soaring space. Entrees cost $22–35. Dinner only.

FIG 232 Meeting St ⓣ843/805-5900. Small, minimalist, yet unpretentious neighborhood bistro with an emphasis on fresh regional fare.

fish 442 King St ⓣ843/722-3474. Small, upscale seafood place a block west of the city visitor center. The menu is simple in the extreme, with $18–28 entrees labeled as "salmon", "trout." Closed Sat lunch & all Sun.

Gaulart and Maliclet aka *Fast and French*, 98 Broad St ⓣ843/577-9797. Idiosyncratic French bistro, popular with locals. While not necessarily authentic, the food is very good, ranging from cheap snacks like a $4 croque-monsieur to $13 specials such as bouillabaisse or chicken du jour.

Hominy Grill 207 Rutledge Ave ⓣ843/937-0930. This stylish neighborhood restaurant is a favorite for gourmet Low Country cooking – try the brunches. Closed Sun eve.

Hyman's Seafood 213 Meeting St ⓣ843/723-6000. Sprawling, family-owned restaurant serving great seafood in a convivial, casual setting.

estine's Kitchen 251 Meeting St ⓣ843/722-7224. Authentic black Low Country cooking, served in a simple dining room in the heart of downtown. Go for the superb fried chicken or meat-and-three-veggie deals. Closed Mon.

Magnolia's 185 E Bay St ⓣ843/577-7771. Nouvelle Southern cuisine – shrimp with grits and such – in a buzzy monochrome setting with a circular bar.

Poogan's Porch 72 Queen St ⓣ843/577-2337. Delicious local food in a big old Charleston house, including Low Country Boils, crabcakes, and catfish. Very popular for Sunday brunch. Dine on the porch or on the shady patio.

Slightly North of Broad 192 E Bay St ⓣ843/723-3424. Another smart nouvelle Southern restaurant – scallops with smoked sausage, blue crab salad, and the like. It's lively with downtown business folk at lunchtime (Mon–Fri only), when they offer a $10 *prix-fixe* menu.

Nightlife and entertainment

Charleston has lots of **music venues**, **clubs**, and **bars**. For listings, see the free weekly *City Paper* (ⓦwww.charlestoncitypaper.com). Ask at the visitor center about the city's many **festivals**: chief among them is the **Spoleto Festival** (ⓣ843/722-2764, ⓦwww.spoletousa.org), an extraordinarily rich extravaganza of international arts for such a relatively small city. Inspired by its Italian namesake, the festival runs for seventeen days in May/June. October's **Moja Arts**

Festival (Ⓦwww.mojafestival.com) celebrates African-American and Caribbean theater, dance, and film.

Blind Tiger 38 Broad St Ⓣ843/577-0342. Local bar with hidden entrance, busy deck, and regular live music.

Music Farm 32 Ann St Ⓣ843/577-6989, Ⓦwww.musicfarm.com. This warehouse-like building alongside the visitor center is the best place in Charleston to see regional and national touring bands.

Rooftop Bar at the Vendue Inn (see p.476). Elegant rooftop bar and restaurant with great views over the city, and live music of all kinds daily.

Tin Roof 1117 Magnolia Rd Ⓣ843/571-0775. This small and unpretentious bar In the West Ashley neighborhood highlights rock, punk, and underground bands weekly.

Around Charleston

The **river road**, Hwy-61, leads **west** from Charleston along the Ashley River, past a series of magnificent **plantations**. **Drayton Hall**, closest to Charleston at 3380 Ashley River Rd (daily: March–Oct 8.30am–5pm; Nov–Feb 8.30am–4pm; Ⓦwww.draytonhall.org; $14), is an elegant Georgian mansion with handcarved wood and plasterwork; there is little furniture on show, and the hourly guided tours of the house concentrate on the fine architecture. At 11.15am, 1.15pm and 3.15pm, however, special talks, backed up by photographs and artifacts, emphasize the role of **African-Americans** in the Low Country, tracing the story of slavery and emancipation and how it related to Drayton Hall.

The nearby **Magnolia Plantation and Gardens** is most notable for its stunning ornamental gardens, particularly in spring when the azaleas are blooming (daily March–Oct 8am–dusk; Nov–Feb call, hours vary; $15, ticket valid for six days; Ⓣ1-800/367-3517, Ⓦwww.magnoliaplantation.com). Admission gives you access to the gardens, which include a tropical greenhouse, a petting zoo, a maze, and a wildlife observation tower, but you have to pay extra for **house tours** (daily 9.30am–4.30pm; $7). You don't have to pay the general admission charge to explore the **Audubon Swamp Garden** ($7), a preserved swamp complete with alligators and lush flowers. If you've paid general admission you can also take a "nature train" tour of the grounds, or a "nature boat" tour of the swamp; both cost $7 and last 45min.

Across the Ashley River, on Hwy-171, west of the Ashley River Bridge, **Charles Towne Landing** is a 663-acre state park, located on the site where in 1670 the English colonists established the first permanent settlement in the Carolinas (daily 9am–5pm; $5). As well as the landing site itself, you can see a living history settlement, a replica of a seventeenth-century merchant ship, and a zoo, home to species the colonists would have encountered when they landed here – pumas, bison, alligators, black bears, and wolves.

East of Charleston, **beaches** such as **Isle of Palms** and **Sullivan's Island** are heavily trafficked by locals on weekends. The further from town, the more likely you are to find a stretch to yourself. If you want to stay, there are plenty of motels and **eating** options. On Isle of Palms, head for the *Sea Biscuit Café*, 21 J.C. Long Blvd (Ⓣ843/886-4079; closed Mon), for great Southern breakfasts, and *Windjammer*, 1008 Ocean Blvd (Ⓣ843/886-8596), a late-night bar with live music at weekends. On Sullivan's Island, *Bert's Bar*, 2209 Middle St (Ⓣ843/883-3924), is a friendly bar and grill.

The sea islands

South of Charleston toward Savannah, the coastline dissolves into small, marshy islands. On pretty **Edisto Island**, south of US-17 on Hwy-174, huge live oaks festooned with drapes of Spanish moss line the roads, beside bright green marshes with rich birdlife, and fine beaches on the seaward side. If you want to stay, there are no budget motels, but the **campground** at **Edisto Beach State Park** (Ⓣ843/869-2756, Ⓦwww.southcarolinaparks.com; $19 to camp) is near a beach lined with palmetto trees and other semitropical plants. They have a few air-conditioned cabins that fill up months in advance (❸).

The largest town in the area, **BEAUFORT** (pronounced "Byoofert"), has a lovely old district – offset somewhat by racial tensions and the baleful proximity of the Parris Island US Marine Base, notorious for the brutality of its training regime. Think *The Big Chill* meets Kubrick's *Full Metal Jacket*; both movies are set here. The Greyhound **bus** station is two miles north of town on US-21. The **visitor center** at 1106 Carteret St (Ⓣ843/525-8531, Ⓦwww.beaufortsc.org) has details of tours around the historic district and discount coupons for the **motels** out on US-21. In town, the *Best Western Sea Island Inn*, near the water at 1015 Bay St (Ⓣ843/522-2090, Ⓦwww.bestwestern.com/seaislandinn; ❻), has nice rooms with an old-fashioned feel. For a luxurious **B&B**, head for the *Beaufort Inn*, 809 Port Republic St (Ⓣ843/379-4667, Ⓦwww.beaufortinn.com; ❻), which also has a superb Low Country/New American **restaurant**. Breakfast is best at *Blackstone's*, 205 Scott St (Ⓣ843/524-4330); if you're after coffee and a light meal, there's *Firehouse Books and Espresso*, 706 Craven St (Ⓣ843/522-2665).

St Helena Island and Hunting Island Beach

Across the bridge to the southeast of Beaufort, **ST HELENA ISLAND**, dotted with small shrimp- and oyster-fishing communities, is among the least spoiled of the eastern sea islands. The further south you go the more gorgeous the **landscape** gets: amazing Spanish moss hangs from ancient oaks, while enormous, wide views stretch out across bright marshes. Occasionally you see what looks like a fleet of ships in the middle of a field, only to realize that in fact the boats are anchored in a small salt creek, hidden by bright green marsh reeds.

This is an area of strong **black communities**, descended from slaves, who were given parcels of land when they were freed by the Union army in February 1865; they speak a dialect known as Gullah, an Afro-English vernacular with many West African words. The **Gullah Institute**, in the **Penn Center Historic District** off US-21 (Ⓣ843/838-2432, Ⓦwww.penncenter.com), houses the **school** started for freed slaves by Charlotte Forten, a black Massachusetts teacher. The school was an important retreat for civil rights leaders in the 1960s. Nearby, off US-21, the ruined black **Chapel of Ease**, with seashell-adorned interior walls, was built in 1742.

There are some great **places to eat** around here. *Ultimate Eating*, 859 Sea Island Parkway (Ⓣ843/838-1314), serves Low Country and Gullah-style dishes, while at 1929 Sea Island Parkway, before the bridge across to Hunting Island, the tiny *Shrimp Shack* (March–Dec Mon–Sat from 11am; Ⓣ843/838-2962), is a fresh **seafood** joint serving up shrimp burgers.

St Helena's main **beach**, at **Hunting Island State Park** on the east shore (daily dawn–dusk: $4), can get crowded. Pelicans come here to feed; it's also a turtle-nesting site. You can **stay** near the beach, although you need to book at least a week in summer, and reserve about a year in advance (Ⓣ843/838-2011, Ⓦwww.southcarolinaparks.com; ❹).

Georgia

Away from the bright lights of its capital Atlanta, **GEORGIA**, the largest of the Southern states, is primarily rural. Its highly indented coastline holds some beaches and towns, but mostly the state is composed of slow, easygoing communities, where the best way to enjoy your time is to sip iced tea and have a chat on the porch.

Settlement in Georgia, the thirteenth British colony (named after King George II), started in 1733 at Savannah, intended as a haven of Christian principles for poor Britons, with both alcohol and slavery banned. However, under pressure from planters, **slavery** was introduced in 1752, and by the time of the **Civil War** almost half the population were black slaves. Little fighting took place on Georgia soil until Sherman's troops marched in from Tennessee, burned Atlanta to the ground, and, in the infamous "March to the Sea," laid waste to all property on the way to the coast.

Today, bustling **Atlanta** stands as the unofficial capital of the South. The city where **Dr Martin Luther King Jr** was born, preached, and is buried bears little relation to *Gone With the Wind* stereotypes, and its forward-thinking energy is upheld as a role model. Atlanta's main tourist destination rival is the **Georgia coast**, stretching south from old **Savannah** via the **sea islands** to the semitropical **Okefenokee Swamp**, inland near Florida. In the **northeast**, the **Appalachian foothills** are particularly fetching in fall, while the college town of **Athens** has a reputation for producing rock groups such as R.E.M. and the B-52s.

Getting around Georgia

Georgia's main points of interest are easily accessible, but local transportation is poor. Amtrak **trains** from Washington, DC, to New Orleans and Florida call at Atlanta and Savannah, respectively. **Bus** services in most areas are patchy and infrequent, though Atlanta has regular connections to the major cities, and several daily buses along the coast call at Savannah. Atlanta has the world's largest passenger **airport**, and Savannah has a reasonable service, but airfares between the two are high.

Atlanta

ATLANTA is a relatively young city. It began in 1837, when an almost random dot on the map was named "Terminus" during plans for railroad construction. After the railroads arrived, the renamed Atlanta proved to be a crucial transportation center in the Civil War. Home to the huge Confederacy munitions industry, it was **burned** by Sherman's Union army in 1864, an act immortalized in *Gone With the Wind*. Recovery after the war was quick: Atlanta was the archetype of the industrial "New South," championed by "boosters" – newspaper owners, bankers, politicians, and city leaders. Giants who based themselves here included **Coca-Cola**, source of a string of philanthropic gifts to the city. **Black** immigration increased its already considerable African-American population and led to the establishment of the thriving community, centered on **Auburn Avenue**, which was to produce **Martin Luther King Jr**.

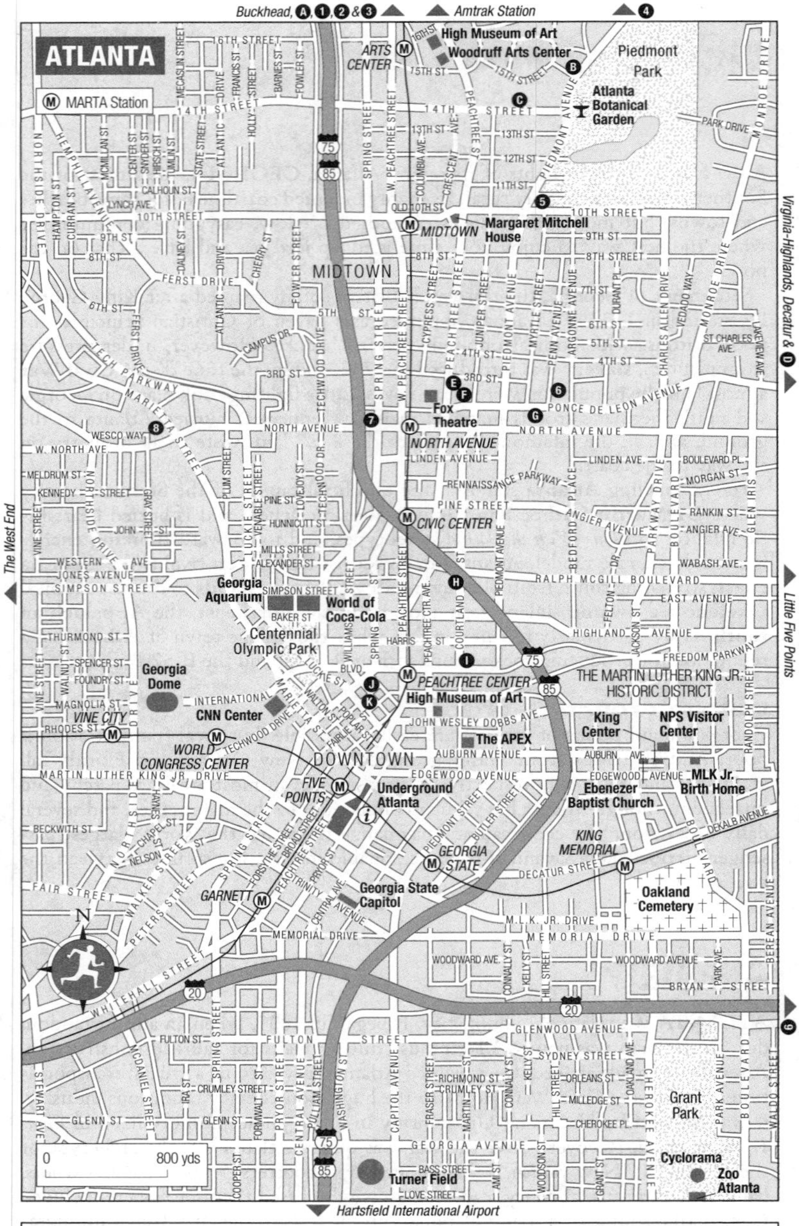

ACCOMMODATION

Ansley Inn B
Atlanta International Hostel G
Georgian Terrace Hotel F
Hampton Inn & Suites J
Highland Inn D
Hotel Indigo E
Ritz-Carlton Buckhead A
Sheraton I
Super 8 K
Travelodge H
W Atlanta-Midtown C

RESTAURANTS

Ann's Snack Bar 9
Atlanta Fish Market 2
Colonnade 3
Fat Matt's Rib Snack 4
Flying Biscuit 5
Mary Mac's Tearoom 6
R Thomas' Deluxe Grill 1
Thelma's Kitchen 8
The Varsity 7

Today's Atlanta is at first glance a typical large American city, but no visitor could fail to notice its progressive feel. The city elected the nation's first black mayor, the late Maynard Jackson, and African-American politicians continue to reach success here. Its hosting of the 1996 **Olympics** is just the highest profile success in a sustained catalogue of entrepreneurial achievements. Tourists come to Atlanta for its vibrant arts, dining, and nightlife scenes, but must-see tourist attractions include the various sites associated with Dr King to cultural institutions like the High Museum of Art and Atlanta History Center.

The flip side of the fact that there was no great reason to put a city here is that neither are there any obvious geographical factors to prevent Atlanta from **growing** indefinitely. The population of the entire metropolitan area now exceeds five million. Cut off by roaring freeways, Atlanta's neighborhoods tend to have distinct identities; lavish **Buckhead** is only a short drive away from grungier, punky **Little Five Points**, but the two neighborhoods have little in common.

Arrival and information

The colossal **Hartsfield-Jackson International Airport** (Ⓣ 1-800/897-1910), the busiest passenger airport in the US, is ten miles south of downtown Atlanta, just inside I-285 ("the perimeter"). It marks the southern terminus of the south line of the **subway** (see below), a 15min ride from downtown, and is also served by the Atlanta Link **shuttle buses** (daily 6am–midnight; $16.50 to downtown; Ⓣ404/524-3400 or 1-866/545-9633, Ⓦwww.theatlantalink.com) and Checker Cab **taxis** (Ⓣ404/351-1111; $30 to downtown).

Atlanta's **Amtrak** station, 1688 Peachtree St NW, is at the north end of Midtown, just under a mile north of the nearest subway station, Arts Center; catch a cab or bus #23 to connect. Greyhound **buses** arrive south of downtown at 232 Forsyth St, near the Garnett Street subway station.

Atlanta's principal **visitor center** is downtown in the Underground Mall (50 Upper Alabama St) at Pryor and Atlanta streets (Mon–Sat 10am–6pm, Sun noon–6pm; Ⓣ404/523-2311, Ⓦwww.atlanta.net). The adjoining **AtlanTIX** (Tues 11am–3pm, Wed–Sat 11am–6pm, Sun noon–3pm; Ⓣ678/318-1400, Ⓦwww.atlantaperforms.com) sells tickets for local events and performances, with half-price discounts available every day. Other **visitor centers** are located in the Lenox Square mall in **Buckhead** (Tues–Sat 11am–5pm, Sun noon–4pm), which also holds an AtlanTIX booth, and in the North Terminal at the **airport** (Mon–Fri 9am–9pm, Sat 9am–6pm, Sun 12.30–6pm).

The city's **subway** system consists of two distinct lines, one east–west and one north–south; they intersect downtown at Five Points (Mon–Fri 5am–1am, Sat–Sun 5am–12.30am; single fare $1.75, weekly pass $13). The system is run by the Metropolitan Area Rapid Transit Authority (MARTA; Ⓣ404/848-5000, Ⓦwww.itsmarta.com), which also operates a wide network of **buses**.

The Atlanta Preservation Center runs ninety-minute **walking tours** of Atlanta neighborhoods, including Sweet Auburn (with emphasis on the churches), and an architectural tour of downtown (March–Nov only, daily except Tues; $10; Ⓣ404/688-3350, Ⓦwww.preserveatlanta.com).

Accommodation

The most economical **accommodation** options in **downtown** Atlanta are the chains, but with so many conventions in town even these aren't particularly inexpensive; weekend rates can be better, but just to park costs at least $15 per night. **Midtown** is generally cheaper, and puts you nearer the nightlife, while **Buckhead** boasts some of the swankiest hotels in the country. The B&B Atlanta agency can reserve **B&B**

rooms (Ⓣ404/875-0525 or 1-800/967-3224, Ⓦwww.bedandbreakfastatlanta.com).

Ansley Inn 253 15th St Ⓣ404/872-9000 or 1-800/446-5416, Ⓦwww.ansleyinn.com. Lovely, friendly Midtown B&B, in a century-old Tudor-style mansion near Ansley Park where the 22 rooms have stripped-wood floors, antique furnishings, wet bars, and whirlpool tubs. ❺

Atlanta International Hostel 223 Ponce de Leon Ave Ⓣ404/875-9449 or 1-800/473-9449, Ⓦwww.hostel-atlanta.com. Around a hundred $22 beds in male, female, and mixed dorms, in a central Midtown location close to the North Ave MARTA station. Also a pool table, kitchen, and laundry room.

Georgian Terrace Hotel 659 Peachtree St NE Ⓣ404/897-1991 or 1-800/651-2316, Ⓦwww.thegeorgianterrace.com. Stylish century-old hotel in prime Midtown location across from the Fox Theatre. Very classy rooms and suites – some bedrooms are round, offering great views – plus fine restaurants and a rooftop pool. ❼

Hampton Inn and Suites Atlanta Downtown 161 Spring Street NW Ⓣ404/589-1111 or 1-800/426-7866, Ⓦhamptoninn.hilton.com. This six-storey downtown chain hotel may look unspectacular, but all its rooms have been renovated to a surprisingly high standard, making it one of the best-value central options. Rates include breakfast. ❻

Highland Inn 644 N Highland Ave Ⓣ404/874-5756, Ⓦwww.thehighlandinn.com. Hipsters flock to this budget hotel nestled conveniently near Little Five Points and Virginia Highlands. The ballroom and bar hosts live music and djs many nights.

Hotel Indigo 683 Peachtree St at Ponce de Leon Ⓣ404/874-9200, Ⓦwww.hotelindigo.com. Plush but well-priced boutique hotel near the Fox Theatre in the heart of Midtown. ❺

Ritz-Carlton Buckhead 3434 Peachtree Rd NE Ⓣ404/237-2700, Ⓦwww.ritzcarlton.com. Exquisite, elegant hotel, one of the finest in the Ritz-Carlton group, with one of Atlanta's best haute cuisine restaurants. ❼

Sheraton Atlanta Hotel 165 Courtland St NE Ⓣ404/659-6500 or 1-800/833-8624, Ⓦwww.sheratonatlantahotel.com. Luxury downtown hotel with wonderful indoor pool surrounded by foliage, plus its own mini-shopping mall. ❻

Super 8 111 Cone St Ⓣ404/524-7000 or 1-800/800-8000, Ⓦwww.super8atlanta.com. Very atypical *Super 8*, housed in a converted downtown hotel and offering bargain rates for a great spot near Centennial Park. ❹

W Atlanta - Midtown 188 14th St NE Ⓣ404/892-6000, Ⓦwww.starwoodhotels.com/whotels. Posh boutique from the W empire in the heart of Midtown. In addition to the lavish amenities are a Bliss spa and Jean-Georges restaurant. ❾

The City

Atlanta's layout is confusing, with its roads following old Native American trails rather than a logical grid. An unbelievable number of streets are named "Peachtree"; be sure to note whether you're looking for Avenue, Road, Boulevard, and so forth. The most important, **Peachtree Street**, cuts a long north–south swath through the city. Sights are scattered, but relatively easy to reach on public transportation. Most individual neighborhoods, including **downtown**, the Martin Luther King Jr Historic District along **Auburn Avenue**, and trendy **Little Five Points** and **Virginia-Highland**, are easy to explore on foot.

Downtown Atlanta

Downtown Atlanta centers on the railroad terminus for which the city was founded. During the late nineteenth century, its original core was effectively buried by the construction of railroad viaducts; businesses moved their commercial activities up to the new street level and used their former premises as cellars. Twice now, in 1969 and 1989, the city has attempted to revitalize the underground labyrinth of cobbled streets as an entertainment, shopping, and dining complex. Known as **Underground Atlanta** (or "the Underground"), it remains a gimmicky mall.

By contrast, tourists and locals alike are flocking to **Centennial Olympic Park,** a quarter-mile northwest of Underground Atlanta. Created when several downtown blocks were razed prior to the 1996 Olympics, and intended as a focus for public festivities during the Games, the park was forced into temporary closure by the pipe-bombing that killed two people. Now relandscaped, it's the city's most popular open space.

On the north side of the park, **Georgia Aquarium**, 225 Baker St (Sun–Fri 10am–5pm, Sat 9am–6pm; $26, under-13s $19.50; Ⓣ404/581-4000, Ⓦwww.georgiaaquarium.org), claims to be the world's largest such site. A state-of-the-art facility aimed at children, it's been such a success that unless you reserve tickets in advance for a specific time slot, you may well not be able to get in at all.

Immediately east of the aquarium, the **World of Coca-Cola** museum has recently moved from its former home at Underground Atlanta. Explore high-tech displays on Coca-Cola's history and quench your thirst with Coke products from all over the world (daily hours vary, $15; Ⓣ404/676–5151, Ⓦwww.worldofcoca-cola.com).

At Centennial Park's southwest corner, the **CNN Center** is the headquarters of the largest news broadcaster in the world. Adrenaline-fueled, 55-minute guided tours (Mon–Fri 9am–5pm, $12; reservations essential; Ⓣ404/827–2300).rush visitors past frazzled producers and toothy anchorpersons.

Sweet Auburn

A half-mile east of downtown, **Auburn Avenue** stands as a monument to Atlanta's black history. During its heyday in the 1920s, "**Sweet Auburn**" was a prosperous, progressive area of black-owned businesses and jazz clubs, but it went into a decline with the Depression, from which, despite repeated attempts at revitalization, it has never truly recovered.

Nonetheless, several blocks have been designated as the **Martin Luther King Jr National Historic Site**, in honor of Auburn's most cherished native son. This short stretch of road is the most visited attraction in all Georgia. Head first for the Park Service's **visitor center**, 450 Auburn Ave NE (daily: mid-June to mid-Aug 9am–6pm; mid-Aug to mid-June 9am–5pm; Ⓣ404/331-5190, Ⓦwww.nps.gov/malu). If you're looking for an account of the civil rights years, the museum at Memphis is much more comprehensive (see p.514), but this provides a powerful summary.

When you arrive at the visitor center, register for a free tour of King's **Birth Home**, a short walk east at 501 Auburn (same hours as visitor center). As only fifteen people can visit at a time, and school groups often visit en masse, you may have to settle instead for a "virtual tour," utilizing the computers at the visitor center. The home itself is a 14-room Queen Anne-style shotgun house, restored to its prosperous 1930s appearance. Home to King until he was twelve, it remained in his family until 1971.

Across from the visitor center, the **King Center**, 449 Auburn Ave NE (daily 9am–5pm; Ⓦwww.thekingcenter.org), is privately run by King's family. Chiefly an educational and research facility, it also features displays of artifacts such as King's Bibles. King's mortal remains, guarded by an eternal flame, are held in a plain marble **tomb**, inscribed with the words "Free at last, free at last, thank God Almighty I'm free at last," which stands in the shallow Reflecting Pool outside.

Next door, the **Ebenezer Baptist Church**, where King's funeral took place – and where his mother was assassinated while playing the organ in 1974 – has been converted into another museum (closed at time of press for renovation, visit Ⓦwww.nps.gov/malu for latest information), staffed by volunteers eager to share their memories. It's now only used for special occasions, while its congregation has decamped to a much larger church alongside the visitor center.

Midtown

Midtown stretches from Ponce de Leon Avenue to 26th Street. In recent years, it has become dominated by massive skyscrapers – look out for the spiky **One**

Dr Martin Luther King Jr (1929–68)

Martin Luther King Jr was born in Atlanta at 501 Auburn Avenue on January 15, 1929. The house was then home to his parents and his grandparents; both his maternal grandfather, Rev A.D. Williams, and his father, Martin Luther King Sr, served as pastor of the nearby **Ebenezer Baptist Church**. Young Martin was ordained at 19 and became co-pastor at Ebenezer with his father, but continued his studies at Crozer Theological Seminary in Pennsylvania, where he was influenced by the ideas of Mahatma Gandhi, and at Boston University.

Returning to the South, King became pastor of Dexter Avenue Baptist Church in **Montgomery**, Alabama, in 1954, where his leadership during the bus boycott a year later (see p.538) brought him to national prominence. A visit to India in 1957 further cemented his belief in non-violent resistance. He returned to Atlanta in 1960, becoming co-pastor at Ebenezer once more, but also taking on the presidency of the **Southern Christian Leadership Conference**. There he became the figurehead for the **civil rights** struggle, planning strategy for future campaigns, flying into each new trouble spot, and commenting to the news media on every latest development. His apotheosis came in August 1963, when he addressed the **March on Washington** with his famous "I Have a Dream" speech. He was awarded the Nobel Peace Prize in 1964.

Despite King's passionate espousal of non-violence, J. Edgar Hoover's **FBI** branded him "the most dangerous and effective Negro leader in the country," and attempted to discredit him over his personal life. King himself became more overtly politicized in his final years. Challenged by the stridency of Malcolm X and the radicalism of urban black youth, he came to see the deprivation and poverty of the cities of the North as affecting black and white alike, and only solvable by tackling "the triple evils of racism, extreme materialism, and militarism." In the South, he had always been able to appeal to the federal government as a reluctant ally; now, having declared his opposition to the war in **Vietnam**, he faced a lonelier struggle. His **Poor People's Campaign** had barely got off the ground before King was assassinated in Memphis on April 4, 1968.

Atlantic Center, at 15th and Peachtree streets, designed by Philip Johnson and John Burgee. The flamboyant Art Deco **Fox Theatre**, 660 Peachtree St NE, at Ponce de Leon (Ⓣ404/881-2100, Ⓦwww.foxtheatre.org), with its strong Moorish theme, should also not be missed. Unless you buy a ticket for one of its fairly mainstream shows, the only way to see the theater is on an organized tour (Mon, Wed & Thurs 10am, Sat 10am & 11am; $10; Ⓣ404/688-3353).

Three blocks north of the theater, the only ordinary brick home left on Peachtree Street, at no. 990, is the **Margaret Mitchell House** (Mon–Sat 9.30am–5pm, Sun noon–5pm; $12; Ⓣ404/249-7015, Ⓦwww.gwtw.org). Mitchell and her husband lived in the small basement apartment during the ten years she took to write the best-selling novel of all time, *Gone With the Wind*. Published in 1936, it took just six weeks to sell enough copies to form a tower fifty times higher than the Empire State Building; the 1939 movie escalated its popularity. Guided tours and various exhibits tell the whole story. More memorabilia is displayed in the separate but linked **movie museum** (same hours and ticket).

A little further up Peachtree, at no. 1280, the enormous **Woodruff Arts Center** is home to Atlanta's **High Museum of Art** (Tues, Wed, Fri & Sat 10am–5pm, Thurs 10am–8pm, Sun noon–5pm; $18; Ⓣ404/773-4444, Ⓦwww.high.org). In 2005 the High unveiled three new buildings designed by Renzo Piano, around its central piazza. Now with double the exhibition space, it's a truly world-class museum. Permanent collections include the "Art and Life in Africa" displays at street level, American folk art by outsider artists like Howard Finster and Mose Tolliver, and extensive European galleries covering five centuries from Renaissance Italy to the French Impressionists. The High also has a top-notch restaurant, *Table 1280*.

A few blocks east of Peachtree St, best approached via 14th St, the highlight of **Piedmont Park** is the landscaped **Atlanta Botanical Garden** (daily except Mon: April–Oct 9am–7pm, Nov–March 9am–5pm; $12). In addition to holding conservatories of tropical and desert plants, the garden hosts summer-long sculpture exhibitions.

Buckhead

North of Midtown, where Peachtree meets Paces Ferry Road, the affluent **Buckhead** neighborhood has long been a trendy area of glitzy malls and swanky hotels. In recent years, it has acquired an unwanted reputation as "party central" and even witnessed several murders. However the area is likely to continue as the city's premier **nightlife** and **shopping** district, becoming even more exclusive than ever.

Tucked away a short distance west of central Buckhead are the permanent exhibits at the **Atlanta History Center**, 130 W Paces Ferry Rd (Mon–Sat 10am–5.30pm, Sun noon–5.30pm; $15; ⓣ404/814-4000, ⓦwww.atlantahistorycenter.com). One section covers Atlanta history in exhaustive detail; black and women's history is well represented, though there's very little on Dr King. Several other rooms display a remarkable collection of Civil War artifacts. You can also tour two houses on the grounds: the 1920s mock-classical mansion **Swan House** and the antebellum **Tullie Smith Farm** and garden.

The West End

The **West End**, Atlanta's oldest quarter, is a reviving district southwest of downtown. Historically a black residential area, it continues as a more upbeat counterpoint to Sweet Auburn. Here, you'll find Georgia's only museum dedicated to African-American and Haitian art, the **Hammonds House**, 503 Peeples St SW (Tues–Fri 10am–6pm, Sat & Sun 1–5pm; ⓣ404/752-8730), as well as the 1910 Beaux Arts **Herndon Home**, 587 University Place NW (Tues–Sat 10am–4pm; $7), which was designed and lived in by Alonzo Herndon, a former slave who went on to become the city's first black millionaire.

You can also visit the **Wren's Nest**, at 1050 R.D. Abernathy Blvd, the former home of Joel Chandler Harris, the white author of *Brer Rabbit* (Tues–Sat 10am–2.30pm; $8). The house remains much as Harris left it upon his death in 1908. Storytelling sessions take place Saturdays at 1pm in the garden.

Grant Park

A mile southeast of downtown, **Grant Park** – named for a Confederate defender of Atlanta, not the victorious Union general – is home to two neighboring attractions. A theater houses the **Cyclorama**, a huge circular painting depicting the Civil War Battle of Atlanta. You may sit inside the circle of the painting while the entire auditorium slowly rotates around you. An accompanying **museum** (Tues–Sun 9am–4.30pm; $8) treats the war from the viewpoint of the average soldier. Nearby, **Oakland Cemetery**, the largest and oldest in the city, is the resting place of famous Atlanta citizens including Margaret Mitchell. In 2008 a tornado touched down on the grounds that host a Jewish cemetery nestled up against a Confederate one.

The adjacent **Zoo Atlanta** (daily 9.30am–5.30pm; $18; ⓦwww.zooatlanta.org) features a pair of giant pandas from Chengdu, gorillas, and several orangutans, plus recreations of various habitats.

Little Five Points to Emory University

Northeast of Auburn Avenue, around Euclid and Moreland avenues, the youthful **Little Five Points** district is a tangle of thrift stores, secondhand record stores, funky restaurants, body-piercing parlors, bars, and clubs. By way of contrast, just a few blocks north at 1 Copenhill Ave, on the hill where Sherman is said to have watched Atlanta burn, the **Jimmy Carter Presidential Library and Museum** (Mon–Sat 9am–4.45pm, Sun noon–4.45pm; $8; ⓣ404/865-7100, ⓦwww.jimmycarterlibrary.org) is devoted to the peanut farmer who rose to become Georgia state governor and the 39th president of the USA.

Northeast, beyond the **Virginia-Highland** restaurant district, the trek to **Emory University**'s campus is rewarded by the airy **Michael C. Carlos Museum**, 571 S Kilgo Circle (Tues–Sat 10am–5pm, Sun noon–5pm; $7 donation; ⓣ404/727-4282, ⓦcarlos.emory.edu), which hosts a collection of fine art and antiquities from all six inhabited continents.

Stone Mountain

Half an hour's drive east of Atlanta's city center, **Stone Mountain State Park** is arrayed around the base of what's said to be the world's largest natural granite monolith, part of which holds a massive **bas-relief sculpture**, measuring 90ft by 190ft that depicts Confederates Jefferson Davis, Robert E. Lee, and Stonewall Jackson. Started in 1924 by Gutzon Borglum, who went on to carve Mount Rushmore in South Dakota, it was not completed until 1970. You can see it by paying the $8 per vehicle park entrance fee, but an additional $25 per adult or $20 per child aged 3–11 (reduced 'twilight' fare is $15 for everyone after 4pm) entitles you to a host of attractions including a 30min **train ride** around the mountain, **paddlewheel** and **pedal-boat** rides on the nearby lake, two **mini-golf** courses, and the Crossroads **theme park**, which features a "4D" movie theater. It's also possible to **hike** up the mountain on a 45min trail, or ride a skylift to the top. Contact ⓣ1-800/401-2407 or ⓦwww.stonemountainpark.com for full details on seasonal operating hours.

Eating

Atlanta has scores of good **restaurants** to suit all budgets. Most downtown options are upmarket, while Buckhead is even glitzier. Southern **soul food** is best around Auburn Avenue.

Ann's Snack Bar 1615 Memorial Drive ⓣ404/687-9207. Locals wait in line in this tiny diner for the immensely popular Ghetto Burger, which is topped with fried onions, chilli, coleslaw, bacon, and cheese. Closed Sun.

Atlanta Fish Market 265 Pharr Rd NE ⓣ404/262-3165. Buckhead's top seafood specialist, at the sign of the giant fish, with ultra-fresh oysters and crabs; dinner can get expensive, but lunch is great value.

Colonnade 1879 Cheshire Bridge Rd NE at Wellborne ⓣ404/874-5642. Long-established, inexpensive Southern restaurant adjoining Midtown's *Cheshire Motor Inn*. Specializes in fried chicken made just the way it's supposed to be.

Fat Matt's Rib Shack 1811 Piedmont Ave NW ⓣ404/607-1622. Atlanta's best barbecue, halfway between Midtown and Buckhead, plus live blues at 8pm nightly. It makes little difference if you choose a plateful of juicy pork or chicken, or a "sandwich" (a slab of ribs piled on a slab of bread) – everything here is delicious.

Flying Biscuit 1001 Piedmont Ave ⓣ404/874-8887. A pleasing diner at a lively Midtown intersection. Renowned locally for its healthy/organic breakfasts, it also serves medium-priced New American lunches and dinners, all with a Southern twist. Four other Atlanta outposts exist.

The Glenwood 1263 Glenwood Ave ⓣ404/622-6066. Eclectic neighborhood gastro-pub fare in a cozy East Atlanta setting. Full bar and large selection of beers.

Holy Taco 1314 Glenwood Ave SE ⓣ404/230-6177. Moderately priced freshly prepared Mexican fare in a hip East Atlanta setting. Locals come for the spacious patio and the organic agave margaritas.

Mary Mac's Tearoom 224 Ponce de Leon Ave ⓣ404/876-1800. Cute little Midtown restaurant, straight out of the 1940s, famous for its cheap traditional Southern cuisine, served for lunch and dinner daily.

R Thomas' Deluxe Grill 1812 Peachtree St NW ⓣ404/872-2942. Quirky 24hr Midtown place where all the seating is outdoors, albeit sheltered by rattan screening. The varied menu ranges from Thai stir-fries with quinoa to fish tacos and it makes a healthy and cheap option.

Thelma's Kitchen 302 Auburn Ave ⓣ404/688-5855. Inexpensive soul-food institution in a new setting, now housed in the former Auburn Avenue Rib Shack building; try the salmon and grits for breakfast, and, of course, fried chicken for lunch. Mon–Sat 8am–8pm.

The Varsity 61 North Ave NW ⓣ404/881-1706. Vast, packed Midtown fast-food drive-in diner: a true Fifties throwback, with chili dogs for under $2. Open until at least 11.30pm nightly.

Nightlife

Atlanta is a place where you can have a very good time. The main concentrations are in overlapping **Virginia-Highland**, **Little Five Points**, and **Midtown**, the center of Atlanta's thriving **gay and lesbian** scene. **Buckhead** can be fun if you are prepared to spend a lot of money. Major venues for touring acts include the *Tabernacle* at 152 Luckie St (ⓣ404/659-9022), and the *Variety Playhouse*, 1099 Euclid Ave (ⓣ404/524-7354, ⓦwww.variety-playhouse.com). Up-to-the-minute listings can be found in the free weekly *Creative Loafing* (ⓦwww.creativeloafing.com).

Apache Café 64 Third St NW ⓣ404/876-5436, ⓦwww.apachecafe.info. This busy downtown café serves up Latin and Caribbean favorites, but is most loved for its ever-stimulating nightly program of live R & B and soul artists, jazz funk and hip-hop dance nights, and spoken-word performances.

Blind Willie's 828 N Highland Ave NE ⓣ404/873-2583, ⓦwww.blindwilliesblues.com. The best blues venue in town, with appearances by major artists, this Virginia-Highland hangout is also a lively bar. Open Mon–Sat from 7pm.

Django Gypsy Kitchen and Saloon 495 Peachtree St ⓣ404/347-8648, ⓦwww.djangoatlanta.com. "The Belly," the funky basement of this smart, contemporary restaurant at the south end of midtown, is the nightly venue for wildly eclectic dance parties, with music from house to hip-hop to soca to Afro-Cuban jazz. Closed Sun.

The Drunken Unicorn 736 Ponce de Leon Pl. NE, no phone, ⓦwww.thedrunkenunicorn.net. This unmarked downstairs all-ages music venue hosts hot indie bands and dance parties where the D.I.Y. vibe is still very much alive.

The Earl 488 Flat Shoals Rd ⓣ404/522-3950, ⓦwww.badearl.com. Atlanta's finest rock club, in East Atlanta, just south of I-20, puts on proper live acts pretty much every night. Be sure to ask for a basket of free boiled peanuts.

Eddie's Attic 515-B N McDonough St, Decatur ⓣ404/377-4976, ⓦwww.eddiesattic.com. Nightly acoustic music, from traditional fiddlers to contemporary singer-songwriters, plus occasional stand-up comedy.

Manuel's Tavern 602 N Highland Ave ⓣ404/525-3447, ⓦwww.manuelstavern.com. Memorabilia lines the walls of this classic neighborhood bar known as a favorite watering hole for journalists, writers, and politicians. Jimmy Carter announced his run for governor here in 1970. Superb pub fare served until late.

Star Community Bar 437 Moreland Ave NE ⓣ404/681-5740, ⓦwww.starbar.net. Enjoyable Little Five Points watering hole, in a former bank bursting with Elvis memorabilia, and offering live music Wed–Sat. Closed Sun.

North from Atlanta: the mountains

Some spectacular **Appalachian mountain scenery** – at its best in October, when the leaves turn a brilliant red and gold – lies just a short drive from Atlanta. Hwy-

348 ascends a particularly impressive pass at the White County line, crossed at the top by the **Appalachian Trail**. Of the various towns, **Dahlonega** makes the best base. The rest – like **Helen**, 35 miles northeast, now a pseudo-Bavarian village – get pretty kitschy. However the region abounds in **state parks**.

Dahlonega

Attractive **DAHLONEGA**, in the Appalachian foothills fifty miles northeast of Atlanta on US-19, owes its origins to the first-ever **Gold Rush** in the US. In 1828 Benjamin Parks discovered gold at Auraria, six miles south. Five years later Dahlonega was established as the seat of Lumpkin County. Soon enough gold was excavated for Dahlonega to acquire its own outpost of the US Mint, which produced over $6 million in gold coins before termination by the Civil War. The story is recounted in the **Gold Museum**, housed in the former courthouse on the square (Mon–Sat 9am–5pm, Sun 10am–5pm; $4; ⓣ706/864-2257). You can also pan for gold at small mines in the area. The town hosts one of Appalachia's biggest annual **bluegrass** festivals in late June, while late October sees the **Gold Rush Days**, a downhome festival.

Dahlonega's **visitor center** is across from the courthouse (daily 9am–5.30pm; ⓣ706/864-3711 or 1-800/231-5543, ⓦwww.dahlonega.org). The *Smith House*, just down from the square at 84 S Chestatee St (ⓣ706/867-7000 or 1-800/852-9577, ⓦwww.smithhouse.com), is a classic Southern **restaurant**, serving all-you-can-eat meals at low prices, and also offering comfortable double **rooms** (❹).

Amicalola Falls State Park

Twenty miles west of Dahlonega on Hwy-52, **Amicalola Falls State Park** (daily 7am–10pm; $3 per vehicle, $25 to camp; ⓣ706/265-1969) focuses on a dramatic waterfall that cascades down a steep hillside. After driving to the overlook, continue another half-mile to the park's modern **lodge** (ⓣ706/265-8888 or 1-800/573-9656, ⓦwww.amicalolafalls.com; ❹), which holds comfortable double rooms and a restaurant with panoramic views. For even more seclusion, hike five miles toward the start of the **Appalachian Trail**, to reach *Len Foote Hike Inn* (reservations required, ⓣ1-800/581-8032, ⓦwww.hike-inn.com; ❻), accessible only on foot, which offers basic rooms and serves breakfast and dinner family-style, included in the overnight rates.

Athens

Charming **ATHENS**, almost seventy miles east of Atlanta, is home to the thirty-thousand-plus students of the University of Georgia, and has a liberal feel. Its compact downtown north of campus is alive with book and record stores, clubs, bars, restaurants, and cafés; **Broad Street** in particular is lined with sidewalk tables.

Although Athens holds few conventional tourist attractions, it has become internationally famed as the home of rock groups such as R.E.M. and the B-52s. R.E.M. started out playing at the *40 Watt Club*, originally at 171 College Ave, but repeatedly relocated until it found its current premises at 285 W Washington St (ⓣ706/549-7871, ⓦwww.40watt.com), where it continues to host an eclectic array of musicians. Bigger names tend to appear at the *Georgia Theatre*, 215 N Lumpkin St (ⓣ706/549-9918, ⓦwww.georgiatheatre.com), a converted movie theater that also shows films on quiet nights. Up-and-coming bands can be heard at the *Caledonia Lounge*, 256 W Clayton St (ⓣ706/549-5577, ⓦwww.caledonialounge.com). The free weekly *Flagpole* (ⓦwww.flagpole.com) carries full **music listings**.

Practicalities

From Atlanta, Greyhound arrives at 220 W Broad St; the Athens Transit System operates **buses** (approx. every 30min; $1.25¢ flat fare). Housed in the 1820 Church-Waddel-Brumby House, the city's oldest surviving home, the **visitor center** is near campus at 280 E Dougherty St (summer Mon–Sat 10am–6pm, Sun noon–6pm, otherwise Mon–Sat 10am–5pm, Sun 2–5pm; ⓣ706/353–1820, ⓦwww.athenswelcomecenter.com). Historic bus tours leave at 2pm Mon–Wed and Fri–Sun ($15; ⓣ706/208-8687).

Lodging can be a problem during football games and other big university functions. Choices include the good-value *Courtyard by Marriott Athens Downtown*, 166 N. Finley St (ⓣ706/369-7000, ⓦwww.marriott.com/ahncy; ❹); the *Hilton Garden Inn*, 390 E Washington St (ⓣ706/353-6800, ⓦwww.hi-athens.com; ❹); or the ten-room *The Colonels* B&B on Angel Oaks Farm just 15min from downtown at 3890 Barnett Shoals Rd (ⓣ706/559-9595, ⓦwww.thecolonels.net).

As you would expect from a college town, there is a diverse array of cuisine available at reasonable prices. R.E.M. devotees head straight for the original home of their **Automatic for the People** album title – *Weaver D's* soul-food café, a short walk east of downtown at 1016 E Broad St (lunch only; ⓣ706/353-7797), which serves delicious fried chicken and veggies. *The Grit*, similarly close to downtown on the northwest side, at 199 Prince Ave (ⓣ706/543-6592), offers inexpensive eclectic vegetarian dishes, while *Mama's Boy*, just south of downtown at 197 Oak St (ⓣ706/548-6249), serves the best breakfast in town. Athens has a thriving **bar** scene, although Georgia's blue laws require drinks-only bars to close on Sundays. *The Globe* at 199 Lumpkin Street is a casual bar that also serves tasty food. For a classic dive bar, head to *The Georgia Bar*, 159 W. Clayton St (ⓣ706/546-9884), where cheap beer and good conversation come in equal proportions.

Central Georgia

South of Atlanta, **central Georgia** is famous more for its people than places. **Otis Redding**, **James Brown**, **Little Richard**, and the **Allman Brothers** were all born or grew up here. Former president **Jimmy Carter** came from little Plains, roughly 120 miles due south of the capital. .

The small towns hold little in the way of conventional sights, although **Juliette**, twenty miles north of Macon, is where the *Whistle Stop Café* dishes up the fried green tomatoes of book and movie fame (ⓣ478/992-8886; Sun–Fri 11am–4pm, Sat 11am–8pm). **Vidalia,** further east, is the "Sweet Onion Capital of the World." The largest communities are Columbus, a dull army center, and likeable **Macon**.

Macon

MACON, eighty miles southeast of Atlanta on I-75, makes an attractive stop en route to Savannah, especially when its 280,000 **cherry trees** erupt with blossoms, celebrated by a festival in late March. Set along the **Ocmulgee River**, Macon was founded in 1823 and became a major cotton port.

Home to **Little Richard**, **Otis Redding**, and the **Allman Brothers**, Macon is also where **James Brown** recorded his first smash, the epoch-making "Please Please Please," in an unlikely-looking mansion at 830 Mulberry St. Otis is commemorated by a bronze statue beside the Otis Redding Memorial Bridge. Duane Allman and Berry Oakley, killed here in motorcycle smashes in 1971 and 1972 respectively, are buried in **Rose Hill Cemetery** on Riverside Drive, the inspiration for several of the band's songs. These lives are celebrated in the **Georgia**

Music Hall of Fame, next to the visitor center (see below) at Martin Luther King Jr Blvd and Walnut St (Mon–Sat 9am–5pm, Sun 1–5pm; $8; ⓣ478/751-3334, ⓦwww.gamusichall.com). Georgia musicians are recalled by displays including a gospel chapel, a rock'n'roll soda shop, and a country café. Also worth a visit is the **Tubman African American Museum**, at 340 Walnut St (Mon–Sat 9am–5pm; $5; ⓣ478/743-8544, ⓦwww.tubmanmuseum.com), named for Underground Railroad leader Harriet Tubman, and dedicated to African American arts, culture, and history.

Ocmulgee National Monument

Between 900 and 1100 AD, a Native American group migrated from the Mississippi Valley to a spot overlooking the Ocmulgee River a couple of miles east of modern downtown Macon, where they leveled the site that is now **Ocmulgee National Monument** (daily 9am–5pm; free; ⓦwww.nps.gov/ocmu). Their settlement of thatched huts has vanished, though two grassy mounds, each thought to have been topped by a temple, still rise from the plateau. Near the visitor center, you can enter the underground chamber of a ceremonial **earthlodge**, the clay floor of which holds a ring of individually molded seats, and a striking bird-shaped altar.

Practicalities

Macon's **visitor center**, in the Terminal Station at the foot of Cherry Street (Mon–Sat 9am–5.30pm; ⓣ478/743-3401 or 1-800/768-3401, ⓦwww.maconga.org), is also the base for guided **trolley tours** ($15).

Greyhound pulls into town at 65 Spring St, where Little Richard is said to have written "Tutti Frutti" while washing dishes. The best **accommodation** is downtown: for old-fashioned Southern hospitality, head for the *1842 Inn*, 353 College St (ⓣ478/741-1842 or 1-800/336-1842, ⓦwww.1842inn.com; ❻), which offers a full Southern breakfast in its lovely courtyard. For the budget-conscious, the *La Quinta Inn & Suites*, 3944 River Place Drive (ⓣ478/474-8107 or 1-800/531-5900, ⓦwww.lq.com;) offers well-kept rooms and free high-speed internet.

Although the most **dining** options are Southern, *Bert's*, downtown at 442 Cherry St (ⓣ478/742-9100; closed Sun), is a nice little place where the food ranges from cheap Greek feta burgers at lunch to pricey wasabi tuna at dinner. Go to Macon institution *H & H*, 807 Forsyth St (ⓣ478/742-9810; Mon–Sat 6.30am–4pm) for mouth-watering Southern soul food. Authentic Southern **barbecue** is a 45min drive away, north of town on US-23 to *Fresh Air Barbecue*, near Jackson (ⓣ478/775-3182); it's a roadside shack serving pork that's been hickory-smoked for 24 hours.

Savannah

American towns don't come much more beautiful than **SAVANNAH**, seventeen miles up the Savannah River from the ocean, and twenty miles south of the South Carolina state line. The **historic district**, arranged around Spanish-moss-swathed garden squares, formed the core of the original city and boasts examples of just about every architectural style of the eighteenth and nineteenth centuries. The cobbled **waterfront** on the Savannah River is edged by towering old cotton warehouses.

Savannah was founded in 1733 by **James Oglethorpe** as the first settlement of the British colony of Georgia. His intention was to establish a haven for debtors, with no Catholics, lawyers, or hard liquor – and, above all, no slaves. However,

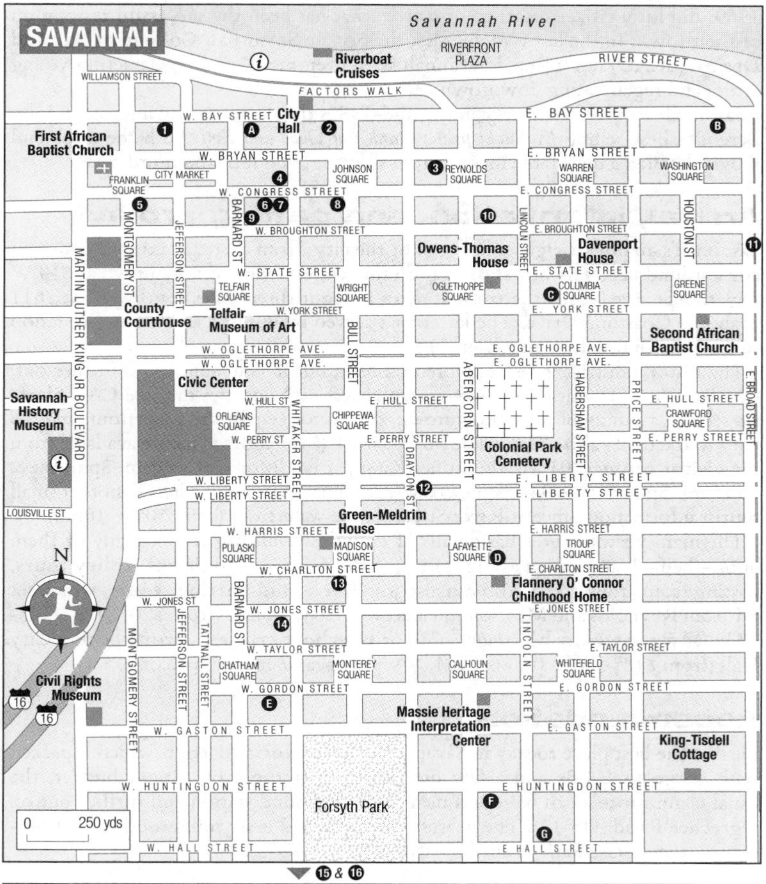

ACCOMMODATION

17 Hundred 90	C	The Mulberry	B
Azalea Inn	F	Savannah Pensione	G
Bed and Breakfast Inn	E		
Days Inn	A		
Hamilton-Turner Inn	D		

RESTAURANTS & BARS

Bacchus Wine Lounge	12	Hang Fire	8	Mercury Lounge	6
Back in the Day Bakery	15	Jazz'd Tapas Bar	9	Moon River Brewing Co.	2
Cha Bella	11	The Jinx	7	Mrs Wilkes' Dining Room	14
Club One	1	Lady and Sons	4	The Olde Pink House	3
Garibaldi Café	5	Leopold's Ice Cream	10	Sentient Bean	16
Gryphon Tea Room	13				

with the arrival of North Carolina settlers in the 1750s, plantation agriculture, based on slave labor, took off. The town became a major export center at the end of important railroad lines in which **cotton** was funneled from far away. General Sherman arrived here in December 1864 at the end of his "March to the Sea." At Lincoln's urging he set to work apportioning land to freed slaves. This was the first recognition of the need for "reconstruction," though such concrete economic provision for slaves was rarely to occur again.

After the Civil War, the plantations floundered, cotton prices slumped, and Savannah went into decline. There was little industry beyond the port and Savannah's graceful townhouses and tree-lined boulevards fell into decay. Not until the

1960s did local citizens start to organize what has been the successful restoration of their town. In the last two decades, the private **Savannah College of Art and Design** (SCAD) has injected Savannah with even more vitality, attracting young artists and regenerating downtown.

Savannah acquired notoriety in the mid-1990s thanks to its starring role in John Berendt's best-selling *Midnight in the Garden of Good and Evil*; both the book and movie detailed a delectable mix of cross-dressing, voodoo, and murder.

Arrival, information, and getting around

Savannah's **airport** is eight miles west of the city; from there, a taxi to downtown costs around $28. The **bus station** is on the western edge of downtown at 610 W Oglethorpe Ave, while the **train station** is about three miles southwest, at 2611 Seaboard Coastline Drive. The latter isn't served by buses; a taxi from the station to downtown usually costs about $12.

The historic district is best explored on foot, but if you want to go further out, Chatham Area Transit (CAT; ⓦwww.catchacat.org) operates the free **CAT Shuttle** service, running between downtown, the visitor center, the waterfront, and the City Market, and also a reasonable **bus** network ($1). Route maps are available from the **visitor center**, 301 Martin Luther King Jr Blvd (Mon–Fri 8.30am–5pm, Sat & Sun 9am–5pm; ⓣ912/944-0455,ⓦwww.savannahvisit.com). There's another small tourist information office at River Street on the waterfront (daily 10am–10pm).

The main visitor center has details of countless **walking tours**, many of them ghost-themed, and serves as the starting point for several different **trolley tours**, costing from around $20. You can also join **horse-and-carriage tours**, which set off from Reynolds and Madison squares every 20 to 30min (from $20; ⓣ912/443-9333, ⓦwww.savannahcarriage.com), or **riverboat cruises**, starting behind City Hall (from $18; ⓣ1-800/786-6404, ⓦwww.savannahriverboat.com).

Accommodation

Ideally, the best place to stay in Savannah is the **historic district**, which is packed with gorgeous **B&Bs** and a few nice hotels. For those on a tight budget, the usual chain **motels** can be found near the Greyhound station and further out on Ogeechee Road (US-17). The nearest **campground** is six miles southeast, at Skidaway Island State Park (from $25; ⓣ1-800/864-7275).

17 Hundred 90 307 E President St ⓣ912/236-7122, ⓦwww.17hundred90.com. The oldest inn in town, said to be haunted, with an atmospheric bar and elegant restaurant. Rooms are small, but many come with original brick fireplaces. ❻

Azalea Inn 217 E Huntingdon St ⓣ912/236-2707 or 1-800/582-3823, ⓦwww.azaleainn.com. Charming, friendly B&B, with ten bright, delightfully furnished en-suite rooms and a very welcome pool in the garden. Superb Southern breakfasts are served daily, formal dinners much more occasionally. ❻

Bed and Breakfast Inn 117 W Gordon St ⓣ912/238-0518, ⓦwww.savannahbnb.com. Great-value B&B, in two 1853 townhouses overlooking shady Chatham Square – reservations are essential. ❹

Days Inn 201 W Bay St ⓣ912/236-4440, ⓦwww.daysinn.com. Though it lacks the character of a B&B, it is an affordable, central choice. ❹

Hamilton-Turner Inn 330 Abercorn St ⓣ912/233-1833 or 1-877/468-8849, ⓦwww.hamilton-turnerinn.com. Opulent, 1873 French Second Empire–style B&B with 17 rooms on Lafayette Square. ❼

The Mulberry 601 E Bay St ⓣ912/238-1200 or 1-877/468-1200, ⓦwww.savannahhotel.com. Friendly Holiday Inn–operated hotel with a B&B feel. Rooftop Jacuzzi, pool, courtyard, and luxurious riverview rooms. ❻

Savannah Pensione 304 E Hall St ⓣ912/236-7744. This former hostel, in a historic Victorian District building, no longer offers individual dorm beds. The basic rooms are rented at very inexpensive rates – meaning it's a cheap option for friends or couples traveling together. ❷

The Town

Savannah's **historic district** is flanked by the river to the north, Martin Luther King Jr Boulevard to the west, and Broad Street – which has long been replaced by Broughton Street as downtown's main commercial thoroughfare – to the east. You can get an overview at the **Savannah History Museum**, adjoining the visitor center in the restored Railroad Station at 303 Martin Luther King Jr Blvd (Mon–Fri 8.30am–5pm, Sat & Sun 9am–5pm; $4.25).

The best way to get a feel for the place is simply to wander its streets. They're lined with shuttered Federal, Regency, and antebellum houses, embellished with intricate iron balconies and intriguing details. The subtropical **greenery** is as stun-

▲ La Fayette Square

ning as the buildings. More than twenty shady residential **garden squares**, ablaze with Spanish-moss-tangled trees, offer shade from the summer's intense heat. Forrest Gump told his life story from a bench in **Chippewa Square**, but eager movie-buffs will find the bench long gone, and just an imposing statue of James Oglethorpe to admire instead.

Most visitors take in a few old **mansions**, such as the Georgian **Davenport House**, at 324 E State St (Mon–Sat 10am–4pm, Sun 1-4pm; $8; Ⓦ www.davensporthousemuseum.org), which boasts an elliptical staircase. The **Green-Meldrim House**, on Madison Square (Tues, Thurs & Fri 10am–4pm, Sat 10am–1pm; $7), is a Gothic Revival mansion that General Sherman used as his headquarters. Its ironwork is a rare example of pre-Civil War craftsmanship; most iron in Savannah was melted down during the Civil War. Many of the balconies and railings you see today are later copies. The impressive **Sorrel Weed House**, at West Harris and Bull streets across from Madison Park (daily 10am–5pm; $10), was one of the first two houses to be named a landmark by the state of Georgia. There are also ghost tours at night in this house alleged to be one of the city's most haunted.

A Regency mansion designed by English architect William Jay on Telfair Square forms the original core of the **Telfair Museum of Art**, 121 Barnard St (Mon, Wed, Fri & Sat 10am–5pm, Sun noon–5pm; $10; Ⓦ www.telfair.org), the South's oldest art museum. In 2006 the Telfair's **Jepson Center for the Arts** opened. The center hosts changing exhibitions that showcase the work of Southern and Savannah-based artists. Kids will love the high-tech gadgets of the ArtZeum. Another Jay edifice, the **Owens-Thomas House** at 124 Abercorn St – designed when Jay was just 24 – forms a third component of Telfair (Mon noon–5pm, Tues–Sat 10am–5pm, Sun 1–5pm, $10 admission includes entrance to all three sites).

Not an imposing example of antebellum architecture, but still well worth visiting is the **Flannery O'Connor Childhood Home** at 207 E Charlton St (Sat & Sun 1–4pm; $4). This legendary Southern Gothic novelist and short-story writer lived here from her birth in 1925 until 1938.

At the southern edge of the historic district, on Calhoun Square, the **Massie Heritage Center**, 207 E Gordon St (Mon–Fri 9am–4pm; $3), is housed in Savannah's first public elementary and illuminates the city's architecture with displays on its neighborhoods and development.

Savannah's **waterfront**, at the foot of a steep bluff below Bay Street, resembles an eighteenth-century European port. The main thoroughfare, **River Street**, is cobbled with the ballast carried by long-vanished sailing ships, while its tall brick cotton warehouses are said to be haunted by ghosts of the slave stevedores. It's now a touristy district, lined with seafood restaurants and bars filled with partying crowds.

Two blocks south of the visitor center, at 460 Martin Luther King Jr Blvd, the **Ralph Martin Gilbert Civil Rights Museum** (Mon–Sat 9am–5pm; $4) explores Savannah's significant role in **black history**. With a sustained program of sit-ins, "wade-ins" at whites-only Tybee Island beaches, and a fifteen-month boycott of local department store Levy's – the longest-running store boycott in the history of the movement – Savannah was active in the campaigns of the 1960s; by 1964, Dr King called it "the most integrated city south of the Mason-Dixon Line."

African-American history is also recalled at the 1775 **First African Baptist Church** at 23 Montgomery St. This is the oldest black church in North America, built by slaves. Downstairs, the diamond shapes made by holes in the floor were ventilation holes for slaves hiding in the 4ft subterranean crawl spaces while waiting to escape to safe havens via the Underground Railroad. At the **Second African Baptist Church**, 123 Houston St, General Sherman read the Emancipation

Proclamation in December 1864, and issued the famous **Field Order #15**, which granted each freed slave forty acres and a mule.

Southeast of downtown, the **Victorian District** is being slowly restored, and has a couple of good museums. The center of this process is the **King-Tisdell Cottage**, 514 E Huntingdon St (Tues–Sat noon–5pm; $4; Ⓦwww.kingtisdell.org). In addition to a collection of Gullah baskets and African woodcarving, it illustrates the history of African Americans both before and after the Civil War. The **Beach Institute**, 502 E Harris St (Tues–Sat noon–5pm; $4), Georgia's first school for freed slaves, today houses an African-American art gallery with a permanent display of woodcarvings by folk artist Ulysses Davis.

A ten-minute drive east from Savannah is **Bonaventure Cemetery**, 330 Bonaventure Rd, swathed in trees and sloping down to the Wilmington River. The final resting place of local luminaries such as Johnny Mercer and Conrad Aiken, it's also a major sight in *Midnight in the Garden*, in which it's written about to great effect.

Eating

Savannah has lots of **restaurants**. Most places on the **waterfront** are unremarkable. Far better to head for the **City Market** – four blocks of restored grain warehouses just a few blocks back from the river – which is downtown's prime restaurant and nightlife district.

Back in the Day Bakery 2403 Bull St Ⓣ912/495-9292. A recently opened artisan bakery where everything is made from scratch, including moist red velvet cupcakes. It also serves savory treats like the jambon royal panini. Tues–Fri 8am–4pm, Sat 8am–3pm.

Cha Bella 102 E Broad St Ⓣ912/790-7888. Contemporary Italian restaurant at the eastern edge of downtown, serving high-quality, Mediterranean cuisine with a strong commitment to organic ingredients. Tues–Sun 5.30–10pm.

Garibaldi Cafe 315 W Congress St Ⓣ912/232-7118. This atmospheric City Market restaurant, all gold mirrors and pressed-tin ceiling, serves great Northern Italian dishes, nouvelle cuisine, and seafood.

Gryphon Tea Room Bull and Charlton sts Ⓣ912/525-5880. There's an atmospheric mix of art students, lecturers, and ladies-that-lunch in this sweet tearoom, housed in an old pharmacy with its original counter, tiled floor, and mirrors. Hundreds of special teas, genteel gourmet lunches, and mouthwatering cakes; high tea is served 4–6pm. Closed Sun.

Lady and Sons 102 W Congress St Ⓣ912/233-2600. Thanks to heavy TV exposure, Paula Deen's Southern restaurant sees daily lines around the block for its buffets of fried chicken, Low Country Boil, and the like. Many locals insist it's not a patch on *Mrs Wilkes*.

Leopold's Ice Cream 212 E Broughton St Ⓣ912/234-4442. Hollywood producer Stratton Leopold has revamped his family's traditional ice-cream parlor, originally opened in 1919, and serves homemade ices, plus a full menu of sandwiches, salads, and burgers.

Local 11 Ten 1110 Bull St Ⓣ912/790-9000. The term locavore is taken seriously at this hip, buzzy interpretation on seasonal Low Country, Italian and French fare (pastas are made from scratch). Thorough wine list and inventive cocktails. Reservations recommended. Open for dinner Tues–Sat.

Mrs Wilkes' Dining Room 107 W Jones St Ⓣ912/232-5997. This local institution offers a real Southern experience, serving all-you-care-to-eat lunches for $16. Diners sits around large tables for mounds of fried chicken, sweet potatoes, spinach, and spaghetti. There's no sign outside so get there early and join the line. Mon–Fri 11am-2pm. No credit cards.

The Olde Pink House 23 Abercorn St Ⓣ912/232-4286. With its pink Regency facade, this place looks a bit too good to be true, but its Low Country, fish-heavy food is actually superb. Open for dinner only.

Sentient Bean 13 E Park Ave Ⓣ912/232-4447. This spacious yet cozy coffee shop overlooking Forsyth Park serves great vegetarian fare in addition to a good cup of fair trade joe. The space has become a meeting ground for local activists, D.I.Y. enthusiasts and singer/songwriters alike.

Entertainment and nightlife

Savannah's **nightlife** is decidedly laid-back. Everything is fairly close together, between City Market and the river. Almost uniquely in the US (New Orleans is another exception) you can drink **alcohol** on the streets in open cups. For **listings**, pick up the free weekly *Connect* newspaper (ⓦ www.connectsavannah.com).

Savannah has the largest Irish population per capita in the US, and **St Patrick's Day** (March 17) is a big deal. Nowadays nearly a million visitors descend here to guzzle copious amounts of Guinness; many of the 130,000 permanent residents choose this weekend to leave town.

Bacchus Wine Lounge 102 E Liberty St ⓣ912/235-4447. This trendy, sleek space with floor to ceiling glass windows offers an extensive wine list specializing in boutique labels.

Club One 1 Jefferson St ⓣ912/232-0200. Decadent gay club, where drag acts once a month include Lady Chablis, from "The Book"; everyone is welcome.

Hang Fire 37 Whitaker St ⓣ912/443-9956. A hipster haven downtown where PBR flows freely with DJs some nights. Late nights see this little place packed with a jovial 20-and-30-something crowd.

Jazz'd Tapas Bar 52 Barnard St ⓣ912/236-7777, ⓦ www.jazzdsavannah.com. Postmodern City Market lounge in the basement of the former Kress department store. Serves Southern-style (as opposed to being particularly Spanish) tapas snacks and puts on live, no-cover jazz or blues nightly (except Mon).

The Jinx 127 W Congress St ⓣ912/236-2281, ⓦ www.thejinx.net. Savannah's premier rock club, in City Market, also puts on dance nights.

Mercury Lounge 125 W Congress St ⓣ912/447-6952. Super-hip lounge, with kooky decor, regular swing music, and live jazz.

Moon River Brewing Co. 21 W Bay St ⓣ912/447-0943. Popular brewpub near the waterfront.

Out from Savannah

Tybee Island, eighteen miles east of the city on US-80, has the area's best **beach**, as well as a 154ft **lighthouse** from 1736 (daily except Tues 9am–5.30pm; $6). Old Savannah Tours run daily **shuttle buses** in summer ($10 round-trip; ⓣ912/234-8128 or 1-800/517-9007, ⓦ www.oldsavannahtours.com). **Accommodations** include the 1930s oceanfront *DeSoto Beach Hotel*, 212 Butler Ave (ⓣ912/786-4542 or 1-877/786-4542, ⓦ www.desotobeachhotel.com; ⑤). For **Low Country food**, try *The Crab Shack*, 40 Estill Hammock Rd (ⓣ912/786-9857), for fresh crabs and shrimp by the creek – if you can find it. Take a right off the main road to the beach, about two miles before the lighthouse turnoff.

Fort Pulaski National Monument, off US-80 E en route to Tybee Island (daily, summer 9am–5.30pm, rest of year 9am–5pm; $3; ⓦ www.nps.gov/fopu), is the most interesting of several forts. At one point an impressive Confederate stronghold, it was the first masonry fortress to be pierced by rifled cannon fire.

Ten miles south of Savannah, at 7601 Skidaway Rd, is the **Wormsloe State Historic Site** (Tues–Sat 9am–5pm, Sun 2–5.30pm; $4; ⓦ www.wormsloe.org). In the eighteenth century this was an important plantation; the tabby ruins of the fortified house of British settler Noble Jones are now overgrown with palms and forest. Inside, a museum covers the early settlement of Savannah.

Much of the Georgia coast consists of a string of **National Wildlife Refuges**, on the small marshy islands of the **barrier island chain**. It's well worth detouring to visit **Blackbeard Island**, **Wolf Island**, **Pinckney**, or **Wassaw**, where swamps are filled with nesting birds and offer great fishing.

Brunswick and the southern coast

BRUNSWICK, the one sizeable settlement south of Savannah, is a hop-off point for the offshore **sea islands**. The town in itself is industrial, though the shrimp docks can be quite interesting when the catch is brought in. If you stay a night here, the **visitor center**, 4 Glynn Ave (daily 8.30am–5pm; ⓣ912/265-0620 or 1-800/933-2627, ⓦwww.bgivb.com), has lists of budget **motels** and central **B&Bs**. A more unusual alternative is the wonderful *Hostel in the Forest*, a couple of miles west of I-95 exit 6, reached via a muddy driveway on the south side of US-82 (ⓣ912/264-9738, ⓦwww.foresthostel.com). For $20 per person you'll get either a dorm bed in a geodesic dome or a private room in one of eight treehouses. The price includes a communal dinner, and all guests are expected to perform a small chore. The best **food** nearby is at the superlative *Georgia Pig*, in an unlikely setting next to a gas station at exit 6 on I-95 to Hwy 17 (ⓣ912/264-6664), where smoky barbecue comes with the local Brunswick stew, coleslaw, and baked beans.

The sea islands

Several of Georgia's **sea islands**, like those of South Carolina, were divided among freed slaves after the Civil War. However, these islands remained poor agricultural communities, with little in the way of tourist destinations. Today they make handy alternatives to Florida as seashore breaks for tired inlanders.

Jekyll Island

The **southern islands** are the most developed, thanks largely to **Jekyll Island**, which was originally bought in 1887 for use as an exclusive "club" by a group of millionaires including the Rockefellers, the Pulitzers, the Macys, and the Vanderbilts. A small **Welcome Center** stands on the causeway (daily 9am–5pm; ⓣ912/635-3636 or 1-877/453-5955, ⓦwww.jekyllisland.com), though the **Jekyll Island Museum Center** (daily 9am–5pm) provides a more useful overview of the island's history. Reached by turning left after you pay the $3 island toll, and then heading along Riverview Drive onto Stable Road, it also runs hourly guided tours of the mansions for $10. The "historic district" centers on the rambling old original club building, which, as the *Jekyll Island Club Hotel*, now offers elegant and surprisingly affordable **accommodation** (ⓣ912/635-2600 or 1-800/535-9547, ⓦwww.jekyllclub.com; ➎). There's a **campground** a little further north (ⓣ1-866/658-3021; starting at $21), near the nesting sites of loggerhead turtles.

St Simon's Island and Cumberland Island

Most of **St Simon's Island**, reached across a green marsh (35¢ toll), is still an evocative landscape of palms, and live oaks covered with Spanish moss. The village is pleasantly quiet, and the nearby beach is nice for strolling, but fierce currents render **swimming** unsafe: head instead for the east side of the island, where the sand stretches for miles. Southeast Adventure Outfitters, 313 Mallory St (ⓣ912/638-6732, ⓦwww.southeastadventure.com), rents **kayaks** and runs bird- and dolphin-watching tours. **Fort Frederica National Monument**, seven miles north of the causeway (daily 9am–5pm; $30 per vehicle), was built by General Oglethorpe in 1736 as the largest British fort in North America, and has since been left to deteriorate.

As well as **resorts** like the lovely *Sea Palms*, 5445 Frederica Rd (ⓣ912/638-3351 or 1-800/841-6268, ⓦwww.seapalms.com; ➍), whose rooms overlook the marshes, **accommodation** options include *Saint Simon's Inn*, 609 Beachview Drive, a block from the beach near the village (ⓣ912/638-1101, ⓦwww

.stsimonsinn.com; ④). The best place to **eat** is at *Frannie's Place Restaurant*, 318 Mallory St (Ⓣ912/638-1001), famed for its Brunswick stew; try also the specialty sandwiches, crabcakes, and desserts.

To the south, **Cumberland Island** is a wildlife refuge of marshes, beaches, and semitropical forest roamed by wild horses, with the odd deserted planter's mansion. You can get here by ferry from the village of St Mary's, back on the mainland near the Florida border (March–Nov daily 9am & 11.45am; Dec–Feb Thurs–Mon 9am & 11.45am; 45min; $15 round-trip).

Okefenokee Swamp

The dense **Okefenokee Swamp** stretches over thirty miles down to Florida from a point roughly thirty miles southwest of Brunswick. Tucked away among lush plants and trees are over thirty species of snakes, as well as bears, pumas, and alligators. The only entrance is the **Okefenokee Swamp Park**, a private charity-owned concession at the northeast tip, on Hwy-177 off US-23/1 (daily 9am–5.30pm; $15; Ⓣ912/283-0583, Ⓦwww.okeswamp.com). Admission grants access to an interpretive center on wildlife, an observation tower, and reconstructed pioneer buildings; $12–30 extra will get you **boat tours** through the swamp (be sure to slick yourself with bug repellent). Nearby accommodation in **Waycross**, ten miles north, holds bargain **motels** such as the *Pinecrest*, 1761 Memorial Drive (Ⓣ912/283-3580; ①). Nearby Laura Walker State Park, just north of the swamp at 5653 Laura Walker Rd (Ⓣ912/287-4900 or 1-800/864-7257), has 44 tent and RV campsites for $23 a night.

Kentucky

Two hundred years after it was wrested from Native Americans, **KENTUCKY** still hasn't quite decided whether it belongs in the North or the South. Both of the rival presidents during the Civil War, Abraham Lincoln and Jefferson Davis, were born here, and divisions were acute between slave-owning farmers and the merchants who depended on trade with the nearby cities of the industrial North. While the state remained officially neutral, more Kentuckians joined the Union army than the Confederates. After the war, Kentucky sided with the South in its hostility to Reconstruction, and has tended to follow southern political trends.

Kentucky's rugged beauty is at its most appealing in the mountainous **east** and the small historic towns of the **Bluegrass Downs**, where visits can be enlivened by the varied attractions of bourbon whiskey, thoroughbred horses, and bluegrass music. Most of these are within easy reach of reserved **Lexington**, a major horse-breeding market, while hipper **Louisville**, home of the **Kentucky Derby**, lies eighty miles west and is a busy manufacturing and arts center.

Getting around Kentucky

Kentucky's limited **public transportation** can be a real headache. There's full Greyhound service along the interstates south of Louisville and Lexington, but that's about it. Amtrak doesn't operate here at all. **Cycling** is a pleasant and manageable option but **driving** is the only way to cover much ground.

Lexington, Bluegrass Country, and eastern Kentucky

The fertile **Bluegrass Downs**, just eighty miles across, form the base of America's thoroughbred racing industry, with **Lexington** quietly prospering at its heart. The name comes from the unique steel-blue sheen of the buds in the meadows, only visible in early morning during April and May. Kentucky's first white pioneers, who trekked in the 1770s through the 150 miles of wilderness now called the **Daniel Boone National Forest**, were amazed to find this "Eden" deserted while the Indians lived in much less attractive terrain. Archeologists later discovered this was due to mineral deficiencies in the soil causing fatal bone diseases. The area around Lexington holds some of the oldest towns west of the Alleghenies. Eastern Kentucky, however, suffers from acute rural poverty despite the fine scenery of the **Natural Bridge** and **Cumberland Gap** regions.

Lexington

The productivity of the bluegrass fields has kept **LEXINGTON**'s economy ticking over since 1775, though the lack of a navigable river has always made its traders vulnerable to competition from Louisville. However, its current affluence dates from after World War I, when Lexington emerged as the world's largest **burley tobacco** market, although its most conspicuous activity these days is the **horse** trade, with an estimated 450 farms in the vicinity. Consequently, Lexington feels quasi-rustic despite a population exceeding two hundred thousand and boasts many fine antebellum houses.

Arrival and information

Lexington's **airport** is six miles west of town on US-60 W, near Keeneland Racetrack. **Greyhound** drops off about a mile northeast from downtown at 477 New Circle Rd across the street from the local bus station (bus #3 goes downtown). Lex-Tran (Ⓣ859/253-4636, Ⓦwww.lextranonthemove.org) operates a good service to the university and suburbs, but you'll need a **car** to reach the horse-related attractions. The **visitor center** is at 301 E Vine St (Mon–Fri 8.30am–5pm, Sat 10am–5pm, Sun May–Aug noon–5pm; Ⓣ859/233-7299 or 1-800/845-3959, Ⓦwww.visitlex.com) and gives out handy walking- and driving-tour maps. Check the free *ACE Weekly* (Ⓦwww.aceweekly.com) for local **listings** and events.

Accommodation

Lexington has limited downtown accommodation, though there are budget **motels** around the I-75 and the visitor center can help find rooms. The best **campground** is north of downtown at the Horse Park (Ⓣ859/233-4303, Ⓦwww.kyhorsepark.com; from $15).

Gratz Park Inn 120 W Second St Ⓣ859/231-1777 or 1-800/752-4166, Ⓦwww.gratzparkinn.com. Downtown's oldest and most prestigious hotel, with rooms decorated in nineteenth-century style and a gourmet restaurant. ❼

Holiday Inn North 1950 Newtown Pike Ⓣ859/233-0512, Ⓦwww.hilexingtonnorth.com. Vast and very upscale affiliate of the Holiday Inn chain northeast of downtown, complete with a covered "Holidome" holding a swimming pool, sports hall, and gym. ❺

Homewood Suites 249 Ruccio Way Ⓣ859/223-0880 or 1-800/225-5466, Ⓦwww.homewoodsuites.com. Good-value, spacious suites, set in mall territory around four miles south of downtown. Fairly quiet considering the proximity of major highways. ❺

La Quinta 1919 Stanton Way, junction of I-64 & I-75, exit 115 Ⓣ859/231-7551 or 1-800/531-5900. Handily placed motel with comfortable rooms and free continental breakfast. ❸

Swann's Nest B&B 3463 Rosalie Lane ⓣ859/226-0095, ⓦwww.swannsnest.com. An appealing rural retreat, offering five comfortable guest suites on a thoroughbred farm. ❺

Downtown Lexington

The glass office blocks, skywalks, and shopping malls of Lexington's city center, set in a dip on the Bluegrass Downs, crowd in on fountain-filled **Triangle Park**. There are few attractions beyond the **University of Kentucky Art Museum**, in the Singletary Center for the Arts, at Rose Street and Euclid Avenue (Tues–Sun noon–5pm, Fri until 8pm; ⓣ859/257-5716 ⓦwww.uky.edu/ArtMuseum; free), which displays contemporary American art and Native American artifacts. The city's best photo opportunity can be found in the form of **Thoroughbred Park**, at Main Street and Midland Avenue, where an impressive life-sized bronze sculpture depicts a horse race in progress.

Lexington's horses

Along **Paris** and **Ironworks pikes**, northeast of Lexington in an idyllic Kentucky landscape, sleek thoroughbred horses cavort in bluegrass meadows, some still penned in by immaculate white-plank fences,. To the west, you can watch the horses' early-morning workouts at **Keeneland** racetrack (April–Oct daily dawn–10am; free; ⓣ859/254-3412 or 1-800/456-3412, ⓦwww.keeneland.com). Tasteful dark-green grandstands emphasize the crisp white rails around the one-mile oval track, where meetings are held for three weeks in April (Wed–Sun 7.30pm) and three weeks in Oct (Wed–Sun 1pm). Book reserved tickets ($6–15) by phone or online.

Tours of horse farms used to be very popular, but owners are increasingly reluctant to allow them. The easiest way to see a farm is to take a guided bus tour out of Lexington; **Blue Grass Tours** (daily 9am & 1.30pm; $30; ⓣ859/252-5744 or 1-800/755-6956, ⓦwww.bluegrasstours.com) offer a three-hour, fifty-mile itinerary that includes a stop at **Old Friends Farm** (ⓦwww.oldfriendsequine.org), plus a visit to Keeneland. One of the few farms still conducting its own tours is **Three Chimneys** (ⓣ859/873-7053 ⓦwww.threechimneys.com) on Old Frankfort Pike, about fifteen minutes west of downtown; tours are free but places must be booked in advance. The **Thoroughbred Center**, 3380 Paris Pike (April–Oct Mon–Sat 9am; Nov–March Mon–Fri 9am; $10; ⓣ859/293-1853, ⓦwww.thethoroughbredcenter.com), allows you to watch trainers at work. The enjoyable 1032-acre **Kentucky Horse Park**, a little further along at 4089 Ironworks Parkway (mid-March to Oct daily 9am–5pm; Nov to mid-March Wed–Sun 9am–5pm; $9–15; ⓣ859/233-4303, ⓦwww.kyhorsepark.com) features over thirty different equine breeds, a working farm, and guided **horseback rides** ($22 extra); its fascinating **International Museum of the Horse** traces the use of horses throughout history. In nearby Georgetown, at **Whispering Woods**, experienced equestrians can ride unsupervised, while novices can ride with a guide ($25 for 1hr, up to $80 per day; ⓣ502/570-9663, ⓦwww.whisperingwoodstrails.com).

Eating, drinking, and nightlife

Lexington's large student population means it has several lively, youth-oriented **places to eat**, besides the steakhouses catering to the horse crowd and conventioneers. The streets around the corner of Broadway and Main Street hold a few lively bars, such as the *Horse & Barrel*.

Alfalfa Restaurant 141 E Main St ⓣ859/253-0014. Hippyish café featuring wide range of inexpensive international food, with an emphasis on vegetarian dishes and famous buckwheat pancakes. Live music some evenings, plus temporary art exhibits.

Atomic Café 265 N Limestone St ⓣ859/254-1969. Fun Caribbean ambiance, with good spicy food and potent cocktails. Live reggae Thurs–Sat and a pleasant outdoor space.

Common Grounds 343 High St ⓣ859/233-9761. Popular downtown coffeehouse, open until at least midnight daily with live music at weekends. A great rendezvous for coffee, sandwiches, and simple snacks.

Keeneland Track Kitchen 4201 Versailles Rd ⓣ859/254-3412. The place to eat hearty home-style breakfasts for next to nothing in the company of jockeys and other horsey folk.

Kentucky Theatre 214 E Main St ⓣ859/231-6997, ⓦwww.kentuckytheater.com. Evocatively restored 1920s movie palace showing offbeat and art-house films, as well as being a great venue for rock, blues, and jazz concerts. Serves alcohol and decent snacks.

Metropol 307 W Short St ⓣ859/381-9493. Intimate downtown restaurant, housed in an 1825 brick building, that serves upscale cuisine such as lobster ravioli.

Ramsey's Diner 496 E High St ⓣ859/259-2708. Very popular and atmospheric diner, with four other outlets in town, all serving tasty sandwiches, burgers, and meals for $5–12. Open until 1am.

Bluegrass Country

Other than the horse farms directly to the north, most places of interest near Lexington lie southwards, including the fine old towns of **Danville** and **Harrodsburg**, and the restored **Shaker Village** at Pleasant Hill. After about forty miles, the meadows give way to the striking **Knobs** – random lumpy outcrops, shrouded in trees and wispy low-hanging clouds, that are the eroded remnants of the Pennyrile Plateau.

The Shaker Village at Pleasant Hill

The utopian settlement of **PLEASANT HILL**, hidden among the bluegrass hillocks near Harrodsburg, 26 miles southwest of Lexington, was established by **Shaker missionaries** from New England around 1805. Within twenty years, nearly five hundred villagers here were producing seeds, tools, and cloth, for sale as far away as New Orleans. During the Civil War, the pacifist Shakers were obliged to billet Union and Confederate troops alike. Numbers thereafter declined until the last member died in 1923, but a nonprofit organization has returned the village to its nineteenth-century appearance.

The Shaker values of absolute celibacy, hygiene, simplicity, and communal ownership have left their mark on the thirty-four gray and pastel-colored dwellings, which women and men entered via different doors. Visitors can watch demonstrations of broom-making, weaving, quilting, and other traditional handicrafts (April–Oct daily 10am–5pm; $14; Nov–March 10am–4.30pm, reduced program of events; $7), and also take river excursions on the sternwheeler *Dixie Belle* (late April to Oct daily noon, 2pm & 4pm; $6). An on-site **inn** offers good-value rooms, and also houses a superb **restaurant** specializing in boiled ham, lemon pie, and other Kentucky favorites (ⓣ859/734-5411 or 1-800/734-5611, ⓦwww.shakervillageky.org; ④); reserve well in advance to either eat or sleep.

Berea

BEREA, thirty miles south of Lexington, just off I-75 in the foothills where Bluegrass Country meets Appalachia, is home to unique **Berea College**, which gives its fifteen hundred mainly local students free tuition in return for work in any of 120 crafts, ranging from needlework to wrought ironwork. It was founded in 1855 by abolitionists as a vocational college for the young people of East Kentucky – both white and black, making it for forty years the only integrated college in the South. The college's reputation has attracted many private art and craft galleries to little Berea. For details on these and a chance to buy representative local crafts, visit the **Kentucky Artisan Center** at exit 77 off I-75 (daily 8am–8pm; ⓣ859/985-5548, ⓦwww.kentuckyartisancenter.ky.gov). Free tours of both the campus and assorted student craft workshops leave from the sumptuous *Boone Tavern Inn*, a student-run inn and restaurant at Main and Prospect streets (Ⓣ859/985-3700 or 1-800/366-9358, Ⓦwww.berea.edu/boonetavern; ⑤). If you're on a tight **budget**, *Mario's Pizza*, 636 Chestnut St (Ⓣ859/986-2331), is a good option.

Daniel Boone National Forest

Almost the entire eastern length of Kentucky is taken up by the steep slopes, narrow valleys, and sandstone cliffs of the unspoiled **DANIEL BOONE NATIONAL FOREST**. Few Americans can have been so mythologized as **Daniel Boone**, who first explored the region in 1767, and thus ranks as one of Kentucky's earliest fur-trapping pioneers. Perhaps the most famous legend tells of the time he was captured by Shawnee Indians and initiated as "Sheltowee," or Big Turtle. Learning of their plans to attack pioneer communities, Big Turtle escaped just in time to warn the citizens of his own settlement at Boonesborough, southeast of Lexington. Sadly, Boone failed to legalize his land claims, and was forced to press further west to Missouri, where he died in 1820 at the age of 86.

If you want to **camp** in the area, *Twin Knobs,* in Salt Lick at the north end of the forest, is a good option with a range of facilities (mid-March to Oct; $16; Ⓣ1-877/444-6777).

Natural Bridge and around

The geological extravaganza of the **Red River Gorge**, sixty miles east of Lexington via the Mountain Parkway, is best seen by driving a thirty-mile loop from the **Natural Bridge State Resort Park** on Hwy-77, near the village of Slade. Natural Bridge itself is a large sandstone arch surrounded by steep hollows and exposed clifflines; for those reluctant to negotiate the half-mile climb, there is a chairlift ($7 round-trip). As well as hiking trails, canoeing, fishing, rock-climbing, and camping, there's **accommodation** at the secluded *Hemlock Lodge* (Ⓣ606/663-2214 or 1-800/325-1710, Ⓦwww.naturalbridgepark.com; ④), where weekends can be reserved a year in advance.

Toward the south

In 1940, "Colonel" Harland Sanders, so titled as a member of the Honorable Order of Kentucky Colonels, opened a small clapboard diner, the *Sanders Café*, alongside his motel and gas station in tiny **Corbin**, ninety miles south of Lexington on I-75. His **Kentucky Fried Chicken** empire has since spread all over the world. The original 100-seat restaurant, near the junction of US-25 E and US-25 W, has been restored with 1940s decor and an immense amount of memorabilia (daily 10am–10pm; Ⓣ606/528-2163). The food served is usual KFC, but it's an atmospheric little spot.

On the tristate border of Kentucky, Tennessee, and Virginia, the **Cumberland Gap National Historic Park** is one of the most visited parts of the area. A natural passageway used by migrating deer and bison, the area served as a gateway to the West for Boone and other pioneers. **Pinnacle Overlook**, a 1000ft lookout over the three states, is near the **visitor center**, on US-25 E in Middlesboro (daily 8am–5pm; Ⓣ606/248-2817, Ⓦwww.nps.gov/cuga).

Louisville, central, and western Kentucky

In such a heavily rural state, the manufacturing giant of **Louisville** stands out, with its lively cultural and racial mix. Only occasionally does it bother with the laid-back Southern image other parts of the state are so keen to promote. In the **southern** hinterland, numerous small towns retain their tree-shaded squares and nineteenth-century townhouses – and their strict Baptist beliefs – while the endless caverns of **Mammoth Cave National Park** attract spelunkers and hikers in the thousands. The **west**, where the Ohio River meets the Mississippi, is flat, heavily forested, and generally less attractive.

Louisville

LOUISVILLE, just south of Indiana across the Ohio River, is firmly embedded in the American national consciousness for its multimillion-dollar **Kentucky Derby**. Each May, the horse race attracts over half a million fans to this cosmopolitan and well-diversified industrial city, which still bears the traces of the early French settlers who came upriver from New Orleans. Louisville also produces a third of the country's **bourbon**.

The city's history revolves around a perennial rivalry with Cincinnati, a mere one hundred miles upstream. Thus, despite being pro-Union during the Civil War, it promoted itself thereafter – erecting Confederate statues and so on – as *the* place for Southern business to invest. Today, besides a lively arts scene and lots of citywide festivals, Louisville boasts an excellent network of public parks. One native son who took advantage of the recreation facilities was three-times world heavyweight boxing champion **Muhammad Ali**, who used to do his early-morning training in the scenic environs of Chickasaw Park.

Arrival and information

Most major US airlines fly into **Louisville International Airport** (Ⓣ502/368-6524), five miles south of downtown on I-65; take bus #2 or pay an $18 cab fare to get into the city center. **Greyhound** terminates at fairly central 720 W Muhammad Ali Blvd. Downtown **trolleys** run from 7.30am to 8pm/10pm on weekdays and until 6pm on Saturdays for 50¢. The **visitor center** is at Fourth and Jefferson streets (Mon–Sat 10am–6pm, Sun noon–5pm; Ⓣ502/379-6109 or 1-888/568-4784, Ⓦwww.gotolouisville.com) and offers discounts on some of the attractions. For news of upcoming events, pick up a copy of the free **listings** publications *LEO* (*Louisville Eccentric Observer*) or *Velocity*.

Accommodation

Louisville's **accommodation** is plentiful, although downtown prices have been creeping up and of course it's solidly booked up for the Derby. You can **camp** just over the river in Clarksville, Indiana at the central *KOA*, 900 Marriott Drive (Ⓣ812/282-4474, Ⓦwww.koa.com).

Central Park B&B 1353 S Fourth St Ⓣ502/638-1505 or 1-877/922-1505, Ⓦwww.centralparkbandb.com. Opulent seven-room Victorian B&B in the heart of the Historic District. ❺

The Columbine B&B 1707 S Third St Ⓣ502/635-5000 or 1-800/635-5010, Ⓦwww.thecolumbine.com. Six-room B&B, all with private baths, in a colonnaded mansion close to the university. Great garden and gourmet breakfasts. ❺

Econo Lodge 401 S Second St Ⓣ502/583-2841, Ⓦwww.econolodge.com. About as cheap an option as you'll find right downtown. Most rooms are simple but perfectly adequate, while the priciest have hot tubs. ❸

Galt House 140 N Fourth St ⓣ502/589-5200 or 1-800/626-1814, ⓦwww.galthouse.com. This massive, 25-storey, twin-tower hotel on the Ohio riverfront has an unmistakable Kentucky feel, with grand ballrooms, sweeping staircases, and avenue-like corridors. 7

Hampton Inn Downtown Louisville 101 E Jefferson St ⓣ502/585-2200, ⓦwww.louisvilledowntown.hamptoninn.com. Comfortable rooms plus a free buffet breakfast, an indoor pool, and fitness center. 6

Downtown Louisville

Downtown Louisville rolls gently toward Main Street, then abruptly lunges to the river. **Riverfront Plaza**, between Fifth and Sixth streets, is a prime observation point for the natural **Falls of the Ohio** on the opposite side of the river. Two sternwheelers, the *Belle of Louisville* and the *Spirit of Jefferson*, cruise from the wharf at Fourth Street and River Road in the summer (Mon–Sat noon–2pm & 7–9pm; summer only Sun noon–2pm; $16; ⓣ502/574-2355 or ⓦwww.belleoflouisville.org). Even non-baseball fans will likely be impressed by the **Louisville Slugger Museum**, at 800 W Main St (Mon–Sat 9am–5pm; Sun noon–5pm; $9; ⓣ502/588-7228, ⓦwww.sluggermuseum.com). Frequent **tours** start with a short, emotive movie featuring prominent shots of Louisville Slugger bats being used to good effect, then take in displays honoring key players and giving a lucid explanation of how wooden bats are made. All visitors receive a souvenir miniature bat.

The town's newest museum is the excellent **Muhammed Ali Center**, beside the river at 144 N Sixth St (Mon–Sat 9.30am–5pm, Sun noon–5pm; $9; ⓣ502/584-9254, ⓦwww.alicenter.org), which, apart from chronicling the local hero's boxing career with entertaining multimedia displays, provides insight into his political activism and Muslim faith, refreshingly presented in a positive light. The **Speed Art Museum**, at 2035 S Third St on the University of Louisville campus (Tues, Wed & Fri 10.30am–4pm, Thurs 10.30am–8pm, Sat 10.30am–5pm, Sun noon–5pm; free; ⓣ502/634-2700, ⓦwww.speedmuseum.org), hosts traveling exhibits and has a small, but interesting, permanent collection of art and sculpture from medieval to modern times, featuring works by Rembrandt, Monet, Rodin, and Henry Moore.

The Kentucky Derby

The **Kentucky Derby** is one of the world's premier horse races; it's also, as Hunter S. Thompson put it, "decadent and depraved." Derby Day itself is the first Saturday in May, at the end of the two-week **Kentucky Derby Festival**. Since 1875, the leading lights of Southern society have gathered at **Churchill Downs**, three miles south of downtown, for an orgy of betting, haute cuisine, and mint juleps in the plush grandstand, while tens of thousands of the beer-guzzling proletariat cram into the infield. Apart from the $40 infield tickets available on the day – offering virtually no chance of a decent view – all seats are sold out months in advance. The actual race, traditionally preceded by a mass drunken rendition of "My Old Kentucky Home," is run over a distance of one and a quarter miles, lasts barely two minutes, and offers around a million dollars in prize money. Churchill Downs also hosts thoroughbred races from May to July, and from October to November (ⓣ502/636-4400 or 1-800/283-3729).

The excellent hands-on **Kentucky Derby Museum** (mid-March to Nov Mon–Sat 8am–5pm, Sun noon–5pm; Dec to mid-March Mon–Sat 9am–5pm, Sun 11am–5pm; $10; ⓣ502/637-7097, ⓦwww.derbymuseum.org), next to Churchill Downs at 704 Central Ave, will appeal to horseracing enthusiasts and neophytes alike. Admission includes a magnificent audiovisual display that captures the Derby Day atmosphere on a 360° screen and you can take a tour of the stables and racecourse for an extra $10.

Eating

Louisville's **restaurants** cater to all tastes, though downtown prices are fairly high.

Bristol Bar & Grille 1321 Bardstown Rd ⓣ502/456-1702. A perennial Louisville favorite, offering good bistro-style salads and entrees, as well as great desserts. Two other locations at 300 N Hurstbourne Parkway and 614 W Main St.

Café Kilimanjaro 649 S Fourth St ⓣ502/583-4332. Dishes and drinks from the Caribbean, Africa, and South America in relaxed surroundings with tropical decor.

Lynn's Paradise Café 984 Barrett Ave ⓣ502/585-5966. Nationally acclaimed chef Lynn Winter serves up homestyle cooking in an offbeat, friendly atmosphere.

Ramsi's Café on the World 1293 Bardstown Rd ⓣ502/451-0700. Atmospheric café open nightly until late and offering eclectic and very tasty selections from around the world. A downtown branch, at 215 S Fifth St, opens for weekday lunches only, served cafeteria-style.

Seviche 1538 Bardstown Rd ⓣ502/473-8560. Stylish Latin restaurant in the busy Deer Park district, featuring ceviche as well as seafood and steak entrees cooked to South American recipes. Most dishes are over $20.

Vietnam Kitchen 5339 S Mitscher Ave ⓣ502/363-5154. A small, basic restaurant with a huge menu, fifteen minutes' drive down Third St, behind the Iriquois Manor mall. This is where the city's Asian chefs eat on their days off. Closed Wed.

Nightlife and entertainment

Fronted by several outlandish sculptures, the **Kentucky Center for the Arts**, 501 W Main, between Fifth and Sixth avenues (ⓣ502/562-0100 or 1-800/775-7777, ⓦwww.kentuckycenter.org), is Louisville's main venue for high culture. Meanwhile, the **Actors' Theatre of Louisville**, 316 W Main St (ⓣ502/584-1205 or 1-800/428-5849, ⓦwww.actorstheatre.org), has a national reputation for its new productions. As for **drinking** and **live music**, the two-mile strip around Bardstown Road and Baxter Avenue (take bus #17) is punctuated by fun bars and restaurants; the best **gay** clubs are on the eastern edge of downtown.

Connections 130 S Floyd St ⓣ502/585-5752. The pick of Louisville's gay scene. At weekends, this giant club, complete with terrace garden, holds over 2000.

Headliners 1386 Lexington Rd ⓣ502/584-8088, ⓦwww.headlinerslouisville.com. Lively club that showcases local, national and even international indie bands.

Molly Malone's 933 Baxter Ave ⓣ502/473-1222. Enjoyable Irish pub and restaurant, with live music on the weekends and Euro soccer on TV.

Phoenix Hill Tavern 644 Baxter Ave ⓣ502/589-4957, ⓦwww.phoenixhill.com. Big bar with four separate areas; occasionally hosts national touring acts.

Stevie Ray's 230 E Main St ⓣ502/582-9945, ⓦwww.stevieraysbluesbar.com. As the name suggests, a loud, rocking blues bar.

Out from Louisville

South from Louisville to Tennessee, **central Kentucky** offers great scope for a driving tour. There's small-town charm and well-aged bourbon in **Bardstown** and Abraham Lincoln's birthplace of **Hodgenville**, while the top natural attraction is the amazing **Mammoth Cave National Park**, the largest underground cave system in the world.

Fort Knox

Legendary **FORT KNOX** straddles one hundred thousand acres on either side of US-31 W, thirty miles southwest of Louisville. The bomb-proof **Bullion Depository**, on Gold Vault Road, surrounded by security fences, machine-gun turrets, patrol guards, and huge floodlights, stores nine million pounds of the federal gold reserve behind doors weighing twenty tons apiece. No visits are allowed at the depository; you can only stop by the road for a maximum of five minutes.

Bardstown and bourbon country

Forty miles south of Louisville on US-31 E, attractive **BARDSTOWN** is the place to get acquainted with Kentucky **bourbon whiskey**, created in early pioneer days, so the story goes, when Elijah Craig, a Baptist minister, added corn to the usual rye and barley. Named for Bourbon County near Lexington, Kentucky's whiskey soon gained a national reputation, thanks to crisp limestone water, strict laws concerning ingredients and production, and the skills of small-scale distillers.

Get into the spirit at Bardstown's free **Oscar Getz Museum of Whiskey History** in Spalding Hall, 114 N Fifth St (Mon–Fri 10am–5pm, Sat 10am–4pm, Sun noon–4pm; Jan & Feb closed Mon & Tues; March & April closed Mon; free; Ⓣ502/348-2999, Ⓦwww.whiskeymuseum.com). Fourteen miles west at **Clermont**, you can stop at the **Jim Beam American Outpost** (Mon–Sat 9am–4.30pm, Sun 1–4pm; free; Ⓣ502/543-9877), which has an informative museum, a film on the whiskey-making process, an outdoor moonshine still and barrel-making museum, and a Beam family home. **Maker's Mark Distillery**, twenty miles south of Bardstown on Rte-49 near **Loretto**, is an out-of-the-way collection of beautifully restored black, red, and gray plankhouses, in which whiskey is still made manually (Mon–Sat 10.30am–3.30pm, Sun March–Dec 1.30–3.30pm; free; Ⓣ502/865-2099, Ⓦwww.makersmark.com). However, don't expect a sample, as most of rural Kentucky is **dry**.

Abraham Lincoln's birthplace

On February 12, 1809, **Abraham Lincoln**, the sixteenth president of the US, was born in a one-room log cabin in the frontier wilds, son of a wandering farmer and, if some accounts are to be believed, an illiterate and illegitimate mother. Three miles south of Hodgenville, on US-31 E, the **National Historic Site** (summer daily 8am–6.45pm; rest of year daily 8am–4.45pm; free; Ⓣ270/358-3137, Ⓦwww.nps.gov/abli) has a symbolic cabin of his birth, enclosed in a granite and marble Memorial Building with 56 steps, one for each year of Lincoln's life. You can stay on the site in one of the three rustic *Nancy Lincoln Inn Cabins* (Ⓣ270/358-3845; ❸). The family moved ten miles northeast in 1811 to the **Knob Creek** area, where Lincoln's earliest memory was of slaves being forcefully driven along the road. Here you can visit another recreation of his boyhood home (daily April–Oct varying hours; free).

Mammoth Cave National Park

The three hundred and sixty-five miles of labyrinthine passages (with an average of five new miles discovered each year) and domed caverns of **MAMMOTH CAVE NATIONAL PARK** lie ten miles off I-65, around ninety miles south of Louisville. Its amazing geological formations, carved by acidic water trickling through limestone, include a bewildering display of stalagmites and stalactites, a huge cascade of flowstone known as **Frozen Niagara**, and **Echo River**, 365ft below ground, populated by a unique species of colorless and sightless fish. Among traces of human occupation are Native American artifacts, a former saltpeter mine, and the remains of an experimental tuberculosis hospital, built in 1843 in the belief that the cool atmosphere of the cave would help clear patients' lungs. It's possible to take a limited-access self-guided tour, but by far the best way to appreciate the caves is by joining one of the lengthy **ranger-guided tours** (2–6hrs. $5–48). Tickets are available from the **visitor center** (mid-April–Nov daily 8am–6.15pm; Dec–mid-April 9am–5pm; Ⓣ270/758-2328, Ⓦwww.nps.gov/maca). Make reservations (Ⓣ1-877/444-6777, Ⓦwww.recreation.gov) in advance, especially in summer, and keep in mind that the temperature in the caves is a constantly cool 54°F.

The park's attractions are by no means all subterranean. You can explore the scenic **Green River**, as it cuts through densely forested hillsides and jagged limestone cliffs, by following hiking trails or renting a canoe from Green River Canoeing (ⓣ270/597-2031 or 1-800/651-9909). **Camping** is free in the backcountry; however, a permit must be picked up first at the visitor center; the rustic *Mammoth Cave Hotel* (ⓣ270/758-2225, ⓦwww.mammothcavehotel.com; ❹) has cottages and motel **rooms**.The privately owned caves all around, many of which ruin the sights with garish light shows, and the "attractions" in nearby Cave City and Park City, are best ignored.

Tennessee

Stretching almost five hundred miles from east to west, **TENNESSEE** is full of contrasts. The traditional mountain culture of the Smoky Mountains could not be further from the blues-soaked, cotton culture of the Mississippi valley.

Only one sizeable settlement has found a foothold above the marshlands that line the Mississippi – the expansive port of **Memphis**. Tennessee's largest city, it is the birthplace of urban **blues**, and long-time home of **Elvis Presley**, and is cherished by music fans. The fine plantation homes and tidy towns of **middle Tennessee**'s rolling farmland reflect the comfortable lifestyle of its pioneers; and smack in the heart of it sprawls **Nashville** – synonymous with **country music**. The mountainous **east** shares its top attraction with North Carolina – the peaks of **Great Smoky Mountains National Park**.

Some history

Tennessee's first white settlers, most of them British Protestants, crossed the mountains in the 1770s to settle in the hills and hollows of the Appalachians. Initially relations with the **Cherokee** were good. However, demand for land increased, and confrontations throughout the state culminated in 1838 with the forced removal of the Indians on the "Trail of Tears." When the **Civil War** came, the plantation owners of the west maneuvered Tennessee into the Confederacy, against the wishes of the non-slaveholding farmers in the east. The last state to secede became the site of 424 battles and skirmishes.

Despite economic development, soil erosion and farm mechanization led to a mass migration to the cities in the years before World War I. The fundamentalist beliefs of these transplanted hill-dwellers influenced a **prohibition** movement that kept Tennessee bone-dry until 1939. Many counties still forbid the sale of alcohol. The New Deal of the 1930s brought significant changes. In particular, the **Tennessee Valley Authority**, created in 1933, harnessed the flood-prone **Tennessee River**, providing much-needed jobs and cheap power, and ignited the transition from an agricultural to an industrial economy.

Getting around Tennessee

The **airports** at Memphis and Nashville have extensive connections throughout the US, though fares between the two are high. If you harbor fantasies of traveling by **boat** along the Mississippi, note that only luxury craft make the trip these days, at prohibitive prices (see p.517). **Amtrak** calls at Memphis, and while Greyhound provides a reasonable service to major towns and cities, traveling **by bus** through the small towns in the east is very difficult. **Driving** though, is the best option, with I-40 running East to West. The mountain landscape couldn't get more breathtaking than a drive through Newfound Gap Road, which cuts a sinewy curve through the Smoky Mountains.

Memphis

Perched above the Mississippi River, **MEMPHIS** welcomes visitors to celebrate the city that gave the world **blues**, **soul**, and **rock 'n' roll**, as well as to chow down in the unrivaled **barbecue** capital of the nation. If it's the **Elvis** connection that draws you here, you won't leave disappointed. But even the King represents just one small part of the rich musical heritage of the home of **Sun** and **Stax studios**.

Culturally and geographically, Memphis has always had more in common with the delta of Mississippi and Arkansas than with the rest of Tennessee. Founded in 1819 and named for Egypt's ancient Nile capital, its fortunes rose and fell with **cotton**. The Confederate defeat that ended slavery briefly plunged the city into economic chaos, but thanks to its potential for river and rail transportation it soon bounced back. The nation's second largest inland port became a major stopping-off point for **black migrant** farmers and sharecroppers escaping the poverty of the Delta, and many stayed, significantly shaping the city's identity.

In the 1950s and 60s, Memphis had a confidence that belied its size. The city reached its lowest ebb, however, when **Dr Martin Luther King Jr** was **assassinated** here in 1968, and for a couple of decades thereafter it tottered on the brink of terminal decline, with downtown blighted by white flight. In the 1990s the city regenerated itself, pouring money into projects like the transformation of **Mud Island** and the construction of the 321ft stainless-steel **Pyramid**. More recently, downtown has seen the arrival of not only the huge **Peabody Place** mall, but also a handsome minor league baseball stadium – **Autozone Field**, home of the Redbirds – and a major performance arena, the **Fed Ex Forum**. The fabled **blues** corridor of **Beale Street** is booming once more, while the recent **Rock'n'Soul Museum**, **Gibson Guitar Plant** and **Stax Museum** keep true to the city's musical heritage. Then there is **Graceland** – a refreshing change from the usual "gracious southern home" – which provides an intimate glimpse of the city's most famous son.

Arrival and information

Memphis is on I-40 as it runs east–west and I-55 from the south. Both join I-240, which loops around the city, and cross the Mississippi River. **Memphis International Airport** is twelve miles south of downtown – a long and complicated bus trip for $1.50, but just fifteen minutes by the Yellow Cabs **limo/van** service ($15; ⓣ901/577-7700 or 1-800/796-7750, ⓦwww.premierofmemphis.com) or **taxi** ($20–25). Greyhound **buses** stop at 203 Union Ave in the heart of downtown, while the restored **Amtrak** station at 545 S Main St is on the southern edge of downtown.

The spacious **Tennessee Welcome Center**, just off I-40 downtown at 119 N Riverside and Adams – facing Mud Island at river level – is open 24 hours a day (ⓣ901/543-5333, ⓦwww.memphistravel.com). There's another **visitor center** at 3205 Elvis Presley Blvd, on the way to Graceland (same hours and phone).

City transportation and tours

The **Memphis Area Transit Authority** (Ⓣ901/274-6282, Ⓦwww.matatransit.com) operates a useful downtown **trolley** along Main Street and Riverside Drive, connecting the Pyramid and neighboring Pinch District with Beale Street, the Civil Rights Museum, and the South Main Arts District. Another trolley heads along Madison Avenue to the medical centers midtown, but this is less useful for visitors. **Fares** are the same for both ($1, Mon–Fri 11am–1.30pm 50¢, 2-trip pass $1.50, day-pass $3.50, 3-day pass $8).

Horse-drawn **carriage tours** abound downtown – prices vary but you're looking at around $45/30min. Somewhat funkier, **American Dream Safari** (Ⓣ901/527-8870, Ⓦwww.americandreamsafari.com) offers **driving tours** in a 1955 Cadillac. Ranging from a 3hr "greatest hits" jaunt ($40 per person, max 5 people) to a Sunday gospel and fried chicken outing ($75); they're pricey, but enjoyable. Another way to see the city is to float along the mighty Mississippi: **sternwheelers** leave from Riverside Drive at Monroe Avenue (April–Oct at least one daily, 2.30pm; more in summer and fewer Nov–March; 90min; $20; Ⓣ901/527-2628, Ⓦmemphisriverboats.net).

The hip folks at Shangri-La Projects – an off-shoot of the must-visit midtown record store – offer the **Ultimate Rock'n'Roll Tour** (Ⓦwww.memphisrocktour.com). This might take the form of an overview of all of Memphis's best music sites (1hr, $75 for up to two people; 3hr, $180) or be customized to your specific interests ($75/hr).

Accommodation

Downtown Memphis is the most convenient place to **stay**, with a good choice of historic hotels and upscale chains; you'll be lucky to find anything for less than $100 a night, however. There are cheaper options near Graceland on Elvis Presley Boulevard to the south. The visitor center can help you find a room, though it's best to book in advance at busy times, such as the anniversary of Elvis's death in mid-August and during the month-long Memphis in May festival (see p.520).

Days Inn Graceland 3839 Elvis Presley Blvd Ⓣ901/ 346-5500 or 1-800/329-7466. Reliable option near Graceland, with Elvis memorabilia and videos in the lobby, along with – bliss! – a guitar-shaped pool. Rates include continental breakfast. ❹

Elvis Presley's Heartbreak Hotel 3691 Elvis Presley Blvd Ⓣ901/332-1000 or 1-877/777-0606, Ⓦwww.elvis.com. An ideal choice for Elvis fans, this boutique hotel – next to Graceland – features a (small) heart-shaped pool, 24hr in-room Elvis videos, and peanut butter sandwiches in the *Jungle Room* lounge. The larger rooms come with kitchenettes, or you could splash out and stay in one of the lavish Elvis-themed suites, which sleep up to eight (and start at around $500 per night). Free downtown shuttle and breakfast. ❹

Holiday Inn Select 160 Union Ave Ⓣ901/525-5491, Ⓦwww.hisdowntownmemphis.com. In an unbeatable location opposite the *Peabody*, with good rooms at reasonable prices, an outdoor pool, and a sushi bar. ❺

Kings Court Hotel-Downtown Memphis 265 Union Ave Ⓣ901/527-4305, Ⓦwww.kingscourtmemphis.net. This newly renovated motel just off Beale Street has well-kept basic rooms at an economy rate.

The Peabody 149 Union Ave Ⓣ901/529-4000 or 1-800/732-2639, Ⓦwww.peabodymemphis.com. This opulent hotel near Beale Street is the place to stay in Memphis. Don't miss the legendary mascot ducks, who waddle from the elevator promptly at 11am, spend the day in the lobby fountain and then return to their penthouse at 5pm. Rooms are comfortably elegant, while the glorious lobby is an attraction in itself, with a friendly, relaxed bar. ❽

Sleep Inn at Court Square 40 N Front St Ⓣ901/522-9700, Ⓦwww.choicehotels.com. Offering the best value downtown, this upscale motel faces the river near Mud Island and backs onto Main Street and the trolley line. Rates include continental breakfast. Parking $8. ❹

Talbot-Heirs Guesthouse 99 S Second St Ⓣ901/527-9772 or 1-800/955-3956, Ⓦwww

.talbothouse.com. Characterful, friendly, and comfortable accommodations close to Beale Street. Each of the nine themed suites has modern furnishings, a kitchenette, CD player, and internet access. Rates include continental breakfast. ⑥

The City

With its revitalized downtown, Memphis has a friendly scale that's uncommon in cities of comparable size. **Downtown** still retains a healthy ensemble of buildings from the cotton era, best admired either along the riverfront or from the trolley route down **Main Street**. Today these edifices are more likely to have been converted into expensive apartments than house thriving businesses, but the city streets are once again busy with pedestrians. Tourist activity is concentrated around the enormous **Peabody Place** mall – which has succeeded in luring locals back downtown, even if it could really be anywhere in the US – only a hop away to the bars and clubs of **Beale Street**, the **Civil Rights** and **Rock'n'Soul** museums just beyond that, and **Sun Studio** not far east. Elsewhere, **Mud Island** on the river itself merits half a day, as does the **Stax** museum, while **Graceland**, ten miles south, should not be missed.

Beale Street and around

Beale Street began life in the mid-nineteenth century as one of Memphis's most exclusive enclaves; within fifty years its elite residents had been driven out by yellow fever epidemics and the ravages of the Civil War to be replaced by a diverse mix of blacks, Greeks, Jews, Chinese, and Italians. But it was **black culture** that gave the street its fame. Beale Street was where black roustabouts and travelers passing through Memphis immediately headed. In the Jim Crow era, Beale served as the center for black businesses, financiers, and professionals.

As the black Main Street of the mid-South, Beale in its Twenties' heyday was jammed with vaudeville theaters, concert halls, bars, and juke joints (mostly white-owned). Along with the frivolity came a reputation for heavy gambling, voodoo, murder, and prostitution. Although Beale still drew huge crowds in the Forties, the drift to the suburbs and, ironically, the success of the **civil rights** years in opening the rest of Memphis to black businesses, almost killed it off. The **bulldozers** of the late Sixties spared only the grand Orpheum Theatre, at 203 S Main St, and a few commercial buildings between Second and Fourth streets.

Beale Street has now been restored as a handsome **Historic District**. Its souvenir shops, music clubs, and cafés are bedecked with retro facades and neon signs, while a Walk of Fame with brass musical notes embedded into the sidewalk honors musical greats such as B.B. King and Howlin' Wolf. Blues fans in particular will be drawn to its music venues, which showcase top regional talent. At Beale's western end, no. 126 – the former home of the iconic **Lansky's**, tailor to the Memphis stars – was remodeled in 1997 to become an Elvis-themed restaurant; the site now stands empty, though Lansky's itself continues to thrive in a new location in the historic *Peabody* hotel (see p.511).

A. Schwab's Dry Goods Store remains at 163 Beale. Little changed since it opened in 1876. It's a treasure trove, with an incredible array of paraphernalia – best-sellers include Mojo Hands and High John the Conqueror lucky roots (closed Sun). Further east, at no. 352, the tiny former home of **W.C. Handy** – moved here from its original site at 659 Janette St – offers another evocative sense of old Memphis. In 1910, Handy was the first man to publish blues tunes (often blues in name only; see p.542).

One block south of Beale, in the plaza of the enormous FedEx Forum, the **Rock'n'Soul Museum** (daily 10am–7pm, last admission 6.15pm; $10), is an ideal place to start a musical tour of Memphis. Presenting the story of the city's musical

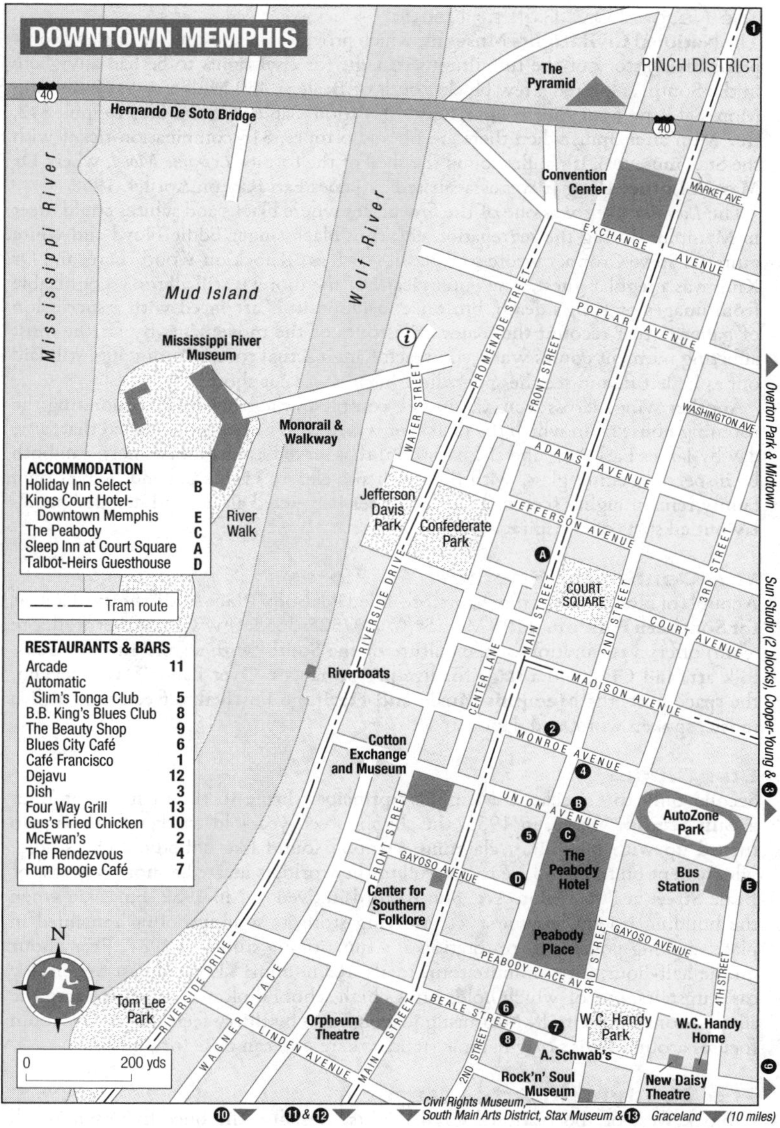

heritage scrapbook-style, it makes connections between such issues as migration, racism, civil rights, and youth culture, with a host of artifacts ranging from Elvis's stage gear and one of B.B. King's "Lucille" guitars to Al Green's Bible.

Also in the plaza, the **Gibson Guitar Factory** offers guided tours that allow you to watch the manufacture of those classic six-string and bass guitars so beloved by musicians like King and Chuck Berry (Mon–Sat hourly 11am–4pm, Sun hourly noon–4pm; $10; must be 5 or older; ⓦ www.gibsonmemphis.com).

The National Civil Rights Museum

The **National Civil Rights Museum**, which provides the most rewarding and comprehensive history of the tumultuous struggle for civil rights to be had anywhere in the South, is located a few blocks south of Beale at 450 Mulberry St (June–Aug Mon–Sat 9am–6pm, Sun 1–6pm; Sept–May Mon–Sat 9am–5pm, Sun 1–5pm; $12, free Mon after 3pm, when there are no audio tours; $15 combination ticket with the Stax museum). It's built around the shell of the former *Lorraine Motel*, where **Dr Martin Luther King Jr** was assassinated by James Earl Ray on April 4, 1968.

The *Lorraine* itself was one of the few places where blacks and whites could meet in Memphis during the segregation era; thus black singer Eddie Floyd and white guitarist Steve Cropper wrote soul classics such as "Knock on Wood" here, and Dr King was a regular guest. The outer facade of the motel is still all too recognizable from images of King's death, but once inside visitors are faced with a succession of galleries that recount the major milestones of the movement. By far the most affecting moment comes when you reach King's actual room, Room 306, still laid out as he left it, and see the spot where his life was cut short.

Another wing, across from the motel, completes the story by incorporating the rooming house from which the fatal shot was fired. The bedroom rented that same day by James Earl Ray, and the bathroom that served as his sniper's nest, can both be inspected behind glass, with the death site clearly visible beyond. King's own family remain highly sceptical as to whether Ray acted alone, and detailed panels lay out all sorts of conspiracy theories.

The Center for Southern Folklore

A couple of blocks west of the chain store-filled **Peabody Place Mall**, the tiny **Center for Southern Folklore**, 119 S Main St (Ⓣ901/525-3655, Ⓦwww.southernfolklore.com) offers a celebration of the culture of the South, with a store full of books, folk art, and CDs, and a stage for live performances. Over Labor Day weekend, the space hosts the **Memphis Music and Heritage Festival**, a free event of live music, spoken word, and dance.

Sun Studio

Second only to Graceland, Memphis's principal shrine to the memory of Elvis is **Sun Studio**, where, in 1953, the shy eighteen-year-old trucker from Tupelo turned up with his guitar, claiming, "I don't sound like nobody." The studio, which went on to introduce rock'n'roll to the world, is located a short way east of Beale Street at 706 Union Ave. Sun Records moved out in 1959, but even when the building briefly became a scuba-diving store its soundproofing remained in place, making possible its restoration as a functioning studio in 1987. Every hour on the half-hour, forty-minute tours (daily 10am–6pm; $12) lead past the display cases upstairs, one of which holds Elvis's high school diploma, and down into the single-room studio itself. Measuring just eighteen by thirty feet, the shabby room focuses around Elvis's original mic stand, where you can pose for photos.

The South Main Arts District

A block west of the National Civil Rights Museum, the once flyblown South Main Street has been given a new lease of life. Spanning the eight or so blocks along Main between Vance and G. E. Patterson avenues, the **South Main Arts District** (Ⓦwww.southmainmemphis.org) is a burgeoning area of galleries, boutiques and restaurants, complete with a crop of condos and lofts. It's particularly buzzing on the last Friday of the month, when the free "Art Trolley" (6–9pm) runs along Main and the parallel Tennessee Street, and stores offer complimentary snacks and drinks. Look out for *D'Edge* gallery, 550 Main St (Ⓣ901/521-0054,

▲ Sun Studio

Ⓦwww.d-edgeart.com), which features the folk art-inspired work of African-American artist George Hunt.

The Stax Museum of American Soul Music

In 2003 one of the city's most famous addresses, 926 E McLemore Ave, was resurrected. In 1960, this spot was occupied by the Capitol Theater, the central landmark of a neighborhood where blacks had just started to outnumber whites. The theater went on to become the headquarters of the **Stax** record label, where over the next fifteen years artists such as Otis Redding, Isaac Hayes, and Albert King achieved 237 entries in the top 100. The studio was a veritable powerhouse of funky soul; by 1990, however, with Stax long since defunct, 926 E McLemore Ave was no more than a derelict lot.

Now the complex has been reconstructed larger than ever, with a music academy sitting next to the **Stax Museum of American Soul Music**, also known as **Soulsville** (March–Oct Mon–Sat 9am–4pm, Sun 1–4pm; Nov–Feb Mon–Sat 10am–4pm, Sun 1–4pm; $10, $15 combination ticket with the Civil Rights Museum). Visits start with a film history of the label, using stunning footage to illuminate both the triumphs and the tensions that arose from its status as a joint black-white enterprise in the segregated South. The first exhibit beyond, designed to emphasize the gospel roots of soul music, is an entire Episcopal Church, transported here from Duncan, Mississippi. Showpiece artifacts include Isaac Hayes's peacock-blue and gold Cadillac. The actual Stax studio has been recreated in detail, featuring the original two-track tape recorder used by Otis Redding to record "Mr Pitiful" and "Respect." A map of the immediate neighborhood, still largely rundown, shows what an amazing assembly of talent lived nearby; Aretha Franklin was born at 406 Lucy Ave.

The riverfront

The northern boundary of downtown Memphis is marked by the 32-storey, 321ft **Pyramid**, two-thirds the size of Egypt's Great Pyramid. Completed in 1991, it was intended to create a symbolic link with Egypt's Nile Delta. After a decade and a half hosting major exhibitions, concerts, and games it has since been overshadowed by the FedEx Forum and lain empty since 2005. While it remains to be seen what the future holds for this marvelous folly – at the time of press there is talk that it will become a Bass Pro Shop – its symbolism is undeniable. The surrounding neighborhood, the historic **Pinch District**, is named for the impoverished – "pinched" – Irish immigrants who settled here in the mid-1800s.

From Riverside Drive, which runs south from the Pyramid, **monorail trains** and a walkway head across the Mississippi's Wolf Channel to **Mud Island** (Tues–Sun: April, May, Sept & Oct 10am–5pm; June–Aug 10am–6pm; park access free, monorail $4 or included in museum admission, $8). Highlights of the island's **Mississippi River Museum** include a full-sized reconstructed steam packet squeezed into the core of the building, a morbidly fascinating "Theater of Disasters," and tales of characters like keelboatman Mike Fink, who in 1830 styled himself "half horse, half alligator." **River Walk**, which runs to the southern tip of the island is a scale replica of the lower Mississippi River. From the pavilion nearby, it's also possible to rent canoes ($20/hr) and kayaks ($15/hr); in summer, you can even bring a sleeping bag and join a mass campout where the tent, dinner, breakfast and entertainment is laid on (second Fri of each month April–Oct; ⓣ901/576-7241).

Back on the mainland, south of the monorail, **Jefferson Davis** and **Confederate parks** hold little of interest. Heading south along **Front Street**, however, brings you to the imposing buildings of **Cotton Row**. This area might have seen busier days, but it is still the largest spot cotton market (meaning actual cotton is sold here, for cash) in the world. Memphis's **Cotton Museum**, in the grand old Cotton Exchange at Front Street and 65 Union Ave, outlines the history of the "white gold" that has had such a huge influence on the economy and culture of the South (Tues–Sat 10am–5pm, Sun noon–5pm; $5).

Further south, **Tom Lee Park**, the venue for major outdoor events such as the **Memphis in May** festival (see p.520), runs for about a mile and a half along the river. The park commemorates a black boatman who rescued 32 people from a sinking boat in 1925 – despite not being able to swim.

Graceland

In itself, Elvis Presley's **Graceland** was a surprisingly modest home for the world's most successful entertainer – it's certainly not the "mansion" you may have imagined. And while Elvis was clearly a man who indulged his tastes to the fullest, Graceland has none of the pomposity that characterizes so many other showpiece

The Big Muddy

I do not know much about gods; but I think that the river
Is a strong brown god – sullen, untamed and intractable.

St Louis–born T.S. Eliot, *The Four Quartets*

North America's principal waterway, the **Mississippi** – the name comes from the Algonquin words for "big" and "river" – starts just ninety miles south of the Canadian border at Lake Itasca, Minnesota, and winds its way nearly 2400 miles to the Gulf of Mexico, taking in over one hundred tributaries en route and draining all or part of thirty-one US states and two Canadian provinces.

The **"Big Muddy"** – it carries 2lb of dirt for every 1000lb of water – is one of the busiest commercial rivers in the world, and one of the least conventional. Instead of widening toward its mouth, like most rivers, the Mississippi grows narrower and deeper. Its **delta**, near Memphis, more than three hundred miles upstream from the river's mouth, is not a delta at all, but an alluvial flood plain.

In the words of Mark Twain, who spent four years on it as a riverboat pilot, the Mississippi is also "the **crookedest** river in the world." As it weaves and curls its way extravagantly along its channel, it continually cuts through narrow necks of land to shape and reshape oxbow lakes and meander scars, cutoffs, and marshy backwaters. A nightclub could operate one day in Arkansas and then find itself in dry Tennessee the next, thanks to an overnight cutoff.

A more serious manifestation of the Mississippi's power is its propensity to **flood**. Although the river builds its own levees, artificial embankments have, since as early as 1717, helped to safeguard crops and homes. After the disastrous floods of 1927, the federal government installed a wide range of flood-protection measures; virtually the entire riverfront from Cape Girardeau, Missouri, to the sea is now walled in, and it's even possible to drive along the top of the larger levees.

While it's no longer feasible to sail Twain's route for yourself, **riverboat excursions** operate in most sizeable river towns, including Memphis (see p.511). Longer cruises, between St Louis and New Orleans – or even further afield – on the luxurious *Delta Queen*, *American Queen*, and *Mississippi Queen* **paddlewheelers**, are expensive; contact the Delta Queen Steamboat Company (Ⓣ1-800/543-1949, Ⓦwww.deltaqueen.com).

Southern residences. Visits are affectionate celebrations of the man; never exactly tongue-in-cheek, but not cloyingly reverential either.

Elvis was just 22 when he paid $100,000 for Graceland in 1957. Built in 1939, the stone-clad house was then considered one of the most desirable properties in Memphis, though today the neighborhood is distinctly less exclusive, its main thoroughfare – **Elvis Presley Boulevard** – lined with discount liquor stores, ancient beauty parlors, fast-food joints, and surprisingly few Elvis-related souvenir shops. Tours start opposite the house in **Graceland Plaza**; excited visitors, kitted out with headphones, are ferried across the road in minibuses, which depart every few minutes and sweep through the house's famous "musical gate," etched with musical notes and Elvis's silhouette. No stops are made at the perimeter "Wall of Love," scrawled with tens of thousands of messages from fans, but you are free to walk back there after the tour.

The audio tours, peppered with spoken memories from Elvis's daughter, Lisa Marie, and rousing choruses from the King himself, allow you to spend as long as you wish, although the upstairs rooms are out of bounds to visitors. The interior is a frozen tribute to the taste of the Seventies; choice viewings include the Hawaiian-themed **Jungle Room**, with its waterfall and green shag-carpeted ceiling, where Elvis recorded "Moody Blue" and other gems from his latter years, the **Pool**

Room, whose walls and ceiling are covered in bright paisley fabric suggesting a little documented psychedelic phase, and the navy-and-lemon **TV Room**, mirrored and fitted with three screens that now show classic 1970s TV shows. A former garage allows you to see many personal items that Elvis kept upstairs, ranging from a spectacular white, circular, fur bed to his very ordinary bedroom slippers, and including philosophy books scrawled with his musings, his extensive gun collection, and whippet-slim suits from the 1960s.

In the separate **Trophy Room**, you parade past Elvis's platinum, gold, and silver records, stage costumes, and outfits from many of his 31 films; footage of his early TV performances offers breathtaking reminders of just how charismatic the young Elvis was. The tour of the interior ends with the **racquetball room**, where he played on the morning he died. In the attached lounge, the piano where he sang for the last time (apparently "Unchained Melody") stands eerily silent, while in the court itself his resplendent, bejeweled capes and Vegas jumpsuits stand sentinel beneath huge monitors showing his later performances. Here, perhaps more than anywhere else, you can feel the huge presence of the man who changed the face of music forever.

Elvis (Jan 8, 1935–Aug 16, 1977), his mother, Gladys, his father, Vernon, and his grandmother, Minnie Mae, lie buried in the **Meditation Garden** outside, their graves strewn with flowers and soft toys sent from fans. Elvis's body was moved here two months after his death, when security problems at the local cemetery became unmanageable. There's often a log-jam here, as visitors crane to read the messages sent by fans, take moments to offer their own prayers, and snap photos of the bronze memorial plaques.

Graceland Plaza, resounding with nonstop Elvis hits, holds several enjoyable extra attractions: don't miss the wittily edited film *Walk a Mile in My Shoes*, the "**Sincerely Elvis**" timeline, which follows 1956, the year he made it big, month by month, and Elvis's personal **airplanes**, including the *Lisa Marie*, customized with 24-carat gold washroom sink and blue suede furnishings. End your tour with a sit-down in the **Elvis Presley Automobile Museum**, which, quite apart from a Harley-Davidson golf cart and powder-pink Cadillac, shows action-packed and vaguely car-related clips from his movies. **Elvis After Dark**, in the shabby mall next door, ostensibly covers the notoriously playful Presley's leisure time, but compared to the rest of the complex it feels like little more than an add-on to the neighbouring gift store. Completists, however, will not want to miss the TV punctured by a bullet fired by Elvis himself (he also shot his fridge, his stereo, and even Lisa Marie's slide). The Plaza's many **gift stores** and its clutch of Elvis-themed **diners** (try to seat yourself in the 1950s Cadillac for the barbecue at the *Chrome Grill*) make it easy to stay all day.

Graceland practicalities

Graceland is ten miles southeast of downtown Memphis, at 3734 Elvis Presley Blvd. The ticket office is open March–Oct Mon–Sat 9am–5pm, Sun 10am–4pm; Nov daily 10am–4pm; Dec–Feb Mon & Wed–Sun 10am–4pm. The last house tour starts at the ticket office's closing time, while the other attractions remain open for roughly another two hours.

A combined Platinum **ticket** to all the main attractions (allow three hours) is $32; house tours only, $27; parking $8. The $68 VIP tour is barely worth it, only granting access to a room with a few extra personal items and allowing you to by-pass queues. **Reservations** are recommended, especially in August (Ⓣ 901/332-3322 or 1-800/238-2000, Ⓦ www.elvis.com).

Midtown and East Memphis

The centerpiece of wooded **Overton Park**, three or so miles east of downtown on Poplar Avenue, is the **Memphis Zoo** (daily: March–Oct 9am–6pm; Nov–Feb 9am–5pm; last admission 1hr before closing; $13, $3 parking). If the usual array of gorillas, orangutans, and giraffes doesn't satisfy you, you can visit with a pair of giant pandas. The park also holds the **Memphis Brooks Museum of Art** (Tues & Wed, 10am–4pm, Thurs 10am–8pm, Fri 10am–4pm, Sat 10am–5pm, Sun 11.30am–5pm; $7), whose array of fine art features a strong collection of medieval and Renaissance works.

A mile or so south of the park, the **Cooper-Young** intersection boasts a handful of funky espresso bars and restaurants, along with a good crop of vintage stores. It's a lively place, quite different from downtown but still distinctly Memphis, where blues and barbecue rub along with poetry readings and yard sales, art exhibits and antique auctions. Its one-day **festival** (Ⓦ www.cooperyoungfestival.com), held in September, attracts huge crowds for its folk arts, regional crafts, and local music.

A couple of miles further southeast, the **Memphis Pink Palace Museum and Planetarium** at 3050 Central Ave (Mon–Sat 9am–5pm, Sun noon–5pm; $8.75) centers on the marble mansion of Clarence Saunders, who founded America's first chain of self-service **supermarkets**, Piggly-Wiggly, in 1916. Saunders went bankrupt in 1923 and never actually lived here; instead, the building acquired several new wings in the process of becoming an appealingly old-fashioned and rather quirky museum of Memphis history. It holds all kinds of stuffed animals and oddities, including a gory exhibit on the city's early years and a fascinating walk-through model of the first Piggly-Wiggly store. There's also an IMAX cinema and the **Sharpe Planetarium**.

Eating

Memphians are fond of their food, and proclaim their city to be the **pork barbecue** capital of the world. There's far more to Memphis than BBQ, however – **soul food** fans will be delighted, as will anyone who likes inventive **contemporary Southern cuisine**. You'll have no problem finding somewhere good **downtown** – note that several of the Beale Street clubs reviewed under "Nightlife" on p.520 also serve food – or in the eclectic **Cooper-Young** district.

Arcade 540 S Main St ⓣ 901/526–5757. Said to be Memphis's oldest restaurant, this landmark diner – Elvis ate here! – in the South Main District was featured in Jim Jarmusch's movie *Mystery Train*, among many others. Come here for large Southern breakfasts, pizzas, and home cooking. Daily 8am–3pm.

Automatic Slim's Tonga Club 83 S Second St ⓣ 901/525-7948. A Memphis institution in the heart of downtown, where you can eat Southwestern-tinged global cuisine – coconut-crusted fish served with jicama slaw and avocado, for example – in comfortably hip surroundings. Closed Sun.

The Beauty Shop 966 S Cooper ⓣ 901/272-7111. The witty retro fittings – glass brick partitions, mismatched crockery, 1940s hairdryer chairs – are perfectly in tune with Cooper-Young's funky vintage-store flair, while the eclectic fusion food (lunch, dinner and Sunday brunch) is tasty and satisfying.

Café Francisco 400 N Main St ⓣ 901/578-8002. Hunker down on an overstuffed velvet sofa or at a rickety table in this cavernous, effortlessly boho and very relaxing coffeehouse that also serves good light meals. It's on the trolley route, near the Pyramid in the Pinch district. Free wi-fi.

Dejavu 936 Florida ⓣ 901/942-1400. Chow down on Creole soul food and vegetarian fare at this healthy and affordable downtown spot, which used to be a small church. Entrees change daily with a seasonal focus. Closed Sunday.

Dish 948 S Cooper ⓣ 901/276-0002. Right in the heart of the trendy Cooper-Young district, this minimalist restaurant serves tapas and sushi to a fashionable crowd. After 10pm live DJ's get the dancing started.

Four Way Grill 998 Mississippi Blvd ⓣ 901/507-1519. Convenient for the Stax museum, this spotless little soul food joint – a favourite haunt of Martin Luther King Jr – dishes up unbeatable blue plate specials at unbelievably low prices. Closed Mon.

Gus's Fried Chicken 310 S Front St ⓣ901/527-4877. This tiny downhome place near the South Main Arts District has caught the attention of the national press for its delicious, crackling-crisp and spicy chicken – don't miss it.

Interstate Bar-B-Que 2265 S Third St ⓣ901/775-2304, ⓦwww.jimneelysinterstatebarbecue.com. Legendary barbecue restaurant, south of downtown (leave I–55 at exit 7) on the way to the Delta. Try the barbecue spaghetti. Closed Sun.

Java Cabana 2170 Young Ave ⓣ901/272-7210. Friendly alternative coffeehouse in the Cooper-Young district, with poetry readings and live music. Closed Mon.

McEwan's 122 Monroe Ave ⓣ901/527-7085. At the heart of downtown, four blocks north of Beale, McEwan's has the ambiance of a cosy neighborhood bistro, serving inventive and delicious modern Southern cooking in a brick-walled room. The laid-back adjoining bar is also a local favorite.

Otherlands 641 S Cooper Ave ⓣ901/278-4994. Funky Midtown coffeehouse that's good for espresso, juices and fresh sandwiches. The laid-back crowd hangs out for hours in the warren of rooms, with their jumble of tatty sofas, armchairs, and even desks. Open until 8pm Mon–Sat, 7pm weekends.

The Rendezvous General Washburn Alley, 52 S Second St ⓣ901/523-2746, ⓦwww.hogsfly.com. Downtown Memphis's most famous pork barbecue joint, tucked away in a back alley, is colossal and very crowded. Enjoy the inexpensive meat feasts in a hectic atmosphere. Open Tues–Sat.

Nightlife and entertainment

Memphis's thriving **live music** scene is at its best during the city's many **festivals**, especially the month-long **Memphis in May** (ⓦwww.memphisinmay.org), where big-name music performances run side by side with the World Championship Barbecue Cooking Contest, and August's **Elvis Tribute Week**.

At other times touristy **Beale Street**'s close-packed assortment of music clubs actually has plenty to offer. The whole enclave is successful both architecturally and atmospherically, with street musicians adding to the ambiance. On Friday nights, a $10 wristband offers admission to all the major clubs. The stage in **W.C. Handy Park**, on Beale at Third Street, also features live bands – most nights for free. At the other end of the scale, the city's vibrant punk and garage scene sees **alternative bands** playing hole-in-the-walls.

Beyond its music, Memphis is also a good place for movie lovers, with classic films shown at the grand old Orpheum during the summer, an increasingly popular international **film festival** in April, and, in October, the edgy **Indie Memphis**, which focuses on low-budget Southern movies.

The best source of **listings** is the free weekly *Memphis Flyer* (ⓦwww.memphisflyer.com). You could also pop into Shangri-La Records, a treasure trove of Memphis music, midtown at 1916 Madison Ave (ⓣ901/274-1916, ⓦwww.shangri.com), for flyers and news of upcoming gigs.

B.B. King's Blues Club 147 Beale St ⓣ901/524-KING. Despite accusations from purists of having "sold out," this remains Beale's most popular club. It's spacious and lovely, with regular blues (among other music) – and the barbecue's not bad, either. B.B. himself appears once or twice a year.

Blues City Café 138 Beale St ⓣ901/526-3637, ⓦwww.bluescitycafe.com. Popular Beale Street barbecue joint where musicians from nearby clubs dine on well-priced ribs, catfish, tamales, and gumbo. Live music nightly until late, in a down-home atmosphere. Open daily 11am–3am (5am at weekends).

Buccaneer Lounge 1368 Monroe Ave ⓣ901/278-0909. This grungy midtown venue – with a kind of pirate-themed junk store ambiance – is one of the city's best places to see local underground bands.

Earnestine and Hazel's 531 S Main St ⓣ901/523-9754. A legendary brothel-turned-juke joint, this spot was the haunt of everyone from Elvis to the Stax musicians. It's especially good late at night, when the Memphis music juke box blasts and the famed burgers start sizzling.

HiTone Café 1913 Poplar Ave ⓣ901/278-8663, ⓦwww.hitonememphis.com. From Memphis garage bands to comedians to Elvis impersonators, this eclectic Midtown bar/club is always worth checking out.

Hollywood Raiford's 115 Vance Ave ⓣ901/528-9313. Considered the most happening after-hours dance club, the hotspot was sold and gut-renovated with the previous owner's blessing. Raiford still comes In to DJ and the party continues to be the place to get down to funk jams from the 1970s, 80s, and 90s.

New Daisy Theater 330 Beale St ⓣ901/525-8981, ⓦwww.newdaisy.com. Restored movie theater at the east end of Beale that attracts a young, pierced crowd for its punk, metal, boxing, and hardcore wrestling.

P&H Café 1532 Madison Ave ⓣ901/726-0906. ⓦwww.pandhcafe.com. Legendary hole-In-the-wall. The coldest pitchers of beer are poured here, where the local hipsters, artists, and musicians rub shoulders.

Rum Boogie Café 182 Beale St ⓣ901/528-0150. ⓦwww.rumboogie.com. Live blues is staged in the main room, while the smaller and more intimate Blues Hall, adjoining, is a mocked-up juke joint that regularly hosts anything from boogie blues to frenetic punkabilly.

Wild Bill's 1580 Vollintine Ave ⓣ901/726-5473. Neighborhood juke joint where visitors are welcome to join locals at the long tables for laid-back live blues and soul Fri–Sun. Located three miles northeast of downtown, in North Memphis.

Young Avenue Deli 2119 Young Ave ⓣ901/278-0034, ⓦwww.youngavenuedeli.com. Misleadingly named Cooper-Young favorite, featuring almost nightly local and national rock, folk, punk, and alt bands.

Shiloh National Military Park

Approximately 110 miles east of Memphis and twelve southwest of Savannah, Tennessee, via US-64 and Hwy-22, **Shiloh National Military Park** (daily 8am–5pm; $5 per vehicle; ⓣ731/689-5696, ⓦwww.nps.gov/shil) commemorates one of the most crucial battles of the Civil War. After victories at Fort Henry and Fort Donelson, General Grant's confident Union forces were all but defeated at Shiloh by a surprise early-morning Confederate attack on April 6, 1862. A stubborn rump of resistance held on until around 5pm, and the Confederates elected to finish the task off the next morning rather than launching a twilight assault. However, Grant's decimated regiments were bolstered by the overnight arrival of reinforcements, and instead it was their dawn initiative that forced the tired and demoralized Confederates to retreat. In the end, over twenty thousand men had been killed.

The **visitor center** displays artifacts recovered from the battlefield. A self-guided ten-mile driving tour takes in the **National Cemetery**, whose moss-covered walls contain thousands of unidentified graves.

Nashville

Set amid the gentle hills and farmlands of central Tennessee, sprawling **NASHVILLE** attracts millions of visitors each year. The majority come to immerse themselves in **country music**, whether at mainstream showcases like the **Country Music Hall of Fame** and the **Grand Ole Opry**, or in the smaller clubs and honky-tonks found not only downtown but also in Nashville's many neighborhoods.

Behind the rhinestone glitter and showbiz exists a hard-working conservative city. Nashville has been the leading settlement in middle Tennessee since **Fort Nashborough** was established in 1779. A state capital since 1843, it is now the **financial** and **insurance** center of the mid-South. Rapid development since World War II has transformed a once-compact town into a maze-like conurbation, stretching out in all directions along the undulating roads, here known as **pikes**.

For all its "Nash-Vegas" image, the city has maintained a strong reputation for **learning** since planter times. As well as holding over a thousand **churches** – more

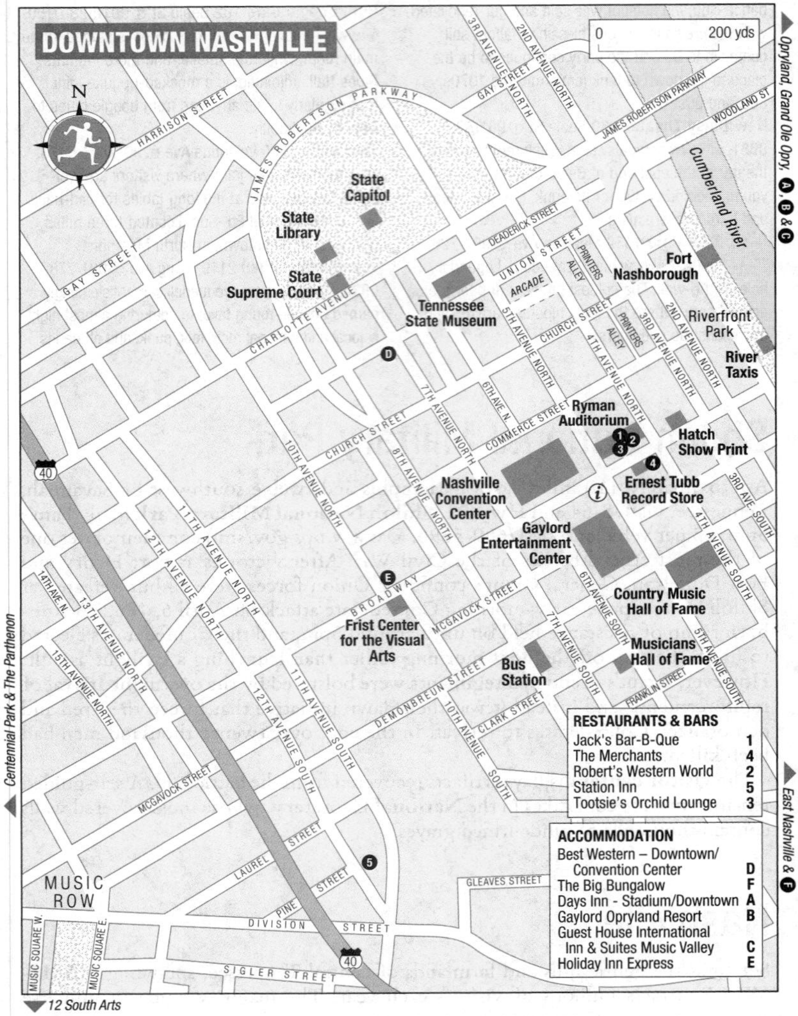

per capita than anywhere else in the country – it has been tagged the "Protestant Vatican" for its proliferation of training colleges for preachers and missionaries, church administrative offices, and Bible-publishing plants.

Arrival, information, and getting around

Nashville International Airport is eight miles – around a $25 **taxi** ride – southeast of downtown. The Gray Line shuttle (every 15–20min 5am–11pm; $12 one way, $20 round-trip; ⓣ 615/883-5555) drops off at most downtown hotels; Metropolitan Transit Authority **buses** leave hourly ($1.60; ⓣ 615/862-5950, ⓦ www.nashvillemta.org). The **Greyhound** station is in a seedy part of downtown at 200 Eighth Ave S. There's no Amtrak service.

The best place to pick up information on the city is the excellent **visitor center**, downtown at Fifth and Broadway, in the massive Gaylord Entertainment Center (Mon–Sat 8.30am–5.30pm, Sun 10am–5pm; ⓣ615/259-4747 or 1-800/657-6910, ⓦwww.visitmusiccity.com); the second branch, 150 4th Ave N (Mon–Fri 8am–5pm; ⓣ615/259-4731), is also good.

If you like your country music laid on with lots of campy fun, hop aboard the "Big Pink Bus" and let the singing guides of **Nash-Trash Tours** dish the dirt on all your favorite stars (Wed–Sat, 90min; $29.50; reservations essential; ⓣ615/226-7300 or ⓣ1-800/342-2132, ⓦwww.nashtrash.com).

Accommodation

The CVB's **Central Reservations Center** (ⓣ1-800/657-6910) offers discounted rates on most city hotels; the budget **motels** are concentrated a couple of miles north of downtown, off the I-65 Trinity Lane/Brick Church Pike exit. Rates are usually higher in June during the CMA Music Festival (formerly Fan Fair; see p.526). There's RV and tent **camping** at *Opryland KOA*, 2626 Music Valley Drive (ⓣ615/889-0286 or 1-800/562-7789, ⓦwww.nashvillekoa.com), set in 27 attractive acres and with free live music shows in the summer.

Best Western – Downtown/Convention Center 711 Union St ⓣ615/242-4311 or 1-800/627-3297. Cheap motel on the north side of downtown, facing the capitol. Rates include continental breakfast. ❸

The Big Bungalow 618 Fatherland St ⓣ615/256-8375, ⓦwww.thebigbungalow.com. An artistically-kept funky B&B in the heart of East Nashville. Amenities include a massage therapist on the premises and occasional live music performed by local Nashville musicians in the living room. Rates include a breakfast prepared by the innkeeper.

Days Inn – Stadium/Downtown 211 N First St ⓣ615/254-1551 or 1-800/251-3038, ⓦwww.daysinn.com. Inexpensive hotel near downtown with basic rooms. The area can feel unsafe at night, so take a cab. ❸

Gaylord Opryland Resort 2800 Opryland Drive ⓣ1-888/777-6779. Unbelievably vast, 3000-room place – included here not because it's recommended, but simply because it's used by so many tour groups. It takes an age simply to get to or from your luxurious rooms decorated with modern Southern flair, let alone drive the nine miles downtown. Suites can cost as much as $3500. ❼

GuestHouse International Inn & Suites Music Valley 2420 Music Valley Drive ⓣ615/885-4030. Clean, comfortable and good-value option near the Gaylord Opryland and Grand Ole Opry. Rates include continental breakfast. ❹

Holiday Inn Express 920 Broadway ⓣ615/244-0150. A good downtown option with a pool and free breakfast buffet. ❺

The City

Other than the venerable structures you'd expect in a state capital, such as the Capitol building itself, the major landmarks of **downtown Nashville** are the **Country Music Hall of Fame**, at Fifth and Demonbreun streets, and the gigantic **Gaylord Entertainment Center** sports and entertainment complex (formerly the Nashville Arena), at Fifth Avenue and Broadway.

Further afield, **Music Row**, which centers on Demonbreun Street a mile southwest of downtown, forms the heart of Nashville's recording industry, with companies like Warner Bros., Mercury, and Sony operating out of plush office blocks – there's little of interest to tourists.

Nine miles northeast of downtown in the **Opryland** area and along **Music Valley Drive**, you'll find not only the **Grand Ole Opry** – which still hosts its famed live radio show – but also several old-fashioned country music-related sights.

The Country Music Hall of Fame

Nashville's premier visitor attraction is the **Country Music Hall of Fame**, 222 Fifth Ave S (daily 9am–5pm; $19.95, $25.95 including admission to Studio B, $32.95 including admission to both). The building itself is an architectural tour de force, laden with musical symbolism – the whole thing is in the shape of a bass clef – but what really makes it special are the exhibits. Alongside paraphernalia from countless stars, including Elvis's gold Cadillac, you get a detailed history of the genre from its earliest roots. As well, songwriters and musicians give regular live demonstrations of their skills. The **Hall of Fame** itself is somewhat anticlimactic, simply consisting of a circular chamber filled with plaques.

The Hall of Fame also offers short **bus tours** that provide the only way to visit RCA's legendary **Studio B** on Music Row. Between 1957 and 1977, forty gold records were cut here, including Dolly Parton's "Jolene," but it's probably most famous for a thirteen-year run of Elvis hits. Recently restored and rewired, it's once again open for business, but only the most dedicated of fans are likely to find walking through the bare rooms interesting.

▲ Ernest Tubb Record Shop

Downtown Nashville

Most of **downtown Nashville** looks much like any other regional business center, though it's worth strolling along both **Broadway** and **Second Avenue** to enjoy the assortment of honky-tonks, bars, restaurants, and gift stores. In business since 1879, the unmissable **Hatch Show Print**, 316 Broadway (Mon–Fri 9am–5pm, Sat 10am–5pm; Ⓣ615/256-2805), prints and sells posters from the early days of country and rock 'n' roll, using the original blocks, and continues to produce new work. Opposite, another institution, **Ernest Tubb Record Shop** (Ⓣ615/255-7503, Ⓦwww.etrecordshop.com), sells vintage and rare country and bluegrass music, and displays Grand Ole Opry costumes.

The original home of the Grand Ole Opry, the **Ryman Auditorium**, 116 Fifth Ave, can be seen on self-guided tours (daily 9am–4pm; $12.50; $16.25 for occasional backstage tours; Ⓦwww.ryman.com). A church-like space, its wooden pews illuminated by stained glass, it really evokes the heyday of traditional country. You can still catch the odd live evening performance by big-name bands.

Spreading its remit beyond country music, the **Musicians Hall of Fame** (Mon–Thurs 10am–6pm, Fri & Sat 10am–5pm; $14.95; Ⓦwww.musicianshalloffame.com), a few blocks away at 301 Sixth Ave S, pays homage to the session musicians often overlooked. Instruments, photos, film footage, and recordings tell the story of the generations of players who provided the backbone for some of the most famous songs ever recorded.

Downtown also has some non-music-related diversions. Housed in a gorgeous Art Deco building, the **Frist Center for the Visual Arts**, 919 Broadway (Mon–Wed 10am–5.30pm, Thurs & Fri 10am–9pm, Sat 10am–5:30pm, Sun 1–5pm; $8.50; Ⓦwww.fristcenter.org), features everything from sculpture and photography to ancient art. At the other end of Broadway, **Riverfront Park** dips down to the **Cumberland River**. Immediately north, a replica of the wooden **Fort Nashborough** serves as a monument to the city's founders of 1779. A few blocks north again, **Tennessee State Museum**, 505 Deaderick St (Tues–Sat 10am–5pm, Sun 1–5pm; free), is strongest on Civil War history, highlighting the hardships suffered by the soldiers on both sides, of whom 23,000 out of 77,000 died at Shiloh (see p.521).

West of Downtown

In 1897, Tennessee celebrated its Centennial Exposition in **Centennial Park**, two miles southwest of downtown at West End and 25th avenues. Nashville honored its nickname as the "Athens of the South" by constructing a full-sized wood-and-plaster replica of the **Parthenon**. That proved so popular that it was replaced by a permanent structure in 1931, that's now home to Nashville's premier **art museum** (Tues–Sat 9am–4.30pm; June–Aug also Sun 12.30–4.30pm; $5). The upper hall is dominated by a gilded 42ft replica of Phidias's statue of the goddess Athena – said to be the largest indoor statue in the Western hemisphere.

Just across West End Avenue from Centennial Park, weather-beaten Gothic structures sit alongside more modern buildings on the campus of the prestigious **Vanderbilt University**. South of here, 21st Avenue S runs through the heart of the colorful **Hillsboro Village**, abounding in cafés, restaurants, and antique stores. Half a mile northeast of Centennial Park, **Fisk University** is one of the nation's oldest black colleges. The excellent **Van Vechten Gallery**, on campus at Jackson St and 18th Ave N (Tues–Fri 10am–5pm, Sat & Sun 1–5pm; closed Sun in summer; donation), holds works by Picasso, Cézanne, Renoir, and Georgia O'Keeffe; it also has changing exhibits on African-American themes. Just east, 12th Avenue South from Wedgewood Avenue to Sevier Park is the bustling **12 South Arts** district, with a multitude of hip boutiques, coffee shops, galleries and bars.

Eating

Nashville has its share of awful chains, but it also offers many down-home Southern joints, as well as upscale places well suited for expense-account dining. Many live music venues (see below) also serve food.

Arnold's 605 8th Ave S ⓣ615/256-4455. Classic canteen for Southern meat-and-three meals (featuring meat, three vegetables, and cornbread and/or rolls). The delicious country cooking includes fried chicken, ham, or pork chops with side dishes for around $7. Get there early for lunch to avoid a long wait. Mon–Fri 10.30am–2.45pm.

Frothy Monkey 2509 12 Ave South ⓣ615/292-1808, ⓦwww.frothymonkeynashville.com. At the epicenter of the edgy 12 South Arts district, this cafe serves up locally and organically driven sandwiches and soups in an eclectic setting. Free wi-fi.

Jack's Bar-B-Que 416 Broadway St ⓣ615/254-5714, ⓦwww.jacksbarbque.com. Conveniently located across the street from Ernest Tubb's, *Jack's* consistently ranks as the top barbecue in town. Moist pork shoulder and mac 'n' cheese is piled high by friendly servers on a Styrofoam plate.

Jimmy Kelly's 217 Louise Ave ⓣ615/329–4349. Nashville's favorite steakhouse for seventy years, just off West End Ave near Vanderbilt. Dinner only Mon–Sat.

The Loveless Café 8400 Hwy-100, 20 miles south of town ⓣ615/646-9700, ⓦwww.lovelesscafe.com. Friendly café famed for its country food. Breakfast is the best meal of the day: hunks of salty ham with gravy, eggs, toast, and fluffy biscuits. Reservations recommended.

Marché Artisan Foods 1000 Main St ⓣ615/262-1111, ⓦwww.marcheartisanfoods.com. Dine on impeccably prepared European fare in the up-and-coming and edgy East Nashville nabe. Homemade brioche and croissants make brunch particularly satisfying. Prepared artisanal meats, cheeses, and antipasti are available for purchase. Closed Mon, dinner breakfast and lunch daily, dinner Tues–Sat.

Merchants 401 Broadway ⓣ615/254-1892. Historic downtown building housing two dining rooms; the casual grill downstairs, which is ideal for a tasty lunch – crabcakes, grilled portabello sandwiches, and the like – and the more formal restaurant upstairs, serving classic American favorites.

Pancake Pantry 1796 21st Ave ⓣ615/383-9333. With more than 20 pancake choices, and wonderful flapjacks, this cheery Hillsboro Village institution is a popular breakfast spot – expect to wait, maybe hours, for a table at the weekend. Mon–Fri 6am–3pm, Sat & Sun 6am–4pm.

Radius10 1103 McGavock St ⓣ615/259-5105, ⓦwww.radius10.com/. Culinary Institute of America alum Chef Jason Brumm brings Nashville delectable haute fish tacos and kobe flank steak in a slick interior. Lunch Mon–Fri, dinner Mon–Sat. Reservations recommended.

Nightlife and entertainment

The two obvious ways to experience **live country music** in Nashville are either to head for the cluster of **honky-tonks** that line Lower Broadway between Second and Fourth avenues or to buy a ticket for a show at the **Grand Ole Opry**. If you're in town for a few nights, however, it's worth making the effort to catch up-and-coming or more specialized acts at places like the *Bluebird Café* and the *Station Inn*; look out, too, for special events, including bluegrass nights, at **Ryman Auditorium** (see p.525). Just west of downtown, the hip residential neighborhood **Elliston Place** boasts a number of music venues. With its tacky clubs and vacant storefronts, **Printers Alley** is best avoided.

In June, the **CMA Music Festival** (formerly known as **Fan Fair**) is a four-day series of concerts and opportunities to meet the stars (ⓦwww.cmafest.com).

For **listings**, check the free weeklies *Nashville Scene* (Wed) and *All The Rage* (Thurs), or Friday and Saturday's *Tennessean*.

12 South Taproom 2318 12th Ave South ⓣ615/463-7552, ⓦwww.12southtaproom.com. Decent pub fare and a multitude of beers on tap, including locally brewed Yazoo in the hip 12 South Arts district.

Bluebird Café 4104 Hillsboro Rd ⓣ615/383-1461, ⓦwww.bluebirdcafe.com. Having launched the careers of superstars like Garth Brooks and Faith Hill, this intimate café, six miles west of downtown in the Green Hills district, is the place to see the latest country artists. Early evening entertainment by up-and-coming songwriters is free, but a cover of $8–15 is charged for the second show.

Douglas Corner Café 2106 Eighth Ave S ⓣ615/298-1688, ⓦwww.douglascorner.com. The *Bluebird's* main competitor has live music – Americana, rock, and country – six nights a week, often with no cover, and regular open-mike songwriters' nights.

Ernest Tubb Record Store Midnight Jamboree Texas Troubadour Theatre, 2414 Music Valley Drive ⓣ615/885-0028. A live radio show, recorded every Sat from midnight to 1am, in a theater adjoining the Music Valley branch of the Tubb store (there's another on Broadway). Features promising newcomers as well as major Opry stars. Free.

Exit/In 2208 Elliston Place ⓣ615/321-3340, ⓦwww.exitin.com. Venerable venue for rock, reggae, and country, with the occasional big name – not to mention beer and pizza.

Nashville Palace 2611 McGavock Pike ⓣ615/889-1540, ⓦwww.nashvillepalace.net. Opposite the *Gaylord Opryland* resort, with music all day every day, big name C & W stars, talent nights, and post-Opry shows.

Robert's Western World 416 Broadway ⓣ615/244-9552, ⓦwww.robertswesternworld.com. Some of the best country music on Broadway, plus rockabilly and Western swing, in a lively honky-tonk that doubles as a cowboy boots store.

Station Inn 402 12th Ave S ⓣ615/255-3307, ⓦwww.stationinn.com. Very popular bluegrass and acoustic venue near Music Row. Shows 9pm nightly. No smoking.

The Sutler 2608 Franklin Pike ⓣ615/292-5254. Aspiring singer-songwriters make a beeline for this bar/club, south of downtown, that's hosted everyone from Nanci Griffith and Emmylou Harris to Guy Clark.

Tootsie's Orchid Lounge 422 Broadway ⓣ615/726-0463, ⓦwww.tootsies.net. Downtown honky-tonk, with a raucous atmosphere and good, gutsy live performers.

South from Nashville

Southeast of Nashville, nineteenth-century plantation homes line US-31 between suburban Brentwood and historic **Franklin**, eighteen miles out. One of the bloodiest battles of the Civil War was fought here on November 30, 1864, when 8500 men fell in less than an hour. Twenty-two thousand Confederates forced a Union retreat to Nashville, but incurred such heavy casualties as to shatter their Army of Tennessee beyond further use. Among strategic buildings open to visitors is **Carnton Plantation**, a former Confederate hospital where bloodstains are still visible on the floor, a mile southeast of town on Hwy-431 (Mon–Sat 9am–5pm, Sun 1–5pm; $12; ⓦwww.carnton.org).

Jack Daniel's at Lynchburg

The change-resistant village of **LYNCHBURG**, seventy miles southeast of Nashville, is home to **Jack Daniel's Distillery** (daily 9am–4.30pm; free). Founded in 1866, this is the oldest registered distillery in the country. Seventy-minute **tours** lead through every step of the sour-mash whiskey-making process; ironically, you can't actually sample the stuff, as this is a dry county.

Lynchburg itself is laid out around a neat town square with a redbrick courthouse and a number of old-fashioned stores. One enjoyable throwback is *Miss Mary Bobo's Boarding House*, which serves enormous **Southern dinners** (fried chicken, turnip greens, and the like) at group tables in an 1805 home (reservations essential; ⓣ615/759-7394).

Eastern Tennessee

Until the creation of the Tennessee Valley Authority, the opening of **Great Smoky Mountains National Park**, and the construction of the interstate highways, life had remained all but unchanged in the remote hills and valleys of **eastern Tennessee** since the arrival of the earliest pioneers. Now visitors flock here for the natural beauty; and as a result, especially in the fall, the Smokies can get very clogged with traffic. Most communities in the area are small, and either overly touristy or just bland. Of the two main cities – modern **Knoxville** and picturesque **Chattanooga**, both of which have benefited from considerable industrial growth thanks to cheap TVA power – only Chattanooga holds much appeal for tourists.

Smoky Mountain gateway towns

Most visitors who approach the Smokies from the north or west leave I-40 twenty miles east of Knoxville, or two hundred miles east of Nashville, and sweep south on **Hwy-66** and **US-441** through the 25-mile procession of heavily commercialized "**gateway towns**" that leads to the national park. This is Tennessee's most conspicuously touristed area, with its endless motels and expensive novelty "attractions" geared toward vacationing families.

Pigeon Forge

With so many themed **attractions**, ranging from Dollywood (see below) to the Black Bear Jamboree Dinner and Show, there's ostensibly lots to do in the dry town of **PIGEON FORGE** – though almost everything is appealing only on a kitschy level. Tucked in the relentless strip of discount outlets and motels, Pigeon Forge's **welcome center** is at 1950 Parkway (Ⓣ865/453-8574 or 1-800/251-9100, Ⓦwww.mypigeonforge.com). Reasonable **motels** include the well-kept *Best Western Toni Inn*, 3810 Parkway (Ⓣ865/453-9058; ❸), and the comfortable, friendly *Shular Inn*, 2708 Parkway (Ⓣ1-800/451-2376; ❸), both of which have pools. The *Smoky Mountain Pancake House*, 4050 Parkway (Ⓣ865/453-1193), is good for **breakfast**.

Gatlinburg

If you can't bring yourself to stop in Pigeon Forge, you'll probably end up in **GATLINBURG**, another five miles south on US-441. Squeezed amid the foot-

Dolly Parton's Dollywood

Born in 1946, one of twelve children, **Dolly Parton** grew up in several modest homes around Pigeon Forge, the most isolated of them two miles from the nearest neighbor and over four miles from the mailbox. As a child she sang every week on local radio, before leaving for Nashville on the day she finished at Sevier County High School. Her first success, duetting with Porter Wagoner, came to an acrimonious end in the early Seventies, but she scored a major country hit in 1976 with "Jolene." She then crossed over to a poppier sound, and, with her charismatic presence, was a natural in Hollywood films like *9 to 5* and *The Best Little Whorehouse in Texas*. Her songs have been acclaimed for their readiness to address issues like rural poverty, and as a woman, a singer, and a songwriter she has always been a strong-minded and inspirational figure.

Dollywood, Parton's "homespun fun" theme park at 700 Dollywood Lane in Pigeon Forge (April–Dec; call or visit the website for schedule; April–Oct $51.30, children 4–11 $40.15; Ⓣ865/428-9488, Ⓦwww.dollywood.com), blends ersatz mountain heritage with the glamour of its celebrity shareholder. One section showcases Appalachian **crafts**, making everything from lye soap to horse-drawn carriages; a museum looks at Dolly herself in entertaining detail; and music shows are constantly on the go. The thrill rides offer plenty for adrenaline-junkies and kiddies alike, but after a full day it can all start to feel a bit precious. A water park, **Dolly's Splash Country** (late May to mid-Sept; call for schedule; adults $43.50, children $37.90; same phone, Ⓦwww.dollywoodssplashcountry.com), is adjacent.

hills of the Smokies, its Germanic heritage still shows through. As well as being a little more upmarket, it's also "wet," so its restaurants serve alcohol. While there is at least a town center to stroll through, it's once again bursting with overpriced, gimmicky tourist attractions. It also offers a couple of chairlifts up the surrounding peaks, one of which leads to the year-round Ober Gatlinburg **ski resort** and **amusement park**.

Gatlinburg's central Parkway holds three **visitor centers** (Ⓣ1-800/588-1817, Ⓦwww.gatlinburg.com). This being the closest town to the park, **accommodation** is relatively expensive. The good-value *Sidney James Mountain Lodge*, slightly up from the mayhem at 610 Historic Nature Trail (Ⓣ1-800/876-6888, Ⓦwww.sidneyjames.com; ❸), offers comfortable rooms, some of them creekside, and two pools. Central **eating** options include *Lineberger's*, 903 Parkway (Ⓣ865/436-9284), which serves decent seafood.

Townsend

A less frenetic approach to the Smokies, if you're driving in from the east, is to follow the Foothills Parkway and then take US-321 for the final seven miles to **TOWNSEND**, twelve miles west of Pigeon Forge. There's no town to speak of, just a peaceful strip where the motels are laid-back and the air is clear. The *Highland Manor*, 7766 E Lamar Alexander Parkway (Ⓣ865/448-2211 or 1-800/213-9462, Ⓦwww.highlandmanor.com; ❸), has a nice grounds, great views, and a pool. You can **eat** fresh trout and crispy fried chicken in a country-store atmosphere at the *Hearth and Kettle*, opposite the hotel at 7767 E Lamar Alexander Parkway (Ⓣ865/448-6059).

Great Smoky Mountains National Park

The northern boundary of **GREAT SMOKY MOUNTAINS NATIONAL PARK**, which stretches for seventy miles along the Tennessee–North Carolina border (see also p.470), lies just two miles south of Gatlinburg on US-441. Don't expect immediate tranquility, however: the roads, particularly in the fall, can be lined with cars. If you're not staying in Gatlinburg it's best to use the well-marked bypass rather than drive through the town.

The Smokies attract over ten million visitors per year, more than twice as many as any other national park. These peaks are named for the **bluish haze** that hangs over them, made up of moisture and hydrocarbons released by the lush vegetation. Since the Sixties, however, **air pollution** has been adding sulphates to the mix, which has cut back visibility by thirty percent. Sixteen peaks rise above 6000ft, their steep elevation accounting for dramatic changes in climate.

Camping in the Smokies

Hikers intending to stay out overnight must obtain free **backcountry permits**, available from visitor centers (except in Cades Cove), campground offices, and ranger stations. Advance reservations are required for some areas. For information, call Ⓣ865/436-1231. Note that if you want to camp on the **Appalachian Trail** you'll need to stick to the designated areas, caged in behind iron bars to keep out the bears.

The park also has ten developed ("frontcountry") **campgrounds**, of which only two, *Cades Cove* and *Smokemont*, remain open year-round. Most of the rest are open mid-March through October. The three most popular grounds – *Cades Cove*, *Elkmont*, and *Smokemont* – are always fully booked in advance. If you want a space in the summer or fall, you should make **reservations** on Ⓣ877/444-6777 or at Ⓦwww.recreation.gov.

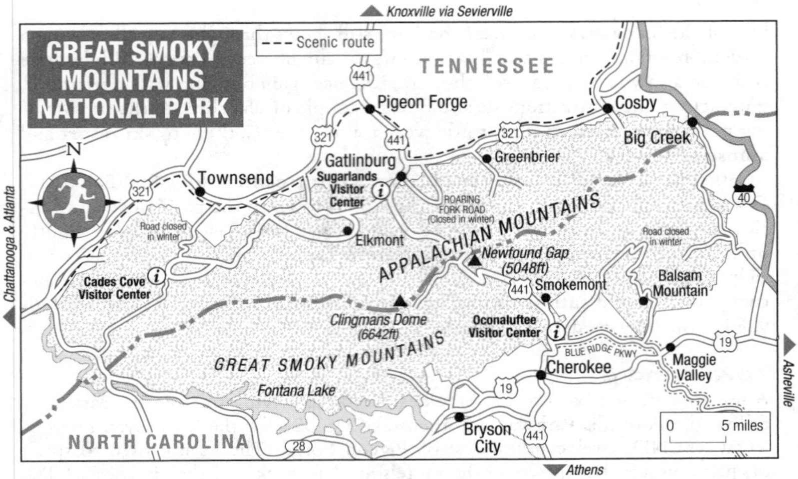

While late March and mid-May is a great time to visit for spring flowers, the **busiest periods** in the park are midsummer (mid-June to mid-Aug), and, especially, October, when the hills are shrouded in a canopy of reds, yellows, and browns. Perhaps the best way of all to escape the crowds is to sample the park's eight hundred miles of **hiking** trails.

Just inside the park on US-441, **Sugarlands Visitor Center** (daily: March 8am–5pm, April & May/Sept & Oct 8am–6pm, June–Aug 8am–7pm, Dec–Feb 8am–4.30pm Ⓣ865/436-1200, Ⓦwww.nps.gov/grsm) has leaflets covering hiking trails, driving tours, forests, and wildlife, and can provide details on each day's program of ranger-led tours and activities. Many visitors, however, do no more than follow **US-441**, here known as the Newfound Gap Road, all the way to North Carolina. From the gap itself, ten miles along on the state line, a spur road to the right winds for seven more miles up to **Clingman's Dome**, at 6643ft the highest point in Tennessee. A spiral walkway on top affords a panoramic view of the mountains, rather spoiled by the fact that virtually all the mature firs in the area have been killed off by insect infestation.

If you want to stay longer, the main focus of visitor activity is in the **Cades Cove** area, which can be reached either by branching west at Sugarlands along the scenic **Little River Road**, or directly from Townsend via **Rich Mountain Road** (closed in winter). The eleven-mile driving loop here, always jam-packed with cars in summer and fall, passes deserted barns, homesteads, mills, and churches that stand as a reminder of the farmers who carved out a living from this wilderness, before they were forced to move out when National Park status was conferred in 1934. Halfway along, there's another **visitor center** (daily: Apr–Aug 9am–7pm, Sept & Oct 9am–6pm, call for winter hours). This loop is reserved for **cyclists** on Saturday and Wednesday mornings in summer, from dawn until 10am; bikes can be rented at the Cades Cove Store near the *Cades Cove Campground* (Ⓣ865/448-9034).

Chattanooga

Few places can be so identified with a single song as **CHATTANOOGA**, in the southeast corner of Tennessee. Though visitors expecting to see Tex Beneke's and Glenn Miller's "Chattanooga Choo-Choo" will be disappointed (the town is not even served by Amtrak), the place has a certain appeal, not least its beautiful location on a deep bend in the **Tennessee River**, walled in by forested plateaus on three sides. This setting led John Ross, of Scottish and Cherokee ancestry, to found a trading post here in 1815, and its strategic importance made it a prize during the Civil War.

The Town

The centerpiece of Chattanooga's twenty miles of reclaimed riverfront is **Ross's Landing** (the town's original name), a park at the bottom of Broad Street. Here the five-storey **Tennessee Aquarium** traces the aquatic life of the Mississippi from its Tennessee tributaries to the Gulf of Mexico, and also shows giant IMAX movies (daily 10am–6pm; longer hours in summer; $19.95, IMAX $8.50, combined ticket $25.95; ⓣ1-800/262-0695, ⓦwww.tnaqua.org). **Cruises** on the *Southern Belle* **riverboat** (ⓣ423/266-4488, ⓦwww.chattanoogariverboat.com) leave from the foot of nearby Chestnut Street. Prices start from $15 for a ninety-minute daytime sightseeing tour.

Perched above the river, the **Bluff View Art District**, where High meets Second, comprises a handful of galleries, workshops, museums and cafés in lovely old buildings. The **Hunter Museum of American Art** is worth a look, with a changing roster of exhibitions covering photography, painting, sculpture, folk art and crafts from the nineteenth century to present (Mon, Tues, Fri & Sat 10am–5pm, Wed & Sun noon–5pm, Thurs 10am–8pm; $8; ⓦwww.huntermuseum.org).

Keep walking to find grand century-old buildings in the lively **business district**, such as the Tivoli Theatre at 709 Broad St; as a general rule, however, the further you get from the river, the more run-down Chattanooga becomes.

To ride a Chattanooga choo-choo, the authentic **steam trains** of the **Tennessee Valley Railroad** offer a variety of trips, from 55-minute local jaunts to stunning six-mile rides, crossing the river, running through deep tunnels, and turning round on a giant turntable (March–Oct Tues–Sat; Nov & Dec limited days; from $14; ⓣ423/894-8028, ⓦwww.tvrail.com). The two main stations, restored to their 1930s look, are at 2202 N Chamberlain Ave in east Chattanooga and 4119 Cromwell Rd (I-75 exit 4 to Hwy-153).

Lookout Mountain

The 2215ft **Lookout Mountain** (ⓦwww.lookoutmountain.com), looms six miles south of downtown. To reach the top, either drive the whole way along a complicated road or use the world's steepest **incline railway**, which grinds its way up through a narrow gash in the forest from 3917 St Elmo Ave, near the foot of the mountain, tackling gradients of up to 72.7 percent (daily: Jan–Mar, Nov & Dec 10am–6pm; April & May, Sept & Oct 9am–6pm; June–Aug 8.30am–9.30pm; 3 trips/hr, 45min; $14 round-trip; children $7; ⓣ423/821-4224).

At the top, a short steep walk through **Point Park** brings you to **Point Lookout**, which commands a view of the city and the Tennessee River below. This forms part of the **Chickamauga and Chattanooga National Military Park**, covering several sites around the city and in nearby Chickamauga, Georgia, that witnessed fierce Civil War fighting in 1863. Among the many memorials in Point Park is the only **statue** in the country to show Union and Confederate soldiers shaking hands.

For something a little less serious, join generations of road-trippers and "See Rock City" – the iconic sign, painted on roadside barns as far away as Georgia and Texas, was the result of an aggressive 1930s marketing campaign. **Rock City** is basically a walking trail along the mountain that offers not only the pleasure of scrambling through narrow gaps and swinging on rope bridges, but also delights such as **Fairyland Caverns**, holes carved into the rock and populated by fairy-

The Cherokee and the Trail of Tears

During the eighteenth and early nineteenth centuries, the **Cherokee** were the most powerful Indian tribe in the tri-state region of Tennessee, Georgia, and North Carolina. They forged close links with white pioneers, adopting white methods in schooling and agriculture, intermarrying, and even owning African slaves. The only Native Americans to develop their own written alphabet, they had a regular newspaper, *The Cherokee Phoenix*.

Against a background of aggressive territorial claims by settlers, the Cherokee produced a written constitution modeled on that of the US, stating their intention to continue to be a self-governing nation. John Ross, founder of Ross's Landing, and at most one-eighth Cherokee, was elected as their first Principal Chief in 1828 in an effort to negotiate with national and state governments over their lands. However, as white encroachment increased, their former ally Jackson, now US president, was pressured by the Georgians into "offering" the Cherokee western lands in exchange for those east of the Mississippi. Although the tribal leadership refused, a minority faction accepted, giving the government the opportunity they required. The Cherokee were ordered to leave within two years, and fourteen thousand were forcefully removed to Oklahoma in 1838 along the horrific **Trail of Tears**: four thousand died of disease and exposure on the way. In the meantime, their land was sold by lottery, and Ross's Landing was renamed Chattanooga. Descendants of the one thousand Cherokee who managed to avoid removal by escaping into the mountains now occupy a small reservation in North Carolina (see p.470).

The **Red Clay State Historic Park**, twenty miles east of Chattanooga off Hwy-317, recounts the old Cherokee way of life, with replica houses, tools, and household implements. Its balsamic Sacred Council Spring was once a meeting place for Cherokee elders.

tale characters. Inside Lookout Mountain itself, **Ruby Falls**, a 145ft waterfall, is heralded by a mock medieval castle entrance (Rock City $15.95, children $8.95; Ruby Falls $14.95, children $7.95; combination ticket $29/$15, combination with Incline Railway $42/$23).

Practicalities

Greyhound connections with Nashville, Knoxville, and Atlanta arrive on Broad Street, downtown. The **visitor center** (daily 8.30am–5.30pm; ⓣ423/756-8687 or 1-800/322-3344, ⓦwww.chattanoogafun.com) is next to the Tennessee Aquarium, near the river. Countless cheap **motels** line the interstates, but for something special head to the elegant *Bluff View Inn*, 412 E Second St (ⓣ423/265-5033 or 1-800/725-8338; ❺), which offers a variety of rooms – some with lovely views – spread across three restored houses in the appealing Bluff View Art District. There's **camping** at *Raccoon Mountain Campground*, 319 West Hills Drive (ⓣ423/821-9403, ⓦwww.raccoonmountain.com; cabins ❶–❷, tent sites $18).

As for **eating**, the Bluff View Art District has the romantic, bistro-style *Back Inn Café*, 412 E 2nd St (ⓣ423/265-5033), which serves Mediterranean food and has a terrace with river views. Elsewhere, the *Big River Grille & Brewing Works*, 222 Broad St (ⓣ423/267-2739), is a cavernous brewpub and restaurant near the Aquarium. For upmarket seafood try *Easy Seafood Bistro and Pub*, 203 Broad St (ⓣ423/266-1121). The nearby *Hair of the Dog Pub*, 334 Market St (ⓣ423/265-4615) serves food nightly until late and has a roomy terrace for soaking in the natural setting while drinking one of their fifty beers on tap. For scrumptious pancakes in an offbeat setting try *Aretha Frankensteins*, 518 Tremont St (ⓣ423/265-7685).

Alabama

Just 250 miles from north to south, **ALABAMA** ranges from the fast-flowing rivers, waterfalls, and lakes of the **Appalachian foothills** to the bayous and beaches of the **Gulf Coast**. Industry is concentrated in the **north**, around **Birmingham** and **Huntsville**, first home of the nation's space program. Farmlands of middle Alabama envelop **Montgomery**, the state capital. Away from the French-influenced coastal strip of **Mobile**, fundamentalist attitudes have traditionally backed right-wing demagogues, such as **George Wallace**, the four-time state governor. The state has emphasized industrial growth and now ranks second, only behind Detroit in U.S. automobile manufacturing.

Getting around Alabama

Daily Amtrak **trains** from New York and Atlanta to New Orleans stop at Anniston, Birmingham, and Tuscaloosa, while the line from Jacksonville to New Orleans passes through Mobile. Amtrak **buses** connect Birmingham and Mobile by way of Montgomery, while Greyhound serves the major towns and cities. A **drive** on the Talledega Scenic byway will take you through the southernmost portion of the Appalachian Mountains and the highest point in the state, Cheaha Mountain.

Northern Alabama

Northern Alabama, on the edges of the Appalachians, is brightened by the **Tennessee River Valley**. The area's first white settlers were small farmers who had little in common with plantation owners further south, and attempted to dissociate from the Confederacy during the Civil War. Substantial mineral finds led to an industrial boom that peaked in the early Thirties.

Huntsville

Many Southern cities aspire to blend the old with the new; few achieve it as dramatically as **HUNTSVILLE**, a hundred miles south of Nashville, just inside the Alabama border. Its center recalls the days of cotton merchants and railroad owners with the **Huntsville Depot Museum**, 320 Church St NW (March–Dec Tues–Sat 10am–4pm; Jan Wed–Sat 10am–4pm; $10; Ⓦwww.earlyworks.com). Nearby, **Alabama Constitution Village**, 109 Gates Ave (same hours as Depot Museum; $10, or $15 combined ticket), evokes earlier history, with reconstructed Federal-style buildings.

In World War II the army consolidated **rocket and missile research** efforts here. Heading the project were **Dr Wernher von Braun** and 118 other German scientists, who came to Huntsville after a token period of rehabilitation. Von Braun's contribution to the Nazi war effort is ignored by the city, which prefers to laud his Space Age achievements, such as **Explorer I**, the nation's first satellite, and the **Saturn V** rocket.

The giant **US Space and Rocket Center**, five miles west of downtown on Hwy-20, off I-65 (daily 9am–5pm; $20, $25 with IMAX; Ⓦwww.spacecamp.com/museum), contains a mind-boggling array of technological exhibits, as well as an IMAX cinema. Outdoors, in the Rocket and Space Shuttle parks, rockets protrude skywards in the blazing Alabama sunshine.

Practicalities

Huntsville's **visitor center** is at 500 Church St, at the northern edge of downtown, (Mon–Sat 9am–5pm, Sun noon–5pm; ⓣ256/551-2370, ⓦwww.huntsville.org). Chain **motels** on the outskirts include a *Best Value Inn*, near the Space Center at 2201 N Memorial Parkway (ⓣ256/536-7441; ❷). As for **restaurants**, *Jazz Factory*, 109 Northside Sq (ⓣ256/539-1919), offers San Francisco-style fine dining, while *Little Paul's Barbecue*, 815 Madison St SE (ⓣ256/536-7227; closed Sun), serves good, cheap barbecue.

Birmingham

The transformation of farmland into **BIRMINGHAM** began in 1870. Speculators were attracted to a mixture of iron ore, limestone, and coal, perfect for making iron and steel. Industry expansion ended with the Depression; iron and steel now account for only a few thousand jobs. Service and medical industries have helped transform what was once a smog-filled metropolis.

Arrival and information

Birmingham Airport is four miles from downtown; call Yellow Cabs (around $20) on ⓣ205/252-1131. The Greyhound station is at 19th Street N, between Sixth and Seventh avenues – a rough area – while **Amtrak** pulls in downtown at 1819 Morris Ave. **Public transportation** is poor. The main **visitor center** is just off I-20/59 at 2200 Ninth Ave N (Mon–Fri 8.30am–5pm; ⓣ205/458-8000, ⓦwww.birminghamal.org). Birmingham has two free **listings** magazines: *The Birmingham Weekly* (ⓦbirminghamweekly.com) and the *Black and White* (ⓦwww.bwcitypaper.com).

Accommodation

Although downtown **hotels** are pricier than the chains near the highway, many offer weekend specials.

Civil rights in Birmingham

Early in 1963, civil rights leaders chose Birmingham as the target of "Project C" (for confrontation), aiming to force businesses to integrate lunch counters and employ more blacks. Despite threats from Police Chief **"Bull" Connor** that there would be "blood running down the streets of Birmingham," the pickets, sit-ins, and marches went forward, resulting in mass arrests. Dr Martin Luther King Jr wrote *Letter from a Birmingham Jail* after being branded an extremist by local white clergymen. Connor's use of high-pressure hoses, cattleprods, and dogs against demonstrators catalyzed support. Pictures of German shepherds sinking their teeth into schoolkids were transmitted around the world, and led to a settlement that June. Success in Birmingham sparked demonstrations in 186 other cities, which culminated in the 1964 **Civil Rights Act** prohibiting racial segregation.

The headquarters for the campaign, the **16th Street Baptist Church**, was the site of a sickening Klan bombing on September 15, 1963, which killed four young black girls attending a Bible class. Two of the three murderers were finally jailed in 2000.

Nearby, the admirable **Civil Rights Institute**, 520 16th St (Tues–Sat 10am–5pm, Sun 1–5pm; $9; ⓦwww.bcri.org), is an affecting attempt to interpret the factors that led to such violence and racial hatred. Exhibits recreate life in a segregated city, complete with a burned-out bus and heart-rending videos of bus boycotts and the March on Washington.

Hotel Highland at Five Points South 1023 20th St S ⓣ205/933-9555, ⓦwww.thehotelhighland.com. This modern boutique within walking distance of Five Points South features luxury one-bedroom suites with handcrafted Brazilian furniture. All rooms have LCD TVs and free DSL internet. Complimentary continental breakfast and free airport shuttle. 6

Redmont Hotel 2101 5th Ave N ⓣ205/324-2101, ⓦwww.theredmont.com. Handsome historic hotel with a classic 1920s feel, a few blocks northeast of Amtrak. 4

Tutwiler Hotel 2021 Park Place N ⓣ205/322-2100, ⓦwww.thetutwilerhotel.com. Luxurious restored 1920s hotel near the Civil Rights Institute operated by Hampton Inn & Suites. Each room has a unique layout and features huge dark-wood framed windows. 6

The City

Downtown Birmingham extends north from the railroad tracks at Morris Avenue to Tenth Avenue N, between 15th and 25th streets. The main interest is the powerful **Civil Rights Institute** and the **16th St Baptist Church** (see box opposite). Visit the **Carver Theatre for the Performing Arts**, 1631 Fourth Ave N, where the **Alabama Jazz Hall of Fame** (Tues–Sat 10am–5pm; $2; ⓦwww.jazzhall.com) is a memorial to legends ranging from boogie-woogie maestro Clarence "Pinetop" to avant jazzist Sun Ra. **Five Points South**, on 20th St and 11th St S, is livelier than downtown thanks to the proximity of the university. The narrow streets are packed with bars and restaurants.

Northwest of downtown, the Birmingham-Jefferson Civic Center, 22nd St and Tenth Ave N, houses the **Alabama Sports Hall of Fame** (Mon–Sat 9am–5pm; $5; ⓦwww.ashof.org), a tribute to greats like 1936 Olympic hero **Jesse Owens**, **Le Roy "Satchel" Paige**, and boxer **Joe Louis**. The nearby **Museum of Art**, 2000 Eighth Ave N (Tues, Thurs–Sat 10am–5pm, Wed 10am–9pm, Sun noon–5pm; free), is strong on American landscapes and Wedgwood pottery.

East of downtown, at First Ave N and 32nd St, stand chimney stacks of **Sloss Furnaces** (Tues–Sat 10am–4pm, Sun noon–4pm; free; ⓦwww.slossfurnaces.com), which produced iron to feed the city's mills and foundries from 1882 until 1971. Self-guided **tours** portray the harsh working conditions endured by the ex-slaves, prisoners, and unskilled immigrants who labored here.

Eating and drinking

Birmingham has some fantastic **barbecue** joints; for something a little more upmarket, the best bet is to ignore downtown in favor of **Five Points South**. The diverse **nightlife** scene offers up hip and classic in equal proportions.

Bottega 2240 Highland Ave S ⓣ205/939-1000. Elegant 1920s clothing store that now houses one of Five Points South's classiest restaurants, serving luscious, garlic-rich Mediterranean cuisine with entrees at $25 and up; prices are slightly lower in the adjoining café.

Bottle Tree Cafe 3719 3rd Ave S ⓣ205/533-6288, ⓦwww.thebottletree.com. Catch the hottest indie bands seven nights a week at this gallery/club/bar/café decked out with comfy retro couches.

Dreamland Barbecue 1427 14th Ave S ⓣ205/933-2133. Enjoy a big plate of ribs with sliced white bread and sauce in a bright setting.

Garage Cafe 2304 10th Terr S ⓣ205/332-3220. A converted garage turned ephemera-strewn hip nightspot. Cash only.

Highlands Bar and Grill 2001 11th Ave S ⓣ205/939-1400. Top-notch French and Southern fare in an exquisite setting with a menu that changes daily. Classic cocktails, like their signature Highlands Martini – Bombay with a splash of dry vermouth and olives – are mixed to perfection. Tues–Sat dinner only. Reservations recommended.

West of Birmingham

Just west of Birmingham I-20/59 passes **Bessemer**, a likeable small town. The **Hall of History Museum**, in the railroad depot at 1905 Alabama Ave (Tues–Sat

9am–4pm; free), displays Native American artifacts alongside exhibits from the pioneer years. *Bob Sykes*, at 1724 Ninth Ave (Ⓣ205/426-1400), serves mouth-watering **barbecue**.

Tuscaloosa, home of the lively main campus of the University of Alabama, is 32 miles southwest of Bessemer. If you're hungry, combine eating with a view of the **Black Warrior River** at *Cypress Inn*, 501 Rice Mine Rd N (Ⓣ205/345-6963), which specializes in reasonably priced seafood and catfish. If you're not in the mood for fancy, *Nick's in the Sticks*, 4018 Culver Rd (Ⓣ205/758-9316), an unmarked hole-in-the-wall about ten minutes outside of town, dishes up the finest steak around in an unforgettable shack-like setting. Be prepared to wait.

South central Alabama

Southern Alabama – memorably depicted in Harper Lee's child's-eye view of racial conflict, *To Kill a Mockingbird* – still consists mostly of small, sleepy, God-fearing rural communities. Only state capital **Montgomery**, with a population of just over two hundred thousand, achieves metropolitan status. The **Black Belt**, originally named for the rich loamy soil, is now usually taken to refer to the region's ethnic make-up. Cotton was the major earner until the boll weevil infestation of 1915. Now it has been supplanted (officially) by soybeans, corn, and peanuts.

Montgomery

MONTGOMERY's location, ninety miles south of Birmingham and 160 west of Atlanta, made it a natural political center for the plantation elite, and led to its adoption as state capital in 1846 and temporary capital of the Confederacy fifteen years later. Despite its monumental downtown buildings, Montgomery is strangely quiet. Most neighborhoods are either exclusively white or totally black; integration sadly does not appear to be on the social agenda in the city that saw the first successful mass civil rights activity in 1955–56.

Arrival, information, and accommodation

Dannelly Field Airport is fifteen miles from downtown on US-80; the Greyhound station is at 950 W South Blvd. The **visitor center** is in the old train station at 300 Water St (Mon–Sat 9am–5pm, Sun noon–4pm; Ⓣ334/262-0013, Ⓦwww.visitingmontgomery.com). As for accommodation, there are a couple of homey **B&Bs** in town, plus the usual **motels** alongside the highways.

Capitol Inn 205 N Goldthwaite St Ⓣ334/265-3844 or 1-866/471-9028, Ⓦwww.capitolinnhotel.com. Old-fashioned motel perched on a small hill fifteen minutes' walk from downtown; its location is somewhat bleak at night. ❷

Lattice Inn 1414 S Hull St Ⓣ334/262-3388. Lovingly restored 1906 house offering four B&B rooms and a pool, a mile or so southeast of downtown in the Cloverdale neighborhood. ❹

Red Bluff Cottage 551 Clay St Ⓣ334/264-0056 or 1-888/551-2529, Ⓦwww.redbluffcottage.com. Friendly B&B near the capitol, with comfortable rooms, a big porch, and good food. ❹

The City

Although 1993 saw Alabama's state flag finally replace the Confederate flag over the **State Capitol** at the top of Dexter Avenue, downtown Montgomery still bears reminders of its white-supremacist past. You can tour the capitol (Mon–Fri 9am–5pm, Sat 9am–4pm; free), where a bronze star marks the spot where Jefferson Davis was sworn in as president of the Confederacy on February 18, 1861

▲ Civil Rights Memorial

(see p.452) – a hundred years later Governor George Wallace stood here and proclaimed "Segregation forever!"

Montgomery was jammed with mourners in 1954 for the funeral of 29-year-old country star **Hank Williams**, who died of a heart attack on his way to a concert on New Year's Eve 1953. An Alabama native, Williams was as famous for his drink- and drug-sustained lifestyle as he was for writing classics like "I'm So Lonesome I Could Cry." The **Hank Williams Memorial** dominates the Oakwood Cemetery Annex, 1304 Upper Wetumpka Rd, near downtown; Hank's statue stands at Lister Hill Plaza on N Perry Street. There's also the **Hank Williams Museum**, at 118 Commerce St (Mon–Fri 9am–4.30pm, Sat 9am–4pm, Sun 1–4pm; $8; Ⓦwww.thehankwilliamsmuseum.com), complete with the 1952 Cadillac in which he made his final journey.

Just off Woodmere Boulevard, ten miles southeast of the city, **Blount Cultural Park** is a regional center for the arts, as home to the **Alabama Shakespeare Festival** (Ⓣ1-800/841-4273, Ⓦwww.asf.net) and the **Montgomery Museum of Fine Arts** (Tues–Sat 10am–5pm, Sun noon–5pm; free), which spans more than two hundred years of American art and has an impressive collection of European masters.

Eating and drinking

Downtown Montgomery has some especially good soul food. A few minutes' drive southeast, suburban **Cloverdale** offers a selection of fancier restaurants. With its bars and jazz clubs, Cloverdale is also the place for **nightlife**; downtown is quiet at night.

Farmers' Market Café 315 N McDonough St Ⓣ334/262-1970. Montgomery's best spot for Southern-style breakfasts, just off downtown, next to the busy marketplace. Mon–Fri 5.30am–2pm.

Lek's Railroad Thai 300b Water St Ⓣ334/269-0708. Next to the visitor center, this elegant downtown oddity serves tasty pad Thai, sushi, noodles, and soups, along with lots of good veggie options. Closed Sun.

Martha's Place 458 Sayre St Ⓣ334/263-9135. Superb Southern food, from collard greens to fried chicken. Lunch only; closed Sat.

Vintage Year 405 Cloverdale Rd Ⓣ334/264-8463. One of Alabama's best restaurants, with haute nouvelle Southern cuisine in a bistro setting. Dinner only, reservations recommended; closed Sun & Mon.

Civil rights in Montgomery

In the Fifties, Montgomery's **bus system** was a miniature model of segregated society. The regulation ordering blacks to give up seats to whites came under repeated attack from black organizations, culminating in the call by the Women's Political Council for a mass boycott after seamstress **Rosa Parks** was arrested on December 1, 1955, for refusing to give up her seat, stating that she was simply too tired. Black workers were asked to walk to work, while black-owned taxis carried those who lived further away for the same 10¢ fare as buses. The protest attracted over ninety-percent support, and the Montgomery Improvement Association (MIA), set up to coordinate activities, elected the 26-year-old pastor **Dr Martin Luther King Jr** as its chief spokesperson. Meanwhile, the laid-off white bus drivers were employed as temporary police officials. Despite personal hardships, bombings, and jailings, the boycott continued for eleven months, until in November 1956 the US Supreme Court declared segregation on public transportation to be illegal.

King remained pastor at the small brick **Dexter Avenue King Memorial Baptist Church**, in the shadow of the capitol at 454 Dexter Ave (email to request tours a week in advance; ⓦwww.dexterkingmemorial.org), until his move back to his hometown of Atlanta in 1960. The upstairs sanctuary, left much as it was during his ministry, contains his former pulpit.

One block away at the corner of Washington Avenue and Hull Street, in front of the Southern Poverty Law Center (which specializes in helping victims of racial attacks), the moving **Civil Rights Memorial**, designed by Maya Lin, consists of a cone-shaped black granite table. It's inscribed with a timeline of events structured around the deaths of forty martyrs murdered by white supremacists and police; the circle ends with the assassination of Dr King. Water flows throughout. The wall behind is engraved with the quotation employed so often by Dr King: "(We will not be satisfied) until justice rolls down like waters and righteousness like a mighty stream." Displays in the **Civil Rights Memorial Center** (Mon–Fri 9am–4.30pm, Sat 10am–4pm; $2; ⓦwww.splcenter.org) tell the story of the campaigns.

A few blocks west of the memorial, the **Rosa Parks Museum**, 252 Montgomery St (Mon–Fri 9am–5pm, Sat 9am–3pm; $5.50), commemorates "the mother of the civil rights movement." Exhibits cover her life, the bus boycott, and other major civil rights figures.

Selma

The market town of **SELMA**, fifty miles west of Montgomery, became the focal point of the civil rights movement in the early Sixties. Black demonstrations and attempts to register to vote were repeatedly met by police violence, before the murder of a black protester by a state trooper prompted the historic **march from Selma to Montgomery**. On "Bloody Sunday," March 7, 1965, six hundred unarmed marchers set off across the narrow **Edmund Pettus Bridge**. As they went over the bridge, a line of state troopers fired tear gas without warning, lashing out at the panic-stricken demonstrators with nightsticks and cattle prods. This violent confrontation, broadcast all over the world, is credited as a direct influence in the passage of the **Voting Rights Act**. The story is told in the **National Voting Rights Museum**, beside the bridge at 1012 Water Ave (Mon–Fri 9am–5pm, Sat 10am–3pm, closed daily from 12.30–1.30pm; $6; ⓦwww.nvrm.org).

Lined with independently owned stores and cafés, **Broad Street** is the town's main thoroughfare, running into the wide riverfront **Water Avenue**, with its frontier-style storefronts and garages. Just a few blocks away are the beautiful homes of Selma's **historic district**.

Practicalities

Selma's **visitor welcome center** is at 2207 Broad St, north of town at the junction with Hwy-22 (daily 8am–8pm; ⓣ334/875-7241, ⓦwww.selmaalabama.com). Downtown is short on inexpensive **places to stay**. The historic *St James Hotel*, close to the Pettus Bridge at 1200 Water Ave (ⓣ334/872-3234 or 1-800/678-8946; ⑤), is a Historic Hotel of America. The best of several soul-food **restaurants** is the *Downtowner*, 1114 Selma Ave (Mon–Fri 7am–2.30pm; ⓣ334/872-5933).

Alabama's Gulf Coast

Alabama's narrow **Gulf coastline** sustained little damage from Hurricane Katrina in 2005, and remains blessed with white sand beaches, lapped by clear blue waters. The coast veers sharply inward to the port city of **Mobile**, which features antebellum buildings in a tree-shaded center. Away from the water's edge, agriculture, dominated by pecans, peaches, and watermelons, flourishes on the gently sloping coastal plain.

Mobile

The port city of **MOBILE** (pronounced "Mo-beel") traces its origins to a French community founded in 1702 by Jean-Baptiste Le Moyne, who also established Biloxi and New Orleans. Early white settlers brought with them **Mardi Gras**, which has been celebrated here since 1704, before New Orleans was even founded. With its Spanish and Colonial-style buildings, parallels with New Orleans are everywhere, from street names like Bienville and gumbo specials – though there's little in the way of traditional attractions.

Mobile survived the torches of the Union army in the Civil War to preserve enough antebellum buildings to designate four areas as historic districts. A good starting point is **Fort Condé**, 150 S Royal St (daily 8am–5pm; free), a reconstruction of the city's 1724 French fort. Dioramas cover local history. Nearby, you can tour the World War II battleship **USS Alabama** (daily: April–Sept 8am–6pm; Oct–March 8am–4pm; $12, parking $2). North of the fort is the **Church Street Historic District**, which holds fifty-nine, mostly pre–Civil War buildings. Don't miss the **Museum of Mobile**, in the old City Hall at 111 S Royal St (Mon–Sat 9am–5pm, Sun 1–5pm; $5; ⓦwww.museumofmobile.com), which tells the story of the town from its earliest days. Twenty miles south, off I-10, the 65 acres that make up **Bellingrath Gardens** (daily 8am–5pm; $10, $18 with house tour; ⓦwww.bellingrath.org) include a quarter of a million azaleas.

Practicalities

Downtown Mobile is under the shadow of I-10. The **Greyhound** station is centrally located at 2545 Government St. Mobile's **visitor center**, in Fort Condé (see above), can help with accommodation (daily 8am–5pm; ⓣ251/208-7569 ⓦwww.mobile.org). Cheap **motels** cluster at exit 3 of I-65; it's nicer to stay downtown. The *Malaga Inn*, 359 Church St (ⓣ251/438-4701, ⓦwww.malagainn.com; ④), has huge rooms and a pretty courtyard. Another historic **hotel**, the *Admiral Semmes*, 251 Government St (ⓣ251/432-8000, ⓦwww.radisson.com; ⑤), is a Radisson-owned property.

Mobile has quite a few **places to eat fish**: *Wintzells' Oyster House*, 605 Dauphin St (ⓣ251/432-4605; a second outpost is in West Mobile), serves good-value fresh oysters. To add water views to the mix, take Hwy-98 across the bridge; the *Original Oyster House*, on the bay (ⓣ251/626-2188) serves delectable fried blue-crab claws.

Nightlife is concentrated along Dauphin Street. *The Bicycle Shop*, at no. 661, is a laid-back **pub**; at *Grand Central*, no. 256, an array of bands play for no cover; *Soul Kitchen*, no. 219, hosts jazz, blues, and reggae on the weekends. *Lagniappe* is the free weekly **listings** paper (Ⓦ www.lagniappemobile.com).

Mississippi

Before the Civil War, when cotton was king and slavery remained unchallenged, **MISSISSIPPI** was the nation's fifth wealthiest state. Since that war, it remains the poorest, its dependence on cotton a handicap that leaves it victim to the vagaries of the commodities market.

From Reconstruction onwards, Mississippi was also infamous as the strongest bastion of segregation in the South. It witnessed some of the most notorious incidents of the **civil rights** era, from the lynching of Chicago teenager Emmett Till in 1955 to the murder of three activists during the "Freedom Summer" of 1964. Not until the early Seventies did the church bombings and murders end. Even today, **racial tension** is palpable and difficult to deny, and the **poverty** hidden down rural backroads - or clearly visible just across the railroad tracks - may come as a shock to many visitors.

The legalization of gambling during the early 1990s stimulated the economy, with the giant casinos of Biloxi drawing visitors to the Gulf Coast. However, the shoreline suffered such appalling devastation from Hurricane Katrina in 2005 that it is will be undergoing major reconstruction for years.

Mississippi's principal city is its capital, **Jackson**, but historic river towns like **Vicksburg** and **Natchez** provide good reasons to stray off the interstates. Literary **Oxford** has an appealing ambiance, while **blues** fans will need no encouragement to go exploring sleepy **Delta settlements** such as Alligator or Yazoo City.

Getting around Mississippi

Although **Greyhound** serves most of Mississippi, including the Delta, only along the coastal stretch are services at all frequent. Jackson has the only **airport** of any size, while Amtrak **trains** from New Orleans head north to Memphis by way of Jackson and Greenwood; northeast to Atlanta, passing through a succession of unexciting small towns; and along the coast to Florida, stopping at Biloxi. Trips on the Mississippi itself are run on expensive luxury **cruisers** (see p.511).

The Delta

That Delta. Five thousand square miles, without any hill save the bumps of dirt the Indians made to stand on when the River overflowed.

William Faulkner, *Sanctuary*

"That Delta" is not in fact a delta at all; technically it's an alluvial flood plain, a couple of hundred miles short of the mouth of the Mississippi. The name stems from its

▲ Fishing on the Mississippi

resemblance to the fertile delta of the Nile (which also began at a city named Memphis); the extravagant meanderings of the river on its way to **Vicksburg** deposit enough rich topsoil to make this one of the world's finest cotton-producing regions.

Though the main thoroughfare south is the legendary **Hwy-61**, the backroads, characterized by huge empty views, interrupted by roadside shacks, tiny churches and the sound of the blues, provide the best route for exploring.

Clarksdale

CLARKSDALE, the first significant town south of Memphis, has an unquestionable right to claim itself the home of the blues. Its phenomenal roll-call of former residents – stretching from Muddy Waters, John Lee Hooker, Howlin' Wolf, and Robert Johnson up to Ike Turner and Sam Cooke – is celebrated in the **Delta Blues Museum**, housed at 1 Blues Alley (March–Oct Mon–Sat 9am–5pm, Nov–Feb Mon–Sat 10am–5pm; $7 adults, $5 children 6–12, under 6 free; ⓣ662/627-6820, ⓦwww.deltabluesmuseum.org).

Long a rundown rural community, Clarksdale received an influx of money and visitors triggered by the large complex of **casinos** a dozen miles north at **Tunica**. Attempts to revitalize the town's blues heritage currently focus on the **Blues Alley** district, a general name for the area around the restored passenger depot of the Illinois Central Railroad, where many black Mississippians, including Muddy, started their migration to the cities of the north. Each year, in early August, the town holds the **Sunflower River Blues and Gospel Festival** (free; ⓣ1-800/626-3764, ⓦwww.sunflowerfest.org).

Practicalities

The hippest and quirkiest **accommodation** near Clarksdale is at **Hopson Plantation**, two miles south of town on US-49, where, from the outside, old sharecroppers' cabins and a cotton gin appear much as they did when this was a working cotton plantation. Inside, however, is a different story. The *Shack Up Inn* (ⓣ662/624-

The Delta blues

In 1903, W.C. Handy, often credited as "the Father of the Blues," and then a leader of a vaudeville orchestra, waited for a train in Tutwiler, fifteen miles southeast of Clarksdale. During the wait, a ragged black man carrying a guitar sat down next to him and began to play what Handy called "the weirdest music I had ever heard." Using a pocketknife pressed against the guitar strings to accentuate his mournful vocal style, the man sang that he was "Goin' where the Southern cross the Dog."

This was the **Delta blues**, characterized by the interplay between words and music, with the guitar aiming to parallel and complement the singing rather than simply provide a backing. Though a local, place-specific music – the "Southern" and the "Dog" were railroads that crossed a short way south at Moorhead – it did not simply spring up from the ground, but combined traditional African instrumental and vocal techniques with slave "field hollers," as well as the reels and jigs then at the basis of popular entertainment.

The blues started out as young people's music; the old folks liked the banjo, fife, and drum, but the younger generation were crazy for the wild showmanship of bluesmen such as **Charley Patton**. Born in April 1891, Patton was the classic itinerant bluesman, moving from plantation to plantation and wife to wife, and playing Saturday-night dances with a repertoire that extended from rollicking dance pieces to documentary songs such as "High Water Everywhere," about the bursting of the Mississippi levees in April 1927. Another seminal artist, the enigmatic **Robert Johnson**, was rumored to have sold his soul to the Devil in return for a few brief years of writing songs such as "Love in Vain" and "Stop Breakin' Down." His "Crossroads Blues" spoke of being stranded at night in the chilling emptiness of the Delta; themes carried to metaphysical extremes in "Hellhound on My Trail" and "Me and the Devil Blues" – "you may bury my body down by the highwayside / So my old evil spirit can catch a Greyhound bus and ride."

Both Patton and Johnson died in the 1930s. Within a few years the Delta blues had been carried north to **Chicago** by men such as **Muddy Waters** and **Howlin' Wolf**. Their electrified urban blues was the most immediate ancestor of rock 'n' roll.

In addition to towns such as Clarksdale (see p.541) and Helena, Arkansas (p.549), blues enthusiasts may want to search out the following rural sites:

Stovall Plantation Stovall Road, 7 miles northwest of Clarksdale. Where tractor-driver Muddy Waters was first recorded; a few cabins remain standing, though Muddy's own is now in the museum at Clarksdale.

Sonny Boy Williamson II's Grave Outside Tutwiler, 13 miles southeast of Clarksdale.

Parchman Farm Junction US-49 W and Hwy-32. Mississippi State Penitentiary, immortalized by former prisoner Bukka White.

Dockery Plantation On Hwy-8, between Cleveland and Ruleville. One of Patton's few long-term bases, also home to Howlin' Wolf and Roebuck "Pops" Staples.

Charley Patton's Grave New Jerusalem Church, Holly Ridge, off US-82, 6 miles west of Indianola.

Robert Johnson's Grave Payne Chapel in Quito, off Hwy-7, roughly 6 miles southwest of Greenwood, where he was poisoned.

8329, Ⓦwww.shackupinn.com; ❸), where B&B stands for "bed and beer," has half a dozen cabins and ten rooms at the *Cotton Gin Inn*. All rooms are comfortably appointed and the cabins all have a kitchenette and a small porch. Another option is the very basic *Riverside Hotel*, 615 Sunflower Ave (Ⓣ662/624-9163, Ⓦwww.cathead.biz/riverside.html; ❷), formerly a hospital famous as the site of **Bessie Smith**'s death in 1937. If you spend the night, talk to local legend, Frank "Rat" Ratliff, the son of the original owner, and learn the "true history of the blues."

As for **eating**, *Abe's*, 616 S State St (Ⓣ662/624-9947, Ⓦwww.abesbbq.com), is a good central barbecue joint. The more upscale *Madidi*, 164 Delta Ave (Ⓣ662/627-7770; closed Sun & Mon), offering a classy French take on Southern cuisine, is owned by a consortium that includes Morgan Freeman; the group also operates the *Ground Zero Blues Club*, nearby at 0 Blues Alley (Ⓣ662/621-9009, Ⓦwww.groundzerobluesclub.com), which books top local musicians on weekends. Otherwise, catching a live blues show takes a bit of luck, as long-standing juke joints find it impossible to compete with the Tunica casinos. Ask at the Delta Blues Museum about upcoming events at more authentic venues like *Red's*, Sunflower Ave & MLK Drive (Ⓣ662/627-3166 or 662/302-1600) or *Sarah's Kitchen*, 278 Sunflower Ave (Ⓣ662-627-3239).

Delta towns

Seventy miles south of Clarksdale, **GREENVILLE** is the largest town on the Delta. Still an important riverport, it hosts the **Mississippi Delta Blues Festival** (Ⓣ1-888/812-5837, 662/335-3523, Ⓦwww.deltablues.org) every year on the third weekend of September. One good, safe **accommodation** option near the river is the *Greenville Inn*, 211 Walnut St (Ⓣ662/332-6900; ③). For a **meal**, stop by *Doe's Eat Place*, 502 Nelson St (Ⓣ662/334-3315), which serves arguably the best down-home cooking in the entire Delta, and has become a franchise with restaurants in Arkansas, Oklahoma, Louisiana, Missouri, Kansas, and Kentucky.

INDIANOLA, 23 miles east of Greenville on US-82, each year in June has a "Home-Coming" celebration for **B.B. King**, who was born here. The open-air concert is organized by *Club Ebony*, 404 Hannah Ave (Ⓣ662/887-9915, Ⓦwww.clubebony.biz); King bought the club in 2008.

Forty miles east of Indianola on US-82, **GREENWOOD**, a sleepy town of twenty thousand people, is the country's second largest cotton exchange after Memphis. Greenwood plays up its connection to Robert Johnson (he died here), though the **Cotton Capital Blues Festival** in October remains the city's current contribution to the Delta Blues music legacy.

Of the many **motels** along US-49 and US-82, the *Travel Inn* at 623 US-82 W (Ⓣ662/453-8810; ②) is basic, clean, and good value, with an outdoor pool. By far the best **food** in Greenwood is the Italian/Cajun cuisine at *Lusco's*, on the wrong side of the railroad tracks at 722 Carrolton Ave (Ⓣ662/453-5365). Each table in this eccentric old place is hidden away in a small booth, veiled by chintz curtains – an arrangement dating from the days of Prohibition, when *Lusco's* was the haunt of cotton barons who came here to drink moonshine.

Northeastern Mississippi

Cutting its way south through Mississippi, I-55 acts as a boundary between the Delta and the luscious forests of the **northeast**. Of the area's small market towns, the most appealing are the old-style shopping center of **Columbus** and **Holly Springs**. Other places of interest iinclude the genteel **Oxford** and tidy blue-collar **Tupelo**, birthplace of **Elvis Presley** and **John Lee Hooker**.

Oxford

Twelve thousand residents and eleven thousand students enable **OXFORD**, an enclave of wealth in a predominantly poor region, to blend rural charm with a busy nightlife. Its central square is archetypal smalltown America, but the leafy streets have a vaguely European air – the town named itself after the English city as part of its campaign to persuade the **University of Mississippi**, known as Ole Miss, to locate its main campus here.

An undeniably appealing place today, this was the site of one of the bitterest displays of racial hatred seen in Mississippi in 1962. After eighteen months of legal and political wrangling, federal authorities ruled that **James Meredith** be allowed to enroll as the first black student at Ole Miss. The news that Meredith had been "sneaked" into college by federal troops sparked a riot that left three dead and 160 injured. Despite constant threats, Meredith graduated the following year, wearing a "NEVER" badge, the segregationist slogan of Governor Ross Barnett, upside down. A memorial commemorating his achievement was finally unveiled in September 2002, on the fortieth anniversary of his admission. Also on campus, the **Blues Archive** (Mon–Fri 8am–5pm; free; ⓣ662/915-7753) holds thousands of recordings and B.B. King's personal memorabilia, while the **Center for the Study of Southern Culture** looks at Southern folkways (Mon–Fri 8am–5pm; free; ⓣ662/915-5993).

From Ole Miss, a ten-minute walk through lush Bailey Woods leads to secluded **Rowan Oak**, the former home of novelist **William Faulkner**, preserved as it was on the day he died in July 1962 (Tues–Sat 10am–4pm, Sun 1–4pm; $5; ⓣ662/234-3284). The fictional Deep South town of Jefferson in Yoknapatawpha County, where the Nobel Prize-winner set his major works, was based heavily on Oxford and its environs. Each year, during the last week in July, the University holds a Faulkner and Yoknapatawpha Conference.

In town, a walk around the **square** brings you to Neilson's, the oldest department store in the South – delightful and little changed since 1897. Continuing your walk, you can pick up a piece of quirky Mississippi folk art or join students sipping lattes on the balcony of the exemplary Square Books, at Van Buren and Lamar streets.

Practicalities

Oxford's **visitor center** (Mon–Fri 9am–5pm, Sat 10am-4pm, Sun 1–4pm; ⓣ662/232-2367 or 1-800/758-9177, ⓦwww.oxfordcvb.com), next to Neilson's in the town square, hands out good walking-tour leaflets. **Accommodation** options include the *Downtown Oxford Inn and Suites*, 400 N Lamar Blvd (ⓣ662/234-3031 or 1-800/606-1497; ❹), and the comfortable B&B *The Five Twelve Bed and Breakfast*, 512 Van Buren Ave (ⓣ662/234-8043; ❸). On the town square, you can **eat** homestyle meals at the *Ajax Diner* (ⓣ662/232-8880; closed Sun), or more sophisticated Southern cuisine at *City Grocery* (ⓣ662/232-8080; closed Sun). The *Bottletree Bakery*, 923 Van Buren Ave (ⓣ662/236-5000; closed Mon), is a friendly café with soups and sandwiches.

Tupelo

On January 8, 1935, **Elvis Presley** and his twin brother Jesse were born in **TUPELO**, an industrial town in northeastern Mississippi. Jesse died at birth, while Elvis grew up to be a truck driver. Their parents, Gladys and Vernon Presley, who lived in poor, white East Tupelo, struggled to survive. The family's financial strain was bad enough that Elvis' sharecropper father, in a desperate attempt to raise cash, resorted to forgery and was jailed for three years. Their home was repossessed, and the family moved to Memphis in 1948.

The Tupelo **CVB**, at 399 E Main St (Mon–Fri 8am–5pm; ⓣ662/841-6521 or 1-800/533-0611, ⓦwww.tupelo.net), has details of a four-mile driving tour that takes in Elvis's first school and the shop where he bought his first guitar. The town doesn't go in for overkill, however; Main Street is a long, placid stretch of nondescript buildings, with nary a gift shop to be seen. The actual **Elvis Presley Birthplace**, 306 Elvis Presley Drive (May–Sept Mon–Sat 9am–5.30pm, Sun 1–5pm; Oct–April Mon–Sat 9am–5pm, Sun 1–5pm; $4; ⓦwww.elvispresley-birthplace.com; ⓣ662/690-6623), is tiny. A two-room shotgun house, built for $150 in 1934, it's been furnished to look as it did when Elvis was born. The separate **museum** alongside (same hours; $8, or $12 combined admission) is filled with memorabilia and includes poems about, and shrines to the King.

Among local **motels**, there's a central *Comfort Inn*, 1190 Gloster St (ⓣ662/842-5100, ⓦwww.comfortinn.com; ❸), while the *Wingate Inn*, just off Hwy-78 at 186 Stone Creek Blvd (ⓣ662/680-8887 or 1-800/228-1000, ⓦwww.tupelowingateinn.com; ❸), is a more upscale, business-oriented option. *Park Heights*, 335 E Main St (ⓣ662/842-5665; only open for dinner and closed Sun & Mon), serving seafood, salads, steak, and pasta, is one of the better **restaurants** in town.

South central Mississippi

South of the Delta, the rich woodlands and meadows of **central Mississippi** are heralded by steep loess bluffs, home to engaging historic towns such as **Vicksburg** and **Natchez**. Driving around the area is a pleasure, especially along the **Natchez Trace Parkway** – devoid of trucks, buildings, and neon signs.

Jackson

Set two hundred miles from both Memphis and New Orleans, **JACKSON** has been Mississippi's state capital since 1821. In the twentieth century it became the largest conurbation in the state, and, as such, it is the collection point for much of Mississippi's cultural and historical legacy.

Following extensive damage caused by Hurricanes Katrina and Rita, the **Old Capitol** closed for more than three years for repair. The Capitol and its museum at 100 S State St reopened in January 2009 (Mon–Fri 9am–5pm, Sat 9am–1pm), and the **Museum of Mississippi History**, once housed in the Old Capitol, is awaiting the construction of a new building on North Street. The **Mississippi Museum of Art** (Tues–Sat 10am–5pm, Sun noon–5pm; adults $5, students $3) at 380 South Lamar St is the newest incarnation of the state's largest art museum. The MMA houses collections of the state's best-known artists and has frequent exhibitions of regional, national and international art. At 528 Bloom St, the **Smith-Robertson Museum and Cultural Center** (Mon–Fri 9am–5pm, Sat 10am–2pm, Sun 2–5pm; adults $4.50), housed in what was Jackson's first public school for blacks (open from 1894–1971), tells the story of black Mississippians since the French first imported slaves in 1719.

As counterpoint to these institutions, there is also a small but vibrant art scene in Jackson. The eclectic **Artichoke** gallery (Mon–Fri 10am–5.30pm, Sat 10am–3pm) at 1012 E Fortification St displays and sells works by current Mississippi artists.

Practicalities

Greyhound **buses** arrive at 201 S Jefferson St, and Amtrak **trains** at 300 W Capitol St. The Jackson **CVB** is at 111 E Capitol St, Suite 102 (Mon–Fri 8.30am–5pm; ⓣ601/960-1891 or 1-800/354-7695, ⓦwww.visitjackson.com).

Central **rooms** can be had close to the State Capitol at the *Old Capitol Inn*, a tastefully converted former YMCA at 226 N State St (ⓣ601/359-9000 or 1-888/359-9001, ⓦwww.oldcapitolinn.com; ❹), while the strip along the I-55 corridor has the usual selection of chain hotels and motels. Downtown Jackson more or less closes down at 6pm, with the exception of *Hal & Mal's Restaurant & Brewery*, 200 S Commerce St (Ⓦwww.halandmals.com, Ⓣ601/948-0888; closed Sun), which specializes in New Orleans cuisine and puts on **live bands** throughout the week.

Vicksburg

Forty-four miles west of Jackson, the historic port of **VICKSBURG** straddles a high bluff on a bend in the Mississippi. During the Civil War, the town's domination of the river halted Union shipping and led Abraham Lincoln to call Vicksburg the "key to the Confederacy." A crucial target for General Grant, he eventually landed south of the city in the spring of 1863 and attacked from the east. After a 47-day siege, the outnumbered Confederates surrendered on the Fourth of July – a holiday Vicksburg declined to celebrate for the next hundred years – and Lincoln was able to rejoice that "the Father of Waters again goes unvexed to the sea."

Entered via Clay Street (US-80) just northeast of town, **Vicksburg National Military Park** preserves the main Civil War battlefield (daily: summer 8am–5pm; $8 per vehicle; Ⓣ601/636-0583, Ⓦwww.nps.gov/vick). A sixteen-mile loop drive through the rippling green hillsides traces every contour of the Union and Confederate trenches, punctuated by statues, refurbished cannon, and over 1600 state-by-state monuments. Nearby, in the **Vicksburg National Cemetery**, 13,000 of the 17,000 Union graves are simply marked "Unknown."

As the Mississippi has changed course since the 1860s, it's now the slender, canalized Yazoo River that flows alongside the battlefield and most of downtown Vicksburg. The core of the city has changed little, however, despite the arrival of four permanently moored **casinos**. Paying homage to the steamboat history of the town, **Catfish Row Art Park** (downtown Vicksburg on Levee St, between Clay St and Grove St) is free, open daily from 9am–8pm and provides an interactive tour complete with a children's "splash fountain" and seasonal Farmer's Market. The downtown area is progressively being restored to its original late-Victorian appearance, though most of its finest buildings were destroyed during the siege.

The fascinating **Old Court House Museum**, 1008 Cherry St (summer Mon–Sat 8.30am–5pm, Sun 1.30–5pm; rest of year closes at 4.30pm; $5; Ⓦwww.oldcourthouse.org), covers the Civil War era in great depth, even selling genuine minié balls (bullets) for $2. The museum also holds displays on Vicksburg's first settlement, Nogales, which was founded in 1796, as well as the postwar years. A small museum at the **Biedenharn Candy Company**, 1107 Washington St (Mon–Sat 9am–5pm, Sun 1.30-4.30pm; $3; Ⓦwww.biedenharncoca-colamuseum.com), marks the spot where Coca-Cola was first bottled, with vivid displays on how it all came about.

Practicalities

Vicksburg has two major **visitor centers**, both just off I-20: the Mississippi Welcome Center, at exit 1A beside the river (daily 8am–6pm), and the town's own tourist information center near exit 4, opposite the battlefield entrance on Clay Street (daily: summer 8am–5.30pm; winter 8am–5pm; Ⓣ601/636-9421 or 1-800/221-3536, Ⓦwww.visitvicksburg.com).

The military park is the prime area for **motels**, such as the spartan *Hillcrest*, 4503 Hwy-80 E (Ⓣ601/638-1491; ❶), which has a pool, and the comfortable *Battlefield Inn*, at 4137 I-20 Frontage Rd (Ⓣ601/638-5811 or 1-800/359-9363, Ⓦwww.battlefieldinn.org; ❹), which includes use of the pool, two free cocktails, and a free breakfast buffet. Among appealing central **B&Bs** are *Anchuca*, housed in the town's first colonnaded mansion, at 1010 First East St (Ⓣ601/661-0111 or 1-888/686-0111, Ⓦwww.anchucamansion.com; ❺), which has seven guestrooms, including a gorgeous suite extending through the former slave quarters, as well as a pool and fine breakfasts; and the 1868 Victorian-Italianate *Annabelle*, 501 Speed St (Ⓣ601/638-2000 or 1-800/791-2000, Ⓦwww.annabellebnb.com; ⑤).

When it's time to **eat**, tuck into superb all-you-care-to-eat "round table" lunches of fried chicken and other Southern delicacies at *Walnut Hills*, 1214 Adams St at Clay (Ⓣ601/638-4910; Mon–Sat 9am–11pm, Sun 11am–2pm). At *The Biscuit Company*, 1100 Washington St (Ⓣ601/631-0099), you can eat pizza or po'boys and hear **live jazz** or **blues** most weekends.

Natchez

Sixty miles south of Vicksburg, the river town of **NATCHEZ** is the oldest permanent settlement on the Mississippi River. By the time it first flew the Stars and Stripes in 1798, it had already been home to the Natchez people (see below) and their predecessors, as well as French, British, and Spanish colonists. Unlike its great rival, Vicksburg, Natchez was spared significant damage during the Civil War, ensuring that its abundant Greek Revival antebellum mansions remained intact, complete with meticulously maintained gardens. Interspersed among them are countless simpler but similarly attractive white clapboard homes, set along broad leafy avenues of majestic oaks, making Natchez one of the prettiest towns in the South. **Horse and carriage** tours (see p.596) explore the downtown area, while fourteen individual mansions stay open all year round, among them the elaborate, octagonal **Longwood**, 140 Lower Woodville Rd (daily 9am–4.30pm; $8), with its huge dome, snow-white arches and columns, and the palatial **Stanton Hall**, 401 High St (daily 10am–4pm; $8). Tours set off from 200 State St during the twice-yearly **Natchez Pilgrimage** (mid-March to mid-April & first two weeks in Oct; $34; Ⓦwww.natchezpilgrimage.com).

While Natchez proper perches well above the river, a small stretch of riverfront at the foot of the bluff constitutes **Natchez Under-the-Hill**. Once known as the "Sodom of the Mississippi," it now houses a handful of bars and restaurants, plus the 24-hour *Isle of Capri* riverboat **casino**, a cacophony of slot machines and craps tables (Ⓦwww.isleofcapricasinos.com/natchez/).

Natchez takes its name from the **Natchez Indians** who survived here until 1729, when they rose against the French. Joined by African slaves, they killed 250 colonists before the French and their Choctaw allies crushed the rebellion. The former Natchez spiritual center known as the **Grand Village**, home to a leader revered as the "Great Sun," can now be explored at 400 Jefferson Davis Blvd (Mon–Sat 9am–5pm, Sun 1.30–5pm; free). See the visitor center and reconstructed dwellings, as well as a large park-like area with an imposing ceremonial mound at either end. Another Natchez site, the much larger **Emerald Mound**, stands just off the Natchez Trace northeast of town (free 24hr access).

Natchez's rich **African-American** heritage – Richard Wright, the author of *Native Son*, was born nearby and lived in the town as a small boy – is chronicled in an excellent 26-page free booklet.

Practicalities

Natchez's vast **Visitor Reception Center** occupies a panoramic location overlooking the river at 640 S Canal St, alongside the Mississippi River bridge (March–Oct Mon–Sat 8.30am–6pm, Sun 9am–4pm; Nov–Feb Mon–Sat 8.30am–5pm, Sun 9am–4pm; Ⓣ601/446-6345 or 1-800/647-6724, Ⓦwww.visitnatchez.com). It's the starting point for **trolley ($2)** and **bus tours** (minimum 2 people, $20 for the hour-long tour) and sells tickets for **ghost tours** (daily 7:30pm; minimum 6 people; $20) and **carriage rides** ($15; 45 min) that leave from Canal and State streets.

Mississippi's Gulf Coast

Previous editions of this book have included an extensive description of **Mississippi's Gulf Coast**, where fine beaches, and the resort atmosphere of **Biloxi** in particular, attracted considerable numbers of summer visitors. However, the storm surge that accompanied Hurricane Katrina in August 2005 caused such extensive damage to the region that, years later, it is still being reconstructed. Here, unlike in New Orleans, the coastline was battered by colossal waves, and entire towns were simply obliterated from the map. Businesses like the giant casinos of Biloxi have reopened, and, according to the Biloxi Visitors Center (Mon–Fri 9am–5pm; ⓣ228/374-3105; 136 Lameuse St) 80–90 percent of the area's hotels are open. Though desolate gaps along the coast remain, in time a full recovery will be achieved, and, in the meantime, great deals can be found. For informed tourists, vacationing on the Gulf Coast can be a rich and rewarding experience that will have a positive impact on the region's economy.

As for **accommodation**, the *Ramada Inn*, across from the visitor center at 130 John R. Junkin Drive (ⓣ601/446-6311 or 1-800/256-6311, ⓦwww.ramada.com; ❹), enjoys much the same magnificent views, while the *Natchez Eola*, 110 N Pearl St (ⓣ601/445-6000 or 1-866/445-3652, ⓦwww.natchezeola.com; ❺), is a venerable downtown hotel of considerable charm. The *Mark Twain Guesthouse*, 33 Silver St (ⓣ601/446-8023, ⓦwww.underthehillsaloon.com; ❸), is down by the river; its three simple rooms share a bathroom and its proximity to the *Under the Hill Saloon* make for a boisterous and festive atmosphere. For a quintessential Natchez experience, consider staying in a more upmarket **B&B**, such as the opulent *Burn*, 712 N Union St (ⓣ601/442-1344, ⓦwww.theburnbnb.com; ❻), with a beautiful pool.

For **food**, *Cock of the Walk*, on the bluff at 200 N Broadway (ⓣ601/446-8920), serves irresistibly tasty catfish, while the *Marketplace Café*, 613 Main St (ⓣ601/304-9399; closed Mon), occupying most of a large open-sided market building downtown, sells good, inexpensive breakfasts and lunches. *Biscuits and Blues*, 315 Main St (ⓣ601/446-9922), combines burgers and barbecue with **live blues** on weekends.

Arkansas

Southeast to northwest, **ARKANSAS'** geography undulates, rising from the alluvial floodplains of the Delta to the forested hills of the Ozark Mountains and ultimately giving way to the Great Plains. Unlike the Southern states on the east side of the Mississippi River, Arkansas (the correct pronunciation is "Arkansaw" according to a state law from 1881) remained sparsely populated until the 1880s when railroads opened up the interior and settlers began to move toward urban centers. The combined forces of the Great Depression and industrial mechanization eventually forced thousands of farmers to leave their fields in the early decades of the 1900s, allowing Arkansas to begin to develop an industrial economic base. Historically, Arkansas belongs firmly to the American South. It sided with the Confederacy during the Civil War, and its capital, Little Rock, was, in 1957, one of the most notorious flashpoints in the struggle for civil rights. But it was in 1992 that local boy Bill Clinton's accession to the presidency catapulted Arkansas to national prominence. Four towns lay claim to him: Hope, his birthplace; Hot Springs, his "home town"; Fayetteville, where he and Hillary married; and, of course, Little Rock. Each of these sites is included in the "Billgrimage": a tour, complete with an Arkansas Passport (also available at Arkansas Visitors Centers and the Clinton Presidential Library) that is stamped at each site.

Though Arkansas encompasses the **Mississippi Delta** in the east, oil-rich timber lands in the south, and the sweeping **Ouachita** ("Wash-ih-taw") **Mountains** in the west, the cragged and charismatic **Ozark Mountains** in the north are its most scenic asset, abounding with parks, lakes, rivers and streams.

Getting around Arkansas

While **driving** the state's greenery-lined highways is a pleasure, it's difficult to venture beyond Little Rock and Hot Springs using **public transportation**. Greyhound runs intermittent services and Amtrak cuts diagonally northeast–southwest through the state, calling at Little Rock and a few smaller towns. Little Rock Airport and the Northwest Arkansas Regional Airport near **Rogers** are the only sizeable **airports**. To see the Ozarks you'll certainly need a **car**.

Eastern Arkansas

What's surprising about the eastern Arkansas delta lands is that they are far from totally flat: **Crowley's Ridge**, a narrow arc of windblown loess hills, breaks up the uniform smoothness, stretching 150 miles from southern Missouri to the atmospheric river town of **Helena**. Helena has plenty to recommend it, not least its strong **blues** heritage.

Helena

The small Mississippi port of **HELENA**, roughly sixty miles south of Memphis, was once the shipping point for Arkansas' cotton crop; Mark Twain described Helena as occupying "one of the prettiest situations on the river." A compact **historic district** bordered by Holly, College, and Perry streets reflects that brief period of prosperity, before the arrival of the railroad. Nowadays it feels the strain of living in the shadow of the enormous casinos across the river. Nonetheless, Helena is a laid-back place, with great appeal for fans of the **Delta blues and** most of the town's activity takes place along run-down **Cherry Street** on the levee.

In 1941, Helena was the birthplace of the celebrated **King Biscuit Time Show**, broadcast on radio station KFFA (1360 AM). Featuring performances from legends like boogie pianist Pinetop Perkins and harmonica great **Sonny Boy Williamson II** ("Rice" Miller), the show was the first in the nation to broadcast live Delta blues. With a huge influence that belies its tiny size – musicians from B.B. King to Levon Helm quote it as a major inspiration – the show has been on air continuously ever since, hosted since 1951 by living legend "Sunshine" Sonny Payne. Broadcasts on KFFA 1360 AM radio (Mon–Fri 12.15–12.45pm; Ⓦwww.kingbiscuittime.com; Ⓣ870/338-4350) are recorded from the foyer of the excellent **Delta Cultural Center Visitor Center**, 141 Cherry St (Tues–Sat 9am–5pm Ⓣ870/338-4350); observers are welcome. If you miss the show, make sure to stop by the visitor center's **music exhibit**, complete with listening stations and great video footage.

Blues fans can also buy – and hear – a thrilling assortment of records at **Bubba Sullivan's Blues Corner**, in the mall at 105 Cherry St (Ⓣ870/338-3501). Bubba is a mine of information on local gigs, not least the town's superb free **Arkansas Blues and Heritage Festival** (formerly the King Biscuit Blues Festival; Ⓦwww.bluesandheritage.com). Held every fall on the weekend before Columbus Day, it attracts big-name blues, acoustic, and gospel performers.

The **Delta Cultural Center** has another site a block south of the visitor center, in a restored train depot at 95 Missouri St (Tues–Sat 9am–5pm; free). Exhibits cover all aspects of the region's history, from the first settlers of this soggy frontier to contemporary racism, with, of course, lots of good stuff about the region's musical heritage. From here you can walk along the levee to **River Park,** which has fabulous views of the Mississippi.

Practicalities

The 1904 *Edwardian Inn*, 317 Biscoe St, on the main highway into town north of the Mississippi Bridge (Ⓣ870/338-9155 or 800/598-4749, Ⓦwww.edwardianinn.com; ④), is an opulent **B&B** with large oak-paneled rooms, whose only drawback is the nearby industrial building that partially obstructs the view of the river. For **food**, *Cherry Street Deli*, 420 Cherry St (Ⓣ870/817-7706), has good soup and sandwiches, while *Oliver's*, 101 Missouri St (Ⓣ870/338-7228), serves catfish, steak, and the like. The *Roadkill Grill*, 523 Cherry St (Ⓣ870/995-2881) serves up burgers and fries. If you want to hear some live **blues**, stay on Cherry Street and check out *Sonny Boy's Music Hall*, no. 301 (Ⓣ870/338-3501), or *Fonzie's*, no. 400 (Ⓣ870/817-7736).

Central Arkansas

Little Rock sits in the centre of the state, just fifty miles west of the quirky spa town of **Hot Springs** that marks the eastern gateway to the remote **Ouachita Mountains**. The rippling farmland of the **Arkansas River Valley** is sandwiched by the Ouachita crests on the south side and the craggy ridges of the Ozarks to the north. Mining and logging communities dot the east–west roads in the hill country, and the fastest growing region in the state is the I-540 corridor between the college town of **Fayetteville** and Wal-Mart's company town, **Bentonville**.

Little Rock

The geographical, political, and financial center of Arkansas, **LITTLE ROCK** is at the meeting point of the state's two major regions, the northwestern hills and the eastern Delta. The town today has a relaxed, open feel, a far cry from the dramatic time of 1957 (see below), and, since the election of William J. Clinton to the presidency in 1992, it's held a certain cachet that's unique in the state.

The city's newest attraction, the **William J. Clinton Presidential Library and Museum**, directly east of downtown at 1200 President Clinton Ave (Mon–Sat 9am–5pm, Sun 1–5pm; $7; Ⓦwww.clintonlibrary.gov), is housed in an elevated, glass-and-metal building attractively set on the river. A dazzling structure, the Clinton Library is a visual metaphor for Clinton's oft-repeated avowal to build a bridge to the twenty-first century. Revitalizing a once-depressed district of abandoned warehouses, the environmentally-friendly building is part of a campus of federally certified "green" buildings which also include the headquarters of **Heifer International**, a international non-governmental organization dedicated to alleviating world hunger. Heifer provides free tours in addition to a host of ever-changing community programs (Mon–Fri 9am–5pm).

Crisis at Central High

In 1957, Little Rock unexpectedly became the battleground in the first major conflict between state and federal government over **race relations**. At the time, the city was generally viewed as progressive by Southern standards. All parks, libraries, and buses were integrated, a relatively high thirty percent of blacks were on the electoral register, and there were black police officers. However, when the Little Rock School Board announced its decision to gradually **desegregate** its schools – the Supreme Court having declared such segregation unconstitutional – James Johnson, a candidate for governor, started a campaign opposing interracial education. Johnson's rhetoric began to win him support, and the incumbent governor, **Orval Faubus**, jumped on the bandwagon himself.

The first nine black students were due to enter **Central High School** that September. The day before school opened, Faubus, "in the interest of safety," reversed his decision to let blacks enroll, only to be overruled by the federal court. He ordered state troopers to bar the black students; soldiers with bayonets forced Elizabeth Eckford, one of the nine, away from the school entrance into a seething crowd, from which she had to jump on a bus to escape. As legal battles raged during the day, at night blacks were subject to violent attacks by white gangs. Three weeks later, President Eisenhower reluctantly brought in the 101st Airborne Division, and, amid violent demonstrations, the nine entered the school. That year, they experienced intense intimidation; when one retaliated, she was expelled. The graduation of James Green seemed to put an end to the affair, but Faubus, up for re-election, renewed his political posturing by closing down all public schools in the city for the 1958–59 academic year – and thereby increased his majority.

Today Central High School – an enormous brown, crescent-shaped structure, bearing no little resemblance to a fortress – is on the National Register of Historic Places and has been designated as a National Park site. It's at 1500 S Park Ave, about a mile from the capitol. Across the street in a restored former gas station at 2125 Daisy L. Gatson Bates Drive, the **Central High Visitor Center** was the spot from which reporters filed stories on the only public payphone in the neighborhood. The **Visitor Center** (Mon–Sat 9am–4.30pm, Sun 1–4.30pm; free; Ⓦ www.nps.gov/chsc/), expanded to a second building in 2007 at 2120 Daisy L. Gatson Bates Drive to commemorate the 50th Anniversary of the events, and has a good exhibition about the 1957 crisis.

The Clinton Library also acts as a canny way to draw visitors to Little Rock's vibrant **River Market District**, with its splash of restaurants and bars, farmers' market, and thriving and eclectic food hall. Down the street from the library, at 610 President Clinton Ave, the **museum store** (Ⓦ www.clintonmuseumstore.com) sells some marvelous gifts – from "I Miss Bill" stickers and Socks the cat mousepads to compilation CDs of the former president's favorite music. Also nearby, at 500 President Clinton Ave, the **Museum of Discovery** is a favorite with kids (Mon–Sat 9am–5pm, Sun 1–5pm; adults $8, children $7), while, along the river, **Riverfront Park** runs for several blocks. A commemorative sign here marks the "little rock" for which the city is named (not particularly striking, but then the name gives that away).

Surrounded by smooth lawns and shaded by evergreens, the **Old State House Museum** (Mon–Sat 9am–5pm, Sun 1–5pm; free), in the old capitol building at 300 W Markham St, is well worth a visit. The displays – everything from Civil War battle flags to African-American quilts – do an admirable job of covering Arkansas history, with strong sections on women and political history. Here, Clinton announced his bid for the presidency on October 3, 1991, and made his acceptance speech thirteen months later – and then again in 1996.

The **Historic Arkansas Museum's** Hinderliter Grog Shop, 200 E Third St (Mon–Sat 9am–5pm, Sun 1–5pm; $2.50), Little Rock's oldest standing building, dates from around 1827. A **gallery** at the museum displays locally made crafts from the last two centuries, temporary historical exhibits, and contemporary Arkansas art.

Another point of interest, MacArthur Park, features the elegant **Arkansas Arts Center** (Tues–Sat 10am–5pm, Sun 11am–5pm; free; Ⓦwww.arkarts.com), with rotating exhibits (the MFA in Boston will lend its Egyptian Masterpieces in 2009-2010), a collection of drawings dating from the Renaissance to the present, and a nice selection of contemporary crafts. The Arts Center also features local and locally-born artists in juried competitions like **The Delta Exhibition**.

West of Downtown, north of Markham Street along Kavanaugh Boulevard is the historic neighbourhood of **Hillcrest**. Filled with early 20th century bungalows, Hillcrest is a hip, hilly and eminently walkable neighborhood whose center, between Van Buren Avenue and Walnut Street, features a cozy collection of boutique shops and stylish restaurants.

The Heights, running west along Kavanaugh from the intersection with Cantrell is similar to Hillcrest, although it enjoys a higher elevation on a ridge whose most exclusive streets command stunning views of the river. Down the hill from The Heights walkers, joggers and cyclists make their way along the river's edge at **Murray Park**, a pretty expanse of green parkland bookended by the **Big Dam Bridge** on the west and **Rebsamen Park Golf Course** on the east.

Practicalities

Greyhound arrives at 118 E Washington Ave in North Little Rock, across the river. **Amtrak** has a more central location at Markham and Victory streets. The **visitor center** is at 615 E Capitol Ave, near the post office (Mon–Fri 8.30am–4.30pm; Ⓣ501/376-4781 or 1-800/844-4781, Ⓦwww.littlerock.com).

Finding **accommodation** downtown should be no problem. The luxurious *Rosemont B&B*, 515 W 15th St (Ⓣ501/374-7456, Ⓦwww.rosemontoflittlerock.com; ❹–❻) offers home comforts like a full breakfast and a stocked pantry, while at the *Comfort Inn & Suites Downtown*, a short walk from the Clinton Center at 707 I-30 (Ⓣ501/687-7700; Ⓦwww.comfortinnlittlerock.com; ❹) has large rooms, a pool, and a hearty free breakfast.

There are plenty of good places to grab a bite to **eat** in town. The bustling **River Market District food court** (Mon–Sat 7am–6pm) provides a wealth of choice unheard of in these parts, with stalls dishing up organic soups, Middle Eastern salads, down-home BBQ, and pad Thai. *Boulevard Bread Co.*, adjoining the food court at 400 President Clinton Ave (Ⓣ501/374-1232), has a sister location 1620 N Grant St in The Heights. Both locations provide a cornucopia of taste treats with a conscience – from fair trade organic coffee to locally grown ingredients. *The Rumba Revolution* in the River Market area at 300 President Clinton Ave (Ⓣ501/823-0090, Ⓦwww.rumbarevolution.com) is a newer, less-divey complement to a couple of Little Rock's other live music venues with a Mexi-Cuban restaurant on one side and a music venue on the other that are both equally successful and equally eclectic. *Vino's*, 923 W Seventh St (Ⓣ501/375-8466, Ⓦwww.vinosbrewpub.com), is an unpretentious, friendly brewpub serving ales and pizza; a popular spot for office lunches, after dark it takes on a more alternative edge, featuring live punk music. There's more music at *Juanita's*, 1300 S Main St (Ⓣ501/372-1228, Ⓦwww.juanitas.com; closed Sun), a fairly typical Tex-Mex restaurant and a fixture on the Little Rock music scene, hosting live rock shows most nights. Perhaps Little Rock's most renowned restaurant is *Doe's Eat Place*, 1023 W Markham St (Ⓣ501/376-1195), a branch of the Greenville, Mississippi, restaurant, serving excellent steak and tamales in unpretentious surroundings; it's a longtime favorite of former president Clinton and still a hotspot for hungry politicos. Possibly the best restaurant in town, though, is *Brave New Restaurant*, just a little outside of downtown at 2300 Cottondale Lane (T 501/663-2677, W www.bravenewrestaurant.com), which serves delicate combinations of fresh meats and seafood and intuitive sauces against the backdrop of the Arkansas River.

In Hillcrest, *Ciao Baci*, a wine and tapas bar and restaurant in a converted bungalow at 605 Beechwood St (Sun–Fri 5pm–2am, Sat 5pm–1am; T 501/603-0238), has delectable food and drinks and stays open late. *Za Za* at 5600 Kavanaugh in Hillcrest (Mon–Thurs 10.30am–9pm, Fri & Sat 10.30am–10.30pm; T 501/661-9292) is an excellent spot to stop for adventurous salads, wood-fired brick oven pizzas, and homemade gelato for dessert.

Hot Springs

Fifty miles southwest of Little Rock, the low-key, historic, and somewhat surreal spa town of **HOT SPRINGS** nestles in the heavily forested Zig Zag Mountains on the eastern flank of the Ouachitas. Its **thermal waters** have attracted visitors since Native Americans used the area as a neutral zone to settle disputes. Early settlers fashioned a crude resort out of the wilderness, and after the railroads arrived in 1875 it became a European-style spa; its hot waters are said to cure rheumatism, arthritis, kidney disease, and liver problems. The resort reached its glittering heyday during the Twenties and Thirties, when the mayor reputedly ran a gambling syndicate worth $30 million per annum, and players included Al Capone and Bugsy Siegel. Movie stars and politicians, aristocrats and prize-fighters flocked to "quaff the elixir," and Hot Springs became *the* place to see and be seen. The resort's popularity waned when new cures appeared during the Fifties, though its faded grandeur and small-town sleepiness give it a distinctive appeal.

Downtown Hot Springs threads through a looping wooded valley, barely wide enough to accommodate the main thoroughfare of Central Avenue. Eight magnificent buildings behind a lush display of magnolia trees, elms, and hedgerows make up the splendid **Bathhouse Row**. Between 1915 and 1962, the grandest of them all was the **Fordyce Bathhouse**, at the 300 block of Central, which reopened in 1989 as the **visitor center** for **Hot Springs National Park** – the only national park to fall within city limits. Apart from the Buckstaff (see below), this is the only bathhouse you can actually enter: the interior, restored to its former magnificence, is an atmospheric mixture of the elegant and the obsolete. The heavy use of veined Italian marble, mosaic-tile floors and stained glass lend it a decadent feel, while the gruesome hydrotherapy and electrotherapy equipment, including an electric shock massager, seem impossibly brutish (daily 9am–5pm; free; T 501/624-2701, W www.nps.gov/hosp).

It's still possible to take a "**bath**" – an hour-long process involving brisk rubdowns, hot packs, a thorough steaming, and a needle shower – on Bathhouse Row. The only establishment still open for business is the 1912 **Buckstaff**, 509 Central Ave, where a thermal mineral bath costs $22, and traditional bathing package with massage $50 (March–Nov Mon–Sat 7–11.45am & 1.30–3pm, Sun 8–11.45am; Dec–Feb Mon–Fri 7–11.45am & 1.30–3pm, Sat 7–11.45am; T 501/623-2308, W www.buckstaffbaths.com). Swathed in cotton sheets, you are marched by no-nonsense guides from bath to shower to massage table in a municipal, rather prosaic, atmosphere. Full bathing facilities are also available at several hotels. Hot Springs' water lacks the sulfuric taste often associated with thermal springs; fill up a bottle at any of the drinking fountains near Central Avenue. Most of them pump out warm water – if you prefer it cold, head for the Happy Hollow Spring on Fountain Street.

Behind the Fordyce, two small **springs** have been left open for viewing. The **Grand Promenade** from here is a half-mile brick walkway overlooking downtown. Trails of various lengths and severity lead up the steep slopes of **Hot Springs Mountain**. To reach the summit, take a short drive or any of several different trails, including a testing two-and-a-half-mile hike through dense woods of oak, hickory, and short-leafed pine. The observation decks of the 216ft **Mountain Tower** at the top (daily: summer 9am–9pm; spring and fall 9am–6pm; winter 9am–5pm; $6) offer superb views of the town, the Ouachitas, and surrounding lakes.

Quite apart from its waters, Hot Springs prides itself on its small **galleries**, plenty of which line Central Avenue interspersed with some good examples of wonderfully weird Americana.

Practicalities

Greyhound pulls in to 1001 Central Ave; most places of interest, including good **accommodation** options, are within easy distance of Central Avenue, the city's main thoroughfare. Though rates can rise during the lengthy high season (Feb–Nov), luxury accommodation is surprisingly inexpensive, ranging from spa hotels with their own bathhouses to chain motels and B&Bs. Dominating the town center, the atmospheric 1920s *Arlington Resort/Spa*, 239 Central Ave (T 501/623-7771, W www.arlingtonhotel.com; 4; bath and whirlpool $26, massage $34), is by far the nicest place to stay, oozing faded grandeur – Al Capone rented the entire fourth floor and President Clinton attended his junior and senior proms in the ballroom. The tasteful rooms are airy and comfortable, if a little small. The nearest place to **camp** is *Gulpha Gorge Campground* in the national park, two miles northeast on Hwy-70 B, off Hwy-70 E (T 501/624-3383, W www.nps.gov/hosp; $10 per night).

Hidden among the cheap family **restaurants** along Central Avenue, *Rolando's* at no. 210 is a cheery Nuevo Latino place serving up delicious, creative food (T 501/318-6054). Nearby, the *Arlington*'s restaurant presents Hot Springs' version of haute cuisine – including a fine Sunday brunch – in elegant environs. *Mollie's*, near downtown in an old house at 538 Grand Ave, specializes in tasty comfort foods like chicken in the pot and matzo ball soup (T 501/623-6582; closed Sun), while at *McClard's Bar-B-Q*, three miles south of downtown at 505 Albert Pike (T 501/624-9586; closed Sun & Mon), the mouthwatering pork ribs, slaw, beans, and hot tamales are all handmade. *McClard's* is not to be missed; even Bill and Hillary stopped by here on their wedding day.

As you might expect, Hot Springs' **nightlife** is marvellously cheesy, ranging from variety shows and jamborees to *The Witness*, an outdoor musical of Christ's life as sung by the Apostle Peter; it's held six miles from downtown at 1960 Millcreek Rd (June–Sept Fri & Sat 8pm; $13.50; T 501/623-9781, W www.witnessproductions.com). Those with more secular tastes might prefer *The Maxwell Blade Magic Lantern Theater*, 121 Central Ave (summer Tues–Sat 8pm; adults $15, children 15 and under $10; T 501/623-6200, W www.maxwellblade.com), starring "Master of Illusion" Maxwell Blade. On a different note, there's a prestigious **documentary film festival** put on each October by the Hot Springs Documentary Film Institute (W www.hsdfi.org), and a well-known classical **music festival** during the first two weeks of June (W www.hotmusic.org).

The Ozark Mountains

Although the highest peak fails to top two thousand feet, the **Ozark Mountains**, extending beyond northern Arkansas into southern Missouri, are characterized by severe steep ridges and jagged spurs. Hair-raising roads weave their way over the precipitous hills, past rugged lakeshores and pristine rivers. When ambitious speculators poured into Arkansas in the 1830s, those who missed the best land etched out remote hill farms. They remained isolated until the last few decades; the Ozarks has now become the fastest-growing rural section of the US, a major tourist and retirement destination. Much-needed cash flooded in and has converted centers such as **Harrison** into cookie-cutter American towns.

The word "Ozark" is everywhere, used to entice tourists into music shows or gift emporia. With all the hype, it's increasingly difficult to tell the genuine article from imitations – a good reason to visit the **state park** at **Mountain View,** which preserves traditional Ozark skills and music. The region's most popular destination, **Eureka Springs**, just inside the Missouri border, is a pretty mountainside Victorian spa town that has developed a laid-back and rootsy bohemian scene.

Mountain View and around

Roughly sixty miles north of Little Rock, the state-run **Ozark Folk Center**, two miles north of the town of **MOUNTAIN VIEW** on Hwy-14, is a good living history museum that features how life used to be in these remote hills. Homestead skills are displayed in reconstructed log cabins, and folk musicians and storytellers perform throughout the park. Special events, including regular Ozark and roots music **concerts**, are held most evenings (craft displays mid-April to end Sept Wed–Sat 10am–5pm, Oct Tues–Sun 10am–5pm, $10; concerts mid-April to end Sept Wed–Sat 7.30pm, Oct Tues–Sat 7.30pm, $10; combination ticket $17.50; Ⓣ870/269-3851, Ⓦwww.ozarkfolkcenter.com).

Mountain View's **visitor center**, 107 N Peabody Ave (April–Oct Mon–Fri 9am–5pm, Sat 10am–4pm; Nov–March Mon–Fri 10am–4pm, Sat 10am–2pm; Ⓣ870/269-8068 or 1-888/679-2859, Ⓦwww.ozarkgetaways.com), can help with **accommodation**; there is plenty of choice, particularly if you like the personal service of a B&B or the rustic charm of a mountain cabin. The *Dry Creek Lodge* (Ⓣ1-800/264-3655; ❸) is a good-value option on the grounds of the Folk Center, while the friendly *Inn at Mountain View*, 307 W Washington St (Ⓣ870/269-4200, Ⓦwww.innatmountainview.com; ❹), is a pretty B&B owned by folk musicians; they serve a full country breakfast. Good **restaurants** include the Folk Center's *Iron Skillet* (Ⓣ870/269-3851) and *Tommy's Famous...*, an award-winning pizzeria and rib joint at 205 Carpenter St, four blocks west of the town square (Ⓣ870/269-3278). For entertainment, even in winter, it's hard to beat the friendly **jam sessions** in the square, and naturally there are also a number of good music **festivals**. Reserve a room well in advance for the venerable **Arkansas Folk Festival** (music, crafts, food stalls, parades), held in April, and the **Bean Festival** (beans, cornbread, music, outhouse races), held on the last Saturday in October.

In the **Ozark National Forest**, fifteen miles northwest of Mountain View off Hwy-14, you can take a variety of tours (times and rates vary; Ⓦwww.fs.fed.us/oonf/ozark/recreation/caverns.html) of the **Blanchard Springs Caverns**, an eerily beautiful underground cave system with a crystal-clear swimming hole surrounded by towering rock bluffs .

The **Buffalo River** – a prime destination for white-water canoeing – flows across the state north of Mountain View. In the sweet little settlement of Gilbert, off Hwy-65 at the end of Hwy-333 E, **Buffalo Camping and Canoeing**

(ⓣ870/439-2888, ⓦwww.gilbertstore.com) rents canoes for trips on the mid-section of the river, at its most spectacular around **Pruitt Landing**. A few log **cabins**, most of which sleep at least four, are available (ⓦwww.buffalorivercabin.com; ❹–❽).

Eureka Springs

Picturesque **EUREKA SPRINGS**, set on steep mountain slopes in Arkansas' northwestern corner, began life a century ago as a health center. As that role diminished, its striking location turned it into a tourist destination, filled with Victorian buildings and streets linked by flights of stone stairs. Today it has a relaxed, progressive feel, with kitsch outdoor movie events (ⓦwww.lucky13cinema.org), special "Diversity Weekends" (ⓦwww.eurekapride.com), and plenty of places offering alternative therapies. Take a ride on the **Eureka Springs and North Arkansas Railway**, whose rolling stock includes a magnificent "cabbage-head" wood-burning locomotive; trips depart from the depot at 299 N Main St (mid-April to Oct Mon–Sat 10.30am, noon, 2pm & 4pm; $10; ⓦwww.esnarailway.com).

Three miles east of town on US-62 E, a seven-story **Christ of the Ozarks** – a surreal statue of Jesus with a 60ft arm span – sets the tone for a jawdropping religious complex known as the **Great Passion Play** (end April to end Oct), the brainchild of Elna M. Smith, who, worried that Mid East holy sites would be destroyed by war, decided to build replicas in the Ozarks. The complex includes a **Bible Museum** and a **Sacred Arts Center** (both open the same days the play is performed, 10am–8pm; admission included in price of tour). The **Passion Play** re-enacts Christ's last days on earth with a cast of 250, including live animals, in a 4100-seat amphitheater (same months; nightly except Sun and Wed 8.30pm, after Aug 7.30pm; $23.25, includes Bible Museum and Sacred Arts Center; ⓣ1-866-566-3565, ⓦwww.greatpassionplay.com).

Practicalities

In town, US-62 becomes Van Buren with the **visitor center** at 137 W Van Buren (daily 9am–5pm; ⓣ479/253-8737, ⓦwww.eurekasprings.com). Log cabins and B&Bs abound, many with staggering views, and there is plenty of inexpensive **lodging** along Hwy-62 E. There are two particularly delightful options downtown: *Trade Winds*, next to the visitor center at 141 W Van Buren, is a funky, gay-friendly place with wittily decorated theme rooms and a pool (ⓣ479/253-9774 or 1-800/242-1615; ⓦwww.eurekatradewinds.com; ❸); ten minutes' walk away, at 27 Glenn (Hwy-62 W), the superb *Sherwood Court* offers individually decorated cottages, some with Jacuzzis, surrounding flower-filled courtyards (ⓣ479/253-8920 or 1-800-268-6052, ⓦwww.sherwoodcourt.com; ❷–❺ including continental breakfast).

For **food**, the artsy *Mud Street Café,* 22 S Main St, serves good espresso, light lunches and desserts, plus dinner on Friday and Saturday (ⓣ479/253-6732; closed Wed). The friendly local institution *Chelsea's Corner*, 10 Mountain St, off Spring St (ⓣ479/253-6723), features **live music** most evenings. Eureka Springs holds the fine **Ozark folk festival** in October (ⓣ501/253-7788), and the acclaimed **blues festival** in June (ⓦwww.eurekaspringsbluesfestival.com).

7

Florida

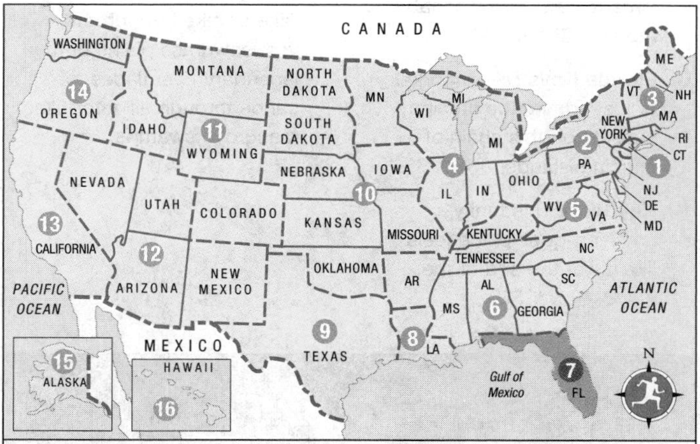

AL - ALABAMA	IN - INDIANA	MN - MINNESOTA	RI - RHODE ISLAND
AR - ARKANSAS	LA - LOUISIANA	MS - MISSISSIPPI	SC - SOUTH CAROLINA
CT - CONNECTICUT	MA - MASSACHUSETTS	NC - NORTH CAROLINA	VA - VIRGINIA
DE - DELAWARE	MD - MARYLAND	NH - NEW HAMPSHIRE	VT - VERMONT
FL - FLORIDA	ME - MAINE	NJ - NEW JERSEY	WI - WISCONSIN
IL - ILLINOIS	MI - MICHIGAN	PA - PENNSYLVANIA	WV - WEST VIRGINIA

CHAPTER 7 Highlights

* **Kennedy Space Center, Space Coast** Some of the world's most high-tech machinery just a stone's throw from a wildlife refuge. See p.587

* **Ocean Drive, Miami** South Beach's finest Art Deco showpiece, buzzing with cosmopolitan cafés, flashy vintage cars, and wannabe models. See p.566

* **Florida Keys** Dive, snorkel or just admire the flaming sunsets off this chain of enticing islands. See p.575

* **Key West** This funky, anything-goes place feels like it's at the end of the world. See p.578

* **St Augustine** Sixteenth-century Spanish town packed with historic interest and a handful of lovely beaches. See p.589

* **Walt Disney World** Pure entertainment, planned down to the last detail. Simply irresistible. See p.597

* **Everglades National Park** Bike or hike through the vast sawgrass plains of the legendary Everglades, or canoe through alligator-filled mangrove swamps. See p.614

▲ Key West

7

Florida

Brochure images of tanning tourists and Mickey Mouse give an inaccurate and incomplete picture of **FLORIDA**. Although the aptly nicknamed "Sunshine State" is indeed devoted to the tourist trade, it's also among the least-understood parts of the US. Away from its overexposed resorts lie forests and rivers, deserted strands filled with wildlife, vibrant cities, and primeval swamps. Contrary to the popular retirement-community image, new Floridians tend to be a younger, more energetic breed, while Spanish-speaking enclaves provide close ties to Latin America and the Caribbean.

By far, the essential stop is cosmopolitan, half-Latin **Miami**. A simple journey south from here brings you to the **Florida Keys**, a hundred-mile string of islands known for sports fishing, coral-reef diving, and the sultry town of **Key West**, legendary for its sunsets and liberal attitude. Back on the mainland, west from Miami stretch the easily accessible **Everglades**, a water-logged sawgrass plain filled with camera-friendly (but otherwise unfriendly) alligators.

Much of Florida's **east coast** is disappointingly urbanized, albeit with miles of unbroken beaches rolling alongside. The residential stranglehold is loosened further north, where **Kennedy Space Center** launches NASA shuttles. Farther along, historical **St Augustine** stands as the longest continuously occupied European settlement in the US.

In **central Florida** the terrain turns green, though it's no rural idyll, thanks in most part to **Orlando** and **Walt Disney World**, which sprawls out across the countryside. From here it's just a skip west to the towns and beaches of the **Gulf Coast**, and somewhat further north to the forests of the **Panhandle**, Florida's link with the Deep South.

Weather-wise, warm sunshine and blue skies are almost always the norm. The state does, however, split into two **climatic zones**: subtropical in the south and warm temperate in the north. Orlando and points south have a mild season from October to April, with warm temperatures and low humidity. Down here, this is the **peak tourist season**, when prices are at their highest. Conversely, the southern summer (May to Sept) brings high humidity and afternoon storms; the rewards for braving the mugginess are lower prices and fewer tourists.

North of Orlando, winter is the off-peak period, even though daytime temperatures are generally comfortably warm (although snow has been known to fall on the Panhandle). During the northern Florida summer, the crowds arrive, and the days and nights are hot and sticky. Keep in mind that June to November is **hurricane season**, and there is a strong possibility of big storms.

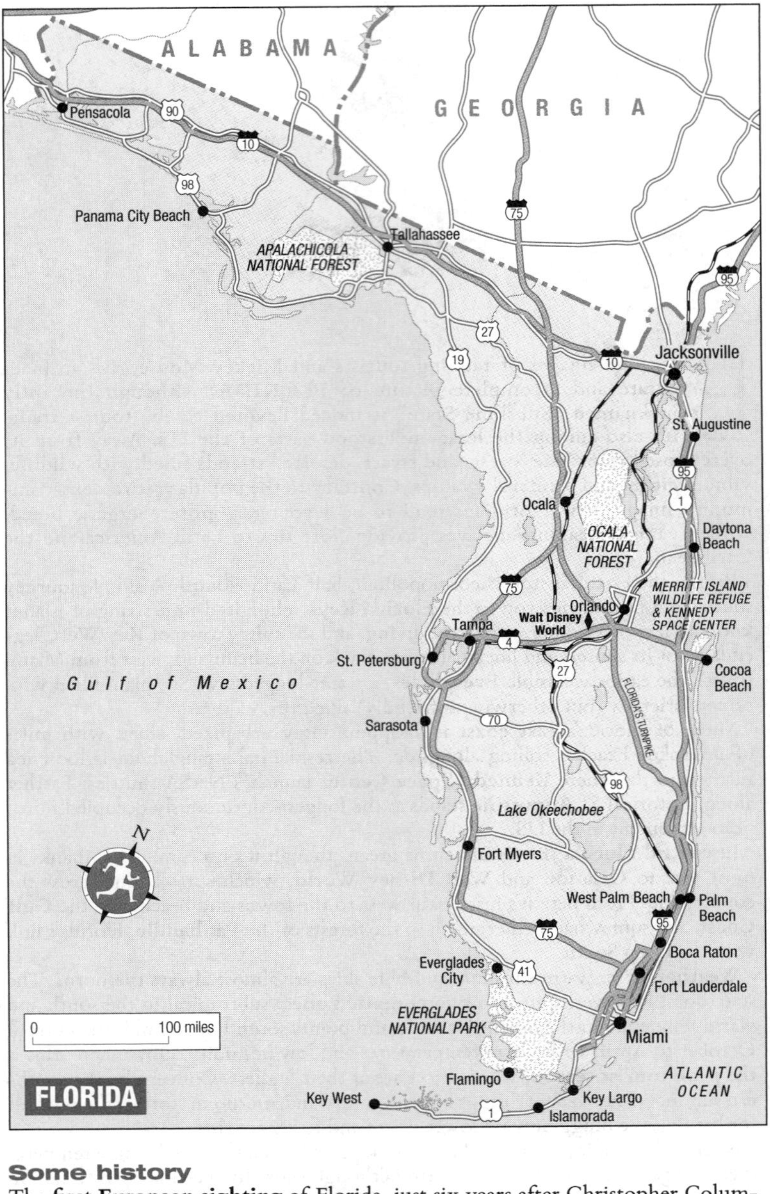

Some history

The **first European sighting** of Florida, just six years after Christopher Columbus reached the New World, is believed to have been made by John and Sebastian Cabot in 1498, when they spotted what is now Cape Florida, on Key Biscayne in Miami. At the time, the area's one hundred thousand inhabitants formed several distinct **tribes**: the Timucua across northern Florida, the Calusa around the southwest and Lake Okeechobee, the Apalachee in the Panhandle, and the Tequesta along the southeast coast.

In 1513, a Spaniard, **Juan Ponce de León**, sighted land during *Pascua Florida*, Spain's Easter celebration; he named what he saw *La Florida*, or "Land of Flowers." Eight years later he returned, the first of several Spanish incursions prompted by rumors of gold hidden in the north of the region. When it became clear that Florida did not harbor stunning riches, interest waned, and it wasn't until 1565 that conquistador Pedro Menéndez de Avilés founded **St Augustine** – site of the longest continuous European habitation in North America. In 1586, St Augustine was razed by a British naval bombardment led by Francis Drake. The ensuing bloody confrontation for control of North America was eventually settled when the British captured the crucial Spanish possession of Havana, Cuba; Spain willingly parted with Florida to get it back. By this time, indigenous Floridians had been largely wiped out by disease. The area's Native American population now largely comprised disparate tribes that had arrived from the north, collectively known as the **Seminoles**, who were generally left undisturbed in the inland areas.

Following American independence, Florida once more reverted to Spain. In 1814, the US general (and future president) Andrew Jackson – on the pretext of subduing the Seminole, but with the actual intention of taking the region – marched south from Tennessee, killing hundreds of Indians and triggering the **First Seminole War**. Following the war, in 1819, Spain **ceded Florida** to the US, in return for American assumption of $5 million of Spanish debt. Not long after, Jackson was sworn in as Florida's first American governor, and Tallahassee was selected as the new administrative center.

Eleven years later, the **Act of Indian Removal** decreed that all Native Americans in the eastern US should be transferred to reservations in the Midwest. Most Seminole were determined to stay and, as a result, the **Second Seminole War** broke out, with the Indians steadily driven south, away from the fertile lands of central Florida and into the Everglades, where they eventually agreed to remain. Florida became the **27th state** on March 3, 1845, coinciding with the prosperity brought by the railroads. As a member of the Confederacy during the **Civil War**, Florida's primary contribution was the provision of food – a foretaste of its post-war economic role after being re-admitted to the Union.

At the beginning of the twentieth century, the country's newspapers extolled the curative virtues of Florida's climate, and northern speculators began to invest in the state. These early efforts to promote Florida as a **tourist destination** brought in the wintering rich: the likes of Henry Flagler and Henry Plant extended their railroads and opened luxury resorts on the east and west coasts, respectively. After World War I, it seemed that everyone in America wanted a piece of Florida, and chartered trains brought in thousands of eager buyers. But most deals were on paper only, and in 1926 the banks began to default. The **Wall Street Crash** then made paupers of the millionaires whose investments had helped shape the state.

What saved Florida was **World War II**. During the war, thousands of troops arrived to guard the coastline, providing them with a taste of Florida that would entice many to return. Furthermore, in the mid-Sixties, the state government bent over backwards to help the Disney Corporation turn a sizeable slice of central Florida into **Walt Disney World**, the biggest theme park ever. Its enormous commercial success helped solidify Florida's place in the international tourist market: directly or indirectly, tourism now makes up twenty percent of the total state economy.

Behind the optimistic facade, however, lie many **problems**. There's a broadening gap between the relative liberalism of the big cities and the arch-conservatism of the northern Bible Belt. Gun laws remain notoriously lax, and the multimillion-dollar **drug trade** shows few signs of abating – at least a quarter of the cocaine entering the US is said to arrive via Florida. Increased protection of the state's **natural resources** has been a more positive feature of the last decade and impressive amounts of land are under state control – overall, wildlife is less threatened now than at any time since white settlers first arrived.

Getting around Florida

Surprisingly compact, Florida is **fairly easy to navigate** if you have a car: crossing between the east and west coasts takes just a couple of hours, and determined drivers can make one of the longest trips – between the western extremity of the Panhandle and Miami – in a full day's drive. Getting around by **public transportation**, on the other hand, requires adroit advance planning. Major towns and cities are linked by Greyhound **buses** – and, in some cases, infrequent Amtrak **trains** – but many rural areas and some of the most enjoyable sections of the coasts are not covered. Although inadvisable in the cities, **cycling** is a great way to see large parts of Florida – miles of cycle paths follow the coasts, and long-distance bike trails cross the state's interior.

Miami

Far and away the most exciting city in Florida, **MIAMI** is an often intoxicatingly beautiful place, with palm trees swaying in the breeze and South Beach's famous Art Deco buildings stunning in the warm sunlight. Away from the beaches and the tourists, the gleaming skyscrapers of downtown herald Miami's proud status as the headquarters of many US corporations' Latin American operations. Even so, it's the people, not the climate, the landscape, or the cash, that makes Miami so noteworthy. Two-thirds of the two-million-plus population is Hispanic, the majority of which are **Cuban,** and Spanish is the predominant language almost everywhere.

Just over a hundred years ago Miami was a swampy outpost of mosquito-tormented settlers. The arrival of Henry Flagler's railroad in 1896 gave the city its first fixed land-link with the rest of the continent, and cleared the way for the Twenties property boom. In the Fifties, Miami Beach became a celebrity-filled resort area, just as thousands of Cubans fleeing the regime of Fidel Castro began arriving here as well. The Sixties and Seventies brought decline, and Miami's dangerous reputation in the Eighties was well deserved – in 1980 the city had the highest murder rate in America.

Since then, with the strengthening of Latin American economic links and the gentrification of South Beach – which helped make tourism the lifeblood of the local economy again in the early Nineties – Miami is enjoying a surge of affluence and optimism.

Arrival and information

Miami International Airport (ⓣ305/876-7000, ⓦwww.miami-airport.com) is six miles west of the city. A cab from the airport costs $22–52, depending on your destination. You can opt for one of the 24-hour SuperShuttle minivans, which will deliver you to any address in Miami for $15–20 per person (ⓣ305/871-2000, ⓦwww.supershuttle.com). Via **public transportation**, take the #7 Metrobus (ⓣ305/770-3131) to downtown, a trip of 40 to 50 minutes ($1.50; every 30mins), or the #J Metrobus ($1.50; every 20–40mins) to Miami Beach farther on. Shuttle buses also leave from the airport to the nearby **Tri-Rail** (ⓣ1-800/TRIRAIL) station, with onward services to West Palm Beach.

A short taxi ride ($10) from the airport will deliver you to the Miami Greyhound station, at 4111 NW 27th Street (ⓣ305/871-1810). Most buses, however, also pull in at the downtown stop, at 1012 NW 1st Avenue (ⓣ305/374-6160). The **Amtrak** station, at 8303 NW 37th Ave, is seven miles northwest of the city center. Three blocks south lies the Tri-Rail Metrorail Station at 1125 E 25 St (coming from Amtrak take a taxi, as this area can be unsafe), where Tri-Rail connects with **Metrorail services to downtown Miami. Bus #L also makes a stop here.** Note that by 2011, all trains and buses should arrive at the new Miami Intermodal Center, next to the airport.

For tourist information head to the Downtown Welcome Center in the lobby of the Olympia Theater, 174 E Flagler St (Mon noon–5pm, Tues–Sat 10am–5pm; ⓣ305/379-7070, ⓦwww.downtownmiami.com); otherwise, try the Miami Beach Chamber of Commerce, 1920 Meridian Ave (Mon–Fri 9am–6pm, Sat & Sun 10am–4pm; ⓣ305/672-1270, ⓦwww.miamibeachchamber.com), which is crammed with leaflets and staffed by helpful locals. Also in South Beach, the Art Deco Welcome Center, 1001 Ocean Drive, is undergoing a major renovation which should be complete by early 2010. Until then the **Miami Design Preservation League** (ⓣ305/672-2014, ⓦwww.mdpl.org) walking tours (see below) will run from the gift shop on 12th Street, just off Ocean Drive.

City transportation and tours

Downtown and South Beach, the two main tourist areas, are eminently walkable – and, indeed, are best enjoyed **on foot**. However, if you want to see more of the city, **driving** is the most practical option. An integrated **public transportation network** run by Metro-Dade Transit (ⓣ305/770-3131, ⓦwww.miamidade.gov/transit) covers Miami, making the city easy – if time-consuming – to get around, at least by day (nighttime services are more skeletal). **Metrorail** trains ($1.50) run along a single line between the northern suburbs and South Miami; useful stops are Government Center (for downtown), Vizcaya, Coconut Grove, and Douglas Road or University (for Coral Gables). Downtown Miami is also ringed by the **Metromover** (free), a monorail that doesn't cover much ground but gives a great bird's-eye view. **Metrobuses** ($2, with a 50¢ surcharge for transfers) cover the entire city, but services dwindle at night.

Taxis are abundant in Miami (**meters** start at $2.50); either hail one on the street or call Central Cab (ⓣ305/532-5555) or Metro Taxi (ⓣ305/888-8888). If you want to rent a **bike**, try the Miami Beach Bicycle Center, 601 5th St, South Beach (Mon–Sat 10am–7pm, Sun 10am–5pm; $8/hr, $24/24hr; ⓣ305/674-0150, ⓦwww.bikemiamibeach.com).

For an informed stroll, take one of **Dr Paul George's Walking Tours** from the Historical Museum of Southern Florida (call for schedule; no tours July & Aug; $20 and up; ⓣ305/375-1621, ⓦwww.hmsf.org). In South Beach, don't miss the ninety-minute **Art Deco Walking Tour** (Tues & Wed, Fri–Sun 10.30am; Thurs 6pm; $20; ⓣ305/672-2014), which runs from the gift shop on 12th Street, until the Art Deco Welcome Center reopens in 2010. The shop also offers a self-guided audio walking tour of the district (available daily 9.30am–5pm; 90min; $15).

Accommodation

Accommodation is rarely a problem in Miami – though you should expect **rates** to go up on weekends, holidays, and in the main winter tourist season (Dec–April), when you'll pay $120–150 (or upwards of $250 in the swankier places) per night. Though it can be great fun to stay in one of the numerous Art Deco **South Beach** hotels, note that they were built in a different era, and, as such, rooms can be tiny. For most visitors, there's little reason not to stay on the beach, though you may get slightly cheaper internet deals elsewhere in the city.

Albion Hotel 1650 James Ave, South Beach ⓣ1-877/RUBELLS, ⓦwww.rubellhotels.com. A sensitive conversion of a classic Nautical Deco building, this is one of the best-value hotels on the beach. Rooms are hip but simple; the raised pool – with portholes cut into its sides – is also a big draw. ❹

Cadet Hotel 1701 James Avenue ⓣ305/672-6688, ⓦwww.cadethotel.com. Tranquil boutique hotel, with a fresh, clean look enhanced with bamboo floors and a patio-garden where you can enjoy a glass of wine; the fresh strawberries and chocolate in the rooms upon arrival are nice touches. ❺

Catalina 1732 Collins Ave ⓣ305/674-1160. Simple white rooms are filled with luxe touches like flatscreen TVs and marble bathrooms, plus there's an outdoor pool, a sundeck, and a bamboo-filled zen courtyard for reading or meditating. ❹

Clay Hotel Hostel-Miami Beach International Youth Hostel 1438 Washington Ave, South Beach ⓣ1-800/379-2529, ⓦwww.clayhotel.com. This beautiful converted monastery serves as the city's best budget hotel and youth hostel. Private rooms with bath from $75, without bath from $60; dorm rooms $25 IYH members, $26 others including linens, with rates dropping to $20 for all dorm guests in the summer.

The Hotel 801 Collins Ave ⓣ 305/531-2222 or 1-877/843-4683, ⓦwww.thehotelofsouthbeach.com. Designer Todd Oldham oversaw every element in the renovation of this hotel, and his colorful yet thoughtful makeover makes it one of the best luxury options on the beach. Don't miss the rooftop pool, shaped like a gemstone in honor of the hotel's original name. ❻

Miami Beach International Travelers Hostel 236 9th St, South Beach ⓣ305/534-0268, ⓦwww.hostelmiamibeach.com. Friendly hostel with beds in four-person dorms starting at $25, as well as private singles (from $89) and doubles ($49 per person). Offers free breakfast, internet facilities, kitchen, laundry, a movie-lounge, and also books tours.

Park Central 640 Ocean Drive, South Beach ⓣ305/538-1611, ⓦwww.theparkcentral.com. Colonial-safari-style rooms (soundproofed against the noise from nearby clubs) with reasonable rates for South Beach. ❺

Pelican 826 Ocean Drive, South Beach ⓣ1-800/7-PELICAN, ⓦwww.pelicanhotel.com. Each room at this campy, quirky hotel is individually themed and named – try the lush red bordello known as the "Best Little Whorehouse." ❻

The Shore Club 1901 Collins Ave, South Beach ⓣ305/695-3100, ⓦwww.shoreclub.com. Ultra-trendy hotel on the beach, with minimalist, brightly colored rooms and several swanky bar-restaurants, like the poolside *Sky Bar* (see review p.574). ❾

The Standard Miami 40 Island Ave, South Beach ⓣ305/673-1717, ⓦwww.standardhotels.com/miami/. The Miami outpost of hip hotelier André Balazs's Standard chain has transformed a forlorn hotel on Belle Isle into spa accommodation complete with Turkish baths and a yoga center. ❻

Townhouse 150 20th St, South Beach ⓣ1-877/534-3800, ⓦwww.townhousehotel.com. Small but stylish white rooms, great staff, free breakfast, and squishy rooftop waterbeds – all at a fraction of most boutique hotel prices. ❺

The City

Each of Miami's **districts** has a character very much its own. Separated from the mainland by Biscayne Bay, the most popular is **Miami Beach**, especially the world-famous **South Beach** portion. In addition to an enticing stretch of sand, this is where many of the city's famed Art Deco buildings can be found, all pastels, neon, and wavy lines.

▲ Art Deco building

Back on the mainland, **downtown** has a few good museums, though the district is being transformed by one of the largest concentrations of residential skyscrapers in the US. To the north, the art galleries and showrooms of **Wynwood** and the **Design District**, and even the earthy, Caribbean enclave known as **Little Haiti** are gradually starting to attract more visitors. Meanwhile, southwest of downtown, there's nowhere better for a Cuban lunch than **Little Havana**. Immediately south, the spacious boulevards and ornate public buildings of **Coral Gables** are as impressive now as they were in the 1920s, when the district set new standards in town planning. Lastly, sun-worshipers should make time for **Key Biscayne**, a smart, secluded island community with some beautiful beaches, an easy five miles off the mainland by causeway.

Miami Beach

A long slender arm of land between Biscayne Bay and the Atlantic Ocean, **MIAMI BEACH**, three miles off the mainland, has been a headline-grabbing resort town

Miami beaches

With twelve miles of calm waters, clean sands, swaying palms, and candy-colored lifeguard towers, you can't go wrong with Miami's choice of **beaches**. The young and the beautiful soak up the rays between 5th and 21st streets, a convenient hop from the juice bars and cafés on Ocean Drive. From 6th to 14th streets, **Lummus Park** – much of whose sand was shipped in from the Bahamas – is the heart of the South Beach scene; there's an unofficial gay section roughly around 12th Street. North of 21st, things are more family-oriented, with a **boardwalk** running between the shore and the hotels up to 46th. To the south, **First Street Beach** and **South Pointe** are favored by Cuban families, and are especially convivial at weekends. For good **swimming**, head up to 85th, a quiet stretch that's usually patrolled by lifeguards.

for almost a hundred years, from its first heyday in the Art Deco-dominated 1920s, through a slick-as-Vegas era in the 1950s, to the hip hedonism of today. Until the 1910s – when its Quaker owner, John Collins, formed an unlikely partnership with a flashy entrepreneur, Carl Fisher – it was nothing more than an ailing fruit farm. With Fisher's money, Biscayne Bay was dredged, and the muck raised from its murky bed was used as landfill to transform this wildly vegetated barrier island into a carefully sculptured landscape of palm trees, hotels, and tennis courts. After a hurricane in 1926 devastated Miami (and especially the beach), damaged buildings were replaced by grander structures in the new Art Deco style, and Miami Beach as we know it appeared. Since then, its history has been checkered: by the 1980s, crack dens and retirement homes were equally commonplace in South Beach, but the 1990s saw a renaissance spearheaded by a few savvy hoteliers and Miami's gay community.

South Beach

Occupying the southernmost three miles of Miami Beach is gorgeous **SOUTH BEACH**, with its hundreds of dazzling pastel-colored 1920s and 1930s Art Deco buildings. By day, the sun blares down on sizzling bodies on the sand – though it's worth braving an early morning wake-up call to catch the dawn glow, which bathes the Deco hotels in pure, crystalline white light. By night, the ten blocks of Ocean Drive become one of the liveliest stretches in Miami, as terrace cafés spill across the specially widened sidewalk and crowds of tourists and locals saunter by the beach.

Loosely bordered north/south by 5th and 20th streets, and west/east by Lenox Avenue and the ocean, the area referred to as the **Deco District** actually incorporates a variety of styles: take one of the excellent walking tours offered by the **Miami Design Preservation League** (see p.563) to learn the difference between Streamline, Moderne, and Florida Deco, not to mention Mediterranean Revival.

The most famous buildings lie along **Ocean Drive**, where revamped hotels make much of their design heritage. Amid the hotels, **Casa Casuarina** (Ⓣ305/672-6604, Ⓦwww.casacasuarina.com) at the corner of 11th Street, was the former home of the murdered fashion designer Gianni Versace. It's now an invitation-only members club, but in 2008, falling revenues prompted an open-door policy for the first time: daily **tours** (9am, 11am, and 2pm) of the lavish interior cost $50.

If the tourist hordes get to be too much, head a block west to **Collins Avenue**, lined with more Deco hotels and fashion chains, or on to **Washington Avenue**, which tends more toward funky thrift stores and cool coffee bars. At 1001 Washington Ave, the Mediterranean-Revival **Wolfsonian–FIU** (Mon, Tues, Sat & Sun noon–6pm, Thurs & Fri noon–9pm; $7; free after 6pm on Fri; Ⓣ305/531-1001, Ⓦwww.wolfsonian.fiu.edu) houses an eclectic collection of decorative arts from

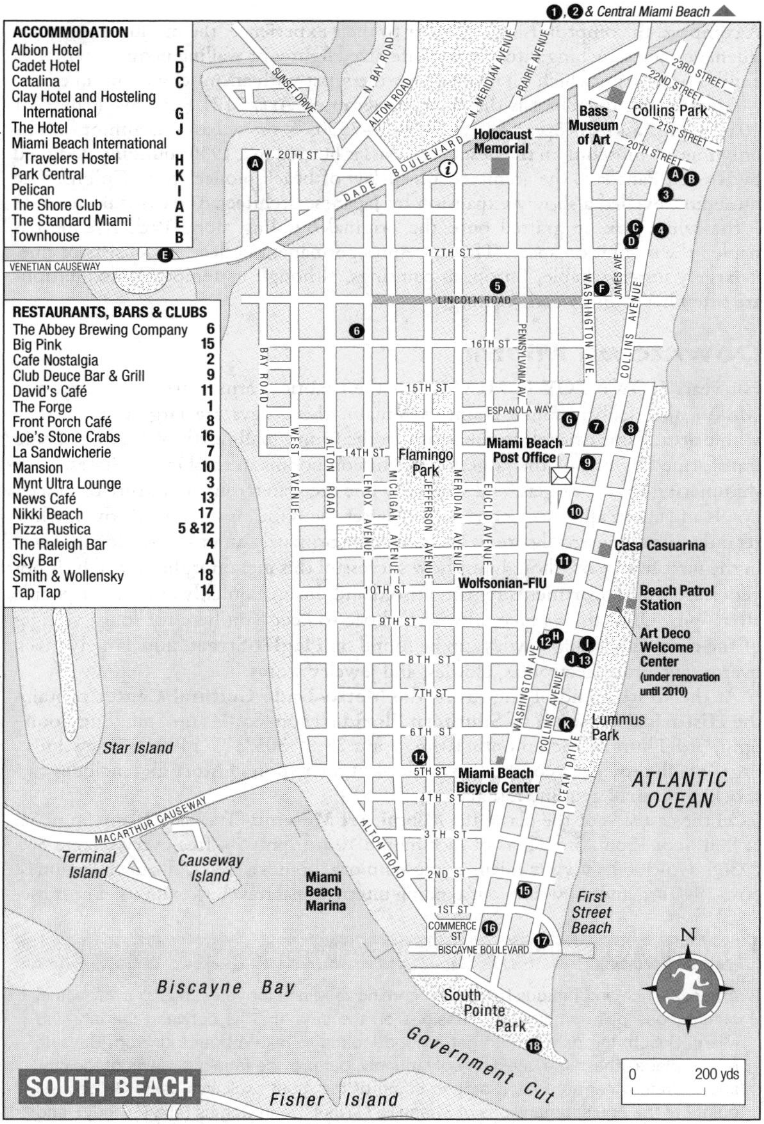

the late nineteenth century to 1945. The displays of old books, photos, paintings, posters, and all manner of domestic objects are impressive, if a bit muddled.

Throughout Miami Beach's history, one group that has kept a constant presence is its sizeable Jewish population, which includes many Holocaust survivors and their families. This contingent is the reason for the moving **Holocaust Memorial**, near the north tip of South Beach, at 1933–1945 Meridian Ave (daily 9am–9pm; $2 suggested donation for brochure; ⓣ 305/538-1663, ⓦ www.holocaustmmb.org).

A complex, uncompromising reminder to their experience, the monument depicts a defiant hand punching into the sky. Life-sized figures of wailing people attempt to climb up the arm, which is tattooed near the wrist with an Auschwitz number.

A few blocks northeast is the **Bass Museum of Art**, 2121 Park Ave (Tues–Sat 10am–5pm, Sun 11–5pm; $8; Ⓣ305/673-7530, Ⓦwww.bassmuseum.org). The only fine art museum on the beach, the Bass is housed in a 1930s building designed by Russell Pancoast, the architect son-in-law of beach pioneer John Collins. The museum unveiled a showy expansion by Japanese architect Arata Isozaki in 2002 – the white box he grafted onto the original building along Park Avenue has tripled the exhibition space. The museum's permanent collection consists of fine, if largely unremarkable, European paintings, although its temporary exhibitions are often lively and worth visiting.

Downtown Miami

For years **DOWNTOWN MIAMI** was the chaotic, Latin heart of the city, and while a few Cuban coffee counters remain, those days are largely gone. The whole area, from Brickell in the south to the Omni mall north of I-395, is being transformed by one of the largest construction booms in the United States. Vast, shimmering towers of glass and steel now line the waterfront, a mixture of offices, hotels and above all, pricey condos. The latter focus means that Downtown, while retaining its commercial core, is set to become primarily an upscale residential area in the next few years, though just how successful this metamorphosis will be is not yet clear – most apartments remain unsold and the area quickly empties of people after 6pm. Until things take off, there's little to keep you here for long; vestiges of the center's bustling heyday can be found on **Flagler Street**, now largely given over to cut-price electronics, clothes, and jewelry stores.

At the western end of the street, the **Metro-Dade Cultural Center** contains the **Historical Museum of Southern Florida** (Mon–Sat 10am–5pm, Sun noon–5pm, 3rd Thurs of each month 10am–9pm; $8; Ⓣ305/375-1492, Ⓦwww.hmsf.org), which provides a comprehensive look at the region's history and includes two shockingly small genuine refugee rafts.

On the east side of the plaza, the **Miami Art Museum** (Tues–Fri 10am–5pm, Sat & Sun noon–5pm, 3rd Thurs of each month 10am–9pm; $8, free every second Sat; Ⓣ305/375-3000, Ⓦwww.miamiartmuseum.org) houses a well laid-out collection of post-1940 art, and showcases outstanding international traveling exhibits. The muse-

Biscayne Bay's million-dollar mansions

America's rich and famous have been coming to Miami for years, hiding away within ostentatious palm-smothered mansions on the cays that lie between the city and Miami Beach; the only way to get a good look is to take a boat tour from Bayside Marketplace. These are unashamedly touristy, but provide fabulous views of the city, and include a narrated jaunt around some of the most exclusive cays. Guides will point out the opulent mansions of Shaquille O'Neal, Sean Combs (aka P Diddy), and Oprah Winfrey, among numerous others.

Operators include Island Queen Cruises (Ⓣ305/379-5119, Ⓦwww.islandqueencruises.com), which runs daily 1.5hr tours (11am-7pm, on the hour) for $22. You can also tour the same islands by kayak, though it pays to take the boat tour first so you know which celebrity backyard you're paddling past. Try South Beach Kayak (Wed–Sat 10.30am–sunset, Sun & Mon 11am–sunset; $25/2hr, $80/day; Ⓣ305/332-2853, Ⓦwww.southbeachkayak.com), 1771 Purdy Ave, Miami Beach, near the Venetian Causeway.

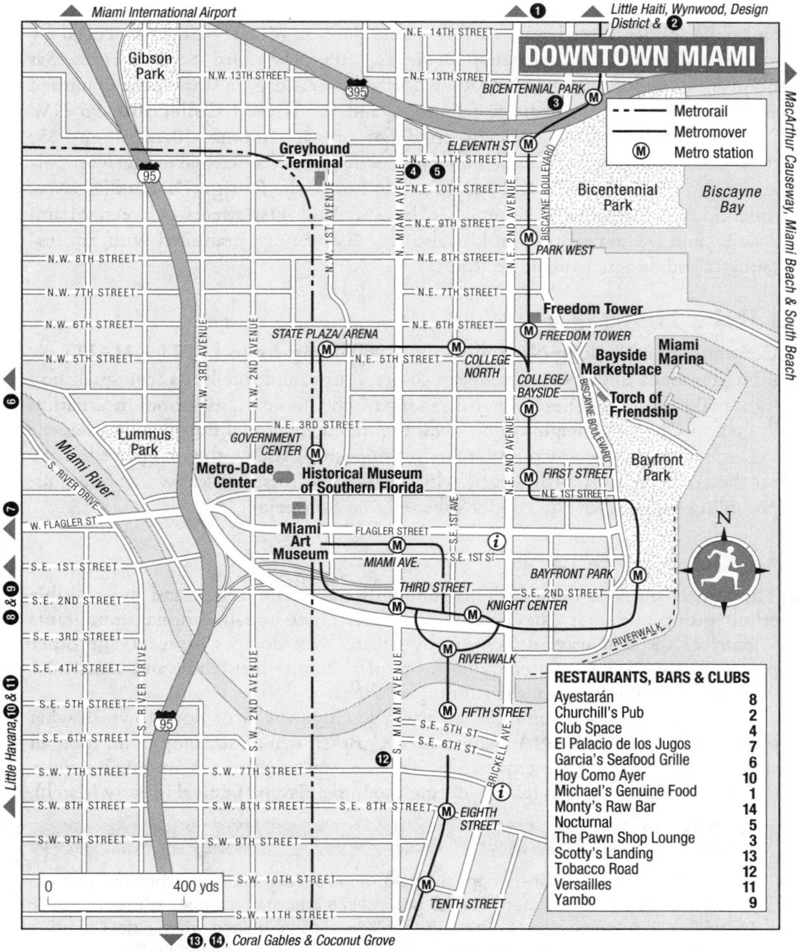

um is expected to relocate to a waterfront space close to I-395 to be called Museum Park, sometime in early 2012; call or check the museum website for details.

The eastern edge of downtown is bounded by Biscayne Boulevard, near which is the **Bayside Marketplace**, a large pink shopping mall with pleasant waterfront views from its terrace – take a **boat tour** of Biscayne Bay from here (see box opposite). Across the boulevard, the striking **Freedom Tower** built in 1925 and modeled on a Spanish belltower, earned its name by housing the Cuban Refugee Center in the 1960s. It is now owned by nearby Miami-Dade Community College, and sometimes opens for special exhibitions.

Wynwood and the Design District

North of downtown and 20th Street, the **Wynwood Art District** is home to one of the largest and most dynamic concentrations of **art galleries** in the nation. Though it's relatively safe to explore, the area remains sketchy at night, and galleries are spread out, so this is one part of Miami best experienced by car. Highlights include **Locust Projects**, 105 NW 23rd Street (Thurs–Sat noon-5pm; ⓣ305/576-8570, ⓦwww.locustprojects.org), a warehouse crammed with tantalizing multimedia installations, and the **Rubell Collection**, 95 NW 29th St (Wed–Sat 10am–6pm, second Sat of each month 10am–10pm; $5; ⓣ305/573-6090, ⓦwww.rubellfamilycollection.com), a massive modern art collection housed in an old warehouse. Further north, the **Design District** (ⓦwww.miamidesigndistrict.net), hemmed in by 36th and 41st streets between Miami Avenue and Biscayne Boulevard, is also worth a wander, crammed with hip restaurants and designer furniture stores.

Little Haiti

Continuing north along NE 2nd Avenue, you'll cruise into **LITTLE HAITI**, an immigrant area filled with Caribbean colors, music, and smells, its trilingual shop signs making sales pitches in English, French, and Creole. In its former incarnation as Lemon City, this neighborhood was the oldest inhabited European settlement in the area, alongside Coconut Grove (see opposite). Today, the best place to soak up the atmosphere is 54th Street, which is lined with stores known as *botánicas*, providing supplies for the voodoo-like religion **Santería**.

Little Havana

The impact on Miami by **Cubans**, unquestionably the largest and most visible ethnic group in the city, has been incalculable. These non-traditional immigrants – many of the first wave driven out by Castro were doctors, lawyers, and other professionals – were soon enjoying more of the same in Miami, and some now wield considerable clout in the running of the city.

The initial home of Miami Cubans was a few miles west of downtown in what became **LITTLE HAVANA**, whose streets, parks, memorials, shops, and food all stand to reflect the Cuban experience. Note, though, that streets are much quieter than those of South Beach (except during the Little Havana Festival in early March),

Cubans in Miami

During the mid-Fifties, when opposition to Cuba's Batista dictatorship began to assert itself, a trickle of Cubans started arriving in a predominantly Jewish section of Miami that was then called Riverside. The trickle became a flood when Fidel Castro took power in 1959, and the area became **Little Havana**, populated by the affluent Cuban middle classes who had the most to lose under communism.

These original immigrants were joined by a second influx in May 1980, when the **Mariel boatlift** brought 125,000 islanders from the port of Mariel to Miami in only a few days. These arrivals were poor and uneducated, and a fifth of them were fresh from Cuban jails – incarcerated for criminal rather than political crimes. Bluntly, Castro had dumped his misfits on Miami. The city reeled and then recovered from this mass arrival, but it left Miami's Cuban community utterly divided. Even today, older Cuban-Americans claim that they can pick out a Marielito from the way he or she walks or talks.

That said, local division gives way to fervent agreement when it comes to Castro: he's universally detested. In Miami, Cubans have been killed for being suspected of advocating dialogue with Castro. Despite failing to depose the dictator, Cuban-Americans have been far more successful at influencing the US government. Since the 1980s, Cubans have been vociferous supporters of the Republican party in what has traditionally been a crucial swing state – and therefore one of the main reasons that the US embargo of Cuba (imposed in 1962), remains in place.

and today, many successful Cuban-Americans have moved elsewhere in the city, to be replaced by immigrants from parts of Central America, especially Nicaragua.

Make a beeline here for lunch at one of the many small restaurants on SW 8th Street, or Calle Ocho, the neighborhood's main drag. Check out also **Cuban Memorial Boulevard**, the stretch of SW 13th Avenue just south of Calle Ocho, where a cluster of memorials underscores the Cuban-American presence in Miami. Here, the simple stone **Brigade 2506 Memorial** remembers those who died at the Bay of Pigs on April 17, 1961, during the abortive invasion of Cuba by US-trained Cuban exiles. Veterans of the landing, aging men dressed in combat fatigues, gather here for each anniversary to make all-night-long pledges of patriotism.

Coral Gables

All of Miami's constituent neighborhoods are fast to assert their individuality, though none does it more definitively than **CORAL GABLES**, located southwest of Little Havana. Twelve square miles of broad boulevards, leafy side streets, and Spanish and Italian architecture form a cultured setting for a cultured community.

Coral Gables's creator was a local aesthete, **George Merrick**, who raided street names from a Spanish dictionary to plan the plazas, fountains, and carefully aged stucco-fronted buildings here. Unfortunately, Coral Gables was taking shape just as the Florida property boom ended. Merrick was wiped out, and died as Miami's postmaster in 1942. But Coral Gables never lost its good looks, and it remains an impressive place to explore. Merrick wanted people to know they'd arrived somewhere special, and as such, eight grand **entrances** were planned on the main approach roads (though only four were completed). Three of these stand along the western end of Calle Ocho as you arrive from Little Havana.

The best way into Coral Gables is along SW 22nd Street, known as the **Miracle Mile**. Long dominated by fusty, no-name ladies'-wear boutiques, it's been redeveloped to attract some funkier, livelier tenants. Note the arcades and balconies, and the spirals and peaks of the **Omni Colonnade Hotel**, at 180 Aragon Ave, one block north, completed in 1926 to accommodate George Merrick's office. Further west, along Coral Way, the **Merrick House** (by 45min tour only on Sun & Wed 1pm, 2pm & 3pm; $5; ⓣ305/460-5361) was George's boyhood home. In 1899, when he was twelve, his family arrived here from New England to run a 160-acre farm, which was so successful that the house quickly grew from a wooden shack into an elegant dwelling of coral rock and gabled windows (thus inspiring the name of the future city).

While his property-developing contemporaries left ugly scars across the city after digging up the local limestone, Merrick had the foresight to turn his biggest quarry into a sumptuous swimming pool. Opened in 1924, the **Venetian Pool**, 2701 De Soto Blvd (June–Aug Mon–Fri 11am–7.30pm; Sept & Oct and April & May Tues–Fri 11am–5.30pm; Nov–March Tues–Fri 10am–4.30pm; year-round Sat & Sun 10am–4.30pm; April–October $10, November–March $6.75; ⓣ305/460-5356, ⓦwww.venetianpool.com), is an essential stop on a steamy Miami afternoon. Its pastel stucco walls hide a delightful spring-fed lagoon, with vine-covered loggias, fountains, waterfalls, coral caves, and plenty of room to swim.

Wrapping its broad wings around the southern end of De Soto Blvd, Merrick's crowning achievement was the fabulous **Biltmore Hotel**, 1200 Anastasia Ave (ⓣ1-800/727-1926, ⓦwww.biltmorehotel.com). With a 26-storey tower visible across much of low-lying Miami, everything about the *Biltmore* is over-the-top: 25-foot fresco-coated walls, vaulted ceilings, immense fireplaces, custom-loomed rugs, and a massive swimming pool hosting shows by such bathing belles and beaux as Esther Williams and Johnny Weissmuller. Today, it costs upward of $200 a night to stay here, but a fascinating free tour leaves from the lobby every Sunday at 1.30, 2.30, and 3.30pm; meet at the birdcages. You can also take **afternoon tea** in the lobby for $17 (Mon–Fri 3pm & 4.30pm sittings).

Villa Vizcaya

In 1914, south of downtown, farm-machinery mogul James Deering blew $15 million on recreating a sixteenth-century Italian villa within the tropical jungle. A thousand-strong workforce completed his **Villa Vizcaya**, 3251 S Miami Ave (daily 9.30am–4.30pm; free house tours every 20min; $12; ⓣ305/250-9133, ⓦwww.vizcayamuseum.org), in just two years. Deering's madly eclectic art collection, and his desire that the villa should appear to have been inhabited for four hundred years, result in a thunderous clash of Baroque, Renaissance, Rococo, and Neoclassical fixtures and fittings. The fabulous landscaped **gardens**, with their many fountains and sculptures, are just as excessive.

Key Biscayne

A compact, immaculately manicured community, **KEY BISCAYNE**, five miles off mainland Miami, is a great place to live – if you can afford it. The only way onto the island is along the four-mile **Rickenbacker Causeway** ($1.50 one-way toll), which runs from SW 26th Road just south of downtown.

Crandon Park Beach, a mile along Crandon Boulevard (the continuation of the main road from the causeway), is one of the finest landscaped beaches in the city, with crystal-clear waters, barbecue grills, and sports facilities (daily 8am–sunset; $5 per car; ⓣ305/361-5421). Three miles of yellow-brown beach fringe the park, and give access to a sand bar enabling knee-depth wading far from the shore.

Crandon Boulevard terminates at the entrance to the **Bill Baggs Cape Florida State Recreation Area**, four hundred wooded acres covering the southern extremity of Key Biscayne (daily 8am–sunset; $5 per car, pedestrians and cyclists $1; ⓣ305/361-5811). An excellent swimming **beach** lines the Atlantic-facing side of the park, and a boardwalk cuts around the wind-bitten sand dunes toward the 1820s **Cape Florida lighthouse**. Climb the 95-foot-high structure for mesmerizing views of the whole island and downtown Miami. For more detailed information, take a ranger-led tour (Thurs-Tues 10am & 1pm; free) and check out the exhibits and video in the nearby **keeper's cottage**.

Eating

Cuban food is what Miami does best, and it's not limited to the traditional haunts in **Little Havana**. The hearty comfort food – notably rice and beans, fried plantains, and shredded pork sandwiches – is found in every neighborhood, and you'll also want to try Cuban coffee: choose between *café cubano*, strong, sweet, and frothy, drunk like a shot with a glass of water; *café con leche*, with steamed milk, and particularly good at breakfast with *pan cubano* (thin, buttered toast); or *café cortadito*, a smaller version of the *con leche*. Cuban cooking is complemented by sushi bars, American homestyle diners, as well as Haitian, Italian, and New Floridian (sometimes known as Floribbean; a mix of Caribbean spiciness and fruity Florida sauces), among a handful of other ethnic cuisines.

Coral Gables, South Beach and the Design District are best for upmarket cafés and restaurants. **Seafood** is abundant: succulent grouper, yellowfin tuna, and wahoo, a local delicacy, are among five hundred species of fish that thrive offshore. **Stone-crab claws**, served from October to May, are another South Florida specialty.

Ayestarán 706 SW 27th Ave, Little Havana ⓣ305/649-4982. This sprawling Cuban restaurant offers hearty and cheap daily specials and superb *café con leche* that you can mix to your liking.

Big Pink 157 Collins Ave, South Beach ⓣ305/532-4700. Come here for large portions of comfort food: mashed potatoes, ribs, macaroni and cheese, and classic "TV dinners," all served at long communal tables.

David's Café 1058 Collins Ave ⓣ305/534-8736. Eat deep-fried delicacies and daily Cuban specials like chicken with rice and beans ($6) on the tables outside, wedged between businessmen and teens, or grab a *café Cubano* (95¢) at the take-out window. There's dining room-style seating at the second branch, 1654 Meridian Ave, just off Lincoln Road: try staples like Cuban sandwiches ($7.95) and pork chops ($12.45). Open 24hr.

El Palacio de los Jugos 5721 W Flagler Ave, Little Havana ⓣ305/264-1503. A handful of tables at the back of a Cuban produce market, where the pork sandwiches and shellfish soup from the takeout stand are the tastiest for miles. Also serving refreshing *jugos* (juices).

The Forge 432 41st St, Miami Beach ⓣ305/538-8533. A memorable upscale dining spot where the hearty traditional food and huge wine cellar combine appealingly with a vibrant atmosphere and eclectic clientele.

Front Porch Café 1418 Ocean Drive, South Beach ⓣ305/531-8300. This local hangout is refreshingly low-key, considering its location: the delicious, dinner-plate-sized pancakes will easily take care of both breakfast and lunch.

Garcia's Seafood Grille 398 NW N River Drive, downtown ⓣ305/375-0765. Wonderful waterfront café with ramshackle wooden benches and superb, fresh fish dishes for around $15. Usually closes at 9.30pm.

Joe's Stone Crabs 11 Washington Ave, South Beach ⓣ305/673-0365. Specializing in succulent stone crabs and always packed – if you're impatient, do as the locals do and head to the takeout window. Crabcakes, fresh fish, and the crispy fried chicken are also good. Open Oct–May.

La Sandwicherie 229 W 14th St, South Beach ⓣ305/532-8934. Gigantic sandwiches stuffed with gourmet ingredients such as prosciutto and imported cheeses and starting at around $5.30. It's open until 5am, so good for a post-clubbing refuel.

Michael's Genuine Food 130 NE 40th St, Design District ⓣ305/573-5550. One of the hottest restaurants in town, with seasonal, local ingredients whipped into eclectic creations by lauded chef Michael Schwartz; sizes range small to extra large (medium and large entrees $10–27).

News Café 800 Ocean Drive, South Beach ⓣ305/538-NEWS. This mid-priced sidewalk café has front-row seating for the South Beach promenade – although the food's unremarkable. Open 24hrs.

Pizza Rustica 863 Washington Ave, South Beach ⓣ305/674-8244. Mouthwateringly fresh gourmet pizza, with slab-like slices costing around $5. Also at 667 Lincoln Rd.

Scotty's Landing 3381 Pan American Drive, Coconut Grove ⓣ305/854-2626. Tasty, inexpensive seafood and fish 'n' chips consumed at marina-side picnic tables. It's tucked away on the water by City Hall, and so can be hard to find – ask if you get lost.

Smith & Wollensky 1 Washington Ave (at South Pointe Park) ⓣ305/673-2800. This steakhouse chain deserves a try for its superb location; sit overlooking the mouth of the Miami River and watch cruise ships navigate the harbor.

Tap Tap 819 5th St, South Beach ⓣ305/672-2898. Tasty, attractively presented and reasonably priced Haitian food. Most dishes are less than $10 – the goat in a peppery tomato broth is a knockout. Dinner only.

Versailles 3555 SW 8th St, Little Havana ⓣ305/444-0240. Local families, Cuban businessmen, and backpackers congregate here for the wonderfully inexpensive Cuban dishes, served by friendly staff amid kitsch decor of chandeliers and mirrored walls.

Yambo 1643 SW 1st St, Little Havana ⓣ305/642-6616. Step out of the USA and into Central America at *Yambo*, an undiscovered gem serving up good, inexpensive Nicaraguan food.

Nightlife and entertainment

Miami's **nightlife** is still unsurpassed in Florida. Almost every dancefloor is attached to a restaurant or a bar, so you could end up dancing anywhere. At the fully-fledged **clubs**, house and techno beats are most popular, followed by salsa or merengue played by Spanish-speaking DJs. Most of the action is centered in South Beach, and **cover charges** are around $20. Door policies are notoriously fierce at current in-spots; the places listed below include laid-back local haunts as well as some of the hotter bars and clubs. The free *New Times* magazine, published every Thursday, offers **listings** of what's going on where and when – including **gay and lesbian info**.

If you want to try out the local **sports** scene, the Marlins major league baseball team and the Dolphins, Miami's pro football team, play at Dolphin Stadium, 2269 Dan Marino Blvd, sixteen miles northwest of downtown Miami (Ⓣ305/623-6100, Ⓦwww.dolphinstadium.com; take bus #27 from the main bus station). Note that the Marlins are due to move to a new stadium in 2011, at 1400 NW 4th St, Little Havana.

Bars and live music venues

The Abbey Brewing Company 1115 16th St, South Beach Ⓣ305/538-8110. This small, unpretentious microbrewery serves the best beers on South Beach. Try the creamy Oatmeal Stout – their best and most popular brew. Open until 5am.

Churchill's Pub 5501 NE 2nd Ave, Little Haiti Ⓣ305/757-1807, Ⓦwww.churchillspub.com. A British enclave within Little Haiti, with soccer and rugby matches on TV, UK beers on tap, and live rock music. Check website for schedule.

Club Deuce Bar & Grill 222 14th St, South Beach Ⓣ305/531-6200. This grimy, noisy grunge bar is a remnant from pre-fabulous South Beach. Drinks are cheap, the crowd's indie, and there's a dartboard and pool table. Open until 5am.

Hoy Como Ayer 2212 SW 8th St, Little Havana Ⓣ305/541-2631, Ⓦwww.hoycomoayer.net. Despite the city's sizeable Cuban population, this dark, smoky joint is about the only place in Miami to hear decent Cuban music. Check website for schedule.

Jimbo's inside the park at Virginia Key Beach, Virginia Key Ⓣ305/361-7026. Renowned ramshackle bar where you can help yourself to a beer from a wheelbarrow filled with ice. A good place to chat with the old-timers.

Monty's Raw Bar 2550 S Bayshore Drive, Coconut Grove Ⓣ305/858-1431. Drinkers often outnumber the diners (it's also a restaurant) at this tiki-style bar, drawn here by the gregarious mood and the views across the bay; the loud reggae music can be a bit overpowering, though.

Purdy Lounge 1811 Purdy Ave, South Beach Ⓣ305/531-4622. An unheralded beachside gem, this large neighborhood bar avoids clogging crowds of out-of-towners by its location on the less-touristed western side of South Beach. Open until 5am.

The Raleigh Bar inside the *Raleigh Hotel*, 1775 Collins Ave, South Beach Ⓣ305/534-6300. This elegant 1940s hotel bar, with its lushly restored wood paneling, is a throwback to the heyday of cocktail culture.

Sky Bar inside the *Shore Club* hotel, 1901 Collins Ave, South Beach Ⓣ786/276-6772. Sprawling outdoor bar draped around the hotel pool, with giant overstuffed square seats: dress up and expect a tough door unless you're staying at the hotel. Check out the smaller, attached *Sandbar*, with its view of the beach and ocean.

Tobacco Road 626 S Miami Ave, downtown Ⓣ305/374-1198, Ⓦwww.tobacco-road.com. This friendly dive bar – Miami's oldest, from 1912 – is a favorite with locals for its exceptional live R&B. Check website for schedule.

Nightclubs

Cafe Nostalgia inside the *Versailles Hotel*, 3425 Collins Ave, Miami Beach Ⓣ305/531-6092, Ⓦwww.cafenostalgia.com. This legendary (and itinerant) Cuban club offers live music for an older crowd early on; from 1am it's Latin hip-hip for 20-somethings.

Club Space 34 NE 11th St, downtown Ⓣ305/375-0001, Ⓦwww.clubspace.com. This downtown pioneer has a rough decor and an illicit ambiance: most people migrate here when the other venues shut down, for after-hours dancing until dawn – expect a friendly, loved-up, youngish crowd and big-name DJs.

Mansion 1235 Washington Ave, South Beach Ⓣ305/532-1525, Ⓦwww.mansionmiami.com. Large nightclub complex with six VIP areas, nine bars, and five dancefloors, each with its own style of music, hip-hop being the most popular.

Mynt Ultra Lounge 1921 Collins Ave, South Beach Ⓣ786/276-6132, Ⓦwww.myntlounge.com. Lounge/dance club, washed in green light, with an enormous bar and large, black leather sofas. Expect a fierce door any night of the week.

Nikki Beach 1 Ocean Drive Ⓣ305/538-1111, Ⓦwww.nikkibeach.com/miami.

Located right on the beach, this sprawling club features loungers, beds and palm trees, offering a real iconic South Beach experience. The restaurant is open daily, but the dancing gets going on the weekends with international and local DJs spinning till dawn.

Nocturnal 50 NE 11th St, downtown ⓣ305/576-6996, www.nocturnalmiami.com. The spaced-out will enjoy the trippy images projected on the rooftop terrace's 360-degree IMAX-style screen as the deep house music thumps in their ears.

The Pawn Shop 1222 NE 2nd Ave, between 12th and 13th sts ⓣ305/373-3511, ⓦwww.thepawnshoplounge.com. Massive, converted 1930s pawn shop with an interior best described as Alice in Wonderland on acid, including an entire school bus and chandeliers and boots dangling from the ceiling.

The Florida Keys

Folklore, films, and fiction have given the **FLORIDA KEYS** – a hundred-mile chain of islands that runs to within ninety miles of Cuba – an image of glamorous intrigue they don't really deserve; at least, not now that the go-go days of the cocaine cowboys in the 1980s are long gone. Rather, the Keys are an outdoor-lover's paradise, where fishing, snorkeling, and diving dominate. Terrific untainted natural areas include the **Florida Reef**, a great band of living coral just a few miles off the coast. But for many, the various keys are only stops on the way to **Key West**. Once the richest town in the US, and the final dot of North America before a thousand miles of ocean, Key West has vibrant, Caribbean-style streets with plenty of convivial bars in which to while away the hours, watching the spectacular **sunsets**.

Wherever you are on the Keys, you'll experience distinctive **cuisine**, served for the most part in funky little shacks where the food is fresh and the atmosphere laid-back. Conch, a rich meaty mollusk, is a specialty, served in chowders and fritters. There's also **key lime pie**, a delicate, creamy concoction of special Key limes and condensed milk, that bears little resemblance to the lurid green imposter pies served in the rest of the US.

Getting around the Keys could hardly be easier. There's just one route all the way through to Key West: the **Overseas Highway** (US-1). The road is punctuated by **mile markers** (MM), starting with MM127 just south of Miami and finishing with MM0 in Key West, at the corner of Whitehead and Fleming streets. As per Keys convention, addresses are given by the closest mile marker, along with the appellation of either "Oceanside" or "Bayside," depending on whether the place in question faces the Atlantic Ocean or Florida Bay.

Key Largo

The first and largest of the keys, **KEY LARGO**, is a disappointing jumble of filling stations, shopping plazas, and fast-food outlets. The town does, however, provide a fine opportunity to visit the Florida Reef, at the **John Pennekamp**

Coral Reef State Park, at MM102.5-Oceanside (daily 8am–sunset; $3.50 per car and driver, plus $2.50 for first passenger, 50¢ for each additional passenger, pedestrians and cyclists $1.50; ⓣ305/451-1202, ⓦwww.pennekamppark.com). This protected 78-square-mile section of living coral reef is rated as one of the most beautiful in the world. If you can, take the **snorkeling tour** (9am, noon & 3pm; 2hr 30mins; $29.95, plus $7 for equipment), or the **guided scuba dive** (9.30am & 1.30pm; 1hr 30mins; $60; diver's certificate required). The **glass-bottom boat tour** (9.15am, 12.15pm & 3pm; 2hr 30mins; $24) is less demanding. For information and to make reservations for all of these tours, call ⓣ305/451-6300. On any of them, you're virtually certain to spot lobsters, angelfish, eels, and jellyfish along the reef, and shoals of silvery minnows stalked by mean-looking barracuda. The reef itself is a delicate living thing, comprising millions of minute coral polyps extracting calcium from the seawater and growing from one to sixteen feet every thousand years. Sadly, it's far easier to spot signs of death than life: white patches show where a carelessly dropped anchor, or a diver's hand, has scraped away the protective mucous layer and left the coral susceptible to terminal disease.

Practicalities

Key Largo has some of the widest selections of reasonably priced **accommodation** in the Keys, with many of the motels offering diving packages. Among the cheaper options, there's the basic but clean *Ed & Allen's Lodgings*, MM103.5-Oceanside (ⓣ1-888/333-5536; ⓦwww.ed-ellens-lodgings.com; ③–④), or the gloriously quirky, adult-only *Largo Lodge*, MM101.5-Bayside (ⓣ1-800/468-4378, ⓦwww.largolodge.com; ⑤–⑥); for something more luxurious, try the huge, stylish chalets at the *Kona Kai Resort*, MM97.8-Bayside (ⓣ1-800/365-7829, ⓦwww.konakairesort.com; ⑨). Delicious, fresh **seafood** – as well as chunks of alligator served like chicken nuggets – is available at *Snapper's*, 139 Seaside Ave, at the end of Ocean View Ave off US-1 at MM94.5-Oceanside (ⓣ305/852-5956), while *Harriette's*, MM95.7-Bayside (ⓣ305/852-8689, open till 2pm) serves good breakfasts.

Islamorada

Comprising a twenty-mile strip of separate islands, including Plantation, Windley, and Upper and Lower Matecumbe keys, **ISLAMORADA** (pronounced "eye-lah-more-RAH-da) is a much more welcoming place to dawdle than Key Largo, fifteen miles to the north. Most visitors come here to **fish** (you'll see charter boats advertised all along the highway), but you can also explore **Indian Key Historic State Park**, one of many small, mangrove-skirted islands off Lower Matecumbe Key. Once a thriving settlement founded by wrecker Jacob Houseman, it now boasts a riot of exotic plants and evocative ruins. Kayak rentals ($20/hr, $50/day) are available from **Robbie's Marina** (ⓣ305/664-9814) at MM78.5-Oceanside (there are no ferries).

Good-value **accommodation** in Islamorada includes the very cheap *Key Lantern/Blue Fin Inn*, MM82-Bayside (ⓣ305/664-4572, ⓦwww.keylantern.com; ③) – ask for a room at the *Blue Fin* (same price), since these were more recently renovated – and the serene *Drop Anchor Resort*, MM85-Oceanside (ⓣ1-888/664-4863, ⓦwww.dropanchorresort.com; ⑤). As for **eating**, *Hungry Tarpon*, MM77.5-Bayside (ⓣ305/664-0535), serves excellent fresh fish as well as tasty breakfasts, while the pricier – and often packed – *Islamorada Fish Company*, MM81.5-Bayside (ⓣ1-800/258-2559), is also good for seafood.

The Middle Keys

Once over Long Key Bridge, you're into **THE MIDDLE KEYS**. At the not-for-profit **Dolphin Research Center**, MM59-Bayside (daily 9am–4.30pm; ⓣ305/289-1121, ⓦwww.dolphins.org), you can swim with the dolphins for $180 (reservations at ⓣ305/289-0002).

The largest of several islands in the Middle Keys, **Key Vaca** holds the nucleus of the area's major settlement, **Marathon**. Here you'll find great **fishing** and **watersports** opportunities, as well as a couple of small beaches. **Sombrero Beach**, along Sombrero Beach Road (off the Overseas Highway near MM50-Oceanside), has good swimming waters and shaded picnic tables.

Opposite the turning to the beach is the entrance to the 64-acre tropical forest of **Crane Point** (Mon–Sat 9am–5pm, Sun noon–5pm; $8; ⓣ305/743-9100, ⓦwww.cranepoint.net). This includes the **Museum of Natural History of the Florida Keys**, which presents an excellent introduction to the history and ecology of the area. Follow the 1.5-mile **nature trail** past the hammock forest, an area of dense hardwood trees characteristic of the Keys, until you reach the end. Here, you'll find the hundred-year-old **Adderley House Historic Site**, established by settlers from the Bahamas.

Marathon has some well-equipped **resorts**, such as the lush *Banana Bay*, MM49.5-Bayside (ⓣ1-800/226-2621, ⓦwww.bananabay.com; ⑤), which has a private beach. The best **budget option** is the *Flamingo Inn*, MM59.3-Bayside (ⓣ1-800/439-1478, ⓦwww.theflamingoinn.com; ④–⑤), a lovingly maintained retro motel with large rooms. For **eating**, there's terrific seafood – including succulent beer-steamed shrimp – at *Castaway*, 15th Street near MM47.5-Oceanside (ⓣ305/743-6247). The tiny, laid-back *Seven Mile Grill*, by the bridge of the same name at MM47.5-Bayside (ⓣ305/743-4481), serves delicious conch and creamy key lime pie to locals, sea salts, and tourists alike. For good, cheap Cuban food and fresh snapper, try *Taino*'s, MM53-Oceanside (ⓣ305/743-5247).

The Lower Keys

Starkly different from their neighbors to the north, **THE LOWER KEYS** are quiet, covered in dense vegetation, and predominantly residential. Built on a limestone rather than a coral base, these islands have a flora and fauna all their own, most notably the **Key deer** (see below).

The first place of consequence you'll hit after crossing Seven Mile Bridge is one of the Keys' prettiest spots: **Bahia Honda State Park**, at MM37-Oceanside (daily 8am–sunset; $3.50 per car and driver, plus $2.50 for first passenger, 50¢ for each additional passenger; pedestrians and cyclists $1.50; ⓣ305/872-2353, ⓦwww.bahiahondapark.com). It has the best stretch of sand in the Keys, and pristine, two-tone ocean waters, which can be enjoyed on a leisurely **kayak ride** ($10/hr, $30/day). You can also take snorkeling trips out to the **Looe Key Marine Sanctuary** from here (daily 9.30am and 1.30pm; $29.95, $7 for equipment; ⓣ305/872-3210), a five-square-mile protected reef, easily the equal of the John Pennekamp Coral Reef State Park (see p.575). If you want to spend more time in the water, drive on to **Ramrod Key** and the Looe Key Dive Center (ⓣ1-800/942-5397, ⓦwww.diveflakeys.com), which offers daily 5hr scuba ($70) and snorkeling ($30) excursions to the sanctuary.

Delightfully tame Key deer can be found ambling around the **National Key Deer Refuge** on Big Pine Key. Visit the refuge center (Mon–Fri 8am–5pm, park open daily sunrise–sunset; ⓣ305/872-2239, Ⓦnationalkeydeer.fws.gov), tucked away in a shopping mall off Key Deer Boulevard, just north of US-1 at MM30, to get a map of the best viewing spots.

Big Pine Key is the main Lower Keys settlement. Nearby you'll find most of the **accommodation** in these parts – which is generally more limited and expensive than in the Middle and Upper Keys. *Looe Key Reef Resort*, MM27.5-Oceanside (ⓣ1-800/942-5397, Ⓦwww.diveflakeys.com; ④–⑤), is an ideal base for visiting the marine sanctuary, while for a real splurge, stay at the idyllic, adult-only *Little Palm Island*, MM28.5-Oceanside, Little Torch Key (ⓣ1-800/343-8567, Ⓦwww.littlepalmisland.com; ⑨), a private islet whose thatched cottages are set in lush gardens a few feet from the beach.

For **food**, the dollar-bill-decorated *No Name Pub*, a mile or so from MM30-Bayside down North Watson Boulevard (ⓣ305/872-9115) is known for its superb thin-crust pizza. Further on down the Overseas Highway, on Sugarloaf Key at MM20-Bayside, the friendly *Mangrove Mama's* (ⓣ305/745-3030; closed Sept) serves stupendous local cuisine in a cheery shack with a tropical garden.

Key West

Closer to Cuba than to mainland Florida, **KEY WEST** often seems rather tenuously bound to the rest of the US. Famed for their tolerant attitudes and laid-back lifestyles, the thirty thousand islanders seem adrift in a great expanse of sea and sky, and – despite a million tourists a year – the place resonates with an individual spirit. In particular, liberal attitudes have stimulated a large gay influx, estimated at two in five of the population. Although Key West today has been heavily restored and revitalized for the tourists, the town has retained some of its sense of individualism and isolation, especially away from the main drag of Duval Street. To best absorb this atmosphere – and the mellow pace of local life – take time to amble the gorgeous, lushly vegetated streets, make meals last for hours, and pause regularly for refreshment in the numerous bars.

Arrival and information

The **airport** (ⓣ305/296-5439) is four miles east of town, with the **Greyhound** bus station (ⓣ305/296-9072) adjacent to its entrance. There are no shuttle buses into town; a **taxi** (ⓣ305/296-6666) costs around $16.

The best place to head for **information** is the Greater Key West Chamber of Commerce, in the center of town next to Mallory Square at 402 Wall St (Mon–Fri 8.30am–6.30pm, Sat & Sun 9am–6pm; ⓣ305/294-2587, Ⓦwww.keywestchamber.org). The Chamber can give precise dates for Key West's annual **festivals**, the best of which are the Conch Republic Celebration in April and Fantasy Fest in late October, which feels like a gay Mardi Gras crossed with Halloween. A good source of **gay information** is the Key West Business Guild, 513 Truman Ave (daily 9am–5pm; ⓣ305/294-4603, Ⓦwww.gaykeywestfl.com).

It's best to explore the narrow streets of the mile-square Old Town – which contains virtually everything that you'll want to see – **on foot**. You could do it in little more than a day, though dashing about isn't the way to enjoy the place. Cycling is another good way of getting around: **bikes** can be rented from Adventure Scooter & Bicycle Rentals, with locations at 1 Duval St (ⓣ305/293-0441) and 617 Front St ($15 per day; ⓣ305/293-9955).

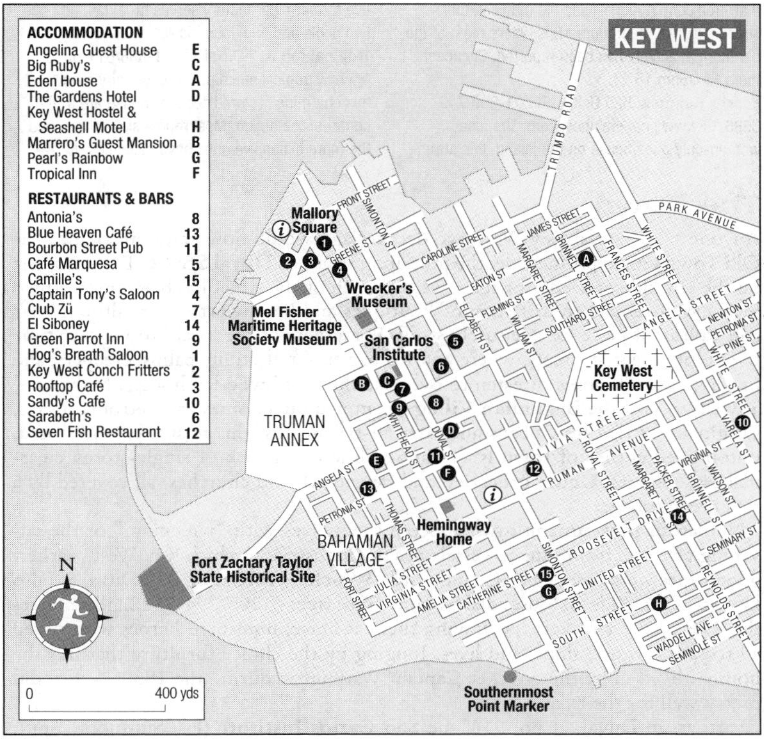

Accommodation

During the winter, it's essential to make a **reservation** for accommodation in Key West; the Fantasy Fest festival at the end of October is another extremely busy time. In summer, competition for rooms is less fierce, and prices drop by up to thirty percent.

Angelina Guest House 302 Angela St ⓣ1-888/303-4480, ⓦwww.angelinaguesthouse.com. This charming guesthouse, tucked away in the back-streets of the Bahamian Village, has a cool, Caribbean feel, and is one of the best deals in town. Room with shared bath 3–4, room with private bath 4–5

Big Ruby's 409 Applerouth Lane ⓣ1-800/477-7829, ⓦwww.bigrubys.com. Gay guesthouse with stylish rooms clustered round a lagoon pool and patio that's perfect for peaceful lounging. 7

Eden House 1015 Fleming St ⓣ305/296-6868, ⓦwww.edenhouse.com. Here, a grotty lobby hides one of the city's best deals – large rooms, free parking, free happy hour every night, and a shaded pool. Room with shared bath from 4–6, room with private bath from 6–7

The Gardens Hotel 526 Angela St ⓣ1-800/526-2664, ⓦwww.gardenshotel.com. One of the swishest hotels in town, this graceful inn has only 17 suites decked out in an airy Malaysian style with flat-screen TVs, fresh flowers, and enormous beds. Groves of greenery and orchids envelop the building and hide it from prying eyes. 7–9

Key West Hostel & Seashell Motel 718 South St ⓣ305/296-5719, ⓦwww.keywesthostel.com. The hostel has cheap dorm beds ($34), a sunny patio, and no curfew, while the Seashell Motel (3) offers standard rooms at the lowest rates in the neighborhood.

Marrero's Guest Mansion 410 Fleming St ⓣ305/294-6977 or 1-800/459-6212, ⓦwww.

marreros.com. Antique-filled old mansion that's supposedly haunted; room 18 is where most of the paranormal activity has been reported. Cheapest room ❻, room 18 ❼

Pearl's Rainbow 525 United St ⓣ1-800/749-6696, ⓦwww.pearlsrainbow.com. The lone women-only guesthouse on the island, this attractive former cigar factory serves breakfast and has two pools and two Jacuzzis. ❺

Tropical Inn 812 Duval St ⓣ1-888/611-6510, ⓦwww.tropicalinn.com. The large, airy rooms in this charming restored "conch" house are at the center of the action. Most rooms sleep three, and the more expensive ones have balconies. ❻–❼

The Town

Anyone who visited Key West two decades ago would now barely recognize the Old Town's main promenade, the mile-long swath of **Duval Street**. Teetering just on the safe side of seedy for many years, much of the street has been transformed into a well-tended tourist strip of boutiques and beachwear shops, although it's still a pleasant place for a leisurely stroll. For a sense of the locals' town, take time to explore the side streets, where gnarled banyans, tall skinny palms, creepers, and unruly, exotic blooms threaten to overtake the faded wooden houses. Make sure, as well, to visit the **Bahamian Village**, centered on Thomas and Petronia streets. Originally settled by Cubans and African-Bahamians, this relatively unrestored, untouristed corner of town is an atmospheric patchwork of single-storey cigar-makers' cottages, Cuban groceries, and ramshackle old churches, all covered by a rich green foliage.

Numerous **museums** in town concern themselves with "wrecking," or the salvaging of cargo from sunken vessels; it's the industry on which Key West's earliest good times were based. The friendly little **Wreckers Museum**, 322 Duval St (also known as the Oldest House; daily 10am–4pm; free; ⓣ305/294-9502), illuminates the lives of the wreckers, portraying them as brave, uninsured heroes who risked all to save cargoes, ships, and lives. Judging by the choice furniture that fills the house – lived in by the wrecker Captain Watlington during the 1830s – they did pretty well for their pains.

Farther up Duval, at no. 516, the **San Carlos Institute** (Fri–Sun noon–6pm; $3 donation; ⓣ305/294-3887) has played a leading role in Cuban exile life since it opened in 1871. Financed by a grant from the Cuban government, the present building dates from 1924. Cuban architect Francisco Centurion designed the two-storey building in the Cuban Baroque style of that period. Soil from Cuba's six provinces covers the grounds, and a cornerstone was taken from the tomb of Cuban independence campaigner José Martí. There's a passable exhibition on Cuban heritage here, and they also distribute the free Cuban Heritage Trail pamphlet, which details sites of interest around town.

The **southernmost point** in Key West, and consequently in the continental US, is at the intersection of Whitehead and South streets. A daft-looking buoy marks the spot.

Back up and just west from the northern end of Duval Street is **Mallory Square**. In the early 1800s, thousands of dollars' worth of salvage was landed at the piers, stored in the warehouses, and flogged at the auction houses here. Nowadays, however, it is dominated by tourist shops and worth only a brief linger.

Head rather to the nearby **Mel Fisher Maritime Heritage Society Museum**, 200 Greene St (Mon–Fri 8.30am–5pm, Sat–Sun 9.30am–5pm; $12; ⓣ305/294-2633, ⓦwww.melfisher.org), which showcases the diamonds, pearls, and daggers, as well as countless vases, an impressive emerald cross, and the obligatory cannon, that Fisher pulled up from two seventeenth-century shipwrecks in the 1980s – a haul said to be worth at least $200 million.

Finally, further down Whitehead Street, you'll find Key West's most popular tourist attraction: the **Ernest Hemingway Home & Museum**, at no. 907 (daily

▲ Key West

9am–5pm; $12, tours leave every 10-30min and last approximately 30min; ⓣ305/294-1136, ⓦwww.hemingwayhome.com). Hemingway owned this large, vaguely Moorish house for thirty years, but lived in it for barely ten, and even the authenticity of the furnishings is disputed. That said, some of his most acclaimed novels, including *A Farewell to Arms* and *To Have and Have Not*, were written in the study (the hayloft of a carriage house, which the author entered by way of a rope bridge). Divorced in 1940, Hemingway boxed up his manuscripts and moved them to a back room at the original *Sloppy Joe's* (see p.582), before heading off for a house in Cuba with his new wife, journalist Martha Gellhorn. Today, some fifty cats – many of them with six toes, traditionally employed as ship's mascots – pad contentedly around the gardens. Whatever the guides say, Hemingway kept his feline harem while living in Cuba, not Key West, so it's unlikely that these cats are in any way related to Papa's pets.

Eating

There's no shortage of chic venues for fine French, Italian, and Asian cuisine in Key West, but most menus, not surprisingly, feature fresh **seafood**, and you should sample **key lime pie** and **conch fritters** – Key West specialties – at least once.

Antonia's 615 Duval St ⓣ305/294-6565. Expensive but excellent northern Italian cuisine served in a formal but friendly environment. Sit in the old front room rather than the characterless modern extension out back. Dinner only.

Blue Heaven Café corner of Thomas and Petronia sts ⓣ305/296-0867. Sit in a dirt yard and enjoy fresh fish, jerk chicken, and fabulous lobster Benedict breakfasts as chickens peck around your feet.

Café Marquesa inside the *Marquesa Hotel* at 600 Fleming St ⓣ305/292-1244. This chichi restaurant with its imaginative and pricey New American menu is the town's best fine dining spot.

Camille's 1202 Simonton St ⓣ305/296-4811. Great, affordable breakfasts and brunches – menu options in the past have included cashew nut waffles and banana buttermilk pancakes. The dinner menu changes every night, but usually features fresh fish and fancy steaks.

El Siboney 900 Catherine St ⓣ305/296-4184. Come to this no-frills family diner for copious, inexpensive, and good-quality Cuban dishes.

Key West Conch Fritters Mallory Sq (no phone). This salmon and white shack, immediately in front of the Aquarium, is the best place to try conch fritters in town (you can really taste the conch here). A dozen fritters costs $11 (six for $6.25), and the coconut shrimp is also worth a try. Daily 10.30am–6pm.

Rooftop Café 310 Front Street ⓣ305/294-2042. This is the insider's choice for key lime pie; it's served with a top layer of fluffy meringue and a gooey graham cracker crust which oozes with a tangy syrup made with lime juice and traces of melted butter. Slices are $7.

Sandy's Cafe inside the M&M Laundry, 1026 White St ⓣ305/295-0159. Dingy café offering cheap and excellent Cuban sandwiches and the best *café con leche* this side of Miami.

Sarabeth's 530 Simonton St ⓣ305/293-8181. Satisfying homestyle cooking served in the appropriately welcoming setting of an old wooden clapboard house.

Seven Fish Restaurant 632 Olivia St ⓣ305/296-2777. This little-known, mid-priced bistro, easy to miss in its tiny white corner building, serves some of the best food – shrimp scampi, meatloaf, and the like – in town. There are just over a dozen tables, so it pays to call ahead.

Nightlife and entertainment

The anything-goes nature of Key West is exemplified by the convivial **bars** that make up the bulk of the island's **nightlife**. Gregarious, rough-and-ready affairs, many stay open as late as 4am and feature regular **live music**. The most popular places are grouped around the northern end of Duval Street, no more than a few minutes' stagger from one another.

Bourbon Street Pub 724 Duval St ⓣ305/296-1992. This huge pub complex is the largest gay-friendly place to drink in the center of town; there's a pleasant garden out back, complete with a large hot tub.

Captain Tony's Saloon 428 Greene St ⓣ305/294-1838. This rustic saloon was the original *Sloppy Joe's*, where Hemingway hung out (see p.581). Today, it's one of the less cheesy choices for live music.

Club Zü 422 Applerouth Lane ⓣ305/295-2498, ⓦwww.clubzu.com. The closest Key West comes to a traditional nightclub, albeit with a sexually-charged atmosphere. Open every night to a mixed but mostly gay crowd; check the website for special theme nights and guest DJs. Happy hour daily 8–10pm.

Green Parrot Inn 601 Whitehead St ⓣ305/294-6133, ⓦwww.greenparrot.com. This Key West landmark, open since 1890, draws plenty of locals to its pool tables, dartboard, pinball machine, and on the weekends, live music.

Hog's Breath Saloon 400 Front St ⓣ305/292-2032, ⓦwww.hogsbreath.com. This bar's one of the best places to catch live music in town, mostly for a nominal cover – just don't be put off by the boozed-up patrons circling its entrance.

The East Coast

Facing the Atlantic Ocean, Florida's **East Coast** runs north for more than three hundred miles from the suburbs of Miami. Each of the communities near the city – all boasting the palm-dotted beaches and warm ocean waves typical of southern Florida – have something unique to offer. **Fort Lauderdale**, no longer the party town of popular imagination, is today a sophisticated cultural center with a bubbling, increasingly upscale social scene. To the north, **Boca Raton** and **Palm Beach** are quiet, exclusive communities, their Mediterranean Revival mansions inhabited almost entirely by multimillionaires. Beyond Palm Beach, the coast is still mostly undeveloped; even the **Space Coast**, anchored by the extremely popular **Kennedy Space Center**, is smack in the middle of a nature preserve. Just north, **Daytona Beach** attracts race car- and motorcycle-enthusiasts with its festivals and the Daytona International Speedway. Lastly, enchanting **St Augustine** is the spot where Spanish settlers established North America's first foreign colony.

By car, the scenic route along the coast is **Hwy-A1A**, which sticks to the ocean side of the **Intracoastal Waterway**, formed when the rivers dividing the mainland from the barrier islands were joined and deepened during World War II. When necessary, Hwy-A1A turns inland and links with the much less picturesque **US-1**. The speediest road in the region, **I-95**, runs about ten miles west of the coastline, and is only worthwhile if you're in a hurry.

Fort Lauderdale

Following the 1960 teen-exploitation movie *Where the Boys Are*, **FORT LAUDERDALE**, with its seven miles of palm-shaded white sands, instantly became the number-one Spring Break destination in the US. However, having fueled its economic boom on underage drinking and lascivious excess, the city promptly turned its back on the revelers. By the end of the 1980s, it had imposed enough restrictions on boozing and wild behavior to put an end to the bacchanal. Since then, Fort Lauderdale has transformed itself into a thriving pleasure port, catering to individual yacht-owners and major cruise liners alike. It's also one of the fastest-growing residential areas in the country, and has for years been known as one of **gay** America's favorite holiday haunts.

Arrival and information

Both of Fort Lauderdale's public transit terminals are in or close to downtown. Greyhound **buses** pull in at 515 NE 3rd St, while the Amtrak and Tri-Rail **train** station (Ⓣ1-800/TRI-RAIL, Ⓦwww.tri-rail.com) is two miles west at 200 SW 21st Terrace – take bus #22 into town ($1.50). The main local **visitor center** is at 100 E Broward Blvd, Suite 200 (Mon–Fri 8.30am–5pm; Ⓣ1-800/22-SUNNY, Ⓦwww.sunny.org).

Local bus #11 runs twice hourly along Las Olas Boulevard between downtown and the beach. You can also use the **water taxi** (all-day pass $13; Ⓣ954/467-6677, Ⓦwww.watertaxi.com), which can take you almost anywhere along Fort Lauderdale's many miles of waterfront.

Accommodation

Although Fort Lauderdale is moving inexorably upscale, plenty of **motels** near the beach still offer a reasonable room for around $50 in summer (more like $90 in winter).

The Atlantic Resort & Spa 601 North Fort Lauderdale Beach Blvd Ⓣ954/567-8020, Ⓦwww.theatlantichotelfortlauderdale.com. The first of a projected series of luxury residence properties facing the ocean, this Mediterranean-style hotel features elegant rooms and suites, a spa, an oceanfront pool, and a superb restaurant. ⑨

Backpackers Beach Hostel 2115 N Ocean Blvd Ⓣ954/567-7275, Ⓦwww.fortlauderdalehostel.com. Clean, well-equipped hostel with free parking, Internet, and local calls. Dorm beds $20, private rooms ③

Pillars at New River Sound 111 N Birch Rd Ⓣ954/467-9639, Ⓦwww.pillarshotel.com. Quiet, intimate British-colonial-style hotel in the heart of the beach area (though facing the waterway rather than the ocean). 7

Riverside Hotel 620 E Las Olas Blvd ⓣ1-800/325-3280, ⓦwww.riversidehotel.com. Pricey but elegant option in the heart of downtown. 6

Tropi Rock Resort 2900 Belmar St ⓣ1-800/987-9385, ⓦwww.tropirock.com. Funky, family-owned hotel a block from the beach, where the good-value rates include use of tennis courts and a small gym. 4–5

Downtown Fort Lauderdale

Downtown Fort Lauderdale focuses on a few blocks between E Broward and E Las Olas boulevards, which cross US-1 a couple of miles east of I-95. Heavily prettified with parks and promenades, it's a pleasant place for a stroll, especially if you follow the mile-long pedestrian **Riverwalk** along the north shore of the New River into the **historic district**. Las Olas Boulevard itself, the main **shopping district**, remains busy day and night, with boutiques, galleries, restaurants, bars, and sidewalk cafés in abundance. It's also home to the stimulating **Museum of Art**, 1 E Las Olas Blvd (daily 11am–5pm, closed Tues June–Sept; $10; ⓣ954/525-5500, ⓦwww.moafl.org), whose largely modern collection features the emotionally powerful expressionistic work of the CoBrA movement of artists from Copenhagen, Brussels, and Amsterdam. Not far west, the simulators and interactive displays at the **Museum of Discovery & Science**, 401 SW 2nd St (Mon–Sat 10am–5pm, Sun noon–6pm; $10, $15 includes IMAX; ⓣ954/467-6637, ⓦwww.mods.org), should pacify kids pining for Disney. There's also a 3D IMAX theater; call or visit the website for showtimes.

The beach

Although downtown has its charms and attractions, most visitors come to Fort Lauderdale for its broad, clean, and undeniably beautiful **beach**. You'll find it by crossing the arching Intracoastal Waterway Bridge, about two miles along Las Olas Boulevard from downtown. Along the seafront, Fort Lauderdale Beach Boulevard once bore the brunt of Spring Break partying, though only a few beachfront bars suggest the carousing of the past. Today, an attractive promenade draws an altogether healthier crowd of joggers, in-line skaters, and cyclists.

Eating and drinking

The two main drags for **eating** and **drinking** in Fort Lauderdale are Las Olas and Sunrise boulevards.

Casablanca Café 3049 Alhambra St ⓣ954/764-3500. An American piano bar in a Moroccan setting, serving a good, eclectic, and moderately priced menu of Mediterranean-influenced American fare. Live music Wed–Sun nights.

Ernie's BBQ Lounge 1843 S Federal Hwy (US-1) ⓣ954/523-8636. Scruffy but likeable place, south of downtown, famous for its glorious conch chowder.

The Floridian 1410 E Las Olas Blvd ⓣ954/463-4041. Retro decor and outstanding diner food – especially the mammoth breakfasts – at rock-bottom prices. Open 24hr.

Mangos 904 E Las Olas Blvd ⓣ954/523-5001. Decent dining, though most people go for the people-watching along Las Olas, and the energetic workout, dancing to roaring nightly live rock/R&B/jazz jams at this singles scene.

Seasons 52 2428 E Sunrise Blvd at the Galleria Mall ⓣ954/537-1052. Health-conscious regional restaurant chain where every one of the fresh and tasty seasonal dishes has less than 475 calories. There's also a good wine list.

Southport Raw Bar 1536 Cordova Rd ⓣ954/525-2526. South of downtown, near Port Everglades, this boisterous local bar specializes in succulent crustaceans and well-prepared fish dishes.

Taverna Opa 3051 NE 32nd St ⓣ954/567-1630. A raucous good time can be had at this fun Greek establishment, complete with flowing ouzo and crashing dishes. Dinner only.

Boca Raton

BOCA RATON (literally, "the mouth of the rat"), twenty miles north of Fort Lauderdale, is noteworthy mostly for its abundance of **Mediterranean Revival architecture**. This style, prevalent here since the 1920s, has been kept alive in the downtown area by strict building codes. New structures must incorporate arched entranceways, fake bell towers, and red-tiled roofs whenever possible, ensuring a consistent and distinctive "look."

This all goes back to architect Addison Mizner, who swept into Boca Raton on the tide of the Florida property boom in 1925. Mizner was influenced by the medieval architecture he'd seen around the Mediterranean, and the few public buildings he completed (along with close to fifty homes) left an indelible mark on Boca Raton (Mizner also shaped the look of nearby Palm Beach). His million-dollar *Cloister Inn*, for example, grew into the present **Boca Raton Resort and Club**, 501 E Camino Real, a pink palace of marble columns, sculptured fountains, and carefully aged wood (Ⓣ1-888/491-BOCA, Ⓦwww.bocaresort.com; ❼–❾). Mizner's spirit is also invoked at **Mizner Park**, off US-1 between Palmetto Park Rd and Glades Rd, a stylish open-air shopping plaza adorned with palm trees and waterfalls. The park is home to the **Boca Raton Museum of Art**, 501 Plaza Real (Tues, Thurs & Fri 10am–5pm, Wed 10am–9pm, Sat & Sun noon–5pm; $8; Ⓣ561/392-2500, Ⓦwww.bocamuseum.org), worth a stop for its drawings by modern European masters – Degas, Matisse, Picasso – and a formidable collection of African art.

A mile north of Hwy-798 (which links downtown Boca Raton with the beach), at 1801 N Ocean Blvd/Hwy-A1A, the **Gumbo Limbo Nature Center** (Mon–Sat 9am–4pm, Sun noon–4pm; $3 donation; Ⓣ561/338-1473, Ⓦwww.gumbolimbo.org) covers twenty acres inhabited by osprey, brown pelicans, and sea turtles. Reserve well in advance for the night turtle-watching tours offered between May and July.

A couple of miles north of downtown, Boca Raton's most explorable **beachside** area is **Spanish River Park** (daily 8am–sunset; cars $16 weekdays, $18 weekends, pedestrians and cyclists free). Most of these fifty acres of lush vegetation and high-rise greenery are only penetrable on trails through shady thickets.

Practicalities

Greyhound does not serve Boca Raton. **Tri-Rail** stops off I-95, at 680 Yamato Rd (Ⓣ1-800/TRI-RAIL); there's a connecting shuttle to the town center. The **Chamber of Commerce** is at 1800 N Dixie Hwy (Mon 9.30am–5pm Tues–Fri 8.30am–5pm; Ⓣ561/395-4433, Ⓦwww.bocaratonchamber.com). The *Townplace Suites by Marriott*, 5110 NW 8th Ave (Ⓣ561/994-7232, Ⓦwww.towneplacebocaraton.com; ❺), and *Ocean Lodge*, 531 N Ocean Blvd (Ⓣ561/395-7772, Ⓦwww.oceanlodgeflorida.com; ❸), are two **hotels** providing reasonable value for money. For **eating**, the upscale *Max's Grill*, 404 Plaza Real, Mizner Park (Ⓣ561/368-0080), has appealing American dishes with Asian influences, while the *Boca Diner*, 2801 N Federal Hwy (Ⓣ561/750-6744) serves a little bit of everything, including Greek and Italian standards.

Palm Beach

A small island town of palatial homes and gardens, **PALM BEACH** has been synonymous for nearly a century with the kind of lifestyle only limitless loot can buy. The nation's wealthy began wintering here in the 1890s, after Henry Flagler brought his East Coast railroad south from St Augustine, building two luxury hotels on this then-secluded, palm-filled island. Since then, the rich and famous have flocked here to become part of the Palm Beach elite.

Lined with designer stores and high-class art galleries, **Worth Avenue**, close to the southern tip of the island, is a good place to see some of the town's Addison Mizner-inspired **architecture**: stucco walls, Romanesque facades, passageways leading to small courtyards, and spiral staircases climbing to the upper levels.

To the north, just off Cocoanut Row, white Doric columns front Whitehall, also known as the **Flagler Museum** (Tues–Sat 10am–5pm, Sun noon–5pm; $15; Ⓣ561/655-2833, Ⓦwww.flagler.org). This, the most overtly ostentatious home on the island, was a $4 million wedding present from Henry Flagler to his third wife, Mary Lily Kenan. As in many of Florida's first luxury homes, the interior design was lifted from the great buildings of Europe: among the 73 rooms are an Italian library, a French salon, and a Louis XV ballroom. All are stuffed with ornamentation, but they lack aesthetic cohesion.

Built in 1926 in the style of an Italianate palace, **The Breakers** hotel, on South County Road off the main strip (Ⓣ561/655-6611 or 1-888/BREAKERS, Ⓦwww.thebreakers.com; ⑨), operates as the last of Palm Beach's swanky resorts. Its design includes elaborate painted ceilings and huge tapestries. Take the guided tour on Tuesdays at 2pm (free for guests, $15 for the public; for information, call Ⓣ561/655-6611).

Practicalities

In keeping with the upper-crust atmosphere, **public transportation** options around Palm Beach are limited. The West Palm Beach Amtrak (Ⓣ1-800/USA-RAIL), Tri-Rail (Ⓣ1-800/TRI-RAIL), and Greyhound (Ⓣ561/833-8534) stations are all located at 205 S Tamarind Ave in West Palm Beach on the mainland. To get to Palm Beach from here, take any PalmTran bus ($1.50; Ⓣ561/841-4BUS) terminating at Quadrille Blvd, and transfer to the #41, or the #42 (no Sun service). The **Convention and Visitors' Bureau** is at 1555 Palm Beach Lakes Blvd, Suite 800 (Mon–Fri 9am–5pm; Ⓣ561/233-3000, Ⓦwww.palmbeachfl.com).

You'll need plenty of money to **stay** here: prices of $200 a night are not uncommon (rates are cheapest between May and Dec). The elaborate, antique-furnished *Palm Beach Historic Inn*, 365 S County Rd (Ⓣ561/832-4009, Ⓦwww.palmbeachhistoricinn.com; ⑦), offers some of the best rates in town, but you'll need to reserve early. The equally opulent *Chesterfield*, 363 Cocoanut Row (Ⓣ561/659-5800, Ⓦwww.chesterfieldpb.com; ⑦), is another good choice. *Charley's Crab*, 456 S Ocean Blvd (Ⓣ561/659-1500), is the place to go for reasonably priced **seafood**, while the lunch counter at *Hamburger Heaven*, 314 S County Rd (closed Sun; Ⓣ561/655-5277), has been serving its delicious **burgers** since 1945. If money is no object – and you're dressed to kill – make for *Café L'Europe*, 331 S County Rd (closed Mon; Ⓣ561/655-4020): spend less than $50 a head in this super-elegant French restaurant and you'll walk away hungry.

The Space Coast

About two hundred miles north of Palm Beach, the so-called **Space Coast** is the base of the country's space industry. The focal point is the much-visited **Kennedy Space Center**, which occupies a flat, marshy island bulging into the Atlantic. In stark contrast, the rest of the island is taken over by a sizeable nature preserve, the

Merritt Island National Wildlife Refuge, offering great opportunities for seeing wildlife, especially birds.

The Kennedy Space Center

The **Kennedy Space Center** is the nucleus of the US space program: it's here that space vehicles are developed, tested, and blasted into orbit. **Merritt Island** has been the center of NASA's activity since 1964, when the launch pads at Cape Canaveral US Air Force base, across the water, proved too small to cope with the giant new Saturn V rockets used to launch the Apollo missions.

To reach the **Visitor Complex** (daily 9am–6pm; $38 adults, $28 children; Ⓣ321/449-4444, Ⓦwww.kennedyspacecenter.com), take exit 212 off I-95 to Hwy-405, and follow the signs; you can also get here by connecting with Hwy-3 off Hwy-A1A. The best **times to visit** are on weekends and in May and September, when crowds are thinner – but at any time, you should still allow an entire day for everything the Space Center has to offer and try to arrive early in the morning. Check the weather, too, as thunderstorms may force some attractions to close.

The various exhibits in the Visitor Complex – mission capsules, space suits, lunar modules, a mock-up Space Shuttle flight deck – will keep anyone with the slightest interest in space exploration interested for a couple of hours. Afterwards, be sure to watch the two impressive IMAX movies dealing with some space theme or other and take a stroll around the open-air **Rocket Garden**, full of deceptively simple rockets from the 1950s, cleverly illuminated to show how they looked at blast-off. The newest attraction is the **Shuttle Launch Experience**, a simulation ride, where passengers get to see what it's like to be an astronaut, vertically "launching" into space and orbiting Earth aboard the Space Shuttle. The remainder of the visit is comprised of a two-hour guided **bus tour**. The bus passes the 52-storey Vehicle Assembly Building (where Space Shuttles are prepared for launch), stops to view the launch pad, and winds up with an opportunity to inspect a Saturn V rocket and witness a simulated Apollo countdown. For the dates and times of **real-life launches**, call Ⓣ321/449-4444 or check the website listed above.

Near the Space Center, on Hwy-405 in Titusville, the **Astronaut Hall of Fame** (included with regular $38 admission) is one of Florida's most entertaining interactive museums, where exhibits allow you to experience G-force and a bumpy ride along the surface of Mars.

Practicalities: Cocoa Beach

The closest **motels** to the Kennedy Space Center are on the mainland along US-1 (in Titusville, for example) – or, if you're looking for a more picturesque location, in **COCOA BEACH**, a few miles south on a ten-mile strip of shore washed by some of the biggest surfing waves in Florida. Options include the *Luna Sea*, 3185 N Atlantic Ave (Ⓣ1-800/586-2732; Ⓦwww.lunaseacocoabeach.com; ❹), *Days Inn*, 5500 N Atlantic Ave (Ⓣ321/784-2550; Ⓦwww.daysinncocoabeach.com; ❹), and *Fawlty Towers*, 100 E Cocoa Beach Causeway (Ⓣ321/784-3870; Ⓦwww.fawltytowersresort.com; ❸–❹). For great oysters and super riverfront views, head for *Sunset Café*, 500 W Cocoa Beach Causeway (Ⓣ321/783-8485) – but go early, as it's frequently mobbed. A good **dinner** option is *Atlantic Ocean Grille*, on the Cocoa Beach Pier (Ⓣ321/783-7549), which has a quality, somewhat expensive menu that's especially strong on seafood.

Merritt Island National Wildlife Refuge

NASA doesn't have Merritt Island all to itself: the agency shares it with the **Merritt Island National Wildlife Refuge** (daily sunrise–sunset; free). Alligators, armadillos, raccoons, and bobcats – as well as one of Florida's greatest gatherings of birdlife – live right up against some of the human world's most advanced hardware. Winter (Oct–March) is the best time to visit, when the skies are alive with birds migrating from the frozen north and mosquitoes are nowhere to be found. At any other time, especially in summer, the island's Mosquito Lagoon is worthy of its name: bring repellent.

Eight miles off I-95's exit 220, Hwy-406 leads to the seven-mile **Black Point Wildlife Drive**, which gives a solid introduction to the basics of the island's ecosystem; pick up the free leaflet at the entrance. Be sure to walk in the refuge, too: off the Wildlife Drive, the five-mile **Cruickshank Trail** weaves around the edge of the Indian River. Drive a few miles farther east along Hwy-402 – branching from Hwy-406 just south of the Wildlife Drive and passing the **visitor center** (Mon–Fri 8am–4.30pm, Sat & Sun 9am–5pm; closed Sun April–Oct; ⓣ321/861-0667) – and then hike the three-fourths-of-a-mile **Oak Hammock Trail** or the two-mile **Palm Hammock Trail**, both accessible from the visitor center parking lot.

Daytona Beach

The consummate Florida beach town, with its T-shirt shops, amusement arcades, and wall-to-wall motels, **DAYTONA BEACH** owes its existence to twenty miles of enticing light brown sands. Once a favorite Spring Break destination, Daytona Beach has been trying to cultivate a more refined image in recent years. This has only been partially successful, with the partying students replaced by bikers and racecar fanatics. The town hosts three major annual events: the legendary **Daytona 500** stock-car race in February (tickets from $99; call ⓣ877/306-RACE or visit ⓦwww.daytonainternationalspeedway.com); **Bike Week**, in early March, which attracts tens of thousands of leather-clad bikers; and the relatively new **Biketoberfest**, in October, a scaled down, more family orientated version of Bike Week.

The origin of Daytona's race-car and motorcycle obsession goes back to the early 1900s, when pioneering auto enthusiasts including Louis Chevrolet, Ransom Olds, and Henry Ford came to Daytona's firm sands to race prototype vehicles beside the ocean. In fact, the world land speed record was smashed here five times by the British millionaire Malcolm Campbell. As increasing speeds made racing on the sands unsafe, the **Daytona International Speedway**, an ungainly configuration of concrete and steel holding 150,000 people, was opened in 1959 three miles west of downtown along International Speedway Boulevard (buses #9, #10 and #60).

Though they can't capture the excitement of a race, **guided trolley tours** (daily except race days 9.30am–5.30pm, every half-hour; included in general admission) do provide a first-hand look at the remarkable gradients that help make this the fastest racetrack in the world. Occupying a large building next to the Speedway, the interactive exhibits that comprise **Daytona 500 Experience** (daily 9am–5pm; $24; ⓣ386/947-6800; www.daytona500experience.com) let you have a virtual try at jacking a race-car off the ground during a pit-stop and commentating on a race, while an engaging wide-screen film complete with excellent 3-D effects tells you all about NASCAR (National Association of Stock Car Auto Racing).

For all the excitement that racing generates, the best thing about Daytona is the seemingly limitless **beach**: it's five hundred feet wide at low tide, and fades dreamily off into the heat haze. Daytona is also one of the few beaches in

Florida you can drive on – eleven of the area's 23 miles of beach are open to motor vehicles. Pay $5 (Feb–Nov only) at the various entrances and follow the posted procedures. Another, less heralded but worthwhile thing to do in Daytona Beach is visit the eclectic **Museum of the Arts and Sciences**, a mile south of the Speedway at 352 S Nova Rd (Tues–Fri 9am–4pm, Sat-Sun noon–5pm; $13; ⓣ386/255-0285, ⓦwww.moas.org), whose diverse collection includes the reassembled remains of a million-year-old giant ground sloth and the first Coca-Cola can sent into space.

Practicalities

US-1 (called, in town, Ridgewood Avenue) plows through mainland Daytona Beach, passing the **Greyhound** station at 138 S Ridgewood. **Trolleys** ($1.25) run the length of the beach until midnight from mid-January to early September. The **visitor center** is at 126 E Orange Ave (Mon–Fri 9am–5pm; ⓣ1-800/854-1234, ⓦwww.daytonabeach.com). If you're going to be in Daytona during any of the big events, **accommodation** should be booked at least six months ahead; and expect minimum stays and prices to at least double. Any of the **motels** along the oceanfront Atlantic Avenue makes a good beach base: there's *Audrey's Tropical Manor*, 2237 S Atlantic Ave, slightly south of town in Daytona Beach Shores (ⓣ386/252-4920, ⓦwww.tropicalmanor.com; ④–⑤); or the welcoming, British-run *Ocean Court*, 2315 S Atlantic Ave (ⓣ386/253-8185, ⓦwww.oceancourt.com; ③). Away from the beach, and close to lively Beach Street, the *Coquina Inn*, 544 S Palmetto Ave (ⓣ386/254-4969; ⓦwww.coquinainndaytonabeach.com; ⑤), is a cozy B&B.

Atlantic Avenue is lined with the predictable fast food outlets, but for more inspiring **eating** options head to Beach Street on the mainland, where the fifties-style *Daytona Diner* at no. 290 1/2 N (ⓣ386/258-8488) dishes up huge breakfasts for around $6 and *Angell & Phelps Café* at no. 156 S (ⓣ386/257-2677) offers creative American-style gourmet cuisine in an informal setting. For fresh fish and seafood, head south toward Ponce Inlet, where you'll find the equally good *Lighthouse Landing*, beside the Ponce Inlet Lighthouse at 4940 S Peninsula Drive (ⓣ386/761-9271), and *Inlet Harbor*, overlooking a marina at 133 Inlet Harbor Rd (ⓣ386/767-5590). Daytona's excellent **nightlife** scene centers on Seabreeze Boulevard with its Spring Break-style discos such as *Razzles* at no. 611 (ⓣ321/257-6236) and Main Street with its raucous biker bars including *Boot Hill Saloon* at no.310 (ⓣ386/258-9506).

St Augustine

Forty miles north of Daytona Beach, US-1 passes through the heart of charismatic **ST AUGUSTINE**. Few places in Florida are as immediately engaging as this old city, with the size and even some of the looks of a small Mediterranean town. The oldest permanent settlement in the US, with much from its early days still intact along its narrow streets, it also offers two alluring lengths of **beach** just across Matanzas Bay.

Though Ponce de León touched ground here in 1513, European settlement didn't begin until half a century later, when Spain's Pedro Menéndez de Avilés put ashore on St Augustine's Day in 1565. The town developed into a major social and administrative center, soon to be capital of east Florida. Subsequently, Tallahassee (see p.617) became the capital of a unified Florida, and St Augustine's fortunes waned. Since then, expansion has largely bypassed the town – a fact inadvert-

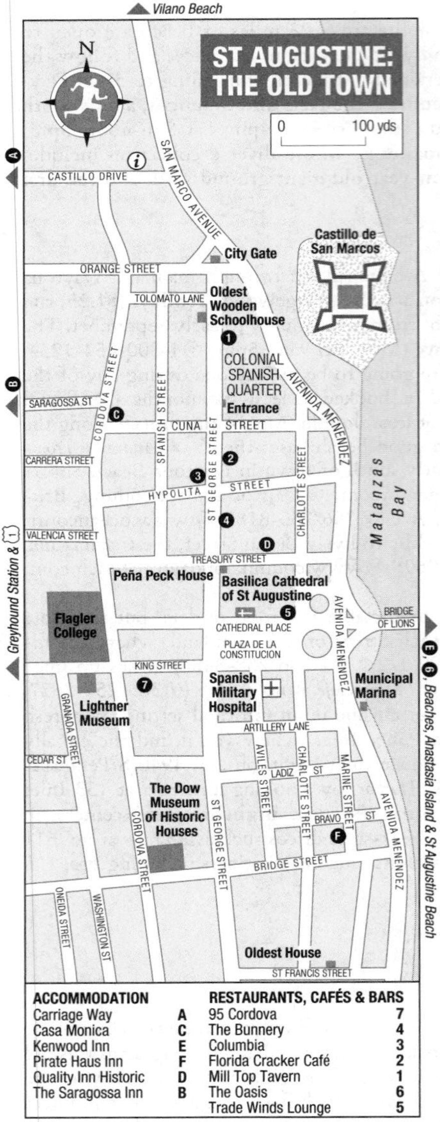

ently facilitating the restoration program that has turned this quiet community into a fine historical showcase.

Arrival and information

The Greyhound **bus** station, 1711 Dobbs Rd, is a couple of miles from the center of town. The **visitor center**, 10 Castillo Drive (daily 8.30am–5.30pm; ⓣ1-800/653-2489, ⓦwww.visitoldcity.com), shows a film on the history of the town, has recommendations for a variety of tours (see below), and information on numerous local festivals, including torch-lit processions and a Menorcan Fiesta.

St Augustine is best seen **on foot**, though two **sightseeing trains** tour the main landmarks (daily 8.30am–5pm; $21; get tickets from the visitor center or at many B&Bs and hotels). There's **no public transportation**, so if you want to get to the beaches two miles away and you don't have a car you'll have to take a **taxi** (Ancient City Cabs; ⓣ904/824-8161). The Old Town Trolley sightseeing train includes free transport on the **Beach Bus**. As for organized **tours**, harbor cruises by Scenic Cruise ($15.75; ⓣ904/824-1806) leave four to six times a day from the Municipal Marina, near the foot of King Street. The well-organized and informative Tour St Augustine ($12; ⓣ1-800/797-3778) leads historical walking tours, while various spooky sites are visited during the "A Ghostly Experience" evening walking tour ($12; ⓣ904/461-1009).

Accommodation

The Old Town has many excellent restored **inns** offering bed-and-breakfast, and there are cheaper chain **hotels** outside the center of town along San Marco Avenue and Ponce de León Boulevard. Note that rates generally rise by $15–50 on weekends.

Carriage Way 70 Cuna St ⓣ1-800/908-9832, ⓦwww.carriageway.com. Canopy and four-poster beds, clawfoot tubs, and antiques add to the period feel of this 1880s house. 5–6

Casa Monica 95 Cordova St ⓣ1-800/648-1888, ⓦwww.casamonica.com. Elegant, beautifully restored Spanish-style hotel that has hosted the king and queen of Spain. Book well in advance. 7–8

Kenwood Inn 38 Marine St ⓣ904/824-2116, ⓦwww.thekenwoodinn.com. Peacefully situated near the waterfront, this charming B&B has a pretty pool and offers complimentary use of bikes for guests. 5

Pirate Haus Inn 32 Treasury St ⓣ904/808-1999, ⓦwww.piratehaus.com. The town's only hostel accommodation, near the Plaza, is popular with backpackers. It has a giant kitchen and a common room stuffed with guidebooks. Beds in air-conditioned dorms are $20; five private rooms. 2

Quality Inn Historic 1111 Ponce de León Blvd ⓣ904/824-5554 or 1-800/575-5288. Although it's on busy Hwy-A1A and the rooms are nothing out of the ordinary, this place is only a 20-minute walk from the center, has reasonable rates, free internet, and continental breakfast. 4

The Saragossa Inn 34 Saragossa St ⓣ904/808-7384 or 1-877/808-7384, ⓦwww.saragossainn.com. This lovely little pink cottage began life in 1924 as a Sears Craftsman bungalow and now holds four comfortable guest rooms and two suites, just a bit west of the beaten path. 5–6

The Old Town

Bordered on the west by St George Street, and on the south by Plaza de la Constitución, St Augustine's **Old Town** holds the well-tended evidence of the town's Spanish period. It may be small, but there's a lot to see: an early start, around 9am, will give you a lead on the tourist crowds, and should allow a good look at almost everything in one day.

Given the fine state of the **Castillo de San Marcos National Monument**, on the northern edge of the Old Town beside the bay (daily 8.45am–4.45pm; $6; ⓦwww.nps.gov/casa), it's difficult to believe that the fortress was built in the late 1600s. Its longevity is due to its design: a diamond-shaped rampart at each corner maximized firepower, and fourteen-feet-thick walls reduced its vulnerability to attack. Inside, there's not a lot to see besides a small museum and echoing rooms, though venturing along the 35-foot ramparts gives good views across the city and the bay.

A hundred yards west of the monument, the eighteenth-century **City Gate** marks the entrance to **St George Street**, once the main thoroughfare and now a tourist-trampled, though genuinely historic, pedestrianized strip. You'll find a bunch of places called "The oldest..." in St Augustine; the **Oldest Wooden Schoolhouse**, set in lush gardens at 14 St George St (daily 9am–5pm; $3.50), is one of the most atmospheric – a restored wooden shack with speaking wax dummies portraying nineteenth-century schoolchildren.

Heading south on St George Street, a fair-sized plot between Tolomato Lane and Cuna Street is taken up by the excellent **Colonial Spanish Quarter** (daily 9am–5.30pm, last ticket sold at 4:45pm; $7). In its nine reconstructed homes and workshops, volunteers dressed as Spanish settlers go about their business at anvils and foot-driven wood lathes.

For a more intimate look at local life during a slightly later period, head a little further south to the **Peña Peck House**, 143 St George St (Sun–Fri 12.30pm–4.15pm, Sat 10.30am–4.15pm; donation requested; ⓣ904/829-5064). Thought to have originally been the Spanish treasury, by the time the British took over in 1763 this was the home of a physician and his gregarious spouse, who turned the place into a high-society rendezvous.

In the sixteenth century, the Spanish king decreed that all colonial towns must be built around a central plaza; thus, St George Street runs into the **Plaza de la Constitución**, a marketplace from 1598. On the plaza's north side, the **Basilica Cathedral of St Augustine** (daily 7am–5pm; donation) adds a touch of gran-

▲ Oldest Wooden Schoolhouse

deur, although it's largely a Sixties remodelling of the late eighteenth-century original.

Tourist numbers lessen as you cross **south of the plaza** into a web of quiet, narrow streets, all just as old as St George Street. West of the plaza along King Street, opposite Flagler College, the opulent **Lightner Museum** (daily 9am–5pm, last admission 4pm; $10; ⓣ904/824-2874) displays fine and decorative arts in the former building of one of the most fabulous resorts of the late nineteenth century. More substantial history is available a ten-minute walk southeast from here, at 14 St Francis St, in the form of the fascinating **Oldest House** (daily 9am–5pm, last admission 4.30pm; $8), which is indeed the oldest house in town, dating from the early 1700s. Its rooms are furnished to show how the house – and people's lives – changed as new eras unfolded.

The beaches

Some fine **beaches** – busiest at weekends – lie just a couple of miles east from the Old Town. Crossing the bay via the Bridge of Lions, and continuing east on Hwy-A1A will bring you to the **Anastasia State Recreation Area**, on Anastasia Island (daily 8am–sunset; cars $3–5, cyclists and pedestrians $1), which offers a thousand protected acres of dunes, marshes, and scrub, linked by nature walks. A few miles further south, **St Augustine Beach** is family terrain, with some good restaurants and a fishing pier. North of Old Town (take May St, off San Marco Ave), the broad **Vilano Beach** pulls a younger crowd.

Eating, drinking, and entertainment

Eating in the Old Town can be expensive, and a number of its cafés and restaurants are closed in the evening. Of those that stay open, several double as **drinking** spots and some have **live music**.

95 Cordova at the *Casa Monica* hotel, 95 Cordova St ⓣ904/810-6810. This luxurious and elegant restaurant's menu features expensive but masterful nouvelle continental cuisine.

The Bunnery 121 St George St ⓣ904/829-6166. Good coffee and economical breakfasts, plus tempting sandwiches and paninis, served in an old Spanish bakery.

Columbia 98 St George St ⓣ904/824-3341. Enjoy paella, tapas and other traditional Spanish/Cuban food in a sumptuous setting of fountains and candlelight.

Florida Cracker Café 81 St George St ⓣ904/829-0397. Offering an eclectic and reasonably priced mix of combo salads, conch fritters and homemade desserts.

Mill Top Tavern 19 1/2 George St ⓣ904/829-2329. There's a terrific, funky atmosphere at the top of this nineteenth-century mill, where you'll hear live music and get a great, open-air view of the Castillo.

The Oasis 4000 Ocean Trace Rd, St Augustine Beach ⓣ904/471-3424. This beach bar is famous for its burgers with their multitude of tasty toppings.

Trade Winds Lounge 124 Charlotte St ⓣ904/826-1590. Convivial bar where you can tap your feet to country and western and rock 'n' roll bands.

Jacksonville

Situated in the great double loop of the St Johns River, **JACKSONVILLE** struggled for years to throw off its longstanding reputation as a dour industrial port city with a deeply conservative population. During the 1990s, the city began to gain standing as a new service industry center, bringing a spate of construction projects and new homebuyers to the area. And in the lead-up to the city's hosting of the 2005 Super Bowl football championship, efforts were made to enhance Jacksonville's beauty by creating parks and riverside boardwalks. However, the sheer size of the city – at 841 square miles, the largest in the US – serves to dilute its easygoing character.

The most noteworthy building in the downtown area, which occupies the north bank of the St Johns River, is the **Florida Theater**, 128 E Forsyth St (box office ⓣ904/355-2787, ⓦwww.floridatheatre.com). Elvis Presley arrived here in 1957 for his first appearance on an indoor stage, an event presided over by a juvenile court judge to ensure that it wasn't too suggestive. The theater's interior has since been restored with a dazzling gold proscenium arch, and today it's used for a variety of performances. Five minutes' walk from the theater, at 333 N Laura St, the **Museum of Contemporary Art** (Tues, Weds, Fri & Sat 10am–4pm, Thurs 10am–8pm, Sun noon–4pm; $8, free Wed 5–9pm; ⓣ904/366-6911, ⓦwww.mocajacksonville.org) has paintings, sculptures, and photography of surprising scope and depth, including large Ed Paschke and James Rosenquist canvases.

Crossing over to the south bank via the River Taxi ($3 one way; $5 round-trip), you'll find the **Museum of Science and History**, 1025 Museum Circle (Mon–Fri 10am–5pm, Sat 10am–6pm, Sun 1–6pm; $9, children 3–12 $6; ⓣ904/396-6674, ⓦwww.themosh.org), with its hands-on exhibits and planetarium.

Just south of the Fuller Warren River bridge (I-95), the **Cummer Museum of Art and Gardens**, 829 Riverside Ave (Tues 10am–9pm, Wed, Thurs, Fri 10am–4pm, Sun noon–5pm; $10, free Tues after 4pm; ⓣ904/356-6857, ⓦwww.cummer.org), has spacious rooms and sculpture-lined corridors containing works by prominent European and American masters. The two acres of lovely Italianate and English gardens that overlook the river are an added bonus.

From all over Jacksonville you can see the 73,000-seat Alltel Stadium, home to the **Jacksonville Jaguars** football franchise (tickets from $50–250; ⓣ1-877/4JAGS-TIX). It's also the scene of the Florida–Georgia college football clash each fall – an excuse for 48 hours of citywide drinking and partying. Next door is **Metropolitan Park**, a pleasant swath of riverside greenery.

Practicalities

From the Greyhound **bus station** downtown at 10 N Pearl St, it's an easy walk to the **Convention and Visitors Bureau**, 550 Water St, suite 1000 (Mon–Fri 8am–5pm; ⓣ904/798-9111 or 1-800/733-2668, ⓦwww.visitjacksonville.com). The **train station** is an awkward six miles northwest of downtown at 3570 Clifford Lane. The cheapest **accommodation** can be found at the chain hotels on the city's perimeter, such as *Comfort Suites*, 1180 Airport Rd (ⓣ904/741-0505; ⑤). Downtown, the *Hyatt Regency Jacksonville Riverfront*, 225 Coastline Drive (ⓣ1-800/233-1234, ⓦwww.jacksonville.hyatt.com; ⑦), has a great riverfront location. Alternatively, head to the Riverside-Avondale residential neighborhood (near the Cummer Museum) for a choice of good B&Bs, including the riverfront *The House on Cherry Street*, 1844 Cherry St (ⓣ904/384-1999, ⓦwww.houseoncherry.com; ④–⑤). For **eating**, you'll find several places for a quick and filling lunch at the Jacksonville Landing mall, downtown between Water St and the river. On the south bank, the *River City Brewing Co.*, 835 Museum Circle (ⓣ904/398-2299), offers great steaks, home-brewed beer, and river views, while Riverside-Avondale has some appealing cafés such as *Biscotti's*, 3556 St Johns Ave (ⓣ904/387-2060).

Jacksonville's beaches

Traveling south from Jacksonville on I-95, then east on Hwy-202, you'll first hit **Ponte Vedra Beach**, whose crowd-free sands and million-dollar homes form one of the most exclusive communities in northeast Florida. A few miles north from here on Hwy-A1A is the much less snooty **Jacksonville Beach**. If you tire of watching the novice surfers, **Adventure Landing**, 1944 Beach Blvd (Sun–Thurs 10am–10pm, Fri & Sat 10am–midnight; ⓣ904/246-4386, ⓦwww.adventure-landing.com), offers an amusement park where each diversion is individually priced, like batting cages ($2), a water park ($27), and go-carts ($7). Two miles north of Jacksonville Beach's old pier, the more commercialized **Neptune Beach** blurs into the identical-looking **Atlantic Beach**; both are more family-oriented, and are best visited for eating and socializing.

Practicalities

The best (and most expensive) **accommodation** is at the artsy boutique hotel *One Ocean*, 1 Ocean Blvd, Atlantic Beach (ⓣ904/247-0305, ⓦwww.oneoceanresort.com; ⑦–⑧), while across the street but also beachfront is the *Sea Horse Oceanfront Inn*, 120 Atlantic Blvd, Neptune Beach (ⓣ904/246-2175, ⓦwww.seahorseoceanfrontinn.com; ⑤). Good **eating options** at the beaches are *Ragtime Tavern Seafood Grill*, 207 Atlantic Blvd, Atlantic Beach (ⓣ904/241-7877), with its extensive seafood menu; *Sun Dog Diner*, 207 Atlantic Blvd, Neptune Beach (ⓣ904/241-8221), offering above-average, creative diner fare; and *Beach Hut Café*, 1281 S 3rd St, Jacksonville Beach (ⓣ904/249-3516), serving huge, delicious breakfasts.

Central Florida

Encompassing a broad and fertile expanse between the east and west coasts, most of **Central Florida** was farming country when vacation-mania first struck the state's beachside strips. From the 1970s on, this picture of tranquility was shattered: no section of the state has been affected more dramatically by modern tourism. As a result, the most visited part of Florida can also be one of the ugliest. A clutter of highway interchanges, motels, and billboards arch around the sprawling city of **Orlando**, where a tourist-dollar chase of Gold Rush magnitude was sparked by **Walt Disney World**, the biggest and cleverest theme-park complex ever created. The rest of central Florida is quiet by comparison.

Orlando and the theme parks

Once a quiet farming town, **ORLANDO** now welcomes more visitors than any other place in the state. The reason, of course, is **Walt Disney World**, which, along with **Universal Orlando**, **SeaWorld Orlando**, and a host of other attractions, of varying degrees of quality, attracts millions of people a year to a previously featureless plot of scrubland. Most of the hotels are found along International Drive, Hwy-192 or in and around Disney World, all of which lie several miles south of the downtown area, which has the city's best nightlife.

Arrival and information

The **international airport** is nine miles south of downtown Orlando; local buses (see below) link the airport with downtown (#11 or #51) and International Drive (#42). Alternatively, **shuttle buses** operated by Mears Transportation (24hrs; ⓣ407/423-5566) charge a flat fee of $16 to any hotel in downtown; $17 to International Drive; and $19 to Hwy-192. Those staying at Disney can take advantage of the free airport transfer offered by **Disney's Magical Express Transportation** (ⓣ1-866/599-0951). **Taxis** to these destinations cost between $30 and $60. **Buses** and **trains** arrive, respectively, downtown at the Greyhound terminal, 555 N John Young Parkway (ⓣ407/292-3424), and the Amtrak station, 1400 Sligh Blvd (ⓣ407/843-7611). The efficient **Official Visitor Center**, 8723 International Drive (daily 8.30am–6.30pm; ⓣ407/363-5872, ⓦwww.orlandoinfo.com) has a plethora of brochures and discount coupons.

Getting around

You have to be determined to get to the theme parks without a car, but it can be done. Local Lynx **buses** (ⓣ407/841-5969, ⓦwww.golynx.com) converge at the downtown Orlando terminal, 455 N Garland Ave. Route #50 heads to Walt Disney World, while route #8 or the limited stop #38 go to International Drive. Along International Drive (including SeaWorld Orlando), the **I-Ride Trolley** (ⓣ1-866/243-7483, ⓦwww.iridetrolley.com) operates every twenty minutes daily from 8am to 10.30pm, costing $1 one way. **Taxis** are the best way to get around at night – try Diamond Cab (ⓣ407/523-3333). All the main **car rental** firms have offices at or close to the airport.

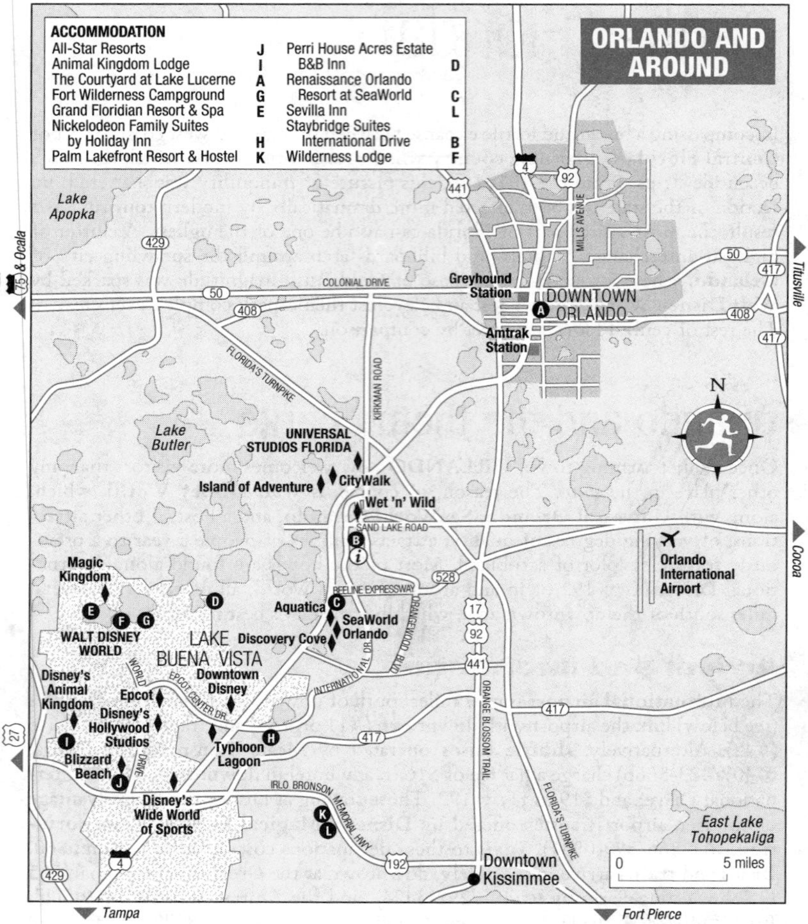

Accommodation outside Walt Disney World

If you're on a budget, or want to spend time visiting the other parks, you'd do best to stay **outside Walt Disney World**. The chain hotels on **International Drive** are close to Universal Orlando and SeaWorld Orlando, with numerous restaurants and shops within walking distance. Plenty of hotels are dotted around Disney property in an area called **Lake Buena Vista**, while budget hotels – and even a hostel – line **Hwy-192** (which is also close to Disney). **Downtown** Orlando has some charming, privately run hotels and B&Bs.

The Courtyard at Lake Lucerne 211 N Lucerne Circle E ⓣ407/648-5188, ⓦwww.orlandohistoricinn.com. Choose from Victorian- and Edwardian-era rooms or airy Art Deco suites at this charming downtown hotel. ❺

Nickelodeon Family Suites by Holiday Inn 14500 Continental Gateway, Lake Buena Vista ⓣ1-877/642-5111, ⓦwww.nickhotel.com. The leader in kid-friendly resorts, with one, two-, and three-bedroom suites, two pools with water slides, and even a spa for the little ones. ❻

Palm Lakefront Resort & Hostel 4840 W Hwy-192 ⓣ407/396-1759, ⓦwww.orlandohostels.com. The obvious choice for backpackers, this resort-style hostel has six-bed, single-sex dorms ($19), private rooms, a pool, and a pleasant lakefront location. ❷

Perri House Acres Estate B&B Inn 10417 Vista Oaks Court, Lake Buena Vista ⓣ1-800/780-4830, ⓦwww.perrihouse.com. The incongruous presence of an eight-room B&B hidden on four wooded acres just five miles from the Magic Kingdom is the perfect antidote to all the theme-park frenzy. ❺

Renaissance Orlando Resort at SeaWorld 6677 Sea Harbor Drive ⓣ1-800/327-6677. An upscale hotel off International Drive directly opposite Sea World Orlando, with spacious rooms and an attractive atrium. ❼

Sevilla Inn 4640 W Hwy-192 ⓣ407/396-4135, ⓦwww.sevillainn.com. Privately owned, unpretentious, and cheap motel (especially in off-season) providing a refreshing change from the chain hotels. ❷

Staybridge Suites International Drive 8480 International Drive ⓣ407/352-2400 or 1-800/866-4549, ⓦwww.sborlando.com. Friendly and popular hotel smack in the middle of I-Drive, with well-equipped suites, free Internet, and buffet breakfast. ❻

Accommodation within Walt Disney World

Prices at the fabulously designed **Disney World resorts** (reservations for all: ⓣ407/939-6244 or ⓦwww.disneyworld.com) scattered around Disney property are much higher – sometimes more than $300 per night – than you'll pay elsewhere. However, the benefits (top-notch facilities, free airport transfers and parking, early access to the parks) can make it worth the extra cash. Though rooms may be available at short notice during the quieter times, you should **reserve as far in advance** – nine months is not unreasonable – as possible.

A good option if you're **camping**, the *Fort Wilderness Campground* is set on a lovely 700-acre forested site near the Magic Kingdom. Here you can hook up your RV or pitch your tent from $43, or rent a six-berth cabin from $265, and still enjoy the privileges of being a Disney guest.

All-Star Resorts Three resorts near the Blizzard Beach water park, with themes based on sports, music, and movies. The most affordable options in Disney, but still perfectly comfortable. ❹

Animal Kingdom Lodge Wake up to see African wildlife grazing outside your window at one of Disney's most spectacular and luxurious resorts. ❽

Grand Floridian Resort & Spa Gabled roofs, verandas, crystal chandeliers, and a full-service spa make this Disney's most elegant – and expensive – resort. ❾

Wilderness Lodge This convincing recreation of a frontier log cabin features a wood-burning fire in the lobby and welcoming rooms. ❽

Walt Disney World

As significant as air-conditioning in making the state what it is today, **WALT DISNEY WORLD** turned a wedge of Florida farmland into one of the world's most lucrative vacation destinations. The immense and astutely planned empire also pushed the state's media profile through the roof: from being a down-at-heel mixture of cheap motels, retirement homes, and alligator zoos, Florida suddenly, in 1971, became a showcase of modern international tourism.

Disney World is the pacesetter among theme parks. It goes way beyond Disneyland (see p.981), which opened in Anaheim, California, in 1955, delivering escapism at its most technologically advanced and psychologically brilliant, across an area twice the size of Manhattan. Its four main theme parks are quite separate entities and, ideally, you should allow at least a full day for each. The **Magic Kingdom** is the Disney park of popular imagination, where Mickey mingles with the crowds – very much the park for kids, though at its high-tech best capable of captivating even the most jaded of adults. Known for its giant, golfball-like geosphere, **Epcot** is Disney's celebration of science, technology, and world cultures; this sprawling area involves a lot of walking, and may bore young children. The

▲ The Magic Kingdom

smaller **Disney's Hollywood Studios** takes its inspiration from movies, TV, and music, offering some good thrill rides and live shows that will appeal to adults and kids alike. The newest of the four, **Disney's Animal Kingdom Park**, brings all manner of African and Asian wildlife to the theme-park setting.

Along with the main parks, other forms of entertainment have been created to keep people on Disney property for as long as possible. There are two excellent water parks, **Blizzard Beach** and **Typhoon Lagoon**, a sports complex called **Disney's Wide World of Sports**, and **Downtown Disney**, where you can eat, drink, and shop to your heart's content.

The Magic Kingdom

The **Magic Kingdom**, dominated by **Cinderella's Castle**, a stunning pseudo-Rhineland palace, follows the formula established by California's Disneyland, dividing into several themed sections: **Tomorrowland**, **Frontierland**, **Fantasyland**, **Adventureland**, **Liberty Square**, and **Mickey's Toontown Fair**. Fantasyland and Mickey's Toontown Fair are very much for the kids, while the other lands, and in particular Tomorrowland and Frontierland, have the edgier rides. Some attractions are identical to their California forebears, while others are unique or greatly improved. In Tomorrowland, the old favorite **Space Mountain** is in essence an ordinary rollercoaster, although its total darkness still manages to terrify younger riders. **Splash Mountain** employs water to great effect, culminating in a stunning 52-foot drop guaranteed to get you wet. **Big Thunder Mountain Railroad** puts you on board a runaway train, which trundles through Gold Rush California at a moderately fast pace.

Away from the thrill rides, many of the best attractions in the park rely on "Audio-Animatronics" characters – impressive vocal robots of Disney invention – for their appeal. Some of the finest are seen in **Stitch's Great Escape**, where the mischievous monster wreaks havoc on the audience, who feel, hear, and smell strange things in the dark. A large cast of AudioAnimatronics characters is also used to good effect in the **Haunted Mansion**, a mildly spooky ghost ride memorable for its spectacular holograms; the leisurely **Jungle Cruise** down the Amazon, Nile, Congo, and Mekong, past ferocious animals and cannibal camps; and **Pirates of the Caribbean**, the classic boat ride around a pirate-infested Caribbean island.

Fantasyland is mainly full of rather dated, juvenile rides, but does have the superb **Mickey's PhilharMagic**, an enchanting 3D journey with Daffy Duck and other well-known characters, set to classic Disney soundtracks. Equally magical is the **Wishes** firework display, which takes place at park closing time.

Epcot

Even before the Magic Kingdom opened, Walt Disney was developing plans for **Epcot** (Experimental Prototype Community of Tomorrow), conceived in 1966 as a real community experimenting with the new ideas and materials of the technologically advancing US. However, the idea failed to shape up as Disney had envisioned: Epcot didn't open until 1982, when global recession and ecological concerns had put a dampener on the belief in the infallibility of science. One drawback of this park is simply its immense size: it's twice as big as the Magic Kingdom, and very sapping on the feet.

The unmissable 180-foot geosphere (unlike a semicircular geodesic *dome*, the geosphere is completely round) sits in the heart of **Future World**, which keeps close to Epcot's original concept of exploring the history and researching the future of agriculture, transport, energy, and communication. Future World is

Information, tickets, and how to beat the crowds

For general Disney World **information**, call ⓣ407/939-6244 or visit ⓦwww.disneyworld.com. **Tickets** cost $75 (children aged 3–9 $63), and allow unlimited access to all shows and rides in one park only, for that day only. The **Magic Your Way** ticket saves money if you spread your visit over a number of days – for example, a seven-day ticket would cost $228 (children 3–9 $193). You can buy a Magic Your Way ticket for a maximum of ten days and you can only visit one park per day. If you want to move from park to park in the same day, you must add the **Park Hopper** option for an additional flat fee of $50. The **Water Park Fun & More** option allows you to add from two to ten extra admissions (the exact number depends on the length of your basic Magic Your Way ticket) to Blizzard Beach, Typhoon Lagoon, DisneyQuest, and Disney's Wide World of Sports for a flat fee of $50. The **parking** lots cost $12 a day, but are free if you're staying at a Walt Disney World resort.

Each park is generally **open** daily from 9am to between 6pm and 10pm, depending on the time of year; pick up the current schedule when you arrive. Note that Disney's Animal Kingdom Park closes at 5pm year round. At their worst, waiting times for the most popular rides can be well over an hour. The best way to **beat the crowds** is to use Disney's FASTPASS system. Place your admission ticket into a machine at the entrance of the attraction; the machine returns it with another ticket that gives you a time to return to the attraction, usually about two hours later. When that time arrives, you can join the FASTPASS line, which gets you in to the attraction with little or no wait. Another good tactic upon arrival is to rush to the far end of the park and work backwards, or to head straight for the big rides, getting them out of the way before the crowds arrive.

divided into several pavilions (including the geosphere, with its classic, recently modified **Spaceship Earth** ride), each corporate-sponsored, and featuring its own rides, films, interactive exhibits, and games. The best of the attractions are **Soarin'**, using the latest flight-simulator and IMAX movie technology to sweep you off on a breathtaking hang-glider ride over California; **Mission: SPACE**, a realistic recreation of a mission to Mars, including real G-force on take-off; **Test Track**, a rollercoaster-style ride where you test a high-performance car; and the **3D** cinematic thrill of **Honey, I Shrunk the Audience**.

Occupying the largest area in the park is **World Showcase**, with eleven different countries represented by recognizable national landmarks or stereotypical scenes. The **restaurants** here are among the best in Disney World; and it's a great place to watch the spectacular nighttime sound- and light-show, **IllumiNations: Reflections of Earth**.

Disney's Hollywood Studios

After signing an agreement in the 1980s with Metro-Goldwyn-Mayer (MGM) to exploit MGM's many movie classics, Disney had an ample source of instantly recognizable images to mold into rides suitable for adults as much as for kids. The park opened in 1989 as Disney-MGM Studios, but since then, the addition of attractions encompassing music, television, and theater led to the decision to rename the park **Disney's Hollywood Studios** to reflect the broader focus on "entertainment."

Most of the things to do at Disney's Hollywood Studios take the form of rides or shows, and there are fewer exhibit-style attractions when compared with the other Disney parks. Thrill-seekers will enjoy the gravity-defying drops (including moments of weightlessness) in the outstanding **The Twilight Zone Tower of Terror** or the slightly more ordinary **Rock 'n' Roller Coaster** with its breakneck-speed launch.

Don't miss the half-hour behind-the-scenes **Backlot Tour**, climaxing with the dramatic special effects on the *Catastrophe Canyon* movie set; the funny **Muppet Vision 3-D** show; and **The Great Movie Ride**, where Audio-Animatronics figures from famous movies interact with real-life actors.

The world of Walt Disney

When the brilliant illustrator and animator Walt Disney devised the world's first theme park, California's **Disneyland** (see p.981), he left himself with no control over the hotels and restaurants that quickly engulfed it, preventing growth and erasing profits Disney felt were rightly his. Determined not to let that happen again, the Disney corporation secretly bought up 27,500 acres of central Florida farmland, acquiring by the late Sixties a site a hundred times bigger than Disneyland. With the promise of a jobs bonanza for Florida, the state legislature gave the corporation the rights of any major municipality – empowering it to lay roads, enact building codes, and enforce the law with its own security force.

Walt Disney World's first "land," the Magic Kingdom, which opened in 1971, was a huge success. Unveiled in 1982, the far more ambitious Epcot represented the first major break from cartoon-based escapism – but its rose-tinted look at the future received a mixed response. Partly due to this, and to some bad management decisions, the Disney empire (Disney himself died in 1966) faced bankruptcy by the mid-1980s. Since then, the corporation has sprung back from the abyss, and despite being subject to a (failed) hostile takeover bid by Comcast in 2004, steers a tight and competitive business ship. It may trade in fantasy, but when it comes to money, the Disney Corporation's nose is firmly in the real world.

The most popular of the live shows are **The Indiana Jones Epic Stunt Spectacular!**, which re-enacts and explains many of the action-packed set pieces from the Steven Spielberg films; and the **Lights, Motors, Action! Stunt Show**, featuring equally eye-catching stunts involving cars, motorbikes, and jet skis.

Disney's Animal Kingdom Park

Disney's Animal Kingdom Park was opened in 1998 as an animal-conservation theme park with Disney's patented over-the-top twist. The park is divided into six "lands" – **Africa**, **Asia**, **Discovery Island**, **Camp Minnie-Mickey**, **DinoLand U.S.A.**, and **Rafiki's Planet Watch** – with Africa and Asia being the most visually impressive, each recreating the natural landscapes and exotic flavors of these two continents with admirable attention to detail.

The best-realized attraction is Africa's **Kilimanjaro Safaris**, where a jeep transport takes you on what feels very much like a real African safari, viewing giraffes, zebras, elephants, lions, gazelles, and rhinos, as well as taking part in anti-poacher maneuvers. Elsewhere in Africa, the troop of lowland gorillas at the **Pangani Forest Exploration Trail** are definitely worth a look. Crossing over to **Asia**, you'll get an astoundingly up-close look at the healthiest-looking tigers in captivity at the **Maharajah Jungle Trek**. Asia also has the thrilling **Expedition Everest** rollercoaster, where a train whizzes (both forward and backward) around a well-detailed replica of a Himalayan mountain. DinoLand U.S.A.'s **DINOSAUR** is a slower but still exciting ride full of small drops and short stops in the dark while scary dinosaurs pop out of nowhere.

The remainder of the park requires no more than casual exploration. The charming Flights of Wonder bird show showcases falcons, owls, and other wonderful birds, while two large-scale stage productions, Festival of the Lion King and **Finding Nemo – The Musical**, are notable for their elaborate sets and costumes, and catchy music.

Universal Orlando

For some years, it seemed that TV and film production would move away from California to Florida, which, with its lower taxes and cheaper labor, was more amenable. The opening of Universal Studios in 1990 appeared to confirm that trend. So far, though, for various reasons, Florida has not proved to be a fully realistic alternative. Even so, this hasn't stopped the Universal enclave here, known as **Universal Orlando**, off I-4, half a mile north of exits 74B or 75A (park opens daily at 9am, closing times vary; one-day, one-park ticket $73, children 3–9 $61, under-3s free; two-day, two-park ticket $104.99/$94.99; parking $12; Ⓣ1-407/363-8000, Ⓦwww.uescape.com), from becoming a major player in the Orlando theme-park arena. Though Disney World still commands the lion's share of attention, Universal has siphoned off many visitors with **Universal Studios**' high-tech movie-themed attractions and the excellent thrill rides at **Islands of Adventure**. And with all the nightclubs at Disney now closed, **CityWalk** has become the main competition to downtown Orlando for nightlife dollars (see "Nightlife and entertainment," p.604). Furthermore, Universal has achieved full-fledged resort status with its three luxurious on-site **hotels**: *Loews Portofino Bay*, *Hard Rock*, and *Loews Royal Pacific Resort* (all three Ⓣ1-888/273-1311, Ⓦwww.uescape.com; ⑨). Universal's equivalent to Disney's FASTPASS (see box, p.599) is called **Universal Express** and it works in virtually the same way. By purchasing **Universal Express Plus** ($25.99–50.99 depending on the time of year), you can enter the Universal Express line whenever and wherever you like for the whole day in both parks.

Universal Studios

Like its competitor Disney's Hollywood Studios, the four-hundred-acre Universal Studios is a working production studio. The newest attraction, **The Simpsons Ride**, combines cutting-edge flight-simulator technology with the irreverent humor of the Simpsons. The park's only rollercoaster, **Revenge of the Mummy**, takes you on a medium-paced journey through scenes from the eponymous movie. Don't miss **Shrek 4-D**, a delightful 3D presentation brought even more to life by an overdose of superb "feelies" (including a few too many water sprays). Also worthwhile, **Disaster** gives you an intensely claustrophobic two minutes of terror as you experience what it's like to be caught on a subway train when an 8.0 Richter-scale quake hits. Along the same lines, **TWISTER...Ride It Out** is a suffocating but gripping experience in which you stand beside an imitation tornado.

If you want to watch a live show, opt for the amusing Universal Horror Make-Up Show, which reveals movie-makeup secrets amidst enjoyably tasteless comic repartee, or try **Fear Factor Live!** (advanced registration required for contestants), which mimics the popular TV show.

Islands of Adventure

Islands of Adventure is Orlando's leader in state-of-the-art, edge-of-your-seat thrill rides: though there are plenty of diversions for the less daring, these rides are what brings the crowds. The park is divided into five sections – **Marvel Super Hero Island**, **The Lost Continent, Jurassic Park, Toon Lagoon**, and **Seuss Landing** – all surrounding a lagoon.

The very best of the rides is **The Amazing Adventures of Spider-Man**, which uses every trick imaginable – 3-D, sensory stimuli, motion simulation, and more – to spirit you into Spider-Man's battles with villains. **Dueling Dragons** is the park's scariest ride: twin rollercoasters ("Fire" and "Ice" – separate lines for each) engineered to provide harrowing head-on near misses with one another; for this reason, the front-row seats are especially sought after. Less intense but still exciting is the **Incredible Hulk Coaster**, with its catapult start and plenty of loop-the-loops and plunges. **Doctor Doom's Fearfall** provides a panoramic view of the park, but the very short controlled drop, during which you experience a few seconds of weightlessness, is anticlimactic. In a similar vein, **Jurassic Park River Adventure** is a generally tame river-raft trip, where the highlight is an 85-foot drop at the end.

Offerings for kids include **Dudley Do-Right's Ripsaw Falls** and **Popeye & Bluto's Bilge-Rat Barges**, both good for getting a midday drenching; and the whole of Seuss Landing, where everything is based on Dr Seuss characters. There's one **live performance** offered throughout the day: **The Eighth Voyage of Sindbad Stunt Show**, where the set, stunts, and pyrotechnics are as good as the jokes are bad.

SeaWorld Orlando and Discovery Cove

SeaWorld Orlando, at Sea Harbor Drive, near the intersection of I-4 and the Beeline Expressway, is the cream of Florida's sizeable crop of marine parks, and should not be missed; allocate a full day to see it all (park opens daily at 9am, closing times

The Orlando Flexticket

Universal Orlando, SeaWorld Orlando, and two water parks – Wet 'n Wild and Aquatica – have teamed together to create a pass that permits access to each park over a period of fourteen consecutive days. The **Orlando Flexticket** costs $234.95 (children 3–9 $194.95), or $279.95/$233.95, including Tampa's Busch Gardens, with a free shuttle from Orlando to Busch Gardens.

vary; $69.95, children 3–9 $59.95; Ⓣ407/351-3600, Ⓦwww.seaworld.com). The big event is *Believe* – thirty minutes of tricks performed by playful killer whales (you'll get drenched if you're sitting in the first fourteen rows of the stadium). Also, try not to miss the kid-orientated sea lion extravaganza, Clyde and Seamore Take Pirate Island. The **Wild Arctic** complex, complete with artificial snow and ice, brings you close to beluga whales, walruses, and polar bears, while a flight-simulator ride takes you on a stomach-churning helicopter flight through an Arctic blizzard.

The park's first thrill ride, **Journey to Atlantis**, travels on both water and rails, and has a sixty-foot drop (be prepared to get very wet). Much more exhilarating, however, is **Kraken**, a rollercoaster that flings you around at speeds of up to 65 miles per hour, free-flying and looping-the-loop at great heights. A brand new rollercoaster, **Manta**, is due to open in 2009.

With substantially less razzmatazz, plenty of smaller aquariums and displays offer a wealth of information about the underwater world. Among the highlights, **Penguin Encounter** recreates Antarctica, with scores of the waddling, flightless birds scampering over an iceberg; **Manatee Rescue** gives you a close-up look at these endangered mammals; and **Shark Encounter** includes a walk through an acrylic-sided and -roofed tunnel.

Discovery Cove, next to SeaWorld Orlando on Central Florida Parkway (daily 9am–5.30pm; $169–189 without dolphin swim, $269--289 with dolphin swim; Ⓣ1-877/4-DISCOVERY, Ⓦwww.discoverycove.com) limits visitors to about a thousand a day (reserve well in advance). The main reason for coming here is to swim and play with the dolphins, while other activities include snorkeling with tropical fish, wading in a pool full of harmless sting rays, and feeding exotic birds. Note that the admission charge includes seven-day access to SeaWorld Orlando or Busch Gardens.

Orlando's water parks

Disney World has two excellent **water parks**. **Blizzard Beach**, north of the *All-Star Resorts* (see p.597) on World Drive (daily 10am–5pm; slightly longer hours in summer; $40, children 3–9 $34; Ⓣ407/560-3400), is based on the fantasy that a hapless entrepreneur has opened a ski resort in Florida and the entire thing has started to melt. The star of the show is **Summit Plummet**, which shoots you down a 120-foot vertical drop at more than fifty miles per hour. Gentler rides include toboggan-style slalom courses and raft rides. As well as the slides, **Typhoon Lagoon**, just south of Downtown Disney (daily 10am–5pm; slightly longer hours in summer; $40, children 3–9 $34; Ⓣ407/560-4141), features a huge surfing pool and a shark reef where you can snorkel amongst tropical fish. Keen to get in on the act, SeaWorld Orlando has recently opened **Aquatica**, across the road from SeaWorld on International Drive (daily 9am–5pm; longer hours in summer; $41.95, children 3–9 $35.95; Ⓣ1-888/800-5447, Ⓦwww.aquaticabyseaworld.com), which combines live animal attractions with wave pools, slides, and beaches. Finally, **Wet 'n Wild**, 6200 International Drive (daily 10am–5pm; longer hours in summer; $41.95, children 3–9 $35.95; Ⓣ1-800/992-9453, Ⓦwww.wetnwildorlando.com), defends itself admirably in the face of the stiff competition, with a range of no-nonsense slides including the almost vertical **Der Stuka**.

Eating in the Orlando area

Downtown and its environs hold the pick of the locals' **eating** haunts; most visitors, however, head for International Drive's inexpensive all-day buffets and gourmet restaurants. You are not allowed to take food into any of the theme parks, where the best restaurants are in **Epcot's World Showcase**, particularly the French- and Mexican-themed establishments.

Bahama Breeze 8849 International Drive ⓣ407/248-2499. Decent Caribbean food ($15–20) in an upbeat atmosphere. Dinner only.
Café Tu Tu Tango 8625 International Drive ⓣ407/248-2222. Original, imaginative dishes ($7–11) served in small portions. All the artwork on the walls is for sale.
Dexter's of Thornton Park 808 E Washington St, downtown ⓣ407/648-2777. Trendy yet informal eatery in downtown's hip Thornton Park neighborhood. Moderately priced.
The Globe 25 Wall St Plaza, downtown ⓣ407/849-9904. Inexpensive snacks and light meals with an Asian twist; the tables outside are ideal for people-watching.
Ming Court 9188 International Drive ⓣ407/351-9988. An exceptional Chinese restaurant, with dim sum and sushi available. Not as costly as you might expect.
Panera Bread 227 N Eola Drive, downtown ⓣ407/481-1060. One of an inviting local chain, with a wide array of baked goods, soups, salads, and sandwiches. Also a WiFi Hotspot.
Punjab 7451 International Drive ⓣ407/352-7887. Reasonably priced curries spiced to your personal taste. A wide vegetarian choice.
Roy's 7760 W Sand Lake Rd, near International Drive ⓣ407/352-4844. Founded in Hawaii, *Roy's* specializes in Hawaiian fusion cuisine. Try the $35 three-course menu.
Seasons 52 7700 W Sand Lake Rd, near International Drive ⓣ407/354-5212. Offering healthy, low-calorie dishes and a popular piano bar for evening cocktails.
White Wolf Café 1829 N Orange Ave, downtown ⓣ407/895-9911. Down-to-earth café/antique store known for creative salads and sandwiches.

Nightlife and entertainment

The closure in 2008 of the nightclubs at Disney's shopping and entertainment complex, **Downtown Disney**, means that Orlando`s **nightspots** are now concentrated in two main areas, each offering a quite different atmosphere.

For wholesome, packaged and somewhat sterile entertainment, head to Universal Orlando's **CityWalk**, 6000 Universal Boulevard ($11.95 for all-night access to every club, plus free parking after 6pm; ⓣ407/363-8000, ⓦwww.citywalkorlando.com), thirty acres of restaurants, dance clubs, and shops wedged between Universal Studios and Islands of Adventure. Here you'll find live reggae at **Bob Marley – A Tribute to Freedom**; an energetic, margarita-fuelled atmosphere at **Jimmy Buffett's Margaritaville**; and a good sound system and flashing lights at the fully-fledged nightclub, **the groove**.

Away from the theme parks, **downtown Orlando** has a large, eclectic, and much more appealing crop of bars, lounges, and clubs. Most of the after-dark action focuses along **Orange Avenue**: *The Social*, no. 54, is a well-known venue for live alternative rock, grunge, and the like; *Tabu*, no. 46, is a large-scale dance club in an old theatre; and *Pulse*, no. 1912, a mile or so south of downtown, is a popular **gay** nightspot.

The West Coast

In the three hundred miles from the state's southern tip to the junction with the Panhandle (see p.617), Florida's **West Coast** embraces all the extremes. Buzzing, youthful towns rise behind placid fishing hamlets; mobbed holiday strips are just minutes from desolate swamplands, and world-class art collections vie with glitzy theme parks. Surprises are plentiful, though the coast's one constant is proximity to the Gulf of Mexico – and sunset views rivaled only by those of the Florida Keys.

The west coast's largest city, **Tampa**, has more to offer than its corporate towers initially suggest – not least the lively nightlife scene in the Cuban enclave of **Ybor City**, and the Busch Gardens theme park. For the mass of visitors, though, the Tampa Bay area begins and ends with the **St Petersburg beaches**, whose miles of sea and sand are undiluted vacation territory. South of Tampa, a string of barrier-island beaches run the length of the Gulf, and the mainland towns that provide access to them – such as Sarasota and Fort Myers – have enough to warrant a stop. Inland, the wilderness of the **Everglades** is explorable on simple walking trails, by canoeing, or by spending the night at backcountry campgrounds, with only the gators for company.

Tampa

A small, stimulating city with an infectious, upbeat mood, **TAMPA**, the business hub of the west coast, is well worth a stop. As one of the major beneficiaries of the flood of people and money into Florida, Tampa boasts an impressive cultural infrastructure envied by many larger rivals. In addition to its fine **museums** and **Busch Gardens**, one of the most popular theme parks in the state, the city holds, in the Cuban-influenced **Ybor City**, just northeast of the city center, the west coast's hippest and most culturally eclectic quarter.

Tampa began as a small settlement beside a US Army base that was built in the 1820s to keep an eye on the Seminoles. In the 1880s, the railroad arrived, and the Hillsborough River, on which the city stands, was dredged to allow seagoing vessels to dock. Tampa became a booming port, simultaneously acquiring a major tobacco industry as thousands of Cubans moved north from Key West to the new cigar factories of neighboring Ybor City. The Depression ended the economic surge, but the port remained one of the busiest in the country and tempered Tampa's postwar decline. Today, little seems to stand in the way of Tampa's continued emergence as a forward-thinking and financially secure community.

Arrival and information

Tampa's **airport** (ⓣ813/870-8700, ⓦwww.tampaairport.com) is five miles northwest of downtown: local HART bus #30 is the least costly connection (see p.606). **Taxis** (try United ⓣ813/253-2424) to downtown or a Busch Boulevard motel cost $25–50; to St Petersburg or the beaches, $45–75. Greyhound **buses** arrive downtown at 610 Polk St (ⓣ813/229-2174); trains at 601 N Nebraska Ave (ⓣ813/221-7600).

The downtown **Visitor Information Center**, 615 Channelside Drive, suite 108A (Mon–Fri 9.30am–5pm, ⓣ1-800/44-TAMPA, ⓦwww.visittampabay.

com), and the **Ybor City Visitor Information Center**, 1600 E 8th Ave, suite B104 (Mon–Sat 10am–6pm, Sun noon–6pm; ⓣ813/241-8838, ⓦwww.ybor.org), give out useful leaflets and maps.

Although both downtown Tampa and Ybor City are easily covered on foot, to travel between them without a car you'll need to use the HART **local buses** ($1.75, one-day pass $3.75; ⓣ813/254-4278, ⓦwww.hartline.org) or the TECO Line **Streetcar System** ($2.50; ⓣ813/254-4278, ⓦwww.tecolinestreetcar.org), a vintage replica streetcar which runs between downtown and Ybor several times an hour. Useful HART bus routes are #8 to Ybor City, #5 to Busch Gardens, #6 to the Museum of Science and Industry.

Accommodation

Tampa is not generously supplied with low-cost **accommodation**; you'll almost certainly save money by staying in St Petersburg (see p.608) or at the beaches (see p.610). There are some good deals, though, at the motels near Busch Gardens.

Best Western All Suites 301 University Center Drive, behind Busch Gardens ⓣ813/971-8930 or 1-800/780-7234. A reasonable base for seeing the city by car, and so close to Busch Gardens that the parrots escape into their trees. Features a happy hour every afternoon and free breakfast. 5

Don Vincente de Ybor Historic Inn 1915 Avenida Republica de Cuba ⓣ1-866/206-4545, ⓦwww.donvicenteinn.com. A luxurious B&B option in Ybor City. Features sixteen beautifully restored suites and swing dancing on Tuesday nights. 6

Gram's Place 3109 N Ola Ave ⓣ813/221-0596, ⓦwww.grams-inn-tampa.com. This funky motel-cum-hostel offers both private rooms – all themed in different musical styles – and rather tatty youth-hostel-style accommodation. $23 for a dorm bed; private rooms 3

Hilton Garden 1700 E 9th Ave ⓣ813/769-9267, ⓦwww.tampayborhistoricdistrict.gardeninn.com. Comfortable digs, even if the decor is a little sterile to be in the heart of Tampa's most historically rich neighborhood. 7–8

Sheraton Tampa Riverwalk 200 N Ashley Drive ⓣ813/223-2222, ⓦwww.tampariverwalkhotel.com. Very convenient downtown location, nicely situated on the banks of the Hillsborough River. 7

Wingate by Wyndham 3751 E Fowler Ave ⓣ813/979-2828. With a free shuttle bus to Busch Gardens (5 minutes away), great free breakfast, clean rooms and a solicitous staff, you can't go wrong here. 5–6

Downtown Tampa

At the time of writing, the highly regarded **Tampa Museum of Art**, temporary location at 2306 N Howard Ave (Tues–Sat 10am–4pm, donation requested; ⓣ813/274-8130, ⓦwww.tampamuseum.org) was in transition. The museum is set to open a new facility at the Curtis Hixon Waterfront Park in fall of 2009, with 66,000 square feet of gallery space, making it 150 percent larger than the former location. The new museum will still specialize in classical antiquities and twentieth-century American art, as well as playing host to traveling exhibits.

From the river, you'll see the silver minarets and cupolas on the far side of the river, sprouting from the main building of the University of Tampa. These architectural ornaments adorn what was formerly the 500-room **Tampa Bay Hotel**, financed by steamship and railroad magnate Henry B. Plant. To reach it, walk across the river on Kennedy Boulevard and descend the steps into Plant Park.

The structure is as bizarre a sight today as it was when it opened in 1891. Since the Civil War, Plant had been buying up bankrupt railroads, steadily inching his way into Florida to meet his steamships unloading at Tampa's harbor. Eventually, he became rich enough to put his fantasies of creating the world's most luxurious hotel into practice. However, lack of care for the fittings and Plant's death in 1899 hastened the hotel's transformation from the last word in comfort to a pile of crumbling plaster. The city bought it in 1905 and leased it to Tampa University 23 years later. In one wing, the **Henry B. Plant Museum**, 401 W Kennedy Blvd (Tues–Sat 10am–4pm, Sun noon–4pm; $5; Ⓣ813/254-1891, Ⓦwww.plantmuseum.com), holds what's left of the hotel's original furnishings.

In Tampa's dockland area, a mile or so southeast of the Tampa Bay Hotel, the splendid **Florida Aquarium**, 701 Channelside Drive (daily 9.30am–5pm; $19.95; Ⓣ813/273-4000, Ⓦwww.flaquarium.org), houses lavish displays of Florida's fresh- and saltwater habitats, from springs and swamps to beaches and coral reefs. Animal residents include an impressive variety of fish, birds, otters, turtles, and alligators.

Ybor City

In 1886, as soon as Henry Plant's ships had ensured a regular supply of Havana tobacco into Tampa, cigar magnate Don Vincente Martínez Ybor cleared a patch of scrubland three miles northeast of present-day downtown Tampa and laid the foundations of **YBOR CITY**. About twenty thousand migrants, mostly Cuban, settled here and created a Latin American enclave, producing the top-class, hand-rolled cigars that made Tampa the "**Cigar Capital of the World**." However, mass production, the popularity of cigarettes, and the Depression proved a fatal combination for skilled cigar-makers: as unemployment struck, Ybor City's tight-knit blocks of cobbled streets and redbrick buildings became surrounded by drab, low-rent neighborhoods.

Ybor City today buzzes with tourists, and at night the atmosphere can get raucous, especially on the weekends. The town is trendy and culturally diverse, yet its Cuban roots are immediately apparent, and explanatory background texts adorn many buildings. The **Ybor City State Museum**, 1818 9th Ave (daily 9am–5pm; $3; Ⓣ813/247-1434, Ⓦwww.ybormuseum.org), helps you grasp the main points of Ybor City's creation and its multiethnic make-up. The museum also offers cigar-rolling demonstrations (Fri–Sun 11am–1pm) and historic walking tours (Sat 10.30am; $6).

Busch Gardens and the Museum of Science and Industry

Busch Gardens, located two miles east of I-275, or two miles west of I-75, exit 54, at 3000 E Busch Blvd (opening hours vary day to day but generally daily 10am–6pm; $67.95, children $57.95; parking $10; Ⓣ1-888/800-5447, Ⓦwww.buschgardenstampabay.com) is one of Florida's most popular theme parks, based on a recreation of Colonial-era Africa and offering some of the fastest, largest, most nerve-jangling rollercoasters in the country. A sedate pseudo-steam train or cable car journey allows inspection of a variety of African wildlife, but by far the most popular of the twenty-odd rides are the roller coasters: **Sheikra**, with its terrifying 200-foot, 90-degree dive; **Montu**, where your legs dangle precariously in mid-air; **Gwazi**, a giant wooden coaster; and **Kumba**, with plenty of high-speed loop-the-loops. After this excitement, retire to the Hospitality House for two free cups of Budweiser beer.

Two miles northeast of Busch Gardens, the colossal **Museum of Science and Industry**, 4801 E Fowler Ave (9am–5pm Mon–Fri, 9am–6pm Sat–Sun; $20.95; Ⓣ813/987-6100, Ⓦwww.mosi.org), demystifies the scientific world through hands-on exhibits and a program of shows where you'll get to feel what it's like to sit in a 74mph wind or ride a bicycle along a tightrope. Several different **IMAX** movies screen throughout the day for an additional $7.95.

Eating

There are plenty of good places to **eat** in Tampa, with a huge concentration of lively restaurants in Ybor City.

Bernini 1702 7th Ave, Ybor City ⓣ813/248-0099. In the lovely old Bank of Ybor City, an Italian joint serving up wood-fired pizza and pasta.

Café Dufrain 707 Harbour Post Drive, Harbour Island, ⓣ813/275-9701. This great, moderately priced place overlooking the water on Harbour Island serves a variety of contemporary cuisine with both mouth-watering meat and seafood dishes – try the Latin grilled salmon or the Argentinean skirt steak.

Cephas 1701 E 4th Ave, Ybor City ⓣ813/247-9022. A funky Jamaican restaurant offering jerk chicken and curried goat, chicken, and fish.

Columbia 2117 E 7th Ave, Ybor City ⓣ813/248-4961. A Tampa – and tourist – institution, the city's oldest restaurant serves fine Spanish and Cuban food. Reservations recommended.

La Creperia Café 1729 E 7th Ave, Ybor City ⓣ813/248-9700. A wide choice of delicious sweet and savory crepes, plus free WiFi Internet access.

Shells 11010 N 30th St ⓣ813/977-8456. Convenient to the hotels near Busch Gardens, this cheap and cheerful seafood restaurant serves consistently good fresh fish.

Nightlife and entertainment

Ybor City's renowned **nightlife** tends to be younger and more raucous than the city's other entertainment areas of Channelside, downtown next to the Florida Aquarium, and the International Plaza and Bay Street, near the airport at the junction of West Shore and Boy Scout boulevards. The free *Weekly Planet* (ⓦwww.weeklyplanet.com) has **listings**, as does Friday's *Tampa Tribune*.

Blue Martini at the International Plaza and Bay Street ⓣ813/873-2583. Good-looking, professional crowd at this trendy lounge bar.

Green Iguana 1708 E 7th Ave, Ybor City ⓣ813/248-9555. Rock bands play nightly, and DJs keep the young crowd very much in the party mood.

Side Splitters 12938 N Dale Mabry Hwy ⓣ813/960-1197. One of the best comedy clubs in the area.

Skipper's Smokehouse 910 Skipper Rd ⓣ813/971-0666. Blues and reggae rule at this family-oriented live music venue.

Tampa Theatre 711 Franklin St ⓣ813/274-8981. Foreign-language, classic, and cult films shown in an atmospheric 1920s theater. Tickets $9.

St Petersburg

Situated on the eastern edge of the Pinellas Peninsula, a bulky thumb of land poking between Tampa Bay and the Gulf of Mexico, **ST PETERSBURG** is a world away from Tampa, even though the two cities are just twenty miles apart. Declared the healthiest place in the US in 1885, St Petersburg wasted no time in wooing the recuperating and the retired, at one point putting five thousand green benches on its streets to take the weight off elderly feet. Although it remains a favourite of retirees, the city has worked hard to attract young blood, as well. In addition to rejuvenating the pier, which now offers something for all ages, St Petersburg's diverse selection of museums and plethora of art galleries have contributed to its emergence as one of Florida's richest cultural centers. Most remarkable of all, the town has acquired a major collection of works by Salvador Dalí.

The **Salvador Dalí Museum**, 1000 S 3rd St (Mon–Wed & Sat 9.30am–5.30pm, Thurs 9.30am–8pm, Fri 9.30am–6.30pm, Sun noon–5.30pm; $15, Thurs after 5pm $5; ⓣ727/823-3767, ⓦwww.salvadordalimuseum.org), stores more than a thousand paintings from the collection of a Cleveland industrialist, A. Reynolds Morse, who struck up a friendship with the artist in the 1940s. Hour-long **free tours** that run continuously throughout the day trace a chronological path around the works, from the artist's early experiments with Impressionism and Cubism to the seminal Surrealist canvas *The Disintegration of the Persistence of Memory*.

Once you've done Dalí, the quarter-mile-long **pier**, jutting from the end of 2nd Avenue North, is the town's focal point. The pier often hosts arts-and-crafts exhibitions, and the inverted-pyramid-like building at its head holds five storeys of restaurants, shops, and fast-food counters. At the foot of the pier, the **Museum of History**, 335 2nd Ave NE (Tues–Sat 10am–5pm, Sun 1pm–5pm; $12; Ⓣ727/894-1052, Ⓦwww.spmoh.org), recounts using modest displays St Petersburg's early twentieth-century heyday as a winter resort. Nearby, the **Museum of Fine Arts**, 255 Beach Drive NE (Tues–Sat 10am–5pm, Sun 1–5pm; $12, including free guided tour; Ⓣ727/896-2667, Ⓦwww.fine-arts.org), holds a superlative collection ranging from pre-Columbian art through Asian and African to the European Old Masters as well as rotating exhibits in the new airy and modern Hazel Hough wing, which more than doubles the museum's space. The **Florida International Museum**, 244 2nd Ave N (during exhibition periods only, Tues–Sat 10am–5pm, Sun noon–5pm, last entry 4pm; $10; Ⓣ727/341-7900, Ⓦwww.floridamuseum.org), occupies an entire block and displays three exhibitions a year on subjects ranging from Ancient Egypt to the Beatles.

Practicalities

The Greyhound **bus** station is downtown at 180 9th St N (Ⓣ727/898-1496). The **Chamber of Commerce** is at 100 2nd Ave N (Mon–Fri 8am–7pm, Sat 9am–7pm; Ⓣ727/821-4715, Ⓦwww.stpete.com). **Accommodation** in St Petersburg can be less costly than at the beaches (see p.610). The area is also rich in charismatic B&Bs, such as *Dickens House*, 335 8th Ave NE (Ⓣ1-800/381-2022, Ⓦwww.dickenshouse.com; ⑥). For sheer luxury, stay at *Renaissance Vinoy Resort*, 501 5th Ave NE (Ⓣ1-888/303-4430, Ⓦwww.renaissancehotels.com/tpasr; ⑧). Hearty, economical Cuban **food** can be had at *Tangelo's Grill*, 226 1st Ave N (Ⓣ727/894-1695). Alternatively, try *Moon Under Water*, 332 Beach Drive NE (Ⓣ727/896-6160); overlooking the waterfront, this inexpensive British tavern is well known for its cocktails and curries.

The St Petersburg beaches

Framing the Gulf side of the Pinellas Peninsula, a 35-mile chain of barrier islands forms the **St Petersburg Beaches**, one of Florida's busiest coastal strips. When the resorts of Miami Beach lost some of their allure during the 1970s, the St Petersburg beaches grew in popularity with Americans and have since evolved into an established destination for package-holidaying Europeans. The beaches are beautiful, the sea warm, and the sunsets fabulous – yet this is not Florida at its best: the whole area is a little tacky, with large portions lacking in charm and character.

All **buses** ($1.75; Ⓣ727/540-1900, Ⓦwww.psta.net) to the beaches originate in St Petersburg, at the Williams Park terminal, on 1st Avenue North and 3rd Street North; an **information booth** there has route details. **Route #35** runs daily to St Pete Beach on Gulf Boulevard, which links all the St Petersburg beach communities. At St Pete Beach, you can change for the **Suncoast Beach Trolley**, which links Passe-a-Grille in the extreme south to Sand Key in the north.

The southern beaches

In twenty-odd miles of heavily touristed coast, only **Pass-a-Grille**, at the very southern tip of the barrier island chain, has the look and feel of a genuine community – two miles of tidy houses, cared-for lawns, small shops, and a cluster of bars and restaurants. During the week, the town is blissfully quiet, while on weekends informed locals come here to enjoy one of the area's liveliest stretches of sand.

A mile and a half north of Pass-a-Grille, the painfully luxurious **Don CeSar Hotel**, 3400 Gulf Blvd (ⓣ727/360-1881 or 1-866/728-2206, ⓦwww.doncesar.com; ❾), is a grandiose pink castle, filling seven beachside acres. Opened in 1928, and briefly busy with the likes of Scott and Zelda Fitzgerald, it enjoyed a short-lived glamour. During the Great Depression, part of the hotel was used as a warehouse, and later as the spring training base of the New York Yankees baseball team.

Continuing north from the *Don CeSar* on Gulf Boulevard brings you into the main section of **St Pete Beach**, a string of uninspiring hotels, motels, and eating establishments. Further north, **Treasure Island** is even less varied tourist territory. An arching drawbridge leads to **Madeira Beach**, essentially more of the same – although, if you can't make it to Pass-a-Grille, the beach here justifies a weekend fling.

The northern beaches

Much of the northern section of **Sand Key**, the longest barrier island in the St Petersburg chain, and one of the wealthier portions of the coast, is taken up by stylish condos and time-share apartments. The island terminates in the pretty **Sand Key Park**, where tall palm trees frame a silky strip of sand. The park occupies one bank of **Clearwater Pass**, across which a belt of sparkling white sands marks the holiday town of **CLEARWATER BEACH**, where a recent condo boom has all but obliterated the small-town feel. The staff at the family-run *Barefoot Bay Motel*, 401 East Shore Drive (ⓣ727/447-1016, ⓦwww.barefootbayresort.com; ❹) couldn't be friendlier. The rooms are clean and well-kept, and the beach is a five minute walk. Regular **buses** (#80) provide links to the mainland town of Clearwater, across the two-mile causeway.

Beach practicalities

The **motels** that line mile after mile of Gulf Boulevard tend to be cheaper than the **hotels** – typically $75–100 in winter, $15–20 less in summer. You'll pay $5–10 extra for a room on the beach side of Gulf Boulevard compared with an identical room on the inland side. At the southern beaches, good, cheap accommodation can be found at the peaceful *Lamara Motel & Apartments*, 520 73rd Ave, St Petersburg Beach (ⓣ1-800/211-5108, ⓦwww.lamara.com; ❸), while the pick of the hotels at the northern beaches is *Sheraton Sand Key*, 1160 Gulf Blvd, Sand Key (ⓣ727/595-1611, ⓦwww.sheratonsandkey.com; ❽). It's easy to find a decent place to **eat** around the beaches. Overlooking the sea, *Hurricane*, 807 Gulf Way, Pass-a-Grille (ⓣ727/360-9558), has a well-priced menu of the freshest seafood. *Fetishes*, 6690 Gulf Blvd, St Pete Beach (ⓣ727/363-3700), is ideal for a more upscale and intimate dining experience, serving expensive American cuisine. In Clearwater Beach, *Frenchy's Café*, 41 Baymont St (ⓣ727/446-3607), cooks up good grouper sandwiches and seafood gumbo.

Sarasota

Rising on a gentle hillside beside the blue waters of Sarasota Bay, **SARASOTA**, 35 miles south of St Petersburg, is one of Florida's better-off and better-looking towns. It's also one of the state's leading cultural centers, home to numerous writers and artists, and the base of several respected performing arts companies. The community is far less stuffy than its wealth might suggest, and downtown Sarasota is fairly lively, with cafés, bars, and restaurants complementing the excellent grouping of bookstores.

The Ringling Museum Complex

John Ringling, one of the owners of the fantastically successful Ringling Brothers Circus, which toured the US from the 1880s, acquired during his lifetime a fortune estimated at $200 million. Recognizing Sarasota's investment potential, he built the first causeway to the barrier islands and made this the winter base for his circus. His greatest gift to the town, however, was a Venetian Gothic mansion and an incredible collection of European Baroque paintings – regarded as one of the finest collections of its kind in the US – displayed in a purpose-built museum beside the house.

The **Ringling Museum Complex**, which includes the mansion (daily 10am–5.30pm; $19; Ⓣ941/359-5700, Ⓦwww.ringling.org), is at 5401 Bay Shore Rd, three miles north of downtown beside US-41. Begin your exploration by walking through the gardens to the former winter residence of John and Mable Ringling, **Ca' d'Zan** ("House of John," in Venetian dialect), built in 1926 for $1.5 million, and furnished with New York estate sale castoffs for an additional $400,000. A gorgeous piece of work and a triumph of taste and proportion, it's serenely situated beside the bay. The artwork is displayed in the spacious **museum**, built around a mock fifteenth-century Italian palazzo. Five enormous paintings by Rubens, commissioned in 1625, and the painter's subsequent *Portrait of Archduke Ferdinand*, are highlights, though there's also a wealth of talent from Europe's leading schools of the mid-sixteenth to mid-eighteenth centuries. Free guided **tours** depart regularly from the entrance.

The Sarasota beaches

Increasingly the stamping ground of European package tourists spilling south from the St Petersburg beaches, the white sands of the **Sarasota beaches** are worth a day of anybody's time. The two islands on which they lie, Lido Key and Siesta Key, are accessible from the mainland, though there is no direct link between them. A third island, Longboat Key, is primarily residential.

The Ringling Causeway crosses the yacht-filled Sarasota Bay from the foot of Sarasota's Main Street to **Lido Key**. The causeway flows into **St Armands Circle**, a roundabout ringed by upmarket shops and restaurants dotted with some of Ringling's replica classical statuary. Continuing south along Benjamin Franklin Drive, you come to the island's most accessible beaches, ending after two miles at the attractive **South Lido Park** (daily 8am-sunset; free).

The bulbous northerly section of tadpole-shaped **Siesta Key**, reached by Siesta Drive off US-41, about five miles south of downtown Sarasota, attracts a younger crowd. The soft sand at the pretty but busy **Siesta Key Beach** (beside Beach Road) has a sugary texture due to its origins as quartz (not the more usual pulverized coral). To escape the crowds, continue south past Crescent Beach and follow Midnight Pass Road for six miles to **Turtle Beach**, a small, secluded stretch of sand.

Practicalities

In downtown Sarasota, Greyhound **buses** stop at 575 N Washington Blvd (☎941/955-5735). The **Amtrak bus** from Tampa pulls in at 1993 Main Street. The local bus terminal is a few blocks west at 1565 1st St (at Lemon St): catch buses here for the Ringling estate or the beaches ($0.75). Call at the **Information and History Visitor Center**, 701 N Tamiami Trail (Mon–Sat 10am–4pm, ☎1-800/522-9799, Ⓦwww.sarasotafl.org), for discount coupons and leaflets.

On the mainland, **motels** run the length of US-41 (N Tamiami Trail) between the Ringling estate and downtown Sarasota, typically charging around $60–90 a night: try the *Best Western Midtown*, 1425 S Tamiami Trail (☎941/955-9841, Ⓦwww.bwmidtown.com; ❸). Prices are higher at the beaches: the friendly *Lido Vacation Rentals*, 528 S Polk Drive, Lido Key (☎1-800/890-7991, Ⓦlidovacation-rentals.com; ❸–❹), is one of the more reasonably priced choices.

Eating options along Main Street include the reasonably priced sandwiches at *Main Bar Sandwich Shop*, no. 1944 (☎941/955-8733), as well as the excellent Tex-Mex favorites at *Two Señoritas*, no. 1355 (☎941/366-1618). On Siesta Key, check out *The Broken Egg*, 140 Avenida Messina (☎941/346-2750), popular with locals for the all-American breakfasts and lunches.

Fort Myers

Fifty miles south, **FORT MYERS** may lack the elan of Sarasota, but it's nonetheless one of the up-and-coming communities of Florida's southwest coast. Fortunately, most of its recent growth has occurred on the north side of the wide Caloosahatchee River, which the town straddles, allowing the traditional center, along the waterway's south shore, to remain relatively unspoiled.

Once across the river, US-41 strikes **downtown** Fort Myers, picturesquely nestled on the water's edge. For a thorough insight into the town's history, head to the **Southwest Florida Museum of History**, 2300 Peck St (Tues–Sat 10am–5pm; $9.50; ☎239/332-5955), which also has an eye-catching 84-foot-long Pullman rail car.

In 1885, six years after inventing the light bulb, **Thomas Edison** collapsed from exhaustion and was instructed by his doctor to find a warm working environment or face an early death. Vacationing in Florida, the 37-year-old Edison bought fourteen acres of land on the banks of the Caloosahatchee and cleared a section of it to spend his remaining winters. This became the **Edison Winter Estate**, 2350 McGregor Blvd, a mile west of downtown (daily 9am–5.30pm; $20 for homes and gardens tour, every 30mins; ☎239/334-3614, Ⓦwww.efwefla.org). The tours begin in the gardens, planted with such exotics as African sausage trees and wild orchids. However, the house, which you can glimpse only through the windows, is anticlimactic – its plainness probably due to the fact that Edison spent most of his waking hours inside the **laboratory**, attempting to turn the latex-rich sap of *Solidago edisonii* (a strain of goldenrod weed he developed) into rubber. However, when the tour reaches the engrossing **museum**, the full impact of Edison's achievements becomes apparent: you'll see several examples of the phonograph that Edison created in 1877, as well as some of the ungainly cinema projectors derived from Edison's Kinetoscope – which brought him a million dollars a year in royalties from 1907. Next door, you can also traipse through the plain **Ford Winter Estate**, bought by Edison's close friend Henry Ford in 1915. Much more awe-inspiring is the enormous banyan tree outside the ticket office – the largest of its kind in the continental US.

The Fort Myers beaches

The **Fort Myers beaches** on **Estero Island**, fifteen miles south of downtown, are appreciably different in character from the west coast's more commercialized beach strips, with a cheerful seaside mood. Accommodation is plentiful on and around Estero Boulevard – reached by San Carlos Boulevard – which runs the seven-mile length of the island. Most activity revolves around the short fishing pier and the **Lynne Hall Memorial Park**, at the island's north end.

Estero Island becomes increasingly residential as you press south, Estero Boulevard eventually swinging over a slender causeway to **Lovers Key State Recreation Area** (daily 8am–sunset; $3–5 per car, $1 for pedestrians and cyclists; ⓣ239/463-4588), where a footpath picks a trail over a couple of mangrove-fringed islands and several mullet-filled creeks to **Lovers Key**, a secluded beach. If you don't fancy the walk, a free trolley will transport you between the park entrance and the beach.

Reached only by crossing a causeway (with a $6 toll), the islands of **Sanibel** and **Captiva**, 25 miles southwest of Fort Myers, are virtually impossible to visit unless you have a car. However, if you have a spare day, these islands offer a wildlife refuge, mangroves, and shell-strewn beaches – for which they are widely renowned. In contrast with the smooth beaches along the gulf side of Sanibel Island, the opposite edge comprises shallow bays and creeks, and a vibrant wildlife habitat under the protection of the **J.N. "Ding" Darling National Wildlife Refuge** (daily except Fri 7.30am–sunset; cars $5, cyclists and pedestrians $1; ⓣ239/472-1100). The main entrance and **information center** are just off the Sanibel–Captiva Road. If you intend to stay here for a night or two, contact the Fort Myers visitor center beforehand for lodging ideas. By doing so, you'll be treated to a beach experience unlike those in most of Florida – lovely yet with an acute sense of isolation.

Practicalities

Greyhound pulls in at the Rosa Parks Transportation Center, 2250 Peck St, while daily **Amtrak buses** from Tampa arrive at 6050 Plaza Drive, about six miles east of downtown. The **Chamber of Commerce** is at 2310 Edwards Drive (Mon–Fri 9am–4.30pm; ⓣ1-800/366-3622, ⓦwww.fortmyers.org). Distances within Fort Myers, and from downtown to the beaches, are large, and you'll struggle without a car, though it is possible – just – to reach the beaches on local LeeTran **buses** (ⓣ239/533-8726, ⓦwww.rideleetran.com; $1.25). You can pick up most LeeTran services **at the** Greyhound terminal.

Accommodation costs in and around Fort Myers are low between May and December, when 30–60 percent gets lopped off the standard rates. However, in high season, prices skyrocket, and spare rooms are rare. Downtown, look along 1st Street: the riverfront *Sea Chest Motel*, at no. 2571 (ⓣ1-800/438-6461; ❸), is among the cheapest. At the beaches, Estero Boulevard is your best bet: the *Beacon*, no. 1240 (ⓣ239/463-5264, ⓦthebeaconmotel.com; ❸), and *Casa Playa*, no. 510 (ⓣ1-800/569-4876, ⓦwww.casaplayaresort.com; ❹–❼), are both clean and reliable. Of the **campgrounds**, only *Red Coconut*, 3001 Estero Blvd (from $40; ⓣ239/463-7200, ⓦwww.redcoconut.com), is right on the beach.

For downtown **food**, try *The Veranda*, 2122 Second St (ⓣ239/332-2065), where the Old South lives on in two 1902 houses and a lush courtyard of mango trees, or *Oasis Restaurant*, 2260 Dr Martin Luther King Jr Blvd (ⓣ239/334-1556), for large, cheap breakfasts and lunch specials. At the beaches, sample the seafood and live music at the *Beach Pierside Grill & Blowfish Bar*, 1000 Estero Blvd (ⓣ239/765-7800), or grab a beer at *Top O' The Mast*, 1028 Estero Blvd (ⓣ239/463-9424), where there's also live music and DJs.

Everglades National Park

One of the country's most celebrated natural areas, **the EVERGLADES NATIONAL PARK** is a vast, tranquil wildlife reserve, with a subtle, raw appeal that makes a stark contrast to America's more rugged national parks. The most dramatic sights are small pockets of trees poking above a completely flat sawgrass plain, yet these wide-open spaces resonate with life, forming part of an ever-changing ecosystem, evolved through a unique combination of climate, vegetation, and wildlife.

Though it appears to be flat as a table-top, the limestone on which the Everglades stands actually tilts very slightly towards the southwest. For thousands of years, water from summer storms and the overflow of nearby Lake Okeechobee has moved slowly through the Everglades towards the coast. The water replenishes the sawgrass, which grows on a thin layer of soil formed by decaying vegetation. This gives birth to the algae at the base of a complex food chain that sustains much larger creatures, most importantly **alligators**. After the floodwaters have reached the sea, drained through the bedrock, or simply evaporated, the Everglades are barren except for the water accumulated in ponds – or "gator holes" – created when an alligator senses water and clears the soil covering it with its tail. Besides nourishing the alligator, the pond provides a home for other wildlife until the summer rains return. Sawgrass covers much of the Everglades, but where natural indentations in the limestone fill with soil, fertile tree islands – or **"hammocks"** – appear, just high enough to stand above the floodwaters.

In the nineteenth century, the Seminole and Miccosukee **Native American tribes** were forced to live hunter-gatherer existences in the Everglades, and still maintain a sizeable presence here. By the late 1800s, a few towns had sprung up, peopled by settlers who, unlike the Indians, looked to exploit the land. As Florida's population grew, the damage caused by hunting, road building, and draining for farmland gave rise to a significant **conservation** lobby. In 1947, a section of the Everglades was declared a national park, which today bestows federal protection to a comparatively small area at the southern tip of the Florida peninsula. The Everglades' boundaries have been steadily pushed back by urban development over the last century, and unrestrained commercial use of nearby areas continues to upset the region's natural cycle. The 1200 miles of canals built to divert the flow of water away from the Everglades and toward the state's expanding cities, the poisoning caused by agricultural chemicals from local farmlands, and the broader changes wrought by global warming could yet turn Florida's greatest natural asset into a wasteland.

Arrival and information

There are **three entrances** to the park: Everglades City, at the northwestern corner; Shark Valley, at the northeastern corner; and the one near the Ernest Coe Visitor Center, at the southeastern corner. **US-41** skirts the northern edge of the park, providing the only land access to the Everglades City and Shark Valley entrances. There is **no public transportation** along US-41, or to any of the park entrances.

Park entry is free at Everglades City, although from here you can travel only by boat or canoe. At the other entrances it's $10 per car and $5 for pedestrians and cyclists. Entry tickets are valid for seven days.

The park is **open year-round**, but the most favorable time to visit is **winter**, when the receding floodwaters cause wildlife to congregate around gator holes, ranger-led activities are frequent, and the mosquitoes are bearable. In **summer**, afternoon storms flood the prairies, park activities are substantially reduced, and the mosquitoes are a severe annoyance. Visiting between seasons is also a good bet.

Accommodation

There are a handful of places to stay in the towns just outside the park's perimeter. In Everglades City, try the charming and clean *Ivey House*, 107 Camellia St (ⓣ239/695-3299, ⓦwww.iveyhouse.com; ❹), or head five miles south to the *Chokoloskee Island Resort* (ⓣ239/695-2881), where you can rent an **RV** by the night for $69–89. Ten miles east of the park, you'll find plenty of **motels** in Homestead and Florida City, as well as the *Everglades International Hostel*, 20 SW 2nd Ave, off Palm Drive (ⓣ1-800/372-3874, ⓦwww.evergladeshostel.com); this is the best option for budget-minded travelers who don't want to camp. Beds go for $25–28 a night and private rooms are available for $55–75. The hostel rents canoes ($30/day) and bikes ($15/day); bike rental plus roundtrip transport to the park entrance is $30. They also offer excellent tours (minimum 4 people; $80). There are well-equipped **campgrounds** (both $16/night; reservations at ⓣ1-800/365-CAMP or ⓦwww.nps.gov) at Flamingo and Long Pine Key, six miles from the Coe entrance. There are also many free backcountry spots on the longer walking and canoe trails (permits are issued at the visitor centers for $10, plus $2 per person). Note that the hurricane-damaged hotel in Flamingo is unlikely to reopen until 2011.

Everglades City and around

Purchased and named in the 1920s by an advertising executive dreaming of a subtropical metropolis, **EVERGLADES CITY**, three miles south off US-41 along Route 29, now has a population of just under five hundred. Most who visit are solely intent on diminishing the stocks of sports fish living around the mangrove islands – the aptly titled **Ten Thousand Islands** – arranged like scattered jigsaw-puzzle pieces around the coastline.

For a closer look at the mangroves, which safeguard the Everglades from surge tides, take one of the park-sanctioned **boat trips**. Try either the Everglades National Park Boat Tours (ⓣ239/695-2591; from $26.50), which depart from the visitor center, or Everglades Rentals and Eco Adventures (ⓣ239/695-3299, ⓦwww.evergladesadventures.com), at the *Ivey House* (see above). The dockside **Gulf Coast Visitor Center** (daily: May–Oct 9am–4.30pm, Nov–April 8am–4.30pm; ⓣ239/695-3311) provides details on the cruises, as well as the excellent ranger-led **canoe trips**.

Shark Valley and the Miccosukee Indian Village

Around forty miles east of Everglades City, **Shark Valley** (entrance open daily 8.30am–6pm) epitomizes the Everglades' "River of Grass" moniker. From here, dotted by hardwood hammocks, the sawgrass plain stretches as far as the eye can see. Aside from a few simple walking trails close to the **visitor center** (daily: May–Oct 9.15am–5.15pm, Nov–April 8.45am–5.15pm; ⓣ305/221-8776), you can see Shark Valley only from a fifteen-mile loop road, ideally covered by renting a **bike** ($6.50 an hour; must be returned by 4pm). Alternatively, a highly informative two-hour **tram tour** (daily; $15.25; reservations on ⓣ305/221-8455) stops frequently to view wildlife, but won't allow you to linger in any particular place, as you'll certainly want to do.

You'll pass real Indian villages all along US-41, with most belonging to the **Miccosukee tribe**, descendents of the survivors of the last Seminole War (1858). Today the tribe runs a small but relatively prosperous reservation in the heart of the Everglades, though the kitschy souvenirs and displays at the **Miccosukee Indian Village** (daily 9am–5pm; $10; ⓣ305/223-8380) are rather contrived – grab some homemade chili instead at nearby *Billie's Restaurant*.

Pine Island and Flamingo

The **Pine Island** section of the park – from the Coe Visitor Center entrance to Flamingo, perched at the end of the park road on Florida's southern tip – holds virtually everything that makes the Everglades tick. Spend a day or two in this southerly portion of the park and you'll quickly grasp the fundamentals of its complex ecology.

Route-9336 (the only road in this section of the park) leads past the comprehensive **Ernest Coe Visitor Center** (daily: May–Oct 9am–5pm, Nov–April 8am–5pm; ⓣ305/242-7700) to the main park entrance. A mile further on, the **Royal Palm Visitor Center** (open 24hrs) usually features ranger activities and events (but little information). The large numbers of park visitors who simply want to see an alligator are usually satisfied by walking the half-mile **Anhinga Trail** here: the notoriously lazy reptiles are easily seen during the winter, often splayed near the trail, looking like plastic props. All manner of birdlife can also be spotted, from snowy egrets to the bizarre, eponymous anhinga, an elegant black-bodied bird resembling an elongated cormorant. To beat the crowds, go early to the Anhinga Trail; after that, peruse the adjacent, but very different, **Gumbo Limbo Trail**, a hardwood jungle hammock packed with exotic subtropical growths.

If you're game, continue along Rte-9336 for thirty-seven miles (past many short hiking-trail opportunities) to the tiny coastal settlement of **FLAMINGO**, a former fishing colony now comprising a marina and campground servicing the needs of sports-fishing enthusiasts. Stop in at the **visitor center** (9am–4.30pm; ⓣ239/695-2945) before heading to the marina, where the informative **Backcountry Cruise** (minimum six people; daily 10am, 1pm & 3.30pm $18; reservations on ⓣ239/695-3101) makes a two-hour foray around the mangrove-enshrouded Whitewater Bay, north of Flamingo.

▲ Turtle in Everglades National Park

The Panhandle

Rubbing hard against Alabama in the west and Georgia in the north, the long, narrow **Panhandle** has much more in common with the states of the Deep South than with the rest of Florida. Hard to believe, then, that just over a century ago, the Panhandle *was* Florida. At the western edge, **Pensacola** was a busy port when Miami was still a swamp. Fertile soils lured wealthy plantation owners south, helping to establish **Tallahassee** as a high-society gathering place and administrative center – a role which, as the state capital, it retains. But the decline of cotton, the chopping-down of too many trees, and the coming of the East Coast railroad eventually left the Panhandle high and dry. Much of the inland region still seems neglected, and the **Apalachicola National Forest** is perhaps the best place in Florida to disappear into the wilderness. The **coastal Panhandle**, on the other hand, is enjoying better times: despite rows of hotels, much is still untainted, boasting miles of blinding white sands.

Tallahassee and around

State capital it may be, **TALLAHASSEE** is nevertheless a provincial city of oak trees and soft hills that won't take more than two days to explore in full. Around its small grid of central streets – where you'll find plenty of reminders of Florida's formative years – briefcase-clutching bureaucrats mingle with some of Florida State University's 35,000 students, who brighten the mood considerably and keep the city awake at night.

Tallahassee was built on the site of an important prehistoric meeting place, and takes its name from the Apalachee Indian: *talwa* meaning "town," and *ahassee* meaning "old." The city's **history** really begins, though, with Florida's incorporation into the US, and Tallahassee's selection as the state's administrative base; the first Florida government convened here in 1823. Since then, Tallahassee has been the scene of every major wrangle in Florida politics, including the controversial ballot recount of the 2000 presidential election. Today, in contrast to the lightning-paced development of south Florida, Tallahassee has a slow tempo and a strong sense of the past, evoked in its historic buildings and museums.

Arrival and information

Tallahassee's Greyhound **bus terminal** is at 112 W Tennessee St (Ⓣ850/222-4249), within easy walking distance of downtown, which can easily be explored on **foot**. For stacks of background information, drop by the **Visitor Information Center**, 106 E Jefferson St (Mon–Fri 8am–5pm, Sat 9am–1pm; Ⓣ1-800/628-2866, Ⓦwww.visittallahassee.com).

Accommodation

Accommodation in Tallahassee is in short supply only during the sixty-day sitting of the state legislature, from early March, and on fall weekends during home football games of the Florida State Seminoles and Florida A&M Rattlers. **Hotels** and **motels** on N Monroe Street, about three miles from downtown, are far cheaper than those downtown.

Comfort Suites 1026 Apalachee Parkway ⓣ850/224-3200, ⓦwww.comfortsuites.com. The beds are heavenly at this comfortable, spotless motel, within walking distance of the capital. There's also a delicious, free continental breakfast. ❻

Governors Inn 209 S Adams St ⓣ1-800/342-7717, ⓦwww.thegovinn.com. Every room in this splendid downtown inn is decorated with antique furniture reflecting the period of the governor each is named after. ❽–❾

Super 8 2801 N Monroe St ⓣ850/386-8286. A good option for the budget traveler, this motel offers simple rooms with basic amenities. ❸

The Town

A fifty-million-dollar eyesore dominates the square mile of **downtown Tallahassee**: the vertical vents of the towering **New Capitol Building**, at Apalachee Parkway and Monroe Street (Mon–Fri 8am–5pm; free). Florida's growing army of bureaucrats had previously been crammed into the more attractive 1845 **Old Capitol Building** (Mon–Fri 9am–4.30pm, Sat 10am–4.30pm, Sun noon–4.30pm; free), which stands in the shadow of its replacement.

For easily the fullest account of Florida's past anywhere in the state, visit the **Museum of Florida History**, 500 S Bronough St (Mon–Fri 9am–4.30pm, Sat 10am–4.30pm, Sun noon–4.30pm; free; ⓣ850/245-6400, ⓦwww.museumoffloridahistory.com). Detailed accounts of Paleo-Indian settlements, and the significance of their burial and temple mounds, some of which have been found on the edge of Tallahassee, are valuable tools in comprehending Florida's prehistory. The colonialist crusades of the Spanish are outlined with copious finds, though there's little on the nineteenth-century Seminole Wars – one of the bloodier skeletons in Florida's closet. There is plenty on the building of the railroads, however.

The **Black Archives Research Center and Museum**, in the nineteenth-century Union Bank Building, along Apalachee Parkway from the Old Capitol's entrance (Mon–Fri 9am–5pm; free; ⓣ850/599-3020), holds one of the largest and most important collections of African-American artifacts in the nation, with oral histories and music stations, as well as some chilling Ku Klux Klan memorabilia.

Eating

With so many politicos and students, there's plenty of good **food** for all budgets in Tallahassee.

Andrew's Capital Grill & Bar/Andrew's 228 228 S Adams St ⓣ850/222-3444. Casual grill and bar serving a variety of sandwiches and burgers all day; the chic downstairs *Andrew's* 228 prepares delicious nouveau Italian dishes like gorgonzola cheesecake and grouper piccata.

Barnacle Bill's 1830 N Monroe St ⓣ850/385-8734. Inexpensive fresh fish and seafood served in a riotous atmosphere.

Capital Steak House in the *Holiday Inn Select*, 316 W Tennessee St ⓣ850/222-9555. Even confirmed white-meat-eaters are giving this steakhouse rave reviews for its high-quality Angus beef.

La Fiesta 2329 Apalachee Pkwy ⓣ850/656-3392. The very best Mexican food in the city.

Mom and Dad's 4175 Apalachee Pkwy ⓣ850/877-4518. Delicious homemade Italian food. Closed Sun & Mon.

Po' Boys Creole Café 224 E College Ave ⓣ850/224-5400. A range of Creole delights; also one of Tallahassee's most popular live music venues.

Wakulla Springs State Park

Fifteen miles south of Tallahassee, off Route-61 on Route-267, **Wakulla Springs State Park** (daily 8am–sunset; cars $4, pedestrians and cyclists $1; ⓣ850/926-0700) holds what is believed to be one of the biggest and deepest natural springs in the world. It pumps up half a million gallons of crystal-clear pure water from the bowels of the earth every day – though you'd never guess it from the calm surface.

It's refreshing to **swim** in the cool pool (in a small roped-off area – this is gator territory), but to learn more about the spring, take the thirty-minute **glass-bottom boat tour** ($6), and peer down to the swarms of fish hovering around the 180-foot cavern through which the water flows. Forty-minute **river cruises** ($6) let you glimpse some of the park's inhabitants: deer, turkeys, turtles, herons, egrets, and the inevitable alligators. Built in 1937 beside the spring, the lovely wooden *Wakulla Lodge* (Ⓣ850/926-0700; ❹–❺) is a serene hotel, with an excellent **restaurant** serving home-cooked country food for breakfast, lunch, and dinner.

The Apalachicola National Forest

With swamps, savannas, and springs dotted liberally about its half-million acres, the **Apalachicola National Forest**, which fans out southwest of Tallahassee, is the inland Panhandle at its natural best. Several roads enable you to drive through a good-sized chunk, with many undemanding spots for a rest and a snack. To see deeper into the forest you'll need to make more of an effort, by following one of the hiking trails, canoeing on the rivers, or simply spending a night under the stars at one of the basic campgrounds. On the forest's southern edge, the large and forbidding **Tate's Hell Swamp** is a breeding-ground for the deadly water moccasin snake; you're well advised to stay clear.

The main **entrances** to the forest (free) are off Hwy-20 and Hwy-319; three minor roads, routes 267, 375, and 65, form cross-forest links between the two highways. **Accommodation** is limited to camping; apart from *Camel Lake* and *Wright Lake* ($10 per night for both; hot showers available), all the campgrounds are free (except for a $3 daily vehicle charge), with very basic facilities (no running water). For more information, call the **ranger stations** at Apalachicola (Ⓣ850/643-2282) or Wakulla (Ⓣ850/926-3561).

Panama City Beach

Follow Hwy-98 fifty miles west from Apalachicola and you'll hit the orgy of motels, go-kart tracks, mini-golf courses, and amusement parks that is **PANAMA CITY BEACH**. Entirely without pretension, the area capitalizes blatantly on the appeal of its 27-mile stretch of white sand. The whole place is as commercialized as can be, but with the shops, bars, and restaurants all trying to undercut one another, there are some great bargains to be found. That said, throughout the lively summer (the so-called "100 Magic Days"), accommodation costs are high and reservations essential. In winter, prices drop and visitors are fewer; most are Canadians and – increasingly – Europeans, many of whom have no problem sunbathing and swimming in the cool temperatures.

Getting a tan, running yourself ragged at beach sports, and going all-out on the nightlife are the main concerns in Panama City Beach, one of the country's foremost Spring Break destinations. Go-karting, jet-skiing, and parasailing are all available at many locations along the coastal strip; otherwise, splash around at the water park ($32 for a go-on-everything day-ticket). For scuba-divers, several accessible shipwrecks litter the area; get details from any of the numerous dive shops.

Practicalities

Places to stay, while plentiful, fill with amazing speed, especially at weekends. As a general rule, **motels** at the east end of the beach are smarter and slightly pricier than those in the center. Those at the west end are quieter and more family oriented. The *Sugar Sands Motel*, 20723 Front Beach Rd (Ⓣ1-800/367-9221,

Ⓦ www.sugarsands.com; ❺–❻), is an excellent-value oceanfront motel away from the noise. The cheapest places to **eat** are the buffet restaurants on Front Beach Road, which charge $8–12 for all you can manage. Alternatively, try one of the regular lunch or dinner restaurants: *Shuckum's Oyster Pub & Seafood Grill*, 15614 Front Beach Rd (Ⓣ850/235-3214); *Mike's Diner*, 17554 Front Beach Rd (Ⓣ850/234-1942), which is also open for breakfast, and until late at night; or the *Boatyard*, 5323 N Lagoon Drive (Ⓣ850/249-9273), for alfresco dining beside a lagoon. **At night**, party-goers congregate at *Club La Vela*, 8813 Thomas Drive (Ⓣ850/235-1061), or *Spinnaker*, 8795 Thomas Drive (Ⓣ850/234-7892), each with dozens of bars, several discos, and a young crowd.

Pensacola and around

You might be inclined to overlook **PENSACOLA**, tucked away as it is at the western end of the Panhandle. The city, on the northern bank of the broad Pensacola Bay, is five miles inland from the nearest beaches, and its prime features are a naval aviation school and some busy dockyards. Pensacola is, however, worth a visit. The nearby white beaches are relatively untouched, and it boasts a rich history, having been occupied by the Spanish as early as 1559. The town repeatedly changed hands between the Spanish, the French, and the British before becoming the place where Florida was officially ceded by Spain to the US in 1821.

Pensacola was already a booming port by 1900, when the opening of the Panama Canal was expected to boost its fortunes still further. The many new buildings that appeared in the **Palafox District**, around the southerly section of Palafox Street, in the early 1900s – with their delicate ornamentation and attention to detail – reflect the optimism of the era.

In earlier times, Native Americans, pioneer settlers, and seafaring traders had gathered to swap, sell, and barter on the waterfront of the **Seville District**, just east of Palafox Street. Those who did well took up permanent residence here, and many of their homes remain in fine states of repair, forming – together with several museums – the **Historic Pensacola Village** (Mon–Sat 10am–4pm; $6; Ⓣ850/595-5985, Ⓦwww.historicpensacola.org). Tickets are valid for one week, and allow access to all of the museums and former homes in an easily navigated four-block area. Inside the US naval base on Navy Boulevard, about eight miles southwest of central Pensacola, the **Museum of Naval Aviation** (daily 9am–5pm; free, IMAX movie $8; Ⓣ1-800/327-5002, Ⓦwww.navalaviationmuseum.org) exhibits US naval aircraft. They range from the first flimsy seaplane, acquired in 1911, to the Phantoms and Hornets of more recent times.

Pensacola Beach

On the other (south) side of the bay from the city, glistening beaches and wind-swept sand dunes fringe the fifty-mile-long **Santa Rosa Island**. On the island directly south of Pensacola, **PENSACOLA BEACH** has everything you'd want from a Gulf Coast beach: fine white sands, watersports rental outlets, a busy fishing pier, and a sprinkling of motels, beachside bars, and snack stands.

Practicalities

The Greyhound **bus station** is seven miles north of the city center, at 505 W Burgess Rd (Ⓣ850/476-8199); ECAT buses #50 and #45 ($1.75; Ⓣ850/595-3228, Ⓦwww.goecat.com) link it to Pensacola proper. A good local **taxi** firm is Yellow

Cab (Ⓣ850/433-3333). ECAT **buses** serve the city, while #61 goes to the beach twice daily; the main terminal is at 1515 W Fairfield Drive. At the foot of the city side of the three-mile Pensacola Bay Bridge, the **visitor center**, 1401 E Gregory St (8am–5pm Mon–Fri, 9am–4pm Sat and 11am–4pm Sun; Ⓣ1-800/874-1234, Ⓦwww.visitpensacola.com), has the usual worthwhile handouts.

Plenty of budget chain **hotels**, charging $50–65 per night, line North Davis and Pensacola boulevards, the main approach roads from I-10. Central options are the *Days Inn*, 710 N Palafox St (Ⓣ850/438-4922; ❸), and *Noble Manor*, 110 W Strong St (Ⓣ850/434-9544, Ⓦwww.noblemanor.com; ❺), a charming B&B. At Pensacola Beach, try the comfortable *Hilton Pensacola Beach*, 12 Via De Luna Drive (Ⓣ850/916-2999; ❼–❽). For **eating** in town, *Fish House*, 600 S Barracks St (Ⓣ850/470-0003), has sushi and steaks along with the seafood. For beachside dining, *Peg Leg Pete's*, 1010 Fort Pickens Rd (Ⓣ850/932-4139), is known for its Cajun food and excellent raw bar.

8

Louisiana

AL - ALABAMA	IN - INDIANA	MN - MINNESOTA	RI - RHODE ISLAND
AR - ARKANSAS	LA - LOUISIANA	MS - MISSISSIPPI	SC - SOUTH CAROLINA
CT - CONNECTICUT	MA - MASSACHUSETTS	NC - NORTH CAROLINA	VA - VIRGINIA
DE - DELAWARE	MD - MARYLAND	NH - NEW HAMPSHIRE	VT - VERMONT
FL - FLORIDA	ME - MAINE	NJ - NEW JERSEY	WI - WISCONSIN
IL - ILLINOIS	MI - MICHIGAN	PA - PENNSYLVANIA	WV - WEST VIRGINIA

CHAPTER 8

Highlights

* **Swamp tours** Watch out for alligators lurking in the ghostly, Spanish-moss-shaded bayous. See pp.630 & 659

* **Napoleon House, New Orleans** Steeped in old New Orleans elegance, this gorgeous family-owned bar has stayed the same for generations, complete with flickering gas lamps and a deeply romantic courtyard. See p.643

* **Vaughan's on a Thursday, New Orleans** Kermit Ruffins on the trumpet, beans and rice on the stove, and riotously happy music fans tearing the roof off this tiny tumbledown neighborhood bar. See p.647

* **Mardi Gras** From the masking and dancing of New Orleans's urban spectacular, to Cajun country's pagan rituals, Louisiana's Fat Tuesday is unlike any other. See pp.648 & p.651

* **Laura Plantation** By far the River Road's most intriguing and illuminating account of Creole plantation life. See p.652

* **Southwest Louisiana Zydeco Music Festival** Just one of the region's many superb festivals, the perfect place to enjoy Cajun and Creole music, crafts, and food. See p.651

* **Angola prisoner rodeo** An unbelievable spectacle, with lifers slugging it out for guts and glory in this notorious maximum-security prison. See p.660

▲ Celebrating Mardi Gras

8

Louisiana

Swathed in the romance of pirates, voodoo, and Mardi Gras, **LOUISIANA** is undeniably special. Its history is barely on nodding terms with the view that America was the creation of the Pilgrim Fathers; its way of life is proudly set apart. This is the land of the rural, French-speaking **Cajuns** (descended from the Acadians, eighteenth-century French-Canadian refugees), who live in the prairies and swamps in the southwest of the state, and the Creoles of jazzy, sassy **New Orleans**. (The term **Creole** was originally used to define anyone born in the state to French or Spanish colonists – famed in the nineteenth century for their masked balls, family feuds, and duels – as well as native-born, French-speaking slaves, but has since come to define anyone or anything native to Louisiana, and in particular its black population.) Louisiana's distinctive, spicy **cuisine**, **festivals**, and, above all, its **music** (**jazz**, **R&B**, **Cajun**, and its bluesy black counterpart, **zydeco**) draw from all these cultures and more. Oddly enough, **northern Louisiana** – Protestant Bible Belt country, where old plantation homes stand decaying in vast cottonfields – feels more "Southern" than the marshy bayous, shaded by ancient cypress trees and laced with wispy trails of Spanish moss, of the Catholic south.

The **French** first settled Louisiana in 1682, braving treacherous swamps and plagues to harvest the abundant cypress. Its first permanent settlement, the trading post of **Natchitoches**, was established in 1714, followed by New Orleans in 1718. In 1760, Louis XV secretly handed New Orleans, along with all French territory west of the Mississippi, to his **Spanish** cousin, Charles III, as a safeguard against British expansionism. Louisiana remained Spanish until it was ceded to Napoleon in 1801, under the proviso that it should never change hands again. Just two years later, however, Napoleon, strapped for cash to fund his battles with the British in Europe, struck a bargain with President Thomas Jefferson known as the **Louisiana Purchase**. This sneaky agreement handed over to the US all French lands between Canada and Mexico, from the Mississippi to the Rockies, for a total cost of $15 million. The subsequent "Americanization" of Louisiana was one of the most momentous periods in the state's history, with the port of New Orleans, in its key position near the mouth of the **Mississippi River**, growing to become one of the nation's wealthiest cities. Though the state seceded from the Union to join the Confederacy in 1861, there were important differences between Louisiana and the rest of the slave-driven South. The **Black Code**, drawn up by the French in 1685 to govern Saint-Domingue (today's Haiti) and established in Louisiana in 1724, had given slaves rights unparalleled elsewhere, including permission to marry, meet socially, and take Sundays off. The black population of New Orleans in particular was renowned as exceptionally literate and cosmopolitan, with a significant number of **free people of color** who owned businesses, property, and even slaves.

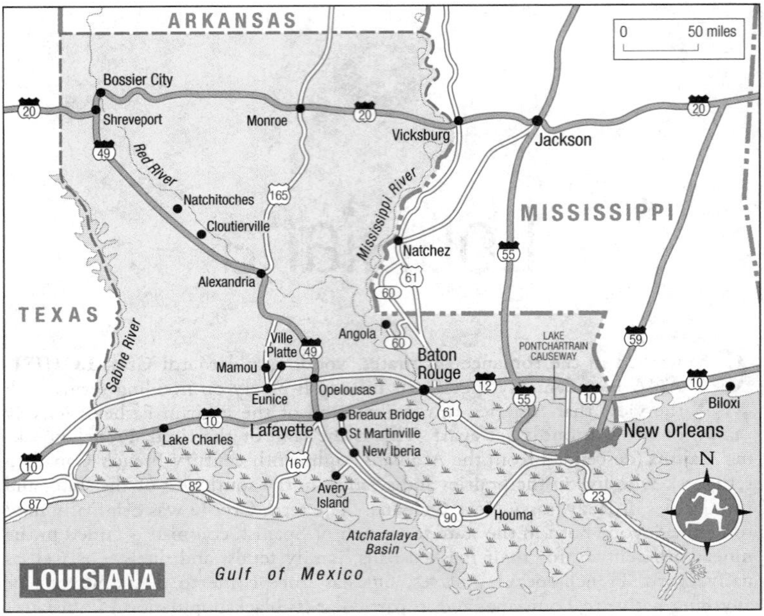

Houston

Though Louisiana was not badly scarred physically by the Civil War, with few important battles fought on its soil, its economy was ravaged, and its social structures all but destroyed. The **Reconstruction** era, too, hit particularly hard here, with the once great city of New Orleans suffering a period of unprecedented lawlessness and racial violence. In time, the economy, at least, recovered, benefiting from the key importance of the mighty Mississippi and the discovery of offshore oil in the 1950s – but during the twentieth century Louisiana came to rely heavily upon **tourism**, centered on New Orleans and Cajun country.

In August 2005, the double whammy of **Hurricane Katrina**, which swept in through the coastal wetlands, and the horrific after-effects of the levee breaks in New Orleans, seemed as if it might put an end to all that. Slowly but surely, however, recovery continues. Though no thinking person can visit southern Louisiana today without feeling a deep sense of loss, the state still has a huge amount to offer. Whether you're canoeing along a cypress-clogged bayou, dining on spicy, buttery crawfish in a crumbling Creole cottage, or dancing on a steamy starlit night to the best live music in the world, Louisiana remains unique – and a place that now, more than ever, needs your support.

Getting around Louisiana

Louisiana is crossed east–west by two major **interstates**, I-20 in the north and I-10 in the south. New Orleans is the hub, traversed by I-10 and served by I-55 and I-59 from Mississippi. I-49 sweeps across the state southeast to northwest, connecting Cajun country with the north.

The international **airport** is in New Orleans; regional airlines serve the rest of the state and surrounding areas. Amtrak **trains** link New Orleans with New York, Chicago, and Memphis, as well as Los Angeles, via Lafayette. Greyhound **buses** connect the major towns with the rest of the country, and are supplemented by smaller local lines. In addition to the Mississippi's bridges and causeways, **ferries** cross the river at New Orleans, St Francisville in Cajun country, and at various points along the River Road to Baton Rouge.

New Orleans

It is painfully clear, since the events of August 2005, that there's a lot more to **NEW ORLEANS** – the "Big Easy," the "city that care forgot" – than its image as a nonstop party town. And while this very special place has lost none of its power to bewitch, visiting New Orleans after the floods requires sensitivity and compassion. Even at the best of times this was a contradictory city, repeatedly striking you with the stark divisions between rich and poor (and, more explicitly, between white and black); years after Katrina, with the emotional and physical scars still running deep, those contradictions are writ larger than ever. While you can still party in the French Quarter and the Faubourg Marigny till the early hours, dancing to great jazz bands and gorging on delicious Creole food, just ten minutes away entire neighborhoods struggle to rebuild, blanketed, despite all the best intentions of their pioneering returnees, by a ghostly silence. That's not to say that enjoying life is inappropriate in today's New Orleans – while it was dealt a crippling blow, let down not only by nature but also by the federal and local governments, the city's vitality and *joie de vivre* remain real, buffeted but not beaten. The melange of cultures and races that built the city still gives it its heart; not "easy," exactly, but quite unlike anywhere else in the US – or the world.

New Orleans began life in 1718 as a **French-Canadian** outpost, its improbable, swampy setting overridden by its prime location near the mouth of the **Mississippi River**. Development was rapid, and with the first mass importation of African **slaves**, as early as the 1720s, its unique demography began to take shape. Despite early resistance from its francophone population, the city benefited greatly from its period as a **Spanish** colony between 1763 and 1800. By the end of the eighteenth century, the **port** was flourishing, the haunt of smugglers, gamblers, prostitutes, and pirates. Newcomers included Anglo-Americans escaping the American Revolution and aristocrats fleeing revolution in France. The city also became a haven for refugees – whites and **free blacks**, along with their slaves – escaping the slave revolts in Saint-Domingue (Haiti). As in the West Indies, the Spanish, French, and free people of color associated and formed alliances to create a distinctive **Creole** culture with its own traditions and ways of life, its own patois, and a cuisine that drew influences from Africa, Europe, and the colonies. New Orleans was already a many-textured place when it experienced two quick-fire changes of government, passing back into French control in 1801 and then being sold to **America** under the Louisiana Purchase two years later. Unwelcome in the Creole city – today's French Quarter – the Americans who migrated here were forced to settle in the areas now known as the **Central Business District** (or **CBD**) and, later, in the **Garden District**. **Canal Street**, which divided the old city from the expanding suburbs, became known as "the neutral ground" – the name still used when referring to the median strip between main roads in New Orleans.

Though much has been made of the antipathy between Creoles and Anglo-Americans, in truth economic necessity forced them to live and work together. They fought side by side, too, in the 1815 **Battle of New Orleans**, the final battle of the War of 1812, which secured American supremacy in the States. The victorious general, **Andrew Jackson**, became a national hero – and eventually US president; his ragtag volunteer army was made up of Anglo-Americans, slaves, Creoles, free men of color, and Native Americans. They were joined by pirates supplied by the notorious buccaneer **Jean Lafitte**, whose band of privateers made good use of the labyrinth of secluded bayous in the swamp-choked delta of the Mississippi River.

New Orleans's antebellum **golden age** as a major port and finance center for the cotton-producing South was brought to an abrupt end by the Civil War. The economic blow wielded by a lengthy Union occupation – which effectively isolated the city from its markets – was compounded by the social and cultural ravages of **Reconstruction**. This was particularly disastrous for a city once famed for its large, educated, free black population. As the North industrialized and other Southern cities grew, the fortunes of New Orleans took a downturn.

Jazz exploded into the bars and the bordellos around 1900, and, along with the evolution of **Mardi Gras** as a tourist attraction, breathed new life into the city. And though the Depression hit here as hard as it did the rest of the nation, it also – spearheaded by a number of local writers and artists – heralded the resurgence of the **French Quarter**, which had disintegrated into a slum. Even so, it was the less romantic duo of **oil** and **petrochemicals** that really saved the economy – until the slump of the 1950s pushed New Orleans well behind other US cities. The oil crash of the early 1980s gave it yet another battering, a gloomy start for near on two decades of high crime rates, crack deaths, and widespread corruption.

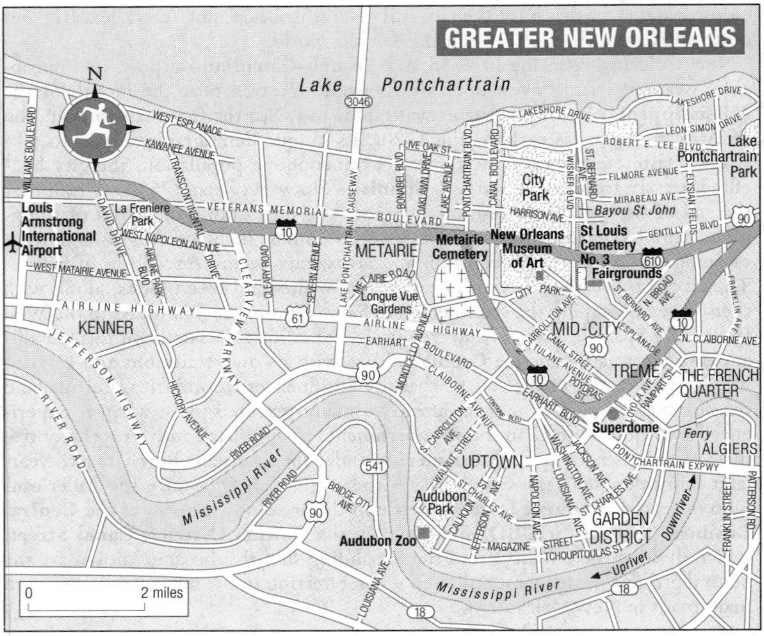

By the turn of the millennium things were improving, until, of course, **Hurricane Katrina** hit ground in 2005. At first it seemed as though the city had done relatively well, in light of the full-scale damage wrought along the Mississippi coast. On August 29, however, New Orleans' **levees** were breached, and rising floodwaters soon covered eighty percent of the city, destroying much of it in their wake. Most damage was sustained by residential areas – whether in the suburban homes around the lakeside, from where most residents had been evacuated, to the less affluent neighborhoods of the east, like the **Ninth Ward** and Gentilly, where those too poor or ill or old to move were trapped in attics and on rooftops for days. The French Quarter, which, as the oldest part of the city was built on the highest ground, was physically unhurt by the flooding, although the economic blow – not least the loss of a huge number of the neighborhood's work force – was tremendous. The city's population remains drastically diminished, due to fatalities and displacement, and many of those who were able to return still face enormous difficulty repairing their lives. While the grass-roots commitment to rebuilding remains, it is clearly going to take time – patience in New Orleans has become not only a virtue but also a survival mechanism. And as the number of volunteers arriving to help dwindles, the city needs its tourists more than ever. A visit to New Orleans today, while giving an enormous amount of joy, is also a show of support, a defiant assertion that, despite the contempt shown it by George Bush's federal government, this beautiful and beleaguered place – and every single person who calls it home – matters.

Arrival and information

Louis Armstrong New Orleans International Airport (**MSY**), eighteen miles northwest of downtown on I-10, has an information booth in its baggage claim area, along with hotel courtesy phones. Flat-rate **taxi** fares into town are $28 for up to two people, or $12 each for three or more; **shuttles** can also take you to your hotel (every 10min; tickets available from 8am to 11pm in the baggage claim area or from the bus driver otherwise; $15 to downtown hotels; ⓣ504/522-3500). **Greyhound** buses arrive next to **Amtrak** at the Union Passenger Terminal, 1001 Loyola Ave, near the Superdome. This area, in the no-man's-land beneath the elevated Pontchartrain Expressway, is not great; book a **cab** in advance to take you to your lodgings. United Cabs is the best firm (ⓣ504/522-9771).

Before you leave home, check **New Orleans CVB** online (ⓦwww.neworleanscvb.com); the site is full of helpful information and news, along with discount coupons. Once you've arrived, the best information, including self-guided walking tours, free **maps**, and still more discount vouchers can be found at the **Welcome Center**, on Jackson Square, at 529 St Ann St in the French Quarter (daily 9am–5pm; ⓣ504/566-5031).

Staying safe in New Orleans

Although the heavily touristed French Quarter is comparatively safe, to wander unwittingly beyond it – even just a couple of blocks – can place your **personal safety** in serious jeopardy. While walking from the Quarter to the Marigny is usually safe enough during the day, it's not a good idea to stray far from the main drag of Frenchmen Street. Wherever you are, take the usual common-sense precautions, and at night always travel by cab when venturing any distance beyond the Quarter.

City transportation

Though New Orleans's most-visited neighborhoods are easy to **walk** around, getting from one to another is not always easy on foot, and if you're traveling anywhere outside the Quarter after dark you'd be better off calling a **cab** (see p.629). The Regional Transit Authority (RTA) runs a network of **buses** and **trolleys** ($1.25, exact fare required; Ⓣ504/248-3900, Ⓦwww.norta.com). The most useful **bus routes** include "Magazine" (#11), which runs between Canal Street in the CBD and Audubon Park uptown, "Canal" (#42), from North Peters up to City Park along Canal Street, and "Jackson-Esplanade" (#91), from Rampart Street on the edge of the Quarter up to City Park.

Far more romantic is the handsome sage-green **St Charles streetcar** (a National Historic Monument, dating back around one hundred years) that rumbles a thirteen-mile loop from Carondelet Street at Canal Street, along St Charles Avenue in the Garden District, past Audubon Park to Carrollton uptown. Service is limited after dark. There's also a newer, **riverfront** trolley, which runs between the Convention Center and Esplanade Avenue, and a third line that runs from Esplanade Avenue up Canal Street, either to City Park (#47) or Carrollton Avenue (#48).

VisiTOUR **passes**, which you can use on the bus and the streetcar, cost $5 for one day, or $12 for three. The RTA website lists vendors.

Accommodation

New Orleans has some lovely **places to stay**, from rambling old guesthouses seeping faded grandeur to stylish boutique hotels. **Room rates**, never low (you'll be

City tours and river cruises

Walking tours are especially popular in New Orleans, with its wealth of gorgeous hidden courtyards and fine architectural details. The **Jean Lafitte National Historic Park Service** offers scholarly and accessible overviews of the Quarter (daily 9.30am & 2.30pm; 90min; free; Ⓣ504/589-2636; tickets given out at the NPS visitor center, 419 Decatur St, 30min before the tour begins). Many visitors, especially with kids in tow, take a narrated trot through the Quarter in one of the **mule-drawn carriages** that wait behind Jackson Square on Decatur. These can be fun, though you should take the "historic" commentary with a grain of salt (30–45min; $12–15 per person).

Another lazy way to while away a steamy afternoon is on a **river cruise**. Leaving from the Toulouse Street wharf behind the Jackson Brewery mall, the *Natchez* steamboat heads seven miles or so downriver before turning back near the Chalmette battlefield. The captain gives a running historical commentary while a jaunty Dixieland band plays in the dining room (Mon–Thurs 2.30pm, Fri–Sun 11.30am & 2.30pm; 2hr; $24.50, $34.50 with lunch; evening cruise 7pm, $40, $64.50 with dinner; Ⓣ504/586-8777, Ⓦwww.steamboatnatchez.com). Tickets are sold at booths behind Jackson Brewery and the aquarium.

New Orleans's local **swamps** – many of them protected areas just a thirty-minute drive from downtown – are otherworldly enclaves that provide a wonderful contrast to the city itself. Dr Wagner's Honey Island Swamp Tours, based ten miles north of Lake Pontchartrain, venture onto the delta of the Pearl River, a wilderness occupied by nutrias, black bears, and alligators, as well as ibis, great blue herons, and snowy egrets. Wildlife is most abundant from April to May and September to November (2hr; $25 adults, $15 children, not including transport from downtown; Ⓣ985/641-1769, Ⓦwww.honeyislandswamp.com).

For details on **ghost**, **voodoo** and **cemetery** tours, see p.635.

pushed to find anything half decent for less than $75 a night), increase considerably for Mardi Gras and Jazz Fest, when prices can go up by as much as two hundred percent and rooms are reserved months in advance. This is not a city in which you want to be stranded without a room, and though it's possible to take a chance on last-minute cancellations and deals, you should ideally make **reservations**. If you do turn up on spec, head immediately for the **welcome center** (see p.629), where you'll find racks of **discount leaflets** offering savings on same-day bookings (generally weekdays only).

Most people choose to stay in the **French Quarter**, in the heart of things. Many accommodations here are in atmospheric **guesthouses**, most of them in old Creole townhouses. In any one place, rooms can vary considerably in size, comfort, and amenities, so be specific if you have certain preferences – and ask for a room away from the street if you want peace and quiet. Outside the Quarter, the **Lower Garden District** offers a couple of budget options, while the **Faubourg Marigny** specializes in B&Bs, and the **Garden District** proper has a couple of gorgeous old hotels. The **CBD** is the domain of the city's upmarket chain and business hotels.

In the French Quarter

Cornstalk Hotel 915 Royal St ⓣ504/523-1515 or 1-800/759-6112, ⓦwww.cornstalkhotel.com. Casually elegant, somewhat faded place in a turreted Queen Anne house, surrounded by a landmark cast-iron fence decorated with fat cornstalks. The appealing, high-ceilinged rooms – each of them different – have lots of period detail, and the location is great. Free wi-fi. ❺

A Creole House 1013 St Ann St ⓣ504/524-8076 or 1-800/535-7858, ⓦwww.acreolehouse.com. Basic but acceptable guesthouse, bordering on shabby in places, with rooms ranging from cozy nooks with shared bath to suites. Rates include continental breakfast. ❸

Hotel Monteleone 214 Royal St ⓣ504/523-3341 or 1-800/535-9595, ⓦwww.hotelmonteleone.com. This handsome French Quarter landmark is the oldest hotel in the city, owned by the same family since 1886, and hosting a fine array of writers and luminaries since then. At sixteen storeys, it's something of a giant on Royal Street, with an elegant Baroque facade, stunning old marble lobby, luxurious rooms, a revolving bar, and a rooftop pool. ❻

Olivier House 828 Toulouse St ⓣ504/525-8456 or 1-866/525-9748, ⓦwww.olivierhouse.com. Though a bit dark in places, this atmospheric, quintessentially New Orleans guesthouse offers real character. The 42 rooms (all with bath) vary widely, but most have funky antique furniture and shutters. There's a tropical courtyard, and a tiny pool. ❻

Omni Royal Orleans 621 St Louis St ⓣ504/529-5333, ⓦwww.omnihotels.com. Landmark French Quarter hotel, stylish and swanky, with an old-fashioned New Orleans elegance that never intimidates. The rooftop pool is lovely. ❼

Hotel Provincial 1024 Chartres St ⓣ504/581-4995 or 1-800/535-7922, ⓦwww.hotelprovincial.com. This sprawling – yet somehow intimate – place is set in a quiet part of the Quarter, with rooms around five peaceful, gaslit courtyards. Some rooms are filled with antiques, others are more ordinary. There are two nice outdoor pools, a bar, and a fancy restaurant, Stella, on site. Good value. ❺

Hotel Villa Convento 616 Ursulines St ⓣ504/522-1793, ⓦwww.villaconvento.com. Friendly, family-run guesthouse that has won a loyal crowd of regulars. Don't expect luxury – these are no-frills rooms with bath; some have balconies, while others open onto a patio. ❹

Outside the French Quarter

Columns Hotel 3811 St Charles Ave ⓣ504/899-9308 or 1-800/445-9308, ⓦwww.thecolumns.com. Characterful Garden District hotel in a stately 1883 mansion on the streetcar line. The whole place seeps louche bordello glamour, especially the Victorian bar (see p.646) with its live jazz bands; the porch, with its namesake columns, is one of the nicest places in the city for a drink. Some rooms come with a balcony, some are bordering on shabby; none have TV. Rates include full breakfast. ❻

The Frenchmen 417 Frenchmen St ⓣ1-800/831-1781, ⓦwww.frenchmenhotel.com. Funky and friendly Faubourg Marigny guesthouse in a great location (though avoid streetside rooms if you are bothered by noise at night), with a variety of rooms spread across two 1860 townhouses. There's a patio, a small pool, and a jacuzzi. Rates include continental breakfast. Free wi-fi. ❹

HI-New Orleans Marquette House 2249 Carondelet St ⓣ504/523-3014. Basic but not bad hostel near the streetcar line in the Garden District. It's not one of the nicest HI properties, but the staff are friendly. Single-sex dorm beds go for $16–20; there are less good-value double rooms (from $30) in a separate building. Day use allowed. Reservations recommended. ❶–❸

Royal Street Inn 1431 Royal St ⓣ504/948-7499, ⓦwww.royalstreetinn.com. Hip Faubourg Marigny lodging above the *R-Bar* (see p.646), and run by the same people. Quirky New Orleans style meets big-city boutique aspirations in the five "suites" (all with bath, and some with balcony) with their stripped floors, bare brick walls and leather furnishings; all have DVD players, Ipod docks and wi-fi. It's favored by a young crowd who hang out in the bar. ❹

St Charles Guest House 1748 Prytania St ⓣ504/523-6556, ⓦwww.stcharlesguesthouse.com. Simple Lower Garden District guesthouse offering a variety of rooms, none with phone or TV. Backpackers choose the basic 6ft by 8ft rooms (shared bath) for $45, but for the pricier en-suite doubles you can get better value elsewhere. It's friendly enough, though, with a hostel-like atmosphere, a pool, and free breakfast. They ask for deposits with reservations. No smoking. ❹

The City

New Orleans is sometimes called the **Crescent City**, because of the way it nestles between the southern shore of Lake Pontchartrain and a dramatic horseshoe bend in the Mississippi River. This unique location makes the city's layout confusing, with streets curving to follow the river, and shooting off at odd angles to head inland. Compass points are of little use here – locals refer instead to **lakeside** (toward the lake) and **riverside** (toward the river), and, using Canal Street as the dividing line, **uptown** (or upriver) and **downtown** (downriver).

Most visitors spend their time in the battered, charming old **French Quarter** (or *Vieux Carré*), site of the original settlement. While the Quarter remains economically and psychically bruised by the Katrina effect, on lively weekends you could imagine that the storm had never happened. On the Quarter's fringes, the funky **Faubourg Marigny** creeps downriver from Esplanade Avenue, while the Quarter's lakeside boundary, **Rampart Street**, marks the beginning of the historic, run-down African-American neighborhood of **Tremé**. On the other side of the Quarter, across **Canal Street** – which, in its scruffier stretches away from the river, is still visibly suffering from storm and flood damage – the **CBD** (Central Business District), bounded by the Mississippi and I-10, spreads upriver to the Pontchartrain Expressway. Dominated by office buildings, hotels, and banks, it also incorporates the **Warehouse District** and, toward the lake, the gargantuan **Superdome**. A ferry ride across the river from the foot of Canal Street takes you to the suburban west bank and the residential district of old **Algiers**.

Back on the east bank, upriver from the CBD, the rarefied **Garden District** is an area of gorgeous old mansions, some of them in delectable ruin. The **Lower Garden District**, creeping between the expressway and Jackson Avenue, is quite a different creature, its run-down old houses filled with impoverished artists and musicians. You can get to either neighborhood on the rumbling streetcar (see p.630) along swanky **St Charles Avenue**, the Garden District's lakeside boundary, or approach using **Magazine Street**, a six-mile stretch of galleries and antique stores that runs parallel to St Charles riverside. Entering the Garden District, you've crossed the official boundary into **uptown**, which spreads upriver to encompass **Audubon Park and Zoo**.

The Mississippi River

A resonant, romantic, and extraordinary physical presence, the **Mississippi River** is New Orleans's lifeblood and its raison d'être. In the nineteenth century, as the port boomed, the city gradually cut itself off from the river altogether, hemming it in behind a string of warehouses and railroads. But, as the importance of the port has diminished, a couple of downtown parks, plazas, and riverside walks, accessible from the French Quarter, the CBD, and uptown, have focused attention back onto the **waterfront**.

Crossing Decatur Street from Jackson Square brings you to the **Moon Walk**, a paved promenade studded with benches and raised flower boxes, where buskers serenade you as you gaze across the water. Upriver from here, long, thin **Woldenberg Park** makes a good place for a picnic, watching the river traffic drift by; it's also the location of a number of free music festivals. At the upriver edge of the park, the **Aquarium of the Americas**, near the Canal Street wharf (Tues–Sun 10am–5pm; $17.50, IMAX $8.50, aquarium and IMAX $22, aquarium, and zoo $25.50, aquarium, IMAX and zoo $28.50), features a huge glass tunnel where visitors – rampaging infants, mostly – come face-to-face with rays and sawfish. There's also a Mississippi River habitat complete with Spots, a white gator, along with an Amazonian rainforest, petting tank, and IMAX theater.

For details of **river tours**, see p.630. and to read more about the Mississippi River itself, see p.517.

The French Quarter

The beautiful **French Quarter** is where New Orleans began in 1718. Today, battered and bohemian, decaying and vibrant, it remains the spiritual core of the city, its fanciful cast-iron balconies, hidden courtyards, and time-stained stucco buildings exerting a haunting fascination that has long caught the imagination of artists and writers. Official tours are useful for orientation, but it's most fun simply to wander – and you'll need at least a few days to do it justice, absorbing the jumble of sounds, sights, and smells. Early morning, in the dazzling light from the river, is a good time to explore.

The Quarter is laid out in a grid, unchanged since 1721. At just thirteen blocks wide – smaller than you might expect – it's easily walkable, bounded by the Mississippi River, Rampart Street, Canal Street, and Esplanade Avenue, and centering on lively **Jackson Square**. Rather than French, the famed **architecture** is predominantly Spanish Colonial, with a strong Caribbean influence. Most of the buildings date from the late eighteenth century; much of the old city was devastated by fires in 1788 and 1794. Shops, galleries, restaurants and bars are concentrated in the blocks between Decatur and Bourbon streets, while beyond Bourbon, up toward Rampart Street, and in the Lower Quarter, downriver from Jackson Square, things become more peaceful. Here, you'll find quiet, predominantly residential streets where the Quarter's **gay** community lives side by side with elegant dowagers, part-time condo-dwellers, and scruffy artists.

Jackson Square

Ever since its earliest incarnation as the Place d'Armes, a dusty parade ground used for public meetings and executions, **Jackson Square** has been at the heart of the Quarter. Presiding over it, an **equestrian statue** – the first in the nation, constructed by Clark Mills in 1856 – shows Andrew Jackson in uncharacteristically jaunty mode, waving his hat. The hectoring inscription, "The Union Must and Shall be Preserved," was added by Union General "Beast" Butler during the Civil War occupation.

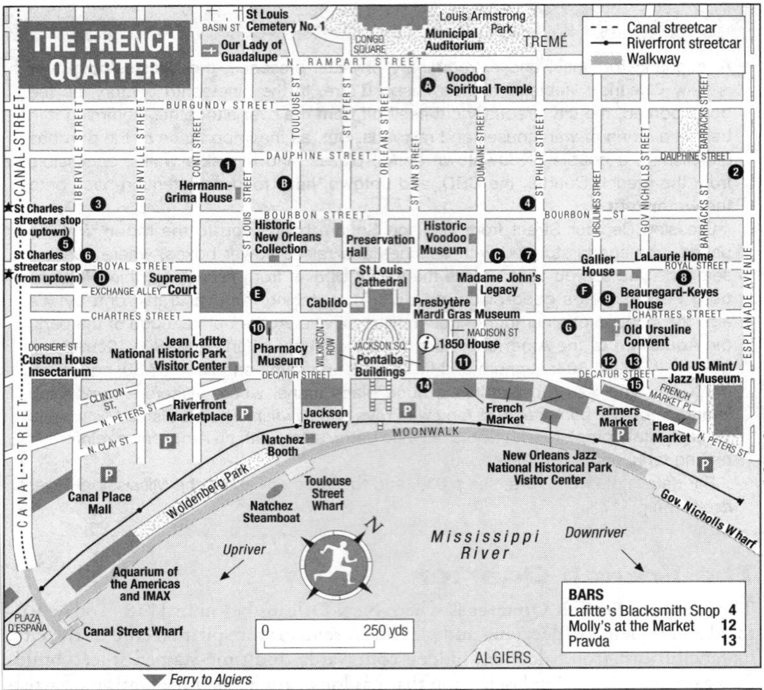

ACCOMMODATION				RESTAURANTS & CAFÉS					
A Creole House	A	Hotel Villa Convento	F	Acme Oyster House	5	CC's	7	Mr B's	6
Cornstalk Hotel	C	Olivier House	B	Bayona	1	Croissant d'Or	9	Napoleon House	10
Hotel Monteleone	D	Omni Royal Orleans	E	Bennachin	8	Fiorella's	15	Port of Call	2
Hotel Provincial	G			Café du Monde	14	Galatoire's	3	Tujague's	11

During the day, everyone passes by at some time or another, weaving their way through the tangle of artists, Lucky Dog hot-dog vendors, palm readers, shambolic brass bands, and blues musicians. A postcard-perfect backdrop for the Jackson statue, **St Louis Cathedral** is the oldest continuously active cathedral in the United States. It's the third church on this spot, built in 1794 after the first two were destroyed by fire and hurricane. Dominated by three tall slate steeples, the facade, which marries Greek Revival symmetry with copious French arches, is oddly two-dimensional, like some elaborate stage prop for the street drama below.

On the upriver side of the cathedral, the **Cabildo** (Tues–Sun 9am–5pm; $6) was built as the Casa Capitular, seat of the Spanish colonial government. The building – which cuts an impressive dash with its colonnade, fan windows, and wrought-iron balconies – is now part of the **Louisiana State Museum** (see p.635). Inside, exhibits illuminate the cultures, classes, and races that bind together Louisiana's history, starting with the Native Americans and winding up with the demise of Reconstruction. Black history is well represented throughout, with as much emphasis on the free people of color as on the city's role as the major slave-trading center of the South. The haunting bronze **death mask of Napoleon** has its own display case, while on the the second floor you can see the reconstructed **Sala Capitular**, where the Louisiana Purchase was signed in 1803, and where, in 1892, the historic *Plessy v. Ferguson* case, which effectively legalized segregation throughout the South, was first argued.

The Louisiana State Museum

The **Cabildo** (see p.634) and the **Presbytère** (see below), along with the **1850 House** (see below), the **Old US Mint** (see p.637), and **Madame John's Legacy** (see p.638), together make up the **Louisiana State Museum**. At present Madame John's Legacy is free following a post-Katrina reorganization; combination tickets for the other sites give a **discount** of twenty percent to two or more sites, and are good for three consecutive days.

Forming a matching pair with the Cabildo, the **Presbytère** (Tues–Sun 9am–5pm; $6), on the downriver side of the cathedral, was designed in 1791 as a rectory. It was never used as such, however, and after completion in 1813 went on to serve as a courthouse. Today, it's an unmissable **Mardi Gras museum**, covering carnival from every conceivable angle. Full of odd treasures – jewel-encrusted costumes, primitive masks, posters, bizarre dance cards – it also features videos, interactive themed rooms, and music stations, managing perhaps more than any other museum to give a real sense of what makes New Orleans tick.

The elegant three-story **Pontalba Buildings**, which line St Peter and St Ann streets where they border the square, were commissioned by the formidable Baroness Pontalba. When Pontalba returned from France in 1849 to find her real estate palling in comparison to the American sector across Canal Street, she dreamed of replacing the shabby buildings around the Place d'Armes with elegant colonnaded structures resembling those she'd seen in Paris. Planned as both business and residential units, they are still used as such, and remain some of the city's most desirable places to live. These were not, as is commonly claimed, the first apartment buildings in the US, but they were innovative in their use of mass-produced materials and, in particular, of **cast iron** – indeed, it was these very balconies that sparked the citywide fad for lacy ironwork, which soon came to replace the plainer iron hand-wrought locally by African slaves. At 523 St Ann St there's an excellent **bookstore**, run by the Friends of the Cabildo, filled with titles and gifts of local interest; upstairs, as part of the state museum (see above), the cordoned-off rooms of the **1850 House** (Tues–Sun 9am–5pm; $3), recreate the tastes of the well-to-do Creole families who lived in these fashionable apartments.

Decatur Street and Esplanade Avenue

Something of an anomaly among Upper Decatur's brassy T-shirt shops and theme restaurants, the **Jean Lafitte National Historical Park and Preserve Visitor Center**, 419 Decatur St (daily 9am–5pm), is not only a starting point for excellent **walking tours** (see p.630), but also a great one-room introduction to Louisiana's delta region. Panels outline local history, architecture, cultural traditions, festivals, cuisine and ecology, and a noticeboard provides Katrina information. There are also listening stations that let you eavesdrop on natives expounding, in a variety of accents, on the meaning of local phrases and expressions, while touch-screen monitors feature classic footage of Louis Armstrong, Mahalia Jackson, and Professor Longhair, among others.

Downriver along Decatur Street, the specialty shops of the restored **French Market** – said to be on the site of a Native American trading area and certainly active since the 1720s – sell tourist knick-knacks; for stalls, head toward the old **Farmers' Market**, just off Decatur on N Peters Street, where fresh produce, spices, hot sauce, and the like are sold around the clock. Next door, a flea market abounds in trashy tack and bargain oddities; for vintage curiosities, head to the cavernous thrift and rummage stores across the way on Decatur.

Spooky New Orleans

Voodoo

Voodoo, still a significant presence in New Orleans, was brought to the city by African slaves via the French colonies of the Caribbean, where tribal beliefs were mixed with Catholicism to create a cult based on spirit worship. French, and later, Spanish authorities tried to suppress the religion (voodoo worshipers had played an active role in the organization of slave revolts in Haiti), but it continued to flourish among the city's black population. Under American rule, the weekly slave gatherings at **Congo Square** (in what is now Louis Armstrong Park; see p.639), which included ritual ceremonies, turned into a tourist attraction for whites, fueled by sensationalized reports of hypnotized white women dancing naked to throbbing drum beats.

Unlike in the West Indies, where the cult was dominated by male priests, New Orleans had many voodoo priestesses. The most famous was **Marie Laveau**, a hairdresser of African, white, and Native American blood. Using shrewd marketing sense and inside knowledge of the lives of her clients, she was in high demand for her **gris-gris** (pronounced "gree gree") – spells or potions – which she prepared for wealthy Creoles and Americans, as well as Africans. Laveau died in 1881, after which another Marie, believed to be her daughter, continued to practice under her name. The legend of both Maries lives on, and their crumbling **tombs** are popular tourist attractions (see below).

Today, voodoo is big business in New Orleans, with a glut of gift shops and a pricey museum in the French Quarter selling ersatz *gris-gris* and exotic voodoo dolls; if you're interested in the real thing, head instead to the **Voodoo Spiritual Temple**, 828 N Rampart St (Ⓣ504/522-9627, Ⓦwww.voodoospiritualtemple.org), where the charismatic Priestess Miriam offers open services, tours, and consultations.

The Cities of the Dead

So much of New Orleans is at, or below, sea level that early settlers who buried their dead – and there were many of them – found that during the frequent flooding great waves of moldy coffins would float to the surface of the sodden earth. Eventually, graves began to be placed, European-style, in above-ground brick and stucco vaults, surrounded by small fences. These **cemeteries** grew to resemble cities, laid out in "streets"; today, as the tombs crumble away amid the overgrown foliage, they have become atmospheric in the extreme. The creepiness isn't totally imaginary, either – though armed muggers, rather than ghosts, are the danger these days; you should **never** venture into a cemetery alone. Nearly all the city tours (see p.630) include a trip around one of the most interesting of the cemeteries – Lafayette #1 in the Garden District, St Louis #1 and #2 in Tremé, or St Louis #3 in Mid-City – some specialize in them.

Ghost tours

New Orleans's image as a Gothic, vampire-stalked city has spawned a variety of **tours** promising **magic**, **voodoo**, **ghouls**, and **ghosts**. Among the campy, the overpriced, and the just plain silly, there are, nonetheless, a couple worth joining. **Save Our Cemeteries** (Ⓦwww.saveourcemeteries.org) is a nonprofit restoration organization leading tours of Lafayette #1 (Mon, Wed, Fri, & Sat 10.30am; 1hr; $6; meet at the Washington Avenue Gate, 1400 block of Washington Ave) and St Louis #1 (Sun 10am; 1hr; $12; meet at the Basin Street Station Visitor Center, 501 Basin St). No reservations are required, but it's worth calling Ⓣ504/525-3377 to double-check that tours are running.

The **New Orleans Jazz National Historical Park Visitor Center** (Tues–Sat 9am–5pm; free; Ⓣ504/589-4841, Ⓦwww.nps.gov/jazz), tucked away in the French Market at 916 N Peters St, is a must for music fans. Light and airy, with

▲ The French Market

good acoustics and an intimate scale, it's a superb, informal place to attend frequent free jazz concerts, talks, movies, and workshops; afterwards, check out the photo displays, self-guided jazz walking tour brochures, and bookstore.

Continuing downriver, you'll come to the outer boundary of the Quarter, **Esplanade Avenue**, an exquisite, oak-shaded boulevard lined with crumbling nineteenth-century Creole mansions. Part of the state museum (see p.635), the **Old US Mint** (Tues–Sun 10am–5pm; $6), on the 400 block near the river, sustained considerable storm damage to its roof. Pre-Katrina, it housed a fascinating **Jazz Museum** – featuring old instruments, sheet music, photos, and personal effects – which is due to reopen, bigger and better, by 2010. Until then the Mint will host major touring shows of local interest (recent highlights have included a Napoleon exhibition and another of African-American photography).

Across Esplanade from the Quarter, the funky **Faubourg Marigny** is an appealingly mixed, low-rent area of Creole cottages and shotgun houses. Though the neighborhood is gentrifying, and its gaggle of music venues, coffeeshops, bars, and restaurants expanding further and further beyond the Quarter, it's best **not to wander** too far away from the blocks around Decatur and **Frenchmen Street**, the district's main drag. Even Elysian Fields – the street where Stanley and Stella lived in Tennessee Williams's *A Streetcar Named Desire* – can feel distinctly dodgy, despite its heavenly name.

Chartres and Royal streets

A left turn at the 600 block of Esplanade Avenue brings you to the **Old Ursuline Convent**, at 1114 Chartres St (Mon–Sat 10am–4pm; $5). Built in 1752, this is the only intact French Colonial structure in the city, and quite possibly the oldest building in the Mississippi valley. Established by an order of nuns from Rouen, it's one of the many places in the Quarter that are said to be haunted, its corridors roamed by specters of the "casket girls" – white virgins shipped over in the early days of the colony, who were kept here before being sold off as wives in an attempt to stop the increasing number of couplings between French settlers and African or Native American women. The admission fee allows you to wander through the old rooms, lined with wordy old information panels explaining the history of the convent and the grueling existence of the nuns who lived here. You'll also see a few icons and finely embroidered vestments, but the real interest is in the time-worn rooms and the lovely herb garden at the back.

A block north at 1132 Royal St, the handsome **Gallier House**, dating from 1857, is a fascinating little place (tours Mon, Tues, Thurs, & Fri 10am, 11am, noon, 2pm, & 3pm, Sat hourly noon–3pm; $10, or $18 with the Hermann-Grima House, see p.639). James Gallier Jr was a leading architect of the day, and the innovative features he designed for his home, such as the outdoor cistern, cooling system and indoor plumbing, soon became essential for anyone wanting to live in comfort in this swampy climate. Meanwhile, the house's filigree cast-iron balconies would have been the last word in chic. Tours, while pricey, are some of the best in the Quarter, focussing as much on social history as fine furniture.

A rare example of the French Quarter's early West Indies-style architecture, with a deep, wraparound gallery, **Madame John's Legacy**, just off Royal Street at 628 Dumaine St (Tues–Sun 9am–5pm; free), was rebuilt after the fire of 1788 as an exact replica of the 1730 house that had previously stood on the site. The building was constructed using the *briquette entre poteaux* technique, in which soft red brick is set between hand-hewn cypress beams, and raised off the ground on stucco-covered pillars. There never was a real Madame John – the name was given to the house by nineteenth-century author George Washington Cable in his tragic short story "'Tite Poulette," and it simply stuck, attracting hundreds of tourists to the city and spawning a nice line in Madame John souvenirs. You are free to wander around the main building, which has a simple exhibition detailing the house's various changes in fortune.

Back on Royal Street, beyond Jackson Square at no. 533, the **Historic New Orleans Collection** stands proud among the neighboring antique stores and chi-chi art galleries. Entry to the streetfront gallery (Tues–Sat 9.30am–4.30pm, Sun 10.30am–4.30pm; Ⓦwww.hnoc.org), which holds excellent temporary exhibitions, is free, but to see the bulk of the collection you'll need to take a guided tour (Tues–Sat 10am, 11am, 2pm, & 3pm; $5). Tours might take in the galleries upstairs, where fascinating exhibits – including old maps, drawings, and early publicity posters – fill a series of themed rooms, or they might venture into the Williams House, beyond a courtyard behind the museum. The Williamses, prominent citizens in the 1930s, filled their home with unusual, exotic objects, and the house is a must for anyone interested in design and decorative arts.

The quirky **Historical Pharmacy Museum**, in an old apothecary a block toward the river at 514 Chartres St ($5), offers great insights into the history of medicine. On the ground floor, hand-carved rosewood cabinets are cluttered with *gris-gris*, a fine range of Creole "tonics" used to cure "all the various forms of female weakness," dusty jars of leeches for blood-letting ("to remove irritability"), and various unpleasant-looking drills and corkscrews. Upstairs you can see a nineteenth-century sick room, and a surprisingly intriguing collection of vintage spectacles from around the world. Due to staffing shortages post-Katrina, the museum is currently only open by appointment, but this may change; call Ⓣ504/565-8027.

Bourbon Street

Continuing lakeside up Conti Street brings you to world-renowned **Bourbon Street**. Though you'd never guess it from the hype, there are two faces to this much-mythologized drag. The touristy, booze-drenched stretch spans the seven stinky blocks from Canal to St Ann: a frat-pack cacophony of trashy daiquiri stalls, novelty shops, and dimly lit girlie bars. This enclave is best experienced after dark, when a couple of its **bars** and **clubs** – though by no means all – are worth a look, and the sheer mayhem takes on a bacchanalian life of its own. When the attraction of fighting your way through the crowds of weekending drunks starts to pall, however, it's easy to dip out again into the quieter parallel streets to regain some sort of sanity. If you do manage to make it as far as St Ann, you come to a distinct crossroads, marked by a brace of raucous gay clubs, beyond which Bourbon transforms into an appealing, predominantly gay, residential area.

Above Bourbon Street: toward Rampart Street

Above Bourbon Street, tourists are outnumbered by locals walking their dogs, jogging, or chatting on stoops. Half a block north of Bourbon, at 820 St Louis St, the restored 1831 **Hermann-Grima House** (tours Mon, Tues, Thurs, & Fri 10am, 11am, noon, 2pm, & 3pm, Sat hourly noon–3pm; $10, or $18 with the Gallier House, see p.638) does a nice job illustrating the lifestyle of middle-class Creoles in antebellum New Orleans; otherwise, though these quiet streets are fringed by some of the Quarter's finest **vernacular architecture**, "sights" as such are few.

Rampart Street, the run-down strip separating the Quarter from **Tremé**, is a boundary rarely crossed by tourists. Though it's home to a good little jazz club (*Donna's*, see p.647), which is just a short walk from the heart of the Quarter, it can feel hairy at night, and only slightly less so during the day. It's not recommended to wander around **Louis Armstrong Park** in daylight hours, either, though it's a different story during the occasional weekend **music festivals**, many of which, continuing its long tradition of black music and celebration, are held in **Congo Square** (see p.636), the small paved area to the left of the entrance arch.

Outside the French Quarter

Tremé, the historic African-American neighborhood where jazz was developed in the bordellos of **Storyville** – long since gone – is named for Claude Tremé, a free black hatmaker who in the nineteenth century owned a plantation on what is now St Claude Street. In the 1800s this was a prosperous area, its shops, businesses, and homes owned and frequented by New Orleans's significant – and unique – free black population, but by the late twentieth century, blighted by neglect and crime, Tremé became a no-go area. Despite this, its rich tradition of jazz funerals, music, and street parades continued, and the turn of the millennium saw signs of gentrification. Though Tremé was largely unscathed by flooding, Katrina nonetheless dealt a severe blow to this poor but culturally rich neighborhood, and many of its houses remain in bad shape.

One way to see the best of Tremé is to make a beeline for the fascinating **Backstreet Cultural Museum**, in an old funeral parlor at 1116 St Claude St (Tues–Sat 10am–5pm; $8; ⓦwww.backstreetmuseum.org). This labor of love celebrates local street culture, including jazz funerals and the traditions of the Mardi Gras Indians; it also hosts excellent music events, and acts as a social hub during the city's many festivals.

Directly across the road, **St Augustine's Church**, 1210 Governor Nicholls St, is the earliest African-American church in the nation, active since 1842. Of crucial significance to the local black community, St Augustine's welcomes tourists to its occasional jazz masses and fundraising events. The spruce, light interior is well worth a look, with its stained-glass windows portraying French saints, and its flags printed with affirmations (Unity, Creativity, Self-Determination, Purpose) in English and Swahili. In the garden, the **Tomb of the Unknown Slave**, a toppled metal cross entwined with balls-and-chains and shackles, honors all African and Native American slaves buried in unmarked graves.

The CBD and Warehouse District

Mark Twain had a point when he dismissed the foreboding Classical interior of the **Custom House** as "inferior to a gasometer," but the dour granite colossus, in the Central Business District – or **CBD** – at 423 Canal St, was key to New Orleans's grand antebellum building program, a hymn to the city's optimism and aspirations. In summer 2008, after more than a decade of delays, a similar optimism was in the air with the opening of the **Audubon Insectarium** (Tues–Sun 10am–5pm; $15) on the ground floor. The first big attraction to open post-Katrina, it's certainly an ambitious project, if mainly of appeal to kids, but there's genuine interest in the exhibits on local breeds, and some exquisite beauty in the butterfly house.

The lakeside edge of the CBD, a tangle of busy gray highways, is dominated by the colossal home of the New Orleans Saints football team, the **Superdome**. At 52 acres, with 27 stories and a diameter of 680ft, this is one of the largest buildings on the planet, and has been etched upon the world's consciousness after housing more than twenty-five thousand Katrina evacuees in unthinkable conditions for six days in August and September, 2005. Though lurid tales of gang rapes, murders, and suicides were later discovered to have been urban myths, the Superdome remains a monument to the horror of the flooding. Standing sentinel over the battered CBD for a year after Katrina, it finally re-opened in fall 2006 with a star-studded rock concert and a triumphant defeat by the Saints over the Atlanta Falcons. The high-profile event provided a huge boost of confidence, and marked a turning point in the city's sense of its own recovery.

Spreading upriver from the foot of Canal Street, New Orleans's **Warehouse District** has a handful of attractions. Most of the sights are concentrated in the **Arts District**, the outcrop of galleries concentrated around Julia and Camp streets. The hub of the scene is the **Contemporary Arts Center**, 900 Camp St (Thurs–Sun 11am–4pm; ground-floor galleries free, changing exhibitions $5; ⓦwww.cacno.org), which has temporary shows on the ground floor and major exhibitions upstairs. Around the corner, the colossal **National World War II Museum**, 945 Magazine St (Tues–Sun 9am–5pm; $14), opened on June 6, 2000, the 56th anniversary of D-Day. Though its collection concentrates on the events of that devastating day, the museum also covers the home front and the D-Day invasions in the Pacific. Its relentless concentration on the American amphibious landings renders the museum's name somewhat inaccurate, however, and there is little room to reflect on the human impact of war.

It can be easy to forget that easy-living New Orleans has its roots entrenched in the Deep South; anyone who needs reminding should take a look at the **Civil War Museum**, 929 Camp St at Lee Circle (Mon–Sat 10am–4pm; $5). A gloomy Romanesque Revival hulk, designed in 1891 as a place for Confederate veterans to display their mementos, this so-called "Battle Abbey of the South" is a relic from a bygone age. Inside the church-like hall, glass cases are filled with swords, mess-kits, uniforms, and fragile sepia photos – there remains a funereal air about the place, with its bittersweet remembrances of long-lost Confederate generals and their forgotten families.

A world away but just next door, at 925 Camp St, the sleek, purpose-built **Ogden Museum of Southern Art** (Thurs–Sun 11am–4pm, Thurs also 6–8pm with live music; $10; ⓦwww.ogdenmuseum.org) has an impressive collection that runs the gamut from rare eighteenth-century watercolors through self-taught art to photography and modern sculpture. While many of the artists are lesser known, it's a fascinating place, evoking a strong sense of this distinctive region.

The Garden District and uptown

Pride of uptown New Orleans, the **Garden District** drapes itself seductively across a thirteen-block area bounded by St Charles Avenue, Magazine Street, Loui-

▲ Garden District villa

siana Avenue and Jackson Avenue. Two miles upriver from the French Quarter, it was developed as a residential neighborhood in the 1840s by an energetic breed of Anglo-Americans who wished to display their accumulating cotton and trade wealth by building sumptuous mansions in huge gardens. Today, shaded by jungles of subtropical foliage, the glorious houses – some of them spick-and-span showpieces, others in ruins – evoke a nostalgic vision of the Deep South in a profusion of porches, columns, and balconies. It's a ravishing spectacle, if somewhat Gothic; while it's a pleasure simply to wander around, you can pick up more detail about the individual houses on any number of official or self-guided tours.

The historic **St Charles streetcar** (see p.630) is the nicest way to get to the Garden District and uptown, affording front-row views of "the Avenue" as St Charles is locally known. Just before the streetcar takes a sharp turn at the riverbend, it stops at peaceful **Audubon Park**, a lovely space shaded by Spanish-moss-swathed trees and looped by cycling and jogging paths. Its top attraction, **Audubon Zoo**, a ten-minute walk from the park's St Charles entrance (Tues–Sun 10am–5pm;

$12.50; zoo and aquarium, $25.50), boasts, among other habitats, a beautifully re-created **Louisiana swamp**, complete with Cajun houseboats, wallowing alligators (including the milky white, blue-eyed "Two-Spot"), and knobbly cypress knees poking out of the emerald-green water.

Algiers and Blaine Kern's Mardi Gras World

A free **ferry** from Canal Street (every 30min 6am–midnight) chugs across the dramatic bend in the Mississippi, bringing you within five minutes or so – depending on the current – to the west bank and the old shipbuilding community of **Algiers**. A quiet residential neighborhood of pastel stucco Creole architecture and subtropical terraces, Algiers's main attraction is **Blaine Kern's Mardi Gras World**, 233 Newton St (daily 9.30am–4.30pm; $17), where year-round you can see artists building and painting the enormous floats used in the Mardi Gras parades. It's a surreal experience wandering these massive warehouses past piles of dusty, grimacing has-beens from parades gone by; in keeping with the carnival spirit, there's plenty of opportunity to dress up, fool around, and take photos. A complimentary minibus picks up and drops off at the ferry landing.

Elsewhere in the city

Toward the lake, in the vast area known as **Mid-City** – much of which was severely damaged in the storm – New Orleans's 1500-acre **City Park** is criss-crossed with roads, and is by no means as peaceful as Audubon Park. It's a welcome green space nonetheless, streaked with lagoons and shaded by centuries-old live oaks. The chief attraction, the excellent **New Orleans Museum of Art** (Wed noon–8pm, Thurs–Sun 10am–5pm; $10), includes pre-Columbian pieces, African works, Asian ceramics and paintings, and contemporary art and photography. The five-acre **sculpture garden** (free) is a must-see, its works – by Louise Bourgeois, Barbara Hepworth, Henry Moore, and others – beautifully dotted among oaks, magnolias, and lush gladioli.

The **Chalmette battlefield**, six miles downriver from Canal Street, is where Andrew Jackson's ragtag army defeated the British at the Battle of New Orleans in 1815 (grounds: Thurs–Mon 9am–4.30pm, Tues & Wed 7am–3pm; visitor center: Thurs–Mon 9am–4.30pm). The attached cemetery is still being repaired after storm damage; check Ⓦ www.nps.gov/jela for updates.

Eating

New Orleans is a gourmand's dream. Gratifyingly, **prices** are not that high compared to other US cities – even at the swankiest places you can get away with $40 per head for a three-course feast with wine. **Lunch**, in particular, can be a bargain, especially at the more upmarket establishments. Due to staffing shortages since Katrina, many restaurants close early, around 9pm, but this may well change. **Opening hours** tend to get extended during the big festivals.

In the French Quarter

Acme Oyster House 724 Iberville St Ⓣ 504/522-5973, Ⓦ www.acmeoyster.com. This noisy French Quarter hangout has been the place for raw oysters and cold beers for generations. Tourists, cops, and office workers alike wait patiently in line for these, as well as the inexpensive po-boys, salty fresh crawfish, and gumbo.

Bayona 430 Dauphine St Ⓣ 504/525-4455, Ⓦ www.bayona.com. Splendid, romantic restaurant – the lovely courtyard feels more relaxed than the formal dining room. Local staples are given a global twist – the simple garlic soup, sweetbreads, and lamb dishes are fantastic – and there's a 250-plus wine list. Lunch is a real bargain – try the grilled cashew butter, smoked duck, and pepper

New Orleans food

New Orleans **food**, commonly defined as **Creole**, is a spicy, substantial, and usually very fattening blend of French, Spanish, African, and Caribbean cuisine, mixed up with a host of other influences including Native American, Italian, and German. Some of the simpler dishes, like red beans and rice, reveal a strong West Indies influence, while others are more French, cooked with long-simmered sauces based on a **roux** (fat and flour heated together) and herby stocks. Many dishes are served **étouffée**, literally "smothered" in a tasty Creole sauce (a roux with tomato, onion, and spices), on a bed of rice. Note that what passes for **Cajun** food in the city is often a modern hybrid, tasty but not authentic; the "blackened" dishes, for example, slathered in butter and spices, made famous by chef Paul Prudhomme. The mainstays of most menus are **gumbo** – a thick soup of seafood, chicken, and vegetables – and **jambalaya**, a paella jumbled together from the same ingredients. Other specialties include **po-boys**, French-bread sandwiches overstuffed with oysters, shrimp, or almost anything else, and **muffulettas**, the round Italian version, crammed full of aromatic meats and cheese and dripping with garlicky olive dressing. Along with **shrimp** and **soft-shell crabs**, you'll get famously good **oysters**; they're in season from September to April. **Crawfish**, or mudbugs (which resemble langoustines and are best between March and October), are served in everything from omelets to bisques, or simply boiled in a spicy stock. To eat them, tug off the overlarge head, pinch the tail, and suck out the juicy, very delicious flesh.

For an only-in-New-Orleans snack, look out for the absurd, giant, hot-dog-shaped **Lucky Dogs** carts set up throughout the Quarter. Featured in John Kennedy Toole's farcical novel *A Confederacy of Dunces*, they've become a beloved institution, though in truth the dogs themselves are nothing great.

jelly sandwich for $11. The pricier dinner menu is well worth it.

Bennachin 1212 Royal St ⓣ504/522-1230. Historically, New Orleans owes a lot to West Africa, including much of its traditional cuisine. And in this tiny, family-run, neighborhood restaurant, the hefty portions of inexpensive, delicious African food – black-eyed-bean fritters, peanut-infused stews, grilled fish in ginger sauce, spinach with plantains – bring Creole food right back to its roots. The iced ginger-honey tea is a treat on a steamy New Orleans night. BYOB; no credit cards. Closes Sun–Thurs 9pm, Fri & Sat 10pm.

Croissant d'Or 617 Ursulines St ⓣ504/524-4663. Tranquil little local place in a pretty, tiled old building. Lines form down the street for the delicious French pastries and stuffed croissants, plus quiches, salads, and steaming *café au lait*, all at the lowest prices in the Quarter. Wed–Mon 7am–2pm.

Fiorella's 45 French Market Place/1136 Decatur St ⓣ504/528-9566. A rough and ready French Quarter classic, this down-home café has long been a local hit for its cheap blue-plate specials, crawfish dishes, and amazing crispy fried chicken. Closes 9pm.

Galatoire's 209 Bourbon St ⓣ504/525-2021, ⓦwww.galatoires.com. Tennessee Williams's favorite restaurant, this grand Creole establishment, with its landmark mirror-lined dining room, is quintessential New Orleans and not at all stuffy. It's best at lunchtime, on Fri or Sun especially, when you can join the city's old guard (gents in seersucker, Southern belles in pearls) spending long, convivial hours gorging on turtle soup, oysters en brochette, crabmeat maison, and filet mignon. No reservations, so expect a wait. Jacket and tie required after 5pm and all day Sun. Closed Mon.

Mr B's 201 Royal St ⓣ504/523-2078, ⓦwww.mrbsbistro.com. Buzzy Creole bistro with dark-wood and etched glass booths, a relaxed, chatty ambiance, and spectacular food. The garlic chicken is the city's finest; the same accolade could go to the signature barbecue shrimp. It can be pricey, but lunch is good value. Walk-ins are welcome. Closes 9.30pm.

Napoleon House 500 Chartres St ⓣ504/524-9752. This ravishing old bar (see p.645) – all crumbling walls and shadowy corners – exudes a classic, relaxed New Orleans elegance. The eighteenth-century building was the home of Mayor Girod, who schemed with Jean Lafitte to rescue Napoleon from exile, but since 1914 it has been owned and run by the same Italian family. Though their fabulous bistro has yet to reopen post-Katrina, bow-tied waiters continue to serve their nice café menu, including warm muffulettas with melted cheese, gumbo, Mediterranean salads, and antipasto. Currently closed evenings and Sun, but call to check.

Tujague's 823 Decatur St ⓣ504/525-8676, ⓦwww.tujaguesrestaurant.com. With one of the loveliest dining rooms in the city, the beloved "Two Jacks," both relaxed and elegant, is a must-visit. Little has changed here over the last 150 years, not least the five-course prix-fixe menu, which always includes shrimp remoulade and tender beef brisket appetizers. If money's tight, simply order the tasty chicken "Bonne Femme" (fried chicken with garlic and parsley) at the beautiful old bar (see p.646).

Outside the French Quarter

Adolfo's 611 Frenchmen St ⓣ504/948-3800. Locals go crazy for the Italian-Creole food, prepared by an Argentine with New Orleans flair. With its ceiling fans, Christmas tree lights, and brick walls, the cozy room – hidden away above the tumbledown *Apple Barrel* pub – is a romantic, relaxed setting for robust pasta, fish and seafood. The kitchen is tiny, so service can be slow – BYOB and hunker down for the evening. Cash only.

Café Reconcile 1631 Oretha Castle Haley Blvd ⓣ504/568-1157, ⓦwww.cafereconcile.com. Something special: a grass roots, nonprofit venture, spearheaded by a Jesuit church, where local at-risk teens are trained for jobs in the hospitality industry. The bustling dining room, in the blighted but slowly recovering neighborhood of Central City, north of the Lower Garden District, is warm and welcoming, prices are ridiculously low, and the food – fried chicken, catfish, daily specials like pot roast or shrimp Creole – beyond delicious. Mon–Fri breakfast & lunch only.

Casamento's 4330 Magazine St ⓣ504/895-9761, ⓦwww.casamentosrestaurant.com. Spotless and old-fashioned, this uptown oyster bar serves inexpensive ice-fresh oysters, fried crab claws, and overstuffed trout "loaves," or sandwiches (to die for). Tues & Wed 11am–2pm, Thurs–Sat 11am–2pm & 5.30–9pm. Closed June–Aug. Cash only.

Jacques Imo's 8324 Oak St ⓣ504/861-0886. Funky, noisy uptown restaurant with a colorful patio. The cooking, a delicious Creole–Cajun take on soul food, is very good value – from the fried oysters and chicken livers to the buttery, blackened redfish. It's a great place to fill up before a gig at the *Maple Leaf* (see p.647), and well worth a trip any time. Dinner only; closed Sun. Reservations only for groups of five or more; you may have to wait a while at the bar.

Mona's 504 Frenchmen St ⓣ504/949-4115. Popular, no-fuss Middle Eastern restaurant in a handy Faubourg Marigny location. The food – kebabs, flatbread pizzas, meze, split red lentil soup – is fresh, zingy, and inexpensive, with lots of delicious vegetarian options. BYOB.

Coffee bars

Café du Monde 800 Decatur St ⓣ504/581-2914. Despite the hype, the crowds, and the sugar-sticky tabletops, this old market coffeehouse, with a large outdoor patio covered by a striped awning, is an undeniably atmospheric place to drink steaming *café au lait* with chicory, and snack on piping hot beignets – the city's distinctive sweet donuts – for just a couple of dollars. Particularly fun after a night out. Daily 24hr.

Café Rose Nicaud 632 Frenchmen St ⓣ504/949-3300. Friendly, delightfully mixed Faubourg Marigny coffeehouse that's a firm favorite with local academics, artists, and musicians who gather around the marble-topped tables, in the capacious armchairs, or outside. Light meals and pastries are served.

CC's 941 Royal St ⓣ504/581-6996. Quarterites linger for hours at the counter or in the leather armchairs, chatting or people-watching through the open French windows. Try their Mochasippi, a creamy iced espresso. Free wi-fi. Other branches around town.

Kahve 2001 Royal St. With its gleaming brass coffee machine, syrupy baklava, rose-and-honey lattes and espresso served in tiny Turkish glasses, this tranquil corner coffeehouse offers funky Faubourg style at its welcoming, life-affirming best. They host occasional live jazz and swing, too.

Rue de ia Course 3121 Magazine St ⓣ504/899-0242. With its pressed-tin walls, *café au lait*-colored decor, ceiling fans, and reading lamps, the *Rue* coffeehouse has an Old Europe ambiance, buzzing with a mixed local crowd and lots of students.

Entertainment and nightlife

New Orleans has long been one of the best places in the world to hear **live music**. From lonesome street musicians, through shambling, joyous brass bands, to international names like Dr John and the Neville Brothers, music remains the heartbeat and lifeline of the Crescent City. The devastation wrought by the post-Katrina flooding hit many musicians – among the less wealthy of the population – particularly hard. Though the effects of the storm on the music scene cannot be underestimated, the quality of what does exist – the bulk of it around weekends and festivals – remains high. The city continues to heal its wounds the best way it knows how: mourning, remembering, celebrating, and surviving by making and dancing to music.

While the French Quarter has its share of atmospheric clubs and bars, there are plenty of good places elsewhere. Visitors who make a beeline for **Bourbon Street**, hoping to find it crammed with cool jazz clubs, will be disappointed. That said, even this tawdriest of streets has a couple of good spots to hear live jazz. A better bet, however, is **Frenchmen Street** in the Faubourg Marigny, lined with bars and music venues that get packed on the weekends. In general, it can be hard to separate the drinking scene from the live music scene – most bars feature music at least one night of the week. Those listed below under "Bars" tend not to have live music, but many of the places reviewed as live music venues (see p.647) are great bars in their own right, too.

To decide where to go, check the free weekly *Gambit* (Ⓦ www.bestofneworleans.com) and the music monthly *Offbeat* (Ⓦ www.offbeat.com), which can be picked up at restaurants and bars all around town. Fliers can be found in French Quarter **record stores** such as Louisiana Music Factory, 210 Decatur St, and the fabulous local **radio station** WWOZ (90.7 FM) features regular gig information and ticket competitions.

Bars

As befits its image as a hard-drinking, hard-partying town, New Orleans has scores of truly great **bars**. However, though **24hr drinking licenses** are common, don't expect every bar to be open all night; even on Bourbon Street, many places close whenever they empty, which can be surprisingly early during slow periods. It is also legal to **drink alcohol in the streets** – for some visitors it's practically de rigueur – though not from a glass or bottle. Simply ask for a plastic **"to go"** cup in any bar and carry it with you. You'll be expected to finish your drink before entering another bar, however.

In the French Quarter

Lafitte's Blacksmith Shop 941 Bourbon St Ⓣ 504/523-0066. Lively, tumbledown bar that's a favourite for tourists. A front for pirate Lafitte's plottings, the building's practically unchanged since the 1700s – despite its exterior sprucing – and retains its beamed ceilings and blackened brick fireplace.

Molly's at the Market 1107 Decatur St Ⓣ 504/525-5169. Once famed for being a haunt of politicos and media stars, Molly's is a French Quarter institution – remaining open through Katrina, the flooding, and subsequent evacuation – and pulls a rowdy crowd of locals, tourists, off-duty waitstaff, and grungy street punks.

Napoleon House 500 Chartres St Ⓣ 504/524-9752. If you visit just one bar in New Orleans, let this ravishing old place be it. Flickering with gaslight, its time-stained walls crammed with ancient oil paintings and on a warm night its tropical courtyard is one of the best places to be.

Port of Call 838 Esplanade Ave Ⓣ 504/523-0120. Strung with tatty nets and life rings, this unpretentious drinking hole is haunted by a noisy crowd who put the world to rights around the large wooden bar or the small tables. Great burgers, too, served with mushrooms or cheese and a buttery baked potato.

Pravda 1113 Decatur St ☎504/525-1818. Though the postmodern, czarist-cum-Social-Realist decor tries a little too hard, with its dim red lighting and comfy banquettes this relaxed cocktail bar makes a nice alternative to the down-and-dirty Decatur bars, especially if you want a quiet drink. They serve quality absinthe, prepared the traditional way, for $20, and have a pretty courtyard out back.

Tujague's 823 Decatur St ☎504/525-8676. Old guard New Orleans restaurant (see p.644) with an equally atmospheric, stand-up bar. It's particularly lively on Sun afternoons, when regulars gather to catch up and gossip.

Elsewhere in the city

Columns Hotel 3811 St Charles Ave ☎504/899-9308. This gorgeous Garden District hotel bar seeps faded Southern grandeur; on warm evenings, make for the columned veranda, which overlooks the streetcar line. For more on the hotel, see p.631.

Ernie K-Doe's Mother-in-Law Lounge 1500 N Claiborne Ave ☎504/947-1078, Ⓦwww.kdoe.com. Since the untimely death of local R&B legend Ernie in 2001, his formidable wife Antoinette has kept their Tremé lounge open as something of a shrine to the self-styled "Emperor of the Universe" – complete with an "Ernie in Heaven" mannequin holding court. Hop in a cab and join the combination of arty hipsters and unimpressed locals that make this place unique.

R-Bar 1431 Royal St ☎504/948-7499. Hip Faubourg Marigny bar with funky thrift-store decor and a pool table frequented by some of the coolest sharks in town. It's popular with a youngish set, which includes visitors staying at the guesthouse upstairs (see p.632). On Monday night you can pay $10 for a haircut and a hand-steadying shot.

Snake and Jake's 7601 Oak St ☎504/861-2802. Dim, debauched and derelict, strewn with ancient Christmas tree lights, a quintessential New Orleans dive bar that is beloved of uptown students and locals. Go very late.

Jazz

Jazz was born in New Orleans, shaped in the early twentieth century by the twin talents of **Louis Armstrong** and **Joe "King" Oliver** from a diverse heritage of African and Caribbean slave music, Civil War brass bands, plantation spirituals, black church music, and work songs.

In 1897, in an attempt to control the prostitution that had been rampant in the city since its earliest days, a law was passed that restricted the brothels to a fixed area bounded by Iberville and Lower Basin streets. The area, which soon became known as **Storyville**, after the alderman who pronounced the ordinance, filled with newly arrived ex-plantation workers, seamen and gamblers, and, from the "mood-setting" tunes played in the brothels to bawdy saloon gigs, there was plenty of opportunity for musicians, in particular the solo piano players known as "professors," to develop personal styles. Children too young to enter the bars set up makeshift "spasm bands" in the streets. Their legacy lives on in the streetwise kids on every corner, tap dancing and playing trumpet.

After Storyville was officially closed in 1917, there was a mass exodus of musicians to Chicago and New York. Many more jazz artists left the city or gave up playing altogether during the Depression (King Oliver died an impoverished janitor); but in the 1950s, the city fathers literally changed their tune and began to promote jazz as a tourist attraction. Nowadays jazz remains an evolving, organic art form, and you're spoiled for choice for places to hear it, whether in parades, at the city's many festivals, in dive bars, or sophisticated lounges. Local, world-class **musicians**, including the multitalented Marsalis family and trumpeters Terence Blanchard, Irvin Mayfield, and Nicholas Payton, all perform regularly. Of the pianists, don't miss Henry Butler, whose superb, superfast modern jazz is matched by his mean R&B and blues repertoire. One of the city's best-loved performers, trumpeter Kermit Ruffins can always be counted on for a good show with his Barbecue Swingers. Other favorites include the ReBirth, whose earsplitting spin on anything from trad jazz to hip-hop goes down as well in student bars as in parades; the more traditional Tremé and Olympia bands; the younger Lil Rascals and New Birth; and the Soul Rebels and the Stooges, who mix a cacophony of horns with hard funk, hip-hop, carnival music, and reggae.

Donna's 800 N Rampart St ⓣ504/596-6914. Hosting smooth jazz and blues, this scruffy barbecue joint on the fringe of the Quarter feels like a locals' place but attracts a loyal out-of-town crowd. Cover varies; one-drink minimum.

Le Bon Temps Roulé 4801 Magazine St ⓣ504/895-8117. A spirited mix of locals and hard-drinking students fill this convivial uptown neighborhood bar – complete with pool tables and good bar food – where the weekly Soul Rebels gig (Thurs) has become an institution. No cover.

Preservation Hall 726 St Peter St ⓣ504/522-2841, ⓦwww.preservationhall.com. This tumble-down old building – with no bar, a/c, or toilets, and just a few hard benches for seating – has long been lauded as the best place in New Orleans to hear trad jazz. The music is lively and joyous, building steam as the night goes on – lines form well before the doors open. Thurs is brass band night. Wed–Sun sets every 45min 8–11pm. $10 cover.

Ray's Room 508 Frenchmen St ⓣ504/309-7137. Local musicians are always hanging out in this loose and easy Faubourg Marigny club, co-owned by Kermit Ruffins; jazz, brass, funk, and soul are on the schedule, along with drummer Bob French's legendary house party, the only place to be on a Monday night in New Orleans. Cover around $10.

Snug Harbor 626 Frenchmen St ⓣ504/949-0696, ⓦwww.snugjazz.com. Sophisticated Faubourg Marigny jazz club in an intimate, two-story space. If money is tight, settle for the bar, where the gigs are shown on a tiny closed-circuit TV. Nightly shows 8pm & 10pm, cover $8–25.

Spotted Cat 623 Frenchmen St ⓣ504/943-3887. With a regular menu of roots music, the Spotted Cat has become the place to see the New Orleans Jazz Vipers, who dish up a high-octane twist on jubilant swing and trad.

Vaughan's 4229 Dauphine St, in the Bywater ⓣ504/947-5562. Rickety old neighborhood bar that fills to bursting point on Thurs, Kermit Ruffins's night. The band is crammed up against the audience – a mixed bunch of locals, students, and the players' friends and family; between sets, help yourself to free beans and rice. Take a cab and prepare for a magical New Orleans evening. Cover $10 on Thurs.

Other live music

There's far more to New Orleans than jazz alone. Though the "**New Orleans sound**," an exuberant, carnival-tinged hybrid of blues, parade music, and R&B, had its heyday in the early 1960s, many of its stars are still gigging, from Al "Carnival Time" Johnson to Irma "It's Raining" Thomas. Their shows, crowded with devoted locals, make for a quintessentially New Orleans night out.

Since the 1960s the city has also been famed for its homegrown **funk** – top acts include Galactic and Papa Grows Funk – while New Orleans's version of hip-hop, known as **bounce**, took the nation by storm. While **Cajun** music is not indigenous to the city, many locals – and tourists – do love to *fais-do-do* (the Cajun two-step) and there are a couple of fantastic places to dance to **zydeco**, its raunchier black relation. The Zydepunks, who mix zydeco with Klezmer, gypsy and Irish music, will always put on a great show. **Blues** fans should look out for guitarists Snooks Eaglin and Walter "Wolfman" Washington, and, for powerful gospel-blues, the formidable Marva Wright. For something unique, scour the listings for **Mardi Gras Indians** (see p.648) such as the Wild Magnolias, whose rare gigs – you're most likely to catch them around Mardi Gras or Jazz Fest – are the funkiest, most extraordinary performances you're ever likely to see.

Circle Bar 1032 St Charles Ave ⓣ504/588-2616, ⓦwww.circlebarnola.com. Painfully hip bar in a crumbling old house at Lee Circle. With an eclectic booking policy, from alt rock to bluegrass, it's renowned for resurrecting R&B legends from oblivion, and always pulls a gorgeous, hard-partying crowd.

Maple Leaf 8316 Oak St ⓣ504/866-9359. Legendary uptown bar with pressed-tin walls, a large dancefloor, and a patio. It's a New Orleans favorite for really great blues, R&B, funk, and brass bands; ReBirth's Tues-night gigs are a must. There's chess and pool, too.

Mid-City Lanes Rock 'n' Bowl 4133 S Carrollton Ave ⓣ504/482-3133, ⓦwww.rockandbowl.com. Its location, in a Mid-City mall, may be unprepossessing, but this eccentric and fun bowling alley-cum-music venue is an institution. Though it's especially heaving on Thurs – zydeco night – they also book great local R&B, blues, and swing, and the crowd is always lively. Take a taxi.

Mardi Gras and other New Orleans festivals

New Orleans's **carnival season** – which starts on Twelfth Night, January 6, and runs for the six weeks or so until Ash Wednesday – is unlike any other in the world. Though the name is used to define the entire season, **Mardi Gras** itself, French for "Fat Tuesday," is simply the culmination of a whirl of parades, parties, street revels, and masked balls, all inextricably tied up with the city's labyrinthine social, racial, and political structures. Mardi Gras was introduced to New Orleans in the 1740s, when **French** colonists brought over the European custom, established since medieval times, of marking the imminence of Lent with masking and feasting. Their slaves, meanwhile, continued to celebrate **African** and **Caribbean** festival traditions, based on musical rituals, masking, and elaborate costumes, and the three eventually fused. From early days carnival was known for cavorting, outrageous costumes, drinking, and general bacchanalia – and little has changed. However, although it has become the busiest tourist season, when the city is invaded by millions, Mardi Gras has always been, above all, a party that New Orleanians throw for themselves. Visitors are wooed, welcomed, and shown the time of their lives, but without them carnival would reel on regardless. **Post-Katrina**, Mardi Gras has become more important than ever, offering not only celebration but also catharsis. As a symbol of what makes this unique city tick, it can't be bettered, and as a lifeline for a beleagured population, it is essential.

Official carnival took its current form in 1857, with the appearance of a stately moonlit procession calling itself the "Krewe of Comus, Merrie Monarch of Mirth." Initiated by a group of Anglo-Americans, the concept of the "**krewes**," or secret carnival clubs, was taken up enthusiastically by the New Orleans aristocracy, many of them white supremacists who, after the Civil War, used their satirical float designs and the shroud of secrecy to mock and undermine Reconstruction. Nowadays about fifty official krewes equip colorful floats, leading huge processions with different, often mythical, themes. Each is reigned over by a King and Queen (generally an older, politically powerful man and a debutante), who go on to preside over the krewes' closed, masked balls. There are women-only krewes; "super krewes," with members drawn from the city's new wealth (barred from making inroads into the gentlemen's-club network of the old-guard krewes), and important **black** groups. The best known and most important of these is **Zulu**, established in 1909 when a black man mocked Rex, King of Carnival, by dancing behind his float with a tin can on his head; today the Zulu parade on Mardi Gras morning is one of the most popular of the season. There are also many alternative, or **unofficial krewes**, including the anarchic **Krewe du Vieux** (from *Vieux Carré*, another term for the French Quarter), whose irreverent parade and "ball" (a polite term for a wild party, open to all) is a blast. The **gay** community plays a major part in Mardi Gras, particularly in the French Quarter, where the streets teem with strutting drag divas. And then there's the parade of the **Mystic Krewe of Barkus**, made up of dogs, hundreds of whom, during what is surely the campest parade of the season, can be seen trotting proudly through the French Quarter all spiffed up on some spurious theme. Tourists are less likely to witness the **Mardi Gras Indians**, African-American groups who, in their local neighborhoods, organize themselves into "tribes" and, dressed in fabulous beaded and feathered costumes, gather on Mardi Gras morning to compete in chanting and dancing. Made up predominantly of poor black men, many of whom lost their homes and their communities in the flooding, this is the Mardi Gras group that has been most diminished by the devastation of Katrina. One important New Orleans Mardi Gras ritual is the flinging of "**throws**" from the parade floats. Teasing masked krewe members scatter beads, beakers, and doubloons (toy coins) into the crowds, who beg, plead, and scream for them. Even outside the parades, tourists embark upon a frantic **bead-bartering** frenzy, which has given rise to the famed "Show Your Tits!"

phenomenon – young co-eds pulling up their shirts in exchange for strings of beads and roars of boozy approval from the goggling mobs. Anyone keen to see the show should head for Bourbon Street.

The two weeks leading up to Mardi Gras are filled with processions, parties, and balls, but excitement reaches fever pitch on **Lundi Gras**, the day before Mardi Gras. Some of the city's best musicians play at **Zulu**'s free party in Woldenberg Park, which climaxes at 5pm with the arrival of the king and queen by boat. Following this, you can head to the **Plaza d'España**, where, in a formal ceremony unchanged for over a century, the mayor hands the city to Rex, King of Carnival. The party continues with more live music and fireworks, after which people head off to watch the big **Orpheus** parade, or start a frenzied evening of clubbing. Most clubs are still hopping well into Mardi Gras morning.

The fun commences early on Mardi Gras day, with **walking clubs** striding through uptown accompanied by raucous jazz on their ritualized bar crawls. Zulu, in theory, sets off at 8.30am (but can be as much as two hours late), followed by **Rex**. Across town, the surreal **St Ann walking parade** gathers in the Bywater, arriving in the Faubourg at around 11am, while the gay costume competition known as the **Bourbon Street awards** gets going at noon. In the afternoon, hipsters head back to the Faubourg, where **Frenchmen Street** is ablaze with bizarrely costumed carousers. The fun continues throughout the Quarter and the Faubourg until **midnight**, when a siren wail heralds the arrival of a cavalcade of mounted police that sweeps through Bourbon Street and declares through megaphones that Mardi Gras is officially over. Like all good Catholic cities, New Orleans takes carnival very seriously. Midnight marks the onset of Lent, when repentance can begin.

Other New Orleans festivals

St Joseph's Day, March 19. Sicilian saint's day, at the mid-point of Lent. Massive altars of food, groaning with bread, fig cakes, and stuffed artichokes, are erected in churches all around town, including St Louis Cathedral, and there's also a parade. The Sunday closest to St Joseph's ("**Super Sunday**") is the only time outside Mardi Gras that the Mardi Gras Indians (see above) take to the streets.

French Quarter Festival, early April. Free three-day music festival that rivals Jazz Fest for the quality and variety of music on offer. Stages and food stalls, free evening gigs, parades, and talent contests. Ⓦ www.fqfi.org.

Jazz and Heritage Festival (Jazz Fest), two weekends (Fri–Sun & Thurs–Sun) end April/early May at the Fairgrounds Race Track, Mid-City. Enormous festival, with stages hosting jazz, R&B, gospel, African, Caribbean, Cajun, blues, and more, with evening performances in clubs all over town. Crafts stalls and phenomenal food stands. Ⓦ www.nojazzfest.com.

Satchmo Fest, end of July/early Aug. Free four-day weekend festival, staged to celebrate Louis Armstrong, at the Mint. Talks focus on Satchmo and his legacy, while the best local jazz and brass bands play live. Plus food stalls, Second Lines and a jazz mass at St Augustine's Church. Ⓦ www.fqfi.org.

Southern Decadence, six days around Labor Day weekend. Huge gay extravaganza, bringing nearly 100,000 party animals to the gay bars and clubs of the Quarter and the Faubourg, with an unruly costume parade of thousands on the Sunday afternoon. Ⓦ www.southerndecadence.com.

Halloween, Oct 31. Thanks to its long-held obsession with all things morbid, and the local passion for partying and dressing up, New Orleans is a fabulous place to spend Halloween, with haunted houses, costume competitions, ghost tours, and parades all over town.

One Eyed Jack's 615 Toulouse St ⓣ504/569-8361, ⓦwww.oneeyedjacks.net. Loosely conceived as a decadent cabaret lounge in old Bourbon Street style, this hip bar and club presents a wide range of shows, including burlesque, trad jazz, rap battles, indie rock, and punk to a friendly crowd.

Tipitina's 501 Napoleon Ave ⓣ504/895-8477, ⓦwww.tipitinas.com. Venerable uptown venue, named after a Professor Longhair song, with a consistently good funk, R&B, brass, and reggae line-up. The Sun Cajun *fais-do-do* is fun, too.

Cajun country

Cajun country stretches across southern Louisiana from Houma in the east, via **Lafayette**, the hub of the region, into Texas. It's a region best enjoyed away from the larger towns, by visiting the many old-style hamlets that, despite modernization, can still be found cut off from civilization in soupy bayous, coastal marshes, and inland swamps.

Cajuns are descended from the French colonists of Acadia, part of Nova Scotia, which was taken by the British in 1713. The Catholic **Acadians**, who had quietly fished, hunted, and farmed for more than a century, refused to renounce their faith and swear allegiance to the English king, and in 1755 the British expelled them all, separating families and burning towns. About 2500 ended up in French Louisiana, where they were given land to set up small farming communities, enabling them to rebuild the culture they had left behind. Hunting, farming, and trapping, they lived in relative isolation until the 1940s, when major roads were built, immigrants from other states poured in to work in the **oil** business, and **Cajun music**, popularized by local musicians such as accordionist Iry Lejeune, came to national attention. Since then, the history of the Cajuns has continued to be one of struggle. The erosion of coastal wetlands threatens the existence of entire communities; the silting up of the Atchafalaya Basin is having adverse effects on fishing and shrimping; and many coastal towns are in the firing line of devastating hurricanes, like Katrina, that hurtle up from the Gulf of Mexico. After Roosevelt's administration decreed that all American children should speak English in schools, French was practically wiped out in Cajun country, and the local patois of the older inhabitants, with its strong African influences, was kept alive primarily by music. Since the 1980s, CODOFIL (the council for development of French in Louisiana) has been devoted to preserving the region's indigenous **language** and culture, and today you will find many signs, brochures, and shopfronts written in French.

Cajun **fais-do-dos** – dances, with live bands, held mostly on weekends – are good places to encounter the culture at close hand. Visitors here will find plenty of opportunity to dance, whether at a restaurant, a club, or one of the region's many **festivals**. Although **Baton Rouge**, the capital of Louisiana, is not actually in Cajun country, heading out this way from New Orleans, via the **plantations** on the banks of the Mississippi, makes an easy approach.

Cajun festivals

Cajun festivals, held almost weekly it seems, provide an enjoyable way to experience the food and music of the region. Note that for the larger events, it's a good idea to reserve a room in advance. The following is merely a sampler; for full details, check with any tourist office in the area.

Mardi Gras, Feb/March. Cajun Carnival differs from its city cousin; although there are private balls, parties, and formal parades, it is a far more countrified and very family-oriented affair. There's plenty of music and street dancing, of course, and villages like Eunice, Church Point, and Mamou are the scene of the mischievous *Courir du Mardi Gras* (see p.658). Ⓦwww.lsue.edu/acadgate/mardmain.htm.

World Championship Crawfish Étouffée Cookoff, last Sunday in March (the third Sun, if Easter falls on the last Sun), Eunice. *The* place to taste the very best mudbugs, accompanied by great local music and a fierce spirit of competition among the scores of teams. Ⓣ337/457-2565, Ⓦwww.eunice-la.com/festivals.html.

Festival International de Louisiane, last full week in April. Huge, free five-day festival in Lafayette, with big-name participants from all over the French-speaking world, celebrating a wealth of indigenous music, culture, and food; Ⓣ337/232-8086, Ⓦwww.festivalinternational.com.

Breaux Bridge Crawfish Festival, first full weekend of May (Fri–Sun), Breaux Bridge. Crawfish-eating contests, étouffée cookoffs, and mudbug races, along with music, crafts stalls, and dancing. $5 Fri & Sun, $10 Sat, $15 for three days; Ⓣ337/332-6655, Ⓦwww.bbcrawfest.com.

Southwest Louisiana Zydeco Music Festival, Sat before Labor Day, Plaisance, near Opelousas. A month of zydeco-related events culminates in a full day of top zydeco performers playing turbo-fuelled "black Creole" music. Also regional cuisine, African-American arts and crafts, talks, dancing, and workshops. $10, $2 for kids; Ⓣ337/942-2392, Ⓦwww.zydeco.org.

Mamou Cajun Music Festival, last weekend Aug or first weekend Sept (Fri & Sat), Mamou, ten miles north of Eunice. Traditional live music, food, crafts, beer-drinking and boudin-eating contests, greasy pole-climbing, and a Cajun Queen beauty pageant for the over-65s. $5. Ⓦwww.mamoucajunmusicfestival.com.

Festivals Acadiens, late Sept or early Oct, Lafayette. Huge three-day festival, with Cajun, zydeco, and traditional French bands, as well as indigenous crafts and food. Ⓦwww.festivalsacadiens.com.

Louisiana Prairie Cajun Capital Folklife Festival fall, Eunice. The Prairie Acadian Cultural Center organizes this free two-day festival with bands, arts and crafts, storytellers, and a wide variety of food stalls; Ⓣ337/457-2565.

Louisiana Yambilee, last week in Oct. Opelousas goes all out to celebrate the sweet potato, with food stalls, silent sweet potato auctions, music, and the marvelously named Lil' Miss Yum Yum contest; Ⓣ337/948-8848, Ⓦwww.yambilee.com.

Northwest from New Orleans: plantation country

The fastest roads out from New Orleans toward the west are the major I-10 and US-61; you can also drive along the **River Road**, which hugs both banks of the Mississippi all the way to Baton Rouge, seventy miles upriver. It's not a particularly eventful drive, winding through flat, fertile farmland, but a series of bridges and ferries allows you to crisscross the water, stopping off and touring several restored antebellum **plantation homes** along the way. Before the Civil War, these spectacular homes were the focal points of the vast estates from where wealthy planters – or rather, their slaves – loaded cotton, sugar, or indigo onto steamboats berthed virtually at their front doors. Generally, the superb Laura plantation excepted (see below), **tours**, often led by belles in ball gowns, skimp on details about the estates as a whole, and in particular their often vast slave populations, presenting them instead as showcase museums filled with priceless antiques. The cumulative effect of these evocations can be stultifying, so it's best to pick just one or two. Many of the houses also offer luxurious **B&B** rooms (rates often include tours), which as well as being rather wonderful places to sleep, allow you to absorb more of the atmosphere of the plantations than is possible on the walk-throughs.

To get to the River Road from New Orleans, take I-10 west to exit 220, turn onto I-310 and follow it to **Hwy-48**, on the east bank (*above* the river on the map). This shortly becomes **Hwy-44**, or the River Road. For the west bank (*below* the river), cross Destrehan Bridge onto **Hwy-18** rather than branching onto Hwy-48. Note that the levee runs the length of the banks, blocking the river from view, and though you'd never guess it from the tourist brochures, hulking chemical plants dominate the River Road landscape. There are rural stretches where wide sugarcane fields are interrupted only by moss-covered shacks – the prettiest views are to be found around the small town of **Convent**, on the east bank – but you'll more often find yourself driving through straggling communities of boarded-up lounges and laundromats, scarred by scrap piles and smokestacks.

From **Edgard**, 25 miles along on Hwy-18, you can cross the river to the **San Francisco House** (daily 10am–4pm; $15), two miles upriver of **Reserve** on Hwy-44. Built in a style dubbed "Steamboat Gothic" by novelist Frances Parkinson Keyes, its rails, awnings, and pillars were designed to recreate the ambiance of a Mississippi showboat. The elaborate facade is matched by a gorgeous interior – a riot of pastoral trompe-l'oeils, floral motifs, and Italian cherubs. Crossing the river at **Lutcher**, the settlement a few miles beyond San Francisco, brings you to Vacherie and the fascinating **Laura plantation** (six tours daily 10am–4pm; $15). Rather than dwelling lovingly on priceless antiques, the tours here, which draw upon a wealth of historical documents – from **slave accounts** and photographs to private diaries – sketch a vivid picture of day-to-day plantation life in multicultural Louisiana. Nine miles upriver from Laura, **Oak Alley** is the quintessential image of the antebellum plantation home. It's a splendid Greek Revival mansion dating from 1839 – and the magnificent oaks that form a canopy over the driveway are 150 years older (Mon–Fri 10am–4pm, Sat & Sun 10am–5pm; $15). The **restaurant** (8.30–10am & 11am–3pm) serves Cajun food, and you can **stay** in pretty B&B cottages in the grounds (Ⓣ225/265-2151, Ⓦwww.oakalleyplantation.com; ❻). Eighteen miles south of Baton Rouge on the west bank, **Nottoway** (1859) is the largest surviving plantation home in the South, a huge, white Italianate edifice with 64 rooms (daily 9am–5pm; $15). The house also has fifteen fancy **B&B** rooms (Ⓣ1-866/527-6884, Ⓦwww.nottoway.com; ❼) and a **restaurant** (daily 11am–2pm & 6–8.30pm).

Also on the west bank, in the small town of **Donaldsonville** at 406 Charles St, the **River Road African American Museum** (Wed–Sat 10am–5pm, Sun 1–5pm; $4) offers an intriguing and alternative view of the region's history, highlighting its cuisine, music, the Underground Railroad, Reconstruction, and the culture of the free blacks.

Baton Rouge

When French explorers first came upon the site of **BATON ROUGE** in 1699, they found poles smeared in animal blood to designate the separate hunting grounds of the Houmas and Bayougoulas Indians. The area on these shallow bluffs therefore appeared on French maps as *Baton Rouge* – "red stick." Now capital of Louisiana and the fifth biggest port in the US, Baton Rouge is an easy-going city for its size. Even the presence of the state's largest **universities**, LSU and Southern, has done surprisingly little to raise the town anywhere much above "sleepy" status.

Surrounded by fifty acres of showpiece gardens, the magnificent Art Deco **Louisiana State Capitol** (daily 9am–4pm; free) serves as a monument to **Huey Long**, the "Kingfish," the larger-than-life Democratic governor who ordered its construction in 1931 and was assassinated in its corridors just four years later.

Mark Twain referred to Baton Rouge's **Old State Capitol** (in use from 1850 to 1932), 100 North Blvd, as "that monstrosity on the Mississippi." A crenellated, pseudo-Gothic pile on a mound overlooking the river, it's worth a look for the **Museum of Political History** (Tues–Sat 10am–4pm, Sun noon–4pm, also Mon 10am–4pm in April & May; $5), which illuminates Louisiana's scandal-ridden political history. The **LSU Rural Life Museum**, 4560 Essen Rd, just off I-10 southeast of downtown (daily 8.30am–5pm; $7), recreates pre-industrial Louisiana life through its carefully restored buildings – among them a plantation house, slave cottages, and a grist mill – spread over 25 acres in a sultry garden setting.

Practicalities

Greyhound **buses**, as well as connecting buses from New Orleans's Amtrak station, come in at 1253 Florida St, fifteen minutes from downtown. For Yellow **Cabs**, call ⓣ225/926-6400. The **visitor center** is downtown at 359 Third St, three blocks from the river between Main and Florida (daily 8am–4.30pm; ⓣ225/383-1825 or 1-800/LA-ROUGE, ⓦwww.visitbatonrouge.com). There are plenty of chain **motels** on and off I-10; *Best Western Richmond Suites*, near LSU at 5668 Hilton Ave (ⓣ225/924-6500, ⓦwww.bestwesternlouisiana.com; ❺) is a cut above many, with a pool, evening drinks and a substantial complimentary breakfast.

For **eating**, *Avoyelles*, three blocks from the river at 333 3rd St (ⓣ225/381-9385), serves blue-plate lunch specials (Mon–Fri) and great shrimp po-boys, and has an outdoor patio for night-time drinking. Most of the city's **bars** and **clubs** are near the **LSU campus** – along College Drive, Chimes Street, and Highland Road – and on Third Street downtown.

Lafayette and around

LAFAYETTE, 135 miles northwest of New Orleans on I-10, is geographically central in Cajun country, and the key city for its oil business. Originally named Vermilionville, after the orange-hued bayou nearby, it was renamed in 1844 in honor of the Marquis de Lafayette, the aristocratic French hero of the American Revolution. Today it's a sprawling city with a small-town feel. Lafayette is particularly vibrant during the superb **Festival International de Louisiane**, in April, and **Festivals Acadiens**, in the fall; at other times, though, you could use it as a base for exploring the swamps, bayous, and dance halls of the region. There are plenty of smaller places nearby, especially in and around **Breaux Bridge**, that offer something a little more personal.

Arrival, information, and getting around

Greyhound arrives in Lafayette at 315 Lee Ave; **Amtrak** pulls in a few blocks north at 133 E Grant St at Jefferson Street. The **airport** is south of town on Hwy-

90. Pick up essential maps and brochures from the Lafayette Parish **visitor center** at 1400 NW Evangeline Thruway, exit 103A off I-10 (Mon–Fri 8.30am–5pm, Sat & Sun 9am–5pm; ⓣ 1-800/346-1958, ⓦ www.lafayettetravel.com). To get the best from the area you'll need a **car**, as the dance halls, restaurants, and hotels are spread out, and the local bus system is of little use to visitors. If you need a **taxi**, try Quality Cab (ⓣ 337/235-8993).

Accommodation in and around Lafayette

Chain **hotels** line Evangeline Thruway just south of I-10, and US-90 and Hwy-182 toward New Iberia, but if you are after something with more character you'll need to head further out. The friendly hamlet of **Breaux Bridge**, just eight miles east, makes another appealing base.

Bayou Cabins 100 W Mills Ave/Hwy-94, Breaux Bridge ⓣ 337/332-6158, ⓦ www.bayoucabins.com. Thirteen rustic cabins – most of which date from the nineteenth century – backing onto Bayou Teche, a 125-mile long waterway. Run by the owners of *Bayou Boudin and Cracklin'* (see p.654); rates include a free taster of their fantastic Cajun food and breakfast served in the café next door. ❸

Bayou Teche B&B 205 Washington St, Breaux Bridge ⓣ 337/332-1049, ⓦ www.aubayoutechebedandbreakfast.com. Appealing guesthouse right on the bayou, in an 1812 Creole cottage expanded in the 1880s to become a boarding house. Rates can include a full breakfast at *Café des Amis* (see p.657) or simply coffee and pastries; the welcoming host leaves you to treat the place like home. ❸–❹

Blue Moon Guest House and Saloon 215 E Convent St, Lafayette ⓣ 337/234-2422, ⓦ www.bluemoonhostel.com. Cheerful hostel and guesthouse, in a nineteenth-century home on a nice street downtown, with two dorms ($18–21) and four private rooms. Regular Cajun, zydeco, and bluegrass gigs and a full bar in the back porch saloon; check ⓦ www.bluemoonpresents.com for schedule. Rates increase for festivals. Free wi-fi. ❶–❹

Juliet Hotel 800 Jefferson St, Lafayette ⓣ 337-261-2225, ⓦ www.juliethotel.com. Though it offers nothing distinctively Cajun, this stylish boutique hotel has a good downtown location and luxurious touches for a good price. ❺

Plantation Motor Inn 2810 NE Evangeline Thruway, Lafayette ⓣ 337/232-7285. Good-value motel north of town near the interstate, with plain rooms and free continental breakfast. ❸

The Town

In the center, such as it is, of Lafayette stands the Romanesque **Cathedral of St John the Evangelist**, 914 St John St, and the old **cemetery**, where the crumbling, raised graves include that of Jean Mouton, the town's Cajun founder. Each of the magnificent branches of the five-hundred-year-old **Cathedral Oak**, spreading over 200ft, weighs seventy tons. Three blocks away, the small **Lafayette Museum**, 1122 Lafayette St (Tues–Sat 9am–4.30pm, Sun 1–4pm; $3), was the "Sunday home" – a townhouse used after Mass, before the family returned to their plantation – of Jean's son Alexandre, Louisiana's first Democratic governor. It's now filled with family memorabilia, Civil War relics, and Cajun Mardi Gras costumes.

Lafayette has two excellent reconstructions of early Cajun communities. **Vermilionville**, 300 Fisher Rd across from the airport, is the most accessible and impressive of the two, extending its scope to explore the culture of the early Creoles as well as the Cajuns (Tues–Sun 10am–4pm; $8). Set in 23 attractive acres on the Bayou Vermilion, it's a living history site, filled with authentic old buildings occupied by craftspeople using traditional skills. A large replica of an old cotton gin serves as a **theater**, hosting storytellers, plays, and noisy *fais-do-dos*. The **restaurant** serves good Cajun lunches.

Next to Vermilionville, at 501 Fisher Rd, the **Acadian Cultural Center**, in the **Jean Lafitte National Historical Park and Preserve** (daily 8am–5pm; free), offers a thorough background on the displaced Cajuns, with a wealth of artifacts

▲ Cathedral of St John the Evangelist

and a forty-minute film shown on the hour. Further southwest, ten miles or so from the Lafayette visitor center, Lafayette's other folk-life museum, the smaller **Acadian Village**, 200 Greenleaf Drive (daily 10am–4pm; $8), depicts early nineteenth-century Cajun life along the bayous.

Eating in and around Lafayette

It's commonly said that a Cajun cooks every part of a pig but its squeal. Though Cajun food bears resemblances to the Creole cuisine you'll find in New Orleans – lots of seafood, rice, rich tomatoey sauces, and gumbos – this is rustic food, often spicy, and pork is indeed a frequent ingredient. At lunchtime, takeout boudin (spicy sausage made with rice) is a treat, as are rich pork cracklin' and salty hogshead cheese.

Cajun music venues

It's easy to "pass a good time" in Cajun country, especially if you're here on the weekend, when the *fais-do-dos* are traditionally held. **Cajun music** is a jangling, infectious melange of nasal vocals backed by jumping accordion, violin, and triangle, fueled by traces of country, swing, jazz, and blues. **Zydeco** is similar, but sexier, more blues-based, and usually played by black Creole musicians. Though songs are in French, the patois heard in both bears only a passing resemblance to the language spoken in France. Music is never performed without space for dancing; everyone can join in. As well as the popular restaurants *Café des Amis*, *Mulate's*, *Prejean's*, and *Randol's* (reviewed on p.657), plus the *Blue Moon Guest House* (see p.654), **venues** include record stores, river landings, and the streets themselves. Sadly, old-time zydeco dance halls are dying out, but a few still exist. Check the music **listings** in the free weekly *Times of Acadiana* (Ⓦwww.timesofacadiana.com) or *Independent* (Ⓦwww.theind.com) – both out on Wednesdays. Look also at the zydeco listings page Ⓦceezees.com/CurrentEvents.htm, or simply look for signs saying "French dance here tonight."

Angelle's Whiskey River Landing 1365 Henderson Levee Rd, Henderson, Breaux Bridge Ⓣ337/228-8567, Ⓦwww.whiskeyriverlanding.net. Lively Cajun and zydeco parties at *Angelle's* – the starting point for a swamp tour – on Sun afternoons. It's around 25min from Lafayette.

El Sid O's 1523 N St Antoine St, Lafayette Ⓣ337/237-1959. Dancing Fri–Sun, with great zydeco and blues bands plus Creole food.

Fred's Lounge 420 6th St, Mamou, 10 miles north of Eunice Ⓣ337/468-5411. Welcoming home of the locally famed radio show "Live from Fred's Lounge" (KVPI 1050 AM; Sat 9–11am), with music, dancing, and lots of drinking. Sat only, 7am–2pm.

Grant Street Dancehall 113 W Grant St, Lafayette Ⓣ337/237-8513, Ⓦwww.grant-streetdancehall.com. Eclectic music barn in downtown Lafayette hosting hip-hop, swamp pop, New Orleans jazz, and blues, as well as Cajun and zydeco.

La Poussière 1215 Grand Point Rd, Breaux Bridge Ⓣ337/332-1721. The old folks' favorite, this venerable dance hall – where most people speak French – hosts *fais-do-dos* (Sat night & Sun afternoon).

McGee's Landing 1337 Henderson Levee Rd, Breaux Bridge Ⓣ337/228-2384, Ⓦwww.mcgeeslanding.com. Another swamp tour outfit-cum-café-cum-music venue hosting live music on Sun afternoons.

Pat's Atchafalaya Club 1008 Henderson Levee Rd, Henderson, Breaux Bridge Ⓣ337/228-7512, Ⓦwww.patsfishermanswharf.com. Large dance hall on the levee, linked to *Pat's* seafood restaurant, and hosting Cajun, zydeco, and swamp pop bands Fri–Sun.

Rendezvous des Cajuns Liberty Center for Performing Arts, S 2nd St and Park Ave, Eunice Ⓣ337/457-7389, Ⓦwww.eunice-la.com/libertyschedule.html. Family-oriented and hugely popular live Cajun/zydeco radio and TV show, mostly in French. Sat 6–7.30pm. Cover $5.

Savoy Music Center 4413 Hwy-190 E, 3 miles east of Eunice Ⓣ337/457-9563, Ⓦsavoymusiccenter.com. Free jam sessions (Sat 9am–noon) at this Cajun record store and accordion workshop are a local institution. Store closed Sun & Mon.

Bayou Boudin and Cracklin' 100 Mills Ave, Hwy-94, Breaux Bridge, exit 109 from I-10 Ⓣ337/332-6158. Rustic Cajun cottage on Bayou Teche, serving fantastic boudin – including a seafood variety – hogshead cheese-smothered chicken, crawfish balls, and beignets, all prepared on the spot. Closed Mon.

Blue Dog Café 1211 W Pinhook Rd, Lafayette Ⓣ337/237-0005, Ⓦwww.bluedogcafe.com. Dine on classy Cajun-Creole food – the crawfish étouffée is great – surrounded by the distinctive blue dog paintings of Cajun artist George Rodrigue. Lunch Mon–Fri, dinner Mon–Thurs, plus Sun brunch.

Café des Amis 140 E Bridge St, Breaux Bridge ⓣ337/332-5273, ⓦwww.cafedesamis.com. This friendly, arty restaurant is a buzzing community hub. The Cajun/Creole food, with lots of creamy crawfish concoctions, is very tasty. Live zydeco breakfasts Sat 8.30–11.30am. Closed Mon; lunch only Tues & Sun.

Dwyer's 323 Jefferson St, Lafayette ⓣ337/235-9364. Downtown community favorite for huge, inexpensive breakfasts and plate lunches, home-cooked burgers, and local specialties. You'll hear a lot of French spoken here. Sun & Mon 6am–2pm, Tues–Sat 6am–8pm.

Mulate's 325 Mills Ave, Breaux Bridge ⓣ337/332-4648 and 1-800/422-2586. This is the original Cajun restaurant and dance hall and, though touristy, is frequented by locals, too. Seafood, catfish, and gumbo go for less than $15; dancing nightly at 7pm, and at noon on weekends.

Poche's Market 3015A Hwy-31, north of Breaux Bridge ⓣ337/332-2108, ⓦwww.pochesmarket.com/. One of the best places to pick up boudin, cracklin', andouille, and old-fashioned pies, as well as tasty home-cooked plate lunches.

Prejean's 3480 I-49 N, Lafayette ⓣ337/896-3247, ⓦwww.prejeans.com. Barn-like restaurant offering delicious food – try the Mardi Gras oyster bake – nightly live music (from 7pm), and dancing. Daily 7am–9pm or 10pm.

Randol's 2320 Kaliste Saloom Rd, Lafayette ⓣ337/981-7080, ⓦwww.randols.com. Dine on Cajun seafood dinners (barbecued softshell crabs are a specialty) in this famed barn-like restaurant, while listening to live Cajun and zydeco. Nightly from 6.30pm.

Robin's 1409 Henderson Hwy, Henderson, Breaux Bridge ⓣ337/228-7594. Innovative Cajun food, with lots of use of Tabasco hot sauce – even in the ice cream – and a killer crawfish étouffé.

Touring Cajun country

You could easily drive through **BREAUX BRIDGE**, eight miles east of Lafayette, and miss it, which would be a shame. Quite apart from its sweet, old-fashioned main street, its unusual crawfish-emblazoned steel bridge over the Bayou Teche, and its handful of B&Bs, restaurants, and music venues, it also makes an appealing base for some of the region's best **swamp tours** (see p.659), and for exploring the **Lake Martin nature reserve**, three miles south on Hwy-31. There's an end-of-the-earth feel to the reserve, where land turns to water, and it's a great experience to drive – or walk the trails – past vistas of tangled cypress flickering with Spanish moss and encroaching greenery creeping onto the narrow road. From February to June tens of thousands of birds nest at the lake, and there's a huge abundance of **birdlife** year-round, including egrets, herons, and spoonbills, not to mention busy nutria splashing through the undergrowth and scores of **alligators** dozing in the sun. If you fancy paddling a **canoe** through this lonely wilderness, contact Pack and Paddle in Lafayette (ⓣ337/232-5854, ⓦwww.packpaddle.com; closed Sun).

North of Lafayette, the **Cajun Prairie** has been described by folklorist Alan Lomax as the "Cajun cultural heartland." A patchwork of rice and soybean fields scattered with crawfish ponds, the region has a few tiny towns of interest. Sleepy old **OPELOUSAS**, twenty miles north of Lafayette on I-49, was capital of Louisiana for a short period during the Civil War, and now has several claims to fame. It was the boyhood home of Jim Bowie, Texas Revolutionary hero and inventor of the Bowie knife; the birthplace of the great zydeco musician **Clifton Chenier**; and is the **yam** capital of the universe (see p.651 for a festival celebrating this achievement). You can find out more about the town at the quirky **Opelousas Museum**, 315 N Main St (Mon– Sat 9am–5pm; free), which displays such relics of local history as the barber's stool on which outlaw Clyde Barrow got his last shave before being shot dead by the FBI in northern Louisiana. Head for the 1950s *Palace Café*, on the central square at 135 W Landry Ave (ⓣ337/942-2142), for shrimp, crawfish, and gumbo in immaculate **diner** surroundings. Chain **hotels** line I-49; the *Holiday Inn* (ⓣ337/948-3300, ⓦwww.hiopelousas.com; ⑤), just north of town, is a good bet.

To learn a little about the Cajun prairie, head for friendly **EUNICE**, about twenty miles west of Opelousas. The exemplary **Prairie Acadian Cultural Center** at the **Jean Lafitte National Historical Park**, 250 W Park Ave (Tues–Fri 8am–5pm, Sat 8am–6pm; free), holds far-reaching displays on local life, ranging across family, language, food, and farming, with regular live Cajun music, storytelling, and cookery demonstrations. There's more music at the **Cajun Music Hall of Fame**, 240 S C.C. Duson Drive (Tues–Sat: summer 9am–5pm, winter 8.30am–4.30pm; free), which features accordions, steel guitars, fiddles, and triangles among its memorabilia. If time is limited, choose these two over the **Eunice Museum**, next to the Hall of Fame at 220 S C.C. Duson Drive (Tues–Sat 9am–5pm; free) – though this too has its charms; it's an old train depot crammed with a ragbag of toys, musical instruments, farming implements, and Native American artifacts. However long you're in town, don't miss out on Eunice's splendid **food**. *Allison's Hickory Pit*, 501 W Laurel Ave (Fri–Sun 11am–2pm; ⓣ337/457-9218), and *Mathilda's Country Kitchen*, 611 St Mary St (closed Sun & Mon; ⓣ337/546-0329), specialize in tasty, home-smoked barbecue and plate lunches, while at *Ruby's*, downtown at 221 W Walnut St (closed Sun; ⓣ337/550-7665), you can eat home-cooked soul food in a vintage setting. Eunice is also central to the region's **music scene**. The regular Savoy Music Center and Liberty Center bashes (see p.656) are supplemented by the riotous annual **Courir du Mardi Gras**, when masked horsemen gallop through the countryside before parading through downtown, where the drinking and dancing continues all day. *Potier's Prairie Cajun Inn*, at 110 W Park Ave (ⓣ337/457-0440, ⓦpotiers.net; ❹), next door to the Liberty Center, is a 1920s hospital restored as a friendly **place to stay**.

From here it's twenty miles north to **VILLE PLATTE**, and the fabulous Floyd's Music Store, 434 E Main St (Mon–Sat 8.30am–4.30pm; ⓦwww.floydsrecords.com), owned by Floyd Soileau, the world's chief distributor of **South Louisiana music**, and stocking everything from zydeco reissues to contemporary swamp pop. A couple of doors down at the *Pig Stand*, 318 E Main St (ⓣ337/363-2883), giant plates of fried chicken, smothered sausage, and ribs come heaped with rice, gravy, black-eyed peas, and potato salad.

South of Lafayette

South of Lafayette, the towns are less immediately welcoming than those in the Prairie, but the surroundings are undeniably atmospheric: this is **bayou country**, a marshy expanse of rivers and lakes dominated by the mighty Atchafalaya swamp, where the soupy green waters creep right up to the edges of the highway. Unsurprisingly, the economy is based on fishing and shrimping, with hunting in the forests and sugar fields, but it's also a semi-industrial landscape, with a web of oil pipelines running beneath the waterways, and refineries and corrugated-iron shacks sharing space with white Catholic churches.

Settled in 1765, old **ST MARTINVILLE** on the Bayou Teche, off US-90 and 18 miles south of Lafayette, was a major port of entry for exiled Acadians. Hard to believe now, but in the nineteenth century this country town grew to become known as "le petit Paris," filled with French Royalists fleeing the Revolution. It was later decimated by yellow fever, fire, and hurricane, and is now a peaceful hamlet, kept going by a trickle of tourists. You'll see a lot of references to "Evangeline;" to find out why, head for **Evangeline Oak Park**, on Evangeline Boulevard where it meets the bayou. Here stands the **Evangeline Oak**, where real-life Acadian **Emmeline Labiche**, the inspiration for Longfellow's epic poem *Evangeline*, disembarked after her hard journey from Nova Scotia, only to hear that her lover, Gabriel, was engaged to another. The park, which has a boardwalk

Swamp tours

Swamp tours are available from many landings in the **Atchafalaya Basin**; you'll pass numerous signs pinned to the old cypress trees along the roadside. The basin is an eerie place: in some places cars cut right across on the enormous concrete I-10 above, and old houseboats lie abandoned. The best tours take you further out, to the backwoods; wherever you go you'll see scores of fishing boats and plenty of wildlife, including sunbathing alligators. The tours below are conducted by Cajuns who see the basin as more than just a tourist attraction and provide fascinating personal commentaries.

The Atchafalaya Experience 338 N Sterling St, Lafayette ⓣ337/261-5150, ⓦwww.theatchafalayaexperience.com. The son in this father-son team is a geologist; both guides are lifelong explorers of the swamp, and tours are ecologically sensitive. Daily 9.30am; 3hr 30min (2hr touring the swamp itself); reservations required; $50.

Bryan Champagne Lake Martin Landing, Rookery Rd, Breaux Bridge ⓣ337/845-5567, ⓦwww.champagnesswamptours.com. Champagne navigates a small crawfish skiff through the bird-rich Cypress Island Swamp – lots of opportunity for alligator-spotting. Tours daily; call for schedules; 2hr; $20.

McGee's Swamp Tours McGee's Landing, 1337 Henderson Levee Rd, Breaux Bridge ⓣ337/228-2384, ⓦwww.mcgeeslanding.com. Twenty-five minutes from Lafayette (take I-10 to exit 115, then highways 347 and 352), this quiet landing offers leisurely tours run from Henderson Swamp, a top fishing spot, as well as live music (see p.656). Daily 10am, 1pm & 3pm; 90min; reservations recommended; $20.

along the bayou, also features the **St Martinville Cultural Heritage Center** (daily 10am–4.30pm; $2), where the **Museum of the Acadian Memorial** pays tribute to the thousands of refugees displaced from Canada to Louisiana between 1764 and 1788, and the **African-American Museum** focuses on the arrival of enslaved Africans into southwest Louisiana during the 1700s, the emergence of free people of color, and the violence of Reconstruction. The nineteenth-century St Martin de Tours **Catholic church**, at 133 Main St, contains a carved font said to have been a gift from Louis XVI and Marie Antoinette, and a peculiar replica of the Grotto of Lourdes, built in the late 1870s; next door, the off-beat **Petit Paris Museum** exhibits local Mardi Gras costumes (daily 9.30am–4.30pm; $1). On the bayou just north of town on Hwy-31, the **Longfellow-Evangeline State Historic Site** (daily 9am–5pm; $2) features a couple of simple **Acadian dwellings** and, in contrast, an 1815 **Creole Plantation House**, made with the *bousillage* mixture (mud, Spanish moss, and animal hair) characteristic of early Louisiana buildings. If St Martinville's sleepy charm wins you over, and you want to **stay**, try the *Old Castillo*, 220 Evangeline Blvd, next to the Evangeline Oak (ⓣ318/394-4010 or 1-800/621-3017, ⓦwww.oldcastillo.com; ④), a B&B with huge rooms. *Le Petit Paris Café*, opposite the church at 116 S Main St (ⓣ337/394-7159), serves light lunches and gourmet coffee. For evening **meals**, you'll do better off around Lafayette and Breaux Bridge.

Northern Louisiana

Northern Louisiana is at the heart of the region known as the **Ark-La-Tex**, where the cottonfields and soft vocal drawl of the Deep South Bible Belt merges with the ranches, oil, and country music of Texas and the forested hills of Arkansas. Settled by the Scottish and Irish after the Louisiana Purchase, the area is strongly Baptist, with less of a penchant for fun than southern Louisiana, though it does share its profusion of **festivals**.

Angola Prison

Isolated at the end of the long and lonely Hwy-60, hemmed in by the Tunica foothills and the Mississippi River some sixty miles northwest of Baton Rouge, **Angola** – or "the farm" as it is commonly known – is the most famous maximum-security prison in the United States, its very name a byword for brutality and desperation. Famous inmates have included blues singer **Leadbelly**, who, as Huddy Ledbetter, served here in the 1930s; today it holds about five thousand prisoners, 77 percent of whom are black. Most of the men are lifers, and around a hundred of them are on Death Row. Outside the main gate, the **Angola Museum** (Tues–Fri 8am–4.30pm, Sat 9am–5pm; free) offers a fascinating insight into this unhappy place. Fading photos and old newspapers reveal appalling prison conditions; the prodding sticks and belts used to beat convicts bring it closer to home.

Since 1970, Angola has staged a **prisoner rodeo** every Sunday in October, an unsettling gladiatorial spectacle which draws thousands (there is also a two-day rodeo in April; both $10; reservations required; ⓣ225/655-2030, ⓦangolarodeo.com). These are extraordinary affairs, the crowds baying while lifers are flung, gored, or trampled in their struggle for glory or maybe just a simple change of scene.

Natchitoches

Tiny **NATCHITOCHES** (pronounced "Nakitish"), in the sleepy cottonfields of the Cane River, is the oldest European settlement in Louisiana, having begun life as a French trading post in 1714. A Catholic oasis, it was swiftly fortified when its Spanish and Native American customers started to combine aggression with commerce.

With lovingly restored Creole architecture, Natchitoches's **Front Street**, on the river, bears a passing resemblance to New Orleans's French Quarter – its lacy iron balconies, spiral staircases, and cobbled courtyards are complemented by friendly, old-style stores. Fleurs-de-lis on the **St Denis Walk of Honor** commemorate celebrities with local connections, such as John Wayne, Clementine Hunter (see p.661), and the cast of the movie *Steel Magnolias*, which was set and filmed here in 1988. It's worth a trip to nearby **CLOUTIERVILLE** (pronounced "Cloochy-ville"), where the quirky **Bayou Folk Museum** (Mon–Sat 10am–5pm, Sun 1–5pm; $5), housed in novelist **Kate Chopin**'s old home, is filled with all manner of local oddities. There's plenty relating to Chopin herself, whose nineteenth-century works, in particular her novel *The Awakening*, about a married woman's desire for independence, shocked the nation.

Practicalities

Natchitoches lies 140 miles northeast of Lafayette, on Hwy-6 off I-49. Greyhound buse stop at a gas station where the two highways meet; note that the town has **no public transportation** or taxis. This is **B&B** territory: one of the most luxurious is the *Judge Porter House*, 321 Second St (ⓣ318/352-9206, ⓦwww.judgeporterhouse.com; ⑤).

The helpful **visitor center**, 781 Front St (daily 9am–5pm; ⓣ1-800/259-1714, ⓦwww.historicnatchitoches.com),_provides self-guided **walking tours** of the historic downtown. The best place to **eat** is *Lasyone's* (ⓣ318/352-3353), around the corner at 622 Second St, which specializes in delicious meat pies, cream pies, red beans and sausage, and fresh, crumbly cornbread.

Cane River National Heritage Area

The **Cane River National Heritage Area**, a collection of restored plantation homes, churches, and forts, stretches for 35 miles south from Natchitoches. Head first for the fascinating **Melrose Plantation**, on Hwy-119 (daily noon–4pm; $8), which was granted in 1794 to Marie Therese Coincoin, a freed slave, by her owner, Thomas Metoyer – the father of ten of her fourteen children. Coincoin assembled the original grounds and additional land grants into an eight-hundred-acre plantation; she was later able to buy freedom for two of her children and one of her grandchildren. Around 1900, enterprising Melrose owner "Miss Cammie" Henry turned the crumbling plantation into an arts community, visited by painters and writers such as William Faulkner and John Steinbeck. In the 1940s, a black Melrose cook, **Clementine Hunter**, began to paint vivid images of life on and around the plantation; her works have since become valuable pieces of folk art. Many of them are on show in the 1800 **African House**, originally used as the slave jail, and in the **Big House**, a typical plantation home, made from brick and *bousillage*.

9

Texas

AL - ALABAMA	IN - INDIANA	MN - MINNESOTA	RI - RHODE ISLAND
AR - ARKANSAS	LA - LOUISIANA	MS - MISSISSIPPI	SC - SOUTH CAROLINA
CT - CONNECTICUT	MA - MASSACHUSETTS	NC - NORTH CAROLINA	VA - VIRGINIA
DE - DELAWARE	MD - MARYLAND	NH - NEW HAMPSHIRE	VT - VERMONT
FL - FLORIDA	ME - MAINE	NJ - NEW JERSEY	WI - WISCONSIN
IL - ILLINOIS	MI - MICHIGAN	PA - PENNSYLVANIA	WV - WEST VIRGINIA

CHAPTER 9 **Highlights**

* **The Menil Collection, Houston** A staggering collection of ancient and modern artworks – plus the somber Rothko Chapel – in a lovely, leafy setting. See p.670

* **The Rio Grande Valley** Tiny, historic border towns dot one of the least-visited regions of the state. See p.676

* **Fort Worth** From cattle drives in the rootin'-tootin' Stockyards, to world-class galleries in the Cultural District, Fort Worth is Texas' best-kept secret. See p.696

* **Marfa** An improbable minimalist arts community in the middle of the West Texas desert. See p.705

* **Big Bend National Park** The Rio Grande rushes through astonishing canyons in this remote wilderness, criss-crossed by well-maintained trails. See p.706

▲ Big Bend National Park

9

Texas

Still cherishing the memory that it was from 1836 to 1845 an independent nation in its own right, **TEXAS** stands **proudly** apart from the rest of the United States. While its 23 million residents are firmly bound together by a shared history, culture, and ideology, the sheer size of Texas – seven hundred miles from east to west and more than eight hundred from top to bottom – gives it a great geographical diversity.

The swampy, forested **east** is more like Louisiana than the pretty **Hill Country** or the agricultural plains of the northern **Panhandle**, and the tropical **Gulf Coast** has little in common with the mountainous **deserts** of the west. Changes in **climate** are equally dramatic: snow is common in the Panhandle, whereas the humidity of Houston is only made bearable by nonstop, high-powered air conditioning.

There are 128 cities with populations of 100,000 or more, and each of the major tourist destinations is unique. Hispanic **San Antonio**, for example, with its Mexican population and rich history, has a laidback feel absent from **Houston** or **Dallas**, while trendy **Austin** revels in a lively music scene and intellectualism found nowhere else in the state.

One thing shared by the whole of Texas is the constant boasting: everything has to be bigger and better than anywhere else. Such chauvinism is tempered both by the state's melting pot of cultures and by a very healthy dose of self-parody.

Some history

Early inhabitants of Texas included the Caddo in the east and nomadic Coahuiltecans further south. The **Comanche**, who arrived from the Rockies in the 1600s, soon found themselves at war when the **Spanish** ventured in looking for gold. In the 1700s, the Spanish began to build **missions** and forts, although these had minimal impact on the indigenous population's nomadic way of life. When Mexico won its independence from Spain in 1821, it took Texas with it as part of the deal. At first, the Mexicans were keen to open up their land, and offered generous incentives to settlers. Stephen F. Austin established Anglo-American colonies in the Brazos and Colorado River valleys. However, the Mexican leader, Santa Anna, soon became alarmed by Anglo aspirations to autonomy, and his increasing restrictions led to the eight-month **Texas Revolution** of 1835–36. The romance of the Revolution draws legions of tourists to **San Antonio**, site of the legendary **Battle of the Alamo**, which, though a military disaster, presaged independence.

The short-lived **Republic of Texas**, which included territory now in Oklahoma, Kansas, New Mexico, Colorado, and Wyoming, served to define the state's identity, and in 1845 Texas joined the Union on the understanding that it could secede whenever it so wished. The influence, especially in the north and east,

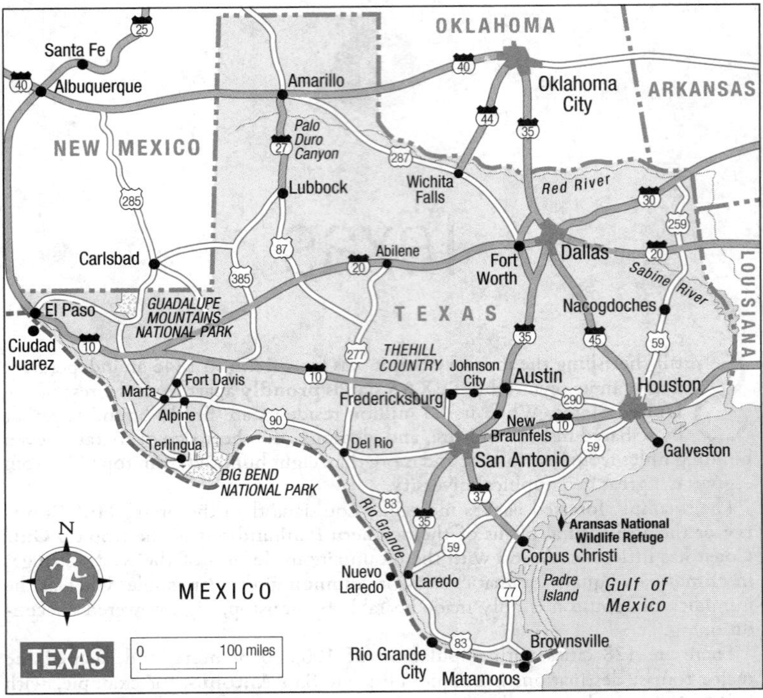

of settlers from the Southern states and their attendant slave-centered cotton economy resulted in Texas joining the **Confederacy**. During Reconstruction, settlers from both the North and the South began to pour in, and the phrase "Gone to Texas" was familiarly applied to anyone fleeing the law, bad debts, or unhappy love affairs. This was also the period of the great cattle drives, when the longhorns roaming free in the south and west of Texas were rounded up and taken to the railroads in Kansas. The Texan – and national – fascination with the romantic myth of the **cowboy** has its roots in this era, and still prevails; today his regalia – Stetson, boots, and bandana – is virtually a state costume.

Along with ranching and agriculture, **oil** has been crucial. After the first big gusher in 1901, at Spindletop on the Gulf Coast, the focus of the Texas economy shifted almost overnight from agriculture toward rapid industrialization. Boom towns flew up as wildcatters chased the wells, and millions of dollars were made as ranchers, who had previously thought their land only fit for cattle, sold out at vast profit. Texas today produces one-fifth of all the domestic oil in the United States, and the sight of nodding pump jacks is one of the state's most potent images. Even **George W. Bush** was a West Texas oilman before ascending to the governor's office and then to the presidency. But the state's commitment to renewable energy is becoming a part of the landscape, too, as gleaming white **wind turbines** sprout up like mushrooms in the Panhandle-Plains region.

Getting around Texas

Texas distances are best negotiated by **car**, and in Houston driving is all but essential. Mass transit has proved impractical in a state with long commuting distances and gasoline prices that are historically lower than the national average. **Cycling** makes sense within cities like Austin and San Antonio, and rentals are available from bike shops. **Greyhound** routes are concentrated between the major cities of the east and the central region, though buses also serve the Gulf Coast, the Rio Grande Valley, West Texas, and the Panhandle. Two **Amtrak** trains pass through Texas: *The Texas Eagle* travels between Chicago and San Antonio, stopping in Dallas and Austin; while the *Sunset Limited* stops in Beaumont, Houston, San Antonio, Alpine, and El Paso on its way between New Orleans and Los Angeles. Given the vast distances, **flying** can save time and is relatively cheap if price wars flare up.

Southern Texas and the Gulf Coast

The coastline of **Texas** curves more than 300 miles from Port Arthur on the Louisiana border (a shipping and petrochemical town and the birthplace of Janis Joplin) to the Rio Grande, which acts as the border with Mexico. **Houston**, with its cosmopolitan population and thriving arts scene, dominates the region, while the smaller population centers of Galveston, Corpus Christi and South Padre Island offer easy beach access. Houston and Galveston were both hit hard by **Hurricane Ike** in September 2008. Although much of the coast is feeling the strain of rapid property development for retired "Winter Texans" from the Midwest, there are still unspoiled stretches of compact, fine sand, particularly south of Corpus along the **Padre Island National Seashore**.

Houston

HOUSTON is a city whose very existence has always depended on wild speculation and boom-and-bust excess. Founded on a muddy mire in 1837 by two real estate-booster brothers from New York – their dream was to establish it as the capital of the new Republic of Texas – Houston was soon superseded by the more promising site of Austin, even while somehow establishing itself as a commercial center. **Oil**, discovered in 1901, became the foundation, along with cotton and real estate, of vast private fortunes, and over the next century wildly wealthy philanthropists poured cash into swanky galleries and showpiece skyscrapers. That colossal self-confidence helped Houston weather devastating oil crises in the 1980s, and more recently it has endured the **Enron** corporate scandal and, in September 2008, **Hurricane Ike**, which pounded the city and sucked windows out of downtown skyscrapers.

Houston has also developed a small but growing workforce eager to bring **alternative energy** to scale, while several **megachurches** headquartered downtown – with celebrity pastors like the non-denominational Joel Olsteen – have become powerful social, cultural, and, in some cases, political forces. Some churches draw as many as 16,000 people to their Sunday services, which are open to the public. There are also several highly regarded **medical centers** in the city.

The fourth-largest city in the United States, Houston is an ungainly beast of a place, choked with successive rings of highways and high on humidity. Despite this, its sheer energy, its relentless Texas pride, and above all, its refusal to take itself totally seriously, lends it no small appeal. For visitors, its well-endowed museums, highly regarded performing arts scene, and decent nightlife mean there is always something to do.

Arrival and information

Downtown Houston lies at the intersection of I-10 (San Antonio–New Orleans) and I-45 (Dallas–Galveston), with most of what you'll want to see encircled by Loop 610. **George Bush Intercontinental Airport** (Ⓣ281/230-3100), 23 miles north, is the main hub for Continental Airlines, while the smaller, domestic **William P. Hobby Airport** (Ⓣ713/640-3000), seven miles southeast of downtown, just west of I-45, is a major hub for Southwest. You'll need to **rent a car** to see the best of Houston; all the major companies are represented at the airports. **Taxis** downtown cost about $50 from Intercontinental, $35 from Hobby. The SuperShuttle **van** (starting at $23 from Intercontinental, $19 from Hobby; Ⓣ1-800/BLUE-VAN, Ⓦwww.supershuttlehouston.com) drops off at hotels downtown and near the Galleria mall, west of downtown. **METRObus** also offers routes from both airports.

Amtrak arrives at 902 Washington Ave, on the western fringes of downtown. The modern **Greyhound** terminal is at 2121 Main St.

For brochures and maps, the **tourist office** is located on the first floor of City Hall, 901 Bagby St (Mon–Sat 9am–4pm; Ⓣ713/437-5200, Ⓦwww.visithoustontexas.com). If you want to connect to the internet, downtown has free wi-fi, and a library branch is adjacent to City Hall.

City transportation

While Houston's **public transit** system is woefully inadequate for a city of its size, visitors might get use out of its downtown **METRORail tram,** which runs north-south for about eight miles – mostly along Main and Fanin streets, between UH and Reliant Park. The Museum District stop is in the middle. Many riders don't bother purchasing $1 honor system tickets. METRO also operates dozens of **bus** routes (Ⓣ713/635-4000, Ⓦwww.ridemetro.org). **Taxis** are expensive, and the humid climate and huge distances make walking unappealing. If you can, rent a **car**. With Houston's wide shoulders, **bikes** are another option. The Houston Bicycle Company at 404½ Westheimer (Ⓣ713/522-4622, Ⓦwww.houstonbicyclecompany.com) rents three-speeds for $25 a day. Bikes can be placed on the front of buses.

Accommodation

Inexpensive **hotels** are concentrated in three areas: near Reliant Stadium, and outside the Loop along either I-45 or I-10. **Upmarket**, business-oriented chains abound downtown and near the Galleria. **Bed-and-breakfasts** offer a welcome alternative in a city as potentially alienating as Houston, and there are a few **budget options**.

Downtown YMCA 1600 Louisiana St ⓣ713/758-9250. Clean single rooms with shared shower start at $35. A great location if you don't have to park a car.

Houston International Hostel 5302 Crawford St ⓣ713/523-1009, ⓦwww.houstonhostel.com. Guests are asked to help clean, so this hostel is grubby. But it's in a decent neighborhood, with the Museum District tram stop six blocks away; dorm beds from $15.

La Colombe d'Or 3410 Montrose Blvd ⓣ713/524-7999, ⓦwww.lacolombedor.com. With just six rooms and an ideal location near the museums, this quaint but luxurious property may be the best hotel in town. If you can't afford a room, grab a cocktail at the small bar. ❼

The Lancaster 701 Texas Ave ⓣ1-800/231-0336, ⓦwww.thelancaster.com. Lady Bird Johnson's Houston hotel of choice is situated in the heart of the Theater District. ❻

Lovett Inn 501 Lovett Blvd ⓣ713/522-5224, ⓦwww.lovettinn.com. On a leafy avenue on the edge of the Montrose district, this historic house offers large, comfortable rooms, first-class service, and an abundant continental breakfast. ❹

The City

It's unwise to try and see too much of Houston in one go. If you have just a short time, concentrate on the superb galleries of the **Museum District** and **Hermann Park**, which are linked to **downtown**, some five miles northeast, by light rail. The city's human face is most evident in the **Montrose** area, which lies west of downtown and overlaps with the Museum District.

Uptown, also called the **Galleria** district after its massive upscale mall, is three miles west. Just outside the Loop, between West Alabama and Westheimer roads, the Galleria's three hundred or so shops and restaurants spread north along Post Oak Boulevard; there is little to do around here except shop and eat.

Downtown Houston

Houston's skyline remains a dramatic monument to capitalism, ambition, and glitz. The observation deck on the sixtieth floor of the **Chase Tower**, 600 Travis

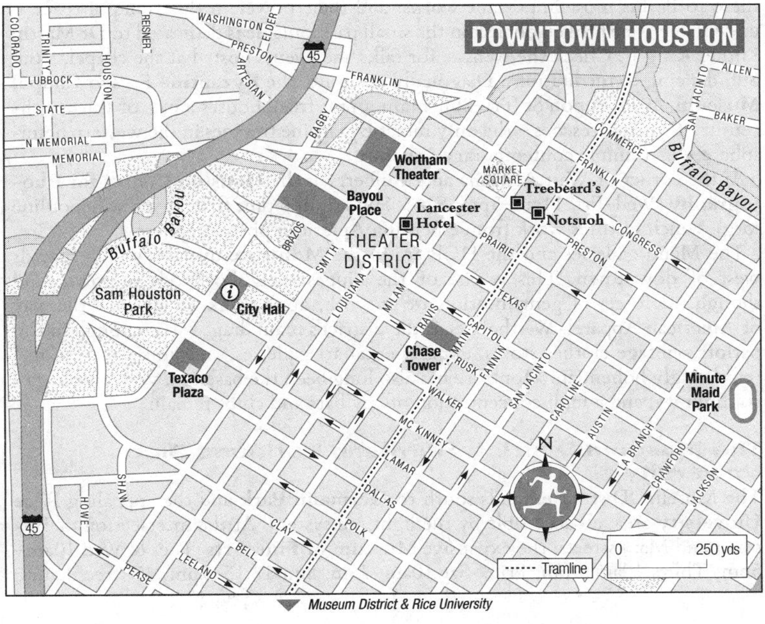

Museum District & Rice University

St, the highest building in the state, offers staggering views of Texas-sized sprawl. Also notable is the nearby Philip Johnson-designed **Penzoil Place**, 711 Louisiana St, while the lobby of the historic **JP Morgan Chase Building**, 712 Main St, is an Art Deco masterpiece.

Nestled below the skyscrapers, **Sam Houston Park** on Bagby Street (Tues–Sat 10am–4pm, Sun 1–4pm) is an appealing green space dotted with restored historic structures from all walks of nineteenth-century life (house tours leave from 1100 Bagby St; $6). Across the street is a reflecting pool that frames the postcard-perfect **City Hall**.

Many residents escape Houston's heat by staying underground, in the nearly seven miles of air-conditioned **tunnels** accessible from most downtown hotels and the visitor center. However, despite their shops and restaurants, they're a confusing and visually unappealing way to get around.

The Museum District: The Menil galleries and Montrose

Five miles southwest of downtown, the quiet oak-lined streets of the **Museum District** are enjoyable to explore on foot, a rarity for Houston. There are two main concentrations of exhibition spaces, with one entire complex dominated by the collections of oil millionaires **John and Dominique de Menil**. At 1515 Sul Ross St, a magnificent purpose-built gallery, designed by Renzo Piano, houses the private **Menil Collection** (Wed–Sun 11am–7pm; free; Ⓦ www.menil.org). Displayed in spacious naturally lit white-walled rooms, the superb works range from Paleolithic carvings to Surrealist paintings. Artists with rooms to themselves include Picasso, Max Ernst, and René Magritte. There's also a fine array of African art. A block east, the minimalist Ecumenical **Rothko Chapel**, 3900 Yupon St (daily 10am–6pm; Ⓦ www.rothkochapel.org), contains 14 somber paintings commissioned by the Menils from Mark Rothko shortly before his death. The artist, who worked with architect Philip Johnson in designing the chapel, considered these to be his most important works, and their power in this tranquil space is undeniable. The broken obelisk in the small park outside is dedicated to Dr Martin Luther King Jr. Check the website for talks and events hosted at the chapel, from Sufi dancing to meditations. Diagonally opposite, the **Byzantine Fresco Chapel Museum**, 4011 Yupon St (Fri–Sun 11am–6pm; free), houses a pair of thirteenth-century Cypriot frescoes – the only intact Byzantine frescoes in the western hemisphere – in a simple contemporary structure.

At the corner of West Alabama and Mulberry is the **Houston Center for Photography** (Wed–Fri, 11am–5pm; Sat & Sun noon–6 pm; free; Ⓦ www.hcponline.org), which features work from emerging American photographers.

The Menil galleries and the HCP are in the **Montrose** district, which spreads west of downtown. This is one of the hippest neighborhoods in town, and though the forces of gentrification are at work, don't think it's all gone the way of American Apparel. Westheimer is the district's main drag. It has enough tattoo parlors, vintage clothes stores, experimental art galleries, and junk shops to feel refreshingly bohemian. Montrose has also long been the base of a very visible **gay** community, and a high concentration of gay bars and clubs remain.

The Museum District: Hermann Park and Rice University

The Museum District extends south to **Hermann Park** and the appealing **Rice University** area, all accessible by the light rail system. At the intersection of Bissonet and Main streets, the expansive **Museum of Fine Arts** (Tues & Wed 10am–5pm, Thurs 10am–9pm, Fri & Sat 10am–7pm, Sun 12.15–7pm; $7, free Thurs;

ⓦwww.mfah.org) features an eclectic collection from all eras, filling its impressive buildings with everything from Renaissance art to rare African gold, with a couple of wings entirely devoted to decorative arts. Crane your neck upward from the Matisses and Rodins in the pine-shaded **Cullen Sculpture Garden** outside for a view of the downtown skyline.

The **Contemporary Arts Museum**, across Main Street at 5216 Montrose Blvd (Tues, Wed, Fri, & Sat 10am–5pm, Thurs 10am–9pm, Sun noon–5pm; free; ⓦwww.camh.org), is housed in yet another of Houston's showpiece buildings: a low-slung windowless corrugated-steel parallelogram. It hosts strong temporary exhibitions, with artists sometimes on hand to answer questions.

Pleasant **Hermann Park**, a few blocks south just beyond **Mecom Fountain**, has a Japanese meditation garden and is a nice place to grab an ice cream and go for a stroll. At the park's **Houston Museum of Natural Science** (Mon & Wed–Sun 9am–5pm, Tues 9am–9pm; $10; ⓦwww.hmns.org), near the Sam Houston monument, most exhibitions are geared toward kids. But at the museum's **Wiess Energy Hall**, you can pour crude oil over a cluster of clear marbles to learn, for example, that Middle East light crude is similar in viscosity to West Texas intermediate crude. As well, you can decide for yourself what technologies – such as solar, wind and geothermal – are most likely to ease the world's energy crunch. The museum's **Cockrell Butterfly Center** (daily 9am–5pm; $8) is a giant three-story greenhouse where you can walk among exotic butterflies as they flutter around a muggy rainforest environment. In a city built to such an inhuman scale, watching delicate butterflies dance about is a refreshing change of pace.

East Houston: The Orange Show and the Port of Houston

The Orange Show (Sat & Sun noon–5pm, summer also Wed–Fri 9am–1pm; $1; ⓦwww.orangeshow.org), five miles east of Hermann Park at 2402 Munger St, just off I-45 at the Telephone Road exit, is a strange affair. A triumph of folk art, it's not really a show but a suburban house transformed into a paean to the orange by the monomaniacal former postal worker and would-be inventor Jeff McKissack. With one simple purpose – "to get more people to eat more oranges" – McKissack spent twenty years covering his home with celebratory tiles, ironwork, and slogans. Run by the same folks but located on the opposite side of town is the **Beer Can House**, 222 Malone (Sat & Sun noon–5pm; $1, guided tour $5). Retired Southern Pacific Railroad upholsterer John Milkovisch and his friends guzzled some 50,000 beers to help give his home its shiny aluminum siding.

The **Port of Houston,** 7300 Clinton Drive, offers free boat tours of the fourth-largest port in the US (ⓣ713/670-2416, ⓦwww.portofhouston.com; Tues & Wed, Fri & Sat 10 am & 2:30 pm; Thurs & Sun 2:30 pm). The boat conducting the tour, the *M/V Sam Houston,* has an outside deck and air conditioning. Security is tight, and reservations are essential.

Eating

Houston's mixed population has left its mark on its **cuisine**: look for Mexican and Vietnamese restaurants, as well as steak and BBQ joints that rival any in the state.

Breakfast Klub 3711 Travis St ⓣ713/528-8561. Obama campaign staffers favored this busy breakfast spot when their office was located across the street. Serves unique dishes like wings and waffles, as well as more traditional morning fare.

Café Annie 1728 Post Oak Blvd ⓣ713/840-1111. If you've got the money, head to the best restaurant in Houston, which plates innovative Southwestern cuisine.

Goode Company 5109 Kirby Rd ⓣ713/522-2530. Good barbecue, with big portions of sliced beef brisket and outdoor seating.

Mai's 3403 Milam St ⓣ713/520-7684. Basic, cheap, and tasty Vietnamese and Chinese food.

Mi Sombrero 3401 N Shepard ⓣ713/862-7244. An authentic mom-and-pop Tex-Mex joint a few miles north of downtown. It's good value, with dinner plates that start at $6, and it's been around since 1978.

Pappas Bros. Steak House 5839 Westheimer Rd ⓣ713/780-7352. Leather booths, marble columns, mahogany paneling, and brass trim set the stage for you to devour an in-house, dry-aged slab of beef.

Nightlife and entertainment

There's no shortage of things to do in Houston; just check the listings in the free *Houston Press* (ⓦwww.houstonpress.com). Downtown's much-trumpeted **Theater District** (ⓦwww.houstontheaterdistrict.org), a 17-block area west of Milam Street between Congress and Capitol streets, includes the **Alley Theater** at 615 Texas Ave (ⓣ713/228-8421, ⓦwww.alleytheatre.org), which offers various discount seats, and the stunningly elaborate **Wortham Theater Center**, 510 Preston St (ⓣ713/237-1439, ⓦwww.worthamcenter.org), home to Houston's opera and ballet, among a host of others. The **Angelika Film Center**, 510 Texas Ave (ⓣ713/225-1470), shows art movies and has a sister screen in New York City.

AvantGarden 411 Westheimer Rd ⓣ832-519-1429, ⓦwww.avantgardenhouston.com. Small, classy bar with a commitment to live music. Listen to local neo-folk bands like the Sideshow Tramps blow the roof off the joint or sit outside by the outdoor fountain constructed out of recycled bottles.

Catbird's 1336 Westheimer Rd ⓣ713/523-8000. Laidback creative types swill Lone Star Beer at this convivial bar with a pleasant patio.

Continental Club 3700 Main St ⓣ713/529-9899, ⓦwww.continentalclub.com/houston. Cousin to the original in Austin, a classic live music venue on the light rail line.

Etta's 5120 Scott St ⓣ713/528-2611. Smokin' Sunday blues jams are the stuff of legend at this bar in a predominantly black neighborhood.

Leon's Lounge 1006 McGowan St ⓣ713/659-3052. The oldest continually operating bar in Houston, this unpretentious neighborhood dive has a friendly staff and a slightly feminine touch.

Notsuoh 2425 314 Main St ⓣ713-409-4750 Young artists and hipsters congregate at this downtown bar with regular live music, poetry readings, and wi-fi. Look for the old neon sign outside that reads "The Home of EASY CREDIT."

Around Houston

Houston's main attraction, **Space Center Houston** (Mon–Fri 10am–5pm, Sat & Sun 10am–6pm; $18.95, parking $5; ⓦwww.spacecenter.org) actually lies some 25 miles south of the city, off I-45 at 1601 NASA Parkway. **NASA** has been controlling space flight from the **Johnson Space Center** here since the launch of Gemini 4 in 1965 – locals love to point out that the first word ever spoken on the moon was "Houston." A working facility, the nerve center of the International Space Station, it offers insight into modern space exploration, with tram tours giving behind-the-scenes glimpses into various NASA compounds. But the crowds are overwhelming, and, with all the kids running around, it at times feels like Disney World.

San Jacinto Battleground (daily 9am–6pm), 22 miles east of Houston off the La Porte Freeway, was the site of an 18-minute fight in 1836 when the Texans all but wiped out the superbly trained Mexican army. The battle is commemorated by the tallest stone-column **monument** in the world (570ft, topped by a 34ft Lone Star). For $5 an elevator takes you to the top, which provides views of the battlefield.

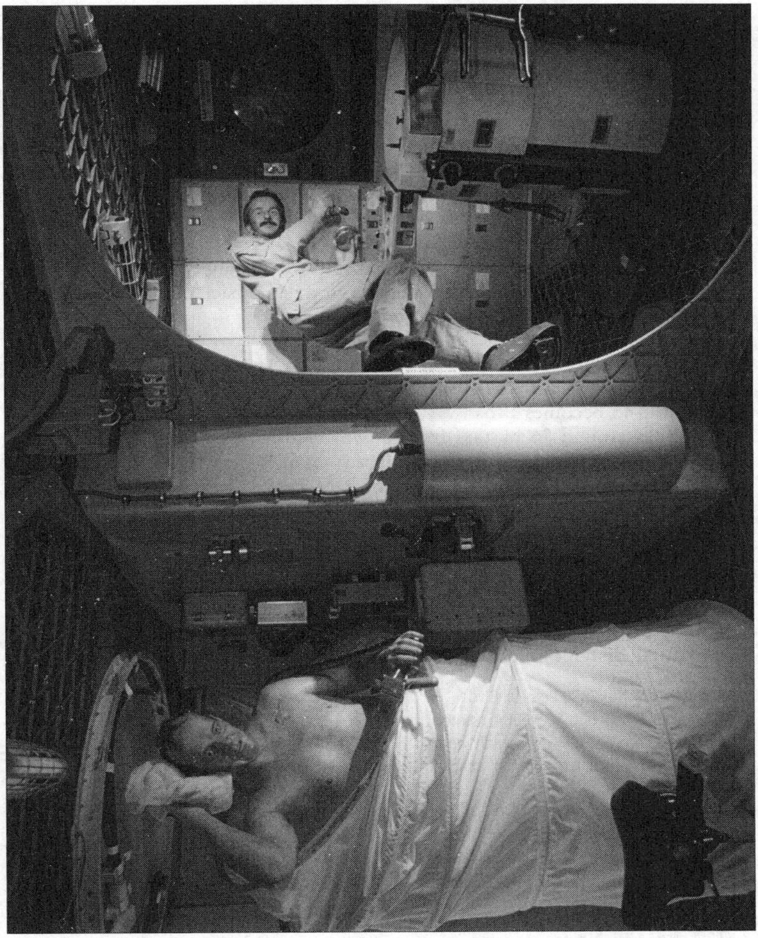

▲ Space Center Houston

The Gulf Coast

You only have to look at the number of condo developments along the **Gulf Coast** to see that this is a major getaway destination, one that was battered in 2008 by **Hurricane Ike**. The climate ranges from balmy at **Galveston** to subtropical at the Mexican border, but everywhere it's windy: **Corpus Christi** rivals Chicago as the gustiest city in the States, and devastating hurricanes in 1900 and 2008 all but leveled the city of Galveston. Recovery from the 2008 storm is ongoing, but Galveston still offers history, shopping, and low-key relief from Houston. Corpus Christi to the south makes the best base for the beaches of **Padre Island National Seashore. Rockport**, a weathered resort on Hwy-35, is convenient to the **Aransas National Wildlife Refuge**, a haven for endangered whooping cranes.

Galveston

In 1890 **GALVESTON** – on the northern tip of Galveston Island, the southern terminus of I-45 – was a thriving port, far larger than Houston fifty miles northwest; many newly arrived European immigrants chose to stay here in the so-called "Queen of the Gulf." However, the construction of Houston's Ship Canal, after the hurricane of 1900 killed more than 6,000 people and washed away much of the land, left the coastal town to fade slowly away. Thanks to its pretty historic district and its popularity with Houston residents seeking a summer escape, Galveston underwent a revitalization. Today its historic district echoes New Orleans, while its bars and edgy beach bums recall what Key West was when Jimmy Buffett began his career there. Still, things have changed since Ike swamped the seawall with a twenty-foot storm surge, and the town is trying to get back on its feet. Check all listings here to make sure they are current.

Arrival, information, and accommodation

Driving from Houston to Galveston is straightforward: once it crosses over to the island, I-45 becomes Broadway, the town's main drag. Greyhound arrives at 714 25th St (around $6 by taxi from downtown). There is no Amtrak service. The main **visitor center** is south of Broadway at 2027 61st St, with a smaller office in the historic **Strand** district, north of Broadway at 2215 Strand (both daily 8.30am–5pm; ⓣ1-888/425-4753, ⓦwww.galveston.com). **Trolleys** (daily 10.20am–6pm; $1; ⓣ409/797-3900, ⓦwww.islandtransit.net) rattle past the historic homes and main sights.

Hotels in Galveston are pricey in summer and on weekends, but bargains can be found at other times; rates along the coastal strip, **Seawall Boulevard**, can drop below $50 per night. Within easy walking distance of the Strand, the town's **East End historic district** holds some relaxing and luxurious **B&Bs**.

Gaido's Seaside Inn 3828 Seawall Blvd ⓣ409/762-9625 or 1-800/525-0064, ⓦwww.gaidosofgalveston.com. A clean, friendly, no-frills choice, with two good fish restaurants attached. ❷–❼

Galveston Island State Park 14901 F.M. 3005, ⓣ409/737-1222, ⓦwww.tpwd.state.tx.us/park/galvesto. Six miles from downtown, with 150 campsites, some facing the Gulf, starting at $20 a night. There are also ten secluded, screened-in lean-to shelters ($20) on the bay side.

HI Galveston 201 Seawall Blvd ⓣ409/765-9431. A good location and a stunning deck. Prices range from $19 for a dorm bed to $45 for a single room.

Hotel Galvez 2024 Seawall Blvd ⓣ409/765-7721, ⓦwww.galveston.com/galvez. Classy hotel, built in 1911, restored by the Wyndham group, with a beautiful pool and swim-up bar. ❺–❼

The City

The **Strand** downtown, the nineteenth-century "Wall Street of the Southwest," has been fitted with gaslights, upmarket shops, restaurants, and galleries. The **Texas Seaport Museum** nearby, in a complex of shops and restaurants on Pier 21, just off Water Street (daily 10am–5pm; $6), focuses on the port's role in trade and immigration during the 19th century; admission includes boarding the *Elissa*, an 1877 tall ship.

Between the Strand and the beaches to the south, Galveston boasts a profusion of historic homes open for guided tours. A standout is the ostentatious **Bishop's Palace**, 1402 Broadway (summer Mon–Sat 10am–4pm, Sun noon–4pm; rest of year daily noon–4pm; $8), with its stained glass, mosaics, and marble. Galveston's old Santa Fe depot, at 25th Street and the Strand, is now the town's **Railroad Museum** (March–Dec daily 10am–4pm, closed Mon Jan–Feb; $7), displaying steam trains, Pullman cars, and train-travel-related artifacts in a skillful evocation of a lost era. Look for the eerie white statues of travelers past in the waiting room.

Moody Gardens, Galveston's biggest attraction – for families, at least – lies on the west side of town, at I-45 off the 61st Street exit. The complex (daily: summer 10am–8pm; winter 10am–6pm) centers on three giant glass pyramids.

The downtown **beaches** of Seawall Boulevard are murky, rocky, and protected behind a 10-mile-long seawall from the ever-encroaching tides and the threat of further hurricanes. Slowly pedaling a **beach cruiser bike** along the seawall is a classic Galveston experience. Contact Island Bicycle Company, 1808 Seawall Blvd, for rentals (ⓣ409/762-2453; $28 per day). A few miles from downtown, **Jamaica Beach** is relatively quiet and a local favorite.

Eating and drinking

Dining out in Galveston will likely mean settling in at one of the many low-key seafood restaurants along Seawall Boulevard – their mix of fresh fish dishes and kitschy decor is strangely appealing. As Galveston likes to party, there are several **nightlife** options.

Casey's Seafood Café 3802 Seawall Blvd ⓣ409/762-9625. Very good local seafood dishes, like iced Gulf shrimp, start at $8 at this busy family restaurant. Also linked to *Gaido's* motel (see p.674) and the more upmarket *Gaido's* seafood restaurant.

MOD 2126 Postoffice St ⓣ409/765-5659. Hipster coffee shop downtown with free wi-fi .

Mosquito Cafe 628 14th St ⓣ409/763-1010. A local favorite, this tasty breakfast and lunch joint opened in 1999 and serves good salads and iced teas.

Old Quarter Acoustic Café 413 20th St ⓣ409/762-9199, ⓦ www.oldquarteracousticcafe.com. A great venue for folk, alt-country and blues; the late Texas singer-songwriter Townes Van Zandt wrote Rex's Blues about the café's owner, musician Rex Bell.

Poop Deck 2928 Seawall Blvd ⓣ409/763-9151. Great bar, if lame name. Sunsets are the specialty at this dive named after the nautical term for the roof atop the aft cabin.

Corpus Christi

The unabashed resort town of **CORPUS CHRISTI** is reached along the coast on Hwy-35 from Houston or Galveston, or on I-37 from San Antonio. Originally a rambunctious trading post, it too was hit by a fierce hurricane, in 1919, but recovered, transforming itself into a center for naval air training, petroleum, and shipping. Much of the population is Hispanic, and the community was devastated in March 1995, when the 23-year-old singer **Selena** was shot dead in a Days Inn parking lot by the former president of her fan club. Selena was on the verge of becoming the first major cross-over star of **Tejano** music, and 50,000 fans turned out for her funeral. The **Selena Museum**, 5410 Leopard St, is stuffed with Selena memorabilia, from her famously extravagant gowns to her red Porsche (Mon–Fri 9am–noon & 1–6pm; $2).

Corpus Christi is an outdoor destination, but apart from fishing, sailing, and watersports across the channel on Padre Island, there are a few diversions. The impressive collection of the **Art Museum of South Texas**, 1902 N Shoreline Blvd (Tues–Sat 10am–5pm, Sun 1–5pm; $6; ⓦwww.stia.org), focuses on fine arts and crafts of the Americas. The white Philip Johnson-designed building, renovated in 2005, is stunning, with windows that give close-up views of freighters navigating Corpus Christi Bay; look for dolphins riding the bow wake. The museum also has an excellent small lunch restaurant called the *Dobson Café*. Nearby at 1581 N Chaparral is tranquil **Heritage Park** (Mon–Thurs 9am–5pm, Fri 9am–2pm, Sat 11am–2pm; free), a collection of twelve Victorian homes and gardens and a nice place to sit a read a book.

Practicalities

There is a greyhound dog racing track in Corpus, but don't get that confused with the Greyhound bus station, which is located at 702 N Chaparral St downtown.

The **visitor center** is further along N Chaparral at No. 1823 (Mon–Fri 9am–5pm; ⓣ1-800/766-BEACH, ⓦwww.corpuschristi-tx-cvb.org). A daytime **trolley** (25¢; ⓣ361/289-2600, ⓦwww.ccrta.org) connects the major attractions with area hotels (except Sun); other services include a free downtown "Beach Shuttle" **tram** service (summer only) and a harbor ferry from Peoples Street to the Texas State Aquarium ($3).

Budget **motels** line tacky Corpus Christi Beach across the Hwy-181 bridge. Downtown at 601 N Shoreline Boulevard, the *Bayfront Inn* (ⓣ1-800/456-2293, ⓦwww.bayfrontinncc.com; ❸–❺) has average rooms and a good location. Downtown Corpus's main concentration of **restaurants** is on Water Street, and at No. 309 the busy *Water Street Oyster Bar* (ⓣ361/881-9448) serves fresh seafood. But the best place to eat is a few miles away at *The Yardarm*, a bayfront restaurant located in a cute yellow house at 4310 Ocean Drive (ⓣ361/855-8157). Two worthy downtown bars are the *Executive Surf Club*, 309 N Water St, and the three-year-old *House of Rock,* 511 Starr St, both of which have packed live music calendars.

Padre Island National Seashore

Padre Island National Seashore is not quite as unspoiled these days as its reputation might suggest, with its ranks of condos advancing steadily and a surprising amount of vehicular traffic on the beach itself, but it remains a good destination for birdwatching, fishing, beachcombing, and camping. Pick up details at the **visitor center**, 20402 Park Rd 22 (daily: summer 9am–5pm; rest of year 8.30am–4.30pm; ⓣ361/949-8068, ⓦwww.nps.gov/pais). The park is open 24 hours, with a $10 admission charge per vehicle, $5 for pedestrians and cyclists, good for one week. Camping on the beach is free, but permits cost $5 for the primitive Bird Island Basin and $8 for the semi-primitive *Malaquite Campground*. Note that an impassable channel divides the island, meaning that the pricier and much more touristy **South Padre Island** (see page 000) in the south can only be reached from the mainland – it's a three-hour drive from Corpus Christi.

The Rio Grande Valley

The **Rio Grande Valley**, at the southern tip of Texas, is one of the least visited but most fascinating regions of Texas. Actually a delta prone to flooding, the Rio Grande Valley is rural and historic country – two-hundred-year-old downtowns remain in many of the border towns sprinkled throughout the region.

Laredo

If you traveling toward the Gulf of Mexico, the best spot to start a tour of the Rio Grande Valley is in **LAREDO**, south of San Antonio. A busy bridge connects the US to Mexico at the bottom of Convent Avenue, where there is a major Border Patrol presence. Laredo has garnered a violent reputation in recent years as battles between Mexican drug cartels have escalated. Its main square is focused around the pretty St Augustin Cathedral, which has a modernist mural of the crucifixion inside and a stone grotto outside. Also on the main square, the historic and sprawling three-star *La Posada Hotel* at 1000 Zaragoza St (ⓣ956/722-1701, ⓦwww.laposadahotel.com; ❺), has comfortable rooms. There is a lobby bar favored by cocktail-drinking businessmen conducting cross-border deals and two courtyard pools. *El Mason* at 908 Grant St is a popular place to eat nearby, though you have to look hard to find the door. It has a daily menu and $5 meals.

Southeast along the Zapata Highway

Southeast down US Hwy-83, the two-lane **Zapata Highway**, is sleepy and friendly **SAN YGNACIO**, where yapping chihuahas roam the streets. The tiny town was once part of the Republic of the Rio Grande and remains a reminder of the independent streak that contributes to the complexity of the region. **ROMA**, 55 miles down the highway, has a strong architectural heritage and its downtown is home to several structures that were built in the 1800s in a nine-square block area; some date to Spanish rule in the 1750s. A birdwatching platform on sandstone cliffs near downtown looks across the Rio Grande toward Mexico; try to eye with your field glasses one of 500 species like the groove-billed ani. You can also hear children playing across the river once plied by steamboats. **RIO GRANDE CITY**, down the highway another twenty miles, has several motels and the *La Borde House* (Ⓣ956/487-5101; ❷), a non-profit historic hotel at 601 E Main St. It has clean, comfortable rooms decorated with period furniture, and the restaurant *Che's*, which serves breakfast. Run by the same family for seventy years, *Caro's*, 607 W 2nd St (Ⓣ956/487-2255), also serves excellent Mexican food.

Further southeast along the river toward the Gulf of Mexico is a booming **urban region**. With a population of 180,000, **BROWNSVILLE** is the biggest town, though **HARLINGEN**, 25 miles to the northwest, is the most pleasant to visit. Its downtown is walkable and active, with several art galleries, coffee shops, and cafés. The *Rio Grande Grill*, 417 W Harlingen, is a popular local diner, and Chop Shop Records, 103 W Jackson St, has a good selection of CDs from local hip-hop artists.

Port Isabel and South Padre Island

The graceful Queen Isabella Causeway connects **PORT ISABEL**, home to one of the biggest commercial fishing fleets in Texas, to **SOUTH PADRE ISLAND**, one of the biggest spring break destinations in the country. As you might expect, much of the island's activities don't extend beyond getting in the water or soaking up the sun's rays near it. Just off the beach, though, you can glean local knowledge from the friendly owners of the Beachcomber's Museum, 104 W Pompano St (Ⓣ956/761-5231), which is also a bookstore and coffee shop rolled into one. Ask Kay Lay to tell you about sea beans that wash ashore after drifting north from South American forests.

Though most visitors to the area make straight for the island, you can stay in Port Isabel at the elegant *Port Isabel Yacht Club and Hotel*, 700 Yturria (Ⓣ956/943-1301; check first to confirm that ongoing renovations are complete; ❹). On SPI a good option is the beachfront *Wanna Wanna*, 5100 Gulf Blvd (Ⓣ956/761-7677, Ⓦwww.wannawanna.com; ❹), which also has a friendly bar popular with locals. A more sedate choice is the *South Beach Inn* (120 E Jupiter; Ⓣ956/761-2471, Ⓦwww.southbeachtexas.com; ❸), which is a few blocks from the beach and has a pool. Watch the sunset and eat dinner at the secluded *Palm Street Pier* restaurant, which has west-facing views of the Laguna Madre and serves fresh shrimp dinners for about $10 (204 W Palm; Ⓣ956/772-PALM; Ⓦwww.palmstreetpier.com). After dinner, old salts and bikers belly up to the *Coral Reef Bar*, 5401 Padre Blvd, to groan, drink beer, and tip the pretty bar maid.

Central Texas

Central Texas stretches from the prairies of the northeast through the green and fertile Hill Country into the chalky limestone landscape of the west, and includes two of Texas' most pleasant cities: Hispanic **San Antonio** and the music-oriented state capital city of **Austin**.

Agriculture has been the economic mainstay here ever since the resistant Comanche population was finally packed off to reservations in the 1840s. The slave-driven cotton plantations of the south and east are gone, but the small communities set up by Polish, Czech, Norwegian, German, and Swedish immigrants in the **Hill Country** maintained, even until very recently, the traditions, architecture, and languages of their homelands. Great cattle drives came trampling through after the Civil War and played a large part in the development of San Antonio.

San Antonio

With neither the modern skyline of an oil town, nor the tumbleweed-strewn landscape of the Wild West, attractive and festive **SAN ANTONIO** looks nothing like the stereotypical image of Texas – despite being pivotal in the state's history. Standing at a geographical crossroads, it encapsulates the complex social and ethnic mixes of all Texas. Although the Germans, among others, have made a cultural strong contribution, today's San Antonio is predominantly **Hispanic**. Though now the seventh largest city in the US, it retains an unhurried, organic feel and is one of the nicest places in Texas to spend a few days.

Founded in 1691 by Spanish missionaries, San Antonio became a military garrison in 1718, and was settled by the Anglos in the 1720s and 1730s under Austin's colonization program. It is most famous for the legendary **Battle of the Alamo** in 1836, when General Santa Anna wiped out a band of Texas volunteers seeking independence from Mexico. After the Civil War, it became a hard-drinking, hard-fighting "sin city," at the heart of the Texas **cattle** and **oil** empires. Drastic floods in the 1920s wiped out much of the downtown area, but the sensitive WPA program that revitalized two of the city's prettiest sites, **La Villita** and the **River Walk**, laid the foundations for its future as a major tourist destination. Recently several massive hotels (think Vegas) have been constructed to accommodate the booming tourism and convention industries. The **military** has a major presence in San Antonio, too, with four bases in the metropolitan area.

Arrival, information, and getting around

San Antonio International Airport (Ⓣ210/207-3411, Ⓦwww.sanantonio.gov/airport) is just north of the I-410 loop that encircles most of the sights. **SA Trans Shuttle** (Ⓣ210/281-9900, Ⓦwww.saairportshuttle.com) makes the twenty-minute journey downtown ($18 single, $32 round-trip; every 10–15min 7am–1:30am), while **taxis** cost about $22 (Yellow Cabs Ⓣ210/222-2222). **Amtrak** arrives centrally at 350 Hoefgen St, while **Greyhound** operates from 500 N St Mary's St.

Pick up maps and information from the **visitor center** at 216 Alamo Plaza, in the *Menger Hotel* (daily 9am–5pm; Ⓣ210/225-8587 or 1-800/447-3372, Ⓦwww.visitsanantonio.com). **Driving** in San Antonio, which is Texas' second largest

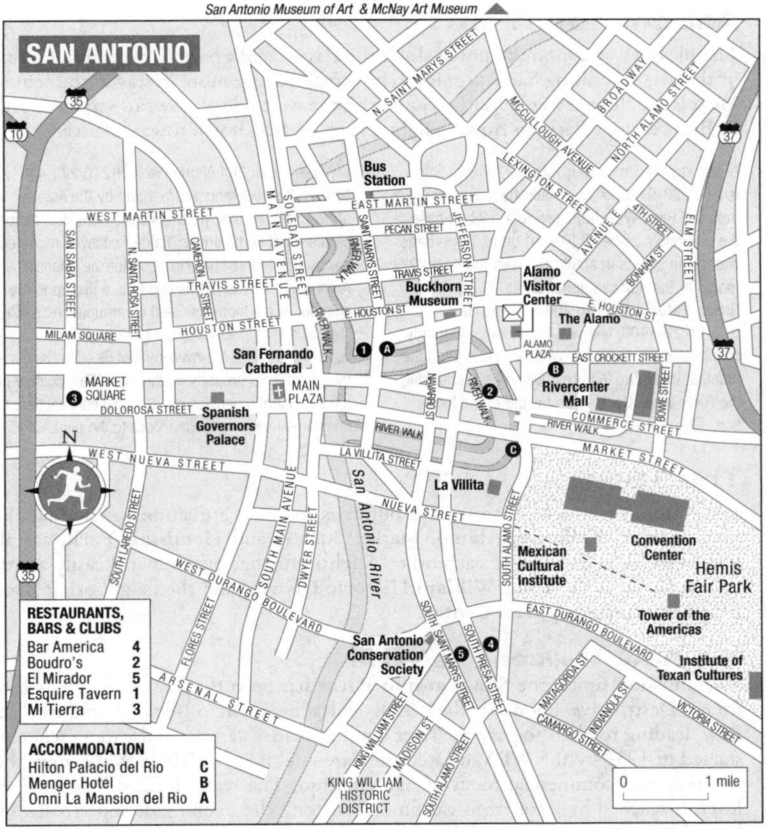

city, can be stressful and expensive – thankfully, most of the main attractions are in walkable distance from each other. Also, in addition to a relatively good bus network, four downtown **streetcar** routes from Alamo Plaza serve the major attractions (every 10min; $1). A one-day pass, available from the VIA Downtown Information Center, 260 E Houston St (Mon–Fri 7am–6pm, Sat 9am–2pm; ⓣ210/475-9008, ⓦwww.viainfo.net), costs $3.75 and can be used on all buses and streetcars. The **Alamo Trolley** offers a sixty-minute historic tour ($19.95; daily 9:30am–5pm; ⓣ1-800/868-7707, ⓦwww.sacitytours.net). A hop-on, hop-off pass costs $10 more and is a good way to spend time at some of the distant missions.

Boat tours (daily 9am–9pm; $7.75; ⓣ1-800/417-4139, ⓦwww.riosanantonio.com) make a 35-minute circuit of the San Antonio River's River Walk, departing from three locations: just below the bridge on Market Street opposite the *Hilton*; below the Commerce Street bridge near the Rivercenter mall; and behind the *Holiday Inn Riverwalk*. The same company also runs a **boat taxi**, which costs $4 single or $10 for a day-pass. The boats run on compressed natural gas.

Bikes can be rented from a small shop above the Blue Star Brewing Co. at 1414 S Alamo (ⓣ210-212-5506, ⓦwww.bluestarbrewing.com) and are an excellent option for exploring neighborhoods beyond the River Walk.

Accommodation

The pleasure of a moonlit amble along the **River Walk** back to your hotel is one of the joys of visiting San Antonio, so it's worth paying more to stay in the center. **Motels** are clustered near Market Square on the west side of downtown; just north of Brackenridge Park on Austin Highway; or on I-35 north toward Austin.

Bullis House Inn and Hostel 621 Pierce St ⓣ210/223-9426, ⓦwww.bullishouseinn.com. Far from the River Walk but close to a military base, the grounds smell a bit like cat urine. Dorm beds with clean sheets in an old Quonset hut cost $23; rooms at the adjacent inn start at $65.

Hilton Palacio del Rio 200 S Alamo St ⓣ210/222-1400, ⓦwww.hilton.com. Modularly constructed for the 1968 World's Fair in just nine months, this hotel features balconies overlooking the River Walk. Good value for the prime location. ❻

Menger Hotel 204 Alamo Plaza ⓣ210/223-4361, ⓦwww.historicmenger.com. Bang by the Alamo, this atmospheric historic hotel was a famous destination on the great cattle drives; Teddy Roosevelt recruited his "Rough Riders" here in 1898 for the Spanish–American War. The rooms don't quite live up to the glamour of the lobby, bar, and communal areas. ❻

Omni La Mansion del Rio 112 College St ⓣ210/518-1000, ⓦwww.omnihotels.com. Rooms at the nicest hotel property on the River Walk come with a full range of amenities and Spanish colonial decor, and some have courtyard access to the pool. ❽–❾

The Town

San Antonio is a delight to walk around, as its main attractions, including the pretty **River Walk**, the **Alamo**, Market Square, and **Hemisfair Park**, are all within strolling distance of each other. Slightly further out, but still easily accessible on foot, is the **King William Historic District** and the neighboring **Blue Star Contemporary Arts Center**.

The River Walk and La Villita

Since mission times, the **San Antonio River** has been the key to the city's fortunes. Destructive floods in the 1920s and subsequent oil-drilling reduced its flow, leading to plans to pave the river over. Instead, a careful landscaping scheme, started in 1939 by the WPA, created the Paseo del Rio, or **River Walk**, now the aesthetic and commercial focus of San Antonio. The walk, located below street level, is reached by steps from various spots along the main roads and crossed by humpbacked stone bridges. Cobbled paths, shaded by pine, cypress, oak, and willow trees, wind for two and a half miles beside the jade-green water, with much of the city's dining and entertainment options concentrated along the way.

La Villita ("little town"), on the River Walk opposite Hemisfair Park, was San Antonio's original settlement, occupied in the mid- to late eighteenth century by Mexican "squatters" with no titles to the land. Only when its elevation enabled it to survive fierce floods in 1819 did this rude collection of stone and adobe buildings become suddenly respectable. It is now a National Historic District, turned over to a dubious "arts community" consisting mostly of overpriced craftshops.

The Alamo

San Antonio's most distinctive landmark, **the Alamo** (Mon–Sat 9am–5.30pm, Sun 10am–5.30pm; free), lies smack in the center of downtown. Inextricably associated with the **battle** that took place here in 1836, a defining moment in the Texas struggle for independence against Mexico, the Alamo has been immortalized in movies and songs, and exists now as a rallying cry for Texas spirit.

Its fame, however, has little to do with its original purpose. It was built in the eighteenth century by the Spanish, the first in a trail of **Catholic missions** established along remote stretches of the San Antonio River. Each was laid out like a small fortified town, with the church as aesthetic and cultural focus. The goal was to strengthen Spanish control by "converting" the indigenous Coahuiltecan – in practice, using them as workforce and army. The missions flourished from 1745 to 1775, but couldn't survive the ravages of disease and attack from the Apache and Comanche, and fell into disuse early in the nineteenth century.

The infamous Alamo battle occurred on March 6, 1836, when 5,000 Mexican troops wiped out 189 rebels dreaming of Texas autonomy. Driven by the battle cry of "Victory or Death!", the besieged band – a few native Hispanic-Texans, adventurers like Davy Crockett and Jim Bowie, and aspiring colonists from other states – held out for thirteen days against the Mexicans before their demise.

Considering its fame, the Alamo is surprisingly small. All that is left of the original complex is its **chapel**, fronted by a large arched sandstone facade, and the **Long Barracks**. A stream of bus tours makes visits crowded and hectic, but for anyone curious about the state's unique brand of pride and stubbornness, the Alamo is unmissable. No response but absolute reverence is permitted – effectively this is a shrine, and a sign insists visitors remove their hats. The grounds, with four acres of lush blooms, palms, and cacti, are a haven from the commotion.

Other downtown attractions

For a jawdropping slice of kitsch Americana, the **Buckhorn Saloon and Museum**, 318 E Houston St (daily: summer 10am–6pm or later, winter 10am–5pm or later), can't be beat. During San Antonio's heyday as a cowtown, cowboys, trappers, and traders would bring their cattle horns to the original *Buckhorn Saloon* in exchange for a drink. The entire bar, a vast and lively Old West-themed space, has since been transplanted to this downtown location, where you can enjoy a mug of beer and a steak in the presence of hundreds of mounted horns. An extra floor ($12.99, with a money-back guarantee) displays a staggering collection of wildlife trophies and includes an informative and entertaining museum of Texas history.

It's a long walk on a hot day through the enormous **Hemisfair Park** – a sprawling campus of administrative buildings with scant lawns – to the **Institute of Texan Cultures**, 801 S Bowie St (Tues–Sat 10am–5pm, Sun noon–5pm; $7), but it's worth the trip. Mapping the social histories of 26 diverse Texas cultures, this lively museum has especially pertinent African-American and Native American sections. Also in the park, the **Mexican Cultural Institute** (Tues–Fri 10am–6pm, Sat & Sun 11am–5pm; free) hosts temporary exhibitions of historic and contemporary Mexican art, and the 750ft **Tower of the Americas** (Sun–Thurs 10am–10pm, Fri & Sat 10am–11pm) offers big views from its observation deck ($10.95).

San Antonio's Hispanic heart beats strongly west of the river. At 115 Main Plaza, the handsome **San Fernando Cathedral** is one of the oldest cathedrals in the US, established in 1731. Mariachi masses are held on Saturday at 5:30pm, when crowds overflow onto the plaza. **Market Square** (daily: summer 10am–8pm; rest of year 10am–6pm), a couple of blocks further northwest on W Commerce Street, dates from 1840. Its festive outdoor restaurants and stalls make it an appealing destination, especially during fiestas like Cinco de Mayo and the Day of the Dead. Fruit and vegetables are on sale early in the morning, while the shops are a compelling mix of color and kitsch. **El Mercado**, an indoor complex, sells tourist-oriented gifts, jewelry, and oddities.

The 25-block **King William Historic District**, between the river and S Alamo Street, offers a different flavor, its shady streets lined with the elegant late nineteenth-century homes of German merchants. It remains a fashionable residential area and has some stylish B&Bs; pick up **self-guided walking tours** outside the headquarters of the San Antonio Conservation Society, 107 King William St. The grassroots **Blue Star Contemporary Art Center**, further south at 116 Blue Star St, makes an appealingly rakish contrast to the rest of the neighborhood with its brewpub, workshops, galleries, and funky crafts stores. This cool complex is the center of the San Antonio arts scene, and it's a wonderful place to spend a few hours.

San Antonio Museum of Art and McNay Art Museum

The **San Antonio Museum of Art**, 200 W Jones Ave (Tues 10am–9pm, Wed–Sat 10am–5pm, Sun noon–6pm; $8, free Tues 4–9pm), occupies the old Lone Star Brewery north of downtown. It's full of treasures, with comprehensive Western Antiquity and Latin American collections.

A little further north, the **McNay Art Museum**, 6000 N New Braunfels Ave at Austin Highway (Tues, Wed & Fri 10am–4pm, Thurs 10am–9pm, Sat 10am–5pm, Sun noon–5pm; $8) is another treat. This exquisite Moorish-style villa, complete with tranquil garden, was built in the 1950s to house the art collection of millionaire and folk artist Marion Koogler McNay, and includes works from major players like Hopper and O'Keefe.

The Mission Trail

Any trip to San Antonio will include a visit to the Alamo, but for a real taste of early Spanish influence in Texas, make an effort to see the more distant, less visited missions. The **Mission Trail** (ⓦ www.nps.gov/saan) runs eleven miles south along the river from Alamo Street, down S St Mary's Street and onto Mission Road. Missions Concepción and San José are covered on the hop-on, hop-off **Alamo Trolley** tour (see p.679). Both can also be reached via bus 42 down Roosevelt Avenue; to get to the others you need to drive. Each mission has its own character, and acts as an **interpretive center**, illustrating some aspect of mission life (daily 9am–5pm; free); the churches themselves still serve active parishes. The main **visitor center** (daily 9am–5pm; ⓣ 210/932-1001) is at Mission San José.

Eating

San Antonio has good **Tex-Mex** food in all price ranges. Many visitors head straight for the restaurants on the River Walk, but, charming as it is to eat alfresco

▲ Mission San José

beside the river, don't be seduced to such an extent that you never venture above ground.

Boudro's 421 E Commerce St Ⓣ210/224-8484. This stylish River Walk Tex-Mex bistro serves creative New American/Southwestern entrees, a wonderful guacamole made at your table, and killer prickly-pear margaritas.
Casbeers 1150 S Alamo St Ⓣ210/271-7791 and 1719 Blanco Rd Ⓣ210/732-3511. Both locations offer good, cheap eats – enchiladas are a specialty – and happening bars.
El Mirador 722 S St Mary's St Ⓣ210/225-9444. Popular family-owned cantina serving very cheap Mexican breakfasts and lunches, and pricier Southwestern cuisine in the evening.
The Guenther House 205 E Guenther St Ⓣ210/351-6306. Light lunches, cookies, and cakes in an airy flour-mill-cum-museum in the King William Historic District.
La Reve 152 E Pecan St Ⓣ210/212-2221. One of the fanciest and best options in town, with an eight-course, $100 tasting menu.
Liberty Bar 328 E Josephine St Ⓣ210/227-1187. This inexpensive restaurant is so old that the building actually leans. Rotating menus feature specials like wild boar sausage.
Mi Tierra 218 Produce Row Ⓣ210/225-1262. With its bedazzlement of *piñatas*, fairy lights, and fiesta flowers, this festive 24hr institution is the highlight of Market Square, serving good, inexpensive Tex-Mex staples and delicious sugary cakes at their *panadería*. Great bar, too.

Nightlife and entertainment

With its abundance of picturesque settings, San Antonio is a great city for **festivals**. The year's biggest event is April's ten-day **Fiesta San Antonio** (Ⓦwww.fiesta-sa.org), marking Texas's victory in the Battle of San Jacinto, with parades, cookouts, and Latin music.

Downtown, the **River Walk** offers rowdy bars and clubs. Somewhat less touristy, **Houston Street** is fast becoming a party strip with a crop of slick yuppie bars, while **S Alamo Street** has a smattering of great dives and live music joints. Just a short drive away in the Hill Country you'll find some great old **rural dance halls,** including *Gruene Hall* in New Braunfels (see p.689).

Other possibilities are the outdoor **Arneson River Theatre**, on the River Walk opposite La Villita, where you can watch Mexican folk music and dance on a stage separated from the audience by the river, and **Aztec on the River**, 201 E. Commerce St, an opulent Art Deco theater that was renovated in 2008.

For **listings**, check the free weekly *Current* (Ⓦwww.sacurrent.com).

Bar America 723 S Alamo St Ⓣ210/223-1285. Three pool tables, two rows of booths with well-worn orange vinyl seating, and the best jukebox in town make this 30-year-old family-run dive a favorite for a cross-section of local residents. Lone Star pounders cost $1.50.
Beethoven Beer Garden 422 Pereida St Ⓣ210/222-1521. Just off of S Alamo St in the King William District, this private club (regularly open to the pubic) is devoted to the preservation of German song, music, and language. On the first Fri of each month, stop by for cheap beer and heaping portions of delicious potato salad.
Blue Star Brewing Company 1414 S Alamo St Ⓣ210/212-5506, Ⓦwww.bluestarbrewing.com. Home brews, food, and live music – from Texas swing to Latin – in a funky arts complex in the King William District.
Esquire Tavern 155 E Commerce St Ⓣ210/222-2521. This colorful old bar with dim lighting has been in operation since 1933. The jury is still out on whether a 2008 renovation will rob it of its charm.
John T. Floore Country Store 14464 Old Bandera Rd, downtown Helotes Ⓣ210/695-8827, Ⓦwww.liveatfloores.com. Old country dance hall 20 miles northwest of San Antonio, with great *tamales* and outdoor dancing on the weekend. The best bands in Texas play here regularly.
Menger Bar 203 Alamo Plaza Ⓣ210/223-4361. Cigar-smoking whiskey drinkers will feel right at home in this bar attached to the *Menger Hotel*, steps from the Alamo.

Austin

AUSTIN was a tiny community on the verdant banks of the (Texas) Colorado River when Mirabeau B. Lamar, president of the Republic, suggested in 1839 that it would make a better capital than swampy and disease-ridden Houston. Early building had to be done under armed guard, while angry Comanche watched from the surrounding hills, but despite its perilous location, the city thrived.

These days it wears its status as state capital lightly. Since the 1960s, this laid-back and progressive city – an anomaly in Texas – has been a haven for artists,

LBJ Library & Museum

AUSTIN

Harry Ransom Center

University of Texas

22ND ST · THE DRAG · UNIVERSITY · WICHITA · SPEEDWAY · SAN JACINTO
21ST ST
20TH ST

MARTIN LUTHER KING JR.
Blanton Museum of Art

W. 18TH · E. 18TH
W. 17TH · E. 17TH
W. 16TH · E. 16TH
W. 15TH · E. 15TH · E. 15TH
W. 14TH · E. 14TH
W. 13TH · E. 13TH · E. 13TH
W. 12TH · E. 12TH

RIO GRANDE · NUECES · SAN ANTONIO · GUADALUPE · LAVACA · COLORADO · CONGRESS · BRAZOS · SAN JACINTO · TRINITY · SABINE · NECHES · RED RIVER · DRISKILL

HOSPITAL
35
E. 12TH

State Capitol

W. 11TH · E. 11TH
Governor's Mansion
W. 10TH · E. 10TH
W. 9TH · E. 9TH
W. 8TH · E. 8TH
RED RIVER DISTRICT
W. 7TH · E. 7TH
Driskill Hotel
W. 6TH · SIXTH STREET · 6TH ENTERTAINMENT DISTRICT
W. 5TH · E. 5TH
WAREHOUSE
W. 4TH · E. 4TH
DISTRICT
Mexic-Arte Museum
W. 3RD · E. 3RD
W. 2ND · E. 2ND

Shoal Creek

W. CESAR CHAVEZ · E. CESAR CHAVEZ
DRISKILL
35

● **Stevie Ray Vaughan statue**

Colorado River
S. 1ST
Bat Colony
Town Lake

0 — 500 yds

RESTAURANTS, BARS & CLUBS

Antone's Blues Club	7
Bouldin Creek Coffee House	10
Cisco's	3
Continental Club	11
Esther's Follies	6
Guero's	9
Lambert's	8
Long Branch Inn	4
Sam's BBQ	2
Stubb's BBQ	5
Texas Chili Parlor	1
Threadgill's	12

ACCOMMODATION

Austin Motel	B
Driskill Hotel	A
Hi-Austin	C
Hotel San Jose	D

Book People & Waterloo Records

◀ Zilker Park ▼ South Congress, **B**, **C**, **D**, **9**, **10**, **11** & **12**

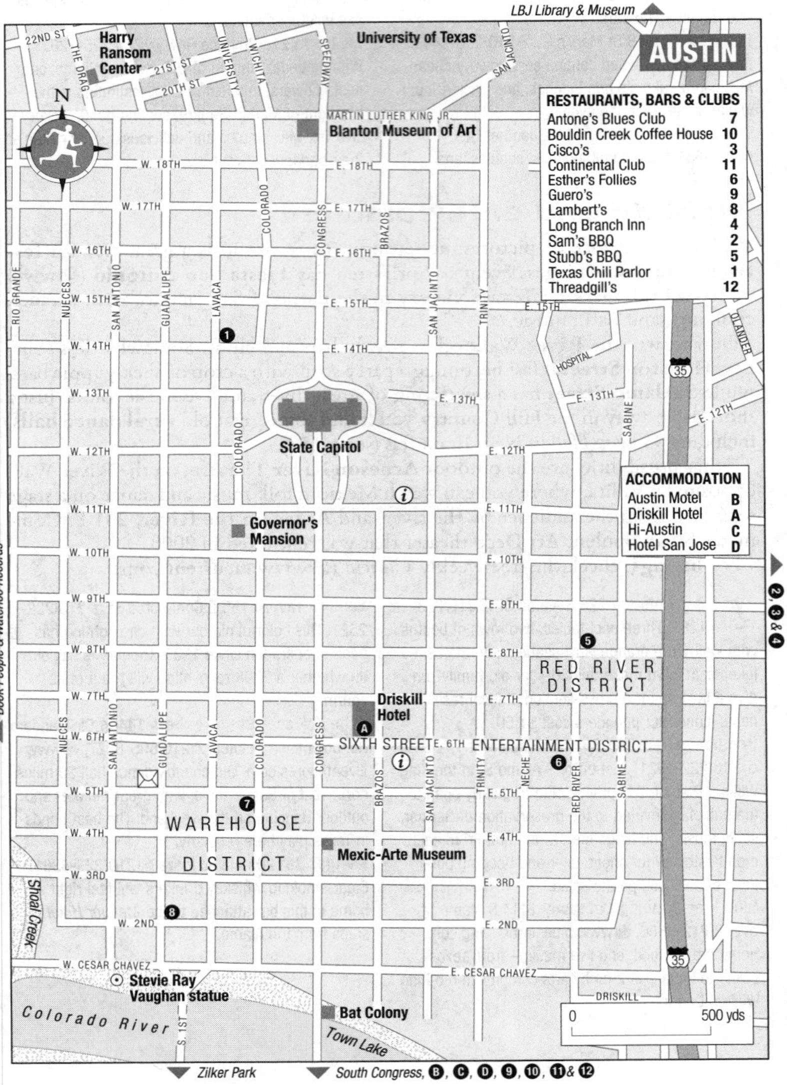

musicians, and writers, and many visitors come specifically for the **music**. And while a certain complacency has crept in, its "alternative" edge being packaged as just another marketing tool, artists hungry for fame are still attracted to this creative hotbed. Local musicians are renowned for their innovative reworkings of Texas' country, folk, and R&B heritage, using Austin's enthusiastic environment as a springboard to national recognition.

Due to a sizeable tech-fueled population leap, brand-new towering condo complexes have shot up to threaten Austin's small-town ambiance. Still, it remains one of the best cities in the state for **cycling** (Lance Armstrong lives here), and the presence of the vast and pretty University of Texas campus adds to the pleasant atmosphere. Within the city limits a great park system offers numerous hiking and biking trails and a wonderful spring-fed swimming pool. Looking further afield, Austin makes a fine base for exploring the green **Hill Country** that rolls away to the west.

Arrival and information

Austin spreads about 20 miles north-south and 18 miles east-west, severed by I-35 (between Dallas and San Antonio) to the east. The dammed Colorado River – called Lady Bird Lake (formerly Town Lake) where it abuts Congress Avenue – runs just south of downtown. Flights arrive at the **Austin-Bergstrom International Airport** (ⓣ512/530-2242, ⓦwww.ci.austin.tx.us/austinairport), eight miles southeast of downtown. From here it's about twenty minutes to downtown by **taxi** (Yellow Cab; ⓣ512/452-9999; around $28) or by SuperShuttle **vans** (ⓣ512/258-3826, ⓦwww.supershuttle.com; $12). **Bus** no. 100 runs from the airport to downtown. **Car rentals** are available at the airport.

The **visitor center** (Mon–Fri 9am–5pm, Sat & Sun 9.30am–5.30pm; ⓣ866/GO-AUSTIN, ⓦwww.austintexas.org) is located at 209 E 6th St.

City transportation and tours

Austin has a good **public transportation** system. The Capital METRO (ⓦwww.capmetro.org, ⓣ512/474-1200) runs **buses** downtown, crosstown, and through the campus for a flat fare of 50¢, or $1 for express buses. The Dillo, also run by METRO, is a free downtown **trolley** that snakes through downtown and the UT campus. A newly-opened **MetroRail** route runs north from downtown. You can rent **bicycles** from Bicycle Sport Shop, 517 S Lamar, just south of Barton Springs (Mon–Fri 10am–7pm, Sat 9am–6pm, Sun 11am–5pm; ⓣ512/477-3472, ⓦwww.bicyclesportshop.com) – reserve in advance if possible. Cruisers cost $22 for a 24-hour rental. Downtown Austin is a pleasant place to take a stroll; pick up free self-guided **walking tours** from the visitor center.

Accommodation

Austin offers a good variety of **places to stay**, with the usual budget hotels on I-35, some classy hotels downtown, a couple of hip choices on South Congress, a **hostel**, and a variety of **B&Bs**.

Austin Motel 1220 S Congress Ave ⓣ512/441-1157, ⓦwww.austinmotel.com. Basic rooms – each one different, many with kitschy murals – in a hip old motel in the funky South Congress district. A favorite with visiting musicians, it's across the street from the venerable Continental Club. 4

Driskill Hotel 604 Brazos St ⓣ512/474-5911, ⓦwww.driskillhotel.com. This handsome and historic downtown hotel is Austin's swankiest choice, with an opulent marble lobby and updated rooms. If you can't afford to stay here, drop by the lobby bar for a mid-afternoon whiskey sour. 8

HI-Austin 2200 Lakeshore Blvd ⓣ1-800/725-2331, ⓦwww.hiaustin.org. Bargain rates right on Lady Bird Lake. No curfew, and most of the young guests head out to 6th St at night. Dorm beds start at $19.

Hotel San Jose 1316 S Congress Ave ⓣ512/444-7322, ⓦwww.sanjosehotel.com. Chic and funky boutique hotel in the South Congress district. Restored from an old motel, it has a variety of minimalist rooms, some with shared bath, along with lovely gardens, a tiny pool, and a cool coffee shop, Jo's, on site. The courtyard happy hour attracts a local crowd for Micheladas, a spicy beer cocktail on the rocks. 4–9

The City

The **Texas State Capitol**, at 12th Street and Congress Avenue (Mon–Fri 8am–5pm, Sat & Sun 9am–5pm; free public tours usually every 15min Mon–Fri 8.30am–4.30pm, Sat 9.30am–3.30pm, Sun noon–3.30pm – but call to check on ⓣ512/305-8400), is over 300 feet high, taller than the Capitol in Washington, with a red sunset granite dome that accents the downtown skyline. The chandeliers, carpets, and even the door hinges of this colossal building are emblazoned with Lone Stars and other Texas motifs. Nearby, the antebellum **Governor's Mansion**, 1010 Colorado St, is the governor's official Texas residence. Arsonists torched the place in June 2008, and tours have been temporarily suspended.

Congress Avenue, an attractive stretch of shops and office buildings that slopes south from the capitol down to the lake, is worth a look. At 700 Congress is the **Arthouse** (Tues, Wed & Fri 11am–7pm, Thurs 11am–9pm, Sat 10am–5pm, Sun 1–5pm), a small space that features emerging Texas artists. **Sixth Street** crosses Congress one block south of here, and at night it is crowded with bar-hopping party people. If you're touring downtown during the day, cool off in the elegant lobby of the *Driskill Hotel*, at Sixth and Brazos, or visit the tiny **O'Henry Museum,** 409 East Fifth St (Wed–Sun noon–5pm; free), a period home dedicated to one of the literary lions of Texas; note the rosewood piano with mother-of-pearl inlay. A few blocks away, at 419 Congress, the **Mexic-Arte Museum** has a nice collection of traditional and contemporary Latin American art, (Mon–Thurs 10am–6pm, Fri & Sat 10am–5pm, Sun noon–5pm; $5; ⓦwww.mexic-artemuseum.org). If you're visiting between March and November, take a walk at dusk down to where Congress Avenue crosses Lady Bird Lake to watch 1.5 million **Mexican free-tailed bats** – the world's largest urban bat colony – emerge in a large black cloud from their hangouts under the bridge. You can smell the guano, and the best views are from the tour boats. Across the bridge, **South Congress** is a hip neighborhood of funky stores, bars, and restaurants. Southwest of here, the 350-acre **Zilker Park** is one of the best of the city's many fine green spaces, a perfect retreat on sultry Austin afternoons. One of its main attractions is the spring-fed (and deliciously cold) **Barton Springs Pool** ($3). Another appealing outdoor space, south of the Barton Springs Pool on Robert E. Lee Road, the **Umlauf Sculpture Garden** (Wed–Fri 10am–4.30pm, Sat & Sun 1–4.30pm; $3.50) is a tranquil, grassy enclave dotted with over a hundred works in bronze, terracotta, wood, and marble.

Back north of the Capitol, the **Bob Bullock Texas State History Museum,** adjacent to the University of Texas at Martin Luther King Jr Boulevard and N Congress, is a massive treasure trove of Texas arcane (Mon–Sat 9am–6pm; $7). Just west of downtown, at the intersection of N Lamar Boulevard and Sixth Street, are Waterloo Records (ⓣ512/474-2500, ⓦwww.waterloorecords.com) and Book People, the best music store and bookstore in town.

The University of Texas

The **University of Texas** – and its fiercely supported Longhorn football team, which plays on fall Saturdays at 94,000-seat Darrell K. Royal-Texas Memorial Stadium – has a tangible, almost defining, presence in Austin. You'll find most student activity in the restaurants, vintage clothing shops, and bookstores on the "Drag", the stretch of **Guadalupe Street** running along campus north from Martin Luther

King Boulevard to 24th. The campus itself has a number of attractions, too. Oil has made this one of the world's richest universities, and its purchasing power is almost unmatched when it comes to rare and valuable books. The university's collection of manuscripts is available to scholars amid tight security in the **Harry Ransom Center**. The Center, in the southwest corner of campus, houses a **gallery** (Tues, Wed & Fri 10am–5pm, Thurs 10am–7pm, Sat & Sun noon–5pm; free; Ⓦ www.hrc.utexas.edu) whose permanent collection includes a Gutenberg Bible and the world's first photograph. A quiet place on campus to sit and read a book is **Battle Hall**, which houses UT's architecture library; note the stenciled open-truss ceiling. The best views in Austin are at sunset from the top of the **Texas Tower**, near the corner of 24th and Guadalupe. (Ⓣ 1-877/475-6633, Ⓦ www.utexas.edu/tower; reservations for the $5 tours are required).

The **LBJ Library and Museum** (daily 9am–5pm; free; Ⓦ www.lbjlib.utexas.edu), on the northeast edge of campus at 2313 Red River St, traces the career of the brash and egotistical Lyndon Baines Johnson from his origins in the Hill Country to the House of Representatives, the Senate, and the White House. Forty-five million documents are housed here, and it's well worth a visit. JFK is said to have made Johnson his vice president to avoid his establishing a rival power base; but in the aftermath of Kennedy's assassination, Johnson's administration (1963–69) was able to push through a far more radical social program than Kennedy ever attempted. Johnson's nemesis, Vietnam, is presented here as an awful mess left by Kennedy for him to clear up, at the cost of great personal anguish.

Eating

Austin has some of the best restaurants in the state, and many have a focus on local ingredients. The greatest concentration is on **South Congress**; budget restaurants popular with students are scattered along the **Drag**.

Bouldin Creek Coffee House 1501 S 1st Ⓣ 512/416-1601. Breakfast made from scratch is served all day at this spot not far from South Congress. It has reasonable prices (a free-range, three-egg omelet with two sides costs $6.75) and friendly staff.

Cisco's 1511 E 6th Ⓣ 512/478-2420. This second-generation Mexican family restaurant is open for breakfast and lunch. Order the *migas* ($7) to chase away your hangover.

Guero's 1412 S Congress Ave Ⓣ 512/447-7688. *Tacos al pastor* are a specialty for about $9 at this busy, sprawling restaurant located across the bridge south of downtown.

Lambert's 401 W 2nd St Ⓣ 512/494-1500. Exercise your taste buds at this self-described fancy BBQ restaurant that puts a modern twist on the old Texas staple. Produce and meats are sourced from local farms and ranches.

Magnolia Café 1920 S Congress Ave Ⓣ 512/445-0000. A 24hr joint that's a local favorite for Tex-Mex and pancake breakfasts, and a great place to refuel after a night living it up on South Congress.

Sam's BBQ 2000 E 12th Ⓣ 512/478-0378. Austin residents will warn you about the neighborhood, but don't be scared when food like this is on the line – heaping portions of tender beef brisket and big glasses of sweet tea for $8.50.

Texas Chili Parlor 1409 Lavaca St Ⓣ 512/472-2828. Rub elbows with pols and their staffers at this venerable lunch spot downtown near the state capitol.

Threadgill's 6416 N Lamar Blvd Ⓣ 512/451-5440, Ⓦ www.threadgills.com. An Austin institution, north of downtown, established when Kenneth Threadgill was given the first license to sell beer in the city after Prohibition. Bringing together hippies and rednecks in the 1960s, Threadgill's was an incubator for the Austin sound, and still features live bands, as well as basic Southern cuisine.

Nightlife and entertainment

Austin's **nightlife** is legendary, and you're spoilt for choice for places to enjoy it. Though the clubs and bars of 6th Street have become touristy, there are plenty of good places elsewhere **downtown**, and it's easy enough to hop into a cab to some of the further-flung classic joints. Three local newspapers carry listings: the *Austin American-Statesman* (Ⓦ www.austin360.com); the *Austin Chronicle* (Ⓦ www.austinchronicle.com); and the *Daily Texan*, the UT paper (Ⓦ www.dailytexanonline.com).

Live music

Although Austin's folk revival in the 1960s attracted enough attention to propel Janis Joplin on her way from Port Arthur, Texas, to stardom in California, the city first achieved prominence in its own right as the center of **outlaw country** music in the 1970s. **Willie Nelson** and **Waylon Jennings**, disillusioned with Nashville, spearheaded a movement that reworked sentimental country and western with an incisive injection of rock 'n' roll. Venues in Austin, far removed from the hard-drinking honky-tonks of the Plains, provided an environment that encouraged and rewarded risk-taking, experimentation, and a lot of cross-breeding. These days the predominant "**Austin sound**" is a melange of country, folk, and blues, with strong psychedelic and "alternative" influences – but the scene is entirely eclectic. The tradition of black Texas bluesmen such as Blind Lemon Jefferson and Blind Willie Johnson, as well as the rocking bar blues of Stevie Ray Vaughan, still lives on, with a top-notch **blues** club in the form of *Antone's*.

Austin's ten-day **SXSW (South by Southwest) Festival** (Ⓦ www.sxsw.com), held in mid-March, has become one of the biggest music and film conferences/festivals in the nation. Attending a showcase of the best bands from Texas and around the world, along with tons of movies, is not cheap: passes for all film, music, and interactive events cost $850 in advance, increasing to $1200 for a walk-up rate; a music-only pass is $550 ($650 walk-up). Even if you can't afford to attend, the city is an exciting place to be during SXSW, with hundreds of unofficial gigs and events open to all. Another major event, showcasing folk, bluegrass, acoustic, blues, country, jazz, and Americana, is the **Kerrville Folk Festival** (Ⓦ www.kerrville-music.com), which lasts nearly three weeks in May and June. It's held on a ranch one hundred miles west of Austin in the small town of Kerville. You can camp and listen to live music under the stars.

Antone's Blues Club 213 W 5th St Ⓣ 512/320-8424, Ⓦ www.antones.net. This old Austin joint in the Warehouse District is the best blues club in the city, a hot and sweaty haunt showcasing national and local acts.

The Broken Spoke 3201 S Lamar Blvd Ⓣ 512/442-6189, Ⓦ www.brokenspokeaustintx.com. Neighborhood restaurant (good chicken-fried steak) and stomping honky-tonk dance hall in south Austin. The barn-like dance floor attracts great country acts; it's a lot of fun. Two-stepping begins at 9pm.

Continental Club 1315 S Congress Ave Ⓣ 512/441-2444, Ⓦ www.continentalclub.com. This longstanding classic is the city's premier place to hear hard-edged country or bluesy folk sung the Austin way.

Stubb's BBQ 801 Red River St Ⓣ 512/480-8341, Ⓦ www.stubbsaustin.com. Indoor and outdoor stages feature eclectic bands of national repute – including a Sun gospel brunch – which you can watch while chewing through great Texas-style brisket, sausage, and ribs.

Victory Grill 1104 E 11th St Ⓣ 512/902-505. Ike and Tina Turner played here, and a Brooklyn artists' collective spray-painted a soulful mural on its main outside wall in 2008. The old building, noted for its heavy blues history, hangs on despite nearby condo development.

Bars

Note that, like some of the restaurants listed, many of Austin's **bars** double as music venues.

Hole in the Wall 2538 Guadalupe St Ⓣ 512/477-4747. A dive near the UT campus with pool tables and live Americana music.

Horseshoe Lounge 2034 S Lamar Blvd Ⓣ 512/442-9111. This beer joint is a survivor from a not-too-distant, rough-and-tumble South

Austin past. Look for the red and green neon lights.

Long Branch Inn 1133 E 11th St ☎512/472-5477. This dark, artsy dive with a small stage, a nice old wooden bar, and slowly turning ceiling fans is located smack dab in the middle of a quickly gentrifying neighborhood.

Scoot Inn 1308 E 4th St ☎512/478-6200. Owned by the same folks who own the *Long Branch Inn*, the *Scoot Inn* attracts a similar but slightly younger crowd and has a nice outdoor beer garden.

Other nightlife

The independent and highly recommended **Alamo Drafthouse** (☎512/476-1230, Ⓦwww.drafthouse.com) has several locations and offers one of the best cinematic experiences in the US. The theaters feature everything from award-winning documentaries to air guitar competitions, plus pints of local beer and made-to-order food are served at your seat. There's usually something to catch on campus, either at the **UT Performing Arts Center**, 23rd Street and Robert Dedman Drive (Ⓦwww.utpac.org), or the **Cactus Café**, a bar and folk-oriented live music venue in the student union building. *Esther's Follies*, 525 E 6th St (Ⓦwww.esthersfollies.com) is Austin's hippest **cabaret**, which combines spoofs of local and national politicians with Texas-style singing and dancing.

The Hill Country

The rolling hills, lakes, and valleys of the **HILL COUNTRY**, north and west of Austin and San Antonio, were inhabited mostly by Apache and Comanche until after statehood, when German and Scandinavian settlers arrived. Many of the log-cabin farming communities they established are still here, such as **New Braunfels** (famous for its sausages and pastries, and, more recently, its watersports) and Luckenbach. You may still hear German spoken, and the German influence is also felt in local food and music; *conjunto*, for example, is a blend of Tex-Mex and accordion music. The whole region is a popular retreat and resort area, with some wonderful hill views and lake swimming, and a lot of good places to camp.

New Braunfels

NEW BRAUNFELS, just 30 miles north of San Antonio on I-35, was founded by German immigrants – mostly artisans and artists – in 1845 and quickly became a trade center. Nowadays, the community, along with its equally historic satellite, **Gruene**, just northeast, makes its living from tourism. The town's two rivers – the Comal and the Guadalupe – are ideal for easy **rafting** and tubing, making this a popular weekend destination.

If outdoor activities don't appeal, downtown's historic district has enough antique stores, galleries, and restored buildings to fill a couple of hours. New Braunfels' **visitor center**, off I-35 at exit 187 (Mon–Fri 8am–5pm; 1-800/572-2626, Ⓦwww.nbjumpin.com), provides a list of accommodation, as well as information on renting rafts and tubes. Should you need **to stay**, the *Heidelberg Lodges* (☎830/625-9967, Ⓦwww.heidelberglodges.com), 1020 N Houston St, are rustic, and their riverfront location makes them a bargain. For **food**, head for *Huisache Grill*, 303 W San Antonio St (☎830/620-9001), for sophisticated, reasonably priced contemporary cuisine, or *Pat's Place* at 202 South Union (☎830/629-1491) for cheese enchiladas in a more casual setting.

There's good though touristy nightlife at the atmospheric clapboard **Gruene Hall**, 1281 Gruene Rd (☎830/606-1281, Ⓦwww.gruenehall.com), where you can see top country stars perform.

The Lyndon B. Johnson Historical Park

Sixty-five miles west of Austin on US-290, the **Lyndon B. Johnson State and National Historical Park** preserves LBJ's birthplace (1908) and the ranch house where Lady Bird Johnson continued to live long after her husband's death in 1973 (90min tours leave from the visitor center, daily 10am–4pm; $6).

The **visitor center** (daily 8.45am–5pm; Ⓣ830/868-7128, Ⓦwww.nps.gov/lyjo) and Johnson's boyhood home (daily 9am–4pm; free guided tours every 30min) are at sleepy **Johnson City**, fourteen miles further east; for a good lunch – chicken fried steak, BBQ, catfish and the like – stop off at the *Hill Country Cupboard*, at the junction of US-281 and US-290 (Ⓣ830/868-4625).

Fredericksburg

On weekends in **Fredericksburg**, crowds of day-trippers from San Antonio and Austin throng Main Street's cutesy specialty stores and fancy tearooms. Several original structures make up the **Pioneer Museum** at 309 W Main St, including a church and a store (Mon–Sat 10am–5pm, Sun 1–5pm; $5). A little more incongruous, the **National Museum of the Pacific War**, 340 E Main St (daily 9am–5pm; $7), features a Japanese garden of peace, and lays out a historical trail past aircraft, tanks, and heavy artillery.

Practicalities

The **CVB**, one block off Main St at 302 East Austin St (Mon–Fri 8.30am–5pm, Sat 9am–5pm, Sun noon–4pm; Ⓣ830/997-6523, Ⓦwww.fredericksburg-texas.com), has details of budget **hotels** along E Main Street; of these, the pool-equipped *Sunday House* at no. 501 (Ⓣ830/997-4484, Ⓦwww.sundayhouseinn.com; ⑤) is one of the more luxurious. **Bed-and-breakfast** is big in historic Fredericksburg; *The Full Moon Guesthouse*, ten miles southeast of Fredericksburg at 3234 Luckenbach Rd (Ⓣ1-800/997-1124, Ⓦwww.luckenbachtx.com; ⑤), offers accommodation in rural cottages and cabins in the sleepy musical hamlet of **Luckenbach**, immortalized in song by both Willie Nelson and Waylon Jennings. There's **camping** in the lovely surrounds of Lady Bird Johnson Municipal Park ($9), three miles southwest on Hwy-16 S.

Restaurants and bakeries line Main Street. *Dietz Bakery*, at no. 218 (Ⓣ830/997-3250), is the oldest family-owned bakery in town. You can eat more substantially at *Friedhelm's Bavarian Inn* at no. 905 (closed Mon; Ⓣ830/997-6300), which specializes in starchy plates of dumplings and sauerkraut.

North and east Texas

Early immigration into **north and east Texas**, during the days of the Republic and following the devastation of the Civil War, was largely from the Southern states. In the 1930s, the northeastern oil fields near **Tyler** proved to be the richest ever found in the US. In addition to oil, agriculture has become a prime source of commerce, with logging important in the densely forested east. The grand exception is, of course, the **Metroplex** – the area that includes **Dallas** and **Fort Worth**.

The main tourist attractions and cultural life of the region are concentrated here, but if you enjoy exploring small-town America, and have a car, the north and east can yield more subtle pleasures. The **national forests** of Angelina, Davy Crockett, Sabine, and Sam Houston in the east are delightful: the forest supervisor (Ⓣ936/639-8501) in Lufkin, midway between Davy Crockett and Angelina on US-59, has details of free and private **camping** facilities. Fans of Wim Wenders' movie will want to check out **Paris, Texas**, northeast on US-82.

East Texas

The tall pine forests of **East Texas** bear more relation to Louisiana than to the rest of the state; while undeniably Texan, the locals also identify themselves culturally and geographically with the adjacent corners of Arkansas and Louisiana – the "**Arklatex**" – and you'll find jambalaya and gumbo in restaurants along with standard Texas dishes.

Burial sites and reconstructed dwellings of the sophisticated **Caddo** Indians, an early southeastern mound-building culture, can be seen at the **Caddoan Mounds State Historic Site**, 30 miles west of **Nacogdoches** on Hwy-21. Active between the ninth and fourteenth centuries, the site includes a self-guided walking tour and displays on Caddoan history (Tues–Sun 8.30am–4.30pm; $2; Ⓣ936/858-3218).

Big Thicket National Preserve

The **Big Thicket National Preserve** on US 69-287, is a remarkable composite of natural elements from the southwestern desert, central plains, and Appalachian Mountains, with swamps and bayous to boot. The area once offered refuge for outlaws, runaway slaves, and gamblers; now it just hides a huge variety of plant and animal life, including deer, alligators, armadillos, possums, hogs, and panthers, and nearly 200 species of birds. Wild flowers, orchids, and towering trees share space with cacti and yucca.

Before entering the site, check in at the visitor center (daily 9am–5pm; Ⓣ409/951-6725, Ⓦwww.nps.gov/bith). There is hiking, canoeing, and back-country camping.

Dallas

Contrary to popular belief, there's no oil in status-conscious **DALLAS**. Since its founding in 1841 as a prairie trading post, by Tennessee lawyer John Neely Bryan and his Arkansas friend Joe Dallas, successive generations of **entrepreneurs** have amassed wealth here through trade and finance, using first cattle and later oil reserves as collateral. One early group of European settlers of the 1850s – French intellectuals and artists known as the La Réunion co-operative – had to pack up and move on after a series of summer droughts and a harsh winter; the few who stayed included a future mayor of Dallas. The city still prides itself on its legacy of arts and culture.

The power of **money** in Dallas was demonstrated in the late 1950s, when its financiers threw their weight behind integration. Potentially racist restaurant owners and bus drivers were pressured not to resist the new policies, and Dallas was spared major upheavals. The city's image was, however, tarnished by the **assassi-**

nation of President Kennedy in 1963, and it took the building of the Dallas/Fort Worth International Airport in the 1960s, and the twin successes of the *Dallas* TV show and the Cowboys football team in the 1970s, to restore confidence. These days its occasional stuffiness is tempered by a typically Texas delight in self-parody – this is the city that calls itself "Big D," after all.

Arrival and information

Dallas is served by two major **airports**. **Dallas/Fort Worth** (DFW; ⓣ972/574-8888, ⓦwww.dfwairport.com) is exactly midway between the two cities (around 17 miles from each). You can catch one of a variety of different **shuttle buses**, such as Super Shuttle (ⓣ817/329-2000, ⓦwww.supershuttle.com), which costs about $17 to get downtown; **taxis** cost around $50 (Yellow Cab ⓣ214/426-6262). The other major airport, **Love Field** (ⓣ214/670-6073, ⓦwww.dallas-lovefield.com), used mostly by Southwest Airlines, lies about nine miles northwest of Dallas, from where **taxis** to downtown cost around $17, shuttles around $11. **Greyhound** is at 205 S Lamar St downtown, while **Amtrak**'s 1916 Union Station is further west at 400 S Houston St. The **Trinity Railway Express** (ⓣ214/979-1111, ⓦwww.trinityrailwayexpress.org) service runs regular commuter trains to Fort Worth for $2.50.

The downtown **visitor center** is in the "Old Red" Courthouse, 100 S Houston St, near the Kennedy-related sights (Mon–Fri 8am–5pm, Sat & Sun 9am–5pm; ⓣ214/571-1300, ⓦwww.visitdallas.com).

City transportation

Dallas proper is circled by Inner Loop 12 (or Northwest Highway) and the Outer Loop I-635 (which becomes LBJ Freeway). Downtown's main sights are easy to tour on foot. **DART**, the Dallas Area Rapid Transit system (ⓣ214/979-1111, ⓦwww.dart.org), is a **light rail** network that operates downtown and travels further afield to places like Mockingbird Station, a laudable example of New Urbanism. Unlike other cities in Texas, Dallas is pouring resources into light rail, and future expansion of the system is planned. Day passes cost $3, and they are also good for the city's **buses**. The **McKinney Trolley** (ⓣ214/855-0006, ⓦwww.mata.org) runs north from the downtown Dallas Museum of Art up McKinney Avenue to the West Village, a complex of restaurants and bars (every 30min Mon–Fri 7am–10pm, Sat 10am–10pm; free).

Accommodation

Hotels in downtown Dallas are geared toward business travelers. Chain **motels** are concentrated on the freeways; there are lots on LBJ Freeway near the Galleria mall, 12 miles north, and there is a friendly **hostel** in Irving.

The Adolphus 1321 Commerce St ⓣ214/742-8200, ⓦwww.hoteladolphus.com. Stunning historic downtown hotel, decorated with antiques. Said to be the most beautiful building west of Venice, Italy, when it was built in 1912, it's still by far Dallas's most glamorous place to stay. ⑧

Dallas Irving Backpackers Guest House 214 W 6th St, Irving ⓣ214/682-9636 or 972/255-9636. Located in Irving, ten miles west of Dallas. Ivan Ivanov, the owner, is friendly and welcoming, and the hostel is clean enough. From downtown, take the TRE train to South Irving Station.

Hotel Belmont 901 Fort Worth Ave ⓣ1-866/870-8010, ⓦwww.belmontdallas.com. Renovated 1940s motel located a short drive from downtown. Feels more like LA than Dallas, with a hip, casual bar and a pool with stunning city views. ⑤

Hotel Lawrence 302 S Houston St ⓣ1-877/396-0334, ⓦwww.hotellawrencedallas.com. Very central European-style hotel in a 1920s building. Small, comfortable rooms, a good continental breakfast, and milk and cookies every evening. ⑤

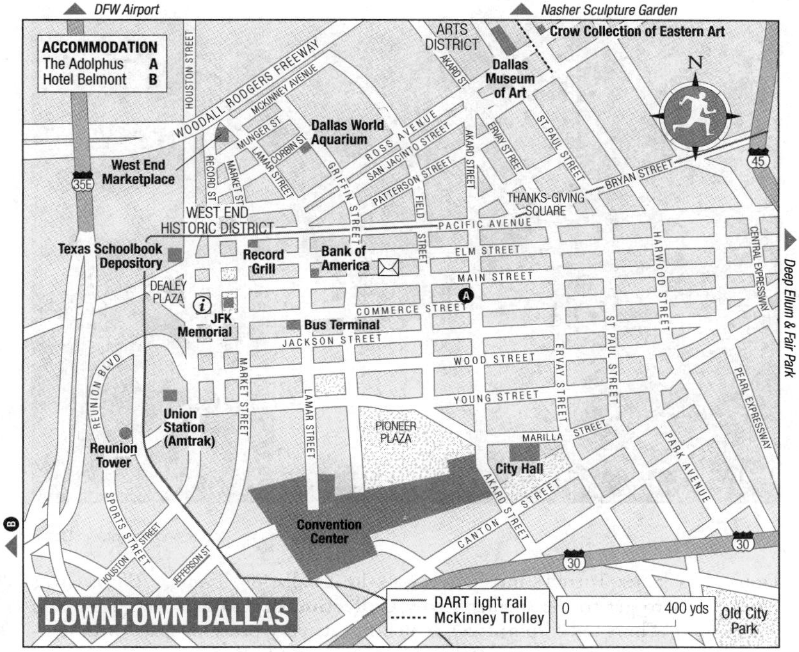

The City

Downtown Dallas is a paean to commerce. Studding the elegant modern skyline, many of its skyscrapers are landmarks in themselves. The most noteworthy is **Fountain Place Tower**, 1445 Ross Ave. Designed by I.M. Pei, its sharp edges are reminiscent of a blue crystal. At night, two miles of green argon tubing delineate the 72-story **Bank of America** building at Lamar and Main, while the **Reunion Tower**, 300 Reunion Blvd, on the west side of downtown next to the Amtrak station, looks like a giant microphone. For big views of the Big D, head to the 40th floor of the **Chase Tower** at 2200 Ross Ave (Mon–Fri 8am–5pm; free).

Main Street and the Arts District

One refuge from the downtown hubbub is the Philip Johnson-designed **Thanks-Giving Square** (Mon–Fri 9am–5pm, Sat–Sun 10am–5pm), at the intersection of Akard, Ervay, and Bryan streets and Pacific Avenue, with its fountains, garden, and modern spiraling chapel.

On the north edge of downtown, the **Arts District** boasts an excellent gaggle of galleries. The **Dallas Museum of Art**, 1717 N Harwood St (Tues–Sun 11am–5pm, Thurs until 9pm; $10, free Thurs 5–9pm, $16 combination ticket with Nasher Sculpture Center; Ⓦwww.dallasmuseumofart.org), has an impressive pre-Columbian collection in the Gallery of the Americas, along with artifacts from Africa, Asia, and the Pacific and works by European artists. Across Harwood Drive, the **Nasher Sculpture Center** (Tues–Sun 11am–5pm, Thurs until 9pm; $10, $16 combination ticket with the DMA; Ⓦwww.nashersculpturecenter.org) has a few galleries inside, but saves the best of its collection for the garden.

▲ The Reunion Tower and downtown Dallas

Don't miss James Turrell's meditative walk-in installation *Tending (Blue)*. Cross Flora Street to get to the smaller **Crow Collection of Eastern Art** (Tues–Sun 10am–5pm, Thurs until 9pm; free), which fills its very peaceful space with delicately hewn works from China, Tibet, Cambodia, and India.

West End, Dealey Plaza, and around

The restored red-brick warehouses of the **West End Historic District**, the site of the original 1841 settlement on Lamar and Munger streets, are filled with specialty stores and theme restaurants; it's a touristy place, thronged at weekends. A few blocks south and west lies **Dealey Plaza**, forever associated with the Kennedy assassination. A small green space beside Houston Street's triple underpass, it has become one of the most recognizable urban streetscapes in the world. Whenever you come, you will find tourists snapping pictures. The **Texas Schoolbook Depository** itself, at 411 Elm St, is now the Dallas County Administration Building, the penultimate floor of which houses **The Sixth Floor Museum** (Mon noon–6pm; Tues–Sun 10am–6pm; $13.50). Displays build up a suspenseful narrative, culminating in the infamous juddering 8mm footage of Kennedy crumpling into Jackie's arms; the images remain deeply affecting. The "gunman's nest" has been recreated and, whatever you believe about Oswald's guilt, it is chilling to look down at the streets below and imagine the mayhem the shooter must have seen that day. One block east of Dealey Plaza, in the **Dallas County Historical Plaza** on Main and Market streets, is the striking **John F. Kennedy Memorial**. Walk inside the simple, open-air concrete structure, and you will feel removed from the city.

Pioneer Plaza and Old City Park

The city's main administrative district, on the south side of downtown, is focused around **City Hall**, a cantilevered upside-down pyramid designed in 1972 by I.M. Pei. The **library** is located near here, while **Pioneer Plaza**, at Young and Griffin streets, holds the world's largest bronze sculpture, a monument to the mighty cattle drives of the West. It depicts forty life-size longhorn steers marching down a natural landscape under the guidance of three cowboys. It is a peaceful space, with an adjacent old cemetery.

Further southeast, across I-30 at 1515 S Harwood St, Dallas's first park, **Old City Park**, is now both a recreational area and home to the **Dallas Heritage Village**, a living museum that charts the history of north Texas from 1840 to 1910. More than 30 buildings have been relocated here from towns in north Texas, among them a farmhouse, a bank, a train station, a store, a church, and a schoolhouse (Tues–Sat 10am–4pm; $7).

Deep Ellum

Deep Ellum – five blocks east of downtown between the railroad tracks and I-30 at Elm and Main streets – is the city's struggling alternative district. Famous in the 1920s for its jazz and blues clubs (and supposedly named by Blind Lemon Jefferson, though it's more likely to stem from the Southern pronunciation of "elm"), the old warehouse district has fallen on tough times in recent years. It is one of the few examples in the US of a gentrifying urban area that began to fail just as it was taking off. It earned an undeserved violent reputation, partly because of a misinformed mayor, and people stayed away. It may have reached bottom, though, and its bars, music clubs, galleries, and restaurants – including some of the best in the city – are starting to lure the crowds back. It is walkable and not nearly as dangerous as some would lead you to believe.

Fair Park

Not far southeast of Deep Ellum, **Fair Park**, a gargantuan Art Deco plaza bedecked with endless Lone Stars, was built to house the Texas Centennial Exposition in 1936, and hosts the annual State Fair of Texas, the biggest event of its kind in the US. Its plethora of fine museums include the lively **Women's Museum** (Tues–Sun noon–5pm; $5; Ⓦwww.thewomensmuseum.org), full of intriguing facts and figures (women smile eight times a day more than men, apparently) and with temporary exhibits exploring subjects as varied as Marilyn Monroe, female photographers, and the lure of the shoe. The nearby **African-American Museum** (Tues–Fri noon–5pm, Sat 10am–5pm, Sun 1–5pm; free; Ⓦwww.aamdallas.org) is also terrific, with a superb collection of **folk art**. The **Museum of Nature and Science** (Mon–Sat 10am–5pm, Sun noon–5pm; $8.75) boasts exhibits on everything from fossils to dental hygiene.

The centerpiece of the park is the magnificent **Hall of State Building**, an Art Deco treasure of bronze statues, blue tiles, mosaics, and murals, with rooms decorated to celebrate the different regions of Texas (Mon–Sat 9am–5pm, Sun 1–5pm; free). The park also holds the **Cotton Bowl** stadium, home of the annual college football classic, and the largest Ferris wheel in the US. For three weeks in October, Fair Park swells with more than three million revelers enjoying the riotous **State Fair** (Ⓦwww.bigtex.com) itself.

Eating

Dallas has a number of **restaurant** districts. Downtown, the **West End Historic District** is lively, if touristy, with rowdy chains; in hipper **Deep Ellum** you can chow down on anything from sushi to Mexican. Uptown, chic **West Village**, accessible on the McKinney trolley, is a squeaky-clean cluster of bars and eateries catering to youthful loft-dwellers; to the northeast of downtown, parallel to I-75, **Lower Greenville Avenue** has a funkier feel.

All Good Café 2934 Main St ⓣ214/742-5362, ⓦwww.allgoodcafe.com. Fresh home-style cooking at this cheery Deep Ellum haunt, which is more evocative of Austin than Dallas and transforms into a live Texas music venue in the evenings.

Local 2936a Elm St ⓣ214/752-7500. Upscale but unpretentious modern restaurant in a historic Deep Ellum building. The chef is the owner.

Record Grill 605 Elm St ⓣ214/742-1853. A small, downtown greasy spoon wedged between a building and a parking lot. A double-meat bacon cheeseburger costs $4. Not far from the Sixth Floor Museum.

Sonny Bryan's 2202 Inwood Rd ⓣ214/357-7120. The original location – it still looks like a shack – of this favorite local barbecue chain lies uptown. Get there in good time as the deliciously tender, smoky meat can be all snapped up by early afternoon.

Entertainment and nightlife

The best **nightlife** destinations in Dallas are **Deep Ellum** and **Lower Greenville**, and there is a small cluster of good bars on **Perry Avenue** near Fair Park. Elsewhere nightlife is pretty formal. The **Dallas Symphony Orchestra** performs at the showpiece Morton H. Meyerson Symphony Center (ⓣ214/670-3600, ⓦwww.dallassymphony.com), while the Dallas Opera is preparing to move into a new $275-million Arts District location in the fall of 2009.

Full **listings** can be found in Thursday's free *Dallas Observer* (ⓦwww.dallasobserver.com) or in the *Dallas Morning News* (ⓦwww.dallasnews.com).

Adair's 2624 Commerce St ⓣ214/939-9900, ⓦwww.adairssaloon.com. A Deep Ellum hole-in-the-wall that attracts both old-timers and students with its hard-edged live honky-tonk music and shuffleboard and pool tables.

Amsterdam Bar 831 Exposition Ave ⓣ214/824-9933. The best of a cluster of great bars right next door to Fair Park with occasional live jazz. Also check out the *Meridian Room*, practically next door at 3611 Parry Ave.

Granada Theater 3524 Greenville Ave ⓣ214/824-9933, ⓦwww.granadatheater.com. Lovely old movie theater hosting big name acts.

Lee Harvey's 1807 Gould St ⓣ214/428-1555, ⓦwww.leeharveys.com. PBR flows like water at this dive situated between downtown and Deep Ellum.

The Prophet Bar 2548 Elm St ⓣ214/939-4321, ⓦwww.theprophetbar.com. Erykah Badu's band plays at this Deep Ellum live music spot every Wed night.

Sons of Hermann Hall 3414 Elm St ⓣ214/747-4422, ⓦwww.sonsofhermann.com. Delightfully old-school country venue, just beyond Deep Ellum, where the Texas masters come to play, and respectful young outfits pay tribute. Plus swing lessons, open-mike nights and acoustic jams.

Fort Worth

Often dismissed as some kind of poor relation to Dallas, friendly **FORT WORTH** in fact has a buzz largely missing in its neighbor 30 miles to the east. Fort Worth is one of the most western cities in Texas. In the 1870s it was a stop on the great cattle drive to Kansas, the **Chisholm Trail**, and when the railroads arrived it became a livestock market in its own right. Cowboys and outlaws populated the city in its early years, and much of that character remains. But while the **cattle** trade is still a major industry, and the **Stockyards** provide a stimulating, atmospheric slice of Old West life, Fort Worth also prides itself on excellent **museums** – the best in the state – and a bustling **downtown** that exists on a human scale. Looking toward the future, the city is also undertaking the massive **Trinity River Master Plan**, which will include one of the largest urban parks in the US and trails and greenways along the Trinity River.

Arrival, information, and getting around

The main road between Fort Worth and Dallas is **I-30**. It runs east-west through the city, while **I-35W** runs north-south. **Loop 820** encircles all the major sights. The

Yellow Checker **shuttle** service (Ⓣ817/267-5150, Ⓦwww.yellowcheckershuttle.com) runs to and from DFW International Airport, seventy miles northeast, for about $19. The **Amtrak** (Ⓣ817/332-2931) and **Greyhound** (Ⓣ817/429-3089) stations are both located southeast of downtown at 1001 Jones St. Fort Worth's public transportation system, **The T** (Ⓦwww.the-t.com, Ⓣ817/215-8600), operates useful **buses and shuttles** ($1.50), with the Trinity Railway Express (Ⓣ817/215-8600, Ⓦwww.trinityrailwayexpress.org) running a longer **commuter service to Dallas** for $2.50. The downtown Sundance Square and Stockyard areas are well patrolled and safe to **walk** around after dark; for a **taxi** between the two, call Yellow Checker (Ⓣ817/426-6262).

There are three **visitor centers** (Ⓦwww.fortworth.com): downtown in the CVB at 415 Throckmorton St, in the Cultural District at the Will Rogers Memorial Center at 3401 W Lancaster Ave, and in the Stockyards at 130 E Exchange Ave.

Accommodation

The liveliest places to stay are around **Sundance Square** downtown, or in the cowtown atmosphere of the **Stockyards**; standard motel rooms can be found along I-35.

The Ashton Hotel 610 Main St Ⓣ1-866/327-4866, Ⓦwww.theashtonhotel.com. Small luxury hotel with 39 rooms appointed with custom furniture and a great location. 9

Courtyard Fort Worth Downtown/Blackstone 601 Main St Ⓣ1-817/885-8700, Ⓦwww.marriott.com/property/propertypage/dfwms. Friendly hotel in a downtown Art Deco building. Rooms on the upper floor have great views, and there's a pool. 6

Hotel Texas 2415 Ellis Ave Ⓣ817/624-2224, Ⓦwww.hoteltexasdfw.com. Great value on the edge of the Stockyards; you can stumble from the rowdy beer hall to your room. Popular with touring country musicians. 3

The City

Fort Worth's main attractions fall tidily into a triangle anchored by downtown, with the Cultural District and the Stockyards two miles away to the west and north respectively. The chief focus of **downtown** Fort Worth is **Sundance Square**, a leafy, red-brick-paved fourteen-block area of shops, restaurants, and bars between First and Sixth streets, ringed by glittering skyscrapers and pervaded with a genuine enthusiasm for the town's rich history. Filling the block bounded by Commerce, Calhoun, Fourth, and Fifth streets, the **Bass Performance Hall** (free tours Sat 10:30am, Ⓦwww.basshall.com) is a showpiece for the district. It's a breathtaking building that recalls the great opera houses of Europe, and it is fronted by angels blowing golden trumpets. Elsewhere, notice the trompe-l'oeil murals – especially the Chisholm Trail mural on Third Street between Main and Houston. Fans of cowboy art should head for the **Sid Richardson Museum of Western Art**, tucked away at 309 Main St (Sun–Thurs 9am–5pm; Fri & Sat 10am–8pm; free; Ⓦwww.sidrichardsonmuseum.org), which has an excellent collection of late works by Frederic Remington, including some of his best black-and-white illustrations, and early elegiac cowboy scenes by Charles Russell; it also hosts temporary exhibitions. If you want to stock up on top-of-the-line rhinestone Western wear or cowboy hats, Leddy's Ranch at 410 Houston St dresses some of the biggest acts in country music.

The Cultural District

Fort Worth has the best galleries and museums in Texas, most of them concentrated in the **Cultural District**, two miles west of downtown on the No. 2 bus. The **Kimbell Art Museum**, 3333 Camp Bowie Blvd (Tues–Thurs & Sat 10am–5pm, Fri noon–8pm, Sun noon–5pm; free, admission charged for special exhibits; Ⓦwww

.kimbellart.org), is considered one of the top small art museums in the US. The vaulted, naturally-lit structure was designed by Louis Kahn, and the impeccable collection includes pre-Columbian and African pieces, with some noteworthy Mayan funerary urns, unusual Asian antiquities, and a handful of Renaissance masterpieces.

The most recent addition to the area, the **Modern Art Museum**, 3200 Darnell St (Tues–Sat 10am–5pm, Sun 11am–5pm, Tues hrs are extended to 7pm between Sept–Nov and Feb–April; $10; free Wed and first Sun of each month; Ⓦwww.themodern.org), is a Tadao Ando-designed modernist building whose light-flooded rooms hold the largest collection of modern art in the nation after New York's Museum of Modern Art. The **Amon Carter Museum**, just up the hill at 3501 Camp Bowie Blvd (Tues, Wed, Fri, & Sat 10am–5pm, Thurs 10am–8pm, Sun noon–5pm; free; Ⓦwww.cartermuseum.org), concentrates on American art, with stunning photographs of Western landscapes, as well as a fine assortment of Remingtons and Russells, and works by Winslow Homer and Georgia O'Keeffe.

The Stockyards

With its wooden sidewalks, old storefronts, dusty rodeos, and beer-soaked saloons, the 10-block **Stockyards** area – centered on Exchange Avenue, two miles north of downtown – offers an evocation of the days when Fort Worth was "the richest little city in the world." There are daily cattle drives, a huffing, shuffling cavalcade of fifteen or so Texas Longhorns, that occur, weather permitting, at 11.30am. The cattle drives begin at the corrals behind the Livestock Exchange Building, and the herd returns around 4pm. The visitor center at 130 E Exchange Ave is the starting point for lively **walking tours** of the Stockyards (around 1hr; from $6).

Along with the steakhouses and honky-tonks, the **stores** in Fort Worth are heaven for Wild West fans. Check out M.L. Leddy's hat, boot, and saddle shop on Exchange Avenue. **Stockyards Station** is a bit touristy, but it houses the Ernest Tubb Record Shop, which sells Americana, folk, and country and western CDs.

Museums in the Stockyards have an appealing small-town feel. Try the **Stockyards Museum** (Mon–Sat 10am–5pm; free), in the huge **Livestock Exchange Building** at 131 E Exchange Ave. It offers a lovingly compiled jumble of local memorabilia including steer skulls, pre-Columbian pottery, and rodeo posters. Next door the **Cowtown Coliseum** (ticket prices vary; Ⓣ817/625-1025, Ⓦwww.cowtowncoliseum.com), holds rodeos, Wild West shows, and country music hoedowns every weekend. It's fronted by a statue of Bill Pickett, the black rodeo star who invented the unsavory but effective practice of "bulldogging" – stunning the bull by biting its lip.

Eating

If you love **steak**, Fort Worth is for you, and especially the Stockyards area, where the many good steakhouses are frequented as much by cattle ranchers as by visitors.

Angelo's Barbecue 2533 White Settlement Rd Ⓣ817/332-0357. Venerable westside barbecue joint, north of the cultural district. Locals declare the brisket here to be the best in the city.

Cattlemen's Steak House 2458 N Main St Ⓣ817/624-3945. Dim lighting and wall-sized portraits of prize steers set the scene at this Stockyards institution, beloved for its juicy steaks – from T-bones to sirloin – and icy margaritas.

Kincaid's Hamburgers 4901 Camp Bowie Blvd Ⓣ817/732-2881. This place used to be a grocery store, but since 1966 it serves the best 8-ounce hamburgers in Texas.

Paris Coffee Shop 700 W Magnolia Ave Ⓣ817/335-2041. Busy southside breakfast and lunch spot that serves basic, fresh grub.

Reata 310 Houston St Ⓣ817/336-1009. One of the nicest places to eat in downtown's Sundance Square, with a tempting Southwestern menu that ranges from upscale cuisine to home-style comfort food. Named after the ranch in the movie *Giant*, James Dean's last.

Nightlife and entertainment

You'd be hard pressed not to find something to your taste in after-dark Fort Worth, a city where roustabouts happily down beers next to modern jazz fans and metalheads. Bar crawling is fun, and there's a great mix of live music venues. Check the *Fort Worth Weekly* (ⓦwww.fwweekly.com) or the *Fort Worth Star-Telegram* (ⓦwww.star-telegram.com) for listings. If you're after a rambunctious Wild Western night out, head for the **Stockyards**. For the performing arts, there's the stunning **Bass Performance Hall** downtown (see p.697; ⓣ817/212-4325, ⓦwww.basshall.com), home to the city's orchestra, opera, and theater companies. Big-name touring musicians like Lyle Lovett and k.d. lang also make the rounds here.

Billy Bob's Texas 2520 Rodeo Plaza ⓣ817/624-7117, ⓦwww.billybobstexas.com. The jewel in Cowtown's crown, this is the largest honky-tonk in the world, down in the Stockyards, with pro bull-riding, pool tables, bars, restaurants and stores, weekly swing and country dance lessons, and big-name concerts.

White Elephant Saloon 106 E Exchange Ave ⓣ817/624-8273, ⓦwww.whiteelephantsaloon.com. Notoriously wild and authentic old Stockyards saloon with a cowboy hat hall of fame.

Toward the Panhandle

Routes west from central Texas lead you through the state's "backyard," where farmlands and rough-cut, juniper-covered hills give way to treeless, sandy landscapes that recently have seen a wind energy boom. Of the towns, **Abilene** and **Sweetwater**, both on I-20 toward El Paso, are interesting enough to be possible stopovers for long-distance drivers; both have a reasonable selection of budget motels.

The Panhandle

The inhabitants of the **Panhandle**, the southernmost portion of the Great Plains, call it "the real Texas;" a starkly romantic landscape strewn with tumbleweeds and mesquite trees, it certainly fulfills the fantasy of what Texas should look like. When Coronado's expedition passed this way in the 16th century, the gold-seekers drove stakes into the ground across the vast and unchanging vista, despairing of otherwise finding their way home. Hence the name **Llano Estacado**, or staked plains, which still persists today.

Once the buffalo – and the natives – had been driven away from what was seen as uninhabitable frontier country, the Panhandle began in the 1870s to yield great **natural resources**. Helium, especially in Amarillo, as well as oil and **agriculture**, have brought wealth to the region, which is also home to large **ranches**.

The region holds few actual tourist attractions – its real appeal is its ends-of-the-earth feel and its stark, rural beauty. **Music** has particular significance in an area famous for songwriters such as Bob Wills, Buddy Holly, Roy Orbison, Waylon Jennings, Terry Allen, Joe Ely, Jimmie Dale Gilmore, and Natalie Maines of the Dixie Chicks.

Lubbock

The largest city in the Panhandle, **LUBBOCK** was built on cotton. In recent years, with farming in decline, the town's economy has come to rely on manufacturing, health care, and Texas Tech University.

With its faceless block buildings and simple homes, Lubbock is at first glance unremarkable. Dig a little deeper, though, and you will find a complex city, one that accommodates Southern Baptism, the high-scoring Texas Tech Red Raiders football team and its philosophical head coach, and a songwriting history unmatched in Texas.

Arrival, information, and accommodation

Loop 289 circles Lubbock proper, with the **airport** (ⓣ806/775-2044, ⓦwww.flylia.com) a few minutes north on I-27; taxis to downtown cost around $18 (Yellow Cab ⓣ806/765-7777). **Citibus** (ⓣ806/712-2000, ⓦwww.citibus.com) runs commuter routes within the Loop, stopping at around 7.45pm (Mon–Sat only; $1.25). The **visitor center** is on the sixth floor of 1600 Broadway (Mon–Fri 8am–5pm; ⓣ 1-800/692-4035, ⓦwww.visitlubbock.org).

Prices for **accommodation** are reasonable, and rooms are plentiful; Avenue Q has a string of reliable chain **hotels**.

Lubbock Inn 3901 19th St ⓣ806/792-5181, ⓦwww.lubbockinn.com. Well-located and recently renovated independent motel with no-frills rooms, a restaurant, and a pool with waterfalls. ❸

Woodrow House B&B 2629 19th St ⓣ806/793-3330 or 1-800/687-5236, ⓦwww.woodrowhouse.com. Seven rooms, each with a different theme – there's even one in a restored caboose – in a mansion-style modern house opposite Texas Tech. ❹

The Town

Downtown Lubbock and Texas Tech University are on the northern side of town. Few buildings of interest survive, thanks to the construction boom of the 1950s and a fierce tornado that ripped through Lubbock in 1970, killing 26 people. However, you can get an interesting overview of local history at the university's

Buddy Holly

Lubbock's claim to world fame is as the birthplace of **Buddy Holly**. Inspired by the blues and country music of his childhood – and a seminal encounter with the young Elvis Presley, gigging in Lubbock at the Cotton Club – Buddy Holly was one of Rock 'n' Roll's first singer-songwriters. The Holly sound, characterized by steady strumming guitar, rapid drumming, and his trademark hiccuping vocals, was made famous by hits such as *Peggy Sue*, *Not Fade Away*, and *That'll Be the Day*. Buddy was killed at 22 in the Iowa plane crash of February 3, 1959 ("the day the music died") that also claimed the Big Bopper and Ritchie Valens. Don't leave town without visiting the **Buddy Holly Center**, 1801 Crickets Ave (Ave G; Tues–Sat 10am–5pm, Sun 1–5pm; ⓦwww.buddyhollycenter.org; $5), an impressive space that holds a collection of Holly memorabilia, including the black glasses he wore on the day he died.

Other sites include the **Buddy Holly Statue** at 8th Street and Avenue Q; it's scheduled to move to a new location by 2011. This eight-foot bronze figure towers over a **Walk of Fame** with plaques to local performers like Waylon Jennings, who played bass at Buddy's final concert. **Buddy's grave** is in Lubbock's cemetery at the end of 34th Street. Take the right fork inside the gate, and the grave, decorated with flowers and guitar picks, is on the left.

Ranching Heritage Center, 3121 Fourth St (Mon–Sat 10am–5pm, Sun 1–5pm; free), where 38 original buildings show the evolution of ranch life. But don't think that ranchers were the first to populate the region – humans have lived in the area for 12,000 years. The **American Wind Power Center**, 1701 Canyon Lake Drive (Tues–Sat 10am–5pm, summer also Sun 2–5pm; $2) showcases more than 120 windmills, many collected by Billie Wolf, a Texas Tech home economics faculty member who spent much of her life interviewing Great Plains farmers and purchasing their rare windmill models. The center also has a towering new turbine: the $1-million Vestas V47, which powers the museum as well as 75 nearby homes. (For more on wind energy in Texas, see box, p.702).

Eating

Lubbock has a variety of **places to eat**, with especially good barbecue and steak joints. Note that many establishments close before 10pm.

Cagle Steaks 2605 Corner of W Fourth and F.M. 179 ⓣ806/795-3879. Classic Texas Plains steak restaurant. A 16-ounce ribeye with all the fixings costs $25.

Gardski's 2009 Broadway ⓣ806/744-2391. Popular American restaurant for Texas Tech students and alumni. Historic photos line the walls. Onion strings are a specialty.

Home Cafe 3131 34th St ⓣ806/687-1466. A new breakfast and lunch spot, with good coffee served all day. Owned and operated by young, friendly Lubbock natives.

Llano Estacado Winery 3131 34th St ⓣ806/687-1466. A few miles southeast of town, the biggest winery in Texas offers tours and free tastings Mon–Sat 10am–5pm and Sun noon–5pm.

Tom and Bingo's 3006 34th Street ⓣ806/799-1514. Tiny eatery churns out the best chopped beef sandwich in Lubbock.

Entertainment and nightlife

Designated the "Music Crossroads of Texas" by the state legislature in 1999, Lubbock exerts surprisingly little energy supporting young local musicians; many decamp to Austin. A new annual **music festival** (ⓣ806/747-5232), held in September, is attempting to rectify that.

The **Depot District** downtown, which spreads for a few blocks from 19th Street and Hwy-27, has a mix of bars and clubs popular with students. At the heart of the area, the lovely old **Cactus Theater**, 1812 Buddy Holly Ave (ⓣ806/762-5233, ⓦwww.cactustheater.com), features nostalgic musicals and variety shows. **The Strip**, located off the 98th Street exit of the Slaton Highway, is where Lubbock residents buy their booze and has a rich honky-tonk history. The local *Lubbock Avalanche-Journal* (ⓦwww.lubbockonline.com) carries listings.

Rodeos are always fun: Texas Tech holds one each year, and there's the **ABC Rodeo** at the Municipal Coliseum every spring. In the same spirit, the **Panhandle South Plains Fair** in late September offers bull-riding, big-name country performers, and livestock exhibits.

Amarillo and around

AMARILLO may seem cut off from the rest of Texas, up in the northern Panhandle, but it stands on one of the great American cross-country routes – I-40, once the legendary **Route 66**. The city's name comes from the Spanish word for "yellow," the color of the soil characteristic to these parts. Sitting on ninety percent of the world's helium and hosting a world-class cattle market, Amarillo is a

Wind energy in Texas

Texas knows booms, most famously oil. Now the energy industry is supporting another classic American boom, this one **wind**. Since white settlement, the parched Texas Panhandle-Plains region has relied on windmills to tap the subterranean Ogallala Aquifer and pump water for livestock, crops, and farm families. In fact, though they may seem dated, many of the simple wooden and aluminum windmill structures that dot the landscape are still spinning, albeit a bit creakily. So it seems only natural that with the recent national focus on renewable energy, Texas would once again turn to wind.

There are more than 5000 modern wind turbines in the state and the largest collection can be found in the Panhandle-Plains region, near Sweetwater. Here motels can't be built fast enough and convoys of oversized trucks cart elongated, alien-white turbine blades one at a time down I-10. At West Texas A&M University in Canyon, the **Alternative Energy Institute** will tell you that Texas wind produces energy for almost 2.5 million homes, but inefficiencies in the grid system create energy bottlenecks. Nevertheless businessmen like billionaire T. Boone Pickens – who is building the largest wind farm in the world near Pampa – flock to the region for wind that blows at an average annual speed of 15mph. Canyon is also home to the **Panhandle-Plains Museum** (see p.703), which features exhibits on how Texans have harnessed the wind. But for the most comprehensive survey of the role wind energy has played, and will continue to play, in Texas, head to the **American Wind Power Center** in Lubbock (see p.701).

prosperous, laid-back city with a nice mix of cowtown appeal, and arty eccentricity, and mouth-watering steaks.

Arrival, information and accommodation

I-40 cuts through Amarillo, running south of downtown; the old Route 66 (Sixth Street) runs parallel to the north. **Greyhound** arrives downtown at 700 S Tyler St (Ⓣ806/374-5371), and there's a small **airport** (Ⓣ806/335-1671) seven miles east. You can pick up information from the downtown **visitor center** in the Civic Center (entrance 2), 401 S Buchanan St (May–Sept Mon–Fri 9am–6pm, Sat & Sun 10am–4pm; Oct–April Mon–Fri 8.30am–5.30pm, Sat noon–4pm; Ⓣ806/374-8474, Ⓦwww.visitamarillotx.com).

Innumerable **chain hotels** are concentrated along I-40 – for cowboy kitsch, you can't beat the *Big Texan Steak House Motel*, 7701 E I-40 at exit 75 (Ⓣ1-800/657-7177, Ⓦwww.bigtexan.com), with its Texas flag shower curtains, cowhide bedcovers and saloon doors – and famed restaurant (see below).

The Town

Amarillo's small "**old town**" consists of a few tree-lined streets and some staid homes. More interesting is the **Route 66 Historic District**, known locally as **Old San Jacinto**, a quirky stretch of restaurants, bars, and stores that runs west along Sixth Street (the old Route 66) from Georgia for about a mile to Western Street.

For more classic Americana, drive 10 miles west of town on I-40 to exit 60 (Arnot Road) and **Cadillac Ranch**. An extraordinary vision in the middle of nowhere, ten battered cars stand upended in the soil, their tail fins demonstrating the different Cadillac designs from 1949 to 1963. Since the cars were installed in 1974, they have been subject to countless makeovers at the hands of graffiti artists, photographers, and members of the public – all encouraged by owner Stanley Marsh 3 (he prefers to use 3 rather than III), eccentric helium millionaire and bon-vivant, on whose land the cars are planted, and who is also responsible for

▲ Big Texan Steak House

the wacky signs ("Strong drink!") dotted around Amarillo and the art installation **Floating Mesa**.

Amarillo is also host to the world's stompingest, snortingest **livestock auction** (Ⓣ806/373-7464, Ⓦwww.amarillolivestockauction.com), held on Tuesdays in the stockyards at 100 S Manhattan off Third, on the east side of town – it's a great show.

Eating and drinking

Carnivores will be in heaven – this is **steak** country through and through.

Big Texan Steak House 7701 E I-40, exit 75 Ⓣ1-800/657-7177. Rip-roaring Wild Western fun in this famed old restaurant, which as well as serving fried rattlesnake and ostrich burgers, offers the 72oz steak challenge: if you can eat it within an hour, you get it free (losers pony up around $70).

Golden Light Café and Cantina 2908 West Sixth Ave Ⓣ806/374-9237. Tasty food at a good value restaurant in a prime location. The cantina regularly draws some of the best touring musicians in Texas.

Outlaws Supper Club 10816 SE Third Ave Ⓣ806/335-1032. Practically surrounded by ranch land, this friendly, casual restaurant is a must for steak connoisseurs.

Canyon

In the former cattle town of **CANYON**, 15 miles south of Amarillo on I-27, the superb **Panhandle-Plains Historical Museum**, 2503 4th Ave, has engaging exhibits on, among other things, Texas ranching, geology, Southern Plains Indians, the automobile, and guns. One recent temporary exhibition explored the years Woody Guthrie spent in the region (daily: June–Aug Mon–Sat 9am–6pm, Sun 1–6pm, Sept–May Mon–Sat 9am–5pm, Sun 1–6pm; $12; Ⓦwww.panhandleplains.org).

Palo Duro Canyon State Park

Palo Duro Canyon, 12 miles east of Canyon and 20 miles southeast of Amarillo, is one of Texas' best-kept secrets. Plunging 1,000 feet from rim to floor, it splits the plains wide open and offers breathtaking views and colors, especially at sunset and in spring, when the whole chasm is scattered with wild flowers.

The park (daily 8am–10pm; $4 per person; Ⓣ806/488-2227, Ⓦwww.palodurocanyon.com) is in the most scenic part of the 120-mile canyon. You can explore the depths on **horseback** (Ⓣ806/488-2180), though backpackers and hikers may want to escape the tourist busloads by following the Prairie Dog Town fork into more remote sections of the park. To **camp**, or to stay in one of the rustic **cabins**, call Ⓣ512/389-8900.

You may balk at heart-warming musical extravaganzas, but the outdoor production *TEXAS*, about the settling of the Panhandle in the 1800s, has an undeniable pull in an area not exactly throbbing with nightlife, with the dramatic prairie sky as a ceiling, a 600-foot cliff as a backdrop, and genuine thunder and lightning (June–Aug Tues–Sun 8.30pm; $11–27; pre-show steak dinner 6pm, $10; Ⓣ806/655-2181, Ⓦwww.texas-show.com).

West Texas

West Texas is the stuff of Wild West fantasy: parched deserts, ghost towns, looming mesas, and, above all, a sense of utter isolation. Although the area south from the Panhandle down to Del Rio on the Rio Grande is, for convenience, also known as West Texas, the fantasy really begins west of the Pecos River; you can drive for hours without seeing another soul to **El Paso**, Texas' westernmost city. Many travelers venture into the desolation to explore **Big Bend National Park**, nearly 300 miles southeast of El Paso in the bend of the Rio Grande, but the region also boasts several small towns that provide delightfully **offbeat stopovers**.

Minimal rainfall and harsh land were not the only hindrances to settlement. The **Apache** and **Comanche**, though accustomed in the 1820s to trading with Mexican *comancheros*, were infuriated when hapless white pioneers began to trickle in during the 1830s. With their horsemanship and ability to find scarce water supplies, the Native Americans posed a real threat; upon statehood, a string of cavalry forts was set up with the help of federal money to protect Mexican and Anglo settlers from attack. As trading posts and cattle ranges began to spring up after the Civil War, the paramilitary **Texas Rangers** were sent out on violent vigilante missions. Eventually, as in the Panhandle, a brutal program of buffalo slaughter, supported by the US Army, starved the natives out. Not long afterward, oil was discovered in West Texas and boom towns appeared, with all the attendant lawlessness, gunslinging, and brawling. Those days are long gone, but the area has been capitalizing on its Wild West image ever since.

The Davis Mountains

The temperate climate of the verdant **Davis Mountains**, south of the junction of I-10 and I-20, makes them a popular summer destination for sweltering urban Texans, while the glassy, starry nights facilitate the work of the **McDon-**

ald Observatory about 20 miles northwest of Fort Davis on Hwy-118 (daily 10am–5.30pm, free; ⓣ432/426-3640, ⓦwww.mcdonaldobservatory.org). Nocturnal "star parties" here provide the opportunity to look at the constellations for yourself (Tues, Fri, & Sat, time depends on sunset; $10). **Davis Mountains State Park** ($5 per person; ⓣ1-800/792-1112, ⓦwww.tpwd.state.tx.us/spdest/findadest/parks/davis_mountains), which starts four miles northwest of Fort Davis, offers good hiking. Rooms at its romantic 1930s adobe-style *Indian Lodge,* restored in 2007, are clean and comfortable – and often booked up, so call in advance (ⓣ432/426-3254 or 1-800/792-1112; ❹). The **Nature Conservancy** also owns 32,000 acres in the area, but public access is limited to one weekend a month (ⓣ432/837-5954).

Fort Davis itself, a one-street town at the junction of highways 118 and 17, is a peaceful base for exploring the state park. The **visitor center**, on Memorial Square (ⓣ432/426-3015, ⓦwww.fortdavis.com) offers road maps for the 75-mile scenic loop of the Davis Mountains. The historic *Hotel Limpia* (ⓣ432/426-3237 or 1-800/662-5517, ⓦwww.hotellimpia.com; ❹) is full of character and serves home-cooked dinners in its cozy dining room. There's delightfully little to do in Fort Davis at **night**, though you can buy "membership" to the hotel's bar for $3.

Marfa and around

MARFA, a small ranching town and arts community 21 miles south of Fort Davis on Hwy-17, has three claims to fame. Firstly, James Dean's last film, the 1956 epic, *Giant*, was filmed here; the cast stayed at the historic and swanky **Hotel Paisano** downtown on Hwy-17 (ⓣ432/729-3669 or 1-866/729-3669, ⓦwww.hotelpaisano.com).

Next, there's the "**Marfa Lights**": mysterious bouncing lights that have been seen in the town's flat fields since the 1880s, attracting conspiracy theorists and alien-hunters. The town's **visitor center**, in the *Hotel Paisano*, can give advice on good vantage points to see the ghostly illuminations; if in doubt, head for the viewing center, nine miles east of town, between two and four hours after sunset.

Marfa's third attraction, just outside town, is the extraordinary **Chinati Foundation** (tours Wed–Sun 10am & 2pm; $10; ⓣ432/729-4362, ⓦwww.chinati.org). Founded by minimalist Donald Judd, the avant-garde works on show here include some of the world's largest permanent art installations, set in dramatic contexts both indoors and out. The **Judd Foundation** at 104 S Highland also has art spaces open to the public (Mon–Fri 9am–5pm; ⓣ432/729-4406).

Besides the *Paisano*, another lodging option is the *Thunderbird Hotel* (601 W San Antonio; ⓣ432/729-1984, ⓦwww.thuderbirdmarfa.com; ❺), a renovated motor court turned hipster hotel. Also check on the progress at *El Cosmico,* (ⓦwww.elcosmico.com) where a "magical tribe of dirt wizards" is constructing an avant-garde development of renovated Air Stream trailers and yurts on fifteen acres. The cheapest place to stay is the *Riata Inn* on Hwy-90 east of town (ⓣ432/729-3800; ❸).

For such a small town, good eats abound in Marfa, led by *Maiya's* downtown at 103 N Highland St (ⓣ432/729-4410, ⓦwww.maiyasrestaurant.com). The *New York Pizza Foundation*, 102 E San Antonio (ⓣ432/729-3377, ⓦwww.pizzafoundation.com), has the best pizza in the Trans Pecos region, while *Adobe Moon*, 200 S Abbot (ⓣ432/729-3030, ⓦwww.adobemoon.com), has good BBQ. For breakfast, try the *Brown Recluse* at 111 W San Antonio (ⓣ432/729-1811, ⓦwww.brownreclusemarfa.com).

There are innumerable, high-end galleries in Marfa that wouldn't be out of place in New York or LA. At the friendly *Marfa Book Co*, 105 S Highland St (Wed–Sun 10am–7pm; ⓣ432/729-3906), you can browse its selection of art, architecture, and Texana titles.

East of Marfa, the friendly college town of **Alpine** is worth a quick stop. It is served by an Amtrak train several times a week and has reasonable rooms at the rustic and clean *Antelope Lodge*. Alpine boasts a rowdy music club called *Railroad Blues*, and good Mexican breakfasts at *Magoo's Place*. Further east, **Marathon** is best known for the luxurious *Gage Hotel* (101 Hwy-90 W; ⓣ432/386-4510, ⓦwww.gagehotel.com; ❹), which has a nice restaurant and bar on site; try the buffalo burger.

Big Bend National Park

The **Rio Grande**, flowing through 1500-foot canyons, makes a ninety-degree bend south of Marathon to form the southern border of **BIG BEND NATIONAL PARK** – thanks to its isolation one of the least visited of the US national parks.

The Apache, who forced the Chisos Indians out three hundred years ago, said this hauntingly beautiful wilderness was used by the Great Spirit to dump all the rocks left over from the creation of the world; the Spanish, meanwhile, called it *terra desconocida,* "strange, unknown land." A breathtaking 800,000-acre expanse of forested mountains and ocotilla-dotted desert, Big Bend has been home to ranchers, miners, and smugglers, a last frontier for the true-grit pioneers of the American West. Today there is camping in designated areas, but much of the park remains barely charted territory. Ruins of primitive Mexican and white settlements are testament to Big Bend's power to defeat earlier visitors. Wild animals have fared somewhat better: mountain lions, black bears, roadrunners, and javelinas (an odd-looking, bristly grey hog-like creature with a pointy snout) all roam free. Violent contrasts in topography and temperature result in dramatic juxtapositions of desert and mountain plant and animal life. Despite the dryness, tangles of pretty wild flowers and blossoming cacti erupt into color each March and April. In the heightened security measures since September 11th, it has become illegal to cross the Rio Grande into **Mexico**, except on certain river trips.

The most interesting route into Big Bend is from the west. You can't follow the river all the way from El Paso, but Hwy-170 – the **River Road**, reached on Hwy-67 south from Marfa (see p.705) – runs through spectacular desert scenery west from Ojinaga, Mexico, which was practically wiped off the map due to floods in 2008. Before reaching the park boundary just beyond **Study Butte**, you pass through **Big Bend Ranch State Park** and the hauntingly beautiful community of **Terlingua** (see p.708).

Once in the park, unless you're prepared to do some strenuous hiking, there are few opportunities to see the river itself; the main road is obliged to run across the desert, north of the outcrop of the Chisos Mountains. West of the headquarters at **Panther Junction** a spur road leads south for about six miles, up into the **Chisos Basin**, ringed by dramatic peaks. The one gap in the rocky wall here is the **Window**, looking out over the Chihuahuan Desert. A twelve-mile loop hike to the **South Rim** is one of the most popular in the park, and the views are humbling. Driving twenty miles southeast of Panther Junction brings you to the riverside **Rio Grande Village** – unless you choose to detour just before, to bathe in natural **hot springs** that feed into the river.

At three separate stages within the park boundaries the river runs through gigantic **canyons.** The westernmost, **Santa Elena**, is the most common **rafting trip**; outfitters are available at Terlingua (see p.708).

For the serious backpacker, a thirteen-mile loop hike to the river on the **Marufo Vega trail** is one of the most stunning in the park. It offers views of the Sierra del Carmen mountain range in Mexico and a descent into a rarely visited slick-rock canyon. Feral burros sometimes wail here at sunset. A more accessible trail leads to the **Upper Burro Mesa pour-off**; it's about five mostly flat miles.

Practicalities

The park headquarters at **Panther Junction** (daily 8am–6pm; Ⓣ432/477-2251), where you can pay the $20-per-vehicle entrance fee (good for seven days), has recently updated orientation exhibits and a daytime gas station. Most **camping** at the park's three developed campsites ($10; pay at a visitor center) is first-come, first-served, though some reservations can be made for the high season (Nov–April ; Ⓣ1-877-444-6777,Ⓦwww.recreation.gov). Primitive **campgrounds** are scattered along the many marked hiking trails. These have no facilities, and you'll need a wilderness permit ($10 fee) from a visitor center. The sites at **Juniper Flats** are only about a three-mile hike and are located in a nice meadow. Other good sites in

▲ Canoeing in Big Bend

the Chisos Mountains are **SE-3, SW-3 and NE-4.**

The **Chisos Basin** has a **visitor center** and is the site of the park's only roofed accommodation. The *Chisos Mountains Lodge* (reservations essential; ⓣ432/477-2291, ⓦwww.chisosmountainslodge.com) offers motel-style rooms with balconies and a few stone cottages (nos. 102 and 103 are the best). The on-site restaurant has a good all-you-can-eat salad bar for $8.

There are additional **visitor centers** at Persimmon Gap and Castolon.

Terlingua

TERLINGUA, a magical little ghost town scattered across the low hills along Hwy-170, used to be populated by the hard-scrabble folks who worked in the mercury mines. But in the 1970s, river guides began moving into the abandoned stone structures, and now Terlingua is home to friendly outdoors enthusiasts, artists, miscreants, and drifters lured by the stunning sunsets and remote environs.

For such a tiny place, Terlingua has a lot to recommend it. Desert Sports offers a variety of **rafting trips**, from one to twelve days (ⓣ432-371-2727, ⓣwww.desertsportstx.com). It also leads group hikes, rents rafts and bikes, and provides shuttles into the backcountry. Allow $135 for a full day's guided trip along Santa Elena Canyon. During the first weekend in November, the community hosts its world championship **chili cookoff** (ⓦwww.chili.org/terlingua.html), when the place turns into the "Redneck Mardi Gras."

La Posada Milagro, at the top of the hill, offers four luxuriously rustic **rooms** (ⓣ432/371-3044, ⓦwww.laposadamilagro.com) in a restored dry-stack stone building, along with a four-bed bunkhouse. Just down the road is *Las Ruinas Camping Hostel*. Stop by the Boathouse bar for info. Near Terlingua's fly-blown cemetery, set against a backdrop of evocative ruins, an old movie house has been converted into the welcoming *Starlight Theater* (ⓣ432/371-2326, ⓦwww.starlighttheatre.com), which in fact is a bar and restaurant. Just outside the theater, locals linger on the **porch** to drink beer, gossip, and marvel at the mountains. You can buy six-packs and browse a fantastic selection of local books at the *Terlingua Trading Company*. There's good food at *Rio Bravo, Kathy's Kosmic Kowgirl Kafe* and the *Ghost Town Café*. For rowdy late-night action, head to *La Kiva* (ⓣ432/371-2250, ⓦwww.lakiva.net), on Hwy-170 at Terlingua Creek, or the *Boathouse* in the Ghost Town.

El Paso

Back when Texas was still Tejas, **EL PASO**, the second oldest settlement in the United States, was the main crossing on the Rio Grande. It still plays that role today, its 600,000 residents joining with another 1.7 million across the river in **Ciudad Juarez**, Mexico, to form the largest binational (and bilingual) megalopolis in North America. At first sight it's not an especially pretty place – massive railyards fill up much of downtown, the belching smelters of copper mills line the riverfront, and the northern reaches are taken up by the giant Fort Bliss military base. Its dramatic setting, however, where the Franklin Mountains meet the Chihuahuan Desert, gives it a certain bold pioneer edge, bearing more relation to old rather than new Mexico, with little of the pastel softness of the Southwest US.

Arrival and information

El Paso's **airport** is about five miles east of downtown; a **taxi** to the center will cost about $22, although many downtown hotels offer free van rides. Greyhound buses stop at 200 W San Antonio Ave (☎915/532-2365), while Amtrak (☎915/545-2247) pulls in at the Daniel Burnham-designed Union Station at 700 San Francisco St, slightly to the west on the other side of the El Paso Convention Center.

The **visitor center** (Mon–Fri 8am–5pm, Sat 10am–3pm; ☎1-800/351-6024, ⓦwww.visitelpaso.com) is at 1 Civic Center Plaza in the convention center complex.

Accommodation

Room rates in El Paso tend to be reasonable. The usual cheapie chains line I-10.

Camino Real 101 S El Paso St ☎915/534-3000, ⓦwww.caminoreal.com/elpaso. Downtown hotel in a grand old 1912 building with a romantic bar topped with a colorful Tiffany glass dome and surrounded by rose and black marble. ❹

Gardner Hotel & Hostel 311 E Franklin St ☎915/532-3661, ⓦwww.gardnerhotel.com. Rooms in this atmospheric hotel – where John Dillinger bedded down in the 1920s – vary from dorms ($22) through singles with shared bath to simple en-suite doubles furnished with antiques. ❶–❹

Quality Inn & Suites 6099 Montana Ave ☎915/772-3300, ⓦwww.choicehotels.com. Convenient for the airport, this spick-and-span place has huge, comfortable rooms, free coffees and pastries and a free full breakfast. ❹

The Town

Downtown El Paso's character is shaped by the **US–Mexico border**. In times past outlaws and exiles from either side of the border would take refuge across the river, and today's traffic remains considerable and not entirely uncontroversial. Manual workers come north to find undocumented jobs, and US companies secretly dump their toxic waste on the south side. Drugs are a major issue, too. The border itself, the Rio Grande, has caused its share of disagreements: the river changed course quite often in the 1800s, and it was not until the 1960s, when it was run through a concrete channel, that it was made permanent. An attractive, 55-acre park, the **Chamizal National Memorial**, on the east side of downtown off Paisano Drive, was built to commemorate the settling of the border dispute; it has a small museum (Tues–Sat 10am–5pm; free) and provides a pleasant green space for walks and picnics. The small but engrossing **Border Patrol Museum**, 4315 Transmountain Drive (Tues–Sat 9am–5pm; free), explains the work of the patrollers and highlights the ingenuity of smugglers.

On the river itself, the **Cordova Bridge** – or Bridge of the Americas – heads across into **Mexico**, where there's a larger park and a number of museums; there are no formalities, so long as you have a multiple-entry visa for the US and don't travel more than 20 or so miles south of the border. Crossing here is free; at the three other bridges – two downtown and one near the Ysleta Mission – you have to pay a 35-cent fee. But be warned: Juarez has been a violent place lately, with about 1000 mostly drug-related murders in 2008 alone.

Although El Paso is predominantly Hispanic, there is also a substantial population of **Tigua Indians**, a displaced Pueblo tribe, based in a reservation (complete with the almost statutory **casino**) on Socorro Road, southeast of downtown. The reservation's arts-and-crafts center sells pottery and textiles. Adjacent to the reservation, the simple **Ysleta del Sur**, the oldest mission in the United States, marks the beginning of an eight-mile **Mission Trail** (☎915/534-0630), with three missions – still active churches – set among scruffy cotton, alfalfa, chili, onion, and pecan fields.

In **Concordia cemetery**, just northwest of the I-10 and Hwy-54 intersection, a shambling collection of crumbling stones and plain wooden crosses commemorates assorted pioneers and desperados. The grave of romanticized gunslinger **John Wesley Hardin** is marked by a crooked headstone northwest of the Chinese graveyard, a section walled off since the Chinese built the railroads in the 1880s. El Paso is also the home of Tony Lama, makers of top-quality **cowboy boots**, available at substantial discounts at outlets across town. There is good hiking in the **Franklin Mountains** west of town, and to the east **rock climbing** is popular at the **Heuco Tanks State Historic Site**.

Eating and nightlife

Dining is, naturally, mostly Mexican. **After dark**, downtown practically expires; try the university area (UTEP), northwest of downtown. Check the free monthly *El Paso Scene* (ⓦwww.epscene.com) for listings. The *Plaza Theater* downtown is gorgeous and hosts big-name acts.

Ardovino's Desert Crossing 1 Ardovino Drive, Sunland Park, NM ⓣ575/589-0653. Just across the state line in New Mexico, this enchanting restaurant serves up pasta dishes and hosts a summer farmers' market.

Casa Juardo 226 Cincinnati Ave ⓣ915/532-6429. Great Mexican food – try the tortilla soup.

H&H Coffee Shop & Car Wash 701 E Yandell Drive ⓣ915/533-1144. Quirky time-warp diner dishing up tasty Tex-Mex – reputed to be a favored stop for President Bush and assorted governors. Stop by in the morning for their wicked huevos rancheros.

Tap Bar and Restaurant 408 E San Antonio St ⓣ915/532-1848. A diverse local crowd hangs out at this downtown dive, which serves good, cheap food.

Guadalupe Mountains National Park

Roughly 100 miles east of El Paso, Hwy-62/180 climbs toward Carlsbad Caverns along the southern fringes of the **Guadalupe Mountains**, once a stronghold of the Mescalero Apache. The national park here ($5; park headquarters in Pine Springs ⓣ915/828-3251, ⓦwww.nps.gov/gumo) is a hiking and camping destination, barely penetrated by roads and without accommodation, food, or gas. It's possible to hike right to the top of Guadalupe Peak, at 8749ft the highest point in Texas, but most walkers head instead for the flat trek through **McKittrick Canyon**, passing from bare desert into lush mountain forests beside sheer canyon walls. Camping within the park ($8 per night per tent site) is allotted on a first-come, first-served basis.

10

The Great Plains

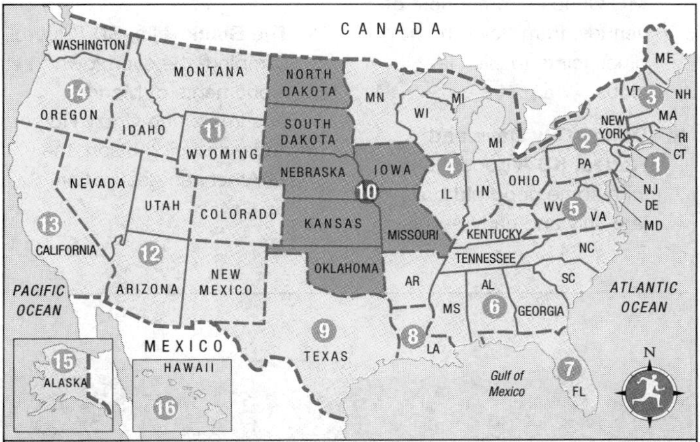

AL - ALABAMA	IN - INDIANA	MN - MINNESOTA	RI - RHODEISLAND
AR - ARKANSAS	LA - LOUISIANA	MS - MISSISSIPPI	SC - SOUTH CAROLINA
CT - CONNECTICUT	MA - MASSACHUSETTS	NC - NORTH CAROLINA	VA - VIRGINIA
DE - DELAWARE	MD - MARYLAND	NH - NEW HAMPSHIRE	VT - VERMONT
FL- FLORIDA	ME - MAINE	NJ - NEW JERSEY	WI - WISCONSIN
IL - ILLINOIS	MI - MICHIGAN	PA - PENNSYLVANIA	WV - WEST VIRGINIA

CHAPTER 10

Highlights

✱ **Woolaroc Ranch, Bartlesville, OK** Fascinating museum of Western art and history. See p.717

✱ **Hannibal, MO** This delightful Mississippi River town is still recognizable as the setting for Mark Twain's epic tales of boyhood. See p.723

✱ **Live music in Kansas City, MO** Choose from a host of venues, from down-home blues joints to slick jazz clubs. See p.733

✱ **Dodge City Days and Rodeo, KS** A good old time with some good old boys in late July and early August. See p.741

✱ **Carhenge, Alliance, NE** America's crazy vehicular Stonehenge, planted in a Nebraska wheat field. See p.749

✱ **The Badlands, SD** This spooky moonscape offers great camping and hiking – and a monument to the Ghost Dancers at Wounded Knee. See p.753

✱ **The Black Hills, SD** Superb camping, the overblown monuments of Mount Rushmore and Crazy Horse, and wandering bison: the all-American destination. See p.754

▲ The Badlands

10

The Great Plains

Stretching west of the Mississippi through **Oklahoma**, **Missouri**, **Kansas**, **Iowa**, **Nebraska**, **South Dakota**, and **North Dakota**, **THE GREAT PLAINS** are lumped together in the popular imagination as an unappealing expanse of unvarying flatness and conservative "Middle American" values. Once, however, this was the **West**, an empty canvas on which outlaws, fur trappers, buffalo hunters, and cowboys painted their dreams. In the 1870s, the wide-open range of the lone prairie, which had originally been known as the **Great American Desert**, promoted as a bountiful Garden of Eden, inspired such fascination that General Custer was moved to call it "the fairest and richest portion of the national domain."

The Plains share a troubled history. The systematic destruction by white settlers of the awesome herds of **bison** presaged the virtual eradication of the **Plains Indians**. Reservations, agencies, and "assigned lands" dwindled as the natural resources of the area attracted white settlement; after 1874, when **gold** was discovered in the Black Hills, the fate of the Native Americans was practically sealed. However, thanks to warriors like **Crazy Horse** and **Sitting Bull**, the struggle for control of the Plains was by no means easy..

The Plains are most comfortable glorying in a romantic myth of the Wild West and flaunting sanitized versions of wicked old cowtowns like **Deadwood** in South Dakota, **Dodge City** (once called the Beautiful, Bibulous Babylon of the Frontier) in Kansas, and **St Joseph**, Missouri, the birthplace of the Pony Express. **Calamity Jane**, **Wild Bill Hickok**, **Billy the Kid**, and **Annie Oakley** all left their marks here when this was the wild frontier, and today, in the sandy scrublands of the Plains, you can still see real cowboys and cattle country.

There is also evidence of nineteenth-century **Russian** and **German** settlement here. Many of the oldest families on the Plains are descendants of European Mennonites who escaped religious persecution in the 1870s, bringing with them new farming methods that heralded the region's great agricultural prosperity. The Plains still provide the nation with much of its food and export two-thirds of the world's **wheat**, seas of which wave over the flat fields of Nebraska and Kansas. The economy has also long been dependent on **oil**, especially in Oklahoma, and gold in the Dakotas.

Defining the geographical limits of the Plains is difficult, and the term itself is almost a misnomer – there are vast flat expanses and long uninterrupted roads, but there are also canyons, forests, and splashes of unexpected color, as well as two of the nation's mightiest **rivers**: the **Missouri**, which weaves its course southeast from North Dakota, and the **Mississippi**, which it joins at St Louis.

The woods, caves, and springs of the **Ozarks**, the lunar landscapes of South Dakota's **Badlands**, and stately **Mount Rushmore** are the region's most visited areas. Drama comes in the form of such unpredictable **weather** as freak blizzards, dust storms, lightning storms, and the notorious "twister" tornadoes. Images of

the devastating Thirties' dustbowl Depression (when topsoil was whisked as far away as Washington DC) remain as potent as the fantasy of Dorothy and Toto being swept up from Kansas by a tornado to the land of Oz.

Getting around the Great Plains

A **car** is practically obligatory in the Plains, where distances are long, roads straight and seemingly endless, and the population sparse. The main routes (I-94, I-90,

I-80, I-70, and I-40) cross from east to west, while north–south travel is often limited to quiet, curving byways. Greyhound **buses** travel the Interstates, but often bypass the small towns that provide a real sense of the region. Subsidiary bus lines include Jack Rabbit in South Dakota, and the Jefferson Line, which covers at least the urban areas in all the Plains states, and sometimes small towns too. Amtrak **trains** cross the Plains almost exclusively at night, with South Dakota not covered at all. St Louis, Missouri, has the major **airport**, while Wichita, Kansas, is a regional hub.

Oklahoma

Often ridiculed by the rest of the country as dust-filled and boring, **OKLAHOMA** has had a traumatic and far from dull history. In the 1830s all this land, held to be useless, was set aside as **Indian Territory** – a convenient dumping ground for the so-called Five Civilized Tribes who blocked white settlement in the southern states. The Choctaw and Chickasaw of Mississippi, the Seminole of Florida, and the Creek of Alabama were each assigned a share, while the rest (though already inhabited by indigenous Indians) was given to the Cherokee from Carolina, Tennessee, and Georgia, who followed in 1838 on the notorious four-month trek known as "the Trail of Tears" (see box, p.532). Today the state has a large Native American population – "oklahoma" is the Choctaw word for "red man" – and even the smallest towns tend to have museums of Native American history.

Once white settlers realized that Indian Territory was, in fact, well worth farming, they decided to stay. The Indians were relocated once more, and in a series of manic free-for-all scrambles starting in 1889, entire towns sprang up literally overnight. Those who jumped the gun and claimed land illegally were known as Sooners; hence Oklahoma's nickname, the **Sooner State**. White settlers didn't have an easy life, however; they faced, after great oil prosperity in the 1920s, an era of unthinkable hardship in the 1930s. The desperate migration, when whole communities fled the dust bowl for California, has come to encapsulate the worst horrors of the Depression, most famously in John Steinbeck's novel (and John Ford's film) **The Grapes of Wrath**, but also in Dorothea Lange's haunting photos of itinerant families, hitching and camping on the road, and in the sad yet hopeful songs of Woody Guthrie. After the slump of the early Thirties, improved farming techniques brought life, and people, back to Oklahoma.

Oklahoma, however, is not all plains. Most of its places of interest, including **Tulsa**, lie in the hilly wooded northeast; the far side of the central "tornado alley" prairie grassland holds the state's revitalized capital, **Oklahoma City**. The lakes and parks of the south, which bears more than a passing resemblance to neighboring Arkansas, have made tourism Oklahoma's second industry after oil.

Getting around Oklahoma

Car travel is the only way to get around. **Amtrak** serves Oklahoma City with one train a day from Fort Worth, Texas, and **Greyhound** buses speed along I-35 and I-40, which converge on Oklahoma City – but public transportation within the towns is minimal. Tulsa and Oklahoma City have **airports**. **Route 66**, which passes through both cities on its way from Missouri to Texas, is no longer a national highway, but if you have plenty of time, it makes a nostalgic alternative to the interstates. **Travel literature** detailing small communities and ghost towns is plentiful at roadside **information centers**; or, you can contact the Oklahoma Route 66 Association (ⓣ405/258-0008, ⓦwww.oklahomaroute66.com).

Eastern Oklahoma

Eastern Oklahoma includes the "Green Country" of the northeast, patterned with the foothills of the Ozarks, as well as woods, streams, lakes, and rivers that make it a popular camping destination. Tulsa is its cultural center; Tahlequah and Pawhuska are the capitals of the Cherokee and Osage nations respectively.

Tulsa

TULSA had its heydey as a wealthy oil town in the Twenties, and the otherwise sedate downtown is worth a tour for its Art Deco architecture alone. Despite – or possibly because of – its liveable, hometown atmosphere, two excellent museums, and thriving art scene, the city tends towards complacency.

Downtown Tulsa's most obvious landmark is the ornate **Art Deco Union Depot**, on the First Street and Boston Avenue Overpass, built in the early 1930s and now housing offices. One distinctive Twenties skyscraper, the **Philtower**, 527 S Boston Ave, has a green- and red-tiled sloping roof and crouching gargoyles, a lobby richly decorated in brass and marble, and a small gallery of Tulsa history. At 1301 S Boston Ave, the huge and gloriously exuberant Art Deco **Boston Avenue Methodist Church** offers good views of the city from its fourteenth story.

The **Greenwood Historic District**, a small section of narrow streets north of downtown, is where most of the town's black population once lived. In 1921, a brutal race riot erupted after a black man was accused of assaulting a white woman in a downtown elevator and houses, businesses, and churches in Greenwood were burned to the ground. Other properties fell victim to urban renewal in the mid-1960s, but a small grouping of buildings remains along Greenwood Avenue and Archer Street. The **Oklahoma Jazz Hall of Fame** at 111 E First St (Mon-Fri 9am-5pm: free; ⓣ918/596-1001) breathes life into this American genre with its tribute to jazz greats who were either residents of the state (Wardell Gray, Charlie Christian) or passed through on national tours (Cab Calloway, Dizzy Gillespie, Count Basie) to jam with local talent.

The airy and stylish **Philbrook Museum of Art**, 2727 S Rockford Rd (Tues–Sun 10am–5pm, Thurs 10am–8pm; $7.50), in the house of oilman Waite Phillips in the well-heeled suburb of Mapleridge, is a Florentine-style mansion set amid an oasis of fountains and greenery. Though displays include Native American pottery, African sculpture, and Renaissance paintings, the house itself is every bit as decorative as the art, with ostentatious marble floors, indoor fountains, and sweeping staircases.

Just northwest of downtown, the **Gilcrease Museum**, 1400 N Gilcrease Museum Rd (Tues–Sun 10am–5pm; $8; ⓣ918/596-2700), is set in the gently rolling Osage Hills, with a fine vista of the verdant valley sprawling into the horizon from the back and a good view of downtown from the front. Thomas Gilcrease, of Indian heritage, grew very rich after oil was found on his land. His private collection of Western art includes Native American works, as well as excellent Remingtons, Russells, and Morans.

Practicalities

Tulsa International Airport lies a few minutes east of downtown. Hwy-169 from Kansas City skirts the city's east side; I-44, which gives access from the south, is also the main route east–west across town. **Greyhound** comes in downtown at 317 S Detroit Ave. The **CVB**, Williams Center Tower II, 2 W Second St, suite 150 (Mon–Fri 8am–5pm; ⓣ918/585-1201 or 1-800/558-3311, ⓦwww.visittulsa.com), provides information on a self-guided **walking tour** of downtown. Local bus service operates between 5am and 8.30pm, with no Sunday service ($1.25).

Most of Tulsa's budget **hotels** are on the interstates and along W Skelly Drive, forking southwest from I-44. Try the *Ramada Inn Tulsa* (3175 E 51st St ⓣ918/743-9811) which serves up comfortable rooms at the roadside, with an indoor pool. There's camping at the *KOA*, 19605 E Skelly Drive (ⓣ918/266-4227; $24). There are a few **B&Bs** in town, including the *McBirney Mansion* (ⓣ918/585-3234; ⑥), perched overlooking the Arkansas river; check the CVB website (see above) for other listings.

Tulsa's **restaurants** are diverse and scattered; good options can be found along E 15th Street and S Peoria Avenue in the **Brookside** district like *Camerelli's* (1536 E 15th St, ⓣ918/582-8900) featuring inexpensive but tasty Italian pasta dishes, with a heavy carnivorous bent, Downtown holds several down-home diners. The Fifties-style *Metro Diner* at 3001 E 11th St (ⓣ918/592-2616) serves up tasty home-baked pies and chicken-fried steaks, as well as ice cream sodas.

Bartlesville

For forty miles north of Tulsa, the monotony of the plains is relieved only by clumps of spindly scrub oaks. Then comes quiet **BARTLESVILLE**, dominated by the extraordinary, anachronistic **Price Tower** (Tues–Sat 10am–5pm, Sun noon–5pm; tours Tues–Sat 11am and 2pm, Sun 2pm). This cantilevered green oddity, at Sixth Street and Dewey Avenue, was designed by Frank Lloyd Wright in 1956 and resembles a tall tree. Today it holds art galleries, the stylish *Copper Restaurant + Bar*, on its 15th and 16th floors, and the modern *Inn at Price Tower*, an Arts and Crafts-style hotel (ⓣ1-877/424-2424; ⑥). The **Frank Phillips Home**, 1107 SE Cherokee Ave (Wed–Sat 10am–5pm, Sun 1–5pm; $3 suggested donation), built in 1908 by the founder of Phillips Oil, displays oil wealth at its gaudiest, with gold faucets, mirrored ceilings, and marble floors. More impressive is his **Woolaroc Ranch**, thirteen miles southwest in the Osage Hills, now a wildlife refuge and museum of Western art and history (daily 10am–5pm; Sept–May closed Mon; $8; 4.30pm last admission; ⓣ1-888/966-5276, ⓦwww.woolaroc.org), where over sixty thousand artifacts are scattered throughout seven huge rooms. Paintings and decorative art, from Native American works to the epic Western scenes of Remington and Russell, line the walls, while artifacts belonging to various tribes, pioneers, and cowboys are gathered in too great an abundance to take in. Look out for the 95-million-year-old dinosaur egg, exquisite Navajo blankets, scalps taken by Native Americans, and Buffalo Bill's weathered saddle. If the pricey tower downtown is out of your lodging budget, opt for the bare bones lodging *Travelers Motel*, 3105 SE Frank Phillips Blvd (ⓣ918/333-1900; ①).

Muskogee

In the 1830s, the Creek Indians relocated fifty miles southeast of Tulsa to **MUSKOGEE**. After establishing the town as the central meeting place of the Civilized Tribes, in 1905 Native American leaders gathered here to draw up a plan for their own separate state, which was never to be. The arrival of the railroad in the 1870s

Storm chasing

With such unpredictable weather, it's no surprise that **storm chasing** has become big business in Oklahoma and surrounding "tornado alley" states. If you're either very foolhardy or very brave, you can spend a week or two driving around the prairies chasing tornadoes and some wicked, wild weather. Companies such as Storm Chasing Adventure Tours (Ⓣ303/888-8629, Ⓦwww.stormchasing.com) and Cloud 9 (Ⓣ405/323-1145, Ⓦcloud9tours.com) claim that their operations are perfectly safe and all but guarantee you an up-close and personal encounter with a tornado. Tours run from one to two weeks, cover many Midwestern states and will set you back anywhere from $2500 to $3000.

and the discovery of oil in 1903 both guaranteed that the white settlers would usurp the town. The **Five Civilized Tribes Museum**, Honor Heights Drive, Agency Hill (Mon–Sat 10am–5pm, Sun 1–5pm; $3; Ⓦwww.fivetribes.org), tells the Native Americans' story through costumes, documents, photographs, and jewelry. The other unlikely attraction in town is the USS *Batfish*, a World War II–era submarine moored in the Oklahoma grass at 3500 Batfish Rd (Thurs–Sat 10am–5pm, Sun 1–5pm, extended summer hours; $6).

Muskogee is an appealing place, with a dozen **motels** within a few blocks along US-69, including a *Days Inn* at 900 S 32nd St (Ⓣ918/683-3911; ③). It also makes a good base for the crystal-clear **Lake Tenkiller**, thirty miles southeast on US-64. Surrounded by woods, cliffs, and quiet beaches, the lake is perfect for fishing, boating, swimming, and scuba diving. Camping facilities are available at Lake Tenkiller State Park; call Ⓣ918/489-5641 for full details.

Oklahoma City and beyond

One hundred surprisingly green miles along the Will Rogers Turnpike and the famed **Route 66** separate Oklahoma City and Tulsa. Along this historic highway, known as the "mother road," the Blue Whale in Catoosa and the Round Barn in Arcadia are classic American **roadside attractions**. West of the state capital, I-40 carries you across empty agricultural communities, the tedium only broken by the worthwhile **Route 66 Museum** in Clinton. I-44 to Wichita Falls passes near the ruggedly beautiful **Wichita Mountains Wildlife Refuge**; to the north, in the Oklahoma Panhandle, ranches and tiny hamlets are the only signs of life.

Oklahoma City

OKLAHOMA CITY was created in a matter of hours on April 22, 1889, after a single gunshot signaled the opening of the land to white settlement. What was barren prairie at dawn was by nightfall a city of ten thousand. In 1911 the capital was moved here from nearby Guthrie, and in 1928 oil was discovered. Sitting on one of the nation's largest oilfields, the city was brought up short by the slump in the 1980s, though it remains the largest stocker and feeder cattle market in the world. The economy came alive again in the 1990s, aided by tourism development and an inflated sales tax that funded redevelopment in run-down neighborhoods.

The devastating **bombing** of the Alfred P. Murrah Federal Building on April 19, 1995, which killed 168 people, nineteen of them children, literally tore the heart out of the city; the massive community rescue effort has since helped Oklahoma City regain some of its self-confidence, though it will be a while before the city

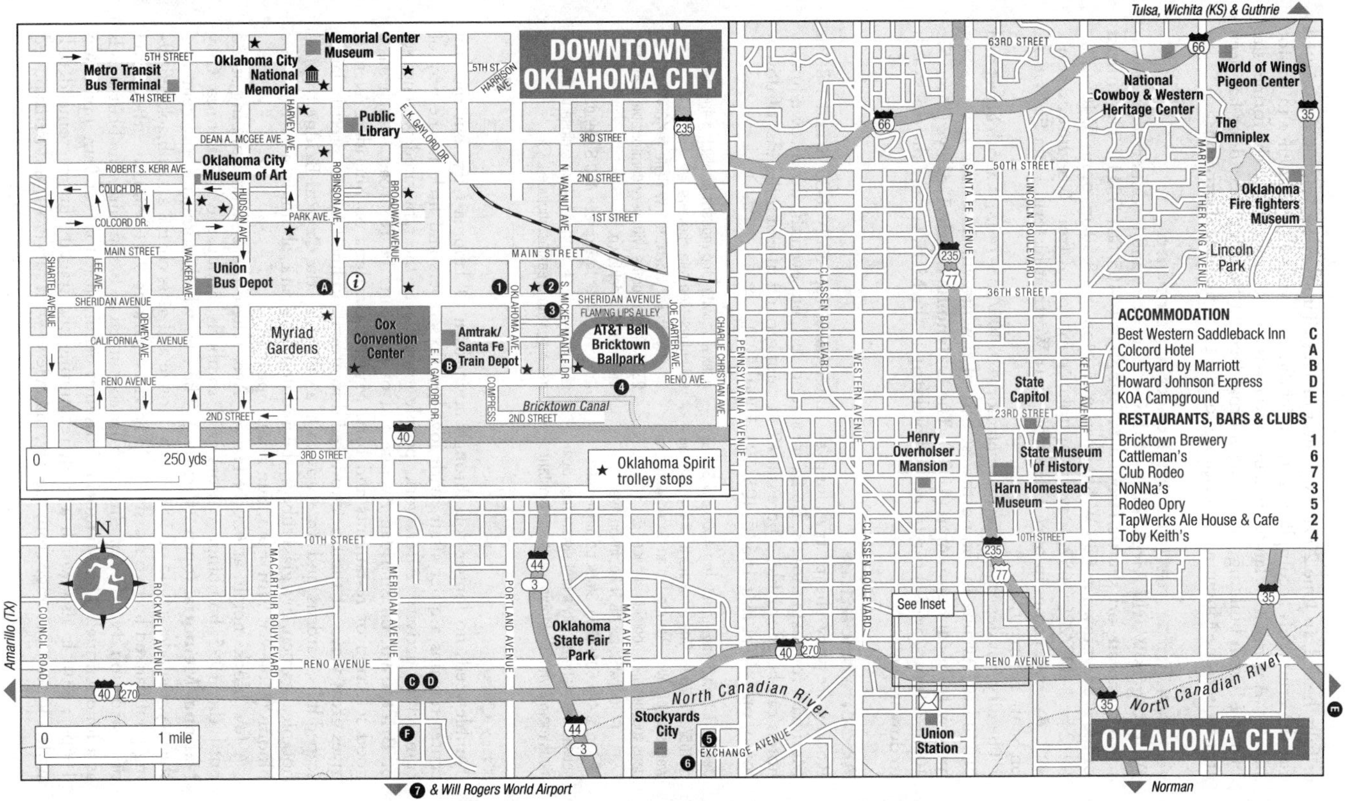
DOWNTOWN OKLAHOMA CITY
OKLAHOMA CITY
Tulsa, Wichita (KS) & Guthrie
Amarillo (TX)
7 & Will Rogers World Airport
Norman
E
ACCOMMODATION
Best Western Saddleback Inn C
Colcord Hotel A
Courtyard by Marriott B
Howard Johnson Express D
KOA Campground E
RESTAURANTS, BARS & CLUBS
Bricktown Brewery 1
Cattleman's 6
Club Rodeo 7
NoNNa's 3
Rodeo Opry 5
TapWerks Ale House & Cafe 2
Toby Keith's 4
Oklahoma Spirit trolley stops
0 250 yds
0 1 mile
N
Memorial Center Museum
Oklahoma City National Memorial
Metro Transit Bus Terminal
Public Library
Oklahoma City Museum of Art
Union Bus Depot
Myriad Gardens
Cox Convention Center
Amtrak/ Santa Fe Train Depot
AT&T Bell Bricktown Ballpark
Bricktown Canal
5TH STREET
4TH STREET
3RD STREET
2ND STREET
1ST STREET
5TH ST
HARRISON AVE.
E.K. GAYLORD DR.
DEAN A. MCGEE AVE.
ROBERT S. KERR AVE.
COUCH DR.
COLCORD DR.
MAIN STREET
SHERIDAN AVENUE
CALIFORNIA AVENUE
RENO AVENUE
RENO AVE.
SHARTEL AVENUE
LEE AVE.
DEWEY AVE.
WALKER AVE.
HUDSON AVE.
HARVEY AVE.
PARK AVE.
ROBINSON AVE.
BROADWAY AVENUE
OKLAHOMA AVE.
S. MICKEY MANTLE DR
N. WALNUT AVE
FLAMING LIPS ALLEY
JOE CARTER AVE.
CHARLIE CHRISTIAN AVE.
COMPRESS
National Cowboy & Western Heritage Center
World of Wings Pigeon Center
The Omniplex
Oklahoma Fire fighters Museum
Lincoln Park
State Capitol
State Museum of History
Harn Homestead Museum
Henry Overholser Mansion
Union Station
Oklahoma State Fair Park
Stockyards City
See Inset
63RD STREET
50TH STREET
36TH STREET
23RD STREET
10TH STREET
MARTIN LUTHER KING AVENUE
LINCOLN BOULEVARD
SANTA FE AVENUE
KELLEY AVENUE
CLASSEN BOULEVARD
WESTERN AVENUE
PENNSYLVANIA AVENUE
MAY AVENUE
PORTLAND AVENUE
MERIDIAN AVENUE
MACARTHUR BOULEVARD
ROCKWELL AVENUE
COUNCIL ROAD
EXCHANGE AVENUE
North Canadian River

is fully healed. In June 2001, ex-military recluse Timothy McVeigh was executed for the crime; his accomplice, Terry Nichols, is serving a life sentence in jail for his part. A permanent landscaped memorial has been constructed at the former site of the Murrah building, while the Journal Record Building next door has been turned into the Museum and Institute for the Prevention of Terrorism.

Arrival, information, and getting around

Will Rogers World Airport lies southwest of the city and is connected to downtown by an airport shuttle (around $17 single; ⓣ405/681-3311). The **tourist office** is downtown at 189 W Sheridan Ave (Mon–Fri 8.30am–5pm; ⓣ405/297-8912 or 1-800/225-5652, ⓦwww.visitokc.com), not far from **Greyhound** at no. 427. **Amtrak** comes in once a day from Fort Worth at historic Santa Fe Station, on Santa Fe Street.

The **city bus** depot (ⓦwww.gometro.org, ⓣ405/235-7433) is at 5th Street and N Hudson Avenue in the northwest part of downtown. Buses run daily except Sunday from 6am until 6pm ($1.25). The **Oklahoma Spirit Trolleys** (Mon–Sat 10am–11pm; 25¢–$1) run from the hotel strip in the Meridian and the stockyards to downtown.

Accommodation

Rooms are very cheap; try along the interstates, especially I-35 S and I-40 at Meridian, for chain **motels**. B&Bs are a good deal, but even the downtown luxury hotels can be affordable. There is a *KOA* campground fifteen miles east of downtown, on I-40 at exit 166 (ⓣ405/391-5000; $23).

Best Western Saddleback Inn 4300 SW 3rd St ⓣ405/947-7000. One block north of I-40, on the west side of town. Pseudo-Indian decor, with luxurious touches like poolside service. ⑤

Colcord Hotel 15 N Robinson Ave ⓣ405/601-4300. Sleek boutique hotel housed in Oklahoma City's first skyscraper. Spacious rooms with Bricktown views spell instant relaxation with chic modern furnishing and heavenly glass-tiled rain showers. ⑥

Courtyard by Marriott 2 W Reno ⓣ405/232-2290. Smart rooms with very comfortable beds in the heart of Bricktown. ⑥

Howard Johnson Express 400 S Meridian Ave ⓣ405/943-9841. Standard rooms close to the freeway, with breakfast included. ③

The City

Tumbleweeds no longer roll through downtown Oklahoma City, but the city center remains a quiet affair, with low-key skyscrapers and little in the way of commercial activity. After work, people gravitate to the renovated warehouses of **Bricktown**, on Sheridan Avenue east of the Santa Fe Railroad, which has a good selection of restaurants and bars. **Myriad Gardens** on Sheridan Avenue, gives great views of the brick-towered downtown skyline from its prettily landscaped hills, gardens, and waterways. On a sunny day the **Crystal Bridge** tropical botanical garden, in a glass tube in the middle of the park, abounds in garish exotic blooms (Mon–Sat 9am–6pm, Sun noon–6pm; $6).

A few blocks north, at 620 N Harvey Ave, where the Federal Building stood until the 1995 bombing, visitors mill somberly about the **Oklahoma City National Memorial** (open 24hr; free). The site, which dominates the center of the city, includes a field of 168 empty bronze and glass chairs, and a black reflecting pool flanked by two massive gold barriers marking 9.01–9.03am – the period of destruction. Nearby, an elm tree that continued to bloom after the blast stands as a lone sentinel. The **Memorial Museum** behind it (Mon–Sat 9am–6pm, Sun 1–6pm; $10) is also worth a visit, recounting the tragedy in gruesome detail, with TV news coverage from the day, interviews with survivors, and items pulled from the wreckage, such as shredded clothing, cracked coffee mugs, and twisted filing cabinets. Other sections describe the ensuing FBI investigation and McVeigh trial, and on the ground floor are tributes to the victims. Outside, the complex is surrounded by a chain-link fence weighed down by tokens and talismans left by mourners.

Close to the memorial, at 415 Couch Drive, is the new **Oklahoma City Museum of Art** (Tues–Sat 10am–5pm, Thurs 10am–9pm, Sun noon–5pm; $12; Ⓦwww.okcmoa.com). The lobby is host to a 55ft blown-glass tower by Dale Chihuly, as well as a permanent exhibition of his work. Other galleries hold European and American art, as well as numerous traveling exhibitions.

Just northeast of downtown, a working oil well pumps crude from underneath the **Capitol Building** at 2300 N Lincoln Blvd (Mon–Fri 8am–4.30pm; free). The Capitol Complex includes the **Oklahoma History Center** (Mon–Sat 9am–5pm, Sun noon–5pm; $5), across from the Governor's Mansion. The **Heritage Hills** area to the south, where the cattle barons, oil millionaires, and bankers used to live, is worth a visit for the luxurious Victorian **Overholser Mansion**, 405 NW 15th St (Tues–Sat 10am–3pm; hourly tours $3); nearby, the **Harn Homestead Museum**, 313 NE 16th St (Mon–Fri 10am–4pm; guided tours only; $5), is also worth a wander for its old barn and wagons, and general pioneer spirit.

Sitting atop Persimmon Hill overlooking Route 66, the **National Cowboy Museum and Heritage Center**, 1700 NE 63rd St (daily 9am–5pm; $8.50; Ⓦwww.nationalcowboymuseum.org), is a real treat, combining "high art" and popular art in one loving collection. In the works of Remington and Russell the link between Western art and Western movies is very clear. The paintings look like film stills, and titles such as *Waiting for Trouble* evoke the cinema's endlessly reworked myths of the West. Large exhibitions focus on contemporary Native American work, much of it colorful, bitter, and subversive. John Wayne's collection is a delight for the cowboy fetishist, and the Western Performers Hall of Fame pays homage to movie cowboys and cowgirls in hilariously reverent oil paintings and memorabilia.

Squeezed between Martin Luther King Drive and Hwy-35 are the **Firefighters Museum**, the **City Zoo**, and the **Omniplex** (ten acres of futuristic exhibits, with an aquarium, planetarium, and IMAX).

Oklahoma City's **stockyards**, on Agnew Avenue and Exchange Street, are the busiest in the world, having sold over one hundred million cattle since 1910. They're well worth a visit, though vegetarians and animal-lovers should steer clear. This is the real thing, stomping, snorting, and smelly, with scrawny animals shunted in and out of tiny pens for auction. The roughnecks who spend their lives here – smoking, chatting, even sleeping – take no apparent notice of the quick-fire auctioneer, but nonetheless millions of head of cattle are bought and sold each year, and it can make for addictive entertainment. Morning sales, starting at 6am (Mon & Tues only), are the most intense, fizzling out by late afternoon.

Eating

Beef is, of course, good in Oklahoma City, especially around the stockyards. The warehouse restaurants of **Bricktown** are popular with the after-work and singles crowds.

Catfish Cabin 6317 N Meridian Ave ⓣ405/721-7553. This local joint serves up legendary catfish to a loyal crowd.

Cattleman's Steakhouse 1309 S Agnew Ave ⓣ405/236-0416. Cattlemen from the adjacent stockyards eat in this comfortable, pub-like restaurant, which has served great steaks since 1910. The place was allegedly won in a craps game. Lunchtime specials are a good deal.

Nonna's 1 Mickey Mantle Way ⓣ405/235-4410. High-end American eats with a European flair. Diners delight in choice cuisine like pan-seared blackberry duck served over candied sweet potatoes and balanced with a savory Yukon gold galette

TapWerks Ale House and Café 121 E Sheridan Ave ☎405/319-9599. Very popular Bricktown restaurant with a British-influenced menu and over one hundred beers on tap.

Toby Keith's I Love This Bar And Brill 310 Johnny Bench Drive ☎405/231-0254. Country crooner Toby Keith's down-home joint dishes up burgers and fries as well as live country music.

Nightlife and entertainment

If you're into **country music**, Oklahoma City will set you right, with quite a few live music and dance venues. Beyond that, there are a few **pubs** and some progressive **clubs** – especially those in **Bricktown**, which attempt to part Oklahoma City from its cowtown image. Wednesday's *Oklahoma Gazette*, along with lively articles, carries good **listings**.

Bricktown Brewery 1 Oklahoma Ave ☎405/232-BREW. Large brewpub, with giant tanks of beer on show in its restaurant. Live music most nights.

Club Rodeo 2301 S Meridian Ave ☎405/686-1191. Popular dance hall and saloon with nightly live music. Can get a little cheesy some nights, other nights are rollicking fun. Quite a way south-west of downtown, but worth the trip. Hours and cover vary.

Rodeo Opry 221 Exchange Ave ☎405/297-9773. Popular venue for authentic country music shows, in the style of Nashville's Grand Ole Opry. One show a week, Sat 7.30pm.

Missouri

The state of **MISSOURI**, where the forest meets the prairie and the Mississippi River meets the Missouri River, has two significant cities: dominant **St Louis** sits midway down the state's eastern fringe; **Kansas City** is almost directly across on the western border. The pair are linked by I-70, but there's not much in between. In contrast, the south features the beautiful hillsides, streams, and ragged lakes of the **Ozark Mountains**, as well as the booming tourist haven of **Branson**. In the east, small river towns such as **Hannibal** and **Ste Genevieve** brighten the course of the Mississippi.

Although the first French colonists honored the claims of local Native Americans, such as the original Missouri, when the area was sold to the US in 1803 as part of the **Louisiana Purchase**, the Indians were driven west by a great rush of settlers. In the 1840s and 1850s immigrants from Germany and Ireland flooded into eastern Missouri. Outnumbering their pro-slavery predecessors, they swung the balance in favor of staying in the Union during the **Civil War** – however, Confederate guerrilla forces attracted considerable support among slave-owners in the west of the state. Meanwhile, Missouri, and St Louis in particular, was establishing itself as an important **gateway to the West**. Today, the "Show Me State" (so called because of the supposed skepticism of the typical Missourian) retains a **conservative** air.

Getting around Missouri

It takes **Greyhound** about six hours to traverse the central corridor between St Louis and Kansas City. Infrequent Greyhound buses run through the southeast, to Springfield and a few Ozark towns, but you'll need a **car** to see the mountains and the river towns in the north. St Louis and Kansas City have major **airports**. Daily Amtrak **trains** from Chicago run to St Louis, from where direct connections can be made to points west. For keen **cyclists**, there's the popular Katy Trail, which stretches 230 miles from St Charles to Clinton.

Eastern Missouri

The Mississippi defines Missouri's eastern border, absorbing as major tributaries the Missouri, Ohio, Illinois, and Des Moines rivers. Over the years, innumerable towns have sprung up along the river, their aspirations reflected by such classical names as Alexandria, Antioch, and Athens. **Hannibal**, the boyhood home of **Mark Twain**, is the largest in the northeast, while Gallic **Ste Genevieve** is the prettiest in the south. All have, however, decreased in importance with the growing pre-eminence of **St Louis**. Away from the river, the land rises to the Ozark Plateau, whose deep green valleys are cut by swift, clear streams.

Hannibal

HANNIBAL might well have been just another medium-sized river settlement, had not Samuel Langhorne Clemens spent his boyhood here. (Clemens renamed himself **Mark Twain**, after the depth-marking cry of pilots on the Mississippi.) Although Hannibal does have other industries, downtown is little more than a Twain theme park of museums, period buildings, and wax displays.

Twain wrote surprisingly little about his hometown in his extensive nonfiction works; you could say he spoke with his feet when he left for good at seventeen to become a journeyman printer, riverboat pilot, journalist, and writer. However, although he calls the rowdy frontier river port "St Petersburg" in *The Adventures of Tom Sawyer* and the sequel *The Adventures of Huckleberry Finn*, Hannibal is the inspiration for the novels.

The Town

Hannibal's riverside location and historical buildings make it almost disturbingly picturesque. Squeezed between two steep bluffs – *Tom Sawyer*'s **"Cardiff Hill"** to the north and **Lover's Leap** to the south – the once-busy community is now quiet except for the occasional creaking of a crane loading cement. You can get an intimate look at the Mississippi aboard the slow-moving **Mark Twain riverboat** (1hr tours 11am, 1.30pm & 4pm, $12; 2hr dinner cruise by reservation 6.30pm, $33; ⓣ573/221-3222). Twain's youthful stomping-ground was the short, cobbled incline of **Hill Street**, at the north end of town. Adjoining the restored **Mark Twain Boyhood Home**, a simple white-clapboard house where Twain lived between 1844 and 1853, the **Mark Twain Museum** (summer daily 8am–6pm; rest of year times vary; $8; ⓣ573/221-9010) includes such memorabilia as first editions, letters, photos, original artwork, and one of the author's trademark white coats. Immediately opposite, there's a bookstore in the original home of Laura Hawkins (the model for Tom Sawyer's first love, Becky Thatcher), who visited Twain in Connecticut in 1908 and lived on in Hannibal until 1928. Nearby stands the law office of Twain's father, a justice of the peace who died of pneumonia while the writer was still a boy. Antique, souvenir, and gift stores stretch away from here down **Main Street**, which also holds the **New Mark Twain Museum** (summer daily 9am–6pm; rest of year times vary; same phone as above). Included in the admission price to the original museum and home, the exhibits here re-create scenes from Twain's books, the cave and Huck Finn's raft among them. Upstairs at the gift shop are the fifteen original **Norman Rockwell paintings** commissioned for limited editions of Twain's most popular titles.

About two miles south of town is the **Mark Twain Cave** (summer daily 9am–8pm; times vary rest of the year; $15; ⓣ573/221-1656), where one-hour tours recall Tom and Becky's frightening misadventure in the dark. Further south, Hwy-79 towards St Louis offers one of the most **scenic drives** along the Mississippi, continually broken by thin, elongated, thickly wooded islands, and bounded by towering limestone bluffs.

Practicalities

Pick up full details on Hannibal from the **visitor center**, 505 N Third St (April–Oct daily 8am–6pm; Nov–March Mon–Fri 8am–5pm, Sat & Sun limited hours; ⓣ573/221-2477, ⓦwww.visithannibal.com). **Motel** rates vary wildly according to season. The very central *Hotel Clemens*, 401 N Third St (ⓣ573/248-1150; ❸–❺), has a pool. One of nearly a dozen **B&Bs**, *LulaBelle's*, 111 Bird St (ⓣ573/221-6662 or 1-800/882-4890; ❸–❻), has rooms of varying degrees of luxury, including some with river views, and serves tasty food. The *Mark Twain Family Restaurant*, just up from the Mark Twain Museum at 400 N Third St (ⓣ573/221-5300), serves classic American fare. A mile south of town on Hwy-79, you can **camp** at the shaded *Mark Twain Campground* (ⓣ573/221-1656 or 1-800/527-0304; $19).

St Louis

Perched just below the confluence of the Mississippi and Missouri rivers, three hundred miles south of Chicago and the same distance north of Memphis, cosmopolitan **ST LOUIS** (pronounced, whatever any song might say, "Saint Lewis") owes its vaguely European air to its history and cultural infrastructure. Any city capable of producing one of the twentieth century's greatest poets, as well as one of its greatest rock 'n' rollers – namely, **T.S. Eliot** and **Chuck Berry** – probably has a lot going for it.

St Louis was founded in 1764 by the French fur trader Pierre Laclede. However, the American immigration that followed its sale to the US under the **Louisiana Purchase** all but extinguished the refinement it had gained during French and Spanish rule. It subsequently became crucial as the major gateway for pioneers on the wagon trails westward. **Transportation** – first steamboats, then trains, and now air haulage – has long been the basis of its considerable industrial strength. However, St Louis has not always had an easy ride. Downtown reached a nadir during the 1970s, but the years since have seen a remarkable turnaround, with attractions on the revitalized **riverfront** including the magnificent **Gateway Arch** and the restored warehouses of **Laclede's Landing**.

Try not to leave without sampling the **outlying districts**. To the west lie arty **Central West End** and young **University** (or "U") **City**, on either side of prodigious **Forest Park**, with its museums and playing fields. The blue-collar **Southside** features the markets, antique shops, and jazz pubs of **Soulard** and the Italian shops and cafés of **the Hill**. Directly across the river in Illinois, **East St Louis**, once the stomping ground of jazz stars like Miles Davis and John Coltrane, has very little to offer visitors.

Arrival, information, and getting around

Lambert-St Louis International Airport is a dozen miles northwest of downtown – $36 by taxi or $3.50 by bus or MetroLink. Some **Greyhound** buses call at the airport, though you cannot buy tickets there. You can either purchase tickets by mail, or you can board at the airport without a ticket and pay for one when you arrive in the bus main terminal downtown at 1450 N 13th St. **Amtrak** stops at 551 S 16th St.

The city has **visitor centers** at the America Center in the massive Cervantes Convention Center (Mon–Fri 9am–5pm, Sat 9am–2pm; ⓣ1-800/916-0092), and at Kiener Plaza (Mon–Fri 9am–5pm, Sat 9am–2pm; closed Jan & Feb; ⓣ314/231-0336). For the latest **events**, visit ⓦwww.explorestlouis.com.

The Bi-State Transit System (ⓣ314/231-2345) operates the **MetroLink**, a light-rail system serving the airport and most significant tourist sights ($1.75; free in downtown Mon–Fri 11.30am–1.30pm). BSTS buses also go to all of the city's suburbs, though service can be slow and infrequent.

Accommodation

Good-value **lodging** can be found downtown, with appealing weekend rates. The CVB will have information on the area's numerous **B&Bs**.

Best Western Inn at the Park 4630 Lindell Blvd ⓣ314/367-7500 or 1-800/373-7501. Good chain motel on the northeast corner of Forest Park, right by the cafés of Central West End. 4–5

Chase Park Plaza 212 Kingshighway Blvd ⓣ314/633-3000. Stately historic high-rise hotel overlooking Forest Park offering richly appointed one- and two-bedroom suites. 7–8

Drury Inn – Union Station 201 S 20th St ⓣ314/231-3900 or 1-800/325-8300. Very tastefully restored accommodation with a grand historic lobby and serviceable, if not somewhat small guest rooms. 4–6

Embassy Suites 901 N 1st St ⓣ314/241-4200. Comfortable suites in the heart of Laclede's Landing. Buffet breakfast included. 6

HI-Great Rivers Hostel 2800 Normandy Drive, Bel-Nor ⓣ314/241-4200, ⓦwww.greatrivershostel.org. This clean hostel, two blocks from a MetroLink stop, is in a former dormitory on the south campus of UMSL. Dorms are $20, private rooms are $30.

The Huckleberry Finn Youth Hostel 1904-1908 S 12th St ⓣ314/644-4660. Dorms ($20) on the edge of a dodgy area in Soulard, so take bus #10 or #30 from downtown. Office hours 8–10am & 6–10pm.

Hyatt Regency St Louis 1820 Market St ⓣ314/231-1234. Located inside the Romanesque Union Station Depot, the Hyatt is centrally located and offers guests modern amenities in a historical setting. 5–7

Park Avenue Mansion 2007 Park Ave ⓣ314/588-9004. Attractive, homey B&B on Lafayette Square, with friendly service and a lovely outdoor patio and garden. 5

The riverfront

The one-and-a-half-mile cobbled granite **wharf** along the Mississippi used to lie in the shadow of a dense tangle of warehouses and factories. When river trade decreased, most were ripped down. However, some restored structures between the Eads and Martin Luther King bridges now form **Laclede's Landing Historic District**, their cast-iron facades fronting touristy antique stores, restaurants, and live music venues. In early September, the district hosts the **Big Muddy Blues Festival**, featuring artists of national prominence and a great party atmosphere (information on ⓣ314/241-5875, ⓦwww.lacledeslanding.org).

On the waterfront itself, where roustabouts once handled cargoes of cotton and ores, assorted permanently moored vessels hold museums, theater shows, a heliport, and casinos. **Cruises** aboard replica paddle-wheelers leave from under the Gateway Arch (April–Nov daily 10am–4.30pm; $12; dinner cruises depart at 7.30pm; call for pricing; ⓣ314/621-4040 or 1-800/878-7411).

Ten minutes' walk south, more than thirty blocks of derelict buildings were torn down to clear space for the **Jefferson National Expansion Memorial**, dedicated

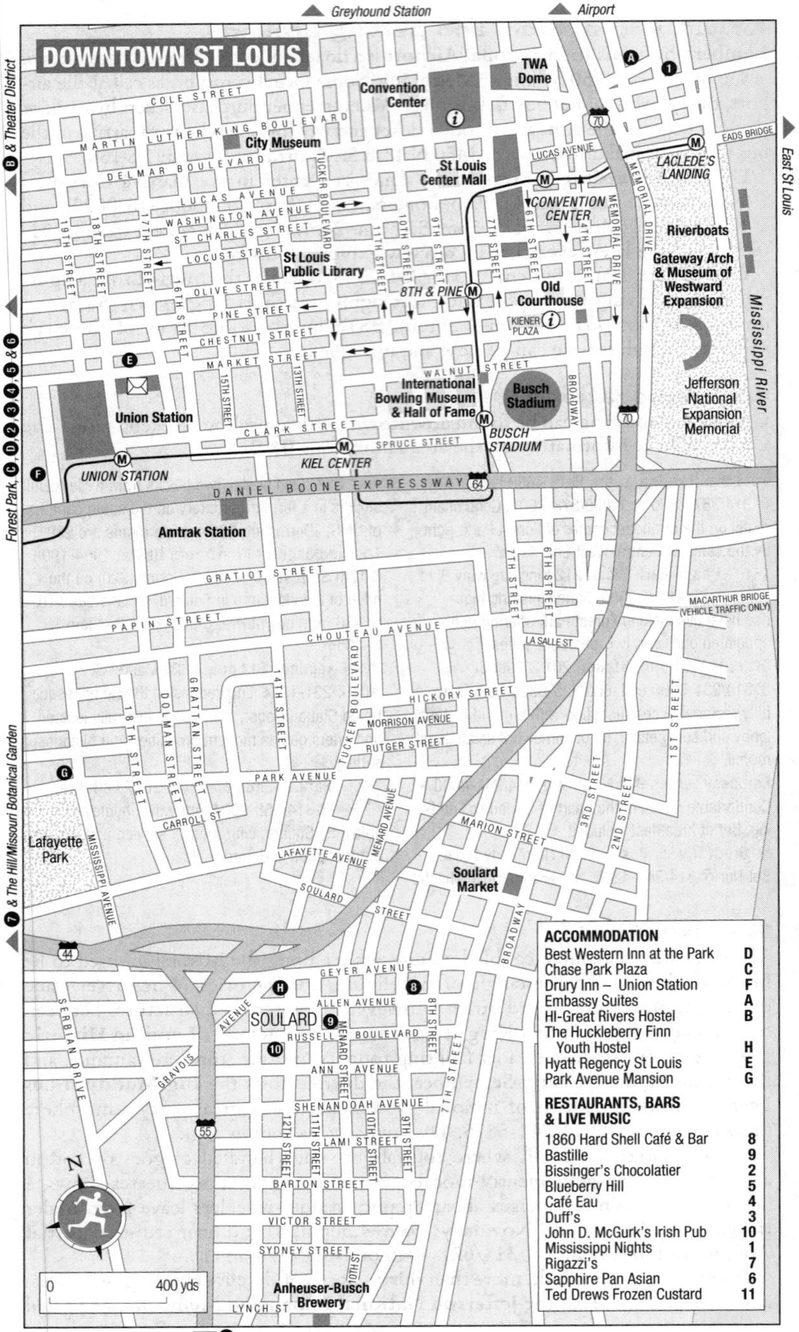
DOWNTOWN ST LOUIS
Greyhound Station
Airport
B & Theater District
East St Louis
Forest Park, C, D, 2, 3, 4, 5 & 6
7 & The Hill/Missouri Botanical Garden
11
Convention Center
TWA Dome
City Museum
St Louis Center Mall
LACLEDE'S LANDING
CONVENTION CENTER
Riverboats
Gateway Arch & Museum of Westward Expansion
St Louis Public Library
8TH & PINE
Old Courthouse
KIENER PLAZA
Mississippi River
Jefferson National Expansion Memorial
International Bowling Museum & Hall of Fame
Busch Stadium
BUSCH STADIUM
Union Station
UNION STATION
KIEL CENTER
DANIEL BOONE EXPRESSWAY
Amtrak Station
EADS BRIDGE
MACARTHUR BRIDGE (VEHICLE TRAFFIC ONLY)
COLE STREET
MARTIN LUTHER KING BOULEVARD
DELMAR BOULEVARD
LUCAS AVENUE
WASHINGTON AVENUE
ST CHARLES STREET
LOCUST STREET
OLIVE STREET
PINE STREET
CHESTNUT STREET
MARKET STREET
WALNUT STREET
CLARK STREET
SPRUCE STREET
TUCKER BOULEVARD
MEMORIAL DRIVE
BROADWAY
GRATIOT STREET
PAPIN STREET
CHOUTEAU AVENUE
LA SALLE ST
HICKORY STREET
MORRISON AVENUE
RUTGER STREET
PARK AVENUE
CARROLL ST
MARION STREET
LAFAYETTE AVENUE
MENARD AVENUE
SOULARD STREET
DOLMAN STREET
GRATTAN STREET
MISSISSIPPI AVENUE
Lafayette Park
Soulard Market
SOULARD
GEYER AVENUE
ALLEN AVENUE
RUSSELL BOULEVARD
ANN AVENUE
SHENANDOAH AVENUE
LAMI STREET
BARTON STREET
VICTOR STREET
SYDNEY STREET
LYNCH ST
GRAVOIS AVENUE
SERBIAN DRIVE
Anheuser-Busch Brewery
0
400 yds
N
ACCOMMODATION
Best Western Inn at the Park D
Chase Park Plaza C
Drury Inn – Union Station F
Embassy Suites A
HI-Great Rivers Hostel B
The Huckleberry Finn Youth Hostel H
Hyatt Regency St Louis E
Park Avenue Mansion G
RESTAURANTS, BARS & LIVE MUSIC
1860 Hard Shell Café & Bar 8
Bastille 9
Bissinger's Chocolatier 2
Blueberry Hill 5
Café Eau 4
Duff's 3
John D. McGurk's Irish Pub 10
Mississippi Nights 1
Rigazzi's 7
Sapphire Pan Asian 6
Ted Drews Frozen Custard 11

▲ The Gateway Arch

to the US president who negotiated the Louisiana Purchase and thereby opened up the West, and to the pioneers who journeyed along the Oregon and Santa Fe trails. The highlight of the expansive green space is the **Gateway Arch**. Designed by Eero Saarinen and completed in 1965, the arch is a 630ft stainless steel parabola of majestic symmetry; in technical terms it's a weighted catenary curve, the outline formed by a heavy cable hanging freely from two points. So long as you're not claustrophobic, it's fun to take the four-minute **tram ride** up the hollow curving arch. Tiny five-seater capsules carry you to a viewing gallery at the top of the arch, where you can linger as long as you like – the views of St Louis, the Midwestern plains, and the mighty Mississippi are spectacular. Lengthy lines are inevitable in the summer, but you can pick up a numbered ticket earlier in the day and come back at an appointed time. Still, you'll have to wait in another line for the elevator, so expect an hour round-trip (daily: summer 8am–9.15pm departures; rest of year 9am–5.15pm; $10).

In a massive bunker beneath the arch, the **visitor center** (daily: summer 8am–10pm; rest of year 9am–6pm; ⓣ314/982-1410) shows a riveting **film** about the construction of the monument, and another on the **Lewis and Clark Expedition**, which set off from St Louis in 1804 to explore the Missouri River, as well as potential water passages to the Pacific Ocean ($7 for one film, $11 for two). The expedition returned two years later with details of trade routes, Native American settlements, and observations on animal and plant life. Also in the visitor center complex, the spacious **Museum of Westward Expansion** (free) recounts the Lewis and Clark story, drawing heavily on the pair's very readable journals.

Nearby, engineering buffs will take note of the extraordinary (if not all that attractive) **Eads Bridge**. Completed in 1876, the massive steel structure was St Louis' first bridge across the Mississippi, doing much to facilitate the railroad boom of the gilded age. Pedestrians and cyclists can cross the bridge for excellent views of the city's **skyline**.

Central downtown

One block from the arch along St Louis' main east–west thoroughfare, Market Street, old photographs at the stately **Old Courthouse Museum** (daily 8am–4.30pm; free) record the development of the city and the settling of the West. Two restored courtrooms were the site of the trial of **Dred Scott**, a black slave who argued that having spent time with his owner in non-slave Illinois and Wisconsin, he had the right to be set free. His case was upheld in 1850, but overturned two years later. On appeal, the Supreme Court declared that Scott, born a slave in a slave state, might, like any other chattel, be taken anywhere his master chose to go. The decision, which meant that the US Constitution saw slaves as legitimate personal property, sent shock waves through the corridors of government and hastened the onrush of the **Civil War**. Scott himself, by now a nationally known figure, was voluntarily freed by his new owner, though he died a year later.

See the world's largest pair of underpants and witness the mystic power of the corndog at the whimsical **City Museum**, 701 N 15th St (hours vary, call ⓣ314/231-2489 for details; $12; ⓦwww.citymuseum.org). The exhibits, made almost entirely of junk, often border on the bizarre, as one floor is devoted to secret passages and dead-ends. There's also a small, but worthwhile, aquarium on-site ($6). Over on Market Street at 18th, the focal point of the giant Romanesque **Union Station** is a 230ft clock tower. The station, erected in 1884, was transformed in the early 1980s into a huge complex of mostly tacky shops, chain restaurants, and a hotel. An artificial lake, where you can rent boats, is in the back.

West of downtown

Three miles west of downtown, the **theater district**, called **Grand Center**, is staked out with ornate street lamps along Grand Avenue between Lindell and Delmar Boulevards. Bright posters advertise the current shows at the **Fabulous Fox Theater**, 527 N Grand Ave (tours Tues, $5; Thurs & Sat, $8, including a special organ performance at 10.30am; ⓣ314/534-1111), where you can have a look at the magnificent Siamese-Byzantine interior and massive Wurlitzer organ.

About a mile further west, on the edge of **Forest Park**, trendy shops, wine bars, and c.1900 mansions line the leafy thoroughfares of the **Central West End** district. A few blocks away at 4431 Lindell Blvd, the Romanesque-Byzantine **Cathedral of St Louis** houses the world's largest collection of mosaic art (daily 10am–4pm; tours Mon–Fri 10am–3pm, Sun 1pm; free).

The decision to put Forest Park four miles directly west of downtown (served by MetroLink every ten to thirty minutes depending on time of day) aroused much criticism during the 1870s, with opponents claiming that its inaccessibility would make it merely a pleasure ground for the local rich. It's larger than New York's Central Park, and every bit as full of attractions; in summer, the 12,000-seat amphitheater is regularly filled for the Broadway-style **musical theater productions** (Ⓣ314/361-1900, Ⓦwww.muny.com).

Standing on **Art Hill** in the central western section of the park, the striking **Beaux Arts Saint Louis Art Museum** (Fri 1–9pm, Tues–Sun 10am–5pm; tours at 1.30pm; free), is the only surviving structure from the 1904 World's Fair. Its mission – to cover international art from prehistoric times onwards – is ambitious. It houses one of the world's most extensive collections of **German Expressionism**, devoting an entire gallery to the powerful, spiraling, jagged images of Max Beckmann, and its pre-Columbian artworks cover every significant style, medium, and culture from Mexico to Peru.

In addition to the animals in its "cageless displays," the **St Louis Zoo** (daily summer 8am–7pm, 9am–5pm rest of year; free), set in beautiful grounds in the park, boasts a "Living World" exhibit, in which an animatronic robot of Charles Darwin gives synopses of his theories.

The main strengths of the **History Museum**, on the northern fringe of the park (Tues 10am–8pm, Wed–Sun 10am–6pm; free), are its thematic collections of old photos of St Louis, documenting river life, black music in the city, and Charles Lindbergh's 1927 flight in the *Spirit of St Louis* (sponsored by the city's aircraft industry) from New York to Paris. The **St Louis Science Center** (Mon–Thurs & Sat 9.30am–5.30pm, Fri until 9.30pm, Sun 11.30am–5.30pm; free) straddles I-64 and can be entered from either side of the freeway; use one of the radar guns on the covered access bridge to check the speed of cars on the freeway below. General admission is free, but it costs a few dollars to get into the planetarium, the OMNIMAX Theater, and other major exhibits.

Southside

The tens of thousands of Germans who came to St Louis in the mid-eighteenth century settled mostly in the **Southside**, where the Teutonic influence is noticeable. These immigrants were skilled brewers; only one of the breweries they opened from the 1850s onwards still stands, but it does happen to be the largest in the world. The one hundred intricate red-brick buildings of the **Anheuser-Busch plant**, 12th and Lynch streets (hours vary seasonally; free; Ⓣ314/577-2626 or Ⓦwww.budweisertours.com for details), produce annually a sizeable proportion of the company's 14.3 million barrels of beer, including Budweiser and Michelob. Free **tours** (80min) are mostly company PR, but they're still good fun, and you get two glasses of beer before being shunted into the gift shop.

A few blocks towards downtown, the colorful **Soulard Market**, at Broadway and Lafayette avenues (Wed–Fri 8am–5.30pm, Sat 6am–5.30pm), is a great place to pick up picnic items and fresh fruit, especially on a Saturday. The terraced streets behind it hold the city's best blues and jazz pubs.

Red-white-and-green fire hydrants let you know that you're in the thirty-square-block **Hill District**, a small, neat Italian community three miles west of Soulard. At its heart, **St Ambrose Church** displays a statue of Italian immigrants; all around, the aroma of freshly baked bread drifts out of the small specialty bakeries that share the area with one-room grocery stores and many restaurants.

Just east of the Hill District, at 4344 Shaw Blvd, the 79-acre **Missouri Botanical Garden** (daily 9am–5pm; $8; Ⓦwww.mobot.org) is a haven of peace and tranquility, just a few hundred yards from busy I-44. The grounds contain everything from a magnificent Japanese garden through scented rose and English woodland gardens to the Climatron, a huge greenhouse that recreates a tropical rainforest complete with waterfalls and cliffs.

Eating

Thanks to heavy Italian immigration in the early twentieth century, **Italian food** predominates in St Louis, from humble salami sellers upwards. Otherwise, there are many friendly **Irish pubs**, serving beef sandwiches and stew, while University City's **Delmar Boulevard** offers African, Middle Eastern, Chinese, Indian, and other ethnic places. More expensive cafés are located in **Laclede's Landing**, and the **Central West End** has a scattering of upmarket espresso bars such as the *Coffee Cartel*, 2 Maryland Plaza.

Bissinger's Chocolatier 32 Maryland Plaza ☎314/367-7750. A must for dessert lovers, offering a delicious variety of chocolate concoctions, both edible and drinkable in addition to well paired spirits.

Duff's 392 N Euclid Ave, Central West End ☎314/361-0522. Small, relaxed, and moderately priced, with a French-flavored international menu, as well as home-made desserts and Sunday brunch. Outdoor seating available.

John D. McGurk's Irish Pub 1200 Russell Blvd, at 12th St, Soulard ☎314/776-8309. Freshly baked soda bread, corned beef and cabbage, Irish stew, and imported Guinness on offer. Live Irish music every night and great outdoor seating.

Rigazzi's 4945 Daggett Blvd, the Hill ☎314/772-4900. Popular trattoria, famous for "frozen fish-bowls" of beer. Over thirty different pasta dishes on the menu plus pizzas, veal, chicken, and steak.

Sapphire Pan Asian 4753 McPherson Ave ☎314/361-0013. Innovative pan-Asian cuisine including fresh sushi in the hip Central West End with lunches starting under $10 and dinner ranging up to $22.

Ted Drewes Frozen Custard 6726 Chippewa Ave ☎314/481-2652; also 4224 S Grand Blvd ☎314/352-7376. A legendary slice of Americana. Try a "concrete" – an ice cream so thick it won't budge if you turn your cup upside down. Open March–Dec.

Nightlife and entertainment

Downtown St Louis' highest concentration of **bars** and **clubs** can be found in **Laclede's Landing**, with nightly jazz, blues, rock, and reggae. Some of the outlying districts are well worth checking out; these include **the Loop** in U City, whose bars and cafés are not only popular with students, and the slightly more upmarket cafés and wine bars of **Central West End**. Unpretentious **Soulard** is the place to go for good jazz and blues. You should also check out **Grand Center**, centered on North Grand Boulevard in midtown, home to stage shows and the **St Louis Symphony Orchestra** (☎314/534-1700). Excellent **listings** can be found in the free weekly *Riverfront Times*.

1860 Hard Shell Café & Bar 1860 S 9th St, Soulard ☎314/231-1860. One of the liveliest bars in Soulard with dancing to blues, R&B, and soul bands. Also serves good Cajun and fish dishes.

Bastille 1027 Russell Blvd, Soulard ☎314/664-4408. Built by Anheuser Busch during prohibition, every square inch of the walls is plastered in random bric-a-brac and in addition to a full rainbow trendy cocktails, this boy bar serves up a full pub fare menu.

Blueberry Hill 6504 Delmar Blvd, U City ☎314/727-4444, Ⓦwww.blueberryhill.com. Crammed full of memorabilia, with the downstairs dedicated to Elvis and a jukebox acclaimed by Cashbox magazine as the best in the country. The drinks and burgers are good, and live entertainment is offered every weekend – Chuck Berry himself comes in for monthly cameos.

Cafe Eau 212 N Kingshighway Blvd, Central West End ☎314/454-9000. Housed in the posh *Chase Park Plaza Hotel*, *Eau* has more than 300 wines stashed in its cellars, and for those who aren't into wine, *Eau* indulges cocktail lovers with an ice bar to keep the night chill.

Mississippi Nights 914 N 1st St, Laclede's Landing ☎314/421-3853. The city's top venue for nonstadium bands.

Ste Genevieve

Sixty miles south of St Louis, Missouri's oldest community, the tiny, French- and German-heritage **STE GENEVIEVE** retains its eighteenth-century charm through historic cottages, a red-brick square, and summer festivals. A perennial favorite of Mississippi flood waters, the town, with a population of 4500, has recently been sheltered by a $50-million levee, a measure taken to ensure the safety of homes that pre-date the American Revolution. The *St Gemme Beauvais*, 78 N Main St (Ⓣ573/883-5744; ④–⑦), is a nineteenth-century Greek Revival inn downtown. Home-cooked catfish, chicken, and seafood are on the menu in the *Anvil Saloon*, 43 S Third St (Ⓣ573/883-7323).

Western Missouri

As the Mississippi River defines Eastern Missouri, its tributary the Missouri (which gave the state its name) dominates the northwest border. Here along the river, jazz and barbeque flourish in **Kansas City**, while the small town of **Independence** lays on the homespun charm made famous by its favorite son, President Harry S. Truman. Further south, surrounding the hokey family-entertainment center of **Branson**, cool lakes and forested hills provide some breathtaking natural beauty.

Kansas City

KANSAS CITY, 250 miles due west of St Louis, straddles the state line between Kansas and Missouri. Virtually all its main points of interest are on the Missouri side, where the fountains, boulevards, Art Deco and Mediterranean-style buildings, and the encouraging revitalization of downtown, are welcome features in a Midwestern city.

Kansas City was a convenient staging post for 1830s wagon trains heading west. Its consequent prosperity

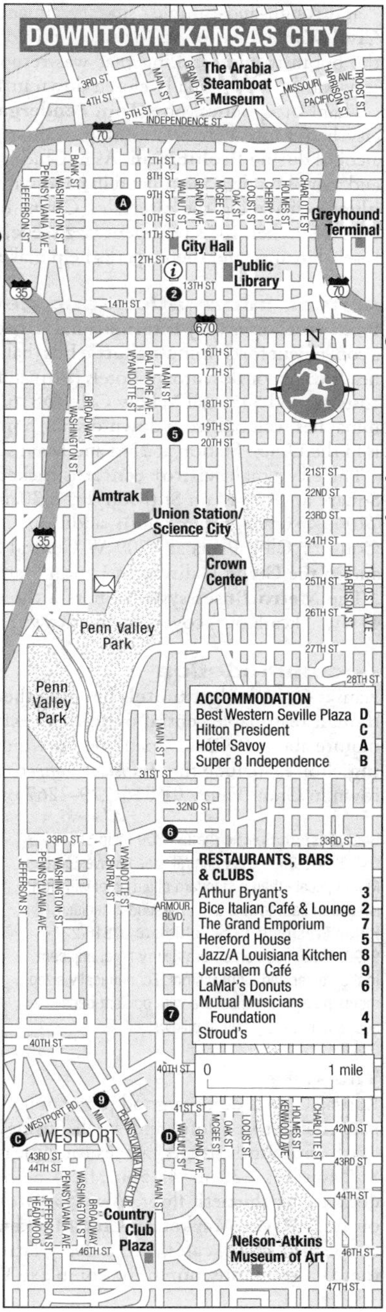

– and rough-and-tumble "sin city" image – was brought to an abrupt end by the **Civil War**. However, its fortunes revived in the 1870s, when the railroads brought the boom in meatpacking that was responsible for the development of the huge stockyards, which finally closed down in 1992.

Thanks to political boss **Tom Pendergast**, an outrageous figure with whom the city had a love-hate relationship, Kansas City's many jazz clubs continued to sell alcohol during **Prohibition**. As in Chicago and New Orleans, speakeasies, brothels, and gambling dens went hand in hand with superlative **jazz** – and, to a lesser extent, **blues** – spawning the careers of Count Basie, Duke Ellington, and, in the Fifties, Charlie Parker. KC's resurgent jazz scene, fine restaurants, professional football and baseball teams, and theme parks help make it a popular short-break destination.

Arrival, information, and getting around

From the **Kansas City International Airport**, twenty miles northwest of downtown, a convenient forty-minute **shuttle bus** (half-hourly 6am–11.55pm; ⓣ816/243-5000) heads to major downtown hotels ($16) and Westport ($17). The equivalent taxi-ride costs around $45; call Yellow Cab (ⓣ816/471-5000). The isolated **Greyhound** terminal lies well out from downtown in a miserable area at 1101 Troost Ave. **Amtrak** is in the Union Station at 23rd and Main streets, opposite Crown Center.

The city's main **visitor center** is tucked away on the 22nd floor of City Center Square at 1100 Main St (Mon–Fri 8.30am–5pm; ⓣ816/221-5242 or 1-800/767-7700, ⓦwww.visitkc.com); additional information offices are housed in the Country Club Plaza at 4709 W Central St (daily 8am–6pm; ⓣ1-800/767-7700) and in the Grand Hallway of Union Station.

The **Metro Buses** system offers a three-day visitor pass ($8; ⓣ816/221-0660, ⓦwww.kcata.org) covering downtown, and routes out to Independence.

Accommodation

Kansas City's budget **motels** lie along the interstates or out towards Independence, though reasonable central options do exist. The visitor center is the best place to inquire about **B&Bs**. Depending on which direction you are coming from, **camping** choices include the *Trailside Camper's Inn*, I-70 exit 24, 24 miles east of downtown in Grain Valley (ⓣ816/229-2267 or 1-800/748-7729; $17 for tents).

Best Western Seville Plaza 4309 Main St ⓣ816/561-9600. Very central, close to Westport. More upscale than a standard chain hotel with Turkish cotton bath towels and upgraded amenities. ❺

Hilton President 1329 Baltimore ⓣ816/221-9490. Rehabbed Forties-era luxury hotel adjacent to the Power and Light District. Economically sized rooms pack in the pleasure with opulent beds adorned in a mountain of pillows. ❼–❽

Hotel Savoy 219 W Ninth St ⓣ816/842-3575 or 1/800-728-6922. Opened in 1888, this Garment District hotel has been beautifully renovated into a 22-room B&B offering a gourmet breakfast. ❺–❻

Super 8 Independence 4032 S Lynn Court ⓣ816/833-1888. Clean budget motel, east of the city in Independence. ❷–❹

The City

Kansas City is doing a good job of reinvigorating its **downtown**, and wandering past the restored lofts and small businesses of the **Garment District**, between Sixth and Ninth streets, makes for a pleasant way to reach **City Hall**, 414 E 12th St (Mon–Fri 8.30am–4.15pm; free), a fine Art Deco building with an observation deck on its thirtieth floor. Also downtown is the **historic district** known variously as **River Market** or **City Market**, on the banks of the Missouri. As well as colorful shops, cafés, and a lively farmers' market at Fifth and Walnut streets, there's a good museum in the complex, **The Treasure of the Steamboat Arabia**, which tells the story behind the 1988 salvaging of a side-wheeler that sank on its way to Council Bluffs in 1856 (400 Grand Blvd; Mon–Sat 10am–5.30pm, Sun noon–5pm; $12.50; Ⓦwww.1856.com). Perfectly preserved artifacts – china, guns, gold, and Kentucky bourbon, to name a few – afford unexpected and intriguing insights into frontier life.

The sprawling concrete **Crown Center**, on Grand Avenue and Pershing Road, owned by Hallmark Cards, calls itself "a city within a city," and houses apartments, shops, restaurants, offices, a hotel, cinemas, and an ice rink. Interesting displays in its splendidly awful **Hallmark Visitors Center** (Tues–Fri 9am–5pm, Sat 9.30am–4.30pm; free) trace styles of greeting cards alongside political and cultural changes; designs from the 1940s, for example, featured stars and stripes and Uncle Sam. The nearby **Union Station**, built in 1914, is a Kansas City landmark: huge, beautifully renovated, and home to **Science City** (Tues–Fri 9.30am–5pm, Sat 10am–5pm, Sun noon–5pm; $19.95 for all attractions; Ⓦwww.sciencecity.com), an incredible arena of futuristic games, movies, and exhibits.

The **18th and Vine Historic Jazz District**, south of I-70 as it sweeps east–west, was the hub of the city's 1930s jazz scene. A huge revitalization project in the 1980s culminated with the opening of the **Negro Leagues Baseball Museum**, 1616 E 18th St (Tues–Sat 9am–6pm, Sun noon–6pm; $6; Ⓦwww.nlbm.com) – an enthralling collection of photographs, interactive exhibits, and game equipment that traces the turbulent history of black baseball in America, which was segregated from the white major leagues for the first half of the twentieth century. In the same complex is the **American Jazz Museum** (Tues–Sat 9am–6pm, Sun noon–6pm; $6), which tells the history of jazz through interactive exhibits that profile some of its greatest performers, including Kansas City native Charlie Parker and others who cut their teeth in the smoky halls of 18th and Vine. The *Blue Room* functions as a working jazz bar, with Thursday through Saturday and Monday-night jam sessions bringing many stars out of the woodwork. If you're going to visit both museums, the $8 combo ticket is your best bet.

Westport, an attractive district of good restaurants, cafés, and trendy shops between 39th and 45th streets, was the original jumping-off point for the Santa Fe Trail. Stop in for a drink at the city's oldest building, *Kelly's Westport Inn*, 500 Westport Rd (Ⓣ816/561-5800), a shabby but friendly red-brick bar. Five miles south of downtown, beginning at 47th and Main streets, the elegant **Country Club Plaza** dates from the early 1920s. Tree-shaded and upmarket (with branches of stores like Anthropologie and Saks), its tiling, mosaics, fountains, and orange trees evoke the streets of Spain; a replica of Seville's La Giralda tower completes the effect.

Highlights at the extensive **Nelson-Atkins Museum of Art**, a few blocks east at 4525 Oak St (Wed 10am–4pm, Thurs & Fri 10am–9pm, Sat 10am–5pm, Sun noon–5pm; free), include superb Oriental exhibits, with figurines from Tang and Egyptian tombs, plus canvases by Titian, Caravaggio, and Monet, as well as twelve Henry Moore sculptures in a landscaped setting.

Eating and nightlife

Barbecue, once the unfashionable food of the poor, is big news in Kansas City – cheap, cheerful, hickory-smoked, and served with tasty sauces. The **Country Club Plaza** has some decent places to sample the spicy cuisine, but they tend to be overpriced and some require formal dress. The restaurants in **Westport** are more casual while the hip **Power and Light District** located downtown at 14th Street and Grand Avenue offers a wide range of cuisines interspersed with nightlife hotspots. Check out Kansas City's **jazz** and **blues** scene, especially the authentic dives holding wonderful jam sessions into the early hours. The Friday and Sunday editions of the *Kansas City Star* carry **listings**, as does the freebie *Pitch Weekly*.

Arthur Bryant's 1727 Brooklyn Ave ☎816/231-1123. The place for barbecue, a mile east of downtown in a desolate area. Serving the largest portions you've ever seen of barbecue and beans; the combo plate easily feeds two hefty appetites. This is serious business – don't take too much time deciding, as rookies aren't given any hand-holding.

Bice Italian Café and Lounge 14 E 14th St ☎816/569-2310. Classic cocktails, happy hour specials, and delicious Italian fare with panoramic views of the Power and Light District.

The Grand Emporium 3832 Main St ☎816/561-2560. Longstanding and dependable blues standby, with live sets, DJs, and salsa dancing weekly.

Hereford House 20th and Main streets ☎816/842-1080. KC's top steakhouse, in a handy downtown spot.

Jazz/A Louisiana Kitchen 1823 W 39th St ☎816/531-5556. Cajun cuisine and live jazz and blues.

Jerusalem Café 431 Westport Rd ☎816/756-2770. Small Middle Eastern restaurant serving superb falafel and kebabs.

LaMar's Donuts 3395 Main St ☎1-800/533-7489. A KC institution, now with branches in several states; this one is the original.

Mutual Musicians Foundation 1823 Highland Ave ☎816/471-5212. National historic landmark in the 18th and Vine district. Fierce jam sessions begin at 1am Fri & Sat and last till 5am, with musicians competing in a frenzy. Things can get a bit rough, and it's recommended that women not attend solo.

Stroud's 5410 NE Oakridge Rd ☎816/454-9600. Renowned fried chicken in a converted farmhouse well worth the drive north of downtown.

St Joseph

Sixty miles north of Kansas City, **ST JOSEPH** boomed as a supply depot for the California Gold Rush, and today is a busy manufacturing town. For a brief eighteen months, beginning in 1860, it was the home of the legendary **Pony Express**, which delivered mail to Sacramento, California, by continuous horseback relay in ten days. The Pony Express was a financial disaster, driven out of business by its inability to compete with the transcontinental telegraph, but riders such as Buffalo Bill Cody went on to become legends. Charlie Miller, the last of the riders, rode from New York to San Francisco in 1931, and died aged 105 in 1955. The full story is told in lively dioramas at the **Pony Express Museum**, 914 Penn St (Mon–Sat 9am–5pm, Sun 1–5pm; $4), which is attractively set in the company's original stables.

It was in St Joseph, on April 3, 1882, that the notorious **Jesse James** was shot in the back by Robert Ford, a 20-year-old member of his own gang who had negotiated a $10,000 reward from the governor. Countless books and films have portrayed Jesse James as a latter-day Robin Hood; in fact, he spent most of the Civil War riding with a band of Confederate guerrillas. The **Jesse James Home Museum** (June–Nov Mon–Sat 10am–5pm, Sun 1–5pm; Nov–May Mon–Sat 9am–5pm, Sun 1–5pm; $4), the one-story frame cottage where James was living incognito while he planned his next bank job, now stands at 12th and Penn streets, having been moved closer to the main highway in the hope of attracting sightseers. A ragged hole in the wall is pointed out as the spot where the bullet supposedly hit, after striking James as he was hanging a picture; you can also see where bloodstained splinters were chiseled from the floor to be sold as souvenirs. As for the assassin, Ford was himself gunned down ten years later, and his killer in turn was also shot.

There are thirteen **museums** in town, most about the Old West, but none really warrants lingering, though the one next to the James home does purport to contain the world's largest ball of twine. If you do want to leave the drive to Kansas City or Omaha for another day, you'll find **motels** strung along I-29 as it passes east of downtown, including a *Motel 6* (☎816/232-2311; ❷) and a *Days Inn* at the intersection with Frederick Boulevard (☎816/279-1671; ❸).

Southwest Missouri – Ozark country

There's little to see south of Kansas City before the **Ozark Mountains**. Occupying most of southern Missouri and northern Arkansas (see p.555), the area remained frontier territory until the timber companies moved in at the end of the nineteenth century. When they moved on, the hill-dwellers were left to eke out a living from the denuded terrain; severe droughts forced many to leave for the cities. For those who remain, fishing resorts and tourist attractions supply some work, though the region remains poor. None of the Ozark peaks are particularly high, though the roads through them switch, dip, climb, and swerve to provide **stunning views** of steep hillsides thick with oak, elm, hickory, and redbud, all quite resplendent in the fall. **Springfield** is the region's main city, 130 miles south of Kansas City, but the gateway to the Ozarks, the country music town of **Branson**, is more popular by far.

Branson

Nestled among beautiful Ozark lakes, the resort of **BRANSON**, forty miles south of Springfield on US-65, is one of the top tourist destinations in the United States. Over seven million visitors a year are attracted to what's become known as the "Ozark Disneyland" for its forty-nine music venues (almost all of a country or nostalgia bent), a few theme parks, and lots of good old family fun.

"The Strip," is populated by a wide range of neon-licked tourist traps and entertainment venues. The spectrum ranges from Japanese fiddler Shoji Tabuchi and ancient crooner Andy Williams to superb acts like Alison Krauss and Union Station. **Tickets** for a two-hour show are fairly priced at around $20. There's no shortage of takers in summer for most, if not all, of the town's 57,000 seats – a figure said to exceed that of Nashville. Branson shows are firmly geared toward families; you won't find anything remotely edgy or avant-garde, although the *Ripley's Believe It or Not* performance is a step in a new direction.

The newly constructed **Branson Landing** offers up waterfront shopping, dining and entertainment highlighted by an impressive hourly water and light show (noon–10pm) designed by the same team that erected the fountains at the Bellagio hotel in Las Vegas.

When you've had it with Branson, escape to nearby **Table Rock Lake**, a scenic area offering hiking, biking, camping, water-skiing, and world-class fishing.

Practicalities

Greyhound connects Branson with Springfield, Kansas City, and Memphis. Call ahead, or drop in at the local **Chamber of Commerce**, at the intersection of Hwy-65 and Hwy-248 (Mon–Sat 8am–6pm, Sun 10am–4pm; ⓣ417/334-4084 or 1-800/214-3661, ⓦwww.explorebranson.com), or at the **North Welcome Center** (Mon–Sat 8am–5pm, Sun 10am–4pm) at 4910 Hwy-65, for a copy of their show guide detailing performance schedules of all the theaters.

During the high season (May–Oct), **hotel** prices rise, especially on weekends, but you can still find some bargains. Branson Vacation Reservations (ⓣ1-800/221-5692) will try to sell you a package deal, but can also book you into a motel, including one of three *Best Westerns* (ⓣ1-800/528-1234; ❹). Experience rustic luxury in one of the well-appointed suites at the *Keeter Center Lodge* on the campus of the **College of The Ozarks** (ⓣ417/239-1900; ❼). Known as "hard work U," every student has a job on campus, and they earn their keep lavishing guests at the lodge. Table Rock State Park three miles southwest of downtown Branson (ⓣ417/334-4704) has **campgrounds** for $8–17. Calorically-loaded country **eats** abound. *Joe's Crab Shack* at Branson Landing (☎417/337-7373), and the down-home cookin' at *The Farmhouse Restaurant*, downtown (☎417/334-9791), are both good options.

Kansas

KANSAS may be associated with quaint, gingham-pinafore images from *Little House on the Prairie* and *The Wizard of Oz*, but the region was at one time known as "bleeding Kansas." The 1854 **Kansas-Nebraska Act**, which gave both territories the right to self-determination over slavery, led to fierce clashes between Free Staters and pro-slavery forces. Runaway slaves from the South were given passage through the area, aided by abolitionist John Brown, and Kansas eventually joined the Union as a free state.

After the Civil War, the mighty cattle drives from Texas made towns like Abilene, Wichita, and Dodge City centers of the "**Wild West**." The debauched, masculine image of the West, spawning such "heroes" as Wyatt Earp and Wild Bill Hickok, is, however, challenged in Kansas, which, as well as being the first state to give women the vote in municipal elections, boasts the nation's first female mayor and senator – though its politics have taken a decidedly conservative turn in recent years, with the Kansas school board removing evolution from the science curriculum.

In 1874, Russian Mennonites brought the grain that was to transform the state into the bountiful "breadbasket" that now harvests most of the nation's wheat. However, only in the west do miles of golden stalks sway in Kansas's infamous gusty wind. The green and hilly northeast, patterned with woods and lakes, is home to the unattractive, industrial capital city of Topeka, liberal college town **Lawrence**, and the dull suburbs of Kansas City (though downtown lies across the state line in Missouri). The once-wicked cowtown of **Dodge City** is in the south-west, while **Wichita**, the state's largest city, lies in the south-central area.

Getting around Kansas

Greyhound **buses** run to all Kansas's main cities, supplemented by erratic smaller companies; services to the west and southwest are especially poor. Amtrak **trains** head east–west between LA and Chicago through the center of the state, calling, usually in the middle of the night, at Lawrence, Topeka, Newton (for Wichita, but without a connecting service), Hutchinson, Dodge City, and Garden City. Wichita has the state's biggest **airport**, but you may find flights to **Missouri's Kansas City International Airport** more convenient.

East Kansas

Undulating **east Kansas** is laced with lakes, streams, and rivers. The northeast, once crossed by the Oregon, Santa Fe, and Smoky Hill trails, and now home to both Topeka and Lawrence, is more heavily visited than the southeast, where the major attraction is the Little House on the Prairie historical site, located 13 miles southwest of Independence on Hwy-75. The heritage of Kansas's four Indian tribes comes alive in annual powwows, held in major towns as well as the northwestern reservations.

Lawrence

The mellow town of **LAWRENCE** lies on the Kansas River, roughly halfway between Kansas City and Topeka. Tree-lined streets, a welcoming historic downtown, and an aura of old-hippie artsiness make it an appealing destination, with a cultural energy owed in part to the **University of Kansas** (home of the Jayhawk, the mythical bird which is the emblem of its sports teams), and a long liberal and intellectual history. Founded by the New England Emigrant Aid Company in 1854, and a center of Free State activities, Lawrence was the site of a violent Civil War skirmish in 1863, when Missouri Confederate guerrilla William Quantrill led about three hundred men against the town, killing over 150, wounding hundreds more, and setting the place ablaze. Rebuilding was quick, however, as evidenced by the limestone and brick buildings of today's downtown, centered on Massachusetts Street, and the KU campus, which stands on a steep, tree-covered grassy bank known as Mount Oread.

Arrival, information, and accommodation

Amtrak comes into Lawrence at 413 E 7th St, and **Greyhound** arrives at 2447 W 6th St. The **visitor center** is north of downtown in the renovated Union Pacific Depot, at N 2nd and Locust streets (Mon–Sat 8.30am–5.30pm, Sun 1–5pm; ⓣ785/865-4499 or 1-888/LAWKANS, ⓦwww.visitlawrence.com).

Comfy **rooms**, which include a good breakfast, can be found near the bus station at the *Hampton Inn*, 2300 W 6th St (ⓣ785/841-4994; ④). If you have a little extra cash, head instead to the lovely all-suite *Eldridge Hotel*, at 7th and Massachusetts streets (ⓣ785/749-5011 or 1-800/527-0909; ⑥); twice burned down by proslavery forces, it has been restored to an evocative elegance, and houses the stylish *Ten* restaurant (ⓣ785/749-5011) and the atmospheric *Jayhawker* bar in the lobby. You can camp three miles out of town along W 23rd St at *Clinton Lake State Park*, where the vehicle fee is $7 and a tent site $8.50 (ⓣ785/842-8562).

The Town

Studded with cafés and eclectic shops, downtown Lawrence is a delight to walk around – and just as busy outside of term time, when day-trippers flock in from less congenial Kansas cities. However, most of the town's formal attractions are clustered on campus. The **University of Kansas Natural History Museum**, on Jayhawk Boulevard at 14th Street (Mon–Sat 9am–5pm, Sun noon–5pm; $5), holds a chronological panorama of North American flora and fauna, as well as the now-stuffed horse Comanche, the lone survivor of Custer's cavalry at the Battle of Little Bighorn. The **Spencer Museum of Art**, 1301 Mississippi St (Tues, Wed, Fri, & Sat 10am–5pm, Thurs 10am–9pm, Sun noon–5pm; free), specializes in world art, with an Oriental gallery, Old Masters, and a pre-Raphaelite masterpiece.

Native American traditions are preserved and packaged for the public each year by the exhibitions of the **Lawrence Indian Arts Show**, held the second weekend in September at the **Haskell Indian Nations University** at 23rd and Massachusetts streets. Also on campus are the **Hiawatha Visitor Center** and **American Indian Athletic Hall of Fame**, open year-round (ⓣ785/749-8404).

Eating, drinking, and entertainment

As befits a college town, the **restaurant** scene in Lawrence is dominated by inexpensive eats. Try *La Parilla*, 814 Massachusetts St (ⓣ785/841-1100), where there's always a line out the door at this tasty, reasonably priced Latin American joint. If cheap college eats aren't your scene, indulge at *Pachamama's* at 800 New Hampshire (Ⓣ785/841-0990, Ⓦwww.pachamamas.com) where an ever-changing seasonal menu includes fork-licking specialties like a tamarind glazed lamb loin and petite filet au poivre. Dinner runs in the mid-$20s and lunch can be had for under $10. **Nightlife**, too, is defined by the students, who can be found in droves along Massachusetts Street. The *Free State Brewing Company* at 636 Massachusetts St (Ⓣ785/843-4555) pulls pints of its award-winning amber beer. As for the **performing arts**, one of the better places to investigate is Liberty Hall, 642 Massachusetts St (Ⓣ785/749-1972). Once a social and political center, this building housed Lawrence's first newspaper until pro-slavery agitators burned it down in 1863. Today it puts on art-house films, plays, and concerts.

West through Kansas

Further west across Kansas, three towns recreate the state's Wild West heritage, although only in the westernmost, **Dodge City**, does the scrubby landscape conform to the cowboy-movie image. **Abilene**, if less famous than Dodge City, has as many outlaw and gunslinger stories, and **Wichita**, about two hundred miles southwest of Kansas City, holds an excellent, authentic reconstruction of frontier days in its Old Cowtown Museum.

Abilene

Like all the old cattle-trail cowtowns, **ABILENE**, 115 miles west of Lawrence on I-70, claims to have been the most riproaring of the lot. By the time legendary lawman Wild Bill Hickok became its marshal in 1871, the unruly behavior was already dying down, and there is little today to remind you of those raucous days.

These days, Abilene prefers to stress its connections with **Dwight Eisenhower**. The **Dwight D. Eisenhower Presidential Library and Museum**, 201 SE Fourth St (daily: May to mid-Aug 8am–5.45pm; mid-Aug to April 9am–4.45pm), encompasses his boyhood home, with its original furnishings, the obligatory film, and many photos and papers on display in the spacious museum ($8). The former president and his wife are buried in the meditation chapel.

Abilene's **visitor center** is at 201 NW Second St (Mon–Sat 9am–6pm, Sun noon-6pm; Ⓣ785/263-2231 or 1-800/569-5915). Most of the town's budget **motels** are off I-70 at Hwy-15. The *Holiday Inn Express*, 110 E Lafayette (Ⓣ1-877/863-4780; ❸) offers comfortable rooms close to the I-70 exit.

Wichita

WICHITA, about 165 miles southwest of Lawrence on I-35, is the largest city in Kansas, split by the Arkansas River, which forks just north of downtown into the Big and Little Arkansas rivers (incidentally, Kansans take umbrage if you pronounce it "Arkansaw"; pronounce it here the way it is spelled). Originally settled by the Wichita Indians, who by 1865 had been relocated to Oklahoma Indian Territory, Wichita grew up as a stop on the Chisholm Trail, a Texas-to-Kansas cattle route. Its glory days were to be short-lived, however, as farmers, angry about the damage done by stampeding cattle, erected fences, which forced the drives onto different trails further west, creating new cowtowns such as Dodge City. Today the city, already supporting a rich arts scene, has been invigorated with a downtown revival.

The City

Downtown Wichita is enlivened mainly by the public art and sculpture that pops up unexpectedly all over the place, in empty lots and even in tree stumps. The exceptional **Wichita-Sedgwick County Historical Museum**, 204 S Main St (Tues–Fri 11am–4pm, Sat & Sun 1–5pm; $4; ⓦwww.wichitahistory.org), is in **Old City Hall**, a heavy stone building decorated with turrets, gargoyles, and arches. The cozy interior is crammed with exhibits on everything from the Wichita Indians through decorative art to Carry Nation, who campaigned against everything from tobacco to corsets. The stately church with vivid stained-glass windows at 601 N Water St houses the **Kansas African American Museum** (Tues–Fri 10am–5pm, Sun 2–6pm; $2; ⓦwww.thekansasafricanamericanmuseum.org), an eclectic antidote to more mainstream views of Great Plains history, with

▲ The Keeper of the Plains

details on Buffalo Soldiers, inventors from across the country, early black Wichitans, and some African art.

The riverside parks are home to a hiking and biking trail system as well as the 44ft *Keeper of the Plains* statue, which faces east at the confluence of the Little and Big Arkansas rivers. It was designed in the 1970s by a Kiowa-Comanche artist, Blackbear Bosin. Native Americans and city officials smoked the peace pipe at its dedication ceremony.

Western artist C.M. Russell is the best represented of the veritable who's who of American painters assembled at the **Wichita Art Museum**, 1400 West Museum Blvd (Tues–Sat 10am–5pm, Sun noon–5pm; $5, Sat free; Ⓦwww.wichitaartmuseum.org).

Old Cowtown Museum, 1871 Sim Park Drive (April–Oct Mon–Sat 10am–5pm, Sun noon–5pm; $7.75), is a seventeen-acre riverside exhibit recreating the buildings of 1870s Wichita. Looking and feeling like a movie set, the area includes – along with some docile longhorns – the city's first one-room jail, a schoolroom, a store, a smithy, churches, stables, and old homes.

Practicalities

Domestic **flights** arrive at the Mid-Continent Airport, five miles southwest of downtown on Hwy-54 (W Kellogg Drive). **Amtrak** stops at Newton, a small Mennonite town 25 miles north, with a local bus connection to Wichita throughout the day; **Greyhound** comes in to 312 S Broadway Ave, two blocks east of Main Street. **City transportation** consists of **buses** (WMTA; $1 per ride; Ⓣ316/265-7221) and, more appealingly, **trolleys**, which run from 11am–3pm during the week and on Saturdays for just 25¢. The resourceful **CVB** is in the heart of downtown at Douglas Avenue and Main Street (Mon–Fri 7.45am–5.15pm; Ⓣ316/265-2800 or 1-800/288-9424, Ⓦwww.visitwichita.com). City trolley **tours** ($10; June–Aug Thurs–Sat 10am) depart from CityArts, 334 N Mead, as well.

Inexpensive **lodgings** in Wichita are plentiful, especially near the airport on W Kellogg Drive – try the *Super 8* at no. 6245 (Ⓣ316/945-5261; ❸). More upscale, the *Hotel at Oldtown*, at First and Mosley streets (Ⓣ316/267-4800; ❼–❽), has a stylish turn-of-the-twentieth-century flavor and perfect location. Nine miles from town, *Blasi Campground*, 11209 W Hwy-54 (Ⓣ316/722-2681), offers tent sites for $24.

There are a horde of **restaurants**, **clubs**, and **bars** around the quaint Old Town Marketplace. Good places to eat include the *River City Brewing Co*, 150 N Mosley St (Ⓣ316/263-2739), which has good Kansas steaks, locally brewed beer, and sandwiches. The *Old Mill Tasty Shop*, by the railroad tracks at 604 E Douglas Ave (Ⓣ316/264-6500), serves great sandwiches and Southwestern food. Visitors can get a taste for the old West at Old Cowtown's *Diamond W Chuckwagon Supper* (April–Oct Thurs–Sat 6.30pm; $30; Ⓣ316/729-4825) where authentic cowboys hoot and holler while diners stuff their gullets with smoked beef brisket, baked beans, honey cornbread, and peach cobbler.

Dodge City

DODGE CITY, 150 miles west of Wichita, is perhaps the most famous of all America's cowtowns. It has certainly been committed to celluloid more times than any other, especially in 1930s Westerns like *My Darling Clementine* and *Dodge City*. However, this wildest of Wild West cities had a heyday of only a decade, from 1875 until 1886. Established in 1872 along with the Santa Fe Railroad, which transported the hides of millions of Plains buffalo, by 1875 the town of traders, trappers, and hunters had to find a new economic base – the buffalo had been exterminated. The era of the great cattle drives was already under way, and Dodge City became a den of iniquity where gambling, drinking, and general lawlessness were the norm. Such wickedness led to gunfights galore, and the notorious Boot Hill cemetery (where the villains were buried with their boots on) was kept busy by charismatic, morally suspect lawmen such as Bat Masterson and Wyatt Earp.

The Town

Dodge City today is rather more staid, with its old downtown area enveloped by a hinterland of railroad tracks and giant silos. Outside of the **Dodge City Days and Rodeo** (Ⓦwww.dodgecityroundup.com), held in late July or early August, the town is content to replay its movie image in the **Boot Hill Museum**, 400 Front Street (June–Aug daily 8am–8pm; Sept–May Mon–Sat 9am–5pm, Sun 1–5pm; $7, $8 in summer). The museum centers on the single-sided **Historic Front Street**, which was constructed in 1958 and has been acquiring old buildings from all over the West ever since. There's a bank and a grocer, stagecoach rides, a funeral parlor, a smithy, and even a full-sized railroad station, as well as the *Long Branch Saloon*, scene of a variety show with cancan dancers every night at 7.30pm ($7.95; summer only). **Boot Hill cemetery** is higher up the hill, still on museum grounds; there's just a sorry little patch of lawn on one corner of the original site, which was in any case abandoned in 1879 after just six years and thirty-four burials. The bodies were reinterred elsewhere, and as the graves were never marked in the first place, the wooden crosses in the cemetery are more than a little bogus.

Other sights in town include the **Mueller-Schmidt Home of Stone**, 112 E Vine St (June–Aug Mon–Sat 9am–5pm, Sun 2–4pm; free), an emotive memorial to pioneer mothers, often forgotten amid the macho Wild West myth-making. The house looks pretty much as it would have when built in 1881, with domestic memorabilia that belonged to early plainswomen. **El Capitan**, at Second Street and Wyatt Earp Boulevard, is a massive bronze longhorn, facing south towards an identical north-facing statue in Abilene, Texas. Together they mark the beginning and the end of the cattle drives.

Practicalities

Amtrak comes right into downtown, to the historic and renovated Santa Fe Station at Central Avenue and Wyatt Earp Boulevard. The **CVB** at 400 W Wyatt Earp Blvd (summer daily 8.30am–6.30pm; winter Mon–Fri 8.30am–5pm; Ⓣ620/225-8186 or 1-800/653-9378, Ⓦwww.visitdodgecity.org) can offer advice on tourist activities. The Dodge City Trolley runs narrated town **tours** ($7) four times a day, in summer only, from a booth on the Boot Hill parking lot.

Most of Dodge City's **motels** are spread out roughly a mile west of downtown along US-50, still known here as Wyatt Earp Boulevard. The *Dodge House* at no. 2408 (Ⓣ620/225-9900; ❸) has a reliable restaurant; and the *EconoLodge* at no. 1610 (Ⓣ620/225-0231; ❷–❸) has an indoor pool and sauna area. **Camping** is an option even for the car-less: the lakeside *Water Sports Campground Recreation*, 500 Cherry St (Ⓣ620/225-8044; $17 tent sites), lies ten blocks south of Front Street.

As for **food**, the pickings are somewhat slim; your best bet may be the chuck-wagon eats at *Beatty & Kelley's* inside the Boot Hill museum (Ⓣ620/227-8188).

Iowa

Boasting undulating hills, and acre upon acre of verdant pastures, **IOWA** lacks the glitz and glamour of America's more popular tourist traps. While nothing about the state truly stands out, that's not to say there aren't a few places worth pulling off the highway to see. Iowa is the very essence of smalltown America, close to the geographical center of the mainland US, and ranking decidedly average in size, population, and level of personal income.

Iowa's history, too, has been relatively uneventful. It was opened for settlement after the **Black Hawk Treaty** of 1832, a one-sided exercise in negotiation with the Sauk Indians, conducted after many of them had been chased down and slaughtered in neighboring Wisconsin and Illinois. The Northern European immigrants who replaced them made agricultural development their prime concern, turning the Iowa countryside into the rolling corn farms so common today.

The state's most visited destination is the throwback Germanic enclave of the **Amana Colonies**. However, Iowa does hold a few oddball sites, such as the original locations for the movies *The Bridges of Madison County* (in south-central **Winterset**, birthplace of **John Wayne**) and *Field of Dreams* (near **Dubuque** in the northeast). You can also see, but not enter, the original house that featured in Grant Wood's much-parodied *American Gothic* painting (at **Eldon** in the southeast, and now owned by the state).

Getting around Iowa

Greyhound buses out of Chicago call at all of Iowa's major towns. Daily buses also run from St Louis to Des Moines and Iowa City; these towns are connected less frequently with Minneapolis/St Paul. **Amtrak**'s east–west route misses the cities, stopping instead at assorted small communities in the south. The only sizeable **airport** is in Des Moines.

Iowa's hills and valleys are a mecca for **cycle touring**. Each year the extremely popular cross-state bike ride – the Register's Annual Great Bike Ride Across Iowa, or the **RAGBRAI** – attracts thousands of entrants, any of whom can tell you that the Plains aren't always flat (tour details Ⓣ1-800/474-3342, Ⓦwww.ragbrai.org).

Eastern Iowa

Eastern Iowa, in the Mississippi River hinterland, is liberally sprinkled with agribusiness towns that display the continuing influence of their central and northern European pioneers, plus **religious communities** – Amish, Mennonite, and the Amana Colonies. All are easily accessible from **Iowa City**; as home to a huge university it's one of the state's livelier centers. Riverside towns such as northerly **Dubuque** and Burlington, near the Missouri state line, have been enlivened since 1991 by **gambling**, though so far games can only be played on board Mississippi paddle-wheelers, decked out in less-than-authentic Mark Twain–era trimmings.

Dubuque

The handsome town of **DUBUQUE**, overlooked by rocky bluffs on the Mississippi around 150 miles west of Chicago, was founded as the first white settlement in Iowa by French-Canadian lead miners in 1788. In the nineteenth century it became a boisterous river port and logging center. Buildings from this era still stand, but the companies that use them are in meatpacking and other food industries.

The National Mississippi River Museum & Aquarium (daily 10am–5pm; $10.50) at Third Street in the old Ice Harbor area, tells the story of Mississippi navigation from the days of Robert Fulton's first commercial steamboat in 1807 until the floods of 1993. The fifteen-minute introductory film *River of Dreams* is a good starting point for your explorations. The complex completed a $188-million renovation in 2003 and includes the aquarium, hotel, and entertainment complex, among other attractions.

Once your appetite has been whetted, you can travel along the high-banked Mississippi on a *Spirit of Dubuque* **paddle-wheeler cruise** (May–Oct daily; ⓣ563/583-8093 or 1-800/747-8093; ⓦwww.dubuqueriverrides.com). Alternatively, what's said to be the world's shortest and steepest **cable-car ride** (April–Nov daily 8am–10pm; $1 single, $2 round-trip) grinds its way from Fourth Street downtown up a sheer bluff to **Fenelon Place**, a residential street of old money and Victorian architecture. The top offers a sweeping view across the Mississippi to Illinois and Wisconsin. Film buffs who enjoyed the 1989 baseball fantasy *Field of Dreams* can meet like-minded souls in surprising numbers at the original movie location, three miles north of Dyersville, which is 25 miles west of Dubuque on US-20. True to the movie's catchphrase – "if you build it, they will come" – crowds still gather on the bleachers to watch phantom games at the edge of the cornfields (April–Nov daily 9am–6pm).

Practicalities

The **Iowa Welcome Center** at 300 Main St (daily 9.30am–5.30pm; ⓣ563/556-4372 or 1-800/798-8844, ⓦwww.traveldubuque.com) is the best place to pick up information on Dubuque. As for places to **stay**, try the *Redstone Inn B&B*, 504 Bluff St (ⓣ563/557-1492; ❹–❻), which was constructed by A.A. Cooper, one of early Dubuque's earliest benefactors, as a wedding gift to his daughter. The 150-year-old *Julien Inn*, 200 Main St (ⓣ563/556-4200 or 1-800/798-7098; ❹–❼), was once owned by mobster Al Capone; he used it as his safe house when trouble was brewing in Chicago. A complete renovation in 2008 restored the Julien to its original splendor, while giving guests the modern amenities they crave. Picturesque **campgrounds** can be found at Miller Riverview Park, off Greyhound Park Road (ⓣ563/589-4238; $10 per tent site). *Café Manna Java*, 269 Main St (ⓣ563/588-3105), offers great sandwiches, brick over pizzas, baked goods and coffee.

Cedar Rapids

Seventy miles southwest of Dubuque, **CEDAR RAPIDS**, home of Quaker Oats, is Iowa's industrial leader. The city is still in recovery from the devastating floods of 2008; The Iowa River, which snakes through the heart of Cedar Rapids, crested at 31.5 feet forcing 24,000 of the city's 60,000 residents to evacuate. The very modern **Museum of Art**, 410 Third Ave SE (Tues, Wed, Fri, & Sat 10am–4pm, Thurs 10am–8pm, Sun noon–4pm; $7), boasts a comprehensive collection of paintings by Grant Wood, best known for his depictions of 1930s farm life. The 21-room Queen Anne Style **Brucemore Estate**, 2160 Linden Drive SE (Feb–Dec, Tues–Sat 10am–3pm, Sun noon–3pm; $7) is preserved by the National Trust for Historic Preservation, and visitors are swept up in the exotic lifestyle of the Sinclair and Hall families. Locals still recall the roars of the Hall's beloved Leo the lion.

Cedar Rapids' **CVB** is based at 119 First Ave SE (Mon–Fri 8am–5pm; ⓣ319/398-5009 or 1-800/735-5557, ⓦwww.cedar-rapids.com). For reasonably priced **rooms**, there's the straightforward *Best Western Cooper's Mill*, 100 F Ave NW (☎319/366-5323 or 1-800/858-5511; ④).

The Amana Colonies

The **Amana Colonies** are situated at the intersection of Hwy-151 and Hwy-220, midway between Cedar Rapids and Iowa City. They were founded in 1855 by the **Community of True Inspiration**, pacifist German refugees (not linked to the Amish or Mennonites) who believed that God spoke through prophets – themselves, for example – rather than ordained ministers. Members led a simple, collective lifestyle: each family lived in its own home, but they all ate together and shared profits from the farms. During the Depression, communal ownership became increasingly difficult to maintain, and in 1932 stock was redistributed among all the adults. However, they did keep up their commitment to close family ties, a sense of community, and religious principles.

The Amana Colonies today consist of seven separate villages set in an immaculate, serene valley. Their prosperity is very evident, though in addition to tasteful clapboard houses standing on well-groomed lawns, and neat plank fences dividing rolling meadows, you'll also come across factories, pizza parlors, and even a golf course. It's geared less toward families and more toward elderly Iowan couples on a weekend getaway. The streets of the largest village, **Amana**, are lined with restaurants and craft shops, a brewery, several wineries (don't get too excited about the wine, grapes are by and large eschewed in favor of berries and dandelions, resulting in sweet medicinal concoctions), and a woolen mill – plus a small **Museum of History** (Mon–Sat 10am–5pm, April–Nov also Sun noon–5pm; $7). The **visitor center**, in Amana at 622 46th Ave (Mon–Sat 9am–5pm, Sun 10am–5pm; ☎319/622-7622 or 1-800/579-2294, Ⓦwww.amanacolonies.com) has details on the many local **B&Bs**.

Probably the most compelling reason to visit the colonies is their undeniably excellent old-style **German food**. The *Ox Yoke Inn* (☎319/668-1443) in Amana village dishes up family-style meals of weiner schnizel, potatoes, spatzel and the like.

Iowa City

IOWA CITY, on I-80 55 miles west of the Mississippi, is refreshingly young at heart. The gold-domed **Old Capitol** is a reminder of its days as state capital, before government was transferred to the more central Des Moines. Residents were placated by getting the **University of Iowa** instead. The arty shops and sidewalk cafés of the compact downtown touch the east end of campus, but its red and gray buildings, closeted by tall dark trees, remain aloof from the rest of the town.

Greyhound stops at 170 E Court St, right downtown. The **CVB** is at 900 First Ave in Coralville, a little over a mile northeast of downtown (☎319/337-6592 or 1-800/283-6592, Ⓦwww.icccvb.org). *Iowa House* is a comfortable central **hotel** in the student union building, beside the river on Madison Street (☎319/335-3513; ③–⑤). Inexpensive **food** is easy to find, be it the pastries and espressos served on long inviting sofas at *Java House*, 211 E Washington St (☎319/341-0012); or the burgers at *Micky's*, 11 S Dubuque St (☎319/338-6860), a friendly, dimly-lit Irish bar. For something a little more upscale, the *Atlas World Grill*, 127 Iowa Ave (☎319/341-7700) serves great eclectic dishes, from macaroni and cheese to Jamaican jerk chicken.

Central and western Iowa

Pigs outnumber people in **central Iowa**. The only city among the cornfields, state capital **Des Moines**, struggles to lift the monotony, and many visitors may prefer the college town of **Ames**. The humdrum west has little to offer.

Des Moines

The steel-and-glass skyline of **downtown DES MOINES**, most of which shot up during the 1980s, is testimony to the town's ever-growing insurance business. For such a fast-track financial center, the streets are curiously empty; pedestrians instead use the **Skywalk**, a three-mile network of temperature controlled corridors linking twenty blocks of offices, banks, parking lots, restaurants, hotels, and movie theaters.

Most businesses stand on the west bank of the Des Moines River, which cuts downtown in two. In 1857, a group of speculators attempted to shift the commercial hub to the east side by bribing commissioners to site the **state capitol** at E Ninth Street and Grand Avenue. Their hopes of huge spin-offs were dashed when the nationwide financial crash later that same year saw property prices collapse. As a result, the five-domed Italian Renaissance–style mass, on the crest of a steep hill, is now detached from the heart of the city (Mon–Fri 8am–4.30pm, Sat 9am–4pm; free; call for tour times ⓣ515/281-5591). A short walk downhill, in the futuristic pink-and-brown **State of Iowa Historical Building**, E Sixth and Locust streets (Tues–Sat 9am–4.30pm, Sun noon–4.30pm; free), are displays covering Indian civilization, pioneer times, and the development of Iowa farming, along with plenty of solemn portraits of former governors.

While an extended stay in Des Moines is not a likely proposition – all of its sights can easily be taken in during the course of an afternoon – if you do find yourself in town overnight, try the *Hotel Fort Des Moines* 1000 Walnut Ave (ⓣ515/243-1161, ⓦwww.hotelfortdesmoines.com; ❹–❼) or if you're looking for a more budget-friendly stopover swing into airport adjacent *Motel 6*, 4817 Fleur Drive (ⓣ515/287-6364; ❷). That Iowans eat well is reflected in the quality – and quantity – of food on offer in Des Moines' many **restaurants**. *Iowa Beef Steakhouse*, 1201 E Euclid Ave (ⓣ515/262-1138) delivers massive slabs of beef supplemented with a salad bar, baked potato and a generous helping of garlic bread. *Stella's Blue Sky Diner*, 3281 100th St (ⓣ515/727-4408), is decked out in lurid pink, turquoise and yellow, and while the retro interior might assault your eyes, the food is a salve to your nostalgia: wash down burgers and fries with divine chocolate, peanut butter, and banana malts.

Around Des Moines

Ten miles west of downtown Des Moines, at I-80 exit 125, the **Living History Farms** in Urbandale (May–Oct daily 9am–5pm; $11) trace the evolution of agriculture on the Plains. Self-guided **tours** progress through five historic sites, from the oval bark homes of an eighteenth-century Iowan settlement, through an 1850s homestead, to a look at the high-tech methods of today. If you want to continue the rural theme, **eat** colossal portions of meat loaf and chops at the *Iowa Machine Shed Restaurant* (ⓣ515/270-6818).

Thirty miles north of Des Moines, **Ames** is the home of **Iowa State University**. Smaller and slightly less trendy than Iowa City, it's still a lively little community (by Iowa standards, at least). The **visitor center**, 1601 Golden Aspen Drive, suite 110 (ⓣ515/232-4032 or 1-800/288-7470, ⓦwww.acvb.ames.ia.us), can advise on concerts and area attractions. **Room** rates are reasonable out at the *Super 8*, three miles from campus at I-35 and Hwy-30 (ⓣ515/232-6510; ❸–❹).

Nebraska

Though modern transcontinental travelers tend to see **NEBRASKA** in much the same light as those heading west during the Gold Rush did – as just another dreary expanse of prairie to get through as fast as possible – this flat and sparsely populated state in fact holds a few places of interest. However, a good three hundred miles of underwhelming, livestock-rearing flatlands separate its most appealing cities, commercial **Omaha** and the livelier state capital, **Lincoln**, from the western Panhandle, where the landscape erupts into giant sand hills and valleys, broken by towering rocky columns and hemmed in by sheer-faced buttes.

Western Nebraska was still embroiled in vicious and bloody battles against Native Americans long after the east had been settled; from the first serious uprising in 1854, it was thirty-six years before the US Army could make white control unchallengeable. Close to the South Dakota state line, **Fort Robinson**, where Crazy Horse was murdered, remains one of the West's most evocative historic sites.

Without navigable rivers, Nebraska had to rely on the **railroads** to help populate the land. During the 1870s and 1880s, rail companies, encouraged by grants that allowed them to accumulate one-sixth of the state, laid down such a comprehensive network of tracks that virtually every farmer was within a day's cattle drive of the nearest halt. Thus the buffalo-hunting country of the Sioux and Pawnee was turned into high-yield farmland, which today has few rivals in terms of beef production.

Getting around Nebraska

The Omaha **airport** offers the best domestic links, though planes from other cities in the region also fly to Lincoln. Several Greyhound **buses** traverse I-80 each day on the coast-to-coast marathon, stopping at all the major towns. Amtrak **trains**, traveling through the night, follow a similar route, calling at Omaha, Lincoln, Hastings, Holdrege, and McCook. **Driving** on I-80 can get tedious; if you're not in a rush, Scenic Hwy-2 (see p.748) is an otherworldly alternative.

Eastern Nebraska

The silt-laden Missouri River separates Nebraska from Iowa and Missouri to the east. There are few natural ports on this stretch, and **Omaha** remains the only riverfront community of any size. **Lincoln**, 58 miles southwest, is the state's capital and seat of its university.

Omaha

OMAHA, Nebraska's largest and most easterly city, has a great zoo, several museums, and a lively entertainment district. As a major terminus on the first transcontinental railroad, Omaha made a logical alternative to distant Chicago as a marketplace for Wyoming and Nebraska ranchers to sell their herds of **cattle**. By the end of the 19th century, massive stockyards had spread along the southern edge of town, and the city still handles well over one million head of livestock per year.

In downtown Omaha you'll find good bars and cafés along the cobbled streets of the **Old Market district**. Train buffs will be impressed with the **Durham**

Western Heritage Museum, converted from the Union Pacific Railroad station, at 801 S 10th St (Tues 10am–8pm, Weds–Sat 10am–5pm, Sun 1pm–5pm; $7), where old train cars and huge model train sets are featured alongside a gallery of Omaha history.

The **Henry Doorly Zoo**, 3701 S 10th St (daily 8.30am–5pm June–Aug, 9.30am–5pm Sept–May; $10.50), rightfully considers itself one of the best zoos in America and is well worth a visit. It started off with two buffalo borrowed from Buffalo Bill; now there's a gigantic aviary, a magnificent bear canyon, the large Kingdoms of the Seas aquarium, and a towering Imax screen.

Twenty-nine miles southwest of Omaha, at exit 426 on I-80, is the **Strategic Air and Space Museum** (daily 9am–5pm; $7; Ⓦ www.strategicairandspace.com), inside two huge hangars containing giant 1950s- and 1960s-era warplanes, some of which were designed and built by the Martin Bomber Company of Omaha. Films, photos, and exhibits concentrate on World War II and the Cold War, the latter highlighted by various weapons including an Atlas-D Intercontinental Ballistic Missile, located outside the museum entrance.

Practicalities

Omaha's **Greyhound** station is at 1601 Jackson St; **Amtrak** trains depart very late at night, and arrive long before the city wakes up, at 1003 S Ninth St. Both depots are well placed for downtown; however, local **public transportation** is poor. The **CVB** is at 1001 Farnam, right downtown (Mon–Sat 9am–4.30pm; Ⓣ 402/444-4660 or 1-866/937-6624, Ⓦ www.visitomaha.com). There's also a **welcome center** for Nebraska as a whole, just off I-80 exit 454, across from the zoo at Tenth Street and Bob Gibson Boulevard (May–Oct daily 9am–5pm, Nov–April Mon–Fri 9am–5pm; Ⓣ 402/595-3990).

Hotel rates are reasonable, except in mid-June when the college baseball World Series comes to town. Rooms at the downtown *Hilton Garden Inn*, 1005 Dodge St (Ⓣ 402/341-4400; ❺–❽), are clean and comfortable. Located next to the SAC Museum, the Eugene T. Mahoney State Park (Ⓣ 402/944-2523) has **campgrounds** ($21), **cabins**, and a **lodge** (❸–❹), in a family-oriented setting.

The Old Market district, centered on Tenth and Howard streets, has the liveliest **restaurants** and **bars**. *Vivace*, 1108 Howard St (Ⓣ 402/342-2050), serves up fresh, contemporary Italian cuisine. Grilled panini's start at $8 or try the seasonal risotto for $16. *The Upstream Brewing Company*, 514 S 11th St (Ⓣ 402/344-0200), has excellent beers and a standard American menu. *The Slowdown*, 729 N 14th St (Ⓣ 402/345-7575), is the epicenter of Omaha's blossoming **indie rock** scene.

Lincoln

Tiny Rochester was selected to be state capital in 1867 – on the condition that it change its name to **LINCOLN** in honor of the recently assassinated president. Such was the disappointment in the territorial seat of government, Omaha, that state officials had to smuggle documents, books, and office furniture out of the city in the middle of the night to avoid armed gangs.

At night, when the students emerge, its compact downtown comes into its own. Of its alphabetical array of broad boulevards, **O Street** (the subject of Allen Ginsberg's poem "Zero Street") is the main drag; 13th and 14th streets are packed with bars and places to eat.

Dwarfing the rest of **downtown**, the central tower of the 1932 Nebraska **state capitol**, 1445 K St (Mon–Fri 8am–5pm, Sat 10am–5pm, Sun 1–5pm; tours every hour; free), protrudes 400ft into the sky. Topped by a 20ft statue of a sower on a pedestal of wheat and corn, its remarkably phallic appearance has prompted the nickname "penis of the prairies." The superb iridescent murals in the foyer are a welcome alternative to old portraits, flags, and emblems, and from the fourteenth-floor observation deck you can survey the flatness of the surrounding farmland.

Twelve thousand years of life on the plains are covered at the **Museum of Nebraska History**, Centennial Mall at 15th and P streets (Tues–Fri 9am–4.30pm, Sat & Sun 1–4:30pm; $2 suggested donation), where displays focus on anthropology rather than history. The Elephant Hall, a gallery of towering mammoth, mastodon, and four-tusker skeletons, is the highlight of the **University of Nebraska State Museum** at 14th and U streets (Mon–Sat 9.30am–4.30pm, Sun 1.30–4.30pm; $5). A few blocks away, the **Sheldon Memorial Art Gallery**, 12th and R streets (Tues–Thurs 10am–5pm, Fri 10am–8pm, Sat & Sun 10am–5pm; free), traces the development of American art, and has a twenty-piece sculpture garden.

Practicalities

Lincoln's **Greyhound** station is downtown at 2400 NW 12th St, while **Amtrak** passes through 201 N 7th St at crazy early-morning hours. StarTran (Ⓣ402/476-1234) runs good **local buses** ($1.25). The **visitor center** is in Lincoln Station, right next to Amtrak (June–Sept Mon–Fri 9am–8pm, Sat 8am–2pm, Sun noon–4pm; rest of year Mon–Fri 9am–6pm, Sat 10am–2pm; Ⓣ402/434-5348 or 1-800/423-8212, Ⓦwww.lincoln.org).

Except on football weekends, it's easy to find inexpensive **accommodation** out by the airport, off I-80 exit 399 – at the *Days Inn* (Ⓣ402/475-3616; ❸), for example. Downtown, the recently remodeled *Holiday Inn*, 9th and O streets (Ⓣ402/475-4011; ❺–❻), is a stumble away from Lincoln's lively entertainment district.

Restaurants downtown tend to be less than compelling, with grills, pizzerias, and family diners predominating. The *Oven*, 201 N 8th St (Ⓣ402/475-6118), offers Indian cuisine with a range of cheap breads and inventive specials. The *Zoo Bar*, 136 N 14th St (Ⓣ402/435-8754), attracts big-name **jazz** and **blues** acts en route between Chicago and Kansas City; *Duffy's Tavern*, 1412 O St (Ⓣ402/474-3543), pulls in a younger crowd and some good **rock bands**. The **Historic Haymarket District**, by the Amtrak station, holds more bars and restaurants, including *The Mill*, at 800 P St (Ⓣ402/475-5522), which has good coffee and internet access.

Western Nebraska

After the unerringly flat journey across eastern Nebraska, the far west comes as a refreshing change. In the **Panhandle**, as it's often called, wave upon wave of rumpled sandy hills, thinly coated with prairie grass, back off toward the horizon like a sea in constant turmoil. Early pioneers wrote the area off as unproductive, and it remained barren until massive irrigation work at the start of the twentieth century enabled agricultural settlement. In the **northwest** the sand hills yield to classic John Ford–style Western scenery: pancake-flat valleys, crisscrossed by dry meandering riverbeds and corralled by crusty, contorted bluffs, all under the constant shadow of fast-moving clouds. Emigrants on the **Oregon Trail** used the bizarre outcrops, which sprout along the way, as "road signs."

Scenic Hwy-2 and Alliance

Scenic Hwy-2 meanders and dips for over 330 miles from I-80 to South Dakota's Black Hills. It passes through the **Sandhills** – a martian landscape carpeted with short-grass prairie and softened by delicate wild flowers and shiny ponds. Apart

▲ Carhenge

from a few farmsteads, grain silos, and tiny churches, all you're likely to see on the open road are lazing cattle, a few sluggish rivers, and the occasional mile-and-a-quarter-long freight train weaving its way through the hills. It's a long, desolate, yet strangely beautiful drive through an anachronistic corner of the US.

The road dawdles for miles through scattered villages before drifting into **ALLIANCE**, which pulls in over fifty thousand visitors per year for its one big attraction. **Carhenge**, two and a half miles north on State Hwy-87 (dawn to dusk; free; Ⓦwww.carhenge.com), is a rough copy of Stonehenge – but made with old cars rather than stone. Erected in a cornfield during a family reunion in 1987, this intriguing collection of Chevys, Cadillacs, and Plymouths, painted a brooding battleship grey and tilted at unusual angles, has to be the best picnic site in America's heartland. To some it's an ingenious piece of Pop Art; others view it as great black humor, or an appalling eyesore. The Nebraska Department of Roads rapidly declared it a junkyard, and ordered the city of Alliance to remove it, forcing locals to form **Friends of Carhenge**, whose work seems to have secured the monument's future.

There is no reason to linger in Alliance, but if you arrive late, try the *Days Inn*, 117 Cody Ave, just off Third Street (Ⓣ308/762-8000; ❸). As food options are limited, its not a bad idea to bring a sack lunch from the big city on your trek across the Sandhills.

The Oregon Trail landmarks

Two of the first landmarks encountered by travelers on the **Oregon Trail**, which in western Nebraska paralleled the route of modern US-26, were the lumpy **Courthouse** and **Jail rocks**, which lie four miles beyond the likeable little town of **Bridgeport**. Fourteen miles west, along Hwy-92, the **Chimney Rock National Historic Site** (daily 9am–5pm; $3; tours available; Ⓣ308/586-2581) rises almost 500ft above the North Platte River. Although this phallic outcrop's nineteenth-century stature may have been chipped away by erosion and lightning, it remains one of the most recognizable and memorable landmarks in the West.

The twin towns of **GERING** and **SCOTTSBLUFF**, 25 miles further west, are the commercial center for the farmlands of western Nebraska. Southwest of Gering, the rugged 800ft rampart of **Scotts Bluff National Monument** (daily: summer 8am–7pm; rest of year 8am–5pm; $5 per car) stands like a Nebraska Gibraltar. Known to the Sioux as Me-a-pa-te ("hill that's hard to get around"), it earned its anglicized name in 1828 after fur trader Hiram Scott was mysteriously found dead at its base. Trips to the top (by foot or free shuttle bus) are rewarded with a magnificent view, and the entrance fee includes the absorbing **Oregon Trail Museum**, which relates the experiences of the early emigrants.

Follow the ruts of bygone wagon trains to *Barn Anew*, 170549 County Rd L, four miles west of Scottsbluff (ⓣ308/632-8647, ⓦwww.barnanew.com; ❹–❺). The 19th century farmstead was converted into an inviting **B&B** in 1997. It sits on the original route out West and delights visitors with its sweeping views of the monument as it erupts from the prairie floor. History buffs will be delighted at this western-themed homestead and its keepers who colourfully relate their own adventures along the Oregon Trail. Grab a **meal** at the *Emporium Coffeehouse & Cafe*, 1818 1st Ave (ⓣ309/632-6222). More than just a purveyor of espresso and scones, the *Emporium* presents diners with a wide range of fare from ricotta stuffed ravioli to medallions of beef, The towns' **visitor center** can be found at 1517 Broadway, Scottsbluff (daily 8am–5pm; ⓣ308/632-2133).

Crazy Horse

The life of Oglala Sioux leader **Crazy Horse** is shrouded in confusion, misinterpretation, and controversy. So thoroughly did the most enigmatic figure in Plains Indian history avoid contact with whites (outside battle, at least) that no photograph or even sketch of him exists; unlike other Indian chiefs, he refused to visit Washington DC, or talk to reporters.

Crazy Horse earned his title as a youth, after he single-handedly charged rival Arapahoe and took two scalps. The finest moment in a brilliant military career came in June 1876, when he led a thousand warriors in inflicting a stinging defeat on the superior forces of General George Crook at the Battle of the Rosebud River. Just eight days later Crazy Horse headed the attack at the **Battle of Little Bighorn**, where Custer and his entire company were killed (see p.825).

After Little Bighorn, US Army efforts to round up the Indians were redoubled. In May 1877, Crazy Horse surprised friend and foe alike by leading nine hundred of his people into Fort Robinson. They gave up their weapons, and Crazy Horse, keen to stay in his native land (unlike Sitting Bull, who had retreated to Canada), demanded that the buffalo grounds along the Powder River should remain in Indian hands. Tensions at the army camp rose after a rumor went around the barracks that the Sioux chief had come to murder General Crook. Crazy Horse was arrested on September 5, 1877; during a tussle outside the fort jail, he was bayoneted three times, and died the next morning.

Quite why this undefeated warrior should have surrendered without a fight, and whether he fell victim to a deliberate assassination, remains unclear. What is certain is that his death signaled the closing chapter of the Indian Wars. The Oglala Sioux were forcibly moved to the poor hunting country of Missouri, and settlers immediately swept in their thousands into western Nebraska, South Dakota, Wyoming, and Montana.

Crazy Horse, so one story goes, was buried by his family in an unmarked grave in an out-of-the-way creek called **Wounded Knee** – the very place where thirteen years later three hundred Sioux men, women, and children were slaughtered in the bloody finale to over half a century of barbarism (see p.754).

Fort Robinson State Park

Some eighty miles north of Scottsbluff, just west of Crawford village, **Fort Robinson State Park**, beside 1000ft crenelated cliffs in the inhospitable White River Valley, preserves the spot where the US Army coordinated its campaign to rid the gold-rich Badlands of the native Sioux. Today, it's a cross between a dude ranch and a living history village – a smoothing over that makes the memories of the obliteration of an entire way of life all the more poignant.

Restored fort buildings contain period furnishings, and there are two small museums. The State Historical Society Museum traces the fort's history from 1874-1946, and the Trailside Museum interprets the geology and natural history of the region. A simple stone marks the spot where **Crazy Horse** was killed (see box, p.750); the **horse-drawn tour** (six per day; $4) acknowledges it with a mere ten-second halt. Good-value **horseback rides** pass some wondrously weird rock formations, and *Fort Robinson Lodge* (Ⓣ308/665-2900; ❷-❹) has nice **rooms** as well as bargain cottages; the *Lodge*'s **restaurant** serves cheap buffalo tacos and other beef and bison dishes. There is good **camping** for $11-19 per person, or you could really rough it at the beautiful but remote Toadstool Geological Park, 25 miles to the north.

The town of **Chadron**, 23 miles east of Fort Robinson, is worth a visit principally for the small **Museum of the Fur Trade**, four miles east on US-20 (summer daily 8am–5pm; $5). The museum is a valuable historical archive illustrating the unique barter system that operated between fur traders and local Native Americans.

South Dakota

The wide-open spaces of the Great Plains roll away to infinity on either side of I-90 in **SOUTH DAKOTA**. Though the land is more green and fertile east of the Missouri River, vast numbers of high-season visitors speed straight on through to the spectacular southwest, site of the **Badlands** and the adjacent **Black Hills** – two of the most dramatic, mysterious, and legend-impacted tracts of land in the US. For whites, they encapsulate a wagonload of American notions about heritage and the taming of the West; to Native Americans, they are ancient, spiritually resonant places.

The science-fiction severity of the Badlands resists fitting into easy tourist tastes. The bigger, more user-friendly Black Hills, home of that most patriotic of icons, **Mount Rushmore**, have been subjected to greater exploitation (dozens of physical, historical, and downright commercial attractions, as well as the mining of gold and other metals), but encourage more active exploration, via hiking trails, mountain lakes and streams, and scenic highways.

Time and Hollywood have mythologized the larger-than-life personalities for whom the Dakota Territory served as a stomping-ground: **Custer** and **Crazy Horse** battled here for supremacy over the Plains, while **Wild Bill Hickok** and **Calamity Jane** were denizens of the once-notorious Gold Rush town of **Deadwood**.

Sioux tribes dominated the plains from the eighteenth century, having gradually been pushed westwards from the Great Lakes by the encroaching whites. To these nomadic hunters, unlike the gun-toting Christian settlers and federal politicians, the concept of owning the earth was utterly alien. They fought hard to stay free: the Sioux are the only Indian nation to have defeated the United States in war and forced it to sign a treaty (in 1868) favorable to them. Even so, they were compelled, in the face of a gung-ho gold rush, to relinquish the sacred Black Hills, and ultimately the choice lay between death or confinement on reservations. For decades their history and culture were outlawed; until the 1940s it was illegal to teach or even speak their language, Lakota. More Sioux live now on South Dakota's six reservations than dwelled in the whole state during pioneer days, but their prospects are often grim. Nowhere is the legacy of injustice better symbolized than at **Wounded Knee**, on the Oglala Sioux **Pine Ridge Reservation** – scene of the infamous 1890 massacre by the US Army, and also of a prolonged "civil disturbance" by the radical American Indian Movement in 1973.

Today Native American traditions are celebrated by music, dance, and socializing at **powwows**, held in summer on the reservations; the state tourist office can supply dates and locations. The outdoors-minded state also has 170 parks and recreation areas for hikers and campers. In winter, downhill **skiing** is limited to Terry Peak and Deer Mountain, outside **Lead** in the Black Hills; cross-country skiing and snowmobiling are more prevalent.

Getting around South Dakota

You'll be hard put to see much of South Dakota without a **car**. Amtrak routes bypass the state entirely, though Jefferson (Ⓣ1-800/444-6287) **bus lines** serve points between Rapid City and Sioux Falls, sites of the two major **airports**. To see iconic attractions such as Mount Rushmore and the Crazy Horse Memorial, you might hook up with Discovery Tours (Ⓣ605/722-5700), which runs lively minibus **tours** from Rapid City and Deadwood.

East of the Missouri

For tourists, little in eastern or central South Dakota can be considered essential. **Sioux Falls**, the state's biggest city, is faceless but handy. As one of the country's quietest and smallest capitals, **Pierre** has its charms, while **Mitchell** boasts the palatial Corn Palace, an arena adorned with the cash crop reconstructed on an annual basis, and **Yankton** has the excellent Lewis and Clark Recreation Area on its doorstep. The town marks the start of an alternative cross-state route to I-90, trundling through nearby **Vermillion**, home to the exceptional Shrine to Music Museum, plus the Rosebud and Pine Ridge reservations. About sixty miles northwest of Sioux Falls, **De Smet** is known as "Little Town on the Prairie" thanks to the autobiographical books of Laura Ingalls Wilder. You can tour eighteen sites she mentions for smatterings of history, pretty scenery, and homely pride. **Chamberlain** holds the worthwhile Akta Lakota Museum and Cultural Center.

Pierre

Straggling along the east bank of the Missouri River at the center of South Dakota, **PIERRE** is the second smallest and by far the least sophisticated of all the US state capitals; it is instead a typical South Dakota town, whose fifteen thousand residents do their best to ignore the fact that it's the seat of state government.

Apart from the black-domed **capitol building** itself, which sits in a pleasant park at the northeast edge of downtown and is open for tours (daily 8am–10pm; free), there's not a lot to detain you here. One exception is the worthwhile

Cultural Heritage Center (Jun–Aug Mon–Sat 9am–6.30pm, Sun 1–4.30pm; Sept–May Mon–Sat 9am–4.30pm, Sun 1–4.30pm; $4), located high on a hill half a mile north of the capitol, and modeled on traditional Plains Indian dwellings. Repository for the usual barrage of pioneer implements and prehistoric artifacts, the museum is one of few such places that does more than pay lip service to the state's significant Native American cultures.

Pierre's **visitor center** is at 800 W Dakota St (Ⓣ605/224-7361 or 1-800/962-2034, Ⓦwww.pierre.org). *Pier 347*, 347 S Pierre St (Ⓣ605/224-2400), offers bagels and coffee drinks, while the fast-food chains line up along Sioux Avenue, which also holds the bulk of the town's **motels**, including the clean and comfortable *Governor's Inn*, 700 W Sioux Ave (Ⓣ605/224-4200, Ⓦwww.govinn.com; ❸).

The Badlands

The White River **BADLANDS** could be considered a pocket-sized cousin to Arizona's Grand Canyon. What's most impressive about the "Badlandscape" is not its scale, as at the Canyon, but rather its sheer strangeness. More than 35 million years ago this area of southwest South Dakota was a saltwater sea; later it became a marsh, into which sank the remains of such prehistoric mammals as sabre-toothed cats and three-toed horses, to be covered with white volcanic ash. Drying as it evolved, the terrain became unable to support the deep-rooted shrubs or trees that might have preserved it, and over the last few million years erosion has slowly eaten away layers of sand, silt, ash, mud, and gravel, to reveal rippling gradations of earth tones and pastel colors. The crumbly earth is carved into all manner of shapes: pinnacles, precipices, pyramids, knobs, cones, ridges, gorges, or, if you're feeling poetic, lunar sandcastles and cathedrals. While the Sioux cherished these incredible contortions of nature for harboring bighorn sheep, mule, deer, and other tasty prairie fare; early French trappers didn't share the natives enthusiasm, dubbing these white hills the *Mauvaises Terres à Traverser*, or "bad lands to travel across;" they have also been brutally described as "hell with the fires out."

The most spectacular formations can be found within the **Badlands National Park**, particularly its northern sector, while the poverty-stricken Pine Ridge Indian Reservation encompasses the southern stretches. Clean-cut **Wall**, just a few miles north of the park boundaries, is the most–visited commercial center in the region.

Badlands National Park

About one-tenth of the most spectacular Badlands were declared a national park in the 1970s. The two most accessible entrances are off I-90 at exits 131 (northeast entrance) and 109-110 (at the town of Wall), connected by the forty-mile paved loop of Hwy-240, peppered with scenic overlooks; see p.755 for a map of the area. Visitors can backpack or climb just about anywhere; among the best of the marked **hiking trails** are the Door Trail, a half-hour loop that enters the eerie wasteland through a natural "doorway" in the rock pinnacles ten miles south of the northeast entrance, and the even shorter Fossil Exhibit Trail, ten miles further on. The Badlands' rainbow colors are most vibrant at dawn, dusk, and just after rainfall.

Adjoining the Ben Reifel **visitor center**, five miles from the northeast entrance (daily: 8am–5pm, call ahead for extended summer hours; $15 per vehicle for seven days; Ⓣ605/433-5361), is the only in-park **accommodation** option, *Cedar Pass Lodge*, which has its own **restaurant** (Ⓣ605/433-5460; cabins ❸, cottages ❹; mid-

April to Oct). Another **visitor center**, White River (June–Aug daily 9am–5pm), stands on Hwy-27 in the less-visited and less spectacular southern end of the park. A handful of seasonal **campgrounds** operate in the park.

Wall

The town of **WALL**, eight miles north of the Badlands owes its notoriety to **Wall Drug**, which began modestly in 1931 as a pharmacy and veterinary supplies shop on Main Street, it's now one of the largest tourist traps in the world. Over five hundred billboards along I-90 tout the store's wares, including the free ice water that was its original sales gimmick, are likely to pique your interest; by the time you get to exit 110 (the one with the 85ft Wall Drug dinosaur), you'll be compelled to pull off and see what all the fuss is about.

Behind the hype lies a kitschy emporium that serves up to twenty thousand visitors per day. You can fill up on a wide range of serviceable fare ranging from buffalo hot dogs to freshly fried doughnuts in the 520-seat café-cum-Western art gallery, or simply enjoy the wall-to-wall collection of photos, memorabilia, animal trophies, and mechanical automata like the Cowboy Orchestra and the Chuckwagon Quartet. The merchandise, separated into individual stores, runs the gamut from quality (see the Western bookstore and trail outfitters) to junk (anyone for a rattlesnake mold?).

An overnight in Wall positions travelers for a dawn dino trek in the Badlands. Try the rough-hewn, fully *Frontier Cabins* located conveniently at exit 110 (Ⓣ605/279-2619; ❺). Those who prefer a tent to four walls can pitch it for the night at *The Sleep Hollow Campground* (Ⓣ605/ 279-2100). The *Cactus Café and Lounge* on Main Street (Ⓣ605/279-2561) offers a mixed menu of reasonably priced Mexican, Italian, and American **food**.

Wounded Knee

No other atrocity against Native Americans remains so potent and poignant as the massacre at **WOUNDED KNEE**. On December 29, 1890, the US Army delivered a coup de grace to the vestiges of Plains Indian resistance, killing several hundred unarmed Sioux men, women, and children. The massacre was triggered by a misunderstanding during a tribal round-up: a deaf Indian, asked to surrender his rifle along with his peers, instead held it above his head, shouting that he'd paid a lot for it. An officer grabbed at the gun, it went off, and the troops started shooting.

A commemorative stone **monument**, surrounded by a chain-link fence, marks the victims' collective gravesite, off Hwy-27 in the Pine Ridge Reservation. The tribe has so far refused federal funds to turn the site into a national monument, wanting instead to leave it uncommercialized; a concrete block nearby offers a few souvenirs and local knowledge.

The Black Hills

Our people knew there was yellow metal in little chunks up there, but they did not bother with it, because it was not good for anything.

Black Elk, Oglala Sioux holy man

The timbered, rocky **BLACK HILLS** rise like an island from a sea of rolling hills and flat, grain-growing plains, stretching for a hundred miles between the Belle Fourche River in the north and the Cheyenne to the south, and varying in width from forty to sixty miles. For many generations of Sioux, their value was and still

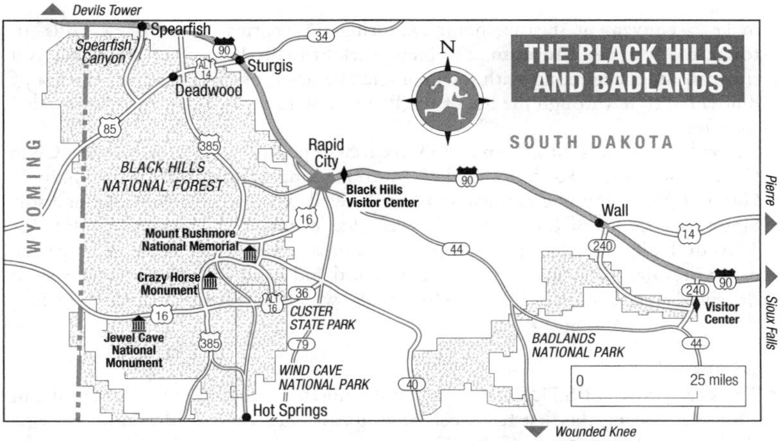

is immeasurable. The Hills are "the heart of everything that is," a kind of spiritual safe, a place of gods and holy mountains where warriors went to speak with Wakan Tanka (the Great Spirit) and await visions. They were dubbed *Paha Sapa*, or Black Hills, even though they are actually mountains (the highest, Harney Peak, rises 7242ft), and the blue spruce and Norway pine trees that cover them only appear to be black from a distance.

Assuming the Hills to be worthless, the United States government drew up a treaty in the mid-nineteenth century that gave these mountains and most of the land west of the Missouri River to the Indians. All such treaties were eventually broken once the discovery of **gold** turned the Indians' Eden into the white explorers' El Dorado, and fortune-hunters came pouring in.

The Hills these days are a major tourist destination, but despite the T-shirt stores, pseudo-historical wax museums, cowboy supper shows, and water slides, the Hills have not been robbed of all their beauty and dignity. Rustic walk-in campgrounds are available throughout the national forest, and you can get away from it all in a mountain-top lodge. No place in the Hills is much farther than ninety minutes from the four presidential heads carved into **Mount Rushmore** or the remarkable **Crazy Horse Memorial**, one of the world's most ambitious works-in-progress. In the shade of these great monuments, the less spoiled southern hills are home to the bison of **Custer State Park** and **Wind Cave National Park**, along with the town of **Hot Springs**.

The North Hills

The predominantly privately owned **northern Black Hills** are more commercialized than their southern siblings, with **Rapid City**, the hub, surrounded by a smattering of smaller towns, such as **Sturgis**, **Spearfish**, and **Deadwood**. The back roads, especially in the **Spearfish Canyon** area, form a network of prime driving and cycling country. The Black Hills **Information Center**, exit 61 off I-90 (June-Aug daily 8am–8pm; rest of year daily 8am–5pm; ⓣ605/355-3700), is just outside of Rapid City and has an abundance of information on the Black Hills, the Badlands, and Native American points of interest.

Rapid City

South Dakota's second largest town, **RAPID CITY**, is swamped with family-fun, and even if you aren't interested in its myriad rated G attractions, the city makes a convenient starting point exploring the charms of the Black Hills. In town, the **Journey Museum**, 222 New York St (daily 9am–5pm; $7), leads you through time, beginning with the geologic evolution of the Plains and the era of dinosaurs, right through the life of the Plains Indians to the pioneers who invaded their territory.

Greyhound pulls into town at 333 Sixth St. The **visitor center** is in the Civic Center, 444 Mount Rushmore Rd N (Mon–Fri 8am–5pm; ⓣ605/343-1744 or 1-800/487-3223, ⓦwww.rapidcitycvb.com). Well-worn wood trimmings and soft Sioux furnishings of the delightful *Hotel Alex Johnson*, 523 Sixth St (ⓣ605/342-1210 or 1-800/888-2539; ❺–❻), provide a great escape from the dull corporate decor prevalent in Rapid City, Both the **food** and hand-crafted **beer** at *Firehouse Brewing Co.*, 610 Main St (ⓣ605/348-1915) – which has plenty of outdoor seating – are worth sampling.

Sturgis

The sleepy town of **STURGIS**, thirty miles north of Rapid City, comes to life in a big way during the first full week of August, when the world-famous **Sturgis Rally and Races** (ⓣ605/720-0800, ⓦwww.sturgismotorcyclerally.com) packs out virtually every motel, campground and even the locals bedrooms and backyards with motorcycle enthusiasts. Where else in the West will pasties and chaps pass for formal attire? An abundance of Harley souvenirs stock the downtown stores year-round, and even if you've rolled into Sturgis on four wheels, the **Sturgis Motorcycle Museum and Hall of Fame**, 999 Main St (Mon–Fri 9am–5pm, Sat & Sun 9am–4pm; $5) is worth a visit.

The Sturgis **visitor center** (ⓣ605/347-2556, ⓦwww.sturgis-sd.org) lies off I-90 exit 32. For a taste of the biker culture that pervades Sturgis year-round, head to the *Full Throttle Saloon*, 12997 E Hwy-34 (ⓣ605/423-4584), a raucous venue with dubious activities including mechanical bull riding.

Deadwood

One of the West's wildest Gold Rush towns, **DEADWOOD**, in a deep gulch high in the hills 42 miles northwest of Rapid City, has the rare accolade of being a **National Historic Landmark** in its entirety. Within a year of the discovery of **gold** here in 1876, six thousand gold-diggers had swarmed in to stake their claims; con artists, outlaws, and other dubious frontier types were not far behind. Among them were James Butler, aka **Wild Bill Hickok** – sometime spy, scout, bullwhacker, stagecoach driver, sheriff, and gambler, who spent only a few weeks in Deadwood prior to his murder here by a young drifter in 1876. Martha **"Calamity Jane"** Canary Burke, an illiterate alcoholic whose checkered career included stints as scout, prostitute, nurse, and Wild West Show performer arrived the same time as Hickok. She died penniless in 1903; despite barely knowing him, her last wish was to be buried beside Hickok in **Mount Moriah Cemetery**, a short but blustery hike from town.

Gambling was outlawed in Deadwood in 1889, the year South Dakota achieved statehood, but betting parlors and brothels flourished well into the twentieth century. Now the old ghosts have been revitalized, since the passing of limited-stakes gambling legislation in 1980 and every spare square inch of saloon space is packed with the ubiquitous one-armed bandits. Corny but entertaining gunfights, singalongs, and community theater are shown sporadically; for details, check with the **CVB**, 767 Main St (ⓣ1-800/999-1876, ⓦwww.deadwood.org). For an overview of Deadwood past and present, start by visiting the **History and Information Center**, in the heart of town at 3 Siever St (daily: June–Sept 8am–7pm; rest of year 9am–5pm; ⓣ605/578-2507). Main Street boasts several grand old **hotels**, including the *Bullock* at no. 633 (Ⓣ605/578-1745 or 1-800/336-1876; ❹–❻), and the *Franklin Hotel* at no. 700 (Ⓣ605/578-2241 or 1-800/688-1876; ❺). The *Main Street Manor Hostel,* 515 W Main St, in Lead (Ⓣ605/717-2044, Ⓦwww.mainstreetmanorhostel.com), offers cozy, homey accommodation five minutes from Deadwood. *Saloon #10*, 657 Main St (Ⓣ605/578-3346), has cold **beer**, sawdust floors, and lots of memorabilia. Above the door is the chair in which Hickok was sitting when he was shot dead, while holding two aces, a pair of eights, and the nine of diamonds – forever after christened the Dead Man's Hand. While the *Saloon* represents the wilder side of town, the elegant dining room upstairs at the *Deadwood Social Club* presents the more sophisticated side of Deadwood with hand-crafted northern Italian fare, a well-planned wine list and some of the best darn cheesecake in the West.

Spearfish Canyon area

Aspen, birch, and white spruce spread over the towering limestone cliffs above the nineteen-mile **Spearfish Canyon National Scenic Highway**, which starts on Hwy-14A half an hour's drive west of Deadwood, and threads past sights such as Bridal Veil and Roughlock falls. The route reveals almost as many **gastronomic pleasures** as it does scenic ones. Twenty minutes out of Spearfish, the *Latchstring Restaurant* (Ⓣ605/584-3333) serves steaks, pasta, shrimp, and excellent rainbow trout almandine. Marking the southern mouth of the canyon at Hwy-14A and Hwy-85, the *Cheyenne Crossing Store* (Ⓣ605/584-3510) is a must if you have a hearty appetite; popular menu items include all-day breakfasts with buffalo sausage, enormous Indian tacos, and traditional Indian fry bread.

Marking the canyon's north end, the more subdued **SPEARFISH** is only worth a visit for the **Black Hills Passion Play**, a re-enactment of the death and resurrection of Jesus Christ (June–Aug Tues, Thurs & Sun 8pm; tickets $20–25; Ⓣ605/642-2646 or 1-800/457-0160). The **visitor center** is at 106 W Kansas St (Ⓣ605/642-2626 or 1-800/626-8013, Ⓦwww.spearfish.sd.us). For **accommodation**, *Yesterday's Inn B&B*, 735 Eighth St (Ⓣ605/644-0210; ❹–❻), offers lovely rooms downtown in a restored 1889 Victorian home. As far as food goes, try *Roma's*, 701 Fifth St (Ⓣ605/722-0715), a classy, modern Italian restaurant serves a tasty selection of pastas and entertains diners with live piano music.

The South Hills

The **southern Black Hills** encompass lower foothills and wooded pastureland; from a purely physical standpoint they draw visitors for their scenery and wildlife rather than kitsch or gambling. **Mount Rushmore** and **Crazy Horse**, mark the northern end of the region; **Custer State Park** and **Wind Cave National Park** account for much of the central zone; while the pleasant town of **Hot Springs** sits on the southern edge.

Mount Rushmore National Memorial

America's two largest stone carvings are a mere seventeen miles apart – no more than spitting distance when you consider the scale on which they're conceived. The better-known **Mount Rushmore National Memorial** (daily: summer 8am–10pm; rest of year 8am–5pm), originally dubbed "The Shrine of Democracy," is the linchpin of the Hills' tourist circuit. It's an easy 24-mile drive southwest of Rapid City, though by far the most impressive approach is to take **Iron Mountain Road** (US-16A) from **Custer State Park** (see p.759), which runs for seventeen miles up and over 5500ft Iron Mountain.

In 1923, state historian Doane Robinson and the sculptor **Gutzon Borglum**, known for carvings such as the leaders of the Confederacy in Stone Mountain,

Georgia (see p.488), talked over the possibility of turning the imposing fingers of granite known as the Needles into a dramatic patriotic sculpture. They discussed depictions of such heroic figures of the West as Lewis and Clark, Buffalo Bill Cody, and Jim Bridger. Borglum opted for a nearby mountain named after New York attorney Charles E. Rushmore, upon which he would fashion the faces and heads of four certifiably great American presidents: **George Washington**, **Thomas Jefferson**, **Abraham Lincoln**, and Borglum's buddy, **Theodore Roosevelt**.

Borglum talked, dreamed, and worked big. "American art ought to be monumental, in keeping with American life," he opined. Sixty when the project began in 1927, he died fourteen years later, $200,000 in debt, just a few months prior to the dedication of the last head – Roosevelt's – in 1939. Inclement weather and uncertain funding had meant that the actual sculpting took about six and a half years, at a total cost of $993,000.

The Big Four gaze out impassively, cheek by jowl, arguably a greater engineering feat than an artistic one. Each head is about sixty feet from chin to crown – by way of comparison, the Statue of Liberty's head is only seventeen feet. Lincoln, Borglum's favorite, has an eighteen-foot-long nose and the glint in each eleven-foot-wide eye is thirty inches. If he and his fellow presidents had been done full-figure to scale, they'd stand 465ft tall and be able to stride across the Potomac River in Washington DC, without getting their knees wet.

The best time to view Rushmore is dawn or dusk, when there are fewer people and better lighting. Patriots flock here for a massive **fireworks display** on July 3. Although there is no admission charge, a $10 **parking fee** has been introduced since the construction of a multilevel parking lot and high-tech **visitor center**. The **café** here, complete with panoramic windows, as seen in Hitchcock's *North by Northwest*, serves full meals and "Monumental Breakfasts" of hash browns, eggs, country-fried steak with gravy, and a biscuit piled on one plate.

Crazy Horse Memorial

In 1939, prompted by the sight of the Rushmore monument, Sioux leader Henry Standing Bear wrote to **Korczak Ziolkowski**, who had just won first prize for sculpture at the New York World's Fair, telling him that Indians "would like the white man to know that the red man has great heroes, too." The chief invited Ziolkowski to take on a similar project – and, less than a decade later, pushing forty and with just $174 to his name, the New Englander moved permanently to the Black Hills to undertake a vastly more ambitious mission than Rushmore – the **Crazy Horse Memorial**, on US-16, five miles north of Custer.

The subject, the revered warrior Crazy Horse on horseback, so appealed to Ziolkowski that he set out to make his monument the biggest statue in the world, higher even than the Great Pyramid. The work he began on **Thunderhead Mountain** in 1948 – five Native American survivors of the Battle of Little Bighorn attended the dedication ceremony – didn't stop with his death in 1982; his widow, children, and grandchildren continue to realize his vision. National and international interest has greatly increased as the monument finally starts to take recognizable shape; the 90ft-high face was completed in time for the fiftieth anniversary celebrations in 1998, although it will easily be another fifty years before the project is finished. The main viewing terrace at the **visitor center** is nearly a mile from the carving itself and the 20ft scale model on show there is 34 times smaller than the end result, which will be 563ft high and 641ft long.

Ziolkowski himself raised and spent $4 million on the non-profit project, refusing to accept federal or state funds, instead relying entirely on admissions and contributions. The site, open dawn to dusk year-round (and illuminated for an hour each night), is free to Native Americans. **Admission** costs $10, though you

The bison of the Great Plains

In the fifteenth century, the Great Plains were roamed by one hundred million shaggy, short-sighted American **bison** (popularly known as buffalo, a corruption of the French *boeuf*). Apart from eating their flesh, Native Americans used the fur and hide for clothing and shelter, the bones for weapons, utensils, and toys, and the droppings for fuel. Eliminating the bison en masse was a mercilessly effective way to deplete the Indians as well. By 1900 there were fewer than one thousand bison left in North America.

Custer State Park was instrumental in helping to raise that meager number to a head count of 250,000 in the US and Canada. The park's own 1200 bison constitute the country's second largest publicly owned herd, surpassed only by Yellowstone National Park (see p.812). However, over ninety percent of bison in the US are now privately owned – the meat, higher in protein and lower in cholesterol than either chicken or tuna, is becoming something of a cross between a novelty and a delicacy item in restaurants (you can try it in burger form at the *State Game Lodge* in Custer State Park, as well as dozens of other places around South Dakota). The Triple U Ranch, outside Pierre, South Dakota, boasts a herd of 3500 strong, though Ted Turner owns around twenty thousand, split between his ranches in several western states.

The Custer State Park bison are free to roam where they please until either the last Monday of September or the first Monday in October, when the park stages its annual **roundup**. From selected viewing points, the public is welcome to witness one of the Midwest's more thrilling occasions: helicopters, jeeps, and pickup trucks, as well as riders on horseback, steer the often recalcitrant herd down a six-mile "corridor" and into a series of pens. There the calves are branded and vaccinated, and the whole herd sorted to determine which five hundred will be auctioned off on the third Saturday in November. Proceeds from the sale account for twenty percent of the park's annual revenue.

Don't let the tranquil, easygoing appearance of North America's biggest mammal lull you into a false sense of security. An average bull can stand six feet high at the hump, weigh up to a ton, outrun a horse, turn on a dime, and gore a human most efficiently.

can see the face just as well if you're passing by from the highway. The premises include an exhibit of Native American artifacts and crafts, a Native American Cultural Center, a restaurant (May–Oct), and a gift shop. **Private tours** of the construction site at the top of the mountain are given in exchange for a high-level contribution.

Custer State Park

The 73,000 sublime, billboard-free acres of **Custer State Park** fill much of the southern-central Black Hills, a perfect antidote to the commercial crassness elsewhere. The **Needles Highway** (Hwy-87; open mid-April to mid-Oct) winds for fourteen miles through pine forests and past the eponymous jagged granite spires in the park's northwestern corner, between Sylvan and Legion lakes. Not far from Sylvan Lake, as you pass close to the summit of Harney Peak (South Dakota's highest point, at 7242ft), look south to spot the **Needle's Eye**, a slender gap in one of the pinnacles that measures three to four feet wide and fifty to sixty feet tall. The eighteen-mile **Wildlife Loop** (separate from the Needles Highway) undulates through the rolling meadows along the park's southern edge. Sunrise and sunset are prime times to spy such critters as elk, bighorn sheep, antelope, deer, burros, and the most plentiful species, bison. Finally, **Iron Mountain Road** (US-16A), to the northeast, makes a dramatic route to Mount Rushmore (see p.757). This is the most likely place to bump into the park's famous "begging burros": tame and disarming four-legged panhandlers who stick their snouts through the windows of passing vehicles in search of handouts.

For a fuller appreciation of the beauty of Custer State Park, forsake your car and set off into the wilderness. Rangers at the park entrances – where you're required to pay **entrance fees** of $5 per person, or $12 per vehicle (the pass remains valid for a week, and admits you to all other South Dakota state parks) – can advise on **hiking** and **biking trails**, while concession firms offer horseback rides, boat rental, and cross-country drives in open-topped jeeps. Good short hikes include the one-hour **Stockade Lake Trail** in the west, which climbs to give distant views across the lake to Harney Peak and the Needles, and the two-hour **Lovers Leap Trail**, which starts from the park's main Peter Norbeck **visitor center**, on Hwy-16A in the east (daily: summer 8am–8pm; rest of year 9am–5pm, closed Dec–March; ⓣ605/255-4464).

The park's four state-run resorts make it a splendid **place to stay** (for reservations call ⓣ1-800/658-3530). The finest is the *State Game Lodge* (ⓣ605/255-4541) on Hwy-16A not far from the visitor center, which operates a motel-style lodge and also has some lovely individual cabins (❹–❺) at the edge of the woods; the *Pheasant Dining Room* offers hearty meals starting with to-die-for flapjacks and French toast layered with fresh bananas and strawberries. A breakfast buffet is available, but the menu choices present diners with a fresher selection. Tucked in the northwest corner on its own artificial lake, the *Sylvan Lake Resort* (ⓣ605/574-2561; ❹–❻) similarly offers comfy cabins, more traditional rooms in its tasteful main building, and the upscale *Lakota Dining Room*. Custer State Park also has eight **campgrounds** (ⓣ1-800/710-2267), which cost $16–21 a night, plus park entrance fees.

Wind Cave National Park

Beneath wide-open rangelands, **Wind Cave National Park**, fifteen minutes north of Hot Springs, comprises over one hundred miles of mapped underground passages etched out of limestone. One of the largest caves in the US, it was discovered in 1881 when a loud whistling noise on the plains led a settler to a hole in the ground – the cave's only natural opening. Nowadays rangers lead a variety of cave **tours** ($7–23 based on length of tour) from the **visitor center** (hours vary seasonally; ⓣ605/745-4600, ⓦwww.nps.gov/wica/), pointing out delicate features such as frostwork and boxwork along the way. If you come in summer, forget the standard walking tours and opt for the ones that allow you to crawl around in the smaller passages, or explore the caves by candlelight (call ahead).

Even if you lack the time or inclination to delve into the Dakotas' dank bowels, simply **driving** through the park is yet another unmissable Black Hills experience. Its native grass prairieland is home to deer, antelope, elk, coyote, prairie dogs, and a sizeable herd of buffalo. There's also a primitive campground in the park ($12 per night).

Hot Springs

The Black Hills' southern anchor, **HOT SPRINGS**, differs from other regional towns in that it hasn't tarted up its downtown to look like a movie set. It doesn't need to. Several dozen utilitarian yet handsome sandstone structures dominate its center, through which flows the sprightly Fall River.

Battles over the town's thermal pools have caused as much grief as the clamor for gold. Before white settlement, the Sioux drove out the Cheyenne, and later landowners, speculators, and settlers dodged and outwitted each other for ownership of the springs. The disputes ceased in 1890 when Fred Evans incorporated numerous small springs and one mammoth hot-water pool into a spa center. Today, **Evans Plunge**, on the north edge of town at 1145 N River St (summer Mon–Fri

5.30am–10pm, Sat & Sun 8am–10pm; rest of year Mon–Fri 5.30am–8pm, Sat & Sun 10am–8pm; $11; ⓣ605/745-5165), is a popular family-fun center, where three great slides zoom down into the 87° waters.

The unique **Mammoth Site** on the Hwy-18 bypass is the only in situ display of mammoth fossils in the US (daily mid-May to Aug 8am–8pm; rest of year times vary; $7.50). In 1974, building on a housing project here came to an abrupt halt when a tractor driver unearthed a seven-foot tusk. Paleontologists soon declared that the workers had discovered the 26,000-year-old grave of Columbian and Woolly mammoths – to date, 55 animals, all male, have been found. Inside the dome, fascinating guided **tours** explain how these ten-ton mammoths, along with camels, bears, and rodents, were trapped in a steep-sided sinkhole (a pond formed by a collapsed underground cave) and were gradually covered by sediment. Complete skeletons are easy to pick out in the excavation site, which is still being uncovered slowly by groups of summer volunteers.

Information for visitors to Hot Springs is available from the old train depot (June–Aug only Mon–Fri 8am–7pm, Sat 8am–6pm, Sun noon–7pm) at 630 N River St. The *Super 8*, 800 Mammoth St (ⓣ605/745-3888 or 1-800/800-8000; ❹), offers comfortable rooms adjacent to the mammoth site; alternatives include the sumptuous *The Flat Iron*, 745 N River St (ⓣ605/745-6439), which serves great coffee, **sandwiches** and salads on a sunny terrace or in a cozy dining room, as well as offering five suites upstairs from the restaurant (ⓣ605/745-5301; ❺–❻).

North Dakota

NORTH DAKOTA has no nationally recognizable landmarks, nor is the state's history particularly lurid or glamorous. It seems like somebody's quiet afterthought, a place to pass through. Grain silos loom on the horizon, and the haystacks resemble loaves of bread. In the summer, with the sun baking in a defiantly blue sky and the wind raking strong fingers through tall fields of golden wheat and flax, North Dakota epitomizes all things rural American. Charming, picturesque – and a bit maddening.

The influx of Europeans into the Dakota Territory, spurred by the **Homestead Act of 1862**, precipitated a population and agricultural boom that lasted into the twentieth century. As in South Dakota, the fertile east is more thickly settled than the west, where vast cattle and sheep ranges predominate.

From **Fargo**, the state's largest city, I-94 passes through the central capital of **Bismarck**, and on to the **Bad Lands** of the west, once cherished by President Theodore Roosevelt. Though the national park bearing his name is the state's key tourist destination, Roosevelt would surely not be pleased about the continuing disfiguration of much of western North Dakota by strip-mining operations.

Getting around North Dakota

Amtrak runs one **train** per day in each direction between Fargo and Williston in the northwest, via Grand Forks. Greyhound operates one interstate **bus** per day, making the ten-hour trip from Minneapolis/St Paul to Bismarck, via Grand Forks and Fargo, before heading west along I-94 into Montana.

East of the Missouri River

Far more of North Dakota lies east of the big winding **Missouri River**, the state's uneven dividing line, than west. The **Red River Valley**, the state's furthest eastern strip, is home to two sizeable cities, easygoing **Grand Forks** and the less attractive **Fargo**. Pelicans, geese, swans, prairie chickens, and ring-necked pheasants live off the sloughs and potholes of the rolling, glaciated prairie of south-central North Dakota, while lakes and woodlands dominate the north and the Canadian border. **Spirit Lake Sioux Indian Reservation** at Devils Lake is midway between Grand Forks and the low-slung Turtle Mountains, which are topped by Lake Metigoshe and the **International Peace Garden** (more of a political symbol than a compelling sight).

Grand Forks

GRAND FORKS sits eighty miles north of I-94, right next to Minnesota and a mere 75 miles south of the Canadian border. Even before its foundation a century ago, fur traders had used the area to rest and barter during their travels between Winnipeg and Minneapolis. It's a small, friendly, outdoorsy city, with nineteen parks and several tree-lined avenues of fine homes. Furious construction has rebuilt the downtown area, ravaged in the 1997 floodwaters, which now holds a smattering of interesting shops and restaurants.

The most interesting distractions can be found on the red-brick main campus of the **University of North Dakota**. The **North Dakota Museum of Art** (Mon–Fri 9am–5pm, Sat & Sun 11am–5pm; donation) offers an eclectic assortment of contemporary art and top touring exhibits. Fascinating tours of the **John D. Odegard School of Aerospace Sciences** (ⓣ701/777-2791, ⓦwww.aero.und.edu; weekday tours offered 8am–4.30pm by appointment), one of the largest civilian pilot-training schools in the world, take in flight simulators, the air-traffic control room, and an altitude chamber.

Grand Forks' **visitor center** is at 4251 Gateway Drive (ⓣ701/746-0444 or 1-800/866-4566, ⓦwww.visitgrandforks.com). **Greyhound** stops at US-81 and Hwy-2 and on the UND campus, while **Amtrak** pulls in at no. 5555 W Demers Ave. Downtown's *Guesthouse International Inn*, 710 First Ave N (ⓣ701/746-5411; ④), is a comfortable, nicely situated **motel**; if you want to spend less, the *Super 8*, 1122 N 43rd St (ⓣ701/775-8138; ③), has clean, serviceable rooms near the UND campus. The most serene place to **camp** is twenty miles west on US-2, in the grounds of pretty Turtle River State Park (ⓣ701/594-4445; $15; reservations recommended). For **dining**, *Dakota Harvest Bakers*, 17 N Third St (ⓣ701/772-2100), serves good soups and sandwiches, as well as tasty baked goods.

Devils Lake

The scruffy town of **DEVILS LAKE**, ninety miles west of Grand Forks on US-2, shares its name with the state's largest natural body of water, which boasts a state park and a number of private campgrounds along more than three hundred sprawling, irregular, and growing miles of shoreline. Downtown holds a smattering of nineteenth-century buildings and a few rough-and-ready bars. Most of the places to stay, such as the *Super 8* (ⓣ701/662-8656; ③), are strung along US-2. The *Woodland Resort*, on Creel Bay, about six miles from town (ⓣ701/662-5996, ⓦwww.woodlandresort.com; ②–⑧), includes cabins, a motel, a campground, and a restaurant, and you can also rent boats, pontoons, and fishing gear. Expert fishing guides are available for hire year round as once the ice pack stiffens, ice-fishing season is in full swing. For other camping options, head 25 miles southwest of town to Grahams Island State Park (☎ 1-800/807-4723; $10 per tent site); contact the Devils Lake CVB, 208 W US-2 (Mon–Fri 8am–5pm; in summer also Sat 9am–5pm & Sun 10am–4pm; ☎ 701/265-8188), for more information.

Fifteen miles south of town, **Spirit Lake Sioux Indian Reservation** is the site of **Fort Totten Military Post** (daily 8am–5pm in summer; $4), one of the best-preserved frontier military posts in the country. During the last weekend in July, the reservation hosts the thrilling **Spirit Lake Oyate Wacipi Powwow and Rodeo.** It's an impassioned, alcohol-free, multitribal party at which hundreds of magnificently clothed dancers of all ages compete for cash prizes.

The West

Anyone with a hankering to play cowboy could do worse than follow in the footsteps of **Theodore Roosevelt**, who declared "I never would have been president if it had not been for my experiences in North Dakota." Roosevelt initially came to the state in search of spiritual and physical renewal after the deaths (on the same day) of his mother and first wife. He dubbed what he discovered during his few years in this "grimly picturesque" area, with its clear skies, panoramic views, and weird, colorful landforms, a "perfect freedom." The national park named after him is the choicest destination in the **North Dakota Bad Lands** (distinct from South Dakota's Badlands) that dominate the state's western half.

The **Missouri River** wriggles like a giant raggedy worm out of Montana, down past North Dakota's capital, **Bismarck**, and into South Dakota. En route it is transformed into **Lake Sakakawea**, a virtual inland sea nearly two hundred miles long that's the state's premier water playground. **Scenic state highways 1804 and 1806** follow the routes mapped out by the Lewis and Clark expedition in those respective years.

Bismarck and Mandan

The West seems to begin as soon as you cross the Missouri River from **BISMARCK**, a capital city with a small-town feel, to Mandan. Both were founded in 1872, Bismarck as a military camp to protect railroad crews from hostile Indians and outlaws. Named in honor of German Chancellor Otto von Bismarck in the hope of attracting Germanic settlers, the scheme failed, but the name stuck. The city survived an early lawless period (present-day Fourth Street was once dubbed "Murderers' Gulch") and a major fire to become first the territorial and then the state capital.

Contemporary Bismarck is pretty much contained within the oblong between I-94 in the north and Main Avenue to the south. Locals are proud of their nineteen-story limestone **capitol building**, 600 E Boulevard Ave, dating from the mid-1930s and set at the crest of a public park. The interior, a model of spatial economy and marbled Art Deco elegance, is open for free guided **tours** (Mon–Fri 8–11am & 1–4pm; in summer also Sat 9–11am & 1–4pm & Sun 1–4pm). Across the street, the superb **North Dakota Heritage Center** (Mon–Fri 8am–5pm, Sat–Sun 10am–5pm; donation suggested) divides the state's past into six sections, from the dinosaurs onwards. Look out for Sitting Bull's painted robe and the bison "smell box," which offers curious tourists a whiff of buffalo dung.

The major reason to venture into **MANDAN** is **Fort Abraham Lincoln State Park** ($5 per vehicle), five miles south of downtown via Hwy-1806, where the centerpiece is the **Custer House** (daily: summer 9am–7pm; Sept 9am–5pm; Oct 1–15 1–5pm; Nov–April by appointment; $6), an admirable reconstruction of the

1874 original designed by the brutally ambitious, indefatigable horseman himself. The guided tour supplies nuggets of quirky information about Custer (he loved to eat raw onions), his wife, and their household prior to his death at Little Big Horn in 1876. Nearer the river, four earth lodge reconstructions stand on the site of the once-vast **On-A-Slant village**, occupied by the Mandan (or River-Dweller) tribe from about 1610 to the late 1700s. After the Mandan abandoned On-A-Slant, they moved upstream and settled on the site that became Fort Mandan, where in 1804 the explorers Lewis and Clark came into contact with the Shoshone woman **Sakakawea** (aka Sacajawea), who helped guide them west towards the Pacific. The site and adjacent **historical museum** (daily: summer 9am–7pm; Sept 9am–5pm; Oct daily 1–5pm; Nov–April by appointment; free with purchase of Custer House ticket) sit below a bluff topped with replicas of the Fort Lincoln infantry post.

Practicalities

Bismarck's **Greyhound** terminal is at 3750 E Rosser Ave; its **visitor center** is at 1600 Burnt Boat Drive (summer Mon–Fri 8am–7pm, Sat 8am–6pm, Sun 10am–5pm; winter Mon–Fri 7:30am–5pm; Ⓣ701/222-4308 or 1-800/767-3555, Ⓦwww.bismarckmandancvb.com). For clean rooms near downtown, try the *Expressway Inn*, 200 E Bismarck Expressway (Ⓣ701/222-2900; ❸). For **camping**, try the excellent Cross Ranch State Park, thirty minutes north of Bismarck on Hwy-1806 (Ⓣ701/794-3731; vehicle fee $5, campgrounds $10). Overlapped by a six-thousand-acre nature preserve, the park features sixteen miles of **trails**. Closer to town, you can camp in Fort Abraham Lincoln State Park (Ⓣ1-800/807-4723; $10).

There is limited **dining** and **nightlife** in Bismarck. *Peacock Alley*, 422 E Main St (Ⓣ701/255-7917), serves tasty Italian and American cuisine. There is fine dining at *Meriwether's Restaurant* at the Port of Bismarck (Ⓣ701/258-0666), where the *Lewis & Clark* riverboat takes visitors on narrated **historical rides** ($16 excursion, $41 Sat dinner cruise; Ⓣ701/255-4233, Ⓦwww.lewisandclarkriverboat.com).

Theodore Roosevelt National Park

The **Theodore Roosevelt National Park**, a huge tract of multihued rock formations, rough grassland, and lazy streams, is split into north and south units approximately seventy miles apart; the area between comprises a checkerboard of federal, state, and privately owned territory. Exploring the park's seventy thousand acres is like entering different rooms, from desert to woods to mountains. Both units (daily dawn–dusk; $5 per person, maximum $10 per car) are at their most subtle at sunrise or sundown, the best times to observe such fauna as elk, antelope, bison, and several fascinating, closely-knit prairie dog communities.

Your first taste of the larger, more popular **southern unit** is likely to be at the breathtaking **Painted Canyon**, seven miles east of the town of Medora off I-94 exit 32. Here and elsewhere in the park, the land is like a sedimentary layer cake that for millions of years has been beaten by hard, infrequent rains, baked by the sun into a kaleidoscope of colors, and cut through to its base by erosive streams and rivers. A mile-long **nature hike**, accessible in the summer months, begins at the end of the canyon's boardwalk.

The southern unit's main **visitor center** in Medora (June to early Sept Mon–Fri 8am–6pm, Sat & Sun 8am–8pm; early Sept to May Mon–Fri 8am–4.30pm; Ⓣ701/623-4466) counts as park headquarters, and runs tours, nature walks, and lectures by campfire in high season. Out back, the simple cabin was used by the young Roosevelt while a partner in the Maltese Cross Ranch (free guided tours daily). A highlight of the scenic 36-mile loop road is the sublime view from **Wind Canyon**, ten miles out of Medora. Peaceful Valley Ranch (Ⓣ701/623-4568),

▲ Painted Canyon, Roosevelt National Park

seven miles from Medora and a mile from the park's first-come, first-served *Cottonwood Campground* ($10 per tent site), arranges horseback tours in summer for $25 for 90 minutes.

The smaller **northern unit**, off Hwy-85 near Watford City, receives only a tenth as many visitors, though it's more spectacular than its southern counterpart; the highlight is **Oxbow Overlook**, at the end of a 15-mile scenic drive. The **visitor center** here is open daily (9am–5.30pm; ⓣ701/842-2333). Keep in mind that the northern unit is on Central time, while the southern unit is on Mountain time (see p.61).

Medora

MEDORA, the southern gateway to Theodore Roosevelt National Park, languished in obscurity until the early 1960s, but has become one of North Dakota's principal attractions, an inoffensively touristy place with enough to keep you busy, and reasonably interested, for most of a day. The biggest noise in town is the **Medora Musical** (daily 8.30pm; $28.50–32.50; ⓣ1-800/633-6721, ⓦwww.medora.com), a pseudo-Western, super-Americana variety show staged beneath the stars in a vast, modern amphitheater. The extravaganza is preceded by a fantastic feed whereby 240 steaks are simultaneously fondued on pitchforks inside giant oil vats (6.30pm; $24.50).

Before you stuff your gullet, feel the burn on a mountain bike along the 96-mile **Maah Daah Hey Trail**. Rent wheels from Dakota Cyclery in Medora (ⓣ701/623-4808; $25 for a half-day). The *Medora Campground* (ⓣ701/623-4435) caters to both tents ($18) and RVs ($25–30). For something a little more rural, try the *Buffalo Gap Guest Ranch* (ⓣ701/623-4200, ⓦwww.buffalogapguestranch.com; ❶–❹), six miles west of Medora at the trailhead of the Buffalo Gap Trail. The ranch offers **accommodation** ranging from tent sites to cabins and has stables and a restaurant as well, which is handy as **eating** options are limited to a few taverns and restaurants clustered in the downtown with menus limited to burgers, fries and the like.

11

The Rockies

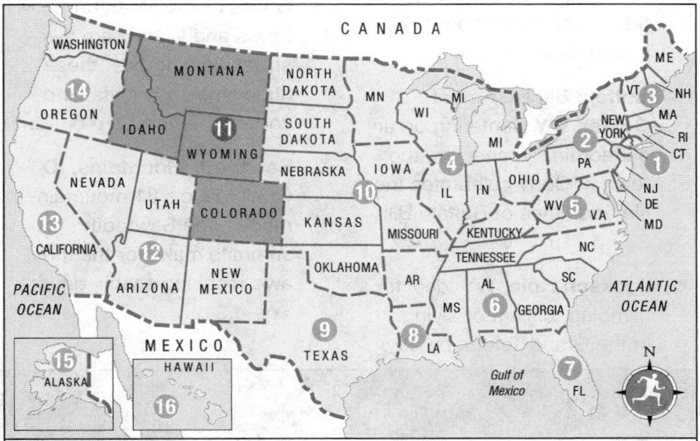

AL - ALABAMA	IN - INDIANA	MN - MINNESOTA	RI - RHODE ISLAND
AR - ARKANSAS	LA - LOUISIANA	MS - MISSISSIPPI	SC - SOUTH CAROLINA
CT - CONNECTICUT	MA - MASSACHUSETTS	NC - NORTH CAROLINA	VA - VIRGINIA
DE - DELAWARE	MD - MARYLAND	NH - NEW HAMPSHIRE	VT - VERMONT
FL - FLORIDA	ME - MAINE	NJ - NEW JERSEY	WI - WISCONSIN
IL - ILLINOIS	MI - MICHIGAN	PA - PENNSYLVANIA	WV - WEST VIRGINIA

CHAPTER 11 # Highlights

✱ **Durango & Silverton Narrow Gauge Railroad, CO** This steam-train ride corkscrews through spectacular mountains to the mining town of Silverton. See p.799

✱ **Mesa Verde National Park, CO** Explore the thirteenth-century cliffside dwellings of the Ancestral Puebloans, the first major civilization in the region. See p.795

✱ **Buffalo Bill Historical Center, WY** Centering on an extraordinary museum, the town of Cody celebrates the life and times of Buffalo Bill. See p.810

✱ **Jackson Hole, WY** Ideal for climbing, biking, or skiing in the Grand Tetons by day, followed by eating, drinking, or stomping in the cowboy bars by night. See p.819

✱ **Going-to-the-Sun road, Glacier National Park, MT** The hairpin turns along this fifty-mile stretch offer staggering views near the Continental Divide. See p.838

✱ **Gates of the Mountains, MT** Lewis and Clark were awe-struck floating past these huge limestone cliffs, and you will be, too. See p.832

✱ **Sawtooth Mountains, ID** Of all Idaho's 81 mountain ranges, the Sawtooth summits make for the most awe-inspiring scenic drive. See p.842

▲ Mesa Verde National Park

11

The Rockies

Exploring the **Rocky Mountain** states of **Colorado**, **Wyoming**, **Montana**, and **Idaho** could literally take a lifetime. Stretching over one thousand miles from the virgin forests on the Canadian border to the deserts of New Mexico, America's rugged spine encompasses an astonishing array of **landscapes** – geyser basins, lava flows, arid valleys, and huge sand dunes – each in its own way as dramatic as the region's magnificent white-topped peaks. The geological grandeur is enhanced by wildlife such as bison, bear, moose, and elk, and the conspicuous legacy of the miners, cowboys, outlaws, and Native Americans who fought over the area's rich resources during the nineteenth century.

Apart from the **Ancestral Puebloan** cliff-dwellers, who lived in southern Colorado until around 1300 AD, most **Native Americans** in this region were nomadic hunters. They inhabited the western extremities of the Great Plains, the richest buffalo-grazing land in the continent. Spaniards, groping through Colorado in the sixteenth century in search of gold, were the first whites to venture into the Rockies. But only after the territory was sold to the US in 1803 as part of the **Louisiana Purchase** was it thoroughly charted, starting with the **Lewis and Clark expedition** that traversed Montana and Idaho in 1805. As a result of the team's reports of abundant game, the fabled "**mountainmen**" had soon trapped the beavers here to the point of virtual extinction. They left as soon as the pelt boom was over, however, and permanent white settlement did not begin until gold was discovered near Denver in 1858. Within a decade, speculators were plundering every accessible gorge and creek in the four states in the search for valuable ores. The construction of transcontinental rail lines and the establishment of vast cattle ranches to feed the mining camps led to the slaughter of millions of buffalo, and conflict with the Native Americans became inevitable. The **Sioux** and **Cheyenne**, led by brilliant strategists like Sitting Bull and Crazy Horse, achieved decisive victories over the US Army, most notably at Little Bighorn – "**Custer's Last Stand**." However, a massive military operation had cleared the region of all warring tribes by the late 1870s.

Most of those who came after the Native Americans saw the Rockies strictly in terms of profit: they took what they wanted and left. Small communities in this isolated terrain remain exclusively dedicated to coal, oil, or some other single commodity, and all too often the uncertain tightrope walk between boom and bust is evident in their run-down facades.

Each of the four states has its own distinct character. **Colorado**, with fifty peaks over 14,000ft, is the most mountainous and populated, as well as the economic leader of the region. Friendly, sophisticated **Denver** is the only major metropolis in the Rockies. It's also the most visited city, in part because it's that much more accessible, and it plays the role of gateway to some of the best ski resorts in the

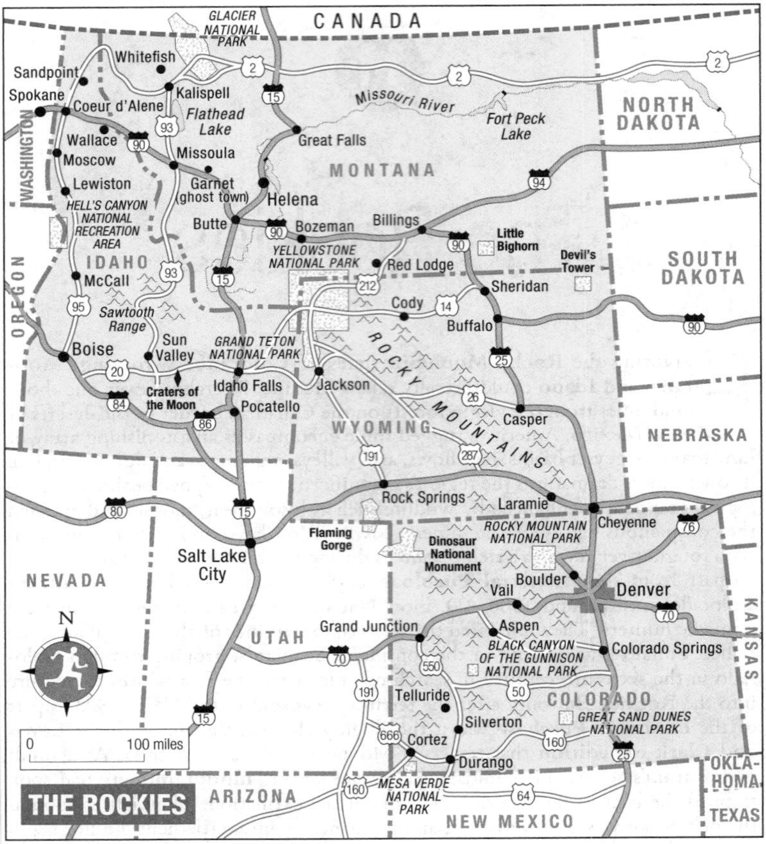

country. Less touched by the tourist circus is vast, brawny **Montana**, where the "Big Sky" looks down on a glorious verdant manuscript scribbled over with gushing streams, lakes, and tiny communities.

Vast stretches of scrubland fill **Wyoming**, the country's least populous state, best known for gurgling, spitting **Yellowstone**, adjacent **Grand Teton National Park**, and the nearby **Bighorn Mountains**. Rugged, remote, and desolate **Idaho** holds some of the Rocky Mountains' last unexplored wildernesses, most notably the mighty **Sawtooth** range.

Between early June and early September you can expect **temperatures** in the high sixties all the way up to a hundred degrees Fahrenheit, depending on whether you are in the high desert of Wyoming, the plains of Idaho, or the mountains of Colorado. In the mountains, you should be prepared for wild variations – and, of course, the higher you go the colder it gets. The altitude is high enough to warrant a period of acclimatization, while the intensity of the sun at these elevations can be uncomfortably fierce. In fact, parts of Wyoming and Colorado bask in more hours of sunshine per year than San Diego or Miami Beach. Spring, when the snow melts, is the least attractive time to visit the Rockies, and while the delicate golds of quaking aspen trees light up the mountainsides in early fall, by October things are generally a bit cold for enjoyable hiking or sports. Most **ski** runs are open by late November and operate well into March – or even June, depending on snow conditions. The coldest month is January, when temperatures below 0°F are common.

Attempting to rush around every national park and major town is a sure way to miss out on one of the Rockies' real delights – coaxing your car along the tight switchback roads that wind up and over precipitous mountain passes, especially through the majestic **Continental Divide**. Remember to check in the rear-view mirror as you go, though – you might be missing that perfect photo for your album. At some point it's worth forsaking motorized transportation, though, to see at least some of the area by **bike**; the Rockies contain some of the most challenging and rewarding cycling terrain on the continent. And of course, you cannot count yourself a visitor to the area without embarking on a hike or two.

Colorado

Geographically diverse **COLORADO** veers from the outstretched flats of the east and the colossal mountains of its central region to the arid canyons and plateaus of the west. In the north, **Native Americans** hunted and trapped in lush mountain valleys in summer, and returned to the prairies for the winter; in the south, the Ancestral Puebloans of Mesa Verde grew corn on their isolated mesas and shared in the great early civilization of the Southwest.

Parts of what is now Colorado accrued to the US at different times: the east and north were acquired under the **Louisiana Purchase** in 1803, while the south was won 45 years later in the war with **Mexico**. (Land grants issued under Mexican rule were honored by the Americans, which accounts for a still-strong Latin American influence.) Gold-hungry Spaniards came through in the sixteenth century, and US Army Colonel Zebulon Pike ventured into the mountains on an exploratory expedition in 1806, but the Native American way of life only became seriously threatened with the discovery of **gold** west of Denver in 1858. At that time, Colorado was still part of Kansas Territory; it became a territory in its own right in 1861, and a state in 1876. The distractions of the Civil War gave the Native Americans the opportunity to fight back, but they were soon overwhelmed. From then until the end of the century, Colorado boomed; the quantities of gold and silver extracted from the mountains did not compare with the riches found in California, but they were sufficient to fuel a rip-roaring frontier lifestyle.

For the modern visitor, the obvious first stop is **Denver**, at the eastern edge of the Rockies and the biggest city for several hundred miles around. Outside Denver, the northern half of the state holds many of the most popular destinations, starting with the dynamic college town of **Boulder** and spectacular **Rocky Mountain National Park**. The majority of the resorts that have made Colorado the continent's foremost **skiing** destination snuggle into the mountains west of Denver: **Summit County** attracts the most visitors, **Vail** is considered best for terrain, and **Aspen** boasts the glitziest apres-ski scene. The far west of the state stretches onto the red-rock deserts of the Colorado Plateau, where the dry climate has preserved the extraordinary natural sculptures of **Colorado National**

Monument. **Pikes Peak** towers over the state's second-largest city, **Colorado Springs**, but beyond that, the state's **southeast** quarter is mostly agricultural plains. In the **southwest**, **Mesa Verde National Park** preserves perhaps the most impressive of all the cliff cities left by the ancient Ancestral Puebloan civilization, while the old mining towns of **Durango** and **Crested Butte** stand revitalized in the mountains.

Getting around Colorado

By far the largest **airport** in Colorado is in Denver. Shuttle buses radiate from here to all the main towns and ski resorts – as do commuter-style aircraft. Denver is also a major hub for Greyhound **buses** to all neighboring states. Amtrak **trains** run straight across the middle of Colorado, and while they can be frustratingly slow, they're timed in both directions to pass through magnificent Glenwood Canyon in daylight hours.

Colorado is also one of the best destinations in the world for **cyclists**, hosting numerous on- and off-road championships. For excellent **maps and guides** to cycle routes in the state, contact the Colorado Department of Transportation (Ⓣ303/639-1111 or 1-877/315-7623, Ⓦwww.cotrip.org).

Denver

Its skyscrapers marking the final transition between the Great Plains and the American West, **DENVER** stands at the threshold of the **Rocky Mountains**. Despite being known as the "**Mile High City**," and serving as the obvious point of arrival for travelers heading into the mountains, it is itself uniformly flat. The majestic peaks of the Front Range are clearly visible but begin to rise roughly fifteen miles west of downtown, allowing Denver plenty of room to spread out.

Mineral wealth has always been at the heart of the city's prosperity, with all the fluctuations of fortune it entails. Though local resources have been progressively exhausted, Denver has managed to hang on to its role as the most important commercial and transportation nexus in the state. Its original "foundation" in 1858 was by pure chance; this was the first spot where small quantities of **gold** were discovered in Colorado. There was no significant river, let alone a road, but prospectors came streaming in, regardless of prior claims to the land – least of all those of the **Arapahoe**, who had supposedly been confirmed in their ownership of the area by the Fort Laramie Treaty of 1851.

There was actually very little gold in Denver itself; the infant town swarmed briefly with disgruntled fortune-seekers, who decamped when news came in of the massive gold strike at Central City. Denver survived, however, prospering further with the discovery of **silver** in the mountains. All sorts of shady characters made this their home; Jefferson "Soapy" Smith, for example, acquired his nickname here, selling bars of soap at extortionate prices under the pretence that some contained $100 bills. When the first railroads bypassed Denver – the death knell for so many other communities – the citizens simply banded together and built their own connecting spur.

These days, Denver is a welcoming and enjoyable city, with a fairly liberal outlook. Tourism is based on getting out into the great outdoors rather than on sightseeing in town, but somehow the city's isolation gives its 2.5-million population a refreshing friendliness; and in a city that is used to providing its own entertainment, there always seems to be something going on.

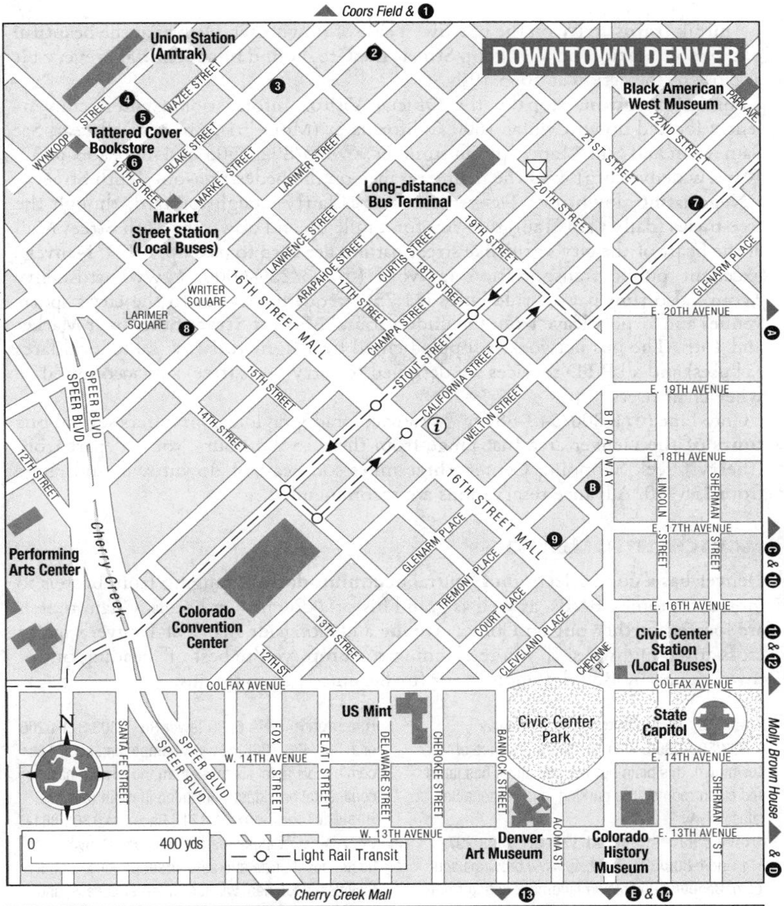

ACCOMMODATION		RESTAURANTS				BARS & CLUBS			
Broadway Plaza Motel	E	Bump and Grind	10	Tom's Diner	12	Breckenridge Brewery	1	Mercury Café	7
Brown Palace Hotel	B	El Azteca	9	Vesta Dipping Grill	3	The Church	14	Wynkoop Brewing Co.	4
Capitol Hill Mansion	D	Palace Arms	B	Wazee Supper Club	6	Comedy Works	8		
Hostel of the Rockies	C	Racine's	13			Cruise Room Bar	5		
Queen Anne Inn	A	Taki's	11			El Chapultepec	2		

Arrival, information, and getting around

The gigantic, ultra-high-tech **Denver International Airport** (Ⓣ303/342-2000 or 1-800/247-2336, Ⓦwww.flydenver.com) lies 24 miles northeast of downtown. Regular RTD SkyRide **buses** can take you downtown ($7–11 single, $13–20 round-trip) and to Boulder ($11 single). Buses leave from outside Door 511 on the East Side of Jeppesen Terminal, Level 5, Island 5. There are also a number of independent shuttles that, for $20–25, will drop you off at a downtown hotel; shuttles to many of the state's major ski resorts can also be arranged within the terminal, though advance reservations are recommended.

Amtrak **trains** arrive on the northwest side of downtown Denver at the beautiful old **Union Station** on Wynkoop Street; the Greyhound **bus terminal** is every bit as close to the action at 1055 19th St.

For **information**, stop by the Official Visitor Information Center, conveniently located downtown at 1600 California St (Mon–Fri 9am–6pm all year, Sat 9am–5pm and Sun 11am–3pm in summer; ⓣ303/892-1505 or 1-800/233-6837, ⓦwww.denver.org) with the main entrance on the pedestrian-only 16th Street.

Negotiating downtown Denver **on foot** is fairly straightforward, though the free **buses** (daily 6am–1am) that run for a mile up and down the 16th Street Mall at the heart of the city's grid-like street pattern are hard to pass up. RTD, Denver's excellent public transportation network (ⓣ303/229-6000, ⓦwww.rtd-denver.com), also runs pay-to-ride buses ($1.75); frequent services to the city's sports venues and airport leave from the underground **Market Street Station** at Market and 16th. The bus network is supplemented by a **light railway** (same local fares as buses) and all RTD services are designed to carry bikes (free) and accommodate wheelchair users.

Gray Line (ⓣ1-800/348-6877, ⓦwww.coloradograyline.com) offers several **bus tours** of the Denver area that range from three to ten hours; tours depart from Cherry Creek Shopping Center, three miles southeast of downtown, and range from $35–90. Advance reservations are recommended.

Accommodation

Denver has a good selection of central **accommodation**, ranging from hostels to motels to homey B&Bs, as well as grand historic downtown hotels. Chain motels are located further out on Colfax Avenue and alongside many of Denver's major cross-town highways. If you're planning to **camp**, you're best off heading out of town to nearby Boulder, Golden, or further into the mountains.

Broadway Plaza Motel 1111 Broadway ⓣ303/893-0303. Within walking distance of downtown, this plain but friendly motel has large and clean rooms, free parking, and reasonable rates. 3–4

Brown Palace Hotel 321 17th St ⓣ303/297-3111 or 1-800/321-2599, ⓦwww.brownpalace.com. Beautiful downtown landmark dating from 1892, with elegant dining rooms and public areas, as well as impeccable rooms. The eight-story cast-iron atrium is particularly stunning. 8–9

Capitol Hill Mansion 1207 Pennsylvania St ⓣ303/839-5221 or 1-800-839-9329, ⓦwww.capitolhillmansion.com. This luxurious B&B in a turreted Victorian sandstone mansion is on a leafy street near the state capitol. Each of its eight antique-furnished rooms is delightful, and several include large whirlpool tubs. 5–7

Hampton Inn DIA 6290 Tower Rd ⓣ303/371-0200 or 1-800/426-7866, ⓦwww.hamptoninn.com. A comfortable hotel six miles from the airport; basic continental breakfast is included in room rate. 4

Hostel of the Rockies 1717 Race St ⓣ303/861-7777, ⓦwww.innkeeperrockies.com. Denver's top hostel boasts free and safe street parking, laundry facilities, a kitchen, wireless internet access, and a TV room. Dorm beds go for $24 a night, while private rooms ($30–35) are in a separate building five blocks from the hostel. Sociable cookouts take place each Saturday in the back garden.

Queen Anne Inn 2147 Tremont Place ⓣ303/296-6666 or 1-800/432-4667, ⓦwww.queenannebnb.com. Central and very hospitable 1879 B&B near a peaceful park where you can catch a carriage ride; each of the fourteen rooms is tastefully and individually decorated. 6–8

The City

If you're not here to work, **downtown's** main draw is the shops and restaurants of **16th Street**, a pedestrian zone also served by free buses. There's a range of galleries, brewpubs, shops, and lofts in **LoDo**, or Lower Downtown, a revitalized late-Victorian district bordered by 14th, 20th, Wynkoop, and Larimer streets; it was here, between 14th and 15th streets, that William Larimer built Denver's original log cabin. The structure burned down in a general conflagration within a few years, whereupon a city ordinance decreed that all new construction be in brick. Opposite the venerable Union Street train station is a branch of one of the best independent **bookstores** in the US: the Tattered Cover at 1628 16th St and Wynkoop.

Denver's black community is most prominent in the old **Five Points** district, northeast of LoDo, created to house black railroad workers in the 1870s. The **Black American West Museum** at 3091 California St (June–Aug Tues–Sat 10am–5pm; Sept–May Tues–Sat 10am–2pm, closed holidays; $8; ⓣ303/482-2242, ⓦwww.blackamericanwestmuseum.com) has intriguing details on black pioneers and outlaws, and debunks certain Western myths: one-third of all nineteenth century cowboys were black, and many were former slaves who left the South after the Civil War.

Three blocks from the southeastern end of 16th Street, the **State Capitol** at Broadway and E Colfax Avenue (Mon–Fri 7am–5.30pm) offers a commanding view of the Rockies swelling on the western horizon. The thirteenth step up to its entrance is exactly one mile above sea level. The capitol is a rather predictable copy of that in Washington DC, but the free tours (every 45min Mon–Fri, closed holidays; 9am–3.30pm in summer, 9.15am–2.30pm rest of year) are pleasantly informal, and you can climb its dome for an even better view.

Civic Center Park, right in front of the capitol, is flanked by two of Denver's finest museums. The glass tile-covered **Denver Art Museum** at 100 W 14th Ave (Tues–Thurs & Sat 10am–5pm, Fri 10am–10pm, Sun noon–5pm; $13; ⓣ720/865-5000, ⓦwww.denverartmuseum.org) has a solid collection of paintings from around the world, but is most noteworthy for its superb examples of Native American craftwork. Some of its pre-Columbian art from Central America – particularly the extraordinary Olmec miniatures – is also spectacular. Also flanking the park is the **Colorado History Museum** at 1300 Broadway (Mon–Sat 10am–5pm, Sun noon–5pm; $7; ⓣ303/866-3682, ⓦwww.coloradohistory.org), where the most interesting exhibits are the historical dioramas in the downstairs galleries.

A few miles east of downtown, the enormous **City Park** is home to the **Denver Museum of Nature and Science**, 2001 Colorado Blvd (daily 9am–5pm; museum $11, IMAX $8, museum plus IMAX or planetarium $16, all three $21; ⓣ303/322-7009 or 1-800/925-2250, ⓦwww.dmns.org). Its exhibits extend beyond the very good dinosaur exhibits and wildlife displays to include anthropological material on Native Americans. There's also a large **zoo** nearby (daily: April–Oct 9am–5pm, Nov–March 10am–4pm; admission April–Oct $12, Nov–March $9; ⓣ303/376-4800, ⓦwww.denverzoo.org), whose four thousand inmates include a couple of huge lowland gorillas in a large, thickly wooded sanctuary.

Denver's **Elitch Gardens** theme park, on the western edge of downtown at 2000 Elitch Circle (June–Sept daily 10am–10pm; Oct–May weekends only, irregular hours; $35, parking $10; ⓣ303/595-4386, ⓦwww.elitchgardens.com), is surprisingly close to the city center (a ten-minute walk along the Cherry Creek cycle path) and has some great white-knuckle rides, as well as a decent **waterslide park**.

Finally, twenty miles west of downtown (though essentially a Denver suburb) lies the town of **Golden,** linked by regular buses to Market Street Station. Since the 1860s, the town has been virtually synonymous with beer giant **Coors**, the world's largest brewery (Mon–Sat 10am–4pm; free; ⓣ303/277-2337, ⓦwww.coors.com). Located three blocks east of Washington Avenue, Golden's main thoroughfare, the brewery serves up 90-minute tours heavy on corporate shill and punctuated with a tasting session of Coors' numerous products; you'll have the chance to sample its alternately maligned and loved Coors Light (aka Silver Bullet), the lower-calorie beer for which the company is most famous. On the opposite side of Golden's downtown, mountains rise sharply from the plains, among them

Lookout Mountain, site of the **Buffalo Bill Museum** (May–Oct daily 9am–5pm, Nov–April Tues–Sun 9am–4pm; $3; Ⓦwww.buffalobill.org) and final resting place of William Cody, the famed frontiersman, buffalo-hunter, army scout, and showman who died in Denver in 1915 (see also p.811). Though now surrounded by huge electricity pylons, the gravesite offers great views in both directions, over the city and out to the mountains. The adjacent museum does a thorough job of outlining Buffalo Bill's past, and one of the more gruesome elements on display is a pistol whose handle has been fashioned from human bone.

Eating

Along with plenty of Western-themed steak and barbecue eateries, Denver has a modest selection of international restaurants. Several of the city's famed **brew-pubs** serve good quality meals as well. Of the several distinct restaurant districts, the **Larimer Square** area is the most easily accessible on foot.

Bump and Grind 439 E 17th Ave ⓣ303/861-4841. Cheap café/bistro just outside downtown that's the flamboyant hub for the local gay social scene, particularly during weekend brunch when the waitstaff is almost exclusively transvestite. The food is excellent, creative, and inexpensive – the eggs Benedict on sourdough bread costs just $7.

El Azteca 301 16th St ⓣ303/534-4222. At lunchtime, office workers arrive en masse for authentic, top-notch Mexican food served in this small eatery in the basement of a dreary food-court. Prices are low, service quick, and the food – particularly the *carne asada* – excellent. Closed evenings.

Palace Arms 321 17th St ⓣ303/297-3111. This intimate, classy restaurant tucked in the *Brown Palace* hotel (see p.774) is the ultimate splurge in town, with a menu of mostly seasonal game specialties and decor of Napoleonic period antiques – including a pair of Napoleon's dueling pistols.

Racine's 650 Sherman St ⓣ303/595-0418. Housed in a former auto showroom, this large, laid-back place is a Denver institution. The inexpensive menu features excellent egg-based breakfasts, with imaginative pastas, reliably good sandwiches, and serviceable Mexican entrees later in the day.

Taki's 341 E Colfax Ave ⓣ303/832-4440. Giant, inexpensive portions of Japanese food are served in this friendly and longstanding local family business, with cafeteria-style ordering that gets you the food fast. The miso soup is too good to miss and the salmon bowl – a sizeable piece of salmon smothered in a mustard sauce, with rice – is exceptional.

Tom's Diner 601 E Colfax Ave ⓣ303/861-7493. Wonderfully gritty and authentic 24hr diner, providing cheap deals on big portions of stock diner food in a seedy part of town.

Vesta Dipping Grill 1822 Blake St ⓣ303/296-1970. Attractive restaurant in a renovated LoDo warehouse serving tasty food in unusual combinations. The menu is based on the concept of dipping meat or veggies in a spectrum of flavors (Mediterranean, Asian, and Mexican).

Wazee Supper Club 1600 15th St ⓣ303/623-9518. Established LoDo dining room doling out good cheap burgers, deli sandwiches, and superb pizzas, plus a full range of beers, all in an Art Deco atmosphere. The kitchen serves until 1am most nights.

Nightlife and entertainment

The congregation of brewpubs and sports bars in the LoDo district, particularly near baseball park Coors Field, have made this the city's liveliest nightlife area. There are plenty of other more stylish or relaxing places to drink here, too. Most bars close around 1am. For news of **musical** happenings, consult the free weekly *Denver Westword*, found in sidewalk dispensers and cafés around downtown.

The remarkable **Red Rocks Amphitheater** (ⓣ303/694-1234, Ⓦwww.redrocksonline.com), fifteen miles west of downtown Denver via I-70 (exit 259), has been the setting for thousands of rock and classical concerts; U2 filmed its landmark *Under a Blood Red Sky* here in 1983. The 9000-person capacity venue is squeezed between two 400ft red-sandstone rocks that seem to glow in early morning and late evening. The surrounding Red Rocks Park is open to visitors free of charge during the day.

The great outdoors

From the otherworldly outcrops of Monument Valley to the churning surf of California's Big Sur shoreline, the USA abounds in stupendous scenery. Many first-time visitors are staggered by the immensity and diversity of the country's wide-open spaces, and even if you think of yourself as a "city person," you should seize the opportunity to venture into that spectacular wilderness. While not all of the USA's finest landscapes lie within their boundaries, its fifty-plus national parks, which combine practical amenities with environmental stewardship, make the obvious focus for an unforgettable outdoors itinerary.

Rock climbing in Yosemite National Park ▲

Hiking in Mount Rainier National Park ▼

Hiking

America's national parks offer the perfect opportunity to experience the thrills of hiking in genuine wilderness while minimizing the risks. Almost all can be explored on networks of maintained trails, on which you can escape the crowds and face real physical challenges.

Rather than simply ticking off the hardest trails at the biggest-name parks, hiking is all about taking the time to engage with the landscape, and to appreciate where you are. That said, certain truly fabulous trails are worth seeking out. At the **Grand Canyon**, clear time for the two-day hike down to the Colorado River and back. Set off before dawn on the steep, exposed South Kaibab Trail, to avoid the midday heat; spend the night at Phantom Ranch on the canyon floor; and climb back the next day along the gentler, shadier Bright Angel Trail. Spell-binding **Zion National Park**, further north, offers a wider range of trails, from the easy but spectacular Riverside Walk to the more demanding West Rim Trail, up to the awesome Angel's Landing viewpoint. Great mountain hikes include the Skyline Trail in Washington's **Mount Rainier National Park**, and the Hidden Lake Trail through the wildflowers of **Glacier National Park**. Hikers on Maui in Hawaii descend the Sliding Sands Trail into the multi-colored volcanic crater in **Haleakala National Park**, while fearless adventurers in California's **Yosemite** climb the amazing Half Dome, for vertiginous views over the awesome valley below.

Before you attempt any long trail, ask park rangers about current conditions. Don't underestimate the difficulties posed by desert or mountain terrain, or adverse weather, but don't let them put you off either. Just be sure to take all proper precautions.

Scenic drives

While the ideal way to experience the American wilderness is on foot, if you choose your route carefully, you can have just as much fun on the road. Time your trip to coincide with the fall colors, for example, which arrive at different times in different areas, and you won't regret it.

Great scenic drives can be found all over the US. The serpentine **Blue Ridge Parkway** crests the Appalachian mountains for hundreds of miles through Virginia and North Carolina, curving through endless forests with barely a sign of human habitation. Similarly, the **Natchez Trace Parkway** follows a native American trail from Tennessee down to the Mississippi, through dense woodland scattered with ancient settlements, while further north, the **Pictured Rocks National Lakeshore** skirts the dramatic cliffs of Michigan's Upper Peninsula.

The further west you go, the more spectacular the scenery. Even the interstates can serve up stupendous views, while less-used roads like US-14, which climbs Wyoming's **Wapiti Valley** to Yellowstone, are often magnificent. In Idaho, Hwy-75 heads north from Ketchum through the stunning serrated peaks of the **Sawtooth National Recreation Area**; further south in Utah, Scenic Hwy-12 spends a hundred miles dipping into the northern fringes of remote **Grand Staircase-Escalante National Monument**, with its extraordinary red-rock formations. Colorado's **Million Dollar Highway** connects a string of atmospheric old mining towns via 11,000-foot mountain passes, while down in Texas the **River Road** parallels the Rio Grande along the Mexican border, passing through quirky ghost towns like Terlingua. And in California, Hwy-1 makes an utterly superb coastal drive from San Francisco south towards Los Angeles,

▲ Blue Ridge Parkway

▼ Grand Staircase-Escalante National Monument

with the sublime canyon-cut landscape of the **Big Sur Coast** as its undisputed highlight.

Bryce Canyon National Park ▲

Denali National Park ▼

Hawaii Volcanoes National Park ▼

Top ten national parks

▸▸ **Acadia**, Maine. Tiny Mount Desert Island, just off northern New England, is where the sun first hits the US each morning. A narrow fjord teems with wildlife, while rugged hills offer fine hiking. p.268

▸▸ **Big Bend**, Texas. A colorful, high-desert wilderness on the Mexican border, cradled within a sweeping curve of the Rio Grande that's a white-water rafter's paradise. p.706

▸▸ **Bryce Canyon**, Utah. A totally bizarre sight: a throng of sandstone pinnacles, glowing red, yellow, and orange, and burning like flames into a remote Utah hillside. p.915

▸▸ **Canyonlands**, Utah. The Colorado and Green rivers thread through this mind-boggling labyrinth of contorted canyons and desiccated plateaus, explored by hundreds of miles of hiking trails. p.919

▸▸ **Crater Lake**, Oregon. A staggeringly beautiful blue lake, filling a collapsed volcanic caldera – with another cinder cone rising from its depths. p.1128

▸▸ **Denali**, Alaska. Visitors flock to America's highest peak, Mount McKinley, for rafting, skiing, hiking, and the virtual certainty of seeing a bear. p.1161

▸▸ **Glacier**, Montana. With its spectacular waterfalls, lush Alpine meadows and mighty massifs, Glacier is the crown jewel of the Rockies. p.836

▸▸ **Hawaii Volcanoes**, Hawaii. Where the Big Island grows bigger before your very eyes, as torrents of incandescent lava explode into the steaming Pacific. p.1185

▸▸ **Yellowstone**, Wyoming. A true natural wonder, best known for its spurting geysers and bubbling mud pots, but also filled with lakes and mountains, wolves and bison. p.812

▸▸ **Yosemite**, California. Whether you stroll the valley floor or climb its soaring cliffs, this geological wonderland is a must-see for any California visitor. p.1007

Denver's other pride and joy, the modern **Denver Performing Arts Complex** on 14th and Curtis streets (ⓣ303/893-4100, ⓦwww.artscomplex.com), is home to the Denver Center Theater Company, Colorado Symphony Orchestra, Opera Colorado, and the Colorado Ballet, and hosts performances nightly. Facilities in the complex include eight **theaters**, as well as the acoustically superb, in-the-round **Symphony Hall**.

In the hunt for **tickets** to all cultural and sporting events, Ticketmaster (ⓣ303/830-8497, ⓦwww.ticketmaster.com) can usually help. You can also try the Ticket Bus, parked on 16th and Curtis, in person (daily 10am–6pm), where you'll often find last-minute **deals** on shows that have yet to sell out.

Breckenridge Brewery 2220 Blake St ⓣ303/297-3644. Cozy and lively brewpub opposite Coors Field, with quality craft beer and a terrific range of delicious barbecue plates.

The Church 1160 Lincoln St ⓣ303/832-3528. A dance club inside a gutted cathedral that combines a downtown nightlife landmark, wine bar, sushi bar, and three invariably busy dance floors. Programming varies from hard house to garage to hip-hop, and the crowd can be equally eclectic. $5–15 cover.

Comedy Works 1226 15th St ⓣ303/595-3637. Right off Larimer Square, Denver's major comedy venue is the most likely place to find big-name stand-up acts on tour. Shows kick off nightly at 8pm, with several performances on weekend nights.

Cruise Room Bar *The Oxford Hotel*, 1600 17th St ⓣ303/628-5400. A replica of the Art Deco bar on the *Queen Mary* ocean liner, this is worth a stop for the atmosphere alone.

El Chapultepec 1962 Market St ⓣ303/295-9126. Tiny, but popular LoDo stalwart with nightly live jazz and occasional big names. No cover, but there's a two-drink minimum.

Grizzly Rose 5450 N Valley Hwy ⓣ303/295-1330. Celebrated Country and Western venue that's a 10-minute drive north of downtown on I-25 (exit 215). The huge venue has bands nightly and attracts famous names regularly. There's even a mechanical bull. Cover $5–20.

Mercury Cafe 2199 California St ⓣ303/294-9281. When there's not jazz on at *The Merc*, there are tango dance classes, poetry readings, or some other form of entertainment. The club is combined with a good-value restaurant serving healthy choices (many vegetarian) as well as high tea.

Wynkoop Brewing Co. 1634 18th St ⓣ303/297-2700. Opposite Union Station, the state's first brewpub serves up solid home-brewed beers and great bar food; there's an elegant pool hall upstairs. Brewery tours, with free samples, are given on Sat (1–5pm) – call ahead to confirm.

Northern Colorado

The major attraction for visitors in the Denver area is **Rocky Mountain National Park** to the northwest. Though on the map the distances involved may not look that great, it would be a mistake to attempt to see the whole park on a day-trip from Denver. Segments of its loop drive can be very slow and laborious, and in a single day it's more realistic just to dip a few miles into the park's eastern fringes.

The lively foothill town of **Boulder** can be used as a base, though the smaller mountain towns give you more time in the wilds: **Grand Lake**, near the park's western entrance, makes a more attractive stopover than **Estes Park** in the east, while back on the west side, **Winter Park** is an affordable, enjoyable ski resort. Further west, midway across the state on either side of the I-70 freeway, you'll find the famous Rocky Mountain ski resorts of **Vail**, **Aspen**, and the rest, as well as the evocative mining town of **Leadville**. Continuing toward the Utah border, the landscape dips and rises in a patchwork of granite peaks, raging rivers, and red-sandstone canyons, through **Glenwood Springs** and winding up at **Grand Junction** and the striking scenery of **Colorado National Monument**.

Boulder

BOULDER, just 27 miles northwest of Denver on US-36, is one of the liveliest college towns in the country, filled with a young population that seems to divide its time between phenomenally healthy daytime pursuits and almost equally unhealthy night-time activities – the town is sometimes referred to as "seven miles surrounded by reality." It was founded in 1858 by a prospecting party who felt that the nearby Flatiron Mountains, the first swell of the Rockies, "looked right for gold;" in fact they found little, but the community grew anyway.

With an easygoing, forward-looking atmosphere and plenty of great places to eat and drink, Boulder makes an excellent place to return to each night after a day in the mountains. Downtown centers on the leafy pedestrian mall of **Pearl Street**, lined with all sorts of lively cafés, galleries, and stores – including several places where you can rent **mountain bikes**. The most obvious short excursion is to drive or hike up nearby **Flagstaff Mountain** for views over town and further into the Rockies; any road west joins up with the Peak to Peak Highway, which heads through spectacular scenery to Estes Park and Rocky Mountain National Park. For rock climbing, **Eldorado Canyon State Park** offers many opportunities; the excellent Neptune Mountaineering, south of town in the Table Mesa shopping center at 633 S Broadway (Ⓣ303/499-8866, Ⓦwww.neptunemountaineering.com), can answer questions and provide gear.

The adventurous **University of Colorado** offers regular **arts events**, including the classical-focused Colorado Music Festival (Ⓣ303/449-1397, Ⓦwww.coloradomusicfest.org), held each summer in the Chautauqua Auditorium; two campus theaters also host the seven-week Colorado Shakespeare Festival (Ⓣ303/492-0554, Ⓦwww.coloradoshakes.org). Even the small **Naropa University** (Ⓣ303/444-0202, Ⓦwww.naropa.edu), founded in 1974 by a Tibetan Buddhist, has a notable presence in this progressive, alternative-thinking town, sponsoring events throughout the year.

Practicalities

The main point of entry for local and long-distance **buses** is the Transit Center, 14th and Walnut streets (Ⓣ303/299-6000). Regular services to and from Denver International Airport ($10 single) and the city of Denver itself ($5) arrive here as well. For city information, visit the hospitable, low-key **Boulder Convention & Visitors Bureau**, 2440 Pearl St (Mon–Fri 9am–5pm; Ⓣ303/442-2911 or 1-800/444-0447, Ⓦwww.bouldercoloradousa.com). For information on public lands around Boulder, contact the City of Boulder Open Space and Mountain Parks (Ⓣ303-441-3440, Ⓦwww.ci.boulder.co.us/openspace). One of Boulder's chief attractions is that it's easy and pleasant to get around on foot or bicycle, but the town's **bus service** is also excellent: the frequent HOP and SKIP services link the University Hill area with downtown and a major mall (approximate hours: Mon–Fri 5.30am–midnight, Sat 7.30am–11pm, Sun 7.30am–10.30pm; $1.25). For **taxi service**, try Boulder Yellow Cab (Ⓣ303/777-7777).

Even if you're not **staying** in the historic *Hotel Boulderado*, located near Pearl Street at 2115 13th St (Ⓣ303/442-4344 or 1-800/433-4344, Ⓦwww.boulderado.com; ❻–❼), wander in for a drink and free evening jazz. The *Foot of the Mountain Motel*, 200 W Arapahoe Ave (Ⓣ303/442-5688 or 1-866/773-5489, Ⓦwww.footofthemountainmotel.com; ❹), is a friendly, log-cabin-style motel, nine blocks from downtown beside Boulder Creek. There's also the welcoming *Boulder International Hostel* near the campus in a Victorian building at 1107 12th St (Ⓣ303/442-0522, Ⓦwww.boulderhostel.com), with both dorm beds ($27) and private rooms ($55) available.

Plenty of **bars** and **restaurants** mark the Pearl Street area. The free *Boulder Weekly* newspaper is replete with the latest dining and boozing information. Student favorite *Traling's Oriental Cafe*, 1305 Broadway (☎303/449-0400), is a grungy canteen-style restaurant with tasty and amazingly cheap Chinese food. A far more sophisticated choice is *Sunflower*, 1701 Pearl St (☎303/440-0220), where you'll find a healthy (if high-priced) menu of organic and free-range items. Another local splurge is the *Flagstaff House*, 1138 Flagstaff Drive (☎303/442-4640), where the menu changes daily but invariably includes seafood, game, and vegetarian pasta dishes. The *Hotel Boulderado* (see p.778) also houses two popular **nightspots**: the *Corner Bar*, with armchair seating and creative, reasonably priced dishes served until late at night on the patio; and the more casual *Catacombs Bar*, which features nightly live blues, jazz, and acoustic guitar music. *West End Tavern*, 926 Pearl St (☎303/444-3535), is a nice spot for live roots music, locally brewed beer, and spectacular views of the Flatirons from the roof terrace. For getting your groove on, *Round Midnight* at 1005 Pearl St (☎303/442-2176) with its packed weekend dance floor is your best bet.

Rocky Mountain National Park

You don't have to go to **ROCKY MOUNTAIN NATIONAL PARK** to appreciate the full splendor of the Rockies; it's simply one small section of the mighty range, measuring roughly twenty-five by fifteen miles. A tenth of the size of Yellowstone, it attracts around the same number of visitors – around three-and-a-half million per year, and with the bulk of those coming in high summer, the one main road through the mountains can get incredibly congested. However, the park is undeniably beautiful, straddling the Continental Divide at elevations often well in excess of ten thousand feet. A full third of the park is above tree line, and large areas of snow never melt; the name of the **Never Summer Mountains** speaks volumes about the long, empty expanses of arctic-style tundra. In the park's lower reaches, among the rich forests, are patches of lush greenery; you never know when you may stumble upon a sheltered mountain meadow flecked with flowers. Parallels with the European Alps readily spring to mind – helped, of course, by the heavy-handed Swiss and Bavarian themes of the region's motels and restaurants.

Approaching the park

Coming from the **east**, you barely penetrate the foothills of the Rockies before arriving at the unattractive but bustling gateway town of **Estes Park**, 65 miles northwest of Denver. At the end of the nineteenth century, Estes Park was the private hunting preserve of the Irish Earl of Dunraven; once he was squeezed out, the town took on the more democratic function it still serves: providing visitors with food, lodging, and other services. The **park headquarters** and **Beaver Meadows Visitor Center** (daily 8am–5pm; park admission $20 per vehicle, good for seven days; information ☎970/586-1206, Ⓦwww.nps.gov/romo) is a couple of miles north, on US-36.

To reach the **western** entrance, 85 miles from Denver, turn north off I-70 onto US-40, which negotiates **Berthoud Pass** en route to **Grand Lake**, a more low-key version of Estes Park. This unlikely yachting center, high in the mountains, consists of one main boardwalk-lined street featuring family amusements, lodgings, and restaurants beside the lake. The **Kawuneeche Visitor Center** of Rocky Mountain National Park is a mile north of town (daily 8am–4.30pm; ☎970/627-3471).

Exploring the park

The showpiece of the park is **Trail Ridge Road** (generally open late May to mid-October), between Estes Park and Grand Lake. This 45-mile stretch of US-34, the highest-elevation paved road in any US national park, affords a succession of tremendous views, and several short trails start from parking lots along the way. There are no services on the route, which generally takes three to four hours to drive. The definite highlight is the stretch of road on either side of the **Alpine Visitor Center**, halfway along Trail Ridge Road at Fall River Pass (late May–early Oct 10.30am–4.30pm); the peaks and alpine tundra here are breathtaking. The visitor center is really the only requisite stop for anyone happy enough to view the alpine tundra by car, as its **exhibits** relate to the flora and fauna of the tundra. Good areas for wildlife viewing are a little further east along Trail Ridge Road.

The other scenic drive in the park is along the unpaved, summer-only **Old Fall River Road,** which was the park's first road, completed in 1920. Running east–west along the bed of a U-shaped glacial valley, it doesn't have open mountain vistas, but it's much quieter than its paved counterpart, and there's far more chance of spotting **wildlife**: roaming the area are moose, coyote, mountain lions, and black bears, which with the park's plentiful natural food supply, tend to avoid contact with humans.

While many people do little more than the drive along Trail Ridge Road, the park is best appreciated on foot. As there are dozens of superb **hikes** to choose from, think about the kind of experience you're after – photographing a particular animal, for instance, or hiking across the Continental Divide – and enlist a ranger to help plan your excursion. Bear in mind that the delicate ecosystem of the wild, wind-blown tundra makes it essential to stay on the paths. Be watchful of your own system at this altitude as well; plan hikes conservatively and drink plenty of water to avoid altitude sickness and dehydration.

▲ Mountain goat, Rocky Mountain National Park

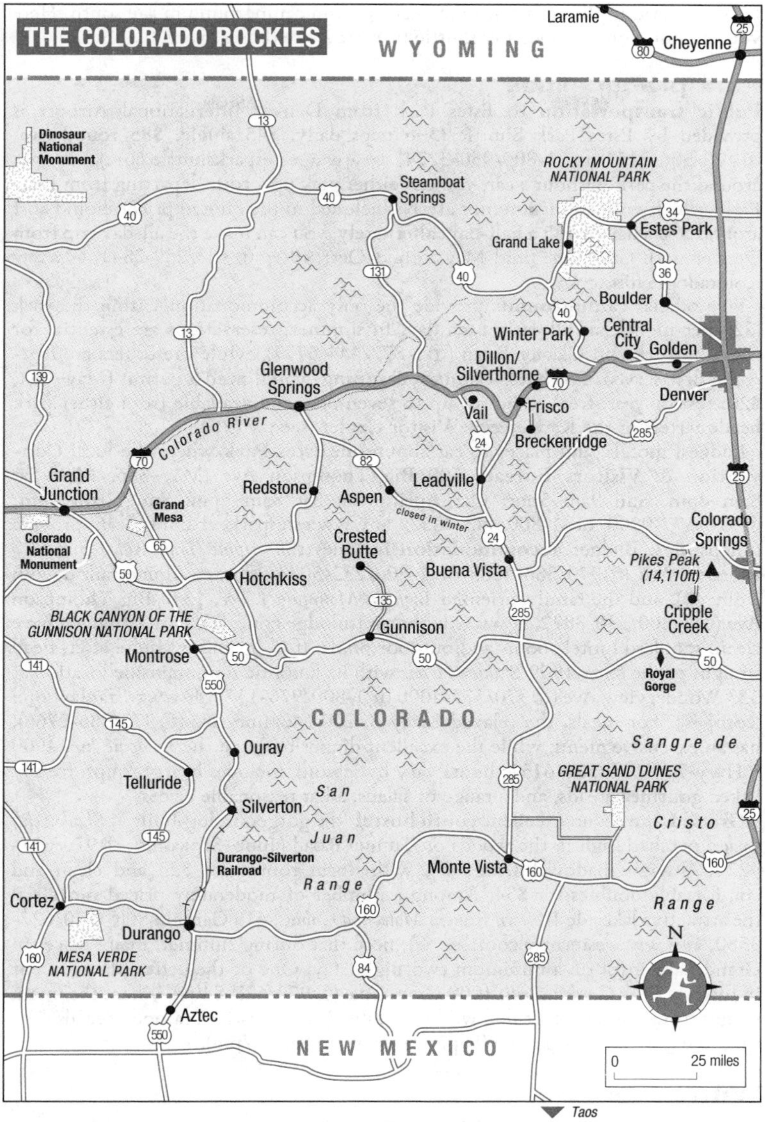

The obvious launching point for numerous day and overnight hikes is **Bear Lake**, a pretty spot at the end of a spur road from Estes Park where the mountains are framed to perfection in its cool, still waters. On the way, the road passes **Moraine Park Museum** (summer only, daily 9am–4.30pm; free), where smart exhibits explain the park's natural history. To ease traffic, free **shuttle buses** (late May–late Sept, daily 7am–7.30pm) operate beyond the museum. The museum itself is on the Moraine Park Route (buses every 30min), which connects the Fern

Lake trailhead in the west with the Glacier Basin campground in the south. Here you can jump on a connecting shuttle to **Bear Lake** (buses every 10–15min).

Park practicalities

Public transportation to Estes Park from Denver International Airport is provided by Estes Park Shuttle (3–6 trips daily, $45 single, $85 round-trip; ⓣ970/586-5151 or 1-800/950-3274, ⓦwww.estesparkshuttle.com). To get around the park without a car, you can either pick up a **tour** departing from Estes Park, which with admission (not always included in the quoted price) should cost around $70 a day or $35 a half-day; alternately, you can make the all-day trip from Denver with Gray Line (mid-May to mid-Oct; $90; ⓣ303/289-2841, ⓦwww.coloradograyline.com).

Five official **campgrounds** provide the only accommodation within the park ($20 per night); all fill early each day. In summer, reservations are essential for Moraine Park and Glacier Basin (ⓣ1-877/444-6777), while the others are first-come first-served. For **back-country camping**, you'll need a permit (May–Oct, $20; rest of year, free), valid for up to seven days and available from either park headquarters or the Kawuneeche Visitor Center (see p.779).

Lodges, motels, and places to eat abound in **Estes Park** where the local **Convention & Visitors Bureau**, 500 Big Thompson Ave (May–Sept Mon–Sat 8am–8pm, Sun 9am–5pm; Oct–April Mon–Sat 8am–5pm, Sun 10am–4pm; ⓣ970/577-9900 or 1-800/443-7837, ⓦwww.estesparkcvb.com), can provide full listings. Budget **accommodation** includes the *Alpine Trail Ridge Inn*, 927 Moraine Ave (ⓣ970/586-4585 or 1-800/233-5023, ⓦwww.alpinetrailridgeinn.com; ❺), and the family-oriented *Bighorn Mountain Lodge*, 1340 Big Thompson Ave (ⓣ1-800/530-8822, ⓦwww.bighornmtnlodge.com; ❺), both of which have clean, standard motel rooms and outdoor pools. If it's glamour you're after, head straight to the circa-1909 *Stanley Hotel*, with its fantastic mountainside location at 333 Wonderview Ave (ⓣ970/577-4000 or 1-800/976-1377, ⓦwww.stanleyhotel.com; ❼). For meals, the relaxed *Molly B*, 200 Moraine Ave (ⓣ970/586-2766), has an extensive menu, while the excellent dinner buffet at the *Baldpate Inn*, 4900 S Hwy-7 (ⓣ970/586-6151; hours vary by season), includes hearty soups, freshly baked gourmet breads, and a range of salads, all at reasonable prices.

Grand Lake has an excellent **youth hostel**: the gorgeous, log-built *Shadowcliff Lodge*, perched high in the woods on Tunnel Road (June–Sept only; ⓣ970/627-9220; ⓦwww.shadowcliff.org; ❷), with dorm rooms for $23 and clean and comfortable doubles for $54. Among a number of moderately priced **motels** is the attractive lakeside *Western Riviera Motel and Cabins*, 419 Garfield St (ⓣ970/627-3580, ⓦwww.westernriv.com; ❺–❻); note that during summer, many places in Grand Lake insist on a minimum two-night stay. One of the better places to **eat** in town is *EG's Garden Grill*, 1000 Grand Ave (ⓣ970/627-8404), where the menu ranges from burgers to grilled wild boar sausages to creative seafood specials – be sure to enjoy the beer garden (happy hour Mon–Sat 5–7pm).

Winter Park

The former railroad center of **WINTER PARK**, 67 miles northwest of Denver, may not be Colorado's trendiest resort, but its wide, ever-expanding variety of ski and bike terrain, friendly atmosphere, and good-value lodgings draw over one million visitors a year. Its namesake **ski resort** (three-day lift ticket $189; ⓣ970/316-1564, ⓦwww.skiwinterpark.com) also has exceptional facilities for kids and disabled skiers, as well as the 200-acre Discovery Park, an excellent, economical area for beginners. Experienced skiers, in turn, relish mogul runs on

Mary Jane Mountain, the fluffy snows of the Parsenn Bowl, and the back-country idyll of Vasquez Cirque.

In addition to skiing, you can **snowmobile** the Continental Divide on a one-hour tour with Trailblazers in Fraser ($60; ⓣ970/726-8452 or 1-800/669-0134, ⓦwww.trailblazersnowmobile.com) or around a 25-mile course just north of town with Mountain Madness ($40/hr; ⓣ970/726-4529). Summer visitors enjoy six hundred miles of excellent **mountain biking** trails, the best of which are accessible from the chair lift ($24 for an adult day bike pass; from $58 with bike rental), in addition to the exhilarating mile-and-a-half-long **Alpine Slide** sled ride ($12) and several contemporary music festivals.

Practicalities

Year-round service to Winter Park is provided by Amtrak, five miles north in Fraser, and by Home James shuttles from Denver International Airport ($60 single; ⓣ1-800/359-7503, ⓦwww.homejamestransportation.com). The **Winter Park Ski Train** makes round-trips from Denver every Saturday and Sunday during ski season, leaving at 7.15am and starting back at 4.15pm ($60; 2hr; reservations required; ⓣ303/296-4754, ⓦwww.skitrain.com). An excellent network of free **shuttle buses** renders a car inessential in town. Trail maps and general outdoor information are available at the Chamber of Commerce, 151 W Lyman Ave.

As well as the **hotels** and **condos** surrounding the ski area that can be booked through Winter Park Central Reservations (ⓣ303/316-1564, ⓦwww.skiwinterpark.com; ❺ and up), inexpensive **motels** line the main street of Winter Park itself, including the comfortable *Viking Lodge* (ⓣ970/726-8885 or 1-800/421-4013; ❷–❸). Places to **eat and drink** downtown include *Carlos and Maria's* in Cooper Creek Square (ⓣ970/726-9674), good for inexpensive margaritas and Mexican food, and *Deno's* (ⓣ970/726-5332), with its hundred-plus beers, tasty pasta plates, and Cajun seafood dishes.

Steamboat Springs

Surrounded by wide valleys, **STEAMBOAT SPRINGS**, 65 miles north of I-70 via Hwy-131, looks like no other Colorado mountain resort. Its roots are in ranching rather than mining, and its downtown area still evokes a pioneer feel – until you spot the upmarket boutiques. In this ski-mad town, ranchers judge the quality of snowfall by the number of fence wires it covers; they're usually satisfied with a three-wire winter, which roughly corresponds to Steamboat's average annual snowfall of 334 inches.

The town's namesake, top-notch **ski resort** (one-day lift ticket $91; ⓣ970/879-6111, ⓦwww.steamboat.com), snuggled into Mount Werner four miles south of downtown, is boosted by such activities as dogsled expeditions, hot-air ballooning, and snowmobiling, available in and around town. A favorite year-round activity is soaking in the secluded 105°F **Strawberry Park Hot Springs** (Sun–Thurs 10am–10.30pm, Fri & Sat 10am–midnight; $10; ⓣ970/879-0342, ⓦwww.strawberryhotsprings.com), seven miles north of town but only accessible by four-wheel-drive vehicles in winter. In town, **Old Town Hot Springs** (Mon–Fri 5.30am–9.45pm, Sat 7am–8.45pm, Sun 8am–8.45pm; pools, waterslides, and fitness center $12 each; ⓣ970/879-1828) offers a range of water-based activities and facilities, as well as child care. During Steamboat Springs' summer season, opportunities for **mountain biking**, **whitewater rafting**, and **horseback riding** abound; a number of outfitters in town can assist you with gear and guides.

Practicalities

Most winter visitors fly into **Yampa Valley Airport**, 22 miles from Steamboat Springs, though it's possible to drive, weather permitting, from Denver on Hwy-40 over scenic Rabbit Ears Pass, or take the Alpine Taxi shuttle direct from Denver International Airport ($80 single; ⓣ970/879-2800 or 1-800/343-7433; ⓦwww.alpinetaxi.com). Visitor information can be found at 1255 Lincoln Ave, two miles east of downtown (Mon–Fri 8am–5pm, Sat 10am–3pm, Sun 9am–6pm during peak times in summer and winter only; ⓣ970/879-0880, ⓦwww.steamboatchamber.com). From town, free SST **buses** run the four miles to and from the ski resort.

Slopeside **lodging**, such as the comfortable *Ptarmigan Inn* (ⓣ970/879-1730 or 1-800/538-7519, ⓦwww.steamboat-lodging.com; winter ❺–❾, summer ❺–❻), costs more than downtown options like the *Rabbit Ears Motel* (ⓣ970/879-1150 or 1-800/828-7702, ⓦwww.rabbitearsmotel.com; winter ❹–❻, summer ❹–❺). **Tent camping** is available at the year-round *Steamboat Campground*, two miles west of downtown on US-40 (ⓣ970/879-0273, ⓦwww.steamboatcampground.com; sites $17–24, depending on season).

For **food**, *Azteca Taqueria*, 116 9th St (ⓣ970/870-9980), has tasty, inexpensive Mexican grub; elsewhere, *Antares*, 57 1/2 8th St (ⓣ970/879-9939), is one of Steamboat's finest restaurants, serving a wide range of fish and meat dishes. Another possibility for delicious (but expensive) dining is *Hazie's* on the mountain (ⓣ970/871-5150; call for seasonal hours of operation), which includes a free gondola ride; its Sunday brunch (9.30am–1.30pm) is particularly excellent. Microbrews and decent pub food are available near the ski area at *The Tugboat Grill and Pub* (ⓣ970/879-7070), which also has live music and a dance floor; *Wolf Den Tavern*, 703 Lincoln Ave (ⓣ970/871-0008), is another good downtown venue for live bands.

Summit County

The purpose-built ski resorts, old mining towns, snow-covered peaks, alpine meadows, and crystal lakes that make up **Summit County** lie alongside I-70, around seventy miles west of Denver. Before white settlement, the Ute hunted here every summer: the swanky Keystone Ranch Golf Club now occupies a meadow where they once pitched their tepees. During the late nineteenth century, the county witnessed several gold-mining booms; today, dilapidated **ghost towns** cling to the mountainsides, but one settlement that has survived is **BRECKENRIDGE**, where streets are lined with brightly painted Victorian houses, shops, and cafés. This is the liveliest of Summit County's four towns; **FRISCO**, stretching sedately along a quiet valley, appeals to those looking for a less hectic pace. Both the other towns, **DILLON** and **SILVERTHORNE**, are dull, though the latter contains dozens of cut-price factory outlet stores. The formulaic ski resort villages of **Keystone** and **Copper Mountain** are also unexciting unless you're here for snowsports.

Arrival and information

By **car**, Summit County is less than two hours from Denver. Greyhound **buses** stop at the Frisco Transit Center, 1010 Meadow Drive from where free buses radiate to the surrounding ski resorts. There are also **shuttles** from Denver International Airport: Colorado Mountain Express serves the county's ski resorts ($84; ⓣ970/926-9800 or 1-800/525-6363, ⓦwww.cmex.com), while Supershuttle (ⓣ1-800/258-3826) operates a similarly priced door-to-door service to hotels. Summit Stage (6.30am–1.30am; ⓣ970/668-0999, ⓦwww.summitstage.com) provides free **local transportation** around the county, and Town Trolley

(Ⓣ970/547-3140) runs through Breckenridge and up to the resort every 20 minutes during ski season. Summit County's main **visitor center** (daily 9am–5pm; Ⓣ970/668-2051 or 1-800/424-1554) is by the lake at the end of Frisco's Main Street; there's also a small welcome center in Breckenridge at 309 N Main St (Ⓣ970/453-6018).

Accommodation

Lodging in Summit County covers all price ranges, with prices doubling in winter. Frisco has the best-priced inns and **motels**. There are also a few downtown **B&Bs** in Breckenridge, where otherwise accommodation usually means an expensive slopeside condo; the Breckenridge Resort Chamber (Ⓣ970/453-2918 or 1-888/251-2417, Ⓦwww.gobreck.com) can advise on prices and package deals. Resort accommodation at both Copper Mountain (Ⓣ970/968-2882 or 1-800/458-8386, Ⓦwww.coppercolorado.com) and Keystone (Ⓣ970/496-4500 or 1-877/753-9786, Ⓦwww.keystoneresort.com) is first class, and so too are the prices, although package deals can occasionally be unearthed.

Fireside Inn 114 N French St, Breckenridge Ⓣ970/453-6456 Ⓦwww.firesideinn.com. Homey little B&B with floral, antique-filled bedrooms (all with private bath) and several cramped dorm rooms ($28–43); the latter all share a TV lounge and kitchenette. Winter ❹–❻, summer ❹–❺

Frisco Lodge 321 Main St, Frisco Ⓣ970/668-0195 or 1-800/279-6000, Ⓦwww.friscolodge.com. Creaky B&B in an old railroad inn, usually the cheapest deal in town. Units have kitchenettes and access to an outdoor hot tub, and cooked buffet breakfast and teatime snacks are served in the cluttered lounge. Winter ❹–❺, summer –❺

Ridge Street Inn 212 N Ridge St, Breckenridge Ⓣ970/453-4680. Comfortable, comparatively affordable B&B in the heart of Breckenridge's lively downtown area. Winter ❺–❻, summer ❹–❺

Outdoor activities

Winter is still the busiest time in Summit County. **Breckenridge Ski Resort** (Ⓣ970/453-5000, Ⓦwww.breckenridge.snow.com), the oldest of the area's four top-class resorts, spans four peaks and offers ideal terrain for all skiers (and snowboarders, with a six-acre park with half-pipe), as does the plush **Keystone** (Ⓣ1-800/354-4386, Ⓦwww.keystone.snow.com), where the biggest night-ski operation in the US permits skiing until 8.30pm. The smallest resort in the county, **Arapahoe Basin** (generally known as "A-Basin;" Ⓣ970/468-0718, Ⓦwww.arapahoebasin.com), offers great above-treeline bowl skiing. The slopes at **Copper Mountain** (Ⓣ1-866/841-2481, Ⓦwww.coppercolorado.com), are divided into three clear sections to separate beginners, intermediates, and experts.

In summer, mountain-bikers and road-racers alike will be happy with the opportunities for **cycling**, particularly the stretch between Frisco and Breckenridge; Colorado Freeride at 114 N Main St in Breckenridge (Ⓣ970/453-0995) is good for rental bikes. Each resort runs a chair lift or **gondola** to the top of the mountains for access to great **hiking** and cycling trails. Keystone is particularly outstanding for its mountain bike trails with world-class downhill and cross-country trails accessed by its lifts (mid-June to early Sept, daily 10am–5pm; day-pass $32). Breckenridge offers exciting toboggan rides down the dry **Superslide**, as well as miniature golf and a giant maze. The slide was closed for construction at the time of writing, but is expected to reopen for the 2009 season; call for hours and prices.

Eating

Summit County doesn't maintain much of a reputation for fine **dining**, though there's no end of good-value places to eat, especially in Breckenridge.

Alpenglow Stube Keystone ☎970/496-4386. The best dining experience in Summit County – take the free gondola ride to the top of 11,444ft North Peak and feast in beautiful surroundings on New American cuisine with a Bavarian edge. It doesn't come cheaply, though: multi-course meals run $90 and up.

Backcountry Brewery 710 Main St, Frisco ☎970/668-2337. Sizeable brewpub where the upstairs deck – with its choice view of the nearby peaks – is the best spot to kick back. Own-brewed beers and dishes such as porter beer-braised ribs ($15) anchor the ample menu.

Butterhorn Bakery & Cafe 408 Main St, Frisco ☎970/668-3997. Superb bakery churning out huge and delicious breads, bagels, cookies, and cakes. It's also well-known for its breakfast burrito, frittatas, and good range of sandwiches or soup lunches (all under $10). Daily until 2.30pm.

The Prospector 130 S Main St, Breckenridge ☎970/453-6858. Traditional home-cooked breakfasts (try the spicy and excellent *huevos rancheros*) and lunches, including roasts and meatloaf. Prices are among the lowest in town.

Drinking

Apres-ski **drinking** is alive and well at the slopeside bars of all four resorts. As the night wears on, head to Breckenridge for several late-night music venues, though Frisco also has some good options.

Breckenridge Brewery 600 S Main St, Breckenridge ☎970/453-1550. This huge brewpub, one of the first in Colorado and now a landmark at the southern edge of town, serves good-quality microbrews and hearty pub food.

Chill 610 Main St, Frisco ☎970/668-9930. Late-night venue complete with debonair decor, low lighting, and billiards. Nightly events include live music, dance lessons, karaoke, and poker tournaments.

Dillon Dam Brewery 100 Little Dam St, Dillon ☎970/262-7777. Good, own-brewed ales and inexpensive quality bar food – salads, burgers, and pastas – with entrees from around $10.

Leadville

Standing at an elevation of over ten thousand feet, south of I-70 and eighty miles west of Denver, the atmospheric old mining town of **LEADVILLE** is the highest incorporated city in the US, with a magnificent view across to broad-shouldered mounts **Elbert** (14,440ft) and **Massive** (14,421ft), Colorado's two highest peaks. As you approach from the south, your first impression is likely to be of giant slag heaps and disused mining sheds, but don't let this put you off: Leadville is rich in character and history, its old red-brick streets abounding with tales of gunfights, miners dying of exposure, and graveyards being excavated to get at the seams.

For an illuminating romp through the town's grim early history, head for the **Heritage Museum**, 102 E Ninth St (summer daily 10am–6pm; $3.50; ☎719/486-1878). Glass cases hold snippets on local fraternal organizations, quack doctors, music-hall stars, and the like, while a host of smoky photographs portray the lawless boomtown that in two years grew from a mining camp of two hundred people into what was then Colorado's second largest city.

Of all Leadville's extraordinary tales, perhaps the most compelling is that of **Horace Tabor**, a storekeeper who supplied goods to prospectors in exchange for a share in potential profits. He hit the jackpot when two prospectors developed a silver mine that produced $20 million within a year. Tabor collected a one-third share and left his wife to marry local waitress "**Baby Doe**" McCourt in the society wedding of 1883 in Washington DC. However, by the time of his death in 1899, Tabor was financially ruined. Baby Doe survived Tabor by 36 years, living a hermit-like existence in the godforsaken wooden shacks on his only remaining mine – the **Matchless Mine**. The buildings still stand, two miles out on Seventh Street, and in the crude wooden shack in which she died, emaciated and frostbitten, guides recount the story of Baby Doe's bizarre life in full, fascinating detail

(May–Sept 9am–4.15pm, Oct–April call for hours; $4; ⓣ719/486-4918, ⓦwww.matchlessmine.com).

Back in town, don't miss the **Tabor Opera House**, 308 Harrison Ave (summer daily 10am–5pm; $4; ⓣ719/486-8409, ⓦwww.taboroperahouse.net), where you're free to wander onto the stage, through the ranks of red velvet and gilt seats, and around the eerie, dusty old dressing rooms. Recorded oral histories tell tales of the theater's golden days. They give no details, sadly, of the time in 1882 when Oscar Wilde, garbed in black velvet knee britches and diamonds, addressed a host of dozing miners on the "Practical Application of the Aesthetic Theory to Exterior and Interior House Decoration with Observations on Dress and Personal Ornament."

Practicalities

Leadville's **visitor center** is at 809 Harrison Ave (June–Sept daily 10am–5pm; ⓣ719/486-3900 or 1-888/532-3845, ⓦwww.leadvilleusa.com). A good place to **stay** is the historic landmark *Delaware Hotel*, 700 Harrison Ave (ⓣ719/486-1418 or 1-800/748-2004, ⓦwww.delawarehotel.com; ❺), a Victorian hotel where rates include continental breakfast. For **food and drink** in Leadville, *Cloud City Coffee House and Deli*, 711 Harrison Ave (ⓣ719/486-1317), serves bagels, buns, and espresso in a grand old hotel lobby, while further along the street at no. 612, *Columbine Cafe* (ⓣ719/486-3599) features an imaginative menu with several vegetarian options, served in familiar diner surroundings. Across from Tabor Opera House, you'll find simple, saucy Mexican fare at *Manuelita's*, 311 Harrison Ave (ⓣ719/486-0292). Leadville's finest **bar** is the wood-paneled *Silver Dollar Saloon*, 315 Harrison Ave (ⓣ719/486-9914), a welcoming watering hole filled with Irish memorabilia.

Aspen

Glossy magazines might have you believe that a tollgate outside **ASPEN** only admits film stars and the super-rich. This elite **ski resort** town, 160 miles west of Denver, is indeed the part-time home of Cher, Jack Nicholson, Michael Douglas, and other celebrities, and while it's not as typically welcoming as the rest of the Rockies, it can be an appealing place to visit in summer – unless you're on an absolute shoestring budget. Visiting in winter requires more cash, though you can save money by commuting to the slopes from Glenwood Springs (see p.792), less than fifty miles away.

From inauspicious beginnings in 1879, this pristine, mountain-locked town developed slowly, thanks to its remote location, to become one of the world's top **silver** producers. By the time the silver market crashed fourteen years later, it had acquired tasteful residential palaces, grand hotels, and an opera house. In the 1930s, when the population slumped below seven hundred, it was, ironically, the anti-poverty WPA program that gave the struggling community the cash to build its first crude ski lift in 1936. Entrepreneurs seized the opportunity presented by the varied terrain and plentiful snow, and the first chair lift was dedicated on Aspen Mountain (also still known by its former name, **Ajax**, among locals) in 1947. Skiing has since spread to three more mountains – Aspen Highlands, Snowmass, and Buttermilk, and the jet set arrived in force during the 1960s. **Development** is a burning political issue: tight architectural constraints have been placed on businesses (*McDonald's* is forbidden to have a neon sign), but the last decade has seen the arrival of yet more Scandinavian-style lodges, condo blocks, and giant houses that remain empty for most of the year.

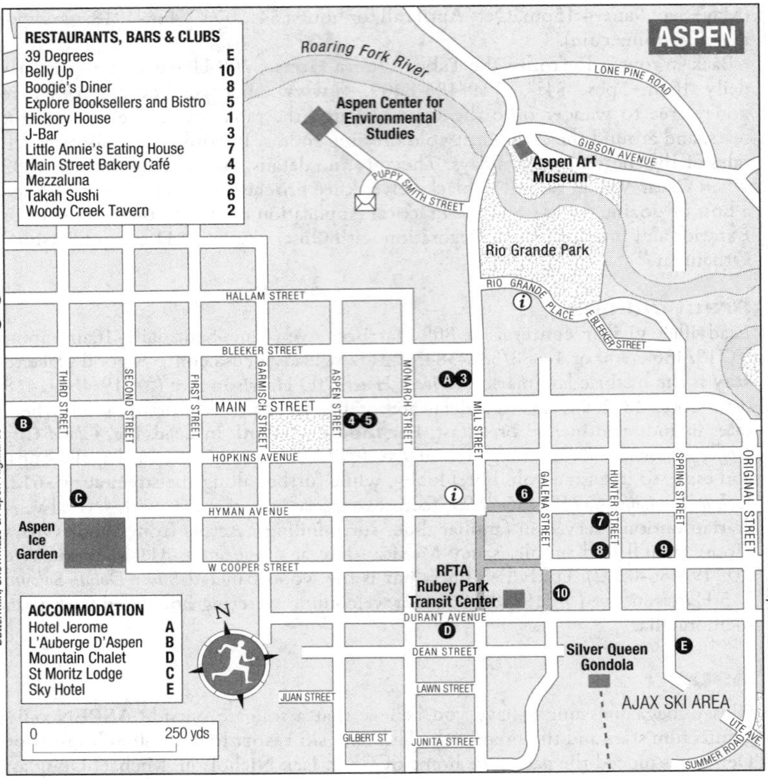

Arrival and information

Towering **Independence Pass**, which provides the most direct access to Aspen via Hwy-82, closes each winter, and the detour through Glenwood Springs adds an extra seventy miles to the trip from Denver. Many instead choose to fly into tiny **Aspen–Pitkin County Airport** (Ⓣ970/920-5384, Ⓦwww.aspenairport.com), four miles north of town; if you fly into Denver, connecting flights may only cost another $100 or so. Alternately, you can take a **shuttle** (book in advance) from Denver International Airport; your best option is Colorado Mountain Express (Ⓣ970/926-9800 or 1-800/525-6363, Ⓦwww.cmex.com; $104). Another option is to fly into Eagle County Airport near Vail, an eighty-minute drive away and also served by Colorado Mountain Express.

Once in Aspen, there's no problem **getting around**: the Roaring Fork Transit Agency (Ⓣ970/925-8484, Ⓦwww.rfta.com) runs a free skiers' shuttle between the four mountains and serves the airport and outlying areas. The main **Rubey Park transit center** terminal is in the center of town on Durant Avenue.

Aspen's **visitor center** is at 425 Rio Grande Place (Mon–Fri 9am–5pm; Ⓣ970/925-1940 or 1-800/262-7736, Ⓦwww.aspenchamber.org). The free *Aspen Daily News* ("If you don't want it printed, don't let it happen") is an excellent source of local gossip, news, and food and drink offers.

Accommodation

Stay Aspen Snowmass Central Reservations (T 970/925-9000 or 1-888/649-9582, W www.stayaspensnowmass.com) runs a helpful service and doesn't balk if you ask for the cheapest available room; it also arranges package deals combining accommodation with lift tickets. Rates vary considerably even in winter; the least expensive times to come are in the "**value seasons**" (last week in Nov, first two weeks of Dec, and first two weeks of April). If you're traveling in a group, you can save money by renting a **condominium**; McCartney Property Management (T 1-800/433-8465, W www.mc-cartneyprop.com) is a good source for condo accommodations. Prices in the entire area at least halve during the **summer**, when **camping** is also a good cheap option; there are nine USFS campgrounds around Aspen, of which only a handful of sites can be reserved (T 1-877/444-6777, W www.recreation.gov). Several campgrounds are on Maroon Creek Road south of Aspen, while smaller options abound east of town toward Independence Pass.

Hotel Jerome 330 E Main St T 970/920-1000 or 1-800/331-7213, W www.hoteljerome.com. Stately downtown landmark built at the height of the 1880s silver boom, with a gamut of modern amenities. Spacious rooms feature period wallpaper, antique brass, and cast-iron beds. The elegant lobby is worth a look even if you're not staying here. ⑨

L'Auberge D'Aspen 435 W Main St T 970/925-8297, W www.preferredlodging.com. Idyllic little cabins close to downtown, superbly outfitted with kitchens and fireplaces. Reserve well in advance in ski season. Winter ⑦, summer ④–⑥

Mountain Chalet 333 E Durant Ave T 970/925-7797 or 1-800/925-7797, W www.mountainchaletaspen.com. Friendly mountain lodge with large, comfortable rooms, pool, hot tub, gym, and fine buffet breakfast. Some dorm-style beds ($55–85) are available in winter, along with a variety of more straightforward rooms. Winter ⑥–⑨, summer ④–⑥

Sky Hotel 709 E Durant Ave T 970/925-6760 or 1-800/882-2582, W www.theskyhotel.com. Funky slopeside hotel sporting chic, 1970s-style decor; playful rooms have faux-fur throws, wi-fi, and video game consoles. There's also a hot tub, fitness room, and outdoor pool, while its *39 Degrees* bar (see p.791) is one of Aspen's choicest apres-ski spots. ⑧

St Moritz Lodge 334 W Hyman Ave T 970/925-3220 or 1-800/817-2069, W www.stmoritzlodge.com. Five blocks from downtown, the dorms ($36–52) and private rooms here are some of the best bargains in town – and suitably hard to get. Facilities include a small heated pool and a comfortable common room. Continental breakfast included in winter. Winter ⑤–⑨, summer ④–⑦

The town and the mountains

Activities in Aspen itself pale in comparison to the virtually limitless recreation opportunities in the neighboring mountains, but hanging out on benches around the town's leafy pedestrianized streets or browsing in the chichi stores and galleries is a pleasant way to spend a couple of hours.

In summer, the Aspen Historical Society, which runs the excellent **Wheeler/Stallard Museum**, 620 W Bleeker St (Tues–Sat 1–5pm; $6; T 970-925-3254, W www.heritageaspen.org), offers **walking tours** of Aspen and nearby ghost towns (guided $10; self-guided, free). The free **Aspen Art Museum** at 590 N Mill St (Tues–Wed & Fri–Sat 10am–6pm, Thurs 10am–7pm, Sun noon–6pm; T 970/925-8050, W www.aspenartmuseum.org) holds changing exhibits and puts on lectures and special events, while the **Aspen Center for Environmental Studies (ACES)**, 100 S Puppy Smith St (May–Nov Mon–Sat 9am–5pm; Dec–April Mon–Fri 9am–5pm, $2; T 970/925-5756, W www.aspennature.org), is a wildlife sanctuary at nearby Hallam Lake offering a range of guided hikes and ski and snowshoe tours (bring your own gear), including a number of nature programs designed for kids.

Aspen's four mountains are run by the **Aspen Skiing Company** (T 970/925-1220 or 1-800/308-6935, W www.aspensnowmass.com; snow report T 1-

888/277-3676). The mogul-packed monster of **Aspen Mountain**, looming over downtown, is for experienced skiers only. On the other hand, **Buttermilk** is great for beginners, with an excellent ski school that offers a three-day guaranteed "Learn to Snowboard" program; the wide-open runs of **Snowmass**, though mostly for intermediate skiers, feature some testing routes. **Aspen Highlands** has high-speed lifts and offers excellent extreme skiing terrain. **Rental** of skis or snowboard gear runs $25–45, with discounts on multi-day rentals or if you book online a week in advance; you can also rent snowshoes if you want to trek up and down the mountains. However, the town's best value has to be its fifty miles of groomed **Nordic ski trails** – one of the most extensive free cross-country trail networks in the US. If you don't want to wait for the snow, consider **mountain boarding** – lessons on these snowboards with wheels are offered in summer by the Ski & Snowboard Schools of Aspen (ⓣ877/282-7736).

Cycling is the main **summer** pursuit around Aspen; Timberline Bike Tours, 730 E Cooper Ave (ⓣ970/274-6076, ⓦwww.timberlinebike.com), offers mountain bikes for hire, organized tours, and guidance on routes and difficulty levels. The Roaring Fork River, surging out of the Sawatch Range, is excellent for **kayaking** and **rafting** during a short season that's typically over by early to mid-July. Beware, though, as sections of Class V rapids here are dangerous and every summer sees fatalities. Blazing Adventures, 48 Upper Village Mall in Snowmass Village (ⓣ970/923-4544 or 1-800/282-7238, ⓦwww.blazingadventures.com), offers guided trips.

If you fancy **walking** in the mountains, pick up the free *Ute Scout Hiking and Biking Guide*, available from the visitor center (see above). An easy way to quickly get your bearings along with great valley views is to take the Silver Queen **gondola** from 601 Dean St to the summit of **Aspen Mountain** (mid-June to early Sept daily 10am–4pm; $23–26 for day-pass, $46 for week pass; ⓣ970/925-1220, ⓦwww.aspensnowmass.com), where ACES regularly offers guided nature walks. Occasional free lunchtime concerts and talks are also held, and there's a good restaurant, the *Sundeck*, as well. Even more alluring is the landscape around the twin purple-gray peaks of the **Maroon Bells**, fifteen miles southwest, soaring above dark blue Maroon Lake. The Bells are reached via the eleven-mile-long Maroon Creek Road, accessible to only overnight campers with permits, disabled travelers, bikers, in-line skaters, and RFTA buses 8.30am–5pm; buses depart from the Aspen Highlands Ski Area (mid-June to Sept 9am–4.30pm; $6 round-trip). A combination ticket ($27) good for both the Maroon Bells bus and the Silver Queen gondola is available at Four Mountain Sports in Aspen Highlands Village or at the Rubey Park Transit Center.

Eating and drinking

Many of Aspen's classy **cafés and restaurants** charge over $25 for a main course, but good budget places exist and competition can be keen. Note, too, that many of Aspen's bars serve good, reasonably priced food (see p.791).

Boogie's Diner 534 E Cooper Ave ⓣ970/925-6610. Inexpensive 1950s-style diner occupying an airy second-floor atrium lined with vinyl and chrome. The menu includes great meatloaf, thick shakes, and even a one-pound burger, as well as a few imaginative tofu options.

Explore Booksellers and Bistro 221 E Main St ⓣ970/925-5336. Fantastic bookstore with a shady roof terrace and a kitchen serving creative vegetarian dishes, good espresso, and pastries.

Hickory House 730 W Main St ⓣ970/925-2313. Popular rib house that also turns out terrific breakfasts, from buttery waffles to meaty, southern-style platters.

Little Annie's Eating House 517 E Hyman Ave ⓣ970/925-1098. Lively, popular, and unpretentious saloon-style restaurant serving potato pancakes and hearty stews at lunch, and huge trout, chicken, beef, or rib dinner platters for under $20.

Main Street Bakery Cafe 201 E Main St ⓣ970/925-6446. Inventive New American cuisine in a casual, chatty setting. A good breakfast alternative to Hickory House for its massive, fresh fruit-packed breakfasts.

Mezzaluna 624 E Cooper Ave ⓣ970/925-5882. Mid-priced Northern Italian dishes (including wood-fired pizzas), served in a vivacious setting.

Takah Sushi 320 S Mill St ⓣ970/925-8588. Phenomenally good sushi and pan-Asian cuisine amidst a cheerful atmosphere. Highly recommended, but quite expensive.

Entertainment and nightlife

Going out in Aspen, the capital of **apres-ski**, is possible year-round and need not drain your pocketbook. In summer, downtown hosts several top-notch festivals – the flagship event is the summer-long **Aspen Music Festival** (ⓣ970/925-9042, ⓦwww.aspenmusicfestival.com), when orchestras and operas feature well-known international performers, as well as promising students who come to learn from masters. The annual, if brief season of the reliably good **Aspen Santa Fe Ballet** runs from mid-July to early August (ⓣ970/925-7175, ⓦwww.aspensantafeballet.com), while a year-round program of concerts, plays, and dance performances runs at the Wheeler Opera House, 320 E Hyman Ave (ⓣ970/920-5570 or 1-866/449-0464, ⓦwww.wheeleroperahouse.com).

39 Degrees *Sky Hotel*, 709 E Durant Ave ⓣ970/925-6760. This bar-club feels as if it could be set in Manhattan or Berlin; amidst its geometric curves, low lights, flickering fires, and leather sofas, ski boots tap to DJ-spun ambient music.

Belly Up 450 S Galena St ⓣ970/544-9800. Cavernous basement venue hosting everything from big-name artists to calendar-girl contests, with an almost cinema-sized screen for televised sports. Not a bad place for a drink on busy nights; otherwise, you tend to rattle around in the space.

J-Bar *Hotel Jerome*, 330 E Main St ⓣ970/920-1000. This grand bar, dating from 1889, is a good place to soak up the old building's atmosphere, well-heeled hotel guests and all.

Woody Creek Tavern 1858 Woody Creek Rd, Woody Creek ⓣ970/923-4585. Rustic tavern where ranch hands, Aspen visitors, and the occasional celebrity local (Hunter S. Thompson was a frequent patron) shoot pool, guzzle fresh lime-juice margaritas, and eat good Tex-Mex. It's in tiny Woody Creek, seven miles northwest of Aspen along Hwy-82.

Vail

Compared to most other Colorado ski towns, **VAIL**, 97 miles west of Denver on I-70, is a new creation: only a handful of farmers lived here before the resort opened in 1952. Built as a relatively unimaginative collection of Tyrolean-style chalets and concrete-block condos, at least the town is a compact and pedestrian-friendly place, albeit pockmarked by pricey fashion boutiques and often painfully pretentious restaurants. Vail Resorts, which operates the ski area at Vail, also owns an even more exclusive gated resort, **Beaver Creek**, eleven miles further west on I-70. Lift tickets between the two are interchangeable, which – given the exceptional quality of the snow, and the sheer size and variety of terrain available – produces a formidable winter sport destination. In summer, you can use the lifts at both resorts to go **mountain biking** – best at Vail, given its former World Cup Downhill and cross-country courses (lifts run mid-June to Aug daily 10am–4.30pm; $20–25) – and **hiking**, best at the quieter Beaver Creek.

Practicalities

From Denver International Airport, several companies offer **shuttles** to Vail and Beaver Creek, including Colorado Mountain Express (ⓣ970/926-9800 or 1-800/525-6363, ⓦwww.cmex.com; $89). More convenient (and therefore, more expensive) flights are available to **Eagle County Regional Airport** (ⓣ970/524-8246, ⓦwww.eaglecounty.us/airport), 35 miles west of Vail. Ground transportation from the airport to either resort is just $3 on Eagle County Transit (Ⓣ970/328-3520), while Airlink Shuttle (Ⓣ970/845-7119 or 1-800/554-8245, Ⓦwww.airlinkshuttle.com) charges $39 per person.

Vail spreads for eight miles along the narrow valley floor, with successive nuclei from east to west at Vail Village, Lionshead, Cascade Village, and West Vail. Each is pedestrianized and linked by free shuttle buses to one another and to the lifts; central parking lots are free in summer, but steeply priced in winter. **Vail Transit** (Ⓣ970/479-2178, Ⓦwww.vailgov.com) also runs regular free shuttles year-round between different areas of town.

For information on skiing and accommodation, contact the **Vail Valley Chamber Tourism Bureau** (Ⓣ970/476-1000, Ⓦwww.visitvailvalley.com), which can help you reserve a room, as well as provide assistance with organized transportation and ski packages. **Accommodation** rates in and around **Vail Village**, the area's main social center, are invariably high; try *Tivoli Lodge*, 386 Hanson Ranch Rd (Ⓣ970/476-5615 or 1-800/451-4756, Ⓦwww.tivolilodge.com; winter ❽, summer ❻), where rates include a continental breakfast and use of an outdoor pool, whirlpool, and sauna. If you're looking to live it up, check into the seamless *Sonnenalp Resort of Vail,* 20 Vail Rd Village (Ⓣ970/476-5656 or 1-866/284-4411, Ⓦwww.sonnenalp.com; ❾), a luxury hotel straight out of a snowy European Christmas card, bang in the center of Vail with a full complement of facilities and an excellent spa. In the nearby hamlet of **Minturn**, the *Eagle River Inn*, 145 N Main St (Ⓣ970/827-5761 or 1-800/344-1750; winter ❼, summer ❻), is a B&B decked out in tasteful Santa Fe style, seven miles south of Vail on US-24.

Eating out in Vail can also prove expensive. *Vendetta's*, 291 Bridge St (Ⓣ970/476-5070), offers fine Italian lunch specials, as well as pizza and pasta dinners, for mostly under $20. Elsewhere in the village, *La Cantina* (Ⓣ970/476-7661), with its first-class Mexican food, seriously potent margaritas, and few tables crammed into a corner of Vail Transportation Center, won't break your bank.

Nightlife revolves around **The Circuit** on Vail Village's Bridge Street; most people tour between the bars and discos. The checklist of places to see and be seen includes *The Club* (Ⓣ970/479-0556), a basement bar playing boisterous rock; loud music also rules upstairs at *Vendetta's* (see above).

Glenwood Springs

Bustling, touristy **GLENWOOD SPRINGS** sits at the western end of impressive Glenwood Canyon, 157 miles due west of Denver on I-70 and within striking distance of both Vail and Aspen; as such, it offers those with their own vehicle a budget base for either destination. Just north of the confluence of the Roaring Fork and Colorado rivers, the town was long used by the Ute people as a place of relaxation thanks to its **hot springs,** which became the target for unscrupulous speculators who broke treaties and established resort facilities in the 1880s. North from downtown and across the Eagle River is the town's main attraction, the behemoth **Hot Springs Pool**, 410 N River St (daily: summer 7.30am–10pm; rest of year 9am–10pm; $13.25–18.25; Ⓣ970/945-6571 or 1-800/537-7946, Ⓦwww.hotspringspool.com), offering spa services in addition to two large pools, a pair of fun water slides, and a humble mini golf course. More intimate are the natural, subterranean steam baths of the nearby **Yampah Spa Vapor Caves** at 709 E Sixth St (daily 9am–9pm; $12; Ⓣ970/945-0667, Ⓦwww.yampahspa.com), where you can relax on cool marble benches set deep in ancient caves. Also on the north side of town is the **Glenwood Caverns Adventure Park**, 508 Pine St (hours vary by season; $37; Ⓣ970/945-4228 or 1-800/530-1635, Ⓦwww.glenwoodcaverns.com), where you'll find thrill rides, horseback rides, and the park's namesake caverns that extend for two miles, with some chambers reaching a height of fifty feet. Two tours are available for the caverns: the ninety-minute Adventure Tour ($30) and the three-hour, dimly lit Wild Tour ($60).

Some of the West's most colorful characters came to Glenwood Springs in the early days, including Dr John R. **"Doc" Holliday**, a dentist better known as a gambler, gunslinger, and shooter in the gunfight at the OK Corral (see p.884). A chronic tuberculosis sufferer, Holliday came to the springs for a cure but died just a few months later in November 1887, at the age of 35; he's buried on a bluff overlooking the town in the picturesque Linwood Cemetery. In the paupers' section lies the grave of Harvey Logan, alias bank robber Kid Curry, a member of Butch Cassidy's notorious Hole-in-the-Wall gang.

Practicalities

Amtrak trains arrive at 413 7th St, at the end of a scenic route through the canyons, gorges, and valleys of central Colorado. Greyhound, traveling along a stunning, riverside stretch of I-70, stops close to downtown at the Phillips 66 station at 51171 US-6. The **visitor center**, 1102 Grand Ave (open 24hr, staffed Mon–Fri 8.30am–5pm, Sat & Sun 9am–3pm; Ⓣ970/945-6589, Ⓦwww.glenwoodchamber.com) is easily found in the middle of town at Savre Park. RFTA's Zipline express bus route links the town with Aspen (1hr; $6; Ⓣ970/925-8484, Ⓦwww.rfta.com).

For a place to stay, the beatnik *HI-Glenwood Springs Hostel*, near downtown at 1021 Grand Ave (closed 10am–4pm; Ⓣ970/945-8545 or 1-800/946-7835, Ⓦwww.hostelcolorado.com), has spacious dorms ($16), private rooms ($25–33), plus kitchen facilities, a giant record collection, and a wealth of local knowledge. The friendly staff will also arrange tours and whitewater trips. The *First Choice Inn*, 51359 6th St (Ⓣ970/945-8551 or 1-800/332-2233; ❷–❹), at the west end of town boasts reasonably priced lodging and features striking mountain views, laundry facilities, and free breakfast. Those wishing to maximize their soak time will want to bed down at the comfortable, but pricier *Hot Springs Lodge* (Ⓣ970/945-6571 or 1-800/537-7946, Ⓦwww.hotspringspool.com; ❻–❽), the accommodation arm of the city's popular hot springs resort; room rates include unlimited use of the pools, as well as either continental breakfast or a discounted cooked breakfast.

For **food and drink**, the *Daily Bread Cafe and Bakery*, downtown at 729 Grand Ave (Ⓣ970/945-6253), has delicious breakfasts, soups, and salads. Inside the nearby *Hotel Denver*, the *Glenwood Canyon Brewing Company*, 402 7th St (Ⓣ970/945-1276), will sate your appetite and quench your thirst with its solid pub grub and excellent handcrafted microbrews.

Grand Junction

The immediate environs of **GRAND JUNCTION**, 244 miles west of Denver on I-70, are awash in outdoor opportunities, and within a fifty-mile stretch you can trace the transition from fertile Alpine valley to full-blown desert. Another town that sprang into life in the 1880s with the arrival of the railroad, Grand Junction now makes its living primarily through the oil and gas industries. Although initial impressions are bound to be unfavorable – an unsightly sprawl of factory units and sales yards lines the I-70 Business Loop – the tiny downtown is much nicer, with leafy boulevards hemming in a small, tree-lined historic district dotted with sculptures and stores.

Although the Colorado section of Dinosaur National Monument is ninety miles north of Grand Junction along Hwy-139, the neighboring town of **Fruita** holds the intriguing **Dinosaur Journey Museum**, 550 Jurassic Court (Mon–Sat 10am–4pm, Sun noon–4pm; $7; Ⓣ970/858-7282, Ⓦwww.dinosaurjourney.org).

▲ Cathedral Rock, Dinosaur National Monument

The interactive museum features robotic displays of several kinds of dinosaurs, as well as a collection of giant, locally excavated bones – all helping to create a vivid picture of these prehistoric beasts. The affiliated Dino Digs program (Ⓣ970/242-0971 or 1-888/488-3466, Ⓦwww.dinodigs.org) offers one- to five-day **digs** nearby.

The main attraction of the Grand Junction area, however, is the splendid local network of **hiking and biking trails** and **rock climbing sites**, in and through parched, rugged, and spectacular high desert country. All activities are possible year-round, and are in fact generally more pleasant in the winter months, given the area's often suffocating summer heat. The only truly seasonal activity here is the sampling of Colorado **wine** and the excellent local peaches; contact the visitor center (see below) for information on touring the several wineries in the surrounding Grand Valley.

Particularly enticing for hikers is the remarkable scenery of **Colorado National Monument**, just west of Grand Junction. More than two hundred million years of wind and water erosion have gouged out rock spires, domes, arches, pedestals, and balanced rocks along a line of cliffs; the colorful result makes for an enthralling painted desert of warm reds, stunning purples, burnt oranges, and rich browns. The park has two entrances ($7, good for one week) at either end of twisting, 23-mile **Rim Rock Drive**, which links a string of spectacular overlooks with the **visitor center** at the north end of the park (summer 8am–6pm; rest of year 9am–5pm; Ⓣ970/858-3617, Ⓦwww.nps.gov/colm). Short hikes along the way afford unencumbered views of several monoliths, while longer treks get right down to the canyon floor. Nearby but outside the park, rock climbers should investigate excellent **Unaweep Canyon**, southeast of Grand Junction on Hwy-141; back in Grand Junction itself, Summit Canyon Mountaineering, 461 Main St (Ⓣ970/243-2847 or 1-800/254-6248, Ⓦwww.summitcanyon.com), can supply necessary information and gear.

Fruita, twelve miles west of Grand Junction, is also a big magnet for **mountain bikers**, who flock to its nearby smooth, rolling single-track trails. Trail information and rental bikes (from $45/day) are to be had from Over the Edge Sports, 202 E Aspen Ave (ⓣ970/858-7220, ⓦwww.otefruita.com), a block east of the roundabout at the center of Fruita.

Practicalities

Amtrak stops in Grand Junction at Second Street and Pitkin Avenue; Greyhound buses serve Durango, Denver, and Salt Lake City from 230 S Fifth St. The town's friendly **visitor center** at 740 Horizon Drive (ⓣ970/244-1480 or 1-800/962-2547, ⓦwww.visitgrandjunction.com) can provide information on daytime excursions and nightlife.

Budget **accommodation** near the interstate offers reasonable rates – try the dependable *Best Western Sandman Motel*, 708 Horizon Drive (ⓣ970/243-4150; ③–⑤), with pool and free breakfast; an alternative is the *HI-Melrose House* at *Hotel Melrose* downtown, 337 Colorado Ave (ⓣ970/242-9636), where bunks cost about $24 and private rooms start at a paltry $28. If you want to camp, try Colorado National Monument's sole campground, *Saddlehorn*, high above Grand Junction, where sites go for $10 and space is always available.

You can **dine** inexpensively at the busy *Blue Moon Bar & Grill*, 120 N 7th St (ⓣ970/242-4506), which serves sandwiches, salads, and pub food; meanwhile, serviceable breakfasts and lunches are available at *Main St Cafe*, 504 Main St (ⓣ970/242-7225), a 1950s-nostalgic diner with a few sidewalk tables outside.

Southern Colorado

The richly varied landscape of **southern Colorado** ranges from the grassy, farm-rich plains of the state's sparsely populated southeast to the **San Juan Mountains** in the southwest region, of which vibrant **Durango** is the beating heart. Along the Denver–Albuquerque highway corridor is subdued **Colorado Springs**, which sits at the foot of towering **Pikes Peak**; west of here, lofty mountain passes lead into deep, river-cut valleys and classic mining territory. Mineral riches brought in the land's original white settlers (first illegally, but eventually supported by the US government), who drove the Ute people away into the poorer **Four Corners** region of Colorado's far southwest.

North of Durango, the dramatic **San Juan Skyway** completes a loop of over two hundred miles through the mountains, north along US-550 and then back via Hwy-145 and US-160. The stretch of road north of Durango, negotiating its way through stunning alpine scenery, is known as the **Million Dollar Highway** for the supposedly gold-laden gravel that was used in its construction; it passes over multiple 10,000ft-plus summits and through the picturesque mining villages of **Silverton** and **Ouray**. West of Durango is popular **Mesa Verde National Park**, home to Ancestral Puebloan dwellings and a large cache of archeological remains. Remote **Crested Butte**, north of the San Juans, is a gorgeously preserved late-Victorian frontier town reborn in the twentieth century as one of Colorado's major ski resorts.

Colorado Springs and around

Seventy-one miles south of Denver on I-25, **COLORADO SPRINGS** was originally developed as a vacation spot in 1871 by railroad tycoon William Jackson Palmer. He attracted so many English gentry to the town that it earned the nickname "Little London." Despite sprawling for ten miles alongside I-25, modern Colorado Springs, a bastion of conservatism compared to liberal Denver, still retains much of Palmer's vision, thanks to a high military presence (most notably the US Air Force Academy), fundamentalist religious organizations, exclusive Colorado College, and an affluent Anglo-American community.

The most entertaining man-made attraction in the area is the **Pro Rodeo Hall of Fame**, 101 Pro Rodeo Drive (summer daily 9am–5pm, rest of year Wed–Sun 9am–5pm; $6; ⓣ719/528-4764, ⓦwww.prorodeohalloffame.com), where videos and displays explain the sport's various disciplines – calf roping, barrel racing, and the like. West of town and off US-24 W is the incredible **Garden of the Gods**, where gnarled and warped red sandstone rockery was lifted up at the same time as the nearby mountains (around 65 million years ago), but has since eroded into finely balanced overhangs, jagged pinnacles, massive pedestals, and mushroom formations. The **visitor center** (daily: summer 8am–8pm, rest of year 9am–5pm; free; ⓣ719/634-6666, ⓦwww.gardenofgods.com) at the park's eastern border has details on hiking and mountain-biking **trails**, as well as **rock-climbing** routes.

Practicalities

From **Denver International Airport**, there are a number of inexpensive **flights**, or you can book a ride on Colorado Springs Shuttle (ⓣ719/687-3456 or 1-877/587-3456, ⓦwww.coloradoshuttle.com; $50). Greyhound **buses** stop at 120 S Weber St downtown. Colorado Springs' **visitor center** is at 515 S Cascade Ave (daily: summer 8.30am–6pm, rest of year Mon–Fri 8.30am–5pm; ⓣ719/635-7506 or 1-800/888-4748, ⓦwww.experiencecoloradosprings.com). For **accommodation**, there's the elegant, rustically themed *Old Town GuestHouse*, 115 S 26th St (ⓣ719/632-9194 or 1-888/375-4210, ⓦwww.oldtown-guesthouse.com; ❻–❽), where hors d'oeuvres at check-in and an evening guest reception are among the personal touches. The tidy and busy *Garden of the Gods Campground*, 3704 W Colorado Ave (ⓣ719/475-9450, ⓦwww.coloradocampground.com), has $51 cabins for two – a much better deal than the grossly overpriced sites ($39) at the campground.

Appealing places to **eat** downtown include the excellent *Olive Branch*, 23 S Tejon Ave (ⓣ719/475-1199), which features a breadth of low-priced dishes, from Greek chicken to vegetarian chilli. One block away, *Phantom Canyon Brewing Co.*, 2 E Pikes Peak Ave (ⓣ719/635-2800), is a great place for own-brewed beer and filling pub fare. Although not much of a party town, one of Colorado Springs' best **bars** is *Meadow Muffins*, 2432 W Colorado Ave (ⓣ719/633-0583), festooned with movie memorabilia, hosting live entertainment, and serving good burgers, sandwiches, and salads.

Pikes Peak and the Royal Gorge Bridge

Though there are thirty taller mountains in Colorado alone, **PIKES PEAK**, just west of Colorado Springs, is probably the best known – largely because the view from its crest inspired Katharine Lee Bates to write the words to "America The Beautiful." The 14,110ft peak was first mapped by American soldier and explorer Zebulon Pike in 1806, who never climbed it himself. By the end of the nineteenth century, gondola trails had been built to carry wealthy tourists like Ms Bates to the top; its unlikeliest summit, however, came in 1929, when a Texan named Bill Williams spent twenty days (and made 170 trouser changes) scaling the mountain, all the while pushing a peanut with his nose.

Less insane souls can reach the peak by a long **hike**, or via a difficult **toll road** (May–early Sept 7am–7pm; rest of Sept 7am–5pm; Oct–April 9am–3pm; $10/person up to $35/car; ⓣ719/385-7325 or 1-800/318-9505, ⓦwww.pikespeakcolorado.com) that becomes unpaved halfway up the mountain. The thrilling **Pikes Peak Cog Railway** ($31–33, reservations advised; ⓣ719/685-5401, ⓦwww.cograilway.com) runs year-round and grinds its way up an average of 847ft per mile on its ninety-minute journey to the summit; from 11,500ft onward it crosses a barren expanse of alpine tundra, scarred by giant scree flows. From the bleak and windswept peaktop, it's possible to see Denver seventy miles north and the endless prairie to the east, while to the west, mile upon mile of snowcapped Rockies peaks soar into the distance. The train leaves from 515 Ruxton Ave in **Manitou Springs**, six miles west of Colorado Springs.

About 45 miles south of Pikes Peak, beside the town of Cañon City – via Hwy-115 and US-50 from Colorado Springs – is the rather rickety **ROYAL GORGE BRIDGE** (daily 7am–dusk; $24; ⓣ719/275-7507 or 1-888/333-5597, ⓦwww.royalgorgebridge.com), the world's highest wooden suspension bridge, spanning a vertiginous 1053ft crack over the roaring Arkansas River. The gorge is the focus of several other attractions, which though quite commercialized, can still terrify you; these include an aerial tram, an incline railway, and the Royal Rush Skycoaster – a bungee swing that for $25 will send you reeling over the canyon.

Great Sand Dunes National Park

Composed of fifty square miles of silky shifting sand, **GREAT SAND DUNES NATIONAL PARK** huddles against the craggy Sangre de Cristo Mountains, about 170 miles southwest of Colorado Springs. Over millions of years, fine glacial sands have been blown east from the San Juan Mountains and deposited at the base of the Sangre de Cristo range to help create a place of strange and eerie beauty. Most visitors go little further than the "beach" beside Medano Creek, which runs along the eastern and southern side of the dune mass. However, the climb up the dunes themselves, though incredibly tiring, is not to be missed for the fun **slide** down (bring your own dune board), as much as the views of the amazing scenery. Also worthwhile is a walk along sandy trails, squeezed between the dunes and the mountains, or a night spent out at one of the underused back-country campsites.

The **visitor center** (daily: summer 9am–6pm, rest of year 9am–4.30pm; ⓣ719/378-6399, ⓦwww.nps.gov/grsa) is three miles beyond the park entrance ($3 per vehicle, good for one week), behind which lies the **Mosca picnic area** – the main gateway for exploring the dunes. A free **back-country permit** is required for the park's seven primitive back-country sites and is available at the visitor center. Most campers, however, stay at the large *Pinyon Flats Campground* ($14), the only camping area in the park accessible by car, and usually full with tents and RVs alike in summer; sites are available on a first-come, first-served basis. *Great Sand Dunes Oasis Store* (April–Oct; ⓣ719/378-2222, ⓦwww.greatdunes.com), just before the monument entrance, offers showers, laundry, and tent sites ($18), as well as a small number of basic **cabins** (❹). Behind the store, *Great Sand Dunes Lodge* (ⓣ719/378-2900, ⓦwww.gsdlodge.com; ❹), has pleasant rooms with dunes views, an indoor pool, and gas grills for cooking out.

Mesa Verde National Park

The only national park in the US devoted exclusively to archeological remains, **MESA VERDE NATIONAL PARK** is set high on a densely wooded plateau south of US-160, 225 miles west of Great Sand Dunes and about fifty miles past Durango. Well worth the trip, it's nevertheless so far off the beaten path that its extensive **Ancestral Puebloan ruins** were not fully explored until 1888, when a local rancher discovered them on his land.

Between the time of Christ and 1300 AD, Ancestral Puebloan civilization expanded to cover much of the area known as the "**Four Corners**." These earliest dwellings were simple pits in the ground, but before they vanished from history they had developed the architectural sophistication needed to build the extraordinary complexes of Mesa Verde. Over centuries, Ancestral Puebloan housing had evolved from pithouses to spectacular multistory apartments, nestled in rocky alcoves high above the sheer canyons that bisect the southern edge of the Mesa Verde plateau. Why they did so remains unclear, although recent evidence suggests that Ancestral Puebloan culture was not quite as peaceful as previously imagined; in any event, the soil at Mesa Verde ultimately appears to have been depleted, and the natives are thought to have migrated into what's now New Mexico to establish the pueblos where their descendants still live.

Touring the park

The access road to Mesa Verde climbs south from US-160, ten miles east of Cortez. Once past the entrance station ($15 in summer, $10 rest of year, good for one week), the road climbs and twists for fifteen miles to the **Far View Visitor Center** (late April–mid-Oct daily 8am–5pm; ⓣ970/529-4465), where exhibits cover Navajo, Hopi, and Pueblo crafts and jewelry. Immediately beyond, the road forks south to the two main constellations of remains: **Chapin Mesa** to the south, and **Wetherill Mesa** to the west. To tour any of the major ruins, you must buy timed **tickets** ($3; purchase at Far View in summer, Chapin Mesa Archeological Museum rest of year). On Chapin Mesa, Cliff Palace is usually open 9am–5pm daily from late April until early November, and Balcony House for the same hours between late April and mid-October; at busy times, you won't be able to tour both on the same day. On Wetherill Mesa, generally open late May to early September, tours of Long House operate between 9am and 4pm daily.

Six miles toward Chapin Mesa from the visitor center, the **Chapin Mesa Archeological Museum** (daily: April–mid-Oct 8am–6.30pm; mid-Oct–March 8am–5pm) holds the park's best displays on Ancestral Puebloans. It's also the starting point for the short, steep hike down to **Spruce Tree House**, the only ruin open in winter (via guided tour) – a neat little village of three-story structures, snugly molded into a rocky alcove and fronted by plazas.

Beyond the museum, **Ruins Road** (daily April–early Nov, 8am–dusk) consists of two one-way, six-mile loops. If you're pressed for time, follow the eastern one to reach **Cliff Palace**, the largest surviving Ancestral Puebloan cliff dwelling anywhere. Tucked one hundred feet below an overhanging ledge of pale rock, its 217 rooms once housed over two hundred people. Even without a tour ticket (see above), you can get a great view from the promontory where tour groups gather, beside the parking lot. Entering the ruin itself, especially on a quieter day, provides a haunting evocation of a lost and little-known world, as you walk through the empty plazas, peer down into the mysterious *kivas* (circular, stone-lined ceremonial pits), and glimpse fading murals inside some of the structures.

Balcony House, a little further on, is one of the few Mesa Verde complexes clearly geared towards defense; access is very difficult, and it's not visible from above. Guided tours involve scrambling up three hair-raising ladders and crawling through a narrow tunnel, teetering all the while above a steep drop into Soda Canyon. If you don't have a head for heights, consider giving it a miss.

At the end of the twisting twelve-mile drive onto Wetherill Mesa (daily late May to early Sept 8am–4.30pm; no RVs), you can catch a free miniature train around the tip of the mesa to the **Long House**, the park's second largest ruin, set in its largest cave. Hour-long tours descend sixty or so steps to reach its central plaza, then scramble around its 150 rooms and 21 *kivas*.

Park practicalities

Mesa Verde gets very crowded in high summer; the best months to visit are May, September, and October. The park is open all year, but most structures are inaccessible in winter, and services such as gas, food, and lodging only operate between late April and mid-October. Most visitors stay in nearby towns; the only **rooms** in the park itself are at the visitor center-adjacent *Far View Motor Lodge* (mid-April–late Oct; ⓣ1-800/449-2288, ⓦwww.visitmesaverde.com; ❺–❻), where the balconies have superb views and the absence of phones and TVs makes for a tranquil stay. There are 435 **campsites** from which to choose at gigantic *Morefield Campground*, four miles after the park entrance (mid-May–mid-Oct; $20 and up), and you'll find several more commercial campgrounds nearby. The lodge's upmarket *Metate Room* provides fabulous **meals** incorporating buffalo and elk meat into main courses, and sides such as beans, flat bread, and roasted corn. Food is also available year-round at *Spruce Tree Terrace* cafeteria near the Chapin Mesa museum.

Durango

Friendly, ebullient **DURANGO** is the largest town in southwest Colorado and the best hub for exploring the Four Corners region. Such is the attractiveness of the town and surrounding San Juan Mountains that it has attracted an influx of new residents in recent years, here to enjoy its year-round outdoor activities, excellent range of restaurants, and flourishing arts scene. The energetic city of 16,000 plays big but still retains a small-town feel, thanks in part to the student populace from **Fort Lewis College**, high on a hill above town.

Durango was founded in 1880 as a refining town and rail junction for Silverton, 45 miles north. Steam trains continue to run along the spectacular old mining route through the Animas Valley, though nowadays tourists, not sacks of gold, are the money-making cargo. **The Durango & Silverton Narrow Gauge Railroad** runs up to three round-trips daily ($75–159 round-trip; ⓣ970/247-2733, ⓦwww.durangotrain.com) between May and October, from the depot at 479 Main Ave at the south end of town. The views from the train are spectacular as it chugs by rocky cliffs and through huddles of lush aspen, framed by the rugged Animas River below. (The trains are slow, however, so if you're hoping to save time, consider the return-bus option offered by the railroad ticket office.)

A memorable, if pricey way to combine the train ride with above-ground thrills is to book a day's visit to remote **Soaring Tree Top Adventures** (daily, mid-May–mid-Oct; $339; ⓣ970/769-2357, ⓦwww.soaringtreetopadventures.com; reservations necessary), north of Durango along the Animas River and only accessible by the railroad (or for the super-wealthy, helicopter). The fee includes train fare, harness equipment, training, and a fine lunch atop one of the resort's elevated tree platforms, from which guests zip through aspen and pine groves and high over the rushing river while attached to a network of industrial-strength cables; the longest of the course's 20-odd spans runs an exhilarating 1400ft. The cheery staff includes eco-specialists happy to share detailed knowledge of the forest and meadow flora.

Practicalities

Greyhound services between Denver and Albuquerque call in at 275 E 8th Ave. Durango's **tourism office**, 111 S Camino del Rio (summer Mon–Fri 8am–7pm, Sat 10am–6pm, Sun 11am–5pm; rest of year Mon–Fri 8am–6pm, Sat 8am–5pm, Sun 10am–4pm; ⓣ970/247-0312 or 1-800/525-8855, ⓦwww.durango.org), has full lists of **accommodation**, topped by the stalwart *Strater Hotel* at 699 Main Ave (ⓣ970/247-4431 or 1-800/247-4431, ⓦwww.strater.com; summer ❻–❼, winter ❺–❻, includes breakfast), where Louis L'Amour wrote several of his novels in room 222 directly above the hotel's *Diamond Belle Saloon*. One block off Durango's main artery, the red-brick *Rochester Hotel* at 721 E Second Ave (ⓣ970/385-1920 or 1-800/664-1920, ⓦwww.rochesterhotel.com; summer ❼–❽, winter ❺–❼, includes breakfast), co-managed with the cozy *Leland House Bed & Breakfast* across the street, is decked out with memorabilia from western films made in the Durango area over the years. For cheaper rates a couple miles north of downtown, try the *Siesta Motel* at 3475 Main Ave (ⓣ970/247-0741 or 1-877/314-0471, ⓦwww.durangosiestamotel.com; summer ❸–❻, winter ❷–❺).

Among the multitude of **restaurants** in downtown Durango, head to *Cyprus Cafe* (ⓣ970/385-6884), 725 E Second Ave, for excellent Mediterranean-inspired dishes and a robust wine list; there's also a lovely patio and, on many evenings, a live jazz combo. Back on Main Avenue at no. 1022, the fun *Carver Brewing Co* (ⓣ970/259-2545) opens early for breakfast, serves Southwestern lunches and dinners, and buzzes late into the night in its brewpub role. For terrific baked goods and sandwiches, try *Bread* at 42 Hwy-250 (ⓣ970/247-5100), a few miles northeast of the city center.

Silverton

The turnaround point for the narrow gauge railroad from Durango comes at **SILVERTON**: "silver by the ton," allegedly. Spread across a small flat valley and hemmed in entirely by the tall peaks of the San Juan Mountains, it's one of Colorado's most evocative (and secluded) mountain towns, where wide, dirt-paved streets lead off toward the surrounding heights. Silverton's zinc- and copper-mining days only came to an end in 1991, and the population has dropped since then, with those who remain generally relying on the seasonal tourist train – winters here are harsh and largely quiet. Although the false-fronted stores along "Notorious Blair Street" may remind one of the days when **Wyatt Earp** dealt cards here, the town is defined by the restaurants and gift shops that fill up between 11am and 2pm, when train tourists are deposited into town.

Silverton offers inexpensive **accommodation** at the *Triangle Motel*, 848 Greene St (ⓣ970/387-5780, ⓦwww.trianglemotel.com; summer ❸–❹, winter ❷–❸), at the south end of town, which also offers good-value two-room suites and jeep rental. For a little extra cash, you can enjoy one of the forty creaky, antique-furnished rooms at the *Grand Imperial Hotel*, 1219 Greene St (ⓣ970/387-5527 or 1-800/341-3340, ⓦwww.grandimperialhotel.com; ❹). The thin-walled *Silverton Inn & Hostel*, 1025 Blair St (ⓣ970/387-0115; ❷–❸), has dorm beds for $26–30. For **food and drink**, duck into rip-roaring *Handlebars* at 117 13th St (ⓣ970/387-5395), where the menu is full of hearty bar food and mustache-infused decor is king.

Ouray

The equally attractive mining community of **OURAY** lies 23 miles north of Silverton, on the far side of 11,018ft **Red Mountain Pass**, where the bare rock beneath the snow really is red, thanks to mineral deposits. The Million Dollar Highway twists and turns to get here, passing abandoned mine workings and rusting machinery in the most unlikely and inaccessible spots; trails and back roads into the San Juans offer rich pickings for hikers or drivers with four-wheel-drive vehicles.

Ouray itself is squeezed into a verdant sliver of a valley, with the commercially run **Ouray Hot Springs** beside the Uncompahgre River at the north end of town. A mile or so south, a one-way-loop dirt road leads to Box Canyon Falls Park (daily 8am–8pm; $3), where a straightforward 500ft trail, partly along a swaying wooden parapet, leads into narrow Box Canyon and the namesake falls that thunder through a tiny cleft in the mountain at the far end.

The local **visitor center** (daily 8am–6pm; closed Mon & Tues in winter; ⓣ970/325-4746 or 1-800/228-1876, ⓦwww.ouraycolorado.com) is on the northern edge of town beside the hot springs. At *Box Canyon Lodge*, an old-style timber **motel** at 45 Third Ave below the park (ⓣ970/325-4981 or 1-800/327-

5080, Ⓦwww.boxcanyonouray.com; ❹–❻), you can soak in natural hot tubs. The luxurious *St Elmo Hotel*, 426 Main St (Ⓣ970/325-4951 or 1-866/243-1502, Ⓦwww.stelmohotel.com; ❹–❼), features a good **restaurant** (the *Bon Ton*), while the *Grounds Keeper Coffee House*, 524 Main St (Ⓣ970/325-0550), is a central café serving espresso drinks and healthy and light lunches.

Telluride

Lying at the flat base of a bowl of vast steep-sided mountains, **TELLURIDE**, 120 miles northwest of Durango via an indirect highway route, is located in one of the Rockies' most picturesque valleys. The former mining village was briefly home to the young Butch Cassidy, who robbed his first bank here in 1889. These days, the town is better known as the home of a top-class **ski resort** that rivals Aspen for celebrity allure. Happily, it has achieved its status without losing its character, exemplified by the low-slung buildings on the wide main street, beautifully preserved as a National Historic District. Healthy young bohemians with few visible means of support but top-notch ski or snowboarding equipment seem to form the bulk of the twelve hundred inhabitants, while most visitors tend to dwell two miles above the town in **Mountain Village**; the two places are connected by a free, year-round gondola service. In summer, the **hiking** opportunities are excellent; one three-mile round-trip walk leads from the head of the valley, where the highway ends at Pioneer Mill, up to the 431ft **Bridal Veil Falls**, the tallest in Colorado. Come winter, nearly half the ski terrain in Telluride is geared for experts, with its steep mogul fields particular favorites.

Accommodation is much less expensive in summer than during ski season, though prices do go up on summer holidays, as well as for the Bluegrass Festival in June, the Jazz Festival in early August, and the Film Festival in early September. As well as being the town's official **information service**, the Telluride Visitor Information Center, 630 W Colorado Ave (summer daily 9am–7pm; rest of year Mon–Fri 9am–5pm; Ⓣ970/728-4245 or 1-888/355-8743, Ⓦwww.telluridevisitorguide.com), can recommend local lodging. Of specific places, the recently remodelled landmark 1895 *New Sheridan Hotel*, 231 W Colorado Ave (Ⓣ970/728-4351 or 1-800/200-1891, Ⓦwww.newsheridan.com; ❾) has handsome rooms and a cozy library, as well as an in-house bar and restaurant. Elsewhere in Telluride, *The Victorian Inn* at 401 W Pacific Ave (Ⓣ970/728-6601 or 1-800/611-9893 Ⓦwww.tellurideinn.com; summer ❺–❻, winter ❺–❽) has clean, motel-style doubles. For **eating**, *Honga's Lotus Petal*, 135 E Colorado Ave (Ⓣ970/728-5134), offers a variety of fine sushi and pan-Asian entrees in stylish surroundings, while *Smuggler's Brewpub and Grille* at 225 S Pine St (Ⓣ970/728-0919) is a lively evening hangout with a wide-ranging menu and good local brews.

Black Canyon of the Gunnison National Park

More than living up to its bleak-sounding name, **BLACK CANYON OF THE GUNNISON NATIONAL PARK** is seventy miles southeast of Grand Junction and reachable from US-50 to the south or Hwy-92 from the north. The view down into the fearsome, black rock canyon to the foaming Gunnison River below is about as foreboding as mountain scenery gets. Over two million years, the river has eroded a deep, narrow gorge, leaving exposed cliffs and jagged spires of crystalline rock more than 1.7 billion years old. The aspen-lined road leading to the top of the canyon winds uphill until the trees abruptly come to an end, the road

▲ Skiing at Crested Butte

levels out, and the scenery takes a dramatic turn – stark black cliffs, with the odd pine clinging to a tiny ledge in desperation. Snowshoeing and cross-country skiing are possibilities here in winter, while in summer there are good opportunities for fishing, hiking, and advanced-level climbing and kayaking.

The park's **entrance fee**, good for one week, is $15 per vehicle. The **visitor center** (daily: summer 8am–6pm, rest of year 8.30am–4pm; ⓣ970/249-1914, ⓦwww.nps.gov/blca) on the south rim has details on the two first-come, first-served **campgrounds**, one on each side of the canyon, as well as information on activities – particularly watersports, hunting, and fishing – in the nearby **Curecanti National Recreation Area** and **Gunnison Gorge National Conservation Area**.

Crested Butte

The beautiful Victorian mining village of **CRESTED BUTTE**, 150 miles northeast of Telluride and 230 miles southwest of Denver, almost died off in the late 1950s when its coal deposits were exhausted. However, the development of 11,875ft **Mount Crested Butte** into a world-class **ski resort** in the 1960s, and a **mountain-bikers**' paradise two decades later, means that today it can claim to be the top year-round resort in Colorado. The old town is resplendent with gaily painted clapboard homes and businesses, and zoning laws ensure that condos and chalets are confined to the resort area, three miles up the road behind the foothills.

In skiing and snowboarding circles, **Crested Butte Mountain Resort** (one-day lift tickets $59 early season, $82 rest of season; ⓣ970/349-2333 or 1-800/810-7669, ⓦwww.skicb.com) is best known for its extreme terrain, with lifts serving out-of-the-way bowls and faces that would only be accessible by helicopter at other resorts; unsurprisingly, the resort hosts both the US extreme skiing and snowboarding championships. That said, there are plenty of long beginner runs mixed in over the mountain's one thousand skiable acres, keeping the slopes accessible to all. Fifteen chair lifts link 106 runs, which are usually uncrowded thanks to the resort's isolated location. Cross-country (especially telemark) skiing attracts thousands, as does snowmobiling.

In summer, **mountain bikes** all but outnumber cars around the town, especially during **Fat Tire Week** in July, one of the oldest festivals in the young sport and one that, according to local legend, evolved from a race over the rocky 21-mile **Pearl Pass** to Aspen in the 1970s. You can still ride this route – 190 miles shorter than the road – but some of the most exciting trails are much nearer the town and include the gorgeous 401 trail with its wide-open vistas; the thickly wooded Dyke Trail; and the long, varied, and occasionally challenging Deadman's Gulch. The visitor center (see below) can help with a basic map and route descriptions for the main trails, and local shop The Alpineer, 419 6th St (ⓣ970/349-5210 or 1-800/223-4655, ⓦwww.alpineer.com), offers a selection of rental bikes.

Practicalities

A five-hour drive southwest from Denver along mostly minor highways, Crested Butte is not an easy place to reach, though the roads are almost always open. Most skiers arrive on regular daily **flights** from Denver, which touch down at Gunnison Airport, 28 miles and a forty-minute trip to Crested Butte via the Alpine Express Shuttle ($34 single; ⓣ970/641-5074 or 1-800/822-4844, ⓦwww.alpineexpressshuttle.com). A car is unnecessary once in town; free **buses** ply the three-mile route between the town and resort every fifteen minutes 7.10am–11.50pm, while the inexpensive Town Taxi (ⓣ970/349-5543) covers the same route after hours. The **visitor center** at 601 Elk Ave (daily 9am–5pm; ⓣ970/349-6438 or 1-800/545-4505, ⓦwww.visitcrestedbutte.com) produces a regular events guide for the area.

The choice of **accommodation** is between the ski area or downtown; you're likely to flit between the two areas every day, so it's only worth staying at the generally more expensive mountainside lodgings if you're obsessed with getting first tracks. *Crested Butte Mountain Resort* (see above) can book rooms and advise on money-saving package deals – be sure to reserve a room well in advance during winter. Down in town, the log-built *Claim Jumper Bed and Breakfast*, 704 Whiterock Ave (ⓣ970/349-6471; ❺–❻), with its six themed rooms amid a jumble of Americana, is one of the most enjoyable in Colorado. *Old Town Inn*, Hwy-35 and Belleview Ave (ⓣ970/349-6184; ❺), offers standard motel rooms along the main road at the southern edge of town, while the large and friendly *Crested Butte International Lodge and Hostel*, 615 Teocalli Ave (ⓣ970/349-0588 or 1-888/389-0588 ⓦwww.crestedbuttehostel.com; ❹–❺), offers dorm beds for $25–38.

Crested Butte lays claim to a surprising number of gourmet **restaurants**, with better average prices than those at Colorado's glitzier resorts. Among the more expensive, the inviting *Bacchanale*, 209 Elk Ave (ⓣ970/349-5257), features two-tiered dining and a varied Northern Italian menu, including good veal and cannelloni. For lower prices and the town's liveliest atmosphere, try the *Powerhouse*, 130 Elk Ave (ⓣ970/349-5494), which serves punchy Mexican cuisine in a fondly restored 1880s generating station; the huge wooden bar stocks 65 varieties of tequila.

The early **apres-ski** center is *Rafters*, adjacent to the lifts at 12 Snowmass Rd (ⓣ970/349-2298); down in Crested Butte itself, Elk Avenue is lined with no-nonsense bars such as *Kochevars* at no. 127 (ⓣ970/349-6745) and *Talk of the Town* at no. 230 (ⓣ970/349-6809). If you'd rather sink back into a black microsuede sectional sofa and sip a martini, drop into *Lobar* at 303 Elk Ave (ⓣ970/349-0480), a hipster enclave that's part lounge and part sushi bar.

Wyoming

Pronghorn antelope all but outnumber people in wide-open **WYOMING**, the ninth largest but least populous state in the union, with just 515,000 residents. Above all, this is classic **cowboy country** – the inspiration behind *Shane*, *The Virginian*, and countless other Western novels – replete with open range, rodeos, and country-and-western dance halls. The state emblem, seen everywhere, is a hat-waving cowboy astride a bucking bronco.

Well over three million tourists per year head to the state's northwest corner for the simmering geothermal landscape of **Yellowstone National Park**, and the craggy mountain vistas of adjacent **Grand Teton National Park**. Between Yellowstone and South Dakota to the east are the helter-skelter **Bighorn Mountains**, likeable Old West towns such as **Cody** and **Buffalo**, and the otherworldly outcrop of **Devils Tower**.

The meager supply of buffalo in early Wyoming caused fierce intertribal wars and kept the **Native American** population down to around ten thousand. However, the Sioux, Cheyenne, and Blackfoot combined to inflict notable defeats on the US Army before it could clear the way for pioneer settlement in the 1870s. The cattle ranchers and sheep-farming homesteaders who followed engaged in violent **range wars** over grazing rights to the wiry grasslands.

Unlikely as it may seem, this rowdy state was the first to grant women the right to vote in 1869 – a full half-century before the rest of the country, on the grounds that the enfranchisement of women would attract settlers and increase the population, thereby hastening statehood. A year later Wyoming appointed the country's first women jurors, and the "Equality State" elected the first female US governor in 1924.

The absence of rivers to irrigate farmland has put a lid on agricultural growth. Any weather-beaten, denim-clad stranger is just as likely to be an oil roustabout as a genuine cowboy, with **mineral extraction** having replaced livestock as the mainstay of the state's economy in the early twentieth century; today, Wyoming's coffers overflow with profits from the booming coal, oil, and natural gas industries.

Getting around Wyoming

Greyhound **buses** run along I-80 through the south. The rest of the state is covered only patchily by regional bus companies, so having your own car is definitely the best option. Jackson has the state's busiest **airport**, though flights also go to Casper and Cheyenne. **Cycling** across northern Wyoming can be great fun, although if you're crossing the Bighorns you'll need to pick your routes carefully, as roads here have incredibly steep gradients.

South and central Wyoming

State capital **Cheyenne** is one of the few towns of real note in the lower two-thirds of Wyoming. Set in the heart of rich prairie – a surprise after the scrubland, mountain, and desert of most of the region – it has closer economic ties with Omaha or Denver than with the rest of Wyoming. West of Cheyenne, smaller **Laramie** gathers energy from being home to the state's only four-year university, while the spectacular wilderness of the **Wind River Range**, accessible from **Lander** and **Pinedale**, accounts for much of Wyoming's west-central portion.

Cheyenne

The eastern approach into **CHEYENNE**, dropping into a wide dip in the plains, leaves enduring memories for most travelers. With the snow-crested Rockies looming in the distance and short, sun-bleached grass encircling the town, the sky appears gargantuan, dwarfing the city's outlying neighborhoods. Even a quick exploration reveals a diverse community shaped by railroads, state politics, and even nuclear arms. Union Pacific's sprawling yards and fine old terminus now mark the eastern edge of downtown, while to the west, the city's longstanding military installation was expanded in 1957 to house the first US intercontinental ballistic missile base.

Cowboy culture is big here, too, as the ranchwear stores and honky-tonks dotted around town attest. Along with hosting the world's largest outdoor rodeo, the ten-day **Cheyenne Frontier Days** festival (ⓣ1-800/227-6336, ⓦwww.cfdrodeo.com) in late July attracts thousands of people to its concerts with top country stars, parades, chuckwagon races, air shows, and cook-outs. The rest of the year, things are pretty quiet. **Sixteenth Street**, or Lincolnway, is the retail and entertainment heart of Cheyenne, while the **Wyoming State Museum**, 2301 Central Ave, takes a sober look at Wild West history (May–Oct Mon–Sat 9am–4.30pm; Nov–April Mon–Fri 9am–4.30pm, Sat 10am–2pm; free; ⓣ307/777-7022, ⓦwww.wyomuseum.state.wy.us). The **Cheyenne Frontier Days Old West Museum**, five minutes' drive from downtown at 4610 Carey Ave (Mon–Fri 8.30am–5.30pm, Sat & Sun 9am–5pm; $7; ⓣ307/778-7290, ⓦwww.oldwestmuseum.org), is more lighthearted, telling how the railroad came to town, with some great old engines and well-presented temporary exhibits. Much space is devoted to the Frontier Days celebrations, with photos, costumes, and videos evoking the annual frenzy.

Practicalities

Greyhound **buses** run east and west along I-80 and south to Denver; the local station is at 5401 Walker Rd. You can find a free detailed map of the city, along with lodging and restaurant recommendations, at Cheyenne's **visitor center** at 1 Depot Square (May–Sept Mon–Fri 10am–6pm, Sat 9am–6pm, Sun 10am–4pm; Oct–April Mon–Fri 8am–5pm; ⓣ307/778-3133 or 1-800/426-5009, ⓦwww.cheyenne.org).

Although places to **stay** are normally inexpensive, prices increase sharply during the Frontier Days festival. Budget motels line West Lincolnway; try the austere but clean *Atlas Motel* at no. 1524 (ⓣ307/632-9214; ❷–❸). Classier surroundings are found at the *Plains Hotel*, 1600 Central Ave (ⓣ307/638-3311 or 1-866/275-2467, ⓦwww.theplainshotel.com; ❹–❺) and the *Nagle Warren Mansion*, 222 E 17th St (ⓣ307/637-3333 or 1-800/811-2610, ⓦwww.naglewarrenmansion.com; ❻), which offers superb bed-and-breakfast accommodation in opulent surroundings. Cheyenne has no shortage of **eateries** serving cowboy-sized meals, with the best of the lot being *Sanford's*, 115 E 17th St (ⓣ307/634-3381), a lively brewpub with fine food, as well as comedy and live music downstairs.

Laramie and around

LARAMIE lies fifty miles west of Cheyenne via either I-80 or the spectacular Hwy-210 (Happy Jack Road), the latter slicing through plains studded with bizarrely shaped boulders and outcrops. At first Laramie seems typical of rural Wyoming, but behind downtown's Victorian facades lurk hard-rocking record stores, day spas, vegetarian cafés, and secondhand bookstores – unusual for rodeo land, and a direct by-product of the **University of Wyoming**, whose campus spreads east from the town center. Free museums and sights of interest on campus include the Anthropology Museum, the Museum of Geology, and the Rocky Mountain Herbarium.

The centerpiece of the ambitious **Wyoming Territorial Prison State Park**, west of town at 975 Snowy Range Rd (May–Sept daily 9am–6pm, call for winter hours; $5; ⓣ307/745-6161, ⓦwww.wyoparks.state.wy.us), is the old **prison** itself. A touch over-restored, it nonetheless holds informative displays on the Old West and women in Wyoming, as well as huge mugshots of ex-convicts – among them Butch Cassidy, who was incarcerated here for eighteen months in 1896 for the common crime of cattle-rustling.

Practicalities

Greyhound pulls into Laramie at the Phillips 66 station at 375 W Lyon St; the **visitor center** is at 210 Custer St (Mon–Fri 8am–5pm; ⓣ1-800/445-5303, ⓦwww.laramie-tourism.org). **Rooms** are clean and rates are reasonable at the downtown *Travel Inn*, 262 N 3rd St (ⓣ307/745-4853 or 1-877/310-7381; ❷–❸). If you're looking for a more rural place to lay your head, head about 20 miles west out of Laramie on Hwy-130 to the *Vee Bar Guest Ranch*, 2091 Hwy-130 (one-night stays on Sat only; ⓣ307/745-7036 or 1-800/483-3227, ⓦwww.veebar.com; ❻), where you can relax in a cozy creekside cabin overnight and enjoy a hearty cooked breakfast in the morning. For **dining**, *Corona Village*, 421 Boswell Drive (ⓣ307/721-0167), serves tasty and inexpensive Mexican dishes, while buzzing *Lovejoy's Bar and Grill*, 101 E Grand Ave (ⓣ307/745-0141), is a friendly student hangout that serves good espresso, bagels, muffins, and lunch specials.

The Medicine Bow Mountains and Saratoga

West of Laramie, **Hwy-130** dips into the huge wind-gouged bowl of **Big Hollow**, passes through the tiny community of **Centennial**, and starts the steady climb up through the **MEDICINE BOW MOUNTAINS**, one of Wyoming's most picturesque drives. Overlooks at the top of the 10,847ft Snowy Range Pass (closed in winter) reveal alpine lakes and meadows set tightly against steep mountain faces.

Forty-nine miles west of Centennial, sleepy **Saratoga** sits in a valley between the Snowy and Sierra Madre ranges. Though not much to look at, **Hobo Hot Springs** on Walnut Avenue is a free outdoor pool fed by natural hot springs, available 24 hours a day. Saratoga's most evocative **hotel** is the slightly musty, but antique-furnished *Wolf Hotel*, 101 E Bridge St (ⓣ307/326-5525, ⓦwww.wolfhotel.com; ❸–❹), which also has a restaurant and bar (closed Sun). Other **dining** opportunities around the Medicine Bows are limited, but you'll find suitably rustic meals back at Centennial's *Old Corral Steak House*, 2750 Hwy-130 (ⓣ370/745-5918 or 1-866/653-2677), where the appetizer menu boldly features deep-fried pickle spears.

Rawlins

There would be little reason to stop at the tiny prairie town of **RAWLINS**, one hundred miles west of Laramie on I-80, but for the unmissable **Wyoming Frontier Prison**, 500 W Walnut St (hourly tours April–Oct daily 8.30am–6.30pm, Nov–March Mon–Fri 9am–5pm; $4.50; ⓣ307/324-4422). In service until 1981, this huge jail with dark cells, peeling walls, and echoing corridors can make for a creepy experience – not least due to the fascinating anecdotes told with aplomb by the exceptional guides. The darkest moment comes as the gas chamber (in use from 1937 until 1965) is revealed.

Butch Cassidy and the Sundance Kid

Without a doubt the two most engaging characters to roam the Rocky Mountains of northern Colorado and southern Wyoming, **Butch Cassidy and the Sundance Kid** remain legends not only of the Old West, but of a romantic outlaw existence in which breaking the law became an expression of personal freedom. Thanks in large part to the 1969 Hollywood film *Butch Cassidy and the Sundance Kid* (which starred Paul Newman and Robert Redford), these two former thieves and cattle rustlers continue to cast a long shadow across the Rockies.

Butch Cassidy was born **George LeRoy Parker** in Beaver, Utah, on 6 April, 1866. Taught the art of cattle-rustling by ranch-hand Mike Cassidy, Parker borrowed his mentor's last name, then picked up the handle "Butch" while working as a butcher in Rock Springs, Wyoming. He pulled his first bank job in Telluride, Colorado, in 1889, and soon found himself in the company of a like-minded group of outlaws known as the **Wild Bunch**. Among them was one **Harry Longabaugh** – the Sundance Kid – who picked up his nickname following a jail stint in Sundance, Wyoming. The Wild Bunch were eclectic in their criminal pursuits, and the gang's resumé would include horse-rustling as well as the robbing of trains, banks, and mine payrolls; between them, they gave away a fortune in gold to friends and even strangers in need, hence their reputation as latter-day Robin Hoods.

The gang took to laying low through the winter months in **Brown's Hole**, a broad river valley in remote northwest Colorado, and they were also known to visit the southern Wyoming towns of Baggs, Rock Springs, and Green River. Their saloon excesses were tolerated, however, because at the end of a spree they would meticulously account for every broken chair and bullet hole, making generous restitution in gold. The gang, however, was eventually undone by their own vanity and love of a good time: during a visit to Fort Worth, Texas, five of the men posed for a photo in smart suits and derby hats, looking so dapper that the photographer proudly placed the photo in his shop window, where it was seen the following day by a detective from the famous Pinkerton agency.

Wearying of life on the run, Butch and Sundance sailed for **South America** in 1902, and were soon trying their hand at gold-mining, while robbing the occasional bank or train. The Hollywood version was true enough to this point, but Butch Cassidy did not die in a hail of bullets at the hands of Bolivian soldiers in 1909 as depicted in the film – although it seems that Harry Longabaugh did. The last say belongs to Josie Morris, an old girlfriend from Butch's Brown's Hole days, who insisted that he came to see her on his return from South America, and claimed furthermore that he died an old man in Johnny, Nevada, sometime in the 1940s.

Just to the west, the Continental Divide briefly splits into two in the **Great Divide Basin**. Theoretically, rain that falls here should remain here, unable to flow toward either ocean; in reality, virtually all of it evaporates, as the brick-red dirt of the **Red Desert** stretches implacably away toward the horizon.

The Wind River Range

Roads to Grand Teton and Yellowstone national parks from southern Wyoming skirt the **WIND RIVER RANGE**, the state's longest and highest range; some of the Rockies' most beautiful and challenging hiking terrain is found in the **Bridger Wilderness** area, accessible from the west. No roads cross the mountains; you can either see them from the east by driving through the Wind River Indian Reservation on US-26/287, or from the less accessible west, by taking US-191 up from I-80 at Rock Springs.

Wind River Indian Reservation and Lander

The 1.7 million acres of **WIND RIVER INDIAN RESERVATION** occupy a largely forgotten swath of west-central Wyoming, overshadowed by the high snowcapped peaks to the west and south. It is the only Indian reservation in Wyoming, and extends roughly seventy miles from the natural spa town of **Thermopolis** in the east, through arid grasslands and desiccated uranium-rich badlands, to **Dubois** in the west, with the rich fishing grounds of the cottonwood-lined Wind River at its heart.

Near **Fort Washakie** – named for the centenarian Chief Washakie, who held the Shoshone together throughout the period of white expansion – is the likely grave of **Sacagawea**, the guide of Lewis and Clark's expedition. **Powwows** – gatherings that have both spiritual and social significance to Native Americans – are held mainly in summer, and are open to the public. Contact the Shoshone Tribal Cultural Center in Fort Washakie (Mon–Fri 9am–4pm; ⓣ307/332-9106) for details.

The friendly one-horse town of **LANDER** on US-287 makes an appealing base, with a string of cheap **motels** along Main Street and an excellent **B&B** at the Art Nouveau–style *Blue Spruce Inn*, 677 S Third St (ⓣ307/332-8253 or 1-888/503-3311, ⓦwww.bluespruceinn.com; ❹). A good place to **eat** is *Gannett Grill* at 126 Main St (ⓣ307/332-7009), which serves half-pound burgers and New York-style pizza.

Dubois

The former logging town of **DUBOIS** ("pronounced dew-BOYS"), squeezed into the northern tip of the Wind River valley and an oasis among the badlands, turned to tourism after its final sawmill closed in 1987; it doesn't hurt that it's located sixty miles southeast of Grand Teton National Park via dramatic **Togwotee Pass**. Dubois is home to the biggest herd of bighorn sheep in the lower 48 states, and celebrates that fact with the impressive **National Bighorn Sheep Interpretative Center**, a half-mile northwest of town on US-26/287 (daily: summer 8am–7pm; rest of year 9am–5pm; closed for part of winter; $2; ⓣ307/455-3429 or 1-888/209-2795, ⓦwww.bighorn.org). Along with running 4WD spotting tours ($25; reservations required), the center contains several dioramas and exhibits on the majestic mascot of the Rockies.

Dubois is a smart stop thanks to clean and affordable **lodging** such as the beautifully restored historic *Twin Pines Lodge*, 218 Ramshorn St (ⓣ1-800/550-6332, ⓦwww.twinpineslodge.com; ❸). A popular local evening pastime is listening to country crooners in classic Western **bars** like the *Rustic Pine Tavern*, 121 E Ramshorn St (ⓣ307/455-2772), where the bar menu includes pork ribs and rib eye chili; it's co-managed with a full-scale steakhouse next door.

Pinedale

On the west side of the Wind River Range, a beautiful 77-mile drive away from Jackson on US-189/191 along the Hoback River, **PINEDALE** offers excellent access to a variety of outdoor pursuits; once a major logging center, it's now a growing hub for the natural gas industry. The **Museum of the Mountain Man**, 700 E Hennick Rd (May–Sept, daily 9am–5pm; Oct, Mon–Fri 10am–noon and 1–3pm; rest of the year by appointment only; $5; ⓣ307/367-4101 or 1-877/686-6266, ⓦwww.museumofthemountainman.com), commemorates the town's role as a rendezvous for fur trappers in the 1830s.

A sixteen-mile road winds east from Pinedale past Fremont Lake to **Elkhart Park Trailhead**, from where horse-worn paths lead past beautiful **Seneca Lake** and up rugged Indian Pass to glaciers and 13,000ft peaks; the Pinedale Ranger Station office at 29 E Fremont Lake Rd (Ⓣ307/367-4326) has maps to help you plan a hiking route. More so even than in most areas of the Rockies, mosquito repellent is an absolute necessity in the Wind River Range in summer.

The best place to **stay** in Pinedale is *The Log Cabin Motel*, 49 E Magnolia St (Ⓣ370/367-4579, Ⓦwww.thelogcabinmotel.com; summer ❺–❼, rest of year ❸–❻), which maintains several 1920s cabins, many with kitchens. When you're ready to **eat**, breakfast is best taken at the *Patio Grill*, 35 W Pine St (Ⓣ307/367-4611), where buttery pancakes are the specialty and servers sure to call you "sweetie" circle the room. Come afternoon and evening, *Bottoms Up Brewery* at 402 Pine St (Ⓣ307/367-2337) serves hefty pub grub and own-brewed beers.

Northeast and north central Wyoming

Northern Wyoming has more to offer than just a handy route between the Black Hills and Yellowstone: the surreal volcanic outcrop of **Devils Tower**, the massive **Bighorn Mountains**, and the desertscape of the **Bighorn Basin** are notable natural attractions in a land steeped in the history of Native American wars, outlaw activity, and pioneer hardships. The striking Bighorns soar abruptly from the plains to over 9000ft; the loftiest peaks, protruding well above timberline, seem bald beside their dark-coated neighbors. The small town of **Cody**, eighty miles east of the heart of Yellowstone, is one of the more commercialized settlements around here, and worth a stopover for its Western-theme museums.

Devils Tower National Monument

Though Congress designated **DEVILS TOWER**, in far northeastern Wyoming, as the country's first national monument in 1906, it took Steven Spielberg's inspired use of it as the alien landing spot in *Close Encounters of the Third Kind* to make this eerie 1267ft volcanic outcrop a true national icon. Plonked on top of a thickly forested hill above the peaceful Belle Fourche River, it resembles a giant wizened tree stump; however, it can be hauntingly beautiful when painted ever-changing hues by the sun and moon.

Four short trails loop the tower, beginning from the **visitor center** (early April–late Nov, hours vary by season; Ⓣ307/467-5283, Ⓦwww.nps.gov/deto) at its base, three miles from the main gate. The **entrance fee** is $10 per car (good for one week), and until late October you can **camp** for $12 a night – arrive early or you'll end up paying more than twice that at one of the nearby commercial campgrounds.

Buffalo

Snuggled among the southeastern foothills of the Bighorn Mountains, easy-going **BUFFALO** remains largely unaffected by the bustle of the nearby I-90/I-25 junction; winters here are comparatively mild to other areas of Wyoming, thus prompting locals to refer to the town as the state's "banana belt." Although Main Street, now lined with frontier-style stores, used to be an old buffalo trail, the place was actually named after Buffalo, New York. The **Jim Gatchell Museum**, 100 Fort St (mid-April–mid-Oct, Mon–Fri 9am–4pm; $5; Ⓣ370/684-9331, Ⓦwww.jimgatchell.com), houses a fine collection of Old West curiosities pertaining to soldiers, ranchers, and Native Americans.

Pick up local information from the **visitor center**, 55 N Main St (Mon–Fri 8am–5pm; Ⓣ307/684-5544 or 1-800/227-5122, Ⓦwww.buffalowyo.com). At the immaculately restored *Occidental Hotel*, 10 N Main St (ⓣ370/684-0451, ⓦwww.occidentalwyoming.com; summer ❹–❼, rest of year ❸–❺), you can **stay** in the multi-room Owen Wister Suite, where the famed writer wrote a chunk of *The Virginian*. The sumptuous lobby is a feast for the senses, and many rooms feature vintage radios tuned to old-time music on the hotel's own micro-frequency.

The Bighorn Mountains and Bighorn Basin

Of the three scenic highways that wind through the **Bighorn Mountains**, US-14A from **Burgess Junction**, fifty miles west of **Sheridan**, is the most spectacular. The road, typically closed November to May due to snow, edges its way up **Medicine Mountain**, on whose windswept western peak the mysterious **Medicine Wheel** – the largest such monument still intact – stands protected behind a wire fence. Local Native American legends offer no clues as to the original purpose of these flat stones, arranged in a circular "wheel" shape with 28 spokes and a circumference of 245ft – though the pattern suggests sun-worship or early astronomy. For more information, drop into the **Burgess Junction Visitor Center** (late May–mid-Sept, 8am–5.30pm), one-half mile east of Burgess Junction on US-14.

The Alps-like route down the highway's west side, with gradients of ten to twenty percent, is said to have cost more to build per mile than any other road in America. Tight hairpin bends will keep drivers' eyes off the magnificent overlooks down into the **Bighorn Basin**, a sparsely vegetated valley walled in by mighty mountains on three sides and ragged foothills to the north. North of here up Hwy-37 is **Bighorn Canyon National Recreation Area** and its Yellowtail Reservoir, a favorite of watersports enthusiasts.

Cody

Plenty of noisy pickup trucks cruise the main streets of **CODY**, the "rodeo capital of the world," located along US-14 and the North Fork of the Shoshone River. The town was the brainchild of investors who, in 1896, persuaded "Buffalo Bill" Cody to become involved in their development company, knowing his approval would attract homesteaders and visitors alike. During summer, tourism is huge business here, but underneath all the Buffalo Bill–linked attractions and paraphernalia, Cody manages to retain the feel of a rural Western settlement.

The town's wide main thoroughfare, **Sheridan Avenue**, holds souvenir and ranchwear shops and is the scene of parades during the annual **Cody Stampede Rodeo** (ⓣ307/587-5155 or 1-800/207-0744, ⓦwww.codystampederodeo.com), held annually in early July. During summer months, the **Cody Nite Rodeo** happens nightly at the open-air arena on the western edge of town (8pm; $17; same contact info as Cody Stampede Rodeo); there's a $5 shuttle bus from town.

Just east of the rodeo grounds off US-14 is **Old Trail Town** (mid-May–mid-Sept, 8am–8pm; $8; ⓣ307/587-5302), a collection of buildings dating from 1879–1901 and salvaged from the surrounding region; among them are cabins and saloons frequented by Butch Cassidy and the Sundance Kid, as well as Curly, the Crow scout of George Custer. Additionally, famed mountain man **Jeremiah "Liver Eatin'" Johnston** is buried here.

Buffalo Bill Historical Center

Holding the nation's most comprehensive collection of Western Americana, Cody's **Buffalo Bill Historical Center** at 720 Sheridan Ave comprises five distinct museums (hours vary by season; $15; ⓣ307/587-4771, ⓦwww.bbhc.org). At the **Buffalo Bill Museum,** artifacts trace William Cody's life through his years involved with the Pony Express, Civil War, Indian Wars, and his own Wild West shows (see box below). The lives of western Native Americans are celebrated in the **Plains Indian Museum**, where many of the ceremonial garments remain in stunning condition. In the **Whitney Gallery of Western Art**, the contrasting styles of Frederic Remington and Charles M. Russell command the most attention; the propagandist Remington dwells on conflict, depicting the Indian as a savage in the path of progress, while Russell's work shows a consistent respect for the Native American way of life. The largest known collection of American-made firearms in the world is housed in the **Cody Firearms Museum**, while the **Draper Museum of Natural History** is lined with interactive exhibits and beautiful taxidermy displays, all of which highlight the geology, wildlife, and human history of the Greater Yellowstone region.

Practicalities

For information and lodging reservations, contact Cody's **visitor center** at 836 Sheridan Ave (late May–Sept Mon–Fri 8am–6pm, Sat 9am–5pm, Sun 10am–3pm; rest of year, daily 8am–5pm; ⓣ307/587-2777, ⓦwww.codychamber.org). Cody Trolley Tours (ⓣ307/527-7043, ⓦwww.codytrolleytours.com; $22) offer corny hour-long **tours** of town, while **whitewater rafting** and **kayak** trips on the Shoshone are handled by Wyoming River Trips ($27–67; ⓣ307/587-6661 or 1-800/586-6661, ⓦwww.wyomingrivertrips.com).

Buffalo Bill

The much-mythologized exploits of **William Frederick "Buffalo Bill" Cody**, born in Iowa in 1846, began at the age of just eleven, when the murder of his father forced him to take a job on a wagon train. An early escape from ambush brought Cody fame as the "Youngest Indian Slayer of the Plains;" four years later, he became the youngest rider on the **Pony Express**, averaging a blazing 15mph on his leg of the legendary mail route. After a stint fighting for the Union in the Civil War, Cody found work – and a lifelong nickname – supplying buffalo meat to workers laying the transcontinental railroad. He claimed to have killed over 4200 animals in just eighteen months, before rejoining the army in 1868 as its chief scout.

By the 1870s, exaggerated accounts of Cody's adventures were appearing back east in the "dime novels" of Ned Buntline, and with the Indian Wars all but over he took to guiding Yankee and European gentry on buffalo hunts; the theatrical productions he laid on for his rich guests developed into his world-famous **Wild West Show**. First staged in 1883, these spectacular outdoor carnivals usually consisted of a re-enactment of an Indian battle such as Custer's Last Stand (featuring Sioux who had been present at Little Bighorn), trick riders, buffalo, clowns, and exhibition shooting and riding by the man himself. The show spent ten of its thirty years in Europe, and dressed in the finest silks and sporting a well-groomed goatee, Cody stayed in the grandest hotels and dined with heads of state; Queen Victoria was so enthusiastic in her admiration that rumors circulated of an affair between them.

Later in life, a mellower Cody played down his past activities, to the point of urging the government to respect all Native American treaties and put an end to the wanton slaughter of buffalo and game. Although the Wild West Show was reckoned to have brought in as much as one million dollars per year, many of his investments failed badly, and, in January 1915, a penniless 69-year-old Buffalo Bill died at his sister's home in Denver. His grave can be found atop Lookout Mountain, outside Golden, Colorado (see p.775).

Cody's showpiece Western **hotel**, the *Irma* at 1192 Sheridan Ave (Ⓣ307/587-4221 or 1-800/745-4762, Ⓦwww.irmahotel.com; ❸–❻), was named for Buffalo Bill's daughter in 1902, and retains a superb original cherrywood bar (a gift to Buffalo Bill from Queen Victoria) in its namesake downstairs restaurant. Among local good-value motels, the clean and comfortable *Buffalo Bill's Antlers Inn*, 1213 17th St (Ⓣ1-800/388-2084, Ⓦwww.antlersinncody.com; ❸–❹) stands out. Sheridan Avenue is Cody's central place for **eating** and **drinking**: after a stout meal at the *Irma Hotel* (see above), call in for a drink at the *Proud Cut Saloon* (Ⓣ307/527-6905) at no. 1227. A top spot for breakfast is *Our Place* (Ⓣ307/527-4420), out on the west end of town at 148 Yellowstone Ave.

Yellowstone National Park

Millions of visitors arrive yearly at **YELLOWSTONE NATIONAL PARK**, America's oldest national park, to glory in its magnificent mountain scenery and abundant wildlife, and to witness hydrothermal phenomena on a grand scale. Measuring roughly sixty by fifty miles, and overlapping slightly from Wyoming's northwestern corner into Idaho and Montana, the park centers on a 7500ft-high plateau, the caldera of a vast volcanic eruption that occurred a mere 600,000 years ago. Into it are crammed more than half the world's **geysers**, plus thousands of **fumaroles** jetting plumes of steam, **mud pots** gurgling with acid-dissolved muds and clays, and of course, **hot springs**.

A visit to Yellowstone can amount to an extraordinary experience, combining the **colors** of the Grand Canyon of the Yellowstone, massive and deep-azure Yellowstone Lake, wildflower-filled meadows, and rainbow-hued geyser pools; the **sounds** of subterranean rumblings, belching mud pools, and steam hissing from the mountainsides; the constant **smells** of drifting sulfurous fumes; and, the **sights** of shambling bears, heavy-bearded bison, herds of elk, and more than a dozen elusive wolf packs on the prowl. The key to appreciating the park is to take your time, plan carefully, and – particularly if you visit in summer – exercise patience with the inevitable crowds and auto traffic; if you allow for a stay of at least three days, you should be suitably rewarded.

Arrival and information

Two of the five main **entrances** to Yellowstone are in Wyoming, via **Cody** to the east and **Grand Teton National Park** to the south. The others are in Montana: **West Yellowstone** (west), **Gardiner** (north), and **Cooke City** (northeast). Due to winter snow, most roads are open from early May to October only (see box, p.814). **Admission** ($25 per car, good for one week) includes entry to adjacent Grand Teton National Park (p.819).

Albright Visitor Center at **Mammoth** is the park's sole year-round information center, near the north entrance (daily: early May–Aug 8am–7pm, Sept 8am–6pm, Oct–early May 9am–5pm; Ⓣ307/344-2263, Ⓦwww.nps.gov/yell); other, summer-only **visitor centers** are located approximately every 25 miles along the main **Loop Road**. Most issue back-country hiking permits, and each hosts an exhibit on a different aspect of the park.

Consult the free park publication *Yellowstone Today* for activities and current regulations. Excellent National Park Service leaflets (50¢ each), which can be found at major sights as well as visitor centers, cover the important landmarks, marking trails and points of interest. The nonprofit *Yellowstone Association* (Ⓣ307/344-2293, Ⓦwww.yellowstoneassociation.org) is an invaluable resource, and is

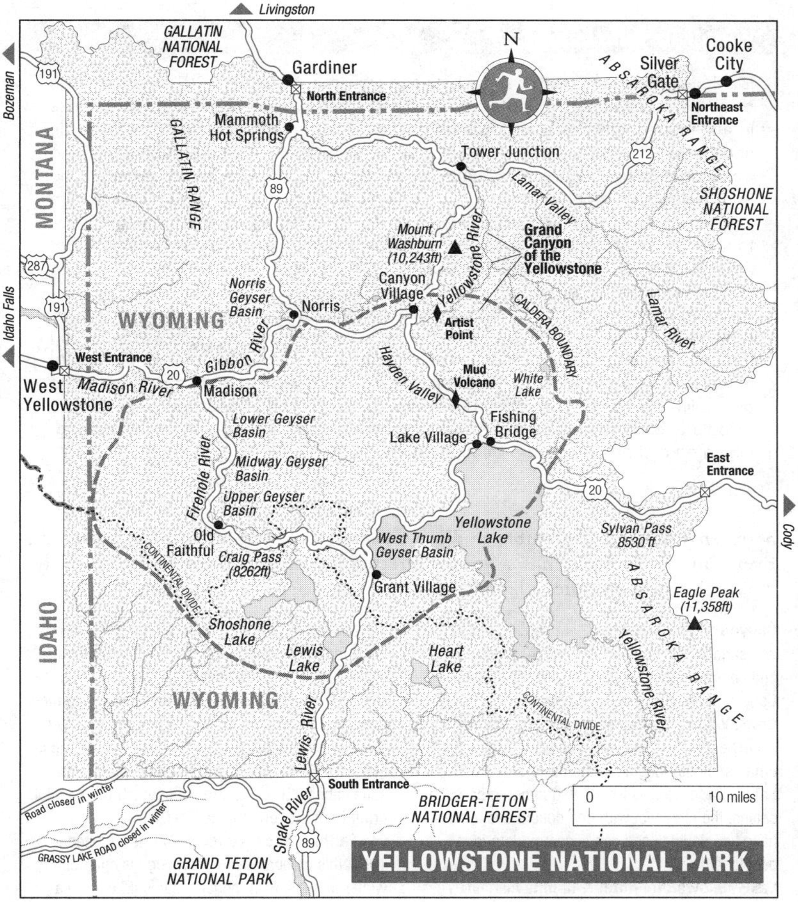

especially noteworthy for its excellent courses that range from wolf watching and back-country excursions to science-and-nature writing.

A car is virtually essential to properly visit Yellowstone. If you need to get to the park by **bus**, Karst Stage (ⓣ406/556-3500 or 1-800/845-2778, ⓦwww.karststage.com; reservations essential) operates shuttle **buses** that run from the Bozeman, Montana airport to West Yellowstone and Mammoth. Several companies offer hurried **tours** of the park from inside the park as well as from the gateway towns; these include Xanterra (ⓣ1-866/439-7375, ⓦwww.travelyellowstone.com), West Yellowstone's Buffalo Bus Tours (ⓣ1-800/426-7669, ⓦwww.yellowstonevacations.com), and Jackson's Gray Line (ⓣ307/733-4325 or 1-800/443-6133, ⓦwww.graylinejh.com).

Accommodation in the park

All indoor **lodging** within Yellowstone is run by Xanterra (ⓣ1-866/439-7375, ⓦwww.travelyellowstone.com). **Reservations** are strongly recommended

Winter in Yellowstone

Blanketed in several feet of snow between November and April, Yellowstone takes on a new appearance in **winter**: a silent and bizarre world where waterfalls freeze in mid-plunge, geysers blast towering plumes of steam and water into the crisp air, and bison – beards matted with ice – stand in huddles. It's undeniably cold, and transportation can require some hefty pre-planning, but crowds are non-existent and wildlife-spotting opportunities are superb. Only the fifty-mile road from Gardiner to Cooke City via Mammoth Hot Springs is kept open (although beyond that, the Beartooth Highway is closed). The park's sole winter lodging is available at *Mammoth Hot Springs Hotel* or *Old Faithful Snow Lodge & Cabins* (accessible only by snowcoach and snowmobile).

Xanterra (Ⓣ1-866/439-7375, Ⓦwww.travelyellowstone.com) operates **snowcoach** trips and tours of the park over the closed roads from West Yellowstone, Flagg Ranch to the south, Old Faithful, and Mammoth Hot Springs ($55–145). **Snowmobile** rental, generally cheapest in West Yellowstone, costs around $135 a day; note that only a limited number of snowmobiles are allowed in the park at any one time, so reserve ahead. Much less expensive is **cross-country skiing** and **snowshoeing**, with groomed or blazed trails throughout the park.

between June and September and are essential over public-holiday weekends. Every major location has a lodge offering dining facilities (most close by 9.30pm), and sometimes a laundromat, grocery store, and gift shop.

Canyon Lodge & Cabins Plain hotel rooms ($172) and simple frame cabins ($74–156), all en-suite and centrally located one half-mile from Grand Canyon of the Yellowstone. 4–7

Grant Village Spartan en-suite motel rooms on the southwest shore of Yellowstone Lake – the southernmost indoor lodging in the park. 6

Lake Lodge Cabins Nearly two hundred en-suite cabins, the cheapest with one double bed; others have two doubles and can accommodate four people. 4–6

Lake Yellowstone Hotel & Cabins Alarmingly yellow, this Grand colonial-style hotel features ordinary rooms ($150–227) and dark, dingy en-suite cabins ($134). Its *Sun Room*, overlooking the lake, is a terrific spot for an evening drink. 6–8

Mammoth Hot Springs Hotel & Cabins Circa 1930s lodging at the north end of the park, offering a range of cabins ($79–222) and hotel rooms ($89–121). Open year-round. 4–8

Old Faithful Inn & Lodge Cabins One of the most beautiful lodges around, this 1904 inn – said to be the world's largest log building – has a wide range of rooms ($98–216), in addition to budget and en-suite cabins ($68–112). You can watch Old Faithful erupt from the terrace bar. 3–8

Old Faithful Snow Lodge & Cabins Opened in 1999, this comparatively new lodge is open during winter months, with modern rooms ($201). Adjacent cabins ($99–147) are slightly older, but attractive and well-sealed against the cold. 4–7

Roosevelt Lodge Cabins Over eighty cabins ($67–112) a short drive from the Lamar Valley, from sparsely furnished to motel-like. 3–5

Accommodation in gateway towns

In addition to **Jackson** (see p.810) and **Cody** (p.822) in Wyoming, the small towns just outside the park's western and two northern gates offer somewhat cheaper lodging. **West Yellowstone**, the largest town, is somewhat disfigured by gift stores and fast-food joints but manages to retain a certain charm, and its surrounding national forest lands are well worth exploring. Friendly **Gardiner** lies just five miles from Mammoth Hot Springs. Less developed, the one-street town of **Cooke City** is three miles from the isolated northeast entrance on US-212, which just east of town becomes a dead-end road in winter.

Elk Horn Lodge 103 Main St, Cooke City ⓣ406/838-2332, ⓦwww.elkhornlodgemt.com. Two cabins and six motel rooms, all with full bath, TV, mini-fridges, microwaves, and coffeemakers. ❹–❺

Headwaters of the Yellowstone Bed & Breakfast Hwy-89, Gardiner ⓣ406/848-7073 or 1-888/848-7220, ⓦwww.headwatersbandb.com. A fantastic B&B on the banks of the Yellowstone River, less than four miles north of Gardiner. All five guestrooms have their own private bathroom, while the two cabins – one sleeping up to four, the other up to six – have excellent views. ❻–❼

Madison Hotel 139 Yellowstone Ave, West Yellowstone ⓣ406/646-7745 or 1-800/838-7745, ⓦwww.madisonhotelmotel.com. This historic hotel includes an adjacent motel (with cabin-themed rooms) and one of the few hostels in the region; the attractive, log-hewn building dates back to 1912 and has dorm rooms ($32 per person) that accommodate up to four people. Open late May–early Oct. ❸–❹

Three Bear Lodge 217 Yellowstone Ave, West Yellowstone ⓣ406/646-7353 or 1-800/646-7353, ⓦwww.three-bear-lodge.com. Large motel housing 75 sizable rooms and two-bedroom family units that sleep six. On-site amenities include a friendly diner, and snowmobile packages are usually available. ❺–❻

Yellowstone Village Inn 1102 Scott St, Gardiner ⓣ1-800/228-8158, ⓦwww.yellowstonevinn.com. On the edge of town, this high-end motel has 43 tidy rooms, most themed around wildlife or Western Americana, including a John Wayne room. High season runs mid-June–mid-September, with substantially lower rates available at other times. ❸–❻

Camping

Xanterra operates five of the twelve campgrounds in Yellowstone. The other seven operate on a first-come, first-served basis; arrive early in the day to get a site during summer months, as most are full by 11am. It might be worth booking your first night at one of the reservation-only sites (ⓣ1-866/439-7375, ⓦwww.travelyellowstone.com) – Bridge Bay, Canyon, Grant Village, Madison, and Fishing Bridge (RVs only) – just to make sure there's a place for you the day you arrive. **Fees** range from $12–18.50 per night for tent camping and $36 for RVs, and campgrounds operate anywhere from early May and late June through mid-September and early November; the only year-round campground is Mammoth, at 6200ft. Though all campgrounds have toilet facilities, few have showers.

To camp in the **back country**, you'll need a permit – free from visitor centers, information stations, and ranger stations; these can be collected no earlier than 48 hours in advance of your camping trip. You can also camp at commercial grounds in the gateway towns, and in neighboring national forests Gallatin (ⓣ406/587-6701) to the northwest and Shoshone (ⓣ307/527-6241) to the east.

Touring the park

The majority of Yellowstone's top sights are signposted within a few hundred yards of the 142-mile **Loop Road**, a figure-eight circuit fed by roads from the park's five entrances. Although the **speed limit** is a radar-enforced 45mph – important, given the number of bison and other oversize mammals that regularly cross the roads – journey times are often difficult to predict. **Wildlife traffic jams**, usually caused by stubborn herds of bison parking themselves on the pavement, are not unusual and should be expected; also for this reason, it's advisable to avoid night driving in Yellowstone.

To get the most out of a visit, even if you're short of time, choose one or two areas of the park to thoroughly explore. Only in the early morning is **cycling** truly bearable or safe; there are only a few mountain-bike trails, and all accessible to hikers and horses as well. Of course, no trip to Yellowstone is complete without at least one **hike**, be it to a waterfall or geyser; each visitor center has free day-hiking handouts for their areas.

▲ Mammoth Hot Springs

The following account runs clockwise around the Loop Road, from Old Faithful to the Yellowstone Lake area; both sights are in the southern half of the park.

Geyser country: from Old Faithful to Mammoth Hot Springs

For well over a century, the dependable **Old Faithful** has erupted more frequently than any of its higher or larger rivals, making it the most popular geyser in the park. As a result, a half-moon of concentric benches, backed by a host of visitor facilities, now surround it at a respectful distance on the side away from the Firehole River. On average, it "performs" for expectant crowds every 78 minutes; approximate schedules are displayed in the nearby visitor center and in the lobby of the inn. The first sign of activity is a soft hissing as water splashes repeatedly over the rim; after several minutes, a column of water shoots to a height of 100 to 180ft as the geyser spurts out a total of eleven thousand gallons.

Two miles of boardwalks lead from Old Faithful to dozens of other geysers in the Upper Basin. If possible, try to arrive when **Grand Geyser** is due to explode. This colossus blows its top on average just twice daily, for twelve to twenty minutes, in a series of four powerful bursts that can reach 200ft. Other highlights along the banks of the Firehole River, usually lined with browsing bison, include the fluorescent intensity of the **Grand Prismatic Spring** at **Midway Geyser Basin**, particularly breathtaking in early evening when human figures and bison herds are silhouetted against plumes of mineral spray.

Thirty miles north of Old Faithful in the less crowded **Norris Geyser Basin**, two separate trails explore a pallid landscape of whistling vents and fumaroles. **Steamboat** is the world's tallest geyser, capable of forcing near-boiling water over 300ft into the air; full eruptions are entirely unpredictable. The **Echinus Geyser** is the largest acid-water geyser known; every 35 to 75 minutes it spews crowd-pleasing, vinegary eruptions of forty to sixty feet.

At **Mammoth Hot Springs**, at the northern tip of the Loop Road, terraces of barnacle-like deposits cascade down a vapor-shrouded mountainside. Tinted a marvelous array of grays, greens, yellows, browns, and oranges by algae, they are composed of travertine, a form of limestone which, having been dissolved and carried to the surface by boiling water, is deposited as tier upon tier of steaming stone.

Tower and the Lamar Valley

The main landmark of Yellowstone's **Tower** and **Roosevelt** areas, east of Mammoth Hot Springs, is **Mount Washburn**, one of the park's highest peaks; its lookout tower can be reached by an enjoyable hike (five or six miles round-trip, depending on the trailhead) or a grueling cycle ride. If you are looking for an easier hike, try the trail that leads down to the spray-drenched base of **Tower Fall**. From Tower Junction, the Northeast Entrance highway wanders east through the meadows of serene **Lamar Valley** – often called "North America's Serengeti" for its **abundant wildlife**, where life-and-death struggles between predators (grizzlies, wolves, mountain lions) and prey (elk, bison, pronghorn, mule deer) play out daily. Beyond Lamar Valley tower the classic, icy peaks of the **Absaroka** (pronounced "ab-SORE-kuh") **Mountains**.

The Grand Canyon of the Yellowstone

The Yellowstone River roars and tumbles for twenty miles between the sheer golden-hued cliffs of the **Grand Canyon of the Yellowstone**, its course punctuated by two powerful **waterfalls**: 109ft **Upper Falls** and its downstream counterpart, thunderous 308ft **Lower Falls**. On the south rim, **Artist Point** looks down hundreds of feet to the river canyon, where frothing water swirls between mineral-stained walls. Nearby, **Uncle Tom's Trail** descends steeply to a spray-covered platform in the canyon, gently vibrating in the face of pounding Lower Falls. A few miles south, the river widens to meander through tranquil **Hayden Valley**, one of the finest spots in Yellowstone to view wildlife from the road.

Yellowstone Lake

North America's largest alpine lake, deep and deceptively calm **Yellowstone Lake** fills a sizeable chunk of the eastern half of the Yellowstone caldera. At 7733ft above sea level, it's high enough to be frozen half the year, and its waters remain perilously cold through summer. Rowboats ($9.50 per hour) and slightly larger outboard motorboats ($47 per hour), along with 22ft ($76 per hour) and 34ft ($96 per hour) powerboats, can be rented from the Bridge Bay Marina (May–Sept; ⓣ307/242-3876) near Lake Village.

A brief human history of Yellowstone

Although Native Americans had long hunted in what is now **Yellowstone National Park**, they were here only in limited numbers by the 1807 arrival of the first white man – **John Colter**, a veteran of the Lewis and Clark expedition (see also p.829). Colter's account of the exploding geysers and seething cauldrons of "Colter's Hell" (located east of Yellowstone, near Cody) was widely ridiculed at the time. However, as ever more trappers, scouts, and prospectors told similar tales, three increasingly larger expeditions set out to chart the region each year beginning in 1869. In 1872, Yellowstone was set aside as the first **national park**, in part to ensure that its assets were not entirely stripped by hunters and miners, and also to appease railroad interests looking for a new destination to which they could shuttle visitors.

At first, management of the park was beset by problems, and Congress devoted enthusiasm, but little funding, toward its protection. Irresponsible tourists stuck soap down the geysers, damaging their intricate plumbing; bandits preyed on stagecoaches carrying rich excursionists; and, the Nez Percé even killed two tourists as they were chased through the park (see p.845). By 1886, Congress had taken the park out of civilian hands and put the army in charge.

Once the army handed Yellowstone over to the newly created **National Park Service** in 1917, automobiles had become a prevalent presence in the park. The conflict between tourism and wilderness preservation has raged ever since. Ecologists now warn that the park cannot stand alone as some pristine paradise; rather, it must be seen as part of a much larger "Greater Yellowstone Ecosystem" encompassing Yellowstone, the Tetons, the Snake River Valley (which stretches south of Jackson to just over the Idaho border), and the northern reaches of the Wind River Mountains. In 1995, amid vociferous complaints from local ranchers fearing a subsequent loss of livestock, **wolves** were reintroduced to the park. They've since made an emphatic comeback, and from the original fourteen animals released, there are now around 150 wolves comprising some fifteen packs roaming the Greater Yellowstone area.

Finally, the **fires** that razed 36 percent of the park throughout the summer of 1988 also brought Yellowstone's environmental policies into focus. Park authorities considered the burn a natural part of the forest's eco-cycle, in which 200-year-old trees were cleared to make way for new growth; the scarred mountainsides – now covered with squat, youthful pines – are in the midst of recovery. 2003 saw the most fires in the park since 1988, but they left nowhere near as much destruction in their wake.

At **West Thumb Geyser Basin**, where hot pools empty into the lake's tranquil waters and fizz away into nothing, it's easy to see why early tourists would have made use of the so-called **Fishing Cone** by cooking freshly caught fish in its boiling waters. To the south, the highway leads towards Grand Teton past **Lewis Lake**, the third largest lake in the park, with **Shoshone Lake** and **Heart Lake** hidden in the backcountry to the west and east respectively; both lakes are well worth a hike.

Eating in the park

Snack bars and **restaurants** inside the park aren't cheap, but given where you are, they're not hideously expensive either. Buying food at the general stores can get pricey, though. There's not much menu variation among Yellowstone's several **restaurants**, but you'll find that the ones at *Old Faithful Inn*, *Old Faithful Snow Lodge*, and *Lake Yellowstone Hotel* are the clear standouts for location, mood, and ambiance; entrees ($15–32) typically range from salmon and steak to pasta and Caesar salads. Yellowstone restaurants are also open for **breakfast** – usually a buffet that includes fresh fruit, cereals, pastries, and standard cooked items, for under

$10 – and **lunch**. More workaday **cafeterias** are dotted around the park as well, as are **soda fountains** inside several general stores, where burgers and fries along with ice cream and shakes are served to rows of customers on stools.

Eating in the gateway towns

While Yellowstone's gateway towns hold few culinary delights, they do offer cheaper prices and more variety. In **West Yellowstone**, *Running Bear Pancake House*, 538 Madison Ave (Ⓣ406/646-7703), is the first place to come for an enjoyable breakfast, while *Bullwinkles* at 19 Madison Ave (Ⓣ406/646-7974) is tops for lunch and dinner, with huge salads and delicious pan-fried fish. **Gardiner**'s *Sawtooth Deli*, 220 Park Street (Ⓣ406/848-7600), serves breakfasts and barbecue, while the *Corral Drive-Inn* at 711 Scott Street (Ⓣ406/848-7627) makes a terrific burger. The impossible-to-miss *Beartooth Cafe* (Ⓣ406/838-2475) is **Cooke City**'s best eatery throughout the day.

Grand Teton National Park and Jackson Hole

The classic triangular peaks of **GRAND TETON NATIONAL PARK**, stretching for fifty miles between Yellowstone and Jackson, are more dramatic than the mountains of its superstar neighbor park to the north. These sheer-faced cliffs make a magnificent spectacle, rising abruptly to tower 7000ft above the valley floor. A string of gem-like lakes is set tight at the foot of the mountains; beyond them lies the broad, sagebrush-covered **Jackson Hole** river basin (a "hole" was a pioneer term for a flat, mountain-ringed valley), broken by the gently winding Snake River.

The Shoshone people knew the mountains as the *Teewinot* ("many pinnacles"), but their present name, meaning "large breast," was bestowed by over-imaginative French-Canadian trappers in the 1830s. After Congress set the mountains aside as a national park in 1929, it took another 21 years of legal wrangling for Grand Teton to attain its current size – local ranchers protested that the economy of Jackson Hole would be ruined if further land was surrendered to tourism. During this time, John D. Rockefeller Jr bought up large parts of Jackson Hole and presented them gratis to the government for the strict purpose of conversion to parklands, on the condition that his Grand Teton Lodge Company be the park's primary concessionaire, which it remains today.

Seeing the park

No road crosses the Tetons, but those that run along their eastern flank were designed with an eye to the mountains, affording stunning views at every bend. Two excellent side-trips are the **Jenny Lake Scenic Loop**, leading to a face-to-face encounter with towering, partly hunchbacked 13,770ft **Grand Teton**, and the narrow track up **Signal Mountain**, which offers a breathtaking panorama including the Tetons and Jackson Hole.

Hiking trails have been laid out so that no time is wasted in getting to the highlights. One easy and popular walk is along the sandy beaches of **Leigh Lake**, where the imposing 12,605ft **Mount Moran** bursts out dramatically from the lake shores. Also accessible is cascading **Hidden Falls**, reachable by a two-mile walk along the south shore of Jenny Lake; an even easier option is to take the shuttle boat ($9 round-trip) across the lake and walk the remaining eight hundred yards.

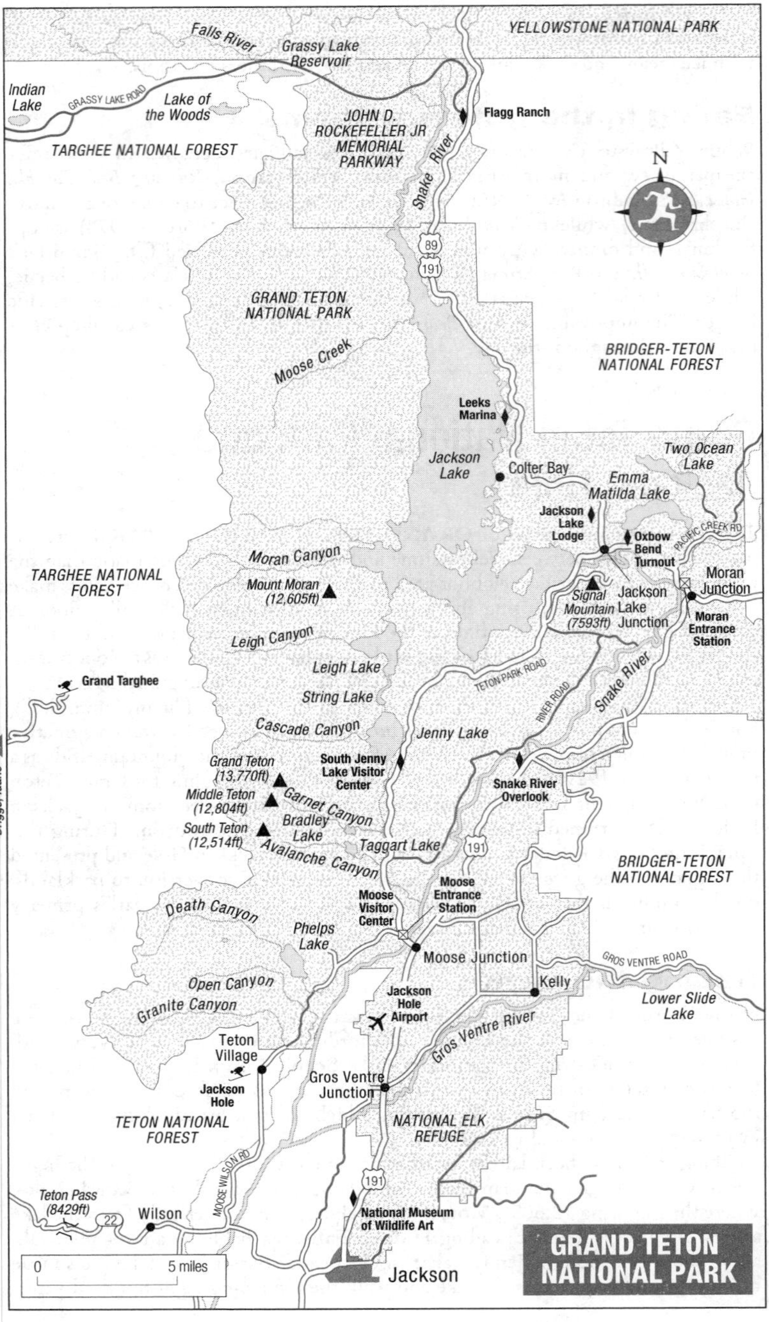
YELLOWSTONE NATIONAL PARK
Falls River
Grassy Lake Reservoir
Indian Lake
GRASSY LAKE ROAD
Lake of the Woods
JOHN D. ROCKEFELLER JR MEMORIAL PARKWAY
Flagg Ranch
TARGHEE NATIONAL FOREST
Snake River
N
89
191
GRAND TETON NATIONAL PARK
BRIDGER-TETON NATIONAL FOREST
Moose Creek
Leeks Marina
Jackson Lake
Colter Bay
Two Ocean Lake
Emma Matilda Lake
Jackson Lake Lodge
Oxbow Bend Turnout
PACIFIC CREEK RD
Moran Canyon
Mount Moran (12,605ft)
TARGHEE NATIONAL FOREST
Signal Mountain (7593ft)
Jackson Lake Junction
Moran Junction
Moran Entrance Station
Leigh Canyon
Leigh Lake
TETON PARK ROAD
RIVER ROAD
Snake River
Grand Targhee
String Lake
Cascade Canyon
Jenny Lake
Grand Teton (13,770ft)
South Jenny Lake Visitor Center
Snake River Overlook
Middle Teton (12,804ft)
Garnet Canyon
South Teton (12,514ft)
Bradley Lake
Taggart Lake
Avalanche Canyon
191
BRIDGER-TETON NATIONAL FOREST
Driggs, Idaho
Moose Visitor Center
Moose Entrance Station
Death Canyon
Phelps Lake
Moose Junction
GROS VENTRE ROAD
Open Canyon
Kelly
Lower Slide Lake
Granite Canyon
Jackson Hole Airport
Gros Ventre River
Teton Village
Jackson Hole
Gros Ventre Junction
TETON NATIONAL FOREST
NATIONAL ELK REFUGE
MOOSE WILSON RD
191
Teton Pass (8429ft)
22
Wilson
National Museum of Wildlife Art
0
5 miles
Jackson
GRAND TETON NATIONAL PARK

A more adventurous, but suitably rewarding amble heads up the macabrely named **Death Canyon**, up which you hike to reach a verdant plateau after four miles on a well-graded trail adjacent to crashing creek waters.

On the flat roads of the Hole, **cycling** is a joy; bikes can be rented at Adventure Sports within the Dornan's complex in Moose Junction ($12/hour, $34/day; ⓣ307/733-3307, ⓦwww.dornans.com). To admire the Tetons from **water**, take a float trip along the Snake River or rent a **canoe** or **kayak** from the marinas at Jenny Lake, Colter Bay, or Signal Mountain Lodge. In winter, all hiking trails are open to **cross-country skiers**, and **snowmobiles** can be rented in Jackson. Given the composition of the Tetons, excellent **rock climbing** opportunities exist within the park; Exum Mountain Guides (ⓣ307/733-2297, ⓦwww.exumguides.com) runs classes and guided trips from a summer office located steps from Jenny Lake.

Practicalities

Handed out at all entrance stations, the free *Teewinot* park newspaper offers details of trails, facilities, and ranger-led activities. The park **entrance fee** of $25 per car (good for one week) also covers Yellowstone. Grand Teton's main **visitor center** is just off the main road in **Moose** (daily: early June–early Sept 8am–7pm, rest of year 8am–5pm; ⓣ307/739-3399, ⓦwww.nps.gov/grte) in the south; others are at **Jenny Lake** (daily: late May–early June and early Sept–late Sept 8am–4.30pm, early June–early Sept 8am–7pm; ⓣ307/739-3392) near the park's center, **Colter Bay** (daily: early May–early June and early Sept–mid-Oct 8am–5pm, early June–early Sept 8am–7pm; ⓣ307/739-3594) halfway up the east shore of Jackson Lake, and **Flagg Ranch** (daily: early June–early Sept 9am–4pm; ⓣ307/543-2861) at the park's northern end. The free **Indian Arts Museum** within the Colter Bay Visitor Center has an extensive collection of native craftwork from the area.

The majority of **rooms** and **activities** within the park are managed by Grand Teton Lodge Company (ⓣ307/543-2811 or 1-800/628-9988, ⓦwww.gtlc.com); reservations are absolutely essential in summer. Prices for the comfortable rooms and cottages at *Jackson Lake Lodge* (❽–❾) depend on whether or not you want a mountain view. *Colter Bay Village Cabins* (❸–❼) are more utilitarian; in high summer, $43 "tent cabins" – canvas cabins with bunk beds (bed linen available for hire), wood-burning stove, and outdoor barbecue grill – are also available. Independently run *Signal Mountain Lodge* (ⓣ307/543-2831, ⓦwww.signalmtnlodge.com; ❺–❽) has a wide range of lodging, from bland motel-style units (❼–❽) to much nicer rustic log cabins (one- or two-room units available; ❻–❼). All five park **campgrounds** are only open in summer and operate on a first-come, first-served basis ($17–19 per site). Individual campgrounds tend to fill in July and August in roughly the following order: Jenny Lake (50 tent/10 walk-in sites; no RVs), Signal Mountain (81 sites), Colter Bay (370 sites), Lizard Creek (60 sites), and Gros Ventre (355 sites). For **back-country camping**, you'll need a permit, available free from the Moose and Colter Bay visitor centers and the Jenny Lake Ranger Station.

The park **restaurants and snack bars**, especially at *Jackson Lake Lodge*, are good but a little pricey. Within the Dornan's complex in Moose, the *Pizza Pasta Company* (ⓣ307/733-2415) serves good pizzas, salads, and sandwiches, best chased down with a bottle from *Dornan's Wine Shoppe* next door. Be sure to earmark time for an evening **drink** at the *Blue Heron Lounge* inside *Jackson Lake Lodge*, where you can recline in comfortable chairs and ogle through huge picture windows the warm blues, grays, purples, and pinks of a Teton sunset.

Jackson

More Mild West than Wild West thanks to an overflow of art galleries and high-end lodging, **JACKSON** makes for an enjoyable base, tucked in at the end of **Jackson Hole**, five miles from Grand Teton National Park's southern boundary. Centered around a tree-shaded square marked by an arch of tangled elk antlers at each corner, the Old West–style boardwalks of **downtown** front boutiques, galleries, and a range of restaurants and bars. In winter, time is best spent visiting the 25,000-acre **National Elk Refuge** on the north edge of town (the source of the town square's antler arches), where you can take a horse-drawn sleigh ride among a 7000-strong herd of elk (daily early Dec–early April 10am–4pm; $16; ⓣ307/733-9212, ⓦwww.fws.gov/nationalelkrefuge); rides depart from the Jackson Hole & Greater Yellowstone Visitor Center along US-26/89/191 (see below) several times an hour. Across the highway from the elk refuge, the **National Museum of Wildlife Art** (daily: summer 9am–5pm; winter Mon–Sat 9am–5pm, Sun 1–5pm; ⓣ307/733-5771 or 1-800/313-9553, ⓦwww.wildlifeart.org; $10) houses an impressive global collection that trails only Cody's Buffalo Bill Historical Center (see p.810) for best museum in the region.

While busiest in summer with road-tripping national park visitors, Jackson remains a year-round draw thanks to **Jackson Hole Mountain Resort** (lift tickets $87; ⓣ307/733-2292 or 1-888/333-7669, ⓦwww.jacksonhole.com), a twenty-minute drive from downtown to **Teton Village** at its base. Justifiably famous, the resort's 2500 acres of terrain are some of the best in the US for confident intermediates and advanced skiers and boarders. Within town, **Snow King** ($41; ⓣ307/733-5200 or 1-800/522-5464, ⓦwww.snowking.com) is an affordable, family-friendly hill that's also lit for night skiing, while **Grand Targhee Resort** ($66; ⓣ307/353-2300 or 1-800/827-4433, ⓦwww.grandtarghee.com), an hour's drive away on the Wyoming/Idaho border, is renowned for fresh powder. Come summer, all three resorts offer limited lift-accessed mountain biking, along with a host of other outdoor activities, including hiking and paragliding.

Arrival, information, and activities

Jackson's **airport** is actually within Grand Teton National Park, eight miles to the north; it's linked to town by AllTrans **shuttle service** ($15 single to Jackson, $23 to Teton Village; ⓣ307/733-3135 or 1-800/443-6133, ⓦwww.jacksonholealltrans.com). **Taxi** fare from the airport is $25–30 into town and $45–50 to Teton Village, the latter taking 45 minutes to reach in winter due to closed roads. If you're flying into neighboring Idaho or Utah, AllTrans operates its direct **shuttle service** daily between Jackson and Idaho Falls (2hr; $40 single), Pocatello (3hr; $48), and Salt Lake City (5.5hr; $75).

Visit the excellent **Jackson Hole & Greater Yellowstone Visitor Center** at 532 N Cache St (daily: late May–late September 8am–7pm, rest of year 9am–5pm; ⓣ307/733-3316, ⓦwww.jacksonholechamber.com) for all kinds of information on northwest Wyoming. Nearby, the staff at **Bridger-Teton National Forest Headquarters**, 340 N Cache St (Mon–Fri 8am–4.30pm; ⓣ307/739-5500), can help you plan hiking and camping trips in the Gros Ventre Mountains, east of town.

Transportation around Jackson Hole is provided by START buses (ⓣ307/733-4521, ⓦwww.startbus.com), operating from roughly 6.30am to 10pm daily; rides within town are free, while trips to Teton Village are $3 single. Gray Line (ⓣ307/733-4325 or 1-800/443-6133, ⓦwww.graylinejh.com; $85) offers hurried, single-day **bus tours** of Grand Teton, though you're better off renting a car and touring at your own pace. Guided **bike tours** in the area are run by Teton

Mountain Bike Tours (T 1-800/733-0788, W www.tetonmtbike.com) and start at $60 for a half-day tour, including equipment.

Dozens of **rafting** companies in Jackson offer float trips within Grand Teton and whitewater trips on the Snake River south of town; expect to pay about $55 for a half-day trip, including transportation and outerwear. Two longtime local guide companies are Dave Hansen Whitewater, 435 N Cache St (T 307/733-6295 or 1-800/732-6295, W www.davehansenwhitewater.com), and Mad River at 1255 South Hwy-89 (T 1-800/458-7238, W www.mad-river.com).

Accommodation

Accommodation in Jackson is fairly expensive in summer; rates drop by around 25 percent in winter and are good value for a ski vacation. It's the opposite case in Teton Village, where the ski-in ski-out accommodation is at a premium come winter. If **camping** is your goal, you're best off staying at Grand Teton's enormous *Gros Ventre Campground* a few miles to the north (see p.823).

The Alpine House 285 N Glenwood St T 307/739-1570, W www.alpinehouse.com. You won't receive better service at five-star resorts than what you'll get at this cozy, 22-room B&B on a quiet street a few blocks from the town square. Breakfasts are equally extraordinary. 7–9

Anvil Motel 215 N Cache St T 307/733-3668, or 1-800/234-4507, W www.anvilmotel.com. Situated at one of Jackson's busier intersections, it's not the quietest spot, but the smallish rooms are in good shape. A bunker below the motel contains the "Bunkhouse," a joyless dorm space ($25) that's only worth considering if traveling solo. Winter 3–4, summer 4–5

The Inn at Jackson Hole 3345 W Village Drive, Teton Village T 307/733-2311 or 1-800/842-7666, W www.innatjh.com. 83 mid-size rooms, along with a few lofts. Amenities include heated outdoor pool and hot tub, laundry, on-site tuning shop, and a popular restaurant, *Masa Sushi*. Winter 8, summer 7

Four Seasons Resort Jackson Hole 7680 Granite Loop Rd, Teton Village T 307/732-5000 or 1-800/914-5110, W www.fourseasons.com/jacksonhole. Teton Village's largest slopeside structure features a main lounge cast in rough-hewn stones and native artifacts. Elegant suites come with marble bathroom counters and leather couches, while the heated outdoor pool, massive fitness center and spa, and full ski concierge services are all to be expected for nightly rates starting in the $500 range. 9

The Hostel 3315 Village Drive, Teton Village T 307/733-3415, W www.thehostel.us. Excellent slopeside hostel features a lounge with fireplace, TV and game room, and laundry, as well as ping-pong and pool tables. Note that each private room, either with king bed or four twin beds, is rented as a unit, and sometimes requires a five-night minimum stay. Winter 5, summer 4

The Wort Hotel 50 N Glenwood St T 307/733-2190 or 1-800/322-2727, W www.worthotel.com. Built in 1941, the Wort is the most venerable high-end property in town, combining old-world style with modern facilities that include two large hot tubs, a grill-bistro, and the attractive *Silver Dollar Bar & Grill*. 9

Eating and nightlife

The year-round tourist trade makes Jackson the best town in Wyoming for nightlife, with its ever-changing roster of **restaurants** and **bars**.

Mangy Moose Teton Village T 307/733-4913. Legendary ski-bum hangout, famed for its apres-ski sessions that segue into evenings of live rock or reggae. The bustling upstairs dining room does decent burgers, chicken, and pasta. Cover charge for live music $7–25.

Million Dollar Cowboy Bar 25 N Cache St T 307/733-2207. Everyone at least ducks once into this hugely touristy watering hole to sit on one of the saddles at the bar; there are also four pool tables and frequent live bands. Cover most nights $5–8.

Nani's Genuine Pasta House 242 N Glenwood St T 307/733-3888. Charming, if overpriced Italian restaurant serving up enormous platters of pasta. Red and white checkered tablecloths and a pleasant outdoor patio add to the ambiance.

Pearl Street Bagels 145 W Pearl St T 307/739-1218. Popular local spot for fresh bagels and coffee beverages.

Rendezvous Bistro 380 S Broadway T 307/739-1100. Moderately priced bistro on the outskirts of town, where a clever menu of main courses includes chili-rubbed pork chops and crispy risotto cake. An impressively diverse wine list accompanies.

Shades Cafe 82 S King St ⓣ307/733-2015. Unpretentious and affordable spot, with excellent breakfasts early and light, healthy lunches (soups, sandwiches, burritos) come afternoon. The lovely deck is a popular hangout on mild-weather days. Closed evenings.

Snake River Brewing Co 265 South Millward St ⓣ307/739-2337. Great locals' brewpub a few blocks southwest of the town square. Reasonably priced pastas and wood-fired pizzas are well worth trying, but it's the award-winning beers that pack 'em in.

Montana

MONTANA's wondrous Big Sky country, along the northernmost edge of the US portion of the Rocky Mountains, is a region of snowcapped summits, turbulent rivers, spectacular glacial valleys, heavily wooded forests, and sparkling blue lakes. The scenery is at its most dramatic in the **western** side of the state, especially **Glacier National Park**. By contrast, the **eastern** two-thirds is high prairie: sun-parched in summer and wracked by blizzards in winter. Grizzly bears, elk, and bighorn sheep are found in greater numbers in Montana than just about anywhere else on the continent.

Each of Montana's small cities has its own proud identity. The enjoyable town of **Missoula** is a laidback college town; the historic copper-mining hamlet of **Butte** is a hardscrabble union stronghold; the elegant state capital **Helena** harkens back to its prosperous gold-mining years; and **Bozeman**, just to the south, is one of the hippest mountain towns in the US.

Wheat, lumber, and (coal) mining form the contemporary base of Montana's economy. Tourism is the state's second biggest earner; however, apart from skiing, the harsh climate generally restricts tourist activities to the summer months.

Getting around Montana

Considering Montana's hulking size and sparse population, transportation connections could be worse. **Flights** can be booked to Kalispell, Billings, Bozeman, Great Falls, and Missoula, while Amtrak **trains** run across the north on the *Empire Builder* route, stopping east and west of Glacier National Park, and at Essex in the summer. Greyhound runs a number of **bus** lines on I-90 and I-15, while Rimrock Stages (ⓣ1-800/255-7655, ⓦwww.rimrocktrailways.com) runs regular routes through the major towns (except for Bozeman). Western Montana, in particular, is great **cycling** territory; the Adventure Cycling organization (ⓣ1-800/755-2453, ⓦwww.adventurecycling.org), whose national headquarters are in Missoula, can provide special maps. Clearly, the best way to get around is by **car**, with practically every interstate exit in the west leading to mountain retreats, striking landmarks, or pleasant hamlets.

Eastern Montana

Before ranchers and farmers settled the flat prairie of **eastern Montana**, it was prime **buffalo** territory: one early traveler waited three nights while a massive herd crossed his path. Native Americans fought hard to hold onto their land; the crushing defeats they inflicted on the US Army include the legendary victory at **Little Bighorn**. However, the ongoing spectre of white colonization was enforced with heartless martial rigor – the military nearly wiped out the buffalo by the 1870s, thus depleting the natives' major food source. The result ensured that by the end of the nineteenth century the native peoples would be marginalized, ultimately confined to reservations and without a voice (or often, a stake) in the lucrative mineral exploitation of the land – a depressing and all-too-common occurrence in the triumphalist "Manifest Destiny" America of the time.

The plains are intermittently broken by mountains, of which the most impressive are the icy **Beartooth Range**, crammed between the town of Red Lodge and Yellowstone National Park. Most of the region's towns are sleepy agricultural centers, stopovers on the way to outlying historical or natural attractions. Even **Billings**, Montana's largest city, would feel like a small town anywhere else.

Little Bighorn Battlefield National Monument

By the middle of the 1870s, the bloody and exhausting **Indian Wars** had been going on for decades in the American West, fueled by white colonists' desires for land and, increasingly, **gold**. Unfortunately for the native Lakota and Cheyenne, the valuable ore was discovered on their Black Hills land, and the predictable onrush occurred. With tensions mounting, in June 1876, massive army detachments were sent to southeastern Montana led by the crack **Seventh Cavalry** and, at its head, flamboyant **General George Custer** — who had first commanded the exploratory expedition that discovered the gold. Perhaps unrivaled in American history for fame or opprobrium, he then led the military to one of its most enduring defeats at **Little Bighorn** (see box).

Located on the current Crow Indian Reservation in the Little Big Horn Valley, the **monument** is 56 miles southeast of Billings, with the entrance one mile east of I-90 on US-212. You can trace the course of the battle on a five-mile, self-guided driving tour through the grasslands (daily 8am–dusk; $10 per car, $5 for pedestrians and motorcycles; Ⓦwww.nps.gov/libi), below the high ridge overlooking the valley, or on a narrated bus tour (spring–fall 10am-3pm; $8, kids $2). White-marble tablets mark where individual soldiers fell, and a sandstone obelisk stands above their mass grave on "Last Stand Hill" (Custer himself was buried at the West Point Military Academy in New York). Dioramas in the **visitor center and museum** (Ⓣ406/638-3204) outline the battle, while the US military **cemetery** nearby holds soldiers from all of America's wars.

Hardin, thirteen miles northwest, makes its living from tourists seeking authentic native artifacts and Western mementos. Each year, on the weekend closest to the battle's anniversary, the **Little Bighorn Days** festival centers on re-enactments of the battle at a site eight miles west of the town (*not* the original battlefield; Ⓦwww.custerslaststand.org). Other activities include tribal dancing, downtown parades, dinner dances, and a rodeo.

The least expensive place to **stay** is the *Western Motel*, off Hwy-313 at 830 W Third St (Ⓣ406/665-2296, Ⓦwesternmotel.net; ❸), and the *Kendrick House Inn*, 206 N Custer Ave (Ⓣ406/665-3035; ❺), is a worthwhile B&B offering five rooms rich with old-time antique decor. *The Purple Cow*, 1485 Hwy-47 N (Ⓣ406/665-3601), is a cheerful family **diner** serving home-cooked feasts.

Custer's Last Stand

During an erratic career, **George Armstrong Custer** was one of the central American military icons of the late nineteenth century. Though he graduated last in his class at West Point in 1861, he became the army's youngest-ever brigadier general, seeing action at Gettysburg and national fame through his presence at the ultimate Union victory at Appomattox, with his own troops blocking the Confederate retreat. However, he was also suspended for ordering the execution of deserters from a forced march he led through Kansas, and found notoriety for allowing the murder in 1868 of almost one hundred Cheyenne women and children. His most (in)famous moment, though, came on June 25, 1876, at the **Battle of the Little Bighorn**, known to native tribes as the **Battle of the Greasy Grass**.

Custer's was the first unit to arrive in the **Little Bighorn Valley**. Disdaining to await reinforcements, he set out to raze a tepee village along the Little Bighorn River – which turned out to be the largest-ever gathering of Plains Indians. As a party of his men pursued fleeing women and children, they were encircled by two thousand Lakota and Cheyenne warriors emerging from either side of a ravine. The soldiers dismounted to attempt to shoot their way out, but were soon overwhelmed; simultaneously, Custer's command post on a nearby hill was wiped out. Although American myth through the 1960s established Custer as an unquestioned hero, archeologists and historians have since discounted the idea of **Custer's Last Stand** as a heroic act of defiance in which Custer was the last cavalryman left standing; the battle lasted less than an hour, with the white soldiers being systematically and effortlessly picked off. This most decisive Native American victory in the West – led by Sitting Bull – was also their final great show of resistance. An incensed President Grant piled maximum resources into a military campaign that brought about the effective defeat of all Plains Indians by the end of the decade.

Billings

By Montana standards, **BILLINGS** is a big city. It has a dramatic setting, bounded on its north and east sides by the 400ft crumpled sandstone cliffs of the **Rimrock**, and has made an attempt to spruce itself up with an attractive and lively row of galleries, bars, and restaurants along Montana Avenue. The most prominent historical gem is the **Moss Mansion**, 914 Division St (June–Sept Mon–Sat 9am–4pm, Sun 1–3pm; Oct–May daily 1–3pm; $7; Ⓦwww.mossmansion.com), a sturdy 1903 red-sandstone manse that appeals for its late-Victorian decor and glimpse at how comfortably a handful of Western elites – in this case, a publisher and industrialist – lived a century ago. Another striking structure, a former Romanesque Revival library at 2822 Montana Ave, now houses the **Western Heritage Center** (Tues–Sat 10am–5pm; $3; Ⓦwww.ywhc.org), where you can bone up on the region's history through antique documents, relics and photographs.

Just north of Montana Avenue, you can dress like a cowboy thanks to Lou Taubert Ranch Outfitters, 123 N Broadway (Ⓣ406/245-2248), which has an enormous selection of hats, boots, shirts, jeans, and jackets. A couple of blocks northeast, the **Yellowstone Art Museum**, 401 N 27th St (Tues–Sat 10am–5pm, Thurs closes 8pm, Sun noon–5pm; $7; Ⓦyellowstone.artmuseum.org), partly housed in the town's 1910 jail, specializes in Western exhibits, including absorbing book illustrations, paintings, and posters by cowboy illustrator Will James.

Billings' **bus station** is at 2502 First Ave N (Ⓣ406/245-5116). For **accommodation**, try the cheery *C'mon Inn*, 2020 Overland Ave S (Ⓣ1-800/655-1170, Ⓦwww.cmoninn.com; ❺), an agreeable spot whose rooms variously offer fireplaces, jacuzzis, and fridges, plus continental breakfast; or the five cozy rooms and suites of the always-reliable *Josephine B&B*, 514 N 29th St (Ⓣ406/248-5898,

Ⓦwww.thejosephine.com; ❹), which has the added draw of free wi-fi and passes to a nearby gym. For **eating**, the town is strong on meat-and-potatoes fare, but the height of classic dining may be *The Rex*, 2401 Montana Ave (Ⓣ406/245-7477), which has top-flight steaks and serviceable seafood in a structure dating back nearly a hundred years.

Red Lodge and the Beartooth Scenic Highway

The atmospheric town of **RED LODGE** is sixty miles south of Billings at the foot of the awe-inspiring **Beartooth Mountains** – whose jagged peaks and outcrops contain some of the oldest rocks on earth – and in winter acts as a base for skiers using the popular **Red Lodge Mountain**, six miles west on US-212 (lift tickets $46; Ⓣ406/446-2610 or 1-800/444-8977, Ⓦwww.redlodgemountain.com). Originally founded to mine coal for the transcontinental railroads, Red Lodge's future was secured by the construction of the 65-mile **Beartooth Scenic Highway**, connecting to Cooke City at the northeastern entrance to Yellowstone National Park (see p.812), a striking series of tight switchbacks, steep grades, and exciting overlooks. Even in summer the springy tundra turf of the 10,940ft **Beartooth Pass** is covered with snow that (due to algae) turns pink when crushed. All around are gem-like corries, deeply gouged granite walls, and huge blocks of roadside ice. Contact the **Beartooth Ranger District** of Custer National Forest (office in Billings at 1310 Main St, Ⓣ406/657-6200, Ⓦwww.fs.fed.us/r1/custer), for more information on the rugged options for hiking and **camping** (free or $5–12) in this chilly, wind-scoured terrain, and taking in the fine views of the Beartooth area and the abundant bighorn sheep, elk, and bear.

Though Red Lodge has plenty of cheap motels south of town, the nicest **place to stay** is the lovely *Pollard Hotel*, 2 N Broadway (Ⓣ406/446-0001 or 1-800/POLLARD; ❺), an 1893 brick building with some rooms offering jacuzzis and balconies, plus pool, sauna, and comfortable old library, where Western icons Buffalo Bill, Calamity Jane, and others have stayed. Slightly cheaper, the *Lupine Inn*, 702 S Hauser (Ⓣ1-888/567-1321, Ⓦwww.lupineinn.com; ❺) has on-site pool and spa, rooms with wi-fi and kitchenettes, and continental breakfast. Some of the best **food** in town is served in *Pollard*'s dining room, which offers fresh, local fare – leaning toward beef and fish – while on Broadway, *Bridge Creek Backcountry Kitchen*, no. 116 S (Ⓣ406/446-9900), serves fine clam chowder alongside steak and burgers, and *Carbon County Steakhouse*, no. 121 S (Ⓣ406/446-4025), has hearty pasta, ribs, steak, and seafood, as well as Rocky Mountain Oysters — bull testicles, to the uninitiated.

Fort Peck Lake

Some two hundred miles north of Billings, lonely Hwy-2 is an isolated, both bleak and beautiful stretch that runs from Glacier National Park to North Dakota, peppered with remote villages, Indian Wars battlefields, and striking vistas. The highlight is the irregular, massive expanse of 130-mile-long **Fort Peck Lake**, with 1500 miles of erratic shoreline, which the New Deal created in the 1930s by damming the Missouri River. The main draw is **fishing** for trout, bass and pike (licenses $5–15, see Ⓦfwp.mt.gov/fishing). In the adjacent million-acre **Charles M. Russell Wildlife Refuge** (Ⓣ406/438-8706, Ⓦwww.fws.gov/cmr) you can spot pronghorn antelope, elk, deer, and bighorn sheep. Fossils — among them *T rex* and *triceratops* bones discovered around the site — are on view in the dam's **interpretive center** (May–Sept daily 9am–5pm, Oct–April Mon–Fri 10am–4pm;

free; ⓣ406/526-3493). On the lake's south side, about 25 miles north of Jordan, off Hwy-200, **Hell Creek State Park** is a popular, serviceable spot for **camping** ($15–18; ⓣ406/234-0900, ⓦwww.recreation.gov), and has some of the best walleye fishing in the country. As with the other campgrounds in the area, this one is quite remote and only accessible by rugged country road. Use a four-wheel-drive vehicle to explore these parts.

Western Montana

Western Montana offers a beautifully expansive, almost unreal, setting where the big skies must be seen to be believed, and you'll encounter entirely different weather from one horizon to the next. The region is replete with outdoor adventures, especially in glorious **Glacier National Park**, one of America's greatest natural wonders. The only old-time mining camps that have grown into substantial settlements are the genteel state capital **Helena** and craggy **Butte**, which made its money from copper. Between them, they conjure up more of a feel for the rambunctious times, the lust for profit, and the hardships of the industrial era than all the ghost towns in the Rockies combined.

Bozeman and around

Fetching **BOZEMAN** lies at the north end of the lush Gallatin Valley, 142 miles west of Billings and ninety miles north of Yellowstone. The stately Victorian storefronts along busy **Main Street** are some of the most historic in the West (with some seven hundred on the National Register of Historic Places), and it's here where you can find many solid choices for dining, drinking, and shopping.

South of downtown, the huge **Museum of the Rockies** 600 W Kagy Blvd at S Seventh Avenue (summer daily 8am–8pm; rest of year Mon–Sat 9am–5pm, Sun 12.30–5pm; $10; ⓦwww.museumoftherockies.org) features Native American weapons, biology exhibits, a planetarium, Western landscape paintings, and a well-preserved, walk-in 1889 farmhouse constructed from logs and built from a catalog design. The collection is best known, though, for its stunning dinosaur finds — among them the world's largest-known skull of a *T rex*, one of the museum's twelve sets of bones from that species. Smaller in scale, the **Pioneer Museum**, 317 W Main St (June–Aug Mon–Sat 10am–5pm, rest of year Tues–Sat 11am–4pm; $3; ⓦwww.pioneermuseum.org), is also worth a look, housed in a crenellated old jail from 1911, with an intriguing selection of historic objects, including a replica log cabin, scale-model pioneer wagons and army forts, and a gallows for hanging town miscreants. From the museum you can take **walking tours** (brochures from visitor center, below) of Main Street's elegant structures, its districts strewn with grand nineteenth-century mansions, and even the local cemetery where the town's bigwigs are buried. More unexpectedly, the **American Computer Museum**, Bridger Park Mall, 2304 N 7th Ave, suite B (June–Aug daily 10am–4pm; Sept–May Tues–Sat noon–4pm, Thurs closes 8pm; $5; ⓦwww.compustory.org), follows the evolution of computers, from their bulky, awkward beginnings to today's tiny, lightning-fast marvels.

Practicalities

Greyhound stops at 1205 E Main St, and the **visitor center** is at 224 E Main St (ⓣ406/586-4008, ⓦwww.historicbozeman.com), providing maps and information plus limited free internet access. **Hotels** in Bozeman tend toward the familiar chain variety, so you may be better off at a distinctive **B&B** like *Lehrkind Man-*

sion, 719 N Wallace Ave (Ⓣ1-800/992-6932, Ⓦwww.bozemanbedandbreakfast.com; ❻), which occupies a delightful Queen Anne home and nearby garden house, together offering nine rooms richly appointed with Victorian antiques and Old West-styled furniture. Alternatively, those searching for an authentic Montana experience might enjoy the *Howlers Inn*, 3185 Jackson Creek Rd (Ⓣ1-888/469-5377, Ⓦwww.howlersinn.com; ❺), which, true to its name, sits next to a small wolf sanctuary and features jacuzzi, sauna, and rooms with DVD players and microwaves. For budget travellers, the basic but friendly *International Backpackers Hostel*, 405 W Olive St (Ⓣ406/586-4659, Ⓦwww.bozemanbackpackershostel.com), has six bunk beds for $20 each and a pair of private rooms for $42.

Bozeman boasts plenty of good **places to eat**. The *Community Co-op*, 908 W Main St (Ⓣ406/587-4039, Ⓦwww.bozo.coop), serves terrific vegetarian dishes, deli sandwiches, and mouth-watering desserts. Other favorites include the *McKenzie River Pizza Co.*, 232 E Main St (Ⓣ406/587-0055) and eight other Montana locations, which has twenty different kinds of pizza - try the chili-laden Branding Iron for a kick – and *John Bozeman's Bistro*, 125 W Main St (Ⓣ406/587-4100), with its fine duck, lamb, and elk dishes, plus a nice array of tapas. For **drinking** *Montana Ale Works*, 611 E Main St (Ⓣ406/587-7700), has dozens of regional microbrews along with solid steaks and burgers.

Outdoor activities

Bozeman is well placed for those seeking **outdoor activities**, particularly in rugged Hyalite Canyon just south of town (Ⓦwww.hyalitecanyon.com), which has top-notch hiking and mountain biking in summer and excellent ice climbing in winter, or at the challenging ski area, **Bridger Bowl** (lift tickets $45; Ⓣ406/587-2111, Ⓦwww.bridgerbowl.com). An hour's drive south down the beautiful Gallatin Valley is the much pricier **Big Sky Resort** (lift tickets $78; Ⓣ1-800/548-4486, Ⓦwww.bigskyresort.com; hotel rooms ❺+), popular for its top-quality powder and steep slopes on 11,166ft Lone Mountain.

Three miles north of I-90, thirty miles west of Bozeman, **Missouri Headwaters State Park** ($5 per vehicle; camping $12–15; Ⓣ406/994-4042), marks the place where the Missouri River begins its circuitous journey to the Mississippi. Its marshy grasslands beneath a shallow bluff were seen by Lewis and Clark in July 1805; fur trappers who followed in their wake included Kit Carson, and traces remain of the nineteenth-century town they created. These days the park has plenty of good fishing, hiking, and birdwatching. Another fifteen miles west, **Lewis & Clark Caverns State Park** (tours 9am–4.30pm, summer until 6.30pm; $10; Ⓣ406/287-3541) offers a fascinating underworld of limestone spires and pillars, which you can see on rugged two-hour, two-mile **walking tours**; bring sturdy shoes and a jacket – the temperature is a consistent 50°F. To stay in the park, three **cabins** ($40) are available. For details on more outdoor activities, check with the **ranger office**, in Bozeman at 3710 Fallon St (Mon–Fri 8am–4.30pm; Ⓣ406/522-2520, Ⓦwww.fs.fed.us/r1/gallatin), which also provides information on hiking trails.

Butte and around

Eighty miles west of Bozeman, the former copper-mining colossus of **BUTTE** (as in "root") sits on a steep hillside where massive black headframes – "gallows frames" to miners – of long-abandoned pits soar up among dirty-yellow slag heaps, making it one of the most polluted parts of the US. Still, it's an oddly compelling landscape, best appreciated at dusk, when the golden light casts a glow on the mine-pocked hillsides, and the old neon signs illuminate historic brick buildings. Among immigrants to leave their mark here were miners from **Ireland** – Butte still hosts the biggest St

Patrick's Day celebrations in the Rockies – and **Cornwall**; the traditional meat-and-potato pasty (*PASS-tee)* is still served in many cafés — and tough enough to survive being dropped for lunch to miners in their shafts.

From its early days, Butte was a pillar of unionism, as miners obtained a minimum wage and an eight-hour day, and it became impossible to get work without a union card. By the 1950s the focus had switched from traditional mining in shafts to ugly open pits. Today only the Continental Pit mine is in use. To take a look at the ecological disaster that is the 1800-foot-deep, 5600-foot-wide, and 7000-foot-long **Berkeley Pit**, head for Continental Drive. Here, a viewing platform surveys the most toxic stretch of water in the United States (more information at Ⓦwww.pitwatch.org).

Butte is both rich with toxins and with Victorian architecture, its six thousand preserved buildings putting it firmly on the National Historic Register. On West Park Street, the excellent **World Museum of Mining** (April–Oct daily 9am–6pm; $7; Ⓦwww.miningmuseum.org) is packed with fascinating memorabilia, and outside, beyond the scattered collection of rusting machinery – from jackhammers to mine carts – the museum's 50-building **Hell Roarin' Gulch** re-creates a cobbled-street mining camp, complete with saloon, bordello, church, schoolhouse, and Chinese laundry. Above it all looms the blackened, 100ft headframe of the 3200-foot-deep **Orphan Girl** mineshaft. To get a handle on the town's colorful history, take a **walking tour** with Old Butte Historical Adventures, 117 N Main St (May–Oct daily; $10; Ⓣ406/498-3424, Ⓦwww.buttetours.info), which covers the area's architecture, mines, railway lines, a speakeasy, and even journeys to the region's ghost towns (prices vary; by appointment only).

Few of Butte's mining baron residences are grander than the 34-room **Copper King Mansion**, 219 W Granite St (tours May–Sept daily 9am–4pm; $7; Ⓣ406/782-7580, Ⓦwww.thecopperkingmansion.com). Along with frescoed ceilings, handcrafted woodwork, and chandeliers and fireplaces, the mansion also has the draw of being a B&B, where you can stay amid tasteful old-time luxury for as little as $65 a night. Another curiosity is the 26-room **Arts Chateau**, 321 W Broadway (June-Sept Mon–Fri 7.30am–4pm, also Fri 7–11pm, Sat 9am–4pm, Sun 10am–2pm; $5; Ⓣ406/723-7600), nothing less than a mock-French castle — splendid with its spiral staircase, exotic-wood-inlaid rooms, and wrought-iron decor. It now holds Victorian furniture and antiques, as well as a rotating selection of contemporary regional art. By contrast, in an old noodle parlor at 17 W Mercury St, the **Mai Wah Museum** (June–Sept Tues–Sat 11am–5pm; donation; Ⓦwww.maiwah.org) focuses on the history of the Chinese community with an intriguing collection of photos, cooking implements, kites, fireworks, menus, and books. The community was six hundred strong at the end of the nineteenth century, but by the 1940s widespread racism had reduced it to just a few families.

At night the 90ft **Our Lady of the Rockies** statue, 3100 Harrison Ave (Ⓦwww.ourladyoftherockies.org), is illuminated by floodlights. Built entirely by voluntary labor, it was set in place on top of the Continental Divide, some 3500ft above Butte, by helicopter.

Practicalities

Greyhound **buses** drop off downtown at 1324 Harrison Ave. From June to August, ninety-minute **trolley tours** of town (9am, 11am, 1.30pm, & 3.30pm; $7) leave from the **Chamber of Commerce**, 1000 George St (June–Aug daily 8am–6pm; Sept daily 8am–5pm; Oct–May Mon–Fri 9am–5pm; Ⓣ406/723-3177, Ⓦwww.buttecvb.org). Good **accommodation** (along with Copper King Mansion; see above) includes the 1924 *Finlen Hotel*, 100 E Broadway (Ⓣ406/723-5461, Ⓦwww.finlen.com; ❸), which has basic but functional rooms in a classic 1924 building;

and *Toad Hall Manor*, 1 Green Lane (1-866/443-TOAD, Ⓦwww.toadhallmanor.com; ❹), a quite stylish B&B in a stately neo-Georgian house, whose four units variously come with jacuzzis, fridges, microwaves, and courtyards.

Butte has plenty of good places to **eat and drink**, most of them uptown. *Joe's Pasty Shop*, 1641 Grand Ave (Ⓣ406/723-9071), serves up the hearty, meat-filled Cornish dish with vigor, while the *Pekin Noodle Parlor*, at 117 S Main St (Ⓣ406/782-2217), is an old-fashioned Cantonese joint with a menu that stretches from chow mein and fried wontons to sandwiches and steaks. A bit more upscale, the *Uptown Café*, 47 E Broadway (Ⓣ406/723-4735), serves pizza, pasta, and sandwiches, but is best known for its steak-and-seafood dinner entrees and inexpensive, fixed ($12.50) five-course meals, while *Lockett's Bakery*, 2000 Farragut Ave (Ⓣ406/723-8569) has a nice range of Danishes and pastries, bread and doughnuts for a morning pick-me-up.

The Grant-Kohrs Ranch

The National Historic Site of **GRANT-KOHRS RANCH**, 266 Warren Lane in the town of Deer Lodge (June–Aug 8am–5.30pm, Sept–May 9am–4.30pm; free; Ⓦwww.nps.gov/grko), lies forty miles west of Butte on I-90. In operation since 1860, this true West cattle ranch, under the guidance of "Montana Cattle King" **Conrad Kohrs**, was once the hub of ten million acres of range property and many thousands of Hereford and Shorthorn cows. Though its holdings are substantially reduced these days, the ranch still has its share of cows and draft horses on view. It also displays authentic buggies and wagons around its preserved old barns, and **wagon tours** around the site are available in the summer (Thurs–Mon 9am–5pm on the hour; $5). In its blacksmith shop you can watch horseshoes and irons being worked over an anvil (summer only). Compare the pleasant Victorian environs of the house of the first owner, John Grant, with the much humbler conditions the ranch hands tolerated in Bunkhouse Row.

Helena and around

An hour north of Butte on I-15, **HELENA** offers a fine view over the golden-brown **Prickly Pear Valley**, and was founded in 1864 when a party of prospectors hit the jackpot at what is now **Last Chance Gulch**, the town's attractive main street, whose stately Romanesque and Neoclassical buildings are now home to gift shops, diners, and bars. Above it all looms the **Old Fire Tower**, off-limits to interlopers but still worth a short walk to see the latest in fire prevention, circa 1876. During the boom years, more than $20 million of gold was extracted from the gulch, and fifty successful prospectors remained here as millionaires. Their palatial residences grace the west side of town in the **Mansion District**. Contrast this with the far more modest digs southwest of town in **Reeder's Alley**, a collection of miners' cabins, wooden storehouses, and other humble working-class structures, now refurbished into smart shops and restaurants. Helena has an unexpected Hollywood connection, too: Gary Cooper was born and raised here, and Myrna Loy lived here as a child. Honoring the actress is the **Myrna Loy Center for the Performing Arts**, based out of a former jail at 15 N Ewing St (Ⓣ406/443-0287, Ⓦwww.myrnaloycenter.com), which screens indie films and presents concerts, plays, comedy and more.

Another worthwhile stop is the **Original Governor's Mansion**, 304 N Ewing St (May–Sept Tues–Sat noon–3pm on the hour, rest of year Sat only; $4; Ⓣ406/444-4789), which housed the state's chief executive during the first half of the twentieth century and still impresses with its Queen Anne style and broad decorative-arts collection. The legislative branch has worked since 1902 out of the massive Neoclassical **state capitol**, 1301 E Sixth Ave (Mon–Sat 8am–5pm; free; Ⓦwww.montanacapitol.com), covered with a copper-clad dome and featuring, in the House chamber, a huge mural by "cowboy artist" Charles M. Russell depicting a dramatic encounter between native tribes and Lewis and Clark. You can see more of Russell's work at the excellent **Montana Historical Society Museum**, 225 N Roberts St (Mon–Sat 8am–5pm, Thurs closes 8pm; $5; Ⓦmontanahistoricalsociety.org), as well as early photographs of Montana life, early pioneer and tribal artifacts, and an array of costumes and textiles. True Charles Russell enthusiasts should venture up to Great Falls to see his eponymously named **museum** at 400 13th St N (May–Sept daily 9am–6pm, rest of year Tues–Sat 10am–5pm, Sun 1–5pm; $9; Ⓦwww.cmrussell.org), which displays his many evocative landscape paintings and offers tours of the artist's elegant house.

The majestic red spires of the **Cathedral of St Helena** rise 230ft at 530 N Ewing St (Ⓣ406/442-5825, Ⓦwww.sthelenas.org); the inside is adorned with elaborate Bavarian stained glass, white-marble altars, and gold leaf. Also interesting is the **Holter Museum of Art**, 12 E Lawrence St (Tues–Fri 10am–5.30pm, Sat 10am–4pm, Sun 11.30am–4.30pm; free; Ⓦholtermuseum.org), most notable for its contemporary sculpture and decorative works, and west of downtown, the **Archie Bray Foundation**, 2915 Country Club Ave (Mon–Sat 10am–5pm, Sun 1–5pm; free; Ⓦarchiebray.org), which hosts world-renowned ceramic artists who work while you watch, and displays a broad variety of pottery.

Practicalities

Greyhound connects at Helena's **transit center** at 630 N Last Chance Gulch. In the summer the Historical Society runs hour-long **tours** in an imitation steam train (actually a tram) from the corner of Sixth and Roberts (June–early Sept 11am & 3pm, June also 1pm, July & Aug also 1pm & 5.30pm; $7.50; Ⓦwww.lctours.com). The visitor center is at 225 Cruse Ave (Mon–Fri 9am–5pm; Ⓣ406/447-1530), where you can pick up a free map. Information and maps on local hiking trails are available from **Helena National Forest Ranger Station**, 2001 Poplar St (Mon–Fri 8am–4.30pm, Ⓣ406/449-5490, Ⓦwww.fs.fed.us/r1/helena), which can also direct you to **campgrounds** (summer only; free or $5-8) near the Continental Divide, as well as any of six remote, primitive **cabins** ($25–30; reserve at Ⓣ1-877/444-6777, Ⓦrecreation.gov). However, Helena's most stylish **lodging** is its B&Bs, including *Barrister Bed & Breakfast*, 416 N Ewing St (Ⓣ406/443-7330 or 1-800/823-1148; ⑤), a lovely 1874 Victorian mansion near the cathedral and originally used as priest's quarters, now offering five graceful rooms; *Sanders B&B*, 328 N Ewing St (Ⓣ406/442-3309, Ⓦwww.sandersbb.com; ⑤), whose seven old-fashioned rooms come with Western decor and antiques, some with claw-footed tubs and fireplaces.

Decent places to **eat** include *Bert and Ernie's*, 361 N Last Chance Gulch (Ⓣ406/443-5680), for its deli sandwiches and nice array of pizzas, plus mid-priced seafood and pasta; the *Windbag Saloon*, at no. 19 S (Ⓣ406/443-9669), a big old barn of a place – and former brothel – that serves rib-stuffing seafood, burgers and steaks; and *Miller's Crossing*, 52 S Park Ave (Ⓣ406/442-3290), which has microbrews and eclectic live music.

Gates of the Mountains

For a look at the local topography in all its rugged, unspoiled glory, take a two-hour **boat tour** through the stunning **Gates of the Mountains**, 25 miles north of Helena off Hwy-287 (June-Sept hours vary, generally hourly Mon–Fri 11am–2pm or 3pm, Sat & Sun 10am–4pm; $11; Ⓣ406/458-5241, Ⓦwww.gatesofthemountains.com). This dramatic stretch of the Missouri River, which enters a gorge between sheer 1200ft limestone cliffs that rise abruptly from the northern shores of a tranquil lake, was named by Meriwether Lewis of the Lewis and Clark expedition. The area offers unmatched scenic splendor and plenty of excellent hiking and backpacking opportunities, not to mention an eye-opening array of wildlife, including black bears, eagles, bighorn sheep, beavers, and mountain lions.

Missoula

Framed by the striking Bitterroot and Sapphire mountains, vibrant and friendly **MISSOULA** is full of contrasts – truck-sales yards and bookstores, continental cafés and gun shops – and where students from the local University of Montana provide much of the town's energy. In James Crumley's *Dancing Bear*, it's depicted as "the town with the best bars in a state of great bars."

One sign of Missoula's dynamism is its **Missoula Art Museum**, 335 N Pattee St (Tues–Sat 11am–5pm; free; Ⓦwww.missoulaartmuseum.org), which shows challenging, risk-taking work in digital photography, modern painting and sculpture, and a range of eye-opening pieces by contemporary Native American artists. Elsewhere, on the university campus at Main Hall, the **Montana Museum of Art & Culture** (Wed–Sat 11am–3pm, donation suggested; Ⓦwww.umt.edu/montanamuseum), has a scattershot collection of art highlighted by interesting Renaissance-era Flemish tapestries, modern ceramics, a few gems from William Merritt Chase, Rockwell Kent, and Eugene Atget, and prints by Chagall, Delacroix, Picasso, Toulouse-Lautrec and Ed Ruscha, among others.

For another interesting cultural experience, head out to the 1914 **Fort Missoula** off Hwy-93 S, on whose grounds the **Historical Museum**, in building 322 (summer daily 10am–5pm, Sun opens at noon; $3; mid-Sept–mid–June Tues–Sun noon–5pm; Ⓦwww.fortmissoulamuseum.org), holds rather dry displays on military and agricultural history, but is best for its relocation of a dozen buildings from the Old West days, including a railroad depot, church, and schoolhouse. Unexpected are the World War II internment barracks for Italian nationals and Japanese-Americans, recalling the grim days when the fort was used for confining perceived "enemies," many of whom were US citizens.

Finally, the Forest Service **Smokejumper Center**, ten miles out of town on US-93 at 5764 W Broadway, discusses methods used to train smokejumpers – highly skilled firefighters who parachute into forested areas to stop the spread of wildfires. Fires are legion in this part of the country during the dry season. A small **visitor center** further explains their work (summer 8.30am–5pm; Ⓣ406/329-4934).

Practicalities

Greyhound pulls in at 1660 W Broadway. The more distinctive **accommodation** choices include *Goldsmith's Inn*, 809 E Front St (Ⓣ406/721-6732, Ⓦwww.goldsmithsinn.com; ❺), a quaint 1911 Victorian B&B with nice riverside views, whose units variously offer balconies and fireplaces, and sitting rooms in the suites. The *Doubletree Missoula Edgewater*, 100 Madison St (Ⓣ0 pt06/728-3100, Ⓦwww.doubletree.com; ❼), is near the university right on the Clark Fork River – on which you can conveniently fly-fish – with nice rooms and suites and gym, pool, and hot tub. Some of the cheapest adequate lodging is at *Ruby's Inn*, 4825 N Reserve St (Ⓣ0 pt06/721-0990, Ⓦrubys.montana.com; ❹), which aside from its serviceable rooms also has free high-speed internet, pool, spa, and laundry.

You can **eat** well in Missoula: *The Shack*, 222 W Main St (Ⓣ406/549-9903), is good for its inventive soups and sandwiches, plus some tasty omelets for breakfast; *Mustard Seed*, 2901 Brooks St (Ⓣ0 pt06/542-7333), is popular for its pan-Asian food, including sushi — no mean feat in Montana; the ✱ *Staggering Ox*, 123 E Main

St (Ⓣ406/327-9400), offers the most bizarre take on conventional fare – sub sandwiches baked in a can and presented vertically – but does it very well; and if for some reason you want to go fancy in this most casual of towns, try the *Red Bird*, 111 N Higgins St (Ⓣ406/549-2906), for its pricey vanilla pork loin and grilled bison.

Outdoor activities

Missoula is particularly good for its outdoor activities. The **visitor center**, across the river from the campus, 825 E Front St (Ⓣ406/543-6623, Ⓦwww.missoulachamber.com), can provide details on **trails**, such as the grueling two-mile one leading from its office up **Mount Sentinel**, embellished by the huge concrete letter "M." The top gives a great view of the area, especially the rugged Hellgate River Canyon. Other worthwhile trails traverse **Rattlesnake National Recreation Area**, which, despite the name, claims to be serpent-free; find more information at the local **ranger station**, at Fort Missoula, Building 24 (Mon–Fri 7.30am–4pm; Ⓣ406/329-3750, Ⓦwww.fs.fed.us/r1/lolo). Missoula is excellent for cycling, too, and another good source of information and **trail maps** is the Adventure Cycling Association, 150 E Pine St (Ⓣ406/721-1776); the Bicycle Hangar, 1801 Brooks St (Ⓣ406/728-9537), rents out good-quality bikes.

The most developed of the city's small ski areas is **Montana Snowbowl**, twelve miles northwest, which has a range of slopes for all abilities (lift tickets $36) and boasts a summer **chair lift** (July–early Sept daily noon–5pm; $7, kids free, $2 for bikes; Ⓣ406/549-9777). For state-park **camping** you'll need to backtrack east, either 25 miles on I-90 to small **Beavertail Hill** (May–Sept; $15; Ⓣ406/542-5500), which also has replica tepees to stay in ($25), or forty miles on Hwy-200 and a brief jog on Hwy-83 north to **Salmon Lake** (May–Sept; $15; Ⓣ406/677-6804), which is great for its fishing and swimming in the Clearwater River.

Around Missoula: Garnet Ghost Town

To get a more in-depth look at the rugged days of the Old West, travel east from Missoula some forty miles on I-90, then another ten miles by single-lane gravel road, to **Garnet Ghost Town** (road open May–Dec; summer daily 10am–5pm, rest of year Sat & Sun 11am–3pm; $3; Ⓦwww.garnetghosttown.net), a slice of industrial history that rewards a long look. A century ago, the site was home to hundreds of hard-rock gold miners doing a tough, perilous job. Since the buildings have been kept in their semi-decayed state, the atmosphere is quite arresting: the quiet and lonely specter of vacant, wood-framed saloons, cabins, stores, and a jail. Most intriguing are the three evocative, creaky levels of the **Wells Hotel**, where you can contrast the once-chic parlor and dining area on the ground floor with the bare, spartan floors of the unheated top level, where miners would lay out their bedrolls and bodies in lined, human-sized parking spaces.

Flathead Lake and around

The sheer splendor of the awe-inspiring, 28-mile-long **Flathead Lake** – the largest freshwater lake west of the Mississippi – provides a welcome diversion on the long route north toward Glacier National Park, reached by following US-93 north from I-90. Before getting to the lake, stop off and view the five hundred residents of the 18,500-acre **National Bison Range**, accessible near the town of Moiese, twenty miles west of St Ignatius off Hwy-212 (visitor center: May–mid-Oct daily 8am–6pm, opens 9am on weekends, mid-Oct–April Mon–Fri 8am–4pm; driving concourse: daily 7am–dusk; $5; Ⓦwww.fws.gov/bisonrange). You drive through the striking mountainside scenery past the great horned beasts traveling in herds – best appreciated from the safety of your slow-moving car.

Once you get to the south lakeshore, boats can be rented in **Polson** at Flathead Lake Boat Co, 4 8th Ave (Ⓣ406/883-0999), while summertime lake cruises are offered aboard the *Port Polson Princess* ($17–23; Ⓣ406/883-2448) from *Best Western KwaTaqNuk Resort*, 49708 Hwy-93 E in Polson (Ⓣ406/883-3636 or 1-800/882-6363, Ⓦwww.kwataqnuk.com; ❺), which also has a marina with boat rentals, as well as a grubby casino. As alternate chain accommodation, the *Port Polson Inn*, also overlooking the lake from 502 Hwy-93 E (Ⓣ406/883-5385 or 1-800/654-0682, Ⓦwww.portpolsoninn.com; ❹), is a better, cheaper bet.

Between Polson in the south and Somers in the north, US-93 follows the lake's curving western shore, while the smaller Hwy-36 runs up the east, scrunched beneath the **Mission Mountains**, and is the summer roadside home to countless roadside cherry and berry vendors. Both routes offer superb views of the deep alpine waters, though US-93 is closest to conical **Wild Horse Island** (daily dawn-dusk; free), the lake's largest island, which you can reach by boat. Dozens of bighorn sheep here make regular appearances to hikers on the moderate-to-steep trails – though the untamed equines are rarely seen.

Fishing and pleasure boats also launch at the small resort of **Bigfork** in the northeast, and you can **stay** in town at the smart and cozy *Grand Hotel Bigfork*, 425 Grand Dr (Ⓣ406/837-7377, Ⓦwww.grandhotelbigfork.com; ❻), which is best for its central location, or at the *Candlewycke Inn*, 311 Aero Lane (Ⓣ406/837-6406, Ⓦwww.candlewyckeinn.com; ❼), an antique-laden B&B whose five pleasant units variously come with jacuzzis, skylights, and fridges. For **dining**, there's fine nouveau-French fare at *La Provence*, 408 Bridge St (Ⓣ406/837-2923), or the adequate bars and diners along Electric Avenue. However, don't miss the sugary temptations at *Eva Gates*, 456 Electric Ave (Ⓣ406/837-4356), the town's prime draw for its fudges, jams, and sweets made with **huckleberries**. The quasi-official fruit of the region, the berries show up in everything from ice cream to beer.

Fifteen miles north of the lake, drab **Kalispell** is out of sight of the water, but is a good jumping-off point for trips around the lake or up to Glacier National Park. You can find out more about the attractions of the Flathead Valley at the **visitors center**, 15 Depot Park (Ⓣ406/756-9091, Ⓦwww.fcvb.org). **Accommodation** options around Kalispell include the stylish 1912 *Kalispell Grand Hotel*, 100 Main St (Ⓣ406/755-8100, Ⓦwww.kalispellgrand.com; ❺), whose rooms have free high-speed internet access and continental breakfast; and the *Garrison Inn*, five miles west of Kalispell off Hwy-2 (Ⓣ406/752-5103, Ⓦwww.thegarrisoninn.com; ❻), with three cozy log-cabin-type rooms with rustic decor and nice views. For decent **food**, try the decent Chinese dishes at the *Alley Connection*, 22 1st St W (Ⓣ406/752-7077), or *MacKenzie River Pizza*, 1645 Hwy-93 S (Ⓣ406/756-0060), which has a good range of tasty, savory pies. *Montana Coffee Traders*, 328 W Center St (Ⓣ406/756-2326), along with fine java, has nice wraps, salads, pasta, and burritos.

Whitefish

The tasteful resort of **WHITEFISH**, seventeen miles north of Kalispell, lies on the south shore of beautiful **Whitefish Lake** in the shade of the Whitefish Mountain Ski Resort (lift tickets $54; Ⓣ406/862-2900, Ⓦwww.skiwhitefish.com), one of the area's big-name winter-sports draws, which is also excellent for its **summer hiking**. You can trudge four hard miles up to a restaurant on top of the mountain and take a free chair-lift ride for the descent (uphill it's $12), or **cycle** the narrow roads around the lake and foothills – bikes can be rented from Glacier Cyclery, 326 E 2nd St ($25–30 a day; Ⓣ406/862-6446).

Amtrak drops off downtown, off Central Avenue at 500 Depot St, en route to and from Glacier National Park. There's a useful tourist **information** counter in the depot; the local **Chamber of Commerce** is at 520 E 2nd St (Ⓣ406/862-3501, Ⓦwww.whitefishchamber.com). Try **staying** at one of the 22 homey log cabins of the *North Forty Resort*, 3765 Hwy-40 W (Ⓣ406/862-7740, Ⓦwww.northfortyresort.com; ❻–❼ by season), which come equipped with fireplaces, kitchens, free wi-fi and outdoor barbeques, or one of the nicer **B&Bs**, such as the friendly little *Duck Inn*, by the river at 1305 Columbia Ave (Ⓣ406/862-3825 or 1-800/344-2377, Ⓦwww.duckinn.com; ❺), whose units have soaking tubs and fireplaces; or the timber-chic *Hidden Moose Lodge*, 1735 E Lakeshore Dr (Ⓣ1-888/733-6667, Ⓦwww.hiddenmooselodge.com; ❻), excellent for its outdoor hot tub, hearty breakfasts, and rooms with jacuzzis or private decks. At Whitefish Mountain, *Kandahar, The Lodge* (Ⓣ406/862-6098, Ⓦwww.kandaharlodge.com; ❻), is a stylish affair with spa, sauna, gym, and jacuzzi, and wide range of rooms, suites, lofts, and studios.

For **dining**, the *Tupelo Grille*, 17 Central Ave (Ⓣ406/862-6136), is probably the most esteemed place around, giving your stomach a (pricey) Southern spin with crawfish cakes, andouille ravioli and good ol' shrimp and grits, while you can power down cheaper, but still solid, burgers and pasta at the *Craggy Range Bar & Grill*, 10 Central Ave (Ⓣ406/862-7550). *Great Northern Brewing*, 2 Central Ave (Ⓣ406/863-1000), is Whitefish's finest craft brewer – you may just want to try everything on offer – and if you're looking for a lively **night out**, the *Hellroaring Saloon & Eatery* (Ⓣ406/862-6364) at Whitefish Mountain is the place to be – especially during ski season.

Glacier National Park

Two thousand lakes, a thousand miles of rivers, thick forests, breezy meadows, and awe-inspiring peaks make up one of America's finest attractions, **GLACIER NATIONAL PARK** – a haven for bighorn sheep, mountain goats, black and grizzly bears, wolves, and mountain lions. Although the park does hold 25 small glaciers, it takes its name from the huge flows of ice that carved these immense valleys 20,000 years ago. Outside of summer, the crisp air, freezing-cold waterfalls, and copious snowfall give the impression of being close to the Arctic Circle; in fact, the latitude here is lower than that of London.

Arrival and information

There are several **visitor centers.** One is at the park's main, **western entrance** at **Apgar**, on the shores of gorgeous McDonald Lake, twenty miles east of Whitefish and just 35 miles south of the Canadian border (mid-May–Oct hours vary, often daily 9am–4.30pm, closes 8pm in summer; Nov–April Sat & Sun only), and another at the **east gate** at **St Mary**, seventy miles west of Shelby (daily: mid-May to late June & early Sept to mid-Oct 8am–5pm; late June to early July 8am–9pm; early July to early Sept 7am–8pm). **Logan Pass** (mid-June to mid-Sept; hours vary, often daily 10am–5pm) visitor center stands at the top of the Going-to-the-Sun Road – the one through-road between the two entrances, usually passable between early June and mid-October, though in recent years the park staff have been closing the road in mid-September for maintenance. The park itself is open year-round, however, and it's well worth trekking as far as Lake McDonald or St Mary's Lake even when the road is blocked and the visitor centers are closed. The **entrance fee** of $25 per vehicle (or $12 per individual on foot, bike or motorcycle) is good for seven days, but for an extra $10 you can get a year-round vehicle pass. For **park information** call Ⓣ406/888-7800 or go to Ⓦwww.nps.gov/glac.

Glacier, together with the adjacent, much smaller Waterton Lakes National Park (ⓣ403/859-2224) in Canada, is part of **Waterton-Glacier International Peace Park**, though Going-to-the-Sun Road does not enter Canada. Both parks operate their own fees and regulations, and to get to Waterton's separate entrance, north of St Mary, you have to pass customs and pay a $7 entrance fee (camping is $14–33 per night).

The southern border of Glacier is skirted by US-2, which remains open all year and is an attractive alternative drive. Amtrak **trains** follow the same route, stopping at West Glacier, a short walk from the west gate; East Glacier, thirty miles south of St Mary; and Essex (summer only), in between.

Travelers arriving by **public transportation** can travel around the park via the bright-red vintage "**jammer**" buses (so called because of the need to jam the gears into place) that provide narrated sightseeing tours from the main lodges (June–Sept; $30-90; 2–8hr; ⓣ406/892-2525, ⓦwww.glacierparkinc.com). There's also a functional, one-way **Hiker's Shuttle** (July & Aug; $8) that covers the popular west side of the park and traverses the Going-to-the-Sun Road, while the **East Side Shuttle** (June–mid Sept; $8-40) connects Glacier Park Lodge to Waterton; the transfer point between the two lines is at *Many Glacier Hotel*. **Sun Tours** (June–Sept; ⓣ406/226-9220 or 1-800/786-9220, ⓦwww.glaciersuntours.com) offers guided tours led by members of the Blackfeet tribe.

Accommodation within the park

Accommodation within the park is run by Glacier Park Inc. (all reservations at ⓣ406/892-2525, ⓦwww.glacierparkinc.com), and most of the lodges are open from June into September. The striking *Glacier Park Lodge* in East Glacier (❻) is known for the massive Douglas-fir pillars in its huge lobby, while near West Glacier, the lovely *Lake McDonald Lodge* has an ideal shoreline location and simple motel rooms (❺), more spacious lodge rooms for $36 more, or small rustic cottages outside the complex (❺). More upscale are the *Prince of Wales Hotel* in Waterton, which has mountain-view and lake-view units ($275–345) and luxurious suites ($799). The *Many Glacier Hotel* has pricey suites, with value rooms for half that price (❻–❾). The park's cheapest accommodation is the *Swiftcurrent Motor Inn* at Many Glacier (❺, cabins ❸–❹), good for its access to trails on the northeast side. A bit nicer is the lakeside *Rising Sun Motor Inn* (❺), seven miles in from the east gate at St Mary, as well as the *Village Inn at Apgar* (❺), fronting Lake McDonald with great views.

The park's thirteen **campgrounds** – most ranging from $10 to $20 – often fill up by late morning during July and August; ask at any visitor center for locations and availability or call ⓣ406/888-7800. Most are open from June to mid-September, though there are also several cheap **primitive campgrounds** ($10), which may not include water but do tend to be open longer, in some cases April to November. All sites are first-come, first-served, though you can reserve Fish Creek and St Mary in advance (ⓣ1-800/365-CAMP, ⓦwww.recreation.gov). For overnight backpacking, get a permit from any visitor center.

Accommodation outside the park

The places to **stay** outside Glacier are a bit removed from the park. The quaint 1910 *Belton Chalet*, two miles outside the western entrance (June-Oct; ⓣ406/888-5000, ⓦwww.beltonchalet.com; ❻), offers very basic digs with few amenities other than a few antiques, though the three-bedroom cottages (❾) have fireplaces and balconies; no phone or TV. One- and two-bedroom cabins are rented by the *Glacier Outdoor Center*, off Hwy-2 a half-mile from the west entrance (ⓣ406/888-5454, ⓦwww.glacierraftco.com; ❾); they offer nice modern decor, decks, kitchens, and fireplaces, though at steeper prices than elsewhere.

Halfway between the east and west park gates is **Essex**, where the atmospheric 1939 *Izaak Walton Inn* (Ⓣ406/888-5700, Ⓦwww.izaakwaltoninn.com; ❻) is the site of the Amtrak stop. Beside cozy wood-paneled rooms, four remodeled cabooses offer three-night stays for $690. The inn has a serviceable restaurant for fish and burgers. In the village of **East Glacier Park**, near another Amtrak station, the simple *Backpacker's Inn* hostel (May–Sept; Ⓣ406/226-9392), behind *Serrano's Mexican Restaurant* at 29 Dawson Ave, has three cabins: two are private with bathrooms ($30) and a third offers shared dorm space ($12 per person). Up in **Polebridge**, 28 miles north of the park's west entrance, largely via gravel road, the *Northfork Hostel* (Ⓣ406/888-5241, Ⓦwww.nfhostel.com) is extremely cozy, with no electricity. Campsites go for $10, dorm beds cost $15 and small private cabins start at $35, while log cabins are $80.

Information on other **lodging** in the park's vicinity is available from Glacier Country (Ⓣ1-800/338-5072, Ⓦwww.glaciermt.com), while popular alternative bases to the west of the park include Whitefish and Kalispell (see p.835).

Exploring the park

The fifty-mile **Going-to-the-Sun Road** is one of the most awe-inspiring scenic drives in the country, and driving it from west to east can take several hours (even when summer restrictions on vehicle size effectively ban RVs), creating the illusion that you'll be climbing forever – with each successive hairpin bringing a new colossus into view. At the east end of ten-mile **Lake McDonald**, the road starts to climb, as snowmelt from waterfalls gushes across the road, and the winding route nudges over the **Continental Divide** at **Logan Pass** (6680ft) – a good spot to step out and enjoy the views. Four miles on, there's an overlook at **Jackson Glacier**, one of the few glaciers visible from the roadside. Once you get to the east gate, continue about five miles southeast on US-89 for an expansive view of the Great Plains.

Glacier is a true hiker's paradise, with beautiful views at every turn — though you will have to be in shape to get to the end of the best trails. Good short **trails** start from **Avalanche Creek** on the west flank of the Divide. The mile-long **Trail of the Cedars** loop leads through dark forest to a wall of contoured vivid red sandstone, from where a four-mile path continues gently uphill, past several waterfalls, to glacier-fed **Avalanche Lake**. The most popular trail in the park begins at Logan Pass, following a boardwalk for a mile and a half across wildflower-strewn alpine meadows framed by extraordinary craggy peaks, en route to serene **Hidden Lake**.

At **Swiftcurrent Lake**, north of the east entrance and reached by the Many Glacier entrance, an easy two-mile loop trail runs along the lakeshore, and an exciting five-mile, one-way trail heads to **Iceberg Lake**, so called for the blocks of ice that float on its surface even in midsummer.

From **St Mary Lake**, you can weave a mile and a half up through fir forest to the crashing, frothing **St Mary Falls** and on to the taller **Virginia Falls**; combined with an early-morning boat trip from the Rising Sun launch to the trailhead (see below), this can be a sublime experience.

Down in the quiet southeastern end of the park, the two-mile **Aster Park** trail starts at Two Medicine Lake, framed by the majestic massifs, and leads through spruce forest into flower-filled meadows, passing a couple of beaver ponds and a nice waterfall before ascending steeply for a half-mile through the forest to a small outcrop. From here there are fantastic views of the mighty Sinopah and Rising Wolf mountains, and the calm lakes below.

Tour boats explore all of the large lakes, starting at $10 for one-hour trips, including sunset cruises on Lake McDonald and St Mary Lake. You can also rent canoes, rowboats, and outboards. The lakes, teeming with cutthroat trout, are excellent for **fishing**; regulations are available from visitor centers. Both Glacier Raft Co. (Ⓣ406/888-5454 or 1-800/235-6781, Ⓦwww.glacierraftco.com) and Wild River Adventures (Ⓣ1-800/700-7056, Ⓦwww.riverwild.com), based outside the west gate, offer vigorous half-day ($46) and full-day ($78) **whitewater rafting** trips down the middle fork of the Flathead River, running along the western park boundary.

Finally, pay heed to the signs marking most of the trails as **grizzly bear** country – there's no guarantee of your safety. Avoid traveling alone, being overly quiet, wandering off trails, wearing perfume. The park provides literature and maps that give details on safety issues, but if you avoid hiking at dusk or in the early morning (prime time for bear activity) and carry bear spray (available from gun dealers), you're less likely to be the victim of an unwanted encounter.

Eating and drinking

Food in the park, served in hotel dining rooms, is nothing special. You have to hit the *Izaak Walton Inn* in Essex (see p.838) for something tastier, but the best place to head is **East Glacier Park**, where *Serrano's*, 29 Dawson Ave (May–Sept; Ⓣ406/226-9392), serves decent Mexican food and microbrews, and *Glacier Village*, 306 Hwy-2 (Ⓣ406/226-4464), is the place to come for all things huckleberry, in traditional jams and pancakes, or even ladled on pork chops, along with buffalo ribs, steaks, and burgers, and a solid selection of regional beers. On the northeast side of Glacier, the *Two Sisters Café* on Hwy-89 in Babb (June–Sept; Ⓣ406/732-5535) is a funky roadhouse famous for its outlandish decor, as well as its breakfasts, burgers, chili, and desserts. Not too far away in Babb, the *Cattle Baron* on Hwy-89 (Ⓣ406/732-4033) provides a distinctive, upscale north Montana experience, doling out high-end slabs of meat – cattle, bison, lamb, etc. – in heaping proportions.

Idaho

IDAHO was the last of the states to be penetrated by white settlers, and still has many square miles of barely explored **wilderness**. Though much of its scenery deserves national-park status, its citizens have long been suspicious of federal authorities and tourists alike, and so it remains one of the country's most environmentally compelling places, despite widespread anti-environmental attitudes. Indeed, the name "Idaho" was promoted by a mining lobbyist, who claimed it was a Shoshone word meaning "gem of the mountains;" he later admitted to making it up.

Idaho is very much a destination for the outdoors enthusiast: Natural wonders in its five-hundred-mile stretch include **Hells Canyon**, America's deepest river gorge, the dramatic **Sawtooth National Recreation Area**, and the black, barren **Craters of the Moon** – not to mention the skiing mecca of **Sun Valley**. Beyond these, hikers and backpackers have the choice of some eighty mountain ranges, interspersed with virgin forest and lava plateaus, while the mighty **Snake** and **Salmon rivers** offer endless **fishing** and **whitewater rafting**.

In 1805, **Lewis and Clark** declared central Idaho's bewildering labyrinth of razor-edged peaks and wild waterways the most difficult leg of their epic trek. To this day, there is no east–west road across the heart of the state, and the central wilderness divides the state into halves. The heavily forested **north** is interspersed with glacial lakes fronted by resorts like **Sandpoint** and **Coeur d'Alene**; in the **south**, irrigation begun in the 1880s – partly instigated by the still-dominant Mormons – has transformed the scrubland along the Snake River into the fertile fields responsible for the state's license-plate tag of "Famous Potatoes."

Getting around Idaho

Bus services between northern and southern Idaho are very poor, and a **car** is essential for travel. Only one **Amtrak** route — the *Empire Builder* — crosses the state, linking Seattle with Chicago, and stopping only at Sandpoint in northern Idaho. Boise has an **airport**, though Spokane and Salt Lake City can be more convenient for northern and southeastern Idaho, respectively.

Southern Idaho

Dropping down into **southern Idaho** from western Montana can be dispiriting: Though the initial leg on I-15 is visually compelling, with the magnificent **Mesa Falls** as a worthwhile detour along Hwy-47 and Yellowstone only a short distance east, the scenery along the interstate soon consists of farming plots and a few deserted stretches of sand and rocks. Only state capital **Boise** provides any urban interest, as Idaho Falls and Pocatello are both drab. However, a trip into the interior along US-20 brings you to the spectacular ragged outcrops of the **Sawtooth Mountains**, and an hour away is the forbidding landscape of **Craters of the Moon**. Also, during summer, the much-hyped **Sun Valley** ski resort is a good base for mountain bikers, rafters, and hikers, with many good bars and restaurants.

Craters of the Moon National Monument

At first sight, the eerie, 83-square-mile **Craters of the Moon National Monument**, ninety miles west of Idaho Falls, looks like a sooty-black wasteland. Closer inspection reveals a surreal cornucopia of lava cones, tubes, buttes, craters, caves, and splatter cones, with trees battered by the fierce winds into bonsai-like contortions. All these features were caused by successive waves of lava pouring from gaping wounds in the earth's crust throughout the millennia; the most recent event occurred 2,000 years ago.

The park **visitor center** is on US-20 (daily summer 8am–6pm, rest of year 8am–4.30pm; Ⓣ208/527-1300, Ⓦwww.nps.gov/crmo); entrance for seven days is $8 per car, or $4 per bicycle and pedestrian, and spaces at the 52-site, first-come, first-served *Lava Flow* **campground** cost $10 (May–Oct). A seven-mile **loop road**, open late April to mid-November, takes you around myriad lava fields, where trails of varying difficulty lead past assorted cones and monoliths – don't stray from the paths, as the rocks are razor-sharp and can reach ovenlike temperatures. Highlights include the one-mile trail past hollow **tree molds** where the ancient wood ignited, leaving craggy holes; the steep half-mile trek to the top of the **Inferno Cone**, with commanding views of the region; and the eight-mile **Wilderness Trail** (wilderness permit required, from the visitor center), which leads deep into the back country past cinder cones, ropy lava flows, and the blown-out expanse of **Echo Crater**. In winter, the road is open for groomed **cross-country skiing**; for a conditions report, call Ⓣ208/527-3257.

There are also **caves** here and elsewhere in the monument, molten lava tubes that can be explored alone or on ranger-led tours – the short **Cave Trail** takes you past four of them, notably the lengthy and spacious **Indian Cave** and the innocent-sounding **Boy Scout Cave** – involving a entry crawl over broken rock and a wet, icy floor that invites at least a twisted ankle.

Sun Valley

East of Boise and 150 miles west of Idaho Falls, **Sun Valley** is the common label for the entire Wood River Valley area – though technically it is just the name of a **ski resort** (Ⓦwww.sunvalley.com). The 1930s brainchild of Union Pacific Railroad chairman (and later politician and diplomat) Averell Harriman, this alpine ski center was sited on **Dollar** and **Bald mountains**, here in the relatively gentle foothills of the Sawtooths near the old sheep-ranching village of **KETCHUM**. The Sun Valley name was chosen because the snow withstood even the brightest winter sun. The world's first chairlift was built here in 1936, and the resort was an instant success, attracting the likes of Clark Gable and Gary Cooper, who came to hunt and fish. **Ernest Hemingway** completed *For Whom the Bell Tolls* as a guest of the resort in 1939, and lived in Ketchum for the last two years of his life before his shotgun suicide; his very plain grave can be found in the town cemetery. A **festival** for the influential author is held every September (Ⓦwww.ernesthemingwayfestival.org).

Sun Valley's **season** runs from late November to April; as well as downhill skiing (daily lift pass $55–80 by season at Bald Mountain, $32–38 at Dollar Mountain), you can also set off cross-country. Ketchum itself is a lively little town with plenty of accommodation, and an oasis of nightlife in an otherwise thinly populated zone. Among summer outdoor activities are **cycling** along thirty miles of excellent trails, as well as **mountain biking** on the superb lift-accessed trails on Bald Mountain (lift ticket $20 per day), and **rafting** on the rivers to the north.

Practicalities

There's **transportation** on the KART bus system (rides $3; Ⓣ208/788-RIDE, Ⓦwww.kart-sunvalley.com), and Ketchum's **visitor center**, 371 N Main St, runs a free reservation service for **accommodation** (Ⓣ1-866/305-0408 or 1-800/234-0599, Ⓦvisitsunvalley.com).

Room rates are highest in summer and winter, but you can save a bundle by staying in nearby Hailey, twelve miles south. The luxurious 600-room *Sun Valley Lodge* resort is as expensive as you'd expect (Ⓣ208/622-4111 or 1-800/786-8259, Ⓦwww.sunvalley.com; ❽), with in-room flat-screen TVs, high-speed internet access, and DVD players. For similar prices, the resort's *Sun Valley Inn* (same contact; ❼) offers mock-Swiss Alps design. Most spots in Ketchum are pricey, though the *Tamarack Lodge*, 291 Walnut Ave (Ⓣ1-800/521-5379, Ⓦwww.tamaracksunvalley.com; ❻), provides clean, functional rooms with wi-fi, fridges and microwaves for about the cheapest you're going to find for adequate digs in town. A bit less expensive in **Hailey** is the *Inn at Ellsworth Estate*, 702 Third Ave S (Ⓣ1-866/788-6354, Ⓦwww.ellsworthestate.com; ❺), with clean and tasteful B&B rooms, some with fireplaces and DVD players.

The dining room at the *Sun Valley Lodge* (Ⓣ208/622-2150) serves some of the best upscale **meals** in Idaho, typically nouveau French using fresh local ingredients, while in Ketchum the midpriced *Ketchum Grill*, 520 East Ave (Ⓣ208/726-4460), has tasty, eclectic options, from meatloaf and hamburgers to quail and duck breast. More expensive is the breakfast-and-lunch hangout *Cristina's*, 520 Second St E (Ⓣ208/726-4499), which also offers a nice Sunday brunch. *Whiskey Jacques*,

251 N Main St (Ⓣ208/726-5297), is a good local bar, with **live music** by mid-level national acts, and a solid range of pizzas and burgers.

The Sawtooth Mountains and around

North of Ketchum and Sun Valley, Hwy-75 climbs through rising tracts of forests and mountains to top out after twenty miles at the spectacular panorama of **Galena Summit**. Spreading out far below, the meadows of the Sawtooth Valley stretch northward. The simple road meanders beside the young **Salmon River**, whose headwaters rise in the forbidding icy peaks to the south, as the serrated ridge of the **Sawtooth Mountains** forms an impenetrable barrier along the western horizon. Backpackers are guaranteed solitude in these climes, dotted with some five hundred remote alpine lakes – pick up details of **camping** sites and hiking trails at the **Sawtooth National Recreation Area headquarters**, eight miles north of Ketchum (daily 8.30am–5pm; Ⓣ208-727-5000, Ⓦwww.fs.fed.us/r4/sawtooth). Fly-fishing for brown trout, steelhead, and salmon is a popular pastime here as well.

At tiny **STANLEY**, a few miles north, dirt roads radiating from the junction of Hwy-75 and Hwy-21 have assorted **motels**, the better of which include the Western-flavored *Valley Creek Motel* (Ⓣ208/774-3606, Ⓦwww.stanleyidaho.com; ④), whose nice rooms have kitchenettes and wi-fi; and the large, cozy *Mountain Village Lodge* (Ⓣ208/774-3661, Ⓦwww.mountainvillage.com; ④), which has sixty comfortably furnished rooms with fridges and microwaves and a natural hot-springs spa. In summer, Stanley's main activity is organizing **rafting trips**. Operators include The River Company (Ⓣ208/788-5775, Ⓦwww.therivercompany.com), which charges $71–91.

Twelve miles west of Stanley at the town of **Sunbeam**, you begin the 45-mile scenic drive that leads into the historic settings preserved at the **Land of the Yankee Fork State Park**, whose **interpretive center** (summer daily 9am-5pm; free; Ⓣ208/879-5244) at the park's eastern junction, near Challis at the intersection of highways 75 and 93, gives you the opportunity to try your luck panning

▲ Sawtooth National Recreation Area

gold. Along the route you can explore the preserved ghost towns of **Custer** and **Bonanza**, the **Yankee Fork Gold Dredge**, a 112-foot, nearly thousand-ton barge that mined gold from stream gravel, and the **Custer Motorway** (also known as Forest Road 070), an old, rustic toll road, curving northwest away from Hwy-75, with numerous historic attractions and rugged trails leading off from it. Camping, rafting, fishing, and cross-country skiing are good options in this remote wilderness.

Boise

One of the few highlights of otherwise bleak and arid southwestern Idaho is the verdant, likeable community of **BOISE** (pronounced *BOY-see*), straddling I-84 some 350 miles from Salt Lake City. Boise was established in 1862 for the benefit of pioneers using the Oregon Trail. After adapting (or misspelling) the name originally given to the area by French trappers – *les bois*, the woods – the earliest residents boosted the town's appearance by planting hundreds more trees.

The centerpiece of Boise's compact **downtown**, the **State Capitol**, Jefferson Street and Capitol Boulevard, is a stately Neoclassical structure that exhibits gemstones such as the star garnet, found only in southeast Asia and Idaho. It's currently under renovation, so check Ⓦwww.capitolcommission.idaho.gov for current progress. Nearby, **Old Boise Historic District** (Ⓦwww.oldboise.com) is an elegant area of stone-trimmed brick restaurants and shops built in the tasteful commercial Victorian style of the time. The **Basque Museum and Cultural Center**, 611 Grove St (Tues–Fri 10am–4pm, Sat 11am–3pm; $3; Ⓦwww.basquemuseum.com), is in a former boarding house that was for many years home to Basque immigrants, who shepherded in mountainous central Idaho, and traces their cultural heritage through antiques, relics, photographs, and key manuscripts.

Amid the humpy desert hills around it, the city is rightly proud of its **Greenbelt**, some nineteen miles of paths that crisscross the tranquil **Boise River** to link nine separate parks. In **Julia Davis Park**, the **Idaho Historical Museum** (May–Sept Tues–Sat 9am–5pm, Sun 1–5pm; Oct–April Tues–Fri 9am–5pm, Sat 11am–5pm; $4; Ⓦwww.idahohistory.net/museum.html) displays artifacts from Native American and Basque peoples, details the difficult experience of the Chinese miners of the 1870s and 1880s, and expounds on Idahoans from furriers to gold miners and ranchers. Also, the **Pioneer Village** preserves cabins and houses dating from as early as 1863, among them an adobe that belonged to the mayor in the 1870s.

The **Old Idaho Penitentiary**, at 2445 Old Penitentiary Rd, off Warm Springs Avenue (daily summer 10am–5pm; rest of year noon–5pm; $5; Ⓦwww.idahohistory.net/oldpen.html), is an imposing sandstone citadel that feels like a desolate outpost, despite being just a mile from downtown. Constructed in 1870, it remained open until 1974. Self-guided tours take you through the cramped solitary-confinement unit, and the gallows where the last hanging in Idaho was carried out a half-century ago. A small museum displays confiscated weapons and mugshots of former inmates, including one Harry Orchard, who blew up the state governor in 1905. Oddly situated beside the prison, the **Idaho Botanical Gardens** (Mon–Fri 9am–5pm, Sat & Sun noon–4pm, May–Oct Sat & Sun closes 6pm; $4; Ⓦwww.idahobotanicalgarden.org) has a dozen themed gardens adorned with irises, roses, herbs, and cacti, with one of them based around native plants that Meriwether Lewis reported in his 1805 explorer's journal.

Finally, at the **Idaho Shakespeare Festival**, 5657 Warm Springs Ave (May–Sept; tickets $29–38; Ⓣ208/336-9221, Ⓦwww.idahoshakespeare.org), performances can be inspired and tickets are usually cheap and available. Around five plays are presented per season, with two or three of them penned by the Bard.

Practicalities

Greyhound **buses** stop at 1212 W Bannock St, and Valley Ride (tickets $1; Ⓣ208/846-8547, Ⓦwww.valleyride.org) runs a fairly extensive local **bus** service. The **visitor center** is at 312 S 9th St, suite 100 (April–Sept Mon–Sat 10am–6pm; Oct–March Mon–Fri 10am–3pm; Ⓣ208/344-7777, Ⓦwww.boise.org). Downtown **hotels** include *The Grove*, 245 S Capitol Blvd (Ⓣ208/333-8000 or 1-888/961-5000, Ⓦwww.grovehotelboise.com; ❺), offering large, well-appointed rooms, many with great views over the city and mountains beyond. The restaurant-hotel *Leku Ona* (Ⓣ208/345-6665, Ⓦwww.lekuonaid.com; ❸), has boutique rooms that are basic but tasteful, and has the advantage of one of the city's finest Basque restaurants, serving up a range of seafood. The nicest **B&B** is the *Idaho Heritage Inn B&B*, 109 W Idaho St (Ⓣ208/342-8066, Ⓦwww.idheritageinn.com; ❹), a lovely Victorian building that was once the residence of Governor Chase Clark and later Senator Frank Church, with six agreeable rooms.

Good options for **eating** in Boise include *Goldy's*, 108 S Capitol Blvd (Ⓣ208/345-4100), where you can create your own excellent breakfast combos for less than $10, and the *Grape Escape*, 800 W Idaho St (Ⓣ208/368-0200), a fine bistro offering gourmet cheeses, sandwiches, quiches, and salads and wine tastings. *Bar Gernika*, 202 Capitol Blvd (Ⓣ208/344-2175), is excellent for its authentic Basque specialties – particularly the range of stews and lamb dishes. Appealing downtown **bars** include the bustling *Bittercreek Alehouse*, 246 N 8th St (Ⓣ208/345-1813), with its dozens of microbrews, and *Bardenay Restaurant & Distillery*, 610 Grove St (Ⓣ208/426-0538), which distills its spirits and features a nice range of affordable, tasty beef and seafood.

Northern Idaho

The stark wilderness of the Sawtooth, Salmon River, and Clearwater mountains make traveling through the heart of Idaho impossible. There are only two routes between south and north: up the eastern fringe from Idaho Falls, or, more enjoyably, along US-95 via Hwy-55 out of Boise. At first barren and infertile, just before Lewiston the scenery unfolds into pastoral farmland. The **Nez Percé** hunted buffalo, gathered berries, and fished here for hundreds of years, until gold was discovered and they were forced to beat a bloody retreat. The heavily forested far north of the Idaho Panhandle is broken by hundreds of deep glacial lakes, the largest of which host resort towns such as **Coeur d'Alene** and **Sandpoint** – not major destinations, but good stopovers.

Hells Canyon region

From the busy little water-sports and ski resort of **McCALL**, 110 miles north of Boise, Hwy-55 climbs steadily to merge with US-95 and follow the turbulent **Little Salmon River**. Just south of the hamlet of Riggins, thirty miles on, comes a good opportunity to see **Hells Canyon** from Idaho. With an average depth of 5500ft this is the deepest river gorge in the US, though due to its broad expanse and lack of sheer walls it doesn't quite have the impact of the more precipitous Grand Canyon. Nevertheless, it is impressive, with Oregon's Wallowa and Eagle Cap ranges rising behind it and the river glimmering far down below. Hwy-241 leads toward the overlooks; the final few miles of dirt road require a four-wheel-drive vehicle and permission from the Riggins forest ranger office on Hwy-95 (Mon–Fri 8am–5pm; Ⓣ208/628-3916, Ⓦwww.fs.fed.us/hellscanyon). The canyon is also accessible by road from Oregon (see p.1131) and by boat from Lewiston.

The hamlet of **RIGGINS** reclines in a steeply rising T-shaped canyon. This is prime **whitewater-rafting** and **kayaking** country, and outfitters, spread along a one-mile stretch of the one-street village, outnumber cafés and shops. The **Chamber of Commerce** (Ⓣ208/628-3778 or 1-866/221-3901, Ⓦwww.rigginsidaho.com) has details. From Riggins, US-95 heads north along the Salmon River Valley for thirty miles to the rumpled terrain around even smaller **White Bird**, the start of Nez Percé country.

Industrial **LEWISTON**, 110 miles north of Riggins, is best known for its **Lewiston Round-up**, a massive rodeo held in early September (Ⓣ208/746-6324, Ⓦwww.lewistonroundup.org), and as a starting point for journeys through Hells Canyon on the Salmon River. Boats sail past abandoned mine shafts and tribal caves, with mountain goats, bobcats, snakes, and birds of prey adding further interest. Snake River Adventures, 227 Snake River Ave (Ⓣ1-800/262-8874, Ⓦwww.snakeriveradventures.com), offers an all-day whitewater-rafting trip costing around $220 including lunch, or $500 for combination rafting and jet boat trips spread over two days. Contact the Lewiston **Chamber of Commerce**, 111 Main St (Mon–Fri 8am–4.30pm, Ⓣ208/743-3531, Ⓦwww.lewistonchamber.org) for information on other outfitters.

The Nez Percé

The first whites to encounter the **Nez Percé** people were the weak, hungry, and disease-ridden Lewis and Clark expedition in 1805. The natives gave them food and shelter, and cared for their animals until the party was ready to carry on westward.

Relations between the Nez Percé (so called by French-Canadian trappers because of their shell-pierced noses) and whites remained agreeable for over fifty years – until the discovery of gold, and white pressure for property ownership led the government to persuade some renegade Nez Percé to sign a treaty in 1863 that took away three-quarters of tribal land. As settlers started to move into the hunting grounds of the Wallowa Valley in the early 1870s, the majority of the Nez Percé, under the leadership of **Chief Joseph**, refused to recognize the agreement. In 1877, after much vacillation, the government decided to enact its terms and gave the tribe thirty days to leave.

Ensuing skirmishes resulted in the deaths of a handful of settlers, and a large army force began to gather to round up the tribe. Chief Joseph then embarked upon the famous **Retreat of the Nez Percé**. Around 250 warriors (protecting twice as many women, children, and old people) outmaneuvered army columns many times their size, launching frequent guerrilla attacks in a series of narrow escapes. After four months and 1700 miles, the Nez Percé were cornered just thirty miles from the safety of the Canadian border. Chief Joseph then (reportedly) made his legendary speech of surrender, "From where the sun now stands I will fight no more forever."

The Nez Percé had been told that they would be put on a reservation in Idaho; instead, they were taken to Oklahoma, where the marshy land caused a malaria epidemic. Chief Joseph died in 1904 on the Colville reservation in Washington, but decades later the Nez Percé were allowed to return to the Northwest, where today some 1500 live in a reservation between Lewiston and Grangeville – a minute fraction of their original territory.

Nez Percé National Historic Park, containing 38 separate sites, is spread over a huge range of north-central Idaho, eastern Oregon, and western Montana. At the visitor center in Spalding, ten miles east of Lewiston (daily 8am-4.30pm, summer closes 5pm; free; Ⓣ208/843-7001, Ⓦwww.nps.gov/nepe), the onsite Museum of Nez Percé Culture focuses on tribal arts and crafts. The heavily ravined White Bird Battlefield, seventy miles further south on US-95, was where the Native Americans inflicted 34 deaths on the US Army, in the first major battle of the Retreat. Further exhibits on Nez Percé history can be found in the Wallowa County Museum in Joseph, Oregon (see p.1131).

Moscow

The thirty miles of US-95 between Lewiston and **MOSCOW** wind through the beautiful rolling hillsides of the fertile Palouse Valley. Moscow itself is a friendly, culturally rich town that makes a good overnight stop, with students from the **University of Idaho** providing some color. Bookstores, galleries, bars, and cafés line the tree-shaded and partly pedestrianized **Main Street**, while theater, music, and independent cinema are on offer throughout the year, and summer sees a sprinkling of arts festivals: the **Moscow Artwalk** (Ⓣ208/883-7036, Ⓦwww.moscow-arts.org/artwalk.html) brings together dozens of artists, galleries, and the public for diverting summertime exhibits, and the **Lionel Hampton Jazz Festival** (Ⓣ208/885-6765, Ⓦwww.jazz.uidaho.edu) is named after the classic bandleader and showcases big names new and old.

Moscow's **visitor center** is at 411 S Main St (Ⓣ208/882-1800, Ⓦwww.moscowchamber.com). Greyhound stops at the ultra-basic *Royal Motor Inn*, 120 W Sixth St (Ⓣ208/882-2581; ❸), though you're better off at one of the half-dozen **B&Bs** in the area, the most distinctive of which is *Mary Jane's Farm*, 1000 Wild Iris Lane (Ⓣ208/882-6819, Ⓦwww.maryjanesfarm.org/bb; ❻), a pleasant spot with primitive facilities, where you're expected to get in touch with your pastoral side by working the farm like an authentic rustic. Good places to **eat** include *Wheatberries Bake Shop*, 531 S Main St (Ⓣ208/882-4618), which has nice sandwiches, espresso drinks, soups, and panini, and the stylish *Red Door*, 215 S Main St (Ⓣ208/882-7830), excellent for its upscale seafood, game, and steak.

Coeur d'Alene

No longer strictly identified with the neo-Nazis who made their home in nearby Hayden Lake, **COEUR D'ALENE**, fifty miles north of Moscow on US-95, is now best known for its phenomenally expensive **Coeur d'Alene Resort**, which dominates the unremarkable downtown and is well worth the money if you want to spend most of your time golfing (Ⓣ208/765-4000, Ⓦwww.cdaresort.com; ❼). West of the resort at Independence Point, **cruises** ($18–35; Ⓣ208/765-2300) range from ninety-minute jaunts that give you a closer view of the lake to six-hour journeys through the scenic St. Joe River corridor, where all kinds of wildlife are on view.

Greyhound **buses** stop at 137 E Spruce Ave, and free local **transit** is available on Idaho City Link (Ⓣ1-877/941-RIDE, Ⓦwww.idahocitylink.com). The **visitor center** is at 100 N First St (Mon–Fri 8am–5pm; Ⓣ1-877/782-9232, Ⓦwww.coeurdalene.org), which has a good range of free, helpful publications. Aside from the resort, you could do much worse than to stay at the cheap and clean *Flamingo Motel* (Ⓣ1-800/955-2159, Ⓦwww.flamingomotelidaho.com; ❹), which, along with its fridges and wi-fi, offers kitschy theme rooms kitted out in classic cowboy, tropical cabana, and ultra-patriotic stylings, among many other eye-opening choices. By contrast, the *McFarland Inn*, 601 E Foster Ave (Ⓣ208/667-1232, Ⓦwww.mcfarlandinn.com; ❻), offers a more tasteful, though much less fun, B&B setting with DVD players and wi-fi. For **eating** out, *Beverly's*, is a chic choice for seafood and meat in the *Coeur d'Alene Resort* (Ⓣ208/765-4000), serving up the likes of king crab and rack of elk; and *Brix*, 317 E Sherman Ave (Ⓣ208/665-7407), is good for its tasty sandwiches for lunch and more expensive steak, quail and seafood for dinner.

Silver Mountain and Wallace

About forty miles east of Coeur d'Alene on I-90, you'll come to Kellogg and the surprisingly good ski hill of **SILVER MOUNTAIN** (Ⓣ208/783-1111 or

1-866/344-2675, Ⓦwww.silvermt.com). It has the world's longest single-stage **gondola** (3.1 miles; rides $18), and is open year-round for fine skiing in winter (lift tickets $49), and some good mountain biking (rental $30–50 per day) and hiking in summer; there's also lodging (❼), rates for which include use of the sizeable indoor waterpark facility.

A further ten miles east are the authentic Western streets of friendly **WALLACE**, where most of the town's buildings are federally protected and evoke strong images of silver-mining days. A fun, 75-minute trolley-car ride, the **Sierra Silver Mine Tour**, leaves from 420 N Fifth St (May-Sept daily tours on the half-hour 10am-4pm, until 2pm May & Sept; $10.50; Ⓣ208/752-5151, Ⓦwww.silverminetour.org) lets you descend a thousand feet to appreciate the hard labor endured by miners a century ago. To find out more about how they dug for shiny metal, drop by the **Wallace District Mining Museum**, 590 Bank St (summer daily 9am-6pm; $2; Ⓣ208/556-1592), which has replicas, photos, and artifacts from the golden and silvery days; to find out what they did on their days off, visit the **Bordello Museum**, 605 Cedar St (tours on the half hour Mon–Sat 9.30am–6.30pm, Sun 10am–5pm; $5; Ⓣ208/753-0801), giving the hundred-year history of a certain local "institution." Wallace isn't a place to linger for long, but if you want to **stay** here, the *Wallace Inn*, 100 Front St (Ⓣ208/752-1252, Ⓦwww.wallaceinn.net; $119), has a pool, hot tub, sauna and gym, though pretty basic rooms. For **dining**, the enjoyable *Jameson*, 304 6th St (Ⓣ208/556-6000), has mid-priced seafood and steak, and you can eat surrounded by vintage decor.

Sandpoint

Forty-four miles north of Coeur d'Alene, little **SANDPOINT** lies at the northwestern end of **Lake Pend Oreille** (pronounced "PON-duh-ray"), with its downtown overlooking placid Sandy Creek but its main attractions somewhat further out. At the south end of the lake, **Farragut State Park**, 13400 Ranger Rd (Ⓣ208/682-3814), has 4,000 acres for hiking, camping ($12–20), and the like. To the northeast, the spiky Selkirk Mountains hold the **Schweitzer Mountain Resort**, northern Idaho's best ski resort (Ⓣ208/263-9555, Ⓦwww.schweitzer.com). Lift tickets are $59 and night skiing is $15; in summer you can use one of the lifts for hiking and mountain biking, all day for $15. **Lodging** choices at the resort start at $225. If you're looking for more old-fashioned entertainment, venture 25 miles south on Hwy-95 to **Silverwood Theme Park** (May–Oct hours vary; $37, kids $20; Ⓣ208/683-3400, Ⓦwww.silverwoodthemepark.com), one of the rare theme parks in the northern Rockies, where you can indulge in roller coasters, water slides, and some 65 rides and attractions.

Amtrak **trains** on the *Empire Builder* line pass through late at night in Sandpoint — the only stop in Idaho — at 450 Railroad Ave. **Accommodation** includes the elegant *Inn at Sand Creek*, 105 S First Ave (Ⓣ208/255-2821, Ⓦwww.innatsandcreek.com; ❺), whose suites come with internet access, fireplaces, and smart modern decor; and the *Coit House*, 502 N Fourth Ave (Ⓣ208/265-4035, Ⓦwww.coithouse.com; ❸), a tasteful 1907 Victorian B&B within walking distance of downtown and the lake. Good **dining** can be found at the *Sand Creek Grill* at the *Inn at Sand Creek* (see above), which serves upscale Northwest cuisine. For **drinking**, *Eichardts*, 212 Cedar St (Ⓣ208/263-4005), has a dozen microbrews and local rock bands on weekends.

12

The Southwest

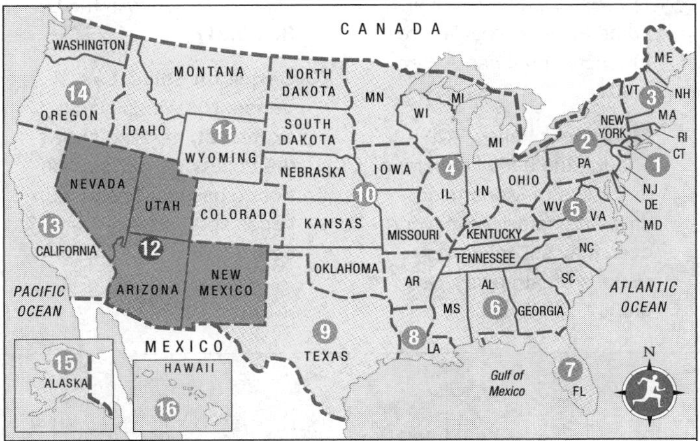

AL - ALABAMA	IN - INDIANA	MN - MINNESOTA	RI - RHODE ISLAND
AR - ARKANSAS	LA - LOUISIANA	MS - MISSISSIPPI	SC - SOUTH CAROLINA
CT - CONNECTICUT	MA - MASSACHUSETTS	NC - NORTH CAROLINA	VA - VIRGINIA
DE - DELAWARE	MD - MARYLAND	NH - NEW HAMPSHIRE	VT - VERMONT
FL - FLORIDA	ME - MAINE	NJ - NEW JERSEY	WI - WISCONSIN
IL - ILLINOIS	MI - MICHIGAN	PA - PENNSYLVANIA	WV - WEST VIRGINIA

CHAPTER 12

Highlights

✱ **Santa Fe, NM** Great museums, fascinating history, atmospheric hotels – New Mexico's capital is a must on any Southwest itinerary. **See p.855**

✱ **The Havasupai Reservation, AZ** Glorying in its turquoise waterfalls, this little-known offshoot of the Grand Canyon remains home to its original Native American inhabitants. **See p.901**

✱ **Monument Valley, AZ** Though the eerie sandstone monoliths of Monument Valley are familiar the world over, they still take every visitor's breath away. **See p.905**

✱ **Canyon de Chelly, AZ** Ancestral Puebloan "cliff dwellings" pepper every twist and turn of this stupendous sheer-walled canyon. **See p.906**

✱ **Scenic Hwy-12, UT** Crossing the heart of Utah's red-rock wilderness, Hwy-12 is perhaps the most exhilarating drive in the US. **See p.917**

✱ **Cirque du Soleil, Las Vegas, NV** With several exuberant, dazzling shows, the postmodern Canadian troupe has redefined Las Vegas spectacle for the century. **See p.941**

▲ St Francis Cathedral, Santa Fe

12

The Southwest

The four sparsely populated Southwestern desert states of **New Mexico**, **Arizona**, **Utah**, and **Nevada** are extraordinary and unforgettable. They stretch from Texas to California across an elemental landscape ranging from towering monoliths of red sandstone to snowcapped mountains, on a high desert plateau that repeatedly splits open to reveal yawning canyons. This overwhelming scenery is complemented by the emphatic presence of numerous Native American cultures, and the palpable legacy of America's Wild West frontier.

Among the region's earliest inhabitants were the **Ancestral Puebloans**. While their settlements and cliff palaces, abandoned seven centuries ago, are now evocative ruins, their descendants, the **Pueblo** peoples of New Mexico and the **Hopi** in Arizona, still lead similar lifestyles. Less sedentary tribes, such as the **Navajo** and the **Apache**, migrated into the Southwest from the fourteenth century onwards. Adopting local agricultural and craft techniques, they appropriated vast tracts of territory, which they in turn were soon defending against European immigrants. The first such, in 1540, were Coronado's **Spanish** explorers, who spent two years fruitlessly searching for cities of gold. Sixty years later, Hispanic colonists founded the province of **New Mexico**, an ill-defined region that covered not only all of the Southwest but much of modern California and Colorado. Not until 1848 – by which time New Mexico had spent thirty years as a neglected backwater of the newly independent Mexico – was the region forcibly taken over by the **United States**. Almost immediately, large numbers of outsiders began to pass through on their way to Gold Rush California.

Thereafter, violent confrontations increased between the US government and the Native Americans. The entire **Navajo** population was rounded up and forcibly removed to barren eastern New Mexico in 1864 (though they were soon allowed to return to northeastern Arizona), while the **Apache**, under warrior chiefs Cochise and Geronimo, fought extended battles with the US cavalry. Though the nominal intention was to open up lands to newly American settlers, few ever succeeded in extracting a living from this harsh terrain.

One exception were the **Mormons** (the Church of Jesus Christ of Latter-Day Saints), whose flight from religious persecution brought them by the late 1840s to the alkaline basin of Utah's **Great Salt Lake**. Through sheer hard work, they established what amounted to an independent country, with outlying communities all over the Southwest. They still constitute seventy percent of Utah's population, and maintain effective control of the state's government.

Each of the four Southwestern states remains distinct. New Mexico bears the most obvious traces of long-term settlement, the Native American pueblos of the north coexisting alongside former Spanish colonial towns like **Santa Fe**, **Albu-**

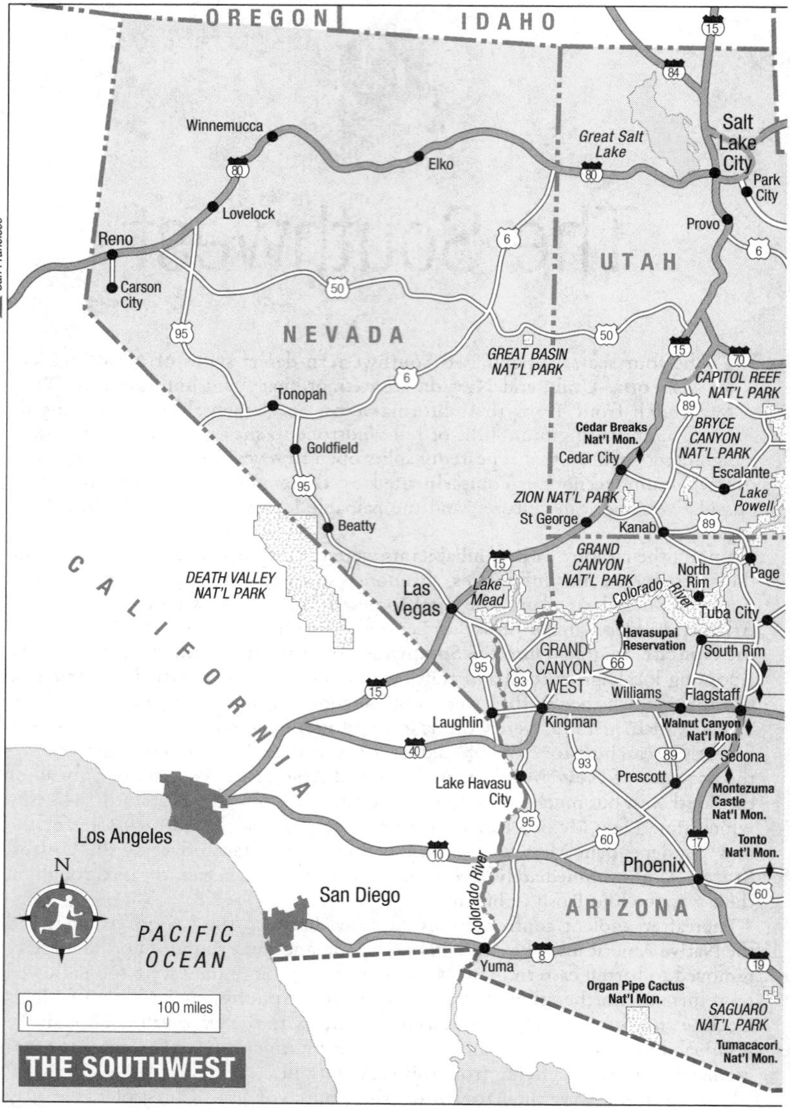

querque, and **Taos**. In Arizona, the history of the Wild West is more conspicuous, in towns such as **Tombstone**, site of the OK Corral. Over a third of the state belongs to Native American tribes, including the Apache, Hopi, and Navajo; most live in the red-rock lands of the northeast, notably amid the splendor typified by the **Canyon de Chelly** and **Monument Valley**.

The canyon country of northern Arizona – even the immense **Grand Canyon** – won't prepare you for the uninhabited but compelling landscape of southern Utah,

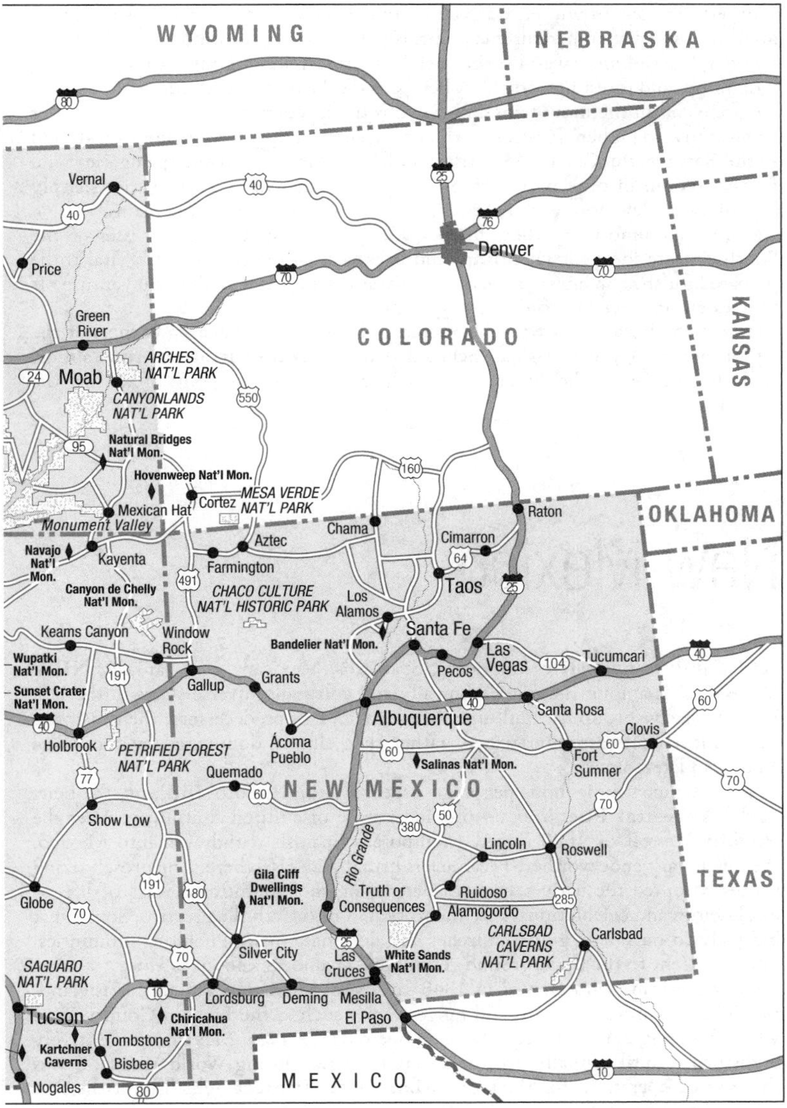

where **Zion** and **Bryce** canyons are the best known of a string of national parks and monuments. **Moab**, poised in the east between majestic **Canyonlands** and the surreal **Arches**, is the top destination for youthful outdoors enthusiasts. Nevada, on the other hand, is nothing short of desolate; gamblers are lured in the millions by the bright lights of **Las Vegas**, but away from the casinos there's little to see or do.

You can count on warm sunshine anywhere in the Southwest for nine months of the year, with incredible sunsets most evenings. Although "snowbirds" flock to southern Arizona in winter, elsewhere summer is the peak tourist season, for no good reason – air temperatures topping 100°F can make the outdoors unbearable, while in late summer awesome thunderstorms sweep in without warning, causing flash floods and forest fires. By October, perhaps the best time to come, the crowds are gone and in the mountains and canyons the leaves turn red and gold. Winter brings snow to higher elevations – there's excellent skiing in **northern Utah** and in the **Sangre de Cristo Mountains** of New Mexico – while spring sees wild flowers bloom in otherwise barren desert. Note that the climate varies sharply according to elevation, with mountains often 30°F cooler than the plains.

More than almost anywhere in the US, the backcountry wildernesses of the Southwest are ideal for **camping** and backpacking expeditions. It's vital to be prepared for the harshness of the desert: always carry water, and if you venture off the beaten track let someone know your plans.

Unless you have your own vehicle, many of the most fascinating corners of the region are utterly inaccessible. Scheduled public **transportation** runs almost exclusively between the big cities – which are not at all the point of visiting the region.

New Mexico

Settled in turn by Native Americans, Spaniards, Mexicans, and Yankees, **NEW MEXICO** is among the most ethnically and culturally diverse states in the US. Each successive group has built upon the legacy of its predecessors; their histories and achievements are intertwined, rather than simply dominated by the white American late-comers.

New Mexico's indigenous peoples – especially the **Pueblo Indians**, the heirs of the **Ancestral Puebloans** – provide a sense of cultural continuity. After the **Pueblo Revolt** of 1680 forced a temporary Spanish withdrawal into Mexico, the missionary endeavor here became less brutal than elsewhere. The proselytizing padres co-opted the natives without destroying their traditional ways of life, as local deities and celebrations were incorporated into Catholic practice. Somewhat bizarrely to outsiders, grand churches still dominate many Pueblo communities, often adjacent to the underground ceremonial chambers known as *kivas*.

The Americans who arrived in 1848 saw New Mexico as a useless wasteland. But for a few mining booms and range wars – such as the Lincoln County War, which brought **Billy the Kid** to fame (see p.875) – New Mexico was relatively undisturbed until it finally became a state in 1912. During World War II, it was the base of operations for the secret **Manhattan Project**, which built the first atomic bomb, and since then it has been home to America's premier weapons research outposts. By and large, people here work close to the land, mining, farming, and ranching.

Northern New Mexico holds the magnificent landscapes of the **Rio Grande Valley**, which cradles both **Santa Fe**, the adobe-fronted capital, and the artists' colony of **Taos**, with its nearby pueblo. The broad swath of **central New Mexico** along I-40 – the interstate that succeeded the old **Route 66** – pivots around the state's biggest city, **Albuquerque**, with the extraordinary mesa-top Pueblo

Adobe

For many visitors, the defining feature of New Mexico is its **adobe architecture**, as seen on homes, churches, and even shopping malls and motels. Adobe bricks are a sun-baked mixture of earth, sand, charcoal, and chopped grass or straw, set with a mortar of similar composition, and then plastered over with mud and straw. The soil used dictates the color of the final building, so subtle variations are seen all across the state. However, adobe is a far from convenient material: it needs replastering every few years and turns to mud when water seeps up from the ground. These days, most of what looks like adobe is actually painted cement or concrete, but even this looks attractive enough in its own semi-kitsch way, while hunting out such superb genuine adobes as the remote **Santuario de Chimayó** on the "**High Road**" between Taos and Santa Fe, the formidable church of **San Francisco de Asis** in Ranchos de Taos, or the multi-tiered dwellings of **Taos Pueblo**, can provide the focus of an enjoyable New Mexico tour.

village of **Ácoma** ("Sky City") an hour's drive west. In wild, wide-open **southern New Mexico**, deep **Carlsbad Caverns** are the main attraction, while you can still stumble upon mining and cattle-ranching towns barely changed since the end of the Wild West.

Getting around New Mexico

Though public transportation is minimal in New Mexico, Albuquerque, pit stop for transcontinental Greyhound **buses** and Amtrak **trains**, and site of the only major **airport**, is now connected to Santa Fe by the new **Rail Runner** commuter service.

Northern New Mexico

The mountainous north is the New Mexico of popular imagination, with its pastel colors, vivid desert landscape, and adobe architecture. Even **Santa Fe**, the one real city, is hardly metropolitan in scale, and the narrow streets of its small, historic center, though thronged with tourists, retain the feel of bygone days. The amiable frontier town of **Taos**, 75 miles northeast, is remarkable chiefly for the stacked dwellings of neighboring **Taos Pueblo**.

An hour's drive west from Taos or Santa Fe brings you to **Bandelier National Monument**, where ancient cliff dwellings were carved out of the volcanic plateau that now holds the laboratories of **Los Alamos**. Alternatively, the hills east of the Rio Grande hold characterful Hispanic hamlets, threaded along a scenic mountain highway known as the **High Road**.

Santa Fe

SANTA FE has long ranked among the chic-est cities in the US, a favorite destination for upmarket travelers in particular. Its romantic appeal rests on a very solid basis: it's one of America's oldest and most beautiful cities, founded by Spanish missionaries a decade before the Pilgrims reached Plymouth Rock. Spread across a high plateau at the foot of the stunning Sangre de Cristo Mountains, New Mexico's capital still glories in the adobe houses and Baroque churches of its original architects, while its newer museums and galleries attract art-lovers from all over the world.

As upward of a million and a half tourists descend yearly upon a town of just seventy thousand inhabitants, Santa Fe has inevitably grown somewhat overblown.

Long-term residents bemoan what's been lost, while first-time visitors may be surprised by the depressing urban sprawl on the edge of town. There's still a lot to like about Santa Fe, however, Once you get used to the rigorous insistence that every building should look like a seventeenth-century Spanish colonial palace, strolling around its compact, peaceful downtown is a real pleasure.

Arrival, information, and getting around

Almost all visitors to Santa Fe arrive by **car**, most driving an hour north on I-25 from **Albuquerque**. The new Rail Runner **train** line connects Albuquerque, both the airport and downtown, with Santa Fe's Railyard district, half a mile southwest of downtown (journey time 1 hr 30min; $7 one-way, $9 all-day pass; Ⓣ 1-866/795-7245, Ⓦ www.nmrailrunner.com). Schedules are primarily designed for commuters, with no services on Sundays.

Amtrak trains do not serve Santa Fe, though arrivals at **Lamy**, 17 miles south-

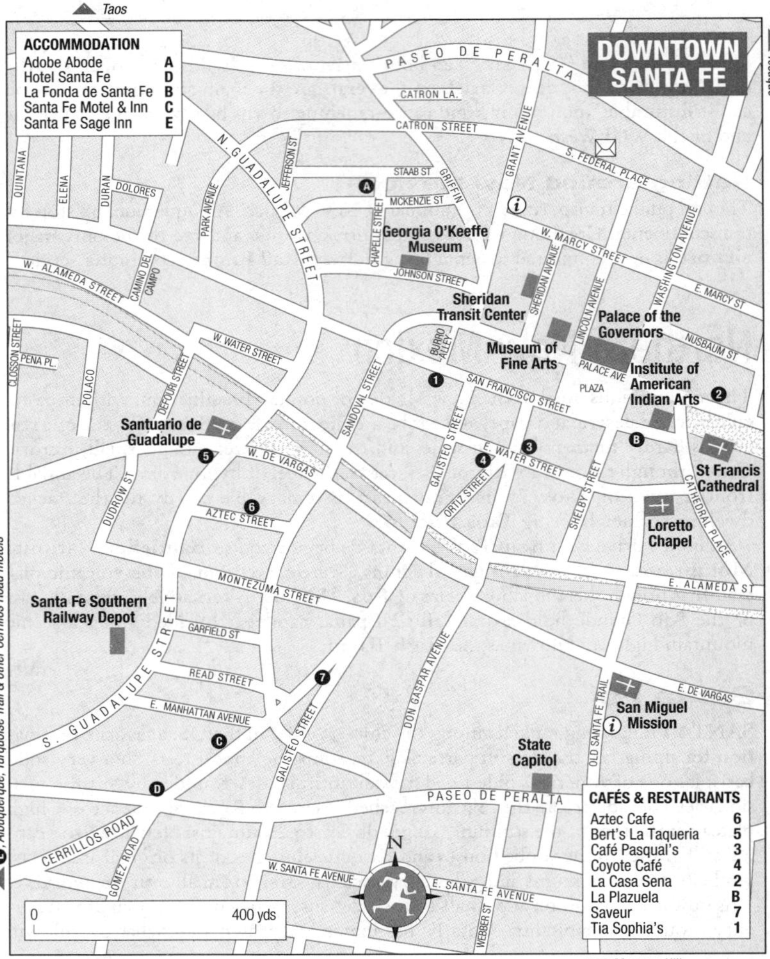

east, are met by Lamy Shuttle vans ($18 one-way; ⓣ505/982-8829). **Buses** from all over the Southwest call at the Greyhound terminal at 858 St Michael's Drive (ⓣ505/471-0008), a long way from the plaza.

By far the most useful **visitor center** is run by the New Mexico Department of Tourism, at 491 Old Santa Fe Trail (daily: June–Aug 8am–7pm; rest of year 8am–5pm; ⓣ505/827-4000 or 1-800/545-2040, ⓦwww.newmexico.org).

Most of what there is to see lies within walking distance of the central plaza, but to get there from your hotel, or to see the farther-flung attractions, you may need to use the Santa Fe Trails **bus service** (ⓣ505/955-2001). Route #2 runs up Cerrillos Road, while route #M loops between the plaza and the outlying museums, for the standard flat fare of $1. Santa Fe's only **taxi** company is Capital City Cabs (ⓣ505/438-0000); **bikes** can be rented at Mellow Velo, 638 Old Santa Fe Trail (ⓣ505/995-8356, ⓦmellowvelo.com). Two-hour **walking tours** of town set off from the blue gate of the Palace of the Governors on Lincoln Avenue (May–Oct Mon–Sat 10.15am; $10; ⓣ505/476-5109).

Accommodation

Even in winter, you won't find a **room** within walking distance of downtown for under $80, and in summer – when every bed is frequently taken – there's little under $125. The main road in from I-25, Cerrillos Road, holds most of the motels and the one hostel.

The most appealing **campgrounds** nearby are in the Santa Fe National Forest, starting seven miles up Hwy-475, northeast of town (summer only; ⓣ505/438-7840, ⓦwww.fs.fed.us/r3/sfe).

Adobe Abode 202 Chapelle St ⓣ505/983-3133, ⓦwww.adobeabode.com. Small, playfully themed, central B&B, offering folk-art-filled rooms both in a century-old house and in a separate newer building. ❼

El Rey Inn 1862 Cerrillos Rd at St Michael's Drive ⓣ505/982-1931 or 1-800/521-1349, ⓦwww.elreyinnsantafe.com. Most characterful of the Cerrillos Rd motels, with stylish Southwestern-style rooms, nice suites, and a pool. ❺

Hotel Santa Fe 1501 Paseo de Peralta at Crerillos Rd ⓣ505/982-1200 or 1-800/825-9876, ⓦwww.hotelsantafe.com. Attractive, elegant and very comfortable adobe hotel, within walking distance of the plaza, owned and run by Picuris Pueblo Indians and holding a good restaurant, *Amaya*. ❼

La Fonda de Santa Fe 100 E San Francisco St; ⓣ505/982-5511 or 1-800/523-5002, ⓦwww.lafondasantafe.com. Gorgeous old inn on the plaza, which features hand-painted murals and stained glass throughout. Each lavishly furnished room is different, and there's a good restaurant, plus a lounge with live entertainment and a rooftop bar. ❾

Santa Fe International Hostel 1412 Cerrillos Rd at Alta Vista ⓣ505/988-1153, ⓦwww.hostelsantafe.com. Some travelers find this old-fashioned HI-AYH hostel, housed in a ramshackle former motel a couple of miles southwest of the plaza, unfriendly, poorly furnished and dirty, and damp and cold in winter; others are totally satisfied, and don't mind the compulsory chores. Dorms beds cost $18, en-suite rooms $35 single, $45 double. ❶/❷

Santa Fe Motel & Inn 510 Cerrillos Rd ⓣ505/982-1039 or 1-800/930-5002, ⓦwww.santafemotel.com. Delightfully stylish little adobe complex where even the most conventional rooms are appealingly furnished. Some have their own kitchens, while there are also several gorgeous little *casitas*. The staff are very friendly, and rates – great for such a quiet, central location – include cooked breakfast. ❺

Santa Fe Sage Inn 725 Cerrillos Rd at Don Diego; ⓣ505/982-5952 or 1-866/433-0355, ⓦwww.santafesageinn.com. The most central chain motel, a mile or so from the plaza; large, clean, and functional if not inspiring. ❹

Downtown Santa Fe: around the plaza

Santa Fe's old central **plaza** is still the focus of town life, especially when filled with buyers and craftspeople during the annual **Indian Market**, on the weekend after the third Thursday in August, and during the first weekend in September for the **Fiestas de Santa Fe**. Apart from an influx of art galleries and stylish restaurants, the web of narrow streets around the plaza has changed little through the centuries. When the US took over in 1848, the new settlers neglected the adobes and chose instead to build in wood, but many of the finer adobe houses have survived. Since the 1930s, almost every non-adobe structure in sight of the plaza has been designed or redecorated to suit the Pueblo Revival mode, with rounded, mud-colored plaster walls supporting roof beams made of thick pine logs. Central Santa Fe today, in fact, looks much more like its original Spanish self than it did a hundred years ago.

The low-slung, initially unprepossessing **Palace of the Governors** fills the entire northern side of the plaza (Mon–Thurs, Sat, & Sun 10am–5pm, Fri 10am–8pm; closed Mon in winter; $8, free Fri 5–8pm; Ⓦ www.palaceofthegovernors.org). Originally sod-roofed, the oldest public building in the US was constructed in 1610 as the headquarters of Spanish colonial administration. Until 1913, it looked like a typical, formal, territorial building, with a square tower at each corner; its subsequent adobe "reconstruction" was based on pure conjecture. The well-preserved interior, organized around an open-air courtyard, holds excellent displays on the history of Hispanic New Mexico, and a well-stocked bookstore. Outside, its arcaded veranda serves as a market for Native American crafts-sellers.

Just west of the palace, the **Museum of Fine Arts** (same hours and prices; Ⓦ www.mfasantafe.org) is housed in a particularly attractive adobe, with ornamental beams and a cool central courtyard, and focuses on changing exhibits of contemporary painting and sculpture by mostly local artists. Of greater appeal to most visitors is the **Georgia O'Keeffe Museum**, a block northwest at 217 Johnson St (same hours and prices; Ⓦ www.okeeffemuseum.org). This boasts the largest collection of O'Keeffes in the world, including many of the desert landscapes she painted near **Abiquiu**, forty miles northwest of Santa Fe, where she lived from 1946 until her death in 1986. In its permanent collection, some New York cityscapes make a surprising contrast to her trademark sun-bleached skulls and iconic flowers.

Across the tiny Santa Fe River to the southwest, three blocks along **Guadalupe Street**, you'll find an attractive little district centered around the small eighteenth-century **Santuario de Guadalupe** (May–Oct Mon–Sat 9am–4pm; Nov–April Mon–Fri 9am–4pm; donation). Former warehouses and factories in the **Railyard** nearby house boutiques, art galleries, and restaurants.

Two blocks south of the plaza along the Old Santa Fe Trail stands the ancient **San Miguel Mission** (Mon–Sat 9am–5pm, Sun 1.30–4pm; $1). Only a few of the massive adobe internal walls survive from the original 1610 building, most of which was destroyed in the 1680 Pueblo Revolt.

Not far east, gallery-lined **Canyon Road** – which stakes a claim to being the oldest street in the US, dating from Pueblo days – climbs a steady but shallow incline along the riverbed and is lined by fine adobes.

The outlying museums

On a plateau two miles southeast of the town center, with extensive views of the surrounding hills and mountains, stands Santa Fe's other museum cluster. The delightful **Museum of International Folk Art** (daily 10am–5pm; closed Mon

The Museum of New Mexico

A combination ticket, costing $18 and valid for four days, grants admission to five leading Santa Fe museums: the Palace of the Governors, the Museum of Fine Arts, the Museum of Indian Arts and Culture, the Museum of International Folk Art, and the Museum of Spanish Colonial Art.

in winter; $8; Ⓦ www.moifa.org), focuses on a huge collection of clay figurines and models from around the world, arranged in colorful dioramas that include a Pueblo Feast Day with dancing *kachinas* and camera-clicking tourists. Its Hispanic Heritage Wing is an engaging reminder of just how close New Mexico's ties have always been with Mexico itself, while the gift shop sells unusual ethnic souvenirs. The neighboring **Museum of Indian Arts and Culture** (same hours and prices; Ⓦ www.miaclab.org) holds superb Native American pottery, ranging from **Ancestral Puebloan** pieces up to the works of twentieth-century revivalists, and covers contemporary Southwestern cultures in fascinating detail.

In the same complex, the **Museum of Spanish Colonial Art** displays traditional Hispanic religious artworks, such as the *santos* (naïve painted images) and *bultos* (carved wooden statues of saints) that are so pervasive in the iconography of Santa Fe (daily 10am–5pm; closed Mon in winter; $6; Ⓦ www.spanishcolonial.org).

Eating

Santa Fe has been renowned as a culinary hot spot since the 1980s, when a stupendous feat of marketing managed to make dishes such as banana-crusted sea bass seem quintessentially Southwestern, and is now said to have more quality **restaurants** per head than any other US city.

Aztec Cafe 317 Aztec St Ⓣ 505/820-0025. Counterculture hangout in the Galisteo Street district, serving coffees, pastries, and light meals until 7pm nightly, with occasional live music.

Bert's La Taqueria 416 Agua Fria Ⓣ 505/474-0791. Very good, very stylish Mexican restaurant, housed in a former convent. Delicious specialties include spiced corn truffles with cheese, and even *chapulines* (grilled grasshoppers); little costs over $10. Closed Sun.

Café Pasqual's 121 Don Gaspar Ave Ⓣ 505/983-9340. Lovely, lively Old/New Mexican restaurant, serving top-quality food (including breakfast) in an attractive tiled dining room a block south of the plaza. Entrees include vegetarian enchiladas ($19) and chile-rubbed filet mignon ($38); as an appetizer, try the delicious Pigs and Figs salad, made with bacon, figs, and mozzarella ($14).

Coyote Café 132 W Water St Ⓣ 505/983-1615, Ⓦ www.coyotecafe.com. Celebrity chef Mark Miller sold his showcase restaurant, just off the plaza, in 2007, but under new owners it remains as trendy as ever. The à la carte prices can be ferocious, with entrees like pan-seared white miso sea bass or elk tenderloin costing close to $40, and appetizers like scallop carpaccio for $15. Lunch, especially at the rooftop *Cantina* upstairs, is a better deal. It's possible to plot a vegetarian course through the menu, with a vegetable torta at $23, though you'll have to cope with the cowhide seats. Daily 11.30am–9pm.

La Casa Sena 125 E Palace Ave Ⓣ 505/988-9232. Charming courtyard restaurant, a block from the plaza; zestful Southwestern lunches, with entrees around $12–15, are the best deal, though the set dinners are consistently good. *La Cantina*, adjoining, is a little cheaper and its staff performs Broadway show songs.

La Plazuela La Fonda de Santa Fe, 100 E San Francisco St Ⓣ 505/982-5511. Delightful, beautifully decorated Mexican restaurant in the heart of La Fonda, open daily for all meals, and with an open-air feel despite the glass ceiling. All the usual Mexican dishes are nicely prepared and sold for reasonable prices.

Saveur 204 Montezuma St Ⓣ 505/989-4200. High quality cafe-cum-salad bar not far west of the State Capitol, serving delicious cooked and raw specialties by the pound, and offering major discounts after 3pm. Mon–Sat 8am–3.45pm.

Tia Sophia's 210 W San Francisco St Ⓣ 505/983-9880. Spicy, very inexpensive Mexican diner west of the plaza that's a huge hit with lunching locals. Daily except Mon 7am–2pm.

Nightlife and entertainment

Unlike its abundance of restaurants, Santa Fe has the limited range of **nightlife** you'd expect in a small city, though its cultural scene livens up in summer. For full listings, check the free weekly *Reporter* (Ⓦ sfreporter.com). Year-round, musical and theatrical performances take place downtown at the **Lensic Performing Arts Center**, a striking former movie theater at 211 W San Francisco St

(Ⓣ505/988-1234, Ⓦwww.lensic.com). The much-anticipated Santa Fe Opera season runs from late June through August in a magnificent amphitheater seven miles north of town (Ⓣ505/986-5900, Ⓦwww.santafeopera.org).

Some of the most atmospheric places to **drink** in town are in the old hotels – such as the downstairs lounge and rooftop bar of *La Fonda* on the plaza (see p.857) – but otherwise conventional bars are few and far between.

Catamount Bar 125 E Water St Ⓣ505/988-7222. Downtown bar with plenty of microbrews on tap, and live rock or blues most nights.

Cowgirl Hall of Fame 319 S Guadalupe St Ⓣ505/982-2565. Very busy country-themed restaurant and bar, with regular live music.

El Farol 808 Canyon Rd Ⓣ505/983-9912. Historic bar-cum-restaurant that serves Spanish tapas to musical accompaniment from blues to flamenco.

Evangelo's 200 W San Francisco St Ⓣ505/982-9014. The only good bare-bones bar in easy walking range of the plaza, with a pool table, a jukebox, and occasional live music.

Bandelier National Monument

The Ancestral Puebloan ruins of **Bandelier National Monument** cut into the forested mesas of the Pajarito Plateau, 35 miles northwest of Santa Fe. Around 1300 AD, itinerant groups, seeking sanctuary from drought and invasion, gathered here to build a community that amalgamated their assorted cultures.

A paved 1.5-mile trail through the prime site, **Frijoles Canyon**, starts from the **visitor center**, at the end of the narrow switchbacking road down from Hwy-4 (daily: June–Aug 8am–6pm; March–May, Sept & Oct 9am–5.30pm; Nov–Feb 9am–4.30pm; $12 per vehicle; Ⓣ505/672-3861, Ⓦwww.nps.gov/band). Not far along, a side path from the circular, multistorey village of **Tyuonyi** leads up to dozens of **cave dwellings**, their rounded chambers scooped out of the soft volcanic rock; you can scramble up to, and even enter, some of them, to peer out across the valley. The main trail continues to the **Long House**, an 800-foot series of two- and three-storey houses built against the canyon wall. Rows of petroglyphs are clearly visible, carved above the holes that held the roof beams. Half a mile beyond, protected by a rock overhang 150ft above the canyon floor, a reconstructed *kiva* sits in **Alcove House**. To reach it you have to climb rickety ladders and steep stairs cut into the crumbly rock.

Los Alamos

Immediately east of Bandelier, **Los Alamos National Laboratory** is the main US center for the research and development of **nuclear weapons** (as well as neurobiology, computer science, and solar and geothermal energy). Most of the complex is off-limits; the small and over-simplified **Bradbury Science Museum** (Tues–Fri 9am–5pm, Sat–Mon 1–5pm; free) is the only part you can visit. Guides glow with excitement as they describe their weapons' devastating power.

From Santa Fe to Taos: the High Road

The quickest route between Santa Fe and Taos follows US-84 as far as the Rio Grande, then continues northeast along the river on Hwy-68. US-84 passes through the heartland of the **northern pueblos**, a cluster of tiny Tewa-speaking communities that have survived for over five centuries, but unless your visit coincides with a feast day (see box), there's little to see.

However, a circuitous alternative route known as the "**High Road**" leaves US-68/84 a dozen miles north of Santa Fe, near Nambe Pueblo. Leading high into the wooded **Sangre de Cristo Mountains**, it passes a number of pueblos and Hispanic villages.

The Ancestral Puebloans

Few visitors to the Southwest are prepared for the awesome scale and beauty of the desert cities and cliff palaces left by the **Ancestral Puebloans**, as seen all over the high plateaus of the "**Four Corners**" district, where Colorado, New Mexico, Arizona, and Utah now meet.

The earliest humans reached the Southwest around 10,000 BC, but the Ancestral Puebloans first appeared as the **Basketmakers**, near the San Juan River, about two thousand years ago. Named for their woven sandals and bowls, they lived in pits in the earth, roofed with logs and mud. Over time, the Ancestral Puebloans adopted an increasingly settled lifestyle, becoming expert farmers and potters. Their first freestanding houses on the plains were followed by multistoried **pueblos**, in which hundreds of families lived in complexes of contiguous "apartments." The astonishing **cliff dwellings**, perched on precarious ledges high above remote canyons, which they began to build around 1100 AD, were the first Ancestral Puebloan settlements to show signs of defensive fortifications. Competition for scarce resources became even fiercer toward the end of the thirteenth century, and recent research suggests that warfare and even cannibalism played a role in their ultimate dispersal. Moving eastward, they joined forces with other displaced groups in a coming-together that eventually produced the modern **Pueblo Indians**. Hence the recent change of name, away from "Anasazi," a Navajo word meaning "ancient enemies," in favor of "Ancestral Puebloan."

Among the most significant **Ancestral Puebloan sites** are:

Mesa Verde Magnificent cliff palaces, high in the canyons of Colorado; see p.797.

Bandelier National Monument Large riverside pueblos, and cave-like homes hollowed from volcanic rock; see opposite.

Chaco Canyon The largest and most sophisticated freestanding pueblos, far out in the desert; see p.871.

Wupatki Several small pueblo communities, built by assorted tribal groups; see p.892.

Walnut Canyon Numerous canyon-wall houses above lush Walnut Creek; see p.892.

Betatakin Canyon-side community set in a vast rocky alcove in Navajo National Monument; see p.905.

Canyon de Chelly Superbly dramatic cliff dwellings in glowing sandstone canyon now owned and farmed by the Navajo; see p.906.

Hovenweep Enigmatic towers poised above a canyon; see p.925.

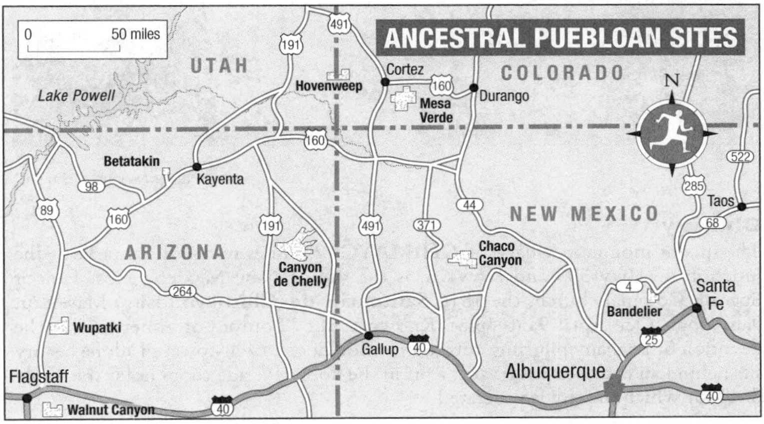

▲ Bandelier National Monument

Chimayó

The quaint mountain village of **CHIMAYÓ**, 25 miles north of Santa Fe at the junction of Hwy-503 and Hwy-76, is the site of New Mexico's most famous Spanish Colonial church, the 1816 **Santuario de Chimayó** (daily: May–Sept 9am–6pm; Oct–April 9am–4pm). Known as the "Lourdes of America" for the devotion of its many pilgrims, this round-shouldered, twin-towered adobe beauty sits behind an enclosed courtyard; a pit in the floor of a side room holds the "holy dirt" for which the site is venerated.

The Rio Grande Pueblos

The first Spaniards to explore what's now New Mexico encountered a settled population of one hundred thousand so-called **Pueblo Indians**, living in a hundred villages and towns (*pueblo* is Spanish for "village"). These people soon grew to resent the imposition of Catholicism and their virtual enslavement. In the **Pueblo Revolt** of 1680, the various tribes banded together and ousted the entire colonial regime, killing scores of priests and soldiers and sending hundreds more south to Mexico. After the Spanish returned in 1693, the Pueblos showed little further resistance, and they have coexisted surprisingly amicably ever since, accepting aspects of Catholicism – most pueblos hold a large adobe church – without giving up their traditional beliefs and practices. New Mexico is now home to around forty thousand Pueblo Indians; each of its nineteen autonomous pueblos has its own laws and system of government.

The Pueblos celebrate Saints' days, major Catholic holidays such as Easter and the Epiphany, and even the Fourth of July with a combination of Native American traditions and Catholic rituals, featuring elaborately costumed dances and massive communal feasts. The spectacle of hundreds of costumed, body-painted tribal members of all ages, performing elaborate dances in such timeless surroundings, is hugely impressive.

However, few of the pueblos should be regarded as the tourist attractions they're touted to be. While the best known, **Taos** and **Ácoma**, retain their ancient defensive architecture, the rest tend to be dusty adobe hamlets scattered around a windblown plaza. Unless you arrive on a feast day, or are a knowledgeable shopper in search of Pueblo crafts, visits are liable to prove disappointing. In addition, you'll certainly be made to feel unwelcome if you fail to behave respectfully – don't "explore" places that are off-limits to outsiders, such as shrines, *kivas*, or private homes.

Fifteen of the pueblos are concentrated along the Rio Grande north of Albuquerque, with a longstanding division between the seven **southern pueblos**, south of Santa Fe, most of which speak Keresan, and the group to the north, which mostly speak Tewa (pronounced *tay-wah*). Visitors to each are required to register at a visitor center; some charge an admission fee of $3 to $10, and those that permit such activities at all typically charge additional fees of $5 for still photography, $10–15 for video cameras, and up to $100 for sketching. There's no extra charge for feast days or dances, but photography is usually forbidden on special occasions.

Half a mile further north on Hwy-503, the *Rancho de Chimayó* is the best traditional New Mexican **restaurant** in the state, serving superb *flautas* and a mouthwatering *sopaipilla*, stuffed with meat and chilis, on a lovely sun-drenched outdoor patio, and it also offers reasonable **rooms** in a separate building (closed Mon Nov–April; ⓣ505/351-4444; ⓦwww.ranchodechimayo.com; ❹).

Taos

Still home to one of the longest-established Native American populations in the US, though transformed by becoming first a Spanish colonial outpost, and more recently a hangout for bohemian artists and New Age dropouts, **TAOS** (which rhymes with "mouse") has become famous out of all proportion to its size. Just seven thousand people live in its three component parts: **Taos** itself, around the plaza; sprawling **Ranchos de Taos**, three miles to the south; and the Native American community of **Taos Pueblo**, two miles north.

Beyond the usual unsightly highway sprawl, Taos is a delight to visit. Besides museums, galleries, and stores, it still offers an unhurried pace and charm, and the sense of a meeting place between Pueblo, Hispanic, and American cultures. Its reputation as an **artists' colony** began at the end of the nineteenth century. Not

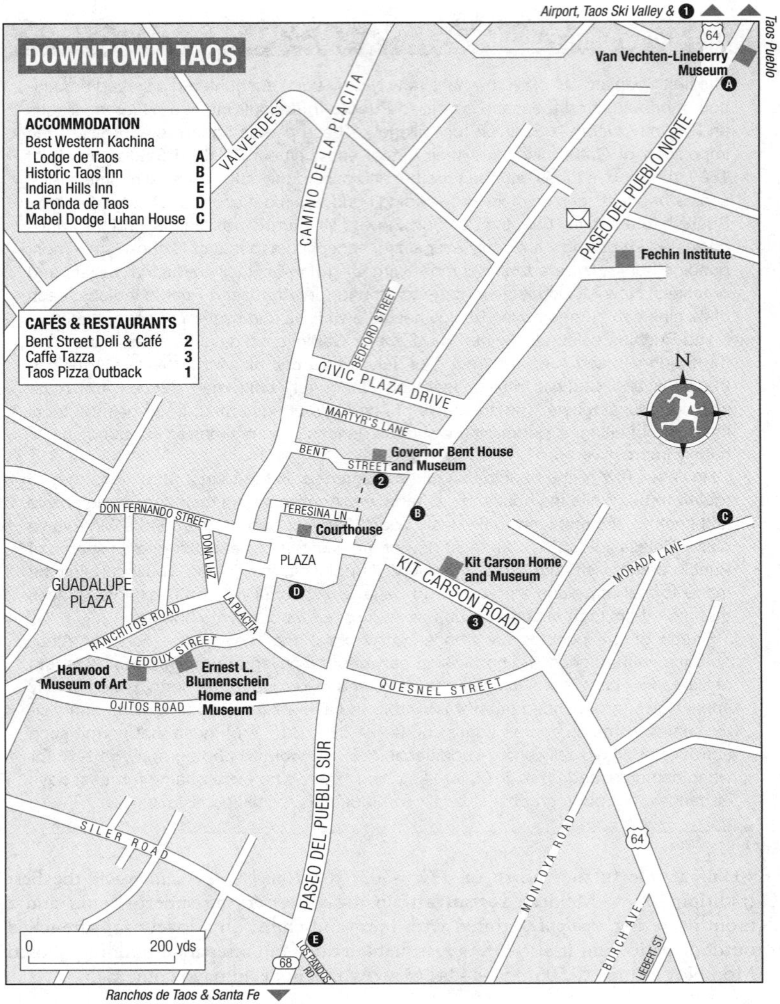

long afterward, society heiress Mabel Dodge arrived and married an Indian from the Pueblo to become Mabel Dodge Luhan. She in turn wrote a fan letter to English novelist **D.H. Lawrence**, who visited three times in the 1920s; his widow Frieda later made her home in Taos. New generations of artists and writers have "discovered" Taos ever since, the most famous of all being **Georgia O'Keeffe**, who stayed for a few years at the end of the 1920s.

Arrival and information

Two daily Greyhound and TNM&O **buses** from Albuquerque ($38) and Santa Fe ($28) arrive at **Taos Bus Center** (ⓣ505/758-1144), opposite the well-equipped local **visitor center**, two miles south of the plaza at the intersection of Hwy-68 and US-64 (daily 9am–5pm, closed Sun in winter; ⓣ505/758-3873 or 1-800/732-8267, ⓦwww.taoschamber.com).

Accommodation

Taos has **accommodation** to meet all needs, at prices well below those of Santa Fe (though thanks to the local ski resort rates don't drop in winter). The best places to **camp** are the nine summer-only campgrounds in **Carson National Forest** (ⓣ505/758-6200, ⓦwww.fs.fed.us/r3/carson), reached by following Kit Carson Road east until it becomes US-64.

Abominable Snowmansion Hostel/HI-Taos Taos Ski Valley Rd, Arroyo Seco ⓣ505/776-8298, ⓦwww.abominablesnowmansion.com. Pleasant, friendly HI-AYH hostel-cum-ski lodge, on a tight curve in the road up to the Ski Valley, five miles north of downtown. Office open daily 8–11am & 4–10pm. Dorm beds $15 in summer, $22 in winter, when rates include breakfast; teepees, and camping space out back; bargain private rooms and cabins, with and without en-suite facilities. ❶/❸

Best Western Kachina Lodge de Taos 413 Paseo del Pueblo Norte ⓣ505/758-2275 or 1-800/522-4462, ⓦwww.kachinalodge.com. Large, tasteful, family motel at the Taos Pueblo turn-off, with Southwestern art, a reasonable restaurant, a pool, live music, and small-scale Pueblo dances every summer night. ❹

Historic Taos Inn 125 Paseo del Pueblo Norte ⓣ505/758-2233 or 1-888/519-8267, ⓦwww.taosinn.com. Rambling, ravishing – and very Southwestern – central hotel. Each of its 44 rooms plays a variation on the Pueblo theme, while *Doc Martin's* restaurant (see p.867) and the *Adobe Bar* are packed nightly. ❹–❼

Indian Hills Inn 233 Paseo del Pueblo Sur ⓣ505/758-4293 or 1-800/444-2346, ⓦwww.newmex.com/indianhillsinn. The only cheap-ish highway motel within walking distance of the plaza; be sure to get a room away from the street. ❹

La Fonda de Taos 108 South Plaza ⓣ505/758-2211 or 1-800/833-2211, ⓦwww.lafondataos.com. Vintage 1930s hotel on the plaza that's been revamped to hold 24 luxurious suites, with Southwestern furnishings and tiled bathrooms. ❺

Mabel Dodge Luhan House 240 Morada Lane ⓣ505/751-9686 or 1-800/846-2235, ⓦwww.mabeldodgeluhan.com. Gorgeous 200-year-old adobe B&B complex, not far northeast of the plaza, where the lovely guestrooms are named for former guests like Willa Cather and Ansel Adams. Two rooms, including the light-filled solarium, share a bathroom painted by D.H. Lawrence; a cheaper lodge annex has more modern fittings. ❹–❽

Taos plaza and the museums

The old Spanish **plaza** at the heart of Taos is now ringed by jewelry stores, art galleries, and restaurants; all conform to the predominant Pueblo motif of rounded brown adobe. Specific sights are few – a small **museum** in the *La Fonda de Taos* hotel has a collection of sexy but amateurish paintings by D.H. Lawrence, and the tree-filled square itself is often animated by guitar-toting buskers – but the surrounding streets are perfect for an aimless stroll. Some of the best places to eat or drink, as well as a number of top-notch art and crafts galleries, are on **Bent Street**, a block north of the plaza. The street takes its name from the first American governor of New Mexico, Charles Bent; his house here, in which he was murdered in 1847, has been preserved as a ramshackle little museum of frontier life (daily April–Oct 9.30am–5pm, Nov–March 10am–4pm; $2).

Just east of the plaza, across the highway at the end of Taos's sole surviving stretch of wooden boardwalk, is the dusty adobe dwelling that was home to mountain man, mason, and part-time US cavalry officer **Kit Carson** (see p.867) in the mid-1800s. It too is now a small **museum**, commemorating Carson's many adventures (daily 9am–6pm; $5).

Two miles north of the Taos Pueblo turn-off, reached by a dirt road that angles into a tricky five-way intersection, the **Millicent Rogers Museum** (April–Oct daily 10am–5pm; Nov–March Tues–Sun 10am–5pm; $10; ⓦwww.millicentrogers.org) holds superb Ancestral Puebloan and Mimbres pottery; the more recent black-on-black ceramics of San Ildefonso Pueblo potter Maria Martínez; and beautiful Navajo blankets.

Ranchos de Taos

South of the plaza, either side of Hwy-68, **Ranchos de Taos** was originally a separate farming community. Each *rancho* had its own main house, or *hacienda*; one has been restored as a **museum** of colonial life. The **Hacienda Martínez** (daily April–Oct 9am–5pm, Nov–March 10am–4pm; $7), two miles southwest of the plaza on Ranchitos Road, was built in 1804. Within its thick, windowless, adobe walls – sealed like a fortress against Indian raids – two dozen rooms are wrapped around two patios, holding animal pens and a well. Trade goods of the kind its first owner, Taos mayor Don Antonio Martínez, once carried south along the Rio Grande are displayed alongside tools, looms, and simple furnishings.

In Ranchos' own small plaza, the mission church of **San Francisco de Asis** squares its broad shoulders, or more accurately its massive adobe buttresses, to the passing traffic. Built around 1776, it's one of colonial New Mexico's most splendid architectural achievements, with subtly rounded walls and corners disguising its underlying structural strength. Though the ever-changing interplay of light and shade across its golden exterior has fascinated painters from Georgia O'Keeffe onward, the interior is equally intriguing, with a magnificently ornate green-and-red reredos framing several naïve paintings.

Taos Pueblo

Continuously inhabited for nearly one thousand years, the two multistorey adobes at **Taos Pueblo**, two miles north of Taos plaza and half a mile east of Hwy-68, jointly constitute the most impressive Native American dwelling place still in use. Hlauuma, the north house, and Hlaukwima, the south house, are separated by the Rio Pueblo de Taos, which flows down from the sacred Blue Lake, inaccessible to outsiders. Pueblo residents make few concessions to the modern world, living without toilets, running water, or electricity.

The pueblo is generally open to visitors from 8am until 5.30pm from Monday to Saturday, and between 8.30am and 5pm on Sunday, but it often closes for tribal events such as festivals or funerals, and remains closed between mid-February and early April (ⓣ505/758-1028, ⓦwww.taospueblo.com). Assuming the pueblo is open, park at the edge of the plaza, and pay an **entrance fee** ($10 per person, plus $5 per still or video camera), that entitles you to join the guided **walking tours**, led by Pueblo residents, which leave at regular intervals.

For most of the year, Pueblo life continues with scant regard for the intrusion of tourists, but feast days and dances, held throughout the summer, can be spectacular. The biggest parties are the **Corn Dances** in June and July, and the **Feast of San Gerónimo** at the end of September.

Taos Ski Valley

Fifteen miles north of Taos lie the challenging slopes of **Taos Ski Valley**, reached via an attractive road that winds up from the village of Arroyo Seco. Located on the north flank of **Wheeler Peak**, the highest point in New Mexico at 13,161ft, the demanding runs are usually open to skiers and snowboarders between late November and early April (daily lift tickets late Nov to mid-Dec and late March to early April $40, mid-Dec to late March $66; information ⓣ505/776-2291, reservations ⓣ1-800/776-1111, ⓦwww.skitaos.org).

Eating, drinking, and nightlife

Taos is too small to offer much **nightlife**, but it does have a fine selection of **restaurants** in all price ranges, and several coffeehouses. If your main priority is to **drink**, the *Adobe Bar* in the *Taos Inn* (see p.865) is the coziest spot in town.

Bent Street Deli & Cafe 120 Bent St ☎505/758-5787. Airy, partly outdoor place, just north of the plaza with good-value breakfasts, sandwich lunches, and tasty dinners for under $20.
Caffè Tazza 122 Kit Carson Rd ☎505/758-8706. Trendy, central café with nice sunlit terrace, selling coffees and light veggie meals to students and assorted eccentrics.
Doc Martin's *Taos Inn*, 125 Paseo del Pueblo Norte ☎505/758-1977. Delicious, inventive New Mexican food in a romantic adobe inn, just east of the plaza. All meals daily; most dinner entrees, such as piñon-crusted salmon or roast chicken, cost $20–24.

Joseph's Table *La Fonda de Taos*, 108 South Plaza ☎505/751-4512. This delightful restaurant serves wonderful (if rich) food in a lovely setting, with very friendly service. A fabulous parma ham risotto appetizer is $14, while full entrees like crispy duck leg or pan-seared scallops cost around $30. You can also order smaller portions from the separate *Joe's Bar* menu, like a $14 buffalo burger for $12. Lunch served May–Aug only.
Taos Pizza Outback 712 Paseo del Pueblo Norte ☎505/748-3112. Hard-to-find pizzeria, a mile north of town, with a welcoming, youthful ambience and huge portions of great food – the $10 veggie calzones are amazing.

Albuquerque and central New Mexico

Most travelers simply race through **central New Mexico**, but it does hold isolated pockets of interest. Dozens of small towns hang on to the last remnants of the winding old "Chicago-to-LA" **Route 66**, long since superseded by I-40. **Albuquerque** – New Mexico's largest city, and site of its only major **airport** – sits dead center, at the intersection of I-40 and I-25. The area to the **east**, stretching toward Texas, is among the most desolate parts of the Southwest, but the mountainous region **west** has more to see – above all **Ácoma Pueblo**, the mesa-top "Sky City."

East of Albuquerque: Tucumcari and Fort Sumner

The long line of truck stops, diners, and motels at **TUCUMCARI**, the biggest town between Albuquerque and Amarillo, Texas (see p.701), has made it a favorite I-40 pit stop. To enjoy one of the world's greatest collections of barbed wire, drop in at the mind-boggling **Tucumcari Historical Museum,** 416 S Adams St (May–Aug Mon–Sat 8am–5pm; Sept–May Tues–Sat 8am–5pm; $2). Literally hundreds of inexpensive **rooms** lie along this stretch of old Route 66, including the classic *Blue Swallow* **motel**, 815 E Route 66 (☎505/461-9849, Ⓦwww.blueswallowmotel.com; ❷). For **food**, *Del's Restaurant*, 1202 E Route 66 (☎505/461-1740; closed Sun), is as good a diner as you're going to find, serving both Mexican and American dishes.

FORT SUMNER, southwest of Tucumcari, is where frontiersman and US Army colonel **Kit Carson** dragged the Navajo from Arizona in 1864 (see p.904). On the site of their former reservation, at **Fort Sumner State Monument**, seven miles southeast of the modern town, the **Bosque Redondo Memorial** honors the Navajo and Apache who died during their imprisonment (daily 8.30am–5pm; $5; Ⓦwww.nmmonuments.org). Wild West fanatics come to Fort Sumner because outlaw **Billy the Kid** was gunned down here by Pat Garrett in 1881. His grave stands behind the jumbled **Old Fort Sumner Museum** (daily 9am–5pm; $4), his tombstone shielded from memento-seekers by a steel cage.

Albuquerque

Sprawling at the heart of New Mexico, where the main east–west road and rail routes cross both the Rio Grande and the old road south to Mexico, **ALBU-**

QUERQUE is, with half a million people, the state's only major metropolis. Though many tourists head straight for Santa Fe, ignoring Albuquerque, the "**Duke City**" has a good deal going for it. Like Phoenix, it's grown a bit too fast for comfort, but the original Hispanic settlement is still discernible at its core, and its diverse population gives it a rare cultural vibrancy. Even if its architecture is often uninspired, the setting is magnificent, sandwiched between the Rio Grande and the dramatic, glowing **Sandia Mountains**. Specific highlights include the intact **Spanish plaza**, the neon-lit **Route 66** frontage of Central Avenue, and the excellent **Indian Pueblo Cultural Center**, while every October Albuquerque hosts the nation's largest **hot-air balloon** rally.

Arrival and information

Public transportation in Albuquerque has been transformed by the new **Rail Runner** light-rail system (fares from $1; ⓣ1-866/795-7245, ⓦwww.nmrailrunner.com). Commuter trains from its Downtown Albuquerque station, in the **Alvarado Transportation Center** at First and Central on the eastern edge of downtown, run south to Belen and north to Bernalillo, but the main appeal for tourists is that services also continue all the way north to Santa Fe, as detailed on p.856. The first Rail Runner stop south of downtown, the Bernalillo County/International Sunport station at 113 Rio Bravo SE, is a short ride from the airport on ABQ Ride bus #222; alternatively, bus #50 runs straight from the airport to the Downtown station.

Both Amtrak **trains** between Los Angeles and Chicago, and long-distance Greyhound buses (including 4 daily **buses** to Santa Fe; ⓣ505/243-4435; $28), also use the Alvarado Transportation Center.

Finally, the Alvarado Transportation Center is also the hub of the ABQ Ride **city bus** network (ⓣ505/843-9200, ⓦwww.cabq.gov/transit). Its free D-Ride route circles downtown, while commuter buses further afield cost $1 a ride.

Accommodation

The twenty-mile length of **Central Avenue**, the old Route 66, is lined with the flashing neon signs of $40-per-night **motels**. You'll have to pay a little extra to stay in the heart of Old Town or downtown. Larger convention **hotels** are congregated along the interstates, and near the airport.

Ambassador Inn 7407 Central Ave NE ⓣ505/265-1161. There's nothing fancy or exciting about the *Ambassador*, and east of the liveliest part of Central Avenue, but for a clean, presentable, ordinary motel room, the price is great. ❷

Casas de Sueños 310 Rio Grande Blvd SW ⓣ505/247-4560 or 1-800/665-7002, ⓦwww.casasdesuenos.com. Beautifully furnished, exotic, and friendly B&B, very close to Old Town, with themed cottages and smaller rooms. ❺

Comfort Inn – Airport 2300 Yale Blvd SE ⓣ505/243-2244 or 1-800/221-2222, ⓦwww.comfortinn.com. Good-value motel, served by free shuttles from the airport across the road, and with complimentary breakfasts. ❹

La Quinta Inn Albuquerque Airport 2116 Yale Blvd SE ⓣ505/243-5500. Large, upscale motel, served by frequent shuttles from the nearby airport, and offering safe, good-value accommodation. ❹

Monterey Nonsmokers Motel 2402 Central Ave SW ⓣ505/243-3554 or 1-877/666-8379, ⓦwww.nonsmokersmotel.com. Clean, fifteen-room motel, two blocks west of Old Town, with pool, laundry, and a strict nonsmoking policy. ❷

Route 66 Hostel 1012 Central Ave SW ⓣ505/247-1813, ⓦhttp://members.aol.com/route66hos/htmlRT66/. Albuquerque's only hostel, a friendly place between Old Town and downtown, offers dorm beds for $17, kitchen facilities, and very plain but bargain-priced private doubles. Office hours daily 7.30–10.30am & 4–11pm. ❶

Old Town

Once you've cruised up and down **Central Avenue**, looking at the flashing neon and 1940s architecture of this twenty-mile stretch of Route 66 (Sun Tran buses do it all day for $1), most of what's interesting about Albuquerque is concentrated in **Old Town**, the old Spanish heart of the city. As the billboards on the interstate nearby rightly proclaim, "it's darned old and historic." The tree-filled **main plaza** is overlooked by the twin-towered adobe facade of **San Felipe de Neri church**; it's a pleasant place to wander or have a meal, even if there's not a whole lot to do. Among the more bizarre of the many knick-knack shops, the **Rattlesnake Museum**, southeast of the plaza at 202 San Felipe St NW, has live rattlers on display (June–Aug Mon–Sat 10am–6pm, Sun 1–5pm; Sept–May Mon–Fri noon–6pm, Sat 10am–6pm, Sun 1–5pm; $3.50; Ⓦwww.rattlesnakes.com).

In the cluster of museums five minutes northeast of the plaza, the **Albuquerque Museum of Art and History**, 2000 Mountain Rd (daily except Mon 9am–5pm; $4, free Sun 9am–1pm; Ⓦwww.cabq.gov/museum), holds impressive weapons carried by the Spanish conquistadors as well as delicate religious artifacts, and paintings and photos depicting Albuquerque through the centuries. Across the street, the **National Atomic Museum** at 1905 Mountain Rd NW (daily 9am–5pm; $6; Ⓦwww.atomicmuseum.org), traces the history of nuclear science and weapons from the discoveries of Madame Curie up to robotic devices such as the "truck-killing standoff weapon" Fireant. It's currently due to expand and become the **National Museum of Nuclear Science and History**.

Nearby, the **New Mexico Museum of Natural History**, 1801 Mountain Rd NW (daily 9am–5pm; closed Mon in Jan & Sept; $7; Ⓦwww.nmnaturalhistory.org), has full-scale models of dinosaurs, and a replica of a Carlsbad-like snow cave. Its fascinating "Start Up" exhibition uses Microsoft's origins in Albuquerque in 1977 as the springboard for a history of the computer revolution.

The riverfront

The Rio Grande having shifted its course over time, there's a low-key gap west of Old Town, much of it left undeveloped in deference to the unruly river. Along the wooded eastern riverbank, the **Bio Park** holds two attractions. The **Albuquerque Aquarium** (June–Aug Mon–Fri 9am–5pm, Sat & Sun 9am–6pm; Sept–May daily 9am–5pm; $7; Ⓦwww.cabq.gov/biopark) offers the chance to dine beside a glass-walled tank filled with live sharks, or walk through a tunnel surrounded by fierce-eyed moray eels. Across the way, the **Rio Grande Botanic Garden** (same hours; same ticket) consists of two large conservatories – one holding rare plants from the Sonoran and Chihuahua deserts, the other more temperate Mediterranean species – plus a series of walled gardens.

Indian Pueblo Cultural Center

The **Indian Pueblo Cultural Center**, at 2401 12th St NW, one block north of I-40, is a stunning museum (daily 9am–4.30pm; $8; Ⓣ505/843-7270, Ⓦwww.indianpueblo.org) and crafts market (daily 9am–5.30pm; free), co-operatively owned and run by the diverse Pueblo Indians of New Mexico.

In New Mexico's one major museum about Native Americans that's curated by Native Americans, the displays have a clear and distinct point of view. The shared Ancestral Puebloan heritage at the root of Pueblo culture is explained in detail, as is the impact of the Spanish conquistadors. There's also a good explanation of a topic Pueblo Indians rarely discuss with outsiders: how indigenous religion has managed to coexist with imported Catholicism. Videos illustrate modern Pueblo life, and the stores upstairs sell outstanding pottery and jewelry, while a good-quality **café** serves Pueblo specialties.

Sandia Crest

The forested 10,500-foot peaks of the **Sandia Crest** soar east of Albuquerque, affording beautiful views during and after sunset. In summer it's a good 25°F cooler up here than in the valley, while in winter you can go downhill or cross-country **skiing** (mid-Dec to mid-March; lift tickets $48; ⓣ505/242-9052, ⓦwww.sandiapeak.com). If you don't want to drive the scenic but twisting twenty-mile route from Albuquerque, take the stunning **Sandia Peak Tramway** (summer daily 9am–9pm; winter Mon & Wed–Sun 9am–8pm, Tues 5–8pm; $17.50), the world's longest single-span tramway at 2.7 miles; it leaves from the end of Tramway Road at the city's northeast edge.

Eating

Albuquerque is the place to get to grips with what real New Mexico food is all about. Family diners all over the city compete to create the spiciest chiles rellenos and enchiladas.

Artichoke Café 424 Central Ave SE ⓣ505/243-0200. Simple but classy restaurant in the heart of downtown, serving a good, varied menu of California-influenced modern American cuisine; typical entrees cost $18–30. Dinner only on weekends.

Flying Star 3416 Central Ave SE ⓣ505/255-6633. Lively, crowded University District café serving eclectic international cuisine to a largely student clientele. The vast menu ranges through breakfast specialties, salads, and blue-plate specials such as Vietnamese noodles or pasta pomodoro for $10. Open daily from 6am until late.

Frontier 2400 Central Ave SE ⓣ505/266-0550. Legendary 24-hour diner across from the university, where an unceasing parade of characters chow down on burgers, burritos, and great vegetarian enchiladas.

Pueblo Harvest Cafe Indian Pueblo Cultural Center, 2401 12th St NW ⓣ505/843-7270. Unusual Native American restaurant, serving Pueblo specialties like fry-bread at lunchtime, plus fine dinners, with braised bison ribs among the tasty $20–30 entrees.

Satellite Coffee 3513 Central Ave NE ⓣ505/256-0345. University District coffee bar, marked by the sign of the flying saucer, which also serve daily specials like split pea soup.

Scalo 3500 Central Ave SE ⓣ505/255-8781. Large but romantic and stylish Northern Italian restaurant near the university. Appetizers like steamed mussels or beef carpaccio cost $10, entrees such as roasted salmon are more like $25, and there are plenty of pasta and vegetarian options.

Drinking and nightlife

Many of downtown Albuquerque's **bars** and **nightclubs** have long doubled as small theaters or music venues, though a disastrous fire in February 2008 saw *Puccini's Golden West Saloon* destroyed and other clubs severely damaged. The free weekly *Alibi* magazine (ⓦwww.alibi.com) carries full listings of what's coming up or going down.

Burt's Tiki Lounge 313 Gold Ave SW ⓣ505/247-2878, ⓦwww.burtstikilounge.com. Tuesday is the big tiki-bar cocktail night here, though the Polynesian décor makes a good backdrop for live bands for the rest of the week. Mon–Sat 8pm–2am.

Caravan East 7605 Central Ave NE ⓣ505/265-7877. Enormous honky-tonk, where tenderfeet can do the two-step with throngs of urban cowboys.

KiMo Theater 423 Central Ave NW ⓣ505/768-3522, ⓦwww.cabq.gov/kimo. Gorgeous, city-owned "Pueblo Deco" theater, dating from the late 1920s, which puts on an eclectic program of opera, dance, and theater performances, kids' movies, and also regular live bands.

The Launchpad 618 Central Ave SW ⓣ505/764-8887, ⓦwww.launchpadrocks.com. Dance and live music space that showcases touring indie and world music bands; there's also a cluster of pool tables.

West of Albuquerque: I-40 to Arizona

As you drive between Albuquerque and Arizona, don't let the tacky parade of billboards and hoardings offering cut-price cigarettes and Indian jewelry cause you to miss such interesting side trips as **Ácoma Pueblo** and **Chaco Canyon**, which lie south and north of I-40 respectively.

Ácoma Pueblo

The amazing **Ácoma Pueblo**, a dozen miles south of I-40 fifty miles west of Albuquerque, encapsulates a thousand years of Native American history. Its focus is the ancient village known as "**Sky City**," perched 367ft high atop a magnificent isolated mesa. Probably occupied by Chacoan migrants between 1100 and 1200 AD, when the great pueblos of Chaco Canyon were still in use, Ácoma has adapted to repeated waves of invaders ever since, while retaining its own strong identity. As the Ácomans have long been happy to take the tourist dollar, visitors seldom feel the awkwardness possible at other pueblo communities. Nonetheless, Ácoma is the real thing, and its sense of unbroken tradition can reduce even the least culturally sensitive traveler to awestruck silence.

To visit Sky City, you have to join one of the hour-long guided **tours** (daily: May–Oct 8am–6.30pm, Nov–April 8am–4.30pm; last tour leaves one hour before closing; $12, plus $10 for photo permit, no camcorders or video; ⓣ505/470-0181 or 1-800/747-0181, ⓦwww.skycity.com), which leave regularly from the excellent visitor center and museum ($4) at the base of the mesa. The main stop is at the **San Esteban del Rey** mission, a thick-walled adobe church completed in 1640. The visual impact of the building is undeniable, and it's striking that the Ácomans obviously never felt inclined to follow its architectural example. Instead they went on constructing the multistorey stone and adobe houses around which the tour then proceeds. Only thirteen families live permanently on the mesa; most Ácomans reside down below, where they can get electricity, running water, and jobs. Villagers do, however, come up here during the day to sell pottery and fry-bread.

Grants

The old Route 66 town of **GRANTS**, fifteen miles west of Ácoma, holds half a dozen budget motels, including a good *Super 8*, 1604 E Santa Fe Ave (ⓣ505/287-8811; ❸). In the heart of town, the *Mission at Riverwalk*, 422 W Santa Fe Ave (ⓣ505/285-4632; ❹), a café in a former church, serves sandwiches, smoothies, and coffee, and has a separate guest house for rent. The local **visitor center,** in the enjoyable **New Mexico Museum of Mining** at 100 N Iron Ave (Mon–Sat 9am–4pm; $3; ⓣ505/287-4802, ⓦwww.grants.org), offers a chance to make a virtual descent into a mock-up of one of the region's many **uranium mines**.

El Morro National Monument

Hidden away on Hwy-53 south of the Zuni Mountains, 42 miles west of Grants, **El Morro National Monument** feels as far off the beaten track as it's possible to be. Incredibly, however, this pale-pink sandstone cliff was a regular rest stop for international travelers before the Pilgrims landed at Plymouth Rock, thanks to a perennial pool of water that collects at the base of a tumbling waterfall. This spot was first recorded by Spanish explorers in 1583 – *el morro* means "the headland" – and in 1605, Don Juan de Oñate, the founder of New Mexico, carved the first of many messages that earned it the American name of **Inscription Rock**.

Translations of El Morro's graffiti are displayed in the **visitor center** (daily: summer 8am–7pm; spring & fall 9am–6pm; winter 9am–5pm; $3 per person; ⓣ505/783-4226, ⓦwww.nps.gov/elmo). You can see the real thing on a half-mile trail, which stays open until an hour before the visitor center closes.

Chaco Canyon

Few casual visitors brave the long, bumpy ride to the Ancestral Puebloan ruins of **Chaco Canyon**, north of I-40 between Grant and Gallup. Although **Chaco Culture National Historical Park** holds North America's largest pre-Columbian city, for beauty and drama it can't compete with lesser settlements such as

Canyon de Chelly (see p.906), and the low-walled canyon itself is a mere scratch in the scrubby high-desert plains.

However, there's still plenty about Chaco to take your breath away. Over 3600 separate sites have been logged here, of which thirteen are open to visitors. Six, arrayed along the canyon's north wall, are so-called "Great Houses" – self-contained pueblos, three or four storeys high, whose fortress-like walls concealed up to eight hundred rooms.

Both the routes to Chaco Canyon entail driving twenty miles over rough but passable dirt roads, and should not be attempted during or within a day of a rainstorm. Whether you approach from the south, by following Hwy-57 up from **Seven Lakes**, eighteen miles northeast of **Crownpoint**, or from the north or east, by turning off US-550 at **Nageezi**, 36 miles south of **Bloomfield,** you enter the park at its southeast corner, close to the **visitor center** (daily 8am–5pm; $8 per vehicle; Ⓣ505/786-7014, Ⓦwww.nps.gov/chcu). The basic first-come, first-served *Gallo* **campground** ($10), a short way east, is the only visitor facility in the park; from April to October it's usually full by 3pm.

The gates of the canyon's eight-mile one-way **loop road** are open from dawn to dusk. The major stop is at the far end, where **Pueblo Bonito** ("beautiful town") – said to have been the biggest building in America until structural steel was developed in 1898 – can be explored on an easy half-mile trail. Work on this four-storey D-shaped structure started in 850 AD and continued for three hundred years. Entering the ruin via its lowest levels, the path reaches its central plaza, which held at least three **Great Kivas** – ceremonial chambers used by entire communities rather than individual clans or families.

Gallup

Half an hour from Arizona, 65 miles west of Grants, the famous Route 66 town of **GALLUP** is a handy but uninteresting I-40 pit stop. Though the former Route 66 frontage contains some incredibly inexpensive **motels**, such as the *Colonial*, 1007 W Coal Ave (Ⓣ505/863-6821; ❶), the only place really worth stopping for is the lovely ★ *El Rancho Hotel*, 1000 E 66 Ave (Ⓣ505/863-9311 or 1-800/543-6351, Ⓦwww.elranchohotel.com; ❹, built in 1937 to serve the many Hollywood stars filming nearby. Nowadays you can ogle their signed photos in the spacious Spanish Revival lobby, grab a bite in its decorative restaurant, or spend the night in the Ronald Reagan Room, the Marx Brothers Room, or the Mae West Room. The best guestrooms are in the original ranchhouse, the rest in a two-storey motel building.

The Navajo and other Native Americans come together in **Red Rock State Park**, four miles east of Gallup, on the second weekend in August for the **Inter-Tribal Indian Ceremonial**, the largest such gathering anywhere (information and tickets Ⓣ505/863-3896; Ⓦgallup-ceremonial.org). Four days of dances and craft shows have as their highlight a Saturday morning parade through the town.

Southern New Mexico

Most travelers who come to **southern New Mexico** are here to visit **Carlsbad Caverns National Park**. Crassly commercialized it may be, but it's too amazing a geological spectacle to miss. Northwest of Carlsbad, the **Sacramento** and **Jicarilla mountains** are home to the **Mescalero Apache** reservation as well as some rough-and-ready resorts. The desolate dunes of the **White Sands** monument spread west of the mountains, with the rolling hills of the **Rio Grande Valley** beyond.

Carlsbad Caverns National Park

CARLSBAD CAVERNS NATIONAL PARK consists of a tract of the Guadalupe Mountains that's so riddled with underground caves and tunnels as to be virtually hollow. Tamed in classic park-service style with concrete trails and electric lighting, this subterranean wonderland is now a walk-in gallery, where tourists flock to marvel at its intricate limestone tracery. Summer crowds can get pretty intense, but in a strange way that's part of the fun – Carlsbad feels like a real throwback to the great 1950s boom in mass tourism. Before you decide to join in,

▲ Carlsbad Caverns National Park

however, be sure to grasp that it's a *long* way from anywhere else – three hundred miles southeast of Albuquerque and 150 miles northeast of El Paso, Texas.

To reach the park, follow the narrow, twisting seven-mile road that leaves US-62/180 at **White's City**, twenty miles southwest of **CARLSBAD** itself. This ends at the **visitor center**, where you can pick up a schedule of tours (daily: June to late Aug 8am–7pm; late Aug to May 8am–5pm; Ⓣ505/785-2232, Ⓦwww.nps.gov/cave).

Almost all visitors confine their attention to the main cave, **Carlsbad Cavern** itself, which is the only one covered by the standard park fee of $6 per person for three days. Direct elevators drop to the Cavern's centerpiece, the **Big Room**, 750 vertical feet below the visitor center, but you can choose instead to walk down via the **Natural Entrance Route** (last entry summer 3.30pm; rest of year 2pm). This steep paved footpath switchbacks into the guano-encrusted maw of the cave, taking fifteen minutes to reach the first of the formations and another fifteen to reach the Big Room. All visitors must ride the elevator back out.

Measuring up to 1800ft long and 250ft high, the Big Room is festooned with stalactites, stalagmites, and countless unnameable shapes of swirling liquid rock. All are a uniform stone gray; the rare touches of color are provided by slight red or brown mineral-rich tinges, improved with gentle pastel lighting. It takes an hour or so to complete the level trail around the Room's perimeter. Whatever the weather up top – summer highs exceed 100°F – the temperature down here is always a cool 56°F, so dress warmly.

Adjoining the Big Room, the **Underground Lunchroom** is a vast formation-free side cave, paved in the 1950s to create a diner-cum-souvenir-shop that sells indigestible lunches in polystyrene containers, plus Eisenhower-era souvenirs like giant pencils and Viewmaster reels.

Guided tours from the Big Room explore beautiful side caves such as the **King's Palace**, filled with translucent "draperies" of limestone (daily summer 10am, 11am, 2pm & 3pm; winter 10am & 2pm; $8). Additional tours can take you along the **Left Hand Tunnel** route down from the visitor center ($7), or on a much more demanding descent into either **Spider Cave** or the **Hall of the White Giant** (both $20).

Practicalities

No matter how you get to Carlsbad Caverns, you have to cross seemingly endless miles of the **Llano Estacado**, the deathly flat rangeland that covers southeast New Mexico and the Texas Panhandle. The route from El Paso, Texas, has the advantage of passing through **Guadalupe Mountains National Park** (see p.710).

WHITE'S CITY is not a town but a privately owned tourist complex, which as well as a little water park holds the closest **accommodation** and **camping** to the park, including the mock-adobe *Best Western Cavern Inn* (Ⓣ505/785-2291 or 1-800/228-3767, Ⓦwww.whitescity.com; ❸; the *White's City RV Park* (same number), which has tent camping space; and the *Velvet Garter Restaurant* (same number). There's little in **CARLSBAD** itself, 25 miles north of White's City, beyond its many motels, such as the large *Best Western Stevens Inn*, 1829 S Canal St (Ⓣ505/887-2851 or 1-800/730-2851, Ⓦwww.stevensinn.com; ❹). Rates here include a full breakfast at the *Flume Room* **restaurant**, which is pretty much the best in town.

Roswell

Seventy-five miles north of Carlsbad, the small ranching town of **ROSWELL** is renowned as the spot where an alien spaceship supposedly crash-landed on July 4, 1947. The commander of the local air force base announced that they had retrieved the wreckage of a flying saucer, and despite a follow-up denial within a day the story has kept running, with TV series like *X-Files*, *Roswell* and *Taken* stoking the imaginations of UFO theorists.

Despite the wishful thinking of the truly weird clientele who drift in from the plains, the **International UFO Museum**, 114 N Main St (daily 9am–5pm; $5; ⓣ505/625-9495, ⓦwww.roswellufomuseum.com), inadvertently exposes the whole tawdry business as transparent nonsense. By way of contrast, the **Roswell Museum**, 100 W 11th St (Mon–Sat 9am–5pm, Sun 1–5pm; free), boasts an excellent, multifaceted collection, with a section celebrating pioneer rocket scientist Robert Goddard (1882–1945). Historical artifacts elsewhere range from Spanish armor to astronaut Harrison Schmitt's spacesuit, while a gallery displays Southwestern landscape paintingss including a solitary Georgia O'Keeffe.

Roswell's **visitor center** is at 426 N Main St (Mon–Sat 9am–5pm; ⓣ505/624-0889, ⓦwww.roswellnm.org). The finest **motel** in town, the *Best Western Sally Port Inn*, 2000 N Main St (ⓣ505/622-6430 or 1-800/548-5221, ⓦwww.bestwestern.com; ❸), also has a good **restaurant**. The *Cattle Baron*, 1113 N Main St (ⓣ505/622-2465), is a large, good-value **steakhouse**, while *Farley's*, just up the hill at 1315 N Main St (ⓣ505/627-1100), is a livelier sci-fi-themed pub and diner.

Lincoln

Perhaps the most enduring of New Mexico's many legendary Wild West figures is Brooklyn-born William Bonney, better known as **Billy the Kid**. He first came to fame as an 18-year-old in 1878, when the **Lincoln County War** erupted between rival groups of ranchers and merchants in the frontier town of **LINCOLN**, on Hwy-380 halfway between Carlsbad and Albuquerque. Since those days, no new buildings have joined the venerable false-fronted structures that line Main Street, and the entire town is now the **Lincoln State Monument**. Visitors can stroll its length at any time, and visit various historical sites (each site $3.50, joint admission to all sites $5; not all sites remain open throughout the winter; ⓣ505/653-4372, ⓦwww.nmmonuments.org & ⓦwww.hubbardmuseum.org).

Displays in the **Historic Lincoln Visitors Center**, at the east end of town (daily 8.30am–5pm), cover Hispanics, cowboys, "Buffalo Soldiers" – the black cavalrymen stationed at nearby Fort Stanton – and Apaches, as well as the Lincoln County War. Billy the Kid's most famous jailbreak is commemorated at the **Lincoln County Courthouse** (daily 8.30am–5pm), at the other end of the street; waiting here under sentence of death, he shot his way out and fled to Fort Sumner, where Sheriff Pat Garrett eventually caught up with him (see p.867). On the first weekend of August the streets echo with gunfire once again, during the three-day **Old Lincoln Days** festival.

Near the courthouse, the *Wortley Hotel* – once owned by Pat Garrett – offers seven simple but appealing **hotel** rooms (ⓣ505/653-4300, ⓦwww.wortleyhotel.com; April to mid-Oct only; ❹), and its **dining room** serves simple stews and sandwiches at lunchtime only.

Ruidoso

The **Sacramento**, **Capitan,** and **Jicarilla mountains**, which rise at the western edge of the Llano Estacado, 85 miles northwest of Carlsbad, form a rare respite from the scrubby flatness. Spread out along winding roads that cut through dense groves of pine, fir, and aspen, the main town here is the fast-growing resort of **RUIDOSO**.

The **Ruidoso Downs** racetrack, just east of town, plays host to a 77-day racing season that culminates on Labor Day with the **All-American Futurity**, one of the world's richest horse races. Alongside, the **Hubbard Museum of the American West** (daily 9am–5pm; $6; Ⓦwww.hubbardmuseum.org) holds displays on all aspects of Western history, with an especial emphasis on horses. In winter, attention turns to the 12,000-foot slopes of **Ski Apache** (Ⓣ505/464-3600, Ⓦwww.skiapache.com), a downhill ski area northwest of town on Hwy-532 where lift tickets cost around $50 per day.

Ruidoso's **visitor center** is at 720 Sudderth Ave (Mon–Sat 9am–5pm, Sun 1–4pm; Ⓦwww.ruidoso.net), while **motels** include the inexpensive *Apache*, 344 Sudderth Ave (Ⓣ505/257-2986 or 1-800/426-0616, Ⓦwww.ruidoso.net/apache; ❸). The glitzy *Inn of the Mountain Gods*, three miles southwest on Carrizo Canyon Road (Ⓣ505/257-5141 or 1-888/324-0348, Ⓦwww.innofthemountaingods.com; ❺) is, like the ski resort, owned by the Mescalero Apache, and holds a lucrative casino as well as fine dining and luxury accommodation. Other eating possibilities range from the classy French cuisine of *Le Bistro*, 2800 Sudderth Drive (closed Sun; Ⓣ505/257-0132), to the sandwiches and coffee at the *Ruidoso Roastery*, 113 Rio St (lunch only, closed Sun; Ⓣ505/257-3576).

White Sands National Monument

Filling a broad valley west of Ruidoso and the Sacramento Mountains, the **White Sands** are 250 square miles of glistening, three-storey-high dunes, not of sand, but of finely ground gypsum eroded from the nearby peaks. Most of the desert valley is under the control of the military, who use it as a missile range and training ground, and as a landing site for the **space shuttle**; only the southern half of the dunes is protected within **White Sands National Monument** (and even that is often closed for an hour or two at a time while missile tests are under way). The best place to start is at the **visitor center**, just off US-70, which illuminates the unique plants and animals that dwell here (daily: late May to early Sept 8am–7pm; early Sept to late May 8am–6pm; Ⓣ505/479-6124, Ⓦwww.nps.gov/whsa). An eight-mile paved road ($3 per person) stretches into the heart of the dunes, where you can scramble and slide in the sheer white landscape.

ALAMOGORDO, which sits at the base of the Sacramento Mountains, sixteen miles east of the Monument along US-54, holds the nearest food and lodging.

Las Cruces and Mesilla

From White Sands, US-70 heads southwest across the Tularosa Valley to **LAS CRUCES** – "the Crosses" – a large, modern farming community on the Rio Grande at the junction of I-10 and I-25. The town takes its name from the dozens of white crosses set up in the sands to mark the graves of early travelers killed by the Apache, but any sense of its history is pretty well buried by motels and fast-food franchises. It's a prosperous place, though, and likely to become more so if, as anticipated, **Spaceport America**, currently being built in the empty desert roughly 45 miles northeast, becomes the base for the first-ever passenger spaceflights, due to be operated by Virgin Galactic (Ⓦwww.virgingalactic.com) from 2010 onwards.

The little-changed Hispanic village of **MESILLA**, just south of I-10 two miles west, was until the 1870s one of the Southwest's largest towns, with eight thousand inhabitants. During the Civil War, it even served briefly as the Confederate capital of New Mexico and Arizona, but it went into swift decline when the railroad bypassed it in 1881. Mesilla's delightful Old West **plaza** has a real frontier feel, even though most of its old adobes, like the former courthouse where Billy the Kid was sentenced to death in 1881, now house art galleries and souvenir shops.

Restaurants include the steak-oriented *Double Eagle* (ⓣ575/523-6700), while the *Mesón de Mesilla*, 1803 Av de Mesilla (ⓣ575/525-9212, ⓦwww.mesondemesilla.com; ❺), is a gorgeous "boutique resort" **hotel** five minutes' walk east.

The southwest corner

I-10 heads west from Las Cruces across southwestern New Mexico, also known as the "**Boot heel**" for the way it steps down toward Mexico. In this wide-open rangeland, so sparsely inhabited that there are roughly three square miles per person, towns are few and far between. Both **DEMING**, sixty miles west of Las Cruces, and **LORDSBURG**, on I-10 twenty miles short of Arizona, hold Amtrak stations, plus a string of gas stations, cafés, and motels, but little else.

Silver City

Almost entirely wilderness, the semi-arid, forested, volcanic **Mogollon** and **Mimbres mountains** soar to ten thousand feet above the high desert plains, and remain little altered since Apache warrior **Geronimo** was born at the headwaters of the Gila River.

Halfway up the mountains, the biggest settlement, **SILVER CITY**, lies 45 miles north of I-10 where US-180 from Deming meets Hwy-90 from Lordsburg. The Spanish came here in 1804, sold the Mimbreño Indians into slavery, and opened the **Santa Rita copper mine**, just east of town below the Kneeling Nun monolith. The town was re-established in 1870 as a rough-and-tumble silver camp – **Billy the Kid** spent most of his childhood here. A fine selection of ornate old buildings is scattered along elm-lined avenues and across the hills. The **Western New Mexico University Museum**, 12th and Alabama (Mon–Fri 9am–4.30pm, Sat & Sun 10am–4pm; free), holds the world's finest collection of beautiful **Mimbres pottery**, produced locally around 1100AD.

In downtown Silver City, the *Palace Hotel*, 106 W Broadway (ⓣ575/388-1811, ⓦwww.zianet.com/palacehotel; ❷), is a small, nicely restored nineteenth-century hotel. Just outside town, the large 1920s *Bear Mountain Guest Ranch* (ⓣ575/538-2538 or 1-877/620-2327, ⓦwww.bearmountainlodge.com; ❺), makes a great base for bird-watching, cycling, mountain biking, or cross-country skiing. Bullard Street in the heart of town holds **saloons and cafés** like the *Jalisco Café* at no. 100 (ⓣ575/388-2060).

Arizona

The tourism industry in **ARIZONA** has, literally, one colossal advantage – the **Grand Canyon** of the Colorado River, which is the single most awe-inspiring spectacle in a land of unforgettable geology. In comparison to the inhuman scale of the Grand Canyon, however, several other Arizona destinations have a more abiding emotional impact, thanks to the sheer drama of human involvement in this forbidding but deeply resonant desert landscape.

Over a third of the state still belongs to the **Native Americans** who have lived here for centuries, and who outside the cities form the majority of the population. In the so-called **Indian Country** of northeastern Arizona, the

Navajo Nation holds the stupendous **Canyon de Chelly** and dozens of other **Ancestral Puebloan ruins**, as well as the stark rocks of **Monument Valley**. The Navajo surround the homeland of the stoutly traditional **Hopi**, who live in remote **mesa-top villages**. The third main tribal group is the **Apache**, in the harshly beautiful southeastern mountains – the last Native Americans to give in to the overwhelming power of the American invaders.

Away from the reservations, **Wild West** towns like **Tombstone**, site of the famed OK Corral, give a clear sense of Arizona's rough-and-ready, pioneer mentality; this was the last of the lower 48 states to join the Union, in 1912. The **cities**, however, are not nearly so much fun. In **Phoenix**, the capital, well over a million souls are scattered over a five-hundred-square-mile morass of shopping malls and tract-house suburbs; **Tucson** is rather more appealing, but is still liable to wear thin after a couple of days.

Though the open spaces of southern Arizona can be harsh, the bleakness is balanced somewhat by the many reserves that protect its amazing flora and fauna, such as **Saguaro National Park**, just outside Tucson, with its giant cactuses, real-life roadrunners, and rare Gila monsters.

Getting around Arizona

Greyhound **buses** stop at Arizona's major cities and most towns along the interstates, while Amtrak **trains** cross the state on two transcontinental routes (via Tucson in the south, or Flagstaff further north). Seeing the backcountry, however, is all but impossible without a car. The largest airport is in Phoenix.

Tucson, Phoenix, and southern Arizona

While most of Arizona's compelling natural attractions are in its northern reaches, the **southern** half of the state holds ninety percent of its people, all its significant cities, and several important historic sites. **Phoenix**, the state capital, is huge, sprawling, and dull; **Tucson** makes a livelier base; and there's some great frontier Americana in the southeast corner, especially in **Tombstone**.

Tucson and around

After serving as a Spanish and Mexican outpost, and then as territorial capital for both the US and Confederate governments, **TUCSON** (pronounced *too-sonn*) – a mere sixty miles north of Mexico on the cross-country I-10 – has grown into a modern metropolis of 900,000-plus people without entirely sacrificing its historic quarters. Equal parts college town and retirement community, it's one of the more attractive big cities of the Southwest – which admittedly isn't saying much. Although it suffers from the same Sunbelt sprawl as Albuquerque and Phoenix, it has a compact center, some enjoyable restaurants, and pretty good nightlife, energized by the 37,000 students at the University of Arizona. There's also some superb landscape within easy reach, from the forested flanks of **Mount Lemmon** to the rolling foothills of **Saguaro National Park**.

Arrival and information

Tucson International Airport, eight miles south of downtown (Ⓣ520/573-8100), receives far fewer long-distance flights than Phoenix. It's connected to central Tucson by the slow Sun Tran **bus** #11 or #6 ($1), and the $25 shuttle vans of Arizona Stagecoach (Ⓣ520/889-1000, Ⓦwww.azstagecoach.com). For **taxi** service, call Allstate Cab (Ⓣ520/798-1111). The Amtrak station, downtown at

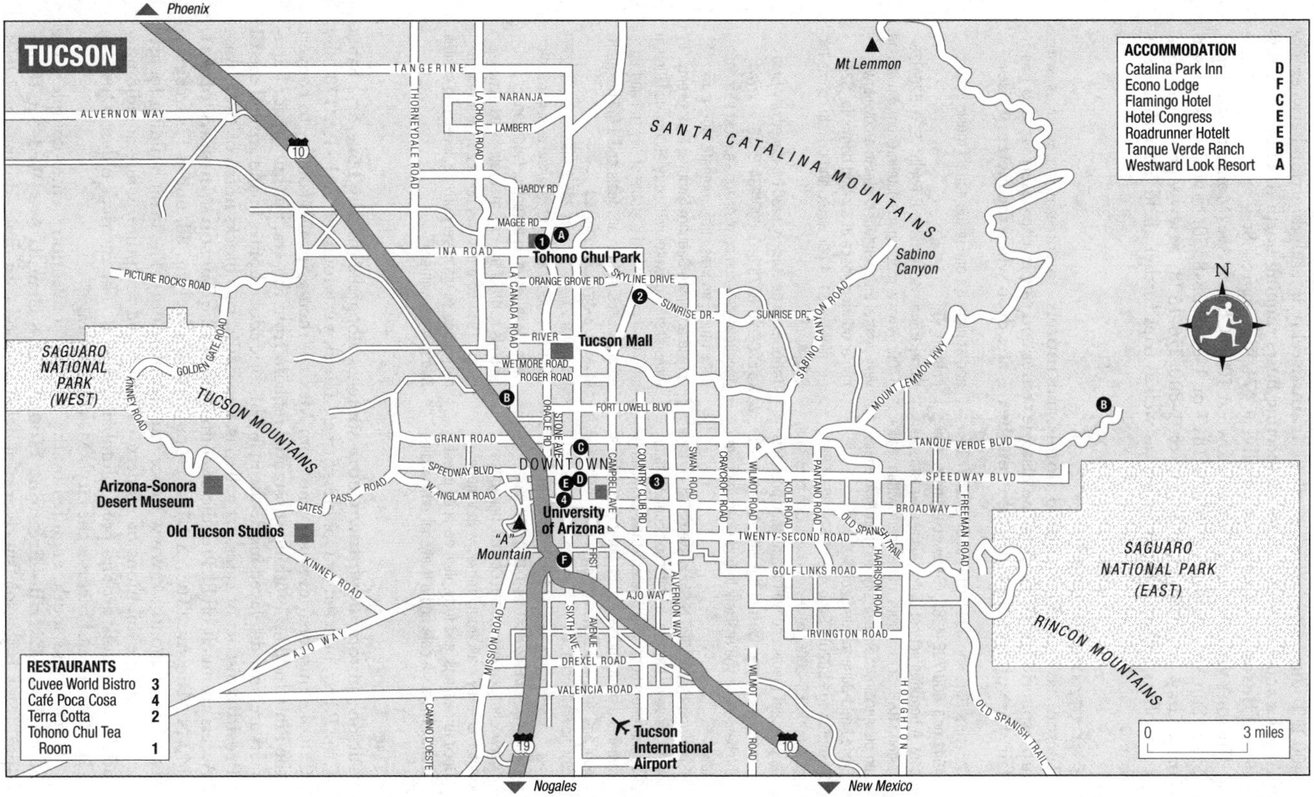
TUCSON
Phoenix
Nogales
New Mexico
ACCOMMODATION
Catalina Park Inn D
Econo Lodge F
Flamingo Hotel C
Hotel Congress E
Roadrunner Hotelt E
Tanque Verde Ranch B
Westward Look Resort A
RESTAURANTS
Cuvee World Bistro 3
Café Poca Cosa 4
Terra Cotta 2
Tohono Chul Tea Room 1
Mt Lemmon
SANTA CATALINA MOUNTAINS
Sabino Canyon
TUCSON MOUNTAINS
RINCON MOUNTAINS
SAGUARO NATIONAL PARK (WEST)
SAGUARO NATIONAL PARK (EAST)
Tohono Chul Park
Tucson Mall
DOWNTOWN
University of Arizona
"A" Mountain
Arizona-Sonora Desert Museum
Old Tucson Studios
Tucson International Airport
TANGERINE
ALVERNON WAY
NARANJA
LAMBERT
LA CHOLLA ROAD
THORNEYDALE ROAD
HARDY RD
MAGEE RD
INA ROAD
PICTURE ROCKS ROAD
ORANGE GROVE RD
SKYLINE DRIVE
SUNRISE DR.
SABINO CANYON ROAD
MOUNT LEMMON HWY
LA CANADA ROAD
RIVER
WETMORE ROAD
ROGER ROAD
FORT LOWELL BLVD
GRANT ROAD
ORACLE RD
STONE AVE
SPEEDWAY BLVD
W. ANGLAM ROAD
GATES PASS ROAD
GOLDEN GATE ROAD
KINNEY ROAD
CAMPBELL AVE
COUNTRY CLUB RD
SWAN ROAD
CRAYCROFT ROAD
WILMOT ROAD
KOLB ROAD
PANTANO ROAD
TANQUE VERDE BLVD
BROADWAY
OLD SPANISH TRAIL
TWENTY-SECOND ROAD
HARRISON ROAD
FREEMAN ROAD
GOLF LINKS ROAD
AJO WAY
ALVERNON WAY
FIRST AVENUE
SIXTH AVE.
IRVINGTON ROAD
DREXEL ROAD
VALENCIA ROAD
MISSION ROAD
CAMINO D'OESTE
HOUGHTON
10
19
N
0 3 miles

400 E Toole Ave, is served by three **trains** weekly in each direction between Los Angeles and points east, with connecting buses running north to Phoenix. Greyhound **buses** also stop very centrally, at 471 W Congress St.

Tucson's **visitor center** is downtown at 100 S Church Ave (Mon–Fri 8am–5pm, Sat & Sun 9am–4pm; ⓣ520/624-1817 or 1-800/638-8350, ⓦwww.visittucson.org). Gray Line (ⓣ520/622-8811 or 1-800/276-1528; ⓦwww.graylinearizona.com) offers $59 **city tours** by bus, as well as trips further afield in southeast Arizona.

Accommodation

Tucson has reasonably priced **hotels** and **motels** downtown, as well as some atmospheric **B&Bs** both in the historic center and out in the desert. It also has its fair share of **resorts** and **dude ranches**. Rates drop when the mercury rises.

Catalina Park Inn 309 East First St ⓣ520/792-4541 or 1-800/792-4885, ⓦwww.catalinaparkinn.com. A beautiful yet not overly fussy six-room historic B&B, across from a quiet park within walking distance of the university and Fourth Avenue. Closed mid-June to late Sept. ❻

EconoLodge 3020 S Sixth Ave ⓣ520/623-5881 or 1-800/553-2666, ⓦwww.econolodge.com. With its pleasant rooms and well-maintained pool, this inexpensive motel, west of the airport, represents the best value you're likely to find close to downtown. ❷

Flamingo Hotel 1300 N Stone Ave ⓣ520/770-1910, ⓦwww.flamingohoteltucson.com. Despite recent renovations, this Western-themed motel remains a plain budget option, but it does have a pool and spa, and stands barely a mile north of downtown Tucson. ❸

Hotel Congress 311 E Congress St ⓣ520/622-8848 or 1-800/722-8848, ⓦwww.hotelcongress.com. Central, bohemian hotel, an easy walk from Amtrak, with vintage Art Deco furnishings, and forty plain en-suite guest rooms. There's a café and a lively bar downstairs, and at night it's one of the hottest music venues in town. ❹

Roadrunner Hostel 346 E Twelfth St ⓣ520/628-4709, ⓦwww.roadrunnerhostelinn.com. Small and very central independent hostel in a downtown home, offering space in six-bed dorms for $24 per night or $144 per week, and private rooms for $48. ❶/❷

Tanque Verde Ranch 14301 E Speedway Blvd ⓣ520/296-6275 or 1-800/234-3833, ⓦwww.tanqueverderanch.com. Arizona's most authentic dude ranch, an irresistibly romantic 400-acre spread adjoining Saguaro National Park twenty miles east of downtown. Luxury accommodation in individual casitas and a stable of over a hundred horses. Rates include all meals and a full program of rides. 3-day minimum. ❾

Westward Look Resort 245 E Ina Rd ⓣ520/297-1151 or 1-800/722-2500, ⓦwww.westwardlook.com. Plush resort, in attractive landscaped grounds north of the city, that retains its atmospheric 1912 core but now holds 250 extra-large rooms and suites in very private, low-slung casitas. Summer ❺, winter ❼

The City

Tucson's historic **downtown core** stretches along the (usually bone-dry) Santa Cruz River, bisected by Congress Street. The city was founded in the late 1700s by Catholic missionaries who came from Mexico, then a Spanish colony, to convert the Pima Indians. Nothing substantial remains from this era, but hundreds of artifacts are now displayed inside the many historic adobe homes in and around the **El Presidio** district of cafés, art galleries, and B&Bs, two blocks north of Broadway. Access to much of El Presidio is controlled by the **Tucson Museum of Art**, 140 N Main Ave (Tues–Sat 10am–4pm, Sun noon–4pm; $8, under-13s free; free first Sun of month; ⓦwww.tucsonmuseumofart.org). The main building focuses on changing exhibitions of modern paintings and sculpture, while an adjoining adobe holds folk art and pre-Columbian artifacts. The district's oldest house, La Casa Cordova, showcases the city's Mexican heritage.

Three blocks south, engulfed by the Tucson Convention Center complex, the adobe **Sosa-Carrillo-Frémont House**, 151 S Granada Ave (Wed–Sat 10am–4pm; free), is the sole survivor of a neighborhood torn down during the 1960s.

Built for merchant Leopoldo Carrillo in 1858, it was rented by former explorer turned Arizona governor John C. Frémont in 1878, and offers a vivid sense of the more civilized side of frontier life.

Tucson's other main area of interest, around the University of Arizona, spreads between Sixth Street and Speedway Boulevard, a mile east of downtown. Its chief highlight is the on-campus **Arizona State Museum** (Mon–Sat 10am–5pm, Sun noon–5pm; $3; Ⓦwww.statemuseum.arizona.edu), where a comprehensive assembly of Native American pottery and other works traces the stories of the various Southwest tribes.

Arizona-Sonora Desert Museum

Part zoo, part garden, the top-notch **Arizona-Sonora Desert Museum** is fourteen miles west of the university along Speedway Boulevard, in Tucson Mountain Park (daily: June–Aug Sun–Fri 7.30am–5pm, Sat 7.30am–10pm; March–May & Sept 7.30am–5pm; Oct–Feb 8.30am–5pm; $9.50, ages 6–12 $2 June–Aug; $13, ages 6–12 $4 Sept–May; Ⓦwww.desertmuseum.org). Indoor displays highlight regional geology and history, and a series of glass-fronted cages are occupied by tarantulas, rattlesnakes, and other creepy-crawlies. Along the looped path beyond – a hot walk in high summer – bighorn sheep, mountain lions, jaguars, and other seldom-seen desert denizens prowl in credible enclosed simulations of their natural habitats, and a colony of impish prairie dogs goes about its impenetrable business. Hawks and bald eagles fly about their own large aviary, thankfully separated from a greenhouse full of hummingbirds.

Saguaro National Park

Flanking Tucson to either side, the two sections of **Saguaro National Park** offer visitors a rare opportunity to stroll through desert "forests" of monumental, multi-limbed **saguaro** (pronounced *sa-wah-row*) cactuses. Each saguaro can grow up to fifty feet tall and weigh up to eight tons, but takes around 150 years to do so. Whatever you may have seen in the movies, you can drive a long way in Arizona without seeing one; saguaro are unique to the Sonora Desert, and the thrill when you finally encounter a thousand at once is deeply satisfying. Both segments of the park can be seen on short forays from the city: in summer, it's far too hot to do more than pose for photographs, and there is no lodging, or even permanent campground. **Admission** to either or both sections of the park, valid for a week and payable at the visitor centers (Ⓦwww.nps.gov/sagu), costs $10 per vehicle. **Backcountry camping** is by permit only; contact park rangers for details.

The **Tucson Mountain District** stretches north from the Desert Museum around fifteen miles west of downtown Tucson, on the far side of the mountains. Beyond the **visitor center** (daily 8am–5pm; $10; Ⓣ520/733-5158, Ⓦwww.nps.gov/sagu), the nine-mile **Bajada Loop Drive** loops through a wonderland of weird saguaro, offering plentiful short hiking trails. Signal Hill is especially recommended, for its petroglyphs and superb sunset views.

To reach the eastern section of the park, the **Rincon Mountain District** (Ⓣ520/733-5153), drive seventeen miles east of town, first along Broadway Boulevard and then Old Spanish Trail. Here, too, short trails such as the quarter-mile Desert Ecology Trail lead off the eight-mile **Cactus Forest Drive** (daily: April–Oct 7am–7pm; Nov–March 7am–5pm), but many visitors come specifically to hike far from the road, up into the mountains. The saguaro cactuses thin out almost as soon as you start climbing the Tanque Verde Ridge Trail, which leads in due course to a hundred-mile network of remote footpaths through thickly forested canyons.

Eating and drinking

Though downtown Tucson shuts down pretty early each evening – it's hard to find anywhere to eat after 9pm – the city has a fine selection of **restaurants**. Mexican joints and cowboy-style Wild West steakhouses abound in the central districts, while fancier places congregate further north in the Foothills.

Cafe Poca Cosa 110 E Pennington St ⓣ520/622-6400. Popular and stylish downtown café that serves tasty, inexpensive Mexican – or to be more precise, Sonoran – cuisine with contemporary Southwestern flair. Typical menu highlights include shredded beef, or cod with clams. Lunch entrées cost around $10; at dinner they're more like $20. Closed Sun & Mon.

Cup Cafe *Hotel Congress*, 311 E Congress St ⓣ520/798-1618. Jazzy downtown café, straight out of the 1930s but updated to include an espresso bar, which makes a good breakfast rendezvous and stays open late nightly.

Cuvee World Bistro 3352 E Speedway Blvd ⓣ520/881-7577. The eclectic menu at this playfully opulent yet casual bistro samples pretty much any tasty world cuisine. Entrees from crispy sea bass to mahogany roasted duck are priced at $18–25, and there's live music at weekends. Closed Sun.

Terra Cotta 3500 Sunrise Drive ⓣ520/577-8100. Inventive Southwestern cuisine, served for dinner only way north of downtown in the Foothills. The menu ranges from gourmet pizzas cooked in a wood-burning oven to meats grilled with chiles, with typical entrees at around $20.

Tohono Chul Tea Room Tohono Chul Park, 7366 N Paseo del Norte ⓣ520/797-1222. Attractive adobe café in small desert park on the northern fringes of town that's ideal for breakfast, a $10 lunch special, or a scones-and-jam afternoon tea.

Nightlife

Most of the arty **cafés** and **nightclubs** on Congress Street downtown double as bars and restaurants, while several student-oriented places can be found in the university area. There are half a dozen country-and-western saloons on the outskirts of town as well. For a full rundown, check the listings in the free *Tucson Weekly* (ⓦwww.tucsonweekly.com).

Choice options include *Club Congress*, inside *Hotel Congress* at 311 E Congress St (ⓣ520/622-8848), a hectic, late-opening bar with live music a couple of nights each week. For microbrews and simple food, head for *Gentle Ben's Brewing Co*, 865 E University Blvd (ⓣ520/624-4177), which is regularly packed with students. A 1920s vaudeville palace, the *Rialto Theatre*, 318 E Congress St (ⓣ520/740-0126, ⓦwww.rialtotheatre.com), is the hottest venue for touring bands.

South to the border: the Mission Trail

South from Tucson, I-19 heads straight for the Mexican border, 65 miles away, passing reminders of the region's Spanish and Mexican heritage. The **Mission San Xavier del Bac** – the best-preserved mission church in the United States – lies just west of the freeway, nine miles south of downtown Tucson on the fringe of the vast arid plain of San Xavier Indian Reservation (daily 9am–6pm; donation suggested). It was built for the Franciscans between 1783 and 1797, and even today its white-plastered walls and towers seem like a dazzling desert mirage; how much more dramatic they must have been two centuries ago. No one knows the name of the architect responsible for its Spanish Baroque, even Moorish lines – it consists almost entirely of domes and arches, making only minimal use of timber – let alone the identities of the O'odham craftsmen who embellished its every feature. The ideal time to come is on Sunday morning, when masses draw large congregations from the reservation.

Forty miles further south, the evocative ruin of another eighteenth-century mission church is preserved as **Tumacácori National Historical Park** (daily 9am–5pm; $3 per person). Topped by a restored whitewashed dome, the mission is home only to the birds that fly down from the Patagonia Mountains. Behind its red-tinged, weather-beaten facade, the plaster has crumbled from the interior walls to reveal bare adobe bricks. A few traces of a mural can still be discerned in the raised sanctuary. The small **visitor center** houses an informative museum.

Nogales, Arizona, and Nogales, Mexico

Twenty miles south of Tumacácori, an hour from Tucson, sits the largest of the Arizona–Mexico border towns, **NOGALES** – in effect two towns, one in the US and one across the border in Mexico, known jointly as *Ambos Nogales* (both Nogales). There's nothing particular to see, either side of the border, though the contrast between the orderly streets of the frankly dreary little American town, and the jumbled white-washed houses that cling to the slopes in Nogales, Mexico, which is basically a large-scale street market, is striking.

Crossing the border is straightforward, as only travelers heading further south of the border require Mexican visas. US citizens should, however, carry their passports, while foreign visitors should check that their visa status entitles them to re-enter the US; if you're on or eligible for the Visa Waiver Scheme (see p.54), you're fine. If driving, leave your car on the US side. There's no need to change money: businesses across the border accept US dollars.

None of the Arizona-side **motels** stands within a mile of the border; the closest is the *Best Western Siesta Motel*, 673 N Grand Ave (Ⓣ520/287-4671; ❸). Most visitors prefer to **eat** in Mexico, where abundant cafés and diners line the busy central streets. Classier dining is offered by *La Roca*, hollowed into the rocky hillside just east of the railroad, a couple of blocks from the border at calle Elias 91, where a full meal costs under $20.

The southeast corner

Among thousands of acres of unspoiled and magnificent wilderness, southeast Arizona contains numerous well-preserved and highly atmospheric **ghost towns**. I-10 buzzes across the region toward New Mexico; to enjoy a grand tour, detour south instead along the more scenic US-80.

Kartchner Caverns State Park

Arizona's newest state park – **Kartchner Caverns**, seven miles south of Benson – centers on caves in the Whetstone Mountains that were discovered in 1974. Unlike Carlsbad Caverns, they're unusual in being "live," or still growing, but they're not really worth traveling across the country to see, and with a visit for a family of four costing at least $60 in admission fees alone, they're also wildly overpriced.

Admission to the park costs $5 per vehicle, but visitors can only see the caves on either of two **guided tours**. The shorter tour lasts over an hour, including a tram ride to the cave entrance and 45 minutes underground, threading through the caverns' two upper "rooms," the **Throne Room** and the **Rotunda Room** (adults $19, $10 ages 7–13). The ninety-minute **Big Room** tour delves deeper into the cave system, and requires visitors to pass through no fewer than six airlock doors (mid-Oct to mid-April only; adults $23, $13 ages 7–13).

Tours are often fully booked, so make advance **reservations** if you can (Mon–Fri 8am–5pm; Ⓣ520/586-2283, Ⓦwww.azstateparks.com). You have to pay the full, non-refundable fee when you book, but you can change precise timings subsequently. If you turn up without a reservation and fail to get in, content yourself with the displays in the large **Discovery Center** (daily 7.30am–6pm).

Tombstone

The legendary Wild West town of **TOMBSTONE** lies 22 miles south of I-10 on US-80, 67 miles southeast of Tucson. More than a century has passed since its mining days came to an end, but "The Town Too Tough to Die" clings to an afterlife as a tourist theme park. With its dusty streets, wooden sidewalks, and swinging saloon doors, it's surprisingly unchanged. While it's much more commercialized than its counterpart in New Mexico, Lincoln (see p.875), it's also more fun. The moody gunslingers who stroll the streets these days are merely rounding up customers to watch them fight, but there's enough genuine rivalry between groups to give the local council ongoing headaches, and give the place an oddly appealing edge. The ideal time to visit is during **Helldorado Days** in late October, when the air is cooler and the sun less harsh.

Tombstone began life as a silver-boomtown in 1877, and by the end of the 1880s it was all but deserted again. However, on the day that gave it the notoriety that's kept it alive, its population stood at more than ten thousand. It was 2pm on October 26, 1881, when **Doc Holliday**, along with **Wyatt Earp** and his brothers Virgil and Morgan (who all served as local sheriffs), confronted a band of suspected cattle rustlers, the Clantons, in the legendary **Gunfight at the OK Corral**. Within a few minutes, three of the suspects were dead. The Earps were accused of murder, but charges were eventually dropped.

Although the gunfight in fact took place on Fremont Street, the **OK Corral** itself remains the major attraction, especially for its 2pm gunfight (daily 8.30am–5pm; $5.50; Ⓦwww.ok-corral.com). In a baking-hot adobe-walled courtyard, crude dummies show the supposed locations of the Earps and the Clantons, in complete contradiction to contemporary reports of the fight.

Just off the main drag at Toughnut and Third streets, the one-time seat of Cochise County now serves as **Tombstone Courthouse State Historic Park** (daily 8am–5pm; $3). Several well-known trials of the time took place in its little-changed courtroom. Excellent exhibits include two detailed alternative versions of what might have actually happened at the OK Corral.

Central **motels** include the *Tombstone Motel*, 502 E Fremont St (Ⓣ520/457-3478 or 1-888/455-3478, Ⓦwww.tombstonemotel.com; ❸), while the classier

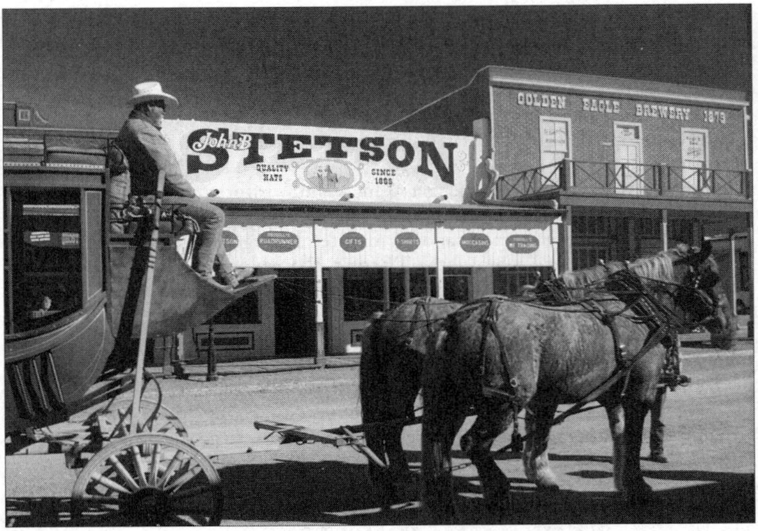

▲ Stagecoach, Tombstone

Holiday Inn Express is a mile north on US-80 W (Ⓣ520/457-9507 or 1-800/465-4329; Ⓦwww.ichotelsgroup.com; ❹). Among old-style **saloons** serving burgers and beer in a raucous atmosphere are the *Crystal Palace* at Fifth and Allen streets, and *Big Nose Kate's* at 417 E Allen St.

Bisbee

Crammed into a narrow gorge 25 miles south of Tombstone, the town of **BISBEE** is rivaled only by Jerome, near Sedona, as Arizona's most atmospheric Victorian relic. Like Jerome, its fortunes were built on a century of mining mundane copper from the mountains, rather than a few ephemeral years of gold and silver. Its solid brick buildings testify to the days when Bisbee's population of twenty thousand outstripped both Phoenix and Tucson to make it the largest city between New Orleans and San Francisco. Phelps Dodge finally closed down its Bisbee operations in 1975, having extracted more than six billion dollars' worth of metals. As the miners moved away, however, artists and retirees moved in, preserving Bisbee's original architecture while turning it into a thriving, friendly little community that caters to tourists without being overwhelmed by them.

Walking Bisbee's narrow central streets, lined with galleries and antiques stores, is a pleasure in itself. If you'd like to know more of the background, call in at the **Bisbee Mining and Historical Museum**, 5 Copper Queen Plaza (daily 10am–4pm; $7.50).

The fanciest **place to stay** is the venerable *Copper Queen Hotel*, 11 Howell Ave (Ⓣ520/432-2216, Ⓦwww.copperqueen.com; ❻), which has a plush bar and a good **restaurant** with terrace seating. On the southern outskirts, just beyond the Lavender Pit, the *Shady Dell RV Park*, 1 Douglas Rd (Ⓣ520/432-3567, Ⓦwww.theshadydell.com; ❸–❻), offers a unique opportunity to sleep in one of nine beautifully restored, irresistibly kitsch 1950s trailers.

Southwest Arizona: Yuma

There's virtually nothing in the vast desert plain of southwest Arizona to tempt you off the twin freeways that sprint to California. The largest town, **YUMA**, is little more than an oversized pit stop for freight trains and cross-country truckers. **Yuma Territorial Prison**, now a state park (daily 8am–5pm; $4) beside the Colorado River, was known a century ago as the "Hell Hole of Arizona," holding over a hundred of the Wild West's most violent criminals. Its first inmates were forced to build the adobe walls that later contained them; you can wander around the grounds and cell blocks at will, and visit the small museum.

Neon-lit budget **motels** along the main drag include the good-value *Yuma Cabana*, 2151 S Fourth Ave (Ⓣ928/783-8311 or 1-800/874-0811, Ⓦwww.yumacabana.com; ❷), while the **River City Grill**, downtown at 600 W Third St (Ⓣ928/782-7988), is a bright "international" restaurant that's Yuma's most fashionable hangout.

Phoenix

The state capital and largest city in Arizona, **PHOENIX** holds minimal appeal for tourists. When it began life in the 1860s, the sweltering little farming town stood in the heart of the large Salt River Valley, with a ready-made irrigation system left by ancient Indians (the name Phoenix honors the fact that the city rose from the ashes of a long-vanished **Hohokam** community). Within a century, however, Phoenix had turned into what writer Edward Abbey called "the blob that is eating Arizona," acquiring the money and political clout to defy the self-evident absurdity of building a huge city in a virtually waterless desert. Now the fifth largest city in the US, it has filled the entire valley; over 1.5 million people live within its boundaries, while four million people inhabit the twenty separate incorporated cities, such as **Scottsdale**, **Tempe**, and **Mesa**, which together make up the metropolitan area.

Above all, Phoenix is **hot**; between June and August daytime highs average over 100°F, making it the hottest city outside the Middle East. Even in winter, temperatures rarely drop below 65°F, and snowbirds from colder climes pay vast sums to warm their bones in the luxury resorts and spas, concentrated especially in Scottsdale, that are the modern equivalent of the 1930s dude ranches that first attracted visitors here. Apart from the **Heard Museum**'s excellent Native American displays, the cactuses at the **Desert Botanical Garden**, and Frank Lloyd Wright's architecture studio at **Taliesin West**, Phoenix is short of must-see attractions. In fact, if you're on a touring vacation, you'd miss little if you bypassed it altogether.

Arrival, information, and getting around

Phoenix is so vast, and so utterly dependent on car travel, that it's much easier to drive than to use **public transport** – even driving, it can take hours to get across town. However, the **Metro Light Rail System** (Ⓣ602/253-5000, Ⓦwww.valleymetro.org) commenced operations in 2008, along a twenty-mile route, from Camelback Road north of downtown Phoenix to Apache Boulevard in

Mesa. There's a station close to **Sky Harbor International Airport**, three miles east of downtown, at 44th and Washington, and fares are the same as for local **buses**, at $1.25 for a one-way ride. Alternatively, SuperShuttle vans charge around $10 from the airport to downtown destinations, and more like $20 for Scottsdale (Ⓣ602/244-9000 or 1-800/258-3826, Ⓦwww.supershuttle.com). Arizona Shuttle Services runs frequent buses south to **Tucson** (daily 6.30am–11.30pm; one-way $30 with 7-day advance reservation; Ⓣ520/795-6772 or 1-800/888-2749, Ⓦwww.arizonashuttle.com). There's no Amtrak **train** service, but Greyhound **buses** arrive at 2115 E Buckeye Rd (Ⓣ602/389-4200), close to the airport.

Phoenix's main **visitor center** is downtown at 125 N Second St (Mon–Fri 8am–5pm; Ⓣ602/254-6500 or 1-877/225-5749, Ⓦwww.visitphoenix.com), while **Scottsdale** has its own visitor center at 4343 N Scottsdale Rd (Mon–Fri 8am–5.30pm; Ⓣ480/421-1004 or 1-800/782-1117, Ⓦwww.scottsdalecvb.com).

Accommodation

Metropolitan Phoenix is so huge that it's important to stay near the places you want to visit. Downtown Phoenix is not one of the more expensive areas, with cheap motels lining the somewhat run-down W Van Buren Street a few blocks north of the center. The summer room rates given below rise significantly in winter.

Best Western Central Phoenix Inn & Suites 1100 N Central Ave Ⓣ602/252-2100 or 1-800/780-7234; Ⓦwww.bestwestern.com. Rates remain constant year-round at this good-value business-oriented hotel, close to downtown a quarter-mile north of the Heard Museum. ❺

Budget Lodge Motel 402 W Van Buren St Ⓣ602/254-7247 or 1-800/780-5733; Ⓦwww.budgetinn.com. Reasonably attractive rooms at very attractive rates, in an unexciting motel within walking distance of the downtown core, though you won't want to walk here after dark. ❸

Days Inn Scottsdale Resort at Fashion Square Mall 4710 N Scottsdale Rd Ⓣ480/947-5411 or 1-800/329-7466, Ⓦwww.scottsdaledaysinn.com. Though not all that prepossessing, this two-storey motel, immediately north of Fashion Square Mall – just stroll across the street – has perfectly acceptable rooms, plus an outdoor pool. ❸

Four Seasons Resort Scottsdale at Troon North 10600 East Crescent Moon Drive Ⓣ480/515-5700, Ⓦwww.fourseasons.com/scottsdale. Magnificent desert resort, with very luxurious rooms and suites arrayed around spacious swimming pools in the cactus-studded mountains north of Scottsdale, plus a good spa. ❼

Hotel San Carlos 202 N Central Ave Ⓣ602/253-4121 or 1-866/253-4121, Ⓦwww.hotelsancarlos.com. To appreciate this historic, very central 1920s hotel, you have to prefer an old-fashioned, frazzled and often noisy downtown hotel to a crisp, new deathly-quiet motel. That said, rooms are very tastefully furnished, and there's a nice café, and a rooftop pool. ❼

Hyatt Place Tempe 1413 W Rio Salado Parkway Ⓣ480/804-9544, Ⓦphoenixairport.place.hyatt.com. Handy for both the airport and downtown Tempe – and connected to both by free shuttles – this crisp, new hotel offers upscale facilities at surprisingly affordable prices. ❹

Metcalf House Hostel 1026 N Ninth St above Roosevelt Ⓣ602/254-9803, Ⓦhttp://home.earthlink.net/~phxhostel/. Dorm beds at $18 for HI/AYH members, $25 non-members, in a slightly rundown location in a residential district, 15min walk north of downtown. No phone reservations, but space is usually available. No curfew. Check in 5–10pm, or, usually but not always, 7–10am. Closed July & Aug. ❶

Central Phoenix

Although **Downtown Phoenix** – the few blocks east and west of Central Avenue and north and south of **Washington Street** – remains too hot and too spread out to walk around in any comfort, determined efforts have been made to revitalize the area. A ninety-block district, focusing on two massive side-by-side sports stadiums, the **US Airways Center** and **Chase Field** (home respectively to the Phoenix Suns and Arizona Diamondbacks; see p.889) has even been re-branded with a new name – **Copper Square**. Adjoining the two is the one significant downtown **mall**, the **Arizona Center**, on Van Buren Street between Third and Fifth.

What little remains of Phoenix's nineteenth-century architecture now constitutes **Heritage Square**, a couple of blocks southeast at 115 N Sixth St. Rather than original adobe ranch houses, however, it preserves a quaint assortment of Victorian homes, converted into tearooms and toy museums. You can get a better impression of the early days at the **Phoenix Museum of History**, across the street at 105 N Fifth St (Tues–Sat 10am–5pm; $6; Ⓦwww.pmoh.org), which features the city's first jail – a rock with a chain attached.

Two more significant attractions lie a mile or so north of downtown. The vast and hugely rewarding **Phoenix Art Museum**, 1625 N Central Ave (Tues 10am–9pm, Wed–Sun 10am–5pm; adults $10, ages 6–17 $4; free Tues 3–9pm; Ⓦwww.phxart.org), is rooted in an extensive array of Western art, though its temporary exhibitions range through all eras and styles. Three blocks north, the **Heard Museum**, 2301 N Central Ave (daily 9.30am–5pm; $10; ages 6–12 $3; Ⓦwww.heard.org), has also been greatly enlarged, while still showcasing the lovely old buildings in which it was founded, and offers a good introduction to the culture of the **Native Americans** of the Southwest. Its superb pottery collection ranges from stunning Mimbres bowls to modern Hopi ceramics, but best of all is a wonderful array of Hopi **kachina dolls**.

In **Papago Park** at the south end of Scottsdale, the fascinating **Desert Botanical Garden** (daily: May–Sept 7am–8pm; Oct–April 8am–8pm; adults $10, ages 3–12 $4; Ⓦwww.dbg.org), is filled with amazing cactuses and desert flora from around the world. Prime specimens include spineless "totem pole" cactuses from the Galápagos Islands, and "living stone" plants from South Africa. Separate enclaves are devoted to **butterflies** – at their best in August and September – and **hummingbirds**, of which Arizona boasts fifteen indigenous species.

Taliesin West

Whatever its general appearance may suggest, Phoenix has attracted some visionary designers. **Frank Lloyd Wright** came to the city to work on the *Biltmore Hotel*, and stayed for most of the 25 years before his death in 1959. His winter studio, **Taliesin West** – at 114th Street and Frank Lloyd Wright Boulevard, at Scottsdale's northeastern edge – is now an architecture school and a working design studio, with multimedia exhibits of the man's life and work (Oct–May daily 10am–4pm, June & Sept daily 9am–4pm, July & Aug Mon & Thurs–Sun 9am–4pm; Ⓣ480/860-2700; Ⓦwww.franklloydwright.org). It's still a splendidly isolated spot, and one where his trademark "organic architecture" makes perfect sense. The site can only be seen on **guided tours**; you can join either an hour-long "Panorama Tour" ($27) or a ninety-minute "Insight Tour" ($32), which are offered at frequent intervals. The expertise and enthusiasm of the guides makes the experience well worth the price.

Eating

Unless you're prepared to pay resort prices, it's hard to find a good **restaurant** in Phoenix with much atmosphere. Apart from a block or two in central Scottsdale, and Tempe's lively Mill Avenue, no areas of the metropolis are small enough to walk around while you look for a place to eat, but if you're happy to drive, neighborhood diners – especially Mexican – can still be found.

Alice Cooper'stown 101 E Jackson St Ⓣ602/253-7337. Barbecue restaurant-cum-sports bar, owned by the rock star and alongside downtown's US Airways Center. While far from fine dining, the food's better than you might expect, and the atmosphere is fun, with waiters in full Alice make-up. Lunch and dinner daily.

Bandera 3821 N Scottsdale Rd, Scottsdale Ⓣ480/994-3524. Chicken cooked in the wood-burning oven is the specialty in this busy, inexpensive rotisserie in downtown Scottsdale, but other meats and fish are almost as good. Daily, dinner only.

Barrio Café 2814 N 16th St ⓣ602/636-0240, ⓦwww.barriocafe.com. Reservations are not taken at this popular little place, but it's worth the wait to enjoy authentic southern Mexican food.

Cibo Restaurant 603 N Fifth Ave ⓣ602/441-2697. Downtown house, with a nice patio, serving gorgeous saltimbocca sandwiches and salads for lunch, then $12 pizzas plus a wide range of antipasti for dinner. Closed Sun.

Cowboy Ciao 7133 E Stetson Drive at Sixth, Scottsdale ⓣ480/946-3111, ⓦwww.cowboyciao.com. Hip Scottsdale roadhouse serving "modern American food with global influences." Lunchtime burgers, salads or sandwiches cost around $13; dinner entrees like stuffed pork rib chop or lamb loin $25–30.

House of Tricks 114 E Seventh St, Tempe ⓣ480/968-1114. Tiny, romantic modern-American place in the university district, with lots of vegetarian options. Closed Sun.

Monti's La Casa Vieja 3 W First St, Tempe ⓣ480/967-7594. Tempe's oldest adobe house, built in 1873, is now a Western-themed diner serving a conventional steak-and-chicken menu at extraordinarily low prices. Lunch and dinner daily.

Pizzeria Bianco Heritage Square, 623 E Adams St ⓣ602/258-8300. High-quality pizzas in a very convenient downtown location; no wonder it's so popular. Tues–Sat 5–10pm.

Nightlife, entertainment, and sports

For a rundown of what's on musically in Phoenix, pick up the free weekly *New Times* (ⓦwww.phoenixnewtimes.com). Both the **Phoenix Symphony Hall**, 225 E Adams St (ⓣ602/495-1999; ⓦwww.phoenixsymphony.org, and the **Scottsdale Center for the Arts**, 7380 E Second St (ⓣ480/994-2787, ⓦwww.scottsdalearts.org), put on classical music, theater, and ballet. The **Arizona Diamondbacks** play major league baseball beneath the retractable roof of air-conditioned Chase Field (ⓣ602/514-8400, ⓦwww.azdiamondbacks.com), while the **Phoenix Suns** play NBA basketball at the US Airways Center, 201 E Jefferson St (ⓣ602/379-7900, ⓦwww.suns.com), and football's **Arizona Cardinals** are based at Glendale's new, state-of-the-art University of Phoenix Stadium (ⓣ602/379-0102, ⓦwww.azcardinals.com).

Bar Smith 130 E Washington St, Phoenix ⓣ602/229-1265, ⓦwww.barsmithphoenix.com. This best thing about this stylish downtown bar and lounge is its fabulous outdoor dancefloor, upstairs. Closed Sun.

Bikini Lounge 1502 Grand Ave, Phoenix ⓣ602/252-0472. A real gem of a dive bar, this veteran tiki joint attracts a fascinating, eclectic mix of local characters.

Chez Nous 915 Grand Ave ⓣ602/266 7372, ⓦwww.cheznouscentral.com. Dark, deeply atmospheric old-style cocktail lounge, with a steady soul and Motown soundtrack and live R&B bands.

e4 4282 N Drinkwater Blvd, Scottsdale ⓣ480/734-9181, ⓦwww.e4-az.com. Massive, eye-popping dance club, designed around air, earth, fire and water, and holding a Vegas-style "ultra-lounge" downstairs as well as the *Liquid* dance club with cascading waterfalls. Closed Sun, Mon & Thurs.

Last Exit Bar & Grill 1425 W Southern Ave, Tempe ⓣ480/557-6656, ⓦwww.lastexitlive.com. Rock-oriented live music venue in an unpromising mall, where acts range from country-rock to local punks.

Marquee Theatre 730 N Mill Ave, Tempe ⓣ480/829-0607, ⓦwww.luckymanonline.com. The best venue to see big-name touring acts, with an open floor rather than seating, and good beer.

Central Arizona

The I-40 interstate crosses the center of Arizona, skirting the **Navajo Reservation** that fills the northeastern corner of the state. Though the narrow strip of land to either side can be extraordinarily beautiful, with double rainbows reaching across the desert plain and fiery dawns blazing along the horizon, it holds few specific places worth stopping. The one exception is the pleasant town of **Flagstaff**, which makes a base for excursions to ancient **Native American sites** and the New Age center of **Sedona**, as well, above all, as the **Grand Canyon**.

East of Flagstaff: Holbrook and Winslow

East of Flagstaff, two old Route 66 towns, **WINSLOW** and **HOLBROOK**, are kept alive by transcontinental truckers. Each town consists of little more than a strip of motels, such as the concrete teepees of the *Wigwam Motel* at 811 W Hopi Drive in Holbrook (Ⓣ928/524-3048, Ⓦwww.galerie-kokopelli.com/wigwam; ❷). However, Winslow is now graced once more by the restored splendor of *La Posada Hotel*, at 303 E Second St (Ⓣ928/289-4366, Ⓦwww.laposada.org; ❺), which is such a totally magnificent place that it's worth going a very long way out of your way to spend a night here. A glorious fake, it was designed by Mary Jane Colter, of Grand Canyon fame, in the 1920s to emulate an 1860s hacienda. It also holds a great **restaurant**, the *Turquoise Room* (Ⓣ928/289-2888), open for all meals daily.

Petrified Forest National Park

At **Petrified Forest National Park**, which straddles I-40 a dozen miles east of Holbrook, a fossilized prehistoric forest of gigantic trees has been unearthed by erosion. The original cells of the wood have been replaced by multicolored crystals of quartz. Cross-sections, cut through with diamond saws and polished, look stunning, and can be seen in the two **visitor centers**, thirty miles apart at the north and south entrances. On the ground, however, along the various trails that set off from the park's **27-mile Scenic Drive**, the trees themselves are not always all that exciting. Segmented, crumbling, and very dark, they can seem like a bunch of logs lying in the sand; the best viewing is when the setting sun brings out rich red and orange hues.

The northern section of the national park – site of the main visitor center and **entrance station** (daily: summer 7am–7pm; winter 8am–5pm; $10 per vehicle; Ⓣ928/524-6228, Ⓦwww.nps.gov/pefo) – is renowned for its views of the **Painted Desert**, an undulating expanse of solidified sand dunes, which at different times of day take on different colors (predominantly bluish shades of gray and reddish shades of brown).

Flagstaff

Northern Arizona's liveliest and most attractive town, **FLAGSTAFF** occupies a dramatic location beneath the San Francisco Peaks, halfway between New Mexico and California. Straddling the I-40 and I-17 interstates, it's both a way station for tourists en route to the Grand Canyon, eighty miles northwest, and a worthwhile destination in its own right.

Downtown, where barely a building rises more than three storeys, oozes Wild West charm. Its main thoroughfare, Santa Fe Avenue, used to be **Route 66**, and before that the pioneer trail west. A stroll around Flagstaff's central few blocks is gloriously evocative of the past. The tracks of the Santa Fe Railroad still cut downtown in two, so life remains punctuated by the mournful wail of passing trains.

Ever since it was founded, in 1876, Flagstaff has been a diverse place, with a strong black and Hispanic population, and Navajo and Hopi heading in from the nearby reservations. Now home to just over fifty thousand, it makes an ideal base for travelers. As well as the abundant hotels, hostels, restaurants, bars, and shops downtown, food and lodging chains line the interstates.

Arrival and information

Daily Amtrak **trains** stop in the center of town, where the station doubles as a helpful **visitor center** (Mon–Sat 8am–5pm, Sun 9am–4pm; ⓣ928/774-9541 or 1-800/379-0065, ⓦwww.flagstaffarizona.org).

Open Road Tours and Transportation (ⓣ928/226-8060 or 1-800/766-7117, ⓦwww.openroadtours.com), based at the station, runs twice-daily **bus services** via Williams to the Grand Canyon (8am & 3.45pm; adults $27, under-12s $19). Greyhound is a few blocks south of downtown at 399 S Malpais Lane (ⓣ928/774-4573).

Accommodation

Flagstaff's dozens of **motels** and **B&Bs** provide reasonable value, while budget travelers can benefit from a couple of high-quality **hostels**. Most of the chain motels are congregated well to the east, but staying nearer downtown is much more fun.

DuBeau International Hostel 19 W Phoenix Ave ⓣ928/774-6731 or 1-800/398-7112, ⓦwww.dubeauhostel.com. Welcoming independent hostel just south of the tracks, whose converted en-suite motel rooms serve as four-person dorms at $20 per bed, or private doubles at $45. Weekends only, Nov–Feb. ❶/❷

Grand Canyon International Hostel 19 S San Francisco St ⓣ928/779-9421 or 1-888/442-2696, ⓦwww.grandcanyonhostel.com. Independent hostel, under the same friendly management as the *DuBeau*. Dorm beds $20, private rooms $38–45. Free pick-up from Greyhound, car rental discounts, and Grand Canyon tours (March–Oct Mon, Wed, Fri & Sat; Nov–Feb Tues, Thurs & Sat; $75). ❶/❷

Hotel Weatherford 23 N Leroux St ⓣ928/779-1919, ⓦwww.weatherfordhotel.com. Attractive old downtown hotel, with elegant wooden fittings; tasteful accommodation in restored rooms, not all en-suite. Can be noisy. ❸–❻

Monte Vista 100 N San Francisco St ⓣ928/779-6971 or 1-800/545-3068, ⓦwww.hotelmontevista.com. Attractive 1920s hotel and downtown landmark. Rooms, not all en-suite, are named for celebrity guests; Paul McCartney stayed here in 2008. Weekend rates rise by up to $20. ❸–❺

Super 8 Flagstaff Downtown 602 W Route 66; ⓣ928/774-4581 or 1-800/800-8000, ⓦwww.super8.com. Attractive chain motel centered on an enclosed swimming pool, adjacent to a Barnes & Noble bookstore less than a mile southwest of downtown. ❹

The Town

Flagstaff's appealing **downtown** stretches for a few redbrick blocks north of the railroad. Filled with cafés, bars, and stores selling Route 66 souvenirs and Indian crafts, as well as outdoors outfitters, it's a fun place to stroll around, but holds no significant tourist attractions or historic buildings. Your most lasting impression is likely to be of the magnificent San Francisco Peaks, rising smoothly from the plains on the northern horizon, and topped by a jagged ridge.

The exceptional **Museum of Northern Arizona**, however, is three miles northwest of downtown on US-180 (daily 9am–5pm; $7, under-18s $4; ⓣ928/774-5213, ⓦwww.musnaz.org). Its main emphasis is on documenting Native American life, with an excellent run-through of the Ancestral Puebloan past and contemporary Navajo, Havasupai, and Hopi cultures, but it also actively encourages the development of traditional and even new skills among Native American craftworkers.

Eating and nightlife

While surprisingly short of high-end **restaurants**, central Flagstaff holds a lively assortment of both old-style Western **diners** and eclectic **budget** options. Thanks to all those students, the area around San Francisco Street, both north and south of the tracks, is filled with vegetarian cafés and espresso bars.

Beaver Street Brewery & Whistle Stop Café 11 S Beaver St ⓣ928/779-0079. Inventive sandwiches and salads, wood-fired pizza, and outdoor barbecue in the beer garden in summer.

Dara Thai 14 S San Francisco St ⓣ928/774-0047. Large Thai place just south of the tracks, where the service is great and a plate of delicious pad Thai noodles costs just $8 for lunch, $10 for dinner.

Downtown Diner 7 E Aspen Ave ⓣ928/774-3492. Classic Route 66 diner a block north of the main drag, featuring leatherette booths and hefty burgers and sandwiches.

Macy's European Coffee House & Bakery 14 S Beaver St ⓣ928/774-2243. Not merely superb coffee, but heavenly pastries to go with it, plus more substantial vegetarian dishes such as black bean pizza, and even couscous for breakfast.

The Museum Club 3404 E Route 66 ⓣ928/526-9434, ⓦwww.museumclub.com. A real oddity; this log-cabin taxidermy museum is somehow transmogrified into a classic Route 66 roadhouse, saloon, and country-music venue, now a second home to hordes of dancing cowboys.

Sunset Crater and Wupatki national monuments

North of Flagstaff, the **San Francisco Volcanic Field** holds around four hundred volcanoes. Some are still active, though the most recent eruption was that of **Sunset Crater**, twelve miles from Flagstaff on US-89, in 1066 AD. The crater was named by John Wesley Powell for the many colors of its cone, which swells from a black base through reds and oranges to a yellow-tinged crest. It's too unstable for walkers to be allowed onto the rim, but a trail passes through lava tubes around its base. The **visitor center** is nearby (daily 8am–5pm; ⓣ928/526-0502, ⓦwww.nps.gov/sucr; $5 per person), opposite the *Bonito* **campground** (ⓣ928/526-0866; $16; early May to mid-Oct).

A dozen miles further north stand the ancient ruins of **Wupatki National Monument** (daily: summer 8am–7pm; winter 8am–5pm; $5 per person, including Sunset Crater; ⓣ928/679-2365, ⓦwww.nps.gov/wupa). The **Sinagua** were joined by many others, including the **Ancestral Puebloans**, after the Sunset Crater explosion deposited a rich new layer of topsoil. The specific site known as Wupatki ("big house"), set proud on its natural foundations of red sandstone, is the largest of numerous ruins.

Walnut Canyon National Monument

Between 1100 and 1250 AD, **Walnut Canyon**, ten miles east of Flagstaff just south of I-40, was home to a thriving Sinagua community. Literally hundreds of their **cliff dwellings** nestle beneath overhangs in the sides of the canyon. They simply walled off natural alcoves, and then put up partitions to make separate rooms. No single dwelling is on the same scale as at Wupatki, and only a handful are accessible to visitors, but cumulatively they make for an impressive spectacle.

A scenic window in the **visitor center** (daily: June–Aug 8am–6pm; March–May & Sept–Nov 8am–5pm; Dec–Feb 9am–5pm; $5 per person; ⓣ928/526-3367, ⓦwww.nps.gov/waca) gives an excellent overall view. No accommodation, and only minimal snack food, is available.

Sedona and Red Rock Country

US-89A threads its way south from Flagstaff through spectacular **Oak Creek Canyon** to emerge after 28 miles at **Sedona**, on the threshold of the extraordinary **Red Rock Country**, where giant mesas and buttes of stark red sandstone soar from the valley floor. The boom-and-bust mining town of **Jerome** looks down from a mountainside to the south.

Vortex Tours of Red Rock Country

As few of the side roads around Sedona are paved, there's a booming business in **off-road tours**, and especially those that visit so-called "**vortexes**." These are run by companies such as the garish Pink Jeep Tours (from $55; ⓣ928/282-5000 or 1-800/873-3662, ⓦwww.pinkjeep.com) and Earth Wisdom Tours ($68 and up; ⓣ928/282-4714 or 1-800/482-4714, ⓦwww.earthwisdomtours.com), who teach their clients "the ancestral secrets of the Medicine Wheel." Many of the jeep roads are perfectly passable in ordinary vehicles. So long as you're happy to remain in ignorance as to which rocks are really electromagnetic tuning forks vibrating in harmony with Alpha Centauri, there's no great need to take a commercial tour. If you *really* want to get off-road, you can also head for Legends of Sedona Ranch (ⓣ928/282-6826 or 1-800/848-7728), where "horses are free . . . but rides ain't." An hour on **horseback** costs around $65.

Sedona

There's no disputing that the New Age resort of **SEDONA** enjoys a magnificent setting, amid definitive Southwestern canyon scenery. Sadly, however, the town itself adds nothing to the beauty of its surroundings, with mile upon mile of ugly red-brick sprawl interrupted only by hideous malls. While Europeans tend to be turned off by Sedona, many American travelers love it for its combination of luxurious accommodations and fancy restaurants, and its almost limitless opportunities for active outdoor vacationing. In particular, artists, healers, and wealthy retirees have flocked here in the last few decades. Whether you love it or hate it may depend on whether you share their wide-eyed awe for angels, crystals, and all matters mystical – and whether you're prepared to pay over-the-odds prices for the privilege of joining them.

Established in 1902 by one Theodore Schnebly, Sedona's big break came in 1981, when author Page Bryant "channeled" the information that Sedona is in fact "the heart *chakra* of the planet." Since she pinpointed her first **vortex** – a point at which psychic and electromagnetic energies can supposedly be channeled for personal and planetary harmony – the town has achieved its own personal growth, and blossomed as a focus for **New Age** practitioners of all kinds. It's also where **John McCain** has his Arizona ranch.

If you don't have much time to explore, you can see most of the sights, albeit from a distance, from US-89A; the best parts are south along Hwy-179 within Coconino National Forest. The closest **vortex** to town is on **Airport Mesa**; turn left up Airport Road from US-89A as you head south, about a mile past the downtown junction known as the **"Y"**. The vortex is at the junction of the second and third peaks, just after the cattle grid. Further up, beyond the precariously sited airport, the **Shrine of the Red Rocks** looks out across the entire valley.

Sedona's **visitor center**, just north of the "Y," has full listings of lodgings and tour operators (Mon–Sat 8.30am–5pm, Sun 9am–3pm; ⓣ928/282-7722 or 1-800/288-7336, ⓦwww.visitsedona.com). This is an expensive place to **stay**; what pass for budget **motels** include the *Sedona Motel*, close to the "Y" at 218 Hwy-179 (ⓣ928/282-7187, ⓦwww.thesedonamotel.com; ❸), and *Los Abrogados Lodge*, a little further north at 270 N US-89A (ⓣ928/282-7125 or 1-800/521-3131, ⓦwww.ilxresorts.com; ❹).

Fournos, 3000 W Hwy-89A (reservations required; ⓣ928/282-3331), is a nice little Greek **restaurant**, open for dinner at 6pm and 8pm from Thursday to Saturday, and for brunch on Sunday at noon; the *Coffee Pot Restaurant*, 2050 W Hwy-89A (ⓣ928/282-6626), is a large old-style diner, serving all the burgers, Mexican dishes, and fried specials you could hope for.

Jerome

The former mining town of **JEROME**, high above the Verde Valley on US-89A thirty miles south of Sedona, is conspicuous from far and wide: an enormous letter "J" is etched deep into the hillside above it, while a large chunk of that hillside is missing altogether, having been blown apart for **opencast copper mining**. Serious exploitation of the mineral wealth here started when the **United Verde** mine opened in 1876. Until the current tortuous road was built, the only way up to Jerome was the precipitous rail line connecting the mine with the world's largest copper smelter at Clarkdale.

From the 1950s, when the mines closed down, until the 1970s, Jerome was a **ghost town**. Many of those who simply moved into its empty houses are still here, making a living from arts and crafts, while the town itself has made a dramatic recovery. The hillside is so steep that many houses have two storeys at the front and four or five at the back. Under the concussion of two hundred miles of tunnels being blasted into the mountainside, the whole town used to slip downhill at the rate of five inches per year; the **Sliding Jail** on Hull Avenue came to rest 225ft from where it was built.

At the highest point in town, the *Jerome Grand Hotel*, 200 Hill St (Ⓣ928/634-8200 or 1-888/817-6788; Ⓦwww.jeromegrandhotel.com; ❺), is a restored Spanish Mission hotel with fabulous views. The rooms are atmospheric rather than particularly luxurious, and there's a good on-site restaurant, *The Asylum*.

Montezuma Castle National Monument

In an idyllic setting just above Beaver Creek and just east of I-17, 25 miles from Sedona, **Montezuma Castle National Monument** preserves a superb Sinagua **cliff dwelling** (daily: summer 8am–6pm; winter 8am–5pm; $5; Ⓣ928/567-3322, Ⓦwww.nps.gov/moca). Filling an alcove in the hillside with a wall of pink adobe, its five storeys taper up to fit the contours of the rock. Apparently, the fingerprints of the masons are still visible on the bricks, and the sycamore beams remain firmly in place, but visitors are not permitted to climb up.

West of Flagstaff: I-40 to California

Everything along I-40 west of Flagstaff is dominated by the road's function as the main route between Las Vegas and the Grand Canyon. The first town you reach, **WILLIAMS**, seems to exist solely to capture the passing tourist trade, with a historic **railroad** running north to the Canyon (see p.895). From **SELIGMAN**, 45 miles further west, a long stretch of the old Route 66 loops northward through the **Hualapai Indian Reservation** and a dozen fading towns, **PEACH SPRINGS** in particular, that look straight out of *The Grapes of Wrath*. This makes a great detour on what is otherwise a very dull drive; it also provides the best access to the less visited western reaches of the Grand Canyon, around **Havasu Canyon** (see p.902).

There's little reason to stop at **KINGMAN**, the largest town in western Arizona, from where US-93 branches north to Las Vegas and I-40 continues to Los Angeles.

Lake Havasu City

Forty miles southwest of Kingman, ten miles from California, a detour south leads to one of the more bizarre sights of the American desert – the old gray stone of **London Bridge**, reaching out to an artificial island across the stagnant waters of the dammed Colorado River at **LAKE HAVASU CITY**. The resort's developer, Robert P. McCulloch, bought the bridge (under the impression it was Tower Bridge – or so the story goes) for $2.4 million in the 1960s, shipped it across the Atlantic chunk by chunk, and reassembled it over a channel dug to divert water from Lake Havasu. Lake Havasu City holds an undeniable attraction for the parched urbanites of Phoenix, who flock to fish on the lake or race on jet-skis, but minimal appeal for travelers from further afield. Moreover, between March and June, it's filled with students on **spring break**, drinking and partying around the clock.

Motels abound, ranging from the perfectly adequate *Americas Best Value Inn*, 101 London Bridge Rd (Ⓣ928/855-5559 or 1-888/315-2378; ❷), to the extravagant riverfront *London Bridge Resort*, 1477 Queen's Bay Rd (Ⓣ928/855-0888 or 1-866/331-9231, Ⓦwww.londonbridgeresort.com; ❺), where the lobby is all but filled by a gilt replica stagecoach. *Shugrue's* (Ⓣ928/453-1400), across the bridge in the Island Fashion Mall, serves good fresh fish – even sushi – as well as salads and pasta.

The Grand Canyon

Although almost five million people visit **GRAND CANYON NATIONAL PARK** every year, the canyon itself remains beyond the grasp of the human imagination. No photograph, no statistics, can prepare you for such vastness. At more than one mile deep, it's an inconceivable abyss; varying between four and eighteen miles wide, it's an endless expanse of bewildering shapes and colors, glaring desert brightness and impenetrable shadow, stark promontories and soaring sandstone pinnacles. Somehow it's so impassive, so remote – you could never call it a disappointment, but at the same time many visitors are left feeling peculiarly flat. In a sense, none of the available activities can quite live up to that first stunning sight of the chasm. The **overlooks** along the rim all offer views that shift unceasingly from dawn to sunset; you can **hike** down into the depths on foot or by mule, hover above in a **helicopter**, or raft through the **whitewater rapids** of the river itself; you can spend a night at **Phantom Ranch** on the canyon floor, or swim in the waterfalls of the idyllic **Havasupai Reservation**. And yet that distance always remains – the Grand Canyon stands apart.

The vast majority of visitors come to the **South Rim** – it's much easier to get to, it holds far more facilities (mainly at **Grand Canyon Village**), and it's open year round. There is another lodge and campground at the **North Rim**, which by virtue of its isolation can be a lot more evocative, but at one thousand feet higher it is usually closed by snow from mid-October until May. Few people visit both rims; to get from one to the other demands either a tough two-day hike down one side of the canyon and up the other, or a 215-mile drive by road.

Admission to the park, valid for seven days on either rim, is $25 per vehicle or $12 for pedestrians and cyclists.

The South Rim

When someone casually mentions visiting the "Grand Canyon", they're almost certainly referring to the **South Rim**. To be more precise, it's the thirty-mile stretch of the South Rim that's served by a paved road; and most specifically of all, it's **Grand Canyon Village**, the small canyon-edge community, sandwiched between the pine forest and the rim, that holds the park's **lodges**, **restaurants**, and **visitor center**. Nine out of every ten visitors come here, however, not because it's a uniquely wonderful spot from which to see the canyon, but simply

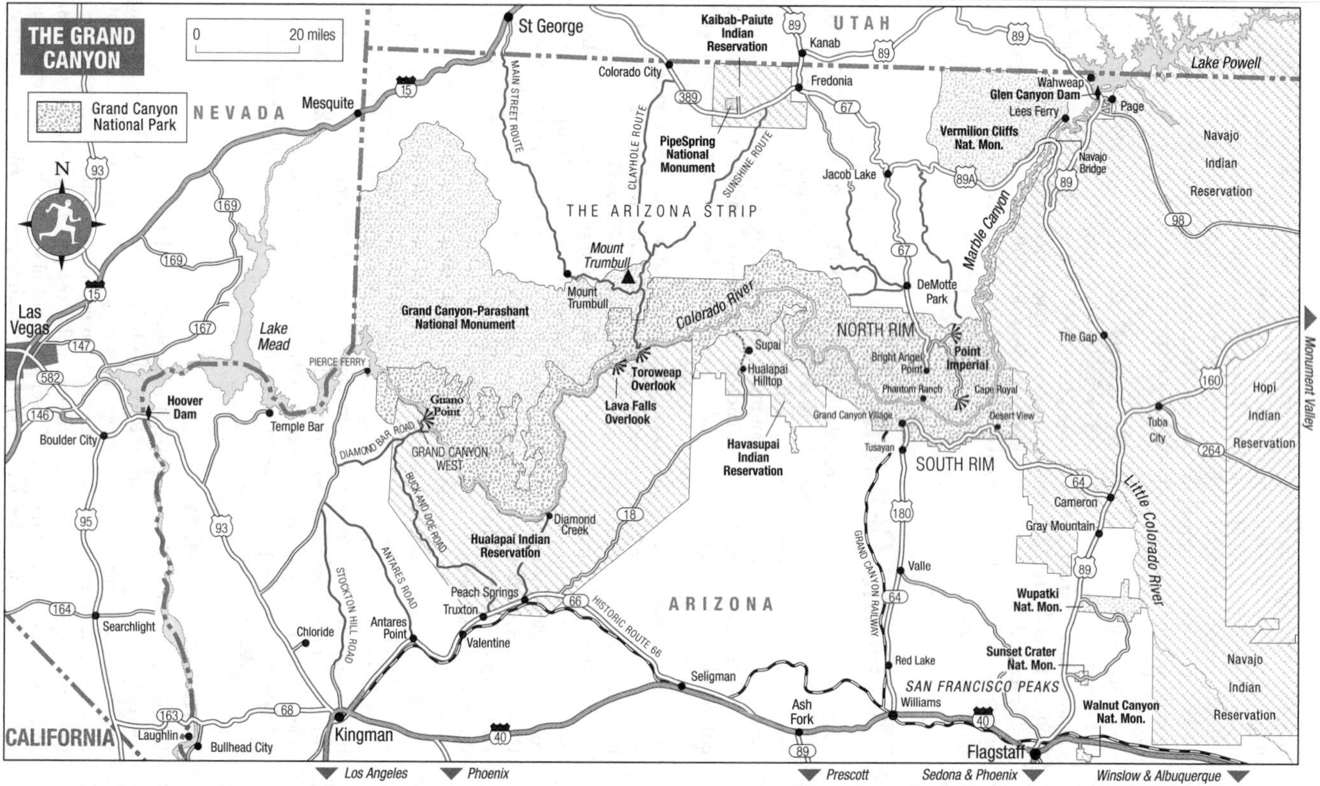
THE GRAND CANYON
Grand Canyon National Park
0 20 miles
N
NEVADA
UTAH
ARIZONA
CALIFORNIA
THE ARIZONA STRIP
St George
Mesquite
Las Vegas
Boulder City
Hoover Dam
Lake Mead
Temple Bar
PIERCE FERRY
Colorado City
Kanab
Fredonia
Kaibab-Paiute Indian Reservation
PipeSpring National Monument
MAIN STREET ROUTE
CLAYHOLE ROUTE
SUNSHINE ROUTE
Mount Trumbull
Grand Canyon-Parashant National Monument
Jacob Lake
DeMotte Park
Vermilion Cliffs Nat. Mon.
Wahweap
Glen Canyon Dam
Lees Ferry
Page
Lake Powell
Navajo Bridge
Marble Canyon
Navajo Indian Reservation
Hopi Indian Reservation
The Gap
Tuba City
Colorado River
NORTH RIM
SOUTH RIM
Point Imperial
Bright Angel Point
Phantom Ranch
Cape Royal
Desert View
Grand Canyon Village
Tusayan
Supai
Hualapai Hilltop
Havasupai Indian Reservation
Toroweap Overlook
Lava Falls Overlook
Guano Point
GRAND CANYON WEST
DIAMOND BAR ROAD
BUCK AND DOE ROAD
Diamond Creek
Hualapai Indian Reservation
Peach Springs
Truxton
Valentine
Antares Point
ANTARES ROAD
STOCKTON HILL ROAD
Chloride
Kingman
Searchlight
Laughlin
Bullhead City
HISTORIC ROUTE 66
Seligman
Ash Fork
Williams
GRAND CANYON RAILWAY
Valle
Red Lake
Cameron
Gray Mountain
Little Colorado River
Wupatki Nat. Mon.
Sunset Crater Nat. Mon.
SAN FRANCISCO PEAKS
Walnut Canyon Nat. Mon.
Flagstaff
Monument Valley
Los Angeles
Phoenix
Prescott
Sedona & Phoenix
Winslow & Albuquerque
15
93
169
167
147
582
146
95
164
163
68
40
66
18
389
67
89
89A
98
160
264
64
180

because tourist facilities just happen to have been concentrated here ever since the railroad arrived a century ago.

However, it's as good a place to start as any. The canyon can be admired from countless vantage points, not only within the village but also along the eight-mile **Hermit Road** to the west and the 23-mile **Desert View Drive** to the east. The village is more attractive than you might imagine, and once the day-trippers have gone, does not feel overly crowded.

Getting to the South Rim

Nearly all visitors make their way to the South Rim by heading north of I-17 from either **Williams** (52 miles south) or **Flagstaff** (75 miles southeast). Most of the route is through ponderosa pine forests, so the route followed by the restored **steam trains** of the Grand Canyon Railway up from Williams is not especially scenic, even if it does make a fun ride (departs Williams daily, usually at 9.30am; from $65 round-trip; ⓣ928/773-1976 or 1-800/843-8724, ⓦwww.thetrain.com). For details of buses from Flagstaff, see p.891.

The small **airport** at Tusayan – six miles from the South Rim, and used primarily by "flight-seeing" tour companies (see p.900) – also welcomes scheduled services, especially from Las Vegas, with operators such as Scenic Airlines (sometimes as low as $80 one-way; ⓣ702/638-3300 or 1-800/634-6801, ⓦwww.scenic.com).

Arrival and information

Long-proposed schemes to ban private vehicles from the canyon area look unlikely to be implemented. **Canyon View Information Plaza**, well short of the village center near Mather Point, which was supposed to be the hub of a new light rail system, serves instead as the main information point for visitors. Its open-air dis-

Geology and history of the canyon

Layer upon layer of different rocks, readily distinguished by color, and each with its own fossil record, recede down into the Grand Canyon and back through time; the strata at the riverbed are among the oldest exposed rocks on earth. And yet how the canyon was **formed** is a mystery. Though the Colorado runs through the heart of an enormous hill (known to Native Americans as the Kaibab, "the mountain with no peak"), experts cannot agree how that could happen. Studies show that the canyon is still slowly deepening, at 50ft per million years. Its fantastic sandstone and limestone formations were not literally carved by the river, however; they're the result of erosion by wind and extreme cycles of heat and cold. These features were named – **Brahma Temple**, **Vishnu Temple**, and so on – by Clarence Dutton, who wrote the first Geological Survey report on the canyon in 1881.

While it may look forbidding, the Grand Canyon is not a dead place. All sorts of desert **wildlife** survive here – sheep and rabbits, eagles and vultures, mountain lions, and, of course, spiders, scorpions, and snakes. **Humans** have never been present on any great scale, but signs have been found of habitation as early as 2000 BC, and the **Ancestral Puebloans** were certainly here later on. A party of **Spaniards** passed through in 1540, and a Father Garcés spent some time with the Havasupai in 1776, but **John Wesley Powell**'s expeditions along the fearsome uncharted waters of the Colorado in 1869 and 1871–72 were what really brought the canyon to public attention. Entrepreneurs made a few abortive attempts to mine different areas, then realized that facilities for tourism were a far more lucrative investment. With the exception of the Indian reservations, the Grand Canyon is now run exclusively for the benefit of visitors, although as recently as 1963 there were proposals to dam the Colorado and flood 150 miles of the Canyon, and the Glen Canyon dam has seriously affected the ecology downstream.

In-park accommodation reservations

All in-park **accommodation reservations** – for the lodges on both the South and the North rims, as well as for *Phantom Ranch* and RV camping – are handled by Xanterra Parks & Resorts (same-day ⓣ928/638-2631, advance ⓣ303/297-2757 or 1-888/297-2757, ⓦwww.grandcanyonlodges.com). The best rooms are often booked as much as a year in advance, and your chances of turning up without a reservation and finding a place in summer are minimal.

plays and trail guides are complemented by a good bookstore and a visitor center staffed by helpful rangers (daily: May to mid-Oct 7.30am–6pm; mid-Oct to April 8am–5pm; ⓣ928/638-7888, ⓦwww.nps.gov/grca).

Grand Canyon Village is still accessible to private vehicles, as is the road east from the village to Desert View. Both the road west from the village to **Hermit's Rest**, however, and the short access road to **Yaki Point** – the first overlook east of Mather Point, and the trailhead for the **South Kaibab Trail** – are only open to private vehicles during December, January, and February. Free **shuttle buses** run on three routes: the ponderous **Village Route**, which loops between Grand Canyon Village and the information plaza; the **Kaibab Trail Route** between the plaza and Yaki Point; and the eight-mile **Hermit's Rest Route**, which heads west to eight canyon overlooks.

South Rim accommodation

All the "lodges" in Grand Canyon Village are operated by the park concessionaire, Xanterra. In terms of seeing the canyon, it makes little difference where in the village you stay. Even in the "rim-edge" places – the magnificent 1905 *El Tovar Hotel* (❼) and the *Bright Angel* (rooms ❹, rim-side cabins ❻), *Thunderbird*, and *Kachina* lodges (both ❼) – few rooms offer much of a view, and in any case it's always dark by 8pm. Further back are *Maswik Lodge* (❹), and the two-part *Yavapai Lodge* not far from the information plaza (❺). For details on making reservations at all of these options, see the box, above.

Tent and RV camping (without hookups) is available at the year-round **Mather Campground**, south of the main road through Grand Canyon Village. Sites for up to two vehicles and six people cost $18 per night between March and mid-November, when it's possible, and strongly recommended, to make a reservation (ⓣ1-877/444-6777, ⓦwww.reservations.nps.gov). Between mid-November and Feb, sites are first-come, first-served, and the fee drops to $15 per night. The adjacent **Trailer Village** consists exclusively of RV sites with hookups, costing $30 per site per night for two people; reserve through Xanterra (see box).

The summer-only *Desert View* campground, 26 miles east, is first-come, first-served, costs $12, and has no hook-ups. You can also camp inside the canyon itself, with a permit from the **Backcountry Reservations Office** near *Maswik Lodge* (daily 8am–noon & 1–5pm; see ⓦwww.nps.gov/grca/backcountry); permits cost $10, plus $5 per person per night.

If all the park accommodation is full, the nearest alternative is the underwhelming service village of **Tusayan**. *Seven Mile Lodge* (ⓣ928/638-2291; no advance reservations; ❹) offers the least expensive rooms, while the *Holiday Inn Express* (ⓣ928/638-3000 or 1-888/473-2269, ⓦwww.gcanyon.com; ❻) is more stylish.

South Rim eating

Grand Canyon Village holds a reasonably wide range of places to **eat**. Both *Yavapai* and *Maswik* lodges have basic cafeterias, open until 9pm and 10pm

▲ The Grand Canyon

respectively. *Bright Angel Lodge* has its own **restaurant**, as well as the *Arizona Steakhouse*; both are open until 10pm and offer entrees costing $15–25. At *El Tovar*, where the dining room looks right out over the canyon, the sumptuous menu is enormously expensive. Breakfast is the most affordable meal; lunch and dinner can easily cost upwards of $40. Most of the hotels in **Tusayan** have their own dining rooms.

Exploring the South Rim

Most South Rim visits start near the Canyon View Information Plaza, but the canyon panorama that spreads out below **Mather Point** here is more comprehensive than any obtainable from Grand Canyon Village. The views to the east in particular are consistently stupendous; it's hard to imagine a more perfect position from which to watch the **sunrise** over the canyon.

Various vantage points along the rim-edge footpath nearby offer glimpses of the Colorado River. Walk west for around ten minutes – turn left along the rim from the information plaza – and you'll come to **Yavapai Point**. From here, you can see two tiny segments of the river, one of which happens to include both the suspension footbridge across the Colorado and *Phantom Ranch* (see p.901). Nearby, the **Yavapai Observation Station** (daily: hours vary from 8am–8pm in summer down to 8am–5pm in winter; free) has illuminating displays on how the canyon may have formed.

The **West** and **East Rim drives** extend along the South Rim for several miles in either direction from the information plaza and Grand Canyon Village, paralleled to the west by the **Rim Trail** on the very lip of the canyon. No one overlook can be said to be the "best," but there are far too many to stop at them all. **Sunset** is particularly magical at Hopi Point, to the west.

South Rim tours

Xanterra (contact the "transportation desk" in any lodge, or call ⓣ928/638-2631) runs at least two short daily **coach tours** along the **rim** to the west ($23) and east ($40) of the village, **sunrise** and **sunset** trips to Yavapai Point ($18)**,** and **mule** rides to Plateau Point ($154) and *Phantom Ranch* (from $420; see overleaf).

Multi-day **whitewater rafting trips** in the canyon proper – such as those run by Western River Expeditions (ⓦwww.westernriver.com) or Canyoneers (ⓦwww.canyoneers.com) – are often booked up years in advance, while no **one-day** raft trips are available within Grand Canyon National Park. For a trip along the river at short notice, there are however two alternatives, at either end of the canyon. Colorado River Discovery, based in Page, Arizona, offers one-day trips that start below **Glen Canyon Dam** and take out at **Lees Ferry** ($70; ⓣ928/645-9175 or 1-888/522-6644; ⓦwww.raftthecanyon.com), while further west, the tribal-run Hualapai River Runners arrange pricey one-day trips on the Hualapai Reservation, starting at Diamond Creek ($328; ⓣ928/769-2219 or 1-888/255-9550, ⓦwww.destinationgrandcanyon.com).

Airplane tours cost from around $85 for 30min up to as long as you like for as much as you've got. Operators include Air Grand Canyon (ⓣ928/638-2686 or 1-800/247-4726, ⓦwww.airgrandcanyon.com) and Grand Canyon Airlines (ⓣ928/638-2359 or 1-866/235-9422, ⓦwww.grandcanyonairlines.com). **Helicopter tours**, from something over $100 for 30min, are offered by Maverick (ⓣ928/638-2622, ⓦwww.maverickhelicopter.com) and Papillon (ⓣ702/736-7243 or 1-888/635-7272, ⓦwww.papillon.com), who also operate amazing $555 day-trips to the Havasupai Reservation. All the companies are in **Tusayan**, at or near the airport.

Driving or taking a shuttle bus along the East Rim Drive opens up further dramatic views. **Desert View**, 23 miles out from the village, is, at 7500ft, the highest point on the South Rim. Visible to the east are the vast flatlands of the **Navajo Nation**; to the northeast, **Vermillion** and **Echo Cliffs**, and the gray bulk of **Navajo Mountain** ninety miles away; to the west, the gigantic peaks of **Vishnu** and **Buddha temples**, while through the plains comes the narrow gorge of the **Little Colorado**. The odd-looking construction on the very lip of the canyon is **Desert View Watchtower**, built by Mary Jane Colter in 1932 in a conglomeration of Native American styles and decorated with Hopi pictographs.

Into the canyon

Hiking any of the trails that descend **into the Grand Canyon** allows you to pass through successive different landscapes, each with its own climate, wildlife, and topography. While the canyon offers a wonderful wilderness experience, however, remember that it can be a hostile and very unforgiving environment, grueling even for expert hikers.

That the South Rim is 7000ft above sea level is for most people fatiguing in itself. Furthermore, all hikes start with a long, steep descent, and unless you camp overnight you'll have to climb all the way back up again when you're hotter and wearier.

For day-hikers, the golden rule is to keep track of how much time you spend hiking down, and allow twice that much to get back up again. Average summer temperatures inside the canyon exceed 100°F; to hike for eight hours in that sort of heat, you have to drink an incredible thirty pints of water. Always carry at least a quart per person, and much more if there are no water sources along your chosen trail. You must have food as well, as drinking large quantities without also eating can cause deadly water intoxication.

Bright Angel Trail

The **Bright Angel Trail**, followed on foot or mule by thousands of visitors each year, starts from the wooden shack in the village that was once the Kolb photographic studio. The trail switchbacks for 9.6 miles down to **Phantom Ranch**, but under no circumstances should you try to hike down and back in a single day. It might not look far on the map, but it's harder than running a marathon. Instead, the longest feasible day-hike is to go as far as **Plateau Point** on the edge of the arid Tonto Plateau, an overlook above the Inner Gorge from which it is not possible to descend any further. That twelve-mile roundtrip usually takes at least eight hours. In summer, water can be obtained along the way.

Miners laid out the first section of the trail a century ago, along an old Havasupai route. It has two short tunnels in its first mile. After another mile, the **wildlife** starts to increase (deer, rodents, and ravens), and there are a few **pictographs,** all but obscured by graffiti.

At the lush **Indian Gardens** almost five miles down, site of a ranger station and campground with water, the trails split to Plateau Point or down to the river via the **Devil's Corkscrew**. The latter route leads through sand dunes scattered with cactuses and down beside **Garden Creek** to the Colorado, which you then follow for more than a mile to *Phantom Ranch*.

Phantom Ranch

It's a real thrill to spend a night at the very bottom of the canyon, at the 1922 **Phantom Ranch.** The **cabins** are reserved exclusively for the use of excursionists on two-day mule trips ($420 per person for one night, $592 for the winter-only two-night trips), booked through Xanterra (see p.900). Beds in the four ten-bunk **dorms** ($36) are usually reserved way in advance, also through Xanterra, but it's worth checking for cancellations at the Bright Angel transportation desk as soon as you reach the South Rim. Do not hike down without a reservation, and even if you do have one, reconfirm it the day before you set off. All supplies reach *Phantom Ranch* the same way you do (an all-day hike on foot or mule), so **meals** are expensive, a minimum of $18.50 for breakfast and up to $38 for dinner. **Camping** at the beautiful *Bright Angel Campground*, a little closer to the Colorado River, is by **permit** only, as detailed on p.898. Again, do not hike down without a reservation.

Grandview Trail

The **Grandview Trail**, down from Grandview Point, was built during the 1890s to aid copper mining on **Horseshoe Mesa**, still littered with abandoned mine workings. Although it's possible (by connecting with other trails) to use the Grandview to find your way down to the Tonto Platform and thus, eventually, the Colorado River, it's not itself a rim-to-river route. Instead, the hike down to the mesa and back is a popular **day-hike**, though that doesn't mean it's easy; now officially "unmaintained," it's a very demanding trail. Several of its switchbacks were constructed by inserting metal rods deep into the canyon wall, then covering them with juniper logs, stones, and dirt. At times it can be a little hair-raising, but it has stayed surprisingly sturdy for over a century. Reckon on six hours for the round-trip.

The Havasupai Reservation

The **Havasupai Reservation** really is another world. Things have changed a little since a 1930s anthropologist called it "the only spot in the United States where native culture has remained in anything like its pristine condition," but the sheer magic of its turquoise waterfalls and canyon scenery makes this a very special place.

Havasu Canyon is a side canyon of the Grand Canyon, 35 miles as the raven flies from Grand Canyon Village, but almost two hundred miles by road. Turn off the interstate at Seligman or Kingman, onto AZ-66 (which curves north between the two), stock up with food, water, and gas, and then follow Arrowhead Hwy-18 to **Hualapai Hilltop**. An eight-mile trail zigzags down a bluff from there, leading through the stunning waterless Hualapai Canyon to the village of **SUPAI**. Riding down on horseback with a Havasupai guide costs $70 one-way, $120 round-trip, and there's often a helicopter service as well ($85 one-way; Ⓣ623/516-2790). Hiking is free, but all visitors pay a $35 entry fee on arrival at Supai.

Beyond Supai the trail leads to a succession of spectacular waterfalls, including **Havasu Falls**, which is great for swimming, and **Mooney Falls**, named after an unfortunate prospector who dangled here for three days in the 1890s, at the end of a snagged rope, before falling to his death.

A **campground** ($17; Ⓣ928/448-2141) stretches between Havasu and Mooney Falls, and Supai itself holds the **motel**-like *Havasupai Lodge* (Ⓣ928/448-2111; ❻), along with a **café**, a **general store**, and the only **post office** in the US still to receive its mail by pack train. Supai is frequently hit by freak floods, as in August 2008, which can result in the temporary closure of the campground and lodge.

The Hualapai Reservation: the "West Rim"

Immediately west of the Havasupai reservation, and also inhabited by descendants of the Pai people, the **Hualapai Indian reservation** spreads across almost a million acres, bounded to the north by a 108-mile stretch of the Colorado River.

Fifty miles northwest of the reservation's only town, **PEACH SPRINGS**, itself 35 miles northwest of **Seligman** on Route 66, a cluster of overlooks above the Colorado river is cannily promoted as **Grand Canyon West**, or the "**West Rim**" of the Grand Canyon. This is the closest spot to Las Vegas where it's possible to see the canyon, and most of its visitors are day-trippers who fly here unaware that that they're not seeing the canyon at its best. The massive Hualapai program to attract tourists culminated in 2007 in the unveiling of the heavily publicized **Skywalk**, a horseshoe-shaped glass walkway out over a 4000-ft drop above a side arm of the canyon. It's so extraordinarily expensive, limited in scope, and time-consuming to visit – having driven a minimum of forty miles on dirt roads from the nearest highway, you have to pay $20 to park at the end, plus at least $57 per person to reach and walk on the Skywalk – that it can't be recommended over a trip to the national park.

To the North Rim

The 215-mile route by road from Grand Canyon Village to the **North Rim** follows AZ-64 along the East Rim Drive to Desert View, then passes an overlook into the gorge of the Little Colorado, before joining US-89 fifty miles later at **CAMERON**. The Cameron Trading Post, still a trading center for the Navajo Nation, holds a good **motel** and **restaurant** (Ⓣ928/679-2231 or 1-800/338-7385, Ⓦwww.camerontradingpost.com; ❺).

Lees Ferry

The direct route to the North Rim, now US-89A, crosses **Navajo Bridge** seventy barren miles north of Cameron, five hundred feet above the Colorado river. There are in fact two Navajo Bridges, the 1929 original, now reserved for pedestrians, having been supplanted by a wider facsimile in 1995. Until the first was built, a ferry service operated six miles north at **LEES FERRY**. Established in 1872 by Mormon pioneer John D. Lee, it was the only spot within hundreds of miles to offer easy access to the banks of the river on both sides. Lee himself was on the run after the **Mountain Meadows Massacre** in Utah in 1857, in which he led a white band clumsily disguised as Indians in their slaughter of a wagon train of would-be settlers.

Lees Ferry is the sole launching point for **whitewater rafting** trips into the Grand Canyon – the first point where boats can get out again is at Diamond Creek, twelve days away by muscle power. The ferry site still holds the atmospheric remains of Lee's Lonely Dell ranch, as well as a basic **campground** (Ⓣ928/355-2334; $12). Back on US-89A, beneath the red of the **Vermilion Cliffs**, a succession of **motels** all have their own restaurants – *Marble Canyon Lodge* (Ⓣ928/355-2225 or 1-800/726-1789; Ⓦwww.leesferryflyfishing.com; ❸), *Lees Ferry Lodge* (Ⓣ928/355-2231 or 1-800/451-2231, Ⓦwww.vermilioncliffs.com; ❸), and *Cliff Dweller's Lodge* (Ⓣ928/355-2261 or 1-800/962-9755; Ⓦwww.cliffdwellerslodge.com; ❹).

The turning south to get to the North Rim, off US-89A onto AZ-67, comes at **JACOB LAKE**, home to the welcoming *Jacob Lake Inn* (Ⓣ928/643-7232, Ⓦwww.jacoblake.com; ❹) and the lovely *Jacob Lake Campground*, open to tent campers only (Ⓣ928/643-7395; mid-May to Oct; $12), but not much else. From here – along a road that's closed in winter – it's 41 miles to the canyon itself.

The North Rim

Higher, more exposed, and far less accessible than the South Rim, the **NORTH RIM** of the Grand Canyon receives less than a tenth as many visitors. A cluster of venerable Park Service buildings stand where the main highway reaches the canyon, and a handful of rim-edge roads allow drivers to take their pick from additional lookouts. Only one hiking trail sees much use, the **North Kaibab Trail**, which follows Bright Angel Creek down to *Phantom Ranch*.

Tourist facilities on the North Rim, concentrated at **Bright Angel Point**, open for the season in mid-May and close in mid-October. **Accommodation** at *Grand Canyon Lodge* is in cabins and motel-like structures that spread back along the ridge from the lodge entrance, very few of which have canyon views; advance reservations are essential. (Ⓣ480/337-1320 or 1-877/386-4383, Ⓦwww.grandcanyonlodgenorth.com; ❺). The *Lodge* also holds a good **restaurant** (Ⓣ928/638-2611), plus a saloon, and an espresso bar, and arranges **mule rides** (1hr $30, half-day $65, full-day canyon expeditions $125; Ⓣ435/679-8665, Ⓦwww.canyonrides.com). Just over a mile north is the *North Rim Campground*, where space is usally available to backpackers, but can be reserved ($18; Ⓣ1-877/444-6777; Ⓦwww.recreation.gov).

The park itself remains open for day-use only after mid-October, but no food, lodging, or gas is available, and visitors must be prepared to leave at a moment's notice. It's shut down altogether by the first major snowfall of winter, which in recent years has come as late as December.

Northeastern Arizona: Indian Country

The deserts of northeastern Arizona, popularly known as **INDIAN COUNTRY**, hold some of the most fascinating **pre-Columbian ruins** in North America, in the most striking settings imaginable. The cliff palaces of **Canyon de Chelly**, and **Betatakin** and **Keet Seel** in the Navajo National Monument, are among the greatest architectural achievements of the **Ancestral Puebloans**, made that much more special by the fact that the lands on which they stand are still lived on and worked by their heirs, the Hopi and Navajo.

The **NAVAJO NATION**, the largest Native American reservation in the US, extends into western New Mexico and stretches to include the majestic sandstone pillars of Monument Valley in southernmost Utah. The Navajo may drive pickup trucks and wear baseball caps, but you get a very real sense that you're traveling through a foreign country here. Everyone can speak English, but Navajo, a language so complex that it was used as a secret code during World War II, is still the lingua franca. The reservation follows its own rules over Daylight Savings; in frontier-style towns like Tuba City, the time on the clock can vary according to whether you're in an American or a Navajo district.

When the Americans took over this region from the Mexicans in the mid-nineteenth century, the Navajo – who call themselves *Dineh*, "The People" – almost lost everything. In 1864, Kit Carson rounded up every Navajo he could find and forced them all to move to Fort Sumner in desolate eastern New Mexico (see p.867). A few years later, however, the Navajo were allowed to return. Most of the 300,000-plus Navajo today work the land as shepherds and farmers on widely scattered smallholdings, though craftspeople also sell their wares from roadside stands and tourist stops.

Visiting this region, it's important to respect the people and places you encounter. Though the Ancestral Puebloans have long since vanished, many of the relics

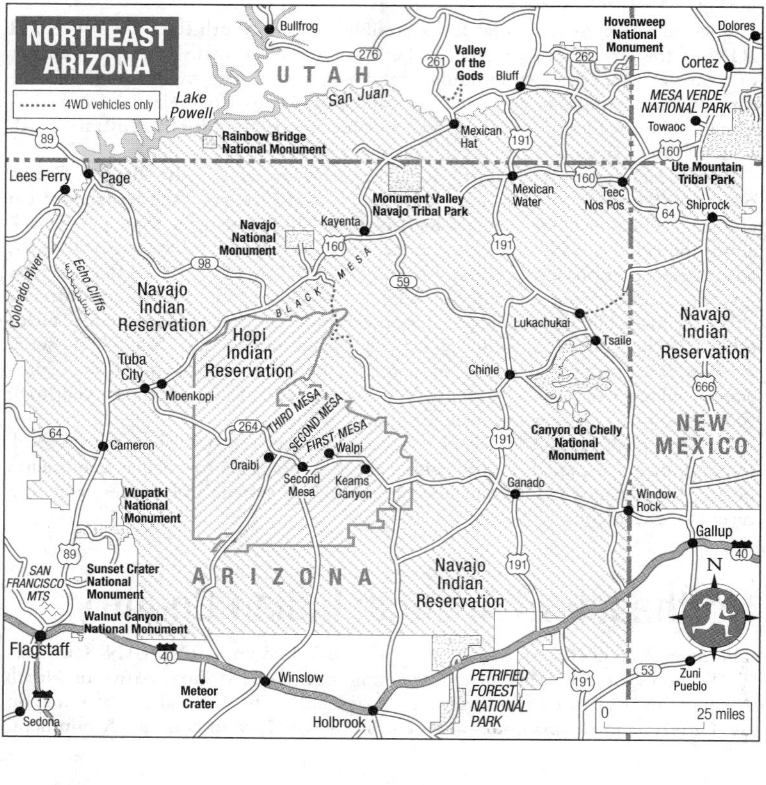

they left behind are on land that still holds spiritual significance to their modern counterparts. Similarly, it is offensive to photograph or otherwise intrude upon people's lives without permission; one reason why the Hopi, for example, banned photography was because it was such an interfering nuisance.

On a practical note, don't expect extensive **tourist facilities**. Most towns exist solely as bureaucratic outposts that only come alive during the annual tribal fairs and rodeos, and have little to offer visitors beyond a handful of places to eat and even fewer hotels and motels. For more information, check out the official **websites** Ⓦwww.discovernavajo.com and Ⓦwww.explorenavajo.com.

Navajo National Monument

Navajo National Monument, in the northwest quarter of the reservation, protects two of Arizona's biggest and most beautifully sited cliff dwellings. You'll find the useful **visitor center** (daily 8am–5pm; free; Ⓣ928/672-2700, Ⓦwww.nps.gov/nava) at the end of paved Hwy-564, ten miles north of US-160. Behind it, a ten-minute trail crosses the plateau to a viewpoint overlooking **Betatakin**, an exceptionally well-preserved 135-room masonry structure tucked in a large natural alcove halfway up the 700-foot-high, brilliant-red sandstone cliff on the far side of a canyon. It's only possible to hike down to Betatakin – which feels as though it was abandoned seven years, not seven centuries, ago – by joining one of the unforgettable five-hour ranger-guided hikes (schedule varies, typically summer daily 8.15am & 10am, winter daily 10am). Numbers are limited, so call ahead and get to the visitor center as early as possible on the day – or stay the previous night at the very attractive free **campground** in the forest alongside.

In summer, you can also visit the even larger Ancestral Puebloan site of **Keet Seel**. However, the seventeen-mile round-trip hike from the visitor center is too grueling to attempt in a single day, so you'll have to stay overnight in the small **campground** near the site, having obtained a permit from the visitor center at least a day in advance.

There are few **places to stay** nearby. However, **TUBA CITY**, west of the monument, has the large, modern *Quality Inn Tuba Trading Post* (Ⓣ928/283-4545 or 1-800/644-8383; Ⓦwww.qualityinntubacity.com; ❺), while **KAYENTA**, 22 miles northeast of the monument at the junction of US-160 and US-163, holds the similarly anonymous but adequate *Best Western Wetherill Inn* (Ⓣ928/697-3231, Ⓦwww.gouldings.com; ❺), and the *Hampton Inn–Navajo Nation* (Ⓣ928/697-3170 or 1-800/426-7866, Ⓦwww.hamptoninn.com; ❻), which has a surprisingly good **restaurant**.

Monument Valley

The classic southwestern landscape of stark sandstone buttes and forbidding pinnacles of rock, poking from an endless expanse of drifting red sands, is an archetypal Wild West image. Only when you arrive at **MONUMENT VALLEY** – which straddles the Arizona–Utah state line, 24 miles north of Kayenta and 25 miles southwest of Mexican Hat – do you realize how much your perception of the West has in fact been shaped by this one spot. Such scenery does exist elsewhere, of course, but nowhere is it so perfectly distilled. While moviemakers have flocked here since the early days of Hollywood – this is where John Ford made John Wayne a star – the sheer majesty of the place still takes your breath away. Add the fact that it remains a stronghold of **Navajo** culture, and Monument Valley can be the absolute highlight of a trip to the Southwest.

The biggest and most impressive of the monoliths are a pair called **The Mittens**, one East and one West, each of which has a distinct thumb splintering off from its central bulk. Over a dozen other spires are spread around nearby, along with **rock art panels** and an assortment of minor but nicely sited **Ancestral Puebloan ruins**.

You can see the buttes for free, towering alongside US-163, but the four-mile detour to enter **Monument Valley Tribal Park** is rewarded with much closer views (daily: May–Sept 6am–8pm; Oct–April 8am–5pm; $5; ⓣ435/727-5870; ⓦwww.navajonationparks.org). A rough, unpaved road drops from behind the visitor center and *View* hotel to run through Monument Valley itself. The 17-mile **self-drive route** makes a bumpy but bearable ride in an ordinary vehicle, and takes something over an hour (daily: summer 6am–8.30pm; rest of year 8am–4.30pm). However, the Navajo-led **jeep** or **horseback tours** into the backcountry are very much recommended; a 90-minute jeep trip costs from around $50 per person if arranged on the spot, with plenty of longer and potentially much more expensive alternatives. As well as stopping at such movie locations as the **Totem Pole**, most tours call in at a Navajo *hogan* (eight-sided dwelling) to watch weavers at work.

This guide went to press shortly before the opening of a stunning new Navajo-owned **hotel** alongside the main viewpoint at Monument Valley. Appropriately named *The VIEW* (ⓣ928/727-3470, ⓦwww.monumentvalleyview.com; ❽), it offers luxurious rooms with absolutely magnificent views, plus a reasonable **restaurant** and its own extensive program of well-priced tours. Nearby, the exposed *Mitten View* **campground** is first-come, first-served, with water available in summer only (summer $10, winter $5). Just outside the park, six miles west in Utah, the veteran *Goulding's Lodge* (ⓣ435/727-3231, ⓦwww.gouldings.com; ❼), is a 1920s trading post that offers pricey motel rooms and an unexceptional restaurant, plus its own campground ($24).

Canyon de Chelly National Monument

A short distance east of **CHINLE**, sixty miles southwest of Kayenta and seventy miles north of I-40, twin sandstone walls emerge abruptly from the desert floor, climbing at a phenomenal rate to become the awesome thousand-foot cliffs of **CANYON DE CHELLY NATIONAL MONUMENT**. Between these sheer sides, the meandering course of the Chinle Wash can be discerned by its fringe of cottonwoods as it winds through grasslands and planted fields. Here and there a Navajo *hogan* stands in a grove of fruit trees, a straggle of sheep is penned in by a crude wooden fence, or ponies drink at the water's edge. And everywhere, perched above the valley on ledges in the canyon walls and dwarfed by the towering cliffs, are the long-abandoned adobe dwellings of the **Ancestral Puebloans**.

Two main canyons branch apart a few miles upstream: **Canyon de Chelly** (pronounced *de shay*) to the south and **Canyon del Muerto** to the north. Each twists and turns in all directions, scattered with vast rock monoliths, while several smaller canyons break away. The whole labyrinth threads its way northward for thirty miles into the Chuska Mountains.

Canyon de Chelly is a magnificent place, on a par with the best of the Southwest's national parks. Its relative lack of fame owes much to the continuing presence of the **Navajo**, for whom the canyon retains enormous symbolic significance (although they did not build its cliff dwellings). Visitors are largely restricted to peering into the canyon from above, from overlooks along the two "rim drives." There's no road in, and, apart from one short trail, you can only enter the canyons with a Navajo guide.

Some history

The canyon's first known inhabitants, **Ancestral Puebloan Basketmakers**, dwelled here from around 300 AD. During the next thousand years, they advanced from living in pit houses dug into the soil to building elegant cliff dwellings, and developed fine pottery and weaving. For some centuries after they left, the **Hopi** came here to farm each summer, but **Navajo** migrants eventually displaced the Hopi altogether.

From 1583 onward, the Navajo were locked with the Spanish in a bloody cycle of armed clashes and slave raids. The US Army in turn failed repeatedly to dislodge the Navajo, but no treaty could restrain the rapacious hunger for land by New Mexican settlers. The end appeared to have come with the brutal round-up and deportation (the "**Long Walk**") of the entire Navajo people, completed by Kit Carson in 1864 when he starved the last of them down from Navajo Rock and destroyed their homes and livestock. So barbaric was the Navajo's imprisonment at Fort Sumner, however, that Congress soon allowed them to return. To this day, 25 Navajo families still farm the Canyon de Chelly in summer.

The view from above: the rim drives

Each of the two "rim drives" offers a succession of spectacular overlooks; allow two to three hours for each forty-mile round-trip.

The first significant stopping point along the South Rim Drive is **Junction Overlook**, after four miles, far above the point where the two main canyons branch their separate ways; as you scramble across the bare rocks you can see Canyon de Chelly narrowing away, with a *hogan* immediately below. Two miles further along, by which time the canyon is 550ft deep, **White House Overlook** looks down on the highly photogenic **White House Ruins**. This is the only point from which unguided hikers can descend to the canyon floor, taking perhaps 30 to 45 minutes to get down and a good hour to get back up. The beautiful if precarious trail, at times running along ledges chiseled into the slick rock, culminates with a close-up view of the ruins; the most dramatic dwellings, squeezed into a tiny alcove sixty feet up a majestic cliff, were once reached via the rooftops of now-vanished structures. Visitors are forbidden to walk for more than a hundred yards in either direction beyond the site. Back up on the South Rim Drive, twelve miles along, the view from **Sliding House Overlook** reveals more Ancestral Puebloan ruins seemingly slipping down the canyon walls toward the ploughed Navajo fields below, while eight miles further on the road ends above the astonishing **Spider Rock**, where twin 800-foot pinnacles of rock come to within 200ft of the canyon rim.

The **North Rim Drive** runs twenty miles up Canyon del Muerto to **Massacre Cave**, where a Spanish expedition of 1805 killed around one hundred Navajo

Into the canyons

Tours of the canyon floor, organized by *Thunderbird Lodge* (see overleaf), zigzag along the washes, which vary from two- or three-feet deep during the spring thaw to completely dry in summer. For most of the year, the bone-shaking tours are in open-top flatbed trucks that lurch over the rutted earth, and the heat can be incredible; in winter they carry on in glass-roofed army vehicles with caterpillar tracks. To reach as far as Spider Rock, you have to take the full-day tour ($74; no reductions for children), but the half-day trip at $46 (under 13s $34.50) still enables you to see a wide variety of sites and terrain, including the White House Ruins.

The visitor center also arranges highly recommended 4.5-mile, four-hour **group hikes**, which cost $15 per person. The precise schedule varies, but usually includes a morning trip via the White House Trail and an afternoon hike in the Canyon del Muerto; separate **night hikes** last just two hours but cost slightly more. Tsotsonii Ranch (Ⓣ928/755-2037, Ⓦwww.totsoniiranch.com) organize horseback trips for $15 per person per hour, plus $15 an hour for a guide.

women, children, and old men. The "cave" is just a pitifully exposed ledge, upon which the huddled group was easily picked off by the Spanish, using ricochets off the overhang above. Visible from the nearby **Mummy Cave Overlook** is the **House Under The Rock**, with its central tower in the Mesa Verde style – the single most striking ruin in the monument. Of the two viewpoints at **Antelope House Overlook**, one is opposite Navajo Fortress, an isolated eminence atop which the Navajo were besieged for three months in 1863, while the other looks down on the twin ruined square towers of Antelope House. In the **Tomb of the Weaver** across the wash, the embalmed body of an old man was found wrapped in golden eagle feathers.

Practicalities

The Canyon de Chelly **visitor center**, on the road from Chinle (daily 8am–5pm; no entrance fee; ⓣ928/674-5500, ⓦwww.nps.gov/cach), has informative displays, and provides guides for unorthodox hiking or motorized expeditions. Facilities nearby are overstretched, so it's essential to book your **accommodation** well in advance. The most appealing options are the *Thunderbird Lodge* (ⓣ928/674-5841 or 1-800/679-2473, ⓦwww.tbirdlodge.com; ❺), very near the canyon entrance, which arranges the standard sightseeing tours and has an adequate cafeteria, and the *Chinle Holiday Inn* (ⓣ928/674-5000, ⓦwww.holiday-inn.com/chinle-garcia; ❺), slightly further back toward Chinle, where the food is a lot better. The free, minimally equipped *Cottonwood* **campground** has pleasant sites among the trees alongside *Thunderbird Lodge*.

Window Rock

The reservation's governing body, the Navajo Tribal Council, has its seat near the New Mexico border. It was based for fifty years at Fort Defiance, a US cavalry outpost, until in the 1930s **WINDOW ROCK** was established as a new capital. Named for the natural stone arch on its northern side, it's not a great place to get a grasp of Navajo culture, but it does at least have gas stations, shops, and a **motel**, the showpiece *Quality Inn Navajo Nation Capital*, at 48 W Hwy-264 (ⓣ928/871-4108 or 1-800/662-6189; ⓦwww.qualityinnwindowrock.com; ❹). The nearby **Navajo Nation Museum and Visitor Center** (ⓣ928/871-7941; summer Mon & Sat 8am–5pm, Tues–Fri 8am–8pm; winter Mon–Fri 8am–5pm; donation) gives the background on tribal history and displays high-quality crafts.

The Hopi Mesas

Almost uniquely in the United States, the **Hopi** people have lived continuously in the same place for over eight hundred years. Some invaders have come and gone in that time, others have stayed; but the villages on **First**, **Second**, and **Third mesas** have endured, if not exactly undisturbed then at least unmoved.

To outsiders, it's not immediately obvious why the Hopi should have chosen to live on three barren and unprepossessing fingers of rock poking from the southern flanks of **Black Mesa** in the depths of northeast Arizona. There are two simple answers. The first lies within the mesa itself: its subterranean rocks are tilted to deliver a tiny but dependable trickle of water, and also hold enough coal to give the Hopi limitless reserves of fuel. The second is that the Hopi used to farm and hunt across a much wider area, and were only restricted to their mesa-top villages by the encroachment of their Navajo neighbors. While the Hopi are celebrated for their skill at "**dry farming**," managing to preserve enough precious liquid to grow corn, beans, and squash on hand-tilled terraces, this precarious and difficult way of life has nonetheless been forced upon them.

By their very survival, and the persistence of their ancient beliefs and ceremonies, the Hopi have long fascinated outsiders. While visitors are welcome, the Hopi have no desire to turn themselves into a tourist attraction. Although stores and galleries make it easy to buy crafts such as pottery, basketwork, silver overlay jewelry, and hand-carved *kachina* dolls, tourists who hope for extensive sight-seeing – let alone spiritual revelations – are likely to leave disappointed, and quite possibly dismayed by what they perceive as conspicuous poverty.

Visiting the Hopi Mesas

The essential first stop is the modern, mock-Pueblo **Hopi Cultural Center** below Second Mesa, which holds a **museum** (summer Mon–Sat 8am–5pm, Sun 9am–4pm; winter Mon–Fri 8am–5pm; $3; ⓣ928/734-6650), as well as a **cafeteria** and **motel** (ⓣ928/734-2401, ⓦwww.hopiculturalcenter.com; ❹). In summer, its plain but adequate rooms are usually booked solid a week or more in advance.

Unless your visit coincides with one of the very few social events that's open to tourists (ask at the cultural center), the only way to see the mesa-top villages is to take a **guided tour** of the most impressive one, **WALPI** (daily: winter 10am–4pm, summer 9.30am–6pm; $8; ⓣ928/737-2262). By Hopi standards, Walpi is not in fact that old; it was hastily thrown together in the immediate aftermath of the Pueblo Revolt of 1680, when the people of First Mesa moved to a more secure site in the face of possible Spanish or Navajo attack. The spot they chose is absolutely stunning, standing alone at the narrow southernmost tip of the mesa, and connected to the other First Mesa villages by the merest slender neck of stone, with a drop of three hundred feet to either side. It's now home to around 35 people, who live without electricity or running water.

To see Walpi, take Hwy-264 to modern **POLACCA**, at the foot of First Mesa, then drive a mile up the twisting paved road until it ends in **SICHOMOVI**. Tours assemble in Sichomovi's small community center, setting off at regular intervals for a half-hour walk to and around Walpi. There's plenty of opportunity to ask questions, and to buy pottery, *kachina* dolls, and fresh-baked *piiki*, a flatbread made with blue cornflour.

Utah

With the biggest, most beautiful, and most pristine landscapes in North America, **UTAH** has something for everyone: from brilliantly colored canyons, across endless desert plains, to thickly wooded and snow-covered mountains. Almost all of this unmatched range of terrain is public land, making Utah *the* place to come for **outdoor pursuits**, whether your tastes run to hiking, mountain biking, whitewater rafting, or skiing.

Southern Utah has more **national parks** than anywhere else in the US; it has often been suggested that the entire area should become one vast national park. The most accessible parts – such as **Zion** and **Bryce Canyon** – are by far the most visited, but lesser-known parks like **Arches** and **Canyonlands** are every bit as dramatic. Huge tracts of this empty desert, in which fascinating pre-Columbian pictographs and Ancestral Puebloan ruins lie hidden, are all but unexplored; seeing them requires self-sufficiency and considerable planning.

Though **northwestern** Utah is predominantly flat and dry, the granite mountains of the **Wasatch Front** tower over state capital **Salt Lake City** – an attractive and enjoyable stopover – while the resorts around **Park City** offer some of North America's finest **skiing**.

Led by Brigham Young, Utah's earliest white settlers – the **Mormons** – arrived in the Salt Lake area in 1847, and set about the massive irrigation projects that made their agrarian way of life possible. At first they provoked great suspicion and hostility back East. The Republican Convention of 1856 railed against slavery and polygamy in equal measure; had the Civil War not intervened, a war against the Mormons was a real possibility. Relations eased when the Mormon Church decided in 1890 to drop polygamy on its own terms before being forced to do so. Statehood followed in 1896, and over a century on, seventy percent of Utah's two-million-strong population are Mormons. The Mormon influence is responsible for the layout of Utah's towns, where residential streets are as wide as interstates, and all are numbered block-by-block according to the same logical if ponderous system.

Mormon businessmen became renowned as fiercely pro-mining and anti-conservation. Only since the 1980s has tourism been appreciated as a major industry, and former mining towns such as **Moab** developed facilities for wide-eyed travelers smitten by the allure of the desert. Increased tourism has also led to a relaxation of Utah's notorious **drinking laws**. In most towns, at least one restaurant is licensed to sell beer, wine, and mixed drinks to diners, and maybe even to sell beer in its bar or lounge.

Getting around Utah

Although Amtrak and Greyhound serve Salt Lake City and a few provincial towns, it's nearly impossible to get anywhere in Utah without your own **car**. However, various firms offer **bus tours** of the national parks, while southern Utah also has an unbeatable range of mountain biking and river rafting: see p.921 for a list of companies.

Southern Utah: the national parks

Southern Utah is a peculiar combination of the mind-boggling and the mundane. Its **scenery** is stupendous, a stunning geological freakshow where the earth is ripped bare to expose cliffs and canyons of every imaginable color, unseen rivers gouge mighty furrows into endless desert plateaus, and strange sandstone towers thrust from the sagebrush. By contrast, however, the tiny **Mormon towns** scattered across this epic landscape are, almost without exception, boring in the extreme, so most visitors spend as much time as possible **outdoors**.

While Southern Utah's five national parks are complemented by many lesser-known but equally dramatic wildernesses, they make the most obvious targets for travelers. In the southwest, **Zion National Park** centers on an awe-inspiring canyon, backed by barren highlands of white sandstone, while **Bryce Canyon** is a blaze of orange pinnacles. To the east, **Arches** holds an eroded desertscape of graceful red-rock fins and spurs, all on a more manageable scale than the astonishing hundred-mile vistas of neighboring **Canyonlands**. Both lie within easy reach of **Moab**, a disheveled former mining town turned Utah's hippest destination. The fifth park, **Capitol Reef**, stretches through the middle of the state, pierced by slender, ravishing canyons.

The defining topographical feature of southwest Utah is the **Grand Staircase**. Named by pioneer river-runner John Wesley Powell, it consists of a series of plateaus,

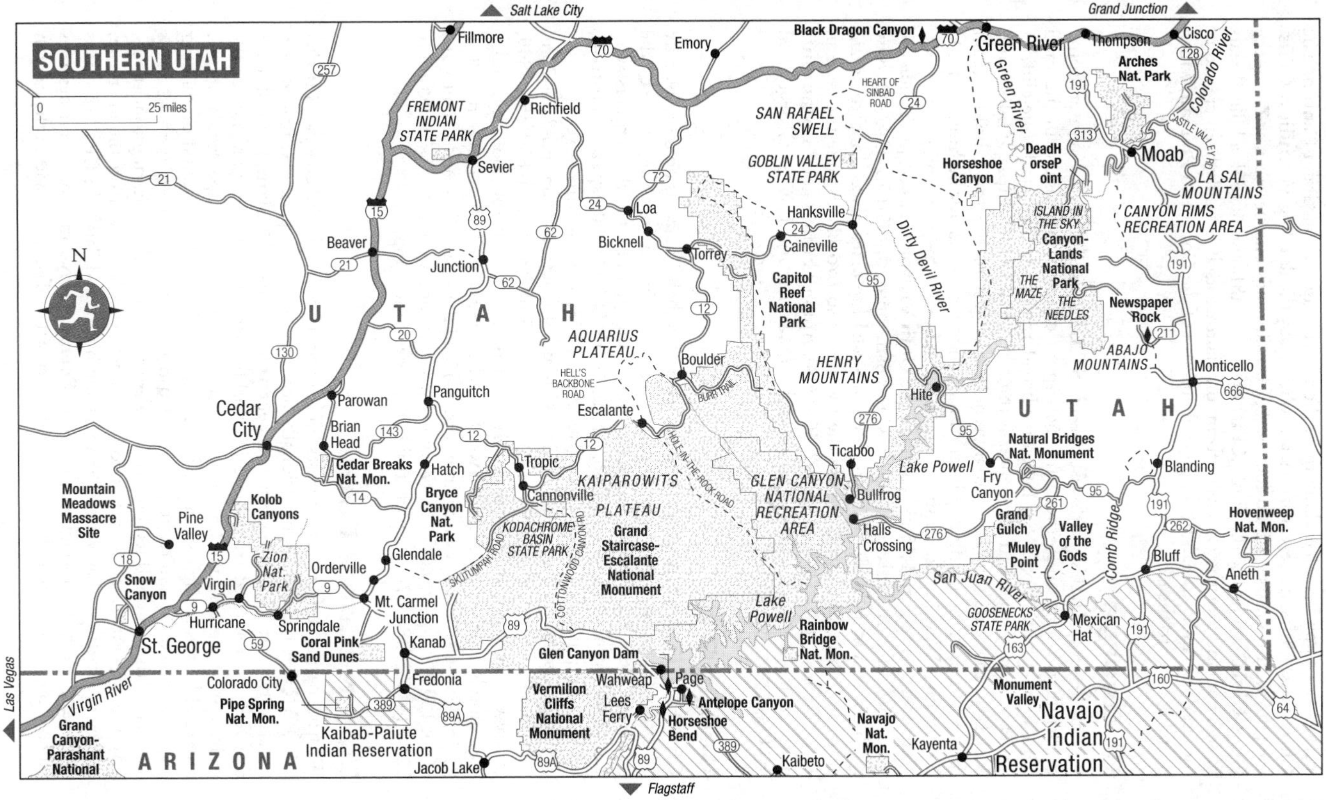

SOUTHERN UTAH
0
25 miles
N
Salt Lake City
Grand Junction
Las Vegas
Flagstaff
Fillmore
Emory
Black Dragon Canyon
Green River
Thompson
Cisco
Colorado River
Arches Nat. Park
Moab
CASTLE VALLEY RD
LA SAL MOUNTAINS
CANYON RIMS RECREATION AREA
FREMONT INDIAN STATE PARK
Richfield
Sevier
HEART OF SINBAD ROAD
SAN RAFAEL SWELL
GOBLIN VALLEY STATE PARK
Horseshoe Canyon
DeadH orseP oint
Green River
ISLAND IN THE SKY
Canyon-Lands National Park
THE MAZE
THE NEEDLES
Newspaper Rock
ABAJO MOUNTAINS
Monticello
Loa
Bicknell
Torrey
Hanksville
Caineville
Capitol Reef National Park
Dirty Devil River
Beaver
Junction
U T A H
AQUARIUS PLATEAU
HELL'S BACKBONE ROAD
Boulder
BURR TRAIL
HENRY MOUNTAINS
Hite
Cedar City
Parowan
Brian Head
Panguitch
Escalante
HOLE-IN-THE-ROCK ROAD
Ticaboo
Lake Powell
Natural Bridges Nat. Monument
Fry Canyon
Blanding
Cedar Breaks Nat. Mon.
Hatch
Tropic
Cannonville
KAIPAROWITS PLATEAU
GLEN CANYON NATIONAL RECREATION AREA
Bullfrog
Halls Crossing
Grand Gulch
Valley of the Gods
Comb Ridge
Hovenweep Nat. Mon.
Mountain Meadows Massacre Site
Pine Valley
Kolob Canyons
Bryce Canyon Nat. Park
KODACHROME BASIN STATE PARK
COTTONWOOD CANYON RD
Grand Staircase-Escalante National Monument
SKUTUMPAH ROAD
Muley Point
Bluff
Aneth
Snow Canyon
Virgin
Zion Nat. Park
Orderville
Glendale
Mt. Carmel Junction
Springdale
Hurricane
St. George
Coral Pink Sand Dunes
Kanab
Lake Powell
Rainbow Bridge Nat. Mon.
San Juan River
GOOSENECKS STATE PARK
Mexican Hat
Glen Canyon Dam
Wahweap
Page
Antelope Canyon
Horseshoe Bend
Colorado City
Fredonia
Virgin River
Pipe Spring Nat. Mon.
Kaibab-Paiute Indian Reservation
Vermilion Cliffs National Monument
Lees Ferry
Navajo Nat. Mon.
Kayenta
Kaibeto
Monument Valley
Navajo Indian Reservation
Grand Canyon-Parashant National
A R I Z O N A
Jacob Lake

stacked tier upon tier, that climb from the North Rim of the Grand Canyon. The **Chocolate Cliffs**, nearest Arizona, are followed by the dazzling **Vermilion Cliffs**, then the **White Cliffs** – a 2000-foot wall of Navajo sandstone, best seen at Zion – the **Grey Cliffs**, and finally the **Pink Cliffs** of Bryce. Although it took a billion years of sedimentation for these rocks to form, the staircase itself has only been created in the last dozen million years by the general upthrust of the **Colorado Plateau**, which stretches away to the east.

St George

Just off 1–15 in Utah's southwest corner, **ST GEORGE** was the winter home of Brigham Young and other early Mormon leaders, who basked in the mild climate of "Utah's Dixie." Set beneath a broad, reddish-brown sandstone cliff, it's a pretty enough town. At the center is the fine 1877 **LDS Temple** at 440 South 300 East, the oldest still in use anywhere. The rest of the town holds quaint pioneer homes, including Brigham Young's much-restored **adobe house** on 200 North First West (daily: summer 9am–8pm, winter 9am–5pm; free).

Travelers driving up I-15 can call in at the **Utah Visitor Center**, just inside the state line (daily: summer 8am–9pm; winter 8am–5pm; ⓣ435/673-4542, ⓦwww.utah.com). Virtually all St George's commercial life takes place along the main drag, St George Boulevard, where the twenty or so **motels** include the veteran *Dixie Palm* at no.185 E (ⓣ435/673-3531; ❷). Among various good **restaurants** in the Ancestor Square development is the *Pizza Factory*, 1 W St George Blvd (ⓣ435/628-1234; closed Sun).

Cedar City

CEDAR CITY, 53 miles north of St George and half its size, is no more worthy of a stop. Founded as an iron-mining town in the 1850s, it's now kept alive by the Southern Utah State College on its western fringe, and by the theatergoers who watch the enthusiastic productions of summer's **Utah Shakespeare Festival**, held on campus (late June to Oct; ⓣ435/586-7878, ⓦwww.bard.org).

A large **visitor center** stands at 581 N Main St (summer Mon–Fri 8am–7pm, Sat 9am–1pm; winter Mon–Fri 8am–5pm; ⓣ435/586-5124 or 1-800/354-4849, ⓦwww.scenicsouthernutah.com). **Main Street** is handy for food and lodging; motels with pools include two *Best Westerns*, the *El Rey Inn* at no. 80 S (ⓣ435/586-6518, ⓦwww.bwelrey.com; ❹), and the smart *Town and Country Inn* at no. 189 N (ⓣ435/586-9900, ⓦwww.bwtowncountry.com; ❹). *Sullivan's* at no. 301 S (ⓣ435/586-6761) is part steakhouse, part coffeeshop.

Zion National Park

With its soaring cliffs, riverine forests, and cascading waterfalls, **ZION NATIONAL PARK** is the most conventionally beautiful of Utah's parks. At first glance, it's also the least "Southwestern"; its centerpiece, **Zion Canyon**, is a lush oasis that feels far removed from the otherworldly desolation of Canyonlands or the weirdness of Bryce. Like California's Yosemite Canyon, it's a spectacular gorge, squeezed between mighty walls of rock and echoing with the sound of running water; also like Yosemite, it can get claustrophobic in summer, with its roads clogged with traffic and its limited facilities crammed with sweltering tourists.

Too many visitors see Zion Canyon as a quick half-day detour off the interstate, as they race between Las Vegas (158 miles southwest) and Salt Lake City (320 miles northeast). Beautiful though the canyon's **Scenic Drive** may be, Zion deserves much more of your time than that. Even the shortest hiking trail within the canyon

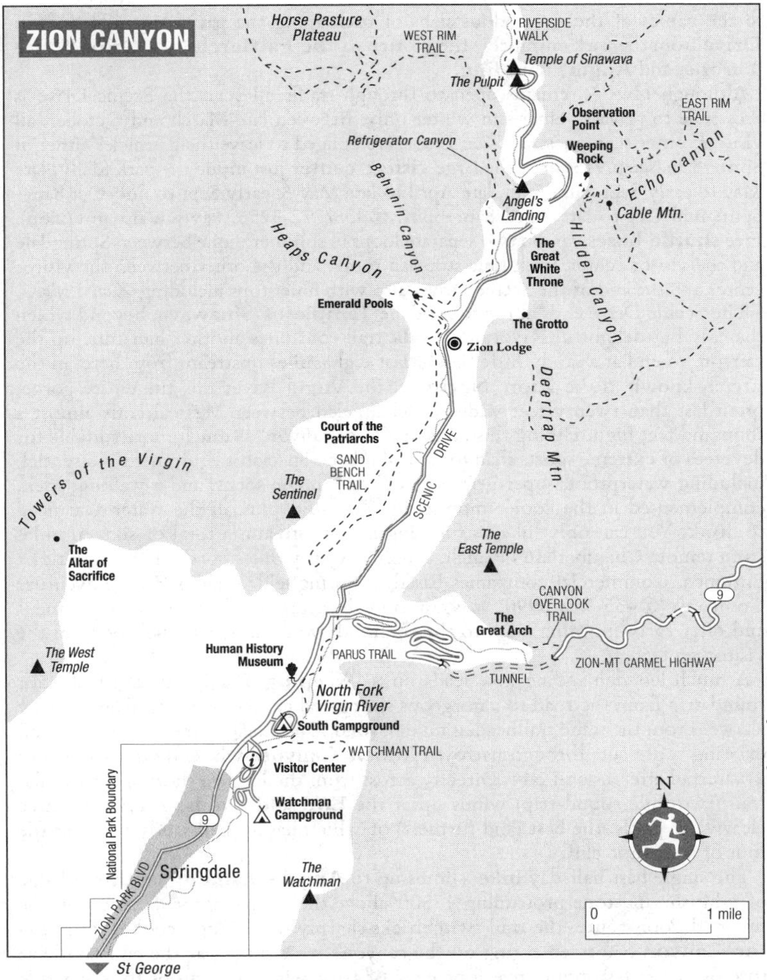

can escape the crowds, while a day-hike will take you away from the deceptive verdure of the valley and up onto the high-desert tablelands beyond.

Summer is by far the busiest season. That's despite temperatures in excess of 100°F, and violent thunderstorms concentrated especially in August. Ideally, come in April or May, to see the spring flowers bloom, or in September and October, to enjoy the fall colors along the river. The **admission charge** for Zion, valid in all sections of the park for seven days, is $25 per vehicle, or $12 for motorcyclists, cyclists, and pedestrians.

Visiting Zion Canyon

In **Zion Canyon**, mighty walls of Navajo sandstone soar half a mile above the groves of box elders and cottonwoods that line the loping North Fork of the **Virgin River**. The awe of the Mormon settlers who called this "Zion" is reflected in the names of the stupendous slabs of rock along the paved six-mile **Scenic Drive** from the park entrance – the **Court of the Patriarchs**, the **Great White Throne**, and **Angel's Landing**.

Although Hwy-9 remains open to through traffic all year, the Scenic Drive is accessible to private vehicles in winter only. Between late March and October, all visitors, other than guests at *Zion Lodge*, are obliged to leave their vehicles either in Springdale (see p.915) or at the large **visitor center** just inside the park (daily: late May to early Sept 8am–7pm, late April to late May & early Sept to mid-Oct 8am–6pm; mid-Oct to late April 8am–5pm; ⓣ435/772-3256, ⓦwww.nps.gov/zion). Free **shuttle buses** run on two separate loops in summer – one between Springdale and the visitor center, with nine stops en route, and the other between the visitor center and the end of the Scenic Drive, also with nine stops including *Zion Lodge*.

The Scenic Drive ends at the foot of the **Temple of Sinawava**, beyond which the easy but delightful **Riverside Walk** trail continues another half-mile up the canyon, to end at a sandy little beach. For eight miles upstream from here, in the stretch known as the **Zion Narrows**, the Virgin River fills the entire gorge, often less than twenty feet wide and channeled between vertical cliffs almost a thousand feet high. Hiking this ravishing "slot canyon" is much more suitable for devotees of extreme sports than for casual hikers. Specialist equipment is essential, including waterproof, super-grip footwear, neoprene socks, and a walking stick, complemented in the cooler months by a drysuit, plus all the water you need to drink. You can only hike its full length downstream, a total of sixteen miles from remote Chamberlain's Ranch, roughly twenty miles north of the park's East Entrance. Commercial companies based in Springfield, such as Zion Adventure Company (ⓣ435/772-0990, ⓦwww.zionadventures.com), rent out equipment and offer early-morning rides to the trailhead; you also need a permit from the visitor center.

A much less demanding hike leads up to **Weeping Rock**, an easy half-hour round-trip from the road to a gorgeous spring-fed garden dangling from a rocky alcove. From the same trailhead, a mile beyond *Zion Lodge*, a more strenuous and exciting route cuts through narrow **Hidden Canyon**, whose mouth turns into a waterfall after a good rain. Directly across from the lodge a short and fairly flat trail (two-mile round-trip) winds up at the **Emerald Pools**, a series of three clearwater pools, the best (and furthest) of which has a small sandy beach at the foot of a gigantic cliff.

The single best half-day **hike** climbs up to **Angel's Landing**, a narrow ledge of whitish sandstone protruding 1750ft above the canyon floor. Starting on the Emerald Pools route, the trail switchbacks sharply up through cool **Refrigerator Canyon** before emerging on the canyon's west rim; near the end you have to cross a heart-stopping five-foot neck of rock with sheer drops to either side (there's a steel cable to grab hold of). That round-trip takes a good four hours, but backpackers can continue another twenty miles to the gorgeous Kolob Canyons district (see p.915).

The high dry plateau above and to the **east** of Zion Canyon, reached by continuing on Hwy-9 at the Scenic Drive turnoff, stands in a complete contrast to the lush Virgin River gorge. Its most dramatic sight is the **Great Arch**, best seen from the turnouts before the mile-long tunnel, beyond which the **Canyon Overlook** trail gives a good introduction to the park's flora and fauna, such as the speedy lizards that race from rock to rock.

Practicalities

The only **food and lodging** within Zion itself is at *Zion Lodge* (open all year; same-day ⓣ435/772-7700, reserve through Xanterra at ⓣ303/297-2757 or 1-

888/297-2757, Ⓦwww.xanterra.com or Ⓦwww.zionlodge.com; ❻), set amid rolling and well-shaded lawns near the Great White Throne. The terrace of its fine old wooden dining room makes a great lunch stop. The *Lodge* is also the base for **horseback** excursions, with regular one-hour rides costing $30 per person (Ⓣ435/679-8665, Ⓦwww.canyonrides.com). Two good **campgrounds**, both charging $18 per night, are located alongside the visitor center; the *Watchman* accepts reservations in summer (Ⓣ1-877/444-6777, Ⓦwww.recreation.gov), while the summer-only *South* is first-come, first-served.

The best alternatives to the in-park lodge are in the appealing small town of **SPRINGDALE**, set among the riverbank cottonwoods half a mile south of the park entrance. Budget **motels** along Hwy-9, known here as Zion Park Boulevard, include the friendly *El Rio Lodge*, no. 995 (Ⓣ435/772-3205 or 1-888/772-3205, Ⓦwww.elriolodge.com; ❸), while two pricier modern alternatives, the *Best Western Zion Park Inn* at no. 1215 (Ⓣ435/772-3200 or 1-800/934-7275, Ⓦwww.zionparkinn.com; ❺), and the extremely stylish *Desert Pearl Inn*, no. 707 (Ⓣ435/772-8888 or 1-888/828-0898, Ⓦwww.desertpearl.com; ❻), offer good views and pools. The *Spotted Dog Café*, 428 Zion Park Blvd (Ⓣ435/772-3244), is the finest local **restaurant**, while apart from being the liveliest **bar** for miles, the dinner-only *Bit and Spur Saloon*, opposite the *Zion Park Inn* (Ⓣ435/772-3498), serves very good Mexican food.

The Kolob Canyons

Although the immaculate **Kolob Canyons** are just three miles off I-15, twenty miles south of Cedar City, this section of Zion receives far fewer visitors than Zion Canyon itself. Here, too, the focus is on **red-rock canyons**, which in the Kolob seem somehow redder, and the trees greener, than those down below.

The view from the five-mile paved road that heads up from the small **visitor center** (daily: late April to mid-Oct 8am–5pm, mid-Oct to late April 8am–4.30pm; Ⓣ435/772-3256) is amazing, while the two main hiking trails are highly recommended. One starts two miles from the visitor center and follows Taylor Creek on a five-mile round-trip to **Double Arch Alcove**, a spectacular natural amphitheater roofed by twin sandstone arches. The other trail sets off from the north side of the parking area at Lee Pass, four miles beyond the visitor center, and follows a well-marked route for seven miles past LaVerkin Falls to **Kolob Arch**, which at over 300ft across rivals Landscape Arch in Arches (see p.923) as the world's longest natural rock span.

Bryce Canyon National Park

The surface of the earth can hold few weirder-looking spots than **BRYCE CANYON**, a two-hour, 86-mile drive northeast of Zion. Named for Mormon settler Ebenezer Bryce, who declared that it was "a helluva place to lose a cow," it is not in fact a canyon at all. Along a twenty-mile shelf on the eastern edge of the thickly forested **Paunsaugunt Plateau**, 8000ft above sea level, successive strata of dazzlingly colored rock have slipped and slid and washed away to leave a menagerie of multihued and contorted **stone pinnacles**.

In hues of yellow, red, and flaming orange, the formations here have been eroded out of the muddy sandstone by a combination of icy winters (the temperature drops below freezing two hundred nights out of the year) and summer rains. The top-heavy pinnacles known as "**hoodoos**" form when the harder upper layers of rock stay firm as the lower levels wear away beneath them. **Thor's Hammer**, visible from Sunset Point, is the most alarmingly precarious. These hoodoos look down into technicolor ravines, all far more vivid than the Grand Canyon and much more human in scale. The whole place is at its most inspiring in winter, when the figures stand out from a blanket of snow.

The park approach road runs south from Hwy-12 about twenty miles east of the small town of Panguitch; the **entrance fee** is $25 per vehicle, per week. There's a free (summer-only) **shuttle bus** system, but visitors can drive to all the scenic overlooks year round.

The two most popular viewpoints into **Bryce Amphitheater**, at the heart of the park, are on either side of *Bryce Canyon Lodge*: the more northerly, **Sunrise Point**, is slightly less crowded than **Sunset Point**, where most of the bus tours stop. **Hiking trails** drop abruptly from the rim down into the amphitheater. One good three-mile trek switchbacks steeply from Sunset Point through the cool 200-foot canyons of **Wall Street**, where a pair of 800-year-old fir trees stretch to reach daylight. It then cuts across the surreal landscape into the **Queen's Garden** basin, where the stout and remarkable likeness of Queen Victoria sits in majestic condescension, before climbing back up to Sunrise Point. A dozen trails crisscross the amphitheater, but it's surprisingly easy to get lost, so don't stray from the marked routes.

Sunrise and Sunset points notwithstanding, the best view at both sunset and dawn (which is the best time for taking pictures) is from **Bryce Point**, at the southern end of the amphitheater. From here, you can look down not only at the Bryce Canyon formations but also take in the grand sweep of the whole region, east to the **Henry Mountains** and north to the Escalante range. The park road then climbs another twenty miles south, by way of the intensely colored **Natural Bridge**, an 85-foot rock arch spanning a steep gully, en route to its dead end at **Rainbow Point**.

Practicalities

The **visitor center**, just past the entrance, carries information on current weather and hiking conditions (daily: May–Sept 8am–8pm; April & Oct 8am–6pm; Nov–March 8am–4.30pm; ⓣ435/834-5322, ⓦwww.nps.gov/brca). Much the

▲ Bryce Canyon National Park

best place to **stay** is the venerable *Bryce Canyon Lodge*, 100 yards from the rim between Sunrise and Sunset points (April–Oct only; reserve through Xanterra ⓣ303/297-2757 or 1-888/297-2757, ⓦwww.brycecanyonlodge.com; ❻), where rustic cabins cost a few dollars more than basic doubles. It also has a **dining room**, a grocery store, a laundry, and public showers.

Two ugly year-round **motels** guard the approach to the park, just off Hwy-12; the large *Ruby's Inn* (ⓣ435/834-5341 or 1-866/866-6616, ⓦwww.rubysinn.com; ❺), which has a dreadful restaurant, and the cheaper, newer (and misleadingly named) *Bryce View Lodge* (ⓣ435/834-5180 or 1-888/279-2304, ⓦwww.bryceviewlodge.com; ❹). *Ruby's Inn* has its own **campground** ($24), and there are also two first-come, first-served campgrounds within the park ($15): *Sunset Campground*, close to Sunset Point, and *North Campground*, near the visitor center. To camp below the rim, backpackers require permits from the visitor center.

Bryce Canyon to Capitol Reef: Highway 12

Turning its back on the grand amphitheater of Bryce Canyon, tiny **TROPIC**, straggling along Hwy-12 eight miles east of the park entrance, seems almost embarrassed about the flamboyant geological phenomena ranged above it. As well as a few motels, this Mormon farming community holds Ebenezer Bryce's restored log cabin, alongside the **Bryce Pioneer Village** motel-cum-restaurant (ⓣ435/679-8546 or 1-866/657-8414, ⓦwww.bpvillage.com; ❸).

Hwy-12 next curves along the edge of the Table Cliff Plateau before dropping into the remote canyons of the **Escalante River**, the last river system to be discovered within the continental US and site of some wonderful **backpacking** routes.

At the west end of **ESCALANTE**, 38 miles east of Tropic, a **visitor center** holds information on the vast **Grand Staircase-Escalante National Monument** (mid-March to mid-Nov daily 7.30am–5.30pm; mid-Nov to mid-March Mon–Fri 8am–4.30pm; ⓣ435/826-5499, ⓦwww.ut.blm.gov/monument). The most accessible highlight is **Calf Creek**, sixteen miles east of Escalante, where a trail leads just under three miles upstream from a nice undeveloped **campground** ($7) to a gorgeous shaded dell replete with a 125-foot waterfall. More ambitious trips start from trailheads along the dusty but usually passable **Hole-in-the-Rock Road**, which turns south from Hwy-12 five miles east of town. A trio of slender, storm-gouged **slot canyons**, including the delicate, graceful Peek-a-Boo Canyon and the downright intimidating Spooky Canyon, can be reached by a mile-long hike from the end of Dry Fork Road, 26 miles along. From **Hurricane Wash**, 34 miles along, you can hike five miles to reach Coyote Gulch, and then a further five miles, passing sandstone bridges and arches, to the Escalante River. Under normal conditions, two-wheel-drive vehicles should go no further than **Dance Hall Rock**, 36 miles down the road, a superb natural amphitheater sculpted out of the slickrock hills. The pick of Escalante's **motels** is unquestionably the *Prospector Inn*, 380 W Main St (ⓣ435/826-4653, ⓦwww.prospectorinn.com; ❸).

Thirty miles beyond Escalante, at **BOULDER**, the Burr Trail, all except twenty miles of which is paved, heads east through the southern reaches of **Capitol Reef National Park** and down to **Lake Powell**. Where it leaves Hwy-12, the modern *Boulder Mountain Lodge* (ⓣ435/335-7460 or 1-800/556-3446, ⓦwww.boulder-utah.com; ❹) holds twenty comfortable rooms. It also has a reasonable **restaurant**, but a few yards further east, the spotless *Boulder Mesa Restaurant* (ⓣ435/335-7447) is better.

North of Boulder, Hwy-12 makes a gorgeous drive up onto the Aquarius Plateau, with marvelous vistas to the east across waves of gold and red sandstone outcrops; the lovely Oak Creek **campground** is fifteen miles along (ⓣ435/425-3702; $9).

Capitol Reef National Park

CAPITOL REEF might sound like something you'd find off the coast of Australia, but its towering ochre, white, and red-**rock walls** and deep **river canyons** are of a piece with the rest of the Utah desert. The outstanding feature is a multilayered, 1000-foot-high reef-like wall of uplifted sedimentary rock. Stretching over a hundred miles north to south, but only a few miles across, the seemingly impenetrable barrier of the **Waterpocket Fold** was warped upward by the same process that lifted the Colorado Plateau, and its sharply defined sedimentary layers display two hundred million years of geological activity. The Fold is repeatedly sliced through by deeply incised river canyons – some only twenty feet wide, but hundreds of feet deep – often accessible only on foot.

Motorists who stick to the one paved road through the park, Hwy-24, which cuts across the northern half of the Fold, following the canyon of the **Fremont River**, do not incur an entrance fee. Beneath the enormous rock outcrop known as the **Castle**, you'll find the **visitor center** (daily: June–Sept 8am–7pm; Oct–May 8am–4.30pm; ⓣ435/425-3791, ⓦwww.nps.gov/care) and an irresistible campground ($10), set amid the cherry, apple, and peach orchards of the abandoned Mormon community of **FRUITA**. To the west, the **Goosenecks Overlook** gazes down 500ft into the entrenched canyons cut by Sulphur Creek. Further east, beyond Fruita's former schoolhouse, are some extraordinary **Fremont petroglyphs**, figures of bighorn sheep and stylized space-people chipped into the varnished red rock a thousand years ago. Another four and a half miles along, a beautiful **day-hike** heads up along the gravelly riverbed through **Grand Wash** – a cool canyon where Butch Cassidy and his gang used to hide out.

Alternatively, the paved **Scenic Drive** ($5 per vehicle) heads twelve miles south from the visitor center, past the top of Grand Wash, to **Capitol Gorge** and back. A more adventurous sixty-mile loop trip explores **Cathedral Valley** in the north, while a 125-mile southern route starts at the foot of the volcanic **Henry Mountains**, then follows the Burr Trail through **Muley Twist Canyon**, and continues west to Boulder.

The nearest **food and lodging** to Capitol Reef is eleven miles west, around **TORREY**. The *Capitol Reef Inn & Café*, 360 W Main St (ⓣ435/425-3271, ⓦwww.capitolreefinn.com; ❸), is a crisply maintained little motel, just off the highway in the heart of town, while the *Rim Rock Inn*, three miles east at 2523 E Hwy-24 (March–Nov; ⓣ435/425-3388 or 1-888/447-4676, ⓦwww.therimrock.net; ❸) is a newer, wood-built hotel, with a good dining room.

Goblin Valley

Fifty desolate miles east of Capitol Reef along Hwy-24, you reach the tiny crossroads of **Hanksville**. Twenty miles north on Hwy-24, a right turn takes you onto a 32-mile dirt road to the rock art of **Horseshoe Canyon**, a remote subsection of Canyonlands National Park (see below).

Half a mile further north on Hwy-24, a side road to the west veers off to **Goblin Valley State Park** (open 24hr; $7), where thousands of gnome-like figures loom out of the soft Entrada sandstone. The **Carmel Canyon** trail loops for over a mile through a throng of misshapen rock pillars, many of which seem to have eyes and other human features. Stay at the well-equipped **campground** (ⓣ1-800/322-3770; $16) if you want to see the place by moonlight, when it looks especially spooky.

Green River

The uneventful riverside town of **GREEN RIVER**, just east of the Hwy-24 junction on I-70, is the largest community on a 200-mile stretch of interstate.

Its **John Wesley Powell River History Museum**, 885 E Main St, doubles as the local visitor center (daily: April–Oct 8am–8pm, Nov–March 9am–5pm; $3; ⓣ435/564-3427; ⓦwww.jwprhm.com).

As well as various cheap **motels**, Green River holds a few classier options, including the *Best Western River Terrace*, 880 E Main St (ⓣ435/564-3401 or 1-800/780-7234, ⓦwww.bestwestern.com; ❺), which has a pool, river views, and a decent restaurant.

Canyonlands National Park

At 527 square miles the largest and most magnificent of Utah's national parks, **CANYONLANDS NATIONAL PARK** is as hard to define as it is to map. Its closest equivalent, the Grand Canyon, is by comparison simply an almighty crack in an otherwise relatively flat plain; the Canyonlands area is a bewildering tangle of canyons, plateaus, fissures, and faults, scattered with buttes and monoliths, pierced by arches and caverns, and penetrated only by a paltry handful of dead-end roads.

Canyonlands focuses on the Y-shaped confluence of the **Green** and **Colorado rivers**, buried deep in the desert forty miles southwest of Moab. The only spot from which you can see the rivers meet, however, is a five-mile hike from the nearest road. With no road down to the rivers, let alone across them, the park therefore splits into three major sections. The **Needles**, east of the Colorado, is a red-rock wonderland of sandstone pinnacles and hidden meadows that's a favorite with hardy hikers and four-wheel-drive enthusiasts, while the **Maze**, west of both the Colorado and the Green, is a virtually inaccessible labyrinth of tortuous, waterless canyons. In the wedge of the "Y" between the two, the high, dry mesa of the **Island In The Sky** commands astonishing views, with several overlooks that can easily be toured by car. Getting from any one of these sections to the others involves a drive of at least a hundred miles.

Canyonlands does not lend itself to a short visit. With no lodging, and little camping, inside the park, it takes a full day to have even a cursory look at a single segment. Considering that summer temperatures regularly exceed 100°F and most trails have no water and little shade, the Island In The Sky is the most immediately rewarding option. On the other hand, if you fancy a long day-hike you'd do better to set off into the Needles.

Island In The Sky and Dead Horse Point State Park

Reached by a good road that climbs steadily from US-191, 21 miles south of I-70, the **Island In The Sky** district looks out over hundreds of miles of flat-topped mesas that drop in 2000-foot steps to the river. Four miles along from its **visitor**

Canyonlands fees and permits

Canyonlands National Park charges an **entry fee** of $10 per vehicle, $5 for cyclists or hikers, valid for seven days in all sections of the park. **Backpacking** permits, covering a maximum party of seven persons in the Needles and Island In The Sky districts, or five persons in the Maze, cost $15. Permits for **four-wheel-drive** or **mountain-biking** expeditions that involve backcountry camping, issued for groups of up to three vehicles with a total of fifteen people in the Island In The Sky, ten in the Needles, or nine in the Maze, are $30. **Reservations** are essential for the most popular areas, especially in spring and fall. Permits must be picked up in person – with every member of the group present – from the appropriate park visitor center. For full details, see ⓦwww.nps.gov/cany.

center (daily: March–Oct 8am–6pm; Nov–Feb 9am–4.30pm; ☎435/259-4712), the enjoyable **Mesa Arch Trail** loops for a mile around the mesa-top hillocks to the edge of the abyss, where long, shallow Mesa Arch frames an extraordinary view of the **La Sal Mountains**, 35 miles northeast. The definitive vantage point, however, is **Grand View Point Overlook**, another five miles on at the southern end of the road. An agoraphobic's nightmare, it commands an endless prospect of layer upon layer of bare sandstone, here stacked thousands of feet high, there fractured into bottomless canyons. The Island In The Sky's only developed **campground**, the first-come, first-served and waterless *Willow Flat* ($10), is just back from the **Green River Overlook**, along the right fork shortly after the Mesa Arch trailhead.

A turnoff long before the Island In The Sky visitor center cuts south to the smaller but equally breathtaking **Dead Horse Point**, located at the tip of a narrow mesa, which looks straight down 2000ft to the twisting Colorado River. Cowboys used the mesa as a natural corral, herding up wild horses then blocking them in behind a piñon pine fence that still marks its 90-foot neck. One band of horses was left here too long and died – hence the name. As a Utah state park, Dead Horse Point charges its own $7 admission fee. The **visitor center** (daily: summer 8am–6pm; winter 8am–5pm; ☎435/259-2614) stands two miles short of the point itself, and there's also a **campground** ($15).

The Needles and Newspaper Rock

Taking its name from colorful sandstone pillars, knobs, and hoodoos that punctuate its many lush canyons and basins, the **Needles** district allows a more intimate look at the Canyonlands environment than does Island In The Sky. Here you're not always gazing thousands of feet downward or scanning the distant horizon; instead you can wander through seemingly endless acres of stone figures.

The road ends with a great collection of mushroom-shaped hoodoos at the **Big Spring Canyon Overlook**. A memorable and demanding eleven-mile round-trip hike from here remains the only way to get to the **Confluence Overlook**, 1000ft above the point where the Green River joins the muddy waters of the Colorado, to flow together, parallel but separate, toward fearsome **Cataract Canyon**. Various short walks head off the road at selected viewpoints; one of the best is **Pothole Point**, a mile before **Big Spring Canyon**. A longer day-trip, or a good overnight hike, leaves from near the *Squaw Flat* **campground** ($15) to the green meadow of **Chesler Park**, cutting through the narrow cleft of the Joint Trail. Pick up information and backcountry permits at the **visitor center** (daily: March–Oct 8am–6pm; Nov–Feb 9am–4.30pm; ☎435/259-4711).

The pretty 35-mile drive in to the Needles from US-191 winds along Indian Creek through deep red-rock canyons lined by pines and cottonwoods. At **Newspaper Rock**, twelve miles in, hundreds of tiny **petroglyphs**, many of which show deer, antelope, bear claws, and helmeted human figures, have been etched in the jet-black desert varnish of a red-sandstone boulder by centuries of passing hunters and travelers. There's a lovely (free) streamside **campground** just across the road.

The Maze and Horseshoe Canyon

Of Canyonlands' half-million annual visitors, only one in a hundred penetrates the harsh and remote **Maze** district. Filling the western third of the park, on the far side of the Colorado and Green rivers, the Maze is noted for its ancient rock-art panels and for many-fingered box canyons, accessible only by jeep or by long, dry hiking trails. If you're tempted, call in to the Hans Flat **ranger station**, 46 miles east of Hwy-24 (daily 8am–4.30pm; ☎435/259-2652).

Tree-lined **Horseshoe Canyon**, reached halfway down a long, long dirt road that loops south from Green River itself to join Hwy-24 just south of Goblin Valley, contains the greatest concentration of **ancient rock art** in the Southwest. Allowing at least an hour's driving from the highway both before and after, plus five hours for the six-mile round-trip hike down into the canyon itself, you'll need to set aside a full day, but it's well worth the effort, both for the joy of the walk and for the sight of the "**Great Gallery**" at the far end. Hundreds of mysterious, haunting pictographs – mostly life-sized human figures, albeit weirdly elongated, or draped in robes and adorned with strange, staring eyes – were painted onto these red-sandstone walls, probably between 500 BC and 500 AD. Rangers from Hans Flat lead guided hikes into Horseshoe Canyon on summer weekends (April–Oct Sat & Sun 9am).

Arches National Park

The writer Edward Abbey, who spent a year as a ranger at **ARCHES NATIONAL PARK** in the 1950s, wrote in *Desert Solitaire* that its arid landscape was as "naked, monolithic, austere, and unadorned as the sculpture of the moon." It

Adventure travel in southeast Utah

River trips

Moab operators offering **motorized** half- and one--day Colorado River trips for $45 and up include Worldwide River Expeditions (ⓣ435/259-7515 or 1-800/231-2769, ⓦwww.worldwideriver.com), Adrift Adventures (ⓣ435/259-8594 or 1-800/874-4483, ⓦwww.adrift.net), and Tag-a-Long Expeditions (ⓣ435/259-8946 or 1-800/453-3292, ⓦwww.tagalong.com). Trips start northwest of Moab, near the butte known as Fisher Towers, and head back to town; many companies let passengers float quieter stretches in two-person kayaks. The same operators run **oar-powered** trips that are slower but much quieter, and less expensive than motorboat trips. Longer (2- to 7-day) trips head through Cataract Canyon and other wild Canyonlands spots.

Mountain biking

Only experienced riders should attempt Moab's most challenging mountain-bike route, the **Slickrock Bike Trail**. This ten-mile, half-day loop threads its way among the sandstone knobs atop the mesa three miles east of Moab. A more relaxing alternative is to explore the dirt roads leading through the red-rock country of Kane Creek, west of town.

Among **bike shops** offering daily rental and guided tours, including trips into Canyonlands National Park, are Rim Tours (ⓣ435/259-5223 or 1-800/626-7335, ⓦwww.rimtours.com), and Poison Spider (ⓣ435/259-7882 or 1-800/635-1792, ⓦwww.poisonspiderbicycles.com).

Jeep tours

Most of the thousands of miles of **jeep trails** around Moab were built by miners and haven't been maintained since. Collect a free map and guide at the visitor center, and rent a four-wheel-drive jeep or pickup truck for around $115 per day from Canyonlands Jeep Adventures at 225 S Main St (ⓣ435/259-4413, ⓦwww.moab-utah.com/canyonlandsjeep). Tag-a-Long Expeditions, see above, offer **guided jeep tours** from $80.

Scenic flights

From a small airfield twenty miles north of Moab on US-91, Redtail Aviation (ⓣ435/259-7421 or 1-800/842-9251, ⓦwww.redtailaviation.com) and Slickrock Air Guides (ⓣ435/259-6216, ⓦwww.slickrockairguides.com) run unforgettable **flights** over the Canyonlands area, starting at $135 per person for one hour.

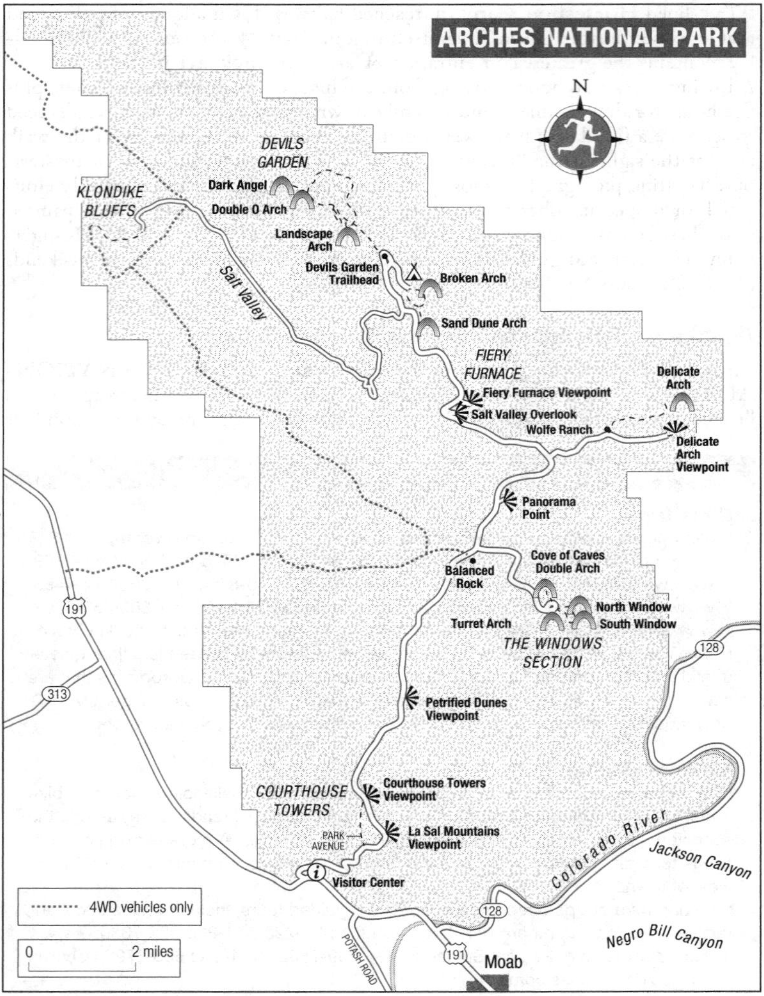

certainly is one of the least terrestrial places on this planet. Massive fins of red and golden sandstone stand to attention out of the bare desert plain, and over eighteen hundred natural arches of various shapes and sizes have been cut into the rock by eons of erosion. Apart from the single ribbon of black asphalt that snakes through the park, there's nothing even vaguely human about it. The narrow, hunching ridges are more like dinosaurs' backbones than solid rock, and under a full moon, you can't help but imagine that the landscape has a life of its own.

While you could race through in a couple of hours, plan to spend at least a day here to do Arches justice. A twenty-mile road cuts uphill sharply from US-191 and the **visitor center** (daily: April–Oct 7.30am–6.30pm; Nov–March 8am–4.30pm; $10 per vehicle or $5 for motorcyclists, cyclists, and pedestrians; ⓣ435/719-2299,

Ⓦwww.nps.gov/arch). The first possible stop is the south trailhead for **Park Avenue**, an easy trail leading one mile down a scoured, rock-bottomed wash. If you stay on the road, the **La Sal Mountains Viewpoint** provides a grandstand look at the distant peaks rising over 12,000ft above the desert, as well as the huge red chunk of **Courthouse Towers** closer at hand.

From **Balanced Rock** beyond – a 50-foot boulder atop a slender 75-foot pedestal – a right turn winds two miles through the **Windows** section, where a half-mile trail loops through a dense concentration of massive arches, some over 100ft high and 150ft across. A second trail, fifty yards beyond, leads to **Double Arch**, a staunch pair of arches that together support another arch overhead.

Further on, the main road drops downhill for two miles past Panorama Point and the turnoff to **Wolfe Ranch**, where a century-old log cabin serves as the trailhead for the wonderful three-mile round-trip hike up to **Delicate Arch**, which, as a freestanding crescent of rock perched at the brink of a deep canyon, is by far the most impressive arch in the park. Crowds congregate here each evening for the superb sunset views; coming back down in the dark can be a little hair-raising, though. Three miles beyond the Wolfe Ranch turnoff, the deep, sharp-sided mini-canyons of the **Fiery Furnace** section form a labyrinth through which rangers lead regular hikes in spring, summer, and fall ($10; reserve in advance at the visitor center).

The road continues on to the **Devil's Garden** trailhead, from which an easy one-mile walk leads to a view of the astonishing 306-foot span of **Landscape Arch**, now too perilously slender to approach more closely. Several other arches lie along short spur trails off the route, though one, Wall Arch. finally collapsed in August 2008. Seeing them all, and returning from **Double O Arch** via the longer primitive trail, requires a total hike of just over seven miles. Arches' only **campground** ($15; water only available mid-March to Oct) is across from the trailhead, 24 of its 52 sites are first-come first-served, and are usually taken by early morning, while the rest can be reserved March–Oct only, between four and 180 days in advance (Ⓣ518/885-3639 or 1-877/444-6777, Ⓦwww.recreation.gov).

Moab

Founded in the late 1800s, **MOAB** was hardly a speck until the 1950s, when prospector Charlie Steen discovered uranium in the nearby hills. When the ensuing mining boom finally waned, the hold of Moab's mine-owners and businessmen waned with it. The town threw in its lot with tourism, and has become the Southwest's number one adventure-vacation destination.

Moab still isn't a large town, though – the population has yet to reach ten thousand – and neither is it an attractive one. The setting is what matters. With two national parks on its doorstep, plus millions more acres of public land, Moab is an ideal base for outdoors enthusiasts. At first, it was a haven for **mountain bikers** lured by the legendary **Slickrock Bike Trail**. Then the **jeep** drivers began to turn up, and the **whitewater-rafting** companies moved in, too. These days it's almost literally bursting, all year, with legions of Lycra-clad vacationers from all over the world.

Perhaps the main reason Moab has grown so fast is that out-of-state visitors tend to find Utah's other rural communities so boring. As soon as Moab emerged from the pack, it became a beacon in the desert, attracting tourists ecstatic to find a town that stayed up after dark – even if it does amount to little more than a few miles of motels, restaurants, and bars.

Arrival and information

Moab's **visitor center** is at Center and Main streets (daily: summer 8am–9pm; winter 9am–1pm & 2–5pm; Ⓣ435/259-8825 or 1-800/635-6622, Ⓦwww

.discovermoab.com). Bighorn Express (Ⓣ801/417-5191 or 1-888/655-7433, Ⓦwww.bighornexpress.com) runs daily shuttle **buses** between Salt Lake City and Moab, via the Amtrak station at Green River, and continuing on to Monticello.

Accommodation

Though Moab holds around thirty **motels** and a dozen **B&Bs**, all of its 1500-plus rooms are frequently taken between mid-March and October – when you'd be lucky to find anything below $80 – so reservations are strongly recommended.

Commercial **campgrounds** nearby include the shaded *Slickrock Campground*, 1301 N Hwy-191 (Ⓣ435/259-7660 or 1-800/448-8873, Ⓦwww.slickrockcampground.com; $20), a mile north of town; if you're happy to put up with far more primitive facilities to escape the crowds, head for the BLM's **Sand Flats Recreation Area**, along the top of the mesa east of town, near the Slickrock Bike Trail, at 1924 S Roadrunner Hill (Ⓣ435/259-6111; $10).

Adobe Abode 778 W Kane Creek Blvd Ⓣ435/259-7716, Ⓦwww.adobeabodemoab.com. Attractive, Pueblo-style home a few hundred yards from downtown Moab, offering six comfortable and tastefully furnished B&B rooms. ❺

Best Western Greenwell Inn 105 S Main St Ⓣ435/259-6151 or 1-800/780-7234, Ⓦwww.bestwesternmoab.com. Central, modern hotel that offers spacious good-value rooms with tasteful furnishings and fittings. ❺

Gonzo Inn 100 W 200 South Ⓣ435/259-2515 or 1-800/791-4044, Ⓦwww.gonzoinn.com. Luxurious if rather self-consciously hip inn, complete with kitsch-retro furnishings, quirky artworks, and an espresso bar. ❻

Inca Inn Motel 570 N Main St Ⓣ435/259-7261 or 1-866/462-2466, Ⓦwww.incainn.com. Clean, minimally equipped but adequate budget motel, with pool. ❸

Lazy Lizard International Hostel 1213 S Hwy-191 Ⓣ435/259-6057, Ⓦwww.lazylizardhostel.com. Amiable, very laid-back independent hostel, a mile south of the center, with $10 beds in six-person dorms, $7 camping, and private cabins for $30-plus, plus hot tub, kitchen, and Internet access. ❶

Red Rock Lodge 51 North 100 West Ⓣ435/259-5431 or 1-877/207-9708, Ⓦwww.red-rocklodge.com. Though entirely lacking the flair of Moab's fancier inns, this simple traditional motel offers clean rooms in a supremely central location. ❸

Eating and drinking

Moab offers by far the greatest range of **restaurants** in southern Utah, most of which cater to vegetarians. With two pubs and a winery, there's also no problem getting a **drink**, while **coffee bars** are springing up everywhere.

Buck's Grill House 1393 N Hwy-191 Ⓣ435/259-5201. Belying its stockade-like exterior, this dinner-only "American Western Food" joint is actually a sophisticated affair, serving rich, classy Southwestern food, such as game hen or pork ribs, at very reasonable prices.

Desert Bistro 1266 N Main St Ⓣ435/259-0756. Top-notch dinner-only restaurant, set in a ranch home with a patio that's perfect for summer nights. On the modern bistro menu, entrees like venison medallions or smoked rabbit agnolotti cost up to $38.

Eddie McStiff's 57 S Main St Ⓣ435/259-2337. Central pub that serves interesting beers, including raspberry and blueberry varieties, and inexpensive salads, pizzas, and pasta.

Jailhouse Café 101 N Main St Ⓣ435/259-3900. Very popular central café, open for breakfast only. Indoor and outdoor seating year-round, and great specials like ginger pancakes and eggs Benedict. Daily except Tues 7am–noon.

The Peace Tree 20 S Main St Ⓣ435/259-8503. Very central juice bar and café that serves good sandwiches, wraps, and smoothies to take out or eat on the small outdoor patio, until 6.30pm daily.

Natural Bridges National Monument

Hwy-95 runs for over a hundred miles southeast from Capitol Reef, through dozens of red-rock canyons, and across the Dirty Devil and Colorado rivers, before topping out on the sagebrush plains of San Juan County. En route it gives access to the marvelous sandstone spans at **Natural Bridges National Monument**, forty miles west of US-191. The **visitor center** is four miles off Hwy-95 (daily 9am–5.30pm; $6 per vehicle; Ⓣ435/692-1234, Ⓦwww.nps.gov/nabr), near a small **campground** ($10).

Three canyons come together in the monument. At each junction, the streams that carved them have also formed sandstone bridges. The largest, **Sipapu Bridge**, is 268ft across and over 200ft high, and can be seen from the nine-mile paved road that loops through the monument; hike less than a mile down into the canyon for a closer look. **Kachina Bridge**, the next along, is nearly as high but twice as thick, and has Ancestral Puebloan pictographs at its base. The oldest, slimmest, and most fragile bridge – **Owachomo**, a mile and a half up Armstrong Canyon – spans 180ft but is only nine feet thick at its thinnest point. A strenuous eight-mile trail along the canyon bottom leads past all three.

Monticello

The small town of **MONTICELLO** stands 56 miles south of Moab on US-191, sixteen miles beyond the turnoff for the Needles section of Canyonlands. Its strip of **motels** includes a smart *Days Inn*, 549 N Main St (Ⓣ435/587-2458, Ⓦwww.daysinn.com; ❸). Good, large, standard **meals** can be had at the *MD Ranch Cookhouse*, 380 S Main St (Ⓣ435/587-3299). The **visitor center** at 232 S Main St doubles as a small frontier **museum** (daily except Tues 9am–6pm; Ⓣ435/587-3235 or 1-800/574-4386, Ⓦwww.southeastutah.org).

The San Juan River, Mexican Hat, and Bluff

From Natural Bridges, Hwy-261 runs south for 25 miles to the edge of Cedar Mesa, high above the eerie sandstone towers of the **Valley of the Gods**. It then turns to gravel and drops over a thousand feet in little over two twisting, hairpin-turning miles down the "**Moki Dugway**." Six miles from the foot of the switchbacks, the barely marked Hwy-316 branches off to yet another overlook, high above the **San Juan River** at the extraordinary and aptly named **Goosenecks State Reserve** (open 24hr; free). A thousand feet below, the river snakes around in such convoluted twists and turns that it flows six miles in total for every one mile west.

Back on Hwy-261, sleepy **MEXICAN HAT**, just twenty miles north of Monument Valley, takes its name from a riverside **sandstone hoodoo** that looks like a south-of-the-border sombrero. Right on the river, the *San Juan Inn* (Ⓣ435/535-2210 or 1-800/447-2022; Ⓦwww.sanjuaninn.net; ❹), has its own grocery store, restaurant, bar and trading post.

The rafts you may see emerging from the water at Mexican Hat went in at **BLUFF**, twenty miles upstream. The road between the towns, US-163, doesn't follow the river very closely but is still an enthralling drive, while the backstreets of Bluff hold a number of **Mormon pioneer houses**. Places to **eat** include the friendly outdoor *Cottonwood Steakhouse* (Ⓣ435/672-2282), while an excellent **motel** at the south end of town, the *Desert Rose Inn*, 701 W Hwy-191 (Ⓣ435/672-2303 or 1-888/475-7673, Ⓦwww.desertroseinn.com; ❹), holds thirty attractively decorated rooms.

Hovenweep National Monument

Hidden in the no-man's-land that straddles the Utah–Colorado border, the remote **Ancestral Puebloan ruins** at **Hovenweep National Monument** offer a haunting sense of timeless isolation. Located 25 miles east of US-191 along Hwy-262, which branches off halfway between Bluff and Blanding, and 35 miles west of Cortez, Colorado, Hovenweep preserves six distinct conglomerations of ruins sprouting from the rims of shallow desert canyons. Easy access is restricted to **Little Ruin Canyon**, behind the **visitor center** (daily: April–Sept 8am–6pm; Oct–March 8am–5pm; $6; Ⓣ970/562-4282, Ⓦwww.nps.gov/hove). A mile-long loop trail offers good views of the largest ruins, including the grandly named **Hovenweep Castle**, constructed around 1200 AD. No accommodation, gasoline, or food is available at or anywhere near Hovenweep, but a **campground** remains open all year ($10; no reservations).

Lake Powell and Glen Canyon Dam

The mighty rivers and canyons of southern Utah come to an abrupt and ignoble end at the Arizona border, where the **Glen Canyon Dam** stops them dead in the stagnant waters of **Lake Powell**. Ironically, the lake is named for John Wesley Powell, the first person to run the Colorado River through the Grand Canyon. The roaring torrents with which he battled, along with magnificent Glen Canyon itself, are now lost beneath these placid blue waters, and the blocked-up Colorado, Green, Dirty Devil, San Juan, and Escalante rivers are now a playground for houseboaters and water-skiers. The construction of the dam in the early 1960s outraged environmentalists and archeologists, and created a peculiar and utterly unnatural landscape, the deep and tranquil lake a surreal contrast with the surrounding dry slickrock and sandstone buttes.

Lake Powell has 1960 miles of shoreline – more than the entire US Pacific coast – and 96 water-filled side canyons. The water level fluctuates considerably, so for much of the time the rocks to all sides are bleached for many feet above the waterline, with a dirty-bath tidemark sullying the golden sandstone. Many summer visitors bring their own boats, or rent a vessel from one of the marinas that fringe the lake.

If you're passing through, by far the most accessible stop is **Wahweap Marina**, just off US-89 on the way between Zion and the Grand Canyon, where the plush *Lake Powell Resort* (Ⓣ928/645-2433 or 1-888/896-3829, Ⓦwww.lakepowell.com; ❻) has comfortable lakeside rooms and good food. The same company arranges **houseboat rental** from Wahweap and other Lake Powell marinas, and there's **camping** on the lakeshore at each of the marinas. Otherwise, the nearest **accommodation** is across the Arizona border in the chain motels of **PAGE**, like the good-value *Best Western at Lake Powell*, 208 N Lake Powell Blvd (Ⓣ928/645-5988 or 1-888/794-2888, Ⓦwww.bestwestern.com; ❹).

GLEN CANYON DAM itself, in between Page and Wahweap, can be seen from the **Carl Hayden Visitor Center** (daily: March–Oct 8am–6pm; Nov–Feb 8.30am–4.30pm; Ⓣ928/608-6404, Ⓦwww.nps.gov/glca) on the west bank, which also arranges free 45-minute dam tours.

The cheapest way to get out on the waters of Lake Powell is to take the **ferry** ($20 per car) between **Halls Crossing** and **Bullfrog** marinas, two-thirds of the way up the lake, from where the Burr Trail heads west toward Capitol Reef, while Hwy-276 runs northeast to Natural Bridges.

Northern Utah

Although northern Utah holds less to interest the tourist than the south, **Salt Lake City**, the capital, is by far the state's largest and most cosmopolitan urban center, and is overlooked by the dramatic Wasatch Mountains. The **northeast corner** has coal mines, old railroad towns and, along the Wyoming border, the **Uinta Mountains**, uncrossed by road and showing hardly a sign of civilization. From the **northwest**, the harshly alkaline **Great Basin** plain stretches uneventfully west across Nevada to California.

Salt Lake City

Disarmingly pleasant and easygoing, **SALT LAKE CITY** is well worth a stopover of a couple of days. Its setting is superb, towered over by the **Wasatch Front**, which marks the dividing line between the comparatively lush eastern and the bone-dry western halves of northern Utah. The area offers great hiking and cycling in summer and fall and, in winter, some of the world's best **skiing**. People elsewhere in the US still tend to imagine Salt Lake City as decidedly short on fun, but so long as you're willing to switch gears and slow down, its unhurried pace, and the positive energy of its people, can make for a surprisingly enjoyable experience.

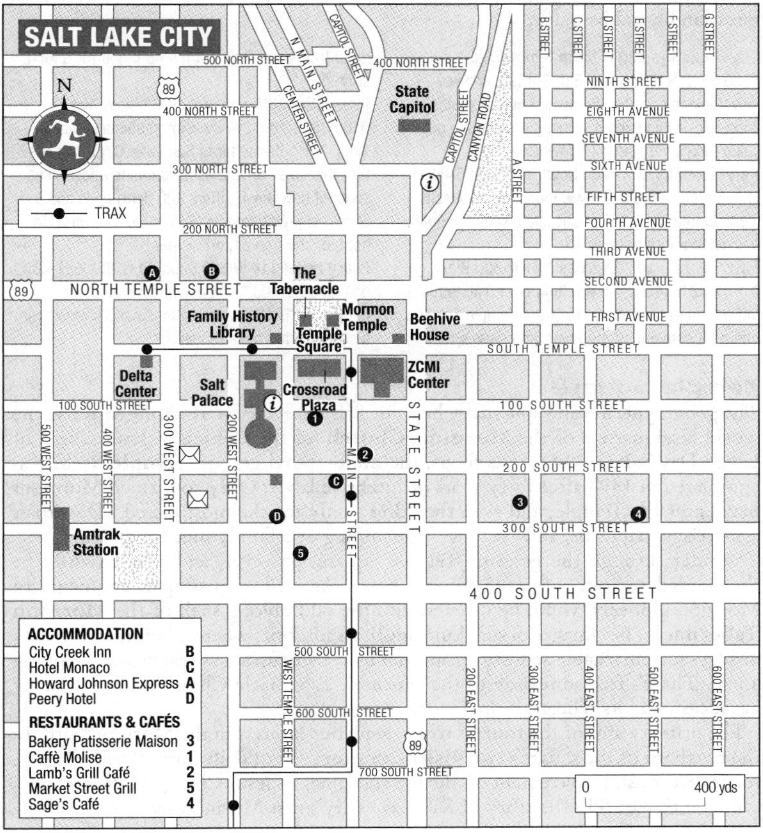

Arrival, information, and getting around

Salt Lake City International Airport is a mere four miles west of downtown. A **taxi** into town costs around $20; cheaper **shuttle vans** to downtown destinations are run by Xpress Shuttles (ⓣ801/596-1600 or 1-800/397-0773, ⓦwww.xpressshuttle.com), while Canyon Transportation (ⓣ801/255-1841, ⓦwww.canyontransport.com) serves the ski areas. Long-distance Greyhound-Trailways **buses** arrive downtown, at 300 S 600 West (ⓣ801/355-9579), as do Amtrak **trains**, at 320 S Rio Grande Ave. Local buses, and also TRAX trams, are operated by the Utah Transit Authority (ⓣ801/743-3882, ⓦwww.rideuta.com); journeys within the immediate downtown area are free.

The **visitor center** is downtown at 90 S West Temple Blvd in the Salt Palace Convention Center (Mon–Fri 9am–6pm, Sat & Sun 9am–5pm; ⓣ801/534-4490, ⓦwww.visitsaltlake.com). For details on the rest of Utah, stop by the Utah Travel Council, in the imposing Council Hall across from the capitol at 300 N State St (Mon–Fri 8am–5pm, Sat & Sun 10am–5pm; ⓣ801/538-1030, ⓦwww.utah.com).

Accommodation

Salt Lake City is well equipped with **accommodation**, with downtown options that range from budget motels and B&B inns to rather more luxurious hotels, and the usual mid-range places near the airport and along the interstates. Weekend rates can be real bargains.

City Creek Inn 230 W North Temple Blvd ⓣ801/533-9100 or 1-866/533-4898, ⓦwww.citycreekinn.com. Family-owned budget motor court, old-fashioned but spruced up, offering good-value rooms very close to downtown. ③

Hotel Monaco 15 W 200 South ⓣ801/595-0000 or 1-800/805-1801, ⓦwww.monaco-saltlakecity.com. Extremely hip, very upscale downtown hotel, housed in a former bank. ⑨

Howard Johnson Express 121 N 300 West ⓣ801/321-3450, ⓦwww.hojo.com. This ageing but adequate motel, not far from Temple Square, makes a convenient stopover, and serves a good free breakfast, but it's no place for a long stay. ③

International Ute Hostel 21 E Kelsey Ave ⓣ801/595-1645, ⓦwww.internationalutehostel.com. Much the better of Salt Lake City's two hostels, this small private establishment, a few miles south of downtown, offers $20 dorm beds and a couple of private rooms ($45), plus bike rental, a hot tub, and free airport pickup. ①/②

Peery Hotel 110 W 300 South St ⓣ801/521-4300 or 1-800/331-0073, ⓦwww.peeryhotel.com. Renovated 1910 downtown landmark, offering very tasteful, comfortable rooms. ⑥

Temple Square

The geographical – and spiritual – heart of Salt Lake City is **Temple Square**, the world headquarters of the **Mormon Church** (or the Church of Jesus Christ of Latter-Day Saints – LDS). Its focus, the multi-spired granite **Temple** itself, was completed in 1893 after forty years of intensive labor. Only confirmed Mormons may enter the Temple, and even they do so only for the most sacred LDS rituals – marriage, baptisms, and "sealing," the joining of a family unit for eternity.

Wander through the gates of Temple Square, however, and you'll swiftly be shepherded to join a free 45-minute **tour**. As well as passing monuments to Mormon pioneers, you'll be ushered into the odd oblong shell of the **Mormon Tabernacle**. No images of any kind adorn its interior, where a helper laconically displays its remarkable acoustic properties by tearing up a newspaper and dropping a nail. There's free admission to the Mormon Tabernacle Choir's 9.30am Sunday broadcast, and its rehearsals on Thursday evenings at 8pm.

The primary aim of the tours is to awaken your interest in the Mormon faith. In the northern of the square's two **visitor centers** (both daily 9am–9pm), displays focus to a considerable extent on the life and times of Jesus Christ, while its southern counterpart tells the story of Salt Lake City's first Mormon settlers.

Downtown Salt Lake City

A block east of Temple Square along South Temple Boulevard, the **Beehive House** (Mon–Sat 9am–9pm; free) is a plain white New England–style house, with wraparound verandas and green shutters. Erected in 1854 by church leader **Brigham Young**, it's now a small museum of Young's life, restored to the style of the period. Free twenty-minute tours set off at least every half-hour.

The **Family History Library**, across West Temple Boulevard from Temple Square (Mon 8am–5pm, Tues–Sat 8am–9pm; free; Ⓣ801/240-2584 or 1-800/346-6044, Ⓦwww.familysearch.org), is open to everyone, but primarily intended to enable Mormons to trace their ancestors and then baptize them into the faith by proxy. The world's most exhaustive genealogical library gives immediate access to birth and death records from over sixty countries, some dating back as much as five hundred years. All you need is a person's place of birth, a few approximate dates, and you're on your way; volunteers provide help if you need it, but leave you alone until you ask. Next door to the library, the **Museum of Church History and Art** (Mon–Fri 9am–9pm, Sat & Sun 10am–7pm; free) charts the rise of the Mormon faith in art and artifact.

The area southwest of Temple Square centers on the massive **Salt Palace** convention center and sports arena (home of the Utah Jazz basketball team). The surrounding district of brick warehouses around the Union Pacific railroad tracks is filled with designer shops and art galleries, signs that even Mormons can be yuppies.

The neighborhood on the gentle hill that stands above today's Temple Square, around the imposing, domed **Utah State Capitol** (summer Mon–Sat 8am–8pm; rest of year Mon–Sat 8am–6pm; free), is known as **Capitol Hill**. It holds some of Salt Lake City's grandest Victorian homes, with dozens of ornate houses lining Main Street and Quince Street to the northwest.

Eating

Salt Lake City may have perfectly good **restaurants**, but it lacks an atmospheric – let alone hip – dining district. If you like to compare menus, the only downtown area with much potential is the block or two to either side of West Temple Street, south and east of the Salt Palace.

The Bakery Patisserie Maison 250 S 300 East Ⓣ801/328-3330. Not surprisingly, it's the pastries that draw downtown devotees in droves, but this cafe also does great, cheap, lunchtime salads and sandwiches. Closed Sun.

Bambara Hotel Monaco, 202 S Main St Ⓣ801/363-5454, Ⓦwww.bambara-slc.com. Chic, post-Deco, and pricey downtown restaurant, with a fabulous menu ranging from crab-stuffed peppers to cider-glazed duck breast. Breakfast and dinner daily, lunch weekdays only.

Caffè Molise 55 W 100 South Ⓣ801/364-8833, Ⓦwww.caffemolise.com. Authentic, high-quality, great-value Italian food downtown, with tables in a nice little courtyard in summer, and jazz on Fridays.

Lamb's Grill Cafe 169 S Main St Ⓣ801/364-7166, Ⓦlambsgrill.com. Great breakfasts, best eaten at the long shiny counter, and excellent-value set meals throughout the day. Closed Sun.

Market Street Grill 48 W Market St Ⓣ801/322-4668, Ⓦwww.marketstreetgrill.com. As close as Salt Lake City comes to a New York City bar and grill, with fresh seafood, especially oysters, plus steaks in all shapes and sizes. $13 lunch specials, full dinners $18 and up.

Ruth's Diner 2100 Emigration Canyon Rd Ⓣ801/582-5807, Ⓦwww.ruthsdiner.com. Good-value indoor and patio dining, often accompanied by live music, set in and around old railroad carriages in a narrow canyon just three miles east of town. There's a wide selection of fresh dishes, great salads, and Utah's best breakfasts.

Sage's Café 473 E 300 South Ⓣ801/322-3790, Ⓦwww.sagescafe.com. Salt Lake's finest vegetarian restaurant, with an all-organic menu that ranges from pizza to raw salads. Closed Sun.

Drinking and nightlife

Salt Lake City doesn't roll up the sidewalks when the sun goes down. To find out about the broad range of **fringe** art, music, and clubland happenings, pick up the free *City Weekly* (Ⓦwww.slweekly.com). Many **drinking** venues are technically private clubs, in which a nominal membership fee entitles the cardholder and up to five guests to two weeks' use of the facilities, but there are also a handful of **brewpubs** for which membership is not required. Good options for an evening out include the *Dead Goat Saloon*, 119 S West Temple Blvd (Ⓣ801/328-4628, Ⓦwww.deadgoat.com), a raucous, semi-subterranean saloon, with live loud music most nights. The casual, friendly *Squatters Pub*, 147 W 300 South (Ⓣ801/363-2739), offers a range of beers available until at least midnight every day, plus a simple menu. The best place to hear **live music**, surprisingly enough, has to be *The Depot*, in the Union Pacific Station at 400 W South Temple Blvd (Ⓣ801/456-2888, Ⓦwww.depotslc.com), though *Zanzibar*, 677 S 200 West (Ⓣ801/746-0590, Ⓦwww.zanzibarslc.com), also programs good jazz and blues.

Park City

Despite Brigham Young's strictures against prospecting for precious metals – he feared a Gentile Gold Rush – the first mining camp at **PARK CITY**, just thirty miles east of downtown Salt Lake City along I-80 through the mountains, was established in the late 1860s. In 1872 George Hearst laid the foundations of the Hearst media empire by paying $27,000 for a claim that became the Ontario Silver Mine, worth $50 million. These days, the **Park City Mountain Resort** (Ⓣ435/649-8111 or 1-800/222-7275, Ⓦwww.parkcitymountain.com), and the nearby **The Canyons** (Ⓣ435/649-5400, Ⓦwww.thecanyons.com) and (skiers-only) **Deer Valley** (Ⓣ435/649-1000 or 1-800/424-3337, Ⓦwww.deervalley.com) resorts constitute Utah's largest **ski area**, with the season usually running from mid-November to mid-April. Daily lift passes for each resort cost upwards of $85; equipment rental outlets include Park City Sport (Ⓣ1-800/523-3922, Ⓦwww.parkcitysport.com). In addition, Park City hosts the prestigious **Sundance Film Festival**, held during the second half of January each year (Ⓣ435/658-3456, Ⓦwww.sundance.org).

Spurred in part by its role in hosting the 2002 Winter Olympics, Park City these days seems determined to remodel itself on the chic resorts of Colorado. Amid the ever-growing sprawl of new condos and factory outlets, **Main Street** pays only the occasional token gesture towards maintaining its former identity as a mountain mining community.

Practicalities

Park City has an information kiosk at 333 Main St (Mon–Fri 10am–7pm, Sat & Sun noon–6pm; Ⓣ435/649-6100 or 1-800/453-1360, Ⓦwww.parkcityinfo.com). Lewis Bros Stages (Ⓣ801/359-8677 or 1-800/826-5844, Ⓦwww.lewisstages.com) runs scheduled **shuttles** from downtown Salt Lake City ($30) and the airport (up to $60).

Accommodation rates double in the ski season; the visitor center can provide full listings of resorts and other lodgings. The down-to-earth *Chateau Apres*, 1299 Norfolk Ave (Ⓣ435/649-9372 or 1-800/357-3556, Ⓦwww.chateauapres.com; ❺), is a cozy lodge motel. *Café Terigo*, 424 Main St (Ⓣ435/645-9555), is a good Mediterranean **restaurant** in the heart of town, while *Windy Ridge*, 1250 Iron Horse Drive (Ⓣ435/647-2906), serves deli snacks and sandwiches. The *Wasatch Brew Pub*, 250 Main St (Ⓣ435/649-0900), is open until midnight daily and serves good food as well as microbrewed beer.

Nevada

Without doubt the most desolate US state, **NEVADA** consists largely of endless tracts of bleak, empty desert, its flat sagebrush plains cut intermittently by angular mountain ranges. Apart from the huge acreages given over to mining and grazing, much of Nevada is used by the **military** to test aircraft and weapons systems. While dozens of intriguing small communities are scattered around the state, many more are decrepit roadside ghost towns.

Though millions of people pass through, there's only one real reason why anyone ever *visits* Nevada, and that is to **gamble**: the second you cross the state line, you're attacked by a 24-hour onslaught of neon signs and gimmicky architecture, each advertising the best odds and biggest jackpots, nowhere more than in the surreal oasis of **Las Vegas**. Even the smaller and more down-to-earth settlements of **Reno** and state capital **Carson City** revolve around the casino trade.

Getting around Nevada

Traveling Nevada's vast empty spaces is nearly impossible without a car. Las Vegas is no longer served by Amtrak, but Reno still welcomes daily trains between San Francisco and Salt Lake City. Both Las Vegas and Reno have airports, and buses connect the two cities – though they're well over four hundred miles apart.

Las Vegas

Shimmering from the desert haze of Nevada like a latter-day El Dorado, **LAS VEGAS** is the most dynamic, spectacular city on earth. At the start of the twentieth century, it didn't even exist; now it's home to two million people, and boasts nineteen of the world's twenty-five largest hotels, whose flamboyant, no-expense-spared **casinos** lure in thirty-seven million tourists each year.

Las Vegas has been stockpiling superlatives since the 1950s, but never rests on its laurels for a moment. Many first-time visitors expect the city to be kitsch, but the casino owners are far too canny to be sentimental about the old days. Yes, there are a few Elvis impersonators around, but what characterizes the city far more is its endless quest for **novelty**. Long before they lose their sparkle, yesterday's showpieces are blasted into rubble, to make way for ever more extravagant replacements. A few years ago, when the fashion was for fantasy, Arthurian castles and Egyptian pyramids mushroomed along the legendary Strip; next came a craze for constructing entire replica cities, like New York, Paris, Monte Carlo, and Venice; and the current trend is for high-end properties that attempt to straddle the line between screaming ostentation and "elegant" sophistication.

While the city has cleaned up its act since the early days of Mob domination, it certainly hasn't become a **family** destination. Neither is Vegas as **cheap** as it used to be. It's still possible to find good, inexpensive rooms, and the all-you-care-to-eat buffets offer great value, but the casino owners have finally discovered that high-rollers happy to lose hundreds of dollars per night don't mind paying premium prices to eat at top-quality restaurants, while the latest developments are charging room rates of more like $300 than $30 per night.

Although Las Vegas is an unmissable destination, it's one that palls for most visitors after a couple of (hectic) days. If you've come solely to gamble, there's not much to say beyond the fact that all the casinos are free, and open 24 hours per day, with acres of floor space packed with ways to lose money: million-dollar slots, video poker, blackjack, craps, roulette wheels, and much, much more.

A history of Las Vegas

The name Las Vegas – Spanish for "the meadows" – originally referred to a group of natural springs that from 1829 onward served as a way-station for travelers on the Old Spanish Trail. In 1900, the valley had a population of just thirty people. Things changed in 1905, with the completion of the now-defunct rail link between Salt Lake City and Los Angeles.

Though Nevada was the first state to outlaw gambling, in 1909, it was made legal once more in 1931, and the workers who built the **Hoover Dam** flocked to Vegas to bet away their pay packets. Providing abundant electricity and water, the dam amounted to a massive federal subsidy for the infant city. Hotel-casinos such as the daring 65-room *El Rancho* began to appear in the early 1940s, and mobster Bugsy Siegel raised $7 million to open the *Flamingo* on the Strip in 1946.

By the 1950s, Las Vegas was booming. The military had arrived – mushroom clouds from **A-bomb tests** in the deserts were visible from the city, and visitors drove out with picnics to get a better view – and so too had big guns like **Frank Sinatra**, who debuted at the *Desert Inn* in 1951, and **Liberace**, who received $50,000 to open the *Riviera* in 1955. As the stars gravitated toward the Vegas honeypot, nightclubs across America went out of business, and the city became the nation's undisputed live-entertainment capital.

The beginning of the end for Mob rule in Vegas came in 1966, after reclusive airline tycoon **Howard Hughes** sold TWA for $500 million and moved into the *Desert Inn*. When the owners tired of his non-gambling ways, he simply bought the hotel, and his clean-cut image encouraged other entrepreneurs to follow suit. **Elvis** arrived a little later; the young rock 'n' roller had bombed at the *New Frontier* in 1956, but started a triumphant five-year stint as a karate-kicking lounge lizard at the *International* (now the *Las Vegas Hilton*) in 1969.

Endless federal swoops and stings drove the Mob out of sight by the 1980s, in time for Vegas to reinvent itself on a surge of junk-bond megadollars. The success of Steve Wynn's *Mirage* in enticing a new generation of visitors, from 1989 onward, spawned a host of imitators. *Excalibur* and the *MGM Grand* were followed by *Luxor* and *New York–New York* and then, as the millennium approached, by the opulent quartet of *Bellagio*, *Mandalay Bay*, the *Venetian*, and *Paris*. Although the twenty-first century started with shockwaves, when Steve Wynn was forced to sell *Bellagio* and the *Mirage* to the MGM group, and 9/11 triggered a major downturn, Las Vegas bounced back. The *Venetian* has gone from strength to strength as the flagship for all that the city does best; Wynn himself opened his biggest casino yet, *Wynn Las Vegas*; and MGM pressed ahead with the colossal CityCenter development even as the storm clouds of the latest recession were appearing on the horizon.

Arrival, information, and getting around

Las Vegas's busy **McCarran International Airport** is a mile east of the southern end of the Strip, and four miles from downtown. Some hotels run free shuttle buses for guests, while Bell Trans (ⓣ 702/739-7990, ⓦ www.bell-trans.com) runs **minibuses** to the Strip ($6.50) and downtown ($8). From the airport, a **taxi** to the Strip costs from $15 for the southern end up to $30 for casinos further north, though fares can vary enormously depending on the time taken. Amtrak **trains** don't serve Las Vegas, but Greyhound's long-distance **buses** arrive at 200 S Main St downtown.

Traffic is so bad in Las Vegas that if you've just come to explore the Strip, it's not worth renting a car. Be warned, though, that on summer days it's too hot to walk more than a couple of blocks along the Strip. **Public transport** does exist. The **Las Vegas Monorail** runs along the eastern side of the Strip from the *MGM Grand* to the *Sahara* (Mon–Thurs 7am–2am, Fri–Sun 7am–3am; single trip $5, 1-day pass $12; Ⓦ www.lvmonorail.com), but doesn't go to the airport or downtown. Separate, free monorail systems also link *Mandalay Bay* with *Excalibur* via *Luxor*, the *Monte Carlo* with *Bellagio* via *CityCenter*, and the *Mirage* with *TI*. In addition, the city-run, 24-hour **Deuce bus** ($2; Ⓦ www.catride.com) connects the Strip with downtown, while the oak-veneered streetcars of the **Las Vegas Strip Trolley** ($2.50; Ⓦ www.striptrolley.com) ply the Strip between *Mandalay Bay* and the *Stratosphere*.

The **visitor center** at the Convention Center, 3150 Paradise Rd, is not worth visiting (daily 8am–5pm; Ⓣ 702/892-7575 or 877/847-4858, Ⓦ www.visitlasvegas.com). You'd do better to buy the daily *Las Vegas Review-Journal*, which always incorporates a four-page guide to the city.

Accommodation

Although Las Vegas has well over 140,000 motel and hotel rooms, it's best to book **accommodation** ahead if you're on a tight budget, or arriving on Friday or

Saturday; upwards of two hundred thousand people descend upon the city every weekend. Las Vegas hotels no longer offer cheap deals at the drop of a hat. It is true that serious gamblers can get their accommodation free, but to count as "serious" you'd have to commit yourself to gambling several thousand dollars.

Even if you stay in the same room for several days, you'll be charged a different rate for each day, depending on the day of the week, and what's going on in town. The only sure-fire way to get a cut-price room is to **visit during the week** rather than on the weekend. Rates rise enormously on Friday or Saturday, by at least $50 extra in a lower-end property, well over $100 in the big-name casinos. On top of that, many hotels won't accept Saturday arrivals.

Bellagio 3600 Las Vegas Blvd S ⓣ702/693-7111 or 1-888/987-6667, ⓦwww.bellagio.com. Extremely luxurious rooms, with plush European furnishings and marble bathrooms, an amazing pool complex, and some great restaurants. Sun–Thurs ❼, Fri & Sat ❾

Caesars Palace 3570 Las Vegas Blvd S ⓣ702/731-7222 or 1-866/227-5938, ⓦwww.caesars.com. Right in the heart of the Strip, the epitome of 1960s luxury continues to offer the last word in pseudo-Roman splendor, with top-class restaurants and shops. ❼

California Hotel 12 Ogden Ave at First St ⓣ702/385-1222 or 1-800/634-6505, ⓦwww.thecal.com. Almost all the guests in this mid-range downtown casino are Hawaiian, and Hawaiian food and drink dominate the bars and restaurants. The actual rooms are plain but adequate. Sun–Thurs ❷, Fri & Sat ❸

Circus Circus 2880 Las Vegas Blvd S ⓣ702/734-0410 or 1-800/634-3450, ⓦwww.circuscircus.com. Venerable Strip hotel popular with budget tour groups. Kids love the theme park and (almost) nonstop circus acts, while adults love the low room rates. Sun–Thurs ❷, Fri & Sat ❹

Imperial Palace 3535 Las Vegas Blvd S ⓣ702/731-3311 or 1-800/351-7400, ⓦwww.imperialpalace.com. While the *Imperial Palace* is showing its age, considering its central location its plain rooms still offer some of the best value on the Strip. Sun–Thurs ❷, Fri & Sat ❹

Luxor Las Vegas 3900 Las Vegas Blvd S ⓣ702/262-4444 or 1-877/386-4658, ⓦwww.luxor.com. All two thousand rooms in this vast glass pyramid have tremendous views – and they're much larger than usual. Unlike the extra two thousand rooms in the newer tower next door, however, most have showers, not baths. Sun–Thurs ❸, Fri & Sat ❹

Main Street Station 200 N Main St at Ogden ⓣ702/387-1896 or 1-800/713-8933, ⓦwww.mainstreetcasino.com. Downtown's best-value option, with 400 large rooms plus a brewpub and good restaurants. Ask for a room on the south side, rather than next to the freeway. Mon–Thurs & Sun ❷, Fri & Sat ❹

MGM Grand 3799 Las Vegas Blvd S ⓣ702/891-7777 or 1-877/880-0880, ⓦwww.mgmgrand.com. Waiting for any kind of service, especially check-in, at the largest hotel in the US – 5044 rooms and counting – can be horrendous, but you get a great standard of accommodation for the price. Sun–Thurs ❹, Fri & Sat ❻

New York–New York Hotel & Casino 3790 Las Vegas Blvd S ⓣ1-866/815-4315, ⓦwww.nynyhotelcasino.com. Rooms at the most exuberantly fun Strip casino are very nice, if a bit small, and filled with Art Deco furnishings and flourishes. Sun–Thurs ❸, Fri & Sat ❺

Paris–Las Vegas 3655 Las Vegas Blvd S ⓣ702/946-7000 or 1-877/796-2096, ⓦwww.parislasvegas.com. If not the absolute pinnacle of luxury, rooms and services at the flamboyant French-themed *Paris* are still pretty good, and for location, views, and ambience it more than holds its own. Sun–Thurs ❺, Fri & Sat ❽

USA Hostels Las Vegas 1322 E Fremont St ⓣ702/385-1150 or 1-800/550-8958, ⓦwww.usahostels.com. Former motel, in a slightly forbidding neighborhood ten blocks east of downtown. It's much the better of the city's two independent hostels, with dorm beds from $21 and private double rooms from $58. Rates include free breakfast; cheap dinners are also available. There's also a heated swimming pool. The friendly staff arrange city and national-park tours, as well as a weekly clubbing night. ❶/❸

The Venetian 3355 Las Vegas Blvd S ⓣ702/414-1000 or 1-877/883-6423, ⓦwww.venetian.com. Even the standard rooms at this upscale Strip behemoth are split-level suites, with antique-style canopied beds atop raised platforms, plus spacious living rooms. Sun–Thurs ❻, Fri & Sat ❾

Wynn Las Vegas 3131 Las Vegas Blvd S ⓣ702/770-7100 or 1-877/321-9966, ⓦwww.wynnlasvegas.com. Steve Wynn has once again rewritten the Strip's definition of luxury, but the very stylish rooms, most of which offer great views of the "Lake of Dreams," come of course at a substantial price. Sun–Thurs ❼, Fri & Sat ❾

The City

Though the Las Vegas sprawl measures fifteen miles wide by fifteen miles long, the only area of interest to tourists is the six-mile stretch of **Las Vegas Boulevard** that includes both **downtown**, near where I-15 meets US-95, and the **Strip**, home to the major casinos. In between lie two seedy miles of gas stations, fast-food drive-ins, and wedding chapels, while the rest of town is largely residential.

The Strip

For its razor-edge finesse in harnessing sheer, magnificent excess to the deadly serious business of making money, there's no place like the **Las Vegas Strip**. It's hard to imagine that Las Vegas was once an ordinary city, and Las Vegas Boulevard a dusty thoroughfare scattered with the usual edge-of-town motels. After six decades of capitalism run riot, with every new casino-hotel setting out to surpass anything its neighbors ever dreamed of, the Strip remains locked into a hyperactive craving for thrills and glamour, forever discarding its latest toy in its frenzied pursuit of the next jackpot.

Mandalay Bay

The Strip's procession kicks off at its southern end with the glowing gilded tower of **Mandalay Bay**, which boasts a vaguely Burmese theme. Financed through the profits from its neighbors, *Luxor* and *Excalibur*, *Mandalay Bay* is more upmarket than either, and its excellent restaurants, as well as the *House of Blues* music venue, keep it lively at night. During the day, all it has to offer the casual sightseer is the **Shark Reef** aquarium, right at the back of the property (daily 10am–11pm; $16), a disappointingly small mock-up of a steamy, half-submerged temple complex, inhabited by crocodiles, jellyfish, and, of course, sharks.

Luxor

A block north of *Mandalay Bay* stands the 36-storey pyramid of **Luxor**. While it remains an astonishing building, it has recently been stripped off most of its

▲ The Strip

ancient-Egyptian trappings, in favor of rebranding as the sort of "hip", upscale casino resort that now dominates the Strip. As part of the process, it now houses two expensive permanent exhibitions: **Bodies** (daily 10am–10pm; $31, under-15s $23), maverick German anatomist Gunther Von Hagens' collection of genuine but "plastinated" human corpses, and **Titanic**, featuring not merely artifacts but a huge piece of the doomed liner, recovered from two miles down in the Atlantic Ocean (same hours and prices).

Excalibur and the MGM Grand

Luxor's architect, Veldon Simpson, had previously designed the less sophisticated **Excalibur**, immediately north. A mock medieval castle, complete with drawbridge, crenellated towers, and a basement stuffed with fairground-style sideshows, it's usually packed out with low-budget tour groups. Its brief reign as the world's largest hotel, from 1990 to 1993, ended when the five-thousand-room **MGM Grand** – another Simpson creation – opened across the street. There, the main attraction, the **Lion Habitat**, is a walk-through wooded zoo near the front entrance, where real lions lounge around a ruined temple beneath a naturally lit dome (daily 11am–10pm; free).

New York–New York

Opposite the *MGM Grand*, **New York–New York** is an exuberantly meticulous recreation of the Big Apple. This miniature Manhattan boasts a skyline featuring twelve separate skyscrapers and is fronted, naturally, by the Statue of Liberty. Unusually, the interior is every bit as carefully realized, with a lovely rendition of Central Park at dusk (not perhaps somewhere you'd choose to be in real life). In one respect, it even surpasses New York itself: for $14 you can swoop around the whole thing at 65mph on the hair-raising Manhattan Express **roller coaster**.

Planet Hollywood

Planet Hollywood is a remodelled version of the former Aladdin, which hit the rocks in 2004. In keeping with the latest generation of casinos, it's all geared towards a young crowd, with a screaming loud décor it calls "Hollywood Hip". The mile-long Miracle Mile Shops, wrapped in a figure-eight around the casino and its theater, is under different ownership, and is looking quite a mess, having attracted some frankly tacky stores, diners and bars.

City Center

The enormous **CityCenter** complex, unveiled in 2009 between the *Monte Carlo* and *Bellagio*, is a bold attempt by MGM-Mirage to reshape Las Vegas's urban landscape. The exciting new theme here is that there is no theme; CityCenter is supposedly the kind of project that might be built in any city. Whether it's a sign that the city has finally come of age, or a disastrous blunder in the face of impending recession, remains to be seen. CityCenter consists of the twin, residential **Veer Towers**, each leaning five eye-catching degrees off vertical in opposite directions; three non-gaming hotels, the **Harmon Hotel**, the **Mandarin Oriental**, and the completely condo **Vdara**; the 61-storey, 4000-room **Aria** resort and casino; and the **Crystals**, a high-end retail, dining and entertainment "district", topped by a spikey angular roofscape. At the time this book went to press, construction was all but completed, but nothing had yet opened. Almost the only specific feature promised by MGM Mirage was that Aria will host a new Cirque du Soleil show, setting out to do for Elvis Presley what *Love* has done for the Beatles (see p.941).

Paris

Paris was the 1999 handiwork of the same designers as *New York–New York*. With a half-size Eiffel Tower straddling the Arc de Triomphe and the Opera, it all feels a little compressed, but once again the attention to detail is a joy. There's also a fine assortment of top-notch French restaurants. Elevators soar through the roof of the casino and up to the summit of the Eiffel Tower, for stunning views of the city, at their best after dark (daily 9.30am–12.30am; $10).

Bellagio

Paris' Eiffel Tower was cheekily positioned to enjoy a perfect prospect of **Bellagio**, opposite. In 1998, Steve Wynn unveiled the *Bellagio* as his attempt to build the best hotel in world history. *Bellagio* is undeniably a breathtaking achievement, striving to be somehow more authentic than the original town on Lake Como. The trouble is that *Bellagio* is not in Italy; it's in Las Vegas, and stuffed full of slot machines. The main hotel block, a stately curve of blue and cream pastels, stands aloof from the Strip behind an eight-acre artificial lake in which hundreds of submerged fountains erupt every half-hour in Busby-Berkeley water-ballets, choreographed with booming music and colored lights.

Otherwise, *Bellagio*'s proudest boasts are the **Via Bellagio**, a covered mall of impossibly glamorous designer boutiques, and its opulent **Conservatory**, where a network of flowerbeds beneath a Belle Epoque canopy of copper-framed glass is replanted every few weeks with ornate seasonal displays.

Caesars Palace

Across Flamingo Road from *Bellagio* – this is the intersection where Tupac Shakur was gunned down in 1996 – **Caesars Palace** still encapsulates Las Vegas at its best. Here, a moving walkway delivers you past grand marble staircases that lead nowhere, and full-size replicas of Michelangelo's *David*, into a vast labyrinth of slots and green baize, peopled by strutting half-naked Roman centurions and Cleopatra-cropped waitresses. Above the stores and restaurants of the **Forum**, the blue-domed ceiling dims and glows as it endlessly cycles from dawn to dusk and back again. The mall itself is now three storeys tall, but you may have to hurry to see the gloriously kitsch "living statues" who inhabit its various fountains; they seem to be disappearing into the netherworld at an alarming rate.

The Mirage and TI

Nighttime crowds jostle for space on the sidewalk outside the glittering **Mirage**, beyond *Caesars*, to watch the recently rebuilt volcano that erupts every fifteen minutes, spewing water and fire into the lagoon below. Although veteran magicians Siegfried and Roy were finally driven into retirement by Roy's near-fatal accident in 2003, their trademark white tigers can still be seen in the *Mirage*'s spacious **Secret Garden & Dolphin Habitat** (Mon–Fri 11am–5.30pm, Sat & Sun 10am–5.30pm; $15, under-10s free).

Next door, a pirate galleon and a British frigate, crewed by actors, continue to do noisy battle outside **TI**, the former *Treasure Island*, though ludicrously enough the sailors these days are no longer gnarled buccaneers but the scantily-clad **Sirens of TI** (every 90min after dark; free). *Treasure Island* used to be pirate-themed throughout, but having abandoned all thoughts of appealing to children, its lovingly crafted fripperies have been stripped away.

The Venetian and the Palazzo

Across the Strip from *TI*, the facade of the **Venetian** includes loving facsimiles of six major Venice buildings, as well as the Rialto Bridge and the Bridge of Sighs.

The main emphasis in the casino itself is on the **Grand Canal Shoppes**, reached via a stairwell topped by vivid frescoes copied from yet more Venice originals. The ludicrous recreation of the **Grand Canal** at the top, complete with gondolas and singing gondoliers ($15 a ride), is quintessential Las Vegas, and as such utterly irresistible – it's *upstairs*, for God's sake.

When the Venetian first opened, it held two much-publicized outposts of the Guggenheim Museum. Both, sadly, have now closed, leaving just a ridiculously expensive branch of **Madame Tussaud's** waxwork museum (daily 10am–10pm, some seasonal variation; $24, under 13s $14). 2008 did however see the opening of the adjoining **Palazzo**, which can be entered either via the Grand Canal Shoppes or directly from the Strip. Officially, it's regarded as being a resort in its own right, but so far it seems remarkably devoid of any identity, and just feels like a big, bland mall.

Wynn Las Vegas

Wynn Las Vegas, next door to the *Venetian*, was built by Steve Wynn on the site of the vanished *Desert Inn*, using all the fortune he accrued by building and selling the *Mirage* and *Bellagio*. In a nutshell, it's *Bellagio* reimagined for a younger, hipper and even richer crowd, with a shift away from European elegance in favor of contemporary Asian design. The resort is partly obscured behind an artificial tree-covered mountain; once you find your way inside, you find that's the backdrop for the enormous **Lake of Dreams**, an "environmental theater" in which ethereal sculpted figures emerge from a large expanse of water, in front of a massive waterfall that continually changes color.

The interior of *Wynn Las Vegas* is a riot of color, with spectacular patterns and motifs sprawling all over carpets, mosaics, and tiles, and a central atrium filled with sparkling trees and dazzling flowers. It has all proved profitable enough for the original hotel tower to be joined by a second, taller tower, dubbed **Encore** and clad in the same glossy "Wynn Bronze".

The North Strip: Circus Circus and the Stratosphere

North of *Wynn Las Vegas*, the long-neglected northern segment of the Strip was until the recession hit widely expected to be the city's next growth area. Both the veteran *New Frontier* and *Stardust* casinos have been demolished, but it now seems uncertain whether the promised *Echelon* and *Fontainebleau* mega-resorts will materialize.

Instead, the main landmarks here are the family-oriented **Circus Circus**, which holds an indoor theme park, the **Adventuredome** (Mon–Thurs 11am–6pm, Fri & Sat 10am–midnight, Sun 10am–9pm; all-day pass adults $25, kids $15), and the **Stratosphere**, which at 1149ft is the tallest building west of the Mississippi. The outdoor deck near its summit offers amazing panoramas across the city ($14), while three wonderfully demented thrill rides can take you even closer to heaven (Sun–Thurs 10am–midnight, Fri & Sat 10am–2am; $34 all-day rides). Insanity and X-Scream dangle riders over the edge, strapped into individual seats and in a precarious gondola respectively; and the terrifying Big Shot is an open-air couch that shunts to the top of an additional 160-foot spire, then free-falls down again. Half a mile east, at 3000 Paradise Rd, the **Las Vegas Hilton** is, since it closed its **Star Trek Experience** theme ride, no longer worth visiting.

Downtown and the Liberace Museum

As the Strip has evolved from strength to strength, **downtown** Las Vegas, the city's original core, has been neglected. Long known as "Glitter Gulch," it never really was a "downtown" in the conventional sense, having never held many stores or businesses apart from its few compact blocks of lower-key casinos. It has however repeatedly attempted to revive itself. In the **Fremont Street Experience**, five entire blocks of its central street have been roofed over to form a "Celestial Vault", studded with over twelve million LED nodules to create a screen that's illuminated in dazzling nightly displays (hourly, sunset–midnight; free).

The only off-Strip museum worth visiting is the **Liberace Museum**, two miles east of the Strip at 1775 E Tropicana Ave (Tues–Sat 10am–5pm, Sun noon–4pm; Ⓦwww.liberace.org; $15). Liberace, who died in 1987, started out as a classically trained pianist playing the bars of Milwaukee during the 1940s. His subsequent career is recalled by a yellowing collection of cuttings and family photos, along with an electric candelabra, bejeweled quail eggs with inlaid pianos, rhinestone-covered fur coats, glittering cars, and more.

Eating

Less than twenty years ago, Las Vegas's **restaurant** scene was governed by the notion that visitors were not prepared to pay for gourmet food. Now, however, the casinos compete to attract culinary superstars from all over the country to open Vegas outlets. Many tourists now come specifically to sample the best restaurants in the US; the choice on the Strip is overwhelming, and every hotel seems to have at least one good restaurant.

Buffets

Almost every casino features an all-you-can-eat **buffet**. At its best, the traditional buffet experience is like being granted unrestricted access to the food court in an upmarket mall: you'll get good fast food, but not great cooking. While some high-end casinos like *Bellagio* and *Paris* have raised prices to a level that makes it possible to provide true gourmet feasts, the cheapest buffets, especially at the largest Strip casinos, like *Excalibur* and the *MGM Grand*, can still be very poor.

The Buffet *Bellagio*, 3600 Las Vegas Blvd S ⓣ702/791-7111. Far and away Las Vegas's best buffet. Breakfast is $15; lunch is $20, and can include sushi, sashimi, and dim sum; and dinner, with choices like lobster claws, fresh oysters, and venison, is $28, or $36 on Fri & Sat.

Garden Court Buffet Main Street Station, 200 N Main St ⓣ702/387-1896. Downtown's best-value buffet, ranging from fried chicken and corn at the "South to Southwest" station, to tortillas at "Ole," and pork chow mein and oyster tofu at "Pacific Rim." Breakfast is $7, lunch $8, and dinner varies $11–16.

Le Village Buffet *Paris*, 3655 Las Vegas Blvd S ⓣ702/946-7000. Superb French cuisine, with great seafood, succulent roast chicken, and super-fresh vegetables. The setting is a little cramped, squeezed into a very Disney-esque French village, but the food is *magnifique*. Breakfast is $15, lunch $18, and dinner $25.

Todai Seafood Buffet Miracle Mile Shops, *Planet Hollywood*, 3663 Las Vegas Blvd S ⓣ702/892-0021. *Todai* specializes in magnificent all-you-can-eat Japanese spreads. It's seafood heaven, with unlimited sushi and sashimi plus hot entrées, noodles, and barbecued and teriyaki meats. Lunch Mon–Fri $18, Sat & Sun $20; dinner Mon–Thurs $28, Fri–Sun $30.

Restaurants

America *New York–New York*, 3790 Las Vegas Blvd S ⓣ702/740-6451. Cavernous 24-hour diner, with a vast 3D "map" of the United States curling from the ceiling, and a staggeringly eclectic menu. At any hour of the day or night, there really is something for everyone, and it's all surprisingly good.

Bouchon Venezia Tower, *The Venetian*, 3355 Las Vegas Blvd S ⓣ702/414-6200. Despite its sky-high reputation and exclusive setting, Thomas Keller's spacious French bistro is friendly and affordable. A delicious French onion soup costs $8.50 and a roast chicken with onions and lentils costs $27.50. Breakfast is a Francophile's dream of croissants, pastries, yogurt and coffee, and sitting outside on the huge piazza is a real joy. Breakfast and dinner daily.

Dos Caminos Mexican Kitchen *The Palazzo*, 3355 Las Vegas Blvd S ⓣ702/577-9600. For flair as well as food, this huge, beautifully designed Mexican restaurant is highly recommended, from the deliciously creamy guacamole onwards. Dinner might start with roasted plantain empanada ($10) followed by avocado-leaf-crusted big-eye tuna ($25); at weekends, lunch is replaced by a well-priced, relaxed brunch. Lunch and dinner daily.

Il Fornaio *New York–New York*, 3790 Las Vegas Blvd S ⓣ702/650-6500. The nicest place to enjoy the atmosphere of the casino, this rural-Italian restaurant is a real joy. Choose from pizzas for around $14, or entrees like seafood linguini ($22) or rotisserie chicken ($19.50). Delicious olive breads, pastries, and espresso coffees are also sold in a separate deli nearby.

Mon Ami Gabi *Paris*, 3655 Las Vegas Blvd S ⓣ702/944-4224. The first and the finest casino restaurant to offer open-air seating right on the Strip has the feel of a proper French pavement bistro. At lunch, try the gloriously authentic onion soup ($8), the mussels ($11), or the thin-cut steak frites ($20). Dinner features more expensive steak cuts and fish entrées. Lunch and dinner daily.

Paymon's Mediterranean Cafe and Market 4147 S Maryland Pkwy at Flamingo ⓣ702/731-6030. This highly recommended Middle Eastern restaurant, with attractive Cretan murals, is simple but also Vegas's best vegetarian option. Salads, pita sandwiches or spinach pie cost $8–10, while dips such as hummus or the eggplant-based *baba ganoush* are $5. Closed Sun.

Phô at the Coffee Shop *TI*, 3300 Las Vegas Blvd S ⓣ702/894-7111. If you're looking for a simple, cheap and tasty meal, there's no faulting the Strip's only Vietnamese restaurant. Its specialty here is hearty bowls of phô soup, available in chicken, beef or vegetable flavors for $10, while rice or vermicelli noodle dishes start at $10.50.

Red 8 *Wynn Las Vegas*, 3131 Las Vegas Blvd S ⓣ702/770-9966. Airy, relaxed Asian bistro where the food is traditional Southeast Asian, predominantly Chinese, with Malaysian and Mongolian thrown in. Subtle, aromatic flavors abound – dim sum ($6–10) include tasty pan-fried turnip cakes and steamed buns – and you'll also find perfectly executed classics like spicy shredded jellyfish ($9), barbecued duck or pork ($16), or Kung Pao shrimp ($19).

Zefferino Grand Canal Shoppes, *The Venetian*, 3355 Las Vegas Blvd S ⓣ702/414-3500. Very romantic, and yet utterly playful Italian restaurant, with its ornate balconies overlooking the Grand Canal. Dinner entrees can be pricey, with fish dishes at $37–70, but the $25 three-course set lunch, served daily except Sun, is exceptional value. Lunch and dinner daily.

Bars and clubs

All the casinos have plenty of bars, but if you want a drink, there's no need to look for one; instead, a tray-toting waitress will come and find you. The old-fashioned **Las Vegas lounge** has returned in force, whether knowingly retro-styled for twenty-something rockers, glammed up as an "ultra-lounge," or lovingly recreated for older visitors looking to recapture the quieter but still decadent flavor of the Rat-Pack era. In addition, Las Vegas has finally come of age as an international **clubbing** capital. The success of nightclubs at hipper casinos like the *Hard Rock* and *Mandalay Bay* has prompted all their major rivals to follow suit, often with spectacular results.

The Beatles Revolution Lounge *Mirage*, 3400 Las Vegas Blvd S ⓣ702-692-8383, ⓦwww.thebeatlesrevolutionlounge.com. Once you get past the somewhat silly claim that this ultra-lounge truly reflects an artistic collaboration between the Beatles and the Cirque du Soleil, you can enjoy the psychedelic lightshow and fab 1960's décor. DJ sets most nights, live indie bands Tues. Closed Sun.

Gipsy 4605 Paradise Rd ⓣ702/731-1919, ⓦwww.gipsylasvegas.com. High-profile gay dance club, where there's normally some form of live entertainment to justify the $5 post-midnight cover charge, with go-go boys performing Friday, and beer busts most nights. The elaborate lost-city decor attracts young ingénues and local celebs. Daily 10pm–6am.

Horse-a-Round Bar *Circus Circus*, 2880 Las Vegas Blvd S ⓣ702/734-0410. Tiny but truly bizarre, this perfect replica of a children's merry-go-round overlooks the clowns and acrobats of *Circus Circus*'s Midway. Fri & Sat 4.30pm–midnight.

House of Blues *Mandalay Bay*, 3950 Las Vegas Blvd S ⓣ702/632-7600, ⓦwww.hob.com. The Strip's premier live-music venue, the voodoo-tinged, folk-art-decorated House of Blues has a definite, but not exclusive, emphasis toward blues, R&B, and the like. Typical prices range from $35 up to $100 for stars like Aretha Franklin.

Liquidity *Luxor*, 3900 Las Vegas Blvd S ⓣ702/262-4591. Very blue, very modern, water-themed ultra-lounge in the center of *Luxor*, with waterfalls both real and virtual cascading from the ceiling.

Nine Fine Irishmen *New York–New York*, 3790 Las Vegas Blvd S ⓣ702/740-6463. The affinity between New York and all things Irish finds expression in this wood-paneled pub, shipped from Ireland and featuring Irish musicians, singers, and dancers nightly.

rumjungle *Mandalay Bay*, 3950 Las Vegas Blvd S ⓣ702/632-7408. You have to run a gauntlet of go-go dancers and volcanic gas jets just to get into this bar-restaurant-nightclub. Inside, the leopardskin-clad staff serve well-priced cocktails, plus a vast menu of rums. It's too loud to do anything more than watch, or join, the dancefloor action.

Entertainment

In the early 1960s, when Frank Sinatra's Rat Pack were shooting the original *Ocean's 11* during the day then singing the night away at the *Sands*, the city could claim to be the capital of the international entertainment industry. After that, the world moved on, but in the last few years, Las Vegas has come back into its own. The cheesy, feathers-and-tassels revues have closed down, to be replaced by surprisingly stimulating, postmodern shows by the likes of the **Cirque du Soleil** and the **Blue Man Group**. A new generation of big-name stars are taking up the kind of long-term residencies we all thought had vanished with Elvis. **Cher, Bette Midler** and **Elton John** at *Caesars'* huge Colosseum are the most conspicuous, but more are expected to follow.

The Amazing Johnathan Harmon Theater, Miracle Mile Shops, *Planet Hollywood*, 3667 Las Vegas Blvd S ⓣ702/836-0833, ⓦwww.amazingj.com. Far from the unbridled craziness his advertising might lead you to expect, Johnathan is a lovable magician whose emphasis on comedy means he barely completes a trick all evening. That's probably for the best, as carefully honed patter and hilarious skits like "Bad Karate Theater" make this one of Las Vegas's funniest shows. Tues–Sat 9pm. $66.

Blue Man Group *The Venetian*, 3355 Las Vegas Blvd S ⓣ702/414-7469, ⓦwww.blueman.com. Enter a strange and unfamiliar world, in which three bald, blue performance artists sell out a 1750-seat theater every night of the week. Don't expect stars, or a plot, or even words; instead, you get synchronized eating of breakfast cereal and live endoscopies on audience members, plus deafening, exhilarating drumming from the Men themselves, and some stunning special effects. Mon, Wed, Thurs & Sun 8pm; Tues, Fri & Sat 7pm & 10pm. $72–132.

Kà *MGM Grand*, 3799 Las Vegas Blvd S ⓣ702/769-9999, ⓦwww.ka.com. For anyone interested in theater, Las Vegas's fourth Cirque du Soleil production, Kà, is an absolute must-see. The most expensive theatrical production ever staged, anywhere, it boasts a quite extraordinary set; the stage floor not only rises, but can swivel and pivot in every direction. Kà is much more plot-driven than other Cirque shows, telling a complex saga about two Asian twins separated by enemy kidnappers, so although it's still basically a succession of truly breathtaking stunts, with extraordinary puppetry and sumptuous costumes, there's scope for darkness and emotional impact alongside the usual whimsy. Tues–Sat 7pm & 9:30pm. $69–150.

Lance Burton *Monte Carlo*, 3770 Las Vegas Blvd S ⓣ702/730-7160. The best family show in Las Vegas, featuring master magician Lance Burton. Most of it consists of traditional but very impressive stunts with playing cards, handkerchiefs, and doves, but large-scale illusions include the disappearance of an entire airplane and a narrow escape from hanging. Tues & Sat 7pm & 10pm, Wed–Fri 7pm. $67 & $73.

Legends in Concert *Imperial Palace*, 3535 Las Vegas Blvd S ⓣ702/794-3261. Enjoyable celebrity-tribute show, with a changing roster of impersonators posing as stars from Dolly Parton to Barry White. Mon–Sat 7pm & 10pm. $50, including two drinks; ages 12 and under $35.

Love *The Mirage*, 3400 Las Vegas Blvd S ⓣ702/796-9999. In which the Cirque du Soleil do their stuff to a remixed Beatles soundtrack, in an auditorium that's intimate at some moments and exuberantly all-embracing at others. Nostalgic and visionary in equal measure, Love celebrates the Beatles' achievement while avoiding anything too literal. The costumes, lighting and staging are all magnificent, and some of the setpieces are astonishing. When all's said and done, it's a dance show more than anything else, but don't let that put you off. Daily except Tues 7pm & 10pm. $103–165.

Mystère *TI*, 3300 Las Vegas Blvd S ⓣ702/796-9999. Fabulous Cirque du Soleil showcase, with tumblers, acrobats, trapeze artists, pole climbers, clowns, and strongmen, but no animals apart from fantastic costumed apparitions. Sat–Wed 7pm & 9.30pm. $66–105.

O *Bellagio*, 3600 Las Vegas Blvd S ⓣ702/796-9999. From the synchronized swimmers onward, the Cirque du Soleil display their magnificent skills to maximum advantage. Any part of the stage at any time may be submerged in water of varying depths – one moment a performer can walk across a particular spot, the next someone may dive head-first into it from the high wire. Wed–Sun 7.30pm & 10.30pm. $103–165.

Lake Mead and the Hoover Dam

The vast reservoir thirty miles southeast of the city, **LAKE MEAD**, was created by the construction of the Hoover Dam. A bizarre spectacle, its blue waters a vivid counterpoint to the surrounding desert, it gets excruciatingly crowded all year round. Though the Lake Mead National Recreation Area straddles the border between Nevada and Arizona, the best views come from the Nevada side. Even if you don't need details on how to sail, scuba-dive, water-ski, or fish from the marinas along the five-hundred-mile shoreline, call in at the Alan Bible **visitor center** (daily 8.30am–4.30pm; ⓣ702/293-8990, ⓦwww.nps.gov/lame), four miles northeast of Boulder City on US-93, to enjoy a sweeping prospect of the whole thing.

Eight miles on, US-93 reaches the **Hoover Dam** itself, completed in 1935. Designed to block the Colorado River and provide low-cost electricity for the Southwest, it's among the tallest dams ever built (760ft high), and used enough concrete to build a two-lane highway from the West Coast to New York. Three levels of visit are possible; you can simply explore the **Hoover Dam Visitor Center** (daily April–Sept 8.30am–5.45pm, Oct–March 9.15am–4.15pm) for $8, or take a half-hour ($11) or two-hour **guided tour** ($30).

Crossing Nevada

The bulk of Nevada is made up of dry plains, sliced by knife-edge volcanic mountain ranges. Called the **Great Basin** because its rivers and streams have no outlet to the ocean, the land has a certain eerie, even hypnotic, beauty. The main route across the state, **I-80**, shoots from Salt Lake City to Reno, skirting dozens of bizarrely named small towns packed with casinos, bars, brothels, motels, and little else. The other main route, **US-50**, has a reputation as the loneliest highway in America. Older and slower than I-80, it follows much the same route as did the Pony Express in the 1860s, but many of the towns have faded away or been entirely abandoned.

Great Basin National Park

Just across the border from Utah, **Great Basin National Park** encapsulates the scenery of the Nevada desert, from angular peaks to high mountain meadows cut by fast-flowing streams. The limestone **Lehman Caves** may not be as large as Carlsbad Caverns, but if anything are more densely packed with intriguing formations. Guided tours leave regularly throughout the day, costing $8 for 1hr, or $10 for 90min, from the **visitor center** near the mouth of the caves (daily: summer 8.30am–4pm; winter 9.30am–3pm; ⓣ775/234-7331, ⓦwww.nps.gov/grba), five miles west of the hamlet of **Baker**.

From the Lehman Caves, a twelve-mile road climbs the east flank of the bald and usually snowcapped **Wheeler Peak**, and trails lead past alpine lakes and through a grove of gnarled, ancient bristlecone pines to the 13,063ft summit. Off-track cross-country skiing is excellent in winter. The nearest real town, **ELY**, an hour's drive away, has two worthwhile museums – the entertaining **Nevada Northern Railway Museum** (Mon & Wed–Sat 8am–5pm, Sun 8am–4pm; $4; Ⓦnevadanorthernrailway.net), which offers $24 rides on a restored steam train, and the **County Museum** (daily 9am–4pm; free) – as well as a dozen **motels** (like *Motel 6*, 770 Avenue O; Ⓣ775/289-6671; ❷) and a handful of casinos and restaurants.

Elko

ELKO, the self-proclaimed last real cowtown in the West, straggles alongside I-80 a hundred miles west of Utah. Amid huge open cattle ranges, it's a fitting home for January's annual **Cowboy Poetry Gathering** (Ⓦwww.westernfolklife.org), a get-together to celebrate folk culture and keep alive the traditions and tales of the Wild West.

During the 72-hour **National Basque Festival** (Ⓦwww.elkobasque.com), each Fourth of July weekend, hulking men throw huge logs at each other amid a whole lot of carousing and downing of platefuls of Basque food. Northern Spanish food is available year-round in **restaurants** like the *Star Hotel*, two blocks south of the main drag at 246 Silver St (Ⓣ775/753-8696). Greyhound and Amtrak both stop in Elko, while the many **motels** include the *Gold Country Inn*, 2050 Idaho St (Ⓣ775/738-8421; ❹). Elko's **visitor center** is at 700 Moren Way (Mon–Fri 9am–5pm; Ⓣ775/738-4091 or 1-800/248-ELKO, Ⓦwww.elkocva.com).

Reno and around

The self-proclaimed "biggest little city in the world," **RENO**, on I-80 near the California border, is a somewhat downmarket version of Las Vegas, with miles of gleaming slot machines and poker tables, along with tacky wedding chapels and quickie divorce courts. While the town itself may not be much to look at, its setting – at the foot of the snowcapped **Sierra Nevada**, with the Truckee River winding through the center – is superb. The **casinos** are concentrated downtown, along Virginia Street on either side of the railroad tracks.

Burning Man

Nevada's legendary **Burning Man Festival** is celebrated in a temporary, vehicle-free community known as **Black Rock City**, way out in the Black Rock Desert, twelve miles north of tiny Gerlach, which is itself a hundred miles north of Reno. It takes place at the end of August each year, in the week leading up to Labor Day. That's a very, very hot time to be out in the Nevada desert, particularly if, like approaching half of the fifty thousand revelers, you're completely naked.

The festival takes on a different theme each year, always with a strong emphasis on spontaneity and mass participation. An exhilarating range of performances, happenings and art installations culminates in the burning of a giant human effigy on the final Saturday. After that, in theory at least, Black Rock City simply disappears without trace.

For full information, and the latest ticket prices, typically around $250 for the week, access Ⓦwww.burningman.com. All visitors must buy tickets in advance; you can't pay at the gate, and neither will you be admitted unless you can prove total self-sufficiency. You have to bring everything, including all your water, food and shelter. The site holds no public showers or pools, and its economy is almost entirely based on barter. No money can change hands, with the single exception of the sale of coffee and ice.

Practicalities

Reno's **Cannon International Airport** is a couple of miles southeast of downtown. Greyhound **buses** arrive at 155 Stevenson St, while daily Amtrak **trains between** San Francisco and Salt Lake City call at 135 E Commercial Row downtown.

The local **visitor center** is in the Reno Town Mall at 4001 S Virginia St (daily 8am–5pm; ⓣ1-800/367-7366, ⓦwww.renolaketahoe.com). All the big casinos offer accommodation, with rates doubling at weekends; the best are the *Atlantis*, 3800 S Virginia St (ⓣ775/825-4700 or 1-800/723-6500, ⓦwww.atlantiscasino.com; ❷); *Silver Legacy*, 407 N Virginia St (ⓣ775/325-7401 or 1-800/687-8733, ⓦwww.silverlegacyreno.com; ❷); and *Circus Circus*, 500 N Sierra St (ⓣ775/329-0711 or 1-800/648-5010, ⓦwww.circusreno.com; ❷. Reno's best-value **buffet** is at the *Eldorado*, 345 N Virginia St (ⓣ775/786-5700 or 1-800/879-8879, ⓦwww.eldoradoreno.com; ❸).

Carson City

US-395 heads south from Reno along the jagged spires of the **High Sierra**, en route to **Death Valley**. After just thirty miles, state capital **CARSON CITY** – named after frontier explorer Kit Carson in 1858 – holds a number of elegant buildings, the excellent **Nevada State Museum**, at 600 N Carson St (daily 8.30am–4.30pm; $5), which covers the geology and natural history of the Great Basin, and a handful of world-weary casinos.

Carson City's **visitor center** is on the south side of town at 1900 S Carson St (Mon–Fri 8am–5pm, Sat & Sun 10am–3pm; ⓣ775/687-7410, ⓦwww.visitcarsoncity.com). *Bliss Bungalow* is a luxurious **B&B** in a restored Arts-and-Crafts house, downtown at 408 W Robinson St (ⓣ775/883-6129, ⓦwww.blissbungalow.com; ❹), while *Hardman House* at 917 N Carson St (ⓣ775/882-7744; ❹) is an attractive, well-priced **hotel**.

Virginia City

Much of the wealth on which Carson City – and indeed San Francisco – was built came from the silver mines of the **Comstock Lode**, a solid seam of pure silver discovered in 1859 beneath Mount Hamilton, fourteen miles northeast of Carson City off US-50. Raucous **VIRGINIA CITY** grew up on the steep slopes above the mines, and a young writer named Samuel Clemens made his way here with his brother, the acting Secretary to the Governor of the Nevada Territory, to see what all the fuss was about. As **Mark Twain**, he later published his descriptions of the wild life of the mining camp in the hilarious *Roughing It*. There's not much to Virginia City nowadays, as all the old storefronts have been taken over by hot-dog vendors and tacky souvenir stands, but the surrounding landscape of arid mountains still feels remote and undisturbed.

13

California

AL - ALABAMA	IN - INDIANA	MN - MINNESOTA	RI - RHODEISLAND
AR - ARKANSAS	LA - LOUISIANA	MS - MISSISSIPPI	SC - SOUTH CAROLINA
CT - CONNECTICUT	MA - MASSACHUSETTS	NC - NORTH CAROLINA	VA - VIRGINIA
DE - DELAWARE	MD - MARYLAND	NH - NEW HAMPSHIRE	VT - VERMONT
FL- FLORIDA	ME - MAINE	NJ - NEW JERSEY	WI - WISCONSIN
IL - ILLINOIS	MI - MICHIGAN	PA - PENNSYLVANIA	WV - WEST VIRGINIA

CHAPTER 13 **Highlights**

* **San Diego Zoo** About as humane and "natural" as a zoo can get, with a vast collection of rare species. See p.955
* **Disney Hall** LA's foremost example of modern sculpture—which also happens to be a terrific symphony hall. See p.968
* **Mono Lake** A strange and remote sight that's well worth the trip – prime bird-watching territory amid blue waters and gnarled tufa columns. See p.1001
* **Joshua Tree National Park** The eerily twisted "arms" of Joshua trees beckon visitors to explore this long-abandoned mining country. See p.996
* **Highway 1** A thrilling, circuitous drive along the US's West Coast, with pounding Pacific surf and dramatic cliffside vistas. See p.1017
* **Yosemite National Park** Giant sequoias, towering waterfalls, the sheer face of Half Dome – your eyes will hardly get a rest. See p.1007
* **Alcatraz** Eerie, legendary one-time maximum-security prison stuck out on "the Rock" in San Francisco Bay. See p.1034

▲ Mono Lake

13

California

Publicized and idealized all over the world, **CALIFORNIA** has a formidable reputation as a terrestrial paradise of sun, sand, and surf, added to fast-paced, glitzy cities, primeval old-growth forests, and vast stretches of deserts. All this, however, lies under the constant threat of the **Big One** – a massive earthquake of unimaginable destruction – along with the floods, fires, droughts, and other disasters. And although once the power base for taxpayer revolts and reactionary stalwarts such as Ronald Reagan and Richard Nixon, it has also been the source of some of the country's most **progressive movements**, from the protests of the Sixties to modern environmentalist, civil rights, and various reform activities. **Economically**, the region is crucial, whether in film, music, finance, shipping, or the all-consuming sector of real estate.

California is much too large to be fully explored in a single trip – much will depend on what you're looking for. **Los Angeles** is far and away the biggest and most stimulating city: a maddening collection of freeways, beaches, suburbs, and extreme lifestyles. To the south, the more conservative metropolis of **San Diego** has broad, welcoming beaches and a renowned zoo, while further inland, the **deserts**, most notably **Death Valley**, make up a barren and inhospitable landscape of volcanic craters and salt pans that in summer becomes the hottest place on earth. Heading north, the **central coast** is a gorgeous run that takes in lively small towns such as **Santa Barbara** and **Santa Cruz**.

California's second city, **San Francisco**, is about as different from LA as it's possible to get: a European-styled jewel whose wooden Victorian houses and steep hills make it one of the world's most distinctive and appealing cities. To the east, excellent national parks include **Yosemite**, where waterfalls cascade into a sheer glacial valley, and **Sequoia/Kings Canyon** with its gigantic trees, as well as the ghost towns of the **Gold Country**. North of San Francisco the countryside becomes wilder, wetter, and greener, peppered with volcanic tablelands and verdant mountains.

The **climate** in **southern California** features seemingly endless days of sunshine and warm, dry nights, with occasional bouts of winter flooding. **Coastal** mornings can be hazily overcast, especially in May and June; in the Bay Area around San Francisco it can be chilly all year, and fog rolls in to spoil many a sunny day. Much more so than in the south, winter in **northern California** can bring rain for weeks on end. Most hiking trails in the **mountains** are blocked between October and June by the snow that keeps California's ski slopes among the busiest in the nation.

The rise of America's most populous state

Spaniard **Juan Cabrillo** first sighted San Diego harbor in 1542, naming it **California** after an imaginary island inhabited by Amazons, from a Spanish novel. **Sir Francis Drake** landed near Point Reyes, north of San Francisco, in 1579, where the "white bancks and cliffes" reminded him of Dover. In 1602 **Sebastián Vizcáino** bestowed most of the place names that still survive; his exaggerated description of **Monterey** as a perfect harbor led later colonizers to make it the region's military and administrative center. The Spanish occupation began in earnest in 1769, combining military rule with **missionary** zeal. Father **Junípero Serra** first established a small mission and *presidio* (fort) at San Diego, and by 1804 a chain of 21 missions, each a long day's walk from the next along the dirt path of *El Camino Real* (The Royal Road), ran from San Diego to San Francisco. Native Americans were either forcibly converted into Catholicism or killed; disease ensured that they were soon wiped out.

Mexico gained its independence in 1821, but **Americans** were already starting to arrive, despite the immense difficulty of getting to California – three months by sea or four months by covered wagon. The growing belief that it was the **Manifest Destiny** of the United States to cover the continent from coast to coast, evident in the imperialist policies of President James K. Polk, soon led to the **Mexican–American War**. By January 1847 the Americans controlled the entire West Coast.

A mere nine days before the signing of the treaty that ended the war, flakes of **gold** were discovered in the Sierra Nevada, leading to a rush of prospectors from all parts of the world and California's 1850 entry into the US as the **31st state**. It took just fifteen years to pick the land clean of visible gold, and the **transcontinental railroad** was completed in 1869, linking the gold fields to the rest of the US. Hordes of newcomers came from the Great Plains to Southern California and helped make Los Angeles the state's biggest city. Thanks to this migration, along with periodic real-estate booms and the rise of the **film industry**, California became the nation's fastest-growing state. Heavy industry followed during **World War II**, in the form of shipyards and airplane factories.

As home to the **Beats** in the Fifties and the **hippies** in the Sixties, California was at the leading edge of cultural change. The Vietnam-era protests ended with the abolition of the draft, followed by the rise of the indulgent, cocaine-fueled "Me Generation" of the 1970s. The economic counterpart of this shift also developed when **Proposition 13**, in 1978, augured a national trend to dramatically cut taxes at the cost of government solvency. The 1980s saw further right-wing gains, with a string of laissez-faire Republican governors, and the Nineties crash-landed in economic scandal, a depressed real-estate market, rising unemployment, gang violence, and race riots in LA – compounded by **earthquakes**, **drought**, and **flooding**.

Some of the glow has come off the golden state in the twenty-first century, but countless new **migrants** continue to arrive – many from Latin America. One of these migrants, Austrian **Arnold Schwarzenegger**, had the good fortune to become a well-paid action movie hero before taking his place as 38th California governor. Inspired by the example of "Conan the Barbarian," many residents imagine that if a linguistically challenged bodybuilder can rule the state, then they too might be capable of great things here in this land of golden opportunity, real or imaginary.

Getting around California

Despite America's rising gas prices, a **car** is still necessary for exploring much of California. A city such as Los Angeles couldn't exist without the automobile, and in any case driving down the coastal freeways in a sleek convertible is too fun to resist.

Amtrak **Pacific Surfliner trains** link **San Diego** and **LA** (and up to San Luis Obispo), with a stop at Fullerton for buses to Disneyland. The **Coast Starlight** runs up the coast from LA, stopping at **Oakland** and **Emeryville**, the nearest

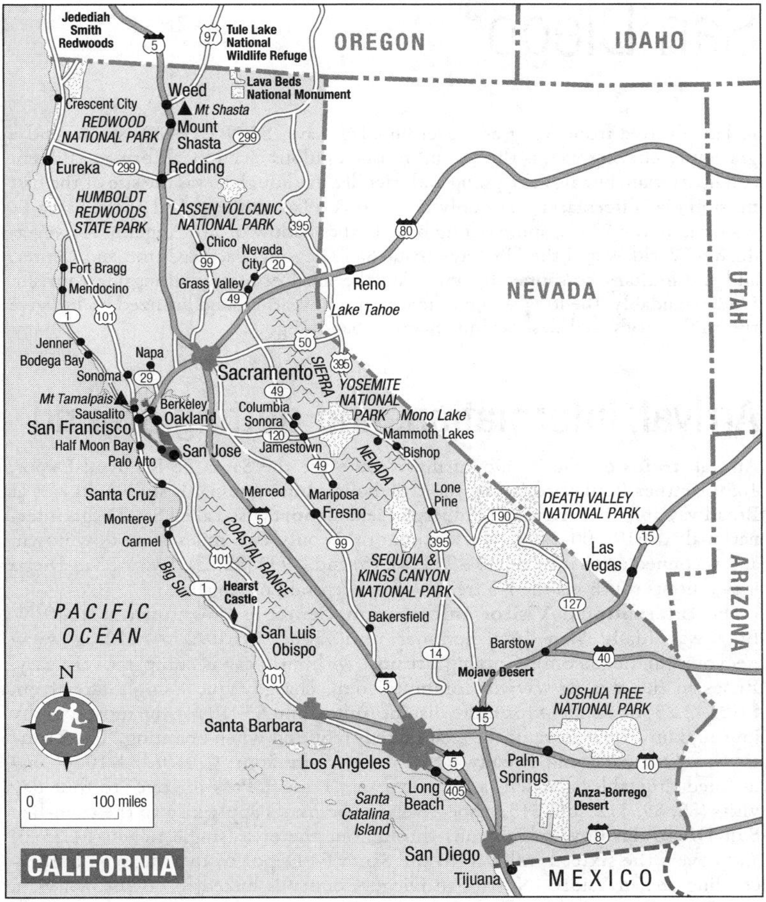

stations to San Francisco, and continues on via Sacramento to Seattle. The **San Joaquins** from Oakland runs along the Central Valley, connecting with LA by bus. Greyhound **buses** link all the main towns. Keep in mind that in some cases, depending on route, **flying** may be a better bet between the major cities.

If you plan to do any **long-distance cycling**, traveling from north to south can make all the difference – the wind blows this way in the summer, and the ocean side of the road offers the best views. Be careful if you cycle along the coast on Hwy-1: despite the stunning views, the highway has heavy traffic, tight curves, and is prone to fog.

San Diego

Relatively free from smog and overbuilt freeways, **SAN DIEGO**, set around a gracefully curving bay, is the second most-populous city in California – affluent and libertarian, but also easygoing and friendly. Although it was the site of the first mission in California, the city only really took off with the arrival of the Santa Fe Railroad in the 1880s, and has long been in the shadow of Los Angeles. However, during World War II the US Navy made San Diego its Pacific Command Center, and the military continues to dominate the local economy, alongside tourism. Understandably, the long white beaches, sunny weather, and bronzed bodies give rise to the city's well-deserved nickname, "Sandy Ego."

Arrival, information, and getting around

Amtrak **trains** on the Pacific Surfliner route use the Santa Fe Railroad Depot, 1050 Kettner Boulevard, while the Greyhound **bus** terminal is six blocks east at Broadway and First Avenue. Lindbergh Field **airport** (also called San Diego International; Ⓣ619/400-2400, Ⓦwww.san.org) is only two miles from downtown, and is connected to it by buses #923 ($1.75) and #992 ($2.25). By car, San Diego is two hours south via the I-5 freeway from central Los Angeles.

The **International Visitor Information Center** is downtown at 1040 W Broadway (daily 9am–4pm, summer until 5pm; Ⓣ619/236-1212, Ⓦwww.seeyouinsandiego.com). **Getting around** without a car is comparatively easy. **Buses** in the area (Ⓦwww.sdcommute.com), charge typical single fares from $1.25–2.25, or $2.50–4 for more distant routes, and $5–10 for the most lengthy journeys into rural terrain; the exact fare is required when boarding. The **Transit Store**, at First and Broadway (Mon–Sat 9am–5pm; Ⓣ619/234-1060), has detailed timetables and sells a **Day Tripper Transit Pass** for one- to four-day visits ($5, $9, $12, and $15, respectively). The passes apply also to the tram-like **San Diego Trolley**, which runs throughout the area (single tickets $1.25–3) and covers the sixteen miles from the Santa Fe Depot to the Mexican border-crossing at San Ysidro. North San Diego County is linked to downtown via a simple commuter light-rail system called **The Coaster**. Fares range from $4.50 to $6 single (Ⓣ1-800/COASTER, Ⓦwww.gonctd.com). For **bicycle** rentals, try Cheap Rentals, 3685 Mission Blvd, Mission Beach (Ⓣ858/488-9070, Ⓦwww.cheap-rentals.com).

Accommodation

Accommodation is plentiful throughout San Diego. The best-placed, though mall-like, **campground** is **Campland on the Bay**, 2211 Pacific Beach Drive (Ⓣ1-800/422-9386, Ⓦwww.campland.com), linked to downtown by bus #30, where a basic site starts at $60, with more elaborate sites running up to $160. For a more serene camping option, there's **San Elijo Beach State Park**, Rte-21 south of Cardiff-by-the-Sea ($11–25; Ⓣ1-800/444-7275, Ⓦwww.reserveamerica.com).

Hotels, motels, and B&Bs

Bahia Resort 998 West Mission Bay Drive, Mission Bay ⓣ1-800/576-4229 or 858/488-0551, ⓦwww.bahiahotel.com. Beachside accommodation with expansive ocean views, watersport rentals, pool, and jacuzzi. Rooms range from cozy but pleasant rooms in a palm-garden setting to pricier bayside suites. ❽

Balboa Park Inn 3402 Park Blvd, Hillcrest ⓣ619/298-0823, ⓦwww.balboaparkinn.com. Spanish Colonial, gay-oriented B&B, within walking distance of Balboa Park and museums. Offers 26 romantic themed suites (with Parisian, Impressionist, and jungle motifs, to name a few) with microwaves and mini-fridges. ❹

Bed and Breakfast Inn at La Jolla 7753 Draper Ave ⓣ858/456-2066 or 1-800/582-2466, ⓦwww.innlajolla.com. A collection of fifteen themed rooms with tranquil gardens, great service, and nice proximity to the beach and art museum. ❼

Bristol 1055 First Ave, downtown ⓣ619/232-6141, ⓦwww.thebristolsandiego.com. Nice boutique hotel with stylish modern decor and tasteful amenities, plus in-room CD players and internet access. ❼

Crystal Pier Hotel and Cottages 4500 Ocean Blvd, Pacific Beach ⓣ858/483-6983 or 1-800/748-5894, ⓦwww.crystalpier.com. Beautiful, deluxe cottages built in the 1920s, situated right on Pacific Beach pier. All units are suites with private deck, and most have kitchenettes. ❽

Heritage Park B&B 2470 Heritage Park Row, Old Town ⓣ619/299-6832 or 1-800/995-2470, ⓦwww.heritageparkinn.com. Restored Queen Anne mansion in Heritage Park, chock-full of Victorian trappings. Breakfast and afternoon tea are included. Rooms and suites are in the usual lace-and-chintz style. ❺

Horton Grand 311 Island Ave at 3rd Ave, downtown ⓣ619/544-1886 or 1-800/542-1886, ⓦwww.hortongrand.com. Classy amalgam of two century-old hotels, with fireplaces in most of the 132 antique-flavored rooms (some with balconies), an on-site restaurant, a piano bar, and Saturday-afternoon high tea. ❻

Hotel del Coronado 1500 Orange Ave, Coronado ⓣ619/522-8000 or 1-800/468-3533, ⓦwww.hoteldel.com. The luxurious place that put Coronado on the map in 1888 and is still the area's major tourist sight (see p.954). The striking rooms and suites, expansive bay views, and old-fashioned Victorian charm give the place much appeal. ❾

La Pensione 606 W Date St at India St ⓣ619/236-8000, ⓦwww.lapensionehotel.com. Good-value hotel within walking distance of the city center. Rooms are small but equipped with microwaves, fridges, and cable TVs, and there's an on-site laundry. ❸

Manchester Grand Hyatt One Market Place, at Harbor Drive ⓣ619/232-1234, ⓦwww.manchestergrand.hyatt.com. The most prominent hotel along the waterfront, a pair of gleaming white slabs of luxury with pool, spas, health club, several restaurants and lounges, and rooms with expansive views of the bay. Ground zero for conventioneers. ❾

Park Manor Suites 525 Spruce St, near Balboa Park ⓣ619/291-0999 or 1-800/874-2649, ⓦwww.parkmanorsuites.com. Renovated complex that's nearly a hundred years old. Tasteful hotel suites feature kitchens and nice, large sitting areas. Continental breakfast included. ❺

Tower23 723 Felspar St, Pacific Beach ⓣ1-866/TOWER-23, ⓦwww.tower23hotel.com. Despite being named for a lifeguard tower, this is among the most chic of the local boutique hotels, offering stylish rooms with flatscreen TVs, internet access, and designer furnishings. The stylish suites variously come with balconies, cabanas, and whirlpool tubs. ❾

US Grant 326 Broadway, downtown ⓣ619/232-3121 or 1-800/237-5029, ⓦwww.usgrant.net. Downtown's poshest address since 1910, with a grand Neoclassical design, chandeliers, marble floors, and cozy but comfortable guestrooms and more capacious suites. The elegant ballrooms and swank conference rooms are worth a peek. ❾

Hostels

Banana Bungalow 707 Reed Ave, Pacific Beach ⓣ858/273-3060 or 1-800/5-HOSTEL, ⓦwww.bananabungalow.com/sub/bbsd.html. Friendly if scruffy place with access to the beach, offering volleyball, BBQ cookouts, and lively atmosphere. Breakfast, internet access, and a communal kitchen are included. Dorm beds $20-25, private rooms $65–105. Take bus #30, then it's a five-minute walk.

HI-Pt Loma 3790 Udall St, Ocean Beach ⓣ619/223-4778, ⓦwww.sandiegohostels.org. A couple of miles back from the beach and minus the relentless party atmosphere of other hostels, offering free breakfast, patio, and weekly bonfires. Well-run and friendly, with dorms for $20–31 and private rooms $45–63. Take bus #923.

HI-San Diego Downtown 521 Market St at 5th Ave, downtown ⓣ619/525-1531, ⓦwww.sandiegohostels.org. Handy for the Gaslamp District, with free breakfast and high-speed net access, plus a library and organized trips. Dorm beds $22–27, private doubles $50–57.

Ocean Beach International Backpackers Hostel 4961 Newport Ave, Ocean Beach ⓣ619/223-7873 or 1-800/339-7263. Lively spot a block from the beach, offering barbecues, bike and surfboard rentals, airport transport and nightly movies. Dorm beds $17–24, with free wi-fi, sheets, showers, and continental breakfast.

USA Hostels – San Diego 726 5th Ave, downtown ⓣ619/232-3100 or 1-800/438-8622, ⓦwww.usahostels.com/sandiego. Well-placed hostel on the edge of the Gaslamp District. Converted 1890s building, with six to eight beds per room, sheets, and continental breakfast, for $23–29. Private rooms $62–74. Free breakfast, free wi-fi, and organized tours to Tijuana make this one of the best city hostels.

The City

With its mix of laid-back libertarians and rock-ribbed conservatives, San Diego embodies a work-hard, play-hard ethic, although it leans more towards the latter. Featuring an easily navigable downtown, scenic bay, 42 miles of beaches, and plentiful parks and museums, the city is hard not to like from the moment you arrive.

Downtown San Diego

Loosely bordered by the curve of San Diego Bay and the I-5 freeway, **downtown** is, for those not headed straight to the beach, the inevitable nexus of San Diego and the best place to start a tour of the city. Various preservation and restoration projects, kick-started in the late 1970s, have improved many of the area's older buildings, resulting in several pockets of stylishly renovated turn-of-the-century architecture, while the corporate towers left over from the boomtown 1980s and 90s showcase the city's bustling trade with the Pacific Rim as well as its inflated real-estate market.

The tall Moorish archways of the **Santa Fe Railroad Depot**, at the western end of Broadway, built in 1915 for the Panama-California Exposition, still evoke a sense of grandeur. The depot is contiguous with the downtown branch of the **Museum of Contemporary Art**, or MCA San Diego, 1001 Kettner Blvd (Fri–Mon & Wed 11am–5pm, Thurs 11am–7pm; $10; ⓣ858/454-3541, ⓦwww.mcasd.org), a fine first-stop for anyone interested in contemporary art with a California twist. Although its permanent collection focuses on American minimalism, Pop Art, and the indigenous art of Mexico, its temporary shows are the real appeal here, often involving quirky pop-culture surrealism and daring agit-prop manifestos. Further west, **Broadway** slices through the middle of downtown, at its most hectic between Fourth and Fifth avenues. Many visitors linger around the fountains on the square outside **Horton Plaza**, between First and Fourth avenues south of Broadway (hours vary; often Mon–Fri 10am–9pm, Sat 10am–8pm, Sun 11am–7pm; ⓦwww.westfield.com/hortonplaza), a giant roofless mall of some 140 stores and, for better or worse, San Diego's de facto city center. The complex's whimsical, colorful postmodern style, loaded with quasi-Art Deco and southwestern motifs, is inevitably a colossal tourist draw.

Gaslamp District

South of Broadway, a few blocks from Horton Plaza, lies the sixteen-block **Gaslamp District**, San Diego's original city center before it became a notorious red-light district, but now filled with smart streets lined with cafés, antique stores, art galleries, and, of course, "gas lamps" – powered by electricity. A tad artificial it may be, but its late-nineteenth-century buildings are intriguing to explore, especially on the two-hour **walking tour** (Sat 11am; $10; ⓣ619/233-4692, ⓦwww.gaslampquarter.org/tours) that begins from the small cobbled square at Fourth and Island avenues. The square is within the grounds of the **William Heath Davis**

Map labels (Downtown San Diego):

Airport ▲ | ❶ & ❷ ▲ ▲ ▲ Ⓐ & Little Italy (1 block) | ▲ Hillcrest (25 blocks)

DOWNTOWN SAN DIEGO

Balboa Park

CEDAR STREET
BEECH STREET
ASH STREET
A STREET
B STREET
C STREET
BROADWAY
E STREET
F STREET
G STREET
MARKET STREET
ISLAND AVENUE
J STREET
K STREET

Maritime Museum ❸
San Diego Ferry
USS Midway
Santa Fe Railroad Depot & American Plaza ❺
Greyhound Station
Museum of Contemporary Art
Newtown Park
Transit Store
Horton Plaza ❼
Copley Symphony Hall ❻
Tram line
Library
GASLAMP DISTRICT
William Heath Davis House Ⓔ
Seaport Village Ⓖ ❶❹
Embarcadero Marina Park
San Diego Convention Center
Petco Park

0 — 200 yds

Coronado ◄
East San Diego & Coronado ▼ | ▼ Petco Park

ACCOMMODATION

Bristol	B
HI-San Diego Downtown	E
Horton Grand	F
La Pensione	A
Manchester Grand Hyatt	G
US Grant	C
USA Hostels – San Diego	D

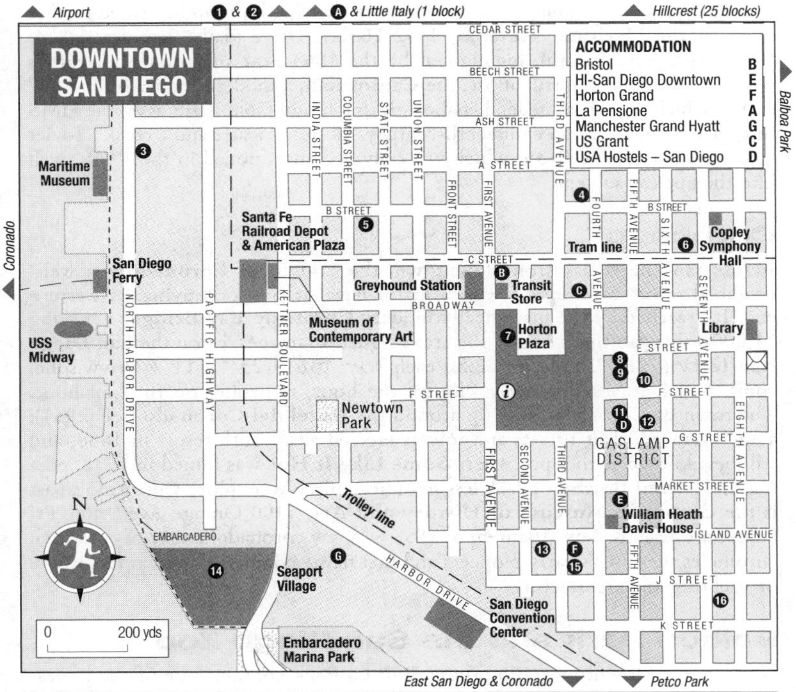

RESTAURANTS, BARS & CAFÉS

4th and B	4	Bitter End	11	Croce's	10	Filippi's Pizza	
Anthony's Fish		Café 222	13	de' Medici	8	Grotto	1
Grotto	3	Candelas	15	Dizzy's	16	Karl Strauss	
Bella Luna	12	Casbah	2	Dobson's	7	Brewery	5
On Broadway	6						
Onyx Room	9						
Upstart Crow	14						

House, 410 Island Ave (Tues–Sat 10am–6pm, Sun 9am–3pm; $5), whose owner founded modern San Diego and in 1850 built this saltbox-styled home – copious with photographs, with each room commemorating a different historical period.

The focus of San Diego sporting activity, especially on the weekend, is **Petco Park**, Seventh Avenue at Harbor Drive (☎619/795-5000, ⓦsandiego.padres.mlb .com), which draws plenty of Padres baseball fans but has more limited options for parking. If you've come to play spectator, make an early trip on the Blue Line trolley (which passes alongside) – mass transit around game time resembles a rail-bound journey into deepest tourist hell.

The bayfront

Along San Diego's curving, enjoyable **bayfront**, the pathway of the **Embarcadero** runs a mile or so along the bay, curling around to the western end of downtown; along this stretch, the expansive green lawn of **Embarcadero Marina Park South** provides some summertime amusement for its mainstream concerts. Beyond this, if you can't get enough of the US military on your TV set at home, clamber aboard for a tour of the **USS Midway**, 910 N Harbor Drive (daily 10am–5pm, last admission 4pm; $17; ⓦwww.midway.org), which shows off its formidable collection of naval hardware and weapons to the public, along with flight simulators and various old-time planes. Seven, more vintage ships can be visited further north at the **Maritime Museum**, 1492 Harbor Drive (daily 9am–8pm; $14; Ⓦwww.sdmaritime.com), highlighted by the 1863 **Star of India**, the world's oldest iron sailing ship still afloat; the **Californian**, a modern replica of an 1847 cutter, which served as a federal lawboat during heady Gold Rush days; the **HMS Surprise**, a replica of an eighteenth-century, 24-gun frigate; and a creaky Soviet diesel submarine, the **B-39**, which was only decommissioned in the 1990s, well into the nuclear-sub era.

Coronado

Across San Diego Bay from downtown, the isthmus of **Coronado** is a well-scrubbed resort community with a major naval station occupying its western end. It's reached by the majestically modern **Coronado Bay Bridge**, a curving 11,000-foot span that's one of the area's signature images, or on the **San Diego Bay ferry** (daily 9am–9pm; $3.50 each way; Ⓣ619/234-1111, Ⓦwww.sdhe.com), which leaves Broadway Pier on the hour, returning on the half-hour. The town of Coronado grew up around the **Hotel del Coronado** (see p.951), a Victorian whirl of turrets and towers erected as a health resort in 1888, and still best known as the spot where **Some Like It Hot** was filmed in 1958, posing as a Miami Beach hotel. A less grandiose place to explore Coronado's past is the **Coronado Museum of History and Art**, 1100 Orange Ave (Mon–Fri 9am–5pm, Sat & Sun 10am–5pm; $5; Ⓦwww.coronadohistory.org), which chronicles the town's early pioneers and first naval aviators, as well as its history of yachting and architecture.

Balboa Park and the San Diego Zoo

Northeast of downtown, sumptuous **Balboa Park** contains one of the largest groups of **museums** in the US, as well as charming landscaping, traffic-free promenades, and stately Spanish Colonial–style buildings. The park is large but easy to get around **on foot** – if you get tired, there's always the free tram. The **Balboa Park Passport**, a week-long pass that allows one-time admission to all fourteen of the park's museums and its Japanese garden (plus the San Diego Zoo, for an extra $26), is available for $39 from the **visitor information center** (daily 9.30am–4.30pm; Ⓣ619/239-0512, Ⓦwww.balboapark.org), inside the on-site House of Hospitality. Near the center, the **Spreckels Organ Pavilion** (concerts June-Aug Sun 2pm; free; Ⓦwww.serve.com/sos-organ), is worth a look as the home of one of the world's largest organs, with some 4500 pipes.

Most of the major museums flank El Prado, the pedestrian-oriented road that bisects the park. There's plenty to see, so plan on spending at least a full day here, especially if you bought a Passport. Highlights include the stirring collection of Russian icons at the **Timkin Museum of Art** (Tues–Sat 10am–4.30pm, Sun 1.30–4.30pm; closed Sept; free; Ⓦwww.timkenmuseum.org); the **San Diego Museum of Art**'s (Tues–Sun 10am–6pm, Thurs closes 9pm; $10; Ⓦwww.sdmart.org) solid stock of European paintings from the Renaissance to the nineteenth century, highlighted by Hals and Rembrandt; the exhibitions of the **Museum of Man** (daily 10am–4.30pm; $10; Ⓦwww.museumofman.org) that may involve replicas of huge Mayan stones, Native American artifacts, and Egyptian relics; the child-oriented amusements and IMAX theater of the **Reuben H. Fleet Science Center** (Mon–Thurs 9.30am–5pm, Fri 9.30am–9pm, Sat 9.30am–8pm, Sun 9.30am–6pm; $12.50, kids $9.75; Ⓦwww.rhfleet.org); the **Natural History Museum** (daily 10am–5pm; $13; Ⓦwww.sdnhm.org) and its great collection of fossils, hands-on displays of minerals, and exhibits on dinosaurs and crocodiles; the history of aviation on view at the **Air & Space Museum** (daily 10am–4.30pm, summer closes 5.30pm; $15; Ⓦwww.aerospacemuseum.org), whose dozens of planes include the **Spitfire**, **Hellcat**, and the mysterious spy plane **Blackbird**; and the **Automotive Museum** (daily 10am–5pm; $8; Ⓦwww.sdautomuseum.org), where car enthusiasts will enjoy scads of classic motorcycles and cars, among them a 1948 Tucker Torpedo – one of only fifty left.

Immediately north of the main museums, the enormous **San Diego Zoo** (daily mid-June to early Sept 9am–8pm; early Sept to mid-June 9am–4pm; Ⓦwww.sandiegozoo.org) is one of the world's most renowned, with hundreds of different species, among them rare Chinese pheasants, Mhorr gazelles, and a freakish two-headed corn snake. It's an enormous place, and you can easily spend a full day here, soaking in the major sections devoted to the likes of chimps and gorillas, sun and polar bears, lizards and lions, and habitats such as the rainforest. Regular **admission** ($24.50, kids $16.50) only covers entry to the main zoo and the children's zoo; to add a 35-minute bus tour and a round-trip ticket on the Skyfari aerial tram, you'll need the $34 package (kids $24). A $60 ticket (kids $43) also admits you to the San Diego Wild Animal Park near Escondido (daily 9am–4pm, summer closes 8pm; $28.50, $17.50 kids), a two-thousand-acre preserve for big cats, rhinos, giraffes, and the like, which roam about outside your car's windows.

On the border of Balboa Park, **Hillcrest** is a lively and artsy area at the center of the city's **gay community** – about as close as San Diego gets to having a bohemian air. Go there either for something to eat – there's a selection of interesting cafés and restaurants around University and Fifth streets – or simply to stroll around the fine gathering of Victorian homes.

Old Town San Diego and Presidio Hill

In 1769, Spanish settlers chose **Presidio Hill** as the site of the first of California's missions, later to be dominated by Mexican officials and then by early arrivals from the eastern US. **Old Town San Diego**, reachable from downtown via the Trolley, is now a state historical park and the site of several original adobe dwellings. These are generally open 10am to 5pm and have free admission, but most things in the park that aren't historical – shops and restaurants – open around 10am and close at 9 or 10pm. Highlights include the **Casa de Estudillo** on Mason Street, built by the commander of the **presidio**, José Maria de Estudillo, in 1827, one of the poshest of the original adobes. Next door, the **Casa de Bandini** was the home of the politician and writer Juan Bandini and acted as the social center of San Diego during the mid-nineteenth century. Details on the many structures here are available from the **visitor center**, inside the Robinson-Rose House, near Taylor and Congress streets (daily 10am–5pm; Ⓦwww.oldtownsandiego.org).

The Spanish-style building now atop Presidio Hill is only a rough approximation of the original mission – moved in 1774 – but its **Junípero Serra Museum**, 10818 San Diego Mission Rd (daily 10am–4.30pm; Sept–May Mon–Fri 11am–3pm, Sat & Sun 10am–4.30pm; $5), offers an intriguing examination of Junípero Serra, the padre who led the Spanish colonization and Catholic conversion of California. The **Mission San Diego de Alcalá** itself was relocated six miles north to 10818 San Diego Mission Rd (daily 9am–4.45pm; donation; Ⓦwww.missionsandiego.com), to be near a water source and fertile soils – and to be safer from attack. The present building is still a working parish church, with a small **museum**; among the craft objects and artifacts from the mission is the crucifix held by Serra at his death in 1834.

Ocean Beach and Point Loma

Ruled by the Hell's Angels in the 1960s, **OCEAN BEACH**, six miles northwest of downtown via bus #35 or #923, is a fun and relaxed beach town whose quaint, old-time streets and shops have preserved some of their ramshackle appeal and funky character. The two big hangouts include **Newport Street**, where backpackers slack around at snack bars, surf and skate rental shops, and **Voltaire Street**, which true to its name has a good range of independent-minded local businesses. There is often good surf, and the beach itself can be quite fun – especially on weekends, when the local party scene gets cranking. South from the pier rise the dramatic **Sunset Cliffs**, a prime spot for twilight vistas.

South of Ocean Beach, at the southern end of the hilly green peninsula of **Point Loma**, the **Cabrillo National Monument** (daily 9am–5pm; seven-day pass $5 per car, pedestrians and cyclists $3; Ⓦwww.nps.gov/cabr) marks the spot where Juan Cabrillo and crew became the first Europeans to land in California, albeit briefly, in 1542. The startling views from this high spot, across San Diego Bay to downtown and down the coast to Mexico, easily repay a trip here. A platform atop the western cliffs of the park makes it easy to view the November-to-March **whale migration**, when scores of gray whales pass by en route to their breeding grounds off Baja California, Mexico. The nearby visitor center (same as park hours) contains more information, and lies near the **Old Point Loma Lighthouse** (daily 9am–5pm; free), which offers tours that showcase replica Victorian furnishings and equipment from the 1880s.

Sea World, Mission Beach, and Pacific Beach

North of Ocean Beach, **Mission Bay** is the site of San Diego's most popular tourist attraction: **SeaWorld** (hours vary, often mid-June to Labor Day 9am–dusk; rest of year 10am–dusk; $61, children $51, parking $10; Ⓦwww.seaworld.com), reachable by bus #9 from downtown. SeaWorld is San Diego's most popular attraction for its undeniable, if expensive, kid-friendly appeal. Some of the spectacles include the Shamu Show and Shamu Rocks! (orcas paired with flashing lights and rock music); Forbidden Reef, stocked with moray eels and stingrays; the Wild Arctic, populated by walruses, beluga whales, and polar bears; and the Shark Encounter, where sharks circle menacingly around visitors walking through a viewing tunnel.

The biggest-name public beaches in San Diego are **Mission Beach**, the peninsula that separates Mission Bay from the ocean, and its northern extension, **Pacific Beach**. Nurse a beer at one of the many beachfront bars, or rollerblade or bike down **Ocean Front Walk**, the concrete boardwalk running the length of both beaches, and observe the toasty sands overrun with scantily clad beach babes and surfer dudes. A mile north of Pacific Beach's Crystal Pier, **Tourmaline Surfing Park**, La Jolla Boulevard at Tourmaline Street, is reserved exclusively for the sport, as well as windsurfing – but no swimmers are allowed. If you don't have a board, a good alternative is a few miles north, **Windansea Beach**, a favorite surfing hot spot that's also fine for swimming and hiking alongside the oceanside rocks and reefs.

Near the southern end of Ocean Front Walk at 3146 Mission Blvd (hours vary, often Mon–Thurs 11am–8pm, Fri–Sun 11am–10pm; most rides $2–6; Ⓦwww.belmontpark.com), once-derelict **Belmont Park** has been renovated with modern rides, though the two main attractions are both from 1925: the **Giant Dipper** rollercoaster, one of the few of its era still around, and the **Plunge**, once the largest saltwater plunge in the world, and a regular film set for old-time Hollywood swim spectaculars.

La Jolla

A more pretentious air prevails in **La Jolla** (pronounced "La Hoya"), an elegant beach community just north. Stroll its immaculate, gallery-filled streets, fuel up on some California cuisine at one of the many sidewalk cafés, or visit the local site of the **Museum of Contemporary Art**, 700 Prospect St (Fri–Tues 11am–5pm, Thurs 11am–7pm; $6, students $2; Ⓦwww.mcasd.org), which has a huge, regularly changing stock of paintings and sculptures from 1955 onwards, highlighted by California pop and minimalism. On the seaward side of the museum lies the small and tasteful **Ellen Scripps Browning Park**, named for the philanthropist whose home now houses the museum. Where the park meets the coast is the popular **La Jolla Cove**, much of it an ecological reserve whose clear waters make it perfect for snorkeling (if you can find a parking space).

Just up the road, architecture fans won't want to miss a chance to tour one of the citadels of high modernism in the US, the **Salk Institute for Biological Studies**, 10010 N Torrey Pines Rd (Mon–Fri 8.30am–5pm; tours Mon–Fri noon; free; reserve at Ⓣ858/453-4100 ext 1287, Ⓦwww.salk.edu), a collection of rigid geometric concrete blocks and walls featuring stark vistas that look out over the Pacific Ocean, while further north, the **Stephen Birch Aquarium and Museum**, 2300 Expedition Way (daily 9am–5pm; $11, Ⓦaquarium.ucsd.edu), provides up-close views of marine life. Highlights include the Hall of Fishes, a huge kelp forest home to countless sea creatures, and the Shark Reef, displaying a nice range of the fearsome creatures, including a few pint-sized versions. Altogether, the museum is a much more edifying experience than anything at SeaWorld, and a lot cheaper, too.

Eating

Wherever you are in San Diego, you'll have few problems finding something good to **eat** at reasonable prices. Everything from crusty coffee shops to stylish ethnic eateries are in copious supply here, with seafood at its best around the beaches and the Gaslamp District, and the latter also home to the greatest concentration of restaurants of all kinds.

Anthony's Fish Grotto 1360 Harbor Drive, downtown Ⓣ619/232-5103. Fish-and-chips and other affordable seafood favorites are the draw at this longstanding bayside haunt, with a good range of prices. Lunch or dinner; one of several area locations.

Bella Luna 748 5th Ave, downtown Ⓣ619/239-3222. A romantic, moon-themed bistro with an artsy feel, serving up wonderful, mid-priced dishes from different regions of Italy, with hefty servings of pasta and calamari.

Berta's 3928 Twiggs St, Old Town Ⓣ619/295-2343. A far cry from a conventional south-of-the-border restaurant, offering well-priced, authentic cooking from all over Latin America. The affordable and savory dishes include chimichurri steak, paella, and other dishes.

Café 222 222 Island Ave, downtown Ⓣ619/236-9902. Hip café serving great breakfasts and lunches, with excellent pancakes, French toast, and pumpkin waffles. Also has inventive twists on traditional sandwiches and burgers (including vegetarian), all at reasonable prices.

Candelas 416 3rd Ave, downtown Ⓣ619/702-4455. Gaslamp District restaurant offering swank, pricey Mexican fare with inventive combinations of seafood and meat dishes demonstrating a California-cuisine influence. Try the halibut, Serrano ham, or any dessert.

Chez Loma 1132 Loma Ave, Coronado Ⓣ619/435-0661. Delicious upscale French cuisine; especially strong on old-line favorites, though with nouvelle influences too. Good for its rack of lamb, sea scallops, black mussels, onion soup, and, of course, filet mignon.

Chilango's Mexican Grill 142 University Ave, Hillcrest Ⓣ619/294-8646. Regional Mexican food mostly for under $10, highlighted by tasty shrimp, ceviche, enchiladas, tortilla soup, among other solid choices.

Cody's La Jolla 8030 Girard Ave ⓣ858/459-0040. Innovative California cuisine; especially notable are the ling cod, duck breast, and scrumptious burgers. Dinner entrees are about twice as expensive as the affordable lunch dishes.

Croce's Restaurant and Jazz Bar 802 5th Ave, Gaslamp District ⓣ619/233-4355. Pricey but excellent range of pasta, desserts, and salads; the Sunday jazz brunch is a popular event.

de' Medici 815 5th Ave, downtown ⓣ619/702-7228. Upscale Italian fare that draws plenty of suits for its scrumptious cuisine, with the oysters rockefeller, langostino lobster, crab legs, and saltimbocca rounding out a fine menu.

Dobson's 956 Broadway Circle, downtown ⓣ619/231-6771. A chic restaurant in a venerable old building whose cuisine leans toward Continental, and ranges from crab hash and oyster salad to flat-iron steak and rack of lamb.

Filippi's Pizza Grotto 1747 India St at Date St, downtown ⓣ619/232-5094. A good spot for devouring affordable favorites like thick, chewy pizzas and various pasta dishes, including a fine lasagna. Meals are served in a small room at the back of an Italian grocery.

Ichiban 1449 University Ave, Hillcrest ⓣ619/299-7203. Fine Japanese cuisine for a reasonable charge, featuring good rolls, *bentos*, soups, and sushi, in an unpretentious and popular setting.

Karinya 4475 Mission Blvd, Pacific Beach ⓣ858/270-5050. Hot and spicy soups, firecracker shrimp and coconut curry to set your mouth ablaze, with a good range of Thai staples such as noodle dishes and satays as well. A rib-stuffing, affordable bet.

Kono's 704 Garnet Ave, Pacific Beach ⓣ858/483-1669. Crowded, touristy place for breakfast or lunch on the boardwalk, with hefty and inexpensive portions of eggs, sandwiches, hamburgers, burritos and other favorites.

Mission Café and Coffeehouse 3795 Mission Blvd, Mission Beach ⓣ858/488-9060. A wide range of eclectic choices, from French toast and pancakes, to tamales with eggs and roast beef hash, to "roll-ups" stuffed with meat and pasta.

Old Town Mexican Café 2489 San Diego Ave ⓣ619/297-4330. Lively and informal Mexican diner where the crowds expect to queue up before dining on Mexican ribs and steak Azteca; only at breakfast are you unlikely to have to wait for a table.

Point Loma Seafoods 2805 Emerson St, Ocean Beach ⓣ619/223-1109. Fast, cheap counter serving up San Diego's freshest fish in a basket, along with mean crabcake and squid sandwiches that make the locals cheer.

Primavera 932 Orange Ave, Coronado ⓣ619/435-0454. Swank and scrumptious Italian cuisine that's among the best in town. There's carpaccio, pasta, and risotto for those a little lighter in the wallet and steak and lamb chops for the big spenders.

Sportsmen's Seafood 1617 Quivira Rd, Mission Beach ⓣ619/224-3551. A combo diner/market offering cheap and delicious fare – the shrimp cocktail, squid steak, tuna burger, fish-and-chips, crab or lobster platter, and fish tacos are all worth a try.

Taste of Thai 527 University Ave, Hillcrest ⓣ619/291-7525. Terrific Thai staples – spicy noodles, marinated shrimp, pad thai, and so on – for reasonable prices; expect a wait on weekends.

Nightlife

San Diego's upscale cultural focus is **classical music** and **opera**, the big names of which are downtown: **San Diego Opera**, based at the Civic Theatre, 1200 Third Ave (ⓣ619/533-7000, ⓦwww.sdopera.com), and **San Diego Symphony**, Copley Symphony Hall, 750 B St (ⓣ619/235-0804, ⓦwww.sandiegosymphony.com). Half-priced tickets and information are at the **Arts Tix** booth, Broadway at Third Avenue (Tues–Thurs 11am–6pm, Fri & Sat 10am–6pm, Sun 10am–5pm; ⓣ619/497-5000, ⓦwww.sandiegoperforms.com). Elsewhere, the crowds flock to beachside **dance clubs** and boozy Gaslamp District **music venues** for evening amusement. For full listings, pick up the free **San Diego Reader** (ⓦwww.sdreader.com), the Thursday edition of the **San Diego Union-Tribune** (ⓦwww.signonsandiego.com), or the youth-oriented **San Diego CityBeat** (ⓦwww.sdcitybeat.com).

Bars, coffeeshops, and clubs

Bitter End 770 5th Ave, Gaslamp District Ⓣ619/338-9300. Three-story venue in the Gaslamp, complete with lower-level dance floor, martini bar, and upstairs, a private VIP lounge for the sophisticated poseur who doesn't mind paying top dollar for an appletini.

Caffé Calabria 3933 30th St, Hillcrest Ⓣ619/291-1795. Serious coffee drinks for serious coffee drinkers, serving up some fine espresso and French and Italian roasts from their own roasted beans, which you can also buy to take home.

Karl Strauss Brewery & Grill 1157 Columbia St, downtown Ⓣ619/234-2739; see Ⓦwww.karlstrauss.com for other locations. Reasonable selection of ales and lagers – from the Windansea Wheat to the Red Trolley Ale – brewed here on the premises, and an adequate array of bar food.

Kensington Club 4079 Adams Ave, Kensington District, north of Hillcrest Ⓣ619/284-2848. Also called "The Ken" – a great divey joint for beer, wine, and cocktails, but also for wide-ranging live music selections from thumping-dance DJs to head-banging rockers.

Live Wire 2103 El Cajon Blvd, just east of Hillcrest Ⓣ619/291-7450. An impressive selection of imported beers, plus pinball, pool, great jukebox, and funky sub-bohemian atmosphere make this a fine choice for boozing and mixing it up with interesting crowd.

On Broadway 615 Broadway, downtown Ⓣ619/231-0111. The apotheosis of posing in San Diego, a velvet-rope scene that attracts the local celebrity elite (such as they are) willing to fork over steep cover charges to see world-league DJs and minor-league up-and-comers.

Onyx Room 852 5th Ave, Gaslamp District Ⓣ619/235-6699. Groovy underground bar with lush decor, where you can knock back a few cocktails, then hit the back room for live jazz and dance tunes. The swanky lounge upstairs has pricier drinks and bigger attitudes.

Thrusters Lounge 4633 Mission Blvd, Pacific Beach Ⓣ858/483-6334. Sleek bar and club where the dance beats come hard and heavy, and jazz and rock make the odd appearance, too.

Upstart Crow 835 W Harbor Drive, downtown Ⓣ619/232-4855. This coffee bar fused with a bookstore makes for one good reason to come to the dreary shops of Seaport Village, offering a lively cross-section of customers, primo java, and well-chosen reading material.

Live-music venues

4th and B 345 B St, downtown Ⓣ619/231-4343. One of the city's top venues for live pop, rock, Latin and other music, with good sightlines if a barebones atmosphere, and a mix of up-and-comers with frenetic energy and old-timers playing out the string.

Belly Up Tavern 143 S Cedros Ave, Solana Beach Ⓣ858/481-9022. Mid-sized hall that plays host nightly to an eclectic range of live music – anything from grizzled faves like Leon Russell to salsa spectaculars and tub-thumping DJs.

Brick by Brick 1130 Buenos Ave, Mission Bay Ⓣ619/675-5483. Aggressively hip lounge that's one of the better-known indie spots around town, attracting alternative, blues, and hard rock acts.

Casbah 2501 Kettner Blvd, downtown Ⓣ619/232-4355. A grungy joint that nevertheless hosts a solid, varying roster of blues, funk, reggae, rock, and indie bands. Local popularity contrasts with cramped environs.

Dizzy's 344 7th Ave, downtown Ⓣ858/270-7467. As the name suggests, this spot is devoted to straight-up jazz and little else – literally, because the place is quite spartan and doesn't serve alcohol, forcing you to focus on the music instead of gossiping over cocktails.

Humphrey's by the Bay 2241 Shelter Island Drive, Point Loma Ⓣ619/220-8497. Mainstream concert venue draws a range of mellow, agreeable pop, blues, jazz, country, folk, and lite-rock acts, and its restaurant is a solid choice for seafood.

Winston's Beach Club 1921 Bacon St, Ocean Beach Ⓣ619/222-6822. A former bowling alley turned semi-dive bar, this local club has rock bands most nights, with occasional reggae and 1960s-style acts as well.

Los Angeles

The rambling metropolis of **LOS ANGELES** sprawls across the thousand square miles of its great desert basin, knitted together by an intricate network of freeways between the Pacific Ocean and snowcapped mountains. Its colorful melange of shopping malls, palm trees, and swimming pools is both surreal and familiar, thanks to the potent celluloid self-image it has spread all over the world.

Although founded by the Spanish in the eighteenth century, only after the completion of the transcontinental railroad, starting in the 1870s, did LA really begin to grow, as a center for good health, clean living, plentiful sunshine, and endless acres of citrus groves. By the mid-twentieth century, the enduring symbol of the city had become the family-sized suburban house, with requisite swimming pool and two-car garage. Although the movie industry, beginning locally in the 1910s, attracted its share of new arrivals, the biggest boom came after World War II with the mushrooming of the aerospace industry. Since then, despite the regular cycles of boom and bust, the city's been driven by finance, media, and real estate.

The first-time visitor may find Los Angeles thrilling and threatening in equal proportions; it's a place that picks you up and sweeps you along whether you like it or not. While it has its fine-art museums, unexpected swaths of parkland, and a few old-fashioned urban plazas, what people really come here for is to experience the fantasy worlds of **Disneyland** and **Hollywood**, as well as the gilded opulence of **Beverly Hills** and **Malibu**. And as you might expect, if you want to experience as much as possible, you'll need a set of wheels.

Arrival, information, and city transportation

All European and many domestic **flights** use LA International Airport – almost always **LAX** – sixteen miles southwest of downtown along Santa Monica Bay (Ⓣ310/646-5252, Ⓦwww.los-angeles-lax.com). Shuttle bus A is for intra-airport connections, while buses B and C serve their respective parking lots around the clock, with parking lot C being the place to board city buses. Minibuses such as SuperShuttle (Ⓣ1-800/BLUE-VAN, Ⓦwww.supershuttle.com) and Prime Time Shuttle (Ⓣ1-800/RED-VANS, Ⓦwww.primetimeshuttle.com), run all over town; fares depend on your destination but are often around $25–40 (plus tip), with a journey time of between thirty and sixty minutes. **Taxis** charge at least $35 to West LA or $40 to Hollywood, $100 to Disneyland, and a flat $46.50 to downtown; a $2.50 surcharge applies for all trips starting from LAX. For more information check out Ⓦwww.taxicabsla.org.

If you're arriving from elsewhere in the US, or from Mexico, you might just land at one of the **other airports** in the LA area – at Burbank, Long Beach, Ontario, or Orange County's John Wayne Airport in Costa Mesa. **MTA buses** (Ⓣ1-800/COMMUTE, Ⓦwww.mta.net) serve them all – phone on arrival and tell them where you are and want to go.

The main **Greyhound** bus terminal, at 1716 E Seventh St (24hr; Ⓣ213/629-8401, Ⓦwww.greyhound.com), is in a seedy section of downtown, but access is restricted to ticket-holders, so it's safe enough inside. If arriving in LA by **train** you'll be greeted with the Mission Revival architecture of Union Station, 800

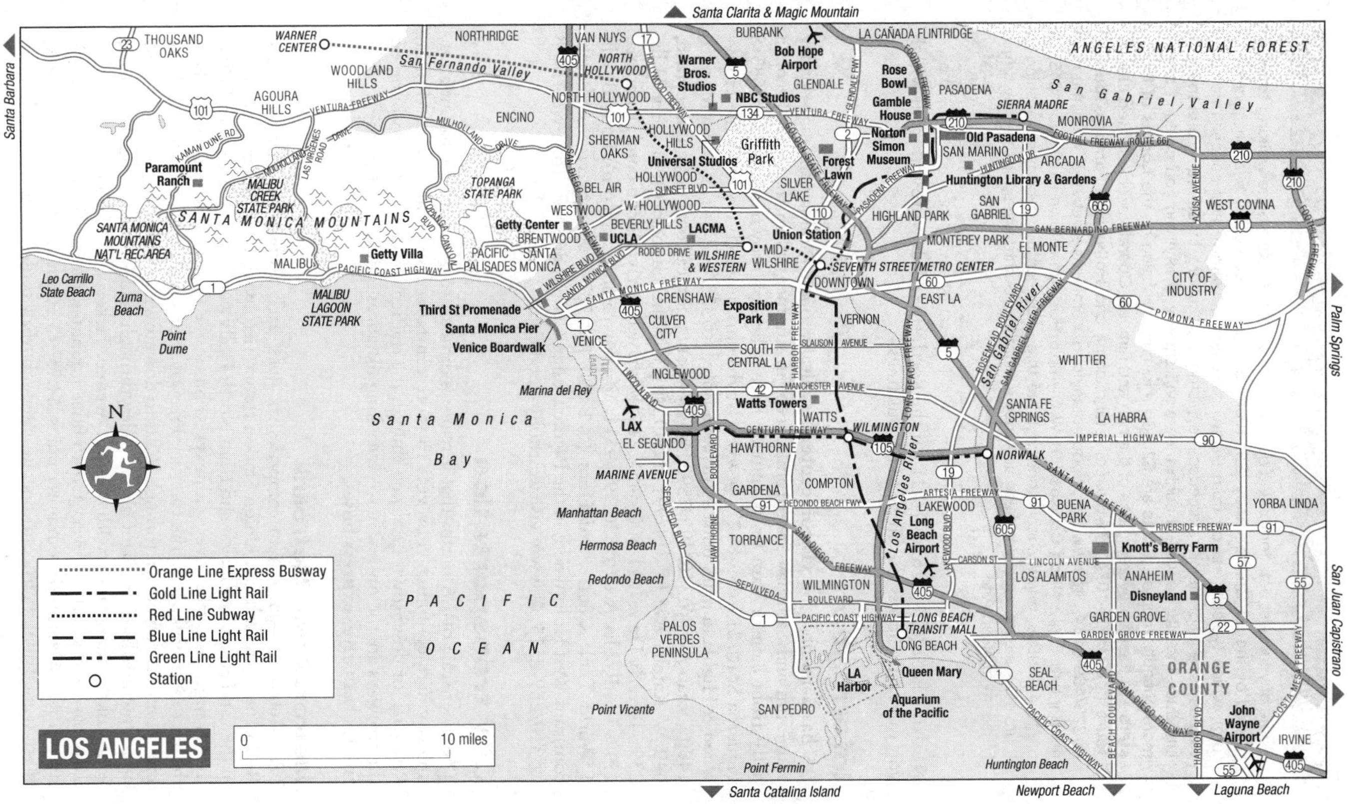
LOS ANGELES
Santa Clarita & Magic Mountain
Santa Barbara
Palm Springs
San Juan Capistrano
Santa Catalina Island
Newport Beach
Laguna Beach
ANGELES NATIONAL FOREST
San Gabriel Valley
San Fernando Valley
SANTA MONICA MOUNTAINS
THOUSAND OAKS
WARNER CENTER
NORTHRIDGE
VAN NUYS
NORTH HOLLYWOOD
WOODLAND HILLS
AGOURA HILLS
ENCINO
SHERMAN OAKS
BURBANK
Bob Hope Airport
LA CAÑADA FLINTRIDGE
Warner Bros. Studios
NBC Studios
GLENDALE
Rose Bowl
Gamble House
PASADENA
SIERRA MADRE
MONROVIA
Norton Simon Museum
Old Pasadena
SAN MARINO
ARCADIA
Huntington Library & Gardens
Forest Lawn
Griffith Park
HOLLYWOOD HILLS
Universal Studios
HOLLYWOOD
SILVER LAKE
HIGHLAND PARK
SAN GABRIEL
WEST COVINA
Paramount Ranch
MALIBU CREEK STATE PARK
TOPANGA STATE PARK
SANTA MONICA MOUNTAINS NAT'L REC.AREA
BEL AIR
WESTWOOD
W. HOLLYWOOD
Getty Center
BEVERLY HILLS
UCLA
LACMA
Union Station
MONTEREY PARK
EL MONTE
BRENTWOOD
RODEO DRIVE
WILSHIRE & WESTERN
MID-WILSHIRE
SEVENTH STREET/METRO CENTER
Getty Villa
PACIFIC PALISADES
SANTA MONICA
MALIBU
Leo Carrillo State Beach
Zuma Beach
Point Dume
MALIBU LAGOON STATE PARK
Third St Promenade
Santa Monica Pier
Venice Boardwalk
DOWNTOWN
EAST LA
CITY OF INDUSTRY
CRENSHAW
Exposition Park
CULVER CITY
VERNON
VENICE
SOUTH CENTRAL LA
WHITTIER
INGLEWOOD
Marina del Rey
Watts Towers
WATTS
SANTA FE SPRINGS
LA HABRA
LAX
EL SEGUNDO
HAWTHORNE
WILMINGTON
NORWALK
MARINE AVENUE
GARDENA
COMPTON
LAKEWOOD
BUENA PARK
YORBA LINDA
Manhattan Beach
Long Beach Airport
Hermosa Beach
TORRANCE
Knott's Berry Farm
Redondo Beach
LOS ALAMITOS
ANAHEIM
Disneyland
GARDEN GROVE
LONG BEACH TRANSIT MALL
LONG BEACH
PALOS VERDES PENINSULA
ORANGE COUNTY
SEAL BEACH
LA Harbor
Queen Mary
Aquarium of the Pacific
Point Vicente
SAN PEDRO
John Wayne Airport
IRVINE
Point Fermin
Huntington Beach
Santa Monica Bay
PACIFIC OCEAN
Los Angeles River
San Gabriel River
VENTURA FREEWAY
FOOTHILL FREEWAY (ROUTE 66)
SAN BERNARDINO FREEWAY
POMONA FREEWAY
SANTA MONICA FREEWAY
SAN DIEGO FREEWAY
CENTURY FREEWAY
SANTA ANA FREEWAY
LONG BEACH FREEWAY
HARBOR FREEWAY
GOLDEN STATE FREEWAY
PASADENA FREEWAY
HOLLYWOOD FREEWAY
GLENDALE FWY
SAN GABRIEL RIVER FREEWAY
ARTESIA FREEWAY
REDONDO BEACH FWY
RIVERSIDE FREEWAY
GARDEN GROVE FREEWAY
COSTA MESA FREEWAY
IMPERIAL HIGHWAY
PACIFIC COAST HIGHWAY
MULHOLLAND DRIVE
LAS VIRGENES ROAD
KANAN DUNE RD
TOPANGA CANYON BLVD
SUNSET BLVD
WILSHIRE BLVD
SANTA MONICA BLVD
LINCOLN BLVD
SLAUSON AVENUE
MANCHESTER AVENUE
ROSEMEAD BOULEVARD
HUNTINGTON DR
AZUSA AVENUE
HAWTHORNE BOULEVARD
SEPULVEDA BLVD
CARSON ST
LINCOLN AVENUE
LAKEWOOD BLVD
WILMINGTON BOULEVARD
BEACH BOULEVARD
HARBOR BLVD
N
Orange Line Express Busway
Gold Line Light Rail
Red Line Subway
Blue Line Light Rail
Green Line Light Rail
Station
0
10 miles

Guided tours

Some of your best bets for touring downtown and other spots are the **walking tours** offered by the **LA Conservancy** (Sat 10am; $10; ⓣ213/623-CITY, ⓦlaconservancy.org), which typically set off from Pershing Square downtown and concentrate on various aspects of the city's architecture, history, and culture. Innumerable **bus tours** introduce the city as well, though they won't show you anything you couldn't see more cheaply yourself. Costs are $20–30 minimum, focusing on the **homes of the stars** – ie the ivy-covered gates of the rich and famous. Operators include **Red Line Tours** (ⓣ323/402-1074, ⓦwww.redlinetours.com), and **Hollywood Fantasy Tours** (ⓣ323/469-8184, ⓦwww.hollywoodfantasytours.com). Alternatively, and much more interestingly, **Neon Cruises** 501 W Olympic Blvd, downtown (June-Nov; $45; ⓣ213/489-9918, ⓦwww.neonmona.org), are three-hour-long, eye-popping evening tours of LA's best remaining neon art, once a month on Saturdays, sponsored by the Museum of Neon Art.

N Alameda St (ⓣ213/624-0171), on the north side of downtown, from which you can easily access the city's MTA bus lines.

Information

LA has a number of **visitor centers**, typically open Monday through Friday 9am–5pm and Saturday 9am–1pm, except in summer, when they may be open daily from 8am or 9am until 6pm or later. The downtown center is at 685 S Figueroa St (ⓣ213/689-8822, ⓦwww.lacvb.com); in Hollywood, at the Hollywood & Highland mall, 6801 Hollywood Blvd (ⓣ323/467-6412); Santa Monica, 1400 Ocean Ave (ⓣ310/393-7593, ⓦwww.santamonica.com); near Disneyland, 640 W Katella Ave (ⓣ714/991-INFO, ⓦwww.anaheimoc.org); Beverly Hills, 239 S Beverly Drive (ⓣ1-800/345-2210, ⓦwww.beverlyhillscvb.com); Pasadena, 171 S Los Robles Ave (ⓣ626/795-9311, ⓦwww.pasadenacal.com); Long Beach, 1 World Trade Center, 3rd Floor (ⓣ1-800/452-7829, ⓦwww.visitlongbeach.com) and West Hollywood, in the Pacific Design Center, 8687 Melrose Ave #M38 (ⓣ310/289-2525, ⓦwww.visitwesthollywood.com).

City transportation

The sheer scale of LA means that it really is difficult to get around without a car, unless you're confining your visit to more centralized spots like Santa Monica, Pasadena, or downtown LA. Even though the traffic is often bumper-to-bumper, the freeways are the only way to cover long distances quickly. Otherwise, try the fastest alternative, **express buses**.

Metrorail and Metrolink

LA's **Metrorail** train system comprises six lines, each distinguished by color: the **Red Line** stretches from Union Station through Hollywood to North Hollywood in the San Fernando Valley – and from North Hollywood on to the western Valley, the **Orange Line** takes over with express buses; the **Green Line** goes from Hawthorne to Norwalk along the Century Freeway (but stops short of LAX); the **Blue Line** connects downtown through Watts to downtown Long Beach; the **Gold Line** links downtown to the San Gabriel Valley through Old Pasadena; and the **Purple Line** links Union Station with Western Avenue. Tickets cost $1.25 single, or $5 for a day pass, and trains run every five to fifteen minutes (more infrequently at night). By contrast, **Metrolink** commuter trains ($4.75–13.50 single; ⓣ1-800/371-LINK, ⓦwww.metrolinktrains.com) operate inter-suburban routes on weekdays, but can be useful if you find yourself at the fringes of the metropolis (for example, Anaheim to LA Union Station is $7.50).

Buses and taxis

Carless Angelenos are still most well served, however, by **buses**, most of which are run by the LA County Metropolitan Transit Authority (MTA or Metro; ⓣ213/626-4455 or 1-800/COMMUTE, ⓦwww.mta.net). Information can also be obtained in person at downtown's Gateway Transit Center, Chavez Avenue at Vignes Street (Mon–Fri 6am–6.30pm), and 5301 Wilshire Blvd, Mid-Wilshire (Mon–Fri 9am–5pm). Buses on the major streets between downtown and the coast run roughly every fifteen minutes between 5am and 2am; other routes, and the **all-night services** along the major streets, are less frequent. At night, be careful not to get stranded alone downtown waiting for a connection.

The standard single **fare** is $1.25; **transfers** cost 30¢ more, but must be made within an hour; **express buses**, and any others using the freeway, are $1.85 up to $2.45 (and usually run 6–8.30am & 4–7pm, every 20–60min). If you're staying a while, you can save some money with a **daily**, **weekly** or **monthly pass**, which cost $5, $17 and $62, respectively. There are also the mini **DASH** buses (ⓣ808-2273 for area codes 213, 310, 323, and 818, ⓦwww.ladottransit.com), with a flat fare of 25¢, and broad coverage throughout downtown and limited routes elsewhere in the city. You'll be hard pressed to find an available **taxi** cruising the streets, so call ahead; among the more reliable companies are the Independent Cab Co (ⓣ1-800/521-8294), Yellow Cab (ⓣ1-800/200-1085), and United Independent Taxi (ⓣ1-800/411-0303). Fares include a base charge of $2.85; add $2.70 per mile, and tack on another $2.50 if you're getting picked up from LAX.

Cycling

Cycling in LA may sound perverse, but in some areas it can be one of the better ways of getting around. There are beachside bike paths between Santa Monica and Redondo Beach, and from Long Beach to Newport Beach, and many equally enjoyable inland routes, notably around Griffith Park and Pasadena. Contact AAA, 2601 S Figueroa St (Mon–Fri 9am–5pm; ⓣ213/741-3686), or the California Department of Transportation, known as CalTrans, 100 S Main St (Mon–Fri 8am–5pm; ⓣ213/897-3656, ⓦwww.dot.ca.gov), for maps and information. The best place to **rent a bike** for the beaches is around the Venice Boardwalk. Prices range from $10 a day for a clunker to $20 a day or more for a mountain bike. Many beachside stores also rent roller skates and rollerblades.

Accommodation

There's a wide range of **places to stay** in LA: Downtown has both upscale and midrange hotels, Hollywood has plenty of cheap motels, West Hollywood is a swanky boutique zone, and the Westside and Malibu are mid- to upper-range territory. If you're not driving, choose your base carefully to avoid lengthy cross-town journeys between these areas, or divide your stay between them. The best **campgrounds** in the LA area are along the Orange County coast, such as Bolsa Chica in Huntington Beach (ⓣ714/846-3460) and the state parks at San Clemente and Crystal Cove (both ⓣ1-800/444-7275), and in the mountains and beaches around Malibu, notably Malibu Creek State Park (ⓣ818/706-8809) and Leo Carrillo State Beach (ⓣ1-818/706-1310). Campgrounds run around $25, though some may cost as much as $45 in the high season.

Hotels, motels, and B&Bs

Hotels and **motels** are listed by neighborhood. If you're arriving on a late flight, or leaving on an early one, hotels near LAX are blandly similar and generally cost around $75–100 a night, but do offer complimentary shuttle service to and from the terminals. Prices increase at many tourist-oriented establishments during peak travel periods, especially those near major attractions like Disneyland and Universal Studios. However, weekday rates at business-oriented hotels, especially during conventions, can be just as expensive, or even more so, than weekend prices.

Downtown and around

Downtown LA Standard 550 S Flower St ⓣ213/892-8080, ⓦwww.standardhotels.com. The downtown branch of LA's uber-trendy chain features sleek, modern furnishings and quirky decor, but is best for its rooftop bar. Although billed as a "business hotel," the party scene is pretty much constant. Avoid the posy, depressing West Hollywood branch. ❼

Hilton Checkers 535 S Grand ⓣ213/624-0000 or 1-800/HILTONS, ⓦwww.hiltoncheckers.com. One of the great LA hotels, with sleek modern appointments in historic 1920s architecture, and nicely furnished rooms, rooftop pool and spa, and sleek Checkers restaurant. Terrific downtown views, too. ❽

Millennium Biltmore 506 S Grand Ave ⓣ213/624-1011 or 1-800/222-8888, ⓦwww.thebiltmore.com. Renaissance Revival architecture from 1923, with a health club modeled on a Roman bathhouse, cherub and angel decor, and a view overlooking Pershing Square. The well-appointed rooms match the stateliness of the design. Downtown LA's best deal for luxury. ❼

Miyako Inn 328 E 1st St ⓣ213/617-2000, ⓦwww.miyakoinn.com. Despite the grim, concrete-box exterior, this mid-priced hotel offers comfortable rooms with fridges, plus on-site gym, spa, massage room, and internet access, and there's a karaoke bar. ❻

Omni 251 S Olive St at Fourth St ⓣ213/617-3300 or 1-800/327-0200, ⓦwww.omnilosangeles.com. Fancy Bunker Hill hotel with plush, elegant rooms, swimming pool and weight room. Adjacent to MOCA and the Music Center. A good deal. ❼

Westin Bonaventure 404 S Figueroa St ⓣ213/624-1000 or 1-800/228-3000, ⓦwww.westin.com. Modernist luxury hotel with five glass towers that resemble cocktail shakers, a six-story atrium with a "lake," and elegant, conic-shaped rooms. A breathtaking exterior elevator ride ascends to a rotating cocktail lounge. ❼

Hollywood Celebrity 1775 Orchid Ave ⓣ323/850-6464 or 1-800/222-7017, ⓦwww.hotelcelebrity.com. Good choice on the affordable boutique scene, with great location in central Hollywood and rooms with charming furnishings and high-speed internet. ❻

Hollywood Roosevelt 7000 Hollywood Blvd ⓣ323/466-7000, ⓦwww.hollywoodroosevelt.com. The first hotel built for the movie greats in 1927, now with a boutique flair. The place reeks of atmosphere, with boutique rooms, cabanas and suites, plus a jacuzzi, fitness room, and swimming pool. ❼

Orchid Suites 1753 Orchid Ave ⓣ323/874-9678 or 1-800/537-3052, ⓦwww.orchidsuites.com. Roomy, if spartan, suites with cable TV, kitchenettes, and heated pool. Very close to the most popular parts of Hollywood – adjacent to the massive Hollywood & Highland mall. ❺

Renaissance Hollywood 1755 N Highland Blvd ⓣ323/856-1200, ⓦwww.renaissancehollywood.com. The hotel centerpiece of the Hollywood & Highland mall complex, with arty flair in the overall design, upscale rooms and suites, and a prime location in the heart of tourist central. ❾

West Hollywood

Chamberlain 1000 Westmount Drive ⓣ310/657-7400, ⓦwww.chamberlainwesthollywood.com. Sumptuous hotel just off the Strip, within easy walking distance of major clubs and attractions. The impressive suites include sunken living rooms, internet access, DVD players, fireplaces, balconies, and refrigerators. ❾

Chateau Marmont 8221 Sunset Blvd ⓣ323/626-1010, ⓦwww.chateaumarmont.com. Exclusive Norman Revival hotel resembling a dark castle or fortress that's hosted all manner of celebrities. Largely suites and bungalows, up to $3000. Cheapest rooms are around $380.

Grafton 8462 Sunset Blvd ⓣ323/654-6470, ⓦwww.graftononsunset.com. Mid-level boutique hotel with bright and trendy furnishings, CD and DVD players, plus a pool, fitness center, and complimentary shuttle to nearby malls and businesses. ❽

Sunset Marquis 1200 N Alta Loma Rd, West Hollywood ⓣ310/657-1333 or 1-800/858-9758, ⓦwww.sunsetmarquishotel.com. A lush hangout for musicians, with private cabanas around two pools, plus a hot tub, sauna, and weight room. There are very pricey villas set in gardens; most rooms are smart suites with kitchens, balconies, and patios. ⑨

West LA and Beverly Hills

Avalon 9400 W Olympic Blvd ⓣ310/277-5221, ⓦwww.avalonbeverlyhills.com. Located in south Beverly Hills, this hipster hotel boasts retro-stylish rooms with mid-modern furnishings, along with in-room CD players, fax machines, and balconies. The chic poolside bar is where Entourage types pose and cut actual Hollywood deals. ⑨

Bel Air 701 Stone Canyon Rd ⓣ310/472-1211 or 1-800/648-1097, ⓦwww.hotelbelair.com. The nicest hotel in LA bar none – and the only business in Bel Air – in an overgrown canyon above Beverly Hills. If you can't afford the rooms, which can reach thousands of dollars a night, go for a beautiful brunch by Swan Lake. ⑨

Beverly Hills Hotel 9641 Sunset Blvd ⓣ310/276-2251, ⓦwww.beverlyhillshotel.com. The classic Hollywood resort, with a bold pink-and-green color scheme and Mission-style design, surrounded by its own exotic gardens. Rooms feature marbled bathrooms, hot tubs, and other such luxuries, and the famed Polo Lounge restaurant is also on site. ⑨

Maison 140 140 S Lasky Dr ⓣ310/281-4000, ⓦwww.maison140.com. High-profile entry decorated in dark-tinged pan-Asian style, boasting rooms with CD and DVD players, internet, plus salon, bar, fitness room, and complimentary breakfast. ⑧

Santa Monica and Malibu

Ambrose 1255 20th St, Santa Monica ⓣ310/315-1555, ⓦwww.ambrosehotel.com. Excellent recent arrival in inland Santa Monica that beats the coastal spots for value and luxury. Craftsman-styled décor and boutique rooms have internet access and include continental breakfast. ⑧

Bayside 2001 Ocean Ave at Bay St, Santa Monica ⓣ310/396-6000, ⓦwww.baysidehotel.com. Just a block from the beach and Main Street. Bland exterior, but generally comfortable rooms; higher-priced units offer ocean views, fridges, internet access, and kitchenettes. ⑥

Cal Mar 220 California St, Santa Monica ⓣ310/395-5555, ⓦwww.calmarhotel.com. Good for its central location (two blocks from the beach, one from the Promenade). Garden suites have CD/DVD players and dining rooms, kitchens, and balconies, and there's a heated pool, fitness room, and airport shuttle. ⑦

Casa Malibu Inn 22752 PCH ⓣ310/456-2219. Located opposite Carbon Beach and featuring superb, well-appointed rooms – facing a courtyard garden or right on the beach – with great modern design and some in-room fireplaces, jacuzzis, and balconies. ⑥

Channel Road Inn 219 W Channel Rd, Pacific Palisades ⓣ310/459-1920, ⓦwww.channelroadinn.com. Romantic getaway nestled in lower Santa Monica Canyon, with ocean views, hot tub, and free bike rental. Enjoy complimentary grapes and champagne in the sumptuous rooms, each priced according to its view. rooms ⑧, suites ⑨

Ritz-Carlton Marina del Rey 4375 Admiralty Way ⓣ310/823-1700, ⓦwww.ritzcarlton.com. The only good reason to stay in this nautical district is this excellent harborside property, chock full of all the luxurious amenities you'd expect, including spa, pool, and whirlpool, plus a prime location right on the water. ⑨

Shutters on the Beach 1 Pico Blvd at Appian Way, Santa Monica ⓣ310/458-0030 or 1-800/334-9000, ⓦwww.shuttersonthebeach.com. The seafront home to the stars, a white-shuttered luxury resort south of the pier. Amenities include hot tubs (with shuttered screens), pool, spa, sundeck, ground-floor shopping, and ocean views. ⑨

The LA suburbs

Beach House at Hermosa 1300 Strand, Hermosa Beach ⓣ310/374-3001, ⓦwww.Beach-House.com. The height of South Bay luxury, offering two-room suites with fireplaces, wet bars, balconies, hot tubs, stereos and fridges, with many rooms overlooking the sea. ⑨

Disneyland Hotel 1150 W Cerritos Ave, Anaheim ⓣ714/956-6400, ⓦwww.disneyland.disney.go.com. Cookie-cutter rooms without much charm, but still an irresistible stop for many. The Disneyland monorail does stop outside (theme park admission is separate). Ultra-basic rooms begin at $235, simple one-bedroom suites at $500.

Graciela Burbank 322 N Pass Ave ⓣ818/842-8887, ⓦwww.thegraciela.com. Modern boutique rooms with fridges, DVD and CD players, and high-speed internet. Also with on-site pool, gym, sauna, and rooftop sundeck with jacuzzi. ⑧

Ritz-Carlton Huntington 1401 S Knoll Ave, Pasadena ⓣ626/568-3900, ⓦwww.ritzcarlton.com. Landmark 1906 hotel, luxuriously designed and tucked away in residential Pasadena. Palatial grounds, ponds, and courtyards, three restaurants, expansive rear lawn, and terrific San Gabriel Valley views. ⑨

Safari Inn 1911 W Olive St, Burbank ⓣ818/845-8586, ⓦwww.safariburbank

.com. A classic mid-century motel, renovated but still loaded with Pop-architecture touches. Features a pool, fitness room, Burbank airport shuttle and in-room fridges, plus continental breakfast. ❻

Stovall's Inn 1110 W Katella Ave, Anaheim ⓣ714/778-1880, ⓦwww.stovallsinn.com. Tasteful, clean chain accommodation near Disneyland, with fitness center, pools, and two spas, and in-room fridges and microwaves. ❹

Westin Long Beach 333 E Ocean Blvd, Long Beach ⓣ562/436-3000, ⓦwww.westin.com. A solid bet for bayside luxury at affordable prices, right by the convention center, with a spa, fitness center, and pool. ❽

Hostels

Hostels are dotted all over the city, many of them also offering cut-rate single and double rooms. Some hostels also offer tours of theme parks, shopping malls and stars' homes, while others organize events, such as volleyball and pizza parties.

Banana Bungalow 2775 Cahuenga Blvd W, in Cahuenga Pass ⓣ323/851-1129 or 1-800/446-7835, ⓦwww.bananabungalow.com. Popular hostel near Universal City and US-101, with free airport shuttles, internet, tours to Venice Beach and theme parks, and outdoor pool and free parking. Dorms $18–27, private doubles $55–89.

HI-Anaheim/Fullerton 1700 N Harbor Blvd, Fullerton ⓣ714/738-3721, ⓦwww.hihostels.com. Convenient and comfortable, five miles north of Disneyland. The excellent facilities include a grass volleyball court, golf driving range, and picnic area. There are only twenty dorm beds, so reservations are a must. $25.

HI-LA/Santa Monica 1436 2nd St, Santa Monica ⓣ310/393-9913, ⓦwww.hilosangeles.org. A few blocks from the beach and pier, this was LA's Town Hall from 1887 to 1889, now renovated with pleasant inner courtyard, internet café, movie room, and 260 beds. $32–35. Reservations essential in summer; open 24hr.

HI-LA/South Bay 3601 S Gaffey St #613 ⓣ310/831-8109, ⓦwww.hihostels.com. Sixty beds in old US Army barracks, with a panoramic view of the Pacific Ocean. Ideal for seeing San Pedro, Palos Verdes, and the whole LA Harbor area. Dorms $25, private rooms $47.

Hollywood International 6820 Hollywood Blvd, Hollywood ⓣ323/463-0797 or 1-800/750-6561, ⓦwww.hollywoodhostels.com. Centrally located, with game room, gymnasium, patio garden, kitchen, and laundry. Offers tours of Hollywood, theme parks, Las Vegas, and Tijuana. Dorms $17, private rooms $40.

Orbit Hotel 7950 Melrose Ave, West Hollywood ⓣ323/655-1510 or 1-877/ORBIT-US, ⓦwww.orbithotel.com. Retro-1960s hotel and hostel with sleek Day-Glo furnishings and ultra-hip modern decor, offering complimentary breakfast, movie screening room, patio, café, private baths in all rooms, and shuttle tours. Dorms $30, private rooms $89–119.

Venice Beach Cotel 25 Windward Ave, Venice ⓣ310/399-7649, ⓦwww.venicebeachcotel.com. In a historic beachside building, this colonnaded hostel (or "cotel") has dorm rooms for $22–26, and private rooms for $52–70.

The City

If LA has a heart, it's **downtown**, which offers a taste of almost everything you'll find elsewhere around the city, from upscale art to freewheeling commercial zones. West from downtown, **Hollywood** has streets imbued with movie myths and legends – and adjoining **West LA** is home to the city's newest money, shown off in Beverly Hills and along the Sunset Strip. **Santa Monica** and **Venice** further to the west are the quintessential seafront LA of palm trees, white sands, and laid-back living, while twenty miles northwest, glamorous **Malibu** is home to the movieland elite.

Suburban **Orange County**, to the southeast, holds little of interest apart from **Disneyland**, a few museums, and a handful of libertine beach towns. On the far side of the northern hills lie the **San Gabriel and San Fernando valleys**, or simply “the Valley,” tract homes and strip malls enlivened by occasional sights of interest, many of them in the genteel burg of **Pasadena**.

Downtown LA

Downtown LA embraces the city’s every social, economic, and ethnic division, and the whole area can easily be seen in a day on foot, considering the walkable scale of the place. LA’s original settlement at **The Plaza** is the obvious first stop, before crossing into the corporate zone of **Bunker Hill**, and continuing through the free-spirited chaos along **Broadway**.

The Plaza

El Pueblo de Los Angeles Historic Park, 845 N Alameda St (daily 9am-5pm; free; Ⓣ213/628-2381, Ⓦwww.ci.la.ca.us/ELP), comprises thirty buildings, a third of them open to the public, and is an essential stop on any history trek through LA. The square known as **the Plaza** was roughly the site of the city’s original 1781

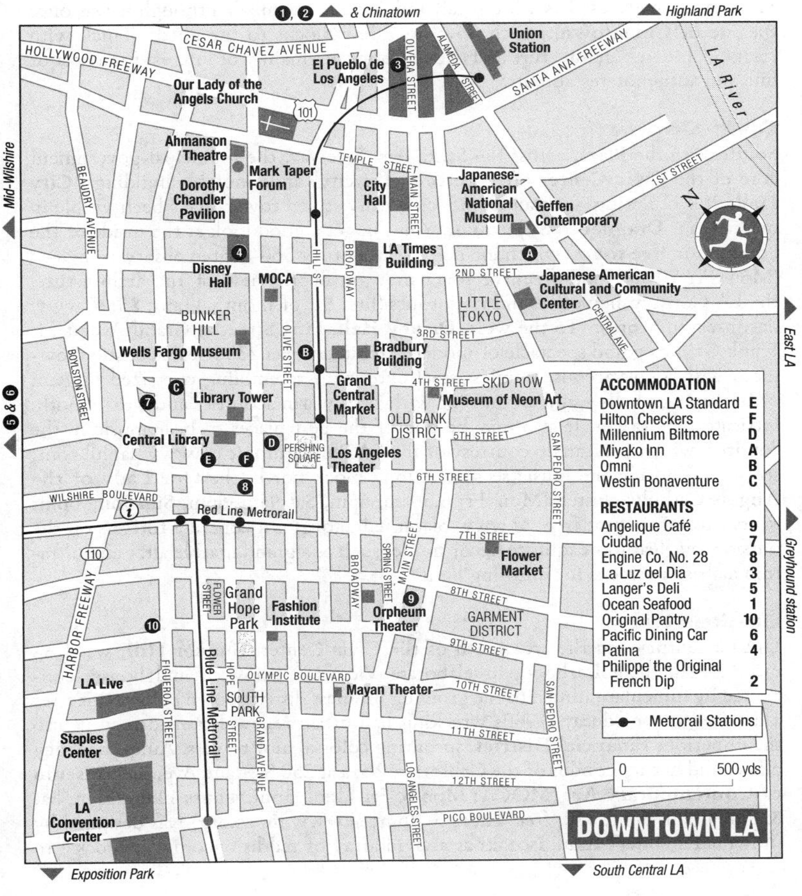

townsite, and the plaza church **La Placita**, 535 N Main St (daily 6.30am–8pm; Ⓦ www.laplacita.org), is the city's oldest, a small adobe structure with a gabled roof, though from 1861 to 1923 it was remodeled or reconstructed four times. If you'd like to take part in one of the church **masses** (occasionally with Mariachi bands), they occur three or four times daily, with twelve Eucharist services on Sunday. **Olvera Street**, which runs north from the plaza (daily 10am–7pm; free; Ⓦ www.olvera-street.com), contrived in part as a pseudo-Mexican village market, offers a cheery collection of food and craft stalls and the historic **Avila Adobe** (Wed–Sun 10am–3pm; free), technically the city's oldest building, though it's been completely rebuilt in the last thirty years. Other worthwhile sights include the **Sepulveda House** (Mon–Fri 9am–4pm; free), an 1887 Eastlake Victorian structure that has rooms highlighting different periods in Mexican-American history, and the **Garnier Building**, now the **Chinese American Museum**, 425 N Los Angeles St (Wed–Sat 10am–3pm; $5; Ⓦ www.camla.org). Inside, local Chinese history, society, and culture is detailed, including revealing letters, photos, and documents, as well as a smattering of contemporary art and the re-creation of a Chinese herb shop c.1900.

Across Alameda Street from the Plaza, the magnificent Mission Revival **Union Station** is chiefly used as a Metrorail and Amtrak terminal, although it was once the site of **Chinatown**, which now sits a few blocks to the north. Thick with ersatz "Chinese" architecture and trinket shops, it's mainly of interest for a host of fine and authentic restaurants.

Civic Center

South from the Plaza, across the Santa Ana Freeway, the municipal-government core of the **Civic Center** offers three of the city's most notable buildings. **City Hall**, 200 N Spring St, is an iconic, classically styled tower that's been visible in media from **Dragnet** to **Superman**. You can get a good look at the inside of the building on free **tours**, which include its 28th-story 360-degree observation deck (Mon–Fri 10am–4pm; free), or for a more in-depth view of the architecture, the LA Conservancy offers monthly tours (first Sat of month 11am; $5; Ⓦ www.laconservancy.org). To the west, **Disney Hall**, First Street at Grand Avenue, is Frank Gehry's grand spectacle of modern architecture, a 2300-seat acoustic showpiece with a curvaceous, stainless-steel exterior – resembling oversized origami or broken eggshells – and an interior with rich, warm acoustics and a mammoth, intricate pipe organ. It also may be one of the best places to hear music in the country, which you can do courtesy of the LA Philharmonic (Ⓦ www.laphil.com; see p.989) during the music season. A long block north, the **Our Lady of the Angels** Catholic church (Mon–Fri 6.30am–6pm, Sat 9am–6pm, Sun 7am–6pm; tours Mon–Fri 1pm; free; Ⓦ www.olacathedral.org) is a concrete fortress on the outside, but features exquisite decor inside, such as a grand marble altar and ultra-thin alabaster screens for diffusing light.

Bunker Hill

Until a century ago the area south of the Civic Center, **Bunker Hill**, was LA's most elegant neighborhood, its elaborate Victorian mansions and houses connected by funicular railroad to the growing business district down below. But after a half-century of decay, 1960s wrecking-ball urban renewal transformed it into the imperious **Financial District**, sprouting colossal new towers. Amid the fancy offices and luxury condos of the California Plaza at 250 S Grand Ave, the **Museum of Contemporary Art** (MOCA; Mon & Fri 11am–5pm, Thurs 11am–8pm, Sat & Sun 11am–6pm; $10, free Thurs 5–8pm; Ⓦ www.moca.org) was designed by showman architect Arata Isozaki as a vivid array of reddish geometric blocks. In addition to work by Franz Kline, Mark Rothko, Robert Rauschenberg, and Claes Oldenburg, and some eye-opening temporary exhibits, it features an impressive selection of **Southern California artists**, ranging from Lari Pittman's spooky, sexualized silhouettes to Robert Williams' feverishly violent and satiric comic-book-styled paintings.

Catercorner to MOCA, the diverting **Wells Fargo Museum**, 333 S Grand Ave (Mon–Fri 9am–5pm; free; Ⓦ www.wellsfargohistory.com). displays old mining equipment, antiques, photographs, a two-pound chunk of gold, a re-created assay office from the nineteenth century, and a simulated stagecoach journey from St Louis to San Francisco. A few blocks southwest rise the sparkling glass tubes of the **Westin Bonaventure Hotel**, 404 S Figueroa St (see "Accommodation," p.964), whose lobby is an Escher-style labyrinth of spiraling ramps and balconies, worth negotiating for a ride in the glass elevators that rise along the building's facade, giving splendid views over much of the downtown. A short distance away, the **Richard J. Riordan Central Library**, 630 W 5th St (Mon–Thurs 10am–8pm, Fri & Sat 10am–6pm, Sun 1–5pm; Ⓦ www.lapl.org/central), dates back to 1926, when its striking, angular lines set the tone for many LA buildings, most obviously City Hall.

Little Tokyo and around

East of Bunker Hill, **Little Tokyo** is an appealing collection of historic sites, restaurants, and galleries, centered around the **Yagura Tower**, First Street at Central Avenue, a small canopy sitting atop slender wooden beams, built in the style of a traditional Japanese fire tower used to spot forest fires. Nearby, the comprehensive **Japanese American National Museum**, 369 E First St (Tues–Sun 11am–5pm, Thurs closes at 8pm; $8; Ⓦ www.janm.org), is housed in a former Buddhist temple constructed in 1925. The museum offers everything from origami to traditional furniture and folk craftwork to the story of the internment of Japanese-Americans during World War II. Just north along a pedestrian plaza, **The Geffen Contemporary**, 152 N Central Ave, is a former police garage now used for the edgier temporary shows of the Museum of Contemporary Art (same hours as above), for which a ticket also entitles you to same-day entry; however, call ahead (Ⓣ 213/621-1745) to make sure the space is actually open when you arrive, since it can be closed for weeks at a time for exhibit installation. Finally, a few blocks south, the latest home for the ever-itinerant **Museum of Neon Art** is at 136 W 4th St (Thurs–Sat noon–7pm, Sun noon–5pm; $7; Ⓦ www.neonmona.org), and is worth a stop to check out some enchanting neon signs, kinetic displays, and an array of oddball artworks that may glow, move, sparkle and otherwise behave in ways foreign to most conventional galleries.

Broadway and the Old Bank District

Although it's hard to picture now, **Broadway** was once LA's most fashionable shopping and entertainment district. Today it's largely taken over by the hustle and bustle of Hispanic clothing and trinket stores, all to a soundtrack of blaring salsa music. You can sample a vivid taste of the area at the broadly ethnic **Grand Central Market**, between Third and Fourth streets (daily 9am–6pm; Ⓦ www.grandcentralsquare.com), where you'll find everything from apples and oranges to pickled pig's feet and sheep's brains. Right alongside, the whimsical terracotta facade of the 1918 **Million Dollar Theater** mixes buffalo heads with bald eagles, and was seen in the film **Blade Runner**, as was the neighboring 1893 **Bradbury Building**, no. 304 (lobby open Mon–Sat 9am–5pm; free), highlighted by a magnificent sunlit atrium surrounded by stylish wrought-iron balconies and open-cage elevators. While the moviehouse has since closed, the extravagant arches and marble columns of the **Los Angeles Theater**, 615 S Broadway, and the **Orpheum**'s neo–French Renaissance grand staircases and chandeliers, at no. 630, are still on view during the annual "Last Remaining Seats" film festival in June (details at Ⓦ www.laconservancy.org).

If you venture a few blocks west of Broadway, you'll come to the most recent focus of LA's urban-revival efforts, the **Old Bank District**, as developers have named it, based around Spring Street from Seventh to Third streets. Although there are no official sights, these stately, hundred-year-old Beaux Arts buildings are now being converted into upscale housing, fancy shops, chic eateries, and the like.

Around downtown

The LA sprawl begins as soon as you leave downtown, diverse environs cut through by freeways and boulevards, with large distances separating the points of interest. As such, it makes little sense to see them consecutively.

Exposition Park

South of downtown, across Exposition Boulevard from the fortress-like USC campus, **Exposition Park** is, given the bleak nature of the surrounding area, one of the better parks in LA, incorporating lush gardens and several modest museums. The **California Science Center**, off Figueroa Street at 700 State Drive (daily 10am–5pm; free; Ⓦ www.californiasciencecenter.org), contains enough enjoyable working models and thousands of gadgets to keep kids absorbed, with an **IMAX Theater** ($8, children $4.75) and an **Air and Space Gallery** marked by a sleek jet stuck to its facade and showcasing satellites, telescopes, airplanes, and rockets. To the south, the **California African American Museum**, 600 State Drive (Tues–Sat 10am–5pm, Sun 11am–5pm; free; Ⓦ www.caamuseum.org), has stimulating exhibits on the history and culture of America's black communities.

The **Natural History Museum of Los Angeles County**, 900 Exposition Blvd (Mon–Fri 9.30am–5pm, Sat & Sun 10am–5pm; $9; Ⓦ www.nhm.org), with its echoey domes and travertine columns, has a tremendous stock of dinosaur skeletons that includes the skull of a Tyrannosaurus rex, and the frame of a Diatryma – a huge flightless bird. Other fascinating displays include Mayan pyramid murals, the reconstructed contents of a Mexican tomb, several roomfuls of crystals, and a tempting display of three hundred pounds of gold, safely off-limits to prying fingers. The last major sights in the park are the **LA Coliseum**, familiar as the site of the 1932 and 1984 Olympics and for its towering headless statues, and the **Rose Garden** (mid-March to Dec daily 9am–dusk; free; Ⓣ 213/765-5397), whose 16,000 bushes are at their most fragrant in April and May, when the bulk of the visitors come for a stroll and a sniff.

The Watts Towers

Now more Hispanic than black, **WATTS** provides only one (very) compelling reason to visit, and only during the day: the Gaudí-esque **Watts Towers**, sometimes called the Rodia Towers, at 1765 E 107th St, a half-mile north off the 105 freeway on Wilmington Avenue. Constructed from iron, stainless steel, old bedframes, and cement, and adorned with bottle fragments and some 70,000 crushed seashells, these striking pieces of folk art are shrouded in mystery. Their maker, Italian immigrant **Simon Rodia**, had no artistic background or training, but labored over the towers' construction from 1921 to 1954, refusing offers of help and unable to explain their meaning or why he was building them. Unfortunately, the 30-minute **tours** (Thurs & Fri 11am–3pm, Sat 10.30am–3pm, Sun 12.30–3pm; $7; ⓣ213/847-4646) don't let you get too close, but can be interesting for the full story of the site. One especially good time to come is during the late-September weekend that hosts the Saturday Day of the Drums Festival and Sunday Watts Towers Jazz Festival. Both take place at the adjoining **Cultural Crescent Amphitheater**; call the Watts Tower Arts Center, 1727 E 107th St (ⓣ213/847-4646, ⓦwww.wattstowers.org), for details and program listings.

Hollywood

Hollywood encapsulates the LA dream of glamour, money, and overnight success, with millions of tourists arriving on pilgrimages every year. Although many of the big film companies long ago relocated to blander digs in Burbank, and you're still more likely to see a homeless person than a movie star, recent attempts at renovation have added a bit of the old glitz to a downtrodden scene. But despite the spate of new malls and hotels and renovated movie palaces, the district will doubtless never attain the mythical status it continues to hold in the minds of its many star-struck visitors.

Central Hollywood

The corner of Hollywood Boulevard and Highland Avenue is the hub of **Central Hollywood**, and there the **Hollywood and Highland** mall (ⓦwww.hollywoodandhighland.com) hosts a major hotel, chain boutiques, and chic restaurants, plus colossal pseudo-film-set architecture and the **Kodak Theater** where the Oscars are held annually. Otherwise, this towering beacon of commerce is no better than your average suburban shopping mall.

A better place to really begin exploring Hollywood Boulevard is in the shadow of the iconic "record stack" of the **Capitol Records Tower**, at the junction of **Hollywood and Vine** – the legendary location for budding stars to be "spotted" by big-shot directors and whisked off to fame and fortune. Few aspiring stars actually loiter in this gritty environment, but many visitors do come to trace the **Walk of Fame**, which officially begins here with a series of gold-inset stars honoring famous and forgotten names of radio, TV and movies – among them Marlon Brando (1717 Vine St), Michael Jackson (6927 Hollywood Blvd), Elvis Presley (6777 Hollywood Blvd), and Ronald Reagan (6374 Hollywood Blvd). For the full rundown, visit ⓦwww.hollywoodchamber.net. Nearby, at 6233 Hollywood Blvd, the 1929 **Pantages Theater** (ⓣ323/468-1770) has a bland facade but one of the city's greatest interiors, a melange of Baroque styling and ornate Art Deco friezes, while next door, the **Frolic Room** is an old-time watering hole that has appeared in countless movies, notable for its neon sign and interior mural of the stars drawn by cartoonist Al Hirschfeld.

Several blocks west, the **Egyptian Theater**, at no. 6708, was built in a modest attempt to re-create the Temple of Thebes, and the very first Hollywood premiere (**Robin Hood**) took place here in 1922. Now restored in glorious fashion, movie-lovers should make a special trip here to view an art, foreign, or indie film, or at least the documentary chronicling the rise of Hollywood (Sat & Sun 11.40am; $7; ⓣ323/466-FILM, ⓦwww.egyptiantheatre.com); you can also take a basic, 60-minute tour of the facility (Tues–Sun 10.30am–4pm; $7; by reservation only at ⓣ323/461-2020 ext 121). Also worth a look, on the west end of the mall, is the **Chinese Theatre**, 6925 Hollywood Blvd (ⓣ323/464-8111, ⓦwww.manntheatres.com/chinese), an odd version of a classical Chinese temple, replete with dubious Asian motifs and upturned dragontail flanks. For $5 you can take in a **tour** of the theatre, and afterward, on the street outside, see the famous forecourt (free access)

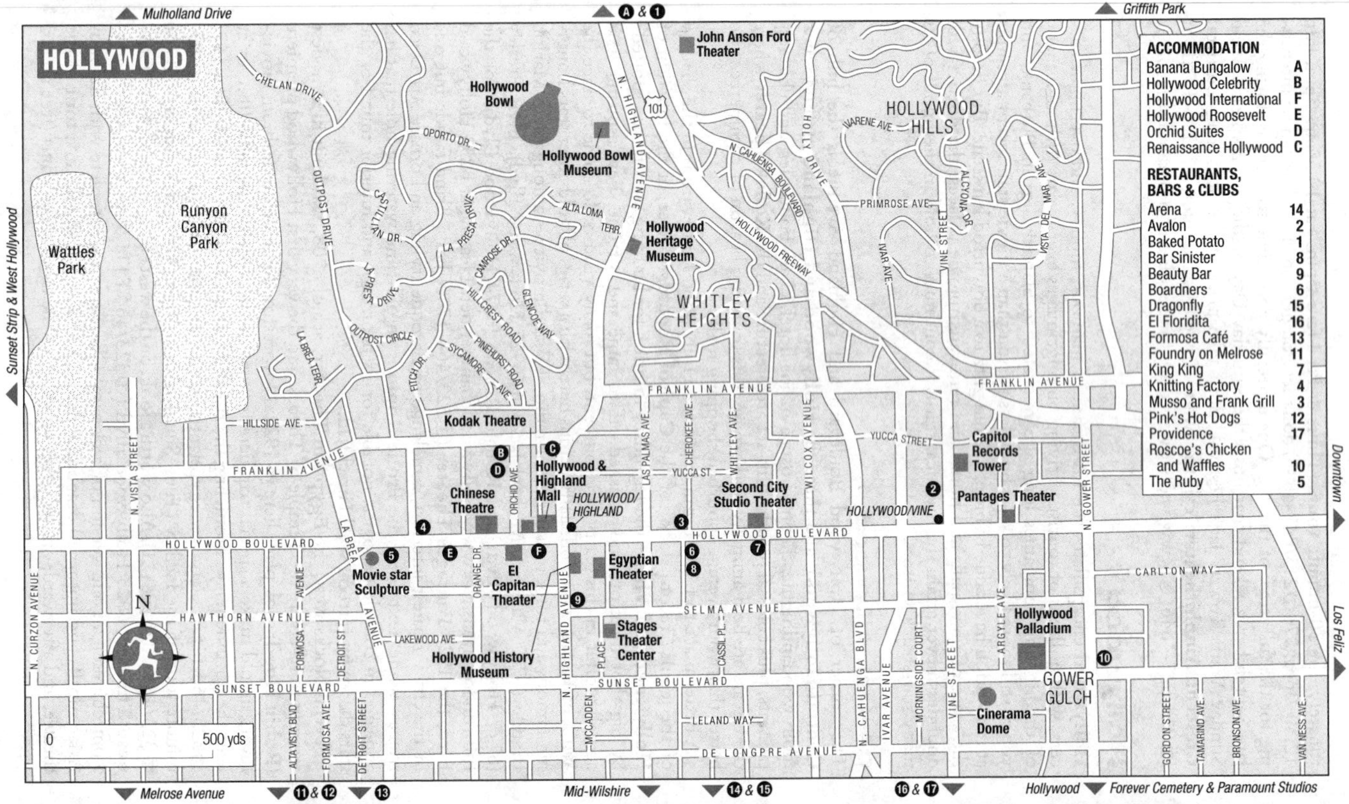

HOLLYWOOD
ACCOMMODATION
Banana Bungalow A
Hollywood Celebrity B
Hollywood International F
Hollywood Roosevelt E
Orchid Suites D
Renaissance Hollywood C
RESTAURANTS, BARS & CLUBS
Arena 14
Avalon 2
Baked Potato 1
Bar Sinister 8
Beauty Bar 9
Boardners 6
Dragonfly 15
El Floridita 16
Formosa Café 13
Foundry on Melrose 11
King King 7
Knitting Factory 4
Musso and Frank Grill 3
Pink's Hot Dogs 12
Providence 17
Roscoe's Chicken and Waffles 10
The Ruby 5
Mulholland Drive
A & 1
Griffith Park
Sunset Strip & West Hollywood
Downtown
Los Feliz
Melrose Avenue
11 & 12
13
Mid-Wilshire
14 & 15
16 & 17
Hollywood
Forever Cemetery & Paramount Studios
Wattles Park
Runyon Canyon Park
Hollywood Bowl
Hollywood Bowl Museum
John Anson Ford Theater
HOLLYWOOD HILLS
Hollywood Heritage Museum
WHITLEY HEIGHTS
Kodak Theatre
Chinese Theatre
Hollywood & Highland Mall
HOLLYWOOD/HIGHLAND
Second City Studio Theater
HOLLYWOOD/VINE
Capitol Records Tower
Pantages Theater
Movie star Sculpture
El Capitan Theater
Egyptian Theater
Hollywood History Museum
Stages Theater Center
Hollywood Palladium
GOWER GULCH
Cinerama Dome
CHELAN DRIVE
OPORTO DR.
OUTPOST DRIVE
CASTILLIAN DR.
LA PRESA DRIVE
ALTA LOMA TERR.
CAMROSE DR.
HILLCREST ROAD
GLENCOE WAY
PINEHURST ROAD
SYCAMORE AVE.
FITCH DR.
OUTPOST CIRCLE
LA BREA TERR.
HILLSIDE AVE.
N. HIGHLAND AVENUE
N. CAHUENGA BOULEVARD
HOLLYWOOD FREEWAY
HOLLY DRIVE
WARENE AVE.
PRIMROSE AVE.
IVAR AVE.
VINE STREET
ALCYONA DR.
VISTA DEL MAR AVE.
FRANKLIN AVENUE
YUCCA STREET
YUCCA ST
LAS PALMAS AVE
CHEROKEE AVE.
WHITLEY AVE
WILCOX AVENUE
ORCHID AVE.
HOLLYWOOD BOULEVARD
LA BREA AVENUE
ORANGE DR.
CARLTON WAY
SELMA AVENUE
HAWTHORN AVENUE
LAKEWOOD AVE.
PLACE
CASSIL PL.
N. CAHUENGA BLVD
IVAR AVENUE
MORNINGSIDE COURT
ARGYLE AVE
N. GOWER STREET
SUNSET BOULEVARD
LELAND WAY
DE LONGPRE AVENUE
MCCADDEN
N. CURZON AVENUE
N. VISTA STREET
FORMOSA AVENUE
DETROIT ST
ALTA VISTA BLVD
FORMOSA AVE.
DETROIT STREET
GORDON STREET
TAMARIND AVE.
BRONSON AVE.
VAN NESS AVE.
N
0
500 yds

▲ Walk of Fame

adorned with the hand- and footprints of Hollywood celebs from the silent era to the present, or linger with hundreds of other sightseers amid the celebrity impersonators — Elvis, Marilyn and Darth Vader among them — low-rent magicians, and assorted oddballs vying for your amusement and money.

Across the street, the similarly impressive **El Capitan Theater**, no. 6834 (see p.992), is a colorful 1926 movie palace, with Baroque and Moorish details and a wild South Seas–themed interior of sculpted angels and garlands, while a few doors down, at no. 7000, the **Hollywood Roosevelt** was movieland's first luxury hotel (see p.964). Just south of the Hollywood and Highland crossing, the **Hollywood Museum**, 1660 Highland Blvd (Wed–Sun 10am–5pm; $15; Ⓦ www.thehollywoodmuseum.com), has four floors of fashion, sets, make-up, and other artifacts taken from a broad swath of movie history, though it has less a feel of a museum than a hodgepodge of castoffs in an overstuffed attic.

Further south, near Santa Monica Boulevard and Gower Street, **Hollywood Forever Cemetery** (daily dawn–dusk; free; Ⓦ www.hollywoodforever.com) is the district's most famous graveyard, and features all manner of buried stars such as Rudolph Valentino and Douglas Fairbanks Sr, as well as more unexpected grave markers, such as Johnny Ramone playing one last guitar riff. South of the cemetery, **Paramount Studios**, 5555 Melrose Ave (2hr tour, Mon–Fri 10am & 2pm; $35; by reservation at ⓣ323/956-1777), is famous for its grand **gate**, though the original studio entrance – which Gloria Swanson rode through in **Sunset Boulevard** – is now inaccessible. The tour isn't quite up to the standard of other studio tours, but if you want to poke around empty soundstages and a mildly interesting backlot, it may be worth it.

Griffith Park

The greenery and mountain slopes that make up vast **Griffith Park** northeast of Hollywood (daily 6am–dusk; ⓣ323/913-4688) offer lush fern and azalea gardens, splendid views, and many miles of fine trails – though if you come at the wrong time, you might just find the park on fire. Hillside conflagrations regularly menace the park during the summer, when it may remain closed for weeks to visitors. One notable sight here, the **LA Zoo**, 5333 Zoo Drive (daily 10am–5pm; $12; ⓦwww.lazoo.org), pales in comparison to its San Diego counterpart (see p.954), though the landmark Art Deco **Griffith Observatory**, 2800 E Observatory Rd (Tues–Fri noon–10pm, Sat & Sun 10am–10pm; free; ⓦwww.griffithobservatory.org), is well worth a visit, highlighted by the twelve-inch Zeiss refracting telescope, solar telescopes for viewing sunspots and solar storms, and modern exhibits covering the history of astronomy and human observation. The observatory has been used as a backdrop in innumerable Hollywood films, most famously **Rebel Without a Cause**, and the surrounding acres are marked by paths that lead into desolate but unspoiled terrain with great views over the LA basin and out to sea (provided the smog isn't too thick). Also meriting a stop is the **Museum of the American West**, near the junction of the Ventura and Golden State freeways at 4700 Western Heritage Way (Tues–Sun 10am–5pm, Thurs closes 8pm; $9; ⓦwww.autrynationalcenter.org), whose comprehensive collection of artifacts includes sections on native peoples, European exploration, nineteenth-century pioneers, the Wild West, Asian immigrants and, of course, Hollywood's versions of all of the above.

The Hollywood Hills

The canyons and slopes of the **Hollywood Hills**, which run from Hollywood itself into Benedict Canyon above Beverly Hills, are best seen from the winding concourse of **Mulholland Drive**, threading the crest of the mountains and accessible by any north-south connector such as Laurel Canyon or Caheunga Boulevard. With its striking panorama after dark of the illuminated city-grid, stretching nearly to the horizon, the road is a prime axis for the LA good life, with mansions so commonplace that only the half-dozen fully blown castles really stand out. Guided tours (see p.962) can point out which is which in these hills, but for the most part you can't get close to them anyway. For a more up-close look at landmark architecture, take in a concert at the **Hollywood Bowl**, 2301 N Highland Ave (ⓣ323/850-2000, ⓦwww.hollywoodbowl.org), the massive concrete bandshell whose summer music offerings tend toward the crowd-pleasing variety – it's as good a spot as any to hear the festive roar of the **1812 Overture**.

Throughout Hollywood, you can see the **Hollywood Sign**, erected as a property advertisement in 1923 (when it spelled "Hollywoodland," until 1949) and illuminated with four thousand light bulbs. Nowadays, infrared cameras and radar-activated zoom lenses have been installed to catch graffiti writers. Curious tourists who can't resist a close look are liable for a steep fine.

West LA

LA's Westside begins immediately beyond Hollywood in **West LA**, roughly bordered by the foothills of the Hollywood Hills to the north and the Santa Monica Freeway (I-10) to the south. West LA is the place where the city's nouveau riche flaunt their fortunes most conspicuously, from the trendy confines of West Hollywood and shadowy wealth of Bel Air to the high-priced shopping strips of Beverly Hills.

The Museum Mile

On the commercial axis of Wilshire Boulevard, the **Miracle Mile**, between La Brea and Fairfax avenues, was the premier property development of the 1930s, and recent development has created a "**Museum Mile**" in their place, also known as **Museum Row**. The first is sited at the **La Brea Tar Pits**, where for thousands of years, animals who tried to drink from the thin layer of water covering this rank pool of tar became stuck fast and preserved for posterity. It's now surrounded by life-sized replicas of such victims as mastodons and saber-toothed tigers, some of them reconstructed next door at the impressive **George C. Page Museum**, 5801 Wilshire Blvd (daily 9.30am–5pm, Sat & Sun opens 10am; $7; Ⓦwww.tarpits.org). Across the street, the **Craft and Folk Art Museum**, 5814 Wilshire Blvd (Tues, Wed & Fri 11am–5pm, Thurs 11am–7pm, Sat & Sun noon–6pm; $5; Ⓦwww.cafam.org), has a small selection of handmade objects – rugs, pottery, clothing, and more. The limited gallery space also hosts a few rotating exhibitions, including vintage circus posters, ceramic folk art, and highly detailed Japanese paper arts-and-crafts. At the intersection with Fairfax Avenue, the **Petersen Automotive Museum**, 6060 Wilshire Blvd (Tues–Sun 10am–6pm; $10; Ⓦwww.petersen.org), pays homage to motorized vehicles of all kinds on three floors, with rotating exhibits such as the Golden Age of customizing, Hollywood prop cars, and "million-dollar" vehicles.

Los Angeles County Museum of Art

On the west side of the La Brea Tar Pits, the enormous **LA County Museum of Art (LACMA)**, 5905 Wilshire Blvd (Mon, Tues & Thurs noon–8pm, Fri noon–9pm, Sat & Sun 11am–8pm; $12; Ⓦwww.lacma.org), is one of the least-known of the important museums in the US, dwarfed in national prestige by the Getty Center even though its collection is considerably broader and, in fact, one of the largest west of the Mississippi. The **Art of the Americas Building** is home to the museum's somewhat spotty collection of **American art**; highlights include the work of John Singleton Copley (the regal **Portrait of a Lady**), Winslow Homer (the dusty realism of the **Cotton Pickers**), Albert Pinkham Ryder (the murky, alluring landscape of **The River**) and Thomas Eakins (the writhing, nude **Wrestlers**). There's also an impressive assortment of American and Western **furniture**, including bureaus from the Federal period and rough-hewn Craftsman designs, and a striking selection of Central and South American art, the highlight of which is the **Fearing Collection**, consisting of funeral masks and sculpted guardian figures from the early civilizations of pre-Columbian Mexico.

The adjacent **Ahmanson Building** has a broad array of exquisite and priceless works of **Asian art** from China and Korea to India and Tibet, as well as an assortment of American **costumes** and **textiles**, occasionally with a nod to Hollywood. However, its central attractions are undoubtedly the **European art rooms**, which begin with a good overview of Greek and Roman art and continue into the medieval era with religious sculptures and various shards of ecclesiastical architecture such as Romanesque capitals, Gothic reliefs, and so on. The Renaissance and Mannerist eras are represented by compelling works such as Veronese's *Two Allegories of Navigation*, great Mannerist figures filling the frame from an imposing low angle; El Greco's *The Apostle Saint Andrew*, an uncommonly reserved portrait; and Titian's *Portrait of Giacomo Dolfin*, a carefully tinted study by the great Venetian colorist. Aficionados of Rodin will also delight in a room full of his small, vigorous sculptures, and elsewhere the likes of Rembrandt, Degas, Renoir and others make their appearances.

On its eastern end LACMA offers the **Pavilion for Japanese Art**, elegant with its sloping ramp and walls styled after shoji screens, and at its western end **LACMA West**, featuring kids' art and temporary shows, but it's in the center building – the **Broad Museum for Contemporary Art** – that LACMA has really come into its own. This new, four-level creation houses some of the best modern art in town, much of it by LA stalwarts such as John Baldessari, Mike Kelley and Chris Burden. The real eye-openers, though, are by Cindy Sherman, whose self-portrait photographs stacked four and five high in one huge gallery are striking to say the least; Jeff Koons, whose various pop-culture-kitsch pieces are centered around a huge blue-metallic "balloon animal"; and Richard Serra, whose giant, rusted, curving steel walls have the entire ground floor all to themselves.

West Hollywood

North along Fairfax Avenue from the Museum Mile, **West Hollywood** is home to Los Angeles's prominent – and affluent – gay community, seen most prominently along the chic blocks from Doheny Drive to La Cienega Boulevard. Just south, **Melrose Avenue** is LA's trendiest shopping street and one of the unmistakable symbols of Southern California, where neon and flashy signs abound among a fluorescent rash of designer and secondhand boutiques, antique shops, and high-end diners. **La Brea Avenue** runs perpendicular to the east side of the Melrose district, offering more space, fewer tourists, and chic clothiers, upscale restaurants and even trendier galleries.

On the north edge of West Hollywood, on either side of La Cienega Boulevard, is the two-mile-odd mix of restaurants, hotels, billboards, and nightclubs on Sunset Boulevard known as the **Sunset Strip**, one of LA's best areas for nightlife. The scene hit its stride in the 1960s around the landmark **Whisky-a-Go-Go** club, no. 8901, which featured seminal psychedelic rock bands such as The Doors, Love, and Buffalo Springfield, and later in the 1970s around the **Sunset Hyatt** hotel, no. 8401, the infamous "Riot House" where Led Zeppelin raced motorcycles in the hallways and drugged-out rock stars committed unspeakable acts of debauchery. The music venues (see p.988 for more choices) are still worth a visit, whether you want to rock, headbang or just dance.

Beverly Hills and around

Beverly Hills is one of the world's wealthiest residential areas, patrolled by more cops per capita than anywhere else in the US. Glorified by the elite shops of **Rodeo Drive**, squeaky-clean streets, and ostentatious displays of wealth, the city is undoubtedly the height of LA pretension. Some of the bigger names include Barney's, 9570 Wilshire Blvd, and, all on Rodeo itself, Chanel, no. 400; Giorgio Armani, no. 436; Gucci, no. 347; Christian Dior, no. 309; and Prada, no. 343. As yet, none of the stores charges for admission, though some do require an invitation. Still, there are a number of decent and unassuming spots for visitors interested in things other than commodities. The **Paley Center for Media**, 465 N Beverly Drive (Wed–Sun noon–5pm; $10, kids $5; Ⓦ www.mtr.org) is one such place, vividly chronicling eighty years of our media-saturated age, and best for its voluminous library of shows, where you can take in everything from **I Love Lucy** to **Seinfeld**, and many more obscure offerings as well. For an overview of Beverly Hills' shopping and the area's art and architecture, take a trip on the **Beverly Hills Trolley** (40min ride; 11am-4pm: Sat & Sun year-round, also July–Aug & Dec Tues–Sun; $5; ⓣ310/285-2442), departing hourly from the corner of Rodeo and Dayton Way.

In the northern hills and canyons, increasingly curvaceous roads head into the hills and become more upmarket, converging on the pink-plaster **Beverly Hills Hotel**, on Sunset and Rodeo (see p.965), constructed in 1912 to attract wealthy settlers to what was then a town of just five hundred people. Will Rogers, W.C. Fields, and John Barrymore were but a few of the celebrities known to frequent the bar here, and the hotel's social cachet still makes its *Polo Lounge* a prime spot for movie execs to power-lunch. Elsewhere, a number of well-concealed gardens and parks offer a respite from the shopping frenzy below. One such place, the wooded **Virginia Robinson Gardens**, 1008 Elden Way (tours Tues–Fri 10am & 1pm; $10; by appointment only at ⓣ310/276-5367), spreads across six acres of flora, with more than a thousand varieties, including some impressive Australian King Palm trees. To the east, the grounds of the biggest house in Beverly Hills, **Greystone Mansion**, 905 Loma Vista Drive, are now maintained as a public **park** by the city (daily 10am–5pm; free). The fifty-thousand-square-foot manor was once the property of oil titan Edward Doheny, whose story was loosely chronicled in the film **There Will Be Blood**, which also shot some interiors here. You can't go inside, but you can admire the mansion's limestone facade and intricate chimneys, then stroll through the sixteen-acre park, with its koi-filled ponds and expansive views of the LA sprawl.

Westwood and UCLA

West of Beverly Hills and the corporate box-towers of Century City, and north of Wilshire Boulevard, **Westwood** is the home of the **University of California at Los Angeles (UCLA)**, and is known to many as "Westwood Village." Once LA's prime movie-going district, Westwood has lost some of its eminence due to a lack of parking, but remains the most densely packed movie-theater district in town, and its 1931 **Westwood Village Theater**, crowned with a grand neon spire at 961 Broxton Ave, is still used for Hollywood premieres and "sneak previews" to gauge audience reactions.

The university itself has a number of good gardens, buildings and museums worth exploring. The highlights include the central **quadrangle**, a greenspace bordered by UCLA's most graceful buildings, including **Royce Hall**, modeled on Milan's Church of St Ambrosio, with high bell-towers, rib vaulting, and grand archways; and the **Powell Library**, featuring a spellbinding interior with lovely Romanesque arches, columns, and stairwell. The **Fowler Museum of Cultural History**, Bruin Walk at Westwood Plaza (Wed–Sun noon–5pm, Thurs closes 8pm; free; ⓦwww.fowler.ucla.edu), offers an immense range of multicultural art – including ceramics, religious icons, paintings, and musical instruments – and its highlights include a worldwide selection of native masks, more than ten thousand textile pieces from different cultures, an extensive collection of African and Polynesian art, and various folk designs. The **Franklin Murphy Sculpture Garden**, in the northeast corner of campus, is LA's best outdoor display of modern sculpture, featuring pieces by Henry Moore, Barbara Hepworth, Henri Matisse, Jacques Lipchitz and Isamu Noguchi; while the **Hannah Carter Japanese Garden**, 10619 Bellagio Rd (Tues, Wed & Fri 10am–3pm; free; by appointment only at ⓣ310/794-0320; ⓦwww.japanesegarden.ucla.edu), is an idyllic spot featuring magnolias and Japanese maples, and traditional structures and river rocks brought directly from Japan. Finally, art lovers shouldn't miss a trip to the **UCLA Hammer Museum**, 10899 Wilshire Blvd (Tues–Sat 11am–7pm, Thurs 11am–9pm, Sun 11am–5pm; $7, kids free, Thurs free to all; Ⓦwww.hammer.ucla.edu), where the minor Rembrandts and Rubens may be less than stunning, but there are some impressive early-American works from Gilbert Stuart, Thomas Eakins, and John Singer Sargent, and insightful, sometimes risk-taking contemporary and avant-garde exhibits – quite a leap from what the conservative Hammer had in mind when he built the art enclave.

The Getty Center

Towering over the surrounding area, the **Getty Center**, near the Sepulveda Pass north of Wilshire Boulevard (Tues–Thurs & Sun 10am–6pm, Fri & Sat 10am–9pm; free, parking $8; Ⓦwww.getty.edu), is Richard Meier's towering modernist temple to high art, clad in acres of travertine, its various buildings devoted to conservation, acquisition, and other philanthropic tasks, and its surrounding gardens arranged with geometric precision. You can get here by MTA bus #761, on its route from UCLA, stopping on Sepulveda Boulevard, near the lower parking lot.

Obliged by law to spend part of its multi-billion-dollar endowment every year, the Getty can outbid anyone to get what it wants, which is usually anything except contemporary art – a real deficiency in the museum's collections. Still, the quality of the **exhibits** is extraordinary, especially in the rooms devoted to decorative arts, where you can see a formidable array of ornate French furniture from the reign of Louis XIV, with clocks, chandeliers, tapestries, and gilt-edged commodes filling several overwhelmingly opulent chambers. The painting collection features all the major names from the thirteenth century on, including Van Gogh's **Irises** and a trio of evocative Rembrandts: *Daniel and Cyrus before the Idol Bel*, in which the Persian king tries foolishly to feed the bronze statue he worships; *An Old Man in Military Costume*, the exhausted, uncertain face of an old soldier; and *Saint Bartholomew*, showing the martyred saint as a quiet, thoughtful Dutchman – the knife that will soon kill him visible in the corner of the frame. Elsewhere in the museum, photography is well represented by Man Ray, Moholy-Nagy and other notables, and there's also a rich assortment of classical, Renaissance, and Baroque sculpture – highlighted by Bernini's **Boy with a Dragon**, depicting a plump, possibly angelic toddler bending back the jaw of a dragon with surprising ease.

Venice, Santa Monica, and Malibu

Set along an unbroken twenty-mile stretch of beaches, the cozy, quirky communities that line **Santa Monica Bay** feature some of the best vistas LA has to offer, with little of the smog or searing heat that can make the rest of the metropolis unpleasant. The entire area is well served by public transportation, near enough to the airport, and a wide choice of accommodation makes it a good base for seeing the rest of the city.

Venice

Venice was laid out in 1905 by developer Abbot Kinney as a romantic replica of the northern Italian city, complete with a twenty-mile network of canals. Over the decades it then became an amusement-park zone, grungy oil-drilling site, ground zero for hippies, drugs, and crime, and finally today's arty district drawing a mix of hipsters, yuppies and real-estate speculators – as well as a smattering of thugs and homeless people. The town's main artery, **Windward Avenue**, runs from the sands into what was the Grand Circle of the canal system. An original Neoclassical **arcade**, around the intersection with Pacific Avenue, is now home to diners and low-rent hotels. Nearby, the few remaining **canals** display renovated white bridges and pedestrian-friendly footpaths (best accessed northbound on Dell Avenue from Washington Boulevard).

Nowhere else does LA parade itself quite so openly as along the wide pathway of **Venice Boardwalk**, packed year-round at weekends and every day in summer with musicians, street performers, trinket vendors and many others; avoid the place after dark, though, when shades of the old Venice appear. South of Windward is **Muscle Beach**, a legendary outdoor weightlifting center where serious-looking dudes (and a few women) pump serious iron, and budding basketballers hold court on the concrete. If you've time, other Venetian sights worth a peek are Jonathan Borofsky's grotesque and looming sculpture **Ballerina Clown**, at Main Street and Rose Avenue; the chic restaurants and boutiques lining **Abbot Kinney Boulevard**; and, south of the Boardwalk, the latest in sleek modern architecture along **Ocean Front Walk**.

Santa Monica

North of Venice, **Santa Monica** is perched on palm-tree-shaded bluffs above the blue Pacific. Once a wild beachfront playground, it's now a self-consciously healthy and very liberal community with a large expatriate British and Irish contingent.

Santa Monica reaches nearly three miles inland, but most spots of interest are within a few blocks of the beach, notably **Palisades Park**, the pleasant, cypress-tree-lined strip along the top of the bluffs which makes for striking views of the surf below. Two blocks east of Ocean Avenue, the **Third Street Promenade**, a pedestrianized stretch with street vendors, buskers, and itinerant evangelists, is the closest LA comes to having a dynamic urban energy, and by far the best place to come for alfresco dining, beer-drinking, and people-watching.

The real focus of Santa Monica is down below, on the **beach**, which is better for sunbathing than swimming, and on the refurbished **Santa Monica pier**, boasting a well-restored 1922 wooden **carousel** (late March–Sept Mon–Thurs 11am–5pm, Fri–Sun 11am–7pm; Oct–early March Thurs–Mon only; 50¢ per ride) and crowds of tourists, teenagers and anyone else seeking a mild carnival thrill by the water. Although the familiar rides of **Pacific Park** (hours vary, often summer daily 11am–11pm, Sat & Sun closes 12.30am; $17, kids $9; ⓦwww.pacpark.com) may catch your eye, save your money for the **Santa Monica Pier Aquarium** (Tues–Fri 2–6pm, Sat & Sun 12.30–6pm; $5, kids 12 and under free; ⓦwww.healthebay.org/smpa), below the pier at 1600 Ocean Front Walk, where you can get your fingers wet touching sea anemones and starfish.

Getty Villa

If you really want to indulge in some serious (ancient) art, head five miles north along the beautiful, curving **Pacific Coast Highway (PCH)**, to the opulent **Getty Villa**, 17985 PCH (Thurs–Mon 10am–5pm; free; by reservation only at ⓣ310/440-7300, ⓦwww.getty.edu), modeled after a Roman country house buried by Mount Vesuvius in 79 AD, and built around its own fetching gardens. Inside, the museum is based around a two-story peristyle and courtyard, where a quaint pool is surrounded by more austere black statues. Highlights include the **Getty Kouros**, a rigidly posed figure of a boy that conservators openly state could be a forgery, a **Cult Statue of Aphrodite** from the Golden Age of Greece (fifth century BC), a voluptuous limestone figure with flowing robe, and a Hellenistic

Statue of a Victorious Youth, wearing only an olive wreath, that was carefully restored after having been recovered from the sea floor. Athenian vases are also well represented, many of them the red-ground variety, as are ancient kylikes, or drinking vessels, and ceremonial amphorae, or vases, given as prizes in athletic contests. Not to be missed is a wondrous Roman skyphos, a fragile-looking blue vase decorated with white cameos of Bacchus and his friends, properly preparing for a bacchanalia.

Malibu and the Santa Monica Mountains

Twenty miles north of Santa Monica at the top of the bay, **Malibu** is synonymous with luxurious celebrity isolation, along with hillside wildfires, which routinely smoke those same celebrities out of their gilded confines. **Surfrider Beach** here was the surfing capital of the world in the 1950s and early 1960s, and is still a big attraction (the surf is best in late summer; check the surfing report at Ⓦ www.surfrider.org). Just beyond is **Malibu Lagoon State Park** (daily 8am–dusk), a nature reserve and bird refuge, and nearby is the **Adamson House**, 23200 PCH (grounds 8am–sunset, house Wed–Sat 11am–3pm; $5; Ⓦ www.adamsonhouse.org), a stunning, historic Spanish colonial–style home featuring opulent decor and colorful tilework.

Most Malibu homes are tucked away in the narrow canyons on the fringes of town. You'd do better to explore the huge **Santa Monica Mountains National Recreation Area** (Ⓦ www.lamountains.com), north of town, which is wilderness in many places, and you can still spot a variety of deer, coyotes, and even the odd mountain lion. If you'd like to find out more about this marvelous protected area, the Santa Monica Mountains **visitor center**, in neighboring Thousand Oaks, 401 W Hillcrest Drive (daily 9am–5pm; Ⓣ 805/370-2301, Ⓦ www.nps.gov/samo), has maps and information. Other good spots here include the 4000-acre **Malibu Creek State Park**, on Las Virgenes Road near Mulholland Drive, where 20th Century-Fox filmed many Tarzan pictures, as well as the TV show **M★A★S★H**, and the park includes a large lake, waterfalls, and nearly fifteen miles of hiking trails. Further west, the **Paramount Ranch**, 2813 Cornell Rd, is another studio backlot with a phony rail crossing and cemetery, and Western movie set used in countless productions.

Five miles up the coast from Malibu Pier, **Zuma Beach** is the largest and most crowded of the Los Angeles County beaches, but adjacent **Point Dume State Beach**, below the imposing promontory of Point Dume, is a lot more relaxed, and the rocks at its southern tip, **Pirate's Cove**, are a good place to view seals and migrating gray whales in winter. At the northwestern edge of LA County, **Leo Carrillo** ("ca-REE-oh") **State Beach Park**, 35000 PCH, has a mile-long sandy beach divided by Sequit Point, a bluff with underwater caves and a tunnel you can pass through at low tide, and is also one of LA's best campgrounds (see p.963).

The South Bay and LA Harbor

South from LA along PCH is an eight-mile coastal strip of quiet South Bay beach towns: **Manhattan Beach**, **Hermosa Beach**, and **Redondo Beach**. Each has a beckoning strip of white sand – much more open to the public than those around Malibu – and Manhattan and Hermosa are especially well equipped for surfing and beach sports; a good time to come is during the **Fiesta Hermosa** (Ⓦ www.fiestahermosa.com), a three-day event held twice over Memorial Day and Labor Day. They're also well connected by the regular bus lines to downtown LA. To the south are **Long Beach** – site of the LA Harbor – and the natural gem of **Catalina Island**.

Long Beach

The massive port of **Long Beach** – part of the biggest such complex in the US – is largely off the tourist trail, though it does offer an enjoyable stretch of restored architecture and antique stores around **Pine Avenue** (linked by the Blue Line light rail to downtown LA; see p.962). Some tourists do come to see the **Queen Mary** (daily 10am–6pm; $25 self-guided tours; Ⓦwww.queenmary.com). The Cunard flagship from the 1930s until the 1960s, the boat is now a luxury hotel chock full of Art Deco amenities, décor and fixtures, and the guided tours ($3–8 extra) are oriented around supposed ghosts that haunt the ship. There's also an on-site **Scorpion submarine** ($11), if you're in the mood to poke around a creaky Russian diesel sub. Across the bay along Shoreline Drive, the **Aquarium of the Pacific** (daily 9am–6pm; $21, children $12; Ⓦwww.aquariumofpacific.org) is a terrific exploration of aquatic flora and fauna from geographic and climatic zones around the world, more than ten thousand species in all, from sea lions and otters, to tide-pool creatures, to exotic leopard sharks and giant Japanese spider crabs. Further east, the **Long Beach Museum of Art**, 2300 E Ocean Blvd (Tues–Sun 11am–5pm; $7; Ⓦwww.lbma.org), is the home of LA-based modern artworks and tasteful displays of early-20th-century California furniture and sculpture.

Orange County

Throughout the US, **Orange County** is synonymous with anodyne, white suburbia – most famously as the site of fun, sanitized **Disneyland** – but in recent years it's begun to change, with many new Hispanic arrivals and much more cultural (and culinary) diversity. Still, most tourists come just for the theme parks and for the easy-going, upscale beach towns of the **Orange County Coast**.

Disneyland

The pop-culture colossus of **Disneyland**, in Anaheim at 1313 Harbor Blvd (summer daily 8am–midnight; rest of year Mon–Fri 10am–6pm, Sat 9am–midnight, Sun 9am–10pm; $69, kids $59, parking $11; Ⓦwww.disneyland.com), is one of America's most iconic sights, as well as one of its most expensive – most of the park's hotels are ridiculously overpriced (see p.965) and there's little quality cuisine in the area. The park is 45 minutes by **car** from downtown LA on the Santa Ana Freeway. Arrive early, as traffic and ride lines quickly become nightmarish, especially in the summer.

Disneyland's best **rides** are in **Adventureland**: the Indiana Jones Adventure, an interactive archeological dig and 1930s-style newsreel show leading up to a giddy journey along 2500ft of skull-encrusted corridors; the Pirates of the Caribbean, a boat trip through underground caverns full of singing rogues; and the Haunted Mansion, a riotous "doom buggy" tour in the company of the house spooks. By contrast, **Frontierland** has mainly lower-end Wild West–themed carnival attractions, **Fantasyland** low-tech fairy-tale rides, notably the treacly It's a Small World; and **Toontown**, a cartoonish zone aimed at the kindergarten set. It's more worthwhile to zip right through to **Tomorrowland**, Disney's vision of the future, where the Space Mountain roller coaster plunges through the pitch-blackness of outer space, the Star Tours ride simulates a journey into the world of George Lucas, and Innoventions offers a fun opportunity to look at, and play with, the latest special effects.

Technically a separate park, the **California Adventure** is a lot less worthwhile. Aside from its slightly more exciting roller coasters and better food, the Adventure is really just another "land" to visit on your Disney trek, albeit a much bigger and more expensive one: you'll have to shell out another $25 for a one-day pass that covers both this and the main park.

Knott's Berry Farm

If you're a bit fazed by the excesses of Disneyland, you might prefer the more down-to-earth **Knott's Berry Farm**, four miles northwest, off the Santa Ana Freeway at 8039 Beach Blvd (hours vary, often summer Sun–Thurs 9am–11pm, Fri & Sat 9am–midnight; rest of year Mon–Fri 10am–6pm, Sat 10am–10pm, Sun 10am–7pm; $52, kids $23; Ⓦwww.knotts.com), whose roller coasters are far more exciting than anything at its rival. The best rides are the GhostRider roller coaster, with its old-fashioned wooden design and "haunted mine train" theme; Jaguar, a high-flyer that spins you around the park concourse; the Boomerang, a forward-and-back coaster that spends a lot of time upside-down; Supreme Scream, a delightfully terrifying freefall drop; Xcelerator, a coaster with a stomach-churning catapult mechanism; and the Perilous Plunge, a hellish drop at a 75-degree angle that's far more thrilling than any old log-flume ride. Knott's also has its own adjacent water park, **Soak City USA** (June–Sept only, hours vary but generally daily 10am–5pm or 6pm; $30, $20 for children or adult entry after 3pm), offering dozens of drenching rides of various heights and speeds.

Orange County Coast

Stretching from the edge of the LA Harbor to the border of San Diego County 35 miles south, the **Orange County Coast** is chic suburbia with a shoreline, the ambiance easygoing, libertarian, and affluent. As the names of the main towns suggest – **Huntington Beach**, **Newport Beach**, and **Laguna Beach** – most of the good reasons to come here involve sea and sand, though a handful of museums and festivals can also make for an interesting trip. Check out the **International Surfing Museum**, 411 Olive Ave, Huntington Beach (Mon–Fri noon–5pm; Sat & Sun 11am–6pm; $3; Ⓦwww.surfingmuseum.org), loaded with famous legends of the waves; Newport Beach's excellent **Orange County Museum of Art**, 850 San Clemente Drive (Wed–Sun 11am–5pm, Thurs closes 8pm; $10; Ⓦwww.ocma.net), focusing on modern California art and presenting regular lectures, events, and art and architecture tours; and Laguna Beach's **Pageant of the Masters** (July & Aug daily shows begin at 8.30pm; $20–100; Ⓣ1-800/487-3378, Ⓦwww.foapom.com), a strangely compelling spectacle in which participants dress up as characters from famous paintings. To the far south, **San Juan Capistrano** merits a stop as the site of the best-kept of all the Californian **missions**, Ortega Highway and Camino Capistrano (daily 8.30am–5pm; $9; Ⓦwww.missionsjc.com). It's also noted for its **swallows**, popularly thought to return here from their winter migration every March 19.

The San Gabriel and San Fernando valleys

The northern limit of LA is defined by two long stretches – the **San Gabriel and San Fernando valleys** – lying over the hills from the central basin, starting close to one another a few miles north of downtown, spanning outwardly in opposite directions – east to the deserts, west to the Central Coast – and featuring a few worthwhile points of interest at considerable distance from each other.

The San Gabriel Valley

Ten miles northeast of downtown LA, the **San Gabriel Valley**'s main appeal is the genteel community of **Pasadena**, best known for its **Rose Parade** in January and **Rose Bowl** stadium west of town. Also distinctive is the historic shopping precinct of **Old Pasadena** along Colorado Boulevard, now fashionable for its restaurants and boutiques (and accessible on the Gold Line light rail).

Pasadena's other best offerings are the splendid collection of the **Norton Simon Museum**, 411 W Colorado Blvd (Wed–Mon noon–6pm, Fri closes 9pm; $8, students free; Ⓦwww.nortonsimon.org), one of LA's best and most little-known art institutions, with a prime selection of Old Masters like Rubens and Rembrandt and modern works by Klee and Picasso, and the **Gamble House**, 4 Westmoreland Place (hour-long tours Thurs–Sun noon–3pm; $10; Ⓦwww.gamblehouse.usc.edu), a famed Craftsman mansion with Arts and Crafts decor and Japanese-inspired design elements – one of many fine works in the vicinity built by Craftsman masters Charles and Henry Greene. Maps and booklets on Pasadena, available at the visitors' bureau (see p.962), detail worthwhile self-guided tours of the city's excellent architecture, historical sites, and museums. The engaging **Pacific Asia Museum**, a mile east at 46 N Los Robles Ave (Wed–Sun 10am–6pm; $7; Ⓦwww.pacificasiamuseum.org), is modeled after a Chinese imperial palace, showcasing historical treasures from Korea, China, and Japan, including decorative jade and porcelain, various swords and spears, and a large cache of paintings and drawings.

South of Pasadena, in dull, upper-crust **San Marino**, the **Huntington Museum and Library**, off Huntington Drive at 1151 Oxford Rd (Mon & Wed–Fri noon–4.30pm, Sat & Sun 10.30am–4.30pm; $15; Ⓦwww.huntington.org), is worth seeking out, as it contains many historic documents and rare books, such as a Gutenberg Bible and the Ellesmere Chaucer – the latter an illuminated manuscript of **The Canterbury Tales** dating from around 1410. Paintings include Gainsborough's **Blue Boy** and Reynolds' **Mrs Siddons as the Tragic Muse**, and the whole complex is set off by acres of beautiful themed **gardens**.

The San Fernando Valley and Magic Mountain

The **San Fernando Valley**, spreading west, is a vast, uninspiring sprawl of tract homes, mini-malls, and fast-food diners, but merits a trip to see **Forest Lawn Cemetery**, in Glendale at 1712 S Glendale Ave (daily 9am–5pm; free; Ⓦwww.forestlawn.org), a fascinating, often kitschy, display of death, Hollywood style. Those buried here include Errol Flynn, Walt Disney, Clara Bow, Nat King Cole, Chico Marx, Clark Gable, and Jean Harlow, among other notables, many under grave markers so garish and tacky they must be seen to be believed.

North of the San Fernando Valley, the three-hundred-acre theme park of **Magic Mountain**, Magic Mountain Parkway at I-5 (hours vary, often summer daily 10am–10pm; rest of year Sat & Sun only 10am–8pm; $60, kids $30, $15 parking; Ⓦwww.sixflags.com), holds the region's wildest roller coasters, with a new fright-ride unleashed nearly every summer.

Burbank and the studios

Miles from Hollywood proper, the nitty-gritty business of actually making films goes on over the hills in otherwise boring **BURBANK**. The studio tours include a peek inside **NBC**, 3000 W Alameda Blvd (box office open Mon–Fri 9am–4pm; $8; reserve at Ⓣ818/840-3537), and a fun trek into the soundstages and studio lots of **Warner Brothers**, 3400 Warner Blvd (Mon–Fri 8.30am–4.30pm; $45; Ⓦwww.wbstudiotour.com), but Disney's fortress-like compound, at 500 S Buena Vista St, is strictly off-limits.

The largest of the backlots belongs to **Universal Studios**, whose lengthy tours (hours vary, often summer daily 9am–8pm or 9pm; rest of year 10am–6pm; $67; Ⓦwww.universalstudioshollywood.com) are more like a trip around an amusement park, with high-tech thrill rides and "evening spectaculars" based on current movies. The shows are without exception cheesy, but for fans of explosions and pratfalls, they're an absolute must.

Eating

Eating in LA covers every extreme, whatever you want to eat and however much you want to spend. Try to take at least a few meals in the higher-end restaurants, many of which serve superb California Cuisine in consciously cultivated surroundings. At the cheaper end of the scale, the options are almost endless, and include terrific burger stands where you can scarf down mountains of fries, primo ethnic diners, and free food available for the price of a drink at **happy hours**.

Downtown and around

Angelique Café 840 S Spring St ⓣ213/623-8698. Affordable Continental eatery in the middle of the Garment District, where you can dine on well-crafted pastries for breakfast or savory sandwiches, rich casseroles, and fine salads for lunch.

Ciudad 445 S Figueroa St ⓣ213/486-5171. Ceviche and paella are some of the highlights at this colorful, if pricey, Mexican-influenced spot, where the live Latin music competes with the delicious food for your attention.

Dong Il Jang 3455 W 8th St ⓣ213/383-5757. Cozy little Korean restaurant where the meat is cooked at your table and the food is consistently good, especially the grilled chicken and BBQ beef. Tempura dishes and a sushi bar are an added draw.

Engine Co. No. 28 644 S Figueroa St ⓣ213/624-6996. Longtime favorite for all-American fare, featuring expensive grilled steaks and seafood, served with great fries in a renovated 1912 fire station.

La Luz del Dia 107 Paseo de la Plaza ⓣ213/628-7495. Authentic Mexican eatery on Olvera Street, worth seeking out for the fiery burritos, enchiladas, and stews, all served in sizeable portions.

Langer's Deli 704 S Alvarado ⓣ213/483-8050. Offers twenty ways of eating what is LA's best pastrami sandwich. Open daylight hours only; curbside pick-up available in a grim area.

Ocean Seafood 747 N Broadway ⓣ213/687-3088. Busy Cantonese restaurant serving cheap and excellent food – dim sum, crab, shrimp, and duck among many standout choices.

Pacific Dining Car 1310 W 6th St ⓣ213/483-6000. Since 1921, this would-be English supper club is where the downtown elite used to cut secret deals. Located inside an old railroad carriage, it's open 24hr for very expensive and delicious steaks.

Patina 141 S Grand Ave ⓣ213/972-3331. One of LA's signature eateries, a fancy, ultra-swank spot in Disney Hall, where you can devour pheasant, pork medallions, and other rotating items on the menu if you're prepared to drop a wad of cash.

Philippe the Original French Dip 1001 N Alameda St ⓣ213/628-3781. Renowned cafeteria with long communal tables, a decor unchanged since 1908, and juicy, artery-clogging French dips – first invented here – loaded with turkey, pork, beef, or lamb for around $6.

Hollywood

Casa Carnitas 4067 Beverly Blvd ⓣ323/667-9953. Delicious and cheap Mexican food from the Yucatán, inspired by Cuban and Caribbean cooking, and including lots of seafood.

The Foundry on Melrose 7463 Melrose Ave ⓣ323/651-0915. Among the greatest of pricey Cal-cuisine spots in the neighborhood, serving such succulent and unexpected dishes as skate wing, black cod with mussels, glazed pork belly, and persimmon salad.

Fred 62 1854 N Vermont Ave ⓣ323/667-0062. Designed like something out of the 1950s, this restaurant offers stylish, affordable Cal-cuisine twists on familiar staples like salads, burgers and fries, and a tempting array of pancakes and omelets, too.

Mario's Peruvian & Seafood 5786 Melrose Ave ⓣ323/466-4181. Good and authentic Peruvian fare: supremely tender squid, rich and flavorful mussels, with a hint of soy sauce in some dishes. Inexpensive, too.

Mexico City 2121 Hillhurst Ave ⓣ323/661-7227. Spinach enchiladas and other Californian versions of Mexican standards, including a mean pollo verde chicken dish, with prices that are easy to stomach.

Pink's Hot Dogs 709 N La Brea Ave ⓣ323/931-4223. Depending on your taste, these famous hot dogs – topped with anything from bacon and chili cheese to pastrami and swiss cheese – are lifesavers or gut bombs. Open until 2am, or 3am weekends.

Providence 5955 Melrose Ave Ⓣ323/460-4170. Near the top of the LA food heap, and for good reason: the place is swarming with foodies, who come for the upscale black sea bass, lobster risotto, lump blue crab, and plenty of other tremendous choices.

Roscoe's Chicken and Waffles 1514 N Gower St Ⓣ323/466-7453. This diner attracts all sorts for its fried chicken, greens, goopy gravy, and thick waffles. One of five area locations.

Shibucho 3114 Beverly Blvd Ⓣ323/387-8498. Seriously tasty, affordable sushi bar where the squid and eel are quite fine, along with the famed toro, an expensive but delicious tuna delicacy.

vermont 1714 N Vermont Ave Ⓣ323/661-6163. One of the better Cal-cuisine eateries in the area. The entrees are predictable enough – such as roasted chicken, crab cakes, and ravioli – but the culinary presentation is effective and, on occasion, inspired.

West LA

Apple Pan 10801 W Pico Blvd Ⓣ310/475-3585. Grab a spot at the counter and enjoy freshly baked apple pie and greasy hamburgers at an old-time joint that opened just after World War II.

Ca' Brea 346 S La Brea Ave Ⓣ323/938-2863. One of LA's best-known, and best, choices for Italian cuisine, with especially solid *osso buco* and risotto. Getting in is difficult, so reserve ahead and expect to pay a bundle.

Campanile 624 S La Brea Ave Ⓣ323/938-1447. Incredible but very expensive Northern Italian food. If you can't afford a full dinner, just try the dessert or pick up some of the city's best bread at *La Brea Bakery* next door.

Canter's Deli 419 N Fairfax Ave Ⓣ323/651-2030. Waitresses in pink uniforms and running shoes serve kosher soup and sandwiches in a kitsch, white-vinyl setting, with its own bizarre cabaret.

Cut 9500 Wilshire Blvd, Beverly Hills Ⓣ310/276-8500. This Wolfgang Puck steakhouse looks sleek and modern like the Getty Center cafeteria – nonetheless, if you like (and can afford) $50 steaks, Kobe short ribs, and Maine lobsters, this is the place.

Frankie & Johnnie's 8947 Sunset Blvd Ⓣ310/275-7770. Amid all the big rock clubs, an old favorite for its sizable pizzas loaded with greasy and healthy ingredients alike. Check out the ink-scrawled messages on the walls, which include praise from famous regulars.

Grace 7360 Beverly Blvd Ⓣ323/934-4400. Expensive but delicious Cal-cuisine that inspires great confidence, not least for its red pork belly, wild-boar tenderloin, and inventive desserts, from butterscotch doughnuts to passion-fruit caramel cake.

Hatfield's 7458 Beverly Blvd Ⓣ323/935-2977. A staple of the upmarket scene that's whipped up a big (deserved) reputation for rotating favorites like rack of lamb, duck breast, smoked pork belly, and outstanding desserts. The seven-course menu ($79) is great.

Jar 8225 Beverly Blvd Ⓣ323/655-6566. An upper-end steakhouse featuring all the usual red-meat fare – prime rib, T-bone, even a pot roast – with an inspired Cal-cuisine flair, throwing in different spices and exotic flavors.

L'Orangerie 903 N La Cienega Blvd Ⓣ310/652-9770. Super-upscale nouvelle California–style French cuisine; if you can't afford around $50 per entrée (or the proper formal wear), enjoy the view from the bar.

Mishima 8474 W 3rd St Ⓣ323/782-0181. Great *miso* soup, softshell crab salad, and *udon* and *soba* noodles, at very affordable prices, at this popular Westside eatery.

Nate 'n' Al's 414 N Beverly Drive Ⓣ310/274-0101. The best-known deli in Beverly Hills, popular with movie people and one of the few reasonable places for dining in the vicinity. Get there early to grab a booth.

Vito's Pizza 846 N La Cienega Blvd Ⓣ310/652-6859. A neighborhood staple that, while not large, draws crowds for its delicious pies, which include a tasty Margherita and slices that recall East Coast pizza in all its glory.

Santa Monica, Venice, and Malibu

Babalu 1002 Montana Ave, Santa Monica Ⓣ310/395-2500. The pumpkin pancakes at this pan-ethnic, Caribbean-influenced restaurant are delightful, as are the sweet potato *tamales* and fried plantains. Service can be erratic, especially at peak times.

Benito's Taco Shop 11614 Santa Monica Blvd Ⓣ310/442-9924. Beef, pork, or fish rolled up in a flour tortilla, for just a few bucks. Most combos are also under $5, making this a good spot to gulp and run. One of three area 24hr joints.

Border Grill 1445 4th St, Santa Monica Ⓣ310/451-1655. Good mid-priced place to sup on delicious shrimp, pork, plaintains, and other nuevo Latin American-flavored fixings, with excellent desserts, too.

Chaya Venice 110 Navy St Ⓣ310/396-1179. Elegant mix of Japanese and Mediterranean foods in an arty sushi bar, with plenty of Cal-cuisine elements and a suitably snazzy clientele.

Chinois on Main 2709 Main St, Santa Monica

☎310/392-9025. One of LA's most renowned, and most expensive, restaurants, run by chef Wolfgang Puck, and serving nouvelle Chinese dishes.

Hal's 1349 Abbot Kinney Blvd, Venice ☎310/396-3105. Popular restaurant in a hip shopping zone in Venice, with a range of well-done, somewhat expensive American standards, including marinated steaks, turkey burgers, and salmon dishes.

LA Farm 3000 W Olympic Blvd, Santa Monica ☎310/453-2204. Delicious, though very expensive, California cuisine, with an accent on crab cakes and lobsters. The main draw is the celebrity-watching: here the stars dine in peace, away from the flashier precincts.

Michael's 1147 3rd St, Santa Monica ☎310/451-0843. Longstanding favorite for California cuisine, served amid modern art, with succulent steak, pasta, and fowl. Reservations are essential, prices steep.

Valentino 3115 Pico Blvd, Santa Monica ☎310/829-4313. Some call it the finest Italian restaurant in the US – traditional Northern Italian dishes, with an infusion of California Cuisine, including a fine grilled veal chop and boneless quail. Expect to max out your credit card.

South Bay and LA Harbor

Bluewater Grill 665 N Harbor Dr, Redondo Beach ☎310/318-3474. Solid seafood spot featuring a slew of mid-priced fresh fish – salmon and catfish to crabs and oysters.

El Pollo Inka 1100 PCH, Hermosa Beach ☎310/372-1433. Cheap Peruvian-style chicken, catfish, and hot and spicy soups to make your mouth water.

George's Greek Café 318 Pine Ave, Long Beach ☎562/437-1184. Centrally located and affordable eatery where you can indulge in tasty gyros, dolmas, and souvlaki, as well as several fine combo plates.

King's Fish House 100 W Broadway #500, Long Beach ☎562/432-7463. Esteemed seafood restaurant with a full selection of salmon, tuna, oysters, and sea bass. One in a local chain of upmarket eateries.

Lasher's 3441 E Broadway, Long Beach ☎562/433-0153. Set in a little house east of downtown, a New American choice for steak, rack of lamb, seafood, and pasta, at the upper end of what you'll pay in this port town.

Orange County

Angelo's 511 S State College Blvd, Anaheim ☎714/533-1401. Straight out of TV's Happy Days, a drive-in complete with roller-skating car-hops, vintage cars, and juicy burgers. Open until 1am on weekends.

Claes Seafood in the Hotel Laguna, 425 S Coast Hwy, Laguna Beach ☎949/376-9283. One of the county's best seafood eateries, where you can sample pricey and delicious *ahi* tuna and halibut with a Cal-cuisine spin, indoors with a fine view of the Pacific.

Favori 3502 W First St, Santa Ana ☎714/531-6838. Worth the long drive out for what may be LA's best Vietnamese food, including delicious garlic shrimp, curried chicken with lemon grass and savory noodles, all for decent prices.

Ruby's 1 Balboa Pier, Newport Beach ☎949/675-RUBY. A solid spot for burgers and fries – the only eatery on this popular pier and one of the few cheap spots in this upscale burg.

Sage 2531 Eastbluff Drive, Newport Beach ☎949/718-9650. Fancy eatery catering to Cal-cuisine lovers, featuring tasty delights like blue crab cakes, steelhead trout, flatiron steak, and roasted duck breast.

The San Gabriel and San Fernando valleys

Art's Deli 12224 Ventura Blvd, Studio City ☎818/762-1221. Long-time film-industry favorite with a good range of hefty, scrumptious sandwiches and soups.

Porto's Bakery 315 N Brand Blvd, Glendale ☎818/956-5996. Popular and cheap café serving flaky Cuban pastries, scrumptious sandwiches, cheesecake soaked in rum, croissants, tarts and tortes, and cappuccino.

Saladang 363 S Fair Oaks Ave, Pasadena ☎626/793-8123. Don't miss out on the pad thai, curry, and salmon at this chic and delicious spot, or the spicy noodles that would pass muster anywhere. The annex, Saladang Song, offers even spicier Thai concoctions.

Shiro 1505 Mission St, South Pasadena ☎626/799-4774. One of the few top-notch restaurants in South Pasadena, perhaps the only one. The top-notch seafood – particularly the grilled catfish and smoked salmon – is prepared in rich, tangy flavors.

Wolfe Burgers 46 N Lake St, Pasadena ☎626/792-7292. A great place for chili, *tamales*, burgers, and *huevos rancheros*, not to mention south- and north-of-the-border burritos.

Nightlife and entertainment

Exploring the jungle of LA **nightlife** can be great fun. Even the quietest venue offers a chance to eavesdrop on a bit of vapid dialogue; the most raucous ones will take your breath away. In all the bars, clubs, and discos, you'll need to be 21 and will be asked for ID. The best sources of **listings** are **LA Weekly** (ⓦwww.laweekly.com) and "The Guide" section in Friday's **LA Times** (ⓦtheguide.latimes.com).

Bars and coffeehouses

LA's **bars** provide a wide range of choices, from the funky dives of Hollywood to the chic enclaves of West LA and Santa Monica. As elsewhere along the West Coast, **coffeehouses** are established all over the city as popular meeting places.

Barney's Beanery 8447 Santa Monica Blvd, West Hollywood ⓣ310/654-2287. Well-worn pool room/bar, stocking over 100 beers, with a solid, Rock'n'Roll-hedonist history. It also serves all-American, rib-stuffing food.

Beauty Bar 1638 N Cahuenga Blvd, Hollywood ⓣ323/464-7676. A drinking spot devoted to hair, nails, and cosmetics, featuring a welter of 1950s-style retro-decor and a cocktail list to match.

Boardners 1652 N Cherokee Ave, Hollywood ⓣ323/462-9621. Formerly one of Hollywood's premier dive bars, now remade into more yuppie-friendly digs to reflect this more sanitized and gentrified stretch of Tinseltown.

El Carmen 8138 W Third St, West LA ⓣ323/852-1552. Groovy faux dive-bar with a south-of-the-border theme pushed to the extreme, with black-velvet pictures of Mexican wrestlers, steer horns, stuffed snakes, and much tongue-in-cheek grunge, as well as signature margaritas.

Formosa Café 7156 Santa Monica Blvd, Hollywood ⓣ323/850-9050. Started in 1925 as a watering hole for Charlie Chaplin's adjacent United Artists studios, this creaky old spot is still alive with the ghosts of Bogie and Marilyn. Imbibe in the spirits; stay away from the food.

Good Luck Bar 1514 Hillhurst Ave ⓣ323/666-3524. A hip Los Feliz retro-dive, this hangout is popular for its cheesy Chinese decor and tropical drinks straight from the heyday of *Trader Vic's*.

Insomnia 7286 Beverly Blvd, West LA ⓣ323/931-4943. A chic spot for chugging cappuccinos while sitting in comfortable sofas and admiring the vivid art on the walls, or tapping out a screenplay on a laptop like some of the regulars.

Intelligentsia 3902 W Sunset Blvd, Silver Lake ⓣ323/663-6173. A new arrival that's more stylish than your average coffeehouse, and linked to a fine seller of beans, which come in many varieties and from many places.

Library Alehouse 2911 Main St, Santa Monica ⓣ310/314-4855. Presenting the choicest brews from West Coast microbreweries and beyond, this is a good spot to select from a nice range of well-known and obscure labels.

Molly Malone's Irish Pub 575 S Fairfax Ave, mid-Wilshire ⓣ323/935-1577. One of LA's drinking staples: an authentic Irish bar, with a crowd of regulars who look like they've been there for ages, plus nightly music, shamrock decor, and the requisite pints of thick Guinness.

Musso and Frank Grill 6667 Hollywood Blvd ⓣ323/467-7788. Simply put, if you haven't had a drink in this landmark 1919 bar, you haven't been to Hollywood. You can also have a pricey bite of diner food to eat.

Nova Express 426 N Fairfax Ave, south of West Hollywood ⓣ323/658-7533. Designed with retro-futuristic sci-fi decor, with weird colors and lighting, and additional curiosities like lava lamps and alien lounge and dance music most nights. Other than the design, coffee and pizza are the main draws.

Novel Café 212 Pier Ave, Santa Monica ⓣ310/396-8566. Used books and high-backed wooden chairs set the tone; good coffees, teas, and pastries, though with many self-consciously studious patrons.

Ye Olde Kings Head 116 Santa Monica Blvd, Santa Monica ⓣ310/451-1402. British-heavy joint with jukebox, dartboards, and signed photos of all your favorite rock dinosaurs; don't miss the steak-and-kidney pie, afternoon tea, or the fish-and-chips.

Clubs and discos

LA's **clubs** range from posy hangouts to industrial noise cellars. The trendier side of the club scene is, as always, elusive, with some venues changing names and clientele every six months (those below are among the more established). Check the **LA Weekly** before setting out.

Avalon 1735 N Vine St, Hollywood ⓣ323/462-3000. Major dance club spinning old-school faves, along with the usual techno and house, with the occasional big-name DJ dropping in. Prices are among the most expensive in town.

Bar Sinister 1652 N Cherokee, Hollywood ⓣ323/769-7070. A collection of sprightly dance beats most nights of the week, then spooky goth music and anemic-looking vampire types on Sat ($10 if in costume). Connected to *Boardners* bar (see p.987).

Bordello 901 E First St, downtown ⓣ213/687-3766. An extravagantly decorated, plush set for serious drinking and partying, where the nightly entertainment might be anything from an up-and-coming indie band to a DJ set to a cabaret freakshow.

Carbon 9300 Venice Blvd, West LA ⓣ310/558-9302. Though hardly near anywhere central, a good spot for eclectic nightly DJs, whose turntables glow with Latin, retro, jungle, drum'n'bass, hip-hop, soul, and rock beats, depending on the night.

Dragonfly 6510 Santa Monica Blvd, Hollywood ⓣ323/466-6111. Unusual decor, two large dance rooms, and house and disco club nights and live music; also presents oddball cabaret shows and various retro-themed evenings.

King King 6555 Hollywood Blvd ⓣ323/960-5765. A solid Hollywood bet for live dance music, with house, funk, rap, and retro-pop all on the DJ docket.

Little Temple 4519 Santa Monica Blvd ⓣ323/660-4540. East Hollywood scene themed around moody Asian decor, with tasty beverages like coconut martini; an expressive, shmoozy clientele, with some of the smarter club-hoppers around town.

Mayan 1038 S Hill St, downtown ⓣ213/746-4287. Formerly a pre-Columbian–styled movie palace, now hosting Latin rhythms and nonstop disco and house tunes on three dancefloors.

The Ruby 7070 Hollywood Blvd ⓣ323/467-7070. A wide range of feverish dance nights take turns Thurs–Sun, covering everything from gothic and grinding industrial to perky house and garage.

Gay and lesbian bars and clubs

7969 7969 Santa Monica Blvd, West Hollywood ⓣ323/654-0280. A landmark for its frenetic assortment of gay-themed (but straight-friendly) shows, from go-go girls to male strippers to drag queens. Always one of LA's most colorful spots for dancing and grinding.

Arena 6655 Santa Monica Blvd, Hollywood ⓣ323/462-0714. Work up a sweat to funk, hip-hop, Latin, and house sounds on a massive dancefloor inside a former ice factory. Plays host to many different club nights.

Jewel's Catch One 4067 W Pico Blvd, Mid-Wilshire ⓣ323/734-8849. Sweaty barn catering to a mixed crowd of gays and straights and covering two wild dancefloors. A longtime LA favorite, located in the middle of nowhere.

Mother Lode 8944 Santa Monica Blvd, West Hollywood ⓣ310/659-9700. Strong drinks, wild dancing to house and "hi-NRG" music, karaoke, and periodic drag antics make this one of the liveliest area clubs.

Rage 8911 Santa Monica Blvd, West Hollywood ⓣ310/652-7055. Very flashy gay men's club and neighborhood favorite, playing the latest house to a long-established crowd.

Ultra Suede 661 N Robertson Blvd, West Hollywood ⓣ310/659-4551. The spot for superior retro-dancing, heavy on 1970s disco and 1980s technopop, with a mixed gay and straight crowd.

Live music

LA has an overwhelming choice for **live music**: ever since the 1960s, the local **rock** scene has been excellent, with up-and-comers getting their first break in clubs on the Sunset Strip; **jazz** is played in a few authentic locales; and **salsa** is immensely popular, and not just among LA's Hispanics. Cover charges can vary widely, so call ahead.

Babe and Ricky's Inn 4339 Leimert Blvd, South Central LA ⓣ323/295-9112. One of LA's top spots for blues, attracting plenty of quality, nationally known acts.

Baked Potato 3787 Cahuenga Blvd West, North Hollywood ⓣ818/980-1615. A small but legendary contemporary jazz spot, where many reputations have been forged. Don't come looking for bland lounge jazz/muzak – instead, expect to be surprised.

Catalina Bar & Grill 6725 W Sunset Blvd ⓣ323/466-2210. This central Hollywood jazz institution offers a wide range of sounds from many big-name performers, as well as good acoustics, filling meals and potent drinks. It can get pricey, though.

El Floridita 1253 N Vine St, Hollywood ⓣ323/871-8612. Decent Mexican and Cuban food plus a fine line-up of Cuban and salsa artists, who play on weekends and jam on other nights.

El Rey Theater 5515 Wilshire Blvd, Mid-Wilshire ⓣ323/936-4790. Although not as famous as its Sunset Strip counterparts, this rock and alternative venue is possibly the best spot to see explosive new bands and still-engaging oldsters.

Jazz Bakery 3233 Helms Ave, Culver City ⓣ310/271-9039. More performance space than club, where the best local musicians play alongside big-name visitors in a former bakery building.

Gabah 4658 Melrose Ave, Mid-Wilshire ⓣ323/664-8913. Eclectic spot serving up a mix of reggae, funk, dub, and rock, with a mix of club and live-music nights. The dicey neighborhood leaves much to be desired, though.

Harvelle's 1432 4th St, Santa Monica ⓣ310/395-1676. Near the Promenade, a stellar blues joint for more than seven decades offering different performers nightly and a little funk, R&B and burlesque thrown in as well.

Key Club 9039 Sunset Blvd, West Hollywood ⓣ310/274-5800. Attracts a young, hip group for its regular concerts in the rock, punk, and metal vein, with lighter fare as well.

Knitting Factory 7021 Hollywood Blvd, Hollywood ⓣ323/463-0204. West Coast branch of landmark New York club (see p.110), located in a strip mall, with a wide range of interpretation, much of it avant-garde.

Largo 432 N Fairfax Ave, Mid-Wilshire ⓣ323/852-1073. Cozy cabaret with some unusual live acts, though mostly jazz, rock, and pop, often of the acoustic variety.

McCabe's 3101 Pico Blvd, Santa Monica ⓣ310/828-4497. LA's premier acoustic guitar shop; long the scene of some excellent and unusual folk and country shows, with the occasional alternative act.

The Roxy 9009 Sunset Blvd, West Hollywood ⓣ310/276-2222. The showcase of the rock industry's new signings, intimate and with a great sound system.

Spaceland 1717 Silver Lake Blvd, Hollywood ⓣ213/833-2843. Excellent spot to catch up-and-coming local and national rockers and other acts, including punk and alternative.

Temple Bar 1026 Wilshire Blvd, Santa Monica ⓣ310/392-1077. A popular, if chaotic, mix of styles can be heard here, from funk and soul to rap and R&B, as well as forays into rock, pop, and world beat.

The Troubadour 9081 Santa Monica Blvd, West Hollywood ⓣ310/276-6168 An old 1960s mainstay that's been through a lot of incarnations. Used to be known for folk and country rock, then metal, now for various flavours of indie rock.

Viper Room 8852 Sunset Blvd, West Hollywood ⓣ310/358-1880. Great live rockers and a headline-grabbing past have helped boost this club's hip aura.

Whisky-a-Go-Go 8901 Sunset Blvd, West Hollywood ⓣ310/652-4202. For many years LA's most famous Rock'n'Roll club, nowadays featuring mainly hard rock.

Classical music, opera, and dance

LA has a number of choices for **classical music**. The Los Angeles Philharmonic (ⓣ213/850-2000, ⓦwww.laphil.org), the city's big name, and Los Angeles Master Chorale (ⓣ213/972-2782, ⓦwww.lamc.org) perform regularly during the year at Disney Hall; the Los Angeles Chamber Orchestra (ⓣ213/622-7001, ⓦwww.laco.org) performs at assorted venues; and the Da Camera Society (ⓣ213/477-2929, ⓦwww.dacamera.org) offers chamber works in stunning settings, from grand churches to legendary modernist homes.

As for **opera**, LA Opera (ⓣ213/972-8001, ⓦwww.losangelesopera.com) stages productions at Downtown's Music Center, while Orange County's Opera Pacific in Costa Mesa (ⓣ1-800/34-OPERA, ⓦwww.operapacific.org) is a similar, classics-oriented alternative. The city's most exciting company is Long Beach Opera

(Ⓣ562/439-2580, Ⓦwww.lbopera.com), which puts on challenging but well-regarded performances of modern and lesser-known operas. Finally, Los Angeles Ballet (Ⓣ310/998-7782, Ⓦwww.losangelesballet.org) arrived in 2006, a belated attempt to fill a serious hole in the LA cultural scene, performing at rotating venues around town.

Disney Hall 1st St at Grand Ave, downtown Ⓣ213/850-2000. Home of the LA Philharmonic, a striking Frank Gehry design (see p.968) hosting many kinds of arts groups.

Dorothy Chandler Pavilion in the Music Center, 135 N Grand Ave, downtown Ⓣ213/972-7211, Ⓦwww.musiccenter.org. Warhorse of the arts world, used by LA Opera and other top names.

Greek Theatre 2700 N Vermont Ave, Griffith Park Ⓣ323/665-1927 Ⓦwww.greektheatrela.com. A broad range of mainstream music acts at this outdoor, summer-only venue.

Hollywood Bowl 2301 N Highland Ave, Hollywood Ⓣ323/850-2000, Ⓦwww.hollywoodbowl.org. Hosts LA Philharmonic concerts, usually of the pops variety, and various jazz and world-beat groups, for open-air concerts during the summer.

John Anson Ford Theater 2850 Cahuenga Blvd, Hollywood Ⓣ323/461-3673, Ⓦwww.fordamphitheatre.org. An open-air venue that has eclectic productions by local classical and operatic groups as well as sporadic pop and rock concerts.

Orange County Performing Arts Center 600 Town Center Drive, Costa Mesa Ⓣ714/556-ARTS, Ⓦwww.pacificsymphony.org. Home of the Pacific Symphony Orchestra and Opera Pacific, as well as touring big names in pop and jazz.

Pasadena Dance Theater 1985 Locust Ave, Pasadena Ⓣ626/683-3459, Ⓦwww.pasadenadance.org. Prominent San Gabriel Valley dance venue, hosting many diverse groups during the year.

Shrine Auditorium 665 W Jefferson Blvd Ⓣ213/749-5123, box office at 655 S Hill St. Huge 1926 Moorish-domed curiosity that hosts touring pop acts, choral gospel groups, and countless award shows.

UCLA Center for the Performing Arts Ⓣ310/825-4401, Ⓦwww.uclalive.org. Coordinates a wide range of touring companies in music, theatre, and dance (Sept–June), and runs a fine dance series between Sept and June, often with an experimental bent.

Comedy

The **comedy** scene in LA has long been a national proving ground for aspiring jokesters and inspired clowns, and it's also a good place to catch live performances by established names as well as up-and-comers. The better-known places are open nightly, but are often solidly booked on weekends. Cover typically ranges from $10–20.

Comedy & Magic Club 1018 Hermosa Ave, Hermosa Beach Ⓣ310/372-1193, Ⓦwww.comedyandmagicclub.com. Strange couplings of magic acts and comedians, highlighted by Jay Leno occasionally testing material here. Tickets can run up to $30.

Comedy Store 8433 W Sunset Blvd, West Hollywood Ⓣ323/650-6268, Ⓦwww.thecomedystore.com. LA's premier comedy showcase and popular enough to be spread over three rooms – which means there's usually space, even at weekends.

Groundlings Theater 7307 Melrose Ave, Hollywood Ⓣ323/934-4747, Ⓦwww.groundlings.com. Only the gifted survive at this pioneering improvisation venue, where Pee Wee Herman and many Saturday Night Live cast members got their start.

The Improv 8162 Melrose Ave, West Hollywood Ⓣ323/651-2583, Ⓦwww.improv.com. Long-standing brick-walled joint known for hosting some of the best acts working. One of LA's top comedy spots, and the forerunner of a national chain.

Improv Olympic West 6366 Santa Monica Blvd, Hollywood Ⓣ323/962-7560, Ⓦwww.iowest.com. A spot for those who like their improv drawn out and elaborate, with comedy routines more like short theater pieces than wacky one-liners.

Laugh Factory 8001 Sunset Blvd, West Hollywood Ⓣ323/656-1336, Ⓦwww.laughfactory.com. Nightly stand-ups of varying standards and reputations, with the occasional big name.

Second City Studio Theatre 6560 Hollywood Blvd, Hollywood Ⓣ323/464-8542, Ⓦwww.secondcity.com. Groundbreaking comedy troupe with numerous branches, in LA hosting nightly improv and sketch comedy sometimes built around lengthy routines.

Theater

Not surprisingly, LA has a very active **theater** scene, with countless venues large and small spread all over town; ticket services like LA Stage Alliance (ⓣ213/614-0556, ⓦwww.lastagealliance.com) offer discount tickets for given shows, under its LA Stage Tix program. The **LA Weekly** and the **LA Times** Friday "Calendar" section both have full listings and reviews.

Ahmanson Theatre/Mark Taper Forum in the Music Center, 135 N Grand Ave, Downtown ⓣ213/972-0700, ⓦwww.taperahmanson.com. Institutional, mainstream theater, with agreeable classics and, less frequently, new plays.

Alex Theater 216 N Brand Blvd, Glendale ⓣ818/243-ALEX, ⓦwww.alextheatre.org. A gloriously restored movie palace – with a great neon spike and quasi-Egyptian forecourt – hosting a fine range of musical theater, dance, comedy, and film.

The Complex 6476 Santa Monica Blvd, Hollywood ⓣ323/465-0383, ⓦwww.complexhollywood.com. An association of five small theaters and five studios putting on innovative works you may not see anywhere else.

Matrix Theater 7657 Melrose Ave ⓣ323/852-1445, ⓦwww.matrixtheatre.com. Lower Hollywood theater offering good, uncompromising productions that often feature some of LA's better young actors and playwrights.

Odyssey Theatre Ensemble 2055 S Sepulveda Blvd, West LA ⓣ310/477-2055, ⓦwww.odysseytheatre.com. Well-respected Westside theater company with a modernist bent, offering a range of quality productions on three stages for decent prices

Pantages Theater 6233 Hollywood Blvd ⓣ323/468-1770, ⓦwww.nederlander.com/wc. An exquisite, atmospheric Art Deco theater, in the heart of historic Hollywood, hosting major touring Broadway productions.

Powerhouse Theatre 3116 Second St, Santa Monica ⓣ310/396-3680, ⓦwww.powerhousetheatre.com. On the border of Venice, this alternative theater presents risk-taking experimental shows; perhaps the best of its kind in town.

Stages Theater Center 1540 N McCadden Place, Hollywood ⓣ323/465-1010, ⓦwww.stagestheatrecenter.com. With three stages offering twenty to one hundred seats, this is an excellent place to catch a wide range of comedies and dramas.

Theatre West 3333 Cahuenga Blvd W, Hollywood ⓣ323/851-7977, ⓦwww.theatrewest.org. A classic venue that's always a good spot to see inventive, sometimes odd, productions with a troupe of excellent young up-and-comers.

Film

Many films are often released in LA months (or years) before they play anywhere else. You can catch **mainstream releases** in any mall-based multiplex, but if you're after golden-age-of-film **atmosphere**, head for one of the historic movie palaces

Pro sports in LA

Baseball: the **LA Dodgers** (ⓣ323/224-1-HIT, ⓦwww.dodgers.com) play at Dodger Stadium near downtown; the **LA Angels of Anaheim** (ⓣ1-888/796-4256, ⓦwww.angelsbaseball.com) at Anaheim Stadium in Orange County; seats for both $8–50.

Basketball: the **Lakers** (tickets $25–275; ⓣ213/480-3232, ⓦwww.lakers.com), **Clippers** ($12–250; ⓣ213/742-7430, ⓦwww.clippers.com), and women's **Sparks** ($5-50; ⓣ1-877/44-SPARKS, ⓦwww.wnba.com/sparks) all play at the Staples Center, south of downtown.

Football: the 102,000-seat **Rose Bowl** (ⓣ626/577-3100, ⓦwww.rosebowlstadium.com) is the site of Pasadena's New Year's Day college football game, but LA hasn't had a pro franchise in 15 years.

Hockey: the **Kings** are based at Staples Center ($30–128; ⓣ1-888/KINGS-LA, ⓦwww.lakings.com), and Orange County's **Anaheim Ducks** play at Honda Center ($20–175; ⓣ714/704-2500, ⓦwww.ducks.nhl.com).

Soccer: the **Galaxy** ($20-75; ⓣ1-877/3-GALAXY, ⓦwww.lagalaxy.com) plays at the Home Depot Center in the South Bay city of Carson.

or evocative second-run houses listed below – or check out the Last Remaining Seats festival in June (W www.laconservancy.org).

Aero 1328 Montana Ave, Santa Monica T 310/395-4990, W www.aerotheatre.com. Thanks to a nice restoration, you can watch classic and art-house movies in this fine old venue from 1940.
ArcLight 6360 Sunset Blvd, Hollywood T 323/464-1478. W www.arclightcinemas.com. All-reserved seats, top-of-the-line projection, good sightlines, wide seats, and — best of all — amid the 14 screens, the iconic Cinerama Dome, a white hemisphere that has the biggest screen in California.
Avalon 1 Casino Way, Santa Catalina Island T 310/510-0179. Located in the stunning Casino building, this great old moviehouse is a riot of mermaid murals, gold-leaf motifs, and an overall design sometimes called "Aquarium Deco."
Bing at the LA County Art Museum, 5905 Wilshire Blvd, Mid-Wilshire T 323/857-6010. Offers engaging retrospectives of famed actors and directors, as well as full-priced evening programs of classic, independent, foreign, art-house, and revival cinema.
Chinese 6925 Hollywood Blvd, Hollywood T 323/464-8111. Landmark cinema showing mainstream fare with a large main screen, six-track stereo sound, and wild chinoiserie interior (see p.971).
Egyptian 6712 Hollywood Blvd, Hollywood T 323/466-FILM. Renovated showcase for classic and foreign films, in the middle of historic Hollywood (see p.971).
El Capitan 6834 Hollywood Blvd, Hollywood T 323/467-7674. Legendary Hollywood venue restored to full glory and renovated a second time. Expect to see plenty of animated and live-action Disney fare.
Nuart 11272 Santa Monica Blvd, West LA T 310/281-8223. Rarely seen classics, documentaries, and edgy foreign-language films, and the main option for independent filmmakers testing their work. Sometimes offers brief Dec previews of Oscar contenders.
Silent Movie 611 N Fairfax Ave, West LA T 323/655-2520, W www.silentmovietheatre.com. Enjoyable mix of silent comedies and adventure flicks – Douglas Fairbanks swashbucklers and the like – along with darker fare like Fritz Lang's *Metropolis* and the occasional talkie.
Village 961 Broxton Ave, Westwood T 310/248-6266. One of the best places to watch a movie in LA, equipped with a giant screen, fine seats, and modern sound system, and a frequent spot for Hollywood premieres.
Warner Grand 478 W 6th St, San Pedro T 310/548-7672, W www.warnergrand.org. Well worth a trip to the LA harbor to see the glory of this 1931 Art Deco masterpiece. Having been restored twice, the theater is now a repertory cinema and performing arts hall.

Shopping

Not surprisingly for a city identified with mass consumerism, you can **buy** virtually anything in LA. The big department stores and exclusive **Rodeo Drive** are the first options for many tourists, along with the city's massive **malls**. Big names in central LA include West Hollywood's **Beverly Center**, at Beverly and La Cienega boulevards (T 310/854-0070); **Westside Pavilion**, Pico and Westwood boulevards, West LA (T 310/474-6255); the **Century City Marketplace**, 10250 Santa Monica Boulevard, West LA (T 310/553-5300); **The Grove**, 6301 W 3rd St, West LA (T 323/571-8830), and **Hollywood and Highland**, at the Hollywood intersection (T 323/960-2331). Many chic boutiques line **Melrose Avenue** between La Brea and Fairfax avenues.

Books

Acres of Books 240 Long Beach Blvd, Long Beach T 562/437-6980. LA's largest, and most disorganized, secondhand collection. You may not be able to find the exact title you're looking for, but chances are you'll stumble across something good.
Book Soup 8818 Sunset Blvd, West Hollywood T 323/659-3110. Great selection, right on Sunset Strip, with narrow, winding aisles stuffed with books. Celebs are sometimes known to come in, attempting to look studious.
Dutton's 11975 San Vicente Blvd, Brentwood

☎310/476-6263. One of the better general-interest stores in town, an ungainly complex built around a central courtyard.

Larry Edmunds Book Shop 6644 Hollywood Blvd, Hollywood ☎323/463-3273. Stacks of books on every aspect of film and theater, plus movie stills and posters.

Hennessey and Ingalls 214 Wilshire Blvd, Santa Monica ☎310/458-9074. An impressive range of coffee-table art and architecture books makes this among the best of its kind in LA. Many cut-rate remainders, but the best are priced at premium.

Samuel French Theatre & Film Bookshop 7623 Sunset Blvd, Hollywood ☎323/876-0570. LA's broadest selection of theater books is found in this local institution, along with a good collection of movie and media-related titles.

Taschen 354 N Beverly Drive, Beverly Hills ☎310/274-4300. Fun, weird, and edifying titles that focus on everything from Renaissance art to kitsch Americana to fetish photography.

Vroman's 695 E Colorado Blvd, Pasadena ☎626/449-5320. One of the San Gabriel Valley's largest retailers for new books, and a good place to browse.

Wacko 4633 Hollywood Blvd, Hollywood ☎323/663-0122. East Hollywood favorite that stocks a great array of titles leaning toward the alternative, covering topics from art and architecture to bizarre fetishes to music guides to conspiracy rants.

Music

Amoeba Music 6400 W Sunset Blvd, Hollywood ☎323/245-6400. Popular record store highlighted by a vast selection of titles – supposedly numbering around half a million – on CD, tape, and vinyl. Also presents occasional in-store live music.

Backside Records 139 N San Fernando Rd, Burbank ☎818/559-7573. With a bent toward the vinyl-minded, this two-level, DJ-oriented store stocks both LPs and CDs with a broad range of electronica, plus some jazz, rap, and soul.

Counterpoint 5911 Franklin Ave, Hollywood ☎323/957-7965. Provides a terrific smorgasbord of used vinyl, CDs, movies on cassette and DVD, books, and even antique 78 records. Also connected to its own underground art gallery.

Fingerprints 4612 E Second St, Long Beach ☎562/433-4996. A formidable indie outfit in the South Bay, offering alternative-leaning CD and vinyl, plus in-store performances from local rockers, and a mellow, soft-sell attitude.

Record Surplus 11609 W Pico Blvd, West LA ☎310/478-4217. The best spot for used music in LA (or anywhere for that matter), loaded with ancient LPs, out-of-print CDs, new releases, and all manner of assorted junk you strangely want to own.

Vinyl Fetish 1614 N Cahuenga Blvd, Hollywood ☎323/957-2290. Loaded with punk, alternative and indie sounds – plus plenty of vinyl for budding DJs – this is also a good place to discover what's new on the ever-changing LA music scene.

The Deserts

California's **deserts** occupy a quarter of the state. Largely untouched outside the scattered military bases, this hot and forbidding landscape exerts a powerful fascination for venturesome travelers. The two distinct regions are the **Low Desert** in the south, the most easily reached from LA, containing the opulent oasis of **Palm Springs** and the primeval expanse of **Joshua Tree National Park**; and the **Mojave** or **High Desert**, dominated by **Death Valley** and stretching along Hwy-395 to the sparsely populated **Owens Valley**, infamous as the place from which LA stole its water.

It is impossible to do justice to this area without a car. Palm Springs can be reached on public transit from LA, but only the periphery of Joshua Tree is accessible, and it's a long hot walk to anywhere worth seeing. You can get as far as dreary Barstow on Greyhound and Amtrak, but no transportation traverses Death Valley, understandably so in the summer.

The Low Desert

Most visitors to the **Low Desert** head straight for its capital, that sun-scorched refuge of the Hollywood and golfing elite, **Palm Springs**. It's the first major town east from LA on I-10, at the center of the **Coachella Valley**, an agricultural empire that grows dates and citrus fruits in vast quantities and is the toasty location of one of the country's best outdoor music festivals, **Coachella** (Ⓦwww.coachella.com), in the spring. Even more compelling, an hour's drive east of Palm Springs is the eerily sublime landscape of **Joshua Tree National Park**.

Palm Springs

Amid lush farmland replete with golf courses, condos, and millionaires, **PALM SPRINGS** embodies a strange mix of Spanish Colonial and mid-twentieth-century modernist architecture. Massive Mount San Jacinto looms over its low-slung buildings, casting a welcome shadow over the town in the late-afternoon heat. Ever since movie stars first appeared here in the 1930s, laying claim to ranch estates and holing up in fancy hotels, the clean dry air and sunshine, just 120 miles east of LA, have made Palm Springs irresistible to the California upper, and the upper middle, class. In recent years, the city has also become a major **gay and lesbian** resort (Ⓦwww.gaypalmspringsca.com has the full rundown of options).

Arrival, information, and getting around

Arriving by car, you drive into town on N Palm Canyon Drive, passing the **visitor center** at no. 2901 (daily 9am–5pm, Sun closes 4pm; Ⓣ1-800/347-7746, Ⓦwww.palm-springs.org), a classic piece of pop architecture with an upswept roof and boomerang design. Greyhound **buses** (4 daily from LA; 2–4hr) pull in downtown at 311 N Indian Canyon Drive, while Amtrak **trains** from LA (2 daily; 2hr 30min) stop just south of I-10 at N Indian Avenue, about ten minutes from downtown. The local operator SunBus (6am–8pm; tickets $1, day passes $3; Ⓣ1-800/343-3456, Ⓦwww.sunline.org) circulates in all the local resort towns. Guided tours of Palm Springs' stash of notable **modernist architecture**, among them designs by R.M. Schindler, Albert Frye and Richard Neutra, are organized by PS Modern Tours (2hr 30min; $65–75; Ⓣ760/318-6118, Ⓔpsmoderntours@aol.com).

Accommodation

Luxury **hotels** outnumber the cheaper variety in Palm Springs, but prices drop by as much as seventy percent as temperatures soar in the summer. The north end of town, along Hwy-111, holds many of the lower-priced places, including countless motels, virtually all of which have pools and air-conditioning. The prices below are **spring** and **autumn rates**; expect to pay about $20-50 more or less for winter and summer, respectively.

Casa Cody 175 S Cahuilla Rd Ⓣ760/320-9346 or 1-800/231-2639, Ⓦwww.casacody.com. Built in the 1920s, this historic, but updated, Southwestern-style B&B offers attractive rooms and a shady garden. A bit more comfortable than higher-priced retro-motels. ❺

Ingleside Inn 200 W Ramon Rd Ⓣ760/325-0046 or 1-800/772-6655, Ⓦwww.inglesideinn.com. Historic downtown option, where the guest list has included Dalí, Garbo, and Brando. Many rooms have antiques, fireplaces, whirlpool tubs, and patios, for double the price of a standard unit. ❻

Orbit Inn 562 W Arenas Rd Ⓣ1-877/996-7248, Ⓦwww.orbitin.com. About the best that can be expected when remaking a 1957 motel into a suave, yuppie-friendly hotel – where you can drink cutely named cocktails by the pool and lounge in stylish, arch-modern rooms. ❽

Palm Court Inn 1983 N Palm Canyon Drive Ⓣ760/416-2333, Ⓦwww.palmcourt-inn.com. Nice motel with two pools, a jacuzzi and gym, plus free continental breakfast and comfortable rooms. ❹

Rendezvous 1420 N Indian Canyon Drive ⓣ760/320-1178, ⓦwww.palmspringsrendezvous.com. Remodeled motel with modern luxuries and sporting retro-1950s designs in its themed rooms (Rat Pack, Marilyn, surfing, etc). ❼

Villa Royale 1620 S Indian Trail ⓣ760/327-2314, ⓦwww.villaroyale.com. Elegant inn with nicely furnished rooms and suites, as well as in-room jacuzzis and a good restaurant. ❼

The Willows 412 W Tahquitz Canyon ⓣ760/320-0771, ⓦwww.thewillowspalmsprings.com. The very reason celebrities were first attracted to Palm Springs in the 1930s: a stunning hangout for the Hollywood elite that provides great views and opulent rooms. ❾

Downtown Palm Springs

Downtown Palm Springs stretches for half a mile along **Palm Canyon Drive** from Tamarisk to Ramon roads, much of it a wide, bright, and modern strip of chain stores that has engulfed the town's quaint Spanish Colonial–style buildings. Shops run the gamut from upscale boutiques and middlebrow art galleries to tacky T-shirt emporia and bookstores devoted exclusively to dead celebrities. In the vicinity you'll find the **Agua Caliente Cultural Museum**, 219 S Palm Canyon Drive (Wed–Sat 10am–5pm, Sun noon–5pm; summer Fri–Sun only; free; ⓣ760/778-1079, ⓦwww.accmuseum.org), with a fine selection of native baskets and pottery craftwork, as well as household objects from the local Cahuilla tribe, such as tools and utensils made from bone, reeds, and stone.

The luxuriously housed **Palm Springs Desert Museum**, 101 Museum Drive (Tues, Wed, & Fri–Sun 10am–5pm, Thurs noon–8pm; summer Fri–Sun only, 10am–5pm; $12.50, children $5; ⓦwww.psmuseum.org), is strong on Native American and Southwestern art, as well as grand American landscaping painting from the nineteenth century. There is a modern art gallery and some lovely sculpture courts on the grounds, and the museum hosts performances of music, theater, comedy, and dance in the 450-seat **Annenberg Theater** (tickets ⓣ760/325-4490).

There's an anarchic piece of landscape gardening at **Moorten Botanical Gardens**, 1701 S Palm Canyon Drive (Mon–Sat 9am–4.30pm, Sun 10am–4pm; $3; ⓦwww.palmsprings.com/moorten), an odd cornucopia of desert plants and cacti, in settings designed to simulate their natural environments. Collections of flora include native agaves, barrel cacti and other succulents, as well as regional plants from as far away as South Africa and South America. Finally, near the airport, the **Palm Springs Air Museum**, 745 N Gene Autry Trail (daily 10am–5pm; $10; ⓦwww.palmspringsairmuseum.org), has an impressive collection of World War II fighters and bombers, including Spitfires, Tomcats, and a B-17 Flying Fortress.

Around Palm Springs

Most visitors to Palm Springs never leave the poolside, but desert enthusiasts still visit to hike and ride in the **Indian Canyons** (daily 8am–5pm, summer Fri–Sun only; $8; ⓦwww.indian-canyons.com), three miles southeast of downtown along S Palm Canyon Drive, where centuries ago, ancestors of the Cahuilla developed extensive agricultural communities. The Palm Canyon Trading Post, 380 N Palm Canyon Drive (same hours as canyons; ⓣ760/323-6018), is a gift shop that serves as the de facto visitor center, from which mile-long guided hikes (90min; $3) leave during regular canyon hours. The canyons are about fifteen miles long, and can be toured by car, although it's worth walking at least a few miles; the easiest trails lead past the waterfalls, rocky gorges, and copious palm trees of **Palm Canyon** (3 miles) and **Andreas Canyon** (1 mile). Some areas are set aside for **trailblazing** in jeeps and four-wheel-drive vehicles: you can rent one from Off-Road Rentals, four miles north of town at 59511 Hwy-111 (Sept–June only; $40 per hour;

ⓣ760/325-0376, Ⓦwww.offroadrentals.com), or take a guided jeep adventure around the Santa Rosa Mountains with Desert Adventures, 67555 E Palm Canyon Drive, Cathedral City (3–4hr; $129–169; ⓣ760/340-2345, Ⓦwww.red-jeep.com).

If the desert heat becomes too much to bear, large cable cars grind and sway over eight thousand feet up the **Palm Springs Aerial Tramway**, Tramway Road, just off Hwy-111 north of Palm Springs (daily 10am–9pm; $22.25, children $15.25; Ⓦwww.pstramway.com), heading to the striking 10,815ft summit of Mount San Jacinto. In the opposite direction from Palm Springs, a few miles east of town, **PALM DESERT** is, like the sun-baked towns further east, riddled with golf courses and elite resorts. Its other claim to fame is the mile-long **El Paseo**, a boutique-rich strip known for its kitschy annual golf-cart parade (Ⓦwww.golfcartparade.com). Palm Desert is also home to the **Living Desert**, a combination garden and zoo at 47900 Portola Ave, Palm Desert (daily: summer 8.30am–1pm; rest of year 9am–5pm; $12, summer $8.75; Ⓦwww.livingdesert.org), rich with cactus and palm gardens, but throwing in incongruous African desert animals such as giraffes, zebras, cheetahs, and warthogs.

Eating and drinking

Although most of the better **restaurants** in Palm Springs are ultra-expensive, more reasonable options can be found with a little effort; the spots preferred by locals are, as ever, to be favored over the slick, often banal cuisine served up by places catering to the tourist trade. Some of the better ones are listed below.

Copley's on Palm Canyon 621 N Palm Canyon Drive ⓣ760/327-9555. Hang out in Cary Grant's old digs while you sup on upscale, smartly prepared California Cuisine, which may include lobster pot pie, rack of lamb, tandoori chicken, and *ahi* tacos

El Mirasol 140 E Palm Canyon Drive ⓣ760/323-0721. Reasonable, affordable Mexican dining that offers a mix of familiar, affordable staples and more authentic fare from Zacatecas and other regions.

Europa 1620 S Indian Trail ⓣ1-800/245-2314. Located in the *Villa Royale Inn* (see p.995), a solid bet for romantic appeal, and known for its delicious, upscale French and Italian offerings, with the added charm of intimate seating and a cozy fireplace.

Las Casuelas 368 N Palm Canyon Drive ⓣ760/325-3213. Local, affordable Mexican favorite that's been around since 1958, and remains popular for its hefty portions and laid-back atmosphere.

Le Vallauris 385 W Tahquitz Canyon Way, next to the Desert Museum ⓣ760/325-5059. Decent contemporary California-Mediterranean cuisine in a gorgeous setting, with sky-high prices and the occasional b-list celebrity dropping in. Reservations only.

Native Foods 1775 E Palm Canyon Drive ⓣ760/416-0070. One of the town's better choices for cheap vegetarian cuisine – with veggie pizzas, burgers, and tacos, plus bean soups, rice bowls and *tempeh* burgers for true initiates.

Shame on the Moon 69950 Frank Sinatra Drive, Rancho Mirage ⓣ760/324-5515. Upscale California cuisine and excellent service are the draw here, attracting a loyal gay clientele. Located eight miles east of downtown Palm Springs.

Tyler's 149 S Indian Canyon Drive ⓣ760/325-2990. The tasty burgers are what send residents tramping out here, but the potato salad, fries, and sandwiches aren't bad, either.

Joshua Tree National Park

Where the low Colorado Desert meets the high Mojave northeast of Palm Springs, **JOSHUA TREE NATIONAL PARK** (Ⓦwww.nps.gov/jotr) protects 1250 square miles of grotesquely gnarled plants, which aren't trees at all, but a type of **yucca**, an agave. Named by Mormons in the 1850s, who saw in their craggy branches the arms of Joshua pointing to the promised land, Joshua trees can rise up to forty feet tall, but have to contend with extreme aridity and rocky soil.

This unearthly landscape is ethereal at sunrise or sunset, when the desert floor is bathed in red light; at noon it can be a furnace, with temperatures sometimes topping 125°F in summer. Still, the park attracts campers, day-trippers, and rock-climbers for its unspoiled beauty, gold-mine ruins, ancient petroglyphs, and incredible rock formations. When hiking, stick to the trails: Joshua Tree is full of abandoned gold mines, so watch for loose gravel and never trust the safety of ladders or timber. Even on the simpler trails, allow around an hour per mile.

One of the easiest hikes (3 miles, foot-travel only) starts one-and-a-half miles from Canyon Road, six miles from the visitor center at Twentynine Palms, at **Fortynine Palms Oasis**. West of the oasis, quartz boulders tower around the **Indian Cove** campground; a trail from the eastern branch of the campground road heads to **Rattlesnake Canyon**, where, after rainfall, the streams and waterfalls break an otherwise eerie silence among the monoliths.

Moving south into the main body of the park, the **Wonderland of Rocks** features rounded granite boulders that draw rock-climbers from around the world. One particular fascinating trail climbs four miles past abandoned mines, where some buildings and equipment are still intact, to **Lost Horse Mine**, 450ft up – which once produced around $20,000 in gold a week, and now consists of antiquated foundations and equipment.

You can find a brilliant desert panorama of badlands and mountains at the 5185ft **Keys View** nearby, from where Geology Tour Road leads down to the east through the best of Joshua Tree's **rock formations** and, further on, to the **Cholla Cactus Garden**.

Practicalities

Less than an hour's drive northeast from Palm Springs, Joshua Tree National Park (always open; $15 per vehicle for 7 days, $5 per cyclist or hiker) is best approached along Hwy-62, which branches off I-10. You can enter the park via the **west entrance**, on Park Boulevard in the town of Joshua Tree (daily 8am-5pm; ⓣ760/366-1855), or the **north entrance** at Twentynine Palms, where you'll also find the **Oasis Visitor Center**, 74485 National Park Drive (daily 8am–5pm; ⓣ760/367-5500). Alternatively, if you're coming from the south, there's another entry at the **Cottonwood Visitor Center** (daily 9am–3pm; ⓣ760/367-5500), seven miles north of I-10.

The park has nine established **campgrounds**, all in the northwest except for one at Cottonwood. Only two have water – **Black Rock Canyon** and **Cottonwood** (both $15) – and except for **Indian Cove** ($15), all the others are $10. You can reserve sites at **Black Rock** and **Indian Cove** by contacting the park reservation center (ⓣ1-877/444-6777, ⓦwww.recreation.gov). The rest are operated on a first-come, first-served basis. Come prepared – gathering firewood is not allowed, and you should stock up on water. **TWENTYNINE PALMS**, a small desert town two minutes' drive from the park, has low-grade motels aplenty, but more pleasant is the historic **Twentynine Palms Inn**, 73950 Inn Ave (ⓣ760/367-3505, ⓦwww.29palmsinn.com; ❺), with its nice wooden cabins and adobe bungalows, and fine **restaurant** where the bread is home-made and the vegetables are fresh from an on-site garden. Morongo Basin Transit Authority **buses** (ⓣ760/366-2395, ⓦwww.mbtabus.com) run between Palm Springs and Twentynine Palms (1 hr 15min; $10 single, $15 roundtrip), but not into the park itself.

The High Desert

The stretches of the **Mojave Desert** that most people see from the road are predictably desolate. Consequently few visitors are inspired to explore further, but this **High Desert** – sited above 2000ft – offers some of the most dramatic scenery in Southern California, rolling with lush grasses, startling volcanic formations, large stands of Joshua trees, and even, in spots, piñon pines.

Death Valley National Park

DEATH VALLEY – the hottest place on earth – is almost entirely devoid of shade, much less water, so carry plenty for both car and body. Its sculpted rock layers form deeply shadowed, eroded crevices at the foot of silhouetted hills, their exotic minerals turning ancient mudflats into rainbows of sunlit iridescence. Throughout the summer, the **temperature** averages 112°F, and the hot ground can reach near boiling. Better to come during the spring, when wildflowers are in bloom and it's generally mild and dry. The central north–south valley contains two main outposts, **Stovepipe Wells** and **Furnace Creek**, where the **visitor center** (daily 9am–5pm; seven-day park pass $20 per vehicle, $10 per pedestrian or cyclist; ⓣ760/786-3200, ⓦwww.nps.gov/deva) is located.

Dante's View, twenty-one miles south on 190 and ten miles along a very steep access road, offers a fine morning vista in which the pink-and-gold Panamint Mountains are highlighted by the rising sun. Near Stovepipe Wells, some thirty miles northwest of Furnace Creek, spread fifteen rippled and contoured square miles of ever-changing **sand dunes**. The most popular site, though, is the surreal luxury of **Scotty's Castle** (50min tours daily 9.30am–4pm, winter 8.30am–5pm; $11; reservations ⓣ760/786-2392), forty miles north of Stovepipe Wells, built in the 1920s as a $2-million desert retreat, tours of which take in the decorative wooden ceilings, indoor waterfalls, and a remote-controlled player piano.

Practicalities

If you plan to **stay**, you must reserve ahead. Furnace Creek Resort (ⓣ760/786-2345, ⓦwww.furnacecreekresort.com) operates two hotels on natural oases – the gorgeous 1920s adobe **Furnace Creek Inn** (❾), and the ordinary **Furnace Creek Ranch** (❺), which has two **restaurants** and a nice bar. More reasonable is **Stovepipe Wells Village** (ⓣ760/786-2387, ⓦwww.stovepipewells.com; ❺) on Hwy-190 about thirty miles northwest of Furnace Creek, offering its own mineral-water pool and restaurant. **Camping** in one of the many park-service campgrounds costs $12–14, depending on facilities and location, or is free if you don't mind being up in the Panamint Range, far from the valley's sights: the only campground that takes reservations is **Furnace Creek** ($12–18; ⓣ1-877/444-6777, ⓦwww.recreation.gov), just north of town.

The High Sierra and Owens Valley

The towering **eastern** peaks of the **HIGH SIERRA** drop abruptly to the empty landscape of the **OWENS VALLEY**, sixty miles west of Death Valley. Almost this entire section of the Sierra Nevada is wilderness: well-maintained roads lead to trailheads at over eight thousand feet, providing access to the stark terrain of spires, glaciers, and clear mountain lakes. US-395 is the lifeline of the area connecting several small towns, all with plenty of budget motels. As there is virtually **no public transportation** in this area (except for CREST and YARTS; see p.1001), you'll really need a **car** to get around.

Mount Whitney and Lone Pine

Rising out of the northern Mojave Desert, the mountainous backbone of the Sierra Nevada announces itself with a bang two hundred miles north of Los Angeles at 14,505-foot **Mount Whitney**, the highest point in the lower 48 states. A silver-gray ridge of pinnacles forms a nearly sheer wall of granite, dominating the small roadside town of **LONE PINE** nearly eleven thousand feet below. **Motels** here include the *Dow Villa Motel* at 310 S Main St (ⓣ760/876-5521 or 1-800/824-9317, ⓦwww.dowvillamotel.com; ❺), where John Wayne always stayed when filming in the area, and the *Best Western Frontier Motel*, 1008 S Main St (ⓣ760/876-5571 or 1-800/780-7234; ❺). Those headed north might want to push on sixteen miles to Independence, where you'll find the slightly run-down but atmospheric *Winnedumah Hotel*, 211 N Edwards St (ⓣ760/878-2040, ⓦwww.winnedumah.com; B&B ❹). You can **camp** at *Tuttle Creek* campground ($5; no water) on Horseshoe Meadow Road some four miles west of Lone Pine beyond the Alabama Hills (see below). The *Pizza Factory*, 301 S Main St (ⓣ760/876-4707), and the diner-style *Mt Whitney Restaurant*, 227 S Main St (ⓣ760/876-5751), are decent places to **eat**. The **Eastern Sierra Interagency Visitor Center**, a mile south of town on US-395 at the junction of Hwy-136 (daily 8am–5pm; ⓣ760/876-6222), is a great source of information about the Owens Valley.

Many early Westerns, and the epic *Gunga Din*, were filmed in the **Alabama Hills** to the west, a rugged expanse of bizarrely eroded sedimentary rock. Some of the oddest formations are linked by the **Picture Rocks Circle**, a paved road that loops around from Whitney Portal Road, passing rocks shaped like bullfrogs, walruses, and baboons.

Two thousand eager souls make the strenuous 22-mile roundtrip **hike** (12–16hr; 6100ft ascent) to the summit of Mount Whitney each summer and fall (generally snow-free June–Oct), some doing it in a day, others sleeping along the way at one of two trail camps. The excellent **Mount Whitney Trail** passes a few lakes before following roughly one hundred switchbacks up to 13,600-foot Trail Crest Pass; it then weaves its way through an often-windy landscape of jagged boulders to the epic summit. Trail permits are awarded by lottery: applications (ⓦwww.fs.fed.us/r5/inyo) are only accepted in February. Any permits left after the lottery are available from the Wilderness Permit Office, Inyo National Forest, 351 Pacu Lane, Suite 200, Bishop, CA 93514 (ⓣ760/873-2400). All hikers pay a $15 fee.

One-day ascents start before dawn from near the excellent *Whitney Portal* **campground** (late May to mid-Oct; ⓣ1-877/444-6777; $16); another nearby camping option is the one-night-only first-come, first-served *Whitney Trailhead* site ($8) at the end of twisting Whitney Portal Road.

Big Pine and the White Mountains

Nearly fifty miles north, hikes lead from the end of Glacier Lodge Road, ten miles west of nondescript **BIG PINE**, up to the **Palisades Glacier**, the southernmost glacier in the northern hemisphere. Along the opposite wall of the five-mile-wide Owens Valley, the ancient, bald, and dry **White Mountains** are home to the gnarled **bristlecone pines**, the oldest living things on earth, some first sprouting over four thousand years ago. Battered and beaten by the harsh environment into contorted but beautiful shapes, even when dead the wood can withstand the wind-driven ice and sand for another thousand years.

The most accessible trees are in 10,000-foot **Schulman Grove**, 24 miles east of Big Pine in **Ancient Bristlecone Pine Forest** (late May–Oct; $3 per person or $5 per vehicle; recorded info on ⓣ760/873-2500), where two trails radiate out from the visitor center. The mile-long **Discovery Trail** passes some photogenic examples, while the four-mile **Methuselah Trail** loops by but intentionally fails to identify the oldest tree, the 4750-year-old Methuselah. An even higher and hardier group of bristlecones stands at Patriarch Grove, accessed by an unpaved road twelve miles beyond the **Bristlecone Pine Forest Visitor Center** at Schulman Grove.

In the White Mountains there's the waterless *Grandview* **campground** (year-round; $5 per night suggested donation), or you can **stay** back in Big Pine at the *Big Pine Motel*, 370 S Main St (ⓣ760/938-2282; ❷).

Bishop

The largest town (population 3500) in the Owens Valley, **BISHOP** is an excellent base for cross-country skiing, fly-fishing, and especially rock climbing. Recommended local **motels** include the *El Rancho*, 274 W Lagoon St (ⓣ760/872-9251 or 1-888/872-9251; ❸), and the *Thunderbird*, 190 W Pine St (ⓣ760/873-4215; ❸). For **eating**, grab a sandwich and any of a number of delicious, own-baked cakes and breads at **Erick Schat's Bakkerÿ**, 763 N Main St (ⓣ760/873-7156); a half-mile south through town on US-395, try the charmingly rustic **Bar-B-Q Bill's**, 187 S Main St (ⓣ760/872-5535), which features an all-you-can-eat salad bar alongside all the usual meaty suspects on the menu. The **visitor center** at 690 N Main St (Mon–Fri 9am–4.30pm, Sat & Sun 10am–4pm; ⓣ760/873-8405 or 1-800/395-3952, ⓦwww.bishopvisitor.com) can provide details of the many **adventure travel specialists** based in town, including Sierra Mountain Center at 174 W Line St (ⓣ760/873-8526; ⓦwww.sierramountaincenter.com). For **hiking** and **camping** information, the White Mountain Ranger Station, 798 N Main St (May–Oct daily; rest of year Mon–Fri; call for hours; ⓣ760/873-2500), will be of more use.

Mammoth Lakes

Forty miles north along US-395 from Bishop, then three miles west on Hwy-203, the resort town of **MAMMOTH LAKES** offers the state's premier ski slopes outside the Lake Tahoe basin, and in summer hosts on- and off-road bike races. The setting is stunning, but the town is pricey and prone to testosterone overload. To ski **Mammoth Mountain** (ⓣ1-800/MAMMOTH, ⓦwww.mammothmountain.com), which looms up behind the resort, pick up **lift tickets** ($78 a day) from the Main Lodge on Minaret Road, where you can also rent **equipment** ($32 for basic skis, boots, and poles; $25 for snowboard and boots), and book **lessons** ($55–67 per half-day). In summer, fifty miles of snow-free slopes transform themselves into the 3500-acre **Mammoth Mountain Bike Park** (one-day pass with unlimited rides on the bike shuttle and gondola $37; $76 with bike rental).

One appealing summer-only destination is **Devil's Postpile National Monument**, seven miles southwest of Mammoth Mountain ($7, includes shuttle bus; ⓦwww.nps.gov/depo). This collection of slender, blue-gray basaltic columns, some as tall as sixty feet, was formed as lava from a volcanic eruption cooled and fractured into multi-sided forms. From here, a two-mile hike along the San Joaquin River leads to the 101-foot **Rainbow Falls**, which refract the midday sun perfectly.

Practicalities

Year-round CREST **buses** (Ⓣ760/872-1901 or Ⓣ1-800/922-1930) stop in the *McDonald's* parking lot on Hwy-203. For summer visitors traveling to or from Yosemite, YARTS (Ⓣ1-877/989-2787, Ⓦwww.yarts.com) operates buses daily from **Mammoth Mountain Inn** in July and August, and on weekends only in June and September; a single fare between Mammoth and Yosemite Valley is $15. During the ski season, get around on the five-line Mammoth Shuttle (Ⓣ760/934-3030). For information, go to the combined US Forest Service **ranger station** and Mammoth Lakes **visitor center**, 2520 Main St, one half-mile east of the town center (daily 8am–5pm; Ⓣ760/924-5500, Ⓦwww.visitmammoth.com).

Mammoth's plentiful **accommodation** is cheapest in summer (and is what we've quoted here); expect one price range higher during ski season. For a reasonably priced B&B close to downtown, visit the rambling *Cinnamon Bear Inn*, 113 Center St (Ⓣ1-800/845-2873, Ⓦwww.cinnamonbearinn.com; midweek ❺, weekends ❻). The *Swiss Chalet Lodge*, 3776 Viewpoint Rd (Ⓣ1-800/937-9477, Ⓦwww.mammoth-swisschalet.com; ❹) offers motel accommodation with mountain views, while the hostel-style *Davison St. Guesthouse*, 19 Davison St (Ⓣ760/924-2188; Ⓦwww.mammoth-guest.com; dorms $25, rooms ❸), has comfortable rooms, four-bed dorms and a kitchen. There are developed **campgrounds** ($16–19) close to Devil's Postpile National Monument, and a number of free waterless campgrounds in the Crestview region of Inyo National Forest about ten miles north of Mammoth.

With the most **restaurants** in the Eastern Sierra, odds are strong you'll find a good meal in Mammoth. Visit *The Stove*, 644 Old Mammoth Rd (Ⓣ760/934-2821), for country cooking served in gargantuan portions; elsewhere, *Whiskey Creek*, at Main and Minaret (Ⓣ760/934-2555), is a lively **bar** and restaurant pouring its own Mammoth Brewing Company beer. For a fancy night out, try *The Lakefront Restaurant* at Tamarack Lodge (Ⓣ760/934-2442), which offers superb lake views and French-Californian dishes for $25–30 each.

Mono Lake, Lee Vining, and Bodie

The blue expanse of **Mono Lake** sits in the midst of a volcanic desert tableland at the north end of the valley. It looks like a science-fiction landscape, with two large islands, one light-colored, the other black, surrounded by salty, alkaline water. Strange sandcastle-like formations of **tufa** – calcium deposited from springs – were exposed after the City of Los Angeles extended an aqueduct (which carries water diverted from the lake's feeder streams) into the Mono Basin through an eleven-mile tunnel. From 1941 until the 1990s the **water level** gradually dropped by over forty feet, creating the biggest environmental controversy in California; emergency action was finally taken, and the lake's level is finally on the way back up. Mono Lake is the primary nesting ground for the state's **California gull** population – twenty percent of the world total – and a prime stopover point for hundreds of thousands of grebes and phalaropes.

For more details about Mono Lake and the fight for its survival, stop by the **Mono Lake Committee Information Center** (daily: late Jun–Aug 8am–9pm; rest of year 9am–5pm; Ⓣ760/647-6595, Ⓦwww.monolake.org) in the small town of **LEE VINING** on US-395, or a mile north at the excellent **Mono Basin Scenic Area Visitor Center** (May–Oct daily 9am–5.30pm; Ⓣ760/647-3044). **Motels** along US-395 include *El Mono Motel* (open late April–late fall; Ⓣ760/647-6310; ❸) and *Murphey's* (Ⓣ1-800/334-6316, Ⓦwww.murpheysyosemite.com; ❹). A new **eating** hotspot in the area is the **New York Times**-lauded *Whoa Nellie*

▲ Bodie

Deli, at the Mobil gas station at the junction of US-395 and Hwy-120 just south of Lee Vining (Ⓣ 760/647-1088). In town itself, try *Bodie Mike's* (open summer only; Ⓣ 760/647-6432) along Lee Vining's brief business strip, for barbecue lunches and dinner.

Northeast of Lee Vining, in a remote, high desert valley, stands a well-preserved relic of the gold-mining 1870s. **Bodie State Park** (open all year but often inaccessible by car in winter; $3 per person; Ⓦ www.parks.ca.gov) is perhaps the most evocative **ghost town** in the US, with many of its structures still intact but not gussied up for tourists. Boasting sixty saloons and dance halls and a population of nearly ten thousand at its peak, it was once the raunchiest and most lawless mining camp in the west; over 150 wooden buildings survive in a state of arrested decay around the intact town center, littered with old bottles, bits of machinery, and old stagecoaches. The ruins of the mines themselves, in the hills east of town, are off limits to visitors except on the frequent tours. Note that the last three miles of the 13-mile drive east from US-395 are unpaved.

The San Joaquin Valley

The vast **interior** of California is split down the middle by the **Sierra Nevada** (Spanish for "snowy range"), or High Sierra, a sawtooth range of snow-capped peaks that stands high above the semi-desert of the Owens Valley. The wide **San Joaquin Valley** in the west was made super-fertile by irrigation projects during the 1940s, and is now almost totally agricultural. Even if the nightlife begins and ends with the local ice-cream parlor, after the big cities of the coast the downshift can be quite refreshing. However, the real reason to come here is to reach the **national parks** of **Sequoia** and **Kings Canyon** – whose huge trees form the centerpiece of a rich natural landscape – and **Yosemite**, where waterfalls cascade down towering walls of silvery granite. Few roads penetrate the hundred of square miles of wilderness, but the entire pristine alpine backcountry is crisscrossed by hiking trails.

The arrow-straight I-5 barrels directly from LA to San Francisco. Six daily **trains** and frequent Greyhound **buses** run through the valley, calling at the towns along Hwy-99, in particular Merced, which has bus connections to Yosemite but otherwise doesn't merit a look-in.

Bakersfield

The first town you come to across the rocky peaks north of Los Angeles is the flat and featureless oil town of **BAKERSFIELD**. This is the unlikely home of one of the liveliest **country music** scenes in the nation, stemming from the arrival during the Depression of Midwestern farmers, with their hillbilly instruments and campfire songs. In the mid-1960s, the gutsy honky-tonk style of Bakersfield artists such as Merle Haggard and Buck Owens challenged the slick commercial output of Nashville, but hopes of luring the major country-music record labels to "Nashville West" foundered with the emergence of rivals like Austin, Texas.

Nevertheless, Bakersfield's honky-tonks are still jumping every Friday and Saturday night. Stetson hats and rhinestone shirts are the sartorial order of the day, and audiences span generations. Most venues are hotel lounges or restaurant backrooms; don't miss the country bar *Trouts*, 805 N Chester Ave (Ⓣ661/399-6700), for a down-to-earth honky-tonk experience. Closer to town, you might also try the *Buck Owens Crystal Palace*, 2800 Buck Owens Blvd (Ⓣ661/328-7560, Ⓦwww.buckowens.com; closed Sun evenings & Mon), where for under $10 you get a live show, dancing, and access to a museum of Buck Owens memorabilia. Buck died in 2006, but his band, The Buckaroos, continue to play on Friday and Saturday nights.

Practicalities

From LA, the Amtrak Thruway bus goes to Bakersfield, where you can catch the train through the valley toward San Francisco and northern California. Several Greyhound **bus** routes require changes here too, calling at 1820 18th St. The **CVB** is at 515 Truxtun Ave (Mon–Fri 8.30am–5.30pm; Ⓣ661/425-7353; Ⓦwww.bakersfieldcvb.org). Bargain overnight stays include the *EZ-8*, 2604 Buck Owen Blvd (Ⓣ661/322-1901; ❷), and the adjacent *La Quinta*, 3232 Riverside Drive (Ⓣ661/325-7400 or 1-800/642-4271; ❹), both pool-equipped and a short stagger from *Buck Owens Crystal Palace* (see see p.1003). For **food**, *Zingo's* at 3201 Buck Owen Blvd (Ⓣ661/321-0627) is a 24-hour truckstop where frilly-aproned waitresses deliver plates of diner staples; and the *Noriega Hotel*, 525 Sumner St (Ⓣ661/322-8419; closed Mon), offers excellent all-you-can-eat Basque meals at long communal tables.

Sequoia and Kings Canyon

The southernmost of the Sierra Nevada national parks, preserving ancient forests of giant sequoia trees, are Sequoia and Kings Canyon. As you might expect, **Sequoia National Park** contains the thickest concentration – and the biggest specimens – of sequoias to be found anywhere, tending (literally) to overshadow its assortment of meadows, peaks, canyons, and caves. **Kings Canyon National Park** has few big trees but compensates with a gaping canyon gored out of the rock by the Kings River as it cascades down from the High Sierra. The few established sights of both parks are near the main roads, leaving the vast majority of the landscape untrammeled and unspoiled, but well within reach for willing hikers.

Arrival and information

A summer **shuttle bus** (late May–early Sept, 4 daily; $15 round-trip) runs into Sequoia NP from the transit center, 425 E Oak St, in the Central Valley town of **Visalia**, where there are Greyhound connections. The two-hour, fifty-mile journey along Hwy-198 ends at Giant Forest from where two free shuttle services call at Sequoia's main sights. There's no **public transportation** into King's Canyon, though both parks are easily reached by **car** either from **Visalia**, or on a slightly longer but faster route along Hwy-180 from Fresno: note that there is **no gas** available in the parks. The **entrance fee** ($20 per car, $10 per cyclist:, free for bus passengers; valid seven days) entitles you to a detailed map of the paired parks, and a copy of *The Guide*, a free seasonal newspaper which details accommodation, guided hikes, and other activities. The two parks are separate but jointly run; for **information** call Ⓣ559/565-3341 or visit Ⓦwww.nps.gov/seki.

Accommodation and eating

The least expensive **rooms** are in the motels near the park entrances: *Sierra Inn Motel* (Ⓣ559/338-0678, Ⓦwww.thesierrainn.com; ❸), fourteen miles west of the southern entrance on Hwy-180 and, near the southern entrance on Hwy-198, *Gateway Lodge* (Ⓣ559/561-4133, Ⓦwww.gateway-sequoia.com; ❺). Inside the parks, all facilities are managed by SKC (Ⓣ1-866/522-6966, Ⓦwww.sequoia-kingscanyon.com; ❹–❼) who operate cabins and hotel units at Stony Creek, Grant Grove, and Cedar Grove; and DNC (Ⓣ1-866/807-3598, Ⓦwww.visitsequoia.com; ❻–❼) who run the upmarket *Wuksachi Lodge* in Sequoia. Space is at a premium during the high season (May to mid-Oct), but you can usually pick up cancellations on the day. In winter you can still camp, but the cheapest roofed accommodation is in cabins at Grant Grove for $130.

Campgrounds are dotted all over both parks, most charging $20 a pitch. In **Sequoia**, the busiest campground is *Lodgepole*, which you can reserve up to five months in advance through the National Park Reservation System (Ⓣ1-800/444-

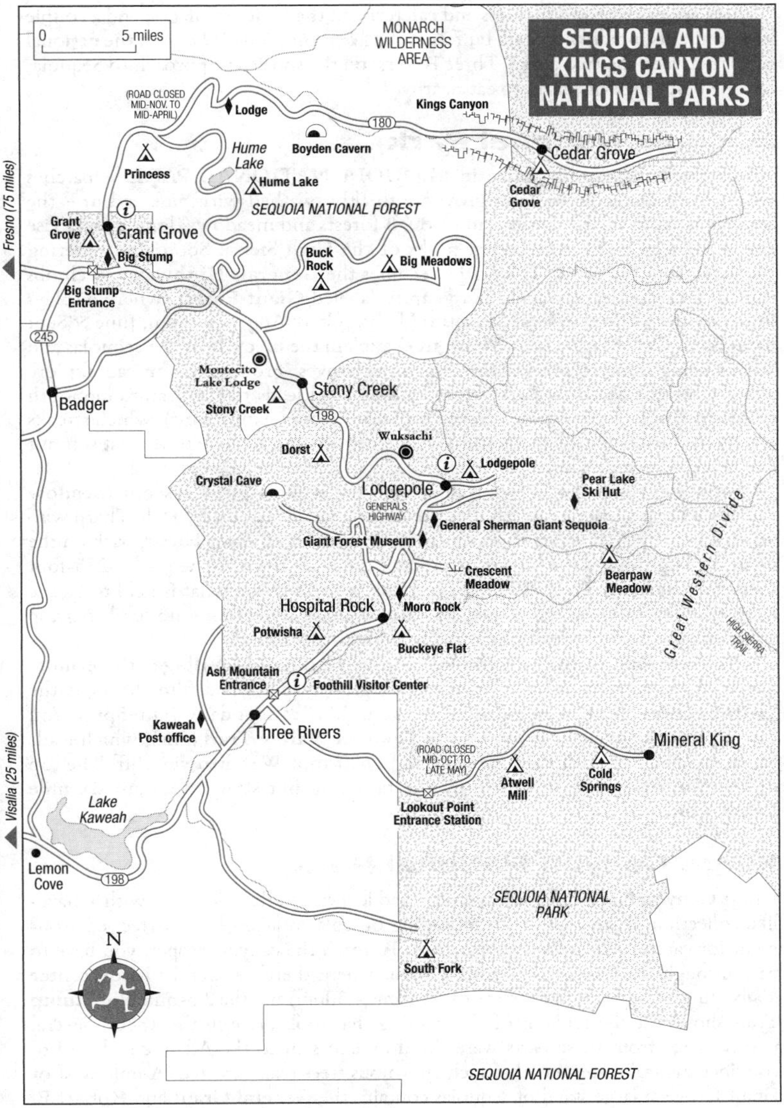

6777, ⓦwww.recreation.gov). In **Kings Canyon**, the bulk of the sites are around Grant Grove, with another at Cedar Grove – all cost $18. For **back country** camping, pick up a free permit from a visitor center or ranger station. And remember this is **bear country**: in established campgrounds use the bearproof food boxes; in the back country rent bear canisters from the stores in Cedar Grove, Grant Grove, and Lodgepole.

There are pricey **food** markets and cafeterias in the various villages, and a couple of restaurants, notably bargain buffets at the *Montecito-Sequoia Lodge* in the national forest between the two parks. Three Rivers, on the southern approach to Sequoia, has the best range of places to eat nearby.

Sequoia National Park

While trees are seldom scarce in **SEQUOIA NATIONAL PARK** – patches where the giant sequoias can't grow are thickly swathed with pine and fir – the scenery is quite varied. Paths lead through forests and meadows; longer treks rise above the tree line to the barren peaks of the High Sierra. Soon after entering the park from the south, Hwy-198 becomes the **Generals Highway** and climbs swiftly into the dense woods of the aptly labeled **Giant Forest**, where displays in the modern **Giant Forest Museum** (daily: July & Aug 8am–6pm, June & Sept 8am–5pm, Oct–May 9am–4.30pm; free) explain the lifecycle of the sequoias and what's being done to protect the remaining groves. From here you can explore along Crescent Meadow Road where a loop road leads to the granite monolith of **Moro Rock** (a three-mile marked trail leads from Giant Forest), which streaks wildly upward from the green hillside. A steep 15-minute hike to the flat summit can reveal 150-mile views.

Continuing east, a perimeter trail around the sequoia-girt **Crescent Meadow** leads to **Tharp's Log**, a cabin hollowed out of a fallen sequoia by Hale Tharp who was led here by Native Americans in 1856. Just north of Giant Forest, back on the Generals Highway, is the biggest sequoia of them all, the 2200-year-old, 275-foot **General Sherman Tree**. While it's certainly a thrill to see what is held to be the largest living thing on the planet, its extraordinary dimensions are hard to grasp alongside the almost equally monstrous sequoias all around.

Whatever your plans, you should stop at **Lodgepole Village**, three miles north of the Sherman Tree, for the geological displays and film shows at the **visitor center** (June to Aug daily 7am–6pm; May & Sept daily 7am–5pm). You can explore the glacial canyon on the **Tokopah Valley Trail** (2hr), which leads to the base of Tokopah Falls, beneath the 1600-foot **Watchtower** cliff. The top of the Watchtower is accessible by the fatiguing but straightforward six-mile **Lakes Trail**.

Kings Canyon National Park

Kings Canyon National Park is wilder and less visited than Sequoia, with a maze-like collection of canyons and a sprinkling of isolated lakes – the perfect environment for careful self-guided exploration. To reach the canyon proper, you have to pass through the hamlet of **Grant Grove**, where there's a useful **visitor center** (daily: June–Aug 8am–6pm; rest of year 9am–4.30pm) and the 2.5-mile **Big Stump Trail** shows off the remains of the logging that took place in the 1880s. Several massive trees from these parts were sliced up and sent to the Atlantic seaboard to convince cynical easterners that such enormous trees really existed. A mile west of Grant Grove, a large stand of sequoias contains the **General Grant** and **Robert E. Lee** trees, which rival the General Sherman in size.

Kings Canyon Highway (Hwy-180; May–Oct only) descends from Grant Grove into the steep-sided Kings Canyon, cut by the furious gushings of various forks of the Kings River. Its wall sections of granite and gleaming blue marble, and the yellow pockmarks of blooming yucca plants (May and early June, in particular), are magnificent. A word of warning: don't be tempted by the clear waters of the river; people have been swept away even when paddling close to the bank in a seemingly placid section.

Once into the national park proper, the canyon sheds its V-shape and gains a floor. **Cedar Grove Village** here is named for its proliferation of incense cedars. There's a **ranger station** across the river (mid-June to Aug daily 9am–5pm; May & Sept hours reduced). Apart from the scenery, you should look out for the **flowers** – leopard lilies, shooting stars, violets, lupins, and others – and **birdlife**, too. Wander around the green **Zumwalt Meadow**, four miles from Cedar Grove Village, which spreads beneath the forbidding gray walls of Grand Sentinel and North Dome.

Just a mile further on, Kings Canyon Road comes to an end at **Copper Creek**. Beyond, the multitude of canyons and peaks that constitute the Kings River Sierra are networked by **hiking paths**, almost all best enjoyed armed with a tent, provisions, and a wilderness permit from the trailhead ranger station.

The Sierra National Forest

The entire gaping tract of land between Kings Canyon and Yosemite is taken up by the **Sierra National Forest**, where you can hike and camp in complete solitude. Don't try lone exploration without thorough planning – public transportation is nonexistent here, and roads and trails are often closed due to bad weather. The best-placed source for free back country permits, and camping and wilderness information is the **ranger station** (daily 8am–4.30pm; ⓣ559/855-5360), on Hwy-168 at Prather, five miles west of the forest entrance.

The popular Shaver Lake and Huntington Lake, rich in campgrounds (reserve in summer on ⓣ1-877/444-6777), soon give way to the isolated alpine landscapes beyond the 9200-foot Kaiser Pass. The sheer challenge posed by the rugged, unspoiled terrain of the adjoining **John Muir Wilderness** can make the national parks look like holiday camps. You can bathe outdoors at the nearby **Mono Hot Springs**, or for the full hot springs experience, head for the *Mono Hot Springs Resort* here (mid-May to Oct; ⓣ559/325-1710, ⓦwww.monohotsprings.com; ❹–❺), which has indoor mineral baths along with self-catering cabins.

Yosemite National Park

More gushing adjectives have been thrown at **YOSEMITE NATIONAL PARK** (ⓦwww.nps.gov/yose) than at any other part of California. However excessive the hyperbole may seem, the instant you turn the corner that reveals **Yosemite Valley**, you realize it's actually an understatement – this is one of the world's most dramatic geological spectacles. Just seven miles long and never more than one mile across, it is walled by near-vertical three-thousand-foot cliffs, streaked by tumbling waterfalls and topped by domes and pinnacles that form a jagged silhouette against the sky. At ground level, grassy meadows are framed by oak, cedar, and fir trees; deer, coyotes, and even black bears are often seen. Tourists are even commoner, but the park is big enough to absorb the crowds: you can visit at any time of year, even in winter when the waterfalls ice up and the trails are blocked by snow, and, excepting summer, the valley itself is rarely overcrowded.

Yosemite Valley was made by glaciers gouging through the canyon of the Merced River: the ice scraped away the softer granite leaving soaring cliffs. The lake that formed when the glaciers melted eventually silted up to create the present valley

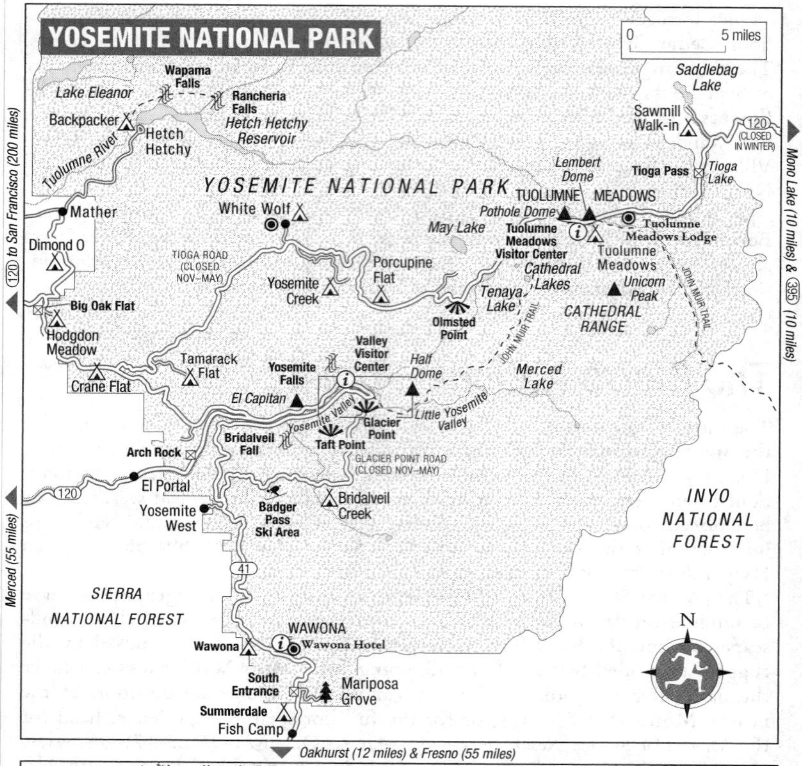

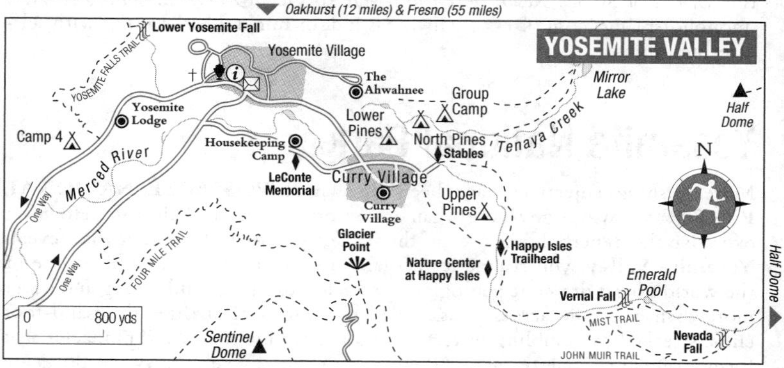

floor. Native Americans lived here in comparative peace until 1851, when the Gold Rush settlers of the **Mariposa Battalion** trailed the Native Americans into the foothills and beyond, becoming the first whites to set foot in Yosemite Valley. The native community was soon forced out to make way for farmers, foresters, and tourists. Thanks to the campaigning work of naturalist **John Muir**, in 1864 Yosemite Valley and Mariposa Grove were set aside as America's first protected wilderness. A Scottish immigrant who traveled the entire area on foot, Muir spearheaded the conservation movement that led to the founding of the Sierra Club, with the express aim of preserving Yosemite. In 1913, the construction of a dam in the Hetch Hetchy Valley just north, to provide water for San Francisco, was a setback; but the publicity actually aided the formation of the present National Park Service in 1916, which promised – and has since provided – greater protection. **Park entry** costs $20 per vehicle, $10 per pedestrian or cyclist, and is valid for seven days. Bus passengers get in free.

Getting there

Getting to Yosemite by car is straightforward, though the only road in from the east, Hwy-120 from Lee Vining, is closed from early November to around the beginning of June. **Gas** is not available in Yosemite Valley. **Public transportation** into the park centers on the Amtrak-accessible Central Valley town of Merced, from where YARTS **buses** (Ⓣ1-877/989-2787, Ⓦwww.yarts.com) make the two-hour run to Yosemite Valley five or six times a day, charging $13 each way. All services call at Merced Transpo, 710 W 16th St, for Greyhound connections, and at the Amtrak station, 324 W 24th St at K Street, where two of the services connect with trains from San Francisco. YARTS also runs a once-daily summer-only service over the Tioga Pass road from Mammoth Lakes and Lee Vining ($15 each way).

There's also the Yosemite Bug Bus (Ⓦwww.yosemitebugbus.com), which picks up from San Francisco hostels and hotels (Mon, Wed, Fri) for two-day-two-night tours to Yosemite with nights at the Yosemite Bug (see below) in a dorm ($205 total) or private room ($225pp total). Bus fares are inclusive of park entry and meals.

If you need somewhere to stay overnight before heading to Yosemite, consider the *HI-Merced Home Hostel* (Ⓣ209/725-0407; members $16, others $19), where the staff pick you up from the train or bus and drop you off at the appropriate station the following morning. If you'd rather be closer to the park, try the lively *Yosemite Bug*, 6979 Hwy-140 (Ⓣ1-866/826-7108, Ⓦwww.YosemiteBug.com; rooms ❷–❹, bunks HI $20, nonmembers $23), at **Midpines**, on the YARTS bus route, where there's a wide range of accommodation and an excellent bar and café.

Yosemite Valley

The three roads from the Central Valley converge on **Yosemite Valley**, roughly in the center of the park's 1200 square miles, and home to its most dramatic scenery. This is the busiest part of Yosemite, with **Yosemite Village** holding the main shops and the useful **visitor center** (daily: June–Sept 9am–7pm; Oct to May 9am–5pm; Ⓣ209/372-0299).

There's little in the village of any great interest; the reason to come here is to explore the major cliffs that dominate Yosemite Valley. The 3600-foot **El Capitan** is one of the world's biggest pieces of exposed granite, so large that rock-climbers on its face are virtually invisible to the naked eye. The truncated face of **Half Dome** is the sheerest cliff in North America, just seven degrees off the vertical.

You can hike to rounded summit of Half Dome by initially following the popular **Mist Trail to Vernal Fall** (3 miles round-trip; 2–3hr; 1100ft ascent), which winds up so close to the sensual waterfall that during the spring snowmelt period (mid-April to mid-June) hikers are drenched by the spray, but rewarded by vivid rainbows. Vernal Fall never completely dries up, but like all those in the valley, it is best seen in spring; by August, falls can be reduced to a trickle, and others dis-

▲ Yosemite National Park

appear altogether. Continuing on the Mist Trail past Vernal Fall, it's a strenuous ascent, the final section aided by a steel staircase hooked on to Half Dome's curving back (late May to mid-Oct only); if you plan a one-day assault, you'll need to start at the crack of dawn.

An early start is also recommended for the trail to **Upper Yosemite Fall** (7 miles round-trip; 4–7hr; 2700ft ascent) leads up along a steep switchback path from behind the *Camp 4* campground, near *Yosemite Lodge*. This almost continuous ascent strains the quads, but you get fine views over the valley on the way up, and after about two miles, a chance to appreciate the power (and volume) of the water as it crashes almost 1500ft in a single cascade. A mile and a half further on the same trail, you reach the top of the fall, more spectacular views, and riverside spots for a much deserved picnic.

The most spectacular views of Yosemite Valley are from **Glacier Point**, the top of a 3200ft almost-sheer cliff, 32 miles by road from the valley. It's possible to get there on foot using the vertiginous **Four-Mile Trail** (4.8 miles one-way; 3–4hr; 3200ft ascent) though slackers prefer to take the bus up (details below) and the trail down. The valley floor lies directly beneath the viewing point, and there are tremendous views across to Half Dome and the distant snowcapped summits of the High Sierra.

Practicalities

Prices within Yosemite are higher than outside the park, but not unaffordable. Of the **hotels** in the valley, try *Yosemite Lodge* (❽) or *Curry Village*, a mile from Yosemite Village, which has similarly priced rooms, plus fixed tent cabins (❹) and cabins ❺–❻); it also offers showers for nonguests ($3). For hotel information and reservations, call Ⓣ801/559-4884 or visit Ⓦwww.yosemitepark.com.

Camping in the valley is only permitted in campgrounds, such as *Camp 4 Walk-in* ($5 per person), just west of *Yosemite Lodge*, which is popular with rock-climbers and has a bohemian reputation; it lacks showers and can only be reserved on the day at the kiosk on-site. Other valley campgrounds cost $20 per site, and you can reserve up to five months ahead in summer (Ⓣ1-877/444-6777; Ⓦwww.recreation.gov): reserve as far in advance as you can, though there are occasionally cancellations.

Food in Yosemite is expensive for what you get, though there is reasonable choice. Yosemite Village has a small supermarket and snack bars, the best of which is *Degnan's Deli*, where massive sandwiches cost around $7. The *Yosemite Lodge Food Court* offers filling and inexpensive meals, and the *Pavilion Buffet* at *Curry Village* has an all-you-care-to-eat feast for $13. There's also a great deck at *Curry Village* where you can order pizza and margaritas. The baronial-style *Ahwahnee Dining Room* (Ⓣ209/372-1489) has the best (and most expensive) food in Yosemite and a great $36 Sunday brunch.

Once in Yosemite Valley, **getting around** is easy. If you drive in for the day, park at *Yosemite Village* and ride the frequent, free **shuttle buses** that loop around the valley in summer (daily 7am–10pm), calling at all points of interest. A number of bicycle paths cross the valley floor but **bike rental** is limited to outlets at *Yosemite Lodge* and *Curry Village* ($26 a day). There are also **guided tours** (Ⓣ209/372-1240), hikes, and horseback trips. Pick up a copy of *Yosemite Today* or browse Ⓦwww.yosemitepark.com for details.

Outside the valley

Mariposa Grove, close to the park's southern entrance, is the biggest and best of Yosemite's groves of **giant sequoia** trees, accessed by a 2.5-mile loop trail. The most renowned of the grouping is the **Grizzly Giant**, thought to be over 2700 years old.

On the eastern edge of the park, **Tuolumne Meadows** (June–Oct only) has an atmosphere quite different from the valley; here, at 8600 feet, you almost seem to be level with the tops of the surrounding snow-covered mountains. The air always has a crisp bite and early summer reveals a plethora of colorful wildflowers. It's a better starting point than the valley for backcountry hiking into the High Sierra, with eight hundred miles of trails, both long and short, crisscrossing their way along the Sierra Nevada ridges. To spend a night in the backcountry, you must get a **wilderness permit**. You can obtain one up to 24hr in advance (free) at the nearest visitor center, but places are limited so it is best to reserve online (Ⓦwww.nps.gov/yose/wilderness; $5 per person) up to 24 weeks in advance. There are tent cabins at *Tuolumne Meadows Lodge* (Ⓣ801/559-4884, Ⓦwww.yosemitepark.com; ❹) and camping at the *Tuolumne Meadows* campground for $20 per site if you have a vehicle, $5 per person if you're hiking and have a wilderness permit.

The Central Coast

Between the busy sprawl of LA and San Francisco, the four hundred miles of the **Central Coast** come as a welcome respite, home to just a few modestly sized cities and lined by clean sandy beaches. The topography is at its most dramatic along

Big Sur, one of the most rugged and beautiful stretches of coastline in the world, while to the south, **Santa Barbara** is a wealthy resort full of old and new money, and **Santa Cruz** in the north is a coastal town redolent of the Sixties. In between, languorous **San Luis Obispo** makes a good base for visiting **Hearst Castle**, the hilltop palace of publishing magnate William Randolph Hearst. Almost all of the towns grew up around the original Spanish Catholic **missions**, once enclosed within thick walls to prevent native attacks. Still featuring attractive nineteenth-century architecture, **Monterey**, a hundred miles south of San Francisco, was California's capital under Spain and Mexico, and briefly the state capital in 1850.

Amtrak's **Coast Starlight** and **Pacific Surfliner trains** run along the coast up to San Luis Obispo, with the former continuing on to the Bay Area and up to Seattle. Greyhound **buses** stop at most coastal towns, especially along the main highway, US-101.

Santa Barbara

Beautifully sited on gently sloping hills above the Pacific, **SANTA BARBARA**'s low-slung Spanish Revival buildings feature red-tiled roofs and white stucco walls, while its golden beaches are wide and clean, lined by palm trees along a curving bay. **State Street**, the main drag, is home to an appealing assortment of diners, bookshops, coffeehouses, and nightclubs.

The few remaining genuine mission structures are preserved as **El Presidio de Santa Barbara**, two blocks east of State Street at 123 E Canon Perdido St (daily 10.30am–4.30pm; $5; Ⓦ www.sbthp.org/presidio.htm), at the center of which are the barracks of the old fortress **El Cuartel**, the second-oldest building in California, and now housing historical exhibits and a scale model of the small Spanish colony. Nearby, the **Santa Barbara Historical Museum**, 136 E De la Guerra St (Tues–Sat 10am–5pm, Sun noon–5pm; donation; Ⓦ www.santabarbaramuseum.com), is built around an 1817 adobe, presenting aspects of the city's past from Ice Age geology to artifacts, from native settlements to modern photo studies. Three blocks north of El Presidio, the still-functional **County Courthouse**, 1100 Anacapa St (Mon–Fri 8.30am–4.30pm, Sat & Sun 10am–4.30pm; free), is a Spanish Revival gem, an idiosyncratic 1929 variation on the Mission theme with striking murals, tilework, and fountain. Take a break in the sunken gardens, explore the quirky staircases, or climb the seventy-foot-high "**El Mirador**" clock tower for a nice view out over the town. Afterwards, drop by the nearby **Santa Barbara Museum of Art**, 1130 State St (Tues–Sun 11am–5pm; $9; Ⓦ www.sbmuseart.org), which features some classical Greek and Egyptian statuary, a smattering of French Impressionists, an Asian collection of some note, and interesting modern photography. Its main appeal, though, comes from its **American collection**, from nineteenth-century landscape painters such as Albert Bierstadt to postwar California modernists like Richard Diebenkorn. Also engaging, the beautifully decorated **Karpeles Manuscript Library**, 21 W Anapamu St (daily 10am–4pm; free; Ⓦ www.rain.org/~karpeles), is home to a diverse array of original documents, such as the Constitution of the Confederate States of America, Napoleon's battle plans for his Russian invasion, and manuscripts by figures such as Twain, Edison, Locke, and Borges.

State Street leads half a mile down from the town center to **Stearns Wharf** (Ⓦ www.stearnswharf.org), the oldest wooden pier in the state, built in 1872. Restoration efforts have now made it home to shopping stalls, food vendors, and the **Ty Warner Sea Center** (daily 10am-5pm; $8), which showcases whale bones and tot-friendly tide pools.

In the hills above the town is the engaging **Museum of Natural History**, 2559 Puesta del Sol Rd (daily 10am–5pm; $10; Ⓦwww.sbnature.org), which showcases intriguing artifacts from native culture, various dioramas of mammals, birds, reptiles, and insects, a planetarium, and actual skeletons of such extinct creatures as the pygmy mammoth. Nearby at 2201 Laguna St, **Mission Santa Barbara** (daily 9am–5pm; donation; Ⓦwww.sbmission.org), dating from 1820, has a colorful twin-towered facade facing out over a perfectly manicured garden towards the sea, combining Romanesque and Spanish Mission styles for a formidable character lacking in some of the prettier missions in the chain. If you continue on into the hills from the mission, you come to the splendid **Botanic Garden**, 1212 Mission Canyon Rd (March–Oct daily 9am-6pm, summer closes 5pm; $8; Ⓦwww.sbbg.org), whose 65 acres are laced with pleasant hiking trails amid endemic cacti, manzanita, trees, and wildflowers - a relaxing respite through hillside meadows and glades.

Arrival, information, and accommodation

Greyhound **buses** stop every few hours downtown at 34 W Carrillo St; Amtrak **trains** arrive at the old Southern Pacific station at 209 State St, right by US-101. A few blocks away is the **visitor center**, at 1 Garden St, (Mon–Sat 9am–5pm, Sun 10am–5pm; Ⓣ805/965-3021, Ⓦwww.santabarbara.com). You can walk to most places, although a frequent **shuttle bus** (25¢) loops around Santa Barbara during the day, with regional buses ($1.25; Ⓣ805/683-3702, Ⓦwww.sbmtd.gov) covering the outlying areas into the evening.

While there are no **campgrounds** in Santa Barbara proper, there are several spots along the coast to the north, including El Capitan and Refugio state beaches (both at Ⓣ1-800/444-7275; $20–25), and to the south, Carpinteria State Beach (same phone and price); all are accessible through Ⓦwww.reserveamerica.com.

Blue Sands Motel 421 S Milpas St Ⓣ805/965-1624, Ⓦwww.bluesandsmotel.com. Looks like your average roadside motel at first, but it's actually a great bet for accommodation: Clean rooms with gas fireplaces, free wireless internet, kitchenettes, and flatscreen TVs – along with a heated pool. ❺

Cheshire Cat 36 W Valerio St Ⓣ805/569-1610, Ⓦwww.cheshirecat.com. Loaded with precious Victorian decor, this B&B has twelve rooms, two cottages, and a coach house, and features a hot tub, bikes for guests' use, and an Alice in Wonderland theme. ❼

Four Seasons 1260 Channel Drive Ⓣ805/969-2261, Ⓦwww.fourseasons.com/santabarbara. The apex of swanky resort style in the area, where the opulent rooms boast fireplaces and wrought-iron balconies, and the complex has a spa, pool, and fitness center. ❾

Inn at East Beach 1029 Orilla del Mar Ⓣ805/965-0546, Ⓦwww.innateastbeach.com. A motel-like appearance but clean, good-value rooms with free wireless internet, microwaves and fridges, and some suites with kitchens, built around a kidney-shaped pool. ❻, summer ❾

Inn of the Spanish Garden 915 Garden St Ⓣ805/564-4700, Ⓦwww.spanishgardeninn.com. Elegant boutique rooms with designer furnishings, fireplaces, high-speed internet connections, and French presses for morning coffee. ❾

Marina Beach Motel 21 Bath St Ⓣ1-877/627-4621, Ⓦwww.marinabeachmotel.com. Clean and modern motel rooms, with continental breakfast and options for bike rentals, kitchenettes, and jacuzzis. A bit cheaper than comparable spots in the area. ❺, summer ❼

Montecito Inn 1295 Coast Village Rd Ⓣ1-800/843-2017, Ⓦwww.montecitoinn.com. Spanish Revival inn with a wide range of rooms and rates, from quaint, basic units to elaborate suites, plus pool, sauna, and jacuzzi. ❽

Santa Barbara Tourist Hostel 134 Chapala St Ⓣ805/963-0154, Ⓦwww.sbhostel.com. Centrally located hostel near the beach and State St, with bicycle and surfboard rentals, complimentary breakfast, and internet access. Dorm rooms go for $22–30, with private rooms also available ($69–89), some with private bath (extra $10).

Eating, drinking, and nightlife

Although Santa Barbara has plenty of places for munching on comfort food and swilling beer, the unquestioned center for local and tourist activity is **State Street**, which is lined with a number of good **restaurants**, **bars**, and **clubs**.

Arigato Sushi 1225 State St ⓣ805/965-6074. The main draw for sushi in town, this boutique Japanese spot is a bit on the pricey side – with the requisite modernist chic and hipster diners – but the fresh, delicious raw fish tends to justify the expense.

Bouchon 9 W Victoria St ⓣ805/730-1160. Elite California cuisine favorite, presenting a rotating menu of dishes such as citrus-marinated quail, rack of lamb or venison, maple-glazed duck breast, and a full selection of fresh seafood.

Ca' Dario 37 E Victoria St ⓣ805/884-9419. Although there are a number of upscale Italian haunts in town, this is one of the few that lives up to its prices, with fine cheeses and pasta, and main dishes that include roasted quail, veal chops, and fresh fish.

Natural Café 508 State St ⓣ805/962-9494. Scrumptious, cheap veggie meals – with pasta, sandwiches, salads, falafel, and desserts - in a prime spot for people watching.

Pacific Crepes 705 Anacapa St ⓣ805/882-1123. About as close to a decent crêpe as you're going to get here, prepared by real French cooks, who do an especially good job on the dessert crêpes.

Q's Sushi-a-Go-Go 409 State St ⓣ805/966-9177. Four bars – including one for sushi – plus a dancefloor in a three-story location make this lounge and restaurant a big draw if you're ready to drink and boogie; the sushi, though, is just average.

Tupelo Junction Cafe 1218 State St ⓣ805/899-3100. One of the town's best spots for breakfast, focusing on items like bacon-spinach-onion scrambles, crab cake and potato hash, vanilla French toast, and pumpkin waffles. Also with lunch and dinner.

Velvet Jones 423 State St ⓣ805/965-8676. Among the few good places in town to catch a show, typically of the indie variety, on the weekends and perhaps comedy and reggae at other times, drawing the usual crowd of students and would-be hellraisers.

Wildcat Lounge 15 W Ortega St ⓣ805/962-7970. A good spot for seeing electronica DJs and various bands, in a chic atmosphere with a mix of locals, students, and out-of-towners.

San Luis Obispo

SAN LUIS OBISPO, 160 miles north of Santa Barbara and halfway between LA and San Francisco, is a few miles inland, but makes a good base for exploring the coast. Still mainly an agricultural center, it holds a nice selection of nineteenth-century architecture, especially around **Buchon Street**, as well as good restaurants, pubs, and – outside summer weekends – plenty of accommodation.

The compact core of San Luis is eminently walkable, centered on the late-eighteenth-century **Mission San Luis Obispo de Tolosa**, 751 Palm St (daily: Jan–May 9am–4pm; June–Dec 9am–5pm; donation; ⓦwww.missionsanluisobispo.org), which was the prototype for the now-ubiquitous red-tile roof church. Between the mission and the visitor center, **Mission Plaza**'s terraces step down along San Luis creek, along which footpaths meander, crisscrossed by bridges every hundred feet, and overlooked by shops and outdoor restaurants on the south bank. **Higuera Street**, a block south of Mission Plaza, is the main drag, and springs to life on Thursday nights (5–9pm; free) for the **Farmers' Market**, when the street is closed to cars and filled with vegetable stalls, barbecues, and street musicians. The highlight of the area, though, is the historic **Fremont Theater**, 1035 Monterey St, an Art Deco marvel that becomes a riot of splashy neon at night and still plays movies. A few blocks southeast of the theater, the **Dallidet Adobe and Gardens**, 1185 Pacific St (Fri 10am–1pm; donation; ⓣ805/543-6762), is a handsome 1860s residence and one of the area's oldest buildings, with a pleasant garden sitting in the shadow of a pair of 125ft-tall redwood trees.

Arrival, information, and accommodation

The Greyhound **bus** depot is at 150 South St, half a mile from the center of town, while Amtrak **trains** stop at the end of Santa Rosa Street, half a mile south of the business district. The **Chamber of Commerce**, 1039 Chorro St (Ⓣ805/781-2670, Ⓦwww.visitslo.com), provides brochures for self-guided walking tours of town. The local transit company, San Luis Obispo Regional Rideshare (Ⓣ805/541-2277, Ⓦwww.rideshare.org), has information on transit options in the region, including shuttles and taxis; area **bus** rides cost $1–3.

Rates for **accommodation** are generally low, though if you want a nice view of the ocean, you're better off taking a short drive south to **Pismo Beach**, a beach town that makes a pleasant stopover.

Apple Farm 2015 Monterey St Ⓣ805/544-2040, Ⓦwww.applefarm.com. Agreeable inn with Victoriana furnishings, including canopy beds and fireplaces, and excellent B&B-style breakfasts. Rates are lower in the Trellis Court building than the Inn proper. ❹

Garden Street Inn B&B 1212 Garden St Ⓣ1-800/488-2045, Ⓦwww.gardenstreetinn.com. B&B in a restored 1887 Victorian with comfortable themed rooms and suites (Ireland, China, Mozart). There's complimentary wine on arrival and gourmet cooked breakfasts. ❼

Hostel Obispo 1617 Santa Rosa St Ⓣ805/544-4678, Ⓦwww.hostelobispo.com. At $25 a night, this hostel is the best value around, offering a convenient central location, cheap bike rentals, and complimentary breakfasts. Private rooms $45–80.

Petit Soleil 1473 Monterey St Ⓣ805/549-0321, Ⓦwww.petitsoleilslo.com. Very stylish French-themed B&B offering modish decor in each uniquely designed room, an even more elegant "Joie de Vivre" suite, and truly continental breakfasts that can be quite tasty. ❽

San Luis Creek Lodge 1941 Monterey St Ⓣ1-800/593-0333, Ⓦwww.sanluiscreeklodge.com. Offers 25 smart rooms in three buildings, each in a vaguely Greek Revival, Tudor, and Craftsman style, with microwaves and internet access. Some units have fireplaces, jacuzzis, or balconies. ❻, but rates jump by $60 on summer weekends.

Eating and drinking

Higuera Street is the prime place to **eat**, with a nice range of unassuming restaurants and **bars**. Other good dining choices can also be found throughout town, along with a few microbreweries.

Buona Tavola 1037 Monterey St Ⓣ805/545-8000. Serviceable bistro featuring a good selection of Northern Italian food and wine.

Downtown Brewing Company 1119 Garden St Ⓣ805/543-1843. The major venue on the SLO nightlife scene, featuring two bars spread over two floors and hosting regular performances by Southern California bands and DJs.

Koberl at Blue 998 Monterey St Ⓣ805/783-1135. Swanky lounge/bar/restaurant with chic modern decor. Graze on snacks in the lounge or, in the restaurant, opt for dinner portions of items like seafood, strip steak, and rack of lamb.

Linnaea's 1110 Garden St Ⓣ805/541-5888. Café that serves good espresso and offers live music, from indie rock and acoustic to variety shows, on its small stage on weekend nights.

Mondeo 893 Higuera St Ⓣ805/544-2956. Asian-styled fast-food joint with inventive wraps and bowls, some of the better ones served with swordfish and shrimp.

Oasis 675 Higuera St Ⓣ805/543-1155. Unexpectedly delicious Middle Eastern eatery that features weekend belly dancing – and the set lunches are especially good value.

Hearst Castle

Forty-five miles northwest of San Luis Obispo, the hilltop **Hearst Castle** is one of the most extravagant estates in the world. The former holiday home where publisher **William Randolph Hearst** held court for such guests as Winston

The real Citizen Kane

Often portrayed as a power-hungry monster – most memorably by Orson Welles in his thinly veiled *Citizen Kane* – **William Randolph Hearst** was born in 1863 as the only son of a multimillionaire mining engineer, and learned the newspaper trade in New York under Joseph Pulitzer, the inventor of "**Yellow Journalism**," of which Hearst became the greatest practitioner. When he published his own *Morning Journal*, Hearst fanned the flames of American imperialism to ignite the Spanish–American War of 1898. As he told his correspondents in Cuba: "You provide the pictures, and I'll provide the war." Hearst eventually controlled an empire which during the 1930s sold twenty-five percent of the nation's newspapers – and sixty percent of those sold in California.

Despite his war-mongering nationalism, Hearst was otherwise a lifelong Democrat who served two terms in the House of Representatives but failed to be elected mayor of New York, let alone president. Besides his many newspapers, Hearst owned eleven radio stations and two movie studios, which he used to make his longtime mistress, **Marion Davies**, a star. Both were aboard Hearst's yacht when in 1924 the famed silent-movie producer Thomas Ince – a party guest – died amid suspicious circumstances. Hearst was never prosecuted, but the charge of murder, combined with the more familiar ones of jingoism and corporate monopoly, only helped reinforce the man's dark legend. When the Depression hit, he was forced to sell off most of his holdings, but he continued to exert power and influence – including opposing US involvement in World War II and trying to suppress Welles's film and burn the original negative – until his death in 1951, aged 88.

Churchill, Charlie Chaplin, George Bernard Shaw, and Charles Lindbergh brings in more than a million visitors a year. Its interior combines walls, floors, and ceilings torn from European churches and castles with Gothic fireplaces and Moorish tiles. Nearly every room is bursting with Greek vases and medieval tapestries, and even the many pools are lined with works of art.

Work on Hearst's nearly four-hundred-square-mile ranch began in 1919, managed by architect Julia Morgan, but the castle was never truly completed: rooms were torn out as soon as they were finished to accommodate yet more booty. The main facade, a twin-towered copy of a Mudejar cathedral, stands atop steps curving up from the world's most photographed swimming pool, the **Neptune Pool**, which is filled with spring water and lined by a Greek colonnade and marble statues – the height of aesthetic glory, or irredeemably vulgar, depending on your taste.

The most dramatic time to visit is in the morning, when coastal fog often enshrouds the slopes below the castle, making it resemble **Citizen Kane**'s eerily evocative Xanadu, which was modeled on the estate. Five different, two-hour guided **tours** – which are essential, as are reservations – leave from the visitor center just off Hwy-1 (daily 8.20am–3.20pm; Ⓣ1-916/414-8400, Ⓦwww.hearstcastle.com). New visitors are directed to the Experience Tour ($24), which includes a lush film on the building's construction plus an introductory spin around the Casa del Sol guesthouse and the main rooms of the Casa Grande, while the Garden Tour ($24) offers a peek at the castle's blooms, as well as the guest house and wine cellar. From April to October, docents in period dress take visitors on an Evening Tour of the castle ($30), speaking of master Hearst in the present tense.

Architecture

Architecture has helped to define America's cultural and political life since the country's inception. Today the desire to craft an identity through architecture is still on view, whether it's the over-the-top, larger-than-life designs on the Las Vegas strip or the soaring, ambitious skyscrapers of New York City. But beyond these showstoppers, there are countless structures that honor both the country's native and immigrant populations – from the starkly beautiful adobe homes of Taos Pueblo in New Mexico to the stunning Spanish missions along the California coast.

Historic houses in Charleston, SC ▲

Rockefeller Center ▼

Rise of an American style

The **National Mall** in Washington DC, was envisioned according to Masonic principles of balance and geometric order, with Neoclassical buildings, grand boulevards, and radial axes. Though the city took 150 years to fully realize, its imperial design was prescient. But far removed from the budding capital, the early US was still a country of frontier log cabins, wooden forts and clapboard farmhouses.

In the nineteenth century, the US was awash in imported designs. The stately **Georgian manors** of the northeast gave the impression of British gentry, the neo-Gothic cathedrals suggested an old Catholic order, and mock Egyptian temples, Swiss chalets, and Tudor mansions were conspicuous sights on a Midwest prairie or New England township.

The greatest influence, of course, was the colorful **Victorian** style, which defined the cityscape of places from San Francisco to Boston to Butte, Montana. By 1900, though, the growing ambitions of the US brought forth a more triumphalist element: stunning banks and libraries modeled as temples, robber baron mansions as the palaces of emperors, and train stations like the old Penn Station as the Baths of Caracalla.

Native invention

The 1920s and 30s were a peak of American architectural creativity – best exemplified by the **Art Deco** towers of the Empire State and Chrysler buildings, a descendant of the work done in Chicago by Louis Sullivan, credited with inventing the skyscraper. Elsewhere, **Frank Lloyd Wright** had a long career and Europeans like Mies van der Rohe did some of their best work here.

Although architectural trends can change like haute couture – modern glass-and-steel boxes giving way to tongue-in-cheek Postmodernism, and so on – the greatest builders have preserved their individuality. The concrete austerity of Louis Kahn, the sharp white angles of Richard Meier, and the sculptural fantasies of Frank Gehry are just a few of the homegrown creations that have had a distinct and lingering impact on the wide American landscape.

Frank Lloyd Wright

Possibly the greatest American architect, Frank Lloyd Wright enjoyed a career spanning more than seven decades. His influence was huge: with his use of horizontal volumes, he evoked the native landscape; with his inventive materials like glass brick, Pyrex tubes and precast concrete "knit-blocks," he gave rise to architecture as sculpture; with his "Usonian" homes, he hoped to devise affordable housing. The most familiar of his landmarks are:

Oak Park, IL (see p.333). His most concentrated collection of early-modern gems, including the stunning Unity Temple and his own house and studio.

The Robie House (see p.334). The single most important signpost for the coming suburban ranch home, as well as a lovely piece of design.

Fallingwater (see p.167). Innovative environmental architecture built around an enchanting site of forested beauty and cascading water.

Taliesin (see p.351 & p.888). Two branches, from his marvelous Wisconsin studio and home to his Scottsdale architecture and design school.

Guggenheim Museum (see p.95). A piece of abstract design in the form of a circular beehive with a famous sloping interior ramp.

▲ Stata Center at MIT, Boston

▼ Interior of the Robie House

▼ Looking skyward at the Guggenheim Museum

The Paris Hotel and Casino, Las Vegas ▲

Art Deco facade, Miami ▼

America's architecture

If you're really into seeing the variety of designs the US has on offer, these enclaves of architectural form, function, and style are a good start.

▸▸ **The Painted Ladies, CA** From Haight-Ashbury to Pacific Heights to Alamo Square, a resplendent reminder of the good old Victorian days of the Italianate, Queen Anne, and Eastlake styles.

▸▸ **Charlottesville, VA** Thomas Jefferson's work as the founder and builder of the University of Virginia and Monticello is the classical style at its most refined and elegant.

▸▸ **Anasazi Country, in the Southwest** America's indigenous peoples were some of its most inventive architects, none more so than the Anasazi, whose cliff dwellings, *kivas*, and Great Houses are easily accessible in the Four Corners region of the Southwest.

▸▸ **South Beach, FL** In Miami's fabulous Art Deco District, oceanfront buildings are alive with zigzag lines, neon-rimmed curves, and dynamic letters – all bathed in a warm, modern glow.

▸▸ **The Serra Missions, CA** Father Junipero Serra and his Catholic missionaries left behind a chain of 21 striking, late-eighteenth-century Spanish missions along the coast of California.

▸▸ **Boston, MA** The cauldron of the American Revolution's most eye-catching attractions are the gilded-dome-topped Massachusetts State House and H.H. Richardson's rusticated-stone Romanesque Trinity Church.

▸▸ **Charleston, SC and Savannah, GA** Two ideal towns to see the comfort and gentility of the Old South as well as its darker aspects, from fetching town squares and grand plantations, to grim slave quarters and auction blocks.

▸▸ **Las Vegas, NV** Sin City has long been an icon of pop architecture, with its ersatz castles, pyramids, tropical islands, and pint-sized versions of Paris, Venice, and New York.

The Big Sur Coast

Starting just north of Hearst Castle, the ninety wild and undeveloped miles of rocky cliffs along the **Big Sur Coast** form a sublime landscape where redwood groves line river canyons in the shadow of the Santa Lucia Mountains. Running through this striking terrain is the exhilarating route of **Hwy-1**, carved out of bedrock cliffs 500ft above the ocean, though **public transport** is limited to the Monterey-Salinas Transit (MST) bus (Ⓣ831/899-2555, Ⓦwww.mst.org), which runs between Monterey to Nepenthe four times daily during the summer (Rte-22; $4 each way). Summer weekends are sunny, and winters turbulent, but the southern coastline of Big Sur is comparatively gentle, with sandy beaches hiding below crumbling ochre cliffs. Note that in summer 2008, rampant **wildfires** ravaged the surrounding area, torching some 70,000 acres. To find out more about the current state of the area, and what facilities are open or closed, contact the regional **Chamber of Commerce** (Ⓣ831/667-2100, Ⓦwww.bigsurcalifornia.org).

Heading north on Hwy-1, the acreage on the east side of the highway by **Julia Pfeiffer Burns State Park** (daily dawn–dusk; Ⓣ831/667-2315) was damaged in the conflagration, but closer to the shore still offers some of the best day-hikes in the Big Sur area, including a short walk along the cliffs to an overlook of McWay Falls, which crash onto a beach below. A less-traveled path leads down from Hwy-1 two miles north of the 80ft waterfall through a 200-foot-long tunnel to the remains of a small wharf at **Partington Cove**, one of the few places in Big Sur where you can get to the sea. Once you get there, check out the fascinating, 1700-acre **underwater preserve** where scuba drivers can explore the natural topography and marine life (contact the park for details). As with other Big Sur parks, Pfeiffer Burns provides campgrounds for $20–30 per night (reserve at Ⓣ831/667-2315, Ⓦwww.reserveamerica.com), while private operations like nearby **Ventana Campground** ($35; Ⓣ831/667-2712, Ⓦwww.ventanawildernesscampground.com) offer campgrounds with bath houses equipped with hot water and electricity. Seven miles north of Pfeiffer Burns, lovely old ✱ **Deetjen's Big Sur Inn** (Ⓣ831/667-2377; Ⓦwww

▲ Hwy-1 and the Big Sur Coast

.deetjens.com; ④) has log cabins with rooms hand-crafted from thick redwood planks and in-room fireplaces, plus fine breakfasts and dinners on site.

Further north at **NEPENTHE**, the rooftop **Nepenthe** restaurant, just off Hwy-1 (ⓣ831/667-2345), offers pricey steaks and seafood, though you can find similarly striking views at **Café Kevah** (ⓣ831/667-2344), which serves more affordable organic breakfasts and lunches on its terrace. Across the highway, the **Henry Miller Library** (Wed–Mon 11am–6pm; donation; ⓦwww.henrymiller.org), displays and sells books by the author, who lived elsewhere in the area intermittently until the 1960s. Two miles north along Hwy-1, unmarked Sycamore Canyon Road leads a mile west to Big Sur's best strip of coast, **Pfeiffer Beach** (daily dawn–dusk; $5 per car; ⓣ831/667-2315), a white sandy stretch dominated by a large rock whose color varies from brown to red to orange in the changing light.

Big Sur River Valley

Immediately north of the Pfeiffer Beach turnoff, Hwy-1 drops into the valley of the Big Sur River, where many of the accommodation and restaurants are dotted sporadically along six miles of highway. The area was hit hard by the 2008 fires, especially the outlying trails, so contact the **ranger station** (daily dawn–dusk; ⓣ831/667-2315) for current information and for wilderness permits. When fully open, sheltered **Pfeiffer Big Sur State Park** features deep, clear swimming holes that form in the steepwalled river gorge during late spring and summer, and a hiking trail that leads half a mile up a canyon shaded by redwoods to the 60ft **Pfeiffer Falls**. The **campgrounds** here charge $25 and are often full on summer weekends (ⓣ831/667-2315 or 1-800/444-7275, ⓦwww.reserveamerica.com).

Just north of Pfeiffer Big Sur, the cluster of shops, lodgings, and restaurants known as **The Village** is the most feasible base for seeing the area. **Accommodation** fills up in summer, but if you can afford it, it's worth spending a night in one of the rustic riverside rooms at the **Big Sur River Inn Resort** (ⓣ831/667-2700 or 1-800/548-3610, ⓦwww.bigsurriverinn.com; ⑥), which has an upscale **restaurant** with decent seafood and American cuisine. There are also spacious cabins in the **Big Sur Lodge** (ⓣ831/667-3100 or 1-800/424-4787, ⓦwww.bigsurlodge.com; ⑦), where some of the rooms have kitchenettes and porches, but no phones or TVs. Alternatively try the basic cabins ($95) or campgrounds ($48) at **Big Sur Campgrounds and Cabins**, a mile north of Pfeiffer Big Sur State Park (ⓣ831/667-2322; ⓦwww.bigsurcamp.com).

The Monterey Peninsula

At the northern edge of the Big Sur coast, a hundred miles south of San Francisco, are the rocky headlands of the **Monterey Peninsula**, where gnarled cypress trees mark the collision between the cliffs and the sea. The lively harbor town of **Monterey** was the capital of California under the Spanish and briefly under the Mexicans and Americans, and retains many old adobes and historic structures alongside the usual tourist traps. **Carmel**, on the other hand, three miles to the south, is a self-consciously quaint village of million-dollar holiday homes and art galleries, while pleasant **Pacific Grove** is known mainly for its lighthouse and resident butterflies.

Arrival, information, and getting around

Amtrak and Greyhound avoid the peninsula entirely, so you'll have to arrive by bus at the sprawling agricultural town of **Salinas** inland, then take a further hour-

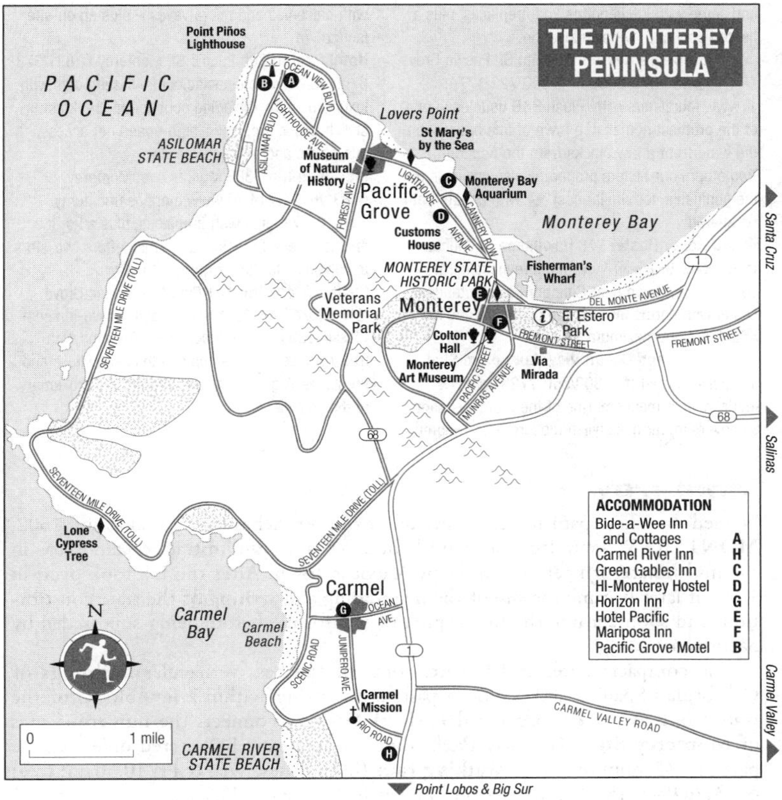

long trip on local bus #20 or 21 on Monterey-Salinas Transit buses (Ⓣ1-888/MST-BUS1, Ⓦwww.mst.org). The base charge is $2, though for Salinas is $4. There's also a free shuttle from downtown to the Aquarium on Cannery Row. Pick up information on Monterey at the **visitor center**, 401 Camino El Estero at Franklin St (Ⓣ1-877/MONTEREY, Ⓦwww.montereyinfo.org); or on the entire peninsula from the **Monterey County Visitor Center**, 150 Olivier St (Ⓣ831/657-6400), which can also help with hotel reservations.

Accommodation

Hotels and **B&Bs** can get pricey, but cheap **motels** are clustered along Fremont Street and Munras Avenue, two miles north of the center. The nearest **camping** is in Veterans Memorial Park ($5 per pedestrian, $25 per vehicle; Ⓣ831/646-3865), site of Steinbeck's fictional **Tortilla Flat**, in the hills above town.

Bide-a-Wee Inn and Cottages 221 Asilomar Ave, Pacific Grove Ⓣ831/372-2330, Ⓦwww.bideaweeinn.com. Good value for the area, with some of the units featuring kitchenettes and microwaves. Short walk to the ocean. ❻

Carmel River Inn Hwy-1 at Carmel River Bridge, Carmel Ⓣ831/624-1575 or 1-800/966-6490, Ⓦwww.carmelriverinn.com. A mix of comfortable hotel rooms (❻) and charming cottages (❼), some of which come with patios or private decks, and some with kitchenettes and fireplaces, plus a heated pool and riverside location.

Green Gables Inn 104 5th St, Pacific Grove ⓣ831/375-2095 or 1-800/722-1774, ⓦwww.foursisters.com. Plush B&B doubles in one of the prettiest homes in a town of fine houses, on the waterfront a few blocks from the Aquarium. Two other Four Sisters properties also available on the peninsula, for similar cost. ❼ with private bath, ❻ shared

HI-Monterey Hostel 778 Hawthorne St, Monterey ⓣ831/649-0375, ⓦwww.montereyhostel.org. Located downtown near Cannery Row, a standard hostel with dorms for $26 and private rooms for $62. Six-night maximum stay.

Horizon Inn and Ocean View Lodge 3rd St at Junipero, Carmel ⓣ1-800/350-7723, ⓦwww.horizoninncarmel.com. One of the more pleasant stopovers in Carmel: stylish modern units – some with balconies and microwaves – plus an on-site jacuzzi. ❼

Hotel Pacific 300 Pacific St, Monterey ⓣ831/373-5700, ⓦwww.hotelpacific.com. All-suite digs with luxury to spare, including continental breakfast, stylish decor, fireplaces, high-speed net access, and patios and/or balconies. ❾

Mariposa Inn 1386 Munras Ave, Monterey ⓣ831/649-1414, ⓦwww.mariposamonterey.com. Cozy rooms with fireplaces, plus a hot tub and continental breakfast. ❺. Also offers two-story townhouses for larger groups, for ❾.

Pacific Grove Inn 581 Pine Ave, Pacific Grove ⓣ1-800/732-2825, ⓦwww.pacificgrove-inn.com. Classic 1904 Victorian boasting 16 rooms with free wi-fi; some units come with ocean views and fireplaces. A good deal, considering the proximity to the sea. ❼

Monterey

Named by the Spanish merchant and explorer Sebastian Vizcaíno in 1602, **MONTEREY** went from a Spanish military and administrative center to, in the mid-nineteenth century, a sleepy Mexican town. After the US took over, in 1846, it later became the site of the negotiating and writing of the state constitution, and soon became the first capital of California, before being superseded by Sacramento.

The compact center still features some of the best vernacular **buildings** of California's Spanish and Mexican past, most sitting within a few blocks of the waterfront. A loosely organized **Path of History** connects the numerous sites of **Monterey State Historic Park**, though most can't be entered unless you're part of a 45-minute guided **walking tour** (Mon, Tues, Wed & Fri 10.30am; free; ⓣ831/649-7118) that leaves from the Pacific House (see below).

The best place to get a feel for life in old Monterey is the **Larkin House**, Pacific and Jefferson streets (45min tour; Tues, Wed, Sat & Sun 2pm; free), home of Thomas Larkin, the first and only American consul to Mexican California, who developed the now-common Monterey style of architecture. The house, the first two-story adobe in California, is filled with antiques and memorabilia, and is surrounded by gorgeous gardens. Larkin also helped organize the would-be state's **constitutional convention**, which took place just around the corner at **Colton Hall** (daily 10am–4pm; free; ⓦwww.monterey.org/museum), furnished as it was during the event, with an early map of the West Coast on view – used by delegates to form the long boundaries of the 31st state. For a break from history, drop by the **Monterey Art Museum**, across the street at 559 Pacific St (Wed–Sat 11am–5pm, Sun 1-4pm; $5; ⓦwww.montereyart.org), which along with good regional photography and painting has excellent rose gardens. The museum's related **La Mirada** house, 720 Via Mirada (same hours and admission), is a charming nineteenth-century stone adobe furnished in the decor of the time, with some nice seaward views.

The **Stevenson House**, three blocks east of the main museum, at 530 Houston St (45min tours; Mon & Fri 2pm, Sat & Sun 10.30am; free), is filled with memorabilia belonging to Robert Louis Stevenson, who passed through in 1879. Six blocks north, tacky **Fisherman's Wharf** is a tourist trap loaded with disused wharves and canneries, some of them converted into boutiques and diners. At the foot of the wharf, the **Custom House** (Sat–Thurs 10am–4pm, Fri 10.30am–4pm; free) is the oldest governmental building on the West Coast, with portions variously built by Spain, Mexico, and the US, and now displaying ancient crates of seized coffee and liquor. Two blocks south, the **Pacific House** (daily 10am–4pm; free) has been a courthouse, boarding house, and dance hall since its construction in 1847, and it now has exhibits on Monterey history and a decent collection of native artifacts.

Heading north from the wharf, a **bike path** runs two miles to Pacific Grove along **Cannery Row** – named after John Steinbeck's literary portrait of the rough-and-ready workers of its seafood plants. Since abandoned, the canneries reopened in the 1970s as malls and restaurants, and now teem with tourists instead of fish (more info at Ⓦwww.canneryrow.com). Along the route, the engaging **Monterey Bay Aquarium**, 886 Cannery Row (daily 10am–6pm, summer opens 9.30am; $25, kids $16; Ⓦwww.montereybayaquarium.org), has a spectacular display of sealife, including a huge Kelp Forest tank, a touch pool (where you can pet bat rays), a two-story sea-otter exhibit, and a large, evocative tank filled with bluefin tuna and hammerhead sharks.

Pacific Grove

Just north of Monterey, **PACIFIC GROVE** – or "Butterfly Town USA," as it likes to call itself – began as a nineteenth-century campground and Methodist retreat, and still holds ornate wooden **cottages** from those long-forgotten days, along 16th and 17th streets. One other reminder of that pious period is the deep-red wooden Gothic church **St Mary's by the Sea**, Central Avenue at 12th St (Mon–Fri 8.30am-4.30pm; Ⓦwww.stmarysbythesea.org), with a simple interior of polished redwood beams and an authentic signed Tiffany stained-glass window.

Ocean View Boulevard circles the coast around the town, passing the headland of **Lovers Point** (originally called Lovers of Jesus Point), where preachers used to hold sunrise services – indeed, it's one of the peninsula's best **beaches**. Every year, from October through early March, hundreds of thousands of golden Monarch **butterflies** come here to escape the winter chill, forming orange and black blankets on the **Butterfly Trees**, on Ridge Road, a quarter of a mile inland on Lighthouse Avenue. At the end of the avenue, near the tip of Monterey Peninsula, stands the 150-year-old **Point Piños** lighthouse (Thurs–Mon 1–4pm; $2), the oldest continuously operating lighthouse on the California coast, though basically a quaint farmhouse with a revolving light poking out of its roof. To find out more about the stunning topography and biology of the area, head to the **Pacific Grove Museum of Natural History**, downtown at Forest Street and Central Avenue (Tues–Sat 10am–5pm; free; Ⓦwww.pgmuseum.org), where you can learn all about the area's birds and butterflies, among other wildlife, and cultural artifacts of the peninsula's native tribes.

If you have time, consider taking the **Seventeen Mile Drive** (daily dawn–dusk; $9.25 per car), a privately owned, scenic toll road that loops along the coast south to Carmel and provides beautiful vistas of rugged headlands and the glistening shoreline. One particular highlight along the way is the **Lone Cypress Tree**, whose solitary silhouette has been the subject of many a postcard in these parts.

Carmel

Set on gently rising bluffs above a sculpted rocky shore, the boutique town of **CARMEL** is well known for its inflated real-estate prices, neat rows of quaint shops and miniature homes along Ocean Avenue, and a largely untouched coastline. Unfortunately, the place also has a thick air of pretension, peppered with tacky middlebrow galleries and mock-Tudor tearooms. Don't expect to see street addresses, mail delivery, or franchise businesses in town: they're all officially banned. Despite the cramped atmosphere, **Carmel Mission Basilica**, 3080 Rio Rd (Mon–Sat 9.30am–5.30pm, Sun 10.30am–5pm; $5; Ⓦwww.carmelmission.org), provides a hint of genuine interest as the second of the California Spanish missions, built in 1771. Three small museums in the mission compound trace its history with antiques and memorabilia, while the darker side of the dainty building becomes apparent via the graves of more than three thousand local Indians in the adjacent **cemetery**.

The town's best feature, however, is the largely untouched nearby coastline. **Carmel River State Beach**, west of town, is a tranquil cove of blue water near a bird sanctuary and bordered by soft white sand and cypress-covered cliffs, though the tides are deceptively strong and dangerous, so be careful if you chance a swim. **Point Lobos State Reserve**, two miles south of the Carmel Mission on Hwy-1 (daily 8am–dusk; $10 per vehicle; Ⓣ831/624-4909), is spread over two square miles, and has more than 250 bird and animal species along its hiking trails, and the sea here is one of the richest underwater habitats in California. Gray whales are often seen offshore - from as little as a hundred yards away - migrating south in January and returning with young calves in April and early May.

Eating

There are many excellent places to **eat** on the peninsula. However, if you're on anything like a tight budget, the best cheap eats are on the north side of Monterey, along Fremont Street and just south of Cannery Row on and around Lighthouse Avenue.

Fishwife 1996 Sunset Drive at Asilomar Blvd, Pacific Grove Ⓣ831/375-7107. Longstanding fixture on the seafood scene, where the dishes come at reasonable prices (around $15 a plate) and the green-lip mussels are worth a try.

Little Napoli Dolores St between Ocean and 7th St, Carmel Ⓣ831/626-6335. Scrumptious mid-priced Italian eatery that offers fresh pasta in sizable portions and an agreeably comfortable setting.

Old Monterey Café 489 Alvarado St, Monterey Ⓣ831/646-1021. Hearty belly-stuffing breakfasts with solid pancakes and omelets, plus tasty sandwiches. Breakfast and lunch only.

Paolina's San Carlos St between Ocean & 7th streets, Carmel Ⓣ831/624-5599. Fresh homemade Italian fare in a casual courtyard setting, mostly pizza, pasta and other usual suspects.

Papa Chano's 462 Alvarado St, Monterey Ⓣ831/646-9587. Affordable Mexican fare with juicy, authentic south-of-the-border specialties, highlighted by a mean chorizo.

Robata Grill & Sake Bar 3658 The Barnyard, Carmel Ⓣ831/624-2643. One of the few good local choices for sushi and tempura, though it can be pricey.

Sardine Factory 701 Wave St, Monterey Ⓣ831/373-3775. Despite the dreadful name, this is prime California seafood – from oysters to crab cakes to the rare abalone – served in French château splendor, with entrees starting at $25.

Stokes 500 Hartnell St, Monterey Ⓣ831/373-1110. The quintessence of California cuisine – all fresh and delicious, including locally raised produce and meat, fine cheeses and herbs, and a blend of international influences – as well as the expected high prices.

The Works 667 Lighthouse Ave, Pacific Grove Ⓣ831/372-2242. A book and newspaper dealer and decent café where you can pick up information about the area while snacking on pastries and drinking coffee or tea.

Drinking and nightlife

Pacific Grove and Carmel offer few decent **nightlife** options, so all listings below are for Monterey. Mid-September's **Monterey Jazz Festival** ($35 and up; Ⓣ1-800/307-3378, Ⓦwww.montereyjazzfestival.org) is the oldest of its kind in the world, dating from 1958 – though 1967's even more famous Monterey Pop Festival was unfortunately only a one-time event. Check out the **Monterey County Weekly** (Ⓦ www.montereycountyweekly.com) for **listings**.

Brittania Arms 444 Alvarado St ⓣ 831/656-9543. British pub with a range of hearty food on offer – shepherd's pie to sandwiches and burgers – along with karaoke and dozens of beers on tap.
Crown and Anchor 150 W Franklin St ⓣ 831/649-6496. All your English favorites, from fish-and-chips to bangers'n'mash, at this unpretentious local pub, best known for its wide array of brews.
The Hippodrome 321 Alvarado St, suite D ⓣ 831/646-9244. Trendy nightclub spread over three floors and boasting a variety of club nights – everything from hillbilly twang to ass-pounding DJ sets – and a young, pulsing crowd.
Lallapalooza 474 Alvarado St ⓣ 831/645-9036. Swank martini bar – also serving midpriced surf 'n turf and pasta – for relaxed social-climbing, with well-mixed, trendy drinks with names like "Pink Panty" and "Purple Haze."
Monterey Live 414 Alvarado St ⓣ 831/375-5483. Engaging spot devoted to all manner of arts, from concert performances to theater and comedy to poetry. Decent meals also served to the eager crowd.

Santa Cruz

In many ways the quintessential California beach town, **SANTA CRUZ**, 75 miles south of San Francisco, is sited at the foot of thickly wooded mountains beside a clean sandy beach. With a strong leftover 1960s vibe, it's also surprisingly untouristy: no hotels spoil the miles of coastline, and roadside stands are more likely to sell apples or sprouts than postcards and trinkets. The **Santa Cruz Boardwalk**, 400 Beach St (June–Aug open daily, rest of year Sat & Sun only; hours vary, often 11am-7pm; $2.25–4.50 per ride, unlimited rides $30; Ⓦ www.beachboardwalk.com), is one of the last surviving beachfront amusement parks on the West Coast, where barefoot hippies mix with farmers and tourists. The highlight is the 1924 **Giant Dipper**, a wild wooden roller coaster that doubles in the movies as a Coney Island ride.

The **beach** next to the boardwalk is popular, but can get rowdy and dirty. For more peace and quiet, follow the coast out of town to one of the smaller beaches such as Capitola or New Brighton. From **West Cliff Drive**, you'll see some of the biggest waves in California, not least at **Steamer Lane**, beyond the Municipal Pier, where surfing in California allegedly began in the nineteenth century. **Cowell's Beach**, just north of the Municipal Pier, is the best place to give surfing a try. The ghosts of surfers past are animated at the **Surfing Museum**, in the old Abbott Memorial lighthouse on the point (Thurs–Mon noon–4pm; free; Ⓦ www.santacruzsurfingmuseum.org), where the boards on display range from early 12ft redwood planks to modern high-tech multifinned cutters. A clifftop cycle path runs two miles out from here to **Natural Bridges State Beach** (daily 8am–dusk; $6 per car; Ⓦ www.santacruzstateparks.org), where waves once cut holes through the cliffs and formed delicate stone arches – though only one remains.

In the hills above Santa Cruz, the local branch of the **University of California** famously has as its mascot the **banana slug**, but is best for its **Arboretum**, near Bay and High streets (daily 9am–5pm; $5; Ⓦ www2.ucsc.edu/arboretum), world famous for its experimental techniques of cultivation and stocked with numerous plants from around the world.

Arrival, information, and accommodation

Greyhound **buses** stop five times a day at 425 Front St, in the center of town, and Santa Cruz has an excellent public transit system known as the **Metro** (tickets $1.50; day pass $4.50; ⓣ831/425-8600, ⓦwww.scmtd.com). Electric Sierra Cycles, 302 Pacific Ave (ⓣ831/425-1593), rents **bikes** for $25-35 per day. The **visitor center** is at 1211 Ocean St (Mon–Sat 9am–5pm, Sun 10am–4pm; ⓣ831/425-1234 or 1-800/833-3494, ⓦwww.santacruz.org).

Santa Cruz has plenty of places to **stay**, though rates can be much higher on summer weekends. Of the many **campgrounds** in the area, the best is at **New Brighton State Beach** (ⓣ831/464-6330, ⓦwww.reserveamerica.com; $25), three miles south at 1500 Park Ave, near the town of Capitola.

Capitola Venetian 1500 Wharf Rd, Capitola ⓣ831/476-6471, ⓦwww.capitolavenetian.com. Aging beach hotel with one- to three-bed rooms, some with stoves, fridges, fireplaces, and ocean views. Rates vary wildly, from ❸ on a winter weekday to ❾ on a summer weekend.

Carousel Motel 110 Riverside Ave, Santa Cruz ⓣ831/425-7090, ⓦwww.santacruzmotels.com. Clean and centrally located units, all with microwaves and continental breakfasts, and some with spas, near the boardwalk. Rates are cheap (❹), but double in summer.

HI-Santa Cruz 321 Main St, Santa Cruz ⓣ831/423-8304, ⓦwww.hi-santacruz.org. Well-situated hostel set in 1870s cottages, offering dorm beds from $28, private rooms for $60. Often booked up in advance.

Pleasure Point Inn 2-3665 E Cliff Drive, Santa Cruz ⓣ408/291-0299, ⓦwww.pleasurepointinn.com. Stylishly modern B&B boasting four rooms with clifftop views, a roof sundeck, and hot tub; rooms have stereos and jacuzzis. ❾ year-round.

Eating, drinking, and nightlife

The main drag of **Pacific Avenue** is peppered with many relaxed **restaurants** and **bars**, while the town itself has the Central Coast's rowdiest **nightlife**, ranging from coffeehouses to nightclubs where the music varies from surf-punk and reggae to Sixties-styled rock. Consult the free **Good Times** magazine (ⓦwww.gtweekly.com) for listings.

The Catalyst 1011 Pacific Ave ⓣ831/423-1336. Happening club with nightly entertainment and one of the best bets for catching mid-level touring artists and up-and-coming locals.

The Crepe Place 1134 Soquel Ave ⓣ831/429-6994. Local institution that serves up mid-priced crêpes with a tasty assortment of both savory and sweet fillings, as well as a few surprises, like jambalaya crêpes.

Kuumbwa Jazz Center 320 Cedar St ⓣ831/427-2227. Friendly and intimate spot in a garden setting showcasing both traditional and modern jazz. Cover anywhere from $5 to 25.

Rio Theatre 1205 Soquel Ave ⓣ831/423-8209, ⓦwww.riotheatre.com. Historic theater that presents cult films, oddball performances, and eclectic music concerts, some from big names.

Saturn Café 145 Laurel St ⓣ831/429-8505. A good place to enjoy the (self-consciously) eccentric flair of Santa Cruz, a vegetarian diner serving tasty items like faux burgers and nachos. Open 'til 3am, or 4am weekends.

Taqueria Vallarta 1101 Pacific Ave #A ⓣ831/471-2655. Authentic, rib-stuffing Mexican fare with a self-serve salsa bar. Mighty good, pretty cheap and closes at midnight.

San Francisco

SAN FRANCISCO proper occupies just 48 hilly square miles at the tip of a slender peninsula along the Northern California coast. Arguably the most beautiful, and likely the most liberal major city in the US, it remains true to itself: a funky, individualistic, surprisingly small place whose people pride themselves on being the cultured counterparts to their cousins in LA. It's a compact and approachable place, where downtown streets rise on impossible gradients to reveal stunning views of the city, the bay, and beyond, and blanket fog rolls in unexpectedly to envelop the city in mist. This is not the California of monotonous blue skies and slothful warmth – the temperature rarely exceeds 80°F and usually hovers in the 60s between May and August, until summer weather finally arrives in autumn's early weeks.

The original inhabitants of this area, the **Ohlone Indians**, were all but wiped out within a few years of the establishment in 1776 of the **Mission Dolores**, the sixth in the chain of Spanish Catholic missions that ran the length of California. Two years after the Americans replaced the Mexicans in 1846, the discovery of gold in the Sierra foothills precipitated the rip-roaring **Gold Rush**. Within a year fifty thousand pioneers had traveled west, and east from China, turning San Francisco from a muddy village and wasteland of sand dunes into a thriving supply center and transit town. By the time the **transcontinental railroad** was completed in 1869, San Francisco was a lawless, rowdy boomtown of bordellos and drinking dens, something the moneyed elite – who hit it big on the much more dependable silver Comstock Lode in Nevada – worked hard to mend, constructing wide boulevards, parks, a cable car system, and elaborate Victorian redwood mansions by century's end.

In the midst of the city's golden age, however, a massive **earthquake**, followed by three days of fire, wiped out most of the town in 1906. Rebuilding began immediately and resulted in another magnificent city; in the decades that soon followed, many of the city's landmarks were built, including Coit Tower and both the Golden Gate and Bay bridges. By World War II San Francisco had been eclipsed by Los Angeles as the West Coast's most populous city, but it achieved a new cultural eminence with the emergence of the Beats in the 1950s and the hippies in the 1960s, when the fusion of music, protest, rebellion, and of course, drugs made international headlines.

It's estimated that over half of San Francisco's population originates from somewhere else. It is a city in a constant state of evolution, fast gentrifying itself into one of the most high-end towns on earth – thanks, in part, to the disposable incomes pumped into its coffers from its sizeable singles and gay contingents. Gay capital of the world, San Francisco has also been the scene of the dot-com revolution's meteoric rise, fall, and steadier recovery; the resultant wealth has pushed housing prices sky-high. Despite the city's economic ebbs and flows, your impression of the city will be that of a proudly distinct place.

Arrival and information

All international and most domestic flights arrive at **San Francisco International Airport** (SFO), located about fifteen miles south of downtown San Francisco proper. Regular BART (see p.1027) trains get you downtown in thirty-five minutes ($5.35 single). San Mateo County Transit (SamTrans) **buses** (Ⓣ1-800/660-4287, Ⓦwww.samtrans.org) leave every half-hour from the lower level of the airport; the KX express ($4) takes around thirty minutes to reach the Transbay Terminal downtown. A number of private **minibus shuttles** depart every five to ten minutes from the lower level of the circular road and take passengers to any San Francisco destination; try SuperShuttle (Ⓣ1-800/258-3826, Ⓦwww.supershuttle.com), which charges $17 per person but only $10 for each additional person in your party. **Taxis** from the airport cost $35–45 (plus tip) for any downtown location, more for the East Bay and Marin County – only worth considering if you can split the charges with others. If you're planning to drive, the usual **car rental** agencies operate free shuttle buses to their depots, leaving every fifteen minutes from the upper level.

Several domestic airlines (JetBlue and Southwest are two) and United fly into **Oakland International Airport** (see p.1049), across the bay. Frequent AirBART shuttle buses ($3, exact change only) connect Oakland International with the Coliseum BART station, where you can hop onto any Daly City- or Millbrae-bound BART train and be in downtown San Francisco in about twenty minutes ($3.55 one-way).

By bus and train

All of San Francisco's **Greyhound** services (ⓣ 1-800/231-2222, ⓦ www.greyhound.com) use the **Transbay Terminal** at 425 Mission St at Fremont, a short walk from the Embarcadero BART station. **Green Tortoise** (ⓣ 1-800/867-8647, ⓦ www.greentortoise.com) buses also use the Transbay Terminal. **Amtrak** trains stop across the bay in **Richmond** (the most efficient BART transfer point) and continue to **Emeryville**, from where free shuttle buses run across the Bay Bridge to downtown San Francisco.

Information

The **San Francisco Visitor Information Center**, on the lower level of Hallidie Plaza adjacent to the end of the cable car line at 900 Market St (Mon–Fri 9am–5pm, Sat & Sun 9am–3pm, Nov–April closed Sun; ⓣ 415/283-0177, ⓦ www.onlyinsanfrancisco.com) at Powell has free maps of the city and the Bay Area, and can help with lodging and travel plans. Its free **San Francisco Book** provides detailed, if a little selective, information about accommodation, entertainment, exhibitions, and stores. The good value **City Pass** (ⓦ www.citypass.com; $54), which allows entry into various attractions, free MUNI rides, and other discounts for seven days, is also available here.

Post offices, with telephone and general delivery facilities, are located all around the city. Two convenient locations near downtown are Sutter Street Station, 150 Sutter St at Kearny, in the Financial District (Mon–Fri 8am–5pm), and Rincon Finance Station, 180 Steuart St at Mission, SoMa (Mon–Fri 7am–6pm, Sat 9am–2pm).

City transportation

San Francisco is the rare American city where you don't need a car to see everything. In fact, given the difficult parking, dense traffic, zealous meter attendants, and treacherous hills, going carless makes sense. The public transportation system, **MUNI**, though maligned by locals for its unpredictable schedule, covers every neighborhood inexpensively. Marked bike routes direct riders to all major points of interest. Walking the compact metropolis is the best bet, with turns often revealing surprises like stunning homes and bustling marketplaces. Wear comfortable shoes for the killer hills, some of them angled at a steep 30 degrees.

For a wealth of information on all forms of Bay Area transportation, including real-time traffic maps, visit ⓦ www.511.org.

MUNI and BART

San Francisco's public transportation is **MUNI** (Ⓣ415/673-6864, Ⓦwww.sfmta.com), which operates a comprehensive network of buses and cable cars that trundle up and over the city's hills; its trains become streetcars when they emerge from downtown's Market Street subway to split off and serve outlying neighborhoods. The flat **fare** is $1.50 on buses and trains (exact change only); with each ticket you buy, make sure you get a **free transfer** – good on all lines (except cable cars) for at least ninety minutes from the time you receive it. A single **cable car** fare is as steep as the hills the vessels climb: $5, with no free transfers.

BART (Bay Area Rapid Transit; Ⓣ415/817-1717, Ⓦwww.bart.gov) is the Bay Area region's electric rail transport system. Although access is limited within San Francisco to Market and Mission streets and a few neighborhoods in the southern part of the city, it does a good job of connecting the city with myriad Easy Bay communities and both the San Francisco and Oakland international airports. Trains operate out of 43 Bay Area stations and are generally timely, clean, and comfortable.

If you're staying a few days, the MUNI **Passport** is available in one-day, three-day, and seven-day denominations ($11, $18, $24, respectively) and is valid for unlimited travel on both MUNI and BART within San Francisco. A **Fast Pass** costs $45 for a full calendar month and is also accepted by both MUNI and BART within city limits; a similar weekly pass is available for $15. MUNI trains run until about 1am nightly; **buses** run all night, but services are greatly reduced between 1am–5am. For **more information**, purchase a handy MUNI map ($3) from the Visitor Information Center. **Bikes** are allowed on MUNI buses equipped with bicycle racks (on the front of the bus) and on BART, except during peak hours.

Other transportation services

Taxis ply the streets, although they can be quite difficult to find outside of downtown, especially on weekends. If you're phoning ahead, try Veterans Cab (Ⓣ415/552-1300) or Yellow Cab (Ⓣ415/626-2345). Fares within the city are roughly $1.85 for the first mile and $1.90 per mile thereafter, plus a customary fifteen-percent tip.

If you fancy **cycling**, the handiest option for rentals is Blazing Saddles (Ⓣ415/202-8888, Ⓦwww.blazingsaddles.com), which has several locations – two of the most convenient are at 1095 Columbus Ave at Francisco Street, in North Beach, and Pier 41 at Fisherman's Wharf. Rates for a standard bike are $7 per hour, $28 per day (tandem $11 per hour and $48 per day). Another option, with similar rates, is Bike & Roll, 899 Columbus Ave (Ⓣ415/771-0392, Ⓦwww.bikeandroll.com).

Organized tours

One-hour **bay cruises** are operated by Blue & Gold Fleet (Ⓣ415/773-1128, Ⓦwww.blueandgoldfleet.com) from piers 39 and 41 – though be warned that everything may be shrouded in fog, making the price ($22, but check for discount fares online) less than worth it.

The best of San Francisco's considerable choices of **walking tours** include City Guides, which features a sprawling roster of ambles sponsored by the San Francisco Public Library (free, but small donation requested; Ⓣ415/557-4266, Ⓦwww.sfcityguides.org); Cruisin' the Castro ($35; Ⓣ415/255-1821, Ⓦwww.cruisinthecastro.com), an absorbing and witty tour of the gay community; the Victorian Home Walk, which swings past the pick of the city's posh old homes ($20; Ⓣ415/252-9485, Ⓦwww.victorianwalk.com); and the Barbary Coast Trail, highlighting the oldest parts of the city and marked by bronze medallions set in the sidewalk (audio tours $14; guided tours $20; ⓣ415/454-2355, ⓦwww.sfhistory.org). There are also two-hour tours of the Mission's murals given by Precita Eyes (see p.1037 for details) that take in the district's distinctive street art.

Accommodation

San Francisco certainly isn't short on lodging, but to get the best pick be sure to reserve well in advance, especially in summer and fall; expect to pay $100–120 per room in any decent **hotel** or **motel** in high season. For **B&Bs**, the city's fastest-growing source of accommodation, contact a specialist agency such as Bed and Breakfast California (ⓣ408/867-9662, ⓦwww.cabbi.com) or Bed and Breakfast San Francisco (ⓣ1-800/452-8249, ⓦwww.bbsf.com). If funds are tight, look into one of the many excellent **hostels**, where beds start at around $20.

San Francisco Reservations (Mon–Fri 6am–11pm, Sat–Sun 8am–11pm; ⓣ1-800/677-1500, ⓦwww.hotelres.com) will find you a room from around $120 for a double. British visitors can reserve rooms through Colby International (Mon–Fri 10am–5pm UK time; ⓣ0151/220 5848, ⓦwww.colbyintl.com). Bear in mind that all quoted room rates are subject to a **fourteen-percent room tax.**

Hotels, motels, and B&Bs

Adagio Hotel 550 Geary St at Jones, Union Square ⓣ415/775-5000, ⓦwww.jdvhotels.com. The decor at this hotel echoes its ornate Spanish Revival facade with deep reds and ochres. Rooms are spacious and exude a calming feng-shui vibe. ❼

Fairmont Hotel 950 Mason St at California, Nob Hill ⓣ1-800/441-1414, ⓦwww.fairmont.com/sanfrancisco. The most famous of the top-notch hotels, with several restaurants and lounges, as well as fantastic views from the rooms. Don't miss the terrace garden, overlooking Powell Street, and the splendor of the *Tonga Room* in the basement (see p.1043). ❼

Golden Gate Hotel 775 Bush St at Mason, Union Square ⓣ1-800/835-1118, ⓦwww.goldengatehotel.com. Friendly, European-style B&B with warmly furnished rooms, some with shared baths. Beautiful original iron elevator and Edwardian interior. Excellent value. ❹

Hotel Bohème 444 Columbus Ave at Vallejo, North Beach ⓣ415/433-9111, ⓦwww.hotelboheme.com. Smack in the middle of the city's Italian quarter, this small, 15-room hotel has tiny but dramatic rooms, with canopied beds. Columbus Ave can be noisy, so light sleepers should ask for a room at the back. ❻

Hotel Del Sol 3100 Webster St at Lombard, Cow Hollow ⓣ1-877/433-5765, ⓦwww.jdvhotels.com. Funky updated motor lodge with a tropical theme and a swimming pool; the best place for budget cool in the city. ❺

Hotel Diva 440 Geary St at Mason, Union Square ⓣ1-800/553-1900, ⓦwww.hoteldiva.com. Trendy modern art hotel with spacious rooms, as well as sleek metal and leather furniture. Touts itself as the sexiest hotel in the area. ❺

Hotel Monaco 501 Geary St at Taylor, Union Square ⓣ1-800/214-4220, ⓦwww.monaco-sf.com. Quirky boutique hotel in a handsome Beaux Arts building. There are canopied beds and goldfish in each room, while the Grace Slick suite features her art for wealthy Jefferson Airplane fans. ❽

Ocean Park Motel 2690 46th Ave at Wawona, Parkside ⓣ415/566-7020, ⓦwww.oceanparkmotel.ypguides.net. Fully across the city from downtown, San Francisco's oldest Art Deco motel is convenient for the coast and the zoo. There's an outdoor jacuzzi and on-site kids' play area. ❹

Phoenix Hotel 601 Eddy St at Larkin, Tenderloin ⓣ1-800/248-9466, ⓦwww.thephoenixhotel.com. This raucous hipster-retro motor lodge feels more like Los Angeles than San Francisco, and is a favorite with touring rock bands. There's a small pool, and the rooms are decorated in tropical colors and rotating local artwork. ❺

Queen Anne Hotel 1590 Sutter St at Octavia, Western Addition ⓣ1-800/227-3970, ⓦwww.queenanne.com. Gloriously excessive restored Victorian that's a quiet bargain. Each room is stuffed with gold-accented Rococo furniture and bunches of silk flowers: the parlor (where afternoon sherry is served) is stuffed with museum-quality period furniture. ❹

Red Victorian Bed, Breakfast & Art 1665 Haight St at Cole, Haight-Ashbury ⓣ415/864-1978, ⓦwww.redvic.com. Homey B&B, decorated with the owner's ethnic arts and exuding her desire for world peace. The best features are the shared bathrooms, which include goldfish-filled toilet cisterns. ④

San Remo Hotel 2237 Mason St at Chestnut, North Beach ⓣ1-800/352-7366, ⓦwww.sanremohotel.com. Quirky option not far from Fisherman's Wharf. Rooms in this warren-like converted house are cozy; all share spotless bathrooms, while a few have sinks. ③

Sir Francis Drake Hotel 450 Powell St at Sutter, Union Square ⓣ1-800/227-5480, ⓦwww.sirfrancisdrake.com. The opulent lobby of this old standby is a riot of marble grandeur with red and purple furnishings; rooms are calmer, with a gentle apple-green color scheme and full facilities. ⑥

Stanyan Park Hotel 750 Stanyan St at Waller, Haight-Ashbury ⓣ415/751-1000, ⓦwww.stanyanpark.com. Adjacent to Golden Gate Park, this small hotel has 35 sumptuous rooms busily decorated in country florals, heavy drapes, and junior four-poster beds. ⑥

Surf Motel 2265 Lombard St at Pierce, Cow Hollow ⓣ415/922-1950, ⓦwww.surfmotorinn.com. This old-school motel has two tiers of bright, simple rooms that are sparklingly clean. Unbeatable prices. ③

Hostels

Adelaide Hostel 51 Isadora Duncan Lane off Taylor St at Geary, Union Square ⓣ415/359-1915, ⓦwww.adelaidehostel.com. 100-bed hostel that includes four-, six-, and ten-person dorms; some have en-suite bathrooms, others share bathrooms. Bunks are built into the wall, much like rail sleeper cars, complete with their own curtains. There's a big, sofa-filled lounge, backyard deck, clean kitchen, and free wireless. Hefty continental breakfasts and cheap laundry. Open 24hr. Dorm beds $23–26.

Green Tortoise 494 Broadway at Montgomery St, North Beach ⓣ1-800/867-8647, ⓦwww.green-tortoise.com. Laid-back destination with dorm beds and double rooms (with shared bath). Both options include free internet, use of the small on-site sauna, and complimentary breakfast. No curfew. Dorm beds from $20.

HI-San Francisco Fisherman's Wharf Building 240, Fort Mason ⓣ415/771-7277, ⓦwww.hiayh.org. High on a bluff between Fisherman's Wharf and the Golden Gate Bridge, this is a choice option for the outdoorsy budget traveler – a standard hostel housed in a nineteenth-century barracks. The drawback is that it's a little out of the way. Beds from $23.

USA Hostel 711 Post St at Jones, Tenderloin ⓣ415/440-5600, ⓦwww.usahostels.com. A friendly and fun place on a safe edge of a gritty neighborhood. There's a kitchen with complimentary tea and coffee all day, and free all-you-can-make pancakes in the morning. Dorm beds (four to a room) run $25–28, with a $1 discount for online booking.

Gay and lesbian accommodation

Inn on Castro 321 Castro St at Market, Castro ⓣ415/861-0321, ⓦwww.innoncastro.com. This luxurious B&B is spread across two nearby houses: It has eight rooms and three apartments available, all of which are brightly decorated in individual styles and have private baths. ⑤

Noe's Nest 3973 23rd St at Noe, Noe Valley ⓣ415/821-0751, ⓦwww.noesnest.com. Seven-room B&B (six with private bath) on a quiet street one mile south of the heart of the Castro. Lavish breakfasts are served each morning, and there's a jacuzzi. ⑤

The Parker House 520 Church St at 18th, Castro ⓣ1-888/520-7275, ⓦwww.parkerguesthouse.com. This 21-room converted mansion is set in beautiful gardens and features ample common areas, a sunny breakfast room, and even a sauna. ⑤

The City

San Francisco is a city of distinct neighborhoods. It's second in the US to only New York in terms of population density, so provided you don't mind a few hilly sidewalks, it's more navigable on foot than other sprawling metropolises around the country. Commercial square-footage is surprisingly small and mostly confined to the downtown area, and the rest of the city is made up of primarily residential neighborhoods with street-level shopping districts easily explored on foot. Armed with a good map and strong legs, you could plough through much of the city in a day or two, but the best way to get to know San Francisco is to dawdle.

Union Square

The city's heart can be found around recently redesigned **Union Square**, located north of Market Street and bordered by Powell and Stockton streets; it takes its name from its role as gathering place for stumping speechmakers during the US Civil War. Cable cars clank past shoppers and theater-goers who gravitate to the district's many upscale hotels, department stores, and boutiques. The square witnessed the attempted assassination of President Gerald Ford outside the **Westin St Francis Hotel** in 1975, and was also the location of Francis Ford Coppola's film *The Conversation*, where Gene Hackman spied on strolling lovers. Many of **Dashiell Hammett**'s detective stories are set partly in the *St Francis*; in fact, during the 1920s, he worked there as a Pinkerton detective.

Along Geary Boulevard, not far from the south side of the square, the **Theater District** is a pint-sized Broadway of restaurants, tourist hotels, and naturally, stage theaters. On the eastern side of the square, **Maiden Lane** is a chic urban walkway that before the 1906 earthquake and fire was one of the city's roughest areas, where prostitution ran rampant and homicides averaged around ten a month. Nowadays, aside from some prohibitively expensive boutiques, the main feature is San Francisco's only **Frank Lloyd Wright-designed building**, an intriguing circular space at no. 140 that, when it opened in 1948, was a prototype for the Guggenheim Museum in New York. Today it's occupied by Xanadu Gallery, which specializes in premium Asian art pieces.

The Financial District and the Embarcadero

North of the city's main artery, Market Street, the glass-and-steel skyscrapers of the **Financial District** have sprung up in recent decades to form the city's only real high-rise area. Sharp-suited workers clog the streets and coffee kiosks during business hours, but the area's canyons of skyscrapers quiet down considerably by evening. Along Montgomery Street, grand pillared entrances and banking halls of the post-1906 earthquake buildings era jostle for attention with a mixed bag of modern towers. The best known is undoubtedly the **Bank of America Center** monolith, 555 California St at Kearny; this broad-shouldered hulk was hugely unpopular when completed in 1969, and continues to divide the city into fans

Cable cars

It was the invention of the **cable car** that put the high in San Francisco's high society, as it made life on the hills both possible and practical. Since 1873, these little trolleys have been an integral part of life in the city, supposedly thanks to Scots-born Andrew Hallidie's concern for horses. Having watched a team struggle and fall, breaking their legs on a steep San Franciscan street, Hallidie designed a **pulley system** around the thick wire rope his father had patented for use in the California mines (the Gold Rush was slowing, and so the Hallidies needed a new market for their product). Despite locals' initial doubts, a transportation revolution followed. At their peak, just before the 1906 earthquake, over six hundred cable cars traveled 110 miles of track throughout the city at a maximum 9.5mph; over the years, usage dwindled and, in 1964, nostalgic citizens voted to preserve the last seventeen miles (now just ten) as a moving historic landmark.

The cars fasten onto a moving two-inch cable which runs beneath the streets, gripping on the ascent then releasing at the top and gliding down the other side. You can see the huge motors that still power these cables at the fun **Cable Car Museum and Powerhouse**, 1201 Mason St at Washington (daily: April–Sept 10am–6pm; Oct–March 10am–5pm; free; ⓣ415/474-1887, ⓦwww.cablecarmuseum.org).

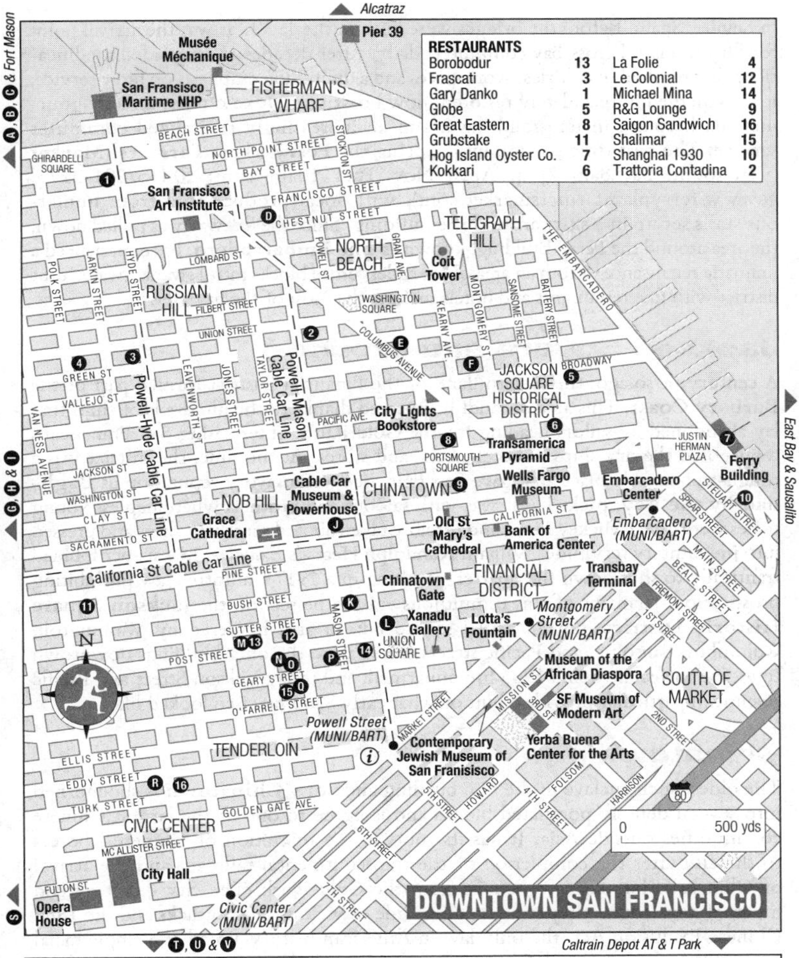

ACCOMMODATION

Adagio Hotel	N	Hotel Bohème	E	The Parker House	V	Sir Francis Drake Hotel	L
Adelaide Hostel	O	Hotel Del Sol	A	Phoenix Hotel	R	Stanyan Park Hotel	I
Fairmont Hotel	J	Hotel Diva	P	Queen Anne Hotel	G	Surf Motel	B
Golden Gate Hotel	K	Hotel Monaco	Q	Red Victorian Bed, Breakfast & Art	H	USA Hostel	M
Green Tortoise	F	Inn on Castro	U	San Remo Hotel	D		
HI-San Francisco Fisherman's Wharf	C	Noe's Nest	T				
		Ocean Park Motel	S				

and those who would like to see it razed to the ground. The **Wells Fargo History Museum**, 420 Montgomery St at California (Mon–Fri 9am–5pm; free; ⓣ415/396-2619, ⓦwww.wellsfargo.com), traces the far-from-slick origins of San Francisco's big money right from the days of the Gold Rush, with mining equipment, gold nuggets, photographs, and a genuine retired stagecoach.

Once cut off from the rest of San Francisco by the double-decker Embarcadero Freeway – damaged in the 1989 earthquake and torn down two years later – the **Ferry Building**, at the foot of Market Street, was modeled on the cathedral tower in Seville, Spain. Before the bridges were built in the 1930s, it was the arrival point for fifty thousand cross-bay commuters daily. After decades of misguided modifications that resulted in colorless workspaces and a dwindling emphasis on ferry service, it has emerged immaculately restored, now boasting deluxe offices, an airy gourmet marketplace in its grand nave, and an increasingly revitalized commuter service. The best time to stop by is during the **Ferry Plaza Farmers' Market** (year-round Sat 8am–2pm, April–Nov Tues 10am–2pm; Ⓣ415/291-3276, Ⓦwww.ferryplazafarmersmarket.com), with local produce sold from numerous stalls set up in a skirt around the building. Since the freeway was pulled down, the area around the Ferry Building, known as **The Embarcadero**, has experienced a dramatic renaissance – from an area of charmless office blocks into a swanky waterfront district with fine restaurants and hotels making the most of the bay views.

Jackson Square and around

A century or so ago, the eastern flank of the Financial District formed part of the **Barbary Coast**. This area of landfill appeared thanks to the hundreds of ships that lay abandoned by sailors heading for the Gold Rush; enterprising San Franciscans repurposed the dry ships as hotels, bars, and stores. At the time, the district was a rough-and-tumble place that gave San Francisco an unsavory reputation as **Baghdad by the Bay**, packed as it was with saloons and brothels where hapless young males were given Mickey Finns and forcibly taken aboard merchant ships and pressed into involuntary servitude. William Randolph Hearst's *Examiner* newspaper lobbied frantically to shut down the quarter, resulting in a 1917 California law prohibiting prostitution. Remains of this tumultuous era can be seen in the **Jackson Square Historic District**, not an actual square but an area bordered by Washington, Columbus, Sansome, and Pacific streets; these were the only buildings downtown to escape the catastrophic 1906 fire unharmed, and today Jackson Street and Pacific Avenue in particular provide a hint of what early San Francisco looked like.

Chinatown

The oldest such enclave in the US, bustling and noisy **Chinatown** is shoehorned into several densely populated blocks and is home to one of the largest Chinese communities outside Asia. It has its roots in the migration of Chinese laborers to the city after the completion of the transcontinental railroad, and the arrival of Chinese sailors keen to benefit from the Gold Rush. The city didn't extend much of a welcome: they were met by a tide of vicious racial attacks and the 1882 Chinese Exclusion Act (the only law in American history aimed at a single racial group), which prevented Chinese immigration and naturalization. Nowadays, Chinatown boasts some of the tackiest stores and facades in the city, making it more akin to shopping in a bad part of Hong Kong than in Beijing. Nonetheless, it bristles with activity despite its increasingly elderly population base and, in sharp contrast to the districts that surround it, a clear lack of wealth.

Enter through **Chinatown Gate** at the intersection of **Grant Avenue** (the district's tourist thoroughfare) and Bush Street. Gold-ornamented portals and brightly painted balconies sit above Grant's crass souvenir stores, while canned crickets chirp above several shop entrances. A few blocks up, **Old St Mary's Cathedral**, 660 California St at Grant, was one of the few San Francisco buildings to survive the 1906 earthquake and fire, and there's a good photo display of the damage to the city in its entranceway.

A half-block east of Grant between Washington, Clay and Kearny streets stands **Portsmouth Square**, San Francisco's first real city center in the mid 1800s and now, for all intents and purposes, Chinatown's living room. When John Montgomery came ashore in 1846 to claim the land for the United States, he raised his flag here and named the square after his ship; the spot where he first planted the US flag is marked today by the one often flying in the square. The plaza is primarily worth visiting to simply absorb everyday Chinatown life, with spirited card games played atop cardboard boxes and other makeshift tables, and neighborhood children letting off steam in the playground.

Parallel to Grant Avenue, **Stockton Street** is the commercial artery for Chinatown locals, its public housing tenements looming overhead and sidewalks full to bursting with locals on the hunt for that day's meat, fish, and produce. **Ellison Enterprises**, 805 Stockton St at Sacramento, is known as Chinatown's best-stocked herbal pharmacy, where you'll find clerks filling orders the ancient Chinese way – with hand-held scales and abaci – from drug cases filled with dried bark, roots, cicadas, ginseng, and other restorative staples. Down adjacent Ross Alley, anyone with even a moderate sweet tooth will want to duck into the fragrant **Golden Gate Fortune Cookie Factory** (daily 7am–8.30pm; free; ⓣ415/781-3956) at no. 56. True to its name, the cramped plant has been churning out 20,000 fresh fortune cookies a day since 1962 – by hand.

North Beach

Resting in the hollow between Russian and Telegraph hills, and bisected by busy Columbus Avenue, **North Beach** has always been a gateway for immigrants, especially Italians who flocked here during the Gold Rush. It became the center of alternative culture in 1953, after the opening of the **City Lights Bookstore**, 261 Columbus Ave at Broadway (see p.1047), the first paperback bookstore in the US and still owned by poet and novelist Lawrence Ferlinghetti. The **Beat Generation** briefly made the store (and the city) the literary capital of America, achieving overnight notoriety when charges of obscenity were leveled at Allen Ginsberg's poem *Howl* in 1957. It was the hedonistic antics of the Beats as much as their literary merits that struck a chord, and North Beach came to symbolize a wild and subversive lifestyle.

Next to City Lights, **Vesuvio**, an old North Beach bar where the likes of Dylan Thomas and Jack Kerouac would drink, remains a haven for lesser-knowns to pontificate on the state of the arts. At the crossroads of Columbus and Broadway, poetry meets porn in a neon-lit assembly of strip joints, the most famous of these being the **Condor Club,** 300 Columbus Ave, where a well-endowed waitress named Carol Doda slipped out of her top one night and kickstarted the concept of topless waitressing in the summer of 1964.

As you continue north on Columbus Avenue, you enter the heart of the old Italian neighborhood, an enclave of narrow streets and leafy enclosures. Explorations lead to small landmarks like **Caffé Trieste**, 609 Vallejo St at Kearny (ⓣ415/982-2605, ⓦwww.caffetrieste.com), where the jukebox often blasts opera classics to cappuccino-sipping artists and other neighborhood denizens; legend has it that Francis Ford Coppola wrote the screenplay for *The Godfather* here. Dawdle in **Washington Square**, where dozens of older, local Chinese practice tai chi on and around the expansive lawn each morning, then head east up the very steep steps on Filbert Street to reach **Telegraph Hill** and **Coit Tower**, which affords grand views of the city and beyond (daily 10am–5pm; lobby free, $3.75 for elevator to top; ⓣ415/362-0808, ⓦwww.coittower.org). Also worth a stroll are the **Greenwich and Filbert steps**, a pair of canopied pedestrian paths that cling to Telegraph Hill's steep eastern flank.

Rising a few blocks west of Columbus, **Russian Hill** was named for six unknown Russian sailors who died here on an expedition in the early 1800s. In the

Alcatraz

Before the rocky islet of **Alcatraz** became America's most dreaded **high-security prison** in 1934, it had already served as a fortress and military jail. Surrounded by the freezing, impassable water of San Francisco Bay, it made an ideal place to hold the nation's most wanted criminals – men such as Al Capone and Machine Gun Kelly. The conditions were inhumane: inmates were kept in solitary confinement, in cells no larger than nine by five feet, most without light. They were not allowed to eat together, read newspapers, play cards, or even talk; relatives could visit for only two hours each month. Escape really was impossible: nine men managed to get off "The Rock," but none gained his freedom, and the only two to reach the mainland (using a jacket stuffed with inflated surgical rings as a raft) were soon apprehended.

Due to its massive running costs, the prison finally closed in 1963. The island remained abandoned until 1969, when a group of Native Americans staged an occupation as part of a peaceful attempt to claim the island for their people, citing treaties that designated all federal land not in use as automatically reverting to their ownership. Using all the bureaucratic trickery it could muster, the US government finally ousted them two years later, claiming the operative lighthouse qualified it as active.

At least 750,000 tourists each year take the excellent hour-long, self-guided audio **tour** of the abandoned prison, which includes sharp anecdotal commentary as well as re-enactments of prison life featuring improvised voices of the likes of Capone and Kelly. Note that the island's name is a corruption of the Spanish word for pelicans (*alcatraces*), although the only reason the current islet is known as Alcatraz is thanks to a muddle-headed English mapmaker and captain who confused the names of several outcrops in the bay in 1826 – what we know as Yerba Buena Island was in fact the original Alcatraz.

Ferries to Alcatraz leave from Pier 33 (frequent departures from 9am–3.55pm May–Oct, 9am–1.55pm Oct–May; last ferry returns at 6.15pm May-Oct, 4.15pm Oct-May; day tour $24.50, night tour departs Pier 33 at 6.10pm and 6.50pm, $31.50; ⓣ415/981-7625, ⓦwww.alcatrazcruises.com); allow at least three hours for a visit, including cruise time. Advance reservations are essential – in peak season, it's impossible to snag a ticket for same-day travel, and ideally you should allow two weeks.

summer, there's always a long line of cars waiting to drive down the tight curves of **Lombard Street** from the precipitous perch on Hyde Street. Surrounded by palatial dwellings and herbaceous borders, Lombard is an especially thrilling drive at night, when most tourists are gone and the city lights twinkle below.

Fisherman's Wharf

If the districts of San Francisco are a family, then **Fisherman's Wharf** is the boisterous uncle who showed up at the reunion in a ghastly shirt, put a lampshade on his head, and never left. The city doesn't go dramatically out of its way to court and fleece tourists, but the scores of tacky souvenir shops and overpriced restaurants that crowd the Wharf expose this area's mission of raking in disposable tourist dollars. The area flourished as a serious fishing port well into the twentieth century, although these days, the few fishermen that can afford the exorbitant mooring charges have usually finished their trawling by early morning and are gone by the time most visitors arrive.

The most endearing sight here is the large colony of barking **sea lions** that has taken over a number of floating platforms between piers 39 and 41. Another entertaining pick is the **Musée Mécanique** on Pier 45 (Mon–Fri 10am–7pm, Sat & Sun 10am–8pm; free; ⓣ415/346-2000, ⓦwww.museemechanique.org), which houses an extensive collection of vintage arcade machines.

Immediately west of the Wharf is **San Francisco Maritime National Historic Park**, a low-key complex that includes restored sailing vessels, curving jetties, impressive nautical architecture, and a sandy spit. Drop into the fine Visitor Center, 499 Jefferson St at Hyde (late May to late Sept 9.30am–7pm; rest of year 9.30am–5pm; Ⓣ415/447-5000, Ⓦwww.nps.gov/safr), which sells tickets for touring the park's docked ships.

Civic Center, SoMa, and the Tenderloin

While parts of San Francisco can almost seem like an urban utopia, the adjoining districts of **the Tenderloin** and **Civic Center** are gritty reminders that not everybody has it so easy. **SoMa**, the district South of Market Street, meanwhile, was transformed by the dot-com boom of the 1990s from an industrial wasteland to a hive of loft offices and granite-walled eateries, centered on the lovely Yerba Buena Gardens. The internet business crash of the early 2000s ended much of its economic upswing, though the area has revived in recent years.

The majestic federal and municipal buildings of **Civic Center** can't help but look strangely out of sync, both with their immediate neighbors and with San Francisco as a whole. Their grand Beaux Arts style is at odds with the quirky wooden architecture of much of the rest of the city – little wonder, as they're the sole remnant of a grand architectural plan to transform the city's downtown into a boulevard-dotted, Parisian-inspired place after the original buildings were leveled by the 1906 earthquake. It was at the huge, domed **City Hall**, across from grassy **Civic Center Plaza**, that Mayor George Moscone and gay Supervisor Harvey Milk were assassinated in 1978. The recently restored gold plate dome is an impressive relic of Gold Rush-era largesse. If you want to take one of the free, fascinating tours around its interior, sign up at the Docent Tour kiosk on the Van Ness Avenue side of the building (tours Mon–Fri 10am, noon & 2pm, Ⓣ415/554-4799, Ⓦwww.ci.sf.ca.us/cityhall).

Formerly one of San Francisco's least desirable neighborhoods, SoMa has enjoyed a rebirth that's seen many of its warehouses converted to offices for internet businesses. The area's anchor attraction is the **SF Museum of Modern Art**, 151 Third St at Mission (Mon, Tues & Fri–Sun 11am–5.45pm, Thurs 11am–8.45pm, closed Wed; $12.50, $6.25 Thurs 6–8.45pm, free the first Tues of the month; Ⓣ415/357-4000, Ⓦwww.sfmoma.org), which opened in January 1995. Major works include paintings by Jackson Pollock, Frida Kahlo, and Diego Rivera, though the temporary exhibitions are the museum's strongest suit. The building, designed by Swiss architect Mario Botta, is flooded with natural light from a striking cylindrical skylight, while the upper galleries are connected by a vertigo-inducing metal catwalk.

San Francisco's burgeoning arts district features a pair of provoking recent additions. The first, the **Museum of the African Diaspora**, 685 Mission St at Third (Wed–Sat 11am–6pm, Sun noon–5pm; $10, free; Ⓣ415/358-7200, Ⓦwww.moadsf.org), spotlights traditional African art, work inspired by the horrors of slavery, and modern pieces in a range of media. Next to a nearby former power substation, you'll see a striking askew blue cube, which is an atrium gallery attached to the new **Contemporary Jewish Museum of San Francisco**, 736 Mission St (Thurs 1–8.30pm, Fri–Tues 11am–5.30pm, $10, under-18s free; Ⓣ415/655-7800, Ⓦwww.thecjm.org). Opened in summer 2007, the museum has no permanent collection; instead, it hosts cleverly curated exhibitions spanning Jewish history and culture, such as a retrospective of the work of *Shrek* creator William Steig.

▲ Dolores Park, the Mission

The Mission

Vibrant, hip, and ethnically mixed, the **Mission** is arguably San Francisco's most intriguing neighborhood. Beginning a few miles southwest of downtown, nestled in a basin, it's also one of the warmest, and the summer fog that blankets the rest of the city usually leaves this area alone. The traditional first stop for immigrants, the Mission was initially predominantly Scandinavian, then Irish, before becoming a sizeable Latin American settlement. Though white hipsters have in recent years swarmed to its old buildings and affordable (by San Francisco standards) rents, it's still a joyously Latino place and one of the unmissable sights of the city.

The area takes its name from the old **Mission Dolores**, 3321 16th St at Dolores (daily 8am–noon, 1–4pm; $3; ⓣ415/621-8203), the oldest building to survive the 1906 earthquake and fire. It was founded in 1776 as Spain staked its claim to California; the graves of the Native Americans it tried to "civilize" can be seen in the cemetery next door, along with those of white pioneers.

The heart of the Mission lies east of Mission Street between 16th and Cesar Chavez streets. Here you'll absorb the district's original Latino flavor among a bevy of stores and salons, as well as *taquerias* cooking hearty Mexican (and Cal-Mex) fare, markets selling tropical fruits, and *panaderias* baking traditional pastries. Head over to the same stretch along Valencia Street, one block west of Mission, where a profusion of independent bookstores and thrift stores makes for a fun afternoon of browsing.

What really sets the Mission apart from the city's other neighborhoods are its **murals** – there are over two hundred in all, though many are more heartfelt than skilled or beautiful. The densest concentration is along **Balmy Alley,** between Folsom and Harrison streets off 24th Street, which is especially known for its politically charged paintings depicting the agonies of many Central American countries. For a more detailed recap of the murals' history and meaning, join one of the **tours** run by mural organization Precita Eyes, 2981 24th St at Harrison (tours Sat & Sun 1.30pm; $12; ⓣ415/285-2287, ⓦwww.precitaeyes.org).

The Castro

Progressive and celebratory, but also increasingly comfortable and wealthy, the **Castro** is the city's center of gay culture, providing a barometer for the state of the grown-up and sobered gay scene. Some people maintain it's still the wildest place in town, while others insist it's a shadow of its former self. Most of the same bars and hangouts still stand from its 1970s heyday, but these days they're host to a different and more conservative breed, while cute shops and restaurants lend a young professional feel to the place. A visit to the district is a must if you're to get any idea of just what San Francisco is all about – the liveliest time to stroll around is on Sunday afternoons, when the streetside cafés are packed.

The neighborhood's one major sight is the **Castro Theater**, 429 Castro St at Market (ⓣ415/621-6120, ⓦwww.thecastrotheatre.com), a stunning example of the Mediterranean Revival style, and flagged by the neon sign that towers above surrounding buildings. Inside, its foamy balconies, wall-mounted busts of heroic figures, and massive ceiling ornamentation lend an air of affirmed glamour, though you'll have to come for a movie showing to get in.

The junction of **Castro and 18th Street**, known as the "gayest four corners of the earth," marks the Castro's center, cluttered with bookstores, clothing stores, cafés, and bars. Neighborhood side streets offer a slightly more exclusive fare of exotic delicatessens, fine wines, and fancy florists amid manicured and leafy residential roads.

Haight-Ashbury

The fame of **Haight-Ashbury**, a few miles west of downtown San Francisco, is synonymous with the hippie movement of the 1960s – which brought the area the notoriety it has capitalized on ever since. Centered on the junction of Haight and Ashbury streets, "The Haight" was a run-down Victorian neighborhood until it was transformed into the hub of counterculture cool during the 1960s. These days, it's an explosion of overt capitalism, a sort of boho theme-park where shops shill hippie memorabilia like tie-dye clothing, hand-blown hookahs, and Grateful Dead Beanie Babies, with a number of brightly colored, youthful clothing boutiques interspersed. It also remains a mecca for runaway youth looking for their own "Summer of Love," so expect to be repeatedly hit up for spare change as you roam Haight Street's sidewalks.

The hippies

The first **hippies** were an offshoot of the Beats, many of whom had moved out of their increasingly expensive North Beach homes to take advantage of the low rents and large spaces in the Victorian houses of the Haight. The post-Beat bohemia that subsequently began to develop here in the early 1960s was initially a small affair, involving drug use and the embrace of Eastern religion and philosophy, together with a marked anti-American political stance and a desire for world peace. Where Beat philosophy had emphasized self-indulgence, the hippies, on the face of it at least, stressed such concepts as "universal truth" and "cosmic awareness." Characters like **Ken Kesey** and his Merry Pranksters set a precedent of wild living and challenging authority. The use of drugs was seen as an integral – and positive – part of the movement. **LSD**, especially, which was not then illegal, was claimed as an avant-garde art form, pumped out in private laboratories and distributed by **Timothy Leary** and his supporters with a prescription – "Turn on, tune in, drop out" – that galvanized a generation into inactivity. Life in the Haight took on a theatrical quality: Pop Art found mass appeal, light shows became legion, and dress flamboyant. The psychedelic music scene, spearheaded by the Grateful Dead, Jefferson Airplane, and Janis Joplin, became a genuine force nationwide, and it wasn't long before kids from all over America started turning up in **Haight-Ashbury** for the free food, free drugs, and free love. Money became a dirty word, the hip became "heads," and the rest of the world were "straights." During the heady days of the massive "be-in" in Golden Gate Park in 1966 and the revolutionary, peace-promoting "Summer of Love" the following year, no fewer than 75,000 pilgrims turned the busy little intersection of Haight-Ashbury into the center of alternative culture.

Toward the eastern end of Haight Street, around Fillmore Street, is the area known as the **Lower Haight**. Mellow by day, and primarily an African-American neighborhood since World War II, it has been slightly transformed over the past decade-plus into a stomping ground for the city's rave culture, and its bars and restaurants are some of the most vibrant in town.

Golden Gate Park

The largest and most diverse greenspace in a city rich in parklands, **Golden Gate Park** is the one above all that's not to be missed. Stretching three miles west from the Haight all the way to Ocean Beach, it was constructed in the late 1800s on what was then an area of wild sand dunes buffeted by sea spray. Today, despite throngs of daily visitors, you can always find some solitude here.

Of the park's museums, the best is the newly (2005) rebuilt **M. H. de Young Museum**, 50 Tea Garden Drive (Tues–Thurs, Sat & Sun 9.30am–5.15pm, Fri 9.30am–8.45pm; $10, free first Tues of each month; Ⓣ415/750-3600, Ⓦwww.thinker.org), which hosts temporary exhibits and a hit-and-miss collection of American art from colonial times up to the present day, although the boxy building's alluring interior is the real star on display. Across the Music Concourse from the de Young, the **California Academy of Sciences** (Mon–Sat 9.30am–5.15pm, Sun 11am–5pm; $24.95, free third Wed of each month; Ⓣ415/379-8000, Ⓦwwwcalacademy.org) reopened in 2008 after a lengthy closure; its new, grass-roofed structure is a bold nod toward twenty-first century sustainable building practices and has been an instant hit with the region's eco-minded public. Inside the grand, glass-walled entrance, exhibits from the planetarium, natural history museum, and aquarium are smartly intertwined and make for an entertainingly educational day's visit.

Next to the de Young, the **Japanese Tea Garden** (Nov–Feb daily 9am–5pm, Mar–Oct daily 8.30am–6pm; $4, free daily for first and last hours of opening) is dominated by a massive bronze Buddha, while carp-filled ponds and bonsai and cherry trees lend a tranquil feel; arrive early to beat the busloads of tourists that pour in regularly. Nearby, the immaculately restored **Conservatory of Flowers** (Tues–Sun 9am–5pm; $5; ⓣ415/666-7001, ⓦwww.conservatoryofflowers.org) and **Strybing Arboretum** (Mon–Fri 8am–4.30pm, Sat & Sun 10am–5pm; free; ⓣ415/661-1316, ⓦwww.sfbotanicalgarden.org), the latter a 75-acre botanic garden that's home to more than seven thousand varieties of plants and trees, are each worthwhile destinations for exotic foliage examination or just quiet reflection.

The Golden Gate Bridge

The orange towers of the **Golden Gate Bridge**, perhaps the best-loved symbol of San Francisco, are visible from almost every high point in the city. Its color was originally intended as a temporary undercoat before a gray topcoat was to be applied, but locals liked the primer so much upon the bridge's 1937 opening that it's remained ever since. Driving or bicycling across it is a real thrill, while the walk across its 1.7-mile span allows you to take in its enormous size and absorb the views of the Marin headlands, as well as those of the city itself. The view is especially beautiful at sunset, when the waning glow paints the city a delicate pink – unless of course everything's shrouded in fog, when the bridge takes on a patently eerie quality.

Eating

San Francisco has long been known for its fine-dining restaurants, and more recently for its wealth of low-end marvels like **taquerias, dim-sum eateries**, and **curry houses**. Indeed, the greatest asset of the city's food scene is its staggering variety – not only in types of cuisine, but in price ranges and overall experiences. These listings reflect the city's dining diversity, from gourmet **vegetarian** restau-

Late-night eating

Although it can be a minor struggle to find a good San Francisco restaurant that serves food after 11pm, the following choices should satiate your **late-night** cravings.

Globe 290 Pacific Ave at Battery, Jackson Square ⓣ415/391-4132. A favorite for local restaurant industry folks, with a Cal-Ital menu heavy on pizzas and fresh fish. Entrees $15–25.

Great Eastern 649 Jackson St at Kearny, Chinatown ⓣ415/986-2500. Elegant and traditional restaurant serving favorites such as sauteed squab with Chinese broccoli. Entrees over $20.

Grubstake 1525 Pine St at Polk, Polk Gulch ⓣ415/673-8268. Old-fashioned diner dishing out all the American basics, although the real draw is the ten or so Portuguese specialties on offer. Entrees $8–15.

Liverpool Lil's 2942 Lyon St at Lombard, Cow Hollow ⓣ415/921-6664. One of the few pub-restaurants in San Francisco to offer a bracingly British menu: liver and onions, lamb shepherd's pie, fish and chips. Entrees $15–25.

Taqueria Can-cún 2288 Mission St at 19th, Mission ⓣ415/252-9560. Standby taqueria boasting some of the finest grilled tortillas in the Mission. The *horchata* (a rice-cinnamon drink) is the ideal foil for one of the terrific super burritos. Burritos and plate meals $5–9.

rants, **steakhouses**, and **oyster bars**, to **Spanish tapas** joints, **Asian bakeries**, and **Czech fare**, for everyone from big spenders to budget-minded visitors.

The local slant of cooking, dubbed **California cuisine**, is a development of French *nouvelle cuisine*, preserving the *nouvelle* focus on a wide mix of fresh, locally available foods, but widening the scope of influences considerably. Of course, with the vineyards of Napa and Sonoma on the city's doorstep, quality **wines** often play a major role on the menus of San Francisco restaurants.

Downtown and around

Borobudur 700 Post St at Jones, Tenderloin ☎415/775-1512. Indonesian powerhouse fuses Indian and Thai influences with often extraordinary results. Don't pass up the *roti prata* (grilled, flaky bread) and curry dipping sauce appetizer. Entrees about $10.

Frascati 1901 Hyde St at Green, Russian Hill ☎415/928-1406. Vividly romantic, bi-level bistro on a prime corner. Uniquely paired California dishes such as maple-leaf duck breast with herb *spaetzle* and huckleberry sauce retain a level of comfort, and the wine list is impressive. Dinner only. Entrees $20–30.

Gary Danko 800 North Point St at Hyde, Fisherman's Wharf ☎415/749-2060. This understated California cuisine oasis regularly vies for the title of best restaurant in town. Granted, this is performance food served with a flourish, but it's utterly splurge-worthy. Arrange well ahead for a reservation. Dinner only. Five-course prix fixe options $65–96.

Greens Building A, Fort Mason Center ☎415/771-6222. San Francisco's original vegetarian restaurant remains popular thanks in no small part to a picturesque pier setting and an airy, pine furniture-filled interior. Oddly casual given the quality and price of the food. Entrees over $20.

Hog Island Oyster Co. 1 Ferry Building, Embarcadero ☎415/391-7117. This outpost of the Tomales Bay (Marin County) farm hosts mollusk devotees who sit elbow to elbow at the wrap-around granite bar. Menu items $10–25.

Kokkari 200 Jackson St at Front, Financial District ☎415/981-0983. The top Greek restaurant in town relies on Hellenic staples such as lamb and eggplant, and its huge open fireplace heats two bedazzling dining rooms decorated with Oriental rugs and goatskin lampshades. Entrees $20–30.

La Folie 2316 Polk St at Green, Russian Hill ☎415/776-5577. Magnificent Provençal food served without attitude or pretension. There are five different five-course prix fixe options to choose from, worth it if you fancy a gourmet treat. Dinner only. $75–105 per person.

Le Colonial 20 Cosmo Place at Taylor, Union Square ☎415/931-3600. Franco-Vietnamese restaurant boasts lush, 1920s-themed dining quarters decked out with tile floors, palm fronds, and ceiling fans, while the upstairs lounge is a salon with rattan couches and faded rugs. Inventive dishes arrive in generous portions. Dinner only. Entrees over $30.

Michael Mina Westin St Francis, 335 Powell St at Geary, Union Square ☎415/397-9222. Postpone the diet and pack your credit card if you want to enjoy the adventurous New American menu at this grandly columned restaurant run by the namesake local chef. Dinner only. Expect to fork out $90–135 per person.

R&G Lounge 631 Kearny St at Commercial, Chinatown ☎415/982-7877. Behind frosted windows looms this enormous Hong Kong–style spot, where family-style dishes lean heavily toward seafood. Entrees under $20.

Saigon Sandwich 560 Larkin St at Eddy, Tenderloin ☎415/474-5698. Closet-sized, lunch-only shop selling sizable, made-to-order *bahn mi* (Vietnamese sandwiches). Expect a line out the door every afternoon. Cash only. Sandwiches under $3.

Shalimar 532 Jones St at O'Farrell, Tenderloin ☎415/928-0333. The chicken tikka masala is the main attraction at this austere South Asian joint, while the lamb saag is just as exceptional (and generous in its portion). Afterward, expect to smell as if you yourself have been doused in spices and baked in the tandoor oven. Entrees under $10.

Trattoria Contadina 1800 Mason St at Union, North Beach ☎415/982-5728. Family-owned, warm, and charming, with white cloth-swathed tables and photograph-covered walls. The rigatoni with eggplant and smoked mozzarella is a top option, and the Powell-Mason cable car will drop you off steps from the front door. Entrees under $20.

SoMa, the Mission, and around

Acme Chophouse 24 Willie Mays Plaza at AT&T Park (Third St at King), Mission Bay ☎415/644-0240. Enormous restaurant at the local ballpark that's one of San Francisco's finest steakhouses. Star items are the grass-fed filet ribeye, and sides like comically buttery mashed potatoes. Entrees over $30.

Asia SF 201 Ninth St at Howard, SoMa ⓣ415/255-2742. Notorious hotspot where gender-illusionist servers perform cheeky dance routines on the bar, while the equally crossbred pan-Asian food is surprisingly successful. Popular with large groups; best avoided by quiet types. Dinner only. Entrees under $20.

Bi-Rite Creamery 3692 18th St at Dolores, Mission ⓣ415/626-5600. Tiny ice cream shop hits all the right notes with its artisanal flavors. Usual suspects like mint chip and chocolate share freezer space with unique concoctions such as toasted coconut and honey lavender. Inexpensive.

Crepes A-Go-Go 350 11th St at Folsom, SoMa ⓣ415/503-1294. Locally beloved crêperie with several savory and sweet varieties available – and in the true Parisian tradition, there's plenty of Nutella on hand. Inexpensive.

Delfina 3621 18th St at Guerrero, Mission ⓣ415/552-4055. Continually buzzing, dinner-only restaurant that attracts nearly every sort of San Franciscan and features light, Cal-Ital dishes that rarely miss. Entrees over $20.

Dosa 995 Valencia St at 21st, Mission ⓣ415/642-3672. *Dosa*'s namesake crêpe-like item – and its close cousin, the thicker *uttapam* – dominate its South Indian menu, while the terracotta dining room is welcoming and not too noisy. Dinner only. Entrees $10–20.

Goood Frikin Chicken 10 29th St at Mission, Mission ⓣ415/970-2428. Superbly seasoned poultry that warrants the extra 'o' in this airy restaurant's goofy name. The dining room is cast in various earthtones, with the ceiling and walls covered in soothing landscape murals. Entrees under $10.

Just for You 732 22nd St at Third, Potrero Hill ⓣ415/647-3033. Out-of-the-way gem produces some of the finest, fluffiest (and largest!) beignets outside of New Orleans. All breads are housemade (try the raisin cinnamon toast), while the enormous pancakes are the stuff of legend. Breakfast and lunch only. Entrees under $10.

Le P'tit Laurent 699 Chenery St at Diamond, Glen Park ⓣ415/334-3235. Carnivores won't want to miss the meaty cassoulet (complete with full leg of duck) and memorable desserts; service and overall vibe are equally warm. Conveniently, it's steps from the Glen Park BART station. Dinner only. Entrees over $20.

Mochica 937 Harrison St at Fifth, SoMa ⓣ415/278-0480. Diminutive Peruvian hideaway specializing in small plates, ceviche, and punch-packing sangria. Many dishes benefit from uncommonly flavorful sauces and marinades. Menu items $10–20.

Papalote 3409 24th St at Valencia, Mission ⓣ415/970-8815. Peerless Cal-Mex cuisine – there's nary a poor menu choice to be made, from the marinated tofu burrito to anything that includes the perfectly grilled carne asada. The warm chips and otherworldly chipotle salsa is the real *coup de grace*. Burritos and plate meals under $10.

Shanghai 1930 133 Steuart St at Mission, SoMa ⓣ415/896-5600. Sleek, downstairs destination designed like a supper club with plenty of sexily decadent decor. It's become one of the city's most respected Chinese restaurants; there's live jazz nightly, and a cigar bar adjacent to the main room. Entrees $10–20.

Taqueria San Francisco 2794 24th St at York, Mission ⓣ415/641-1770. The quintessential San Francisco taqueria (look no further than its name), where burritos are characterized by generous heft, flaky grilled tortillas, and rustic meats like *al pastor* (rotisserie-grilled pork) – and for the especially adventurous, *lengua* (tongue) and *sesos* (brain). Expect bouncy tuba-pop from the jukebox. Cash only. Burritos and plate meals under $10.

Walzwerk 381 S Van Ness Ave at 15th, Mission ⓣ415/551-7181. Cramped German eatery serving hearty comfort food. Framed East German pop records and large portraits of twentieth-century Eastern Bloc industry evoke past eras behind the Iron Curtain. Dinner only. Entrees under $20.

Western Addition, Haight-Ashbury, and around

Burgermeister 86 Carl St at Cole, Cole Valley ⓣ415/566-1274. Increasingly popular spot that broils excellent gourmet half-pound burgers. All the mainstream choices are available, as well as a handful of unusual options for the adventurous (like the mango burger). Burgers under $10.

Frankie's Bohemian Cafe 1862 Divisadero St at Pine, Western Addition ⓣ415/921-4725. Amber wood-lined bar-restaurant where the house specialty is a burly Czech mess called *brambory*, which piles meat and/or veggies atop a pan-fried bed of potato and zucchini. Burgers, salads, and 20-oz beers fill out the menu. Entrees $10–15.

Little Star Pizza 846 Divisadero St at McAllister, Western Addition ⓣ415/441-1118. One of San Francisco's top pizzerias, dimly lit and packed nightly with hipsters enjoying its lively bar and jukebox blasting American and British indie rock. The kitchen bakes deep-dish and thin-crust pizzas with equal aplomb. Dinner only. Large pies run $15–23.

Massawa 1538 Haight St at Ashbury, Upper Haight ⓣ415/621-4129. Terrific East African eatery where you shouldn't expect to keep your hands clean as you stab at deliciously gloopy confections with spongy *injera* bread, presented together family-style on a gigantic platter. Entrees $10–15.

Nopa 560 Divisadero St at Hayes, Western Addition ⓣ415/864-8643. Exceptional California cuisine served at long, amber tables. The baked pasta with spicy fennel sausage is a proven winner, as is the simple but near-perfect grass-fed hamburger (served with fries). Dinner only. Entrees under $20.

Rosamunde Sausage Grille 545 Haight St at Fillmore, Lower Haight ⓣ415/437-6851. Tiny storefront grill serving top-grade grilled sausages on sesame rolls. Savvy customers place their order, head next door to the *Toronado* (see p.1043), and await their sausage's delivery over a beer. Inexpensive.

Sociale 3665 Sacramento St at Spruce, Presidio Heights ⓣ415/921-3200. Intimate Italian bistro worth seeking out at the end of its verdant pedestrian lane. Go for the heated dining courtyard, cozy atmosphere, fontina-crammed fried olives appetizer, and Italian-leaning wine list. Entrees $20–30.

The Cheese Steak Shop 1716 Divisadero St at Sutter, Western Addition ⓣ415/346-3712. Odds are slim you'll bite into a finer cheesesteak sandwich in San Francisco than what you'll get at this immensely popular shop, where the menu includes a bacon cheesesteak and several chicken varieties. Sandwiches well under $10.

The Sunset and the Richmond

Arizmendi 1331 Ninth Ave at Irving, Inner Sunset ⓣ415/566-3117. The artisanal breads and pastries are reason enough to head to this small, earthy bakery, but its regular rotation of gourmet pizza is the true surprise treat. Baked goods and pizzas vary daily. Inexpensive.

Aziza 5800 Geary Blvd at 22nd, Outer Richmond ⓣ415/752-2222. Moroccan fine-dining destination with opulent decor, a superb wine list, and fun touches like a rose water-filled pewter basin presented for pre-meal handwashing. The menu's packed with California-accented North African specialties. Dinner only. Entrees $20–30.

Brothers Korean BBQ 4128 Geary Blvd at Sixth, Inner Richmond ⓣ415/387-7991. The décor here is nothing to get excited about, but the moderately priced feasts of marinated meats and myriad, pungent side dishes are worth the visit. Certain tables have sunken *hibachis* on which you can cook your own meats. Entrees $12–20.

Gordo Taqueria 1233 Ninth Ave at Lincoln, Inner Sunset ⓣ415/566-6011. Burrito shop that lives up to its name (which translates to "fat" in English) by specializing in hefty, stumpy slabs that never miss the mark. The menu's as simple as can be, including only tacos, burritos, and quesadillas. Cash only. Menu items under $6.

Koo 408 Irving St at Fifth, Inner Sunset ⓣ415/731-7077. Japanese fusion restaurant featuring a combination of cooked plates designed to be shared, as well as plenty of sushi, sashimi, and specialty rolls. Dinner only. Menu items under $20.

Marnee Thai 1243 Ninth Ave at Lincoln, Inner Sunset ⓣ415/731-9999. Humming spot where the kitchen's home-style central Thai cooking rolls with the seasons – winter visitors may see a markedly different menu than those in summer. Entrees about $10.

Park Chow 1240 Ninth Ave at Lincoln, Inner Sunset ⓣ415/665-9912. Surprisingly huge space with a menu that's all over the globe, from salads, American comfort food, pizzas, and pastas to artisan cheese plates and even a handful of Asian noodle dishes. Entrees $10–15.

Pluto's 627 Irving St at Seventh, Inner Sunset ⓣ415/753-8867. Custom salads are the big draw here, as they're among the biggest, best, and cheapest in town. The turkey and stuffing is a soul-warming option any day of the year. Menu items under $10.

Nightlife and entertainment

Compared to **nightlife** in other major cities, where you need money and attitude in equal measure, San Francisco's scene demands little of either. This is no 24-hour city, however, and the approach to socializing is often surprisingly low-key, with little of the pandering to fads and fashions that goes on elsewhere. The club scene may not be nationally recognized as one that's cutting-edge, but it's inexpensive compared to those elsewhere: a decent night out might run you $40–50, including cover charges and a few drinks. As is the case in restaurants, smoking is illegal in bars and clubs.

The *Chronicle Datebook* (ⓦ www.sfgate.com) pull-out supplement (available in the Sunday paper), along with the free weeklies *San Francisco Bay Guardian* (ⓦ www.sfbg.com), *SF Weekly* (ⓦ www.sfweekly.com), and *The Onion* (ⓦ www.theonion.com), are the best sources of **listings.** Ticketmaster (ⓣ 415/421-8497, ⓦ www.ticketmaster.com) is the major **ticket** agency, while Tickets.com (ⓣ 415/776-1999, ⓦ www.tickets.com) is also worth a try.

Bars

San Francisco, while famous for its restaurants, has a huge number of **bars**, ranging from comfortably scruffy jukebox joints to chic watering holes.

111 Minna 111 Minna St at Second, SoMa ⓣ 415/974-1719. Loft space that's a combination bar, art gallery, and performance venue, located in a vibrant area of SoMa. It gets busier, noisier, and more raucous as the evening wears on, so go early if you want to chat. Cover free–$5.

The Alembic 1725 Haight St at Cole, Haight-Ashbury ⓣ 415/666-0822. With its wooden bar and mustard-yellow walls, this classy spot has perhaps the best alcohol selection in the city, with a vast range of spirits as well as locally brewed beer and fancy cocktails.

The Attic 3336 24th St at Mission, Mission ⓣ 415/643-3376. Beloved dive that's so dark, it takes your eyes time to adjust to the low lighting. Decor is clearly inspired by a vintage attic, with oddball antiques in random places.

Bambuddha Lounge *Phoenix Hotel*, 601 Eddy St at Larkin, Tenderloin ⓣ 415/885-5088. Sleek, South Pacific-inspired cocktail lounge with terrific DJs and strong drinks. Skip the overly self-aware interior and head outside for drinks by the pool.

Edinburgh Castle 950 Geary Blvd at Polk, Tenderloin ⓣ 415/885-4074. Evocative Scottish bar filled with heraldic Highland memorabilia. The room upstairs regularly hosts live performances, while the pub food comes straight from the co-owned nearby chippie *The Old Chelsea*.

Latin American Club 3286 22nd St at Valencia, Mission ⓣ 415/647-2732. A cozy place that retains a neighborhood feel. The ceiling space above is crammed with piñatas, Mexican streamers, and assorted trinkets, and there's a pool table in the middle of the room.

Li Po 916 Grant Ave at Jackson, Chinatown ⓣ 415/982-0072. Named after the Chinese poet, this narrow haunt is a little grotty, although that's part of its charm. One of the few places to go for a drink in Chinatown.

Lucky 13 2140 Market St at Church, Castro ⓣ 415/487-1313. Straight bar on the outskirts of the Castro with an extensive selection of international beers. It's filled with pool-players chomping on free popcorn; there's a humble patio out back.

Mad Dog in the Fog 530 Haight St at Fillmore, Lower Haight ⓣ 415/626-7279. Aptly named by two lads from Birmingham, England who own the joint, this is one of the Lower Haight's most loyally patronized bars, with darts, English beer, and footie on TV.

Place Pigalle 520 Hayes St at Gough, Hayes Valley ⓣ 415/552-2671. Decorated in plush, deep reds, this friendly lounge boasts rotating art on the walls and the neighborhood's most popular pool table.

Spec's Twelve Adler Museum Café 12 Saroyan Place off Columbus at Broadway, North Beach ⓣ 415/421-4112. Amiable watering hole packed with an older, eccentric local crowd and known for its chatty bar staff.

Tonga Room *Fairmont Hotel*, 950 Mason St at California, Nob Hill ⓣ 415/772-5278. Ultra-campy bar styled like a Polynesian village, complete with pond, simulated rainstorms, and grass-skirted band strangling jazz and pop covers to death upon a floating raft. The cocktails are outrageously overpriced, but a $7 happy hour buffet makes up for it.

Toronado 547 Haight St at Fillmore, Lower Haight ⓣ 415/863-2276. Renowned for its vast selection of international ales and lagers, this cacophonous tavern should be the first stop on any beer aficionado's itinerary.

Trad'r Sam's 6150 Geary Blvd at 26th, Outer Richmond ⓣ 415/221-0773. San Francisco's original Tiki bar is a bit of an excursion from the central neighborhoods, but it's worth it for the enormous (and occasionally flaming) bowls of colorful cocktails.

Tunnel Top 601 Bush St at Stockton, Union Square ⓣ 415/986-8900. Fun spot atop the Stockton Tunnel that boasts stiff drinks and a terrific balcony.

Zeitgeist 199 Valencia St at Duboce, Mission ⓣ 415/255-7505. San Francisco's version of a biker bar (it's particularly popular with bicycle messengers) with a gigantic patio that's a smoker's dream. There's also a short food menu consisting mostly of barbecue chicken and burgers.

Gay and lesbian bars

San Francisco's **gay and lesbian bars** are many and varied, ranging from cozy cocktail lounges to no-holds-barred leather-and-chain hangouts. The scene may no longer be quite as wild as its reputation would have you believe, but at its best it can still be hard to beat.

The Café 2369 Market St at 17th, Castro ⓣ415/861-3846. Longtime staple of the local club scene that remains a crowd-pleaser. It's classic out-and-proud Castro, from the thumping beats to the rainbow-colored socks strategically placed on male dancers.

Eagle Tavern 398 12th St at Harrison, SoMa ⓣ415/626-0880. A good old-fashioned leather bar mostly popular with 30-somethings and older, although its Sun beer bust ($10 until 6pm) brings in a slightly more diverse crowd. Expect a mud wrestling night here and there.

Esta Noche 3079 16th St at Valencia, Mission ⓣ415/861-5757. A fun, if dingy and smelly Latino drag bar that attracts a youngish, racially mixed clientele. There's a raucous drag revue every Fri and Sat night, and drink specials until 9pm nightly.

Pilsner Inn 225 Church St at Market, Castro ⓣ415/621-7058. Mature watering hole filled with a diverse crowd playing pool and darts. There's a large patio out back, and a generally welcoming, open vibe.

The Stud 399 Folsom St at Ninth, SoMa ⓣ415/252-7883. Legendary club that's been on the scene since the mid 1960s. It's still as popular as ever, attracting a diverse, energetic, and uninhibited crowd. Don't miss the fabulously freaky drag queen cabaret at *Trannyshack* every Tues.

Wild Side West 424 Cortland Ave at Andover, Bernal Heights ⓣ415/647-3099. Unpretentious and friendly tavern at the center of the Bernal Heights lesbian scene, with plenty of kitsch Americana to gaze at. There's a lovely garden out back, but without heatlamps, you'd be well advised to stay inside on a cold evening.

Live music: rock, jazz, and folk

San Francisco's **live music scene** reflects the character of the city: laid-back, eclectic, and not a little nostalgic. Options for shows are wide and the scene is strong, with the city regularly spawning good young bands; in recent years, it's helped launch acid jazz, a swing dancing revival, and more than a few nationally known acts.

12 Galaxies 2365 Mission St at 21st, Mission ⓣ415/970-9777, ⓦwww.12galaxies.com. This industrial-style club centers on a low-rise stage for live performances – whether metal, indie rock, country, comedy, or vaudeville – most nights; the best views are from the mezzanine. The bar also hosts dance parties, including nights that celebrate dub and Brazilian grooves. $6–16.

Boom Boom Room 1601 Fillmore St at Geary, Western Addition ⓣ415/673-8000, ⓦwww.boomboomblues.com. Once owned by late blues legend John Lee Hooker, this small, intimate bar with a checkerboard floor delivers blues and roots acts nightly. $6–15.

Bottom of the Hill 1233 17th St at Missouri, Potrero Hill ⓣ415/621-4455, ⓦwww.bottomofthehill.com. Well off the beaten path, San Francisco's celebrated indie rock stronghold still draws a late-twenty- to thirty-something crowd nightly. $6–14.

Bruno's 2389 Mission St at 20th, Mission ⓣ415/648-7701, ⓦwww.brunoslive.com. Like something from a Scorsese film, this retro-1960s restaurant is also home to an intimate live venue featuring local jazz or new-school R&B acts. $5–10 (no cover for diners).

Café du Nord 2170 Market St at Sanchez, Castro ⓣ415/861-5016, ⓦwww.cafedunord.com. This old subterranean speakeasy is a terrific place to enjoy touring or local rock bands, with the occasional swing and folk act booked for good measure. $6–12.

Elbo Room 647 Valencia St at 17th, Mission ⓣ415/552-7788, ⓦwww.elbo.com. A local cradle of acid jazz in the early 1990s, it's now home to international music performers and DJs. $5–12.

The Fillmore 1805 Geary St at Fillmore, Western Addition ⓣ415/346-6000, ⓦwww.thefillmore.com. This landmark auditorium was the musical heart of the 1960s counterculture, masterminded by legendary local promoter Bill Graham. Today, it continues to draw rising touring acts to its large ballroom, and there's a free apple and commemorative poster for every showgoer. Ticket prices vary wildly, depending on the headliner.

Great American Music Hall 859 O'Farrell St at Polk, Tenderloin ⓣ415/885-0750, ⓦwww.musichallsf.com. A former bordello converted long ago into a beloved (by locals and performers alike) venue for rock, blues, international, and comedy acts. $12–25.

The Independent 628 Divisadero St at Hayes, Western Addition ⓣ415/771-1421, ⓦwww.theindependentsf.com. As the name suggests, this mid-sized club with disarmingly friendly staff and exceptional sound specializes in booking local and international indie outfits. $7–18.

Yoshi's 1330 Fillmore St at Eddy, Western Addition ⓣ415/655-5600, ⓦwww.yoshis.com. Oakland's fabled jazz club has expanded across the bay, with a round stage, balcony, and sizable dancefloor. Opened in late 2007, this chic venue already draws the biggest names in jazz. $12–32.

Clubbing

Still trading on a reputation for hedonism earned decades ago, San Francisco's **nightclubs** in fact continue to trail those of other large American cities. That said, the compensations are manifold – it's rare to encounter high cover charges, ridiculously priced drinks, feverish posing, or long lines. The greatest concentration of clubs is in **SoMa** and, recently, the **Mission**. Unlike most other cities, where the action never gets going until after midnight, many San Francisco clubs have to close at 2am during the week, so you can usually be sure of finding things well underway earlier.

1015 Folsom 1015 Folsom St at Sixth, SoMa ⓣ415/431-1200, ⓦwww.1015.com. Multi-level superclub, popular across the board for late-night dancing. The music's largely house and garage, and you can expect marquee names like Sasha & Digweed and Paul Hardcastle on the main floor. $15–20.

Cat Club 1190 Folsom St at Eighth, SoMa ⓣ415/431-3332. This dark, loud space remains one of the city's hotspots; popular throwback parties throughout the month include *Hot Pants* and *1984*. $5–10.

The Endup 401 Sixth St at Harrison, SoMa ⓣ415/357-0827, ⓦwww.theendup.com. Longtime favorite attracts hardcore clubbers of all sexual walks for after-hours dancing on its cramped dance floor. It's best known as the home of Sunday's all-day *T-Dance* party (6am-8pm); if you want a break from the beats, there's an outdoor patio with plenty of seating. $6–10.

Pink 2925 16th St at Capp, Mission ⓣ415/431-8889. Looking like a romance novelist's hideaway with billowing curtains and candles, this is nevertheless a serious place to dance. Expect high-quality deep house DJs, a friendly gay/straight crowd, and pricey drinks. Tuesday's *Taboo* is especially popular. $5–10.

Skylark 3089 16th St at Valencia, Mission ⓣ415/621-9294, ⓦwww.skylarkbar.com. Popular for its intimate vibe, low lightiing, strong drinks and varied DJs, this spot makes for an inexpensive night out. No cover.

Space 550 550 Barneveld Ave at Oakdale, Bayshore ⓣ415/289-2001, ⓦwww.space550.com. An enormous warehouse club known for its trancey, industrial dance programming. Although it's set in an otherwise culturally desolate area of town, crowds of local clubbers routinely make the trip. $5–15.

Ballet, opera, and symphony

San Francisco rightfully has a reputation for embracing the performing arts. The top-form **San Francisco Ballet** (ⓣ415/865-2000, ⓦwww.sfballet.org), the oldest such troupe in the US, performs January to May, with *The Nutcracker* showing each holiday season; tickets begin at $30, while standing-room tickets are sold two hours before each performance for $10–12. The Ballet shares its stage at **War Memorial Opera House**, 301 Van Ness Ave at Grove, with the **San Francisco Opera** (ⓣ415/864-3330, ⓦwww.sfopera.org), whose season runs Septtember to December, with a short summer season in June and July; tickets are $25–200, while same-day rush tickets become available for students, seniors, and military personnel at 11am. The Opera's opening night gala is one of the biggest social events on the West Coast.

Adjacent to the War Memorial, the **Louise M. Davies Symphony Hall,** 201 Van Ness Ave at Hayes, is the permanent home of the **San Francisco Symphony** (ⓣ415/864-6000, ⓦwww.sfsymphony.org), a once-musty institution that has catapulted to the first rank of American symphonies under the guidance of conductor Michael Tilson Thomas. The season runs September to May, while ticket prices range wildly from $35–125, with day-of-performance rush tickets often available for $20.

If you visit San Francisco between June and August, check the schedule of the annual **Stern Grove Festival** (ⓣ415/252-6252, ⓦwww.sterngrove.org), which presents free symphony, opera, and ballet performances every summer at its namesake park at 19th Avenue and Sloat Boulevard in the city's outlying Parkside district.

Theater

Theater is plentiful in the city, though unfortunately many of the larger venues often fall prey to a schedule of Broadway reruns. The bolder **fringe circuit** stages new plays with greater frequency, and while quality can be uneven, these smaller concerns are more interesting than the crowd-pleasers staged at major San Francisco houses. For half-price bargains, try the **Tix Bay Area** booth (Tues–Thurs 11am–6pm, Fri 11am–7pm, Sat 10am–7pm, Sun 10am–3pm; ⓣ415/430-1140, ⓦwww.theatrebayarea.org) in Union Square.

American Conservatory Theater (ACT) 415 Geary St at Taylor, Theater District ⓣ415/742-2228, ⓦwww.act-sf.org. Leading resident group that mixes newly commissioned works and innovative renditions of the classics, with inventive set design and staging. Tickets can cost as little as $14 for a preview show, though you'll pay $30–70 most of the time; rush tickets are generally available from noon on performance days.

BATS Improv Bayfront Theater, Fort Mason Center ⓣ415/474-6776, ⓦwww.improv.org. Celebrated long-form improv company (its titular acronym stands for Bay Area Theatresports) that hosts classes, guest groups, and an improv competition every Sun night; it also stages its own shows year-round. Tickets $5–20.

Beach Blanket Babylon *Club Fugazi*, 678 Green St at Powell, North Beach ⓣ415/421-4222. This legendary musical revue, filled with celebrity impersonations and towering hats, has been running continuously since 1974. Recommended, but reserve in advance. Tickets $25–78.

Exit Theater 156 Eddy St at Taylor, Tenderloin ⓣ415/673-3847, ⓦwww.theexit.org. One of the best spots in town for cutting-edge theater. It's known for April's DivaFest, devoted to women-centric plays and performances, as well as producing and being an anchor venue for Sept local Fringe Festival. Tickets $20–25.

Magic Theatre Building D, Fort Mason Center ⓣ415/441-8822, ⓦwww.magictheatre.org. The busiest and largest local company after *ACT* specializes in the works of contemporary playwrights, as well as those by emerging new talents. Tickets $40–45.

Theater Rhinoceros 2926 16th St at S Van Ness, Mission ⓣ415/861-5079, ⓦwww.therhino.org. The city's prime gay-oriented theater space includes two auditoria, each hosting productions that range from heartfelt political drama to raunchy cabaret acts. Tickets $15–25.

Shopping

While boasting the large-scale stores and international names you'd expect in a major city, San Francisco's **shopping scene** is, by and large, low-key and unpretentious. If you want to run the gauntlet of designer labels, or just watch the style brigade consume, **Union Square** is ground zero for serious dollar-dropping. The city being so neighborhood-oriented, however, a number of boutique-laden streets around town invite browsing and spending, from tidy **Union Street** in Cow Hollow to funkier outposts like **Valencia Street** in the Mission and **Hayes Street** in Hayes Valley.

Books

Abandoned Planet Bookstore 518 Valencia at 16th, Mission ⓣ415/861-4695. Eccentric and utterly San Francisco bookstore that crams its shelves with left-wing and anarchist volumes.

Argonaut Bookshop 786 Sutter St at Jones, Tenderloin ⓣ415/474-9067. Best choice by far for local history, specializing in volumes on California and the West, from the Gold Rush to the dot-com era. The knowledgeable staff is a major plus.

City Lights Bookstore 261 Columbus Ave at Broadway, North Beach ☎415/362-8193. America's first paperback bookstore, and still one of San Francisco's best; the range of titles includes house publications.

A Different Light 489 Castro St at 18th, Castro ☎415/431-0891. Well-stocked shop featuring gay and lesbian titles, with an especially strong fiction section, and even a kids' lit corner. Readings and events occur regularly.

Get Lost 1825 Market St at Valencia, Mission ☎415/437-0529. Tiny, travel bookstore crammed with unusual titles alongside all the standard guidebooks; it also stocks a decent assortment of maps and gear for the adventure traveler.

Green Apple Books & Music 506 Clement St at Sixth, Inner Richmond ☎415/387-2272. Relaxed and welcoming store in the city's unofficial Chinatown West that features new and used books (including rare, out-of-print volumes), plus a smart selection of CDs and vinyl.

Modern Times 888 Valencia St at 20th, Mission ☎415/282-9246. Progressive community bookstore, with a fine selection of Latin American literature and publications on women's issues and contemporary cultural studies.

Stacey's Booksellers 581 Market St at Second, Financial District ☎415/421-4687. A larger store for shoppers who want a broad selection of titles and genres without having to support a national retail giant. The interior's rather sterile, but not unwelcoming.

Music

Amoeba Records 1855 Haight St at Stanyan, Haight-Ashbury ☎415/831-1200. Massive independent music retailer that got its start in Berkeley in 1990, with one of the largest and widest-ranging collections you'll ever find; best of all, prices are geared towards the everyday shopper, rather than the deep-pocketed collector. Also plays frequent host to free in-store performances.

Aquarius Records 1055 Valencia St at 21st, Mission ☎415/647-2272. Neighborhood store with knowledgeable staff and a good range of indie rock and experimental titles.

Jack's Record Cellar 254 Scott St at Haight, Lower Haight ☎415/431-3047. The city's best vinyl source for American roots music – R&B, jazz, country, and rock and roll.

Jazz Quarter 1267 20th Ave at Lincoln Blvd, Outer Sunset ☎415/661-2331. Dusty and musty, this tiny shop a block off the N-Judah streetcar line will appeal to jazz fiends on the prowl for rarities.

Mikado 1737 Post St at Buchanan, Japantown ☎415/922-9450. Enormous Japanese record store sprawled across the Japan Center, with an exhaustive selection of Asian music.

Open Mind Music 2150 Market St at Church, Castro ☎415/621-2244. A more peaceful alternative to the hordes who throng to Amoeba, this excellent shop boasts loads of vinyl across genres, along with CDs and other assorted memorabilia.

Ritmo Latino 2401 Mission St at 20th, Mission ☎415/824-8556. The place to head for all varieties of Latin music: salsa, bolero, mariachi, reggaeton, merengue, and Latin indie rock.

Tweekin Records 593 Haight St at Steiner, Lower Haight ☎415/626-6995. A haven for DJs that stocks all the hottest house, downtempo, and techno releases, as well as disco, reggae, funk and soul.

The Bay Area

Of the six million people who make their home in the vicinity of San Francisco, only a lucky one in eight lives in the city itself. Everyone else is spread around the **Bay Area**, a sharply contrasting patchwork of very rich and very poor towns dotted down the peninsula or across one of the three impressive bridges that span the chilly waters of the exquisite natural harbor. In the **East Bay** are industrial Oakland and intellectual Berkeley, while south of the city, the **Peninsula** holds the gloating wealth of Silicon Valley, which gained its nickname from the multibillion-dollar technology industry. To the north across the Golden Gate Bridge is the woody, leafy landscape and rugged coastline of **Marin County**, an elitest pleasure zone of conspicuous luxury and abundant natural beauty.

The East Bay

The largest and the second-most-traveled bridge in the US, the **Bay Bridge** connects downtown San Francisco to the East Bay, part graceful suspension bridge and part heavy-duty steel truss. Currently being replaced along half its span, the Bay Bridge works a lot harder for a lot less respect than the more famous Golden Gate: a hundred million vehicles cross it each year. The heart of the East Bay is **Oakland**, a resolutely blue-collar city that spreads north to the progressive university town of **Berkeley**; the two communities all but merge into one city, and the hills above them are topped by a twenty-mile string of forested **regional parks**.

Arrival, information, and getting around

Flights direct to the East Bay touch down at **Oakland Airport**, just outside town (ⓣ510/577-4015 or 1-800/992-7433 for automated flight info, ⓦwww.oaklandairport.com). The AirBART shuttle van (every 15min; $2; ⓣ510/577-4294) runs to the Coliseum BART station from where you can hop on BART (see below) to Berkeley, Oakland, or San Francisco. There are numerous door-to-door **shuttle buses** from the airport, such as A1 American (ⓣ1-877/378-3596, ⓦwww.a1americanshuttle.com) – expect to pay around $18 to downtown Oakland, $30–40 to San Francisco. Note that the **Greyhound** station is in a dodgy part of northern Oakland on San Pablo Avenue at 21st Street. **Amtrak** terminates at 2nd Street near Jack London Square in West Oakland, where you can catch a free shuttle bus to downtown San Francisco (a smoother alternative is to get off at Richmond and change onto the nearby BART trains).

There are two main **visitor centers**: Oakland CVB is at 463 11th St (Mon–Fri 8.30am–5pm; ⓣ510/839-9000, ⓦwww.oaklandcvb.com), while Berkeley's office

Sports in San Francisco and the Bay Area

San Francisco's dedication to its **professional sports** teams can verge on the obsessive. Tickets for the big events can sell out, but it's usually possible to show up on the day, and it needn't cost all that much: an outfield seat to watch baseball from the "bleachers" goes for around $8, while promotional specials like Wednesday Dollar Days, run by the Oakland team, can reduce prices of seats and hotdogs to only a couple of bucks. Advance tickets for all Bay Area sports events are available through Ticketmaster's charge-by-phone ticket service (ⓣ415/421-8497, ⓦwww.ticketmaster.com), or through the teams' headquarters.

Baseball: The **Oakland A's** play at the usually sunny Coliseum (ⓦwww.oaklandathletics.com), which has a BART stop in front. The **San Francisco Giants** play at AT&T Park, where home runs sometimes land in the bay (ⓣ415/972-2000, ⓦwww.sfgiants.com). There are five hundred bleacher-seat tickets made available two-and-a-half hours before game time and long lines form early and often. Walk up to the ticket booths at 24 Willie Mays Plaza, near Third and King streets, to get them.

Football: The **San Francisco 49ers**, five-time Super Bowl champions, also play at 3Com Park, where you may have to pay as much as $100 per seat (ⓣ415/656-4900, ⓦwww.sf49ers.com), and the **Oakland Raiders**, blue-collar heroes and runners-up in the 2003 Super Bowl, bash heads at the Oakland Coliseum (ⓦwww.raiders.com).

Basketball: The gradually resurgent **Golden State Warriors** play at the newly renovated Oakland Arena (ⓣ510/986-2200, ⓦwww.nba.com/warriors).

Ice hockey: The always competitive **San Jose Sharks** (ⓣ408/287-7070, ⓦwww.sj-sharks.com) play at their own arena in San Jose.

Soccer: The **San Jose Earthquakes** (ⓣ408/985-4625, ⓦwww.sjearthquakes.com), MLS champs in 2001, draw large crowds at San Jose State's Spartan Stadium.

is at 2015 Center St (Mon–Fri 9am–1pm & 2–5pm; ⓣ510/549-7040, ⓦwww.visitberkeley.com).

The underground **BART** system links the East Bay with San Francisco (Mon–Fri 4am–midnight, Sat 6am–midnight, Sun 8am–midnight; $1.40–7.65; ⓣ510/465-2278, ⓦwww.bart.gov). **AC Transit** (ⓣ510/891-4777, ⓦwww.actransit.org) buses cover the entire East Bay area, with a more limited service running to Oakland and Berkeley from the Transbay Terminal in San Francisco; they're the only option for crossing the Bay when BART shuts down for the night.

East Bay accommodation

The East Bay's **motels** and **hotels**, which cost from $55 a night, are barely better value for money than their San Francisco counterparts.

Bancroft Hotel 2680 Bancroft Way, Berkeley ⓣ510/549-1000 or 1-800/549-1002, ⓦwww.bancrofthotel.com. Small hotel – just 22 rooms – with good location and service. Breakfast included. ⑤

The Claremont Resort & Spa 41 Tunnel Rd, Berkeley ⓣ510/843-3000 or 1-800/551-7266, ⓦwww.claremontresort.com. The lap of luxury among Berkeley hotels in a 1915 building. Even the basic rooms are a treat, but you'll pay for the privilege. Spa sessions start around $100/hour for facials or massages. ⑧

Downtown Berkeley YMCA 2001 Allston Way at Milvia St, Berkeley ⓣ510/848-9622, ⓦwww.baymca.org. Berkeley's best bargain accommodation, just one block from the Berkeley BART stop. Rates, starting at around $39 for a single, $50 for a double, include use of gym and pool. ②

The French Hotel 1538 Shattuck Ave, North Berkeley ⓣ510/548-9930. There's a touch of European class about this small and comfortable hotel with 18 simple but pleasant rooms in the heart of Berkeley's Gourmet Ghetto. ④

Jack London Inn 444 Embarcadero West, Oakland ⓣ510/444-2032, ⓦwww.jacklondoninn.com. Kitschy 1950s-style motor lodge next to Jack London Square. ④

Maya Motel 4715 Telegraph Ave, North Oakland ⓣ510/654-5850. Basic motel but neat enough and better than most in this area, which is within walking distance of trendy Rockridge. ②

Shattuck Plaza 2086 Allston Way, Berkeley ⓣ510/845-7300, ⓦwww.hotelshattuckplaza.com. Comfortable, central rooms in a well-restored older hotel. ⑤

Waterfront Plaza Hotel 10 Washington St, Oakland ⓣ510/836-3800 or 1-800/729-3638, ⓦwww.waterfrontplaza.com. Plush, modern hotel moored on the best stretch of the Oakland waterfront. ⑥

Oakland

OAKLAND, the workhorse of the Bay Area, is one of the largest ports on the West Coast. It has also been the breeding ground of revolutionary **political movements**. In the Sixties, the city's fifty-percent black population found a voice through the militant Black Panthers, and in the Seventies the Symbionese Liberation Army, kidnappers of heiress Patty Hearst, obtained a ransom of free food for the city's poor. It's not all hard graft, though: the climate is often sunny and mild when San Francisco is cold and dreary, and there's great hiking in the redwood- and eucalyptus-covered hills above the city.

There's not much to see within the city. The major concession to the tourist trade is the waterfront Jack London Square, an aseptic cluster of national chains that have nothing to do with the writer. At the far eastern end of the promenade, however, you will find **Heinhold's First and Last Chance Saloon**, a slanting tiny bar built in 1883 from the hull of a whaling ship. Jack London really did drink here, and the collection of yellowed portraits of him on the wall are the only genuine thing about the writer you'll find on the square. A half-mile north up Broadway from the waterfront, Oakland's restored downtown is anchored by chain stores and the gargantuan open-air **City Center** complex of offices and fast-food outlets. Beside it, at Broadway and 14th Street, the massive space of **Frank Ogawa Plaza** is a pleasant place to eat lunch outdoors, while further east on 10th and Oak streets, the **Oakland Museum of California** (Wed–Sat

10am–5pm, Sun noon–5pm; $8, free second Sun of month; Ⓣ510/238-2200, Ⓦwww.museumca.org) has good exhibits of California's ecology and history, including the Beat Generation.

Writer **Gertrude Stein** was born in Oakland at around the same time as the macho and adventurous London, but she's barely commemorated anywhere. Perhaps it's because it was Stein who wrote "what was the use of me having come from Oakland...*there is no there there*" – a quote that has haunted the city ever since. Oakland residents argue that there is indeed a *there* there, notably in the small, trendy community of **Rockridge** and the lively neighborhoods around Piedmont and Grand avenues, the latter near pleasant **Lake Merrit**.

Joaquin Miller Park, the most easily accessible of Oakland's hilltop parks, stands above East Oakland (take AC Transit bus #64 from downtown) and includes a small white cabin called The Abbey, former abode of the "Poet of the Sierras," Joaquin Miller. Also in the nearby hills but reached by AC Transit bus #53, the Chabot Space & Science Center, 10000 Skyline Blvd (Wed & Thurs 10am–5pm, Fri & Sat 10am–10pm, Sun 11am–5pm; $13; Ⓣ510/336-7300, Ⓦwww.chabotspace.org) features excellent interactive displays and a fine planetarium.

Berkeley

BERKELEY (named for the English philosopher-theologian George Berkeley) is dominated by the **University of California**, one of America's most famous – and infamous – universities. Its grand buildings and thirty thousand students give off an energy that spills south down raucous **Telegraph Avenue**, where aging hippies peddle rainbow bracelets in front of vegetarian restaurants, music stores, and pizza joints. The very name of Berkeley conjures up images of dissent and it remains a solidly left-wing oasis. **Sproul Plaza**, in front of the school's entranceway, Sather Gate, is where the Free Speech Movement began, and, as some historians would argue, the experience known as the Sixties. Among the sites of the almost-daily pitched battles of the Sixties and early Seventies, part of the broad campus revolt against the Vietnam War, is the now-quiet **People's Park**. Today the campus prides itself on its high academic rankings and Nobel-laureate-laden faculty. Stroll the campus's tree-shaded pathways or join the free student-led **tours** that leave from the visitor services office, 101 University Hall (Mon–Sat 10am, Sun 1pm; Ⓣ510/642-5215, Ⓦwww.berkeley.edu/visitor).

Telegraph Avenue holds most of the student hangouts, and several excellent bookstores. Older students congregate in **Northside**, popping down from their woodsy hillside homes to partake of goodies from Gourmet Ghetto – the restaurants, delis, and bakeries on Shattuck Avenue like the renowned *Chez Panisse* (see p.1051). North of here, on the hills, **Tilden Regional Park** has good trails and a fine rose garden. Along the bay itself, at the **Berkeley Marina**, you can rent windsurfing boards and sailboats, or just watch the sun set behind the Golden Gate.

Eating

As befits the birthplace of California cuisine, the East Bay offers a choice of good **restaurants**. Berkeley is both an upmarket diner's paradise and a student town where you can eat cheaply and well, especially on and around Telegraph Avenue.

Bay Wolf 3853 Piedmont Ave, North Oakland Ⓣ510/655-6004. Chic restaurant whose menu is influenced by the cuisine of Tuscany, Provence, and the Basque country. Entrees like double mustard-tarragon chicken cost mostly over $20.

Brennan's 720 University, West Berkeley Ⓣ510/841-0960. Great down-home self-service meals like roast beef and mash. Also a solidly blue-collar hangout that's a great place for drinking inexpensive beers and watching sports on TV, including European soccer.

Cha-Am 1543 Shattuck Ave, North Berkeley Ⓣ510/848-9664. Climb the stairs to this unlikely, always crowded small restaurant for deliciously spicy Thai food at bargain prices.

Cheeseboard Pizza 1512 Shattuck Ave, North Berkeley ⓣ510/549-3055. Incredibly good gourmet pizza at $2.50 a slice. Irregular hours, but usually open for lunch and dinner Tues–Sun.

Chez Panisse 1517 Shattuck Ave, North Berkeley ⓣ510/548-5525. First and still the best of the California cuisine restaurants, overseen by legendary chef Alice Waters. Dinner is served at two sittings, 6pm and 8.30pm; the prix fixe menu costs $50–75 depending on the day of the week. The Café upstairs is comparatively inexpensive. Reservations recommended for the Café, essential for the main restaurant.

Homemade Café 2454 Sacramento St, Berkeley ⓣ510/845-1940. Nontraditional California-style Jewish and Mexican breakfasts and lunches – at shared tables when it's crowded.

Juan's Place 941 Carleton St, West Berkeley ⓣ510/845-6904. The original Berkeley Mexican restaurant, with great food (tons of it) and an interesting mix of people.

Kirala 2100 Ward St, Berkeley ⓣ510/549-3486. Many argue that *Kirala* serves the best sushi in the Bay Area, if not the whole USA. Moderate pricing, too – expect to pay around $20 to get your fill.

La Mediterranee 2936 College Ave, Berkeley ⓣ510/540-7773. Great Middle Eastern food in a relaxed atmosphere.

La Note 2377 Shattuck Ave, Berkeley ⓣ510/843-1535. The appropriately sunny, light cuisine of Provence isn't the only flavor you'll find in this petite dining room: students and teachers from the jazz school next door routinely stop in for casual jam sessions.

Le Cheval 1007 Clay St, Oakland ⓣ510/763-8595. Downtown Vietnamese place serving exquisitely spiced food at reasonable prices in comfortable surroundings.

Tropix Backyard Café 3814 Piedmont Ave, North Oakland ⓣ510/653-2444. Large portions of fruity Caribbean delicacies at reasonable prices, with authentic jerk sauce and thirst-quenching mango juice. Outside seating on the patio.

Vik's Chaat Corner 726 Allston Way, West Berkeley ⓣ510/644-4412. Fantastic lunchtime spot, where you can feast cheaply on authentic South Indian dishes such as *masala dosa* in a huge, no-nonsense self-service canteen.

Cafés and bars

The many bohemian **cafés** in Berkeley are full from dawn to near midnight with earnest characters wearing their intellects on their sleeves; if you're not after a caffeine fix, you can generally get a glass of beer or wine. For serious drinking you're better off in one of the many **bars**, particularly in rough-hewn Oakland. Grittier versions of what you'd find in San Francisco, they're mostly blue-collar, convivial, and almost always less expensive.

The Alley 3325 Grand Ave, Oakland ⓣ510/444-8505. Ramshackle old-timers' piano bar where locals come specifically to sing. Music starts at 9pm. Closed Mon.

Ben 'n' Nick's 5612 College Ave, Rockridge ⓣ510/933-0327. Lively bar with good taped rock music and tasty pub food.

Caffè Mediterraneum 2475 Telegraph Ave, Berkeley ⓣ510/841-5634. Berkeley's oldest café, straight out of the Beat Generation archives: beards and berets optional, books de rigueur.

Coffee Mill 3363 Grand Ave, Oakland ⓣ 510/465-4224. This café near Lake Merritt doubles as an art gallery and often hosts poetry readings, too.

Heinhold's First and Last Chance Saloon 56 Jack London Square, Oakland ⓣ510/839-6761. Authentic waterfront bar that's hardly changed since around 1900, when Jack London drank here. They've never even bothered to fix the slanted floor that was caused by the 1906 earthquake.

Jupiter 2181 Shattuck Ave, Berkeley ⓣ510/843-8277. Many, many beers to select from at this local favorite, which offers live jazz on weekends and an outdoor beer garden.

Pacific Coast Brewing Co 906 Washington St, Oakland ⓣ510/836-2739. The only real microbrewery downtown, where you can also get decent grub to wash down with your ale.

Pub (Schmidt's Tobacco & Trading Co) 1492 Solano Ave, North Berkeley ⓣ510/525-1900. This small, relaxed bar lures a mixture of bookworms and game players with a good selection of beers. They even get away with a semi-open smoking area out back, perhaps because their other speciality is selling the evil weed.

Triple Rock Brewery 1920 Shattuck Ave, Berkeley ⓣ510/843-2739. Lively student bar with fine burgers and beers – be sure to check out which two revolving cask-conditioned ales are on.

The White Horse Inn 6551 Telegraph Ave at 66th St, North Oakland ⓣ510/652-3820. Oakland's oldest gay bar – a small, friendly place with mixed dancing for men and women nightly.

Live music and entertainment

Nightlife is where the East Bay really comes into its own. Though traditional **clubs** are virtually nonexistent, there are plenty of **live music venues**, from smoky jazz cafés to sweaty R&B dives. Live dance music thrives here; there's also plenty of joints hosting poppy, punky guitar bands that echo Green Day and Nirvana.

The range of **films** screened here is top-notch. Berkeley's **Pacific Film Archives** at 2575 Bancroft Ave ($8; Ⓣ510/642-5249 for tickets, Ⓦwww.bampfa.berkeley.edu), one of the finest film libraries in California, puts on contemporary international films, plus old favorites. The free *East Bay Express* has the most comprehensive listings of what's on.

924 Gilman 924 Gilman St, West Berkeley Ⓣ510/525-9926, Ⓦwww.924gilman.org. On the outer edge of the hardcore punk, indie, and experimental scene, this institution helped launch Green Day and Sleater-Kinney. No alcohol, all ages. Weekends only; cover $5–10.

Ashkenaz 1317 San Pablo Ave, Berkeley Ⓣ510/525-5054, Ⓦwww.ashkenaz.com. World music and dance café hosting acts from modern Afro-beat to the best of the Balkans. Kids and under-21s welcome. Cover $10–15.

Blake's on Telegraph 2367 Telegraph Ave, Berkeley Ⓣ510/848-0886, Ⓦwww.blakesontelegraph.com. Funky student club featuring a variety of live acts from blues and soul through rock to punk and rap. $3–15

Freight and Salvage 2020 Addison St, West Berkeley Ⓣ510/548-1761, Ⓦwww.freightandsalvage.org. Singer-songwriters perform in a coffeehouse setting. Cover mostly under $20, open-mike nights $5.

Starry Plough 3101 Shattuck Ave, Berkeley Ⓣ510/841-2082, Ⓦwww.starryploughpub.com. Lively Irish bar that features bargain-price live rock, country and folk many nights of the week. Free to $8.

Stork Club 2330 Telegraph Ave, Oakland Ⓣ510/444-6174, Ⓦwww.storkcluboakland.com. Presently a favorite with DJs and indie bands, this historic club features a jukebox that specializes in country tunes. Closed Mon; cover usually $5.

Yoshi's World Class Jazz House 510 Embarcadero W, Oakland Ⓣ510/238-9200, Ⓦwww.yoshis.com. The centerpiece of Oakland's revived Jack London Square, this combination jazz club and sushi bar routinely attracts the biggest names in jazz. Cover $10–50.

The Peninsula

The city of San Francisco sits at the tip of a five-mile-wide neck of land commonly referred to as the **Peninsula**. Home of old money and new technology, the Peninsula stretches for fifty miles through relentless suburbia south from San Francisco along the Bay, winding up in the futuristic roadside landscape of the Silicon Valley near **San Jose**.

There was a time when the region was largely agricultural, but the computer boom – spurred by Stanford University in **Palo Alto** – has replaced the orange groves and fig trees of yesteryear with office complexes and parking lots. Most of the land along the **coast** – separated from the bayfront sprawl by a ridge of redwood-covered peaks – remains rural; it also contains some of the best **beaches** in the Bay Area.

Palo Alto

Palo Alto, home of preppy, conservative **Stanford University** (Ⓣ650/723-2560, Ⓦwww.stanford.edu), has become somewhat of a social center for Silicon Valley's nouveau riche and wealthy students, as evidenced by the trendy cafés and chic new restaurants along its main drag, **University Avenue**. The town doesn't offer a lot in terms of sights other than Spanish Colonial homes, but it's a great place for a lazy stroll and a gourmet meal. Wash down a California-style Greek dish from *Evvia*, 420 Emerson St (Ⓣ650/326-0983), or Left Bank Parisian cuisine from *La*

Cheminée, 530 Bryant St (Ⓣ650/328-2722), with a microbrewed beer from the *Gordon Biersch Brewery*, 640 Emerson St (Ⓣ650/323-7723), or a latte from *Caffè del Doge*, 419 University Ave (Ⓣ650/323-3600). Cheaper but still delicious ethnic fare can be enjoyed at the Thai *Krung Siam* (Ⓣ650/322-5900) and Indian *Hyderabad House* (Ⓣ650/327-3455) restaurants, located at nos. 423 and 448 University Ave, respectively. Reasonably affordable **rooms** are available at the *Cardinal Hotel*, 235 Hamilton Ave, in the heart of downtown (Ⓣ650/323-5101, Ⓦwww.cardinalhotel.com; shared bath ❹, private bath ❺).

San Jose

Burt Bacharach could easily find **SAN JOSE** today by heading south from San Francisco and following the heat and smog that collects below the Bay. Although one of the fastest-growing cities in California, it is not strong on identity – though in area and population it's close to twice the size of San Francisco. Sitting at the southern end of the peninsula, San Jose has in the past 25 years emerged as the civic heart of Silicon Valley, surrounded by miles of faceless high-tech industrial parks where the next generations of computers are designed and built. Ironically, it's also acknowledged as the first city in California, though the only sign of this is the unremarkable eighteenth-century **Mission Santa Clara de Asis**, on the pleasant campus of the Jesuit-run Santa Clara University.

The area's most famous landmark is the **Winchester Mystery House**, 525 S Winchester Blvd, just off I-280 near Hwy-17 (daily 9am–5pm, 9am–7pm in summer; Mansion Tour $23.95, Guided Behind-the-Scenes Tour $20.95, combo $28.95; Ⓣ408/247-1313, Ⓦwww.winchestermysteryhouse.com). Sarah Winchester, heiress to the Winchester rifle fortune, was convinced upon her husband's death in 1884 that he had been taken by the spirits of men killed with Winchester rifles, and believed that unless a room was built for each of the spirits, the same fate would befall her. Work on the mansion went on 24 hours a day for the next thirty years – stairs lead nowhere, windows open on to solid brick. Today it's a relentlessly hyped commercial cash cow, but is still worth a detour. The **Rosicrucian Museum**, 1342 Naglee Ave (Tues–Fri 10am–5pm, Sat & Sun 11am–6pm; $9; Ⓣ408/947-3636, Ⓦwww.rosicrucian.org), houses a brilliant collection of Assyrian and Babylonian artifacts, while the revamped **Tech Museum of Innovation** (daily 10am–5pm; $8; Ⓣ408/294-8224, Ⓦwww.thetech.org), downtown at 201 S Market St, contains hands-on displays of high-tech engineering as well as an IMAX theater (one show included in admission; extra show $4).

San Jose's **visitor center** is next to the huge Convention Center at 408 S Almaden Blvd (Mon–Fri 8am–5pm, Sat & Sun 11am–5pm; Ⓣ408/295-9600 or 1-800/726-5673, Ⓦwww.sanjose.org), though it is geared more to business people than travelers. Downtown **accommodation** is grossly overpriced, so it's best to try further out. Options include the *Valley Inn*, 2155 The Alameda (Ⓣ408/241-8500, Ⓦwww.valleyinnsanjose.com; ❸), and the *Howard Johnson Express*, 1215 S 1st St (Ⓣ408/280-5300 or 1-800/509-7666, Ⓦwww.hojo.com; ❸). Good old-fashioned American **food** is dished up at *Original Joe's*, 301 S First St (Ⓣ408/292-7030). Grab a stool at the counter or settle into one of the comfy booths at this San Jose institution, where $10 still goes a long way. For a snack and touch of hubbly-bubbly, head to *Hookah Nites*, 371 S 1st St (Ⓣ408/286-0800). The same stretch of S 1st St is also home to most of the city's bustling **nightlife**.

The coast

The **coastline** of the Peninsula south from San Francisco is a world away from the valley of the inland: mostly undeveloped, with a few small towns, and countless beaches that run 75 miles down to the mellow cities of Santa Cruz and Capitola. Just south of San Francisco, Hwy-1 hugs the precipitous cliffs of Devil's Slide, passing the decent mini-resort of **Pacifica** en route to the clothing-optional sands of **Gray Whale Cove State Beach** (daily 8am–sunset; ⓣ650/728-5336, ⓦwww.parks.ca.gov). Despite the name, it's not an especially great place to look for migrating gray whales, but there is a stairway from the bus stop down to a fine strand of sand. Two miles further on Hwy-1, the red-roofed buildings of the 1875 **Point Montara Lighthouse**, set among the wind-swept Monterey pine trees at the top of a steep cliff, have been converted into a **youth hostel** (ⓣ650/728-7177, ⓦwww.norcalhostels.org; dorm $20–25; ❸). Just beyond the hostel, down California Street, the **Fitzgerald Marine Reserve** (ⓣ650/728-3584; free) has three miles of diverse oceanic habitat, peaceful trails, and, at low tide, the best tidal pools. But continue a tiny bit further for the historic **Moss Beach Distillery** (ⓣ650/728-5595), a great place to grab a snack and a beer on its windswept patio – they provide enormous blankets to help brave the fog.

A few miles further south on Hwy-1 is **Princeton-by-the-Sea**, where you can wash down a full meal or cheaper bar snack with the finely crafted ales of the excellent **Half Moon Bay Brewing Company**, 390 Capistrano Ave (ⓣ650/728-2739). Next up is the wonderful strand of **Miramar**, also the unlikely location of the *Douglass Beach House* (ⓣ650/726-4143, ⓦwww.bachddsoc.org), an informal jazz pub that attracts some big names. The next town, constantly expanding **Half Moon Bay,** offers camping behind its eponymous state beach (ⓣ650/726-8820; $20), as well as fancier accommodation such as the *Old Thyme Inn*, 779 Main St (ⓣ650/726-1616 or 1-800/720-4277, ⓦwww.oldthymeinn.com; ❺), and a few eating options – try **Cetrella**, 845 Main St (ⓣ650/726-4090), a large and snazzy Mediterranean place that serves delicious upscale fare. Gas up here; fuel stations are rare for the next fifty miles to Santa Cruz.

Marin County

Across the Golden Gate from San Francisco, **Marin County** is an unabashed introduction to Californian self-indulgence: a pleasure zone of conspicuous luxury and abundant natural beauty, with sunshine or fog, sandy beaches, high mountains, and thick redwood forests. Though in the past the region served as logging headquarters, the county is now one of the wealthiest in the US, attracting young professionals to its swanky waterside towns.

The modern **ferries** that travel across the bay from San Francisco can make a great start to a day out. Boats to the chic bayside settlement of **Sausalito** leave from the Ferry Building on the Embarcadero, run by Golden Gate Ferry (Mon–Fri 7.40am–7.55pm, frequency varies; reduced timetable at weekends; $7.10 each way; ⓣ415/455-2000, ⓦwww.goldengate.org) or Pier 39 at Fisherman's Wharf, run by Blue & Gold Fleet ferries (6–7 trips daily; $9.50 each way; ⓣ415/705-8200, ⓦwww.blueandgoldfleet.com). **Biking** over here means a beautiful ride over the Golden Gate Bridge (unless there's fog) and allows you to explore the headlands freely. Golden Gate Ferries accommodate up to 25 bikes, first-come, first-served.

Across the Golden Gate: the Marin Headlands

The largely undeveloped **Marin Headlands**, across the Golden Gate Bridge from San Francisco, afford some of the most impressive views of the bridge and the city behind. The coastline is much more rugged than it is on the San Francisco side, and it makes a great place for an isolated clifftop scramble among the concrete remains of old forts and gun emplacements. Heading west on Bunker Hill Road takes you up to the brink of the headlands before the road snakes down to Fort Barry and wide, sandy **Rodeo Beach**, from which numerous hiking trails branch out. Check in at the Marin Headlands Visitor Center (daily 9.30am–4.30pm; ⓣ415/331-1540, ⓦwww.nps.gov/goga) above Rodeo Lagoon for free maps. The largest of the fort's old buildings has been converted into the spacious but homely *HI-Marin Headlands* **hostel** (ⓣ415/331-2777 or 1-800/979-4776 ext 168, ⓦwww.norcalhostels.org; dorm $21; ❸), an excellent base for more extended explorations of the inland ridges and valleys.

Sausalito

Attractive, smug little **SAUSALITO**, along the Bay below US-101, was once a gritty community of fishermen and sea traders, full of bars and bordellos. Now exclusive restaurants and pricey boutiques line its picturesque waterfront promenade, and expensive, quirky houses climb the overgrown cliffs above Bridgeway Avenue, the main road and bus route through town. Ferries from San Francisco arrive next to the Sausalito Yacht Club in the town center. If you have sailing experience, split the $172–375 daily rental fee of a four- to ten-person sailboat at Cass's Marina, 1702 Bridgeway Ave (ⓣ415/332-6789, ⓦwww.cassmarina.com).

Aside from walking, shopping, and sucking in the sea air, Sausalito has a one-of-a-kind exhibit in the **Bay Model Visitor Center**, 2100 Bridgeway (Tues–Sat 9am–4pm; donation suggested; ⓣ415/332-3870, ⓦwww. spn.usace.army.mil/bmvc), where elevated walkways in a huge building lead you around a scale model of the entire bay, surrounding deltas, and its aquatic inhabitants, offering insight on the enormity and diversity of this area.

If you decide **to stay**, *Casa Madrona* at 801 Bridgeway Ave (ⓣ415/332-0502 or 1-800/288-0502, ⓦwww.casamadrona.com; ❽) is a deluxe **hotel** that climbs up the hill opposite the bay and also houses *Mikayla*, a delectable seafood **restaurant** (ⓣ415/331-5888). For less expensive food, head for *Tommy's Wok*, 3001 Bridgeway Ave (ⓣ415/332-1683), a largely organic Chinese restaurant, or try terrific, low-cost curries at *Sartaj India Cafe*, 43 Caledonia St (ⓣ415/332-7103). The *Bar With No Name*, 757 Bridgeway Ave (ⓣ415/332-1392), is an ex-haunt of the Beats, hosting frequent live jazz.

Mount Tamalpais and Muir Woods

Mount Tamalpais dominates the skyline of the Marin peninsula, looming over the cool canyons of the rest of the county and dividing it into two distinct parts: the wild western slopes above the Pacific Coast and the increasingly suburban communities along the calmer bay frontage. The Panoramic Highway branches off from Hwy-1 along the crest above Mill Valley, taking ten miles to reach the center of **Mount Tamalpais State Park** (ⓣ415/388-2070, ⓦwww.mtia.net), which has some thirty miles of hiking trails and many campgrounds. While most of the redwood trees that once covered its slopes have long since been chopped down to build San Francisco's Victorian houses, one towering grove remains, protected as the **Muir Woods National Monument** (daily 8am–sunset; $5; ⓣ415/388-2595, ⓦwww.nps.gov/muwo). It's a tranquil and majestic spot, with sunlight filtering three hundred feet down from the treetops to the laurel- and fern-covered canyon below. Being so close to San Francisco, Muir Woods is a popular target, and the paved trails nearest the car park are often packed with coach-tour hordes; more secluded hiking paths include the Matt Davis Trail, leading south to Stinson Beach and north to Mount Tamalpais.

Mill Valley

From the east peak of Mount Tamalpais, a quick two-mile downhill hike follows the Temelpa Trail through velvety shrubs of chaparral to the town of **MILL VALLEY**, the oldest and most enticing of the inland towns of Marin County. For many years the town has made a healthy living out of tourism and October's annual **Mill Valley Film Festival**, a world-class event that draws Bay Area stars and up-and-coming directors alike.

The restored town centers on the redwood-shaded square of the *Depot Bookstore and Café* (Ⓣ415/383-2665), a popular bookstore, café, and meeting place at 87 Throckmorton Ave. The **Chamber of Commerce** is next door at 85 Throckmorton Ave (Mon–Fri 10am–noon and 1–4pm; Ⓣ415/388-9700, Ⓦwww.millvalley.org). Far and away the best place to **stay** is the *Mill Valley Inn*, 165 Throckmorton Ave (Ⓣ415/389-6608 or 1-800/595-2100, Ⓦwww.millvalleyinn.com; ❼), a gorgeous European-style inn with elegant rooms and two private cottages. *Avatar's Punjabi Burrito's*, at 15 Madrona St (Ⓣ415/381-8293), serves a unique range of burritos with spicy curry fillings, while the *Toast Café*, 31 Sunnyside Ave (Ⓣ415/388-2500), serves large, affordable breakfasts and lunches.

Point Reyes National Seashore

The westernmost tip of Marin County comes at the end of the **Point Reyes National Seashore**, a near-island of wilderness bordered on three sides by over fifty miles of isolated coastline – pine forests and sunny meadows hemmed in by rocky cliffs and sandy, windswept beaches. This wing-shaped landmass is a rogue piece of the earth's crust that has been drifting steadily northward along the San Andreas Fault, having started out some six million years ago as a suburb of Los Angeles. When the great earthquake of 1906 shattered San Francisco, the land here, at the epicenter, shifted over sixteen feet in an instant, though damage was confined to a few skewed cattle fences.

The **Bear Valley visitor center** (Mon–Fri 9am–5pm, Sat & Sun 8am–5pm; Ⓣ415/464-5100, Ⓦwww.nps.gov/pore), two miles southwest of Point Reyes Station in Olema, has engaging displays on local geology and natural history, plus details of hiking trails. Just to the north, Limantour Road heads six miles west to the *HI-Point Reyes* **hostel** (closed 10am–4.30pm; Ⓣ415/663-8811, Ⓦwww.norcalhostels.org; dorm from $20; ❸) in an old ranch house. Nearby **Limantour Beach** is good (and cold) for swimming.

Eight miles west of the hamlet of Inverness, a small road leads down to **Drake's Beach**, the presumed landing spot of Sir Francis Drake in 1579. Appropriately, the coastline resembles the southern coast of England – cold, wet, and windy, with chalk-white cliffs rising above the wide sandy beach. The road continues southwest another four miles to the very tip of Point Reyes, where a precarious-looking **lighthouse** (Thurs–Sun 10am–4.30pm, tours first and third Sat of each month; free; Ⓣ415/669-1534) stands firm against the crashing surf. The bluffs here are excellent for watching sea lions and, from mid-March to April and late December to early February, migrating gray whales.

The Gold Country

More than 150 years before techies from all over the world rushed to California in search of Silicon gold, rough-and-ready forty-niners invaded the **GOLD COUNTRY** of the Sierra Nevada, about 150 miles east of San Francisco, in search of the real thing. The area ranges from the foothills near Yosemite to the deep gorge of the Yuba River two hundred miles north, with **Sacramento** as its largest city. Many of the mining camps that sprang up around the Gold Country vanished as quickly as they appeared, but about half still survive. Some are bustling resorts, standing on the banks of whitewater rivers in the midst of thick pine forests; others are just eerie ghost towns, all but abandoned on the grassy rolling hills. Most of the mountainous forests along the Sierra crest are preserved as near-pristine wilderness, with excellent hiking, camping, and backpacking. There's also great skiing in winter, around the mountainous rim of **Lake Tahoe** on the border between California and Nevada, aglow under the bright lights of the nightclubs and casinos that line its southeastern shore.

Sacramento

California's state capital, **SACRAMENTO**, in the flatlands of the Central Valley, was founded in 1839 by the Swiss John Sutter. He worked hard for ten years to build a busy trading center and cattle ranch, only to be thwarted by the discovery of gold at a nearby sawmill in 1848. His workers quit their jobs to go prospecting, and thousands more flocked to the goldfields of the Central Mother Lode, without any respect for Sutter's claims to the land. Sacramento became the main supply point for the miners, and remained important as the western headquarters of the transcontinental railroad. Flashy office towers and hotel complexes have now sprung from its rather suburban streetscape, enlivening the flat grid of leafy, tree-lined blocks.

There's not a great deal to see, though the wharves, warehouses, saloons, and stores of the historic core along the **riverfront** have been restored and converted into the touristy shops and restaurants of **Old Sacramento**. On the northern edge of the old town, the **California State Railroad Museum** (daily 10am–5pm; $8; ⓣ916/445-6645, ⓦwww.csrmf.org) brings together a range of lavishly restored 1860s locomotives, with "cow-catcher" front grilles and bulbous smokestacks.

A mile or so east of downtown, the dome of the **state capitol** (ⓣ916/324-0333, ⓦwww.capitolmuseum.ca.gov) stands proudly in a spacious green park two blocks south of K Street Mall. Recently restored to its original elegance, the luxurious building brims over with finely crafted details. Although you're free to walk around, you'll see a lot more on one of the free hourly **tours** (daily 9am–4pm); ID is required to enter the building. Further east at 27th and L streets, **Sutter's Fort State Historic Park** (daily 10am–5pm; $3; ⓣ916/445-4422) is a re-creation of Sacramento's original settlement. An adobe house displays relics from the Gold Rush, and on summer weekends costumed volunteers act out scenes from the 1850s.

Practicalities

Most tourists arrive in Sacramento by car, taking a logical break from driving on Rte-80. **Trains** come in at 4th and I streets, near Old Sacramento, while Greyhound **buses** arrive at 7th and L streets. The **airport** is twelve miles northwest of the city: SuperShuttle Sacramento vans ($14; ⓣ1-800/258-3826, ⓦwww.supershuttle.com) take you directly to your downtown destination.

Sacramento's most accessible **visitor information center** is at 1002 2nd St (daily 10am–5pm; ⓣ916/442-7644, ⓦwww.oldsacramento.com). Besides the central *HI-Sacramento Hostel*, 900 H St (ⓣ916/443-1691, ⓦwww.norcalhostels.org; dorm $23; ❸), there are plenty of **places to stay** within walking distance of the city center – the best value being the *Econo Lodge*, 711 16th St (ⓣ916/443-6631 or 1-800/553-2666, ⓦwww.econolodge.com; ❷), while a fancier option is *Amber House B&B* (ⓣ916/444-8085 or 1-800/755-6526, ⓦwww.amberhouse.com; ❼). Further away, the *Vizcaya Mansion*, 2019 21st St (ⓣ916/455-5243 or 1-800/456-2019, ⓦwww.sterlinghotel.com; ❻), offers historic luxury in a quiet residential area. *Paesano's*, at 1806 Capitol Ave (ⓣ916/447-8646), is a deservedly popular pizza **restaurant**; *Tapa the World*, at 2115 J St (ⓣ916/442-4353), serves delicious *tapas* until midnight, often accompanied by live flamenco guitar; and *Centro Cocina Mexicana*, 454 28th St near J Street (ⓣ916/442-2552), offers innovative Californian-Mexican fusion cuisine. For alternative **live music** try *Old Ironsides*, 1901 10th St (ⓣ916/443-9751, ⓦwww. theoldironsides.com). Pick up the free weekly *Sacramento News & Review* (ⓦwww.newsreview.com) for more entertainment details.

The Mines

In the romantically rugged landscape of the Gold Country, overshadowed by the 10,000ft granite peaks of the Sierra Nevada, fast-flowing rivers cascade through steeply walled canyons. During the fall, the flaming reds and golds of poplars and sugar maples stand out against an evergreen background of pine and fir. The camps of the **southern mines** were the liveliest and most uproarious of all the Gold Rush settlements, and inspired most of the popular images of the era: Wild West towns full of gambling halls, saloons, and gunfights in the streets. Freebooting prospectors in these "placer" mines sometimes panned for nuggets of gold in the streams and rivers; further **north**, the diggings were far richer and more successful, but the gold was (and still is) buried deep underground, and had to be pounded out of hardrock ore.

Sonora, Columbia, Jamestown, and Mariposa

The center of the southern mining district is **SONORA**, set on steep ravines roughly a hundred miles east of San Francisco. This friendly and animated logging town boasts Victorian houses and false-fronted buildings on its main Washington Street. The Tuolumne County Visitors Bureau, 542 West Stockton St off Hwy-49 (April–Sept Mon–Fri 9am–7pm, Sat 10am–6pm, Sun 10am–5pm; Oct–March Mon–Fri 9am–6pm, Sat 10am–6pm; ⓣ209/533-4420 or 1-800/446-1333, ⓦwww.thegreatunfenced.com), is the best source of information.

Sonora's onetime arch-rival, **COLUMBIA**, three miles north on Parrots Ferry Road, is now a ghost town (and a state historic park), with a carefully restored Main Street that gives an excellent – if slightly contrived – idea of what Gold

Rush life might have been like. In 1854 it was California's second largest city, and it missed becoming the state capital by two votes – just as well, since by 1870 the gold had run out and the town was abandoned.

In **JAMESTOWN**, three miles south of Sonora, the **Railtown 1897 State Historic Park** (daily April–Oct 9.30am–4.30pm, Nov–March 10am–3pm; free, tours $2; ⓣ209/984-3953, ⓦwww.railtown1897.org), on the corner of 5th and Reservoir streets, holds an impressive collection of old steam trains, including the one used in *High Noon,* and offers rides some weekends. Further south, after a breathtaking drive over the Don Pedro Lake and Merced River, is **MARIPOSA**, gateway to Yosemite and one of the last Gold Rush towns on Hwy-49. Its **California State Mining and Mineral Museum**, a mile or so south of the historic downtown (May–Sept daily 10am–6pm; Oct–April Wed–Mon 10am–4pm; $2; ⓣ209/742-7625), has a working 1860s stamp mill model and hundreds of mineral samples.

Practicalities

In downtown Columbia, the best **place to stay** is right on the historic Main Street in the balconied *City Hotel* (ⓣ1-800/532-1479, ⓦwww.cityhotel.com; ❺); in Sonora, *Sterling Gardens* is a comfortable B&B with four guestrooms among ten acres at 18047 Lime Kiln Rd (ⓣ209/533-9300 or 1-888/533-9301, ⓦwww.sterlinggardens.com; ❺), while the well-placed *Gunn House Hotel* (ⓣ209/532-3421, ⓦwww.gunnhousehotel.com; ❸) is right in town at 286 S Washington St; motels on Hwy-49 between Sonora and Jamestown include the good-value *Miner's Motel* (ⓣ209/532-7850 or 1-800/451-4176; ❸). Jamestown's Main Street is lined by old Gold Rush hotels such as the fantastic *Jamestown Hotel* at no. 18153 (ⓣ209/984-3902 or 1-800/205-4901, ⓦwww.jamestownhotel.com; ❹), which boasts an impressive restaurant while being close to other good options, including *Morelia Mexican* (ⓣ209/984-1432), across the street at no. 18148. Sonora has a wide variety of **places to eat or drink** along Washington Street: *Alfredo's* at no. 123 (ⓣ209/532-8332) is a local favorite for Mexican food, while the *Diamondback Grill*, at no. 110 (ⓣ209/532-6661), has tapas and Mediterranean dishes; the retro *Iron Horse Lounge* at no. 97 (ⓣ209/532-4482) maintains a Wild West saloon image.

Grass Valley, Nevada City, and Downieville

The compact communities of **GRASS VALLEY** and **NEVADA CITY**, four miles apart in the Sierra Nevada Mountains, were the most prosperous and substantial of the gold-mining towns. Since the 1960s, artists and craftspeople have settled in the elaborate Victorian homes of the surrounding hills and gorges. In Grass Valley, the **North Star Mining Museum** (May–Oct daily 10am–5pm; donation suggested; ⓣ530/273-4255) at the south end of Mill Street is housed in what used to be the power station for the North Star Mine. Its giant water-driven **Pelton wheel**, fitted with a hundred or so iron buckets, once powered the drills and hoists of the mine. Dioramas show the day-to-day working life of the miners, three-quarters of whom had emigrated here from the depressed tin mines of Cornwall (bringing the Cornish pasty with them).

The last mine in California to shut down was its richest, the **Empire Mine** (May–Aug 9am–6pm; Sept–April 10am–5pm; $3; ⓣ530/273-8522, ⓦwww.empiremine.org), now preserved as a state park in the pine forests a mile south-east of Grass Valley off Rte-49. It closed in 1956, after more than six million ounces of gold had been recovered, when the cost of getting the gold out of the ground exceeded $35 an ounce, the government-controlled price at the time. Machinery sold off when the mine closed has been replaced from other disused workings and now augments the excellent and very informative **museum** at the entrance.

The excellent Grass Valley **visitor center** at 248 Mill St (Mon–Fri 9.30am–5pm, Sat 10am–3pm; ⓣ530/273-4667 or 1-800/655-4667, ⓦwww.grassvalleychamber.com) is housed in a replica of the original home of Lola Montez, an Irish entertainer and former mistress of Ludwig of Bavaria, who retired here after touring America with her provocative "Spider Dance" and kept a grizzly bear in her front yard.

Towns don't get much quainter than **Nevada City**. Amid all its shops and restaurants, the lacy-balconied and bell-towered **Old Firehouse** at 214 Main St houses a small **museum** of social history of the region (May–Oct daily 11am–4pm; Nov–April Fri–Sun noon–3pm; donation).

Both towns are very compact and connected every thirty minutes by the Gold Country Stage **minibus** (Mon–Fri 7am–6pm, Sat 10am–5pm; $1, $3 for a day pass; ⓣ1-888/660-7433, ⓦwww.goldcountrystage.com).

North on Rte-49, an hour's drive from Nevada City, you'll head into the most rugged and beautiful part of the Gold Country, where waterfalls tumble over black rocks bordered by pines and maples. **DOWNIEVILLE** is in the midst of an idyllic setting and particularly popular with mountain bikers; it abuts an extensive trail system with moderate to extreme bike trails. Oddly, as the only mining camp to have ever hanged a woman, the town has restored a gallows to commemorate that grisly passage of its history.

Accommodation

Accommodation in the revamped old Gold Rush **hotels** doesn't come cheap, but if you can afford to splash out on a B&B, Nevada City has some excellent options.

Holbrooke Hotel 212 W Main St, Grass Valley ⓣ530/273-1353 or 1-800/933-7077, ⓦwww.holbrooke.com. Historic hotel, once visited by Mark Twain, and right in the center of town. Breakfast included. ④

Holiday Lodge 1221 E Main St, Grass Valley ⓣ530/273-4406 or 1-800/742-7125, ⓦwww.holidaylodge.biz. Comfortable, basic accommodation with perks such as a swimming pool, free breakfast, and free local calls. ③

National Hotel 211 Broad St, Nevada City ⓣ530/265-4551, ⓦwww.thenationalhotel.com. Oozing faded glory, this historic landmark is the oldest continuously operating hotel in the West and still provides decent rooms. ④

Outside Inn 575 E Broad St, Nevada City ⓣ530/265-2233, ⓦwww.outsideinn.com. Quiet, 1940s motel with swimming pool, and only a 10min walk from the center of town. ③

Swan-Levine House 328 S Church St, Grass Valley ⓣ530/272-1873, ⓦwww.swanlevinehouse.com. Attractively decorated, sunny rooms in an old Victorian hospital run by two artists. ④

Eating and drinking

Both Grass Valley and Nevada City have good places to **eat**, as well as many **bars** and **saloons**, where you'll often be treated to free live music.

Café Mekka 237 Commercial St, Nevada City ⓣ530/478-1517. Relaxed, stunningly decorated coffeeshop, popular with arty locals.

Cirino's 309 Broad St, Nevada City ⓣ530/265-2246 and 213 W Main St, Grass Valley ⓣ530/477-6000. Casual Italian place serving filling deli sandwiches and a range of tasty entrees.

Marshall's Pasties 203 Mill St, Grass Valley ⓣ530/272-2844. Stunning array of freshly filled Cornish-style pasties. Takeout only.

Sopa Thai 312 Commercial St, Nevada City ⓣ530/470-0101. Beautifully decorated place that dishes up authentic Siamese fare and has become a local favorite.

Swiss House 535 Mill St, Grass Valley ⓣ530/273-8272. The central European decor seems out of place here but the hearty food, such as schnitzel and apple strudel, will fill you up.

Lake Tahoe

One of the highest, deepest, cleanest, and coldest lakes in the world, **Lake Tahoe** is perched high above the Gold Country in an alpine bowl of forested granite peaks. Longer than the English Channel is wide, and more than a thousand feet deep, it's so cold that perfectly preserved cowboys who drowned over a century ago have been recovered from its depths. The lake straddles the Nevada stateline as well and lures weekenders with sunny beaches in the summer, snow-covered slopes in the winter, and bustling casinos year-round.

Arrival, information, and getting around

The nearest you can get to Lake Tahoe on Greyhound or Amtrak from San Francisco and Sacramento is Truckee, fifteen miles north (see p.1065). From there, local TART **buses** (ⓣ530/581-3922 or 1-800/736-6365, ⓦwww.laketahoetransit.com) run to Tahoe City and around but, frustratingly, not onwards to South Lake Tahoe. Transport around the south shore is provided by BlueGo buses and trolleys (ⓣ530/541-7149, ⓦwww.bluego.org). There are shuttles from both ends of the lake to Reno airport: North Lake Tahoe Express (ⓣ530/541-4892, ⓦwww.laketahoetransit.com) and South Tahoe Express (ⓣ1-866/898-2463, ⓦwww.southtahoeexpress.com); prices vary according to the number of passengers. You can rent **bicycles** from numerous outlets, including the Mountain Sports Center (ⓣ530/542-6584, ⓦwww.camprichardson.com) in South Lake Tahoe's *Camp Richardson Resort*, and from Olympic Bike Shop (ⓣ530/581-2500) in Tahoe City.

There are four official **visitor centers** around the lake: in California at 3066 US-50, South Lake Tahoe (daily 9am–5pm; ⓣ530/541-5255 or 1-800/288-2463, ⓦwww.tahoeinfo.com), and 380 North Lake Blvd, Tahoe City (daily 9am–5pm; ⓣ530/581-6900 or 1-800/824-6348, ⓦwww.gotahoenorth.com); and in Nevada at 969 Tahoe Blvd, Incline Village (Mon–Fri 8am–5pm, Sat & Sun 10am–4pm; ⓣ1-800/468-2463, ⓦwww.gotahoe.com), and at 168 Hwy-50 in Stateline (ⓣ775/588-4591, ⓦwww.tahoechamber.org).

Accommodation

There are dozens of bargain **motels** along the Southshore, though weekday rates from $50 can easily more than double on weekends and in summer. In Tahoe City, there are fewer budget choices. If you're stuck, any of the visitor centers will try to help.

Doug's Mellow Mountain Retreat 3787 Forest Ave, South Lake Tahoe ⓣ530/544-8065, ⓦwww.hostelz.com. Basic hostel-style accommodation in what is essentially Doug's home, with cooking facilities and cheap bike rental. Beds $18 per person and double rooms available. ❷

Driftwood Lodge 4115 Laurel Ave at Poplar, South Lake Tahoe ⓣ530/541-7400, ⓦwww.tahoedriftwood.com. The heated pool and private beach access make this otherwise very basic accommodation particularly appealing in summer; very close to casinos of Stateline. ❷

Inn by the Lake 3300 Lake Tahoe Blvd, South Lake Tahoe ⓣ1-800/877-1466, ⓦwww.innbythelake.com. Nicely furnished rooms, a heated swimming pool and jacuzzi, free breakfast, and use of bicycles render this a relaxing spot; good value for money. Free shuttle bus to the casinos. ❺

River Ranch Lodge Hwy-89 and Alpine Meadows Rd, Tahoe City ⓣ530/583-4264 or 1-800/535-9900, ⓦwww.riverranchlodge.com. Historic lodge on the Truckee River with a casual atmosphere and one of the lake's best restaurants. ④

Royal Valhalla 4104 Lakeshore Blvd, South Lake Tahoe ⓣ530/544-2233 or 1-866/493-4603, ⓦwww.tahoeroyalvalhalla.com. Not exactly regal but one of the better motels, with balconies overlooking the lake and kitchenettes. ④

Tahoma Meadows B&B 6821 W Lake Blvd, Tahoma ⓣ1-866/525-1553, ⓦwww.tahomameadows.com. Well-furnished rooms in a lovely setting at this friendly place on the west shore, 7 miles south of Tahoe City. ⑤

Tamarack Lodge 2311 North Lake Blvd, Tahoe City ⓣ530/583-3350 or 1-888/824-6323, ⓦwww.tamarackattahoe.com. One of the best deals anywhere on the lake, with comfortable and clean cabins and rooms. ③

South Lake Tahoe and around

In **South Lake Tahoe**, the lakeside's largest community, ranks of restaurants, modest motels, and pine-bound cottages stand cheek by jowl with the high-rise gambling dens of **Stateline**, just across the border in Nevada. If you happen to lose your money at the tables and slot machines, you can always explore the beautiful hiking trails, parks, and beaches in the surrounding area.

Lake Tahoe skiing

Lake Tahoe has some of the best **downhill skiing** in North America, and its larger resorts rival their Rocky Mountain counterparts. Although skiing is not cheap – the largest ski areas charge well over $60 for a single day – most resorts offer decent-value rental/lift ticket/lesson packages or multiday discounts, especially if booked in advance online. **Snowboarding** has caught on in a big way, and the same resorts that once scoffed at the sport have now installed massive snow parks with radical half-pipes and jumps. **Cross-country skiing** is also popular. Most resorts **rent** skis for about $30 and snowboards for $35 or more.

Downhill skiing

Heavenly reachable by shuttle from Southshore, two miles from the casinos, or via the gondola on Hwy-50, next to the state line (ⓣ775/586-7000 or 1-800/243-2836, ⓦwww.skiheavenly.com). Prime location and sheer scale (85 runs and 29 lifts) make this one of the lake's most frequented resorts, and it also offers the highest vertical skiing served by a lift.

Kirkwood Ski Resort 35 miles south of South Lake Tahoe on Hwy-88 (ⓣ209/258-6000, ⓦwww.kirkwood.com). A bit out of the way if you're in Tahoe but worth the trip as a destination in itself for its recreational possibilities, including excellent hiking and biking trails.

Squaw Valley USA Squaw Valley Road, halfway between Truckee and Tahoe City (ⓣ530/583-6955 or 1-888/766-9321, ⓦwww.squaw.com). Thirty-three lifts service over four thousand acres of unbeatable terrain at the site of the 1960 Winter Olympics. Non-skiers can take the cable lift ($19) and use the ice-skating/swimming pool complex for the day.

Cross-country skiing

Royal Gorge in Soda Springs, ten miles west of Truckee (ⓣ530/426-3871 or 1-800/666-3871, ⓦwww.royalgorge.com). The largest and best of Tahoe's cross-country resorts has 204 miles of groomed trails. Trail fee $25–29, rental fee $21, and lessons (group $25, private $40).

Spooner Lake in Nevada at the intersection of Hwy-50 and Hwy-28 (ⓣ775/749-5349, ⓦwww.spoonerlake.com). The closest cross-country resort to South Lake Tahoe has lake views and 63 miles of groomed trails. Trail fee $12–21, rental fee $19, and lessons $47, including pass and rental.

The **Heavenly Gondola**, in the heart of town, rises to an elevation of 9136ft (summer daily 10am–5pm; $30). From there, enjoy breathtaking views from East Peak Lake, East Peak Lookout, or Sky Meadows. Hikes are graded from easy to strenuous. Closer to the water, the prettiest part of the lake is along the southwest shore, at **Emerald Bay State Park**, ten miles from South Lake Tahoe, which has a number of good shoreline **campgrounds**. A mile from the parking lot, **Vikingsholm** is a reproduction of a Viking castle, built as a summer home in 1929 and open for hourly tours (summer daily 10am–4pm; $6). In **Sugar Pine Point State Park**, two miles north, the huge **Ehrman Mansion** (daily 11am–4pm; $6) is decorated in Thirties-era furnishings; the extensive lakefront grounds were used as a location in *The Godfather II*.

The rest of the 75-mile **drive** is lovely enough, though certainly not the "most beautiful drive in America," as one locally produced brochure touts. Another way to see the lake is to take a paddlewheel **boat cruise** on the *MS Dixie II* or *Tahoe Queen*, from Zephyr Cove (timetable varies; $39–69; ⓣ775/589-4906, ⓦwww.zephyrcove.com), reached on a free shuttle from South Lake Tahoe. You can sign up for other boat tours through one of the casinos.

Tahoe City

Tahoe City, the hub on the lake's northwestern shore manages to retain a more relaxed small-town attitude than South Lake Tahoe. Hwy-89 meets Hwy-28 at Lake Tahoe's only outlet, the **Truckee River**. At the mouth of the river, the **Gatekeeper's Museum** (May to mid-June Wed–Sun 11am–5pm; mid-June to mid-Oct daily 11am–5pm; $2), contains a well-presented hodgepodge of artifacts from the nineteenth century, and a good collection of native basketware. **Rafting** down the Truckee is a common activity in summer, with raft rental companies (prices start around $35 per person) clustered at the junction of highways 28 and 89.

Squaw Valley, the site of the 1960 Winter Olympics, is situated five miles west of Tahoe City off of Hwy-89, although the original facilities (except the flame and the Olympic rings) are now swamped by the rampant development that has made this California's largest ski resort (see box, p.1062).

Eating and drinking

Fast food and casino all-you-care-to-eat buffets are standard in Southshore, while Tahoe City has a better range of moderately priced **restaurants** and a couple of good **bars**, all within a few minutes of each other.

The Brewery at Lake Tahoe 3542 Lake Tahoe Blvd, South Lake Tahoe ⓣ530/544-2739. Microbrewery with decent ales ranging from pale to porter, and food specials such as beer-steamed shrimp and quality steaks.

Bridgetender Bar & Grill 30 West Lake Blvd, Tahoe City ⓣ530/583-3342. Friendly rustic bar with good music, a fine range of beers, and huge portions of ribs and burgers.

Lakehouse Pizza 120 Grove St, Tahoe City ⓣ530/583-2222. Tahoe's best place for pizza is also a popular spot for cocktails on the lake at sundown.

Pierce Street Annex in the back of the Safeway complex, Tahoe City ⓣ530/583-5800. The place for drinking and dancing on the Northshore, but with sometimes-cheesy music. Popular with the younger Tahoe City crowd.

River Ranch Hwy-89 and Alpine Meadows Rd, Tahoe City ⓣ530/583-4264 or 1-800/535-9900. Historic lodge on the Truckee River serving excellent New American cuisine in a relaxed atmosphere.

Sprouts 3123 Lake Tahoe Blvd near Alameda Ave, South Lake Tahoe ⓣ530/541-6969. Almost, but not completely, vegetarian, with good organic sandwiches, burritos, and smoothies.

Sunnyside 1850 West Lake Blvd, near Tahoe City ⓣ530/583-7200. One of the most popular places to have cocktails at sunset on the deck overlooking the lake.

Tahoe House Bakery Hwy-89, half a mile south of Hwy-28, Tahoe City ⓣ530/583-1377. Family-style bakery and deli, popular with locals.

Taj Mahal 3838 Lake Tahoe Blvd, in the *Quality Inn*, South Lake Tahoe ⓣ530/541-6495. Basic Indian fare with a daily eleven-dish lunch buffet.

Tep's Villa Roma 3450 Hwy-50, South Lake Tahoe ⓣ530/541-8227. Longstanding Southshore institution that serves large portions of hearty Italian food.

Truckee and Donner Lake

Fifteen miles north of Tahoe City, the pleasant town of **TRUCKEE** is not only a jumping off point for Lake Tahoe, but a developing tourist destination in its own right. It is well placed for outdoor excursions and it retains a fair amount of nineteenth-century wooden architecture along its main drag, Donner Pass Road, still referred to as Commercial Row by locals. This strip holds a good choice of **eating** and **drinking** joints, such as *Dragonfly* (ⓣ530/587-0557), a Pacific Rim and Asian fusion restaurant at no. 10118, and *OB's* (ⓣ530/587-4164), a relaxed pub with decent food at no. 10046. Around the corner at 10007 Bridge St, the *Truckee Hotel* (ⓣ530/587-4444 or 1-800/659-6921, ⓦwww.thetruckeehotel.com; ④) is a central **place to stay** with a wide range of rooms. The Chamber of Commerce, 10065 Donner Pass Rd (Mon–Fri 8.30am–6pm, Sat & Sun 9am–6pm; ⓣ530/587-2757, ⓦwww.truckee.com) is very helpful and friendly.

Several miles west of Truckee, **DONNER LAKE**, surrounded by alpine cliffs of silver-gray granite, was the site of a gruesome tragedy in 1846, when the **Donner Party**, heading for the Gold Rush, found their route blocked by early snowfall. They stopped and built crude shelters, hoping that the snow would melt; it didn't. Fifteen of their number braved the mountains in search of help from Sutter's Fort in Sacramento; only two men and five women made it, surviving by eating the bodies of the men who died. A rescue party set off immediately, only to find more of the same: thirty or so half-crazed survivors, living off the meat of their fellow travelers. The horrific tale is recounted in the small **Emigrant Trail Museum** (daily 9am–4pm; free; ⓣ530/582-7892), just off Donner Pass Road in Donner State Park (parking $6 and camping May–Sept; $25; ⓣ1-800-444-7275, ⓦwww.reserveamerica.com).

Northern California

The massive and eerily silent volcanic lands of **northern California** have more in common with Oregon and Washington than with the rest of the state. Its small settlements live by farming and an ever-decreasing number by logging and fishing, though locals have been joined in recent years by New Agers, ex-hippies, and a growing contingent of tourists. Once you're past the atypically lush valleys of the **Wine Country**, the coast stretches for four hundred miles of rugged bluffs and forests. Aside from the beautiful deserted beaches that stripe the coast, trees are the big attraction, thousands of years old and hundreds of feet high, dominating a landscape swathed in swirling mists. The **Redwood National Park** teems with campers and hikers in summer, but out of season it can be idyllic. The remote wildernesses of the interior can be enchanting, especially around the **Shasta Cascade** and **Lassen Volcanic National Park**.

Public transportation is, not surprisingly, scarce, though Greyhound buses run from San Francisco and Sacramento up and down I-5 into Oregon and US-101 as far as Arcata.

The Wine Country

The warm and sunny hills of **Napa** and **Sonoma valleys**, an hour north of San Francisco, are by reputation at the center of the American wine industry. In truth, less than five percent of California's wine comes from the region, but what it does produce is America's best. In summer, cars jam Hwy-29 through its heart, as visitors embark on a day's hectic tasting.

The Napa Valley

Thirty miles of gently landscaped hillsides, the **Napa Valley** looks more like southern France than a near-neighbor of the Pacific Ocean. The one anomaly is the town of **Napa** itself, a sprawling, ungainly city of 60,000 best avoided in favor of the wineries and small towns north on Hwy-29. Nine miles north is **YOUNTVILLE**, anchored by **Vintage 1870**, 6525 Washington St (daily 10.30am–5.30pm; ⓣ1-800/946-3487, ⓦwww.vintagewinecellar.com), a shopping and wine complex in a converted winery that's home to Napa Valley Aloft (ⓣ1-800/944-4408, ⓦwww.nvaloft.com), which specializes in sunrise hot-air balloon tours from $245 per person.

Of the large wineries at the valley's southern end, **Robert Mondavi**, at 7801 St Helena Hwy in Oakville (daily 10am–5pm; ⓣ1-888/766-6328, ⓦwww

▲ Vineyard in Napa Valley

.mondavi.com) offers the most informative and least sales-driven tours ($25) and tastings (from $15).

Up the valley past the pretty village of **ST HELENA**, **Beringer Vineyards**, at 2000 Main St (daily 10am–5pm; tasting $5, tours $10–35; ⓣ707/963-7115, ⓦwww.beringer.com), is modeled on a German Gothic mansion and has graced the cover of many a wine magazine. Spacious lawns and a grand tasting room heavy with dark wood make for quite a regal experience.

Homey **CALISTOGA**, at the very northern tip of the valley, is well known for its mud baths, whirlpools, and mineral water, though its wineries are just as appealing. South of town, **Clos Pegase**, 1060 Dunaweal Lane (daily 10.30am–5pm; $5; ⓣ707/942-4981, ⓦwww.clospegase.com), is a flamboyant, high-profile winery that draws a link between fine wine and fine art, with an excellent sculpture garden; there are tours at 11am and 2pm. The **Chateau Montelena**, 1429 Tubbs Lane (daily 9.30am–4pm; $15–25; ⓣ707/942-5105, ⓦwww.montelena.com), just north of town, is one of the valley's oldest and smallest wineries, with an impressive medieval facade and a reputation for first-class chardonnays. A mile further up the road, the **Old Faithful Geyser** (daily 9am–6pm; $8; ⓣ707/942-6463) spurts boiling water sixty feet into the air at forty-minute intervals. The water source was discovered during oil drilling here in the 1920s, when search equipment struck a force estimated to be up to a thousand pounds per square foot. In time, landowners turned it into a high-yield tourist attraction, using the same name as the famous spouter in Yellowstone National Park (see p.816).

Practicalities

From San Francisco there are daily Gray Line **bus tours** ($68; ⓣ1-888/428-6937, ⓦwww.grayline.com) to the Wine Country; otherwise you will need a car. The main **Visitors Bureau** (daily 9am–5pm; ⓣ707/226-7459, ⓦwww.napavalley.com) is at 1310 Napa Town Center, off First Street in Napa itself, but most towns have their own information outlet.

In **St Helena**, the *El Bonita Motel*, 195 Main St (ⓣ707/963-3216 or 1-800/541-3284; ⑥), is a smart Art Deco hotel on the south side of town, while the nearby *Ambrose Bierce Inn* (ⓣ707/963-3003, ⓦwww.ambrosebiercehouse.com; ⑦), is a luxury B&B at 1515 Main St. St Helena's **restaurants** range from the inexpensive Mexican of *Armadillo's*, 1304 Main St (ⓣ707/963-8082), to the haute cuisine and four-hundred-plus wine list at the gigantic *Wine Spectator Greystone Restaurant*, 2555 Main St (ⓣ707/967-1010), owned by the Culinary Institute of America.

In **Calistoga**, *Dr Wilkinson's Hot Springs*, 1507 Lincoln Ave (ⓣ707/942-4102, ⓦwww.drwilkinson.com; ⑤), is a legendary health spa and hotel, while less expensive lodgings (and spa facilities) lining the main drag, Lincoln Avenue, include the quiet, modern *Comfort Inn* at no. 1865 (ⓣ707/942-9400, ⓦwww.comfortinn.com; ④). Downtown's most enticing hotel can be found at 1457 Lincoln Ave in the historic *Mount View Hotel and Spa* (ⓣ707/942-6877 or 1-800/816-6877, ⓦwww.mountviewhotel.com; ⑧ double, ⑨ cottage with patio and jacuzzi). Creative cuisine, featuring unheard-of combinations such as *chile rellenos* with walnut pomegranate sauce, makes **dining** at the *Wappo Bar & Bistro*, 1226 Washington St (ⓣ707/942-4712), a delicious adventure. *Brannan's Grill*, 1374 Lincoln Ave (ⓣ707/942-2233), serves fresh oysters, salmon, and pecan-stuffed quail in an airy wood-interior bistro. The less expensive *Calistoga Inn*, 1250 Lincoln Ave (ⓣ707/942-4101), offers great seafood appetizers, including wheat-ale steamed clams and mussels, plus a wide range of wines, microbrewed beers, and excellent desserts.

Sonoma Valley

On looks alone, the crescent-shaped **Sonoma Valley** beats Napa hands down. This altogether more rustic valley curves between oak-covered mountain ranges from the Spanish Colonial town of **SONOMA** to Glen Ellen, a few miles north along Hwy-12. It's far smaller than Napa, and many of its wineries are informal, family-run businesses, where a charge for tasting is still frowned upon and visitors are few.

The restored **Mission San Francisco Solano de Sonoma** (daily 10am–5pm; $2), just east of the spacious plaza in Sonoma, was the last and northernmost of the California missions, and the only one established in northern California by the nervous Mexican rulers, who were fearful of expansionist Russian fur-traders. The plaza was also the sight of the Bear Flag Revolt, the 1846 action that propelled California into independence from Mexico, and then statehood. Many of Sonoma's wineries are concentrated a mile east, within walking distance, and include the grand old **Buena Vista Carneros**, 18000 Old Winery Rd (daily 10am–5pm; tasting $5–10; various tours free–$50; ⓣ1-800/678-8504, ⓦwww.buenavistacarneros.com), which has champagne cellars, tunnels of oak caskets, and a high-ceilinged tasting room. A ten-minute drive further north, in charming Glen Ellen, is the **Benziger Family Winery**, 1883 London Ranch Rd (daily 10am–5pm; tasting $10–15; ⓣ1-888/490-2739, ⓦwww.benziger.com). A self-guided tour explains how wine grapes are cultivated and flavored, and nine times daily a tram tour ($15) takes you around the vineyard along the side of Mount Sonoma. A half-mile up London Ranch Road, **Jack London State Park** (daily 9.30am–5pm, until 7pm in summer; $6 per car) sits on the 140 acres of ranchland owned by the famed author of *The Call of the Wild*. Here you'll find the author's final resting place, along with a decent museum that houses a collection of souvenirs that he picked up while traveling the globe.

Practicalities

Public transportation to the valley is available through Golden Gate Transit's bus services from San Francisco to Petaluma and Santa Rosa (ⓣ707/541-2000, ⓦwww.goldengate.org). For useful **info**, head for the Visitors Bureau (daily summer 9am–6pm, winter 9am–5pm; ⓣ707/996-1090, ⓦwww.sonomavalley.com), in a cute building right on Sonoma's plaza. **Accommodation** is pricey, though the *Sonoma Hotel*, 110 W Spain St (ⓣ1-800/468-6016, ⓦwww.sonomahotel.com; ❺), has French country-style doubles and a great bar, and the *Swiss Hotel*, 18 W Spain St (ⓣ707/938-2884, ⓦwww.swisshotelsonoma.com; ❻), is in a landmark building on the plaza with four-poster beds in each room. Good shopping and cafés abound on and around the square; *The Girl and the Fig*, 110 W Spain St (ⓣ707/938-3634), is a highly rated French **restaurant**, while at 400 E First St, *Cucina Viansa* (ⓣ707/935-5656) serves creative Italian cuisine at reasonable prices.

The northern coast

The fog-bound towns and windswept, craggy beaches of the **northern coast** that stretches to the Oregon border is better suited for hiking and camping than sunbathing, with cool temperatures year-round and a huge network of national, state, and regional parks preserving magnificent **redwood** trees. Throw on your hiking boots and get out onto the trails that sweep past lolling seals, migrating whales, and some of the oldest, tallest trees on earth.

The Sonoma Coast and Russian River Valley

Despite the weekend influx from San Francisco, the villages of the **Sonoma Coast** and **Russian River Valley** seem all but asleep for most of the year. Tucked along the slow, snaking Hwy-1, towns include **BODEGA BAY**, where Hitchcock filmed *The Birds*. From here, a great thirteen-mile hike leads along the rugged cliffs to busy **Goat Rock Beach**, where the Russian River joins the ocean. A prime seal- and whale-watching spot, the beach is less than a mile from equally pleasing **JENNER**, which is a good place for clam chowder and ocean-staring.

About ten miles inland on Hwy-116, toward the warm and pastoral Russian River Valley, **GUERNEVILLE** is a well-established gay resort. It offers plenty of **places to stay** – though many are expensive. The *New Dynamic Inn*, 14030 Mill St (ⓣ707/869-1563, ⓦwww.newdynamicinn.com; ❹), is one of the more modest places, while the **campground** at *Johnson's Resort* (ⓣ707/869-2022, ⓦwww.johnsonsbeach.com; ❷) on 1st Street also has cabins, rentable by the week. The popular *Pink Elephant*, 9895 Main St (ⓣ707/865-0500), offers live music, as well as cheap booze and snacks, while *Main St Station*, 16280 Main St (ⓣ707/869-0501), is a great pizzeria with nightly live jazz. The **Armstrong Redwoods State Reserve** ($6 per car), two miles north, contains 750 very dense acres of enormous redwoods interspersed by trails – one of the best ways to see it is on horseback. Guided expeditions run by Horseback Adventures (ⓣ707/887-2939, ⓦwww.redwoodhorses.com) vary in length from half a day ($70) to overnight pack trips (from $250) with tented accommodation.

MONTE RIO, four miles back down the river toward the coast, is a lovely old resort town, at the entrance to the 2500-acre **Bohemian Grove**, where the richest and most powerful men in the country traditionally gather in privacy each July for two weeks of (supposedly male-only) high jinks.

The Mendocino coast

The coast of **Mendocino County**, 150 miles north of San Francisco, is a dramatic extension of the Sonoma coastline – the headlands a bit sharper, the surf a bit rougher, but otherwise more of the same. **MENDOCINO** itself looks like a transplanted New England fishing village: weathered and charming, with plenty of art galleries and boutiques. Just south of town, hiking and cycling trails weave through the unusual **Van Damme State Park**, on Hwy-1 ($6 per car; ⓣ707/937-5804), where the ancient trees of the Pygmy Forest are stunted to waist height because of poor drainage and soil chemicals. Two-hour sea cave tours through the park are available through Kayak Mendocino (three times daily; $50; ⓣ707/964-7480, ⓦwww.kayakmendocino.com).

Bigfoot Country

Willow Creek, forty miles east of Arcata, is the self-proclaimed gateway to "**Bigfoot Country**." Reports of giant 350- to 800-pound humanoids wandering the forests of northwestern California have circulated since the late nineteenth century, fueled by long-established Indian legends, but weren't taken seriously until 1958, when a road maintenance crew found giant footprints. Thanks to their photos, the Bigfoot story went worldwide. However, in 2002, the bereaved family of Ray L. Wallace claimed he made the 1958 footprints, a hoax they had promised to keep secret until after his death. But the number and variety of prints (over forty, since 1958) still points to a Bigfoot mystery, and the small **visitor center** in Willow Creek has details of Bigfoot's alleged activities.

The best of the affordable **accommodations** in the center of town is the *Sea Gull Inn*, 44960 Albion St (☎707/937-5204 or 1-888/937-5204, Ⓦwww.seagullbb.com; ❺), though the antique-filled *The Mendocino Hotel*, 45080 Main St (☎707/937-0511 or 1-800/548-0513, Ⓦwww.mendocinohotel.com; ❹), offers some rooms with shared baths and more luxurious suites. The town's oldest **bar** is *Dick's Place* on Main Street, the closest thing you'll find to a local hangout. Of Mendocino's **restaurants**, the most famous is *Café Beaujolais*, 961 Ukiah St (☎707/937-5614), which specializes in organic California cuisine. *955 Ukiah Street* (closed Tues; ☎707/937-1955) serves some of the best food in town: entrees are considered a steal for $15–25 a plate. For slightly cheaper fare with a great view, try the *Mendocino Café*, 10451 Lancing St (☎707/937-4197), which serves sandwiches, salads and pasta.

The Humboldt coast

Humboldt is by far the most beautiful of the coastal counties: almost entirely forestland, overwhelmingly peaceful in places, in others plain eerie. The impassable cliffs of **Kings Range** prevent even the sinuous Hwy-1 from reaching the "Lost Coast" of its southern reaches. To get there you have to detour inland via US-101 through the deepest redwood territory as far as **GARBERVILLE**, a one-street town with a few good bars that is the center of the "Emerald Triangle," which produces the majority of California's largest cash crop, marijuana.

Redwood country begins in earnest a few miles north, at the **Humboldt Redwoods State Park** (☎707/946-2409, Ⓦwww.humboldtredwoods.org), California's largest redwood park. The serpentine **Avenue of the Giants** weaves for 33 miles through trees that block all but a few strands of sunlight, but you can exit at numerous points to get back on US-101. This is the habitat of *Sequoia sempervirens*, the coastal redwood, with ancestors dating back to the days of the dinosaurs, and some are over 350ft tall. Three campgrounds fill up quickly in summertime (☎1-800/444-7275, Ⓦwww.reserveamerica; $20).

Tiny **SAMOA**, a few minutes by car over the bay from sprawling Eureka, holds the last remaining cookhouse in the West. Lumbermen came to the *Samoa Cookhouse* (☎707/442-1659) to eat gargantuan meals after a day of felling redwoods; the oilskin tablecloths and burly workers have gone, but the lumber-camp style remains, with long tables and colossal portions of red meat. Many people bypass **EUREKA** itself but the Old Town is worth a wander, especially during the Arts Alive! nights on the first Saturday of each month, when almost a hundred businesses open their doors for arts – much of it performing – along with plenty of drinking and frivolity.

ARCATA, seven miles north of Eureka, a small college town with an earthy, mellow pace, has a grassy central plaza surrounded by good restaurants, and some excellent white-sand, windswept beaches to the north. The *Fairwinds Motel*, 1674 G St (☎707/822-4824 or 1-866/352-5518, Ⓦwww.fairwindsmotelarcata.com; ❸), is probably the best deal in town. More upscale, the *Hotel Arcata*, 708 Ninth St (☎707/826-0217 or 1-800/344-1221, Ⓦwww.hotelarcata.com; ❹), is central and offers standard rooms and nicer suites. *Humboldt Brewery*, 856 10th St, no longer makes its own ale but stocks a good range, has low-priced food and often hosts live music.

Redwood National Park

Thirty miles north of Arcata, the small town of **ORICK** marks the southern limit, and busiest section, of the **Redwood National Park. Tall Trees Grove** here is home to one of the world's tallest trees – a mighty 367-footer. Many visitors hike to it on the 8.5-mile trail from Bald Hill Road near Orick, but make sure to visit the **Kuchel information center** (daily 9am–5pm; Ⓣ707/464-6101), from which you can obtain the needed free permit to drive along the access road to the trailhead.

Of the three state parks within the Redwood National Park area, **Prairie Creek** is the most varied and popular, and while bear and elk roam in plain sight, rangers lead **tours** through the wild and damp profusion. Highlights include the meadows of **Elk Prairie** in front of the **ranger station** (daily: summer 9am–6pm; rest of year 9am–5pm; Ⓣ707/464-6101), where herds of Roosevelt Elk – massive beasts weighing up to twelve hundred pounds – wander freely.

Spectacular coastal views can be had from trails in the Klamath area, especially the **Klamath Overlook**, two miles up Requa Road and about three-quarters of a mile above the sea. You can jump over, lumber under, or glide through all the naturally contorted and sculpted **Trees of Mystery** (daily: summer 8am–7pm; winter 9am–5pm; $13.50; Ⓣ1-800/638-3389, Ⓦwww.treesofmystery.net), except the impressive **Cathedral Tree**, where nine trees have grown from one root structure to form a spooky circle. Further north in a stupendous coastal setting just off US-101, the *HI-Redwood National Park* **hostel** (Ⓣ707/482-8265, Ⓦwww.norcalhostels.org; ❸) has dorm beds from $21 and two private rooms.

The park headquarters are in otherwise missable **Crescent City** at 1111 Second St (summer daily 9am–5pm, winter Mon–Sat 9am–5pm; Ⓣ707/464-6101, Ⓦwww.nps.gov/redw), but you can pick up information all over the park. There are **campgrounds** everywhere; three that have showers and water are *Prairie Creek* on US-101, *Mill Creek*, five miles south of Crescent City, and *Jedediah Smith*, eight miles north of Crescent City on the Smith River. If you do come in summer, make reservations through ReserveAmerica (Ⓣ1-800/444-7275, Ⓦwww.reserveamerica.com), and if things get really desperate, head up US-101 to the numerous **motels** around Crescent City.

The northern interior

The remote **northern interior** of California, cut off from the coast by the **Shasta Cascade** range and dominated by forests, lakes, and mountains, is largely uninhabited. Interstate 5 leads through the heart of this near-wilderness, forging straight through the unspectacular farmland of **Sacramento Valley** to **Redding** – the region's only buses follow this route. Redding makes a good base for the **Whiskeytown-Shasta-Trinity area** and the more demanding **Lassen National Volcanic Park**. Mountaineers and the spiritually-minded flock to **Mount Shasta**, which is close enough to the volcanic **Lava Beds** at the very northeastern tip of the state for them to be a long but feasible day's car trip.

Chico

Charming little **CHICO**, about midway between Sacramento and Redding, some twenty miles east of I-5, is a good stopoff if you don't want to cover the whole valley from top to bottom in one day, or if you're here to visit Lassen Volcanic National Park (see p.1071) and need somewhere to stay. Home to **Chico State University**, the laid-back town is loved by mountain bikers for its many trails. Cheap rooms near downtown can be found at the *Matador Motel*, 1934 The Esplanade (Ⓣ530/342-7543; ❷), and there are several good restaurants, notably the 24-hour *Jack's Family Restaurant*, 540 Main St (Ⓣ530/343-8383), a great down-home diner.

Redding and Shasta

A sprawling expanse of chain stores with a shopping mall at its heart and a poured-concrete convention center at its gate, **REDDING** appears to be an anomaly amidst the natural splendor of the northern interior. The region's largest city, with over 70,000 people, it has acted as a northern nexus since the late nineteenth century, when the Central Pacific Railroad came through. Today it remains a crossroads, bulging with cookie-cutter motels and fast food outlets, but the superb **Turtle Bay Exploration Park**, 800 Auditorium Drive (March–Oct daily 9am–5pm, Nov-Feb closed Tues; $13; Ⓣ530/243-8850, Ⓦwww.turtlebay.org), full of fascinating interactive exhibits, and stunning Sundial Bridge, designed by Spanish architect Santiago Calatreva, have greatly enhanced the town's image. If you have a car and need **to stay**, try the *Best Western Hilltop Inn*, 2300 Hilltop Drive (Ⓣ530/221-6100 or 1-800/336-4880, Ⓦwww.bestwestern.com; ❹); the *Bridgehouse B&B*, 1455 Riverside Drive (Ⓣ530/247-7177, Ⓦwww.reddingbridgehouse.com; ❺), is a friendly and good-value option, only a short walk from downtown. **Buz's Crab** (Ⓣ530/243-2120), 2159 East St, is a local institution, serving a huge range of moderately priced fish and seafood.

SHASTA, four miles west of Redding and not to be confused with Mount Shasta, is somewhat a ghost town. The row of half-ruined brick buildings here represent a once booming gold-mining town, literally at the end of the road from San Francisco and on the very edge of the wilderness. The **Courthouse** has been turned into a museum (Wed–Sun 10am–5pm; $2), full of historical California artwork and mining paraphernalia, while the gallows and prison cells are a grim reminder of the daily executions that went on here.

Lassen Volcanic National Park

About fifty miles over gently-sloping plains east from Red Bluff on Hwy-36, or forty miles east from Redding on Hwy-44, the 106,000 acres that make up the pine forests, crystal-green lakes, and boiling thermal pools of the **LASSEN VOLCANIC NATIONAL PARK** are one of the most unearthly parts of northern California's forbidding climate, which receives up to fifty feet of snowfall each year, keeping the area pretty much uninhabited outside the brief summer season. **Mount Lassen** itself last erupted in 1915, when the peak blew an enormous mushroom cloud some seven miles skyward, tearing the summit into chunks that landed as far away as Reno; scientists predict that it is the likeliest of all the West Coast volcanoes to blow again.

The thirty-mile tour of the park along Hwy-89 from **Manzanita Lake** in the north should take no more than a few hours but is often not fully open until the snows have melted in June. There is a $10 access fee per vehicle to the park, valid for seven days. The Mount Lassen explosion denuded the devastated area, ripping out every tree and patch of grass. Slowly the earth is recovering a green blanket, but the most vivid impression is one of complete destruction. Marking the halfway point, **Summit Lake** is a busy camping area set around a beautiful icy lake, close to which are the park's most manageable hiking trails. From a parking area to the south (8000ft up), the steep, five-mile ascent to Lassen Peak begins. Experienced hikers can do it in four hours, but wilderness seekers will have a better time pushing east to the steep trails of the **Juniper Lake** area.

Continuing south along Hwy-89, Lassen's indisputable show-stealers are **Bumpass Hell** and **Emerald Lake**, the former (named for a man who lost a leg trying to cross it) a steaming valley of active pools and vents that bubble away at a low rumble all around. The trails are sturdy and easy to manage, but you should never venture off them. The crusts over the thermal features are often brittle, and breaking through could plunge you into very hot water. Before leaving the park at **Mineral**, make an effort to stop at **Sulphur Works**, an acrid cauldron of steam vents. A magnificent but grueling trail leads for a mile around the site to the avalanche-prone summit at **Diamond Peak**, which affords great views over the entire park and forestland beyond.

The Park Service has its **headquarters** in Mineral (summer daily 8am–4.30pm, winter Mon–Fri 8am–4.30pm; ⓣ530/595-4444, ⓦwww.nps.gov/lavo), where you can get free maps and information (there's a box outside when it's closed, and they'll leave your back country permits here if you arrive late), including the *Lassen Park Guide*. Another **visitor center** (summer daily 9am–5pm; ⓣ530/595-4444 ext 5180) is at Manzanita Lake, just inside the northern entrance, and includes the Loomis Museum, which documents the park's eruption cycle.

Mount Shasta City and Mount Shasta

Roughly sixty miles north of Redding, a scenic road branches off I-5 to the tiny town that describes itself as "the best kept secret in California": **MOUNT SHASTA CITY**, hard under the enormous bulk of the 14,162-foot **Mount Shasta**. Still considered active despite not having erupted for two hundred years, this lone peak dominates the landscape for a hundred miles around, and its "energies" attract New Agers by the score. If you want to climb to the summit (10hr; crampons and ice axe needed most of the year), or simply to explore the flanks of the mountain along the many trails, you must obtain a free permit from the **ranger district office**, 204 W Alma St (April–Oct Mon–Sat 8am–4.30pm; rest of year Mon–Fri 8am–4.30pm; ⓣ530/926-4511), or you can self-issue one at the main trailheads.

The nearest Greyhound stop is at Weed, nine miles north, whence local STAGE **buses** (ⓣ530/842-8295 or 1-800/247-8243) connect to Mount Shasta City. The **Chamber of Commerce** is at 300 Pine St (daily: summer 9am–5.30pm, winter 10am–4pm; ⓣ530/926-3696 or 1-800/926-4865, ⓦwww.mtshastachamber.com). There's friendly **accommodation** at the excellent *Alpenrose Cottage Guest House*, 204 E Hinkley St (ⓣ530/926-6724, ⓦwww.snowcrest.net/alpenrose; ❸), among other choices. Within ten miles to the southeast and south respectively, the *McCloud Hotel Bed & Breakfast*, 408 Main St, McCloud (ⓣ530/964-2822 or 1-800/964-2823, ⓦwww.mchotel.com; ❺), has some rooms with jacuzzis, while the *Cave Springs Motel*, 4727 Dunsmuir Ave, Dunsmuir (ⓣ530/235-2721, ⓦwww.cavesprings.com; ❷), has a range of rooms and cabins by a river. *Lake Siskiyou Campground* (ⓣ530/926-2618; $20) is four miles west of town and the most picturesque in the area.

Some of the town's best **meals** can be had at *Trinity Café*, 622 N Mount Shasta Blvd (ⓣ530/926-3372; closed Sun & Mon), which serves quality California cuisine, and *Vivify* (ⓣ530/926-1345), an upmarket Japanese restaurant at 531 Chestnut St. For good bar food and a chance to meet the locals, head for *Billy Goats Tavern*, 107 Chestnut St (ⓣ530/926-0209).

Lava Beds National Monument

Lava Beds National Monument ($10 per vehicle for seven days), in the far north of the state, is one of the most remote and beautiful of California's parks, and also one of its most interesting. The history of these volcanic caves and huge black lava flows is as violent as the natural forces that created them. Before the Gold Rush the area was home to the **Modoc** Indians, but repeated and bloody confrontations with miners led the government to order them into a reservation shared with the Klamath, their traditional enemy. After only a few months the Modocs drifted back to the isolation of the lava beds, and in 1872 the army was sent in. Fifty-five Modoc warriors, under the leadership of "Captain Jack," held back an army ten times the size of theirs for five months from a natural fortress of passageways now known as **Captain Jack's Stronghold**, at the park's northern tip. You can retrace the conflict through well-detailed, self-guided trails in the park and informative exhibits at the **visitor center** (daily: summer 8am–6pm; rest of year 8am–5pm; ⓣ530/667-2282, ⓦwww.nps.gov/labe).

The bulk of the lava tube caves are close to the visitor center from where you can take the free ranger tours (daily 9am & 2pm). With some nerve and a good light source (free loaner flashlights from the visitor center), you can explore the caves alone. You can camp near the visitor center, but there are no shops nearby, so bring everything you'll need with you. Nearby is the **Modoc Ranger Station** (Mon–Fri 8am–5pm; ⓣ530/233-5811), which has general information on the Modoc National Forest. North and west of the Lava Beds region, the **Klamath Basin National Wildlife Refuge** hosts millions of birds migrating along the Pacific Flyway. The **visitor center** (Mon–Fri 8am–4.30pm, Sat & Sun 10am–4pm; ⓣ530/667-2231) is off Hill Road near the northwest entrance for the Lava Beds. Surprisingly, the best way of spotting the wildlife is by driving along designated routes; getting out of the car and walking scares the birds off. If you want to **stay** in the area, the best place is *Fe's B&B* (ⓣ1-877/478-0184, ⓦwww.fesbandb.com; ❸) at 660 Main Street in Tulelake, fourteen miles north of the main park entrance.

14

The Pacific Northwest

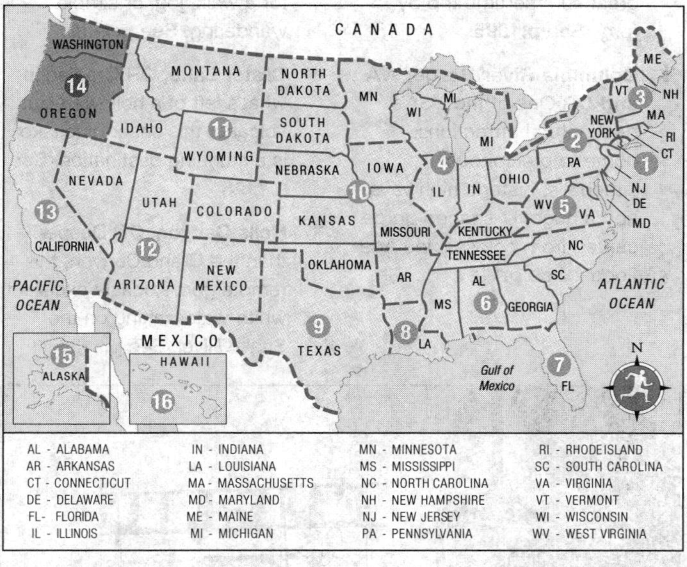

AL - ALABAMA	IN - INDIANA	MN - MINNESOTA	RI - RHODEISLAND
AR - ARKANSAS	LA - LOUISIANA	MS - MISSISSIPPI	SC - SOUTH CAROLINA
CT - CONNECTICUT	MA - MASSACHUSETTS	NC - NORTH CAROLINA	VA - VIRGINIA
DE - DELAWARE	MD - MARYLAND	NH - NEW HAMPSHIRE	VT - VERMONT
FL- FLORIDA	ME - MAINE	NJ - NEW JERSEY	WI - WISCONSIN
IL - ILLINOIS	MI - MICHIGAN	PA - PENNSYLVANIA	WV - WEST VIRGINIA

CHAPTER 14

Highlights

* **Pike Place Market, Seattle, WA** Seattle's lively urban market holds an array of fine restaurants, seafood and produce vendors, and street entertainers. See p.1082
* **San Juan Islands, WA** Perched at the upper corner of America, these three bucolic islands make for a great summertime trip by ferry. See p.1095
* **Columbia River Gorge, WA and OR** One of the USA's best natural attractions, home to precipitous waterfalls, historic highways, and a huge, U-shaped gorge carved from colossal Ice Age floods. See p.1117
* **Mount St Helens, WA** Still a haunting sight nearly three decades after it blew its top, the most renowned volcano in North America. See p.1104
* **Forest Park, OR** A true urban oasis, set near downtown Portland and featuring the Wildwood Trail, one of the Northwest's best routes for a walk, jog, or simple wandering. See p.1112
* **Crater Lake, OR** Cradled in what's left of a hollowed-out volcano, this sheer blue lake is a stunning destination. See p.1128
* **Hells Canyon, OR** Deeper than the Grand Canyon, this remote gorge boasts excellent white-water rafting on the Snake River. See p.1131

▲ Sign above the Pike Place Market, Seattle

14

The Pacific Northwest

The **PACIFIC NORTHWEST** states of **Washington** and **Oregon** are well known as the liberal, green pocket in America's upper-left corner, similar in climate, topography, and environmental politics, but quite different in their attitudes toward growth. Washington's sprawling development, bustling military bases, and notorious freeway gridlock contrast dramatically with Oregon's low-scaled design and easygoing lifestyle, thanks in no small measure to its stringent land-use laws and "urban-growth boundaries" around its larger cities.

Cooler and wetter than California to the south, both states are split by the great north–south spine of the **Cascade Mountains**, where regular rainfall and a moist climate create a verdant landscape, thick with woodlands that on Washington's **Olympic Peninsula** have become small rainforests. This fertile land is where the region's population is most heavily concentrated, yet much of it remains remarkably pristine – especially in Oregon. Both **Seattle** and **Portland** lie roughly fifty miles from the Pacific Ocean along the I-5 freeway. Seattle, the commercial and cultural capital of the Northwest, is a major port known for its high-tech and aerospace industries and signature "grunge" music, and location along the beautiful, island-strewn **Puget Sound.** Portland offers much historic appeal for its old-time terracotta architecture and ten stately bridges crossing the scenic Willamette River, along with its nationally regarded culture of bicycling.

Beyond the Cascades, the land to the **east** is far drier, peppered with desert and scrubland, as well as bleak stretches of lava beds and cinder cones. Of the towns, only **Spokane** in Washington is of any appreciable size, though Oregon's booming resort town of **Bend** has a Cascade-straddling location that makes it a useful base for exploring mountains, deserts, and especially the beautiful **Columbia River Gorge** to the north. Of outstanding interest also is the scarred territory between Seattle and Portland around **Mount St Helens**, which erupted with devastating effect in 1980.

Some history

The **first inhabitants** of the Pacific Northwest may have reached the continent 12,000 to 20,000 years ago by crossing a land bridge over what is now the Bering Strait between Siberia and Alaska. By the late eighteenth century, European sea captains such as James Cook and George Vancouver came in search of the fabled **Northwest Passage**, an ice-free route between the Atlantic and the Pacific. Explorers Meriwether Lewis and William Clark, who reached the Oregon coast near present-day Astoria in 1804, were the first whites to cross the interior of the continent, and within forty years American settlers were streaming in along the **Oregon Trail**. This legendary period of immigration gave de facto control of the region to the United States, and official title followed in 1846 with the signing

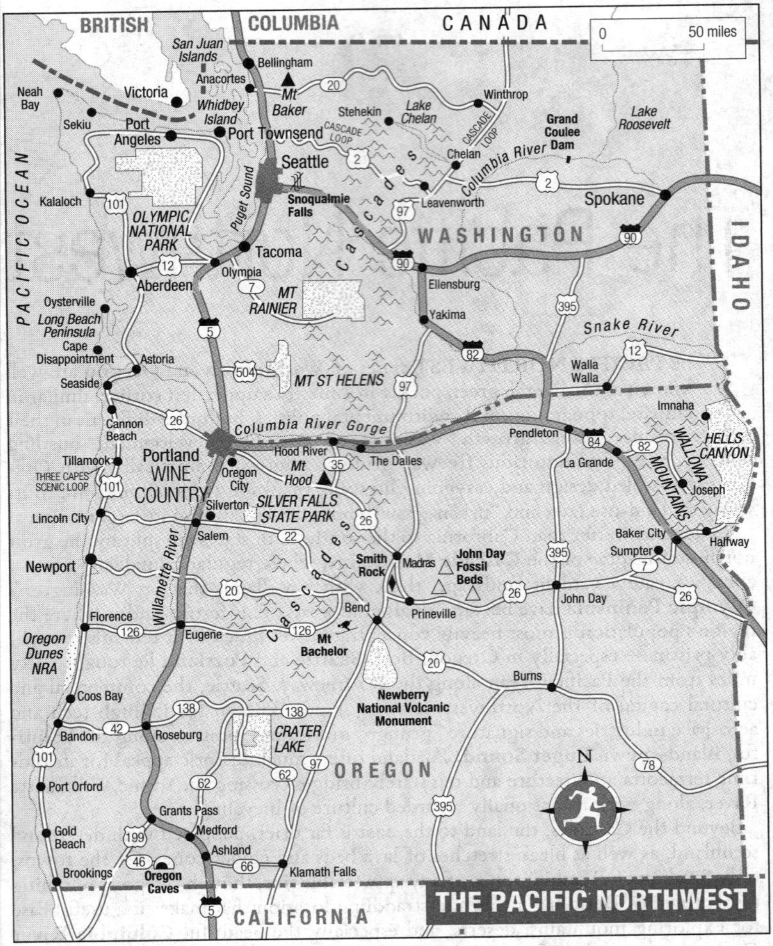

of a land pact with Britain that established a territorial boundary for the US and Canada at the 49th Parallel. In 1859 Oregon became the second **American state** west of the Great Plains (after California). Thirty more years would pass before Washington state entered the Union.

When the railroads reached Portland and Seattle, Oregon and Washington began their economic ascent, aided by timber sales and, in the case of Seattle, the booming trade supplying prospectors on their way to Alaska's Klondike Gold Rush. Later decades would see the rise and fall of the lumber market and the emergence of airplanes and computer software as major local products. Outdoor adventuring and nature tourism have since become big attractions, especially from late May through September, when the region's rains abate enough for the sun to illuminate the striking mountain and forest scenery.

Washington

Likeable and vibrant, Seattle's greatest asset may be its proximity to the glorious **Puget Sound**, the deep-water inlet around which much of the population of Washington lives. Some of the islands here serve as stepping stones to the **Olympic Peninsula** to the west, whose mountains are home to rare elk and lush vegetation that merges into rainforest, and whose rustic beaches have remained pristine and protected. Not quite as rainy as the mountains to the northeast, the **southern coast** is flatter and more accessible but not as appealing. The nearest real attraction lies a few hours south, where you can marvel at the eye-opening volcanic scenery of **Mount St Helens**.

Dry and desolate, the sprawling prairie-plateau and flood-scoured "channeled scablands" that make up most of **eastern Washington** are a great, bleak expanse enlivened by the pleasant burg of **Spokane** and the colossal **Grand Coulee Dam**, along with much fascinating geology. Otherwise you're only likely to come out here if you're traveling the Cascade loop, a memorable four-hundred-mile round-trip drive through the stunning **Cascade Mountains**.

Getting around Washington

From Seattle, Amtrak runs its *Coast Starlight* **train** once daily south to Portland and LA, while its *Cascades* line runs four times per day south to Eugene, Oregon, and twice daily north to Bellingham and Vancouver, BC. Amtrak's daily *Empire Builder* route heads east to Chicago. Greyhound provides **bus** service east across the Cascades to **Spokane** and beyond, with other eastern routes to Wenatchee (for Chelan), Ellensburg, Yakima, and Walla Walla, and north–south routes linking Bellingham and Seattle to Portland.

Getting around Puget Sound is more difficult and requires planning. Washington State Ferries (Ⓣ206/464-6400 or 1-800/84-FERRY; Ⓦwww.wsdot.wa.gov/ferries) run between Anacortes, Washington, to Sidney, BC (for Victoria and Vancouver Island) and the San Juan Islands; from Port Townsend to Keystone on Whidbey Island; and between Seattle and points on the Kitsap Peninsula and Vashon and Bainbridge islands. Reservations are not accepted except for the Port Townsend and Anacortes routes, and they are highly recommended for the latter, especially during the peak summer season; tickets are available from Pier 52, Colman Dock, in Seattle.

Other Washington ferry companies include **M.V. Coho** (Ⓣ360/457-4491, Ⓦwww.cohoferry.com), which runs ferries from Port Angeles to Victoria, BC (2–4 daily, except 1 in Jan), and charges $13.50 for a walk-on one-way ticket and $50 for a car, with a crossing time of 90min and no reservations; and **Victoria Express** (Ⓣ360/452-8088, Ⓦwww.victoriaexpress.com), operating a 1hr trip on the same route (May–Sept 2–4 daily; $25 round-trip), and 2.5 hrs to Friday Harbor on San Juan Island (June–Aug 1 daily; $80 round-trip), both for passengers only.

Seattle

Located on the shore of sparkling Elliott Bay, with the snowy peak of Mount Rainier in the distance, **SEATTLE** has a magnificent setting, with a modern skyline of glass skyscrapers, a friendly charm, and plenty of fun coffeehouses, good restaurants, and engaging clubs.

Flooded out of its first location on Alki Point in what is now the suburb of West Seattle, the town in the 1850s shifted to the present location of Pioneer Square, renaming itself after the Native American **Chief Sealth**, who helped reduce violent tensions between whites and local tribes. As the surrounding forest was gradually felled and the lumber shipped out, Seattle grew slowly until the Klondike Gold Rush of 1897 put it firmly on the national map as a transport and commercial hub. Since the beginning of the twentieth century, the **Boeing** corporation has been crucial to the city's economic strength, and more recent success stories have included **Microsoft**, **Starbucks** and **Amazon.com**, the boom times interrupted only by the occasional dot-com bust, earthquake (in February 2001), or housing crunch.

Despite the changes wrought by Seattle's solid economy as the city grows into an international destination, its more established neighborhoods remain distinctive, and it has a pleasantly down-to-earth ambiance, whether you come here in the summer with the rest of the tourist trade, or make like the locals and brave the steady rains (with many fewer visitors) from October to May.

Arrival and information

Seattle-Tacoma International Airport, or **Sea-Tac** (Ⓣ206/433-5388 or 1-800/544-1965, Ⓦwww.portseattle.org/seatac), is fourteen miles south of downtown Seattle. **Gray Line Airport Express** bus (daily 5.30am–11pm every 30min; $11, $18 round-trip Ⓣ206/624-5077 or 1-800/426-7532, Ⓦwww.graylineseattle.com) drops off at eight major hotels downtown, with connections to other hotels in the area from 5.30am to 9pm, for $3 extra; reserve at least one hour in advance for these connections at Ⓣ206/255-7159. Shuttle Express has door-to-door service (daily 24hr; Ⓣ425/981-7000 or 1-800/487-RIDE, Ⓦwww.shuttleexpress.com) for $30–35 to downtown. **Taxis** charge $35–40 to go downtown and leave from the third floor of the parking garage. **Buses** to Seattle leave from the north end of the baggage claim area. The cheapest option is Metro bus #194 ($1.50, $2.25 during peak hours Mon–Fri 6–9am & 3–6pm).

Trains arrive at the **Amtrak** terminal in King Street Station at Third Avenue and Jackson Street (Ⓣ206/382-4125 or 1-800/872-7245, Ⓦwww.amtrak.com); just to the east along Jackson Street, the International District Station is a hub for frequent Metro buses going downtown. **Greyhound buses** (Ⓣ206/628-5526 or 1-800/231-2222, Ⓦwww.greyhound.com) arrive at Eighth Avenue and Stewart Street, on the eastern edge of downtown, as well as at King Street Station. Located inside the Washington State Convention and Trade Center, Seventh Ave at Pike St (daily 8.30am-5pm; Ⓣ206/461-5840, Ⓦwww.visitseattle.org), the Seattle Convention and Visitors Bureau can provide directions, **information**, bus schedules, and help with accommodation. The free official travelers' brochure, *Washington State Visitors' Guide* (call Ⓣ1-800/544-1800 for a copy, or visit Ⓦwww.experiencewa.com), has a comprehensive list of hotels, motels, B&Bs, and the like.

City transportation

Seattle's mass transit system, known as the **Metro** (Ⓣ206/553-3000, Ⓦtransit.metrokc.gov), runs bus routes throughout the city and King County, extending into the Eastside suburbs across Lake Washington, and south to the airport. Customer service stations are available at King Street Station, 201 S Jackson St (Mon–Fri 8am–5pm), and at 1301 5th Ave in Rainier Square (Mon–Fri 9am–5.30pm); both offer maps and schedules and sell daily passes on weekdays. (You can also purchase passes online at Ⓦbuypass.metrokc.gov.) The Metro's best feature is its

Downtown Ride Free Area, bounded by Battery Street, South Jackson Street, 6th Avenue, and the waterfront. From 6am to 7pm daily, bus trips beginning and ending within this zone are free; cross out of the free zone and you pay the driver as you get off; come back in and you pay as you enter. Buses run weekdays from 5am or 5.30am to midnight or 1am, though some routes may end service as early as 7pm; typically, weekend hours start an hour or two later and end an hour earlier; fares are $1.50, or up to $2.25 during rush hour.

Washington State **ferries** (Ⓣ206/464-6400 or 1-800/84-FERRY; Ⓦwww.wsdot.wa.gov/ferries) dock at Pier 52 (Colman Dock) on downtown's waterfront, with a couple of passenger-only routes using Pier 50. Other ferry routes connect at Fauntleroy in West Seattle. Gray Line (Ⓣ206/626-5208, Ⓦwww.graylineseattle.com) organizes three-hour **bus tours** (3hr; $34) of the city, as well as combination bus-and-**boat tours** (6hr; $58) on an Argosy sightseeing cruise (more tours at Ⓣ206/623-1445, Ⓦwww.argosycruises.com).

Accommodation

When it comes to **hotels** in Seattle, the best choices are often downtown. Also of good value are the city's **hostels** and **B&Bs**, the latter of which are abundant on Capitol Hill. Specialist **B&B agencies** include A Pacific Reservation Service (Ⓣ206/439-7677 or 1-800/684-2932, Ⓦwww.seattlebedandbreakfast.com) and Seattle Bed and Breakfast Association (Ⓣ206/547-1020 or 1-800/348-5630, Ⓦwww.lodginginseattle.com).

Hotels, motels, and B&Bs

Ace 2423 First Ave Ⓣ206/448-4721, Ⓦwww.theacehotel.com. A Seattle favorite with modern, slightly arty rooms and a chic white lobby in the heart of Belltown. Hardwood floors, lofty ceilings, and shared bathrooms for $75; double that price for more comfortable and well-appointed suites. ❹

Alexis 1007 1st Ave, downtown Ⓣ206/624-4844 or 1-800/426-7033, Ⓦwww.alexishotel.com. Plush décor at this top-notch hotel, as well as a spa, a steam room, and restaurant. Nearly half the rooms are suites that, at their largest, have luxurious touches like fireplaces and dining rooms. ❾

Bacon Mansion 959 Broadway E, Capitol Hill Ⓣ206/329-1864 or 1-800/240-1864, Ⓦwww.baconmansion.com. Eleven elegant rooms and spacious suites in a grand 1909 Tudor Revival structure, just north of Broadway. Well-decorated if a bit small, the least expensive rooms are cheap for the area, although the price doubles at the high end. Two-night minimum stay on weekends. ❺

Green Tortoise 1525 2nd Ave between Pike and Pine sts, downtown Ⓣ206/340-1222 or 1-888/424-6783, Ⓦwww.greentortoise.net. Old-style hotel now functioning as a hostel, with four-to-eight-to-a-room dorms ($25–30) and some private doubles ($40–42). Free breakfast, wi-fi, and pickups at Amtrak, Greyhound, or ferries; they also do summer walking tours of the city.

Hotel Andra 2000 Fourth Ave Ⓣ206/448-8600 or 1-877/448-8601, Ⓦwww.hotelandra.com. An intimate boutique hotel with chic, modern units – more than half of them suites. Gym, restaurant, and Internet. ❾

Hotel Max 620 Stewart St Ⓣ206/441-4200 or 1-800/426-0670, Ⓦwww.hotelmaxseattle.com. Located in a renovated 1920s building a block from the monorail, with stylish, if cozy, rooms kitted out with vaguely "artistic" themes – with different photographers showcased on each floor and original art in each room. ❼

Hotel Vintage Park 1100 Fifth Ave Ⓣ206/624-8000, Ⓦwww.hotelvintagepark.com. Offering splashy upscale décor, a stylish boutique hotel with rooms themed around wine-drinking and vineyards; amenities include fireplaces, jacuzzis, stereos, and of course, nightly tastings of vino. ❾

MarQueen 600 Queen Ave N, Seattle Center Ⓣ206/282-7407 or 1-800/445-3076, Ⓦwww.marqueen.com. Refurbished 1918 building with 56 rooms and suites, period antiques, and amenities like hardwood floors, kitchenettes, microwaves, and fridges, as well as an onsite spa and free wi-fi. ❽

Monaco 1101 4th Ave, downtown Ⓣ206/621-1770 or 1-800/715-6513, Ⓦwww.monaco-seattle.com. Luxurious boutique hotel with zesty designer furnishings, plus a striking lobby, fitness center, and elegant suites with CD players and fax machines – some with jacuzzis as well. ❾

Pensione Nichols 1923 1st Ave, Belltown ⓣ206/441-7125, ⓦwww.pensionenichols.com. Classy little B&B that's a great deal, with small but clean rooms, shared baths, and simple, tasteful décor in a classic 1904 building. Only $99 for single travelers; add $35 for another person. Two-night minimum during summer. 5

Pioneer Square 77 Yesler Way, Pioneer Square ⓣ206/340-1234, ⓦwww.pioneersquare.com. Restored 1914 brick hotel (now a *Best Western*) built by Seattle pioneer Henry Yesler, and one of the few good establishments in the Pioneer Square area with adequate comfort. Ground-floor saloon with microbrews. 8

Shafer-Baillie Mansion 907 14th Ave E ⓣ206/322-4654 or 1-800/985-4654, ⓦsbmansion.com. This mansion's oak-paneled walls and late-Victorian style echo its 1914 construction. B&B offers three rooms and two suites with antique tubs and refrigerators, plus internet. 6

Sorrento 900 Madison St, First Hill ⓣ206/622-4400 or 1-800/426-1265, ⓦwww.hotelsorrento.com. Modernized, 76-room edifice with a European flair, stylish décor, and posh onsite restaurant, on the east side of I-5 by downtown. The regal exterior surrounds a circular courtyard with palm trees, and some units have views of Puget Sound. 9

University Inn 4140 Roosevelt Way NE, University District ⓣ206/632-5055 or 1-800/733-3855, ⓦwww.universityinnseattle.com. Business-oriented hotel off University Way. Some rooms have kitchens, all have complimentary breakfast; there's also a pool and spa and wi-fi. 6

W Seattle 1112 4th Ave, downtown ⓣ206/264-6000, ⓦwww.whotels.com. Stylish modern tower with a staff of beautiful people and smart rooms in high style. An even better draw is the ambiance: there's a chic lobby bar with often-packed "cocktail couches." 9

The City

Downtown Seattle sits alongside the curve of Elliott Bay just off the I-5 freeway, crowded with plenty of attractions, but none more popular than **Pike Place Market** and its engaging array of stalls and cafés. Further south, the nineteenth-century Victorian townsite of **Pioneer Square** is lined with bars and clubs, while at the **Seattle Center** in the north, the **Space Needle** presides over museums and carnival rides, as well as the showpiece **Experience Music Project**. Several outlying districts are often livelier than downtown: **Capitol Hill**'s cafés and bars are the heart of the city's hipster and gay scene, and the **University District** is a student area with inexpensive cafés and uptempo nightlife.

Pike Place Market and the Seattle Art Museum

Centrally located at Pike Street and First Avenue, **Pike Place Market** (daily Mon–Sat 10am–6pm, Sun 11am–5pm; ⓣ206/682-7453, ⓦwww.pikeplacemarket.org) began in the early twentieth century and is the oldest continuous working public market in the US. It comprises thirteen buildings on a triangular lot covering nine acres, holding three hundred produce and fish vendors, bakeries, craft stalls, and small retailers, many of whom grow or make what they sell. Street entertainers play to crowds, the aroma of organic coffee drifts from cafés, and stalls offers piles of lobsters, crabs, salmon, vegetables, fruit, and flowers. Further inside, handmade jewelry, woodcarvings, and silk-screen prints are on sale, while near the entrance, a favorite meeting place is the **brass pig** in front of the Public Market Center sign – a large, actual piggy bank, with receipts going to charity.

Close to Pike Place Market at 1300 First Avenue, the **Seattle Art Museum** (usually Tues–Sun 10am–5pm, Thurs & Fri until 9pm; $13, free first Thurs of month; ⓣ206/654-3100, ⓦwww.seattleartmuseum.org), is one of the top cultural institutions in the Pacific Northwest. On the top floor, visitors can take a look at various temporary works, or, on the second level, the **Art Ladder**, a stairway featuring numerous large-scale installation and sculptural pieces spread across five

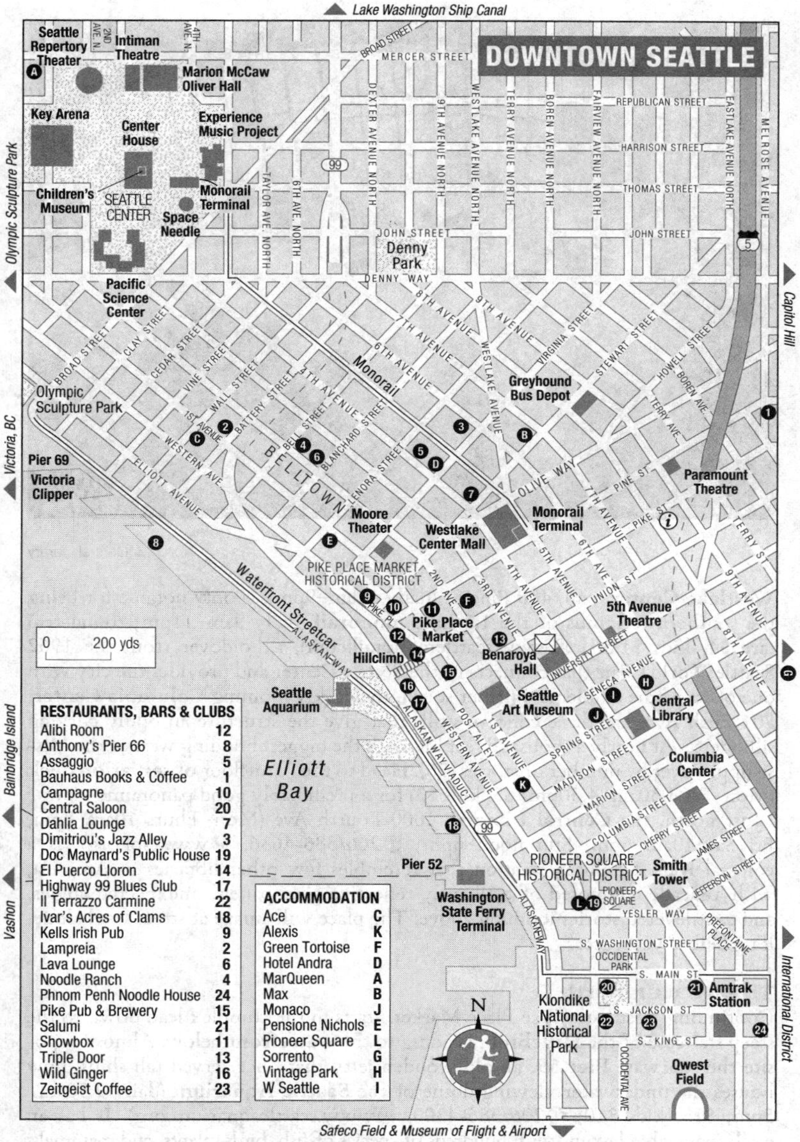

thousand square feet, along with art made by museum visitors. On the third floor are the **Wright Galleries for Modern and Contemporary Art**, where you may see regional modern art from budding Northwest talents.

The Business District

Between Second and Seventh avenues, most of downtown is given over to the steel-and-glass office towers of Seattle's **Business District**. Here, the multi-story

▲ Central Library

Westlake Center mall, 400 Pine St (daily 10am–9pm), is only notable for being the southern terminus of the 1.3-mile **monorail** (daily 9am–11pm; round-trip fare $4, kids $1.50; Ⓦ www.seattlemonorail.com), a holdover from the 1962 Seattle World's Fair that connects to the Seattle Center and provides the city with one of its prime emblems. Further south, the darkly looming **Columbia Center**, 701 Fifth Ave, has three concave walls that give the structure an oddly curving silhouette. At nearly a thousand feet high, it's the biggest building west of the Mississippi River by number of stories (76). Head to the 73rd-floor **observation deck** (Mon–Fri 8.30am–4.30pm; $5, kids $3) for a predictably good panoramic view.

Just north, the **Central Library**, 1000 Fourth Ave (Mon–Thurs 10am–8pm, Fri–Sat 10am–6pm, Sun noon–6pm; Ⓣ 206/386-4636, Ⓦ www.spl.org), is a colossal Rem Koolhaas creation that resembles few other libraries in America, with a facade composed of brilliantly reflective glass panels, unexpected angles, and cantilevered stories looming above. The place will amaze at street level alone, long before you enter.

The waterfront

Continuing west from Pike Place Market, stairs in the complex lead down to the steep staircase of the **Hillclimb**, heading to the **waterfront** below. Almost opposite the stairway, **Pier 59**, an old wooden jetty that once served tall ships, now houses the underwater viewing dome of the **Seattle Aquarium** (daily 9.30am–5pm; $15, kids $10; Ⓣ 206/386-4300, Ⓦ www.seattleaquarium.org). It has an easily navigable layout, with hundreds of species of fish, birds, plants, and mammals. A 400,000-gallon underwater dome recreates life in Puget Sound, its highlights including black-tip sharks; electric eels; octopuses; a functional salmon hatchery and fish ladder, which displays the life cycle of the threatened Pacific salmon.

On the opposite end of the waterfront, at 2901 Western Ave, the 8.5-acre **Olympic Sculpture Park** (daily dawn–dusk; free; Ⓦ www.seattleartmuseum.org/visit/osp) is set around a zigzagging pathway that passes over road and railway before leading down to the water's edge. On the way are showpieces like

Alexander Calder's 39ft *Eagle*, a jagged array of red steel arcs; Louise Bourgeois' disembodied granite *Eye Benches*; Richard Serra's undulating rusty-steel *Wake* slabs; and a Claes Oldenburg typewriter eraser, among other arch-modern pieces – but the greatest piece of sculpture may be the park itself, a bravura example of landscape art.

Pioneer Square

A few blocks inland from the ferry terminal, **Pioneer Square** is Seattle's oldest district, rich with appealing bookshops and galleries amid the old red-brick and wrought-iron buildings.

A good way to find out about the city's seamy past is on a 90-minute **Underground Tour** from *Doc Maynard's* tavern, 610 First Ave (hours vary by month, usually leaving daily on the hour 11am–4pm, sometimes until 6pm; $15, kids $7; ⓣ206/682-4646, ⓦwww.undergroundtour.com), which details how, after a disastrous 1889 fire, this area was rebuilt with the street level raised by one story, so what used to be storefronts are now underground, linked by subterranean passageways. One long block east, the 1914 white-terracotta **Smith Tower**, 506 Second Ave, was the city's first skyscraper, as well as its longtime visual icon well before the 1960s arrival of the Space Needle. These days, it's best for the prime views from its 35th-floor **observation deck** (April–Oct daily 10am–dusk, rest of year Sat & Sun 10am–3.30pm; $7.50; ⓦwww.smithtower.com).

A few blocks south at 117 S Main St, **Klondike Gold Rush National Historical Park** (daily 9am–5pm; free; ⓦwww.nps.gov/klse) houses a small museum celebrating the days when Seattle was the gateway to Alaskan gold, and prospectors streamed in and traders – and con artists – made their fortunes. In the streets around, highbrow culture finds a place on the first Thursday of the month at the **Gallery Walk** (6–8pm; free), showcasing nearly forty local art dealers holding simultaneous openings, while **Art in the Park** (3–9pm; free) features a broad range of visual and performance-art pieces in nearby Occidental Park.

Seattle Center

North of downtown, the **Seattle Center** (ⓦwww.seattlecenter.com) dates from the 1962 Seattle World's Fair and since then the 74-acre complex has become the city's cultural hub, the site of museums, sporting events, concerts, and festivals. The **monorail** from Westlake Center (see p.1084) drops you close to the **Space Needle**, the Space Age-modernist city icon, which is most appealing at night when it's lit up. The panoramic view from the observation deck, where there's a bar, is unmatched (daily 9am–midnight; $16, two trips in 24hr $20; ⓦwww.spaceneedle.com).

Southwest of the Needle, the **Pacific Science Center** 200 2nd Ave N (Mon–Fri 10am–5pm, Sat & Sun 10am-6pm; $11, kids $6–8; ⓣ206/443-2001, ⓦwww.pacsci.org) is full of science-related exhibits for children, and includes a planetarium and IMAX theater. Also good for the kids is the **Children's Museum**, in the Center House complex (Mon–Fri 10am–5pm, Sat & Sun 10am–6pm; $7.50; ⓦwww.thechildrensmuseum.org), which offers tot-friendly activities and attractions like an artificial mountain forest, where kids crawl through logs or simulate a rock climb.

The most recent highlight of the Seattle Center, though, is the Frank Gehry-designed **Experience Music Project**, 325 5th Ave N (daily 10am–7pm, winter closes 5pm; $15, kids $12; ⓦwww.empsfm.org), a giant burst of colored aluminum – into which the monorail passes – that houses an 80,000-piece collection of rock memorabilia divided up into exhibits on different phases of popular music history, as well as rotating exhibits on subjects from Bob Dylan to Brooklyn hip hop.

Capitol Hill

A fifteen-minute bus ride east of downtown takes you to the mildly counterculture-flavored **Capitol Hill**, whose **Broadway** axis offers a solid choice for dining, buying music, clubbing, and drinking coffee from sidewalk espresso carts. On the northern end of Broadway, between E Roy Street and E Highland Drive, the **Harvard-Belmont Historic District**, along with adjacent Millionaires Row, is rich with huge Neoclassical mansions and sprawling period-revival homes; for a tour, contact the Seattle Architectural Foundation ($15; Ⓣ206/667-9184, Ⓦwww.seattlearchitecture.org). East of Broadway from Twelfth to Ninth avenues, the **Pike/Pine Corridor** is filled with all-night coffeehouses, live music venues, and trendy bars. Near its southern end, the **Frye Art Museum**, 704 Terry Ave (Tues–Sat 10am–5pm, Sun noon–5pm, Thurs closes at 8pm; free; Ⓣ206/622-9250, Ⓦfryeart.org), holds works by Winslow Homer, John Singer Sargent, Thomas Eakins, and (anti)modern artists like Andrew Wyeth, as well as a fine selection of the **Munich school**, focusing on the Belle Epoque between 1870 and 1900, when Munich was one of Europe's foremost cultural centers. Recent exhibits have broadened the museum's focus to include more contemporary work, including an array of multimedia, performance, and installation pieces.

The northern end of Capitol Hill is highlighted by **Volunteer Park** 1247 15th Ave (daily 6am–11pm), where you'll find the 1912 **Conservatory**'s hothouses, home to flowers, shrubs, and orchids from jungle, desert, and rainforest habitats (daily 10am–4pm, summer closes 6pm; free; Ⓣ206/684-4743), as well as the old **Water Tower** that provides a free, sweeping view of Seattle, albeit through wire mesh. Also located within the park is the **Seattle Asian Art Museum** (Tues–Sun 10am–5pm, Thurs until 9pm; $5; Ⓣ206/654-3100, Ⓦwww.seattleartmuseum.org), home to one of the most extensive collections of Asian art in the US, encompassing Japanese, Korean, Vietnamese, Chinese, and Southeast Asian art, spread across many centuries and dynasties. Among the more interesting pieces are the meticulously crafted Japanese landscape scrolls and the grim, early Chinese statues of tomb guardians, court attendants, and warriors.

Ten blocks east, on the other side of Capitol Hill, **Washington Park Arboretum** (daily dawn–dusk; free; Ⓦdepts.washington.edu/wpa) is a lush showcase for indigenous vegetation, with many charming footpaths and regional trees, plus the immaculately designed **Japanese Gardens**, where banks of pink flowers sit beside neat little pools with brightly colored carp (March–Nov daily 10am–dusk; $5).

The University District

Across the Lake Washington Ship Canal from Washington Park, the **University District**, or the "U" District, is a busy hodgepodge of coffeehouses, cinemas, and boutiques catering to the University of Washington's forty thousand students. The area centers on University Way, known as **"The Ave,"** and is lined with inexpensive ethnic restaurants and many decent book and record stores.

On campus, the **Henry Art Gallery**, 15th Avenue NE and NE 41st Street (Tues–Sun 11am–5pm, Thurs closes at 8pm; $10, free for any students with ID; Ⓦwww.henryart.org), presents the most imaginative contemporary exhibits to be found in any of Seattle's art museums, and houses American and European paintings and photography from the last two centuries. The **Burke Memorial Museum**, 17th Ave NE and NE 45th St (daily 10am–5pm; $8; Ⓦwww.washington.edu/burkemuseum), holds the US's largest collection of Native American art and artifacts west of the Mississippi – including Tlingit "**grizzly bear house posts**," modern carvings of the native legend of the hunter who married a bear – and presents selections from its huge collection of 2.75 million fossils and Ice Age skeletons, including the remains of a 12,000-year-old sloth.

Along the Lake Washington Ship Canal

As with the "U" District, Seattle's northern neighborhoods are divided from the rest of town by the **Lake Washington Ship Canal**, which connects Lake Union with Elliott Bay to the west and Lake Washington to the east. On the north shore of Lake Union, **Gasworks Park**, 2101 N Northlake Way (daily 6am–11.30pm; free), is a former gas plant turned postmodern park, where children now play on grassy hills that were once slag heaps and decaying, graffiti-covered machines offer surreal evidence of the site's previous industrial incarnation. Further west, a procession of boats passes through the **Hiram M. Chittenden Locks** (daily 7.30am–9pm; free; ⓣ206/783-7059), and a **fish ladder** is laid out with viewing windows, through which you can see enormous fish leaping up (late summer for salmon, fall and early winter for trout).

Beyond the locks is Salmon Bay, with **Fisherman's Terminal** on its south side, 3919 18th Ave W (daily 7am–4.30pm; ⓦwww.portseattle.org/seaport), crowded with Seattle's fishing fleet and diners selling freshly caught fish. On the northern side of Salmon Bay, blue-collar **Ballard** appeals for its historic **Ballard Avenue**, between 17th and 22nd avenues NW, home to galleries, bars, and restaurants behind the stately facades of hundred-year-old buildings.

Fremont and the Woodland Park Zoo

East of Ballard, **Fremont** is a self-consciously hip area with a spate of boutiques, bookshops, and cafés, with its hub around Fremont Avenue N from N 34th to N 37th streets. Just off N 34th Street, the **Fremont Sunday Market** (April–Oct 10am–5pm, Nov–March 10am–4pm; free; ⓦwww.fremontmarket.com/fremont) hosts vendors of secondhand jewelry, furniture, clothing, trinkets, and music. Fremont's other main draws are its quirky **public artworks** scattered around the district, most notably the **Fremont Troll** lurking under the Aurora Bridge, 36th St and Aurora Ave, emerging from the gloom with an actual VW Bug in its clutches, and, at the triangular corner of N 36th Street and Fremont Place, a colossal, Slovakia-built **statue of Vladimir Lenin** thrusting forth toward passing motorists, surrounded by blocky flames. The **Fremont Fair & Solstice Parade** (ⓣ206/297-6801, ⓦwww.fremontfair.com), in mid-June, is Seattle's jolliest celebration, with hundreds of food stalls and arts vendors, plus a parade of naked bicyclists and human-powered floats, followed by a pageant at the end of the route in Gasworks Park.

A bit further north, Aurora Avenue leads toward the **Woodland Park Zoo**, N 55th St and Phinney Ave N (daily 9.30am–4pm, summer closes at 6pm; $11, kids $8; ⓦwww.zoo.org), a sleek facility whose spacious layout and botanical garden–quality trees and plants make it attractive to anyone with a love of nature. Most of the engaging exhibits are arranged to reflect different climates and terrains – Northern Trail, Tropical Asia, Tropical Forest, Temperate Forest, and so on.

The Museum of Flight

The biggest of Seattle's museums, the **Museum of Flight**, a twenty-minute bus ride (#174) south of downtown at 9404 E Marginal Way (daily 10am–5pm; $14, kids $7.50; ⓦwww.museumofflight.org), is partly housed in the restored 1909 "**Red Barn**" that was the original Boeing manufacturing plant, now displaying relics from the early days of flight. Elsewhere, the **Great Gallery** features more than fifty full-sized airplanes, from ancient prototypes to a replica of John Glenn's 1962 Mercury space capsule, to an SR-71 Blackbird spy plane, which once flew 80,000 feet above the jungles of Vietnam. More icons are on display outside in the museum's expansive **Airpark** (daily 11am–3.30pm, summer closes 4.30pm; free with museum admission), which has a walk-in collection of models that include the 727, 737, and jumbo-jet 747, as well as the supersonic, but now discontinued, Concorde.

Boeing Tour Center

Thirty miles north of Seattle, the last major suburb along I-5, **Everett**, is home to the manufacturing plant for **Boeing**, site of the popular **Boeing Tour Center**, whose entrance is on Hwy 526, a few miles west of Exit 189 off I-5 (tours Mon–Fri 9am–3pm on the hour; $15 for same-day tickets, $17.50 in advance; tickets at ⓣ1-800/464-1476, ⓦwww.boeing.com/companyoffices/aboutus/tours). The tour is a smoothly executed PR exercise, focusing on Boeing's impressive technological feats, including the 98-acre **factory** that's listed in the *Guinness Book of World Records* as the largest building in the world by volume (472 million cubic feet). Overhead platforms afford views of much of the floor space, cluttered by new planes in various phases of gestation, and the tour concludes with a bus ride on the "flight line," where finished models are tested.

Eating

Seattle has many fine **restaurants**, from the funky diners of Capitol Hill and ethnic restaurants of the University District to the delicious seafood of Pike Place Market. Moreover, local **coffeehouses** host an engaging cultural scene, and are inexpensive choices for whiling away the time or surfing the internet (starting at $6/hr). Corporate giant *Starbucks* started here in the early 1970s (in an extant location in the Pike Place Market), though you're better off sampling a local brew that you can't find in your hometown mini-mall. Better yet, check out one of the 200-plus **espresso carts** scattered about town, each colorfully styled and uniquely designed.

Restaurants and cafés

The 5 Spot 1502 Queen Anne Ave N, north of Seattle Center ⓣ206/285-SPOT. Southern-style diner whose affordable "Melting Pot Meals" may include fried green tomatoes, fried chicken dipped in buttermilk and honey, and brisket with onion and Coca-Cola marinade.

Anthony's Pier 66 2201 Alaskan Way ⓣ206/448-6688. Waterfront restaurant with good, expensive seafood – such as ahi tuna, crab, octopus, and salmon fillets – the "ocean" part of the equation – but also good for its pasta and steaks.

Assaggio 2010 4th Ave, Belltown ⓣ206/441-1399. Pleasant, midpriced Italian restaurant with a friendly ambiance and a menu featuring such items as arancini rice balls and potato dumplings with gorgonzola, among the expected pizzas, pastas, and veal.

Café Flora 2901 E Madison St, Capitol Hill ⓣ206/325-9100. One of the city's best vegetarian restaurants, attracting even devout carnivores for its creative soups, salads, and entrees, like yucca cakes and sage polenta, for mid- to high prices.

Campagne 1600 Post Alley, downtown ⓣ206/728-2800. Superb French provincial cooking near the Pike Place Market, with excellent pan-roasted beef entrees, steak tartare, squab, and the ever-tasty pommes frites, fried in duck fat. A less expensive branch, *Café Campagne*, can be found downstairs.

Dahlia Lounge 1904 4th Ave, Belltown ⓣ206/682-4142. Upscale restaurant best known for its seafood, featuring delicious main courses like a mean King salmon and Berkshire pork rack. If you can't afford to drop a wad on dinner, try the adjoining, excellent *Dahlia Bakery*.

Dick's Drive-In 115 Broadway Ave E, Capitol Hill ⓣ206/323-1300. Longstanding fast-food institution serving up sloppy but lip-smacking burgers, rich shakes, and fries with just the right crunch. One of five citywide locations, all open daily until 2am.

El Puerco Lloron 1501 Western Ave ⓣ206/624-0541. "The Crying Pig," a rare authentic Mexican restaurant in Seattle – including traditional décor – serving affordable tamales, tostadas, and excellent *chiles rellenos*. Located on the Hillclimb behind the market.

Il Terrazzo Carmine 411 First Ave S, Pioneer Square ⓣ206/467-7797. The height of Italian chic in the city, with splendid risotto, squid, prawn bisque, rack of lamb, gnocchi and a fine range of pastas, for steep prices.

Lampreia 2400 1st Ave at Battery St ⓣ206/443-3301. Very pricey Northwest Cuisine spot specializing in beef and fish, augmented with über-trendy items

like squid-ink pasta and poached veal. Expect plenty of attitude if you're not wearing the right clothes.
Monsoon 615 19th Ave E, Capitol Hill ⓣ 206/325-2111. Upper-end pan-Asian restaurant that's popular for delicious, though rotating, items like drunken crispy chicken, caramelized catfish, duck-stuffed squid, ginger fiddleheads, and prawn salad.
Noodle Ranch 2228 2nd Ave, Belltown ⓣ 206/728-0463. Delicious, Asian fusion cuisine starting at $10 and featuring imaginative noodle-based dishes and other creations, served in a casual atmosphere. The green curry is the chef's specialty and packs quite a punch.
Phnom Penh Noodle House 660 S King St, south of Pioneer Square ⓣ 206/748-9825. Like the name says, an honest-to-God Cambodian noodle joint that doles out rich helpings of noodles in various sauces, as well as traditional favorites like spicy soups and fishcakes.
Piecora's 1401 E Madison St, Capitol Hill ⓣ 206/322-9411. One of the better pizza parlors in a city not known for its pizza, leaning toward the New York style with rich, flavorful, and gooey pies served in a friendly neighborhood environment.
Salumi 309 Third Ave S, Pioneer Square ⓣ 206/621-8772. Old-fashioned sausages served on delicious homemade bread. Succulent ingredients include oxtail, prosciutto, lamb, and numerous hog parts. Ever-popular resto is, however, only open Tuesday-Friday 11am-4pm.
Wild Ginger 1400 Western Ave, downtown ⓣ 206/623-4450. Upscale restaurant with fiery dishes from Southeast Asia, India, and China. Try the barbequed prawns, red curry squid, Dungeness crab, or Angkor Wat chicken.

Coffeehouses

Allegro Espresso Bar 4214 University Way ⓣ 206/633-3030. Longstanding café that's one of the better spots to taste local java brews around the University, with free wireless Internet for customers. Live music on Friday nights.
Bauhaus Books & Coffee 301 E Pine St, Capitol Hill ⓣ 206/625-1600. A hangout for the dressed-in-black crowd with large tables, a used-book section – focusing on art and architecture volumes – and good coffee and tea.
Caffè Ladro 600 Queen Anne Ave N ⓣ 206/282-1549. Near the Seattle Center, this "coffee thief" has an arty flair, with a range of light meals (and some veggie options) in addition to hearty coffees. Eleven other citywide branches.
Elliott Bay Book Company 101 S Main St, Pioneer Square ⓣ 206/682-6664. Seattle's greatest bookstore is also home to its greatest book-friendly cafe, with a nice range of sandwiches, soups and java, and regular readings by notable authors.
Online Coffee Company 1720 E Olive Way, Capitol Hill ⓣ 206/328-3731. Spacious and relaxed Internet café with coffee, beer, wine, and baked goods — plus free wi-fi. The outside patio has a view of Puget Sound. Open until 1am.
Verite Coffee 2052 NW Market St ⓣ 206/782-9557. Fun coffeeshop along Ballard's main drag, with excellent coffee and flavorful cupcakes with offbeat toppings like carrot and lavender.
Vivace Espresso 901 E Denny Way, Capitol Hill ⓣ 206/860-5869. A large haunt for serious java-drinkers and truly run by "espresso roasting and preparation specialists"; their sidewalk café at 321 Broadway E is the prime people-watching perch in the area.
Zeitgeist Coffee 171 S Jackson St ⓣ 206/583-0497. Mostly coffee, a few sandwiches, some pastries, and modern art are found at this pleasant haunt in the heart of Pioneer Square's gallery scene.

Drinking and nightlife

Seattle's **nightlife** revolves around its pounding **live music** venues and convivial **bars**, which pour an excellent selection of microbrewed beers. The tavern scene is most accessible, and touristy, in **Pioneer Square**, where the "joint cover night" plan (weekends $10, weekdays $5) allows you entrance into six different music venues. Other prime turf for hearing music can be found in **Capitol Hill** and, here and there, downtown and Belltown.

Bars and clubs

Alibi Room 85 Pike St ⓣ 206/623-3180. Swank bar tucked in an alley behind the Pike Street Market. Excellent food in café-type rooms upstairs, DJs spinning tunes on the dance floor downstairs, and a good selection of film scripts in the library, along with regular events for area filmmakers.
Central Saloon 207 First Ave S, Pioneer Square ⓣ 206/622-0209. Seattle's oldest (dive) saloon was established in 1892, and is consistently crowded, filled with a mix of slumming tourists and slumming scenesters. Live music ranges from alt-rock to punk to metal and eclectic.
Comet Tavern 922 E Pike St, Capitol Hill

Ⓣ206/323-9853. The oldest bar on Capitol Hill and a grunge institution – not surprisingly a smoky dive and a rocker's hangout, too, with regular shows.

Doc Maynard's Public House 610 1st Ave S, Pioneer Square Ⓣ206/682-4649. Pile-driving rock bands entertain tourists in this worn-at-the-edges 1890s saloon. Meeting place for Underground Tours (see p.1085). Fri and Sat music.

Elysian Brewing 1221 E Pike St, Capitol Hill Ⓣ206/860-1920. Brewpub of one of the best local microbreweries, with flavorful oddities like Zepyrus Pilsner and Dragonstooth Stout. The menu is pretty good, too, offering sandwiches, bangers and mash, and pork tacos.

Kells Irish Pub 1916 Post Alley, Pike Place Market Ⓣ206/728-1916. Spirited Irish bar and restaurant in a central location, with patio seating and performances by Irish-oriented folk and rock groups. Crowd is mostly tourists and business-district types.

Lava Lounge 2226 2nd Ave Ⓣ206/441-5660. Revival of 1950s tiki-lounge kitsch, with a South Pacific–inspired décor of lava lamps and darkly tropical murals. There's eclectic live music and DJs at night, happy hour from 3 to 7pm, and shuffleboard to pass the time.

Linda's Tavern 707 E Pine St, Capitol Hill Ⓣ206/325-1220. Good old tub-thumping watering hole that's popular for its jukebox stocked with classics and indie rock, and quintessential Seattle hedonist vibe.

Pike Pub & Brewery 1415 1st Ave, downtown Ⓣ206/622-6044. Small craft brewery serving its own beers, as well as numerous bottled brands; has a large wine list, adequate food, and touristy atmosphere near the Pike Place Market.

Music venues

Dimitriou's Jazz Alley 2033 6th Ave, downtown Ⓣ206/441-9729. Best big-name jazz spot in town, showcasing international acts, as well as up-and-coming brilliants. Tickets start around $20.

Highway 99 Blues Club 1414 Alaskan Way, downtown Ⓣ206/382-2171. Any nightspot that names itself after a grim highway overpass must be a place worth a visit, and this rootsy joint certainly is, showcasing regional and national performers in a bare-bones space that's all about the music.

Moore Theater 1932 2nd Ave, Belltown Ⓣ206/467-5510. This 1907 former vaudeville auditorium sometimes hosts exciting up-and-coming bands, but more often you'll find established names in pop and rock, along with comedians, dancers, kids' shows, and so on.

Nuemo's 925 E Pike St, Capitol Hill Ⓣ206/709-9467. A hard-thrashing venue that has clawed its way up (almost) to the top of the indie-rock heap. The murals and wall art are splashy and irreverent, and the bands are of the punk, goth, rock, and alt-anything variety.

Showbox 1426 1st Ave, downtown Ⓣ206/628-3151. This 1000-person hall across from Pike Place Market is the best place to catch touring acts that have yet to make the bigger arenas, along with well-regarded regional bands, usually with an indie slant.

Sunset Tavern 5433 Ballard Ave NW, Ballard Ⓣ206/784-4880. Along with being a colorful bar and karaoke spot, the *Sunset's* also a good venue for catching aggressive young rockers and various eclectic acts in nightly performances.

Tractor Tavern 5213 Ballard Ave NW, Ballard Ⓣ206/789-3599. Solid joint in Ballard with great character, good microbrewed beers, and roots music of all kinds – zydeco, Irish, blues, bluegrass.

Triple Door 216 Union St, downtown Ⓣ206/838-4333. Attractive modern complex that's the apogee of the folk, roots, alt-country, and blues scene; the Mainstage has major players and up-and-comers, while the Musicquarium mixes things up with DJs and more experimental fare – it's also free.

Tula's 2214 2nd Ave, Belltown Ⓣ206/443-4221. Jazz of all stripes every evening, mostly from regional unknowns, with live jams Monday evenings. Also open for food and drink starting at 3pm.

Performing arts and festivals

Many of Seattle's **performing arts** venues are based around the Seattle Center; the most prominent of these is **Marion Oliver McCaw Hall**, a sleek, modern facility that hosts the **Seattle Opera** (Ⓣ206/389-7676, Ⓦwww.seattleopera.org). In the same complex, **Pacific Northwest Ballet** (Ⓣ206/441-2424, Ⓦwww.pnb.org) puts on around seven programs from September to June. Away from Seattle Center, **Seattle Symphony Orchestra** performs downtown in the glass-walled **Benaroya Concert Hall**, 3rd and Union streets (Ⓣ206/215-4747, Ⓦwww.seattlesymphony.org), whose acoustics are heralded as being among the finest in the world for classical performances.

For **theater**, Seattle's longest-established small troupe is the **Seattle Repertory Company** (ⓣ206/443-2222, ⓦwww.seattlerep.org) at the Seattle Center, while next door, the **Intiman Theater** (ⓣ206/269-1900, ⓦwww.intiman.org) performs classics and premieres of innovative works. A bit to the north at 100 W Roy St, **On the Boards** presents modern **dance** performances (ⓣ206/217-9888, ⓦwww.ontheboards.org), while big-name musicals open downtown at the **Fifth Avenue Theatre**, 1308 5th Ave (ⓣ206/625-1900, ⓦwww.5thavenue.org), or the **Paramount**, 911 Pine St (ⓣ206/682-1414, ⓦwww.theparamount.com), a large 1928 movie palace, seating around three thousand and hosting lectures, films, comedians, assorted concerts, and more.

Seattle's major events include Bumbershoot, hosting hundreds of artists on dozens of stages around town on Labor Day weekend (ⓣ206/281-7788, ⓦwww.bumbershoot.org), and the Northwest Folklife Festival (ⓣ206/684-7300,

Day-trips to Bainbridge and Vashon islands

For a brief escape from Seattle, the **ferry ride** across Elliott Bay to **Bainbridge Island** provides a relaxing, scenic experience. Washington State Ferries leave from Pier 52 (hourly 5.30am–1.35am; foot passengers $6.70 (collected westbound only in peak season); vehicle and driver $11.25 non-peak, $14.45 peak season; ⓣ206/464-6400 or 1-800/84-FERRY, ⓦwww.wsdot.wa.gov/ferries) for the 35-minute trip to the island, a green and rural spot occupying less than fifty square miles. The island's only conventional attraction, the **Bloedel Reserve**, 7571 NE Dolphin Drive, off the Agatewood Road exit of Hwy-305 (Wed–Sun 10am–4pm; $10; by reservation only at ⓣ206/842-7631, ⓦwww.bloedelreserve.org), is a natural conservatory containing nearly 150 acres of gardens, ponds, meadows, and wildlife habitats. If you want to pitch a tent on the island, there's **camping** at the far end in Fay Bainbridge State Park ($17–24; ⓣ206/842-3931, ⓦwww.parks.wa.gov). Highlighted by **Waterfall Gardens**, 7269 NE Bergman Rd (ⓣ206/842-1434, ⓦwww.waterfall-gardens.com; ❻), a pleasant inn offering expansive grounds with ponds, trails, waterfalls, plus four suites with kitchens, jetted tubs, and refrigerators, area accommodation is limited to **B&Bs**, details of which can be obtained from the **visitor center** in the town of **WINSLOW**, 590 Winslow Way E (ⓣ206/842-3700, ⓦwww.bainbridgechamber.com). Decent choices for eating in Winslow are the *Harbour Public House*, 231 Parfitt Way SW (ⓣ206/842-0969), a renovated 1881 house now used for serving up seafood, salads, burgers, and microbrews, and **Café Nola**, 101 Winslow Way (ⓣ206/842.3822), a popular bistro that's well worthwhile for its tasty pastries, vegetarian fare, and agreeable Sunday brunch.

Other ferries from Seattle and West Seattle make the short trip to easygoing, bicycle-friendly **Vashon Island.** Ferries from downtown Seattle's Pier 50 are passenger-only (Mon–Fri 7.35am–6pm; 35min trip; $8.70), while West Seattle trips are also for vehicles (daily 5.20am–2am; 20min; foot passengers $4.30, vehicle and driver $14.50, $18.50 peak season). A few nice beaches lie along the coast of this island, where the community of **VASHON** is little more than a simple hamlet. The *AYH Ranch Hostel*, 12119 SW Cove Rd (ⓣ206/463-2592, ⓦwww.vashonhostel.com; ❸), six miles from the Seattle–Vashon ferry dock at the north end of the island, offers log-cabin dorm beds and tepees for $20, or private rooms for $65. Phone ahead to make a reservation and arrange a free pickup at the jetty. There are also a number of good **B&Bs**, among them *Artist's Studio Loft,* 16592 91st Ave SW (ⓣ206/463-2583, ⓦwww.asl-bnb.com; ❺), and the *Swallow's Nest Guest Cottages*, 6030 SW 248th St (ⓣ206/463-2646, ⓦwww.vashonislandcottages.com; ❺). Good **places to eat** include *The Hardware Store*, 17601 Vashon Hwy SW (ⓣ206/463-1800), a former tool vendor now given over to tasty nouveau American cuisine, and *Rock Island Pizza*, 17322 Vashon Hwy SW (ⓣ206/463-6814), which has gourmet pizzas and microbrews.

Ⓦwww.nwfolklife.org), a Memorial Day event at the Seattle Center drawing folk musicians from around the world. In late May and early June, the Seattle International Film Festival (Ⓣ206/464-5830, Ⓦwww.seattlefilm.com) centers on classic moviehouses in Capitol Hill, and in July, Seafair (Ⓣ206/728-0123, Ⓦwww.seafair.com), is a colorful celebration held all over town with airplane spectacles, hydroplane events, and milk-carton boat races.

For **listings**, *Seattle Weekly* (Ⓦwww.seattleweekly.com) and *The Stranger* (Ⓦwww.thestranger.com) are free from boxes on the streets and many cafés and stores, and are good for reviews of theater, cinema, and the arts, as is the Friday edition of the *Seattle Post Intelligencer* newspaper (Ⓦseattlepi.nwsource.com).

Puget Sound

The grand waterway of **Puget Sound** hooks far into western Washington, its array of islands and peninsulas the dramatic setting for passing yachts, oceangoing ships, fishing trawlers, and even nuclear submarines. The southern edge of the Sound is increasingly urban, where the formerly industrial **Tacoma** and the small state capital of **Olympia** are worthwhile stopovers, while the waterway itself surrounds many appealing mountains, forests, and lakes. Popular escapes include rural **Whidbey Island** and the beautiful **San Juan Islands** further north.

Tacoma

Sitting on the Seattle–Portland axis of I-5, **TACOMA** is an old industrial town that in the last decade has experienced a resurgence with new museums, theaters, and restaurants. Its centerpiece is the massive blue-and-white **Tacoma Dome**, perched just off the freeway, a major concert venue (Ⓣ253/272-3663, Ⓦwww.tacomadome.org), if something of an eyesore.

Most of Tacoma's attractions sit near each other on the main drag of **Pacific Avenue**, just south of downtown. The most notable of these is art celebrity Dale Chihuly's glittering pedestrian overpass, the **Bridge of Glass** (daily dawn-dusk; free; Ⓦwww.chihuly.com/bridgeofglass), chock-a-block with crystalline blue spires and glass vases and curiosities on view. It leads to the **Museum of Glass**, 1801 E Dock St (Wed–Sat 10am–5pm, Sun noon–5pm, summer also Mon & Tues 10am-5pm; $10; Ⓣ1-866/4-MUSEUM, Ⓦwww.museumofglass.org), which resembles a giant metal kiln and presents Chihuly's work and that of other glassblowers, veering between museum art and industrial design. On the west side of the bridge is the copper-domed **Union Station** (Mon-Fri 8am-5pm; Ⓣ253/863-5173 ext. 223), built in 1911 and now redesigned as a courthouse and display space for some of Chihuly's more extravagant works – especially the 27 orange- and henna-hued glass butterfly shapes in the **Monarch Window**. On the south side of Union Station, the excellent **Washington State History Museum**, 1911 Pacific Ave (Mon–Sat 10am–5pm, Thurs open until 8pm, Sun noon–5pm; $8; Ⓦwww.wshs.org/wshm), has a huge array of exhibits on regional history in its **Great Hall of Washington History**. Large galleries nicely recreate the milieu of frontier towns and early logging industries, as well as a replica general store and native plank house. On the north side of the Station is the **Tacoma Art Museum**, 1701 Pacific Ave (Tues–Sat 10am–5pm, Sun noon-5pm; $7.50; Ⓦwww.tacomaartmuseum.org), a gleaming steel-and-glass creation by Antoine Predock. The temporary exhibits are fairly wide-ranging, anything from native tribal works to classic photography to installation art.

Further north, the historic core of Tacoma is centered around the two-block-long **Antique Row**, Broadway between S 7th and S 9th streets, now in decline from its glory days as a haven for lovers of historic castoffs, and the **Broadway Center for the Performing Arts**, 901 Broadway (ⓣ253/591-5890, ⓦwww.broadwaycenter.org), whose two stunning former moviehouses are landmarks with terracotta facades and much historic-revival décor. If you have time, wander about eight blocks northwest of the Theater District to stately **Wright Park**, Sixth Avenue and S G Street, highlighted by the **Seymour Botanical Conservatory**, 316 S G St (daily Tues–Sun 10am–4.30pm; free; ⓣ253/591-5330), a 1908 glass-and-steel structure that holds some two hundred different species, from orchids and lilies to ferns and bromeliads, and, across the street, the Neoclassical **Karpeles Manuscript Museum**, 407 S G St (Tues–Sun 10am–4pm; free; ⓣ253/383-2575, ⓦwww.karpeles.com), which holds an immense collection of manuscripts, among them the concluding page of Darwin's *Origin of Species* and a study page for Karl Marx's *Das Kapital*, and some excellent temporary exhibits as well.

Finally, four miles north of downtown is picturesque **Point Defiance Park**, Pearl Street off Ruston Way, which at seven hundred acres is one of the largest urban parks in the USA. Its **Five-Mile-Drive** loop has fine vistas of Puget Sound and many appealing trails branching off from it. Also diverting are an on-site zoo, aquarium, and logging museum, but especially **Fort Nisqually** (hours vary, often Wed–Sun 11am–5pm; $4; ⓦwww.fortnisqually.org), a reconstruction of the fur-trading post Hudson's Bay Company set up in 1833, with homes and storehouses that illustrate the stark lifestyles of denizens of the original fort.

Practicalities

Hotels in Tacoma are less expensive than their counterparts in Seattle. If you're sufficiently fired up by all the glass art in town, make a night of it with a stay at the *Hotel Murano*, 1320 Broadway Plaza (ⓣ253/986-8083, ⓦwww.hotelmuranotacoma.com; ❽), which, apart from its designer digs, flat-screen TVs, and the like, has corridors and public spaces loaded with shimmery artworks, many of them glass in the style of local bigwig Dale Chihuly. Tacoma's better **B&B** choices include *The Villa*, about a mile northeast of downtown at 705 N 5th St (ⓣ253/572-1157, ⓦwww.villabb.com; ❻), set in a Renaissance Revival mansion surrounded by luxurious gardens. Some of the rooms have private verandas with prime views. Another is *Geiger Victorian*, 912 North I St (ⓣ253/383-3504, ⓦwww.geigervictorian.com; ❺), loaded with all the chintz and antiques you'd expect, plus a fireplace, and claw-footed tubs in the rooms. For a bite to **eat**, try the *Southern Kitchen*, 1716 6th Ave (ⓣ253/627-4282), whose delicious gumbo, catfish, hush puppies, candied yams, and fried okra are about as close to Dixie as you're going to get in the Pacific Northwest; and *Harmon Pub & Brewery*, 1938 Pacific Ave (ⓣ253/383-2739), a solid choice for quaffing primo microbrews that also has serviceable burgers, salads, and pizza.

Olympia

Picked as Washington's territorial capital in 1853, **OLYMPIA** offers a small but appealing set of attractions that are well worth a look on a stopover between Portland and Seattle. Its compact downtown area is presided over by the **Old Capitol**, Washington St at 7th Ave (Mon–Fri 8am–5pm; free), an 1892 jewel with Gothic turrets and arched windows, while nearby along **East Fourth Avenue** is one of the prime strips for hearing Northwest rock at its best and cheapest (try *Le Voyeur*, no. 404, ⓣ360/943-5710, and the *4th Avenue Tavern*, no. 210, ⓣ360/786-1444). There's also the waterfront **Olympia Farmers Market**, 700 N Capitol Way (April–Oct Thurs–Sun 10am–3pm; Nov–Dec Sat & Sun only; ⓦww.olympiafarmersmarket.com), with a nice selection of fruits, vegetables, herbs, and handicrafts.

Just south of downtown, the neat lawns of the **Capitol Campus** are the setting for the grand Neoclassical **Legislative Building** (tours daily on the hour 10am–3pm; self-guided visits daily 10am–4pm; ⓣ360/902-8880, ⓦwww.ga.wa.gov/visitor), which was completed in 1928 and merits a look for its six gargantuan bronze entry-doors decorated with scenes from state history; a rotunda with a five-ton Tiffany chandelier; and a large circular walnut table in the State Reception Room, whose base was carved from a single tree trunk in the shape of eagles' legs. Across from the Capitol, the classical **Hall of Justice** (Mon–Fri 8am–5pm; same contacts as above), is the home of the state supreme court, its elegant colonnade clad in sandstone and echoing the architectural grandeur of its neighbor.

Practicalities

The **Greyhound** station is at 107 Seventh Ave SE at Capitol Way (ⓣ360/357-5541), just north of the Capitol Campus, and the **Amtrak** station is eight miles southeast, at 6600 Yelm Hwy in the town of Lacey. Intercity Transit runs local **buses** (75¢ ticket, one-day pass $1.50; ⓣ360/786-1881, ⓦwww.intercitytransit.com), also providing a free DASH shuttle service between downtown, the Farmers Market, and the Capitol Campus. Olympia's **visitor center** (Mon–Fri 8am–5pm; ⓣ360/586-3460) is on the Capitol Campus, 14th Ave and Capitol Way.

Beyond the typical motels, distinctive **accommodation** includes the *Swantown Inn*, 1431 11th Ave SE (ⓣ360/753-9123, ⓦwww.swantowninn.com; ⑤), four rooms in a striking 1887 Eastlake Victorian, with wireless internet, savory breakfast, and views of the Capitol; the *Phoenix Inn*, 415 Capitol Way (ⓣ360/570-0555, ⓦwww.phoenixinnsuites.com; ⑤), with fridges and microwaves in each room, plus an onsite pool, jacuzzi, and gym; and the *Inn at Mallard Cove*, 5025 Meridian Road NE (ⓣ360/491-9795, ⓦwww.theinnatmallardcove.com; ⑥), a half-timbered Tudor Revival estate whose three lovely rooms variously come with fireplaces, private decks, and jacuzzis. There's also **camping** at forested Millersylvania State Park, 12245 Tilley Rd ($17–22; ⓣ360/753-1519), south of Olympia, two miles east of I-5, exit 99. Of places to **eat**, the *Urban Onion*, 116 Legion Way (ⓣ360/943-9242), has delicious burgers for vegetarians and carnivores, while a few blocks away, *Spar Café*, 114 Fourth Ave E (ⓣ360/357-6444), is a 1930s diner with music on weekends and a menu thick with hearty burgers and microbrews.

Whidbey Island

With its sheer cliffs and craggy outcrops, rocky beaches and prairie countryside, **WHIDBEY ISLAND** is the second-largest island in the continental US – nearly fifty miles in length from north to south. Although it's possible to reach the island by road – Hwy 20 off I-5 drops into the north end of Whidbey, 85 miles north of Seattle – the **ferry** is usually a more practical option. The quickest route from Seattle is to head thirty miles north to Mukilteo and catch the ferry to **Clinton** on Whidbey's southern tip (daily 5am–1am; 20min trip; foot passengers $3.95, vehicle and driver $8.60). From Port Townsend on the Olympic Peninsula (see p.1098) another ferry goes to **Keystone**, in the middle of the island (5am–midnight; 30min; foot passengers $2.60, vehicle and driver $11.15; ⓦwww.wsdot.wa.gov/ferries). Whidbey's **bus** system, Island Transit (most routes Mon–Fri only; ⓣ360/321-6688, ⓦwww.islandtransit.org), offers eight free routes that collectively run along the length of the island.

Just a few miles away from where the ferry docks in Clinton, the town of Langley is a well-heeled seaside village with an old-West-style stretch of wooden storefronts set on a picturesque bluff overlooking the water. The town's charm is based on its antique stores and galleries, such as the Whidbey Art Gallery,

117 Anthes Ave (Ⓣ360/221-7675), and the Hellebore Glass Studio, 308 First St (Ⓣ360/221-2067). Good places to stay are *Country Cottage of Langley*, 215 6th St (Ⓣ360/221-8709 or 1-800/718-3860, Ⓦwww.acountrycottage.com; ❻), which has six cottages set around in a restored 1920s farmhouse, all units with CD players and fridges, some with jacuzzis and fireplaces; and The Inn at Langley, 400 First St (Ⓣ360/221-3033, Ⓦwww.innatlangley.com; ❾), whose posh rooms have porches, balconies and waterfront views. Among the limited food options in town, The Braeburn, 197D 2nd Street (Ⓣ360/221-3211), is a local favorite for its old-fashioned meatloaf and coleslaw, pot roast and omelettes; and Neil's Clover Patch Cafe, 2850 SR 525 (Ⓣ360/321-4120), is a buffet spot with gut-busting weekly specials of fish 'n' chips and pork ribs.

The middle part of the island contains Ebey's Landing National Historic Reserve (free; Ⓦwww.nps.gov/ebla), compelling for its late nineteenth-century military garrisons Fort Casey and Fort Ebey, which have since been converted into evocative state parks, peppered with gun batteries, whose artillery emplacements can be freely explored, along with the eerie, bomb-shelter-like bunkers. Fort Ebey is also a good spot to camp (March–Oct; $17–22; Ⓣ360/678-4636). Nearby, charming little Coupeville is Washington's second-oldest city and features preserved Victorian mansions, and its Front Street is where you'll find most of the shops and eateries. Good accommodation includes Captain Whidbey Inn, 2072 W Captain Whidbey Inn Rd, two miles west of town at Penn Cove (Ⓣ360/678-4097, Ⓦwww.captainwhidbey.com; ❹), a nautical-themed hotel with a variety of rooms; and the Anchorage Inn, 807 N Main St (Ⓣ360/678-5581, Ⓦwww.anchorage-inn.com; ❹), with seven nice B&B rooms. For eating, try *Knead & Feed*, 4 Front St (Ⓣ360/678-5431), offering homemade bread, pies, and cinnamon rolls; Christopher's, 23 Front St (Ⓣ360/678-5480), with its savory panini, seafood, pastas, and steaks; and Toby's Tavern, 8 Front St (Ⓣ360/678-4222), for its surprisingly tasty seafood, burgers, and microbrews, plus solid, gut-stuffing pastrami sandwiches and French dips.

On the northern edge of the island, **Deception Pass State Park**, 5175 N Hwy-20 (daily 8am–dusk; Ⓣ360/675-2417) is not to be missed, sprawling over four thousand acres of rugged land and sea that's great for hiking, fishing, bird-watching, and scuba diving. You can **camp** here, as it has around 250 tent sites ($17–22; Ⓣ360/657-2417), though it fills up quickly in the summer months, so call ahead.

The San Juan Islands

North and west of Whidbey Island, midway between Seattle and Vancouver, BC, the beautiful **SAN JUAN ISLANDS** are scattered across the northern reaches of Puget Sound. Every summer brings plenty of visitors, especially on the largest ones, San Juan and Orcas, so you're well advised to book your stay and transportation in advance.

Arrival and getting around

Washington State Ferries sails to the islands from the harbor a few miles west of **Anacortes**, a gritty port 75 miles north of Seattle at the end of Hwy-20. The town is reachable via **Airporter Shuttle** (6am–11.30pm; 3hr trip; $33 one-way, $61 round-trip; Ⓣ1-866/235-5247, Ⓦwww.airporter.com), which runs ten buses daily from Sea-Tac Airport and three from downtown Seattle. The ferry runs 12–18 times daily and stops at Lopez, Shaw, Orcas, and San Juan islands (5.30am–10.45pm; Ⓣ1-888/808-7977, Ⓦwww.wsdot.wa.gov/ferries), and the slow cruise through the archipelago is a delight. Motorists should get to the port early, as there's often an hour's wait or more to get vehicles onto a summer crossing. Round-trip **fares** to the islands – $11.85 for foot passengers and $32–50 for a car and driver, depending on the destination and season – are collected only on the westbound journey, and there is no charge for foot passengers on inter-island trips (bringing a bike is an extra $4).

If you want to catch an early ferry from Anacortes, Commercial Avenue is lined with numerous budget **hotels**, the least generic of which is the hot-tub-equipped *Islands Inn*, no. 3401 (ⓣ360/293-4644, ⓦwww.islandsinn.com; ❹), offering bayside views and fireplaces, while the *Majestic Hotel*, no. 419 (ⓣ360/299-1400, ⓦwww.majesticinnandspa.com; ❻), is a lovely option from 1889, recently renovated into an upscale model with spa and a good onsite restaurant and bar.

As an alternative to ferry travel, Kenmore Air (ⓣ1-866/435-9524, ⓦwww.kenmoreair.com) runs hour-long **seaplane flights** from Seattle's Lake Union to six stops in the San Juans ($121 one-way, $242 round-trip). A passenger-only alternative is the *Victoria Clipper* (ⓣ360/448-5000 or 1-800/888-2535, ⓦwww.victoriaclipper.com), which runs from Pier 69 in Seattle to San Juan's Friday Harbor ($42–48 one-way, $65–75 return), with a 5hr layover there.

Orcas Island

Horseshoe-shaped **ORCAS ISLAND** teems with rugged hills and leafy timber that tower over its fetching farm country, craggy beaches, and abundant wildlife. The ferry lands in tiny **Orcas**, and maps and **information** are available from a small visitor center near the ferry. In the summer you can get around the island on the **Orcas Island Shuttle** (June–Aug; $6 per ride; ⓣ360/376-RIDE, ⓦwww.orcasislandshuttle.com). The best spot to stay near the ferry landing is the *Orcas Hotel* (ⓣ360/376-4300, ⓦwww.orcashotel.com; ❹), a restored Victorian inn whose plushest rooms have jacuzzis, balconies, and harbor views, though not in the cheaper ones. You can rent **bicycles** from Dolphin Bay Bicycles, just up from the dock ($30 per day; ⓣ360/376-4157, ⓦwww.rockisland.com/~dolphin).

Ten miles north, in the drab town of Eastsound, you can also rent bikes from Wildlife Cycles, 350 N Beach Rd at A Street ($30 per day; ⓣ360/376-4708, ⓦwww.wildlifecycles.com), while the Chamber of Commerce, on N Beach Rd past Eastsound Square (ⓣ360/376-2273, ⓦwww.orcasislandchamber.com), provides maps and information. Also informative is the Orcas Island Historical Society & Museum, 181 N Beach Rd (late-May–Sept Tues–Sun 11am–4pm; $3; ⓦorcasmuseum.org), which illuminates the island's Native American and pioneer history, and is spread over six interconnected log cabins from the 1880s and 1890s. Fine places to eat include Christina's, 310 Main St (ⓣ360/376-4904), a well-regarded local favorite that offers Northwest cuisine and seafood for around $30 an entree, and *Portofino Pizzeria*, along A Street (ⓣ360/376-2085), for tasty, hand-crafted pizzas and calzones. Nestled at the end of West Beach Road, Beach Haven Resort (ⓣ360/376-2288, ⓦwww.beach-haven.com; ❺) is a great place to stay, its beachfront apartments and log cabins lining a densely wooded, sunset-facing cove; in summer they're only available by the week.

The island's highlight is **Moran State Park**, off Horseshoe Hwy southeast of Eastsound (ⓦwww.orcasisle.com/~elc), where more than thirty miles of hiking trails wind through dense forest and open fields to freshwater lakes, to the summit of **Mount Constitution** – the San Juans' highest point – crowned with a rugged stone observation tower. The park's four **campgrounds** (primitive $7–9, regular $14–20; ⓣ1-888/226-7688) fill up early in summer, so book ahead. Further along, lovely *Doe Bay Village & Resort*, Doe Bay Rd, 18 miles east of Eastsound (ⓣ360/376-2291, ⓦwww.doebay.com), is tucked into a secluded bay and offers everything from hostel beds (❷) to basic campsites (❷) to modern cabins (❹–❼); whatever your choice, there's a minimum stay of two to three nights. In nearby **Olga**, *Café Olga* (ⓣ360/376-5862) serves tasty **meals** and fruit pies and has an adjoining art gallery.

San Juan Island

SAN JUAN ISLAND is the ferry's last stop before Canada, best known as the home of two harbor towns and, at the southern tip, **American Camp** (hours vary, often daily 8am–4.30pm; free; ⓣ360/378-2902, ⓦwww.nps.gov/sajh), a national park whose territory once played a role in the infamous "Pig War," an 1859 border conflict between the US and Britain. More appealing is **English Camp**, to the west (same entry as American Camp), where forests overlook pleasant fields and maple trees near the shore, and four buildings from the 1860s and a small formal garden have been restored.

Friday Harbor, the lone incorporated spot in the San Juans, has cafés, shops, and a waterfront that make for pleasant wandering, and its small **Whale Museum**, 62 First St N (daily: June–Aug 9am–6pm, rest of year 10am–5pm; $6; ⓦwww.whalemuseum.org), which has a small set of whale skeletons and displays explaining their migration and growth cycles, as well as a listening booth for whale songs, along with walrus, seal, and dolphin soundtracks. To see the real thing, head past the coves and bays on the island's west side to **Lime Kiln Point State Park**, 6158 Lighthouse Rd (daily 8am–dusk), named after the site's former lime quarry. Orca ("killer") whales come here in summer to feed on migrating salmon, and there's usually at least one sighting a day. San Juan Safaris (ⓣ360/378-1323 or 1-800/450-6858, ⓦwww.sanjuansafaris.com) is one of several companies offering three-hour **whale-watching cruises** (April–Sept only; $69), plus sea-kayaking trips (June–Sept) for the same price.

From April to September, **San Juan Shuttle** stops at most of the island's principal attractions ($5/one-way, $15/day-pass; ⓣ360/378-8887 or 1-800/887-8387, ⓦwww.sanjuantransit.com), and **bikes** ($9/hr, $36/day, $165/week) can be rented at Island Bicycles, 380 Argyle St (summer daily, Wed–Sat rest of year; ⓣ360/378-4941, ⓦwww.islandbicycles.com). You can also pick up information and **maps** of the island's irregular main roads at the **chamber of commerce** at 135 Spring St (Mon–Fri 10am–5pm, Sat & Sun 10am–4pm; ⓣ360/378-5240, ⓦwww.sanjuanisland.org).

Choices to **stay** include *Bird Rock Hotel*, 35 First St (ⓣ1-800/352-2632, ⓦwww.birdrockhotel.com; ❺), a boutique item with designer furnishings, flat-screen TVs, free wi-fi, morning breakfast, and some units with jacuzzis (the cheapest rooms have shared bath); *Lakedale Resort* (ⓣ1-800/617-2267, ⓦwww.lakedale.com), six miles from the ferry on Roche Harbor Rd (accessible by bus), which has everything from simple campsites (❶) to elegant lodge rooms (❾) to canvas-walled (❻) and log-framed cabins (❾); and *Harrison House*, 235 C St (ⓣ360/378-3587, ⓦwww.harrisonhousesuites.com; ❻), a popular B&B in a verdant setting, with kayaks and mountain bikes for island use, and five sizable suites with jacuzzis, kitchens, fireplaces, and one to three bedrooms each. The local Bed & Breakfast Association (ⓣ360/378-3030, ⓦwww.san-juan-island.net) can also hook you up with a room, though it's essential to reserve ahead. Of Friday Harbor's plentiful places to **eat**, *Downriggers*, 10 Front St (ⓣ360/378-2700), is a long-standing presence for its affordable seafood – everything from lobster quesadillas to crab griddle cakes, while *The Place*, 1 Spring St, (ⓣ360/378-8707) provides upscale crab cakes, oysters, and all types of seafood, as well as savory pasta; and *Steps Wine Bar and Cafe*, First St at Friday Harbor Center (ⓣ360/370-5959), is a chic, highly regarded spot for its fine wines, with Northwest cuisine menu that's also quite tempting.

At the northwest tip of the island is Roche Harbor, established in the 1880s around the limestone trade, and highlighted by the gracious white Hotel de Haro,

248 Reuben Memorial Drive (T 1-800/451-8910, W www.rocheharbor.com; 7–9), an elegant 1886 complex with standard rooms with shared bathrooms, as well as four upscale suites and quaint cottages with antique décor. At the hotel there are several places to eat. The best by far is McMillen's (T 360/378-5757), with good, if pricey, steak and seafood entrees and waterside vistas.

The Olympic Peninsula

West of Puget Sound lies the great **Olympic Peninsula**, accessible by US-101, which loops around its coastal perimeter. Rugged peaks dominate the peninsular core, which rises high above lush subalpine vegetation, giving way to the tangled rain forests of the western valleys, and the wild beaches of the Pacific edge. Fringed with logging communities, the peninsula's most magnificent parts are protected within **Olympic National Park**, with its scores of superb hiking trails, many campsites, and several fine old lodges.

Port Townsend

With its brightly painted mansions, convivial cafés, and easily walkable scale, **PORT TOWNSEND** is a fetching, if somewhat isolated, relic from the 1890s that's a great place to spend a day or two before venturing on to the mountains. There are few "official" sights, but plenty in the way of charm in one of the West Coast's most attractive little towns. Perched on the peninsula's northeastern tip across from Keystone on Whidbey Island, Port Townsend's physical split – half on a bluff, half at sea level – reflects nineteenth-century social divisions, when wealthy merchants built their houses uptown, far above the rowdy clamor of the port below.

The downtown area lies at the base of the hill on **Water Street**, which sports an attractive medley of Victorian brick and stone buildings, now home to stylish restaurants, boutiques, and especially, art galleries. The area's rich history is detailed in the museum of the **Jefferson County Historical Society**, 540 Water St (Mar–Dec daily 11am–4pm; $4; W www.jchsmuseum.org), which has an eclectic assortment of items, from a photographer's chair draped with bear and buffalo skins to unusual late nineteenth- and early twentieth-century two-necked harp guitars.

Though bustling year-round, the town is busiest during its **summer festivals** – principally American Fiddle Tunes in early July, Jazz Port Townsend in late July, and the Wooden Boat Festival in September (T 360/385-4742, W www.woodenboat.org). Some of these take place at the state park at **Fort Worden** (T 360/344-4400, W www.fortworden.org), the remains of a military garrison two miles north of town. It offers a wide range of accommodation from dorm beds ($20–26) to campsites ($19–38) and former officers' houses ($145–365), as well as several museums, a science center, and a lighthouse – not to mention dozens of good hiking trails at the edge of Puget Sound, one of which leads to the massive concrete gun emplacements of the 1890s **Kinzie Battery**. If you're really intrigued by these deadly relics, you can take a trail and go poking around **Artillery Hill**, where the guns sit silently under heavy tree cover.

Practicalities

Although Port Townsend is easily accessed by road, you can also get there by **ferry** from Keystone (see p.1094). The ferry terminal is just south of downtown, off Water Street. Get maps and information at the helpful **visitor center**, 2437 E Sims Way (daily 9am–5pm; ⓣ360/385-2722, ⓦwww.ptguide.com), twelve blocks south of the ferry terminal on Hwy-20.

There's a good choice of places to stay, and the most central is the Palace Hotel, 1004 Water St (ⓣ360/385-0773, ⓦwww.palacehotelpt.com; ④), a Victorian charmer that's seen better days, but still has antique décor, claw-footed tubs, and excellent views of the sound. The town's specialty, though, is its B&Bs, the best of which occupy grand Victorian mansions uptown, such as the *Ann Starrett Mansion,* 744 Clay St (ⓣ360/385-3205 or 1-800/321-0644, ⓦwww.starrettmansion.com; ⑦), an 1889 Queen Anne with ceiling frescoes, spiral staircase, and antique furnishings; Old Consulate Inn, 313 Walker St (ⓣ360/385-6753 or 1-800/300-6753, ⓦwww.oldconsulateinn.com; ⑥), an 1889 villa with spiky tower and wraparound veranda, and seven plush suites (plus one rather small room), as well as a grand piano and an old organ; and the delightful *Manresa Castle,* Seventh and Sheridan streets (ⓣ360/385-5750 or 1-800/732-1281, ⓦwww.manresacastle.com), a quasi-French castle from 1892 that has thirty rooms ranging from affordable cozy single units to swanky suites in the tower (⑤–⑧).

Port Townsend has many fine places to eat, among them Fountain Café, 920 Washington St (ⓣ360/385-1364), with seafood and pasta specialties a short distance from the waterfront; the Silverwater Café, 237 Taylor St (ⓣ360/385-6448), with fresh seafood such as ahi tuna and a range of burgers and pasta; and *Sweet Laurette Patisserie,* 1029 Lawrence St (ⓣ360/385-4886), the best French-style bakery in town, featuring elaborate (and expensive) cakes that resemble artworks, and cheaper scones, pies, and pastries. Drinking is best enjoyed at Water Street Brewing, 639 Water St (ⓣ360/379-6438) showcasing live music and boasting great microbrews, and a wonderful old wooden bar with an enormous mirror.

Port Angeles

PORT ANGELES is the most popular point of entry into Olympic National Park, a few miles to the south. Its working-class harbor is backed by striking mountains, but there are few reasons to linger, except as a stopover to more compelling destinations.

Although it's preferable to stay inside the park, Port Angeles has a number of inexpensive **motels** near its uninspiring one-way main drags, First Street and Front Street. By far the best chain offering is *Best Western Olympic Lodge*, 140 Del Guzzi Drive (ⓣ360/452-2993, ⓦwww.portangeleshotelmotel.com; ⑦), with a pool and spa, and rooms with free wi-fi, fridges, and microwaves. Also good is *Domaine Madeleine,* 146 Wildflower Lane (ⓣ360/457-4174, ⓦwww.domainemadeleine.com; ⑦), an elegant B&B with a lovely five-acre garden and five art-themed rooms, which variously come with jetted tubs, fireplaces, and balconies.

For **eating**, *Michael's Divine Dining*, 117-B E 1st St (ⓣ360/417-6929), is a fine-dining spot that has paella, oysters, pasta, and especially steak; almost as good, the midpriced *Bella Italia,* 118 E 1st St (ⓣ360/457-5442), offers prime seafood, pasta, pizza, and traditional Italian cuisine.

Port Angeles has the peninsula's best **transportation** links. The **bus** depot is beside the waterfront at W Front and Oak streets, and from there it's only a couple of minutes' walk to the main **ferry** terminal. Olympic Bus Lines (ⓣ360/417-0700, ⓦwww.olympicbuslines.com) offers daily trips to Amtrak and Greyhound stations in Seattle ($39) and to Sea-Tac Airport ($49). Black Ball Transport (ⓣ360/457-4491, ⓦwww.cohoferry.com) **car ferries** arrive from – and shuttle over to – Victoria, British Columbia (March–Dec two to four ferries daily; 1 hr 45min trip; one-way fares $13.50 walk-on, $50 per car and driver). Arriving at a neighboring pier at the foot of Lincoln Street, the **passenger ferries** of Victoria Express (ⓣ360/452-8088 or 1-800/633-1589, ⓦwww.victoriaexpress.com) operate a faster service (2–3 daily) for $25 round-trip. Port Angeles' **visitor center**, 121 E Railroad St, beside the ferry terminal (ⓣ360/452-2363, ⓦwww.portangeles.org), has information on the entire peninsula and can put you in touch with river-rafting and sea-kayaking operators.

Olympic National Park

Magnificent **OLYMPIC NATIONAL PARK**, consisting of the colossal Olympic Mountains in the heart of the peninsula plus a separate, isolated sixty-mile strip of Pacific coast farther west, is one of Washington's prime wilderness destinations, with boundless opportunities for spectacular hiking and wildlife watching. Created in 1938 by Franklin D. Roosevelt, it features more than two hundred miles of wild rivers, while the river valleys contain sizeable tracts of **temperate rainforest**.

Natural highlights, which are numerous, include **Hurricane Ridge**, where the jagged peaks and sparkling glaciers of the mountains spread out majestically before you; glacially carved **Lake Crescent**, popular for trout fishing and hiking on shoreline trails; the wild **beaches** of the Pacific coast, where black rocks jut out of the sea, and appealing **Ruby Beach** is named for its red-and-black-pebbled sand. Meanwhile, the **Queets River Rainforest** is worth a visit for its rustic trails, and for the luxuriant flora and fauna, highlighted by the world's tallest Douglas fir – 220ft tall and 45ft around; and **Quinault Rainforest**, the most beautiful of all the peninsula's rain forests, around the shores of glacier-carved **Lake Quinault**.

Practicalities

The main **visitor center**, in Port Angeles at 600 E Park Ave (April–Oct daily 9am–4pm, summer closes 6pm; ⓣ360/565-3100, ⓦwww.nps.gov/olym), has useful brochures and trail maps, while the **Wilderness Information Center**, 3002 Mount Angeles Rd (April–Oct, hours vary by season; ⓣ360/565-3100), supplies information on trail conditions in the area; smaller visitor centers are located at Hurricane Ridge and Hoh Rainforest. The **entrance fee** is $5 for individuals or $15 per car; both fees are good for seven days of park access. The **weather** is consistently erratic and often rainy – there's even a fair amount of snow as late as June. You can stay inside the park at any of the sixteen excellent **campgrounds** ($10–18). Try *Heart o' the Hills*, six miles south of Port Angeles, along Hurricane Ridge Road, or further west, *Altair* – though this is closed in winter along with several others.

Other good places to stay are *Lake Crescent Lodge* (May–Oct; ⓣ360/928-3211, ⓦwww.lakecrescentlodge.com; ❺), well placed among dense forest on the lake's south shore, offering simple rooms to elegant cottages; and *Sol Duc Hot Springs Resort* (March–Oct; ⓣ1-866/4SOLDUC, ⓦvisitsolduc.com; ❻), set deep in the park twelve miles off US-101, whose 26 basic cabins come with spartan but adequate amenities, though the pricier ones have kitchens for just $20–30 more. The resort provides free guest access to **Sol Duc Hot Springs** (otherwise $11) – three pools with mineral-rich waters bubbling up at 100 to 108F°. Elsewhere, impressive *Kalaloch Lodge* (ⓣ360/962-2271, ⓦwww.visitkalaloch.com), has basic lodge rooms (❺) and more upscale cabins (❽); and the charming 1926 *Lake Quinault Lodge* (ⓣ360/288-2900 or 1-800/562-6672, ⓦwww.visitlakequinault.com; ❻), on the shores of Lake Quinault, offers rooms with fireplaces or lakeside views, and an onsite pool and sauna.

The southwest coast

Heading south on US-101 from Lake Quinault, leaving the national park, it's about forty hilly miles to industrial **Aberdeen**, from where there's a choice of routes: US-12/Hwy-8 lead east towards Olympia (see p.1093), while Hwy-101 pushes south over the hills, threading along the shore of muddy Willapa Bay and the **southwest coast** of Washington. Here, the bay is home to the 15,000-acre **Willapa National Wildlife Refuge** (Ⓦwww.fws.gov/willapa), whose various dunes, forests, marshes, and mudflats shelter some two hundred species of migrating shorebirds. Continuing on, the **Long Beach Peninsula** is something of a low-rent resort area, offering the usual chain motels and souvenir shops, but it's worth a trip to the northern tip, where **OYSTERVILLE** is a forested collection of rusting old buildings that's the home of **Ekone Oysters** (Ⓣ360/665-6585), recognizable by its piles of discarded shells and renowned for its fresh smoked oysters. Also good for the palate is the **Pacific Coast Cranberry Museum**, 2907 Pioneer Rd in the town of Long Beach (Ⓣ360/642-5553, Ⓦwww.cranberrymuseum.com), where you can wander through a cranberry bog (daily 8am–dusk) and purchase berry-flavored treats.

Down at the far southwestern tip of Washington, near the mouth of the Columbia River, is scenic **Cape Disappointment State Park** (daily summer 6.30am–10pm, rest of year closes 4pm; Ⓦwww.parks.wa.gov). The evocative 1856 **North Head Lighthouse** (summer daily 11am–3pm; $2.50) still stands watch, and the **Lewis and Clark Interpretive Center** (daily 10am–5pm; $5) can tell you all about the historical hazards of navigating the Columbia River. Fortunately, you'll be spared any such difficulty as you travel south on Hwy-101 over the 1966 span of the **Astoria Bridge**, crossing the state boundary into Oregon (see p.1107).

The Cascade Mountains

The **Cascade Mountains** offer mile upon mile of dense forested wilderness, traversed by a tangle of beautiful trails and vistas. The most popular access point is **Mount Rainier**, set in its own national park ninety miles southeast of Seattle, while the haunting scenery around volcanic **Mount St Helens** compels visitors internationally. Further north, Hwy-20, the high mountain road that crosses the Cascades, is by far the most spectacular route to eastern Washington, traversing the snow-capped wonder of **North Cascades National Park**.

The North Cascades and the Cascade Loop

The magnificent **Cascade Loop** (Ⓣ509/662-3888, Ⓦwww.cascadeloop.com) offers a 400-mile round-trip along highways 20, 153, 97, and 2 – though the full trip is only feasible during the summer, since at other times snow closes the mountain passes; take a few selected treks through the gorgeous environs unless you have at least three days to explore the territory in full. You can find out more information at **North Cascades National Park Headquarters**, 2105 Hwy-20 near Sedro Woolley, located just east of where Hwy-20 begins its journey inland at Burlington (daily 8am–4.30pm; Ⓣ360/854-7200, Ⓦwww.nps.gov/noca).

Winthrop

From the information center, the highway threads through high mountain passes to tiny **WINTHROP**, an old mining town decked out in a Wild West get-up, and the original setting for Owen Wister's *The Virginian*. While the effect is more than a bit cheesy, the false-fronted "saloons" and "dance halls" do make for some good snapshots. If you'd like to **stay**, one good choice is the *Hotel Rio Vista*, 285 Riverside Ave (Ⓣ509/996-3535 or 1-800/398-0911, Ⓦwww.hotelriovista.com; ❻), which offers nice suites with hot tubs, kitchenettes, and DVD players in a fine riverside setting; or the luxurious *Sun Mountain Lodge* (Ⓣ509/996-2211 or 1-800/572-0493, Ⓦwww.sunmountainlodge.com; ❾), with cabins and lodge rooms in a grand spot on the edge of the Cascades, nine miles southwest of town along Twin Lakes and then Patterson Lake Road.

As for **eating** and **drinking** options, *Winthrop Brewing Co*, 155 Riverside Ave (Ⓣ509/996-3183), dispenses solid microbrews, and the *Duck Brand Cantina*, 248 Riverside Ave (Ⓣ509/996-2192, Ⓦwww.methownet.com/duck), serves up cheap and tasty Mexican fare and has six simple, Western-themed rooms in its onsite B&B ($69). The nearby **visitor center**, 202 Riverside Ave (Ⓣ509/996-2125, Ⓦwww.winthropwashington.com), offers information and backcountry permits for hiking and camping.

Chelan and Stehekin

The fetching resort of **CHELAN**, sixty miles south of Winthrop, nestles at the foot of **Lake Chelan**, whose spectacularly deep waters fill a glacially-carved trough nestled in the mountains. Of several good **lodging** options, *Darnell's Lake Resort*, 901 Spader Bay Rd (April-Oct Ⓣ1-800/967-8149, Ⓦwww.darnellsresort.com; ❼), has a pool, tennis courts, boat launch, and other amenities, as well as rooms that variously come with kitchenettes, kitchens, fridges and/or microwaves. Cheaper digs are available at the *Apple Inn Motel*, 1002 E Woodin Ave (Ⓣ509/682-4044, Ⓦwww.appleinnmotel.com; ❹). The **ranger station** at 428 W Woodin Ave (daily 8am–4.30pm; Ⓣ509/682-2576) can ply you with hiking maps when you're ready to hit the trails, while the **visitor center** is near the waterfront at 102 E Johnson Ave (Mon–Fri 9am–5pm, Sat 10am–4pm; summer also open Sun; Ⓣ509/682-3503 or 1-800/4-CHELAN, Ⓦwww.lakechelan.com).

The Lake Chelan Boat Company, 1418 W Woodin Ave (Ⓣ509/682-4584 reservations, Ⓦwww.ladyofthelake.com), runs a passenger ferry service to the head of Lake Chelan. Leaving from the jetty a mile west of town on Woodin Avenue, the *Lady of the Lake II* takes four hours to cruise the 55 miles of the nation's deepest gorge (May–Oct; $23.25 one-way, $39 round-trip); the year-round *Lady Express* (May-Oct $35.75 one-way, $59 round-trip; Nov–April $39 round-trip) reaches Lake Chelan's mountainous western tip in half the time. All cruises feature 60- to 90-minute layovers at **STEHEKIN**, a tiny, isolated village otherwise accessible only by a Chelan Airways **seaplane** ($120 one-way, $165 round-trip; Ⓣ509/682-5555, Ⓦwww.chelanairways.com), which is also available for airborne **tours** of the region ($85–320). At Stehekin there are **campsites** and trailheads leading to some of the best hiking and backpacking in the North Cascades. Bikes and canoes are available from the *Stehekin Landing Resort* (Ⓣ509/682-4494, Ⓦwww.stehekinlanding.com; ❺), where the lakeside rooms are a bit pricier than standard units. For camping and hiking information, visit the **Golden West Visitor Center** near the Stehekin jetty (April–Oct daily 8.30am–4.30pm, Nov-Mar Wed-Mon 12.30-2pm; Ⓣ360/854-7365).

Wenatchee to Snoqualmie Falls

Several miles south of Chelan, the Cascade Loop turns west along US-2 just north of the apple-producing town of **Wenatchee**, where you can munch away on various varieties and guzzle apple juice at the **Washington Apple Commission Visitor Center**, on the northern edge of town at 2900 Euclid Ave (Mon–Fri 8am–5pm; free; Ⓦwww.bestapples.com). Afterwards, head back to

US-2 for pocket-sized **LEAVENWORTH**, a Bavarian theme town where even the fast-food outlets are decked out in high gables and half-timbered woodwork. It's best as a base for taking in the outdoor activities in the spectacular mountain surroundings. The **ranger station**, just off US-2 at 600 Sherbourne St (Mon–Sat 7.45am–4.30pm; ⓣ509/782-1413), provides trail guides and hiking information, and River Rider (ⓣ1-800/448-RAFT, ⓦwww.riverrider.com) is one of the more prominent guides offering tubing on the Wenatchee River ($10 per person) and kayaking and rafting excursions ($55–75) on a range of Cascade rivers. The **visitor center**, 940 Hwy-2 (ⓣ509/548-5807, ⓦwww.leavenworth.org), has copious listings of places to **stay** and **eat**. The cozy rooms and suites of the *Hotel Pension Anna*, 926 Commercial St (ⓣ1-800/509-ANNA, ⓦwww.pensionanna.com; ❺), are decked out in cheerful Teutonic kitsch, but the rooms at the stylish *Enzian Motor Inn*, 590 Hwy-2 (ⓣ509/548-5269 or 1-800/223-8511, ⓦwww.enzianinn.com; ❺), are more tasteful, if blander too. The *Andreas Keller*, 829 Front St (ⓣ509/548-6000), doles out hefty helpings of gut-busting German cuisine like schnitzel and spatzele, as well as lively Bavarian music and beer-bearing barmaids – bring your Tyrolean hat.

West of Leavenworth, US-2 crosses the mountains over Stevens Pass, but the principal east–west highway, I-90, lies further south, connecting Seattle with the Yakima Valley. Near I-90 is the striking, 270ft torrent of **Snoqualmie Falls** (ⓦwww.snoqualmiefalls.com), and behind it the luxurious *Salish Lodge*, 6501 Railroad Ave SE (ⓣ425/888-2556 or 1-800/2-SALISH, ⓦwww.salishlodge.com; ❾), still best known as a location in the David Lynch TV series *Twin Peaks*.

Mount Rainier National Park

Set in its own national park, glacier-clad **MOUNT RAINIER** is the highest (14,410ft) and most accessible peak in the Cascades, and a major Washington landmark. Not until June does the snow melt enough for roads to open, and then the deer and mountain goats appear, dazzling wildflowers illuminate the alpine meadows, and the mountain makes for some perfect hiking. More than three hundred miles of **trails** criss-cross the park, ranging from short walks – such as the 1.2-mile Nisqually Vista Trail loop – to the five-mile Skyline Trail up to Glacier Overlook, to the 93-mile Wonderland Trail that encircles Mount Rainier itself. If you only have a day to explore , visit the south and east sides from the Nisqually entrance to **Paradise**, with a side trip to **Sunrise** – a stunning eighty-mile drive winding through river valleys and lowland forests with glaciated peaks and stunning vistas. (Climbing Mount Rainier, however, is hazardous and should only be undertaken by experienced climbers.)

Practicalities

The park is **located** some seventy miles southeast of Tacoma by way of Highway 7 and a transfer onto minor route 706. Admission to the park is $15 per vehicle, $5 per person, for a one-week pass. The park has four **entrances**: Nisqually in the southwest corner, Stephen's Canyon in the southeast, White River in the northeast, and Carbon River in the northwest. Only the Nisqually entrance is open year-round (for cross-country skiing; the others open June–Sept) and the only one serviced by public **transportation** – a ten-hour day-trip with Gray Line from Seattle (May–Sept; $59; ⓣ360/624-5077 or 1-800/426-7505, ⓦwww.graylineseattle.com). For map and trail conditions, stop by the **visitor centers** at Longmire, Ohanapecosh, Sunrise, White River, and, the most useful, Paradise (May to Sept daily 9am–5pm; ⓣ360/569-2211, ⓦwww.nps.gov/mora).

For official park accommodation (ⓣ360/569-2275, ⓦrainier.guestservices.com; ❺, plus $36–50 for private bath), the classic lodge of the National Park Inn is open

▲ Mount Rainier

year-round with 25 guestrooms and a restaurant, while the Paradise Inn, just underwent a lengthy renovation and appeals for its 1916 rustic charm. Make reservations well in advance. Outside the park, in the town of Ashford, *Whittaker's Bunkhouse*, 30205 SR 706 E (Ⓣ360/569-2439, Ⓦwww.whittakersbunkhouse.com), is an old loggers' bunkhouse with dorm beds (❶) and double rooms with private baths (❹); and Mounthaven, 38210 SR 706 E (Ⓣ360/569-2594 or 1-800/456-9380, Ⓦwww.mounthaven.com; ❺), has nine cabins, some with fireplaces, kitchenettes, fridges, wood stoves, and porches. The park's six campgrounds require reservations ($8–18; Ⓣ1-877-444-6777, Ⓦreservations.nps.gov), which you can obtain up to 24 hours in advance from any hiking center in the park.

Mount St Helens

The looming volcanic mound of **MOUNT ST HELENS** erupted on May 18, 1980, its blast wave flattening 230 square miles of surrounding forests, a massive mudflow sending an avalanche of debris down the river valleys. Since then, the forests and animals have reemerged though the scarred landscape, which still testifies to the awesome force of nature.

The area around the mountain has three entry routes. Many visitors arrive along Hwy-504, off I-5 roughly halfway between Olympia and Portland, which snakes through dark green forests until bald, spiky trees give way to thousands of lifeless gray trees lying in combed-down rows. At the end is the **Johnson Ridge Observatory** (May–Oct daily 10am–6pm; Ⓣ360/274-2140, Ⓦwww.fs.fed.us/gpnf/mshnvm), which offers fine views of the still-steaming lava dome, a film of the eruption, and testimony by survivors. In the summer, expect long highway caravans of SUVs and RVs, and huge numbers of tourists.

One alternative is to take Hwy-503 from Portland (via I-5) to **Cougar**, on the mountain's southern side – dotted with ravines and lava caves, as well as ashen lahars – from where the summer-only forest roads USFS-90, -25, and -99 wind along its flanks to **Windy Ridge** on the northeast side of the mountain. Here you can see entire slopes denuded of foliage, colossal tree husks scattered like twigs, and huge dead zones where anything alive was vaporized. Windy Ridge can also be accessed from the north from **Randle** along USFS-25 and -99, passing through lava flows with numerous viewpoints en route.

Practicalities

The one-day **Monument Pass** ($8) allows entry to the Coldwater Lake Recreation Area and the Johnston Ridge Observatory; the **Northwest Forest Pass** ($5) is good for other sites, and is available through putting money in drop boxes at site parking lots. En route to Windy Ridge from Hwy-503 is **Mount St Helens Volcanic Monument Headquarters** (daily 8am–5pm; t360/449-7800) in Amboy, which has maps and information. Near Silver Lake on Hwy 504 is the **Mount St Helens Visitor Center** (daily 9am–4pm, summer closes 5pm; $3; Ⓣ360/274-0962, Ⓦwww.parks.wa.gov/mountsthelens.asp), complete with informative exhibits and a small-scale model of the volcano.

Though there aren't any campgrounds within the national monument, there are private **campgrounds** in the vicinity of Cougar (June–Aug only; $17; Ⓣ503/813-6666 for reservations): the Cougar campsite, located on Yale Reservoir just north of the village; Beaver Bay, about a mile north on 503; and Cresap Bay, two miles south of 503. Mountain **permits** are required for those interested in climbing above 4800 feet. From April to October, the time you'll most likely want to make the effort, only one hundred permits per day are given out, a fee is charged ($22), and you must reserve your permit ahead of time online at Ⓦwww.mshinstitute.org. You're required to pick up your permit at *Lone Fir Resort*, 16806 Lewis River Rd in Cougar (Ⓣ360/238-5210, Ⓦwww.lonefirresort.com; ❸), which has basic motel rooms, some with kitchens and microwaves, and RV and tent camping for $15–27. Better is the *Silver Lake Motel & Resort*, Hwy-504 six miles east of I-5 in Silver Lake (Ⓣ360/274-6141, Ⓦwww.silverlake-resort.com; ❺), where you can fish for bass from your balcony in waterfront rooms with kitchenettes, or try cabin sites with kitchens. It also has RV hookups ($27) and campsites ($17).

Eastern Washington

Olive-colored sagebrush covers many acres of **eastern Washington** and massive red rocks loom over the prairies, while huge bare patches of basalt and torn-away groundcover testify to the enduring effect of ancient Ice Age floods. To the south lies the lower Yakima Valley, with miles of orchards and farms, which make it one of the largest producers of apples in the world. Of eastern Washington's major towns, only **Spokane** has any degree of cultural life, but some are decent bases for outdoor activities such as fishing, hiking, and skiing.

Ellensburg

East of the mountains along I-90, 130 miles from Seattle, **ELLENSBURG** is the first notable stop. The dusty little burg of fetching nineteenth-century red-brick architecture is mainly known for its **Ellensburg Rodeo** (tickets start at $15; Ⓣ509/962-7831 or 1-800/637-2444, Ⓦwww.ellensburgrodeo.com), held over Labor Day weekend, with Stetson-clad cowhands roping steers, riding bulls, and braving bucking broncos; and the **Clymer Museum of Art**, 416 N Pearl St at 4th Ave (Mon–Fri 10am–5pm, Sat 10am–4pm, Sun noon–4pm; free; Ⓦwww.clymermuseum.com), which displays stylish Old West paintings alongside temporary exhibitions – everything from patchwork quilts and wheat weaving to cowboy poetry.

Greyhound stops at 1512 Hwy-97. The **visitor center**, 609 N Main St (Mon–Fri 8am–5pm, Sat 10am-2pm, also summer Sun 10am–2pm; Ⓣ509/925-3138, Ⓦwww.visitellen.com), provides maps and **hotel** options; one good choice is the *Inn at Goose Creek*, 1720 Canyon Rd (Ⓣ509/962-8030, Ⓦwww.innatgoosecreek.com; ④), whose ten rooms are themed around ideas like hunting, sports, Christmas, the rodeo, and so on, each with Internet access and a fridge. For something more conventional, the *Best Western Lincoln Inn*, 211 W Umptanum Rd (Ⓣ509/925-4244, Ⓦwww.bestwestern.com; ⑤), has rooms with microwaves and fridges, plus a pool, gym, and hot tub. The Art Deco *Valley Café*, 103 W Third Ave (Ⓣ509/925-3050), is a good place to **dine** on eclectic fare, from seafood coconut curry to chicken marsala.

Walla Walla

About 120 miles southeast of Yakima along I-82 and US-12, **WALLA WALLA** is also becoming known for its terrific wines, but is otherwise an uneventful college and agricultural town best known for its sweet onions – eaten raw like apples. This was the place where the missionary **Marcus Whitman** arrived from the East Coast in 1836, only to be martyred eleven years later when a band of natives murdered him, his wife, and eleven others. This was followed by swift action by the U.S Army to deal harshly with the local tribes, culprits or not.

The site where the **Whitman Mission** was burned down (daily 8am–4.30pm, summer until 6pm; $3; Ⓣ509/522-6360, Ⓦwww.nps.gov/whmi), seven miles west of town off US-12, has basic marks on the ground to illustrate its layout. Of more pseudo-historical value, the **Fort Walla Walla Museum**, 755 Myra Rd (April–Oct daily 10am–5pm; $7; Ⓦwww.fortwallawallamuseum.org), is a curious mock-up of a pioneer village, with replica shacks loaded with antiques and Old West dioramas.

Contact the **Walla Walla Wine Alliance** (Ⓣ509/526-3117, Ⓦwww.wallawallawine.com) for locations and opening hours of most area wineries, as well as maps. Walla Walla's **visitor center** is at 29 E Sumach St (Mon–Fri 9am–5pm; Ⓣ509/525-0850, Ⓦwww.wwchamber.com). The most prominent place to **stay** is the 1927 tower of the *Marcus Whitman Hotel*, 6 W Rose St (Ⓣ509/525-2200, Ⓦwww.marcuswhitmanhotel.com; ⑥), with a grand lobby, wine-tasting events, and complimentary breakfast. The best B&B is the *Inn at Blackberry Creek*, 1126 Pleasant St (Ⓣ509/520-7372, Ⓦwww.innatblackberrycreek.com; ⑤), whose three, artist-themed rooms have flat-screen TVs, DVD players, and, in selected rooms, a fireplace, wood stove, and/or jacuzzi. **Dining** is best enjoyed at the *Destination Grill*, 416 N 2nd Ave (Ⓣ509/529-3800), good for its prime rib, cocktails, and microbrews; and *CreekTown Cafe*, 1129 S 2nd Ave (Ⓣ509/522-4777), with tasty sandwiches, pasta, and burgers for lunch, and top-shelf oysters, salmon, and duck for dinner – plus a good selection of Walla Walla wine.

Spokane

A few miles from Idaho on I-90, **SPOKANE** ("spo-CAN"), eastern Washington's only real city of any size, has some grandiose late nineteenth-century buildings – built on the spoils of nearby Idaho silver mines – and its pleasant parks and striking architecture can nicely fill a day. The town's hub, hundred-acre **Riverfront Park**, was the site of the 1974 World's Fair and sprawls over two islands in the middle of the Spokane River, which tumbles down the rocky shelves of **Spokane Falls**. The **attractions** (day passes $14; June–Aug Sun–Thurs 11am–7pm, Fri & Sat 11am–9pm; Ⓦ www.spokaneriverfrontpark.com) include an ice-skating rink, the charming hand-carved **Looff Carousel** ($2), and the **Spokane Falls Skyride** ($7), which rises above the falls to take in a commanding view of the area.

Most of the relics of Spokane's early grandeur can be found several blocks southwest on West Riverside Avenue, where Neoclassical facades cluster around Jefferson Street. One architectural highlight is the **Clark Mansion**, 2208 W Second Ave, an 1897 marvel of lovely classical arcades and red-tiled roofs. Also check out the **Northwest Museum of Art and Culture**, 2316 W 1st Ave (Tues–Sun 11am–5pm; $7; Ⓦ www.northwestmuseum.org), which focuses on regional history and artwork, Native American culture, and fine arts from WPA-era paintings to items from nineteenth-century Japan and seventeenth-century Holland. Make sure to drop by the adjacent **Campbell House** (Tues–Sun 11am–5pm; free with museum admission), a restored Tudor Revival confection dreamed up for a silver baron in 1898.

Practicalities

Amtrak and Greyhound share the **transit center** at 221 W First St, and the **visitor center** is at 201 W Main St (Mon–Fri 9am–5pm, also summer Sat & Sun; Ⓣ 509/747-3230 or 1-800/776-5263, Ⓦ www.visitspokane.com). Nice **accommodations** include the 1914 *Davenport Hotel*, 10 S Post St (Ⓣ 1-800/899-1482, Ⓦ www.thedavenporthotel.com; ⑦), a stately 1914 pile that's been renovated to showcase its wildly ornate lobby and has spacious, well-designed suites; and the stylish *Hotel Lusso*, N One Post St (Ⓣ 509/747-9750, Ⓦ www.hotellusso.com; ⑥), whose rooms have nice amenities and wi-fi access, and whose suites are rich with designer furnishings, CD players, and fireplaces. There's also **camping** in Riverside State Park ($17–24; Ⓣ 509/456-3964), six miles northwest off Hwy-291. For **eating**, *Luna*, 5620 S Perry St (Ⓣ 509/448-2383), serves up delicious, pricey Northwest Cuisine and gourmet pizzas, while *Milford's Fish House*, 719 N Monroe St (Ⓣ 509/326-7251), is a favorite local spot for its chic seafood like pan-fried oysters, lobster tail, tuna cakes, and Manila clams.

Oregon

For nineteenth-century pioneers on the arduous Oregon Trail, the rich and fertile **Willamette Valley** was the promised land, and it's still the heart of the state's social, political, and cultural life. **Portland**, the biggest city, has a cozy European feel; **Salem**, the state capital, maintains a small-town air; and **Eugene**, at the southern foot of the valley, is a likable college community.

East of Portland, waterfalls cascade down mossy cliffs along the **Columbia River Gorge**, south of which looms the imposing presence of **Mount Hood**. Central Oregon is based around the popular recreation hub of **Bend**, while further south around **Grants Pass**, the major rivers carve steep gorges and make for some excellent whitewater rafting, and the liberal hamlet of **Ashland** offers a splash of culture with its annual Shakespeare Festival.

The **Oregon Coast**'s most northerly town, **Astoria**, enjoys a magnificent setting strewn with imposing Victorian homes, while farther south, wide expanses of sand are broken by jagged black monoliths, pale lighthouses look out from stark headlands, and rough cliffs conceal small, sheltered coves. Finally, the rugged deserts and lava fields of **Eastern Oregon** are much more remote, and some small towns still celebrate their cowboy roots with annual rodeos.

Wherever you go, try to pronounce the state's name as "OR-uh-gun"; calling it "or-EE-gone" will mark you as a tourist, and is sure to invite a quick correction.

Getting around Oregon

From Union Station at 800 NW Sixth Ave and an adjacent bus station, **Portland** is well connected by **train** and **bus** to Seattle in the north and California to the south. Amtrak runs its *Coast Starlight* train once daily north to Seattle or south to LA; the *Cascades* four times daily between Eugene and Seattle; and the *Empire Builder* daily east to Chicago. Bus routes radiate from Portland out to western and eastern Washington, across southern and central Oregon and to the coast. Finally, **cycling** throughout Oregon is a popular endeavor, especially along majestic stretches of coastal Hwy-101. Having your own vehicle can facilitate access to many of the state's more remote spots, particularly if you're planning to sample the great hiking and camping options on hand (see Ⓦ www.oregon.gov/OPRD).

Portland

With few major attractions and an unpretentious bohemian flavor, **PORTLAND** makes for an excellent spot to slow down and relax in the wealth of good diners, microbreweries, clubs, bookstores, and coffeehouses. Though sporting grand Beaux Arts architecture, Portland has a small-city feel thanks to a walkable urban core of short city blocks and attractions that cluster close together.

The city was named after Portland, Maine, following a coin toss between its two East Coast founders in 1845 ("Boston" was the other option). Its location on the **Willamette River**, just 78 miles from the Pacific, made it a perfect lumber and trading port, and it grew quickly, replacing its clapboard houses with ornate facades and Gothic gables. As a reminder of those days, the town's quirky **"Benson Bubblers"** – four-headed drinking fountains that are prime fixtures on downtown streets – are constantly flowing.

Arrival and information

Portland International Airport (PDX) is a twenty-minute drive from downtown, also accessed from Terminal C by the **MAX Red Line** light rail (every 5–20min, 5am–midnight; $2.25), which shuttles passengers on a 40min journey along the freeways before heading downtown along SW First Avenue and SW Morrison Street. A **cab** from the airport into town costs $30. Greyhound, 550 NW 6th Ave (Ⓣ503/243-2361), and Amtrak, close by at 800 NW 6th Ave (Ⓣ503/273-4865), are within walking distance of the center; if you arrive at night, take a cab – this part of town is dicey after dark.

The **visitor center**, in Pioneer Square at 701 SW 6th Ave (Mon–Fri 8.30am–5.30pm, Sat 10am–4pm, Sun 10am–2pm; Ⓣ503/275-8355, Ⓦ www.travelportland.com), has plenty of maps and information on both the city and the state. Portland's main **post office** is at 715 NW Hoyt St (Ⓣ503/294-2124; zip code 97205). Unlike most US states, Oregon has **no sales tax**, so buying goods here can be cheaper than in neighboring states.

City transportation

Although you can see much of the compact city center on **foot**, or along the city's impressive, extensive network of **cycling** paths and trails (visit ⓦ www.portlandonline.com/transportation for maps and information), Portland also has an excellent public transit network. Its **MAX light rail** system channels riders around central downtown and Old Town, connects to the western and eastern suburbs and north Portland, and tunnels under Washington Park and the zoo. Tri-Met **buses** are based at the downtown **transit mall** – whose original axis along Fifth and Sixth avenues is under construction to make way for a light-rail extension, so the main lines have temporarily relocated to Third and Fourth avenues. The **Tri-Met Ticket Office** in Pioneer Square (Mon–Fri 8.30am–5.30pm, unstaffed Sat 10am-4pm; ⓣ 503/238-7433, ⓦ www.trimet.org) offers free transit maps and sells all-zone day tickets ($4), regular fares ($1.65-1.95), and other passes.

The colorful **Portland Streetcar** line runs between the south waterfront, Portland State University, the Pearl District, and Northwest Portland, covering many downtown sights on NW and SW 10th and 11th streets. As with buses, **fares** are free inside Fareless Square – basically the downtown core – otherwise $1.95 (ⓦ www.portlandstreetcar.org). At the streetcar's southern terminus, at SW Moody Ave and Gibbs St, the splashy **Aerial Tram** (Mon–Fri 5.30am–9.30pm, Sat 9am–5pm, Sun 1–5pm; $4 round-trip; ⓦ www.portlandtram.org) connects the south waterfront to OHSU hospital 500ft up on Marquam Hill – a 3min ride that's great for viewing the beautiful landscape of trees, skyscrapers, and, on a clear day, Mount Hood. Finally, **taxis** don't stop in the street; get one at a hotel or call Broadway Cab (ⓣ 503/227-1234) or Portland Taxi Co. (ⓣ 503/256-5400).

Accommodation

Scads of flavorless **motels** line the interstates, but for a few dollars more you're far better staying downtown, where you'll find **hostels**, **B&Bs**, and a good range of **hotels**, the pick of which occupy grand and elegantly restored old buildings.

Hotels, motels, and B&Bs

Ace 1022 SW Stark St ⓣ 503/228-2277, ⓦ www.acehotel.com. Affordable boutique hotel with amenities like flat-screen TVs, in-room murals and other fun art, wi-fi Internet, photo booth, and convenient location two blocks from Powell's Books. ④

Benson 309 SW Broadway ⓣ 503/228-2000 or 1-888/523-6766, ⓦ www.bensonhotel.com. The spot for visiting dignitaries and celebs, this classy hotel has a superb walnut-paneled 1912 lobby, swank bedrooms with modern appointments, and a range of rooms, suites, and penthouses. ⑦

Edgefield 2126 SW Halsey St ⓣ 503/669-8610 or 1-800/669-8610, ⓦ www.mcmenamins.com/edge. Fifteen minutes east of the airport in the drab suburb of Troutdale, this unique brewery-resort features restaurants, bars, winery and tasting room, distillery, movie theater, gardens, and golf course. Also with its own hostel, at $40 per dorm bed. The cheapest doubles have shared baths. ③

Governor 611 SW 10th Ave ⓣ 1-800/554-3456 or 503-224-3400, ⓦ www.govhotel.com. Stylish 1923 Italian Renaissance Revival building rich with elegant rooms and suites with fireplaces, spas, sofas, and stylish décor, plus an onsite pool and fitness center. Centrally located a block from MAX and streetcar lines. ⑦

Heathman 1001 SW Broadway ⓣ 503/241-4100 or 1-800/551-0011, ⓦ www.heathmanhotel.com. Occupies a finely restored Neoclassical building, with an elegant, teak-paneled interior and much marble and brass. Splendid rooms and suites, high-def TV, excellent restaurant, and popular lobby-lounge where you can swill among the swells. ⑦

Heron Haus 2545 NW Westover Rd ⓣ 503/274-1846, ⓦ www.heronhaus.com. Stylish 1904 Tudor B&B, with some large suites featuring fireplaces, spas, and cozy sitting areas. Excellent continental breakfast and close hiking access to Portland's expansive Forest Park. ⑥

Hotel DeLuxe 729 SW 15th Ave ⓣ 1-866/986-8085, ⓦ www.hoteldeluxeportland.com. Chic luxury item with smart décor and onsite gym, plus wi-fi, iPod stations, and HDTVs in all the rooms. Well-placed along the MAX tracks, just west of downtown. ⑦

Inn at Northrup Station 2025 NW Northrup St ⓣ503/224-0543, ⓦwww.northrupstation.com. Convenient property poised on the streetcar line in Northwest Portland and offering a range of colorful suites with splashy retro designs, some with kitchens, patios, and wet bars. ❼

Jupiter 800 E Burnside ⓣ503/230-9200, ⓦwww.jupiterhotel.com. Converted chain motel that's now flush with arty minimalism, a party atmosphere, and the uber-cool presence of the adjoining *Doug Fir Lounge* (see p.1116). ❺

Kennedy School 5736 NE 33rd Ave ⓣ503/249-3983 or 1-888/249-3983, ⓦwww.mcmenamins.com/kennedy. Unique B&B rooms in a refurbished 1915 schoolhouse with chalkboards and cloakrooms, plus modern appointments. Excellent breakfast, multiple brewpubs, movie theater, outdoor bathing pool, and "detention bar." ❺

Monaco 506 SW Washington St ⓣ503/222-0001 ⓦwww.monaco-portland.com. Themed around a vaguely Asian-flavored style, this primo luxury spot appeals for its designer décor, free wi-fi, flat-panel TVs and DVD players, and central location in the downtown core. ❾

Vintage Plaza 422 SW Broadway ⓣ503/228-1212 or 1-800/263-2305, ⓦwww.vintageplaza.com. An intimate boutique hotel with tasteful rooms with free wi-fi and a calm, relaxed atmosphere. Wine is offered in the afternoons in the lobby. One of the city's few dog-friendly hotels. ❾

White Eagle 836 N Russell St ⓣ503/335-8900, ⓦwww.mcmenamins.com/eagle. Portland's best deal, a refurbished 1905 hotel and hip brewpub in an industrial-bohemian neighborhood. Rooms are clean, simple and cheap, with shared baths. Live music nightly downstairs – so early sleepers beware. $60, or bunk rooms for $40. ❶–❷

Hostels

HI-Portland Hawthorne 3031 SE Hawthorne Blvd ⓣ503/236-3380 or 1-866/447-3031, ⓦwww.portlandhostel.com. Nice Victorian house in the Hawthorne District, offering free wi-fi, tours of local sights, cheap bike rental, and occasional live music. $25 dorms, $51 private rooms.

HI-Portland Northwest 425 NW 18th Ave ⓣ503/241-2783, ⓦwww.nwportlandhostel.com. Located in a nineteenth-century home in Northwest Portland, near the popular Mission Theatre & Brewpub and just east of the main action on 21st and 23rd streets. Contains espresso bar, free wi-fi, kitchen, and fireplace. $25 dorms, private rooms $57.

The City

The **Willamette** (pronounced "wuh-LAM-it") **River** bisects Portland into its east and west sides, with **Burnside Street** delineating the north from the south; each street address describes its relation to these dividers – SE, NW, and SW, and NE (there's also N, which is everything east of the river and roughly west of I-5) . The **downtown core** lies between the river's west bank and the I-405 freeway, in the city's southwest section; the rest of town is mostly residential.

Downtown

Named after the adjacent **Pioneer Courthouse**, a squat 1868 structure that still maintains its judicial function, **Pioneer Courthouse Square** is the indisputable center of Portland. Surrounded by **downtown**'s historic white terracotta buildings, the square's curving brick terraces are constantly filled with music and people. Just south of the square, at SW Broadway and Salmon, you can take a two-and-a-half hour **walking tour** of city highlights (daily 10am; $19; ⓦwww.portlandwalkingtours.com), a good introduction for first-time visitors.

Broadway epitomizes Portland's mix of early grandeur and new wealth, with prestigious hotels sharing space with cultural institutions, such as the grand old Paramount movie theater, restored as part of the impressive **Portland Center for the Performing Arts**, 1111 SW Broadway (ⓦwww.pcpa.com). One block west, the **South Park Blocks** are a twelve-block green belt and favorite Portland hangout, under the shadow of statues of Teddy Roosevelt riding on to victory at San Juan Hill and a dour Abe Lincoln. Twice a week, the park hosts a popular **farmers' market** (May–Oct Wed 10am–2pm, April–Dec Sat 8.30am–2pm; ⓦwww.portlandfarmersmarket.org) that draws fruit and vegetable growers, and other vendors of bread, pastries, candles, and handicrafts. Looming nearby is the

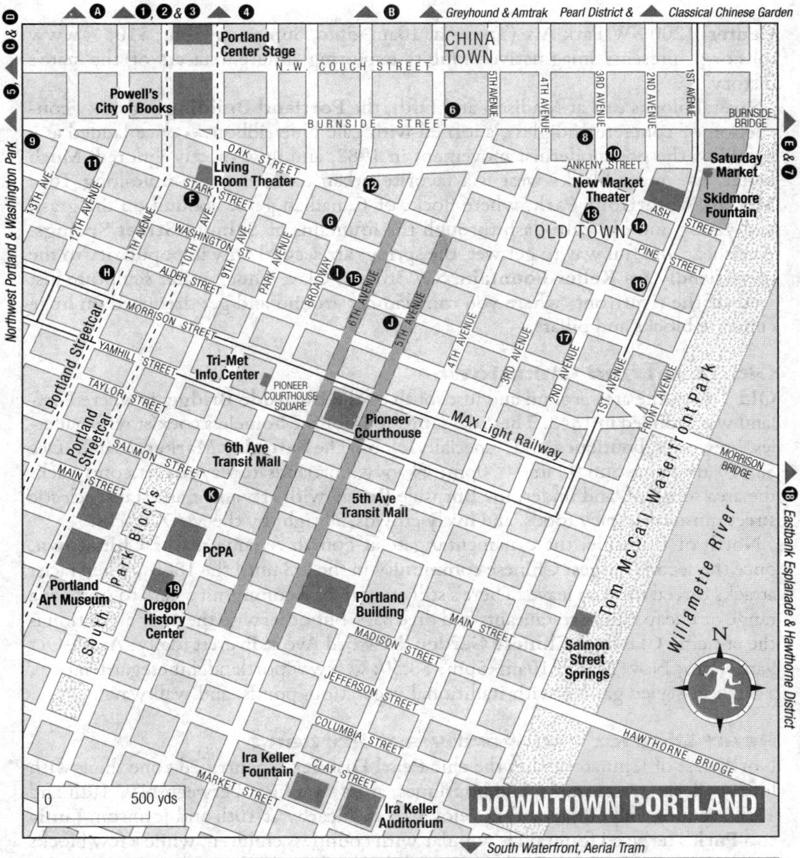

ACCOMMODATION				RESTAURANTS, BARS & CLUBS					
Ace	F	Inn at Northrup Station	A	Berbati's Pan	10	Jake's Famous Crawfish	11	Oba	3
Benson	G	Jupiter	E	Crystal Ballroom	9	Jimmy Mak's	4	Pazzo	15
Governor	H	Monaco	J	Dante's	8	Justa Pasta	1	Produce Row	18
Heathman	K	Vintage Plaza	I	Doug Fir	7	Kells	14	Roseland Theater	6
Heron Haus	D	White Eagle	B	Higgins	19	McCormick and Schmick's	16	Saucebox	12
Hotel DeLuxe	C			Hot Lips Pizza	2			Stumptown Roasters	13
				Huber's	17			Towne Lounge	5

grand **Simon Benson House**, Park at Montgomery St (Mon–Fri 9am–5pm; Ⓣ503/725-4948), a Queen Anne mansion that was the former home of one of the city's famous timber barons, featuring rooms paneled in different regional woods, graceful moon windows and horseshoe arches, and a lovely wraparound veranda.

Several blocks north, the **Portland Art Museum**, 1219 SW Park Ave (Tues, Wed & Sat 10am–5pm, Thurs & Fri 10am–8pm, Sun noon–5pm; $10; Ⓦwww.pam.org), has a wide-ranging collection of Northwest Native American masks, Mexican statues, and ancient Chinese figures. The real reason to visit the museum, though, is the **Mark Building**, which, with its underground entrance (accessed via the old wing) and six floors, holds a fine array of modern and postmodern works in various media, with part of the top floor reserved for temporary shows. Across the park, decorated with huge *trompe l'oeil* pioneer murals, the **Oregon History**

Center, 1200 SW Park Ave (Tues–Sat 10am–5pm, Sun noon–5pm; $10; Ⓦwww.ohs.org), presents imaginative exhibits exploring different facets of the state's history.

Several blocks east at Madison and Fifth, the **Portland Building** is a boxy concoction of concrete and glass, adorned with pale blue ribbons – once lauded as a herald of the postmodernist movement in 1982, and now mostly ignored. Much better, five more blocks west is a favorite urban oasis, the two-mile-long **Tom McCall Waterfront Park**, where flocks of Canadian geese abound on the grass, and young and old alike dash through the fountains of **Salmon Street Springs**. As a cheap and fun way to get wet, the springs are second only in popularity to the user-friendly **Ira Keller Fountain**, SW 3rd and Clay, a huge water sculpture just west of the riverfront, where you can clamber around and get drenched on huge concrete blocks and pillars.

Old Town and Chinatown

Old Town, the area around and just south of the **Burnside Bridge**, is where Portland was founded in 1843. These days, missions for the homeless coexist with galleries, brewpubs, boutiques, and, especially, clubs. The **Saturday Market** (March–Dec Sat 10am–5pm, Sun 11am–4.30pm; Ⓦwww.portlandsaturdaymarket.com) packs the area south of, and under, the Burnside Bridge with arts and crafts stalls, eclectic street musicians, spicy foods, and lively crowds, all right by the MAX tracks.

North of Burnside, the ornamental gate at Fourth Avenue marks **Chinatown**, once the second-largest Chinese community in the US until the 1880s, when racist attacks forced most to leave. There's still enough of a community here to support a range of cheap ethnic restaurants and dive bars, but otherwise the only attraction is the enticing **Classical Chinese Garden**, NW 3rd Ave at Everett (daily: April–Oct 9am–6pm; Nov–March 10am–5pm; $8.50; Ⓦwww.portlandchinesegarden.org), a Suzhou-styled garden with traditional vegetation, ponds, and walkways.

Pearl District and Northwest Portland

Northwest of Chinatown lies the chic **Pearl District**, a gentrified zone thick with lofts, galleries, restaurants, and boutiques, at its swankiest between NW 10th and 12th avenues, and Glisan and Lovejoy streets. Nearby at 10th and Johnson, **Jamison Park**'s terraced fountain is popular with countless children, while a few blocks north, **Tanner Springs Park** is one of the city's most distinctive green spaces, with a western wall of metal girders bordering sloping, marshy turf peppered with benches and indigenous plants. On the southern edge of the Pearl is Portland's biggest draw, the famed **Powell's City of Books**, 1005 W Burnside St (daily 9am–11pm; Ⓦwww.powells.com). With more than a million new, used, and rare books on four floors, Powell's occupies an entire block, as well as separate branches around town, and provides free color-coded maps so customers don't get lost.

Further west, what's known in travel brochures as Nob Hill is called **Northwest Portland** by locals. Stretching between Burnside and Pettygrove streets along NW 23rd and 21st avenues, the neighborhood is choked with fine restaurants and boutiques, the assortment of restored Victorian piles adding a San Francisco tinge.

Forest Park and Washington Park

A few miles west of Northwest Portland, the 5000-acre **Forest Park** (Ⓦwww.forestparkconservancy.org) is the country's largest urban green space, interlaced with countless hiking routes, including the thirty-mile **Wildwood Trail**, which can be accessed around NW 31st Avenue and Upshur Street; otherwise, follow NW Thurman until it dead-ends and take **Leif Erickson Drive** (closed to traffic) deep into the hills. South of Forest Park, the elegant houses of the wealthy include

▲ Powell's City of Books

Pittock Mansion, 3229 NW Pittock Drive (Feb–Dec daily 11am–4pm, opens 10am July & Aug; $7; Ⓦ www.pittockmansion.com), a 1914 French Renaissance Revival gem whose most attractive attribute may be its stunning – and free – view of the city from the front lawn.

Beyond the mansion, the 130-acre **Washington Park** is home to a number of Portland's top attractions. These include the lovely **International Rose Test Gar-**

den (daily 7.30am–9pm; free), planted in 1917 as a distant home for European rose blooms threatened by World War I, and still featuring a huge array of bright summertime blooms; the tranquil **Japanese Garden** (daily: April–Sept 10am–7pm; Oct–March 10am–4pm; $8; Ⓦ www.japanesegarden.com), actually a collection of five traditional gardens with ponds, bridges, foliage, and sand designs; and the **Oregon Zoo** (daily: April–Sept 9am–6pm; Oct–March 9am–4pm; $9.75; Ⓦ www.oregonzoo.org), with the requisite primates, penguins, and, this being the Northwest, beavers; however, the facility's real stars are its Asian elephants, now a herd of seven that in 1962 produced the first birth of an Asian elephant in the Western hemisphere.

Most park attractions have easy access to **MAX light rail** ($1.95 from downtown), whose station is buried deep underground and accessible only by elevator. Once you get here, you can hop on a summertime **shuttle** (every 15min daily: June–Sept 10am–7pm; $1.95) and access all the park's major sights on a day-pass ticket.

The Eastside

Since the end of the nineteenth century, most of the city's population has lived on the **Eastside**. Perhaps the best reason to venture across the river is to walk or bike the three-mile loop of the **Eastbank Esplanade**, which connects from the Hawthorne to the Steel bridges on floating walkways and cantilevered footpaths, offering striking views of downtown with the roar of nearby I-5 as a soundtrack. Near the loop's south end, the interactive exhibits and high-tech toys of the **Oregon Museum of Science and Industry (OMSI)**, 1945 SE Water Ave (hours vary, often Tues–Sun 9.30am–5.30pm; $11; Ⓦ www.omsi.edu), are bright and kinetic, though primarily geared toward children and adults with only a sketchy knowledge of science.

Two miles further east, the **Hawthorne District** is Portland's best alternative culture zone. With Hawthorne Boulevard as its axis between 34th and 45th streets, and dominated by the sparkly, quasi-Moorish 1927 *Bagdad Theater & Pub* at no. 3702 (Ⓣ 503/236-9234), the area teems with bookstores, hip cafés, dive bars, cheap restaurants, and only a handful of corporate chain stores. Six blocks north, **Belmont Avenue** is a short historic corridor thick with boutiques, novelty shops, and ethnic diners, centered around 34th Street, while a mile southwest around 26th Avenue, the pocket of **Clinton Street** is home to a few good restaurants, funky bars, and vintage clothiers.

Finally, intrepid Eastside explorers may wish to venture up to **NE Broadway**, between 12th and 20th streets, good for its ethnic and upscale restaurants; the galleries and diners of the gentrifying **North Mississippi District**, between Beech and Skidmore streets; the gallery- and boutique-rich stretch of **NE Alberta Street**, between 20th and 30th avenues, also on the leading edge of local gentrification; or the antique-buying center of **Sellwood**, several miles south of OMSI along Tacoma Street.

Eating

As in Seattle, Portland's Northwest Cuisine provides a mix of international cooking and fresh regional produce, and the city is becoming nationally famous for its many excellent **dining** options for all palates and pocketbooks. Downtown, the Pearl District and Northwest Portland and places around the Eastside have swank cocktail bars, upscale bistros, and fun brewpubs, while Hawthorne Boulevard and Belmont Avenue have the best cheap grub and ethnic diners.

Bombay Cricket Club 1925 Hawthorne Blvd ⓣ503/231-0740. Terrific mid-range restaurant a mile west of the main Hawthorne scene with some of the town's best Indian food. Dive right into the delicious vindaloos and tandooris.

Clay's Smokehouse Grill 2932 SE Division St, Eastside ⓣ503/235-4755. Among the top barbecue houses in town, serving up hearty brisket, ribs and pork sandwiches, spicy and delicious hot wings, and old-fashioned desserts like pineapple upside-down cake.

Esparza's 2725 SE Ankeny St, Eastside ⓣ503/234-7909. The height of Tex-Mex in the Pacific Northwest, a cheery place loaded with bric-a-brac and offering big plates of traditional fare like burritos with lamb or pork, as well as unconventional entrees like ostrich and alligator.

Higgins 1239 SW Broadway, downtown ⓣ503/222-9070. Fine Northwest cuisine restaurant, where fresh local ingredients and scrumptious desserts are the focus. Menu rotates, but watch for the cider-glazed pork loin and squash lasagne. Main courses around $20–30.

Hot Lips Pizza 721 NW 10th Ave, Pearl District ⓣ503/595-2342. A pizza joint serving what may be the city's best pies – complex, delicious concoctions that use organic, locally grown ingredients. Also at 2211 SE Hawthorne Blvd, Eastside (ⓣ503/234-9999).

Jake's Famous Crawfish 401 SW 12th Ave, downtown ⓣ503/226-1419. A landmark for more than a hundred years, with a staggering choice of fresh local seafood like sturgeon and Dungeness crab and spicy crawfish cakes. Terrific desserts, too. Lunch specials under $10.

Justa Pasta 1326 NW 19th Ave, NW Portland ⓣ503/243-2249. Unassuming spot serving some of the city's best and most affordable fine Italian fare, including savory soups, delicious pastas, and locally grown Painted Hills beef. The coconut cake and assorted ice creams are also a treat.

Lauro Kitchen 3377 Division St, Eastside ⓣ503/239-7000. A local favorite that doesn't need any publicity – even the mayor has to wait for a table on weekends. If you don't mind the delay, come for some of the city's best and most affordable Northwest cuisine.

McCormick and Schmick's 235 SW 1st Ave, downtown ⓣ503/224-7522. The first location of what's become a national chain of fine seafood restaurants, with fresh nightly specials and a lively oyster bar.

Oba 555 NW 12th Ave, Pearl District ⓣ503/228-6161. Flashy, expensive eatery that fuses flavors from all over Latin America and is most inviting during happy hour in the bar, when the succulent bar-menu entrees are mostly around $5.

Pazzo 621 SW Washington St, downtown ⓣ503/228-1515. Top-notch Italian and Northwest cuisine with a solid selection of fresh seafood and inventive pasta, just off the lobby of the *Vintage Plaza Hotel* (see p.1110).

Pix Patisserie 3402 SE Division, Eastside ⓣ503/232-4407. Local hot-spot with a colorful range of French desserts made by a Parisian-trained chef known as the "Pixie." Good for its international beers. Also at 3901 N Williams Ave, North Portland (ⓣ503/282-6539).

Pok Pok 3226 SE Division St, Eastside ⓣ503/232-1387. One of the city's best spots for Thai food – scrumptious curry noodles, green papaya salad, and pad Thai – though portions can be small. The adjoining takeout shack has much cheaper, but still excellent, food.

Siam Society 2703 NE Alberta St, Eastside ⓣ503/922-3675. While there are plenty of excellent, affordable Thai diners around town, this mid-level entry is a welcome sight, doling out innovative versions of Southeast Asian fare in a moody modern setting.

Nightlife

Portland is a beer-drinker's paradise, with more than thirty primo **microbreweries**, including *Rogue Ales Public House*, 1339 NW Flanders St (ⓣ503/222-5910); *Bridgeport Brewing*, 1313 NW Marshall St (ⓣ503/241-3612); and *Widmer Gasthaus*, 929 N Russell St (ⓣ503/281-3333). McMenamins "concept" brewpubs sell their own locally brewed ales in unique settings, such as former schoolhouses and renovated hotels (ⓦwww.mcmenamins.com), and Belmont Station, 4500 SE Stark St (ⓣ503/232-8538), is the town's greatest retail beer seller, featuring a huge range of labels from around the world. For **music**, Portland maintains a small but vital presence on the national map, with countless alternative bands. The coolest venues are located around east and west Burnside.

Bars, brewpubs, and coffeehouses

The Alibi 4024 N Interstate Ave, North Portland ☎503/287-5335. The pinnacle of Polynesian kitsch, a fun and somewhat divey joint that has cheap, powerful drinks, a spirited atmosphere, and a weekend karaoke scene that's among the city's best.

Amnesia Brewing 832 N Beech St ☎503/281-7700. Terrific summertime people-watching in this microbrewer's beer garden, set on a happening stretch of the North Mississippi District. Quaff a flavourful brew or sample a burger or a banger from the pub menu.

Goose Hollow Inn and Tavern 1927 SW Jefferson St ☎503/228-7010. Great microbrews, the city's top Reuben sandwich, and a convenient location near the MAX tracks, a mile west of downtown. Watch for colourful, bearded owner Bud Clark, the city mayor in the 1980s, best known for his slogan "Whoop! Whoop!"

Dot's Café 2521 SE Clinton St, Eastside ☎503/235-0203. Funky late-night spot decked out in garage-sale décor, offering good brews, the classic bacon cheeseburger, cheese fries, and a helluva grilled-cheese sandwich.

Horse Brass Pub 4534 SE Belmont St, Eastside ☎503/232-2202. Offers a voluminous beer list loaded with micro- and Eurobrews – considered one of the best around – and a savory British pub menu of Scotch eggs, bangers and mash, and the like. Fun atmosphere, too.

Huber's 411 SW 3rd Ave, downtown ☎503/228-5686. Portland's oldest bar is an elegant spot with an arched stained-glass skylight, mahogany paneling, and terrazzo floor. Famous for roast turkey sandwiches and flaming Spanish coffees.

Kells 112 SW 2nd Ave, downtown ☎503/227-4057. Longstanding Irish bar, with fine authentic Irish stews and soda bread, and a range of microbrews, imported beers, and of course, Irish (and Scotch) whiskey. Expect loud, drunken hijinks on weekends.

Lucky Labrador 915 SE Hawthorne Blvd, Eastside ☎503/236-3555. Dog-friendly brewpub occupying a large space with an outdoor patio. Fresh ales, great sandwiches, and BBQ specials.

Pied Cow 3244 SE Belmont Ave ☎503/230-4866. An Eastside favorite for its coffee, tea, and dessert. Set in a stately Victorian house, it offers late-night hours, lush garden seating, and the chance to puff fruit-flavored tobacco from a hookah pipe.

Produce Row 204 SE Oak St ☎503/232-8355. Be one of the rare tourists at this local institution. It's stuck in an unglamorous spot by the railroad tracks but is ideal for beer lovers, with dozens of taps and seemingly endless bottled brews. Also has a nice range of live music.

Rimsky-Korsakoffee House 707 SE 12th Ave, Eastside ☎503/232-2640. Excellent place to linger for hours over dessert and coffee. Immensely popular with bohemians and slackers.

Saucebox 214 SW Broadway, downtown ☎503/241-3393. Great pan-Asian cuisine, colorful cocktails, and nightly music that attracts black-clad poseurs and serious hipsters.

Stumptown Roasters 3356 SE Belmont Ave, Eastside ☎503/232-8889. Widely acknowledged as the city's best coffee, made from a blend of seven different types. The most convivial of a local chain, the others are at 4525 SE Division St, Eastside (☎503/230-7702), and 128 SW 3rd Ave, downtown (☎503/295-6144).

Live music and clubs

Berbati's Pan 10 SW 3rd Ave, downtown ☎503/248-4579. Overly large space has a nightly selection of eclectic bands – local to international – usually for $15 or less.

Blue Monk 3341 SE Belmont St ☎503/595-0575. A hip little spot along a rejuvenated Eastside stretch, where you can devour serviceable Italian food upstairs and hear the sounds of local jazz performers downstairs.

Crystal Ballroom 1332 W Burnside St, downtown ☎503/778-5625. Two levels above their *Ringlers* bar, a nineteenth-century dance hall with a "floating" floor on springs. Bands range from hippie to hip-hop and feature the best of Portland's indie rock and retro-DJs in "Lola's Room" on the floor above the bar.

Dante's 1 SW 3rd Ave, downtown ☎503/226-6630. Perhaps the city's hippest nightspot. Cabaret acts and live music mix with the club's signature "Sinferno" Sunday strip shows and "Karaoke from Hell" Mondays.

Doug Fir Lounge 830 E Burnside, Eastside ☎503/231-WOOD. For an underground space with limited room to groove, this is still one of the city's prime venues for alt-country, dance, and indie rock. The adjacent *Jupiter* hotel (see p.1110) can be handy for passing out afterwards.

Goodfoot 2845 SE Stark St, Eastside ☎503/239-9292. Frenetic live-music joint and dance club, always sweaty, smoky, and packed on weekends – but worth it to hear top-notch DJs spinning funk and retro-soul.

Holocene 1001 SE Morrison St, Eastside ☎503/239-7639. Packed with hipsters posing at point-blank range and an essential stop for local DJs and bands, *Holocene* mixes a range of cocktails and even broader spectrum of musical styles.

Jimmy Mak's 221 NW 10th Ave, downtown ⓣ503/295-6542. One of the few choices for nightly jazz in a town not known to swing. Come by to hear local Mel Brown or visiting name acts.

Roseland Theater 8 NW 6th Ave, downtown ⓣ503/224-2038. Located in one of the city's dicier corners, but a top spot for rock and alternative acts – often the last affordable venue for fans before the groups start touring stadiums.

Wonder Ballroom 128 NE Russell St ⓣ503/284-8686. A specially renovated old ballroom that now plays host to some of the more intriguing national and international acts in indie rock and other alternative styles. Just off a gritty stretch of MLK Blvd, so drive or take a cab.

Performing arts and film

The **performing arts** scene revolves around the **Portland Center for the Performing Arts**, 1111 SW Broadway (ⓣ503/248-4335, ⓦwww.pcpa.com), which includes the **Arlene Schnitzer Concert Hall**. The "Schnitz" is a sumptuously restored 1928 vaudeville and movie house that presents musical extravaganzas, dance, and theater, hosting performances by the **Oregon Symphony** (ⓣ503/228-1353, ⓦwww.orsymphony.org) and **Oregon Ballet Theater** (ⓣ503/222-5538, ⓦwww.obt.org), among others. Several blocks away at SW 3rd Ave, between Market and Clay, the **Ira Keller Auditorium** is home to traveling musicals and the **Portland Opera** (ⓣ503/241-1407, ⓦwww.portlandopera.org). **Portland Center Stage**, 128 NW 11th Ave (ⓣ503/445-3700, ⓦwww.pcs.org), is a premier theater troupe that offers contemporary and classical works in the stylish new-old space of a former armory converted into a fancy theatre complex.

If you're interested in catching a **film**, local favorites include Cinema 21, 616 NW 21st Ave (ⓣ503/223-4515, ⓦwww.cinema21.com), for foreign and independent movies; the Clinton, 26th Avenue at Clinton Street (ⓣ503/238-5588, ⓦwww.clintonsttheater.com), for art-house, cult, and underground cinema; the Living Room Theater, SW 10th Avenue at Stark (ⓣ971/222-2010), with a Northwest Cuisine eatery and screening rooms for modern indie works; and the grand Hollywood, 4122 NE Sandy Blvd (ⓣ503/281-4215, ⓦwww.hollywoodtheatre.org), for all of the above. The **Northwest Film Center**, at the Portland Art Museum, 1219 SW Park Ave (ⓣ503/221-1156, ⓦwww.nwfilm.org), shows art-house, foreign-language, and classic movies.

During the summer, **free concerts** are held at Pioneer Courthouse Square, Waterfront Park, the zoo, and the International Rose Test Garden. The free *Willamette Week* (ⓦwww.wweek.com) carries **listings** of what's on and where, as does the free *Portland Mercury* (ⓦwww.portlandmercury.com), and the Friday edition of the main local newspaper, *The Oregonian* (ⓦwww.oregonian.com). *Just Out* is the chief gay/lesbian publication (ⓦwww.justout.com).

Around Portland: the Columbia River Gorge and Mount Hood

East of Portland along the I-84 freeway, the **Columbia River Gorge** is a striking geological setting with gusty winds, craggy rocks, and incredible views. Scoured into a wide U-shape by huge Ice Age–era floods, the gorge is a nationally protected scenic area (ⓦwww.fs.fed.us/r6/columbia), where waterfalls tumble down sheer cliffs, and fir and maple trees turn fabulous shades of gold and red in the fall. Much more rugged in the nineteenth century before the arrival of modern dams, this was the ominous final leg of the Oregon Trail, where many pioneers met a dark end negotiating perilous rapids on flimsy wooden rafts.

The most dramatic part of the gorge is around the town of **Hood River**, where colorful windsurfers in the summer bound over the whitecapped waves, while rising to the south, the snowy peak of Mount Hood provides a romantic, mist-shrouded backdrop. The narrow, winding **Historic Columbia River Highway** (accessible at exits 22 or 35 off I-84) boasts several excellent vantage points, particularly at **Crown Point**, where the 1915 **Vista House** – perched high above the gorge about ten miles east of Troutdale – has restored to its original rustic grandeur (May-Oct daily 9am-6pm; free; ⓦwww.vistahouse.com). Further east, some highway sections are closed to automotive traffic, but open to hikers and cyclists, while down on the Columbia River itself (I-84 exit 25) is **Rooster Rock State Park** ($3; ⓣ503/695-2261), popular with windsurfers but best known for offering one of the few nude, or clothing-optional, beaches in the region.

The most spectacular of the waterfalls in the vicinity is **Multnomah Falls** (daily dawn–dusk; free; ⓣ503/695-2372), the second-tallest year-round waterfall in the US, whose waters plunge 530ft down a rock face, collect in a pool, and then drop another seventy feet. As it is the state's most popular natural attraction, the crowds here can get quite thick. Further east, **Bonneville Dam** (daily 9am–5pm; free; ⓣ541/374-8820) is a huge New Deal project that generates regional electricity and offers a chamber where you can see salmon making their way upstream.

Mount Hood

To the south along Highway 35, **Mount Hood** is a dormant volcano rising about eleven thousand feet, the tallest peak in the Oregon Cascades. The **Mount Hood Loop** – a combination of highways 35 and 26 – takes in both the mountain and the gorge. One of the joys of the area is to explore the mountain via trails radiating out from its slopes; contact Mount Hood Information Center (see below) for information. The highest point on the loop at some 4000ft, **Barlow Pass** is named after Sam Barlow, a wagon-train leader who blazed the first "road" around the mountain, which became the unpleasant, precipitous alternative to the even more dangerous Columbia River route on the Oregon Trail.

Near the intersection of highways 35 and 26, a turn-off leads to the rough-hewn stone of **Timberline Lodge** (ⓣ1-800/547-1406, ⓦwww.timberlinelodge.com; $155), a grand affair, solidly built in rough-hewn stone and timber with an interior loaded with Arts and Crafts–style wooden furniture and antique fittings. This colossal New Deal structure is also a popular ski resort (ⓣ503/622-0717; lift tickets $49), and was the exterior set for Stanley Kubrick's *The Shining*. Two other downhill ski areas – Mount Hood Meadows (ⓦwww.skihood.com; $54) and Mount Hood SkiBowl (ⓦwww.skibowl.com; $39) – are good alternatives, though without the handsome lodge. There are also many miles of cross-country skiing trails throughout the **Mount Hood National Forest**. For more information on mountain activities and lodging, contact Mount Hood Information Center (Mon–Fri 9am–5pm; ⓣ1-888/622-4822, ⓦwww.mthood.info).

Hood River

Adjacent to the Columbia River, north of Mount Hood, charming little **HOOD RIVER** is a hub for river windsurfing and mountain biking, with outfitters' shops lining the hillside streets and **Port Marina Park** to take in the windsurfers traversing the waves. One of the most exquisite **places to stay** in the entire region is the *Columbia Gorge Hotel*, just off I-84 at the far west end of town, at 4000 Westcliff Drive (ⓣ1-800/345-1921, ⓦwww.columbiagorgehotel.com; ❼), where hacienda-style buildings perch on a clifftop right above the gorge, and the hotel's exquisite gardens even have their own waterfalls. More central, *Inn at the Gorge*, 1113 Eugene St (ⓣ541/386-4429, ⓦwww.innatthegorge.com; ❺), is a stately 1908 Colonial Revival home that's been transformed into a tasteful, elegant B&B with minimal Victorian kitsch. For **eating** and **drinking**, *Full Sail Brewing*, 506 Columbia St (ⓣ541/386-2247), is a fine local microbrewery; the *Sixth Street*

Bistro, 509 Cascade Ave (Ⓣ541/386-5737), has some solid burgers and American fare; and *Mike's Ice Cream*, 504 Oak St (Ⓣ541/386-6260), is known for its marionberry milkshakes. The **visitor center**, in Port Marina Park (Ⓣ1-800/366-3530, Ⓦwww.hoodriver.org), provides information on all the regional attractions, including the engaging summertime **fruit loop** (Ⓦwww.hoodriverfruitloop.com), a driving concourse that connects to growers of cheap and delicious apples, pears, cherries, and peaches. Covering the same area, the charming, antique blue-and-red trains of the **Mount Hood Railroad** (Ⓣ541/386-3556 or 1-800/872-4661, Ⓦwww.mthoodrr.com), offer a twenty-mile sightseeing trip (4hr 15min) down along the Hood River Valley, using a railway that was built in 1906 to service the valley's agricultural communities. Trains depart from the old railway station at 110 Railroad Ave, just off Second Street (April–Dec; 2–6 weekly; $25–30; departures at 10am and/or 3pm).

The Willamette Valley

South of Portland, the **WILLAMETTE VALLEY** has a diverse agricultural scene, but is best known for its grapes. The scenic route through wine country, Hwy-99 W, accesses dozens of acclaimed **wineries**, most of which pour superb Cabernets, Rieslings and – attracting international attention – pinot noirs. Pick up a wine-country tour map from any local visitor center (or Ⓦwww.oregonwine.org). In **Dayton**, the renowned *Joel Palmer House*, 600 Ferry St (Ⓣ503/864-2995, Ⓦwww.joelpalmerhouse.com), draws Portland urbanites for its delicious, if expensive, Northwest cuisine; the same excellent fare can be found in tiny **Dundee** at *Tina's*, 760 Hwy 99W (Ⓣ503/538-8880). Solid choices for **accommodation** include *Lobenhaus*, 6975 NE Abbey Rd near Lafayette (Ⓣ1-888/339-3375, Ⓦwww.lobenhaus.com; ⑦), with six modern B&B rooms, some with views of gardens, a pond, and woods, and *Springbrook Hazelnut Farm*, 30295 N Hwy 99W, Newberg (Ⓣ1-800/793-8528 or 503/538-4606, Ⓦwww.nutfarm.com; ⑧), a grand old 1912 estate built around a restored farmhouse with a cottage and carriage house among orchards and vineyards.

While the heart of wine country can be found less than an hour southwest of Portland, due south, Highway 99W passes historic **Oregon City**, the first state capital, at the end of the Oregon Trail. Today, the only reasons to stop are the **John McLoughlin House**, 713 Center St (Wed–Sat 10am–4pm, Sun 1–4pm; donation; Ⓦwww.mcloughlinhouse.org), the 1846 dwelling of a trail pioneer that's loaded with artifacts and details on local history; and the **End of The Oregon Trail Interpretive Center**, 1726 Washington St (March–Oct: Mon–Sat 9.30am–5pm, Sun 10.30am–5pm; Nov–Feb: Tues–Sat 11am–4pm; $8; Ⓦwww.endoftheoregontrail.org), housed in a trio of giant, imitation covered-wagon buildings, which hold dioramas, replica antiques, and documentary films – and staff in period costume.

Continuing south through the valley on I-5, the main reason to stop in **SALEM** is to see the modern, white Vermont-marble **State Capitol**, 900 Court St NE (Mon–Fri 8am–5pm; free; tours at Ⓣ503/986-1388), whose cupola is topped by a large gold-leaf pioneer, axe in hand, eyes to the West, and **Mission Mill Village**, 1313 Mill St SE (Mon–Sat 10am–5pm; $8; Ⓦwww.missionmill.org), a collection of well-preserved pioneer buildings and a gloomy, nineteenth-century woolen mill. If you're **camping**, head for the huge waterfalls and lush forests of **Silver Falls State Park** (Ⓣ503/873-8681; $16–21), 26 miles east of Salem, the state's most popular park – so reserve many weeks (or months) in advance. In the general area, the valley also has some of the best examples of **covered bridges**, with thirty-four in the state spanning creeks from Albany to Cottage Grove (see Ⓦ coveredbridges.stateoforegon.com).

Eugene

Student and hippie central, **EUGENE** is a liberal enclave where Ken Kesey and some of his Merry Pranksters came to live after retreating from California. It's an energetic cultural center, to which the **University of Oregon** in the city's southeast corner lends a youthful bohemian feel, especially along 13th Avenue just west of campus. The campus is most worth visiting for its **Jordan Schnitzer Museum of Art** (Wed 11am–8pm, Thurs–Sun 11am–5pm; $5; Ⓦ uoma.uoregon.edu), the jewels of which are a Cézanne watercolor, Asian art and artifacts (among them Japanese ceramics, lacquerware, textiles, and gowns), and Russian Orthodox icons. Another major attraction is the **Saturday Market**, Eighth Ave and Oak St (April–Nov 10am–5pm; Ⓦ www.eugenesaturdaymarket.org), something of a neo-hippie carnival with live folk music, plenty of handicrafts, and street performers. Eugene is also a prime spot for **sports**, and trails abound in the city center, along the river banks, and up imposing **Spencer's Butte**, a huge basalt monolith south of town. Especially appealing, north of the Willamette River from downtown and the university, is four-hundred-acre **Alton Baker Park**, with running and BMX tracks, rock and other gardens, an amphitheatre for hosting seasonal events and concerts, and a science museum.

Ten miles west of Eugene on US-126, little **Veneta** hosts the **Oregon Country Fair** (tickets $18–21; Ⓣ 541/343-4298, Ⓦ www.oregoncountryfair.org) in July, a countercultural festival of music, art, food, and dancing. Traffic can be heavy, and even if you have a car it's easier to go by bus – the LTD (see below) operates special services.

Practicalities

Greyhound stops at 987 Pearl St, and Amtrak at Fourth Ave and Willamette St. Eugene has a terrific bus system, the LTD ($1.25; Ⓣ 541/687-5555, Ⓦ www.ltd.org), offering day passes for $2.50, and 50¢ rides on the "Breeze" shuttle linking downtown and the university. The **visitor center** is at 754 Olive St (Mon–Fri 9am–5pm, Sat 10am–4pm; Ⓣ 541/484-5307, Ⓦ www.visitlanecounty.org). The best **places to stay** include the *Campbell House*, 252 Pearl St (Ⓣ 541/343-1119 or 1-800/264-2519, Ⓦ www.campbellhouse.com; ❺), an elegant 1892 Victorian home with twenty rooms; and *Excelsior Inn*, 754 E 13th Ave (Ⓣ 541/342-6963 or 1-800/321-6963, Ⓦ www.excelsiorinn.com; ❺), a small hotel with fourteen rooms and suites, plus a fine, onsite Northwest cuisine restaurant. The *Eugene International Hostel*, 2352 Willamette St (Ⓣ 541/349-0589), offers free wi-fi and twenty clean and comfortable dorm beds (❶) and private rooms (❷).

Of Eugene's better places to **eat**, *Café Zenon*, 898 Pearl St (Ⓣ 541/343-3005), has an eclectic menu rich with international fare; *Chanterelle*, 207 E 5th Ave (Ⓣ 541/484-4065), is an intimate French bistro; and *Marché*, 296 E Fifth Ave, ground floor of 5th Street Market (Ⓣ 541/342-3612), provides a successful blend of French and Northwest cuisine, with expensive but exquisite wild salmon, duck, and lamb. Live **music** is also big in town. *Jo Federigo's*, 259 E 5th Ave (Ⓣ 541/343-8488, Ⓦ www.jofederigos.com), has nightly jazz and serves solid Italian cuisine, while funky *WOW Hall*, 291 W 8th Ave (Ⓣ 541/687-2746, Ⓦ www.wowhall.org), showcases up-and-coming rockers. For a taste of the music scene near the university, stroll along **13th Avenue** and hear the indie rock and punk wafting out from the bars and clubs.

South to California

South of Eugene along I-5, unenticing **Grants Pass** is a great base for **whitewater rafting** – the visitor center, just off I-5 at 1995 NW Vine St (Ⓣ541/476-5510, Ⓦwww.visitgrantspass.org), provides brochures from more than a dozen licensed river guides. Beyond Grants Pass, I-5 dips southeast through **Ashland** (see below), taking a mountainous inland route to California, while thirty miles southwest of Grants Pass along US-199, at the dull burg of **Cave Junction**, Hwy-46 veers east twenty miles to the **Oregon Caves National Monument** (90min tours daily April–Nov: hours vary, often 9am–5pm; $8.50; Ⓣ541/592-2100, Ⓦwww.nps.gov/orca). Tucked in a wooded canyon and kept at a temperature of 41°F, it's actually one enormous cave, with small branching passages, where the marble walls are covered with elaborate stalactites, stalagmites, and flowstone. Close to the cave entrance is the appealing *Oregon Caves Chateau*, 2000 Caves Hwy (May-Oct; Ⓣ1-877/245-9022, Ⓦwww.oregoncave.com; ④), an elegant 1930s lodge with grand public rooms. You can also try one of the **campgrounds** along Hwy-46, with *Grayback* and *Cave Creek* being the closest to the monument ($10–16; Ⓣ541/592-2166 for reservations).

Ashland and the Shakespeare Festival

The progressive hamlet of **ASHLAND**, forty miles southeast of Grants Pass, is mainly known for its **Oregon Shakespeare Festival**, held between February and October, packing audiences into the half-timbered **Elizabethan Theatre**. The town's Rogue River Valley setting is magnificent, with good skiing in the winter and rafting in summer. There's also some excellent fringe theater – not to mention pleasant cafés, galleries, and boutiques, especially around the **Historic Railroad District** (Ⓦwww.ashlandrrdistrict.com) a few blocks north of the festival.

The **Angus Bowmer Theatre**, adjacent to the Elizabethan Theatre, stages both Shakespearean and more recent works, while the austere **New Theatre** has a mostly modern repertoire. The three theaters share the same box office, 15 S Pioneer St (tickets $20–81; Ⓣ541/482-4331, Ⓦwww.osfashland.org). For a dose of musical comedy to relieve the drama, try the **Oregon Cabaret Theater**, in a renovated pink church at First and Hargadine ($21–32; Ⓣ541/488-2902, Ⓦwww.oregoncabaret.com).

The **visitor center** is at 110 E Main St (Mon–Fri 9am–5pm; Ⓣ541/482-3486, Ⓦwww.ashlandchamber.com). Greyhound **buses** drop passengers on the edge of town near the I-5 freeway exit. Ashland has more than sixty **B&Bs**, many of which are in charming Victorian homes; the Ashland B&B Network (Ⓣ1-800/944-0329, Ⓦwww.abbnet.com) has information on most of them. The best **hotel** is the grand and centrally located *Ashland Springs*, 212 E Main St (Ⓣ1-888/795-4545, Ⓦwww.ashlandspringshotel.com; ⑦), with its charming two-story lobby, day spa, afternoon tea, and small but nicely appointed rooms; the *Winchester Inn*, 35 S 2nd St (Ⓣ541/488-1113, Ⓦwww.winchesterinn.com; ⑦), has en-suite rooms and attractive gardens; and the top budget option is the well-placed *Ashland Hostel*, 150 N Main St (Ⓣ541/482-9217, Ⓦwww.theashlandhostel.com; ① dorm beds, ③ private rooms). The main choices for **eating** are found along **Main Street**, near the entrance to Lithia Park. The choices vary widely, from the eclectic entrees of the upscale French *Chateaulin*, 50 E Main St (Ⓣ503/482-2264), to the cheap but tasty pasta, burgers, salads, and seafood of *Greenleaf*, 49 N Main St (Ⓣ541/482-2808), to the elite Northwest Cuisine fare of *Larks*, 212 E Main St in the *Ashland Springs* Hotel (Ⓣ1-888/795-4545). If you come in the summer, head twenty miles northwest to the preserved Old West hamlet of **Jacksonville** for the annual **Britt Festival** (June-Aug; tickets $24-52; Ⓣ1-800/882-7488; Ⓦwww.brittfest.org), to hear the top names in jazz, pop, and country music.

The Oregon coast

The **Oregon coast** offers four hundred beautiful, moody, and often secluded miles of stunning terrain, almost all of it public land, where parks and campgrounds abound, and the extensive beaches are open for hiking, beachcombing, shell-fishing, and whale-watching. Although its shoreline hasn't escaped commercialism, the Oregon coast remains one of the least exploited in the entire US.

A number of coastal state parks offer accommodation in the form of seaside **cabins** and **yurts** – domed circular tents with wooden floors, electricity, and lockable doors, as well as bunk beds and a futon (yurts $27–39 per night, cabins $20–66; ⓣ1-800/452-5687, ⓦwww.oregonstateparks.org). Alternatively, you can **camp** for $16–22 at various sites on the coast.

For the most scenic transportation along the waves, **cycling** is always a good option, whether within the state parks, along US-101 (following the coastline to the California border), or on the many smaller "scenic loop" roads. Pick up a coastal bike route map from any major visitor center.

Astoria

Set near the mouth of the Columbia River, the port of **ASTORIA** was founded in 1811 as a base for exporting furs to Asia by John Jacob Astor, but nowadays many of Astoria's rusty canneries and nautical facilities have vanished, as the city has reinvented itself for tourists as a sprightly, well-scrubbed boutique town. From the east, the main road, **Marine Drive**, runs parallel to the waterfront, about eight miles from the Pacific Ocean. Exhibits from Astoria's seafaring past are on display at the **Columbia River Maritime Museum**, 1792 Marine Drive (daily 9.30am–5pm; $8; ⓦwww.crmm.org), which also features impressive displays of scrimshaw, native artifacts, and reconstructed ships, as well as several walrus-tusk Inuit sculptures sold as scrimshaw souvenirs to visiting sailors.

From Marine Drive, numbered streets climb up towards fancy Victorian mansions, many now renovated B&Bs, leading to the top of Coxcomb Hill, where the **Astoria Column** is decorated with a winding mural depicting pioneer history, and offers stunning views for anyone willing to climb its 164 cramped spiral stairs. Back in town, further west, the **Flavel House**, 441 8th St (daily: summer 11am–4pm; rest of the year 10am–5pm; $5; ⓣ503/325-2203), is one of the grandest of the city's mansions, the impressive, 1886 Queen Anne home of sea captain George Flavel, featuring main rooms set up as dioramas featuring period furniture and décor.

Less than ten miles south of Astoria, reached by a turnoff on Hwy-101, **Fort Clatsop National Memorial** (daily: summer 9am–6pm; rest of the year 9am–5pm; $5; ⓦwww.nps.gov/lewi) is the main historic highlight of the North Coast. While it's only a replica of the Lewis and Clark's winter camp, the various exhibits, reconstructions, and activities make it well worth seeking out — though in the summer, off-site parking (to accommodate all the visitors) is often necessary, at the water launch at Netul Landing, a mile south of the site off Fort Clatsop Road, where you can ride a **shuttle** back to the visitor center. Further west, also off US-101, **Fort Stevens State Park** (day-use fee $3; campsites $18–22, yurts $30; ⓣ1-800/452-5687) offers good trails and miles of beaches. The fort was developed as a Union post in the Civil War, and was shelled during World War II by a passing Japanese submarine, which makes it the only military installation on the mainland US to have been fired on by a foreign government since 1812.

Practicalities

Bus or train access to this part of the coast is limited, but Amtrak operates a once-daily bus service that drops off at the **visitor center** at 111 W Marine Drive (summer daily 8am–6pm; winter Mon–Fri 9am–5pm; ⓣ503/325-6311, ⓦwww.oldoregon.com), near the base of the US-101 bridge over the Columbia, which leads into southwest Washington. To make a leisurely trip along the waterfront, hop aboard the **Astoria Trolley** (summer daily noon–7pm; rest of year Fri–Sun 1–4pm; $1), historic rail cars that ply a tourist-oriented route. Many of Astoria's distinctive offerings are its **B&Bs,** many of them in Victorian mansions. Among the best is the *Rosebriar*, 636 14th St (ⓣ1-800/487-0224, ⓦwww.rosebriar.net; ❹), a renovated, modernized 1902 convent with great river views. For fancier digs, the *Hotel Elliott*, 357 12th St (ⓣ1-877/EST-1924, ⓦwww.hotelelliott.com; ❽), is a historic 1924 charmer with upscale amenities in its rooms and suites, some with fireplaces and jacuzzis, while *Cannery Pier*, 10 Basin St, near the Astoria Bridge (ⓣ503/325-4996 or 1-888/325-4996, ⓦwww.cannerypierhotel.com; ❾), is a swank boutique property housed on a waterfront pier, whose sleek modern rooms have high-speed Net access, fireplaces, and balconies.

Good places to **eat** include *Baked Alaska*, 1 12th St (ⓣ503/325-3554), which has fine entrées like sturgeon, oysters, and Dungeness crab, as well as the delicious eponymous dessert, and the *Wet Dog Café*, on the waterfront at 144 11th St (ⓣ503/325-6975), a prominent hangout with reasonable bar food, decent microbrews, and live music; also good for **drinking** is *Rogue Ales*, 100 39th St (ⓣ503/325-5964), which serves up its signature microbrews and burgers and seafood right on the water a bit east of town.

Cannon Beach

Seventeen miles south of Astoria, **Seaside** is a drab resort of carnival rides and chain motels, the one spot on the Oregon coast nature-lovers avoid, but another nine miles south, the more upmarket and pleasant **CANNON BEACH** is most known for its 240ft **Haystack Rock**, a black monolith crowned with nesting seagulls – accessible at low tide, though definitely not climbable. The place is at its liveliest during the mid-June **Sandcastle Competition**, a one-day event that draws artistic sand-crafters and hapless muck-shovelers from around the region. You're apt to see anything from sand dinosaurs and sphinxes to mermaids and monkeys, with Jesus and Elvis also putting in frequent appearances. To escape the town's crush of tourists, head four miles north to **Ecola State Park**, where dense conifer forests decorate the basaltic cliffs of Tillamook Head, or south to **Oswald West State Park**, named after the pioneering governor who helped preserve most of the state's beaches, where there's a beautiful beach, rocky headland, and coastal rainforest. The park's tent-only **campground** (Mar-Oct only; $14) is popular with surfers in wetsuits and provides wheelbarrows to transport your gear to the site.

The **visitor center** is at 207 N Spruce St (ⓣ503/436-2623, ⓦwww.cannonbeach.org). In town, **accommodation** is tight, especially in the summer. *Cannon Beach Hotel*, 1116 S Hemlock St (ⓣ1-800/238-4107, ⓦwww.cannonbeachhotel.com; ❻), is a cozy boutique hotel with smart, modern furnishings and tasteful appointments, while the *Waves Motel*, 188 W Second St (ⓣ503/436-2205 or 1-800/822-2468, ⓦwww.thewavesmotel.com; ❺), has agreeable studios and suites, sited on the seafront for about $100 more. For **food**, *Newman's at 988*, 988 S Hemlock (ⓣ503/436-1151), provides pricey Continental fare that's fresh and succulent, from duck breast and the catch of the day to beef medallions and lobster ravioli, and *Bill's Tavern & Brewhouse*, 188 N Hemlock St (ⓣ503/436-2202), is the town's busiest **bar**, offering bar fare along with their own handcrafted brews.

▲ Haystock Rock, Cannon Beach

Tillamook to Newport

Forty-four miles south of Cannon Beach, **TILLAMOOK** is famous mainly for its **Tillamook Cheese Factory**, just north of town on US-101 (daily 8am–6pm, summer closes 8pm; free; Ⓦwww.tillamookcheese.com), where on a self-guided tour you can watch cheese evolve from milky liquid in large vats to yellow and orange bricks on conveyor belts, and sample ice cream in the process.

South of Tillamook, Highway 101 curves around bucolic inland valleys, but better is the lengthier alternative of the **Three Capes Scenic Loop**, which leads you on a circuitous trip lurching around long bays and jagged promontories, across lowlands and around hillsides, until the road merges with Highway 101 west of the coastal **Siuslaw National Forest**.

Further south, there's no avoiding **Lincoln City**, the ugliest town on the Oregon coast, sprawling along the highway for seven congested, dreadful miles, but hold out for another thirty miles and you'll reach **NEWPORT**, where the **Historic Bayfront** along Bay Boulevard is the obvious first stop for many – with its souvenir shops, seafood diners, and sea lions wallowing on the wharves – along with pleasant **Nye Beach**, a quiet oceanside gem further west. To the south, across the bridge at 2820 SE Ferry Slip Rd, the impressive **Oregon Coast Aquarium** (daily summer 9am–6pm; rest of year 10am–5pm; $14.25; Ⓦwww.aquarium.org) is home to marine mammals like the sea otter and seal, seabirds like the tufted puffin, and a whopping octopus in a glass-framed sea grotto, but its highlight is Passages of the Deep, a shark-surrounded underwater tunnel. Just north of town, Newport's other top attraction is **Yaquina Head** (daily dawn–dusk; $5), an officially, and deservedly, decreed "Outstanding Scenic Area" with informative marine biology center, striking cape lighthouse, manmade tidepools, and jaunty seals and sea lions playing on the shoreline rocks.

Practicalities

Newport's Greyhound station is at 956 SW 10th St, and the chamber of commerce is at 555 SW Coast Hwy (Ⓣ541/265-8801, Ⓦwww.newportchamber

.org). The most prominent place to stay is the well-worn Sylvia Beach Hotel, on Nye Beach at 267 NW Cliff St (541/265-5428, www.sylviabeachhotel.com; 4), whose twenty rooms each bear the name of a famous writer, from Melville to Dickinson. Newport also has some good B&Bs (details at www.moriah.com/npbba), with charming amenities set in historic houses and estates, among the finest being the Tyee Lodge, 4925 NW Woody Way (1-888/553-8933, www.tyeelodge.com; 6); where six comfortable and modern B&B units have expansive oceanfront views. Also worthwhile is Elizabeth Street Inn, 232 Elizabeth St (541/265-9400 or 1-877/265-9400, www.elizabethstreetinn.com; 7), whose sizable rooms have kitchenettes, microwaves, fireplaces, and sea-facing balconies, and there's an onsite spa, gym, and pool.

There's a cluster of first-rate **cafés** and **restaurants** on Bay Boulevard at the bayfront. *Mo's Original*, in the 600 block (541/265-2979), is the most conspicuous chowder house, but better is *Chowder Bowl*, 728 NW Beach Dr (541/265-7477), which, despite its unexceptional look, does serve the best bowl in town. *Rogue Ales Public House*, no. 748 (541/265-3188), is the liveliest spot for food and beer, and also offers one- and two-bedroom "Bed and Beer" hotel units ($90–130, plus two complimentary bottles) so you don't have to risk driving away drunk. Near Nye Beach, *Cafe Stephanie*, 411 NW Coast St (541/265-8082), is a good place to go for sandwiches, fish tacos, and solid salmon chowder, with solid breakfasts, too.

Oregon Dunes National Recreation Area

Beginning at the town of Florence, colossal sand dunes dominate the coast for 45 miles, punctuated with dramatic pockets of forest and lake, and rise up to an incredible 180ft high but are infrequently visible from Highway 101. About half of them, however, are accessible to the public in the **Oregon Dunes National Recreation Area**, part of the Siuslaw National Forest ($5 day-use fee; www.fs.fed.us/r6/siuslaw). The US Forest Service, which manages the dunes, maintains seventeen evocative **hiking trails** that are, for the most part, free of ATVs and proceed through a variety of terrains. The paths are described in a free booklet, *Hiking Trails in the Oregon Dunes*, available from local visitor centers and the **Oregon Dunes National Recreation Area Visitor Center**, 855 Highway Ave (summer daily 8am–4.30pm, rest of the year Mon–Fri same hours; 541/271-6000), at the junction of Highway 101 and Hwy 38, twenty miles south of Florence.

Bandon

At the mouth of the Coquille River along US-101, easygoing **BANDON** has in the last decade been reinvented from a quaint beach town into a successful golf resort, with the usual souvenir shops, chain stores, and motels to choose from. However, the main attraction is still its rugged **beach**, strewn with unusual rock formations and magnificent in stormy weather. In calmer conditions, clam-diggers head off to the river's mudflats, crabbers gather at the town dock, and the whole scene makes for a nice stroll. The **visitor center** is at 300 SE 2nd St (541/347-9616, www.bandon.com), and there's oceanfront **accommodation** just south of town at the *Sunset Motel*, 1865 Beach Loop Drive (541/347-2453 or 1-800/842-2407, www.sunsetmotel.com; 6), which offers decent rooms, condos, and seafront cabins. In town, the place to stay is the harborfront *Sea Star Guest House*, 370 1st St (541/347-9632, www.seastarbandon.com; 5), offering wi-fi, suites, and a penthouse, plus a harbor and sunset view from a deck. You can **camp** just north of town at **Bullards Beach State Park** ($20; 541/347-2209), where the disused Coquille River Lighthouse casts a romantic silhouette over miles of windswept sands. Try the good **seafood** at *Bandon Boatworks*, 275 Lincoln Ave SW (Ⓣ541/347-2111), and *Wild Rose Bistro*, 130 Chicago Ave SE (Ⓣ541/347-4428), which has reliable pasta and steak, too, as well as good homemade bread and desserts. Pick up a tangy treat at *Cranberry Sweets*, 1st St at Chicago SE (Ⓣ541/347-9475) – there are bogs right outside town.

Port Orford to the California border

Towns are fewer and farther apart going south on US-101 from Bandon, with the coastline at its prettiest beyond **Port Orford**, where forested mountains sweep smoothly down to the sea. These mountains mark the western limit of the **Siskiyou National Forest**, a vast slab of remote wilderness best explored by boat along the turbulent Rogue River from workaday **GOLD BEACH**. Here, the **visitor center**, on the main road at 29795 Ellensburg Ave (Ⓣ541/247-0923, Ⓦwww.goldbeachchamber.com), has details of rafting and powerboat excursions plus details for the town's basic motels and hotels. Starting seven miles south of Gold Beach are a trio of very appealing state parks: **Cape Sebastian**, which has a fine viewpoint perched two hundred feet above the surging waves, as well as trails through flowery meadows and ocean bluffs; **Pistol River**, best known for its fabulous collection of sea stacks – monstrous, gnarled behemoths scattered amid the waters – and regular **windsurfing** competitions; and **Samuel H. Boardman**, a twelve-mile coastal strip rich with viewpoints, picnic areas, and scenic paths. Finally, at the state's far southwestern corner, **Brookings** has a warmer climate, and is best used as a base for exploring northern California's **Redwood National Park** (see p.1069). Contact the local **visitor center** (Ⓣ541/469-3181, Ⓦwww.brookingsor.com) for more details.

Central Oregon

East of the Cascades, Oregon grows warmer and drier, as green valleys give way to the high desert with sagebrush, juniper trees, craggy hills, and stark rock formations broken up by the occasional tract of pine forest. **Central Oregon**'s eye-catching volcanic landscape features cracked lava beds, towering cone-like hills, and deep craters such as beautiful **Crater Lake** in the south.

Bend and around

BEND is the most useful base for visiting central Oregon, giving access both to mountain grandeur and eerie volcanic landscapes, and packed with restaurants, microbreweries, and outdoor-gear shops. Bracketing the west side of downtown along the river, **Drake Park** is a popular half-mile stretch with pleasant paths, an outdoor stage, and a setting near fetching **Mirror Pond**, widely acknowledged to be the most picturesque sight within the city. Beyond recreation, the area's main attraction is the **High Desert Museum**, 59800 US-97 (daily: May–Oct 9am–5pm, Nov–March 10am–4pm; $15; Ⓦwww.highdesertmuseum.org), a fascinating collection of artifacts from Native American and pioneer history, along with displays of regional flora and fauna – river otters, porcupines, and so forth – and a reconstructed pioneer homestead and sawmill. There are panoramic views over Bend from **Pilot Butte**, the remains of a small volcano a mile east of downtown off US-20; you can drive or walk to the top. Also worth a visit is **Smith Rock**, about 25 miles north (day use $3, primitive camping $4; Ⓣ541/548-7501), a state park whose towering basalt cliffs draw thousands of urbanites to practice their skills climbing and rapelling; the deep gorge creates perfect conditions for horseback riding, cycling, and hiking.

Practicalities

Greyhound stops at 20545 Builders St, the **visitor center** is at 917 NW Harriman (Ⓣ541/382-8048, Ⓦwww.visitbend.com), and the **Central Oregon Welcome Center**, 661 SW Powerhouse Drive (Ⓣ1-800/800-8334, Ⓦwww.covisitors.com), has brochures and accommodation listings. The best **accommodation** can be found in several smart **B&Bs**, such as the trim and elegant ranch-style digs of the *Cabin Creek*, 22035 Hwy 30 East (Ⓣ541/318-4798, Ⓦwww.cabincreekbedandbreakfast.com; ❻), and the *Sather House*, 7 NW Tumalo Ave (Ⓣ541/388-1065, Ⓦwww.satherhouse.com; ❺), with the usual tasteful period décor. Alternatively, the *St Francis Hotel*, 700 NW Bond St (Ⓣ541/382-5174, Ⓦwww.mcmenamins.com; ❻), is a charmingly renovated, former Catholic school from 1936 that offers rooms with free wi-fi and the chance to stay in a nunnery, friary and parish house (❾). You can also camp ($17–22) or stay in a **yurt** ($29) in **Tumalo State Park** (Ⓣ541/388-6055), a wooded dell by the Deschutes River five miles northwest along US-20.

For **eating** and **drinking**, *Pine Tavern*, 967 NW Brooks St (Ⓣ541/382-5581), serves microbrewed ales and stouts and sturdy American cuisine, while the *Deschutes Brewery and Public House*, 1044 NW Bond St (Ⓣ541/382-9242), brews and serves some of the Northwest's most prominent beers. Upscale diners may enjoy *The Blacksmith*, 211 NW Greenwood Ave (Ⓣ541/318-0588), with pricey but successful experiments in Northwest cuisine like lobster corn dogs, cider-brined pork chops, and "campfire trout."

Mount Bachelor and the Cascades Lake Highway

The Northwest's largest ski resort, **Mount Bachelor**, 22 miles southwest of Bend (mid-Nov to late May; Ⓣ541/382-2442 or 1-800/829-2442, Ⓦwww.mtbachelor.com; lift tickets $54), caters to downhill and cross-country skiers and snowboarders alike, with twelve ski lifts and no fewer than seventy runs. It's also the first stop on the **Cascade Lakes Highway**, a hundred-mile mountain loop road giving access to trailheads into the **Three Sisters** – a trio of spiky peaks visible throughout central Oregon – and passing dense forests and deep-blue lakes, crumbly lava flows and craggy peaks. Further south is the **Diamond Peak** wilderness area and a sprinkling of campgrounds (see Ⓦwww.oregonstateparks.org for information). Get details from **Deschutes National Forest Ranger Station**, in Bend at 1001 SW Emkay Drive (Ⓣ541/383-5300, Ⓦwww.fs.fed.us/r6/centraloregon).

Newberry National Volcanic Monument

The so-called **Lava Lands** cover a huge area of central Oregon, but especially in the Bend area at **Newberry National Volcanic Monument** (dawn–dusk; day pass $5). Dating back seven thousand years to the eruption of Mount Newberry, the monument is actually a huge, gently sloping crater laced with hiking paths, nature trails, campgrounds, and prime fishing spots. Some of the highlights (most free with monument admission) include the chilly, mile-long **Lava River Cave** (May & June Wed–Sun 9am–5pm, July–mid-Sept daily 9am–5pm; $3 for a lamp), an eerie subterranean passage made from a hollow lava tube that remains a steady 42 degrees; the **Lava Cast Forest**, circular, basalt casts of tree trunks burnt by lava before they could fall; and the surreal landscape of the **Big Obsidian Flow**, huge hills of volcanic black glass that native tribes throughout the area once used to make arrowheads. The **Lava Lands visitor center** (same hours as Lava River Cave; Ⓣ541/593-2421), eleven miles south of Bend on US-97, is an excellent source of maps and information on hiking trails, and provides access to the monument's other major sight, **Lava Butte**, a massive 500ft cinder cone, whose narrow rim you can reach by car and traverse in a short walk. There are several seasonal **campgrounds** here, too, mostly around the lakes (generally May–Oct; $10–14; reservations from visitor center or US Forest Service office in Bend; see p.1127)

Crater Lake National Park

Just over a hundred miles south of Bend, the blown-out shell of Mount Mazama holds the resoundingly beautiful **CRATER LAKE** (seven-day access fee $10; Ⓦ www.nps.gov/crla), the deepest lake in the Western hemisphere, formed after an explosion 42 times greater than that of Mount St Helens (see p.1104). The biggest island on the lake, **Wizard Island**, is actually the tip of a still-rising cinder cone, and the so-called **Phantom Ship**, is a jagged volcanic dike that, in dim light or fog, resembles a mysterious clipper on the water. In its snowy isolation, the lake, at a depth of nearly two thousand feet, is awe-inspiring; in summer, wildflowers bloom along its high rim; the waters host a small population of rainbow trout and kokanee (landlocked) salmon, but these were introduced in the early 1900s.

Practicalities

You'll need a **car** to get to the park, though only the southern route (US-62 from Medford) is open year-round. The northern access road (via Hwy-138) is more exciting, emerging from the forests to cut across a bleak pumice desert, though it's closed from mid-October to June, as is the spectacular, 33-mile "Rim Drive" around the crater's edge. Regular **boats** cruise the lake (July to mid-Sept daily 10am–3pm; 1hr 45min; $26), reached via the sheer, mile-long **Cleetwood Cove trail**, which provides the only access to the lake surface. The trail is on the north edge, but visitor facilities are clustered on the south edge at tiny **Rim Village**, where the **visitor center** (June–Sept 9.30am–5pm) is a few steps from *Crater Lake Lodge* (late May to mid-Oct; Ⓣ 541/830-8700, Ⓦ www.craterlakelodges.com; ⑥), a fully refurbished 1915 hotel on the lake's south side. The lodge has a magnificent Great Hall, complete with Art Deco flourishes, and pleasant rooms – get either a corner room or one overlooking the lake. Operated by the same company, the *Cabins at Mazama Village* (June–Oct; same phone; ⑤) are seven miles from the crater, but have an adjoining **campground** ($19) in a quiet wooded setting. Other park campgrounds include the large *Mazama Village* (mid-June to early Oct; $15–18; reserve at Ⓣ 1-888/774-2728) and the much smaller *Lost Creek* (mid-July to early Oct; $10). The **park headquarters** is at the Steel Visitors Center, located three miles south of Crater Lake on Hwy 62 (April–Oct 9am–5pm; rest of year 10am–4pm; Ⓣ 541/594-3100, Ⓦ www.crater.lake.national-park.com), where you can inquire about the activities on offer, including taking a **scuba dive** (June-Sept; free permits) into the depths of the deep blue lake.

Eastern Oregon

The scrubby sageland, bare hills, and stark rock formations of **Eastern Oregon** have an austere beauty that's frequently eye-catching, and there is a real sense of adventure in exploring this vast, sparsely populated land. Much of it is classic **cowboy country**, familiar from some Hollywood films not made in the Southwest. The unexpected colors of the **John Day Fossil Beds**, the remote, snow-capped **Wallowa Mountains**, and the deep slash of **Hells Canyon** are all very dramatic landscapes, and not to be missed if you have the time to explore them. Eastbound on Hwy-126/26 from Redmond, you'll emerge from a brief passage through the **Ochoco National Forest** – also worth a look for its wooded slopes, craggy canyons, and rocky pillars.

John Day Fossil Beds

John Jacob Astor's fur-trapping employee **John Day** provided the moniker for the **John Day Fossil Beds**, preserved in a layer of volcanic ash while the Cascades formed, just after the extinction of the dinosaurs 65 million years ago. There are three fossil sites, the first of which is the **Painted Hills** unit, nine miles northwest of Mitchell, just off US-26. Striped in shades of beige, rust, and brown, the surfaces of these evocative, sandcastle-like hills are quilted with rivulets worn by draining water. Thirty miles east is the **Sheep Rock** unit, on Hwy-19, two miles from its junction with US-26. Here, the **Condon Paleontology Center** (hours vary, usually daily 9am–5pm; free; ⓣ541/987-2333, ⓦwww.nps.gov/joda) provides a good introduction to the local geology and the world of fossils. A mile north is the **Blue Basin**, a natural amphitheater where a mile-long trail leads past various fossil replicas, like that of a saber-toothed cat and a tortoise that hurtled to its death millions of years ago. The last site, the **Clarno** unit, is twenty miles west of the town of Fossil, but doesn't have a visitor center, but does offer the **Trail of the Fossils**, where you can see up-close impressions of the plants and creatures that lived in the junglelike forest conditions, along with huge **palisades** that loom over the setting, massive pillars of rock created by volcanic mud flows some 44 million years ago.

Baker City

In the forested hills east of John Day, US-26 turns southeast for the long run down to Idaho. More enjoyable is the far shorter drive on Hwy-7 through the southern

The Oregon Trail

Between the 1840s and 1870s, more than a quarter-million Americans journeyed by wagon train from the Midwest on the **Oregon Trail**, fueled by an idea of "manifest destiny" to see their country expand from coast to coast, regardless of who or what might be in the way. The first migrants were further inspired by the missionaries who went west to try to Christianize Native Americans in the 1830s, and who sent back glowing reports of the region's temperate climate, fertile soil, dense forests, fish-rich rivers, and absence of malaria.

In spring 1843 more than a thousand would-be migrants gathered at Independence and Westport on the banks of the Missouri, preparing for the "**Great Migration.**" Nearly all were experienced farmers, using ox-pulled wagons with flimsy canvas roofs to transport supplies and often walking alongside their vehicles, instead of riding and adding extra weight to them – as Hollywood would have it.

Traversing almost two thousand miles, the migrants forced their wagons across pristine rivers, forests, and mountains, pausing at the occasional army fort or missionary station to recuperate. After three months on the trail, they arrived at what is now the town of The Dalles. From here the group faced an uneasy choice before reaching the lush Willamette Valley just beyond: build rafts and risk the treacherous currents and whirlpools of the Columbia River or take the equally perilous Barlow Road around Mount Hood (see p.1118), notorious for its swiftly changing weather and steep hillsides.

Over the next thirty years, fifty thousand more settlers arrived in the Willamette Valley, with others moving into California and (what would become) Washington. Along with helping Oregon to become a state in 1859, the migration spawned a cottage industry of specialist suppliers and wagon-builders. Inevitably, except for some isolated wagon-wheel ruts here and there, there are few surviving signs of the migrants, other than the considerable lore of their journey that continues to this day.

reaches of the **Wallowa-Whitman National Forest** to the Gold Rush boomtown of **BAKER CITY**, whose **Main Street** features stylish old structures mostly built of local stone in a potpourri of European styles – from Gothic through Renaissance revivals. The **Oregon Trail Regional Museum**, 2480 Grove St (late Mar–Oct daily 9am–5pm; $5), showcases artifacts from pioneer days, but is most notable for its fine collection of rocks, petrified wood, and fluorescent geodes. More expansive, the **Oregon Trail Interpretative Center**, five well-signposted miles east of town at Flagstaff Hill (daily: April–Oct 9am–6pm; Nov–March 9am–4pm; $5; Ⓦ oregontrail.blm.gov), has extensive dioramas, replicas, relics, and audiovisual displays, and four miles of trails revealing wagon ruts and other points of interest from that historic route (see box).

Greyhound **buses** connect to Portland at 515 Campbell St. The most prominent **hotel** is the opulent *Geiser Grand*, 1996 Main St (Ⓣ 541/523-1889, Ⓦ www.geisergrand.com; ④), a classic 1889 hotel decked out with a stained-glass ceiling and mahogany fixtures. Otherwise, the surrounding Wallowa-Whitman National Forest has many **campgrounds**; get details from the **visitor center**, 490 Campbell St, beside exit 304 on I-84 (Ⓣ 541/523-5855, Ⓦ www.visitbaker.com). Among the limited choices for **eating**, try *Barley Brown's Brewpub*, 2190 Main St (Ⓣ 541/523-4266), for its dependable pub fare and good microbrews; or the *Baker City Cafe*, 1840 Main St (Ⓣ 541/523-6099), for its affordable pizza, pasta, and sandwiches.

Pendleton

The large, flat **Grande Ronde Valley**, north of Baker City on I-84, is based around the dusty burg of **La Grande**, but for local color and history you're better off pushing northwest on I-84, following the route of the Oregon Trail, to **PENDLETON**. It's best known as the home of the popular, week-long **Pendleton Round-Up** in September ($14–18 per event; Ⓣ 1-800/45-RODEO, Ⓦ www.pendletonroundup.com), combining traditional rodeo with extravagant pageantry; the **Round-Up Hall of Fame**, 1205 SW Court Ave (June–Sept Mon–Sat 10am–5pm; free), is stuffed with related memorabilia, and around town you can pick up a cowboy hat or saddle at one of the many Western boutiques catering to tourists as well as locals. Elsewhere, the famed **Pendleton Woolen Mills**, 1307 SE Court Place (tours Mon–Fri 9am–3pm; free; information at Ⓣ 541/276-6911, Ⓦ www.pendleton-usa.com), will mainly appeal to textile fans fascinated by the intricacies of carding, spinning, warp dressing, and weaving, although you can always pick up a sweater, too. The town's star turn, though, is the **Pendleton Underground**, 37 SW Emigrant Ave (March–Oct Mon–Sat 9.30am–3pm, rest of year varies; 90min; $15; Ⓦ www.pendletonundergroundtours.org), which lets you tour the town's subterranean passageways, initially built for shelter from the inclement climate, but used during Prohibition as saloons, card rooms, and brothels, as well as housing, laundries, and opium dens for the local Chinese, who were the object of derision and violence when they dared to walk the streets.

Practicalities

Greyhound **buses** pull in at 801 SE Court Ave, and the **visitor center** at 501 S Main St (Mon–Fri 9am–5pm; Ⓣ 541/276-7411 or 1-800/547-8911, Ⓦ www.pendletonchamber.com) issues free town maps and has details of local attractions and accommodation. For **accommodation**, *Rugged Country Lodge*, 1807 SE Court Ave (Ⓣ 1-877/7-RUGGED, Ⓦ www.ruggedcountrylodge.com; ④), has affordable suites with wi-fi and complimentary breakfast; more unusual is the *Working Girls Hotel*, 17 SW Emigrant Ave (June–Oct; Ⓣ 1-800/226-6398; ③), where four guest rooms and one suite are housed up in what was once – until the 1950s, in fact

– a brothel. Most **restaurants** dole out hefty portions of all-American fare. The best of the lot are the *Rainbow Café and Lounge*, 209 S Main St (Ⓣ541/276-4120), with Round-Up memorabilia plastered over the walls, and doling out rib-stuffing burgers, sandwiches, and chicken-fried steak; and *Raphael's*, 233 SE 4th St (Ⓣ541/276-8500), for its innovative Northwest cuisine, from crab legs and Indian huckleberry salmon to glazed rattlesnake.

Hells Canyon

East of Joseph, marking the Idaho border, the **Snake River** has cut the deepest chasm on the continent – **Hells Canyon**, a 130-mile gorge that's a thousand feet deeper than the Grand Canyon, though it doesn't really look it, since it lacks the vertiginous walls of its Arizona counterpart. With the **Seven Devils** mountains rising above it, the area is preserved as **Hells Canyon National Recreation Area** (day pass $5; Ⓦwww.fs.fed.us/hellscanyon), where deer, otters, mink, and elk live, along with rattlesnakes, black bears, and mountain lions. Motor vehicles are banned in much of the canyon, so you can only explore by foot or on horseback. The forest roads that skirt the area are rough and slippery, and many are closed by snow much of the year. If you intend to use them, first check with the **rangers** in Enterprise, 88401 Hwy-82 (Ⓣ541/426-5546), or Baker City, 1550 Dewey Ave (Ⓣ541/523-6391). Also available is information on the USFS's twenty scattered primitive **campgrounds** (first-come, first-served; free or $5) – eleven in Oregon, nine in Idaho.

From Joseph, Little Sheep Creek Highway leads to **Imnaha**, where a narrow and perilous graveled Forest Service road leads to the ultimate view from **Hat Point**, site of a campground and lookout tower. The easier approach is at the south end of the canyon, along Hwy-86 east from Baker City. Another approach heading into the canyon, from the town of Halfway on Hwy-86, meets the Snake River at Oxbow Dam, where a rough Forest Service road leads to **Hells Canyon Dam**, the launching-point for exhilarating jet-boat and rafting trips through the canyon. *Hells Canyon Adventures* (reserve at Ⓣ541/785-3352 or 1-800/422-3568; Ⓦwww.hellscanyonadventures.com) and other companies run these and other sightseeing **tours** in the summer (2–3hr; $45–55 per person).

15

Alaska

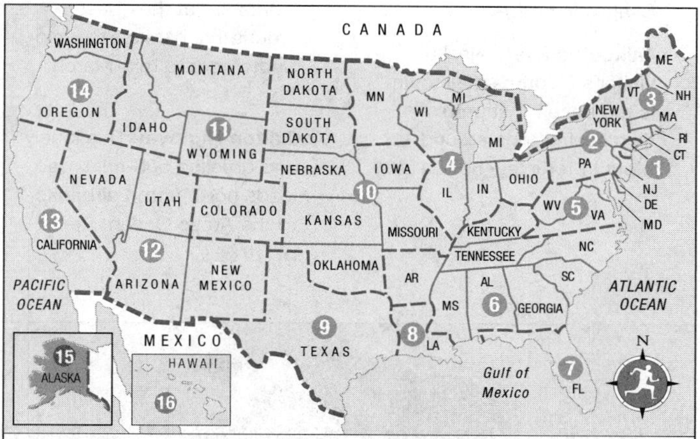

AL - ALABAMA	IN - INDIANA	MN - MINNESOTA	RI - RHODE ISLAND
AR - ARKANSAS	LA - LOUISIANA	MS - MISSISSIPPI	SC - SOUTH CAROLINA
CT- CONNECTICUT	MA - MASSACHUSETTS	NC - NORTH CAROLINA	VA - VIRGINIA
DE - DELAWARE	MD - MARYLAND	NH - NEW HAMPSHIRE	VT - VERMONT
FL - FLORIDA	ME - MAINE	NJ - NEW JERSEY	WI - WISCONSIN
IL - ILLINOIS	MI - MICHIGAN	PA - PENNSYLVANIA	WV - WEST VIRGINIA

CHAPTER 15 Highlights

* **Sitka** Russian influence blended with Native heritage and fabulous coastal scenery, making this one of Alaska's most diverting towns. See p.1141
* **The Chilkoot Trail** Follow in the (frozen) footsteps of the Klondike prospectors on this demanding 33-mile trail near Skagway. See p.1147
* **Talkeetna** Every Alaska visitor's favorite small town is the base for superb flightseeing trips around Mount McKinley. See p.1160
* **Denali National Park** Alaska's finest park offers superb mountain scenery and incomparable wildlife-spotting around the highest peak in North America. See p.1161
* **Aurora borealis** The spectacular after-dark displays of the Northern Lights are at their best around Fairbanks from mid-September to mid-March. See p.1167
* **Dalton Highway** This lonely and grueling 500-mile road leads north from Fairbanks to the Arctic Ocean. See p.1167

▲ Sitka's harbor

15

Alaska

No other region in North America fires the imagination like **ALASKA** – a derivation of *Alayeska*, an Athabascan word meaning "great land of the west." Few who see this land of gargantuan ice fields, sweeping tundra, glacially excavated valleys, lush rainforests, deep fjords, and occasionally smoking volcanoes leave unimpressed. **Wildlife** may be under threat elsewhere, but here it is abundant, with Kodiak bears standing twelve feet tall, moose stopping traffic in downtown Anchorage, wolves prowling national parks, bald eagles circling over the trees, and rivers solid with fifty-plus-pound salmon.

Alaska's sheer size is hard to comprehend. If superimposed onto the Lower 48 states, it would stretch from the Atlantic to the Pacific, while its coastline is longer than the rest of the US combined. All but three of the nation's twenty highest peaks are found within its boundaries, and one glacier alone is twice the size of Wales. In addition, not only does it contain America's **northernmost** and **westernmost** points, because the Aleutian Islands stretch across the 180th meridian, it contains the **easternmost** point as well.

Perhaps surprisingly then, a mere 670,000 people live in Alaska, of whom only one-fifth were born in the state: as a rule of thumb, the more winters you have endured, the more Alaskan you are. Often referred to as the **"Last Frontier,"** Alaska in many ways mirrors the American West of the nineteenth century: an endless, undeveloped space in which to stake one's claim and set up a life without interference – or at least that's how Alaskans would like it to be. Throughout the last hundred years or so, tens of thousands have been lured by the promise of wealth, first by gold and then by fishing, logging, and, most recently, oil. However, Alaska's 100,000 **Native peoples** have been greatly marginalized, though Native corporations set up as a result of pre-oil boom land deals have increasing economic clout.

Traveling around Alaska still demands a spirit of adventure, and to make the most of the state you need to have an enthusiasm for striking out on your own and roughing it a bit. Binoculars are an absolute must, as is bug spray; the **mosquito** is referred to as the "Alaska state bird" and it takes industrial-strength repellent to keep it away. On top of that, there's the **climate** – though Alaska is far from the great big icebox people imagine it to be. While winter temperatures of -40°F are commonplace in Fairbanks, the most touristed areas – the southeast and the Kenai Peninsula – enjoy a maritime climate (45–65°F in summer) similar to that of the Pacific Northwest, meaning much more rain (in some towns 180-plus inches per year) than snow. Remarkably, the summer temperature in the Interior often reaches 80°F.

Alaska is far more expensive than most other states: apart from two dozen hostels and myriad campgrounds, there's little budget accommodation, and **eating** and **drinking** will set you back at least twenty percent more than in the Lower

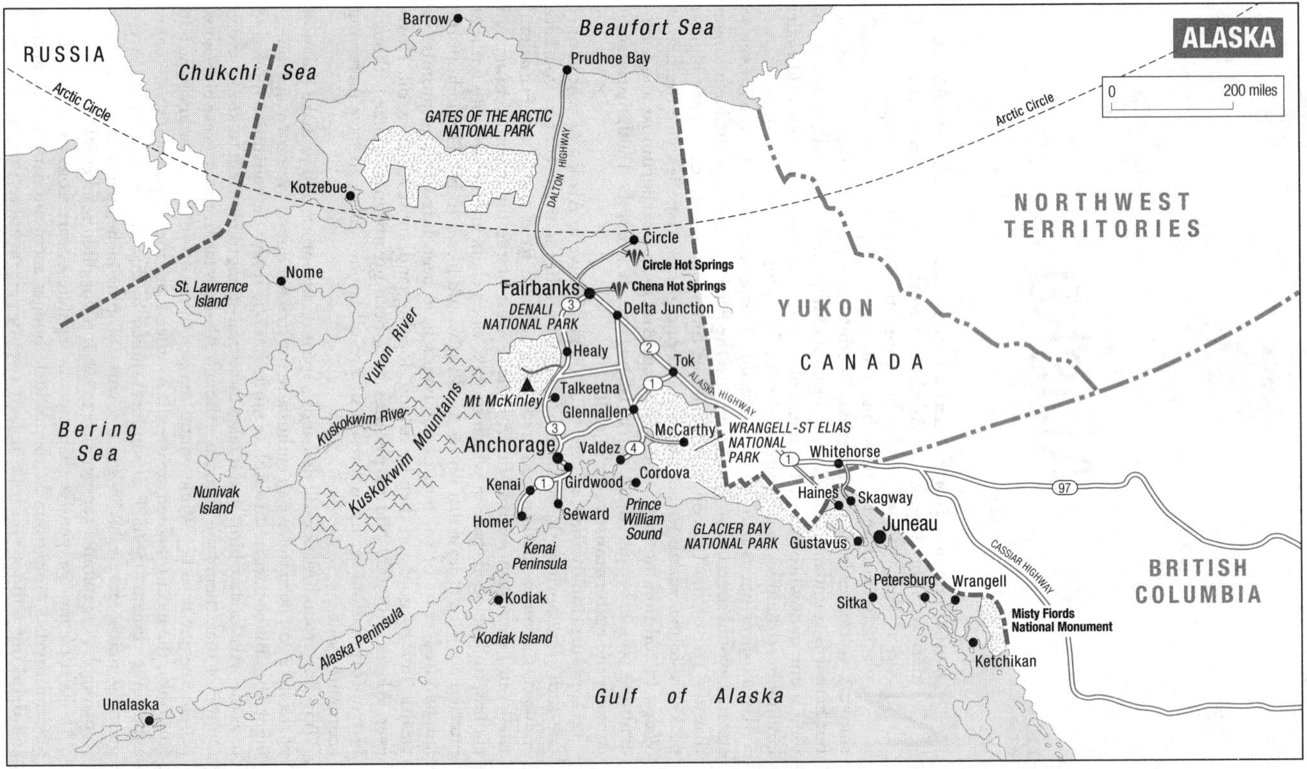
ALASKA
0
200 miles
RUSSIA
Chukchi Sea
Beaufort Sea
Arctic Circle
Arctic Circle
Barrow
Prudhoe Bay
GATES OF THE ARCTIC NATIONAL PARK
DALTON HIGHWAY
Kotzebue
Nome
St. Lawrence Island
Circle
Circle Hot Springs
Chena Hot Springs
Fairbanks
Delta Junction
DENALI NATIONAL PARK
Healy
Tok
ALASKA HIGHWAY
Talkeetna
Mt McKinley
Glennallen
McCarthy
WRANGELL-ST ELIAS NATIONAL PARK
Anchorage
Valdez
Cordova
Girdwood
Kenai
Seward
Homer
Prince William Sound
Kenai Peninsula
Kodiak
Kodiak Island
Yukon River
Kuskokwim River
Kuskokwim Mountains
Bering Sea
Nunivak Island
Alaska Peninsula
Unalaska
Gulf of Alaska
NORTHWEST TERRITORIES
YUKON
CANADA
Whitehorse
Haines
Skagway
Juneau
Gustavus
GLACIER BAY NATIONAL PARK
Petersburg
Wrangell
Sitka
Ketchikan
Misty Fiords National Monument
CASSIAR HIGHWAY
97
BRITISH COLUMBIA

48 (perhaps fifty percent in more remote regions). Still, experiencing Alaska on a **low budget** is possible, though it requires planning and off-peak travel. From June to August room prices are crazy; May and September, when tariffs are relaxed and the weather only slightly chillier, are just as good times to go, and in April or October you'll have the place to yourself, albeit with a smaller range of places to stay and eat. Ground **transportation**, despite the long distances, is reasonable, with backpacker shuttles ferrying budget travelers between major centers. **Winter**, when hotels drop their prices by as much as half, is becoming an increasingly popular time to visit, particularly for the dazzling **aurora borealis** (see box, p.1167).

Some history

It is thought that Alaska has been inhabited for longer than anywhere else in the Americas; it was here that humans first reached the "New World" from eastern Russia, most likely around fourteen thousand years ago. These first settlers can be classified into four groups. The **Aleut**, in the inhospitable Aleutian Islands, built underground homes and hunted sea mammals such as walrus for food and clothing, while the nomadic **Athabascan** herded caribou in the Interior. The warrior **Tlingit** lived in the warmer coastal regions of the southeast, where food was plentiful, while the **Eskimos** (or, more correctly, the Yup'ik and Iñupiat), who inhabited the northwestern coast, lived off fish and larger marine life. Descendants of all these groups can be found in Alaska today, predominantly in remote communities.

In 1741, Danish explorer **Vitus Bering**, working for the Tsar of Russia, became the first Caucasian to set foot on Alaskan soil and found huge numbers of fur seals and **sea otters**, whose treasured pelts were made into hats. Russians, and later British and Spaniards, joined in the ensuing slaughter, both of the otters and the Aleut, who were enslaved and forced to hunt on behalf of the fur traders. By the end of the century, the Russians had established their Alaskan capital at present-day **Sitka**, pushed down the coast as far as Northern California and, in the process, decimated the sea otter colonies.

During the 1860s, limited returns and domestic economic problems forced Russia to sell its lands to America. On October 18, 1867, Secretary of State William Seward purchased what was disparagingly known as **"Seward's Folly"** or "Seward's Icebox" for $7.2 million – less than 2¢ per acre. Alaska soon turned out to be a literal **gold mine** with major discoveries at Juneau (1880), Nome (1898), and Fairbanks (1902). With logging companies and commercial fishing operations soon descending upon Alaska, the government began to take a more active interest in its affairs, and in 1959 Alaska became the **49th state**.

Fortune-seekers headed to Alaska again in the mid-1970s to build the **trans-Alaska pipeline** from Prudhoe Bay to the ice-free port of Valdez. Today, Alaska still derives the majority of its wealth from oil and gas and, consequently, is prone to extreme boom-and-bust cycles. Once-lucrative fishing and lumber industries are fast giving way to tourism as a source of income, and the ethical question of how best to use Alaska lands in the future has led to bitter controversy. Nowhere is this more apparent than in the case of the **Arctic National Wildlife Refuge**, a vast tract of tundra in Alaska's northeast that has some degree of protection, but is constantly under threat from the oil industry and Alaska's Republican governor, senators, and congressman.

Getting to Alaska

Alaska is a long way from the rest of the United States, and however you get there it is going to be **expensive**. Once you accept that, however, there is no question as to the most **enjoyable** method – the memorable ferry trip on the Alaska Marine Highway.

By air

Most **flights** from the Lower 48 are routed via Seattle. The most frequent service is operated by Alaska Airlines (T 1-800/252-7522, W www.alaskaair.com), who charge $500–600 round-trip to Anchorage with optional stop-offs at Ketchikan, Juneau, Sitka, and Cordova at little extra cost.

By sea

The **ferries** of the state-run **Alaska Marine Highway System** (T 1-800/642-0066, W www.ferryalaska.com) reaching many places that cars can't, operates in two separate regions with an occasional "Cross-Gulf" link. The popular **southeast** route runs a thousand miles from Bellingham, north of Seattle, through a wonderland of pristine waters, narrow fjords, and untouched forests to Skagway, at the northern end of the **Inside Passage**, stopping at Ketchikan, Wrangell, Sitka, Juneau, and Haines. The whole trip takes three days and costs $353 for walk-on passengers, $448 for a small car, $57 for bicycles, and $88 for kayaks. It is possible to sleep – and even to pitch a tent – on the "solarium," a covered, heated upper deck, while a two-berth cabin costs from $337. The **southwest** ferry system connects the Kenai Peninsula and Prince William Sound to Kodiak and the Aleutians, and the two systems are linked by "Cross-Gulf" ferries from Juneau to Whittier and Kodiak twice a month in summer. Throughout, section passenger fares depend on distance traveled: $45 from Sitka to Juneau; $83 from Sitka to Ketchikan; or $221 from Juneau to Whittier. While it's a bargain for foot passengers prepared to rough it, an extended voyage with vehicle and a cabin (both of which should be reserved in advance) becomes expensive. If you're driving up from the Lower 48, consider boarding a ferry at Prince Rupert in British Columbia, two days' drive north of Seattle. This saves one day at sea without missing much of the natural spectacle.

By road

For many people, the drive up through Canada is one of the major highlights of a visit to Alaska. The only road is the 1500-mile **Alaska Highway** from Dawson Creek in British Columbia to Fairbanks, which was built by the military in just eight months. It has a fearsome reputation, but is now fully paved with gas stations, campgrounds, and hotels along the way. It remains as beautiful as ever, and still demands a spirit of adventure from drivers who attempt it.

No direct **buses** run to Alaska, though for around $200 you can hop on a Greyhound in Seattle and, after a few transfers over two gruelling days, reach Whitehorse in the Yukon, from where Alaska Direct (T 1-800/770-6652, W www.alaskadirectbusline.com) make the run to Anchorage ($210) or Fairbanks ($180).

The AlaskaPass

Foot passengers planning to travel up the Inside Passage to Anchorage, Denali, and Fairbanks may make considerable savings by purchasing the **AlaskaPass** W www.alaskapass.com), which allows unlimited travel for a certain period on the Alaska Marine Highway ferries, the Alaska Railroad, and the White Pass & Yukon Railroad. There are three passes: 15 consecutive days of travel ($929); 8 travel days out of 12 ($799); and 12 days out of 21 ($979). Kids (2 to 11) travel half-price. Add on a $85 booking fee, which is charged per itinerary (not per person).

Getting around Alaska

Getting around Alaska on the cheap can be tough; **public transportation** is limited, and many areas are only accessible by boat or plane, which is invariably pricey. With the exception of the ferry system (see above), **Anchorage** is very much the hub of Alaska, with several **bus** companies running to major destinations: Seward with The Park Connection (Ⓣ1-800/266-8625, Ⓦwww.alaskacoach.com; $56); Homer with Stage Line (Ⓣ907/868-2607, Ⓦwww.thestageline.net; $65); Talkeetna with Talkeetna Shuttle Service (Ⓣ907/733-1725, Ⓦwww.denalicentral.com; $65) and Denali ($65) and Fairbanks ($91) with Alaska/Yukon Trails (Ⓣ1-800/770-7275, Ⓦwww.alaskashuttle.com). The expensive **Alaska Railroad** (Ⓦwww.akrr.com) runs nearly five hundred miles from Seward north through Anchorage to Fairbanks, with a spur to Whittier for cruise liners and ferries to Valdez and Juneau. One-way summer **fares** from Anchorage are: Denali $135, Fairbanks $194, Whittier $60, and Seward $69.

Driving around Alaska in summer requires no special skills, though minor routes are often gravel, requiring caution. Wildlife, especially moose, can be a danger any time, even on city streets. In spring and fall you should be prepared for snow, and it is wise to carry a **survival kit**, particularly in winter, as traffic can be sparse even on major routes. Road conditions can change rapidly – call Ⓣ511 or 1-866/282-7577 or see Ⓦ511.alaska.gov.

Travel by **plane** is not always more expensive than other methods. Alaska Airlines (see p.30), flies to most major communities and uses partners such as ERA Aviation (Ⓣ1-800/866-8394, Ⓦwww.flyera.com) and PenAir (Ⓣ1-800/448-4226, Ⓦwww.penair.com) to get to smaller towns. **Chartering a plane** might sound extravagant but can be inexpensive for groups of four or more, and may be the crowning glory of an Alaska vacation. To arrange this, contact any 'bush plane' operator (every town has at least one). ERA Aviation and PenAir are good starting points, though they may refer you to another company.

Southeast Alaska

Southeast Alaska is archetypal Alaska: an awesome four-hundred-mile-long tableau of fjords, mountains, glaciers, a thousand islands, and thick conifer forests lining the **Inside Passage**. The area's first settlers were the **Tlingit** (*thling-get*), and it was not until the end of the eighteenth century that Russian expansionists burst into the region. Today, southeast Alaska's small communities resound with tales of endurance, folly, and cruelty.

The state's southernmost town, **Ketchikan**, rich in Native heritage, makes a pretty introduction, while **Sitka** retains a Russian influence. Further north are swanky **Juneau**, the capital; **Haines**, with its mix of old-timers and arty newcomers; and **Skagway**, thoroughly redolent of the old gold-mining days. You could spend months exploring here, but most are content to focus on the towns of Sitka and Skagway, and **Glacier Bay National Park**, an expensive side-trip from Juneau that penetrates one of Alaska's most stunning regions.

With no roads connecting towns, by far the best way to travel is by **ferry**, though at some stage make sure you take a **floatplane** ride. For a true outdoor adventure, you can rent a **cabin** in the huge Tongass National Forest – which encompasses most of southeast Alaska – for around $35 per night; details from the visitor centers in Juneau (see p.1142) and Ketchikan (see p.1140), or through Ⓦwww.recreation.gov.

Ketchikan and around

KETCHIKAN, almost seven hundred miles north of Seattle, is the first port of call for many cruise ships and its historic downtown, wedged between water and forested mountains, becomes saturated in summer. Beyond the souvenir shopping, it can be a delight, built into steep hills and partly propped on wooden pilings, dotted with boardwalks, wooden staircases, and totem poles.

By 1886, the town's numerous canneries made it the "salmon capital of the world," while the forests of cedar, hemlock, and spruce, which had provided timber for Tlingit homes and totems, fed the town's sawmills. Ketchikan now looks to tourism as its savior, with the nearby **Misty Fiords National Monument** as the prime draw.

The state's fourth largest city is a strong contender for the nation's wettest; annual precipitation averages 165 inches, but Ketchikan's perennial drizzle and sporadic showers won't spoil your visit.

Arrival and information

Ferries dock two miles north of downtown on Tongass Highway; city **buses** stop here hourly. Alaska Airlines serves the **airport**, which is on an island and is linked to town by half-hourly ferries ($5 round-trip). The **visitor center** stands downtown at 131 Front St (daily 8am–5pm; Ⓣ1-800/770-3300, Ⓦwww.visit-ketchikan.com), and for information about the surrounding Tongass forests visit the **Southeast Alaska Discovery Center**, 50 Main St (Mon–Fri 8am–5pm Sat & Sun 8am–4pm; Ⓣ907/228-6220, Ⓦwww.fs.fed.us/r10/tongass), a striking cedar-framed building which houses absorbing displays ($5) of the region's natural habitats and native culture.

Accommodation

Hotels in Ketchikan vary widely, and the closest **campgrounds** to town ($10) are in the attractive Ward Lake Recreation Area, five miles northwest of the ferry terminal.

Alderhouse 420 Alder St Ⓣ907/247-2537, Ⓦwww.alderhousebnb.com. Very welcoming B&B an easy walk from the AMHS ferry dock and close to buses running between downtown and Totem Bight. Attention to detail makes everything, especially the breakfast, a treat. Open June–Sept; 2-night minimum. ❺

Eagle View Hostel 2305 5th Ave Ⓣ907/225-5461, Ⓦwww.eagleviewhostel.com. Suburban house shared with the owner, offering great views of the Narrows. Single-sex dorm beds (as well as one double room) cost $25 including bed linen, towel, and use of the kitchen, barbecue, and sauna. No lockout or curfew. Follow Jefferson off Tongass Highway then turn right onto 5th. Open April–Oct.

Ketchikan Youth Hostel in the United Methodist Church, 400 Main St Ⓣ907/225-3319, Ⓔktnyh@eagle.ptialaska.net. Very basic hostel with beds for $15, daytime lockout and curfew. June–Aug only.

The New York Hotel 207 Stedman St Ⓣ1-866/225-0246, Ⓦwww.thenewyorkhotel.com. Tastefully refurbished hotel by the small boat harbor with cozy rooms and a good café. ❺

The Town

The bulk of Ketchikan's historic buildings lie on **Creek Street**, a rickety-looking boardwalk along Ketchikan Creek. This was a red-light district until 1954; now all the former houses of ill-repute are given over to gift shops and galleries. **Dolly's House**, 24 Creek St, once the home and workplace of Dolly Arthur, the town's most famous madam, is now a small museum stuffed with saucy memorabilia (generally daily 8am–5pm; $5).

Most of the totem poles you see around town are authentic replicas, but the **Totem Heritage Center**, 601 Deermount St (daily 8am–5pm; $5), exhibits the largest collection of original totem poles in the US: 33 mostly nineteenth-century examples recovered from abandoned Native villages. The Tlingit-run **Saxman Totem Park**, two miles south of town, displays the world's largest standing collection of poles and an authentic tribal house. For $3 you get to see the poles and exterior of the buildings, but you'll need to join the **Saxman Native Village Tour** (May–Sept daily; 1hr; $40; ⓔinfo@capefoxtours.com; no phone) to see sculptors at work and a dance performance inside the clan house.

Fourteen of the best replica totem poles and a rebuilt tribal house stand in **Totem Bight State Park**, breathtakingly set on a forested strip of coast overlooking the Narrows, ten miles north of town on the Tongass Highway. On the way back, take some time out to do the easy but enjoyable boardwalk trail up to **Perseverance Lake**, starting on Ward Lake Road, four miles north of town.

Eating and drinking

Inexpensive **food** in Ketchikan tends to be rather good, a rare combination in Alaska. The town is also renowned for its hard **drinking**.

Chico's 435 Dock St ⓣ907/225-2833. Bargain authentic Mexican food and pizza with dinners starting at $10, or just grab a $7 burrito to eat in or take out.

Diaz Café 335 Stedman St ⓣ907/225-2257. Great inexpensive diner food with some tasty Filipino dishes. Closed Mon.

First City Saloon 830 Water St. Straightforward boozing bar occasionally featuring bands and shows. Probably the mostly likely place to indulge in a little dancing.

That One Place 207 Stedman St ⓣ907/225-0246. Nonsmoking restaurant and bar with a daytime menu loaded with excellent soups, burgers, wraps, and salads (mostly $9–12), plus some sumptuous desserts. Also open evenings when there's an excellent tapas menu, with most plates $5–7. Closed Sun.

Misty Fiords National Monument

Twenty-two miles east of Ketchikan on the mainland, the awe-inspiring **MISTY FIORDS NATIONAL MONUMENT** consists of 2.3 million acres of deep fjords flanked by sheer 3000ft glacially scoured walls topped by dense rainforest. As befits its name, the monument is at its most atmospheric when swathed in low-lying mists. The best access is with Alaska Travel (ⓣ1-800/325-5757, ⓦwww.mistyfjord.net) who offer a six-hour cruise ($139) and an excellent four-hour cruise/fly combo ($269). Fourteen rustic cabins (mostly $35) are rented out by the Forest Service (ⓣ1-877/444-6777). Access is either by floatplane with Taquan Air (ⓣ1-800/770-8800, ⓦwww.taquanair.com), or kayak with Southeast Sea Kayaks (ⓣ1-800/287-1607, ⓦwww.kayakketchikan.com).

Sitka

Perched on the seaward edge of the Inside Passage, **SITKA** ranks as one of Alaska's prettiest and most historic towns. The Russians established a fort here in 1799 and Sitka subsequently became the capital of Russian America, witnessing transfer of ownership to the US in 1867. Sitka today earns its keep mostly from fishing and tourism and offers a wealth of great outdoor opportunities.

Arrival and information

Traditional **ferries** and a fast catamaran jointly visit Sitka around five times per week, mooring seven miles northwest of town. Sitka Tours **shuttles** (ⓣ907/747-8443; $10 round-trip) run downtown and offer two-hour town tours ($12). Flights arrive a half-hour walk from downtown. You can rent **kayaks** from Sitka Sound Ocean Adventures (ⓣ907/747-6375, ⓦwww.ssoceanadventures.com; $40 a half-day, double $50), who also organize day-long guided trips on the Sound

($145). The **visitor center** is in the Centennial Building, 330 Harbor Drive (daily 8am–5pm; ⓣ907/747-3220, ⓦwww.sitka.org).

Accommodation

Sitka's **accommodation** includes the historic *Sitka Hotel*, 118 Lincoln St (ⓣ907/747-3288, ⓦwww.sitkahotel.com; ❸–❹), which offers a touch of old-fashioned style, some rooms without bathrooms; and the Sitka Youth Hostel, 109 Jeff Davis St ⓣ907/747-8661), with bunks for $24. **Campers** should head less than a mile north of the ferry dock to the gorgeous *Starrigavan* campground, on Halibut Point Road (ⓣ1-877/444-6777; $12), or seven miles east of Sitka to the free but basic *Sawmill Creek Campground*, on Blue Lake Road, at the start of the Beaver Lake Trail.

The Town

The best place to get a grasp of Sitka's Russian past is from diminutive **Castle Hill**, where Alaska was officially transferred to the US on October 18, 1867; a plaque marks the spot. A two-minute stroll to the heart of downtown leads to **St Michael's Cathedral**, a fine piece of Russian church architecture, completed in 1848 and rebuilt after a disastrous fire in 1966. It displays priceless original icons (Mon–Fri 9am–4pm; $2). Nearby is the large, mustard-colored 1842 **Russian Bishop's House** (daily 9am–5pm; $4). Guided tours take in the restored chapel, schoolroom, and bishop's living quarters. Four blocks further along at 104 College Drive, the **Sheldon Jackson Museum** (daily 9am–5pm; $4) houses a compact but extensive display of Native artifacts accumulated by missionary and educationalist Sheldon Jackson.

Nearby, the site of a decisive battle between the Tlingit and the Russians is marked by the **Sitka National Historic Park** with its evocative collection of vividly painted **totem poles**, all replicas of nineteenth-century classic designs. A **visitor center** (summer daily 8am–5pm; $4) features good interpretative displays.

Sitka's **trail system** ranges from coastal strolls to harder climbs up Gavan Hill and steep Mount Verstovia: for more information visit the **Forest Service office**, 204 Siganaka Way (ⓣ907/747-6671).

Eating and drinking

Sitka's **restaurants** aren't exactly going to set gourmet tongues wagging, though there are several decent places to dine out. Coffee and light lunches are best at *Backdoor,* 104 Barracks St ⓣ907/747-8856. For more upscale dining, try *Ludvig's Bistro*, 256 Katlian St (ⓣ907/966-3663), offering expensive but excellent Spanish-, Portuguese-, Italian-, and Moroccan-influenced dishes. Closed Sun. If you're looking for evening drinks, *Pioneer Bar*, 212 Katlian St (ⓣ907/747-3456), is a down-to-earth boozing spot lined with hundreds of black-and-white photographs of fishing boats.

Juneau and around

The sophisticated and vibrant city of **JUNEAU** is the only state capital in the nation not accessible by road. It is exceptionally picturesque, hard against the **Gastineau Channel**, with steep, narrow roads clawing up into the rainforested hills behind. Gold features heavily in its history. In 1880, Joe Juneau made **Alaska's first gold strike** along the banks of the Gastineau Channel. Until the last mine was shut down in 1944, this was the world's largest producer of low-grade ore – all the flat land in Juneau, stretching from downtown to the airport, is landfill from mine tailings. Today, state government provides much of the employment, and tourism plays its part with the drive-to **Mendenhall Glacier** and the watery charms of **Tracy Arm fjord** as temptation.

Arrival, information, and getting around

The **ferry terminal** is fourteen miles northwest of downtown at Auke Bay; ferries often arrive at unearthly hours, so getting into town can be a problem. Apart from taking a $40 taxi ride, the only transport is the city's Capital Transit **bus service** (Mon–Sat hourly 8am–10.30pm, Sun 9am–5pm; ⓣ907/789-6901; $1.50), which stops a mile and a half south outside DeHarts grocery. Buses also pick up from close to the airport, nine miles north of downtown, which sees daily Alaska Airlines flights.

The **visitor center**, Centennial Hall, 101 Egan Drive (Mon–Fri 8.30am–5pm, Sat & Sun 9am–5pm; ⓣ1-888/581-2201, ⓦwww.traveljuneau.com) has stacks of brochures about the Tongass National Forest, Glacier Bay, and around. Popular **hikes** from Juneau include the undemanding Perseverance Trail and, over the bridge on Douglas Island, the Treadwell Mine Historic Trail. *Driftwood Lodge* (ⓣ907/586-2280), rents out **mountain bikes** for $25 a day.

Accommodation

Juneau has the widest range of accommodation in Southeast Alaska, as well as some fine camping.

Alaskan Hotel and Bar 167 S Franklin St ⓣ1-800/327-9374, ⓦwww.thealaskanhotel.com. Pleasant old hotel with a salacious past and a fine bar in the heart of downtown. Doubles with shared or private bath ❸–❹, suites ❺

Juneau Hostel 614 Harris St ⓣ907/586-9559, ⓦwww.juneauhostel.org. Clean, comfortable, and relaxed hostel, in an old home near downtown, with dorm beds ($10) and a family room, but an inconvenient daytime lock-out (9am–5pm) and a midnight curfew.

Mendenhall Lake Campground Montana Creek Rd, 13 miles from downtown. A gorgeous Forest Service campground within sight of the Mendenhall Glacier and with space for RVs ($26) and some lovely lakeside walk-in tent sites ($10).

Silverbow Inn 120 2nd St, downtown ⓣ1-800/586-4146, ⓦwww.silverbowinn.com. Attractive, small hotel with smallish but nicely furnished and tastefully decorated rooms, each with TV, phone and wi-fi, and with a good continental breakfast included. ❻

Thane Road Tent Camping Mile 1 Thane Rd. Primitive site 15min walk south of downtown. $5.

The Town

Many original buildings stand in the **South Franklin Street Historic District** – Juneau managed to avoid the fires that destroyed many other gold towns in Alaska. The onion-domed **St Nicholas Russian Orthodox Church**, on Fifth and Gold (Mon 9am–6pm, Tues & Thurs 9am–5pm, Fri 10am–noon & 3–5pm, Sat 11am–3pm, Sun 1–5pm; $2 suggested donation), contains icons and religious treasures, while the well-presented **Alaska State Museum**, 395 Whittier St (daily 8.30am–5.30pm; $5), covers Native culture, Russian heritage, and the first gold strikes. Its pride and joy is the logbook in which Bering reported his first sighting of Alaska. The smaller **City Museum**, at Main and Fourth streets (Mon–Fri 9am–5pm, Sat & Sun 10am–5pm; $4), displays relics from the mining era. The best views of town are from the top of the **Mount Roberts Tramway** (summer daily 9am–9pm; $25), which careers from the cruise-ship dock 1800 feet up Mount Roberts, where there's a nature center and some easy trails.

Eating and drinking

Downtown has a reasonable selection of places to **eat and drink**, but most fill up very quickly when cruise ships are in town.

Alaskan Hotel Bar 167 S Franklin St. Great old bar, with live music most nights, especially toward the weekend.

The Hanger on the Wharf Merchants Wharf ⓣ907/586-5018. Former floatplane hangar with tremendous waterfront views. There are over twenty beers on tap, plus pool tables and live music on weekends. Also serves wraps and burgers at lunch and the likes of jambalaya and halibut tacos ($13–14) at dinner.

Paradise Café 245 Marine Way. Stylish little café and bakery with excellent soups, salads, phyllo rolls, and wraps, all made from scratch and eaten at tables in an adjacent room. A little pricey but worth it. Open for breakfast and lunch to 3pm.

Rainbow Foods 224 4th St ⓣ907/586-6476. Wholefood and organic grocery serving a limited selection of light lunches (Mon–Fri), plus a salad bar. Try the home-made cookies and espresso.

Silverbow Bakery 120 2nd St ⓣ907/586-4146. Relaxed eat-in bakery and coffee bar with bagels and superb pastries bolstering a menu of homemade breads used in hot and cold deli sandwiches ($7–11).

Mendenhall Glacier and Tracy Arm Fjord

Capital Transit **buses** run 13 miles west of downtown to the one-and-a-half-mile-wide **Mendenhall Glacier**, the state's most accessible. The **visitor center** (daily 8am–7.30pm; $3) is built on a point occupied by the glacier as recently as 1940. Hiking **trails** include the West Glacier Trail, on which, with extreme caution and without official approval, you can explore the ice caves.

One of the best day-trips out of Juneau is up the narrow, twisting **Tracy Arm fjord**, with waterfall-fringed cliffs and common sightings of whales and seals. Take one of the day-long **cruises** with Adventure Bound Alaska (ⓣ1-800/228-3875, ⓦwww.adventureboundalaska.com; $130).

Glacier Bay National Park

Sixteen glaciers spill into the 65-mile-long **GLACIER BAY**, Alaska's finest array of tidewater glaciers located sixty miles northwest of Juneau. Brown and black bears, moose, mountain goats, sea otters, humpback whales, porpoise, seals, and a colorful array of birds have made the area their home. It is an expensive place to visit requiring either an Alaska Airlines flight from Juneau to Gustavus ($100–130 round-trip). Glacier access is by **day-cruise** (8hr; $184) from nearby Bartlett Cove, and you'll also need at least one night's **accommodation**. At Bartlett Cove you can camp for free or stay at *Glacier Bay Lodge* (ⓣ1-888/229 8687, ⓦwww.visitglacierbay.com; ❼), with tasteful rooms and a good restaurant. Accommodation in a room, a cabin, or a small house can be found in Gustavus in the form of *Bear's Nest B&B* (ⓣ907/679-2440, ⓦwww.gustavus.com/bearsnest; ❺–❻), where there's good eating next door at the *Bear's Nest Café*._

Haines

Tiny **HAINES** sits on a peninsula at the northern end of the longest and deepest fjord in the US, Lynn Canal. Somewhat overshadowed by its brasher neighbor, Skagway, it remains a slice of real Alaska with an interesting mix of locals and urban escapees.

The Tlingit fished and traded here for years before 1881, when the first missionaries arrived. Today, the town survives on fishing and tourism, hosting in mid-August the cookouts, crafts, and log-rolling of the **Southeast Alaska Fair**.

Arrival and information

Haines' AMHS **ferry** terminal is five miles north of town, with a daily service to and from Juneau and Skagway. Local **taxis** meet all ferry arrivals; downtown should cost $10, but ask before you board. A convenient passenger-only fast ferry ($31 single; ⓣ1-888/766-2103, ⓦwww.haineskagwayfastferry.com) runs between Haines and Skagway from a dock near Fort Seward. The **visitor center**,

122 Second St (Mon–Fri 8am–7pm, Sat & Sun 9am–6pm; ⓣ 1-800/458-3579, ⓦ www.haines.ak.us), has all kinds of maps and information.

Accommodation

As well as the usual mid-range **accommodation**, Haines has half a dozen handy **campgrounds**.

Bear Creek Cabins and Hostel Small Tract Rd ⓣ 907/766-2259, ⓦ bearcreekcabinsalaska.com. Good hostel over a mile south of Fort Seward with coin-op laundry and no lock-out or curfew. Campers ($14 for two) can use hostel facilities. Dorms $18, cabins $48

Port Chilkoot Camper Park Mud Bay Rd beside Fort Seward ⓣ 1-800/542-6363, ⓦ www.hotelhalsingland.com. Central campsite with pay-showers and a laundromat on site. Full hookup $25, dry RV $16, tents $10.

Portage Cove State Recreation Site Beach Rd, half a mile southeast of Fort Seward. A small site for backpackers and cyclists only. It's right by the beach and has great views and potable water. No overnight parking. $5.

Summer Inn B&B 117 2nd Ave ⓣ 907/766-2970, ⓦ www.summerinnbnb.com. Immaculately kept downtown B&B with shared bathrooms, some with sea views and all including a good cooked breakfast. It has a very homey feel with clawfoot baths, quilts, and fresh flowers. ④

The Town

In the center of town, the **Sheldon Museum & Cultural Center**, 11 Main St (Mon–Fri 10am–5pm, Sat & Sun 1–4pm; ⓦ www.sheldonmuseum.org; $3), shows how Haines fits into its Chilkat environment and the wider Tlingit world, and exhibits fine examples of woodwork, clothing, and the distinctive yellow and black Chilkat blanket in wolf, raven, and killer whale designs.

Half a mile away, grassy **Fort William H. Seward** was established in 1903 to contain general Gold Rush lawlessness, and territorial disputes with Canada. It is now the site of **Alaska Indian Arts** (Mon–Fri 9am–5pm; free), with a back room where you can chat to carvers as they work on huge totem poles.

Nearby, the stuffed birds of the **American Bald Eagle Foundation**, 113 Haines Hwy at Second Avenue (daily 10am–6pm; $3), make a poor substitute for seeing the world's largest gathering of **bald eagles**, which flock to the banks of the Chilkat River each November. Over three thousand birds – as many as two dozen to a tree –gather along a five-mile sand bar at the **Chilkat Bald Eagle Preserve**, nine miles north of town on the Haines Highway.

Haines is also a popular starting point for **rafting trips**: Chilkat Guides on Beach Road (ⓣ 1-888/292-7789, ⓦ www.raftalaska.com) run four-hour **float trips** ($89) down the Chilkat River, ideal for viewing eagles and other wildlife.

Eating and drinking

Haines' most exciting **bars** and **restaurants** can be found in the Fort Seward area, notably at the *Hotel Hälsingland*.

Bamboo Room 11 2nd St near Main ⓣ 907/766-2800. Standard diner popular for its well-prepared meals (especially the locally caught halibut and chip dinner), and fresh-baked pies.

Chilkat Restaurant and Bakery 5th Ave & Dalton St ⓣ 907/766-3653. A great spot for some of their baked goods with an espresso coffee, or more substantial fare. They do everything from tasty breakfasts, salads and halibut sandwiches to regular Thai lunches for $11, all beautifully cooked.

Mountain Market & Café 151 3rd Ave at Haines Hwy ⓣ 907/766-3340. Combined natural-food grocery and espresso bar that's one of the best places in town for a $6 bagel breakfast, a $7 tortilla wrap, or just a muffin with your mocha.

Skagway and around

SKAGWAY, the northernmost ferry stop on the southeast route, sprang up overnight in 1897 as a trading post serving **Klondike Gold Rush** pioneers about to set off on the five-hundred-mile ordeal. Having grown from one cabin to a town of twenty thousand in three months, Skagway, rife with disease and desperado violence, was reported to be "hell on earth." It boasted over seventy bars and hundreds of prostitutes, and was controlled by organized criminals, including **Jefferson "Soapy" Smith**, notorious for cheating hapless prospectors out of their gold.

By 1899, the Gold Rush was over, but the completion in 1900 of the White Pass and Yukon Route railway from Skagway to Whitehorse, the Yukon capital, ensured Skagway's survival. Today, the town's eight hundred residents have gone to great lengths to maintain (or recreate) the original appearance of their home, much of which lies in the **Klondike Gold Rush National Historic Park**, and in summer as many as five cruise ships a day call in to appreciate the effort.

Arrival, information, and getting around

AMHS ferries and an independent operator (see p.1144) arrive daily from Haines and Juneau at the foot of the main thoroughfare, Broadway, and just a block from the **train station** from where WP&YR trains (see p.1147) head inland. Yukon Alaska Tourist Tours (reservations essential ⓣ1-866/626-7383, ⓦwww.yatt.ca), run a bus from Skagway to Whitehorse ($40) and a train-bus combo ($119).

Skagway is very compact, and most of the sights can easily be seen on foot. The Klondike Gold Rush National Historic Park **visitor center**, Broadway at 2nd Avenue (daily 8am–6pm; ⓣ907/983-2223, ⓦwww.nps.gov/klgo), holds talks, leads walking tours, and has historical displays and an impressive movie about the Gold Rush, as well as maps and information on the Chilkoot Trail. Skagway's **visitor center** (daily 8am–6pm; ⓣ1-888/762-1898, ⓦwww.skagway.com) is on Broadway between Second and Third avenues in the Arctic Brotherhood Hall building.

Accommodation

In such a touristy little town, **accommodation** prices run slightly high, and rooms are often reserved far in advance.

At the White House 475 8th Ave at Main St ⓣ907/983-9000, ⓦwww.atthewhitehouse.com. High-standard B&B in one of Skagway's original homes with restored, modernized rooms and substantial breakfasts. ❺

Cindy's Place Mile 0.2 Dyea Rd ⓣ1-800/831-8095, ⓦwww.alaska.net/~croland. Three cabins in the woods two miles from downtown Skagway, one budget, two more luxurious log-built affairs with private bathrooms (one with a wood-burning stove), phone, and cooking equipment. All guests have free use of the hot tub and there are thoughtful touches like a dozen varieties of tea and coffee in the cabins, plus home-made jams and jellies for breakfast. Deluxe ❺, budget ❷

Skagway Home Hostel 3rd Ave and Main St ⓣ907/983-2131, ⓦwww.skagwayhostel.com. In-with-the-family hostel in a century-old building with bunks in single-sex dorms ($20), mixed dorms ($15) and one private room (❷). There's a communal feel, ample supplies for cooking (honesty box), and an 11pm curfew. ❷

Skagway Mountain View RV Park Broadway at 12th Ave ⓣ1-888/323-5757, ⓦwww.bestoflaskatravel.com. Large RV-dominated spot with all the expected facilities, water and electricity hookup ($45), and a few wooded tent sites ($25) that are in high demand.

The Town

Strolling up Broadway you can't miss the eye-catching facade of the 1899 **Arctic Brotherhood Hall**, decorated with almost nine thousand pieces of driftwood and housing the Skagway Visitor Center. Many of the other buildings hereabouts form part of the **Klondike Gold Rush National Historic Park**, notably the former **Mascot Saloon** on Broadway (daily 8am–6pm; free), and **Moore House**, Fifth Avenue at Spring Street (daily 10am–5pm; free), a museum **devoted to** Skagway's original resident that features stories and photos of the Gold Rush. There's further detail in the recently refurbished **City of Skagway Museum** (Mon–Fri 9am–5pm, Sat 10am–5pm, Sun 10am–4pm; $2), which contains Soapy's Derringer pistol and good Tlingit artifacts.

The useful *Skagway Trail Map*, available from the visitor center, details **hikes** in the area, including those in the Dewey Lakes system, which pass pretty subalpine lakes and tumbling waterfalls, and the more difficult scramble up AB Mountain. Sockeye Cycles, Fifth Avenue and Broadway (ⓣ907/983-2851, ⓦwww.cyclealaska.com), rents out well-maintained **mountain bikes** for $25 a half-day, and the neighboring Mountain Shop (ⓣ907/983-2544) rents and sells backpacking supplies.

A lazier way to take in the scenery is on the **White Pass and Yukon Route** railway (early May to late Sept; 2–3 departures daily; ⓣ1-800/343-7373, ⓦwpyr.com), which follows the gushing Skagway River upstream past waterfalls and ice-packed gorges and over a 1000ft-high wooden trestle bridge, stopping at the White Pass summit ($103 round-trip). There's no shortage of riders, so get there early and grab a seat on the left-hand side going up. The company also offers a through bus service to Whitehorse.

Eating and drinking

Most of Skagway's **bars** and **restaurants** line the touristy part of Broadway.

The Haven State St at 9th Ave ⓣ907/983-3553. Relaxed coffee shop with sofas and stacks of magazines, serving good espresso, egg or granola breakfasts, mouthwatering panini and fresh salads – Santa Fe, Greek, Caesar – all available with added chicken ($7–10).

Red Onion Saloon Broadway at 2nd Ave ⓣ907/983-2222. An 1898 bar and former bordello with heaps of character, draft beers, and excellent pizza.

Sabrosa Broadway at 6th Ave ⓣ907/983-2469. Daytime café and bakery tucked in behind the gift shops that's great for breakfast (from $5) and lunches of burritos ($8), vegetarian chili (cup $4, bowl $6), and tarragon, pecan, and chicken salad ($9). Shaded outdoor seating for those hot days.

Stowaway Café 205 Congress Way ⓣ907/983-3463. Stop by in the evening for the likes of lemongrass halibut ($23), back baby ribs ($23), and peach bread pudding ($7), all served in a congenial atmosphere with views of the small boat harbor. Open nightly 4–10pm.

The Chilkoot Trail

Alaska's most famous trail, the 33-mile **CHILKOOT TRAIL**, is a hike through one huge wilderness museum following the footsteps of the original Klondike prospectors. Starting in **Dyea**, nine miles from Skagway, and ending in **Bennett** in Canada, the trail climbs through rainforest to tundra often strewn with haunting reminders of the past, including ancient boilers that once drove aerial tramways, and several collapsed huts.

The three- to five-day hike can be strenuous, especially the final ascent up from Sheep Camp (1000ft) to Chilkoot Pass (3550ft). You must be **self-sufficient** for food, fuel, and shelter, and be prepared for foul weather. Campgrounds line the trail, as well as emergency shelters with stoves and firewood. Dyea is accessible by road, and the White Pass and Yukon Railway runs a service for hikers returning to Skagway (daily except Wed & Sat; $90).

The main hiking season runs from July to early September, when there is a quota system administered by Parks Canada (ⓦwww.pc.gc.ca/chilkoot). First visit the

▲ Hiking the Chillkoot Trail

Skagway **Trail Center**, Broadway at 1st Avenue (early June to early Sept daily 8.30am–4.30pm), where rangers make sure you understand the challenges and dangers, and can advise on weather conditions and current bus and train schedules for the trip back to Skagway. While here, you must also pay Can$50 for a permit.

Anchorage

Wedged between the two arms of Cook Inlet and the imposing Chugach Mountains, **ANCHORAGE** is home to over forty percent of Alaska's population and is the state's transport hub. A sprawling city on the edge of one of the world's great wildernesses, it often gets bad press from those who live elsewhere in the state and deride it as "just half an hour from the real Alaska." However, it has its attractions and, with its beautiful setting, can make a pleasant one- or two-day stopover.

Anchorage was born in 1915 as a tent city for Alaska Railroad construction workers. During the 1930s, hopefuls fleeing the Depression poured in from the Lower 48, and World War II – and construction of the Alaska Highway – further boosted the city. The opening of the airport established Anchorage – midway between New York and Tokyo – as the "Crossroads of the World," and statehood in 1959 and the 1970s oil boom brought in yet more optimistic adventurers.

Arrival and information

Anchorage International Airport, five miles southwest of town, is served by bus #7, part of the citywide **People Mover** system ($1.75 flat fare or $4 day-pass from the driver). Alaska Shuttle (ⓣ907/388-8888) charges $10 to take you downtown and taxis cost around $25. The **train station** is downtown at 411 W 1st Ave (ⓣ1-800/544-0552, ⓦwww.akrr.com), and the major sights are easily reached on foot.

The **Log Cabin Visitor Center**, downtown at 4th and F (daily 8am–6pm; ⓣ907/274-3531, ⓦwww.anchorage.net), is across the street from the **Alaska Public Lands Information Center** (daily 9am–5pm; ⓣ907/271-2737, ⓦwww.nps.gov/aplic) which has an excellent natural history display plus maps and brochures. It'll help plan trips into the Interior, and make reservations both for accommodation and the shuttle bus in Denali National Park – vital in summer.

Accommodation

Inexpensive **accommodation** in Anchorage can be hard to find, especially in summer when many places are fully booked. **Campers** should head for the central *Ship Creek RV Park*, 150 N Ingra (ⓣ1-800/323-5757, ⓦwww.alaskarv.com; $16–24 [ed; depends on season. $16 in May & Sept, $24 June–Aug]), or the more woodsy *Centennial Campground* (ⓣ907/343-6986; $20), five miles north on the Glenn Highway.

Anchorage Guesthouse 2001 Hillcrest Drive ⓣ907/274-0408, ⓦwww.akhouse.com. Upscale hostel, just over a mile from downtown and handy for the Coastal Trail (bike rental available). Other perks include sheets, towels, breakfast, use of kitchen, free gear storage, free local calls, and internet access. Dorm beds cost $30 and there are private doubles and kings. ❹

Anchorage International Hostel 700 H St ⓣ907/276-3635, ⓦwww.anchoragehostel.org. Functional and very central hostel with a daytime lock-out , evening curfew and some private rooms; reserve well ahead in summer. Dorm beds $25, rooms ❸

Earth B&B 1001 W 12th Ave ⓣ907/279-9907, ⓦwww.earthbb.com. Enthusiastically and liberally run, this is home away from home for Denali-bound climbers. It's simple but very accommodating, with a barbecue out back. Bus #7 or #36 from downtown. ❺

Oscar Gill House 1344 W 10th Ave ⓣ907/279-1344, ⓦwww.oscargill.com. Lovely B&B in a 1913 house, restored with understated elegance. Two rooms share a bath while the largest has its own jacuzzi, all tastefully done and managed by very welcoming hosts. Private bath ❻, shared ❺

Qupqugiac Inn 640 W 36th Ave, midtown ⓣ907/563-5633, ⓦwww.qupq.com. Great budget hotel with clean, simple rooms with phone and satellite TV, and a communal lounge with kitchen and free internet. Bus #9 from downtown passes a block away on Arctic Blvd. Rooms with bath ❹, without ❸

Spenard Hostel International 2845 W 42nd Place ⓣ907/248-5036, ⓦwww.alaskahostel.org. Friendly suburban hostel with nearby mall just a mile and a half from the airport (bus #7). Cheap bike rental, no curfew or lock-out, and dorm beds for $21.

Voyager Hotel 501 K St at 5th Ave ⓣ1-800/247-9070, ⓦwww.voyagerhotel.com. The best of the mid- to upper-range hotels featuring spacious rooms (with kitchenette) and most of the facilities of a business hotel at much lower cost. Reserve well in advance in summer. ❼

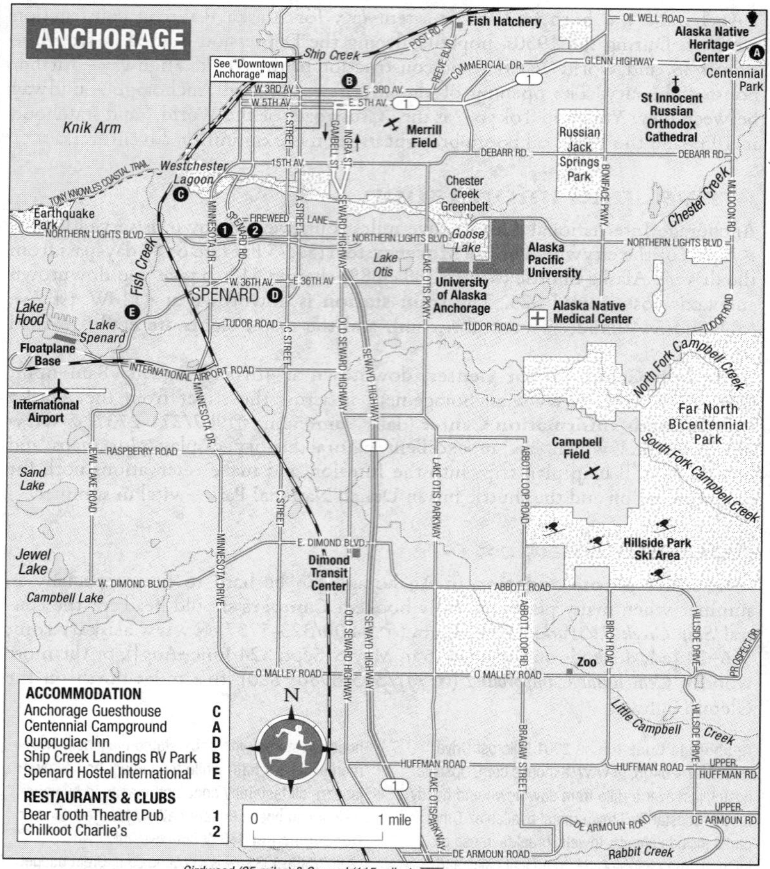
ANCHORAGE
See "Downtown Anchorage" map
Knik Arm
Ship Creek
Fish Hatchery
POST RD.
REEVE BLVD
COMMERCIAL DR.
OIL WELL ROAD
GLENN HIGHWAY
Alaska Native Heritage Center
Centennial Park
Fairbanks (355 miles)
W 3RD AV.
E. 3RD AV.
W 5TH AV.
E. 5TH AV.
C STREET
GAMBELL ST.
INGRA ST.
Merrill Field
St Innocent Russian Orthodox Cathedral
Russian Jack Springs Park
BONIFACE PKWY
DEBARR RD.
15TH AV.
Westchester Lagoon
TONY KNOWLES COASTAL TRAIL
Earthquake Park
Chester Creek Greenbelt
Chester Creek
MULDOON RD
MINNESOTA DR.
SPENARD RD
FIREWEED LANE
A STREET
SEWARD HIGHWAY
NORTHERN LIGHTS BLVD
Goose Lake
Lake Otis
Alaska Pacific University
University of Alaska Anchorage
LAKE OTIS PKWY
Fish Creek
W. 36TH AV.
E 36TH AV
SPENARD
Lake Hood
Lake Spenard
Floatplane Base
TUDOR ROAD
Alaska Native Medical Center
INTERNATIONAL AIRPORT ROAD
International Airport
OLD SEWARD HIGHWAY
North Fork Campbell Creek
Far North Bicentennial Park
RASPBERRY ROAD
JEWEL LAKE ROAD
Sand Lake
Campbell Field
South Fork Campbell Creek
ABBOTT LOOP ROAD
LAKE OTIS PARKWAY
Jewel Lake
E. DIMOND BLVD.
Dimond Transit Center
Hillside Park Ski Area
W. DIMOND BLVD.
Campbell Lake
ABBOTT ROAD
ABBOTT LOOP RD.
BIRCH ROAD
HILLSIDE DRIVE
PROSPECT DR
O MALLEY ROAD
Zoo
Little Campbell Creek
BRAGAW STREET
HUFFMAN ROAD
UPPER HUFFMAN RD
UPPER DE ARMOUN RD
DE ARMOUN ROAD
Rabbit Creek
ACCOMMODATION
Anchorage Guesthouse C
Centennial Campground A
Qupqugiac Inn D
Ship Creek Landings RV Park B
Spenard Hostel International E
RESTAURANTS & CLUBS
Bear Tooth Theatre Pub 1
Chilkoot Charlie's 2
N
0 1 mile
Girdwood (25 miles) & Seward (115 miles)

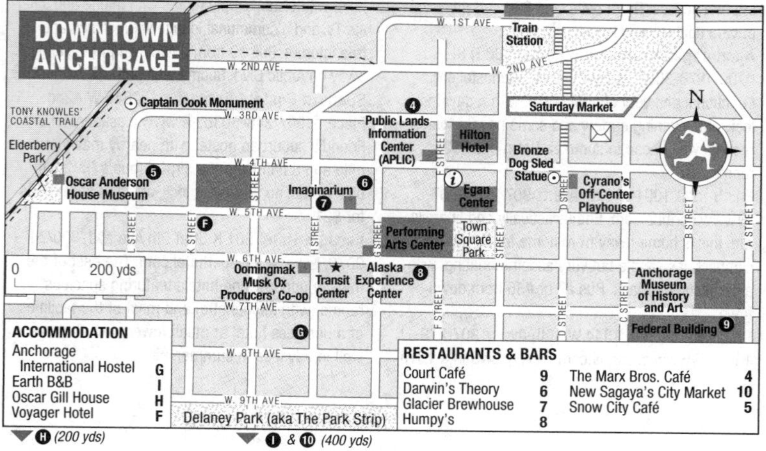
DOWNTOWN ANCHORAGE
W. 1ST AVE.
Train Station
W. 2ND AVE.
Captain Cook Monument
TONY KNOWLES' COASTAL TRAIL
W. 3RD AVE.
Saturday Market
Public Lands Information Center (APLIC)
Hilton Hotel
Elderberry Park
W. 4TH AVE.
Bronze Dog Sled Statue
Oscar Anderson House Museum
Imaginarium
Egan Center
Cyrano's Off-Center Playhouse
W. 5TH AVE.
L STREET
K STREET
H STREET
G STREET
E STREET
D STREET
C STREET
B STREET
A STREET
Performing Arts Center
Town Square Park
W. 6TH AVE.
Oomingmak Musk Ox Producers' Co-op
Transit Center
Alaska Experience Center
Anchorage Museum of History and Art
0 200 yds
W. 7TH AVE.
F STREET
Federal Building
W. 8TH AVE.
W. 9TH AVE.
Delaney Park (aka The Park Strip)
N
ACCOMMODATION
Anchorage International Hostel G
Earth B&B I
Oscar Gill House H
Voyager Hotel F
RESTAURANTS & BARS
Court Café 9
Darwin's Theory 6
Glacier Brewhouse 7
Humpy's 8
The Marx Bros. Café 4
New Sagaya's City Market 10
Snow City Café 5
H (200 yds)
I & 10 (400 yds)

The City

Travelers eager to rush off into the "real" Alaska tend to overlook cosmopolitan Anchorage – a blend of old and new, urban blight and rural parks – but there is plenty to see, and it's worth spending some time experiencing it.

Your first stop should be the **Anchorage Museum of History and Art**, 121 W Seventh Ave (summer daily 9am–6pm; $8), providing an excellent overview of the state and its history through intricate dioramas, alongside beautiful examples of carved ivory and basketware. The art gallery on the ground floor is notable for the works by Alaska's best-known painter, Sydney Laurence, including a monumental oil painting of Mount McKinley.

The rest of the downtown sights are more modest: the **Imaginarium**, 737 W Fifth Ave (Mon–Sat 10am–6pm, Sun noon–5pm; $5.50), has hands-on displays telling you all about glaciers, the Northern Lights, polar bears, and the private life of the dopey-looking moose; the period-furnished 1915 **Oscar Anderson House Museum**, 420 M St (June to mid-Sept Mon–Fri noon–5pm; $3), illustrates early Anchorage life; and the **Alaska Experience Theater**, 333 West 4th Ave (daily 10am–9pm; $10), presents forty minutes of Alaska's best scenery, shot from choppers and beamed onto a 180° wraparound screen; the admission price includes a film of the devastating 1964 Good Friday **earthquake** that leveled much of downtown – North America's strongest-ever quake at Magnitude 9.2.

Seven miles east on the edge of town lies the **Alaska Native Heritage Center**, off the Glenn Highway at Muldoon Road (mid-May to mid-Sept daily 9am–5pm; $23.50). Although pricey, it gives an excellent introduction to the state's five main ethnic groups, each represented by a typical house where Native guides interpret their culture. Throughout the day, cultural groups perform in the main auditorium, where there is also an instructive introductory film. A free shuttle runs to the Center from the Sheraton downtown.

On long summer days it is better to stay outside, perhaps strolling (or biking) along the **Tony Knowles Coastal Trail**, which offers restorative views of Turnagain Arm, or exploring the mountains and lakes of the 495,000-acre **Chugach State Park**, just fifteen minutes' drive east from Anchorage. Challenging trails traversing the park include an often treacherous scramble up 4500ft Flattop Mountain, giving spectacular views of the city and Cook Inlet.

Eating, drinking, and nightlife

Nowhere in Alaska will you find a more diverse range of places to **eat** than in Anchorage. That's not to say you'd make a special journey here for the culinary wonders, but after a few weeks in the wilds, the city can seem like heaven. For groceries, make for Carr's supermarket at the junction of Northern Lights Boulevard and Minnesota Drive (bus #3 or #36), which has a strong deli section.

Good **bars** abound, both downtown and in the lively (and somewhat edgy) neighborhood of **Spenard** – on Spenard Road between Northern Lights Boulevard and International Airport Road. Shows, plays, opera, and concerts take place at the **Center for Performing Arts** (Ⓣ907/263-2787).

Bear Tooth Theatre Pub 1230 W 27th Ave Ⓣ907/276-4200, Ⓦwww.beartooththeatre.net. Top-notch combined restaurant, bar, and cinema where, for $3 on top of your meal price, you can also watch an arthouse movie. The menu has a wide range – Caesar salads ($7), burritos and tacos ($9–11), and gourmet pizzas ($13–19 for a 14-inch), and the microbrews are excellent.

Chilkoot Charlie's 2435 Spenard Rd Ⓣ907/272-1010, Ⓦwww.koots.com. Sawdust-strewn barn that packs them in nightly for pricey drinks, pool, foosball, two floors of DJ-led dance, and live music from 9.30pm.

Court Café 222 W 7th at C St Ⓣ907/277-6736. Breakfast and lunch cafeteria that's about the best budget value downtown, certainly a cut above the fast-food joints and more filling. Steaming clam chowder or an entrée will cost around $6.

Darwin's Theory 426 G St at 4th Ave ⓣ907/277-5322. Straightforward local bar good for moderately priced boozing and neighborly encounters with colorful local characters.

Glacier Brewhouse 737 W 5th St ⓣ907/274-2739 ⓦwww.glacierbrewhouse.com. Hugely popular restaurant, bar, and microbrewery serving wonderful food and drink. At least half a dozen toothsome house-brewed beers accompany alder-wood-baked gourmet pizza ($11), spit-grilled three-peppercorn prime rib ($26), or steamed Alaska King crab legs ($37).

Humpy's 610 W 6th Ave ⓣ907/276-2337, ⓦwww.humpys.com. Popular watering hole with live music and a strong college-bar feel. The likes of charbroiled salmon, burgers, soups, and salads (mostly about $10) slip down with local micro-brews plus English and Belgian bottled beers, and over thirty single malts.

The Marx Bros. Café 627 W 3rd Ave ⓣ907/278-2133, ⓦwww.marxcafe.com. The best all-round fine dining downtown served up in a historic house with views of the water. Start on the likes of Kachemak Bay oysters with pepper vodka and ginger sorbet ($13) or Neapolitan seafood mousse ($15), followed by potato-wrapped halibut with a Provençal sauce ($35). Dinner only.

New Sagaya's City Market 900 W 13th Ave at I St ⓣ907/274-6173. Trendy and expensive grocery store, deli, and café with a great selection ranging from organic vegetables and great cheeses to pizza, wraps, Thai dishes, and good coffee. The nearest groceries to downtown.

Snow City Café 1034 W 4th Ave ⓣ907/272-2489. The best place downtown for breakfast – eggs Benedict or Florentine for $11, yogurt, fruit and granola for $6 – or relaxing over a pot of Earl Grey and a slice of cake. Lunchtime options include soups, salads, pesto chicken pasta ($11), and tofu stir-fry ($11). Daily to 4pm.

Kenai Peninsula

South of Anchorage, the Seward Highway hugs the shore of **Turnagain Arm** past **Girdwood** and the ski resort of **Alyeska**. Just beyond, a side road cuts to the ever-popular **Portage Glacier**, and continues through a tunnel to **Whittier**, little more than a ferry dock for accessing Prince William Sound (see p.1156). Beyond Portage, the Seward Highway enters the **Kenai Peninsula**, "Anchorage's playground," which at over nine thousand square miles is larger than some states. The peninsula offers an endless diversity of activities and scenery, mostly concentrated around major communities such as **Seward**, the base for cruises into the inspirational **Kenai Fjords National Park**, and artsy **Homer**, where the waters and shorelines of the glorious **Kachemak Bay State Park** are the main destination. Most Alaskans come to the Kenai Peninsula to **fish**: the Kenai, Russian, and Kasilof rivers host "combat fishing," with thousands of anglers standing elbow to elbow using strength and know-how to pull in thirty-pound-plus king salmon. **Campgrounds** along the rivers fill up fast, especially in July and August.

Girdwood and Portage Glacier

Outdoorsy **GIRDWOOD**, 37 miles south of Anchorage, lies two miles inland in the shade of the **Alyeska Resort**, Alaska's largest winter sports complex and the lowest-elevation ski resort in the world, starting just 270 feet above sea level. Downhill runs and an extensive night-skiing operation run from November to mid-April (tows $55 a day), and in summer you can ride the Alyeska Tramway ($18) up to stunning views and some good hiking territory. Girdwood Ski and Cyclery, Mile 1.5 Alyeska Highway (ⓣ907/783-2453; closed Mon & Tues), rents city **bikes** ($25 a day) to explore the town and coastal cycle path.

Stay at the grand *Alyeska Prince Hotel* (ⓣ907/754-1111 or 1-800/880-3880, ⓦwww.alyeskaresort.com; ❽); *Carriage House B&B*, Mile 0.2 Crow Creek Rd (ⓣ1-888/961-9464, ⓦwww.thecarriagehousebandb.com; ❺), or *Alyeska Hostel*

(☎907/783-2222, Ⓦwww.alyeskahostel.com; $50), with $20 bunks and rooms. There's tasty, inexpensive **food** at *The Bake Shop* (☎907/783-2831) on Olympic Mountain Loop at the base of the ski tows, and at the unmissable Cajun-influenced *Double Musky Inn* on Crow Creek Road (☎907/783-2822): budget on $40 a head and a meal to remember.

Eleven miles south of Girdwood, a road leads to Whittier, past **Portage Glacier**, a popular day-tour from Anchorage. Frustratingly, you can't see the glacier from the parking lot; instead you must pay Gray Line $29 for a cruise around the lake's corner to the glacier's snout. Two USFS **campgrounds** ($12–18) can be found two or three miles back down the road.

Seward and Kenai Fjords National Park

SEWARD, ringed by glaciers and mountains 127 miles south of Anchorage, sprang to life in 1903 after engineers declared this ice-free port the ideal starting point for railroad tracks to the Interior. Since then it has been a key freight terminal, but tourism – particularly cruises into Kenai Fjords National Park – is now its most conspicuous business.

Seward's main activities are enjoying the scenery and visiting the wonders at the waterfront **SeaLife Center** (summer daily 9am–7pm; $20), a successful marriage of marine research and visitor education partly funded by the Exxon Valdez oil spill settlement. The center offers the chance to watch ongoing cold-water research in action and marvel at the underwater antics of stellar sea lions, harbor seals, and adorable puffins. Also tackle **Mount Marathon** (4hr round-trip) for some glorious views: the trail here is the scene of an annual Fourth of July race, thanks to the antics of two pioneers who, in 1909, bet each other to run up and down the 3022-foot mountain – the current race record is 43 minutes 23 seconds.

Most visitors also drive thirteen miles out to **Exit Glacier** (24hr; free), one of the few in the state you can approach on land. From the **nature centre** at the end of the road (summer daily 9am–8pm; free), a short stroll leads to the still-active glacier, though signs warn you back from the ice wall and its inviting blue clefts. Exit Glacier is part of **KENAI FJORDS NATIONAL PARK**, a magnificent 580,000-acre region of peaks, glaciers, and craggy coastline. Its towering mountains are mantled by the prodigious three-hundred-square-mile Harding Icefield, feeding the three dozen retreating glaciers, which have exposed the dramatic fjords after which the park is named. Eight of these tidewater glaciers "calve" icebergs into the sea with thunderous booms, and the fjords also hold a wealth of **marine wildlife** – sea otters, porpoises, seals, stellar sea lions, plus orca, gray, humpback, and minke whales – as well as the seabird rookeries on the cliffs of the Chiswell Islands. All the Seward-based **cruise** companies do a good job: try Renown Tours (☎1-888/514-8687; $69–139); pay out for the longer day-tours that go right up to the calving tidewater glaciers.

The park's **visitor center**, 1212 Fourth Ave in Seward's small boat harbor (summer daily 8.30am–7pm; ☎907/224-2125), provides maps, film shows, and details on regional hikes.

Practicalities

Get here from Anchorage on daily **trains** (a lovely journey: ☎1-800/544-0552; $69 single, $110 round-trip) or using Seward Bus Line (☎907/224-3608; $50 single). Seward's two hubs of activity, the small boat harbor and downtown, are joined by the mile-long Fourth Avenue, while the main **visitor center** is inconveniently situated at Mile 2 Seward Highway (summer daily 8am–6pm; ☎907/224-8051, Ⓦwww.sewardak.org). There's a shuttle bus (☎907/224-5569; $10 round-trip) running from the small boat harbor hourly to Exit Glacier.

For budget **accommodation** downtown, go to the slightly cramped *Moby Dick Hostel*, 432 3rd Ave (mid-April to Sept; ⓣ907/224-7072, ⓦwww.mobydickhostel.com; ③), with bunks ($18), limited kitchen facilities, and small private rooms, or try the more upscale *Murphy's Motel*, 911 Fourth Ave (ⓣ1-800/886-8191, ⓦwww.murphysmotel.com; ⑤–⑦), close to the small boat harbor. Alternatively, head out of town to the lovely *Alaska's Treehouse* (ⓣ907/224-3867, ⓦwww.seward.net/treehouse; room ④, suite ⑥), a very welcoming B&B in a large timber house with a hot tub out on the deck among the spruce trees seven miles out along the Seward Highway (turn into Timber Lane Drive then Forest Rd). Campers can almost fish from their tent at the excellent, centrally located *Waterfront Campground* (mid-April to Sept; tents $10, RVs $15–30), off Ballaine Boulevard.

Food in Seward is fairly reasonably priced: for good coffee or light meals, head to *Resurrect Art*, 320 3rd Ave, a converted church where you can also play board games, while *Yoly's Bistro*, 220 4th Ave (ⓣ907/224-3295) is a great downtown restaurant and bar serving soups, sandwiches, and the likes of lemongrass chicken ($15) and wasabi halibut ($21). For fine dining (mains around $25), try *Chinook's Waterfront* 1316 4th Ave (ⓣ907/224-2207), which is near the small boat harbor and has great mountain views. If you're looking for a good range of beers, stop at the lively *Yukon Bar*, 201 4th Ave at Washington Street, which also offers live music throughout the summer – jam session, karaoke, live bands, and usually a set or two from Kenai Peninsula legend Hobo Jim on Sunday.

Homer and around

HOMER, 226 miles south from Anchorage, is the Kenai Peninsula's southernmost road-accessible town. It commands a truly magnificent setting, spread beneath gently sloping verdant bluffs with a four-mile finger of land – **The Spit** – slinking out into the dark waters of Kachemak Bay, into which flow crystal-blue glaciers, framed by dense black forest. With abundant activities, a lively nightlife, and a varied, youthful population that supports a thriving arts community, it's so appealing you'll probably want to linger a few days extra.

Russians, drawn by the abundance of coal, were the first whites to reach the area, and by the mid-1800s several American companies had followed suit. In 1896, **Homer Pennock**, a gold-seeker from Michigan, set up the community that still bears his name. Every summer in recent years, young people from the Lower 48 have arrived here in droves to work on the halibut boats, many living in an impromptu tent city on the beach.

Arrival, information, and getting around

The Stage Line (ⓣ907/399-4429) runs a daily **bus** service between Anchorage and Homer for $65 each way. Most hotels, restaurants, and shops are in town, while almost all of the fishing charter and tour operators can be found along the twee boardwalks of The Spit. There is no public transport between the town and The Spit so hitch, grab a cab or rent a bike from Homer Saw & Cycle, 1532 Ocean Drive (ⓣ907/235-8406; $25 a day). The main **visitor center** is at 201 Sterling Hwy (summer Mon–Fri 9am–7pm, Sat & Sun 10am–6pm; ⓣ907/235-7740, ⓦhomeralaska.org).

Accommodation

Homer's good-value **hotels** and **B&Bs** are often fully booked in midsummer; the visitor center, though, can help if you arrive without reservations.

Driftwood Inn 135 W Bunnell Ave ⓣ1-800/478-8019, ⓦwww.thedriftwoodinn.com. Rambling older hotel with an extensive and varied range of rooms, RV parking, and a communal TV lounge with video library. There is free tea and coffee and breakfast is available for a fee. Shared bath ❹, private bath ❹–❼.

Homer Hostel 304 W Pioneer Ave ⓣ907/235-1463, ⓦwww.homerhostel.com. Centrally located hostel in a converted home where you sleep in made-up beds and bunks ($23), in 5- to 6-bed dorms, and relax in a big lounge with a great view of the mountains. There's no curfew or lock-out and they have cheap bike and rod rental. Rooms ❸

Homer Spit Camping ⓣ907/235-1583. The classic Homer experience, either in tents on the beach or in RVs around the fishing hole. Within a short walk of each site, you'll find drinking water, toilets, and fish-cleaning tables. $8 per tent, $15 per RV.

Old Town B&B 106 W Bunnell Ave ⓣ907/235-7558, ⓦwww.oldtownbedandbreakfast.com. Beautiful, three-room B&B in a 1936 building. The rooms have wooden floors and a restrained decor of antiques, quilted bed covers, and old-fashioned bathroom fittings; two have tremendous sea views (one with private bathroom). Shared bath ❹, private ❺

Seaside Farm Hostel Mile 5 East End Rd ⓣ907/235-7850, ⓦwww.xyz.net/~seaside . Small farm hostel with slightly cramped bunks ($20) and a lovely range of rooms, plus small cabins dotted around the property. Open May–Sept. Camping $10, rooms & cabins. ❷

The Town and around

Stop first at the new **Alaska Islands & Ocean Visitor Center**, 95 Sterling Hwy (summer daily 9am–6pm; free; ⓣ907/235-6961, ⓦwww.islandsandocean.org), designed to showcase various facets of the Alaska Maritime National Wildlife Refuge through interactive exhibits, replica seabird cliffs, and sections on the work of biologists in remote locations. Not far away, the **Pratt Museum**, 3779 Bartlett St (daily 10am–6pm; $6), features excellent displays on Kachemak Bay, its people and history along with remote-controlled cameras trained on nesting seabirds and the salmon-feeding bears. Many of Homer's most popular activities, however, revolve around The Spit. To Alaska anglers, Homer is **"Halibut Central"**: a full day's fishing excursion with any of the charter companies begins at around $190. If you don't mind joining the crowds, it's cheaper and simpler to visit the **Fishing Hole**, a tiny bight on The Spit, which is stocked with salmon and offers good fishing from mid-May to mid-September.

The prime tourist attraction in the Homer area is **Kachemak Bay State Park**, directly across the bay, with its 250,000 acres of forested mountains, glaciers, pristine fjords, and inlets. Bird species here include puffin, auklets, kittiwakes, and storm petrels, and marine creatures such as seals, sea otters, and whales are also plentiful. The most popular destination is the gorgeous hamlet of **Halibut Cove**, where boardwalks link art galleries and *The Saltry* restaurant: the *Danny J* **ferry** (ⓣ907/235-7847) makes two daily trips to Halibut Cove, on the south shore of the bay, via Gull Island rookery, for $50 round-trip, $30 if you book in for an evening meal.

The area's best trails, most of them manageable in a day, are those in Kachemak Bay State Park, on the south side of Kachemak Bay: pick up the park's hiking-trails leaflet ($2) and other information from the visitor center. The most-traveled route, up to **Grewingk Glacier**, is an easy three-and-a-half-mile trek above the spruce and cottonwood forest to the foot of the glacier, from where you get splendid views of the bay.

Eating and drinking

Not surprisingly, Homer's culinary scene focuses mostly on fresh fish. For **nightlife**, head out to a colorful bar or to the relaxed **Pier One Theater** (June–Aug; ⓣ907/235-7333), next to the fishing hole on the Spit.

Café Cups 162 Pioneer Ave ⓣ907/235-8330. Relaxing yet vibrant café serving some of the best coffee and great sandwiches and salads.

Fat Olive's 276 Ohlson Lane ⓣ907/235-3448. Chic modern restaurant with strong Italian leanings, excellent pizza, a convivial atmosphere, and a good selection of microbrews.

Lands End Resort at the end of The Spit ⓣ1-800/478-0400. Plush and not-too-pricey restaurant offering an absolutely wonderful view of the bay as well as a fairly standard but tasty Alaska menu. Breakfast is a must.

Salty Dawg The Spit. No self-respecting drinker should pass up a few jars in the *Dawg* with its dark interior, life preservers pinned to the wall, and what is reliably claimed to be the only surveyors' benchmark located in a bar in the US.

Two Sisters Bakery 233 E Bunnell Ave ⓣ907/235-2280. Great little spot for that morning coffee either in the bakery or at tables out on the deck. Good too for pizza, soups, and quiches at moderate prices.

Prince William Sound

Prince William Sound, a largely unspoiled wilderness of steep fjords and mountains, glaciers and rainforest, rests calmly at the head of the Gulf of Alaska. Sheltered by the Chugach Mountains in the north and east, and the Kenai Peninsula in the west, and with its sparkling blue waters full of whales, porpoise, sea otters, and seals, the Sound has a relatively low-key tourist industry. The only significant settlements, spectacular **Valdez**, at the end of the trans-Alaska pipeline, and **Cordova**, a fishing community only accessible by sea or air, are the respective bases for visiting the **Columbia** and **Childs glaciers.**

The region's first settlers, the Chugach Eskimos, were edged out by the more aggressive Tlingit, in their turn displaced by Russian trappers in search of sea otter pelts, and then by American gold prospectors and fishers. The whole glorious show was very nearly spoiled forever on Good Friday 1989, when the **Exxon Valdez** spilled eleven million gallons of its cargo of crude oil. Although the long-term effects have yet to be fully determined, the spill fortunately affected just a fifth of the Sound and today no surface pollution is visible.

Valdez

VALDEZ, 300 road miles from Anchorage and the Western Hemisphere's northernmost ice-free port, lies at the head of a fjord reaching twelve miles inland from Prince William Sound. With its stunning backdrop of mountains, glaciers, and waterfalls, and a record annual snowfall of over forty feet, Valdez (pronounced *val-Deez*) offers great hiking, rafting, sea kayaking, wildlife-viewing, and, of course, fishing.

The 1890s **Gold Rush** transformed Valdez from a remote whaling station into a flourishing settlement, when thousands of prospectors came to cross the deadly Valdez and Klutina glaciers on the Valdez Trail to the mines in the Yukon. Only three hundred of the 3500 miners who set out made it to the goldfield – those that did not perish from frostbite and starvation gave up. Valdez came to depend on fish canneries, logging, and occasional military use for its survival, but nature conspired to finish it off on Good Friday 1964: the epicenter of North America's largest **earthquake** was just 45 miles away. The ground turned to quivering jelly, snapping roads, toppling buildings, and killing 33 residents. However, the citizens of Valdez refused to be intimidated, and moved sixty-odd buildings to the more stable present site four miles away.

The town's fortunes rose again during the 1970s, when oil was found beneath Prudhoe Bay, and Valdez became the southern terminus of the 800-mile **trans-Alaska pipeline**, carrying close to a million barrels of oil per day. Although winds and tides kept the oil from the *Exxon Valdez* out of the port of Valdez, ironically the spill triggered an economic boom as the city became the base for the massive **cleanup.** The operation cost Exxon three billion dollars, and called on eleven

▲ Kayaking in Prince William Sound

thousand workers in over one thousand boats and three hundred planes to scour the beaches. All seems pristine now, though many species have still not fully recovered their former numbers.

Arrival and information

One of the most exciting things about Valdez is getting here; both car and ferry rides are unforgettable. The **Richardson Highway** holds epic scenery: restful alpine meadows, mountain glaciers, the icy summit of **Thompson Pass**, and the waterfall-fringed **Keystone Canyon**. There is no regular bus service, but **ferries** from Cordova or Whittier dock at the end of Hazelet Avenue (Ⓣ907/835-4436). ERA Aviation (Ⓣ1-800/866-8394, Ⓦwww.flyera.com) flies three times daily from Anchorage (from $190 round-trip) to the **airport** five miles north, from where **taxis** (Ⓣ907/835-2500) run downtown for around $10. The **visitor center** (summer Mon–Fri 8am–7pm, Sat 9am–6pm, Sun 10am–5pm; ⓣ907/835-4636, ⓦwww.valdezalaska.org) is at 200 Chenega St.

Accommodation

Valdez's **accommodation** gets snapped up pretty quickly and there's no hostel, but a free phone outside the visitor center connects with some of the fifty-plus **B&Bs**. **Campers** can choose between the central but busy *Bear Paw RV Park* (ⓣ907/835-2530; $25), and the inconvenient *Valdez Glacier Campground* (ⓣ907/873-4058; $12), five miles from town past the airport. The cheapest rooms are at *L&L's B&B*, 533 W Hanagita St (ⓣ907/835-4447, ⓦwww.lnlalaska.com; ❸), with five comfortable shared bathrooms ten minutes' walk from the center, but with free bikes and a good breakfast. Upscale, there's the *Valdez Harbor Inn*, 100 N Harbor Drive (ⓣ1-888/222-3440, ⓦwww.valdezharborinn.com; ❻), a renovated *Best Western*, with a great waterside location, where rooms have cable TV, DVD player, microwave, fridge, and free wi-fi.

The town and around

The **Valdez Museum**, 217 Egan Drive (summer daily 9am–6pm; $6), carries just enough detail on the Gold Rush, oil terminal, glaciation, and *Exxon Valdez* oil spill. The entry price covers you for its **annex**, at 436 S Hazelet Ave (same hours), which covers the 1964 earthquake at length.

The **Maxine & Jesse Whitney Museum** at the Community College, 303 Lowe St (summer daily 9am–7pm; $5) has an astounding collection of carved ivory and an assortment of dead beasts, including a couple of moose hides with Alaskan scenes burned into them by an early pioneer. There's also an instructive documentary on the Alaska Pipeline.

If you fancy something more active, Pangaea Adventures (ⓣ1-800/660-9637, ⓦwww.alaskasummer.com) offer **sea-kayaking** trips to Duck Flats (3–4hr; $60), or a more ambitious coastal paddle to Gold Creek (6–7hr; $89). It is worth making the effort to reach distant paddling destinations, (accessed by water taxi), principally Shoup Glacier (8hr; $180) and Columbia Glacier (10hr; $230). They also offer **kayak rentals** (single $45 per day, double $65), the rates reducing by $5 a day after the first day._

You should also take a cruise out into Prince William Sound, principally to see the spectacular **Columbia Glacier**, three miles wide at its face and towering three hundred feet above the sea. Unfortunately it is receding rapidly and the fjord is now so choked with ice that you can't get close to the face. Weather permitting, you can see it at long range from the AMHS **ferries** running between Valdez and Whittier, but for a closer look go with Stan Stephens Glacier & Wildlife Cruises (ⓣ1-866/867-1297, ⓦwww.stanstephenscruises.com), who pick their way through a floating icefield and point out such sights as Bligh Reef, where the *Exxon Valdez* grounded. Choose between a six-hour cruise at $100 and the nine-hour cruise that also visits the Meares Glacier ($135).

Eating

The **dining** selection in Valdez, while nothing particularly special, should satisfy for the night or two you're here. The *Alaska Halibut House*, 208 Meals Ave (ⓣ907/835-2788) serves budget halibut sandwiches and salmon wedges, but the best all-around dining is at *Alaska's Bistro* (ⓣ907/835-5688, ⓦwww.alaskasbistro.com) in the *Valdez Harbor Inn*. Oil-boom survivor *The Pipeline Club*, 136 Egan Drive (ⓣ907/835-4332), is also worth a try for top-quality steak and seafood, as well as for its lively dark bar.

Cordova and the Copper River Delta

Far quieter than Valdez, and only accessible by sea or air, **CORDOVA** is an unpretentious fishing community on the southeastern edge of the Sound. In 1906 Irish engineer **Michael J. Heney** chose Cordova as the port for the copper mined in Kennicott, a hundred miles northeast, and gambled on cutting a path between two active glaciers for his proposed Copper River and Northwestern Railroad – the CR&NW – ridiculed at the time as the "Can't Run & Never Will." Nonetheless, in 1911 Heney spanned the Copper River with the elaborate "**Million Dollar Bridge**" and the railroad was completed. Even so, the mines were exhausted just 27 years later and Cordova shifted its dependency to fishing, in turn dealt a potentially fatal blow by the grounding of the *Exxon Valdez* in 1989. For the next two seasons, the community reeled from the effects of the **oil spill**; since then fortunes have slowly improved.

Today the "Million Dollar Bridge," battered by the 1964 earthquake, cuts a lonely figure at the end of the Copper River Highway, a 48-mile gravel road across the wondrous wetlands of the **Copper River Delta**, a major breeding ground for America's migratory birds backed by the Chugach Mountains. It is a tranquil spot for fishing, birdwatching, or **hiking** along many of the excellent trails, such as the easy Saddlebag Glacier Trail. The road ends just over the bridge beside the incredibly active **Childs Glacier**.

Copper River and Northwest Tours (Ⓣ907/424-5356) run occasional day-trips to the Million Dollar Bridge ($75 including lunch) , but by far the best way to make the journey is in a **rental car** (from around $70 a day, unlimited mileage) from either Chinook Auto Rentals, in the Airport Depot Diner or at the *Northern Nights Inn* (Ⓣ1-877/424-5279, Ⓦwww.chinookautorentals.com) or Cordova Auto Rental, at the airport (Ⓣ907/424-5982, Ⓦwww.ptialaska.net/~cars).

Cordova itself has few sights; the **small boat harbor** is the core of the town's activity, particularly when the fleet is in, from May until September. The **Cordova Historical Museum**, 620 First St (summer Mon–Sat 10am–6pm, Sun 2–4pm; $1 suggested donation), has quirky exhibits on local history, including the evolution of the little **ice worm** that lives in the glaciers and the funky festival that celebrates its existence each February. The **Ilanka Cultural Center**, by the harbor at 110 Nicholoff Way (Ⓣ907/424-7903; summer Tues–Fri 10am–5pm, Sat noon–4pm; donation), has a complete orca skeleton hanging over the entrance, plus local native arts- and- crafts and a fine bookshop.

Practicalities

There is no road access to Cordova; daily **flights** from Anchorage and Juneau land at the airport twelve miles down the Copper River Highway, to be met by a **bus** ($10). Near-daily **ferries** from Valdez and Whittier dock a mile north of town. For information, contact the **Chamber of Commerce** at 404 First St (Mon–Fri 9am–4pm; Ⓣ907/424-7260, Ⓦwww.cordovachamber.com). Cordova has no **hostel** and the only tent **camping** close to town is at the scruffy *Odiak Campground and RV Park* on Whitshed Road, half a mile south of town (Ⓣ907/424-6200; $20), so you might want to rent a car and camp out along the Copper River Delta. The cheapest option in town is the basic *Alaskan Hotel*, 600 First St (Ⓣ907/424-3299, Ⓔhotelak@ctcak.net; shared bath ❷, private ❸), though you may prefer the *Northern Nights Inn*, 501 Third St (Ⓣ907/424-5356, Ⓦwww.northernnightsinn.com; ❹), or the cosy modern *Cordova Lighthouse Inn*, Nicholoff Way (Ⓣ907/424-7080, Ⓦwww.cordovalighthouseinn.com; ❻), overlooking the small boat harbor. For **food**, try the popular *Killer Whale Café*, 507 First St (Ⓣ907/424-7733). Wash it down afterwards with a drink at the *Alaskan Hotel*'s **bar**.

Interior and northern Alaska

Interior and northern Alaska is the quintessential "great land." For the most part it's a rolling plateau divided by the Alaska and Brooks ranges, crisscrossed by rivers, punctuated by glaciers, and with views of imposing peaks, above all Mount McKinley, the nation's highest. Even in high summer, when RVs clog the George Parks Highway, people are still hugely outnumbered by game: moose, Dall sheep, grizzly bears, and herds of caribou sweep over seemingly endless swathes of taiga (sparse birch woodland) and tundra.

Heading north from Anchorage the first essential stop is tiny **Talkeetna**, which has great views of Mount McKinley and the opportunity to fly around it. The mountain is at the heart of **Denali National Park**, the jewel of the Interior. If you prefer your wilderness with fewer people and regulations, head east to the untrammeled vastness of **Wrangell-St Elias National Park**. Alternatively, **Fairbanks**, Alaska's second city, is diverting in its own right and serves as the hub of the North, with roads fanning out to **hot springs** and five hundred miles north to the Arctic Ocean at **Prudhoe Bay**.

Weather here can vary enormously from day to day, with even greater seasonal variations: in winter temperatures can drop to -50°F for days at a time, while summer days reach a sweltering 90°F. However, the major problem during the warmer months is huge mosquitoes; don't forget the insect repellent.

Talkeetna

A hundred miles from Anchorage, the eclectic hamlet of **TALKEETNA** has a palpable small-town Alaska feel, but is lent an international flavor by the world's mountaineers, who come here to scale the 20,320ft **Mount McKinley**, usually referred to in Alaska by its Athabascan name of **Denali**, "the Great One." Whatever you choose to call it, North America's highest peak rises from 2000ft lowlands, making it the world's tallest from base to peak (Everest et al rise from high terrain). Though central to Denali National Park, the mountain is best seen from the **overlook** just south of Talkeetna, which reveals the peak's transcendent white glow, in sharp contrast to the warm colors all around.

From mid-April to mid-July, climbers mass in Talkeetna to be flown to the mountain: only half of the 1200 attempting the climb each year succeed, usually due to extreme weather. Air-taxi companies such as K2 Aviation (Ⓣ1-800/764-2291, Ⓦwww.flyk2.com) also run **flightseeing** trips ranging from a spectacular one-hour ($190) flight to the full ninety-minute grand tour ($265) all around the mountain. Add half an hour and around $80 for a glacier landing in a plane fitted with skis.

Talkeetna's famed **Moose Dropping Festival** falls on the second weekend of July; little brown balls sell fast (with a sanitary coat of varnish) for use in earrings or necklaces. In addition to these highly desirable lumps of Alaskana, the festival features dancing, drinking, a moose-dropping throwing competition and some more drinking.

Practicalities

Talkeetna is at the end of a fourteen-mile spur off the George Parks Highway, which can usually be hitched. Bus services avoid Talkeetna except for Alaska Park Connection (daily from Anchorage; $56; Ⓣ1-800/266-8625, Ⓦwww.alaskacoach.com); Anchorage to Denali **trains** stop half a mile south of the center of Talkeetna once a day. Information is available from the **Talkeetna Ranger Station**, on B Street (summer daily 8am–6pm; Ⓣ907/733-2231).

For a town of just three hundred, Talkeetna teems with good **accommodation**, including the welcoming *Talkeetna Hostel* on I Street (Ⓣ907/733-4678, Ⓦwww.talkeetnahostel.com; bunks $23, rooms ❸). Dating back to 1917, the central *Talkeetna Roadhouse* (Ⓣ907/733-1351, Ⓦwww.talkeetnaroadhouse.com; ❸–❺) bolsters its old-style atmosphere with great home-cooking, bunks ($21) and rooms with shared bathrooms. Easily the fanciest hotel is the *Talkeetna Alaskan Lodge* (Ⓣ1-877/777-4067, Ⓦwww.talkeetnalodge.com; ❼), on the hill to the south of town. **Campers** can stay at the *Talkeetna River Park* ($12), at the western end of Main Street, but many stroll another hundred yards west and (unofficially) pitch by the river.

Good places to **eat** include the bakery/diner at the *Talkeetna Roadhouse* (see above), and the *West Rib Pub & Grill*, Main Street (Ⓣ907/733-3354), which has good burgers and sandwiches. And make sure you stop for a **drink** in the wonderfully ancient *Fairview Inn* on Main Street.

Denali National Park

The six-million-acre **DENALI NATIONAL PARK**, 240 miles north of Anchorage, is home to **Mount McKinley**, which is often shrouded in cloud. The mountain is far from the park's only attraction, however. Shuttle buses offer a glimpse of a vast world of tundra and taiga, glaciers, huge mountains, and abundant wildlife – the Park Service reports that 95 percent of visitors see **bears**, **caribou**, and **Dall sheep**, 82 percent moose, and over one-fifth **wolves**, along with porcupine, snowshoe hare, red foxes, and over 160 bird species. Visiting Alaska without trying to see Denali is unthinkable for most travelers, and therein lies a problem. In high summer, the visitor center and service areas out on the Parks Highway are a stream of RVs, tour buses, and the like. Things pick up in the park itself, and back-country hiking, undertaken by only a tiny fraction of visitors, remains a wonderfully solitary experience.

In **winter**, Denali is transformed into a ghostly, snow-covered world. Motorized vehicles are banned and transportation, even for park personnel, is by snowshoe, skis, or dogsled as temperatures dive and northern lights glitter over the snows.

▲ Denali National Park

Getting to the park

Driving to Denali Park takes about five hours from Anchorage or three from Fairbanks; **hitching** is quite easy with twenty hours of summer daylight. **Bus** services from Anchorage are run by The Park Connection (ⓣ1-800/266-8625, ⓦwww.alaskacoach.com) and Alaska/Yukon Trails (ⓣ1-800/770-2267, ⓦwww.alaskashuttle.com), charging $65–79, with the latter continuing to Fairbanks ($46). **Trains** (daily in summer) leave at 8.15am from both Anchorage ($135) and Fairbanks ($59), depositing you at 4.10pm and 12.40pm respectively at the train station a mile and a half inside the park entrance. **Park entry** costs $10 per person and is valid for a week.

Sightseeing, hiking, and other activities

The only vehicles allowed on Denali's narrow, unpaved ninety-mile road are a few tour buses and green **shuttle buses**, which you should book well in advance (ⓣ1-800/622-7275, ⓦwww.reservedenali.com) or up to two days ahead at the **wilderness access center** (May–Sept daily 8am–6pm; ⓣ907/683-9274), just inside the park entrance. You can pick up a free copy of the *Alpenglow* paper and a wide range of literature here or at the visitor center, near the train station, or join ranger-led activities including short hikes and the popular, and free, dogsled demonstration held daily at 10am, 2pm, and 4pm.

Shuttle buses run to either the **Toklat River** at Mile 53 ($23), where rangers lead one-hour tundra tours each day at 1.30pm, or to the aptly named **Wonder Lake** at Mile 84 ($40); round-trips take six and eleven hours, respectively. The shuttle drivers don't give guided tours, but with forty pairs of watchful eyes on board, you're almost guaranteed to see the big mammals. You can also hop off at any point for a day-hike (no permits required), returning to the road to flag down the next bus back, if it has room. Buses run at least hourly in season, and there are others used mainly by campers that will pick up stragglers at day's end.

Back-country camping is the best way to appreciate Denali's scenery and its inhabitants. Don't expect it to be easy though, as there are no formal trails, and with thick spongy tundra and frequent river crossings even hardy hikers find themselves limited to five miles a day. The park is divided into 87 units and only a designated number of hikers are allowed into each section at a time. Free permits are available, one day in advance, from the **Backcountry Information Center** (daily 9am–6pm), facing the Wilderness Access Center, though high demand means you should be prepared to hike in the less popular areas. The BIC will also teach you about avoiding run-ins with bears and issue you with bear-resistant food containers. Special camper buses reserved for those with campground or back-country permits cost $29.25. If there's room, buses also carry bikes; cyclists can be dropped anywhere, but are obliged to keep to the road. Another option is to join a **narrated tour** (ⓣ1-800/622-7275) along the park road: either the five-hour Natural History Tour ($56) or the full-day Tundra Wilderness Tour ($94), which penetrates as far as Mile 53, stopping frequently to observe wildlife.

Just outside the park entrance, several **rafting** companies offer two-hour trips down the Nenana River: all offer a gentle "scenic float" and an eleven-mile "Canyon Run" through Class III and IV rapids – they cost around $75 individually and $105 for a joint run. Denali Outdoor Center (ⓣ1-888/303-1925, ⓦwww.denalioutdoorcenter.com) charges a couple of dollars more than some of the others, but offers a quality experience.

Practicalities

With the exception of several exclusive lodges deep in the heart of the park, there are no hotels in Denali, so your choice is between camping, the $160-a-night gaggle of summer-only hotels a mile north of the park entrance, or the cheaper offerings either ten miles further north in the little coal-mining town of **HEALY**, or spots a few miles south along the George Parks Highway. The only cheap option by the park entrance is to camp at *Denali Rainbow Village RV Park* (Mile 238.6, ⓣ907/683-7777, ⓦwww.denalirv.com; from $29) or *Denali Riverside RV Park* (Mile 240.5, ⓣ1-866/583-2696, ⓦwww.denaliriversiderv.com; $22), while the only real hostel hereabouts is the excellent *Denali Mountain Morning Hostel and Lodge*, Mile 224.5, thirteen miles south (ⓣ907/683-7503, ⓦwww.hostelalaska.com; cabins ❸, rooms ❷), set in wooded seclusion and with a bargain shuttle service ($5 round-trip) to the park. Accommodation is in spacious dorms ($25) or separate cabins, there's an efficient kitchen, all manner of games, and the hosts will do everything to facilitate your Denali visit. In Healy there's the high-quality *Motel Nord Haven*, Mile 249.5 Parks Highway (ⓣ1-800/683-4501, ⓦwww.motelnordhaven.com; ❻), and the lovely *Earth Song Lodge*, Mile 4 Stampede Rd (ⓣ907/683-2863, ⓦwww.earthsonglodge.com; ❻), with a cluster of cabins with great mountain views and a café on site.

Camping is the best way to experience Denali up close, with most of the park's six campgrounds open from mid-May to mid-September. The best is **Wonder Lake** ($16), with a stunning view of McKinley; failing that, **Igloo Creek** ($9) is good for spotting Dall sheep, while **Riley Creek** ($12–20), near the entrance, is open year-round. All sites are bookable at the main visitor center or via phone or the web (ⓣ1-800/622-7275, ⓦwww.reservedenali.com). If you don't do this you may have to wait a day or two to get a spot. The best alternative is *Denali Grizzly Bear Resort*, Mile 231.1, seven miles south of Denali (ⓣ1-866/583-2696, ⓦwww.denaligrizzlybear.com; ❶–❼), with $22 campsites set in the trees close to the Nenana River with a wide variety of attractive cabins all around.

Eating is expensive, with only a limited range of grocery stores and a small selection of fairly pricey restaurants close to the park entrance, such as the *Black Bear Coffee House* (ⓣ907/683-1656), serving light meals, and *Lynx Creek Pizza and Pub* (ⓣ907/683-2547), where the menu includes salads and sandwiches as well as pizza and draft microbrews.

Wrangell-St Elias National Park

As Denali becomes more crowded, people are increasingly making the trip to remoter **WRANGELL-ST ELIAS NATIONAL PARK** in the extreme southeast corner of the Interior, where four of the continent's great mountain ranges – the Wrangell, St Elias, Chugach, and Alaska – cramp up against each other. Everything is writ large: glacier after enormous glacier, canyon after dizzying canyon, and nine of the sixteen highest peaks in the US, all laced together by braided rivers and idyllic lakes where mountain goats, Dall sheep, bears, moose, and caribou roam.

The first whites in the area came in search of gold but instead hit upon one of the continent's richest copper deposits. The mines closed in 1938, after 27 frantic years of production, and today **Kennicott**, with over thirty creaking, disused buildings, is a virtual ghost town. You can visit the mill complex on fascinating two-hour **walking tours** run by St Elias Alpine Guides ($25; ⓣ1-888/933-5427, ⓦwww.steliasguides.com), who also run a number of hikes, ice-climbing trips, mountain-bike rides, raft trips, and even glacier skiing adventures out into the virtually trailless park.

Practicalities

Half the fun is getting to McCarthy along 58 rugged miles of the **McCarthy Road**, following the trackbed of the abandoned railroad that once linked the

Kennicott mill to the port at Cordova. Take it slow and stop often to admire the scenery and abandoned trestle bridges. At the end of the road you cross the Kennicott River on a footbridge and continue half a mile to the village of McCarthy on foot, from where a shuttle bus runs along the rough five-mile dirt road to Kennicott. Hitching along the McCarthy Road can be a hit-or-miss affair; if you haven't got a vehicle you can go with Backcountry Connection (Ⓣ1-866/582-5292, Ⓦwww.alaska-backcountry-tours.com), who charge $109 round-trip from Glennallen. The park's **visitor center** is just south of Glennallen at Mile 107 on the Richardson Highway (summer daily 8am–6pm; Ⓣ907/822-5234, Ⓦwww.nps.gov/wrst).

Accommodation around McCarthy and Kennicott isn't cheap, though there are two hostels. *Kennicott River Lodge and Hostel* (Ⓣ907/554-4441, Ⓦwww.kennicottriverlodge.com; ❹), near the road end, has four-bunk cabins ($28 per person) and nice common areas; *Lancaster's Backpacking Hotel*, in McCarthy (Ⓣ907/554-4402, Ⓦwww.mccarthylodge.com; ❸) has simple shared bathrooms costing $48 for one, $68 for two. The associated *Ma Johnson's Hotel* (❻) is very pleasant and atmospheric, and *McCarthy Lodge* across the road serves good food. In Kennicott there's the upscale *Kennicott Glacier Lodge* (Ⓣ1-800/582-5128, Ⓦwww.kennicottlodge.com; ❼), which also has the town's one restaurant (reserve for dinner).

Fairbanks

FAIRBANKS, 360 miles north of Anchorage, is at the end of the Alaska Highway from Canada and definitely at the end of the road for most tourists. Though somewhat bland, its central location makes a great base for exploring a hinterland of gold mines and hot springs, and a staging point for trips into the surrounding wilderness and for journeys along the **Dalton Highway** to the Arctic Ocean oil community of **Prudhoe Bay**.

Alaska's second most populous town was founded accidentally, in 1901, when a steamship carrying trader E.T. Barnette ran aground in the shallows of the Chena River, a tributary of the Yukon. Unable to move his supplies any further, he set up shop in the wilderness and catered to the few trappers and prospectors trying their luck in the area. The following year **gold** was found, a tent city sprang up, and Barnette made a mint. In 1908, at the height of the rush, Fairbanks had a population of 18,500, but by 1920 it had dwindled to only 1100. To thwart possible Japanese attacks during World War II, several huge **military bases** were built and the population rebounded, getting a further boost in the mid-1970s when it became the construction center for the **trans-Alaska pipeline**, causing the population to reach an all-time high. The city's economy dropped dramatically with the oil crash, and unemployment hit twenty percent before government spending put the city back on track.

The spectacular **aurora borealis** is a major winter attraction, as is the **Ice Festival** in mid-March, with its ice-sculpting competition and open-sled dog racing on the frozen downtown streets. Summer visitors should try to catch the three-day **World Eskimo-Indian Olympics** in mid-July, when contestants from around the state compete in the standard dance, art, and sports competitions, as well as some unusual ones like ear-pulling, knuckle hop, high kick, and the blanket toss.

Fairbanks suffers remarkable extremes of climate, with winter temperatures dropping to -70°F and summer highs topping 90°F. Proximity to the Arctic Circle means over 21 hours of sunlight in midsummer, when midnight baseball games take place under natural light, and 2am bar evacuees are confronted by bright sunshine.

Arrival, information, and getting around

Alaska Airlines flies frequently from Anchorage to **Fairbanks Airport**, four miles southwest of downtown; the MACS Yellow Line **bus** (Mon–Sat; $1.50) runs downtown, but the long wait between services means you'll probably want to grab a **taxi** (around $15). Alpenglow (ⓣ1-800/770-2267, ⓦwww.alaskashuttles.com) will take you around town for $5 ($8 round-trip) or to the airport or rail depot. The airport is also a gateway for flights into the bush; Frontier Flying Service (ⓣ1-800/478-6779, ⓦwww.frontierflying.com) operates a reliable service. **Trains** from Anchorage (daily in summer, weekly in winter) stop beside the Johansen Expressway inconveniently far from downtown. It's cheaper to get here by bus with Alaska/Yukon Trails (ⓣ1-800/770-7275, ⓦwww.alaskashuttle.com), who charge $91 from Anchorage, drop off at the visitor center and major hostels and hotels. The best way to get around town is by car, but there's a good riverside cycle trail and the five **bus lines**, run by MACS (ⓣ907/459-1011), provide a reasonable service. Among the companies that can whisk you off into the surrounding bush and fly you to the **Arctic Circle**, the widest choice is with the Northern Alaska Tour Company (ⓣ1-800/474-1986, ⓦwww.northernalaska.com).

The **visitor center**, at 550 First Ave (summer daily 8am–8pm; ⓣ1-800/327-5774, ⓦwww.explorefairbanks.com), carries a vast amount of information on lodging and activities. For information on the area's parks, including Denali, stop by the useful **Alaska Public Land Information Center** (APLIC) at 250 N Cushman St (daily 9am–6pm; ⓣ907/456-0527, ⓦwww.nps.gov/aplic).

Accommodation

Downtown motels and hotels tend to be either quite pricey or pretty dodgy. **B&B**s are plentiful, with rooms from $80 a night; the visitor center offers free phone calls and all the brochures. Thankfully there are a couple of good hostels, and for campers there's the tranquil and convenient *Tanana Valley Campground*, 1800 College Rd at Aurora Drive (mid-May to mid-Sept; ⓣ907/456-7956; $10), on the MACS bus Red line and with free bikes for guests.

Ah, Rose Marie 302 Cowles St ⓣ907/456-2040, ⓦwww.akpub.com/akbbrv/ahrose.html. Small but well-run and justly popular B&B where a hearty breakfast is served on the glassed-in porch. ❹

Billie's Backpackers 2895 Mack Rd ⓣ907/479-2034, ⓦwww.alaskahostel.com. Welcoming though somewhat cramped hostel, in a nice area and handily placed on the bus route between downtown and the university. Free internet access; bikes available. Bunks $35, camping $20.

Golden North Motel 4888 Old Airport Way ⓣ1-800/447-1910, ⓦwww.goldennorthmotel.com. Friendly and spotlessly clean motel near the airport with cable TV and free wi-fi. Courtesy pickups are available, and the Yellow and Blue buses pass nearby. ❹

GoNorth Base Camp 3500 Davis Rd ⓣ907/479-7272, ⓦwww.gonorthalaska.com. A kind of outdoors hostel in a forested area with large fixed tents with five beds ($25; $23 with own sleeping bag). There's also camping ($12–18), space in a tipi ($20) and reasonably priced bike rental.

Minnie Street B&B Inn 345 Minnie St ⓣ1-888/456-1849, ⓦwww.minniestreetbandb.com. Top-line B&B with every luxury, including free wi-fi and a spacious deck with a hot tub. Some rooms have a jacuzzi and there's a full breakfast. Shared bath ❻, private bath ❼, jacuzzi ❽

The Town

The main point of interest **downtown** is the small **Fairbanks Community Museum**, 410 Cushman St at 5th Avenue (Tues–Sat 10am–6pm; donation appreciated), containing locally donated trapping, mining, and dogsled racing equipment. The museum also acts as the public face of the **Yukon Quest** dogsled race – a grueling thousand-mile marathon between Fairbanks and Whitehorse – selling related books, videos, and T-shirts. A similarly wintry theme is pursued at the **Ice Museum**, 500 2nd Ave at Lacey Street (summer daily 10am–8pm; $12), a year-round taster of the Ice Sculpting competition by way of a slide show and walk-in refrigerators housing some small carvings. A couple of miles west on the banks of the Chena River, the touristy **Pioneer Park** (mostly free) celebrates Alaskan history though minor attractions such as pioneer museums, the only large wooden sternwheeler left in the US, and a miniature railway encircles the entire park; there's plenty to amuse the kids. College Road heads west past **Creamer's Field**, thick with sandhill cranes and Canada geese, especially in spring and fall, to the University of Alaska Fairbanks' attractive campus. Here the superb new extension to UAF's **Museum of the North** (summer daily 9am–9pm; $10;, Ⓦ www.uaf.edu/museum) allows it to display its eclectic collection of native and contemporary art, as well as natural and human history displays.

Unashamedly touristy but fun and very popular is a four-hour **cruise** down the Chena River on the "Riverboat Discovery" ($50; Ⓣ 1-866/479-6673, Ⓦ www.riverboatdiscovery.com), which includes a visit to a mock Native village.

Eating and nightlife

Fairbanks' **eating** options are varied, with good Thai particularly prevalent. They're also well scattered, with downtown and College Road, toward the university, having the greatest concentrations. Nowhere downtown sells groceries: the closest are Safeway and Fred Meyer at the eastern end of College Road. Fairbanks has its decent **nightspots**, though none lie in hard-drinking downtown.

Alaska Coffee Roasting Co. West Valley Plaza, 4001 Geist Rd Ⓣ 907/457-5282. Fairbanks' best coffee, roasted daily on the premises served in a cozy café hung with local art. There's a good selection of wraps, cakes, and muffins, too.

Blue Loon Mile 353.5 Parks Hwy Ⓣ 907/457-5666, Ⓦ www.theblueloon.com. Late-closing hotspot five miles west of Fairbanks that's always good for a convivial drink. Hosts local and touring bands (sometimes a DJ) several nights a week, and screens cult and art-house movies. Closed Sun–Tues.

The Diner 244 Illinois St Ⓣ 907/451-0613. Reliable diner fare at good prices.

Gambardella's Pasta Bella 706 2nd Ave, downtown Ⓣ 907/457-4992, Ⓦ www.gambardellas.com. Fairbanks' best Italian and not wildly expensive, with a pleasant outdoor area for those endless summer evenings.

Howling Dog Saloon Mile 11 Old Steese Hwy, Fox Ⓣ 907/456-4695, Ⓦ www.howlingdogsaloon.com. Eleven miles north of town, but perhaps the north's best bar – unassuming, unpretentious, and fun. Live rock and R&B bands perform.

The Marlin 3412 College Rd Ⓣ 907/479-4646. Poky wood-paneled cellar bar at the cutting edge of Fairbanks' music scene with live bands – blues, jazz, and rock – most evenings from around 9pm and only a small cover charge, if any.

Pump House Mile 1.3 Chena Pump Rd Ⓣ 907/479-8452, Ⓦ www.pumphouse.com. A local favorite in a historic pumphouse, stuffed with gold-mining paraphernalia and with a deck to watch life go by on the Chena River. Great for steak, seafood, and burgers, and also pulls in a substantial drinking crowd.

Second Story Café 3525 College Rd Ⓣ 907/474-9574. Pleasant spot above Gulliver's Bookstore, serving wraps, sandwiches, bagels, biscotti, and coffee, all at reasonable prices, Free internet access as well.

Thai House 412 5th Ave, downtown Ⓣ 907/452-6123. A small but ever-popular restaurant serving the usual range of Thai dishes, but all done to perfection and at very modest prices for around $11. Closed Sun.

Around Fairbanks: two hot springs

Chena Hot Springs, the most accessible and developed resort in the area, stands in a clearing sixty miles east of Fairbanks amid a wonderfully bucolic swath of **muskeg** (grassy swampland) and forest traversed by good hiking trails and teeming with moose. For $10 a day non-guests can use the hot pools and large outdoor "rock pool," which are free for those staying at the fully-equipped resort (Ⓣ 1-800/478-4681, Ⓦ www.chenahotsprings.com; ❼–❽), where camping costs $20 and yurts $65. The resort also rents out canoes and mountain bikes, as well as offering rafting float trips.

The Northern Lights

The **aurora borealis**, or "Northern Lights," an ethereal display of light in the uppermost atmosphere, give their brightest and most colorful displays in the sky above Fairbanks. For up to one hundred winter nights, the sky appears to shimmer with dancing curtains of color ranging from luminescent greens to fantastic veils that run the full spectrum. Named after the Roman goddess of dawn, the aurora is caused by an interaction between the earth's magnetic field and the **solar wind**, an invisible stream of charged electrons and protons continually blown out into space by the innate violence of the sun. The earth deflects the solar wind like a rock in a stream, with the energy released at the magnetic poles – much like a neon sign.

The Northern Lights are at their most dazzling from December to March, when nights are longest and the sky darkest, but late September can be good for summer visitors. They are pretty much visible everywhere, but the further north the better, especially around Fairbanks.

The Dalton Highway

Built in the 1970s to service the **trans-Alaska pipeline**, the mostly gravel-surfaced **Dalton Highway**, or Haul Road, runs from Fairbanks five hundred miles to the oil facility of Prudhoe Bay on Alaska's north coast, some three hundred miles beyond the Arctic Circle. It is a long, bumpy, and demanding drive, so take spare tires, gas, provisions, and, ideally, a sturdy four-wheel-drive vehicle: most regular rentals aren't permitted up here. Not far from Fairbanks you start to parallel the pipeline, snaking up hills and in and out of the ground. At 188 miles, a sign announces that you've just crossed the **Arctic Circle**. The **Northern Alaska Tour Company** (Ⓣ 1-800/474-1986, Ⓦ www.northernalaska.com) will drive you up in a minibus and either drive you back to Fairbanks ($169; a long arduous day) or fly you back ($319).

The highway plugs on north through increasingly barren territory, finally dispensing with trees as you climb through the wilderness of the **Brooks Range**, a 9000ft chain mostly held within the **Gates of the Arctic National Park**. From Atigun Pass you descend through two hundred miles of grand glaciated valleys and blasted arctic plains to the end of the road at dead-boring **Deadhorse**. You can't stroll by the ocean or camp here, so your choices are confined to staying in one of the $130-per-night hotels and taking a $39 tour past the adjacent – and off-limits – **Prudhoe Bay** oil facility to the Arctic Ocean where you can dip your toe or go for the full body immersion. By far the best way to do it is with Northern Alaska, who run a three-day fly/drive tour to Prudhoe Bay for $890.

16

Hawaii

AL - ALABAMA	IN - INDIANA	MN - MINNESOTA	RI - RHODE ISLAND
AR - ARKANSAS	LA - LOUISIANA	MS - MISSISSIPPI	SC - SOUTH CAROLINA
CT - CONNECTICUT	MA - MASSACHUSETTS	NC - NORTH CAROLINA	VA - VIRGINIA
DE - DELAWARE	MD - MARYLAND	NH - NEW HAMPSHIRE	VT - VERMONT
FL - FLORIDA	ME - MAINE	NJ - NEW JERSEY	WI - WISCONSIN
IL - ILLINOIS	MI - MICHIGAN	PA - PENNSYLVANIA	WV - WEST VIRGINIA

CHAPTER 16 Highlights

* **Waikiki Beach, Oahu** Learn to surf, or just sip a cocktail, on the world's most famous beach. **See p.1177**
* **Pearl Harbor, Oahu** View a reminder of December 7, 1941 – the "date that will live in infamy" – by visiting the sunken USS Arizona. **See p.1177**
* **Kilauea Eruption, Big Island** The Big Island gets bigger day by day, thanks to the spectacular eruption of its youngest volcano, Kilauea. **See p.1185**
* **Lahaina, Maui** This early nineteenth century whaling port ranks among the most historic towns in Hawaii. **See p.1188**
* **Lumahai Beach, Kauai** This superb beach has been featured in countless movies, but beware the treacherous waters. **See p.1192**
* **Kalalau Trail, Kauai** Admire the magnificent Na Pali coastline of Kauai from one of the world's greatest hiking trails. **See p.1193**

▲ Surfing at Waikiki Beach

16

Hawaii

With their fiery volcanoes, palm-fringed beaches, verdant valleys, glorious rainbows, and awesome cliffs, the islands of **HAWAII** boast some of the most spectacularly beautiful scenery on earth. Despite their isolation, two thousand miles out in the Pacific, they belong very definitely to the United States. Pulling in 7.5 million tourists per year, including honeymooners from all over the world, frequent fliers cashing in their mileage, and 1.5 million Japanese, the fiftieth state can seem at times like a gigantic theme park.

Honolulu, on **Oahu**, is by far the largest city in Hawaii, while Waikiki, its resort annex, is the main tourist center. Three other islands attract sizeable numbers of visitors: **Hawaii** itself, which is also known as the **Big Island** in a vain attempt to avoid confusion, **Maui,** and **Kauai**. All the islands share a similar topography and **climate**. Ocean winds shed their rain on their northeast, **windward** coasts, keeping them wet and green; the southwest, **leeward** (or "Kona") coasts can be almost barren, and so make ideal locations for big resorts. While temperatures remain consistent all year at between 70°F and 85°F, rainfall is heaviest from December to March, which nonetheless remains the most popular time to visit. Although a visit to Hawaii doesn't have to cost a fortune – **budget** facilities do exist – the one major expense you can't avoid, except possibly on Oahu, is car rental.

Some history

Each of the Hawaiian islands was forced up like a vast mass of candle drippings by submarine volcanic action, all fueled by the same "hot spot," which has remained stationary as the Pacific plate drifted above. The process continues at Kilauea on the Big Island, where lava explodes into the sea to add new land day by day, while the oldest islands are now mere atolls way to the northwest. Until two thousand years ago, these unknown specks were populated only by the few plants, birds, and animals carried here by wind or wave. The first known human inhabitants were the **Polynesians,** who arrived in two principal migrations: one from the Marquesas in the eighth century, and another from Tahiti four or five hundred years later.

No Western ship chanced upon Hawaii until **Captain Cook** arrived at Kauai in 1778. He was amazed to find a civilization sharing a culture – and language – with the peoples of the South Pacific. Although Cook himself was killed in Hawaii in 1779, his visit started an irreversible process of change. In reshaping the islands to suit their needs, Westerners decimated most of the indigenous flora and fauna – as well as the Hawaiians themselves. Cook's men estimated that there were a million islanders; the population today is roughly the same, but only eight thousand **pure-blood Hawaiians** are left.

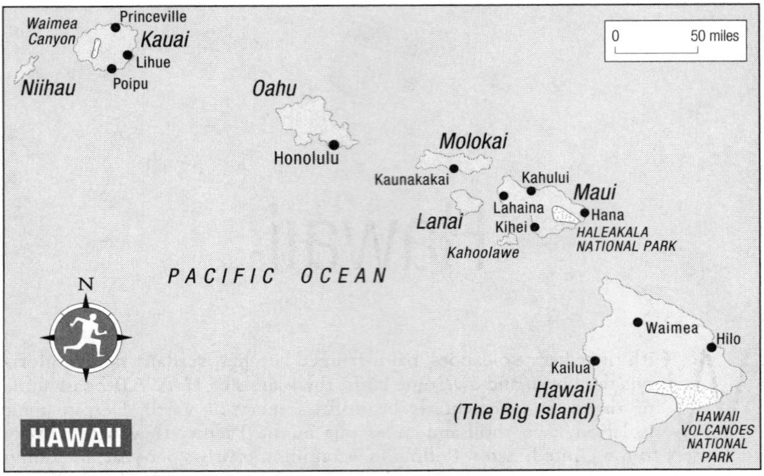

Within a few years of Cook's arrival, **Kamehameha** became the first king to unite all the islands. However, exposure to the world economy swiftly devastated Hawaii's traditional way of life. White advisers and ministers soon dominated the government, and the families of the first missionaries from New England became Hawaii's wealthiest and most powerful class. As the US grew increasingly reliant on Hawaiian-grown **sugar**, Hawaii moved inexorably towards annexation. In 1887 an all-white group of "concerned businessmen" forced King David Kalakaua to surrender power, and subsequently called in the US warship **Boston** and declared a provisional republican government. US President Cleveland (a Democrat) responded that "Hawaii was taken possession of by the United States forces without the consent or wish of the government of the islands . . . (It) was wholly without justification . . . not merely a wrong but a disgrace."

On August 12, 1898, Hawaii was formally **annexed** as a territory of the United States. Its ultimate integration into the American mainstream was hastened by its crucial role in the war against Japan, and the expansion of tourism thereafter. The islands finally became the fiftieth of the United States in 1959, after a plebiscite showed a seventeen-to-one majority in favor. The only group to oppose statehood were the few remaining native Hawaiians.

Modern Hawaii

Roughly sixty percent of the million-plus modern Hawaiians were born here. Around one-third are Caucasian (many of them US military personnel), one-third Japanese, and one-sixth Filipino, with 200,000 claiming at least some Hawaiian ancestry. With agriculture in decline, the need to import virtually all the basics of life results in a high **cost of living**.

Few vestiges of **ancient Hawaii** remain. What is presented as "historic" usually postdates the missionary impact. Ruined temples (**heiaus**) to the old gods still stand in some places, but Hawaii's "old towns" are pure nineteenth-century Americana, with false-front stores and raised wooden boardwalks. While authentic **hula** dancing is a powerful art form, you're most likely to encounter it bastardized in a **luau**. Primarily tourist money-spinners, these "traditional feasts" provide an opportunity to sample Hawaiian **foods** such as **kalua** pig, baked underground, and local fish such as **ono, ahi, mahi-mahi**, and **lomi-lomi** (raw salmon). **Poi** – a paste made from mashed taro root – remains a staple of the diet, much as it was when one of Captain Cook's men described it as "a disagreeable mess."

The Hawaiian **language** endures primarily in place names and music. At first glance it looks unpronounceable – especially as it is written using a mere twelve letters (the five vowels, plus **h, k, l, m, n, p**, and **w**) – but each letter is enunciated individually, and long words often break down into repeated sounds, such as "**meha-meha**" in "Kamehameha."

Getting to and around Hawaii

Honolulu, just under six hours by plane from the US West Coast, is one of the world's busiest centers for air traffic; return fares from **LA, San Francisco**, and **Seattle** start at around $350. There are also direct flights from the mainland to Maui, the Big Island, and Kauai. Many flights to the US from **Australia** – such as those on Continental – include free stopovers in Hawaii. **European** travelers should buy all-inclusive tickets from Europe.

The principal **inter-island airline,** Hawaiian Airlines (Ⓣ1-800/882-8811 or 1-800/367-5320, Ⓦwww.hawaiianair.com), connects all the major islands several times per day, with standard single fares of around $85. A budget competitor, go! (Ⓣ1-888/435-9462, Ⓦwww.iflygo.com), offers less frequent services at cheaper rates. In addition, a high-speed inter-island ferry (Ⓣ1-877/443-3779; Ⓦwww.hawaiisuperferry.com) sails once or twice daily between Oahu and Maui, starting at around $49 per passenger plus $65 per vehicle.

All the airports have **car rental** outlets; with the exception of Oahu, however, **bus** services on the islands barely exist.

Oahu

Three-quarters of Hawaii's population live on **OAHU**, which has monopolized the islands' trade and tourism since European sailors realized that **Honolulu** offered the safest in-shore anchorage for thousands of miles. Eighty percent of visitors to Hawaii arrive in Honolulu, and most remain for their entire vacation. Oahu effectively confines tourists to the tower-block enclave of **Waikiki**, just east of downtown Honolulu; there are few rooms anywhere else.

While overcrowding and development make it hard to recommend Oahu over the **Neighbor Islands** (as the other Hawaiian islands are known), it can still give a real flavor of Hawaii. Oahu has some excellent **beaches**, with those on the North Shore a haven for **surfers** and campers, and the **cliffs** of the Windward side are awesome.

Honolulu

Before the Europeans came, **HONOLULU** was insignificant; soon so many foreign ships were frequenting its waters that it had become Kamehameha's capital, and it remains the economic center of the archipelago. While the city

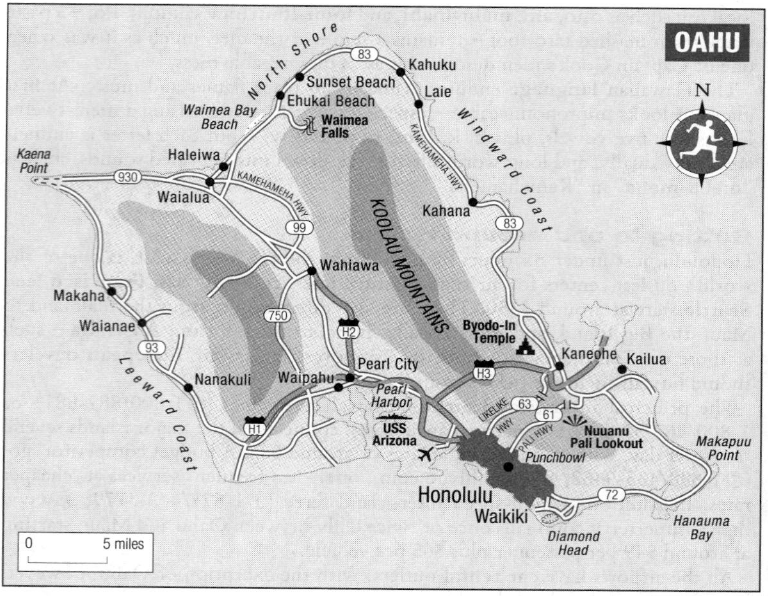

covers a long (if narrow) strip of southern Oahu, **downtown** is a manageable size, and a lot quieter than its glamorous image might suggest. The tourist hotels are concentrated in the skyscrapers of the distinct suburb of **Waikiki**, a couple of miles east.

While its setting is beautiful, right on the Pacific and backed by dramatic cliffs and extinct volcanoes, most visitors are here simply to enjoy the sheer **hedonism** of shopping, eating, and generally hanging out in the sun. It's also the center of an exemplary **public transportation** system that facilitates exploration of the whole island.

Arrival, information, and getting around

Honolulu's **International Airport** is just west of downtown. **Car rental** outlets abound, but a car is not especially desirable in Honolulu, what with city traffic and hefty parking fees in Waikiki. The nine-mile (not at all scenic) drive to Waikiki takes anything from 25 to 75 minutes; Reliable (single $10, round-trip $18; ⓣ1-888/924-9292, ⓦwww.reliableshuttle.com) is one of many **shuttle services** that run to any Waikiki hotel. Regular **buses #19** and **#20** also head to Waikiki, but don't allow large bags, cases, or backpacks. A **taxi** will cost around $25.

Information

The **Hawaii Visitors Bureau** maintains a strong online presence at ⓦwww.gohawaii.com. Free listings magazines and leaflets are everywhere you turn, and all the hotels have information desks. Kiosks around Waikiki offer greatly discounted rates for island tours, helicopter rides, dinner cruises, surfing lessons, and so on.

Getting around

Sixty **bus** routes, collectively named TheBus, cover the whole of Oahu (ⓣ808/848-5555, ⓦwww.thebus.org). All journeys, however long, cost $2, with free transfers onto any connecting route; a 4-day pass costs $20. The most popular routes with Waikiki-based tourists are **#2** to downtown, **#8** to Ala Moana Shopping Center, **#20** to Pearl Harbor, **#22** to Hanauma Bay, and the bargain "Circle Island" buses (**#52** clockwise and **#55** counterclockwise), which take four hours to loop around the central valley and the east coast, passing the legendary North Shore surf spots.

Among companies running **city and island bus tours**, for anything from $27 up to $78 for a full day, as well as off-island packages, are Polynesian Adventure Tours (Ⓣ808/833-3000 or 1-800/622-3011, Ⓦwww.polyad.com).

Accommodation

All the accommodation listed below is in or near **Waikiki**; very little is available in central Honolulu. Waikiki accommodation covers a wide range, and the highest rates will bring absolute luxury, but it's possible to find comfortable lodging for much less. An ocean view costs at least $50 extra; everything is close to the ocean, however.

Aloha Punawai 305 Saratoga Rd Ⓣ808/923-5211 or 1-866/713-9694, Ⓦwww.alternative-hawaii.com/alohapunawai/. This 19-room hotel, opposite the post office, offers clean, air-conditioned apartments and studios, all with kitchenettes. ❺

The Breakers 250 Beach Walk Ⓣ808/923-3181 or 1-800/426-0494, Ⓦwww.breakers-hawaii.com. Small, intimate hotel on the western edge of central Waikiki; all rooms have kitchenettes and TV, and there's a bar and grill beside the pool. ❺

Hawaiiana Hotel 260 Beach Walk Ⓣ808/923-3811 or 1-800/367-5122, Ⓦwww.hawaiianahotelatwaikiki.com. Pleasant little family hotel, abounding in tiki images, where the rooms are ranged around two pools; all have kitchenettes, some have balconies. ❺

New Otani Kaimana Beach Hotel 2863 Kalakaua Ave Ⓣ808/923-1555 or 1-800/356-8264, Ⓦwww.kaimana.com. Intimate, Japanese-toned beachfront hotel half a mile east of central Waikiki. ❼

Outrigger and **Ohana**. Linked hotel chains with numerous locations around Waikiki, mostly high-rises (*Outrigger* Ⓣ1-800/688-7444, Ⓦwww.outrigger.com; *Ohana* Ⓣ1-800/462-6262, Ⓦwww.ohanahotels.com; both also on Ⓣ303/369-7777). *Ohana* hotels like the *Ohana East*, 150 Kaiulani Ave (❺), or the slightly more luxurious *Ohana Waikiki Beachcomber*, 2300 Kalakaua Ave (❺), are generally cheaper than the *Outrigger*s, such as the all-condo *Luana Waikiki*, 2045 Kalakaua Ave (❼), and the flagship *Waikiki on the Beach*, 2335 Kalakaua Ave (❽). ❺–❾

Polynesian Beach Club Hostel 2584 Lemon Rd Ⓣ808/922-1340, Ⓦwww.hawaiihostels.com. Clean, efficiently-run hostel, a block from the sea. Some rooms hold four $25 bunk beds, some hold six at $23, some serve as good-value private doubles, and there are also private suites. Free snorkels and boogie boards are available; there's cheap internet access; and meals are served in the communal area some nights. ❶–❸

The Royal Hawaiian 2259 Kalakaua Ave Ⓣ808/923-7311 or 1-866/716-8109, Ⓦwww.royal-hawaiian.com. This 1920s "Pink Palace," commanding the beach, is one of Waikiki's best-loved landmarks. The entire complex has recently been totally renovated, but the original building, looking out across terrace gardens to the sea, remains irresistible. ❾

Waikiki Beachside Hostel 2556 Lemon Rd Ⓣ808/923-9566 or 1-866/478-3888, Ⓦwww.waikikibeachsidehostel.com. Small hotel block near the park in eastern Waikiki – not literally "beachside" – that has been converted into a popular, lively private hostel, with dorm beds for $26, plus pricier double rooms, and free wi-fi. ❶–❸

The City

Downtown Honolulu is surprisingly small, set back a little from the sea and focused around a spacious plaza on King Street that includes **Iolani Palace** and the **state capitol**. The imposing palace, built for King David Kalakaua in 1882, can be visited on guided tours (by reservation, Ⓣ808/522-0832; Ⓦwww.iolanipalace.org; Tues–Sat 9–11.15am; $20) or self-guided audio tours (Tues–Sat 11.45am–3.30pm; $12); the collection of ancient artifacts in the basement, including feathered royal cloaks, is the most impressive feature. Across the road stands a flower-bedecked, gilt statue of Kamehameha the Great.

To reach the nearby ocean, pedestrians have to negotiate fearsome traffic. The **Aloha Tower** on Pier 9 used to be the city's tallest building; the surrounding area is now a mall, fronting onto the docks and better for dining than it is for shopping. Climb to the top of the tower for an enjoyable overview (Mon–Sat 9am–9pm, Sun 9am–6pm; free). The **Hawaii Maritime Center** just east on Pier 7 (daily 8.30am–5pm; $8.50) documents Hawaii's seafaring past in superb detail, from ancient migrations through to modern tourism. A stunning film from 1922 shows the true-life drama of whaling, and there's a wall of gigantic historic surfboards. In the adjacent dock are the fully rigged four-master **Falls of Clyde** and the replica Polynesian canoe **Hokulea**, whose Pacific voyages have inspired tremendous interest in traditional navigation.

Honolulu residents take great pride in the stunning fine art at the **Academy of Arts**, half a mile east of the capitol at 900 S Beretania St (Tues–Sat 10am–4.30pm, Sun 1–5pm; $10; ⓣ808/532-8700, ⓦwww.honoluluacademy.org). As well as paintings including Van Gogh's **Wheat Field**, Gauguin's **Two Nudes on a Tahitian Beach**, and one of Monet's **Water Lilies**, the Academy also holds fascinating depictions of Hawaii by visiting artists, including vivid, stylized studies of Maui's Iao Valley and Hana coast by Georgia O'Keeffe, plus magnificent ancient **Chinese** ceramics and bronzes.

Chinatown

Just five minutes' walk west of downtown Honolulu, the faded green-clapboard storefronts of **Chinatown**, lining the narrow streets that lead down to Nuuanu Stream, seem like another world. Some of Chinatown's old walled courtyards are now malls, but the businesses remain much the same as ever, and you can still find herbalists weighing out dried leaves in front of vast arrays of bottles. Pig snouts and salmon heads are among the food specialties at **Oahu Market**, on N King and Kekaulike streets.

Bishop Museum

The anthropological collection at the **Bishop Museum** at 1525 Bernice St (daily 9am–5pm; $16; ⓣ808/847-3511, ⓦwww.bishopmuseum.org) – well away from the ocean and downtown, near the foot of the Likelike Highway – showcases real Polynesian culture. Three floors display ancient carved stone and wooden images of gods, magnificent feather **leis** and cloaks, and a full-sized **hale** (traditional hut) from Kauai, in addition to Japanese samurai armor and even a full-sized sperm whale. There are also excellent exhibitions for kids, and a planetarium. TheBus #2 from Waikiki stops two blocks away on Kapalama Street.

Punchbowl

High above Honolulu, lush lawns in the caldera of an extinct volcano are the setting for the **National Memorial Cemetery of the Pacific** (daily: March–Sept 8am–6.30pm; Oct–Feb 8am–5.30pm), which holds casualties from all US Pacific wars, including Vietnam. Once home to an ancient sacrificial temple, it's on TheBus route #15.

Waikiki

Built on a reclaimed swamp, **Waikiki** is very nearly an island, all but separated from Honolulu between the sea and the Ala Wai canal. The site may be venerable, but these days its **raison d'être** is rampant commercialism. You could, just about, survive here with very little money, but there would be no point – there's nothing to see, and the only thing to do apart from surf and sunbathe is to stroll along the seafront **Kalakaua Avenue** and shop.

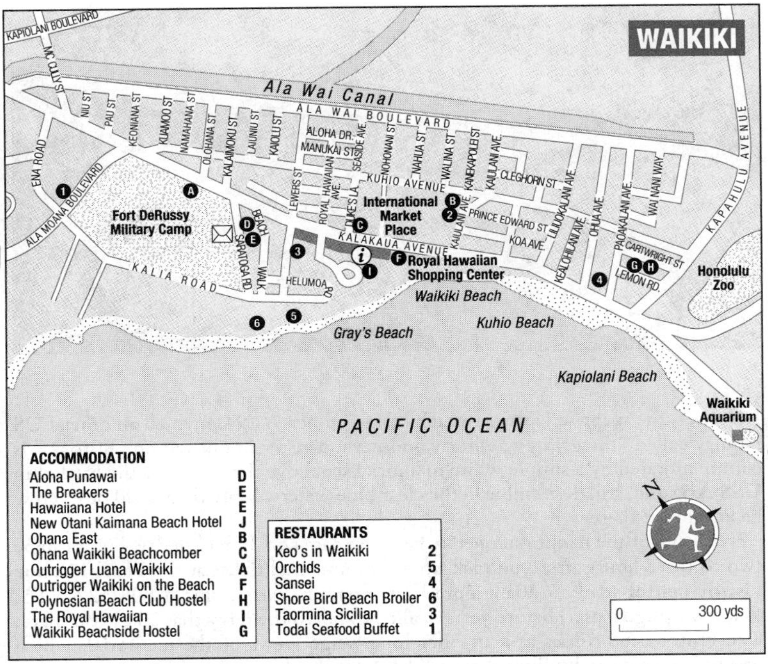

In places, the parallel **Waikiki Beach** narrows to just a thin strip of sand, but it's still a wonderful place to spend a lazy day, and there's always something going on, from surf lessons to outrigger canoe rides. The pedestrian walkway along its edge, lined with pleasant gardens, makes it a refuge from the frenzy nearby, and usually you only have to walk a little west of the centre to find a more secluded spot.

Diamond Head

Waikiki's most famous landmark is the pinnacle of **Diamond Head**, another extinct volcano just to the east. The lawns of the crater interior are oddly bland, but a straightforward hiking trail, passing through a network of tunnels built during World War II, leads up a mile or so to the summit, and a panorama of the whole coast. TheBus #22 and #58 stop on the road nearby.

Hanauma Bay

A few miles to the east, the magnificent crescent-shaped **Hanauma Bay**, formed when the wall of a crater collapsed and let in the sea, is renowned as Oahu's best place to **snorkel** (summer daily except Tues 6am–7pm, 2nd and 4th Sat of month 6am–10pm; winter daily except Tues 6am–6pm, 2nd Sat of month 6am–10pm; $5, under-13s free; ⓣ808/396-4229). Thanks to strict conservation measures, the sea abounds in brightly colored fish. Hourly buses from Waikiki drop passengers at the visitor center.

Pearl Harbor

Almost the whole of **Pearl Harbor**, the principal base for the US Pacific fleet (just over one hour west of Waikiki on TheBus #20), is off-limits to visitors.

▲ Hanauma Bay

However, the surprise Japanese attack of December 7, 1941, which an official US inquiry called "the greatest military and naval disaster in our nation's history," is commemorated by a simple white memorial set above the wreck of the battleship **USS Arizona**, still discernible in the clear blue waters. More than 1100 of its crew lie entombed there.

Free tours of the memorial operate between 8am and 3pm each day, but it can be two or three hours after you pick up your numbered ticket at the **Pearl Harbor visitor center** (daily 7.30am–5pm, last program starts 3pm; Ⓣ808/422-0561; Ⓦwww.nps.gov/usar) before you're called to board the ferry that takes you there. The visitor center does at least offer long-range views of the memorial, which was partly financed by Elvis Presley's 1961 Honolulu concert, his first show after leaving the army. The huge **USS Missouri**, which survived the attack and was used four years later for the ceremony in Tokyo Harbor that ended World War II, is moored alongside the Arizona. Guided visits, by bus from alongside the Pearl Harbor visitor center, include the actual surrender site as well as sweeping views of the harbor from the **Missouri**'s bridge (daily 8.30am–5pm; tours $16–30; Ⓣ1-877/MIGHTYMO, Ⓦwww.ussmissouri.com).

Eating

Honolulu and Waikiki offer an enormous range of **dining** possibilities, and the recommendations below are just a sampling. Excellent and well-priced stalls in the **Maunakea Marketplace** on Maunakea Street in Chinatown sell a wide range of international cuisines; there's a large fast-food mall in the **Ala Moana Center**; and Waikiki's Kuhio Avenue is lined with snack outlets and noodle bars.

Indigo Eurasian Cuisine 1121 Nuuanu Ave, Honolulu Ⓣ808/521-2900. Closed Sun & Mon. Delicious nouvelle "Eurasian" crossover food, as well as dim sum, served in a lovely old Chinatown building.

Kakaako Kitchen Ward Center, 1200 Ala Moana Blvd, Honolulu Ⓣ808/596-7488. Mall diner that dishes up high-quality fast food; pretty much everything, from the hamburger stew to the signature dish chicken linguine, costs $7–10, and there's a menu of daily $8 specials like meat loaf or pot roast.

Keo's in Waikiki 2028 Kuhio Ave, Waikiki Ⓣ808/951-9355. Hawaii's best Thai restaurant. The menu isn't all that unusual, but everything, from the specialty "Evil Jungle Prince" curries onwards, tastes great, and most entrees cost under $15. Breakfast is both American and Asian; lunch and dinner are entirely Thai.

Orchids *Halekulani*, 2199 Kalia Rd, Waikiki Ⓣ808/923-2311. Waikiki's finest gourmet restaurant, facing the beach in the gorgeous, peaceful *Halekulani* hotel, and offering scintillating contemporary Hawaiian cuisine. Open for all meals daily.

Sansei *Waikiki Beach Marriott*, 2552 Kalakaua Ave ⓣ808/931-6286. Wonderful, dinner-only Japanese-inspired restaurant, serving superb sushi at around $10 for a specialty roll, and a full Pacific Rim menu with entrees at $20–40. Late-night dining and free karaoke Fri & Sat.

Shore Bird Beach Broiler *Outrigger Reef*, 2169 Kalia Rd, Waikiki ⓣ808/922-2887. Open-air oceanfront restaurant serving a $12 breakfast buffet, and dinner with an open salad bar for $15–22, depending on choice of entree. Guests cook their own meat or fish on a communal grill.

Taormina Sicilian 227 Lewers St, Waikiki ⓣ808/926-5050. Good Italian restaurant in Waikiki's new Beachwalk area, using local fish as well as traditional Sicilian recipes.

Todai Seafood Buffet 1910 Ala Moana Blvd, Waikiki ⓣ808/947-1000. Stylish all-you-care-to-eat Japanese buffet in western Waikiki. Lunch costs $15 and dinner $29, but the range and quality of the food, including sushi, shrimp, crab, and lobster, makes it a real bargain.

Yakiniku Camellia 2494 S Beretania St ⓣ808/946-7955. Korean buffet restaurant a mile north of Waikiki, where you select slices of marinated beef, chicken, or pork and grill it yourself at the gas-fired burners set into each table. Open daily for lunch ($12) and dinner ($19).

Nightlife

Honolulu's **nightlife** is concentrated in Waikiki, where fun-seeking tourists set the tone. On the whole, the available entertainment is on the bland side. Hawaii tends to be off the circuit for touring musicians, so if you enjoy live music you'll probably have to settle for lesser-known local performers. Look out for special events at downtown's beautifully restored Hawaii Theatre, 1130 Bethel St (ⓣ808/528-0506, ⓦwww.hawaiitheatre.com).

Chai's Island Bistro Aloha Tower Marketplace, 101 Ala Moana Blvd, Honolulu ⓣ808/585-0011. Sumptuous and very expensive Thai restaurant, where the very finest Hawaiian musicians perform for diners nightly 6.45–8.45pm.

House Without A Key *Halekulani*, 2199 Kalia Rd, Waikiki ⓣ808/923-2311. Romantic open-air beach bar, blessed with spectacular ocean sunsets, where the no-cover evening cocktail hour features gentle, old-time Hawaiian classics performed by top-notch musicians and hula dancers.

Hula's Bar and Lei Stand *Waikiki Grand Hotel*, 134 Kapahulu Ave, Waikiki ⓣ808/923-0669, ⓦwww.hulas.com. Waikiki's most popular gay venue occupies a suite of ocean-view rooms across from the Honolulu Zoo. As well as a state-of-the-art dance floor equipped with giant video screens, there's also a more casual lounge area. Daily 10am–2am.

Pipeline 805 Pohukaina St, Honolulu ⓣ808/589-1999, ⓦwww.pipelinecafe.net. Mon–Thurs 9pm–4am, Fri & Sat 10pm–4am. Nightclub, behind the Ala Moana mall, that's a favorite with the surf set. DJs most nights, cover charge for weekly rock or reggae gigs.

Windward Oahu

The most spectacular moment on a tour of Oahu comes as you leave Honolulu on the **Pali Highway** (Hwy-61), and cross the Koolau Mountains to see the sheer green cliffs of the windward side of the island, veiled by swirling mists. The highest spot, four miles northeast of Honolulu, is the **Nuuanu Pali Lookout**. Kamehameha the Great finalized his conquest of Oahu here in 1795, forcing hundreds of enemy warriors over the edge of the cliffs.

Oahu's leading paying attraction, with one million annual visitors, is the **Polynesian Cultural Center** in Laie, ten miles short of the island's northernmost tip (Mon–Sat 12.30–9pm; $55–205; ⓣ808/293-333, ⓦwww.polynesia.com). This haphazard mixture of real and bogus Polynesia – in which the history veers firmly towards the latter – is owned and run by the Mormon Church. After touring "villages" modeled on the various islands of Polynesia, you can stay into the evening for a luau and/or dance performances. TheBus #52 takes roughly two hours to get this far.

Sea sports and safety

The nation that invented **surfing** remains its greatest arena. The sport was popularized early in the twentieth century by Olympic swimmer Duke Kahanamoku, using a 20ft board; these days most are around six feet. As a rule, the best surfing beaches are on the north shore of each island. **Windsurfing and kitesurfing**, too, are hugely popular, in similar locations, while smaller **boogie boards** make an exhilarating initiation. **Snorkeling** and **diving** are top-quality, although Hawaii's **coral** has fewer brilliant hues than those seen in warmer equatorial waters.

Bear in mind, however, that **drownings** in Hawaii are all too common. Waves can sweep in from two thousand miles of open ocean onto beaches that are unprotected by any reef. Not all beaches have lifeguards and warning flags, and unattended beaches are not necessarily safe. Watch the sea carefully before going in, and never take your eyes off it thereafter. If you get swept out, don't fight the big waves; allow yourself to be carried out of the danger zone, then when the current dies down swim back to shore.

North Shore Oahu

The **surfing beaches** of northern Oahu are famous the world over, but they're minimally equipped for tourists. **Waimea**, **Sunset**, and **Ehukai** beach parks are all laid-back roadside stretches of sand, where you can usually find a quiet spot to yourself. In summer, the tame waves may leave you wondering what all the fuss is about; see them at full tilt in the winter, and you'll have no doubts.

HALEIWA, the main surfers' hangout, combines alternative shops and cafés with upfront tourist traps. Much of the **food** around is vegetarian; the **Paradise Found Café**, 66-443 Kamehameha Hwy (Ⓣ808/637-4540), serves breakfast and lunch, both for under $10, while **Haleiwa Eats**, nearer the ocean at 66-011 Kamehameha Hwy (Ⓣ808/637-4247), is a simple, well-priced Thai joint.

For **accommodation**, you'll have to head five miles northeast to the **Backpacker's Vacation Inn**, at 59-788 Kamehameha Hwy by Waimea Bay (Ⓣ808/638-7838, Ⓦwww.backpackers-hawaii.com; ❶–❾), which has dorm beds for $27–30 per night, as well as some great-value ocean-view private rooms and studios.

The Big Island

Although the **Big Island of Hawaii** could hold all the other islands with room to spare, it has the population of a medium-sized town, with just 170,000 people (half what it was in Captain Cook's day). Visitation remains low compared to Oahu and Maui; despite its fair share of restaurants, bars, and facilities, this is basically a rural community, where sleepy old towns have remained unchanged for a century. The few resorts are built on the barren lava flows of the **Kona** coast to catch maximum sunshine; the beaches are great, but these are otherwise the least beautiful areas.

Thanks to the **Kilauea** volcano, which has destroyed roads and even towns, and spews out pristine beaches of jet-black sand, the Big Island is still growing, its southern shore inching ever further out to sea. **Hawaii Volcanoes National Park**, which includes **Mauna Loa** as well as Kilauea (though not **Mauna Kea**, further to the north and higher than either), is absolutely compelling; you can explore steaming craters and cinder cones, venture into the rainforest, and at times approach within feet of the eruption itself.

As befits the birthplace of King Kamehameha, more of the ancient Hawaii survives on the Big Island than anywhere else in the islands. **Puuhonua O Honaunau** preserves a "place of refuge" for defeated warriors and those who ran afoul of society's rules, and there are further temples north along the Kohala coast, while **Waipio Valley**, where Kamehameha spent his youth, remains as lush and green as ever.

Flights to the Big Island arrive at both **Hilo** on the rainy east coast, or near the resort town of **Kailua** (often referred to as Kona) on the west. Public transportation is all but nonexistent.

Windward Hawaii

Almost all the rain that falls on Mauna Kea flows down the eastern side of the Big Island. As a result, myriad streams and waterfalls nourish dense jungle-like vegetation, so the main road north along the coast from Hilo is alive with flowering trees and orchids.

Hilo

Although it's the Big Island's capital and largest town, just 45,000 people live in **HILO**, which remains endearing and unpressured. Mass tourism has never taken off here, mainly because it rains too much. However, the rain falls mostly at night, and America's wettest city blazes with tropical blooms against a backdrop of rainbows.

With its modest streets and wooden stores, Hilo's **downtown** looks appealingly low-key. Sadly, that's largely because all the buildings that stood on the seaward side of Kamehameha Avenue were destroyed by two tsunami, in 1946 and 1960. The story is told in the **Pacific Tsunami Museum**, on Kamehameha Avenue at Kalakaua Street (Mon–Sat 9am–4pm; $7; Ⓣ808/935-0926, Ⓦwww.tsunami.org). A scale model shows how the city looked before 1946; contemporary footage and letters bring home the impact of the tragedy.

The **Lyman Museum**, based in the 1830s home of early missionaries at 276 Haili St (Mon–Sat 9.30am–4.30pm; $10; Ⓣ808/935-5021, Ⓦwww.lymanmuseum.org), holds a fascinating display of ancient weapons and documents Hawaii's various ethnic groups, including the Portuguese who arrived in 1878 from the volcanic Azores.

Five minutes' drive from downtown brings you to the fascinating new **'Imiloa Astronomy Center of Hawaii**, 600 'Imiloa Place (daily except Mon 9am–4pm; $14.50; Ⓣ808/969-9700, Ⓦwww.imiloahawaii.org). This explains the work of the international scientists who use the astronomical observatories at the summit of Mauna Kea, while also outlining traditional Hawaiian beliefs about the site's spiritual importance.

Practicalities

A taxi into town from Hilo International **Airport**, on the eastern outskirts, costs around $10. The **Hawaii Visitors Bureau** is at 250 Keawe St (Mon–Fri 8am–4.30pm; Ⓣ808/961-5797, Ⓦwww.bigisland.org). From Kamehameha Avenue, Hilo's Hele-On **bus** (Ⓣ808/961-8744) operates one daily service to Kailua (Mon–Sat) and down to Hawaii Volcanoes National Park (Mon–Fri).

Two good **hostels** offer both private rooms for around $70 and dorm beds for $25. The attractive **Hilo Bay Hostel** is downtown at 101 Waianuenue Ave (Ⓣ808/933-2771, Ⓦwww.hawaiihostel.net; ❶–❹), while **Arnott's Lodge** is in the woods two miles southeast at 98 Apapane Rd. (Ⓣ808/969-7097, Ⓦwww.arnottslodge.com; ❶–❸), and also offers tent spots for $10, plus island tours. Otherwise, the **Dolphin Bay,** 333 Iliahi St (Ⓣ808/935-1466 or 1-877/935-1466, Ⓦwww.dolphinbayhilo.com; ❹), is a nice, friendly little hotel. The Seaside Restaurant, 1790 Kalanianaole Ave Ⓣ808/935-8825; closed Mon) is a great local fish restaurant with its own aquafarm.

North from Hilo

The **Belt Road** (Hwy-19) follows the **Hamakua coast** north of Hilo, clinging to the hillsides and crossing ravines on slender bridges. For a glimpse into the interior, head into the mountains after fifteen miles to the 450ft **Akaka Falls**. A short loop trail through the forest, festooned with wild orchids, offers views of Akaka and other waterfalls.

Waipio Valley

Highway 240, which turns north off the Belt Road at **HONOKAA**, comes to an abrupt end after nine miles at the edge of **Waipio Valley**. As the southernmost of six successive sheer-walled valleys, this is the only one accessible by land. It's as close as Hawaii comes to the classic South Seas image of an isolated and self-sufficient valley, dense with fruit trees and laced by footpaths leading down to the sea.

It's perfectly possible to walk down the steep, mile-long track into Waipio, but most visitors take tours, either in the four-wheel-drive vehicles of the Waipio Valley Shuttle (Mon–Sat 9am, 11am, 1pm & 3pm; Ⓣ808/775-7121; $55), at the Waipio Valley Art Works in Kukuihaele, a mile from the end of the road, or on horseback (Ⓣ808/775-1007; $85).

The Kona coast

Hawaii's leeward **Kona coast** divides into two distinct areas. North of its only sizeable community, **Kailua**, barren lava trails down to the sea from the third-highest Big Island volcano, Hualalai. Thanks to the relentless sun on its superb beaches, luxury hotels dot the shoreline as incongruous green patches. To the south, the hillsides are more fertile, and although the condos are spreading, you can still get a real feel for the old Hawaii in the land where Captain Cook met his end.

North Kona and the resorts

The best of the spectacular sandy beaches along the Kona coast – safe for summer swimming, though with tempestuous winter surf – lie to the north of Kailua. **Hapuna Beach**, almost forty miles up the coast, is deservedly the most famous, despite being overshadowed by the giant **Hapuna Beach Prince Hotel** (Ⓣ808/880-1111 or 1-888/977-4623, Ⓦwww.hapunabeachprincehotel; ❾).

Several more luxurious **resort hotels** lie in the district of South Kohala, thirty miles north of Kailua (see below). Three separate enclaves – Waikoloa, Mauna Kea, and Mauna Lani – have been landscaped out of this inhospitable lava desert, each one a self-contained oasis holding two or three hotels, a beach or two, and nothing else. Although **Waikoloa** is the least exclusive of the three, it's home to the ostentatious, mile-long **Hilton Waikoloa Village** (Ⓣ808/886-1234 or 1-800/445-8667, Ⓦwww.hiltonwaikoloavillage.com; ❾), where guests travel to and from their rooms by electric boats or monorail.

For idyllic seclusion, head a few miles south, to the turquoise lagoons of **Kiholo Bay**, reached via an unmarked and very bumpy dirt road halfway between mile posts 82 and 83 on Kamehemeha Highway.

Kailua (Kona)

Although the Big Island's main resort is officially called **KAILUA**, it's much more commonly referred to as **Kona**. An attractive little town that has played a major part in Hawaiian history, it's more affected by tourism than any other Big Island community, and its seafront row of fast-food restaurants and souvenir shops could be almost anywhere.

King Kamehameha's funeral rites were performed in the ancient temple of **Ahuena Heiau**, poised beside a little beach at the northern end of the bay. A short way south, **Hulihee Palace** (Mon–Sat 9am–4pm, Sun 10am–4pm; $6) faces out to sea from the center of Kailua. Built as the governor's residence in 1838, it was damaged in an earthquake in 2006, but you can still inspect the massive **koa**-wood furnishings inside, made to fit the considerable girth of the various Hawaiian royals who lived here.

Practicalities

The largely open-air **Kona International Airport**, situated on a field of black lava nine miles north of Kailua, has the usual car rental places; otherwise Speedi Shuttle **buses** into town cost around $20 per person (Ⓣ808/329-5433, Ⓦwww.speedishuttle.com).

Accommodation options in Kailua start in the north with the landmark King Kamehameha's Kona Beach Hotel, 75-5660 Palani Rd (Ⓣ808/329-2911 or 1-800/367-6060, Ⓦwww.konabeachhotel.com; ❻), set around a picturesque little beach. Further hotels line the oceanfront Alii Drive for about five miles south; the pick of them for budget travelers is the simple, three-story Kona Tiki motel, 75-5968 Alii Drive (T808/329-1425, Ⓦwww.konatiki.com; ❸). Recommended sea-view restaurants in the heart of town include Cassandra's Greek Taverna, 75-5669 Alii Drive (T808/334-1066), and Huggo's, 76-6828 Kuhakai St (Ⓣ808/329-1493).

Kealakekua Bay

Kealakekua Bay, a dozen miles south of Kailua, was where Captain Cook was killed on February 14, 1779, during his second visit to Hawaii, after a year spent searching for the fabled Northwest Passage. One of ancient Hawaii's major population centers, it's now barely inhabited, and the white **obelisk** on the death site – legally a small piece of England – is all but inaccessible. You can only get to within a mile of the bay by car, at **Napoopoo Beach**, though you'll get a glimpse of it from the road on the way down. The bay itself is the best place on the Big Island for **snorkeling**, even if there are sharks further out. The catamaran **Fair Wind** offers snorkeling cruises here from Keauhou Bay, just south of Kailua (daily: 9am departure $119, shorter 2pm departure $109; Ⓣ808/345-0268, Ⓦwww.fair-wind.com).

This region, South Kona, is the prime source of **Kona coffee**, which sells here for up to $50 per pound (including shipping). The town of **CAPTAIN COOK**, on the verdant slopes high above Kealekekua, is home to the bargain **Manago**

▲ Carved effigy, Puuhanva O Honaunau

Hotel (Ⓣ808/323-2642, Ⓦwww.managohotel.com; ❶–❸), which offers comfortable ocean-view rooms amid flowering Japanese gardens. A mile south of Captain Cook, the **Coffee Shack** (daily 7am–4pm; Ⓣ808/328-9555) serves wonderfully fresh coffee and smoothies on a terrace that enjoys staggering views all the way down to the bay.

Puuhonua O Honaunau

Puuhonua O Honaunau National Historical Park (daily 7.30am–5.30pm; $5 per vehicle), four miles on from Kealakekua, is the single most evocative historical site in all of the Hawaiian islands, jutting into the Pacific on a small peninsula of jagged black lava. The grounds include a lovely little beach, backed by a fishpond, and three **heiaus** (places of worship), guarded by large carved effigies of gods – reproductions, but still eerie in their original setting. An ancient "**place of refuge**" lies firmly protected behind the mortarless masonry of the sixteenth-century **Great Wall**. Those who broke ancient Hawaii's intricate system of **kapu** (taboo) – perhaps by treading on the shadow of a chief or fishing in the wrong season – could expect summary execution unless they fled to such a sanctuary. As chiefs lived on the surrounding land, transgressors had to swim through shark-infested seas. If successful, they would be absolved and released overnight.

Hawaii Volcanoes National Park

The Big Island's southernmost volcanoes, **Mauna Loa** and **Kilauea**, jointly constitute **HAWAII VOLCANOES NATIONAL PARK**, thirty miles from Hilo and eighty from Kailua. Possibly the most dramatic of all the US national parks, it includes desert, arctic tundra, and rainforest, besides two active volcanoes.

Evidence is everywhere of the awesome power of the volcanoes to create and destroy; no map can keep up with the latest whims of the lava flow. Whole towns have been engulfed, and what were once prized beachfront properties lie buried hundreds of yards back from the sea.

Kilauea Caldera

The main focus of the park is **Kilauea Caldera**, the summit crater of Kilauea, twenty miles up from the ocean. Close to the rim, on the eleven-mile **Crater Rim Drive**, both the **visitor center** (daily 7.45am–5pm; $10 per vehicle; ⓣ808/967-7311, ⓦwww.nps.gov/havo) and the fascinating **Jaggar Museum** of geology (daily 8.30am–5pm; free) offer basic orientation. Kilauea is said to be the home of the volcano goddess **Pele**, who has followed the "hot spot" from island to island. When Mark Twain came here in 1866, he observed a dazzling lake of liquid fire; since a huge explosion in 1924 it's been shallower and quieter, a black dusty expanse dotted with hissing steam vents. Enthusiastic hikers should set time aside to follow the long trails that explore the caldera floor. Both the **Halemaumau Trail**, a seven-mile round-trip, and the **Kilauea Iki Trail**, a total of five miles, involve picking your way from cairn to cairn across an eerie landscape of cracked and jagged lava.

Among shorter routes, the mile-long **Devastation Trail** is a boardwalk laid across the scene of a 1959 eruption. Most of what you see is new growth – fresh lava is full of nutrients, and rainwater and seeds soon collect in the recesses – but a few older trees survived partial submersion in ash by growing "aerial roots" some way up their trunks.

Chain of Craters Road

Chain of Craters Road winds down to the sea from Crater Rim Drive, sweeping around a succession of cones and vents in an empty landscape where the occasional dead white tree trunk or flowering shrub pokes up. Fresh sheets of lava constantly ooze down the slopes to cover the road. When a new road is built on top of the flow, more lava covers it. Along the coast, the scale of the damage since 1983 has been too great to repair – over seven miles have been lost – so now the road is a dead end, and getting shorter year by year. One by one the landmarks along its seafront stretch have been destroyed, and before long it may not follow the shoreline at all.

Check current conditions at the **visitor center** when you arrive, and make sure you have enough gas. The end of the road is a fifty-mile round-trip from the park entrance, and there are no facilities of any kind along the way. For the last few years, depending on where current volcanic activity is concentrated, it has been possible at times to walk across the congealed lava blocking Chain of Craters Road to see molten rock gush from the earth – sometimes directly into the sea. The park's **Volcano Update** (ⓣ808/985-6000, ⓦhvo.wr.usgs.gov) has the latest details; for information on ranger-led tours, call the visitor center.

Practicalities

The national park operates two free **campgrounds** on a first-come, first-served basis, while **Volcano House**, close to the edge of the crater within the park

(☎808/967-7321, Ⓦwww.volcanohousehotel.com; cabins ❸, rooms ❺–❽), has spectacular views, and good food in the evening, although the prices for its simple motel-style rooms are rather high. Otherwise, the small and inconspicuous town of **VOLCANO**, just before the park entrance on the Hilo side, provides the best places to **stay** in the vicinity, with B&Bs such as the lovely **Hale Ohia** (☎808/967-7986, Ⓦwww.haleohia.com; ❻), south of the highway across from the village. **Kilauea Lodge**, on the leafy main street (☎808/967-7366, Ⓦwww.kilauealodge.com; ❼), is a comfortable inn with a very good **restaurant**.

Maui

The island of **MAUI**, the second largest in the Hawaiian chain, is Oahu's principal rival, attracting roughly a third of all visitors to the state. Some say that things have gone too far, with formerly remote, unspoiled beaches, around **Kaanapali** and **Kihei** for example, now swamped by sprawling resorts. On the other hand, the crowds come to Maui for the good reason that it's still beautiful. This is the best equipped of all the islands for **activity** holidays – whale-watching, windsurfing, diving, sailing, snorkeling, and cycling. Temperatures along the coast can be searing, but it's always possible to escape to somewhere cooler. **Upcountry Maui**, on the slopes of the mighty **Haleakala** volcano, is a delight, while the waterfalls and ravines along the tortuous road out west to **Hana** outclass anything on Oahu.

Maui activities

Snorkeling and diving

Maui's best-known **snorkeling** and **diving** spot is the tiny crescent of **Molokini**, poking above the sea – all that's left of a once-great volcano. There's no beach or landfall, but you do see a lot of fish, including deep-water species. Countless cruises leave early each morning (to avoid the heat) from Maalea Harbor; snorkelers can pay anything from $50 to $110 for a morning trip, and from $35 for a shorter afternoon jaunt. Vessels range from the twenty-passenger *Hokua* (☎808/249-2583, Ⓦwww.alohabluecharters.com) up to the 150-seater *Prince Kuhio* (☎808/242-8777, Ⓦwww.mvprince.com).

Downhill cycle rides

One of Maui's more unusual opportunities is to be taken by van to the top of **Haleakala** to watch the sun rise, and then brought back down to the park entrance to ride a bicycle from there 29 miles down to Paia by the sea – without pedaling once. Serious cyclists find the slow pace of the trip frustrating; complete novices or the unfit shouldn't try; in-betweens think it's great. Companies running trips for around $110 (including pickups) include Cruiser Phil's (☎808/893-2332, Ⓦwww.cruiserphil.com) and Maui Downhill (☎808/871-2155, Ⓦwww.mauidownhill.com).

Kahului and Wailuku

Almost half of Maui's 140,000 inhabitants – the workers who keep this fantasy island going – live in the twin towns of **KAHULUI** and **WAILUKU**, to the north of the "neck" connecting its two mountainous sections. Kahului is the main commercial center; Wailuku is one of the few towns on Maui that feels like a genuine community, and the presence of budget accommodation and restaurants – and the stunning **Iao Needle** nearby – make it a good central base.

There's no sightseeing to speak of in either Kahului or Wailuku, though you may become familiar with both while shopping for food and other necessities. Wailuku's Main Street heads straight into the **West Maui Mountains**, stopping three miles in at **Iao Needle**, a stunning 1200ft pinnacle of green-clad lava that stands, head usually in the clouds, at the intersection of two lush valleys. Kamehameha won control of Maui here in 1790, in a battle determined by a cannonade directed by two European gunners.

Practicalities

Virtually all visitors to Maui arrive at **Kahului Airport**. Speedi Shuttle **buses** (Ⓣ808/661-6667 or 1-800/977-2605, Ⓦwww.speedishuttle.com) connect the airport regularly with resorts around the island.

Although Wailuku is nowhere near Maui's main resort areas, and lacks any hotels, thanks to its two lively, friendly **hostels** it's the most popular destination for budget travelers. Both *Banana Bungalow*, 310 N Market St (Ⓣ808/244-5090 or 1-800/846-7835, Ⓦwww.mauihostel.com; ❶–❸) and the *Northshore Hostel*, 2080 Vineyard St (Ⓣ808/986-8095 or 1-866/946-7835, Ⓦwww.northshorehostel.com; ❶–❸) offer dorm beds for $25 and simple private rooms. *Banana Bungalow* also offers free airport shuttles, a changing schedule of free island tours, and cut-price car rental.

Neither Kahului and Wailuku offers much in the way of fine **dining**, but *Kozo Sushi*, at 32 Main St in Wailuku (Ⓣ808/243-5696) is a good, very central sushi

Whale-hunting and whale-watching

The first **whaling ships** arrived in Hawaii in 1820, the same year as the missionaries – and had an equally dramatic impact. With the ports of Japan closed to outsiders, Hawaii swiftly became the center of the industry. Any Pacific port of call must have seemed a godsend to the whalers, who were away from New England for three years at a time, and paid so badly that most were either fugitives from justice or just plain mad. Hawaii was such a paradise that up to fifty percent of each crew would desert, to be replaced by native Hawaiians, born seafarers eager to see the world.

Until the 1840s, Honolulu, which permitted drinking, was the whalers' favorite port. Then potatoes and prostitution lured them to **Lahaina** as well, where the sea was calm enough for ships to dock beside the open road and stock up on provisions at a grassy marketplace beside a central canal.

At the peak of the trade, almost six hundred whaling vessels docked in Honolulu in a single year. Decline came with the Civil War – when many whaling ships were deliberately sunk to blockade Confederate ports – and an 1871 disaster, when 31 vessels lingered in the Arctic too long, became frozen in, and had to be abandoned.

Ironically, the waters off western Maui now rate among the world's best areas for whale-watching and whale research. Between January and March each year, and for up to a month either side of that, **humpback whales** use the ocean channels here as both sanctuary and playground. The whales are often clearly visible from the shore, but specific whale-watching trips can take you much closer (with money-back guarantees if you don't see one). Operators include the nonprofit Pacific Whale Foundation ($20; Ⓣ808/249-8811 or 1-800/942-5311, Ⓦwww.pacificwhale.org).

restaurant, while *Maui Coffee Roasters*, at 444 Hana Hwy, Kahului (Ⓣ808/877-2877) is a relaxed espresso bar that serves good lunch specials.

Lahaina

The only real town along the green but sunny shoreline of West Maui, **LAHAINA** is one of the prettiest communities in all Hawaii. During the early nineteenth century it served as capital of the entire Kingdom of Hawaii, but it has barely grown since then, and still resembles the peaceful tropical village it used to be. Its main oceanfront street is lined with timber-frame buildings; coconut palms sway to either side of the mighty central banyan tree; surfers swirl into the thin fringe of beach to the south; and the mountains of West Maui dominate the skyline.

The view out to sea from Lahaina, towards the island of **Lanai**, is superb. If you have the time, consider taking a ferry there for the day; there's little to see on the island, but the main beach, at Hulopoe Bay, is a delight. Expeditions provides five sailings daily, from Lahaina Harbor ($25 each way; Ⓣ808/661-3756, Ⓦwww.go-lanai.com).

Practicalities

If you have the money to spend on resort-style **accommodation**, Lahaina and the coast to the north have some good options, but there's very little available for under $100 per night. In the heart of town, the *Best Western Pioneer Inn*, 658 Wharf St (Ⓣ808/661-3636 or 1-800/457-5457, Ⓦwww.pioneerinnmaui.com; ❻) is a lively old hotel, while the *Old Lahaina House* to the south (Ⓣ808/667-4663 or 1-800/847-0761, Ⓦwww.oldlahaina.com; ❹), offers good-quality en-suite B&B rooms in a private home, complete with pool.

Good places to **eat** include *Cilantro Fresh Mexican Grill*, in the Old Lahaina Center mall at 170 Papalaua Ave (Ⓣ808/667-5444), but for a gourmet treat you can't beat *The Feast at Lele*, 505 Front St (🏃 Ⓣ808/667-5353), where $105 buys a magnificent Polynesian banquet, served right on the beach and accompanied with live music and hula.

Kihei and Wailea

Maui's other main resort area is south of Kahului, across the isthmus. The long strip of hotels, malls, and condos begins at **KIHEI**, with the road heavily built up on both sides, but thins out beyond the manicured lawns of **WAILEA**, near some superb beaches. **Paluea Beach** is ideal for families, while **Little Beach**, reached by a trail from the gorgeous, enormous **Makena (Big) Beach**, is famous for (illegal) nudism.

Few of the **accommodation** options are geared towards budget travelers, though inexpensive condos are available at **Kihei Akahi**, 2531 S Kihei Rd (Ⓣ808/879-2778, Ⓦwww.crhmaui.com; ❺). For **food**, **Sansei**, at the Kihei Town Center (Ⓣ808/879-0004), offers great-value sushi and Pacific Rim concoctions.

Upcountry Maui

Hawaii is not always a land tarnished by civilization. **Central Maui**, in the nineteenth century "a dreary expanse of sand and shifting sandhills, with a dismal growth . . . of thornless thistles," is now a pastoral idyll, thanks to an ingenious system of irrigation channels.

The highway to the top of **Haleakala** climbs higher, at a faster rate, than any road on earth. Starting in rich meadows, it climbs past purple-blossoming jacaranda, firs, and eucalyptus to reach open ranching land, and then ascends in huge curves to the volcanic desert and the crater itself.

Haleakala

Though **HALEAKALA** – "the House of the Sun" – is the world's largest dormant volcano, you may not appreciate its full ten-thousand-foot majesty until you're at the top. Shield volcanoes are not as dramatic as the classic cones, as lava oozes from fissures along broad flanks to create a long, low profile, and the summit is often obscured by clouds. That it hasn't erupted for two hundred years doesn't necessarily mean it won't ever again.

The higher reaches of the mountain are a **national park**, which never closes (admission $10 per vehicle). Manhattan would fit comfortably into the awe-inspiring **crater**, almost eight miles across, which was for the ancient Hawaiians a site of deep spiritual power. The most popular time to come is for the **sunrise**; the **visitor center** at the top operates from just before dawn until 3pm (Ⓣ808/572-4400, Ⓦwww.nps.gov/hale). Hiking trails of varying difficulty cross the crater floor, where **camping** is permitted in three remote cabins that are awarded by lottery two months in advance. They require a hike of four to ten miles and a $75 fee per night. In addition, fifteen to twenty-five free tent sites outside the crater are available every day (first-come, first-served).

Makawao and Paia

Coming down from Haleakala, Hwy-365 leads north to two laid-back little country towns populated mainly by old Californian hippies: **MAKAWAO**, five miles up from the ocean, and **PAIA**, Maui's first plantation town, near the great windsurfing beach of **Hookipa**. Neither offers any accommodation, but in the center of Makawao, the friendly Italian restaurant **Casanova's**, 1188 Makawao Ave (Ⓣ808/572-0220), puts on live music at night, courtesy of the local community of rock exiles. Fresh fish is the specialty at the oceanfront **Mama's**, a mile east of Paia at 799 Poho Place (Ⓣ808/579-8488), while vegetarians will be glad of the top-quality Vietnamese food at **Fresh Mint**, 115 Baldwin Ave, in Paia (Ⓣ808/579-9144).

The road to Hana

The rains that fall on Haleakala cascade down Maui's long windward flank, covering it in thick, jungle-like vegetation. Convicts in the 1920s hacked out a road along the coast that has become a major tourist attraction, twisting in and out of gorges, past innumerable waterfalls and over more than fifty tiny one-lane bridges. All year round, and especially in June, the route is ablaze with color from orchids, rainbow eucalyptus, and orange-blossomed African tulip trees. The usual day's excursion is roughly fifty miles (three hours) each way from Paia, to gorgeous **Oheo Gulch**, ten miles beyond Hana, where waterfalls tumble down the hillside to oceanfront meadows.

Hana

The former sugar town of **HANA** itself might seem a disappointment at the end of the road; it's a pleasant enough little community that isn't especially interested in attracting tourists. Rooms at the deluxe **Hotel Hana-Maui** (Ⓣ808/248-8211 or 1-800/321-4262, Ⓦwww.hotelhanamaui.com; ⑨) **start** at around $500;

Joe's Place on Uakea Road is a basic but affordable alternative (Ⓣ808/248-7033, Ⓦwww.joesrentals.com; ❷). There's also **camping** beside the black-sand beach at lovely Waianapanapa State Park, four miles short of Hana (Ⓣ808/984-8109; $5).

Kauai

Although no point on the tiny island of **KAUAI** is as much as a dozen miles from the sea, the variety of its landscapes is quite incredible. This is the oldest of the major islands, and the forces of erosion have had more than six million years to sculpt it into fantastic shapes. The mist-shrouded extinct volcano **Mount Waialeale** at its heart is the world's wettest spot, draining into a high landlocked swamp. Nearby is the chasm of **Waimea Canyon**, while the north shore holds the vertiginous green cliffs of the awe-inspiring **Na Pali** coast, familiar to millions from films such as **Jurassic Park** and **South Pacific**, but the sole preserve of adventurous **hikers**. Kauai is a place to be active, on sea and land; and if you only take one **helicopter** flight in your life, this is the place to do it.

Lihue

Flights to Kauai arrive at the capital, **LIHUE**, which stands slightly inland of little Nawiliwili Harbor at the southeast corner of the island. It's roughly at the mid-point of the one main road that encircles the island (prevented from completing a loop by the Na Pali cliffs), but as a base it's undistinguished. The population is just five thousand, and downtown consists of a few tired plantation-town streets set well back from the sea.

The small **Kauai Museum** at 4428 Rice St (Mon–Fri 9am–4pm, Sat 10am–4pm; $7) traces the island's history from the mythical **menehune** (dwarfs said to have been here before the Polynesians arrived) through Captain Cook's 1778 landfall and on to its sugar-growing heyday.

Practicalities

Lihue's **airport** is only two miles from downtown ($8 by **taxi**; Wailua or Kapaa cost closer to $20). Along with the usual **car** rental outlets, it also has **helicopters** – Blue Hawaiian (Ⓣ808/245-5800, Ⓦwww.bluehawaiian.com) is typical, offering tours from $240. The **Hawaii Visitors Bureau** is in town at 4334 Rice St (Mon–Fri 8am–4.30pm; Ⓣ808/245-3971, Ⓦwww.kauaidiscovery.com).

There's no great point staying in Lihue rather than along the coast. However, the **Garden Island Inn**, near the harbor at 3445 Wilcox Rd (Ⓣ808/245-7227 or 1-800/648-0154, Ⓦwww.gardenislandinn.com; ❹), is a lovely refurbished three-story motel, dripping with purple bougainvillea. For a quick meal in the heart of town, call in at **Hamura's Saimin**, 2956 Kress St (Ⓣ808/245-3271), a family-run Japanese food counter which specializes in bowls of **saimin** (noodles) for $5. A mile or two east, the **Hanamaulu Restaurant and Tea House** (Ⓣ808/245-2511) is a delightful old place, complete with fishponds, that serves both Chinese and Japanese food.

East Kauai

Most Kauaians live between Lihue and the overlapping communities of **WAILUA**, **WAIPOULI**, and **KAPAA**, whose malls, condos, and hotels blend into each other a few miles north of the capital. All the way along there's an exposed thin strip of beach; only Wailua is especially scenic, and you have to go further north for snorkeling.

Accommodation

While most East Shore **hotels** are expensive by any other than Hawaiian standards, possibilities on a more affordable scale do exist.

Hotel Coral Reef 1516 Kuhio Hwy, Kapaa Ⓣ808/822-4481 or 1-800/843-4659, Ⓦwww.hotelcoralreefresort.com. This simple little hotel, facing the beach, offers some of Kauai's best rates. ❹

Kauai International Hostel 4532 Lehua St, Kapaa Ⓣ808/823-6142, Ⓦwww.kauaihostel.net. Kauai's only hostel, across from Kapaa Beach and open to everyone except Hawaiian residents, with a maximum one-week stay. $25 dorm beds, and a few private rooms. ❶–❸

Lae Nani 410 Papaloa Rd, Wailua Ⓣ808/822-4938 or 1-800/688-7444, Ⓦwww.outrigger.com. Irresistible complex of luxurious oceanfront apartments and condos, with lovely swimming alongside. ❼

Eating

Kapaa is the only town in East Kauai with anything like a center; you can windowshop for **restaurants** along its street of wooden stores, which are fronted by a beach park.

Caffè Coco 4-1639 Kuhio Hwy, Wailua Ⓣ808/822-7990. Attractively ramshackle café, serving cheap and wholesome, if not entirely vegetarian, breakfasts and lunches for under $10, plus changing dinner specials. Closed Mon.

Lemongrass Grill 4-885 Kuhio Hwy, Kapaa Ⓣ808/821-2288. Smart, lively, upscale restaurant, serving a predominantly Japanese and seafood menu with entrees at $15–28. Dinner only.

Mermaids Cafe 1384 Kuhio Hwy, Kapaa Ⓣ808/821-2026. Small, partly vegetarian café in central Kapaa, serving wholesome breakfasts and bargain Asian-flavored lunches and dinners.

North Kauai

Despite the development elsewhere on the island, the astonishing valleys of Kauai's **Na Pali coast** remain inviolate – though accessible enough by canoe to sustain large Hawaiian populations, their awesome walls shield them from any attempt to build roads.

To reach long, golden **Secret Beach** – one of Kauai's best-looking beaches, though swimming is usually unsafe – drive up Hwy-56 from the south, pass **Kilauea**, and then turn right at Kalihiwai. Take the second right onto a dirt track leading to a parking area, and the beach is a ten-minute walk down through the woods. At the far end, a waterfall of beautiful fresh mountain water cascades down the cliffs, and there are often spinner dolphins just offshore, especially around the picturesque 1913 Kilauea **lighthouse**. The cliffs above are a bird sanctuary.

Hanalei

Major development stops beyond the resort of **Princeville**, mainly because the road then crosses seven successive one-lane bridges. The first is over the Hanalei River, where the valley stretching away inland is a National Wildlife Refuge. Here endangered Hawaiian ducks, coots, and stilts are protected by the preservation of their major habitats – natural wetlands and taro ponds.

The small town of **HANALEI**, set around a magnificent bay, has some low-key apartments for rent, but otherwise little formal accommodation. Of local **restaurants**, the busy **Hanalei Gourmet** in the Hanalei Center mall (Ⓣ808/826-2524) makes an ideal stop for breakfast or a sandwich lunch, and also has live music most nights.

Gorgeous **Lumahai Beach**, at the western edge of Hanalei Bay, has starred in countless movies, among them **South Pacific**, but is too treacherous for swimming. All the roadside beaches from here on, however, are good for snorkeling. Just two miles from the start of the Na Pali coast (see p.1193), the **Hanalei Colony Resort** (Ⓣ808/826-6235 or 1-800/628-3004, Ⓦwww.hcr.com; ⑧) is Kauai's most dramatic waterfront property, within a few feet of the pounding surf; all its units have two bedrooms. The road finally comes to an end at **Kee Beach**, perhaps the loveliest spot of all, with safe inshore swimming.

▲ Hiking the Kalalau Trail

The Na Pali coast

The lush valleys of the **Na Pali coast**, separated by knife-edge ridges of rock thousands of feet high but just a few feet thick, make Kauai one of the world's great hiking destinations. Although many of the best views (other than from a helicopter) are from the trails in Kokee State Park (see below) or boat trips out to sea, the **Kalalau Trail** along the shore is unforgettable. The full eleven miles to Kalalau Valley is arduous and gets progressively more dangerous; in places you have to scramble along a precipitous (and shadeless) wall of crumbly red rock.

However, the first two miles of the trail, to **Hanakapiai Beach**, are the most beautiful. They're steep but straightforward, passing through patches of dense vegetation where you clamber over the gnarled root systems of the splay-footed **hala** (pandanus) tree. From the beach, a further hour's arduous hike (off the main trail) leads inland to the natural amphitheater of the towering **Hanakapiai Falls**. It takes at least four and a half hours to get to the falls and back from the trailhead at Kee Beach, opposite the ten-mile marker at the end of the road. Hikers and campers doing anything more than a day-hike must obtain **permits**, costing $10 per person per night, from the State Parks Office (3060 Eiwa St, Lihue; ⓣ808/274-3444).

South Kauai

POIPU, Kauai's principal beach resort, lies on the south coast roughly ten miles west of Lihue, where sunshine is more consistent and there's great surfing and snorkeling. Its finest **hotel** is the sumptuous **Grand Hyatt Kauai**, 1571 Poipu Rd (ⓣ808/742-1234 or 1-800/554-9288, ⓦwww.kauai-hyatt.com; ⑨), while **Grantham Resorts** (ⓣ808/742-2000 or 1-800/325-5701, ⓦwww.grantham-resorts.com; ⑤–⑨) quotes lower prices for local condos than you'll be offered by individual properties. The best restaurants are two upmarket Pacific Rim options: **Casa di Amici**, 2301 Nalo Rd (ⓣ808/742-1555), and **Roy's Poipu Bar & Grill** (ⓣ808/742-5000), in the Poipu Shopping Village Mall.

West Kauai

Two of the major scenic attractions in all Hawaii – the gorge of **Waimea Canyon** and **Kokee State Park** (with its views of the Na Pali cliffs to one side and the sodden Alakai Swamp to the other) – can only be reached from the **west coast** of Kauai. The coast itself, however, is nondescript. **WAIMEA**, the largest town, is just one short street at the foot of the poorly marked road up to the canyon. The statue of **Captain Cook**, which commemorates his "discovery" of Hawaii here on January 20, 1778, is an exact replica of one in Cook's home town of Whitby, England. Western Kauai's only **accommodation** option is **Waimea Plantation Cottages** (ⓣ808/338-1625 or 1-866/774-2924, ⓦwww.waimea-plantation.com; ⑦), set in an attractive coconut grove, and with a good restaurant and brewpub in the main plantation house.

Waimea Canyon and Kokee State Park

It's not unreasonable to call **Waimea Canyon** the "Grand Canyon of the Pacific." At three thousand feet, it may not be quite as deep as its Arizona rival, but the colors – all shades of green against the bare red earth – are absolutely breathtaking. The road from Waimea climbs beside the widening gorge, until after eight miles the mile-wide canyon can be seen in all its splendor.

Explore **Kokee State Park**, higher up, as early in the day as possible; by late morning the valleys may be filled with mist and clouds. Although the ranger station at **KOKEE**, the park headquarters, is often unstaffed, you can pick up trail information from the small but informative **Kokee Natural History Museum** nearby (daily 10am–4pm; $1 donation), where displays center on the area's indigenous wildlife. Kauai is the only island where mongooses have not killed off most native **birds**, and at this height mosquitoes are no threat either, so some of the world's rarest species survive here and nowhere else.

Kokee Lodge Housekeeping Cabins, next to the park headquarters, are rented by the day (PO Box 819, Waimea, Kauai, HI 96796; ⓣ808/335-6061; ❹), and there's free **camping**, available with a permit from the parks office in Lihue (see p.1190). For **food, Kokee Lodge** has lunch specials for around $7.

A few miles further up, **Kalalau Lookout** stands over the valley where the Kalalau Trail ends. The **Pihea Trail** follows the course of a lunatic attempt to extend the road beyond its current end. At times it narrows to a few feet, with precipitous drops to either side, and visibility can drop to nothing as the clouds siphon across the ridges. Inland lies the **Alakai Swamp**, where the heaviest rainfall on earth collects in the rock; the few humans who manage to penetrate the mists are assailed on all sides by the shrills, whistles, and buzzes of a jungle without mammals or snakes. The trail running through the swamp consists of a boardwalk for almost its entire six-mile length, though in places the planks just rest on cloying black mud. Giant ferns dangle above the trail, and orchids gleam from the undergrowth. If you make it all the way to the end, you're rewarded with a stupendous panorama of Hanalei Bay.

Contexts

Contexts

History

There is much more to the history of North America than the history of the United States alone. In these few pages, however, there's little room to do more than briefly survey the peopling and political development of the disparate regions that now form the USA. Many of the events and issues discussed below are covered in more detail in the relevant chapters, while the books listed on p.1221 onwards are invaluable resources for further study.

First peoples

The first definitely dated trace of human beings in the Americas stems from just 14,000 years ago, when the true pioneers of North America, nomadic hunter-gatherers from Siberia, reached what's now **Alaska**. Thanks to the last ice age, when sea levels were three hundred feet lower than in the modern Bering Strait, a "**land-bridge**" – actually a vast plain, measuring six hundred miles north to south – connected Eurasia to America.

At that time, Alaska effectively formed part of Asia rather than North America, being separated by impenetrable glacier fields from what is now Canada and points south. Much like an air lock, the region has "opened" in different directions at different times; migrants reaching it from the west, oblivious to the fact that they were leaving Asia, would at first have found their way blocked to the east. Several generations might have passed, and the connection back towards Asia been severed, before an eastward passage appeared. When thawing ice did clear a route into North America, it was not along the Pacific coast but via a corridor that led east of the Rockies and out onto the Great Plains.

This migration was almost certainly spurred not by the urge to explore what must have seemed unpromising territory, but the pursuit of large mammal species, and especially **mammoth**, that had already been harried to extinction throughout almost all of Eurasia. A huge bonanza awaited the hunters when they finally encountered America's own indigenous "**megafauna**," such as mammoths, mastodons, giant ground sloths and enormous long-horned bison, all of which had evolved without fear of, or protection against, human predation.

Within a thousand years, both North and South America were filled with a total of ten million people. Although that sounds like a phenomenal rate of spread, only a small group of original human settlers need have been responsible. To achieve that impact, it would have taken a band of just one hundred individuals to enter the continent, and then advance a mere eight miles per year, with a population growth of 1.1 percent each year. The mass **extinction** of the American megafauna coincided so exactly with the advent of humans that humans must surely have been responsible, eliminating the giant beasts in each locality in one fell swoop, before pressing on in search of the next kill.

Quite apart from its ecological impact, the consequences of the elimination of large land mammals were legion. It precluded future American civilizations from domesticating any of the major animal species that were crucial to Old World economies. Without cattle, horses, sheep, or goats, or significant equivalents, they lacked the resources used elsewhere to supply food and clothing to large settlements, provide draft power to haul ploughs or wheeled vehicles, or increase mobility and the potential for conquest. What's more, most of the human diseases later introduced from the rest of the world evolved in association with domesticated animals; the first Americans developed neither immunity to such diseases, nor any indigenous diseases of their own that might have attacked the invaders.

At least three distinct waves of **migrants** arrived via Alaska, each of whom went on to settle in, and adapt to, a more marginal environment than its predecessors. The second, five thousand years on, were the "**Nadene**" or Athapascans – the ancestors of the Haida of the Northwest, and also the Navajo and Apache of the Southwest – while the third, another two thousand years later, found their niche in the frozen Arctic north and became the **Aleuts** and the **Inuits**.

Within the modern United States, the earliest known settlement site, dating back 12,000 years, has been uncovered at Meadowcroft in southwest Pennsylvania. Five hundred years later, the Southwest was dominated by what archeologists call the **Clovis** culture, whose distinctive arrowheads were first identified at Clovis, New Mexico. Subsequent subgroups ranged from the Algonquin farmers of what's now New England to peoples such as the Chumash and Macah, who lived by catching fish, otters, and even whales along the coasts of the Pacific Northwest.

Nowhere did a civilization emerge that could rival the wealth and sophistication of the great cities of ancient Mexico, such as Teotihuacan or Tenochtitlan. However, the influence of these far-off cultures did filter north; the cultivation of crops such as beans, squash, and maize made the development of large communities possible, and northern religious cults, including those that performed human sacrifice, are thought to owe much to Central American beliefs. The so-called **Moundbuilders** of the **Ohio** and **Mississippi** valleys developed sites such as the Great Serpent Mound in modern Ohio and Poverty Point in Louisiana. The most prominent of these early societies, now known as the **Hopewell** culture, flourished between around 1 and 400 AD. Later on, **Cahokia**, just outside present-day St Louis, became the largest pre-Columbian city in North America, centered on a huge mound topped by some form of temple, and reaching its peak between 1050 and 1250 AD.

In the deserts of the **Southwest**, the **Hohokam** settlement of Snaketown, near what's now Phoenix in Arizona, set about grappling with the same problems of water management that plague the region today. Nearby, the **Ancestral Puebloan** "Basketmakers" developed pottery around 200 AD, and began to gather into the walled villages later known as pueblos, possibly for protection against the threat of Athapascan invaders, such as the Apache, who were arriving from the north. Ancestral Puebloan "cities," such as Pueblo Bonito in New Mexico's Chaco Canyon – a center for the turquoise trade with the mighty Aztec – and the "Cliff Palace" at Mesa Verde in Colorado, are the most impressive monuments to survive from ancient North America. Although the Ancestral Puebloans are no longer identifiable as a group after the twelfth century – they probably dispersed after a devastating drought – many of the settlements created by their immediate descendants have remained in use ever since. Through centuries of migration, war, and changes of government, the desert farmers of the **Hopi Mesas** in Arizona (see p.908), and the pueblos of **Taos** and **Ácoma** in New Mexico, have never been dispossessed of their homes.

Estimates of the total indigenous population held by the Americas before the arrival of the Europeans vary widely. Although serious suggestions for North America range between two and twelve million, an acceptable median figure would be around fifty million people in the Americas as a whole, with five million of those in North America, speaking around four hundred different languages.

European contacts

The greatest seafarers of early medieval Europe, the **Vikings**, established a colony in Greenland around 982 AD. Under the energetic leadership of Eirik the Red, this became a base for voyages along the mysterious coastline to the west. **Leif Eiriksson** – also known as Leif the Lucky – spent the winter of 1001–02 at a site that has been identified with L'Anse aux Meadows in northern Newfoundland. Climatic conditions may well have been much better than they are today, though it remains unclear what were the "grapes" that led him to call it **Vinland**. Subsequent expeditions returned over the next dozen years, and may have ventured as far south as Maine. However, repeated clashes with the people the Vikings knew as **Skraelings** or "wretches" – probably Inuit, also newcomers to the area around this time – led them to abandon plans for permanent settlement.

A further five centuries passed before the crucial moment of contact with the rest of the world came on October 12, 1492, when **Christopher Columbus**, sailing on behalf of the Spanish, reached San Salvador in the Bahamas. A mere four years later the English navigator John Cabot officially "discovered" Newfoundland, and soon British fishermen in particular were setting up makeshift encampments in what became known as **New England**, to spend the winter curing their catch.

Over the next few years various expeditions mapped the eastern seaboard. In 1524, for example, the Italian **Giovanni Verrazano** sailed past Maine, which he characterized as the "Land of Bad People" thanks to the inhospitable and contemptuous behavior of its natives, and reached the mouth of the Hudson River. The great hope initially was to find a sea route in the Northeast that would lead to China – the fabled **Northwest Passage**. To the French **Jacques Cartier**, the St Lawrence Seaway seemed a distinct possibility, and successive expeditions explored and attempted (unsuccessfully) to settle the northern areas of the Great Lakes region from the 1530s onwards. Intrepid trappers and traders began to venture ever further west.

To the south, the Spaniards had started to nose their way up from the Caribbean in 1513, when **Ponce de Leon**'s expedition in search of the Fountain of Youth landed at what is now Palm Beach, and named the region of **Florida**. Spanish attentions for the next few years focused on the lucrative conquest of Mexico, but in 1528 they returned under Panfilo de Narvaez, whose voyage ended in shipwreck somewhere in the Gulf. One of his junior officers, **Cabeza de Vaca**, managed to survive, and together with three shipmates spent the next six years on an extraordinary odyssey across Texas into the Southwest. Sometimes held as slaves, sometimes revered as seers, they finally managed to get back to Mexico in 1534, bringing tales of golden cities deep in the desert, known as the **Seven Cities of Cibola**.

One of Cabeza de Vaca's companions was a black African slave called **Estevanico the Moor**, a giant of a man who had amazed the native peoples they encountered. Rather than return to a life of slavery, he volunteered to map the route for a new expedition; racing alone into the interior, with two colossal greyhounds at his side, he was killed in Zuni Pueblo in 1539. The following year, **Francisco Vázquez de Coronado**'s full party managed to prove to everyone's intense dissatisfaction that the Seven Cities of Cibola did not exist. They reached as far as the Grand Canyon, encountering the Hopi and other pueblo peoples along the way. Hernán Cortés, the conqueror of the Aztec, had meanwhile traced the outline of the peninsula of Baja California, and in 1542 Juan Cabrillo sailed right up the coast of California, failing to spot San Francisco Bay in the usual mists.

Although no treasures were found in North America to match the vast riches plundered from the Aztec and Inca empires, a steady stream of less spectacular discoveries – whether new foodstuffs such as potatoes, or access to the cod fisheries of the northern Atlantic – began to boost economies throughout Europe. It was the Spanish who established the first permanent settlement in the present United States, when they founded **St Augustine** on the coast of Florida in 1565 – permanent, at least, until it was burned to the ground by Sir Francis Drake in 1586. In 1598 the Spanish also succeeded in subjugating the pueblo peoples, and founded the colony of **New Mexico** along the Rio Grande. This was more of a missionary than a military enterprise, and its survival was always precarious due to the vast tracts of empty desert that separated the colony from the rest of Mexico. Nonetheless, the construction of a new capital, **Santa Fe**, began in 1609 (see p.457).

The growth of the colonies

The great rivalry between the English and the Spanish in the late sixteenth century extended right around the world. Freebooting English adventurers-cum-pirates contested Spanish hegemony along both coasts of North America. Sir Francis Drake staked a claim to California in 1579, five years before **Sir Walter Raleigh** claimed **Virginia** in the east, in the name of his Virgin Queen, Elizabeth I. The party of colonists he sent out in 1585 established the short-lived settlement of **Roanoke**, now remembered as the mysterious "Lost Colony" (see p.203).

The Native Americans encountered by the earliest settlers were seldom hostile at the outset. To some extent the European newcomers were obliged to make friends with the locals; most had crossed the Atlantic to find religious freedom or to make their fortunes, and lacked the experience or even the inclination to make a success of the mundane business of subsistence farming. Virginia's first enduring colony, **Jamestown**, was founded by Captain John Smith on May 24, 1607. He bemoaned "though there be Fish in the Sea, and Foules in the ayre, and Beasts in the woods, their bounds are so large, they are so wilde, and we so weake and ignorant, we cannot much trouble them;" not surprisingly, six out of every seven colonists died within a year of their arrival in the New World.

Gradually, however, the settlers learned the techniques necessary to cultivate the strange crops that grew in this unfamiliar terrain. As far as the English government was concerned, the colonies were strictly commercial ventures, intended to produce crops that could not be grown at home, and it was inconceivable to them that the colonists might have goals of their own. After early failures with sugar and rice, Virginia finally found its feet with its first **tobacco** harvest in 1615 (the man responsible, John Rolfe, is now better known as the husband of Pocahontas). A successful tobacco plantation requires two things in abundance: land, which intensified the pressure to dispossess the Indians, and labor. No self-respecting Englishman came to America to work for others; when the first **slave** ship called in at Jamestown in 1619, the captain found an eager market for his cargo of twenty African slaves. By that time there were already a million slaves in South America.

The 102 **Puritans** known to history as the "**Pilgrim Fathers**" were deposited on Cape Cod by the *Mayflower* in late 1620, and soon moved on to set up their own colony at Plymouth (see p.203). Fifty of them died during that winter, and the whole party might well have perished but for their fortuitous encounter with the extraordinary **Squanto**. This Native American had twice been kidnapped and taken to Europe and succeeded in making his way home; during his wanderings he had spent four years working as a merchant in the City of London, and had also lived in Spain. Having recently come home to find his entire tribe exterminated by smallpox, he decided to throw in his lot with the English. With his guidance, they finally managed to reap their first harvest, celebrated with the mighty feast of **Thanksgiving** that is still commemorated today.

Of greater significance to the history of New England was the founding in 1630 of a new colony, further up the coast at Naumkeag (which became Salem), by the Massachusetts Bay Company. Its governor, **John Winthrop**, soon moved to establish a new capital on the Shawmut peninsula – the city of **Boston**, complete with its own university of Harvard. His vision of a Utopian "City on a Hill" did not extend to sharing Paradise with the Indians; he argued that they had not "subdued" the land, and it was therefore a "vacuum" for the Puritans to use as they saw fit. While their faith helped individual colonists to endure the early hardships, the colony as a whole failed to maintain a strong religious identity (the Salem witch trials of 1692 did much to discredit the notion that the New World had any moral superiority to the Old), and breakaway groups soon left to create the rival settlements of Providence and Connecticut.

Between 1620 and 1642, sixty thousand migrants – which amounted to 1.5 percent of the population – left England for America. Those who came in pursuit of economic opportunities tended to join the longer-established colonies, where in effect they diluted the religious zeal of the Puritans. Groups hoping to find spiritual freedom were more inclined to start afresh; thus **Maryland** was created as a haven for Catholics in 1632, and fifty years later **Pennsylvania** was founded by the Quakers.

The English were not alone, however. After Sir Henry Hudson rediscovered Manhattan in 1609, it was "bought" by the **Dutch** in 1624 – though the Indians who took their money were passing nomads with no claim to it either. The Dutch colony of New Amsterdam, founded in 1625, lasted less than forty years before it was captured by the English and renamed **New York**; by that time, there was a strong Dutch presence on the lower reaches of the Hudson River.

From their foothold in the Great Lakes region, meanwhile, the **French** sent the explorers Joliet and Marquette to map the course of the Mississippi in 1673. They turned back once they had established that the river did indeed flow into the Gulf of Mexico, but their trip cleared the way for the foundation of the huge and ill-defined colony of **Louisiana** in 1699. The city of **New Orleans**, at the mouth of the Mississippi, was created in 1718.

While the Spanish remained firmly ensconced in Florida, things were not going so smoothly in the Southwest. In the bloody **Pueblo Revolt** of 1680, the pueblo peoples managed to drive the Spanish out of New Mexico altogether, only to have them return in force a dozen years later. Thereafter, a curious synthesis of traditional and Hispanic religion and culture began to evolve, and, but for hostile raids from the north, the Spanish presence was not seriously challenged.

With the arrival of the foreigners, things were also changing in the unknown hinterland. The frontier in the east was pushing steadily forward, as colonists seized Indian land, with or without the excuse of an "uprising" or "rebellion" to provoke them into bloodshed. The major killer of the indigenous peoples, however, was **smallpox**, which worked its way deep into the interior of the continent long before the Europeans. (Scientists speculate that the Native Americans may have had no equivalent "new" diseases to inflict on the newcomers because of the long period their ancestors had spent crossing the Arctic in subzero temperatures.) As populations were decimated, great migrations took place. In addition, around this time the **horse** arrived on the Great Plains. The original inhabitants of the region were sedentary farmers, who also hunted buffalo by driving them over rocky bluffs. The bow and arrow was discovered around the fifth century, but the acquisition of horses (probably captured from the Spanish, and known at first as "mystery dogs") made possible the emergence of an entirely new, nomadic lifestyle. Groups such as the Cheyenne and the Apache swept their rivals aside to dominate vast territories, and eagerly seized the potential offered by firearms when they were introduced in due course. This created a very dynamic, but fundamentally unstable culture, as they became dependent on trade with Europeans for the necessities of life.

The American Revolution

The American colonies prospered during the **eighteenth century**, with the cities of Boston, New York, and Philadelphia in particular becoming home to a wealthy, well educated, and highly articulate middle class. Frustration began to mount at the inequities of the colonies' relationship with Britain. While they were allowed to trade among themselves, the Americans could otherwise only sell their produce to the British, and all transatlantic commerce had to be undertaken in British ships.

Although full-scale independence was not an explicit goal until late in the century, the main factor that made it possible was the economic impact of the pan-European conflict known as the **Seven Years' War**. Officially, the war in Europe lasted from 1756 to 1763, but fighting among the English, French, and Spanish in North America broke out a little earlier. Beginning in 1755 with the mass expulsion of French settlers from Acadia in Nova Scotia (triggering their epic migration to Louisiana, where as the **Cajuns** they remain to this day), the British went on to conquer all of Canada. In forcing the **surrender of Québec** in 1759, General Wolfe brought the war to a close; the French ceded Louisiana to the Spanish rather than let it fall to the British, while Florida passed into British control for a year before reverting to the Spanish. All the European monarchs were left hamstrung by debts, and it became apparent to the British that colonialism in America was not as profitable a business as in those parts of the world where the native populations could be coerced into working for their overseas masters.

There was one other major player on the scene – the **Iroquois Confederacy**. Evidence of Iroquois culture, characterized by military expansionism and even human sacrifice, has been found in the Great Lakes region dating from around 1000 AD onwards. Forever in competition with the Algonquin and the Huron, the southern Iroquois had by the eighteenth century resolved themselves into a League of Five Nations – the Seneca, Cayuga, Onondaga, Oneida, and Mohawk, all in what's now upstate New York. Wooed by both French and British, the Iroquois for most of the century charted an independent course between the two. During negotiations with the colonists in 1744, an Onondaga chief, unimpressed by the squabbling representatives of Pennsylvania, Virginia, and Maryland, had recommended "by your observing the same methods our wise forefathers have taken, you will acquire fresh strength and power." Benjamin Franklin, who was present, wrote in 1751 that "It would be a very strange thing if . . . ignorant savages should be capable of forming a scheme for such a union . . . that has subsisted ages and appears indissoluble; and yet that a like union should be impracticable for ten or a dozen English colonies."

Shortly after the Seven Years' War, an unsuccessful insurrection by the Ottawa tribe in 1763, led by their chief **Pontiac**, led the cash-strapped British to conclude that, while America needed its own standing army, it was not unreasonable to expect the colonists to pay for it.

In 1765, the British introduced the **Stamp Act**, which required duty on all legal transactions and printed matter in the colonies to be paid to the British Crown. Firm in the belief that there should be "no taxation without representation," delegates from nine of the colonies met in the Stamp Act Congress in October 1765. By that time, however, the British prime minister responsible for the Act had already been dismissed by King George III. Only briefly, in Georgia, were the offending stamps ever distributed, and the Act was repealed in 1766.

However, in 1767, Chancellor Townshend made political capital at home by proclaiming "I dare tax America," as he introduced a program of legislation that included the broadly similar Revenue Act. That led the merchants of Massachusetts, inspired by **Samuel Adams**, to vote to boycott English goods; they were subsequently joined by all the other colonies except New Hampshire. Townshend's Acts were repealed in turn by a new prime minister, Lord North, on March 5, 1770. By chance, on that same day a stone-throwing mob surrounded the Customs House in Boston; shots from the guards killed five people in what became known as the **Boston Massacre**. Even so, most of the colonies resumed trading with Britain, and the crisis was postponed for a few more years.

In May 1773, Lord North's **Tea Act** relieved the debt-ridden East India Company of the need to pay duties on exports to America, while still requiring the Americans to pay duty on tea. Massachusetts called for the colonies to unite in action, and its citizens took the lead on December 16 in the **Boston Tea Party**, when three tea ships were boarded and 342 chests thrown into the sea. As John Adams put it, "to let it be landed would be giving up the principle of taxation by Parliamentary authority."

The infuriated British Parliament thereupon began to pass a body of legislation collectively known as both the "Coercive" and the "Intolerable" Acts, which included closing the port of Boston and disbanding the government of Massachusetts. Thomas Jefferson argued that the acts amounted to "a deliberate and systematical plan of reducing us to slavery." To discuss a response, the first **Continental Congress** was held in Philadelphia on May 5, 1774, and attended by representatives of all the colonies except Georgia.

War finally broke out on April 18, 1775, when General Gage, the newly imposed governor of Massachusetts, dispatched four hundred British soldiers to destroy the arms depot at **Concord**, in order to prevent weapons from falling into rebel hands. Silversmith **Paul Revere** was dispatched by the citizens of Boston on his legendary ride to warn the rebels, and the British were confronted en route at Lexington by 77 American "Minutemen." The resulting skirmish led to the "shot heard 'round the world."

Congress set about forming an army at Boston, and decided for the sake of unity to appoint a Southern commander, **George Washington**. One by one, as the war raged, the colonies set up their own governments and declared themselves to be states, and the politicians set about defining the society they wished to create. The writings of pamphleteer Thomas Paine – especially *Common Sense* – were, together with the Confederacy of the Iroquois, a great influence on the **Declaration of Independence**. Drafted by Thomas Jefferson, this was adopted by the Continental Congress in Philadelphia on July 4, 1776. The anti-slavery clauses originally included by Jefferson – himself a slave-owner – were omitted to spare the feelings

The Constitution

As signed in 1787 and ratified in 1788, the **Constitution** stipulated the following form of government:

All **legislative** powers were granted to the **Congress of the United States**. The lower of its two distinct houses, the **House of Representatives**, was to be elected every two years, with its members in proportion to the number of each state's "free Persons" plus "three fifths of all other persons" (meaning slaves). The upper house, the **Senate**, would hold two Senators from each state, chosen by state legislatures rather than by direct elections. Each Senator was to serve for six years, with a third of them to be elected every two years.

Executive power was vested in the **President**, who was also Commander in Chief of the Army and Navy. He would be chosen every four years, by as many **"Electors"** from each individual state as it had Senators and Representatives. Each state could decide how to appoint those Electors; almost all chose to have direct popular elections. Nonetheless, the distinction has remained ever since between the number of "popular votes," across the whole country, received by a presidential candidate, and the number of state-by-state "electoral votes," which determines the actual result. Originally, whoever came second in the voting automatically became **Vice President**.

The President could **veto** acts of Congress, but that veto could be overruled by a two-thirds vote in both houses. The House of Representatives could **impeach** the President for treason, bribery, or "other high crimes and misdemeanors," in which instance the Senate could remove him from office with a two-thirds majority.

Judicial power was invested in a **Supreme Court**, and as many "inferior Courts"as Congress should decide.

The Constitution has so far been altered by 27 **Amendments**. Those that have introduced significant governmental changes include **14** and **15**, which extended the vote to black males in 1868 and 1870; **17**, which made senators subject to election by direct popular vote, in 1913; **18**, introducing women's suffrage, in 1920; **22**, restricting the president to two terms, in 1951; **24**, which stopped states using poll taxes to disenfranchise black voters, in 1964; and **26**, which reduced the minimum voting age to 18, in 1971.

of the Southern states, though the section that denounced the King's dealings with "merciless Indian Savages" was left in.

At first, the Revolutionary War went well for the British. General Howe crossed the Atlantic with around twenty thousand men, took New York and New Jersey, and ensconced himself in Philadelphia for the winter of 1777–78. Washington's army was encamped not far away at Valley Forge, freezing cold and all but starving to death. It soon became clear, however, that the longer the Americans could avoid losing an all-out battle, the more likely it was that the British would over-extend their lines as they advanced through the vast and unfamiliar continent. Thus, General Burgoyne's expedition, which set out from Canada to march on New England, was so harried by rebel guerrillas that he found himself obliged to surrender at Saratoga in October 1777. As the logistical difficulty of maintaining the British war effort became ever more apparent, other European powers took delight in coming to the aid of the Americans. Benjamin Franklin led a wildly successful delegation to France to request support, and soon the nascent American fleet was being assisted in its bid to cut British naval communications by both the French and the Spanish. The end came when Cornwallis, who had replaced Howe, was instructed to dig in at Yorktown and wait for the Royal Navy to come to his aid, only for the French to seal off Chesapeake Bay and prevent reinforcement. Cornwallis surrendered to Washington on October 17, 1781, just fifteen miles from the site of the first English settlement at Jamestown.

The ensuing **Treaty of Paris** granted the Americans their independence on generous terms – the British completely abandoned their Native American allies, including the Iroquois, to the vengeance of the victors – and Washington entered New York as the British left in November 1783. The Spanish were confirmed in their possession of Florida.

The victorious US Congress met for the first time in 1789, and the tradition of awarding political power to the nation's most successful generals was instigated by the election of George Washington as the first **president**. He was further honored when his name was given to the new capital city of **Washington DC**, deliberately sited between the North and the South.

The nineteenth century

In its first century, the territories and population of the new **United States of America** expanded at a phenomenal rate. The white population of North America in 1800 stood at around five million, and there were another one million African slaves (of whom thirty thousand were in the North). Of that total, 86 percent lived within fifty miles of the Atlantic, but no US city could rival Mexico City, whose population approached 100,000 inhabitants. (Both New York and Philadelphia reached that figure within twenty years, however, and New York had passed a million fifty years later.)

It had suited the British to discourage settlers from venturing west of the Appalachians, where they would be far beyond the reach of British power and therefore inclined to carry on independent existences. For George Washington, however, any agreement to follow such a policy had been a "temporary expedient to quieten the minds of the Indians." Adventurers such as **Daniel Boone** started to cross the mountains into Tennessee and Kentucky during the 1770s. Soon makeshift rafts, made from the planks that would later be assembled to make log cabins, were careering west along the Ohio River (the only westward-flowing river on the continent).

In 1801, the Spanish handed Louisiana back to the French, on the express undertaking that the French would keep it for ever. However, Napoleon swiftly realized that any attempt to hang on to his American possessions would involve spreading his armies too thinly. He chose instead to make the best of things by selling them to the United States for $15 million, in the **Louisiana Purchase** of 1803. The new territories extended far beyond the boundaries of present-day Louisiana (see map p.1206), and for President Thomas Jefferson it was a matter of urgency to send the explorers **Lewis and Clark** to map them out. With the help of Sacagawea, their female Shoshone guide, they followed the Missouri and Columbia rivers all the way to the Pacific; in their wake, trappers and "mountain men" came to hunt in the wilderness of the Rockies. The **Russians** had already reached the Pacific Northwest by this time and established a network of fortified outposts to trade in the pelts of beaver and otter.

British attempts to blockade the Atlantic, primarily intended as a move against Napoleon, gave the new nation its first chance to flex its military muscles. Although British raiders succeeded in capturing Washington DC, and burned the White House to the ground, the **War of 1812** most significantly provided the US with a cover for aggression against the Native American allies of the Brit-

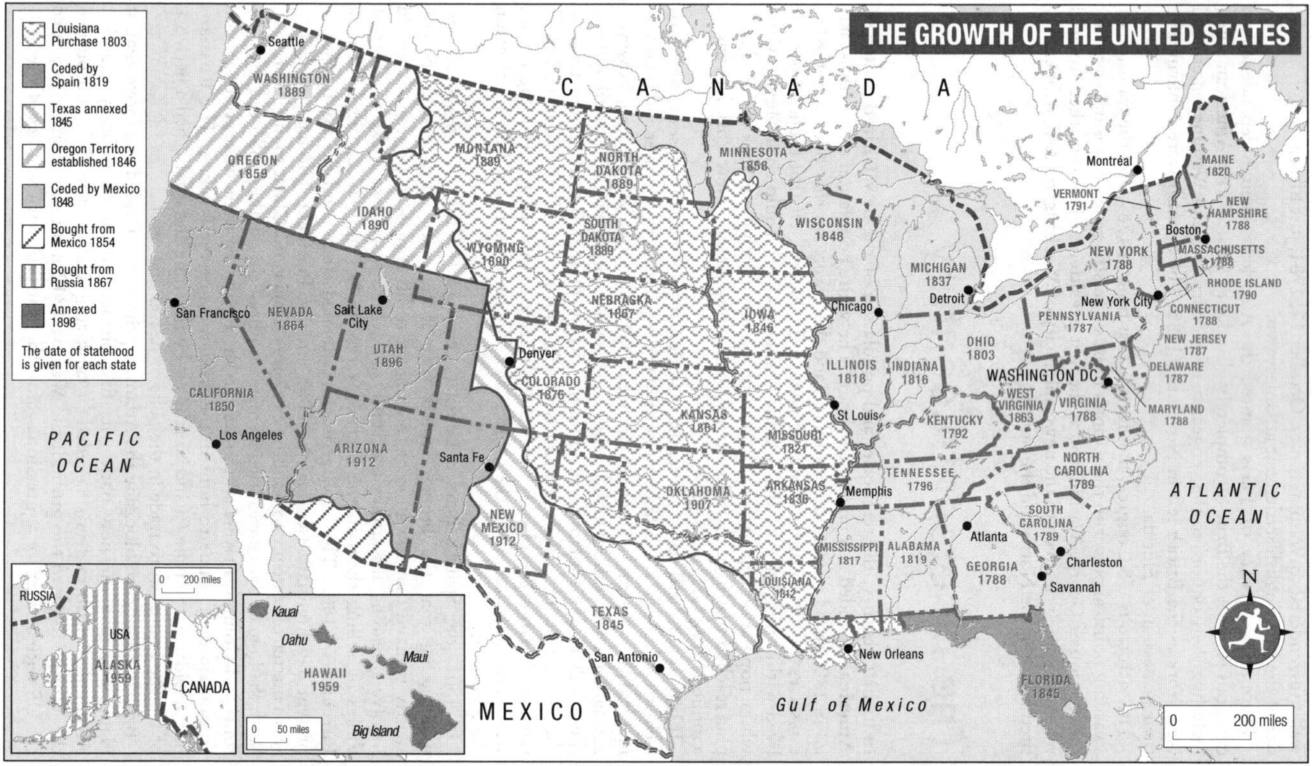
THE GROWTH OF THE UNITED STATES
Louisiana Purchase 1803
Ceded by Spain 1819
Texas annexed 1845
Oregon Territory established 1846
Ceded by Mexico 1848
Bought from Mexico 1854
Bought from Russia 1867
Annexed 1898
The date of statehood is given for each state
CANADA
MEXICO
PACIFIC OCEAN
ATLANTIC OCEAN
Gulf of Mexico
WASHINGTON 1889
OREGON 1859
IDAHO 1890
MONTANA 1889
WYOMING 1890
NORTH DAKOTA 1889
SOUTH DAKOTA 1889
MINNESOTA 1858
WISCONSIN 1848
MICHIGAN 1837
CALIFORNIA 1850
NEVADA 1864
UTAH 1896
COLORADO 1876
NEBRASKA 1867
IOWA 1846
ILLINOIS 1818
INDIANA 1816
OHIO 1803
ARIZONA 1912
NEW MEXICO 1912
KANSAS 1861
MISSOURI 1821
KENTUCKY 1792
WEST VIRGINIA 1863
VIRGINIA 1788
OKLAHOMA 1907
ARKANSAS 1836
TENNESSEE 1796
NORTH CAROLINA 1789
SOUTH CAROLINA 1789
TEXAS 1845
LOUISIANA 1812
MISSISSIPPI 1817
ALABAMA 1819
GEORGIA 1788
FLORIDA 1845
MAINE 1820
VERMONT 1791
NEW HAMPSHIRE 1788
NEW YORK 1788
MASSACHUSETTS 1788
RHODE ISLAND 1790
CONNECTICUT 1788
PENNSYLVANIA 1787
NEW JERSEY 1787
DELAWARE 1787
MARYLAND 1788
Seattle
San Francisco
Los Angeles
Salt Lake City
Denver
Santa Fe
San Antonio
Chicago
Detroit
St Louis
Memphis
New Orleans
Atlanta
Charleston
Savannah
WASHINGTON DC
New York City
Boston
Montréal
N
0 200 miles
RUSSIA
USA
ALASKA 1959
CANADA
0 200 miles
Kauai
Oahu
Maui
HAWAII 1959
Big Island
0 50 miles

ish. Thus **Tecumseh** of the Shawnee was defeated near Detroit, and **Andrew Jackson** moved against the Creek of the southern Mississippi. Jackson's campaign against the Seminole in Florida enabled the US to gain possession of the state from the Spanish; he was rewarded first with the governorship of the new state, and later by his election to the presidency. During his period in office, in the 1830s, Jackson went even further, and set about clearing all states east of the Mississippi of their native populations. The barren region that later became Oklahoma was designated as "Indian Territory," home to the "Five Civilized Tribes." The Creek and the Seminole, and the Choctaw and Chickasaw of Mississippi were eventually joined by the Cherokee of the lower Appalachians there, after four appalling months on the forced march known as the **"Trail of Tears."**

For the citizens of the young republic, it took only a small step from realizing that their country might be capable of spreading across the whole continent to supposing that it had a quasi-religious duty – a **"Manifest Destiny"** – to do so. At its most basic, that doctrine amounted to little more than a belief that might must be right, but the idea that they were fulfilling the will of God inspired countless pioneers to set off across the plains in search of a new life.

Mexico had by now gained its independence from Spain. The Spanish territories of the Southwest had never attracted enough migrants to turn into full-fledged colonies, and the American settlers who arrived in ever-increasing numbers began to dominate their Hispanic counterparts. The Anglos of **Texas** rebelled in 1833, under the leadership of General Sam Houston. Shortly after the legendary setback at the **Alamo** (see p.680), in 1836, they defeated the Mexican army of Santa Anna, and Texas became an independent republic in its own right.

The ensuing **Mexican War** was a bare-faced exercise in American aggression, in which most of the future leading figures of the Civil War received their first experience fighting on the same side. The conflict resulted in the acquisition not only of Texas, but also of Arizona, Utah, Colorado, Nevada, New Mexico, and finally California, in 1848. A token US payment of $15 million to the Mexican government was designed to match the Louisiana Purchase. Controversy over whether slavery would be legal in the new states was rendered academic when it turned out that, on virtually the same day the war ended, gold had been discovered in the Sierra Nevada of California. The resultant **Gold Rush** created California's first significant city, **San Francisco**, and brought a massive influx of free white settlers to a land that was in any case utterly unsuitable for a plantation-based economy.

Proponents of Manifest Destiny seem never to have given much thought to the **Pacific Northwest**, which remained nominally under the control of British Canada. However, once the Oregon Trail started to operate in 1841 (see p.1129), American settlers there swiftly outnumbered the British. In 1846, a surprisingly amicable treaty fixed the border along the 49th parallel, just as it already did across eastern Canada, and left the whole of Vancouver Island to the British.

The Civil War

From the moment of its inception, the unity of the United States had been based on shaky foundations. Great care had gone into devising a **Constitution** that balanced the need for a strong federal government with the aspirations for autonomy of its component states. That was achieved by giving Congress two separate chambers – the **House of Representatives**, in which the number of representatives from each state depended upon its population, and the **Senate**, in which each state, regardless of size, had two members. Thus, although in theory the Constitution remained silent on the issue of **slavery**, it allayed the fears of the less populated Southern states (where although the slaves lacked the vote, each was counted as three-fifths of a person when it came to determining the number of representatives elected per state) that the voters of the North might destroy their economy by forcing them to abandon their "peculiar institution." However, it gradually became apparent that the system only worked so long as there were equal numbers of "Free" and slave-owning states. The only practicable way to keep the balance was to ensure that each time a new state was admitted to the Union, a matching state taking the opposite stance on slavery was also admitted. Thus the admission of every new state became subject to endless intrigue. The 1820 **Missouri Compromise**, under which Missouri joined as a slave-owning state and Maine as a Free one, was straightforward in comparison to the prevarication and chest-beating that surrounded the admission of Texas, while the Mexican War was widely seen in the North as a naked land grab for new slave states.

Abolitionist sentiment in the North was not all that great before the middle of the nineteenth century. At best, after the importation of slaves from Africa ended in 1808, Northerners had vague hopes that slavery was an anachronism that might simply wither away. As it turned out, the profitability of the Southern plantations was dramatically boosted by the development of the cotton gin, and the increased demand for manufactured cotton goods triggered by the **Industrial Revolution**. What ultimately changed the situation was the rapid growth of the nation as a whole, making it ever more difficult to maintain a political balance between North and South.

Matters came to a head in 1854, when the **Kansas–Nebraska Act** sparked guerrilla raids and mini-wars between rival settlers by allowing both prospective states self-determination on the issue. That same year, the **Republican Party** was founded, on the platform of resisting the further expansion of slavery. Escaped former slaves such as Frederick Douglass were by now inspiring Northern audiences to moral outrage, and Harriet Beecher Stowe's *Uncle Tom's Cabin* found unprecedented readership.

In October 1859, **John Brown** – a white-bearded, wild-eyed veteran of some of Kansas's bloodiest infighting – led a dramatic raid on the US Armory at Harpers Ferry, West Virginia, intending to secure arms for a slave insurrection (see p.420). Swiftly captured by forces under the command of Robert E. Lee, he was hanged within a few weeks, proclaiming that "I am now quite certain that the crimes of this guilty land will never be purged away but with blood."

The Republican candidate for the presidency in 1860 was the little-known **Abraham Lincoln** from Kentucky; he won no Southern states, but with the Democrats split into Northern and Southern factions he was elected with 39 percent of the popular vote. Within weeks, on December 20, South Carolina became the first state to secede from the Union; the **Confederacy** was declared on February 4, 1861, when it was joined by Mississippi, Florida, Alabama, Georgia, Louisiana, and Texas. Its first (and only) president was **Jefferson Davis**, also from Kentucky; at their inauguration, his new vice president remarked that their government was "the first in the history of the world based upon the great physical and moral truth that the negro is not equal to the white man." Lincoln was inaugurated in turn in March 1861, proclaiming that "I have no purpose, directly or indirectly, to interfere with the institution of slavery in the States where it exists. I believe I have no lawful right to do so, and I have no inclination to do so." He was completely inflexible, however, on one paramount issue: the survival of the Union.

The **Civil War** began just a few weeks later. The first shots were fired on April 12, when a much-postponed federal attempt to resupply Fort Sumter, in the harbor at Charleston, South Carolina, was greeted by a Confederate bombardment that forced its surrender. Lincoln's immediate call to raise an army against the South was greeted by the further secession of Virginia, Arkansas, Tennessee, and North Carolina. Within a year, both armies had amassed 600,000 men; Robert E. Lee had been offered command of both and opted for the Confederacy, while George McLellan became the first leader of the Union forces. Although the rival capitals of Washington DC, and Richmond, Virginia, were a mere one hundred miles apart, over the next four years operations of war reached almost everywhere south of Washington and east of the Mississippi.

Tracing the ebb and flow of the military campaigns – from the Confederate victories of the early years, via Grant's successful siege of Vicksburg in 1863 and Sherman's devastating March to the Sea in 1864, to Lee's eventual surrender at Appomattox in April 1865 – it's easy to lose sight of the fact that it was not so much generalship as sheer economic (and man) power that won the war. The war pitted the **Union** of 23 Northern states, holding over 22 million people, against the **Confederacy** of 11 Southern states, with 9 million people. As for potential combatants, the North initially drew upon 3.5 million white males aged between 18 and 45 – and later recruited blacks as well – whereas the South had more like one million. In the end, around 2.1 million men fought for the Union, and 900,000 for the Confederacy. Of the 620,000 soldiers who died during the conflict, a disproportionate 258,000 came from the South – representing one quarter of its white men of military age. Meanwhile, not only was the North able to continue trading with the rest of the world as it maintained its industrial and agricultural output, but it also stifled the Confederacy with a devastating **naval blockade**. The Southern war effort was primarily financed by printing $1.5 billion of paper currency, which with neither reserves nor income to support it was so eroded by inflation that it became worthless.

Even so, the Confederacy came much closer to victory than is usually appreciated. The repeated out-maneuvering of federal forces by General **Robert E. Lee**, and his incursions into Union territory, meant that in each of three successive years, from 1862 to 1864, there was a genuine possibility that Northern morale would collapse, allowing opponents of the war to be elected to power and agree to peace. After all, the Revolutionary War had shown how such a war could be won: for the Union to triumph, it had to invade and occupy the South, and destroy its armies, but for the South to win it only had to survive until the North wearied of the struggle.

The dashing tactics of Confederate generals Lee and Jackson, forever counter-attacking and carrying the fight to the enemy, may have been in the finest romantic traditions of the Old South, but they arguably contributed to the Southern defeat. The grim, relentless total-war campaigning of Grant and Sherman eventually ground the South down. There's a particular irony in the fact that had the Confederacy sued for peace before Lee gave it fresh hope, a negotiated settlement might not have included the abolition of slavery. In the event, as the war went on, with Southern slaves flocking to the Union flag and black soldiers fighting on the front line, emancipation did indeed become inevitable. Lincoln took the political decision to match his moral conviction by issuing his **Emancipation Proclamation** in 1862, though the **Thirteenth Amendment** outlawing slavery only took effect in 1865.

Lincoln himself was assassinated within a few days of the end of the war, a mark of the deep bitterness that would almost certainly have rendered successful **Reconstruction** impossible even if he had lived. There was a brief period, after black men were granted the vote in 1870, when Southern states elected black political representatives, but without a sustained effort to enable former slaves to

IN THIS TEMPLE
AS IN THE HEARTS OF THE PEOPLE
FOR WHOM HE SAVED THE UNION
THE MEMORY OF ABRAHAM LINCOLN
IS ENSHRINED FOREVER

▲ The Lincoln Memorial, Washington DC

acquire land, racial relations in the South swiftly deteriorated. Thanks to white supremacist organizations such as the Ku Klux Klan, nominally clandestine but brazenly public, Southern blacks were soon effectively disenfranchised once more. Anyone working to transform the South came under attack either as a carpetbagger (a Northern opportunist who headed South for personal profit) or a treacherous scalawag (a Southern collaborator).

The aftermath of the Civil War can almost be said to have lasted for a hundred years. While the South condemned itself to a century as a backwater, the rest of the re-United States embarked on a period of expansionism and prosperity.

The Indian Wars

With the completion of the transcontinental railroad in 1867, Manifest Destiny became an undeniable reality. Among the first to head west were the troops of the federal army, with Union and Confederate veterans marching under the same flag to do battle with the remaining Native Americans. Treaty after treaty was signed, only to be broken as it became expedient to do so (usually upon the discovery of gold or precious metals). When the whites overreached themselves, or when driven to desperation, the Indians were capable of fighting back. The defeat of **General George Custer** at Little Bighorn in 1876, by **Sitting Bull** and his Sioux and Cheyenne warriors (see p.825), provoked the full wrath of the government. Within a few years, leaders such as **Crazy Horse** of the Oglala Sioux and **Geronimo** of the Apache had been forced to surrender, and their people were confined to reservations. One final act of resistance came in the form of the visionary, messianic cult of the **Ghost Dance**, whose practitioners hoped that by correct ritual observance they could win back their lost way of life, in a land miraculously free of white intruders. Such aspirations were regarded as hostile, and military harassment of the movement culminated in the massacre at **Wounded Knee** in South Dakota in 1890.

A major tactic in the campaign against the Plains Indians was to starve them into submission, by eliminating the vast herds of bison that were their primary source of food. As General Philip Sheridan put it, "For the sake of a lasting peace . . . kill, skin and sell until the buffalo are exterminated. Then your prairies can be covered by the speckled cow and the festive cowboy." More significant than the activities of the much-mythologized cowboys, however, was the back-breaking toil of the miners up in the mountains, and the homesteading families out on the plains.

Industry and immigration

The late nineteenth century was an era of massive **immigration** to North America from the rest of the world, with influxes from Europe to the East Coast paralleled by those from Asia to the West. As in colonial times, national groups tended to form enclaves in specific areas – examples range from the Scandinavian farmers of Minnesota and the northern Plains, to the Basque shepherds of Idaho, and the Cornish miners of Colorado. In the Southwest, where individual hard work counted for less than shared communal effort, the **Mormons** of Utah had fled persecution eastward across the United States to become the first white settlers to eke a living from the unforgiving desert.

The fastest growth of all was in the nation's greatest **cities**, especially New York, Chicago, and Boston. Their industrial and commercial strength enabled them to attract and absorb migrants not only from throughout Europe but also from the Old South – particularly ex-slaves, who could now at least vote with their feet.

Now that it stretched "from sea to shining sea," the territorial boundaries of the US had reached almost their current form. In 1867, however, Secretary of State William Seward agreed to buy **Alaska** from the crisis-torn Russian government for $7.2 million. The purchase was at first derided as "Seward's Folly," but it was not long before the familiar Midas touch of the Americans was revealed by the discovery of gold there as well.

The various US presidents of the day, from the victorious General Grant (a man palpably out of his depth) onwards, now seem anonymous figures compared to the industrialists and financiers who manipulated the national economy. These "**robber barons**" included such men as John D. Rockefeller, who controlled seventy percent of the world's oil almost before anyone else had realized it was worth controlling; Andrew Carnegie, who made his fortune introducing the Bessemer process of steel manufacture; and J.P. Morgan, who went for the most basic commodity of all – money. Their success was predicated on the willingness of the government to cooperate in resisting the development of a strong labor movement. A succession of widely publicized strikes – such as those on the railroads in 1877, in the mines of Tennessee in 1891, and in the steel mills of Pittsburgh in 1892 – were forcibly crushed.

The nineteenth century had also seen the development of a distinctive American voice in **literature**, which rendered increasingly superfluous the efforts of passing English visitors – such as Charles Dickens, and the Trollopes, mother and son – to "explain" the United States. From the 1830s onwards, a wide range of writers set out to find new ways to describe their new world, with results as varied as the introspective essays of Henry Thoreau, the morbid visions of Edgar Allan Poe, the all-embracing novels of Herman Melville, and the irrepressible poetry of Walt Whitman, whose endlessly revised *Leaves of Grass* was an exultant hymn to the young republic. Virtually every leading participant in the Civil War wrote at least one highly readable volume of memoirs, while public figures as disparate as Buffalo Bill Cody and the showman P. T. Barnum also produced lively autobiographies. The boundless national self-confidence found its greatest expression in the vigorous vernacular style of **Mark Twain**, whose depictions of frontier life, whether in the journalistic *Roughing It* and *Life on the Mississippi*, or fictionalized in novels like *Huckleberry Finn*, gave the rest of the world perhaps its most abiding impression of the American character.

Many Americans saw the official "closure" of the Western frontier, announced by the Census Bureau in 1890, as tantamount to depriving the country of the Manifest Destiny that was its *raison d'être*, and were prompted to search for new frontiers further afield. Such **imperialist ventures** reached a crescendo in 1898, with the annexation of the Kingdom of **Hawaii** – which even then-President Cleveland condemned as "wholly without justification . . . not merely wrong but a disgrace" – and the double seizure of Cuba and the Philippines in the **Spanish–American War**, which catapulted **Theodore Roosevelt** to the presidency. Though he took the African proverb "speak softly and carry a big stick" as his motto – and was hardly, if truth be told, noted for being soft-spoken – Roosevelt in office did much to heal the divisions within the nation. While new legislation reigned in the worst excesses of the Robber Barons, and of rampant capitalism in general, it alleviated popular discontent without substantially threatening the business community, or empowering the labor movement. A decade into the twentieth century, the United States had advanced to the point that it knew, even if the rest of the world wasn't yet altogether sure, that it was the strongest, wealthiest country on earth.

The twentieth century

It may not have been apparent to everyone at the time, but the first few years of the twentieth century witnessed the emergence of many of the features that came to characterize modern America. In 1903 alone, Wilbur and Orville Wright achieved the first successful powered **flight**, and Henry Ford established his Ford Motor Company. Ford's enthusiastic adoption of the latest technology in mass production – the assembly line – gave Detroit a head start in the new **automobile** industry, which swiftly became the most important business in America. Both **jazz** and **blues** music came to the attention of a national audience for the first time during that same period, while Hollywood acquired its first **movie** studio in 1911, and its first major hit in 1915 with D. W. Griffith's unabashed glorification of the Ku Klux Klan in *Birth of a Nation*.

This was also a time of growing **radicalism**. Both the NAACP (National Association for the Advancement of Colored People) and the socialist International Workers of the World ("the Wobblies") were founded in the early 1900s, while the campaign for women's suffrage also came to the forefront. Writers such as Upton Sinclair, whose *The Jungle* exposed conditions in Chicago's stockyards, and Jack London proselytized to the masses; contemporary improvements in the educational system suggest this may well have been the most literate period in US history.

President Wilson managed to keep the US out of the **Great War** for several years but, when the time came, American intervention was decisive. With the Russian Revolution illustrating the dangers of anarchy, the US also took charge of supervising the peace. However, although Wilson presided over the postwar negotiations that resulted in the Treaty of Versailles in 1919, isolationist sentiment at home kept the US from joining his pet scheme to preserve future world peace, the League of Nations.

Back home, the 18th Amendment to the Constitution, in 1920, forbade the sale and distribution of alcohol, while the 19th finally gave all American women the vote. Quite how **Prohibition** ever became the law of the land is something of a mystery; certainly, in the buzzing metropolises of the Roaring Twenties, it enjoyed little conspicuous support. There was no noticeable elevation in the moral tone of the country, and Chicago in particular became renowned for the street wars between bootlegging gangsters such as Al Capone and his rivals.

The two Republican presidents who followed Wilson did little more than sit back and watch the Roaring Twenties unfold. At least until his premature death, **Warren Harding** enjoyed considerable public affection, but he's now remembered as probably the worst of all US presidents, thanks to the cronyism and corruption of his associates. It's hard to say quite whether **Calvin Coolidge** did anything at all; his laissez-faire attitude extended to working a typical four-hour day, and announcing shortly after his inauguration that "four-fifths of our troubles would disappear if we would sit down and keep still."

The Depression and the New Deal

By the middle of the 1920s, the US was enough of an industrial powerhouse to be responsible for more than half the world's output of manufactured goods. After leading the way into a new era of prosperity, however, it suddenly found itself dragging the rest of the world down into economic collapse. It's hard to say exactly what triggered the **Great Depression**; the consequences were out of all proportion to any one specific cause. Possible factors include American overinvestment in the floundering economy of postwar Europe, combined with high tariffs on imports that effectively precluded European recovery. Conservative commentators at the time chose to interpret the calamitous **Wall Street Crash** of October 1929 as a symptom of impending depression rather than a contributory cause, but the quasi-superstitious faith in the stock market that preceded it showed all the characteristics of such classic speculative booms as Britain's eighteenth-century South Sea Bubble. On "Black Tuesday" alone, enough stocks were sold to produce a total loss of ten thousand million dollars – more than twice the total amount of money in circulation in the US. Within the next three years, industrial production was cut by half, the national income dropped by 38 percent, and, above all, unemployment rose from 1.5 million to 13 million.

National self-confidence, however shaky its foundations, has always played a crucial role in US history, and President Hoover was not the man to restore it. Matters only began to improve in 1932, when the patrician figure of **Franklin Delano Roosevelt** accepted the Democratic nomination for president with the words "I pledge myself to a new deal for America," and went on to win a landslide victory. At the time of his inauguration, early in 1933, the banking system had all but closed down; it took Roosevelt the now-proverbial "Hundred Days" of vigorous legislation to turn around the mood of the country.

Taking advantage of the new medium of radio, he used his "Fireside Chats" to cajole America out of crisis; among his earliest observations was that it was a good time for a beer, and that therefore the experiment of Prohibition was over. The **New Deal** took many forms and worked through many newly created agencies, but was marked throughout by a massive growth in the power of the federal government, which only now seems to be under threat. Among its accomplishments were the National Recovery Administration, which created two million jobs; the Social Security Act, of which Roosevelt declared "no damn politician can ever scrap my social security program;" the Public Works Administration, which built dams and highways the length and breadth of the country; the Tennessee Valley Authority, which by generating electricity under public ownership for the common good was probably the closest the US has ever come to institutionalized socialism; and measures to legitimize the role of the unions and revitalize the "Dust Bowl" farmers out on the plains.

Roosevelt originally saw himself as a populist who could draw support from every sector of society. By 1936, however, business leaders – and the Supreme Court – were making it clear that as far as they were concerned he had done more than enough already to kick-start the economy. From then on, as he secured an unprecedented four consecutive terms as president, he was firmly cast as the champion of the little man.

After the work-creation programs of the New Deal had put America back on its feet, the deadly pressure to achieve victory in **World War II** spurred industrial production and know-how to new heights. Once again the US stayed out of the war at first, until it was finally forced in by the high-stakes gamble of the Japanese, who launched a pre-emptive strike on Hawaii's Pearl Harbor in December 1941. In both the Pacific and in Europe, American manpower and economic muscle eventually carried all before it. Roosevelt died early in 1945, after laying the foundations for the postwar carve-up with Stalin and Churchill at Yalta, and thus was spared the fateful decision, made by his successor Harry Truman, to use the newly developed atomic bomb on Hiroshima and Nagasaki.

The coming of the Cold War

With the war won, Americans were in no mood to revert back to the isolationism of the 1930s. Amid much hopeful rhetoric, Truman enthusiastically participated in the creation of the **United Nations**, and set up the **Marshall Plan** to speed the recovery of Europe – a task in which it was far more successful than any of the corresponding attempts made 25 years earlier. However, as Winston Churchill announced in Missouri in 1946, an "**Iron Curtain**" had descended upon Europe, and Joseph Stalin was transformed from ally to enemy almost overnight.

The ensuing **Cold War** lasted for more than four decades, at times fought in ferocious combat (albeit often by proxy) in scattered corners of the globe, and during the intervals diverting colossal economic resources towards the stockpiling of ever more destructive arsenals. Some of its ugliest moments came in its earliest years; Truman was still in office in 1950 when war broke out in **Korea**. A dispute over the arbitrary division of the Korean peninsula into two separate nations, North and South, soon turned into a stand-off between the US and China (with Russia, in theory at any rate, lurking in the shadows). Two years of bloody stalemate ended with little to show for it, except that Truman had by now been replaced by the genial **Dwight D. Eisenhower**, the latest war hero to turn president.

The Eisenhower years are often seen as an era characterized by bland complacency. Once Senator **Joseph McCarthy**, the "witch-hunting" anti-Communist scourge of the State Department and Hollywood, had finally discredited himself by attacking the army as well, middle-class America seemed to lapse into a wilful suburban stupor. Great social changes were starting to take shape, however. World War II had introduced vast numbers of women and members of ethnic minorities to the rewards of factory work, and it had shown many Americans from less prosperous regions the lifestyle that was attainable in other parts of their own country. The development of a **national highway system**, and a huge increase in automobile ownership, encouraged people to pursue the American Dream wherever they chose. Combined with increasing mechanization on the cotton plantations of the South, this led to another **mass exodus** of blacks from the rural South to the cities of the North, and to a lesser extent the West. The cities of **California** entered a period of rapid growth, with the aeronautical industries of Los Angeles in particular attracting thousands of prospective workers.

It was also during the 1950s that **television** reached every home in the country. Together with the LP record, it created an entertainment industry that seemed designed to promote mass conformity, but which swiftly showed itself capable of addressing the needs of consumers who had previously been barely identified. **Youth culture** burst into public prominence from 1954 onwards, with Elvis Presley's recording of "*That's Alright Mama*" appearing within a few months of Marlon Brando's moody starring role in *On the Waterfront* and James Dean's in *Rebel Without a Cause*.

The civil rights years

Racial segregation of public facilities, which had remained the norm in the South ever since Reconstruction, was in 1954 finally declared illegal by the Supreme Court ruling on *Brown v. Topeka Board of Education*. Just as a century before, however, the Southern states saw the issue more in terms of states' rights than of human rights, and attempting to implement the law, or even to challenge the failure to implement it, required immense courage. The action of Rosa Parks in refusing to give up her seat to a white man on a bus in Montgomery, Alabama, in December 1955 triggered a successful mass boycott (see p.538), and pushed the 27-year-old **Rev Dr Martin Luther King Jr** to the forefront of the civil rights campaign. Further confrontation took place at the Central High School in Little Rock, Arkansas, in 1957 (see p.551), when the reluctant Eisenhower found himself forced to call in federal troops to counter the state's unwillingness to integrate its education system.

The election of **John F. Kennedy** to the presidency in 1960, by the narrowest of margins, marked a sea-change in American politics, even if in retrospect his policies do not seem exactly radical. At 43 the youngest man ever to be elected president, and the first Catholic, he was prepared literally to reach for the moon, urging the US to victory in the Space Race in which it had thus far lagged humiliatingly behind the Soviet Union. The two decades that lay ahead, however, were to be characterized by disillusion, defeat, and despair. If the Eisenhower years had been dull, the 1960s in particular were far too interesting for almost everybody's liking.

Kennedy's sheer glamor made him a popular president during his lifetime, while his assassination suffused his administration with the romantic glow of "Camelot." His one undisputed triumph, however, came with the **Cuban missile crisis** of 1962, when the US military fortunately spotted Russian bases in Cuba before any actual missiles were ready for use, and Kennedy faced down premier Khrushchev to insist they be withdrawn. On the other hand, he'd had rather less success the previous year, in launching the abortive **Bay of Pigs** invasion of Cuba, and he also managed to embroil America deeper in the ongoing war against Communism in Vietnam, by sending more "advisers," including Green Berets, to Saigon.

Although a much-publicized call to the wife of Rev Martin Luther King Jr, during one of King's many sojourns in Southern jails, was a factor in Kennedy's election success, he was rarely keen to identify himself with the **civil rights** movement. The campaign nonetheless made headway, given added momentum by the global television coverage of such horrific confrontations as the onslaught by Birmingham police on peaceful demonstrators in 1963. The movement's defining moment came when Rev King delivered his electrifying "I Have a Dream" speech during the March on Washington later that summer. King was subsequently awarded the Nobel Peace Prize for his unwavering espousal of Gandhian principles of nonviolence. Perhaps an equally powerful factor in middle America's recognition that the time had come to address racial inequalities, however, was the not-so-implicit threat in the rhetoric of **Malcolm X**, who argued that black people had the right to defend themselves against aggression.

After Kennedy's assassination in November 1963, his successor, **Lyndon B. Johnson**, pushed through legislation that enacted most of the civil rights campaigners' key demands. Even then, violent white resistance in the South continued, and only the long, painstaking and dangerous work of registering Southern black voters en masse eventually forced Southern politicians to mend their ways.

Johnson won election by a landslide in 1964, but his vision of a **"Great Society"** soon foundered. Instead, he was brought low by the war in **Vietnam**, where US involvement escalated beyond all reason or apparent control. Broad-based popular opposition to the conflict grew in proportion to the American death toll, and the threat of the draft heightened the mood of youthful rebellion. San Francisco in particular responded to psychedelic prophet Timothy Leary's call to "turn on, tune in, drop out;" 1967's "Summer of Love" saw the lone beatniks of the 1950s transmogrify into an entire generation of hippies.

From the earliest days of the civil rights struggle, Dr King had argued that social justice could only be achieved through economic equality. That message was given a new urgency by riots in the ghettoes of Los Angeles in 1965 and Detroit in 1967, and the emergence of the Black Panthers, an armed defense force in the tradition of the now-dead Malcolm X. King also began to denounce the Vietnam War; meanwhile, after refusing the draft with the words "No Vietcong ever called me nigger," **Muhammad Ali** was stripped of his title as world heavyweight boxing champion.

In 1968, the very social fabric of the US reached the brink of collapse. Shortly after Johnson's plummeting popularity forced the president to withdraw from the year-end elections, Martin Luther King was gunned down in a Memphis motel.

Next, JFK's brother **Robert Kennedy**, now redefined as spokesman for the nation's dispossessed, was fatally shot just as he emerged as Democratic front-runner. It didn't take a conspiracy theorist to see that the spate of deaths reflected a malaise in the soul of America.

Richard Nixon to Jimmy Carter

Somehow – perhaps because the brutally suppressed riots at the Chicago Democratic Convention raised the specter of anarchy – the misery of 1968 resulted in the election of Republican **Richard Nixon** as president. Eisenhower's vice president while still in his thirties, Nixon had famously told the press after his failed bid for the governorship of California in 1962 that "you won't have Nixon to kick around any more." Now he was back, and it soon became apparent that he had scores to settle with his countless perceived enemies, above all in the media. Nixon's impeccable conservative credentials enabled him to bring the US to a rapport with China, but the war in Vietnam dragged on, to claim a total of 57,000 American lives. Attempts to win it included the secret and illegal bombing of Cambodia, which raised opposition at home to a new peak, but ultimately it was simpler to abandon the original goals in the name of "peace with honor." The end came either in 1972 – when Henry Kissinger and Le Duc Tho were awarded the Nobel Peace Prize for negotiating a treaty, and Tho at least had the grace to decline the award – or in 1975, when the Americans finally withdrew from Saigon.

During Nixon's first term, many of the disparate individuals politicized by the events and undercurrents of the 1960s coalesced into **activist groupings**. Feminists united to campaign for abortion rights and an Equal Rights Amendment; gay men in New York's *Stonewall* bar fought back after one police raid too many; Native Americans formed the American Indian Movement; and even prisoners attempted to organize themselves, resulting in such bloody debacles as the storming of Attica prison in 1971. Nixon directed various federal agencies to monitor the new radicalism, but his real bugbear was the antiwar protesters. Increasingly ludicrous covert operations against real and potential opponents culminated in a botched attempt to burgle Democratic National Headquarters in the **Watergate** complex in 1972. It took two years of investigation for Nixon's role in the subsequent cover-up to be proved, but in 1974 he **resigned**, one step ahead of impeachment by the Senate, to be succeeded by **Gerald Ford**, his own unelected appointee as vice president.

With the Republicans momentarily discredited, former Georgia governor **Jimmy Carter** was elected president as a clean-handed outsider in the bicentennial year of 1976. His victory showed how far the US had come in a decade, let alone two centuries; a crucial constituency for this new-style Southern Democrat was the recently enfranchised black population of the South. However, Carter's enthusiastic attempts to put his Baptist principles into practice on such issues as global human rights were soon perceived as naive, if not un-American. Misfortune followed misfortune. He had to break the news that the nation was facing an **energy crisis**, following the formation of the OPEC cartel of oil producers. Worse still, the Shah of Iran was overthrown, and staff at the US embassy in Tehran were taken hostage by Islamic revolutionaries. Carter's failed attempts to arrange their release were seized upon by the Republicans as a sign of his weak leadership, and all but destroyed his hopes of winning re-election in 1980. Instead he was replaced by a very different figure, the former Hollywood movie actor **Ronald Reagan**.

The Reagan–Bush years

Reagan was a new kind of president. Unlike his workaholic predecessor, Jimmy Carter, he made a virtue of his hands-off approach to the job, joking that "they say hard work never killed anybody, but I figured why take the risk?" That laissez-faire attitude was especially apparent in his domestic economic policies, under which the rich were left to get as rich as they could. The common perception that Reagan was barely aware of what went on around him allowed his popularity to remain undented by a succession of scandals, including the labyrinthine **Iran-Contra** affair, under which illegal arms sales to Iran were used to fund support for the Contra rebels in Nicaragua. When Reagan was finally confronted with proof that he had been wrong in his insistence that "I did not trade arms for hostages," he produced an extraordinary apology: "My heart and my best intentions still tell me that's true, but the facts and the evidence tell me it is not."

Reagan's most enduring achievement came during his second term, when, with his credentials as a Cold Warrior beyond question, the electorate allowed him greater leeway than a Democrat might have received to negotiate **arms-control** agreements with **Mikhail Gorbachev**, the new leader of what he had previously called the "Evil Empire." On the down side, his successors were left to cope with the explosion in the **national debt** that followed the combination of extensive **tax cuts** alongside the deregulation of the financial markets, the collapse of the savings and loan system, and above all, the enormous increases in defense spending that funded such pet projects as the Strategic Defense Initiative ("**Star Wars**").

In 1988, **George Bush** became the first vice president in 150 years to be immediately elected to the presidency. Despite his unusually broad experience in foreign policy (which included a spell as director of the CIA), Bush did little more than sit back and watch in amazement as the domino theory suddenly went into reverse. One after another, the Communist regimes of eastern Europe collapsed, until finally even the Soviet Union crumbled away. Bush was also president when **Operation Desert Storm** drove the Iraqis out of Kuwait in February 1991, an undertaking that lasted 100 hours and in which virtually no American lives were lost. At the moment of triumph in Kuwait, Bush's soaring popularity seemed certain to guarantee his re-election.

And yet the much-anticipated "**peace dividend**" – the dramatic injection of cash into the economy that voters expected to follow the end of the arms race – never materialized. As one Democrat contender for the 1992 presidential nomination, Paul Tsongas, succinctly put it, "the Cold War is over and Japan won." Between 1980 and 1990, the US had gone from being the world's largest creditor to being the world's largest debtor. The national debt had trebled from $908 billion to $2.9 trillion, and much of the borrowing came from Japan, spared from incurring military expenditures on anything like the same scale. With the 1992 campaign focusing on domestic affairs rather than what was happening overseas, twelve years of Republican government were ended by the election of Arkansas Governor **Bill Clinton**.

Clinton and the end of the century

Clinton's initial failure to deliver on specific promises – most obviously, to reform the health-care system – enabled the Republicans to capture control of Congress in 1994, prompting two years of legislative gridlock. The "Comeback Kid" nevertheless managed to assign the blame for the government's ineffectiveness to the

Republicans, and was elected to a second term. Holding on to office proved more of a challenge, when his affair with White House intern Monica Lewinsky led to the disgrace of **impeachment**, but the Senate ultimately failed to convict, sensing perhaps that the American people did not feel Clinton's indiscretions were serious enough to merit removal.

The new millennium

When Clinton left the presidency, the economy was **booming**. The budget deficit had been eradicated far ahead of even the most optimistic schedule, while the Dow Jones had risen by over 260 percent during Clinton's period in office. His former vice president, however, **Al Gore**, contrived to throw away the 2000 presidential election. Both Gore and the Republican candidate, **George W. Bush**, so adeptly followed Clinton's trademark tactic of "**triangulation**" – targeting the center of the political spectrum by adopting elements of their opponents' agenda – that the result was inevitable: a **tie**. With the final conclusion depending on a mandatory re-counting of votes in Florida, where various irregularities and mistakes complicated the issue, the impasse was ultimately decided in Bush's favor by the conservative **Supreme Court**. At the time, the charge that he had "stolen" the election was expected to seriously overshadow his presidency, while the authority of the Supreme Court was also threatened by the perception of its ruling as partisan.

During his first months in office Bush showed little sign of halting the economic slide caused when the bursting of the dot-com bubble drove hundreds of high-tech companies into bankruptcy, and appeared alarmingly indifferent to the concerns of America's friends and neighbors abroad. As well as cutting taxes and federal spending, he alienated environmentalists by rejecting US compliance with the 1997 Kyoto Agreement on global warming.

Then the atrocity of September 11, 2001 made matters infinitely worse, inflicting a devastating blow to both the nation's economy and its pride. Over three thousand people were killed in the worst terrorist attack in US history, when two hijacked planes were flown into the World Trade Center in New York City, and one into the Pentagon. The attacks were quickly linked to the al-Qaeda network of Saudi Arabian terrorist Osama bin Laden, and within weeks President Bush declared an open-ended "War on Terror."

Confronting a new, changed world, Bush set about re-writing the traditional rule-book of diplomacy and international law. In June 2002, he declared that the US has a right to launch pre-emptive attacks: "If we wait for threats to fully materialize, we will have waited too long . . . We must take the battle to the enemy, disrupt his plans, and confront the worst threats before they emerge."

A US-led invasion took control of Afghanistan in 2001, and was followed by a similar incursion into Iraq in 2003, ostensibly on the grounds that Iraqi dictator Saddam Hussein was developing "weapons of mass destruction." Although Saddam was deposed, apprehended, and in due course executed, it became universally acknowledged that no such weapons existed. Iraq both degenerated into civil war and become a major recruiting ground for international terrorism, while bin Laden himself remained unfound.

Despite a wave of financial scandals, spearheaded by the collapse of the mighty energy firm Enron, Bush defeated Massachusetts Senator John Kerry in 2004 to win a second term. That election did little to suggest the country had become any less polarized, however, and the Bush administration was lambasted for its appalling failure to respond promptly or adequately when Hurricane Katrina and consequent floods devastated New Orleans and the Gulf Coast in 2005.

▲ Soldier in Iraq

That the Democrats regained control of both Senate and House in 2006 was due largely to the deteriorating situation in Iraq. Similarly, the meteoric rise of Illinois Senator Barack Obama – and his hard-fought victory over Hilary Clinton in the 2008 Democratic primaries – owed much to his being almost unique among national politicians in his consistent opposition to the Iraq war. However, while Obama's message of change and optimism, coupled with his oratorical gifts and embrace of new technologies, especially resonated with young and minority voters, his ultimate triumph over John McCain in the presidential election later that year was triggered by the abrupt impact of a new recession. After bankers Lehmann Brothers filed for bankruptcy in September 2008 – the largest bankruptcy in US history – it was clear that no element of the economy was safe from the consequences of reckless "subprime" mortgage lending. At press time, the national exhilaration over Obama's astonishing achievement in becoming the first black US president had yet to be tested by the realities of office. In particular, the world waited to see whether he could fulfill his pledge to withdraw US troops from Iraq, and somehow restore US industrial strength while tackling the worsening environmental crisis.

Books

It would be futile to attempt to provide a comprehensive overview of American literature in the limited space available. The following bibliography is, therefore, an idiosyncratic selection of books intended as a starting point for interested readers. Books tagged with the ★ symbol are particularly recommended.

History and society

Dee Brown *Bury My Heart at Wounded Knee*. Approaching forty years on from its first publication, this remains the best narrative of the impact of white settlement and expansion on Native Americans across the continent.

Bill Bryson *Made in America*. A compulsively readable history of the American language, packed with bizarre snippets, which does much to illuminate the history of the nation.

★ **Mike Davis** *City of Quartz*. City politics, neighborhood gangs, unions, film noir, and religion are drawn together in this award-winning, leftist, hyperbolic history of Los Angeles.

John Demos *The Unredeemed Captive*. This story of the aftermath of a combined French and Indian attack on Deerfield, Massachusetts, in 1704 illuminates frontier life in the eighteenth century.

★ **W.E.B. DuBois** *The Souls of Black Folk*. Seminal collection of largely autobiographical essays examining the separation of the races in American society at the start of the twentieth century.

Joseph J. Ellis *Founding Brothers*. Enjoyable and informative essays on the "revolutionary generation" that bring the characters of Washington, Jefferson, et al to life.

Brian Fagan *Ancient North America*. Archeological history of America's native peoples, from the first hunters to cross the Bering Strait up to European contact.

Tim Flannery *The Eternal Frontier*. "Ecological" history of North America that reveals how the continent's physical environment has shaped the destinies of all its inhabitants, from horses to humans.

Shelby Foote *The Civil War: a Narrative*. Epic, three-volume account containing anything you could possibly want to know about the "War Between the States."

John Kenneth Galbraith *The Great Crash 1929*. An elegant and authoritative interpretation of the Wall Street Crash and its implications.

David Halberstam *The Best and the Brightest*. Still-relevant, gut-wrenching examination of how America's finest, most brilliant Ivy Leaguers plunged the nation into the first war it ever lost, disastrously.

Richard Hofstadter The Paranoid Style in American Politics. Though written in the 1960s, it still serves as a valuable guide to the fearful, conspiratorial mindset that governs the extremes of the political spectrum.

Tony Horwitz *Confederates in the Attic: Dispatches from the Unfinished Civil War*. Strange meld of past and present, as journalist Horwitz explores the places in the South where die-hards keep the Civil War very much alive.

Meriwether Lewis and William Clark *The Original Journals of the Lewis and Clark Expedition, 1804–1806*. Eight volumes of meticulous jottings by the Northwest's first inland explorers, scrupulously following President Jefferson's orders to record every detail of flora, fauna, and native inhabitant.

Magnus Magnusson and Herman Pálsson (trans) *The Vinland Sagas*. If you imagine stories that the Vikings reached America to be no more than myths, here's the day-to-day minutiae to convince you otherwise.

James M. McPherson *Battle Cry of Freedom*. Extremely readable history of the Civil War, which integrates and explains the complex social, economic, political, and military factors in one concise volume.

Perry Miller *Errand into the Wilderness*. Though a bit academic, this is still a core text for understanding Puritan culture, society, and politics in seventeenth-century America.

Clyde A. Milner II, Carol A. O'Connor, and Martha A. Sandweiss *The Oxford History of the American West*. Fascinating collection of essays on Western history, covering topics ranging from myths and movies to art and religion.

James Mooney *The Ghost Dance Religion and The Sioux Outbreak of 1890*. An extraordinary Bureau of Ethnology report, first published in 1890 but still available in paperback. Mooney persuaded his Washington superiors to allow him to roam the West in search of first-hand evidence, and even interviewed Wovoka, the Ghost Dance prophet, in person.

Edmund Morgan *American Slavery, American Freedom*. Complex and far-reaching historical account of the cunning means by which white working-class conflict was averted by rich Virginia planters through the spread of black slavery.

Roderick Frazier Nash *Wilderness and the American Mind*. Classic study of the American take on environmental and conservation issues over the past couple of hundred years. Especially good sections on John Muir and his battles to preserve Yosemite.

Stephen Plog *Ancient Peoples of the Southwest*. Much the best single-volume history of the pre-Hispanic Southwest, packed with diagrams and color photographs.

Marc Reisner *Cadillac Desert*. Concise, engaging account of the environmental and political impact on the West of the twentieth-century mania for dam-building and large-scale irrigation projects.

David Reynolds *Waking Giant: America in the Age of Jackson*. Rousing new portrait of America in the first half of the nineteenth century, from its clumsy attempt to take Canada in the War of 1812 to its successful Mexican land grab three decades later, with the figure of Andrew Jackson providing the touchstone throughout.

Alan Taylor *American Colonies*. Perhaps the best book on any single era of American history – a superb account of every aspect of the peopling of the continent, from remote antiquity until the Declaration of Independence.

Henry David Thoreau. Few of today's writers are more relevant than this nineteenth-century stalwart, whose Walden imagined environmentalism 100 years early, and whose Civil Disobedience provided the template for an essential tool of modern activism.

Mark Twain *Roughing It*, *Life on the Mississippi*, and many others. Mark Twain was by far the funniest and most vivid chronicler of nineteenth-century America. *Roughing It*, which covers his early wanderings across the continent, all the way to Hawaii, is absolutely compelling.

Geoffrey C. Ward, with Ric and Ken Burns *The Civil War*. Illustrated history of the Civil War, designed to accompany the TV series and using hundreds of the same photographs.

Richard White *It's Your Misfortune And None of My Own*. Dense, authoritative and all-embracing history of the American West, which debunks the notion of the rugged pioneer by stressing the role of the federal government.

Juan Williams *Eyes on the Prize*. Informative and detailed account of the Civil Rights years from the early 1950s up to 1966, with lots of rare, and some very familiar, photos.

Edmund Wilson *Patriotic Gore*. Fascinating eight-hundred-page survey of the literature of the Civil War, which serves in its own right as an immensely readable narrative of the conflict.

Bob Woodward and Carl Bernstein *All the President's Men and The Final Days*. Although Woodward continues to crank out Washington exposes, his Nixon-era books still can't be beaten for their portrait of diligent young journalists bringing down a corrupt president, and that president's own unique mania.

Biography and oral history

Muhammad Ali *The Greatest*. Powerful and entertaining autobiography of the Louisville boy who grew up to become world heavyweight boxing champion. The most memorable parts deal with his fight against the Vietnam draft and the subsequent stripping away of his world championship title.

Maya Angelou *I Know Why the Caged Bird Sings*. First of a five-volume autobiography that provides an ultimately uplifting account of how a black girl transcended her traumatic childhood in 1930s Arkansas.

Paul Auster (ed) *True Tales of American Life* (UK)/*I Thought My Father Was God* (US). Anthology of true-life stories sent to Auster for a National Public Radio project. Arranged by subject, it's best dipped into at random; among the mawkish and the mundane are just enough quirky, touching, and plain crazy tales to make it worth the while.

Donald A. Barclay, James H. Maguire, and Peter Wild (eds) *Into the Wilderness Dream*. Gripping collection of Western exploration narratives written between 1500 and 1800; thanks to any number of little-known gems, the best of many such anthologies.

Taylor Branch *America in the King Years*. Brilliant three-volume series showing the immense and long-overdue changes that enveloped America in the civil rights struggle of the 1950s and 60s through the lens of Martin Luther King Jr.

William F. Cody *The Life of Hon. William F. Cody, Known as Buffalo Bill*. Larger-than-life autobiography of one of the great characters of the Wild West. Particularly treasurable for the moment when he refers to himself more formally as "Bison William."

Frederick Douglass, et al *The Classic Slave Narratives*. Compilation of ex-slaves' autobiographies, ranging from Olaudah Equíano's kidnapping in Africa and global wanderings to Frederick Douglass's eloquent denunciation of slavery. Includes Harriet Jacobs' story of her escape from Edenton, North Carolina.

Jill Ker Conway (ed) *Written by Herself*. Splendid anthology of women's autobiographies from the mid-1800s to the present, including sections on African-Americans, scientists, artists, and pioneers.

U.S. Grant *Personal Memoirs*. Encouraged by Mark Twain, the Union general and subsequent president wrote his autobiography just before his death, in a (successful) bid to recoup his horrendous debts. At first the book feels oddly downbeat, but the man's down-to-earth modesty grows on you.

Malcolm X, with Alex Haley *The Autobiography of Malcolm X*. Searingly honest and moving account of Malcolm's progress from street hoodlum to political leadership. Written on the hoof over a period of years, it traces the development of Malcolm X's thinking before, during, and after his split from the Nation of Islam. The conclusion, when he talks about his impending assassination, is painful in the extreme.

Edmund Morris *The Rise of Theodore Roosevelt* and *Theodore Rex*. Thoroughly engaging and superbly researched two-volume biography of Theodore Roosevelt, tracing the energetic and controversial president's astonishing trajectory to the White House, and his far-reaching achievements.

Ron Powers *Mark Twain*. Definitive recent biography of America's most compelling literary figure.

Luc Sante *Low Life*. Rip-roaring look at New York vice in the nineteenth century, and how gangsters, prostitutes, machine politicians, and saloon thugs all contributed to the color and character of the city, for better or worse.

Joanna L. Stratton *Pioneer Women*. Original memoirs of women – mothers, teachers, homesteaders, and circuit riders – who ventured across the Plains from 1854 to 1890. Lively, superbly detailed accounts, with chapters on journeys, homebuilding, daily domestic life, the church, the cowtown, temperance, and suffrage.

Studs Terkel *American Dreams Lost and Found*. Interviews with ordinary American citizens. As illuminating a [illegible] to US life as you could hope for.

Frank Waters *Book of the Hopi*. Extraordinary insight into the traditions and beliefs of the Hopi, prepared through years of interviews and approved by tribal elders.

Gary Younge *Stranger In A Strange Land* and *No Place Like Home*. Black British journalist Gary Younge is one of the most acute observers of contemporary America; his experiences in the self-proclaimed New South, chronicled in *No Place Like Home*, make fascinating reading.

Entertainment and culture

Kenneth Anger *Hollywood Babylon*. A vicious yet high-spirited romp through Tinseltown's greatest scandals, amply illustrated with gory and repulsive photographs, and always inclined to bend the facts for the sake of a good story. A shoddily researched second volume covers more recent times.

Joshua Berrett (ed) *The Louis Armstrong Companion: Eight Decades of Commentary*. Broad selection of essays, interviews, letters, reviews, and autobiography, revealing the world's most influential musician in all his complexity. A fine introduction to the subject, featuring lots of previously unpublished material: standouts include Armstrong's own lament about defeatism and negativity in his fellow black men.

Bob Dylan *Chronicles: Volume One*. Far from the kind of endless stream-of-consciousness he wrote in his younger days, Dylan chose in this long-awaited autobiography to focus in almost microscopic detail on three distinct moments in his life, including Greenwich Village in the early 1960s, and New Orleans in the 1980s. The result is a compelling testament to his place at the epicenter of America's cultural life.

Charlotte Greig *Will You Still Love Me Tomorrow?* Enthusiastic feminist appraisal of (predominantly American) girl groups from the 1950s (the Chantels and the Crystals) through to 1980s rap stars like Salt'n'Pepa. Though inevitably somewhat dated, its many photos and personal recollections still make it a great read.

Peter Guralnick *Lost Highways*, *Feel Like Going Home* and *Sweet Soul Music*. Thoroughly researched personal histories of black popular music, packed with obsessive detail on all the great names. His twin Elvis biographies, *Last Train to Memphis* and *Careless Love*, trace the rise and fall of the iconic star in an unsensational but nonetheless gripping documentary manner, while also performing the rare trick of evaluating him seriously as a musician.

Gerri Hershey *Nowhere to Run: the History of Soul Music*. Definitive rundown on the evolution of soul music from the gospel heyday of the 1940s through the Memphis, Motown, and Philly scenes to the sounds of the early

1980s. Strong on social commentary and political background and studded with anecdotes and interviews.

Michael Ondaatje *Coming through Slaughter*. Extraordinary, dream-like fictionalization of the life of doomed New Orleans cornet player Buddy Bolden, written in a lyrical style that evokes the rhythms and pace of jazz improvisation.

Robert Palmer *Deep Blues*. Readable history of the development and personalities of the Delta Blues.

Geoffrey C. Ward, Ken Burns, et al *Jazz: a History of America's Music*. While the story peters out somewhat after bebop, this highly readable volume (linked to the TV series) boasts hundreds of illustrations and rare photographs, first-hand accounts and lively essays to provide a beautifully drawn picture of America's home-grown music and its icons.

Travel writing

Edward Abbey *The Journey Home*. Hilarious accounts of whitewater rafting and desert hiking trips alternate with essays by the man who inspired the radical environmentalist movement Earth First! All of Abbey's many books, especially *Desert Solitaire*, a journal of time spent as a ranger in Arches National Park, make great traveling companions.

James Agee and Walker Evans *Let Us Now Praise Famous Men*. A deeply personal but also richly evocative journal of travels through the rural lands of the Depression-era Deep South, complemented by Evans' powerful photographs.

Bill Bryson *The Lost Continent*. Using his boyhood home of Des Moines in Iowa as a benchmark, the author travels the length and breadth of America to find the perfect small town. Hilarious, if occasionally a bit smug. *A Walk in the Woods* applies his trademark irony to the Appalachian Trail from Georgia to Maine, but suffers from too much nature and too few quirky characters.

Alistair Cooke *Alistair Cooke's America*. The author's thorough, eloquent overview of American life and customs touches on the complexity of its culture and politics. Also worth a look are any of Cooke's other volumes on the American experience.

J. Hector St-John de Crèvecoeur *Letters from an American Farmer and Sketches of Eighteenth-Century America*. A remarkable account of the complexities of Revolutionary America, first published in 1782.

Charles Dickens *American Notes*. Amusing satirical commentary about the US from a jaded British perspective that's still lighter in tone than the author's later, more scabrous *Martin Chuzzlewit*.

Robert Frank *The Americans*. The Swiss photographer's brilliantly evocative portrait of mid-century American life from coast to coast, with striking images contextualized by an introductory essay from Jack Kerouac.

Ian Frazier *Great Plains*. An immaculately researched and well-written travelogue containing a wealth of information on the people of the American prairielands from Native Americans to the soldiers who staff the region's many nuclear installations.

Jack Kerouac *On the Road*. Definitive account of transcontinental Beatnik wanderings, which now reads as a curiously dated period piece. Not as incoherent as you might expect.

James A. MacMahon (ed) *Audubon Society Nature Guides*. Attractively produced, fully illustrated and easy-to-use guides to the flora and fauna of seven different US regional ecosystems, cov-

ering the entire country from coast to coast and from grasslands to glaciers.
Virginia and Lee McAlester *A Field Guide to American Houses*. Well-illustrated and engaging guide to America's rich variety of domestic architecture, from pre-colonial to postmodern.
John McPhee *Encounters with the Arch Druid*. In three interlinked narratives, the late environmental activist and Friends of the Earth founder David Brower confronts developers, miners, and dam-builders, while trying to protect three different American wilderness areas – the Atlantic shoreline, the Grand Canyon, and the Cascades of the Pacific Northwest.
William Least Heat-Moon *Blue Highways*. Account of a mammoth loop tour of the US by back roads, in which the author interviews ordinary people in ordinary places. A good overview of rural America, with lots of interesting details on Native Americans. His next book, *Prairyerth*, opted for the microcosmic approach, taking six hundred loving pages over the story of Chase County, Kansas.
Jonathan Raban *Old Glory*. A somewhat pompous though always interesting account of Raban's journey on a small craft down the Mississippi River from the head-waters in Minnesota to the bayous of Louisiana.
Bernard A. Weisberger (ed) *The WPA Guide to America*. Prepared during the New Deal as part of a make-work program for writers, these guides paint a fairly comprehensive portrait of 1930s and earlier America. Also available are state-by-state guides, most of them out of print but easily found in US libraries and secondhand bookshops.
Edmund White *States of Desire: Travels in Gay America*. A revealing account of life in gay communities across the country, focusing heavily on San Francisco and New York.

Fiction

General Americana

Raymond Carver *Will You Please Be Quiet Please?* Stories of the American working class, written in a distinctive sparse, almost deadpan style that perhaps owes something to Hemingway and certainly influenced untold numbers of contemporary American writers. The stories served as the basis for Robert Altman's film *Short Cuts*.
Don DeLillo *White Noise*; *Underworld*. The former is his best, a funny and penetrating pop culture exploration, while the latter is one of those typically flawed attempts to pack the twentieth-century American experience into a great big novel. Worthwhile, though.
John Dos Passos *USA*. Hugely ambitious novel (originally a trilogy) that grapples with the US in the early decades of the twentieth century from every possible angle. Gripping human stories with a strong political and historical point of view.
William Kennedy *Ironweed*. Terse, affecting tale of a couple of down-on-their-luck drunks haunted by ghosts from a checkered past; excellent evocation of 1930s America, specifically working-class Albany, New York.
Herman Melville *Moby-Dick*. Compendious and compelling account of nineteenth-century whaling, packed with details on American life from New England to the Pacific.
E. Annie Proulx *Accordion Crimes*. Proulx's masterly book comes as close to being the fabled "Great American Novel" as anyone could reasonably ask, tracing a fascinating history of immigrants in all parts of North America through the fortunes of a battered old Sicilian accordion.

New York City

Paul Auster *New York Trilogy*. Three Borgesian investigations into the mystery and madness of contemporary New York. Using the conventions of the detective novel, Auster unfolds a disturbed and disturbing picture of the city.

Truman Capote *Breakfast at Tiffany's* and *In Cold Blood*. The first story is about a fictional social climber in New York called Holly Golightly; the second concerns the true-life stories of two serial killers in the heartland. The subject matter of these two stories could hardly be more different, but the degree of insight drawn from two uniquely American stories is equally high in both accounts.

Michael Chabon *The Amazing Adventures of Kavalier & Clay*. Pulitzer Prize–winning novel charting the rise and fall of comic book-writing cousins in New York City – one a refugee from World War II Prague, the other a closeted Brooklynite.

Chester Himes *Cotton Comes to Harlem, Blind Man with a Pistol*, and many others. Action-packed and uproariously violent novels set in New York's Harlem, starring the much-feared detectives Coffin Ed Johnson and Grave Digger Jones.

Grace Paley *Collected Stories*. Shrewd love-hate stories written over a lifetime by the daughter of Russian-Jewish immigrants, who published dead-on accounts of New York life in three installments: her first book of stories came out in the 1950s, her second in the early 1970s and her third in the late 1980s.

J.D. Salinger *The Catcher in the Rye*. Classic novel of adolescence, tracing Holden Caulfield's sardonic journey through the streets of New York.

New England

Emily Dickinson Rightfully considered one of the pre-eminent poets of her age, though it took many decades for her innovative work, touching on dark emotional themes, to be recognized as such. The Cambridge Companion to her writing is a good place to start.

Nathaniel Hawthorne *The House of the Seven Gables*. Including his familiar Scarlet Letter, this quintessential US novelist's entire oeuvre is worth pursuing, especially this gloomy Gothic tale of Puritan misdeeds coming back to haunt the denizens of a cursed mansion.

John Irving *The Cider House Rules*. One of Irving's more successful sprawling novels, weaving themes of love, suffering, and the many facets of the abortion debate against a Maine backdrop.

H.P. Lovecraft *The Best of H.P. Lovecraft: Bloodcurdling Tales of Horror and the Macabre*. Creepy New England stories from the author Stephen King called "the twentieth century's greatest practitioner of the classic horror tale."

The South

William Faulkner *The Reivers*. The last and most humorous work of this celebrated Southern author. *The Sound and the Fury*, a fascinating study of prejudice, set like most of his books in the fictional Yoknatapawpha County in Mississippi, is a much more difficult read.

Zora Neale Hurston *Spunk*. Short stories celebrating black culture and experience from around the country, by a writer from Florida who became one of the bright stars of the Harlem cultural renaissance in the 1920s.

Harper Lee *To Kill a Mockingbird*. Classic tale of racial conflict and soci-

ety's view of an outsider, Boo Radley, as seen through the eyes of children.
Cormac McCarthy *Suttree*. McCarthy is better known for his "modern Western" works like *Blood Meridian* and *All the Pretty Horses*, but this beautifully written tale, of a Knoxville, Tennessee, scion opting for a hard-scrabble life among a band of vagrants on the Tennessee River, is his best.
Carson McCullers *The Heart is a Lonely Hunter*. McCullers is unrivaled in her sensitive treatment of misfits, in this case the attitude of a small Southern community to a deaf-mute.
Margaret Mitchell *Gone With the Wind*. Worth a read even if you know the lines of Scarlett and Rhett by heart.
Toni Morrison *Beloved*. Exquisitely written ghost story by the Nobel Prize-winning novelist, which recounts the painful lives of a group of freed slaves after Reconstruction, and the obsession a mother develops after murdering her baby daughter to spare her a life of slavery.
Flannery O'Connor *A Good Man is Hard to Find*. Short stories, featuring strong, obsessed characters, that explore religious tensions and racial conflicts in the Deep South.
Alice Walker *In Love and Trouble*. Moving and powerful stories of black women in the South, from the author of the much-acclaimed *The Color Purple*.
Eudora Welty *The Ponder Heart*. Quirky, humorous evocation of life in a backwater Mississippi town. Her most critically acclaimed work, *The Optimist's Daughter*, explores the tensions between a judge's daughter and her stepmother.

Louisiana

James Lee Burke *Black Cherry Blues*. Perhaps the best in Burke's series featuring Cajun cop Dave Robicheaux. Here Robicheaux sets out to expose alliances between government and organized crime in Louisiana and Montana.
George Washington Cable *The Grandissimes*. Romantic saga of Creole family feuds, written c.1900 but set during the Louisiana Purchase. Superb evocation of steamy Louisiana elite, the Creole lifestyle, and the resistance of New Orleans to its Americanization. Apparently shocking at the time for its sympathetic portrayal of blacks.
Kate Chopin *The Awakening*. Subversive story of a bourgeois married woman whose fight for independence ends in tragedy. The swampy Louisiana of a century ago is portrayed as both a sensual hotbed for her sexual awakening and as her eventual nemesis.
Valerie Martin *Property*. A bleak but wonderfully written tale of the brutalizing effects of slavery, on both mistress and slave, on a Louisiana sugar plantation.
Anne Rice *Feast Of All Saints*. Rice's vampire novels are great fun, but her finest portrait of nineteenth-century New Orleans comes in this sensitive examination of race, sexuality, and gender issues in the antebellum period.
John Kennedy Toole *A Confederacy of Dunces*. Anarchic black tragicomedy in which the pompous and repulsive anti-hero Ignatius J. Reilly wreaks havoc through an insalubrious and surreal New Orleans.
Robert Penn Warren *All The King's Men*. This fascinating fictionalized saga of Louisiana's legendary "Kingfish", Huey Long, is also a truly great American novel in its own right.

The Great Lakes and the Great Plains

Willa Cather *My Ántonia*. Stunning book set in Nebraska that provides a great sense of the pioneer hardships on the Plains.
Louise Erdrich *The Beet Queen*. Offbeat tale of passion and obsession among poor white North Dakota folk – particularly women – against the backdrop of an economy and culture changing with the introduction of sugar beet as a crop in the 1940s. Erdrich's other novels play through the tensions between tradition and "progress" in Native American communities.
Garrison Keillor *Lake Wobegon Days*. Wry, witty tales about a mythical Minnesota small town, poking gentle fun at the rural Midwest.
Mari Sandoz *Old Jules*. Written in 1935, this fictionalized biography gives a wonderful insight into the life of the author's pioneer Swiss father on the Nebraskan plains. Sandoz's other major work, *Crazy Horse*, contains great historical overviews but is spoiled somewhat by her insistence on narrating it through Sioux eyes.
Upton Sinclair *The Jungle*. Documenting the horrific unsanitary conditions in Chicago's meat-packing industry, Sinclair's compelling Socialist-tract-cum-novel, first serialized in 1905, ranks among the most influential books in US history.
Richard Wright *Native Son*. The harrowing story of Bigger Thomas, a black chauffeur who accidentally kills his employer's daughter. The story develops his relationship with his lawyer, the closest he has ever come to being on an equal footing with a white.

The Rockies and the Southwest

A.B. Guthrie Jr *Big Sky*. When first published in the Thirties it shattered the image of the mythical West peddled by Hollywood. Realistic historical fiction at its very best, following desperate mountain man and fugitive Boone Caudill, whose idyllic life in Montana was ended by the arrival of white settlers.
Tony Hillerman *The Dark Wind*, and many others. The adventures of Jim Chee of the Navajo Tribal Police on the reservations of northern Arizona, forever dabbling in dark and mysterious forces churned up from the Ancestral Puebloan past.
Barbara Kingsolver *Pigs in Heaven*. A magnificent evocation of tensions and realities in the contemporary Southwest, by a Tucson-based writer who ranks among America's finest prose stylists.
Norman MacLean *A River Runs Through It*. Unputdownable – the best ever novel about fly-fishing, set in beautiful Montana lake country.

California and the West

Raymond Chandler *The Big Sleep* and *Farewell My Lovely*. The original incarnations of archetypal tough guy and iconic private eye Philip Marlowe are far more complex and beautifully written than the related movies would lead you to expect. Pulp fiction at its finest – written by an American raised in London.
David Guterson *Snow Falling on Cedars* and *East Of the Mountains*. Two gripping novels that capture the flavor of the Pacific Northwest; the first is an atmospheric mystery centering on postwar interracial tensions, the second features a dying man looking back on his life.
Jack London *The Call of the Wild and Other Stories*. London's classic tale, of a

family pet discovering the ways of the wilderness while forced to pull sleds across Alaska's Gold Rush trails, still makes essential reading before a trip to the far north.

Armistead Maupin *Tales of the City*. Long-running saga comprising sympathetic and entertaining tales of life in San Francisco, that also work surprisingly well as suspenseful stand-alone novels. That many of its key characters are gay meant that over the years the series became a chronicle of the impact of AIDS on the city. Maupin's *Maybe the Moon* is the poignant true-life story of his friend, the short person who played ET in the movie but was never allowed to reveal her true identity.

Thomas Pynchon *The Crying of Lot 49*. Shorter, funnier, and more accessible than *Gravity's Rainbow*, this novel of techno-freaks and potheads in Sixties California reveals, among other things, the sexy side of stamp collecting.

John Steinbeck *The Grapes of Wrath*. The classic account of a migrant family forsaking the Midwest for the Promised Land. Steinbeck's lighthearted but crisply observed novella *Cannery Row* captures daily life on the prewar Monterey waterfront. The epic *East of Eden* updates and resets the Bible in the Salinas Valley and details three generations of familial feuding.

Nathanael West *The Day of the Locust*. West wrote dark novels wholly vested in the American experience; this one, set in LA, is an apocalyptic story of fringe characters at the edge of the film industry.

Film

The list below focuses on key films in certain genres that have helped define the American experience – both the light and the dark. Films tagged with the ★ symbol are particularly recommended.

Music/musicals

Calamity Jane (David Butler, 1953). The Western gets a rumbustuous musical twist with tomboy Doris Day giving thigh-slapping gusto to the title role and Howard Keel as the rugged hero who (almost) tames her.

Gimme Shelter (Albert and David Maysles, 1969). Excellent documentary about the ill-fated Rolling Stones concert at Altamont. Its searing look at homegrown American violence and Vietnam-era chaos at the end of the 1960s also includes an on-camera stabbing.

Gold Diggers of 1933 (Mervyn LeRoy/Busby Berkeley, 1933). In which genius choreographer Berkeley pioneered his trademark overhead-crane shots of flamboyantly trompe l'oeil dance numbers featuring lines of glamorous chorines. See also 42nd Street and Footlight Parade.

Meet Me in St Louis (Vincente Minnelli, 1944). Most famous for its Judy Garland number "*The Trolley Song*," this charming piece of nostalgia celebrates turn-of-the-century America through the ups and downs of a St Louis family during the 1903 World's Fair.

On the Town (Stanley Donen/Gene Kelly, 1949). An exuberant musical tour of New York City, led by director Kelly and Frank Sinatra, who play sailors on shore leave.

★ **Singin' in the Rain** (Stanley Donen/Gene Kelly, 1952). Beloved musical comedy about Hollywood at the dawn of the sound era, featuring memorable tunes like "*Make 'Em Laugh*" and the title song, along with energetic performances by star Kelly, sidekick Donald O'Connor, and a pixie-ish Debbie Reynolds.

Woodstock (Michael Wadleigh, 1969). Gimme Shelter's upbeat counterpart, documenting the musical pinnacle of the hippie era, showing a half-million flower children peacefully grooving to Jimi Hendrix, The Who, and Sly and the Family Stone while getting stoned, muddy, and wild on an upstate New York farm.

Silent era

Birth of a Nation (D.W. Griffith, 1915). Possibly the most influential film in American history, both for its pioneering film technique (close-ups, cross-cutting, and so on) and appalling racist propaganda, which led to a revival of the KKK.

★ **The General** (Buster Keaton, 1926). A fine introduction to Keaton's acrobatic brand of slapstick and his inventive cinematic approach, in which the Great Stone Face chases down a stolen locomotive during the Civil War.

The Gold Rush (Charlie Chaplin, 1925). Chaplin's finest film: the Little Tramp gets trapped in a cabin during an Alaska blizzard in an affecting story that mixes sentiment and high comedy in near-perfect balance.

Greed (Erich von Stroheim, 1923). An audacious scene-by-scene adaptation of Frank Norris's novel *McTeague*, a tragic tale of love and revenge in San Francisco at the end of the nineteenth century. Slashed from ten to two-and-a-half hours by MGM, the film remains a cinematic triumph for its striking compositions, epic drama, and truly bleak ending.

Sunrise (F.W. Murnau, 1927). Among the most beautiful Hollywood productions of any era. Sunrise's German émigré director employed striking lighting effects, complex traveling shots, and emotionally compelling performances in a tale of a country boy led astray by a big-city femme fatale.

Westerns

McCabe and Mrs. Miller (Robert Altman, 1971). Entrepreneur Warren Beatty brings prostitution to a Washington town and tries to reinvent himself as a gunslinger in this now-classic anti-Western.

Once upon a Time in the West (Sergio Leone, 1968). The quintessential spaghetti Western, actually filmed in Spain by an Italian director, steeped in mythic American themes of manifest destiny and rugged individualism.

Red River (Howard Hawks, 1948). Upstart Montgomery Clift battles beef-baron John Wayne on a momentous cattle drive through the Midwest. Prototypical Hawks tale of clashing tough-guy egos and no-nonsense professionals on the range.

The Searchers (John Ford, 1956). Perhaps the most iconic of Ford's many Westerns; a highly influential production with vivid cinematography and epic scale, in which John Wayne relentlessly hunts down the Indian chief who massacred his friends and family.

The Wild Bunch (Sam Peckinpah, 1969). A movie that says as much about the chaotic end of the 1960s as it does about the West, featuring a band of killers who hunt for women and treasure and wind up in a bloodbath unprecedented in film history.

Americana

Breakfast at Tiffany's (Blake Edwards, 1961). Manhattan never looked more chic, and Audrey Hepburn, dressed in Givenchy, gives a quintessentially stylish performance as vulnerable kept woman Holly Golightly. The theme tune, too, "*Moon River*", penned by Henry Mancini, shines. Based on a novella by Truman Capote (who originally wanted Marilyn Monroe to play Golightly).

Citizen Kane (Orson Welles, 1941). Arguably the greatest American movie ever, inverting the rags-to-riches saga: a poor country boy finds nothing but misery when he inherits a fortune.

The Color Purple (Steven Spielberg, 1985). Based on Alice Walker's Pulitzer prize-winning epistolary novel about an African-American woman's triumph over devastating adversity in the segregated South, the movie is translated by Spielberg into a huge, visually rich experience, boasting splendid performances and a delicious dose of shameless heart-tugging.

E.T. The Extra-Terrestrial (Steven Spielberg, 1982). Reagan-era blockbuster and sentimental variation on 1950s monster flicks, courtesy of the director's ongoing interest in absentee fathers, suburban fantasies, and otherworldly saviors. A fine example of American cinema's never-ending search for lost innocence.

Gone With the Wind (Victor Fleming, 1939). Possibly the most popular movie of all time, this lush, affecting and elegiac look at the Old South provides three hours of expertly wrought historical melodrama. Vivien Leigh dazzles as rebellious Southern belle Scarlett O'Hara, while Hattie McDaniel, as her mammy, won the first Oscar ever to be awarded to an African-American.

Mr. Smith Goes to Washington (Frank Capra, 1939). Tub-thumping populist film that still resonates for its rosy belief in the goodness of the common man, dark view of political elites, and earnest hope for America's future. Though less familiar, the director's Meet John Doe offers a grimmer variation on the tale, while the enduring tearjerker It's A Wonderful Life provides a Christmas take on the same themes.

Nashville (Robert Altman, 1975). A long, woolly epic, typical of Altman's style, about 24 characters adrift in the nation's capital of country music, who come together at a political rally and witness an unexpected assassination.

North by Northwest (Alfred Hitchcock, 1959). Not only an exciting chase film, in which international criminal James Mason hunts down ad-man Cary Grant, but also a fun travelogue that starts on New York's Madison Avenue and ends on the cliff-face of Mount Rushmore in South Dakota.

Rebel Without a Cause (Nicholas Ray, 1955). The apotheosis of adolescent angst, with James Dean lamenting the hypocrisies of family life and engaging in all manner of fisticuffs, deadly drag races, and night-time battles with the cops.

There Will Be Blood (Paul Thomas Anderson, 2007). This unsettling, epic, saga of America's turn-of-the-century oil boom differs from Upton Sinclair's novel, *Oil* in unexpected ways to become dominated by its lead, Daniel Day Lewis. His magisterial performance as the unknowable, monstrous prospector Daniel Plainview raises many disturbing questions about the American Dream.

The Wizard of Oz (Victor Fleming, 1939). A cinematic institution and Technicolor extravaganza that shows Hollywood at its zenith, romanticizing small-town life in the Midwest and offering up eye-popping fantasies of good and evil witches, dancing dwarves, flying monkeys, and Judy Garland sporting ruby shoes on a yellow-brick road.

Road movies

Badlands (Terrence Malick, 1973). Midwest loner-loser Martin Sheen and girlfriend Sissy Spacek take a spellbinding tour of the heartland while on a random murder spree. A dark view of life on the road as a synonym for existential futility.

Easy Rider (Dennis Hopper, 1969). Peter Fonda and director Hopper head out in search of America while riding on a groovy set of wheels, pick up nerdy Jack Nicholson on the way, get high in a New Orleans cemetery, and get killed by gun-toting rednecks. A road movie as a metaphor for political and cultural conflict.

Thelma and Louise (Ridley Scott, 1991). The road movie as feminist manifesto, in which two friends (Susan Sarandon and Geena Davis) wind up on the run after one of them kills a would-be rapist. At last it's the girls who get to tote the guns and swig the whiskey – and director Scott provides plenty of striking images of the American Southwest.

Film noir and gangster films

Bonnie and Clyde (Arthur Penn, 1967). Warren Beatty and Faye Dunaway play Depression-era gangsters in a film that did much to destroy Hollywood's censorship code by ushering in an era of open sexuality and unmitigated blood and violence.

Chinatown (Roman Polanski, 1974). Film noir seventies-style, with Jack Nicholson as Jake Gittes, a morally aloof private eye whose dogged investigations reveal municipal corruption, racism, and incest in LA.

Double Indemnity (Billy Wilder, 1944). In many ways the quintessential film noir: insurance salesman Fred MacMurray is corrupted by femme fatale Barbara Stanwyck, with stylishly dark photography and memorably fatalistic ending.

On location

Although many memorable sights are off limits to the public or exist only on the backlot tours of movie-studio theme parks, there are still countless film-making locations that widely advertise their Tinseltown appearances or make quiet efforts to accommodate visitors. This list provides an overview of notable films; you could conceivably make an entire vacation out of traveling from spot to spot.

2001: A Space Odyssey (Stanley Kubrick, 1968). Monument Valley, Arizona, p.905.

Back to the Future (Robert Zemeckis, 1985). Gamble House, Pasadena, p.983.

Badlands (Terrence Malick, 1973). Badlands National Park, South Dakota, p.753.

Being There (Hal Ashby, 1979). Biltmore Estate, Asheville, North Carolina, p.469.

The Birds (Alfred Hitchcock, 1963). Bodega Bay, California, p.1068.

Blade Runner (Ridley Scott, 1982). Los Angeles: Union Station, p.961, Bradbury Building, p.969.

The Bridges of Madison County (Clint Eastwood, 1995). Winterset, Iowa, p.742.

Citizen Kane (Orson Welles, 1941). Hearst Castle, California, p.1016 – inspiration for film's "Xanadu."

Close Encounters of the Third Kind (Steven Spielberg, 1978). Devils Tower, Wyoming, p.809.

Easy Rider (Dennis Hopper, 1969). New Orleans cemeteries p.636; Sunset Crater, Arizona, p.892.

Five Easy Pieces (Bob Rafelson, 1970). San Juan Islands, Washington, p.1095.

Galaxy Quest (Dean Parisot, 1999). Goblin Valley, Utah, p.918.

Grapes of Wrath (John Ford, 1940). Petrified Forest, Arizona, p.890.

Greed (Erich von Stroheim, 1923). Death Valley, California, p.998.

High Plains Drifter (Clint Eastwood, 1972). Mono Lake, California, p.1001.

Intolerance (D.W. Griffith, 1916). "Babylon" set, Hollywood, California, p.971.

Jaws (Steven Spielberg, 1975). Martha's Vineyard, Massachusetts, p.212.

Little Big Man (Arthur Penn, 1970). Custer State Park, South Dakota, p.759.

Manhattan (Woody Allen, 1978). Central Park, p.91; Brooklyn Bridge, p.82.

Midnight in the Garden of Good and Evil (Clint Eastwood, 1998). Savannah, Georgia, p.492.

Mr. Smith Goes to Washington (Frank Capra, 1939). Lincoln Memorial, p.378.

Mystery Train (Jim Jarmusch, 1989). *Arcade*, Memphis, Tennessee, p.519.

Nashville (Robert Altman, 1975). Parthenon, p.525; Grand Ole Opry, p.523.

North by Northwest (Alfred Hitchcock, 1959). United Nations, New York City, p.89; Mount Rushmore, South Dakota, p.757.

Gangs of New York (Martin Scorsese, 2002). Scorsese's stunning evocation of the gang-ridden world of New York, just before the Civil War, features an unforgettable performance by Daniel Day-Lewis as "The Butcher."

The Godfather (Francis Ford Coppola, 1972). The film that revived the gangster genre for modern times, avoiding the cartoonish mobsters and no-nonsense G-men of its predecessors and focusing instead on the family hierarchy of organized crime and its deep connections to all levels of American society. The Godfather II is if anything, an even better movie, tracing both the genesis of the Corleone family and moving towards its inevitable decline.

Klute (Alan J Pakula, 1971). A feminist film noir, which marked the transformation of Jane Fonda from sex kitten into radical firebrand. She offers a nuanced portrayal of a fiercely

On the Town (Stanley Donen/Gene Kelly, 1949). American Museum of Natural History, New York City, p.97.

Paper Moon (Peter Bogdanovich, 1973). St Joseph, Missouri, p.306.

The Parallax View (Alan J. Pakula, 1974). Space Needle, Seattle, p.1085.

Planet of the Apes (Franklin J. Schaffner, 1968). Page, Arizona: p.900, Lake Powell, Utah, p.926.

Poseidon Adventure (Ronald Neame, 1972). *Queen Mary*, Long Beach, California, p.981.

Rebel Without a Cause (Nicholas Ray, 1955). Griffith Observatory, Los Angeles, California p.974.

Return of the Jedi (Richard Marquand, 1983). Redwood National Park, California, p.1069.

Rocky (John G. Avildsen, 1976). Philadelphia Museum of Art, Pennsylvania, p.150.

The Searchers (John Ford, 1956). Monument Valley, Arizona, p.905.

Shane (George Stevens, 1953). Wyoming: Grand Teton National Park, p.819, Jackson Hole, p.819.

The Shining (Stanley Kubrick, 1980). *Timberline Lodge*, Oregon, p.1118.

Singin' in the Rain (Stanley Donen/Gene Kelly, 1952). Chinese Theatre, Hollywood, p.971.

Some Like It Hot (Billy Wilder, 1959). *Hotel del Coronado*, San Diego, p.954.

The Sting (George Roy Hill, 1973). Santa Monica pier, California, p.979.

A Streetcar Named Desire (Elia Kazan, 1951). New Orleans, Louisiana, p.627.

Sunset Boulevard (Billy Wilder, 1950). Hollywood: Paramount Studios, p.974, Sunset Boulevard, p.974.

Thelma and Louise (Ridley Scott, 1991). Arches National Park, Utah, p.921.

The Thing (Christian Nyby/Howard Hawks, 1951). Glacier National Park, Montana, p.836.

Touch of Evil (Orson Welles, 1958). Venice, California, p.978.

Twin Peaks (David Lynch/ABC-TV, 1990–1991). Snoqualmie Falls/*Salish Lodge*, Washington, p.1103.

Vertigo (Alfred Hitchcock, 1958). San Francisco: Golden Gate Bridge, p.1039, *Fairmont Hotel*, Nob Hill, p.1028.

Witness (Peter Weir, 1985). Lancaster County, Pennsylvania, p.153.

Zabriskie Point (Michelangelo Antonioni, 1969). Death Valley, California, p.998.

independent New York hooker who refuses to be rescued by Donald Sutherland's PI.

Maltese Falcon (John Huston, 1941). A forerunner of a spate of noirs made later in the 1940s, in which Bogart plays his trademark role of Philip Marlowe, the cool and calculating detective who runs up against sexy schemer Mary Astor, low-life Peter Lorre, and evil flesh-pile Sydney Greenstreet.

Mildred Pierce (Michael Curtiz, 1945). Half film noir, half mother-daughter melodrama, with a barnstorming performance from arch diva Joan Crawford in the title role. Both femme fatale and long-suffering heroine, she's as ambiguous as any character you'll find in the noir canon.

Independent and cult movies

Blue Velvet (David Lynch, 1986). A young man (Kyle Maclachlan) peers under the cheery facade of apple-pie America and finds a sinister netherworld of tortured lounge singers, vicious sex games, and nitrous-inhaling perverts.

Bowling for Columbine (Michael Moore, 2002). Maverick director Moore bagged an Oscar for this eye-opening documentary into US gun culture.

Fargo (Joel Coen, 1996). Set amid the snowy landscapes of northern Minnesota and North Dakota, a quirky tale of a scheming car salesman whose plan to kidnap his own wife and keep the ransom money goes terribly wrong. See also Raising Arizona, O Brother, Where Art Thou and No Country for Old Men for more strange and twisted Coen brother visions.

Mystery Train (Jim Jarmusch, 1989). Shock-haired indie darling Jarmusch offers a deeply atmospheric and typically skewed portrayal of the crumbling music city of Memphis, with four stories revolving around different guests in a Gothic motel. Includes cameos from musical icons Rufus Thomas, Screamin Jay Hawkins, and Tom Waits.

Pulp Fiction (Quentin Tarantino, 1994). A touchstone for American independent cinema, composed of three interlocking vignettes and directed with stylish verve and audacity.

Slacker (Richard Linklater, 1990). Emblematic of Generation X ennui in the 1990s, this indie great also manages to highlight 96 characters with episodic monologues over the course of 24 hours in Austin, Texas. Memorable alone for its collection of paranoid conspiracy rants.

Taxi Driver (Martin Scorsese, 1976). Robert De Niro does a memorable turn as Travis Bickle, a psychotic loner and would-be assassin whose infatuation with a teen prostitute (Jodie Foster) inspired a real-life assassination attempt on Ronald Reagan five years later.

Small print and Index

A Rough Guide to Rough Guides

Published in 1982, the first Rough Guide – to Greece – was a student scheme that became a publishing phenomenon. Mark Ellingham, a recent graduate in English from Bristol University, had been traveling in Greece the previous summer and couldn't find the right guidebook. With a small group of friends he wrote his own guide, combining a highly contemporary, journalistic style with a thoroughly practical approach to travelers' needs.

The immediate success of the book spawned a series that rapidly covered dozens of destinations. And, in addition to impecunious backpackers, Rough Guides soon acquired a much broader and older readership that relished the guides' wit and inquisitiveness as much as their enthusiastic, critical approach and value-for-money ethos.

These days, Rough Guides include recommendations from shoestring to luxury and cover more than 200 destinations around the globe, including almost every country in the Americas and Europe, more than half of Africa and most of Asia and Australasia. Our ever-growing team of authors and photographers is spread all over the world, particularly in Europe, the USA and Australia.

In the early 1990s, Rough Guides branched out of travel, with the publication of Rough Guides to World Music, Classical Music and the Internet. All three have become benchmark titles in their fields, spearheading the publication of a wide range of books under the Rough Guide name.

Including the travel series, Rough Guides now number more than 350 titles, covering: phrasebooks, waterproof maps, music guides from Opera to Heavy Metal, reference works as diverse as Conspiracy Theories and Shakespeare, and popular culture books from iPods to Poker. Rough Guides also produce a series of more than 120 World Music CDs in partnership with World Music Network.

Visit www.roughguides.com to see our latest publications.

Rough Guide travel images are available for commercial licensing at www.roughguidespictures.com

Rough Guide credits

Text editor: Steven Horak
Layout: Dan May
Cartography: Jasbir Sandhu
Picture editor: Michelle Bhatia
Production: Rebecca Short
Proofreader: Anita Sach & Stewart Wild
Cover design: Chloë Roberts
Photographer: Susannah Sayler, Paul Whitfield, Greg Ward, Dan Bannister
Editorial: Ruth Blackmore, Andy Turner, Keith Drew, Edward Aves, Alice Park, Lucy White, Jo Kirby, James Smart, Natasha Foges, Róisín Cameron, Emma Traynor, Emma Gibbs, Kathryn Lane, Christina Valhouli, Monica Woods, Mani Ramaswamy, Harry Wilson, Lucy Cowie, Helen Ochyra, Alison Roberts, Joe Staines, Peter Buckley, Matthew Milton, Tracy Hopkins, Ruth Tidball; **Delhi** Madhavi Singh, Karen D'Souza, Lubna Shaheen
Design & Pictures: **London** Scott Stickland, Dan May, Diana Jarvis, Mark Thomas, Chloë Roberts, Nicole Newman, Sarah Cummins, Emily Taylor; **Delhi** Umesh Aggarwal, Ajay Verma, Jessica Subramanian, Ankur Guha, Pradeep Thapliyal, Sachin Tanwar, Anita Singh, Nikhil Agarwal
Production: Rebecca Short, Vicky Baldwin
Cartography: **London** Maxine Repath, Ed Wright, Katie Lloyd-Jones; **Delhi** Rajesh Chhibber, Ashutosh Bharti, Rajesh Mishra, Animesh Pathak, Jasbir Sandhu, Karobi Gogoi, Amod Singh, Alakananda Bhattacharya, Swati Handoo, Deshpal Dabas
Online: **London** George Atwell, Faye Hellon, Jeanette Angell, Fergus Day, Justine Bright, Clare Bryson, Aine Fearon, Adrian Low, Ezgi Celebi, Amber Bloomfield; **Delhi** Amit Verma, Rahul Kumar, Narender Kumar, Ravi Yadav, Debojit Borah, Saurabh Sati, Rakesh Kumar, Ganesh Sharma
Marketing & Publicity: **London** Liz Statham, Niki Hanmer, Louise Maher, Jess Carter, Vanessa Godden, Vivienne Watton, Anna Paynton, Rachel Sprackett, Libby Jellie, Laura Vipond, Vanessa McDonald; **New York** Katy Ball, Judi Powers, Nancy Lambert; **Delhi** Ragini Govind
Manager India: Punita Singh
Reference Director: Andrew Lockett
Operations Manager: Helen Phillips
PA to Publishing Director: Nicola Henderson
Publishing Director: Martin Dunford
Commercial Manager: Gino Magnotta
Managing Director: John Duhigg

Publishing information

This 9th edition published May 2009 by
Rough Guides Ltd,
80 Strand, London WC2R 0RL
14 Local Shopping Centre, Panchsheel Park, New Delhi 110017, India
Distributed by the Penguin Group
Penguin Books Ltd,
80 Strand, London WC2R 0RL
Penguin Group (USA)
375 Hudson Street, NY 10014, USA
Penguin Group (Australia)
250 Camberwell Road, Camberwell, Victoria 3124, Australia
Penguin Group (Canada)
195 Harry Walker Parkway N, Newmarket, ON, L3Y 7B3 Canada
Penguin Group (NZ)
67 Apollo Drive, Mairangi Bay, Auckland 1310, New Zealand
Cover concept by Peter Dyer.

Typeset in Bembo and Helvetica to an original design by Henry Iles.

Printed in Italy by L.E.G.O. S.p.A, Lavis (TN)

1256pp includes index

A catalogue record for this book is available from the British Library

ISBN: 978-1-84836-035-8

The publishers and authors have done their best to ensure the accuracy and currency of all the information in **The Rough Guide to the USA**, however, they can accept no responsibility for any loss, injury, or inconvenience sustained by any traveller as a result of information or advice contained in the guide.

1 3 5 7 9 8 6 4 2

Help us update

We've gone to a lot of effort to ensure that the 9th edition of **The Rough Guide to the USA** is accurate and up to date. However, things change – places get "discovered", opening hours are notoriously fickle, restaurants and rooms raise prices or lower standards. If you feel we've got it wrong or left something out, we'd like to know, and if you can remember the address, the price, the hours, the phone number, so much the better.

Please send your comments with the subject line "**Rough Guide USA Update**" to Ⓔ mail@roughguides.com. We'll credit all contributions and send a copy of the next edition (or any other Rough Guide if you prefer) for the very best emails.

Have your questions answered and tell others about your trip at Ⓦ community.roughguides.com

Acknowledgments

Sam thanks Sal Impastato and all at the Napoleon House; co-authors Jeff and Nick; Paula Neudorf; Steven Horak, for astute editing in a tight spot and an impressively light touch; and fellow traveller Greg, without whom this book, and so many other wonderful things, would never have happened.

Greg: Thanks one last time to everyone at Rough Guides' New York office for their work on the book over the years, and to Steven Horak for steering it so adroitly into port. Thanks to Sam yet again, for everything, and to Nick and Jeff too. On the road, thanks especially to Steve Lewis in Santa Fe, Stephanie Heckathorne and Scott Dunn in Phoenix, and Marian Delay and Callie Tranter in Moab.

JD would like to thank his fellow authors Sam, Greg and Nick, along with editors Steven Horak, Andrew Rosenberg, AnneLise Sorensen, and Paula Neudorf, for all their respective and considerable labors on this book. Also worth a cheer are friends and associates Lisa Scarpelli, Zora O'Neill, and Peter Moskos, as well as corporate contacts/helpers Sara Crocker, Allison Goldstein, Marcia Murphy, Dennis Holifena, Kimberli Partlow, David Cohen, Lauren Zelisko, David Rodriguez, Emmie Lancaster, Doug Camp, Thomas Blaszczyk, and Jane Vorwig, not to mention the helpful hints provided by the Convention and Visitors Bureau staff for numerous cities and regions, but especially Baltimore, Washington, D.C., Los Angeles, San Diego, and Seattle. Finally, thanks to everyone on the RG staff who have worked so assiduously.

Nick would like to thank the various state tourist authority personnel, especially: Ellen Cornfield & Jeanette Pierce in Philadelphia, PA; in NY, Ed Healy & Doug Sitler in Buffalo, Greg Marshall in Rochester, Margaret Marchuk in Lake Placid and Lisa Berger in the Catskills; in Ohio, Tammy Brown & Aimee Zerla in Columbus, Ed McMasters in Cincinnati and Samantha Fryberger in Cleveland; Marge Bateman in Kentucky; and in northern California, Karen Whitaker & Bob Warren of Shasta Cascades, Joanne Steele of Siskiyou Co, Richard Stenger of Humboldt Co, Emily Polsby of Mendocino Co and Kelly Chamberlin of Half Moon Bay. Special thanks for hospitality to Dawa in Brooklyn, Pam, Brendan, Janine, Dan, Drew & Mark in Pittsburgh and the Bonita posse in Berkeley. Gratitude to the American people for finally voting in a President with a brain! Great job, Steve Horak, for riding in like the cavalry for the edit. Finally, heartfelt thanks to Maria for continuing love and support.

The editor would like to thank Sam, Greg, Nick and Jeff, and all the contributors for their enthusiasm and hard work and for making my part so enjoyable. Additional thanks to Dan May, Jasbir Sandhu, Michelle Bhatia, Katie Lloyd-Jones, Alison Roberts, Anita Sach, Mani Ramaswamy, Keith Drew, Stewart Wild, AnneLise Sorensen for pitching in and Paula Neudorf for getting it all started.

Readers' letters

Thanks to all the readers who have taken the time to write in with comments and suggestions (and apologies if we've inadvertently omitted or misspelt anyone's name):

D.T.L. Bairdow, John and Patty Brissenden, P. Cameron, Hank Drayton, Charles Elder, Jean A. Ellen, Blair Granicher, Sarah Hines, Vaughan L. King, Jakub M. Konysz, Jesse Le Blanc, Evan Levy, Linda Liang, Peter Ludlow, Jodi Mullen, Jennifer Nash, Fernando Olea, Ian Schrager, John Waugh.

Photo credits

All photos © Rough Guides except the following:

Title page
Sign of fast food restaurant on Route 66, AZ © Theo Allofs/Corbis

Full page
Glacier lilies and Mount Clements. Glacier Natural Park, MT © John G. Wilbanks/ SuperStock

Introduction
Balcony in the French Quarter, New Orleans, LA © Owaki/Kulla/Corbis
Jazz musicians, New Orleans, LA © PCL /Alamy
Ready for surfing, CA © EGDigital/istock
Plimoth Plantation, MA © Catherine Karnow/Corbis

Things not to miss
01 Monument Valley, AZ © Demetrio Carrasco/DK
02 Pre-game at Yankee Stadium, NY © Richard Levine/ Alamy
03 Pike Place Market, Seattle, WA © Scott Pitts/DK
04 Antebellum home in Savannah, GA © Mike Briner /Alamy
05 Mardi Gras, New Orleans, LA © Mira/Alamy
06 Morning Glory Pool, Yellowstone National Park, WY © iStock
07 Rock and Roll Hall of Fame, Cleveland, OH © Jeff Greenberg/Alamy
09 Aurora Borealis over Fairbanks, AK © Roman Krochuk/iStock
10 Chicago at night, IL © David Elfstrom/iStock
12 Maid of the Mist, Niagara Falls, NY © Francesca Yorke/DK
13 Crazy Horse Memorial, SD © Danita Delimont/Alamy
14 Burning Man Festival, NV © LHB Photo/Alamy
15 The Everglades, FL © Dave King/DK
16 Statue at the MLK Center for Non-Violence in Atlanta, GA © EditorialFotos/Alamy
17 Elvis' gravesite, Graceland, TN © Danita Delimont/ Alamy
18 Skiers on Telluride's Gold Hill, CO © Doug Berry/ iStock
22 Art Deco facade, Miami, FL © Max Alexander/DK
24 Glacier National Park, MT © Joe McDonald/Corbis
25 Gogol Bordello at South by Southwest, Austin, TX © Erich Schlegel/Corbis
26 Kilauea Volcano, HI © SuperStock
27 Highway 1, CA © Look/Die Bildagentur der Fotografen GmbH/Alamy
28 Small pond in the Katahdin Region, ME © Mira/Alamy
31 Bull riding at a rodeo, AZ © Jerry Cooke/Corbis

Black and whites
p.118 Taughannock Falls State Park, NY © Panache Photos/Alamy
p.124 Beach house, East Hampton, NY © Pete Turner/ Getty
p.131 Black Brook, Adirondacks, NY © Phil Degginger/ Alamy
p.141 Niagara Falls, NY © Francesca Yorke/DK
p.154 Amish bakery in Lancaster County, PA © Jeff

Greenberg/Alamy
p.162 The Golden Triangle, Pittsburgh, PA © Alan Schein/Corbis
p.168 Allegheny National Forest, PA © Buddy Mays/Alamy
p.226 The Breakers, RI © Philip C. Jackson/DK
p.239 Centre Harbour on Lake Winnipesaukee, NH © Dan Bannister/DK
p.248 Vermont State House, Montpelier, VT © David Lyons/DK
p.260 The Maine Maritime Museum, Bath, ME © Dan Bannister/DK
p.276 Boundary Waters Canoe Area Wilderness, MN © Raymond Gehman/Corbis
p.284 Rock and Roll Hall of Fame, Cleveland, OH © Jeff Greenberg/Alamy
p.302 The Henry Ford Museum, Dearborn, MI © David R. Frazier Photolibrary, Inc./Alamy
p.311 Pictured Rocks National Lakeshore, MI © Conrad Zobel/Corbis
p.315 The Indianapolis 500, IN © Russell LaBounty/ASP Inc/Icon/Corbis
p.326 The Chicago skyline, IL © DK
p.363 Locator Lake, Voyageurs National Park, MN © Tom Bean/Corbis
p.414 Monticello, Charlottesville, VA © Kevin Shields/Alamy
p.425 River Gorge Bridge, WV © Andre Jenny/Alamy
p.448 Sitting room of Graceland, TN © Patrick Frilet/Hemis/Corbis
p.456 Wright Brothers National Monument, NC © Zach Holmes/Alamy
p.467 Blue Ridge Parkway, NC © Mike Briner/Alamy
p.477 Historic buildings, Charleston, SC © S. Greg Panosian/iStock
p.495 Lafayette Square, Savannah, GA © Richard Cummins/Superstock
p.515 Sun Studios, Memphis, TN © Danita Delimont/Alamy
p.524 Ernest Tubb Record Shop, Nashville, TN © Jon Arnold Images Ltd/Alamy
p.537 Civil Rights Memorial, Montgomery, AL © Peter Wilson/DK
p.541 Fisherman on the Mississippi River © Annie Griffiths Belt/Corbis
p.558 Key West, FL © Peter Wilson/DK
p.581 Duval Street, Key West, FL © Peter Wilson/DK
p.592 Oldest Wooden Schoolhouse, St Augustine, FL © Linda Whitwam/DK
p.616 Everglades National Park, FL © Peter Wilson DK
p.655 Cathedral of St John the Evangelist, LA © Peter Wilson/DK
p.664 Big Bend National Park, TX © Peter Wilson/DK
p.673 Space Center Houston, TX © Witold Skrypczak/SuperStock
p.682 Mission San José, TX © Peter Wilson/DK
p.694 Reunion Tower, Dallas, TX © Richard Cummins/SuperStock
p.703 Big Texan Steak House, Amarillo, TX © Witold Skrypczak/SuperStock
p.707 Canoers in Big Bend National Park, TX © Dave Hughes/iStock
p.712 Badlands National Park, SD © Jon Spaull/DK
p.727 Gateway Arch, MO © Jon Spaull/DK
p.739 Keeper of the Plains, KS © Jon Spaull/DK
p.749 Carhenge, NE © Tom Bean/Corbis
p.765 Painted Canyon, Roosevelt National Park, ND © Jon Spaull/DK
p.816 Mammoth Hot Springs, Yellowstone, WY © Andy Holligan/DK
p.842 Sawtooth National Recreation Area, ID © Andy Holligan/DK
p.850 St Francis Cathedral, Santa Fe, NM © Tony Souter/DK
p.1076 Sign above Pike Place Market, Seattle, WA © Scott Pitts/DK
p.1084 Central Library, Seattle, WA © Daniel Brunner/iStock
p.1104 Mount Rainier National Park, WA © Danny Warren/iStock
p.1113 Hawthorne District, Portland, OR © Bruce Forster/DK
p.1124 Haystack Rock, OR © Bruce Forster/DK
p.1170 Surfing at Waikiki Beach, HI © Devon Stephens/iStock
p.1178 Hanauma Bay, HI © Carolina Garcia Aranda/iStock
p.1220 Soldier in Iraq © Craig DeBourbon/iStock

Color section: American food
Diner on Route 66 © Gerrit de Heus/Alamy
Barbecue at Kerrville, TX © Dave G. Houser/Corbis
Eating a hamburger © SuperStock
Lobster dinner, ME © Bob Krist/Corbis
Hoppin John © Bon Appetit/Alamy
Tex-Mex burritos © foodfolio/Alamy
Katz's Delicatessen, New York City, NY © dbimages/Alamy
Lunch at Galatoire's, New Orleans, LA © Louis Sahuc

Color section: American music
Jazz musician in Preservation Hall, New Orleans, LA © Nicholas Pitt/Alamy
Bluegrass musicians rehearsing, NC © Owen Franken/Corbis
Gillian Welch performing, Mountain View, CA © Tim Mosenfelder/Corbis
John Lee Hooker © Michael Ochs Archives/Corbis
Miles Davis © Hulton-Deutsch Collection/Corbis
Ginger Reyes of the Smashing Pumpkins © Casey Flanigan/FilmMagic/Getty Images
Mary J. Blige and Jay-Z in New York City, NY © Chad Batka/Corbis
B.B. Kings Blues Club, Memphis, TN © John Elk III/Alamy
Preservation Hall, New Orleans, LA © Cosmo Condina /Alamy

Color section: The great outdoors
Kayakers in Havasu Creek, Grand Canyon National Park © Joel W. Rogers/Corbis
Hiking in Mount Rainier National Park, WA © Neta Degany/iStock
Blue Ridge Parkway, NC © Andre Jenny/Alamy
Grand Staircase-Escalante National Monument, UT © True North Images/SuperStock
Bryce Canyon National Park, UT © Jon Arnold Images Ltd/Alamy
Denali National Park, AK © Blick Winkel/Alamy
Kilauea Volcano, Hawaii Volcanoes National Park, HI © Donna and Steve O'Meara/SuperStock

Color section: Architecture
Taos Pueblo, NM © Craig Aurness/Corbis
Homes in Charleston, SC © Mark Lewis /Alamy
Rockefeller Center at twilight, New York City, NY © Rudy Sulgan/Corbis
Interior view of the Robie House © Thomas A. Heinz/Corbis
The Guggenheim Museum © DK
The Paris Hotel and Casino, Las Vegas, NV © Richard Cummins/Corbis
Facade of hotel, Miami, FL © Peter Wilson/DK

Index

Map entries are in color.

Rough Guide favorites

Americana

The Boardwalk, Atlantic City p.174
Carhenge, NE p.749
Coney Island..............................p.100
Crazy Horse Memorial, SD p.758
Dollywood, TN p.528
Graceland, Memphis, TN p.516
The Strip, Las Vegas, NV p.935
Watts Towers, Los Angeles, CA p.970

C

D

Rough Guide favorites

College towns

Ann Arbor, MI p.305
Athens, GA p.490
Berkeley, CA......p.1050
Boulder, CO.........p.778
Burlington, VT p.250
Chapel Hill, NC ...p.464
Madison, WI p.350
Missoula, MT p.833

E

F

G

Rough Guide favorites

Historic sites

The Alamo, San Antonio, TX ....p. 678
Fort Sumter, SC p.476
Ground Zero p.78
Harpers Ferry, WV p.418
Lexington, MA p.201
Lincoln Memorial p.378
Little Bighorn Battlefield, MT p.823
Mesa Verde, CO p.795
MLK Jr National Historic Site, Atlanta, GA p.485
Pearl Harbor, HI p.1177
Roanoke Island, NC p.456
St Augustine, FL p.589
The Sixth Floor Museum, Dallas, TX p.694

N

Rough Guide favorites

Movie locations

The Birds p.1068
The Bridges of Madison County p.742
Close Encounters of the Third Kind p.809
Field of Dreams ...p.743
Giant p.705
Mystery Train p.519
Mystic Pizza p.230
Rocky p.151
The Shining p.1118
Thelma and Louise p.921
Witness p.153

O

P

INDEX

Rough Guide favorites

Ski resorts

Alyeska, AK p.1152
Aspen, CO p.787
Crested Butte, CO p.802
Jackson, WY p.822
Mammoth Lakes, CA p.1000
Park City, UT p.930
Stowe, VT p.249
Summit County, CO p.784
Sun Valley, ID p.843

Rough Guide favorites

Small towns

Belfast, ME p.263
Crested Butte, CO p.802
Edenton, NC p.454
Eunice, LA p.658
Hot Springs, SD ..p.760
Jerome, AZ p.894
Lee Vining, CA ...p.1001
Natchitoches, LA...p.660
Talkeetna, AK p.1160
Taos, NM p.863
Terlingua, TX p.708

Rough Guide favorites

Sports

Angola prisoner rodeo, LA p.660
Cheyenne Frontier Days, WY p.805
Daytona Beach, FL p.588
Fenway Park, Boston, MA p.200
Indianapolis Speedway, IN p.316
Kentucky Derby, Louisville, KY p.506
Rose Bowl, Pasadena, CA p.983
Wrigley Field, Chicago, IL p.332

INDEX

Rough Guide favorites

The Wild West

X

Y

Z

Map symbols

maps are listed in the full index using colored text

- International border
- State border
- Chapter boundary
- 80 Interstate highway
- 30 US highway
- 1 State highway
- Unpaved road
- 4WD road
- Tunnel
- Path/trail
- Railroad
- Ferry route
- River
- Cave
- Mountain range
- Mountain peak
- Waterfall
- Spring
- Marshland/swamp
- Gorge
- Battlefield
- Point of interest
- Airport
- Airfield
- Viewpoint/lookout

- Lighthouse
- Museum
- Monument/memorial
- Ski area
- Restaurant
- Accommodation
- Campsite
- P Parking
- Bus stop
- M Metro
- Hospital/medical center
- i Information center
- Post office
- Statue
- Fountain/gardens
- Wall
- Arch
- Park entrance
- Church (regional maps)
- Building
- Church (town maps)
- Stadium
- Cemetery
- Park/forest
- Beach
- Indian reservation